We would like to thank the website www.dellamoda.it

The archives and publications
that were the sources for certain illustrations
are cited in the captions for those illustrations.

Project Editor, English-Language Edition: Antony Shugaar

Copy Editor: Helen Farrell

The publishing house assumes responsibility for the contents
of this dictionary and their translation.

Translation and adaptation with the support
of ICE-Italian Institute for Foreign Trade

Photocomposition:
Marilena Giammarrusti, Annalisa Possenti,
Tommy Procopio, Cristina Uberini

http://www.bcdeditore.it
e-mail: info@bcdeditore.it

ISBN 88-6073-015-5
ISBN 978-88-6073-015-2

Fashion Dictionary

edited by Guido Vergani

Baldini Castoldi Dalai *editore*, Inc.

Contributors to the entries

Mara Accettura
Lele Acquarone
Gaetano Afeltra
Giulio Alberoni
Maria Vittoria Alfonsi
Antonella Amapane
Denis Artioli
Sandra Artom
Laura Asnaghi
Eleonora Attolico
Gianluca Bauzano
Franco Belli
Marilena Bergamaschi
Fulvio Bertasso
Irene Bignardi
Hélène Blignaut
Ilaria Boero
Daniela Bolognetti
Anne Monique Bonadei
Enrico Bonerandi
Giulia Borgese
Gisella Borioli
Giulia Borioli
Isabella Bossi Fedrigotti
Lorenza Branzi
Cristina Brigidini
Stefano Bucci
Sofia Camerana
Gianluca Cantaro
Maria Vittoria Carloni
Sofia Catalano
Sandra Cecchi
Luigi Chiavarone
Michele Ciavarella
Miriam Cipriani
Marta Citacov
Ilaria Ciuti
Gianni Clerici
Mino Colao
Emma Costa
Aldalberto Cremonese
Valentina Crepax
Giulia Crivelli
Olga D'Alì
Grazia D'Annunzio
Priscilla Daroda
Eva Desiderio
Antonio Dipollina
Laura Dubini
Ginevra Falzoni
Daniela Fedi
Pierangela Fiorani
Aurora Fiorentini
Emanuela Fontana
Anna Gloria Forti
Maddalena Fossati
Marcella Gabbiano
Mariella Gardella
Minnie Gastel
Francesca Gentile
Silvia Giacomoni
Bonizza Giordani Aragno
Roberta Giordano
Sofia Leoncina Gnoli
Dario Golizia
Stefano Grassi
Simonetta Greggio
Gabriella Gregorietti
Pasquale Guadagnolo
Elena Guicciardi
Virginia Hill
Image Fashion & Communication
Emilio Isgrò
Alberto Lattuada
Laura Laurenzi
Laura Lazzaroni
Lorenzo Leonarduzzi
Gianluca Lo Vetro
Cristina Lucchini
Angela Madesani
Antonio Mancinelli
Lucia Mari
Fiorella Marino
Silvia Martinenghi
Pierangelo Mastantuono
Isabella Mazzitelli
Adele Melzi
Ruben Modigliani
Renata Molho
Pier Giorgio Mora
Roberto Mutti
Roberto Nepoti
Roberta Orsi Landini
Mario Pancera
Silvia Paoli
Giuliana Parabiago
Manuela Parrino
Maria Pezzi
Olivella Pianetti
Cloe Piccoli
Benedetta Pignatelli
Paola Pisa
Eleonora Platania
Paola Pollo
Edoardo Ponzoni
Maria Vittoria Pozzi
Alessandra Quattordio
Giampiero Remondini
Stefania Ricci
Mariacristina Righi
Antonella Romano
Roberto Rosati
Marina Rovera

Estefania Ruilope Ruiz
Laura Salza
Anna Santini
Alessandra Scifo
Luca Selvi
Lucia Serlenga
Luigi Settembrini
Beppe Severgnini
Valeria Sico
Lucia Sollazzo
Marilea Somaré
Lina Sotis
Maria Rita Stiglich
Emilio Tadini
Sara Tieni
Isa Tutino Vercelloni
Valeria Vantaggi
Guido Vergani
Maurizio Vetrugno
Giuliana Zabeo Ricca

AAMA (American Apparel Manufacturers Association). An association of American clothing manufacturers. Informs members of new technologies and works on industry-wide problems. Includes more than two thirds of the manufacturing companies in the U.S. and is active in every part of the country. Organizes promotional activities and defends the interests of its members. Supports seminars, publishes reports and sends informational bulletins. Founded in 1933 with the name of SGMA (Southern Garment Manufacturers Association), it was renamed AAMA in 1960.

A&V An abbreviation for Alex Pogrebnojus (1968) and Vida Simanaviciute (1961), designers from Lithuania. Their atelier-studio in Vilnius opened in 1996. They create clothes and costumes for plays and other stage productions. Their clothes are a mix of sports open-work fabrics with pinned flowers. They showed their work at Moscow's Week of Fashion in October 2002.

Abaca Manila hemp. Textile fiber obtained from the leaves of certain tropical plants originating in the Philippines called musaceae. Used unbleached for coarse and hard-wearing fabrics.

Abate Loris (1927). Italian jewellery designer and fashion entrepreneur, born in Mantua. His father boasted of being from an ancient line of goldsmiths in Sicily. He abandoned the study of engineering in Turin to take his first steps in the world of jewellery. In 1960 he began an association with Mila Nutrizio Schön founding the Mila Schön *griffe*, a great business and creative success. In 1978, in Fino Mornasco, he founded Schontess, a company which designs and produces fine fabrics, manufactures ties and foulards, and also works under contract for third parties. In the mid 1980s he sold his shares in Schön to a Japanese group. In 1985 he was appointed president of the Camera della Moda (Chamber of Fashion), a post that he held for six years, during which time he transformed the steps of Trinità dei Monti in Rome into an Italian fashion runway for worldwide evening telecasts. In the same period he devoted himself to the brand carrying his own name which produces ready-to-wear. He opened shops that carry only his own brand in Milan and Porto Cervo, while continuing to create his own line of jewellery. The town of Vicenza dedicated a retrospective show to him as part of the exhibition *Orogemma*.

(*Bonizza Giordani Aragno*)

A Bathing Ape Fashion brand of prêt-à-porter created in 1993 by the Japanese stylist Nigo after working as a journalist for various underground periodicals. The *griffe* style is especially targeted to young people, accompanied by a wide choice of accessories and furniture.

Abbe James (1883-1973). American photographer. A versatile artist, he devoted himself to cinematography, working with the great director D. W. Griffith in Hollywood. During the 1920s he moved to Paris where he began to work in fashion (with a certain preference for the clothes of Patou), showing a very personal style characterized by natural light and the use of mirrors to illuminate areas of shadow. Like other photographers of the time, he used theater and movie actresses as models. His pictures, at once both simple and refined, were published by Vogue France, Vogue America, Harper's Bazaar, L'Officiel de la Couture, Fémina, and Vanity Fair. During the 1930s his attention shifted to photo reportage and he produced important photo features during the Spanish Civil War and the Second World War. He also took the first official portrait of Stalin.

Abbondanza Matos Ribeiro Portuguese brand launched in 1989 by Eduarda Abbondanza and Mário Matos Ribeiro. Their work is characterized by great technical rigor in the cutting of fabric and an image that is romantic and evocative. In 1991 they launch the project ModaLisboa, through which they contribute to the success of Portuguese fashion and to its launch on an international level, presenting their own ideas on runways along with those of other stylists. In 1995 they stop presenting their collections in order to dedicate themselves to the creation of clothes and costumes for the theater. In 1996 they found the Asociación ModaLisboa in order to promote the work of Portuguese designers and the idea of contemporary and interdisciplinary Portuguese fashion.

(*Estefania Ruilope Ruiz*)

Abboud Joseph (1950). Designer born in Lebanon. Lives and works in New York. Though following a rather unusual path (he studied literature at the University of Massachusetts and at the Sorbonne in Paris), he has carved out a considerable niche in the vanguard of American style. He designs women's wear and creates high-fashion fabrics. He combines a casual American style with the colours and fabrics of his native country. His inspiration comes especially from *kilim* carpets, which he collects, even when he made creations for other *griffes*, such as Louis in Boston. He became an established designer working with Ralph Lauren but leaves in 1986 to start his own business. Success is immediate and he later works on women's wear, sportswear, accessories, shoes, perfumes and furniture. His men's wear collections are presented in Europe for the first time in 1990.

❑ 2000, June. Brand takeover. For $65 million, GFT Net, which is the manufacturing arm of the Italian company HDP, becomes the sole owner of Abboud's lines and licensing.

❑ 2002, May. Positive results in the first quarter of the year: in contrast with the results of other HDP brands, Abboud scores a 3% increase.

❑ 2002, September. Abboud is the last remaining fashion brand owned by HDP after the sale of Valentino, Sahzà, Revedi and Facis.

❑ 2002. The year ends with revenues of €80 million and operating results of €10.5 million.

❑ Publication of Abboud's book *Thread*; he is also the official designer for various television networks, the NBC Olympics, CBS's March Madness and NFL Today.

Abraham Silk factory founded in Zurich, Switzerland in 1878 by Jacob Abraham. It became famous after the First World War under the leadership of its president Gustav Zumsteg, transforming itself into Abraham Holding. Its fabrics are of extremely high quality, both for the high fashion and luxury prêt-à-porter lines. These include 250 printed silk fabrics, 100 jacquards and damasks, and about 30 types of plain dyed fabrics, the most well-known of which is *gazar*, a sort of silken gauze created exclusively for haute couture and presented in more than twenty colors.

Abs Fab Knitwear and accessories brand created by Cristina Marcante (Milan, 1966) and Giorgia Fasolino (Varese, 1966). They launched their first knitwear and accessories Collection in 1999. After graduating in Economics from Bocconi University (Marcante) and in Modern Literature (Fasolino), they both worked for advertising agencies before discovering their vocation for fashion.

Absinthe Boutique opened in Paris in 1990 by Marthe Desmoulins with a preference for the fashion of the 1920s and '30s.. She prefers strong colors and shaded tints to black in order to create elegant, poetic and very feminine lines. She offers clothes and accessories such as shoes, hats, jewels and handbags with a preference for artisanal goods. The creations of Dries Van Noten, Julie Skarland, Abe Hamilton, Isabelle Marant and Youneda Kasuko can be found there.

Academy of Fashion and Costume Design School founded in Rome in 1964 by Rosanna Pistolese, a Professor of Costume Design at California State University as well as a journalist, costume designer, fashion designer, historian and fashion expert. The school offers a four-year course in fashion and costume design. Students study the history, technique and theory of both in parallel coursework. The instructors are university and college professors, journalists and industry professionals. Short courses are also scheduled during the year. Admission is at age 18 after graduation from high school. Those who are already college graduates enroll for only the last two years of study. Valentino once called the school "a breeding ground for Italian fashion." Around 70% of the students find a job in the industry. Among its former students who have become famous is Isabella Rossellini.

> ❑ 2003, January. The designs of the students are presented on the runways of the *Altaromaltamoda*.
> ❑ A student of the Academy is appointed design director of Exté. He is the 30 year-old Sergio Ciucci who, after studying at the Academy, worked for two years in Japan and later on with Maurizio Galante. His first men's wear Collection was presented in the Autumn-Winter season of 2003-2004.

Academy's logo by René Gruau.

Academy of Fine Arts of Antwerp Founded in 1663, the school has offered courses in fashion since 1965. Admission is by open competition and the course of study takes five years, including four of classes plus one of stage and specialization. The director of studies is Linda Loppa, an important figure in the emerging world of Belgian fashion who is about to open her ambitious project the Flanders Fashion Institute. She demands the best from her students and can fail 90% of them. Among her well-known former students are Dirk Bikkembergs, Anne Demeulemeester, Dries Van Noten and Martin Margiela.

> ❑ 2000, September. The Flanders Fashion Institute, in cooperation with the Academy of Fine Arts, starts a post-graduate course of design for the footwear industry.

Accademia nazionale dei Sartori A development from the Università dei Sartori (Italian word for 'tailors') founded in Rome by Pope Gregorius XIII in 1575. It had its first premises in Via della Consolazione, at the foot of the Capitol, where the church in which the Guild of Tailors traditionally worshipped (the Church of St. Omobono) still stands. The university building was destroyed and rebuilt many times and went through several restorations. In 1574 the Church of St. Omobono became the social and religious center of the guild. The University of Sartori began its activity right there in 1575 thanks to a yearly sum of 20 *scudi* and 20 *libras* of manufactured wax granted by the Papal State. In 1801 all the guilds, the tailors included, were abolished by Pope Pius VII and consequently the university was closed. In 1938, during Fascism, the church was returned to the tailors and in 1940-42 it underwent restoration financed by the municipality of Rome. In 1947 the master tailor Amilcare Minnucci decided to continue the tradition and founded the present Accademia Nazionale dei Sartori. In 1948, 373 years after the foundation of the ancient university, the building of St. Omobono no longer hosted the academy, which moved to premises in Piazza San Silvestro where the first fashion show was presented. In 1960 the academy moved again, this time to Via Due Macelli, and in 1967 to Largo dei Lombardi, where it still exists. The current President is Sebastiano Di Rienzo, who succeeded Mario Napolitano.

> ❑ At the start of the new century, 250 fashion-houses depend on the Accademia dei Sartori.

Accardi Carla (1924). Italian painter. In 1949 she created for her own use a sculpture-brooch in gold with diamonds, pearls and corals. In the post-war period it is one of the most important pieces of art-jewelry directly inspired by a work in *gouache* from the period of Forma 1, the name by which a group of Italian abstract artists described themselves.

Accessoire Diffusion A brand of French shoes. It made its début in 1978 and was created by Jean Paul Barriol, who discovered his calling and skill as a shoe designer after studying fine arts. His work is a revelation, given that today, associated with a very ancient shoe factory, Bilard, he owns 21 boutiques in France that sell men's wear, women's wear (his ballet flats are very well known), small leather goods and leisure shoes.

Acconci Vito (1940). Italian-American artist born in New York in the Bronx. Among the first exponents of that branch of Conceptual Art known as Behavioral Art, he always considered the experience of the body as fundamental to his work (performance art, photography, and sculpture). For this reason he created sculpture in the shape of garments, such as his installation at the Museo Pecci in Prato in 1991, in which six gigantic brassieres with cups made of wire netting and plastered fabric were adjusted by shoulder straps made of steel cables. In 1993 he created *Shirt/Jacket of Pockets*, a jacket of transparent plastic made of pockets joined together by zippers. *Leaf Shirt* was done in 1985: a green leaf-covered shirt as a symbol of the deep connection between nature and the human body.

Acetate Fabric made of cellulose acetate fiber, used pure or in a blend of cotton, viscose and silk. It was invented in Germany in 1869. The Swiss chemists Camille and Henry Dreyfuss continued the research on spun yarn which, during World War I, was used for tarpaulin covers for airplanes. In the 1920s the English firm Celanese Ltd produced the first fabric using the Swiss method. Acetate is still used in all areas of women's fashion for its silken look. It can be found in taffeta, twill, satin, and *cady*, in linings and ribbons, in synthetic furs and linen. It can be shiny or opaque. Soft and elastic, it doesn't crease or shrink and dries quickly.

Acid House A youth movement that followed disco funk music, very electronic with a psychedelic sound. It appeared in England in 1989-1990. It was minimalist in dress, anti-fashion, featuring strong colors, fluorescent T-shirts, casual clothes, fabrics printed with the symbols of the era, and "a smile". It was, above all, a new way of life, with large musical gatherings in unlikely places and locations (similar to today's "rave parties"). It shared ideals with the hippy movement of the 1960s and '70s, a society parallel to the existing one but outside traditional values and rules, where everything was allowed.

Acid Jazz A movement and a fashion of spontaneous origin. In September 1988, with what many will remember as the second "Summer of Love" gone, after the first and classic one of 1967, Acid was the term most in vogue. Just like punk, zazou, swing, and hip hop, it indicates at the same time both everything and nothing. These words are the empty square necessary to play the game, as in Chinese checkers. Specifically, the term acid jazz aids in the recovery of much material from periods past which would otherwise be in the hands of solitary enthusiasts. For deejays like Gilles Peterson and Edward Piller, in search of valid alternatives for listeners tired of the monotony of Acid House, it was an opportunity to make people dance while mixing Gil Scott-Heron and Aaron Neville with unobtainable and rare discs by obscure jazz vocalists along with Betty Carter and Etta Jones and much else under a new label. Dress codes also became fresh and neat. Shoes could be sneakers or fake crocodile loafers, without worry; polo shirts could be those with openwork by Duffer of St. George or the surfwear-inspired ones by Stussy and Quicksilver; raincoats by Burberrys or ones of suede bought second-hand: but everything was always mixed with extreme taste and with respect for the traditions of the past. In this sense, it was a genuine post-modern style. (*Maurizio Vetrugno*)

Ackermann Heider (1970). A Colombian designer born in Santa Fe de Bogotá and raised in Ethiopia, Chad, France and Algeria. He then moved to the Low Countries where he attended the Academie

Royale of Antwerp in Belgium. While a student he worked with John Galliano but after three years he left the academy because in the meanwhile he had become an assistant for the men's and women's Collections of Wim Neels, a designer and his teacher. He later specialized in drapery. As a designer he worked for Mayerline, a Belgian prêt-à-porter company. Since 2002 he has designed his own women's Collection, inspired by Africa's ethnic influences and by a European metropolitan style. He was also the last designer to work with Ruffo in the creation of the Ruffo Research Collection for Spring-Summer 2003. (*Gianluca Cantaro*)

Acrylic Synthetic fiber created in 1947 in the U.S. It is light, color-fast, acid-resistant, and can be used in any climate condition. It doesn't become matted or creased, dries quickly and doesn't need ironing. Thanks to its property of retaining heat, it is used in winter clothing especially. Its label name changes according to the manufacturer (Courtelle, Orlon, Dupont, Dralon, Bayer).

Active Wear Brand of unisex clothing, from the combined advanced technologies of the Samsonite and Lineapiù of Capalle firms. Lineapiù, founded in 1975, is in the forefront of spun yarn testing with 15 worldwide production centers. The brand made its début in January 1999. Some of its characteristics are extremely innovative, inspired by certain features of Samsonite suitcases and their industrial design. These include an anti-hail treatment on knitwear; a pocket that in every garment can be turned into a case-container for the garment itself; a neck that can be inflated to become a sort of small pillow to allow rest during trips by train or car; an alarm clock that can be carried in the facings of a jacket.

Adam Men's fashion magazine launched in France in 1925. A year later it referred to itself as the "magazine of rue de la Paix." At the time, that street was the symbol for luxury in Paris. For reasons of good taste, it urged caution in the embrace of innovation and oddities. Taken over in 1960 by Condé Nast, it had several ups and downs, changed its name twice (Nouvel Adam and Men Adam) and in 1973 closed for good.

Add Down Brand of casual clothing produced by the Milanese firm Comei and designed by Giovanni Chicco (Biella, 1954), known as John G. Grain. It made its début in 1999, showing shoulder-padded clothes for both men and women, with an emphasis on good tailoring and innovation. It has 200 shops in Italy and 300 in France, Germany, Japan, and the U.S. The core of the Spring-Summer Collection is the Add System, focused on the alternate use of nylon, silk and cotton.

Adidas German brand of shoes, clothing and accessories for all sports. Together with Nike and Reebok, it is a main player in the international market and dictates fashions. For the young generation – although by now this type of shoe has completely destroyed any kind of tradition – the Torsion model shoe has an added fashion value just as those of the English firm Church's do for those over 50. In half a century of life, this brand stood out as the most prominent during some of the most prestigious worldwide sports events. In 1971, as just one of many possible examples, Muhammad Alì and Joe Frazier both wore Adidas shoes during the boxing match called the "fight of the century." The company was born in Herzogenaurach in 1920, founded by Bavarian shoemakers Adolf and Rudolf Dassler. The brand name was registered in 1948 and comes from the contraction of Adolf's first name (Adi) and last name; he was the older brother. A few months after this christening, Rudolf founded the similarly-named Puma. The three-striped Adidas logo made its début in 1949 and was perfected in the trefoil symbol of 1973. Already in 1956 several athletes wore Adidas the Melbourne Olympics. Sixteen years later the company was the official supplier for the Games. Adi Dassler, who died in 1978, was the first foreigner accepted into the *Hall of Fame* of the sporting goods industry of the U.S. One of the most recent innovations in sports shoe manufacturing is the Torsion system, introduced in 1988. In 1997 Adidas, with a workforce of 10,000 employees, took over the French company Salomon and changed its name to Adidas-Salomon AG.

❑ 2000, September. Berlin: opening of the first Adidas Originals store. With about 3200 square feet the store at the Berlin-Mitte is intended only for original collections of shoes and accessories and for special editions such as the Crystal Superstar, of which only 100 pairs were produced.

❑ 2002. The German company takes over the remaining capital shares of Adidas Italia owned by the Colombo Group. The Italian affiliate keeps its premises in Monza. In a record year, earnings increase 10% and sales 7%, reaching €6,5 billion.

❑ 2000, July. The Japanese designer Yohji Yamamoto was appointed Creative Director of Adidas Sport Style. The line, first called Equipment, specialized in sports fashion. The collection comprised 50 articles of clothing for men's and women's wear, and a line of accessories. Before arriving at his new post, the Japanese designer worked for three seasons with Adidas Originals. His shoes were best sellers, with an estimated turnover of €500 million. The Japanese designer made his business relationship with Adidas ever closer, creating a prêt-à-porter line Y3, which was completed in October 2002 and presented in January 2003 at Pitti Uomo.

❑ 2005, January. After ending 2004 with record figures, an increase in sales of 3 percent (equal to 6.47 billion Euros), while profits soared 21 percent over 2003, reaching a level of 314 million Euros.

❑ 2005, July. Agreement between Adidas and Porche Design to create a line in the sector of activewear.

❑ 2005, August. For 3.1 billion Euros, the German company purchased Reebok. The acquisition restabilized the sportswear market where, now, each of the leading companies (the other one is Nike) controls nearly a third of the sports apparel and footwear markets. Adidas is also a sponsor of the World Cup of soccer in Germany in 2006 and the Olympics in Beijing in 2008.

Ad Lib Neo-hippy fashion trend started in Ibiza in the 1970s and '80s. It takes its name from the Latin expression *ad libitum*, meaning "as you wish." It featured bright and fluorescent colors, printed fabrics and soft, loose styles. The exuberance of the style reflected that of the Balearic Islands, a gathering place for hippies during the 1970s and still today the site of night-time follies. In such places this trend is always in vogue.

Adolphe Lafont Brand of work clothing launched in France by 1896 by a tailor of that name in Lyon following his invention of "la poche mètre," a pocket sewn over the pants waist for his father-in-law, a carpenter, who didn't know where to put his tape measure. Overalls soon followed from this. In 1975 Vogue America dedicated a cover to Lafont's colored overalls and they soon became the fashion.

❑ 1999. the brand is taken over by the Danish group Kansas Wenaas.

❑ 2003, April. The crisis at a plant in Villefranche-sur-Soane resulted in the dismissal of 51 workers, with a large part of the production moved to North Africa and Poland. In recent years Adolph Lafont consolidated the production of Textiles Chaussures Export in Tunisia.

Adri (1930). American designer. Adrienne Steckling, who went by the name Adri, was one of the late 20th century American women designers pioneering a wardrobe of functional separates suited to the needs of active, modern women. Born in Missouri, she was a *Mademoiselle* guest editor and later studied fashion at Parson's School of Design, where she studied under Claire McCardell, an important influence. She worked at B.H. Wragge for several years before beginning a collaboration with the design house Anne Fogarty. The basis of her designs was a wardrobe of functional separates often in bold graphic patterns and neutral solids.

Adrian (1903-1959). American designer. Born in Connecticut, Gilbert Adrian Greenburgh was undoubtedly the greatest costume designer of the American cinema's golden age. He studied art at Parson's School of Design and in Paris before designing costumes for the theater in New York in the 1920s. His work was discovered by Natasha

Sketches by Adrian published by *WWD* on 14 February 1945 (Archive of Parsons School of Design).

Rambova, wife of Rudolph Valentino, which led to his first major Hollywood assignment designing costumes for Valentino's film *Cobra* (1925). He became head designer for Metro Goldwyn Mayer from 1928-1939. Adrian was famous for transforming the look of many Hollywood stars: asked to minimize Joan Crawford's muscled shoulders, he did just the opposite, creating the padded look that has signified powerful women throughout the past century. Other costumes he designed for Crawford include the white organdie dress she wore in *Letty Lynton* (1932), and the graphic black dress with white neck and cuffs she wore in *Grand Hotel* (1932). Adrian also turned his magic touch to Greta Garbo, imbuing her with a drama and mystery that added to her stardom. Though her costumes in *Mata Hari* (1932) might have bordered on kitsch, the detail of the historic films is flawless, among them *Anna Karenina* (1935), where he showed off his flair in transforming military uniforms, *Camille* (1936) and *Queen Christina* (1933). His mastery of understated glamour was typified in Jean Harlow's bias-cut white satin evening dresses in *Dinner at Eight* (1933). The arrival of Technicolor, with its pastel colors and brightly cheery shades, made Adrian's purist aesthetic vision obsolete. In 1939 he left Metro Goldwyn Mayer and opened his own couture salon. Sporadically he returned to create for the stage. He died of a heart attack at 57. His boldly modern style, the aggressive proportions, the dramatic and futurist use of black and white continue to inspire fashion designers today.

Adrover Miguel (1965). Spanish designer, living and working in New York since 1991, born in the village of Calonge, on the island of Majorca, in a family of farmers. When only 12 he quit school to work on his parents' farm. Before arriving in the U.S. he spent time in London where was influenced by punk rock and the new romanticism. Although a self-taught man, his first line of clothes, Dugg, launched in 1995, drew the attention of New York's fashion world due to its innovative character and use of color. In that same year, in partnership with Douglas Hobbs, he started Horn, a store in Manhattan's East Village, destined to become in a very short time a meeting place for avant-guard artists and designers such as Alexander McQueen, Bernadette Corporation and Bless. The "urban" style invented by Adrover addresses itself to the typical New Yorker embodying his independent and playful attitude. Still famous is his deconstruction of the Burberry jacket. In Spring 1999 Adrover offered his vision of the urban woman in the show Midtown, earning compliments from Anna Wintour, the director of Vogue America, and Carly Horn, a writer for The New York Times. In 2000 three collections were enough to make him the winner of the *CFDA Perry Ellis* and *Vogue Fashion* awards as the best avant-guard designer. (*Francesca Gentile*)

Aedo Peter. Chilean designer, studied painting at the Academy of Fine Arts in Santiago, Chile. After graduation he travelled in Europe and settled in Barcelona, devoting himself to design. He contributed to the collections of Induyco (El Corte Inglés) and in 1974 he directed the design department at Fred Perry. In 1980 he founded his own business, working exclusively with the best Spanish boutiques and at the same time began to create sportswear Collections for Puma International. Nowadays, every six months he presents a Collection at the Pasarela Gaudì and a bridal Collection at Novia España. In 1999 he launched his first Collection of stockings for Medias Glory. He also created the costumes for several Spanish films. His drawings are warm, delicate and enveloping. He works a great deal with leather and silks, and prefers clean, simple lines fit for every type of woman.

(*Estefania Ruilope Ruiz*)

AEFFE Multi-brand Italian group established in 1980 and active in luxury goods. It owns the Alberta Ferretti, Moschino, Narciso Rodriguez and Pollini brands. It is located in San Giovanni in Marignano, not far from Cattolica. It is among the world's most important companies in the design, production and distribution of luxury goods. The Group manufactures and distributes men's and women's wear, shoes, underwear and beachwear, small leather goods, accessories, perfumes and glasses. The original core of the business was founded in 1975 and named after Alberta Ferretti, the renowned designer. From the beginning, the division of roles within the company was clear: Alberta supervised the design and creative part, while her brother Massimo was president and in charge of management. In 1981 Alberta presented her Collection in Milan for the first time. Two years later she began her partnership with Moschino, a new name in Italian fashion, through an exclusive license agreement for production and distribution. In 1985 the first Alberta Ferretti boutique in Milan opened and the new Philosophy line made its début. Her collaboration with the Turkish-born English designer Rifat Ozbek dates to 1988. In 1994 a production and distribution agreement for the prêt-à-porter lines of Jean-Paul Gaultier was concluded. In order to consolidate the Group's presence in the American market, AEFFE USA Inc. was established in New York with premises on 56th Street. The following year saw an agreement with the American designer Narciso Rodriguez that gave AEFFE an exclusive license for the production and distribution of the prêt-à-porter Collections of his company. That firm, based in New York, is owned half by AEFFE and half by Rodriguez. At the end of 1999 AEFFE acquired 70% of the Moschino *griffe*. In this way the AEFFE Fashion Group was born. In 2000, LDV Holding, part of the Gruppo San Paolo IMI, joined the Group with 20% ownership. This widening of the shareholding base was a prelude to and prepared for the Group's expansion. In 2001, AEFFE took over Pollini's majority stake in order to consolidate its competitive presence in the business of shoes, leathery goods and accessories. In the same year, it acquired 50% of Velmar, a company specialized in underwear and beachwear, in order to complete its line of products. With these acquisitions AEFFE Fashion Group attained a critical mass enabling it to remain at the forefront of a super-competitive world market in luxury goods. The underwear and beachwear Collections made their début under the name of Alberta Ferretti with a strategic position in the medium to high price range. In 2002 Milan saw the début of the first store belonging to the P-Box project. There all the accessories Collections of the entire

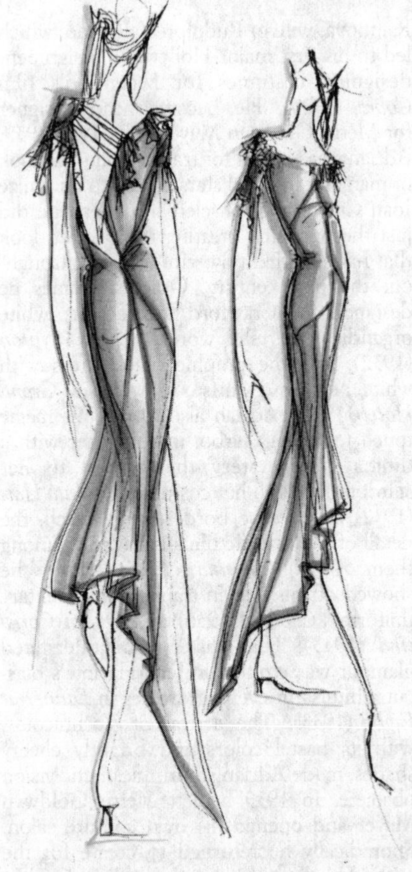

Alberta Ferretti's sketches.

AEFFE group were sold. During 2002 three more P-Box stores were opened, in Cattolica, in Milan and in Modena. Also launched in 2002 was the first Pollini line of men's and women's wear. The Group manufactures its clothing through a network of small firms spread out all over Italy. Shoes and bags are made by Pollini. For the other items there are license agreements with third-party producers and distributors. Particular attention is paid to distribution. Besides the company showrooms in Milan, London, New York, Paris and Tokyo, there are showrooms run by agents and/or importers, sometimes on an exclusive basis. This kind of structure allows the distribution of the Group's products in some 4,500 multi-brand points of sale all over the world. In addition, the Group controls 160 stores, either directly-owned or franchised, with 93 of them selling a single brand and 67 shops in shop. In 2001 the Group showed remarkable growth: revenue reached €242 million with a net profit of €10 million. The turnover grew more than 40% compared to 2000 and was partly due to continued-operations growth and partly due to the acquisition of Pollini, whose turnover of €25 million was consolidated for the first time in 2001. Without taking Pollini's results into account, real growth would have been 18%. In 2002, net revenues would amount to €250.4 million, and net profit €17.3 million. "In a quiet economic situation this would be an unsatisfying result, but bearing in mind the industry's trend of losses, these few percentage points must be considered a positive outcome," said President Massimo Ferretti. In 2003 the Group focused its efforts on retail. The P-Box formula – the sale of accessories from all the brands in one shop – was repeated with other items. "Starting in September 2003 with the opening of the first Italian store, a similar operation will sell clothing. All the lines of AEFFE's brands will be concentrated in the same selling space. The Group's multi-brand approach is perfect for medium to small size towns; "attacking" them with single-brand stores would be tantamount to an extreme standardization of our products", says Ferretti. "In addition, this type of distribution allows us to strengthen the reputation of each brand, another asset upon which the Group is concentrating its resources. At the beginning of 2003 important plans were set in motion with the aim of positioning the business for sustained growth over many years." Among these were a joint-venture for the Moschino lines in the Far East, a distribution agreement for Pollini with Itochu for the Japanese market, and one with Fairton Strategy Limited in Hong Kong. In the U.S., which represents 19% of the total turnover, the aim was to promote new product categories, from accessories to shoes to beachwear, but above all the new Pollini clothing line. *(Dario Golizia)*

❑ 2003, July. After leaving behind a 2002 characterized by growth (both in turnover, of 3.5% to 250.4 million, and in the gross operating margin, of 22.5% to 38.4 million), the group invests 30 million for the period 2003-2007.

❑ 2003. Two agreements are signed with Itochu for the Japanese market: a joint venture for Moschino, and one for the distribution of Pollini. A different strategy in the U.S. "Across the ocean our target is to introduce new categories of product: accessories, shoes, beachwear, underwear and, above all, Pollini's new clothing line."

❑ 2003. A year mainly dedicated to retail. New openings in Moscow and Paris, with the début of three stores in each town, selling Pollini, Moschino and Alberta Ferretti. An intensive schedule for Pollini: re-styling of the boutiques in Bologna, Parma, Florence, Venice, Bergamo and Rimini. Openings in Japan of five corners in as many department stores. Two boutiques opened in China, one in Guangzhou, the other in Shanghai.

❑ 2004, January. Rifat Ozbek, after three years away, is back as creative director of the Pollini Collection of women's wear.

❑ 2004, March. For 2004 the Moschino brand focused its development strategies abroad, especially on the Far East, the U.S. and Russia. In particular in Japan, a joint venture strengthened the company's presence there. In the U.S. the effort is made through the department stores. In Russia, a collaboration with the group Bosco dei Ciliegi allowed the opening of a new boutique.

❑ 2004, November. The AEFFE group produced the Collections of Basso & Brooke and Sinha/Stanic, winners of the Fashion Fringe Campaign 2004.

❑ 2004, December. The Moschino brand has 24 single-brand stores and 50 shop-in-shop and corners all over the world.

❑ 2005, February. The Pollini line works with Georgina Goodman, an English shoe designer. The creative direction of the line remains in the hands of the founders, the brothers Alberto and Antonio Pollini.

❑ 2005, April. After the opening in 2004 of the first point of sale in Korea, in Seoul, Pollini opened a second boutique for clothing and accessories in Pusan.

❑ 2005, June. Moschino and FALC signed an exclusive three-year license to produce Moschino men's shoes. The first Collection is to be in the market in the Spring-Summer 2006. FALC employs 300 people and has a turnover (2004) of 90 million euros.

(*Dario Golizia*)

Aertex Cellular cotton fabric originally invented by Lewis Haslam, a Lancashire, England, mill owner and politician who, inspired by a remark by his elderly aunt, developed the idea for using holes to create a light, warm and breathable fabric, aided by two doctor colleagues. In 1888 the three men founded "The Cellular Clothing Company" to manufacture and distribute garments made from the new fabric, which they called Aertex. Their idea anticipated the introduction of thermal cotton knitwear, and in the 20th century Aertex jackets and shirts became increasingly popular for school, sports and leisure.

Aesthetic Movement Artistic movement begun in England between 1880 and 1900 in which clothing ("aesthetic dress") was inspired by the work of Millais, Holman Hunt, Rossetti, Burne-Jones and other pre-Raphaelite artists. Similar to medieval clothing, it was unstructured, with small details and few accessories. A forerunner of Art Nouveau, the Aesthetic Movement was a variation on other movements of the time which favored the decorative arts then widespread almost everywhere in Europe and the U.S. at the end of the 19th century. Their aim was to encourage a more spontaneous style of clothing which ran counter to the current fashions and "reform" them. Corsets and tight clothing were completely abandoned in favor of soft fabrics and fluid lines which freed the body, with lines in the Empire style and decorated with patterns found in nature, either animal or floral, or with purely decorative motifs, either medieval or post-Renaissance. Particularly important were the patterns for fabric and clothing made by William Morris and sold by Liberty of London. It was a style of clothing especially suited to intellectual women and was part of the movement for women's emancipation.

Afro (Basaldella Afro, 1912-1976). Italian painter. He also designed jewellery, starting with a pair of earrings in yellow gold with emeralds and rubies produced in 1949 by the goldsmith Gherardi of Rome. Among the main figures in the renewal of painting in postwar Italy, Afro – who was born in Udine and died in Zurich – created jewellery until the early 1960s. His pieces are unique and reflect the abstract character of his painting. His work as a goldsmith was exhibited at the International Exhibition of Modern Jewellery 1890/1961 at Goldsmith Hall, Foster Lane, London, in 1962.

A.F Vandervorst Business name of two Belgian designers. Their first women's Collection was presented in Paris in March 1998 with a brand that combined his initials, A.F. for Filip Arickx, with her surname, (An) Vandervorst. With their second Collection they won the Vénus de la Mode award for future great designers. After attending the Royal Academy of Fine Arts of Antwerp together, he joined the atelier of Dirk Bikkembergs and for several years she designed accessories for Dries van Noten. Their work is strongly influenced by contemporary art, especially by the works of the German artist Joseph Beuys. They designed the Ruffo Research line of leather goods. The brand also includes a line of shoes and accessories and a lingerie Collection whch they named Nightfall.

Agassi André (1970). Famous tennis player who often distinguished himself for wearing styles that fascinated a very young and supposedly rebellious audience. Among his fashion choices were denim shorts, a cap with an opening at the back for his bleached ponytail, and the pink-and-black outfit that drew the disapproval of tournament director Roland Garros in Paris in 1990 and an invitation to wear more moderate colors. He immediately complied during the next match at Wimbledon, appearing in a sort of pure-white maternity dress with his forehead covered by a white bandana like a pirate's and showing the logo of Nike, his sponsor. (*Gianni Clerici*)

Agatha French jewellery shop. It presents the basics: two yearly, very trendy, but not too expensive Collections. Opened in Paris in 1974 based on an idea by Michel Quiniou, by 1990 it had 20 boutiques in France. By 1993 the points of sale numbered 130, of which 40 were abroad. By 1998 there were 160 in the most important cities in the world. The firm's logo makes the shops immediately recognizable. Their official color is blue.

❑ At the end of 2000, Agatha had 178 boutiques in 19 countries worldwide.
❑ 2003. Several boutiques are opened in the U.S. Among the most prestigious are those on Madison Avenue in New York, in Beverly Hills and in Las Vegas. There are two shops are in Moscow and eleven Japanese cities have at least one point of sale, some having more.

Agent Provocateur English brand of underwear, started with the opening of the Agent Provocateur shop in London in December 1994 by Joseph Corre (1967), the son of the designer Vivienne Westwood, and Serena Rees (1968). They offer a line of lingerie characterized by eroticism and exhibitionism. Provocation is the leitmotiv of the two designers. Their first publicity campaign used the slogan "The week of fashion is dead, this is the week of passion".

❑ 2000, October. Opening of the new Los Angeles boutique on Melrose Place.
❑ 2001. The perfume created by Azzi Picktall and launched on the English market the August before receives the FiFi Award as best new woman's fragrance.
❑ 2002, July. After shops on Broadwick Street and Pont Street, a third London boutique opens in Royal Exchange.
❑ On the occasion of the release of the Collection *40 LIC* of songs by the Rolling Stones, the lingerie brand launches an underwear and beachwear line with a logo displaying the large tongue created by Andy Warhol for Mick Jagger and his group.

Agenzia per la Moda Public limited-liability company established in Rome in May 1998. The Chamber of Commerce owns 75% and the city of Rome 25%. It has its premises in the very historic center of the city in Piazza Montecitorio. Sofia Loren is the honorary president and the managing director is Mauro Muccio. Its purpose is to re-establish Rome as a center of couture on a national and international level. It was in fact in Rome that many of the country's *griffes* began. And the Camera Nazionale della Moda Italiana (National Chamber of Italian Fashion) was established in Rome in June 1958. Agenzia per la Moda and the Chamber of Commerce cooperate in the organization of exhibitions and cultural events connected to the world of high fashion and, twice a year, in January and July, to the main fashion shows.

❑ 2002, July. The début of AltaRoma, fashion event conceived by the Agenzia to become a focal point for emerging young designers. Funded by a group of high level sponsors, the event takes place in the Parco della Musica Auditorium and is accompanied by a series of exhibitions on artistic themes.
❑ 2002, December. After the resignation of Andrea Mondello, the new president of AltaRoma is Stefano Dominella. Mondello left after leading the company in the direction of privatization.
❑ 2003, January. AltaRoma is held for the second time, at the Temple of Hadrian and the Parco della Musica Auditorium.

Agha Mehemed Fehmy (1896-1978) was one

of the 20th century's most influential magazine art directors. Born in the Ukraine, Agha was educated in Kiev before fleeing the Russian Revolution of 1917. He completed his studies in Paris, and there began his career as an illustrator and photographer at the Dorland Advertising Agency. Aided by his knowledge of five foreign languages (Russian, French, Turkish, English and German), he began submitting illustrations to various foreign magazines, and was hired by German *Vogue* in 1928. Publisher Condé Nast brought him to America the following year where he became art director of *Vogue, House & Garden* and *Vanity Fair*. Agha's groundbreaking approach to graphics, typeface and covers changed not only the look but also the essence of fashion and lifestyle magazines. He was bold in his use of bleed photographs and duotone, sans serif type and asymmetrical photo placement, and was also at the forefront of working with celebrated artists and photographers such as Cecil Beaton. Agha retired from Condé Nast Publications in 1943, and was succeeded by his former assistant Alexander Lieberman.

Agnès French *griffe* of hats, named after the designer considered the inventor of the art deco hat. Agnès made her apprenticeship in the atelier of Caroline Reboux atelier and opened her own boutique in Deauville after W.W. I. Artists such as Léger, Mondrian and Delaunay designed exclusive patterns for her. She then moved to Paris and in the 1930s experimented successfully with new materials such as rubber. She retired in 1949 and died soon after.

Cloche and broad-brimmed hats, from 1928-1930.

Agnès B (1941). French designer. In early 1998 she won her umpteenth case against The Gap, the giant American chain, which was selling an exact copy of her favorite piece: a plush cardigan with snap fasteners and caneté trimmings which in 1999 celebrated its twentieth anniversary. Among her other favorites, much copied but thus far without any court cases, is the heavy cotton long sleeve striped T-shirt. Agnès Troublé, under the professional name Agnès B., opened her first boutique in 1975 in the Paris neighborhood of Les Halles after working as a journalist for Elle magazine and as a designer for Dorothée Bis. Her style, characterized by a small number of practical pieces at reasonable prices, was immediately successful, leading to new stores in addition to those on the rue du Jour. These included men's, women's and children's departments and recently also a space dedicated to travellers showing objects and books from all over the world. She has always combined her love for fashion with a passion for art and next to her boutiques she opened a bookshop-gallery. Since 1987 she has also designed a line of make-up and perfume.

❑ 2001. Thanks to humanitarian events held in Sarajevo and her efforts in the struggle against AIDS, she has received much public recognition, including the Légion d'Honneur.

❑ Her entry in the U.S. market was low-profile, targeting women between 18 and 30 with a campaign for leather goods and cosmetics. In her New York boutique, decorated with photographs and film posters created by the eclectic designer, there is a unisex department along side the men's and women's Collections.

Agnès-Drecoll French fashion house established in 1931 from the merger of Maison Agnès, specialized in underwear and cloaks, with the dressmaker's shop Drecoll, the Paris branch of an atelier founded in Vienna in 1902 by Christoff von Drecoll, a supplier to the imperial Court. To direct the Paris branch, a couple renowned in the world of Parisian elegance was summoned: the Besançon de Wagner. In 1924 they left the leadership of the firm in the hands of their son Pierre and his wife Maggy Rouff, who later started a successful business of her own. It was Pierre who decided to go into partnership with the *griffe* Agnès, which withstood various upheavals in the world of fashion after the Second World War, operating until 1953.

Agnona Italian wool producer. In a consortium with another Italian firm and a Peruvian firm, in 1965 it obtained a quota for vicuña fiber, a trade which Peru liberalized after thirty years in which it was forbidden to shear the small animal that lives in the Andes at 13,000 feet. The firm was established in Agnona (Vercelli) in 1953 by Francesco Ilorini Mo, who aimed for production of the highest quality. In this way he maintained contact with the best producers of fiber in the world, guaranteeing himself the best choice of super-fine wools such as mohair, camel, alpaca, and cashmere in Australia, Peru, China and Tibet. The firm has been vertically integrated, from raw material to prêt-à-porter, since the 1970s: from warehouse to blending, from spinning to spooling, twisting, warping, weaving, raising, clipping and manufacturing, especially knitwear and accessories made with precious fibers. The distribution occurs through single-brand boutiques and selected points of sale all over the world. The firm has 261 workers and in 1998 the turnover was 67 billion Italian lire. In January 1999 it became part of the Zegna Group, but the firm is still run by the children of Francesco Ilorini Mo: Massimo, Alberto (the president) and Federica. Agnona belongs to the world's most important associations of producers and consumers of fine fibres. It is one of three associate members of the International Vicuña Consortium, which holds a worldwide exclusive for that very precious wool. In Peru it has shares in the Incalpaca Txp, a leading business in the production of alpaca.
(*Giuliana Zabeo Ricca*)

❑ 2001, November. After renovations, Agnona's first boutique in Milan reopened in via della Spiga, near the show-room in via Senato. Boutiques in Florence, Venice, Porto Cervo, Shanghai, Tokyo and Seoul soon followed. In 2001 the company installed counters dedicated to its products in some of the world's most prestigious department stores, including a space of 2100 square feet in Harrod's in London. Harrod's became exclusive distributor of the Agnona brand in the U. K. Agnona's impact on the New York market was very large. After the opening of the store near Bergdorf Goodman, this brand belonging to the Zegna Group was among the best sellers on Fifth Avenue, along with Chanel and Oscar de la Renta. The plan is now to firmly establish this *griffe* based in Borgosesia as a kind of "Zegna for women."

Aigle French firm and brand of casual and sportswear. Thc brand began in 1853 when an American, Hiram Hutchinson, moved to France and established in Montargis the Compagnie Nationale du Caoutchouc, the first French factory of rubber boots (in the Indian language the words *caa ou tchou* mean *crying tree*). He registered the Aigle trademark in memory of the American eagle. At the time, France was essentially a rural country and success was almost immediate with the farmers who appreciated a waterproof, comfortable, and strong product. In the 1950s and '60s, the production of tennis shoes was more than 8 million pieces. At the end of the 1960s the factory moved to Ingrandes, near Chatellerault, in the Vienne region, to the site of a former American military base, and the name of the brand was simplified to "Aigle". In 1972, at the Olympic Games in Munich, the firm launched, with Marc Payot, the soon-to-be-famous deck shoe Nautisme, with its two white stripes on a blue, red or yellow ground and an anti-slip suction sole. In 1989, along with the first textile Collection, the firm opened a shop in Saint Germain-de-Près in Paris. Starting in 1990 the factory was no longer part of the Hutchinson group and 80% was acquired by the investment company Apax Partners. It began to be quoted on the stock exchange, widened its market in Japan (20 single-brand and franchise stores), Korea, Hong Kong (5 single-brand stores), Taiwan and France. It opened franchise boutiques in Strasbourg, London and Düsseldorf. By 2000 the brand had a total of 102 stores (46 in Europe and 56 in Asia). A pioneer in France in clothing for the outdoors, is among the industry's leading European brands with more than 700 different products for climbing, sailing, hunting, fishing, riding skiing, travel, and leisure time. Over the years, industrial discipline and continuous research have improved product quality, but Aigle boots are still unique items hand-made of natural rubber. In Summer 2001, the first children's Collection made its début and Winter 2001-2002 saw a high-tech line, Actimum, specially developed to answer the need for comfort and thermal protection in the most extreme climates. In 2003, Aigle celebrated 150 years of activity. For the occasion Eric Bergère was asked to design a new clothing line, a limited series of the brand's "essential" pieces. The famous shoe launched in 1972 with Payot, today renamed Malouine, was selected as "object of the year" for the Première Classe exhibit that is held every March at the Jardin des Tuileries, "dressed" by twelve designers, in a game of metamorphoses of the Third Millennium.

(*Gabriella Gregorietti*)

Aigner Brand of leather goods and clothing established in 1950 by the Hungarian designer Etienne Aigner. He made his début in New York. In 1965, in Munich, a company was formed based on the brand. The main characteristic of Aigner is a special red-colored leather. From then on, the company's horseshoe brand was marketed in 37 countries and quoted on the stock exchange. In 1972 Etienne Aigner Srl was established in Italy and given responsibility for the entire output of leather goods, extending its production to shoes and luggage. In the 1970s and '80s, production expanded goods made of silk, with foulards, and to cosmetics, with the launch of the perfume Etienne Aigner No.1. In 1978 the first line of men's and women's wear was launched, which starting in the 1999-2000 season was produced by Modyva. The Collection for the following Autumn-Winter 2003-2004 season was by the Austrian designer Ines Valentinitsch who took Aigner on the runways. (*Gianluca Cantaro*)

Aigrette Tuft of feathers which adorns the head of some birds, including the egret. It was used to embellish hats, on Empire-style dresses, and put in a lady's chignon in the late 19th century. It was back in fashion during the Art Deco period and used as a hat decoration during the 1940s. On stage it adorned the dresses and heads of theater actresses and cafe singers. The designers called it *spray*.

Ailanto Company established in 1992 by the twins Aitor and Iñaki Munoz (1969). They were born in Algorta (Vizcaya) and graduated in Fine Arts from the University of Barcelona. The distinctive features of their fashion are color and the geometry of forms. At their début, Iñaki, the designer – Aitor is the manager – drew the attention of the Biennale of Fashion of Barcelona and won the Juan Antonio Comin award. Many of their dresses have more than twelve different colors. Since 1995 they have presented their Collections on the runways of Gaudì and Cibeles. In 1999 they made their Paris début at the Salon Atmosphere. Each of their Collections focuses on a different theme. They are modern, but from an aesthetic point of view they clearly follow the art of the 1950s, '60s and '70s. They have a considerable market in Japan, Hong Kong and Italy. (*Estefania Ruilope Ruiz*)

❑ 2000. The Spring-Summer Collection 2001 was presented at the New York Workshop and at London Fashion Week.
❑ 2003. For their Spring-Summer Collection of 2003 the two brothers were inspired by the glamour of the 1970s, with particular attention to especially sophisticated evening dresses.

Airaghi Rita (1944). Or else Gianfranco Ferré: where he is, she is there too; where he is not, she's there anyway. She has supported her designer cousin since 1970, when Ferré began his adventures in the world of fashion designing accessories for Walter Albini. A strange profession, yet a stimulating one, which brings her in touch with a new world, quite different from the world of teaching in which she lived after taking a degree in Modern Litterature with a thesis in medieval Latin. Teaching and fashion went together for a while. Then, in 1978, with the birth of the Ferré *griffe*, her commitment to working there became total. She showed herself to be a winner, a major player. To manage Ferré means dealing with the press, identifying locations for the presentation of the Collections, managing photographers, hiring staff, visiting editors, organizing the office and the archives, inventing the brand. She admits enjoying, in this unexpected role, the precious collaboration of Beppe Modenese. Now, this lady born in Legnano under the sign of Scorpio undoubtedly belongs to the top ranks of women in her role of complete manager. She is responsible for Communications and External Relations at Gianfranco Ferré, Inc., a task which, not so different from what she has done since the beginning, consists of a whole series of responsibilities and positions in all areas: public relations, the organization of presentations and events, promotion, advertising, and the management of the firm's image, all of which are demanding tasks that require her complete attention. She is a woman of strong personality, great energy, and determination, who is reliable and self-effacing, a person of character who is decisive, intuitive and willing to help others.

(*Lucia Mari*)

Ai-Zome Japanese printing technique using only shades of blue from dark blue to light blue. In 1984 it was taken up again by Rei Kawakubo who used it in the flower-patterned clothes of his Spring-Summer Collection.

AJAF (All-Japan Apparel Federation). The most important Japanese clothing association. It combines and represents the greatest names in manufacturing. Established in order to help develop and to defend the clothing industry, it was organized in 1973 through the initiative of six large firms in the industry. It also disseminates information about production and marketing to its members.

Ajour French term meaning "in the daylight" used to describe open-work embroidery because it lets light pass through. Mostly seen on linen or as hemstitches on sheets, tablecloths and towels, it is used as a decoration on dresses, skirts and blouses. It is made by first removing some threads from the fabric's warp (the more threads removed, the higher the hemstitch). Then the weft threads are combined in small bunches using a slipknot thread to create an open-work hem. It is possible to create small groups using the different techniques (simple hemstitch, small lily stitch, etc.). It was very popular in the 1998 Collections of Missoni and Julien MacDonald.

(*Gabriella Gregorietti*)

Akethon A brand inspired by Akhenaton, the first monotheist Egyptian pharaoh, who worshipped the sun god Aton, with whom he identified. The brand, established in the 1990s, was among the first to introduce the ideas of grunge and vintage to the shoe industry. Manufactured by the firm Linea Marche, which also produces O.x.s., Kid, Vic Matié and Paul May, the line also includes accessories, handbags, and large bags.

Akhmadullina Alena (1981). Russian designer, born in Sosnovy Bor, near Leningrad. She studied at the State University of Technology and Design of St. Petersburg. She has observed the entire world of fashion without ever leaving her country, absorbing and adopting the most varied influences. Her Collections mix different styles, such as a street-style addded to a military sensibility. She uses only natural materials, bringing together various shapes inspired by animals but always with perfectly constructed tailoring. She favors quiet tonalities, but with sudden flashes of color that light up the Collections. Her fashions are easy-to-wear and meant for those who like a style that is normal but not banal.

(*Gianluca Cantaro*)

Alaïa Azzedine. French designer of Tunisian origin. Tiny like the genii of Aladdin's lamp (his first name sounds like Aladdin), Alaïa arrived in Paris in 1957 as an apprentice sculptor after graduating from the Ecole des Beaux Arts of Tunis, his hometown. He became a great name in fashion in the 1980s, thanks to an unmistakable style, while remaining a tireless craftsman. His passion for sculpture contributes to the three-dimensional feeling of his dresses, which so often emphasize the back and the bottom ("They are the core of feminine seduction," he likes to say). The study of the history of costume and tailoring in the 1900s, from Madeleine Vionnet to Poiret and Balenciaga, taught him the principles of the highest style. His daily work of cutting and sewing, the long fittings with the most important and demanding clients, from Simone Zehrfuss to Louise de Vilmorin, from Cécile de Rothschild to Arletty, gave him the perfection and self-confidence of a master. In 1965 Alaïa opened his first atelier (two rooms in rue de Bellechasse, on the left bank of the Seine) which became the destination of a cosmopolitan pilgrimage thanks to the most sophisticated word-of-mouth. During these years he attracted and won a young and avant-guard clientele with his wrapped knitted black dresses, zipper-shaped jackets, belts and gloves in studded and open-work leather. In 1980 he presented his first Collection and in 1982, a presentation at the luxury store Bergdorf Goodman in New York opened the doors of America to him and brought international success. In 1985 he moved from rue de Bellechasse to an old youth hostel in the Marais district, restored by his friend the architect-designer Andrée Putman. In 1990 he "fell in love" with an ex-industrial workshop in rue de la Verrerie and transformed it into an atelier with the help of the American artist Julian Schnabel. But, in spite of his great success, the French-Tunisian designer has maintained his distance from organized fashion, the financial market, and show business. On July 14th 1989, for the bicentennial of the French Revolution, Jessye Norman sang the *Marseillaise* while wearing one of his creations, a white, red and blue dress. In 1997 the Dutch Museum of Groningen, designed by Alessandro Mendini, dedicated a large exhibition to him, with works by Andy Warhol, Picasso, Schnabel, Basquiat, and César near his clothes. In 1993 he gave up the runways and the presentation of Collections that have to comply with a calendar set by the Chambre Syndicale which, in Paris, is the law for fashion. (*Maria Vittoria Carloni*)

❑ 2000, September. Patrizio Bertelli, head of the Prada Group, announces the purchase of a majority stake in the French firm. Prada becomes the exclusive owner of the firm's licenses.
❑ 2002, July. After several years, Azzedine returns to the runways of French haute couture.

Alain-Bernard Catherine (1944). French journalist. In January 1992 she became director of the monthly magazine Dépèche Mode, changing both the content and its appearance. She updated the layout and reduced the cover price, dedicating 50% of its pages exclusively to fashion and limiting coverage of the news. She began her career in 1967, working for several magazines, including Mademoiselle. In 1972 Elisabeth Bernigaud appointed her chief-editor of Dépèche Mode Professionel. Four years later, the two of them created Dépèche Mode Grand Public, which they directed together. From 1977 to 1991 she worked with Elle, Madame Figaro and Nouveau Figaro.

Alain Manoukian Brand of prêt-à-porter fashion known and distributed throughout the world, from the U.S. to Japan and from Europe to Russia. Alain's wife, Dany, creates the Collections working with a group of designers that she directs. They made their début with a line of heavily patterned and colored sweaters, of Nordic inspiration, which included matching caps and hats. The Collection was later expanded to also include articles in fabric.

Alan Scott Italian brand of men's and women's prêt-à-porter, named after the designer who created it in January 1998 together with Ino Aguib, the managing director. Since 1999 the company has produced a line of accessories.

❑ 2000, April. Vestimenta employs the designer oversee the line of Hilton men's wear, a brand owned by the Trento group. The first Collection arrived in shops during the Spring-Summer season of 2001.

Alba (Alba Armillei, 1934). Roman hairdresser known for elaborate hairstyles and chignons decorated with flowers and feathers. Since 1964 her salon has been in via Condotti, but she also became well known in Porto Rotondo where, at the beginning of the 1970s, during the most fashionable years of the village built by Nicolò and Luigino Donà dalle Rose on the Costa Smeralda in Sardinia, she opened a beauty salon with her sister Francesca. For eleven years, from 1967 to 1981, Alba worked on the presentation of Collections by Irene Galitzine, Emilio Pucci, and Valentino. During the 1980s and 1990s she worked as a designer of haute couture in partnership with her son.

Albane Camille (1943). French hairdresser. She began to work in 1965 with Jacques Dessange and with him opened the first Camille Albane salon in 1969. She develops a network of franchises, following the example of her teacher, who was the first to introduce it to the world of hairdressers. She concluded an exclusive agreement for the Avon line. She is famous for her colors, above all for a certain red dye obtained from natural ingredients.

Albanese Fortunato. Italian writer. In 1917 he organized the first Congresso Nazionale dell'Industria e del Commercio dell'Abbigliamento (National Congress of Clothing Manufacturers and Merchants) in Rome, in which those invited from Milan did not participate, in order to avoid disputes with the trade unions who were fighting for an eight hour workday. In 1938 he wrote *Profili di un'opera e di un programma* whose purpose was to encourage the development of Italian writing about fashion and, as requested by the Fascist regime, to make the Italian fashion industry more prominent than the French one.

Albers Detlev (1918-1986). German designer. He made his début in high fashion in 1956 in Berlin when he opened his own atelier with experience gained from years of working in the firm of Erich Vogel. In the 1970s he turned to prêt-à-porter creating the brand Mr. Albers. He retired from work only two years before his death.

Alberti Antonio (1927-1986). Journalist and historic editor of the magazine Amica, at the time owned by the Crespi brothers, who were also the owners of the newspaper Corriere della Sera. He directed the woman's weekly with energy and imagination from 1964 to 1972, the year in which he left in order to direct an afternoon paper, the Corriere di Informazione, at a moment that was very difficult for the newspaper itself and for the publishing house. He ended his stay there long before the closing of the paper in 1979-1980. Together with Guglielmo Zucconi and the editor Caprotti, in 1974 he tried to relaunch the weekly Tempo. It was a fruitless attempt both for him and his successor Lino Jannuzzi. He died prematurely a few years later.

Albertina (1921). She defined herself as a real knitter and not as a dressmaker of knitting. Discovered by Schuberth in the 1950s, she proved that wool could be used in high fashion and not only in sportswear. In 1954 she opened an atelier in Rome. Albertina Giubbolini (born in Colle Val d'Elsa) always worked on traditional machines and she owes her success to artisanal craftsmanship. The Metropolitan Museum of Art in New York has 12 of her models, considered masterpieces of creativity and innovation, in its Collection. Several actresses, among them Gloria Swanson, Clara Calamai, Elizabeth Taylor and Lana Turner, have worn her creations. Important fashion designers, such as Alberto Lattuada, worked for her.

Albertina's model in a sketch by Maria Pezzi (1970s).

❑ 2001, February. Albertina, together with the pioneers of Italian fashion, participated in the celebration organized at Palazzo Pitti to mark the 50 years since the first runway presentation organized in Florence by Bista Giorgini.
❑ 2002, December. Lisbon pays tribute to the art of the Roman designer. At the Serra Tropicale, in the center of the Portuguese capital, more than 100 models were presented.

Alberto Guardiani Line of men's and women's shoes manufactured by Nuova Centauro. The firm, whose focus is the comparison between tradition (in style and technique) and innovation, was established with the name Centauro during the 1940s by the brothers Luigi and Dino Guardiani. In 1972 Alberto, Dino's son, took over the business, at a moment when Dino was the sole proprietor. Alberto renamed the company, launched a women's line and, while maintaining production of the firm's classic items, brought out Low Tide, a brand aimed at young people and the sports market. In 1999 in Montegranaro, Ascoli Piceno, the company built a vertically integrated plant that could design, cut, and assemble garments, with an atelier for the finishing touch.
(*Ruben Modigliani*)

Albini Walter (1941-1983). Italian designer. He left his inspired mark on the 1960s and 1970s, anticipating many trends and opening the door to the great success of Italian prêt-à-porter. He was born Gualtiero Angelo Albini in Busto Arsizio, Lombardy, on March 3rd 1941. Against the advice of his parents, he abandoned the study of classics to attend, as the sole male student, the Institute of Art, Design and Fashion in Turin. At 17 he began to work with magazines and newspapers, making sketches of the fashion shows, first in Rome, and then in Paris, where he moved for four years. There he met Chanel, falling under her spell. He studied her creations in detail in the pages of old issues of important fashion magazines which he bought in bulk. In 1963 he created his first Collection. After meeting Mariuccia Mandelli in Paris, he worked three years for Krizia, and in the last season worked with Karl Lagerfeld, who was just starting out. He later designs for Billy Ballo, Cadette and then for Trell. In his work of that time one can already see a tribute to Poiret. Towards the end of the 1960s, by now an established designer, he creates for the most important Italian houses, for Cole of California, and he works with Gimmo Etro on printed fabrics. His parallel research on cutting – ever more lightened – and on fabric is a constant of Albini's work. Thanks to him a new relationship is established between the designer and the textle manufacturer, at long last equal in status, giving birth also to the new idea of "groupages" of advertising pages in specialized magazines. His first proposal, to Montedoro, of the "uni-max" formula dates to the 1970s, when he suggested a uniformity of both cutting and colors for men and women. It is also the period of the famous *Anagrafe* Collection, with eight brides in long pink dresses and eight widows in short black ones. The following season, for Misterfox, he created a *Pre-Raphaelites* Collection, an example of how he could bring his own cultural passions to fashion in an original way. He continued his work for Montedoro, designing loose-fitting men's and women's Collections. He is by far the most celebrated and sought after Italian designer, but also the most intolerant of restrictions. The FTM Group took up the distribution of his Collections, designed with common elements in a single style for five separate fashion houses each specialized in a different product: jackets, knitwear, jersey, dresses, shirts. The houses were Basile, Escargots, Callaghan, Misterfox, and Diamant's (replaced by Sportfox few months later). In this way he obtained a complete line, presented it in Milan instead of Florence, which at that time was the customary place to show a Collection, and had as much space and time as needed. Others who separated from Florence in this way weret Caumont, Ken Scott, Krizia, Missoni and Trell. It was the beginning of Italian prêt-à-porter. But while the international press called him "the new Italian star," "as charismatic as Yves Saint-Laurent", the Italian press proved to be myopic and provincial, as did the distribution system. Albini, disheartened, broke all his contracts but one. He continued his relationship with Misterfox and with them produced a new men's and women's line which carried his name and was presented for the Spring-

Walter Albini's sketch for the Summer 1972 Women's and Men's Collection.

Summer season in London in 1973. It was the first appearance of a new formula, later much imitated, in which a primary line with a strong and driving image, and a limited volume of sales, was economically supported by a second and more simple Collection aimed at a larger market. Albini, who lived (and designed) like a character by F. Scott Fitzgerald, called it *The Great Gatsby*. This was the moment to create that unstructured jacket, the shirt-jacket (sometimes made of the same fabric as the shirt worn below), which was to be so important for the future of fashion in Italy. In 1973 he opened the showroom on via Pietro Cossa in Milan. In that same year he bought a house in Venice, and there, at the Cafe Florian, he mounted a memorable show, presenting clothes which seemed to come out of a timeless dream. The show was later brought to New York. His extraordinary creative talent was by now recognized all over the world, and he was able to give form to his own personal dreams as well as to ideas found in the broader culture, always with a light touch. And yet, Albini didn't receive enough support, he didn't have a solid commercial organization behind him. The crisis arrived in 1974-1975, though his Collections continued to amaze for the particular beauty of his creations, with their refined fabrics printed in patterns such as murrhines and paisley. In this way he relaunched the Kashmir-inspired prints which moved from fashion to home furnishings, with a success that lasted many seasons and still continues. Among the other famous patterns that he created, besides the stars, stripes, and dots, were faces, dancers, Scottish terriers, the zodiac, Madonnas, a hound's-tooth design, and the giant Prince of Wales printed on silk and on velvet. Creator of the total look, he embodied it first of all in a completely personal way, identifying his way of life with his creative style, furnishing his houses to match his fashions and designing in similar style fabrics, objects, furniture, glassware and coordinated interiors for design magazines such as Casa Vogue. An excellent draftsman, when he skips a season, as in Autumn-Winter 1974-1975, he proposed, in a moment of reflection and as an alternative to the Collections, an exhibit of his sketches dating from 1962 on. He travelled a lot, especially to India, the Far-East and Tunisia, where he bought a house in Sidi-fou-Said. The Collections that followed were inspired by those journeys. In 1975 he presented the first solo men's Collection, in this also anticipating the future. In January 1975, in Rome, was his first high fashion runway, in collaboration with Giuseppe Della Schiava, who manufactured the printed silks to one of his drawings. The Collection was inspired by Chanel and the 1930s, his passions as ever. "High fashion is dead, long live high fashion," he said, his ideas always against the trend. His second Collection was totally in pink, inspired once again by Chanel and Poiret, while his prêt-à-porter Collections for Trell were inspired by a revived "bon-ton," contradicted the following season by an "urban guerilla" style. From time to time his men's Collections were presented by male friends, and by female friends, to emphasize the unisex concept, on busts that narcissistically reproduced his own image, through life-size photographic portraits of himself made by all his photographer friends, and on panels carrying a mask reproducing his handsome face. Sometimes, polemically, the Collections were reduced to a grouping of "robes trouvées," as if to state that what really counts is only the *ars combinatoria* (art of combining things). Once he dreamed up a scandalous exhibition of personalized phalluses dressed as a

A Walter Albini's sketch.

devil, Mickey Mouse, and Lawrence of Arabia, and also as Lagerfeld, Fabio Bellotti, and Saint-Laurent. The ever recurrent motif in his fashion was the style of the 1930s, with half-belt jackets, flat necks, large trousers, the shirt-jacket, sandals, two-toned shoes, Bermuda shorts, and later on sleeveless jackets, knitwear caps pulled down over the eyes, and the first heavy-duty boots. In the last years he worked with Helyette, Lanerossi and Peprose. He entrusted Collections bearing his own name to Marzo, a new company, but the manufacturers didn't follow their instructions. Paolo Rinaldi, his most faithful working partner and press agent, was always at his side. In the early 1980s, the press, always concerned with "new entries," ignored him. Albini died at the young age of 42, leaving behind an unforgettable lesson in style, to be studied again only after his death, in the light of his great achievement, nourishing his myth. The designer gave a vigorous push to Italian prêt-à-porter as an expression of design applied to fashion in an innovative way but with solid historical roots. He invented the new image of a woman wearing a jacket, trousers, or a shirtdress. He again suggested that the revival is an intelligent form of research and reinvention, and used irony and dissent as a means of criticism. He affirmed the total look, paying great attention to accessories and details, which to him were even more important than the dress itself, while adopting a maniacal perfectionism that was somehow detached and natural. He worked without holding anything back, but never in haste or roughly or with mediocrity; he never accepted compromises, a diminution of style, or restrictions imposed by the market. *(Isa Tutino Vercelloni)*

Albouny French fashion house specialized in hats and costume jewellery. It was established just before W.W. II by Monsieur Albouny, an original character who, during the German occupation of Paris, attracted attention by using recycled materials, like newsprint, to manufacture a hat-with-veil which had a huge success. Post-war peace didn't stifle his creativity. He invented, with skilful ribbed embroidery, hats that were very light and airy. In 1964 he abandoned the world of fashion to open a second-hand shop in the flea market at Porte de Clignancourt, in Paris.

Alcantara Spanish city on the Tagus river near the Portuguese border. Also a brand of synthetic fabric manufactured in the early 1970s as the result of a collaboration between the Italian firm Anic and the Japanese firm Toray. Very fine and expensive, it has the consistency of velvet or suede, and is treated like leather. Very resistant, it doesn't crease, can be printed and embroidered and is available in an endless range of colors. Water-resistant, it is ideal for fur-lined cloaks.

Alcione Tie manufacturer. The company was established in 1945 and has been managed since 1970 by the sole managing director, Luciano Poppa. This family business is very well known for the high quality of its craftsmanship and conducts a substantial export business.

Alden American shoe and small leather goods company, established in 1884. Although open to new technologies, it maintains its craftsmanship and manufacturing techniques, even if it should mean taking six months to treat a shell made from cordovan, which is a very precious leather, a sort of cashmere for shoes that is obtained from the hind quarters of a horse. Its models are traditional, slightly stretched, with polished uppers. They provide a steel support to sustain the arch of the foot, producing a relaxed effect. The soles, made of natural leather only, are padded with thermal insulating granulated cork to cushion the step.

❑ Introduction of a raincoat line made of polyester and rayon, on sale in the most important American department stores.

Aldmuller Fred (1909). Austrian tailor. The love and respect Austrians have for their national costumes have inspired even their greatest tailors. So it was in the Aldmuller atelier, one of Vienna's oldest and most famous, where it was possible to admire not only the seasonal Collections but also new interpretations of traditional folk garments.

Alea Men's shirt manufacturer and market-leader. Founded in 1952 in Savignano sul Rubicone by Agostino Maremonti and Spartaco Onofri, it took its name from the famous exclamation uttered by Julius Cesar in the center of Savignano, when crossing the Rubicon, more than 2,000 years ago. Characterized by a dynamic business policy and, at the same time, a solid industrial-tailoring tradition, it represented Italy's second wave in the production and distribution of men's shirts. Seventh in size of the European industrial groups, it is a substantial business that employs almost 1,000 workers with a turnover (balance sheet 2002) of more than €20 million. It created three brands: Alea, Harry Brook and The Golf Club, through which the company sells about 1.5 million pieces a year. The Alea brand, sold in more than 600 shops in the main European countries, is manufactured only in Italy and aimed at an upscale market through its Linea Oro line, which is characterized by great attention to style and tailoring. Harry Brook, conceived as a second line and manufactured only in Romania, was created to be accessible to a younger market open to new trends in fashion, and is distributed in 800 shops in Europe. The Golf Club brand, with its casual style and sportswear orientation, is characterized by fashion content decidedly aimed at fans of informal clothing and is distributed mostly in Italy.

(*Sara Tieni*)

❑ 2002. Start of construction for a new plant of 250,000 square feet to be built less than a mile from the original one in Savignano sul Rubicone. Business plans envision the creation of a third industrial hub in northern Romania, in addition to the two already existing there.
❑ 2002, June. The fashion house celebrates its fiftieth anniversary at Palazzo Pitti, with an exhibition of designer shirts by 12 tailors of the Italian school. In the ten days following the event's conclusion, the exhibition is moved to Villa Maiano in Fiesole, and in September to an old fish farm of the 1700s in Savignano sul Rubicone.
❑ 2003, January. Agreement with Enrico Coveri. The Coveri line of shirts, manufactured by Alea, is available in 150 to 200 shops starting with the Collection of Autumn-Winter 2003, with an initial distribution of 45,000 pieces per season, to be increased to 100,000 units in the following years.

Alek Wek 1933 Brand of accessories created by the Sudanese model Alek Wek. The year 1933 is when father was born. After arriving in London with her younger sister to escape the civil war which was devastating her country, she was noticed on a London street by a talent scout. In 1997 she was on the cover of Elle America, and shortly thereafter came her consecration as a star when the monthly i-D declared her "model of the decade." In 1999 People Magazine counted her among the fifty most beautiful people in the world. She is on the runway of many fashion designers and is also involved in humanitarian projects.

(*Maddalena Fossati*)

Aléoutienne Silk fabric, stiff and bright.

Alès Patrick (1935). French hairdresser, a "doctor" for hair. He didn't feel a calling for this line of work, but found it by chance, needing a way to pay for his studies. He found one at age 17 as an assistant to the hairdresser Louis Gervais. Cutting hair and setting it caaught his interest and by age 21 he was already first hairdresser at Carita. In 1967 he went out on his own and opened his first salon in Paris. His studies inspired him to test on the hair certain therapies against plant diseases and ageing. In 1970 the first Phytosolba laboratories were founded and, with the imprimatur of the Faculty of Medicine of Paris, began to produce and distribute treatment products. The Alès Group has important interests in the cosmetics industry and operating offices in Europe and the U.S.

❑ 2001. The group acquired Jean-Louis Renaud Inc., which renamed Alès Group Canada.
❑ The line Une Femme de Caron was launched.
❑ 2003. The Alès Group consists of seven firms producing cosmetics, hair products and perfumes.

Alexandre (1922). French hairdresser. When very young, as assistant to the famous

Antoine in Cannes, he did the hair of Begum, wife of the Aga Khan, and of the Duchess of Windsor. This was enough to give him notoriety and in 1947 Antoine appointed him director of his Paris salon. Divas and members of the jet set placed their heads in his hands. Grace Kelly, Princess of Monaco, relied only on him for 25 years. Elisabeth Taylor called him to Hollywood for a permanent. In 1952 he associated himself with the Carita sisters. He started his solo career rather late, at age 35, opening his own salon first in Faubourg Saint-Honorék and then in avenue Matignon. Countless hairdos by him have been seen on runways. (*Mino Colao*)

Alexandre Matthieu Brand of prêt-à-porter established in 1999 in a partnership between Alexandre Morgado (1975) and Matthieu Bureau (1974). They both graduated from the Atelier Chardon Savart. Morgado was the assistant of Didier Lamarthe and worked with the lace house Vermont. Bureau worked with Dice Kayek. They made their début at the Festival for Young Designers in Hyères.

❑ 2001, October. They design for Ruffo Research. The first line of leather goods for Ruffo is presented during the Spring-Summer 2002. It is a Collection of sleeveless leather vests covered with Swaroski crystals and dark brown leather sweaters.
❑ 2003, March. Alexandre Matthieu returned to the official program of the Paris fashion week.

Alexandrine French glove-factory founded in 1864. Originally from Grenoble, towards the end of the 1920s it opened a shop on the Champs Elysées in Paris. Its fame was due to particularly sophisticated designs which immediately brought the brand into the world of high fashion. Along with gloves it also created accessories such as handbags and stockings. Its shops are almost everywhere in France (from Cannes to Biarritz) and in New York.

AleXsandro Palombo (1973). Italian designer born in the Salento region. At 19 he moved to Milan to study fashion design and also to express and intensify his connection to the culture of Salento through studies of the ethnology and historiography of the Mediterranean region. In March 1998 he created the aleXsandro Palombo brand, with a capital X like the P in his surname to indicate the Christian symbol of *pax Christi*. After his first presentation in March 2001, the international press defined him as the artist-designer of ethno-eroticism. The American newspaper The New York Times of March 3, 2003 called him "a new talent of color and knitwear." His creative path is characterized by the symbols of his land: the *Taranta*, a music and a dance which combine mysticism and sensuality, religious references to Padre Pio and Mother Theresa, and socio-political statements like the wearing of a *kefiah*.

Sketch of an evening dress by AleXsandro Palombo.

Alfaro Victor (1965). Mexican designer. He designed his first Collection in 1991 and in 1995 received the Perry Ellis Award for New Fashion Talent. Very much appreciated in the U.S., he entered into a joint venture with the Italian group Gilmar, starting in the Autumn-Winter season of 1998-1999 and aiming for international distribution.

❑ He concludes an agreement with the luxury kabel Tse to create articles in cashmere.

A model by Victor Alfaro.

Alfieri & St.John Goldsmith's firm from Valenza established in 1977. From the beginning the firm has created jewellery characterized by a marked originality of design, unusual and rich in poetic touches. Since 1999, when it joined the Damiani Group, the firm has reinforced its connection to the world of fashion. Its designs are constantly updated with an eye to making the most of their originality. And yet they maintain the tailor-made aspect of the jewellery, which continues to be rigorously handmade, while aiming for a market segment that has a passion for basic shapes and originality. Among the must-have pieces created after the restyling of the last three years are the X-shaped pendants and the Messaggio rings, which are wedding rings engraved on the inside with quotes taken from celebrated literary masterpieces. To stress its individuality, the company entrusted its advertising and communication campaign to the painter Enzo Esposito, who interpreted the jewels in an artistic way according to contemporary tastes.

Alfonsi Maria Vittoria. Journalist and writer, she began her career working for the magazines Mamme e Bimbi, Marie Claire and Bellezza. She wrote a woman's column for several newspapers such as La Gazzetta di Mantova, la Gazzetta del Sud and Giornale di Sicilia. She worked closely with the television networks, starting with the programe *Personalità* (RAI) directed by Mila Contini and, from 1973 to 1983, directing and hosting *Parliamo di Moda* e *Speciale Donna* (TVR-Rete 4). As a correspondent, she has followed the world of fashion since 1959, with brilliant reporting and a vast knowledge of the field. She was the fashion editor for L'Arena di Verona and Il Giornale di Vicenza, newspapers for which she still works as a correspondent, reporting on the fashion shows and contributing to the culture pages. Her books include *I grandi personaggi della moda* (Cappelli Editore, 1974), *Donne al vertice* (Cappelli, 1983), *Questo è il made in Italy, ovvero la moda dietro la vetrina* (1986), *A tavola con... Stile*, and *Figli d'arte? No, grazie*. In 2001 she donated her personal Collection of clothes, newspapers, magazines, books, photographs and videos documenting the fashion of the 20th century to the Galleria Nazionale d'Arte Moderna di Roma (National Gallery of Modern Art in Rome) to be displayed in the rooms of the Museo Boncompagni Ludovisi.

Alice band A ribbon or band, often of velvet, used to hold one's hair. Popular at the end of the 1800s following the publication of Lewis Carroll's book *Alice In Wonderland* (1872) because the heroine used it to bind her long blond hair.

Alima Line of shoes which got its start with ballet slippers. Designed by Franca Carraro, the Collection offers a flat shoe in every possible variation: rounded, pointed, in an oriental style, decorated, and pop. Produced and distributed by Maliashoes, the factory of Elche, near Alicante, Spain, its lines include Alima Blu for sneakers, Alima Hope for elegant slippers, and Alima New Born for small shoes for infants.

(*Giuliana Parabiago*)

Aliverti and Stecchini Silk factory near Como. It was established in 1921 by Luigi Aliverti and Giovanni Stecchini. In the beginning, manufacturing was at the Bregnano plant, near Como, which was already operating by 1920. Then it expanded with the opening of the weaving mill at Guanzate in 1924. In 1946, with the departure of Luigi Aliverti, the company changed its name to Tessitura Serica Gianni Stecchini e Figli, the figli (sons) being Pier Luigi and Mario. At the death of Giovanni Stecchini in 1950, Pericle Bari was appointed president. In the early 1950s, the factory was close to being shut down, even though production continued until 1956, when liquidation became effective. (*Pierangelo Mastantuono*)

Alix Barton French house of high fashion founded in 1932 by Julie Barton (1883). She was joined one year later by Germaine Krebs, who contributed her artistic talents to the partnership. Madame Krebs had previously sold her designs and fabrics to various houses, and had worked with Premet, but always remained in the background. Her work with Alix – as the house was soon known – quickly made her famous, above all for drapery and the use of fabrics which, as with wax satin, no other dressmaker has ever considered. She became so famous that in 1941 Germaine went out on her own and became Madame Grès.

Allard Linda (1940). American designer. She created the Ellen Tracy brand and was responsible for its success. She was among the first to give women a professional look that addressed their new needs. In 1984 the brand name was changed to her name.

❑ 2003, Spring. She celebrated 40 years of work at Ellen Tracy with a party at the Celeste Bartos Forum of the New York Public Library.

Allegri Leading Italian company in the manufacture of men's and women's raincoats and sportswear. It was founded by Allegro and Renato Allegri in Vinci, the Tuscan village where Leonardo was born, and had an immediate success with a nylon raincoat. It was the late 1950s and early 1960s, a period when their activity began to go beyond simple waterproof items and became part of the international culture of the trench coat, steadily modernizing the line. The operating headquarters are still in Vinci, but they answer to Dismi 92, a public company with a paid-up capital of €5 million. The president is Pietro Allegri and the managing directors are Augusto and Dianora Allegri. In the last decade, their line has become more fashionable and has benefited from research and the testing of new materials, with more productive technology and innovative marketing strategies. This was a process that above all involved an expansion of the very vocabulary of the raincoat, as it became richer in fashion and in style, more innovative in its forms and proportions, and showed a greater concern for detail, resulting in the complete diversity of some 200 Collections a year. In 1990 Allegri was awarded the *Pitti Immagine Uomo* prize for its extraordinary results in rainwear and sportswear, a field in which Italian firms had to compete with more established and traditional manufacturers, especially the British. The year 1999 saw the launching of Ironside, a raincoat fabric made of nylon fiber and steel thread. The company has two factories with 250 workers, plus 1,500 more in the induced activity. Today the Group has some 770 clients in Italy and more than 720 worldwide, among which are the most prestigious stores in the U.S.,

Model *Oslo* for Allegri by Giorgio Armani.

Germany, Japan and England. Allegri has three active licenses. The most long-lived is with Giorgio Armani, started back in 1976 and expanded over the years into a licensing arrangement that is still in force. The license with the young English designer Neil Barrett dates to 1999, and the one with Pirelli for the new P.Zero line began in January 2002. Pirelli entrusted Allegri with the design and commercialization of its new men's and women's wear lines. In addition to the premises in Vinci, the company has an extraordinary showroom in Milan's Palazzo Serbelloni. It also owns the Allegri Weather Points, single-brand boutiques in Milan, Florence and Tokyo (Tokyo opened in 2001), conceived as meeting places where, always in accord with the interactive and technological spirit of the firm, there is a meteorological "totem," made of a new, weather-resistant, washable and recyclable material that provides round-the-clock information on weather conditions and on the astronomical chart of the skies above the main cities of the world. In 2001 Weather Point also became the brand for a line of sportswear and travelwear aimed at a young audience. (*Maria Vittoria Alfonsi*)

❑ 2004, May. In Spring-Summer 2005 the company launched a new line designed by the avant-garde Belgian firm A.F. Vandevorst. The line is to maintain the technical quality of the firms products, but also to convey a more sophisticated allure.

Allis Spun yarn which started the viscose era in knitwear. Launched by Lineapiù in 1980.

Allison Occhiali A brand launched in Padua in 1983 by a small factory specialized in high quality eye-glasses. With a focussed and innovative business strategy, it became a big success. In 1999 Allison joined It Holding, thereby gaining prestigious brands and advanced capabilities in marketing and communication. It merged with Optiproject and acquired its distribution network. New offices were established in Los Angeles and Canada. In 2002 the continued growth is marked by a renovated and futuristic-designed premises in Padua, the heart of the company. The factory manufactures and distributes glasses for privately owned brands such as Gianfranco Ferré, Romeo Gigli, Extè Eyewear, Try, and Desil, and on license from Anna Sui, 0 RH+, Vivienne Westwood, and Les Copains. (*Sofia Catalano*)

Ally Capellino English brand created in 1979. After studying fashion at the Middlesex Polytechnic, Alison Lloyd (London 1956) began her career with her business partner Jono Platt, initially producing only accessories. The brand's curious name was meant to be the Italian translation of Little Hat, but once they realized the spelling mistake they decide to keep it all the same. In the 1980s they added a women's prêt-à-porter line, designed by Lloyd, to the production of accessories. Her style is a free interpretation of English tradition: dressmaking inspired by the 1940s and '50s, the country, tweed, everything reimagined with a modern and humorous touch. For the Summer Collections, they always use linen. In 1986 they launched a men's line, followed in 1990 by a sportswear line called Hearts of Oak. The following year they launched Mini Capellino, a children's line. In 1996 the sportswear line was shut down and they opted for a "diffusion line" called simply "ao." Their first single-brand store opened on Sloane Avenue in Chelsea in 1997. Alison Lloyd has always preferred to work behind the scenes and consolidate her success, the reward of being prudent, rather than subjecting herself to the ups and downs of avant-guard fashion. She sponsored a retrospective dedicated to Jean Michel Basquiat at the Serpentine Gallery in London.

❑ 1999. Alison Lloyd founds Capellino Design, of which she is the sole owner. Her first customer is the BHS chain of stores, for which she creates men's, women's and children's wear lines.
❑ 2003. Goa Corporation is appointed her agent in Italy. For the Autumn-Winter 2003 season, women's hats in leather and wool and cashmere gloves extend the accessories line.

Alma Italian knitwear factory founded in 1945 by Alma Donati. Its premises are in Bareggio (Milan). Today it is a brand of Alma Group S.p.A., which also markets the Spaziolo brand, among others, and manufactures high-fashion prêt-à-porter knit outerwear. The ratio of domestic (Italian) and export (Europe, U.S., Japan) sales is 60/40.

❑ For the Spring-Summer 2003 Collection the designer created a complete wardrobe with crochet-worked skirts, bags and dresses. The wedding dress "La Stella" was completely hand-sewn with 600 star-shaped wefts seamlessly joined to produce a *lace rosette* effect. The bouquet was made of crochet-worked daisies.
❑ Creazioni Alma is the name of the made-to-measure atelier whose showroom in Rome is on via XXIV Maggio.

Alma Aguilar (1976). Spanish designer from Madrid. Her family (her father is a jazz musician, her mother a poet and painter) had a great influence on her artistic education. She began her study of design at the Escuela Superior de Técnica Industriales de la Confecciòn in Madrid. In 1995 she won a competition for young designers and shortly thereafter began to learn her trade in the most important Spanish ateliers, working with Devota y Lomba, Laura Montero and Paco Casado. As a freelancer, she designed various clothing Collections including a children's line for the department store El Corte Inglès. At the same time she worked as an illustrator for magazines and newspapers such as Mia, El Mundo, Epoca and El Diario de Barcelona. In 1998 she created her own brand, named after herself, and presented her first prêt-à-porter Collection in Madrid for the Spring-Summer season in 1999. By the time of her third Collection she began to exporting her merchandise and also opened a flagship store in Madrid.

(*Mariacristina Righi*)

Almeida Ricardo (1955). Brazilian tailor. His father had a thriving business in linens while he grew up with the exciting social and night life of São Paulo, dividing his time between motorbike racing and his job as shop assistant in a shirt store. He joined a contract manufacturer that produced several brands and then in 1994 opened his first shop. Then came his own Collections at the São Paulo Fashion Week. He specializes in men's wear

A sketch by Alma Aguilar.

with a classic style, with quality workmanship and fine fabrics, always keeping a careful eye on the European *griffes*. Among his clients are important figures in show business and politics, such as the president, Lula da Silva. In 2003 he launched RA Sports, a line of casualwear.

Sketch of a men's fashion model by Ricardo Almeida.

Aloisi De Relitern Luciana. Italian designer of jewellery. She began to make a name for herself in the 1930s. From 1946 to 1983 she had an atelier and a shop under her name in Rome. Simple lines and shapes of great purity made her Collections much loved by many, including Elizabeth Taylor and Jacqueline Kennedy.

Alpaca Wool fiber that takes its name from an animal with long woolly hair found in the Peruvian Andes. The woollen thread obtained from its fleece is warm and precious. It is similar to vicuña, even if it doesn't match its nobility and rarity.

Alpha Clothing manufacturer established in the U.S. in 1959 as a supplier to the military. For 35 years the U.S. Dept. of Defense used Alpha to supply all its service branches. Its MA-1 aviator jackets became a cult item. Over the years Alpha produced more than 40 million articles of military-style clothing meeting the most rigorous standards.

❑ 1999. The U.S. Dept. of Defense renewed its agreement for the supply of the MA-1 jacket.
❑ Through a restyling of its classic lines, Alpha remains the leading supplier of heavy jackets to the U.S. Army, Navy, Air Force, and Marines Corps. Its work with the U.S. Army has lasted for more than 40 years.

Alphonsine French hat firm founded by the designer of the same name towards the end of the 1800s. She became the top milliner during the Belle Époque, when the hat was transformed into a triumph of feathers, egrets, and bulk. She arrived in Paris at the age of 15 and became an apprentice to Madame André. It was a good way to learn the business. She was then offered the position of manager at a smaller fashion house. She worked there for 20 years, taking every opportunity to improve herself, with travel, visits to museums, and the careful study of costume in paintings. She was such an extraordinary self-taught woman that, at the beginning of the 1900s, when fashion began to look to the remote past for its inspiration, she, better than her contemporaries, had the ability to interpret and understand that trend. In 1888 she opened her own atelier and then in 1904 moved it to rue de la Paix, at the time the height of elegance.

Altana Italian clothing manufacturer and distributor. A leader in children's wear, it is in the medium to high range of the market. It was founded in 1982 in Padernello (Treviso) by Marina Salamon, the sole managing director of the company, which is controlled by the Alchimia family, which at present also controls Doxa, the largest Italian market survey company. Until 1991 Altana concentrated on men's and children's shirts for the Benetton and 012 Benetton brands. In 1991 Altana launched lines of women's and children's casualwear, finding success in this area. Today, the firm's brands include Amore (3 Collections, for baby, newborn and young girls), Teddy Bear (young boys), and Pepperino (baby and junior Collections), and it produces on license Superga (newborn and junior), Moncler (baby and junior) and Henry Cotton's (baby and junior). Altana also has a women's Collection, marketed under the Amore brand. Shirts, once the company's main offering, is now just one of several product lines together with dresses, suits, sweatshirts, knitwear, jackets, trousers and skirts. Its clothing is sold in about 800 multi-brand shops in Italy and around 300 shops abroad, with an annual production of some 700,000 pieces. In 2002 its turnover was about €19 million (85% in Italy, 15% abroad). One interesting detail: the company's staff, from top managers to workers, is composed entirely of women. (*Maria Vittoria Alfonsi*)

Altea Italian manufacturer of ties, scarves and foulards. In 1892 Giuseppe Sartori opened a tie shop at the intersection of via Verri and via Montenapoleone. His son Felice would completely revolutionize the business which, in 1946, changed its name and became known as Altea. The firm is managed by the fourth generation of the Sartori family. It employs 160 workers with a turnover of 61 billion liras, with 28.7 billion liras from the EU market, 22.4 billion liras from other countries, and 9.9 billion liras from Italy.

Alterio Ruben (1949). Argentine illustrator famous for a particular technique of oil painting on paper. After graduation from the Academy of Fine Arts in Buenos Aires, he earned his living in Brazil and Spain before moving to Paris, where he made a name for himself in advertising and in fashion, working for design firms as well as newsweeklies and monthlies.

Altieri Academy Founded in Rome in 1973, it is in a palazzo on via S. Nicola da Tolentino 50, just steps away from Piazza Barberini and via Veneto. It instructs students in the various creative fields and has expanded its offerings to include the latest job categories, from design to digital photography, from cosmetics to fashion and photo modelling, from graphic design to advertising and web-design. The method is at the same time practical and theoretical. The school's slogan is "Learning while working and working while learning." Since 1983, at the end of each school year, there is a traditional event, *Una sera d'estate* (A Summer Night), organized to facilitate contacts and job offers for the best students. Each year since 1994, timed to coincide with the fashion shows in Rome, the Academy has presented the Collections of its recently graduated designers, and at the same time the school's fashion models make their début. The most creative designer is given the G.B. Giorgini Award, named for the creator of the Italian runway. The Academy has for years promoted the big event "Giovani stilisti internazionali a confronto" (International Young Designers Competition) which has been hosted by, among others, Franco Ciambella, Micol Fontana, Helietta Caracciolo, Bruno Piattelli, Irene Galitzine, Marella Ferrera, Paola d'Onofrio, Camillo Bona, Grace Pearm, and Urbano della Scala. (*Gabriella Gregorietti*)

Alves Dino (1968). Portuguese designer. A graduate of the Academy of Fine Arts, he defines himself as a creator of images who dresses his women with complete irreverence. His aim is to recycle stories and articles of clothing in order to create something completely new, different from the others thanks to its originality, strength and personality. He is inspired by the world that surrounds him and by art, especially sculpture.

Alviani Getulio (1939). Italian artist born in Udine. Considered one of the most interesting Italian practitioners of kinetic-visual experiments, he created printed fabrics, dresses and jewellery based on the same ideas that inspired his artwork. In the same way that his work *Superfici a testura vibratile* displays different patterns according to the light and the movements of the viewer, his printed fabrics, manufactured in different variaions of two contrasting colors by Germana Marucelli in 1964, transform themselves according to the movements of the body. Again in 1964, he and Marucelli created *Positivo/Negativo*, a long, sleeveless evening dress. After his début in Marucelli's atelier in Milan, his designs were presented that same year in New York at Rizzoli and at the Italian Institute of Culture. His dress Cerchio+Quadrato is from 1965, while the swimsuit *Bath Tape* was created in 1966 with Rudi Gernreich. Alviani also created several pieces of jewellery based on matching and contrasting colors and materials, including the disk earring of 1965 and the *1+2+3+4=10=1* ring composed of four gold wedding rings of different colors.
(*Cloe Piccoli*)

❑ 2003, June. Trieste hosts the exhibit Imagerie Art Fashion, organized by the cultural association Gruppo '78, in collaboration with the City Council and the Region of Friuli-Venezia Giulia. The union of fashion and art, the subject of the event, was represented by the artist's "superfici vibratili" (vibrating surfaces) and by the Collections created for Marucelli.

Amadeus Line of men's and women's wear for leisure which reinterpreted traditional Austrian costume in a modern and luxury style. Created in 1987, the line was manufactured by Schneiders, an Austrian firm established in 1946 with plants in Salzburg and Seitenstetten. In 1999 an American office was opened in New York.

Amann Elisa (1964). Spanish designer born in Bilbao. She worked with Ines Monge, her fellow-citizen. They opened their atelier in Barcelona. Vogue Spain gave them two covers. They create their clothes using rags, lace, threads, yarns, fringes, trimmings and remnants of fabric. They believe in a style which is the exact opposite of what they define as "the false splendor of fashion."

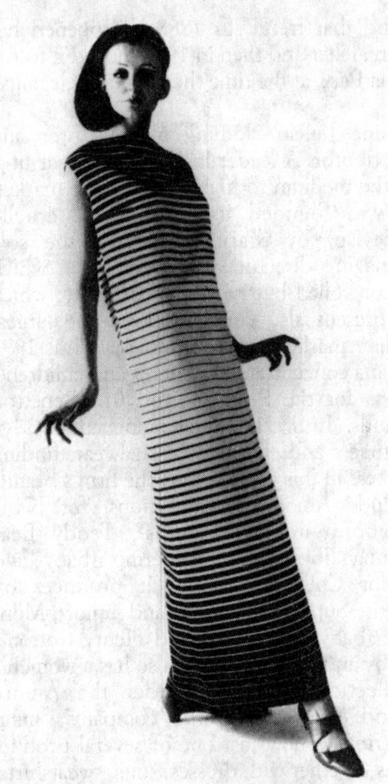

Dress for Germana Marucelli by Getulio Alviani (1964).

Americana A style very fashionable in America during the 1950s, also called "negative shoulder" because it has no sleeves. Its sleeve holes are cut on a bias that is so pronounced that they leave the shoulders completely bare. It can have a crewneck, a high neck or a deep V-neck. It is used on dresses, blouses, and light sweaters for day or evening.

American Apparel American manufacturer of neutral colored T-shirts, established in 1995 in South Carolina and soon moved to Los Angeles. Its marketing strategy depends on product quality rather than price, with clothes made from materials that are lighter and softer than those of its competitors. The company also distinguishes itself for its attention to social problems. Its employees, often coming from difficult environments, have an in-house doctor and dentist, can attend English classes and yoga lessons, and receive counseling in the choice of medical insurance. (*Ruben Modigliani*)

Amey Ronald (1886-1932). American designer born in Arizona. He studied design at the Chouinard School in Los Angeles and began to work in the world of fashion. At the outbreak of the Korea War he enlisted in the Air Force. While in the service, together with another soldier, he designed dresses for the wives of his fellow servicemen living at their airbase in New Mexico. After his discharge, he moved to New York and resumed his studies at Parsons, although he didn't graduate. He worked for several fashion houses but, because of his volatile character, he didn't put down roots anywhere. He started his own business, Burkey-Amey, in 1959, together with his ex army-buddy Joseph Burke. At its peak the business had 40 employees. In 1970 Amey acquired his partner's shares and started Ronald Amery, Inc. As with many other fashion houses in the early 1970s, the new business had difficulties establishing itself, while the critics considered his designs too innovative. Before his death, the designer collaborated with Aurora Ruffolo.

Amica Italian women's weekly news and fashion magazine founded in 1962 by Franco Sartori, Flavio Lucchini and Enrico Gramigna (the first editor-in-chief), and published by Rizzoli. Its name was chosen by Dino Buzzati, after a publication of the 1930s which illustrated the high fashion of Paris. For a period of time, the magazine focused exclusively on fashion and beauty, with the idea that women should "dream" and not be informed. Some years later, though, the "practical" aspect was emphasized with the introduction of paper patterns and advice about updating the wardrobe, leaving high fashion with just a very few pages, although always illustrated by Brunetta. In August 1981, Paolo Pietroni, the editor-in-chief from 1974 1979, returned to his previous post, succeeding Carla Giagnoni. Amica changed its format and target audience, showing a growing interest for products made in Italy. In those years the relationship between information and advertising changed as well. In 1990 Giovanna Mazzetti was appointed editor-in-chief, a position which she had shared with Pietroni since 1988. The addition of women's supplements to *Corriere della Sera* (*Io Donna*) and *la Repubblica* (*D*) brought about a crisis at the magazine. In the Spring of 1998, the editorship was entrusted to Fabrizio Sclavi and Giusy Ferré.

❑ 2002, June. Forty years after its first issue, Amica shut down but was again on newsstands by September, this time edited by Maria Luisa Rodotà with Emanuela Testori as fashion co-editor. The new direction of the magazine was seen in its pursuit of a new aesthetic in graphics and the fashion-image, achieved by photographers such as Jean François Le Page, Kayt Jones, Hans Feurer and Karina Taira. The magazine was converted to a monthly.
❑ 2004, May. Daniela Bianchini became the new director.

Amies Hardy Edwin (1909-2003). English designer and the favorite of Queen Elisabeth. At the start of a long career, by 1934 he was founder and managing director of London's Lachasse Couture House. He went out on his own in 1946 in the field of women's wear, both prêt-à-porter and haute couture. Four years later, Elisabeth, heir to the throne, ordered a dress from him. It is his "consecration." In 1962 he presented a men's Collection. He was the author of the *ABC of Men's Fashion* and *The Englishman's Suit*.

Amir Nourredine (1968). Designer from Morocco. Born in Rabat, she lives and works in Marrakech. Always faithful to the traditional styles and fabrics of her mother country, she has renewed them in a profound way. Some see the style of Issey Miyake in her work. She creates immense bat-like cloaks with hand-woven wool and felt, "haiks" made of veils with inlays of raffia, and cloaks with henna-colored hieroglyphs. The Museum of Fashion in Antwerp, which opened in September 2002, dedicated a large exhibition to her.

Amiralai Nadia. Belgian designer, of a German mother and Syrian father. She completed a four-year course in fashion design at the Royal Academy of Fine Arts of Antwerp, winning several awards for her "end of the year" Collections, among which was the Christine Mathijs Prize for her Ovaron Collection, coming in third. This is a particularly prestigious prize because it is awarded by Dries Van Noten, a very well-known Belgian designer. The Ovaron Collection included clothes inspired by the narrative of a life: written texts were affixed to the garments, along with illustrations, travel documents and small objects. Her style is influenced by her roots and by the colors and fabrics of the Arab world.

(*Giulia Crivelli*)

Amok Brand created by the Swiss designer Sandra Kunatle (1966). After her studies at the École des Beaux Arts in Zurich, she moved to London where she created the first men's skirt, the basis of her future activity.

Anastassios Cartalis (1966). Greek designer. He studied fashion at the Lette-Verein school in Berlin. From 1991 to 1997 he worked for Nina Ricci in Paris. He created his own brand, Cartalis, in 1997. In 2000, Swarovski hired him to create their crystal-ornamented designs. The following year he presented his Autumn-Winter Collection for 2001-2002 at the Tuileries. In 2002 he presented his second couture Collection.

❑ 2003. He opened seven showrooms worldwide, from Tokyo to Toronto.

ANDAM (Association Nationale pour le Dévelopment des Arts de la Mode). Established in 1989 by the French Ministry of Culture and Communication to give stipends to young fashion designers working in couture, prêt-à-porter, men's wear and accessories. Among others, stipends have been given to designers such as Martin Margiela, Jean Colonna and Jeremy Scott.

Anderson Douglas (1958). Canadian designer. He started in the world of fashion by attending the International Academy of Merchandising and Design of Toronto. After graduation, he moved to Europe to test the field. Once in Paris, he obtained his first job, as an assistant designer at Dior. He then moved to Italy and worked for three years in the design studio of Enrico Coveri. At the end of this period in his professional life, he became a freelance consultant for various Italian and German companies, among them Gherardini and Caren Pfleger. Today, after his latest collaboration with the Rena Lange Group of Munich as chief designer for the accessories lines and supervisor of the creative staff for prêt-à-porter, he decided to put his experience to good use designing his own Collection. The dresses are manufactured by Lesina in Padua, while the knitwear is made by Elkay in Monza. He designs for the practical woman, one who likes a simple style of dressing.

(*Valeria Vantaggi*)

Anderson Garrick (1944). American tailor. He opened his atelier in New York in 1978, after working some time for Jones. He began his activity in partnership with Virginia Marshall, focusing on the quality and elegance of imported fabrics. His made-to-measure clothes adapt the English style to the American man. Tailoring is his strong suit, but he recently started a prêt-à-porter line that is on sale in major department stores like Saks.

Anderson Milo (1912-1984). American costume designer, particularly skilled in the creation of historical costumes. He dressed Olivia De Havilland in some of Warner Brothers's greatest successes, such as *Captain Blood*, *The Charge of the Light Brigade*, and *The Adventures of Robin Hood*. He made his début at the age of 20 at Goldwyn Pictures, designing stage costumes for vaudeville artist Eddie Cantor. He later signed a contract with Warner Bros., where he remained until 1952. Many female stars considered him their favorite costume designer. It is enough to remember the red dress that Bette Davis wore in *Jezebel*, Joan Crawford's exciting outfits in *Mildred Pierce*, and Lauren Bacall's charming make-up in *Young Man With A Horn*. After leaving the world of film, he dedicated himself successfully to interior decor. (*Roberto Nepoti*)

Anderson & Sheppard London tailors on Savile Row. Fred Astaire owes his legendary elegance to them. For decades, before and after the two world wars, it was said that their suits had a perfect "drop" because of the softness of their cutting and tailoring.

❑ 2003. The shop, established in 1873, is still one of the "top six tailors" of Savile Row, and counts among its clients Prince Philippe and Prince Charles.

André Adeline (1946). French designer. She created the single-leg skirt, a garment which covers one leg totally and leaves the other completely bare. Some of her designs are on permanent display at the Fashion Institute of Technology. From 1969 to 1972 she was an asssistant to Marc Bohan at Dior. In 1973 she created the women's prêt-à-porter Collection for Louis Féraud. In collaboration with Jean-Charles de Castelbajac, she designed her first complete Collection in 1976. In 1981 she started her own business. Beginning in 1992 she toured the world's most important cities with her *prèmiere* and workers, showing men's and women's made-to-measure clothes. Since 1994 she has been in charge of the knitwear Collection for Nina Ricci.

❑ 1997. She launched her first haute couture Collection and worked for Les 3 Suisses, designing exclusive styles for the 1998 season.
❑ 1999, January. The year of her first prêt-à-porter Collection in Paris. She designed costumes for the theater and also designed the Bettina line.
❑ 2000, July. She worked with the Canadian designer Daniel Storto, famous overseas for his leather gloves. In Paris, Adeline's models wore "Siamese-twin gloves," a single glove which splits from the elbow down.
❑ 2003. For the Autumn-Winter season, as reported by the newspapers, Adeline "seems to return to the origins of fashion."

Andrea Rosati Italian brand of clothing. It was established in 1985 with a women's line that sold 3,000 pieces in the first year. In 1995 the new Andrea Rosati Donna Collection was introduced along with a line of knitwear called Rose Laban. In 1997 a new men's line was added, selling more than 18,000 pieces. In view of its strong distribution in the U.S., Canadian and Mexican markets, the company signed an important agreement with Pak Trading of Los Angeles in 1998. Export sales and promotion were to be handled through this joint venture directly from Los Angeles. The plan for the year 2000 was to double the number of customers in the U.S., going from 70 shops to some 130 or more.

❑ 2003, January. A U.S. presentation by Rosati and one hundred other Italian firms during the fourth edition of I-TexStyle, a trade show dedicated to Italian textiles organized by the Italian Institute for Foreign Trade.

André Bardot French tailor for men, with an atelier in Paris. They clothed Jean Cocteau and Jean Marais. They became famous in the 1950s for their anti-conformist style which broke with classic standards.

André Kim Korean brand connected to Moda e Parfum Beauté and created by the designer of the same name. For years it has been one of the best-known brands from Korea, carrying Korean culture to the world. The designer made his international début in 1962 on the runways of Paris. He followed with presentations in Australia, China, Egypt, Italy, Spain, and the U.S. He was the first Korean designer to be awarded the Medal for Culture of the President of Korea, in 1997 (he had received a similar award from the Republic of Italy in 1982). In 2000 he was a UNICEF special representative and he has since then expanded his charity work. His style is baroque, fanciful, and inspired by a fusion of western elegance and eastern tradition. His brand also includes a line of cosmetics, perfumes and skin care products, all of high quality. (*Laura Lazzaroni*)

Andreu Andres (1940). Catalan designer, born in Tarragona. He did his apprenticeship designing fabrics and working with small prêt-à-porter houses. At the age of 20 he joined the workshop of Pedro Rodriguez, who had an extremely successful atelier in Barcelona. This apprenticeship lasted 6 years and allowed him to start his own business, also in Barcelona. He made his name with fashions that were daring and experimental.

Later, he softened his avant-guard style. Spanish critics rank him among the greatest of Spain's designers.

Andrevie France (1945-1984). Belgian designer. She was self-taught and began her career in the 1970s almost by chance, opening her own small shop in Brussels where she sold only women's prêt-à-porter. That first success took her to Saint-Tropez and then to Paris, where she became famous through clothes which, though classic in style, were highly innovative in their combination of colors.

Andrienne or Andrié. A term again in use to define a loose-fitting and elegant woman's dressing gown. In fashion especially during the 18th and 19th centuries, it owes its name to Baron's *Andrienne* (a remake of the *Andrian* by Terence), in which the gown was worn by Dancourt with great success.

Anfibi Boots of untreated leather, often black, to mid-calf, similar to military boots, with laces in the front.

Angeli Hélène (1945). French designer and painter. After working on two high-fashiion Collections with Saint-Laurent and Chanel, she decided in 1980 to devote herself solely to design. Her atelier in Nice has a wide offering of bags, accessories, leather goods and household furnishings in a mix of fabrics and materials including silk, leather, gold and metal. For several years some of her work has been on display at the Musée de la Mode et du Textile in Paris.

A.n.g.e.l.o. Firm specialized in second-hand clothes. They import, select and, in the slang of the industry, make the garments "hygienic" for bulk and retail sale. Founded in 1979 by Angelo Caroli and Mario Gulmanelli, it has its headquarters in Lugo di Romagna with more than 10,000 square feet in which garments from the late 1800s up to the 1990s are collected. Some 30,000 articles of clothing are available for rent and use in video and film. The firm distributes its recycled clothes through thirteen points of sale, including privately-owned shops, franchises, and kiosks, all over Italy.

❑ 2001, January. Milan hosts an exhibition about camouflage, in which some thirty original pieces from the armies of different countries around the world are reused as fashion accessories.
❑ 2001, February. Special appearance during an episode of the television program *Link* dedicated to vintage clothing. The firm is mentioned as a major resource for second-hand clothes in Italy.
❑ 2001, June. Birth of the line A.n.g.e.l.o. Gold for recycled men's clothing in Spring-Summer 2002.
❑ 2002, March. The Vintage Palace, which is the firm's headquarters, in cooperation with the municipality of Lugo di Romagna, organizes the exhibit *L'eleganza ai tempi della Callas* ("Elegance in the Era of Callas"). On display are garments and accessories of the 1950s.
❑ 2003, July. At the same time as the presenations of Pitti Filati, an exhibit *Vintage Selection A.n.g.e.l.o* takes place at the Stazione Leopolda in Florence. The firm shows its line of men's and women's wear for summer, military-style jackets, swimwear, handbags, and shoes.

Angora Special type of wool named after the Turkish city of Ankara, where a breed of goats with long, silky hair which is the source of mohair was raised. Angora wool comes from the hair of the angora rabbit, reared mostly in China. The white and silky hair produces a fiber that is soft, very light and shiny, and used mainly in knitwear. Fabric made of angora wool is likewise very soft and fuzzy.

Angsana Farah (1973). Swiss designer of Indonesian origin. She studied at the Central School of Fashion in London. She remained in London after graduation, and later went to Paris, where in 1999 she launched her first women's wear Collection. But her goal was to design for men. In 2002 she showed at the Men's Fashion Week in Paris. Her ideal man, warrior-like and also a pleasure-seeker, caught the attention of everyone.

Animal prints A garment, textile or any other type of material, printed with spots like a cheetah or leopard, or with stripes like a tiger or a zebra. The colors are not necessarily the traditional ones but can vary according to the designer's imagination, given that the essential element is the pattern, which reproduces animal skin or fur. This type of print has been a favorite with many designers. During the 1960s, Valentino made it a focal point in his Collections, ennobling it and endowing it with a new elegance and refinement. Azzedine Alaïa uses it on his closely fitted minidresses, Anna Molinari on her unique cashmere sweaters, while Dolce & Gabbana adopt it in more outrageous forms: gilt, laminated and above all very ostentatious.

Anna Italian women's weekly published by Rizzoli. It was started in 1984 from a radical restyling of Annabella, a famous magazine which that suffered a deep crisis at the end of the 1970s. Its troubles were evident in the rapid succession of six editors-in-chief in less than ten years: Benedetto Mosca, Paolo Occhipinti, Luciana Omicini, Maria Venturi, Willy Molco, and Carla Gabetti. In December 1989, another terrible year for the weekly, sales of Anna hit 215,000 copies, their lowest ever. In that year the editorship was given to Mirella Pallotti, who oversaw another restyling of form and content. The magazine became more like the latest version of Grazia, a competing weekly published by Mondadori, with more space for culture and news. Sales began to rise again and reached 367,000 copies in 1992. Then, starting in 1995, there was a new decline, and the editorship was entrusted to Edvige Bernasconi, who had been successful at Donna Moderna, published by Mondadori. With her, sales returned to more than 300,000 copies.

❑ 2003, February. The editorship passes from Edvige Bernasconi to Rosellina Salemi, formerly deputy-editor for news.

Annabella Furrier established in 1960 in Pavia by Giuliano Ravizza (1926-1992) who at the time was 34 years old and had been a doctor. He often said "My father was a tailor. I owe to his work with needle and thread the opportunity to start my career from a solid base. Just before the last war, he sensed that the era of made-to-measure clothing was almost over. And so he made the big leap. First a shop of ready-made clothes, then two. By 1950 he had five, all of them in Pavia. In 1960 he became ill and I was forced to leave the medical field. But I didn't want to follow his exact footsteps. The idea of furs, of a single, large store, began here, along with the intent to demythologize the mink coat, reducing prices and transforming the myth of fur into a consumer good almost as common as a dishwasher." Thanks to an agreement with Angelo Rizzoli Sr., the store was called Annabella, after one of his successful women's magazines. Ravizza was the first to make the revolutionary decision to publish the price of furs in the newspapers and to produce long- and short-format TV commercials, entrusting them to the famous director Franco Zeffirelli, who cast Jerry Hall, the former wife of Mick Jagger, in them. After the death of Giuliano Ravizza, the company was managed by his three children, Simonetta, Ruggero, and Riccardo, who increased the turnover. The main premises are in Pavia, with 14 shop-windows in a store of 20,000 square feet. A shop named Simonetta Ravizza was opened in Milan on via Montenapoleone.

❑ 2002, September. Annabella also becomes a brand of eau de toilette for women.

❑ 2003, February. Naomi Campbell, at one time active in the animal-rights movement, is on Ravizza's runway wearing a *lapin*, a military-style blouse with a foxtail and a precious, long sable fur which can be shortened through zippers.

Annapiù Tricot Italian knitwear factory. Anna Maria Carrer created the brand at the end of the 1970s, putting thirty years of experience in knitwear to good use. The factory is located in Asti where the firm uses fine craftsmanship to produce a "total look" in knitwear, with an eye to fashion and using fine fibers such as cashmere and mohair.

❑ Annapiù is a breeding ground for young designers. Among the ten winners of the Young Emerging Students prize, sponsored by MOMI, the Region of Lombardy, and the Comune and Chamber of Commerce of Milan, was Loris Sensolini, a designer who worked on the firm's creations.

❑ 2003, March. Annapiù models are presented by appointment during Milano Moda Donna.

Annapurna Italian manufacturer of knitwear in cashmere, cashmere-silk and fine natural fibers. The firm was established in Prato, Tuscany, in 1978 by Aida Barni, after the birth of her fourth child from her marriage to Pierluigi Galli, one of the world's leading experts on spun yarns. One half of the production is exported to Germany, Austria and Switzerland, countries in which the company is the market leader. The rest is sold in Italy, France, Japan and the U.S. The brand name recalls the mountains of Kashmir and the peak of Annapurna, more than 26,000 feet and climbed for the first time by a Japanese team composed only by women. The brand is famous also for *Cashmere*, an invaluable book published for the first time in 1986 and reissued in 1997, one of whose authors is Pierluigi Galli. Printed also in French, English and Japanese, the book is an international reference work for technical schools, trade buyers and consumers. The brand's success is due to its fine manufacturing techniques and expert finishing. The Annapurna and Aida Barni Collections are offered each season at the company's Milan showroom at via della Spiga, 46. The philosophy of the firm is based on the work of skilled craftsmen, an attention to detail, and the use of exclusive colors (in recent seasons these included midnight blue, tourmaline, slate green, dry moss). There is a lasting commitment to customer service, and to clothes that suit Italian taste and are highly fashionable.

❑ Aida Barni received the *La Città delle Donne* (*City of Women*) award and was given the keys to the city of Prato. The president of the Republic of Italy, Carlo Azeglio Ciampi, named her a *Cavaliere del Lavoro*.

❑ 2002, September. Annapurna presented its Collection at the third annual Fashion China, an exhibit of clothing and accessories held in Shanghai. The 2002 exhibit was organized by the Italian firm Ingedo, by the China National Garment Association and by Ccpit Tex.

❑ New showrooms were opened in Düsseldorf, Stuttgart and New York.

Anna Rachele Brand of women's prêt-à-porter produced by the Sintesi Group of Carpi (Modena). The brand made its début in 1991 as a knitwear line and was named after Anna Rachele Bedetti, the company's founder. The firm is today directed by her son, Andrea Sacchetti. Active on the foreign market as well as in Italy, today it explores fashion trends by means of a "total look" with a modern slant, and plans to develop an accessories division. For several years it has been supported by BST Milano, a younger and more casual line. (*Laura Lazzaroni*)

Anna Tricot Knitwear factory established in 1976 in Carpi, during an industry boom similar to that of the 1960s. It produces knit outerwear, both cut and sewn and "diminished," as they say in industry jargon. Sales are one half in Italy and one half abroad.

Annenkov Juri Pavlovich (1901-1974). Costume designer from Russia. Born in Petropavlovsk, he worked on the scenery for the first great revolutionary shows and attended the Meyerhold theater school. In 1924 he abandoned Russia for Germany, where he began to work for the cinema, designing the costumes for F.W. Murnau's *Faust*. Later he worked principally in France, changing his first name to Georges. He collaborated with Marcel L'Herbier (*L'Affaire du Collier de la Reine*), Jean Delannoy (*L'Eternel Retour*, *Symphonie Pastorale*) and, above all, with Max Ophüls, designing costumes for his masterpieces (*Le Plaisir*, *Madame de...*, and *Lola Montès*, for which he and Marcel Escoffier designed the costumes of Martine Carol). He also worked in Italy, on Giacomo Gentilomo's *Due Orfanelle*. In 1951 he published an autobiography entitled *En habillant les vedettes* (Dressing the Stars).

Annex Brand of prêt-à-porter clothes launched in 1986 by the Swiss designer Dorothee Vogel with her business partner Urs Kunz. Their Collections accentuate femininity and often recall the creativity of artists such as Bill Viola and Angela Bullock. The company recently extended its market to the United States.

❑ 2003. Annex remained the leading Swiss brand of women's wear, together with Hanro, Ida Gut and Divina of Switzerland. These companies are good exporters, contrary to the rest of the industry in Switzerland, which, in the last decade has suffered a pronounced decline due to competition from Middle and Eastern Europe.

Anorak Hooded jacket, originally made of sealskin, worn by Eskimos, in whose language the word anorak means wind. Over time it has become the most popular item of wind-proof casual wear, now manufactured with high-tech fabrics. The big pocket in front is its characteristic feature.

Anousha Hempel English atelier for high couture and prêt-à-porter fashion, opened in 1988 by the designer of the same name. She won her place in the forefront of the fashion world and also in the wardrobe of the royal family thanks to an ability to balance sensitivity to the past with a taste for the present, with a rigor that is almost Japanese. Her daring hats and evening dresses have given pleasure to many. She furnished Blakes and other exclusive London hotels with a fresh and very personal style.

❑ She focused on hotel and commercial design, working for Van Cleef & Arpels. Her fashion designs were documented in the DVD series *Master of Fashion*.
❑ The Hempel Hotel opened at the Crave Hill Gardens in London. Its minimalist aesthetic is a perfect example of the designer's style.
❑ After her success with the Blakes Hotel in London, she works on the Blakes Hotel in Amsterdam.
❑ 2003. She worked on the interior of Tom Aikens' new restaurant, which opened in Chelsea in March.

Anselmo Dionisio Tie factory founded in 1953 by Vittorio Dionisio. It was originally called Diony's. In 1977 Vittorio's son Anselmo took over from his father and added his own name to the business. Current production, which includes ties, bow ties, scarves and foulards for both men and women, totals 250,000 pieces a year. After manufacturing for Versace, Cacharel, Fath and Ginocchietti, it now produces exclusively for its own brand. The annual turnover is about 6 billion liras and the factory employs 33 workers in-house plus 40 outside workers. It exports everywhere in Europe, to the U.S., and Japan. Its premises are in Origgio, Novara.

(*Fulvio Bertasso*)

Anteprima Italian brand of prêt-à-porter fashion. It is part of Sidefame Italia, a company belonging to the Fenix Group in Hong Kong. All the Collections are coordinated by the Japanese designer Izumi Ogino. It sells 60% of its production in the Far East, where it has 26 single-brand stores. In Europe, it has shops in Paris and Milan.

❑ 2000. The firm opened a single-brand store in Milan, at corso Como, 9. Anteprima entered the new century paying particular attention to accessories. Its top product is the wirebag line, unique bags made of PVC.
❑ 2003. The consolidation of the market in the Far East, with three cities having a total of 15 Anteprima points-of-sale: Tokyo (7), Hong Kong (5) and Taipei (3).

Anthesis Distributor of underwear, of home-wear for men, women and children, corsets, lingerie, and tights. Founded in 1989 by Sergio Bertola and Renzo Sartori, it has offices in Verona and Varese. The turnover went from 300 million liras in 1989 to 60 billion liras in 1999, with total sales of 2 million pieces. This made the company number one among Italian firms in its part of the industry. It has a large network of direct sales agents, or "ambassadors of underwear" which in 1999 numbered some 10,300. It is the first example of an Italian company specialized in direct selling which has been able to utilize its methods abroad, marketing its products in several European countries and overseas.

Anthias Jewellery atelier in Milan opened in 1991 as the result of a partnership between Monica Castiglioni and Natsu Toyofuku. It quickly became known as a creative space in which the design of jewellery was free of the trends of fashion and dictates of the market. Jewels were conceived as small sculptures that one might wear. Each coming from an artistic family, the two lady goldsmiths, after completing their apprenticeship at the Primateria laboratory in Milan owned by Davide De Paoli, dedicate themselves to metalworking, in particular to silver but also to "poor" metals such as bronze and iron. Their personal search for new molded forms ennobles these "inferior" materials and gradually brings the two designers – one with a style that is informal and material-based, the other poetically abstract – toward a stylistic homogeneity that becomes ever more marked. In 2001 they began a collaboration with Mikimoto Japan, a leader in the field of cultured pearls. Their predilection for unusual stones, such as milky aquamarine and red quartz, is today accompanied by a curiosity for traditional materials such as wood and glass, employed in the manufacturing of both decorations and small sculpture. Anthias jewellery is on sale at the Museum of Modern Art in New York, and often shown at international exhibitions. *(Alessandra Quattordio)*

Anthony John (1938). American designer. He uses the most refined fabrics, such as chiffon and satin, to manufacture extremely simple clothes. His designs are meant for a young and sophisticated woman.

❑ 2003. The 65 year-old designer is considered one of the inventors of "easy-to-travel" clothing, garments easy to roll up and pack into bags and suitcases.

Antichi Telai Tailoring shop in Rome. Since 1894 it has created men's suits and accessories with the most perfect and craftsman-like tailoring. An impeccable style and made-to-measure manufacturing characterize the suits, the ties, the shirts with personalized buttons, cuffs, and collars, and the English fabrics, such as woolens from Dormeuil and Holland & Sherry. The firm has an exclusive for clothes of pashmina, shared in Italy only with Brioni. While the style clothing is mainly classic in inspiration, the accessories offer original and more fanciful details, like the breast-pocket handkerchief manufactured according to the cloth and pattern chosen by the client, and the inlay tie, consisting of two ties of different size, color and pattern, sewn one upon the other with silk thread. They have two ateliers, in via Silla and via Alessandri.

Antoine (1884-1977). Hair stylist. Born in Poland, Antek Cierplikowski began his career as a hair stylist while still in his teens at a prominent Warsaw salon. He emigrated to France and landed his first important apprenticeship at Calloux, one of the most famous Parisian hairdressers of the day. Two of the celebrated French actresses, Sarah Bernhardt and Gabrielle Réjane, soon became faithful clients, and in 1909 Antoine was able to open his own salon on Rue Cambon. Antoine was the world's first celebrity hairdresser, shuttling between America and Europe to cater to a roster of stars that included Greta Garbo, Claudette Colbert (he styled her trademark bangs), Danielle Darrieux and Arletty. He was the first to introduce drastically boyish haircuts for women and experimental hair dyes, such as the light blue shade he tinted Lady Elsie Mendl's grey hair, and radically blonde streaks.

Antonella Tricot Famous brand of knitwear from the Carpi region. It was established in 1967 by Luisa Savani and is today a public limited company. It manufactures for women and children. It distributes 40% of its production in Italy, and the rest in France, Germany, Japan, the U.S., and Australia.

Antonelli Maria (1903-1969). Italian haute-couture dressmaker, born in Siena. The daughter of an employee at the Quirinale, as a young girl she was fascinated by fashion and apprenticed at the dressmaker Battilocchi in Rome. She later went out on her own and by the early 1940's had become famous, dressing stars of the Italian cinema who chose her dresses because of their originality. These included Clara Calamai, Alida Valli, and Mariella Lotti. In 1947 she designed a wedding dress for the English actress Dawn Addams, who, to the jubilation of the illustrated magazines and the first paparazzi, married Prince Massimo. Bista Giorgini invited her to participate in the first Made in Italy fashion shows in Florence. She is considered a pioneer of Italian fashion. In her atelier worked designers such as Pino Pascali, Elio Costanzi, Mario Vigolo, Chino

Bert and, for evening dresses, a very young Pino Lancetti. At the end of the 1940s, the set and costume designer Giulio Coltellacci created for her a Collection inspired by the colors of the roofs of Rome. In 1958 she launched a prêt-à-porter line under the name Antonelli Sport. The contribution of her collaborator André Laug was decisive. The Dinamica line, inspired by the world of technoloy, was created in 1963, followed by the Fuso and Optical lines. When Laug quit to go out on his own, his place was taken by Silvano Malta, who designed a very successful retro line with pastel colors and draping fabrics. In the late 1960's Maria became ill, and when she died her shop died with her.

A model by Maria Antonelli. Cover of *Bellezza* magazine, edited by Palazzi.

Antoni & Alison English brand of women's wear. It was founded by Antoni Burakowski and Alison Roberts in order to market T-shirts carrying ironic and surreal slogans. The T-shirts quickly became a cult item and very much sought after, especially as they were vacuum-packed. Their Collection includes traditionally tailored clothes, in sharp contrast with the T-shirts. Among their fans are Nicole Kidman and the actresses of the TV programs *Friends* and *Sex and the City*. For Debenhams the designers have created a line aimed at young girls and based on jeans, knitwear and accessories. They sell to trendy boutiques all over the world.

(*Virginia Hill*)

Antonio Stage name of Antonio Lopez (1943-1986), a designer and illustrator. He was one of the great names of the 20th century. One need only remember that at the time his work first appeared in the New York Times, Women's Wear Daily, and Vogue, drawing and illustration seemed to be finished as a way of documenting the world of fashion, totally supplanted by photography. Antonio made them live again. It was the 1970s. A native of Puerto Rico, the son of a dressmaker and a manufacturer of mannequins, he moved to New York in 1961 to study at the High School of Industrial Design and the Fashion Institute of Technology. Decisive for his career was a meeting with the designer Charles James. He began during the era of Pop Art, and this would influence his style, his method of composition, and the feminine type that is a recurring element in his work. Yet he never put his style above the attention to detail and the concern for legibility that made his illustrations strong, innovative and absolutely his own.

Antonio D'Errico Italian brand of prêt-à-porter. It was created at the end of the 1970s, bringing together in one group several companies active in the manufacturing and marketing of medium quality women's clothing. Its premises are in Casandrino, near Naples. The line is sold in Italy and exported to many countries, including the United Kingdom, Japan, Spain, Switzerland, Belgium, France and Canada.

❑ 2003. The two annual Collections, by Nicola and Assunta, the firm's in-house designers, are sold in showrooms in London, New York, and Dubai.

Antonioli Trendy fashion store opened in Milan in 1987 by Claudio Antonioli. The first shop is in Piazza Lima, near corso Buenos Aires. In 2003 another store opened in the area of the Navigli. Its merchandise

A Missoni's model illustrated by Antonio Lopez, 1985.

consists of established brands as well as a dynamic group of avant-guard styles. Among them are Dior, McQueen, Ann Demeulemeester, Dolce & Gabbana, Martin Margiela, Antonio Marras, and Haider Ackermann,. A new store has also opened in Lugano.

A.P.C. Atelier de Production et de Création, acronym adopted by the designer Jean Touitou (Tunis, 1951). After completing his studies in history and linguistics, fields far away from fashion, he chose fashion and was hired by Kenzo and Agnès B. He made his début with this brand in 1987 and favored a low profile. He became known for the skilled cut of his tailoring, exclusive fabrics, and a taste for historical references. He prefers a basic, minimalist and rigorous style. It is precise in a pure way, with workmanship that can be appreciated only from close up and to which the runways cannot do justice. The atelier also busies itself with things that have nothing to do with fashion, including the production of olive oil. In 1995 he launched his own record company producing, for example, discs by Sofia Coppola and Marc Jacobs. Six years later, he invested in a DVD film by Zoe Cassavetes. In the A.P.C. mail order catalogue, which benefits from the work of Eley Kishimoto and Jessica Ogden, he offers clothes by Anna Sui and Martine Sitbon. Touitou has three boutiques in Paris, one in London and four in Japan.

❑ 1991. The first boutique in Japan and, the following year, another in New York, in Soho. The launch of the mail order catalog. After the opening of a boutique in Paris in the 6th Arrondissement, he also begins to sell on the Internet.
❑ 1998. He arrives in London where he produces several music compilations.
❑ 2002. Opening of the second store in Tokyo, in the Harajuku neighbourhood, popular with people under 20.

Aponte Laura (1906-1990). Italian knitwear designer. She came from a noted Roman family, her father a lawyer and her mother, Pinella Tittoni, a talented mandolin player. She married very young to a nobleman from the Veneto, had the marriage annulled in the mid 1930s, and then happily married the journalist Salvatore Aponte, who had been the Moscow correspondent for Corriere della Sera during Russian Revolution. They lived together in Paris and in Libya, and returned to Italy at the beginning of the war. In 1945, Laura began her activity in the field of fashion, choosing knitwear. Her début was quite adventurous: she put together a group of sweaters made with recycled wool and knitted on a jacquard loom, with patterns inspired by the designs of contemporary artists in Rome. Her first client and supporter was the baroness Gaby di Robilant. She introduced Laura to Elsa Schiaparelli, who wanted Laura's designs for her boutique in Place Vendôme in Paris. It became a major triumph. In America, Harper's Bazaar put her on its cover. Her atelier in Rome was on via Gesù e Maria. In 1959 she was invited to Florence for the Sala Bianca shows. In 1970 she retired to Capri, leaving the company in the hands of her daughter Nora who, as a designer, continued to work under the brand Laura Aponte Tricots until 1983.

(*Bonizza Giordani Aragno*)

Apostopulos Nikolas (1952). French designer of Greek origin. He has multiple degrees, in law and political science from the Univ. of Athens and from the Sorbonne in Paris. In 1985 he opened his *griffe* Nikos, after working as a manager at Alaïa. His special talent was knowing how, with technique and good taste, to mix Lycra and viscose. In 1985, using this especially flexible fabric, he created his first Collection of men's underwear. Since then, he has concentrated on lines of underwear, including lines for women.

❑ The first appearance of Sculpture, a perfume for men.
❑ 2003. The Nikos brand includes a line of jewellery made with gold, platinum and diamonds, plus a line of bodycare.

Aquascutum Founded in 1851 as a tailors' shop in Mayfair, Aquascutum is one of Britain's quintessential clothing brands, best known for its classic luxury raincoats and tastefully restrained English style. Founder John Emary set out to create a waterproof wool that would stand up to the damp

British climate, and by 1853 he had succeeded, branding it Aquascutum (literally "water shield" in Latin). Almost from the beginning his coats found their way into both the military - for officers' coats during the Crimean War and the siege of Sebastopol - and an outdoorsy upper-class wardrobe. By the late 19th century the firm was supplying coats to the British royal family. The company's signature waterproof garment was perfected during World War I when Aquascutum, like Burberry, developed and supplied the army with belted, double-breasted coats, featuring military details such as epaulettes and cuff straps, for officers in the trenches. The design of the lightweight, practical and effortlessly stylish Aquascutum trench coat, which was further developed during World War II when they were donned by Royal Air Force aviators, remains remarkably unchanged to this day. Classic models and new interpretations continue to influence both its men's and women's lines, providing an anchor for the company's brand recognition. In the early 20th century Aquascutum branched into women's clothing, emphasizing notions of solidity and good taste while continually re-inventing its fabrics and design processes. Most notably it launched a water repellent coating that stood up to repeated dry cleanings, called Aqua 5, which was prominently featured in the company's advertising in the 1960s. Fashionable accents included bold new colors, luxurious linings, fur trimmings and distinctive patterns, such as the company's patented Club Check, introduced in the 1970s.

❑ 2000. The company names Michael Herz head designer for women's wear.
❑ 2001. 150th anniversary of the founding of Aquascutum. To celebrate the event, Aquascutum holds a major fashion show in Florence at the Palazzo Corsini, the first such event organized by the company in five years. In January, Nervesa, holder of the Aquascutum license for Italy, shows pieces from the Aquasport line by Aquascutum in a new show room on Corso Venezia in Milan. The company introduces a limited edition of "Heritage Coats" reflecting its century-and-a-half long history of outerwear, and the firm's accessories line is expanded, resulting in a nearly 70% increase in the sales of belts and other leather objects at year's end.
❑ 2004, December. Japanese designer Junya Watanabe is commissioned to re-edit pieces from the Aquascutum archives, which are sold in limited edition in the London store only. Also this year, the flagship store at 100 Regent Street, London, which has been in the same location since 1901, is thoroughly redesigned in the spirit of a Regency townhouse.
❑ 2005, February. Aquascutum Collection, the new younger line of the brand, also designed by Michael Herz and Graeme Fidler, joins the more classic Aquascutum London line.

Ara French fashion house opened in Paris in 1930 by the 28 year-old Armenian tailor Ara Frenkian, who had done long apprenticeships at Cyber and at Jenny. He withdrew from business during W.W. II and the Nazi occupation, and resumed his activity only after Liberation. Fifteen years later, he retired. In 1988 he published his autobiography, *Ara, un artisan de la haute couture.*

Arai Junichi (1932). Japanese fabric designer. He worked with almost every great Japanese designer, including Issey Miyake and Rei Kawakubo. In 1984 he was given the title Designer for Industry of the Royal Society of Art.

❑ Professor at the Institute of Design and Textile in Otsuka.
❑ 2000. He participated in a series of conferences entitled Aluminium by Design at the Carnegie Museum of Art in Pittsburgh. They explored the different uses of aluminum in fashion. Among the speakers was Arai, who had experimented with metals throughout his career. Other conferences were held in New York, Montreal, Miami, Detroit and London.
❑ 2002, March. Arai's first exhibit in England. The walls on three floors of the Harris Museum and Art Gallery in Preston, were covered with his textile designs. The show was a joint effort between Nippon Airways and the Univ. of Central Lancashire, and remained

open through June. Some of Arai's works are also in the permanent Collection of the Victoria and Albert Museum in London.

Arakawa Shinichiro (1967). Japanese designer. He studied fine arts in Tokyo, and then fashion at the Studio Berçot in Paris, where in 1993 he presented his first prêt-à-porter Collection. Two years later he presented in the streets of Tokyo some pieces manufactured only with traditional Japanese materials. This Collection was entitled Koinobori, from the multicolor flag typical of the children's festival in May.

❑ 1999. He launched the first line of "artwork clothing," garments which can be worn or hung on the wall like paintings.
❑ 2001. His Autumn-Winter Collection was inspired entirely by Seiko Matsuda, a pop star of the 1980s, when the designer was a teenager.
❑ His continued his collaboration with Honda for the creation of a line of clothing for motorcyclists called Shinichiro Arakawa Honda, to which a women's line is added. The début of each new Collection became a regular part of Tokyo's Fashion Week.
❑ His three Collections for the new millennium presented in Paris are inspired by the spatial dimensions length, breadth and depth.

Araki Nobuyoshi (1940). Japanese photographer born in Tokyo, the fifth of seven children. In 1963, after graduating in Engineering from the Univ. of Chiba with a concentration in photography and cinematography, he was hired by the advertising agency Dentsu, where he would stay for nine years. Very attentive to the scenographic side of photography, he constantly photographed all aspects of reality with every model of camera. He worked with ease in both color and black and white, with frequent recourse to the expressivity of instant Polaroid film, which he used as a kind of block-notes. In a country such as Japan, which for years banned explicit nudity (until the 1980s every picture showing pubic hair was censored or destroyed), Araki proposed a different and bravely daring vision. His explicit references to sexuality and to bondage, and the immediacy of his nudes, were set in a wider context dominated by the presence of an extremely modern urban landscape as well as by the traditional interior décor of the Japanese house. His most famous work, *Sentimental Journey*, followed his relationship with his wife Yoko Aoki from 1971 to 1990, when she prematurely passed away. The exaltation of the female body and a subtle polemic against its commercialization are traits also present in the many advertising campaigns and fashion reports (always accompanied by haunting short films shot backstage in video by an assistant), carried out by Araki, now considered one of the most famous contemporary Japanese photographers. He began to exhibit his works in Japan in 1965, in Europe in 1994 and in the U.S. in 1995. His most important exhibits were in Paris, in Tokyo and at the Museo Pecci in Prato. (*Roberto Mutti*)

Aramidics The most recent among the families of chemical fibers. They can be considered a type of aromatic polyamide and are available in the shape of a flock or as a continuous thread. The fibers are chemically and heat resistant up to 400°C, while their toughness and fire resistance make them especially fit for high-tech use, for example as space clothing, in aeronautics, and in high-level sports. Among the brands that use it are Kevlar and Nomex by Dupont, Tecnora and Conex by Teijin, and Twaron by Acordis. (*Gabriella Gregorietti*)

Aran Traditional Irish fisherman's sweater. Manufactured with untreated wool, ecru in color, and woven with braids, relief stitches and lozenge shapes, it is also used as a cardigan and jacket. It is named after the Irish islands of the same name.

Arapu Venera (1968). Rumanian designer born in Ploiesti. She studied in Bucharest, first at the School of Plastic Arts, then at the Academy of Fine Arts, in fashion design. In 1997 she moved to Paris to attend the Esmond school, and at the end of her studies she won the Grand Jury's first prize for the graduating classs. This was a turning point and marked the beginning of a fortunate career in the world of fashion, first with a stint at Givenchy Haute Couture at the side of Alexander Mc Queen and then a year with Paul Ka. In 1999 the Venera Arapu line made its début, and in March 2001 it was presented for the first time in Paris.

Arbeid Murray (1935). English designer. He left school at the age of 15 to follow in the footsteps of his father, who was a tailor. After a short course in model-making and a few years as an apprentice, in 1952 he went to work for Michael Sherard as assistant designer. In 1957 he opened his own house, specializing in expensive ball gowns. The firm closed in 1992.

❑ 2002, November. One of Lady Diana's favorite designers, Arbeid was celebrated in the exhibit Royalty and Elegance held in Nashville, Tenn., which brought together more than one hundred dresses and fabrics from the 16th century up to today.

Arbiter Magazine of fashion and style founded in the immediate post-war period. From the start, the contribution that Michelangelo Testa made to the magazine was crucial. He was hired in 1946 as an editor and within a few months became editor-in-chief and director. Testa turned Arbiter into a magazine with great ambitions, working with the most important journalists and illustrators. The covers done by Paolo Garretto are still famous. The traditional emphasis on information and trends, especially in men's fashion, was expanded to include all the most important areas of stylistic and artistic production. In the 1950s the magazine played a prominent role in the industrial development of Italian fashion and design. An important event in that history was a meeting in 1951 between textile mills, clothing manufacturers, journalists, and members of the new advertising industry. They met in order to consider the possibility of an absolutely new initiative, a show devoted to men's fashion. At the end of the 1960s, Arbiter was taken over by Rusconi Editore. But without Testa's enthusiasm and leadership, the magazine lost both readers and credibility, and ceased publication. A few years later it was back on the newsstands with a different name, Il Piacere.

Arbus Diane (1923-1971). American photographer born in New York into a wealthy family of Russian origin – the Nemerovs – that owned the Russeks department store on Fifth Avenue. At the age of 18 she married Allan Arbus and together they opened a photographic studio interested in fashion, doing work for Vogue and Glamour. He concentrated on taking the photos, she on the visual concept. By 1957 their collaboration was beginning to wear thin, just like their marriage. Allan began to take acting lessons while Diane went around the city taking pictures. The studio was officially closed only in 1969. It was in this period that Diane's personality as a photographer came out, partly thanks to the encouragement of her teacher, the great Lisette Model, but also to the influence of photographers such as Weegee and Robert Frank, with their "rough style," and the rigorous August Sander. In the 1960s she worked for Junior Bazaar, Esquire, Nova, The New York Times, and New York Magazine (starting with its very first issues, when it was the Sunday magazine of the Herald Tribune). She published portraits in Infinity and worked with Richard Avedon and Marvin Israel on Picture Newspaper, a large-format photomagazine which published twelve issues from 1968 to 1971. She was also interested in teaching and held several workshops. And finally, she had a column in Harper's Bazaar entitled *At My Age*. She often alternated fashion pieces with images that were harsh, and sometimes violent, in a language that was blunt and basic. After working many years with a Leica, she turned to the square-format Rolleiflex, at the same time changing her aesthetic vision. In 1967 her great solo exhibit at the Museum of Modern Art in New York made the photos famous but also emphasized the anxious and fragile aspects of her character.

(*Roberto Mutti*)

Arcando Alessio (1897). Italian shoemaker. After working as a model cutter for the master shoemakers Marchesi and Bergamaschi, he opened his own shop in 1919. During the 1920s and 1930s, his customers were at first dandies and the smart set, and then later on high society. In the 1950s and until the late 1960s, his clients were the nouveau riche beneficiaries of the economic boom. In 1968 and 1969 he won the Oscar for Best Men's and Best Women's Shoes.

Arche French shoe manufacturer. Established in 1968 in Château-Renault by André Hélaine, its has always emphasized the imagination of its designs and a variety of colors. In 1981 the firm launched an original calfskin ankle-boot with a latex sole, under the Archette label. In 1990 the firm was no. 20 in the top 100 French companies. It employs 160 workers and manufactures 2,000 pairs of shoes a day, in the same plant as at the beginning.

❑ At the beginning of the new millennium the firm remains in the control of the founding family, which owns 81% of the shares. Annual results are still excellent, despite difficult conditions in the industry.
❑ 2001, August. The company's first pilot store opened in Soho in New York.
❑ 2001, December. The Institute of Store Design declared the Arche store "the most beautiful boutique in New York."
❑ 2002, September. The store in Paris opened, on Boulevard de la Madeleine in a space previously occupied by Bally. There were additional openings in Bordeaux, Vincennes, Nimes and Zurich. At the end of 2002 there were 17 stores in France and around 30 in the rest of the world.
❑ 2003. By the end of the year new stores were expected in Milan, Geneva, Brussels, Cologne, Berlin, Singapore and Moscow.

Arcte Italian leader in men's and women's underwear and swimwear. Established in Bologna in 1954, it manufactures and distributes, among others, the lines Argentovivo and Bacirubati. It employs 230 workers.

❑ 2000. The Arcte Group controls six brands: Argentovivo, Azuleja, Bacirubati, Jamas, Allen Cox, and Julipet. Its turnover is €60 million a year, and it has 4,000 points-of-sale all over the world.

Arena Brand of swimwear. In the 1970s, seven-time Olympic swim champion Mark Spitz was its spokesman. In this way the three-lozenge brand became synonymous with swimming, allowing Arena to be the official sponsor of several sports federations. The brand also includes sports underwear, swimming accessories and fitness shoes.

Arena English magazine of news and men's fashion. Founded in London in 1986 by Nick Logan, the very clever inventor of The Face. Logan sensed that a new audience had formed: young urban males with excellent jobs, a lot of money and a desire for the latest trends. Adopting the popular and well-tested editorial model of the women's magazines, he offered articles about fashion, culture, cinema, travel and a bit of news. Top photographers and a winning graphic completed the picture. During the 1990s the magazine was updated and became a bit New Age, more spiritual and more thoughtful about the world, but without dropping its fundamentally consumer orientation.

Arfango Brand belonging to Calzolai e Pellettieri, a public company established in Florence in 1902, and known for its handmade products and its respect for a tradition that made Florence the capital of the art of working in leather. Arfango is celebrated all over the world for its aged leather and its process of tanning leather in a pit. This is a method which goes back to the 15th century: after several operations of cleaning, preparing, and stripping, the hide is placed in very large tubs of water to which are added oak and mimosa bark extract. At the end of this procedure, the hide is greased, softened, and let dry for four months, then pulled in a way to make it smooth and even. Now it is ready to be polished by hand with seaweed and wax.

❑ 2003. Arfango offered a Collection of bags and accessories with matching leather outerwear.

Argence French house for luxury women's shoes, established in 1900. Its first shop was in Paris on rue du Faubourg Saint-Honoré, and then it moved to rue des Pyramides, where it remained until the early 1980s, when the firm closed down. The Argence shoe Collection is kept at the International Museum of Shoes Paris.

Argentina High-necked crewneck sweater, straight and almost rectangular in shape, with wide armholes and long sleeves, manufactured in various yarns such as wool, interlock and cotton.

Argentovivo One of six brands – the others are Bacirubati and Azuleja for women, Julipet, Allen Cox and Jamas for men – belonging to the Arcte Group from Bologna, a leader in the production and distribution of underwear and swimwear. In addition to the Argentovivo line, which presents two Collections a year, one for underwear and corsetry and the other for homewear, plus a Summer Collection of swimwear and beachwear, starting in 2000 Arcte began to enlarge and differentiate its primary line by creating and marketing new lines based on it. These included Argentovivo Project underwear, Argentovivo Moiré beachwear and swimwear, manufactured in basic styles but with high-tech and hypoallergenic materials, and Argentovivo Line-Up, with a design meant to emphasize the curves of the body. At present there is in Italy only one Argentovivo single-brand boutique – owned directly by the Group, in Bologna. But the brand is distributed in the most important cities in Italy and abroad, including France, Great Britain, Belgium, Greece and Spain. For the Italian market, the Arcte business plan includes various partnership agreements.

(*Sara Tieni*)

Argyle A pattern named after a Scottish clan and a geographic area in western Scotland. It is a classic lozenge motif, obtained by inlay or jacquard, typical of Scottish knee socks and sweaters. It is used especially in knitwear for pullovers, cardigans and scarves, and for socks and tights in wool and nylon. It has been back in fashion since 2000. Vivienne Westwood has used it for tights as a contrast under her tartan skirts.

(*Gabriella Gregorietti*)

Arianna Italian monthly published by Mondadori from 1957 to 1973. Starting with its first issue, published in April with Rosanna Armani on the cover, Arianna tried to focus on a readership of young women mostly out on their own and independent of their family. The magazine was one of several innovative editorial initiatives by Mondadori, of which the weekly Epoca was the centerpiece. It was also part of a comprehensive redesign undertaken in order to confront strong competition from the magazines published by Rizzoli. Lamberto Sechi was the founder and director of the magazine, and later would be the director of Panorama. Gianni Baldi became his successor. After a period of moderate success, sales began to drop. The crisis was irreversible and in a sense the magazine practically disappeared, as due to a total restyling the magazine returned to the newsstands with a completely different layout under the name Cosmopolitan-Arianna as a large-format paper taking a teasing look at the moderate areas of feminism.

(*Stefano Grassi*)

Arkadius Brand created by the Polish designer Arkadius Weremczuk (1969), now living in London. He left his native country and the study of teaching in 1992 in order to become a designer. After a picaresque journey through Tuscany, where he worked as a dish washer, and to Munich, where he worked as a commercial artist, he finally arrived in London where he attended the Central St. Martins College of Art and Design. He proved to have a singular determination, just like his decidedly strong and sexy style. His student work was noticed by Isabella Blow, the muse of Alexander McQueen, who would later support his first Collection. Blow herself became his manager. The House of Arkadius was founded in London in 1999. Success was immediate, and among his customers were the hottest names in pop music and international show business. He was given the Elle Magazine award for Best Polish Designer 2000, and was chosen by Placido Domingo to design the costumes of *Don Giovanni*, co-produced by the Los Angeles Opera and the Polish National Opera. His creations can be found in the most daring boutiques in the world, but he also has his own store in the center of London.

(*Virginia Hill*)

Armand Basi Catalan manufacturer of men's, women's and children's wear. In the 1940s, Josep Armand Basi opened a small tailor's shop in Barcelona. In the next twenty years the shop grew to become such a large company that in 1961 it obtained the exclusive license to manufacture the French brand Lacoste in Spain. The 1970s were a turning point for the company, marked by the arrival of Juste de Nin, who was appointed artistic director and brought a modern touch to the Collections. A new plant at Badalona, near Barcelona, was opened in 1987, and in 1994 the firm entered markets in other European countries, in Asia, and in the U.S. The following year it opened its first London store, followed by a store in the Paseo de Gracia in Barcelona. This period saw the brand's first presentations at Men's Fashion Week in Paris, as well the grand opening, once again in London, of an exclusive boutique on elegant Conduit Street in Mayfair.

(*Maddalena Fossati*)

Armani Giorgio (1934). Italian designer, born in Piacenza. By far the dominant figure in the extraordinary flourishing of high fashion prêt-à-porter which spread from Milan throughout the world. An individual who, due to his physical charm, detached manner, and ability to merge work and environment in a vision that is simple, concise, rigorous, and clear, has seemed to express a perfect symbiosis between his own lifestyle and the elegance of his models. His economic empire (a turnover in 1997 of €1,900 and more than 2,000 select shops throughout the world) is the reward not only of creativity and imagination, as it is for many other famous names in fashion. His success expresses a creative power that has been able to interpret desires, reconcile opposing needs and brilliantly reinvent a basic article of clothing. Armani himself embodies the success of his famous jacket which freed men from the old armor of the bourgeois suit, gave women self-confidence in a masculine look, and, as it was said during the 1970s, helped them more than did feminism itself. The designer began his spectacular career in prêt-à-porter at the age of 40, after a long, multifaceted and invaluable apprenticeship in which he learned much, both about taste and about the relationship between fashion and business. After interrupting the study of medicine, in the 1960s he worked at La Rinascente, at the time a true crucible for the creative skills of architects, designers, market researchers and advertising experts. His activity was wide-ranging and went from the buying of men's clothing, and figuring out from the market, with sufficient lead time for manufacturing, how many people wanted a change of wardrobe, to window displays. Even today he can't resist the impulse to spend an entire morning on the windows of one of his many boutiques. In 1965 Nino Cerruti noticed his talent and hired him to redesign his Hitman line. By this time already precise and meticulous, Armani learned the importance of fabrics, both for their creative possibilities and for the economic value of even one inch of material saved in the cost of a garment. He began to design clothes in a way that would afford economies of scale manufacturing. He spent seven years at Cerruti, selecting fabrics that were lighter and lighter, colors that were colder, making everything less structured, changing buttons, and narrowing the shoulders, all in order to give the men's jacket, up to that time a formal and stiff garment, a supple and real-life look, youthful for all ages. It was the 1970s, and the fashion world, on both sides of the Atlantic, adored the early Made in Italy lines, while new social classes were ready for the idea that one needs good clothes in order to emphasize personal success. Sergio Galeotti, a young man from Viareggio who had just left an architecture studio to become a model buyer, realized that Armani couldn't remain a designer who worked for others, but had to have a Collection of his own. Cautious and somewhat distracted, Armani took two years to convince himself, in 1973, to open his own consulting business with Galeotti in Milan, while still working for various firms – from Gibò and Montedoro to Tendresse, Courslande and Sicons – and quickly entered his name in the final fashion shows at Palazzo Pitti in Florence. Scarcely a year later, in 1974, his first men's Collection came out, and, in 1975, the first women's Collection. It was such a triumph that in 1976 the Giorgio Armani company was born. Galeotti conceived the company's structure: no in-house manufacturing, only the production of ideas. The formula was reaffirmed in 1978 in the agreement with GFT, the first to make possible high fashion prêt-à-porter produced in a factory but under the close eye of the designer. Very soon, Armani's shows became the most anticipated, both for the clothes and for the decor. The farsightedness of the new *griffe* was constant, guided by the notion that young people especially would be the consumers of fashion, as long as it remained affordable and did not lose its appeal. Very quickly in comparison with other lines, Emporio Armani became a reality. The eagle became for young men a sign of belonging to a new style of dressing and of being; a loose-fitting, agile, less solemn look attractive to women. Armani's fame grew quickly. In 1981, annoyed by polemics over a Collection inspired by ancient Japanese costumes, following some of Kurosawa's films, he decided to stay away from the fashion shows for a season, and Time Magazine, finding the protest explosive, put his picture on the cover. In 1982 the turnover tripled. Meanwhile, his consulting services were requested by Mario Valentino, for his Collection of leather goods, by Erreuno, and by licensees wanting to use his trademark, such as Bagutta for men's shirts, Hilton for cloaks, and Allegri for raincoats. His unmistakable and ever-varied touch lights up a decade of work, while his fundamental research in high fashion prêt-à-porter leads to results of such refinement that they can no longer be produced in a factory. In 1983 Armani changed his agreement with GFT, which from that point on would produce a new line, Mani, intended essentially for the U.S, while high fashion prêt-à-porter would use the label Borgonuovo 21, the street in Milan where he restored and rented the palazzo that once belonged to Franco Marinotti (Snia Viscosa) and the cotton manufacturers Riva. Shows are mounted in a 513-seat theater that once was the ballroom and swimming pool. Galeotti was barely able to manage the showing of the Spring-Summer Collection for 1985 and would die in August of that very same year. The second decade of activity finds Armani alone but poised, thanks to study and a strong will, to add to his great achievements a real revolution in women's clothing. The world was changing and women no longer needed to camouflage themselves, or to hide their bodies in the looseness of a perfect jacket. The novelty of of the Autumn-Winter 1986 Collection was the evening dress. Armani's woman, a mix of seduction and common sense, could count on an Armani universe: from perfume to timeless high fashion prêt-à-porter, similar to herself with minimal change, from writing paper to lamps, in a line that was more free and well-developed in the various aspects of its diffusion, the Emporio line. Loved by the elite and by mass consumers, adored by the critics, Armani was three times awarded the *Occhio d'Oro* in Italy for the Season's Best Collection, and has received many honors throughout the world. He dressed Catherine Deneuve in *Speriamo che sia femmina*, Richard Gere in *American Gigolo* and provided costumes for the Strauss opera *Elektra* at La Scala, directed by Luca Ronconi with stage-designs by Gae Aulenti. Today Armani has five lines: Borgonuovo 21, G.A., Collezioni Mani, AX (basic fashions sold in the shop of the same name in the U.S.) and Armani Jeans, plus the linen, underwear and swimwear lines. Analyzing the stylistic development over what is by now 25 years of activity, certain constants emerge and some variations from his characteristic rigor can be seen. The taste and logic of his first revolution are never diminished, either in the men's or the women's Collections, with their mutual exchanges of particular elements not only in terms of shape and cut, but also in the selection of interchangeable colors, in their materials, in a masculine appearance, a loose and soft hand or, viceversa, in shirts and jackets with a female touch for a man of a disconcerting freedom. The George Sand of Spring 1976, in the winter of that year wore tweed jackets with a bold pattern, very macsculine, but accompanied by a plissé skirt which, like trousers, allowed a loose and long stride. In Spring 1977 there were two skirts, overlapping, while the men's jacket took on sophisticated accents, and the idea of "doubling" passed to men's clothing as well, when a knitted jacket was put over a blazer. The jacket was destined to join every other element of clothing. In 1978 it went with a bathing suit, in the fall it combined with military colors. There was continuous research into everything to do with the shoulders, and the result was a "Garbo" long-wearing even in crêpe de chine. But the evolution of the jacket in 1983 was based on three items: the blazer in black velvet, the long-sleeve jacket with round shoulders, and the *caban* of Andean origin. There were few trousers and, instead, many varieties of culottes in very new tromp-

A sketch by Giorgio Armani for his Women's Spring-Summer 1997 Collection.

l'oeil designs. The jacket was transformed, becoming an interchangeable item or a piece to be combined freely. Only in 1984 was there a return to the taste for a men's wardrobe with a hint of the feminine, an androgynous Collection like no other. But the following year, for the Autumn-Winter Collection, Armani showed his sweet side, presenting a masculine jacket, but loose and down buttoned, for an easy-going woman with hair up and a neckless blouse. It was a show with 350 different fabrics varying in shades of blue, grey, and brown. In October 1985 the Spring-Summer Collection won extraordinary success with its ethereal, stylized woman, her legs covered by very clear stockings and completely in view, wearing high heels. It was a femininity somewhat difficult and yet in some ways too much on display. It was a change in Armani's usually sober look. The jacket is always the clue to understanding a style, but new suggestions came from the princess dresses in printed silk. In 1986 evening wear outdid day clothes – according to the demands of the American market. The Armani woman, self-confident and without nostalgia, chose a jacket that was no longer rigid and severe, breaking the rules of jacket-and-blouse in favor of daring new combinations (1987). From then on (1988), the Autumn-Winter Collection was characterized by an atmosphere that was soft and light in color, and by the subtle provocation of a jacket resting on the waist and the hips, with long, double skirts. In 1990 once again the jacket was the focal point, slim, wrapped, with small shoulders and a marked waist. The skirts were short or to the calf, the trousers sometimes straight and severe or else full like a man's. It was a choice of dusty, sharp colours, though tempered by the greys and sandy earth tones typical of the Armani palette. In addition, there were the great envelopping overcoats such as the Tunisian *djellaba*. In 1992 smoking was the season's trademark, variously interpreted in combination with extremely feminine fabrics and details. New flexibilities, new concessions, very new luxury. Elegant fabrics used in casual clothes was a special characteristic of 1994, enhanced by a color palette in ruby inspired by Matisse. Waistcoats peep out under jackets; trousers are as long as they can be, and long skirts trimmed with fringes take center stage. Evening dresses display an imperious elegance in their colors and precious fabrics, yet with shapes reduced to the essentials. The Autumn-Winter 1996 Collections showed great refinement and a love for structure which revealed itself in the ankle-length overcoats with velvet facings and *matelassé* lining. The repeated and refined use of fabrics cut on-the-bias, caressing the body, is more popular than ever. Also the favorites of the evening, from the "boldinian" style dress in silk velvet tied at the neck by a necklace of roses, to the sheath dress in black stretch tulle with tatoo embroidery. The year 1997 saw the arrival

A Giorgio Armani's sketch for the Autumn-Winter 1990-91 Men's Collection.

of "sophisticated grege," a new shade between grey and beige. Lean shapes, small proportions, a symbolic simplicity. Refined fabrics such as *plissé* wools, *matelassé*, double *crêpe*. And for evening, everything is precious: graphic embroidery in ivory and ebony, lace and velvet. The style is by now more and more defined and authoritative. It doesn't change. What do change are the methods, the movements, and the details, with greatest importance given to refinement in materials and the finishing touches of master tailoring, which combined to make sophistication the main idea of the season. During 1998-1999 evening is more and more the singular moment, with embroidered dresses inspired by oriental porcelains. The jackets, slim, without lapels, and with fastenings that are hidden and often on the side, have lost the connection with tailored suits and are worn even with long dresses, low-waist trousers, and long, straight skirts in order to accentuate the silhouette. And there are plenty of dustcoats, a series of overcoats cut like jackets, which are long and slinky. For 2000 the image is strong, consistent, glamorous, pure and precise: love at first sight, with English pastel shades and a special regard for black. Ankle-length skirts, short jackets with wide kimono sleeves, jackets cut like Indian blouses, slim trousers under tunics and extra-large trousers with a man's shirt. A refined evening with the new idea of "light catchers" made of stretch tulle worked in the shape of a web, with a deliberately consistent choice of clear and sharp lines on the body. The Armani woman entered the third millennium with an allure that was up to date and sparkling, with one eye on the use and management of style, and the other on the passions of the young, but always aware that the power of her own image lay in the unbeatable Armani style, with his special colors, a skillful line and expert cut. This is a woman gliding with lightness, grace and incomparable class, leaving behind her the inevitable strains of a modernism that is often coarse or simply too ugly. The latest Collection, already looking toward the new millennium, G.A. Man in Spring-Summer 2000, has reconfirmed the primary place Giorgio Armani in the men's wear industry.

(*Lucia Sollazzo*)

❑ Femininity and romanticism: from these two words Armani's new woman was born. The look came out for Winter 2001-2002 and evoked the emotion of a debutante's ball with skirts of frilly tulle and handkerchiefs of organza cut on the bias worn with long pullovers inspired by the sea or with small tops. Graceful girls paraded past, as if dancing on pointe: "Ballet is the apotheosis of elegance", said the designer. Everything was delicate and ethereal, seeming to hint at dreamy sensations. The show's finale was memorable, with 30 real ballet dancers posing like those of Degas. It confirmed what had been seen in the previous season, with tailored pantsuits characterized by an unusual sweetness, a vague reCollection of the manager-woman. The soft mood was also more in evidence in the shows that followed. And the classic blazer? It adapted to the new trend and in Summer 2003 became longer, almost a tailcoat waving on a slender body. Unusual pieces broke the familiar rhythm of the ensembles, sensuality was all on edge without any exotic nostalgia or erotic aggression. In Autumn-Winter 2003-2004 Armani again changed course. His designs gave the body a new outline, emphasizing it and caressing a waist made prominent by short and close-fitting jackets. Then, in a surprise, he pays tribute to women's legs with triangular miniskirts and shorts, a gentle reinterpretation of the hot pants of the 1970s. It was a very stylish woman, almost dipped in ink, in the severity of black broken up by lines of white, for an evocative graphic effect. As usual, his clothes needed to be admired up close, for the sophisticated details and refined fabrics. It was like a heaven of embroidery. He lowered the age of the fashion-conscious, which the Emporio line accentuated through the impertinent and teasing style of the French tomboy, with everything made "short." His men's style was also updated, an image somewhere between reason and sentiment, the silent revolutionary of a new classicism that still observed the rules of comfort, particularly in his knitwear creations.

(*Lucia Mari*)

❑ 1999, September. Giorgio Armani SpA opened the accessories division, with the goal of improving their results in leather goods. Dawn Mello & Associates entrusted with the account for the new division.
❑ 1999, September. The commercial structure of the Group (direct and franchising), operating in 33 countries, includes 53 Giorgio Armani Boutiques, 6 Collezioni stores, 129 Emporio Armani, 48 A/X Armani Exchange, and 4 Armani Jeans.
❑ 2000, January. Giorgio Armani SpA raises its stake in Giorgio Armani Japan Co. Ltd., a joint venture founded in 1995, to 85% of the shares, leaving the remaining 15% to Itochu.
❑ 2000, February. Birth of Armani Collezioni which brings together, in Europe and in Asia, the already-existing Giorgio Armani, Collezioni Uomo and Mani Donna. The new label is also introduced in the U.S., while the Mani Uomo line of suits and shirts remains solely in the American market.
❑ 2000, June. The Armani Group purchases for 55 billion liras from GFT the manufacturing business of the men's line Armani Collezioni as well as its distribution and sales in the U.S.
❑ 2000, July. Armani Group and Zegna Group agree to create a joint venture (51% to Armani, 49% to Zegna) to manufacture and distribute the Armani Collezioni lines. The goal is to exploit to the maximum the potential of the Armani Collezioni Uomo brand throughout the world, and the Mani Uomo brand in the U.S., using the manufacturing and organizational skills of both groups.
❑ 2000, October. The opening of new stores continues. An Armani shop opens at via Manzoni 31, in Milan. Designed by Studio Gabellini Associates, in collaboration with Armani himself, the megastore has some 80,000 square feet on three floors. The 1,000 square foot basement is used to sell electronics, especially by Sony. On the ground floor are Emporio Donna, Emporio Uomo, Emporio Accessori, a space dedicated to perfumes, and Armani Jeans for men and women. On the second floor, in addition to the restaurant Nobu and to Armani Caffé there is Armani Casa.
❑ 2000. The year shows consolidated revenues of 2,002 billion liras, a 20% increase compared to 1999, a gross margin of 374 billion liras, a net consolidated profit of 235 billion liras, an 11% increase, and a net worth amounting to 618 billion liras.
❑ 2001, February. Opening of the first Giorgio Armani Accessori boutique, at via della Spiga 19, in Milan. On sale are high-quality bags, shoes and leather goods.
❑ 2001, May. Giorgio Armani SpA, already owner of 53.2% of the capital stock of Simint Spa – an Italian company listed on the Electronic Stock Exchange – announces a tender offer for the Simint common stock that it does not already own. The price offered per share is €6.2. The goal is to activate a process of internationalizing the production and marketing activities of Armani products within the companies of the Group.
❑ 2001, July. As a result of the bid for Simint, 39.49% of Simint's shares are added to the 53.24% already owned by the Armani Group, thus giving Armani control of 92.73% of the company.
❑ 2001. Giorgio Armani Japan, founded in 1987 as a joint venture with Itochu Corporation, reorganized its retail activities in Japan. The program entailed the reopening, after a thorough renovation, of the world's largest Armani store, in a manner consistent with the image of the new Armani boutiques on via Sant'Andrea in Milan, on Place Vendôme in Paris, and in Kioicho, Tokyo. Then new Emporio Armani stores were opened in Marunouchi and Aoyama, and the Emporio Armani in Midosuji was renovated. The Japanese market ranked third in order of importance after the U.S. (34%) and Italy (15%). Giorgio Armani Japan distributes five lines belonging to the Armani Group: Giorgio Armani, Giorgio Armani Accessori, Armani Collezioni, Emporio Armani and Armani Jeans. The company manages 22 shops; 10 Giorgio Armani boutiques, 1 Armani Collezioni shop and 11 Emporio

Armani. The Giorgio Armani and Armani Collezioni lines are also sold through the shop-within-a-shop formula.

❑ 2001, July. Roberto Pesaro was appointed Chief Operating Officer of Giorgio Armani Corporation.

❑ 2001, October. Armani opened its first boutique in Rusia, in Moscow at no. 1 Tretyakovsky Lane. It was the 33rd point-of-sale opened by Armani in the year 2001, resuming the strategy of expanding the exclusive retail network. Twenty shops were completely renovated.

❑ 2001. A new joint venture, Borgo 21, was created to develop the top line of the Armani brand.

❑ 2001. Consolidated revenues reached €1,272 million, an increase of 23% which included all the geographic areas and all the lines. The turnover was distributed as follows: Europe 45%, North America 28%, Asia-Pacific and rest of the world 27%. The net consolidated profit was €110 million, the net worth €122 million, with investments of €307 million.

❑ 2002, January. Armani acquires 100% of Miss Deanna, a firm specialized the production of high quality knitwear.

❑ 2002, November. The Armani-Chater House megastore in Hong Kong opened, with 30,000 square feet on three floors, second in size only to the one on via Manzoni in Milan.

❑ 2002, November. Armani Group and Luxottica Group ended their licensing agreement for the production and distribution of glasses in the Giorgio Armani and Emporio Armani lines.

❑ 2002. The yearly results showed growth in the main indicators. The consolidated turnover, €1,301 million, showed a 2.3% increase compared to 2001. The induced turnover, €1,691 million, grew 6.4%. There was considerable growth in Emporio Armani Watches, 24%, and in cosmetics, 11%. Profits before tax, €199 million, grew 9.7%. Also noteworthy were investments of €87 million, devoted, among other things, to the expansion of the distribution network (30 new stores and 16 renovations) and to the acquisition of manufacturing plants. Finally, the Group invested 10% of the induced turnover communications.

❑ 2003, February. The Group gave Sàfilo a long-term license for the production and worldwide distribution of the Giorgio Armani and Emporio Armani watch Collections.

❑ 2003, February. The Group's exclusive distribution network comprised 57 Giorgio Armani boutiques, 12 Armani Collezioni shops, 115 Emporio Armani shops, 66 A/X Armani Exchange shops, 10 Armani Jeans shops, 5 Armani Junior shops, and 12 Armani Casa shops, in 35 countries around the world.

❑ 2003, June. The Giorgio Armani boutique on via Condotti in Rome reopened after a total renovation. Armani himself worked on the restyling along with the architect Claudio Silvestrin.

❑ 2003, September. Mercedes-Benz and Giorgio Armani entered into a joint venture for the creation of the Mercedes-Benz CLK Giorgio Armani Design Car. Armani said, "Mercedes-Benz has achieved extraordinary fame for the quality, style and elegance of its cars. For me, it's been very interesting to observe how similar our design philosophies and system of working are. This makes me think that in the future there will be more opportunities to carry out common projects which can develop our respective strengths."

❑ 2003, October. John Hooks was appointed the new President of Giorgio Armani Japan. Armani continued to as commercial director of the group.

❑ 2003, December. The third and largest of Armani's multi-concept stores, the Armani/Funf-Hofe, was opened on Theatinerstrasse in Munich, joining in the Armani on via Manzoni in Milan and the Armani/Chater House in Hong Kong.

❑ 2003, December. The economic-financial results for 2003 were brilliant. The consolidated turnover €1,255 million grew 3% at constant exchange rates. The net profit of €134 million increased 14%. Also excellent was the increase in net worth which grew 149%, In 2002, it grew to €264 million. In the same year the company invested €38 million, mainly in distribution, with 30 new sales points opened and 11 restyled.

❑ 2004, February. The Armani group diversified into luxury hotels. It signed with EMAAR Properties PJSC, the largest real estate company in the Middle East, a memo of understanding for the creation of Armani resorts and luxury hotels. The collaboration called for the opening of ten hotels and four resorts within seven years. The total investment was projected at about 1 billion dollars. EMAAR was to manage the construction and managerial aspects and Armani would be responsible for style and design.

❑ 2004, March. Signed a multi-year license agreement with Wolford AG for the production and worldwide distribution of the Giorgio Armani hosiery line.

❑ 2004, April. The fourth multi-concept store was opened in the Three on the Bund, Shanghai.

❑ 2004, June. An Armani store opened in Dubai.

❑ 2004, July. Fortune Magazine published a list of the 25 most powerful men in European business. Giorgio Armani was the only Italian, ranked number 25.

❑ 2004, August. New Emporio Armani stores opened in Riga and Shanghai.

❑ 2004, September. A shop with the new Emporio Armani concept opened in Paris. "The new design of the Emporio Armani in St. Germain belongs to a strategy aimed at strengthening and differentiating the various product lines and at creating an environment in which the store's architecture lends support to the presentation of the Collections in a way that is modern and accessible to the clients," said Giorgio Armani.

❑ 2004, September. An Armani Jeans shop opened in Corso di Porta Ticinese in Milan. It was designed by the architects Massimiliano and Doriana Fuksas. An Armani Jeans Café was opened inside.

❑ 2004, October. At the Armani boutique on Maidson Avenue, the model Eugenia Silva organized a charity sale for the benefit of the American Museum of Natural History.

❑ 2004, October. Armani was given the Superstar Award at the Night of Stars Awards of Fashion Group International.

❑ 2004, December. The year closed with a turnover of €1,299 billion, an increase of 6.5% at constant exchange rates and 3.5% at current exchange rates. The net profit was €126 million euros, a slight decline -5.2% compared the previous year. The net worth was €397 million, an excellent increase of 50.3% over the €264 million of 2003. Investments were €50 million, of which €35 million was used for the opening of 16 new stores and the restyling of the existing ones.

❑ 2005, January. The designer made his début in haute couture, presenting in Paris the first Giorgio Armani Privé Collection. Thirty-one clothes in pure Armani style, very precious and unique.

❑ 2005, March. The first quarter registered growth in direct sales in company-owned stores of 16% compared to the first quarter of 2004. In particular, sales in China increased 52%, in Japan 15%, in Europe 10%, and in the U.S. 3%.

❑ 2005, March. A new single-brand Armani Casa store opened at via Manzoni, 37 in Milan.

❑ 2005, April. Armani was appointed Designer of the Year by the Fashion Editors Club of Japan.

❑ 2005, April. The Giorgio Armani exhibition moved from the Guggenheim to the Mori Art Museum of Tokyo. For the occasion, the men's and women's Collections of Autumn-Winter 2005-2006 were presented. The show was followed by the first presentation of Armani's haute couture Collection.

❑ 2005, April. The group had 4,700 workers, 13 production plants, 58 Giorgio Armani boutiques, 11 Armani Collezioni stores, 121 Emporio Armani stores, 70 A/X Armani Exchange stores, 12 AJ/Armani Jeans stores, 6 Armani Junior stores, 1 Giorgio Armani Accessories store, and 17 Armani Casa stores, distributed in 37 countries throughout the world. The group's

brand are: Giorgio Armani, Armani Collezioni, Emporio Armani, AJ/Armani Jeans, A/X Armani Exchange, Armani Junior and Armani Casa.
❑ 2005, May. Armani dressed the English national soccer team for its tour of exhibition matches in the U.S.
❑ 2005, June. Armani designed the uniforms of the crew of the Bribon, the new sailing ship of the King of Spain.
(*Dario Golizia*)

Armani Misia (1905-1994). Italian journalist. She was among the first, in the 1930s, to have her own fashion column in a prestigious weekly, L'Illustrazione Italiana. She later worked on the magazines Metropoli and Il Mondo Tessile. In 1947 she moved to I Tessili Nuovi, which, in 1950, accepted her suggestion and changed its name to Linea. In 1962, with the help of colleagues such as Vera Rossi and Elsa Robiola, she created the Premio Critica della Moda award given by Italian jounalists. In 1966 she was among the founders of Linea Italiana, the magazine of the Centro Italiano della Moda (Italian Fashion Centrer), which was later absorbed by Mondadori and became the official magazine of Italian fashion. She was born in Pavia, but spent her life and career in Milan.

Armor-Lux French brand of knitwear. It was created in Quimper, Brittany, in September 1938 – in the days of the false peace signed in Munich – by the Swiss-German Walter Hubacher (1907) and two partners, Daniel Bloch and Charles Perrenot. Hubacher had 16 years' experience working in large factories that made underwear and other articles of clothing. The business had a very good start but in 1942 the lack of raw materials forced the closing of the firm. It was able to reopen in 1945, although starting again from scratch. Results were not good until 1959 when Hubacher obtained control and for nine years invested 7.20% of the turnover in new manufacturing plants. The result was growth of 20% per year. In 1993, the 86 year-old Hubacher sold a majority stake to Jean-Guy Le Floch, who increased the number of brands, took aim at the Asian market, hired the Japanese designer Zucca to create a new Collection, and increased export revenues.

❑ 2002, September. The firm sponsored the around-the-world solo voyage of the sailor Bernard Stamm.
❑ There were 40 Armor-Lux shops in France. The Group employed 635 workers who manufactured about about 20,000 pieces a day. Annual sales were 4 million pieces, with 20% destined for the European and Japanese markets.
❑ Eight Collections per year, including the Terre et Mer line for women, wool garments by Guy de Berac, the Britain Stock line, the new born Armor Kids line, and the Armor Baby line.

Arms Homer notices them. He praises the arms of goddesses who scheme over the fortunes of quarrelsome mortals, when from the sky they descend to earth wrapped in an aura of ambrosia. And what more seductive emotion could there be for the shipwrecked Ulysses at his meeting with "Nausicaa of the white arms"? Slim arms; solemn as the stylized dresses in which they offer themselves to the eye, like those of the women of Egypt; the enchanting arms of Greek girls, round and soft, wrapped in their pleated tunics. Arms that disappear in a vast uproar of cloaks and mantles or, more simply, in sleeves, for which fashion always has its

Dress of 1927: the deep neckline emphasizes arms (Prints Collection A. Bertarelli, Milan).

rules. Large sleeves for ladies who live in medieval castles, doubled and cut so as liberate the puffs of a concealed blouse; close-fitting but worked determinedly upward, between shoulder and forearm, during the Renaissance. If not, what could a lady like Laura Gonzaga have had to talk about when writing to Isabella of Mantua on the subject of Lucrezia Borgia's dress, made all in satin with gold fringes on a black ground, and the sleeves as well ? On the other hand, there was no niggling critic like St. Bernardino, no well-meaning prohibition, to be concerned in some strange way with naked arms, not even when the 17th century, besides its shoulder-to-shoulder necklines, put them on display and revealed them in all their luxuriance. Besides, completely naked arms would appear only during the period of the Directorate when in France a sometimes exasperated interest in the ancient world lived on in every way from clothing to furniture, and the uniform of the elegant woman was the chemise decorated with embroidery in Greek motifs, a tunic in light batiste with a long vent on the side, the waist under the breasts, so light as to be transparent, so that – even if for a short time – corsets and stays disappeared. It was natural that the moralists and enforcers, always lying in wait, would have other things to think about, that nude, almost-available breast, a much aimed-at target, but now women feel comfortable in showing even their legs. The arms, beautiful and chaste, have become calm. So much so that Napoleon would have them covered, at least at court, because spending on luxury could rescue the economy. Then, among crinolines, with chaste clothes during the day and deep necklines at night, arms once again took center stage. Especially in the 1920s when the flapper fashion spread over Europe. The lady, with short hair and a boyish figure, like a butterfly escaped from the most painful corsets in history, finally had arms and legs. Breasts were nonexistent, but in the evening shoulders and arms were bare and bejewelled, not in metal or precious stones, but with the special creations of the goldsmith. Arms sparkled in the very elegant, poised fashion of the 1930s, in the reflection of a naked back. Then women gave up the long gloves that went up to the armpits and devoted themselves to the fashion for toned muscles, free time, with the help of sports, and the desire for a suntan. Besides, the arm-holes of American dresses and T-shirts also involve the armpits, even if between the nostalgia for revivals and the transparencies of the nude look, nudity is so evident that why bother to talk about the arms any more? It's easier for them to be noticed in a stretch T-shirt which shows off the bust and makes them look thinner, in a new, if rehabilitated, frailty.

(*Lucia Sollazzo*)

Armstrong Jones Antony (1930). English photographer, born in Sussex. He began to take photographs when still a student at Eaton and Cambridge, becoming a professional in 1951. He quickly became famous thanks to a refined and rigorous style, publishing photos in Life, Vogue, Geo, Stern, Paris Match, and Look. In 1960 he married Princess Margaret (from whom he was to divorce a few years later), the sister of Queen Elisabeth II, who bestowed on him the title of Lord Snowdon. In 1961 he signed an exclusive contract with the Sunday Times and joined the staff of the Council of Industrial Design. In addition to his fashion photographs, taken almost exclusively for the English edition of Vogue, he shot reportage and social documentaries for the BBC, receiving various prizes and awards.

Army surplus Those who have never walked through a market selling second-hand goods, or army surplus merchandise, on the model of the one in Livorno, will never know how important the surplus jackets, trousers, and heavy boots of the American military wardrobe are for a certain type of Italian man. With these rejects entire generatiions of students dressed themselves (before and after the Eskimo), as a form of protest, for comfort, as a political choice, and to be part of the crowd. More than a fashion, it was a declaration of intent, yet limited to the casual and to the street style of '68.

(*Stefano Bucci*)

Arnault Bernard (1949). French entrepreneur. He leads the LVMH Group, an empire of luxury goods which includes Dior, Lacroix, Vuitton, Moët Hennessy, Kenzo, Guerlain and the Bon Marché department stores. He seemed to be destined for a career as a builder when, as a graduate of the École Polytechnique, he began to manage his father's construction company. The turning point came in the early 1980s. Prompted to do so by the government, he purchased the textile group Boussac Saint-Frères, then in bankruptcy. The group included Dior and Bon Marché, thanks to investments that it had made. This was the beginning. In 1997, the group had a turnover of more than FFr 14,000 billion, with a net profit of FFr 1,336 billion. In Winter 1999, he became the main stockholder of Gucci. But his control was blocked by an alliance between management and the French financier François Pinault. At the end of that year, on October 12, he acquired, together with Prada, 51% of Fendi.

Arnold Janet (1932-1998). English historian of clothing. After her art studies in Bristol, her hometown, she worked for various English theaters as a consultant in historical costumes. She then worked as a commercial model maker in London, first for Frederick Starke and then for Victor Stiebel. Again in London, she taught the history of costume in the theatre. Her meticulous research on the cutting and constructiion of historical garments were published to noteworthy success. The handbook series *Patterns of Fashion*, with its precise and easy-to-follow drawings, is indispensable for costume designers and historians. Among her most important studies was the reconstruction of the garments belonging to Cosmo I and Eleanor of Toledo from a series of fragments found in the Medici tombs in Florence. In England she became the authority on the wardrobe of Queen Elizabeth I thanks to her research published in the 1988 book *Queen Elisabeth's Wardrobe Unlock'd.* In the decade before her death she was invited to give lectures all over the world. The Victoria and Albert Museum dedicated a retrospective to her in 1998-1999. (*Virginia Hill*)

Arrow Long-established American brand of shirts. It began at the end of the 1800s through the merger of Maullin-Blanchard of Troy, New York with Coo & Company. In 1913 the business was relaunched by Cluett-Peabody & Co., which hired the well-known publicity agent J.C. Leyendecker to promote The Arrow Collar Man and shirts that had special removable collars. In the 1920s, the Arrow catalogue included more than 400 collar models. The stiff collar went out of fashion and the company turned to a sewn-collar shirt. In the 1930s the firm was saved by its patent for the "sanforized" process, named after its inventor, Sanford L. Cluett. It is a method to avoid the shrinking of cotton during washing. Arrow was also the manufacturer of the first colored shirts. In 1962 the brand followed a policy of expansion into export markets. Today, as part of the French group Bidermann, it is present in 78 countries.

❑ At the turn of the century Arrow's garments were exported to India, the Middle East, Australia and Hong Kong.
❑ 2000. The new casual lines America's Khakis and America's Golf are launched. Distribution in the Philippines and South Africa was started, along with a new joint venture for the Chinese market.
❑ 2003. Selling figures showed that Arrow dominates the market for white shirts in India. That is traditionally the best selling garment in the country. Some 11% of the brand's 55 million shirts produced in India each year are white. Arrow shares the top spot in the market with Louis Philippe, followed by Van Heusen and Zodiac, A total of 295 million shirts, branded and not branded, are sold in the country each year.

Arsenico & Breakfast Store opened in 1968 in Turin, in via Gaudenzio Ferrari, close to the University, by Roberto Abate and Gina Gennari. In the wake of the events of 1968, they sold second-hand clothes found in London street markets. Within time the store began to specialize in second-hand American clothing, but also offering new clothing. For men there was a wide range of jeans, sweatshirts, and leather jackets for the air force and police, not to mention tuxedos. For women there were long party dresses in glamorous colors. Rock groups and theater companies were among the clientele.

Ars Rosa Women's underwear boutique in Milan. From the shop's first day in 1952, the window displays told passersby that Ars Rosa by Bettina Rossi would be the home of exquisite taste in lingerie, almost all in pure silk, shiny satin and linen blends, embellished by hand embroidery, valencienne lace and *broderies anglaises*. There were made-to-measure dressing gowns of tricot cashmere, warm, soft, and very beautiful in the brightest colors. The shop also offered baptism outfits for babies, and items for the trousseau, all handmade, of course.

(*Marilea Somaré*)

Art Agency Cerratelli Tailor shop providing costumes for the theater and film, opened in Florence in 1919 on the initiative of the baritone Arturo Cerratelli, one of the first performers in La Bohème. It is the oldest in Italy and has always belonged to the Cerratelli family, whose members work there. It has worked on countless plays, operas, and films. Many costume designers have made use of its expertise, among them Sensani, Anna Anni, Maria De Matteis, Danilo Donati, Marcel Escoffier, Ezio Frigerio, and Pier Luigi Pizzi. It first worked in the cinema with *An Adventure of Salvator Rosa*, followed by *El Cid*, *A Room With A View* and many films by Franco Zeffirelli, from *The Taming of the Shrew* to *Brother Sun, Sister Moon*. The firm's story was told in 1972 in an exhibition at Palazzo Strozzi in Florence. It's costumes have been an important part of many other exhibitions, including *Visuality of May* (Florence, Forte di Belvedere, 1979), *Franco Zeffirelli* (Tokyo, Seibu, 1989), *The Enchanting Artifice between Music and Vision. The Melodrama in Cinema* (Milan, Museo della Scala, 1995-1996), *Sensani* (San Casciano dei Bagni, 1998).

Art Déco (École Nationale Supérieure des Arts Décoratifs). It is, with Duperré's École Nationale Supérieure des Arts Appliquées, the only public school devoted to fashion in Paris. Admittance is by open competition and graduates receive a diploma issued by the state. It offers two courses of studies, one for textiles and the other for clothing.

Art-Goût-Beauté French monthly of the 1920s founded by the heirs of Albert Godde Bedin, a famous silk manufacturer in Lyon. At the beginning, the magazine favored articles about fabrics and their manufacture. Then there were stories about the history of costume, fashion, life in Paris, and high society. These alternated with pictures of models and illustrations of furs, hats, children's wear and accessories. At the time, this magazine was the symbol of Parisian elegance. It reproduced the creations of the great designers in their original colors. It was richly produced and printed on glossy paper, with articles written in three languages (French, English and German), and illustrated with small color prints and mezzotint engravings inserted into the text.

Artica Brand of knitwear for women and children established by the Tirelli family in 1956 in Carpi, Modena. Modena is a worldwide center for knitwear, after having been a center for the processing of straw used for hats.

Art Kane (1925-1995). American photographer, born in New York, in the Bronx, to a family of Russian Jewish immigrants. Art Kane, whose real name was Arthur Kanofsky, became famous as a graphic designer at a young age and, when 27, was hired by Esquire, the youngest art director of his time. He decided to become a photographer, and suffered a demanding apprenticeship under Alexey Brodovitch, the legendary art director at Harper's Bazaar. By the end of the 1950s Kane had made a name for himself in photography as well, thanks to a very personal style. He was the first, in fact, to use an extreme wide-angle lens of 21 mm and produced well-known images shot close-up from below of models such as Verushka, Jean Shrimpton, and Margaux Hemingway, published by Vogue, Look, Life, McCall's, Esquire and Harper's Bazaar. In addition to his fame as a fashion photographer, he is known for his photos of musicians, especially jazz musicians.

❑ Since his death, the artist's archive has been managed and preserved by the Art Kane Estate. His son Jonathan is an expert on the work and one of its greatest supporters.

❑ Kane's celebrated photograph in which the rock band The Who is completely wrapped in the flag is imitated by other young groups such as Oasis and repeated twenty years later by the original English band.

❑ 2002, August. The Govinda Gallery of Washington, D.C. mounted a solo exhibition for the artist, in collaboration with his foundation. Fashion photos and pictures of pop idols and various American celebrities were among the exhibited works.

Artom Guido (1931). Textile entrepreneur. He was president of Federtessile from 1975 to 1980, a time when the federation was only getting started and Italian prêt-à-porter was booming. With three vice-presidents, Angelo Pavia, Giancarlo Lombardi and Mario Boselli, at his side, he fought with success against *Progetto 80*, a government plan to help certain industries such as chemicals, electronics and aviation while excluding others such as clothing and textiles which were considered mature and not in need of assistance. He understood, as Beppe Modenese maintained, that the Italian fashion industry had to focus on Milan as the sole location for its shows in order to facilitate the work of journalists and to provide a comprehensive visual experience of the creative and entrepreneurial strength of Italian design. He joined with Modenese in trying (with success) to convince designers to present their Collections at the Fiera di Milano, of which, twenty years later in 1997, he would be appointed president. He resigned from the post in 1998 over a policy disagreement.

Art to Wear American movement founded by Julie Schafler Dale in the 1960s. It was based on the concept of clothes as a form of wearable art. After graduation from the School of Fine Arts of New York University, Dale became interested in the relationship between fashion and avant-guard art. In 1973 in Manhattan she opened the Artisans Gallery where she offered one-off designs quite different from what the clothing industry produced. She was in this way able to influence the most forward-looking fashion designers, often inspired by oriental cultures and primitive societies which didn't separate art from handicraft. The materials used by the artists belonging to this movement were very eclectic, ranging from leather to yarns, but also including feathers, paper, silicon, PVC, and metal, as in the gold blouse created by Mark Mahall in 1978 and made from 25,000 interlaced safety pins to form an iridescent fabric. This blouse is in the Collection of the Metropolitan Museum in New York. Paper hand-painted kimonos, silk tunics with designs printed in silicone – like those created by Carol Motty in 1985 – and sculpture-like ruffs in crochet that reproduced the skyline of Manhattan in three dimensions were all works which, though unique, were strongly linked to each other by a common thread: the idea of art to wear. Commited to skill and craftsmanship, and decidedly against consumer standardization, the members of the Artisans Gallery sought to create harmony between the art-garment and the person who wore it. They designed expressive shapes that were not purely contemplative but were artistic creations in which one could wrap oneself, an act which combined art and life both symbolically and materially. (*Aurora Fiorentini*)

Arzano Mario (1939). Tailor born in Naples who continued the family business. In 1973 he took over his mother's atelier in via dei Mille. He has a staff of 12 assistants. He designs French haute couture, buying patterns and fabrics from Ungaro and Saint-Laurent, among others. In recent years he also created his own line of high fashion for women, taking advantage of the high quality of craftsmanship in Naples.

Arzuaga Amaya (1970). Spanish designer. She followed in the footsteps of her mother, Maria Luisa Navarro, a knitwear designer who controls the largest Spanish group in the field, Elipse. Amaya was born in Lerna, near Burgos. She maked her début in 1994 during the women's prêt-à-porter show in Paris. Her next Collections, presented at the same time in Paris and in Spain, sold 55,000 pieces in 35 countries. Her Collections of women's and men's wear for Autumn-Winter 1997-1998 have been presented on the runways of London Fashion Week.

❑ 2003, February. Second presentation in Milan for the designer loved by Pedro Almodóvar, for whose films she created many of the costumes. In Milan Amaya presented chiffon mini-tunics combined with leather leggings and blouses of boiled wool with large pleats.

Aschengreen Piacenti Kirsten. In 1983 she created the Galleria del Costume for the Palazzo Pitti in Florence. It is one of the few Italian museums dedicated to fashion, and has put on many exhibits, including *The Donation of Tirelli* (1986) and *Fashion at the Court of the Medici: The Restored Costumes of Cosimo, Eleanor and Don Garzia* (1993). She was born in Madras, India to a Danish family. She received a degree in Art History from the Courtauld Institute in London and one in literature from the University of Florence. From 1971 to 1996 she worked for the Soprintendenza per i Beni Artistici e Storici di Firenze, first as a supervisor and then as director of the Museo degli Argenti at the Pitti. She was also in charge of the Museo delle Porcellane, also at the Pitti. Since 1992 she has taught the history of fashion and costume at the Catholic University of Milan. In 1996 she was appointed curator of the Museo Stibbert for which she organized the exhibi *L'abito per il corpo, il corpo per l'abito* (*The Garment Made for the Body, The Body Made for the Garment*). From 1983 to 1997 she was director of the Italian Center for the Study of the History of Textiles. She is presently director of the National Commission for the Conservation and Development of Decorative Arts, Fashion and Costume, and of the Association of Friends of the Galleria del Costume.

Ascher Zika (1910). English fabric designer and manufacturer, born in Prague. In the 1930s he emigrated to England with his wife Lida. She worked as a designer for fashion houses such as Molyneux, while Zika opened in London in 1942, a shop for printing on silk. The quality and originality of their work drew the attention of various designers and resulted in a series of fortunate collaborations. In 1945 they printed designs by Henry Moore on silk for Nina Ricci. From this came the idea that would establish them as innovators in textiles rather than simple artisans. Starting in 1948 they produced the Ascher Squares, square silk foulards printed with designs by the most important artists of the era. Thirty-one artists, among them Matisse, Moore, Dérain and Picabia, participated in the initiative. Immediately successful, the foulards become instant collector's items and are exhibited in galleries as genuine works of art. In the same period, the British government invited the Aschers to participate in an exhibit at the Victoria and Albert Museum called *Britain Can Make It* that was organized to promote British manufactures. This recognized their contribution to the rebirth of the textile industry. In the early 1950s, Princesses Elisabeth and Margaret were among their clients. The most important houses in Paris, among them Dior and Schiaparelli, requested their fabrics. In the following years they developed new types of fabrics. Very successful was their downy mohair, woven in Scotland with the addition of nylon threads in neon colors.

❑ 2003. At the request and through the efforts of Zandra Rhodes, clothes made of fabrics created by the Aschers are kept in an area of the Fashion and Textile Museum in London dedicated to Notable British Textile Designers, together with the work of other great names such as Celia Birtwell, Georgina Von Etzdorf and Liberty Studios.

Ascot A large tie called also a plastron. At the end of the 20th century it also became part of the woman's wardrobe. It is the most elegant tie that can be worn with a morning suit. It is tied around the neck in a double knot and held in place with a pin. It is similar, but not identical, to the *cache-col* (a type of scarf, or cravat), an elegant accessory which can substitute for the tie in an informal situation and is much easier to knot.

Ashida Jun (1930). Japanese designer of Korean origin. He has more than 200 points-of-sale between Japan and Paris. He became known also in Italy and in 1989 he was named a Cavaliere della Repubblica. He made his début in 1951 under the wing of Junichi Nakahara. He began to present in Paris in 1977. He diversified his Collections with three brands: Jun Ashida, Miss Ashida, and Jun Ashida for Men. His daughter Tae works in the company.

❑ 2000. *Nostalgia, a Farewell to the 20th Century* was the title of his Autumn-Winter Collection, a special tribute by the Japanese designer to the century just ended. The wardrobe, presented at the Akasaka Prince Hotel in Tokyo, was a

Collection of designs from previous decades, with luxury fabrics and stylistic echoes. The Collection of the designer's daughter Tae was titled *Transitino*.
❑ 2002. A foulard-shawl created for the 2002-2003 season had great success.
❑ 2003. The 73 year-old Japanese designer counts among his admirers members of the Japanese imperial family. Princess Misaka wears Ashida's designs and always attends his presentations.

Asics Japanese factory of sport shoes. In 1949 Kihachiro Onitsuka (1918) established 1949 the Onitsuka Co. Ltd. in Kobe, Japan. He started with the manufacture of basketball shoes, soon adding shoes for volleyball and track. In 1956, during the run-up to the Olympic Games in Melbourne, the positive result of close cooperatiion between manufacturers and athletes brought about an expansion of production in the areas of track and field, soccer, and skiing. During the three Olympiads of the 1960s, Rome in 1960, Tokyo in 1964 and Mexico in 1968, Onitsuka shoes were worn not only by Japanese athletes, but also by the best from other nations. An interesing story concerns the Ethiopian runner Abele Kibila who won the marathon in Rome running barefoot and was nicknamed "Barefoot Abebe." Four years later, in Tokyo, only Mr. Onitsuka was able to convince him to wear shoes created expressly for him. Since then he became known simply as "Marathon King." Starting in the 1960s, the company enjoyed incredible success and worldwide distribution. It brought to perfection new technologies and new materials, in 1985 creating a large testing laboratory called "R&D Department of Asics." Digital and laser technology allowed the company to produce for each athlete custom shoes that were made-to-measure within a millimeter. At the Olympics in Sidney, Naoko Takahashi, who has one leg shorter than the other by a few centimeters, wore Asics. The three companies Onitsuka, GTO and Jalenk merged in 1977 to form Asics Corporation. In 2000, the designer Hitoshi Mimura became the leader of the company. Asics has points-of-sale and distributors all over the world, from the U.S. to Europe, from Latin America to China, and in Israel, Dubai, India, South Africa, the Philippines and Indonesia. The company has continued the commitment, almost a philosophy, of its founder, who was the author of two books – *If You Fall Down, Just Stand Up* and *Asics: Kihachiro Onitsuka's Philosophy of management* – to form a healthy younger generation through athletics. (*Gabriella Gregorietti*)

Aspesi Alberto (1944). Italian designer. He became successful thanks to a quilted nylon jacket, swollen like the Michelin puppet. He was born in Gallarate, Varese. In 1969 he founded A&D-Camiceria of Alberto Aspesi, which became Bagarre of Alberto Aspesi in 1973, and finally carried only his own name in 1990. He has eight lines, aimed at a clothing style that is clean and severe, with a uni-sex cut. The most recent was shown during the Autumn-Winter season of 1999. It was called LSD and was created in collaboration with the designer Lawrence Steele. Also in this Collection was a quilted jacket, though in a different form (it was silver and could be turned into a sleeping bag), always the specialty of the house and the object of constant updating: no cumbersome proportions, a casual style good also in the city, and three different sizes (to the waist, a vest, and to the ankles). The Aspesi style was always known for the basics, though with the line *This is a door, here is a sea* it adjusted to more trendy needs: high-tech materials, creased velvets, and lots of colours, which certainly didn't characterize the other lines. The company's premises are in Legnano.

❑ 2002, September. An agreement with the designer Lawrence Steele for the manufacture and marketing of the firm's lines took effect with the Spring-Summer season.
❑ 2003, April. Intek, owner of 50% of Alberto Aspesi Inc., sold its shares to Grayling, a company that is part of the group 2G Investimenti. The transfer to the new group, directed by Giuliano Tabacchi, costs €21 million, liabilities included. The remaining half of the capital stock is still owned by Aspesi.

Aspesi Natalia (1929). Journalist and writer. She was born in Milan, and still lives and works there. A columnist for the newspaper

La Repubblica, she has followed fashion for years, with a sharp and ironic pen, and paying special attention to costume. Typical of her style was a 1998 article about Naomi Campbell's bottom, and also her book *Il lusso & l'anarchia* (Rizzoli, 1982), an extraordinary piece of research and a fascinating narrative about fashion during the Fascist regime. Before devoting herself to journalism, she worked as a babysitter in Switzerland and England, as a salesman of machinery for creameries, and as a designer of ties. She worked on the evening daily La Notte, was hired as a reporter for Il Giorno in the early 1960's, and has worked at La Repubblica as a special correspondent since its first issue. She wrote *La donna immobile* (Fabbri Editore, 1976), *Lui! Visto da lei* (1978), *Il trionfo del privato* and *Vivere in tre* (1981).

Asprey English jeweller's shop located at a famous address, 165-169 New Bond Street, known not only by the people of London but by everyone who loves the Anglo-Saxon style. Its history began more than 200 years ago, making its début with a refined Collection of luxury goods, especially articles in leather and art objects. Later on it moved to silverware, porcelain serving sets, precision time pieces, and jewellery. Its readiness to create any kind of object upon request – "It can be done" is the motto of Edward Asprey – led the firm to work with jewellery especially. Asprey's special pride is its long relationship with the royal family, starting with the first patent received in 1862 from Queen Victoria, in addition to a very prestigious clientele among which number princes, maharajas, politicians, diplomats, and show business celebrities. Overseas, the brand had by 1984 already gained a rather respectable address: 725 Fifth Avenue in New York. In 1986 Asprey joined the group of sponsors for Ferrari in the Formula One racing championship, creating a Collection of accessories in gold, silver and enamel, distinguished by mythological references to Ferraris.

❑ 1998. The jewellery shop, already taken over in 1995 by Jefri Bolkiah, brother of the Sultan of Brunei, is merged with its competitor Garrard for the sum of 100 million pounds. Asprey & Garrard was thus born.
❑ 1999, December. The Asprey necklace (diamonds and pearls) worn by Lady Diana in her last public appearance, was sent to auction for charity, with a floor of $500,000.
❑ 2000, July. Tommy Hilfiger purchases Asprey & Garrard from Brunei Investment Group.
❑ 2001, February. Agreement with the business giant LVMH for cooperation in the jewellery market.
❑ 2002. End of the agreement, the two companies go their separate ways.

Assofibre Italian national association of chemical fiber manufacturers. Its members represent 90% of the country's production. The industry's turnover is about 3,500 billion liras with 9,350 employes. The export volume of 482,000 tons is 70% of total production. World-wide production in 1996 was 24.1 million tons. Italy is the only European country with a complete line of textiles covering the entire production chain, from fiber to finished article.

(*Giuliana Zabeo Ricca*)

Assunta Roman fur shop. It was founded by Assunta Aguccioni, who started her career in 1937 at Balzani, and in 1942 opened her own business working with Forquet, Carosa, Lancetti and Valentino. In 1969 received the cinema prize Maschera d'Argento for her "tile" fur inspired by the church of Santa Maria del Popolo in Rome. She made long and flared furs, casual trousers in ermine, flowered inlays and mink Bermuda shorts. In 1969 she worked with the fashion designer Alberto Lattuada. He designed the Eskimo Collection for her, with coats worked in Persian lamb in the shape of inlaid tiles. The Ninotschka Collection of 1971-1972 presented garments made of Crimea lamb. She was also able to offer elegant cloaks of chinchilla, zebra and mink worked horizontally. Among her clients was Romy Schneider.

Asta Olga (1880-1963). A very important figure in the history of embroidery and lace in the 20th century. Born in Venice, Olga Lustig went to work at a very young age as a shop assistant in the lace firm Jesurum, another legendary name in the industry. At 19 she married Giosuè Asta, an officer in the merchant marine. A little later, in the early 1900s, she opened her first small shop in Piazza San Marco. An almost immediate success allowed her to expand the business and gave her three shop windows under the archway of the Procuratie Vecchie. She used to say that she was totally unable to do any sewing work. But she was extremely skilled in designing ensembles for bridal veils, tablecloths, table decorations and sheets. The design department was located in the back of the shop. After making a sketch she prepared a final model that, reviewed and corrected, would be given to the embroiderers and lace makers. Even in the 1920s Olga found herself faced with the problem of a trade – lace embroidery, with bobbin and with needle – that was threatened by progress. Her solution was to open in Burano a school of lacemaking so that the tradition would not die. Before the war, she opened a branch of the school in Milan on Corso Littorio (today Corso Matteotti), directed until its closing at the beginning of the 1960s by Bianca Kalberg and Amalia Vernocchi. Olga sold her products also in the Côte d'Azur and St. Moritz. She was a supplier to the royal family and numbered among her clients Barbara Hutton, King Farouk (who ordered for his wife a trousseau that is still famous for its opulence), the Duke and Duchess of Windsor, Douglas Fairbanks, William Powell, Myrna Loy and the families of the Italian aristocracy and upper class. She always shared the profits of the firm with her employees, long before profit-sharing became part of the strategy of unions. When she died in 1963 the firm was already in trouble, as the times and what people wore had changed. The firm could not survive much longer, and when it closed, her designs were scattered.

Astrakhan Fur made of Persian lamb. On July 17th 1971, at a fashion show in Rome's Grand Hotel, Carlo Tivoli, who had suddenly become famous for his red and blue Persian lamb furs, declared it to be "necessary, the non-superfluous fur." And, to judge only by the fashions of the 1900s, which saw it as something important in every decade, though with many ups and downs and in different ways, one couldn't say that he was wrong. Many faces and many names were given to this kind of fur, so easy to work with

Mantle with astrakhan neck, 1919 (Prints Collection A. Bertarelli, Milan).

and so chic that – still in Tivioli's words – "it confers class and distinction as nothing else can, and creates a strong sense of success because it can be shaped and is easy to use, and allows almost any kind of processing, just like a textile." If it took its French name from Astrakhan, the ancient capital of Turkestan, near present-day Bukhara, it has been called Persian lamb in English, Persianer in German, and persiano in Italian. But the original name of this lamb (Ovis aries platyura) was karakul, which in the Uzbek language meant black lake or black rose and, even before defining a breed of sheep, was a lake in the Pamir region as well as a city in Uzbekistan located south-west of Bukhara. The origin of the karakul was here, and even if it might evoke for us the curled petals of a black rose or the mirror of a lake around which the sheep grazed, it was certainly valued since ancient times. The people of of Syria and Mesopotamia used it and, in more recent times, karakul caps with feathers and precious stones were part of the wardrobe of the Shah of Persia and of the Russian princes. In the early 1900s, attempts were made to introduce it to lands far away from the place of origin and from the nearby regions of Afghanistan, Crimea, and Persia. But these attempts in the U.S., Canada and Poland failed, just as all the attempts by Germans in their colonies failed, with the exception of South-West Africa. Under the burning heat of the southern sun in what is now Namibia, karakul found the ideal conditions of a dry climate and arid environment to grow even more beautiful and became famous under the name of Swakara (from the initials of South West Africa). Splendid, with its light leather and silk-like moiré look, and fine, extremely fine, with its flat fleece, is the Breitschwanz, the aborted or stillborn or newborn lamb. In a variety of patterns, with plays of light and natural colors (black above all, but also white, grey, and various shades of brown), the astrakhan can be dyed in the most vivid colors and can be made into the most daring creations, either a witty pair of bell-bottom trousers or a romantic frock-coat all lace and open-work. *(Maria Rita Stiglich)*

Ateca Manufacturer and marketer of some of the most successful lines of casual clothing, such as the Avirex padded jacket and Chino trousers, both in the image of the U.S. Air Force top pilots. The company has it premises in Carpi and is led by Alfredo Cionti. It has a turnover of about €45 million.

❑ 2002, January. After 15 years the company loses its Avirex licenses. Avirex becomes an independent firm under the name Avirex Europa.

Atkinson Nigel (1964). English designer. Designing textiles is his great passion. After attending very prestigious schools like the Portsmouth College of Art and the Winchester School of Art, in 1987 he opened his own workshop specialized in the production and artisanal printing of fabric at Smithfield Market in London. His special, rich and innovative fabrics found a place in the Collections of interior decorators, fashion designers, costume designers and theater and set designers. In 1991 Atkinson moved to Camden Square, redoubled his efforts and created, in 1994, his own *griffe*, Nigel Atkinson Accessories. In 1996 he was invited to the first Biennale di Firenze and participated in the Visitors Exhibition organized by Luigi Settembrini and Franca Sozzani. His work was shown at the Opificio delle Pietre Dure.

❑ He has worked with Romeo Gigli and Alberta Ferretti. He has designed costumes for the cinema and theater as well as fabrics for interior decoration.

ATMI (American Textile Manufacturers Institute). It brings together American textile firms from about 30 states. The organization promotes the textile industry and defends the interests of its members with the government as regards laws concerning the import of textile goods. It also provides economic and statistical information.

Ato Behind this brand of clothing and accessories for men hides a Japanese designer. He does not wish to show himself so as to avoid influencing the purchase decisions of his clientele. His career began in 1993 with the opening of a shop in the chic neighbourhood of Aoyama in Tokyo. After great success in his native country, in 2000 achieved international success when major department stores bought the firms's designs on an exclusive basis. His Collections do not have specific themes, as a way to maintain creativity, and some members of the staff work 3 days in the boutique in order to stay in tune with clients.

Attaché Case. Rigid valise, usually used by diplomat, businessmen, couriers, or for quick plane trips as carry-on luggage. It was considered indestructible because before being sold, it had to survive the "chute-choc" test, being dropped and pounded.

Audibet Marc (1949). French designer. He made its début in 1971 as an assistant to Ungaro for high fashion. Since 1972 he has designed the men's Collections for Cerruti and in 1975 worked with him on the launch of the first women's Collection. From 1977 to 1981 he designed the men's wear lines of Christian Aujard and collaborated with Basile and Laura Biagiotti. He uses mainly avant-guard fabrics, creating dynamic shapes. In 1984 he launched his own *griffe* for women's prêt-à-porter, which would stay on the market until the Summer of 1988. In 1991, for two seasons, he designed a knitwear line. Since 1992 he has worked with Hermès and Prada on their women's Collections.

❑ 1999. He began to work with Salvatore Ferragamo, designing their women's Collection.
❑ 2001, October. After four seasons he left Ferragamo, and his place was taken by the Scottish designer Graeme Black after a seven year collaboration with Armani.

Auguste The brand conceals the identify of the Belgian designer Christof Beaufays. He attended the École de la Cambre in Brussels and achieved success at the Hyères Festival in 1999.

Aujard Christian (1941-1977). French entrepreneur. In partnership with a group of designers he created a line of prêt-à-porter under his own name. It featured soft and somewhat oversize jackets for men, ample overcoats and long skirts for women. He died after a fall while riding on horseback and left the brand in the hands of his wife Michèle and the designer Jeff Sayre, who had been with the house since 1973. For the last ten years the brand has been part of the firm Alex Cini B., which distributes mainly in the Orient and has a boutique in rue de Tournon in Paris.

Aulenti Gae (1927). Architect and designer. In 1992, together with Luca Ronconi, she organized the exhibit *La Sala Bianca, nascita della moda italiana* (*The White Room: The Birth of Italian Fashion*) at Palazzo Strozzi in Florence. One year later, the exhibit went to the Musée des Arts de la Mode et du Textile at the Louvre in Paris. In 1994, at the Guggenheim Museum in New York, she organized the exhibit *The Italian Metamorphosis*, in which fashion played a large part. In 1996, at the Biennale di Firenze, of which she was Vice-President, she was responsible for the exhibit *Visitors* along with Franca Sozzani and Luigi Settembrini. She studied with Ernesto Rogers. She designed the Musée d'Orsay in Paris, which opened at the end of 1986 and for which President Mitterand awarded her the Legion d'Honneur. In 1985 she was in charge of the renovation of Palazzo Grassi in Venice, and in 1987-1995 she did the same work for the Museu d'Art de Cataluña in Barcelona. She also did the plans for the Musèe National d'Art Moderne inside the Beaubourg in Paris. Among her most well known design objects are the *Pipistrello* (1966) and *Parola* lamps, and a round table for Fontana Arte.

Austin Henri Wilfred (1906). A famous tennis player, known as "Bunny." He was the first to wear shorts on the Central Court at Wimbledon, in 1932. They were made of white flannel, of course. His sister, Joan Winifred, scandalized Wimbledon by not wearing socks.

Avagolf Manufacturer of luxury knitwear, producing mid-price clothes for women in natural fibers. Founded in 1958 by Luisa Poggi, it has had great success year after year. Its premises are in San Colombano al Lambro, near Milan. The firm is managed by Vittorio Manzoni, the founder's son. About 40 people are employed there.

Two Avagolf models. Sketch by Maria Pezzi.

Avedon Richard (1923-2004). American photographer, one of the greatest in the field of fashion. In his photos, which began to appear in the 1940s, the models became actors on unusual sets: the zoo, a circus, a launching pad, a refuse dump. He encouraged his subjects to move as spontaneously as possible in order to obtain images of the greatest naturalness. After studying philosophy at Columbia University, he went to war. On his return, in 1944, he began to be interested in photography and met Alexey Brodovitch, the art director of Harper's Bazaar's, for whom he started to work in 1945. Once he had entered into the atmosphere of Brodovitch's cerebral and deeply intellectual tones, Avedon would never abandon it. His work with the magazine would continue even with the directors who followed, until 1984. From 1966 to 1990 he also worked with Vogue. Many of his photos, in which the lens is focused on the "emotional geography" of a body or face, have been published by the French magazine Égoiste. Very important in his photos, in addition to the particular points of view, the sharp angles, and the stroboscopic lights, is the background, almost always white in order to empty the picture and deprive it of any outside reference. He has discovered and launched the most important models, from Dovima to Suzy Parker to Veruschka, and from Twiggy to Penelope Tree to Lauren Hutton to Benedetta Barzini. The public at large knows his work through the advertising campaigns and TV commercials he has done for Revlon, Chanel, Dior, and Versace. He was the first to photograph a man for the cover of a women's magazine. It was the actor Steve McQueen. He has had several exhibitions of his work. Among them was the one in 1974 with portraits of his father, Jacob Israel, at the Museum of Modern Art. There was a retrospective of his fashion photos at the Metropolitan Museum of Art in 1978. In 1994 his work was the subject of a large traveling exhibition called *Evidence, 1944-1994.*

(*Angela Madesani*)

❑ In 1995 and 1997 he photographed the Pirelli calendars.
❑ In September 2003 the Metropolitan Museum of New York gave him a retrospective.

Avirex American brand of sportswear, characterized by sturdiness and basic designs. Created in the 1940s to manufacture jackets for the U.S. Air Force, the brand has grown to become one of the most popular among young people in American cities. Its signature pieces are the traditional leather bomber jackets and the clothing with logos from the various American colleges and universities. The company began to experience enormous growth starting in 1974 thanks to the efforts of Jeff Clyman and Franck Marchese, two men who, with one eye on the past and the other on the future, were able to understand the tastes of young people.

(*Priscilla Daroda*)

❑ 2000. The new millennium sees the American divided into three parts, with the U.S. operation remaining in the hands of the Clyman family, the Japanese operation controlled by the Edwin family, and the European operation part of a Dutch business group but coordinated by Avirex.
❑ 2001. Avirex turnover in Europe was €30 million.
❑ 2002, January. Avirex Europe became an independent company, freeing itself from the control of Ateca, which had controlled its licenses for 15 years and which was also owned by Edwin, which had 51%.
❑ The first result of this change was the reduction in the number of points-of-sale. In Italy, the number of stores went from 600 to 480, of which 90 were new. In France, the 140 existing stores were completely shut down, and new 7 shops opened. The goal was to give up a business model based on jeans in favor of higher-quality men's wear.
❑ 2003, January. A new license was granted to Portolano Guanti of Naples, which would carry Avirex accessories in the European market.

Avoledo Patrizia (1952). Italian journalist and editor of Donna Moderna, an Italian women's weekly published by Mondadori. Born in Milan, she began to work at the publishing house as a switchboard operator while still quite young, Later, after studies in psychology and pedagogy, and a period as a secretary in the editorial department, she began to work at DuePiù. It was the beginning of a great career. Made editor-in-chief at DuePiù in 1985, she later became director of the specialized magazine Dolly, and in 1989 was at Cento Cose as deputy manager under Kicca Menoni. In 1991 she arrived at the recently-launched Donna Moderna, also a Mondadori magazine. She was the deputy of Edvige Bernasconi, who had brilliantly conceived and launched the magazine and achieved an enormous circulation. In 1995 she becomes the magazine's director. A very intelligent woman, she poured great passion into the magazine, and, assisted by her deputy manager Cipriana Dall'Orto, consolidated the magazine's success, a genuine editorial phenomenon with an audited weekly circulation of 650,000 copies.

❑ 2000. She won the Marisa Bellisario prize in the Special Awards section for the "commitment, perseverance and optimism shown at the helm of the best-selling women's weekly in Italy."

Avolio Giorgio. Milanese tailor. He exhibited, together with Bertoli and Pucci, at the Tessitrice dell'Isola, the fashion boutique at the first show organized by Giorgini in Florence at the birth of Italian fashion on February 12, 1951. His style was completely opposite the very fanciful one of Bertoli: raincoats, women's suits in check patterns, dull colours, and white blouses. Classicism was his trademark. His atelier was in via San Damiano, in Milan.

Avon Celli Italian knitwear factory, already operating in the 1920s and relaunched 30 years later by Pasquale Celli. The firm owes its worldwide success to refinement in manufacturing, a craftsman-like attention to detail, expensive yarns – cashmere, fine wool, pure silk – and an unmistakeable style that combines classic tailoring with just the right touch of fashion.

AWC (Australian Wool Corporation). An association founded in 1973 by Australian sheep farmers. It has taken the place of the Australian Wool Board that was founded in 1936. It promotes the use of wool, communication among the membership, product research and commercial development. As Australia is the world's leading producer of wool, the AWC is the major source of funding of the IWS (International Wool Secretariat), providing 70% of the budget.

Ayazzi-Fantechi Milliner's shop in Florence well known during and 1930s and after. It was active in the period of autarky and during the war. Its models became very famous on May 22nd 1950, in Florence, during the historical presentation at the Teatro della Pergola, among the cream of the local production.

Azagury Jacques (1956). English designer born in Casablanca. At the young age of 20 he launched his own line. It came to a halt two years later, but was stubbornly resumed in 1978. He worked in London with Jane Culliman, who decorated his clothes with flowers. This design partnership has made a name for itself with bridal wear in particular.

❑ 2001, November. Sir Hardy Amies leaves the helm of the historic house on Savile Row bearing his name and is succeeded as chief designer by Jacques Azagury.
❑ 2002, June. The first Collection created by Azagury for Autumn-Winter 2002 is never put on sale and the creative staff is replaced.
❑ The Luxury Brands Group, owner of Hardy Amies, decides to dismiss the designer, breaking the agreement which provided for the preparation of two Collections. His replacement is Ian Garland.
❑ 2003, April. Azagury designs some of the dresses worn by the female stars during the Bafta Award, the annual awards ceremony for British television.

Azagury Partridge Solange (1961). English creative director at Boucheron after its acquisition by Gucci. Of Moroccan origin, she was born and lives in London. She opened a shop in Notting Hill, beginning with jewellery inspired by the 1920s and costume jewellery. Today, she divides herself between London and Paris, where she works in the historical Boucheron premises in Place Vendôme. Studying the house's rich archives, Solange revives the old models in order to present them in a new spirit, though keeping their traditional prestige. So she reinterprets, but doesn't distort, the unmistakeable style of this jeweller to tsarinas and queens, actresses and heiresses. One example of this would be the famous "white" jewels, created with diamonds in a platinum setting, although, at the same time, she also plans a more accessible line for all women. She follows her own instinct for creativity, not the latest trends. She used some two thousand diamonds to make a sort of snake skin, a real temptation for the lapel of a jacket. She has a particular love for sapphires, which she sets in a very personal way, softening their characteristic blue with black gold. In this way they became less showy and could be worn, irreverently, with jeans. She prefers colors that are more mature, such as plum, brown and violet, and forms that are the most wrapped and rounded.

Aziz (1969). Dutch designer. After his victory at the Grand Prix Jeunes Stylistes in Hyères in 1996, he made a name for himself with his "tri-dimensional" Collections for men and women, characterized by deep inquiry into the nature of forms and materials. He lives and works in Amsterdam.

Azzaro Loris (1933). French designer. His dresses glowing with red sequins, the transparent and pleated draped bodices, have been instruments of seduction for many stars – Rachel Welch, Marisa Berenson, Claudia Cardinale, Joan Collins, Isabelle Adjani – between the 1970s and early 1980s. Born in Tunisia of Italian parents, he made his début in Paris in 1962, creating, for a group of friends only, sparkling accessories of lurex and sequins. But it was only in 1968 that he became famous thanks to an openwork dress that appeared in every fashion magazine. From that moment, he became the symbol of a certain overdressed elegance, played out on showy and colorful creations, certainly influenced by the culture of his native land. In 1974 he launched a perfume, the first in a series of successful fragrances that sold extremely well, with 10% of the world market for men's perfumes.

❑ 2003. The firm hires the young designer Jérome Dreyfuss to make its couture more dynamic. The investment company Frey, specialized in real estate and wine, buys a majority stake in Azzaro. In line with the firm's usual practice, the terms of the agreement are not disclosed.

Azzuolo Antonio. French designer of Canadian and Italian origin. He studied in Canada where he majored in fashion at Ryerson University in Toronto (1989). Still a student, he opened his first atelier in Toronto and won several prizes as a "young emerging designer." In the early 1990s he worked in Paris. From 1992 to 1995 he was an assistant designer at Hermès for the men's Collection. He then moved to Kenzo and stayed there until 1997 as designer for the Jeans Uomo line. In 1996 he created A&A Design and showed prêt-à-porter Collections for men and women under his own name. He worked as a freelance designer with the large department store Galeries Lafayette. His simple and modern line is sold in Europe, America and Japan.

B

BAA McArthurGlen Chain of European super-stores. It pays particular attention to fashion, with great designers and large discounts, usually 50%. It offers Versace, Levi's, Calvin Klein, Paul Smith, Donna Karan, Reebok, and Adidas, plus Dunhill accessories and products from Disney and Warner Bros.

Babani Firm offering fabrics and clothing established in 1919 by Madame Babani in a shop on Boulevard Haussmann in Paris. She sold Liberty fabrics as well as the Renaissance-inspired ones created by Mariano Fortuny. Like Maria Gallenga, Babani was an imitative follower of Fortuny, from whom she separated in order to pursue a lesser sophistication and a taste for embroidery. The firm was in business for ten years.

Babini Marina (1956). Italian designer. Upon graduation from the Istituto Marangoni in Milan in 1978 she immediately created her own brand, combining her name with the word Italia in order to emphasize the idea of traditions, roots and taste. From her very first Collection, she offered a total look in which every piece was interchangeable and coordinated. The firm is based in Faenza, where it produces 100,000 pieces per year and employs 250 workers.

> ❑ 2003. The brand opens its own showroom in Faenza, while the headquarters for export is in Milan, near Sari Spazio. Among the American stars who appreciate the simplicity and clean lines of Babini's designs are Halle Berry, Jo Champa, Janet Jackson and Sharon Stone.

Babouche Manufacturer of Morocco-style slippers founded in 2000 by Patrizio Miceli, Cyril Saulnier and Pierre Jacquet. These three men, with the help of the shoemakers of Marrakech, created these babouches by adjusting them to an urban, western style.

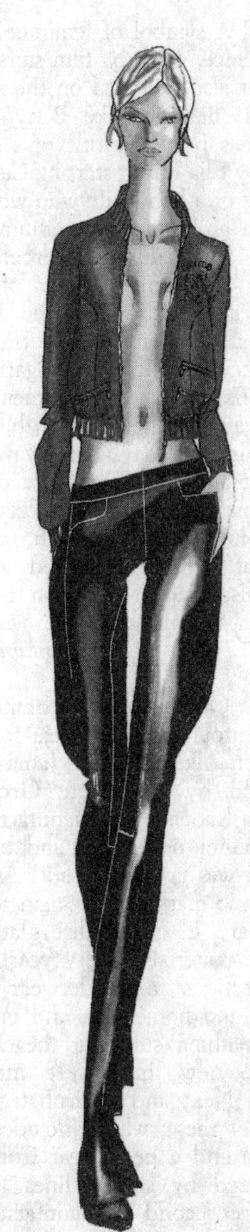

Lady's riding-pants model designed by Marina Babini.

Some of them, in fact, have a slight heel. They can be striped or with flowers, and made of leather, denim, snakeskin, silk, or tweed, even in a camouflage pattern. Sold in France at fifty points-of-sale, Babouche slippers have been quite successful, and are by now on sale in twelve other countries.

Baby Doll A symbol of feminine seduction par excellence, worn by film stars since the 1950s, but also sketched on the silhouettes of cartoon heroines like Betty Boop. Its name comes from the title of a 1956 film directed by Elia Kazan starring Carrol Baker in the role of a baby-wife who wore a short nightgown and sucked her thumb. At the time the film caused a great scandal, provoking the terrible anger of Cardinal Spellman and stirring up the Legion of Decency. Short length and transparency were the key attributes of this garment born in the 1950s at a historical moment in which women again felt the desire to be attractive at any time of day. Half-way between underwear and sleepwear, of a charmingly childish shape, it consists of a sleeveless low-necked blouse short enough to allow a glimpse of panties decorated with bows and lace also used to embellish the neckline and hem of the blouse itself.

(*Gianluca Bauzano*)

Bacirubati One of the six brands which, with Argentovivo and Azuleja for women, and Julipet, Allen Cox and Jamas for men, are owned by the Arcte Group from Bologna, a leader in the manufacturing and distribution of underwear and beachwear. Bacirubati was created to address a young and dynamic market. The main features of the line are its minimalist glamour and innovative materials. Every year there are two Collections for underwear, corsetry, sleepwear and homewear, and one Collection for bathing suits and beachwear. In 2002 two new lines were introduced, Bacirubati Next and Bacirubati Cotonext. The first of these, which includes both an underwear and a beachwear Collection, is characterized by simple lines and basic colors. The second is manufactured with an innovative stretch cotton, under a patent called Futura that is produced exclusively for Arcte by Franzoni Filati, which allows complete freedom of movement. Along with the other brands of the Arcte Group, Bacirubati is distributed in the most important locations in Italy also in France, Germany, Great Britain, Belgium, Greece and Spain.

(*Sara Tieni*)

Backhaus Maria Vittoria (1942). Italian photographer. She works in Milan and is considered one of the best for taking still life photos of accessories, jewels, objects, adn the kitchen. She studied set design at the Accademia di Brera and began her career as a reporter for the weekly magazine Tempo in the second half of the 1960s. Later she worked in fashion, collaborating especially with Vogue Italia and becoming a close friend of Walter Albini. After arriving at the monthly Casa Vogue, under the direction of Isa Tutino Vercelloni, she began to work with still life, quickly demonstrating her talent, taste, and skill at working with lights. She favors large-format photography. She is the niece of Arnaldo Mussolini and the daughter of Vito, the last editor-in-chief of Popolo d'Italia. She married Giorgio Backhaus, the translator of Max Horkheimer and Theodor Adorno, philosophers of the Frankfurt School.

Backpack Schoolchildren used to go to school with a folder or a satchel. Today they all use backpacks, which are more convenient due to their larger size, and are of course more fashionable. This sturdy canvas bag with external pockets and shoulder

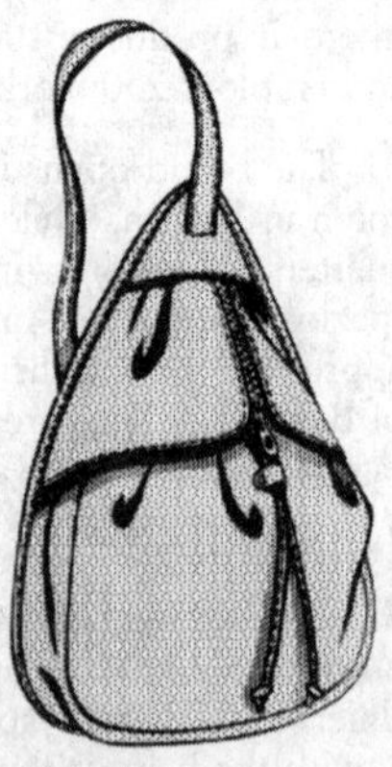

Backpack by Bagagerie.

straps is no longer used only by soldiers, mountaineers, and excursionists, but has become a useful accessory to one and all. Ideal for free time and for students, the backpack has joined the ranks of the handbag as a trendy accessory. Prada launched a nylon model at the beginning of the 1980s. It took until the end of the decade, however, for the phenomenon to really take off and its use to become widespread.

Badgley Mischka American brand founded by Mark Badgley (born in East Saint Louis, Ill., in 1961) and James Mischka (born in Burlington, Wisc., in 1960), who presented their first Collection in New York in 1988, demystifying and simplifying glamour. Their refines afternoon and evening dresses are made in cotton brocade, silk, and wool velvet. Simplicity, wearability and perfect tailoring are their trademark. According to Vogue, Badgley and Mischka created "the perfect black dress, new but without being a novelty."

❑ 1999, March. For the Oscars they dress both Jennifer Lopez and Laura Dern in black.
❑ 2001, September. The two designers decide not to show their Collections at New York Fashion Week, for the first time in 12 years. Among their reasons, the imminent opening of two new boutiques.
❑ 2002. For Spring-Summer 2003, the two designers, included in Vogue's list of the ten best American designers, propose fashion that is "more accessible."

Badulescu Enrique Coròdoba (1961). Mexican photographer who studied photography in Munich. He quickly made a name for himself due to the simplicity with which he worked – one Hasselblad camera and a single tungsten flash – largely offset by his heavy colors and the originality of his daring shots. He was first published by the Mexican magazine Fotozoom, but starting in the 1980s he contributed to a complete renewal of fashion photography in Mexico. At the same time his photos began to appear in foreign magazines such as The Face and L'Uomo, and in the various international editions of Vogue and Harper's Bazaar. Convinced that fashion photography can go beyond the limits of the commercial market and build a bridge in the direction of art, Badulescu worked for Armani, Dolce & Gabbana, Valentino, Nina Ricci, Gap and Galliano.

Baeza Guillermina. Designer born in Tangiers, Morocco, and now about 60. She is a designer possessed of great inspiration, thanks to the mixture of races and culture in her native country and to the education she received in Europe. In the 1960s she moved to Barcelona and created her first swimwear and underwear lines. During the 1980s she made her début at the Pasarela Gaudì in Barcelona and presented her prêt-à-porter line in Paris. At the end of 1998 she joined the industrial group Pulligan Internacional. There she started another swimwear line, called Lola Escobar, and a children's line, called Guillermina Baeza Children. She draws inspiration from recent decades, especially the years of the 1970s, with their abundance of geometric prints. She has been able to give equal importance to underwear and outerwear.

(*Estefania Ruilope Ruiz*)

Bagatt Brand of shoes, bags and leather goods, founded in 1983. In 1999, it had 50 single-brand shops in Italy and 16 abroad. This was the strategy mapped out by Quattroci, the Aragonese company that is part of the Capra Group and controls the entire manufacturing and distribution process through the tannery Nuova Cap and the footwear factory Quattroci.

❑ 2003, February. The Capra Group sold the footwear factory Adamello, in Vigevano. Carlo and Filippo Capra were the majority shareholders.
❑ 2003. Bagatt designs are sold in 110 points-of-sale around the world, including Germany, France, Greece, Cyprus, and Great Britain.

Baggy Style of oversize trousers with many pockets and meant to be worn without a belt. It came back in fashion with the triumph of the "comfortable oversize," which had to allow freedom of movement and, above, all, be practical. It is inspired by the most classic work clothes, as seen in the abundance of pockets, by the rehearsal clothing of dancers, for the freedom of movement they allow, and by the uniforms of prisoners, because they don't need a belt. But, for recent generations, they are above all the symbol of a way of dressing that is rebellious and very trendy. Also influenced by techno-trend, they are worn very low on the hips in order to allow glimpses of underwear. On the other hand, they were worn very high around the waist by Emilio Tadini, the Milanese painter-writer who, starting in the 1970s, was their standard-bearer.

Baguette Mini-bag created by Fendi, named after the traditional French bread because it could also be carried leisurely under the arm, thanks to a handle 16" long. It was presented for the first time in Spring 1996 and since then has become a real cult item. It is collected by celebrities like Caroline of Monaco, Sharon Stone, Sophia Loren, Madonna, Elizabeth Hurley and Catherine Deneuve. Created by Silvia Venturini Fendi, 37 years old, the daughter of Anna and responsible for all the accessory lines at the firm, the Baguette goes through a restyling process every season with the selection of new materials and decorations. The choice has gone from the waterproof fabric Dreso to crocodile skin, with other variations on the theme such as hand-painted leather, cashmere, and flowered brocade copied from Botticelli's painting *Primavera* and manufactured by the Fondazione Lisio of Florence by means of a technique dating back to 1770. The production of this cloth amounts to only 5 cm per day, and as the Baguette's dimensions are approximately 10" x 6" without counting the handle, the Primavera model is a limited edition. Some of the models are one-of-a-kind pieces, decorated with real semi-precious stones, pearls and precious crystals. As a substitute, one can aspire to a multi-colored micro-bag that Fendi calls Croissant.

(*Daniela Fedi*)

Baiadera A printed fabric with multi-color parallel and contrasting stripes. It was first manufactured only in silk, then later with other yarns such as cotton and rayon. It is also the name of the traditional costume of an Indian temple dancer, which goes from the hips to the ground with large skirts open in front and wide draping trousers tied around the ankles.

Bailey Cristopher (1971). English designer. Like a plastic surgeon, he performed a total face lift on a famous brand, Burberry. Respecting the family traditions, he updated them with a fresh touch that was sometimes spirited and even provocative but never bourgeois. This was especially true with respect to Burberry Prorsum, the most important line. The traditional checkered and striped patterns were not up for discussion, but they would often sparkle with lurex in order to make a new customer feel like a rock star. Or they would be matched with rather unconventional but high-impact accessories. After his graduation from the Royal College of Art in London, Bailey worked with Donna Karan from 1994 to 1996 and with Tom Ford at Gucci from 1996 to 2001. As a good Englishman, however, he feels more comfortable now that he works for a British company. He loves to break with tradition by using irreverent combinations, with an eye to the 1970s, his favorite decade. So, under a perfect jacket with impeccably finished tailoring, he puts a cheap T-shirt or a vintage blouse. He is a polite and reserved young man, perhaps even shy. Season after season, his young, fresh and lively presentations win the approval of the public and the critics. Thomas Burberry, who created his famous raincoat in the middle of the 19th century, would be pleased. (*Lucia Mari*)

Bailey David Royston (1938). English photographer. Born in a poor London neighborhood, he was self-taught and became interested in photography while in the army, fascinated by a photo by Henri Cartier Bresson. At the end of the war he began to work as an assistant to the fashion photographer John French, who chronicled the taste of the high bourgeoisie. When barely 22, David, who had already experienced the anxieties of the generation of "angry young men" who were fans of jazz (he is a good trumpet player) and the theater of John Osborne, was discovered by Vogue, which hired him. It was the 1960s and Bailey, who also worked freelance for Elle, Glamour, the

Daily Express, the Sunday Times, and the Daily Telegraph, took his photos with the same spontaneity with which he lived in the swinging London of the time, surrounded by fame, by the friendship of rock stars, and by the love of very beautiful women such as Catherine Deneuve, who he married in 1967 and would be the second of his four wives. All this inspired Michelangelo Antonioni in his film *Blow Up* to base the character of the photographer played by David Hemmings on him and John Cowan. His nonchalance and his rapid style made him part of the counter-culture. With his friends Terence Donovan and Brian Duffy, he was a member of The Terrible Three. His pictures, with their great freshness of execution and extraordinary spontaneity, were very much influenced by film, especially by the Nouvelle Vague. Bailey always worked with a single model, first Jean Shrimpton and then Marie Helvin, always placing great emphasis on the relationship between the dress and the person wearing it. He published several books, including *David Bailey's Box of Pin-Ups* (1965), *Goodbye Baby and Amen* (1969), *David Bailey's Trouble and Strife* (1980), *If We Shadows* (1989), *The Lady Is A Tramp* (1995), *Birth of the Cool* (1999), and *Chasing Rainbows* (2000). He made two films, one about Cecil Beaton (1971), and one about Andy Warhol (1973). He has had many exhibits all over the world, including the great anthological retrospective show at London's Victoria & Albert Museum in 1984. An honorary member of the Royal Photographic Society, he is also a serious collector and counts among his favorites Man Ray, Roger Fenton and Henry Fox Talbot, the Englishman considered, for his calotypes, one of the inventors of photography. (*Roberto Mutti*)

Bailey Xenobia. American milliner. In a career that began in the 1980s, she created the hats for Spike Lee's film *Do The Right Thing* (1989). She favors crochet work for her unisex hats whose shape and color combinations are inspired by Africa and the artists of Brooklyn.

❑ In recent years the designer has moved in the direction of art work and away from the world of fashion, as in the project Paradise Under Reconstruction in the Aesthetic of Funk, in which complicated crochet work is used in a way that recalls the folk art of America and Africa.

Bailly Christiane (1932-2000). French designer, considered one of the pioneers of prêt-à-porter. Born in Lyon, she made her début in the world of fashion as a model: first, in 1957, working almost exclusively for Balenciaga, and later working freelance for Chanel and Dior. When she decided create her own designs, she opted for a style that was functional and reduced to essentials. Her start, in 1959, was similar to that of many other designers of the time: a portfolio under the arm and a lot of time spent in waiting rooms. Thanks to a sketch sold to Marie Chasseng, one of her designs made the pages of Women's Wear Daily. The critics were favorable, but commercial success was still far off, and soon her partnership with Emanuelle Khanh, which had the help of Rabanne, their assistant, came to an end. She was one of the first designers to create a complete knitwear Collection. The American journalist Hebe Dorsey invited her to present her Collection in New York in a group with other new talents. It was 1966, and her clothes caused a sensation. But she was unable to start her own business and worked for others: 4 years for Missoni, 6 for Aujard. From 1981 to 1983 she again tried to start her own *griffe*. She fell back on prestigious collaborations with Cerruti, Rabanne, Hermès, and Scherrer. According to the critics, she had much less success than she deserved. (*Mino Colao*)

Baj Enrico (1912-2003). Italian painter, among the artists who founded the Movimento Nucleare in Milan. In 1961 he designed for the Bruna Bini Collection an outfit made up of a blouse and skirt decorated with inlays of fabric, plastic, and military medals. It represented a lady general and was meant to be placed next to his paintings illustrating the same subject in his *Dame e Generali* period.

Bakelite The ancestor of plastics, a substance invented and patented in 1909 by Leo H. Baekeland. It had many uses, including the manufacture of costume jewellery. It was used from the 1920s until the early 1950s to make billiard balls, telephones, radios, kitchen tools, poker chips, buttons and, of course, costume jewellery. A resinous and dark material, it could be dyed almost any color, though it had the defect of becoming easily faded over time. It was also almost indestructible. Bakelite was able to imitate many other materials, including marble, ivory, amber, coral, and tortoiseshell, as well as various precious and semi-precious stones. It can be transparent, translucent or opaque. Over time it takes on a surface patina and tends to crack. In the U.S. there are already, of course, several books on the subject, as it has become a collector's item, and not at cheap prices. These books include: *Bakelite Bangles: Price and Identification Guide*, *Bakelite Pins*, and *Bakelite in the Kitchen*. Pieces in particular colors are much sought-after. These include Butterscotch, a golden yellow with a touch of brown produced only during the 1930s; End-of-the-Day, a blend of three or more contrasting colors; and Star Dust, transparent with specks of gold, which disappeared at the end of the 1930s. The demand and prevailing prices are such that the vintage items are no longer enough in sufficient supply, and new pieces are manufactured with recycled Bakelite. There is also a fake Bakelite, known as Fakelite. It is important to be able to distinguish it from celluloid and lucite, which are similar materials but lighter and more delicate. (*Gabriella Gregorietti*)

Baker Maureen (1925). British designer. She quickly achieved worldwide fame when, in 1973, the British Royal Family entrusted her with the creation of a wedding dress for Princess Ann. Until then, the official tailor to the Court had been Norman Hartnell.

❑ Baker is the designer of a line of hand-painted accessories for the house. These include small wall clocks, vases, and photo frames, a few of the objects usually sold in the department stores of Great Britain during the Christmas holiday.

Bakst Léon. The professional name of Lev Samojlovic Rosenberg (1886-1924), a Russian painter. A Symbolist, he created together with Diaghilev and Alexandre Benois the avant-guard movement known as The World of Art. He followed Diaghilev to Paris and was the most important costume and set designer of the Ballets Russes. He worked on *Schéhérazade* (1909), *The Firebird* (1910), and *Afternoon of a Faun*. His references to the folk traditions of his native land, charged with exoticism, influenced the French fashions of those years.

Baldan Maria Grazia. Jeweller, born in Udine but settled in Milan, where she started her career as a sales manager at Rubinstein. In 1973 she obtained the license to sell the jewellery of the American firm Kenneth Jay Lane in Italy. Shortly after, she decided to start her own business. She designed jewellery made of galalite and, in 1975, her first pieces in gold and ivory. In 1977, a journey to China was a revelation. While visiting the fair at Canton she discovered the fascination of ancient corals, of imperial jades, and of old coins. She took over a jewellery shop in Sardinia, in Porto Rotondo, and opened her first shop in Milan, in via Fiori Chiari. It was the early 1980s. Her pieces always showed a memory and love of the past, of objects with a story of their own, like an ancient coral or an antique jade. This characterizes her Collections even today, in a combination of old and new, strange and familiar. Her materials and inspiration come from frequent trips to India, Tibet, Afghanistan and China, in a never-ending search for unusual and rare objects and materials, from a 400 B.C. coin to a ruby from the Liao dynasty. The design for the setting comes later, in order to create pieces that are truly unique.

Baldaque Anabela (1964). Portuguese designer. She launched her own brand in 1993. Her Collections are for a modern and decidedly feminine woman, with a fashion sense that is up-to-date and contemporary. She likes a simple cut and favors precious and innovative materials of the best quality. Her clients are mainly women between 20 and 45 years old.

Baldassari Maurizio (1936). Italian designer. Born in Liguria, Maurizio Baldassari launched his first menswear Collection in 1983, at a moment when international demand for subtle Italian men's fabrics and clothing was pushing an entire generation of new Italian designers onto the international scene. Baldassari is a tailor at heart, working contemporary influences, including touches of leather and boldly modern hues, into a classic repertoire. Like many of his contemporaries, Baldassari began his career working for the Italian department store chain La Rinascente, where he served as a buyer and a consultant from 1957 to 1975. He left Rinascente to begin design consulting for fashion companies including Ellesse, Robe di Kappa, Redaelli and Levi's. In the same period he served as a design consultant for the Italian Fashion Committee of the Textile and Clothing Industries. Baldassari followed his menswear line with a lingerie line in 1988, and a women's Collection in 1989. In the 1980s he also designed a complete line for the Japanese department store Takashimaya.

Baldini Gianni. Draftsman and designer. After a brief career as a painter, in the 1950s in Florence he began to create textiles that were extremely graphic in style. Next was the creation of a prêt-à-porter Collection which left a vivid little mark on the flavor of that season. Married to an American model of Armenian origin, he moved to Santa Margherita for family reasons, and there, in the 1970s, he concluded his career. He was the first, in 1962, to show confidence in Walter Albini, entrusting him with his Collection.

Baldinini Italian shoe factory, established in 1910 in San Mauro Pascoli. Each year it manufactures 250,000 pair of shoes, of which at least 60% is exported. It has showrooms in Milan (Montenapoleone), in Düsseldorf (Königsallee), and in London (St. John's Wood). Since 1992 the company has expanded in Eastern Europe, where it has single-brand shops, the most important of which is the Moscow store on Revolution Square, a few steps away from Red Square. For the last thirty years, the company has been managed by Gianni Baldinini.

❑ The brand is today part of the Mariella Burani Fashion Group.
❑ The year 2002 ended with a total turnover of €22 million, with a net profit of 5%.
❑ 2003, April. Opening of a shop on Moscow's fashionable Tverskaya Street.
❑ 2003, Summer. Opening of a men's boutique in via Verri, Milan. The renovation of the historic space in via Montenapoleone starts in the fall.
❑ 2003, June. A presentation at Pitti Immagine of the results of the partnership between Baldinini and the German brand of men's and women's fashion René Lezard created for the manufacture of men's shoes.

Balenciaga Cristobal (1895-1972). Spanish designer. Starting in 1937, he made his career in Paris. Soon after the war I attended the presentation of seven Balenciaga Collections, but I never saw so much as the nose of the great Cristobal peeking out through a door or a curtain of his atelier, not even when the applauses and bravos overwhelmed the select, calm, and well-mannered audience. I had the opportunity to meet him once, by chance, at three in the afternoon in a little bistro. He was alone, sad, and elegant, eating an omelette with black olives and exchanging tender looks with his dog, which, if I remember well, was one of those small bulldogs called "the dogs of the Queen of England." A malicious person told me that in his last years Balenciaga, somewhat obsessive and ever more lonely, kept in his breast-pocket a linen handkerchief with which he would clean his dog's behind every time that the animal pooped in the street. Perhaps I shouldn't

Balenciaga portrayed by Cecil Beaton in 1953 (Prints Collection A. Bertarelli, Milan).

begin a portrait of Balenciaga, this Grandee of Spain, for twenty years considered an authentic, unsurpassed artist and – according to his very few friends – a simple and human man, with some foolish gossip. But I think I had in me, after so many years, the same reaction which makes schoolboys scream, laugh and shove each other when they get out of school after hours of being kept inside. This because in Balenciaga's atelier, the presentations had the atmosphere of a convent ruled by an extremely strict abbess, or that of a boarding school with the wicked headmistresses of certain German movies. Mademoiselle Renée, the implacable directress of the atelier on Avenue George V, had an almost sadistic relationship with journalists. Not only could one not speak, but one couldn't cough and, not for any reason at all, not even the outbreak of a world war, could one leave the room before the end of the presentation. These rules applied also to the models, who were not to speak loudly in the dressing rooms and could not show any facial expression when out on the runway. They were the ugliest models in Paris, but they managed to show great style without even the slightest concession: no jewels, no unusual hairdos, and no curly hair, which was abhorred. The famous Colette, with her Dracula-style walk, a ferocious bulldog look on her broad face, and hatred in her eyes, succeeded in selling more clothes than all the other models put together. One could not really say that these presentations were like parties, as was the case in all the other ateliers, from Dior to Fath. One suffered this torture because it was redeemed by the beauty of the clothes, a real art exhibit that one could not ignore if you wanted to "know" about fashion. "A titan of fashion," is what Cecil Beaton called him, expressing a sense of his greatness and his desire for solitude. He would see only a very few friends and his family, the brothers, sisters, nieces and nephews who managed the ateliers in San Sebastián, Madrid, and Barcelona. He didn't worry about worldliness or about other designers. This extremely proud Spanish man, with a very simple life; this exceptional tailor whose only passion was his craft, who was almost crazily devoted to his work; this artist, who combined the refinement of Paris with the classicism of Spain, the dramatic black-and-white with the reds, turquoises, beiges, and yellows of Goya, was one of the most remarkable personalities of 20th century fashion. And though, like Greta Garbo, always invisible, he was also one of the most praised. If, when talking about many famous tailors, the words "precocious predestination" seem appropriate, in the case of Balenciaga one must truly speak of artistic gifts, of inborn genius like that of Giotto, supposedly a young shepherd when his artistic talent was discovered by Cimabue. The young Cristobal didn't watch over sheep, but in Guetaria, his poor native village on the Basque coast, his future would have been as a fisherman or at the helm of his father's boat. But he preferred to sew at the side of his mother, who did extra work in order to add to the family's meager income. The only grand, rich villa in town was occupied in Summertime by the Torres family, with their old grandmother, a former beauty from Madrid and still an exceptionally elegant woman. Watching the old lady come out of church dressed in a suit of white tussor, with a straw hat covered in brown chiffon knotted under her chin, it seems that the young Cristobal said to her ecstatically "You are so elegant." This aroused the interest of the Marquise, and the young boy continued, "I will create dresses as beautiful as yours." In response came the playful challenge with which the Marquise gave him the task of copying her suit, which was by Poiret, with everything necessary to do so. Within five days, on his mother's old sewing machine, a trembling Cristobal made an almost perfect copy. The Marquise became his patroness and helped him find a job in a fashion house in Madrid in order to learn the profession. In 1915, at the age of 20, Balenciaga opened his first atelier in San Sebastián. After a few years, he opened two more, in Madrid and Barcelona, which he named after his mother, Elisa. Every six months he would travel to Paris to buy patterns from the great designers, Chanel being his favorite. He also began to design his own patterns using those inspired rules of proportion (a jacket could miraculously fit several sizes) that he would never abbandon. In 1937 the Spanish Civil War forced him to flee to Paris where, with a small amount of capital offered him by another Spanish refugee, he opened a head office in Rue

George V. If his début Collection had been a failure, he would not have had the money to create a second. But, instead, he obtained glory and riches. Balenciaga was by this time already 42, and the long years of hardwork and privation had left a bad taste in his mouth, a pessimism in his heart, and presented a painful dilemma between his desire to be recognized and loved and his aversion to any kind of publicity and to journalists. "Dior c'est fou fou," he would say, giving his opinion of that designer's availability to the press and of his position in the spotlight. Strangely enough, he shared with Cardin, who is exactly his opposite, the passion for houses (he had six), not to live in them, but just to collect them. His austere apartment in Madrid was done and redone several times only to have him conclude, after the first night spent there, that it was too noisy. His 16th century country house, the Reinerie, was outfitted with luxury bathrooms, every possible domestic appliance, and precious old rustic French furniture, only to be pronounced "too sad" after just a single day. He would spend some time each Summer in San Sebastián, where his sister Augustina took care of him like a loving mother. In Barcelona, where his atelier was managed by his nephew and godson José Balenciaga, he never set foot. Unlike all the other celebrity couturiers of the time who changed the shape and line of their clothes every six months (e.g. a trapezium, the letter H, a scissors-shape, or a swallow-shape), his changes were imperceptible but fundamental. When he came out with his famous black "sack," a scandal

A dress by Balenciaga in a sketch by Cecil Beaton of 1952 (Prints Collection A. Bertarelli, Milan).

was made of it and the style was openly ridiculed. And yet, that extremely well-proportioned sack became popular, and later, varied ever so slightly and fastened loosely in the front, became a tunic of such purity that it is imitated even today. His most famous tweed suit, with the off-center fringed neck and fastened in front by four large buttons, continues to be a source of lessons for other designers. The off-center neck was his obsession, and if he found himself in front of a lady in a suit with a close-fitting neck, he would instinctively open it. "The stem has to have air all around in order to regally support the flower that is the head." And on those heads, in his hats, he would express his inspired madness. But one has to remember that his pioneering lunacies (the short balloon dress, the immense kimono, the architectural asymmetry) could only be worn by certain women, "those" women of whom there were perhaps only five in the entire world. Among his clients were women such as the Marquise Llanzol, the most elegant lady in Spain; Loel Guinness, a thin, Mexican brunette who wore two strings of very precious pearls that interrupted the black of a jersey-and-mink dress, created exclusively for her by the great master; the Duchess of Windsor, as fanatic as he about the small details; the grey-haired Countess Idarica Gazzoni, with a very distinct elegance known all over Europe; not to mention his royal clients such as Fabiola of Belgium. These were the clients he liked, women who were decisive, confident in their choices and naturally elegant, because one of his few stated beliefs was precisely this: "No tailor can make a woman elegant if she isn't that way naturally." Alhough he was a man little interested in money, as seen in his constant rejection of attractive and commercially lucrative offers, especially from America (he never seriously considered an invitation to design a line of a prêt-à-porter), he had a sure sense of the value of his work, and when buying from him even the most illustrious and titled clients paid for their clothes on delivery. His was the only fashion house without accounts receivable. In 1968, he decided to retire. In his long career, there had also been opportunities to create costumes for the theater and cinema. These included the dresses for Alice Cocea and Suzet Mais in *Histoire de Rire* by Armand Salacrou (1940), the black sequin mantle, the mantle of death, for Christiane Barry in Cocteau's *Orphée*, the costumes for Arletty in *Bolero* by Jean Boyer, and those for Ingrid Bergman in Anatole Litvak's *Anastasia*. In 1973 Diana Vreeland dedicated a retrospective, *The World of Balenciaga*, to him at the Costume Institute of New York's Metropolitan Museum. In 1986, also in New York, the Fashion Institute of Technology organized the exhibit *Balenciaga*, and the following year the designer was commemorated by the town of San Sebastián with an exposit at Miramar Palace. From a chapter that Bettina Ballard, one of his very few intimate friends, dedicated to him in her book *In My Fashion*, three passages will illustrate his exceptional and contrasting character. About his appearance: "In 1937, when I met him for the first time, Balenciaga was a Spanish man with a gentle voice and a skin as white as an egg-shell; his hair was black, straight, shiny and combed backward on the well proportionate head; his thin lips offered a sudden smile only to express a sincere pleasure; his was an instinctive charm which inspired devotion." "He was a simple soul, he knew little of Spain and of its art. I never succeeded in taking him to Prado; he never travelled and he returned from his short journeys to Italy, where he lived by cultivated friends who told him about the country's artistic beauties, with a sense of stupor and coyness." After describing his Paris mansion furnished with Louis XVI furniture, Collections of precious Spanish bronzes or ivory Bilboquets, Bettina Ballard continued: "Not a single painting on the walls, neither music, nor a book." A poor life gathered around his fashion, for which he cried at the end of every Collection, because he missed the air to continue to live.

(*Maria Pezzi*)

❑ 2003, February. The firms's first American boutique opens in New York on West 22nd Street, as decided by the designer of the *maison* Nicolas Ghesquiere. The opening is combined with the *griffe*'s first presentation in America, during Fashion Week.

❑ 2003. Renovation of the firm's only boutique in France, on Avenue George V in Paris.

❑ The Balenciaga Museum of Guetaria,

the designer's hometown, should be completed and activated within 2003. For the time being, hats, dresses, sketches, jewellery and photographs of the designer can be seen at the Cristobal Balenciaga Fondation in an exhibit of 2,400 square feet in the center of the Basque town. (*Pierangelo Mastantuono*)

Balestra Renato. Italian designer. He made his début in the 1950s. His very feminine fashion is characterized by the large use of silk. In his recent Collections he has also used very modern fabrics marked by bright interwoven threads and combined with chiffon. A native of Trieste and a man of central European culture, he joined the world of fashion after studying engineering.

A sketch by Renato Balestra. Evening dress, Spring-Summer 1998.

A bet between friends convinced him to sketch a design, and it was thought so highly of that, without his knowing, it was sent to Milan and he was invited to collaborate on a Collection for the fashion show in Florence. Inspired by Jole Veneziani, the Fontana sisters and Schuberth, he opened his first atelier in Rome in 1960, on via Gregoriana, winning great success in America, in the Middle East, and the Far East. Among his most famous clients were Farah Diba and the Queen of Thailand. Today the house of Balestra is located on via Sistina and is particularly active. It has about thirty lines, from prêt-à-porter to men's wear.

❑ 2002, September. Balestra presents his Collection for Autumn-Winter 2002-2003 in the Royal Palace of Caserta.
❑ 2002-2003. After being appointed honorary professor at the Academy of Fashion in Beijing, he published his book *Alla ricerca dello stile perduto* (Rusconi editore). He designed the uniforms for the pilots of Philippine Airlines and for the Alitalia flight attendants. He hosted the TV program *Rosa Chic* (RAI Uno) and was a regular guest on the evening TV show *Chiambretti c'è*, with great success.

Balla Giacomo (1871-1958). Italian painter. In May 1914 he signed the *Manifesto del vestito maschile futurista* (Manifesto of the Futurist Men's Suit) in which he theorized the *Vestito Trasformabile* (Transformable Suit), a suit that could be modified by attaching fabric of different colors and shapes by means of snap fasteners. The first Futurist suit, "dynamic, aggressive, annoying, strong-willed, violent, flying, agile, joyful, illuminating, phosphorescent," as described by the painter himself, is from that year, while the first clothes created by the artist, in a large or fine checkered pattern, characterized by a basic but dynamic cut, came out in 1912. One of the masters of the Futurist Movement, he was very interested in clothing, considering it as a radical, futurist renewal of life, which would lead to his *Manifesto per la Ricostruzione Futurista dell'Universo* (Manifesto for the Futurist Reconstruction of the Universe), signed in 1915 together with his fellow-artist Depero. Starting in the 1920s, Balla created suits, ties, waistcoats, tapestries, fans, bags and hats in which the lines of velocity in his painting are transformed into extravagant arabesques and geometric decorations of vivid and contrasting colors. Each one is a unique piece and was created by the artist at his home in Rome, with the help of his daughters Luce and Elica. Some very important pieces belong to the Biagiotti-Cigna Collection (Guidonia) and to the Coen and Pieroni Collection in Pescara.

(*Cloe Piccoli*)

Giacomo Balla. Sketch of a dress, 1928 (from "Art Fashion". Biennial of Florence, Skira 1996).

Ballantyne Manufacturer of cashmere knitwear. Established in 1931 in Borders, Scotland, it is a leader in the industry. Production is 400,000 pieces a year. It is part of Dawson International Plc and recently opened Ballantyne Cashmere Italy. In addition to Italy, with 30% of turnover, its biggest market is Japan.

❑ 2002, September. Massimo Alba is the new creative director, while Alfredo Canessa is appointed president. Alba plans the brand's relaunch, relying upon a staff of young collaborators of different nationalities, all based in Milan. The manufacturing plants remain in Scotland.
❑ 2003, January. The new path of Ballantyne Cashmere begins at Pitti Uomo with a Collection designed by Massimo Alba and his staff.

Ballard Bettina. Journalist. During the 1950s she was editor-in-chief of Vogue America. She wrote a memoir called *In My Fashion*. Italian fashion owes her a great deal, as it also owes to Carmel Snow of Harper's Bazaar, Sally Kirkland of Life, Eugene Sheppard and Hebe Dorsey of the New York Herald Tribune, Fay Hammond of the Los Angeles Times, Nancy White of Life, and Matilde Taylor (she was a supporter of the correspondent Elisa Massai) of Women's Wear Daily which, in the season of the first presentations, supported it enthusiastically In February 1951, a few days after the first shows in Florence which gave Made in Italy its start, and at which only five Italian journalists appeared, Giovanni Battista Giorgini, the organizer, received this letter from Bettina Ballard: "Actually your event was too close to the French Collections to allow me to leave Paris. But I received excellent news from Jessica and Franco of Bergdorf Goodman and from Cole of Leto Chon Balbo. They all seem very interested in Italy, and Vogue is too. I'm sure that we will do something together very soon." That "soon" came quickly. On July 19th of the same year, Ballard sat in the first row at the Grand Hotel in Florence for the second *Italian High Fashion Show*. In her memoir, she commented on the success of Italian clothing remembering her time in Rome as a Red Cross nurse right after World War II: "When I saw those aristocratic ladies in Rome wearing dresses that were from before the war but made of flowered silk, with sandals like those worn by friars or else that were jewel-shaped, with large, fringed straw hats, I, who was dressed in the latest Paris fashion, felt very out of fashion. The victory of the Italian style was determined, indeed, by its imagination, by the inspiration of a fashion not made for special occasions, and not for the liturgy, but a fashion inspired by the Mediterranean and by living in its light and midst its colors."

Ballet flats Light, flat and very low-cut footwear, inspired by those worn by ballet dancers. They were introduced in France by Repetto, an American firm specialized in dance wear. The idea was taken up by Capezio, who created the patent-leather ballet flats with ankle ribbons. In the 1950s, launched on the cinema screen by Brigitte Bardot and Audrey Hepburn, they were back in fashion, especially for Summer, in colors matching the dress. In 1977, Saint-Laurent had his models wear ballet flats. Ten years earlier Roger Vivier had created for him the pilgrim's ballet flat, decorated with a gold metal brooch, which sold thousands of pieces.

Ballin Italian shoe factory in Fiesso d'Artico, near Venice. The Ballin brothers began their production of artisan-quality shoes in the immediate post-war period. Starting in 1945, and for more than 50 years, their success was guaranteed by the ever-more refined crafts-man-like perfection of their materials and their design, combined with modern industrial manufacturing techniques. Giorgio Ballin, today the president of the company, is one of the founders of ACRIB (Association of Industrial Shoemakers of the Brenta Region). Today, the company, with an annual production of 200,000 shoes, has won markets all over the world, from France to the U.S., exporting more than 80% of its production. This was made possible by the creation of new Collections, alongside the more traditional ones. The designers Jimmy Choo and Helen Joy have worked for Ballin. An avant-guarde technique and style characterize the new spirit given to the company by Anna Sui, the American designer who is the daughter of Chinese immigrants.

(*Marilea Somaré*)

Balloon Brand of prêt-à-porter fashion. It was created in 1976 by the brother-and-sister Roberto and Gabriella Greco. It was their idea to use artisan-quality yarns made in the Far East – such as silk, cotton and cashmere – to create clothes designed by them. Their line is based on the "total look." Since 1994 the Rome-based company has used the franchise system for its distribution, with 65 points-of-sale in Italy, 2 in Madrid and 1 in London (Covent Garden). The Balloon brand, aimed at the middle market, was soon supported by the Blunauta line, meant for a more demanding clientele. Starting in 2001 Blunauta became the firm's only brand, with Balloon remaining as the name of the company.

Ballu Isabelle (1967). French designer. Born in Brittany, at the age of 18 she left for Paris. Not liking the routine of an apprenticeship or the usual role of assistant to a famous name, she immediately began to design her own brand using her own money.

❑ 2000, April. The most glamorous representatives of French haute couture gather in Singapore for the French Fashion Furor. Ballu presents her Spring-Summer Collection together with Jérôme Dreyfuss, Eric Bergère, Christian Dior and many others.
❑ 2002, October. The designer presents her clothes at Fashion Week in Paris.

Bally Swiss brand of shoes. It dominates the industry, with 6 factories in Switzerland, 2 in France, 1 in England and an extensive distribution network throughout Europe. The brand is proud of being able to combine mass production with great craftsmanship. The company was established by Carl Franz Bally in 1851 in Schönenwerd. Fifty years later it expanded to France and, by the 1930s the company had 56 shops in Paris and the rrest of the country. By 1965 there were 240 Bally shops in 50 foreign countries. In 1978 the firm was taken over by the Swiss holding company Oherlikon Bürhle. In the early 1990s, Bally entered the clothing market, although shoes remain the core business, with about 9 million pairs produced each year.

❑ The managers of the brand don't worry about making a sensation or shocking people at the fashion shows, or about top models presenting their shoes. No, they care only about what is important, which means sales. The shoes are manufactured in leather that is so beautiful and soft as to feel like fabric. They are best appreciated from up close because of the cut, the weave, the folds, and other signs of skilled craftsmanship. It is fashion meant to be worn, a "clean" elegance which starts from below because, let us not forget, Bally is above all a giant in footwear. (*Lucia Mari*)

❑ 1999, November. The Texas Pacific Group (TPG) acquires the company from Oherlikon Bürhle.
❑ 2000. As a result, Scott Fellows is appointed creative director, the first step toward a relaunch as a luxury brand with global distribution.
❑ 2001. Bally celebrates 150 years of business and opens a shop in Berlin.

Bally Shoe Museum Schönenwerd, Switzerland. One of the most important footwear museums in the world, with more than 10,000 shoes, boots, and slippers of all types as well as various materials relating to their manufacture. The Collection began at the end of 1800s, when the Bally family decided to search the world for interesting shoes to use as inspiration for their own manufacturing. They accumulated crates of shoes from North America, Persia, Turkey, the Far East and the lower Nile. The specimens were exhibited for the first time only in 1915 in a show at the Museum of Applied Arts in Zurich. The family also began to collect objects and art work depicting shoes. The museum opened in 1942. The Collection was located in the former residence of Carl Franz Bally, near the factory. The displays document the historical and cultural evolution of the shoe.

Balmain Pierre (1914-1982). French tailor. His style was defined by the expression "Jolie Madame." He became very rich, but died poor. Hubert de Givenchy gave his eulogy in the church of Saint Pierre de Chaillot in front of a white coffin covered with white flowers, surrounded by people who worked in fashion personalities and a very few friends, while the organ played Mahler's Second Symphony. It was Paris' last goodbye to one of its major figures, who died on June 29th 1982 in the very same American Hospital where Fath, his contemporary at the beginning of his career, also died. Like Fath, he didn't have people willing to back him; like him, he was rich only in enthusiasm and skill, rewarded with sudden celebrity from his success. The press had not written about him for quite some time and didn't attend his presentations, which were considered uninteresting and stuck on that theme of the Jolie Madame which had made him famous, to which he would remain faithful, and which, after him, would return many times. And yet, in 1955, in an article for L'Espresso called *Dior, and you know who is Dior, didn't outshine him*, Camilla Cederna, after the surprise of her first meeting with that man who had a physique so at odds with the ideal of a great tailor, wrote: "A vigorous aviator (during the war), with wide, massive shoulders, a broad face with a short, impertinent moustache, and a high, ambitious forehead. This is Pierre Balmain, one of the greatest tailors of the century, his business turnover amounts to one billion liras." And again in 1964, in the preface to the English edition of his autobiography *Pierre Balmain, My Years and Seasons*, one can read: "To be chic, every rich woman who can buy her clothes in Paris must have at least one Balmain piece as the basis of her wardrobe." Fashion was his destiny: he would make dolls out of cardboard and dress them. That is the way many other tailors also began. Except that at the time Pierre was already a grown boy and his hobby was considered a scandal in the small village where he lived, Saint Jean de Maurienne in Haute Savoy: "A boy who wants to do a woman's job!" With an imperious command, his beautiful, strong-willed and adored mother (the only one who had influence over him, who was equally imperious and stubborn) ordered him to move to Paris to study architecture. Fortunately, as he himself would later say, an economic setback in his family obliged him to "earn his living." Therefore, in 1934, he began his time at Molyneux. In this atelier at the peak of success and snobbism, the provincial, ambitious, enthusiastic Balmain not only acquired a trade that was perfect for him, along with an English taste for a very sophisticated simplicity, but also came into contact with the powerful society elite which was Molyneux's clientele, with the tastes, refined lunches, salons, the charm, and the demands of the beautiful women of whom the Duchess of Kent, the most important client of the *maison*, was the representative. This craving for high society, luxury and wealth was to take permanent root in his Savoyard character, creating a dangerous conflict. In 1939 he went to Lelong along with Dior, with whom he became such close friends as to plan to open an atelier together. Finally, on October 12th 1945, came the big

Anonymous sketches at Balmain. Antonelli Collection, 1952 (*La moda italiana / Le origini dell'Alta Moda e della Maglieria*, Electa 1987).

leap. With some small savings, the pawning of his mother's jewellery, and a little borrowed money, he bought the building on Rue de François I which, enlarged and redecorated, would be his permanent place of business. He started with 20 workers, 50 models, and his mother and aunt as supervisors. That first Collection had two special godmothers. One was Gertrude Stein, the companion of Hemingway and Fitzgerald during their Paris years, and the other was her friend Alice B. Toklas. They were old and a little ridiculous in their masculine clothes. Balmain had met them in Savoy, where they stayed during the war. He won them over them with two suits and they became the Paris propagandists for his talent. They were unsightly but they were powerful in the cultural world that at the time mixed perfectly with fashion and high society. They gave him his first push, together with their friends Cecil Beaton and Christian Bérard who would introduce him to the theater world with the great success of the costumes for Giraudoux's *La Folle de Chaillot* (*The Mad Woman of Chaillot*). His first dress was sold to Princess Ghislaine de Polignac, and since then the list of his clients has constituted a true book of Gotha which included the Duchess of Kent, the Duchess of Windsor, the Countess Charles Emmanuel de la Rochefoucauld, Queen Sirikit of Thailand, the wealthiest members of the bourgeoisie, as well as various artists and divas. He dressed Katharine Hepburn in the film *Les Millionaires*, in which the actress played the most elegant woman in the world. He created the first extremely tight-fitting sexy black dress for Juliette Gréco, a dress which became the uniform of existentialism. Later, in the mid 1950s, even Brigitte Bardot, who was anti-fashion, turned to him when she had to go to London to be presented to Queen Elizabeth. They immediately had a violent disagreement, as she didn't want to cover her famous bosom (she was in competition with Marilyn Monroe for the best décolleté) and the tailor didn't want to trample on the etiquette of the Court. She left for London in a high-necked dress, but one which emphasized the curve of her breasts, and the tailor received a telegram which said, "Great success, all the journalists took note of my overflowing modesty." From presentation to presentation, he became more and more in the forefront of celebrity (in 1955 he received the *Neiman Marcus Award*), while his taste for high society, his theatricality, his ostentation when receiving guests at Elba or Croissy, grew in proportion. For a dinner in honor of the Royals of Thailand he ordered a trout weighing some 175 pounds from Lake Chad in Africa, and ordered some Florentine craftsmen to build a kettle almost five feet long. He never missed a season opening at La Scala, to which he offered flowers to decorate the boxes and where he made his entrance wearing a top hat and a bat-like cloak. He was always accompanied by his most spectacular models: the Irish Bronwen Pugh, very tall, swaying, and dreamy; and his favorites, Marie Thérèse and Praline. He was a man who attracted and rejected at the same time. A dualism that was very clear in the pages of the book *It Isn't All Mink*, written by Ginette Spanier, his directress for 20 "He was an extraordinary personality; he loves enthusiasm and emphasis, but he is a stubborn, obstinate perfectionist. He has no half-ways. He loves the very simple and demure blue and white dresses of Molyneux and the most luxurious evening toilettes in which, to create a contrast, he matched lynx fur and tulle, an ermine blouse with a white and black chequered skirt, luxury embroideries and the white foxes so appreciated by his client Marlene Dietrich. He adored very tall women, but small feet, dancing, the rich people and he asked Father Bernardet, from Savoy, to bless all his new boutiques." He knew the highest glory, but he was also the only great tailor to know the downfall. After the death of his mother, a solid Savoyard woman, Balmain lost also his precious friend and partner, a manager, an organizer, as Berger was for Saint-Laurent or Giammetti for Valentino. At the first crisis, he made the great mistake of selling his safest source of income, his perfumes (*Vent Vert* was a big success) to Revlon. Other difficulties followed. On the eve of the 30th anniversary of the house, he faced bankruptcy, which he tried to avoid. A loyal and proud man, he sold everything, from his house in Croissy to his property on Elba, and put all his personal assets into the firm. But it was not enough. The atelier functioned, the number of his clients did not drop, and the luxury prêt-à-porter line went very well, but nothing was organized according to the standards of the time, deliveries were never on time, and there were only two points-of-sale in Paris. The IDI (the Institute of Industrial Development) and some private banks tried to intervene. The *maison* was rescued and relaunched, and even expanded under his successor, the Danish Erik Mortensen, and later with Hervé Pierre, Alistair Blair and Oscar de la Renta. In 1975, Balmain wrote a long letter to his most devoted friend, Giuliano Fratti. It was a sad letter, and like a testament. It was mailed from Marrakech, but written on paper with Elba's initials: "This paper is all I have of my beautiful home. I am nothing but an old rich man."

(*Maria Pezzi*)

❑ 2002, March. Laurent Mercier becomes creative director in place of the outgoing Oscar de la Renta. The line is presented in October together with the new fragrance Balmya.
❑ 2002, July. After 10 years of collaboration with the *maison*, de la Renta presents his farewell Collection at the Paris Haute Couture week.
❑ 2002. The company acquires the factory and four shops of Mugler. The year closes with an operating profit of €1.9 million and a turnover of €25.9 million.

Banana Republic Chain of American stores known for updating and adapting the clothing of exotic travel, safaris, and the military. It became famous for bush jackets, Bermuda shorts, large blouses, overalls, and large multi-pocket jackets. The brand made its début in 1978. It came from an idea dreamed up by Mel and Patricia Ziegler, a married couple that worked for the San Francisco Chronicle, he as a reporter and she as an illustrator. On his various assignments, Mel would purchase military clothes in the shops and Patricia would alter them. They opened their first store in Mill Valley, California. The success was such that they were able to open more locations. In 1983 the brand was purchased by The Gap Inc. and is now their top line.

❑ 2002, October. For the first time after two years of free fall, the brand registers a 6% growth in sales, following the general trend of The Gap Inc, owner of the brand, which in the last quarter saw an increase in sales of $300 million compared to the same period of 2001.
❑ 2003, January. The positive trend in sales is confirmed by an 11% increase at the beginning of the year, due mainly to a reduction in operating costs and an updating of the shops and the brand image.

Bandana Cotton handkerchief in a simple flower pattern on a background of a bold color such as red, yellow, blue, or violet. It is manufactured based on an ancient technique from India known as "tie-dyeing." Adopted by the cowboys of the American West, it was worn on the face after being folded in a triangle in order to protect the nose from dust, or on the head, knotted at the back of the neck. During the 1960s, hippies made it a characteristic feature of their clothing. It was worn at all times and in all places, knotted at the back of the neck, by the American cult photographer Bruce Weber, by the mythical Kurt Cobain of Nirvana, and by Marco Pantani, the winner of the 1998 Giro d'Italia and Tour de France. It is very often worn in the islands of the Mediterranean, in particular on Pantelleria, brought back in fashion by Giorgio Armani and his guests.

Bandeau Band of fabric worn on the forehead in order to hold back the hair, and in sports to wipe away sweat. John McEnroe always wears one during his tennis matches, and hippies wore them during the 1960s. The hairdo of the same name, with a part in the middle and smooth bandeaux on the sides covering the ears and gathered up at the back of the neck, was made famous by Cléo de Merode. Olivia De Havilland had the same hairdo when playing sweet Melanie in the film *Gone With the Wind* and also in the film *The Heiress*, which was based on the novel *Washington Square* by Henry James.

Bandera Strong cotton twill in ivory or ecru, attributed to a probably mythical Monsù Bandera, but certainly manufactured in Piedmont as early as 1600 and, at that time, used universally. The ladies of the House of Savoy, awaiting the arrival from Paris of the second Royal Madame, Giovanna Battista di

Savoia Nemours, reigning after the death of her husband Carlo Emanuele II, used that cotton twill to cover the chairs, armchairs, sofas, worn-out damasks, and velvets that could not be replaced because the treasury had been "impoverished by many wars...." The ladies did even more. Copying designs from the stuccoed walls and the painted flowers in the boudoir, they embroidered a bandera using a herringbone stitch, a stem stitch, and a chain-stitch, thus giving his name to this embroidery that is definitely of Piedmontese origin. Handed down from mother to daughter, and from one lady of the manor to another, the manufacture of this fabric was taught in schools and it was produced to order in workshops up until the 1930s. It was later resumed by Consolata Pralormo who, finding herself in difficulty during the restoration of the bandera-embroidered canopy of a four-poster bed in her own castle, first sent some women of the village who knew plain embroidery to learn the bandera technique from the surviving experts. Then, in 1993, she opened a school in Turin where more than 600 students learned it. Bandera also made a début in fashion. Consolata Pralormo created waistcoats on which were embroidered small bunches of flowers that seemed to come out of the pockets, as well as shopping bags and elegant clutch bags all in a flourish of small fruits and birds.

(*Lucia Sollazzo*)

Bandolier A band made of leather, fabric, or metal worn over the shoulder and across the chest, inspired by military gear, from which hangs a bag known as a bandolier bag or a shoulder bag. The first bag of this type was presented by Chanel in 1920 and became popular because lightweight clothes couldn't have many pockets. At the time of the Second World War, the bag was relaunched by Schiaparelli. Made of rough and heavy leather like that used for a postman's bag, it could hold a great deal and was quickly adopted for use when bicycle riding. But it was above all starting in the 1970s that it became very fashionable and took the place of the more bourgeois handbag with handles. Whether made of untanned leather, tanned leather, suede, canvas, or microfiber, it has become an indispensable accessory for a woman's wardrobe, for its convenience and practicality, just like the small backpack and the pouch.

Bangles Inspired by the traditional women's jewellery of certain African tribes, such as the Masai, who wear them on their arms or around the neck. They are a series of many rigid rings, mostly thin, made of different colors and materials, all mixed together. They are in use in Europe since the beginning of the last century.

Banks Jeff (1943). English designer. Famous not only for his *griffe*, but also for his face: in fact he hosted for British television the only successful program about the world of fashion, *The Clothes Show*. He was born in Wales and then moved to London to study fabric engineering at the Saint Martin's School of Art. Between 1964 and 1974 he presented his designs at the Clobber boutique, where he sold his clothes alongside those of other young designers. Real success arrived in the second half of the 1970s, when he participated in the opening of the Warehouse chain of stores.

❑ 2001, June. The Graduate Fashion Week, an event created by Banks for young talents in fashion, celebrates 10 years of activity. It is one of the most important showcases in the world for new names in fashion, and can attract more than 40,000 visitors. It launched Stella McCartney, Antonio Berardi and Alexander McQueen.

Banlon A process of adding crimp and stretch to synthetic yarns, developed and patented by the U.S. textile manufacturer Joseph Bancroft & Sons. The yarn can be used to make knit or woven fabrics, and was popular for casually fitted shirts and socks in the 1960s.

Banton Travis (1894-1958). American fashion designer and film costume designer. His career began in New York in the fashion houses of Lucile and Madame Frances. In 1920, he designed the wedding dress that Mary Pickford wore when she married Douglas Fairbanks, which introduced him to Hollywood society. His first film sketches were for the femme fatale Pola Negri and for the "It Girl" Clara Bow. In 1927 he became chief costume designer for Paramount, a position that, notwithstanding his eccentric behavior, he would maintain until 1938. Less daring than Adrian – his antagonist at MGM – he had a more multi-faceted creativity. Thus, if for Mae West he could caricature in a felicitous way the genre of "1890s burlesque," for Marlene Dietrich he could invent not only exotic disguises that went to the limits of the absurd (*Morocco*, 1930, and *The Garden of Allah*, 1936), but also sophisticated evening outfits (*Desire*, 1936) and the famous brocade tunic with an undulating skirt (*Angel*, 1937) which influenced even Schiaparelli and anticipated the New Look. Whereas his creations for Claudette Colbert always had a delicious chic Parisian style, those for Carole Lombard had a cold and impeccable elegance. Miraculously balanced between the sublime and the ridiculous were the one thousand yards of cock feathers in a thousand shades of black created for the incredible apparation of Dietrich in *Shanghai Express* (1932), indisputably the icon of Hollywood camp at its highest level. Contrary to Adrian, he aimed to exalt the female figure to the highest, and his period costumes were often confidently anachronistic, more interested in the star's glamour than historical precision. The costumes of Claudette Colbert in *Cleopatra* (1934) were a glittering example of this, not really Egyptian but audaciously sexy and an anticipation of today's nude look, to the point that Banton could be given the credit or the blame for it. His recurrent problem with alcohol forced the end of his contract with Paramount. In 1938 he left his position to his collaborator and protégé Edith Head. Later on he worked for Fox and Universal, but his golden season was over. He is to be remembered for his fanatic attention to details and an obsessive search for perfection. He remains an example of high professionalism and of creativity that was versatile and controlled in a masterly way.

(*Alberto Lattuada*)

Baratta Ubaldo. Italian tailor. At the age of 15 he left his hometown of Salsomaggiore in order to test his abilities in Paris, at that time the capital of fashion. Ten years working in both large and small ateliers added style and professionalism to his craft. With this experience he moved to London and enrolled at the Minister's Tailor and Cutter Academy. He then returned to Italy and settled in Montecatini, whose thermal baths were very popular with high society. Among his clients were members of the Royal Family who granted him a royal patent. Eventually, he arrived in Milan where his atelier in via Borgogna became one of the cardinal points on the map of men's and women's tailoring. In 1956 he presented at Palazzo Pitti's Sala Bianca in Florence and, later, in Rome. He participated, with dresses made of artificial fibers, in the first meeting of *Moda Cinema Teatro* (Fashion Cinema Theatre) organized by the Centro delle Arti e del Costume (Center of Arts and Costume) at Palazzo Grassi in Venice. During the 1960s his workshop employed almost 200 tailors. He created a leisure space suit for NASA astronauts and, in the 1970s, uniforms for Alitalia. In 1967 he was one of the first Milanese tailors to join the National Chamber of Italian Fashion. In 1977, by now old, he sold the firm to Loretta Giovani. She furthered his ideas, updating them with the help of a modern and technologically advanced organization. In 1999 the brand was acquired by Gianni Campagna.

Barbas Raymond (1900-1983). French entrepreneur and president of Jean Patou. He joined that Paris fashion house in 1920 after his marriage to Marie-Magdaleine, the founder's sister. Susanne Lenglen, the six-time Wimbledon champion and dominant player in women's tennis between 1919 and 1926, owed her entry into the world of fashion to Barbas. After the death of his brother-in-law, management of the business was in his hands. He remained in charge until his own death, when he was succeeded by his nephew, Jean de Mouy. In the 1950s, at the head of a trade group of manufacturers, Barbas obtained from the government a series of measures meant to invigorate French fashion and the textile industry.

Barbato Gianni (1953). Artisan designer, born in Naples. After an apprenticeship with the town's most famous shoemakers, he started his own business. He created innovative hand-sewn shoes and used new leathers such as kangaroo, sometimes combining it with as many as twelve other materials, and also ivory horn for the heels. Eclectic, an experimenter, the first to relaunch the cowboy boot, he worked with Sergio Rossi and Fendi, and now works with Stuart Weitzman. His shoes can be found in the most important shops, from Paris to New York and from London to Tokyo, serving a high class clientele. Barbato has opened a company, Serbatoio, and a plant in Civitanova Marche.

(*Maria Vittoria Alfonsi*)

A Model by Gianni Barbato.

Barbeau Serge (1951). Canadian photographer. In 1975 at the age of 24 he obtained a masters in Communication and that same year decided to become a fashion photographer. Two years later he published his first editorial work in New York, and in 1985 he moved to Milan where he worked for the magazines Anna, Donna and Vogue Bellezza. In 1995 he moved to Paris where he still lives and works. His photos have been published in Biba, L'Optimum, Madame Figaro, Marie Claire France, Arena, L'Officiel, and Vogue Spain. Among his clients are Dior, Galeries Lafayettes, Lacoste, Lanvin, La Perla, L'Oréal, and Wella.

Barbeiro Luis (1960). Portuguese designer. He made his name on the international level in 1990, winning the first prize for industrial design at Intermoda. In 1983, after finishing his studies, he founded the fashion house *O Atelier* with Isabel Telinhos. His first Collection was presented at the Castello de Sao Jorge in Lisbon in 1987.

Barberis Canonico Historic textile factory established in Pratrivero (Biella) in 1921. It has become a major international firm and exports 70% of its production of fine fabrics all over the world.

❑ 2003. The factory's approximately 400 workers produce some 6 million yards of fabric per year, with wool coming mainly from Australia. Among the main export markets are the U.S., Germany, China and the United Kingdom.

Barbier Georges (1882-1932). French illustrator and master of Art Deco. Born in Nantes, he learned the trade in the workshop of Lésage. At the age of 26 he arrived in Paris and enrolled, after the start of classes, at the Academie des Beaux Arts, part of a group of friends that included Iribe, Boutet de Movel, Brissaud, and Lepape. Together with them, he worked intensely for La Gazette du Bon Ton, the Journal des Dames and des Modes, Fémina, and Comoedia Illustrée. From 1911 to 1925 he worked with the atelier Worth. His albums of sketches for the Nijinski ballets are very famous. He created sets and costumes for the theater and the cinema, including *Don Juan* by Edmond Rostand, *Monsieur Beaucaire*, a film with Rudolf Valentino, and, together with Erté, for the Folies-Bergère.

Barbieri Gianpaolo (1940). Italian photographer. He produced a theatrical image of fashion, presented in color and in black and white. Influenced by the cinema of the 1940s and '50s, he used that experience in setting-up his photos. For example, if a photograph needed to be full of tension, he found inspiration in the anguished Ingrid Bergman of *Spellbound*. After a start working with his father, an expert in fabrics at Galtrucco, and after an attempt to make his name in the cinema as an actor and as a cameraman, he met Tom Kublin, became his assistant, and chose to be a photographer. It was 1964. He worked for Harper's Bazaar and, in 1965, published his first work for Vogue-Novita. In the course of time, he produced advertising campaigns for some of the major fashion designers, both Italian and non-Italian, from Saint-Laurent to Valentino and from Albini to Versace and Armani. He published the books *Artificiale* (1982), *Silent Portraits* (1984), *Tahiti Tattoos* (1989) and *La mappa del desiderio*, with a text by Antonio Tabucchi, for the jeweller Pomellato.

> ❑ Publication of the book *Tahiti Tattoos*, with 125 black-and-white photographs on the ritual art of the island.
> ❑ 2001, October. The photographer offers his personal interpretation of the calendars which are found all over the walls of Italian homes. For GQ magazine Barbieri portrays the two "handout" girls (ragazze velina) of Striscia la notizia, under the artistic direction of Frankie Mayer.
> ❑ 2002, February. In the Photology gallery on via della Moscova in Milan, an exhibit about the 1960s and '70s called *Gian Paolo Barbieri – A History of Fashion* is dedicated to the photographer's work of that period.

Barbisio Italian hat factory founded in 1862 in Sagliano Micca (Vercelli). Along with Borsalino, it is the most famous brand. Its men's hats, all hand-made of soft felt of very fine quality, are known by the motto "Barbisio, a name, a brand, a guarantee." In the 1940s and '50s, with a return to male elegance inspired by Anglo-Saxon fashion, the hats with a rigid brim met with great success.

> ❑ 2001, February. Barbisio hats, along with the two other brands controlled by owner Giorgio Borrione, Bantam and Cappellificio Cervo, have a new showroom on via Mazzini in Milan.
> ❑ 2001, June. At Pitti Uomo the firm presents three different models of Panama hat manufactured in Ecuador using "toquilla," a particular variety of elastic and shiny straw obtained from the leaves of the *Carludovica Palmata*, or Panama hat palm, a plant typical of Ecuador.

Barbour Waterproof oilskin jacket sold by John Barbour in his shop in South Shields, an English coastal town, starting in 1894. It is an excellent example of the identification of a brand with a product. In fact, now, when one says Barbour, one means a type or a shape, like a loden or a montgomery, independent of who manufactured it. The real Barbour, made of 40 pieces of oilskin fabric sewn together with more than 15,000 stitches, is manufactured in the United Kingdom and has had extensive distribution in Italy since 1983, the year in which WP Lavori of Corso became the exclusive distributor and launched a true fashion trend. The first Barbour shop was under the name J. Barbour & Co., Tailors and Drapers. Today, the word "drapers" is out of fashion. It is related to drapery and in the 1800s indicated anything which had to do with fabric and clothing. In the Barbour shop they produced the first oilskin waterproof jackets, sold under the brand name Beacon, which had as part of its logo the South Shields lighthouse. Barbour raincoats were immediately very popular with sailors and with people who lived ashore. In 1908, Malcom Barbour, the son of John, created the first mail-order catalogs and launched the model and the brand starting with the idea of selling complete oilskin outfits not only to mariners but also to anyone working in the open air. In 1912 Barbour transformed itself into a limited liability company, J. Barbour & Sons Limited. Malcom's son Duncan entered new markets, including clothing for motorcyclists. In 1930 a new type of oiled cotton, Thornproof, less rigid than the earlier material, was introduced. At present Barbour manufactures 11 different varieties of jackets and a wide range of accessories. Since 1965, the company's president has been Margaret Barbour, the widow of John, the son of Duncan.

Bardelli Shop for classic men's clothing in Milan. In 1941 Matilde Bardelli opened her first hat shop in the famous premises at Corso Magenta 13. In the 1950s, she began to be interested in men's clothing. She was helped first by her oldest son Gianco, and later by her two other sons Domenico and Mario, while Bona Orombelli, Gianco's wife, took care of the women's line. Today, Bardelli selects the best from both Italian and foreign manufacturers of classic but up-to-date clothing and is considered an essential stop for elegant clothes, especially for men.

Bardot Brigitte (1934). French film star, but more sex symbol than actress, universally known as B.B., a major figure in the cultural mythology of the 1950s and '60s. She had a look that was both naïve and provocative, made up of several different elements but without specific reference to any particular garment or accessory. It could include long blond hair that fell to the shoulders, or else a long ponytail, plus make-up in different shades of pink, black ballet flats, Capri pants, a tight belt around the waist, a strapless bra in a checked Vichy pattern, and boat-neck blouses. It was, in fact, a total look, one which has influenced generations of women. Often imitated was the lace-trimmed pink wedding dress with a low, round neckline that the actress wore on the day of her second wedding, in 1959. The myth of B.B., which began with her study of dance at a very young age, and continued soon after with her career as a model, posing for magazines such as Elle and Jardin des modes, exploded with her back-lit appearance behind a sheet in *Et Dieu... Créa la femme* (1956), a rather modest film directed by her first husband, Roger Vadim, but one which established Brigitte as someone to be followed and imitated. The most powerful moments of this myth are not connected primarily with the release of other successful films, but mostly with the more titillating moments of her complicated love life. In the collective memory of the culture, Brigitte is also the star who made the cotton bikini into a great success, with that very light cotton also used for aprons and men's shirts celebrated even by Paolo Conte. Among her films are *La verité*, *Le mépris*, *En cas de malheur*, *Le repos du guerrier*.

(*Sofia Leoncina Gnoli*)

Barentzen (de) Patrick (1932). French designer. Born in Paris to a noble family of Danish origin, at the age of 18 he began as a draftsman for Dessés, then worked as a model maker for Jacques Fath until that designer's death. In 1956 he arrived in Italy. In Milan he worked with Fercioni, Jole Veneziani, and Rina Modelli. Along with Monsieur Gilles, he designed hats for Projetti. In Rome, he worked for several fashion houses. His sketches are found in the archives of Schuberth, the Fontana sisters, Antonelli, Fabiani and Simonetta. He designed two Collections for Luciani and Falconetto. He decided to open his own tailor shop on via San Sebastianello in 1958, with the valued cooperation of Monsieur Gilles, the famous milliner and creator of astonishing hats. In 1960 he made his début on the runway in Florence of Palazzo Pitti's Sala Bianca. His French origin is particularly evident in his stylistic references to Balenciaga. In 1966 he started a line of prêt-à-porter. His association with Monsieur Gilles came to a halt when Gilles decided to open an atelier with Rocco Muscariello, the assistant of De Barentzen known by the name Rocco Barocco. In 1972 he shut down his business and left Italy, never to return.

❑ 2000, November. He is among the participants in an exhibit that Malta dedicated to Italian fashion of the period 1950-1970, a show that moved to the Aldobrandini stables in Frascati a month later. Barentzen was of course also involved in the tribute that the most important boutiques on via Borgognona in Rome paid to Monsieur Gilles, showing the hats of that milliner with whom the Danish designer had been professionally linked throughout the 1950s.

Barleycorn Line of casual shoes that is part of Fornari, one of the most important Italian companies for young fashion, with its brands Fornarina, Nose, and Brain. Started with a single men's item in the mid 1990s, it soon added more items and within two years it entered the women's market. The element which makes the brand recognizable is the rubber stripe on the side that wraps around the shoe's entire upper giving the idea of great craftsmanship.

Barnes Emma. English knitwear designer. After a master's degree in Fashion Knitwear at the Royal College of Art, in 2001 she won the Way In Harrods Competition prize. She has designed for Alexander McQueen. Her knitwear Collection for Autumn-Winter 2001-2002 was inspired by Mexico. The natural and synthetic fabrics, all printed by hand, with their lace and ribbons, reproduced the eclectic atmosphere of the messages found on the altars of old Mexican churches, covered with flowers, ribbons and photographs. Mexican clothing, on the other hand, with its sharp contrasts of bright colors, inspired her to match knitwear with other materials like chiffon and cotton.

(*Gabriella Gregorietti*)

Barnes Jhane (1954). American designer. She has adored fashion ever since, when she was very young, her school gave her the task of designing the uniforms for its music band. It was a great success and her teachers encouraged her to enroll at the Fashion Institute of Technology in New York. While still attending that school, she cut and sewed a pair of pants for a friend who was a model. By chance, in a restaurant, the buyer for a department store saw the model and the pants, and ordered 1,000 pairs. This was the beginning of her adventures. It was 1976. She focused on men's clothing and accessories. Her specialty was and remains fabric designed in a photo-realism style, transferring from the computer directly to the weft. This allowed her to make original and unique combinations of designs and colors. This technique has contributed to her creativity and allowed her business to expand to furnishings with a line of fabrics for upholstery and carpets.

(*Priscilla Daroda*)

❑ 1999. Her second fabric Collection, in which she experimented with the photo-realism technique, wins two *NeoCon* awards, a *Gold Award for Textiles*, and a *Most Innovative* award. In that same year she also won four *Good Design* awards from the Museum of Architecture and Design in Chicago for the upholstery she created for Collins & Aikman.
❑ 2000. The opening of her fourth shop in Las Vegas, in the Alladin Hotel, selling men's wear, accessories, carpets and fabric.
❑ 2001. Bernhardt asks her to create a line of items for the home. Among the most important pieces in the Collection is an absolutely minimalist cocktail table in steel and aluminium. Her business partner Eddie Di Russo, a reliable tailor and a friend since the beginning of her career, dies.
❑ The launch of Frequency, a new line of men's casual clothing, and of Oceania, for the carpet division of Collins & Aikman.

(*Pierangelo Mastantuono*)

Barnett Sheridan (1951). English designer of sober style and classic line. Between 1969 and 1973 he was a student at the Hornsey College of Art and the Chelsea College of Art in London. After that he worked as a freelancer and as a teacher. In 1976 he opened a design firm with Sheilagh Brown, but it was unable to establish itself and was shut down 4 years later.

Barneys Department store in New York selling ready-to-wear. It was founded by Barney Pressman who, in order to rent the premises and obtain his first merchandise, pawned his wife's engagement ring. Within a few years this great New York department store became a leader in men's ready-to-wear, and in 1968 it began to sell European designers. In 1976 a new women's department was opened, and within a decade it led to the opening of a new main store. At the beginning of the 1990s a joint venture with the Japanese financial firm Isetan allowed the company to open branch stores in the U.S. and Japan.

Barocco Rocco (1948). Designer from Naples, active in high fashion and prêt-à-porter. He works in Rome and is famous for the refinement of his brocade and lamé fabrics, and for the tiger- and leopard-spotted designs used for dresses, coats and jackets. He has always extolled a sensual, ironic and non-conformist woman. On Summer vacations in Ischia, at a very young age, he worked at Filippo, a boutique near the harbor where Silvana Pampanini, Gianna Maria Canale and Anna Magnani came to buy their dresses. As he recalls, he is the one who suggested to Magnani that she wear the black petticoat which soon became the symbol of her "Mediterranean" appeal. There he met Patrick de Barentzen and Monsieur Gilles, who had a famous atelier in Rome on via San Sebastianello. The two designers convinced him to move to Rome. In 1968 de Barentzen moved to Paris and Barocco entered into a partnership with Gilles. They set up on via Ludovisi, but fairly soon Rocco decided to open his own atelier. Success was almost immediate, thanks to

Rocco Barocco: trousers and evening top (1998).

well-known clients like Claudia Cardinale, Stefania Sandrelli, Ursula Andress, Sandra Milo, Liza Minnelli and Laura Antonelli. In the 1970s his Collections stand out for their optical patterns and bell-bottom trousers. His travels to the East were a great source of inspiration, especially in the search for fabrics, especailly brocades and silks. During the 1980s, though still dedicated to high fashion, the designer began to work in prêt-à-porter and became diversified. It was the start of second lines such as Fashion and RB, of men's suits, oversized clothes, swimwear, shirts, various leather goods, foulards, gloves, umbrellas and perfumes.

(*Eleonora Attolico*)

❑ Unconventional and joyful, and at the same time very chic: these are the clothes of Barocco. Everything is assumed, as in every self-respecting movie script : he is always at the service of a risqué sensuality and, at the same time, offers tailoring that would please even the Duchess of Windsor. He has a passion for research and the working of material. At the Milano Moda Donna for Winter 2003-2004, he enchanted everyone with his prohibitively expensive extra-smooth, diamond-embroidered mink coats, and the hand-knitted lynx coats that were like a pullover. There was a change in course, however, for the men's Collection. After being inspired by the dandies of the past, the Winter 2004 Collection looked to the simplicity of the 1950s and to the myth of James Dean. He amazes by not wishing to amaze.

(*Lucia Mari*)

❑ 2003. For the Summer, the designer turned to jewelled costumes embellished with crystal and paste which recalled American jewellery of the 1950s.
❑ In contrast with many of the big names in fashion, Roccobarocco continues to rely on licensees for the manufacture of his women's wear. Knitwear is manufactured by Sicem, in Soliera (Modena).

Baron Fabien (1959). French graphic designer. He did the graphic restyling of Vogue Italy (1989), Interview, Harper's Bazaar (1992) and laid out the dummy for D-La Repubblica delle Donne in 1996. After proving himself in the graphic studios of Paris, he chose to be in New York, where he moved in 1982, finding a job at G.Q. very quickly. He was part of the launch of New York Woman and was chief graphic designer at Barneys, the department store. He often worked in partnership with the photographer Steven Meisel. They are responsible for the page make-up and the images of *Sex*, the provocative book by Madonna.

❑ 2002, April. After six issues, he abandons the post of editor-in-chief at Arena Homme Plus. For the forthcoming Autumn-Winter 2002 issue his place was taken by Ashley Heath, whose place had been taken by Baron and the art director Art Lloyd in 1998.
❑ He works with Calvin Klein on the new fragrance CKbe, and with Hugo Boss and Issey Miyake. For Klein he produces a commercial with the collaboration of Wayne Maser.

Baron Simone (1909-2000). French journalist and decorator. Born in La Rochelle, she studied at the Academy of Fine Arts, becoming a designer and a decorator. After her studies she began to work with several newspapers, including Jardin des modes and Marie Claire. In 1939 she worked for Aujourd'hui, which was under the direction of Henri Jeanson. In 1948 she was introduced to Hélèn Gordon-Lazareff, the director of Elle, who on seeing her exclaimed: "Your are small, me too, we will get along!" (they were both less than five feet tall), and became chief editor of the magazine. In this period she began her climb to success. Together with Lazareff she would revolutionize the world of the woman's weekly. Starting in 1957 she had a column for women in France-Soir, one of the most important French newspapers. In 1963 she went to Journal du Dimanche as the fashion editor and stayed there until 1995.

(Daniela Bolognetti)

Baroni Italian clothing manufacturer specialized in knitwear, established in Concordia, Modena, in 1966. Established in order to manufacture men's and women's knitwear in a simple and traditional style, in 2003 Baroni entered the field of textiles. Giancarlo and Deanna Baroni, the present leaders of the company, have put together a new team of designers in order to create a new men's line which also includes T-shirts and shirts. Baroni's production is split into five fashion lines: Baroni women's and Baroni men's, both of which connote leisure and elegance; the Deanna Baroni line, more glamorous and dedicated to women; and the Roberta Puccini and Filiblu lines, the first for women and the second for men, which are aimed at a young customer and therefore lean toward the casual but still remain elegant. The Baroni lines are manufactured completely in Italy and distributed in some 1,500 points-of-sale, of which 200 are outside the country. In 2001 the company's turnover was €23 million and the production was 700,000 pieces. *(Daniela Bolognetti)*

Barracan Garment made of camel or goat hair, ankle-length, loose-fitting, and with a hem that wraps around the body. It is typical of North Africa was in fashion in the West during the colonial period.

Barracco Giovanni (1916). Tailor born in Palermo, Sicily. When the Palazzo della Moda di Pillitteri e Merlet opened on Piazza Castelnuovo in 1925, Barracco was only 9 years old, but he went to work there, cleaning the three storey building which was divided into a milliner's, a fur department, and tailor's shop and a shop for daytime wear. In the tailor's shop, Gino Zonca and Piero Ingrassia did the cutting and sewing. They were his teachers. In 1932, at the age of 16, he was ready to enroll in the new Institute of Fashion in Turin, which urged Italian tailors to create fashions that were independent of Paris. During W.W. II, while he earned his living doing fashion sketches for the Calabri firm, he opened his own atelier in Florence on the Lungarno Acciaioli. After the liberation of Florence, he returned to Palermo and set up in via Villafranca. It was the time of dances at Villa Igea. But fabrics were scarce. In order to provide evening wear for some American Red Cross nurses he went to an umbrella factory and purchased forty umbrella cases and used them to make dresses. As soon as the conflict was over, he hurried to Milan in order to supply himself with fabric from the firm Villa, and there he met the dress maker Maria Marzolati. She would become his wife and help him in the atelier which he opened in 1946 and which would close only in 1980. Barracco dressed all the most beautiful and elegant women of Palermo, from Princess Arabella di Scalea to Countess Giovanna Trigona, from Marquise Lucia Pisani to Orietta Ascoli and Vita Zapalì. His competitors were the La Parola brothers and a small group of excellent dress makers: Enrica Stassi, Anna Capodieci and Maria Conigliaro. A great tradition had now ended.

(Antonella Romano)

Barret Bali (1969). French designer of prêt-à-porter. Her real name is Marie Amelie, but her little sister called her Bali, mispronouncing it. From this came the choice of her professional name. She worked for many years with Corinne Delemazure and Laroche. She created Collections for companies that sell by mail-order. She then went out on her own, setting a policy of affordable prices for very creative fashions. Her styles are sold in the Bon Marché chain of department stores, in Japan, and in London, in the trendy boutique The Cross.

❑ 1999. Her new line of women's clothing makes its début. It is made up of only 15 pieces in four basic colors.
❑ 2002, February. The opening of her first boutique in Paris, on Rue de Mont-Thabor. This begins worldwide distribution of her designs, which can now be found in Germany, Italy, Hong Kong and Japan.
❑ 2002. Presentation of her Spring men's wear "mini-Collection."

Barrett Italian manufacturer of classic men's and women's shoes, located in Parma. The firm has a long history. It was established in 1917 under the name Zet. In 1952, as part of a corporate restructuring, it adopted the name Barrett and gradually began to transform itself from an artisanal workshop into a real factory. In 1997 there was further change in the ownership. The son of a former associate, Paolo Putzolu, took control of the company. Under his direction, in 1998, the annual turnover increased 25%, going from 8 billion to 10 billion liras. The company employs 80 workers. In 1999 the firm launched the Blu Barrett line aimed at a more fashionable segment of the market.

Barrett Neil (1965). English designer. He is noticed and chosen by Gucci while studying for his master's in fashion design at the Royal College of Art, which he pursued after graduating from the Central Saint Martin's College of Art. Since then, from 1989 to 1993, he designed 10 men's Collections for Gucci. In 1994, together with Patrizio Bertelli, he set up the men's line of Prada and designed it for the following eight seasons. In 1998 he became the designer for Active Wear, a clothing brand which would make its début the following year, a product of the partnership between the industrial group Prato Lineapiù and Samsonite.

❑ 1999. He decides to settle in Milan, where he opens a showroom in via Savona.
❑ 2000. He launches his first men's and women's Collections during the Milan fashion weeks.
❑ 2001, October. Eyeglasses for men with added details that make the lines softer, thanks to lightweight materials such as glasant. This is the eyewear line designed by Barrett that was presented at the subdued Moda Milano Donna which followed the events of September 11th.
❑ 2002, June. The first result of his collaboration with Puma: a tennis shoe without laces made of canvas in combination with new and aged leather.
❑ 2003, September. The designer is appointed creative director of the new Puma Collections.
❑ 2004. He designs the uniform of the Italian national soccer team for the 2004 European Championship.

Barrett Slim (1960). Irish jewellery designer, born in County Galway. He studied painting at the Regional Technical College in Galway. In 1982 he moved to London where he began to work as a self-taught designer (something of which he is very proud, feeling himself free from any technical or traditional restraints). The following year he presented his first Collection. He has a faithful clientele that is a bit trendy and somewhat high society. He relaunched the fashion for tiaras with precious stones. He has designed jewellery Collections for Lagerfeld, Chanel, Versace, Montana, Ungaro, Galliano and Katharine Hammett. He works with his wife Jules de Bairead in a former match factory near Islington, a trendy area in north London. He is the designer of the small crown with 231 diamonds made for the wedding of Victoria Adams, one of the Spice Girls, to the soccer player David Beckham.

❑ 2000, January. He wins the De Beers Diamond International Award.
❑ 2000. In April the tiara designed by Barrett and worn by Victoria Adams on her wedding day goes to auction for the benefit of the Red Cross. The crown, made of 231 diamonds, has an estimated value of £120,000.
❑ Barrett is listed in the Guinness Book of World Records for a gold tiara, a one-of-a-kind piece manufactured for an exhibit at Wartski in London celebrating 100 years of designs for tiaras.

❑ The creativity of the Irish designer enters the temple of British jewellery, Asprey & Garrard in Old Bond Street, together with the work of 29 other colleagues.
❑ The Victoria and Albert Museum in London and the Ulster Museum in Belfast put some of Barrett's works on permanent display.

Barrie Scott (1946-1993). American designer. His very sexy and impudently provocative dresses brought him quick success. He belonged to a lively group of African-American designers who, at the end of the 1960s, established themselves on Seventh Avenue in New York. The most distinguishing feature of his work is a particularly sensual use of jersey, cut in unusual and fanciful ways. In 1983 in Milan he established Scott Barrie Italy in partnership with the Kinshido Company of Japan.

Barthes Roland (1915-1980). Essayist and critic, among the greatest French exponents of Structuralism. In his work – *Le degree zero de l'écriture* (1953), *Mythologies* (1957) and *Éléments de semiologie* (1964) – he paid attention to fashion, examining and analyzing it on a semiotic level and as a system with philosophical and social content. Barthes examined the world of fashion in his book *Savoir et style*, using linguistic structuralism and the ideas of the Swiss Ferdinand de Saussure as a point of departure, starting with the relationship between language and words. In *Système de la mode* (1967) he examined its intrinsic meaning and connection to society and everyday life.

Barthet Jean (1930-2000). Milliner. Originally from Béarn, the region in southwest France that is also home to the beret, Barthet soon left the provinces for Paris, where he introduced his first hat Collection in 1949. His growing reputation led to his designing for films (*Les Demoiselles de Rochefort*). From the 1960s through the 1980s his exquisitely crafted, witty creations dominated high fashion and high society. His jet-setting clients included Jacqueline Kennedy, Sophia Loren and Elisabeth Taylor, and in this period he also collaborated on Collections with Kenzo, Sonia Rykiel and Ungaro.

Bartlett John (1963). American designer. He has an international reputation as an innovator in men's fashion. Born in Cincinnati, Ohio, he started drawing at the age of 16, inspired by Brooks Brothers clothing and the uniforms of the Salvation Army. He graduated in sociology from Harvard and later he majored in economics in London. In 1986 he returned to the U.S., and, after enrolling at the Fashion Institute of Technology, he started to design for Willi Wear. In 1992 he opened a shop in the West Village and launched his first men's Collection. Fashion columnists reported that his antique linen, silk and denim suits restored to men the traits of a lost masculinity. In April 1997, he presented his first women's Collection inspired by Hollywood film noir of the 1940s. Also in 1997 he concluded an agreement with Genny Holding to produce and distribute his Collections in Italy.

❑ 2000, January. He makes his début at Pitti Immagine Uomo with his collectiion for Autumn-Winter 2001. It is the first time that the young American designer presented his Collections in Europe.
❑ 2002. He presents a new clothing line, John Bartlett Uniform.

Bartley Luella (1974). English designer, born in London. She has the appearance of a young girl and reminds one of a very young Jodie Foster. Her resume includes experience as a journalist for the Evening Standard, British Vogue, and Dazed and Confused. She belongs to the world of the "disorderly." Music and the street are her sources of inspiration. She is a sort of small Westwood and makes fashion in order to distinguish herself, to not go unobserved. After all, she is a great friend of John Galliano. Her leather mini-dresses sprayed with fluorescent graffiti celebrating Iggy Pop, Mick Jagger and Johnny Rotten are cult items. She is very famous in Great Britain and many other countries where young people love her intriguing, feminine and ironic style that is rich in creativity, color and fantasy. An anti-conformist, her clothes show a connection to an elite that she actually opposes and that she can have a very intellectual or extravagant idea of glamour, and exactly the opposite. She often revisits punk, and even grunge. She made her début at Milano Collezioni with the Winter 2001-2002 show. Her Collection is as she is, rich in personality and boldness, qualities which allowed her to win the *Designer of the Year* award in 2000.

(*Lucia Mari*)

Bartolomei Corsi Sandra. Fashion journalist. She began writing in the 1950s for Secolo XIX and Il Globo. She was one of the few journalists present at the début of Italian fashion in the house of Bista Giorgini in Florence on February 12th 1951.

Barzini Benedetta (1943). Top model and cover girl. The daughter of Luigi Barzini, Jr., the famous correspondent of Corriere della Sera, and Giannalisa Feltrinelli, she made her début as a model in 1963 in Rome for Vogue America and was photographed by Leonbruno/Body wearing a necklace by Buccellati. She was discovered by Consuelo Crespi, at the time a fashion editor, who noticed her in the street without knowing that she was the daughter of family friends. She was 20 years old. After that photograph, Diana Vreeland, the director of Vogue, sent a telegram inviting her to New York to work with Irving Penn. She was supposed to be in New York for ten days but stayed for five years. Five years in which, in front of the cameras of Bert Stern, Sokolowsky, and Avedon, her lined, aged face became the sophisticated interpreter of that exotic Mediterranean look that Americans liked so much. When she returned to Italy, she was one of the favorite models of Ugo Mulas. Today she is a journalist and teaches a course on the history of clothing for the School of Fashion Designers at the University of Urbino.

❑ 1999. Publication of her book written with Samuele Mazza, *Aldo Coppola: Talking Heads*, dedicated to the art of the famous hairdresser.
❑ 2001, March. She returned to the Milan runway, for the Autumn-Winter Collection of Stephan Janson.
❑ 2001, April. Viafarini of Milan hosts an exhibit on the German artist Tobias Rehberger, who creates installations using the clothing of personalities in fashion, music and theater who have had an influence on the collective imagination. Next to items worn by Barzini were others worn by Caterina Caselli, Francesco Moser, Rita Pavone, and Paolo Rossi.
❑ 2002, March. Very much in demand, she divides her time between Gucci, Dolce & Gabbana and Gattinoni.

Basf German company and worldwide leader in chemical and pharmaceutical products, coloring agents, and textile fibers. Its president is Jürgen Strube. Among its most well-known brands are Zantrel, Zefran, Vivana, Golden Glow, and Golden Touch. The fiber division of Basf Corporation is based in the U.S., in the state of New Jersey. It produces synthetic fibers in polyamide, polyester and viscose.

Basic English-language term adopted in the 1980s to indicate clothing that is easy-to-wear, practical, loose-fitting, and casual. It refers to garments that are uncomplicated and easily available. A good basic outfit is made up of jeans, a T-shirt, and sneakers.

Basile Italian clothing company. Some of the greatest names of the Made in Italy fashion movement worked here, including Albini, Tarlazzi, Soprani, and Versace. The company was established as a tailor's shop by Remo Basile in 1951. In the 1970s Remo's son Gianfranco joined the business and transformed it into a manufacturing company focused on a refined total look that maintained the firm's tradition of excellent tailoring. Supported by this strong image, in the middle of that same decade, the

Basile. Cardigan and men's shirts (1982).

company became part of the FTM Group, made up of Aldo Ferrante, Gianni Tositti and Gigi Monti. The objective of the group was to produce and distribute various promising lines of prêt-à-porter, especially Italian ones. After a short period of difficulty, Basile's success was consolidated at the end of the 1980s thanks to a partnership with the Japanese company Mitsui and Kimbun, which opened the door to the Japanese market for the Italian firm.

❑ Today the owner of the Basile brand is Reality of Milan, which controls the production of ties, scarves, hosiery, bags, watches and accessories. Gigi Monti is the stylist coordinator.

Basketball sneakers Sports shoes and casual wear. One of the most obvious examples of how a piece of sports gear can become a true fashion phenomenon to the point of turning into a status symbol on a level equal to that of other more formal clothing accessories. Their use as a street shoe began at the beginning of the 1970s, with a real explosion in the decade that followed, thanks in part to the many different styles offered by the three leaders of the international market, Adidas, Nike and Reebok. Continuous technological research (injection soles, ventilation systems, anatomical modelling) and constantly updated styling, in order to offer newer and newer models, with the help of ever-more original advertising campaigns, have focused the attention of the mass media, affecting the clothing styles of young people for the last three decades. The original version of this shoe, high around the ankles, with laces in front, colored fabric, and a rubber sole, was designed for basketball players, in order to provide a functional and comfortable shoe that had clean lines and was affordable. A similar shoe, in fabric and with a rubber sole, but low around the ankles, is used in tennis.

Bassetti Historic firm dealing in linens. It was established in Milan in 1830 by Carlo Baronicini with the opening of a shop for cloth and blankets and would become the foremost Italian company dealing in linens for the home. During the 1840s it became associated with a hand-weaving mill in Rescaldina, a small rural center near Legnano. In 1864 Giovanni Bassetti joined the company and, 20 years later, after taking control of the firm, he began an intense program of travel aimed at expanding the business. One day, crossing the Straits of Messina by boat, he was shipwrecked. Although he was rescued, the cold temperatures gave him fatal pneumonia. His wife Rosa became head of the company and an early example of the female entrepreneur. After a change in company name to Società Giovanni Bassetti, the three heirs, Ermete, Felice and Giovanni, purchased a finishing mill in Trezzo sull'Adda. The boom years of the 1960s saw Bassetti expand in the European market, especially in France, Spain, Germany and England. In 1964 a new continuous process plant was opened in Rescaldina, with production according to a precise coordination of the various sectors, which for the first time were connected to each other. It was the début of the Piumone, Brio, and Teso lines, and of the new sheets with releasable bed corners, the Perfetto line. In the first half of the 1990s, Bassetti took over the French company Jalla, a producer of terry cloth, and also Descamps, which had some 140 points-of-sale in Europe. In early December 2001, the brand was absorbed by the Zucchi Group, who already owned 85% of it.

(*Pierangelo Mastantuono*)

Bassman Lillian (1917). American photographer. In her photographs, the material sense of what she documents finds support in the skillful use of light. Her bold experiments in form have not always been appreciated by her clients. In 1942 she started at Harper's Bazaar working with Brodovitch and, in 1945, she became director of a spinoff, Junior Bazaar. After being forgotten for many years, she was honored at the Festival de la Photo de Mode in 1994, and the New York Institute of Technology dedicated an exhibition to her in 1997 on the occasion of her 80th birthday.

(*Angela Madesani*)

Bastida Asunción (1902-1975). A standard-bearer for high fashion in Spain, she made her début in 1926 in Barcelona, her hometown. In 1934 she moved to Madrid. During the years of the Spanish Civil War (1936-1939), she was forced to stop her work. In 1940, the great dress maker (she was recognized as such even by the great Paris designers) took part in the founding of the Cooperative of High Fashion. In 1970, her atelier, which had as clients many people connected to the Franco regime, shut down, but she continued to work until her death.

Bata Multinational shoe company. Active all over the world with more than 100 subsidiaries in 90 countries, the Bata Shoe Organization today has a network of 6,000 direct points-of-sale. The group's motto is: "Think global, act global," which means to exploit economies of scale and to satisfy local needs. Established in Zlin, Czechoslovakia in 1894 by Thomas Bata, it now has its headquarters in Toronto, Canada. The Bata family still leads the firm with Thomas G. Bata, the founder's nephew, as general director, and his father, Thomas J. Bata, the current president. (*Valeria Vantaggi*)

❑ Bata begins the new millennium under the control of the Hello firm, owned by Francis and Jean-Michel Werling.
❑ 2002, March. The birth of Sportgroup, a non-profit joint venture consortium between Bata Italia and Trops. The partnership, with headquarters in Padua, is open to the participation of new partners and acts as a coordinator for the purchase of shoes, clothing, and sports accessories, and for marketing.
❑ 2002. In the first six months the company had a turnover of €115 million, an increase of 11% over the same period of the previous year, and sold a total of 2.5 million shoes in the four different chains that it owns: Bata City, Bata Superstore, Bata Factory Store and Athletes World.
❑ The multinational has a shoe museum in Toronto, Canada.

Bates John (1938). Designer in the Swinging London of the 1960s. He is considered one of the inventors of the pantsuit and of very short miniskirts. Born in Ponteland, Great Britain, the son of a mine worker, he worked first as a journalist and then as a fashion illustrator. In 1964, together with two partners, he founded the prêt-à-porter firm Jean Varon. It was the beginning of the success which would lead him to design costumes for Diana Rigg, the star of the TV series *The Avengers*. Starting in 1974 he designed his own line.

❑ Perhaps the most famous model created by Bates, the "A-line dress," with the bodice removed and replaced by a simple knit mesh, is on permanent display at the Museum of Costume in Bath, England.

Bathrobe Shaped like a dressing gown. For a long time made only in white cotton smocking, then later mostly in terry cloth, the bathrobe has always been found where there is water. Meant to be used when getting out of the bathtub, it was manufactured in a silk ivory color during the 1930s as a complement to beach pajamas. Today it is an important item that goes along with a set of towels, with which it can match patterns, colors, and embroidery. It receives substantial attention from designers.

Batik Malaysian term meaning a dot or design. It is a method of printing textiles, perfected by the inhabitants of Java since the fifth century A.D. Printed silks in batik patterns were presented for the first time in France at the Universal Exhibition of Paris in 1900. Before dyeing, the parts that are not to be colored are covered with liquid wax. This gives the typical marble or dotted effect, with irregular patterns, more or less worked out, but unique and unrepeatable. Cotton batiks are used for African "pagnes" and Indonesian sarongs; those made of silk are often the work of artists.

Batiste Very thin fabric of cotton or linen, soft and transparent, often used for underwear, but also for shirts and handkerchiefs. According to tradition, its name comes from Baptiste of Cambrai, who was the first to produce this kind of fabric, back in the thirteenth century.

Batlles Ramon (1895-1978). Catalan photographer, famous as a portraitist and as a writer on fashion. During the 1930s he worked with the most prestigious magazine in the field at the time, "D'Acì I D'Allà." He later went into partnership with another important Barcelona photographer, Josep Compte, with whom did various fashion work and created advertising campaigns.

Battaglia Family and brand name of various historic shops dealing in fabric, men's wear, and women's fashions, opened by the brothers Salvatore, Enzo, Amedeo and Ettore Battaglia in the Sicilian cities of Palermo, Catania, and Taormina. The shops were opened gradually over the years according to the family's moods and break-ups. The story began in 1923 with a fabric shop on Palermo's centrally located via Ruggero Settimo. It continued with an alliance between Amedeo and Enzo which gave birth to Battaglia Esquire Fashion (men's wear), with success in Catania, with the first boutique in Taormina, with a second Esquire Fashion in Palermo on via Cavour, and with Battaglia Clubman, which Enzo opened in Piazzetta Ruggero Settimo. There, starting in 1970, together with his own women's boutique, he sold Hermès brand merchandise on an exclusive basis. Enzo Battaglia has been a master of commerce and elegance. Many of his employees have started successful businesses. (*Antonella Romano*)

Battelle Kenneth (1927). American hairdresser. Famous in the 1960s for his impeccable dome-shaped hairdos, he soon became Jackie Kennedy's favorite hairdresser, while his work was immortalized on the cover of Vogue America by models like Veruschka and Jean Shrimpton. His hairstyles are characterized by an impressive formal elaboration and by the frequent use of hairpieces for the most refined effects.

❑ 2001. He leaves the hair salon at the Waldorf-Astoria, by now a New York institution, and the management is taken over by the young Kevin Lee.
❑ 2003, March. Publication of Michael Gordon's book *Hair Heroes*, dedicated to the most important American hair stylists. Kenneth Battelle is remembered as "the one who invented Jackie Kennedy's fluffy hairdo."

Battilocchi High fashion Italian tailor's shop. It was established in the 1920s in Rome, at via Sistina 67, by Aurora Battilocchi. Among her clientele were members of the House of Savoy, of the aristocracy, and of the high bourgeoisie. Many of her clothes were purchased in Paris, while a small part were manufactured to Italian designs. In the strict and severe Battilocchi "bottega," Maria Antonelli and the Fontana sisters developed their skills, learning the refined use of detail and an ability to cut fabric, with an almost fanatic play at putting the finishing touch on something. "It was like living at court," remembers Micol Fontana, "you didn't just learn the job, but also the ways in which to present a finished dress."

Battistoni Boutique in Rome founded by Guglielmo Battistinoni in 1946. A student at the Academy of Fine Arts, he soon became, out of necessity and vocation, a shirt maker. He made the collar points longer and slightly larger than classic models, modernizing men's shirts. His boutique, located in an interior court off via Condotti, became, starting in the 1950s, a meeting place for artists and literary men. Still today, one can see pictures by Picasso, Modigliani, Guttuso, Matta and Cocteau on the walls. Among the most regular clients were Andy Warhol and Marlon Brando, as well as the Duke of Windsor, Charlie Chaplin, Marc Chagall and John Cassavetes. Alberto Moravia collected Battistoni's famous *croatté* ties. Furthermore, the shop was known for its Oxford and *fil à fil* shirts, its sport jackets, morning coats and smoking jackets, both ready-to-wear and made-to-measure. Battistoni is today managed by Guglielmo's children, Gianni and Simonetta, and has been able to diversify with a line of women's prêt-à-porter, four perfumes (the *Marta* and *Mars* bottles were designed by Renato Guttuso), foulards, crocodile-skin belts, and shoes. In Milan, they have a boutique on via della Spiga. (*Eleonora Attolico*)

❑ 1999, November. Presentation of the new fragrance Creation, at the opening of the Giacomo Manzù exhibit at the Maison Battistoni in Palazzo Caffarelli, Rome. It continues the duality of art and fashion that has characterized the firm since its earliest days.
❑ 2002, March. Via Condotti celebrates Rome, cinema, fashion and the chronicles of the 1950s and '60s in the

exhibit *Eleganza e Illusione* (Elegance and Illusion). The designers of via Condotti opened their personal archives and brought out period photographs, files, and catalogues. In the atrium and courtyards of Battistoni, the elegance of Dino Pedrali met the "illusion" of five unpublished shots from Fellini's last film, *La Voce della Luna* (The Voice of the Moon).

Battle jacket Long jacket closed with a zipper and metal buttons, with broad drooping shoulders, used by both men and women as a garment symbolic of casual wear and the army surplus aesthetic. It was an absolutely indispensable item in 1968 and the early 1970s. Like the Eskimo jacket, army boots and multipocket trousers, by the end of the 1990s it was no longer in fashion.

Baudoin-Masson Brand of ready-to-wear launched in 1983 by two Belgian designers, Anne Masson and Eric Baudoin, who had just graduated from the École Nationale des Arts Visuels in Brussels. At their début they won the prize for men's fashion at the Hyères Festival, open to young designers. Their fashion is sober, without any straining after effect.

Baudrillard Jean (1929). French sociologist and writer, born in Reims. He became interested in fashion while studying the production and consumption patterns of modern society. His books include *Les systems des objets* (1968), *La Societé de consommation* (1970), and *De la seduction* (1979). His opinions are strongly critical. Fashion, like the market, is one of the culprits responsible for a decline in societal values, and for their destruction. This is a change allowed by the system so that, in substance, there is no real change. Fashion doesn't move forward, but continues to put forward again what has already been done, it turns on itself, applies modern make-up to what has already been seen.

Bauhaus Weaving workshop (1920-1933). Part of the Bauhaus cultural program starting in 1920, under the direction of Georg Muche, who would preside over it until 1927, it was initially attended only by women, with a small number of men attending later. Set up to teach weaving techniques, hand and machine embroidery, and tailoring, and enjoying a good deal of autonomy, it immediately established a strong connection with the carpenter's workshop, in order to make decorative elements that could be coordinated with furnishings such as carpets, tapestries, cushions and linings. Already in 1923 this department was producing things for sale, experimenting with fabrics blended with cellophane, chenille, and artificial silk, favoring innovative fibers in combination with more traditional ones. The greatest impetus on the level on stylistic innovation came from the lessons of the Bauhaus' great artists. Fundamental was the influence of Johannes Itten on students Otti Berger and Anni Albers, who worked with basic shapes such as the circle, the square, and the triangle, and often in pure colors. Through the studies of the weaving workshop, the typology of the tapestry would be completely revolutionized. There would no longer be a traditional narrative and figurative background, but compositions that were geometric and bidimensional, more in line with the ideas of the new abstract art. Besides, even the lessions of Paul Klee, Kandinskij and Moholy-Nagy favored the progressive affirmation of these tendencies with the result that fabrics and designs would more and more resemble geometric paintings. In 1927 Gunta Stìlzl became director of the textile department and promoted the opening of an in-house dye-works for fabric. In the Dessau era, a new impetus was given to industrial design in order to develop a new and significant professional figure: the textile designer. After the dismissal of Stìlzl in 1931, Mies van der Rohe asked Lilly Reich, an interior designer from Berlin, to coordinate the activities of the workshop, and she would point it towards the production of printed fabrics for fashion and furnishings up until the forced closing of 1933.

(*Aurora Fiorentino*)

Bawa Alpana. Indian designer born in the Punjab and raised in New Delhi. In 1983 she moved to New York (where she still studies and works) in order to attend the prestigious Parsons School of Design. The influence of her native land is evident in her passion for brilliant colors and precious fabrics like silk and brocade, in the service of a contemporary "western" style to be combined, always with original results, with Oriental taste. The men's Collection follows the same ideas. The firm's headquarters is in Soho, New York.

(*Francesca Gentile*)

Bayer German manufacturer. It is one of the most important companies in the production of dyes and synthetic fibers. For many years it has sought the advice of famous designers such as Verner Panton and Olivier Mourgue who, with their creativity, have exploited to the maximum the possibilities offered by the firm's fibers and dyes. It also produces a wide range of auxiliary textile products which are used to improve the quality of fabrics and leathers. The company's oldest division includes 800 dyes, optical blueings and pigments for the dyeing and printing of various materials. Among Bayer's fibers are the following brands: Dralon (polyacrylic), Perlon (polyamide), Dorlastan (elastan), and Dorix (polyamide).

Bayerisches National Museum The national museum of Bavaria, in Munich. It has a Collection of clothing and accessories with thirty thousand pieces. The oldest garments date to the 16th century. There are many regional folk costumes clothes as well as examples of 20th century fashion. The fabric Collection contains pieces dating to the period of early Christianity. Of major importance is the in-house center for research and restoration.

BCBG American manufacturer of women's clothing and accessories, founded by Max Azria in 1989. In 1981, after 11 years of experience in the field, the Parisian designer and entrepreneur moved to the U.S. in order to launch Jess, a chain of French boutiques for the American woman. The success of the initiative pushed Azria to open a fashion house that combined a sophisticated European style with an American spirit. It was the birth of BCBG. In a mode of continuous expansion, the brand has 140 points-of-sale throughout the world, with 80 of them in the U.S. In 1998 Azria acquired the French *maison* Hervr. In 2000 he formed a strategic partnership with Procter & Gamble in order to revitalize Giorgio Beverly Hills, the historic boutique on Rodeo Drive in Beverly Hills. In 2001 he launched the "Giovane" Collection of perfumes and accessories.

(*Francesca Gentile*)

Beach-jamas Large trousers for the beach, named by the American designer Ken Scott, the creator of many styles in the fabulous 1960s.

Beard Peter (1938). American photographer, born in New York. He studied art at Yale. His main interest wasn't fashion, but Africa, its animals, the savannah, elephants, and crocodiles, a passion that "stuck to him" after he met the writer Karen Blixen in 1961. And it was in Africa, on a fashion assignment, that he discovered Iman, an Ethiopian, transforming her into one of the most celebrated top models of the 1970s and '80s. In 1999, the designer Gerard Darel, famous for purchasing Jacqueline Kennedy's pearl necklace at auction in 1996, entrusted to him the advertising campaign that featured Stephanie Seymour.

Beat An existential and literary movement that was interested in the creation of a style that would be the literary equivalent of the be-bop rhythm of Charlie Parker and Thelonius Monk, rather than in the details of tailoring. In his books *The Subterraneans* and *On the Road*, Jack Kerouac, who was the prototype of the beat artist, used the character of Sal Paradise to meet every kind of hipster, zoot-suiter, pachuco and biker, and ever mentioned his dress code. Like a contemporary anthropologist, the beat writer doesn't participate, except as a witness, in the rituals he describes. His personal style remains supremely relaxed and nonchalant in the normality (often super-conscious) of his own clothing and hairstyle. The same applied to all the early members of the group, with the exception of William Burroughs, who was the movement's Buster Keaton, according to Tom Leary, and wore a three-piece grey suit (jacket, trousers and vest) and a felt hat, whether he was in Tangiers in 1958 or London in 1967, in the full bloom of the psychedelic era.

(*Maurizio Vetrugno*)

The Beatles English musical group. They reached the top of the charts not only because of their music but also because of their image, a source of inspiration and a reflection, at different times and in different ways, of the youth culture of the 1960s and 1970s. Originally from Liverpool, John Lennon (1940-1980), Ringo Starr (1940), Paul McCartney (1942) and George Harrison (1943-2001) dressed like kids from the outskirts of town in the 1950s: leather jackets and black T-shirts in the style of Gene Vincent. It was the photographer Astrid Kircherr, German girlfriend of Stuart Sutcliffe (a musician who was briefly associated with the group), who recognized the necessity of a more coordinated image for the band. In Hamburg, during a tour in 1960, she cut all the band members' hair, creating the famous moptop, a sort of helmet of hair with thick bangs, which made them istantly recognizable. A few years later – the Beatles were by now well advanced along the road to fame – their manager Brian Epstein decided to coordinate that image further. He called Dougie Millings, a show biz tailor, and asked him to create for them a modern but not excessively non-conformist look. In 1963 the Beatles began wearing what would become their uniform: Pierre Cardin-style jackets, with a tailored cut, but without collars, cigarette pants, narrow Edwardian style ties, and ankle boots with Cuban heels. Thus adorned, in 1964 they went on tour in the United States and their look had an immediate impact on fashion (as did that of their girlfriends, who wore Mary Quant miniskirts). In the second half of the 1960s, the image of the Beatles changed, keeping pace with the major changes in the youth culture of the times, especially marked by the antiwar political struggle and the terrible advent of drugs. Some of the songs that emerged were *Lucy in the Sky with Diamonds* (L.S.D.) and *All You Need Is Love* (Peace, not war in Vietnam) both from 1967. And so we see their new wardrobe: a hippy psychedelic style, bell bottom jeans, kaftans, embroideries and beads, long and unkempt hair. The image, however, was always well coordinated: the band always got its clothes from popular tailors and designers, such as Tommy Nutter or The Fool, and from the most exclusive boutiques.

(*Virginia Hill*)

Beaton Cecil Walter Hardy (1904-1980). English photographer. For more than half a century he was the portraitist of international high society. He began to take photos while in high school at Harrow in London and later at St. John's College in Cambridge. From the almost Victorian mannerism of his first portraits – Daphne du Maurier, for example – he came to the "angry" poses of the painter Graham Sutherland and the poet W.H. Auden. A great snob, he was attracted by famous people whose portraits he would carefully "construct." In England, he was for decades the court photographer, helping to create an image for Mary, the Queen Mother, and for Elisabeth II. In the meantime, in the 1930s, already famous for his fashion work in Vogue, he discovered Hollywood. Endless was the stream of celebrities who posed for him for Vanity Fair. Among them were Buster Keaton, Gary Cooper, Lillian Gish, Vivien Leigh, Norma Shearer, Johnny Weissmuller, Marlene Dietrich, Marlon Brando – very young, in 1947 – Audrey Hepburn, Sinatra and his clan, Marilyn Monroe and, above all, Greta Garbo. He himself, in his memoirs, wrote that the diva was his only female passion. After idolizing and chasing her for years, he was finally able to meet her again only in 1946 in New York. He fell in love to the point of asking her, in vain, to marry him. In 1940, the man who made frivolity and refinement into a way of life was called to the service of his country. At first, he was asked to take the official photos of the Queen to be sent to the troops, and then to portray Winston Churchill at his very tidy writing-desk, with a giant cigar in his mouth and a crafty look on his face. His photograph of a little girl wounded during a bombing in London and recovering in the hospital was published on the cover of Life and helped convince the American public of the need to enter the war. He photographed the London underground when it was used as a bomb shelter. Then he was asked by the Ministry of Information to document the war in North Africa and the Far East. At the end of the war he returned to high society and to his passions, among which was the design of costumes for the theater and cinema. His designed for *Anna Karenina* with Vivien Leigh in 1947; for *My Fair Lady* on Broadway in 1956 and, later, for the film with Audrey Hepburn, which won him an Oscar; and for *Gigi* in 1957. In 1972, he was knighted. Semi-paralyzed but determined not to give in, he did his last work for Vogue on the Autumn 1979 Collections. The novelist Truman Capote said about him, "What makes Beaton's work so unique is the extraordinary visual intelligence that permeates his photographs. The historians of the next century will be even more grateful and thankful to him than we are." Among his books are *The Book of Beauty* (1930) and *The Best of Beaton* (1968). In 1971, the Victoria and Albert Museum in London exhibited his work as an eye witness to fashion. (*Giulia Borgese*)

Beatrice Modelling agency founded in Milan in 1976 by the Frenchwoman Beatrice Manigoff Traissac, who is still the director. Even though it is quite important, it has always tried to have a limited number of highly select models. Among the most famous in 1999, were the top models Tanga, Karen Elson and Stephanie Seymour.

Beaumenay Joanet Isabelle (1957). French designer of knitwear. She was born in Oasis de Gassin. She studied architecture at the École des Beaux Arts in St. Etienne (1979), and then moved to Paris where she worked for 10 years as a graphic designer for comic strips. She decided to take courses in fashion design at the Studio Berçot in Paris (1992). Between 1993 and 1995 she was the assistant of Veronique Leroy. Later, with Daniel Oblette, she created her own brand. She specializes in knitwear with special attention paid to technique and materials.

❑ 1999. She designed the Autumn-Winter 1999-2000 Collection for Elite Models Fashion. She opened a Paris showroom in Boulevard Saint Denis.
❑ 2001, February. The designer's styles are presented in Milan at Zip Zone.

Beaver Very warm, soft and strong fur, waterproof with a regular and velvety appearance. Honey-colored beaver was very fashionable in the 1960s. Nutria is less expensive version.

Beccaria Luisa (1956). A designer from Milan, and a descendant of Cesare Beccaria, the 18th century jurist and author of *Of Crimes and Punishments*. Another of her ancestors was Giulia Beccaria, the mother of Alessandro Manzoni. Married with four children, she defines herself as a designer who had a calling: "When still quite young, I designed my first ball gowns." In 1989, on the occasion of her début at Milano Collezioni, she amazed the public by presenting a tableau vivant in which young girls from high society participated. But her real début goes back to 1980, when she presented a few of her designs at the Fornasetti art gallery, just for fun. Everything sold within three days. The fun, then, had turned into work. The originality of her creations, rich in details and made with precious fabrics, in unusual and surprising colors, is fascinating. The rest is common knowledge:

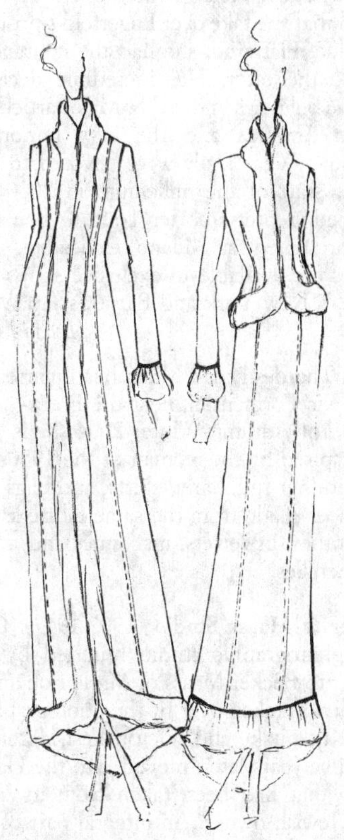

Luisa Beccaria. Indian ink sketches of coat and evening dress.

her Collections became an important part of each season, and she opened a single-brand (mono*griffe*) boutique for women, children and bridalwear. She also opened an atelier handling made-to-measure clothes exclusively. Her success had many aspects: a major figure at the high fashion shows in Rome; a guest of honor in Paris with her presentation during French haute couture week; an invitation by the Italian Institute of Culture in Paris; and more presentations of haute couture in Paris. Her woman of dreams is charming, sometimes frail like a Lalique crystal, or an echo of memories past, wearing clothes inspired by the paintings of Fragonard and Winterhalter. And also, there are references closer in time that remind us of the stars of Hollywood and bring us a contemporary romanticism that is rich in suggestiveness. The Vendôme Group suggested that she take over Lagerfeld's position at Chloé. Flattered, she had the courage to decline the offer. Her incredible decision became big news in the U.S. Major articles in Vogue America and the very important Woman's Wear Daily were devoted to her. At the start of the millenium in 2000 she designed a prêt-à-porter couture line that was presented at Milano Collezioni. Her clothes are available in exclusive shops like Barney's New York and Barney's Japan.

(*Lucia Mari*)

❑ The designer's Milan headquarters is in via Formentini, near the Brera.
❑ For Autumn-Winter 2004 she is inspired by the woman of the 1950s, with her full, flared skirts, and bags and shoes made from the same fabric as the clothes, in velvets, macramés and chenilles.

Becker & Maass Studio (1902-1957). German photographic studio founded by the firm Otto Becker Maass of Marie Bohem. In 1933 it was taken over by the photographers Else Kutznitzki and Victor Fest-Hofenfels who, five years later, moved it to the Harlip studio that had been taken from its legitimate Jewish owner. An integral part of the image-producing propaganda system of the Third Reich, for three decades it played a leading role publishing magazines such as Striwi and Konfektionaer, and managing its own publishing house. After the war, the studio suspended its activities and shut down completely in 1957.

Bédat & C Swiss brand of watches. It was founded in 1997 by Christian Bédat. With the help of his mother Simone, an expert in luxury watches, he decided to create a brand carrying the family name. His intention was to make an exclusive product which distinguished itself from other Swiss products through its identity and excellence. Bédat watches are in fact unique numbered pieces and have enjoyed immediate success in the U.S They offer very refined manufacturing and design. In 2000, the Gucci Group, interested the Bédat image, acquired 85% of the company.

Bedetti Pedraglio Silk factory established in 1925, when, at the death of its co-founder Cesare Maggi and the entry into the business of Ettore Pedraglio, the Bedetti-Maggi firm changed its name to Bedetti Pedraglio. The silk fabrics manufactured in the mill at Casnate (Co), are meant for wholesale and export. Until the post-war period, Bedetti Pedraglio was known especially for the production of "bema," a silk shantung fabric for men's suits. In 1949, Giulio Bedetti, nephew of the founder Arturo, took over from his uncle and became the manager. In 1952, Bedetti Pedraglio was put into liquidation and succeeded by Tessitura Serica Bedetti e Pedraglio, managed by Giulio, with production still at the mill in Casnate. In 1982, at Giulio's death, the management was taken over by one of his daughters. The following year the historic plant in Casnate was closed. From that moment until the day the firm closed, manufacturing was outsourced to third parties. In 1995 the company was put into liquidation.

(*Pierangelo Mastantuono*)

Bedford cord Very resistant ribbed fabric, originally made of wool, nowadays also of cotton, in imitation of corduroy. It derives its name from the Massachusetts town where it was produce in the second half of the '800. It's used in particular to make horse-riding pants.

Bedin Giovanni (1974). Italian designer. He followed a family tradition, as both his

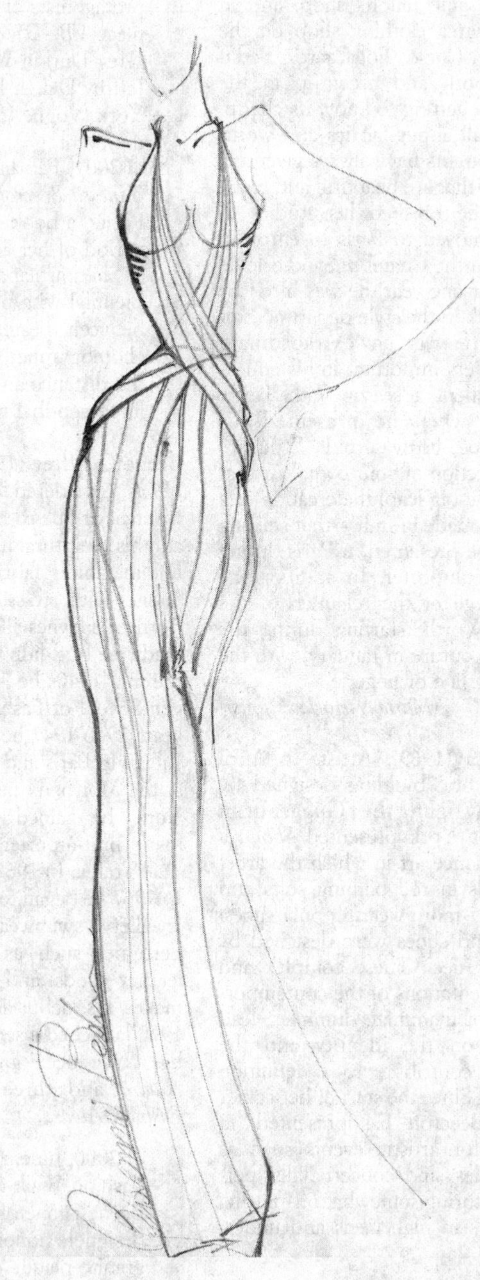

Evening dress by Giovanni Bedin.

mother and his father were clothesmakers specializing in menswear. They met while working in the same tailor's shop, and in Vicenza they own a clothing shop on the centrally-located Corso Fogazzaro. Bedin was therefore born and grew up in the world of fashion, getting to know its charm, its secrets, and all about fabrics and workmanship. "My parents have always given me a taste for things that are beautiful and real," he says. After he finished his studies in accounting, he moved to Paris to enroll in fashion courses at the Chambre Syndicale de la Couture. After one year, he was hired by Lagerfeld to work in the style department of the KL line. It was an extraordinary experience and very important in his education. He then spent a season with Tierry Mugler. Then, when he presented his portfolio at Chloé, he was told: "You are ready for a Collection of your own." At that moment came the big leap: the creation of a line of his own – made in Italy – that starting in 2001 would be presented in Paris during the week of prêt-à-porter. In addition, he was put in charge of the relaunch of the fashion brand Worth, starting during the week of Haute Couture in January, with the presentation of a line of lingerie.

(*Maria Vittoria Alfonsi*)

Beecroft Vanessa (1969). Artist. In April 1998, in its historic building designed by Frank Lloyd Wright, the Guggenheim Museum in New York presented *Show*, a piece of performance art in which the artist lined up 15 girls in red bathing suits and high heels, and 5 more wearing only shoes. The costumes and shoes were designed by Tom Ford for Gucci. These complex and enigmatic representations of the contemporary woman, or of inanimate dummies, lead one to reflect on the identity and the elements which contribute to a definition of her as fashion. Since the start of her career in the 1990s, Beecroft has presented, in places suitable for artistic events such as museums, galleries, and concert halls, performance art featuring somewhat off-putting female characters in high heels and underwear.

❑ 2000. Exhibit at the Kunsthalle in Vienna.
❑ 2000, December. The guests at Beecroft's wedding, celebrated a few weeks before in Portofino, become the protagonists of her performance art piece *VBGDW* (Vanessa Beecroft & Greg Durkin Wedding), shown at the Jeffrey Deitch Projects gallery in New York. Vogue Italia devoted an article to the event.
❑ 2001, February. Publication of *Vanessa Beecroft Performances* by Hatje Kantz, a book dedicated to the first period of her art.
❑ She participated in the Venice Biennial with performance art that was between theater and fashion, using choreographed models looking off into the distance and making almost imperceptible movements.

Beene Geoffrey (1927). American designer. He is considered an imitative follower of Balenciaga due to his perfect skill in cutting and his sculptural use of fabric. He is famous for matching fabrics in an unusual way: flannel with strass, and jersey with taffeta. Born in Haynesville, Louisiana, he studied medicine but didn't complete his degree. In the mid-1940s he is enrolled at the Traphagen School of Fashion in New York. In the years 1946-1947 he studied at the Académie Jullian in Paris and worked as an apprentice at the Molyneux tailor's shop. Back in New York, he gained experience working for many prêt-à-porter fashion houses such as Teal Traina. In 1962 he went out on his own. In 1967 he began to design and produce ties, jewellery, swimwear, eye glasses, watches, perfumes such as *Grey Flannel* cologne, leather goods, and housewares. In 1969 he makes his début in men's fashion and in 1970 launched a second line, Beene Bag. He has twice been given the *Neiman Marcus Award* and three times the *Coty High Fashion Award*.

❑ 2000, June. At the inauguration of the Fashion Walk of Fame in New York, Beene is one of eight American designers honored with a bronze and granite plaque on Seventh Avenue, the street of fashion.
❑ Eight *Coty Awards*, four CFDA prizes, and several career awards from

❑ museums and schools of fashion show how important the 76-year old designer is to the history of American fashion. ❑ The shirtwear brand is under the firm control of the giant Phillips-Van Heusen, which also holds licenses for Donna Karan, Arrow, Kenneth Cole, and others.

Beer Atelier opened in Paris in 1905 by the German tailor Gustav Beer who, ahead of his time and anticipating the relocation of the fashion houses, chose to be in Place Vendôme. He achieved a certain fame, even for his lingerie. His success allowed hi to open branches in Nice and Montecarlo. In 1931 the company name was changed to Agnés-Drecoll, and that firm shut down in 1953.

Beguelin Henry (1968). Swiss designer of accessories, including bags, belts and shoes. His discovery of leather, the material which would be part of his entire creative output, was due to a meeting with a master saddler in Locarno. In 1970 he opened a shop-workshop in Marina di Campo, a small village on the island of Elba. From here, his bags, shoes and belts arrived on the American market, thanks to his collaboration with Barneys in New York. In the mid 1990s the company was purchased by Tullio Marani, who also started the distribution of interior furnishings. In the U.S. he is distributed by Barneys. In 1999 he opened a second shop in Vigevano where his new Collection, Henry Cuir, is produced.

(*Lorenza Branzi*)

❑ 1998. With the split between the two partners, Marani remains sole proprietor. With his wife Claudia responsible for the design department, he gave new energy to the company, which now has 40 artisan-workers. ❑ The new millennium begins with the launch of a line of leather clothing for women. These are hand-made in the tradition of the firm.

A Belfe's model in a sketch by Brunetta (Biki Collection).

Belfe Italian clothing company. The business began in Marostica as a small family firm which manufactured semi-processed straw goods and waterproof garments. The name is an acronym of Pasquale Belloni and Franco Festa, who established the company in 1920. In 1930, as sole owner, Belloni specialized in casual wear and supplied clothing to the Italian army in Africa. Starting in 1950 production was shifted to activewear and leisurewear. Angelo Carlo, the son of Festa, took over management of the company in 1976. In 1990 he opened a leather department (Skinea) which produces Giorgio Armani's lines of leather goods, snow apparel, and sports apparel. Since 1998 the company has been guided by the third generation: Ludovico, Stefano and Francesca Festa Marzotto. The company's figures show more than 2 million pieces manufactured every year, 62 direct points-of-sale, and 40% of the production for export. In order to offer the complete range of its products, the firm has opened the Belfe & Belfe boutiques, with a line that goes from informal city clothes to a specific look for various sports.

❑ 2001. The year ends with a loss, on a net turnover of €77 million and a deficit of €9.37 million.
❑ 2002, January. There is a new stock offering and a new general manager for the historic company located in Marostica. He is Thierry Andreatta, already a member of the board of directors.
❑ 2002, September. An agreement with Raid Gauloises for technical planning, development, distribution and advertising and publicity of the "urban casual" lines of the French *griffe*. The new Collections, starting with Winter 2003-2004, are put on sale in 150 Belfe shops throughout the world.
❑ 2003, February. The year begins with the opening of a new showroom of Milan, on Corso Sempione. In view of a relaunch on the American market, the New York shop is reopened and there is a new shop in Denver.
❑ Stefano Festa Marzotto, the company's vice-president, is to manage the expansion in the Far East. For the time being, Belfe is present in corner shops in Hong Kong, Taiwan, Korea and Japan.

Bella Women's weekly magazine featuring practical articles, specializing in knitwear, published by Rizzoli. It was established in the immediate post-war period as a romance magazine. Giorgio Scerbanenco, a great writer of mysteries and detective stories, was its founder and director. In 1963 the magazine changed its format under the new direction of Emilio De Rossignoli and in 1970, led by Maria Santini, it changed again and became a classic women's magazine, adding the typical columns on fashion and beauty. In 1987 it underwent a radical restyling and became Più Bella. In 1989 Antonella di Scovolo became the new editor-in-chief. In 1995, after some troubled years, the magazine was sold to Editoriale Donna. Since 1998 it has been under the leadersip of Marina Bigi.

❑ 2000, September. Patrizia Caglioni, who worked on the editorial staff of Anna, becomes the new director. The arrival of this editor from Bergamo is a result of the reorganization that followed the acquisition of Editoriale Donna by Alberto Donati.

Bellaish Victor (1968). Israeli designer, slightly older than 30, born in Tel Aviv, where he attended the Academy of Textile Technology majoring in fashion design.He is a newcomer already known in the fashion world for the strong personality of his work, which, in 1996, conquered the public of Gorizia and won the Mittelmoda award. Roberto Cavalli noticed him as well, and Victor would work with him for four years, learning subtle ways to create seductive clothes which, nevertheless, he would interpret in his own way, favoring black over wild patterns. The turning point came in 2000: he collaborated with Les Copains and he went out on his own. His hometown celebrated him as the "first Israeli designer with his own Collection." The idea, of course, was to conquer the public at Milano Moda Donna. He succeeded with the presentation of the Collection for Spring-Summer 2001, when he presented a kind of woman-insect in the grip of disturbing and dangerous fantasies, with scorpions chasing each other, stung by thorns, with rubber prickles undulating on fabrics so sheer that they look like colored air, and winged sleeves. The scorpion wasn't a casual choice, however. It is considered a sacred creature in his country. He is highly skilled in mixing different and unlikely materials: leather, denim, silicon, silk and chiffon, a "blob" which wants to emphasize a femininity that plays with contrasts, hard and soft at the same time.

(*Lucia Mari*)

Bellati Manfredi (1937). Italian photographer. Born in Belluno, he grew up and studied in Venice, where he learned painting and sculpture with his uncle Valerio Bellati, and where he enrolled in the school of architecture. After a period of study in Leeds, he returned to Italy where he worked as an architect on domestic interiors and became familiar with photography in order to document his work. Developing a strong passion for the camera, he worked with Domus and Architectural Review on photos of interiors, and with Vogue, for which he did portraits of actors, writers and directors. With the support of Roberta di Camerino, he entered the world of fashion, lived in the swinging London of the 1960s, worked on the magazine Queen and on the English edition of Vogue. Back in Italy in 1972, he published in the most important fashion magazines. He did campaigns for Marelli, Contax, Campari, and Coin (for which he won the 1980 Clio Award), and presented his work in several personal and collective exhibits. He also knows how to make jokes with fashion, as he showed with *Revivals*, the book-catalogue named after the exhibit in which he posed very young and scantily-clad models among symbols of the 1950s and '60s: the Vespa, the juke-box, the red dispensing machine for Coca-Cola, the battery-operated gas pump, a Beatles record, and Nabokov's book *Lolita* along with a lollipop and the heart-shaped glasses worn by the model.

Bell bottoms The classic trousers of American sailors. Low on the waist, narrow to the knees, from there they flare out in varying widths, sometimes to excess, like the foot of an elephant. Known as bell bottoms and as twisters' pants, they were the rage in the 1960s and 1970s, for both men and women. They have been presented again in recent Collections. These trousers, originally created for sailors, were the symbol of an entire generation in the 1960s and '70s. Bell-bottom trousers (for both men and women, elegant in smooth velvet, and casual in prewashed jeans) crossed easily into an age marked by contradictions fitting, thanks to their unmistakable shape, into a longing for modernity felt by the children of the middle class as much by the young working class. A comfort in fit seen in their recent return to fashion which (while life became ever worse) confirmed the latest rediscovery of the hippie era.

Belleteste French manufacturing company. Established in 1936 by Pierre Belleteste, it became famous immediately but, starting in 1973, it was forced to sell its stock capital little by little because of unexpected difficulties. Started as a simple house for women's fashion, it later expanded, and from 1963 on, it operated on a large industrial scale, opening factories for linen, shirts, children's wear and trousers all over France.

Bellezza Italian fashion magazine. Founded in 1941, it was the official magazine of high fashion until the end of the 1950s. It witnessed the creative perseverance of Italian couture during the war. The architect Giò Ponti and Elsa Robiola, who directed it, were among its founders. All the great tailors and couturiers of the time were contributors, in order to make it a magazine comparable to Vogue and Harper's Bazaar. The graphic design was particularly painstaking, along with the use of different kinds of paper: designs, drawings, and fashion sketches took precedence over photography thanks to the collaboration of the most important artists of the time. The covers were often drawn by artists such as Giò Ponti, De Pisis, Prampolini, Dudovich, Pallavicini and Brunetta, whose contribution to the magazine was of long duration and very valuable. It was aimed at the high middle class. Contributions came from Leonor Fini, Riccardo Magni, René Gruau, Maria Pezzi and Irene Brin. In the 1950s the first photographs by Patellani and Cesano began to appear. The editor at that time was Aldo Palazzi, who published the weekly newspaper Tempo. In order to maintain its role as the official representative of Italian fashion, Bellezza

Cover of the monthly Bellezza designed by René Gruau (April 1949).

devoted particular space to boutiques and prêt-à-porter, to accessories, jewellery, and fabrics. It celebrated its twentieth anniversary in 1961, only to close a few years later.

Belloni Annamaria (1965). Italian photographer. She began her career with a specific interest in the processing of Polaroid instant film. For a while, she managed her own gallery in Piacenza, where she lives and works, exhibiting Italian and foreign artists. In recent years she has approached fashion using very original and creative images by working with Luci di Luci, for which she managed the 2003 Collection, and also with Adriano Callegari.

Bellotti Fabio (1938). Italian textile entrepreneur. He learned the trade in the workshop of his uncle, who manufactured scarves – and who became his guardian at the death of his father, who was an architect. After his studies, he worked for Falconetto, Ken Scott and Mantero. At the end of the 1970s he began his personal adventure in the world of fabrics as the creator of Rainbow, which had a big success with designers such as Lancetti, Valentino, Krizia, Albini, Armani, Lagerfeld, Chanel, Lacroix, Donna Karan and Calvin Klein. During the 1970s and '80s he and his wife Daniela Morera were frequent visitors on the New York scene, with Andy Wharol, the underground clubs, and the group of people who revolved around the emblematic Studio 54 discotheque and its owners. The jet set, and artists such as Haring and Schnabel, and his travels to Bali, Vietnam, India, and Burma were a source of constant inspiration for his creativity. At the end of the 1990s, he sold the company.

Bellucci Italian manufacturer of fabric for luxury prêt-à-porter, headquartered in Prato. It was established in the post-war period to manufacture carded yarn with recycled wools. The famous rags from Prato were for the Lanificio Mario Bellucci the beginning of success in the early 1950s. The rags came from the U.S,, which produced a lot of waste at the time. Hand-selected and processed by ragmen, they allowed the production of heavy carded yarns for overcoats, very much in demand at the time. An increase in the cost of artisanal labor, along with more affordable prices for fine wool, and an increased taste for attractive fashions, combined to cause the almost complete disappearance of recycled fabrics. The firm, which covers the complete manufacturing cycle, from spinning to warping and from weaving to finishing, was able to transform itself, maintaining a top position in skilled design, high quotas for Australian wools, and for linens, silks, cottons and viscose fibers, all subject to accurate quality control. Looking at the numbers, if you put the figures for the turnover in 1996, 1997 and 1998 all in a row, they are like hitting the jackpot: 54, 59 and 63 billion liras. In 1998 the annual production was 3.9 million yards. The benchmark for comparison is that of the big players: Max Mara, Marzotto, and Vestebene in Italy; and abroad, Hugo Boss, Donna Karan, Marks & Spencer, and Zara Inditex. (*Giuliana Zabeo Ricca*)

❑ 2001, February. The company is represented at the 45th edition of Prato Expo by the firm's heir Simone Bellucci.

Bellville Sassoon A brand that, in almost forty years, has organized itself especially for the production of evening dresses in chiffon, organdy and tulle. Today, David Sassoon and Lorcan Mullany control the company, which was founded in London in 1953 by Belinda Bellville. Sassoon became her partner in 1958. In 1997 the brand won the *British Designer Award*, partly for its enhanced reputation from being distributed in the world's most famous department stores, from Harrods to Neiman Marcus.

Belperron Susanne. French designer. In the 1920s and '30s she created jewellery that was considered revolutionary for its often geometric shapes and for unusual materials that were not often used together, such as rock crystal fused to gilded metal. After working with Bouvin, she opened her own space in Paris, and then started a partnership with Jean Hertz. Since that time the firm has been called Hertz-Belperron.

Belstaff English company founded in 1924 by Harry Grosberg in Stoke on Kent, in Staffordshire. It produces waterproof clothing. It uses only Wax Cotton, which is an Egyptian cotton processed with natural oils that let it breathe easily and is still waterproof. The firm has always specialized in the production of technical garments for motorcyclists. It is a matter of record that a Belstaff jacket was worn by Lawrence of Arabia in the years of his final return to England, and also by Che Guevara and Arthur Miller.

❑ 1999. The firm's 75th anniversary signals a strong return to the American market by a brand considered the most long-established in clothing for bikers, together with Harley Davidson.
❑ 2002. Belstaff introduces Sportwool, a new thermal insulating fabric which protects from abrasions in case of a fall.
❑ 2004. The English company belongs to the Clothing Company group and joins the world of cinema, creating, in collaboration with the Hollywood costume designer Sandy Powell, an ad hoc Collection for the film *The Aviator* by Martin Scorsese, whose star is Leonardo Di Caprio.
❑ 2005, February. It makes a decisive entry into the world of fashion, making its début on the runways in Milan.
❑ 2005, June. It continues its adventure in film. This time with the Hero jacket, manufactured on the suggestion of the costume designer Joanna Johnston. The jacket appears on the big screen in the film *The War of the Worlds*, directed by Steven Spielberg and starring by Tom Cruise.

Belt A flexible or rigid string, manufactured in different materials, such as leather and suede, and in a varnish, or fabric, or metal. Worn tight around the waist to make it thinner, or loose on the hips to support a billowy and blousing top, a belt either wraps around clothes or makes them tighter. Sometimes it is sewn within the dress, or else threaded through belt loops. Of very ancient origin, it is perhaps the oldest decoration about which there is any information. Some clues date it to the bronze age. It is like a jewelled decoration for ladies in medieval castles, and was often a small cord loose on the hips during the 14th century. In the 1500s people had a habit of hanging small objects such as keys, mirrors, and tiny scissors from it. Over time it underwent several evolutions and took on different meanings, many of them symbolic. For example, during the Middle Ages its use was forbidden to ladies of the court. From the 1700s up to the 1920s belts were often embellished with ribbons and decorated buckles, which could be varied according to the color and fabric of the dress. It became a necessary accessory for men's clothing, in which it replaced suspenders, and a more and more noticeable ornament on ladies' outfits. Among the famous styles of belts is the chatelaine, a chain belt that is worn on soft and smooth sheath dresses, or, almost a jewel, on a more casual tweed suit. The *hzam* is the belt that women in Morocco wear with caftans as a precious ornament embroidered with both gold and colored thread; it is more a bodice than a belt. The Japanese *obi* is a belt-broad sash, a foot wide and four feet long, often made in richly embroidered silk. In the Japanese tradition there are many ways of knotting and wrapping it high around the waist, and these take on different meanings which are passed on from mother to daughter. The obi is often seen in the models of various western designers. (*Gabriella Gregorietti*)

Beltrami Marie (1945). French designer. Starting in the mid 1970s she made jewellery, items for daily use, and fashion accessories. In 1978, she created her own brand. Between 1980 and 1981 she worked for Fiorucci, and the following year she launched her own line. At the end of 1988 she left her brand *griffe* to work as a costume designer for Jean-Paul Goude, who was responsible for the great, creative parade of 14th July 1989, the bicentennial of the French Revolution. Together with Goude she made advertising spots for Chanel perfumes and Perrier Spring water.

❑ 2001, February. The designer exhibits at BHV Rivoli, in Paris. This artistic event, organized by Andrée Putman, is held on the fourth floor of the entirely renovated department store. Thirteen artists are invited to show their work in this singular alliance between art and shopping.

Belvest Italian company producing ready-to-wear, established in Padua in 1964 by Mino Nicoletto. Today the company is directed by

Maria Teresa Nicoletto, the sole managing director. It has 500 workers and was among the first companies to offer made-to-measure clothing. It works mainly in men's clothing and has established itself in the market due to the high quality of its garments, which is the result of both technical research in materials and great attention to detail. A women's line was planned for Summer 2000.

❑ 1999. The women's line acquires its own look after several years of being a reflection of the men's line.
❑ The firm's first showroom opens on via Sant'Andrea in the fashion district of Milan.
❑ 2003, October. Belvest takes the lead as a sponsor and participant in the educational activities for the three-year degree in the Culture and Technology of Fashion offered by the Faculty of Letters and Philosophy at the University of Padua.

Bemberg A natural fiber also called cuprammonium rayon. Its name comes from the German factory which produced it for the first time. Elastic, resistant and easy to dye, it first appeared at the end of the 1800s as a substitute for silk, and it is used mainly as a lining.

Be.Mi.Va. Spinning mill near Prato. Established in 1960 in Capalle, it has gone through several phases – from viscose in the 1980s to creative yarns in the early 1990s – resulting in a steady specialization in the manufacture of fanciful yarns for knitwear. The creation of Be.Mi.Va.-tex dates to the middle of the last decade. This was a new line of yarns meant for the orthogonal fabrics with which the factory made its début at Filo in 1998. At present the company employs about 40 in-house workers and works with various associated factories in addition to outside consultants. It participates in the major industry trade fairs, including Pitti Filati, Expofil, Filasia and Filo.

Benda Pseudonym of Georges Kugelmann, a French costume designer. His name is linked to several masterpieces of French film as the creator creating magnificent costumes for historical movies and clothes for films set in modern times. At the end of the 1930s he abandoned international theater, where he had a solid reputation, in order to work in films. His knowledge of the way people dressed in the past was of great help when he designed the costumes for Jacques Fayder's *Carnival in Flanders*, taking inspiration from the Flemish painters of the 1600s. One also remembers *Nôtre Dame de Paris*, from Hugo's novel. He designed the costumes for almost all of Sacha Guitry's films, and for René Clair's *Le Million*.

Bender Lee (1939). London designer. He experienced the final days of swinging London and that explosion of young, revolutionary fashion. A graduate of Saint Martin's School of Art and the London College of Fashion, she made her début with the boutique Bus Stop in Kensington Church Street. Her business partner is her husband Cecil. They sold clothes that were rather eccentric, almost extreme in their look, but affordable. The Bus Stop brand was successful in the U.S. also. By 1980 the adventure was over. Two years later, with a more subdued style, Lee Bender returned to the fashion stage with a new boutique in Knightsbridge carrying her name.

❑ 2001. She signs an agreement as fashion consultant for some British and Asiatic firms. In particular, she looked after the penetration of eastern markets by western companies.

Benetton Manufacturer of knitwear and prêt-à-porter, established in 1965 in Ponzano Veneto (Treviso) by the Benetton siblings Luciano, Giuliana, Gilberto and Carlo. At the beginning it was simply an artisan's workshop specialized in knitwear that was well-designed at rather affordable prices. Today, with a turnover of almost 9 trillion liras, company stores and franchisees all over the world, it has become the twelfth largest Italian industrial group in the Mediobanca ranking, and it is one of the most important clothing and textile concerns in Italy. Half of all sales come from the traditional areas – sportswear and accessories under the brands Benetton, Benetton 012, Sisley, Zerotondo, and Tutti i colori del mondo – to which must be added the licenses for accessories, underwear, beachwear, cosmetics and linens. The other half of the turnover comes, on the other hand, from more recent areas of expansion: wholesale distribution, highway restaurants, real estate, and merchant banking. For years, Benetton's advertising campaigns, which are innovative and often provocative, have shown the hand of a great photographer, Oliviero Toscani, a creator not only of images but also of slogans and messages. As to the business, the group produces in-house 80% of the T-shirts, shirts, dresses and trousers which are sold all over the world. The remaining 20% has been manufactured abroad for the last few years. In the plants at Castrette, giant and very modern factory sheds fitted with cables and designed by the architect Tobia Scarpa, one thousand people operate computers and control panels that remind one of the great research centers for advanced technology. They are in fact the heart of a giant production network which starts with wool from sheep in Argentina and goes all the way to distribution in the last Benetton shop in the third world, or in Greenland, where they sell Benetton sweaters and shirts. It is a network which studies the fabric, designs the Collection, and cuts, dyes and controls the quality, of almost 80 million pieces a year, while distributing them, at almost the same moment, and therefore practically without any warehousing, to 7,000 shops in 120 countries. The Robostore logistics system, with a staff of only 14 people sorting 30,000 packages a day and 10 million pieces per month, loading them on trucks and, according to the destination, separating them by country and sales point, looks with its conveyer belts like the luggage sorting center of an airport. The less complicated steps of processing, such as sewing and ironing, are given out by contract: a group of companies in the Veneto work almost exclusively for Benetton and employ 30,000 people. In the clothing industry, Benetton seems to have achieved, in addition to a successful formula, also a sort of squaring of the circle in the industrial organization of Italy. It resembles, in fact, any one of the many "Made in Italy" manufacturing districts, but with only one brain at the top. Everything began almost by chance. "My sister Giuliana," says Luciano Benetton, "made sweaters for a small shop in our area. One day, she gave me a sweater that was very bright yellow. Well, everyone wanted it. They were tired of the sad and dull colors of the time. Then, said: "Come on, let's try it; you, Giuliana, will design and I will sell. We bought an old machine to weave stripes onto net stockings. We sold it cheap, and we transformed it. Since then, no one has been able to stopp us." The global annual turnover amounts to about 4 trillion liras. The company is listed on the stock exchange in Milan, New York and Frankfurt. (*Marcella Gabbiano*)

UNITED COLORS
OF BENETTON.

Benetton's Logo.

❑ 1999. Edizione Holding, the company which controls the Benetton group, had a turnover of 9,028 billion liras (the Austostrade turnover not included) and a net profit of 390 billion liras. Compared to the 268 billion of 1998, there was an increase of 45.7%. During the year, Edizione Holding continued the diversification of the "core business" of clothing, through the following acquisitions (majority and not): Austostrade (Highways), Fondazione Cassa di Risparmio of Turin, Acesa, Ina, UniCredito Italiano, Brisa, American Group Host Marriott Services (now HMS Host), and, finally, a stake in Blu, the fourth-largest Italian mobile phone operator.

❑ 2000, March. An agreement is signed for the transfer of the Formula One Team Benetton to the French automotive company Renault for 120 million dollars. Benetton is to continue as the official sponsor for two more years. In Hamburg, a new four-storey superstore opens in the city center. The development of the sales network continues through direct investments in several German cities, after the shop openings in Berlin, Leipzig, Cologne, Düsseldorf, Stuttgart and Hanover. The

German market is the second in strategic importance and sales volume after Italy.

❑ 2000, September. The first superstore opens in Moscow, at 19 Tverskaya, with 20,000 sq. ft. on three floors. The following month, a new flagship store opens in Cardiff. In December, Benetton concludes an agreement to acquire 12 department stores from the Coin Group, for 25.3 billion liras.

❑ 2000. Fabrica, the center for research and the development of communications strategies owned by the Group, becomes more and more important. The opening of its headquarters in a prestigious architectural complex near Treviso confirms its strategic and creative function.

❑ 2000. The Group's balance sheet shows consolidated revenues of 3,908 billion liras (2.02 billion in Euros) and a net profit of 471 billion liras (243 million Euros). The dividend distributed to shareholders was 90 liras per share. Markets in which it grew most were Korea, the U.S., and Japan. In Japan, the Group pursued a strategy of closing down small points-of-sale and opening new mega-stores.

❑ 2001, May. An agreement is formalized with Txt e-solutions, a company specialized in the design and production of software. The agreement foresees the supply of solutions to make mega-store distribution more efficient on a world-wide basis, through a direct control which would show the changes occurring in every local micro-market and allow a response in real time. The program, known as Txt Sc&Cm For Fashion, coordinates the management of supplier relations with the needs of the distribution network in order to optimize it with respect to consumer demand.

❑ 2001, June. Sisley, a brand owned by Benetton, opens a store in Nantes in order to consolidate its presence in the French market. This is the second store in France, after the one in Paris. Sisley has 800 single-brand stores and it is also present, with large kiosks, in about 300 Benetton stores.

❑ 2001, September. The Group chooses Bologna for its first mega-store which, thanks to the collaboration with Fabrica, will also be an experimental environment focused on creativity and culture.

❑ 2001, September. The subject of the new communication campaign is voluntary service. The initiative was carried out with the support of UNV, the section for voluntary service at the United Nations. The investment of about 24 billion liras covered press services and bill-posting in 60 countries.

❑ 2001, October. Début of a new mega-store in Milan, in Corso Vercelli. Soon after there are openings in Palma de Mallorca and Paris, where 2 new flagship stores open on Place de l'Opéra and Avenue des Champs-Elysées, and also in Lisbon. Benetton invests 52 billion in three mega-stores in Japan, with one in Kyoto and two in Osaka. The turnover in Japan in 2000 is roughly of 580 billion liras.

❑ 2001. The Group has 100 mega-stores all over the world, with a target of 300 within 2004, and a distribution network of 5,000 shops scattered in 120 countries. In the previous two years the Group invested about 500 million Euros for the opening of mega-stores in the historic centers of large cities.

❑ 2001. Benetton had a turnover of 2.098 billion Euros, an EBITDA (Earnings Before Interest, Taxes, Depreciation, and Amortization) of 398 million and a net profit of 148 million, a result not directly comparable with the 243 million of 2000 because that was influenced by a gain on the sale of the Formula One Team. In comparative terms, however, the net profit diminished by 6.5%.

❑ 2002, March. A preliminary agreement is concluded with Viceversa Edizione Design, a company that will create a line for the home under the Benetton brand.

❑ 2002, July. Benetton issued a three-year bond (debenture loan) for 300 million Euros, the second in the history of the company.

❑ 2002, October. Début of two new stores in Venice and Shanghai.

❑ 2002, November. The Benetton

family tries to acquire 100% of Società Autostrade, of which it already has a minority shareholding through Edizione Holding.

❑ 2002. According to Forbes, the Benetton fortune is worth 4.9 billion dollars, corresponding to 62nd place in the ranking of the world's richest people.

❑ 2002. Edizione Holding, the family's safe deposit box, had a consolidated turnover of 5.4 billion Euros (Autostrade not included) in line with the year 2001. Of concern was a slight drop in the Benetton Group: the turnover of 1.9 billion Euros was less than the 2.09 billion of 2001; and there was a net loss of 9.9 million Euros compared to a profit of 148 million in 2001. The sports businesses Nordica, Prince, and Rollerblade had negative results, although the cash flow of 124 million Euros was positive.

❑ 2003, February. The Nordica brand is sold to Tecnica, causing the transfer of 160 workers.

❑ 2003, February. After opening plants in Croatia, Slovakia and Hungary, Benetton invests 16 million dollars in Tunisia. A new mega-store is opened in Osaka, Japan, with an investment of 1.5 billion yen. It is the tenth since the beginning of 2001. The overall sum invested amounts to 12 billion yen, or about 90 million Euros. In 2001 the turnover in Japan is 200 million Euros, in line with the results in 2000.

❑ 2003, February. The theme of the new communication campaign is Food for Life, the problem of hunger in the world. Carried out together with the World Food Program, a U.N. agency, it has a budget of 15.7 million Euros.

❑ 2003, March. A preliminary agreement is concluded with Prime Newco, part of the Tecnica group, for the sale of Rollerblade. This is part of the strategy of concentrating on the core business, which is clothing. The value of the deal is 20 million Euros, to which must be added 1.5% of Rollerblade's turnover for five years. In 2002, Rollerblade had a turnover of 66 million Euros and an operating loss of 1 million Euros. The Group considers the possibility of also selling Prince.

❑ 2003, March. Luigi De Puppi abandons his position as managing director of the Benetton Group.

❑ 2003, March. Benetton sells the Prince brand of tennis rackets and the Ektelon brand of equipment and accessories for badminton to the U.S. private equity fund Lincolnshire. The value of the deal is 36.5 million Euros. The agreement completes Benetton's exit from the sports accessory business and plans for the new strategic architecture of the company, a return to the core business of clothing.

❑ 2003, April. Silvano Cassano is the new managing director of Benetton Group. He joins the company at a historic moment. The unexpected diversification into sports accessories that began in 1997 ended with the recent sale of Nordica, Rollerblade and Prince. In 2002, the Group, of which 70% is controlled by the family, had a net loss of 10 million Euros, the first in its history. Today it has refocused its attention on clothing.

❑ 2003, May. The first quarter results show revenues (casual) of 351 million Euros, net of changes in the exchange rate, a 3.8% increase. Overall turnover is 444 million Euros (compared to 447 million in 2002), due to the anticipated drop in the sporting goods business. The net profit of 25 million Euros showed an increase of 29%. Retained earnings remained at 76 million, while borrowings amounted to 709 million Euros, against 756 million in the first quarter of 2002.

❑ 2003, May. The development of new points-of-sale continues. The Groups has plans to open 22 new stores in Russia this year, and 10 more in 2004. The goal is to reach 100 shops within the end of 2004.

❑ 2003, July. The Benetton Group is present in 120 countries with its brands United Colors of Benetton, Sisley, the Hip Site, Playlife and Killer Loop. It manufactures more than 100 million pieces a year, 90% of which is made in Europe. The distribution network consists of 5,000 points-of-sale. Benetton Group is controlled by the family's finance company, Edizione Holding, consisting of a network of companies active in different sectors: other than clothing, which makes up 69.9% of the combined activity, there is the autostrade (highway) division, plus restaurant services, telecommunications, real estate, agriculture, and minority shareholdings in various companies. In total, Edizione Holding has a turnover of 7 billion Euros and employs 50,000 workers. In eight years the Benetton siblings Luciano, Gilberto, Giuliana and Carlo have assembled, piece by piece, under the umbrella of Edizione Holding, a group which, from its beginnings in the textile sector, has now become a conglomerate. In 1994, textiles represented 100% of the turnover; in 2003 sweaters would represent 30% of the total.

❑ 2003, September. Début of a new mega-store in Hong Kong offering the brands United Colors of Benetton, Sisley, Playlife and Killer Loop.

❑ 2003, September. Début of a new mega-store in Birmingham offering the brands United Colors of Benetton, Sisley and The Hip Site.

❑ 2003, October. Joel Berg is the new director of United Colors of Benetton. He is responsible for the brand's image as well as advertising and the presentation of the Collection.

❑ 2003, December. Benetton Group presents its strategy for the period 2004-2007. Sales are expected to grow 25% and the gross operating margin by 40%. In order to attain such results without having a price war, product quality is to be improved. The strategy is based on a strong distribution network and production know-how.

❑ 2003, December. The year closes with a consolidated turnover of 1.859 billion Euros, a net profit of 108 million Euros and a net financial position of 368 million.

❑ 2004, April. Opening of a new Benetton mega-store in Paris. Taking up five floors inside a historic building of the second half of the 1800s, it sells the United Colors of Benetton and the Sisley Collections.

❑ 2004, June. The 15th anniversary of Benetton's listing in the New York's stock exchange.

❑ 2004, July. The group's expansion in Germany continue with the opening of a mega-store in Berlin, on three floors, offering the entire Collections of United Colors of Benetton and Sisley.

❑ 2004, September. The group's presence on the Internet doubles, with the web-sites www.benetton.com and www.benettongroup.com. The first is a web-site focused on consumers, while the second offers financial information and news about the Group's communication activity.

❑ 2004, December. A new store is opened on the very centrally-located via Maistra in St. Moritz. Covering two floors, it offers the entire United Colors of Benetton Collection.

❑ 2004, December. The year closes with a consolidated turnover of 1.686 billion Euros, 1.504 billion of which is produced by the casual division. The gross operating margin is 757 million Euros, the net profit is 123 million Euros, and the retained earnings is 431 million Euros.

❑ 2005, March. The first quarter shows a turnover of 378 million Euros (compared to 381 million in the same period of 2004) and a net profit of 23 million Euros (compared to 28 million in 2004). The retained earnings position improves, with 470 million Euros, against 497 million the previous year.

❑ 2005, April. A joint venture agreement is signed with the Boyner Group, with the goal of strengthening the Benetton brands in Turkey.

❑ 2005, May. A license agreement is signed with Selective beauty for the worldwide development and distribution of Benetton perfumes.

❑ 2005, June. The group secures, with a syndicate of 10 banks, a revolving line of credit for 500 million Euros, to be due in 2010.

❑ 2005, June. A worldwide licensing agreement is signed with Zorlu Holding for the production and distribution of the Sisley Home Collection.

(*Dario Golizia*)

Benissimo A monthly magazine of sewing and knitwear, founded in March 1983 by Gruppo Editoriale Fabbri, at a moment when magazines of this kind were enjoying great success. Embroidery was no longer the activity of a lace maker, but a hobby or a personal interest. Directed by Edvige Bernasconi, who continued to devote many pages to beauty, cooking and fashion, the magazine had a large circulation in the early 1980s. Every issue was sold with a life-sized paper pattern. In 1985 Bernasconi left the magazine to join Mondadori, and the new director was Grazia Pierangela Chiesa, who increased the space dedicated to fashion. In 1990, Fabbri was taken over by the Rizzoli-Corriere della Sera group, bringing Benissimo along with it. A new director, Maria Santini, was appointed, and she changed both the graphic design and the content. Benissimo returned to being exclusively about women's hobbies. During the 1990s, RCS sold the magazine to Cooperativa Editoriale, which appointed Anna Condemi as director.

❑ 2002. Bruno Quattro was appointed managing director.

Benito Pseudonym of Eduardo García (1891-1953), a Spanish illustrator. As a child he was part of the workshop of the painter Mignon, and later he enrolled at the San Fernando School of Fine Arts in Madrid. He moved to Paris, where he found a job at the Gazette du Bon Ton. It was the 1920s, the years of Art Deco. But Benito was interested in Cubism and his graphic style was favorably influenced by it, bringing a new spirit to the illustrations in fashion magazines such as Goût du Jour and La Guirlande. Vogue understood his art and gave him a platform for it, to the point of becoming identified with his graphic style. He illustrated several books and also made many portraits.

Bennis & Edwards Brand of American shoes, although it might be better to say New York shoes, because the success of the extravagant and paradoxical imagination of Susan Bennis and Warren Edwards, who became shoemakers quite unexpectedly, has all the features of something made popular by word of mouth. The story began in the 1970s, with shoes made by hand, in the traditional way with high quality materials, carefully sewn, and great craftsmanship, but also with a strong and often rather "showy" look characterized by a frantic creative freedom. It is not by chance that the brand's advertising says, "Manhattan's most extravagant shoes, boots and accessories."

Benito: Scheherazade's Model.

❑ The designers' shop is on the 57th Street.

Béranger Dan (1945). French designer. He studied at the school of the Chambre Syndicale de la Couture of Paris, but Germany was his proving ground. A few years later he returned to Paris and worked on a new prêt-à-porter line called Emesse. In 1974, he presented his first Collections which, manufactured in Italy, carried his name. Like many others in those years, his customer was the working woman who didn't want to give up her feminine elegance. He was successful. He designed the costumes for *Emmanuelle*, though the movie was more about nudity than about clothes. Nevertheless, his work on the film gave a boost to his reputation.

Berao Joaquin (1945). Spanish jeweller and designer. Born in Madrid, he designed his first Collection betwween 1970 and 1975, and the Bloomingdale's department store in New York purchased all of it. He opened retail points-of-sale in Spain, Italy and Japan. He doesn't use semi-precious or precious stones and focuses on the plastic quality of the jewels.

❑ 2002, November. The 30th anniversary of his career is celebrated with the Prince Philip Award, a prestigious prize given to Spanish companies that have distinguished themselves during the year. Berao is chosen for the Design category out of a group of six designers and companies.
❑ 2003. The designer's turnover amounts to more than 10 million Euros and he has stores in Tokyo, Milan, Barcelona and Madrid.

Bérard Christian (1902-1949). Painter, illustrator and stage designer. He was born in Paris, and had good teachers, including Maurice Denis and Edouard Vuillard, as well as excellent co-workers, such as Jean Cocteau and the ballet librettist Boris Kochno, who was Diaghilev's secretary. His eclecticism took him away from painting but made him a key player in the worlds of fashion, illustration, fabric design, and theater. His illustrations appeared in Harper's Bazaar and Vogue, with particular influence on Schiaparelli and the young Dior. His style showed traces of Surrealism. He found his true calling in the theater. His stage designs and costumes were the symbols of an era, starting with his début in 1930 working on Kochno's ballet *La Nuit*, which had music by Henri Sauguet and choreography by Serge Lifar. He worked many times with Louis Jouvet, including on *L'école des femmes* (1936), *La folle de Chaillot* (1945) and *Don Juan* (1947). He designed the costumes for Cocteau's film *La belle et la bête*. He died on stage while working on *Fourberies de Scapin*, same as the play's author, Molière. (*Mino Colao*)

Berardi Antonio (1968). English designer. The son of Sicilian immigrants, he graduated from Saint Martin's College of London in 1994 and his end-of-studies presentation was so successful that the Liberty and A La Mode department stores quickly purchased this first, unfinished, Collection. The following year he presented a line of his own and in 1996 he signed a contract with the Italian company Givuesse. In 1997 he won the American prize for Best New Designer and then the British Fashion Award for emerging designers. His clothes are sexy and super-feminine.

❑ 2001. The new century begins in a collaboration with Exté. The materials used for his personal Collection are mostly from Italy, especially the handmade corsets with Murano glass.
❑ For Summer 2003 he offers a procession of spirited and shamelessly elegant women, the kind of super-feminine and super-sexy woman found in a 19th century brothel. To wear his dresses properly, one needs the right age (very young), a particular physique (perfect), and impudence (in abundance). He favors accessories that have a sense of humor. For Winter 2002-2003 his boots were decorated with trinkets of Wedgewood porcelain. In the previous season, on mini-boots made of snakeskin, fabric and string, he sewed dessert cutlery. Sensuality was obviously a key component of the Winter 2003-2004 Collection: with the allure of film noir, his muse was the heiress Patricia Hearst, the wicked soul of the 1960s and 70s. A female-within-a-woman like the Russian dolls intentionally shown one inside the other: the tiny jacket is sewn onto a tapered jacket, and that one in its turn over a very tight-fitting coat. A dramatic dark rose in glossy silk folded like origami grows between the pleats of fabric, blossoming on small jackets, bursting on trousers let out at the hem. Gibò of Florence manufactures for him. It is a collaboration based on the growth of the brand.
❑ 2003, September. An agreement is signed with Dressing Spa, the designer's second line. It is to be named 2die4 and

is to be the crowning achievement of Berardi's style, and also offer some seasonal flashes. Easier to be manufactued than the first line, it is aimed girls between 18 and 25 years of age. Prices are to be lower by about one third. The début is set for the Spring-Summer 2004.

❑ 2005, April. Starting from Spring-Summer 2006, the designer is to take the place of Antonio Marras as the creative director of Trend Les Copains of BVM Italian Spa, a company from Bologna that owns the brand Les Copains.

(*Lucia Mari*)

Bercane Jean Luc (1954). French designer. As a young boy he worked in a women's clothing factory in Toulouse where he learned the fundamentals of couture. Eager to test himself, he left for Paris and the big fashion houses. As a freelancer he worked in haute couture for quality houses such as Jacques Esterel and Chloé. In 1997, he presented his first Collection in an atypical space, outside the official fashion calendar. His style, characterized by high-tech materials such as microfibers and metalic yarns, had a modest success. He lives and works in Toulouse, and his Collections are sponsored by the coutoure house Bruno Saint Hilaire.

(*Maddalena Fossati*)

Berceville Claude. French tailor. His atelier on Rue Malesherbes in Paris was a meeting place for many actors of stage and screen, including Michel Piccoli and Jean-Claude Brialy. Up until the early 1980s he was known as the "tailleur des comédiens," or the actor's tailor.

Berenson Marisa (1948). British model. She had a great first career as a model (with a début at age 6 on the cover of Elle) and a current one as an actress. Niece of Elsa Schiaparelli and grandniece of Bernard Berenson, the famous art critic, she was discovered and launched by the most powerful muse in fashion, Diana Vreeland. Growing up in comfort and with celebrity thanks to her family, she had a sad childhood in boarding schools, including Poggio Imperiale in Florence, and wore a corrective corset for her back. She had a series of famous love affairs, and in 1976 she married the American billionaire Jim Randall, with whom she had a daughter, Starlite Melody. Later she married the lawyer Aaron Richard Golab. Her most well-known films are *Death in Venice*, *Cabaret*, *Barry Lindon* and *Prêt-à-porter*.

Beret A round-shaped hat in soft fabric usually worn with informal clothing. It has a virile, aggressive and somewhat martial image because it is part of the uniform of several military organizations, in different colors depending on the unit, and it also has a bohemian air because it is loved by painters, especially Picasso. The most common derivation links it to the Basque population of the French and Spanish Pyrenees, but it was also used by the Greeks and Romans. In the 16th century men wore it on top of the net that they used to bind their hair and embellished it with jewels and feathers. In 1880, decorated with flowers, bows and feathers, it became part of the female wardrobe. In 1920 it was in great fashion all over Europe and something that fashionable women had to have. Towards the end of the 1960s it was again very popular thanks to the film *Bonnie and Clyde* (1967), in which it was worn by Faye Dunaway, who relaunched the cap on the big screen. (*Gianluca Bauzano*)

Beretta Anne Marie (1937). French stylist, born in Béziers. She often worked in Italy, for Max Mara and Marina Rinaldi. She built her success very slowly, starting at a very young age. From 1958 to 1964 she designed models for Esterel and Castillo; from 1965 to 1974 for Cassini, D'Alby and Bercher. In all those years, she always worked with natural fabrics: alpaca and cashmere for Winter, linen for Summer. Her colors are those of her native land, the Languedoc, between green and dark grey. But her style is seen also in the innovative raincoats that she produced for the Ramosport brand during the 1980s. (*Valeria Vantaggi*)

❑ After 30 years of collaboration, her alliance with Ramosport is ended. Her achievement, acknowledged by everyone, was to have helped the transformation of the company's raincoat into a garment of fashion.

❑ 2003. Her Paris headquarters is in Rue Saint Sulpice.

Beretta Sport Brand of clothing owned by the weapons factory Pietro Beretta. The firm was established in 1526 when Master Bartolomeo Beretta of Gardone first sold 185 gun barrels to the Arsenale of Venice. It is a leader in its field and has many police forces among its clientele. Ten years ago it entered the clothing business with a line of casual wear managed by Tino Girombelli and sold in hunting and fishing shops. Seeing its success, Beretta, managed by Ugo Gussalli, opened sportswear stores in New York, Dallas and Buenos Aires. In 2002, an atelier for sportswear was opened in Paris. The Collection also includes accessories, from bags to watches and from shoes to berets made either of loden cloth or thorn-resistant fabric. Beretta Sport ended the period 2001-2002 with a turnover of 14.5 million Euros and a net profit of around 8.3%. The opening of new shops in Milan, London and Madrid has been scheduled.

(*Daniela Bolognetti*)

Eric Bergère, sketch for Summer 1999's Collection.

Bergdorf Goodman Large American department store. It started as a women's wear store on New York's Fifth Avenue, at the corner of 19th Street, under the name Bergdorf and Voight. In 1889 Herman Bergdorf hired the young tailor Edwin Goodman, in 1901 they became partners, and in 1914 they opened a shop where Rockefeller Center now stands. They were among the first to sell prêt-à-porter, thus eliminating the long waiting period required with tailors. In 1928 they moved to the present address, Fifth Avenue and 58th Street, in the former Vanderbilt mansion, in a shop designed and decorated to look like the Parisian houses of their rich clientele. In 1953, Bergdorf Goodman was New York's most sophisticated department store: it sold luxury ready-to-wear and had an on-site beauty salon. In 1972 it was acquired by Carter Hawley Hale Stores. In 1986 the store opened a department for furniture and household accessories. The following year, ownership changed again, passing to the Neiman Marcus group. Bergdorf Goodman has launched many designers in America, including Missoni, Armani, Ferré, Krizia, and Lacroix, and discovered Donna Karan and Calvin Klein.

Bergé Pierre (1930). Co-founder and president of Yves Saint-Laurent. He lives and works in Paris. To define him only as a manager, as one should for his managerial gifts, would be limiting. He is, in fact, also an author of essays on the theater. At the age of 18 he was the editor of a literary review which had among its authors the most important names of the time, from Camus to Sartre to Queneau. He has been the secretary of Jean Giono. With a passion for art, he contributed to the success of Bernard Buffet. Also having also a passion for music, sometimes to excess, he started Music Mondays at the Théâtre de l'Athéné-Louis Jouvet in Paris, which he purchased and restored. He discovered and launched the career of the soprano Jessye Norman. In 1988, appointed by Mitterand, he became president of the Paris Opera, where he would remain until 1994, overseeing the first seasons at the Opera Bastille. His masterpiece, though, was the alliance with Saint-Laurent who, acclaimed for his *Trapezium* Collection with Dior, he managed to convince to go out on his own, and also arranged the financing. It was 1960. Since that time he has been the entrepreneurial strategist of the house, a support for the designer, and even, with his brusque manners, the guardian of his creativity. Alongside this is his institutional activity as founder in 1973 of the *Chambre Syndicale du Prêt-à-porter des couturiers et des createurs de mode*, of which he remained president until 1993, and as founder in 1986 and president of the French Institute of Fashion.

Bergère Eric (1960). French designer. A graduate of Esmod, he designed his first Collection in October 1995. There are about twenty single-brand stores under his name throughout the world. His concept is to display the body but without forcing it into clothes that are too tight. Before starting his own business, he worked with Erreuno, Hermès, Lanvin and Inés de la Fressange.

❑ 1999. The Mitsubishi group offers him a contract for exclusive distribution in Japan. It is his first step in the Far East. This leads to the opening of a boutique in Tokyo's Aoyama neighborhood and to distribution in more than 40 location in the country.
❑ His puts his versatility in the service of Harel shoes and later of Bruno Magli shoes.
❑ 2000, July. He opens his first boutique in Paris, in Rue de Sourdière.
❑ 2002. There are 42 shops which distribute the designer's creations.
❑ 2003. His Summer Collection is inspired by "Les Italiens des années '70" and the dresses of goddesses such as Lea Massari and Sophia Loren.

Berhanyer Elio (1931). Spanish designer. His given name his Eliseo Berenguer. Born in Cordova, he moved to Madrid at the age of 17 and ten years later began to work in the field of fashion. He is self-taught. In 1960 he presented his first Collection. In 1969 he launched his line, called Elio Berhanyer Vanguardia, with his perfumes Zarabanda and Elio's. Their success allowed him to open a boutique in Madrid, and then one in Barcelona and, in 1983, one in Mexico City. He designed the uniforms for Iberian Airlines and for the croupiers in the Madrid casino.

❑ 2003. At his 70th birthday, Elio is unanimously considered "el mas grande entre los grandes," or the greatest among the greatest, of Spain, in the words of his colleague Juan Rufete.
❑ He is given the task of organizing the Tribute to Manuel Pertegaz, which Spain will present the following year to the one who is considered, together with Balenciaga, a master.

A sketch by Elio Berhanyer. The jackets evokes the costume of Harlequin.

Berhault Louis. Also known as Jean Louis (1907). French costume maker. For 40 years he designed costumes for the stars of Hollywood. He is part of the legend of the long gloves and black satin dress worn by Rita Hayworth in the film *Gilda*. Born in Paris, he studied at the Académie des Arts Decoratifs. He was then hired as an apprentice in the atelier Agnès-Drecoll on Place Vendôme. From 1944 to 1958 he was chief costume designer at Columbia Pictures. He then went to Universal. Nominated several times for an Oscar, he would win in 1956 for *The Solid Gold Cadillac*, creating the entire wardrobe for Judy Holliday. He designed Joan Crawford's costumes for *Queen Bee* in 1955, those for Lana Turner in *Imitation of Life* in 1959 and *Portrait in Black* in 1960. His designs were also seen in many of Sandra Dee's films of the early 1960s, and in some of the Doris Day films that she made with Rock Hudson. No one can forget the mini-dress (the first of its kind) and the bathing suits that he made for Elizabeth Taylor for the film *Suddenly Last Summer*, co-starring Montgomery Clift, in 1960. Diana Vreeland said of him: "He succeeded in giving the film stars an immense charge of sensuality." In the 1960s he established the firm Jean Louis Inc. in Beverly Hills, offering new designs as well as copies of his film costumes. For Marilyn Monroe he designed the cherry-red dress that she wore in *The Misfits* in 1961, bathrobes and bikinis for the unfinished *Something's Gotta Give* of 1962, and the sequin dress that she wore at the birthday party for President Kennedy, when she sang, in front of thousands of people at Madison Square Garden, "Happy Birthday, Mr. President." Among his most well-known clients were the Duchess of Windsor, the actress Irene Dunne, and Nancy Reagan.

Beri Ritu (1971). Indian designer. She says that she became a fashion designer by chance: "Once graduated from the University of Delhi in 1987, I enjoyed myself making my own clothes, then some friends started to ask me to make some for them too, and in a short time, it became a real business." The big leap had been made, and in order to gain more confidence in cutting, she enrolled, in 1988, at the National Institute of Fashion Technology in Delhi, an affiliate of the well-known F.I.T. of New York. In 1990, as part of the defense of her thesis, she created the Lavanya Collection (in Sanskrit it means "charm"), which was later on sale in boutiques on Regent Street. Today her creations are versatile: from T-shirts to high fashion, and the uniforms she designed for the Indian team at the Olympic Games in Atlanta in 1994: a white blazer and navy trousers for men, and a dress inspired by the colors of the national flag for women. But it was her passion for embroidery, often in gold, which is her distinctive feature in the world of fashion, and a desire to specialize even more in this technique, that caused her to go to Paris, where she studied with François Lesage. Her clothes, manufactured with silk, velvet, chiffon and denim, always have a sexy touch, which mixes well with oriental tastes and Parisian refinement. Nicole Kidman, often wearing her clothes, made the Indian designer known in Hollywood. *(Valeria Vantaggi)*

Berin Harvey. American designer. During the 1960s he was the favorite of past and present American first ladies: Mamie Eisenhower, Bess Truman, Pat Nixon, Lady Bird Johnson. Faithful to a style characterized by lace, velvet, different types of silk, and classic silhouettes, he abandoned his work in the early 1970s.

Berluti A boutique for men's shoes in the Rue Marbeuf in Paris. Behind the counter and in the workshop are the heirs of Alessandro Berluti who, born in Senigallia, Italy in 1865, left there at the end of the 1800s to work as a shoemaker in France. The head of the family is Olga Berluti. The boutique is a meeting place for the fans of the Derby model, which comes in bordeaux red, cognac and parchment colors, in leather treated to look antique.

❑ 1993. LVHM acquires the brand.
❑ 2000, May. Opening of the boutique in Milan, on via Verri.
❑ During her management, Olga Berluti, a member of the fourth generation, has created five new lines: Tatoués, Guerrier, Dandy, Esprit de la Couture, and Lasso.

Bermuda shorts Trousers cut above the knees, manufactured in cotton of different weights. As in the case of the bikini, they get their name from a geographic location, in this case the coral archipelago of Bermuda in the North Atlantic, which became an American tourist destination starting in the 1930s and '40s. They were created as a solution to a local law that did not allow women to show their legs completely naked, but they immediately became part of the men's wardrobe, in a model with a cuff. Today, they are worn by the local inhabitants throughout the year, even with a shirt and tie. The knee-length trousers worn by colonial troops in the British Empire are modeled after Bermuda shorts. In the same period as Bermuda shorts appeared, in 1933, other shorts made their appearance, in the beginning similar to Bermudas in length, and later totally different in style and more trendy in their development.

Bernad Antoni (1944). Catalan photographer. Born in Barcelona, he studied the fine arts and worked for five years as an advertising designer. In 1965 he won the first international prize awarded to a documentary about fashion. Starting in 1966 he dedicated himself almost exclusively to photography and worked with Elle, Jardin des Modes, the English and French editions of Vogue, Vanity Fair, and the Spanish magazines Telva and Woman. In 1974 he was awarded the Loewe prize for his fashion photographs. He has published a volume of portraits, *Catalans*, edited by Ediciónes 62, Barcelona.

Bernard Augusta (1886-1946). After opening an atelier in 1920 in Biarritz, her hometown, three years later she settled in Paris and became famous for her simple but well-cut women's suits. During the 1930s she dressed the French aristocracy, and the Marquise of Paris didn't mind posing for Vogue wearing silk pajamas created by her. That was in February 1931, four years before the house closed.

Bernard Jeanne Adèle (1982-1962). French dress maker. A shop assistant at Béchoff-David, in 1909 she opened the *maison* Jenny on the Rue de Castiglione in Paris. Since her very first Collection, the designer distinguished herself for her richly embroidered glass-bead dresses and for a particular antique-rose color that was her signature. In 1915 her success was marked by the opening of an atelier covering six floors on two buildings along the Champs Elysées. Critics have written that some of her clothes influenced Chanel. After a merger with Lucile Paray in 1938, the brand becomes lost in the history of fashion.

Bernardin Kim (1963). Korean designer. He studied at MGM (School of Plastic Arts) in Korea. For his women's prêt-à-porter fabric and knit Collections he was inspired especially by the world of nature.

Bernasconi Italian silk factory. Established in 1899 by Davide Bernasconi, who was managing director and general manager until his death in 1922, when the leadership was taken by his son Leopoldo. In the early 1900s, Bernasconi was known for a very varied product line, ranging from silks for manufacturers of women's wear and linings to ties, scarves, handkerchiefs, and umbrellas meant, to a large part, for the international market. From the three original weaving mills – in Cernobbio (Co), Morbegno (So) and Cantello (Va) – between 1906 and 1925 it expanded with the purchase of plants in Solbiate Comasco, Maccio, Giussano, and Figliaro, and with the opening of new mills in Cagno and Cernobbio (dye-works). In 1936 Emilio Sancassani, the nephew of Leopoldo Bernasconi, was appointed general director. Starting in the 1950s, after Ticosa joined the board of directors, Bernasconi underwent a period of reorganization. Beginning in 1955, local plants were shut down, and by the end of the 1960s only the production units in Cernobbio, Solbiate and the dye-works were operative. In the late 1960s and early '70s, Ticosa acquired the Bernasconi brand and continued to marketing fabrics with the same *griffe*, until it shut down in 1972. Finally, in that year, Bernasconi's weaving mills entered into partnership with the Milanese company Multifibre, bringing as a "dowry" the plant in Solbiate. (*Pierangelo Mastantuono*)

Bernasconi Edvige (1938). Italian journalist. Born in Florence, strong-willed and determined, she started her career in 1961 as a secretary in the editorial office at Successo, a monthly published by Palazzo Editore, and becomes a professional journalist in 1968. A year later, she was already editor-in-chief at Bella and by 1970 she was at Oggi (Rizzoli Editore). In 1980, the publishing group Fabbri appointed her director of the women's division where, in 1982, she launched the magazine Benissimo. She was then given the direction of the magazine Candy Candy. In 1986 Mondadori put her in charge of planning for women's periodicals and made her director of Guida Cucina. The magazine Sale & Pepe was launched in 1987. She then devoted herself to a stimulating new project, Donna Moderna, which would be a great success thanks to her brilliant intuition of what a specific, large audience expects from a service magazine: an absolutely innovative concept with an immediate hold on readers. She was also editorial director of Confidenze and Guida TV. In May 1995, at the top of her career, she quit Mondadori and returned to RCS as director of the magazine Anna and editorial director of Bella and Donna Oggi, a magazine launched with the specific aim of offering a contrast to the great expansion of Donna Moderna. That plan did not go well, but, thanks to her authority and successful coordination of a large team, she was able to revitalize Anna which, with a circulation of more than 300,000 copies, is back on top.

❑ 2003, January. She leaves the direction of Anna. Her place is taken by Roselina Salemi.

Bernasconi Silvana. Italian journalist and illustrator. Passionate and an expert on art, she then devoted herself to fashion. Born in Forlì, she studied stage design in Rome, where she married Umberto Bernasconi, who was well-known through his association with a leading culture magazine, and he helped launch her on a journalism career. She worked with Corriere Lombardo and Settimo Giorno. In 1952 she and her husband founded the magazine Mamma and Bimbi, the first quarterly review of children's fashion, which closed in 1974. From 1969 to '75 she directed Harper's Baazar Italy, and from 1974 to '83 she was correspondent for the French edition of Vogue. She also worked for Vogue Italia, a magazine for which she still does special assignments.

Bernigaud Elizabeth (1943). French journalist. Due to her policies, Dépeche Mode, the magazine of which she became director in February 1976, together with Catherine Alain-Bernard, isn't targeted only on fashion professionals, but also on the public at large. Her formula is to produce a magazine that is objective and clear, based on professional information, and open to young talent such as the photographer Paolo Roversi, who made his début there.

Berro Marcial. Argentine artist and designer, born in La Plata. He started his career in New York and then moved to Paris, where he presently lives, although twice a year he returns to La Plata, a town which, as its name indicates (*plata*, in Spanish, means silver), has a centuries-old tradition of working in precious metals, especially silver. This is, in fact, his favorite material for the creation of high quality jewellery, all unique pieces, sometimes eccentric, and very unusual. For eight years he has been designing a more traditional line for the famous French brand Fred. But his idol is Fulco di Verdura, the Italian jewellery designer who died in 1978, loved by Chanel, and who worked with Dalí toward the end of the 1930s, famous for his surreal and bizarre creations. Berro, who works in his atelier in perfect harmony with three artisans who are his perfect alter-egos, periodically exhibits his jewels in the Naìla de Monbrison Gallery in Paris, on Rue de Bourgogne.

(*Gabriella Gregorietti*)

Bertasso Gianni (1932). Italian journalist. Founder and editor of the weekly Fashion. He was hired by the Italian state TV network RAI in 1956, after winning a national competition, and for six years he worked at the general headquarters. In 1963 he began to work as a consultant for large Italian companies such as Lancia Automotive Industry, Buitoni Alimentari, and Gruppo La Centrale, as well as foreign firms such as Repesa and the State Oil Company of Spain. In 1966 he created the corporate newspaper of the insurance company Ausonia, called Ausorgan. In 1967 he was appointed director of Mark 3, an illustrated periodical of motor racing, later acquired by the Gruppo Editoriale della Gazzetta dello Sport. In 1970 he became director of Giornale Tessile, or Textile Daily, known as G.T. In the 1980s he acquired control, and this was the beginning of Fashion, a weekly dedicated to fashion in Italy. This was the only Italian weekly specialized in the textile-clothing sector, and it was straightforward and professional. In 1999 Fashion was taken over by the German multinational group DFV. In 2000, Bertasso founded Mood, a fortnightly magazine focusing on the emerging trends in the fields of fashion, design, art and contemporary cooking. Characterized by careful attention to graphics, Mood offered itself as an innovative Italian style magazine dedicated to the basic sources of taste and to its evolution which, within the various creative fields, gives birth to fashion, design, lifestyle and the spirit of the things that surround us. Aimed principally at those who are active in the fields of fashion and design, it is addressed also to a wider public that is interested in changing trends. Bertasso has been on the teaching staff of the School of Fashion Designers at the University of Urbino, and of the Marzotto project for fashion journalists. He is general secretary and one of the founders of the Best Seller Club Moda, which gathers together the directors and distributors in the field of fashion and design.

Berteil French hat company. With three boutiques in Paris, it was a favorite of the president of France and of many European royal courts. During the 1950s, when hats went out of fashion, Berteil kept going by focusing on headgear for sports and patenting a waterproof felt.

Bertha Shawl in cotton, linen or lace worn in the mid 1800s with low-neckline dresses in order to cover the breast. It was also worn as a multi-layered cape around the neck. It was worn by Charlemagne's mother, Queen Bertha.

Berthoud François (1961). Swiss fashion illustrator, born in Lausanne. After completing the study of art in his hometown, he moved to Milan in 1982 and immediately went to work for Condé Nast. He created the image of Vanity magazine. He also works with several American magazines.

❑ 2000. Berthoud appears in *Visionaire 9-Faces*, a limited-edition publication which gathers grotesque portraits of photographers, stylists and designers such as Mario Testino, Bruce Weber, and Martin Margiela.

❑ 2003, March. Fashion sketches by the greatest graphic designers are exhibited at Tokyo's Park Museum. Berthoud contributes to the event with a drawing inspired by the work of Gianni Versace, published by Interview magazine in 1993.

Bertin Lyne (1945). French hairdresser. In the 1970s she opened a salon in Paris that was frequented by artists, painters, actors and dancers. She also worked on presentations for Dior and Lanvin. She first trained as a sculptor, which helped her in her new career. Minimalist furnishings, an intimate atmosphere, and classic music in the background are typical of her salon.

Bertoli Franco (1910-1960). Designer. He was among the thirteen people who, ignoring the danger of making enemies of the at-the-time very powerful French, accepted the invitation to show Italian fashions during a presentation to American buyers. It was February 1951. The presentation had a domestic setting, the drawing room of the Villa Torrigiani in Florence, the home of the man who would become the great strategist of the Made in Italy concept, Bista Giorgi. Bertoli already had a great deal of creative experience, intensified by the difficulty of finding fabric and materials during the war. He started as a designer of handbags. He had opened a small atelier in Milan on via Manzoni and there, on the eve of the conflict, he expanded his interests to include clothing. Maria Pezzi, the dean of fashion journalists, remembered she had seen him, around 1942, using dog collars to make bag handles: "In that period of shortages, there was now and then a batch of cheap fabric to be found. One day, Bertoli, who was thin and had the manner of a great gentleman, found yards and yards of lining material of horrendous quality but superb color, in shocking pink. He turned them into very nice umbrella-shaped skirts. If he could find silk or rayon waste, he had his concierge, who had a knitting machine, work on it. He used a batch of gros-grain ribbons to make some very fanciful bags." Beppe Modenese, who witnessed the beginnings of fashion in Florence, said "Bertoli was among the first one to create appliqués, such as cloth flowers on the fabric of large skirts. The Americans were crazy about it. He was really creative and did things completely different from the others." His adoptive son, Enzo Bertoli, continued his father's work until 1995.

(*Roberta Giordano*)

Bess Italian brand of classic knitwear in cotton and wool, but also in blends of cashmere and elasticized yarns. It was created in 1992 in Milan by Andrea Cesati and his wife Valentina Davoli. There isn't a shop that sells only the Bess brand, but its sweaters and clothes (for women only) are distributed in the most prestigious Italian and foreign boutiques. They aim at the medium-high market of women who are 25 to 40 years old. Quite independent of fashion trends, Bess creations change from one year to another only in the use of new sewing stitches and individual necklines.

❑ 2000, July. The 2001 Spring-Summer catalogue is published on CD-ROM. It becomes a regular feature of the seasons following.
❑ 2002. The brand's advertising agency is Team Moda, of Corso Venezia, Milan.
❑ 2002. Bess knitwear is exported to Germany, Belgium, Spain, Korea and Peru. The marketing is entrusted to Mi-To SRL, which has wide experience in the Far East.

Bessie Becker German house of prêt-à-porter established in Munich in 1952 by Irmgard Becker. A stage decorator and costume maker first, and later a fashion illustrator for the newspaper Heute, her Collections are characterized by a decidedly young style.

Best Company Italian brand of prêt-à-porter. It was established in the 1970s thanks to an idea of the designer Olmes Carretti, who wished to bring products made of brushed fabrics into the domestic market. At first it manufactured only men's wear. Then it expanded to include women's prêt-à-porter, children's wear, and a total look that embraced school diaries, note books, shoes, and perfumes. After various difficulties, the brand returned to the Fin.part group which then relaunched it.

❑ 2002, May. Cisalfa, already the brand's exclusive distributor for a couple of years, acquires it from the Milanese holding company Fin.part. The negotiation, started in mid 2001, closes with an expenditure of €2.91 million. Cisalfa plans a decisive relaunch of the brand.

Beth Levine Brand of shoes. In 1958, in a window at Tiffany's in New York, next to a precious jewelled clutch bag by Jean Schlumberger, a triumph was achieved by a pair of low-cut shoes with peacock feathers created for the occasion by Beth Levine. In fact, in the 1960s the most eccentric and unusual shoes were created by American designers, in particular by Beth and Herbert Levine. In 1967 they designed a shoe that became the stuff of legend: the stretch boot with which they won a *Coty Award*. Shortly after, they came out with the short-boot, a unique and inseparable item, considered that shoes were now an article of clothing item and vice versa. And in the early 1970s, the era of folk culture, flowers everywhere, clogs, Indian sandals, and the discovery and adoption of alternate clothing styles from far-away countries, Herbert Levine re-designed and launched for the American market the Hu-Gee, the traditional shoes worn by Chinese women. It was a model in red lacquer with a decidedly stylized shape. It was the time, 1971, when Nixon made his opening with China.

❑ 2000, May. At the Bata Shoe Museum in Toronto, there was an exhibit entitled *Herbert and Beth Levine: An American Pai*, a play on words meant to introduce a 30-year retrospective of their work from 1948 to 1975, including shoes made of light plastic and paper.
❑ Representative samples of Herbert Levine Inc., which closed down in 1975, are kept in several museums in the U.S., and by the Texas Fashion Collection of the School of Visual Arts at North Texas University.

Bettina (1925-2001). French model. Born Simone Bodin, she was renamed in 1947 by Fath. The daughter of a railroader and a kindergarten teacher, in 1946 she settled in Paris to work as a dress designer, but instead was hired as a model first by Costet, and later by Fath. At the time, the newspapers wrote: "If Dior has the new look, Fath has Bettina." From that moment on, she was immortalized by photographers such as Irving Penn, Cartier Bresson and Norman Parkinson. After a failed marriage with the photographer Beno Graziani, in 1955 she started a stormy and expensive love affair with Ali Khan, who died in a car accident in 1960 without marrying her. Thanks to an inheritance received from him, the "little Begum" opened an atelier, turning herself for a few years into a designer and business woman. Later, she led a life that kept her away from photographers.

(*Laura Salza*)

Betty Barclay Brand of clothing. The license obtained from the U.S. in 1954 for the use of this brand was only one small piece of the business activity of Max Berk (1908-1993). Berk was a German manufacturer of women's prêt-à-porter with long experience gained in an underwear factory that was destroyed during the war. The company, located in Nussloch, Heidelberg, developed the business through the opening of many, perhaps 130, boutiques all over the world, and the creation of two additional *griffes*: Vera Mont, dedicated to evening dresses, and Gil Bret, in 1968, for coats, women's suits, and dresses. The turnover in the mid 1990s was more than 500 billion liras.

(*Lucia Serlenga*)

❑ 2002, August. The opening of a new store in Viernheim, in the shopping mall of Rhein-Neckar-Zentrum. The fiscal year ends with an increase in revenues of 5% and an increase in export volume of 46%. The strongest markets are the British, Austrian, Swiss, and French. The launch of the new casual line's 6th season.

❑ 2003, July. A change in the license. After eight years, the collaboration with Scalamandre is ended. Starting with Spring-Summer 2004 the new licensee is the Dutch Intermedium BV.

❑ The German women's team is to wear Betty Barclay at the next Olympics in Athens.

Beuys Joseph (1921-1986). German artist. The image of him wearing a felt hat is perhaps more famous than his paintings. The artist as a work of art, the body as a tangible sign of existence, clothes as a second skin, a precise reflection of identity: these indicate the fields of his experimentation during the 1970s. In his work Beuys has often used fabric, cloth, felt, and wool as references to precise existential conditions. A work consisting of a man's suit with jacket and pants of felt, *Filzanzung*, dates to 1970.

Biagini Roberto (1963). Florentine designer with an avocation for poetry. Since his first Collection in 1994, every Collection is introduced with a poem written by him. It is at the same time a meditation on life and a summary of the sartorial themes that will soon unfold. Up until the presentation of his first men's Collection, Biagini had been interested only in women's wear, which he put aside at the moment he signed an agreement to work with an American distributor who opened that foreign market to him. Present every year at Pitti Immagine and at several American trade fairs in the industry, the designer has been part of the National Chamber of Fashion since 1997.

Biagiotti Laura (1943). A designer and entrepreneur, she has brought a romantic and feminine element into Italian fashion, expressed through the most refined materials like cashmere, linen and taffeta. Laura has followed in the footsteps of her mother Delia, the owner of a famous atelier in Rome in the 1960s. From her she inherited good taste and a knowledge of the world of fashion and French haute couture which at the time were the point of reference of every elegant woman. After her studies in archaeology, which fed her other great passion, and a period of working with Schuberth, Barocco, Litrico and others, she joined her mother in the running of the atelier. Understanding the potential of the emerging luxury prêt-à-porter, in 1965, together with Gianni Cigna, she founded Biagiotti Export, a company which manufactured and exported the high-fashion creations of Rome. In 1972 she entered the knitwear sector directly, acquiring MacPherson of Pisa, a prestigious company specialized in the production of cashmere items. The possibilities offered by cashmere, until then used only for very classic pieces in the English tradition, fascinated young Laura and

Laura Biagiotti: a "Doll's" dress (1977-78).

prompted her to use it as one of the principal materials on which to base the research for her future Collections. The début of her first Collection occurred that same year: a few pieces which revolved around a white jacket that could be transformed by accessories and worn from morning to evening. It was the beginning of a deep love for white, the color which became at that time another distinctive feature of her work. The designer creates for women like herself rather than for the abstract creatures of the runway. She believes in fashion that is easy-to-wear, in clothes for those who want to keep being themselves. During the 1980s her style became more refined and settled. Her cashmere pieces were innovative and sophisticated, and experimented with solutions never tried before, so much so that the New York Times gave her the title "Queen of Cashmere." Her doll's dresses, trapezoidal in shape, cut in linen or taffeta, repeat their success season after season. The white linens, embroidered like grandmother's linen, became very new and elegant solutions for modern life. In 1980 she acquired and restored to its old splendor Marco Simone's castle in Guidonia, in the countryside near Rome, where she established her home and her business. The relaxing atmosphere of the castle, its peace, the serene family life with her daughter Lavinia and her husband Gianni Cigna (who died prematurely in 1996), blended together in an incessant activity that allowed the designer to attain important goals. She has several records: she was the first Italian designer invited to present a Collection in China, in 1988; the first invited to the Kremlin, in 1995; and the first to Cairo, in 1998. She has received many awards: Cavaliere del Lavoro in 1995; Woman of the Year in New York in 1992; and the Marco Polo award in 1993. Her love for art, for culture, and for her hometown have made Laura Biagiotti a sophisticated patron of the arts. Through the Foundation Biagiotti Cigna, established in memory of her husband, she gave 170 paintings by the Futurist artist Giacomo Balla to the city of Rome, sponsored the reconstruction of the curtain of the opera house La Fenice in Venice, and did the same for the restoration of Michelangelo's staircase on the Campidoglio in Rome on the occasion of the Jubilee for the year 2000.

(*Gisella Borioli*)

❑ Everything proceeds according to tradition: her beloved cashmere, the adored color white, the experimentation with materials, and the cultivated quotations; these are the main elements in every Collection of this lady who, in 2002, celebrated 20 years of militancy in fashion. At a presentation on her birthday, she showed cashmere washed at a temperature of 100°C and felted to the point of looking like a luxury plush sweatshirt. Laura-land, in other words, the world of Laura Biagiotti: small great inventions, like the souvenir print of Summer 2003 with lace-trimmed inlays of old postcards. This was not by chance, because the Italian Postal Service issued more than two million stamps with the names and styles of various Italian designers, including hers. Standing at her side was her daughter Lavinia, her valuable collaborator and the one responsible for the Laura Biagiotti Roma line, as well as for the Winter 2003-2004 presentation, which was inspired by the Russian theater. Suggestions presented also in a masculine way, a vagabond man with emptiness in his heart. (*Lucia Mari*)

❑ 2001, February. The designer resigns her position as vice president of the Chamber of Fashion. The board of directors rejects her resignation because of "the importance and high quality of her contribution to the association."
❑ 2001, September. Twelve years after the début of Roma comes the launch of Emotion, a new fragrance created by Biagiotti and her daughter, Lavinia Cigna.
❑ 2002, August. Biagiotti, by now a regular on the Chinese runways, presents her styles along with various Italian, French, Dutch and Chinese designers on Tienanmen Square in Beijing, for the first time after the tragic events of 1989. An agreement is reached with the Mafrat Group for the production and marketing of accessories and eye glasses, as well as girl's shoes under the Dolls brand.

❑ On the occasion of the 10th anniversary of its founding, Laura Biagiotti maintains her post as president of the Comitato Leonardo, an association concerned with safeguarding and promoting Italian style throughout the world.
❑ *Zarin* and *Matrioska* bags are Biagiotti's new accessories for the Autumn-Winter season, inspired by the Russia of the Czars, modular and studded with semi-precious stones, in suede, soft leather, antique leather, and with fur trim.

Biagiotti Cigna Lavinia (1978). Born in Rome, she followed in her mother's footsteps. She was educated at the exclusive Marymount school in Rome. In 1996, after the death of her father, Gianni Cigna, she decided to leave her medical studies in order to work with her mother. She made her début in 1997 on the occasion of a charity event in Cairo. That was her first time on the runway with her mother for the final applause. In 1999 she coordinated the presentation of the new Laura Biagiotti line of eye glasses and the new Tempore and Tempore Donna perfumes. She also organized the event that marked the restoration of the staircase of the Campidoglio in Rome, brought back to its ancient splendor with her mother's patronage. In 2000, she brought to the Milan runways, for the evocative grand finale of the Spring-Summer 2001 Collection, a large number of the champions who triumphed at the 2000 Olympics in Sydney. This was a new link between fashion and sport which is repeated at every Biagiotti presentation. In 2001, she designed along with her mother a new clothing line called Laura Biagiotti Roma. With the collaboration of Maurizio Millenotti, who was nominated for an Oscar for his costumes for the film *The Legend of The Pianist on the Ocean*, Lavinia created the clothes for the play *The Blue Room*.

(*Maria Vittoria Alfonsi*)

Bianchi Silk factory in Como. The firm was established in 1925 when Giuseppe Bianchi decided to continue the marketing of "pure silk and blended fabrics" started by his father under the brand name Seterie Maria Monti. Before the war, to its initial production of fabric for men's wear, the firm added, figured or diapered fabrics for men's accessories, women's corsets, and furniture, as well as flags, liturgical clothing and sacred vestments.

Bianchini-Férier Silk factory established in Lyon in 1888 by the Italian Carlo Bianchini, in partnership with François Aruier and François Férier. It was famous for its crêpe de chine georgette, heavily used by tailors of haute couture, and for hiring artists such as Sonia Delaunay and Raoul Dufy to design their fabrics. Within ten years of its founding, the firm was already a big name. It had offices in Paris and was about to arrive in London. In 1909 it opened an office in New York and, in 1922, one in Montreal. Today, it has an archive with 40,000 original sketches.

❑ 2001, December. "Christmas Exhibition" at Abbott & Holder in London. On sale, together with 600 drawings and watercolors, from the Pre-Raphaelite Sir Joseph Noel Paton to the Shakespearian illustrator John Masey-Wright, were the Art Deco textile sketches of the firm.
❑ 2002. The company is placed under receivership. By the end of the year a liquidation plan was ready.
❑ 2003, March. Damask silks created for Bianchini-Férier by Dufy have a prominent place in an exhibit at the Victoria and Albert Museum in London dedicated to Art Deco and its various expressions.

Biani Alberto (1953). Italian designer. Since 1979 he has designed the women's Collection New York Industrie. A Venetian born in Noventa Vicentina, in 1984 he established Staff International, a house that produced Collections for men and women. The 1996 was a turning point, with the birth of the Alberto Biani *griffe*, presented in Milan, and the opening of his first boutique, also in Milan. The first Collection produced by him and not by Staff International was in Autumn-Winter 1999. His concept of modern tailoring was a success: a strong image for garments which, from a stylistic point of view, must have a life that is longer than the pursuit of short-term ideas and styles.

❑ 2003. After eight years, he again designs for New York Industrie, the brand created by him and later sold to McAdams by Staff International.

Alberto Biani: sketch for men's suit.

Bias Cutting on the bias was hugely popular for dresses and skirts of the interwar years and its popularity has never really faded. By cutting diagonally to the weft of the fabric, a bias cut facilitates the modeling of a garment, by allowing the material to hug the body and then hang in a flowing and loose fashion. It is thought that cutting on the bias was invented by Madame Vionnet. In fact, it already existed but was only used for trims and little collar or wrist details. It is therefore fair to say that it was created by Madame Vionnet, who extended its use when her workshop reopened in 1918 after World War I. She explored and exploited all the creative potential that the bias cut offered, using it mainly for evening dresses and suits. Having invented this new technique, a new curvaceous and flowing silhouette of a women's figure was born, one that was copied throughout the 1930s and still survives today.

Biba A London boutique and name given to a trendy style of clothing linked to the British avant-guard of the 1960s. Biba is the name of the sister of designer Barbara Hulanicki (1936), who thought about this name when, together with her husband Stephen Fitz-Simon, she started a mail order business in 1963. It sold skirts and other items of clothing, and launched the Biba Postal Boutique through advertisements in the Daily Express. It was again with the Biba name that, in 1964, at the height of swinging London, she opened her first shop in Kensington. The shop offered a window for a new style created for the young people of the time, made of clothes which showed the shape of the body and stressed the physical type dominant at the time, that of the top model Twiggy. The daughter of Polish Jews who emigrated to Palestine before the war, at the age of 22 she moved to England and studied at the Brighton School of Art. In 1955 she won a competition for beachwear designs advertised by the Evening Standard newspaper. Encouraged by that adventure, she left college in order to work as a fashion illustrator for Vogue and for Tatler, and then on the London editorial staff of Women's Wear Daily. Thanks to these experiences, she decided to make her début as a designer. Her style is characterized by great attention to everything that goes on around her, from a youthful desire to break the rules of bourgeois style to a look back at the fashions of the 1930s, with some nostalgia. Her styles (maxi and mini-skirts, bikinis with matching blouses, overcoats in velvet or in shiny and colored PVC) have great success, partly because of their low prices. A period of decline begins in the second half of the 1970s.

❑ 1975. Barbara moves to Brazil. The shop, run by her husband, closes shortly after.
❑ After the death of Fitz-Simon, the designer moves to Miami, where she creates architecture for hotels in a tropical-deco style. She did the restyling of various prestigious hotels in South Beach, including The Marlin.
❑ The myth of Biba is today kept alive by the new London shops clearly inspired by it, by very frequent exhibits in the most important British museums,

and by the passion of fans who seek out the work and any memorabilia from the firm's golden age.
❑ 2003, February. The second episode of the BBC documentary *Designing the Decades*, dedicated to British fashion, celebrates the art of Biba along with Clive Sinclair, Charles Hall, Roy Jacuzzi and Malcom McLaren.

Biba French monthly magazine. The first issue was published in January 1980. It was aimed especially at women who work, with the purpose of providing all kinds of information quickly. In addition to fashion and columns on the news, cinema, and books, space was given to inquiries on the world of work and women's rights, and on the various professions. In 1982, Anne Lefèbvre, the chief editor, divided the magazine into three parts, concerning jobs, seduction and lifestyle.

Bibita Clothing brand. It is inspired by the artistic avant-guards of the last century. Its creator is Stefania Baldassarre who, for Autumn-Winter 2003, made reference to the abstract expressionism of Jackson Pollock in clothes decorated with open-work motifs and printed with a sponge-stencil technique. The body-painting effect of light sweaters and T-shirts, manufactured with looms used for lingerie, in Spring-Summer 2003, was due in particular to Georgia O'Keefe. The following Autumn-Winter season was characterized by clothes without seams.

Bickler Sabine and Susanne. Italian designers. Two young Milanese sisters of German descent, after working for a few years in their father's company, decided to produce an underwear line. It was the birth of Sobimil Srl (1983). The basic idea was to create small Collections such that all the proposed pieces could be mixed and matched, both as to color and style. Interpreting a new trend which saw the success of Homewear clothes, the Collection expanded with the creation of their new brand, Sobimilla. It was a practical, comfortable, young and witty way of dressing, but refined in its simplicity, perfect at home and outdoors: T-shirts and tricot tops with contrasting or color-on-color trim were combined with large *coulisse* trousers, long or mini-skirts; small cardigans matched to dresses with frills that are almost child-like; romantic brassieres in flowered stretch-tulle with lace along the neck. The fibers used are natural. There are also accessories, coordinated with the clothing, from slippers to mini bags trimmed with small pearls.

(*Gabriella Gregorietti*)

Bidermann Multinational manufacturing company. Established in France by Maurice Bidermann in 1950, it gradually began to specialize in men's wear. It manufactures for Klein, Hechter, Courrèges, Kenzo and Saint-Laurent, and owns the brands Daniel Crémieux and Bill Robinson. Since 1973 it has had an American subsidiary, Bidermann Industries, which in 1990 gained control of Cluett Peabody, the producer of Arrow shirts and Gold Toe socks that, in terms of global turnover, has the leading share, with more than 70%. In men's manufacturing, the group is a leader in France and ranks 11th in the world. It employs altogether almost 9,000 people.

Bidyut Das (1977). Knitwear designer born in India. In the 1990s he moved to London where he began his studies, first in fashion and textiles at Kingsway College, and then at Central Saint Martin's, where he specialized in knitwear, and finally a masters in Men's Fashion Knitwear at the Royal College of Art. His art in the creation of knitwear consists of combining, blending and experimenting. In order to do so he uses different types of materials and, above all, different techniques of working – embroidery, felting, painting, printing, dyeing, and heat pressing – but without torturing the shapes, which remain quite simple. Great attention is paid to color, often combining brilliant tonalities not often found together, with the idea that color can be used as an expression of individuality. Today Bidyut is a professor at Central Saint Martin's where he pursues a project aimed at learning and using the knitting machine. Students learn knitwear manufacturing and then they are assigned themes which they can develop freely, using also unusual materials. (*Daniela Bolognetti*)

Bie Barzaghi Company organized for the development of specialty high-quality textile products. Its headquarters are in Giussano, near Milan. It has made a name on the international market due to its extraordinary capacity for innovation, especially in its finishing treatments, and for its range of avant-guard fabrics with their technical characteristics that vary according to the particular need (protection, waterproofing, breathability). Its fabrics are light, versatile, easy to handle, and easy to maintain, an alternative to standard fabrics, and absolutely able to meet the new needs of consumers. The company, with its line Barzaghi 1926, also focuses on formal clothing made with exclusive fabrics characterized by refined though very modern armatures. Classicism and tradition joined to high performance in comfort, crease-resistance, and practicality are its strong features.

Biennial of Florence Festival of contemporary culture. It proposes to explore and relate, at the highest international level, and through the most innovative form and content, the affinities, the mutual influences, and the creative relationships between fashion, the visual arts, design, architecture, photography, cinema, music and communications. By the end of the millennium, it had been held twice: the inauguration in 1996 and then in 1998. Starting from an idea of Luigi Settembrini (with the cooperation of Roberto Rosati) and promoted by, among others, the Florence Center for Italian Fashion, the Region of Tuscany, and the Municipality of Florence, the Biennial of Florence (also known as the Biennial of Fashion), has perhaps been the first event in which the work of designers has been met on the same level by different creative languages in an attempt to define the central themes of contemporary life. A new chapter in the culture of fashion was thus opened, going beyond the usual low opinion of its role and its most superficial traits. This was particularly evident during the first festival, which took place from September 1996 to January 1997 under the artistic direction of Germano Celant (art historian and art critic, curator at the Guggenheim Museum in New York), Luigi Settembrini, and Ingrid Sischy (journalist and director of Interview). Entitled *Time and Fashion* (*Il Tempo e la Moda*), the first Bienniale was divided into seven exhibits. More than 140 people, among them fashion designers, artists, architects, designers, photographers and musicians from all over the world, participated, often with work created expressly for the occasion. There were three main exhibits, organized in various museums and places around the city. The first, *Art/Fashion*, consisted of seven large structures designed by Arata Isozaki at the Forte di Belvedere and was a joint project with couples each consisting of a designer and an artist: Gianni Versace/Roy Lichtenstein, Helmut Lang/Jenny Holzer, Azzedine Alaïa/Julian Schnabel, Jil Sander/ Mario Merz, Miuccia Prada/Damien Hirst, Rei Kawakubo/Oliver Herring, and Karl Lagerfeld/Tony Cragg. The second, *New Persona/New Universe*, at Stazione Leopolda and organized by Denis Santachiara, was a meditation on the new boundaries of the human being and of the universe with more than 30 participants split between artists and designers: Robert Mapplethorpe, David Bowie, Cindy Sherman, Kiki Smith, Tony Oursler, Giuseppe Penone, Jurgen Teller, Studio Azzurro, Jake and Dinos Chapman, Ines van Lamsweerde, Vito Acconci and Giorgio Armani, Vivienne Westwood, Calvin Klein, Alexander McQueen, Yohij Yamamoto, and Moschino. The third, *Visitors*, curated by Franca Sozzani and organized by Gae Aulenti, was a remarkable meeting between the works and atmosphere of some of the most beautiful and important museums in the world and original projects by fashion designers: Armani at the Uffizi, Valentino at the Gallerie dell'Accademia, Ferré at the Medici Chapels, Dolce & Gabbana at the Museum of Anthropology, Gaultier at La Specola, Miyake at the Galleria d'Arte Moderna di Palazzo Pitti, Galliano at Casa Buonarroti, Blahnik at Palazzo Vecchio, Atkinson at the Opificio delle Pietre Dure, Donna Karan at the Museo del Bargello, Lacroix at Orsanmichele, Margiela at Museo Bardini, Ozbek at Museo Horne, Saint-Laurent at Palazzo Vecchio, Treacy at Museo degli Argenti, Tyler at the Museum of the History of Science, Gigli at Museo Marini, and Marc Jacobs, Todd Oldham and Anna Sui at the Civic Museum of Prato. After Florence, the exhibit *Art/Fashion*, which also presented a historical section about the relationship between the two languages, opened in March 1997 at the Guggenheim Museum

Soho in New York. The other four exhibits were: a retrospective on Emilio Pucci in the Sala Bianca at Palazzo Pitti, an exhibit of photographs by Bruce Weber at the Museo Salvatore Ferragamo, an exhibit about Elton John's wardrobe at the Royal Postal Office in the Uffizi, and an exhibit-event by Michelangelo Pistoletto with the participation of, in addition to Pistoletto himself, Tina Bepperling, Andrea Branzi, Peter Kogler, Pietra, Enrico Rava, Chris Sacker, Oliviero Toscani, and Franz West, at the Museo d'Arte Contemporanea Luigi Pecci in Prato. More than 100,000 visitors, a strong impact on the international level, the presence of forty fashion designers and as many artists, and heavily favorable critical reviews (with some dissent in Germany and Italy, but enthusiasm in France and the English-speaking countries) testify to the great success of the initiative. The second Biennale, managed by a different staff headed by Leonardo Mondadori, was dedicated to the relationship between fashion and cinema, and was divided into the exhibits *Cine-Moda*, curated by Richard Martin, at Palazzo Strozzi; *Riflessioni* curated by Dante Ferretti and Gabriella Pescucci, also at Palazzo Strozzi; and *2001 (meno3)* curated by Terry Jones at Stazione Leopolda; *Costumes of thebe Oscars* curated by Gabriella Pescucci, at Palazzo Pretorio in Prato; *Casting Livorno* curated by Oliviero Toscani at the former Peroni factory in Livorno. The Biennale also included a showing of the film *L'ultimo grido* ("The Last Cry") by Vieri Razzini and Cesare Petrillo at Cinema Le Laudi in Florence, and an event called *Cinderella* curated by Stefania Ricci, Michael Howells and Jenny Beavan at the Museo Salvatore Ferragamo. The more limited impact of this second Biennale and a worsening financial situation were behind the decision not to have a third.

Biennial of Valencia The first international event dedicated to communication between different creative contemporary languages, including fashion. It presents only new projects, studied and carried out around a central idea every other year. It is sponsored by the Generalidad Valenciana and directed by Luigi Settembrini. The first Biennal took place in June 2001 and it was dedicated to the Passions. It opened with an event at the Fura dels Baus with clothes and costumes designed by Jean Paul Gaultier, Versace, Valentino, and Issey Miyake, among others. The main theme, interpreted by 150 of the most important artists of the time, connects the exhibits curated by Achille Bonito Oliva, Peter Greenway, Emir Kusturica, Mladen Materic, Droog Design, Robert Wilson, Robin Rimbaud, Shiro Takatani, David Pérez, and Santiago Calatrava. There were 250,000 visitors and the event was mentioned 950,000 by critics in various media. In June 2003, the second Biennial, on the theme of *The Ideal City*, presented 13 different events. There were five exhibits, organized by Lorand Hegyi, William Alsop and Bruce Mclean, Mike Figgis, Sebastiao Salgado, Francisco Jaurauta and Jean Luis Maubant. There was social project by Vincente Guallart, and two communications projects by Rafael Sierra. There were five theater events presented together with the City of Stage Arts, directed by Irene Papas: the world premiere of *Your Hand in Mine* by Carol Rocamora, directed by Peter Brook, with Natasha Perry and Michel Piccoli; *Barbaric Comedies* by Valle-Inclan; a trilogy directed by Bigas Luna; *Lysistrata* by Aristophanes, with music by Carles Santos and costumes by Francis Montesino. At the second Biennial of Valencia the participants included architects and designers such as Frank Geary, Toyo Ito, Nigel Coates, Rem Koolhaas, and Vito Acconci, and artists such as Miguel Navarro, Marina Abramovic, Anne and Patrick Poirier, Wim Wenders, Sonja Kim, Clay Setter, Betrand Lavier, Piero Castellini, Pascal Pinaud, Wim Delvoye, Richard Noonas, Maurizio Nannucci, Ilya and Emilia Kabakov, Teresa Chaffer and Gloria Friedman, among others.

Biesen (von) Thierry (1965). Lebanese photographer. He started his career in 1989 as an assistant to Art Kane and, four years later, became interested in photo reportages while working for France Press. Starting in 1999 he worked in the field of fashion photography, publishing his work in Talk, Sleazenation, and Mined.

Biffi Store in Milan. During the 1960s, the sisters Rosy and Adele Biffi opened two shops in Milan, one on Corso Genoa and on via Fabio Filzi. They were the first in Italy to offer the French designer Kenzo and the accessories of Ferré, who was just becoming known. Today, there are five shops, including one in Bergamo (in Milan's fashion quadrilateral, a new boutique, Banner, opened on via Sant'Andrea). The sisters' intuition and critical eye have never made a mistake when launching new talents and young people starting out. They were successful, for example, with Clemens Ribeiro and Antonio Berardi. But first, toward the end of the 1960s, it happened with Gianfranco Ferré, who was hesitating between a career in architecture and one in fashion. Franco Limonta, the husband of Rosy Biffi, asked him to do a small Collection of leather clothes, thus giving him the opportunity to make his début.

Biglidue Brand of prêt-à-porter fashion, founded in Milan in 1984 as a second line of the Italian manufacturing company Verri. It has an easy design for a young and elegant public. It offers natural materials mixed with classics in order to obtain clothes that can be worn on every occasion. The line is widely distributed in Japan.

Big Time A factory that manufactures jeans. It was established in 2001 as the result of a joint venture between ICAM, which produces casual clothing, and Calzaturificio Europeo. The company, with headquarters in Lallio, in the province of Bergamo, started its activity in Spring 2002 in collaboration with Fiorucci, for whom it creates and distributes jeans for men, women, and children. The Fiorucci licence is the third for Big Time, after those of Missoni and Enrico Coveri. In 2002 the company had a turnover of about €70 million.

Biguine Jean Claude (1954). French hairdresser. There are ninety hairdressing salons with his name on them throughout France. He owes his success to a formula which combines fast service and low prices.

❑ 2002, May. Début of the new Biguine sunglass line which is distributed by Magnon. In June, the Pro Beauty line is presented, consisting of a professional set of shampoos, crèmes and various treatments. There are a total of 350 salons, of which 130 are abroad, plus 110 beauty farms in 18 countries throughout the world.

Bikers Youth movement and style. The image of Perfecto, the leather jacket by Schott worn by Marlon Brando in *The Wild One*, directed by Stanley Kramer in 1954, is destined to undergo infinite mutations within the typology of biker culture. The biker, as an archetype, is related to the ground in the way that a surfer is to water. In both, the passion for a sport is interpreted as a lifestyle. Or, put a better way, a lifestyle is inferred by expanding the symbolic limits of a sport. In both, the essential thing is to ride the wave, or the asphalt, in terms of means and purpose at the same time. For bikers, a feeling of dissatisfaction and a desire for escape, seen as a model, have their origin in the inability of some World War II veterans to adapt to domestic life after leaving the service. In the U.S. of the 1940s and '50s, in a climate dominated, also from a media point of view, by increasing conformism, bikers abandoned both every previous model of biker life and any attempt to assimilate themselves into the upper classes. Proudly adopting a genuinely working class style of dress (jeans, T-shirt, and a jacket) they created a model that would endure even for those who would never ride a motorbike. The character type of the rebel was embodied first by James Dean and then by Bruce Byron, an almost mythological character in *Scorpio Rising* (1963) by Kenneth Anger, and they would also serve as models for Dennis Hopper in *Easy Rider* (1968).

(*Maurizio Vetrugno*)

Biki Italian dressmaker (1906-1999). She wore a bright green turban when, in 1996, I saw her for the last time. Elvira Leonardi Bouyeure, known as Biki in the world of fashion, was working in her atelier on the ground floor of her house in via Sant'Andrea in Milan, where she lived and worked. I, the reporter, was almost falling asleep; she, the subject of the interview, and 90 years old, was bursting with energy: "Today I'm starting the Japan Collection. Together with my daughter Roberta, I've finished the children's line and I'm sketching the dresses for my very faithful, special, very rich women, who are allergic to today's bric-a-brac, just like my adored Maria

Biki in her atelier in Milan, in a sketch by Brunetta for the magazine Bellezza.

would have been." Maria was Maria Callas. Biki taught her how to dress, she was her Pygmalion of manners and the wardrobe. The soprano was, as one would say in the fashion language of today, her testimonial, imposing the designer on the world with that strange nickname, Biki, which was an exotic variation of Bicchi, as she was called by Giacomo Puccini, her grandfather in affection if not of blood. "I met Maria in 1951 in the house of Wally Toscanini," she would say. "She was a real mess, a fat 'rich and vain' madam who loved accessories that matched, the shoes with the bag, and so much the better if they were in bright patent leather. She came to my atelier, where I was with my son-in-law, Alain Reynaud, who had been the assistant of Jacques Fath, and made designs for me. She was on a diet, barely under 220 lbs. pounds, but she already moved like a thin person and she had the allure of a thin person. In order that she not make a mistake, Alain numbered every item in her wardrobe, including the dresses, shoes, and accessories, and had written down exactly what to wear with what: evening dress no. 8 with shoes no. 14 and shawl no. 6. Maria was a sponge. Her talent was a great gift. What she learned seemed to have belonged to her always, as something innate. For example, her grace in wrapping herself in a shawl. I remember only one person who could keep up with her, Cardinal Montini, who later became pope. I saw him in the archbishopric of Milan. He would protect himself from the cold with a big scarf. A person of natural chic." Biki became a dressmaker, which was the term she preferred, as she hated to be called a designer, thanks to her initiative, generous intelligence, and what she would call "natural chic," the elegance and style of that world that she, by birth and not by income, she entered as a girl, the daughter of Fosca, the baby girl born from Elvira Puccini's first marriage. For Biki, Puccini was "grandfather Tato," and the composer, who called her "the little fashion snob," almost guessing her future work, told her, "I need silence, Turandot is sleeping." Shortly thereafter, he died in Brussels. Biki was not yet 18. She was out in the big world, at La Scala, with the Viscounts of Modrone, and with the Toscanini family. She witnessed the conductor's great anger when his 17 year-old daughter Wally fell in love and eloped with Emanuele Castelbarco, who was 35, married, and unforgivably "blond and aristocratic." She also got to know Franco Florio, the tailor Lelong, the photographer Horst, and Isadora Duncan. But it wasn't just for fun, or to fulfil herself, that she decided to "look after herself." She really had to roll up her sleeves and she did it through fashion and her "natural chic." On the occasion of a lunch organized by Virginia Agnelli, she met Vera Borea, who had a small atelier in Paris, and proposed that she and Gina Cicogna to take care of her beachwear and sportswear Collections in Italy. It was the end of 1933. The partnership didn't go well. But Bicchi (she changed it to "Biki" when she began to work in the fashion world) and Gina Cicogna decided to work together and design underwear. Gabriele D'Annunzio invented the brand name for their lingerie, Domina. In Spring 1934, in the atelier at via Senato 8, they presented their designs, which were inspired by Paris fashions. D'Annunzio, who was known variously as the Poet and as the Commander, and also had huge debts, took some of their clothes for his latest lover, the pianist Luisa Baccara, but paid for them only with this letter of praise: "Biki, the folds, the gaps, the full fabric, and the airy lace, the stitching, and the trimming, are all elements of a precise rhythm and an indistinct unknown, and thus, of poetry." These were the years in which the Fascist regime, during the drive for self-sufficency in the economy, ordered that fashion houses produce on their own, without purchasing fabric from France, which usually amounted to 50% of every Collection. Biki was a pioneer of the Made in Italy movement when she continued on her own after the partnership with Gina Cicogna ended. She no longer made underwear, but suits, dresses, and evening gowns. Her début was on May 5th 1936, the same day that Mussolini announced the return of the empire "on the fatal hills of Rome." Then came World War II and the post-war economic boom. In the Milan of that time, which was going through its first season of prosperity, with mink coats, very elegant dresses for premieres at La Scala, and the imitation of the styles that Enrichetta Pedrini imported from Paris, Biki was, together with Germana Marucelli and Jole Veneziani, the queen of dressmakers and the dressmaker of a new Italian style, supported in her creativity by Alain Raynaud, her son-in-law. She had meanwhile married Robert Bouyeure, but she

Biki. Jacket of black monkey with yellow velvet ribbons. Sketch by Brunetta for the magazine Bellezza.

kept her name, that nickname, in her work. Following her mother's marriage to Mario Crespi, the eldest of three brothers who were the sole owners of Corriere della Sera, she became heiress to a large part of that newspaper empire located on via Solferino. She was rich, but continued to work in her atelier in Sant'Andrea (it had been near via Montenapoleone, and later would be almost at the corner of via della Spiga), as a Stakhanovist but with the coquetry of not admitting that she was tired, of continuing to be Biki, and possibly to teach Maria that "no, in the evening, at home, one cannot wear a velvet broad-brimmed hat.". She was one the first high fashion dressmakers to work with manufacturers: from 1960 to '66 she designed the Cori-Biki line for the Textile Financial Group. She continued to be a "little fashion snob" even when she became old ("You decide whether or not to write how old I am. I know, after a long life, that age can be a reason for pride. But it's still old age anyway.") and new designers came on the scene. She was, like her mother Fosca, a woman of character and full of energy. Hélène Blignaut wrote a biography of Biki: *La scala di vetro*, published by Rusconi in 1995. (*Guido Vergani*)

Bikini Two-piece bathing suit consisting of a very short bottom and a skimpy top that appeared after the war upon the announced return of a femininity that had endured the privation of war-time shortages. The search for novelties in beachwear was in the air: a similar costume was shown in the Spring of 1946 by a very famous designer, Heim. He named it Atome, hoping that it would result in an explosion like the atom bomb. But on July 3rd of that same year, the almost unknown designer Louis Réard would name his daring two-piece costume after Bikini, the Pacific Ocean atoll where, only four days earlier, the U.S. had started nuclear tests. And so, bikini it was. The first models, often crocheted, were in primary colors and quite proper, despite showing more of the body, and were clearly intended for very young girls. A completely different thing was the monokini, which purposely misunderstood the "bi" of bikini as meaning "double." It was a suimsuit made of only one piece, the bottom (it came out in 1964). Starting in the 1970s, the bikini appeared in more reduced versions. There was the string bikini, with a small triangle-shaped bottom piece in front and just a thin string between the cheeks of the backside; and the "tanga," of Brazilian origin, in which the skirt, thanks to its cut, shows the hips up to the waist. (*Lucia Sollazzo*)

Bikkembergs Dirk (1959). German designer, born in Flamershem. He studied at the Royal Academy of Arts in Antwerp. His career started in 1982. Until 1987 he worked for Fashion Brand, a Belgian company making prêt-à-porter. But the turning point in his career was 1986. He won the third *Golden Spindel* as best fashion designer of the year, and this coincided with a decision to launch his own line. Presented in London in March of that same year, it consisted only of men's footwear. In time, men's shirts and knitwear were added. His début in men's prêt-à-porter occurred in Paris, in January of 1988. The presentation of his first official Collection took place later that year, in September, again in Paris. The year 1996 saw the birth of a line of women's footwear, alongside the men's line, with few but very innovative models. In Spring-Summer of that year he launched Bikkembergs, a fast and dynamic men's line, created for a young market.

❑ 2000. He presents, in quick succession, the women's line White Label, a footwear line, and a jeans Collection for men and women called Red Label.
❑ He wins the *Esprit du Siècle* award, given by Moët & Chandon.
❑ 2002, October. The second day of Moscow's AlboModa is entirely dedicated to Belgian designers. Presenting their Collections are Veronique Branquinho, Dirk Bikkembergs and Walter Bereindonck.
❑ 2003, June. For the 2003-2004 season the uniforms of Inter Football Club are designed by Dirk Bikkembergs. It was an unusual runway for the Belgian designer, at the Inter Football Club headquarters on via Durini. The agreement with the black and blue soccer team is the crowning achievement of his life's passion, a career marked by the presentation of his Collection in soccer stadiums, and of women's knitwear Collections decorated with the numbers of a soccer team.

Bilancioni Umberto. Founder with his brother Alfredo of the men's knitwear and clothing brand that carries his name. The brand is characterized by a combination of the craftsman traditions of Le Marche, their region of Italy, with sophisticated research in materials. It is part of the firm Sacma SpA, which has a staff of 70 workers. The style is comfortable due to its shape, and rich in details. The brand is distributed in 37 countries all over the world, with the strongest markets in Italy, the U.S.A., and Japan. In June 2003 the firm participated in Pitti ImmagineUomo in order to celebrate its 50th anniversary in business.

Bill Amberg English brand of bags and leather goods established in 1984. It is named after its owner and designer, who offers a line of leather accessories for men and women, manages a workshop for the design and creation of leather goods, has a department of interior design, as well as a single-brand store in London. The designer has recently launched a line of accessories for children.

Bill Tornade French brand of men's and children's fashion. It was established in 1977 as a creative partnership between the brothers Francis and José Ronez. Their fashion is very young and colorful, created with a variety of fanciful materials.

❑ 2003, May. The French brand is among the 55 new names invited to Pitti Immagine Bimbo.
❑ The French Group Zannier is to produce and market Bill Tornade children's wear, with design still in the hands of Sylvia Rielle. The Collection is distributed in 66 points-of-sale in France and in 40 stores abroad. There are single-brand boutiques for baby wear in Cannes and Paris.

Binda Silk factory in the Lombardy region of Italy established in 1945 by Gianni Binda and Ferruccio Bernasconi. At the time of the start-up, Binda had already been an apprentice with Guido Ravasi, and an associate and manager with Serica Lombarda. The new company, located in Como, specialized in the manufacture of handkerchiefs, scarves and ties. It included a weaving mill, started in 1946, and a print shop, started in 1947. Between the end of the 1940s and the early 1950s, production was mainly printed fabrics for accessories for the Italian and foreign markets. In 1964, the printing works was moved to Breccia, and in 1972 the weaving mill was consolidated in Binago, but later shut down due to diminished exports of processed cloth to the U.S. After 1985, sales rose again, especially in France, Japan and the U.S. In 1993, the heirs of Gianni Binda (his sons Palmiro and Enrico) founded Tie-Como for the marketing of fabrics for high quality ties, and the following year they acquired Incontro Moda, which works in women's clothing. (*Pierangelo Mastantuono*)

Bini Manufacturer of silk and wool fabric in Como. Armando Bini began the "production and trade in silk fabrics and the like" in 1930, under the name Tessitura Serica Bini.

In 1958, the factory built its own production plant in Montorfano. Between the 1950s and '60s, the business took on more and more of the family imprint, as management passed to Sergio, Armando's son, with the help of his parents and sisters. In 1971, Bini began to expand in the field of printed fabrics, with the acquisition of Stamperia di Gironico. In 1984, the printing and weaving mills were put into liquidation.

Bini Gentucca (1973). Italian designer. She has a degree in architecture. She took her first steps in the world of runways designing accessories for Curiel, Blumarine, Karl Lagerfeld, Ferré and Chanel. She then started her own line, selling it in the shops of the Guggenheim Museum in New York and Palazzo Grassi in Venice. Her slogan is "experimentation," so that during the presentation of her Collection in Milan in 2002 she made a space in the shape of houses cut from cardboard. One of her most well-known lines is the "undersize" line for tiny women who are "out of size." She also created unstitched children's clothes that are held together with a new elastic structure.
(*Daniela Bolognetti*)

Biraghi A boutique in Milan selling underwear. It was opened by Ambrogio Biraghi and his associate Longa in 1875 in the Galleria Vittorio Emanule, selling high quality products made in their knitwear factory, Martin Frères. In 1913 the shop moved to via Berchet. It expanded during the 1920s under the management of Tullio Biraghi, the son of Ambrogio, who decided to abandon manufacturing and to import the best foreign brands such as Hanro, Molli, Elbeo and Handerson. During the war, bombs destroyed the shop. In 1961 Biraghi opened a branch in Padua and in 1964 another one in Milan's Corso Buenos Aires. Among his clientele were the Royal House of Savoy, Gabriele D'Annunzio, the Shah of Iran, the tenor Enrico Caruso, the composer Giacomo Puccini, and the actor Ernesto Calindri. In 1984, Ambrogio, the son of Tullio, died. A few months later, his brother Mario, with whom Ambrogio managed the firm, died too. In 1994 Biraghi shut down permanently.

Birkenstock German shoe factory established more than 200 years ago. It was founded in 1774 in a small German village by Johann Adam Birkenstock. At the turn of century it became a substantial business and, starting in 1902, with the development of the flexible support arch, production was expanded on a national level. But the birth of the Birkenstock, the sandal known all over the world, penetrating all national markets, dates back to 1964 when Karl Birkenstock gave it the flexible arch invented by his father. It was the birth of sandal that is still in production and that is incredibly long-wearing, in that it allows endless walks and is extremely comfortable. Starting from the basic model, with its wide sole in the shape of the foot and two parallel leather bands fastened with a strap, Birkenstock has since the 1960s developed about 300 variants in style and color.

❑ 2000. The birth of Rockford and Calgary, the new shoe line for hiking.
❑ 2002. Birkenstock celebrates 25 years of the Boston model, the classic suede clogs. In October, Margot Fraser, who emigrated from Germany to the U.S. thirty years earlier and founded Birkenstock Footprint Sandals Inc., announces the sale of the last 60% of the company to the employees. Now the U.S. subsidiary of the German parent company is entirely owned by the workers.
❑ The 30th anniversary of the Arizona model. To celebrate the occasion, 19 different musicians, actors, sport champions, chefs, and journalists, among them Robin Williams and Chris Isaak, design their own personal Arizona model. The proceeds go to charity.
❑ 2003, March. The German model Heidi Klum lends her name to the firm's products, launching an exclusive line of orthopaedic sandals.
(*Pierangelo Mastantuono*)

Birnbaum Lillian (1955). Austrian photographer. In 1989, she emigrated from Vienna to Paris, where she now lives and works. She specializes in fashion photography and portraiture. Her work has appeared in Elle, Marie Claire, the Sunday Times Magazine, and Stern. She has published three books: *Fahrende* in 1984, *Die Kunstler von Gugging* in 1990, and *Vier Fraulen* in

1993. She is also known as a director of videos. Her portrait subjects include many musicians, in particular the famous violinist Anne-Sophie Mutter, for whom she shoots all the album covers.

Birtwell Celia (1941). English fabric designer, born in Bury. She married the clothing designer Ossie Clark and for him she creates romantic and exotic prints that match the bohemian style of his Collections. She has highly skilled artisans do the handwork, using the most refined fabric. The pieces are expensive and unique, and adored by the Chelsea Set who are fans of the new hippy styles but very demanding as to quality. The couple were immortalized by David Hockney in the portrait titled "The Clarks with Percy The Cat" dated 1970-71.

❑ 2001. The British market is again interested in Birtwell. The costume makers and set designers for the Harry Potter film go to her shop in Notting Hill for the fabrics with stars, animals, and flowers needed for the little wizard's cape, and, of course, for the interior décor.

❑ The "21st Century Retro Fever" that overwhelms the United Kingdom convinces Cacharel to have her design the fabrics for the Spring 2002 Collection. The designer is back at work, collaborating with the husband-and-wife team Clements-Ribeiro. Their style is classic: chiffon in florals with designs done by hand, and fabrics for the home in silk, velvet, linen and cotton, in a naive style.

❑ 2003, July. Toward the end of the second year of working with Cacharel, the Victoria and Albert Museum honors Ossie Clark and Celia Birtwell with a large exhibit that brings together drawings, photographs, and sixty articles of clothing from the period 1965-1974.

Bishop Hazel (1906-1998). American chemist, the inventor of "kiss proof" lipstick. She wanted to study medicine, but the Wall Street crash of 1929 forced her to study chemistry, which brought money in faster. At the end of the 1940s her kitchen was a laboratory where she conducted tests that were not allowed in the dermatology labs of the Columbia Medical Center where she worked. The new product was created in her kitchen. Sold by a small cosmetics company, it was advertised with the slogan: "Don't lose time wiping your kisses from the faces of friends, relatives, children and sweethearts." It was the Summer of 1950. In the America of the baby-boomers, at a cost of just $1 each, the New York department store Lord and Taylor sold out in just one day.

Bisso A yarn and a fabric, light and very thin, derived from the silky, bright filaments produced by certain bi-valve molluscs such as the mussel and the pinna with which they adhere to the sea floor. The filaments are carded and woven like silk. They yield a soft and delicate fabric. Very expensive and rare, used in ancient times only by kings, bisso is used to manufacture underwear, blouses and Summer dresses. By extension, the term bisso is used for a particularly fine fabric made of silk or linen.

(*Gabriella Gregorietti*)

Bissonnais et Taponnier French photo studio active in the first decade of the 20th century. Many of its photographs had to do with fashion and were published by the magazine Les Modes.

Bizzarro Brand of prêt-à-porter launched in 1972 by the Pivetti firm, which is from Sossano, in the province of Vicenza. Specialized in men's and women's wear, it offers loose-fitting city clothes to be worn at work or at leisure. The colors of the various Collections, for knitwear, shirts, and for leather garments, include black, white, blue, brown, grey, and slate grey. It has a turnover of 5 to 6 million Euros a year, of which 65% is for export, especially to Germany, France, the U.S., Canada and Japan.

Blaak English brand of prêt-à-porter founded in 1998. Aaron Sharif and Sachiko Okada, partners in work and in life, met at Central Saint Martin's school, as design students. They share a common vision of fashion which pushed them to evolve their own very personal theories to do with the color black, a theme which would become the name of their Collection. Tradition, emotion, and attitude are the commandments of their unconventional fashions, which are, however, very refined in the cut of the fabrics. The two designers have three times won the *New Generation* award at London Fashion Week. They design an underwear Collection for Top Shop. The brand is on sale at Browns Focus, Liberty, and Barneys, and in several boutiques in the Far East. (*Virginia Hill*)

Black Sandy (1951). British knitwear designer, known especially for the eccentric taste that often characterizes the details on his clothing. He has worked with the London College of Fashion in their research department. In 2002, he published with Alan Cannon-Jones *A Comparative Study of The British and Italian Textile and Clothing Industries*, with particular attention to knitwear and men's tailoring. For Thames and Hudson publishers he has written *Knitwear in Fashion*, a book rich in photographs which the designer dedicated to the best of international knitwear production.

Black, Star & Frost American jewellery shop, with headquarters in New York. At its start, back in 1810, it specialized in commemorative objects. In 1912, the shop moved to Fifth Avenue and sold expensive jewellery only.

Blahnik Manolo (1943). Shoe designer. His shoes, which are considered works of art, have been shown at the Metropolitan Museum of Art in New York and at the Victoria and Albert Museum in London. He participated in the first Biennial of Florence, *Time and Fashion*. Every year at the Oscars several movie stars "have to have" his shoes. Born in Santa Cruz, in the Canary Islands, to a Czech-Hungarian father and a Spanish mother, he studied in Geneva and his first job was as a set designer. It was Diana Vreeland, leafing through one of his sketchbooks, who suggested to him that he focus his efforts on footwear. So in the early 1970s he opened a tiny shop on Church Road in

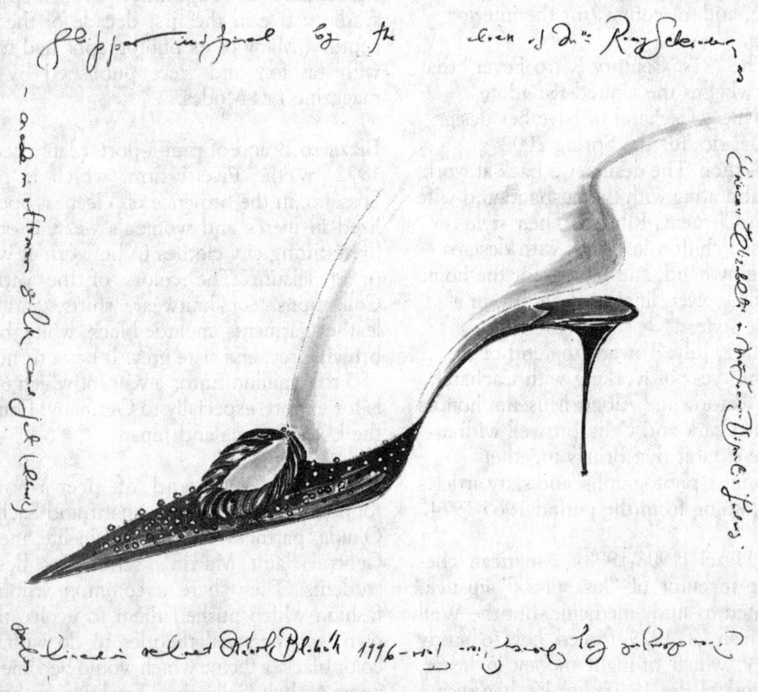

Lace-up ankle-boot by Manolo Blahnik.

Sandal by Manolo Blahnik (1996).

London. It immediately became a meeting place for women such as Loulou de la Falaise, Bianca Jagger, and Tina Show. Today, his eccentric miniature sculptures, balanced on very high heels, and familiarly known in the fashion world as "Manolos," are produced in quantities of no more than 300 to 350 per year. They are all handmade, and almost always with rare and never-before-thought-of materials, such as leaves, tree bark, Venetian beads, and chinchilla. They are still on sale in that very same London shop, which is now a bit larger, and since 1984 also in New York, as well as in about twenty other boutiques, which sell several brands, all over the world. Very sought after by his colleagues is his Brique model of 1971: a sort of clog with a brick-shaped sole and a colored stripe. Always supported by his sister Evangelina, he has collaborated on the Collections of Galliano, Ozbek, and Berardi. (*Giuliana Parabiago*)

❑ 1999, March. To celebrate 50 years of the International Fur Trade Federation, the Marconi Gallery of Milan organizes an exhibition in which Blahnik's rabbit fur boots appear next to a Jean Paul Gaultier dress made of wolf fur with a foxtail, and to Rifat Ozkek's "ratmusqué" bedspreads. During a ceremony at the Museum of Natural History in London, Blahnik is awarded the prize for best designer of accessories for the year.
❑ 2001, October. He designs the shoes for the entire female cast of the TV series Sex and the City. He sells about 100,000 pair of shoes a year just in the U.S. The novelty of the Collection for Spring-Summer 2002 is a 23-inch titanium heel that is only 3 millimeters thick.
❑ 2003, February. The exhibit *Manolo Blahnik, A Retrospective* is dedicated to him by the Design Museum of London.

Blair Alistair (1956). French designer. Educated at the "school" of Dior and Givenchy, he presented his first Collection in Paris in March 1989. He continues the style of the great creators who aren't afraid to use very precious cashmere with grey flannel, with a nostalgic inclination for the fashion of the past, but revisited in a modern key.

❑ In the early 1990s, he took over Erik Mortensen's position as artistic director of haute couture at Balmain. The experience was short, and after few months he was replaced by Hervé Pierre.

Blanchard Elodie (1976). French designer, born in Grenoble. Educated at the Duperre Institute of Paris and at the École Nationale Supérieure des Beaux-Arts, where she won a scholarship to pursue a master's degree in Los Angeles. After spending time serving internships in the fields of fashion and art, and winning several awards, in September 1999 she participated in the Who's Next event in Paris, with the brand Squar-efch, created in collaboration with Fabienna Colombani. Her clothes express the idea of transformation: her skirts become bags, and jackets can be transformed into pockets.
(*Mariacristina Righi*)

Blasi Angelo (1907-1996). Tailor from Naples. Educated in the "school" of Renato De Nicola, he opened his first atelier in the 1920s. The workshop was located in via Calabritto, along the promenade which from Chiaia and Piazza dei Martiri leads to the Villa Comunale and the seafront. The accuracy and elegance of his cutting made Blasi, in the period between the two world wars, a very prestigious tailor who counted among his clients the members of Neapolitan high society. As with many of his colleagues, almost all educated in the workshops of the great tailoring masters such as Morziello and Gallo, De Nicola was above all a very sensible and expert cloth cutter, able to adapt the strict dictates of Anglo-Saxon fashion to the needs and tastes of his clientele. It was his son Nicola (1936), however, who brought the family business into the international market after World War II. During the 1950s, the workshop had about fifty workers who produced for a clientele that ranged from the U.S. to Japan. Starting in the 1960s, the firm sold clothes manufactured by various international companies alongside its own products, in an expanded number of shops. Today, the owner of the company is the founder's nephew, Angelo Blasi (1962).

Blass Bill William Ralph Blass (1922-2002), an American designer famous for knowing how to "sweeten" the women's suit by making it softer and giving it curves that fit the female body. He liked creases, touches of color, and unusual fabrics like tweed, twill, and shirt cloth. He led an empire consisting of, in addition to women's wear, lines for men and licences for beachwear, shoes, furs, candies, and perfumes. He was born in Indiana. Before joining the army during World War II, by the young age of 19 he had already designed for David Crystal Sportswear. He studied at the Parson's School of Design and was later hired to create Collections for Anna Miller and Co. In 1959, that company merged with Maurice Rentner Limited. In 1962 he began to design under his own name, but only in 1970 was he able to acquire the company and name it after himself. In his last Collection he rejuvenated his style, offering on the New York runways a profusion of sheath dresses in cashmere, lace T-shirts, and large twill trousers. He won many awards, including the Council of Fashion Designers' *American Lifetime Achievement Award*.

❑ The new head designer is Lars Nilsson, who took over from Steven Slowik.
❑ 2002, June. The designer dies in his house in New Reston, Connecticut.
❑ 2003, February. Following the presentation for Autumn-Winter 2003-2004, Lars Nilsson quits the firm after six Collections.
❑ In March of the same year Michael Vollbracht is appointed new head designer. He had organized a retrospective exhibit on the work of Blass.
❑ 2003, April. Aretha Franklin wears Bill Blass dresses during what is announced as her final tour. Among the designers who are summoned to the court of the Queen of Soul are Luther Vandross, Valentino, Donna Karan and Halston.

Blatt Anny (1910). French dressmaker. She made her début in Mulhouse, her hometown, working in knitwear. It was knitwear, specifically tricot, that sent her off to Paris, where, in 1933, in her boutique on Rue Faubourg Saint-Honoré, she offered Collections of dresses, sweaters and beachwear that drew the attention of specialized magazines. Not even the very detailed *Dictionnaire de la Mode au XXe Siècle*, published by Editions du Regard 1996, indicates how long this success lasted. Eventually it ended, but by 1958 she was back in business as partner in a chain of shops that distributed wool to be used in knitting her designs. Starting in 1991 her name was used by an old-fashioned French spinning mill.

Blazer The main character in the book *Vestiti, Usciamo* ("Get Dressed, Let's Go Out"), an ironic best-seller on elegance published by Mondadori in 1985, with a women's section by Chiara Boni and a men's section by Luigi Settembrini. This is the most important jacket in the wardrobe. "Dark blue, almost black, absolutely double-breasted, it must be worn in Winter with dark-grey flannel trousers and, sometimes, in a particularly casual version, with cover-coat beige-green trousers." The savage combination of a blazer with blue jeans, adopted sometimes by people otherwise above suspicion, is so obvious and banal as to be deplorable. The shoes must necessarily be brown, better if they are suede. Also acceptable are the so-called Desert Boots. It is a sports jacket but one must never think of picking it up in the American colors of light blue or Olympic red. One must carefully avoid those horrible patches which are applied to the breast pocket, naming the college you never attended or the yacht club you don't belong to. The blazer is the most important jacket of the wardrobe, as much for the Winter as for the Summer. A real wild card, if it is well cut you can wear it confidently on almost any occasion, from casual to the most formal. It should be noted that for evenings that are elegant but not too elegant, these days, especially in Paris, there is a trend of wearing a blazer (with black shoes) instead of a smoking jacket. In Summer, with a beautiful shirt and an amusing handkerchief in the breast pocket, it can even be worn without a tie. It is the only jacket that can do without one. In Summer, a blazer can be matched with white linen trousers, dark-grey light wool trousers, or beige-light green gabardine trousers.

(*Luigi Settembrini*)

Blechman Hardy. English designer, the creator of streetwear and camouflage trousers for leisure time. In the early 1990s, Hardy began to design garments in natural fibers, mainly hemp cloth. In 1994, he established Maharishi, a Hindu term that means "Big Guru." Success arrived with snowpants, trousers that were inspired by military-skateboard clothing and decorated with Japanese embroidery, with reversible camouflage insides. In 1998, they were sold at Barneys, in New York. Over the years his production expanded with lines for men, women, and children under the MHI brand, and with a series of clothes created with recycled fabric. In 2001, he opened a London store at Covent Garden, designed by the architect François Scali in such a way that the entryway leads directly to a bamboo garden. Today, Maharishi has 100 outlets all over the world and employs 25 people in the London headquarters, where work alternates with yoga and meditation lessons. In March 2003, Maharishi presented the results of an unusual collaboration with the Hong Kong toy designer Michael Lau, whose products are on sale in the London store. It is a series of 101 very detailed garden figurines, among which is one that looks like Hardy Blechman. (*Pierangelo Mastantuono*)

Bless Brand created in 1995 by Desirée Heiss and Inez Haag in Paris. Heiss graduated from the University of Applied Arts in Vienna. Kaag, born in Berlin, studied at the University of Art and Design in Hannover. They met in Paris and decided to establish a company to produce objects-clothes and accessories which the two designers manufacture both for themselves and for other designers. They recently worked on some "pieces" (a metallic string with pliers at each end to use as a belt or suspenders) for the Italian firm New York Industrie. During the course of their career they created recycled fur wigs for Martin Margiela, "to-be-personalized" shoes for New Balance and Charles Jourdan, a make-up case filled with small pieces of fabric to apply to the face, and a series of bags which can be transformed into blouses, trousers and skirts. Bless products are updated every three months, can be purchased on the Internet, and are all in limited editions. The two designers say: "We sell ideas, not Collections." Given that their activity cuts across fashion, design, cosmetics, and accessories, it is not an accident that a weekly magazine gave them a very special nickname: "The Unibombers of Chic."

(*Antonio Mancinelli*)

Bliss Brand of jewellery. It belongs to the Damiani Group and is aimed at a younger market, both women and men. It is sold, as are the other brands of the Group – Damiani, Salvini and Alfieri & St. John – in the boutiques on via Montenapoleone in Milan. It is organized in a series of different lines in gold, steel, diamonds, and, sometimes, colored gem stones. Bracelets, earrings, rings, pendants, key-rings are designed so as to be light and worn with each other. The shapes, pure and reduced to basics, are geometric in their inspiration, and show a playful mood in line with the latest fashion trends. Among the themes used are the heart, the cross, shark's teeth, the cube, and the symbols of the continents and the mistral wind of southern France.

(*Alessandra Quattordio*)

Block 60 A line of casual-jeans for youth manufactured and distributed by Gilmar Divisione Industria. The brand, founded in Riccione in 1996 by Oscar Del Bianco and Ilio Pulici, offers more than trendy clothing.

Block 60 has an original showcase in its flagship store in Riccione: an area of 3,200 square feet inspired by the small open air markets that offer a singular mixture of clothes, culture and international foods.

Blommers Anuschka & Nielsschum (1969). Dutch photographer. She studied at the Gerrit Rietveld Akademie of Amsterdam, a city where she lives and works, making a name for herself and building a brand in the fields of fashion and portraiture.

Bloomers Turkish-style trousers worn with a large skirt that goes to the knee. In 1850, the American editor Dexter Bloomer wrote an article for the weekly Seneca Country Courier in which he claimed that the clothing of Turkish women was much more comfortable than that of Americans and Europeans. His wife, Amelia Jenks Bloomer, returned to the subject in her own newspaper, The Lily. A convinced and militant feminist, she waged real war against crinolines, suggesting that women wear oriental-style puffed culottes under shorter and less cumbersome skirts. Bloomers were adopted toward the end of the 1800s and in the early 1900s when bicycle riding became a fashionable activity. Today, they are a kind of short, puffed culottes like knickers.

Bloomingdale's Chain of department stores with 22 locations in 10 states across the U.S. It was established in 1872 by the brothers Lyman and Joseph Bloomingdale on 56th Street in New York City. In 1931, the New York store moved to its present headquarters in the Art Deco building at 59th Street and Lexington Avenue. Starting in the 1960s, the store promoted the sale of imported products, starting with the Casa Bella event for merchandise made in Italy. The big transformation of the store's image came in the 1970s when Bloomingdale's went very upscale with the clothing lines offered, presenting brands that were on the cutting edge and embodied the latest trends.

Blossac Bernard French illustrator. From the 1930s to the 1950s his self-assured and elegant touch documented French haute couture for Vogue and other women's magazines. He was equal in style to the tailors and designers whose creations he presented.

Blouse (1) French term. Originally a shirt made of a coarse material used mainly for work clothes. It became fashionable in the 1950s, both for elegant shirts and jackets and for sport jackets. It is often worn with a small belt at the hips.

Blouse (2) Light jacket or wide, straight shirt worn loose or tucked in with a belt. If longer it can be worn as a tunic or mini-dress. It is one of Saint-Laurent's favorite garments in different versions: from a side-buttoned Russian-style blouse with mandarin collar to a painter's blouse with a lavaliere or lace neck. It is worn by jockeys during the Palio of Siena, each in the color of his district.

Blouson Men's jacket closed by a zipper or snaps. A timeless piece of leather and suede fashion. James Dean, the symbol of rebellious youth of the 1950s in the film *Rebel Without A Cause* (1955), wore one, as did Marlon Brando, in a more aggressive black-leather version, Hell's Angels style, in *The Rebel* (1954). After the success of these movies, it was adopted by young people as a kind of uniform. It is still a cult item in men's fashion.

Blousons Noirs The Summer of 1959 was known in France "the Summer of the blousons noirs." In imitation of English rock-and-roll stars, this spontaneous movement brought together the followers and fanatics of rock-and-roll who idolized, cut their hair, and dressed like James Dean, who died tragically in 1955 wearing blue jeans and the inevitable black leather jacket. They listened to the French rock music of Johnny Halliday and above all to the hard rock played by Vince Taylor and Eddie Cochran. Their gratuitous violence drove them to destroy three concert halls. They drew the scorn and rejection of the French people, and become synonym a alienation. They had definitely disappeared by the early 1960s when hard rock was replaced by the more "gentle" yé-yè' rhythm.

(*Gabriella Gregorietti*)

Blow Isabella (1958). English talent-scout and muse. She has always had her eye on someone very special, be it a designer or a photographer, such as Hussein Chalayan, Philip Treacy, Tristan Webber, and, of course, Alexander McQueen. As with Diana Vreeland and Anna Piaggio, Isabella's look is very original, with a predilection for hats, often eccentric ones. Colin McDowell, who worked at her side in the style section of the London Sunday Times, defined her as "the last woman in the world whom I can imagine wearing jeans and sneakers."

Blumenfeld Erwin (1897-1969). German photographer. His strongly erotic drapery achieved with wet clothes have been copied by many photographers after him. He was born in Berlin. After working in several different fields, he began to work as a professional photographer only in 1936. A friend of Georg Grosz since 1915, he was close to the Dadaist movement, and that would have a strong effect on his artistic and photographic education. Starting in 1938 he worked for the French edition of Vogue, and starting in 1939 for Harper's Baazar. Beaton was his inspirational godfather. In 1941, escaping from occupied France and a concentration camp, he landed in New York. His color and black-and-white pictures, characterized by graphic rigor and a strong poetic ambiguity, are almost always the result of manipulation during developing. Blumenfeld retired from photography at the end of the 1950s to devote himself to his autobiography, *Jadis et Daguerre*. In 1978 he had an exhibit at the Victoria and Albert Museum, and in 1982 one at the Centre Pompidou.

Blunauta Brand of clothing. Its origins have deep roots in the history of Balloon Spa, established in Rome in 1976 thanks to an idea of the siblings Gabriella and Roberto Greco to create extremely refined clothes using artisanal yarns and natural fibers such as silk, linen and cashmere. By 2001 Blunauta had become the company brand, in the wake of a big expansion on the international market and new demand from a more and more sophisticated and demanding clientele. The passage from Balloon to Blunauta was marked by the latter's début on the Milan runways during Milan Collezioni Donna in September 2001. The change of name coincided with improved quality and a rejuvenated, more fashionable product. The philosophy of the company is to offer quality garments at extremely affordable prices, thanks to production which takes place almost exclusively in China through two joint ventures with local partners. There are more than 80 Blunauta shops, divided between directly-owned and franchise stores. They are mainly in Italy, Spain, and the U.S., where a presence was established in December 2002 through Blunauta USA with the opening of 4 directly-owned stores. In that same month, the company decided on a share-offering in the amount of €17.5 million, plus an investment of €25 million to open new single-brands shops. In 2001, Balloon Spa, the holding company controlling the group, had a turnover of €30 million; in 2002, it was 37 million. Some 56% of revenues comes from silk garments, followed by pure cotton, wool and cashmere. *(Dario Golizia)*

Blundell Pamela (1967). English designer working on her own, after separating from her fellow citizen and business partner Copperwheat, with whom she worked during the 1990s. Her strong feature is the timelessness of her creations. Her garments are independent of trends and fashion; this is what makes her style. She doesn't try to astonish, or even less, provoke. Her clothes reflect a long tradition of tailoring and, in fact, she says that what she does is "tailoring for women," in other words, custom made, which is London's new trend. She doesn't do gags on the runway in order to draw the public's attention: what matters to her is the way something is, not what it merely seems to be. She can show good taste, but with irony. And she also does well with casual clothes, because during the performance at Milano Moda Donna (March 2003) the jeans that she designed for Evisu were very successful. *(Lucia Mari)*

Boa Women's accessory of aristocratic origin. It descends from the palatine, a fur scarf worn by the sister-in-law of Louis XIV, the Sun King. It is usually associated with an explicit and direct style of female seduction, and with the frivolity of nights during the era of the Belle Époque, and the musicals and vaudevilles dominated by mythical showgirls like Mistinguette, with movie sets and the immortal platinum blond diva Mae West. It is named after the boa constrictor, because, like that snake, it wraps around the neck and shoulders of the person who wears it. It appeared under that name for the first time at the beginning of the 19th century and was used to cover the necklines and naked shoulders of evening dresses. The fur of the original model disappeared, and was replaced by feathers, especially of the cock and the ostrich, which became typical by the end of the 19th and in the early 20th centuries. The 1920s were the period of its maximum splendor, with a revival in the following decade and during the 1960s, the years of the Italian economic boom.

An ostrich boa matching the dress of Marquise Casati (1909).

Boateng Ozwald (1967). English tailor of Ghanaian background. He works in London, where he was born. He offers himself as a pioneer of what he defines as custom made couture, which he developed transcending the traditional rules of tailoring. He started designing men's Collections in 1988, and in 1995 opened his first shop in London.

❑ 2001. O-Z is the new brand which combines the research for the most modern tailoring solutions with the taste of the moment. It is on sale at Debenhams. Boetang contributes to Pierce Brosnan's wardrobe in his last appearance as 007.

❑ 2003, January. The first classic and casual Collection produced and sold by Marchpole, and designed by Boateng, is available in stores. At first, his creations are to be distributed only in the British market.

❑ 2003, May. Continuing his experience designing for film, Ozwald designs the costumes for the cast of *Matrix Reloaded* for their promotional tour around the world. Starting in July, the designer's line is available in the House of Fraser department stores, while a low-cost line is on sale at Cecil Gee. In Autumn, a flagship store opens in New York.

❑ 2003, December. He is appointed creative director of the men's line of Givenchy. He states that his challenge is to reinvent the French gentleman.

❑ 2004, July. He makes his début on the Paris runways in front of the executive director of LVMH, the holding company which owns the brand.

Bobby Brown American brand of cosmetics created in 1991 by the make-up artist Bobby Brown and his business partner Rosalind Landis. Starting with a line of natural lipsticks it then expanded to include other products for face care and treatment. Characteristic of the entire range of products is the concept of prêt-à-porter make-up, that is to say, light, and with natural shades. It was an invention that revolutionized the cosmetics industry. In 1996, the brand and everything connected to it was taken over by Estée Lauder.

❑ 2001, January. The cosmetic company works with two of the most important firms in digital technology that offer marketing services, TMX Interactive and Cheetahmail.

❑ Bobby Brown products are sold at more than 300 points-of-sale in 20 countries, and on the Internet.

Bobby socks How do you recognize an American movie that is set during the 1950s? That's easy. Just look at the teenagers' socks: short, often white, rolled down to the ankles, matched with ballet flats or heels. The look was completed with very tight sweaters worn with layered skirts. Or, bobby socks could be seen emerging from boots worn under long kilts.

❑ White socks, the symbol of the 1950s, make their appearance at every rockabilly and Happy Days fan club meeting, together with the iconography typical of the time: cars, motorcycles, and juke boxes.

Boccardi Crovato Luciana (1932). Journalist and event organizer. She began her career working for ten years with the theater and music festivals of the Venice Bienniale. After a time as a radio commentator, she then became a journalist specializing in fashion and costume, writing especially for Il Gazzettino di Venezia. The director of the International Biennial of Fashion in Venice, she is the author of several books about the history of costume, among which is *Le scarpe delle feste*.

Boccasile Gino (1901-1952). Painter, poster designer and illustrator. Rather than being a witness to fashion through his drawing, he created a style which, in line with the dictates of the Fascist regime (curvaceous women; the large hips of a farmer's wife for the campaign to increase the population), had an influence on fashion, especially through the covers that he did in 1937 and 1938 for the periodical Signorina Grandi Firme, published by Pitigrilly. There were generous necklines and tight skirts that outlined the bottoms of shapely women, along with exaggerated blouses and women who were "tri-dimensional." A committed fascist, he was loyal to the Republic of Salò and designed propaganda posters. In the post-war period he worked again in advertising.

Body First fashionable in the U.S. during the 1950s, it is by now a necessary accessory. Manufactured with an elasticised and close-fitting fabric, in lace or a light knit, it is ideal under transparent dresses. Used as a dancing or gym garment, it can cover the entire body, down to the ankles, like a leotard, with or without sleeves. During the 1970s it was used as a disco outfit, the so-called body-stocking, worn under a simple skirt.

Body Map English brand of prêt-à-porter designed by Stevie Stewart (1958) and David Holah (1958), both graduates of Middlesex Politech. It was founded in 1982. The name Body Map is reflected in the unconventional creations of the two designers. These are made for young people: unstructured clothes worn in layers. Using mainly white, cream and black, the two designers aim to redefine the traditional body shape by covering it with different fabrics and prints. In 1983 they won an award during the Individual Clothes Show as the "most exiting and innovative young designers of the year."

Boetti Alighiero (1940-1994). Italian artist. In 1967, at the Piper Club of Turin, he presented, with Anne-Marie Sauzeau, Gilardi and others, a Collection of artist clothes. Bizarre and witty, Boetti's women's styles are closely connected to the work that he developed as part of the Arte Povera movement of the period. His Collections consist of three unique pieces: three short sheath dresses, sleeveless, composed of two layers of transparent plastic with inlays of different kinds on the inside. In the first, gold straw and matches; in the second, one lira and half lira coins; in the third, water with detergent green foam and goldfish swimming in it during the time of the presentation. The materials inside the clothes remind one of the stratifications of a work such as *Un metro cubo* (1968). In 1977 he created a T-shirt with a green breast pocket called *Ordine e disordine*, and *Aquilone*, which was practically a foulard (both Edizione 2R, Genoa). In 1990, came the T-shirt *My point of view* (Edizione Parkett).

Boetti Lucia (1909-1985). Theatrical dressmaker. She arrived in Milan from Apulia (Corato di Bari) in 1918 with her entire family. Particularly intelligent and fanciful, self-taught, she started as an embroiderer. After several years in her dressmaker's shop at via Unione 7, she began to specialize in theater costumes, which she created personally for Wanda Osiris and Elena Giusti. She worked for the vaudeville companies of Garinei & Giovannini, for the producer Remigio Paone, for the Legnanesi company, and for the casinos in Las Vegas and Beirut.

She also collaborated with costume makers Giulio Coltellacci, Maurizio Monteverde and Corrado Colabucci.

Bogart Humphrey (1899-1957). American actor. He was the soft-hearted gangster, cynical and romantic at the same time. His tough expression with a cigarette always between his lips became an immediate icon of style, starting with his first movies. His consecration as a star came rather late, at the age of 37, with *The Petrified Forest* (1936), and then, five years later, with the first example of hard-boiled movies like *The Maltese Falcon* (1941). The wrinkled trench coat and the slightly sloping Borsalino hat became his trademark in the vast majority of his films, starting with *Casablanca* (1942). And at the same time, those two items appeared in the wardrobe of millions of men, becoming timeless classics. To prove the extent to which the myth and look of Bogart have entered the collective memory, it is enough to remember the way Woody Allen celebrated him on Broadway in *Play It Again Sam* (1972), or to recall how Belmondo, full of admiration, contemplated a photograph of Bogart in Godard's *A bout de souffle* (*Breathless*, 1959). Even more recently, in the 1980s, Spielberg was inspired by Bogart when he created the wardrobe for his hero Indiana Jones, played by Harrison Ford. (*Sofia Leoncina Gnoli*)

Boggi Chain of clothing stores which, starting in Milan, has opened branches in Spain and Switzerland. "Shop windows are the best advertisement," says Paolo Boggi, the founder. The company was established in Salerno, in 1939, when fashion trends were determined by the V-shape jackets made on Savile Row in London with straight shoulders, a tight waist, and a slightly stiff attitude. Those same jackets would 30 years be successful with the young and not-so-young Milanese who would find at Boggi the opposite of the eccentric, colorful, bellicose, and almost revolutionary clothing that was very much in vogue in those years. Its stores offer excellent fabrics, shirts in solid colors or else judiciously striped, discreet ties, some concessions to sportswear, the triumph of suits in blue, grey, and beige, as well as camel-hair coats and brown leather jackets. Of course, later, during the yuppie era, the Boggi line remained up to date, and in 1984 it expanded its typical classic style to women's clothing. There are 10 shops in Milan, where the company has been headquartered since 1964, plus more in northern Italy and, in othe countries, at Crans-sur-Sierre and in Madrid. The company's turnover is more than 40 billion liras.

❑ 2002. The year ends with a turnover of roughly €25 million.
❑ 2003, February. Boggi and its 29 points-of-sale are sold by Fin.Part, which had acquired the company some time before, to the Monza firm of Brian & Barry. The original shareholder, Paolo Boggi, retains 1% of the shares. The selling price is €13.2 million.

Bogner Brand of clothing launched in 1932 by Willy and Maria Bogner. It made its début with a Collection dedicated to the ski-look: stretch pants were the signature pieces of the line. In 1948, the first presentations made use of famous and free testimonials. Marilyn Monroe, Jane Mansfield and Ingrid Bergman regularly wore their clothes. In 1950 the first men's Collection appeared. In 1960 the company had more than 500 employees, which became 800 in 1968. In 1974 Bogner designed a tennis line. Two years later, the two designers created a golfing line, then small leather goods in 1982, sunglasses in 1983, a cosmetics line in 1985, a bathing suit Collection 1986, the inevitable eau de toilette in 1990, a mountain bike model in 1990, and a series of very precious jewels in 2001. The figures for 2003 proved the company's success, managed by Willy Bogner Jr.: 22 single-brand shops all over the world (with 10 owned by the family and 12 franchised), and 32 kiosks, for a turnover, in 2002, of €133 million. and a production network that includes Germany, Austria, China, Indonesia, Hong Kong, Italy, Portugal, Korea and the U.S.

(*Valeria Vantaggi*)

Bogusch Birgit (1970). Austrian designer. She studied at the Academy of Fine Arts in Linz and at the Academy of Applied Arts in Vienna. At the age of 22 she tried her luck in the world of fashion and started her own business. Her brand is very successful in Austria and Germany.

Bohan Marc (1926). French designer. His given name is Roger Maurice Louis Bohan. Born in Paris, he graduated from high school and then, encouraged by his mother, a milliner, he enrolled in a design course in order to follow an evident interest in fashion. Not yet 20, he was hired by Robert Piguet, and in his atelier he met a young talent, Christian Dior. He remained there four years, then moved on to Molineux and, in 1954, to Patou, who gave him responsibility for the haute couture Collection. But it was the meeting with Dior, who then became a friend, which would influence his career. One year after the death of the man who invented the New Look, he was given the artistic direction of Christian Dior London. It was 1958. Three years later, in 1961, he was back in Paris. This time it was to direct the tailor shop on Avenue Montaigne and to take the place of Dior's favorite assistant, Yves Saint-Laurent, who the designer had designated as his successor but who had been called up to serve with the army in Algeria. It was a fortunate return: his first Collection, called Slim Look, was immediately successful. The line was extended like a pencil sketch, and made lovely. The Collection consisted mainly of suits with tight skirts with the option of an elegant parka. He renewed himself from season to season, designing, inventing, creating, following the steps of his master, and the allure of tradition. In 1966 he brought the style of Dr. Zhivago to the runway: long fur-trimmed greatcoats worn with maxi dresses that fell to the boots. Among his clientele were members of the jet set. In 1967 magazines published photos of Farah Dibah wearing his creations on the occasion of her marriage to the Shah of Iran and her coronation as empress. Princess Grace of Monaco and Princess Alexandra of Yugoslavia, also invited to the royal wedding, wore clothes by Bohan-Dior. More than 100 haute couture garments are created twice a year, with particular attention to evening dresses, as a gentleman likes to see them: ladies of divine elegance, characters in a wide-awake dream. Clothes for every high society event, precious, rich, with big knots draped on a taffeta sheath dress, often creating a puffed effect at the back. And more and more bows resting on a triumph of embroidery, with very refined workmanship in an authentic exercise in luxury. Very aware of color, he uses them all, with a preference for red and black. He doesn't care for green, but doesn't eliminate it entirely. By now, his ideas are part of the collective memory: balaclavas in leopard, little ostrich-trimmed foulards that lend importance to a sober outfit, stockings that have the same patterns as sweaters. Through the accessories he allowed Dior's style to become accessible to everyone. He was famous for his jewels: pins and brooches made of strass, or paste glass, meant for important evenings. A diligent worker, he pays attention to everything: Miss Dior's prêt-à-porter, launched in 1967 by his assistant Philippe Guibourge, for a young clientele; the men's Collection, designed by Bohan himself in 1970; and furs, designed by Frédéric Castet. The white ermine coat that he created for Sophia Loren, with the imprint of her lips on the back, will not be easily forgotten. The infinite licenses, the numberless fragrances, the make-up: Made by Dior conquered the world. Then, in 1989, came the changing of the guard: after some 30 years of honorable service, he left the scene. Gianfranco Ferré was now in charge. *(Lucia Mari)*

❑ Having left Dior, the 63 year-old designer is hired by Hartnell. The house was known as the favorite of the British aristocracy, but closed down for good in 1992.

Boivin Réné French jeweller. When he opened his first shop with his wife, the sister of Paul Poiret, he entrusted the jewellery design to Susanne Belperron. During the 1930s he moved his headquarters to Avenue de l'Opéra and changed the designer to Louis Girare. In 1937, Boivin's creations, designed by his daughter Germaine and Juliette Moutard, were exhibited at the Exposition Internationale des Arts and des Techniques and, in 1946, at the Exposition des Arts Décoratifs.

Bolero Short buttonless jacket that follows the line of the upper body, but hangs loose and does not reach the waist. During the 1860s it was called a Spanish jacket, after the popular Spanish costume. In the last decade of the 1800s, shortened in order to cover only the upper part of the bust, it appeared again, richly decorated, with embroidery, in transparent muslin the same shade as the dress underneath, or in fur for the Winter season. Again in a reduced size it was back in fashion during the late 1950s, used over sleeveless Summer dresses to cover arms and necklines. Worn in Summertime as a small jacket with short sleeves on top of evening dresses, and made of fur, almost always mink, during the 1960s the bolero took the place of the stole.

Bolzoni Monica. Italian designer. A creature of independent and versatile style, she began her journey in the world of fashion, from 1968 to 1974, as the person responsible for the products and image of the French prêt-à-porter line Franck Olivier in Italy. From 1975 to 1980 she was fashion coordinator for Fiorucci, first in Italy and then in America, where she lived at the time of the avant-guard art movement started by Andy Warhol's Factory. In those years she brought to fruition a project that resulted in the opening of the boutique Biancaeblu in Milan in 1982. There she sold dresses as if they were objects of affection, in modular shapes very precise in the cut, and in a style quite contrary to the pomp of fashion in the 1980s. In 1984 she opened a second space which had a big success. It drew the attention of the trade press and of great photographers like Newton, Barbieri and Watson. In 1986, she restored a decaying building in Milan and turned it into the "Sartoria," a kind of workshop where she experimented with innovative materials like metal, nylon, and resined jerseys. Her experience of industrial production with the Japanese giant Mitsubishi dates back to 1989. During the 1990s she developed a more and more intense relationship with the art of the international avant-guard through travelling performances like those of the photographer Vanessa Beecroft, for whom she created an "invisible" lingerie using nylon stockings. She also experimented with a new application for live-cut felt, a process that would become a technical "must-have" for her jersey Collections as well. A stir was created in April 2002 when the Herald Tribune reported on a sign hanging outside her boutique which said that the designer would take some time for herself in order to "reload her own creative energy."

(*Sara Tieni*)

Bombana Manufacturer of stockings. The first factory was established in 1966, but it was during the 1980s that the hosiery factory Franco Bombana became successful in Italy and abroad. It produces mainly for export: 70% of production is absorbed by Northern and Eastern Europe, by the rest of the European Union, and the Middle East.

> ❑ 2003, April. Calzedonia acquires 20% of Franco Bombana. As a result of the agreement, Bombana begins to produce stockings for women and girls to be distributed in the shops of the Veronese company, using its technological and design experience for the benefit of the product. Calzedonia's percentage of ownership will increase over time, even if Bombana continues to offer products under its own brand.

Bomber jacket A short military-style jacket inspired by those worn by World War II aviators and bomber pilots. It became a fashion staple from the 1960s on, particularly for a younger generation who adopted it, along with jeans, as a component of "rebel" fashion. Its basic features include an ample cut, padded lining, zippered front, and a fitted or elasticized waist. Traditionally made from heavy weather-resistant wools or brown leather, bomber jackets have also been broadly interpreted over the decades in black leather and various materials, with decoration including metallic studs, printing and sheepskin linings and collars.

Bombino Domestico (1926). Men's tailor. He learned the trade while still very young, in his home village, Ruvo di Puglia. In 1945 he arrived in Milan, where he opened a workshop on via Fiori Chari. His first clients were among the artists who frequented the Jamaica Bar in the Brera neighborhood of Milan, Gianni Dova, Guido and Sandro Somaré, Crippa, Andrea Cascella, the brothers Pomodoro, the photographer Fontana, the photographer Mulas, and the dandy Piero Sanjust di Teulada. He was successful and opened his first real tailor's shop in 1961 at via Pontaccio 12. In 1971, Loris Abate, who was also his client, asked him to open a men's department for custom-made clothes at Mila Schön, of which he is still in charge.

Bon Nani (1977). Italian designer. He was the first of several offSpring of Sima Fashion, the knitwear company established in 1960 by the Reggio Emilia families Gibertoni and Montanari. The firm offers jerseys, shirts and button-neck sweaters, for men and women, that can be coordinated. The headquarters is in Puianello, near Reggio Emilia.

Bona Camillo (1959). Italian designer of high fashion. His clothes have simple lines in solid colors and refined fabrics like silk. After studying at the Koefia Academy in Rome, he worked in the atelier of the Fontana sisters. His first Collection, presented on the runways of Rome in January 1995, was inspired by the 1930s. He then dedicated his later Collections to the 1920s, the East, Spain, and the Mediterranean.

❑ 2002, July. Bona decides to presents his Collection alone, and does not attend the event Donna Sotto le Stelle (Woman Under the Stars) at Trinità dei Monti. Among the 27 models was Pat Cleveland, in one of her rare appearances on the runway.

Bonanni Paolo (1950). Journalist and the director of Max, a men's monthly focusing on fashion. He began working in the early 1970s at the Corriere della Sera as a proofreader. Then in 1976 he moved to the sports staff of Il Giornale. In 1987 he was hired at Max, where he remained until 1992. After a short period abroad, he returned to Max as deputy manager and in 1995 he became director.

❑ 2002, December. Bonanni is appointed director ff the monthly GQ (Italian edition) after the departure of Andrea Monti, who started it. At Max, his place is taken by Giuseppe Di Piazza.

Bonas Maurizio (1950). Italian designer. Born in Milan, he soon moved to Florence where, at a young age, he began to be interested in fashion and fabrics. Thanks to experience gained in Prato and the outskirts of Florence, he learned the technical aspects of fabrics and yarns which are, after all, the strong point of his style. In 1986 he created the first men's Collection under his own name. The predominant color was black, with a self-assured elegance that was not ostentatious, and a taste for details. It was minimalist but international in the overall image. He was soon considered by critics to be one of the most innovative exponents of the avant-guard. His roots in the tradition of tailoring and his deep knowledge of raw materials allowed him to design fashions for a man with a strong contemporary identity who was not like everyone else and who was not subject to a facile conformity. Minimalism conquered the foreign markets, in particular the Japanese. In 1990 he signed his first agreement with Mitsubishi Corporation for the distribution of his Collections throughout Japan, It was renewed in 1994. That was followed by agreements with the Hong Kong firm Samisa for the opening of a first boutique in that city, and by the opening of a boutique in Taipei in 1995, and of one in Beijing in 1997. At the same time, the designer developed a new interest in women's clothing. His first women's Collection was presented in 1995 in previews in Tokyo, Paris and Milan, showing the same particulars and minimalist chic details as the men's. Bonas is part of the Technical Committee of Pitti Immagine Uomo and is president of the consortium Avanguardia Italia (Avant-guard Italy).

(*Eva Desiderio*)

❑ 2000. He accepts the position of creative director at Franco Ziche, in the early days of the Cleo&Pat line of pants for men and women, and then creates the brand A.Snob, which is an anagram of his own name.

Bonfils Lison (1936). French model and designer. She worked a lot in Italy during the 1960s and 1970s as a designer for Max Mara, Prénatal and Benetton. Very beautiful, with a tomboy attitude, almost always dressed plainly, she was one of the muses at the Jamaica Bar in Milan and of the parties which the brothers Guido and Sandro Somaré, both painters, gave at their studio in via Rossini. Lison made her début in the world of fashion at the age of 17 as a staff model for Dior. In 1958 she began to work for Elle as a reporter. In the 1980s she designed for the brand Mic Mac that was created in Saint Tropez in 1956 by the playboy Gunther Sachs and later taken over by the financier Bernard Tapie. His departure from the scene due to legal difficulties also forced Lison to leave the fashion world.

Bong Lie Sang. Korean designer. He opened his boutique in Seoul in 1985 and his success was such that he didn't need to sell at reduced prices. His "active" woman immediately found a place in the heart of his fellow citizens. In 2002 he arrived in Paris, at in the middle of Fashion Week. His linens, raw cottons, leather, and knitwear seduced the public of the City of Lights.

Bongard Germane (1885-1971). French dressmaker. She was more famous as an art dealer and collector than as a fashion designer. Sister of the renowned Poiret, who in 1909 asked her to design girl's clothes for him, she left her brother's atelier to open her own fashion house, expanding her interest to include the entire woman's wardrobe. After the war, the house took the name Jove. Very keen on contemporary art, in her salon she exhibited the works of Fernand Léger and André Lhote. Later she opened the art gallery Thomas.

Boni Chiara (1949). Italian designer. Born in Florence, she took a degree in languages. At the end of the 1960s, she allied herself with the Group UFO. Through the interaction between architecture, art, and fashion, which at the time was still unknown in Italy, the first boutique of "spontaneous dressing" was born. It was called You Tarzan Me Jane (in partnership with Annalisa Castellini in Milan, and with Elisabetta Ballerini in Florence and Forte dei Marmi), and in 1973 it was honored with the cover of Domus, the historic periodical of architecture and design founded by Gio Ponti. In the beginning, the designer created clothes and accessories for her shops. Then, starting in 1975, using her name as a brand, she became part of the fashion-system with complete Collections and presentations. As opposed to other key figures of the neo-avant-vanguard, in debt to the Futurism of Balla and the Constructivism of Delaunay, her style is sensual and more and more conscious of the body, especially in her use of stretch materials and soft fabrics, such as organzine. In 1985 she signed an agreement with the GFT Group of Turin, which today produces and distributes the new men's line as well. In 1999 she opened a large single-brand boutique in Milan on via del Gesù. (Maria Vittoria Carloni)

❑ At the beginning of the new millennium, she accept the position of district councillor for Culture of the Tuscany Region.
❑ 2003, May. The Inghirami Group acquires 50% of the brand, together with the right to manufacture the men's Collection.

Bonpoint French company of clothing, accessories, furnishings for children. It also has a chain of boutiques. It was established in the 1970s by Marie France Cohen, who started with a shop of 150 square feet in Rue de l'Université in Paris, where the company still has its headquarters. There are now five points-of-sale. The company, which employs 150 people, has a design atelier for the study of colors and for quality control. The chain is by now present all over Europe.

❑ 2003. Its worldwide expansion consists of five shops in the U.S., of which two are in New York, one in Los Angeles on Rodeo Drive, and one each in Miami and Palm Beach. In Italy, Bonpoint has shops in Milan, Rome and Bari.

Boot It can be described simply as footwear comprising a bootleg that reaches up to or over the knee. The ankle boot reaches up to between the ankle and the mid-calf. Originally boots were worn by men. In the 18th century there were elegant models in embroidered leather and plainer models in ox hide. In the mid-1800s, women's fashions demanded little leather or satin boots with a pronounced heel, and laces or a series of buttons up the side. Boots then fell into oblivion, only to reappear short and with elasticated sides in the 1960s. The 1960s and 1970s witnessed a real revival: cowboy boots were worn by men and women alike, while the soft leather "Musketeer" and the suede or patent leather "Barbarella" models that stretched up above the knee were popular.

In the 1990s designer models triumphed: lace boots were designed for a bride by Valentino, they became severe and austere in the hands of Armani, but fun and pop according to Versace. And on the high street denim models were torn and cut (just like jeans), while upmarket evening boots were decorated with either real or fake jewelry.

Boot-cut pants Trousers slightly flared under the knee, falling to the shoes. Not as wide as "trumpet-shaped" flare pants, they are wide enough to be worn comfortably with boots and ankle boots.

Borbonese Company already active in the early 1900s as a supplier of accessories – from ribbons to bows, and from gloves to hats and shawls – to the most prestigious tailoring shops of Turin, a city that was, at the time, very aware couture and a small Italian capital of fashion. Taken over by two young friends, Umberto Ginestrone and Edoardo Calcagno (both of then would later acquire take on the surname of the brand), it had an immediate success in the 1960s with the creation of jewellery that combined great imagination and exquisite workmanship. The ability of the company to establish a harmonious connection between clothing and jewellery is why the most important fashion houses want to work with it. These include Galitzine, Valentino and, immediately thereafter, in Paris, Ungaro and Saint-Laurent, who appreciated the inspiration, experimentation and beauty of its costume jewellery. During the 1970s, there was another extraordinary moment: the firm would find the distinctive element of its *griffe* in a new material that was soft like lamb skin, in a beige or honey color, and treated to reveal a "partridge-eye" dot effect, in bags, cases and a wide range of leather goods manufactured by Redwall. Much imitated, but never equalled, Borbonese bags are light, practical, always elegant, and by now a classic. Also in the line are items manufactured with plasticized fabric, and those showing a dot effect called "graffiti," in beige, very dark brown, blue, light blue, and black. (*Lucia Sollazzo*)

❑ 1992. The "Sexy Bag" celebrates its twentieth birthday. At the big party in

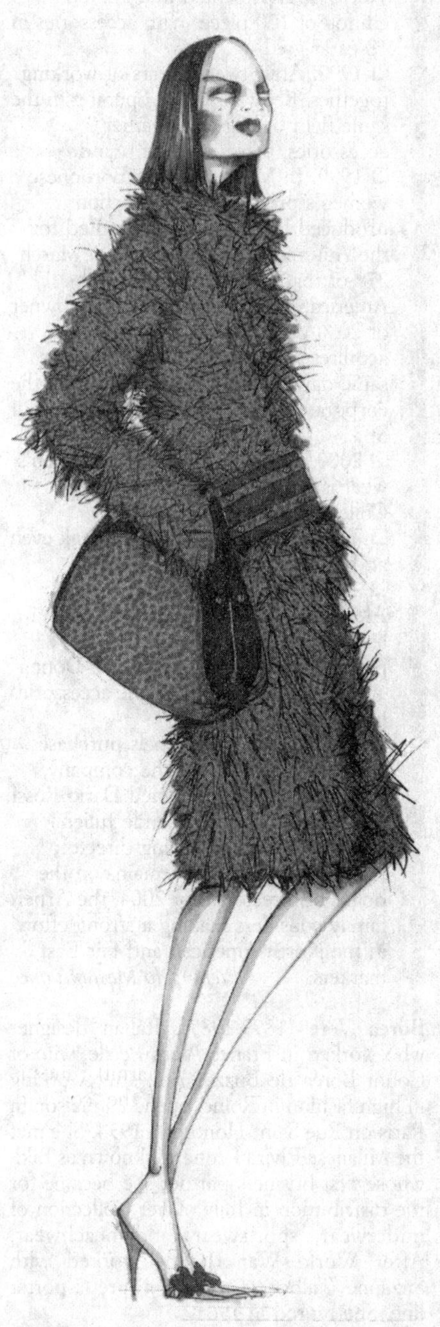

Ermine coat by Borbonese for Autumn-Winter 2001-2002.

Tokyo, it is presented in a limited edition of 100 pieces with accessories in 18-carat gold.
❑ 1992. After twenty years of working together, Redwall, which operates in the same field of bags and leather accessories, takes over the brand.
❑ 1999. In Milan, the first Borbonese women's prêt-à-porter Collection produced by Redwall is presented for the Autumn-Winter season. On March 27th of that same year the French-American family Arpels – current owner of 20% of Van Cleef & Arpels – acquires 50% of the company. That same day at a shareholders' meeting the corporate name is changed to Rossi 1924 Spa.
❑ 2000, September. A line of women's wear is added to the accessories Collection.
❑ The year 2001 ends with a break even and a turnover of €21 million.
❑ 2002. The creative director is Alessandro Dell'Acqua. She designs a line of women's clothing that is presented during Milano Moda Donna and meant to accompany the accessories line.
❑ 2002, November. Arpels purchases the remaining 50% of the company, acquiring the shares owned Dario Rossi and Alberto Vacchi. Claude Julien Arpels becomes managing director, while Alberto Vacchi remains on the board of directors. For 2004, the Arpels family considers making a strong effort in the North American and Far East markets. (*Pierangelo Mastantuono*)

Borea Vera (1899-1985). Italian designer who worked in France. Vera Pecile, wife of Count Borea de Buzzacarini, after working in high fashion in Rome, opened a maison in Paris on Rue Saint-Honoré in 1934. She met the Milanese Elvira Leonardi, known as Biki, whose first business partner she became for the distribution in Italy of her Collection of underwear, sportswear, and beachwear. After World War II, she worked with Suzanne Talbot to create a prêt-à-porter line. She retired in 1963.

Borgognona (Via) Italian street which connects Piazza Grande to the Corso. It is also known as the "street of fashion" because of the high number of prestigious fashion houses which settled there in the last thirty to forty years.

Borioli Gisella (1945). Journalist and art director. In 1980, together with her husband Flavio Lucchini, she created the monthly Donna, which she directed until 1993. Created as a direct competitor of Vogue, it was the first specialized magazine to talk about fashion as a social and cultural phenomenon, including behind the scenes. It was a big editorial success. She started her career in 1966 on the editorial staff of Ottagono, a quarterly of architecture and design. The following year she was hired by Condé Nast as executive editor of Vogue and other magazines in the group. In 1971 she is chief editor of L'Uomo Vogue and, in the same year, co-director of Vogue Bambini. In 1977 she was the head of Lei, the youngest of their magazines. After directing Donna for 13 years, she opened Superstudio Project for consulting, multi-media and international editorial planning. She has published three books: *100 Donne*, *10 Anni di Moda*, and *Gastel*, all with Edimoda. For six years, she was responsible for the fashion section of Annuario Rizzoli. She organized two big photo exhibis (*Gastel* for Donna, 1991, and *Star & Style*, 1992) in the open air at via della Spiga in Milan, and the exhibit *I disegni mai realizzati di Roberto Capucci* (The Unbuilt Designs of Roberto Capucci) at Palazzo Bagatti Valsecchi in Milan (March 1999). She is also the designer and director of Book-Jeans, an innovative series of visual books dedicated to the mythical figures of young people, distributed in an original way in bookshops and jeans stores. The first two titles are *Che Guevara* and *Jim Morrison*. Starting in 1989 she has organized the first course for fashion journalists and editors through her Superstudio.

❑ 2000. She creates, with her husband Flavio Lucchini, the Superstudio project, a large facility available to the city for events in fashion, art, and design, in a former industrial space owned by General Electric. This contributed to the upgrading of the neighborhood around via Tortona in Milan. As an artistic director, she is

interested in theater (and contributes to the project Cittadella dello Spettacolo at the Teatro Franco Parenti in Milan) and television, with consulting clients in Italy and abroad, including her work with Canale 5 for Nonsolomoda, and Donna Sotto le Stelle.
❑ 2002. She directs the first European "fashion award," La Kore-Oscar della Moda, a major event for the State TV network RAI-1.

Borletti Italian sewing machine. Romualdo Borletti established the firm Fratelli Borletti Spa in Milan in 1896. The plant produced on-board instrumentation for motor vehicles, both for industrial and private use. After World War I, in order to create jobs for women, the factory specialized in the manufacture of sewing machines, with the slogan "Borletti, punti perfetti," which means "with Borletti, perfect stitches." The *Superautomatica* model, designed by Zanuso in 1956, was exhibited at the Museum of Design 1945-1990 during Milan's Triennial. The company would later become Borletti-Veglia and be acquired by FIAT.

Umberto Boccioni, *Seamstress*, 1903 (Volonteri Collection, Savona).

Borsalino Not just a hat, but the symbol of a style and a world. Other hats of similar shape are called Borsalinos, as are some obvious imitations, as happens with other articles of clothing that are named after the most famous brands of their type. Synonymous with a certain style, this hat has been worn by very famous actors such as Bogart, Redford, and Sinatra, and it is also the title of a film featuring Jean-Paul Belmondo. The Borsalino hat factory was established in 1857 in Alessandria by Giuseppe Borsalino (1834-1900) and was managed after his death by his son Teresio (1867-1939). At the beginning of the twentieth century, Borsalino already had 1,000 workers and produced 750,000 pieces a year. During the 1980s the company was completely restructured and began to manufacture a clothing line.

❑ In December 1997 Borsalino Spa of Alessandria established Borsalino South, which in January 1998 acquired the hat factory Sabino D'Oria in Maglie.

Borsetta (Handbag) A term derived from the diminutive of the Latin word *bursa*, and more widely used than *borsa*, in accord with the fact that this accessory is used exclusively by women. This has set it apart, especially since the late 1800s and again in the 1920s when it became an article of style and even an object that was subject to change, just like fashion. Its origin is probably connected to the first use of coins, and the bags that the Greeks called *byrsa*, a term meaning leather. The bag, as with any other item connected clothing and fashion, closely mirrors daily life and costume throughout the centuries: from the French *aumonière*, in the period after the Crusades, which was manufactured in cloth but also in silk and velvet, which ladies loved to embroider with their own hands, to purses and pouches decorated with gold and gems, and the Renaissance bags notable for thei very refined fabric. In the 1600s the loose-fitting women's dresses with large, open sleeves, and pockets, eclipsed the bag. In addition, the muff, with its small pockets, served the same purpose. In the mid 1700s, flat bags hanging from belts were open along the top and directly accessible through openings in the dress. But the introduction of baskets and tight dresses caused the disappearance of pockets and bags. But just after the French Revolution, the bag once again became a necessary accessory for the fashionable woman, in a tapered shape worn with light and floating dresses similar to the ancient Roman *reticule*, which were renamed *redicules* by the French, and hung on the arm with silk ribbons. In a similar way, in the 1800s, after rare appearances, frequent disappearances, and precious returns of that ancient harmony in the purses à la Mary Stuart that were meant to hang from belts, bags came back in fashion. It was after the disappearance of crinoline, with the arrival of the famous S-shape, and they began to be differentiated according to their use: for afternoon, travel or shopping. Their real success began after the 1920s. New shapes destined to last were created, almost always rectangular, and they were made in different leathers, such as morocco and kidskin, and were small, sober and precise in their inside details. For evening, it was customary to use a turtle-green or silver *trousse*, necessary for a fresh touch of make-up (absolutely necessary until the 1940s). For daytime, the bag, beyond the by now industrially produced models, was crowned by the fashion world as the most important accessory. Some bags were to make history: the Chanel bag (a tiny soft leather or satin case entirely covered with lozenge stitching, and a gold chain as a handle); the Hermès' day, evening and travel's sets, with details inspired by saddlery; the Gucci bags, starting in 1912; and the Gherardini bags, starting in 1885. The 1930s, probably the most elegant period of the 1900s, saw new paradigms in the relationship between ever-more indispensable accessories and a particular time of day, season, dress, pair of shoes, leather, and color. Bags that would become more and more famous were born: in 1935 Hermès created the bag which, recreated twenty years later, would be loved by Grace Kelly, and it was named after her; in 1936 Elsa Schiaparelli launched a cylindrical leather bucket with a long strap to hang on the shoulders, leaving the hands free; in 1937 Gucci showed a boarskin bucket with a green and red stripe that would become a classic. During that decade, the bag was a real laboratory of style. It was shaped like a ball, a shell, and a watch. It was in maroon, light brown, and various shades of Russian-leather red. There was dyeing of precious leathers like crocodile, every woman's dream before World War II, but during which, due to a shortage of leather, women had to use cloth or velvet bags like those which Giuliana di Camerino, taking refuge in Switzerland, invented, to great success on both sides of the Atlantic after the war. It was an important accessory, closely tied to shoes and gloves. During the 1950s bag was free and formal. But the 1960s had almost arrived, with the effervescence of its many themes and the refinement in detail of styles which cohabit with fashion and set it on fire, from a soft leather case to a varnished jewel case and a shoulder bag. And, like a meteor, the men's bag appeared and disappeared. Then came the hippie's bag, a shapeless and frayed shoulder bag in an oriental style, decorated and very dear to the women who lived in the protest year of 1968. But once she returned to the composed elegance of the 1970s, she preferred the soft, light and roomy Borbonese bags, made of leather treated to produce a dot effect. These were a contrast to more subdued classic bags but still an immediate hit and symbol of the elite, like the bags of Vuitton, and in fact, both were continually subject to forgery. With the introduction of Italian prêt-à-porter, starting in the 1970s, the bag was characterized by new tannery treatments of traditional leathers, great imagination in its transformations, excellent results in the search for substitutes for crocodile and lizard, variety and beauty of colors, and often surprising materials created by chemistry, such as an indestructible nylon, which starting in the 1980s marked the extraordinary success of Prada bags. In addition to all this, the period was marked by great involvement on the part of designers. (*Lucia Sollazzo*)

Borsino Stilisti A privileged space within Momi-Modamilano dedicated to emerging designers, an area in which to find new creative inspirations and to meet young designers who are graduates of the best schools specialized in design. The idea, which made its début in 1998, is sponsored by the Region of Lombardy, Mittelmoda Gorizia, the Municipality of Milan, the Chamber of Commerce of Milan, Unioncamere Lombardy, the Fair of Milan, the Artisans' Association, the Association of Retailers in the Textile-Clothing Sector, Moda Industria, and Federtessile. Also, through the international content brought by Mittelmoda Premio Gorizia, the designers' *coulisse* offers a setting for extreme and avant-guard ideas, giving entrepreneurs in the fabric and clothing field access to new designers.

Borthwick Mark (1970). English photographer. At a young age, he moved to New York, where he now lives and works. He has published in international magazines such as i-D, Interview, Purple Fashion, and Vogue Italy. He works with the brands Hussein Chalayan, Comme des Garçons, Yamamoto, and Martin Margiela.

Bosco Valeria (1962). Italian designer. She went directly from the study of art in high school to being an assistant in the atelier of Enrica Massei. Then she was in the ateliers of Moschino, Ferré, and Etro. She has been a consultant at Basile, Maska, and Genny. Finally, through an agreement with Zamasport, she was able to present the first Collection with her own name, a prêt-à-porter line for Spring-Summer 2000. Behind her designs, tied to the memory of the past, there is a deep knowledge of fabrics and materials that she uses in a very creative way.

Boselli Mario (1941). Textile entrepreneur. His firm, a silk factory in the old tradition, located in Garbagnate Monastero (Co), is today a diversified and technologically advanced group that operates in the various fields of the industry, and remains the only European company that covers the entire process of silk production. Boselli is also active in various national and international institutions in the fashion industry. He has been, among other things, president of Federtessile, of the Club of Exporters, of the Autonomous Institute of the International Fair of Milan, of the International Association of Silk, and of the European Association of Yarn Spinners. He has held various important positions in Confindustria. He was president of Pitti Immagine and in 1998 was appointed vice-president of the National Chamber of Fashion, of which he later became president. His wide international experience (at present he is a member of the Conseille de Surveillance at the Dmc-Dollfus Mieg & C.ie, of the Comité de Strategie of Première Vision, of the Comité de Pilotage of Expofil, of the Board of Directors of the Italian Silk Office, and he is president of the Association Italy/Hong Kong) contributes to his comprehensive vision of the different economic and trading problems in the world of fashion, and to his awareness of the need for internal cohesion within the Italian fashion system. In 1990 he was appointed Cavaliere del Lavoro. France has bestowed on him the Legion of Honor.

Boselli Pier Luigi (1929). Journalist and former director of the women's weekly Grazia. His management experience began in 1966 at Confidenze, the historic women's weekly published by Mondadori. During the four years of his regime, the magazine went through a period of renovation and relaunch, thanks especially to promotional initiatives which caused a rise in circulation. In March 1970, Mondadori put him in charge of Grazia, where he remained for four years. His place was then taken by Nando Sampietro. In April 1974 he was again in charge of a Mondadori weekly, the newborn Guida TV, which opened with a cover dedicated to Mike Bongiorno and a circulation of 1,000,000 copies. But things didn't go well, and a few months later Boselli left his position, to be succeeded by Arrigo Polillo. He worked at Il Giornale and is a member of the jury for the Premiolino award, of which he was one of the founders.

Bosi Guido (1923). Italian tailor for men and women, born in Bologna. He learned his trade in the workshop of Emilio Musicò, who preserved in needle and thread the great tailoring tradition of Naples and Palermo. He opened his own atelier when he was almost 30. He was among the first to soften the lines of men's clothing, with the tricks and techniques used in women's fashion.

Boss Modelling agency opened in 1989. David Bosman is the owner and manager. The staff is composed of twelve people hired in New York and Capetown.

Bottega Veneta Italian manufacturer of bags. It was established in 1967 in Vicenza by Michele Taddei and his wife Laura. After divorcing him and marrying Vittorio Moltedo, she has for some years been sole owner. The bags, in soft leather and even today all hand-made, are typical of the company's production and have always been highly fashionable. The firm has had a single-brand shop in New York in 1971, when it was the first of the Italians to be on Madison Avenue. Its clients Jackie Onassis and Mary

Tyler Moore launched it. Twelve more single-brand shops would later open in America, plus boutiques in Paris, London, Hong Kong, Singapore, Milan, Rome, Venice, and Florence, along with 35 shops in Japan. In 1975 a new shoe line was launched. In 1998 there was a prêt-à-porter Collection inspired by American sportswear which made its début at Milano Collezioni in October of the following year.

❑ The company joins the Gucci Group.
❑ 2003. Début of the unisex sunglasses produced for Bottega Veneta by Sàfilo. The designer was Tomas Maier. The figures for 2002: the company had record revenues, especially in the fourth quarter, when it had a 90.5% increase in comparison to a diminished turnover for the other brands controlled by the Gucci Group.
❑ If Domenico Sole, president of the Gucci Group, declared that "The first quarter of 2003 has been the worst ever," Bottega Veneta proved once again that it could go against the trend, registering a 60% increase in sales.

Bottero Amalia. Journalist. She worked for the most important Italian culture newspapers and periodicals, and for television as an editor of children's programs. A fashion expert, she has followed its news and history. She organized the event at Villa Comunale in Milan in 1964 that commented on the presentation of the *History of Italian Costume* by Rosita Levi Pisetky. In 1979, Mursia published her *Nostra signora la Moda*, a precise and detailed history of the Made in Italy movement, from the period after World War II up to the triumph of the designers. (*Lucia Sollazzo*)

Botti Sisters *Haute couture* dressmaker's shop in Rome opened by Augusta, Carlotta, and Fernanda, the Botti sisters, in 1911 in Via Babuino. After 16 years, the workshop moved to Via Saverio Mercadante, and then from 1959 to 36 Corso Italia until its closure. They used to buy sketches and designs from Paris and then make them up, but some dresses were their own creations. Every six months, they would show at the Grand Hotel di Roma for clients throughout Italy. The history of the Botti sisters is linked to important dresses made for high profile clients such as Queen Elena and her ladies-in-waiting, and for other upper class customers. Their wedding dresses and designs for ceremonial occasions and special evenings, such as premières at the opera house in Rome, were famous. At the end of the 1940s, the house also sold fur coats and garments. The sisters were supplied from Paris. They would visit the *haute couture* French fashion shows, buy interesting garments, and then reproduce them to order for their clients. In Rome, they took part in the fashion shows at the Grand Hotel in Via Veneto. The society magazine, *Le Carnet Mondain*, documented their successes by publishing photographs of the most high profile weddings. The workshop – with 140 workers organized into two shifts – operated almost 24 hours a day. For years, Mario Vigolo was their designer. Immediately after World War II a good part of the bourgeoisie remained loyal customers. The wardrobe of Palma Bucarelli – the superintendent of the National Gallery of Modern Art – was donated to the Museum of Nineteenth and Twentieth Century Decorative Arts: it included two dresses by the Botti Sisters made from sketches by Balenciaga and Elsa Schiaparelli.

Bottom In the Western world, the changing shape of coveted parts of the body has always been linked to different seduction strategies, which alternate the emphasis placed in turn on the bust, hips, waist, legs and arms. Such strategies are not only ingrained in fashion, but affect the body itself, which is affected by all sorts of artificial devices, from the corset to dieting. Masking what was on view until yesterday and showing off what used to be hidden is from time to time the aim of introducing a new style. The S shape of the 19th century gave maximum prominence to the bust and bottom, with the bottom enlarged by a *tournure* and then by a puff. Following a period of slender elegance in the 1920s and 1930s and wartime rationing, after World War II it was only the most curvaceous who were able to compete with the full figures of Sophia Loren or the young Silvana Mangano in the film *Riso amaro*. After the complete and age-old dominance of legs offered by the miniskirt, slowly fashion turned its attention to the bottom. The nude look's wisps of tulle and chiffon were superfluous to the commanding vision of a well-defined bottom, very different from that of the domestic goddess with a wide childbearing pelvis who is therefore blessed with a stately bottom. Today, the most desired form of bottom sits high, is compact and slightly masculine: buttocks that do not divert the curves of the hips, but support the fine top-edge of a skirt that threatens to come slip loose in public. It can happen, as it did at the 1999 Pink Ball in Montecarlo when Naomi Campbell, in a mere slip of a dress, bared her much admired bottom on the runway with an air of bored disinterest.

Botto Poala Spinning mill in Lessona (Biella) established in 1910 in order to manufacture weaving yarns. In the last two decades it has developed a line of knitwear yarns of very high quality. The company, which is part of the Botto Group, is able to manage the entire production cycle of yarns, both combed and carded, for outside weaving mills and knitwear shops. The production is essentially based on high-quality wool fibers such as very fine wool, cashmere and silk.

Boucheron French jeweler. The history of Boucheron begins in 1858 in Paris with Frédéric B. (1830-1903) who chooses as the headquarters of his business the Galérie du Palais Royal, winning the favor of the Second Empire aristocracy with a style inspired by nature. In 1867, his popularity grew with his manufacture of the gold medal for the Universal Exhibition of Paris. Around the same time, he created for Mrs. Clarence H. Mackay a necklace which was destined to be remembered: set between diamonds was a zephyr considered to be the purest, the biggest, and the most beautiful in the world. In 1893, he moved to Place Vendôme 26. Louis Boucheron would continue his father's tradition, hoarding the most extraordinary precious stones, refining the cuts, and using onyx, lapis lazuli, coral, jade, and amber in his creations. He opened a subsidiary firm in London and successfully participated in the famous Art Deco exhibition of 1925. Some of his jewels are today on display at the Victoria and Albert Museum in London and at the Musée des Arts Décoratifs in Paris. Among his clients have been maharajahs, oriental princes, kings of Egypt, and emperors of Persia, along with big American industrialists and movie stars. The new generation, represented by Fred and Gérard Bucheron, returned in the 1940s to a naturalistic and floral inspiration. And immediately after the war, the conquest of the rest of the world began: the Americas, the Middle East and, in the 1970s, Japan and the Far East. In the 1990s the policy of Alain Bucheron was based on prestigious jewellery, in express contrast to less exclusive jewellery, to be worn in everyday life, including also steel watches. The year 1983 saw the launch of the fragrance *Boucheron*, in a bottle shaped like a ring meant for a maharajah. In 1994 there was a second perfume of oriental inspiration, *Jaïpur.*

(*Giuliana Parabiago*)

Bouché René (1894-1963). French illustrator. He is considered to be the last representative of a great tradition that is forgotten because of photography: the use of drawing as a way to record fashion trends and the customs of high society. On his arrival in New York in 1941, he was hired by Vogue, where he would work until his death.

Bouclé Fiber which curls into several small knots. It is used to manufacture sweaters and knitwear dresses and to produce a soft fabric characterized by its peculiar curls, mostly for garments that are fairly heavy. It has often had a comeback in the usual ups and downs of fashion.

Boudicca English brand of prêt-à-porter created in London in 1997 by Zowie Broach and Brian Kikby. They met during their study of fashion at Middlesex Polytechnic. Kikby continued his studies at the Royal College of Art, and then worked with Paul Smith. At their début they distinguished themselves for their intellectual and against-the-trend style. The Guardian defines them as "intellectual tailors." Starting with the Spring-Summer 1998 Collection they gave birth to Boudicca, which is the pronunciation of Bodicea, the female ruler of the first century A.D. who fought to free ancient Britain from the Romans. In fact, freedom, of clothing and of expression, is the basic assumption of their style. They presented their Collection for the first time in February

2000 during Fashion Week in London. Their clothes, conceived as artistic expressions in evident contrast to the standardized style of industrial fashion, are requested for exhibits and events held at the Palais Galliera in Paris and the Barbican Art Gallery in London. (*Virginia Hill*)

Boué Soeurs French dressmakers. The two Boué sisters were born in Toulon, Sylvie in 1880 and Jeanne in 1881. But it was in Paris that they started their dressmaking activity at the turn of the new century, and soon proved to be masters in the creation of lace dresses worked on transparencies. They were careful managers and between 1916 and 1922 opened ateliers in New York, London, and Bucharest. They retired in 1935.

Bouet-Willaumez René (1900-1979). French illustrator. It was Mainbocher, the director of the French edition of Vogue, that hired him at his magazine in 1929, after a short experience in industry as an engineer. He would work with Vogue for three decades, until the end of his career. With him, illustration, still tied to the style of Art Deco, experienced a clear and meaningful shift. His name is associated with one of the most beautiful periods in fashion illustration. Styles simplifed, acquiring spontaneity and lightness, sketched with a pencil that was incisive and personal.

Boulanger Louise (1878-1950). French dressmaker. She opened her atelier in Paris in 1927. She became famous for modifying the styles that were popular at the time, which were straight and short as the fashion *à la garçonne* required, and making them fuller by draping the hips. In 1929 she designed the costumes of Brigitte Helm for the movie *L'Argent* by Marcel L'Herbier, to which she would look for inspiration for a following Collection. By now, her creations belong to the history of costume. In 1998, on the occasion of the 14th edition of the Market Exhibition of Antiques, a kimono of hers that was made in Paris in 1925 was put on sale for 12 million liras.

Bouquin Jean (1936). French designer. He made his début in the world of fashion through the rear door, as a window decorator and shop assistant in men's wear boutiques. At the age of 26, he designed clothes for the John Charles boutique and was noticed by the Renoma brothers, who hired him to manage the styles offered in their department store, which was known for its rich choice of non-French fashion. In 1964, he started his own business with a boutique in Saint Tropez for women's prêt-à-porter, which he himself designed and produced. From that moment on, his ascent would continue, with 24 shops in France. His "fuel" was the idea of offering a luxury hippie style to that segment of the French bourgeoisie which in Italy would have been defined as radical-chic. In 1971 he abandoned the business in order to devote himself to work as a theater manager, and to the rehabilitation of maladjusted young people.

Bourdin Guy (1928-1991). French photographer. His initial passion centered on sketching and painting, and it was as a painter that he made his début, in 1960, in Vogue France. But at that magazine – for which he worked for twenty years – he arrived above all as a photographer when, struck by the aesthetic beauty of the famous picture of a pepper taken by Edward Weston, who captured its sensuality, he decided to interest himself in the field. He rapidly made a name for himself during the 1960s thanks to the personality with which he put together daring advertising campaigns such as the one in 1966 for Charles Jourdan shoes, or the sensual catalogues of underwear for Bloomingdale's in New York. Openly influenced by Surrealism, but also capable of fusing the visions of Man Ray with the vivid chromatism of Pop Art (as proved by the enormous objects, such as hearts and shoes, with which he measured his models), he was an artist almost obsessed with formal perfection. In his study in the Paris neighborhood of Le Marais, the completely black walls, the locked windows, and the absence of a phone showed his willingness to isolate himself from the outside world until his work was finished. Just as careful in the page make-up of his photos, he always refused to use them for exhibits or books, outside the purely commercial purpose for which they had been conceived. It is from this same point of view that one must consider his 1987 rejection of the *Grand Prix National de la Photographie*, which said was "utterly useless." In the last years of his life, in order to avoid depression, he went back to painting, although without abandoning photography. In 2002, the Shine gallery in London dedicated a large retrospective to him, while Bulfinch Publishers issued his only monograph, *Exhibit A: Guy Bourdin*, which offers a complete Collection of his work from the 1950s to 1991.

(*Roberto Mutti*)

Bourette Silk yarn obtained from scrap and waste, characterized by a short and irregular fiber, used to make patterned fabric, generally blended, with a surface noteworthy for its small knots and tiny bows.

Bourgeois Louise (1911). French sculptor. Since 1938 she has lived in New York. Much of her work has as its subject the human body. Clothing is considered like a second skin, a symbol of the body itself. A dress is the symbol of an existential condition: for this reason the artist often makes use of clothes in her installations, as in *Couple* (1996), in which a dummy wearing a men's shirt towers over another wearing only a necklace. In 1978, for the performance *A Banquet/A Fashion Show of Body Parts*, she created latex dress-sculptures worn by the artist herself and others. These clothes, provided with bulges similar to a woman's breasts placed both front and back, were ironical about men and women and invited discussion about ideals of physical beauty.

(*Cloe Piccoli*)

Bourjois Alexandre Napoléon (18345-1893). French creator of cosmetics. He was the founder of one the first cosmetics companies in the world, Bourjois, established in Paris in 1863. At first, he made theatrical make-up. His products were ahead of their time (see *Rouge Fin de Théâtre*, a formula which offered a new powder texture in place of the traditional greasepaint) and allowed him to be appointed official supplier to the imperial theaters. He invented new packaging and, for his *Fard Pastels*, created small cardboard boxes with the legend "Fabrique Spéciale pour la Beauté des Dames." It was the first example of printing on packaging in the history of cosmetics. Among the colors created by him, *Cendre de Rose Brune* is still today a best-seller.

Bousquet Marie-Louise. French journalist She has for a long time been the director of the French edition of Harper's Bazaar. In 1956 she received the Oscar of fashion, for the first time awarded to a French person. Besides being a journalist, she is famous for her literary salons in which, almost every day, great tailors mixed with great artists and writers such as Jean Cocteau, Max Jacob, André Gide and Paul Valéry.

Boussac Marcel (1889-1980). French textile entrepreneur. In the history of fashion, his name is linked especially to the establishment in 1946 of the house of Dior, of which he was not only the financier but indeed the real founder, since the great tailor was undecided about the venture. The son of a small wool entrepreneur, he established his first textile company around 1910. The first world war was a sort of miracle for him because he was selected as the government's supplier of cloth for its pioneering airplanes. At the end of the war, he recycled his remaining inventory by manufacturing shirts. In 1923 he made his début in the world of high fashion by acquiring Pierre Clarence, a house of the second rank. Between the two world wars he built an empire which, when World War II was over, became even stronger more because when consumers started to by again, he was among the few with merchandise in his warehouse. His decline began toward the end of the 1950s, when the entire European textile sector went through a crisis. His group, though in big financial trouble, held out until 1978, when an aged Boussac was forced to appear in court with the company's books. It was bankruptcy. That was when the firm Agaghe-Willot invested 700 million francs and the group was able to breathe again. It remained a giant, with 100 plants and 28,000 workers. As such, it still had dreams of expansion, which would be its ruin. In order to acquire Korvette's, a chain of department stores in the U.S., it accumulated ruinous debt. It was 1981 and the French government urged a bailout, promising special conditions. A consortium led by Bernard Arnault acquired and drastically reorganized the firm. (*Mino Colao*)

Boutet de Movet Bernard (1884-1949). French illustrator. He was an innovator in the use of the fashion sketch as a journalistic tool, less photographic and more interpretative and full of atmosphere. He worked at La Gazette du Bon Ton, Monsieur, Harper's Bazaar and Vogue. His personal wardrobe was quite fashionable.

Boutique French term derived from the term for studio or workshop, in long use to indicate a shop in which clothes are bought, with strong and particular attention to fashion. This is especially the case when the fashion houses support the principal lines of the season with others added on, often known as boutique fashion. In the history of Italian fashion, going back to its famous beginning at the Sala Bianca of Palazzo Pitti, the term boutique refers to small artisan-made Collections, with simple and colorful pieces, fanciful and universally known as the real ancestors of prêt-à-porter. Today the term boutique primarily indicates a shop for high quality clothing, as well as an exclusive place for the purchase of clothes by great tailors and designers, and for merchandise of famous brands. Starting in the 1950s the number of boutiques multiplied dramatically. Every town, and especially every city, has a street, and sometimes more than one, entirely devoted to prestigious boutiques. The famous ones are via Condotti in Rome, via Montenapoleone, via della Spiga and via Sant'Andrea in Milan, Fifth Avenue and Madison Avenue in New York, Faubourg Saint-Honoré in Paris, and, of course, the surrounding neighborhoods.

Boutique de France International French biweekly dedicated to the fashion trade. It was established in 1953 by Maurice Gattégno. Its single-theme issues were, from time to time, dedicated to men's fashion, underwear, fabrics, and so on.

Bouyer Jean Philippe (1959). French designer. He studied at the School of Applied Arts in Paris, majoring in manufacturing techniques. In 1980 he became Lagerfeld's assistant. He was later hired as a designer by the shoe company Charles Jourdan, where he would stay seven years. He worked with Muriel Grateau, Alaïa, and Tarlazzi. Then he returned to Jourdan to launch a clothing line which now sells 25,000 pieces each season.

Bowes Museum Durham, England. Founded in 1892 by the English industrialist John Bowes and his wife Josephine, an actress from Paris. Collectors and philanthropists, in 1860 they decided to create a museum "for people's education and entertainment." They collected clothing and related items and built a French-style castle to house them. The Collection was assembled during the century that followed, mainly through donations, therefore including mainly clothes of local manufacture and origin which can dated from the end of the 1700s on. Other important items of interest include the clothes worn by Empress Eugenie of France between 1850 and 1860; various bridal dresses, complete with accessories, from 1800 to the present time; as well as high fashion pieces designed by Paquin, Hartnell, Fath, and Worth. The Gallery of Costume was inaugurated by the Queen Mother, Mary, in 1976. Also important is the area devoted to fabrics, with examples of lace, embroidery, tapestry, and carpets which can be dated to the 16th century and later. In the library is a Collection of French fashion newspapers from the 1800s that once belonged to Josephine Bowes.

(*Virginia Hill*)

Bowler Hat Typical English hat. It was called a bowler because it was invented by Lord Stock and manufactured by the firm Bowler and Son in 1850, and later by the factory Lock & Co. Made in black felt, rigid and dome-shaped, tight and raised along the edges, it took the place of the silk top hat and was the most important hat in the late 1800s and early 1900s. It is always associated with the businessmen of the City, London's financial district, where it is jokingly called the Billycoke, after the nephew of the second Earl of Leicester, William Coke, who would wear it while hunting. In the U.S. it was called the Derby, after Earl Edward George Derby, who died in 1948, and who wore a grey model of the hat when going to the racetrack. It was made famous in films by Charley Chaplin and by Laurel and Hardy.

It was also "worn" by Liza Minnelli, in *Cabaret*, when she twirled it on the tip of her foot. The bowler is still the preferred hat of London's financiers.

Bow tie According to some, the bow is the most elegant form of tie, and, according to all, the hardest to knot. For those wishing to wear one, it is better to learn how to tie it rather than buy one that is ready-to-wear. It originated in 1894. For menswear it is the natural complement to evening suits: white for tails and black for a tuxedo. It can also be worn in the daytime in a colored or patterned version, as Winston Churchill did. (*Gianluca Bauzano*)

Bow ties worn with different collars.

Boy Billy (1960). American jewellery designer and collector. He has two passions: creating fantasy jewels and collecting high fashion clothes and dolls. Born in Vienna, at a very young age he began to breathe the air of luxury clothes. By the age of 13 he was already collecting them, and today he has more than 11,000 pieces, 2,500 of which are by Elsa Schiaparelli. In 1975 in Paris, on Rue de la Paix, he opened Surreal Couture and, five years later, Surreal Bijoux. It was 1980 and he was only 20. The friend of artists, actors, and important figures in the fashion world, he created "surrealist" bijoux for Thierry Mugler and Charles Jourdan. Among his clientels were Elizabeth Taylor and Lauren Bacall. His works have been shown at the Victoria and Albert Museum, the Museum of Modern Art, and at the Musée des Arts de la Mode. In 1989 he launched his mannequin doll Mdvanii in Europe, and four years later he published his book *Bluette* (Maeght Publishing). In 1990, a traveling exhibition (Le Grand Tra La La) took him abroad and makes his creations famous. He owns the most important Collection of Barbie dolls, the doll which drove millions of little girls and teenagers all over the world crazy. Rather than a traditional doll, the mythical Barbie looks like a model, tall, slender and sexy. Its characteristics are accentuated by the hairdos and accessories, and, especially, by its very rich wardrobe, ranging from sumptuous wedding and evening dresses to furs and bathing suits. From this Billy Boy got the idea of dedicating an exhibition to her at the Musée des Arts Décoratifs in Paris in 1985. There were 300 Barbies dressed by 61 important designers, among them Kenzo, Gaultier, Coveri, Mugler, and Montana. The wedding dress was by Féraud, and the red fur by Dior, while Saint-Laurent dedicated to her as many as 16 models from previous Collections. Inspired by Bettina, his eternal muse, Billy Boy dressed Barbie with a '60s-style black dress, very simple and linear.

Boyd Harvey (1941). American illustrator. He graduated from the Parson's School of Design in New York, where he became a teacher. He started working at the age of 24 and established himself with a style that was not overly realist. He worked with Elle, Vanity Fair, Women's Wear Daily, Mademoiselle, Harper's Bazaar and Gentleman's Quarterly. As an artistic director he managed advertising campaigns for Saint-Laurent, Valentino and Hechter.

Boyle Laura. American designer of accessories in cloth, such tunics and beach robes. She has worked in Paris since 1989. She admits to being very influenced by the art of Marc Rothko, Andy Warhol and Barnett Newman. She belongs to the minimalist school.

Bp Studio Women's knitwear company, known for fine quality and high fashion content. It uses precious fibers such as extra-fine merino, cashmere, silk, cotton, and linen. Its headquarters is in Sesto Fiorentino. It was established in 1959. It has showrooms in Milan and New York, and its main markets are Italy, the U.S., Japan, and Germany.

Braccialini Italian manufacturer of bags and coordinates in leather and fabric, including clothing, accessories, and shoes. In 1953, Carla Braccialini and her first husband Roberto left for Liguria with a very small catalogue of items ranging from bags to clothes and a few hats. It was a simple product line made by a small group of women, all masters of crochet. The firm was a family-run and immediately understood that the Italian market was ready for leather goods and for experiments in combining new materials. The staff, directed by mother Carla, availed itself of the collaboration of her three children, Riccardo (since 1980 taking care of strategy), Massimo (Carla's creative right arm), and Lorenzo (since 2000 taking care of communication). In the last fifty years the distinction between an elegant, exclusive bag and a straw bag (which characterized the 1950s in Italy) has disappeared. Today, it is an accessory and a non-accessory: a piece to wear on its own, and a piece to match with the rest, in which the mix between leather and straw makes it unmistakably a Braccialini creation. The first models were created in a four-room apartment on via delle Pinzochere in Florence, from the sketched model to the *maquette* on which to apply the leather inlays, a job that was given to an outside leather artisan. But during the 1960s this process was recombined into one. Carla opened her first workshop in which every production step was carried out, from the initial sketch to the sewing of straw and leather. She herself admits to have "experimented" with everything and to have tested Vinavil glue. Her workers even taught her how to obtain a better result with normal mastic. The situation was doomed to change drastically with the floods of 1966, which damaged the small workshop, although the tenacity of Mrs. Braccialini allowed her to rise from the ashes like a Phoenix less than a year after the disaster. The fantasy of colors and the liveliness of the chromatic combinations became the company's trademark. And there was more. The boundless experimentation produced results that the market could also enjoy, such as the first wicker baskets, which had delicate lace and embroidery added directly on the leather inlays. Then came the 1980s and Braccialini, by now tops in the field of bags, surprised everyone again and invented a new, fresh and optimistic style, whose key was a constant drive towards experimentation and to being a kind of pioneer in a market that, at the time, was much more competitive than in the 1960s. It was a time of aesthetic revolution with a mix of ribbons and passementeries, small flowers and inlays, and small beads and laces. It was also the start of distribution in Germany, the U.S., and Japan. The product line diversified and in 1986 the company left Florence for Pontassieve, just a few miles away. One year later came a license agreement with Vivienne Westwood for the production and distribution of accessories. The late 1980s saw the establishment of Contromano, an associate company which soon obtained the Roccobarocco license. Time passed and tastes changed. Carla's intuition shifted towards minimalism, which characterized the sobriety of the 1990s, a minimalism reinterpreted by Braccialini, in which liveliness and carelessness appeared through the stiffness of the new lines. Then, the brand decided to focus on the young generation with the line *Tua di Braccialini*. Later, it was the turn of *Metrocity*, a new dynamic line with metal angles aimed at an urban market. In 1993, the company opened a single-brand boutique on via della Vigna Nuova 33/a, in Florence. In 1997 it signed a license agreement with Mila Schön; in 1999 there was one with Contromano Bagutta, and another with Vivienne Westwood for the men's and women's shoe Collections. The year 2000 opened with the merger with Contromano and concluded with the agreement with the Mariella Burani Fashion Group, which had immediately excellent results. Also promising was the opening of new single brand boutiques. It was the start of a luxury pole and evidence of this important partnership were the new stores in Milan and Tokyo. The turnover shot up, reaching as high as 80%, partly thanks to the Braccialini Franchising project and the establishment of Antichi Pellettieri, to which the shares in the firm held by the Burani group were sold. In 2002 there were openings in Treviso and Riccione. There was also one in Shanghai, thanks to a joint venture concluded in Hong

Kong for a distribution network covering the entire Far East. The following year, there were Braccialini showrooms in Milan, Montecatini Terme, and Udine. A further strategic drive took place in 2003, when the French fund L Capital (the LVMH group) purchased shares in Antichi Pellettieri and the Braccialini firm celebrated 50 years of activity. An enviable anniversary which was celebrated in the best way. In 2004, new shops opened in Rome, Dubai, London, Shanghai, Hangzhou, and Chongqing, and these were followed in 2005 by shops in Seoul, Hong Kong, Jeddah, Paris, and Milan. In that same year, the headquarters at Pontassieve was enlarged.

(*Edoardo Ponzoni*)

Braghenti Silk factory near Como. It was established in 1901 by Luigi Braghenti, limited partner and administrator. The factory, with a plant in Malnate (Va) and the headquarters in Como, specializes in the manufacture and trade of silk for ties and women's clothing. In 1921, Alberto Andina, an important figure in Como's financial circles, became president, while Luigi Braghenti kept the role of vice-president and general manager. In 1931, Nico Castellini joined the board of directors and the factory would progressively come under the control of the Castellini family, which for women's clothing preferred linen fabrics to silk and rayon. In 1967, Nico's sons Vittorio and Paolo took over management of the company. In 1988, the acquisition of almost the entire capital stock by Ratti brought on a further evolution: wool and Winter fibers were produced alongside linen up to the end of the 1990s, when Braghenti was completely absorbed within Ratti.

Braglia Lorella (1964). Italian designer. In 1991, she designed her first Collection, produced by Dielle, a knitwear factory which she established in 1984 in Reggio Emilia. Today, production is around 80,000 pieces distributed in Europe and Asia.

❑ The Autumn-Winter 2000-2001 season sees the birth of X, the new women's wear line created by the designer.

Branchini Shoe Factory A brand from Bologna that has produced shoes since 1990. The leathers are sometimes combined in unusual colors, such as yellow, orange, and red. It is also available in a men's line.

Brando Marlon (1924-2004). American actor. A fan of the tight T-shirt and an immediate international success in 1951 with the film *A Streetcar Named Desire* directed by Elia Kazan. Or, perhaps, success was triggered by a great performance and an aggressive and sensual beauty accentuated by the T-shirt which showed off his macho muscles. He was much imitated and women went crazy for him. Three years later, in *On The Waterfront* (1954), Brando launched a fashion for Canadian-style checked jackets. But the movie that would establish him as a trend-setter everywhere was *The Wild One* (1954). Following the début of that movie, jeans and a black leather jacket become a kind of uniform for young people that would last well after the 1950s. That was the beginning of the street-style that is still very fashionable today. (*Sofia Leoncina Gnoli*)

Brandsna Dick (c. 1952). Dutch designer, model maker, and tailor. He has always worked in the shadow of both the great and the minor names, whether they were the creative designers or the industrial manufacturers, as an assistant, a designer, and as aconsultant. Attending the very serious schools of his country he acquired an enormous training in cutting and a tailoring, as if he had learned the job in an artisan's workshop in earlier days. He has worked in the high fashion studio of Saint-Laurent and for many Italian brands and designers.

Brandt Paul Emile (1883-1952). Jeweler of Swiss origin (La Chaux-de-Fonds), but French by adoption. He was a sensitive interpreter of the artistic trends of his time. After studying in Paris under the guidance of Chaplain and Allard, in the early years of the 20th century he was a very original creator of Art Nouveau style jewellery, Immediately after World War I he favored Art Deco, offering rigorous interpretations of accentuated geometric forms. Among the jeweler-artists who distinguished themselves during the Exposition des Arts Décoratifs in Paris in 1926, he had his greatest success in the 1930s. A master of matching unusual materials, he adopted the *coquille d'oeuf*, lacquer and silver. He favored black enamel, platinum, onyx, diamonds, and pearls for his jewellery and for his precious watches with their exacting bi-color scheme organized with a skillful mix of rectangles, triangles, and circles in a pure cubist style.

(*Alessandra Quattordio*)

Branquinho Veronique (1973). Belgian photographer and designer. After high school, she attended a painting course at the Saint Lucas Art School in Brussels. From 1991 to 1995 she studied fashion at the Royal Academy of Fine Arts in Antwerp. She made her début as a designer working with various Belgian manufacturing firms. In 1997, in a gallery in Paris, she presented her first Collection, inspired by Romanticism.

❑ 1998, October. She wins the *VHL Fashion Award* as best fashion designer.
❑ She designs Ruffo Research for Spring-Summer 1999 and for Autumn-Winter 1999-2000. The Collections are presented in Milan.
❑ 1999, July. Exhibit at Colette, in Paris, dedicated to Braquinho and Raf Simons.
❑ 2003, January. She launches her first men's Collection in Paris. In March, she presents in Antwerp the original sketch for the Coke Light can and a can-shaped candle. In Autumn she opens her first boutique in Antwerp, on Nationalstraat.

Brassière In the mid 1800s it was a baby's smock in wool or cotton. Today, it is a tight bodice with or without a neckline, with sleeves or without, which goes to the waist. In is worn in Summer as a top with a skirt or trousers, or as a sexy garment under a tailored jacket.

Bra-top A top shaped like a bra. Launched by Madonna, it is the uniform of all teenage girls, especially in Summer. Very short, just covering the breasts, it leaves the belly-button uncovered.

Breast "Ah, the snows of the breast! Ah, the immodest women of Florence, who go around with their bosom on show," complained Dante. One of the strongest factors influencing the way we dress is our attempt at seduction by using clothes to show off the body's forms. But nothing is more effective than the direct presentation of nudity. Revealing the breasts was nudity's first victory after the austere high-necked garments of the Middle Ages. In Dante's time, necklines were certainly still high, a far cry from the romantic necklines of the nineteenth century which exposed bare arms, back and bosom. In 1342, the legislators in Perugia, who strove to banish any naked skin from the neck down, would have had a heart attack if they had been able to look five centuries into the future and see the nudity of a woman in evening dress at the height of the nineteenth century. As the years passed, chroniclers spoke of breasts being so pushed upwards by the neckline that they seemed about to burst out of the dress. Boccaccio used to wonder why we bother to hide breasts given that nature chose to put them in such a prominent place. The way that clothing has alternated between revealing and hiding breasts doubly underlines their importance. The height of collars rose to the point that they framed the face in the early 15th century: "Watch out for women with bare breasts," roared Savonarola. After a barren period, pretty necklines brightened up the age of Enlightenment, though they no longer ran from one shoulder to the other, and necklines persisted but in a more moderate form. Arcadian shepherdess dresses also allowed glimpses of the breasts through their flimsy material. It was only when the cold winds of the French revolution began to whistle around the door that breasts were hidden by fichu. But breasts returned to sight, having their heyday at the end of the 19th century. The typical housewife, wrapped up in her high-necked everyday clothes, was turned into a woman of showy and glorious buxomness. All the beauty of her breasts was suddenly pushed upwards and displayed in bejewelled necklines of unprecedented lavishness. But amazing décolletages, milk-white skin (a tan would only become fashionable with Chanel), sculpted shoulders, and shapely arms were soon banished by the garçonne look and the ravages of the crisis-ridden 1930s to the extent that, for the first time, the neckline slipped down the back, changing its parameters to reveal a different part of the body. Beautiful necklines were created by the hidden presence of a wide variety of corsets, some more terrifying than others, for example, the cuirass and the bandages that flattened the bust under loose-fitting art deco dresses. Consequently, fetishes for underwear associated with breasts have flourished, as evidenced by the history of the bra, which, for a long time, was designed more to contain the bosom than to show it off. In the golden era of the first Italian ready-to-wear, masculine jackets worn under the banner of feminism – when bras were being burnt in the street – nobody spoke of breasts. It was a real handicap to be naturally well endowed; girls who always needed to add darts – an old technique used to construct curves around breasts – complained that they did not know how to compress their bosom under a linear and revealing jacket. Breasts are a sign of femininity and yet fashion is the godfather of other seduction innovations, from the military to the faux poverty look and from the oriental back to the androgynous. The early 1990s, just as had happened a hundred years earlier, echoed with the unanimous cry of "Designers – show us the body." It began with breasts as the first stage in the renewed glorification of nudity after experiments with transparent materials creating a "now-you-see-me-now-you-don't" effect. And what are we being shown now? The strapless heart-shaped neckline of the 1950s; dresses that lower their neckline at the back down to the base of the kidneys, adding inevitable frissons of excitement with every unexpected fall in the material; jackets slip casually and carelessly over shirts that are not quite done up; peplum dresses are worn undone around the chest. In the 1990s, attention was focused once again on the waist, and both necklines and corsets were reintroduced: confident women, aware of their bodies, are no longer adverse to the idea of the *guêpière*. This latest development in revealing a new area of the woman's upper body was seen, according to a survey in an Italian daily newspaper, as offering women the possibility of discovering a natural spirituality from within. With all the pluralism of fashion, the nude, the scantily veiled, and the completely covered coexist happily together as a repertoire of roles – not just in terms of fashion – that can be drawn upon at different times of day and in different seasons. The invention of stretch fabrics, for example, has overshadowed the fashion for revealing transparencies. With the arrival of the new century, however, a new form of nudity was introduced with the revelation of the bottom.

(*Lucia Sollazzo*)

Brenner Patrizia (1950-2002). With a life led internationally (an Austrian father and an Italian mother, studied in Italy, Switzerland and the U.S.) and with style (Camilla Cederna and Maria Pezzi wrote about her very beautiful and elegant mother, Giulia), she made her début at Milano Collezioni in Spring 2000. She had been in the world of fashion for years as a freelance designer, and worked on Benetton commercials, among other projects. In 1996 she opened a salon-boutique (with two fireplaces) in Milan, on via S. Fermo, for high society clients, to whom she proposed pieces that were very *habillé*, in which the precious material played a very important role (she was known for her kimonos in precious velvet). Her designs were distributed on the international market. She died at the age of 52.

(*Laura Salza*)

Brenot Pierre (1913). French illustrator and designer. He was the creator of the French pin-up after World War II and into the 1950s. On film posters he drew the physical features of the movie character Caroline Chérie, played by Martine Carol. Given his bent for sex appeal, he worked especially in advertising for underwear.

Bresciani Manufacturer of high-quality hosiery for men, made in cotton, wool, silk, cashmere, and linen. The firm is located in Bergamo. The 1998 turnover amounted to 4.5 billions, 80% of which came from exports to the U.S., Europe, South America, the Middle East and the Far East. It started its activity in 1979. It employs 29 workers.

❑ Over the years the basic lines have been enriched by other lines such as Bresciani Sport, Zen by Bresciani, and Cashmere Collection.

❑ The company has sales agents in about 20 countries, including China, the United Arab Emirates, and South

Africa. In the U.S., there are only 6 states out of 50 in which its products are not distributed.

Bricaire Corinne (1944). French designer. In 1973 she launched a prêt-à-porter brand for women: cotton for Summer and pure wool for Winter, pastel-colored with artisan-made dyes. In 1964 she was the assistant of the Italian designer of Yugoslav origin Boza Kosàak. Then she was put in charge of fashion at the Galeries Lafayette. In 1967 she became a designer for Promostyl. In 1974 she opened her own boutique in the area of Les Halles. Starting at the end of the 1980s she was a designer of women's knitwear at Nina Ricci.

Bric's Italian leather manufacturer. It was established in 1952 by Mario Briccola, in Olgiate Comasco. At that time, the corporate name was Industria Valigeria Fine. Eight years later it built its first industrial plant and created a commercial network for distribution. By the early 1970s, the brand was already known on the Italian market for its suitcases, and the firm began the transformation and reorganization that culminated at the end of the 1980s with a generational change that saw the entrepreneurial commitment of Mario's six sons. The company still maintains its customary management. Since that time, the company's growth has been constant. A commercial agreement concluded in the 1990s with the brands The Sac, Kipling, and Tumi completed and expanded the commercial structure. In 1995 the first Bric's stores were opened, with the very first in Milan, on via Dogana. From 1998 to 2002 more stores were opened in Düsseldorf, Catania, Rome, Paris, Kitzbühel, Montercarlo, and Seoul. The most recent is the store on Corso Vittorio Emanuele, the second one in Milan, and a kiosk at Malpensa Airport. For 2002 the turnover was €30,000. Bric's manufactures 500,000 pieces a year, and employs 200 workers. In March 2003 an agreement was concluded with Pininfarina concerning three product lines, rigid suitcases, soft suitcases, and leather goods and briefcases.

The Bridge Florence-based leather goods manufacturer. It has been present on the market since 1969 and in 1996 it passed the 60 billion-lira level in turnover, with nearly half of that in exports. Some 60 percent of sales is split equally between small leather goods and women's handbags. The share for men's leather goods is currently 26 percent.

Brigatti Shop in Milan selling sportswear, clothing, and accessories, in a style that is classic, if not pure English. It is located on Corso Venezia. In Milan, especially for well-off consumers, it is almost an institution, like panettone, or the Galleria Vittorio Emanuele. Established in 1883, Brigatti has always been true to its motto: "Everything for sport.". The original idea belonged to Giulia Brigatti, the mother of the present owner, Giorgio, and the sister of the founders. She created the company's style. A former skating champion, Mrs. Giulia says: "To manage a store of sport articles you have to be a technician, better yet, a champio.". For this reason, as a young man Giorgio Brigatti would climb mountains in Argentina, and now plays golf. At the beginning of the new century, the store was sold to Dolce & Gabbana and Brigatti has ceased operations.

Briggance Tom (1913). American designer. His pieces, of impeccable cut, are considered classics of fashion. After his studies at the Parson's School of Design in New York, and at the Sorbonne in Paris, for 10 years he directed the Collections of the Lord and Taylor department stores. In 1949 he createed his own brand, specializing in beachwear.

Brighton Museum The museum of this British city has a department for clothes, accessories, and fabrics. It owns more than 10,000 pieces and collects mainly material of local manufacture, from the second half of the 18th century up to today. Among the most important items are two costumes from the coronation ceremony of George IV in 1821. Recent acquisitions have been in the sphere of contemporary international fashion, with special attention to British avant-guard.

Brigidini Cristina (1935). She was director of L'Uomo Vogue from 1979 to 1992. She started her career in 1962 as fashion editor at the weekly Marie Claire (Aldo Palazzi

Publishing), which was directed by Antonia Monti, a very demanding editor-in-chief quite capable of having a caption corrected ten times. In 1965 Anna Piaggi and Anna Riva called her to Arianna, a new trendy monthly published by Mondadori. She was also in charge at Quaderni di Arianna (Arianna's Exercise Books) together with chief-editor Fausto Carulli. Still with Mondadori, she moved to Linea Italiana, the official magazine of Italian fashion, and there, in time, she became deputy manager. In 1979 Franco Sartori appointed her director of L'Uomo Vogue. She was the first woman to direct a specialized men's magazine. Under her leadership the monthly had great success in international circulation and advertising revenue. In 1992, after almost 13 years, she left L'Uomo Vogue, and Marco Rivetti, the president of Pitti Immagine, offered her a consulting job as press office and special project supervisor, a position that she still holds alongside Sibilla della Gherardesca, director of public relations.

Brigitte German magazine particularly interested in the new trends of international fashion. Published by Verlag Gruner and Jahr AG Co. of Hamburg, the magazine is aimed at young readers and offers them models and guides with which to make clothes at home. It is descended from Das Blatt Gehört der Hausfrau (The Housewife's Magazine), published in 1886 by Schirmer Edition of Berlin. In 1954 it became a bimonthly, with an average circulation of more than one million copies. In 1970 it merged with the fashion magazine Constanze.

❑ Today, Brigitte, separated from Constanze and transformed into a biweekly, is one of the most popular magazines in Germany. It is directed by Nina Grygoriew.

Brilliantine Fabric, known in French as brillantine, brillanté, or sablé. It has the same characteristics as poplin, but with very tiny patterns made shiny by a varied development of threads against an opaque background. It is usually manufactured in cotton.

Brin Irene. Pseudonym of Maria Vittoria Rossi (1914-1969), an Italian journalist and writer. She was born in Sasso di Bordighera, in the same house where she died at the young age of 55. She belonged to an upper middle-class family, her father a general, her mother an Austrian noblewoman. She started her career as a journalist signing her pieces Mariù, at the Giornale di Genova and at Lavoro. Leo Longanesi appreciated her brilliant, acute, and cultivated articles (her favorite authors, always quoted, were Saint-Simon, Proust, and Musil) so much that he wanted her immediately at Omnibus, the first weekly magazine published in Italy on the eve of World War II and almost immediately shut down by the Fascist regime. He invented the pseudonym by which she would become famous. Her perfect knowledge of foreign languages, a subtle and kind sense of humor added to a special sense of intuition, not to mention her great style, all combined to immediately make her the first great journalist of costume in a small and provincial Italy. These extraordinary qualities of hers are best exemplified in *Usi e Costumi 1920-1940*, published in Rome in 1944 by Donatello De Luigi. She married Gasparo Del Corso, a brilliant officer and owner of the art gallery L'Obelisco. Together, they were the first to introduce Rome to the works of Cocteau, Matta, Magritte, and Dalí. Donna Irene, as her friends called her, was very beautiful and extremely myopic, but abhorred glasses; she always dressed in a sophisticated and nonconformist way. The apartment in Palazzo Torlonia where she lived, furnished with black velvet couches, Coromandel screens, and splendid modern paintings, reflected her refined taste. Other than writing a widely read advice column for the weekly La Settimana Incom, which she signed "Countess Clara," she worked for various Italian magazines such as Bellezza, and for American magazines as well. She was a real talent scout and struggled so that Italian tailors could throw off their Parisian oppressors. Bista Giorgini, the inventor of the Florentine runways that launched the Made in Italy movement, found in her an intelligent ally. In order to make the great Italian tailoring shops of the post-World War II period known across the Atlantic, she organized "8 Countesses 8," a tour through America in which eight very beautiful and aristocratic Roman ladies turned themselves into fashion models. In her book *Lato Debole*, Camilla Cederna wrote about her: "I met her one Summer in Liguria a very long time ago, in a mittel-Europa kind of hotel that no longer exists. She was extremely beautiful with very pale eyes wide open on a world that she observed untiringly. She was very young and already had a column, every Sunday, in Il Lavoro of Genoa. It was just a few sentences about facts, events, and meetings, signed Mariù. Was that half column enough to make it obvious that the first Italian journalist had been born, and to stir admiration, envy, and a lot of suspicion ... in those years when a woman who wrote would imitate Tuscan writers such as Nunziata and Bista while making the bed (*abballinare le matarassa*); or, withdrawn into her own provincialism, would sort out rustic escapes with the farm manager, or crazy run-ins with satanic violinists; if she wasn't telling stories about wretched adventures with aviators and sheiks; or, from the purple pages of some periodical, would suggest for readers a light blue taffeta for a beautiful bed blanket? ... She was the first one to sense and to identify, with painful bitterness, and especially to write about, the mean acts of second-raters and social climbers, and their small balancing acts, the hypocrisies and stupid stratagems of the falsely generous ... She was a modest person, had great dignity, but was extremely discreet; she didn't realize that for Italian journalism she was a master, an example, and a pioneer. No one had ever heard her talking about herself,

Irene Brin portrayed by Fulvio Bianconi (from *La Sala Bianca – La nascita della moda italiana*, Electa – Pitti Immagine 1992). Archive Giovanni Battista Giorgini.

except if just in passing, or with laughter." In 1981 the publishing house Sellerio reissued *Usi e Costumi 1920-1940*, followed in 1991 by *Dizionario del successo, dell'insuccesso e dei luoghi comuni*, and *Le Visite,* and in 1994 by *Cose viste 1938-1939*.

(*Adalberto Cremonese*)

Brioni Men's tailor established in Rome in 1945 under the name Atelier Brioni. The firm grew, transformed itself, and expanded in 1960 with the opening of a factory in Penne, Abruzzi, the hometown of one of the two founders, Nazareno Fonticoli. This was the first example of a tailor's shop organized on industrial lines. The name was Brioni Roman Style. After more than half a century, the firm produces several different lines and continues to manufacture custom-made suits in single-brand boutiques all over the world, from New York to Milan. From the beginning, everything was due to the initiative of Fonticoli, a master tailor from Abruzzi, and of Gaetano Savini, a Roman designer, who decided, after World War II, to restore and revitalize the tradition of Italian men's tailoring. As a child, while attending elementary school, Fonticoli would sew trousers on piecework, one pair a day, to help his family financially. He went to Rome, where he became a master cutter at Satos, a shop in via del Corso. There he met Savini, who managed sales and customer service: a marketing manager, one would say today. It is uncertain which one convinced the other. Probably, Gateano showed some hesitancy in contrast to the outgoing Nazareno. In 1945, they opened a men's tailoring shop in via Barberini and called it Brioni, after the Dalmatian island which had been a fashionable spot during the war and had become synonym for elegance, *la dolce vita,* and dandyism. They had an almost immediate success that was fueled by two extraordinary events. One was the renewed international prominence of Rome, especially with the use of the Cinecittà studios by the big American filmmakers. It was in this atmosphere that the antennas of a monthy magazine attentive to changes in costume and fashion were activated. In the November 1958 issue, a correspondent wrote: "The most surprising phenomenon of post-war men's fashion is the emergence of Italy as the principal center of tailoring on an international level. Rome has replaced London as the most important destination for those who want to dress well." The second event was the launch of the "made in Italy" movement. This came from an idea by Giovanni Battista Giorgini to offer the first presentation of fashions created specifically in Italy and not subject to the dominance of French designers. It took place in February 1951 in Florence. Already by January 1952 clothes made by Brioni "walked" arm-in-arm with those of Simonetta, the Fontana sisters, Germana Marucelli, Jole Veneziani, Noberasco, Schuberth, and Carosa in the Giorgini's third *Italian High Fashion Show*. The buyer for the big department store B. Altman & Co. of New York took notice of this and devoted the store's windows to Brioni's shantung smoking jackets. Some months later, during a very hot July, the runway of the Sala Bianca at Palazzo Pitti, which would become an icon in the history of Italian fashion, hosted the first men's Collections presentation during the fourth *Italian High Fashion Show*. It was at that moment that Brioni became one of the pioneers of "Made in Italy." Since then, for twenty-five years, Brioni, as a tailor shop and as Brioni Roman Style, has been a major figure in more than 400 presentations in 48 countries. In 1955 an article in Life magazine defined Broni as "the Dior of men's clothing." The New York Times spoke of the atelier as the inventor of "a new men's look" and the Boston Herald described it as the leader of a "second Italian Renaissance." In 1980, when tailoring as a profession was beginning to disappear, Brioni Roman Style founded, in Penne, a school to teach cutting, with four-year courses meant to produce master tailors. It was a big investment, not only in terms of money but above all in ideas. The question was how to organize a school which could revive and strengthen traditional tailoring, yet also take into account the twenty-year entrepreneurial culture of Brioni Roman Style which modernized the roots of that tradition. In that time, while keeping manual ability (in drawing, cutting, preparation stitching, basting, hems, button sewing, and finishing) as the focus of its artisanal skill, the firm has been able to reduce the time needed to "build" a suit from 45 to 20 hours, perfecting the division of work according to everyone's particular aptitudes, selecting the personnel, and improving the system. Twenty hours against an average of two and-a-half or three in the manufacturing industry, which explains a lot about the tailoring content of a Brioni suit. In 1988 Brioni was awarded the *Premio Pitti* for its contribution to the development of Italian fashion throughout the world. In 1990, after the acquisition of a series of manufacturing mills and other production units, the Brioni Group was born, consisting of eight plants with 1,700 workers. Half a century of life was celebrated in Florence, on the occasion of Pitti Uomo, with a big retrospective in Palazzo Corsini. In that year of 1995, the atelier was given the task of manufacturing the wardrobe for the newest James Bond, the actor Pierce Brosnan. He was only the most recent of many actors, artists and politicians who have chosen custom-made Brioni suits, including Clark Gable, John Wayne, Henry Fonda, Totò, Robert Wagner, Severino Gazzelloni, and Nelson Mandela. In the last years of the 1990s, the consolidated average turnover of the Group, directed by the general manager Umberto Angeloni, was 100 billion liras.

(*Gianluca Bauzano*)

A Brioni suit, 1956.

❑ 2000. Launch of the first women's Collection on the runway of Spring-Summer 2001.
❑ 2001. The Group's turnover is €150.337 million. It was €118.302 million in 2000 and €105.369 in 1999. The gross operating margin was more than €23 million.
❑ 2002, February. The opening in Milan, at via del Gesù, of a women's boutique. In September, Brioni Donna also opened boutiques in Rome and New York.
❑ 2002, July. The opening of the first men's boutique in Tokyo, on the Ginza.
❑ 2002, August. At the Düsseldorf Salon, Brioni receives the European Fashion Diamond, a prize which Ingedo Company has awarded since 1989 to companies and professionals who distinguish themselves for performance and management.
❑ 2002, December. The premiere of the 20th film in the 007 series. James Bond still wears Brioni creations.
❑ 2002. Brioni ends the year with a consolidated turnover of €157 million. Export represents 80%. The U.S. is the primary market.
❑ 2003, June. Always in the vanguard of industrial "custom made," Brioni opens, on via del Gesù in Milan, a real tailoring workshop that employs 10 people, including workers and cutters. There are 23 single-brand boutiques all over the world. (*Pierangelo Mastantuono*)

Brissaud Pierre (1885-1964). French illustrator, painter and engraver with a marked taste for fashion to the point of being quickly defined as "peintre de l'élégance." Born in Paris, he graduated from the École des Beaux Arts. He then worked with the most prestigious fashion magazines of his time: Vogue, Monsieur, La Gazette du Bon Ton, Fémina, and Jardin des Modes. His sketches, recognizable for their great attention to detail, reveal a classic style and a soft hand. They are created with a peculiar ability to trap the light in a chiaroscuro effect. His activity as an illustrator began in the steps of his older brother Jacques and of his uncle Maurice Boutet, who was famous for his drawings inspired by the fables of La Fontaine. In 1907, he exhibited his first works at the Salon des Independants.

British Warm Military Winter coat. Umpteenth example of clothe deriving from armies' uniforms. It's the overcoat of English officers during the first world conflict. Manufactured in heavy fabric (camel, cashmere or wool) is lightly shaped to fit the silhouette. Dropping at least to knees, if not longer, can be single or double breasted with large pockets, deep lapels and leather buttons. This piece has inspired several designers, both for man and woman.

Britt Jacques Manufacturing company established in 1969 in Bielefeld, Germany. It belongs to the Seidensticker Group and distributes its clothes in twenty different countries. Its most important showrooms, in addition to those in Berlin and Monaco, are in Geneva, London, Zurich, Moscow and Amsterdam, all dedicated to men's clothing. Among its lines are the Silver brand, which indicates the most elegant clothes; the White brand, which is more casual; and the Black, for the trendiest wardrobe.

Brocade Precious fabric that dates to the 15th century, processed on a jacquard loom and relief-embroidered with gold and silver threads. Used first in furnishings, starting in the second half of the 1800s it was very successful in fashion and used to manufacture clothes, cloaks, tunics, and trousers for elegant evening outfits.

Brochier French textile company, established in 1890 by Jean Brochier in Villeurbanne. His son Joseph, in the early 1920s, began a major expansion with the acquisition of a weaving mill. In 1969 the company split into two different units. One was Brochier Silk, now a subsidiary of the Ratti Group. It specialized in textile fibers for high fashion, in the tradition of Lyon. The second unit, Brochier & Sons, is today a subsidiary of the Ciba-Geigy Group. In European it is a leader in chemical compounds, and produces only highly technical fabrics, providing the clothing for space programs.

Broda Doby (1959). French designer. At the

age of 24 she presented her own first Collection, after learning the trade with Andrevie and Gaultier. Since then, she has alternated her own Collections with designer activity for third parties such as Billy Bon, Charles Maudret, Nicole Olivier (bathing suits), and Bergère de France (knitwear). In 1990 she arrived in Japan with a Collection designed expressly for that market.

Brodovitch Alexey (1898-1971). Art director, photographer, painter, illustrator and teacher. Born in Russia (St. Petersburg), he has worked mostly in America. His almost thirty years at Harper's, from 1934 to 1958, left a deep mark on the world of fashion magazines for his choice of daring and innovative solutions in the field of graphic layout and photography. Outstanding was his influence on an entire generation of young art directors and photographers, starting with Irving Penn, his assistant in 1939 when Brodovitch was artistic director at the New York department store Sacks Fifth Avenue. The son of a psychiatrist and a painter, due to the outbreak of World War I he was unable to attend the Academy of Fine Arts in Saint Petersbur and had to enter the military. After the Russian Revolution, he moved to Paris where Diaghilev asked him to paint stage sets for his ballet company. He was, in those years, a theorist of applied art. Then he emigrated to America. The Museum School of Industrial Design in Philadelphia hired him to give classes on advertising. Shortly after, he began his long career at Harper's. In 1945 he published the photography book *Ballet*, which he dedicated to Diaghilev. From 1947 to '49 Richard Avedon made his studio available to him for a workshop on design. In 1959 he worked with Avedon on his book *Observations*, which had a preface by Truman Capote. In 1966 he moved to Paris where, 16 years later, thanks to the photographer Georges Tourdjman, a student of his, there would be a large exhbit dedicated to him. His generous style is recognizable both in the page layout of the magazines he directed and in the concept of space that characterizes the exhibits he organized. There is the use of Bodoni type in capital letters, the idea of not making two similar pages one after the other, and the knowledge that the art director is much more effective when his "signature" is discreet. Though having a very strong character – it was not by chance that Penn would recall his teacher's early experience as an officer in the Czar's army – Brodovitch represented the prototype of the brave and cultivated man, able to instill confidence in young talent, even if not famous yet. In 2002, the publisher Phaidon dedicated a large monograph to him.

(*Roberto Mutti*)

Brody Neville (1957). One of those designers who revolutionized typographic art and graphic design. Educated at the London College of Printing, after graduation he was in charge of graphics for Cabaret Voltaire and became art director at Fetish Records, editing the artwork for the albums of unknown rock bands. As an art director in the early 1980s he was responsible for the image of the magazines The Face, City Limit, and Arena, in the process renewing English graphic design, and not only the "underground" media. In 1987 he opened his own shop, the Research Studio, which in a short time became the indispensable point of reference for anyone interested in graphics. In 10 years of success he designed logos for the German Cable TV Première, Orf, the Dutch Postal Service, the Haus der Kulturen der Welt in Berlin, the Park in Japan, and Greenpeace. In Italy, he was in charge of graphics for various magazines, including the monthly founded by Flavio Lucchini, Lei. Along with the publication of the book *The Graphic Language of Neville Brody* in 1988 there was an exhibit of his work which traveled to the principal European capitals, making him known throughout the world. The contents of the exhibit would form the basis of a monograph. In those years he founded Fuse (Font Works und Font Shop International), an organization which for the last decade of the 1900s dominated the international graphic scene. In 1994 *The Graphic Language of Neville Brody 2* was published. This groups all his work made after 1988. With the advent of computer graphics, he expanded his field of interest and professional experiences, creating the most varied and versatile visual languages used in the world of electronic telecommunications. (*Stefano Grassi*)

❑ Toward the end of the 1990s he

worked with the Austrian DMC in the field of design and TV networks, while in Japan he was hired by Digitalogue for a series of CD-ROM's.

❑ Among recent clients are Nike, Adidas-Salomon, Mont Blanc, and the Museum of Modern Art in New York.

❑ The publication of *The Graphic Language of Neville Brody 2* coincides with an exhibit dedicated to him by the Victoria and Albert Museum in London. It was one of the largest tributes organized by that museum in honor of pop culture.

Brooks Donald (1928). New York designer and costume maker. He was among the first during the 1960s to propose the fashion of pajamas and evening trousers. To him is due, among other things, credit for the relaunch of the blouse. After his studies in English literature at the School of Fine Arts at Syracuse University between 1947 and '49, he attended the Parson's School of Design. His work in theater and cinema is characterized by the creation of costumes for the Broadway comedy *Barefoot in the Park* (1962) and for the movies *The Cardinal* (1963) and *Fireball Jungle* (1968).

Brooks Louise (1906-1985). American actress. She was an icon who influenced fashion, comics, and cinema with a face framed by the neat cut of her black hair. With bangs, deep eyes, and pearly complexion, she was a very beautiful Lulù at the end of the 1920s, in an intense though short appearance. Success arrived after two films shot in Germany thanks to George Wilhelm Pabst, who wanted her as the disturbing main characters of *Pandora's Box* (1928), and *Das Tagebuch einer Verlorenen* (1929). There were more films, of little importance, which didn't last, this time shot in Hollywood. But suddenly during the 1930s she was taken as a model for the character of Dixie Dugan in the comic strip of the same name by John Striebel. Guido Crepax was inspired by her to invent his Valentina. Other cinematographic tributes came from Godard who, in *Vivre sa vie* (1962) used the Louise Brooks hairdo for his protagonist Anna Karina; and from Bob Fosse in *Cabaret* (1972), when he used her "look" as the basis for the character Sally Bowles, played by Liza Minelli. That same hairdo, but in red, was given to the singer Milva by Giorgio Strehler for the character of Pirate Jenny in a new production of Brecht's *The Threepenny Opera* at the Piccolo Teatro dell'Opera.

Brooks Brothers One of the country's oldest retailers, Brooks Brothers was founded in 1818, when Henry Sands Brooks opened his first store, H. & D. H. Brooks & Co., in New York City. Over the years the company developed both retail operations and its own manufacturing business, and in 1845 the firm introduced the country's first ready-made suits. It also continued to create hand-tailored clothing, and supplied suits to dignitaries and presidents including Abraham Lincoln, who was wearing a coat handmade for him by Brooks Brothers the night he was assassinated.

The company revolutionized the American male wardrobe, often drawing for inspiration on classic British designs. Their innovations included silk foulard neckties, polo coats (introduced for men, but soon adopted by girls and women as well), Harris Tweed jackets, Shetland sweaters, Argyle socks and button-down collars on shirts, inspired by British polo shirts, which became the firm's signature product and one of its long-standing best-sellers. When the country introduced British club ties in 1945, they reversed the direction of the diagonal stripes, thus creating the American repp tie. The firm opened its first women's department in 1949, and has since branched into childrenswear and accessories.

Over the years the company dressed male icons from Clark Gable to John F. Kennedy, and became identified, particularly in the late 20th century, with a cosseted conservative east coast style of dressing familiarly known as "preppie" or "Ivy League."

❑ 2001. Claudio Del Vecchio, President and owner of the Retail Brand Alliance, pays Marks & Spencer 225 million dollars for the brand. The agreement includes the acquisition of 242 single-brand shops.

❑ 2003. Brooks Brothers counts 160 shops in the USA, and 67 in Japan, among others. Annual turnover tops 600 million dollars, with 5 million shirts produced yearly.

❑ 2003, April. Brooks Brothers ends its two-year old collaboration with Diego Della Valle, owner of Tod's.

Brooksfield Brand of prêt-à-porter fashion belonging to the Mistral company which, established in 1971 by Umberto Maria Monasteri, initially produced and distributes only men's trousers. The headquarters is in Mocalieri, near Turin. Changes in the market convinced the ownership to expand production in the direction of a British style total look. During the 1980s the company's identity began to be defined around the Brooksfield brand, as part of constant expansion. In 1985 the brand launched a women's line. In the early 1990s, it started a licensing program which developed a perfume (Eurocosmesi), eye glasses (Lastes International), a children's line (Simonetta), and leather goods (Basso Leather). The company, of which 82% is held by the Luxembourg financial company Caesar Finance, has sales of roughly 40 billion liras, 70% of which is in the home market and for the remaining 30% abroad. The annual production of garments, partly commissioned by third parties, amounts to 460,000 pieces. It employs about 50 workers. There are about 300 authorized points-of-sale for men's wear and 140 for women's, distributed in Europe, the Philippines, Japan and Venezuela. There are ten single-brand shops in Europe, including one in Milan.

❑ 2001. Signature of a license agreement with Karichi for manufacture and distribution in Japan. The agreement provides for the opening of 33 points-of-sale and 10 outlets. An agreement is also concluded with the Turkish company Bilsar Tekstil Sanaya, which will open 30 corner shops and 45 outlets within 2006.
❑ 2002. The opening of a headquarters for Mistral in the Soho district of New York foresees an expansion in the U.S. market which should have effects in South America and the Caribbean as well.
❑ 2003. Mistral, of which Brooksfield is the leading brand, ends 2002 with a turnover of around €30 million, an increase of 18% compared to the previous year, thanks in part to the début of the Moncalieri brand in the U.S.

Brosseau Jean-Charles (1929). French milliner and designer. He opened his own maison in 1960, putting his long experience to good use, creating hats for Jean Barthet, for the great couturier Jacques Fath, and for the dressmaker Paulette. He not only worked as an apprentice in a workshop, but also studied at the Chambre Syndicale de la Haute Couture. His flexible chapeau-bonnet was famous. In the 1970s he began to be interested in prêt-à-porter, sketching models for himself and for third parties. Starting in 1990 he had his own boutique in Rue de l'Université.

Brovkina Olga (1970). Russian designer. After graduating from the School of Design in her own country, she received many awards and acknowledgements, until she finally arrived, in 1996, on the coveted prêt-à-porter runways of Milan. She involved herself with avant-guard clothes which amazed and, at the same time, fascinated. She has undoubted talent, is a master of the most disparate fabrics which she skillfully matches while inventing new patchwork. It is a style often taken to the extreme, playing on the alternation of fabrics, patterns, and colors. Hers is a repertory of high-potential seduction, with daringly elegant and witty women. (*Lucia Mari*)

Browns Trendy and avant-guard London boutique. Opened by Joan and Sidney Berstein in 1970, it also manufactures a clothing line. Over 30 years, the first shop on South Molton Street was followed by others on the same street, on Brook Street, and on Sloan Street.

Bruccoleri Franco (1944). Distributor and commercial agent, he opened markets in Germany and northern Europe for Italian clothing manufacturers and contributed to the success of Italian prêt-à-porter. In the mid 1970s he began to introduce groups such as Benetton, GFT, Breco's, and Zamasport to those markets. Near the end of that decade, he was the "ambassador" of great designers such as Armani, Valentino, Fendi, Krizia, and Prada to shops, boutiques and department stores. In 1987 he organized the first exhibition of Italian fashion in Berlin's Reichstag. The Made in Italy movement was fed by the hard work and commercial intuition of people like Bruccoleri.

❑ 2003, March. Together with Franco Pené and Aldo Palmieri he succeeds in convincing Roberto Capucci to return to the runways, although indirectly, after twenty years of absence. It was the birth of Capucci Corporate, of which the maestro owns a portion. The design team, led by the German Bernhard Wilhelm, aimed to reinterpret, in prêt-à-porter, the tradition of the *maison*. Bruccoleri is appointed president of the company.
❑ In May, he is part of the jury of Design Against Fur!, which, during an event at the Capucci showroom in Milan, gives an award to the best advertising campaign against the use of furs, with entries from 559 students at design schools all over the world.

Bruce American brand started in 1998 by designers Nicole Noselli (1971) and Daphne Gutierrez (1971). They both studied at the Parson's School of Design in New York and, after Noselli worked in the atelier of Isaac Mizrahi and Gutierrez worked in the atelier of Donna Karan, they decided to create their own line together. In their studio apartment on the Lower East Side, Bruce came into being, a Collection consisting of only seven pieces. Today, the brand is well known in the world of New York's "alternative" fashion.

Bruce Liza (1955). American designer working in London. She began her career around 1982, designing bathing suits with Rosemary Moore. She became famous (and very much imitated) for her bathing suits in avant-guard fibers such as Lycra which mould the body. Her style, devoid of useless decoration, emphasized the body through neat and precise lines: hers was a modern and aggressive femininity inspired by the bodybuilder Lisa Lyons. She launched the Speedo fashion of stirrup slacks and fluorescent colors which continued through the 1980s. In 1988 she created a women's prêt-à-porter line. With changing fashions and a passage from the cult of the body to the spiritual sensitivity of the 1990s, she lost her status as an innovator and suffered financial difficulties which, in 1999, forced her to close.

❑ In early 1999 she opens, with her husband Nicholas Alvis Vega, a boutique in Los Angeles, on Silver Lake Boulevard.
❑ She launches a new women's line of swimming costumes for Dorothy Perkins.

Bruhel Anton (1900-1982). Australian photographer of German origin. In 1919 he moved to New York where he worked for Western Electric. In 1923, visiting an exhibit of work by students of Clarence White, he became interested in photography. He enrolled in a course and, in 1925, decided to quit his study of engineering in order to become a professional photographer. His first pictures were published in 1926 by The New Yorker, but his fame is tied to his work with Vogue, started in that same year and lasting for four decades. Very famous are the color photos he created with the collaboration of Fernand Bourges, a color technician at Condé Nast who, starting in 1932, invented a process capable of creating very sharp photo transparencies. In January 1936, Vanity Fair, the other magazine with which he worked, published his color portrait of Marlene Dietrich, which for a long time would serve as her iconic image. Among the unusual results of his work were several Christmas cards he created for his editor and for himself. In 1966 he retired to Florida where, in 1970, he published a book about trees with several close-up shots titled *Tropic Patterns*.

Brunel Mireille Etienne (1951). French designer. She captured the attention of the media for her use of very unusual materials such as the jute used for mail bags (the French ones have large red stripes) and railroad sleeper-car blankets. When, in 1979, she and her husband decided to launch the brand Etienne Brunel, which is also the name of her boutique in Lyon, she had already completed her studies at the school of the Chambre Syndicale de la Couture in

Paris. Since 1982 she has had a showroom in Paris, and in 1991 she arrived in Japan with a line created expressly for that market.

> ❑ 2002. At the fifth edition of the design salon Palace d'Or, she presented some treasure-chest-clothes created with materials obtained from luxury manufacturing.
> ❑ 2003, June. Mireille and her collaborator Rachel offer to their clientele the possibility of transforming any white dress into an evening outfit. The process of dyeing, cutting, and sewing has a cost starting at €600.

Brunelleschi Umberto (1879-1949). Italian illustrator, painter and costume maker. He worked for the fashion periodicals Fémina, Gazette du Bon Ton, and the Journal des Dames et des Modes. But his name was above all linked to the vaudeville costumes of Joséphine Baker, the black Venus, and for the shows staged between the two world wars at theatres all over the world, from La Scala of Milan to the Folies Bergères, the Casino, and the Chatelet in Paris, to the Roxy in New York. His style was strongly influenced by the prevailing climate and fashions: Liberty style, orientalism, and Art Deco. The main color of his palette was blue. Once past the exaggerations of Art Deco, he attained a cleaner line, reduced to essentials. He began at the Academy of Fine Arts in Florence, and later concentrated on studies of the nude. In 1900, he moved to Paris where, in order to earn a living he worked as a caricaturist under the pseudonym Harun-al Rashid. He worked at L'Assiette au Beurre together with Paul Iribe. From 1903 to 1910 he participated in the Paris Salons as a painter. In 1914 he returned to Italy, but later settled in Paris for good. In the last part of his life he worked only as a book illustrator, in particular on erotic limited editions.

Brunello Cucinelli Company for prêt-à-porter fashion, specialized in cashmere. It is named after its founder, who established it in Solomeo, Umbria in 1978. It comprises three brands: Brunello Cucinelli (men's and women's knitwear), Rivamonti (women's knitwear), and Gunext (women's skirts and trousers). The company exports 68% of what it manufactures. The turnover is more than 63 billion liras. It has three operating plants and showrooms in Milan, New York, Paris, Düsseldorf, and Osaka. It produces 390,000 pieces a year.

Brunetta Mateldi (1904-1988). Italian sketcher, illustrator and painter. "I knew Brunetta also before the war, I mean, I would meet her here and there, small, thin, and turning left-and-right on high heels, with very green eyes heavily made-up (she reminded me of Colette), hidden by very beautiful and eccentric hats that she often manufactured on her own. But my very first meeting with Brunetta occurred during the first year of the war, in Bagutta, the Milanese trattoria where, in 1927, the ancestor of the Italian literature awards was born. I had been admitted to the famous table shortly before. That evening I wore a cognac-colored velvet tricorn hat with a chenille dotted veil. Seated in front of me, Brunetta

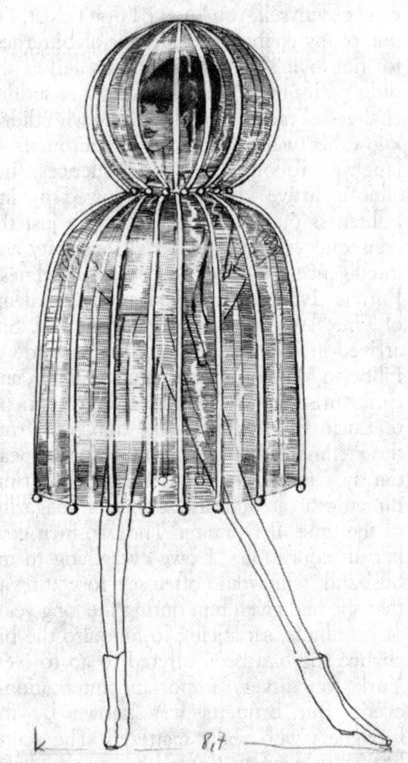

A Sketch by Brunetta (Biki Collection).

asked me to raise the veil and within ten minutes she did a delicious sketch of me without any caricature. "My third eye didn't really capture anything which could give rise to a malicious caricature." She didn't need a third eye, she had radar. She amazed me when I saw her at the presentations, in the theater, or in the street. Her sketches were extremely precise and yet more real than reality. Her drawings of designs by Balenciaga had a more Spanish air than the original drawings done by Cristobal himself. One day, I told her so. She answered: "My eyes are like certain lenses, with the focal point which captures the most unusual, aggressive or hidden detail." For this reason, she was able to transform the most common people into personalities: she undressed them and dressed them again through her pencil, as they wanted and had to be in order to represent that type, that dress, that environment. Perhaps she applied that implacable lens also to herself, because once, looking at herself in a mirror, she told me: "I can't see myself, you know? I don't exist, I'm one of my characters." Humor or bitterness for not loving herself as she was and as she didn't want to be seen? For sure, her sudden changes of mood often left those who didn't know her well confused. Her outbursts of laughter followed by long silences, her almost furtive kindnesses followed by impoliteness or violent protests, were just the consequences of an extreme sensitivity and intelligence, and of a terrible loneliness. Born in Ivrea, she studied at the Academy of Fine Arts in Turin and in Bologna. She arrived in Milan as the very young bride of Filiberto Mateldi, a set designer, painter, and caricaturist. Her husband was a great friend of Lucio Ridenti, who, like him, was from the Piedmont. Ridenti was the last European dandy, and the founder and longtime director of an important theater magazine of the time, Il Dramma. The two men gave her an education. "I owe everything to my husband," she would often say, forgetting all that she had given him during the long years of his illness, sacrificing to him also the big chance she had been offered to go to New York for a very important international event. But Brunetta was known by the foreigners who really mattered. The acute, lively, Irishwoman Carmel Snow, the director of Harper's Bazaar, was the first to open the pages of her beautiful magazine to her. During the presentations in Paris, she wanted Brunetta to make sketches for her, "because there isn't a more inspired interpreter than Brunetta." Pierre Cardin had such high esteem of her that he organized an exhibition of her work at his Espace: "She isn't simply an interpreter of fashion, she can recreate it with genius." He was right because her sketches mirrored the inexorable back and forth of time, the changes and the thefts of these years. She left precious booklets and notes for sketches that are more revealing that the diaries of Goncourt: they are a visual witness that ranges from the society of the Hotel de Paris in Montecarlo to the anonymous people in the Jardin de Luxembourg, from De Chirico to Joséphine Baker, and from Twiggy to the Italian mothers in the time of Mussolini. Orio Vergani wrote: "Drawing and painting are instinctive in her. To draw she would use ash or blush. She would draw using the powder on butterfly wings. But instinct isn't much if it is not guided by a feeling, which isn't that so-called sensitivity, or the beat of a heart. This feeling is our ability to measure life, not in the way drawing mathematically measures an eye, a hand, an arm, but life, the power of that eye, hand, and arm. This is how Brunetta's sketches and watercolors were born. They aren't "women's sketches" or plain references to fashion, but stories of women, tales of an hour of femininity, with the whole mystery of its coquetries and melancholies." *(Maria Pezzi)*

Brunhoff (de) Michel (1892-1958). French journalist. He discovered young talents such as Saint-Laurent and Bourdin, of whom he published the first photograph, in Vogue. In 1912, with Lucien Vogel, he founded the Gazette du Bon Ton. In 1920 he married Cosetta Vogel, Lucien's sister, and with her he founded Illustration de la Mode. Though he kept his position at Illustration de la Mode until 1933, he also worked on Jardin des Modes, and, in 1929, he founded Vogue France, which he would direct until his death.

Bruni Pasquale (1949). Italian jeweler. Born in Calabria, he emigrated to Northern Italy, and at the age of 13 had his first experience in the goldsmiths' workshops of Valenza. In

1969 he opened his own workshop. In 1976 he founded Gioielmoda, creating a jewellery line that is widely distributed, with 300 points-of-sale worldwide. Since 1994 he has had two shops in Tokyo. He has a showroom in Milan's fashion district, on via della Spiga.

> ❑ 2002, December. The opening of the new space on via della Spiga. It is a single-brand shop with 800 square feet, designed by the London firm David Chipperfield Architects.
> ❑ The firm's production is distributed in more than 500 points-of-sale all over Europe, the U.S., and Japan.

Bruni Tedeschi Carla (1968). Top model and singer, born in Turin, with green eyes, brown hair, and 5'8" tall. She started her career as a model at the age of 19, after leaving the study of art and architecture in Paris. She was launched into the firmament of top models by Paul Marciano, who noticed her among several aspiring models and chose her for the Guess campaign. She became a leading model and appeared in advertising campaigns for Bluemarine, Caractère, and Christian Dior. She was on the runways of the greatest designers, especially those in Paris, from Chanel to Valentino and Givenchy. She retired from the runways early, even if she continues to present a Collection in Paris every now and then. In 2001 she had a baby, Ottaviano, with her partner Raphael Enthoven. In 2002 she recorded her first album *Quelqun m'a dit* which immediately went to the top of the French charts. (*Silvia Paoli*)

Bruno Guido (1972). Italian shoe designer, born in Como. His grandfather also created shoes, especially for dancers at La Scala. It was based on his grandfather's models, inherited from him, that Guido began to create his first prototypes. Notwithstanding his education very far outside the world of fashion, and the years of work in his father's computer company, Guido has the work of his grandfather in his DNA. For the Spring-Summer 2000 he presented his first Collection of clogs, shoes, babouches and sandals, very feminine and somewhat inspired by the 1950s. (*Mariacristina Righi*)

Bruno Vanessa (1967). French designer. She continues a family tradition. At the age of 24, she made her début with a line which, in 1995, was followed by the brand Athé. In 1997 Bon Marché dedicated an exclusive space to her and, in that year, she designed a Collection for La Redoute, a company that sells by mail order. In 1998 she opened four boutiques in Japan and her first boutique in Paris. Modernity, simplicity, and color are the keys to her style.

> ❑ She creates a bag manufactured in calfskin that is aged according to the *besace* process (*besace* is French for bag). In order to promote it, she chooses one of the most loved and well-known French actresses, Emmanuelle Béart.

Bruuns Bazar Behind this brand are the Danish brothers Teis and Bjorn Bruun. Their brand and their first Collection of women's prêt-à-porter made their début in 1995, winning immediate success in their homeland and throughout Scandinavia. Their idea of a natural and casual woman was so appreciated that their clothes were quickly purchased by the great boutiques of northern Europe. In 1999 they presented their Collection in Paris, where they would show up punctually every year thereafter. They have 30 points-of-sale all over the world and some single-brand boutiques, such as the one on Rue Herold in Paris. (*Maddalena Fossati*)

Buccellati Mario (1881-1965). Jeweler. Gabriele D'Annunzio called him the "Prince of Goldsmiths" and predicted that he would be remembered as "Mastro Paragon Coppella." As proof of this friendship there is a book containing letters exchanged by the two men entitled *Caro Mario* (Dear Mario) and published by Scheiwiller. But the poet wasn't his only fan. Buccellati counted among his clients the royal families of Italy, Spain, Belgium, and Egypt, as well as the Queen of England and the Vatican courts of Pius XI and Pius XII. Still a young boy, he was an apprentice in the workshop of Beltrami and Besnati, who were among the most important goldsmiths of the time, in Largo Santa Margherita, in Milan. In 1919 he took over the business, giving it his name. His jewels were inspired by the works of the

16th century, by Burano lace, and by lacework fabrics, while original technical solutions characterized their workmanship. Besides jewellery, he also engraved pochettes, powder compacts, cigarette cases, vases, and cups. After his death, the work was continued by four of his five sons: Lorenzo, in Milan, on via Montenapoleone, and in Florence; Luca, in New York, in the shop on 51st Street; Federico, in the shop in Rome, there since 1925; and Gianmaria, in Paris. Each of them heads a business of his own, absolutely independent in commercial decisions and corporate management.

(*Giuliana Parabiago*)

Bucci Ampelio (1936). After his studies at Bocconi University, he opened a company dedicated to strategic consulting and education, named Mies, which worked mostly for the textile and clothing industries. He directed the Management Sector of Domus Academy, Milan's post-university school of fashion, design and, indeed, management. In the 1980s, on behalf of Group Montefibre, he was director of the Design Center, which tried to anticipate trends and innovation in fashion. In 1994 he was placed in charge of the Italian portion of a European Union research project on employment needs in the European textile industry through 2002. He has been a visiting professor at the Institut Français de la Mode, at the Université Dauphiné, and at the University of Art and Design of Helsinki. He coordinated several exhibitions, including *Il senso della moda* (The Sense of Fashion) at the Triennial of Milan in 1979, *Il consumo culturale* (Cultural Consumption) at the Biennial of Venice in 1981, and *La casa italiana* (The Italian House) at Pitti Immagine Casa in 1997.

❑ 2003, July. He is a lecturer at the project seminar *Designing in Between the Ambiguity* at the Domus Academy. The workshop investigates changes in the field of interior furnishings, one in which the barriers between different products are more and more often eliminated.

Buchinho Luis (1969). Portuguese designer. He made a name for himself by winning Intermoda 1989, a contest for young designers. Since 1990 he has worked as a freelancer for Jotex, Traffic, Ferreira, Matos and Rio, Moda Lisboa, and Portex.

❑ 2002, March. The designer opened the presentation at the Carousel du Louvre for Autumn-Winter 2002-2003 that was dedicated to four Portuguese designers. In that same season, the four designers – Paulo Cravo, Nuno Baltasar, Katty Xiomara, and Luis Buchinho – received encouraging signals from the Far East market, and the runways in Japan and Hong Kong had good results.
❑ The general headquarters of the Portuguese designer is in Porto, on Rua Aires de Ornelas.

Bucol French silk company. It was established in Lyon in 1920 by the entrepreneurial couple Bucher and Colcomber, after whom it was named. It exports some 75% of its turnover to Europe, Japan, and the U.S. It manufactures especially for high fashion and furniture. In 1988 it entered into a partnership with the Porcher Textile Group.

❑ Bucol has an archive with 80,000 different styles accumulated during more than 80 years of activity. It has a staff of 64 employees, distributed between the plant at Bussières, in the Loire, which is specialized in colored yarns, and the administrative headquarters in Lyon, where the design department is also located.

Buddahood A shop, an e-commerce site, and a virtual magazine of fashion. The idea is to give space and visibility to new, creative, and innovative designers. A line of extravagant and avant-guard shoes is the starting point. The shop is in London, on Conduit Street, and it offers, in addition to Buddahood shoes, a selection of clothes created by new, young designers. The e-commerce site is the store's on-line mirror, while the on-line fashion magazine wants to be a reference point for the new trends and promising new products of street wear fashion.

(*Sofia Camerana*)

Buhler Muguette. French model maker. A niece of Louis II of Bavaria, from 1922 to 1959 she worked with some of the greatest

French tailoring shops: Poiret, Vionner, Patou, Augusta Bernard, and Mad Carpentier. She often worked with the sketcher Martiale Constantini (1904-1987). She left 15,000 outlines and sketches which her daughter Rosine donated to the Musée de la Mode et du Textile in Paris. From 1944 to 1949 she was in her own business, launching the brand Mug Deval. (*Roberta Giordano*)

Bui Barbara (1956). French designer. Her *griffe* is distributed in more than 180 points-of-sale worldwide. Her success began with a bet in the early 1980s. An actress looking for work, she opened a small atelier-boutique at Les Halles in Paris with her partner William Halimi, distributing the Kabuki brand, with a wink at the Japanese theater. The bet became a business and the Collection was named after her. In 1997 she offered a new line called B.B.

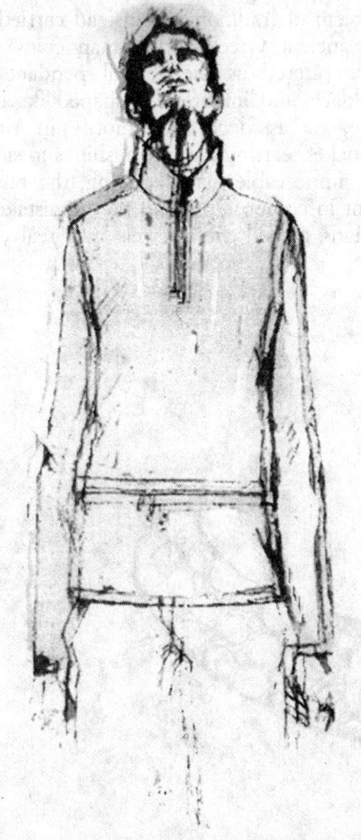

Barbara Bui. Men's Collection, Winter 1999-2000.

❑ She opened boutiques in Paris, on Avenue Montaigne; in Milan, on via Manzoni; and in Soho, in New York. She offered four seasonal Collections: Grande Ligne, Initials, Hommes, and Chaussures. This designer of Vietnamese origin states proudly that she was one of the first to join the new information market.
❑ 2002. The *griffe* has a turnover of €24.5 million compared to €20.3 million the previous year, an increase of 20.6%.
❑ In addition to the fashion activity, there is a Barbara Bui Café, in Rue Etienne Marcel, where it is possible to taste traditional Vietnamese cooking.

Bukowska Krystyna (1936). Polish designer, active especially in France, where she arrived in the early 1960s. Her studies at the School of Decorative Arts in Lodz served as the presentation for a job as sketch artist in the design department of Le Printemps department stores. Shortly after, her sketches were purchased by Zyga Pianko, the creator of the prêt-à-porter brand Pierre D'Alby. She opened a boutique in partnership with other designers at Les Halles, in the premises of an old cheese shop. They sold and mini and maxi skirts, jackets, safari jackets, and artisan-dyed blouses. After the shop was closed, she designed Collections for Japanese manufacturers, presented her designs to the media, and organized the distribution of her products under her own name.

❑ She has a boutique in Paris, in Rue Pont-Louis-Philippe.

Bulega Gianluca (1967). Italian high-fashion designer. His evening dresses are sophisticated in form and materials. He can work with great mastery on metallic organza and stretch tulle. He was born in Rivoli. After a time studying agriculture, in 1993 he went to the European Institute of Fashion Design in Milan, from which he graduated with a thesis written in collaboration with Roberto Capucci. In 1997 he participated in the Biennial of Young Artists of Europe and the Mediterranean that was held in Turin, and in the July of that same year he began to present his models on the high fashion runways of Rome, where he has been a fixed presence ever since. In March 1998 he was at the London Fashion Week. In October 1999 he presented his first prêt-à-porter Collection for Milano Collezioni.

❑ 2002, June. He designs the costumes for the performance of Verdi's opera Luisa Miller which the Toscanini Foundation chose to open the Summer season at Villa Pallavicino in Busseto.
❑ To celebrate the British presidency of the European Union, the Foreign Office and the British Fashion Council organize a fashion presentation to which are invited 27 designers from 14 countries that belong to the Union. Representin Italy are Bulega, Gigliola Curiel, Egon von Fürstenberg, and Antonio Marras.

Bulgari A dynasty of Italian jewelers that started with Sotirio Bulgari, a native of Epirus, who arrived in Italy in 1879 bringing with himself the goldsmith tradition of ancient Greece. In 1885, he opened a shop in Rome, on via Sistina, offering pieces made with both ancient and modern goldsmith techniques. The business developed and, 20 years later, the firm found a new headquarters in via Condotti. Today, the name Bulgari expresses in just one word the concept of classic jewelry modeled according to the new dictates of contemporary taste. Starting in the mid 1900s, the production took on precise and original physical characteristics, the result of the creative commitment and entrepreneurial intuition of Sotirio's two sons, Costantino and Giorgio, who had joined the company's management in the early 1930s. Costantino, interested especially in collecting, started to gather artistic objects, icons, and carved jades, deepening his study of the ancient goldsmith's art. He wrote the book *Argentieri, Gemmari e Orafi* (Silversmiths, Jewelers and Goldsmiths), a fundamental work for knowledge of the Italian goldsmith tradition. Giorgio was put in charge of the commercial management of the company. In the meantime, the jeweler's boutique had become a favorite meeting place of the aristocracy, of rich American tourists traveling to Rome, and of the cinema's international jet set. Introducing the cabochon cut and the use of colored stones set in yellow gold, Bulgari launched a new style of great inventive freedom. The emblem of tradition was instead carried by the ancient Greek and Roman coins that were offered as the central pendants in necklaces and link bracelets shaped like a gas pipe, or as decorative motifs in rings, brooches, earrings, and furnishings in silver. The impeccable manufacturing, the refinement in composition, and the unmistakable designs turned these jewels into real cult-

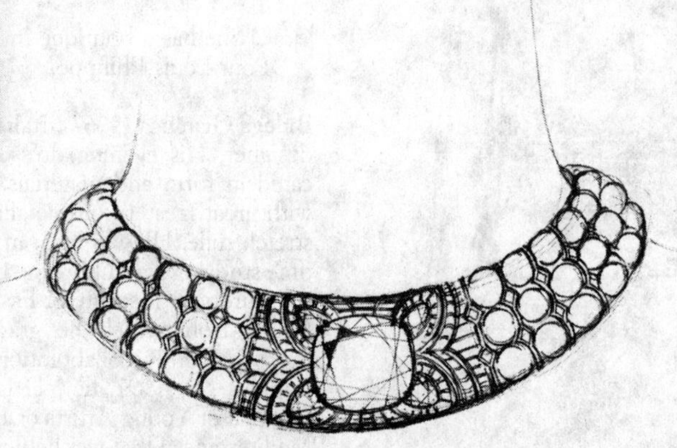

Bulgari. Collier 1988.

objects. In the 1960s, the company was joined by Costantino's daughters Anna and Marina, and by Giorgio's sons Gianni, Paolo and Nicola. These last two are the present heads of the company, together with their nephew Francesco Trapani, who is general director. In the 1970s, the company began to expand on the international market, opening subsidiaries in New York, Paris, Geneva, and Montecarlo. The 1980s and 1990s saw the birth of watches named Parentesi, Bulgari-Bulgari and Quadrato, the creation of a perfume, and the first line of modular jewellery, with a geometric style, called Parentesi. The year 1991 saw the début of the Naturalia Collection, which was inspired by the animal and vegetable world. For the occasion, the film *Anima Mundi* was produced, with the proceeds given to the World Wildlife Fund. The 1990s saw the creation of men's and women's accessories, small leather goods, foulards, ties, and eye glasses. In 1996 Bulgari started an experiment with new materials, in the jewellery line called Chandra, in which porcelain was used together with gold. In 2001 the firm launched Lucea, a Collection that was innovative in style and characterized by a fluid weaving together of gold and precious stones. The advertising for it featured the model Gisele Bündchen. The year 2002 saw the birth of Bulgari Hotel & Resorts, a joint venture between Bulgari and Luxury Group, the luxury hotel division of Marriott International. They envisioned a series of luxury hotels, the first of which would be in the center of Milan, in via privata Fratelli Gabba, near Piazza Scala and the Brera. In Autumn 2003, the company launched the women's fragrance Omnia, the eighth creation in the perfume line for men and women under the Bulgari brand.

(*Alessandra Quattordio*)

Bulleghin Modiano Marisa. Italian designer. From the early days of the *griffe* in 1974, up until 1985, she worked with Giorgio Armani as creative coordinator and participated in the research and selection of fabrics, technical tests on garments, the selection of patterns for each Collection, the organization of presentations, and the photographic sets. She later worked with the Genny Group on the Claude Montana line. From 1987 to 1993, at Krizia, she was responsible for the women's licensing department. From 1993 to 1995 she helped Mila Schön in their creative work.

Bumster Low-waist trousers, low enough to see the "bottom's line." Launched in the 1990s by Alexander McQueen.

Bündchen Gisele (1980). Born in Horizontina, Rio Grande do Sol, Brazil. She has brown hair and blue eyes. She was noticed at the age of 13 while eating in a Sao Paulo MacDonalds by someone with the Elite agency. At 14, she participated in her first modelling contest, and at 16 she ranked second in The Look of the Year organized by Elite. She won the public's attention on the runways and on the covers of the most influential fashion magazines. She models for only a few designers, such as Dolce & Gabbana, and receives huge fees. She was model of the year in 1999, winning the *Vogue/VH-1 Award*. She is featured in advertising campaigns for Versace, Valentino, Dolce & Gabbana, and Ralph Lauren. She is the fiancée of actor Leonardo Di Caprio. (*Silvia Paoli*)

Bundesverband Bekleidungsindustrie (BBI) German National Association of the Clothing Industry. Its headquarters is in Cologne, and it was the first of its kind in Germany. It offers assistance in the solution of political-economic problems.

Bundesverband Der Deutschen Textileinzelhandels German National Association of Textile Retailers. It brings together 30,000 firms and represents their interests on a national level. Its headquarters is in Cologne, and it is the central agency for several regional associations.

Bunka Fashion College Japanese school of fashion and tailoring founded in 1919 in Tokyo by Isaburo Namiki. It produces both fashion designers and managers. Among the most important names who studied there are Kenzo, Yamamoto, Kumagai, Junko Koshino, and Matsuda.

Bunka Gauken Costume Museum Japanese museum established in 1979 on the 60th anniversary of the founding of Bunka College. It brings together 50,000 pieces from all over the world connected to the world of fashion and clothing. Of particular importance are the kimono Collections, clothes and accessories from the Shin dynasty, and ancient fabrics from Japan, India, and Indonesia. Every Autumn, the museum organizes a monothematic exhibition.

Buonanno Anna (1924). Dressmaker from Naples. She continued a family tradition. Her mother Concettina, wife of the English painter Giuseppe Andrower, opened an atelier in Naples in 1917 and, like all the other dressmakers of the time, brought French fashions to Italy. She would purchase paper patterns from the *maisons* of Paris and would reproduce them, adapting them to Italian taste. She was discovered by Jolanda of Savoy, and dressed the hereditary Princess Maria José. Her atelier was in Palazzo Calabritto on Piazza dei Martiri, but she also opened another in Rome. Anna learned the job from her mother. She would have liked to be a painter as was her father, but at the age of 15 she followed Concettina to Paris to buy paper patterns and models. Her destiny was thus decided. She joined her mother's atelier and, in the post-war period, worked beside her, little by little assuming control. She created the wedding dress for Paola of Belgium. She dressed the entire aristocracy of Naples, staying faithful to French fashions. She would remember saying "No" to Sofia Scicolone who, before making her début in the cinema and becoming Sophia Loren, had offered herself as a model: "She had too many curves for us." She later entrusted the direction of the atelier to her daughter Gigliola. In 1994, the atelier was moved to via Chiamone, keeping the brass sign that said Sartoria Concettina Buonanno (Concettina Buonanno Dressmaker).

Burani Mariella (1943). Italian designer. Born in Cavriago, in the province of Reggio Emilia. She had a degree as an elementary school teacher and her dream was to teach. In the early 1960s she married Walter Burani. As she told Gian Luigi Paracchini of Corriere della Sera: "The car had broke down. My father and I had been waiting for hours. One person stopped: it was Walter." Together they give birth to Selene, the first

Evening dress by Mariella Burani.

line of a company that in 1999 had a turnover of 260 billion liras. After the birth of her second son, in 1966, her career as a designer finally took off. First she designed clothes for young girls, and then, in 1975, the company's production expanded to include women's prêt-à-porter. The brands included one that she named after herself, plus others like Amuleti, Selene, and Più Donna. In 1987 the designer made her début at Milano Collezioni. Since that time the Buranis have created a small empire of luxury.

Burberry Registered trademark of raincoats manufactured by the London company of Thomas Burberry 81835-1926). As with the Barbour jacket, Burberry is one of those cases of absolute identification between a brand and its product. With Burberry, today, one automatically thinks of a raincoat-overcoat in beige with a black-and-red tartan lining, with or without a belt at the waist. The prototype was created in 1856 when Thomas Burberry opened his first fabric shop in Basingstoke (Hampshire) under the name T. B. & Sons. Together with the owner of a cotton mill, he produced an overcoat-raincoat that was generously sized with a cotton fabric called gabardine, made waterproof a first time during spinning, and a second time when already closely woven. In 1901, the Department of War commissioned him to make a model fit for military use. It would make his fortune. The new uniform gave a new shape to the person who wearing it. The following year he took out a patent on gabardine, and, in 1909, one on the Burberry trench-coat. At the dawn of World War I, it became the trench-coat of the British Royal Flying Corps. The garment had shoulder straps, a waist belt with rings from which to hang anything a soldier might need in a trench, more small belts to make it a sort of diving suit to protect oneself from water and cold, doubled fabric in the parts most exposed to rain, and many pockets. Starting in 1920, after being tested in that terrible war, Burberry was offered to a middle-class clientele and was immediately successful, a success which has continued until today, without downturns, despite dozens of imitators. At the end of the 1990s, the company hired a designer, Roberto Menichetti, who started a line that was extremely innovative when compared to the company's stable tradition.

❑ 2000, September. The Spring-Summer 2001 Collection designed by Menichetti is presented in London. In the Gubbio workshop where Mrs. Ivonne, the mother of the Italian-American designer, works in an artisanal manner, the garments are manufactured in silk and cotton sewn with carbon threads.

❑ 2001. Menichetti leaves Burberry. His position is taken by Christopher Bailey.

❑ 2002, March. Burberry acquires its own distribution network in the Korean market. In June, they announce that the previous year ended with a 220% rise in operating profit, equal to £.69 million. By the end of the year, shops in San José, California, and New York are opened, the latter after a restyling of its six floors.

❑ 2002, July. Initial public offering of shares of the British group Great Universal Stores (GUS). The share price is fixed at 230 pence, or 3.6 Euros. The total value of the shareholding is £.1.15 billion. For the moment, only 25% of shares will be offered, which will bring £.282 million into the coffers of GUS. At the end of the year, the second single-brand shop opens in Knightbridge, and a new space is opened in Barcelona. Marketing of the Burberry House line begins. The year ends with a 19% increase in revenue.

❑ For Autumn-Winter 2003-2004, the Thomas Burberry brand for leisure and sport is relaunched. This low-price line is offered for young people between 18 and 25 and is inspired by rugby uniforms and jeans.

❑ 2003, June. Rose Marie Bravo of Burberry receives the Eleanor Lambert Award during the annual ceremony organized by the Council of Fashion Designers of America (CFDA).

Burda German women's monthly founded in 1949 by Aenne Burda and published by Verlag Aenne Burda Gmbh & Co., in Offenburg. Its target is a public between 30 and 60 years old, illustrating Collections of high fashion, prêt-à-porter, and styles which can be made at home. In addition to fashion there are large sections dedicated to home activities, cosmetics, and cooking. With a circulation of 2 million copies, Burda International comes out four times a year, presenting high fashion and prêt-à-porter Collections of the entire world.

Buriassi Rossana (1957). Italian jewellery designer, born in Milan. She has given her name to a company devoted to the design and production of jewels and accessories. A graduate of the Academy of Fine Arts of Brera, she also designs leather goods and shoes.

Burka The burka was originally a large waterproof cloak made of loden, worn especially by the people of the Caucasus. It now refers to a garment which covers the entire body and the face, imposed on women by Islamic fundamentalism and, in Afghanistan, by the Taliban.

Burko Black crepe veil used by peasant women of the Nile valley (the Fellah) in the 11th century. It hangs from the turban through a hollow brass quill that goes from the eyebrows to the nose, leaving only the eyes visible. This kind of "scarf-turban," restyled and redesigned, in silk or wool and in a variety of colors, has more than once come back in fashion as a hat.

Burlington Thick socks decorated with the classic Scottish lozenge-shape motif. They had great success during the 1980s, especially in the very brightly colored wool versions. The company was established in the U.S. in 1926. During the 1990s, after being moved to Germany, the company was acquired by the Kunert Group, a European giant in the field.

Burma Costume jewellery company established in France in 1929 by Joe Goldman. The company started off with a very selective production of imitation jewellery. Carefully following the fashion trends, it offered, in fact, reproductions of designs launched from time to time by the most fashionable jewellers. In 1929, when diamonds and platinum were all the rage, established by the success of their exhibit in Paris at the Palais Galliera, the firm made its début with a Collection in silver and Swarovski crystals. The jewels, created using artisanal techniques in limited numbers exclusively for Burma, were initially on sale in boutiques in Paris and the provinces. Later, they were popular in the U.S. and other markets, Italy included, thanks to a very well developed distribution network. The fame of Burma jewels was also tied to the success of actresses of great charm such as Arletty and Michèle Morgan, who often wore them in their films, and to famous personalities who in some cases became spokespersons for the products. Today, Burma's costume jewellery continues to be sold worldwide, in styles that vary according to the taste of individual countries.

Burnoose Over-sized cloak, fluid, loose, sometimes decorated with trimmings or embroidery, often with a hood. It derives from traditional Arab clothing. It is almost always manufactured in cotton, sometimes in very light woolen cloth. It is often used as a beach robe or as an evening dress when made with precious fabrics and embroidery.

Burri Alberto (1915-1994). Italian artist. In the jewels he created starting in 1962 he was able to concentrate on expressing the potentiality of matter, sometimes working directly with a welder, as in some brooches made in 1965. A master of the Material Informal, Burri (born in Città di Castello, which turned a former tobacco tannery into a museum dedicated to him) reflected in jewels the pursuit of Combustions of his artistic work in wood and plastic.

Burro Brand of casual clothing. Created in the early 1990s thanks to an idea of the brothers Olaf and Tim Parker and their friend Su, three young English boys who loved music. For the 1990 World Cup match in Italy, they produced T-shirts on which were printed phrases such as "No to Violence" that had an immediate success. Their T-shirts are sold in night clubs and at concerts. They understood that there is a market for their product and decided to produce a casual clothing line for the young people of the "dance culture." They were also able to produce garments for the members of various music bands, clothes which are worn during the concerts. In 1993 they opened a Burro shop in Covent Garden.

Burrows Stephen Gerald (1943). American designer. A pioneer of the black leather jacket with studs, and of trousers with patchwork and machine stitching with a fluted effect, he contributed a touch of provocative creativity to the fashion of the 1970s, of which he is considered a "guru." Born in Newark, N.J., he studied at the Philadelphia Museum College of Art and at the Fashion Institute of Technology. In 1968 he opened his own boutique, and the following year was hired by the Henry Bendel department store on Fifth Avenue, which was famous for promoting emerging designers. He also started a business of his own. He created casual lines and, in particular, outfits to be worn in discos, very tight on the body, in metallic jersey.

❑ 2002, February. The opening of

Stephen Burrows' World, a boutique within Henry Bendel, in New York. Burrows returns after an absence of some years, during which time he has designed for various friends and for theater sets. In July, the designer is awarded a place on the Fashion Walk of Fame in New York. He is honored with a plaque in bronze and granite fixed in the asphalt of Seventh Avenue, along with Marc Jacobs, Betsey Johnson, and Norma Kamali.

Busby Fur hat, for both men and women. High or flat, of cylindrical form, it was very trendy at the time of *Dr. Zhivago*.

Bush Richard (1973). English photographer. He studied French literature at King's College in London and became interested in photography as an autodidact. This would characterize his instinctive and spontaneous approach to the image, even to this day. He worked with the art director Durren Ellis and published his first work in *Creative Review* in 1999. Two years later he began his collaboration with the designer Jane How, to whom he dedicated a feature published in i-D. Since then, he has worked for magazines such as Nova, Dutch Magazine, Visionaire, Big Magazine, and W Magazine.

Bussi Ferdinando. Italian shoemaker for men and women. In the 1920s his shop in Turin, on via Andrea Doria, was famous for being a supplier to the Royal Family.

Bustier Bodice supported by light lateral whalebones with half-moon cups emphasizing the breast. It made its appearance at the end of the 1800s as an article of underwear. A famous example was the one worn by Scarlet O'Hara in *Gone with the Wind*. Abolished during the 1920s by Poiret, it came back in fashion after the war with Christian Dior's New Look. Today, it is used as an external garment, with bare shoulders, strapless, and often supported at the side by whalebones. It is a "must" for Summertime. In the 1980s, made with fanciful and glittering fabrics, including stretch, it became an important item for evening.

Butan Wool and polyamide fiber combined to make a velour-like yarn, spun with a slight curl. It is offered in light and mixed colors.

Butazzi Grazietta. Historian of fashion with a long career connected to cultural institutions in Milan. From 1976 to 1990 she was a consultant for the Fashion and Costume Collection of the Civiche Raccolte di Arte Applicata (Municipal Collections of Applied Art) at Castello Sforzesco. She collaborated on exhibitions and catalogues of the Museum Poldi Pezzoli (*1922-1943: Twenty Years of Italian Fashion*, and *Italian Velvets of the Renaissance*), and of the Comune di Milano (*The 1700s in Lombardy*). She taught History of Fashion at the Domus Academy from 1985 to 1990. At present she is the editor at the Museum Poldi Pezzoli of *Notizie Soffici*, a newsletter about initiatives in fabric and fashion that includes bibliographic updates. She also worked on the following exhibits: *Fashion Trades of Venice* with the Museo Correr; *Anziehungskrafte. Varieté de la Mode 1876-1986* with the Stadtmuseum of Munich; *The Clothes for the Body, the Body for the Clothes* with the Museo Stibbert of Florence. She has published several books, including: *Il costume in Lombardia* (Electa 1980). *Moda Arte Società Costume* (Fabbri 1982), *La moda italiana* in two volumes edited with Alessandra Mottola Molfino (Electa 1985), *Giornale delle nuove mode di Francia e d'Inghilterra* in three volumes (Allemandi 1989), the *Idee di Moda* series in 9 volumes edited with A. Mottola Molfino (De Agostini), and *Storia della Moda* (Calderini 1995).

Button The most probable etymology reminds one of something particularly gentle: the bud of a plant, in Italian "bocciolo," from the old French "bouton." A second hypothesis refers to the German "botan," remembering that in the fourth century the Germans used a sort of small metallic disc to fasten their clothes. However, to tell the story of the button it is not necessary to go back in the mists of time. Even if archaeology tells of prehistoric buttons, classic antiquity didn't know them. In order to fasten the drapery of peplum, chiton, tunic, stole, and toga, the Greeks and Romans used belts, pins, buckles, and clasps. Not even "lunulae," the small moon-shaped brooches which, for decorative purposes, were pinned or sewn on robes and "calcei" (Roman shoes similar to ankle boots), were real buttons. It is necessary to go to the 12th and 13th centuries to find the ancestor of the modern "small disc" (and not just discs), which, introduced into a buttonhole, unites the two parts of an article of clothing. Perhaps it was the Crusaders who, once back home, spread the Turkish enthusiasm for fastenings that went from chin to waist and from elbow to knuckles. It is certain, though, that the use of buttons started in France where, in the time of Saint Louis, the "boutonniers" were already organized in guilds, and that the vertical, slender, tight, Gothic silhouette was the reason. Along with this fashion, buttons arrived in Italy around the year 1200. Used very frugally to put on clothes which, strangely enough, were still worn up to the neck, they were needed in order to slip on the elegant and very tight sleeves. Paintings and miniatures document the exaggerations, purely ornamental, of numberless rows of such knobs, or "ma spilli" (pins), as they were called, which ran from wrist to shoulder and continued to become, in the centuries that followed, richer and richer, made of gold, silver, pearls, amber and coral, to the point of being affected by sumptuary laws, which limited the excesses of luxury. They were more and more varied (some in the shape of tiny pears, called *peroli*), and more and more numerous, both for women and men. In 1400, one could count from 20 to 50 buttons on a sleeve, usually removable and provided with slits and laces. A Sicilian song of the time tells how the author couldn't find a better comparison with which to address his beloved: "Of gold, of silver, you are my buttons, / buttons of a loving sleeve." There were also buttons that were less rich, made of bone, wood, horn, and brass. Towards the end of the 1500s, buttons made of copper, brass, iron, pewter and tin began to decorate military uniforms. The Renaissance wanted buttons ever more splendid, encrusted with precious stones and made to order. Manufacturers enjoyed the protection of sovereigns and discovered, from time to time, new techniques to make them unusual. The region of Limoges gave birth to enameled buttons: the first examples were meant for François I of France, who was a "maniac" for buttons, considering that on a single piece of clothing he had 13,600 of them, in gold. Louis XIV, The Sun King, wasn't much far behind: in fact, for six buttons he paid an amazing sum, even for a king. From century to century, buttons followed the whims of fashion, multiplying themselves on men's clothing, like the robes of priests in the 1600's, buttoned from neck to ankle, or like the tailcoats and frock-coats of the 1700's. They respected, generally speaking, the needs of national manufacture, so that they were silk-covered in France (to protect the factories of Paris and Lyon), and of metal in England, where, in the late 1500s and early 1600s, the use of fabric was prohibited. In England, in the late 1600s and early 1700s, the first industrial button factories were established, and within a short time Birmingham became a center of world renown. Their "run" was by now unstoppable, both in Europe and in America. There would never again be events, trends, personalities, or expressions of public and private life that buttons could not reflect, or shapes and materials which they could not bend to their will. From the pastoral scenes dear to Marie Antoinette to puzzles, with a weakness for sayings and riddles, from exquisite porcelain to the widow's jet black (ancestor of jet) of Queen Victoria, from celluloid to "very modern" plastic, from the Japanese subjects of Art Nouveau to the straight and squared lines of the 1920s and 1930s, one surprise after another. On the clothes of Elsa Schiaparelli there were "dancing" buttons of such weird shapes that in a biography of the famous couturier one reads: "King button reigns unopposed at Schiaparelli, where no one looks like what a button should look like." And Mademoiselle Coco Chanel, matching metals and precious pearls and colored stones, even invented a style. The Chanel button has remained unmistakable everywhere at every time. Not even World War II stopped the progress of the button, and there was one who, just to manufacture some, was able to make them from the windshields of obsolete bombers. The second half of the 1900s saw ups and downs, but in its decline, the button rediscovered its essence as a piece of jewellery. As a matter of a fact, designers, worthy heirs of Coco Chanel, make them out of jewels. Thus it doesn't surprise one that, just as in the 1800s, five or more buttons, all dissimilar and each with a stone of a different color, embellish, for example, one of the showy white shirts of Gianfranco Ferré. Nor it doesn't amaze one that in his haute couture Collection for Spring-Summer 2003, Jean Paul Gaultier paid a genuine tribute to buttons that run down an entire garment, so that it is studded with them, or, assembled like shells, covered by them entirely. The magic game of a conjurer worthy of his talent, but also of the essense of these decorative and useful "gems."

(*Maria Rita Stiglich*)

Buzzati Dino (1906-1972). Italian writer and journalist. In January 1962, for the Corriere della Sera, of which he was a special correspondent, he followed the high fashion runways of Paris and, in the Summer of the following year, those of Italian ready-to-wear at Palazzo Pitti. He was pushed towards this experience by his friend Maria Pezzi, who at the time wrote a column about fashion for Il Giorno. This Italian writer (*Barnabo of the Mountains*, *The Tartar Steppe*, *Il crollo della Baliverna*, *Terror on the Staircase* and *A Love Affair*) who was the most-translated and loved in France had no squeamishness about it, but looked at fashion with the attention, the participation, and the sharp observation which also made him a great reporter. From Florence he would write: "Forquet. If I were married, I would send my wife to his atelier to be dressed by him." And made his personal ranking: 1) Forquet; 2) De Barentzen; 3) Veneziani; 4) Lancetti; 5) Valentino; 6) Galitzine; 7) Antonelli; 8) Enzo; 9) Marucelli. Then in a group came Guidi, De Luca and Carosa.

Byblos Brand created in 1973 on the initiative of Arnaldo Girombelli, the founder of Genny Holding, and of his brother Sergio. Byblos desires to dress people who are young, in age and spirit, and offers fashion that is fresh and casual. In the history of the line an important role was played by Gianni Versace, who was still a

Byblos. Autumn-Winter 1999-2000 Collection.

newcomer, and who designed the Collections from 1975 to '77. Later, from 1980 to 1996, two English designers, Varty and Allan Clever, were in charge of the design department. From bright colors, lively patterns, daring prints and shapes, the line shifted little by little to a more sober phase, though maintaining a young and sophisticated style. In 1997 the artistic direction was given to an American, Richard Tyler. He was later followed by John Burtlett.

(*Laura Asnaghi*)

❑ 2003. The creative team is composed of Stefano Citron (formerly of Krizia and Milan Schön), Federico Piaggi (formerly of Max Mara, Sportmax, Trussardi, Valentino, and Mila Schön), and Greg Myler (formerly of Erreuno, Krizia, and Mila Schön). A passionate triumvirate for the *griffe* that Swinger acquired from Prada.

Byron Lars (1965). American designer. He made his début with a prêt-à-porter Collection in 1991 and Women's Wear Daily named him "Rookie of the Year." Born in Oakland, he studied at the Brooks Fashion Institute in Long Beach, California, and at the Fashion Institute of Technology in New York. He believes in the spectacular effect of models. The New York Times included him in the group of the "magnificent eight" together with Donna Karan and Calvin Klein.

❑ Starting in 1997, dolls were the real creative passion of the Oakland designer. With the support of Mattel, every year Byron produced a different model of Barbie, inspired by the ethnic Afro-American tradition. Destined to be always "sold out" and the object of fierce collecting were the Indigo Barbie (2000), Mbili (2002), and the most recent, the Tatu Barbie.

C

Caban Large sports jacket in light fabric. Some believe it is descended from the uniforms of English coachmen of the 1800s and named after the term for the carriage, a *cab*. Others believe it is related to a jacket worn by seamen from Brittany in the 1700s. Warm and functional, the caban has been manufactured in very different shapes and materials. In the last decade or so it lost its identity as being for men only and became a unisex garment.

Cacciagrilli The year 2000 saw the birth of a very close collaboration between two photographers who shared a passion for art (they had already participated in various exhibits, both solo and group) and a curiosity about the world of fashion: Alessandra Caccia (1975) and Francesca Grilli (1978). Alessandra, who is from Milan, attended the School of Cinema and the Riccardo Bauer Professional School of Photography there and won the Pezza Award. Fancesca, who is from Bologna, received a university degree from the ISIA of Urbino, and, after moving to Milan, also attended courses at the Bauer school. Their photographs are characterized by a taste for narrative and logical progression, with open tribute paid to a hard-boiled noir style mitigated by irony. For them, clothing is a central fact, around which everything else turns. They work with young designers interested in a new language, such as Serienumerica from Turin, and with famous international brands such as the American cosmetics company Mac. They have published their work in Will, Boiler, and Uovo Zero2.

Cacharel French brand of prêt-à-porter. Behind the name of this famous *griffe*, which was inspired by a nice little duckling typical of the Camargue, is the activity of the entrepreneur and designer Jean-Louis Bousquet (Nimes, 1932). After his first steps as an apprentice tailor, in 1956 Bousquet moved to Paris, where he opened a small atelier of men's shirtwear. In 1962 he established his own company in which he manufactured, in addition to women's and men's shirts, shirtdresses and other women's clothing. He was a pioneer of prêt-à-porter. If the styles were rather classic, quite new was the use, first, of *crepon* (a fabric used up until then for nightgowns) and then, of Art Nouveau cotton, with its famous flowered patterns, two elements which define the style of the house, fresh and romantic, and contributed to its success. The happy idea of using the intimist photographs of Sarah Moon for the advertising campaigns became another characteristic element, constant over time. In the following years, Bousquet invited several young designers who would later become very famous to work with him, including Agnès B., Alaïa, Corinne Cobson, Emmanuelle Khan, Lempicka, and Shimada. His fragrances had great success, starting with the very first, *Anaïs Anaïs*, launched in 1978 and one of the best sellers, and continuing with *Loulou* in 1987, *Eden* in 1994, and *Noa* in 1998. With a worldwide distribution network, the brand today has several licenses for men's, women's, and children's clothing, for accessories, and for the home. (*Gisella Borioli*)

❑ 2000, May. At the end of the 1900s, Jean Busquet has somewhat neglected his brand in order to devote himself to politics, first as a representative, and then as mayor of Nimes. When he decided to relaunch the brand he gave the task to the English designer team Clements-Ribeiro. He saw one of their Collections on TV and knew that they would have the right spirit for the new Cacharel style.
❑ 2002, April. Launch of the new fragrance *Gloria* on the European market.
❑ 2002, November. Publication of the

book *Cacharel. Le Liberty*, a tribute by the *griffe* to the fabric which was at the base of its success.

❑ 2002, December. The continued relaunch of the Cacharel brand, which began in 2000 with a radical change in style. Bousquet now aims at a reorganization of the distribution system and at expansion through new license agreements. The creative restyling by Clements and Ribeiro was a success in those areas where the brand was less well known (England, Asia and the U.S.). On the other hand, there were difficulties in Europe where the memory of the brand's traditional image was strong. The retail plan for 2004 anticipated new single-brand shops in London, New York, and Paris, and for 2005 in Moscow and Brussels. Together with the reorganization of the points-of-sale, Bousquet continued to expand the licenses. He signed an agreement with Mantero for scarves and ties, and with Carré Royal for bags.

❑ 2003, March. A license agreement with the Eminence group for the distribution in Italy of Cacharel underwear (for men and women).

❑ 2004, February. Inspired by its usual themes and symbols, Cacharel launches a new line of jewellery which, like the previous ones, is rich in romantic touches.

❑ 2005, June. Cacharel changes its top management. Chrystel Abadie Truchet is the new general manager. Emmanuel Augustin becomes the new administrative and financial director. Jean Bosquet, main shareholder and founder of the *maison*, is appointed chairman of the board of directors.

Cache-coeur Long-sleeve cardigan, elegant and romantic, which crosses in front in the shape of a V and is knotted in back or on the side with two strings. It was copied from a classic model for children. It evokes the bodices of Biedermeier dresses and appeared for the first time during the 1920s.

Cache-col (Cravat) Small men's scarf usually in silk twill with small patterns, wrapped around the neck and knotted in front. It is worn instead of a tie with a shirt that has two unfastened buttons. It is typical of the English country gentleman, and today considered a little out of fashion.

Cadette Italian prêt-à-porter house. In business since 1966, it was very successful in the early 1980s, thanks to the work of Walter Albini and, later, Moschino, two personalities who, over time, stressed the two-part spirit of Cadette: first, a high level of fashion, realized through the reinterpretation of the past, remembered with longing, in a new key of simple timelessness; and second, an impulse toward the European avant-vanguard, open to the underground trend of the anti-fashion. The brand was created in Milan thanks to a meeting between Enzo Clocchiati (a native of Trieste, someone considered to be a bit mysterious, a student of economics, an executive in industry, a director of Olivetti in Vienna, a member of the staff of the prime minister in Rome) and Christine Tichmarsh, a model for Saint-Laurent, right at the moment when it was necessary to rescue the small business of a friend. The brand would have extraordinary success at Pitti (1967), in the wake of the sophisticated stylism of Albini. The following year, it left the runway of the Sala Bianca after a sudden decision to start high fashion prêt-à-porter in Milan, in order to present and sell its styles directly to Italians and foreigners – a style against luxury, faithful to itself, fashion as culture – in a showroom and in a boutique in the heart of Milan. Another boutique was opened in 1974 in Paris, on Rue Faubourg Saint-Honoré. On the death of Clocchiati, Cadette was taken over by Fantoni, who hired Moschino as designer. The Collection marking the début of that young talent on the runway of the Milan Fair of 1978 brought the *griffe* back to success during the hot stylism of the 1980s.

Cadolle Herminie. Parisian corset maker at the end the 19th and in the early 20th century. She was an ancestor of Poiret in her desire to free women from the constraints of bust and whalebones. At the end of the 1800s, the S body shape was in fashion, obtained thanks to the use of a torture-corset, a real piece of armor which emphasized the breasts and bottom and compressed the waist to the extreme. At the Paris Exposition of 1900, Cadolle was daring enough to present a corset cut in two, a progenitor of today's bra. Of course, the idea caused a scandal and was rejected, for obvious financial reasons as well, by the industry. With women going to work, changes brought by World War I, sports, and new fashion trends, the 1920s brought the end of the corset and the liberation of the female body. Cadolle designed the first bra which reduced and flattened the figure for Chanel's dresses *à la garçonne*.

(*Gabriella Gregorietti*)

Cady A medium weight woven cloth similar to crêpe, usually made of cotton or silk, though it can be wool or synthetic. Commonly used to make women's cocktail or evening dresses.

Caffelatte Italian monthly magazine. It was founded in 2002 in order to give voice to a world balanced between "formal' culture and the underground. Although the subtitle of the magazine reads "fashion, music, art, and anything else," it is mainly interested in fashion and lifestyle. Printed on pleasing recycled paper, it offers an expressly simple graphic design which doesn't, however, overlook images. It publishes young emerging photographers such as Simon, Baby Jane, Ale di Giampietro, and Julian Hargreaves.

Caftan A long cloak, with or without sleeves. Of Turkish origin, it has influenced men's clothing since the 12th century. Today, in the West, the term is also used for distinctive women's dust coats that are long and voluminous, and for outerwear garments in linen or silk.

Cagné Gilles (1939-2003). Make-up artist and image expert, born in Belgium. When still very young, he became creative vice president at Max Factor. He made his name working with photographers such as Avedon and Newton. He reached the peak of fame when taking care of the look of international stars such as Liza Minelli and David Bowie. For several years he taught cosmetology at the Biologic Institutes of the Catholic University of Rome. In 1992, Mondadori published his book *Belle si diventa*, a catalogue of suggestions about make-up and cosmetics based on his professional experience. He also created a Collection of professional make-up under his name.

Cagoule Hood covering the head but not the face. It was used by monks and often attached to the mantle. The hood worn by members of the KKK is a particular form of *cagoule* (from the Latin *cogola*): the face is completely covered, leaving two slits for the eyes. The first to use the cagoule in fashion was Pierre Cardin (Irene Brin called those styles "falconer's berets") in 1968, followed by Paco Rabanne and Courrèges. A further evolution in the cagoule was due to Albini. Causing a scandal in the press, in 1975 he presented a sort of balaclava with holes for the eyes and mouth, in many ways similar to that worn by terrorists and Buddhists.

(*Laura Salza*)

Calabrese Women's large and pointed felt hat, recalling the ones worn by brigands in Calabria a long time ago. In its Summer version it is made of straw.

Calabrese Omar (1949). Scholar of semiotics. He placed visual communication at the center of his research in the field of semiotics and mass communication. Among the founders of the magazines Alfabeta and Carte Semiotiche, a contributor to newspapers and periodicals on the themes of art, fashion, and current events, he has published several books, among which are *L'età neobarocca* (Laterza, 1987) and *Caos and bellezza* (Domus Academy, Milan, 1991).

Calderara Maria (1958). Fashion and jewellery designer. She is a native of Pavia but grew up in Venice. She has a degree in architecture, and creates jewels by combining the tradition of glass-making with that of the new design. Very well known in France (her bracelets and necklaces are on sale at the Musée des Arts Décoratifs), she started some years ago to produce high-fashion garments, continuing her research into fabrics that combine the flavor the past with new technology.

Calico Lightweight woven cotton or cotton-blend fabric usually colorfully printed with a small, allover pattern. The name derives from Calcutta, where the fabric was originally manufactured. The Italian synonym is *cotonina*.

Calignano Gianni (1963). Designer from Lecce. He began to present his Collections on the runways of Rome in January 2000, becoming known for his heavy use of raffia in the appliqued flowers and in crocheted pieces. His light and soft dresses model themselves on the female body thanks to the use of fabrics such as organza, tulle, and crêpe.

Callaghan Italian brand of knitwear. It was established in 1966 as a subsidiary of Zamasport, a company belonging to the Knitwear Group Augusto Zanetti of Novara. An important part of the Made in Italy movement, this brand has been designed by prestigious names such as Albini, 1968 to 1972; Versace, 1972 to 1984; Lebourg, for just one season, Spring-Summer 1985; Tarlazzi, 1985 to 1987; Gigli 1987 to 1995; and Crolla.

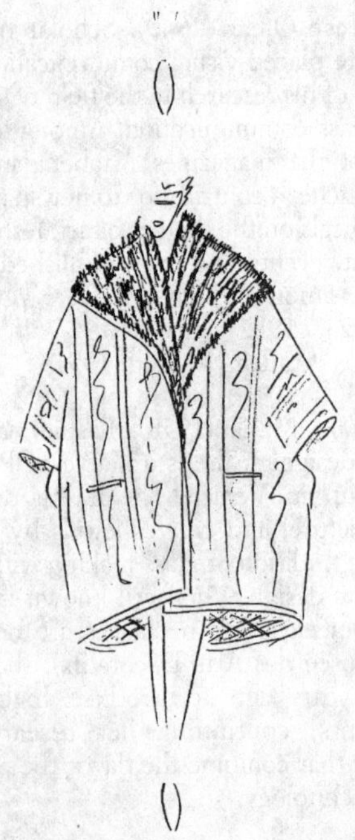

Callaghan: sketch by Romeo Gigli. Autumn-Winter 1988-89 Collection.

Calugi and Giannelli House of prêt-à-porter fashion, especially for men, established in Florence in 1982 by Mauro Calugi (1941) and Danilo Giannelli (1957-1987). In 1985, they presented their creations at Pitti Immagine. An exasperated masculinity and the clerical world are often the subject of their "stylistic satire." Since the death of Giannelli, the house has been guided by Calugi.

Calvenzi Giovanna (1946). Photographer and journalist. She was the director of Lei. A scholar and teacher of the history of photography, she began her career as a photographer working with several periodicals, especially women's magazines. In 1985 she became photo editor at Amica. In 1987 she became editor-in-chief at Max, then was again a photo editor, at Sette, the magazine linked to Corriere della Sera. In 1990 she joined the Condé Nast group as director of photography at Vanity Fair. In 1991 she was put in charge of Lei, where should remain until the magazine closed.

❑ After her time as photo editor at the weekly Lo Specchio della La Stampa, she assumed the same position at Sport Week, the magazine attached to La Gazzetta dello Sport. Considered one of the best Italian photo editors and the recipient of many awards in France, she was artistic director of Rencontres de la Photographie of Arles in 1998, and is artistic consultant for the Fondation CCF pour la Photographie.

Calvert William (1969). American designer. He studied in Italy at the Italian Academy of Fashion in Florence and got his start in the world of Parisian couture, working for Balenciaga. In 1994, he returned to the U.S. and designed a Collection for Diane von Furstenberg. That was followed in 1996 by one for Brooks Brothers. In 1997 he founded his own brand, William Calvert. After the Autumn-Winter 1999 presentations in New York, Time magazine called him one of the most promising designers of 2000. His philosophy is: "My clothes are not made to stay on hangers in the closet."

Calzedonia Hosiery factory that also produces bathing suits and underwear. It was established in 1987 in Vallese di Oppeano, near Verona. The idea for the company came from Sandro Veronesi. The challenge: to make a success out of an initial investment of 500 million liras and the idea of exponential growth in the sale of men's, women's and children's hosiery and clothing through a network of franchise shops. The brand to be promoted was Calzedonia (the same as the company's corporate name). Then, in 1996, the same concept was applied to underwear and sleepwear with the start of a second brand, Intimissimi. Within little more than 16 years, the Calzedonia and Intimissimi network had more than 1,200 shops scattered all over the world, including Spain (with more than 140 points-of-sale), Austria, Portugal, Greece, Poland, Turkey, Mexico, Bosnia, Hungary, Cyprus, Lebanon, and Saudi Arabia. The headquarters is in Vallese, where 400 people are employed, all of them young, with an average age of 25, and mostly women, who represent 85% of the work force. The company's organization is in the avant-guard as concerns its relationship with workers. In 2001 it opened a corporate kindergarten, among the most interesting in Europe, for employees' children between 6 months and 3 years old. Other than the one in the Veneto, there are production units in Avio (Trentino), in Croatia, Bulgaria, Romania, and Sri Lanka. In these last two, the plants produce underwear. Another initiative taken by the firm is the Foundation of San Zeno, created in 1999 with the purpose of giving economic support to projects aimed at the professional education of needy and alienated young people throughout the world. (*Gianluca Cantaro*)

❑ 2003, October. The group launches a new line, Tezenis, with the same franchise strategy used for the Calzedonia and Intimissimi brands. The product line includes women's, men's, and children's underwear, for a younger and more basic market than that of Intimissimi. It was successful due to a self-service formula and aggressive pricing.

❑ 2003, December. The turnover is 341 million euros (against 266 million in 2002), with a pre-tax profit of more than 30 million (against 17 million in 2002). The distribution network has 898 Calzedonia points-of-sale, 620 for Intimissimi, and 12 for Tezenis. In the same year, the company acquired a very large piece of land with the idea of building a logistics hub. According to Veronese, the founder of the company, the reasons for its success are that "We control the entire production process and this saves waste in terms of resources and creates a virtuous cycle. The other reasons are effective advertising and the price-quality ratio."

❑ 2004, December. The group has 1,730 points-of-sale in Italy and throughout the world, consisting of 984 for Calzedonia, 704 for Intimissimi, and 42 for Tezenis.

❑ 2005, April. A Tezenis store opens on the very centrally located Corso Vittorio Emanuele in Milan, next to the large low-price department stores Zara, Conbipel, and H&M. (*Dario Golizia*)

Calzificio Milanese Luigi Ciocca Company established in 1919 by Luigi Ciocca with his business partners Grignaschi, Bertoletti, and Dell'oro. Relocated from Milan to Quinzano d'Oglio, the plant manufactures men's, women's, and children's hosiery and men's and women's light sweaters. The turnover of more than 45 billion liras includes both hosiery sales and a dye-works for yarn. It is in the medium to high end of the market.

Socks of the 1960s in a sketch by Brunetta.

Calzificio Mura Established in 1969 in Asola di Mantova by Luigi Mura, it exported the Mura Collant and Meri Calze-Collant lines to Paris, New York, Moscow, Buenos Aires, Madrid, and Singapore.

Calzini Raffaele (1885-1953). Italian writer and journalist, and special correspondent for Corriere della Sera starting in 1926. For that Milanese daily he covered the fourth presentation of the Italian High Fashion Show organized by Bista Giorgini, to which Florence granted the use of the Sala Bianca in Palazzo Pitti for the first time. It was Tuesday, the 22nd of July, 1952, with a temperature of 42°C in the shade and thunder storms. No one in town paid much attention, as if that gathering of tailors, dressmakers, models, journalists, and buyers from the U.S. and Europe was elitist and of interest only to those in the field, like a meeting of the Carbonari society. But Corriere della Sera didn't feel that way, and it sent a great correspondent, a very refined, Proustian writer (*La tela di Penelope*; *Segantini, romanzo della montagna*) to Florence. Raffaele Calzini wrote a very dignified piece, and it was published on page three: "There were the American buyers, the representatives of the international press, the tailors and dressmakers, and the guests such as Mrs. Churchill, an entire world that was curious, elegant, competent, critical, and refined, composed of shopkeepers and aristocrats, all sitting in three rows on the four sides of a rectangular room that was completely decorated with stuccos like a box of candies and illuminated by eleven rock-crystal lamps among the most beautiful in the world, seemingly doubled in size by the large mirrors hanging on the side walls and at the back. Through two small doors, as in the stage set of a sitting room, models would enter, walking quickly and carefully, one after the other (one of them stumbled and let out a childish cry), performing their ritual presentation: a harmonized and by now classic composition of gestures, steps, pirouettes, curtseys, and swaying, halfway between mime and dance."

Camard Isabelle (1960). French designer and a brand of prêt-à-porter. She was an assistant to Per Spook from 1986 to 1987, and in the meantime completed her studies at the Institut Français de la Mode in Paris and at the Parsons School of Design in New York. In 1988 she worked with Issey Miyake. She made her solo début in October 1990, presenting, in Paris and Tokyo, her first Spring-Summer 1991 Collection.

Camel Woolen fiber. Camel hair produces a precious and well-insulating yarn. It is obtained from the under-hair of the animal, which falls spontaneously every Spring. The gatherers who follow the herds and caravans have an important role in the supply of the fiber. The most precious hairs come from Mongolia and the Persian Gulf. These are the habitats which have, over the millenniums, fortified the animal and its fleece. The characteristics of strength and preciousness which distinguish it are similar to those of the various camelidae of Latin America, the vicuña, alpaca, lama, and guanaco. The wool obtained from camels and dromedaries is soft and reddish in its natural colors.

(*Giuliana Zabeo Ricca*)

Camelhair Precious fabric made from camel hair and wool yarn.

Camelot High quality super-kid mohair produced by Lineapiù in more than one hundred colors. It has the ideal blend for mohair knitting: 67% kid mohair, 3% wool, and 30% polyamide. The cloth obtained from Camelot is light, with a twisted warp made with ordinary wool. When it contains a cotton warp it is called Orléans.

Caminata Sergio (1955). Italian photographer. After he studied photography at the Istituto Rizzoli in Milan, he enrolled in the School of Architecture, but later quit in order to devote himself to professional photography. In 1980 he began his work with Donna, Grazia, Amica, Anna, Gioia, Freundin, Für Sie, and Madame Figaro, as well as with the Japanese edition of Marie Claire, Harper's Bazaar (in Italy, Germany, and Russia), Cosmopolitan, and various editions of Elle. He works, as a director, on the TV broad Nonsolomoda. The publishing house Feltrinelli often uses his photos for the covers of its books. His personal research, tied to his passion for the African continent and to reportage, resulted in the publication of *Himba* (1997) and *Ndebele* (1988). He has had several personal exhibitions.

Camisol A very low-necked short top extending just below the breasts, with very thin straps and a straight neckline. In a longer version, like a dress, it resembles a negligee, in different lengths from mini to maxi, always with thin straps, in light and transparent fabrics.

Cammarata Fabio (1963). Goldsmith and jeweler. Born in Caltanisetta. After obtaining a degree in architecture from the University of Palermo, and a degree in fashion from the Domus Academy of Milan, he began his work in the world of fashion with Diego Della Valle. Then, continuing the goldsmith tradition of his family, he decided to devote himself to jewellery. In 1996 he established Cammarata Gioielli and opened his own atelier in Milan, on via Statuto. There he presented his gold, silver, pearl, and precious-stone Collections of material-informal taste. Keeping in mind the lessons of modern art – Klimt and Mondrian, Abstraction and Surrealism – and revisiting the classic techniques of goldsmithing – granulation as well as a satin finish – he was able to create designs with a very strong personal touch. After moving to a new space in Largo Treves in 2000, he began a lively series of collective expositions involving other goldsmiths besides himself. These included Giovanni Corvaja, Karl Reister, and Jacqueline Ryan. His research put him in touch with new materials such as fur, feathers, and carved wood, while continuing his development of an ever more refined expressive language through the working of precious metals. In 2003 he moved the administrative offices and workshops to via Spalato, devoting himself especially to a stylistic collaboration with the great houses for which he designed jewels and precious accessories. His creations continue to be sold in Milan, in the store on Largo Treves, which is now managed by Haidea, and in New York at Barneys. (*Alessandra Quattordio*)

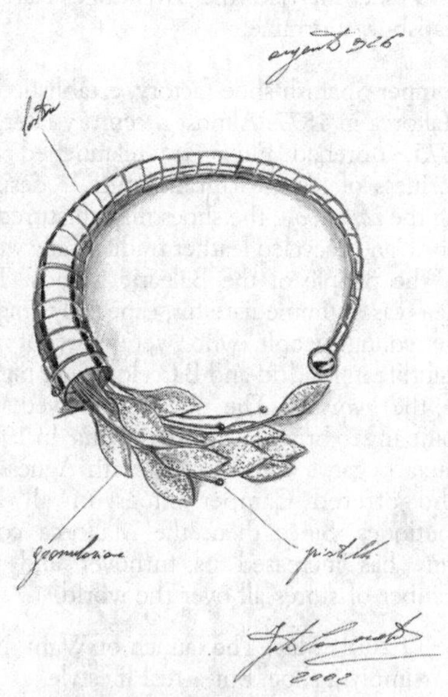

A creation by Fabio Cammarata.

Camomilla Italian company making bags and accessories. It was established in Milan in the early 1980s for the manufacture of backpacks, cases, small and large leather goods. Its customers are teenagers and young women.

Camouflage Look A French term indicating camouflage patterns and colors and irregularly printed fabrics, often in beige and green. For a military look, it was in fashion among the freaks of the 1960s and '70s, and then taken up by the hip-hoppers of the '90s. Today, it is a classic of the Summer Collections.

Camp An expression not referring to any specific time or epoch, used to sum up and represent an extreme form of Dandysm, practically a sort of anti-Dandysm when compared to the historical meaning of that term. It can also be used as an expression of kitsch in the world of fashion. Its roots are in a phantasmagoric language connected both to the homosexual world and to that of transformism and transvestites. It refers to a sort of baroque mannerism or *rocaille* fashion and a certain way of being which, while praising only the most sophisticated details and particulars, mixes them with the classic aesthetic canons of beauty. The result is one of the most spectacular and exuberant ways of dressing and presenting oneself. (*Gianluca Bauzano*)

Campagna Gianni (1944). Italian tailor, born in Roccalumera, Sicily. He arrived in Milan in 1962 to work with his master Domenico Caraceni who, though not belonging to the Caraceni dynasty, knew the trade. In 1972 Pier Giorgio Rivetti hired him at Gruppo

Finanziario Tessile to be in charge of the style and model department. Ten years later, he joins Lubiam in order to redefine their sartorial line. Campagna invented the semi-traditional, a manufacturing system that reduced production time and costs. In 1987 he joined Marzotto, bringing the patent for the semi-traditional method with him, and became responsible for all the lines produced by the company. His return to tailoring occured in 1990, when he accepted a proposal from his friend Ciro Paone, the owner of Kiton. In 1995 he began a campaign to win a clientele in Hollywood and in the U.S., supported by his son Andrea Italia. In the meantime, his tailor shop Sartoria Campagna – with headquarters in Piazza San Babila, Milan – produces about 700 exclusive suits per year, entirely by hand. In the U.S. the Italian tailor dressed actors, bankers, and politicians. In 1999 he opened a new Milan headquarters on via Palestro at the intersection with Corso Venezia. It is a platform for his own production and for the brands Domenico Caraceni and Baratta (another historical *griffe* of Milanese fashion) that he has taken over.

Campanile Shoe factory of Naples, with headquarter in Arzano. The founder, Nicola Campanile, started the firm in 1950, at the young age of 22. In the company are his two sons, Gigi and Cristiano. The turnover is roughly € 15 million a year, with 80% of the production sold in Italy, and the rest exported to Russia, Switzerland, the Far East, and the U.S. The store in Rome occupies five floors and is on via Condotti. The most famous models are the loafer with buckle, the lace-up model, and the Duilio laced shoe with a fringe, which is a men's model that is heavily tooled. In addition to a second line called Casati, a casual brand, Brian Cress, was launched in 1993.

Campbell Naomi (1970). Top model, born in Streatham, London. She has chestnut hair and brown eyes (she wears colored contact lenses, blue and green). She was discovered at the age of 15 while walking in Covent Garden, by Beth Boldt of the model agency Elite. At the age of 18, she was the first black woman to appear on the cover of Vogue France. She is the model of several fashion brands, including Versace, Alessandro Dell'Acqua, Bluemarine, and Ralph Lauren. Known for her whimsical temper and jet set love affairs (the boxer Mike Tyson, the dancer Cortes, the entrepreneur Flavio Briatore), Naomi decided to diversify her activities, and, with her colleagues Elle Mc Pherson and Christy Turlington, started the Fashion Café, which was not very successful. She co-wrote the book *Swan*, recorded a couple of songs, participated in the videos of famous singers, and presented her own fragrance. So far, the thing she does best remains the runways. She has had a doll (and a wax statue at Madame Tussaud) reproducing her features dedicated to her.

(*Silvia Paoli*)

Campbell-Walters Fiona (1932). English model. She was a top model during the 1950s. The daughter of an Admiral of the Royal Navy, she attended a modelling school in London and, still a teenager, she was photographed by Henry Clarke. In a short time her elegance and aristocratic attitude made her an icon in Vogue and one of the favorite models of Cecil Beaton. In 1953, she was on the cover of Life. In 1956 she married Hans Heinrich von Thyssen. They divorced in 1964, after having two sons. In 1993 she married the Archduke Karl of Hapsburg Lorraine.

Camper Spanish shoe factory, established in Mallorca in 1877. Almost a century later, in 1975, Lorenzo Fluxá Jr. relaunched the business of his great grandfather, redesigning the *camaleon*, the shoes manufactured in fabric and recycled leather traditionally worn by the people of the Balearic islands. The idea was an immediate hit, especially among the young people who were part of the nightlife in Madrid and Barcelona, the nights of the *movida.* The success allowed the company to bring out more designs. In 1994, Fluxá began a collaboration with Agnès B., who offered Camper shoes in all her boutiques. Since then, the Mallorca company has increased its turnover and the number of stores all over the world.

❑ 2001, May. The launch of Wabi. Not simply a shoe, but a real lifestyle, inspired by simplicity, tranquility, and meditation. It starts with nature. Wabi, in the Japanese language, means rural. Manufactured in TPU rubber (recyclable, anti-static and resistant) or in felted wool, it has a series of accessories. The internal arch, made of coconut fiber, supports the foot and regulates the temperature.

❑ 2001, June. The Spanish brand's first New York store is one year old and celebrates with great public success. The Soho headquarters, between Wooster and Prince Streets, and designed by Martì Guixé, recreates the atmosphere of Mallorca, where the brand was born. Camper receives the Fashion Brand of the Year 2000 award, organized by the magazine Footwear News.

❑ 2002, June. Four stores are opened in Italy and fifty more around the world. Another single-brand shop opens in Rome. It overlooks Piazza di Spagna and represents a new concept of a store: that of "a walk in progress." In fact, it is a store-department with a temporary look, interactive and made with recycled materials. It is a sort of workshop space where you enter not only to buy but also to leave your signature and thoughts on the walls. The Collection is exhibited on a table supported by shoe boxes, in the store's center. There are four main lines of footwear: Pelotas, inspired by soccer; Twins, an asymmetrical pair; Brothers, with a contoured sole; and, finally, Industrial, hi-tech and comfortable.

❑ 2003, April. The opening of the first European Info-shop, at 28 Old Bond Street, in London.

❑ 2004, April. For the Olympics in Athens, the Spanish firm has created, in a limited edition, the Olympics line. Twins and Less are the two unique models, made in the colors of Olympic medals, gold, silver, and bronze.

Campi Silk factory near Como specialized in fabric for ties. It was established in 1922 by Enrico Campi, who took over the weaving mill in Appiano Gentile (CO) belonging to Verga & Campi, of which he was a partner. At the death of Enrico in 1941, the business was first entrusted to his son-in-law Luigi Guggiari and, in 1948, to his son Giovanni. Around the mid 1950s the brand started to enjoy steady success, with a massive distribution of jacquard fabric for ties on the international market. In that period, Giovanni Campi brought under his own control the shares owned by the heirs of various associates and family members. After his death in 1992, Campi merged, in stages, with the Ratti Group, until its complete takeover in 1998. Among the company's clients are Armani, Dolce & Gabbana, Ferré, and Valentino in Italy; and Calvin Klein, Donna Karan, Ralph Lauren, and Saint-Laurent abroad. (*Pierangelo Mastantuono*)

Camuglio David Vincent (1972). French designer, of Corsican origin. He graduated in 1998 from the Studio Berçot in Paris, but during his school years he worked as an assistant for prestigious houses such as Louis Féraud, Shirtology, and Jeremy Scott. After graduation he was a *stagista* at Costume National. The following year he presented his Collection during the Paris Fashion Week for men's wear. He has presented his haute couture Collections since 2001.

Canadienne Three-quarter jacket that, in fashion jargon is known by the French word "canadienne." It drops to the hips or halfway down the thigh, and is made either in leather or waterproof fabric, with fur on the inside and at the neck. Fastened with buttons or frogs, with a belt around the waist, and roomy pockets, it is inspired by the gear of Canadian hunters.

Canal Nina (1953). Painter of fabric. A nomadic artist is inspired by the world's tribes, she is also a successful rock musician with the group Ut. Born in Cape Town, South Africa, she moved to London in the 1960s. She studied first at the Camberwell School of Art, and then at the Hornsey College of Art. In 1976, after graduation, she painted fabrics for the designer Porter. In New York, she created the brand Nika and, together with other young designers, formed the Under Designer Group. During the 1980s she was in London, working under the pseudonym King Cobra. From 1990 to 1998 she was in Los Angeles, where she painted scarves under her own name. She sells her creations to the most important international boutiques. Since 1998 she has lived in London and Paris, producing her own line of scarves, and working with fashion designers such as Jerome L'Huillier and Paul Smith.

Canali Men's clothing company, established in 1934 by the brothers Giovanni and Giacomo Canali. Its production is mainly in shirts and jackets of excellent tailoring. The entire history of Canali can be seen in a simple comparison between the small tailor's workshop with which it started and the seven manufacturing plants that will bring it into the third millennium. The business began with two owner-operators and just a few workers. Now the company is guided by the third generation and there are 1,000 workers. Within three generations, production has expanded to include accessories, sportswear, and ties.

> ❑ 2003, June. Canali receives the Pitti Immagine Uomo prize. The award, received by Eugenio Canali, general manager of the company, is usually given to those who distinguish themselves in the field of fashion, increasing the success of the Made in Italy movement. Canali clothing is manufactured in seven production centers, all connected to the central headquarters at Sovico, near Milan. About 75% of the turnover is sold abroad. The most important market is North America, followed by Western Europe. Growing markets include those of the former Soviet Union. The year 2002 ended with a turnover of €145 million.

C&A Dutch group active in the manufacture and distribution of clothing. It is among the world's leaders. Its yearly turnover (an average in the early 1990s) amounts to 10,000 billion liras. The acronym is composed of the names of the brothers Clemens and August Brenninkmeijer, who in 1841 in Sneek, Holland established a clothing factory. The first C&A shop was opened in 1861. It was a success because it offered, ahead of its time, ready-to-wear fashion at cheap prices. In 1910 it began expanding throughout Holland and then abroad, where other family members opened new shops: the first was in Germany (1911), followed by England (1922), Belgium (1963), France (1972), Switzerland (1977), Luxembourg (1982), Spain (1983), Austria (1984), Portugal (1991), and, finally, Denmark (1995), for a total of 550 shops and a staff of 40,000 people. It offers clothing for children, men, and women in different styles and at different prices, all in the same location. The brands offered by the company, which is today still owned by the family, are Westbury, Jinglers, Palomino, Clockhouse, Rodeo, Your & Sense, Baby Club, Angelo Litrico, Yessica, Canda, and Here & There.

(Valeria Vantaggi)

Canedi Maria Luisa (1930). High fashion dressmaker from Bologna. She began to sew at the very young age of 12. Up until the mid 1960s she worked in Bologna first as an assistant and then as a department chief in the tailoring shops of Buscardi and Bellini. In 1969 she started her own business, opening an atelier on via Fondazza, the same address where the painter Giorgio Morandi lived. She created evening and bridal dresses, and suits that were custom-made from paper patterns obtained from the French houses of Saint-Laurent and Givenchy. Throughout the years, she specialized in the Ungaro lines, and these are still the foundation of her production.

Canepa Tessitura Serica Italian company which, from its Como headquarters, is active mainly with silk, and to a lesser extent with linen, cotton, viscose, acetate, and nylon. It was established in 1966 by Giovanni Canepa. In 1972, his children Silvia, Francesca, Elisabetta, Michele, and Giovanna joined the business. It produces fabric for clothing such as ties and scarves, and for furniture. In 1993, it acquired Intermoda (silk ties and scarves), which employed 10 workers and had a turnover of 9 billion liras. In 1998 the Group produced 400,000 ties and 4.12 million yards of fabric, with a turnover of 113 billion liras and a working staff of 357 employees. Since that year, the company has been guided by the founder's daughters.

Canette D'Or An award given by the Belgian Textile and Manufacturing Institute. It goes to the best Collection designed in Belgium and manufactured with Belgian materials. The first to receive the award, in 1982, was the designer Anne Demeulermeester, only one year after graduating from the

Royal Academy in Antwerp. Another of the entrants was Dries Van Noten, a student at the time, who by 1985 would win the award twice. In the three years that followed, Walter Van Beirendock was always among the top ten finalists. In 1989, the winner was Veronique Le Roy.

Canfora Workshop in Capri that produces artisan-made loafers and sandals. Famous for its very soft leather, the Canfora family was the first to decorate and embellish its creations with inlays and ornaments made of glass and metal. Their history begins at the end of the 1800s, with a first shop on via Fuorlovado. Between the late 1940s and early 1950s, Amedeo Canfora moved the business to its present location: in a boutique not far from the Quisiana hotel on via Camerelle. Leather thongs were already very successful in this period, but their boom occurred in the 1960s and 1970s. Among its clientele have been Jacqueline Onassis, Soraya, Maria Callas, Dawn Addams, Grace Kelly, and Dado Ruspoli.

Cangioli Italian wool company. Its headquarters are in Prato, near Florence. It was established by Vincenzo Cangioli in 1859: a workshop "to fill the warp" which, eleven years later, would be enlarged by the acquisition of a plant in Vaiano furnished with machines operated by self-produced hydroelectric power. In 1881, the company adopted a kind of law that was strange and unusual for the time. It was the *Worker's Document* and it set down the workers' duties, and, also, though in a limited way, their rights, as, for example, their right to give notice and resign. Toward the end of the century, the inheritor of the company, Alceste, decided to build the plant in Prato. Strong export activity, especially to England, allowed the firm to expand its production to include clothing, with a network of shops, and in 1930 to add blankets. In 1938 a new spinning, dyeing and weaving mill was opened. In 1958, Vincenzo II, named after his grandfather, the founder, was succeeded by his sons Carlo, Gherardo, and Sergio. At the end of the 1970s they decided to make investments in the fabric division which they supported with large imports of alpaca. In 1987 the family business was joined by Gherardo's children, Sabina and Vincenzo. In 1992 further massive investments started a technological modernization process that was followed by a strong increase in the number of products offered. The group consists of six companies: women's fabrics, men's drapery, spinning, industrial weaving, dyeing, and refinishing. It employs 200 workers. The group sells in Italy, Germany, France, Belgium, England, Spain, Japan, and the U.S. When, during World War II, there was fighting in Tuscany, an artillery shell destroyed a chimney of Lanificio Cangioli, but left the rest of the building intact. The image of that chimney became at that time the symbol of Prato. (*Giuliana Zabeo Ricca*)

Cannistrà Giovanni (1969). Sicilian designer. Before the age of 20 he already had his own atelier in Catania. By the 1990s he was participating in the high fashion presentations in Rome, showing evening dresses that were particularly rich with lace and brocades. He pays particular attention to tailoring details and strong color contrasts. For many critics, he is inspired by Christian Lacroix both in technique and style. His creations often recall the traditions and contrasts in color of his native land.

Canonero Milena (1952). Italian costume maker. She often worked with Stanley Kubrick and Francis Ford Coppola, receiving several Oscar nominations (*Out Of Africa* and *Tucker*) and winning the Oscar twice (*Barry Lyndon* and *Chariots Of Fire*). Extremely versatile, she has worked in the stylized universe of *A Clockwork Orange*, on the minute reconstruction of uniforms and costumes of the 1700s, in the obsessive dimension of *Shining*, and on the gangster costumes of *The Godfather III* and *Cotton Club*. Among her most imaginative creations were the Warren Beatty costumes for *Dick Tracy*.

Canovas Isabelle (1945). French designer. Accessories, especially if original and fanciful, can increase the appeal of even the simplest dress, and are the only articles with which it is possible to be extravagant and excessive. This is the philosophy of Isabelle Canovas, the sister of Manuel, the creator of fabrics for furniture. In her three boutiques in Paris, New York, and Madrid, one can find umbrellas, fans, eye glasses, gloves, belts, and bags, all the product of her creative imagination.

Cantarelli Industrial group active in prêt-à-porter fashion. It began with the manufacture of men's wear in the 1960s. The founder was Mauro Ranieri Cantarelli, and he was later joined by his children Rita and Alessandro, responsible for the women's and men's divisions, respectively. The group has two main operating two companies. One is Cantarelli & C., with two plants in the province of Arezzo, one in Rigutino (for menswear) and one in Terentola (womenswear), with a total of 675 employees. The other is Saintandrew's in Bellocchio di Fano, in Pesaro, taken over in 1992 for its menswear production; it has 145 workers. The global turnover of the group, entirely controlled by the family, amounts to roughly 110 billion liras, of which 77 billion are sold in Italy and 32 billion abroad, especially in Europe. (*Fulvio Bertasso*)

❑ 2002, February. The year 2001 ended with a turnover of around €67 million, some 60% of which was in Italy. The company has 800 workers employed in three subsidiary companies.
❑ Cantarelli presents its Collections in the garden of the Hotel Diana in Milan, transformed for the occasion into a market in Zanzibar. Each of the island's spices gives a name and a perfume to a garment, in a colonial atmosphere that introduces a Spring-Summer Collection that plays on the binomial of taste and color, with stripes in cinnamon, curry, saffron, and clove. Midst palm trees, bamboo, and papyrus, the bush jackets, the clothes that remind one of Karen Blixen, the linen blazers in natural colors with a dye extracted from cloves, of which the clothes preserve the perfume.
❑ 2003, June. Two seasons after its début, Cant's, a tailoring project strongly desired by Alessandro Cantarelli, enjoys good commercial success. The turnover comes 50% from Italy and 50% from the East.

Cant's Men's brand and line created by the Cantarelli Group. Designed by Antonio Mazzocco and Alessandro Cantarelli, the first Cant's Collection was created to coincide with the Spring-Summer 2003 Collections and is offered as a men's wardrobe consisting of two sections: a more formal one, characterized by refined tailoring techniques and excellent quality; and a more informal one for leisure time, with pieces in jersey, button-neck T-shirts, and small accessories. The line is produced in Rigutino (Arezzo) and sold in multi-brand boutiques in Italy, Europe, and Asia. After two seasons, the turnover of the brand is €1 million. (*Sara Tieni*)

Canulli Stefano (1959). Italian designer, born in Rome. He works with Lancetti, Valentino, and Capucci. After studying at the Academy of Fine Arts and at the Academy of Costume and Fashion in Rome, he also took courses in photography and advertising. By the age of 20 he was already at the side of Pino Lancetti, working on high fashion Collections. The partnership would last until 1982. Given the job of illustrating the historical archives of Capucci, he worked with the great designer until 1986. From 1989 to 1991 he designed for Thierry Mugler. He createed several advertising campaigns, including those for Valentino Haut Couture, Bruno Piattelli, and Chiara Boni. In 1994 the Museum of Modern Art in New York showed his sketches as part of an exhibit about the Italian shoe.

Canvas Resistant cotton fabric manufactured with twisted yarns in warp and weft. It is the historic fabric of the first jeans, at the time manufactured with sailcloth, that is, in cotton.

C.a.o. (Conception assistée par ordinateur; Computer Aided Concept). Different from D.a. (Dessin assisté par ordinateur; Computer Aided Design), which simulates products in the form of images, C.a.o. conceives a product by taking in account its morphologic limits and the techniques of production. This technology made its appearance in the mid 1960s, and was applied to cutting and paper patterns, and was improved in the early 1970s on textile structure. A computer transforms the data provided (measurements, model, and fabric) into a standard paper pattern on which fabric is then cut with a laser and later sewn. It is therefore possible to create custom-made prototypes in a very short time. C.a.o. provides also an archive which facilitates the work of designers. The system was created by the Alsatian company Vestra.

(*Marilea Somaré*)

Caon Corinna (1952). Italian designer, born in Padua. She has worked in the field of fashion for more than thirty years. In 1976, after her studies and an apprenticeship with a manufacturer of women's prêt-à-porter, she joined the technical staff of Just Fun, a creative structure in which she did research for several brands, including Fiorucci. It was an important period of professional growth, especially for the establishment of her personal style. Before launching her own line, she designed a casual Collection called Casablanca and worked for the firm Sartorie Riunite and its shirtwear brand Équipe. In 1994, after perfecting her tailoring techniques and materials research, she cooperated with Dea to develop a project using her own name and designs, and, in the meantime, small Collections for the Coin Group. Her first Collection was in 1998, presented at Moda Prima in Milan, where she still presents her creations, and also at prêt-à-porter week in Paris. Her style is clean, essential and innovative.

(*Lucia Serlenga*)

Caovilla René (1938). Shoe designer. Called the Cellini of shoes, this designer-entrepreneur, who works in Stra, on the Riviera of the Brenta, inherited a simple artisan's shop from his father. Today, he produces more than 200 pair of shoes a year, can count on a partnership of more than 20 years with Valentino, and works with Ferré, Galliano, and Lauren. Among his most affectionate clients are Caroline of Monaco, Elizabeth Taylor, Sharon Stone, Sofia Loren, Madonna, Nancy Reagan, and Brooke Shields. His shoes are manufactured with unusual and very precious materials, adopting artisanal techniques that are no longer used by others. Very famous is his snake-sandal. It is nothing more than a string studded with crystals around the ankle.

❑ The first and most precious of René's collaborators is his wife, Paola Caovilla Buratto. In addition to being in charge of public relations and communication, she also personally designs the most innovative and important styles.

❑ 2002, October. The brand is launched in the Far East. A series of presentation-events, organized by the distributor Lane Crawford, a big chain of luxury stores, introduces the Caovillas in Hong Kong and Shanghai where they presents their latest luxury models and consolidate the brand's official launch in the Far East.

Capalbio A company which has relaunched the tradition of clothing in the regions of Tuscany and the Maremma. Established in the 1940s as a small factory with the corporate name of Confezioni Tre Torri di Roccasarda, it soon specialized in the manufacture of classic Tuscan jackets. The tradition of Tuscan clothing dates back to the early 1800s. Farmers and noblemen would wear a particular type of jacket that had large side, back, and inside pockets, which were very useful when out in the country or hunting. Jackets for farmers were mainly made from locally-produced fustian and velvet. Those for the rich, however, would use the most precious English and French velvets or moleskin fustian, in addition to Irish tweed and Scottish *chevoir*, which are often custom made. Very well known is the tweed of the Gherardesca family, made in the colors of their coat of arms. By resuming the manufacture of this historical clothing and adapting it to the present day, the Clothing Company, which produces the Capalbio brand, also attends to its preservation. In the 1990s, annual production reached 120,000 pieces, respecting the tradition but also paying particular attention to the ecologic aspects. The brand has been relaunched, and is now protected, by the Global World Foundation, a non-profit association whose president is Count Gaddo della Gherardesca and whose purpose is the defense of the traditions of the Maremma. (*Gianluca Cantaro*)

Capdevilla Massana Manuel (1910). Spanish jeweler and painter. Born in Barcelona, he continued the tradition of his father Joaquim when, in the 1950s, he inherited the jewellery and silver shop that had been opened in 1918. The main features of his creations are often non-precious materials which, thanks to the artist's genius, are ennobled and exalted by their material and chromatic qualities. In order to devote himself completely to painting, some years ago he entrusted the company's management to his own son Joaquim.

(*Cristina Lucchini*)

Cape Large sleeveless mantle, with two side openings for the arms, and a hood, often lined with fur. In the early 1800s, men would wear it as an evening mantle, black with a red lining and a silk collar. Its width allowed women to use it over crinoline skirts.It is often made with precious fur and worn with an evening dress instead of a stole. A variant is the pelerine, which falls only to the waist. Worn on top of an overcoat, it can also be removed. It was the garment of pilgrims and the uniform of French policemen. Following the ups and downs of fashion, the cloak has often been relaunched throughout the twentieth century.

Capellini Lorenzo (1939). Italian photographer. He began his career in the 1950s, ranging from reportage to ballet, from theater to architecture, and art. Toward the end of that decade, he also worked in fashion, working in London with Novità, Vogue, and Queen, and later in Milan with Amica, Gioia, and Vogue Italy. He has exhibit his work at the Centre Pompidou in Paris, at Palazzo Vecchio in Florence, and at New York University.

❑ He is also well-known for portraits of important personalities, including Patty Smith, Giuseppe Ungaretti, Pier Paolo Pasolini, Henry Moore, Maurice Béjart, and Michelangelo Antonioni.
❑ 2003. As part of an event dedicated to that period, Padua featured him in an exhibition entitled *The Sixties by Lorenzo Capellini.*

Capello Jewellery shop in Turin. Established by Vincenzo Capello in 1864, its first headquarters was on via Po. After the Bill of March 14th 1867, it became an official supplier to the Royal House of Savoy, for which it created tiaras and noble ornaments. The family has handed on its tradition from father to son. Today, the owner is Guglielmo Capello, who designs and creates the jewels himself. In the early 1900s, the shop moved to via Accademia delle Scienze, where it is still located today. In 1981, next to the old shop, they opened a boutique which, together with jewellery meant for a younger public, offers a line of silver and gift articles.

Capogrossi Giuseppe (1900-1972). Italian painter. He designed jewellery in the spirit of the abstract compositions of his paintings. In particular, he adopted, both in pictures and brooches, a prong mark which he repeated in different patterns creating color contrasts among the materials used. For a brooch created in the 1950s, he brought together yellow gold, diamonds, coral, and onyx. Among the first Italians to devote himself to informal sign painting, the Roman artist Capogrossi collaborated, in the early 1950s, with the dressmaker Marucelli. In the Collection of Giancarlo Calza, the son of the designer, there are some taffeta dresses accompanied by the artist's original sketches, and an evening dress from the Autumn-Winter 1967-1968 Collection with sequins and abstract trimming.

Capone Guglielmo (1961). Italian designer, born in Caserta. He made his début with Max Mara. In a short time his work was successful and he designed for other important Italian prêt-à-porter companies such as Fendi, Erreuno, and les Copains. In 1991, he had the first men's and women's Collections under his own name, and in 1995 he opened a showroom in Milan.

Caponi Loretta. An embroiderer since the age of 9, she opened in Florence, between the two world wars, a workshop which still carries her name and manufactures women's underwear and trousseaus that are noteworthy for their precious hand-made embroidery. Loretta still works together with her daughter Lucia and other expert embroiderers in her atelier on Piazza Antinori. She tells how she has always been inspired by her clients, the environment they live in, art, and nature. She has always been faithful to the traditional artisanal techniques of her trade. She owns a Collection of embroidery, both detached pieces and pieces that have been applied to clothing, from 1500 to today.

Cappellificio Fagiani Hat factory in the region of Le Marche established by Vincenzo Fagiani in 1976. He soon devoted himself to the manufacture of straw hats with the help of just a very few workers. But already by the early 1980s, thanks to the excellent quality and precision of his manufacturing, he expanded the internal structure and market penetration, reaching a greater number of clients in foreign markets such as Germany, France, Belgium, and Switzerland.

Cappellificio Falcus Hat factory in Tuscany active since the mid 1960s. Its headquarters is in Montevarchi. The factory makes men's hats of all types, from classic to casual models, in fabric, rabbit-hair felt, merino felt, exotic straws, and fur. After 1990, the company became a licensee and producer of the Panizza brand, a very prestigious *griffe* known world-wide that was founded in Piedmont in 1889.

Cappellificio La Familiare Established in 1905, when 10 workers quit the Rossi firm, a company founded in Montevarchi in 1798 that was a pioneer in the working of felt hats, and set up a hat factory which in 1910 took the corporate name of La Familiare. Nino Donati was appointed president (in the 1920s he started his own hat factory), while production management was entrusted to Angelo Masini, an experienced artisan. The production of the new company soon supplanted the Czechoslovak, Austrian, and French companies which had dominated the market for women's millinery. The company's fame increased thanks to the collaboration of milliner Giulio Ponsecchi, known in the world of fashion under the pseudonym Gigi of Florence. After World War II, Ponsecchi designed both La Familiare's felt hats, which since 1952 always opened the fashion presentations at the Sala Bianca of Palazzo Pitti, and Nino Donati's straw hats. (*Stefania Ricci*)

Cappellificio Panizza Historic hat factory established after 1880 in a small building in Verbano on the shore of Lake Maggiore. Thanks to a promising start, in 1882 the owner, Giovanni Panizza, acquired more land in order to expand production. In the early 1900s, Panizza started a business with the Gamba family. This partnership would take the hat factory to such levels as to convince the two partners, in 1933, to build a large new plant for the tacking and blowing department. In October 1954, Giovanni died. Eleven years later, the Gamba family was forced to abandon the business. This began a long period of decline from which the company could not escape, so that in 1981 the factory closed.

Capraro Alberto (1943). American designer. He opened his atelier in 1974 in New York. Part of his success was due to a very important and regular client, Betty Ford, the wife of former President of the U.S. Gerald Ford. After attending the Parson's School of Design, he worked with Oscar De la Renta and designed hats for Lilly Daché.

Capucci Roberto (1930). He is considered the greatest Italian creator of high fashion, understood as a source of unique pieces. He started designing clothes at a very young age.

Evening dress by Roberto Capucci.

In 1951 he presented his first Collections in Florence, under the guidance of Giovanni Battista Giorgini, causing a sensation, kicking up a great fuss, and obtaining enormous success. In 1956, after the presentation in Palazzo Pitti, he was acclaimed by the international press as the best Italian fashion designer. He was complimented even by Christian Dior: "In Italy you have a prodigy named Roberto Capucci; should he turn up in Paris, I hope he comes to visit me." Roberto was unable to accept Dior's invitation because the inventor of the New Look died that very same year. In 1958, with the creation of his box-shaped line, he won the Oscar of Fashion, a prize awarded by Filene's of Boston which, for the first time, gave it to an Italian designer. From 1962 to 1968 he was in Paris where he opened an atelier and would be the first Italian couturier offered a chance to give his name to a perfume. In 1970 he worked with Pier Paolo Pasolini, who chose him to design the costumes of Silvana Mangano for *Teorema*. Over time, his preference for research and his need for freedom from the ruling fashion trends, and also from the repetitiveness of the fashion calendar and the demands of the *griffes*, would increase. In the early 1980s, when Collections could be watched on TV and prêt-à-porter prevailed, he abandoned the Chamber of Fashion and decided to present his Collections according to his own rhythms, always in different towns, and often in museums. In 1986 the Arena of Verona invited him to design the costumes of the priestesses in *Norma* for the *Tribute to Maria Callas*. In 1994 he was awarded the title Academic of Brera. In 1995 he was invited by the China Textile Council to give a series of seminars on the art of fashion at the universities of Beijing and Shanghai. Born in Rome, the son of a doctor, he studied art in high school and then at the Academy of Fine Arts in Rome, where he attended the courses of Mazzacurati, Avenali, and De Libero. He "stumbled" into fashion almost by chance: he had wanted to be a set designer, a costume designer, or perhaps an architect. An outsider since his début, he was scared "by the contagion of vulgarity, by the rule of bad taste, by ugliness" and decided to isolate himself in the *turris eburnea* (the ivory tower) of his atelier in a lonely creativity. He lives a secluded life, looking for stimulus far away from the universe of fashion, which is for him too commercial. He finds it in far-off travels, observing the flight of a bird during an African safari, but also simply by peeling an orange, copying the elegant spiral of the peel. He becomes inspired looking at a painting, a statue, or a suit of armor; or by observing the plissé of a ruff, the voluptuousness of the damask in a portrait by Bronzino, the drapery of a cloak in a statue by Bernini, or the indefinable light-blue of a corset in a painting by Cosimo Tura. Feelings of affinity also have a role in his choice of the most suitable frame in which to show his work: ancient noble palaces, museums, academies, and concert halls. Every presentation is an event, more similar to an artist's personal exhibit than to a fashion runway. To prepare a Collection, he can make as many as 1,200 sketches, first in black-and-white, so as not to be influenced by colors, and then he selects them. Every dress can require as much as four months of work and almost 200 yards of fabric, chosen from among the most precious ones. Capucci is the last to use ermesin taffeta, a fabric that is hand-made on looms from the 1500s. He demands satins that are as soft as crepe, using the *sauvage*, a very sought-after raw silk, the Mikado, the georgette, and fabrics dyed in Lyon. He will reproduce up to 172 shades of one color in the plissé of a cloak, a girdle, or a skirt, as in the dress inspired by the *Oceans* shown on the Italian stand of Lisbon Expo in 1998. He follows a visionary dream of beauty in sculpture-dresses with swirls, crests, and ribs that combine the sumptuousness, the rigor, and the solemnity of Renaissance costumes, fantastic architectures, spectacular allegories, and clothes of very strong personality and nonexistent practicality, much sought after for magnificent balls and particularly important weddings. "I never allowed myself to be influenced by the logic of 'When shall I wear it? On what occasion?' The history of costume wouldn't exist if others, over the centuries, had thought this way." He was the first, in the 1960s, to conceive avant-guard runways on which to introduce elements of extravagant and subtle humor, where he had fun experimenting with every sort of material, such raffia, straw, sea rocks, plastics filled with colored water, bamboo, sackcloth, glass-reinforced plastic, Perspex, and fluorescent rosary beads (Paris, 1965). He rejected the inflated term of designer, preferring to be called a researcher. He was the first to abhor and condemn the phenomenon of top models, who, according to him "suck the blood from clothes. His first client was Isa Miranda, followed by Doris Duranti and Elisa Cegani. Elvina Pallavicini, the princess of the Lefebvre schism, opened the way for the first ladies and the first young ladies of the black aristocracy, the so-called "capuccine" as Irene Brin would define them. For very special occasions he dressed solemn princesses, divas, and first ladies, from Gloria Swanson to Marilyn Monroe, Jacqueline Kennedy, and Silvana Mangano, who Capucci considers the most elegant woman he ever met. Rita Levi Montalcini wore his velvet dress with a short train in Stockholm, during the Nobel ceremony. Among his personal exhibitions: *Roberto Capucci, The Art Of Fashion, Volume, Color, Method* in Florence at Palazzo Strozzi (organized by Pitti Immagine from an idea by Luigi Settembrini), and also in Munich, at the Stadtmuseum, in 1990; *Roberto Capucci, Roben wie Rustungen* at the Kunsthistoriches Museum in 1991, with 80 of his dresses presented next to the same number of ceremonial suits of armor from the 1400s; *Roberto Capucci, The Paths of Creativity* in Rome, at Palazzo delle Esposizioni, in 1994, the year when some dresses from the Capucci archive were exhibited in Montefalco (Perugia) next to paintings by Benozzo Gozzoli and Perugino from the 1400s; *Roberto Capucci's Never-Manufactured Designs*, in Milan, at Palazzo Bagatti Valsecchi,

A design by Roberto Capucci.

in Spring 1999. His clothes are on permanent display in several museums throughout the world, including the Gallery of Costume at Palazzo Pitti in Florence, the Museo-Fortuny in Venice, the Victoria and Albert Museum in London, and the Kunsthistoriches Museum in Vienna.

(*Laura Laurenzi*)

❑ 2001, February. Capucci celebrates 50 years in fashion. Venice dedicates an exhibit to him, organized and curated by Gianluca Bauzano, with the support of the National Chamber of Fashion and designed by Nylstar, on the occasion of the third edition of the Meryl Awards.
❑ 2001, July. Capucci sells part of his empire to Franco Bruccoleri, for twenty years a distributor of great brands in Europe. Bruccoleri is the chief of a syndicate of investors who have decided to relaunch the Capucci brand, without undermining its identity. Roberto Capucci is to remain artistic director of the firm.
❑ 2002, May. To accompany the Capucci exhibit in Tokyo, Fashion System Italy, together with the Italian Textile Association and the Chamber of Fashion, organizes *Flash Made in Italy*. It is an installation with four mega screens, five monitors, and a space for meetings between Italian entrepreneurs and Japanese buyers. The screens broadcast images of the Milano Moda Donna Collections and of Italian events having to do with yarns and clothing. An internet connection let visitors visit the web-sites of more than 600 companies. In 2001, Italian exports of clothes and accessories to Japan amounted to €954 million, an increase of 10% compared to the previous year.
❑ 2003, March. A new creative team, part of the house, will reinvent the style and the image of the prêt-à-porter line, with the help of an archive of 30,000 drawings, sketches, and outlines (half of which are totally new), while respecting the traditions of the firm. The three new designers are: Bernhard Wilhelm, a German; Sybilla, who is from Spain; and Tara Subkoff, an American and a designer at Imitation of Christ.
❑ 2003, May. Clothes as sculpture, true works of art, are those shown by Roberto Capucci during an exhibit organized in a very suitable location, the 18th century Villa Panza, donated to FAI by the contemporary art collector Giuseppe Panza of Biumo. The 80 dresses by Capucci are shown by shape and color in relationship with the art that surrounds them. It is a very wide-ranging retrospective, starting with the box-shaped line of 1958. The pieces exhibited include "Fire," first presented in New York in 1985; the group of clothes for the Biennial of Venice in 1995 that were inspired by the visionary world of mineral and natural elements; the Ocean line created for the Lisbon Expo which combined thousands of pieces of fabric to imitate the colors of the sea; and the Giorgini Collection created to honor 50 years of Italian fashion and the man who launched it in Florence in 1951. The exhibition is curated by Gianluca Bauzano with a catalogue by Skira.
❑ 2003, July. The new Eveningwear Collection, designed by Sybilla, is presented in Paris. The "happening" also sees the début of the new shoe line designed by Franca Maria Carraro. High fashion continues to be the work of Capucci. A selection of clothes anticipating the Spring-Summer 2004 Collection is presented at Rue de Sevigné 46.
❑ 2005, July. Franco Bruccoleri announces in an interview that the planned prêt-à-porter line has ben officially suspended. This happens after the launch of the last Spring-Summer 2005 Collection and in spite of the positive reaction of buyers.

(*Gabriella Gregorietti*)

Capucine Stage name of Germaine Lefèvre (1938), a French actress and model. The daughter of an industrial entrepreneur, she attended school in Samur, where she was discovered by a local photographer and immediately captured by the world of fashion. On the runways she wore clothes by Dior, Balmain and Givenchy. She belongs to the kind of model that has a sacral, sophisticated, and glossy beauty. After a trip to America, she went from the atelier to the movie set, making her début in 1960 in *Song Without End*. Among her other films are *Walk On The Wild Side*, *The Pink Panther*, and *What's New, Pussycat?*

Capuzzolo Massimo (1958). Designer of high fashion and prêt-à-porter from Rome. At first a set designer and an interior decorator, he later became a pupil of Pino Lancetti. In 2000, he presented a Collection of his own for the first time, during the official calendar of Rome's Alta Moda. He also designed a line of accessories. He favors strong colors such as prune, green and bordeaux, and likes asymmetric tops and hems cut vigorously on the bias. He combines very pronounced colors with precious fabrics such as silk, taffeta, and organza. He also distinguishes himself for the high-fashion use of trim in ecologically-friendly fur. In 2002, he presented his Collection at the Art Café. A theme on the runway was the use of elastic bands to compress the waist and knees.

Caracciolo Heliette. Jewellery designer. Refined and cultivated, with a degree from the University of Pisa in the Preservation of the Artistic Heritage, her success came at the same time as that of the new Italian fashion in the years of Palazzo Pitti. In the 1960s her collaboration was sought by several high-fashion designers, including Valentino, Lancetti, and Fausto Sarli. She designed and manufactured jewellery for the cinema and theater. She retired at the end of the 1970s.

Caraceni A family dynasty of men's tailoring known all over the world, with origins in Abruzzi. The head of the family, Tommaso, lived and worked in Ortona (Chieti), where he was born in 1880. Three of his sons learned the art of sewing from him, Domenico, Augusto, and Galliano. They were to make the name of Caraceni famous all over Italy, and later, all over the world. In the beginning it was Domenico, the oldest, in Rome during the 1920s and later followed by Augusto and Galliano, whose work contributed to the success of the enterprise. During the 1930s, Augusto left Rome for Paris, where he opens an atelier on Avenue d'Jena. It was a three-storey building and the location for the entire manufacturing cycle. Galliano remained in Rome with his brother Domenico. During those years from 1930 to 1940, the Caraceni brothers, in Rome and in Paris, worked unceasingly to reach the top, and they succeeded. In fact, from all over the world the most important personalities of the time came to the Caraceni atelier, including politicians, musicians, literary figures, theatrical actors, members of royal houses, and entrepreneurs. In 1940, due to the outbreak of the war, Augusto, as an Italian in enemy territory, was forced against his will to close the Paris atelier and return to Italy. In that same year, Domenico died in Rome. At the end of the war, Galliano reopened the Rome atelier, while Augusto opened a new one in Milan, at via Fatebenefratelli 16. The years between 1946 and 1970 were the family's second artistic period, in which the Caraceni clientele changed and completed itself in accord with the trends of international high society in that time. Between the 1970s and 1980s, first Augusto and then Galliano passed away. With the three pioneers gone, the family continued with renewed vigor. In Rome, Tommy and Giulio, the sons of Galliano, manage the atelier, while in Milan there is Mario, the son of Augusto, who in honor of his father has kept the original sign "A. Caraceni on his atelier. The third Caraceni generation is very successful. Mario has received, among many awards, the St. Omobono prize, the gold medal and certificate of the Milanese Tailor's Guild, and the Great Prize of A Life as a Tailor from the National Academy of Tailors in Rome. During the 1980s and 1990s, the fourth generation prepares itself, while already working in the ateliers in Milan and Rome, learning the secrets of the trade. The great merit of Caraceni is to have introduced, starting with their first appearance on the world stage of artistic tailoring, their own methods of cutting, so that the suit is able to follow, in an anatomical way, the movements of the person wearing it, and thus acquires a perfect wearability that is unattainable in any other way. This is the Caraceni secret, and such it will remain as long as there is a Caraceni who will treasure and transmit it to his successor, and to him only.

(*Gaetano Afeltra*)

Caraceni Domenico (1880-1939). Italian tailor. Together with Ciro Giuliano, he is considered an absolute master. He was the nephew and son of tailors. Tommaso, his father, never left Ortona a Mare, where he was born and inherited the workshop in which he would work until the early 1900s. He was helped by many of his thirteen children, first of all by Domenico and Augusto, who was called Agostino, to whom he taught the trade. It was in this workshop that the first English suits of their fellow citizen Francesco Paolo Tosti made their appearance. The suits were manufactured for the Italian composer by the same London tailor on Savile Row who dressed Edward VII, crowned King of England in 1901 and a symbol of Anglo-Saxon elegance. The musical romances *Malia*, *Vorrei Morir*, and *Non t'Amo Più* stirred the enthusiasm of the extremely stiff Queen Victoria, who named Tosti singing-master at the English Court, "stealing" him from the House of Savoy family and from the Quirinale. Rescued by his talent from a poor life in Ortona, the musician knew that in his homeland even a used suit was a treasure. When he no longer wore a particular jacket or suit, something that happened often, as Edward VII had given him the virus of Dandysm, he would send it to his family in Italy. There it was neccessary to alter them, by taking them in, tightening the sleeves, or lengthening the pants. The suits of "peasant" Tosti, who would be named a baronet, ended up in the tailor's workshop belonging to the Caraceni family. Mario, Tommy and Giulio Caraceni, cousins and heirs of the dynasty, who continue that tailoring tradition, tell how "Domenico would unstitch and disassemble them, to study the cutting, the stitches, the technique. England is the motherland of men's tailoring for the entire world. Domenico Caraceni learned its secrets and 'mixed' that technique, which he also studied deeply in English handbooks, with ours which came from the Abruzzi-Italian tradition and was more complicated and insistent in the stitching. He added, we could say, a Mediterranean softness to the dough, modifying the line of the British tailors, whose suits are always a little stiff, a bit like a military uniform, and have a certain internal substance somewhat like 'armor.' This is why we say that a Caraceni suit has the lightness of a handkerchief. Domenico was so certain to have invented something new that he patented his technique, receiving patent number 28642. Since then, the Abruzzi tailoring school has distinguished itself from the Neapolitan school, which is more marked and exasperated." When, in 1933, Domenico decided to hand on what he had studied, learned, invented, and put into practice during so many years of work, he published the treatise *Orientamenti nuovi nella tecnica e nell'arte del sarto*. The preface was written by the member of the Italian Academy Massimo Bontempelli, one of the greatest minds of the 1900s: "In this treatise Domenico Caraceni places himself among the rationalist or, if you prefer, functionalist architects. It's not so strange. The architect dresses the earth, the tailor dresses the men who walk on it. And tailoring, no matter how little you think of the history of costume through the centuries, always walks in parallel with architecture....Caraceni shows a surprising understanding of his time: 'We are at the height of the 20th century in a marvelous flowering of new forms.' He explains that while the spirit of past centuries fulfilled itself by satisfying a taste for exterior things and had an abundance of decorative motifs, unwisely altering the natural contours of the human figure, today the fundamental essence of proper dress lies in an interpretation of the clothed body that leaves it above all with freedom of movement. For him, the three important qualities of modern manufacturing are softness, lightness, and flexibility. The synthesis of all these requirements is simplicity."

(*Guido Vergani*)

Caraceni Ferdinando (1923). Men's tailor born in Ortona a Mare, same as Domenico Caraceni, the head of the dynasty of great Italian tailors and of the Abruzzi tailoring school. But the two are not from the same family. The story of Ferdinando mingles with that of Augusto Caraceni, the brother of Domenico, in whose tailoring shop in Milan he worked for more than 20 years. When Augusto called him to Milan, Ferdinando was 16 and had already completed his apprenticeship. He was raised on bread and tailoring. As a child, he attended elementary school, and then spent the afternoons "sewing loose stitches" in the shop of the tailor Garzelli. At the age of 13, Alessandro Cavaliere, the best tailor among those who remained in Ortona (the Caraceni brothers had already left for Rome), took him into his shop and taught him the profession. Ferdinando remembers that the trade "had to be in a sense stolen, secretly observing what was done by the 'master,' who was jealous of his secrets, above all when he attached the armhole." The little Caraceni observed and learned: first attaining a "completed apprenticeship" and then, a few years later, becoming a cutter. In 1967 he left Augusto's workshop and started his own business in Milan, on via San Marco. He was helped by Nicoletta, who managed the atelier and referred to herself as "the missing son."

(*Guido Vergani*)

Caraco French term which made its appearance in the 8th century referring to the costume of a French province. The shirt, buttoned in the front, is also called a "robe à la Suzanne" and worn by country women. At the end of 1700s the caraco was also worn in town, launched by the Earl of Avignon, who discovered it in Nantes. In this way it became a garment of the aristocracy, used when traveling, when riding, or as a negligee. Today it refers to a folk blouse with long sleeves, often low-necked and buttoned in the front with laces or hooks, soft and floating, with tails or a skirt from the waist to the hips.

Caractère Italian brand of prêt-à-porter. It was established in 1990, but the manufacturing company, Vestebene, had already been operating for 35 years as an internal division of the Miroglio Group of Alba, whose origins go back to 1884. The brand, which designs neat and linear women's clothes, is distributed throughout Europe, with single-brand boutiques in the most fashionable towns.

❑ 2001, June. The web-site of Caractère receives an award in Cannes on the occasion of the 48th International Festival of Advertising. The result of a collaboration with Q-Turn, the creative workshop of Quam-Narum, the site offers a narrative-sensory path made of images, sound, and noises about the new Autumn-Winter 2001 Collection.

❑ 2002, March. Opening of the first boutique in Moscow.

❑ 2002, September. A new look is given to the Milan boutique for its reopening: sycamore wood and, on the polished floor, the ancient sediment of shells. The brand is distributed in 5 countries through corner shops in Selfridges, Harrod's, and Galeries Lafayette, and through multi-brand stores. For the Miroglio Group, whose 2001 turnover was €824 million (divided between Vestebene and the Division of Fabric and Yarn), Caractère continues to represent the best.

❑ 2003. The opening in Verona, on the very central via Mazzini, of the 13th boutique. In July, another new store opens in Palermo. The 2002 turnover is more than €50 million.

Caramelo Clothing house for men and women named after one of the founders, José Antonio Caramelo. In 1969, three Galicians, Luis Gestal, Javier Cañas, and José Caramelo, opened a factory for high-quality raincoats in La Coruña. The first product was called Antilluvia. Two years later, the production was diversified into three men's lines: Tommy Harrods trousers, Chelton jackets and overcoats, and Yale jerseys. The 1980s saw the distribution of the brand's men's and women's lines in the Spanish market. Today, in the La Coruña plants, the creative staff consists of some thirty designers. There are 718 workers who manufacture 1.5 million pieces a year, distributed in Spain and 27 other countries, including Saudi Arabia, the Philippines, Jordan, and China. In 2002 the turnover was €78 million. (*Pierangelo Mastantuono*)

Carcoat Short overcoat to be worn in cars. It has pockets in the front, two buttons, and loosely-cut sleeves, so as to be comfortable when driving.

Cardigan Woolen jacket, without a neck and buttoned in front. It is a particularly informal garment, whose origin and name are connected to the battle of Balaklava in 1854. In particular, it is associated with the British General J. Th. Brudenel, Earl of Cardigan, who was perhaps its first enthusiast and who commanded the celebrated Charge of the Light Brigade. Very fashionable, especially in the form of a twin set (and better if a Chanel), among boarders and patronesses during the 1970s; it returns to fashion at every cyclical return of the look inspired by the Nouvelle Vague.

Cardin Pierre (1922). French designer. He was born in Sant'Andrea di Barbarana in the Italian province of Treviso. He moved with his family to France in 1926, when he was still in kindergarten. At the age of 14 he began to work in the small workshop of a tailor in Saint Etienne, then he was in Manby during the Nazi occupation. In 1944, after the liberation of Paris, he found a job at Paquin and later, one at Schiaparelli, after working for some time at the Red Cross as an accountant, an experience that would be very useful in the future, as he himself would say. Dior, making his début, hired him as first cutter. Meetings with Cocteau and Bérard push him so much in the direction of the theater that he decided to quit Dior in order to open, together with Marcel Escoffier, a costume atelier. For some years, he hung in the balance between his passion for the literary world and the call of high fashion. Haute couture won out, when, in partnership with André Olivier (his right-hand man in a professional and personal relationship that would end only with André's death in 1993), he presented his styles. It was July 1957. He would return to the theater later, in 1970, not as a costume designer but as a passionate, courageous owner-manager, opening the Espace Cardin ("Je me suis fait plaisir") which, in contrast to his other activities, soaked up millions. He never gave up its program of "avant-guard theater, the launch of young talents," even when critics were not generous. I met Cardin in the Summer of 1957. I was introduced to him by Chino Bert, today a monk but at the time a companion and friend with whom Cardin shared his passion for style and the nightlife. He had just opened an atelier on Rue Faubourg Saint-Honoré, a neighborhood which by now is practically his own property, with nine shops, apartments, and an atelier larger than the Eliseé Palace. I can't remember if I was struck by his first Collection: those were the years of the myth of Dior, of the very mundane Fath and Balmain, of the still astonishing Balenciaga. But I was struck by the man Cardin: beautiful, gentle, sensitive, available. But the pale and cold eyes, and the willful mouth, would reveal an authority and a will that was feverish, almost impatient, and hardly contained by his slow and sweet voice. It was an attractive and disconcerting contrast. I think that precisely in this physical contrast, which expresses the complexity of his nature, is the secret of his amazing success. Yes, because this apparently romantic gentleman, who started out without economic support, without loans, patrons, or producers, built an empire with an enormous business turnover. Cardin has always been faithful to his motto: "High fashion, a source of ideas." Since his début (his absolutely against-the-tide "robe bulles" were a triumph) he has always presented endless Collections as a show of fireworks: 200, 300 models, numberless ideas which would have been enough to make four normal Collections, mixing pieces of sophisticated elegance, of such a purity and genial ability with crazy articles that bordered on kitsch, with avant-guard inventions that would be understood only years later. He was the first to bring the miniskirt on the runway – though he is not mentioned with Courrèges and Mary Quant. His astronauts, later imitated by all department stores, took off before man reached the moon. The very tight skirt, sexy and with a vent, dates to 1966: it was a scandal. As were his prefabricated clothes, for which he used a mould as with a pudding, and his aggressive plastic jewels. One ought to give him credit for all this and also for the fact that he never fell into retro or folklorist temptations. And though dressing women such as Begun, Farah Diba, Lauren Bacall, and, of course, Jeanne Moreau, his great love, he never indulged his clients when creating for them, and he never created for the street. "Clothes have to be worn out in the street, but it's not up to the street to teach the style." He was always alert to changes in society and customs. "I have been the first socialist of fashion," he would proclaim. That explains why in 1958 he signed his first contract with La Rinascente and the German department stores, causing a scandal in the world of haute couture, and why he quit the Chambre Syndicale: "With the money earned from these contracts, which was a lot," he would make clear, "I was able to finance my own activities [this was the real secret of his

Pierre Cardin's styles interpreted by Maria Pezzi.

success: reinvestment], enlarge my ateliers, and take over a shirt factory, which gave me the idea of men's fashion." It was the right, necessary moment for a fashion aimed at young people who were becoming the new leading group in society. And he, a provocateur, in order to have everyone talk and write about him ("When you are talked about, you sell"), he, the best public relations man for himself, created improbably flower-patterned ties and printed shirts, at the moment impossible to sell, but worn by real students. Behind these coups de theatre there was a serious, new production that would culminate in the "dévertebrée" jacket, a triumph that would enable him to conquer America. This American success, and his large private clientele, were due in good part to his ex director Mad, Nicole Alphand, the wife of the former French Ambassador to the U.S., and his ex "right arm" André Olivier. They were of two absolutely opposite tempers: Cardin, a loner, and Oliver, the idol of international café society. Still in 1958, Cardin signed his first license in Japan and returned from there with an excellent photographer, Joshi Takara (a precious member of his team who has been with him ever since), and that idol called Iroko who would be the most important and most photographed exotic mannequin in Paris. From that moment on, trying to follow Cardin was like trying to keep up with lightening. To talking about Cardin as simply a fashion personality is impossible: the man Cardin who travels around the world every year; who deals with queens, presidents, and political personalities; the man who by 1960 was already more famous than Brigitte Bardot ("Ah non; il y avait De Gaulle, Brigitte et moi."); the man who owns a skyscraper in New York, a small village near Cannes, and a tiny palace in Venice ("I go there every year because it's a charming place and the people are friendly."). The Chinese government invites him so that he could see on the spot how China could develop a textile industry. And he is the mad one who brought haute couture to Shanghai and Beijing and, as an advertisement for France, opened Chez Maxim's in Beijing, New York, and Moscow. One day I told him: "You have conquered half the planet as did Napoleon." He answered: "Much more: he would bring mourning, death and war; I bring beauty and work." He works incessantly, but not for the money. "It is my hobby. I don't have cars, yachts, or luxury jets; I have no time for reading, but I know all the world's museums and love the theater and music. I have no vices." He lives alone. He has no servant, no staff. He will make his own bed, eat a sandwich, or open a can simply in order not to lose contact with reality. This is the unique case of a man who, working in order to give life to his ideals and not for money, drowns in it like Uncle Scrooge. Accepted among the Immortals of the Academy of France, laden with honors and money (he is one of the most important real estate owners in Paris), he has no rest. In Summer 1997 I met him in Venice. He was 75: "Je voudrais te dire un tas des choses, chérie, mais je n'ai pas le temps." A plane was waiting for him. He had spent only a few hours there. He moves like lightning. In his work he is a genius able to immerse his fashion within reality, into the present time, into whatever floats on the air or in the wind. In 1980 the Metropolitan Museum of Art dedicated the exhibition *30 Years of Design* to him, and, in 1990, the Victoria and Albert Museum had an exhibit *Pierre Cardin: Past, Present, Future*. At the age of 80, after 60 years of work, Cardin sold his company.

(*Maria Pezzi*)

❑ 2000. To celebrate 50 years of work (he opened his *maison* in 1950 on Rue Richepensée), he organizes a presentation of 100 historic models "as if they were the works of an artist in an art gallery." The presentation takes place in a new space on Booulevard Saint Antoine, at the Concepì Culturel Pierre Cardin. The designer had avoided "open" presentations for years, in order not to be copied.

❑ 2002, December. He plans the sale of his company. The 80 year-old tailor has changed his mind compared to the way he felt seven months before, and recently announced that he wants to sell his empire. It is certain that he doesn't want to deal with the luxury groups, so therefore no negotiation is open with Bernard Arnault (LVMH Group) or François Pinault (Pinault Printemps-Redoute Group). There are 900 Pierre

Cardin licenses scattered in more than 140 countries, and the company has a value of roughly 1 billion dollars. LVMH is still interested in the acquisition. The year 2001 ends with a loss and a turnover of €48.7 million against €53.9 million in 2000. Counter to this trend there is only Pierre Cardin Italy, where the turnover increased more than 10% and the profit was almost €26 million.

❑ 2002, May. From his villa in Cannes, he attended the Festival and gave the press a categorical denial concerning a possible sale of his company. He will not follow the example of Yves Saint-Laurent and has no intention to sell his licenses.

❑ 2003, January. Pitti Immagine gives him the career award during a great party at Palazzo Corsini, ending with a retrospective presentation dedicated to the historic pieces of the designer.

❑ 2003, April. The decision to sell is taken. In Rome, at the Hotel de Russie, where his Chez Maxim's is given the award for best restaurant, the 80 year-old designer declares: "I will sell Cardin to a European banking group which will respect my name. I exclude the luxury groups because they have to manage too many brands. I am not one of many." He excepts only the Marzotto Group, because it is a "pure" company, involved only in the textile-clothing area. Cardin himself, though, leads a very diversified empire which ranges from fashion to restaurants (with 18 restaurants, 8 boutiques, 200,000 employees, 800 products, mineral waters, theaters, and museums). The designer has bought the castle that once belonged to the Marquis De Sade, 64 miles from Avignon, in order to create a museum. On the Cote D'Azur, he has bought the Boule buildings near Cannes.

❑ 2003, July. In the Autumn-Winter Collection, the Cardin man seems to have landed from space. Jackets and coats are without sleeves, which have been eliminated to "allow freedom in the shirts and pullovers." Somewhat similar to waistcoats, and a little robotic, they are worn with rigorously tight trousers.

❑ 2003, July. Solera, a company of underwear and corsetry, has acquired an exclusive Cardin license for underwear for Europe, the U.S., and Mexico, starting with the Spring-Summer 2003 Collection. The company, with headquarters in Occhiobello (Rovigo), ended 2002 with a turnover of about €10 million. At present, the Cardin line is distributed in more than 200 boutiques in Italy and 50 more abroad.

Foulard dresses by Pierre Cardin in a sketch by Maria Pezzi. 1970s.

Cardinale Lidia (1954). Italian designer. She opened her atelier in Brescia 20 years ago. She made her name on the runways in Milan in February 2003. Continuing a family tradition, she cultivated a passion for drawing, a subject which she also teaches. She interprets the trends of the moment, filtering them through her creative sensitivity with very original ideas, combining a very high aesthetic level with steady attention to functionality and comfort. She thinks that the beauty and distinctive features of a garment depend 60% on the choice of fabric. Hers is an elegance that is simple and linear based on refined details: a velvet pantsuit along classic lines, short flower-patterned chiffon dresses with a high belt around the waist, worn with high-heel boots at mid calf. She has also shown small fishnet wool dresses that are seductive and feminine; short Winter coats in black velvet that give a glimpse of shorts and bustiers with laces; a python-patterned trench coat in rabbit skink; and ethnic embroidery on tailored garments. She uses strong colors, often black and brown, and red only in the evening for tailored dresses. At her Milan début, two friends presented her creations: Viviana Beccalossi, the district councilor and vice president of the Lombardy Region, and Patrizia Romani, the wife of the district councilor Paolo Romani. They closed the presentation by coming out together on the runway, one wearing a chalkstripe tailored suit, the other an evening dress. Her atelier in Brescia is often visited by women who are in Italian politics, such as Ombretta Colli.

(*Gabriella Gregorietti*)

Cardona David (1964). American designer, born in Colombia but raised in Los Angeles. He has a degree in engineering. He started designing planes for McDonnel Douglas Corporation. Then, after graduating with the highest marks from a school of design, he entered the fashion industry and worked for five years in the atelier of Richard Tyler. In 1997 he met John Bowman, the founder of Crome Heart, a brand of luxury leather goods and jewellery, and two years later they started Bowman Cardona, which became the manufacturing company for the brand David Cardona. In 2000 he won the *Fashion Award* and, in 2002, he was nominated for the Fashion Group International's *Rising Star Award* Cardona dresses several Hollywood stars, including Angelica Houston, Raquel Welch, Holly Hunter, Britney Spears, and Janet Jackson. He has won an Emmy Award as best costume designer. Besides the world of cinema, he is active in the world of music and his clothes have been worn by stars such as The Backstreet Boys, Carlos Santana, Natalie Cole, and Yolanda. Starting in 2003 he designed the Cerruti women's Collections, though still continuing to work on his own line.

Carel French brand of shoes and prêt-à-porter. The Carel family opened a shop in Paris in 1949 and at the beginning simply sold luxury shoes designed by Séducta and René Cary. The company's first original models date to 1952 (Babies and Marquis, among many). They immediately won the favor of prestigious clients such as Michèle Morgan, Brigitte Bardot, and Sylvie Vartan, and established the success of the brand. Around 1972 Georges, the founder, was joined by his son Tony (1947) who studied design and shoe manufacturing techniques in Milan. Together they established creative partnerships with many designers (Chantal Thomass, De Castelbajac, Gaultier, Mugler, Beretta) and opened one boutique in Neuilly, two in Paris, and three corner shops in the French department stores Printemps, Parly 2, and Galeries Lafayette. The brand mixes materials and colors: zebra stripes and leopard patterns, multicolor crocodile skin, iridescent plastic, studded leather and leather embellished with strass, or glass paste. During the 1980s, Tony broadened the company's horizon: he offered a women's prêt-à-porter line, one marked by masculine influence, and opened another shop, again in Paris, on Avenue Victor Hugo. In the 1990s Carel dressed the working woman, one who needs comfortable clothes but doesn't want to give up her seductiveness, and therefore wears sandals embroidered with small pearls. In this period two more points-of-sale were opened in Paris: one at Bon Marché, on the *rive gauche*, and one at Rue du Cercle 13. On average, the company sells 60,000 pairs of shoes a year. (*Olivella Pianetti*)

Cargo-pants Loosely cut casual trousers, large and comfortable, with large side external pockets and a vent at the waist.

Caribbean Style Fashion inspired by the famous islands. It took center stage in fashion at the end of the 1960s, when Europeans first began to go to the Caribbean for their holidays. Still today a constant source of inspiration for several *griffes* (especially for the Summer Collections),

Caribbean Style is made of just a few essential elements, inspired by the ocean: a colored beach robe, the monokini thong, short T-shirts, and thong shoes decorated in flower-patterns that alternate with cork-soled slippers.

Carioca Maglierie Knitwear and casualwear clothing company that manufactures on the authorization of the High Chiefs of Staff of the Italian Air Force and the Navy, in addition to the General Command of the Guardia di Finanza. The company's lines are called Air Force, Navy Riflemen, and The Guard. Their shape, lines and design are obviously inspired by military style, with original elements as well. The company, established in 1975 by Sauro Mazzola, has been characterized for many years by the general production of casualwear and leisure clothing. In the wake of the success of the Richard Gere film *An Officer and A Gentleman*, the first attempt to give the brand a stronger identity was made with the creation of the Sea Army line: jackets, sweaters, and trousers to be worn whether sailing or in town. The brand was sold to another company in Carpi, but Carioca enlarged its production to include new lines inspired by the military.

Carita French brand of products for face, body, and hair care. It was 1929 when Maria and Rosy Carita, aged 18 and 16, began to work as hairdressers in the space of a former butcher's shop in Toulouse. The small salon became immediately well-known in the area: during World War II and the German occupation of Paris, it was visited by the most elegant women of Paris who took shelter in the free zone. In 1943 the two sisters decided to move to Paris. At the first they worked as apprentices at Gervais, the most famous hairdresser of the time, until they were able to open their own salon. In 1947 they purchased a space at Rue Faubourg Saint-Honoré 5. Within three years they were already employing 50 people and producing their first cosmetics. But success forced them to move again. In 1951 they opened at n.° 11 on the same street (today the headquarters of the Carita Center for Total Beauty), beginning a decade-long collaboration with the coiffeur Alexandre, and later opening a beauty institute where they set up the first complete line of Carita products (face, body, and hair treatments, make-up, and sun products). Towards the end of the 1950s, they attained international fame thanks to the first pineapple-shaped wigs created for the 1958 Spring Collection of Givenchy. The hair styles of the most prominent women in the world at that time were designed by Carita: from the chignon of Maria Callas to the haircut Juliette Gréco, and from the ponytail of Brigitte Bardot to the platinum blond hair of Catherine Deneuve. After the death of the sisters, in 1986 the brand was acquired by Shiseido, which relaunched and modernized the products, focusing on their curative effect.

Carla Carini Line of the clothing company established in 1968 in Moglia (Mantova) by the siblings Elleno and Carla Gasparrini. Carla is the creator of all the lines and president of the Carla Carini Production Company. To the main line, intended especially for young ladies, with classic and casual pieces, they have in recent years added Onli Carini (evening dresses and a more sophisticated wardrobe), Diario (an Anglo-American look for younger women), and Carinissima, a more trendy line.

Carlier French fashion house. Active at the end of the 1800s and in the early 1900s, it was directed by Madame Carlier, who had her greatest success as a milliner, with her very large hats inspired by fashions of the past.

Carlo Barbera & C. Weaving mill in Callabiano (Biella) established in 1949. It works with Australian merino super-refined wool, cashmere, alpaca, and mohair. From the beginning, it has been known for quality. Yarns, before being treated, are stored in a warehouse dug into rock and kept at a constant temperature. In 1971 the Group expanded vertically, launching a prêt-à-porter line for men and women called Luciano Barbera. In 1998 the turnover was 23 billion liras, with exports some 40%. of that. There are 140 employees. The management of the firm is totally in the hands of the family. The president is Carlo Barbera, the founder. Luciano and Giorgio are the general managers. Corrado is the commercial manager.

Carma A historic brand of knitwear, an industry which, after World War II, has contributed to the fame of the small town of Carpi, near Modena. Established in 1952, it manufactures knit outerwear, cut and sewn, for a medium to high clientele. It has never changed ownership.

Carmen Marc Valvo. American designer. In 1989 he established, with an investment of only ten thousand dollars, a clothing and accessory company bearing his own name. Inspired by several trips made around the world, the designer created Collections echoing the Orient and Africa, both in the lines and in the fabrics. A graduate of the Parson's School of Design, before creating his own brand he worked with Atkinson, Nina Ricci, and Dior.

Carnegie Hattie (1889-1956). American designer. In the U.S. her name has been a synonym for high fashion for more than half a century. This was not just for her personal Collections, which aimed, with great refinement, to interpret European styles for American consumers, but rather for her noteworthy ability to select and put the finishing touches on the creations of others. Her empire outlived her up until the 1970s.

Caron French brand of perfumes created in 1904 in Asnières by Ernest Daltroff (1870-1941). The first fragrances, *Royal Caron* and *Chantecler*, in 1906, were followed by many others, including *Narcisse Noir*, *Tabac Blond*, and *Bellodgia*. Starting in 1911, they were always sold in elegant Baccarat crystal bottles. In 1921, the year in which Daltroff found a wise "nose and blending" partner in Michel Morsetti, the perfume *Nuit de Noël* marked the début of the American subsidiary of Caron Corporation on Firth Avenue in New York, an address just as prestigious as that of the Paris salon at Place Vendôme 10. Among Caron's most celebrated fragrances (Caron was the name of a mythical acrobat at the beginning of the last century) are *L'Infini* (created in 1912 and relaunched in 1970), *Fleurs de Rocaille* (1933), and *Le Muguet du Bohneur*, launched, according to the French custom, on May 1st, in 1952. Closer to our time was the success of *Nocturnes* in 1981. The studded boxes of the powder *Peau Fines*, created in the 1930s, have been much-imitated objects of female desire. In 1987, Caron was absorbed by the group Cora-Revillon. (*Emma Costa*)

Carosa Roman house of high fashion whose name was derived from an anagram of the names of two ladies of the nobility who decided, in 1947, to start a business in the field of couture: Princess Giovanna Caracciolo Ginetti (1910-1983) and Barbara Angelini Desalles. The latter quit almost immediately, while Donna Giovanna continued until the mid 1970s. She didn't know how to sew, but she knew how to dress. She had two passions: Balenciaga and the Roman baroque. Thanks to her excellent taste, she was an exceptional talent scout (those who worked in her atelier include Ibi Farkas, De Barentzen, Lancetti, Giambattista Vannozzi, Quirino Conti, and Tarlazzi, her favorite) and was able to command respect in the world of the good Roman bourgeoisie and the international aristocracy. From the windows of her atelier on Piazza di Spagna, pointing out the cupolas, she would exhort her collaborators to look at them and "to appreciate the volumes and proportions." On February 12th 1951 she was invited to the first presentation by Giorgini in Florence. Tarlazzi collaborated with her until 1972. Two years later, the Carosa atelier closed, in large part because of the crisis in high fashion sector caused by the now dominant prêt-à-porter industry. Quirino Conti, who worked with her, writes: "She would get worked up over the flare of a skirt, agonizing over the bias and raving for a certain particular stitch in black."

Carothers Wallace Hume (1896-1937). American chemist and director of research at the American firm Du Pont between 1928 and 1937. He led the team which in 1928 finalized the discovery of nylon, a synthetic material for making yarn first marketed in 1938.

Carpi Town located 29 miles from Modena. It is one of the main centers of European knitwear manufacturing. Economists say that the "Italian Miracle," from the 1950s on, has more of its roots in Carpi and certain small villages of the Veneto, and in strongholds of stocking manufacture such as Castel Goffredo, than in the Turin of Fiat or the

Milan of Pirelli. The "Carpi case" didn't Spring from nothing. It came from a very long and widespread entrepreneurial tradition and a highly-qualified network of artisanal talent deeply embedded in the social-economic reality of the area: hundreds of companies and production units, many family-managed, which made Carpi the capital of the Florentine straw hat, from the production of straw boaters to "magiostrina," and which were hard hit by changes in fashion and the decline of hats. At the end of World War II, all those small factories, firms, and tiny workshops reinvented themselves and started over in the field of knitwear, guessing that after the storm good times would return, and with them a new hunger for clothes. It wasn't something that happened within a few months, as if someone had given the order. Only a handful of straw hat entrepreneurs led the way, but others would soon follow their example. It was a swarm of small, often home-based artisanal operations, with women who passed from knitting to cotton looms, to fulling and raising a nap, and to the double cylinder of circle machines, of families who turned to looms in order to obtain what working with straw or in agriculture could no longer provide them. Year after year, a myriad of companies sprouted up, with people working for third parties, households working at their looms, people toiling under the porticos of buildings, of Lambretta engines backfiring on balconies in order to provide energy to a weaving machine located in the dining-room. At work were grandparents, parents, and children: Mother was the designer, and, quite often, the manager; Father was the loom technician; and children took turns at round-the-clock shifts. As Umberto Severi, a pioneer and real champion of Carpi knitwear, once said: "Giorgio is at the machine in the morning, Maria in the afternoon, and Luciano at night." Selling the goods, with an eye especially on the international market, was something in the DNA of the people of Carpi. "In our veins ran the habit of looking beyond our borders," says Severi. "The name Carpi was a calling card for people like me who traveled around the world to sell. Our hat industry had made a name for itself in many places: the Riuniti firm had headquarters in Paris, London, New York, and Tokyo, and would export to all the continents." The fabric of widespread entrepreneurship favored the formation of a system based on productive decentralization in a territory that, within small distances, grouped all the steps of manufacturing and all the necessary services: spinning, dyeing, weaving mills, manufacturing, ironing workshops, and the maintenance of looms. "Within such a system," wrote Elisa Massai and Paolo Lombardi in their essay *L'industria della maglieria nell'alta moda e nella moda pronta dal 1950 al 1980* (*La moda italiana*, Electa Publishing 1987), "every firm that designs the product and collects the orders organizes around itself a net of weavers who work only against a buyer's order and to which it entrusts the manufacturing of individual articles and every step of production, optimizing times and production costs. Corporate structures are light and reduce fixed costs to a minimum." In March 1962, Giorgio Bocca, in a reportage series for the newspaper Il Giorno about the "miracle" in that Italian province described a Carpi already "miraculously saved": "... Bramante buildings and Este towers surrounded by the pink-blue cubes of factories, hundreds of small firms with their corporate name on the outside: Clorinda, Miriam, CCC, Lucy, Giba, Noemi, Effegi, Globus, Marilyn, and Magic....These were strange factories, small, perhaps without a company car and with just a few workers, but they were able to provide unbelievable quantities of jerseys. More than factories, these were delivery stations and places for sorting goods made at home; oh yes, those long lines of women on bicycles with their bundles resting on the handlebars, skeins of wool if they were going home, jerseys if they were riding in the opposite direction. In the factories, their work was finished and marketed....If Carpi didn't exist, you would have to invent it, in order to explain to future generations what was the 'Italian miracle'. Last year, Italy exported jerseys worth 18 billion lire and as many were sold on the domestic market. If we stick to jersey, Carpi is the third most important city in Europe and the first in Italy. Some can't believe it: ten years ago there was nothing here, just 1,800 workers who would go in search of a job in the Piedmont rice fields. The poverty of the manual workers was a terrible burden on everyone." In that year of 1962, the number of factories was 250. Instead of the Red Revolution (Carpi, like the entire province of Emilia, votes Communist), as Bocca would write, it was the "maier" revolution, a revolution of knitters. In 1996, there were 2,000 companies in Carpi. In 1990, there were 2,258. Between the ups and down, in boom times and difficult periods, Carpi remains a capital of world knitwear and the mirror of that "Italian miracle" that you can understand only if you use the term miracle only with a secular meaning, without any divine or witchcraft aspects: not an event determined from above, but a reality built thanks to human intelligence and intuition, the courage to take risks, creativity, hard work, and entrepreneurial flexibility.

(*Guido Vergani*)

❑ 2001, November. Carpi underlines its "authority" in the field of fashion. On occasion of the 10th World Convention of the Italian Chambers of Commerce abroad, the Town Councillorship for the Politics of Economic Development, with the support of the province of Modena, and the collaboration of the consortium CarpiTrade Italia, presented at the Town Theatre of Modena *A Fashion Night*, an event starring 24 companies from Carpi. The district today has about 1,850 companies employing 11,000 people, with a turnover of more than 2,000 billion liras.

❑ 2001, November. On occasion of Moda Prima in Milan, there is a preview of the Autumn-Winter 2002-2003's presentations from Carpi. Three times a day, 24 Collections are presented on the runway within the exhibit space of CarpiTrade Italia.

❑ 2002, February. Some companies belonging to the Consortium Eco CarpiTrade Italia are to participate in the Magic of Las Vegas, one of the most important American trade shows which will host many brands from all over the world. Twice a year, more than 100,000 experts participate in the development of private brands and of relationships with large distributors.

❑ 2002, February. Present at the Momi Moda Milan are several companies from the Consortium Eco (Export Consulting Organization) of Carpi, which has 50 member firms. The purpose is to make overseas markets better acquainted with the Italian textile industry, of which Carpi is an important manufacturing center, through its new ways of using traditional materials.

Carrera Factory established in Verona in the early 1960s, specialized in the production of jeans. The founders were three brothers, Imerio, Tito, and Domenico Tacchella. In Italy, it is number two in its field. The brand established its reputation at an international level in the 1970s, thanks in part to aggressive advertising. The entire production cycle is carried out in the Calderio plant, an 18th century villa restored according to industrial needs. The spinning is done with the Ring technology, which provides an extremely resistant and silky fabric. The cutting operations are completely automated, allowing the manufacture of very high quality jeans. Their main piece is the basic, produced in different fabrics and in a wide range of brilliant colors. Starting in the 1990s, the company diversified its production line to include shirts, jackets, and accessories, starting a total look of its own. In 1999 it set up a new yarn called Spintech (the inner part of the polyester yarn is covered in soft cotton) for the manufacture of "no ironing" trousers.

Carretti Olmes (1948). A manager in the clothing industry, born in Reggio Emilia. After some years as a "hippy," he worked in the Collection and sale of second-hand clothes. He worked for Spitfire (1975), Fiorucci (1977), and Robe di Kappa (1978). After making a lot of money, he also became famous, in the late 1970s and early 1980s, thanks to cult brands such as Best Company, Henry Lloyd, and Sperry Topsider. He now works on restyling famous but somewhat out-of-date brands, such as the Tyrolese jackets Hofer and the Norwegian clothing line Devold.

Carrilero Pierre (1959). French designer. In 1999 he launched the Pierrot brand, which is, after all, his nickname in everyday life. He learned to knit at a very young age in order to pass the time while recovering from an accident during a soccer match. His experience includes time spent in the textile sector in Lyon, a job at the Paris boutique Magic Circle, a début under this name as a knitwear designer, and a period in New York working for Miguel Adrover and the Horn boutique. His style of fashion proves that everything can be solved with knitwear.

Car Shoe In 1963, Gianni Mostile invented and patented a style of light shoe, a loafer with an upper perforated by very tiny rubber gussets. It was launched as a shoe for automobile drivers, but soon became a fashion accessory of great comfort and practicality. In 2001, the Prada Group acquired the brand and reorganized its style and image. It has a single-brand store in Milan and one in Capri.

Cartalis Anastassios (1966). Greek designer. He studied fashion at the Lette-Verein school in Berlin. From 1991 to 1997 he worked for Nina Ricci in Paris. He created his own brand, Cartalis, in 1997. In 2000, Swarovski hired him to create designs with crystal decorations. The following year he presented his Autumn-Winter 2001-2002 Collection at the Tuilieries. In 2002 he presented his second couture Collection.

Cartier French jeweler. By now in business for more than a century and half, its creative vitality does not decline and it has maintained its right to be considered the leader among the world's great international jewellery designers. Everything began in a small goldsmith's workshop that saw the first examples of a production which would be appreciated, some decades later, by the royal courts of the entire world. In 1847, Louis François Cartier opened his first workshop in Paris, on Rue Montorgueil. Twelve years later, after moving to the Boulevard des Italiens, he began to be appreciated by the most prestigious and demanding clientele of the city. When his son Alfred joined the business, production experienced noteworthy growth. The firm moved to Rue de la Paix in 1899, by which time Cartier jewelry was widely renowned. A year before, in 1898, Alfred's son Louis had concluded a particularly profitable liaison with the Parisian jet set by marrying Andrée Worth, the daughter of the celebrated tailor Charles Frédéric Worth. The jewellery shop, located just a few steps away from the fashion atelier, attracted interest for its extraordinary pieces created in a garland style inspired by the art of the 18th century. Great success was achieved at the English court on occasion of the coronation of Edward VII who, right then, talking about Cartier, uttered the famous sentence "roi des joalliers parce que joaillier des rois" ("king of jewellers because jeweller of kings"), and shortly thereafter a London office was opened on New Burlington Street, under the direction of Jacques Cartier, the younger brother of Louis. It was 1902. In 1908 Pierre was entrusted with the management of the New York boutique in Fifth Avenue. Cartier's most famous watches date to those years of the early 1900s: the Santos, created in 1904 for the aviator Santos-Dumont; the Tonneau (1906); and the Tortue (1912). Louis was the soul of Cartier's jewels, and he was able to shape their image thanks to an artistic sensitivity, an intellectual curiosity, and a creative taste which transcended cultural and geographic borders. He was a great traveler, an habitué at society events, and an aristocratic and self-assured man. After 1907, abandoning the garland style, he invented new geometric motifs which anticipated Art Deco. Influenced by Oriental art, by the Russian ballets introduced in Paris by Diaghilev, and by the dominant neo-Egyptian fashions of the early 1920s, he led the Cartier style to its complete fulfillment. Along with jewellery in onyx, rock crystal, enamel, coral, diamonds, and precious stones, he created the famous "mysterious watches," masterpieces of technical virtuosity played out through the chromatic magic of semi-precious stones. In the 1930s it was the turn of the Tutti Frutti designs, which featured colored precious stones. In the meantime, Louis was joined, in the design department, by Jeanne Toussaint, a very talented designer who would create several famous pieces, including evening bags, cigarette cases, watches, and jewellery. Very famous were the flamingo-shaped brooch of 1940 and the Panthère brooch of 1949, both created for Wallace Simpson, the Duchess of Windsor. In 1945, after the deaths of Louis and Jacques, Pierre Cartier became president of the group, and he would maintain that position until his own death in 1964. The firm was then led by Robert Hocp, who was replaced by Alain Dominique Perrain. He is still at the head of the firm and has attracted a younger clientele. In 1981, the house launched a perfume, named Must, along with a line of deluxe leather goods. The dress swords of the Academy of France are designed by Cartier. In 1988, with the establishment of the Richemont Group, the firm pursued a policy of acquisitions: Baume & Mercier, Piaget, Dunhill, Panerai, and Vacheron Constantin, among others, were all absorbed into the group. In 1994, ten years after its founding, the Fondation Cartier pour l'Art Contemporain was moved to Paris, on Boulevard Raspail, in a space designed by the architect Jean Nouvel, where it has continued an intense activity aimed at the organization of exhibits and avant-guard cultural events. In 1997, Cartier celebrated its 150th anniversary with the retrospective exhibit *Cartier 1900-1939* at the Metropolitan Museum of Art in New York. The exhibit traveled to the British Museum in London as well as other prestigious locations. Since 1999 the Richemont Group has also owned the Parisian jewellery company Van Cleef & Arpels. In 2000 it acquired the LMH group, which has watch brands such as Jaeger LeCoultre, IWC, and A. Lange & Sohne. In 2002, Cartier, which is present throughout the world in more than 200 boutiques, celebrated its connection to art and culture by organizing, under the artistic direction of the architect and designer Ettore Sottsass, the exhibition *Cartier's Design Seen By Ettore Sottsass*. It contained more than 200 pieces, including jewellery, watches, accessories, and precious objects. The show was at the Vitra Design Museum in Berlin and at the Palazzo Reale in Milan.

(*Alessandra Quattordio*)

❑ 2002, October. The reopening in Milan of Cartier's historic headquarters in via Montenapoleone. Conceived by Cartier, and under the artistic direction of Giampiero Bodino, the new boutique occupies three floors. The house first opened in Milan in 1975.

❑ 2003, June. The Compagnie Financière Richemont ends the fiscal year (March 31st) with a steady decline in profits. Also decreasing were the gross margin and sales, but the dividend remains at €0.32 per share. In greater detail, in 2003 net profits went down to €642 million from the previous €826 million. Turnover went down to €3.65 billion from €3.86 billion, a reduction of 5.4%.

❑ 2005, June. The 2004 balance sheet is positive in all respects. Growth is evident in every geographic area and in every sector. At March 31st, the turnover of the Group Richemont was 3.72 billion euros, an increase of 10% compared to the previous year. Also increased were the operative result and the profits, by 77% and 33% respectively.

Cartier brooch, 1887.

Caruso Annalisa. Italian designer. She is definitely a unique case in the panaroma of fashion. Her passion is mixing art and fashion. She has always been inspired by the world of art, ranging from American abstract expressionism to Matisse and contemporary artists. Her 3-year license from the Andy Warhol Foundation for the Visual Arts, obtained after a strict selection process, required her to take the Foundation's needs into account when designing her Collections. For three consecutive seasons she created only a women's line, but now she produces shoes and a men's line as well. In 2002, in the classroom of an auditorium in Rome, she recreated the atmosphere of Warhol's Silver Factory and of the fabulous 1970s in New

York with a performance set in rooms with mirrored walls. Grotesque models, sitting in small plastic swimming pools like dolls or robots, presented a static Collection of evening dresses and skirts in synthetic fabrics covered with silk-screen prints of Marilyn Monroe. There were T-shirts and petticoats with the world's most famous soup can reproduced on a background made of pages from the newspaper that also had Monroe's picture, and black skirts with red-cross embroideries, swollen by layers of chiffon with a picture of Elvis in the background. (*Gabriella Gregorietti*)

Caruso: Ma.Co. Manufacturer of men's tailored clothes, established by Raffaele Caruso, a high-quality tailor, in 1958 in Soragna, in the province of Parma. His clothes are distinctive because they are made with artisanal techniques within an industrialized context at the level of human resources. Jackets are all lined in order to give them a soft and functional feel. The garments also undergo a special washing process that gives them a vintage look. The Raffaele Caruso line is distributed by Ma.Co. throughout the world in several exclusive shops. (*Sofia Camerana*)

Carven French fashion house. The hopes and the sweetness of life in the post-World War II period will always be linked to the very successful perfume *Ma Griffe*, named after the much-praised dress with green stripes on a white background that was in the first Collection by Carmen di Tommaso (1909). On the eve of the success of the film *La bête à l'afflut*, the designer accomplished her intuitive desire to become the dressmaker for tiny women, later extending the freshness of taste and the skill in cutting to clothes for little girls. Among her first clients were Danièle Delorme and Cécile Aubry. A prêt-à-porter line and a knitwear line consolidated the fortunes of the house, thanks also to the launch of new perfumes on the American market. In the 1960s the house would design the uniforms of several international travel agencies. In 1990, Edmond de Rothschild acquired 60% of the company, and three years later the high fashion division was entrusted to the designer Maguy Muzzi. (*Lucia Sollazzo*)

❑ 2002, January. The very famous "Carven green" is always the main feature of the Collection designed by Pascal Millet, with nostalgic models who evoke the style of Jacqueline Kennedy and the more modern and witty tastes of Mouna Ayoub, the Lebanese billionaire patroness of high fashion.

Carvil French shoe brand created in 1953 by Henry Lederman. It produced men's and women's shoes. It entered the history of costume when, in the 1970s, Jacques Dutronc sang in a commercial "les playboy se chaussent chez Carvil," ("playboys wear Carvil shoes"). In 1980, the brand was acquired by Carel, a large company in the French shoe industry. The new owner transformed it and from then on it offered only men's shoes that were soft and comfortable and manufactured in Italy by small-scale artisans using high quality leather.

Cary-Williams Robert (1966). English fashion designer who graduated from the Central Saint Martin's School of Art and Design in London. He showed original talent, when still a young man, in the Collection he created for the Ma graduation at Saint Martin's. It was an eccentric but surprisingly harmonious assemblage of colored leather and khaki fabrics, with spiral zippers around the body. In September 1998, he opened his *griffe* and launched his first Collection during a collateral event at the London Fashion Week. The following year he was included in the official list of London Fashion Week when he received the *British New Generation Award*. The prize included a stipend from Mark & Spencer meant to foster young designers. Notwithstanding these expectations, the presentation didn't meet with any particular success, somewhat curiously in view of the excessive special effects required by the designer: fireworks and smoke from the choreography almost completely obstructed the view. Things went better with in Spring-Summer 2002, when Cary-Williams presented a Collection which renewed the tradition of Victorian-style skirts in crinoline, with references to the fashion of the late 1800s and early 1900s. (*Pierangelo Mastantuono*)

Casadei Italian shoe factory. It was established in S. Mauro Pascoli (Forlì) at the end of the 1950s as an artisanal workshop with particularly skilled production. The 1960s saw the development of a more formal business structure, the beginning of exports to Europe, the U.S. and the Far East, and the start of a full-fledged line dedicated to evening wear and a Collection of bags. Casadei has also produced the shoe Collection of Alessandro Dell'Acqua.

❑ 2002, September. The opening of a two-storey boutique in Milan, on via Sant'Andrea.
❑ 2002, October. The company, which employs 200 people, opens a new single-brand shop in the heart of London, at no. 12 Beauchamp Place, in the Knightsbridge section. In the firm's worldwide activity, Italy is the second market after the U.S., and has 400 points-of-sale, 4 of which are single-brand shops (Milan, Florence, Rimini, and Ferrara). With Germany, it is the most important in Europe. Two more boutiques are opened in Russia, in St. Petersburg and Moscow. The company's choices for expansion are supported by the excellent turnover, which in 2001 reached €32,604 million, an increase of 14.82% in comparison to the previous year.

Evening sandal by Casadei.

Casati Luisa (1881-1957). Great eccentric and icon of elegance. "I want to be a living work of art," the Marquise would say. She was born Luisa Amman into a solid and prosperous bourgeois family. She then married the Marquis Casati in 1900. "To be a living work of art": a declaration of intent which echoed Wilde's aestheticism of existence as a masterpiece, but also anticipated the pop-media exhibitionism of Andy Warhol. She soon became in appearance, with her anti-Leonardesque beauty, the symbol of a fatal, unpredictable, disturbing femininity: tall, very thin, with a pale face dominated by predatory green eyes (always made-up in black and wet with belladonna to make them appear more profound) and framed by a cascade of red locks. She was the dominant figure of the first thirty years of the 20th century, not only of society, but also of the creative effervescence which she gathered around legendary mansions such as the Palazzo dei Leoni in Venice, the Palais de Rose in Paris, the Villa San Michele in Capri, and her native home of Arcore, now the residence of Silvio Berlusconi. She invited artists to parties that have attained the status of myth, very rich and expensive ones. Over the years she asked Boldini, Augustus John, Van Dongen, Brooks, and Zuloaga to do her portrait; she asked Drian, Martini, and Alastair to sketch her; she asked Balla, Barjansky, and Epstein to sculpt her; and she asked Beaton, de Meyer, and Man Ray to photograph her (he would take the very famous portrait in which she has three pairs of eyes). For Bakst, Poiret, Fortuny, and Erté, the request was to create quite improbable clothing-costumes: long furs that fell to the feet in which she walked at night, and that were left open on her naked body, escorted by tigers held on diamond leashes by black servants completely covered in gold foil. Her feverish taste for ego, for the rule of caprice, hide in her a dissonance as pale as her face, the mark of a subterranean extraneousness to herself which pushes her always elsewhere. To places – she was one of the great travelers of her century, and the fifty leopard-and-black-velvet trunks which preceded her arrivals were admired as genuine processions – but above all in the search for emotions. Her passion for black magic, spiritualist séances, and real snakes worn like jewellery, her mania for the "doppelgänger" (in the 1920s she had a reproduction of herself made in wax and she would place it at the table, dressed like herself, having fun by deceiving her guests by remaining immobile for the entire dinner) shows a feverish and self-destructive personality in her shining, redundant decadence. The only one who could stabilize her temper-qua-love was Gabriele D'Annunzio, who called her Coré, and thereby enjoyed many benefits, especially economic ones. But he helped her to cultivate her avant-guard taste: she was the inspiration of Futurists, fascinated Diaghilev, and commissioned musical pieces by Ravel. Movie characters inspired by her would be played by Theda Bara, Ingrid Bergman, Valentina Cortese, and Vivien Leigh. Her persona was celebrated in 1998 by John Galliano for the Haute Couture Spring-Summer Collection. It cost her to become a myth: in 1930 her debts amounted to €25 million. She sold most of her portraits, and in order to avoid creditors she ran to her niece in London, where she died in poverty, but not alone, in 1957. On her grave is a quote from Shakespeare's *Antony and Cleopatra*: "Age cannot wither her, nor custom stale her infinite variety." Her life was a metaphor for a world that will never exist again, one of extreme luxury combined with scorn for every convention.

(*Antonio Mancinelli*)

Luisa Casati, miniature from the 1920s (unknown artist).

Luisa Casati in a sketch by Augustus John (1941 ca.).

Caseley-Hayford Joe (1956). English designer. After an apprenticeship at a London Savile Row tailor and studies at the Tailor and Cutter Academy, at the Saint Martin's School of Art, and at the Institute of Contemporary Art, he made his début in 1983. Ten years later, a line of women's wear that he designed for Top Shop enjoyed excellent sales. Success was guaranteed by his having dressed singers and rock bands. He says about his work: "I think that I would consider fashion a bore if I didn't force myself to constantly ask myself questions."

(*Giulio Alberoni*)

Casentino Heavy woolen fabric, rough to the touch and rustic in appearance, sometimes with little curls on the surface. It is named after its place of origin, the Casentino, a mountainous region of Tuscany in the upper Arno valley. In the beginning, it was dyed in two characteristic colors only: a warm orange and a bright flag green. Used at the end of the 1800s for practical men's casual jackets, for teenagers at the time of the sailor style it was an alternative to the half-belted coat, orange in color, lined with thin pine-green wool, and with a furred neck in fox or beaver. Today, lighter in weight and available in more colors, including black and white, Casentino goes in and out of fashion for prêt-à-porter; in the 1980s it was rediscovered by designers, especially by Enrico Coveri, as a way to emphasize a taste for "moda povera," or the fashions of the poor.

Cashgora A noble fiber obtained from the fleece of Cashgora goats, which come from New Zealand.

Cashin Bonnie (1915). American designer famous for inventing the "layered" dress. She was able to combine different fabrics with great skill. These included leather and organza, as well as poplin, suede, cloth, and tweed. Considered among the most interesting designers, she always offered an independent style fit for active and daring women. Born in Oakland, California, with a dressmaker mother and a photographer father, she made her début at a very young age in a Los Angeles dance company. After going to New York to pursue her dance, she created the costumes for the company at the Roxy Music Hall. In 1937, she began to design for the prêt-à-porter brand Adler & Adler. In 1943, she moved to Hollywood, where she worked for six years at 20th Century Fox. She would dress one of the most elegant actresses of the time, Gene Tierney, in *Laura* (1944). Her great creative period was in the 1950s and 1960s. Some of her most successful designs were the kimono dresses, the high-neck knit dresses, and the several versions of her long-fringed poncho in mohair. She was given the *Neiman Marcus Award* and received the *Coty* prize five times.

Cashin Bonnie. Winter coat model, 1971 (Archives: The Costume Institute, Metropolitan Museum of Art of New York).

Cashmere Precious wool fiber obtained from the Kel goat, which lives in the mountains of Kashmir. Under the animal's long and thick external hair is the *duvet*, or *down*, from which is extracted one of the noblest and most precious fibers in nature. It is worked with very hard combs, and then the duvet is separated from the thick external hair, in order to obtain very thin and soft fibers which are exceptionally warm. Since the time of Caesar, cashmere has been a symbol of refinement. But its distribution in the West occured later, perhaps in the time of Marco Polo and the Silk Road. The Kel goat is bred in small herds. Each goat supplies a small quantity of fiber; a medium jacket consumes the annual production of 20 goats. In Spring, they lose their hair, which shepherds patiently separate from the duvet. Today, the most valuable cashmere doesn't come from Kashmir, but from Mongolia. The yarn is made more valuable by the twisting of two thin yarns, the "two ply," which is possible only with the highest quality. Cashmere is a short carded fiber. (*Giuliana Zabeo Ricca*)

Casnati Manufacturer of silk garments established in 1840 by Basilio Casnati. Its production of silk, wool, and cotton immediately received several tributes and won many prizes at various industrial exhibitions. In 1866, Basilio, the founder, was succeeded by his son Carlo, and then, in 1918, Carlo's son Basilio became sole owner after his brother Ernesto left the firm. In the mid 1920s, the company went through a critical financial period. It turned to Credito Italiano for financial support, which the bank provided, although the bank also took a strong hand in the firm's management. In 1929, Casnati declared bankruptcy, shutting down for good in 1933.

Casquette Beret with a flat cap and large visor in the front. Very famous is one worn by Charlie Chaplin in *The Kid*. A unisex model known as the "gavroche" was worn by young people for sports activities in the 1960s. The model changed toward the end of the 1980s with a rounded cap after the shape of a baseball hat. Of Russian origin, in the second half of the 1800s it was the symbol of the working class and part of a sailor's uniform. During the Belle Époque it was worn by car drivers, cyclists, and sailors.

Cassini Oleg Loiewski (1913). American designer of Russian origin born in Paris. He worked as a costume designer in Hollywood, and also in musicals and TV. He was the tailor for famous women such as Audrey Hepburn and Jackie Kennedy Onassis, for whom he became the official designer in 1961. He designed the First Lady's entire wardrobe for her visit to India in 1962, which caused her to be known as "Ameriki Rani," or the Queen of America. He was very successful due to the simplicity of his cocktail dresses and knitted suits. His provocative sheath dresses were also famous. When very young, he studied in Florence, graduating from the Academy of Fine Arts in 1934. After helping his mother in her boutique there, in 1936 he decided to go to New York. Once here, he worked for the big manufacturing firms of Seventh Avenue (now known as Fashion Avenue), until, in 1940, he accepted a position as costume designer at 20th Century Fox. In 1941 he married the very beautiful actress Gene Tierney, for whom he designed the costumes for the film *The Razor's Edge*, based on the book by Somerset Maugham. The marriage lasted until 1952. Later, Cassini went to the Eagle Lions Studios as head costume designer, although without neglecting the world of Seventh Avenue, with which he maintained a close relationship. He retired a few years ago and lives in Connecticut.

(*Eleonora Attolico*)

An Oleg Cassini's redingote for First Lady Jacqueline Kennedy (1962).

Cassio Paulo (1955). Portuguese designer born in Mozambique. In 1983, he participated in an exhibition for young designers of Portex. The following year he opened his own atelier in Oporto. In 1987 he won, again in Portex, the prize for design. In 1992, with designer Julio Torcato, he created one of the first Portuguese brands of prêt-à-porter.

Castaldi Alfa (1926-1997). Italian photographer. He enrolled in the university but never graduated, following a difficult but fascinating path which took him from the Faculty of Architecture to the Faculties of Italian Literature and Philosophy. Although he was a student of Pietro Longhi, he could be ironic about his sound education: "Culture is useful only to make an excellent figure in salons." He began his career in 1948 with photo reportage. Together with Ugo Mulas, his table companion at the Jamaica Bar in Milan, which was a gathering place for the main figures in some of the most creatively and intellectually vital years in that city, he was among the young people who chose photography as the form of journalism most suitable for reporting on Italy's reconstruction after the war. In the early 1960s he became a fashion photographer, attracted by the great freedom offered by this means of expression. He worked with Arianna, Grazia, Vogue Italy, and many other Italian and foreign magazines, moving with self-assurance from still-life portraits to backstage at the Collections.

(*Luca Selvi*)

❑ He works for Lagerfeld, Valentino, and Krizia. His style is deeply innovative, characterized by an accentuated formal rigor and by clear references to the most refined culture of the time, of which he is also an interpreter. Models appear, under his careful use of light, to be "moldable matter," and must adjust to unusual situations: ironic poses, complex preparations, white backgrounds, an emphasis on clothing used as accessories in order to create the right atmosphere. All these characterize the image of Alfa Castaldi in the 1970s. He was also interested in teaching and worked at the Superstudio of Milan on a project for a school for people interested in photography, design, and the fashion business.

Castelbajac (de) Jean Charles (1949). French fashion designer, born in Casablanca, Morocco. He moved to France in 1955, and in 1968 he created his first prêt-à-porter line for the Ko and Co of Limoges, a company owned by his mother. The following year, he designed for Pierre D'Alby's V. de V. In 1970 he presented his own first Collection: he recycled old fabrics, among which was his old school uniform. Emblematic of his style in that decade are his pieces inspired by leisure such as the poncho for two. Eclectic and sensitive to changes in costume, especially from a social point of view, and a modernist, he anticipated fashion trends and was defined as "the Courrèges of the '70s." His favorite and continuously revisited themes are sports, natural materials, art, and certain characters from the comics. He designed costumes for the cinema (Woody Allen's *Annie Hall*) and the theater, worked with various contemporary artists for the creation of artists' costumes, and was the first designer invited to present his models in an exhibition. During the 1980s, his creativity expanded to include interior design, from furniture to carpets, lamps, and hand-painted porcelain dishes. In 1993 he designed two Swatch watches; in 1997 he created a line of clothes for Pope John Paul II and various ecclesiastic dignitaries. In Italy, he worked with the Max Mara Group on the Sportmax line and, later, on Iceberg.

(*Anna Gloria Forti*)

❑ 2002, December. The designer makes his début in ski fashions, signing an agreement with Rossignol for a new ski wear Collection designed by both firms.

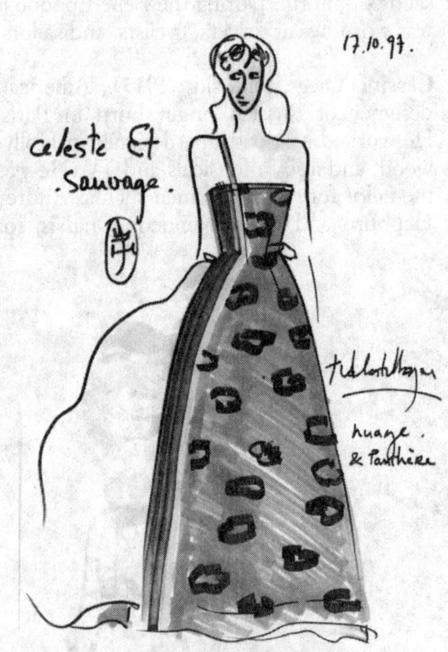

Jean Charles de Castelbajac. Evening dress "Nuage et panthère", 1997.

Castel Goffredo An area famous for the production of stockings and tights, near Mantua. It contains almost 300 companies employing 6,000 workers, with a global turnover of 2,200 billion liras. After the American multinational Sara Lee left the market, this group of companies became the most important in the world for the production of tights. Some 67% of European women depend on exports from Castel Goffredo for their tights. The area enjoys a strategic position thanks to its proximity to the largest companies that manufacture weaving machines for women's stockings, the most important of which is Lonati of Brescia. With the brands Levante, Golden Lady, Omsa, and San Pellegrino, the most important factories in the area are Calzedonia, CSP International (quoted on the stock market), Levante, Franco Bombana, Primamoda, and Calze B.C.

Castellani Ennio (1938). Italian designer from Verona. After his studies at the Academy of Fine Arts in that city, he attended the Koefia Academy of Milan, obtaining a degree in model making and applied arts. Then he worked freelance in tailor shops such as Fercioni, Guidi, and Schubert. In 1960 he was back in Verona where he opened a haute couture atelier, and in a short time his *griffe* became "necessary" for the wedding and ceremonial dresses of the most important women of the town. In those same years he presented a second line during Pitti Donna, worked as an artistic consultant for prêt-à-porter houses, and designed a line for children and a sportswear line. Up until the 1990s he often traveled to Japan to present his Collections in Tokyo and Osaka.

A sketch by Ennio Castellani.

Castelli and Bari Manufacturer of silk products. It was established on the initiative of Emilio Castelli in 1934 from the preexisting company Balbis e Bari. After 1935, the new company acquired the weaving mills in Meda (Milan) and Menaggio (Como), the reeling mill in Brienno (Como), and the twisting mills in Bellusco (Milan) and Clivio (Varese). In the first half of the 1900s, the catalogue of Castelli and Bari included plain-dyed and little-worked fabrics, in addition to some prints. At the death of Emilio Castelli (1942), the weaving mill in Menaggio, the reeling mill in Brienno, and the twisting mills in Clivio and Bellusco were sold. In 1949, the company was put into liquidation.

Castet Frédéric (1929). French designer. In 1953, he was hired at Dior where, after four years of work, he began to design the Dior London Collection. He did it so well that he was awarded first prize by the School of the Chambre Syndicale de la Confection et de la Couture of Paris, the city in which he lived. In 1973 he designed a prêt-à-porter line. In 1988 he quit Dior in order to open his own *maison*.

Castillo Antonio Canovas (1908-1984). A French designer of Spanish origin. He had a versatile career as a designer of scarves, jewellery, and hats for some of the most celebrated couturiers such as Chanel, Schiaparelli, Piguet, and Paquin (from 1938 to 1944); and as a costume designer for the cinema (*Beauty and the Beast*) and at the Metropolitan Opera in New York (1945 to 1950). He had his period of maximum success and happy creativity when he was invited to create haute couture and prêt-à-porter for Lanvin after the death of Jeanne, the founder of the *maison* (1952 to 1963). His styles, with their contoured busts and loose skirts, succeed in renewing, without betraying, the Lanvin style in the lightness of draping and fabric. Spectacular were his evening dresses, in voluptuous satin matched with mink. In 1963, he started his own business with the support of two of the most enthusiastic Lanvin clients, Barbara Hutton and Gloria Guiness. Five years later the *maison* was sold-off.

Knitwear jacket by Antonio Castillo in a sketch by Brunetta (Biki Collection, 1960s).

Castle Irene (1893-1969). American Dancer. Born Irene Foote in New Rochelle, New York, Irene and her husband Vernon Castle formed a celebrated ballroom dance team in the 1910s. Performing first in Europe, at the Café de Paris, and later in theaters throughout America, the Vernon Castles were the pop idols of their times, responsible for such new dance crazes as the one-step and the turkey trot. Castle's slim, effortless chic influenced a generation of young women, who, in particular, widely copied her boyishly bobbed-hair and headbands, her loose, flowing clothes and overall fashion flair.

Casual A term that when used about clothing indicates an informal, practical, self-assured way of dressing, identified with jeans and comfortable garments, mostly for leisure. Typical of the American style of dressing, it was successful in Europe during the 1970s and 1980s, first among young people, and then with a wider and wider public, incorporating into the style various trends coming mostly from the U.S., such as grunge. It includes sportswear, of course, but not in the sense of clothing or outfits in which to practice the sport actively, which instead requires particular fabrics and precise manufacturing. Casual wear doesn't follow any stylistic rules in terms of fabrics, shapes, or colors.

Catalano Elisabetta (1941). Italian photographer. An actress, she began to be interested in photography while on the set of Fellini's film *8* , and she then studied it on her own, with great sensitivity. She started her professional career as a photographer with portraits and worked with *L'Espresso* and *Il Mondo*. During the 1970s she moved to New York and worked for Condé Nast, in particular at Vogue, a collaboration which continued when she moved to Paris. She developed an intense relationship with exponents of conceptual art such as Pistoletto and Chia, and then definitively abandoned the world of fashion in favor of portraits. She published *Uomini* (1973), *Faces and Façades* (1980), and *Tempo di ritratti* (1987), and had several personal exhibits.

Catroux Betty Muse and model. A constant presence in the atelier of Yves Saint-Laurent starting in the 1950s, she was destined to be, with her thin and nervous body, long straight hair, very long legs, and thin lips, the prototype of the Modern Woman: self-assured, at her ease in trousers, which were perhaps stolen from a man's (or woman's) wardrobe. Since that time she has remained one of the great friends and associates of Yves, along with other important icons, such as the rarefied Parisian (Loulou de la Falaise), the woman from the South (Paloma Picasso), the intellectual "comedienne" (Zizi Jeanmarie), and the "jolie madame" of perfect attitude and obscure desires (Catherine Deneuve). It is said that, in Betty's case, the maestro was inspired for that entire part of the creative process which falls under the definition "masculin-feminin": the "grain de poudre" smoking jacket worn on bare skin, the sailor's caban in blue cloth, and the explorer's safari jacket in khaki-colored cotton. It is significant that the first Saint-Laurent Collection without Yves Saint-Laurent, designed in 2000 by Tom Ford, after the acquisition of the brand by the Gucci Group, was dedicated to her: a line of smoking jackets and pantsuits worn by blonde models who around their neck had an orchid as a necklace. But Betty was not there. Faithful, as she is, and as she always has been, to Yves and to his "family."

(*Antonio Mancinelli*)

Catsuit Very tight body suit, in wool or stretch material, similar to the "bodystocking." It gets its name from the success of the famous musical *Cats*.

Cattaneo Silk factory in Como. In 1892, Natale Bosisio, Luigi Comanni, and Giuseppe Cattaneo established a factory specialized in the manufacture of ties and, on a lesser scale, smooth and worked fabrics for women's clothing. In 1903, the three partners split up and the business continues under the guidance of Giuseppe Cattaneo until 1932, when it is put into liquidation. In 1933, Cattaneo participated in the founding of Successori Giuseppe Cattaneo (Heirs of Giuseppe Cattaneo), run by his grandchildren and by the brothers Mario and Carlo Cantaluppi. The representatives of this family are indeed those who directly managed the activity of the company and decided on various changes such as the relocation of the weaving mill in Como to Albese con Cassano (Como) after a fire that devastated the first plant. In the 1960s the Martegani family acquired the company shares that were in the hands of minority stakeholders. Carlo Martegani and Achille Cantaluppi decided to cut the manufacture of fabric for women's clothing and to concentrate on raw materials, especially silk.

Caumont Jean-Baptiste. French designer, active in Italy starting in the 1950s, and among the early important figures, along with Albini, Krizia, and Missoni, in that fortunate period for a prêt-à-porter in Milan. In Paris, where he went in order to study at the School of Fine Arts, he joined the world of fashion at a very young age as a designer for Balmain and, later, for important magazines such as Fémina and Vogue. After a consultant job with La Rinascente, he designed for Amica Manufacturing of Treviso. There, in 1965, he created his first Collection, which earned great approval for its sophisticated, luxurious, and characteristic style, evocative of the 1930s. There were casual suits, but very feminine, for the afternoon and the evening, in the style of 1938, plus short dresses in silk, and loose knitwear characterized by a precise attention to details and to accessories, resulting in a faultless harmony. Starting in 1970, his prêt-à-porter, produced by the Financial Textile Group, was successful especially in America.

Caumont's models sketched by Maria Pezzi.

Cavalli Derna (1912-1999). Dressmaker. Born in Faenza, she began working at a very young age. She started her own business at the age of 22, opening a dressmaker's shop on via Oriani in Faenza. Here she would cut and sew clothes for more than 60 years, often traveling to Milan and Paris to follow the high fashion Collections. She reproduced the styles of Ungaro and Chanel from paper patterns and created custom-made clothes for her clients, always inspired by French fashion. She specialized in the manufacture of wedding dresses. For the families of Emilia Romagna, hers was an atelier of great importance. Among her clientele were actresses and opera singers.

(*Emanuela Fontana*)

Cavalli Roberto (1940). Italian designer. He loves to be defined as "an artist of fashion," perhaps to remember his grandfather who was an illustrious painter, one of the Macchiaioli, and the creator of paintings on display at the Uffizi in Florence, his hometown. He attended the Academy of Fine Arts and soon became interested in the relationship between fashion and painting, investigating various materials in his own print shop, and at the same time experimenting with new technologies. In the 1960s he patented a revolutionary process for printing on leather, and in the decade that followed (1972) he made his début at Palazzo Pitti with his patchworks, which are by now considered a classic of his style, and which are especially typical of his glamorous jeans. Nature is a source of inspiration for him: animal skins, sequins in the shape of fish scales, waves that lose themselves in the transparencies of the fabric. The impact of his Collections is always very strong: ferocious wild beasts, angels and demons that peep out from a jacket or from trousers. Feline and witty women find a confirmation a their personality in Cavalli's style, instinctual and exhibitionist. Every style is breathtaking: shorts and corsets for a Scarlet O'Hara updated to the year 2000, contoured blazers in prints of leopard, crocodile or lynx, and snake skin as a substitute for spotted patterns of every sort. Then the black of the youth gangs, from the jacket of a wild Marlon Brando to punks and heavy metal freaks: his unmistakable, elegant jackets are in very soft deer skin. Something lunar for his micro galactic skirts, and again baroque-patterned jeans: Anna Falchi and Claudia Koll played the winning couple in a prêt-à-porter presentation in Milan in 1995. He turned on the gas in order to stir intense vibrations: sophisticated elegance with a touch of transgression. Stretch became ultra stretch: a master of leather, he treats it like a canvas on which to paint and the body seems tattooed. His brand is distributed in more than 30 countries, directly from the Milan, New York, and Düsseldorf' showrooms. The home market leads with 35% of the turnover (Europe 25%, Asia 20%). The Russian market is expanding and the U.S. market has already been conquered, with his styles in the windows of the most important department stores. The first single-brand boutique opened in Venice in 1996. The principal line is gradually supported by CJ Cavalli Jeans, a men's line, a line of eye glasses produced by Marcolin, and accessories for men and women. The most recent line is women's underwear. His wife, Eva Duringer, who works with him professionally, was Miss Universe. He owns an important art Collection with paintings from the 1400s and 1600s and has a fondness for the painters of Siena. He also likes purebreds.

(*Lucia Mari*)

❑ 2000, October. At Milano Collezioni, an entire day is dedicated to Cavalli. After the Collection is presented in the morning, the afternoon sees the opening of his first boutique in Milan, on via della Spiga. The Cavalli woman has a well-defined silhouette that caresses the body, wraps it, imprisons it in a sort of cobweb of black tulle with often overlapping colored fabrics in fantastic patterns which remind one of scales or feathers.

❑ 2001. The men's shoe line is to be produced and distributed for the next five years by Roberto Botticelli. The Autumn-Winter 2001-2002 Collection is inspired by the Old West, with loafers, ankle boots and, above all, cowboy boots with embroidered details.

❑ 2001, March. Cavalli designs two new lines for the watches produced by Sector. For his beachwear he uses the eclectic and comfortable Sensitive fabric made by Eurojersey, personalizing it with his celebrated prints.

❑ 2001, July. To celebrate his début in Great Britain, Eva and Roberto Cavalli welcome their guests in a Berber tent, thus bringing a piece of Africa to Momo, the historic club in the West End. Among black-and-white striped carpets and copper trays, he presents the new eye glass Collection, which is produced and distributed by Marcolin.

❑ 2001, November. The turnover for the year was expected to be 280 billion liras, but by the end of the year the new estimate is 300 to 350 billion liras. The opening of the next single-brand shops is already planned. After Milan, Rome, Jeddah, Paris, New York, and Venice, one will open on via Tornabuoni in Florence, replacing the historic Caffé Giacosa. But Cavalli is aiming above all at the "new" markets of Hong Kong, Seoul, Taipei, and Moscow.

❑ 2002, January. The new men's Collection for Winter 2002-2003 is refined, precious and extravagant; it renews the style of men's fashion with an irony of excess and fantasy. The inspiration comes from Victorian England. The Collection is presented in Florence at Palazzo Vecchio.

❑ 2002, January. Excess, provocation, color, and fun are the elements of the exhibit *More and More More and More – The Looks Roberto Cavalli Wants for You*, organized by Italo Rota.

❑ 2002, January. Cavalli opens a boutique in "his" Florence in a prestigious location: the ancient Palazzo Viviani della Robbia, with nine large windows on via Tornabuoni. The historic and renovated Caffè Giacosa is connected to the boutique, but it also has independent access.

❑ 2002, February. The exhibition *Men in Skirts* at the Dress Gallery of the Victoria and Albert Museum in London displays work by Cavalli and other designers. Organized with the purpose of celebrating the designers who turned the skirt into a man's garment, the exhibit is divided into five themes: historical styles, the kilt, exoticism, styles vs. culture, and futuristic styles. Roberto Cavalli finds his natural place in the exoticism section where he shows a linen caftan with animal-tribal prints.

❑ 2002, April. An amusing and lively presentation with a touch of self-irony that proposes pieces such as a black tailored suit of Breitschwanz, sophisticated decorated furs, patent-leather overcoats for a cat-woman and calf-length dresses in delicate flower-patterned muslin with long sleeves. Cindy Crawford wore a tight sheath dress in Persian scarlet lamb, a herringbone-patterned fur, and, finally, a long white satin dress embroidered with panther- and tiger-shaped sequins, together with a trench coat in very bright and light snake skin. Something very unusual was a loom-manufactured Scottish fabric in strong colors that was used for tailored suits that had the skirt tight on the hips and then dropped in a flare, and for the tiny jackets worn with jeans. The fabric was also worked in patterned cloths embroidered with silver thread.

❑ 2002, May. For the 85th Giro d'Italia, Cavalli designed the uniforms for Mario Cipollini and his team, in black and white stripes, of course.

❑ 2002, June. Roberto Cavalli Angels, the Collection produced and distributed by Simonetta, is presented at Pitti Bimbo, for Spring-Summer 2003. There are light leather jackets, snake skin patterned jackets, chalkstripe jeans, and oversized overalls in pre-washed fabric. The suede boots on the feet as those of the Navajos, and around the waist are colored raffia belts with plastic beads and feathers.

❑ 2002, July. The opening in Rome, in Piazza di Spagna, of the first boutique dedicated to the youth line Just Cavalli. Roberto Cavalli and Ittierre (It Holding Group) renew, three years in advance, the license for the Just Cavalli line, extending it to 2010.

❑ 2002, August. In the first six months of the year, the watch line designed for Sector has a turnover of €3.9 million, growing 136%. The number of Roberto Cavalli Collections goes from six to nine.

❑ 2002, October. The reopening of the Torre Branca, ex Littorio, in Milan. At the foot of the tower is the Just Cavalli Café, with a counter designed by Ron Arad. Cavalli receives the award *The Provocateurs*, given to "those who dare." The ceremony takes place at Cipriani New York, on the occasion of the 19th edition of the Night of Stars, organized by Fashion Group International.

❑ 2002, November. Roberto Cavalli

A model by Roberto Cavalli.

Devils is a new line dedicated to children and kids from 4 to 14 years. It supports Roberto Cavalla Angels, the Collection for little girls and teenagers produced and distributed by Simonetta, who is to manage the new brand as well.
❑ 2003, April. The fourth point-of-sale in the U.S., in Coral Gables, Florida, is opened: *More More and More By Roberto Cavalli.* All his Collections (with the exception of the first line) can be found there, including the children's, accessories, and household lines. The other American boutiques are in New York, on Madison Avenue; in Bel Harbor, Florida; and in Las Vegas.
❑ 2003, June. Black-and-white striped dishes, gold trimmed glasses, and animal-patterned cushions for the house designed by Cavalli.
❑ 2003, June. A mix between a cowboy and a biker: this is the man presented by Cavalli at Milano Moda Uomo.
❑ 2003, June. The opening of a new boutique in Porto Cervo, Sardinia.
❑ 2004, April. Cavalli hosts *Le Cirque du Soleil* in Milan and organizes an evening for the première of the extraordinary show *Saltimbanco.* The designer, with the creative help of Ettore Scola, transforms a warehouse into an enchanted paradise.
❑ 2004, May. The opening, at number 15 in the Tretyakovskiy Passage in Moscow, of the first single-brand Roberto Cavalli boutique in Russia.
❑ 2004, December. Cavalli is back in New York to host the most exclusive evening of the year on the occasion of the exhibition organized by the Fashion Institute of the Metropolitan Museum of Art in New York, entitled *Wild fashion Untamed.* To celebrate the event, the designer organized an exclusive evening: cocktails and an exhibition preview followed by a dinner for 300 selected international guests.
❑ 2005, January. The opening of the first single-brand Just Cavalli store in Milan. It is an innovative project and the result of collaboration between Roberto Cavalli and Italo Rota for a real "fantasy store."
❑ 2005, April. Roberto Cavalli is the producer, with his friend Dino De Laurentiis, of *The Decameron*, a film directed by David Leland, for which he also designs the costumes. In the cast are Hayden Christensen, Mischa Barton, and Tim Roth.
❑ 2005, July. Roberto Cavalli creates, in collaboration with 3 Italia, the first branded video cell phone. The project includes a donation to the Veronesi Foundation for their cancer research.

(*Gabriella Gregorietti*)

Cavallini Emilio (1945). Italian entrepreneur and designer, born in Tuscany. At the age of 30, after interrupting his study of economics and after gaining some experience in a factory that made stockings, he decided to start his own business making stockings, in more daring colors and with unusual and more fanciful patterns. It was not by accident that he called his company Stilnovo (New Style). Success came quickly, especially abroad. In 1987 he opened a boutique in Milan, on via della Spiga. During the 1990s he also launched a line of shoes, knitwear, and accessories.

Cavalry Hard-wearing fabric similar to covercoat and gabardine. Diagonally woven with marked ribs, usually in wool, it is used to manufacture jackets and trousers, especially sportswear for horseback riding.

Cavanagh John Bryan (1914). Irish designer. He traveled all around the world before settling in Paris in 1947 to work with Pierre Balmain. In 1952 he opened his own atelier in London. Between 1956 and 1959 he was president of the Incorporated Society of Fashion Designers. He retired in 1974.

Cazeneuve Vivianne. French accessories designer. Her début in the world of fashion was unique. A graduate in Financial Sciences at the Sorbonne, she was hired in 1986 by Saint-Laurent as a management consultant. She worked with the designer Peggy Roche and convinced herself that her future was in the design of accessories. Among her designs, in 1994, was a necklace with many tiny religious medals. Her creations are available in more than 50 shops all around the world.

Cecil Hugh. English photographer. He had a photographic studio in London from the end of the 1910s until the early 1930s. His soft style derives from that of the Baron de Mayer. He worked especially for the English edition of Vogue.

Cecil Higgins Art Gallery Bedford, England. The gallery has a Collection created thanks to local donations. It contains more than 2,000 pieces of clothing, especially women's, from the 19th and early 20th century. The textile section contains a great variety of articles, ranging from English 17th century's embroidery to William Morris patterns from the second half of the 1800s to Persian carpets of the 20th century. The lace Collection is very important, and the local lace tradition of Bedfordshire Bobbin Lace is well represented due a donation by the merchant Thomas Lester which includes all the materials necessary for the manufacture and trade of this family business.

Cederna Camilla (1911-1997). Italian journalist. A great name in the period after World War II, she made her début in 1939 on the Milanese newspaper L'Ambrosiano, later working with L'Europeo, L'Espresso, and Il Corriere della Sera. She also published several books. As a result of the massacre at Piazza Fontana in Milan (December 12th 1969), she devoted a large portion of her career to the themes of civil and political commitment, from an investigation of the death of the anarchist Pinelli (1971) to the 1978 files about Giovanni Leone, the president of Italy, to the memories collected in *Il mondo di Camilla* (Feltrinelli Pub., 1980). Fashion has been a leitmotiv throughout her journalism career, and was an interest already apparent in her graduation thesis entitled *Sermons Against the Luxury of Women from the Greek Philosophers to the Church Fathers*. It also figured in her very first piece published by the Corriere della Sera on September 7th 1943 at the end of the Badoglio period and just before the return of the Fascists: *Black Fashion* was a short fashion sketch about the women of the party, starting with Claretta Petacci. Between 1946 and 1956, at L'Europeo under the leadership of Arrigo Benedetti, she followed the activities of the great Milan ateliers: the pioneering phase of Palazzo Pitti, and the Balmain and Dior Collections in Paris. She wrote about Maria Callas and her education in elegance at Biki's atelier. At the same time, and this is what made her original, she observed and recorded "the art of clothing," as she called it, the proprieties of style and the exhibitionist blunders related to fashion. She contributed an essay to the Collection *Milano ha cinquant'anni* published in 1950 by Rinascente with the long article *How Milanese Gentlemen Dress*, in which she praised their "conformism, a result of good traditions," consecrated by the Prandoni jackets "which until a few years ago served as a model for the great tailors of London." Along with Cederna's article there is Irene Brin's *How Milanese Ladies Dress*. In February 1956, she reported for L'Europeo on the cruise to New York made by the "eight Italian ladies" (Consuelo Crespi above all) of noble origin and mannequin size" organized by Giovanni Battista Giorgini to present to American women the styles of the great Milanese and Roman tailors such as Schuberth, Marucelli, Capucci, and Veneziani. Shortly after, she followed the director Benedetti when he founded L'Espresso, and wrote the fashion column *Il Lato Debole* (The Weak Side), which was hers until 1976. Each week, she wrote about the continent of high society, the salons, the years of restoration, profiteering, the deafening economic miracle, and ostentatious clothes for the opera at La Scala: the habits, stereotypes, languages, manias, elegance, and the boorishness of "fashion's men and women." Sketches by Brunetta accompanied her articles. Guido Vergani wrote: "She is a young lady of good family, capable of a smiling nastiness, of acid expressions wrapped in prose only apparently frivolous..- From her stinging blows, devoid of violence and mostly camouflaged by mercy, emerged the healthy moralism of the enlightened Lombardy bourgeoisie, the one of Pietro Verri and Carlo Cattaneo, and the sense of humor of the Milanese people." Besides, the thousand pages (Bompiani, 3 vv., 1977) in which those articles were collected offer not only a source for the social phenomenology of fashion, but also a precious description of trends enriched by a descriptive mastery of fabrics, shapes, cuts, and decoration. These include the still spontaneous fashions of the late 1950s, such as the "wrappers, or scarves, of the English students" worn with tailored suits and satin ankle boots, the advent of reassuring standards such as the "black sheath dress" that was considered "the best rind for a more or less quiet evening," and "the colonial style which in Summer is always ok." She also described anti-fashion ostentations such as the gradual revival of the "rigid and square shoulders of Caraceni's 1950's style," the 'exotic folklore imported by "modernist women" of the 1950s, the "platform shoes instead of Chanel," and the jeans that were considered populist icons, provided they were "gloriously soft and light-blue/white." Several other signs of the careful eye she cast on fashion are scattered in the articles about La Scala premières, a privileged observation point. In the mid 1950s, the large Milanese ateliers favored tapering dresses and chinchilla stoles. In 1963 "one could see ladies wrapped in gold and rust-colored mantles" as in a famous painting by Carpaccio, and "girls wearing a green cape over another longer cloak with boots." During the 1970s, she enumerated: "the Chinese style: blouse and large pants," "the Amazon in tweed jacket," "the 'after-a-day-on-the-ski-runs' woman: open-work knitwear as evening wear," turbans, matelassé patchworks ("producing also a teapot-cover effect"), "real or fake lesbians: sturdy shoes." She rarely expresses esteem, as in a quick objection to the *Système de la Mode* by Roland Barthes, in 1968: "In one respect the fashionable woman differs decisively from the models of mass culture: she doesn't know evil. Fashion never talks about love, it doesn't know unfaithfulness, personal relationships, or flirts: in fashion, you travel only with your husband." Rather, her idea of fashion can be summed up in this "formula for a quiet elegance" offered specifically for a long ago December 7th on the occasion of a première at La Scala: "Then, the dress can be in one single piece but look like it's made of two, but it must always inspire a melancholic and solemn nocturnal grace. A long and tight skirt with two small vents, if not slightly barrel-shaped, of heavy crème, in pearl or smoked gray satin, complete with a jacket or a bolero in black gaietto right to the waist, with drops pouring down like wonderful ink. Boat neck, short sleeves, black pearls sewn like a net, in flowers or stars, on organza or tulle." Camilla Cederna returned to writing about fashion in the 1980s, during the most aggressive phase of the transformation of the clothing industry, of the market, and of its creative trends. Annoyed by exhibitionisms, banalities, and by the abused language of "Made in Italy," she retired from the media-organizing "war" of the Collections and from "contemporary lookism" (*De Gustibus*, Mondadori, 1986). Other works by her include *La voce dei padroni* (1962), *Signore e Signori* (1966), *Maria Callas* (Longanesi, 1968), *Le pervestite* (Immordino, 1968), *Milano in guerra*, with Marilea Somaré and Martina Vergani (Feltrinelli, 1979), and, published by Mondatori in 1987, *Il meglio di Camilla Cederna*.

(*Pasquale Guadagnolo*)

Celeste All That Jazz Clothing line designed by Celeste Pisenti (1979). At the age of 18 she began working with Costume National. In 1999 she was hired by Moschino. Today she is consulting art director and stylist of the Blugirl line (Blufin group). In 2002, for Spring-Autumn 2003, she launched Celeste All That Jazz, her first personal Collection composed of colored and mischievous corsetry inspired by the silent films of the 1920s. The Autumn-Winter 2003-2004 Collection was completed with jackets, coats, dresses, and accessories, although it was purposefully limited to just a few pieces.

Celine French house of leather goods and prêt-à-porter. Celine has a long and deep-rooted history in the world of fashion. Its first boutique was opened in 1946 in Paris, for the design and sale of children's wear. Then, year after year, the maison's success allowed it to expand. In 1963 it presented a women's shoe line, and 1966 saw the début of a leather Collection, while Celine consolidated its position in prêt-à-porter. After being acquired by the Arnault Group, which owned several luxury and fashion brands, the firm, guided by Nan Lergeai, the person at Dior responsible for the Far East, began a policy of opening single-brand boutiques all over the world, with particular attention to the Asian and American markets.

❑ 2001, May. Opening of the first single-brand boutique in London, at the prime address no. 160 is New Bond Street.

❑ 2001, August. The Isetan Museum in Tokyo dedicates a retrospective to

Celine illustrating the maison's style from 1945 to the present day, highlighting the changes made in 1997 with the arrival of artistic director Michael Kors. The celebrated Grant bag, very successful in the 1960s, is the main feature, and it is sewn right in front of visitors in a miniature cardboard version. The pieces on sale are limited and numbered, personalized with the buyer's name.

❑ 2001, September. With the advent of the single European currency, Celine dedicates to the euro a Collection of accessories decorated with the twelve coins which are to be issued.

❑ 2001, November. After London and Antwerp, Club Celine arrives in Italy, in the new boutique opened in Galleria Cavour in Bologna. The firm expects to open 100 more points-of-sale by the end of the year. In Italy, Bologna joins Milan, Rome, and Portofino. Abroad, besides Osaka, London, and Antwerp, there is a new boutique in Costa Mesa, California.

❑ 2003, May. The new Celine bag is called Poulbot. This name is almost unknown, and derives from Francisque Poulbot, an artist contemporary with Toulouse-Lautrec, by whom he was inspired when painting the street urchins of Paris. Since that time, poulbot has meant urchin, and the bag is called an "urchin" or "rascal" bag. It hangs like a shoulder bag, bombé and round with seams held together by metallic rivets, made in leather of bright colors such as orange, fuchsia, and electric blue.

❑ 2003, May. Celine offers a mini-Collection inspired by the streets of Paris. As with the Poulbot bag, the name chosen for the Collection, Macadam, is the name of the paving material put down in 1854, an important element in the stylistic identity of the city. The Collection is to last a single season. Celine has 63 boutiques all over the world.

❑ 2004, October. Roberto Menichetti makes his début in Paris as the creative director of Céline. He replaces the American Michael Kors as the artistic head of the historic French *maison*.

❑ 2005, May. After only two seasons, the collaboration between the Italian designer and the French *maison* comes to an end. The separation is consensual.

❑ 2005, June. After the opening of the boutique on via Condotti in Rome in 2004, another prestigious store is opened on the very central via Tornabuoni in Florence. It is a nice way to celebrate the *griffe*'s 66th anniversary. In the previous four years, the *griffe* shows a growth in turnover of 50%.

❑ 2005, July. The Croatian Ivana Omazic, 32, is appointed new creative director. She will work in the Miu Miu design department and make her début in Paris in October.

Celio Chain of European shops for men's clothing. In 1978, in Paris, Marc and Laurent Grosman took over the management of their father's boutique. It was called Cleo 3000 and sold women's prêt-à-porter. The two brothers started a small revolution: they changed the boutique's sign and pointed it toward's men's fashion, adopting an unmistakable logo: a small blue and green flag. They were so successful that in 1986 they opened six shops. These grew to 13 in 1987, 34 in 1989, 70 in 1991, and 95 in 1992. Three years later, there were 150 shops in France, 6 in Belgium, and 4 in Spain, with a total of 1,400 employees. Their concept is quality at affordable prices.

(*Valeria Vantaggi*)

Cella Giuliana (1943). Italian designer and fabric researcher. After graduating from a school for languages, she completed her education by traveling through India, China, Japan, and Tibet. She made her début in 1997 in Milan. In 1999 she presented her Collection at the House of Culture in Milan which, for the first time, opened its doors to a fashion event. In that same year she designed the dress for the singer Ornella Vanoni's return to the Festival of Sanremo. Her clothes are hand-made with antique and rare fabrics.

❑ 2001, May. She makes her début in the industrial field. For her first knitwear license, she turns to Lineapiù Group.

❑ 2002, June. The personnel of the open-air theater Vittoriale wear uniforms researched and created by the designer. The uniforms evoke the era of D'Annunzio. The Financial Times called her the "queen of ethno-chic."

Cellulose Fibers These exist as acetates and triacetates. They were first obtained by Schutzenberger in 1869 through a chemical process. In 1894 the same researchers who worked on viscose used them for the wings of the planes of World War I. At the end of the conflict, the production of acetate-cellulose was high and demand was low. In 1921, under the brand Celanese, the fiber was marketed as artificial silk. Resistant, robust, and bright, the fashion world liked this fiber and relaunched it.

Cent (100) Idées French magazine founded in 1972 by Marielle Huchiez, and published by the Prouvost group. After two years as a quarterly, it became a monthly in March 1974. The main interest of the magazine is manual work, from that typically for women (like fashion made accessible to everyone, through paper patterns or lessons in cut-and-sew) to do-it-yourself. This winning formula translated into big sales, to the point of reaching a circulation of 300,000 copies in 1984. In an attempt to follow the changing tastes of its readers, the magazine widened the range of its interests, but to the point of losing its identity and the reason-for-being that had given it its initial success. Publication ceased in 1988.

Centinaro Clara (1914-1995). Italian designer. She was known for the artisanal quality of her tailoring. Born in Bedonia (Parma), at the young age of 20 she moved to Rome and began her career as an apprentice in the large ateliers. She also worked at Simonetta. In 1952, she presented her models at the Sala Bianca of Palazzo Pitti, where she was noticed by international buyers. She was an innovator and in 1956 she presented an umbrella-dress in wool and mixed silk with a wide cape neck supported by whalebones. In 1957-58 she designed the pale green embroidered silk dress worn by Miss Universe. In the 1960s, she worked with new materials and offered avant-guard creations such as her short dress with a flared line in transparent plastic and fake fur (1967). In the 1990s, the Centinaro atelier was taken over by Litrico, which also owns the archives. *(Bonizza Giordani Aragno)*

Central Museum Utrecht, Holland. The fashion Collection contains about 7,000 pieces among men's, women's and children's clothes and accessories. They date from the 1600s up to today. The section of contemporary fashion is dedicated to the work of Dutch designers, but also includes representative pieces of international fashion, from Comme des Garçons to Martin Margiela. In addition, there is a section for materials relating to couture such as fashion photographs, sketches, newspapers, and prints.

Centre de Documentaciò Museu Textil Terrassa (Barcelona), Spain. Established as a private Collection in 1946, but today managed jointly by the municipal and provincial governments. Reorganized in 1996, it has 15,000 samples of fabrics of various kinds, from archaeological specimens to pieces from the 11th century. Starting in 1997 the Collection could be consulted on the internet through Image Bank. The specialized library, with more than 6,000 volumes and a wide photographic archive, is open to the public. Thematic exhibits are organized regularly. There is a strong connection to the textile industry which has ancient roots in this Catalan territory.

Centro Design Montefibre This was the first Italian institute for research and forecasting concerning the use of textiles in fashion and in the home. It was active from 1970 to 1985. Every six months it supplied firms in the textile and clothing sector with an analysis of future trends, broken down by colors, threads, fabric patterns, and lines. It promoted meetings, shows, and refresher courses about important issues concerning the Made in Italy movement that, in those years particularly, was developing its industrial dimension. Benefiting from the outside advice of Elio Fiorucci, Popi Moreni, Bé Khan, and other international designers, the Center was coordinated by Ampelio Bucci, Donatella Cerri, Ornella Bignami, Rita Spaggiati, Orlando Lobracciuto, and Nancy Martin.

Centro di Firenze per la Moda Italiana

(Florence Center for Italian Fashion). A public-private, non-profit association which since 1954 has promoted, in Italy and abroad, a series of commercial, cultural, communication, and educational activities in support of Italian fashion. It is the holding company of Pitti Immagine and Ente Moda Italia, operating companies to which the Center gives guidelines for trade shows and promotional efforts, in coordination with the needs of the various business associations of Italian textile and clothing companies and of the local political and economic government institutions which are the Center's shareholders. It has carried out important initiatives in the field of research and in the culture of fashion, often in collaboration with prestigious museums and international cultural institutes. Among the most recent of these was the Biennial of Florence, of which the Center was the principal sponsor.

Centro Internazionale delle Arti e del Costume (International Center of the Arts and Costume). Conceived by Franco Marinotti, the founder of the Snia Viscosa, it was created in Venice, at Palazzo Grassi. From August 21st to August 23rd 1956, the Center organized its first event, entitled *Fashion in Contemporary Costume*, which took place over three days and had the participation of couturiers from Germany, Japan, India, England, Ireland, Spain, and the U.S. The executive committee was composed of Paolo Marinotti (Franco's son), Romeo Toninelli, Bettina Ballard, Brunetta Mateldi, Giulio Rodinò, Francesco Chiarini, and Ferdinando Feliciani. Italy (whose delegates were Brunetta and Irene Brin) was present with 21 fashion houses which created 66 production models, for both boutiques and haute couture. The group was lead by Antonelli, Fabiani, Marucelli, Garnett, Capucci, Carosa, Curiel, Simonetta, Schuberth, and the Pellegrini fur factory. The organization of the Collection had been entrusted to Marida Tecchio and, on the whole, more than 100 brands presented 300 styles in "Man Made" fibers produced by Snia Viscosa. Success was immediate, and there was big international publicity. From year to year, the event became more and more interesting, presenting for the first time great spectacle-presentations (or fashion-spectacles) which saw the participation of directors such as – among others – Filippo Crivelli and of wonderful models, actors, and singers such as Milly, and of very promising young figures such as Mariangela Melato, Giancarlo Giannini, Sandro Massimini, Enzo Tarascio, and Luigi Pistilli. After the death of Franco Marinotti, the Center's activity was continued for some years by his son Paolo until, for several reasons, Palazzo Grassi closed its doors to fashion and, thanks to Gianni Agnelli, opened them to art.

(*Maria Vittoria Alfonsi*)

Centro Italiano della Moda (Italian Fashion Center). It was established in the early 1950s in Milan by Dino Alfieri, the former fascist Minister of Print and Propaganda, and ambassador to Berlin. Its headquarters was in Milan, at Galleria San Babila. It was the Lombardy region's answer to Turin's Fashion Institute. In vain, they both tried to cross the street in order to compete with the Florentine fashion events at Palazzo Pitti. It proposed to promote Italian couture and organized events in Como (Villa Olmo), Venice (Palazzo Grassi), Milan, and Legnano. It also had a school for models.

Centro Studi di Storia del Tessuto e del Costume (Center for the Study of the History of Fabric and Costume). It is located in the Palazzo Mocenigo, Venice, the house-museum that was donated to the city in 1945 by the last descendant of that historic family. Established in 1985 by the municipal government, the Center contains the following Collections: the Civic Museums of Venice (consisting of the Museo Correr and Ca' Rezzonico), the defunct International Center of Arts and Costume at Palazzo Grassi, and the Vittorio Cin Collection. The fabric section contains almost 2,500 pieces, from Coptic finds to Italian hand-work of the first half of the 20th century. The clothing and accessories section has a large quantity of material from the Venetian 1700s, besides Oriental specimens and styles of the early 1900s. Of great importance is the group of sacred vestments from all parts of the Christian world. There are also several examples of locally-produced lace. The specialized library (reopened to the public in 1986 and kept up-to-date) contains rare and ancient books, a Collection of periodicals from the end of the 1700s up to today, and a Collection of 13,000 fashion-plates. In addition to being a source for thematic exhibitions, the Collections are shown on a rotating basis in the halls of the Palazzo. The Center organizes meetings, classes, and publications.

Cercal Specialized service center for the footwear and leather goods industries. It was established in San Mauro Pascoli, in Romagna, in 1983. It supports companies in the leather field by providing information, refresher courses on technological innovation, market monitoring, stylistic research, and education.

Cerini Ernestina (1952). Italian designer. After working as a consultant for several clothing companies, she made her own début in knitwear in 1983. A prêt-à-porter line was created 10 years later. She works in Novara.

Cerio Stefano (1964). Italian photographer. He began his career at the age of 16, while still attending high school in Rome, working with the magazine L'Espresso: it was an important experience which led him to make portraits, still life, and mini-reportages, as well as interior design and fashion photographs. In this last field he made his name working for Moda and King. In 1987 he moved to Milan and created the advertising campaigns for JVC and Honda in which advertising and fashion merged to form a totality, in a style that would be his signature. At the same time he developed a research activity that would result in personal exhibitions. He lives in Milan and Paris.

Cerrato Pina. Boutique in Turin named after its owner who, beginning in the years before World War II, made her name as a milliner and as a woman of excellent taste in her choice of styles from Parisian haute couture that were particularly suitable to the tastes of Turin's ladies. Her millinery creations, very inventive in forms and materials, were a great success until changing fashions sent the hat out of fashion. In the 1950s, the atelier, on the first floor of an ancient building, became Turin's center for prêt-à-porter and later of the luxury ready-to-wear of the most famous Italian and French *griffes*. Her death was quickly followed by the closing of the boutique.

Cerri Pierluigi (1939). Architect, designer, and graphic artist. The Prada Sport "corporate identity," or logo, consisting of a single red line, was his creation. For Pitti Immagine he organized the exhibits *The Eccentric Rule/A Hundred Years of Italian Men's Elegance* (1993) and *Supermarket of Style*. He designed the Caffé Marino and the Marino interior décor at La Scala and at Palazzo Trussardi in Piazza La Scala in Milan. He graduated from the Milan Polytechnic. For many years and since its opening, he was an associate of the Gregotti Studio. In 1998 he opened his own photographic studio. Starting in 1986 he worked on the image of the large cruise ships (Costa Classica, Costa Romantica, and Costa Victoria), designing all the furnishings and interior décor. He designed couches, armchairs, and lamps. For graphic layout, he has often worked in tandem with Gae Aulenti on the organization of exhibits at Palazzo Grassi in Venice.

Cerruti Nino (1930). Entrepreneur and designer, from Biella. If men's fashion in the second half of the past century has become more demanding and casual, if Italian good taste has started on its way to international fame, a great part of this is due to this sensitive and elegant man whose family's wool factory and hometown had become too limiting for him. Nino Cerruti grew up in the Lanificio Fratelli Cerruti (established in 1881 by the brothers Antonio, Quintino, and Stefano Cerruti), among precious fabrics and solid family traditions. He was only 20 when, in 1950, at his father's death, he quit his studies in philosophy and journalism and took the lead of the company. He could have limited himself to the management of that factory but, in 1957, near Corsico, in the Milanese hinterland, he established a manufacturing company, Hitman, to produce high quality men's ready-to-wear. It was, for men's fashion, the début of luxury men's prêt-à-porter (Brioni-Roman Style was founded in 1959). It offered tailoring workshop elegance on an industrial scale. There were ten years of growth, along with an awareness that there was ample opportunity for Italian design, but that the battle had to be fought in the very heart of fashion, in Paris itself. In 1967 he established Cerruti 1881 and opened a boutique in Paris on Place de la Madeleine that was designed by the architect Vico Magistretti. Production remained in Italy. The new line used refined fabrics coming from Lanificio Cerruti, and did the manufacturing at Hitman, Cerruti's Milanese factory, where he had a very promising young assistant named Giorgio Armani and a talented right arm named Pinotto Marelli. His modern, subtly revolutionary but unmistakably elegant style was immediately appreciated by people in the Parisian jet set and by the international clientele gravitating around that city: they liked the mix of design and tradition, the use of colors in shades that were unusual for a men's line, the loosened cuts, the preciousness and softness of the materials. The boutique near the Madeleine became a meeting place for show business personalities and actors. In the early 1970s, one of Cerruti's clients was Jean-Paul Belmondo, the French film star. From the first clothes designed for a Belmondo film, it was just a small step to Hollywood. Cinema became part of the Cerruti universe. His fashions were the most requested, for films and for private life, by personalities such as Michael Douglas, Richard Gere, Jack Nicholson, Robert Redford, Clint Eastwood, Tom Hanks, and Alain Delon, as well as many others. In 1967, together with the men's Collection, Cerruti also presented a women's Collection. For the first time, male rigor was transferred to the female wardrobe, in perfect synchrony with the unisex style of the moment. Women's fashion confirmed and completed the image of the brand: fashion that was never banal, never vulgar, and never excessive, but always attentive to changes in costume. In 1980, Cerruti launched a sports line, in 1986 came the Collection Cerruti 1881 Brothers for leisure time, and, in 1988, the latest of his fragrances, Cerruti Image. The fragrance sector represents about 15% of the turnover. The house also designs watches, accessories, and leather goods.

(*Gisella Borioli*)

A sketch for a Cerruti 1881's dress.

❑ Back to basics: everything in the Spring-Summer 2004 men's Collection is branded Cerruti 1881, the *griffe* including the year the company was founded and carrying its spirit. With this brand also came the Grey first line and the Cobalt distribution line, within which were developed Orange sportswear as well as jeans and licenses to market accessories and perfumes. Fashion that is chic and wearable, for women, continues to be characterized by precious fabrics and excellent tailoring for the "gourmets" of elegance.

(*Lucia Mari*)

❑ 2001, February. Shares worth 51% of the company, valued at €81.3 million, are acquired by the Italian group Fin.part., whose majority shareholder (29.52%) is Gianluigi Facchini. For Cerruti, the strategic objectives are the repositioning of the products, the segmentation into new market niches, and the renegotiation of licenses. The Collections, whose creative director is Nino Cerruti and who remains the company's president, are to go in two directions: formal clothing and sportswear. The distribution network has 4 privately-owned shops and 60 franchises.

❑ 2001, June. For the movie *American Psycho* (U.S., 2000) from the book written by Bret Easton Ellis (1991), the costume designer Isis Mussenden asks Nino Cerruti to produce clothes in the style of the 1980s. In the film, New York's yuppies, and especially the extravagant protagonist, Patrick Bateman, who works on Wall Street, wear only impeccably tailored suits. The very large shoulders, pleated trousers, and narrow ties brought back the style of a past decade. For Bateman, a cashmere Winter coat that longer than usual was used to stress the extremes of his maniacal personality.

❑ 2001. The brand's revenues in the first 9 months are €61.5 million, with a gross operative margin of minus €3 million.

❑ 2002, February. In order to implement the reorganization plan, 32 positions are eliminated. The objective is to rationalize the structure of the Italian and French companies which comprise the Cerruti Group.

❑ 2002, April. The resources of Fin.part are concentrated on Cerruti, which must be managed as a brand and not as a *griffe*. The designer Roberto Menichetti leaves. The new team is composed of Istvan Francer, who is to design the first line, supported by Samantha Sung, who is to work on women's wear, and Adrian Smith, who is to work on men's wear. The brand has three lines: Cerruti, Cerruti 1881, and Cerruti Jeans.

❑ 2002, June. Fin.part acquires the remaining 49% of the firm, for €79 million.

❑ 2002, June. In Florence, during Pitti Immagine Uomo, Cerruti offers, along with the Jeans and 1881 Spring-Summer 2003 Collections, the new distribution service R.E.S., Retail Excellence Service. The objective is superior speed in service plus the firm's high production standards. The entirety is represented by a stage set with 230 small glass bottles containing 230 gold fish signifying the 230 Cerruti points-of-sale around the world.

❑ 2002, June. At Milano Moda Uomo, the Collection returns to its original name, Cerruti 1881. Starting with Spring-Summer 2004, all the lines will have a unique brand, in order to reinforce the tradition connected with the logo 1881. For the time being, the restyling is concerned with Grey (the first line), Cobalt (the distribution line), and Orange (the sportswear line), in addition to the products under license, from accessories to fragrances. Every line is to show the same black label with a different colored mark (grey, cobalt, or orange).

❑ 2002, October. The retail development continues. After Stockholm, Athens, Birmingham, Riyadh, and Cosenza, the first boutique in Madrid is opened, with 3,500 square feet on Calle Velasquez in the total Cerruti style, with white opaque crystal walls. Available are the first men's and women's lines, Cerruti 1881, and the Jeans line, plus accessories and perfumes. The next openings are in Dubai and Chester, and for the following year Panama, Bucharest, and Bordeaux. The boutiques in Abu Dhabi and Paris (4,000 square feet on Avenue de l'Opéra) are reserved only for the men's lines.

❑ 2003, January. Facchini, the principal shareholder of Fin.part, which at June 30th 2002 had accumulated a debt of €510 million, reaffirms that he intends to bet on Cerruti, from which he anticipates new products.

❑ 2003, February. Sophisticated and very feminine, although tough and witty:

that is the woman imagined for Cerruti by Istvan Francer - a tapered and slender silhouette, tight bodices with large necks, stirrup slacks tucked into boots, short black dresses, low-necked and strapless, or else Empire with a gold or crystal-embroidered T-shirt; small and tight soft leather tops to wrap the breasts, with tight skirts. But also, in a game of contrasts: large capes; long redingote cloaks, wide and flared; overcoats that flutter about, covered with feathers.

❑ 2003, March. The revenues for the first quarter of Cerruti clothing are €24.8 million, an increase of 12.2%, while the gross operating margin is €2.7 million, an increase of 58.8%.

❑ 2003, April. After only two seasons, Istvan Francer, the designer of the women's line, quits Cerruti. His place is taken by the young Colombian David Cardona. At the men's line, the position of Adrian Smith is reconfirmed. The Scottish designer had joined Cerruti in 2002, after working for Gianfranco Ferré Uomo, the Gucci Men's Line, and Chiara Boni's women's line. Renewing a relationship with Los Angeles, in May Cerruti opens a boutique on Rodeo Drive that is dedicated to the men's and women's Collections Cerruti and Cerruti 1881, and to fragrances and accessories.

❑ 2003, June. At Milano Moda Uomo, there is a cowboy atmosphere for the Cerruti man interpreted by Adrian Smith who wears a trench coat like those worn by Clint Eastwood, in waxed and pre-washed cotton instead of horsehide. The classic overalls no longer have a front bib but are fastened at the waist like a sash. *(Gabriella Gregorietti)*

Cevese Luisa. Designer. Born in Milan, a textile artist, or better said, a sort of magician, the soul and mind of the company established in the mid 1990s called "Luisa Cevese Riedizioni." A rather irrelevant name, as what it produces, clothing and household items, are authentic inventions made from an innovative and original fabric called "11," which combines textile scraps obtained at no cost from various industries with plastic materials. Obviously, the results are always different. Each product can be considered exclusive, thanks to the nature of the basic elements used and to the manufacturing process, in which the machine, almost like a living artisan, decides from time to time what to do. Therefore, useless and damaged remnants of fabric, called, indeed, "scraps," became an unusual raw material to be molded with plastic selected according to the product to be made, either soft or hard, thick, thin, opaque, transparent, recycled, or not. Truly incredible what she could obtain from this mixture: unique and characteristic patterns for a total brand which doesn't overlook even old and broken carpets, which are restored by the same process. She has client-fans in Europe and the U.S., while her single-brand shop in Milan at via Maurilio 3 is the place to go for those who are looking for something that is one of a kind.

(Lucia Mari)

Chador The Persian name for the long black veil that Muslim women wear to cover the head. Literally, it means "tent," and this is actually its function, to cover like a tent. It represents the encounter between religion, folklore, and Islamic tradition. The Koran admonishes women to dress in a modest way and the chador was originally used to cover the breasts, because in pre-Islamic times women walked with their breasts uncovered. In Arabic, it is called the Hijab, which means hiding. It has other names in the different Middle Eastern countries: abaya, jilbab, kymar, nikab, and rusari. Often, it covers not only the head but also the face, except the eyes. That is not an obligation prescribed by the Koran, or by the Sunnah, but it is part of the tradition of Muslim women: the veil means modesty. In the most orthodox countries, such as Afghanistan, Iran, Iraq, Saudi Arabia, Algeria, and the United Arab Emirates, women are obliged to wear it. The burka is, on the other hand, a total covering, loose-fitting, from head to neck and breasts, and from wrists to ankles, uncomfortable, and cumbersome. It does not expose a single inch of skin. Even the eyes are hidden by a thick mesh. The Taliban regime of Afghanistan, in addition to other restrictions, required women to cover themselves with the burka completely, at the risk of very severe penalties. In February 2002, photographer Shirin Nashat, an American by adoption, held an important exhibition about women and the chador at Castello di Rivoli. In France, Muslim girl made great efforts in order to wear the chador in the classroom. A reinterpretation of the chador and burka with reference to the status of women at certain times is a recurrent theme in fashion Collections: Alexander McQueen, the English designer for Givenchy, in 1997 had already presented a burka which transformed itself into an Andalusian costume. The following year, a designer from Cyprus, Hussein Chalayan, sensitive to the problems in the Middle East, presented three models wearing one chador which could be shortened to become a mask, and another one in a stretch fabric that squeezed the legs and arms, blocking them. Jun Takahashi, an emerging Japanese designer, concluded his Paris Collection with a triumph of burkas in very strong colors burkas worn with sneakers. In 2003, in New York, Miguel Adrover was inspired for his Autumn-Winter Collection by the chadors, turbans, and caftans of the Middle East.

(*Gabriella Gregorietti*)

Chado Ralph Rucci American brand of women's clothing, created in 1994 by Ralph Rucci. The designer, born in Philadelphia in 1957, graduated in Philosophy and English Literature, and not by chance chose for his company the name of the ancient Japanese tea ceremony, a meticulous ritual divided into 331 steps which lead to a state of grace and elegance. In fact, refinery and simplicity characterize his Collections and contribute to his being known as "the most French of the American designers." His attention to detail and the use of high-quality materials complete the picture. He becomes inspired by Balenciaga. Alberto Giacometti is one of his favorite artists. With good reviews in the press (Cathy Horyn of The New York Times has supported him since the beginning), he serves a select clientele willing to spend 15,000 dollars for a dress. The company headquarters is in New York.

(*Francesca Gentile*)

Chaiken and Capone American *griffe* of ready-to-wear fashion, established in 1994 by the Californian Julie Chaiken. Her line is classic, with a metropolitan cut. Her creations are for the contemporary woman who needs clothes for both work and leisure, and for men who want clothes with great attention to detail. In early 1999, Jeff Mahshie was appointed head designer.

Chakkal Roland. French designer. He graduated from the Marangoni Institute in Milan and then moved to Paris where he became an assistant of Saint-Laurent. In 1971 he was hired away by the Group Créateurs and Industriels established by Didier Grumbach and under the art direction of Andrée Putman. Supported by this group, he made his début under his own name. But the success of his Collections was not supported by good management. In 1976 the Group shut down and the designer began to create for third parties, starting with Basile.

Chakra George (1958). Lebanese designer. As a young boy he developed a strong interest in interior decoration, a subject he would study deeply before turning to fashion design. He moved to Canada where he graduated from the Académie des Couturiers Canadiens. At the age of 22 he returned to Lebanon to open his own atelier. With his first Collection, in 1993, he had great success and began to make unique pieces for his clientele in the Arab countries. Today, his business employs 60 people.

(*Maddalena Fossati*)

Chalayan Hussein (1970). Fashion designer, born in Cyprus. His father had a restaurant in the London suburbs. In 1993 he graduated from the Central Saint Martin's College of Art and Design in London, and his Collection was purchased in bulk and shown in the windows of Browns. Introverted and cerebral, he designs experimental clothes (he also uses plexigas) that are on the borderline with art, as in the case of the very famous chador deconstructed in 3 pieces from 1997. For his sure hand in cutting and his intellectual qualities his clothes have often been exhibited at the Victoria and Albert Museum, at the Barbican, and at the Hayward Gallery. In 1999 he was awarded the title *Designer of the Year* at the British Fashion Awards. He also designs the Collection for the American brand Tsé Cashmere.

❑ In recent years, Chalayan's success and good luck have been evident in surprising ways. Franco Pené (of the

Florentine company Gibò), a true fashion talent scout at the international level, included by The Times in a list of the 25 new names that matter, has produced and distributed him. Pené also discovered and produced Alexander McQueen, the duo Victor & Rolf (with whom he established a company), and Julie Verhoven.

❑ 2000, February. Chalayan has invented and produced, together with graphic designers Rebecca Brown and Mike Heart, a dress that, as its name, Airmail indicates, can be put in an ordinary envelope and mailed like a letter. For the time being it is produced only in a run of 200 samples. It is made of tyvek, a material combining the characteristics of paper and fabric.

❑ 2002, July. For the first time Chalayan has presented his Spring-Summer men's Collection in Paris. It is produced on license by Gibò, which already produces the women's line. The line, called Absence et Présence, has 35 garments, most in cotton, denim, and wool, both formal and casual.

❑ 2002, October. The Paris shop Colette, a temple of new trends, dedicates an entire window to the ethnic fashion of Chalayan. For the Spring-Summer season he has abandoned the ethnic, though, in favor of a skillful play of cuts, vents, and glimpses. He has also used the porthole-cut tubular jersey in a multiplicity of overlapping layers, creating the effect of a hole closed by another hole. The same effect is repeated with the chiffon plissé soleil. The Collection is composed of small jackets belted around the waist, vaguely military in shape, worn over skirts with a lateral puff and blouses slightly tucked in the back. On the stage were six musicians (the designer among them) and a very loud techno sound.

❑ 2003, June. The 2004 men's Collection is a striking journey between past and future, based on memory and on the link with one's own roots. It isn't a classic presentation, but an unconventional way to present clothes through a movie shot in Athens, *Temporal Meditations*, in a message made of historical references and metaphors. At the Teatro La Pergola of Florence one sees clothes and symbols taken from his native Cyprus, which are the real protagonists of a 20-minute film directed and conceived by the designer himself. There are suggestive scenes with backgammon players who use pieces of ice and rituals that resemble magic against bad luck on a landing strip.

❑ 2005, April. The Groninger Museum hosts a retrospective dedicated to the last two years of work of this designer of Turkish-Cypriote origins.

❑ 2005, June. He represents Turkey at the 51st edition of the Biennial of Venice with the installation *The Absent Presence*. (*Gabriella Gregorietti*)

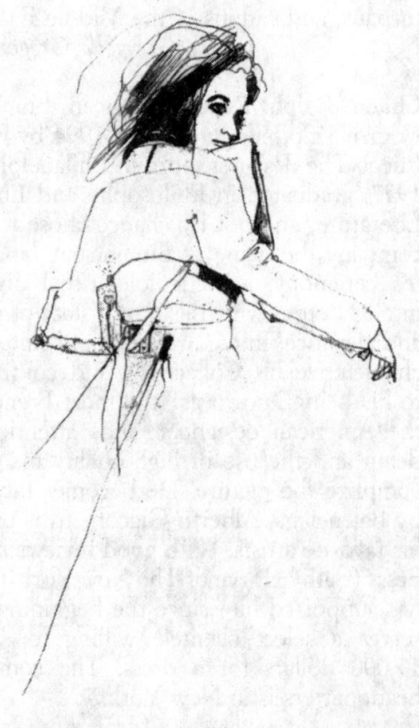

A sketch by Hussein Chalayan: a design from 1999.

Chalkstripe Combed wool or flannel fabric, with thin vertical light stripes which seem to be drawn with chalk. The background is usually dark grey, blue, or black. The men's chalkstripe suit with double-breasted jacket was a classic model of the 1930s, worn by the most famous gangsters of Chicago, with spats and two-tone shoes. For several years, the chalkstripe pattern, which was before purely a "chalk" effect, has widened its palette.

Chambre Syndicale de la Haute Couture Association grouping together French designers of haute couture. It was established in 1910, under the presidency of Léon Réverdot. It has very strict rules. In 1946, the number of registered *maisons* was 106; in 1994 there were only 21.

Chambre Syndicale de la Couture An organization established in 1910 when the labor unions in fashion and manufacturing separated. Today, integrated into the Federation of Couture and Prêt-à-porter of Couturiers and Fashion Designers, this organization offers professional education though its schools.

Chambrey Yesim (1963). Turkish designer, born in Ankara, now working in Paris. At the age of 20 she enrolled in the tailoring school of Esmod, in Paris. In 1989 she participated in the French festival of Hyères, which provides a stage for young fashion talents, and received two important reviews. In 1992 she was awarded the *Beymen Academia*, a prize given by the most important Turkish textile and manufacturing group which, from that moment on, put her in charge of its own Collections. In 1998 she opened a boutique in the Forum des Halles in Paris.

Chamois Leather A mix of rayon, viscose, and polyamide fiber for a soft velvet-like fabric which in touch and look resembles suede.

Champion American brand of sportswear, founded in 1919 in Rochester, New York. It came from an idea by the brothers Abe and Bill Feinbloom, who at first decided to name their business Knickerbocker Knitting Company and later renamed it Champion Knitting Mills. In 1930 Champion invented the plush fabric Reverse Weave: it is 100% cotton and worked horizontally to avoid losing its shape. Around that time the company also offered a distinctive fabric for the uniforms of football teams, the by-now classic grey mélange. Later, it introduced with great success the use of flocked prints on sweaters in order to personalize them with the logos of the various university teams. In the 1950s, Champion invented micromesh, a net fabric for basketball uniforms. In 1979 it established Champion Italy, which in 1984 sponsored Orlando Pizzolato in the New York marathon and Sara Simeoni at the Los Angeles Olympic Games. In 1992, at the Barcelona Olympics, the Champion brand sponsored the Dream Team, the mythic basketball team with Michael Jordan and, in 1996, the entire American Olympic team.

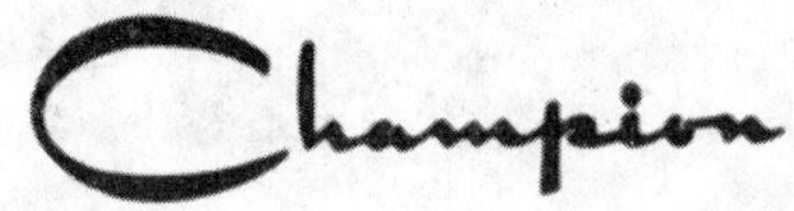

The Champion logo.

Chanel Gabrielle (1883-1971). French dressmaker, known by the nickname Coco. She is the inventor of some of the most important innovations in the fashion of the 20th century. This ambitious and determined woman, who had a poor and unhappy childhood, much of it in an orphanage, represented through her personality a new female model for the 1900s, one devoted to work, a dynamic and informal life, one led without concern for labels but endowed with self-irony. She gave this type of woman the most suitable way of dressing. Through her creations, Chanel completely transformed female elegance, no longer basing it on structural opulence and the ostentation of details and fabrics, but on simplicity and comfort. She modified the day dress, giving it a touch that was markedly casual and functional, and gave the evening dress lines that were fluid and reduced to essentials, introducing more comfortable

Chanel, in a portrait by Cecil Beaton (1953).

and modern fabrics. The high fashion use of knitwear, at first hand-worked and later industrially manufactured, remains one of the sensational novelties proposed by Chanel. The mix of pieces derived from the male wardrobe with elements from the most traditional female wardrobe became a synonym of her style, such as the tailored suit composed of a man's jacket and a straight skirt or trousers, which were until that moment part of men's clothing. Chanel introduced these in every Collection, even for the most formal occasions. Starting in 1924 Chanel showed gaudy low-price jewellery to go with the basic cut of her clothes, disregarding tradition and proposing the democratization of clothing. Pearl costume jewellery, long gold chains, settings of real precious stones with fake ones, and crystals that looked like diamonds were the necessary accessories of Chanel clothing and recognizable signs of her *griffe*. Born on August 19th 1883 in Saumur, southern France, Chanel began her career designing hats, first in Paris, in 1908, and then in Deauville. In these towns, in 1914, she opened her first boutiques, followed in 1916 by a high fashion salon in Biarritz. From her very first offerings, Chanel showed an inclination for casual styles inspired by men's clothing which, in open contrast with prevailing fashions, seemed to apply the healthy living theories of the early part of the century that promoted a healthy life in the open air and clothing that was mindful of the body's needs. Knitwear immediately revealed its tailoring possibilities and in 1916 Chanel obtained from Rodier, a noted French textile industrialist, the exclusive for jersey, a new knitwear fabric made by machine. With it she carried out her program of daytime fashions that were lean and simple, characterized by a skirt, a pullover or cardigan, or a simple tight sheath dress. Her definitive launch in the world of fashion occurred in Paris in 1920, when she established her firm at Rue de Chambon 30. The following year she launched her first and most successful perfume, *Chanel N.°5*, which was followed by many others, such as *N.°22* in 1922, *Gardenia* in 1925, *Bois des Îles* in 1926, *Cuir de Russie* in 1927, *Sycomore, Une Idée* in 1930, *Jasmin* in 1932, *Pour Monsieur* in 1955, and *N.°19* in 1970. In the mid 1920s Chanel introduced a new type of day dress, the *petit noir*. It became a symbol of the decade, a modern version of the modest black dress with white neck and cuffs typical of shop girls and secretaries, and it was a tangible confirmation of an obstinate democratization circulating at the time of which the great dressmaker was a key interpreter. The Chanel tailored suit caught the attention of the female public thanks to the absolute simplicity of its line, the accurary of the cutting and the seams, and the use of soft and well-draping fabrics such as gabardine, cheviot, vicuna, and tweed, in addition to jersey, offered in a shocking mix of understated shades such as beige, grey, and navy blue. Chanel's style is based on the apparent repetition of basic models. Variation is found in fabric patterns and details, according to her belief that "fashion passes, style remains." In 1934 she developed her costume jewellery creations, opening a special atelier where she was supported by the talent of Earl Etienne de Beaumont and Duke Fulco di Ventura, and so, along side high fashion, she increased the production of accessories. In fact, the birth of her quilted bag with shoulder chain, copied by generations of producers, dates to 1930. In the middle of that decade, Chanel enjoyed her greatest fame. The atelier employed 4,000 workers and sold about 28,000 items a year all over the world. But the outbreak of World War II caused a sudden stop. Chanel was forced to close the headquarters on Rue de Chambon, leaving open only the perfume boutique. In 1954, when she returned to the world of fashion, she was 71. The press considered her to be at the end of her career and didn't believe in her. But Coco's new creation, the tailored knit suit of the N.° 5 Collection, was a success. Women all over the world fought to have one. And one of those was Jacqueline Kennedy. Chanel was new again, and she was unique. In 1957, Neiman Marcus honored her with the Oscar of fashion. Her style identified clothes and accessories which have become status symbols, such as the two-color sandal with closed front and open back, created for Chanel in the early 1960s by the French shoemaker André Massaro. After her death on January 10th 1971, the activity of the *maison* was continued by her assistants, Gaston Berthelot and Ramos Esparza, and by their collaborators Yvonne Dudel and Jean Cazaubon. In 1978, alongside the haute couture, the first line of prêt-à-porter, designed by Philippe Guibourgé, was introduced. Since 1983, for high fashion, and 1984, for prêt-à-porter, the brand has been designed by Karl Lagerfeld, the creative director of the *maison*. It is Lagerfeld who deserves the credit for interpreting Chanel's values according to the needs of today, with constant innovation but leaving untouched Chanel's unmistakable style. The Chanel brand has given birth, over the years, to several companies controlled by the family Wertheimer, and to a differentiated production that ranges from cosmetics to jewellery and watches. In 1997 Chanel acquired the French company Erès, specialized in bathing suits, and which has maintained its creative and commercial autonomy.

(*Stefania Ricci*)

❑ 2001, April. The bombé pattern of the famous Chanel matélassé is used on the eye glass frames of Chanel Vision, patterns that are geometric but smooth and rigorously linear, in an alternation of straight angles and sinuous round shapes in dark or metallic colors, with much gold and silver. Simple materials such as acetate and a very light tubular metal are used.

❑ 2001, July. It is the first time that Chanel participates in the Donna Sotto le Stelle (Woman Under the Stars) on the stairs of Santa Trinità dei Monti in Rome.

❑ 2001, December. The reopening in Milan of the historic boutique on via Sant'Andrea. This is part of a renovation of all the Chanel boutiques worldwide (there are 100), carried out by the architect Peter Marino, who wanted to follow Gabrielle Chanel's philosophy that "the most beautiful things are the simplest, and nothing is as beautiful as an empty space." Milan follows the renovations in New York, Paris, Tokyo, Seoul, Vienna, and Mexico City.

❑ 2002, January. The romantic Collection of Karl Lagerfeld for Chanel is presented at the Jardin des Tuileries in Paris, in a completely exceptional setting: a completely transparent tent-structure very similar to a greenhouse, with roses, camellias, clouds of silk, and chiffon. The clothes have a thin and slender line, with extremely tight dresses that extol a very feminine but slim, threadlike, and long-limbed body. Soft and delicate rose petals, sugared or mother-of-pearl, sequin flowers on printed dresses, and on the head a very light camellia in layers of rose-colored chiffon. There are extravagant and original accessories: gold rings made of nails, palm bracelets, and winged shoes with titanium heels.

❑ 2002, February. At an exhibition dedicated to diamonds (organized in Rome from March 1st to the end of June by the Scuderie del Quirinale in collaboration with the Musée National d'Histoire Naturelle of Paris), besides the 30 historic Cartier jewels, and the *De Beers Millennium Star*, and the 30 paintings (among them the *Portrait of Eleonora Gongaza della Rovere* by Titian and the *Portrait of Isabella Brant* by Rubens), there stand out, among the 150 jewels, three masterpieces designed by

Mademoiselle Coco Chanel on the stairs of her atelier. Sketch by Brunetta, 1957.

Coco Chanel: the Étoile, a platinum and diamond brooch from 1932, created for the exhibition *Bijoux de diamants*; the Comète, a necklace composed of 650 diamonds of 70 carats, whose manufacture took more than 9 months; and a set consisting of a ring with 22 diamonds of 2.15 carats and a diamond of 1 carat in the center.

❑ 2002, April. Karl Lagerfeld's prêt-à-porter presented in Paris is made of several pieces that are easy to match, and very young and lively. It is a triumph of waistcoats combined with matching suits in bouclé wool, without sleeves, lined with matélassé (i.e., with quilted linings) in different colors. The Chanel jacket is always a main item, short or long, revisited, perhaps embroidered with sequins, with a tight skirt but also with jeans or leather pants. Lagerfeld has the merit of having maintained the style of the old *griffe* while each time inventing new variants. It is left to the accessories and the details to give a different look to the classic black crepe dress, to the velvet "Spencer," and to the pleated skirt and muslin dress.

❑ 2002, May. Début of the J12 wristwatch, a small jewel of high technology whose perfect circular shape is created in absolute black. Manufactured in the workshops of La Chaux-de-Fonds in Switzerland, it is designed by Jacques Helleu, who conceived it for men, although it also fits a woman's wrist. Available in three different straps, is waterproof to a depth of 60.96 feet.

❑ 2002, July. A prodigious shoe with a flying heel, providing miraculous balance. The sandal has a double sole separating the heel from the back of the shoe, leaving almost an inch of empty space on which the foot floats. To this apparent fragility there corresponds such solidity that the shoe can be worn for dancing a tango, a waltz, or the cha-cha-cha.

❑ 2002, October. The prêt-à-porter for next Summer, more and more aimed at the youth market, has surrendered to the charm of the mini skirt, so improper and short that it hardly covers the bottom. Trousers are very tight and short, clown-like, exaggeratedly wide, in a denim-like fabric. For evening, there are voile dresses, embroidered or decorated with beads, and two-tone shoes with extremely high heels. The Chanel jacket is treated as an accessory to be worn with short skirts in voile printed with graphic motifs or with casual cotton trousers. The favorite colors are white and black, but also pink and brown.

Chanel in a china ink portrait by Cecil Beaton.

❑ 2002, November. For the film *Gosford Park* by Robert Altman, the actress Kristin Scott Thomas (who plays Lady Silvia McCordle) has personally chosen the jewels that she will wear: a necklace and matching earrings from the Fountain series, in platinum with 550 diamonds, and the Cosmos bracelet, with 850 diamonds. From the salons of the Ritz, in November 1932, to Altman's movie, in 2002. Seventy years of history begun with a Collection designed by Coco Chanel, precisely in the year in which the film is set, 1932. The jewels are part of the historical archive of the *maison*.

❑ 2003, March. During the Paris Fashion Week, Lagerfeld's woman isn't simply feminine, but ultra feminine. The classic Chanel tailored suit is smaller, tiny, and very short, in an infinite number of fabrics, including tweed, bouclé, leather, lace, and satin. High heels, black leather spats half way up the leg, and, once again following Mademoiselle's diktat, string upon string of pearls and a cascade of gold chains.

❑ 2005, May. The Metropolitan Museum of New York celebrates the French *maison* with a big retrospective called, simply, *Chanel*. It is a tribute which traces the path of the *maison* established by Gabrielle Chanel in 1920 up to today.

Chantecler Capri's most famous jewels jewellers. The name comes from the founder's nickname: that eccentric and legendary Pietro Capuano, called Chantecler (the name of the old French cock) by his friends, who in the 1930s chose the Parthenopean island as the theater for his wordly and professional life. Already by 1947, Capuano was being helped by Salvatore Aprea. Together they opened the first jeweller's shop with the symbol of the cock as a sign: splendid and original creations of fantasy with pearls, colored precious stones, and diamonds. His boutique soon became a compulsory stop for the international jet set visiting Capri. Today, Chantecler, still owned by the Aprea family, has locations in Cortina D'Ampezzo and Palm Beach.

❑ 2001, November. Two event-exhibitions in Milan and Rome, for a journey through Chantecler's past, first at Milan's Four Seasons Hotel, and immediately after at the Hotel Hassler in Rome. Also shown were the latest pieces of high fashion jewelry designed by the Aprea family, which has owned the *griffe* since 1947. Jewels and history: the family album became an exhibition which tells, through historical pictures, in rigorous black and white, the worldly chronicles of Capri in the 1950s and 1960s.

Chantilly Very light silk lace (just like Chantilly cream), manufactured on a bobbin, usually in black silk with flowered garland patterns. Very precious, it was first manufactured in the town of Chantilly, north of Paris, in the first half of the 1700s. In its traditional crème color it is also called blonde. It was very much in fashion throughout the entire 1800s, especially for shawls and parasols. This type of lace has been back in fashion many times.

Chapelier Hervé (1950). French designer of bags and accessories. Born in Biarritz, he grew up in Bordeaux. He didn't study fashion. In 1976 he designed a traveling bag in nylon and produced it in several colors. Since then he has made backpacks, bags, and suitcases, especially in nylon or nylon and leather. He has four boutiques in Paris and six in Japan. He has a good export business in Italy, England, the U.S. and the Far East. In 1999 the *maison* made its début in high fashion, relying on the young designer Jérôme Dreyfuss.

Chapeux Boutobza French brand of high fashion millinery. It was established in 1996 by the Algerian Hourea Boutobza (1971). After a degree in chemistry taken in France, she moved to Milan to study fashion at the Marangoni Institute. She learned the art of making hats from old Milanese artisans and created a large archive of old shapes and materials that she consults in order to design her own pieces that are between the past and the future, daring but always elegant. In 1997 she came in first at the contest organized by the Museum of the Hat in Chazelles-sur-Lyon, with a tribute to Surrealism. In her atelier in Paris, she works with designers and she manufactures, strictly by hand, custom-made unique pieces.

Charabia Paris Brand of manufacturing and design. Drawing on her experience at Lanvin and Chantal Thomass, toward the end of 1992 Lena Barenton opened a *maison* which began to specialize in a children's line up to 18 months: clothing, bathing accessories, and furnishings. She immediately distinguished herself for a synthesis of practicality and elegance, and for innovative fabrics. Hers was the first company to adopt the color ecru for children's wear, which was then imitated by other big names in children's clothing. The positive reaction of the market prompted Barenton to expand her offers up to 6 years, with the Winter 1996 Collection, and up to 8 years with the Summer 1997 Collection. In August 1999 she opened her first boutique on Rue Madame in Paris, where Chantal Thomass had been located. Today she designs a line for newborns as well as 12-year-olds, using ecological fabrics that are in some cases recycled or recyclable. Charabia produces and distributes the brand Baratin.

Charivari Trendy boutique in New York at 18West 57th Street, opened in 1967 by Selma Wieser. She called it Charivari after leafing through the dictionary. The word is related to the word shivaree, which is a noisy mock serenade to a newly married couple. In 1985 the designer launched her line called Sans Tambours Ni Trompettes. Today her children John and Barbara help in the company's management.

Charles Caroline (1942). English designer. When still young she was a key figure in a season that saw epochal changes in costume,. She was the first to receive the *Swinging London* award for enhancing English fashion with her commitment and talent. She was born in Cairo. She opened her fashion house in London in 1963, after working for Michael Sherard Couture and Mary Quant. An important personality in the London of the 1960s, she dressed pop stars such as Mick Jagger, Ringo Starr, and Dionne Warwick and actresses such as Barbra Streisand. During the 1980s she opened her famous shop on Beauchamp Place, where she was the first to sell clothing and household Collections. Valued as a consultant, she counted among her clients Marks and Spencer and Habitat. Always growing more stylistically refined, she is a favorite of the Royal family and designed the official scarf on the occasion of the 40th anniversary of the coronation of Queen Elizabeth II. In 1998 she launched her own prêt-à-porter line. (*Virginia Hill*)

Charles Kleibacker Brand named after the American designer who, after careers in journalism and advertising, became interested in fashion after a stay in Paris and an apprenticeship with Antonio del Castillo. In 1963 he opened his own shop in New York. His style was characterized by clothes cut on the bias.

Charles of the Ritz American brand of cosmetics established in 1926. Charles was a young French hairdresser who emigrated to the U.S. in the early 1920s. The Ritz was the New York hotel where he opened his salon. Success was such that he went into the preparation and sale of cosmetics. The business grew and, in 1964, when the ownership was in the hands of Richard Salomon, it merged with Lanvin USA. In 1986 it came under the control of Yves Saint-Laurent Inc., which sold the brand to Revlon.

Charles-Roux Edmonde (1920). French journalist and writer, he won the *Goncourt Prize* in 1966 for the novel *Oublier Palermo*. A great friend of Chanel, she published several books about her, among which are *L'Irregulière (Mon itinéraire Chanel)* in 1974 and *Le Temps Chanel* in 1979. In the immediate post-war period (1947-49) she began her journalism career at Elle and for sixteen years, from 1950 to 1966, she was chief editor of the French edition of Vogue. A member of the Goncourt Academy, she received several tributes, including the War Cross (or Croix de Guerre) for her activities during World War II and the *Literary Grand Prix of Provence* in 1977. The daughter of a celebrated French diplomat (her father was the French Ambassador to the Vatican during the 1930s) she married Gastone Deferre, who was for many years the socialist mayor of Marseille.

Charleston American dance very fashionable during the 1920s. Its hopping style deriving from the outward rotation of the leg at the level of the knees lent its name to a particular meaning for the threadlike, adolescent dress characteristic of those "mad" years. This was not so much because the dress was short, something tolerated by the fashion of the time, but rather because of the plastic and metallic-bead fringes which made the dress seem longer than it was and not only didn't hinder one's movements but actually emphasized them with pleasant visual and sound effects. If the tango, imported from Argentina around 1910, had been able to win over a woman recently liberated from the torment caused by corsets, through the flexible verticality of the styles that followed Poiret, the Charleston underlined, with the notes of a fast musical rhythm, the most provocative moment of a woman who had decided on emancipation. An asexual figure, a slender body, bare legs, and short hair: the attributes of an old-model female cast out in favor of attitudes and manners destined to constitute the heritage of future generations.

Charlie (1956). French hairdresser. Very trendy at the end of the 1990s. At the age of 17, she began working with Rosy and Maria Carita in their Paris salon. Appreciating her talent, they passed on to her the wisdom of the profession. For 20 years she would comb and create the hairdos for models for their "poses" in the studios of Avedon, Gilles Bensimon, Isserman, and Newton. She cut the hair of Catherine Deneuve when the actress decided on her "new look." In 1991, the great hairdresser Alexandre offered her a personal space in his atelier. Later, she opened her first salon on Rue Goethe, in the 16th *arrondissement*, and called it "Charlie en particulier." To be combed by her it is necessary to reserve four weeks in advance. Towards the end of the 1990s, a cut cost 600,000 liras, or about $300.00.

Charlier Julien (1927). Belgian manager, born in Liege. His industrial career developed in Belgium and in the U.S. In 1981 he was hired to reorganize the French company DMC by its owners, Thiriez. He did the job, carrying out one of the most prestigious reorganizations in the textile industry.

Charvet Historic shirt shop in Paris. In 1838 Cristophe Charvet opened a shop on Rue de Richelieu where he took measurements and offered fabrics. Shirts were cut and sewn in the back. It was the first shop of its kind. His shirts were known for their high quality of fabric, care in manufacture, and the elegance of the finished product. An official supplier to the Jockey Club, in more than 150 years of existence Charvet has served famous people such as Zola, Eiffel, Edward VII, Offenbach, the Duke of Windsor, De Gaulle, and Kennedy. Since 1965 Charvet has also manufacture shirts for prêt-à-porter. His display windows today at no. 28 Rue de Castiglione.

Chasuble Jacket open at the sides, without a neck and often with a quilted pleating (*chasuble*) which hides the armholes. If the pleating is extended below the line of the shoulders, it makes them look wider. During the 1940s, this technique was used on Winter coats and jackets. Today, it is worn like a cardigan, with or without sleeves, cut straight and closed in front by a zipper.

Chaumet French jewellery shop. The history of one of the most prestigious names in French jewellery starts in 1873 with the goldsmith and watchmaker Marie-Etienne Nitot (1750-1809) who, after the French Revolution, was given the task of cataloging the jewels belonging to Marie Antoinette. It is with his son François Regnault (1779-1853) that the business was moved to Place Vendôme and he created very important works such as the consular sword desired by Napoleon as a symbol of his victories. The name Chaumet appeared again in 1875 when the heiress Marie Morel married Joseph Chaumet (1852-1928), a master goldsmith with an entrepreneurial attitude. Today, the brand, taken over by an Arab financial group, sells small pieces of jewellery, an important Collection of wristwatches for both men and women, a Collection of table clocks, a line of pens, and a line of small leather goods.

❑ 2002, February. The historic French house of high fashion jewelry, now controlled by LVMH, presents its production at the Spazio Bigli in Milan, with many unique pieces.

Chaumont Marcelle (1881-1990). French dressmaker. She anticipated the advent of prêt-à-porter, signing an agreement with the department store Bon Marché towards the end of the 1940s. To avoid expulsion from the Chambre Syndicale de la haute Couture, which would never forgive such a decision, she asked a friend, Juliette Verneil, to represent her in the deal. After few years, illness forced her to retire. Her history is above all that of a great talent discovered by Madeleine Vionnet at the start her own career, in 1912. Until the outbreak of World War II, Marcelle, notwithstanding the fact that she was considered more talented than her boss in cutting on the bias, remained with her. She started her own business only because the Vionnet *maison* decided to close during the Nazi occupation.

Cheap In English, it means "not expensive." In Italian, in recent years, its meaning has widened to include something more devious. In common use the term no longer refers to an object, but to a person. It is a sharp term that in one syllable, cheap, defines a person as being inelegant and graceless. It doesn't quite indicate vulgarity, but just alludes to it. It is something that doesn't have the impact of vulgarity, but is midway between the second-rate and the "I want but I can't." The word is spoken quickly in order to sound more cutting. It is not offensive, but it doesn't permit an answer because it implies a total lack of style in the person attacked. It is almost always some detail or other that causes someone to be considered cheap: a delicious white dress which on a Summer night makes one woman very elegant can look cheap on another who wears it with a jacket in colored snake skin, her lips touched up with brown pencil, like a third-rate television show in the provinces. For women, it's easier to be cheap because they have more accessories with which to indulge themselves. For men, the clear signs of cheapness are usually shoes and ties. Cheap means rich, very rich, or well-off. A poor person always has his style. Typical cheapness, very trendy among gentlemen and young men, is shoes with a buckle. Vulgar are those with big buckles, yuppie-style those with a small buckle, but irremediably cheap both of them. Even if a wardrobe can be updated or changed, it is more difficult to modify one's way of being or behavior, which is learned within the family. Among the most precise indicators of good behavior is the tone of voice when speaking, the very same tone that divides the world in two: the elegant and the cheap. A voice that is too loud, too shrill, too arrogant, too sugary, or too whispering is allowed only in the theater. In the office, at home, or in society, a voice is a voice, not a performing act. Once it is understood that grace can be found in every social class the same as cheapness, and also understood that although money can buy everything no one will ever have enough of it to quiet the naughty gossip that follows those who are unable to deal with it, the cheap person will have only one way to defend himself: simplicity. It is the one thing that you can't label or criticize. The one thing that is never cheap.

(*Lina Sotis*)

Chelsea Boot Ankle boots, launched by the Beatles in the 1960s. They are made in leather, almost always black, with elastic inserts on the side so that they can be worn without laces or zippers.

Chemisier This term first appeared in the 1950s to indicate a dress closed in front by buttons, with or without a neck, with simple lines, just like a man's shirt. Already by the early 1900s, the shirt line had been adopted by Worth and Poiret, and later imitated by several designers such as Chanel, Paquin, and Lanvin.

Chenille Yarn obtained through particular techniques that cause the surface of each ply to retain small tufts of voluminous and straight threads. Invented in France in the 1600s, it can be made of silk, cotton, rayon, or wool. The fabric is similar to velvet or clear-finished fur, but softer. It goes in and out of fashion.

Chen Pascual Maria (1973). Chinese designer active especially in London. She graduated in Men's Design from the Parson's School in New York in 1996, with a scholarship from Hermès, and then followed a master's at the Central Main Martin's, and then finished with another specialization at the Royal College of Art in London. During all this study, she didn't hesitate to obtain work experience with designers such as Anne Klein in New York or with international brands such as Puma and Adidas She won several awards which allowed her to launch her own brand in 1999. Her first Collection was acquired in bulk by Browns Focus of London. She has also designed for the very popular English Top Shop. In addition to making noteworthy experiments in cutting, she is always looking for new techniques that will make materials look older or completely change their appearance. She finds her inspiration in art, photography, and, especially, in the history of costume. Her delicate style and soft lines are appreciated in the world of music: Madonna and David Bowie are great fans. She sells in the most trendy boutiques of Europe, Asia, and America. In 2003, she launched a women's shoe line.

(*Virginia Hill*)

Cheongsam or Qi-pao. Dress of the Chinese folk tradition, in pure Suzy Wong style. In smooth or worked silk, with jacquard or flower patterns, it is very tight to the body, with a mandarin neck and buttons, or frogs and fabric buttons, cut diagonally from the base of the neck to the armhole, and almost always very short. There are deep slits on the side of the skirt or a single deep slit which comes up to the hip. Sometimes the hem and trim are in a different color. Very feminine, it was worn by Jennifer Jones in the tearjerker movie *Love Is A Many Splendored Thing* (1955) which won an Oscar for the costumes by Charles le Maire. In the more recent 1990s, it has displayed the beauty of Gong Li, in films from *Ju Dou* to *Raise The Red Lantern*. It has more than once been used by western designers for short Summer dresses or long evening wear.

Cheruit French house of haute couture active from 1906 to 1935 in Place Vendôme. It was opened by Madeleine Cheruit who had been a première at Raudnitz & Cie. In its almost 30 years of life, the *maison* came to employ some 100 workers.

Chester Barrie. Men's tailor. It was founded in England in 1935 by an American tailor, Simon Ackermann, who moved to Crewe, in Cheshire, in order to have a chance to use the precious fabrics of the area and the expert hands of local artisans. Still today, the garments are made with the same precision and accuracy of detail, with buttonholes in silk and hand-sewn labels. The year 2002 was the start of a new period for the brand, which was divided into The Cheshire Clothing Company for manufacturing and Chester Barrie Ltd. for marketing. The shop on London's Saville Row, the street of the oldest English tailoring workshops, is now owned by The Specialty Retail Group Plc.

(*Sofia Camerana*)

Chesterfield Men's overcoat that was in fashion during the 19th century. It is named after Philip Stanhop, Duke of Chesterfield, who was the first to wear it in the early 1700s. It is straight, with a lapel neck in black velvet and a hidden row of buttons. The Chesterfield line was adopted for women's clothing in the 1900s.

Chetta B American clothing *griffe* created in 1980 by Howard and Sherrie Noviello, with headquarters in New York. It is specialized in cocktail and evening dresses, knitwear, and tailored suits. Under the brand Noviello-Bloom (from the names of the two designers) it has also marketed a men's line.

Chevignon Guy Azoulay created this brand in 1979, and today it belongs to the Naf-Naf Group. As a very young boy he launched himself in the trade of second-hand clothes together with a group of friends in Avignon. A few months later the first line of vintage leather clothes was ready, with such great success among young people that the turnover in the French market quadrupled in just two years. In 1984 he launched Chevignon Kids, for children, and Togs Unlimited. The first mega-store in Paris opened its doors on Place des Victoires. In 1991, the brand came to New York, and that same year saw the first adventures in the Far East, in Japan and Hong Kong. In Summer 1994, Chevignon passed to the control of the Naf-Naf Group: the following year both brands moved their headquarters to Epinay-sur-Seine, closer to the production plants. For Chevignon, it was sportswear time. It opened a flagship store in Nice and a point-of-sale in Moscow. After a 2002 that ended with a turnover of €245.5 million for Naf-Naf's brands, Chevignon started the new year with a new artistic director. The German Mirko Schmitt began a more "fashion-oriented" phase for the twenty-something young man. His first Collection went on sale for the Autumn-Winter 2003-2004 season. There is also a women's mini Collection, presented during the Berlin and Paris fashion weeks.

(*Pierangelo Mastantuono*)

Cheviot Carded wool fabric, which today is also combed, rather rough, with a diagonal or herringbone weave. It comes from the hair of rams living on the Cheviot hills in southern Scotland.

Chiarugi Brand of linen and shirts, created during the 1960s by Dino Chiarugi. About twenty years later, his son Sergio Chiarugi became head of the company, supported by his wife Stefania. Its style, very close to outerwear, has attracted several *griffes* in search of a reliable partner to whom it could entrust the manufacture of underwear and beachwear. The first one of them was Guess, with an initial license signed in 1996, following which there were several others, including one with Emilio Pucci, which along with Chiarugi returned to the historic prints found on bikinis and "external" corsetry. But the soul of the company has remained in the historic brands which today still account for 60% of the turnover: Chiarugi, the top in its sector, characterized by great stylistic research; D, the initial of the early brand Doreal, which embodies the essence of women's underwear; and Nomade, a Collection for the youngest spirits. Their secret for success lies in the use of materials not traditionally associated with underwear, but with very precise guidelines: to offering products with a certain degree of luxury at a cost that is affordable, and not impossible. Therefore, in the Chiarugi vision, a beach robe can be a piece of floating lace under a maxi Alcantara belt; a bra becomes a cubist metaphor built on color geometries; a bikini epitomizes in tiny sizes laser cuts and pre-washed denims.

(*Valeria Vantaggi*)

Chic The origin of the French word "chic" is unclear: the Petit Robert etymologic dictionary says that it derives from the German *schick* (dress) and that French, in the early 1900s, began to use it (spelled *chique*) to indicate self-assurance, savoir-faire, and, finally, elegance. A Larousse dictionary of the early 1900s suggests another hypothesis, totally French, going back to the time of Louis XIII (the early 1600s). At court, the word "chic" was used to characterize a man very skilled in the art of getting past the law. It was a contraction of "chicane" which in old times meant to cavil, quibble, or make a zigzag movement in order to obstruct something (before becoming, today, a series of bends that slow down the cars during a Formula 1 race). It is the source of the English word "chicanery." Over time the word "chic" changed its meaning and in Italy it is now used to indicate elegance. It must have been during the Belle Époque, or perhaps even before, that ladies imbued with French culture, which was needed in order to turn a young girl into a mademoiselle of good society, began to use it to define an unmistakable quality of style and taste. The women of that world owned clothes that could only be named in French: from the charming guêpière, and the peignoir worn when having the hair combed by the maid, to the filmy liseuse, a silk jacket with lace hems, in the same color as the nightgown in chiffon, or even in ostrich, like a powder puff. The trousseau of a "comme-il-faut" bride (that is, from a good family), who wished to have an enviable figure (today, a girl would say "a nice body"), called for a series of outfits to be worn at different times of the day. Besides the long evening dresses, there were the habillés that, over time and with the more widespread use of English, became the cocktail dresses of today. French culture (and, therefore, the idea of "chic") dominated the Italian bourgeoisie up until World War II (the clumsy attempts by the Fascists to substitute ridiculous translations such as "ragazziera" for the French *garçonnière* weren't taken seriously), but it also went beyond Italy because during the 1950s it was still France that set the law for the field of fashion all over the world. Ladies adored Balenciaga, Balmain, Chanel, and Dior, the undisputed masters of Parisian chic, and on their heads, in the evening, they often wore a feathered hat: long thin feathers that followed the curve of the face. The use of the term even after the very late date of 1968 has provided a lot of material for the column on costume written by Camilla Cederna for L'Espresso magazine. Today, the term "poverty chic" still used in some parts of the fashion periphery, while, on the contrary, the word *griffe* is all the rage, especially in the horrible Italian translation "griffato."

(*Sandra Artom*)

Chicco Brand belonging to Gruppo Artsana, established in the early 1950s in Grandate

(Como) as a small family business of pharmaceutical products. Given that children's educational products didn't exist in Italy in those years, the founder of the firm, Pietro Catelli, decided to create the Chicco brand inspired by the nickname of his first son. The brand, today a leader in its field, specialized in the study and production of non-food items for infants, including five lines which are part of the "Chicco Growth Project," suitable for the different phases of a child's development, and also for expectant mothers. For the mothers, in particular, the company offered a shoe and clothing line, the Expectant Mother (Mamma Donna Attesa) Collection, designed to be in line with fashion trends. The Chicco Baby Fashion line, with two theme Collections each year, offers clothes for children from newborn to 10 years old. Launched in 2001 in the American market as well, it is divided into three lines according to the different ages, and it is characterized by practical and joyful clothes and accessories appropriate to the trends of the time (such as the Formula One line of shoes) which have been the cause of Chicco's great commercial success. Sold through a distribution network in 120 countries, Chicco has since 1991 been joined by Neobaby, a widely-distributed brand of children's products. According to recent data, Artsana has a turnover of about €1.250 million and more than 6,000 employees. In addition to its classic shops, Chicco has recently opened the Chiccolands amusement parks (there are now 5 in Italy) within which are the various specialized stores. On the initiative of Pietro Catelli, the Museum of the Toy Horse was opened in Grandate in April 2000, with space to display a Collection of 520 pieces from the 1700s up to today. In the 1950s this was the location of the stables of the mythical trotter Tornese.

(*Sara Tieni*)

Chiffon Light, airy fabric, often in silk, but also in cotton or synthetics. Used mainly for evening dresses and transparent blouses it is also preferred for the manufacture of long scarves and foulards, in soft plain-dyed colors or printed. The chiffon scarf has been interpreted in a variety of ways and it is a recurrent element in fashion, where it has appeared and disappeared ever since the early 1900s.

Chignon In fashion throughout the 1800s and up until the 1920s, it is a hairstyle in which long hair is gathered up in a bun held on the nape of the neck by hairpins, sometimes hidden and sometimes decorated with strass, or glass paste, or jewels. It gets its name from the archaic French term *chaiugnon*, which means nape of the neck. The chignon changed its position in 1865 when a new fashion placed the bun higher up on the head; in fact, the low chignon is called a *catogan*, a term from the 1700s that referred to a hairstyle worn at the time only by men. The drastic change that occurred with the haircut à la garçonne and the prevalence of short and medium length hair, in a ponytail or a page-boy cut, from the 1920s to the 1960s, caused the decline of the chignon (apart from a brief fashion identified with the backcomb). But it often returns to center stage, especially with evening dresses, in frequent and changing revivals.

Chimento Brand of jewellery. In 1964, Adriano Chimento opened a small workshop not far from Vicenza. Today it is one of the most organized Italian firms in the field of jewellry. It is characterized by rigorous craftmanship in the production process.

Chinchilla A type of fur. There were those in Italy after World War II who thought of getting rich with the breeding of chinchillas, because a rumor had circulated – and it was a fraud – that it was a particularly simple thing to do. It was, in fact, very difficult, although very necessary, because this animal that lived in the wild was already in danger of extinction by the early 1900s. Native to the Andes, it was already known in earlier times among the natives who would protect themselves from the cold with its skins and would spin and weave its hair in order to make blankets and extremely soft clothing. The most accepted etymology, among several, says that the name derives from the tribe of the Chinchas. We know that Inca emperors and notables would wear it and that, at the time of the Spanish conquest, it was very widespread in Chile, Peru, Bolivia, and other areas of South America. Two species were common: the short tail (Chinchilla brevicaudata), to which belonged the real, and the long tail (Chinchilla lanigera). The conquistadores brought it to

Europe, where it became the prerogative of kings, nobles, and the highest social classes. In the 1800s, hunters called "chinchilleros" were responsible for the slaughter of great numbers, so that by the second half of the century, when a ranking of the trendiest furs placed chinchilla next to sable, marten, and ermine, its numbers were considerably reduced. In 1930, the last chinchilla skins that appeared on the market went for 200 dollars each, but, spurred by the sophisticated and intellectual fashions of the 1910s and 1920s, it was realized that chinchilla can live in captivity. After the first tests in the U.S. (the pioneer is considered Mathias F. Chapman), and South America, they are today bred on almost every continent, particularly in North America and in Europe. With its changing colors that range from pearl grey, silver-white, grey-blue, and black to rosy-beige, and with its warm, soft, velvet fur swaying at every puff of wind and following every movement of the body, and illuminating the face of the person who wears it, chinchilla continues to represent the greatest luxury, and the voluptuousness of lightness. It is a marvel of high fashion in 2000 just as was in 1820, when the Corriere delle Dame published a fashion-plate with a very elegant *witzchoura* (a type of overcoat) "in clean velvet decorated with chinchilla."

(*Maria Rita Stiglich*)

Chino Since the 1980s it has indicated cotton trousers dropping just below knees, used in sports and free time. Also called slacks.

Chino Bert Pseudonym of Franco Bertolotti (1932). Italian designer and illustrator. Born in Pavia, he attended the Scientific Lyceum Taramelli. At the age of 19 he made his début as a fashion designer with the *maison* Rosandré on via Manzoni in Milan. It was 1951. The following year he tried the great adventure: ten of his styles were presented at Palazzo Pitti. His Box line was appreciated by only a few, such as the painter Brunetta, Giovanni Battista Giorgini, and the journalist Irene Brin. Chino understood that he could not be his own manager and since that time preferred to design for others. Among these was Maria Antonelli, for 4 years. In the meanwhile, discovered by Maria Carita, who managed the most celebrated beauty salon in the world in Paris, he began his career as an illustrator of fashion articles for the newspaper L'Aurore and the monthly L'Art et la Mode. In 1958, Nino Nutrizio, the director of La Notte, Milan's evening newspaper, gave him a weekly column about fashion entitled *Per Voi Signore* (For You, Ladies). At the same time he was back in fashion design, working for both prêt-à-porter and haute couture houses. His clients included Rina Modelli, Jole Veneziani, and Pierre Cardin. In 1963, he began a stylistic partnership with Mila Schön and Loris Abate: he created 20 styles that were presented at Palazzo Pitti and, two years later, he was given the very coveted *Neiman Marcus* award in New York. In 1965 he was asked to work with the débuting Fendi sisters. It was a success again. For Mila Schön he designed the Taroni and Terragni silks, and the wools for the wool mills Nattier and Agnona. After a trip to Hollywood in 1973, he disappeared. Later on it would become known that he had retired to the Benedictine monastery of Santa Scolastica. Chino became Father Franco. He returns to fashion only sporadically between 1984 and 1989 in order to help his friend Schön. In the 1990s he began to paint. He passed from figurative to abstract to informal, on the edge of a very colorful palette.

A sketch by Chino Bert for the Atelier Antonelli, 1956 (from *La Moda Italiana - Le Origini dell'Alta Moda e della Maglieria*, Electa, 1987).

Chintz Printed cotton fabric of Indian origin. A thin layer of starch makes it shiny and waterproof. The name comes from Hindi (*chint*). Already used in furnishings during the 1600s, printed according to the taste of the time (flowers, fruits, and strongly colored birds), chintz, from the time of British rule in India, began to be produced also in England and Ireland, and from there it spread throughout Europe. With the introduction of plastic, chintz began to be used less frequently in practical furnishings, although fashion makes use of its light weight for Summer styles and for raincoats, either in strong colors or solid black, in a waxed version with satin effects.

Chipie A brand of children's shoes belonging to the Zanner Group, a French company that is a leader in the field of children's clothing with 14 licenses for production and distribution. Chipie, with headquarters in Carcassonne, also produces, under license, household linen, leather accessories for school, women's underwear for the bath, wallpaper, stationery, fountain pens, and watches. It has 15 boutiques in France and 200 branches in the most important department stores. The Chipie shoe department made its début at Pitti Immagine Bimbo in June 2003, together with other 54 brands from the industry, for the first time at Fortezza da Basso.

Chloé French high fashion house for prêt-à-porter, created by Jacques, Lenoir, and Gabrielle Aghion in 1952. Since that time, and especially during the 1960s and 1970s, it has shown itself to be a practice field and breeding ground for some of the most famous names in design. The evolution of Chloé is due to the entrepreneurial energy of the founders in their response to the new demand for a prêt-à-porter that would not cause regret over the passing of haute couture. It involved the contributions of different designers, sometimes working on their own, sometimes as a team. These included Gérard Pipart, Graziella Fontana, Christiane Bailly, and Carlos Rodriguez, up until the decisive meeting with Lagerfeld, who was sole designer from 1966 to 1983. His daring, ironic, sometimes exasperated but always surprising style, and the attention paid to accessories as seen in the in-house creation of buttons, jewellery, and hats, and the unusual tone of the presentations, all determined the international success of Chloé and of its young but sophisticated taste with its aggressive femininity. Near the end of the 1990s, Stella McCartney, the daughter of Paul, of Beatles fame, became the *griffe*'s designer.

❑ 2003, March. The French *griffe* celebrates 50 years at the Café de Flore in Paris where it presented its first Collection in 1956. For the occasion, all the designers who contributed to its success have been invited. Lagerfeld left the *maison* in 1983 to go to Chanel. Later, Gaby Aghion sold to Dunhill, now Group Richemont. Stella McCartney went to Gucci, and the new creative director is Phoebe Philo. The prêt-à-porter Collection for Autumn-Winter 2003-2004 presented in Paris is characterized by a young and self-assured line influenced at the same time by vintage, street, and sensuality. Short dresses (or long sweaters) with many frills are worn with leotards in strong colors.

Cho Benjamin (1976). American designer of oriental origin. He studied fashion at the Parson's School of Design, but he left before graduating. He made his début in 1999, presenting his Collection in Paris. His fashion is considered by critics to be more European than American. In Spring 2002 he was selected by Vogue as one of ten emerging young designers.

Choker Also known as a *collier de chien* (literally, dog collar). It can be a string of river pearls or glass beads, or even a passementerie of embroidered velvet, with a jewelled pin, worn tight around the throat. It may derive from the red ribbon displayed by French women whose husbands had been guillotined during the revolution. Very trendy at the end of the 1800s and in the early 1900s, it was an absolute necessity in the wardrobes of ladies who were no longer young. It came back in fashion in the early 1970s as an alternative piece of jewellery. In Florence, it is still possible to find very beautiful and differently shaped hand-made models with glass beads.

Choo Jimmy (1952). English shoe designer. Shoes are in his DNA: the son of shoemakers, he created his first pair at the age of 11. He attended, as did Patrick Cox and Elma Hope, the Cordwainer Technical College, beginning with them a new generation of designers. Within just a few seasons (six, including the Autumn-Winter 2000 Collection) he has reached the covers of the most important fashion magazines. In 1996, he opened his first single-brand boutique in London, followed by others in New York, Los Angeles, Las Vegas, and the most important department stores. The winning characteristics of his shoes are their thin and very elegant line, the very high heels, and their eccentric decoration, sometimes with feathers, macroscopic flowers, or ethnic beads, sometimes in zebra stripes or in pony-skin. To complete them, or to set them off, there are bags, seen as accessories to the shoes. Starting in Autumn-Winter 1999-2000 he also designs men's shoes. All his models are made by hand and his almost manic perfectionism makes them truly unique pieces. His shoes, which were loved by Lady Diana, are also appreciated by the muses of modern glamour such as Elizabeth Hurley, Nicole Kidman, and Elle Macpherson.

A style by Jimmy Choo.

❑ 2003, March. There are eight single-brand boutiques, including London, New York, Beverly Hills, Miami, and Dallas. His new Winter Collection, presented in Milan, is inspired by the East, Art Deco, and the graphic arts. He is inspired by the best of the years between the 1920s and the 1960s, creating shoes in opaque crocodile skin, vintage flattened suede, moiré, and satin, in a range of colors from pink to marine blue, smoke grey, and bright red.
❑ 2003, May. He launches a new bag line, to be produced in Florence.
❑ 2003, June. A tribute from the English Ministry of Commerce and Industry: "Jimmy Choo has made London the world's design center." Of Malaysian origin, Choo arrived in London in the 1980s.

Chopard Manufacturer of high precision watches established in 1860 by Louis-Ulysse Chopard in Soviller, Switzerland. In the beginning it produced pocket watches and chronometers. Then, when the factory moved to Geneva, in 1920, the production turned to luxury models. In 1963 the firm was acquired by Karl Scheufele who, in Germany, already owned the Eszeha factory, which specialized in watches and jewellery. From that moment on the two companies shared production of the Chopard brand. The first presentation of the Happy Diamonds watch was in 1976. It became one of the signature designs of the company, with a dial on which diamonds moved freely between two pieces of sapphire glass. This model was followed by, among others, the Happy Sport and the Ice Cube. In the 1980s the first Chopard boutiques were opened, in Hong Kong, Geneva, and Vienna. In 1993, on the initiative of Karl-Friedrich Scheufele, the son of Karl, a new watch manufacturing plant was opened. It began the production of watch movements named L.U.C., from the initials of Louis-Ulysse Chopard, among which were the L.U.C. Four, the L.U.C. Tonneau 3.97, and the L.U.C. Tourbillon, which was presented at the Basel Fair in 2003. Caroline Gruosi-Scheufele, Karl-Friedrich's sister, is artistic director of the jewellery factory and accessories. She is the creator of several Collections, including the Casmir – a classic of the house –, the La Vie en Rose, and Golden Diamonds. That one, presented in 2003, revolutionized the field of high fashion jewellery because in it gold was made in the shape of precious stones and took their place. Today, Chopard, of which Karl and his wife Karin are presidents, and their children Karl-Friedrich and Caroline are vice-presidents, has 66 single-brand boutiques all over the world. A complete production cycle in the Swiss and German (Pforzheim) factories employs very highly specialized workers who practice 45 different professions, from gold fusion to watch-engineering. Sold exclusively by Chopard are the brand's various accessories (glasses, scarves, decorative objects) and perfumes. Since 1988, Chopard has been the official sponsor of the Mille Miglia (A Thousand Miles), the Italian period car race for which it creates a new watch every year. It also sponsors the International Film Festival of Cannes. (*Alessandra Quattordio*)

❑ 2004, November. Chopard signs a license agreement with De Rigo, a leader in the field of eyewear.

Christo Professional name of Christo Javacheff Grabovo (1935), a Bulgarian artist. Famous key figure of Nouveau Réalisme, he conceives clothes as objects. In 1967 he created the Wedding Dress, an unusual bridal dress, ironic and paradoxical, made of ropes which completely covered the woman's body and pulled a bundle behind. The symbolism was quite explicit: Marriage as a constraint, like a house and a heavy weight to be dragged by the woman.

Church's English brand of shoes. It was created in 1873 by the brothers Thomas, Alfred and William Church. They had a shoemaker ancestor, Stone Church at the beginning of the 1700s. The firm represents the style of the English artisan-made shoe all over the world. There are 250 production steps for each pair and the process takes 8 weeks. The firm's headquarters is in Northampton, the town which provided the boots for Cromwell's army in the Irish War. It also provided 70% of the shoes worn by the British soldiers fighting in the trenches along the Marne in the massacre of World War I. The shoe factory, besides producing the leather shoe, also invented the technique that joins the very high-quality uppers to the futuristic comfort of the rubber used to make the soles. That is how the Goodyear model was born, a lace-up leather shoe with para rubber. The first exports were made in 1887. The début in America came in 1907. There are 200 single-brand boutiques all over the world. The number of employees is about 2,000. In 1998 the turnover was 240 billion liras. The *griffe* is still guided by the family's descendants, even if they no longer control the majority of shares. In Summer 1999 Diego Della Valle, "Mr. Tod's," bought up 8.6% of the shares. Patrizio Bertelli of Prada bought 9% and, at the end of August, launched a friendly takeover bid to acquire control, offering a 20% premium over the share price, of the Stock Exchange's price, worth about 310 billion liras.

❑ 1999. Church's is taken over by Prada Holding, a Dutch company at the head of Gruppo Internazionale, which is among the world leaders in luxury design. The acquisition occurs with the explicit intent of "optimizing" the business opportunities of the brand, with full respect for its English identity. The main strategic plan foresees the rationalization of production criteria and the introduction of marketing logic in the planning of Collections and new products. This is to allow a further expansion of production capacity and the development of a Collection that includes classic categories as well as more contemporary offerings connected to the seasons.
❑ 2002, January. A second single-brand boutique in Milan, after the one on via Sant'Andrea, is opened in September 2000. The 600 square foot shop in Galleria Vittorio Emanuele is on two floors (shop and warehouse), with walls in teak and wengé floors. It was designed by Roberto Baciocchi.
❑ 2002. The Church's Group turnover amounts to €61.2 million, with a return to operating profitability and expected further growth in 2003. There are 48 single-brand points-of-sale, of which 47 are privately owned and 1 is a franchise. The brand is available in 895 multi-brand shops. The group employees a total of 700 people all over the world, with a production centered 95% in England and 5% in Italy for the women's Collection. The expansion policies of the brand have involved the

retail channel and the opening of new single-brand shops in the most important international capitals. The new boutiques are in Milan, in 2001; Paris, on Rue Saint-Honoré; Rome, on via Condotti; St. Moritz, on Palace Arcade, in 2002; and New York, on Madison Avenue, in 2003.

❑ 2003. An agreement is signed between Prada Group and Equinox, an important private equity investment company, to support an ambitious worldwide expansion plan, based on the development of new and complementary categories of merchandise. An important part of the agreement is the complete autonomy of the Prada Group in design decisions and in the strategy concerning the identity of the brand. According to the agreement, Equinox acquired 45% of the capital of the Church's Group.

Ciabattoni Amos (1929). He became secretary of the Rome Center of High Fashion in 1961 and, for 10 years, was also secretary of the National Chamber of Fashion, which he helped to found. He was head of the Italian Institute of Fashion, an old organization for which the state appropriated funds in order to help restart its activities, with a particular desire to coordinate the efforts of the various businesses and organizations in the fashion industry. The national manager of a political party, the Christian Democrats, during the 1950s, he was for 13 years the special secretary to Tupini, who he followed on his journey through the various ministries. He became interested in the politics of fashion on the invitation of Emilio Colombo, who was at the time Minister of Industry. In the 1980s he left most of his positions (although he remained on the Lanerossi board of directors) to devote himself to publishing and advertising.

Ciambella Franco (1966). Italian designer. After enrolling in the faculty of Ancient Letters, he graduated from the European Institute of Design and gained experience working in various fashion houses. In 1992 he opened a small atelier in Civitavecchia, where he designs and produces his Collections with artisanal techniques, researching new forms and testing new materials. A lover of high fashion and its traditions, he makes extensive use of the thin draping and the sumptuous, rigorous shapes of Balenciaga. He is inspired by the perfect line of Mila Schön in the 1960s and 1970s, and by the fluid and bare line of Giorgio Armani: everything filtered, modified, and transformed by his genius and sensitivity. He presented his first high fashion Collection in July 1994, for Autumn-Winter 1994-1995. He had immediate success and his talent was confirmed in July 1995 when he was officially sponsored by the European Institute of Design at an event in the Sala dei Teleri of the Palazzo Ferraioli in Rome, on Piazza Colonna. He is always present at Fashion Week in Rome. His headquarters is in Civitavecchia, where he established the company Opera. In 2000 the designer was present for the first time at Spositalia, with his new bridal Collection.

(*Maria Vittoria Alfonsi*)

An evening dress by Franco Ciambella.

Cianciolo Susan (1969). American designer. She graduates from the Parsons School of Design in New York. With the support of Martin Margiela and art dealer Andrea Rosen, in 1995 she launched the Run Collection brand. In 2001, she decided to close it in order to start creating clothes with her own name. She is an artist (and has presented her work on easels) and a director, receiving an award at the Rotterdam Film Festival in 1997 for the movie *Pro Abortion/ Anti Pink*. She has attracted the interest of critics because she never finishes an article of clothing completely, leaving to her clients the choice of buttons, the length, and possible decorations.

Ciccio Professional name of Francesco Liberto (1936), a made-to-measure shoemaker. He is famous especially in the world of auto races, of Formula One and other rallies, for his very light driving shoes which are comfortable, in colors, sturdy, and fireproof. His workshop is on the seafront of Cefalù, where he was born. He first began to be known among the drivers of the Targa Florio race. Several drivers were among his clients, including Regazzoni, Icks, Alboreto, and Lauda. He also had a place in high fashion: his women's shoes accompanied the dresses of Pucci, Marucelli, and the Fontana sisters in several editions of Maremoda Capri during the 1960s. In particular, he had great success with his cloth-covered boots, *I Muccatturi*, which reproduced patterns from the handkerchiefs of Sicilian carters. He is still at work. (*Eleonora Attolico*)

Cierach Lindka (1952). English designer. She started with evening Collections and bridal dresses. Then she added a line of prêt-à-porter that was younger and more self-assured. As often happens in England with those who work in the fashion field, fame and success were connected to the good fortune of having a member of the royal family among her customers. That's what happened at the end of the 1980s, when she designed the dress for Sarah Fergusson's wedding to to Prince Andrew.

Ciesse Italian clothing firm established in 1976. For 25 years it has studied and manufactured high-tech sportswear for leisure time and for city wear. Always attentive to the needs of the final consumer, the firm has been able to interpret his desires while offering an exclusive total look attuned to present trends and manufactured with avant-guard materials such as Gore-Tex. The company, which operates with regard for and in harmony with nature, has taken up its original logo, the Ligrone, a strange crossbreed with the strength of a lion and the insatiable curiosity of a tiger, in the traditional yellow and blue colors.

(*Maria Vittoria Alfonsi*)

❑ 2000, September. 40 degrees below zero without having to cover up: that is Ciesse's promise thanks to garments that weigh less than 16 ounces and have welded seams. As for the materials, Nylon Tactel by Gore-Tex and Ristop (an internal steel grid reduces the influence of external magnetic fields) are "anti-stress" offerings suitable for urban needs and polluted environmental conditions.

❑ 2001, February. The Ciesse Piumini Collection exploits extremely high-tech principles in order to obtain maximum lightness and protection against wind and water. Paclite is the revolutionary material, light and not bulky, used for jackets and trousers. The new fiber allows clothing in layers and the enjoyment of total comfort through internal waterproofing and thermo-regulation. For more extreme sports, there are welded seams and watertight zippers.

Cifonelli Arturo (1893-1971). Very trendy men's tailor in Rome during the 1960s. He dressed the international playboy Porfirio Rubirosa. His jackets were famous for their loose shoulder line. He opened his first atelier in 1912, together with his father, on via Quintino Sella in Rome. At the end of the 1920s, he moved to Paris. In 1939 he was joined in the profession by his son Adriano, who took over the business at his father's death.

C.I.M. (Comité de coordination des Industries de la Mode). Established in 1955 by Albert Lempereur, it is the only organization for style and fashion recognized by the French government and supported by the textile and clothing federations. It provides important information about future trends to all sectors of the industry. The forecasts (about fabrics, colors, shapes, and styles) are based on the experience of the most famous organizations for style and fashion, among them the three international leaders: Promostyl, Mafia, and Dominique Peclers. Financial difficulties in 1990 required a partial privatization of C.I.M. with the entry of the style office Nelly Rodi.

Cimara Luigi (1891-1962). Italian actor. He was, in life and on the stage, a master of elegance. He would wear only blue ties with white polka-dots, and had one for every day of the year, each different from the other just for the size of the dots. His double-breasted suits were an example for the dandies of the time. At the time of his début he was a member of Tina Di Lorenzo's company. He became a headliner with the Vera Vergani company, directed by Dario Niccodemi. Along with his roles in lighthearted and bourgeois plays such as *L'alba, il giorno e la notte* and *La nemica* (by Niccodemi) he was able to give voice to avant-guard scripts such as *Six Characters In Search of an Author*, of which he was the first interpreter at the Teatro Valle of Rome in 1921. Later, he worked with Kiki Palmer, Laura Adani, and Paola Borboni. (*Valeria Vantaggi*)

Cinelli Company for ready-to-wear fashion. It was established in 1995 as a branch of Cinelli Piume and Piumini at the historic plant in Borgo a Buggiano, near Pistoia (Tuscany), which for more than 40 years has been working with eiderdown. In 1999, with the creation of the brand Cinellistudio, it decided to concentrate on sportswear, mainly for the Winter season. It defines itself as "the tailor shop for down jackets." Today, it is led by Nicola Cinelli. There are more than 800 points-of-sale worldwide, especially in Japan, Switzerland, Austria, and Germany. Among the growth markets are North America, Russia, and Korea.

Cinqetoiles de luxe French brand inspired by luxury hotel linen. It was created in 2001 by Thierry Le Pin, who was already a principal assistant of Joseph. The idea was to offer high-level streetwear and not the reverse, as had already been seen in fashion, and also adding lines for the bath and the home inspired by the great hotels. To advertise his velvet tracksuits, he began with artistic installations linked to the brand at the Hotel Costes in Paris where his creations are on sale. (*Maddalena Fossati*)

Cinzia Rocca Brand of women's ready-to-wear produced by Rodel, whose headquarters are in Dello, near Brescia. It employs 450 people. The line, mainly jackets, coats, etc., is the result of meticulous tailoring applied to mass production: 1,300 pieces a day. The brand is distributed in 40 countries, including the U.S., Japan, Korea, and all of Europe.

Ciofani Raimondo (1960). Born in Trasacco (L'Aquila), he moved to Rome to complete his studies. There he began to live in the world of fashion and show business with a career as a costume maker. Initially, he worked with several ready-to-wear houses in Rome until, in 1991, he contributed to the creation of the brand Swish Jeans as creative director and head of public relations. In this period, he worked with the advertising agency Saatchi&Saatchi and participated in the creation of famous advertising campaigns that featured Naomi Campbell, Monica Bellucci, Yasmeen Ghauri, Carla Bruni, Claudia Schiffer, and Eva Herzigova. In 1997 he left Swish Jeans and was hired by Sixty to relaunch the historic brand Goldie. At the same time, he designed the Phard Collections and the clothing line of Fashion Café in New York. Since 1999 he has worked with the Nyl brand (Lamberti group), presenting it at Milano Collezioni the past two seasons. (*Valeria Vantaggi*)

Cipullo Aldo (1936). Italian goldsmith. Famous for his men's jewellery, this designer collaborated with David Webb, Tiffany, and Cartier before creating a line with his own name in the U.S. in 1974.

CIT Italian factory producing men's and women's wear. It was established in Milan in 1939. The firm's production includes men's shirts, sportswear, knitwear, blouses, dresses, and jackets. Led by Vittorio Polli and Giuseppe Gavazzeni, the company's headquarters are in Arcore, a complex of more than 450,000 square feet. In recent years the turnover has consistently been around 85 to 90 billion liras. Among its brands is the Bagutta Uomo line, created in 1975 due to the need for a high-quality shirt line, to which were added a women's line that in time became a prêt-à-porter Collection; the CIT line, specialized in men's shirts of classic-modern taste; and the Baindouche line, an avant-guard men's Collection.

CITER Centro di Informazione Tessile dell'Emilia Romagna (Textile Information Center of Emilia Romagna), established in the heart of a district where one person out of three is connected to fashion, and where in the early 1990s there were more than 2,000 factories working in textile and knitwear, and at least 1,500 in clothing. Promoted by the Municipality of Carpi – on the initiative of Loredana Ligabue and Silvana Belli – and by ERVET (the Regional Institute for Development), it began its activity in the early 1980s with education and requalification courses, meetings, and workshops, not just for micro-factories but also for already-established entrepreneurs who needed information, updates, and new techniques in addition to research on style, technology and marketing. Today, CITER has a membership of 350 companies in the region plus other firms and clients in the rest of Italy and abroad.

Civiche Raccolte d'Arte Applicata (Municipal Collections of Applied Art). Milan, Castello Sforzesco. The fabric and clothing department was created between 1904 and 1914. The first clothes were purchased, while the accessory Collection began with the discovery of shoes from the 1500s and 1600s in the foundation of the Castle during restoration work. The Collection includes clothes, embroidery, sacred vestments, and fabrics (more than 2,000, from Coptic textiles to the first examples of industrial weaving of the 1900s) of various kinds. The enthusiasm present at the opening of the museum sometimes led to attributions that are now considered incorrect, such as the group of Neoclassic clothes that were believed to belong to the wardrobe of Elisa Bonaparte Baciocchi. Bombings of Milan during World War II destroyed a large part of the Collection. In 1972 the historian of costume Rosita Levi Pizetzky rekindled civic interest in the Collection. In fact, by donating her own private Collection, she sparked a series of other donations that were supported by the municipality with additional purchases, such as the Mora, Regazzoni, and Fortuny Collections and, in 1988, a vast repertory of Milanese fashions from the 1930s and 1940s. Of particular interest is the group of traditional clothes that came mostly from the Industrial Exposition of Milan in 1881. Alongside the somewhat tight space which contains the coat-check and the archives, there is the Bertarelli Print Collection, which has many items related to fashion.

Cividini Brand of knitwear. It was established in 1987, the result of the creativity of Miriam and Piero Cividini and the production ability of Gioacchino Longo's workshop. After their initial success, in 1995 they created the Cividini Collection, a prêt-à-porter line that was exported to the U.S. and Japan. Starting in 1996 the *griffe* has participated at Milano Collezioni. In January 1998 it presented its first men's line. Today, there are single-brand shops in Milan, Hamburg, and Munich.

❑ 2002, June. For the men's Collection, the materials are stretch cotton, wool faille, cotton-metal canvas, creased or waterproof linen, washed poplin, cotton drill, zephyr stretch, and aniline soft leather. The colors are white, beige, black, steel grey, jade, and red ochre.
❑ 2002, September. Cividini, as a visiting professor, has the chair of the Master Class in Fashion Design at the University of the Arts in Berlin (established in 1696 as the Academy of Arts and changing its name only in 2001), one of the oldest in Europe. Thirty years before, the designer had left the Polytechnic of Milan, in his first year of engineering, in order to join the world of fashion as a freelancer for Italian and foreign companies.
❑ 2003, January. For Autumn-Winter 2003-2004, the Cividini men's offerings focus especially on refined fabrics, artisanal details, and innovative workmanship. Without formalism or excess, the garments favor quality, detail, and a tailored cut that is

reinterpreted in a casual way, minimized through unusual workmanship and the use of unconventional materials.

A model designed by Miriam and Piero Cividini.

Claiborne Elisabeth (1929). Belgian designer. In the U.S. she created a very functional prêt-à-porter, easy-to-wear and affordable by the general public. After working for Tina Leser, Omar Kiam, Jonathan Logan, and Youth Guild, she established her own company in 1976. The investment, at the time, was $5,000. Today, the yearly turnover is over $2 billion. A big part of her commercial success is due to continuous adjustment to the styles and trends of the moment. More than an innovator, the designer has been able to be a promoter of the fit-for-every-occasion dress, contributing to the freedom of American fashion from designs that are too right.

❑ 2003, February. The American company will open three boutiques under the Mexx logo (a Dutch clothing brand acquired in 2001) in the U.S. The first will be in New York in Autumn. Six more are expected for the brand Sigrid Olsen. On the other hand, 22 Liz Claiborne stores are to shut down or be moved elsewhere. In 2002, the group had a 7.8% increase in turnover, reaching $3.7 billion (with a net profit of $231.1 million, compared to $192 million in 2001). The results include expenditures of $4.5 million due to store closings. In the fourth quarter, sales increased 12.1% to around $993.9 million.

Clam Digger Tapered trousers in 1950s-style fabric, dropping to mid calf or just below the knee.

Clang John (1977). Photographer from Singapore. He distinguished himself in his native country before moving to the U.S. where he made a name for himself thanks to his style and strong personality. In 2001, he presented his work for the first time in the Studio Diane von Furstenberg in New York, where he lives and works. He has published in Interview, Details, Rank, Surface, The New York Times Magazine, and Nylon. Among his clients are Levi's, Nike, Adidas, Reebok, and Hermès.

Clarins French cosmetics company established in 1954 by Jacques Courtin. It is a leader in Europe. In 1972 it expanded on the international market by open subsidiaries in the U.S. and Japan. It operated in 110 countries with almost 13,000 points-of-sale. In 1990 it launched the perfume line of

Thierry Mugler. Since 1995 it has also produced the Azzaro and Montana fragrances. It has also offered an ecologic line of make-up to protect the skin from atmospheric pollution.

Clark Ossie, pseudonym of Raymond Clark (1942-1996). He was one of the most important designers in Swinging London, the center of gravity for youth fashion and culture in the 1960s, together with Mary Quant, Barbara Hulanicki (Biba), Emmanuelle Kahn, and Zandra Rhodes. Born in Liverpool, he graduated from the Royal College of Arts in London and made his début in 1964 when he started to design clothes for the Quorum boutique in Chelsea, which was visited by the "golden youth" of the London pop scene. He became famous for his long hippie garments, multilayered gypsy clothes, and leather biker jackets. He had great ability in working with fabrics such as crepe, satin, jersey, and chiffon, often printed with patterns designed by his wife, Celia Birtwell. During the 1980s he worked at several different times for English firms, specializing in the creation of evening dresses. He was murdered at the age of 54. *(Minnie Gastel)*

Clarke Henry (1918). American photographer. The book *L'élégances des années '50s*, published in 1986 by Herscher, celebrates his career. His vocation for photography was triggered by the pictures of Beaton and Horst. He attended the classes of Brodowitch at the New School of Design in New York, and did an apprenticeship at Vogue America. In 1949 he moved to Paris where Fath and the Molyneux *maison* chose him as official photographer. In 1950 the art director Libermann hired him at Vogue America but let him stay in Paris. He would work for Condé Nast until 1975.

Clarks Shoes that entered the history of 1968 and the mythology of the protest movement. They are related to the "desert boots" first produced at the suggestion of General Montgomery for British soldiers fighting in Africa during World War II. Nathan Clark, the great-grandson of James Clark, who founded the company C & J Clark together with his brother Cyrus in 1825, saw them worn by fellow soldiers in Burma in 1945. The shoes are characterized by leather tanned in such a way that it becomes soft like velvet and Burma rubber for the sole. Desert boots were launched for the first time in 1950 at the shoe fair in Chicago. At the end of the 1960s they were the favorite of university students who, wearing these shoes and Eskimos, marched in demonstrations to protest. The "regulars" would wear them in light or dark brown suede; "dropouts" like Tiziano Sclavi, the inventor of Dylan Dog, preferred them in blue with red laces. *(Laura Salza)*

Clarks' Desert Boots.

❑ 2001, March. Starting from the historic and revolutionary Desert Boots and from other shoes that have by now become mythic, the British brand offers a fusion of styles for the Spring-Summer Collection. This brings the creation of Shellscape, the Mozie clogs (also printed in ostrich), Slickrock, and Millcreek, which are ideal in the city, and Desert Trek, reissued with new skins.
❑ 2001, June. There is a change of look for the classic models Natalie and Tremont, now made in crocodile-printed calfskin, in brown and red. The aesthetic changes, but the traditional standards of comfort and sturdiness behind the success of the shoes do not.
❑ 2001, September. The opening of the first Italian store, in Padua. It is the beginning of a commercial strategy that expects to strengthen the distribution

network all over the world. It is a company in constant growth, with a turnover in 2000 of 2,276 billion liras thanks to distribution in 150 countries. ❑ 2003, March. A continuation of the corporate policy of strengthening the distribution network and a retail reorganization desired by the British parent company. This time, the choice is an important commercial street in Milan, Corso Buenos Aires. The Clarks brand has been in Italy for more than 30 years. Since 1993 it has been distributed by Asak&Co. of Verona.

Classico Italia Italian consortium grouping together 23 companies that are leaders in men's high fashion. Founded in Florence in 1986, its chairman is Luca Mantellassi, President of the Florentine Chamber of Commerce and Vice-President of Pitti Immagine. Its products (shoes, shirts, ties, jackets, coats, and trousers) are manufactured exclusively in Italy respecting the artisanal tradition of tailoring. The global turnover is more than €350 million. In 2002, it sponsored the Florentine début of the avant-guard theater group Fura dels Baus with the show *The Divine Comedy*, which the Catalan company conceived expressly for the occasion, performing in front of Palazzo Pitti.

Claude Saint-Cyr Pseudonym of Simone Naudet (1911), a French milliner. She did her apprenticeship in the most important workshops of the 1920s and 1930s, where she learned all the secrets of high fashion millinery. In 1937 she opened her own *maison* in Paris, and her creations, thanks to their elegance and rigor, enjoyed immediate success. In 1949, a scandal was caused by her Oblique line, a play of asymmetric drapings invented by chance. She became the official milliner to Queen Elisabeth, working with Norman Hartnell, the queen's tailor. The day of the coronation she was the one who solved a problem caused by a crown that was too large. When, in the 1960s, hats fell out of fashion, she retired to a small boutique. She closed in 1972, but for a while kept working as a consultant.

Claudine The protagonist of several novels by Colette gave her name to a baby-style collar that was flat with rounded points, and almost always white. It was trendy during the 1920s and came back in fashion during the 1960s with the collegiate style.

Claudio Orciani Italian company making leather accessories such as belts, bags, small leather goods, and women's sandals. It was established in Fano in 1979 by Claudio Orciani. In the beginning it made belts of artisanal quality, with great care in the workmanship, high-quality skins, and well-designed buckles. These are the credentials that opened up international markets and allowed the firm to expand with many more products. Belts have remained the most important item. In 1998, Orciani requested the collaboration of sculptors Mario Ceroli, Arnaldo Pomodoro, and Valerio Trubiani for the design of buckles.

Claxton William (1927). American photographer, born in Pasadena. He started photography as a hobby at the age of 7 when he received a camera for his birthday. As a teenager, he took photography lessons from a neighbor. His fiancée, a model in New York, introduced him to Richard Avedon, who gave him his old Rolleiflex. That gift and his love for music became the premises of his career. In the mid 1950s he helped in the founding of the Pacific Jazz record label, and he made all the covers for the albums. He brought sex appeal to the portraits of jazz greats. In 1958 Claxton began to work with Rudi Gernreich and Peggy Moffitt, who would become his wife and introduce him to the world of fashion. He worked with Vogue, Life, Time, Paris Match, and Interview.

Clayden Marian. English designer. Considered a follower of bohemian chic, she combines art and fashion in a funny way. She has always been interested in the painting of fabric painting, and a few years ago decided to transform this passion into a business. She has traveled and lived in various parts of the world, and her fabrics are the result of this mix of cultures. The patterns and colors of her clothes are recognized everywhere, and have been exhibited in great museums such as the Victoria and Albert in London.

Clemencigh Mirella. For 9 years after her début, she was part of the creative group that turned Fiorucci into a big brand and created the Fiorucci phenomenon. In the 1970s and 1980s she traveled through Japan, Korea, China, and Latin America for Fiorucci in search of ethnic objects and inspiration. In 1976 she was in charge, together with artists such as Antonio Lopez, of the image of the Fiorucci store in New York and the first party at Club 54 that was done in pure Fiorucci style. Towards the end of the 1980s, in partnership with the studio of Ettore Sottsass, she designed eye glass Collections for Esprit. She has worked with Casa Vogue and was responsible for Casa Design as part of the editorial staff of Elle Italy. As a consultant, she was responsible for the furnishings in some Max Mara boutiques. In the mid 1990s she began to travel again for research commissioned by Ball, a house specialized in jeans, and by Goldié (accessories). She designs shoes and composes collage books for Camper, a very well-distributed and famous Catalan brand of extravagant shoes.

Clements Ribeiro English brand of ready-to-wear fashion. The British Suzanne Clements (1968) and the Brazilian Inacio Ribeiro (1963) graduated from Central Saint Martin's in 1991, got married, and moved to Brazil, where they established a consultancy business working for several clothing firms. In 1993 they moved back to London, where they settled, and presented their first Collection for Spring-Summer 1994. Their creations are permeated with an eclectic vision that reconciles, thanks to the simplicity of shapes, contrasting elements: here a cashmere T-shirt, or a haute couture fabric used for ready-to-wear. In 1997 they also launched a shoe Collection.

❑ They have received the title *Designer of the Year* five times. In 1996 they won the *British Fashion Awards* in the section "new generation."
❑ 2001, September. The *griffe* makes its début in Paris.
❑ 2002, May. The two designers become directors of the Cacharel prêt-à-porter women's lines.

Cleo Romagnoli Milliner in Rome. The shop was opened in 1937 on via Gregoriana by Cleopatra Costa (1913), using her nickname and her husband's surname. During her career she made hats and hairdos for Lucia Bosé, Leonor Fini, Ava Gardner, and Evita Perón. During the 1950s, she worked with the emerging stars of Italian fashion such as Fabiani, Simonetta, and the Fontana sisters, and later with Barocco, Fendi, Lancetti, and Valentino.

Clergerie Robert. Shoe designer. In 1978 he moved to Romans, the capital of luxury shoes, where the Shoe Museum is one of the most important attractions, and took over the Société Romanaise de la Chaussure, thus starting, at the age of 40, a second life. His family was not in the industry, and he had come from a very different business background when an advertisement by Charles Jourdan captured his attention. For six years Robert would direct the youth line of Xavier Darraud, and during that time he would come to know that he was destined for this career. Then came the one-way ticket from Paris to Romans. Success was immediate. His styles wisely mixed references to the past with non-conformist choices. He says, "It is necessary to create a particular line, finding a third dimension, but when an idea is particularly innovative, you must be able to express it in the simplest way as possible." Starting in 1981 he opened boutiques in Paris, Lyon, Toulouse, Tokyo, New York, Brussels, London, Madrid, and Los Angeles. In 1987 he received an award as the best shoe designer in the U.S. But probably the acknowledgment that moved him the most was the handshake with Roger Vivier, who complimented as the only designer worthy of interest. In 1996, he sold the majority of his shares to a financial group, remaining responsible for the Collections and the economic strategy.

Clergyman English ecclesiastical suit, typical of Protestant pastors, with a black jacket and trousers and a white collar.

Clerici Tessuto Silk factory in the Como area created in 1922 by the married couple Rachele Clerici and Alessandro Tessuto to "trade silk fabrics and the like." From 1925 the sales were supported by in-house production which, starting in 1937, took place in the plant at Grandate (Co). In 1944, their son Eugenio became head of the factory. During the 1950s, a strategy of expansion in the Italian and French prêt-à-porter and high fashion markets led to considerable growth in capital. At the death of Eugenio Tessuto in 1987, the leadership of the company passed to the third generation. In the early 1990s, Clerici Tessuto acquired part of the Sara printing plant in order to diversify production, enlarging it by entering the fields of furnishings and men's accessories.

Cleveland Pat (1950). Model. Originally from New York, Pat Cleveland was discovered on the subway by a *Vogue* editor, and debuted her runway career while still in her teens at Cacharel. Dark haired and exotic, she became an internationally celebrated model in the 1970s and 1980s. Cleveland brought a unique over-the-top quality to her work, sashaying, hopping, miming and dancing down the runway, and generally stealing the show. She often posed for the illustrator Antonio Lopez, and was photographed, among others, by Penn, Barbieri and Toscani.

Cligman Léon (1920). French clothing entrepreneur. Born in Tighina, Russia. When still a child, he arrived in Paris with his family, fleeing the Soviet regime. His father established the firm Indreco Manufacturing. Léon studied at the École Supérieure de Commerce in Paris, worked in the Boussac Weaving Mills and at Galeries Lafayette. Starting in the 1950s he applied new production techniques and new stylistic criteria (an anticipation of prêt-à-porter) to his father's business. The result was a yearly volume of 10 million pieces. Indreco, under his management, took over Newman, Seiligmann, and C. Mendés. Pierre Lévyg, his father-in-law, entrusted him with the relaunch of the Devanlay Group, an operation with which he had great success, especially with the Lacoste brand.

(*Giuliana Zabeo Ricca*)

Clip A piece of jewellery with a Spring attached, used as an earring or to be appled, as a pair, to the edges of a heart-shaped or square neckline. Very trendy during the 1930s on the necklines of Hollywood stars, it is back in fashion thanks to the success of American jewellery. A famous example is Corot's Duet, which can be combined in a single brooch.

Clips Brand of prêt-à-porter. It belongs to the textile group Wanda Mode, established in Carpi (Mo) in 1985 as a company manufacturing women's wear for ceremony. In 1995 the firm opened a showroom in Milan. The following year the Group's turnover reached 20 billion liras.

❑ 2002, February. For Autumn-Winter 2003, in a play of contrasts and superimpositions, a precise cut in tailoring accompanies silk and lace transparencies. It is an alternation of classicism and frivolity, strictness and transgression. The main feature of the entire Collection is fur, used to embellish ankle boots, veiled scarves, the collars of jackets and Winter coats, and the hems of silk skirts. The tones and colors are dark, with a few hints of printed patterns, either floral or spotted.

❑ 2002, September. Daniela Corano, the Clips designer, wants Asia Argento as testimonial.

Clivio Textile factory established in 1918 to manufacture silk for ties, either striped, diapered, printed, or shadow moiré. The founders, Francis Clivio and his brother-in-law Carlo Longoni, executed the first designs for the ties themselves, and then had them produced in the weaving mills at Como, Giussano (Mi), Fino Mornasco (Co), and Minoprio (Co), which were acquired between 1919 and 1921. During the 1930s they began to concentrate on silk and rayon at the plant in Como. In 1934, after the death of Francis Clivio, his widow and the Longoni family continued the business. Starting in the early 1960s, Franco Longoni found himself alone at the head of the company, and decided first to move the printing mill next to the weaving mill and later to sell it to a company, Stamperia Smart, of which he himself was one of the partners. In 1989, the Francis Clivio company was taken over by Dante Prini Spa.

Cloak (1) Full, sometimes floor-length garment, originally of a circular cut, sleeveless and often hooded. Worn hung over the shoulders, it is fastened at the neck with a small chain or else down the entire length of the front. The most sumptuous designs are made of fur or in padded velvet for the evening, with lighter models in satin or taffeta. The male version of the cloak was extremely fashionable throughout the nineteenth century. It almost disappeared entirely or else changed its form to such an extent that the garment became known by different names. It regained popularity from the 1960s onwards.

Cloak (2) Large sleeveless mantle, with two side openings for the arms, and a hood, often lined with fur. In the early 1800s, men would wear it as an evening mantle, black with a red lining and a silk collar. Its width allowed women to use it over crinoline skirts.It is often made with precious fur and worn with an evening dress instead of a stole. A variant is the pelerine, which falls only to the waist. Worn on top of an overcoat, it can also be removed. It was the garment of pilgrims and the uniform of French policemen. Following the ups and downs of fashion, the cloak has often been relaunched throughout the twentieth century.

Cloche Hat Women's hat with a characteristic bell-shape. It is soft, close-fitting and seems to wrap the head. It is worn pulled down on the forehead, with the brim almost covering the eyes. It made its first appearance in the 1920s with the fashion for short hair à la garçonne and the convertible automobile.

Clog Shoes similar to slippers with a thick cork or wooden sole, and a leather or synthetic upper. Very trendy during the 1960s and 1970s, they came back in fashion at the end of the 1990s.

Clone Brand of shoes. His experience in the industry prompted Bruno Bordese to conceive a line: Clone, a name which isn't exactly English or Italian, and therefore immediately international. It was 1994. Two years later, there was a new Collection with the designer's name, and a single-brand store in Milan on Corso Venezia. Bruno Bordese also produces and distributes the shoe line of the English designer Westwood.

❑ 2002, March. The new Autumn-Winter Collection 2002-2003 can be defined as multiethnic. It is a line influenced by the designer's travels. He started with men's shoes, while women's are still a projection, so it is possible to say that the design is unisex. His models are characterized by a mix of styles, casual and elegant, male and female. But his creations are also inspired by the past, by the fashion trends of the 1980s, this time interpreted through draping.

❑ 2002, June. License agreement with the Japanese firm Itochu Fashion System Co., Ltd. for the C line (manufacture and distribution) and the Clone brand (distribution only). The two brands are to be distributed differently: the C brand in department stores, while Clone will be sold in three single-brand stores: the two planned for Tokyo in Spring 2003, and the one for Osaka.

Closed Sportswear brand established in 1979 as the result of a creative partnership between Marithé and François Girbaud who designed it and the industrialist Aldo Ciavatta who produced and distributed it. Success was immediate thanks to the avant-guard style which revolutionized the jeans concept. But the company, unable to provide adequate financial support for expansion, declared bankruptcy in 1992. It was taken over by Bellini, an important group headquartered in Hamburg. Since 1997 Bellini Italy has distributed the brand in Southern Europe.

Cloth A generic term for all types of fabric.

Coast, Weber & Ahaus A single-product brand which made its appearance on the market in 1999. The firm produces shirts, Weber trousers, and Ahaus jerseys. All three labels are inspired by vintage couture and have a very strong image. The creative director is Remo Ruffini (Como, 1961), the founder of Union, which was acquired by the group Fin. Part in March 2001. Distribution for Coast, Weber & Ahaus is concentrated mainly in Italy, France, Germany, and the U.S. The first Coast, Weber & Ahaus boutique was opened in Capri in June 2001. In 2003, new boutiques were opened in Paris, New York (at Bergdorf and Goodman), and Naples.

(*Sofia Catalano*)

Coat Dress (French, *Robe-manteau*). Outfit worn for the most part in Winter and Spring. Straight or flared, buttoned in front, often double-breasted, with men's collar and lapels. Similar in cut and style to an overcoat or a dustcoat.

Cobin Anita (1958). English photographer. She studied at the Polytechnic of Central London and then attended the Royal College of Art. Starting in 1983 she worked as a freelancer for Elle, Observer, New Society, Time Out, and Woman's Own.

Cobson Corinne (1960). French designer. She followed in a family tradition: her parents, Elie and Jacqueline Jacobson, created the brand Dorothée Bis. She made her début in 1986 with a prêt-à-porter line in light fabric and elasticized jersey. She already had experience as a film costume designer for Eric Rohmer and as an apprentice in the family business for which, in 1989, she designed a men's line. In 1992 Cacharel gave her the stylistic direction of the shirts division.

Coca Cola Clothes Line of prêt-à-porter distributed in Europe and the U.S. Young and informal, it is made especially for teenagers, but it also has a children's line (6-12). In addition to clothing, it produces a wide range of accessories, from shoes to watches and eye glasses. When it was established in 1989 it was part of Murjani Enterprises, but three years later it was taken over by the Swiss company STI (Spira Textile Investments).

Coccapani Italian *griffe*. It was established in 1988 under the name Il Marchese di Coccapani, on the initiative of Gianfedele Ferrari, the founder of the Sicem Group, producers of knitwear. The brand was named after the 18th century Villa di Soliera, near the factory, which belonged to the noble family of the Marquises of Coccapani and which has today become the firm's headquarters. The qualitative leap, at least in terms of advertising strategy, occurred in 1993, when the company chose Claudia Schiffer as the model for its products. The brand quickly found its identity, offering a total look to its target of female consumers between 20 and 40 years old. In 1997 the *griffe* made its début at Milano Collezioni, and in 1999 it opened a single-brand boutique on via della Spiga. In 2002, as part of a massive stylistic reorganization, the brand changed its name, leaving the aristocratic aura behind in order to become known as, simply, Coccapani.

❑ 2003, March. At the Milan Collection of Autumn-Winter 2003-2004, the second by the new designer Riccardo Tisci, who radically changed the Coccapani style from classic to trendy, there was great approval, especially from buyers in Japan and the U.S., two markets on which the company depends for its international development, although for the moment only through multi-brand stores. In Japan and Russia, the brand is already well known, but less so in the U.S. In 2002, the turnover was €10 million. Riccardo Tisci joined the company in the Spring of 2002. Born in Como, 27, he now lives in Milan, but lived for more than 9 years in London, where he attended the Saint Martin's School. After graduating in 1998, he returned to Milan and created a small Collection of 28 pieces, handmade with the help of his mother and 8 sisters. The Collection carried his own name and was sold in select boutiques. He also designed a clothing line for Puma. In the meanwhile, Coccapani felt the need to change its style and hired him. Ever since the first Collection, the difference could be seen. The Collection returned to lingerie, with satins, lace, georgettes, and silk organza for light and swaying styles, rich in frills, ruches, and drapings, multilayered, with embroidery and sequins. The colors are those typical for underwear: pale pinks and flesh tones.

❑ 2003, September. The launch of the

AnnamariaB Collection, designed by the designer's wife. It is a ceremony line which has about 120 pieces, aimed at the women's market. The fabrics include silk, cotton, lace, and metallic materials. ❑ 2004, June. Alessandro De Benedetti is asked to create the Spring-Summer 2005 Collection: one hundred pieces which are to be presented in September in the Milan showroom.

Coccinelle Manufacturer of bags and leather goods, established in Parma in 1978 by Giacomo Mazzieri. In 1995 the firm opened its first single-brand store on via Statuto, in Milan. In that same year there were already 80 employees. In 1997 the brand expanded and in Germany the firm established Coccinelle Deutschland GmbH in order to manage showrooms in Hamburg, Munich, and Düsseldorf. In 1998 the product range widened to include sunglasses, watches, jewellery, and shoes. In 2000 Coccinelle started on the path to internationalization, and by the following year there were 27 single-brand stores (Paris, London, and Berlin included) and 1,300 multi-brand points-of-sale, with a foreign turnover that was 30% of the total. Today, Coccinelle has 150 employees and 400 outside associates. A clean style without excess characterizes the brand. There are four Collections per year, with a range of more than 500 articles per Collection.

(*Valeria Vantaggi*)

Coccoli Ugo (1916-1996). Men's tailor and designer. After a youthful apprenticeship with the Roman firm Faré, at the age of 24 he moved to Turin where he opened a custom-made tailor's workshop (1948). Due to his perfect cutting, accuracy in execution, his sober but open-to-modernity taste, he would win and keep the most demanding clientele of Turin. Aware of the expansion of a new mass of consumers and of the growing success of industrial manufacturing, Coccoli was from the beginning part of the group of tailors (Litrico, Piattelli, Brioni, Blasi, and Caraceni) that wanted to establish the Made in Italy movement, in opposition to the prevailing French and English styles. They promoted it at the festival of men's fashion in San Remo and, above all, at the presentations sponsored by the Accademia dei Sartori in Rome in the late 1960s. Expanding outside Italy to Germany, he had great success due to the contrast in his style between classic cutting and modern colors and fabrics: bright blue jackets, smoking jackets with a white jacket and scarlet trousers. During the 1970s Coccoli's style was enriched by a casual accent that could be found in half-belted jackets which often resembled a safari jacket. He was famous for his double-face coats, his light-weight smoking jackets, and his black evening cloak, lined with brightly-colored silk.

(*Lucia Sollazzo*)

Cocteau Jean (1889-1963). French artist and writer. He came into contact with the world of fashion through his friendship and collaboration with Elsa Schiaparelli, who applied his surrealist themes to the accessories she designed. In turn, he illustrated the designer's styles in Harper's Bazaar and other fashion magazines. On some of Schiaparelli's creations, Cocteau's drawings were embroidered by Françoise Lesage. A female bust, with its head thrust back and loose hair, decorates an evening dress from 1937. The ambiguity created by the juxtaposition between the fictional embroidered character and the real person is shocking and provocative. Also from 1937 is a drawing on the back side of another evening dress: it shows two faces looking at each other, and, thanks to an optical effect, suggests the outline of a vase of flowers. In that same year, Cocteau produced for the dressmaker an eye-shaped brooch with a tear dropping from it, and the patterns for the Zicha Arches scarves.

(*Cloe Piccoli*)

Codice Brand of women's knitwear belonging to De Pietri, a company that was already successful in the men's sector. It entered the market aimed at a young woman who would like to wear casual clothing but without changing her classic style too much. It was the 1970s. The company hit its target. But, over the years, management found itself in crisis and sold the brand to Sicem Industriale Spa which, as one of the most important companies in Carpi, was able to relaunche the line.

Coffin Clifford (1916). American photographer, born in Chicago. He moved to Los Angeles, where he studied at the local university. He worked in the advertising departments of MGM and Texaco and, in this way, he entered photography. He got his professional start under the guidance of Cecil Beaton, even though his photographs showed the surrealist influence of George Platt Lynes, with whom he studied in New York. For 14 years, from 1944 to 1958, he worked in New York, London, and Paris (his very elegant sets in Versailles were famous) for the most important fashion magazines, including Glamour, Vogue, and Jardin des Modes. He was also a famous portraitist, as seen in the many photos of writers and artists such as Gore Vidal, Truman Capote, Lucian Freud, and Laurence Olivier.

Cohen Peter. South African designer. He works in the United States, where he arrived at the end of the 1980s. His fashion is casual and indulges in "colonial ethnic," although revisited in a contemporary style. His logo is a gold star: many see it as a Zen symbol.

Coin Italian department store. The founding generation was that of Vittorio Coin who, in 1916, obtained a pitchman's license to sell fabric and haberdashery. Between 1926 and 1933, the firm had its first spurt of growth, with the opening of 4 shops, all of them in Venice and its surroundings, and all specialized in fabric, yarns, and linen. It was in the early 1960s that the Coin family opened its first department stores with sales divided according to merchandise category and a greater variety of goods including toys, small leather goods, fragrances, and household objects. In 1972 the company established Oviesse, aimed at middle to low level consumers. In 1998, the figures showed: 4,200 employees; 2,132 Coin, Oviesse, and Bimbus stores in 64% of the Italian cities with more than 50,000 inhabitants; and 8 million customers. In 1996 sales were more than 1,250 billion liras.

(*Valeria Vantaggi*)

❑ 1999, January. The Group acquires 167 Standa department stores.
❑ 2000, August. It expands in Germany. An agreement with the German Divaco (owned in part by Metro Bank and Deutsche Bank) allows Coin to take over the Kaufhalle selling network, which is present all over Germany, with 99 points-of-sale. Kaufhalle has a turnover of about 1,400 billion liras.
❑ 2000, September. Coin's acquisition strategy is rewarded with a rise in the share price. The company's shares reach a historical high of around €16, an increase of 5.26%. The company has also signed an agreement with Magazine Zum Globus (Migros Group) to open Oviesse department store franchises in Switzerland. At the end of August, the acquisition of Kaufhalle is concluded.
❑ 2001, October. The *Creativity Young Fashion Designer* awards, organized by Coin together with Sistema Moda Italia. It is open to the best students from three schools: Domus Academy, the Marangoni Institute of Milan, and Polimoda of Florence. Piero Costa, the director of the association of textile-clothing and fashion industrialists, has promised to produce the designs of the three winners. First prize goes to a Korean, Kim Jeong-Sun of the Domus Academy; the second prize also goes to a Korean, Kim In Hee; third prize goes to Giorgia Collodoro, from Arezzo, who attends Polimoda.
❑ 2002, October. In the first six months, Coin has consolidated revenues of €689.5 million, with a gross operating margin of €6.3 million. Excluding Germany, the balance sheet is positive compared to the first six months of 2001. In Italy, in fact, the gross operating margin is €44.6 million compared to €31.2 million, with a profit of €15.1 million against €2.2 million, and a pre-tax result of around €14.6 million against a loss of €8.8 million. In Italy things have gone well, both for Coin and Oviesse, while the situation is the opposite in Germany, where the Kaufhalle chain is being changed into Oviesse stores.
❑ 2002, December. After the losses of the first six months, Coin's figures improve. The third quarter shows an increase of 5.6% compared to the same period in 2001, while the profit is around €2.2 million.

Costume by Corrado Colabucci for dancers at the Moulin Rouge in Paris.

Colabucci Corrado (1935-2002). Italian designer and costume maker, born in Legnago (Verona). He graduated with a degree in law, out of a sense of duty to his father, who was a famous judge, but was a designer for his pleasure, creating sportswear and wedding dress Collections. He was the most important costume designer for TV shows, for which he dressed (or undressed) numberless very famous personalities including Mina, Milva, Ornella Vanoni, Gabriella Ferri, Sandra Mondaini, Caterina Valente, and Raffaella Carrà. In the years from 1958 (when he made his début in Paris with the costumes for the show *La Nouvelle Eve*) to 2002, he did important work for *Studio 1*, *Fantastico*, *Canzonissima*, *Scommettiamo Che?*, and *Hallo Word* (in Hamburg with Van Johnson and Rita Moreno in 1968). He also did the *Judy Garland Show* with Sarah Dunes in Las Vegas, and many La Scala performances (in Madrid, Barcelona, and the Canary Islands). Starting in 1984 he often designed costumes for the "grandes revues" at the Moulin Rouge in Paris, including the one that on December 23rd 1999 began the celebrations for the new millennium. Colabucci's imagination and style have often inspired famous tailors and haute couture designers. He twice received awards at the Montreux Festival "for the best costumes seen on TV networks all over the world." (*Maria Vittoria Alfonsi*)

Cole-Haan American brand of shoes. During the 1970s, the Cole-Haan hand-sewn loafer was a must for preppy fashion, along with button-down Oxford shirts, a blue blazer, and khaki pants. Eddie Haan and Trafton Cole founded the brand in Chicago during the 1920s. In 1975 it was acquired by George Denney and production was moved to Maine, where it remains. In 1982, the women's Collection was launched, and the following year, the brand arrived in Europe. In 1988, Cole-Haan became part of the Nike Group.

(*Marilena Bergamaschi*)

Coleman Nick (1961). English designer. He studied at the Saint Martin's School and gained experience working for Burberry. At the age of 24 he made his début in the world of fashion and launched his own *griffe* of ready-to-wear, with an eye on tradition but also with a typically British touch of modernity. In 1987, he designed the unisex line Cocon, with wide distribution in the Far East and the U.S. His first men's Collection came out in 1989. He has a boutique on Neal Street in London. In 1992 he started a second line, Shield.

Cole of California Famous brand of beachwear, from bathing suits to vacation wardrobes. The Group was established in 1923 by Fred Cole. Today, it is directed by Anna Cole.

Colette Italian brand of shoes with a history that goes back to 1886, the year of birth of Enrico Lattuada, the head of a dynasty of artisans. Helped by his wife and son Ambrogio, Enrico opened a workshop in Parabiago (Mi). But it was Ambrogio who would propel the company into the future with the introduction of new machines to assemble the uppers. It was the beginning of the brand La Flessibile, shoes that combined innovative shapes with refined materials. With Vito Lattuada, a member of the third generation, La Flessibile became Colette. From that moment on, Magda Nai, Vito's wife, would follow the administrative part of the business, while Vito dedicated himself to the creative side, giving his shoes lines that were simple and never too "busy." The company launched Collage, a trendy line of comfortable shoes inspired by the American lifestyle, and, in 1975, a line of shoes carrying his own name. The year 1982 saw the début of Laura Biagiotti by Colette. In 1986 Colette became a public limited company and Vito Lattuada received the title Cavaliere del Lavoro. Ten years later, it was time for the fourth generation, Laura and Andrea, who enriched the range of products with the *griffes* Lall by Colette and Andrea Lattuada.

Colette Parisian style boutique. It opened in March 1997 and belongs to Madame Colette and her daughter Sarah. Its 8,000 square feet cover three floors. Designed by the French architect Arnaud de Montigny, the shop offers fashion, design, and food, following a precise method of selection which accepts or rejects products not according to market trends but according to its own ideas. It has a water bar (with a selection of mineral waters), an area dedicated to men's and women's fashion, an exhibition space, and a book/newspaper corner. It is estimated that every day between 500 and 800 people visit the celebrated store at no. 213 Rue Saint-Honoré.

(*Maddalena Fossati*)

Colla Ettore (1896-1968). Italian artist. Among the founders of Gruppo Origine. In 1951, with Burri and Capogrossi, he produced gold jewellery decorated with abstract-geometric shapes influenced by his artistic researches in this field.

Collection Privée Created in 1988 as a shoe line to which was added, in 1996, a clothing Collection. Its designer is Massimo Bizzi, from Bologna, who, after working at Mishap, his family's shoe and clothing company, decided to start Robiz, a line and business of his own. His first shoe Collection was made up of sandals and loafers made with very refined leathers and in new colors, such as matt blacks and very light sand tones. Starting in the mid 1990s, he offered three Collections, for men, women, and children, with a total of 45,000 pairs of shoes produced each year. In 1996 he started a clothing line including high-tech garments and sportswear: windbreakers, safari jackets, and long dustcoats in resinated lien and oiled cotton. Since 1992 there has been a Collection Privée showroom in Milan, on via Monte di Pietà.

College Classic style of clothing for men and women inspired by English college students. It includes blouses, pleated skirts, knitted twin-sets, blazers, and trench coats. During the 1950s everyone wore the famous College shoes: completely flat leather loafers with fringes.

Collier de Chien Necklace worn very tight on the neck, especially if composed of strings of pearls rigidly set and all of the same size. Suitable only for swan-like necks, like those of the femmes fatales of the 1910s. (Literally, "dog collar").

Colmar Brand of sportswear. It was created by Manifattura Mario Colombo which, established in 1923 in Monza (Mi), had been producing hats and gaiters in wool felt for more than 20 years. The, immediately after World War II, with the return of sports events, the company began to produce sportswear with particular attention to skiing. It was the beginning of Colmar which, operating in close collaboration with the Italian Federation of Winter Sports, became famous as a manufacturer of high-tech and specialty garments. For the Olympics of 1952, Colmar equipped the Italian ski team. From that moment on, and for the next 40 years, it dressed the Italian ski and sled teams. Today, the product is distributed in the principal European markets, in North America, and in Japan.

❑ 2003, April. The opening of the new Colmar store, on via Dante in Milan. Inside the 800 square foot space, documentaries about the world of sports are shown. The new Spring-Summer 2003 Collection is for those who want to combine comfort, practicality, and functionality.

Colombo Italo (1922). Italian shoemaker, born in Parabiago (Mi). Right after World War II, he established a small shoe factory (his great-grandfather was also a shoemaker). He was the first to threaten the dominant position in price and quality held by Bologna. A friend of Walter Albini, who acted as his consultant together with Alberto Lattuada, he was the official shoemaker at the high fashion presentations held in the Sala Bianca of Palazzo Pitti in Florence. He has created shoes for Mila Schön and Fendi, and also has a brand of his own.

Colonna Jean (1955). French designer, born in Oran, Algeria. He abandoned his studies in order to seek adventure in the world of Paris fashions. Becoming an assistant to Pierre Balmain in 1977, three years later he opened Le Comptoir du Kit, where he created jewellery and accessories for Gaultier, Montana, and Mugler. His first prêt-à-porter Collection was presented in Paris in 1985 at the French Museum of Modern Art. The success was such that he was invited to Tokyo. His line displays his choice of "poor" materials like skaï and nylon, offering clothes at affordable prices. His style has similarities with grunge, inspired by young people in the streets, with their sneakers and loose clothes. Colonna was among the first to attempt to dispense with the runway, and to present his Collections through catalogues. But very soon, he was back. His shop, rather than looking like a boutique, resembles a supermarket, with a concrete floor and checkouts at the exit. In 1999 he proposed an avant-guard line with asymmetric cuts, fishnet intertwined with cotton, and comfortable street-shoes.

Columbia Sportswear Company American company offering clothing and footwear for the outdoors, sports, and mountain climbing. It is a market leader in the United States, with 16 million pieces sold worldwide, an increase in sales of around 200% over the last ten years, and a turnover that increased from 22 billion liras in 1984 to 600 billion in 1997. The catalogue offers 238 items. It was established in the mid 1930s by Gertrude Boyle who, at the time, had just fled Nazi Germany and is today still featured in Columbia's advertising campaigns. Starting in 1990, the company, with headquarters in Portland, Oregon and subsidiaries in Europe, Japan, Australia, South America, and New Zealand, began to distribute its styles on an international scale through 10,000 retailers. In 1998, it was first quoted on the New York Stock Exchange. The president is Tim Boyle, the founder's son. The design decisions are made by Doug Prentice, Mike Eggeck, and Rodney Gummiringer.

(*Fulvio Bertasso*)

Colvet Sportswear company established in 1991 by Sergio Coletti, who already had 23 years of experience in the field. The headquarters is in Santa Lucia di Piave (Tv). In addition to high-tech mountain clothes, it produces trekking, snowboard, and ski lines. It has also a good export business.

Comense (Ticosa) Manufacturer of yarn and silk fabrics established in Como in 1872 by a group of entrepreneurs, textile dealers, professionals, and property owners. Ticosa, an acronym for Tintoria Comense Sa, was taken over in 1907 by the Lyon firm Gillet &Fils, one of the first European dyeing mills. Charles Marnas was appointed director. In 1911, Comense was divided into 4 departments: thread dyeing, fabric dyeing, finishing, and printing. In the second half of the 1930s, the dominant figure was Augusto Brunner, who had become director of the research laboratory in 1931 and technical director in 1937. In the early 1940s, when Italy declared war on France and England, the company came under government control as it was French property. In 1950, Augusto Brunner became managing director and began several initiatives in order to reorganize the production of fibers and silk. Towards the end of that decade the company offered a new type of elasticized yarn. In 1972, it began the production and marketing of fabric for women's wear under the brand name Bernasconi, and of household fabrics through the Cindy division. In 1976, it launched Tuscany for the shirt sector, the only one not meant for a mass market. The second half of the 1970s saw a period of reorganization which brought a progressive disengagement from the textile sector and the chemical industry. In 1982 Ticosa, sold by the Gillet family to the Schlumberger family, was shut down.

(*Pierangelo Mastantuono*)

Comero Factory making combed fine and extra-fine pure wool fabric for men's clothing. It was established in 1959 by Walter Comero (Vercelli), and has 2 plants producing 3.5 million meters. On the eve of the new millennium, the turnover was 50 billion liras.

Cometti Philippe (1974). French photographer. Considered one of the most interesting emerging figures due to his innovative style, his clients include Emporio Armani, Hermès, Givenchy, H&M, Mila Schön, and Yves Saint-Laurent. His photos have been published in Dutch, Arena, Glamour, Numéro, and Max Moda and in the Italian and Japanese editions of Vogue.

Comme il faut Austrian brand of prêt-à-porter created in 1990 by Franck Wilde and Nicole Blasius, both of whom graduated in 1984 from the Fashion Academy of Vienna. Their creations are on sale in France, Italy, Germany, the U.S, Japan and Switzerland.

Compagnia Tessile Manufacturer in Montemurlo (Prato) specialized in carded and combed fabrics, plain-dyed and patterned. It was established in 1939 with the corporate name of Nerini & Carpini, the surnames of the two founders. During the 1970s, control passed to the Carpini family, who emphasized the creative aspects of the business, to great success. In 1982, the company changed ownership, with the majority of shares going to Brigatti and Pieri, who also changed the name, calling it Compagnia Tessile. They emphasized better quality and service, and began to produce linen as well as cotton, both yarn-dyed and piece-dyed. In 1990, a new Collection, Tuskania, was launched, with the purpose of manufacturing shirts and luxury sportswear. In 1998 the company sold 1.5 million meters of fabric and 300,00 meters of jersey yarn, with a turnover of 55 billion liras.

Comte Michel (1954). Swiss photographer, born in Zurich. He began to travel at the young age of 15, living in England, the U.S., and France. Without going through the classic apprenticeship as an assistant, he immediately became a professional photographer and in 1979 began to work for Condé Nast on Vogue Hommes and Vogue America, and also for Mademoiselles and Marie Claire. He rapidly made a name for himself as one of the best and most consistent photographers, thanks to a style only apparently simple and immediate, reminding one of photo-reportage. In 1981 he moved to New York and then to Los Angeles, publishing in Vogue America and Vanity Fair, and working for Armani, Dolce & Gabbana, Nike, Swatch, and Revlon. He specialized in portraits, creating a style in which the subject is always portrayed frontally, in a direct and clear manner. Starting in 1980, he also devoted himself to reportage, working for the Red Cross in Afghanistan, Iraq, and Bosnia. In 1999, Schirmer/Mosel published his monograph *Michel Comte - Twenty Years 1979-1999*.

Conber Company of women's ready-to-wear fashion established in Vicenza in 1956 by Domenico, Gaetano, and Orazio Rossi, descendants of the textile dynasty of Schio. It was among the pioneers of prêt-à-porter at a time when manufacturing companies displayed little creativity. It was Orazio who decided to change this when, during a trip to Paris, he met a certain Pierre Cardin who was in serious difficulties after having trouble with his general manager, and convinced the great designer to work for Conber. For the first time, a talented designer, though not quite so famous yet, went to work for an Italian company. When Cardin, having improved his financial position, returned to Paris, the Rossi brothers called the dressmaker Maria Antonelli, whose Collections had already been presented in the Sala Bianca. Just before it closed down in 1976, Conber still had some 250 employees.

Concept Paris A consulting service for style and marketing. It was conceived and established in 1991 in Paris by the husband and wife John and Jos Berry. He is English, she is Dutch. Their specific competence goes from yarns and fibers for corsetry, underwear, and home nightwear through to the product's sale. They offer their clients (manufacturing companies in Europe, the U.S., and the Far East, underwear shops, and department stores) an analysis of consumer taste and of changing social and cultural behavior, creative consulting on stylistic trends, development plans for products and brands, and commercial strategies.

(*Mariacristina Righi*)

Conceria Milanese Tannery for fur skins. Established in 1984 by Antonio Panzeri, a tanner with a long experience, it was taken over some years later by Augusto Valsecchi, who is now the sole general manager and whose competence and ability is responsible for its important development. As the company name indicates, the plant is near Milan, specifically in Mazzo di Rho. It employees 122 workers in an industry where it is difficult to find labor because, in addition to the work carried out by highly automated machines, tanning requires delicate manual operations. The company works especially for third parties, mainly wholesalers who then sell the skins to manufacturers. It offers to its clients, who are both Italian and foreign, including prestigious names such as Fendi, a personalized service interpreting their needs and requests, and keeping their business secrets. Always trying to anticipate fashion trends through independent and extensive research, Conceria

Milanese has in recent years given a boost to the dyeing mill in which it uses advanced and special technologies, displaying a coloristic talent that has produced invention after invention, respecting and extolling the characteristics of the fur, its brightness and silkiness, always trying to produce a skin that is lighter and more elastic. Along with the chromatic innovations, there have been new treatments for "always available" fur, which has the advantage of being reversible, in soft leather or suede that can tolerate any atmospheric condition and is rich in relief patterns and motifs. These include tweed prints, sequins, gravel patterns, wax, baguette, leopard, zebra, cheetah, frosted effects, dust, and lacquer. Bleaching, dyeing and dorsatura are the three operations that, alone or combined (two, or all three), have given different results, but always very natural ones, with changing effects, in a very pleasant chiaroscuro. There is also printing by corrosion, impressing, and a type of shearing that is very daring, a "wet effect" that results in an almost metallic brightness. As to the color palette dictated by the whims of fashion, Conceria Milanese has shown incredible creativity with soft tones as well as more lively and provocative ones. There are two-tone effects, tri-colors, mélange, chine, and, for the softer colors, more suffused shadings. One year later, and it is a hymn to color: coral, bright yellow, sorbet, gentian, cedar, mango, with patterns ranging from sheared fox in a *baiadera* (Indian temple dancer; courtesan) pattern to a long-hair fox batik-shade grape cluster. The batik is perfected with flashes of brilliant color sometimes (but not always) on dark backgrounds, true chromatic "arrows"! Another step forward, and there is more color, but veiled, hidden, appearing as a second skin, changing from one shade to another. It is a competition of tones and superimpositions, golden but not showy flashes, a sort of "there is and there isn't," of prints that are so undefined and delicate as to require that they be spoken of in the diminutive (*leopardino, zebretta*, i.e. baby leopard, baby zebra). And then the announcement of a color which no longer fears to be shown: a chic color, even if aggressive in the proposals of the designers who dare the most, together with a series of splendid bleachings (e.g. *Perlato*) and new products such as the one called *Marea* ("Tide"), which has the merit of being handmade. The "path of color" that Conceria Milanese has opened for furrier shops is fantastic, a road it continues to follow in order to preserve for Italy its place at the center of fashion.

(*Maria Rita Stiglich*)

Condotti (Via) A famous street in Rome that provides a showcase for elegance and luxury shopping, via Condotti continues to be the street that is most coveted by the great names of fashion for whom it is, along with Milan's quadrilateral, the most important in Italy. The traditional and established boutiques such as Gucci, Bulgari, and Battistoni, where the Duke of Windsor, Prince Umberto of Savoy, John Steinbeck, Charlie Chaplin, Jean Cocteau, and Renato Guttuso would come to have their shirts custom made, have been joined over time by the most prestigious *griffes* of the Made in Italy movement (and sometimes made elsewhere), such as Armani, Cartier, Ferragamo, Gabrielli, Hermès, La Perla, Prada, Mila Schön, and Trussardi. Then, and not without very animated polemics from the Via Condotti Association, established in the 1960s in order to safeguard the noble street, they were joined by Foot Locker, a fluorescent emporium of sportswear. Over the years, via Condotti, linked with Fifth Avenue, Faubourg Saint-Honoré, and Bond Street, has lost its ancient artisanal vocation, as well as its commercial identity: the old shops have sold their locations to the big brand stores. Also gone, in order to leave its space to a stockings boutique, is the renowned Baretto, which was at the corner of via Belsiana, and which counted Giorgio De Chirico among its habitués. Via Condotti has won its battle against decay and survives in the midst of mass tourism, having being able to keep its identity, if not from a commercial point of view, at least historically. In fact, it mixes consumerism with, for those able to enjoy it, a special spell, an atmosphere of the Grand Tour or a Stendhalian promenade. It gets its name from the acqueduct known as the Acqua Vergine that passed nearby. With the famous stairs of Trinità dei Monti at its back, it constitutes one of the most changeable and picturesque sceneries of the 18th century. An obligatory stop is the historic Caffé Greco, about which Casanova wrote in his memoirs in 1742, but whose golden century was the 19th, when around its small oval tables would gather the most illustrious European painters, sculptors, musicians, and men of letters. Among its eminent patrons were popes and kings, such as Leo XIII and Louis I of Bavaria; painters such as Corot and Ingres; and writers such as Goldoni, Hawthorne, Byron, Chateaubriand, Leopardi, Shelley, Stendhal, Andersen, Gogol, D'Annunzio, Baudeleire, Henry James, Thackeray, and Mark Twain.

(*Laura Laurenzi*)

Connolly English leather factory. It was established in 1878 in London where it still has its display windows on Grosvenor Crescet Mews, in a shop restored by the architect Andrée Putman. Among its prestigious jobs have been the leather seat covers used in Parliament, and the upholstery for some of the most legendary cars in England. It produces shoes, driving gloves, suede jackets, boots, and small leather goods.

Connoly Sybil (1921). Irish designer of Welsh origin. She studied fashion at Bradley's Dressmaking Establishment in London at the end of the 1930s. At the beginning of World War II, she moved to Dublin, Ireland for good. She was hired by Richard Alan and quickly attained a position of responsibility. In 1953 she designed a Collection carrying her own name. She opened her *maison* in 1957. She found a market in America and Australia as well. Her great respect for local artisanal companies caused her to use their products. Her use of Irish tweed, linen, and lace had a great influence in England, where it was sought as an alternative to the supremacy of Paris. Her name became synonymous with the pleated linen typical of local folk costumes, which she turned into very feminine blouses. She also designed tunics and caps for five different orders of nuns.

(*Virginia Hill*)

Conran Jasper (1959). English designer. He comes from a family of artists. His father, Terence Conran, created Habitat. His mother is a successful writer. He made his début in 1979, presenting his first Collection in London. He had just graduated from the Parson's School of Design in New York and later worked for Fiorucci and Wallis. He then started his own business and today his company has a turnover of several million pounds. Starting in 1996 he designed a women's line for the department store Debenham's.

Consagra Pietro (1920). Italian sculptor of large-scale work. He created jewellery with the same rigor and abstract style of his sculpture. The first, from 1959, were brooches in gold and silver, sometimes encrusted with diamonds, that he produced with Mario Masenza in Rome. In 1969, with the goldsmith Gem Montebello, he created masks, the *Face Ornaments*, in gold and coral. Consagra was born in Mazara del Vallo, Sicily.

Consiglio Alessandro (1964). High fashion designer, born in Rome. His work is based on experimentation and the use of unconventional materials such as vegetables, ham, and wood. He presented two Collections at Alta Roma, the first in July 2002 and the second in January 2003. He began his career working for the theater and designing costumes for Gigi Proietti's shows. He has designed bodices for Mira Sorvino, Jessica Lange, Margherita Buy, and Laura Pausini.

Consiglio Maria (1923). Prêt-à-porter and high fashion dressmaker. She opened the atelier Fashion in Naples in 1945. In 1949, she designed the costumes for an *Aida* directed by Roberto Rossellini at the Arena Flegrea in Pozzuoli and after that alternated dressmaking with costume design, working on some 30 productions of opera and ballet at the Teatro San Carlo. She worked with Eduardo De Filippo on plays performed at the San Ferdinando in Naples and for those taken on tour. She retired in 1981 when her atelier was declared uninhabitable after the earthquake in Irpinia.

Constantine Elaine (1965). English photographer. As a very young girl she began to work as a freelancer with the magazine Scooter Scene. She studied at the Statford College of Technology and began her professional career in 1992 as an assistant to Nick Knight before again becoming a freelancer the following year. She has worked on international fashion magazines such as Arena, The Face, Homme Plus, Vogue Italy and, in the U.S., Details, Interview, and Rolling Stone. Among her clients are Levi's, Westwood, and Wrangler. She has been active with exhibitions since 1998, with shows in Paris, New York, and Tokyo, and she won the *Portrait Award* of the John Kobel Foundation.

Constanze German fashion magazine published between 1948 and 1970 by Constanze-Verlag Publishing of Hamburg. It was very successful during the 1950s, especially covering high fashion in Paris and Berlin, showing the outfits of actresses and members of the international jet set. In 1970 the magazine merged with Brigitte.

Constructivism Artistic movement formed in Russia between the end of the 1910s and the early 1920s, before and after the Russian Revolution, from which it absorbed both problems and ideology aiming – as Nicolas Pounine would state – at "the production of material values and objects destined to transform a lifestyle." From this would arise a strong commitment to the applied arts, including clothing, creating a style of dressing suitable to the proletariat, to the new times, and to the new society. Basically, the constructivist artist wanted to finalize the results of his thought and work on behalf of the masses. It dealt, therefore, with social uses, or rather, with the uses of art, even of that art apparently quite far from such purposes, as, for example, abstract, suprematist and symbolist art. Vladimir Tatlin held that art is communication. His idea of constructivism was a synthesis of art and technology. Thus his 1919 project of a Monument to the 3rd International, a distorted spiral pyramid, higher than the Eiffel Tower, in three parts in steel and crystal, meant to host meetings of the Comintern, was at the same time a building, a sculpture, and an ideological expression. Others would follow in this direction. It is important to remember, in particular, besides the brothers Anton and Naum Gabo Pevsner (who would soon detach themselves from it), the three Vesnin brothers, architects, town planners, and set decorators, famous designers of projects for the Palace of Soviets, for Pravda, and for various workers' clubs and auto factories. The official birthday of the movement was in 1921, the year of the New Economic Policy, or NEP, which replaced the war economy. That is when the Constructivist Labor Group of Moscow was formed, composed of Gan, Rodchenko, Varvara Stepanova, Joganson, Medunecky, and the Stenberg brothers. These last three organized the exhibition *Constructivists*, presenting spatial works and sculpture similar to engineering structures. Both within the movement and among its precursors, for example those belonging to the Institute of Artistic Culture in Moscow, or the Inchuk, opposition currents immediately began to form. Kandinsky, accused of subjectivism, because he was more interested in the psychological effects of artistic creation, was forced to resign as director of the Institute. The concept of "composition," affecting the "aesthetic domain" of taste, was considered anachronistic: the aesthetic object, they said, has to be scientifically examined in a laboratory. For Rodchenko, even "every new approach to art comes from technology and engineering and moves towards organization and construction." His exhibition of folding geometric elements cut in concentric circles, presented in May 1921 at the 3rd Convention of Young Architects, is a sort of Constructivist Manifesto. In that same year the exhibit *5x5=25'* opened in Moscow, and in it Rodchenko presented his work together with Stepanova, Aleksandr Vesnin, Ljubov Popova, and Aleksandra Ekster. In 1922, the theoretical and practical essay *Constructivism* by A. Gan was published. In 1923, Ekster (she would flee to Paris the following year), Vera Moukhina, and the designer Lamanova, who by 1919 had already claimed that artists must commit themselves to fashion, started an atelier for mass production as well as a magazine. Rodchenko, Nadejda Oudaltsova, Olga Rozanova, and Varvara Stepanova all participated in this initiative, designing fabrics, work clothes, and sportswear. It was the birth of overalls. In that same year 1923, Popova became the director of the First State Factory of Printed Fabrics. Literature also had its constructivists: the literary movement was founded in Moscow in 1922 by a theoretician, K.L. Zelinsky, and a poet, I.L. Sel'vinsky, and it enjoyed a certain success for some years. In 1924, Vertov shot the constructivist film *Cine-Eye*. Wrapped in the coils of Stalinist politics, with divisions between realists and productivists, accusations of deviationism and bureaucracy, and the flight to the West of artists such as Kandinsky, Gabo, and other intellectuals, the movement faded away in the 1930s. (*Mario Pancera*)

Conte of Florence Italian manufacturer of hats, knitwear, accessories, and prêt-à-porter. The first shop was opened in 1952 in the historic center of Florence. Six years later, the then president, Romano Boretti, decided to specialize in the production and sale of hats. That is how Conte of Florence was established, along with its quilted casual hat, with a capital C and a Lily as a logo, to great success. In 1969 the company was among the first to understand the importance of sponsoring. It began with the Italian ski team. Those were the years of the great victories at Thoeni and Gros. Production was then expanded beyond hats. In the early 1990s, the company focused on golf and sponsored the Italian Open. That first shop has been joined by many more, with a chain of 40 franchise shops in Italy and the rest of Europe.

❑ 2003, April. The company closes 2002 with a turnover of €35 million, an increase of 8% compared to the previous year, and a gross margin of more than 20%.

Conti Liviana (1948). Knitwear designer. She lives in Milan and Rimini, where she works. She is the Italian lady of "inventive knitting." Sensitive to experimentation, she produces very refined knitwear that is strictly artisanal. In 2003, she added a Collection of jackets, trousers, and skirts in stretch materials. Her brand is constantly moving ahead, and growth of 50% was expected in the two-year period 2002 to 2004. The turnover was expected to be around €10 million by 2005. There are 400 points-of-sale worldwide. About 60% of the business is in Italy, and the remaining 40% is export. The development strategy of the company is to increase its presence in foreign markets, especially by strengthening product visibility through press campaigns in the international media.

(*Valeria Vantaggi*)

Conti Quirino (1951). The "Hidden Designer," as Natalia Aspesi has called him. Intelligent, ambitious, educated, crazy for fashion, he was born in Amandola, in the Marche, and since then has lived several lives, divergent and parallel, constantly commuting between Rome and Milan, between fashion, study, the theater, cinema,

"The Revival of Gothic" by Quirino Conti (1997).

and religion. He has excellent results as a set and costume designer, including a memorable *Falstaff* in 1985 in Geneva directed by Gigi Proietti. When in high school, in Rome, he met Orson Welles and helped him prepare the costumes for his *Don Quixote*. While studying architecture (he graduated in 1976 with Bruno Zevi), he collaborated on costumes with Lattuada and Fellini. Then, he discovered high fashion in the Carosa atelier of Princess Caracciolo. Through these youthful encounters, Conti made acquaintances and received stimulation which allowed him to avoid the cliffs of banality while sailing through the ocean of a fashion industry which invited him to collaborate – on prêt-à-porter Collections at different levels, both for men and women – with GFT, Trussardi, Valentino, Inghirami, Mario Valentino, and Krizia. It isn't easy for his resentful sensitivity to accept the limitations of the market. Thanks to this, and to the cultural self-assurance with which he quotes very different sources, from Jean Cocteau to the Amish community, and from Paul Bowles to the Chassidim and the neo-Gothic, he also expresses himself distinctively, if anonymously. And he finds himself playing, totally gratis, a critical role of great importance. (*Silvia Giacomoni*)

Contini Mila (1910-1993). Italian writer and journalist, born in Milan. In 1938, she was appointed director of Grazia, a position she left during the war. Starting in 1945, she worked with Il Corriere Lombardo, La Lettura, L'Illustrazione Italiana, and La Prealpina. Later, she was a correspondent for the weeklies Tempo, Gente, and Oggi. She was director of the Italian edition of Marie Claire from 1958 to 1960, and of the TV program *Personalità*, presented as a women's weekly, from 1960 to '64. She wrote *La Moda nei Secoli* (Mondadori, 1961); *5000 Years of Fashion* (Mondadori, 1976), which was translated into 12 languages, including Russian and Japanese; *Maria José, Regina Sconosciuta*; a medical encyclopedia for the family; and several books on gastronomy. The president of the *Moda Mare* award in Cefalù, and a member of several juries, she was president of the International Press Association for Women and the Family and of the Soroptimist Club of Varese. Very keen on sports, in 1928 she was one of the first women to obtain a driver's license, passing her test at the wheel of an Isotta Fraschini.

Converse American brand of sports shoes, established in 1908 by Marquis M. Converse. Nine years later, he came out with the All Star, the world's most famous basketball sneakers, which would become part of the wardrobe of young people all over the western world. In 1971, Converse Inc. was acquired by Eltra Corporation and, in 1994, it became a public company. For men, women, and children, Converse shoes are manufactured and distributed in more than 90 countries, with a total of more than 9,000 stores. The brand sponsors and dresses the pop band The Spice Girls.

❑ 2001, September. Alongside its high-tech products, Converse launches a line inspired by its past and linked to the brand's history and tradition. It is called Original and offers several vintage pieces.
❑ 2001, November. The All Star (a.k.a. the Chuck Taylor, the American basketball champion for whom the shoes had been created) is more than 80 years old. The model went through several changes over the years, gradually taking up the themes dear to Larry Bird and Magic Johnson (famous players and celebrity spokesmen for Converse) as well as camouflage fashions, up until the 30 new colors and the vintage look of the 1960s and 1970s. The latest style is the "underground," for which various artists have contributed hand-painted unique pieces.
❑ 2002, January. Some new Converse items are presented at Pitti Uomo. The Chuck Taylor All Star is personalized by John Varvatos, a designer from Michigan, who also attended to the restyling of the Jack Purcell model. Varvatos is present at Pitti with a personal Collection as well.
❑ 2003, July. Nike, a multinational based in Portland, Oregon and a leader in sportswear, acquires all of Converse Inc. for $305 million (€268.8 million).

Conway Gordon (1894-1956). Illustrator for Vogue, Harper's Bazaar, and Vanity Fair, and also a costume designer. Born in Claiborne, Texas, she studied in America and Italy. She was discovered by Heyworth Campbell, the art director at Condé Nast publishing. She moved to London in 1920, where she began to work for the theater and the cinema. At the age of 42, she retired to Carbin, Virginia.

Cook Emma (1975). English designer. Born in Manchester, she studied textiles at the University of Brighton and at Central Saint Martin's. The Collection she designed for her graduation drew attention especially for her taste in details. She was an apprentice with Martine Sitbon. She designs for Ghost. She won the Vidal Sassoon award for emerging talent. She made her début at London Fashion Week with the Spring-Summer Collection 2001.

Cooked Wool Knitwear fabric, linz woven, heavily felted. It is the classic fabric used for Tyrolese Walcher jackets, short and straight, in the classic green, blue, and gray for men, and in bright colors, such as red-orange and periwinkle blue, for women, trimmed with a contrasting ribbon and with decorative metal buttons.

Copperwheat Blundell Ready-to-wear brand launched in 1993 by the English designers Lee Copperwheat (1966) and Pamela Blundell (1967). Copperwheat, who studied at the College of Fashion and worked at Aquascutum, designs the men's line; Blundell, who studied fashion at Southampton University and the Epsom School in London, designs the women's. They say that when they create they think of themselves as typical clients.

Coppola Aldo (1940). Women's hairdresser, born in Milan. He followed in his father's footsteps. He began his career at a young age, and in 1964 opened his first salon in Milan, at via Manzoni 25. An avant-guard hair-stylist, he uses new techniques. During the 1970s, with the birth of prêt-à-porter, he became a creator of images for Italian fashion, often designing hairdos for the Collections. As head of the Aldo Coppola Agency, which brings together a staff of excellent hair-stylists and make-up artists, he attends to advertising campaigns and, since 1980, has been an image consultant for L'Oréal.

Coppola & Toppo Italian *griffe* of costume jewellery named after Lyda Coppola (1915-1986). Born in Venice, she studied at the Academy of Fine Arts and joined the workshop of Ada Politzer, a famous creator of jewellery. She created the *griffe* in Milan. The company, named Coppola & Toppo after her marriage to Toppo, captured the attention of the great tailors due to the high quality of its costume jewellery. At first, her creations were especially appreciated by the great French couturiers such as Balenciaga, Balmain, Dior, Fath, Lanvin, and Schiaparelli, who used them as accessories for their Collections. In May 1948, Vogue France dedicated Point de Vue to her. Helped by her brother Bruno, she took a second look at the American market where, thanks to an introduction by Elsa Schiaparelli, her jewellery went on sale in the big New York department stores – Lord & Taylor, Saks Fifth Avenue, and Bergdorf Goodman – and appeared regularly in the most important fashion magazines: Vogue, Harper's Bazaar, and Women's Wear Daily. In fact, the jewellery followed American taste in its spectacular effects of shape and color played out through the flexibility of crystal set on invisible metallic frames. Flowers were typical subjects in the 1960s, by which time Italian designers were entrusting Coppola & Toppo with the manufacture of their jewellery. These included Capucci, Krizia, Pucci, Lancetti, Enzo Fontana, and Valentino. Valentino became the most important client, and gave particular impetus to the company's research on the use of metal and plastic with the various gems. The firm's activity ceased at the death of Lyda Coppola. Maria Pezzi wrote about her in Donna: "She had a total sense of fashion and exceptional aesthetic taste. Hers was an artisanal work by now long gone: before their manufacture in the workshop, she studied her jewels carefully, calculating the weight, examining the workmanship, the lace, and the waterfall effects. It is certain that Italian fashion, from the beginning based on imagination, risk, and personality, found in Lyda a great ambassador."

Corbella Shirt shop established in 1884 by Gaetano Corbella at via San Prospero 1 in Milan. It is number 4 in the city's official chronological register of business establishments. The shop was entirely renovated in 1927 with delightful Art Nouveau furniture in mahogany and bois de rose created by the cabinet maker Egisto Quarti. Personnel assigned to the dressing rooms at La Scala would bring Arturo Toscanini's shirts and tails here to be ironed. The fame of the shop was such that the actor Gilberto Govi would say: "To be born wearing a shirt is a lucky event, wearing a Corbella shirt is worthy of praise." (*Daniela Fedi*)

Corbetta Valeria (1956). Journalist and director of Glamour. She is from Poland, and that is where she went to school. Her journalistic work began during the 1970s. In 1982, she joined Condé Nast as a news editor for the men's monthly Per Lui. In 1987, she went to work for Mondadori and stayed there until 1994, becoming deputy director of Marie Claire. In that year, she was called back to Condé Nast, where she became the director of Glamour. Her management brought circulation of the monthly to about 120,000 copies. Besides new about beauty and fashion, she decided to give more space to everyday news with articles and reports on private life, society and customs.

❑ 2002, March. After Kicca Menoni goes to D la Repubblica delle Donne, she becomes the director of Marie Claire.
❑ 2003, January. When Marie Claire becomes part of Hachette-Rusconi, Mondadori launches a new monthly magazine called Flair and Corbetta becomes the director.

Cordelia Italian magazine created in 1881, it became a sophisticated periodical dedicated to women's fashion. In the 1940s, directed by Emilia Kuster and Vera Rossi Lodomez, it was one of the few publications also interested in men's fashion. In 1942, it became a supplement to the periodical La Donna, but closed few years later.

Coretti Marco (1975). Shoe designer for high fashion and prêt-à-porter. He uses precious materials such as satin, crepe, pearled kidskin, and calfskin. His colors are very lively: red, acid green, violet, and white. And his heels extreme: either very flat or very tall. Among his clients are Fanny Ardant, Caroline of Hanover, Grace Jones, and Madonna. For 8 years he lived in Paris, where he started his career as a model. In 1998, he returned to Rome, graduated from the Institute of Art, and launched an accessories line. During the Rome Fashion Week in January 1999 he presented his first Collection of high fashion shoes. He also designs a prêt-à-porter Collection.

Cornaggia Daniele (1959). Designer specializing in jewellery. After studying set design, he opened a high fashion atelier, joined his business partner Bruno Muheim, and began to produce costume jewellery. He uses gems, skins, and crystals whose originality and harmony guarantee contracts with Christina Dior, Givenchy, and Yves Saint-Laurent. He created a necklace for Jacqueline Kennedy that was later auctioned at Sotheby's, as well as all the jewels that were part of the traveling exhibition organized by the Guggenheim in honor of Giorgio Armani. Daniele Cornaggia also designs a line of bags decorated with the same techniques and semi-precious materials which are by now his trademark.

(*Pierangelo Mastantuono*)

Cornejo Maria. Chilean designer. She graduated from the Ravensbourne College of Design and Communication. She had her professional development in London. For many years, she was "the other half" of the lucky duo Richmond-Cornejo. In 1988, she chose to live and work in Paris. She was appointed artistic director of the *maison* Tehen. She then started her own line, called Zero, on sale in trendy stores such as Colette and 10 Corso Como. Her clothes express a femininity of great potential, with a touch of black humor and transgression, the unavoidable heritage of her partnership with Richmond. She then alternated between bad girl and good girl styles, woman as antagonist and woman as entertainment, all in a game of transformations. It is a work in progress, especially concerning her attention to fabric and workmanship: some cuts appear to be done with a knife, daring slashes that emphasize the hips and nearby parts of the body. (*Lucia Mari*)

Corneliani Company of ready-to-wear men's fashion owned by two brothers. Fratelli Claudio e Carlalberto Corneliani was started in the 1930s in Mantua by their grandfather, and put itself on a solid footing in the second half of the 1950s, after having closed during World War II. The entrepreneurial policy of the two brothers calls for heavy investment in technology in order to improve product quality. In 1974, a license agreement was concluded with the French clothing designer Maurice Renoma, guaranteeing an increase in turnover of 33%. In 1980, the Corneliani brothers acquired Abital, a company from Verona, from Montefibre, after reorganizing and strengthening it, advancing their position in the international market for men's clothing. The company has different lines: Corneliani is a classic Collection; Trend is more in tune with changes in fashion; Set is dedicated to young people; Via Ardigò offers a "formal informal" style of self-assured elegance; and Sportswear Corneliani is focused on sports and leisure time. The Group's products also include other brands, such as Nino Danieli, Full Time, and Browngreen. There are 1,300 employees who each year produce 450,000 jackets and coats, 250,000 trousers, and 200,000 shirts, ties and knitwear garments. The firm has a large turnover (around 180 billion liras in 1998), and by 1974 had already expanded beyond Italy to the American market. In 1998, the company signed an agreement with Polo Ralph Lauren for production and distribution in the U.S., even though it had already in 1986 established Corneliani USA Inc., with headquarters in New York. The plants are in Mantua and Verona. They boast of being technological leaders, and of being pioneers in the "mechanization of the area models." Corrado Corneliani, a member of the fourth generation, studied, together with the staff of Milan Polytechnic, new electronic solutions related to manufacturing and to scanners for custom-made "to-your-measure" products. In 1997, a showroom was opened on via Montenapoleone in Milan, right on the spot where the mythical Salumiere (an old Milanese store) once stood.

A model from the Corneliani line Trend.

❑ 2002, January. The Autumn-Winter 2002-2003 Collection is presented in the frescoed rooms of the palace on via Durini in Milan: classic tailored clothing, with a refined taste for details. Besides the more traditional fabrics, such as herringbone patterns, Prince of Wales, and tweed, Corneliani presents many velvet and chalk-stripe items, with double or dotted lines, as well as many grey, beige, steel, and cognac-colored suits and coats. The styles of the Trend

line are more casual and practical, and less expensive, but equally accurate in the cut and choice of fabrics.
❑ 2002, December. Agreement between Corneliani and the Chinese firm Shanghai Aloai Trade Limited Company calling for the establishment of a plant in Shanghai which is to manufacture men's clothing starting from Spring 2003. In the first year, production is expected to be 100,000 coats and jackets and 100,000 trousers. There will be 350 employees at the start, and more within three years. Corneliani will provide stylistic support, know-how, and technologic guidelines.
❑ 2003, June. The opening of a new boutique in Mexico City, in a building on Avenida Masaryk. After openings in Milan, Paris, and Ekaterinburg, the Group has targeted Central America.

Corona Vittorio (1901). Italian artist. Following the example of the Casa d'Arte Depero in Rovereto, he opened an art gallery in Palermo. It was the second half of the 1920s and Corona, close to the Second Futurism, devoted himself to the design and manufacture of tapestry, fabric, and cushions. In the La Rosa Collection in Rome there is a painted umbrella with patterns influenced by the naturalism of Art Deco and the dynamism of Futurism.

Corona Vittorio (1947). Italian journalist. He was the director of Moda. A graduate in history and philosophy from the University of Catania, he worked since high school with the newspaper La Sicilia. After obtaining his degree, he moved to Milan and Rizzoli Publishing. It was the 1970s. In 1975, he became deputy director of Annabella. In 1981-1982, still at Rizzoli, he was editor of the section "New Products." His first project was the new magazine Amica, which came out in 1982. Corona was deputy director. In 1983, for Eri-Rai Publishing and together with Flavio Lucchini, he created Moda, a women's monthly of which he was in charge for 100 issues. Moda was also the title of a RAI-TV program broadcast for five years under his direction. In 1988, still for Eri, he designed King, a men's monthly that he directed for 50 issues. In 1993, he left the world of periodicals and joined Fininvest, where he contributed to the creation of Studio Aperto, the news program of the Italia 1 TV network, which he produced for some twenty days, until the announcement of his publisher Silvio Berlusconi's début in politics. In 1994, he became deputy director of the newspaper La Voce, under the executive director Indro Montanelli. Between 1996 and 1997 he created and directed the trendy magazine Village. Then he devoted himself to conceiving and producing programs on news and social customs for the RAI and Telemontecarlo TV networks. At present, he is the head of a new company, Corona Productions, which creates initiatives for TV and the press.

Corpo Nove Brand of women and men's jackets for sportswear. It has been the top line of the Paraplu company (1993) since 1995. The jackets and raincoats are very carefully manufactured with distinctive and often unusual fabrics. Corpo Nove produces custom-made items such as pads, necks, cuffs, and hoods in various lengths that can be modified according to the needs of customers.

❑ 2002, September. For its technical and innovative qualities, the American magazine Men's Journal listed Absolute Frontier, the thermo jacket made by Corpo Nove, among the 95 most perfect objects in the world. Steven Spielberg read the news and wanted to wear one for the difficult climatic conditions during the night shots of his latest movie, the fourth episode of *Indiana Jones*. The jacket was created in 1999 for an Antarctic expedition of Adventure Network International. Designed to protect against extreme temperatures, thermally and acoustically insulated, it uses Aereogel, a fabric which also allows one to float.
❑ 2003, May. A selection of garments, manufactured in distinctive fabrics, from nettle to peat, is to be exhibited at the London Science Museum on occasion of the show Treat Yourself. The sponsor is the Wellcome Trust, the largest private foundation interested in avant-guard medical research.

Correani Ugo. Italian jeweler. He created some of the most innovative jewellery for Italian and French prêt-à-porter in the 1970s and 1980s. His made his début in 1973 designing accessories for Albini. From the late 1970s up until his death in 1992, he worked with Versace, Valentino, Lagerfeld, Fendi, Chanel, Lacroix, and Chloé, proposing a revolutionary idea for fashion accessories. He also worked for the theater, contributing to the creation of costumes for the production of *Salomé* by Richard Strauss that was staged by Bob Wilson at La Scala in the 1986-87 season. Today, the designer for Correani is Robert Bruno.

Correggiari Giorgio (1943). Italian designer. Born in Pieve di Cento (Bologna), Correggiari earned a degree in political science and worked in several textile mills before opening his first two Pam Pam boutiques, in Riccione and Milan, in 1967. He continued working as a freelance designer for other fashion brands, including Daniel Hechter, throughout the 1970s, as well as designing the bestselling jeans' lines Ufo, Reporter, Star Point and Colette. By the 1980s he was designing a range of Collections under his own name. His company produces men's and women's lines in addition to accessories.

❑ February 2003. The designer's brother, artist Lamberto Correggiari, provides artistic direction for an innovatively theatrical presentation of the designer's runway show. Correggiari continues to experiment with fabric and fiber technology both in his own lines and in his collaborations with other brands, such as Hechter and Reporter. His men's line is produced by Viva, a division of Vivi Italia Srl.

Corset A tool and a garment belonging to a woman's intimate wardrobe. Designed to protect, support, straighten and, especially, to accentuate the new shapes imposed on the body by fashion, it has been present since the classic era, constantly throughout the centuries since, except in rare periods, in versions that are more or less restrictive, with greater or lesser bulk, in a growing crescendo of violence against natural shapes that would reach its maximum in the first thirty years of the 1800s, until arriving at the image of it that prevails in today's use of the term. In this sense, the exile of the bust, which would be Poiret's great insight, marks the divide between clothing meant to veil and hide the body in a silhouette constructed according to particular erotic-aesthetic standards, and the loose clothing of a woman who was free and no longer enclosed within domestic walls. From the Roman *fasce* (bands) to the *bliaut*, a tight tunic worn in the Middle Ages, and from a doublet made rigid with whalebone (*corps piqué*) for a Renaissance dress to the pointed bodice worn with a large skirt, we arrive at the whalebone corset used for the unique purpose of emphasizing the figure as required by the fashions of the 1700s. The crusade against the bust by doctors, already begun by the end of the 1700s, would be continued with greater vigor when it reappeared, after a period of decline and after the French Revolution, in a form (1810) reduced to a simple bodice meant to separate the breasts. The bust expanded, constricting the waist, especially in the version with straps. The solid whalebones, which compress the body down to the hips, make it a real instrument of torture. Yet it would be fashion, and not any alarm over anatomic deformation or danger to health, that will cause the definite decline of the bust; although, even under the straight dresses of the 1920s, there would be a girdle to flatten the breasts and, extending downward, hold garters for stockings. The diminishing presence, in quantity and quality, of underwear after World War II favors the combination of bra and garter belt, relegating the restrictive girdle to the larger sizes. Later, thanks to tights, the leotard, a very light skin-tight garment with good support covering the entire body from neck to ankles, made in new synthetic fibers, would win its place. And yet, in the ups and downs of fashion, the corset and the lace or fabric girdle (or *guêpière*) have had their revivals, either for function, as in Dior's New Look (1947), or simply for seduction.

(*Lucia Sollazzo*)

Corso Como 10 Cult bazaar for fashion and more, opened in 1990 in Milan at that address by Carla Sozzani. It offers sought-after clothes, accessories, jewellery, books, design objects, and furnishings, all assembled according to a cosmopolitan, refined and exclusive taste. It is a revolutionary model, anticipating the 'boutique as a lifestyle" trend, in contrast to the traditional single-brand store of the 1980s. Along with international *griffes*, including Yamamoto, Comme des Garçons, Prada, Ferretti, Westwood, Lang, Margiela, and Gaultier, there are the NN Studio and OZen lines created by Sozzani herself. Upstairs there is a gallery for photo and art exhibits, and a music room. On the ground floor of this typical Milanese "ringhiera" house (a house with external balconies), there is a restaurant café. This concept-store recently opened the 3Rooms "bed and breakfast": three suites "with some points in common which bring together art initiatives, modern antique collecting, design, and high technology."

Corti Lisa (1940). Italian fashion designer, born in Asmara, Eritrea, when the country was still part of the Italian lands across the Mediterranean Sea, of a very short-lived empire. She works in Milan and began her career in fashion in 1970. In 1986 she created and produced her own line of textile items for the home, such as bedcovers, curtains, tablecloths, and carpets. She also introduced a small clothing line characterized by color, lightness and a personal, modern vision that looked to the East, to India, China, and Japan. The fabrics are printed with stylized flower patterns, and have an ethnic touch, in satin, velvet, silk, and "poor materials" enriched with precious details.

Lisa Corti's styles sketched by Maria Pezzi.

Cose Boutique in Milan. The name on the sign, Cose (Things) was purposefully familiar and evoked small but important objects, dear to women. It opened in 1963, an explosive year for upsetting images, rebellions, and news arriving from London. The store was on via della Spiga, a street which, at the time, was not dominated by fashion and luxury. Open to modernity and new trends, the store soon became a dynamic gathering place for a daring and trendy female clientele. To suggest, stimulate and support that clientele there was a designer and manager of distribution named Nuccia Fattori. Alongside the clothes and knitwear, impossible to find elsewhere, she was able to offer exciting pieces by Biba and Zandra Rhodes, pullovers from Sonia Rykiel, embroidered sweaters from Emmanuelle Khanh, the very feminine avant-guard creations of Chloé, and even the martial self-assertion of Rabanne. At the same time, Nuccia was careful to foster the talent of Walter Albini and the revolutionary and playful genius of Cinzia Ruggeri. The boutique, among the two or three most appreciated in Milan during the 1960s, 1970s, and after, was taken over in 1984.

Cosmis Cyd. French designer. She creates chic-underground clothes. One of several young people in Paris who can create fashion, defending a look which isn't showy, but, on the contrary, lives with the person who wears it. Softly: clothing as a lifestyle, a sort of philosophy which doesn't change personalities, but goes along with them.

Cosmopolitan French women's magazine. It made its début in 1973, in the wake of the American magazine Cosmo. With the first issue, it stated that it wants to be the magazine of women who are not afraid of talking about anything, and are willing to discover something new every day. Cosmopolitan freely discussed, with humor and originality, fashion, beauty, and sexual problems. During the 1970s, the monthly ran articles about couples and genders equality, thus joining the great feminist debate.

Cosmopolitan Monthly published by Giuseppe Della Schiava. First created in the U.S. in 1886 by the Hearst Corporation, the Italian edition made its début almost a century later (1973) for Mondadori, which for two years combined it with the monthly Arianna. The magazine was not very successful, so Mondadori decided to get rid of it and passed it on to Della Schiava, who turned it into a young and unconventional publication. Some of his initiatives were truly shocking. In 1988, with the AIDS epidemic a worldwide concern, the magazine published suggestions about safe sex and included a condom. In 1982, with a similar idea, it offered a Tampax. The magazines held on until 1997 under the direction of Patrizia Pontremoli.

Costa Silk factory established in Genoa on the initiative of some members of the Costa family, an important dynasty of shipowners, who also own some businesses in the textile industry in the area of Cuneo and Asti (Piedmont). On the eve of World War II, Filande e Tessiture Costa rented the weaving mills of Rodero, Casnate and Albate near Como. The Casnate mill was closed in 1954, and the one in Albate was closed in the early 1960s. In 1964, the Costa family became a partner in the Bernasconi silk factories, bringing as a dowry its own silk company which would no longer be independent.

Costelloe Paul (1945). Irish designer and brand of prêt-à-porter. He started his career as an assistant to Jacques Estérel in Paris, then moved to Milan to design models for a manufacturing company, and finally went to New York, where he worked for Ann Fogarty. Then back to Ireland, where he created and distributed two lines: Paul Costelloe and Dressage. Elegant, linear, and of high quality, his creations were for the 1980s "career woman."

Costume Collection and Study Center Norwich, England. This Collection of clothing and accessories is part of the Strangers' Hall Museum located in the same 16th century building. Since the end of the 19th century, it has been collecting and keeping materials of local manufacture. Clothing is divided as follows: men's, women's, and children's fashion, underwear, accessories, uniforms, and ecclesiastic garments. The oldest pieces are from the 16th century. Of particular importance is the Collection of shawls produced in Norwich during the 19th century, imitating the cashmere patterns of shawls imported from India. The fabric Collection includes lace, embroidery, patchwork, and sacred vestments. In addition, there are materials for the manufacture of textiles, both handmade and machine made. For several years the Collection has been housed in a detached building separate from the museum which can be visited by appointment, same as the specialized library.

Costume Designer (Film) The relationship between cinema and fashion has developed along two main paths, but with different chronologies. First, film costume designers influenced fashion, with trends going from films to real life. Later, it was the fashion designers who influenced film; either indirectly (when the cinema adopted their creations) or directly (when fashion designers became costume designers). If until the origins of the seventh art, the birth of a film star often was linked to a style of clothing, a distinctive detail, or a particular hairdo (e.g. Theda Bara and her exotic outfits), the profession of costume designer has had a life of its own only since the 1920s, and it was only in 1948 that they first gave an Oscar for costume design. But within ten years, every movie studio deserving the name had a costume department, and it played an important part in the success of a film. The first costume designer was Howard Geer at Paramount Pictures, which employed 200 professional tailors. Then – just to name a few – Edith Head and Travis Banton worked at Paramount, Charles LeMaire at Fox, Milo Anderson at Warner Bros, Jean-Louis Berthauld at Columbia, and Walter Plunkett at MGM. Compared to a fashion designer, a costume designer must take into account several specific factors, as a film costume is at the same time – as Roland Barthes wrote in his *Système de la Mode* – a "humanity" (it enhances the plausibility of the character) and a theme (it underlines the values and symbols that the character represents). Besides being well informed about the history of costume and fashion, a costume designer must be able to communicate through clothing a character's social position and psychology, he must know the rules of photography and film-making, and be able to work in close relationship with the entire team (he would never design a violet nightgown to be worn in a room painted the same color). The most obvious connection between fashion and the cinema is through the actor who wears particular clothing that gives off an evocative power that makes the public want to dress the same way. Stars such as Joan Crawford, Marlene Dietrich, and Lauren Bacall created the fashions of Hollywood's golden age. In the 1930s, Adrian, the costume designer for Rudolph Valentino and Greta Garbo, sold an evening dress model worn by Crawford in the movie *Return* to Macy's, the famous department store. Once on the market, at the same time the movie opened in theaters, it sold more than half a million pieces in one week. Clothing style also contributed decisively to the aura of Audrey Hepburn. Originating as film costumes, some articles of clothing have dictated fashion styles for entire seasons. Examples include the white chiffon dress worn by Marilyn Monroe in *The Seven Year Itch*, Elizabeth Taylor's dress in *Cat on a Hot Tin Roof*, and Carol Baker's baby doll outfit in the movie *Baby Doll*. The big waves of fashion-revival have started in the cinema, such as Walter Plunkett's creations for Vivien Leigh and Olivia de Havilland in *Gone With The Wind*, the costumes designed by Piero Tosi for Ingrid Thulin in *The Damned*, the 1930s-style mid-calf tweed skirts designed by Theadora Van Runkle for Faye Dunaway in Bonnie and Clyde. The shapes of men's clothing also have a dialogue with the big screen. It is enough to remember the widespread use of raincoats like those worn by Humphrey Bogart, or the leather jackets worn by Marlon Brando in *The Wild Ones*. There are analogies between fashion and the star system, beginning with the fact that both are artificial constructs based on the aestheticization and display of the body. In this way, cinema provides a formidable stage from which to launch and distribute fashion. Maria Pezzi writes: "The influence of the big screen on costume and fashion cannot be doubted. When, in 1923, the film *The Desert Song* came out, with Pola Negri and Rudolph Valentino and love under tents in the desert, the passion for sheiks and the fashion for barracans was huge, especially in England, causing travel agencies that specialized in trips to Africa to flourish. And when the eccentric Lady Mendl arrived in Egypt, she was delighted to discover that pyramids were "beige," her favorite color. The world of fashion was alarmed by this psychological dominion of cinema, especially when it realized that girls of good family were rejecting the elegant bathing suits on sale in the sportswear boutiques that the great designers had just opened, opting instead for the scandalous tight wool tight maillots made fashionable by Carole Lombard. And it was even worse when they realized that high society fiancées were rejecting dresses by Lanvin, the queen of wedding gowns, and sending their little dressmakers to the cinema in order to copy Janet Gaynor's dress in *Seventh Heaven*, with its three-flounce neckerchief and frilled skirt which opened in the back like a lace fan." To the few great Hollywood designer names already mentioned, one must add the Europeans, such as the French Antoine Mago (*Amanti perduti*, *Casco d'oro*) and the Italians Vittorio Nino Novarese, Milena Canonero, Piero Gherardi, Danilo Donati, Gabriella Pescucci, and Giulia Maffai, who were appreciated all over the world, with some of them winning more than one Oscar. The situation concerning the direct cooperation between designers and the cinema is different. Piero Tosi said that the two worlds are completely separate: "Anyone born a costume designer will never be a fashion designer, and vice versa. I have never seen a great fashion designer creating beautiful costumes." The Hollywood failure of some celebrated couturiers, such as Chanel, seems to confirm his opinion. Yet, it is difficult to deny that, starting in the 1960s, designers have had a large influence on the big screen, which has more and more often adopted their styles in order to obtain a "reality effect" (see also the social distribution of branded clothing, with its associated status value). In more recent times, some *griffes* have dressed famous stars or complete films, including Armani (*American Gigolo*, *The Untouchables*) and Gaultier (Peter Greenaway's actors and *The Fifth Element*). Martin Scorsese and Wim Wenders have shot promo-costuming for, respectively, Armani and Yamamoto. Several movies depict the world of fashion and its backstage intrigues, including Michelangelo Antonioni's *Amiche* and *Blow-Up* and Robert Altman's *Prêt-à-Porter*, which included 75 designers and top models. (*Roberto Nepoti*)

Costume Gallery of Palazzo Pitti in Florence. This is the first museum owned by the Italian government entirely dedicated to the study and conservation of costumes, textiles, and clothing. The Gallery was inaugurated in Florence in 1983 under the direction of Kirsten Aschengreen Piacenti. It occupies 13 rooms in the Sundial Pavilion, a long neoclassic building started in 1776 placed, facing south, near the oldest part of Palazzo Pitti, the residence of Vittorio Emanuele II of Savoy during the years that Florence was capital of Italy (1865-1871). The costumes kept here cover a long period of time, with pieces of rare value that are unique in the world. They start with a famous group from the Medici family (coming from the tombs in San Lorenzo), consisting of garments that belonged to Cosimo I Grand Duke of Tuscany, Eleonora of Toledo, and Don Garcia, which are among the oldest still existing, going back to 1562. The Collection arrives in the present with meaningful examples of the work of the most important Italian figures in high fashion and prêt-à-porter, including Capucci, Missoni, Valentino, and Ferré. Since the year of its opening, the Gallery has displayed its great Collection through biennial rotations of costumes and accessories that have become a source of chronological and thematic exhibits on various topics. The Collections grow constantly thanks to the contributions of public and private donors, institutes, banks, and associations, among which is the very active Friends of the Costume Gallery. There were also important donations from the wardrobe of Franca Florio. and authentic costumes and clothes from the period 1700 to 1968 donated by the theater costume designer Umberto Tirelli. For the exhibitions, seven different types of dummies are used, depending on the era and the shape of the garment. There is also a Textile Restoration Workshop, something absolutely necessary for the proper maintenance of the Collection. At present directed by Carlo Sisi, with the collaboration of Caterina Chiarelli, the Gallery has over the years promoted several publications edited by scholars in the field, including *La Galleria del Costume* (5 volumes, from 1983 to 1993), *Lo Splendore di una Regia Corte. Uniformi e livree del Granducato Toscano, 1765-1799* (1983); *I principi bambini. Abbigliamento e infanzia nel Seicento* (1985); *Il guardaroba di Donna Franca Florio* (1986): *La donazione Tornabuoni-Lineapiù. Moda italiana degli anni '50 e '60* (1988): *Spose in Galleria. Abiti nuziali del '900* (1989); *Cerimonia a Palazzo. Abiti di corte tra '800 e '900* (1990); *Umberto Tirelli, un omaggio* (1991); *Anni Venti – La nascita dell'abito moderno* (1991); *La donazione Emilio Pucci: colore e fantasia* (1992); *Moda della corte dei Medici. Gli abiti restaurati di Cosimo, Eleonora e don Garcia* (1993); *La veste del sonno. Letti e abiti da notte alla Galleria del Costume* (1994); *La donazione Roberta di Camerino* (1995); *Abiti in festa. L'ornamento e la sartoria italiana* (1996); *Eleganze della Moda fra '700 e '800* (1997); *Il Salotto alla moda* (1997); and *Eleganze della Moda. La vita in villa* (1998).

(*Aurora Fiorentini*)

❑ 2000, June. The Costume Gallery of Palazzo Pitti reopens, during the 58th edition of Pitti Immagine Uomo. Shown are about forty of the sixty-seven garments, complete with accessories (for a total of 300 pieces), donated to the museum by Gianfranco Ferré. These models are from 1986 to 1999, both high fashion and prêt-à-porter. The exhibit is organized by Margherita Palli, a set designer and collaborator of Luca Ronconi. Along with Ferré's gift, the Gallery offers three other biennial exhibits: a selection of costumes and accessories from the 17th to the 20th centuries; Women's Fashion in the '30s, with paintings by De Chirico, Chessa, Donghi, Bacci and Sironi; and an exhibition of jewellery donated by Flora Wiechmann Savioli.

❑ 2003, July. The Costume Gallery turns 20. and to celebrate the anniversary organizes three exhibits: *The Garment and the Face, Stories about*

Costume from the 18th to the 20th Century; *Alberto Lattuada. A Master at Polimoda*; and *Maurizio Galante. A Donation*.

Costume Institute Part of the Metropolitan Museum dedicated to Costume. The director is Richard Martin, a historian of fashion and the author of *The St. James Fashion Encyclopedia/A Survey of Style/1945 to Present*. It started as the Museum of Costume Art, created in 1937 by the clothes collector Irene Lewisohn when she combined her personal Collection with that of Aline Bernstein. In 1946, the entire Collection passed to the Metropolitan which, over time, enriched it with many acquisitions. Today, it owns more than 50,000 pieces and accessories from the late 1600s up to the present. After reaching retirement age, Diana Vreeland left journalism and, during the 1970s, dedicated her energy and ideas to the Costume Institute, organizing exhibitions in honor of Balenciaga, French haute couture from 1919 to 1939 (*Inventive Clothes*), Saint-Laurent, and the French fashion from the revolution to the Empire.

Costume National Italian brand created by the designer Ennio Capasa, who was born in Lecce in 1960. A graduate of the Academy of Fine Arts of Milan, he traveled for a long time in the Orient, and in 1983 went to Japan to work on the team of an extraordinary designer, Yoshi Yamamoto. In 1987, back in Europe, Capasa designed the first Costume National Collection, minimalist in inspiration, reduced to basics, characterized by a distinctive slender silhouette, close to the body. The New York Times called it "a new chic and cool modernism." In 1993, he presented Costume National Homme. His style was immediately adopted by the emerging trends in music and cinema, which made him a cult designer. Costume National is a family business, located in Milan, for which Ennio Capasa designs the Collections and his brother Carlo is general manager. They both own the brand, which is divided into women's clothing, men's clothing, and accessories.

❑ 2001, March. The brand focuses on a "space-romantic" theme. The Capasa woman wears men's blazers with pointed shoulders, long gloves over sleeves, mini-skirts with soft suede boots, and men's-style trousers, but also lace, leather, and tulle inlays, all cut as in

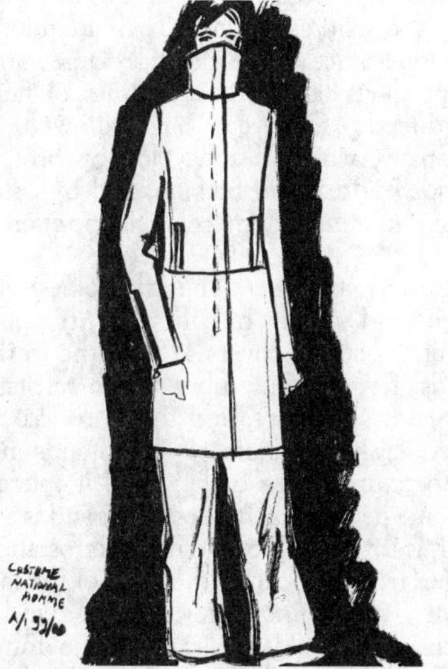

Costume National. Men's and Women's Autumn-Winter 1998-99 Collection.

a painting by Fontana. Black dominates the Collection, lightened only by a few touches of emerald green.

❑ 2002, April. The Collection marks a return to Japanese fashion and the Japanese-style origins of Ennio Capasa, whose master was Yamamoto.

❑ 2002, May. Capasa designs the costumes for a show by Motus, the experimental Italian theater group. The new show, *Splendid's*, opens its tour at the Hotel Elysée in Hamburg.

❑ 2002, November. Costume National opens its first boutique in Paris, for a total of six worldwide. With a total of 2,000 square feet on Rue Cambon at the corner of Rue Mont Thabor, it is designed and furnished like a private house, with unique pieces and carpets. In the Melrose Avenue boutique in Los Angeles, the *griffe* launches *Scent*, its first fragrance.

❑ 2003, March. Eroticism and fiction are to be found in the Collection that Ennio Capasa presents at Paris Fashion Week. The main character is a digital beauty, a heroine of virtual games. Though admitting that eroticism isn't part of the Costume National style, Ennio has given in to it, creating a hyper-contemporary and high-tech Collection which follows the romantic-comics-graphic style begun more than 20 years earlier with the success of the film *Blade Runner*. Obvious, and expressly shown off, are the references to corsetry, rigid stitching, exaggerated padding as a way to stress the lines of overcoats and jackets, belts and bustier dresses, soft leather tight leotards, and spiral-cut fox furs. The Capasa brothers bet on the shoe market, which is now 30% of their turnover. They have just opened a new plant in Strà. At the end of 2002, the company's turnover was €50 million.

❑ 2003, June. Costume National prepares its first youth line, which is to be ready for the Autumn-Winter 2004-2005 season. A 5 year license agreement (renewable for five years more) is signed with Ittierre Spa (Group IT Holding). It provides for the manufacture and distribution of two lines, men's and women's, complete with accessories. Ennio is to control the image and style, and will work directly on the advertising campaigns.

❑ 2003, June. At Milan Moda Uomo, the Spring-Summer 2004 Collection brings back on stage the figure of Casanova, and icon and symbol of womanizers. But a modern Casanova, of course, with some hints of the 1700s: corsetry fasteners, hooks, garters, matelassé (or quilted garments), and night gowns.

❑ 2004, January. It's called C'n'c and is produced by Ittierre, a new line inspired by women's street style that mixes rock & roll and night-clubbing. The Collection is very large, with 400 pieces, plus accessories.

❑ 2005, June. The firm launches, with Ducati, a clothing and accessories Collection inspired by the world of motorcycle racing, called C'n'c for Ducati.

Cotonificio Albini Italian company specialized in the manufacture of shirt fabrics. It was established in 1876 in Albino, near Bergamo, an area which holds the record for its high concentration of textile companies, especially cotton mills. It has always been a family business: the family's fourth generation is supported by a working staff with long and solid experience. Their attention to quality, service to the clientele, large variety of products, and large quantities of fabric produced every year have allowed the company, which is today led by brothers Silvio, Andrea, and Stefano, and by cousin Fabio, to attain an international position.

Cotton Textile fiber. The third oldest after linen and wool, but first in terms of diffusion: cotton covers 47% of the world's needs. It is the only fiber whose resistance increases when wet, and therefore also the most easily washable. It withstands high temperatures, even boiling, and it tolerates alkaline detergents. It doesn't felt and is anti-allergic, hygroscopic, and not electrostatic. It comes from the fruit of the plant of the same name (Gossypium Herbaceum), and is cultivated on a large scale in the former Soviet Union, the U.S., China, India, Egypt, Pakistan, Turkey, and the Sudan. Cottons are classified according to counts, while fiber length determines the quality (from less than 20 mm to more than 40 mm). The most precious cotton is the famous Sea Island from the British West Indies ("West Indian Sea Island Cotton"), already appreciated by Edward VII, whose fibers reach 60 mm in length. Cotton fabrics are mainly used in the manufacture of household linen, in sterilized environments, and in clothing, where they cover all the ranges of use, from underwear and trousers to jackets and coats. Among the best known types are denim, canvas, velvet, fustian, drill, gabardine, poplin, seersucker, and madras. (*Cristina Lucchini*)

Cotton Belt Italian manufacturing brand. It is located in Osmannoro di Sesto Fiorentino (Tuscany). It was intuition that allowed Fiorenzo Fratini to become, during the 1950s, one of the first importers of jeans from the U.S. That same intuition suggested to Corrado and Marcello, Fiorenzo's sons and founders in 1973 of EuroComar, that they create a partnership with the American company Cotton Belt and expand the marketing to a more and more complete range of clothes and accessories.

❑ 2003, June. EuroComar, which belongs to Fingen Apparel, in Tuscany, and is owner of the Cotton Belt brand, has given it under license for 10 years to the Piedmont company Mistral, which already produces the Brooksfield line. Starting with Spring-Summer 2004, Mistral is to produce and market the men's, women's, sportswear, and jeans lines within the European Union.

Coty French perfume house. It was established in 1904 by a young Corsican, François-Joseph-Marie Spoturno (1874-1934), using the surname of his mother, Maria Coti, for the name of the company. In the effervescent Paris of the Universal Exposition of 1900, he discovered at the same time both the exceptional acuteness of his nose and the scarcity of vivacity, fantasy, and daring in the fragrances of the time, which were as anonymous as their bottles. The purpose of his life then became the creation of new and brilliant perfumes which were able to express the multifaceted personalities of women as well as the changes underway in their lives. It was a period of preparation for Grasse, the famous perfume-producing town in southern France, and in 1904 the fragrance *Rose Jacqueminot* was ready. The idea of breaking a bottle of perfume in a shop at the Louvre accelerated an impact which in few months would make a fortune for Coty and his laboratory. But Coty wasn't just a creator of new combinations of essences that have enriched the history of fragrances, the first to experiment with the aroma of spices. Convinced that to be a success a perfume must cover itself with grace and seduction, he entrusted Baccarat and Lalique with the design of his luxury bottles. Aiming at the most precious novelty, during the 1930s Coty would establish a glassworks, a box factory, and a plant for printing gold labels. And he would entrust his magic shop windows to the talent of young artists for the launch of each of his perfumes, some 20 in 25 years. The earnings were exceptional, but the enormous financial burdens – in 1922 he bailed out Le Figaro –, and the crash of 1929 caused the bankruptcy of firm, which would not survive the death of its creator. The assets were taken over by the American company Pfizer in 1966 and by the Benkinsen group in 1992. (*Lucia Sollazzo*)

❑ 2004, September. The group celebrates its 100th anniversary and publishes a book entitled *Coty: Perfumer and Visionary* (Editions Assouline).
❑ 2005, February. The group announces a worldwide licensing agreement with Sarah Jessica Parker for the development of a fragrance line.
❑ 2005, May. The group announces the acquisition, for $800 million, of the fragrance portfolio of Unilever, which controls the perfume licenses of Calvin Klein, Cerruti, Vera Wang, Chloé, and Lagerfeld.

Coulisse Internal belt formed by a string running through two strips of fabric, often used in clothing and accessories. It is handy because it can be adjusted with ease to the width of a garment, either bunching it or not. It is used around the waist or to close the bottoms of sleeves, trousers, and jackets, either casual or elegant.

Country Look A style inspired by the clothing of cowboys, the heroes of western films, from the Gary Cooper of *High Noon* to the John Wayne of *True Grit*. These are the men who inspired a way of being and of dressing that was born from the American dream and narrated in the manner of European designers. From the mixture, more or less successful, of the myth of the Founding Fathers with the aesthetic of the Old World came flared jeans covered with strass, Stetsons worn with shoes that have heels worthy of Madame De Sade, and fringed leather jackets decorated with ostrich feathers à la Josephine Baker. Dreaming, according to ones taste, either of Dolly Parton singing *Poor Lonesome Cowboy* or the most perfidious of J.R.'s.

Courregès André (1923). French designer, born in Pau. He studied civil engineering, but prefered fashion to construction, although his styles seemed designed with a T-square and a compass in order to create a straight and geometric silhouette. His was a minimal chic that was all the rage during the 1960s: the essence of elegance wrapped in trapezium-shaped dresses, skirts stopping above knee anticipating the mini, an elegance stressed through contrast, by the matching of two non-colors, black and white. Opposites reward the simplicity of straight or slightly loose lines, precise in a rigid trapezium-shaped flare. There are dresses that look like paper dolls. Patterns adjust themselves to and prefer stripes and squares derived from op art. There is no reference to the past, although he started his career a long time ago, as a cutter for the mythical Balenciaga, in 1949, before he could afford to open his atelier on Avenue Kleber in Paris. Furthermore, the future is a source of inspiration, as it was for Cardin and Rabanne: his astronauts take off before man's landing on the moon. His Collection called Space Age was famous: projected into tomorrow, it marked the evolution of taste in a triumph of white and silver, to offer the geometries of stars, the suggestions of Star Trek. These are late-in-the-century emotions that Courregès designed 30 years before, a remake for many of his colleagues. This look was also favored for accessories such as the pure white boots and certain square-shaped hats, worn also by Jackie Kennedy, the envied and imitated first lady. The first men's Collection came out in 1973. In 1979 he began to design eye glasses, umbrellas, jewellery, shirts, furniture, children's lines, and perfumes. He was among the first to launch himself into prêt-à-porter, creating the Couture Future line, and entering partnerships with Japanese groups, an experience that led him straight to Tokyo for a decade, from 1984 to 1994, the year in which he returned to work full time at his own *maison*. (*Lucia Mari*)

Courtauld Institute of Art It is part of the University of London University and dedicated to research in the history of art. It is the only insitute in Europe with a Department of the History of Clothing. After the master's degree, it is possible to pursue a Doctorate in Research. The department is directed by Aileen Ribeiro. In order to be given one of the few and coveted places at the Institute, it is necessary to have an honors degree in history, literature, or art history, and to know two or more European languages. The course of study is very academic: it covers the chronology of clothing from Magna Graecia up to the present day. The department is located in Somerset House, also the home of the Institute's celebrated art Collection. There are meetings with people in the trade as well as visits to museums and to the most important English historical Collections. Former students work at the Victoria and Albert Museum, at the National Portrait Gallery, at the Museum of London, at the Bath Museum of Costume, at the Christie's auction house, and at the Saint Martin's School of Art. (*Virginia Hill*)

Courtaulds Textiles English clothing and textile company. It is among the five most important in Europe. Established by George Courtauld, and then expanded by his son Samuel, it began to produce silk in Essex in 1809. By 1850, it was the largest English manufacturer of silk crepe for funerals. When long periods of mourning fell out of favor, the company changed its product line and in 1904 acquired the exclusive rights to rayon. During the 1950s, the group produced the first British acrylic fiber, Courtelle. In the early 1990s, it employed more than 22,000 workers. The company sponsors the Courtauld Institute of Art.

Cover or covercoat. A men's coat characterized by a casual cut, a hidden row of buttons, and large lapels. It was very trendy in the early 1900s. It is made from wool with the same name, in a diagonal or herringbone weave, with ribs in relief, and from twisted yarns. It is often waterproof. Similar to gabardine, but heavier, this fabric is also used for trousers, skirts, jackets, and duster-overcoats.

Coveri Enrico (1952-1990). Italian designer. He was known for his colors: the calling card of a fashion which wants to express joy and optimism and which was the essence of his own life. One is surprised with very vivid reds, brilliant yellows, oranges, greens, fuchsias, and violets, all in competition with one another. The Herald Tribune wrote in 1978: "He has irony and a sense of color, in one of the most beautiful Collections presented in Paris." A sense of color that Coveri often used also for his men's clothing, daring to use pink and violet in blazers with shining lapels. He was, at the same time, the king of sequins, which covered his sparkling suits: "Sequins," commented Le Figaro, "are for Coveri what chains are for Chanel," while the magazine Elle devoted the first of many covers to him, a simple T-shirt on which the name Coveri is written with sequins. It is not by accident that Paris and 1978 are mentioned. This is the city and that is the year in which he presented his first women's Collection, at the Cour Carré in the Louvre, a challenge in this capital of elegance. He arrived in Paris at a young age. He was from Florence (born in Prato), where he attended the Academy of Fine Arts, and worked in the theater as a set and costume designer and as a model. He had a fortunate experience as a designer for Touche, starting in 1976 and lasting 9 years: a period in which he had the opportunity to express and establish his personal talent. It was his key to the conquest of Paris with a single Collection. The rendezvous became seasonal, and in 1987 Paris awarded him the Grande Médaille de Vermeil, while Italy named him a "Commendatore" of the Republic, before the 35 years of age required by the law. His Collection of medals is very rich: tributes and acknowledgments, many international, which honor an adrenaline fashion that often shakes up the long week of French prêt-à-porter and brings clients such as Liza Minnelli, Joan Collins, Sophia Loren, Margot Hemingway, Vanessa Redgrave, La Toya Jackson, and Bianca of Savoy. One success after another: in 1982 the Sportswear, Jeans and Junior (up to 14 years) lines made their début; in 1983 here it was Enrico Coveri baby, followed by Premiers Jours, dedicated to newborns. In 1985, he established You Young, a *griffe* for very young girls (with record sales), and then launched a boy's version. He designed a line for the home, a make-up line, many types of accessories, sportswear, fun furs, and perfumes, among which the most famous was *Paillettes*. In December 1990, he died. His sister Silvana took over the design and management of the company. She is supported by her son Francesco Martini (1975), who, in 1996 began to personally design the You Young Coveri line: provocations caused by bare legs, a taste for color, and jacquard knitwear with a vaguely folk touch, crazy geometric patterns, and patchwork leather. And everything under raindrops of sequins. In autumn 1998, Martini caused a scandal among colleagues opposed to turning the presentations into showy spectacles when he

A sketch by Enrico Coveri for the Men's Spring-Summer Collection 1984.

A sketch by Enrico Coveri for Women's Spring-Summer Collection 1984.

brought onto the runway a transparent bathtub full of milk and, immersed in it, in an attitude of voluptuous relaxation, the TV showgirl Alessia Merz. Starting with the Spring-Summer 2002 Collection, Martini became the head designer of this stimulating *griffe*. There was a terrific range of colors, as ever, along with crazy patterns stolen from the animal world, as well as patterns that expressed an authentic art found in painters more attuned to his fashions. The presentations are uncontainable: there is no transformation, only continuity. And always small provocations that burst into daily life: otherwise, what would Coveri be? Many funny ideas flow into the accessories, transformed into real gags. Inevitably, there are the sequins: making clothes without them would be like serving champagne without the bubbles. One thing is certain: this almost 6'6" tall young man is not a bore: he walks in the streets to catch moods and sensations that will help him find and create designs for a woman whose vocation is freedom. (*Lucia Mari*)

❑ 2001, November. In the Milan headquarters on via Manzoni, Martini presents the Enrico Coveri men's and women's Collections for Spring-Summer 2002. They had already been presented during Milan's Fashion Week. You Young Coveri.com had been seen in previews, but later abandoned Francesco Martini, who at the beginning of the year had gathered his maternal heritage for the primary line, declared: "Making the first two Collections has been very engaging, because they are very different from each other. To design E.C., I let myself be overwhelmed with euphoria. For the first time, I was able to use first-quality materials to give life to colors and geometries."
❑ 2002, January. A new licensing agreement with Big Time, a company that is part of Gruppo Fipar. At Pitti, Francesco Martini offers the new designs of the Autumn-Winter 2002 Collection, both from the Enrico Coveri primary line and the You Young.com line produced by Big Time.
❑ 2002, September. For the Spring-Summer season, the woman imagined by Francesco Martini Coveri is a single woman and happy to be so. "Next Life Single" is the motto proposed with conviction and assurance on T-shirts. The silhouette is formal yet sensual: tight trousers, large blouses, and tailored jackets with pleats and visible seams. According to the house tradition, besides sequins scattered a little bit everywhere, a new print is always present at the Collections. This time it is fish, in a black-and-white version like tropical ones.
❑ 2002, August. At the International Salon of Lingerie in Lyon, the first Enrico Coveri-Cagi Collections of intimate wear are presented.
❑ 2003, June. At Milan Moda Uomo, the Coveri Summer is joyful and full of colors. There are T-shirts with prints of the first videogames from the 1980s and some with the Atari console. Hawaiian shirts are worn open in front and tucked into trousers padded at the knees like those of bikers. There is a comfortable line which uses a necktie as if it were a scarf, and instead of a belt offers a carry-everything string, and borrows a pink plush hood and shell necklace from the female wardrobe. There are chalk-striped linen suits, also in coral, tailored blazers matched with floral trousers, multi-color jackets with thin stripes, and quotes, numbers, acronyms, and sport scores on T-shirts, swim trunks, and pointy-toed loafers.

Cowan John (1929-1979). English photographer. During the 1960s, in England, it was still possible to meet weird and genial characters such as John Cowan. Born in Kent, he left home in search of fortune at the age of 16, got married at 20, worked for an auto dealer, a travel agency, and in a pub. Dazzled by photography, he moved to London and began taking pictures of young people, jazz musicians, and theater actors, rightly convinced that these themes represented the new era of reportage. He was impudent (in 1959 he simply took his photos to Kodak, and thereby obtained the chance to show them in a large personal exhibit), elegant, charming, and exaggerated in his way of life, even in the eyes of an anti-bourgeois photographer friend of his like Terence Donovan. A typical representative of the culture of the early

1960s, Cowan interpreted the style of Mary Quant to perfection, but he identified especially with the world of film: with the James Bond films he shares the choice of the irrepressible beauty of the Bond girls and the dynamism of the shots. Not forgetting his beginnings as an excellent "street photographer," he transmitted everything contained in his reportages by means of a 35mm reflex camera. He often took photos of models who were very young and not yet famous while they carried on in front of various London institutions, for example marching right in front of the Queen's guards at Buckingham Palace or flirting in front of the Stock Exchange. But he also shot true reportages that looked like short films produced all over the world in extreme situations where women ride in the desert, drive cars and motorboats, and appear next to helicopters, as in one celebrated photo feature (a reference to *From Russia With Love*, the second of Bond film, was obvious). He began to publish in Queen and immediately after for The Observer, Sunday Times, Daily Express, Daily Mirror, and Daily Mail. He then went to Vogue, where Diana Vreeland gave him carte blanche. This was the time of his personal and professional relationship with the model Jill Kennington, who he discovered, launched, and simultaneously subjected to his very demanding needs as a photographer. When the relationship ended in 1965, Cowan opened a modelling agency and moved into an enormous loft in Prince Palace where he lived and worked. This was the studio where Michelangelo Antonioni shot *Blow-up* in 1966 and it was evident that the photographer-protagonist was a sort of synthesis between the exaggerations of David Bailey and those of John Cowan. The following year he worked for Kubrick on the initial sequence of the rising sun in *2001: A Space Odyssey*. It was his last important job and his style was no longer popular. He closed his studio and moved to Italy, where he worked with Oliviero Toscani, and then started to travel again. He was soon forgotten by that public which had adored him, and only in 1999 did the beautiful monograph *John Cowan-Through the Light Barrier* give him back his rightful fame. It was too late for the eccentric photographer, whose funeral was also somewhat cinematographic: with all those beautiful ex wives and ex fiancées, it reminded one of the final scene in *L'Homme qui aimait les femmes* by Truffaut. (*Roberto Mutti*)

Cox Patrick (1963). Canadian shoe designer. He works in England and is known for his modern and anti-conformist touch. Since 1997 he has also designed a men's and women's clothing Collection. He studied in London at Cordwainers Technical College

Boot by Patrick Cox.

where, while still a student, he was noticed by Westwood, who invited him to work on her Autumn-Winter 1984-1985 Collection. Upon graduation in 1985, he started his own line, although continuing to work for famous colleagues and houses such as Galliano, Sui, Hamnet, and Lanvin. In 1991, he opened his first shop on Symons Street in London.

C.P. Company Italian brand of sportswear. Its designs are meant mostly for young people, and are inspired by the uniforms of American sports teams. Massimo Osti is the designer who, for some time, has brought the brand success.

Crahay Jules François (1917-1988). French-Belgian designer. He won great approval for the elegance of his evening dresses and the very low necklines proposed in his first Collection in 1959. After an apprenticeship in Lieges, in his mother's atelier, he moved to Paris. In 1947, after a period in the atelier of Jane Regny, he joined Nina Ricci and became the first designer of prêt-à-porter. In 1963 he went to Lanvin, replacing Castillo. Crahay doesn't impose his styles, even the most severe ones, giving the women he dresses the liberty to improvise and recreate his fluttering draping, the cuts on the bias, and the knotted fabrics. Even his luxury minimalism of the 1970s was sweet and feminine. He left the *maison* in 1984 and retired. He would design three more prêt-à-porter Collections for Itokin. (*Olivella Pianetti*)

Crali Tullio (1910). Italian artist. In 1932, he designed men's clothes. Close to the later Futurist wave known as Second Futurism, Crali brought back to clothing that essentiality and modernity of cut typical of the movement. He used contrasting colors. The geometric and asymmetric decorations recalled the dynamism of the Futurists. There were also several dresses during the 1930s with chromatic and geometric backgrounds and with distinctive ideas such as the use of pleats in different colors. Some of his pieces are on display in the La Rosa Collection in Rome.

Cravatterie Nazionali Italian store chain selling only ties from large and small *griffes*. The idea belongs to Francesco Moraewetz, who opened his first boutique on via Verri in Milan's fashion quadrilateral in 1989. By the end of the 1990s, there were 28 boutiques all over Italy. After ten years in business, the number of ties sold was 1 million. The chain has for some time offered clients a custom-made service by which anyone can design his own tie. It is then manufactured and put on sale with the name of the client, who agrees to pick up any unsold ties. On some shelves it is possible to find second-hand ties that shops collect in exchange for new ones, and which are sold at auction as cult objects.

Crawford Cindy (1966). Top model, born in De Kalb, Illinois. She has chestnut hair and brown eyes, and a mole above the right lip. She joined the world of models in 1982, participating in a contest at the Elite agency, even though she didn't come in first. She then abandoned the study of engineering to devote herself to a career as a model. She exemplifies American beauty: clean, physically perfect, spontaneous, and happy. From the late 1980s to the late 1990s she was on the cover of the most important fashion magazines in the world, including Vogue, Elle, and Cosmopolitan. In 1991, she married the actor Richard Gere, but they separated four years later. In the U.S., her fitness videotapes had huge sales. After leaving fashion, she created a company for all her various activities, including Cindy Crawford perfume, contracts with Omega and Pepsi Cola, and many others. In 1998, she married Rande Gerber. She has two children, Presley and Caia.

(*Silvia Paoli*)

Crawford Joan (1908-1977). Had it not been for a particular physical characteristic of Joan Crawford's – who in real life was Lucille Fay La Sueur from San Antonio, Texas – fashion would not, in 1932, have experienced a fundamental shift that woman have enjoyed for more than 60 years. This had to do with her shoulders. When the mythical Adrian first met Joan Crawford in order to design the costumes for the film *Letty Lynton*, directed by Clarence Brown, he could not, evidently being a very extroverted man, refrain from exclaiming (or so the legend goes): "Oh my God, you look like Johnny Weissmuller," which was not very kind indeed. There is no record of her reply, although she was not known to be a diplomatic person. But the clash was fruitful. From the attempt to mask her most evident defect – very broad shoulders, out of proportion to the rest of her figure – a new style was born: that of wide, padded shoulders, with an emphasis on the upper part of the body. Just as he had done for Greta Garbo, who owed the designer much of her charm, Adrian invented for Crawford – who was at a turning point in her career and reinventing what would later be defined as an "image" – a series of dresses with exaggerated shoulders that dropped loose at the hips making her silhouette both unreal and elegant, a line which would be very imitated up to the present day. It was an excellent way to balance imperfect figures but not so good for the effect it had on sales of blouses and similar garments. This was the second "imprint" that Crawford left on current fashions, the first one had to do with her mouth: excessive, cruel, marked with lipstick in a misshapen way that, over the years, would turn her into a tragic mask (how many unhappy characters did she play in her career!) and the bearer of a completely constructed artificial face in which the eyes shone out from under long black eyebrows (another Crawford trademark), a "drag queen" (as Marilea Solbiati and Miro Silvera wrote in *Moda di celluloide*). To get a sense of Adrian's wisdom, it is enough to take a look at the black tailored suit with gold decorations that he created for her in 1938 for the film *Mannequin* by Franz Borzage, and which she would wear with a large brim hat. "If women imitate me, it's for my clothing, and it's Adrian who creates it for me," she admitted. Instead of Adrian's perfectly cut suits, in everyday life she preferred to wear trousers which, according to her, provided the "indispensable modern link to planes, penthouses, and a new way of life" shared with the other girls of the Pants Brigade: Marlene Dietrich, Katharine Hepburn, Sylvia Sidney, and Lupe Velez. What a pity, though, to cover those legs, Adrian must have thought. And he succeeded in making her show them almost completely in the film *Dancing Lady* of 1933 by Robert Z. Leonard, with the help of a marvelous transparent dress which revealed that the dress with the Weissmuller shoulders was just a joke: behind the see-through veils and crystal was the body of a real woman.

(*Irene Bignardi*)

Creed Charles (1909-1966). English designer. The sixth in a line of tailors, he studied in England and Vienna. At the end of a short apprenticeship at Bergdorf Goodman in New York, he returned to the family firm in Paris. At the end of World War II he opened his own shop in London, and it was especially famous for its classic and elegant tailoring characterized by faultless cutting. Alongside the refined tailored clothing, he would later offer sportswear lines created expressly for the American market. The atelier closed upon his death.

Crêpe Fabric made of wool, silk, cotton or synthetic fibers, with a gathered and grainy look. Originally, it was only made of silk. It is used for Summer and evening dresses. It has several variants. Crêpe Georgette is smooth and transparent with a very fine grain. It is the most typical and the lightest of all crêpes, and was named after the French dressmaker Georgette de la Plante, who was famous for evening dresses. Morocco crêpe is the heaviest, with a thick grain and a weft in light relief that creates a thin-ribbed effect. Midway between the two, as regards weight, is crêpe de Chine, which is soft and smooth, either bright or dull, often printed, and non-transparent. In light wool, just slightly gathered, it is called crepella. A different fabric, which doesn't belong to the crêpe family, is *crépon*, with irregular folds that give it an embossed look, similar to tree bark; it has the great advantage of not becoming crumpled.

Crespi Consuelo. American model and later the Italian correspondent for Vogue America, for 15 years from the early 1960s to the mid 1970s. At the time, the magazine's director was Diana Vreeland. Consuelo arrived in Rome together with her sister Gloria O'Connor, also a model, in the early days of Italian fashion. She married Rudy Crespi. Leone, the president of Italy, honored her for her contribution to the success of the Made in Italy movement.

Crespi Rodolfo, Rudy (1924-1985). Public relations man and editor. Born in Sao Paulo, Brazil, he was among the first in Italy to open a public relations agency, Sopec, which worked for many years for Ferragamo and Krizia. From 1975 to 1985, the year of his death, he was the editor of Vogue Brazil and Vogue Mexico.

Cressy Simon. French tailor. Starting from the English tradition of men's clothing, he converted himself, through his children, to a style that was more in tune with the times and with the mood coming out of the London of the Beatles that captured the tase of young people. From this conversion, in 1963, came the Renoma boutique which, anticipating bell-bottoms, was a terrific success for several years.

Cretonne Hard-wearing cloth originating in Normandy, with a hemp warp and linen weft, manufactured in cotton and printed in bright colors.

Cricchi+Ferrante This Dutch brand brings together the photographers Angelo Cricchi and Susanna Ferrante. Their photos are seen more and more often in the most intriguing magazines (Surface, i.-D, Elle France, Stile) due to a very personal sense of glamour, refined taste, particularly elaborate compositions, and a sophisticated use of light. They have done very original campaigns for Galerie Lafayette, Diesel, Byblos, and Energy Jeans.

Crinoline This term derives from a special fabric, the *crinolino*. At first it referred to the stiff petticoat neeeded to swell the skirt, and later to the particular shape of dresses in the 1800s. The hoop skirt was inspired by the need to separate the dress from the body, with the purpose of protecting pregnant women, even if making it too tight around the waist could be dangerous. By 1840, crinoline was already very rigid, more solid than the fabric. In 1860, it was transformed into a cage with rings and Springs and crinoline at the top. Then this tool, hidden under large bulky dresses, became lighter, and it was in these more comfortable forms that crinoline, considered the unsurpassed symbol of femininity, returned to the fashion stage, for example in the 1960s.

(*Lucia Sollazzo*)

Crisci Tanino (1920). Industrialist and shoe designer. He followed in his father's footsteps. In fact, his father, Alfonso Crisci (1876-1937), an artisan shoemaker, opened a factory in 1919 in Casteggio (Pv). At his father's death, Gaetano (Tanino) reorganized the company for the production of military goods, and then, at the end of the war, converted it again for civilian needs. During the 1960s, he decided to enter the retail field on an international level. The first boutique on via Montenapoleone in Milan was soon followed by one in Rome on via Borgognona and one in Florence on via Tornabuoni. His shoes distinguished themselves for the high level of artisanal work at every step of production and for their exclusive materials. In the late 1970s and early 1980s, he established Tanino Crisci France and Tanino Crisci America, and opened boutiques in Paris and New York. In 1988 he established Tanino Crisci Japan with a boutique and a showroom in Tokyo. His son Alfonso (1954) is the current general manager of the company.

Cristiani Antonio (1896-1984). Men's tailor. Born in Maida (Catanzaro), he moved to Paris at the age of 17 to attend the Ladevèze school of cutting. Before opening his own atelier in Rue de la Paix, he worked at Damien and Larsen. Among his future clients were the actor Pierre Fresnay and the painter Pierre Soulages. He was decorated with the Legion d'Honneur. In the 1950s, his sons Christian and Francis would guarantee the future of the atelier up until its closing in 1998.

Cristiano Di Thiene A brand name and a manufacturer of clothing made from leather and ram shearling. The company and the brand are named after their founder, Cristiano Sperotto, and from the village where the company has its headquarters. Sperotto began his activity after World War II with a small atelier that in 1979, when the second generation joined the firm, grew into a major enterprise. The manufacturing cycle is completely in-house, in the Thiene plant, and is characterized by strict quality control. Exports are 50% of total production. The garments have invisible seams and a tailor's finish.

Cristiano Fissore & C. Italian knitwear factory working mostly with cashmere. It was established in Rapallo in 1977 by Cristiano Fissore, head of marketing and administration, and Lucia Bosisio, who is in charge of design. Today, the business is a corporation with a staff of 15 in-house employees and about 100 outside agents. It has an annual turnover of about 12 billion liras, of which 25% comes from export.

Cristina Santandrea Italian *griffe* of prêt-à-porter. Created in the early 1980s and initially produced by CTS of Bologna, it is designed by Cristina herself. In 1995, she launched a second line, Queen & Queen, establishing during the same period a company called Papa Re which today produces both lines. It has been at Milano Collezioni for several seasons.

Crocodile Very precious and expensive skin used in the manufacture of both clothing and accessories. Given its high cost, today it is imitated by printing crocodile patterns on more ordinary skins.

Crolla Scott (1955). Scottish designer. His first passion was sculpture. In 1955 he began to work for Callaghan, imposing a rigorous style aimed at easy-to-wear clothes. His Collections reflect his education in the world of art. Geometry is at the base of his fashion designs.

Crosland Neisha (1960). English textile designer. She studied at the Camberwell School of Art, and then specialized at the Royal College of Art (1986). She works as a consultant for several designers, including Calvin Klein, Ozbeck, and Lacroix. She launched her own line of handmade printed scarves in 1994.

Cruciani Brand of knitwear created in 1993 by Luca Caprai, who left his father's main company, Arnanldo Caprai Gruppo Tessile, which he joined at the age of 18, to invest in another family company, Maglital of Trevi (Perugia), which specialized in knitwear. The objective: to make knitwear, especially in cashmere, that is trendy and of very high quality. The project worked, and Maglital, which in 1994 had a turnover of €750,000, closed 2002 with a turnover of €12 million, with an average annual rate of growth.

(*Gianluca Cantaro*)

Cruz Miguel (1944-1989). Cuban designer. Though Cruz made his name in Italy, he was born in Cuba and began his career studying fashion in Paris at the Chambre Syndicale de la Haute Couture. After finishing his studies he worked at both Castillo and Balenciaga, and in 1963 moved to Italy to work as a freelance designer for several Italian companies. He eventually settled in Rome where he launched his own lines of men's and women's ready-to-wear. Cruz innovatively employed leather, suede and knitwear in his distinctive vision of luxury leisure apparel for a moneyed international set.

Miguel Cruz designs in a sketch by Maria Pezzi ('70s).

C.S.A.C. (Centro Studi e Archivio della Comunicazione). A research center and archive at the University of Parma. It was conceived at the Institute of Art History directed by Carlo Arturo Quintavalle in the late 1960s. The purpose was to create an art Collection on the model of American universities, on the basis of donations of complete archives suitable for illustrating the creative process of the artist and not only the final masterpiece. The initiative was successful. Quintavalle convinced many architects, many designers from Milan, and many stylists to donate their archives. The Collection is divided into 5 sections. The Project section includes a Collection of 70,000 fashion sketches and a large number of clothes. The Walter Albini unit is particularly important, together with that of the illustrator Brunetta. In the 1980s and 1990s, the Center collected materials from the most important Italian *griffes* of the 20th century. The archives can be consulted by scholars and by students with a letter of introduction. The catalogue will soon be available on the Internet. There are exhibitions, seminars, and courses, as well as a publishing program. From its current headquarters in the Nervi Pavilion of Parma, the center will soon move to the Certosa of Valserena. (*Virginia Hill*)

CSP International An industrial group in Ceresara (Mantua) which is a leader in the manufacture of socks, stockings, tights, and underwear for both men and women. It was established in 1983 as a small local business producing tights. After the creation of the historic brand Sanpellegrino, strongly identified with that product, and the creation of an underwear line (in 2000), CSP created Oroblu (1997), a brand aimed at a higher market segment and specialized in tights, corsetry, and seamless underwear. In 1999, the firm acquired the prestigious and historic

French hosiery brand Le Bourget (established in 1927), which ranked third in Europe in terms of production. In 2000, the firm acquired Lepel, another big brand, thanks to which it made its début in the market for underwear and corsetry. Over the years, the company has distinguished itself for the great attention it pays to production technology, its extensive distribution, and a product line that has items for different market segments. At present, with plants also in France and Poland, it has 1,500 employees and a presence in 50 countries. The company produces 100 million pairs of tights each year, and 10 million articles of underwear, for a turnover of more than €160 million. It is the only Italian company in its field that is quoted on the stock exchange. *(Sara Tieni)*

❑ 2003, February. The year 2002 ended with a loss double that of the previous year (882 million liras compared to 426 million liras in 2001) and sharply diminishing net revenue. This was influenced by investments in communication to sustain the stockings sector. The group therefore had net consolidated revenues of €19.6 million, a reduction of 2.3%. The operating margin went from €8.3 million in 2001 to €5.5 million. The recession in the market for tights (both in Italy and abroad) was offset by a favorable trend in underwear and corsetry thanks to the Sanpellegrino and Oroblu brands, which made up 29.2% of the total turnover.
❑ 2003, May. The first quarter saw a reduction in net revenue of €40.8 million, down 11.8% compared to the same period in 2002. The decline doesn't involve Italy, but France and Russia instead. Consolidated net revenues amount to €40.8 million. Sales of seamless underwear and corsetry remain strong, with an increase in turnover from 27.8% to 35.1%, although it doesn't compensate for the 20.5% decline in sales of socks and stockings compared to the first quarter of 2002.

Cucinelli Brunello (1956). Founder and designer of the knitwear factory carrying his name. Established in 1978, it soon became one of the most distinguished brands in the world for cashmere. A multifaceted character, someone who wanted to be an engineer, is a student of philosophy, and the creator of a factory-village, he maintains his company headquarters in the castle of Solimeo, which was restored as part of the village of Corciano, near Perugia, his hometown. Cuccinelli's success – with exports from Europe to Japan and China of 70% of the production, which in 10 years has quadrupled – is connected to the idea of introducing cashmere colors that are different from the usual natural shades of beige and grey, and using distinctive colors. But success is also due to a detailed artisanal attention to manufacturing. A line of refined knitwear (Rivamonti) and a line of trousers and skirts for women (Gunex) have been added to the main line.

❑ 2000, November. Cucinelli acquires 50% of the Saverio Palatella brand. The Autumn-Winter Collection for 2000-2001, presented in Milan, is the result of a double collaboration. Saverio Palatella, who designed the Gentryportofino knitwear line, remains an independent creative director, while Brunello Cucinelli produces the Palatella line through Rivamonti.
❑ 2001, August. The Cucinelli Group has 270 employees and 600 outside agents.
❑ 2002, November. The year ends with a turnover of €62.5 million, an increase of 9.68% compared to the previous year. Also up is the net profit of €3.10 million, compared to €2.65 in 2001, an increase of 9.98%.

Cugnasca Silk factory established by Giuseppe Cugnasca in 1920 and specialized in the manufacture of shawls, hat-veils, handkerchiefs, and fabrics in general. Within 4 years, the weaving mill in Uggiate (Co) would be joined by mills in Como and Paré (Co). Giuseppe's son Giampiero became owner of the company in 1927, and he pursued the opposite policy, concentrating all the production in Como. In 1956, the company passed to the Mantero family who, important figures in the silk industry since 1902, dedicated it mostly to the manufacture of high fashion fabrics for women's clothing in silk, rayon, and nylon. In 1989, Cugnasca was absorbed by Mantero.

Culottes Short pants, or actually a divided skirt, loose-fitting, and comfortable, wide up through the waist. Made of pure silk, they were worn in the 1930s by the most refined women of the time, and since then they have always been in fashion. At the time of the Sun King, on the other hand, culottes were breeches for men at court that went to the knees and were worn with thin silk socks. They would remain unchanged, more or less long and tight, until the early 1800s, when they were replaced by trousers.

Cummings Angela (1944). American goldsmith. Born in Austria, she moved to the U.S. at a very young age. She studied in Perugia and graduated in gemology in Germany. Her first collaboration was in 1968 with Tiffany and then, again with Tiffany, she designed her first Collection in 1972. In 1983, she started her own business and created a line under her name that includes porcelains and silverware. She has a boutique at Bergdorf Goodman in New York. Her designs are available at Bloomingdale's and Neiman Marcus in the U.S., and at Takashimaya in both New York and Tokyo. She has a partnership in Japan with Shiseido.

Cuniolo Gabriella (1945). Italian designer. The daughter of a famous painter, she graduated from the Brera Academy and began as an art teacher But from an early age she had a passion for elegant underwear in the classic style. She abandoned teaching and opened two shops, one in Tortona and the other in Courmayeur. Then she arrived in Milan, where she opened a small shop for elegant and seductive underwear in the fashion quadrilateral. She also offered silk, linen, and cotton embroidered lace nightgowns, including custom-made, as well as petticoats, accessories, and old-fashioned trousseaux. For babies, she had delightful custom-made clothes, plus rompers and small outfits in linen and cotton, embroidered in the most refined style. Household linens weren't lacking: bed-and-bath sets with fancy lace, and embroidered tablecloths in pure linen for important dinners.

(*Marilea Somaré*)

Cuoital A brand of substitute-leather used in Italy during the drive for national self-sufficiency that began in 1935 and during the war years. It was manufactured by Industria Fibre e Cartone and obtained from a mixture of leather scraps, latex, and vulcanized rubber. Competing products were Sapsa, made by Pirelli from ground up leather scrap and rubber latex, and Coriacel, from leather scrap, vegetable fibers, and glue.

Cuprum Fiber obtained from cotton linter and treated with the cuprammonium process. It is produced as a thread and as a raw material. It is non-toxic, non-allergic, and anti-static, and known as "ecologic silk" for its qualities of transpiration and softness. The Cuprum brand is a Bemberg exclusive.

Curiel Raffaella (1943). Italian designer. From her family in Trieste (the atelier owned by Hortense in Palazzo Liberty next to Umberto Saba's bookshop was frequented by the high society of mittel-Europea in the early 1900s) she derived her cosmopolitan taste and a levity tempered by irony. From her uncle Eugenio, an anti-fascist martyr, and from her aunt Grazia, a promoter of the Milanese Casa della Cultura, she inherited a sense of civil and political passion. From her mother Gigliola, a dressmaker in Milan since 1945 and during the 1950s and 1960s an important resource for the rich and elegant ladies of that Italian capital of money, she learned the wisdom of the profession and the difficult art of dressing women in a pleasing way. At first she wanted to be a doctor, but instead, in 1961, Raffaella, nicknamed Lella, designed her first Collection. Since 1970, she has offered a high fashion and prêt-à-porter *griffe*: feminine and balanced lines are typical of her celebrated tailored suits and plissé dresses. For several years she has devoted herself especially to haute couture.

(*Maria Vittoria Carloni*)

❑ 2002, July. The municipality of Rome awards her the Lupa d'Oro prize.
❑ 2002, September. Inspired by Russia

and St. Petersburg, her haute couture Winter Collection is presented at Palazzo Visconti in Milan. It had already been presented in July in Rome at Villa Abamelek on the premises of the Russian Embassy. There were military busbies and cloaks, in silk and precious embroideries. An evening dress, embroidered all over with sequins, reproduced Red Square in Moscow. Some 60% of the turnover comes from exports to the U.S., where she has been doing business for 10 years. Sales were not affected by the downturn, not even after September 11th.
❑ 2002, October. The Milanese designer is the guest of honor and ambassador of the Made in Italy movement in New Delhi, India on the occasion of a two-day celebration dedicated to a half-century of Italian fashion. On October 20th, in Jaipur, she is the guest of her Royal Majesty the Maharani of Jaipur and her daughter Dia, in the Royal Palace that was opened especially in her honor. The designer presented clothes created with antique saris.

Cocktail dress by Raffaella Curiel.

Curiel Castellini Gigliola (1970). She carries the demanding name of her grandmother, who disappeared a year before her birth, and is very much like her mother Lella. In 1997, after graduating in economics from Bocconi University in Milan, she followed in her mother's footsteps as a designer with the *griffe* Gigi by Curiel (using her nickname). Her first Collection, presented in London, where she attended the Central Saint Martin's College of Arts and Design, met with great interest from American buyers. In the following seasons, she confirmed her style: pure lines and great richness of materials, patterns, and colors. Up until her graduation, she had been convinced that her place in the world of fashion was in the role of manager and not of designer.

Cusi Jewellery shop established in Milan in 1886 by Annibale Cusi. The company acquired international fame for its skilled manufacturing and choice of stones. Proof of this can still be found today in the firm's archives which are full of original drawings. In 1915, it was named official supplier to the House of Savoy. Today, Annibale's descendents Ettore, Rinaldo, and Roberto have opened points-of-sale in Milan on via Clerici, Corso Monforte, and via Montenapoleone.

Custo Barcelona A trend that has spread all over the world thanks to the brothers Custo and David Dalmau. The Custo brand was born in the early 1980s and later became Custo Barcelona. Starting in 1996, the Collection has been presented in New York. The printed T-shirt became its symbol when Hollywood celebrities began to wear them in 1997. Some 95% of the production is made up of shirts, a happy combination of innovation and creativity. The Custo brothers began by producing men's shirts and then, in the 1990s, they added women's. The Collection also expanded to include other articles of clothing, such as trousers, dresses, and skirts. They admit to being inspired by surrealist art and by what they see on the streets of Barcelona and New York. They count on a team of graphic designers from Spain and elsewhere. Their manufacturing plants are in Thailand. They work with specially treated and finished combed cotton. *(Estefania Ruilope Ruiz)*

Customizing Habit of personalizing clothes and accessories. In origin it is purely Anglo-Saxon, that is, English and American. A "customized car" is a car modified with accessories according to the owner's preferences. "Custom clothes" and "custom shoes" are made-to-measure clothes and shoes. Customizing belongs, in equal parts, to the atelier tradition as well as to street culture: it ranges from tailor-made suits and high-fashion outfits to punk jackets full of pins, the hand-decorated T-shirts of the Japanese "Ka-gu-ru girls", and the torn jeans of urban youth. Anywhere, in other words, that there is a more or less conscious demand for authenticity and individuality, either aesthetic, cultural, or political. It is not by accident that even mass-produced prêt-à-porter has begun to offer several custom-made lines. These are Collections in which personality becomes something that is expected in advance, in a system that today more and more promotes and sells desire rather than tangible products.

(Antonio Mancinelli)

Cutaway English term. Ceremonial men's suit worn especially by diplomats. It consists of a single-breasted black jacket with a swallow-tail coat, a white shirt and pearl grey waistcoat, and black-and-white striped stove-pipe trousers on a grey ground.

Cutler and Gross English brand of eyewear launched in 1969 with the opening of a boutique in Knightsbridge, London. The objective, subsequently achieved, was to transform the traditional design of eyeglasses so as to give them fashion content. Great success arrived in later years, with the creation and development of a line of sunglasses. The Collection has more than 300 models.

Cyber Atelier in Paris opened in 1921 by Robert Toboul. The Armenian designer Ara Frenkian made his début there. The subsequent launch of a fragrance company (Les Parfums de Paris) was not enough to save it from failure, and Cyber closed in 1930.

Cyberpunk Youth and fashion movement that was more or less spontaneous. In strict tailoring terms, it goes back to 1983, when Westwood and McLaren's Nostalgia of Mup Collection succeeded in influencing a generation of fashion designers, especially Kei Kawakubo, the brilliant heretic at Comme des Garçons, and Yoshi Yamamoto. All that year, and later, it wasn't unusual on the street to see bandages and gauze worn as proud "badges," as signs of survival and indicators of a style to come. This is remembered as the post-atomic style. By definition, cyberpunk style joins cybernetics, a system that studies artificial intelligence from a biological model, and the heritage of punk, with the accent on "heritage" in the sense of "what remains." Then there appeared a group of designers-recyclers who used the useless scraps of a technologically advanced society to form movable "dragster" pieces of sculpture, such as those produced by the members of the *Mutoid Waste Company*, along with body ornaments that emphasized the already-occurred physical and psychic mutations. Obviously, when talking about cyberpunk, one must mention William Burroughs, Bruce Sterling, and J.C. Ballard as the noble fathers of the movement, as well as Guy Debord, who, in the post-situationist version of the phenomenon, expanded his influence to include Clark and Tom Vague, respectively the editors of The Psychedelic Encyclopedia and Vague, the semi-official organs of the movement that were very often visited by enthusiasts looking for more information.

(Maurizio Vetrugno)

D

Daché Lilly (1907-1989). French milliner. After an apprenticeship in Paris with Caroline Reboux, she worked exclusively in New York, opening an atelier in the late 1920s. Up until the 1960s, she was the spokeswoman for European fashion as far as women's hats were concerned: she would buy hat models in Paris and then adjust them according to American taste. In the meantime, she would design her own Collections, looking for inspiration in the hats of far-off African and Asian cultures. She also provided hats for Betty Grable, Marlene Dietrich, and Jacqueline Kennedy. She retired in 1969. She published the books *Talking Through My Hat* (1946) and *Lilly Daché's Glamour Book* (1956).

Daelli Ermanno (1950). Italian designer, born in Florence. He entered the world of fashion as owner of a chain of shops in Florence and Cortina selling clothing and accessories. Through direct contact with the public, Daelli acquired that special sensitivity to trends which allowed him to make his own début in 1985 as a successful designer of women's bags and belts: a casual style of Anglo-Saxon inspiration. In 1990 he organized his first presentation of women's wear in Milan and, six months later, he launched a men's line: metropolitan in inspiration with some ethnic touches and a strong passion for the rigor and essentiality of Japanese design. Afterward, he sold the brand, which continues to be produced, although without any connection to him. Since 1997 he has designed the Ermanno Scervino line.

(*Daniela Fedi*)

❑ 2000, May. Daelli continues to design his Collection for Ermanno Scervino. In 1999, the line has a turnover of 50 billion liras, an increase of 200% over the previous year.
❑ 2002, July. He lands in Southeast Asia thanks to an agreement just concluded with the luxury multinational Joyce, which has some 200 points-of-sale, 50 of them in Hong Kong alone.
❑ 2002, September. The clothing line is expanded by a new line of shoes and bags.
❑ 2003, January. The new men's Autumn-Winter 2003-2004 Collection is presented in the Florence boutique on via Tornabuoni at the time of Pitti Uomo: a Chinese style added to the English dandy of the 1940s, with cuts, shapes and details in military style, and fabrics including velvet, flannel, and tweed as well as nylon and leather. The details are very important, from crocodile-skin frogs to Chinese passementeries. The most precious piece is certainly the dankalia fur, made from a very rare African goat, next to a zebu fur.
❑ 2003, February. The début of the Florentine brand Ermanno Scervino on the Milan runways. The presentation takes place in via della Spiga. It is a collection especially focused on femininity and sensuality, for example with a petticoat-dress manufactured, in the Winter version, in pashmina and woolen lace.

D'Agata Gaetano (1906-1975). Milanese shoemaker, born in Pachino (Siracusa). He began his work as a shoemaker in Rome at Gatto, the workshop of his brother-in-law. He gained more experience during five years in Paris with the famous Perugia and Greco. In 1934, he opened his own shop at via Morone 3, in Milan, where he made ankle boots, evening shoes, laced shoes with a fringe, derby, and loafers, all worked with skill in many kinds of leather, from kidskin to patent leather. From 1969 to 1974, he worked with Emilio Arcando. Among his clients were Tito Carnelutti, all the Falcks, the dandies Massimo Belloni, Leonardo

Vergani, and Luigi Settembrini, and all the elegant salons of Milan. He closed in 1974. (*Marilea Somaré*)

Dagworthy Wendy (1950). English designer. A graduate of the Medway College of Art and Middlesex Polytechnic, Dagworthy launched her ready-to-wear Collection in London in 1972, and quickly developed an international reputation for her casually youthful designs for men and women. Dagworthy often integrated folkloric elements in her clothes, and experimented with contrasting fabrics and patterns, such as ticking and ikat. She closed her company in 1988. She was a member and later director of London Designer Collections, and in September 1998 was named Professor of Fashion at the Royal College of Art.

Dahan Joe. Moroccan designer. He moved to Los Angeles when still a young boy. During the 1980s he designed his first collections, inspired by the New York characters in the film *American Psycho* plus a mix of African atmospheres. Then, the launch of Joe's T-shirts made him famous. In 1991, he threw himself into the jeans business, launching a women's line. But big success arrived in Summer 2000, when Joe's Jeans started to sell like crazy in Manhattan stores. The brand is owned by a large American firm based in Los Angeles with boutiques and showrooms in New York. The jeans have a low waist, legs slightly flared at the ankles, and a tight fit. They are light weight and ideal for Summer, with a vintage look. The Joe's Jeans brand is, little by little, conquering the entire American market.

Dahl-Wolfe Louise (1895-1990). American photographer. Educated in the arts, she became interested in painting as a student at the Art Institute of San Francisco between 1914 and 1922. She attended classes on color given by Rudolph Schaeffer, and these would be of great importance when she distinguished herself in 1937 for being among the first to use warm and elegant colors in fashion photography. In 1927, she began to take commercial photographs for an interior designer, and these recalled the style of the pictorialist photographer Brigman. It was only in 1933 that Vanity Fair first published her landscapes and portraits. In that same year, she opened a studio in New York. She worked for Harper's Bazaar from 1935 up to her retirement in 1958, and distinguished herself for a particularly suggestive taste in composition and ambience for both interiors and exteriors that introduced a modern and dynamic model for the new American woman. (*Roberto Mutti*)

D'Aillencourt Simone (1930). French model. She made her début in 1954 with Hardy Amies. Noticed immediately by the most important fashion magazines, including Vogue, Harper's Bazaar, and Elle, she began a lightning international career. She posed for all the great photographers: Avedon, Bourdin, Hiro, Horvat, Klein, Newton, and Sieff. She retired in 1969 in order to open the model agency Modèle International. A skilled talent scout, she discovered and launched models such as Vibeke Knudsen and Ingmarie Johanson. In the late 1980s, she founded a modeling school.

Daily News Record American magazine devoted to men's clothing, from Fairchild Publications. It is aimed at American retailers and international manufacturers, with news and analysis of the various market segments. Distribution is by subscription only. In 1997, a new tri-weekly edition was launched.

Dainese Sportswear and accessories company established in 1972 by Lino Dainese. It is known mostly for lines dedicated to motorcycle riding and other sports that require protective gear, such as skiing, mountain biking, skating, and hockey. It was among the first to offer motorcycle suits in color, and works with important race car drivers on the testing of new products. One of the most important protections for motorcycle riders came from one of these tests, the back protector. During the 1980s came another important innovation, preformed suits that adjust to a driver's position on the seat. The mid 1990s saw the creation of the "no impact" division, dedicated to sports such as snowboarding and speed skating.

Daks English brand of men's clothing. The traditional English Style is offered in a modern key, with exclusive fabrics made only for the firm. The history of the brand began in 1894 when Simeon Simpson established a company in London offering service that was considered, at the time, extraordinary: custom-made suits in 24 hours. The business was successful to the point that Simeon's son Alexander opened a new company in 1917. The story went on until 1991 when the Simpson family sold the business to the Japanese family Sanyo Seiko, who maintained the brand name and the line without change. The style has, in fact, remained the same up until today, with clothes in velvet, flannel, wool, and alpaca, and a town-country line based on shades of brown, forest green, blueberry, and pewter.

❑ 2002, June. Launch of the Spring-Summer 2003 Collection with a new luxury line for men and women, the Daks Collection. It accompanies the classic Daks Signature line (which goes back to 1894) and the more recent London E1, meant for a younger audience. Timothy Everest, the current creative director, speaks of an accurate and selective choice, both in terms of clientele and points-of-sale (a maximum of 50 single-brand boutiques and kiosks all over the world). Daks opens a showroom on via Vivaio in Milan.

A Daks advertising bill from the 1930s.

Dalal Sandy (1977). American designer. At the age of 21 he astonished the world of New York fashion with his first men's Collection which immediately wons the CFDA award as best young designer for 1998. Celebrated by the best American magazines as a rising star of prêt-à-porter, Sandy Dalal, who was born in New York of Indian origin, learned the art of fashion on the spot. When he was 17, he decided to leave the Parsons School of Design (which is like a university for fashion) and to follow his mother, who worked in the Garment District, a New York neighborhood of textile manufacturers, where he learned the designer's trade. His clothes are designed for a young man, casual with a touch of elegance, or elegant with a touch of madness.

❑ 2002, February. He is appointed creative director of the men's line of International Concept Brand. Up until January, he worked for Genny, where he created the men's line Byblos. The first ICB Collection is expected at the end the year. The ICB women's line is designed by Victor&Rolf.
❑ 2003, January. War and terrorism strongly influence his new collection presented at Milano Moda Uomo: it is a rather bloody presentation, with fake blood which flows into a water basin in the middle of the runway at the end of the event. The clothes show seams that are visible in relief, as symbols of permanent scars.

Dal Co' Alberto (1902-1963). Italian shoemaker, born in Traversetolo (Parma). He learned the trade when still a young boy. Immediately after World War II, supported by his sister Amabile, the mother of the Fontana sisters, he moved to Rome. He opened a store for custom-made shoes and an adjoining workshop at via Crespi 45. In 1951, he moved to Porta Pinciana. He worked with the great *griffes* of Italian fashion of those years, such as Schuberth, Fabiani, Lancetti, and Carosa. Together with the Fontana sisters, he started a line of shoes and bags called *Fontalcò*. Some of the accessories for the trousseau of Maria Pia of Savoy carried this *griffe*. At that time, shoes were manufactured in close contact with the great ateliers: an important dress was matched by shoes and a bag in the same fabric, often decorated with handmade embroidery. Among his clients were Gina Lollobrigida, Soraya, Ava Gardner, Linda Christian, and Audrey Hepburn. He helped spread the fashion for very high heels and stiletto heels on very refined low-cut shoes. He created leather slippers with a grosgrain cockade for Diana Vreeland. Some of his models are shown at the Metropolitan Museum of Art in New York. Among his historic styles is the Paparazzo shoe, created in 1953. It is a low-cut shoe with a slender heel ending in a thinly-plated washer meant to be used against pushy photographers. Today, the store and workshop are at via Vittoria 65 and the tradition is continued by his daughter Nives and his grand-daughter Silvia. (*Bonizza Giordani Aragno*)

Dalla Palma Diego (1950). Italian make-up artist. Called by The New York Times "the prophet of Made in Italy make-up," he branched out over the years from the basic work of his profession and became an image expert for famous and well-known people, both in Italy and abroad. After moving to Milan in 1968, he worked first as a costume and set designer, and then specialized in the art of make-up, becoming famous for the cosmetics he created for many celebrities in the theater and show business. In 1978, in Milan, he opened the Make-Up Studio, an image workshop that was revolutionary in concept, and then created his own line of make-up and facial care products. He wrote six books about make-up and regularly worked with several Italian periodicals. His most-recent project, connected to image and global well-being, concerns accessories.

Dalí Salvador (1904-1989). Spanish artist. Clothes reflect his personality, the duplication of the "Ego," of dreams and desires. Such thinking prompted Dalí to design fashions. The clothes and accessories he designed for Schiaparelli date to 1936. Some of them would be worn by his wife Gala. His creations reproduce the metaphysical and surreal themes of his painting: a white skeleton on a black dress, lobsters painted on an evening dress, ceramic buttons with images of flies on a piece of chocolate, a phone-shaped bag in soft leather and copper; and shoe-, chop-, or inkpot-shaped hats. His pockets were famous, whether real or fake, mouth-shaped and embroidered on a jacket. Same for the drawer-pockets on a tailored suit that have precise references to the drawings and paintings of the period. In 1937, he designed, again with Schiaparelli, a jewelled mermaid. With Folco di Verdura, a famous jewellery designer, he created necklaces in unusual shapes such as an owl, a spider in its cobweb and a St. Sebastian. In 1938, at the International Exhibition of Surrealism in Paris, he presented a mannequin covered in teaspoons. His second jewellery Collection for Schiaparelli came out in 1949. Among the noteworthy pieces was a heart-shaped ruby on which was mounted a crown that, thanks to a small motor, imitated a heartbeat. In 1955, the artists designed 20 pieces of jewellery in gold, rubies, and emeralds that reproduced some of his paintings: an *Atavistic Wound* brooch, a *Venous Hand* box, and a *Light of Jesus Christ* crucifix. In 1965, he designed a swimwear Collection with surrealistic breasts applied on the back. (*Cloe Piccoli*)

Damask A diapered fabric whose effect is obtained through bright patterns on a dull background with geometric and floral motifs. Chinese in origin, it came by way of India and Persia to Damascus, which in the Middle Ages was a very important textile trading center. Damask is always plain-dyed, while damasked fabrics are worked as damask but with threads of different colors, which, besides the chiaroscuro, shiny-opaque effect, create a contrast of colors.

Damiani Italian jewelers. The tradition began in 1924 with Enrico Grassi Damiani, favorite jeweler to the noble families of Valenza Po, the center of the Italian goldsmith tradition. From father to son, the art evolved with a focus on white gold, as the princely metal of the Collections. After a time, the firm became a corporation. It has received several De Beers Diamonds International Awards, which are the Oscars for jewellery. During the 1990s, the advertising spokesperson of the *griffe* was Isabella Rossellini.

❑ 2002, April. The Damiani Manufacturing Company, led by Simone Rizzetto and his brother Christian,

Salvador Dalí. Cover of Vogue America, June 1939 (from *Art fashion*, edited by Germano Celant, Luigi Settembrini, and Ingrid Sischy. Biennial of Florence 1996, Skira).

receives the ISO 9001 quality certification. This certification, recognized at national and international levels, recognizes the quality of precious metals, gems, and pearls selected by expert gemologists according to the place of origin, manufacture, and finishing of the jewellery.

❑ 2002, October. With 130 linear feet of shop windows and two floors at the corner of via Montenapoleone and via Sant'Andrea in Milan, a new Damiani store is opened. This store follows the concept of other stores already opened abroad in Tokyo, Berlin, Dubai, and Honolulu. The project is by the architect Antonio Citterio. Soon there are four stores in Milan, with a total of 25 boutiques all over the world.

❑ 2002, October. After several failed negotiations, the Damiani Group acquires a significant minority stake in the Pomellato Group. The vice president and designer of Damiani, Silvia Damiani, declares her strong confidence in the decades-long experience of Giuseppe Rabolini, the president of Pomellato, whose turnover is about €55 million. For its part, Damiani closes the year 2001 with a turnover of €219 million and profits of €3.1 million. In 2002, investments remain steady at €36 million.

❑ 2002, November. Damiani enters the watch industry. The men's watch Ego Oversize, manufactured in Switzerland, is entirely designed by the *griffe*'s style department. There are three versions with a total of seven models.

❑ 2003, February. Damiani opens two new stores, in Kiev and Moscow.

❑ 2003, May. Some scenes of the soap opera *The Bold and The Beautiful* are shot in Portofino. For the occasion, during a presentation, the actors and personalities show off Damiani watches and jewellery.

❑ 2003, June. The opening in Paris of the international exhibit *Diamonds and the Power of Love*, organized by Diamond Trading Company. There are unique pieces from the most important international jewellers. Damiani presents the Chakra necklace, a two-section cascade of diamonds symbolizing the union between man and woman. The firm opens a new boutique on Place Vendôme. In the boutique is an exhibit of unique pieces by Damiani that have received the De Beers Diamonds International Award, which is the prestigious Oscar for jewellery, and for which Damiani holds the world record, receiving it 18 times. The Damiani group is owned entirely by the family, now in its third generation.

❑ 2004, December. The firm celebrates 80 years of prestige in the world of jewellry with an exhibition. On display are 8 exclusive and unique pieces, including a necklace composed of 1,370 diamonds with 100 carats.

❑ 2005. After ending the previous year with revenue of €180 million, Guido Grassi Damiani, the general manager of the group, talks about the future with an eye on exports and aims at increasing the turnover, of which 80% presently comes from the Italian market.

D'Amico Antonio (1959). His interest in fashion came from his mother, who was a dressmaker. The most important meeting of his life was with Gianni Versace, in whose firm he worked for 13 years up until Versace's death, attending to the design of theater costumes (he worked with Maurice Béjart, Bob Wilson, William Forsythe, and Arnaldo Pomodoro), of the Istante and Versace Sport lines, and of licensing. In 1992, he worked with Versace on the image of The One, Elton John's world tour. In 1998, in partnership with Massimo Leotti, he created the Antonio D'Amico company, offering casual prêt-à-porter for men and women, knitwear, shoes, and accessories.

Dana Buchman American house of women's wear named after its designer, Dana Buchman, a native of Memphis, Tennessee. After graduating from Brown University and attending the Rode Island School of Design, she presented her first Collection of women's wear for work and evening in 1987. Today, she has 5 lines, all known for important fabrics and very precise finishing. The designer also creates eye glasses and accessories. The house is part of the Liz Claiborne group.

Danaud Xavier French brand established at the end of the 1950s as part of the Duchier company (established in 1910 in Annonay) in order to offer a high-level shoe Collection suitable to the the *maison*'s high-fashion clothes. In 1965, 50% of the company was acquired by Charles Jourdan who, in the meanwhile, concluded an agreement with Pierre Cardin for the manufacture and distribution of women's shoes. For a certain time, the Danaud Collection was designed by Robert Clergerie. In 1979, Charles Jourdan completed the acquisition of the brand and the company and then, in 1992, sold them to Yves Desfarges.

D'Ancona Laura (1965). Italian designer, a researcher and fan of vintage. Owner of the design studio Ld'ALab, she also works as a consultant in the fields of clothing and accessories, and teaches at the European Institute of Design, the IED. Born in Rome, after her classical high school studies, she graduated at the top of her class and received a degree in Style and Fashion from the European Institute of Design in Rome (advanced 4-year course) in 1988. She then began a five-year apprenticeship in a design office, where she worked on brands specialized in shirts and jackets, with a preference for the casual and the world of sport. She immediately developed her passion for vintage and her interest for street style in general, traveling in Italy and abroad in search of and buying archival pieces. In 1993, she opened her own design studio and, with the help of a team of collaborators, became a consultant for brands and companies such as Ferretti Studio, Gattinoni, Fendissime, Gas, and Cotton Belt. In 1998, she created, in partnership with the brand A.n.g.e.l.o. of Lugo di Romagna, owner of the largest Italian second-hand clothing archive, a basic Collection of vintage clothes. At the moment, she designs, for the emerging brand Panepinto of Milan, a line focused on knitwear and on small, fanciful, precious, ornate pieces. For the Soffiantini Group of Brescia, she designs the Kiltie line, which is a niche Collection of very high quality that is trendy in its lines, details, and subtle content. (*Maria Vittoria Alfonsi*)

Danes Robert (1961). American designer, specialized in evening clothes. He started by designing men's lines. A graduate of Yale, he moved to New York in 1989 and, in a Chinatown basement, designed his first women's Collection. He presented his clothes for the first time in 1993, enjoying excellent success that allowed him to open a showroom in Soho. His clothes, which enchant Hollywood divas, are characterized by precious fabrics (chiffon, satin, silk) combined with geometric patterns inspired by art and contemporary architecture. His Collection for Winter 1999 evoked the sculpture of Richard Serra and the architecture of Frank Gehry. (*Manuela Parrino*)

Danner Michael (1967). German photographer. In 1995, he moved to England where he studied photography at Brighton University up until 1997. He curates exhibits and photographic events and often presents his own work in both collective and solo exhibits in galleries and important English museums. His photos on fashion and the youth culture, published in Independent on Sunday, the Sunday Telegraph, Spex, Zeit Magazine, Der Spiegel, Suddeuschte Zeitung, and the British Journal of Photography, are always shot in an urban environment.

D'Annunzio Gabriele (1863-1938). Poet, writer, and dramatist. He was one of the most elegant men of Italy, a sort of national Beau Brummel. This was discovered in 1988, when suits, coats, ties, waistcoats, pajamas, nightgowns, spats, underwear, riding outfits, raincoats, hats, handkerchiefs, gloves, starched collars, white piqué scarves to be worn around the neck, a bear skin fur, and suspenders were all taken from the closet of his last home for the exhibit *D'Annunzio's Wardrobe*, organized for Pitti Uomo by Annamaria Andreoli, president of the Fondazione Il Vittoriale degli Italiani. This wardrobe is the most complete document concerning men's fashion in Italy from the late 1800s to the first decades of the 1900s. The labels on those garments represent the very best of those years as to tailoring workshops (De Nicola and Petroni in Naples, Prandoni in Milan); shirt makers (Bonaldi in Venice, Dalmasso in Florence); shoemakers (Quinté in Milan, Montelatici & Volpi in Florence); and boutiques (Pozzi in Milan, Salvatore Morziello in Naples).

When, in 1895, he embarked on the yacht *Fantasia*, owned by Edoardo Scarfoglio, the director of Il Mattino of Naples, for a cruise to Greece, D'Annunzio neatly listed what he was to take on board: "Iron grey suit, black-and-white check suit, brown suit with tait, light brown shirt, three white flannel suits, black tait, light pants, smoking jacket, six white waistcoats." He would say about himself: "I am an animal of luxury." And because of his voracity for luxury he would pile up such a quantity of debt that he was forced to leave Italy in flight from creditors. But his taste and his eye for fashion helped him in his job as a reporter when, in Rome as a young man, he earned his living as a journalist, signing his pieces as Duca Minimo: "Nothing is more voluptuous, in a refined way, than an otter fur that has already been used for a certain period of time." His novel *Pleasure* is full of fashion details. If he had to buy a gift for a woman, he would ask the dressmaker Marta Palmer (it was the late 1920s) to put a label that read *Gabriel Nuntius Vestiarius Fecit* on the dress or cloak. And he was very precise in his requests: "I'd like a large cloak for a very tall lady. I'd like it black, loose, light, with a big bunch of red roses (a very intense color), secretly embroidered on the reverse side....-The roses must be tied with a gold ribbon and a big flourish. Something rich, violent, and done secretly." When, in the mid 1930s, the dressmaker Biki offered him some blouses for the pianist Luisa Baccara, his last partner, he wrote her: "Admiring not in a lifeless shop window but in vital movement the folds, the gaps, the solid fabric and the airy lace, the seams and hems, they have appeared to me as elements of a precise rhythm and a vague unknown, and thus, of poetry."

D'Annunzio Maria Grazia (1956). Journalist. She has been director of Glamour. She owes her career in journalism to Franca Sozzani who, in 1980, asked her to work at Lei. She thus began a collaboration with Condé Nast which went on to include some of their other magazines as well. In 1986, she became chief correspondent at Lei, and in 1988 she was at Vogue Italy as chief editor and later as deputy manager. In 1992, she became director of Glamour, which she left in 1997. At present, she works in New York for the Condé Nast Group.

Dante Prini Italian company that designs, manufactures, and markets silk fabrics for ties on an international level. It works with all the most important *griffes* in the field, and exports 80% of its production. The design work is done in Como and at the subsidiary offices in New York and London. The manufacturing is in Italy. Some of the printing is done in China through a joint venture agreement. Established in 1936 by Dante Prini and developed by his son Enrico, in 1997 the company passed under the joint control of the Miroglio textile group, the Mediocredito Lombardo bank, and the employees.

Dark An urban style, spontaneous in character, dating back to the early 1980s. Black, just black, with some touches of red, this was the only color for this kind of fashion. The main elements of dark clothing are a shaved head dyed black or red, dark and heavy make-up, and lace with studs and crosses.

Darphin Line of high quality cosmetic products. The headquarters is in Place Vendôme, Paris. All the crèmes are still handmade, as the company's founder, the dermatologist Pierre Darphin, began to do in 1958. After his death in 1991, the business passed into the hands of the Benet family, who have continued the tradition.

Dart Term used to describe a very small pleat sewn in relief on the surface of a fabric. It is used to underline the silhouette of a garment, to shape a collar, to outline a shirt. It is decorative and tailored at the same time.

Daryl K American brand of prêt-à-porter created by Daryl Kerrigan. A native of Dublin but a New Yorker by adoption, she opened a boutique in the East Village in Manhattan together with her Irish fiancé Paul Leonard in 1991. In 1992, she designed Joe Pesci's wardrobe for the film *My Cousin Vinny*. In 1997, Kerrigan launched her second line, K-189. Her clothes are inspired by the street and by punk. She often uses original materials, such as the plasticized cloth of parachutes.

❑ 2002, September. After a year of negotiations, the designer is again in possession of her brand, buying it back from Pegasus Appareil. The two brands Daryl K and K-189 had been acquired by them (at the time the Lieber Group) in April 2000. Manufacturing had stopped just one year later, and the two boutiques in New York and Los Angeles closed. The brand would be available at Henri Bendel, sponsored by the Style Section of the New York Times, and was wanted at any cost by the director Ed Burstell, who for years had been a passionate fan of the Irish designer. In 1996, Daryl Kerrigan received the *CDFA Perry Ellis Award* as best woman's fashion designer in the U.S.

Datti Men's tailoring shop in Rome, established after a long apprenticeship by Arocle Datti in 1919. He dressed many great names, from Totò to Eisenhower. He was famous for his cutting of tails and suits. In 1957, he was joined by his son Massimo, only 20, who gave a new stamp to the atelier. In 1959, they participated in the U.S. men's high fashion Collection presentations, winning the attention of critics. In 1974, Massimo Datti opened a boutique on via Bocca di Leone in Rome which is still active.

Daumas Jean-Rémy (1951). French designer who mixes tributes haute couture with vinyl, synthetic furs, and acid colors. Up until the Summer of 1990, when he retired, his Collections represented moments of play and of astonishing taste, with clothes created in contrasting materials such as plastic and tulle, taffeta or sequins with polystyrene and artificial resin. Born in Cannes, he moved to Paris when not yet 20. His first job was at Patou. He then went to Gaultier as an assistant model maker for Tarlazzi. In 1979, one year after opening his own fashion house, he presented with great success his first Collection in the hall of the Théâtre des Champs-Elysées.

D'Avenza Manufacturer of men's wear. Its name comes from the village near Carrara where the company was established in 1957 by the Ackermann family, which had behind it a long tradition of tailoring and of ateliers in New York. In 1994, it was acquired by the Cecchi family from Prato, a textile dynasty that owned the firm Rifinizioni Santo Stefano. The business is directed by Catia Cruciani who, supported by the master cutter Ralph Anania, manufactures clothes that are well tailored and have a strong fashion content. Every garment requires 268 manufacturing steps and 70% of these are done by hand. Every buttonhole is hand-finished with about 70 double-knot stitches. There are 15 steps just to make a collar. Besides Italy, the product sells well in Japan and the U.S.

David Jean-Louis (1934). French hairdresser. Born in Grasse, the son and grandchild of hairdressers, he became first hairstylist at Carita-Alexandre at the age of 21. In 1960, he started his own business, on Avenue de Wagram in Paris. Nine years later, in combination with the photographs of Alice Spring, he was behind the success of the first layered haircut. In the 1980s, he created the androgenic look. In the decade that followed, he offered women a new technique: extreme rapidity of execution and long-lasting wavy hair. Today he heads an important network of franchised hairdressers, with 950 worldwide by 1996, in France, Switzerland, Benelux, Italy, Spain, Poland, Brazil, and the U.S.

David Burnett Line of classic clothing for men produced by Luca's, a company near Brescia with production plants in Gambara. Directed by the Boglioli family, it represents the modern evolution of a tailoring and artisanal project started in the early 1900s by the head of the family Piero and continued by his son Giuseppe. In 1972, Mario Bogioli, Piero's grandson, created the Luca's brand, of which David Burnett is one of three manufactured lines together with Boglioli Italia and Boglioli Sartoria. In mid 1974, the family opened the plant in Gambara, between Brescia and Cremona, and it would eventually employ about 220 people. Today, Burnett suits are distributed throughout Italy, and there is a branch in the Benelux countries, thanks to Pallas Agencies of Antwerp. (*Pierangelo Mastantuono*)

Davide Cenci Boutique in Rome that is a symbol of male elegance, established by Davide Cenci in 1926, with a shop for custom-made shirts on via Campo Marzio. Benedetto Croce was one of the first clients. The philosopher would request soft collars with a low neckband in order to feel comfortable while bent over his books. Sixty years later, a frequent customer at the salon on via Campo Marzio would be Sandro Pertini, president of Italy. Cenci was one of the first to offer ties cut from a roll of fabric chosen by the customer. He also launched the raincoat *Watro*, which was particularly lightweight. Since 1947, the boutique has had a women's department, offering mainly tailored suits and cashmere sweaters. A constant feature is the firm's attention to British fashion, both traditional and casual. During the 1980s, the third generation of the family brought the firm to New York, opening a showroom on Madison Avenue. Starting in 1992, they offered a Davide Cenci line specialized in shirts, jackets, and coats. A boutique was also opened in Milan, on via Manzoni.

Davidson Bruce (1933). American photographer. He bought a camera at the age of 15 and began to take photographs in the style of "street photography" and reportage. After studying at Yale's Design School and at the Rochester Institute of Technology, he purchased a Leica and went to work for Life magazine covering sports. In 1958, he joined the Magnum agency. His work included reportage about life in the circus, about a New York street gang (1959, published in 1999 under the title *Brooklyn Gang* by the International Center of Photography), about Harlem's black community (1966, published and exhibited in 1970 under the title *East 100th Street* by the Museum of Modern Art in New York), about poor immigrants, and about the New York subway. As often happens with photo reporters, he became interested in the world of fashion for just a short period: he was hired by Vogue in 1961 and worked there for three years.

Davies Liz. Designer and artistic director of the Next department stores in England, which opened in 1986 as part of the mini department stores Hepworths & Son. She is inspired by fashion trends, although maintaining a certain simplicity and a precise cut in the tailoring. She avails herself of the collaboration and suggestions of her shop assistants. Before working at Next, she designed linens, in acrylic and rayon fibers, for Courtaulds, the factory which invented the Courtelle fiber, which is light and soft, and often used in linens and homewear.

Dawson International British textile group with headquarters in Edinburgh. It is specialized in carded yarns such as cashmere and lambswool. It also manufactures knitwear and artificial furs. It strengthened its position in the international market by reducing the price of its spun cashmere. It also produces material for furnishings. In the late 1900s it employed almost 12,000 people.

❑ 2002, February. The firm launches a new brand called Dawson Cashmere Company. It is aimed at a middle section of the market and manufactured in China.

❑ 2002, September. Alfredo Canessa is appointed president of Ballantyne, which is controlled by the Dawson Group, and the artistic director is Massimo Alba. The goal is to relaunch the historic brand of knitwear. An international team of young emerging designers works on the new image and the début is at Pitti Uomo in January 2003. The operating headquarters are in Milan, and production is in Scotland. Yarns are provided by another Dawson company, Todd & Duncan.

Day Corinne (1972). English photographer. She left school at the age of 16 and was noticed in 1989 for a series of pictures using her friends as models and portraying them through a conspiratorial and inside look at the world she depicts. A typical representative of the new English photography, she publishes in independent magazines devoted to the youth culture.

Dazed and Confused English magazine devoted to music and fashion launched in 1994 to reach a young, active public wanting to be informed about the latest trends. It is tri-dimensionally conceived: besides a paper version, it has a web-site and an art gallery in London where photo exhibits are held.

Other projects include TV programs, book publishing, music CDs and the organization of various events around the world. The idea is to find a new and alternative way to do journalism.

DEA "Monthly magazine of fashion" published in Milan from November 1933 to September 1948, with a two-year break near the end of World War II, by Giorgio Pierotti Cei, who also published Allegri Bimbi and Almanacco della Casa. It was born as a sort of catalogue of high fashion Paris styles for the well-off Italian bourgeoisie and aristocracy of the 1920s and 1930s. It had great drawings by Boccasile, Brunetta, Dudovich, Edvi, Lucile, Grau, Menni, and Pica, and photos with short captions. Then it had recipes, letters to the editor, and columns on good manners, beauty, bridge, and furnishings signed by, among others, Dino Falconi, Angelo Frattini, Salvator Gotta, and Rina Simonetta. Beginning in 1935 there was a good deal of interference from the Fascist regime urging sobriety, a spirit of sacrifice and discipline, and the praise of Italian products. Transformed by Lia Pierotti Cei, it lost its elitist character and in October 1940 defined itself as "the Magazine of the Italian Fascist family," publishing articles translated into German, Hungarian, and Spanish. In January 1948 it was renamed Fortuna.

(*Stefano Grassi*)

Drawing by Marcello Dudovich for Dea, 1934 (from *Lusso e Anarchia* by Natalia Aspesi, Rizzoli, 1982).

De Alvarez Lilli (1905). Number two tennis player in the world between 1926 and 1928, she was the first to wear, under a skirt, pagoda-shaped trousers in tulle (white, of course), at Wimbledon. This kind of eccentricity, together with her lively chic, earned her the nickname of the Wonderful Señorita.

(*Gianni Clerici*)

Dealy Fiona. English designer. After studying at Lancaster Polytechnic and the Saint Martin's School of Art, she went to work for Zwei, a German prêt-à-porter firm. In close collaboration with another designer, the German Gioia Marcovic, she created a very feminine and sexy Collection for Zwei in the early 1980s. As a result, they both become very famous all over the world.

Dean James (1931-1955). American actor. A myth for an entire generation, he established, in the wake of Marlon Brando, a style of informal clothing made up of jeans, T-shirt, and jacket. His career was very short and he became a celebrity with just three films, all shot in 1955, the year in which he lost his life in a car accident. He was discovered on Broadway by Elia Kazan while performing in a stage adaptation of *The Immoralist* by André Gide. Shortly after, the director chose him for the main character in his movie *East of Eden* (1955), in the role of a sensitive and tormented teenager. Immediately after, came the film that would create the myth: *Rebel Without A Cause* (1955). Finally, with *The Giant* (1955), presented in theaters after his tragic death, came the confirmation of his undisputed cult status.

De Antonis Pasquale (1908-2001). Italian photographer, born in Teramo. He began to take photographs at an early age, documenting the religious celebrations and the folklore of rural Abruzzi. He moved to Rome in 1937 to attend the Experimental Center of Cinematography along with Germi, Antonio, and others. After World War II, he was one of the first photographers to become interested in movie sets, theatrical premieres, fashion runways, and popular celebrations. A friend of painters such as Afro, Cagli, and Guttuso, he took part in the artistic life of the gallery L'Obelisco, where his works were often exhibited between 1951 and 1957. In 1964, as a stage photographer, he began a collaboration with Luchino Visconti that would last a decade. He worked with Irene Brin from the end of World War II up until 1965, documenting the birth and success of Italian high fashion. Still famous is his last fashion reportage on the clothes of Marucelli, photographed for the Roman premiere of the film *2001: A Space Odyssey*. In the theater, he worked with directors such as Strehler, Squarzina, and the young Ronconi. In the essay "Fotografia di Moda negli anni Cinquanta in Italia" for the book *La Moda Italiana* (Electa, 1987), Paolo Barbaro wrote: "In the photos of De Antonis one perceives continuous references to different fields of expression, especially to painting, which remains a constant point of reference in his work; these are references that influence the general composition, as in images in an impressionist style by Carosa and Antonelli, until there is a direct quote, often tinged with a refined irony that is always very pertinent."

De Beers Established in 1888 in South Africa, it is today the world's largest company engaged in the extraction and marketing of raw diamonds. In fact, in its Botswana, Namibia, and Tanzania mines, owned in partnership with the governments of those countries, it produces more than 40% of the diamonds that are on the world market. Extraction occurs in different types of mines: open air, subterranean, on flood plain, coastal, and under water. The search for new mines occurs on six continents. The De Beers' Snap Lake project, which opened in 2000 and is named after the lake in the Northwest Territories of Canada, will lead to the creation of the first Canadian diamond mine. The Diamond Trading Company (DTC), which is part of the De Beers Group and located in London, selects, appraises, and sells about two thirds of the world's annual raw supplies of diamonds. During the 1960s, it supported advertising and promotion campaigns all over the world. This brought benefits to diamond producers, jewellery companies, retailers, and, in the final analysis, consumers. On January 16th 2001, De Beers Group and LVMH announced an agreement providing for the creation of the company De Beers LV. It was given full autonomy in management and operations in order to test and develop the "consumer brand" potential of the name De Beers in the global market.

(*Alessandra Quattordio*)

De Benedetti Alessandro (1970). Designer, born in Genoa. He attended the Marangoni Institute of Milan, and then began to work for Italian and foreign designers. This was his apprenticeship. In 1990, he collaborated with Saverio Patella on his knitwear Collections. In 1992, abandoning the traditional path of fashion, he moved to Australia, where he designed the George Cross Sportswear Collections. Back in Italy in 1994, he designed for Martino Midali. In 1995, he worked for Thierry Mugler in Paris, participating in the organization of the *maison*'s 20th anniversary. Since 1997, he has designed his own Collection, offering woman's prêt-à-porter characterized by a strong concept and a tailored cut. He still continues his collaboration with Saverio Patella and Thierry Mugler.

(*Sofia Catalano*)

❑ 2004, September. He is appointed creative director of the women's Collections of the Exté brand by It Holding.
❑ 2005, February. The Gentex group, specialized in the textile-clothing field, acquires 51% of the brand.
❑ 2005, June. The designer decides to launch a second line in a joint venture with Gentex. The début is expected for September.

De Brecco Brand of ready-to-wear. It is an acronym of the names Filippo Bruno, from Padua (1971), and Simone De Checco, from Milan (1978). They launched their *griffe* of men's wear in 1998, making their début in the U.S., where Filippo was attending the Hollywood Film Institute and Simone was studying at the Fashion Design Institute of California. In February 1999, they established De Brecco Inc., an Italo-American joint venture in which the two Italians have an American partner, who also distributes their Collections in California. Since February 2000, the brand has also had a women's line, which is presented at Milano Collezioni.

(*Laura Salza*)

Decadent Glam A movement and a spontaneous fashion trend. In early 1971, when

Marc Bohan, during an appearance on Top of the Pops, decided to allow the make-up artists to apply some glitter to his eyes and cheeks, he surely didn't realize that he would bring back for an entire new generation of teenagers a long tradition of outrageous behavior and transvestitism. This is a story that, involving creatures dear to Jack Smith and Andy Warhol, goes back to the sources of sexual ambiguity, an obvious device with Mae West and even further back. Even Klossowski's *The Roman Ladies* are mentioned to legitimize a need to appear as something different from one's own self, in order to find one's own authenticity in that other, in the sense of the authentic Greek etymon: "A person acting for oneself." Yet, around 1970, *glam rock* was there, and this time rock stars acted as designers for a generation too young to remember Beatlemania and wanting to give a theatrical sense to their own existence. Thus Bohan and David Bowie are the interpreters of androgyny in a cosmic and alien sense with space suits in satin with sequins and an ostrich boa. Iggy Pop, with bare chest, lamé gloves, and a dog collar, embodied the perfect protopunk. Bryan Ferry and Roxy Music, helped by Anthony Price, gathered together several periods of Hollywood glamour. The brothers Ron and Russell Mall, of Sparks, offered themselves as an amphetamine parody-combination of Charlie Chaplin, Judy Garland, and the New York Dolls in women's clothing both on-stage and off. It should also be remembered that for Bowie's 1973 tour of Japan promoting his album *Aladini Sane*, Kansai Yamamoto designed 9 costumes inspired by traditional Kabuki theater. And obviously, Ossie Clark and Anthony Price designed for rock stars and acquaintances with a lively sense of glam-glitter way before the advent of the phenomenon. Also to be noted is the charming and prevalent obsession over Berlin in the years of the Weimar Republic, explicit in Bob Fosse's 1972 film *Cabaret* with Joel Grey and Liza Minelli, often cited as an influence on the Bromley Contingent, a direct heir of glam. (*Maurizio Vetrugno*)

Decadent-New Romantic A youth movement, a lifestyle, and a style of clothing. New Romantic, Cult With No Name, Thermidoriens (used by the French), Blitzkids: these are just a few names for the movement that started in London in 1978 and '79 and exploded the following year. There were several "punks" in that first moment, such as Marco Pirroni, Chris Sullivan, and the members of the Bromley Contingent, as well as Jordan and Debbie (models and assistants to Westwood and McLaren through the various incarnations of their shop), who had long experience as "natural" designers and who, before the outside world realized that the era of punk was over, gave life to a new vortex of surrealism and experimentation. The Bowie Nights, conceived by Steve Strange and Rusty Egan, were started. Steve Jones was known by everyone as the Mad Hatter, with creations worthy of Dalí's work for Schiaparelli. Vivienne Westwood created a pirate Collection for her new protégés, Bow Wow Wow. And the golden youth of London seem to have been, at that point, somewhat pirate-like in style. Nothing seems excessive: Macaronis ladies of the 1700s, pirates, futurism with reference to the costumes that Thais Galitzy wore in the films of Anton Giulio Bragaglia, new glitterati (with make-up) and new zoot-suiters; in short, anything at all as long as it is stylized and without immediate allusion to the external world. It was right at that moment that the fragmentation of street style, still in fashion at the end of the 20th century, began. Contrary to most previous fashions, the neo-romantics didn't dictate any prescribed wardrobe. There was no tool kit, except the certainty of living in a sort of interregnum where the only norm was obedience to one's ghosts.

De Carlis Fur boutique in Rome. It was opened in 1972 by the two current owners, Carla and Rodolfo De Carlis, who began in a small workshop on via Vittoria, a street of small artisans, cabinet makers, restorers, goldsmiths, and watchmakers. At that time, the business premises were on the second floor of a historic building from the 1800s which during the 1840s was occupied by the most luxurious brothel in Rome. The building, subsequently purchased by De Carlis, has been completely restored and transformed into a mega-store and workshop. With the opening of boutiques which have replaced the old artisan shops, via Vittoria has become a shopping street. And the De

Carlis firm has changed its image. After twenty years of selling just furs, they now offer knitwear, cashmere coats, leather clothing, and accessories. The new manufacturing techniques produce, among other things, ultra-light mini skirts, eel waistcoats with trimmed in fox, sheepskin jackets transformed into astrakhans. The furs are treated, shaved, knitted, and used for the insides of cashmere and leather garments.
(*Gabriella Gregorietti*)

De Clercq Diane (1946). Belgian designer. She is "the one with the stripes": never identical, in geometric shapes and infinite colors, in knitwear, pullovers, and ties. She lived in Côte d'Azur as a child and adolescent, and remembers "I would paint on everything I saw and touched: pieces of cloth, doors, walls, materials, and fabrics." At the age of 17, she enrolled in the School of Decorative Arts in Nice. She traveled and decided to stop in Rome, in order to grow roots there, "because Rome is pink and made for affection." Together with a group of artisan women from Umbria, she created sweater Collections using precious and natural materials. Since 1972, she has been supported for an independent line by her sister Evelyne, and the name of the brand doubled: De Clercq-De Clercq. The Collections are sold in very small numbers in several countries, including France, the U.S., and Japan.

Décolleté A term which entered the French language in the 1700s and has everywhere since then indicated the deep, generous neckline of a bodice, a blouse, or, above all, a dress. A new word was needed to differentiate the term décolleté from the term *encolure*, which was used to define the different shapes of a neckline. In the early 1700s, the so-called *robe à la française* involved a generally square-shaped décolleté, deep almost to half bust, although interrupted by a flat bow (a *parfait*). In the century that followed, the décolleté, reduced and lowered and finally disappearing into the sleeves of evening dresses, offered the eyes a view of the completely bare shoulders of a woman forced, during daylight hours, to wear more chaste clothing. In recent times, nude fashion has gone far beyond its traditional reference to Empire Style dresses and seductive sirens. There is also a type of shoe called décolleté that is closed but tapered and, indeed, low-cut at the ankles. In the mid 1800s it had a large and medium-height heel, but during the 1930s would become decidedly elegant, with a high heel for afternoon and evening. Very much in fashion for high heels of the 1960s, the "décolleté" is at center stage in the latest fashion Collections. (*Lucia Sollazzo*)

Deconstructionism A term that during the 1990s indicated a group of designers whose garments, with visible hems and pale colors, are considered the most intellectual expression of grunge style, a way of dressing that came from a culture of low-cost clothing shops. Deconstructionists, breaking up the various components of fashion in order to later remix them, often without following the traditional logic of shapes, oblige us to reconsider individual pieces of clothing and how to wear them. These designers have a marked artistic inclination to treat their creations as a surface on which to make dye tests. Even if the critics have strongly rejected this artistic expression, expressly calling it ugly and unattractive, there remains the undeniable influence that this style would have on the following phenomenon of garment restructuring.

Dedeyan Claire (1959). French designer. She has designed Collections for the French department stores Printemps and Prisunic, and the Foxton line for Coin in Italy. A graduate in classics from the Sorbonne, at first she worked for several companies, including Mic Mac and Lison Bonfils. She then launched her own brand, characterized by a young and fresh style that was at the same time refined and enriched with retro touches. Thanks to her exuberant creativity, she has won several contests and received many awards, including the *Prix d'Honneur du Défi* (Committee for the Development and Promotion of Textiles and Clothing), and she participated in the second European Fashion Show.

De Donno Manufacturer of hats and berets, classic and casual, in high quality fabrics. The firm opened in 1937 and quickly established its products on the market. Despite its growth in size, the company continues to give great care to quality. The manufacturing process is a wise mix of modern and ancient techniques. The most sophisticated methods of cutting fabric are used right alongside the most traditional instruments of steam ironing, with maximum respect for the artisan's work. In this way, the firm produces both the most classic hats and berets in soft pure wool fabrics such as alpaca and cashmere and the most modern and casual caps in distinctive fabrics and precious leather, truly unique fashion pieces in the Made in Italy tradition. The firm's patient search for fabrics and details and the constant updating of styles are a distinguishing trait of the Collections, which are by now known in Italy and abroad. The factory has a plant in Maglie (Lecce) and exports principally to other countries in Europe.

Dé d'Or The Golden Thimble is the French high fashion award created in 1976 by the journalist Pierre Yves Guillen. Until January 1994, it was given twice a year, at the end of every Collection. Among the winners have been Madame Grés (July 1976), Cardin (January 1977, January 1979), Givenchy (July 1978), Ungaro (January 1980, July 1981), Laroche (July 1985), Lacroix (January 1986 and January 1988), Lagerfeld for Chanel (July 1986), Ferré for Dior (July 1989), Rabanne (January 1990), and Montana for Lanvin (July 1990 and January 1991). Since 1993 it has been called *Dé d'Or Européen de la Mode* and in July 1993 was given to Lauren. In 1994 it was given to Mortensen for Scherrer.

Dee Brett (1964). English photographer. He studied fine arts at Sheffield Polytechnic from 1986 to 1990 and then devoted himself to photography, film making, and exhibitions. He has participated in collective shows and published pictures describing fashion and the lifestyles of young people in magazines such as i-D. He lives and works in London.

De Filippi Fernando (1940). Italian artist. A native of Puglia, he lives and works in Milan. A conceptual artists, he brings to his jewellery, which must be considered sculpture in miniature, the same elements present in his paintings and installations. The *Giano* tie pin, made in gold in just 30 copies, and the *Colonna* brooch in gold and enamel, are from the 1970s. References to classicism, architecture, temples, pediments, and theaters return especially in his jewellery of the 1990s, a period in which De Filippi was working on paintings inspired by the classics but with a clear conceptual content. The artist's research has pushed itself forward even into the field of printed fabrics. Among other things, he designed a printed foulard for the Grossetti Gallery of Milan in 1974.

De Foer Hans (1966). Belgian designer. After trying to be accepted, at the age of 18, at the Académie Royale des Beaux Arts in Antwerp, he studied graphics in Gand and then in 1987 tried for the academy again, and he was admitted. He graduated within four years and began to work for Castelbajac, a *griffe* which also worked on the Courrèges Collections. He later worked with Jean Paul Gaultier. Since October 1998 he has had a *griffe* of his own. His sources of inspiration are mostly ethnic and his creativity is poured into the choice of fabrics. His women's prêt-à-porter line is on sale in Europe, the Middle East, and the U.S.

Degli Innocenti Massimo (1955). Italian designer. He made his début in 1994 and, in 1997, presented his first Collection at Milano Collezioni Donna. Previously, he worked in Paris for Ungaro and Tarlazzi, and in Italy for Valentino, working on the launch of the Oliver line. His business is located in Tuscany, in Chiesa Uzzanese.

De Grisogono Company for high-fashion jewelry, founded in Geneva in 1997 by Fawaz Grumosi, who made a name for his Collections with the introduction of the black diamond as a gem of great preciousness and intense aesthetic appeal. Thanks to the exceptional nature of this type of diamond, other precious stones and pearls that are matched with it, in pieces characterized by designs that are unusual and rather daring from an inventive point of view, assume new expressive values. Every year, new pieces of jewellery are created that combine the Italian artistic tradition – Fawaz Grumosi is Florentine in origin – with the most advanced expressions of contemporary goldsmith design. The company, very innovative as well in the field of watches, has also created various original models such as Instrumento Nº Uno, Instrumentino, and Instrumento Doppio, all the expression of great technical know-how and, in most cases, embellished with diamonds. The launch of a new Collection based on *galuchat* took place in 2003. An ancient material – it had already been used in ancient Egypt, in the 1700s, and during the Art Deco period as a covering for small objects and furnishings – shark skin, or ray skin, properly selected and treated, is matched with gold and precious stones in composite solutions that display the qualities of high-fashion jewellery. There are De Grisogono boutiques in Geneva, Paris, Gstaad, London, Rome, Hong Kong, and Kuwait. (*Alessandra Quattordio*)

❑ 2003, June. The Swiss jewellery brand opens a new boutique in Paris. There are 400 guests, including Kate Moss and Helena Christensen dressed in Dior, Princess Anne, Princess Beatrice di Borbone Sicilia, and the Princes Windish Graetz.

Deimichei Marisa (1951). Journalist. She was a director of Benissimo. Her journalistic work began in 1978. In 1980 she opened a publishing consulting firm and in 1984 was hired at Donnapiù, a new Mondadori monthly where she would stay until the magazine's transformation into Marie Claire. In 1988 she became chief editor at Più Bella and in 1989 deputy director at Anna, under the leadership of Mirella Pallotti. In 1995 she became director of Benissimo, which she would leave after one year in order to become the editorial director of Mondadori's specialized women's magazines.

De Kalb German brand of shirts and accessories launched in Ashaffenburg in 1949 by the brothers Joseph and Theo Kalb, the founders of Kalb GmbH. During the 1950s, thanks to the intuition of Alfred, the youngest member of the family, the firm focused on the production of men's shirts under the De Kalb brand, which in 1972 expanded to include women's blouses and accessories (Kalb Ligne).

Delahaye Jacques (1937). French designer. He was particularly successful in the 1960s, when he designed for various ready-to-wear houses and for Pierre d'Alby. In 1968, he designed the last two high fashion Collections for the *maison* of the recently-deceased Jacques Heim, and then returned to prêt-à-porter working with, among others, Hanae Mori and V de V.

De Lamargé Nicole (1933-1969). French model. She died quite young, when still in the forefront of fashion, much loved by the great photographers of the 1950s and 1960s, especially Peter Knapp, who discovered and launched her in Elle, Bailey, and Bourdin. She had high cheekbones and features that were very fluid and easily transformed by make-up.

De la Renta Oscar (1932). American designer. Born in Santo Domingo, De la Renta left the Dominican Republic to study art at the San Fernando Academy in Madrid. He developed an interest in sketching fashion designs, and his artistic talent led to a job working as an assistant to Balenciaga. In 1961 he moved to Lanvin, in Paris, where he assisted another Spanish-born designer, Cas-

Evening dress by Oscar de la Renta.

tillo. In 1963 De la Renta left Europe for New York, where he began designing the fashion Collections for Elizabeth Arden. Two years later he founded his own fashion house, and, in Collections dedicated to themes such as 'Gypsies' and 'Russia,' quickly acquired a reputation for creating clothes with rich fabrics and a vibrant palette. Since then, and over the ensuing four decades, De la Renta has developed a distinctively American style of luxury that comes through strongly in both tailored daywear and lavishly decorated evening clothes. His fashion house also produces accessories, underwear and fragrances. In 1992 he was named artistic director of Balmain.

❑ 2002, July. After ten years as design director of Balmain, De la Renta resigns his post, citing health reasons, and presents his own haute couture Collection in Paris. Laurent Mercier takes over as creative director of Balmain.
❑ 2002, October. De la Renta is one of 11 designers invited to Beijing for the *Fur Show Beijing 2002*. Other U.S. designers include Vera Wang, Peter Som and Han-Feng, while Cavalli, Ferré and Max Mara represent Italy, and Lacroix, Givenchy, Gaultier and Rykiel are invited from France.
❑ 2003, September. Signs a three-year licensing agreement with Rose Tree Linens of Dallas to launch a line of household linens for Spring-Summer 2004.
❑ 2004, February. A new women's sportswear Collection, O Oscar, is launched under a licensing agreement with the Kellwood Company. The new line includes accessories, lingerie and beachwear, with retail price points lower than the designer's top ready-to-wear lines.
❑ 2004, July. Alex Bolen, the designer's son-in-law and director of corporate development since 2003, is appointed CEO. At the same time, Rachel Barnett resigns as Senior Vice-President after ten years with the firm.
❑ 2004, December. Giuseppe Celio, formerly with Gianni Versace Distribution, is appointed Chief Financial Officer.

Delaunay Sonia (1885-1979). French artist. A great creative personality, committed to both art and fashion, Sophie Stern (her real name) was born in Ukraine and spent her childhood in Saint Petersburg. From 1903 to 1095, she studied in Karlsruhe, right at the time of the flowering of German Expressionism, which would influence her greatly. In 1906, in Paris, she enrolled at the Académie de la Palette, and there she met Robert Delaunay, who she married in 1910. That same year, she began to apply her husband's artistic research on Cubism to embroidery and fabrics. In 1911, she carried out her first abstract work on fabric, making a patchwork blanket for her newborn son Charles. Painting to her was an art that had to expand into the surrounding environment and it had to embrace living forms, according to a concept of the "totality of art" that is common to many avant-guard movements. She developed the idea of creating clothes and furnishings that create a unique whole with painting. In her *Contrastes Simultanés* of 1912, she created a simultaneous abstract language in which pure colors, without any chiaroscuro effect, generated new shapes and depths by means of contrast and

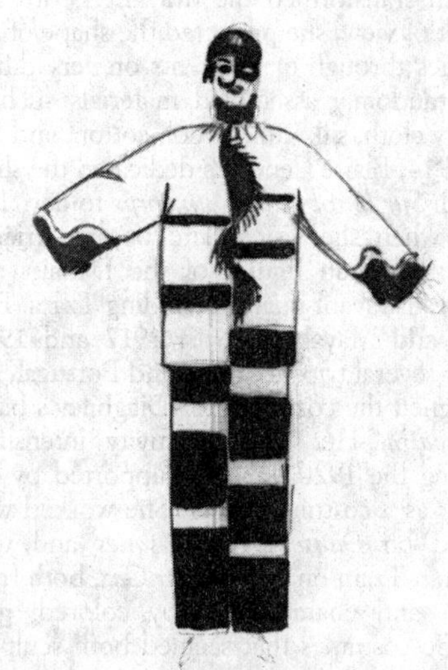

Gouache by Sonia Delaunay (Alviani's Collection).

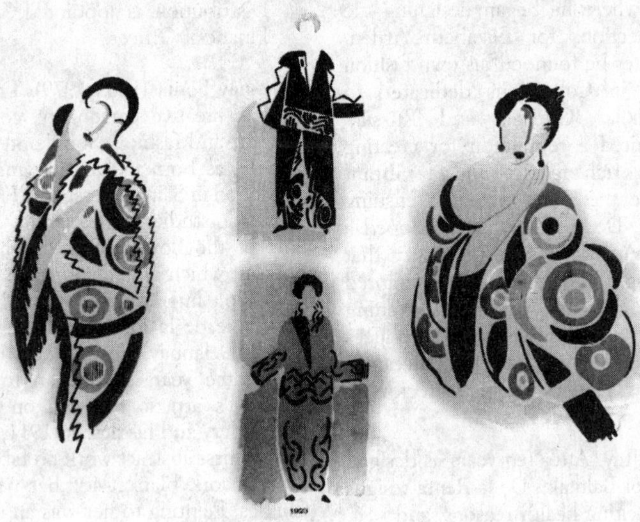

Sketches by Sonia Delaunay (Victoria and Albert Museum, London).

opposition. The following year, she created her first simultaneous dress, which she herself wore for the *Bal Bullier* in Paris: the human body became the support for a traveling paradox, through a dialectic relationship between the abstract and bi-dimensional geometry of the drawing and the tridimensional mobile nature of the figure which transformed the drawing. With this point of view, she projected the shape of her clothes through experiments on very different randomly assembled materials such as heavy cloth, silk, tulle, wool, cotton, and fur. In 1914, Blaise Cendrars dedicated the short poem *Sur la robe elle a un corps* to her. This was when she visited and became friends with the main figures of the Dadaist and Surrealist avant-guard, including Tzara, Breton, and Mayakovsky. In 1917 and 1918, after several trips to Spain and Portugal, she designed the costumes for Diaghilev's ballet *Cleopatra*. Her artistic activity intensified during the 1920s, always supported by her work as a costume maker. She worked with Iliazd on *Danseuse au Disques* and with Tristan Tzara on *Le Coeur a Gaz*, both from 1923 and characterized by colored, geometric costumes that seemed both sculpted and tailored in movement. At the Salon d'Automne in 1924, she opened a *cinematic simultaneous presentation* with fabrics displayed in a special glass case in the large salon of the Grand Palais. They were produced in a kinetic fashion using a device with vertical rollers patented by Robert Delaunay that allowed a simultaneous and infinite movement of the colored lengths of cloth. Her *Boutique Simultanée*, at Boulevard Malesherbes 19, dates to 1925, when she launched an avant-guard fashion that would influence all future textile production, abolishing any themes of naturalistic inspiration in favor of a chromatic and abstract architecture characterized by an easily perceivable rhythm. Again in 1925, she participated in the Exposition des Arts Décoratifs in collaboration with the tailor Jacques Heim. They exhibited clothes and accessories as well as fabrics for both furnishings and clothing (manufactured by Bianchini-Férier) with strong, rhythmic tones. Her experiment in graphic design for the the auto industry, in that same year, was extraordinary. She designed the Citroën B12 model as if it were a printed fabric. In this period she opened boutiques in London and Rio de Janeiro, and, always in search of new means of expression, she set herself the task of making costumes for the films *Le P'tit Parigot* and *Vertigo* by Marcel L'Herbier. In 1927, in acknowledgment of her work, she was invited to the Sorbonne to talk about the influence of painting on the art of clothing, and she was well-received. Instead of speaking in terms of figurative decorativism, she took a decidedly rationalist and simplified approach to textile and fashion design, stimulating the creativity of many great names in international stylism such as Jean Patou and Elsa Schiaparelli, and even anticipating the graphics and colors of op art. Her fame increased during the 1930s, when her clients included Gloria Swanson as well as the wives and companions of intellectuals and designers such as Gropius, Breuer, and Mendelsohn. In 1941, after the death of her husband, she retired to Grasse, in Provence. She no longer worked, but did remain active as a painter. During the 1950s, there were several retrospectives dedicated to her, and in 1975 she received the Legion d'Honneur. After donating sketches and manuscripts to the National Library in Paris, she died in 1979. (*Aurora Fiorentini*)

Del Carlo Fabrizio (1960). Italian designer. The family knitwear business was fundamental for his professional education. In 1986, he opened a knitwear factory with his sister Piera. Under a brand named after himself, he developed a style of refined simplicity, using precious materials and innovative shapes, often adopting a "lived-in" look. In 1996, he opened a new production plant in Capannori (Lucca) which produces 50,000 pieces a year that are distributed to 270 clients all over the world.

Fabrizio Del Carlo: Women's Collection 1998.

Delcourt Xavier (1970). Belgian designer. He graduated from the Royal Academy of Art Tornai in 1988 and continued his studies at the Institute of Visual Arts of Cambers, Brussels. He designs men's wear in a dry and vaguely minimalist style. He presented his Collection for the first time in Paris in 2002, stirring great interest.

Delemazure Corinne (1954). French knitwear designer. She began designing underwear and bathing suits. In the early 1980s, Lanvin appointed her artistic director of knitwear for prêt-à-porter. She made her début under her own name in 1986 with very structured clothes that were devoid of softness except in the fabrics themselves. In those same years she designed a men's line for the Charivari boutique in New York. She called it "Sans tambours ni trompettes," a name she would later use for a women's Collection. In 1991, she designed and produced a more affordable line. Since 1994 she has been the designer of the brand Des Prés Homme et Femme, which belongs to the Japanese group Tomorrowland.

Delfina Swimwear Line of bathing suits designed by Delfina Marmaglia, characterized by artisanal production and matching colors. Success came in 1995 when a journalist for Vogue America, after buying one of her double-face bikinis in Rome, published it in the magazine's November issue. Today, Delfina also offers a line of beachwear and accessories including robes, beaded thong slippers, embroidered bags, and kaftans in Indian gauze. Along with the women's line there is also a mini-Collection for girls which offers the same styles on a smaller scale.

Delgado Lydia (1958). Spanish designer, considered one of the great Iberian names. She came to fashion after classical ballet and a career as a dancer at the Liceu, the opera house of Barcelona. She was part of Antonio Miro's team. In 1990, she opened her first atelier, at first creating a bridal and a high fashion Collection. In 1992, she made her début at Salon Gaudì. In 2000, she designed eye glasses and a shoe line.

Del Hierro Pedro (1948). Spanish designer, born in Madrid. He designs gloves, shoes, hats, suitcases, and ready-to-wear, for both men and women. In the Spain of the 1990s, according to a survey conducted by the newspaper El Pais, he was certainly the best-known designer. He has 30 years of experience. He started in 1966 with Estefan Mill. Ten years later he presented his first Collection. In 1987, he launched a line of more affordable clothes under the Habito label, for sale in department stores.

❑ Since 1990, his Collections have been integrated into Cortefield group, and since 1999 they have been sold in single-brand boutiques under the PdH label.

De Liguoro Lydia. Italian journalist. She defined herself as the "indomitable foot soldier of Italian fashion" for her battles and campaigns against the xenomania of Italian elegance and in favor of clothing, fabrics and accessories created in Italy. She was a supporter of Fascism, and had become a member of the Women's Fascist Groups as early as 1919, immediately after the gathering in Piazza San Sepolcro where the movement was born. In that year, she founded Lidel, a magazine dedicated to "Readings, Illustrations, Drawings, Elegance, and Work." The initials of the corresponding Italian words (Letture, Illustrazioni, Disegni, Eleganze, Lavoro) formed the magazine's title. At first, she attacked any kind of luxury "to bring women, of all social classes, to a sense of moderation....and to limit the ostentatious display that is damaging the country at this time. Then, she changed her tone: if the luxury is Italian, then one must support and favor it, while fighting against the "colonization" of the designers in Paris and against the deeply-rooted habit of buying French styles or reproductions of Lanvin, Paquin, and Poiret. In 1923, Benito Mussolini congratulated her over their common goal: "the success of Italy and of being Italian." In that same year, she left Lidel in order to direct Fantasie d'Italia, the official organ of the National Fascist Federation of the Clothing Industry. Her writings were full of nationalism, and sometimes plunged into the absurdity of the campaign against losing weight, but they never had the virulence of the Giornale della Donna, the official magazine of the Women's Fascist Groups, which ordered people to "banish from Fascist homes the French magazines and newspapers that exalt the strong woman, the main cause of moral imbalance." She strongly supported the policies of the Ente Moda (Fashion Institute) that promoted national self-reliance. She finished her career in the editorial department of the Italian Silk Institute.

The Delineator American fashion periodical. At the beginning of 1870, Ebenezer Butterick, in order to promote the sale of his paper patterns, decided to launch a publishing project, and founded *The Ladies Quarterly Review of Broadway Fashions*. The magazine was very successful, to the point than in 1877 the magazine took over another periodical, *The Metropolitan*, changing its name to *The Delineator* and ultimately becoming one of the most widely sold women's magazines. Until 1894, when it expanded its sphere of interests to include the home as well, *The Delineator* was devoted exclusively to fashion. Later, it included pages devoted to narrative and prose. At the beginning of the 1920s, it reached circulation of about a million copies, with many editions around the world. In 1928, it joined another publication, *The Designer*. In turn, however, *The Delineator* was absorbed in 1937 by the *Pictorial Review*.

De Lisi Ben (1955). American designer, born on Long Island, in New York. He studied painting and sculpture at the Pratt Institute in Brooklyn from 1973 to 1977. His first work experience was at Bloomingdale's, in the children's department. In the late 1970s, he launched a men's line called Benedetto. In 1982, he moved to London where he opened a French restaurant. Two years later, he returned to fashion with a women's Collection. His style is rather distant from the somber London minimalism of the 1990s, something of which he is proud. In 1991, he began a partnership with the Jacques Vert group, manufacturers and distributors of fashion. He won the *British Glamour Designer of the Year* award in 1994 and 1995.

Dell'Acqua Alessandro (1963). Italian designer, born in Naples. After graduating from the Institute of Art, he moved to Milan in the early 1980s and began to collaborate with several fashion *griffes*, including the Genny group, for which he designed the *Malisy* Collection up until 1993. Afterwards, he worked with Pietro Pianforini, Maska, Gilmar, and Alma. In 1994, he presented his first knitwear line, A.A. Milano. In March 1996, he presented his first women's Collection, and today it is sold in 108 boutiques all over the world. On January 8th 1998 he presented his first men's Collection at Pitti Immagine. His style is sensual but not aggressive, with simple shapes that are easy to match in rich materials and decorations, with black and beige the dominant colors.

❑ 2002, December. The designer's début as artistic director of La Perla. Dell'Acqua's inspirational muse is, as always, Courtney Love, but he also makes reference to the elegance of the Hollywood stars of the 1950s.
❑ 2003, January. A syndicate of investors led by the Arpels family acquires 70% of the brand of the Naples designer. Arpels sells a 20% shareholding in Van Cleef & Arpels to the Richemont Group, and acquires the Redwall Group, which produces bags and accessories under the brands Redwall and Borbonese, of which Dell'Acqua has been the designer for a long time. License agreements that are already in effect for the production of fragrances, shoes, and eyewear with the Dell'Acqua brand remain unchanged; these are with, respectively, EuroItalia, Iris, and Visibilia. A new company within the Redwall Group, on the other hand, will obtain a license for clothing under the brand. Claude Arpels, the managing director of Redwall, will have the same post for Dell'Acqua, while the designer remains president and partner, with a 30% stake. Redwall Group closes 2002 with a turnover of about €40 million (€22 million Redwall, €18 million Dell'Acqua).
❑ 2003, March. The début on the Milan runways of the new Dell'Acqua Collection for La Perla. The main piece is in chiffon with cuts, inlays and superimpositions for *pareo* dresses that are fastened around the neck and have precious inlays, broad sashes, lace tops, jackets, and desert boots in ostrich feathers. There is a lot of yellow and black for an extremely feminine Collection that is evanescent and soft and which plays with transparencies and transfers to clothing the refinement that has always characterized the lingerie Collections of La Perla.
❑ 2003, August. Launch of the new men's fragrance.
❑ 2004, February. Launch of the website www.alessandrodellacqua.com, on which it is possible to surf the designer's Collection and to find a lot of information about the firm's licenses, his biography, press releases, the profile of the company, and the distribution network. A single-brand store with the women's and men's Collections, the shoe lines, eye glasses, and bags opens at 149 Fifth Avenue in New York.

A model by Alessandro Dell'Acqua.

Dell'Aquila Mariantonietta (1937-1999). Journalist for specialized periodicals. Hired by Rizzoli in 1958 as a fashion editor for the magazine Annabella, she worked there for almost ten years. In 1969, she went to Mondadori, working first at Arianna, and then at Cosmopolitan. In 1976, she planned and directed the monthly Doppiovù. In 1979, she was at Cento Cose and then went back to Rizzoli, at Amica. She was deputy director at Elle from 1988 to 1994, when she was asked to lead Brava Casa.

Della Schiava Giuseppe (1935). Entrepreneur and editor. From 1990 to 1998, for three successive terms, he was appointed president of the Chamber of Italian Fashion, the association that organizes Milano Collezioni, Roma Collezioni Alta Moda, Donna Sotto le Stelle, and Modamare. He began to work in the world of fashion at a young age, in his family's advertising agency, and then continued with the textile firm Sisan. At the same time, he published and directed, until 1997, Harper's Bazaar Italy, Harper's Bazaar France, Uomo Bazaar, and Cosmopolitan. Since 1999 he has planned and followed the development of his Budapest Collections project, which was to become a point of reference for Hungarian fashion and the countries of Eastern Europe.

Della Spiga (Via). Either the right or the left side of Milan's "fashion quadrilateral," depending on whether you look at it from via Manzoni or Corso Venezia. Guido Lopez and Silvestro Severgnini, in their guide *Milano in mano* (*Easy Milan*, Mursia), wrote: "Before the war, it was the quietest and most charming street in the city center, a kind of back-of-the-shop, tidy and very clean, at the service of buildings whose gardens overlooked the Naviglio. One went there to buy bread, fruits, vegetables, lamps, and passementerie." It is still very clean and tidy, because an association tends to it, and a retired person, relying on the generosity of associates, works with a broom and a duster. But the street's rustic and informal character is now only a memory. Now it is the scene of a fashion explosion, one that took place some years before the one in via Sant'Andrea, because in via della Spiga, during the 1960s, the first trendy boutiques opened their doors, including Cose, Adriana, and Dorothée Bis. The explosion has destroyed, among other things, a lottery ticket kiosk, a tiny pastry shop, the Beneggi pet shop, a fruit store, two stationery stores, the Magugliani haberdashery, the tiny underwear boutique Giuseppina, the Guffanti and Sironi bakeries, a butcher, the Central Drugstore, and a poultry store. That location was until recently a Garzanti bookshop which, as the last command post of culture on the street where the Literary Fair was born 70 years ago, later reopened, still at no 30 via della Spiga, but on the small inside piazza that was created after the building's restoration. From the past, only the Armandola delicatessen has held on along with the most expensive elementary school in town. The invasion, here, has been total, even with some elbowing among the new arrivals.

Della Valle Diego (1953). Entrepreneur. He is the founder of Tod's Spa, an Italian company of shoes, bags, and clothing that, through its brands Tod's and Hogan, has reached first place in the industry. Its origin is in a small factory established in 1940 by Dorino Della Valle, in Sant'Elpidio a Mare, a small village in the Marche. The entire family worked there, and Diego, the son who multiplied its fortunes in the early 1980s by inventing the loafers with small raised rubber spheres on the soles, still smells the leather and skins of his childhood. He has been at the summit of Banca Commerciale Italiana. Since June 2003, with 4.6% of the shares, he has been on the board of directors of Banca Nazionale del Lavoro, on the unanimous vote of its members, taking the seat of Davide Croff on the day of Mario Girotti's appointment as general director. He was the savior of Florence's soccer team, Fiorentina, which, after its financial collapse, almost disappeared. In August 2002, the entrepreneur became the majority shareholder. The shares were acquired for about €7.5 million.

Della Valle Gianni. Italian photographer. He was the first to open, in the mid 1950s, a photo studio specialized in fashion. At first, he worked mainly for publishing houses, and then expanded to advertising.

Dellera Italian fur shop. In 1885, in Pavia, Mattia Dell'Era opened a shop in the city center specialized in the manufacture of drive belts and shoe uppers. At his death, Carlo Lanzani took over the business and changed its name to Dellera and, in 1908, reorganized the Pavia headquarters. The main activity was the manufacture of furs, but suitcases, bags, and belts were also produced and distributed. In 1937, the firm opened a boutique in Milan on via S. Damiano. In the 1950s, the third generation, represented by Giancarlo, joined Tino Lanzani, his father, in the family business. When Elizabeth Taylor ordered a Dellera fur, international interest became focused on the brand. At the end of the 20th century, the company is led by the fourth generation: Andrea takes care of management and purchasing; his sister Gigliola is in charge of advertising and styles. Some of the production is done for third parties, for example the fur line produced for the French designer Erik Schaix in 1999.

Dell'Oglio Men's wear boutique in Palermo. It was opened in 1900 on via Maqueda, near Palazzo Mazarino, by Mario Dell'Oglio, the son of Santi, who in 1890 had founded the Grandi Magazzini del Telegrafo, the most elegant emporium in town. Mario was succeeded by Vincenzo who, in 1957, moved the business to via Ruggero Settimo, where it is still located and where, in 1972, a line of women's wear was launched. At the 100th birthday celebration, in 1990, the family company opened a second boutique on via Parisi. In their archives, the Dell'Oglios keep a card file of the measurements and shapes for the custom-made hats of one hundred clients, beginning with Ignazio and Vincenzo Florio, the last representatives of the celebrated entrepreneurial Palermo dynasty.

(*Antonella Romano*)

Dell'Olio Louis (1948). American designer, born in New York. He has worked at Anne Klein II, the house of casual-elegant fashion established by Anne Klein in 1968. He has always been able, in a career of more than 20 years, to propose outfits that are characterized by simple lines and appropriate for any occasion. A student at the Parson's School of Design until 1969, he has worked for several companies, including Teal Traina. At the death of Anne Klein in 1974, he was appointed co-designer of the house together with Donna Karan. The collaboration lasted 10 years, until Karan decided to start her own business. Once he became the sole head designer,Dell'Olio offered casual-elegant styles for practical and single women. In 1993, the Anne Klein brand was taken over by Richard Tyler. Since then, Dell'Olio has designed three lines for sale in department stores. Typical items are the linen blazers matched with suede trousers and the cashmere jackets with flannel skirts.

Delman Herman B. (1895-1955). American shoe entrepreneur. Delman, a proponent of both glamorous style and innovative craftsmanship, founded one of the oldest and most prestigious U.S. footwear brands. Born in Portersville, California, he launched his shoe company in 1919 after returning from World War I, quickly targeting stars and socialites as his clients. He opened his first store in Hollywood and a second in New York on Madison Avenue, but by 1933 had closed them to focus on manufacturing. In the midst of the Depression, Delman's shoes fetched as much as $500 a pair, and the company was producing 2,500 pairs a week. The company's list of famous clients included Marlene Dietrich, Marilyn Monroe and Jacqueline Kennedy. Delman was known as both an innovator and a keen encourager of young design talent, and was one of the first to hire young shoe designer Roger Vivier in the 1930s. In 1954, Genesco bought the company, resulting in a major expansion. In 1973, Debenham acquired Genesco and with it the Delman brand.

Delmar Manufacturer of corsetry and beachwear. Established in Alserio in 1928, it has a turnover of 45 billion liras (average of the last years of the 1900s). The group's brands are Ritratti, for the highest market segment; Dì sì for young people; Swan Original for beachwear; and Oroblu for underwear.

Del Pezzo Lucio (1933). Italian artist. In 1961, he collaborated with Bruna Bini and created a dress inspired by his artwork of that year. Close to Pop Poetry and Nouveau Realisme, this artist from Naples attached various objects and fragments in wood, cork and plaster, held together by a net, to the dress, which was a white sheath.

Delphi Dress inspired by the Greek chiton. Similar to a tunic, it has a cylindrical shape, drops to the feet, and is tied at the waist by a string. It is in pleated silk, with shoulders and arms fastened by Murano glass beads. The pleating is the famous one created by the genial and eclectic Mariano Fortuny and patented by him in Paris. His wife Henriette would often wear the pleated tunic that he designed, inspired by the Delphi charioteer.

Delpierre Madeleine (1920-1994). Scholar of fashion. She was the first curator of the Musée de la Mode et du Costume at the Louvre. A specialist in the history of costume, especially of the 19th and 20th centuries, she edited a series of small books about the grammar of style for the publishing house Flammarion.

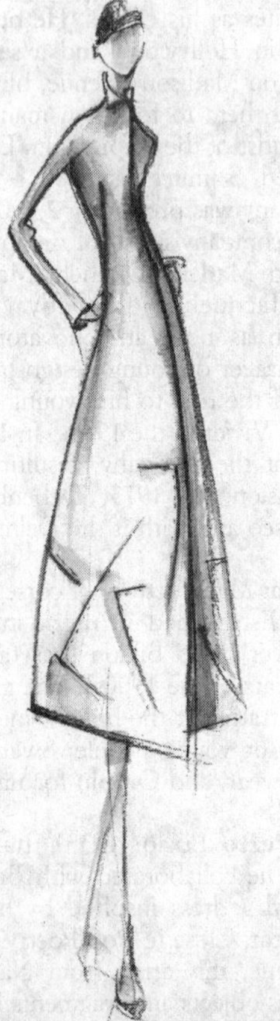

Overcoat by Jesus Del Pozo.

Del Pozo Jesus (1936). Spanish designer. He works mainly in Madrid. In 1980, he presented his first women's prêt-à-porter Collection. In 1981, he was awarded the *Aiguille d'Or* and in 1989 he received the *Cristobal Balenciaga* prize. Del Pozo's Collections favor structured shapes that are played down with touches of fantasy. His men's line is innovative and rigorous. He also designs underwear, scarves and jewellery.

Del Sole Vanessa (1976). Designer, born in Pietrasanta, Tuscany. After graduating from high school, she took a degree in international business at the London School of Economics in Great Britain. She got her start in a family business, Graziano Facchini, in Viareggio, in charge of the design department for a women's clothing line. She made her début with her own Collection in 1999 at Milan Fashion Week. Radiant and creative, she has an empathetic relationship with the fabrics that she works, prints, and decorates in an artistic vein in her workshop in Forte dei Marmi near the sea. She is successful especially in England.

(*Sofia Catalano*)

De Luca Jean-Claude (1948). Designer and brand of prêt-à-porter. He was born in Barcelona, of an Italian father and a French mother. While a law student in Milan, he became assistant costume designer at La Scala. He moved to Paris and worked for Hubert de Givenchy in 1971 and the following year for Dorothée Bis. After a short period at Guy Laroche, he established himself in women's prêt-à-porter as an independent designer, working especially with the Gruppo Finanziario Tessile. From 1976 to 1984 he designed a line of his own that was seductive and sophisticated. Supported financially by the German group Steilmann, he was back with a Collection in 1987.

Del Verme Nicola (1962). Designer. He studied architecture in Naples, and then moved on to fashion working in the ateliers of Lancetti and Gattinoni in Rome. After gaining solid experience in high fashion, he moved to Milan where he was artistic director of Trussardi Marino alla Scala from 1997 to 1999. He also worked at Max Mara.

Three models designed by Vanessa Del Sole.

In 2001, he presented his first prêt-à-porter line. His education in architecture could be seen in the mathematical measurements and geometrical rigor of the line, in his passion for structure, in the lightness of blouses that weighed only 6 ounces, and in the richness of hems and long trains that went on for almost 18 yards. He was put in charge of design for the Hilton men's line by Vestimenta. (*Silvia Paoli*)

❑ 2001, May. He is the only Italian designer invited to the European Museum of the Year Award, a prize created in 1977 to prompt innovation and research in the museum field. At the same time, there was an exhibition *Gesto: Metamorfosi del desiderio* (*Deeds: Metamorphosis of Desire*), in which the sculpture of Stefano Tonelli, the photos of Mario Mulas, and the clothes of Nicola Del Verme interacted one with another, accompanied by music and dance performances.
❑ 2002, September. He becomes artistic director of Hilton by Vestimenta. Besides designing the men's and women's Collections, he assumes creative responsibility for the company's global image, from press campaigns to points-of-sale, with the purpose of modernizing and identifying the brand and its products through a creative and consistent point of view.
❑ 2003, February. An eccentric and non-conformist Collection. Every garment is conceived as a geometric and modular piece, composed of 16-inch squares in a patchwork held together by metallic rivets. Almost every piece is transformable and reversible. The overskirt becomes a sophisticated evening cloak. There are contrasting fabrics mixed with nonchalance, precious brocades combined with cotton, wool with silk, nylon, and goatskin.

Demarchelier Patrick (1943). French photographer. Born in a small village near Paris, he spent his childhood and adolescence in Le Havre. At the age of 17, he began to fool around with his first camera. At 20, he moved to Paris, where he became a photographer, working first as an assistant to Hans Feurer, and then as a freelancer for Elle, Marie Claire, and other periodicals. In 1975, he moved to New York and immediately established himself professionally with work for Vogue, Glamour, Mademoiselle, GQ, and Rolling Stone. He did campaigns for Revlon, Chanel, and Calvin Klein. Since 1992, he has worked steadily for Harper's Bazaar. In 1998 he published the monograph *Forms*.

Demeulemeester Ann (1959). Belgian designer. She is proof of the excellent education offered by the Department of Fashion of the Royal Academy of Fine Arts in Antwerp, from which she obtained her degree in 1981. It is a school which has become a breeding ground for successful designers. After creating the brand B.V.B.A. 32, she presented her first women's wear Collection for Winter 1987-1988 in London. The following year, she was in Milan: her line had expanded to include shoes and accessories. Since 1991, she has been in Paris. Her style is minimalist, with an androgynous silhouette and new harmonies that flow from the contrast and co-existence of elements belonging to both the woman's wardrobe and men's clothing.

Demron It is the fabric of the future, manufactured by Radiation Shield Technologies (headquartered in Miami, with plants all over the U.S.). It guarantees maximum protection from radiation. Technicians have been perfecting their research for ten years, using the latest findings in the field of molecular engineering. They have produced the first radiation-proof fabric in the world, very light and non-toxic. Demron can replace metal for blocking X-rays, and also beta and gamma rays. For the time being, its use is restricted to radiologists and those employed in the nuclear and space industries.

Denim It is the fabric used to make jeans, a garment in which the identification between shape and material is complete. It is usually pure cotton, in a diagonal weave in which the warp yarns are dyed indigo, which is a blue dye of vegetable origin. The name denim comes from the French city of Nîmes. Thanks to its sturdiness, endurance, washability and easy maintenance, it has always been associated with work clothes. The changes in clothing and consumption in the 20th century have made it the casual fabric par excellence, used especially for pants but also for jackets, dresses, skirts, and accessories. The mass production of jeans, starting in the 1970s, made it the favorite uniform of young people. The indigo color has remained number one over the years, but denim can also be natural, black, brightly-colored, pre-washed, bleached, stonewashed, printed, and embroidered, as well as made in stretch fabric. From the pop styles of the hippies to the branded denim of designers, from the most basic styles to the high-tech versions of the new millennium, the use of this fabric has no limits. Present in the Collection of almost every designer, as the motif of a season or as an independent line, denim has known the glory of the haute couture runways thanks to the daring interpretations and sumptuous transformations created by Chanel, Gaultier, Galliano, and Lacroix. (*Cristina Lucchini*)

Dennis Pamela (1960). American designer. She was looking for an evening dress that she could wear to a wedding and, not being able to find something she liked, she decided to design and sew it herself. Thirteen years ago, with that wedding, her career started. In fact, that dress she made was immortalized in a TV commercial and received, within just a few days, orders amounting to $23,000.00. Pamela adores simple lines that show off the body and femininity.

Dépêche Mode French monthly about fashion and its main trends. The first issue came out in February 1967. The title means "Fashion Dispatch." Directed by Jacqueline Bloch, it is published by Verniquet. It was started as a spin-off of the technical monthly of fashion and couture "La Dépêche de la couture et de la mode de Paris," founded by André Vandecrane in 1954.

Depero Fortunato (1892-1960). Italian artist. In 1919, in Rovereto, he founded the Casa d'Arte Futurista (House of Futurist Art) in which he applied the concept of the creative unity of the arts: painting, architecture, decorative arts, and fashion, just as the artist hoped for in his *Manifest for the Futurist Reconstruction of the Universe.* At the Depero House of Art, together with his wife Rosetta, he planned and created, in addition to advertising graphics, interior décor items such as furniture, cushions, tapestries, and clothes, including shawls and scarves with geometric patterns and stylized elements of naturalistic origin, as well as fabrics for furniture. But Depero's most famous article of clothing remains the *Futurist Waistcoat*, expressly conceived for the artists belonging to the movement. They were manufactured in multicolored fabrics with arabesques and naturalistic patterns. The 1923 model for Azari had blue fish in the design; the one for Marinetti, likewise from 1923, had red, yellow, and orange inlays. Also in 1923, he designed shawls and geometric patterns for the Piatti silk factory in Como, and presented his sketches at the Exposition des Arts Décoratifs in Paris. Among the few projects connected to women's clothing were the sketches for Vogue covers during the 1930s. During the 1940s, Depero was influenced by the decorative motifs of *Futurist Aero-Painting* found in the fabrics of the Franco Scalamandré-Silk factory of New York, whose echo can be heard in the 1942 manifesto *The Suit of Victory.* Several of his fashion-works are on display at the Museum of Contemporary Art of Trento and Rovereto, the latter being the town where he died.

(*Cloe Piccoli*)

De Rauch Madeleine (1896-1985). French haute couture dressmaker. She started her own business at the age of 31, using the passion of her three sisters for skating, athletics, and riding as an inspiration for styles appropriate to the sober and practical elegance of a young woman more comfortable in the gym than in a sitting-room. This was a vision to which the *maison* would remain faithful over time, closing down only in 1974. The Collections featured tailored suits in hand-woven, hand-knitted, and crocheted wools. For evening, she proposed a look that was casual-chic. During the 1950s the *maison* received an infusion of energy and imagination thanks to the impeccable cutting style of Marc Bohan, who joined the firm as a designer of haute couture and prêt-à-porter.

Derby Men's laced shoe. It is named after Lord Derby, the English aristocrat who

Fortunato Depero, *Man with Moustaches and Umbrella*, 1924. Collage and tempera (from *Art Fashion*, Biennial of Florence 1996, Skira. Courtesy Galleria Blu).

launched it. The tongue is a single piece with the upper, exactly the opposite of the Oxford model. It exists in a smooth model, which is quite elegant, and a more casual one that is decorated at the toe and heel. Different from the Oxford, there is also a model without laces that is fastened at the side with a buckle.

Derek Rose Pajamas English brand of pajamas, night gowns, and dressing gowns. It is famous for colors and patterns inspired by military regiments and clubs, and for the satin stripes obtained from two-end yarns in the satin part, which produces a brilliant and long-wearing fabric. It was established in 1925 and immediately found a market in London at Harrods, Simpson's, and at the shops on Jermin Street. Shortly after, the pajamas of Mister Derek Rose arrived in New York. Some 70% of the production is exported.

De Ribes Jacqueline (Jacqueline de Beaumont, ca. 1930). French designer. When still in school, between 15 and 17, she was appointed artistic director of the shows at the end of the school year. At the age of 17, she married the Viscount de Ribes, a rich banker and successful man. Then, at 22, she joined the list of the most elegant women of the world. In 1983, she designed a luxury line, After Five, that was launched in the U.S. by Saks Fifth Avenue and is especially remembered for the sumptuousness of the cocktail dresses and the aristocratic elegance of the evening outfits. In 1988, management of the brand was entrusted to the Japanese group Kanebo, which opened a Jacqueline de Ribes boutique in Paris. The firm would last until 1994, when the noble lady, due to health problems, was forced to retire.

De Rigo Italian group at the forefront of the high-quality sunglasses field. In terms of volume, it ranks second in the world, with 30,000 pieces a day. It was established in 1978 by Ennio De Rigo as a simple workshop in Pozzale di Cadore. After 20 years of activity, these the results: 670 models spread over several proprietary brands (Police, Sting, Vogart, Rolling, Charme, Old Italy, and the historic Lozza, created in 1878 and acquired in 1993), brands under license (Fendi, von Fürstenberg, Martini Racing, Fila, and La Perla), and in partnership (as with Prada, since February 19990; 40,000 points-of-sale in 80 countries; 7 production plants; 1,100 employees; and a consolidated turnover, in 1998, of more than 203 billion liras, of which 70% comes from abroad. In 1998, the Group, with headquarters in Longarone (Belluno), acquired the Vantios Group, owner of a chain of 390 shops in England.

❑ 2000, February. The company, quoted on the NYSE, acquires the store chain General Optica, a leader in Spain and the U.S.
❑ 2000, November. The first nine months of the year close with a turnover of 666.4 billion liras, an increase of 40.9%. In 1999, sales had been steady at around 473 billion liras. The growth was due to a new contribution from the Spanish General Optica and from Eyewear International Distribution, a joint venture for the marketing and distribution of Prada-branded eyewear, of which De Rigo owns 51%.
❑ 2001, April. The luxury giant LVMH strengthens its partnership with De Rigo by acquiring 5% of its shares. De Rigo opens a subsidiary in eastern France called Oyannax. Starting in Autumn it distributes Givenchy, another LVMH brand, which joins Loewe, Céline, and Fendi as brands for which the Italian group already manufactures and distributes glasses.
❑ 2002, September. De Rigo acquires the new Furla license. It is to manufacture and distribute sunglasses and frames under the brand of this Italian company that is famous around the world for its shoes, accessories, bags, jewellery, and watches. Furla is present in 64 countries with 178 single-brand stores and kiosks.
❑ 2002, October. De Rigo repurchases its own shares. The company's board of directors will submit to the shareholders a repurchase plan for part of the issued shares, including those offered at the NYSE in the form of American Depository Receipts. The proposed plan covers a maximum of 4.4 million shares, or about 10% of the outstanding stock. If approved, it will set a minimum and

maximum share price and a time period for acceptance. At present, De Rigo owns the brands Police, Sting, and Lozza and owns licenses for the manufacture and distribution of Etro, La Perla, Fila, Onyx, and Furla. It is present in the British market with Dollond & Aitchison.
❑ 2003, April. The profit for 2002 amounts to €10.6 million, compared to €21.2 million in 2001. The strong growth of General Optica in Spain is balanced by a decrease in profits at Dollond & Aitchison in the U.K., in wholesale distribution, and at EID, the joint venture with Prada.
❑ 2003, December. The turnover is €504.8 million, a decline of 1.5% compared to the €512.5 million of 2002. At constant exchange rates, the turnover would have grown by 3.5%. However, the net profit is improved, going from €10.6 million to €18.5 million, an increase of 74.5%.
❑ 2004, January. A two-year license agreement with the BMW group is signed. It calls for the production and distribution of eyeglasses and sunglasses under the Mini brand.
❑ 2004, July. A world-wide license is signed with Escada, for the production and distribution of eyeglasses and sunglasses. "With Escada we have integrated our portfolio, adding a high-level brand with a strong global image, at the same time strengthening our position in the luxury and high-quality segment," declared Ennio De Rigo.
❑ 2004, July. De Rigo purchases 5% of its own shares from the Prada group.
❑ 2004, September. A cross-licensing contract with Viva, the American glasses manufacturer. The brands under license at Viva are Tommy Hilfiger, Guess, and Gant, and will be distributed by De Rigo in Italy and Greece. The De Rigo brands Givenchy, Etro, Fila, and Furla will be distributed by Viva in North America.
❑ 2004, November. A world-wide license agreement with Chopard, a *maison* that manufactures watches and jewellery for the high end market, for the production and distribution of eyeglasses and sunglasses.
❑ 2004, December. The turnover is €514.4 million, an increase of 1.9% compared to the €504.8 million of 2003. The gross operating margin has grown 7.5% to €55.7 million euros, compared to €51.8 million in 2003.
❑ 2005, January. De Rigo obtains from Ermenegildo Zegna a world-wide license for the development, production, and distribution of a line of eyeglasses and sunglasses for men.
❑ 2005, January. A license agreement with Jean-Paul Gaultier for the production and distribution of eyeglasses and sunglasses. "The agreement with Jean-Paul Gaultier expands and strengthens our portfolio of brands and offers an opportunity for growth with the most daring consumers," says Ennio De Rigo.

(*Dario Golizia*)

De Santis Dali Brand of women's wear created in 1998 through a partnership between Carmine De Santis, from Pontecagnano (Sa), and Mohammed Ali Moussa, from Tunis. De Santis attended the European Institute of Design. Moussa received a degree in chemistry and later studied fashion design at Esmod in Paris and at the Carlo Secoli Institute in Milan. After Moussa did some consulting, and De Santis worked in a women's wear factory owned by his father, the two decided to design a prêt-à-porter Collection which would include a shop for both knitwear and tailoring. Their work combines two different cultures: the tailoring tradition of Campania and the minimalist spirit of North Africa.

Descamps Marc Alain (1930). French psychoanalyst. In his book *Psychosociologie de la Mode* he analysed fashion as a structure of systematic and constant elements: the need for change, the game of imitation, belonging to a group, collective taste and trends, the individual's need to differentiate, and the economic aspect. In his view, clothing in itself is a code of communication that is transmitted through fabrics, shapes, and colors. It express the moods, personalities, social classes, professions, cultural levels, and aspirations of those who wear it.

De Senneville Elisabeth (1946). French designer, born in Paris, where she studied the fine arts. She made her début in fashion designing models for the department store Printemps. She designed her first Collection in 1972. She worked as a designer for several manufacturing companies, for the mail order company 3 Suisse, and for Fiorucci. She is considered the French advocate of Pop Art fashion and the one who really shook up the styles of the 1970s and 1980s. She was the most inspired designer of the time in combining art and fashion, and was the first to exhibit the graphic creations of Bazooka, a group formed by Loulou and Kiki Picasso, along with her clothes. Inspired by communist China, she designed the blue overalls for workers that became real bestsellers. She was among the first to use thermal materials which change their color according to the light, and, among the many ideas of those years, she was the one who used materials created for astronauts. After a difficult financial period, she re-emerged on the Paris scene in 1995. *(Simonetta Greggio)*

Desert Boots These are the shoes worn by General Montgomery and his troops in the African desert during World War II. Today, they can be found in any shop. They are very comfortable, usually in suede, above the ankle, with laces, a flat heel, and a rubber sole. They are quite similar to Clarks.

Desforges Jean Louis (1942). French hairdresser. He has three salons in Paris and four in the rest of France. Besides his acknowledged skills, his fame is linked to the concept of independent presentations of new hairdos and cuts at the same time as the seasonal presentation of fashion Collections. Each year since 1985, in his Paris "showroom" near the Bastille, he has presented two Collections, to fashion personnel and designers, as if on a runway. From this came the idea of a school that makes use of fashion presentations, admits only professional hairdressers, and offers courses on cutting and a philosophy of hairdressing that, although bearing in mind current trends and the suggestions of tailors and designers, always gives first importance to the face and personality of the client. A hair academy like this attracts some 20,000 aspiring hairdressers each year.

Déshabillé Women's garment of varied shape, loose and almost always long, made in a light fabric and worn over a nightgown made from the same fabric. It is worn when getting up in the morning or when ready for bed in the evening. The *Gazette du Bon Ton* doesn't allow it to be worn outside the bedroom. With this garment, which appeared in the early 1800s, one can see the meaning of the term – although it did appear before that, in 1677 – used for that comfortable freedom provided by a man's dressing gown, short or long, with sewn-on pockets, loosely fastened with a belt, which in the 1700s took on the characteristics of an everyday article of clothing for the home. The 1772 pamphlet written by Dénis Diderot, *Regrets About My Old Dressing Gown*, in which the garment's comfort is praised together with its long service ("Why didn't I keep it? It was made for me and I was made for it"), is justly famous. A synonym for déshabillé is *peignoir*, from the Latin *pectinare*, but only in its 18th century form as a large dressing gown with long sleeves in a light and warm wool, the equivalent, for women, of a man's dressing gown, although the male garment is worn in more parts of the house. In the early 1800s, in fact, the term *peignoir* also indicated a bathrobe in which one wrapped oneself after a bath. *(Lucia Sollazzo)*

De Simone Livio (1920-1995). Designer from Naples. He had his maximum success in the golden period of the Sala Bianca of Palazzo Pitti in the mid 1960s, remaining faithful to it also in the 1970s, as an imaginative exponent of that boutique fashion which, emphasizing the beauty of fabrics, an enjoyment of shapes, and an explosive capacity for self-renewal, was the flagship of Italian fashion and would become the real basis for the upcoming ready-to-wear luxury styles. Very characteristic was his palette of radiant and intense colors, which, through his silks, made the Mediterranean motifs shine. The designer also made unexpected incursions into a "wax" black that was offset, though, by a daring line that was incurably free and lively.

> ❑ 2000, February. Five years after the designer's death, the *griffe* Livio De Simone continues to live thanks to the talent and designs of his wife Beba.

Faithful to her husband's style, she maintains a continuous search for colors and materials, and has also designed an accessories line (bags, shoulder bags, and haversacks) of her own.

Desmo Italian leather goods company. It was established in 1975 by Mario Fantappié in San Donato in Fronzano (Florence). It offers coordinated lines of bags, shoes, belts, and accessories with a strong design content. The company, which exports 75% of its production, has important single-brand stores in Italy and Japan.

❑ 2002, July. The expansion of the sales network continues. After openings during the last two years in Milan, Florence, St. Bart's, and Taiwan, a shop opens in Forte dei Marmi.
❑ 2002. The Desmo line, split equally between the U.S., Europe, and the Far East, ends the year with a turnover of about €10 million, a slight increase over the previous year.
❑ 2003. A new store in Tokyo, in the New Ginza neighborhood. The space is opened with Bluebell, Desmo's partner in Japan, and completes Desmo's presence in that country: a kiosk at Isetan and single-brand boutiques in Osaka and Nagoya.

D.E.S.S. The Degree of Specialized Superior Studies is a course on fashion and design offered by the Institute of Communication at the University Lumière-Lyon 2 in Lyon, France. It was started in order to provide tools for making observations about fashion, without limiting them just to clothing. It is meant for students who have already obtained their first university degree and show specific interests and skills. Enrollment is limited to 25 students. The course of study lasts one year and includes 350 hours of lessons from October to April that are divided into three areas: technique and design; business enterprise; culture and communication. There is also a three-month practical session with workshops and meetings with people in the trade. Besides the D.E.S.S., the Lumières-Lyon 2 University offers two more specialized courses: the D.U.C.T.H., for design in the textile-clothing sector, and the D.U.E.R.M. which, with one further year of complementary education after the D.E.S.S., grants a degree in fashion studies and research.

(*Mariacristina Righi*)

Dessanges Jacques (1925). French hairdresser. He patented a system for natural permanents. After an apprenticeship with Louis Gervais, he made his début in 1956 in Paris. Within 4 years, he had hired one hundred workers: it was evidence of immediate success, confirmed by the opening of more than 20 salons in France in the 1960s and 1970s, and the start of a franchise system, which was something new in the world of hairdressers. Over time, these franchisees spread his name all over the world through 500 hair salons in which the Dessanges style and technique are practiced. In order to guarantee the same quality in every franchised salon, he opened a school in Paris for cutting and hairdressing as well as make-up, a field in which he launched himself with his own line of products in 1991.

Dessès Jean (1904-1970). French designer. His Greek origin and the childhood and adolescence spent in Egypt influenced the evening dresses that were inspired by the garments on ancient Greek sculpture and by those of the queens of ancient Egypt. After leaving the study of law, he satisfied his passion for design first by providing sketches for the *maison* Madame Jean, and then, for 12 years, as its designer. In 1937, he started his own firm, and his atelier was valued by the most important women of high society and the cinema for his tailored suits, cruise wear, and, especially, his ball gowns, which were richly draped in very lightweight fabrics but also often decorated with pearls and embroidery. In 1963, he retired to Greece, where he opened a boutique: nevertheless, there had been enough time for a very young Valentino, during his beginnings in Paris, to learn from him the trade that would make him famous.

Dessous China Clothing fair dedicated to underwear and beachwear, held in Beijing. Organized by the Igedo Company, it is held every year in March. This is the third event promoted by Igedo in the People's Republic, together with Fashion China (10th to 12th

September, in Shanghai) and Chic (27th to 30th March, in Beijing). At Dessous China in 2003, for the 8th edition, about 100 companies participated, 40 of them from Europe. In 2002, the fair occupied 60,000 square feet in the Beijing Exposition Center, while in 2003 it was at the Shanghai New International Exhibition Center. The fair is not just a way for international companies and Asian buyers to meet, but also a place for forums, debates, and information on fashion.

(*Gabriella Gregorietti*)

Deutscher Fachverlag German group that is a leader in specialized publishing. It has 95 publications, with headquarters in Frankfurt. It ended 2001 with a turnover of €133.5 million (€107.2 million in Germany against €26.3 million abroad). In 2002, for the first time, business came to a standstill, due to the general economic crisis. But the problems were contained, with a loss of only 5.1% compared to the general trend for German advertising which showed a loss of 15.9% for the sector. Among its subsidiaries showing an upward trend were the titles published by Ecomarket, chief among them Fashion, with an increase of 15%, equal to €4.6 million, and Manstein-Verlag in Austria, with an increase of €21.1%, equal to €9.2 million. The results of TextilWirtschaft, a weekly covering textiles and clothing, were not so good, ending 2001 with €20.3 million compared to €23.2 million in 2000.

(*Gabriella Gregorietti*)

Deutsches Institut für Herrenmode Cologne, Germany. Institute for the promotion of German men's fashion. It organizes fashion events, meetings, and research on future trends. It has almost 400 members. It is important historically because it was the first institute of its kind in the world. It was established in Berlin in 1928 from an idea by Baron Hermann Marten von Eelking.

Deutsches Leder und Schuh Museum Offenbach, Germany. Museum of leather and footwear manufacturing, established in 1917. Its Collection includes leather clothing from all over the world, leather goods of all types of the 20th century, 2,500 pairs of shoes from ancient Rome up until today, 80 pairs of gloves, and 300 leather bags. Since 1974, it has regularly re-issued its catalogues in book form.

Deutsches Meisterschule für Mode Munich, Germany. A government-sponsored school of fashion established in 1931. It offers 2-year courses on model-making and, since 1948, 3-year courses on design.

Deutsches Mode-Institut Frankfurt, Germany. Institute for German fashion which offers its members a way to collect and exchange information about fashion and its trends. It was established in Berlin in 1954.

Deutsches Textilmuseum Krefeld, Germany. Opened in 1975, it includes the royal Collection of Mannheim fabrics, the fabric Collection of the Kaiser Wilhelm Museum of Krefeld, and a group of fabrics and garments manufactured by artists belonging to the German Secession movement. There are more than 25,000 pieces from all over the world and from every era. The clothing is mainly from the 20th century. There is a very advanced research and restoration center.

Devcold Sweater in waterproof wool used by Norwegian fishermen. It has a typical yoke pattern, recalling traditional Nordic motifs such as reindeers and snow flakes.

Devil Italian house of women's high fashion, established in Milan in 1958 by Luisa and Enrica De Vecchi, later helped by their sister Angela. It was created with a very elite market segment in mind. Twice a year, but without participating in official events, the firm presents its hand-cut and hand-sewn styles, for which buttons and accessories are expressly designed and manufactured. All the pieces are obviously in limited production. Despite the success of Italian prêt-à-porter, which completely changed the industry, the firm, with headquarters in via Bigli, in the space that once belonged to the historic art gallery Il Milione, has held on, without advertising or a distribution network, by following a careful niche strategy based on extremely high-quality tailoring.

Dévoré Technique that in recent years has often been back in fashion, especially for velvet. It is a method of printing through the corrosion of background threads which dissolve and leave a relief pattern.

Devota y Lomba Spanish brand of ready-to-wear. It began in 1988 when the duo of Luis Devota and Modesto Lomba presented their first Collection in Madrid. A few years later, Devota died. The design heritage was taken over by Lomba, who started his career in the atelier of Angel Muro di Vitoria, studied arts and crafts and moved to Barcelona to further his education. He received the prestigious Cristobal Balenciaga award, and that opened the doors of the fashion world to him. He was recently appointed president of the Association of Spanish Fashion Designers. Today, he has expanded the range of his products, including shoes and bridal Collections. In particular, he loves the classic style, with horizontal vents and classic colors. Brown and black are his preferred colors and he continuously works with these on wool, cashmere, and silk fabrics.

(*Estefania Ruilope Ruiz*)

De Vries Sheila (1952). Dutch designer. Hollywood stars such as Jane Fonda, Linda Evans, and Linda Gray have chosen her glamorous dresses, assuring her success. In 1980, after working for Tony Wagemans, she opened a boutique-atelier in Amsterdam with her husband, Tom de Vries. Seven years later, they opened boutiques in Brussels and Port Beach, California.

De War Kostio French fashion house. Lysta De Rivalo-Mazères, born Kostio de Warkoffska, opened her atelier in Paris in the late 1930s. She specialized in knitwear and tailored clothing. The *maison* closed around 1953.

Diadora International brand that manufactures and distributes sports shoes and clothing. Established in the late 1940s near Treviso for the manufacture of work shoes and hiking boots, it was in the early 1970s among the first Italian brands to start the production of sports shoes, in particular for tennis, running, and basketball. In later years, the plants in Cerano San Marco also produced soccer shoes. In short, the company maintained a leading position in the field by supplying shoes to the most important teams, in particular to such athletes as Baggio, Kuerten, Borg, Van Basten, Zico, Becker, Moser, and Senna. In 1998, it produced 7 million pairs of shoes, to which must be added the 2 million manufactured under license in South America, Japan, and Indonesia. In 1996, the company invested about 12 billion liras in warehouse automation, through which it is possible to stock 2 million pieces and pack up to 30,000 pairs of shoes and 15,000 articles of clothing a day. The distribution network in Italy consists of 2,500 multi-brand points-of-sale, 2 mega stores, 28 single-brand shops, and 50 kiosks. Abroad, it is present in 50 countries. In 1998, the turnover was about 300 billion liras, to which must be added 120 billion liras from licenses. Fifteen years ago, it entered the clothing line with the production of sportswear, whose turnover is about one-third of the total. The company is managed by Giandomenico Lico, president, and Paolo Rota, general manager.

Diamond D English shoe and leather goods company. It was established in 1908 by David Desmond Archibald Rochester, nicknamed Diamond David for his discovery of a very large diamond. Initially, production was limited to polo accessories created in the family's saddle workshop, and later expanded to include shoes. During the 1920s, the firm was very successful with a line of trunks.

Diana A pioneering boutique in that part of Milan which would become the "fashion quadrilateral": first, in 1963, in Montenapoleone and, in 1966, in via della Spiga, where Gulp and Cose were already the rage. Diana Masera (1909) opened it, and since 1957 she had been working successfully under the same name in Forte dei Marmi, offering almost exclusively the creations of Emilio Pucci. The boutique on via della Spiga was a sort of bridgehead to Italy for Dorothée Bis, at the time an emerging *griffe* for young people. It closed in 1986. In 1970, a Diana Bis boutique was opened in Porto Rotondo, Sardinia and it is still open today.

Di Andia Aléjandra Chilean designer. In 1992, she was asked to design the haute couture Collection of the *maison* Carvzen, and being successful continued to do so until the house decided to abandon haute couture completely. Born in Santiago de Chile of a Scottish mother and Chilean father, at the age of 10 she was living in France with her family. She studied at the Art Institute of Florence and at the design school of the Chambre Syndicale de la Confection et de la Couture. She gained her first work experience at Torrente. After that high-level experience with Carvzen, she launched her first Collection, called La Valise d'Aléjandra, in 1997. She isn't so arrogant as to reinvent fashion: her clothes are simple, easy to match, and well cut. She produces in France, except for the knitwear, which is made in Naples. She presented her Collection in Milan in 1999.

Dice Kayek French brand of prêt-à-porter, created by the Turkish designer Ece Ege (1963), daughter of a jeweler from Bursa. She began her career by opening a small jewellery shop in Bodrum, a tourist spot on the coast of Anatolia. She moved to Paris in order to take art courses. In 1992, in partnership with her sister Ayse, she made her début presenting 130 white cotton shirts. She was successful and the following year created her own brand, which was invited to the presentations of the Carousel du Louvre. Since then, her designs have been available at kiosks in Harrods in London, at Henry Bendel in New York, and at Italy Direct in Melbourne.

Dickies American company making work clothes, established in 1922 in Fort Worth, Texas. Its styles are original, well-made, and comfortable, and offer excellent quality for the money. They have also been at the forefront of street style fashion. Besides the U.S., the brand has a large market in England, Germany, France, and Spain, with a developing presence in Italy.

Di Corcia Philip-Lorca (1953). American photographer. He completed his photography studies in 1979 and moved to New York, where he began a series of photos of people encountered in the street chosen for their immediacy and spontaneity, using a technique that required very intense lights and obtaining almost cinematic results. He is also interested in commercial and fashion photography, and has published in Details, Esquire, Fortune, and Harper's Bazaar.

Die Dame German fashion monthly published between 1912 and 1943 by Ullstein-Verlag of Berlin. It succeeded the magazine Illustrierte Frauen-Zeitung, first issued in 1874. It was the first German fashion magazine to publish photographs in combination with drawings and sketches. It carefully followed cultural events, recalled great historical moments, and ran articles written by the most prestigious names of the time, including the novelist Stefan Zweig.

Diesel Italian company making jeans, casual clothing, and accessories. It was established in 1978 by Renzo Rosso together with other textile entrepreneurs in the Veneto. The group, with general headquarters in Molvena, near Vicenza, is present in more than 80 countries, with 10,000 points-of-sale and some 40 privately owned shops. The annual turnover is around 530 billion liras. From Molvena, the firm controls 15 European, Asian and U.S. subsidiaries, with more than 1,000 employees. Most of the manufacturing isn't done in-house, but outside by small to middle-sized companies. The jeans production, in particular, takes place only in Italy. There are license agreements for eyeglasses (Sàfilo), shoes (Global Brand Marketing), perfumes (Marbert), and leather goods (Principe).

❑ 2000, July. Diesel Iberia, the 12th foreign subsidiary, expands further in the Spanish market. In Barcelona, it opens a new showroom with offices in Plaza de Cataluña. In Spain there are 350 single-brand boutiques and 12 more are expected within 2004. The turnover in Spain is equivalent to 17.6 billion liras.

❑ 2000, August. Renzo Rosso, number one and president of the group, announces that Diesel's global turnover for the year is expected to be 700 billion liras.

❑ 2000, September. Kosta Murkudis, a young Greek designer, is appointed creative director of New York Industrie, the casual clothing line produced by Diesel International. In addition to creating the men's and women's Collections, the designer will supervise the advertising campaign. He appears on the cover of W, the monthly of Women's Wear Daily, an honor that fell to Tom Ford in July.

❑ 2001, January. Diesel receives the Made in Italy award, a prestigious American prize in the fashion industry. The company intends to expand further in the U.S. In that market, in 2000, sales increased by one-third over the previous year. Within 2004, from 10 to 35 new shops are expected.

❑ 2002, June. At Pitti Bimbo, the company presents Diesel Kids, a celebration of denim. Against a background of "impossible autos," every imaginable kind of denim is presented, with infinite variation, from stonewashed to torn and color-sprayed models.

❑ 2002, July. Diesel is a sponsor and partner of the Trieste agency Eve, which has conceived and organized the first presentation of an award for young creative designers, called *It's One* (International Talent Support), which is to be followed each year by *It's Two, It's Three*, etc. Wilbert Das, the creative director of Diesel, has worked with Victor Bellaish on the selection of 33 finalists from all over the world. The award, won by Einav Zucker, consists of €13,000 with which the winner can start his own atelier and create a new Collection for the following year's competition. The *Diesel Award*, for €2,500, which went to Daniele Controversio, offers the opportunity to produce and distribute in the best Diesel shops a mini-Collection of 5 pieces labeled with the name of the young designer.

❑ 2002, July. Acquisition of the *maison* Martin Margiela. This Belgian designer, who went to school in Antwerp, already an assistant to Jean-Paul Gaultier, works for Hermés, but since 1988 has also had his own *maison* in Paris. But he needed a strong partner to help him develop further, and he found one in Italy, in the person of Renzo Rosso. The head of Diesel intends to promote a five-year development strategy for the brand.

❑ 2002, September. DieselStyleLab, the men and women's avant-guard line, chooses New York for the first time and returns to the runways of the Bryant Park Pavilion after several years away, for Mercedes-Benz Fashion Week. The line is launched in 1998 but, after having presented in London (September 1998, October 1999) and Paris (October 1999), it undergoes a period of static presentations during Milan's Fashion Week. Forbes magazine lists Diesel among the 32 top luxury brands. The return to the formula of runway presentations and the choice of New York also indicate a strategic change and particular interest in the American market. In 2001, Diesel's U.S. turnover hit $93 million, an increase of 43%. The Collection is often inspired by the aesthetic-cultural contrast between East and West, as in the typical black leather jacket manufactured in a Japanese fabric with kimono-shaped sleeves.

❑ 2002, October. "High profits with double-digit growth in sales, an increase of 10% over the €365 million of 2001, which had already increased 38.8%." This is the Diesel group forecast for 2002, as declared by Renzo Rosso at the Milan Fashion Global Summit. The group plans a thorough review of the points-of-sale, in which the single-brand shops, of which there are 180, including 95 company-owned, are to be favored over the multi-brands.

❑ 2003, June. Daniele Controversio, winner of the *Diesel Award 2002* in Trieste, joins the creative staff of DieselStyleLab.

❑ 2003, June. The women's shoe Collection by Diesel receives a prize at the Sportswear International Fashion Awards (SIFAS). Diesel shoes are manufactured under license by Global Brand Marketing Inc. of Santa Barbara, Calif., which sells its products in more than 130 countries. It owns the Pony and Dry-shod brands and is a licensee for Nautica, Mecca, and Xoxo shoes.

(*Gabriella Gregorietti*)

❑ 2003, September. Australia is Diesel's

new target market. The first store opens in Sidney. Another one is to open soon in Melbourne.

❑ 2003, December. The turnover is €780 million, of which 85% comes from abroad. The gross operating margin of 22%, with a net profit of €74.8 million, almost hits 10%. The cash flow is €120 million.

❑ 2004, June. "Fashion companies must be directed by their managers," is Renzo Rosso's motto. "Real industrial managers must lead their companies and make every single area more professional. That's what I did." As to decentralization, he maintains that "some production cannot continue here: it is the price market's rule. If you go too far away, you won't survive. The important thing is that the brains stay in Italy."

❑ 2004, July. The company's communications strategy continues. A new advertising campaign has also been promoted. "There are 30 acid, dreamy, daily trips, the so-called day dreams," explains Antonella Rossi, the marketing director. "They are the dreams of each one of the 30 protagonists who present the pieces of our Collection; but then, in the video, these dreams shift towards rather uneasy, ironic, atmospheres." Irony, innovation, unpredictability, creativity, desecration: these are the strong elements of Diesel's communication.

❑ 2004, October. Renzo Rosso sells two thirds of his Only The Brave Srl shares, the family holding which controls the Diesel group, to his oldest sons, Andrea and Stefano. "They asked me to teach them how to manage a company: I'm happy because I have always feared that one day they may prefer to stay out of the family business."

❑ 2004, December. Diesel, the owner of Margiela, intends to double the turnover of the Belgian *maison* in the next five years (the present turnover is about €30 million).

❑ 2004, December. Excellent competitive and economic-financial results for the group. The turnover is €1,004.2 million (€909 million from the Diesel brand), up 27.5% over the €788 million of 2003. The pre-tax results are excellent: €204 million, against €128.8 million in 2003, with a net profit of €112.2 million, an increase of 50% compared to the €74.8 million of 2003. The net borrowing has gone down, from €167.5 million to €48.8 million. At December 31st 2004, the group had 173 directly managed stores, of which 21 opened in 2004, while the workforce increased from 2,561 in 2003 to 3,348 in 2004.

In recent years, Diesel has reorganized its market strategy, positioning the brand in a premium segment, investing in research and quality, reorganizing the distribution structure, and reducing the world-wide points-of-sale from 10,000 to 5,000. Also excellent are the results for Dsquared, a brand acquired in 2001. The Martin Margiela brand has also grown consistently.

❑ 2005, May. The conquest of the Spanish market continues. After the opening of a first store in Barcelona in 2002, there are openings in Bilbao, Madrid, and Valencia, and a second one in Barcelona.

❑ 2005, May. A new store opens in Hong Kong. (*Dario Golizia*)

Dietrich Marlene (1901-1992). German actress, born Marie Magdalene Dietrich. Her name is permanently linked to the androgynous style of which she was the inspiration. The non-conformist tailored suits inspired by men's clothing, loved by Dietrich on the set and in her private life, have been a source of inspiration for more than one fashion designer: from Yves Saint Laurent, a great interpreter of the woman's tuxedo, to Giorgio Armani who, more than once, has called Dietrich his inspirational muse. She arrived in U.S. in 1930, after the success of her first film in a major role under the direction of her Pygmalion, Joseph Von Sternberg: *Der Blaue Angel* (The Blue Angel, 1929). Arriving in Hollywood with 25 trunks crammed with clothes and accessories, she signed a contract with Paramount, making her the competitor of Garbo at Metro Goldwyn Mayer. Although the new diva already had a weakness for men's suits – even before moving to America, while still in Berlin, she had a tail-coat made by the tailor of her husband, Rudolf Sieber – the inventor of her look was the great costume designer Travis Banton. He was the one who encouraged her to go on a diet, and he was the one who created a completely different style for her, one that was impudent, winning, aggressive, and immediately fascinating. Banton was the creator of sensational outfits such as the chiffon dress with gold embroidery, so rich with precious stones that it looked as if it had just come from Fabergé, made for the film *Angel* (1937), and the one completely covered by black cock feathers that she wore in *Shanghai Express* (1932). On the set of that movie, Dietrich wore the famous two-tone shoes with a dark toe cap which she claimed was her own creation. Unfortunately, Chanel had already launched that model some time before.

(*Sofia Leoncina Gnoli*)

Di Fonzo Carla (1959). Italian milliner. After completing her studies at the Faculty of Letters and Philosophy in Florence, she moved to New York, where she attended the best design and fashion schools. In 1987, she went back to Italy. After moving to Maremma, she opened a milliner's shop, Carmilia. Inspired by her travels, she adopted high-level artisanal and tailoring techniques to produce hats and accessories in which a typical Italian style is combined with more lively lines that allude to costumes of different cultures, favoring materials of natural origin (straw from Florence, felt, velvet, organza, and raffia) and the world of nature itself (feathers, leaves, and flowers). Her hats are presented in combination with important *griffes*, including Gaultier and Erreuno. Her Collections are presented at various exhibitions and participate in "Alta Roma-Alta Moda."

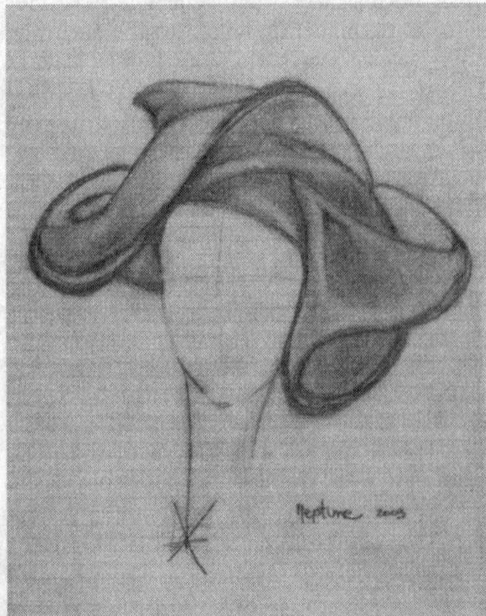

Neptune. Hat designed by Carla Di Fonzo (2003).

Digbay Morton (1906-1983). Irish tailor. He worked in Dublin and is remembered for having revolutionized the "English classic" by simply adding small details such as matching pale colors with tweed, or soft silken fabrics and jerseys to dry wool.

Di Gregorio Lia (1959). Italian goldsmith, born in Bari. After completing her artistic studies, she became interested in the goldsmith's art in Florence, under the guidance of master Bino Bini. After deepening her knowledge metal manufacturing techniques, she moved to Milan, where she opened an atelier and devoted herself to the manufacture of unique pieces emphasizing qualities such as lightness and freshness. This made her creations similar to the weft of a fabric rather than to jewellery as traditionally conceived. Gold, used in thin filaments, was twisted to form precious skeins or modeled in flimsy circles dotted with small pearls or metallic spheres. Completely handmade, the pieces created by Lia Di Gregorio are these days manufactured in goldsmith workshops and are on sale at number 10, Corso Como, in Milan, at Colette, in Paris, and at Barneys, in New York.

(*Alessandra Quattordio*)

Dim French manufacturer of stockings. Since 1989 it has been part of Sara Lee, the giant American manufacturer of tights. It was established in 1953 by Bernard Gilberstein, aimed at a middle-to-high market segment. There are three reasons for the success it has had since the 1970s, and for the volume of sales which allowed it to expand production to include men's and women's underwear: first, a partnership with Publicis, the advertising agency belonging to Marcel Blustein, whose TV campaigns were always successful; second, the jingle by Lalo

Schiffrin which became so popular it was whistled in the street; and third, the fashion for tights, helped especially by the arrival of the mini-skirt.

Dimensione Danza Brand of clothing. It was created in 1983 following the film *Flash Dance*, which was hugely popular partly due to the fitness craze connnected to the acrobatic rhythms of disco dance. Enrico Baroni, with long experience as the director of Fiorucci in New York, and his wife Nadia, a classic dancer, had the intuition not only to open a dancing school, but also to launch a fashion that was easy to wear and easy to invent, whose elements could be matched and layered as one liked: sweaters, T-shirts, tights, sweats, leg warmers, and tops. Success was immediate: the new Collections, two each year, are today the result of the collaboration of their daughter Ginger Baroni and the designer Betty Rossi. Since 1985, the production and distribution have been handled by Meeting, a company in Treviso. More than 500,000 garments are sold every year, all over the world.

(*Gabriella Gregorietti*)

Dina Insignia of Dina Azzolini (1939), a woman's hairdresser in Milan. In 1968, she opened her salon at the crossroads of fashion, at via della Spiga 23, after years of experience as a hairstylist for the most important hairdressers and photographers. Surrounded by a vague new age atmosphere, her salon was a real apartment on two floors where Dina worked with her assistant Francesca, in the company of her mother and a cat. Here, surrounded by plays of light, natural fragrances, and her preferred music, Dina's faithful clients, some of the most elegant women of Milan, in addition to vegetal treatments and a scalp massage, could ask for the "health cut" in order to eliminate split ends. Dina also offers hair-treatment products based on her own personal phyto-therapeutic recipe. In early 2000, Dina moved to via Kramer.

Dinco Dino (1970). American photographer of Italian origin. His first published photo was in 1998 in Surface magazine, and since then he has been considered an artist of some interest due to the avant-guard pictures which allowed him, the following year, to win an award given by the Art Director's Club of New York. He lives and works in Los Angeles.

Dinh Van Jean Brand of jewellery named after its French-Vietnamese designer. He started his own business in 1965 after a long apprenticeship in the Cartier workshops in Paris. It wasn't a quiet début. He was so successful that Cartier New York wanted him on its staff to create a jewellery line with his own name. He worked for Cardin. In 1976, he opened his first shop on Rue de la Paix in Paris. Perhaps his most celebrated creation is *Pi*, a gold disk with a hole in the center. It is worn around the neck with a leather string.

Dinner Jacket Men's formal jacket introduced in the late 1800s by Griswold Lorillard during a party at the exclusive Tuxedo Club, in Tuxedo Park, New York. Since then, Americans have called it the tuxedo. For the Italians and French, it is a smoking, and for the English, a dinner jacket. It is usually black or dark blue, either single or double-breasted, with large silk lapels, trousers with a satin stripe running down the side, a waistcoat that was later replaced by a cummerbund, a white shirt, and a black bow tie. During the exciting '30s, it made its appearance in Côte D'Azur in a Summer version with a white jacket. In those same years, Marlene Dietrich launched the fashion of the woman's tuxedo, an idea taken up more than once by the great names of fashion – among them Saint-Laurent and Chanel – in their Collections.

Dinnigan Colette. Australian designer. She made her début in 1990. Two years later, she opened her first boutique in Sidney, and in 1995 opened another in Melbourne. In that year, she was the first Australian designer accepted as a member of the Chambre Syndicale du Prêt-à-porter in Paris. In October 1996, she presented her Collection at the Hotel Crillon in Paris and was brought to the attention of the international press. Her fashion plays on sensuality and transparencies: very light silks and chiffons, in an evocation of haute couture, that of Paquin in particular.

Dino Erre Italian brand of shirts. It is the

top line of the Frarica factory, which was established in Carpi after World War II thanks to financing by the Marshall Plan. The brothers Clodo and Clomede Righi saw an opportunity and succeeded in expanding the small shirt business of their mother, Fernanda. They are known for the Collofit collar and for the slogan "a shirt and a moustache" in the TV commercials that ran for a long time with Maurizio Costanzo.

Dior Christian (1905-1957). A tailor and a designer who was among the most important figures in all of French haute couture. In the collective memory, he is linked to the New Look, which, on February 12th 1947, made him famous in the space of a single day. It was his first Collection. After the morning presentation, he was pushed out on the balcony of his atelier at Avenue Montaigne 30 to salute a crowd of applauding women. The Paris newspapers were on strike, and so the explosion set off by Dior was felt first in America, where Carmel Snow, the director of Harper's Bazaar, said "It's a new look." The unknown forty year old ("His face and physique made him look like a country priest," wrote Maria Pezzi) who, in an exalted return to femininity, launched immense, long blossoming skirts, with waists squeezed by small bodice-jackets, made half the women in Europe dream and tremble with trepidation. His intuition was striking, but the event which really decided his future was a meeting with Marcel Boussac. The French textile entrepreneur had everything to gain from a lifting of the wartime restrictions on fabrics, and each of Dior's swaying skirts consumed more than 16 yards of fabric, while an evening dress took as much as 27 yards. The object of both praise and invective, Dior had, by now, become Dior: a splendid atelier with a staff of 85 workers. He could change his style, and he did, naming many lines after letters of the alphabet, such as the H, A, and Y lines. He was able to revive the artisanal skills of the "petites mains," and could amaze people with hard-to-figure-out technical devices which could make the cut of a garment

A Dior dress in a sketch by Cecil Beaton (Prints Collection A. Bertarelli, Milan).

crushproof. He launched stiletto heels and excelled in the attention given to accessories such as hats, gloves, and jewellery. For him, ten years were enough, from 1947 up to his death in the Summer of 1957 in Montecatini. He became an immortal, and one of the most admired haute couture empires in the world became a legend. Dior was born in Gramville, in northwestern France. He had a happy childhood in Paris, as well as on holiday in Normandy, in which he was free to abandon himself to his genius for drawing and to a real talent in making costumes for carnival and for informal parties at home. He already had a definite instinct for art and for the joy of living. He clear calling for artistic creation, supported by constant visits to museums and galleries, would emerge only later. After interrupting his university studies in political science, and having put aside the idea of a diplomatic career, which was desired for him by his parents, he started a partnership with his friend Jean Bonjean, the owner of an art gallery in Paris, where the main figures of the various avant-guards of the 20th century exhibited their works. But his mother's death and the bankruptcy of his father's business changed his life, making his tormented youth the exact opposite of his happy childhood. In 1934, he fell seriously ill with tuberculosis. After a year of recovery in Spain, he went back to Paris and began to work on the fashion section of the weekly Le Figaro Illustré. He designed hats and began to sell sketches of clothing and accessories to several fashion houses. This lean period lasted 7 years, until 1938, when he found a steady job as a clothing designer at the *maison* Piguet. One of his first successes was a very full skirt that could be worn even in the daytime. But the outbreak of World War II and his service with the army engineers put a stop to everything. The signing of the armistice found him in the south of France where, in his father's house, he would spend a year and a half enjoying nature and the simple life of a village. Only the insistence of his friends convinced him to return to Paris, in 1941. His place at Piguet wasn't there waiting for him, but he did join the *maison* of Lucien Lelong, where Balmain also worked as an assistant. There, for many seasons, he would design the Collections, creating very tight skirts as well as flared skirts, bringing success not only to Lelong, but to himself as well, because he became the head dress designer. By now, he felt ready to manage a *maison* of his own and knew he could count on an innate talent for business. It was 1946, the year of his partnership with Boussac, who financed him with the considerable sum, for the time, of 60 million francs. In this adventure he was joined by some of Lelong's key people, such as Raymonde Zehnacker, Marguerite Carré, and Mitza Bricard. A young Pierre Cardin was hired as cutter. His team went to work immediately, in the building on Avenue Montaigne, an address which is still today considered magical and pivotal in the expansion and increase in places and regions of a charismatic empire, whose charm was always respectful of the furnishings and atmosphere chosen by Dior: Louis XV armchairs with the grey-and-white medallion that was a symbol of the *maison* on the back. Another motif associated with the *maison* was the lily of the valley, used with Dior's first perfume, *Diorissimo*, in 1948, and later sprayed generously on the pearl grey fitted carpet in the days of Dior's many presentations. It was December 16, 1946 and the début was planned for the presentations of the following February. The women's Collection, offered in the Corolla line, later called the New Look, was extremely new in its accentuated femininity, but with an antique touch: a very tiny waist (the corset and girdle were back, like a sudden jump into the past), high breasts, small shoulders, and long, full skirts with tulle petticoats to increase the bulk. It was a look backwards compared to the liberated body of Poiret and the one caressed by Chanel. It was a return to an aristocratic elegance, and also to a battle of hems, from Collection to Collection, when Dior, already rewarded with the recognition of Neiman Marcus, received in America, adjusted his approach to appeal to a more dynamic post-war woman. He lifted the skirts at the back (in 1948), cutt soft jackets, and presented tapered skirts (in 1949), making them shorter the following year, matching them with sack-shaped jackets with a horseshoe neck. In 1954 the silhouette became softer, waists were no longer squeezed in an H-line, and a love-hate relationship with the sack dress was about to begin. In 1955 came the A line and the Y

Christian Dior in a portrait by Cecil Beaton (Prints Collection A. Bertarelli, Milan).

line, with the dominating motifs the large V necks and dresses matched with immense stoles. In that same year his pursuit of the caftan had a marked effect on fashion, with a delicate high-waist dress in chiffon and a sheath dress as tight as a corset. From perfumes to prêt-à-porter, from accessories to underwear, with licenses and new boutiques in Latin America and Cuba, Dior seemed to want to put every possible avenue of distribution under his own name in order to guarantee its long life. In 1957, the *maison* presented Dior's last Collection, a variation on the theme of the *vareuse*, a kind of blouse with buttoned flap pockets that falls loosely at the sides and is often worn with a khaki bush jacket. The 1958 Collection would be designed by Yves Saint-Laurent, who three years before had become Dior's assistant and heir. The Collection was called *Trapezium* and it was a triumph. Called for military service in 1960, Saint-Laurent would, on his return, create his own atelier, as his place at Dior had been taken by Marc Bohan, someone who, over thirty years, would express the spirit of the founder in a measured and creatively elegant way.. In 1988, a big retrospective at the Pavillon Marsan in the Musée des Arts de la Mode at the Louvre celebrated Dior and the new leadership of Bernard Arnault, the wizard of the luxury goods business. In that same year, the *maison* opened its first boutique in New York, as the number one French company in the U.S. did not yet have a point-of-sale in the Big Apple. The following year, Marc Bohan left. Then the Italian Gianfranco Ferré arrived. In four annual Collections of high fashion and prêt-à-porter – some of which were memorable, starting with revived images of early Dior and gradually emphasizing a timeless luxury that was daring and magic in its opulence – he developed a range of creativity suitable to both the present day and to the prestige of an illustrious *maison*, marked by the perfumes *Dune* and *Dolce Vita*. In more recent times, after Ferré's return to Italy, the impeccable beauty typical of the *griffe* wasn't always apparent in the Collections of John Galliano, which were more prone to irony and excess than to the voluptuous grace of Dior's perfection.

(*Lucia Sollazzo*)

❑ 2000, July. The 32 year old French-Tunisian designer Hedi Slimane takes over the men's prêt-à-porter from Patrick Lavoix.

❑ 2002, January. Dior renews Sàfilo's license to produce and distribute the eyeglass Collection manufactured by them since 1996 and which, in the following year, will also have a men's line.

❑ 2002, March. The year 2001 closes with a deficit. Christian Dior SA Holding, owned 65% by Bernard Arnault, shows a loss of €95 million, on a 6% increase in sales, with revenues of €12.567 billion. The loss is attributed to reorganization costs of the retail operations and to investments needed to reorganize the U.S. business after September 11th. In 2000, the profit was €251 million.

❑ 2002, April. Dior opens a shop in Rome, in one of the most evocative places in the city, the corner of via Condotti overlooking Piazza di Spagna. A small space is reserved for the jewellery designer Victoire de Castellane.

❑ 2002, June. Hedi Slimane is nominated best designer of the year. The prize is given by the Council of Fashion Designers of America.

❑ 2003, March. The year 2002 shows a net profit of €178 million, against a loss of €95 million in 2001. The operating profit has increased 31%.

❑ 2003, March. Vincenzo Moccia, 43, becomes director of Dior Italy, after having been director of Bulgari Italy and of Gucci for northern Italy. The Italian market has contributed a turnover of €492 million (an increase of 41%) and an operating profit of €33 million to Dior.

❑ 2003, March. In Paris, the Dior woman surprises once again and is dressed in latex from head to toe. Galliano has designed the 2004 prêt-à-porter Collection for his usual crazy, sexy, and exaggerated woman, half geisha and half clown, part Japanese and part Chinese. There are skirts and miniskirts in feathered tulle, filmy and billowing, worn with long jackets; latex skirts that look like a second skin but are decorated with a thousand flowers;

blouses that are tight on the hips, similar to mini-dresses and draped like a peplum, with bat-like sleeves; very tight trousers with laces that reach the waist; clouds of silk and chiffon; high heels; platform shoes 8 inches high with ankle laces and very thin strings sparkling with studs; colored fur coats; fake flower-patterned kimonos; and important and over-the-top op-art dresses with women covered up to the nose by a latex muzzle.

❑ 2003, April. Sidney Toledano, the president of Christian Dior SA says that 15 new boutiques will be opened worldwide in addition to the current 145. In 2002 there were 23 new boutiques, and in 2003 there were 15, part of 200 planned within 2007. In Paris, where there already are 15, a new mega-store is opened on Rue Royale.

❑ 2005, January. The centennial of the birth of Christian Dior, on the 21st.

❑ 2005, May. To celebrate the anniversary, the French Minister of Culture, Renaud Donnedieu de Vabres, opens the exhibit "L'Homme du Siècle" in Granville, in Dior's childhood home, which is now a museum, *Les Rumbs*.

❑ 2005, July. The celebrations continue in Paris, during Fashion Week, with a show that covers Dior's entire life, with history, the theater, his mother in an Edwardian-style dress, the little boy Christian in a sailor's suit, and so on, until his success with the divas who visited his atelier. The show is "played" by today's top models, and mentions his passion for dancing and Peru.

(*Maria Vittoria Alfonsi*)

Di Riccio Guido (1950). Designer, born in Lucca (Tuscany). He works and lives in Milan. In 1974, he graduated from the art high school in Florence. In 1975, he worked as a designer and brand manager for many firms in the fashion sector. In 1980, he began to work as a freelancer. In his work, the artisan's craft merges with technology, but in an "ecologically correct" way in the treatment of materials. The fabrics become unique and mouldable in finished pieces, always in the avant-guard. His fashion has the feel of sportswear and the allure of good tailoring. His plans include a total look called Rags, vintage clothing for men and women. He works with several Italian and foreign *griffes*. (*Sofia Catalano*)

Dirndl Traditional costume from the Tyrol. Originally a basic garment of local dress, it became, over the years, once it transcended the narrow confines of yodels and alpine lake metaphors, an essential item (both in country versions and elegant romantic versions) for all ladies with a Nordic taste and frame of mind. After its first 40 years as a hot fashion item, it has remained popular with the ladies of Salzburg and the Milanese ladies in Saint Moritz and Celerina.

Disco Disco fashion. The heritage of funk and glam, the development of new recording techniques (sampling as a method of composition takes its first steps), and the appearance on the musical scene of new stars such as Sylvester, Donna Summer and Gloria Gaynor, give a new boost to two important minorities, blacks and gays, always in the forefront with their common passion for dancing and "attitude." Among the fashion designers of the time, Betsey Johnson, a creator of many modernist extravaganzas, and Norma Kamali are both inspired by this renewed attention to the body. They design clothes, such as jeans in elasticized fabric, shorts, and dancing leotards, in which the basic fabric is combined with new materials like Spandex and Lycra that increase its elasticity and allow greater freedom of movement when going wild to the rhythm of disco music. Typical patterns are black-and-white stripes, snake skin, and streaked patterns, i.e. the exotic and the tropical. As often happens, many of these innovations, initially conceived for a limited public, find success in other areas.

(*Maurizio Vetrugno*)

Di Scovolo Antonella (1947). Journalist and director of Più Bella. She had a complete career at the weekly Annabella, where she arrived in 1967 and would remain for 20 years, going from copy editor for fashion to deputy director. In 1989, she was put in charge at Più Bella, where she renovated the graphics and changed the focus, paying more attention to the world of work and social problems, but without diverging too much from the journal's historic concern for practicality and easy reading.

Dismero Brand of sportswear for women created in Verona in 1987 by Andy d'Auria and produced by Vermoda. The first Collection won widespread attention thanks to a new system which allowed jeans, T-shirts, and shirts to be dyed in the same color. Its practicality and sophisticated casual style are characteristic of a design strategy which, even before Italy, opened markets in Europe, the U.S., and Canada. There are showrooms in Düsseldorf and New York. Only with the Spring-Summer 2000 Collection and the opening, in September 1999, of a boutique on via Montenapoleone in Milan did the Italian firm Dismero "land" in Italy.

Disney Lizzy (1972). English designer. A graduate of the Saint Martin's School in London, in 2002 she became artistic director of Jacques Fath and marked the return to the runways of this prestigious *maison*. In decline in 1998, the *griffe* was relaunched by Mounir Moufarrige, a tycoon and the owner of the France Luxury Group, to which Emmanuelle Kahn and Scherrer belong.

Ditta Villa Italian design house. In the early 1930s, Aristotele Guido, a young entrepreneur from Lecce (Apulia), took over the tailoring workshop at Corso Concordia 12 in Milan and transformed it into the first Casa Modellistica Italiana (Italian Design House). It produced, with its own designers, exclusive styles for large tailoring workshops. The Fascist government had just issued a new law that required ateliers to produce Italian styles that were "independent," i.e. not based on models acquired in Paris, for at least 50% of their Collections, and which foresaw the need for certification by means of a gold seal from the National Institute of Fashion. After World War II, Parisian styles returned to Italy. Led by Eva Arpini, with Giuseppe Biffi as head designer, the firm purchased sketches and patterns at Dior, Balmain, and Givenchy, and original pieces at Chanel and Balenciaga in order to reproduce them with fabric imported by Satam and Gandini. The Collection was made only for large Italian tailoring shops such as Fercioni, Ferrario, Stop Senes, Zecca, Barraco, and Trottmann. Later, Villa also became a furrier's shop with styles by Diro and Fath. In the 1960's, when the firm closed, it was taken over by Krizia and made part of the premises on via Agnello.

Diulgheroff Nicolay (1901-1982). Bulgarian painter. A follower of the Bauhaus in Weimar, he designed fabrics and textiles. In 1923 he designed a silk scarf decorated with abstract motifs which echo both Kandinsky and the popular traditions of his native Bulgaria (Kumstendil). During the 1920s he was part of the Second Futurism group in Turin. As part of this circle, he designed interior furnishings.

Djellabah Cloak, usually in cotton or wool, falling to the knees or lower. It can be plain or decorated with trinkets or passementerie. With its hood and long sleeves, this garment, which can be considered a sort of national costume of Morocco (with its echoes in literature and its use by nationalists), has inspired hundreds of designs, especially in the 1960s and 1970s, and opened the way for the most recent ethnic chic, both before and after Bernardo Bertolucci's film *The Sheltering Sky*.

D-la Repubblica delle Donne Weekly supplement to the daily la Repubblica. It made its début on newsstands on May 21st 1996. The editor-in-chief was Daniela Hamaui, who gave the magazine a new approach compared to traditional women's magazines. Investigations, reportages, and great attention the photographic image soon made it a trendy publication to the point that Wall Paper, a monthly bible of fashion trends, called the magazine a "cult." In 2002, Hamaui was hired by the weekly L'Espresso. Her position at D was taken over by Kicca Menoni, who left Marie Claire (Mondadori) and signed her first issue on March 12th 2002. Over the years, despite changes in graphics and layout, the magazine continued to work with its top collaborators, including Giuseppe Turani, Vittorio Zucconi, and Umberto Galimberti, who wrote a weekly column called Fashion. It was coordinated by Marina Codecasa Cavallo, who became fashion director in 2003, and it featured the work of great photographers such as Wayne Maser, Robert Erdmann, Christophe Kutner, and Diego Uchitel.

DMC French company. Along with its affiliate, the German firm Koecnlin Baurmgartner, and with Texunion, it is a leader in the worldwide market for printed fabrics for clothing. Some 175 million yards are produced and sold each year, contributing more than 50% of a global turnover that, in the first half of the 1990s, was around 270 billion liras. It is also a leader in threads for sewing and embroidery. It employs more than 11,000 people. The company's history is very old and goes back to 1746, when three Alsatian gentlemen, each with different interests in art, finance, and trade, founded a printing works in Mulhouse. They were successful and so were their heirs, who diversified production. In 1961, DMC embarked on a policy of expansion, absorbing Thiriez et Cartier-Bresson, a company in Lille and a competitor in threads for domestic use. Together with the ancient print works, it was up to the threads division to restore the business to good health when, in the 1980s, it went through a long and severe crisis. The firm recovered in the 1990s, and resumed its policy of acquisitions, this time of foreign firms such as the English Donisthorpe, the Hungarian Maya Fashion, and the American companies Greenwood, Fashion-Fabrics of America, and Satexco, plus shares in the Irish firm Atlantic Mills. A brand of polyester and microfiber fabrics called Inoseta came from its partnership with the Japanese group Unitika.

DMR Holding company that controls several firms, especially in the textile field. The headquarters is in Carpi and the firm is led by Renato Crotti and his sons Daniele and Davide. The lead company of the group is Sinanco, established in 1949 to market knitted, diapered, and jacquard fabrics. Today it sells in 29 countries, and exports 80% of its turnover. The other companies in the group, which are Statos, Merak, Sirio, Tecnotex, Torcitura di Novi, and Torotex, basically produce knitwear fabrics differentiated by type, fineness, and diameter that are meant for makers of clothing in particular but also for producers of curtains, sewing-thread sets, ties, and labels. The most recent acquisition is Silanpol, located in Warsaw, which produces and sells mainly in the Polish market and the countries of Eastern Europe. The total turnover of DMR is more than €50 million.

DNR Line of bags created by Dario Rossi, the owner of the Redwall firm, which has been operating since 1973 in Pianoro, near Bologna. Its goal has always been to make a product with strong fashion content through the collaboration of designers. Over time, the company has created an in-house design department.

Dockers This brand, same as Levi's, is a division of Levi Strauss & Co. Launched in the U.S. in 1986, it arrived in Europe in 1993, making its début in Sweden. It arrived in Italy only in 1995. It manufactures more than 2,500 types of casual trousers, both for men and women. In 1998, Dockers Europe surpassed its quota of 4 million trousers sold, with Italy providing about 25% of the European total. There were 740 multi-brand points-of-sale franchises for the men's line and 290 for the women's, launched in Autumn 1998. In Europe, there are 16 Dockers stores, with the most recent the single-brand store opened in Florence in May 1999, the first in Italy.

❑ 2003, Spring. After the big success of its no-iron trousers, Dockers launches another novelty, the Dockers S-Fit, innovative trousers manufactured with the Clean Fabric System, which produces an exclusive no-stain and water-repellant fabric. A long association with DuPont results in a special treatment called Teflon that makes the fabric resistant to the most difficult stains such as wine and coffee. The fabric is no-crease, easy-to-wash, dries quickly, and doesn't need ironing. The styling of the new trousers is also absolutely innovative. The front pockets are closed by zippers and the back pockets have a safety fastening. A side pocket, made specifically for a cell phone, is made of linen with metallic mesh in order to reduce electromagnetic radiation. There is also a model in

cotton, Cramerton, in the traditional khaki color used by the U.S. Army since the 1930s.
❑ 2003, June. Present at the 64th edition of Pitti Immagine Uomo, Dockers celebrates the tenth anniversary of its arrival in Europe. Dockers Italy is third in importance in Europe after Spain and Portugal, with 650 point-of-sale franchises.
❑ 2003, June. Among the offerings for Spring-Summer 2004, Dockers launches the Made in History line, which recalls the clothing of the masons who worked on the Empire State Building. There are trousers and jackets in pale colors such as yellow and ecru, manufactured with natural fabrics and triple seams.

Documento Moda News magazine about the fashion and textile industries published in Turin between 1941 and the Summer of 1942 by the National Institute of Fashion. Despite the fact that the country was at war, the periodical wanted to promote the goals of the Italian textile industry, and of a fashion industry that was based on a government policy of national self-sufficiency, and so Documento Moda was replaced by the technical monthly Pizzi e Pizzi, whose editorial policy was artisanal in tone, favoring cottage industries.

Doeuillet-Doucet French house of haute couture. In 1920, Georges Doeuillet, who learned the profession working for the sisters Callot and trained his eye by writing articles on fashion, opened his own atelier in partnership with some English friends. He built his name as the French subsidiary of an established London mother-company specialized in dresses and cloaks. When, in 1928, a year before his death, Jacques Doucet lost interest in his own firm, Doeuillet didn't let the opportunity slip by and annexed it to his atelier, a avant-guard *griffe* for sophisticated women's clothing. The Doeuillet-Doucet *maison*, despite the addition of new partners, closed in 1937.

Dolara Silk factory with a plant in Fino Mornasco (Como). This company created by Arturo Dolara received unanimous praise from people in the trade at the *Esposizione Voltiana* which took place in Como in 1899, especially for its diapered fabric for clothing. In 1920, Arturo's son Aldo joined the firm, as did Giuseppe Rostagno. After the death of the founder, various industrialists and professionals also joined. In 1946, Dolara merged with FISAC.

Dolce & Gabbana Italian designers. They work as a team and are considered the creators of a new Mediterranean style. Domenico Dolce (1958) was born in Polizzi Generosa (Palermo). As a young man, he followed entered the business of his father Saverio, which was a small clothing company. Stefano Gabbana (1962) was born in Milan. He studied the graphic arts, but soon chose fashion as a profession. The two met and decided to form a professional partnership. For some years, they collaborated with various design studios, until they decided to start their own business, establishing the Dolce & Gabbana *griffe*. Their first participation in a fashion event was in 1985: Beppe Modenese invited them to Milan for the Collezioni Nuovi Talenti (New Talent Collections). They presented a Collection of definite novelty, produced in a series of artisanal Sicilian workshops, which drew the interest of the trade press. But their first self-produced Collection was the following March, in the via Santa Cecilia headquarters of their atelier in Milan. In the intense atmosphere of mini-skirts and squared shoulders and the career woman, the feminine figure proposed by Dolce & Gabbana was the traditional one that could be found among the women of Lampedusa's *Il Gattopardo*, in the streets described by Verga, or in the paintings of Guttuso. The women of Sicily, fiery, seductive, and severe, at the same time God-fearing and attached to family and church; a mix of glamour and verismo, the exaltation of a Mediterranean rediscovery. The inspiring muse was a Santuzza who liked to play the uninhibited girl, with bras and corsets in plain sight, and petticoats, veils, and lace displayed with erotic impudence. The Dolce & Gabbana style was strong and pronounced, and moved away from the panorama of those years. Their Santuzza made her way quickly, wearing a girdle, and a rosary, as if it were a precious necklace, and a man's waistcoat decorated on the back with lace, and a bra over a blouse. In 1988, an agreement was signed providing for the manufacture of the prêt-à-porter by a company in Legnano belonging to the family of Domenico Dolce. Another fundamental step in the career of the two young designers was accomplished in 1990, the year in which they presented their first men's Collection. In 1994 it was the moment of the D & G Collection, a line dedicated to young people, produced and distributed by Ittierre. In order to give a more refined and precise imprint to their style, Dolce & Gabbana put it in the hands of great masters of photography such as Ferri, Scianna, Meisel, Lindbergh, and Newton. The image that emerged seemed to be inspired by the protagonists of films by Germi and Monicelli, women seduced and abandoned, or girls with a gun, in tribute to Anna Magnani, Sophia Loren, Claudia Cardinale, and Stefania Sandrelli. A dominant figure in show business who played a large role in the history of the two designers was Madonna. Their friendship stirred an international outcry with the presence of the American rock star at the D&G party presentation in 1992. Madonna confesses a real passion for Dolce & Gabbana and asks them to design 1,500 costumes for her tour *Girlie Show* in 1993. But, among their fans are many other names as well, such as Demi Moore, Nicole Kidman, Isabella Rossellini, Susan Sarandon, Tina Turner, Gwyneth Paltrow, Liv Tyler, Chiara Mastroianni, Jon Bon Jovi, and Simon Le Bon. In March 1996, D & G celebrated their first important anniversary with a photo book, *10 anni di Dolce & Gabbana* (*10 Years of Dolce & Gabbana*). On the cover was a photo of Monica Bellucci in a remake of the famous striptease in the film *La Dolce Vita*, which was inspired by a real striptease by the Turkish dancer Aiché Nanà in a Roman nightclub at the end of the 1950s. Also in 1996, they launched a CD called *D & G Music,* followed in 1997 by another single *D&G More More More*. For Giuseppe Tornatore, who directed a TV commercial with Monica Bellucci for the first of their fragrances, Domenico Dolce and Stefano Gabbana agreed to play a Sicilian shepherd and a Milanese photographer in the film *L'uomo delle stelle*. Their latest creative step was the D & G Junior line presented at Pitti Bimbo in Florence in June 1999.

(*Laura Asnaghi*)

Dolce & Gabbana: Autumn-Winter 1997-98 Collection.

❑ 2000, July. Dolce & Gabbana open their new boutique on mythical Rodeo Drive in Beverly Hills with a big party. Women's Wear Daily called the event a new touch of Sicily on the West Coast.
❑ 2002, February. After long experience – 15 years – as vice president and manager of Armani, and then as president and managing director of Calvin Klein, Gabriella Forte becomes, at the age of 51, president of Dolce & Gabbana USA and director of Dolce & Gabbana Spa's licensing and accessories.
❑ 2002, June. The junior line expands to include baby wear from 6 to 24 months. The Baby Spring-Summer 2003-2004 Collection is presented against the background of a fake beach. It is basic clothing with the brand name very visible, a lot of denim, and animal prints. Starting at the end of July, the

Collection will be on sale in a kiosk at the Rinascente in Piazza Duomo in Milan. More kiosks will be opened in the single-brand boutiques in Milan, Miami, and Rome (in Piazza di Spagna).

❑ 2002, June. The two designers throw a big party for Kylie Minogue, who is in Italy only at the Filaforum in Assago, at Antologico on via Mecenate. Guests were admitted Only guests wearing the T-shirt with the words "Dolce & Gabbana for Kylie" that was sent with the invitation, and carrying a computer-generated lip-print of the 34 year old Australian pop diva in the shape of a kiss, were allowed to enter. D&G created all the stage costumes for her European tour.

❑ 2002, September. A return to their original style, the one that made them famous in the second half of the 1980s. Ten cult garments, reissued with a Vintage label, open the Collection. Mini-corsets on a white shirt, a black bustier-dress with laces at the hips, and a knitwear sheath are all back on the runways, along with a sexy, very tight black tailored suit which emphasizes the figure. The Collection continues with the new offerings for Spring-Summer 2003. A surreal and nostalgic atmosphere in an old harbor with moorings and rusted chains is the background for the presentation of very tight trousers fastened by buckles, silver cotton jackets, mini-skirts with leather fringes, wide and asymmetric shirts, short peplums in red jersey, and furs with knitwear and chain inlays. "Futurist, super-sexy, extravagant, erotic, warrior, Hellenic, tough": these are the adjectives used by D&G for the new Collection. Unusual details such as décolleté shoes with a chain and lock, very thin and giddy heels, boots with a large studded band, handcuff-bangles, collars with the words sex or love written on them. And then the clothes that transform themselves: a dress, a jacket and even a bag change shapes and sizes at will. By the end of 2002 Dolce & Gabbana expects a turnover of €533 million. No crisis for them.

❑ 2003, January. At the start of the Milan presentations, the new space in Milan is opened, in a building on Corso Venezia that is the historic former headquarters of Brigatti. According to plans by the architect David Chipperfield, frescoes and structures were restored and the three floors contain space not necessarily devoted to selling. One could speak more of a men's club than a shop, with a Sicilian barber (Giovanni Pappalardo, from Gela), a Martini and Rossi bar, and a fitness center with massages, mud packs, and beauty treatments. The furnishings were personally selected by the two designers, with the help of the architect Ferruccio Laviani. Murano lamps, figs from India, baroque thrones, and giant leather bags: everything in D&G style.

❑ 2003, January. For the men's Collection, D&G offers street life fashion which still wishes to maintain its extreme luxury and not become cheap or shabby.

❑ 2003, March. For Winter 2004, D&G invents a techno-romantic woman. It is romanticism revisited in a modern key: a black-and-white dress with computer-printed cat-like spots; an op-art black-and-white dress with antique lace inlay; a sexy dress worn with motocross boots; and classic patent leather open-toed shoes with very high heels, but on a platform sole. And finally, the play of contrasts between man and woman, with jackets and suits that are always different, and colored oversize parachute-parkas.

❑ 2003, March. The first Dolce & Gabbana Vintage boutique opens at via della Spiga 26/a in Milan.

❑ 2003, April. Mary Quant's mini-skirt turns 40. To celebrate the anniversary of a true revolution, a "Mini Pride" event is organized in Riccione. The Dolce & Gabbana brand had to be there, and in fact it closed the train parade with three models in mini-skirts riding an antique car.

❑ 2003, May. D&G boutiques on Old Bond Street and Sloane Street in London are the target of groups associated with London Animal Action. According to reports on the website www.fuk.uk some seventy protesters gathered in front of the reinforced shop windows on Old Bond Street to protest the use of animal skins by the two designers. The protesters say that they will repeat the protest every Saturday until D&G renounces the use of furs.

❑ 2003, May-June. New openings are expected in the near future. After buying a house in Portofino in 2001 – the Villa Olivetta, a mansion rented for years by Mr. Berlusconi, Dolce and Gabbana return to the Gulf of Tigullio. It is now the turn of Santa Margherita Ligure. In June, a boutique measuring 1,300 square feet is opened in the former location of the historic Bima pastry shop, which had closed after 70 years in business. Other recently opened stores are in Venice (September 2002) and Riccione (April 2003). The most important opening is in Munich, in the renovated ancient Fünf Hofe complex. The interior décor, with steel surfaces, mirrors, and boxes of opalescent lights, has been designed, same as the other D&G shops, by the architect Rodolfo Dordoni.

❑ 2003, June. Men's fashion. A small oasis of palm trees and sand, the rhythms of the 1970s, and an exceptional vocalist, Jocelyn Brown. It is Happy Hour Fashion, brought to the runways in a variation of the classic dry martini offered before the presentations. The stylistic focal point could only be David Beckham, the man today considered the new icon of men's fashion. "We dress him," said Domenico Dolce, in an implied polemic against Armani, who dedicated the Beckham Jacket to him.

❑ 2003, October. The launch of *Hollywood*, a book conceived by Stefano and Domenico. A homage to Hollywood and the stars who in the last ten years have chosen Dolce & Gabbana, it has more than 100 photos of the most important film stars of today; the profits from the book will be donated to charity.

❑ 2004, January. The launch of the book *Soccer*. It features 44 players, 3 teams, and 2 coaches, photographed in black-and-white by Mariano Vivanco. The profits will be donated to four charity associations.

❑ 2004, May. A new agreement with Citroën Italy for a D&G version of the C3 Convertible and C3 Pluriel.

❑ 2005, September. The 20th anniversary of the *griffe*. By now it has 80 directly-managed single-brand stores (D&G included), revenues of €700 million at 31st March 2005, and revenues of €1.05 billion. For the future, the plan is to open more single-brand stores and to develop the multi-brand network.

(*Gabriella Gregorietti*)

Dolce & Gabbana: Spring-Summer 1996.

Dolomiten Manufacturer of men's and women's sportswear, established in 1962. The headquarters are in Tesero di Trento. It distributes in specialized stores throughout Italy, the rest of Europe, the U.S., and Japan. It owns the brands Dolomiten, Lodencenter, Dolomiten Sportswear, Pull-d, and Top-Lady. In the 1950s and 1960s the firm had a store on via Montenapoleone in Milan, on the present site of the Valentino boutique.

❑ The brand name is changed to Dolomite. The firm was acquired by the Tecnica group in 1998, and today there is a store on Piazza del Duomo in Milan.

Domenici Anna. Italian designer, born in Milan. She studied in Florence and Rome, where she received her degree. In the mid 1960s she earned her living by selling sketches and drawings to up-and-coming ready-to-wear houses. In 1970, she joined the Krizia design department and became the creative right arm of Mariuccia Mandelli. It was a symbiotic collaboration that lasted 24 years and which, in 1980, gave birth to the fan-shaped plissé. Their work together ended in 1994. Shortly after, she was asked to update the Mila Schön Collections but in a traditional way. She stayed there 4 years.

Dominella Stefano (1952). Managing director of Maison Gattinoni and, since November 2002, president of Alta Roma, the organization which oversees the Rome Fashion Week. He is highly regarded for his excellent managerial ability and a marked artistic spirit. He was born in Ancona. After studying at the Liceo Parini in Milan, and at the San Giuseppe Demerode in Rome, he served in the army as a parachutist. Immediately after, he attended the Academy of Dramatic Arts and, for a semester, the Marangoni Institute. In the late 1970s he worked in the Mila Schön design department in Milan, and then he was a coordinator-assistant to Valentino for prêt-à-porter in Rome. The turning point for him came in 1985 when, together with a schoolmate of his from San Giuseppe, Raniero Gattinoni, he started a restyling project for the Gattinoni *griffe* aimed at developing the prêt-à-porter. After Raniero's death in 1993, Dominella appointed the Venezuelan Guillermo Mariotto, who was already an assistant at Gattinoni, as artistic director of the firm. Gattinoni's High Fashion has won a difficult bet, successfully mixing tradition and technology. It combines, for example, classic embroidery with varied innovative materials such as aluminum sequins and glass splinters. Today, Gattinoni has twelve licenses covering eyeglasses, perfumes, and prêt-à-porter. An indefatigable worker, Dominella is curator of exhibits and educational coordinator at the European Institute of Design. He also deserves credit for the choice of Renzo Piano's Auditorium as the new location for the Alta Roma fashion event, a project which finds him in the forefront of the effort to make the event more and more international.

(*Eleonora Attolico*)

Dominguez Adolfo (1950). Spanish designer and the inventor of Iberian minimalism. After his study of aesthetics and cinematography in Paris, he joined his father's tailoring workshop and transformed it into a fashion atelier. His first Collection was in 1983. A simple and fluid style that is natural, sober, and balanced provides the foundation for his vision of women's and men's fashion. During the 1980s he opened boutiques in Madrid, Barcelona, Paris, and London. He also signed an agreement with a Japanese company for production and distribution in the Far East.

❑ 1999. The U line is launched, aimed at young people over 15. It is fashion that is self-assured, high-tech, and romantic.
❑ 2001. He enters the American market, with a boutique in Miami. Besides the shops in Madrid and Barcelona, which were opened in 1982, there are 181 stores (including 53 single-brand and 79 franchises) scattered throughout Europe, Latin America, China, Japan, and South-East Asia. The company employs 930 people, and the 2001 turnover was 17.5 billion pesetas.
❑ 2003, April. The clothing line is supported by the "Mi casa" Collection, which offers three coordinated lines for bed and bath in natural fibers. A shop called ADC (Adolfo Dominguez Complements) is opened exclusively for accessories. The Unica cosmetics line is launched.

Domino A long, wide hooded cloak, originally only in black and later in precious, sometimes colored, fabrics. Worn with fancy evening clothes. As a unisex item, it is worn during Carnival at masked balls.

Domus Academy Center for post-university study established in 1983 in Milan by a group of professionals, among them the designer Gianfranco Ferré. It is dedicated to professional education, industrial research, and the promotion of cultural activities. It offers a masters in Fashion Design, with a course of study structured as group research. Among the teachers are the entire staff at Moschino, the designer Stephan Janson, the journalists Renata Molho, Titti Matteoni, Aldo Premoli, and Donata Sartorio, the designers Daniela Pupa, and Nancy Martin (for fabrics), and Ampelio Bucci (for marketing). The work is focused on projects covering the various aspects of fashion, from the culture of design to industrial management. Among the other activities of the Domus Academy are the Research Center, for professional research in the field of design; a publishing program; the organization of exhibits, such as the one dedicated to *Italian Fashion* in 1988 in New York; the Domus Design Agency, which since 1991 has provided design projects to various companies; and the Future Fashion Lab, a permanent research laboratory which produces a quarterly abstract of stylistic trends, consumer tastes, and clothing culture for various clients. In 1995, Domus Academy won the *Golden Compass* for its activities.

Donald Christie (1960). Scottish photographer. She studied fine arts at the Polytechnic in Newcastle. Her sensitivity to fashion convinced Levi's, Nike, Diesel, and Converse to entrust her with their advertising campaigns. She lives and works in London.

Donati Nino. Millinery entrepreneur, born in Modena. He was director of the Familiare di Montevarchi. During the 1920s in Florence he established his own straw hat factory. After World War II, it became the most famous in its field in the world of fashion. The author of various publications, he also manufactured felt hats that were produced mostly in the Montevarchi area between Florence and Arezzo.

Don Marshall Brand and pseudonym of the hat designer William Ernest Sydenstriker. He made his début as a costume designer and hairstylist during a show for U.S. troops in the Pacific during World War II. In 1956, Grace Kelly ordered all the hats for her honeymoon with Prince Ranier of Monaco from him, while the hat worn for her wedding, in lace encrusted with pearls, was designed, along with her dress, by the Hollywood designer Helen Rose. At that time, millinery was very popular and served the main figures and great names of show business and high society, even if it wasn't present in the places devoted to fashion and luxury in New York. Marshall's fame was such that he was able to withstand the decline of hats in both high fashion and everyday dress. In 1963 he still had a staff of 55 people between workers and sales personnel. Department stores, especially Bloomingdale's, wanted his help for the mass production of hats, and American designers wanted his advice during their presentations. In the early 1970s, the ever smaller number of women wearing hats forced him to adopt a defensive strategy: an atelier at a prestigious address, Park Avenue and 57th Street, and a staff reduced to just a few workers, serving a small group of elite clients. He was often inspired by Picasso, especially the portraits of Dora Maar and the *Pierrot* paintings.

Donna Women's monthly magazine established in Milan in 1980 by Flavio Lucchini and his wife Gisella Borioli, who for a long time held the positions of managing editor and director, respectively. Carried along on the tide of the Made in Italy movement, Donna's originality lay in its contrast with traditional women's magazines, offering an image of fashion as a social phenomenon, comparable in some ways to industrial design. It launched great Italian photographers such as Ferri, Toscani, and Gastel. It promoted several fashion phenomena and "discovered" Japanese design, as well as new Italian talent such as Dolce & Gabbana. The feminine model it suggested opened the way for a type of woman linked more to the reality of everyday life and less to the images of beauty and elegance in the glossy magazines. In 1998, the Rusconi group relaunched the monthly, entrusting the graphic layout to the head art director, Gianni Brancaccio, the editorial management to Vera Montanari, and the editorial supervision to Marina Fausti. In 1999, the Rusconi group was acquired by Hachette. The management was entrusted to Daria Bignardi. *(Stefano Grassi)*

Donna Moderna Italian women's weekly. The first issue, on the stands March 8th 1988, sold 600,000 copies. After a few weeks, it settled at 350,000 copies and later reached more than 500,000. With 92 pages, columns that were short and others very short, often in side boxes, and written in simple, clear, almost elementary prose, the new magazine, published by Mondadori, was launched with the support of an advertising campaign costing almost 4 billion liras. With Edvige Bernasconi as editor-in-chief, and inspired by a French weekly that was selling more than 1 million copies, it featured useful services and news on classic themes: beauty, fashion, interior decor, health, and current events. At a critical moment for women's magazines, Donna Moderna was aimed at the still intact group of the lower middle-class, the so-called B Target, which until then had been the undisputed territory of gossip magazines such as Bolero and Novella 2000. After one year under Giuseppe Botteri, the magazine was back in the hands of Bernasconi. In the years that followed, the weekly tried to soften its excessively popular characteristics, winning higher-level readers as well. In February 1993, for the first time, circulation surpassed 1,000,000 copies. At the end of 1997, the circulation was about 600,000 copies. Today, it is led by Patrizia Avoledo, assisted with intelligence and professionalism by Cipriana Dall'Orto.

Donovan Terence (1936-1996). English photographer. His first jobs were in London, on Fleet Street, as a lithographer and pressman. At the age of 15, he became interested in photography. In 1959, after an apprenticeship as an assistant to the photographers Adrian Flowers, John Adriaan, and John French, he opened his own studio and started to make a name for himself with advertising campaigns and fashion articles published in Vogue England, Queen, Men About Town, and Nova. He was famous for his choice of London streets as backgrounds for the photos which typified the style of Swinging London and qualified Donovan as the photographer who best interpreted, with his black-and-white images, the spirit of the '60s, along with his colleagues Duffy and Bailey. In addition to his photographic work, he was a noted director of TV commercials. Between 1976, the year of his first film, *Yellow Dog*, and 1996, he made more than 3,000.

Donyale Luna. American model and cover girl. Active in the 1960s and 1970s, she was one of the first Afro-American women to model and pose for the big fashion magazines. She was preceded, in January 1953, by Dolores Francine Rheney, who was discovered by the Roman tailor Ferdinandi and who made her début on the runway of the Sala Bianca in Florence thanks to him. Luna was a star in the ateliers of Paco Rabanne and Courrèges and on the runways of the Italian high-fashion ready-to-wear that was emerging just then. Fellini gave her a small role in *Satyricon*. She married the photographer Ezio Cazzaniga, had a daughter, and died very young.

D'Ora Pseudonym of Philippine Kalmus (1881-1960), an Austrian photographer. In her photos models seem to float on an ethereal background. This blurred effect, used starting in 1916, was made possible by a special lens created by her assistant, Arthur Benda. In 1909, she opened a studio in Vienna and became the portraitist of high society. Invited to work with Vogue France, in 1924 she decided to commute between Vienna and Paris. Until 1939, L'Officiel de la Couture was the platform for her work. Her photos document 15 years of fashion, Collections and alteliers.

D'Orazio Sante (1956). American photographer. After studying painting and the fine arts at Brooklyn College, he devoted himself to photography under the guidance of Lou Bernstein, one of the mythical personalities of the Photo League, from whom he learned the value of immediacy and a sense of street photography. His first photo feature was published in 1981 in Vogue Italy, and then his career continued with Vogue America, Esquire, Town and Country, Interview, Vanity Fair, and D-la Repubblica delle Donne. He created campaigns for Versace, L'Oréal, Revlon, Tommy Hilfiger, and Victoria's Secret, and published the books *A Point of View* (1998) and *Sante D'Orazio* (2000).

Dorazio Piero (1927). Italian artist. His first pieces of jewellery, created during the 1960s at the request of the jeweller Mario Masenza of Rome, were made in cast gold through the lost wax process, the same process used for sculpture. In 1975 and '76, he worked on a small series of jewels in Milan for Gem Montebello. It was a Collection of bracelets, necklaces, and brooches in yellow gold and polychrome enamels which recalled the grids in his paintings of those years.

Doré Doré French stocking factory established in 1819 in Champagne. Thanks to the high level of its products, it has a big market share all over the world. It has a turnover of 220 billion liras per year and employs 700 people. In 1996, it opened a pilot boutique in Milan.

Dorfles Gillo (1910). Scholar of aesthetics and an art critic, he published several books on architecture, design, art, and fashion. Among these, two titles have, since their first publication, aroused international interest. One is *Il Kitsch* (Mazzotta, 1968), an extraordinarily successful book which reintroduced a term that is by now part of the common language. The other is *Mode & Modi* (Mazzotta, 1979), which attempted to explain how it is that among the so many small disorders and changes which are part of man's existence, the only authentic constant is the totality of fashions (and habits). From this book, which is also an anthropological treatise about the clothed body, it would be interesting to quote some of his opinions and analyses of fashion. "Fashion," he says, "isn't simply one of the most important social – an economic – phenomena of our time: it is also one of the safest instruments with which to measure the psychological, psychoanalytic, and socioeconomic motivations of humanity, and thus one of the most sensitive indicators of the particular 'current taste' which always represents the basis for every aesthetic and critical evaluation of a specific historic period." Further on, "In men, differently than in animals, the variety of garments and their multiplicity of shapes are fundamental, and always constitute something that is invented, superimposed, and changeable, in contrast with that perpetuity and lack of 'choice' on the part of animals as to what they wear... In animals, the motifs of sexual attraction (horns, wattles, feathers) are always a fixed component, while in men they are as mutable as fashion itself. And yet, fashion often avails itself of elements that are 'stolen' from nature either as equivalents or as a way to strengthen the elements of sexual attraction." The discussion then touches on the history of costume, when Dorfles affirms that "every revolutionary phenomenon, every upheaval in the politics and morals of a specific country, has always been accompanied by a transformation in its clothing fashions, with a marked change in the exterior look of garrments, almost as a way to emphasize the end of an era... And yet fashion is precisely the kind of revolutionary phenomena that transforms itself, within a short time, into an accepted custom, becoming mannered or affected, and thus anti- or counter-revolutionary." And then: "With the advent of the bourgeoisie as a dominant class, the general population tends to adopt its habits and style of clothing, while the typical clothes of country people disappear... Only in our time does it happen that it is no longer the dominant class which imposes its fashions on others, but, on the contrary, that the lower classes popularize fashions which are later adopted by the bourgeoisie... This is a totally new phenomenon compared to the past, and not simply to a very distant past, but even to a more recent one: the orientation of fashion towards the "low" instead of to the "high." Very out of fashion is the person who will not adjust to the fashions adopted by the lower classes (even if the product of such fashion continues to depend, from an economic-commercial point of view, on those who still control that production, as happens in today's capitalist system)." His conclusion appears to be valid even today, when he says, "The system of fashion (trousers that are tight or flared, jackets that are short or long, low waists and high waists, jackets with or without vents, belted jackets, shirtdresses, blouses that are worn under or over a pullover, and other peculiarities that change over time) will conform to the styles aimed at the great mass of consumers and not at the tiny elites who are still well-off enough to buy custom-made fashions of the great ateliers... These days, even the dominant classes have to take the habits of the masses into account. The purchase of jeans, jackets, overalls, and other trappings of the youth culture represents a huge business that cannot be considered except from both a social and economic point of view." And finally, "Fashion is often identified with kitsch, or it is said that

From the volume *Mode e modi* by Gillo Dorfles (Mazzotta, Milan, 1977).

fashion exploits elements of kitsch by making them trendy. Even more often, something which is not kitsch when it is trendy becomes kitsch the second time around, when it is out of fashion.

(*Franco Belli*)

Dorlostan Elastic fiber. It is produced in the Dormagen and Bushy Park plants of Bayer USA. It is very light, with a particularly soft coat. Demand is greater than supply. A leotard made with dorlostan-polyester weighs less than 2 ounces.

Dormeuil French textile group established in 1842. At first it was a trading company and imported fabrics from England. Then it began to manufacture fabrics for high quality men's clothing. Since 1936, it has been a supplier to haute couture ateliers. It has offices in London and Paris. Since 1993, it has been active in men's prêt-à-porter. The company still belongs to the founding Dormeuil family, now in its fifth generation.

Dorothée Bis Chain of prêt-à-porter boutiques established in Paris in 1962 by Jacqueline Jacobson (1928) and her husband Elie (1925). They opened their first shop on the Left Bank in Rue de Sevrès. Aimed at young people, the ambience was simple, the shop assistants were teenage girls, and the garments on sale (pantsuits and "porthole" dresses) were not available in sizes over 29. In 1964, the shop name became a brand for which Khan, Lagerfeld, Pipart, and Rosier all worked. During the 1970s, Dorothée Bis was very successful thanks to its soft, handmade knitwear. It has 8 stores in France, and they also carry men's clothing and sportswear. In 1997, the chain was acquired by the Naf-Naf group. *(Emma Costa)*

Dorsey Hebe (1925-1987). Journalist. From the 1960s up until her death, she was a fashion editor at the International Herald Tribune. In one of design's most sparkling and creative periods, she was a lucid, independent, and caustic interpreter of its trends. She was well known for her multifaceted **s**, colorful elegance. Nicknamed "the Tunisian from the West" because of her African origins and the dash of her lively, bright style, she made a name for herself as one of the most influential and feared personalities in fashion journalism, and was able to become a critic of shapes and clothing, giving generous and early attention to new talents. Her psychological studies of designers and young stylists remain extraordinary, in timeless portraits ranging from Saint-Laurent to Coveri.

(Lucia Sollazzo)

Dorys Benedikt Jerzy (1901-1990). Polish photographer. A classic example of professional versatility. He was interested in all the aspects of his profession. He started taking pictures when still very young, but only turned it into a real career in 1925. His fame is linked to his talent as a portraitist in his studio in Vienna, and the refinement in his study of processes such as bi-chromed rubber. Over the course of his career he was interested in reportages, landscapes, architecture, and fashion photography.

Dosa Brand of women's clothing created by the Korean designer Christina Kim. She is a singular example of the artisan-designer who rejects the classic circuit of Collections and personally follows the production of clothing in her studio-factory-shop in Los Angeles. Her clean lines, the preference for varieties of white in her silk and taffeta blouses, and her low-profile "Buddhist" approach to fashion have made her the favorite designer of actresses like Nicole Kidman and Cameron Diaz. An advocate of artisanal production, in February 2002 she was invited by Woodbury University in Burbank to give a lecture entitled *Making by Hand*.

Double-breasted A style of closing a jacket, in which one part of the front overlaps the other, with two rows of buttons and one row of buttonholes. Its origin is not certain, but likely connected to the military and possibly the uniforms of Hussars in the 17th century. Later, the double-breasted coat became part of the full-dress uniform during the Napoleonic era. In today's fashion, the double-breasted jacket represents a singular example of the rhetorical figure of speech called metonymy, in which one part stands for the whole. To wear something double-breasted is synonymous – strictly speaking – with a men's suit that has a double-breasted jacket. But on a symbolic level, it immediately brings to mind the business suit. The proportion of the number of buttons is algebraic: 6 to 2 (six buttons, of which two can be buttoned); or 6 to 1; and 4 to 1. The exceptions are models that have either 6 or 8 buttons in which all the buttons can be buttoned, such as navy uniforms and Edwardian-style suits. In modern times, its history is remarkable. In America, after the Depression of 1929, the double-breasted suit became very popular. There was a need for strong masculine images of virile men with broad shoulders and a thin waist. Then, it was adopted as a uniform by the strongest and most powerful men of the 1930s, the gangsters, who preferred chalkstripes and dark fabrics. They were also businessmen, of course, although in a dirty business. Their wealth was secure when economic times were bad. Since then, the double-breasted suit has been surrounded by an aura of formality mixed with an arrogant elegance that is at the same time reassuring. Much loved by politicians of all parties, even as a blue blazer with grey flannel trousers, it caused real debate over the proper way to button models that have two buttons which can be buttoned. Prince Charles diligently buttons both of them. The tailors of Savile Row recommend buttoning only the top one. The Earl of Kent, in the 1930s, opted for an eccentric buttoning of just the bottom one. But there was no debate about the fact that a double-breasted suit cannot be worn unbuttoned. (*Antonio Mancinelli*)

Double-faced A reversible fabric or garment with two faces each having different, often contrasting, colors and patterns. Many designers have elaborated double-faced garments, including Mila Schön.

Double O Brand of ready-to-wear created by Kenichi Nakayama and Rie Watanabe in 1999. The two Japanese designers became partners after meeting at a preview in a London museum. It is a union that combines the worlds of art and fashion. Nakayama graduated in 1994 and worked with Issey Miyake on the Pleats Please line. He designed fabric for Giorgio Armani and for several theatrical productions, and has a past as choreographer. He comes from a tradition of kimono manufacturing and design. Watanabe has worked as an art director in publishing and in Japanese television. They are both keen on art, music, and dance, and presented their first Collection, called Jet Lag, in 1999 at the Royal College of Art, inspired by plane travel. In 2000, they presented the Fog Bound Collection, with real "performances" in places such as subway stops and supermarkets. Following the idea that everyday life has a poetic side, and that every garment can be worn in a different way, they design asymmetric, multifunctional clothes in bright shades and colors, often using denim. (*Daniela Bolognetti*)

Doucet Jacques (1853-1929). French designer. He is considered, together with Worth, the father of French fashion. He was an art collector, a book collector and a patron, all activities that he pursued in perfect harmony from the very start. His career began in 1875 when he first collected furniture, paintings, and drawings of the French 18th century, and created extraordinary dresses which recaptured the shapes and delicate pastel tones of the era. His atelier opened in that same year. The heir of a men's underwear factory established by his grandfather in 1816, he would change it completely in appearance and purpose. Intolerant of the excessively "official" character of fashion design, isolated and very famous, rather than consider himself a designer he preferred to think of himself as, and actually was, a dandy who liked to create clothes that matched the ambience of Art Nouveau furniture for a well-off French and European clientele that shared his tastes. He was among the first designers, at the turn of the 20th century, to reject the corset and the unnatural body shape imposed on women. He availed himself of the collaboration of Paul Poiret and Madeleine Vionnet (1913 to 1925). He favored clothes to be worn at home, casual, not dressed up, in tulle and lace and embroidered in flower-patterned linen, especially with hydrangeas. He became famous for the mother-of-pearl color of his afternoon dresses, for coats trimmed with fur, and for furs used as a soft fabric. He dressed actresses such as the beautiful Otero, Liane De Pougy, and Réjane, his favorite. He had his apartment decorated by avant-guard artists such as Paul Iribe and Martine, the daughter of Poiret. He would help talents such as André Breton, his consultant and assistant in assembling what remains one of the largest art libraries. In 1923, he understood and purchased Picasso's *Les demoiselles d'Avignon*. In 1928, the Doucet atelier merged with Doueillet. (*Lucia Sollazzo*)

Doudoune French term for a waterproof jacket padded with goose feathers or synthetic material. Very warm and light, it is worn in the mountains, but also in town to protect oneself from Winter's frigid temperatures.

Douvier Guy. French designer. He studied painting at the School of Fine Arts and then became interested in fashion. In 1955, he worked for Chanel, and then moved to New York to work for a manufacturing company, and for Dior. Later, he was in Rome at Tiziani and Antonelli, and then back to France at Maggy Rouff. In 1972, in Paris, he was put in charge of the Guy Laroche prêt-à-porter. Starting in 1974 he directed the Laroche design studio and designed the Guy Laroche Diffusion and Guy Laroche Boutique Collections. He died in September 1993, and his position was taken by his assistant Jean-Pierre Marty.

Doyle American manufacturer of sails and

nautical clothing. In 1982, at Harvard University, Robbie Doyle, one of the competitors for the Americas Cup, applied the principle of "elliptical loading" to sails, improving their performance and transforming his company into one of the most technologically advanced, with 40 sails factories all over the world. The sails of the *Amerigo Vespucci* and of solitary sailors such as Giovanni Soldini and Christophe Augin are manufactured by Doyle. In 1995, the firm created a line of nautical clothing and a line for leisure time, thanks to an agreement with Red, a factory specialized in this field. The men's and women's Collections feature high quality technical materials, perfect wearability, functionality, and comfort in sweatshirts, sweaters, jackets, trousers, skirts, T-shirts, and polo shirts, in addition to accessories and travel bags.

Dralon Synthetic fiber. After Bayer's research on acrylonitril starting in 1942, the success of polyacrylic provided the basis for the acrylic Dralon, which was patented in 1954. Marketed first in Europe, and then in the rest of the world, it provides threads for weaving, machine-worked knitwear, auto interiors, and fake furs. It is versatile when blended with other natural or synthetic fibers. It is resistant to, among other things, acid, lye, and alcohol. During combustion it can emit toxic gases. It is bulky, stable, and permeable, and it doesn't swell when wet.

Drap French term for a very thin wool fabric that is soft and shiny with a smooth, silken surface or nap. Originally only carded, it is today also used semi-carded and combed. The combed fabric is used for elegant formal suits such as tuxedos and tail-coats; the carded fabric is used for men's overcoats. Its typical qualities are obtained in the finishing, during which the fabric is fulled, gauzed, clipped, brushed, and pressed.

Dreyfuss Jerôme (1975). French designer. A multifaceted creator, he was noticed for the first time in November 1998 at the Paris Collections. Immediately, his very structured style and his skill, quite noteworthy in such a young man, contributed to the talk about him as someone with authentic promise. His ambition is to design clothes which are at the same time elegant, simple, and modern. This often doesn't exclude a bit of humor, as in a skirt with a lace drawing attached to the bodice with adhesive tape.

(*Simonetta Greggio*)

Drian Pseudonym of Etienne Adrien (1885-1961). French illustrator. With the Liberty or Art Nouveau style fading away, the art world devastated by Cubism, and the decorative arts flying the flag of Art Deco, his style went against the trend, characterized by a conscious classicism. From deep in the provinces, he moved to Paris in 1900. He was one of the names associated with the Gazette du Bon-Ton, Fémina, Nos Elegances, and Harper's Bazaar.

An illustration by Drian published by the Gazette du Bon-Ton (The Costume Institute, Metropolitan Museum of Art, New York).

Drill Very strong and heavy cotton fabric, with a twill weave similar to denim. Manufactured with low-count carded yarns of good quality, it was used in the U.S. in the 1940s for work clothes, usually in white or khaki. It was later used for military and colonial uniforms. Today, it is found in men's and women's Summer clothes.

Dr. Martens Brand of shoe. Dr., or Doc Martens boots were born in the 1940s, at a holiday resort near Munich. A German doctor, Klaus Martens, was recovering from a foot fracture, and he designed and manufactured, together with an engineer friend, an orthopedic boot that was tall and stiff in order to support the ankle. In 1959, he sold the patent to the owners of the English shoe group R. Griggs Ltd., which was established in 1901. Production of the Dr. Martens model AirWair 1460 was started in their Wolloston plant. The name comes from the launch date on the English market: April 1st 1960. Since then, the 1460 model has become the symbol of the most important youth movements, from punk to darks and from pop to the beat generation. The production was then diversified into four lines: Urban, with small logs; Classic, which includes the historic boots; Terrain, the most casual; and Street, with trendy designs. In 1994, London saw the opening of the "sanctuary," the first flagship store. It is in Covent Garden, a large single-brand shop on four floors where it is possible to find everything under the Dr. Martens brand, from shoes to clothing, sunglasses, and stationery items. In Italy, the first single-brand store opened in Florence, on via Tornabuoni, but there are more than 1,000 authorized points-of-sale.

(*Valeria Vantaggi*)

❑ 2002, October. R. Griggs Group Limited, the English company which owns the brand, closes the U.K. plants which employ 1,068 people and moves production to China. The Group's general manager, David Suddens, justifies the decision by calling it a new strategy to overcome recent poor performance and to guide the brand toward a revival of business. Dr. Martens sells about 5 million shoes per year worldwide.

Dr. Scholl Brand created by William Scholl (1922-2003). He was a British-born orthopedist of German descent. In the late 1950s he brought very simple wooden orthopedic sandals with a leather strap at the back to the U.S. from Germany. He intended to start a fashion and launched them with the slogan, "Looking good and doing you good." He succeeded because the girls wearing the first mini-skirts in the Swinging London of the early 1960s liked them. Since then, and for almost two decades, millions of women have worn these very famous sandals.

Drumohr Factory-owned brand of knitwear belonging to Robertson of Dumfries Ltd., founded in 1770 by the Robertson family. In 1992, the company was acquired by the Italian Stefano Angelino who reorganized the Scottish plant and has specialized in the production of cashmere sweaters made in the Shetland islands. The Italian headquarters is in Biella.

Dryden Ernest. Pseudonym of Ernst Deutch (1887-1938), a German illustrator and costume designer. After studying with Gustav Klimt, he made his début in Berlin as a poster illustrator. Shortly after, in the early 1910s, he worked with Die Elegante Welte and the Gazette du Bon Ton, providing drawings and sketches about fashion. He moved to Paris in 1926 and worked for Die Dame. As a costume designer, he is remembered for his costumes for Marlene Dietrich in the Richard Boleslawsky film *The Garden of Allah* (1936).

Dryden Hélène (1887-1934). American designer. Her style was influenced by the Pre-Raphaelites, the symbolism of Beardsley, and Japanese calligraphy. She was a follower of Art Nouveau. She was at the peak of her fame during the 1920s when drawing covers for the American edition of Vogue.

Dry Washing A turpentine-based method of washing clothes. It was discovered and patented by Jolly-Bollin, a French tailor, in 1849. At first the method was empirical. In fact, the stained clothing was unstitched, the dirty section was cleaned with solvent, and the garment was re-sewn. Not until the end of the 1800s was there a way to dry wash garments without disassembling them.

Dsquared Brand of men's ready-to-wear created by the Canadian twins Dean and Dan Caten. The line, to use fashion lingo, is modern basic. The brand made its début in 1994 in Paris, and in 1995 it was presented for the first time at Milano Collezioni Uomo. It's difficult to define the twin's style: rather than just a look, theirs is an unconventional lifestyle which is renewed with every Collection, differentiating itself with fresh and original ideas. Each time, the men's wardrobe is re-created, re-presented, and reinterpreted with irony and irreverence. For Winter 2002-2003, the Collection was, as usual, an invitation to anti-conformity and to a personal and creative style of clothing. It is fashion that comes from the street, and from the freedom to layer garments, combine colors, and mix styles. It only seems to be casual, because it combines tailored garments with casual clothes, layering shirts over sweaters and sweaters over jackets, in a mix of fabrics and clothes that go from denim to leather and from cotton to viscose. Always present, in almost every Collection, are hats and berets of all shapes, and enormous colored scarves. The setting of the Collections mirrors, in extravagance and originality, the "signature" of the two designers. In 2002, at the Winter Collection, one saw garbage bags, recycled materials and a ranch-style wooden house with bales of hay in the background of a city suburb with industrial sheds meant to recreate the mythical world of cowboys. The Summer Collection that year featured country style. The 2003 Autumn-Winter Collection welcomed DSquared2 Airlines on board. In the background was a plane, and down the boarding stairs came pilots and passengers of different types, from a rock star to a dandy to a sportsman. The aviator jackets had leather and gold inserts and were padded with fur. The silk shirts had crystal appliqués and the belt buckles were heavily ornamented. Irreverent and easygoing as always, their last Collection again took up a theme very dear to the Canadian twins: the layering of garments which in an informal way combine T-shirts, sweaters, shirts, multilayered jackets, and the contrast in bulk between very tight trousers and oversize bulky jackets with enormous scarves.

(*Gabriella Gregorietti*)

❑ 2002, September. A three-year partnership with Vicini that, starting with Spring-Summer 2003, will produce and distribute the women's shoe line. The Collection had great success at the last Micam, especially with Asian buyers, in particular those from Korea and Japan. With the agreement between DSquared and Vicini, the shoes are to be sold in the Vicini stores in Milan and New York and in the DSquared stores.

Duccio Del Duca Line of women's shoes created in the mid 1980s by Oregon, a company established in 1970 in Vittore Olona, near Milan.

Ducharne French silk company, with headquarters in Lyon. It is a historic name in the silk industry and was established in 1920 by François Ducharne, who combined in one person a sense of both entrepreneurship and creativity. Both Picasso and Braque designed fabrics for the firm. Ducharne silks helped nourish Schiaparelli's talent. The company closed down in the early 1960s.

Duchein Lome. American designer and collector of gloves. Her boutique La Crasia has been on Fifth Avenue for thirty years, and her clientele includes show business personalities such as Madonna, Brooke Shields, Britney Spears, Michelle Pfeiffer, and Sylvester Stallone, as well as famous names ranging from Jackie Kennedy to Prince, Michael Jackson, and Donna Karan. Together with her team of designers, she manufactures, with artisanal quality, about 60,000 pairs of gloves per year. She has created gloves for several Broadway shows and many Hollywood films. Her gloves can also be custom made. She likes the Victorian style, all lace and mother-of-pearl buttons, as well as the styles of the 1930s and 1940s, when gloves were a necessary part of the wardrobe. The walls of her atelier are covered with gloves, sketches, and photographs. The accumulated material, from 1973 to the present time, is so important in terms of quantity and quality that soon, in that four storey building, there will be a museum devoted to gloves. The historical archive contains unique and rare pieces from all periods.

Duchesse or satin duchesse. A shiny, precious satin, usually in natural silk but also in viscose, acetate, cotton, or rayon, rather heavy, with a sumptuous, glittering look.

Dudovich Marcello (1878-1962). Italian painter, illustrator and poster designer. For more than 50 years, Italians – but also Europeans, because Dudovich, a native of Trieste, worked for a long time at the weekly Simplicissimus, which was printed in Munich and remains one of the best examples of political and social satire expressed through drawings and writing – were able to look at Dudovich's posters. They were like a big open-air exhibit which would describe, on fixed deadline, a drink, a department store, a raincoat, a hat, or a fashion accessory. Dudovich was the inspired interpreter of many eras, from the Belle Époque, and its decline, to World War I, with its Red Cross nurses and women making ammunition, and the Roaring '20s, with its women-in-crisis and its fashionable *garçonnes*, the years of girls playing tennis and trying to emancipate themselves at the wheel of a six-cylinder auto or a Bugatti. The story of Dudovich as an interpreter of his own time is linked to a black hat lying on a yellow armchair. He was little more than a boy. He had arrived in Milan from Trieste, in May 1898, when public gardens were filled with the dead bodies of men killed by artillery, and with Bava Beccari's dragoons. He had been called to Milan by the poster designer Methicoviz, who was also from Trieste, and who worked for the publisher Giulio Ricordi. At Ricordi, Dudovich found a job: he would patiently copy on a lithographic stone the sketches of Terzi and the posters of Capiello. One day, the Borsalino publishing house organized a poster contest. The young apprentice entered (with a black hat on a yellow armchair) and won. As a result he became part of the team of the printer-lithographer Chapuis, in Bologna. In 1911, he was hired by Simplicissimus, as the designer of the high society and fashion column. Together with his wife Elisa Bucchi, an early practitioner of fashion journalism, Dudovich began to move in high society, in order to witness the atmosphere, dissipation, lifestyles, and endless holidays in Deauville, Ostend, and Montecarlo. He wrote in his memoirs: "I would return to the hotel and, my head still full of that elegance, I would pin my drawing paper to the door and sketch from memory the evidence of that time and place. In Paris, we would go to the races at Auteuil and Longschamps; in the evening, to the premières of Tristan Bernard, Sacha Guitry, Max Reinhardt, and Moissi. Together with

Marcello Dudovich, Advertising poster from 1907 (From *L'Italia che cambia*, Artificio, Florence, 1989).

Libero Andreotti and Enrico Sacchetti, my inseparable friends for both painting and revelry – Andreotti was a protégé of Worth, the most illustrious tailor of those years – I would stay up until dawn in bars where the last of the old-time Apaches made you drink from their glasses and stole your women. Gays – at the time they were called vegetarians – began to be trendy and made their eyes up with blue. Mistinguette would dance a tango with the blond Maurice. War changed everything." But it didn't change Marcello Dudovich and didn't take away his skill at depicting an era that the war had suddenly made seem very distant in time and old to the point of decrepitude. His eye, his inspired ability to capture the essence of an outfit, and his graphic intuition, these didn't age and didn't become fossilized while recollecting better days. Just as he had been the interpreter of the Belle Époque, he became, in newspapers and, above all, in posters for La Rinascente, the interpreter of that era which went slightly mad in order to forget the cruel results of the war. He also chronicled the period immediately after, the period of modernism between the two world wars. It was because he couldn't simplete repeat fashions, atmospheres, and realities. He didn't just copy and reproduce, but understood and created. His women weren't like those powerful and almost Michelange-lo-inspired ones painted by Alfredo De Carolis, who engraved the maxims and the bookplates of D'Annunzio. They weren't the panting twin sisters seduced by Andrea Sperelli, the pale protagonists of Pre-Raphaellite mirages, the copies of Anna Fougez, the luxury mammals of Guido Da Verona, or the *garçonnes* who anticipated the gymnastic parades of Achille Starace. His were the eternal women who, with or without cloche hats, in short skirts or long ones, with or without scarves and veils, we might happen to find at our side, even tomorrow. (*Giulio Vergani*)

Duffer of St. George English brand of men's fashions. It was created in 1984 and made successful by designers Michael Cairns, Eddie Prendergast, and Barrie K. Sharpe. They have a store in Covent Garden, London.

Duffle Coat Overcoat worn in the English Navy. At the end of World War II, surplus coats were sold to the public at low cost, a decision that determined their fate. From that moment, the garment became very popular. Falling to the hips or the knees, it is made from a heavy wool and the color is strictly navy blue. In place of buttons, the coat is closed by means of small pieces of shaped wood passed through a cord or a leather loop.

Duffy Brian (1934). Irish photographer. During the 1960s and 1970s he worked for Vogue, Nova, and other fashion magazines. Deploring the excessive influence of the glamour environment, he prefered to make a kind of free photography influenced by what was at the time the positive impact of television, chiefly felt in its immediacy. Together with Bailey and Donovan he was part of a trio of very famous photographers. He lives in London.

Dufour Gilles. French designer. After studying philosophy, he enrolled at the École Supérieure des Arts Décoratifs in Paris. He completed his education at the School of Visual Arts in New York. He was an assistant to André Oliver and, for haute couture, to Pierre Cardin. He then worked with Raymondo de Larrain, the nephew of the Marquis de Cueva, on the costumes and sets for a play. He continued to work in the theatre and cinema, often with Lagerfeld, for whom he would become a close assistant. In 1983, he began his first collaboration with Chanel, where he would become artistic director. Since 1998 he has been the designer at Balmain. (*Valeria Vantaggi*)

Dufy Raoul (1887-1953). French painter. A meeting in 1909 with Poiret, the famous Parisian tailor, would have great influence on Dufy's artistic production. They developed an intense relationship of friendship and collaboration, based on their common taste for decoration and experimentation with different techniques. In 1910, Poiret suggested to Dufy that he apply the system of wood block printing to fabrics. Later, in Poiret's atelier, the Petite Usine, with the help of a chemist, Dufy applied a new technique of printing on fabric which allowed him to transfer to textiles the elements that were typical in his painting, such as brilliant colors and sharp contrasts. In 1911, his relationship with Poiret broken off, Dufy became artistic director of the celebrated textile firm Bianchini-Ferier of Lyon. From 1930 to '33 he created printed silks for Onandaga in New York. Dufy's refined ornaments are flowers: roses, anemones, chrysanthemums, feverfews, daisies, poppies, and fleur-de-lis, on vivid colors or on black-and-white backgrounds. His fabrics also show oriental motifs such as arabesques, embroidered in gold and silver on a black ground, paisley patterns, and flowers and animals in the style of Assyrian iconography.

Dujardin Belgian tailor, specialized in children's clothing, from babies to adolescents and future mothers. Its clientele belongs to the aristocracy. It was created from an idea by the Teurlings brothers. In 1942, they took over the business of Mrs. Welcomme, enlarging it within a short time. By the late 1980s, it employed 470 people and had a turnover of 820 million Belgian francs. One third of the Dujardin shares belong to the holding company Cobepa. The brand is present, in kiosks or boutiques, in department stores such as Harrods and Liberty in London, and Isetan in Tokyo.

Duke Randolph (1958). American designer. He is interested in almost all the areas of leisure time and sportswear, but prefers bathing suits and beachwear.

Duke of Windsor (1894-1972). The romantic Duke of Windsor, who for a few months was Edward VIII, King of England, was the most elegant man of the 20th century. On the other hand, it was the Celts, the ancient inhabitants of Britain, invented the "bracae," or trousers, while the ancient Romans still wore the modest "subligatulae," a kind of underpants of no elegance at all and useless as protection against the cold. This tells a lot about the aptitude of Englishmen when it comes to setting fashions for the rest of the world. With this kind of background, English and Anglophile men's fashion became the most classic and self-assured anywhere. By way of argument, it could also be said that England gave birth to movements and "anti-fashions" which periodically upended the normal laws of elegance, in a kind of short circuit that already glittered in the time of the Regency, when the splendid life of London high society was able to produce a character like George "Beau" Brummel and then immediately mythologize him, to the point that Balzac would define him as "an exceptional man, a prince, and a patriarch of fashion." Possessing the charisma needed in order to invent rules of fashion, with originality, a spirit of independence, and restraint, Brummel, though not an aristocrat, was able to shine in a society that considered fashion to be the province of the aristocracy. His life, his deeds, and his words gave weight and dignity to the search for refinement and elegance, justifying frivolity and vanity (the implied principles of fashion) and creating a relationship of elective affinity between fashion and culture. Not by accident, Brummel and other celebrated dandies such as Byron, Wilde, Beardsley, and Bearbohm were great poets and artists. With these precedents (and despite D'Annunzio and the creations of Armani), the most elegant man of the century had to be an Englishman. The Duke of Windsor, then: what was the source of his elegance? Well, it is appropriate to say that elegance is a gift, one of many bestowed by the gods in ways that may seem unfair, in the same way that someone may be handsome, intelligent, or charming. There are no recipes; elegance is a sort of grace, an inner security which makes you feel comfortable in your clothes. The Duke of Windsor had this grace, this security, at a maximum level. His most celebrated inventions were the dinner jacket (in Italy and France it is called smoking), made in a fabric called "midnight blue," a very dark blue color that under artificial light appears blacker than black, and was worn for the first time in 1920; the Windsor knot, a perfectly triangular large tie knot that was very popular in the 1950s but worn so badly that the Duke repudiated it; and the Windsor collar, with wide, short points, to which the Duke was faithful for his entire life and which is still very popular in Italy, especially in Milan. The Duke of Windsor was the first to regularly wear brown shoes and to wear them in different shades as well. Until that time, in the 1920s, a gentleman would own only very boring black shoes, as brown was meant only for the working class. His unexpected, atypical, creative use of color was surprising: the Duke was the first, long before American preppies, to popularize bright pink and pastel trousers, which, because of the above-mentioned divine injustice, looked wonderful on him. For the preppies, on the other hand, it was a disaster. Which is to say that for the elegance of one it is often necessary to sacrifice the many.

(*Luigi Settembrini*)

Dunhill Alfred. English house of men's clothing and accessories. In 1893, Alfred Dunhill took over the family company, which manufactured trimmings for carriages, and expanded it to include saddles, harnesses, and other accessories. Then, with the spread of motorcars, he began to produce clothing for automobile drivers. In 1904, the firm created the first pocket watch and, three years after that, with the opening of a store on Jermyn Street, Dunhill established its name with its famous smoking pipes (quite celebrated is the anti-wind model) and refined tobacco blends. Also from this period was the birth of the first lighter, Unique. During the 1930s and 1940s, the range of accessories included wristwatches, cuff links, and tiepins for men, and gold cases for women. In the 1960s, Dunhill stores are found all over the world, from North America to Hong Kong, Japan, and Australia. And the products multiply: 1976 was the start of the biennial Collection of men's clothing, to which were added eyeglasses, men's perfume, jewellery, and leather goods. The house has three times won the *Queen's Award* for industry. In the basement of the historic London store on Jermyn Street, renovated in 1997, is the Dunhill Museum, which is open to the public. It collects the most meaningful objects of a century of activity, and organizes theme exhibits. In December 1999, the first store in Italy was opened, on via Manzoni in Milan. The Dunhill brand belongs to the Vendôme Luxury Group. It has 180 points-of-sale in 26 countries.

(*Gabriella Gregorietti*)

Dunkan Nancy. Hall Historian of photography. In 1979, she published the critical survey *The History of Fashion Photography*. The book has a foreword by Yves Saint-Laurent. She was among the curators of the International Museum of Photography at the George Eastman House in Rochester.

Du Pareil au Meme French brand of children's clothing. It is fresh, joyful, and inexpensive, both for day and night, for school and leisure time. In May 2000, a large unisex space for children between 3 months and 14 years was opened in Milan on Largo Cairoli at the corner of via Dante. Another store is in Rescaldina, and it also sells strollers, baby carriages, and accessories. In 2002, the company opened a shoe boutique in France, with new openings (18 stores in 6 years) expected in Belgium and Luxembourg thanks to an agreement with the Belgian company Motek. The first new openings were in Antwerp and Brussels in early 2003. DPAM has 176 points-of-sale all over the world, with 52 of them outside France, consisting of 24 single-brand shops (Spain, Italy, Portugal, Switzerland, Japan) and 28 distribution shops. For 2002, turnover was down 9.1%, to €140.545 million, due to disappointing sales in the fourth quarter. The net profit, on the other hand, was steady. In France the decrease in sales was 10%, while the Italian subsidiary had an increase of 23.6%.

DuPont de Nemours Manufacturer of synthetic fibers. It is one of the most important in the world. It was established in 1802 by Eleuthère DuPont de Nemours, in Wilmington, Delaware, to produce gunpowder. The second generation at Du Pont diversified production to include wool manufacture. In 1920, the company acquired the license to manufacture cellophane and rayon, at the time a French patent. In the late 1930s, it launched nylon, a polyamide material, in which it is still the world leader. Then came Dacron polyester and Orlon acrylic. The Lycra elastomer came out in 1959. A segmented polyurethane generally listed among synthetic fibers, it is always used in a blend with other fibers, and it allows the thread to expand to seven times its length before returning to its original size. Extremely thin, it can be white, opaque, or transparent. A more recent product is Tactel, an innovative polyamide that is extremely soft, light, shiny, and opaque, and particularly suitable for versatile threads, effect threads and fashion textiles. Tactel threads include Aquator, for strong fabrics that have a soft feel ; Diabolo, for brilliance and draping; Micro, for a soft feel and rich texture; and Multisoft, for covering quality and brightness.

(*Giuliana Zabeo Ricca*)

❑ 2002, January. The latest revolutionary bra by DuPont Lycra combines fashion, technology, and cosmetics. It doesn't have hooks or shoulder straps. It adheres to the body thanks to special interchangeable adhesive bands that release a hydrating, toning cream when in contact with the skin. This amazing bra, called Cosmetic Touch Up, has been patented all over the world by Piera Pischedda. It is made in a very light breathable fabric (Sensitive Plus by EuroJersey) that is 28% Lycra. It is available in two models, one with separate cups and another with front and side support bands which end under the arms and leave the back completely bare.

❑ 2003, January. Sales in the textile

division continue to fall, down 3% compared to the previous year. Only in the last quarter of 2002 is there a 5% increase, of $1.6 billion, due to demand for spandex and nylon for clothing, for fibers used in furnishings, and for intermediate products. But the total turnover for 2002 is down, settling around $24 billion.
❑ 2003, April. The "never ending history" concerning the possible sale of the textile division continues.
❑ 2003, May. The big success of the DuPont Textile & Interiors web-site continues. Limits on international travel due to terrorism, war, and, not least, the SARS epidemic, contribute to an increase in activity and business on the web-site, up 900% compared to 2002. The online archive, launched in 2001, makes it possible to request samples of more than 22,000 fabrics manufactured with Du Pont fibers, which are made by 476 partner producers in 64 countries.
❑ 2003, June. A partnership agreement is signed between DuPont Textiles & Interiors and the Korean company Huvis, which is a leader in polyester products. It will enable the development of new innovative products and the mutual use of technologies and brands. Huvis receives a license to use the DuPont brands in the Korean market. The strategic alliance with Huvis follows those already existing with Ciba (for Teflon), Outlast, and DDC Labs.
❑ 2003, June. The Lycra brand escapes the limits of the textile industry and enters cosmetics. DuPont signs a license agreement with the New York company Coty. It is expected that within a short time a specific cosmetics line will be launched. Among the brands owned by DuPont Textiles, which is active in 70 countries with an annual turnover of about $6.3 billion, besides Lycra, are Teflon, Stainmaster, Antron, Coolmax, Thermolite, Cordura, Supplex, and Tacte. (*Gabriella Gregorietti*)

Dupouy-Magnin Tailor's workshop in Paris opened by Félix Dupouy in 1924. There was a merger with the *maison* Magnin in the 1930s. It would remain active until 1948.

Durst André (1907-1949). French photographer. His pictures are closely connected to the formation of Surrealism. After arriving in Paris from Marseilles, he met often with Cocteau and Bérard. In 1934, he documented the Patou Collection for French Vogue. Two years later, the magazine put him in charge of the photo department and made him responsible for photo features on the work of the great Parisian tailors from Balenciaga to Rochas.

(*Angela Madesani*)

Duse Eleonora (1858-1924). Actress. Born in Vigevano, she came from a family of artists. She is still a mythic figure in the collective imagination. She was unconventional, ever since her début, an anti-diva in her acting style, which aimed at "giving voice to the breath and the contradictions of sentiment." Not a vain person, and "indifferent," as Ugo Ojetti would write toward the end of the 1800s, "to other people's judgments," during the day Duse wore rather shabby clothing, characterized by a sort of "pathetic slovenliness typical of the lagoon." But looking at her pictures, one's opinion becomes less severe. Those rare photos of the early 1880s reveal a sober and easy elegance which would become more complicated over the following two decades. Proof of this can be found in the exceptional and numerous original photographs in the Duse archives at the Foundation Giorgio Cini on the island of San Giorgio Maggiore in Venice. These were taken by the greatest wizards of the camera, including Giuseppe Primoli, Giovanni Battista Sciutto, Mario Nunes Vais, Aimé Dupont, Paul Audouard, and Arnold Genthe. Foremost among all the pictures is the splendid portrait of "The Divine Duse" with an ermine stole, taken in New York in 1903 by Edward Steichen who, along with Baron Gayne de Mayer, is considered the inventor of fashion photography. As an artist, Duse was a refined woman, although she could present herself to the public without the slightest trace of make-up and, at a certain age, would show herself with her "white hair, in strident contrast with the character she was playing." She was very attentive to the reconstruction of historical costumes; for contemporary characters, she would choose modern clothes. She wasn't afraid of violet (her surviving clothes are proof of this), she didn't mind spending, and had clear ideas about what she wanted. In 1904, for example, she paid 2,000 liras, the equivalent of about €7,000 today, to buy a special cloak to be worn in *Monna Vanna* by Maurice Maeterlinck. This is what she wrote to Caramba, whose real name was Luigi Scapelli (1865-1936), a journalist, caricaturist, set and costume designer, and director: "I would like, for Monna Vanna, a velvet cloak, in blue... But not precisely blue or... a blue that I know but that I can't explain. Try to understand me, you who are a great costume designer, a true artist. What I would like to have is a blue like the color of the lake in Pallanza (oh, do you remember?) at four in the afternoon!" Among the famous names of fashion in whom she placed her trust were Paul Poiret and, above all, Mariano Fortuny, whose evocative creations she seemed to favor, to judge from the number of pieces that her niece, Eleonora Bullough (who became a nun with the name Sister Mary of St. Mark), donated to the Cini Foundation, as well as to Palazzo Pitti in Florence and the Victoria and Albert Museum in London. Fortuny, a Spanish-Venetian painter, set designer and collector, who became interested in fabrics and fashion in 1907, dedicated the Eleonora model to her. It was made of two smooth and flat panels of printed velvet with deeply pleated satin inlays, of the "Delphi" type. Among the great dressmakers who had the honor to dress Duse, we should remember Bellom S., of Turin and Florence, and Magugliani, of Florence, both suppliers to the Royal House of Savoy, and Redfern, of Paris. But her favorite atelier was the *maison* created in 1857 by Charles Frederick Worth on Rue de la Paix in Paris. In 1921, on the occasion of her return to the theatre, after 12 years of absence, she called upon Jean Philippe, who was known as Luka and was the son of the founder, for help. In the Sister Mary of St. Mark fund, which is part of the Cini Foundation, there is a letter from Luka, dated 6 April 1923, in which he reassured "the great She" (as he would call her), about her debt to him: "You will pay me when you become rich, and if things do not go well and you do not become rich, then I can wait until Judgment Day." (*Maria Rita Stiglich*)

Dustcoat A light overcoat, covering the body from the neck to the ankles, that is usually made of gabardine, wool or cotton. It was first worn at the end of the 19th century when it was adopted by motorcyclists and by the first people to drive cars. The dustcoat has wide sleeves and a pronounced high neck that buttons up, providing suitable protection against the wind and rain. It was often worn with a cloth cap with integral glasses.

Duyos Juan. Spanish designer. His first contact with the world of fashion was in 1992, when he began to work with Manuel Pina, who created clothes for various shops and for his friends. In 1995, he started a partnership with Cecilia Panagua and created the brand Duyos and Panagua. From 1996 to '99 he worked with Antonio Pernas. In September 1997, he presented his first Collection at the Pasarela Cibeles in Madrid. He and Cecilia separated, and he continued to present Collections on his own. His fashion is distinguished by a disillusioned and daring style that is very colorful and original in the printing of fabric.

Dweck Stephen. American jewellery designer. He lives in New York. Silver and very colorful stones are the basis of his work. He made a name for himself in the early 1980s, working with Geoffrey Beene and Donna Karan, gradually assuming more creative autonomy. He cuts stones in very irregular shapes, recalling ancient jewellery. He loves the cameo technique on bakelite, as well as traditional coral, turquoise and jade. Some of his unique pieces are on display at the Costume Institute of the Metropolitan Museum of Art in New York.

D'Ys Julien (1955). French artist and hairdresser. He doesn't like to be called a hairdresser. But his début and the success that followed were the result of his experience in the boutiques of Harlow and Jean-Louis David. In the late 1970s, critics praised the hairstyles he made for Chanel, Comme des Garçons, Galliano, Gigli, Lang, Montana, and Yamamoto. He hasn't created a new hairstyle for a very long time. Instead, he creates sculpture, placing the strangest materials on the head. He paints, sculpts, and photographs, often together with directors, costume designers, and theater choreographers. He lives in Paris and New York.

D'Ys Yannick. French hairdresser. The last name is a pseudonym chosen to form a team with Julien D'Ys. They both did an apprenticeship at Jean-Louis David and Harlow. They work in partnership and separately, for several designers. They do the hair of important personalities such as David Bowie, Inès de la Fressange, Madonna, and Isabella Rossellini.

E

Earl Jean American brand of jeans. It was created in 1996, almost as a game, by the film and television designer Suzanne Costas Freiwald. The clothes are known for being tight-fitting and sexy. The brand really took off in 1997, after the first order placed by Fred Segal, an important department store in Los Angeles. Over the years, the product line has introduced new types of washing and manufacture of the denim fabric. It has also expanded to include knitwear, skirts, and jackets. Since Spring-Summer 2003, the brand has also had a men's line. It has four boutiques, in Los Angeles, Tokyo, New York, and Osaka, and is also present in the most important department stores of the U.S. (*Gianluca Cantaro*)

Echaudemaison Olivier (1942). French make-up artist. At the age of 20, he made his début as assistant to the celebrated *coiffeur* Alexandre in Paris. After moving to London, he worked for Vogue and became interested in make-up, soon becoming the favorite make-up artist of many celebrities, including Catherine Deneuve, Mireille Mathieu, Princess Anne of England, and Caroline of Monaco. He did the make-up worn by Michel Serrault in the play *La Cage aux Folles*. Since 1989 he has been creative director for image and make-up at Givenchy, which became more prominent and up-to-date thanks to him.
(*Ginevra Falzoni*)

❑ 2000. Olivier leaves Givenchy after 10 years working there.
❑ 2000, June. He is among the guests invited by the Sorbonne to the conference "Beauty. Anthropology, Semiology, and Market Strategies," sponsored by the French Confederation of Arts and Trades.
❑ Echaudemaison joins Guerlain, the perfume and cosmetics house that belongs to LVMH. In autumn 2002, he presents the Divinora line of cosmetics.

Ecko American company making urban clothing and sportswear. It was established in 1993 by Marc Ecko, one of the most important figures in the spread of hip-hop fashion among young people. That fashion came out of Afro-American neighborhoods in New York in the 1970s. At first connected to sports, especially skateboarding, today it is the focal point of a global lifestyle that tries to bring together urban youth and their suburban counterparts. The rapper Eminem has helped arouse international interest in the brand. (*Francesca Gentile*)

ECLA The European Clothing Association, with headquarters in Brussels, promotes and defends the interests of the textile and clothing industries within the European Union. It publishes a bulletin, the European Clothing Newsletter, and organizes commercial events abroad.

Eco Umberto (1932). Scholar, writer and essayist. His interests range from medieval aesthetics (he received a degree in philosophy in Turin in 1954, with a thesis on St. Thomas Aquinas), to avant-guard art, including the formulation of a coherent theory of semiotics (he wrote a *Treatise on General Semiotics*) and the themes and phenomena of mass culture. A professor of semiotics at the University of Bologna, he has since the early 1960s been one of the great interpreters of "low" culture, criticizing any apriori condemnations and intellectual devaluations of it. Starting with his "phenomenological" study of the "typical" Mike Bongiorno, Eco has never scorned any "sign" that appeared within the articulated framework of a cultural system. His approach to fashion, which covers its communicative aspect as well as its aesthetics, from the problem of costume to that of increased communication, is wide-ranging and not narrowly focused. Since his early study of aesthetics, in fact, he has set out to understand art as a concrete, empirical act, something done in a material and technical context. From this perspective, every subject can be analyzed according to its signifier, and every form can be understood as the emanation of a function, and the whirling spiral according to which our time fills forms with meaning and then empties them, rediscovering how to decipher a code and then forgetting it, is nothing more, after all, than a continuous operation of design. An operation, in other words, which considers fashion as an exemplary model.

École de la Chambre Syndicale de la Couture Paris. A private fashion school established in 1929 to train workers in the fashion industry. Besides courses in design and model-making, it offers up-to-date courses for journalists and fashion buyers. Certain skills that are on their way to extinction, such as mannequin draping and the hand-finishing of hems and buttons, are still taught here, in the best French tradition. For the privilege of knowing these secrets, tuition is about €7,000 a year, after the presentation of one's portfolio and an interview. Famous former students include Saint-Laurent, Scherrer, Courrèges, Miyake, and Jean Colonna.

École Supérieure des Arts Appliquées Duperré Paris. A state school which offers courses in textile art and design. After an admissions test, some 70 students choose courses of study at different professional levels lasting from 1 to 4 years. Despite the economic constraints on the institute, the education is excellent and puts particular emphasis on culture and creativity. Exchanges are organized with Central Saint Martin's College and the Royal College of Art in London, and the Tokyo School of Fashion in Japan. Former students work in all areas of the industry, from Bon Marché to Printemps and Hèrmes.

Ecomoda A movement in favor of fashions that are compatible with the environment, from the fabrics and dyes that are used to conditions in the workplace. It is sponsored by Legambiente. The first results came in 1994, when about ten companies at the first Exhibition of Ecologic Clothing and Textiles, held in Milan at the Museum of Science and Technology, showed how it is possible to combine environmental concerns with quality and good design. The influence was soon felt and it created new followers among both consumers and researchers. In 1995, Ecomoda published the research of the Allergology Institute at Florence University. In a sample of 20,000 people, 10% were affected by allergic dermatitis due to contact with textile dyes. In 1996, it offered the Eco-Label brand in Europe for environmentally-friendly products and started a public-awareness campaign calling attention to the exploitation of third-world workers. In 1997, it signed an agreement with the labor union Filtea-Cgil in order to promote healthy conditions in the workplace. In 1998, the movement launched an iridescent fiber, a kind of plant silk, obtained from the urticaceous plant Rami, whose cultivation requires a high degree of manual labor.

❑ As part of an exhibit called In The Mood, conceived by Li Edelkoort for Pitti Immagine Filati 2001, for the first time in Europe, Group Lineapiù launched a thread made of ecologic viscose under the Eco-Label brand. All the production processes comply with ecologic standards. Even the outer packaging is eco-compatible.

Eddie Bauer American company making casual clothes and sportswear. It specializes in sales via direct mail catalogues and has sold on the internet since 1996. Established in Seattle in 1920, it has more than 500 shops in the U.S. and Canada, with 11 more in Japan, Germany, and England. Since 1983, it has worked on a line of automobile interiors with Ford. In 1991, it launched a line of home products, and in 1995 it added the new clothing *griffe* A/K/A, which combines the comfort of sportswear with a more classic and professional look suited to the office.

❑ 1999. New lines are launched: first the Baby by Eddie Bauer line, then the Kid-sized line of sleepwear for children, and then the Kid-sized line of outerwear for children.
❑ The Eddie Bauer model Ford automobile is taken out of production, after 16 years and 1 million cars sold.

❑ An Eddie Bauer shop opens in Honolulu, Hawaii.
❑ 2001 is a year of international recognition; the Hispanic College Fund names Eddie Bauer "Company of the Year."
❑ 2003. A fifth agreement is signed between Eddie Bauer and the Lane Company, makers of the Lakeridge brand of products for the home.

Edelstein Victor (1945). English designer. He followed the family trade, in a sense, because his parents had a manufacturing business. After apprenticeships with several important figures in British fashion, including Biba, he worked for the London subsidiary of Dior. He created his own women's line in 1977. After 1982, he worked "custom-made" exclusively. He left the industry in 1993, declaring that there was no more market for luxury.

❑ 1985. The designer creates the blue velvet dress that will be worn by Lady Diana when she dances with John Travolta at the White House later that year. That evening dress was the most important item at the charity auction held in New York in 1997 which brought around $5 million. The same dress was sold again at the Kensington Palace auction held in London in October 1999, together with 13 other models which Maureen Rorech had purchased for more than $1 million at the New York auction.
❑ 2002, November. Edelstein models are shown at the Tennessee State Museum in Nashville. The exhibit *Royalty and Elegance* brings together royal clothes starting with the 17th century wardrobe of Charles I and continuing up to Queen Victoria, the Prince of Wales, Queen Elizabeth II, and Lady D. Different "royal styles" are represented, such as Tipper Gore's for politics and Marilyn Monroe's for Hollywood.

Edling Udo (1965). Designer of Romanian origin. In 1981, he left Romania for Germany, where he worked as an assistant in an advertising agency in Frankfurt. In 1987, he moved to France, where his actual career began. From 1991 to '95 he worked with Galliano, André Walker, Montana, Kecha, Galéries Lafayette, Astorino (in '95 and '96), and Electre. In 1996, he presented his first personal collection. The following year he became director of the New Man line and worked with the *maison* Kenzo. He presented his collection in Paris for the first time in 2002. Today, his clothes, for both men and women, are on sale in Paris and Japan only. "My philosophy," he explains, "consists of introducing small touches of modernity. I don't like to propose shapes that are too extravagant and I don't like sudden changes in the cut of clothes either."

Edward Green Brand of shoes named after the artisan who in 1891 started to produce hand-made shoes for English gentlemen in a small factory in Northampton. In short, he made himself famous as a master shoemaker capable of producing the best shoes in England. Today, that standard of quality is still present in the shoes manufactured by Edward Green; one pair of hand-made shoes requires several weeks of work. In 1983, the company was acquired by John Hlustik, who continued the manufacture of high quality products characterized by classic Goodyear soles, leather uppers made in Italy, and calfskin linings.

❑ More than 110 years after its founding, at its boutique in Burlington Arcade in London, Edward Green remains faithful to the tradition of its four models, the Oxford, Derby, Casual, and Monk.

Edwardian Style Men's fashion launched by King Edward VII in the early 1900s featuring very elegant suits cut and sewn by the tailors of London's Savile Row. There were long, black frock-coat jackets, straight and tight-fitting, and buttoned to the top, with small lapels, as well as embroidered waistcoats, shirts with stiff collars, and stovepipe pants with silk stripes on the sides. It came out again in 1950 as the New Edwardian Style: an elegance that was refined and aristocratic, with a retro-romantic taste which in the years following World War I reflected a desire for hedonism and a return to the happy times in

England in the early 20th century. This fashion had great influence on the popular movement of teddy boys.

Edwin International Japanese manufacturer of jeans, established in Tokyo in 1969. Due to increased specialization in denim products, it soon became one of the leaders in the Japanese market. It is part of the purist vintage tradition which established itself in the late 1990s based on fabrics made on hand looms, dyes used according to ancient procedures, and sophisticated manual finishing. Wearability is often like that of the original denim. The use of fabric less than 29 inches high (less than that usually used for jeans) required rib cutting, because of which every garment shows the characteristic selvage on the side, visible in the turn-up. In 1996, Edwin International acquired a majority stake in Ateca Spa, the owner of the Avirex brand for Europe.

❑ 2001, Autumn. Avirex becomes an independent company. Edwin continues to own the rights for the Japanese market.
❑ 2003, May. Edwin relaunches its partnership with Fiorucci. The Milanese designer says that he intends to work with the Japanese company, which has owned the brand since 1992, in order to identify new licensees and launch new products.

EFIMA An institute for the promotion and organization of specialized trade fairs established by the Italian Association of Clothing Entrepreneurs and the Italian Association of Knitwear and Hosiery Manufacturers, today joined in the Fashion Industry Association. Its purpose is to represent fashion at its highest level of quality and style. Internationalization, innovation and image: this is the strategy around which EFIMA has organized its initiatives aimed at the elite of the fashion trade. It succeeds by arranging coherent, thematic encounters between products and their intended markets: Modit (since 1979), Milano Collezioni (since 1979), Uomomoda New York (since 1978), Anteprima Ideamaglia, Intimo Domani, Acquarium (1981-1982), and Contemporary (1986). After a series of adjustments aimed at finding a balance with Florence and other representative institutes of the fashion world, EFIMA, in Milan, organized three exclusive events of paramount importance, Momi-Moda Milano, Modaprima-Esma, and Sposaitalia.

❑ 2003. Luigi Ciocca, owner of the knitwear company Valdoglio, is the new president of EFIMA. At the 52nd edition of Modaprima, an event created to answer the distribution needs of the big chains, EFIMA launches the Fashion Store Service division, whose purpose is to satisfy the needs of chains and organized retailers.

Eggshell muslin Very fine, but dense and resistant cotton fabric that resembles an eggshell in its color and fineness. Used for women's underwear.

Eisen Mark (1960). American designer. His look is characterized by an urban style with sexy lines and high-tech materials. He defines himself as a post-minimalist in pursuit of detail and quality. He was born in Cape Town. At the age of 18, as desired by his father, he moved to the U S. to attend the University of Southern California, where he designed a helmet for the fans of the Trojans football team which sold 3,000 pieces in just one week. In 1988 he presented Couture Denim, his first collection, which was immediately acquired by the big New York department stores Bergdorf Goodman and Barneys. His inspirations, and at the same time his clients, are Pete Townshend, the guitar player of the Who, Duran Duran, and the Rolling Stones, for whom he designed the costumes for the *Vodoo Lounge* tour. Eisen is famous for his continuous technical research on new fabrics such as laminated chiffon and jersey, resined linen, silk, viscose, cotton, and Lycra, as well as on the insertion of glass fragments into fabric. In 1996 he launched the knitwear line Urchin.

❑ 2000, February. He makes his début at Milano Collezioni after signing an agreement with the Sportswear Company, a firm in Modena owned by Carlo Rivetti.
❑ 2002. Mark Eisen, together with Armani and Calvin Klein, is added to the list of 54 designers who oppose the

use of furs. According to those in the animal rights movement, in the previous year the sale of furs in the U.S. likely collapsed, with losses of $12 million.
❑ 2002, August. The designer joins the management staff of the Ann Taylor Stores Corporation, the company which owns the brand, as vice president for design.

Eisenhower Jacket Military jacket worn by U.S. troops during World War II and associated with General Dwight D. Eisenhower, the Commander-in-Chief of Allied forces in Europe. It is waist-length, with a collar, and sleeves that close with a button at the wrist. For the infantry it is in olive green, for airmen in aviator blue. During the 1980s in Italy it was the symbol par excellence of the "Paninari," young people who liked to meet in fast-food outlets, which at that time were becoming very popular in Europe.

Ekster Aleksandra (1884-1949). Russian painter, born in Kiev. A Constructivist painter, she was part of the group centered around the Fashion Atelier, which opened in Moscow in 1923. A firm supporter of Lamanova and of rational clothing that finds beauty in simplicity, she designed overalls and other clothes for work and sport that were sober and practical. Her "everyday clothes," made in fabrics like linen, cotton, raw silk, and satin, were suited to industrial production and composed of simple geometric figures such as rectangles, squares, and circles. Different shades of color were used to personalize the different garments. She also created one-of-a-kind models inspired by the pictorial aesthetics of Cubism and Futurism. These clothes were in abstract patterns and made exclusively for the Atelier's clientele and for exhibits. But for these models, she didn't care about functionality, but devised inter-connected decorative solutions, choosing only precious fabrics and furs and using daring color combinations such as prune, orange and black, red and black, and silver and violet.

(*Cloe Piccoli*)

❑ 2002, January. More than 50 years after her death, Russia remembers Ekster as one of the "Amazons of the Avant-guard" and the city of Moscow dedicates an exhibit entitled *The Art of the Feminine* to her and other artists from the 16th century up to today.

Elbaz Alber (1961). Israeli designer, born in Casablanca, Morocco. He lived and studied in Tel Aviv until his graduation from the Shenkar College School of Fashion and Textiles. He did a fashion apprenticeship in New York, working seven years with Geoffrey Beene. On March 8th 1999, at the Carousel du Louvre, on an iron runway where models marched like soldiers wearing metal sandals and stiletto heels, he won the right to replace Yves Saint-Laurent (who wished to devote himself to haute couture only) in the design and artistic direction of Yves Saint-Laurent Rive Gauche prêt-à-porter, the most important collection in the entire *maison*. Unlike many other new talents who become the creative head of a historic *griffe*, he didn't distort the house style. He only re-examined it, keeping a perfect balance between tradition and the need to innovate, between himself and the memory of the previous master. He allowed himself some plays on contrast, such as red fox on matted "impoverished" cashmere, and a tuxedo jacket worn with plus fours knickers, a sequined top and a train with a bow on it, as well as some risky colors, including orange and green. Saint-Laurent lent him his good-luck jewellery. Short, not handsome (he says: "I'd love to be handsome and slender. It must feel good to be Tom Cruise."), an indefatigable worker, he arrived at Saint-Laurent after reinvigorating Guy Laroche, for which he designed the 1997 and '98 collections. He left Saint-Laurent in 2000.

❑ 2000, August. Elbaz begins a short collaboration with Krizia.
❑ 2001, Autumn. He signs with Lanvin and becomes creative director in an attempt to improve the prospects of the brand acquired by Shaw-Lan Wang, a leading female media entrepreneur in Asia, in July of that same year. His first collection is presented in 2002 in a triumph of sequins inspired by the style of Jeanne Lanvin.
❑ 2003, Spring. After only three collections, it is evident that Elbaz has

already imprinted his own character on the Lavin style through the use of slim trousers decorated with velvet ribbons and cocktail dresses in black satin.

El Charro Italian brand known especially for leather goods. It had a good piece of the market in the 1980s, offering a country-western urban style with echoes of the Native American Indians: boots, belts with big buckles, jeans decorated with glass beads, heavy jackets in velvet, and jackets with fringes. The brand belongs to a company in Lombardy owned by Giorgio Caravatti, CMF Trading. and has been presented at both Pitti Immagine Uomo and the Salon Mediterraneo in Barcelona. Together with the Benelux countries, Portugal, the Middle East, and Central America, Spain is one of the most important markets for El Charro. The colors, from ecru and beige to walnut and anthracite grey, are never gaudy or showy.

❑ In addition to involvement in car racing and volleyball, sponsorship at the end of the 1990s and the beginning of the new millennium is connected to tourism and leisure time. After the opening of the tourist resort "Hotelito Desconocido" in Mexico, and of Charro Cafés in Rome, Milan, and Modena, comes the opening of the Charro Village in Sharm el Skeik.

El Corte Inglès Spanish chain of department stores. It was established in 1934, two years before the outbreak of the Civil War, by Ramón Rodriguez, who started the business in Madrid with a shop devoted to fabrics and English fashions, a specialty reflected in the company name. This business created an empire: more than 20 stores all over Spain where it is possible to find and buy everything from cooking pots to the ready-to-wear clothes of the great designers, as well as clothes made by the company itself. In fact, El Corte Inglès owns a textile mill and a manufacturing plant which, in the 1970s, used the consulting services of Guido Mantura, the manager of the Textile Financial Group.

El Dique Flotante Spanish brand of men's and women's ready-to-wear. It is now more than 100 years old. The business was started in 1899 and made successful by Joaquim Beleta y Mir. The company name means "The Floating Dock" and it was called that because in the year of its founding the port of Barcelona, the hometown of the owner, received a new breakwater. At first, the company manufactured only garments for children and sailors.

❑ The 100 year-old brand of ready-to-wear is represented at the Textile Museum of Barcelona, in the section dedicated to contemporary clothing, which also includes several great Spanish *griffes* such as Asunción Bastida and Cristóbal Balenciaga.

Elegance Perhaps, as with art, one should not attempt to explain it. Elegance – like class and culture – is usually discussed by people who don't have it. By now, it is rare enough to be like an archeological find and, as such, it enjoys periodic revivals. Contrary to chic, which is sought-after and fashion-dependent, and brings on fatigue and a touch of perversity, true elegance should be unconscious, natural, and oblivious to fashion, indeed, it should be subtly "démodé". A totally and visibly *griffed* look is never elegant. One can look super elegant wearing a men's white shirt, but one has to be Lauren Bacall. The same wearing a T-shirt, if one is Audrey Hepburn. Elegance is a gift – sometimes undeserved – and is independent of social class. Archival photos sometimes show nomadic tribes, native chiefs, or poor peasants, along with depictions of humble trades and activities, and these subjects often possess incredible elegance. While for romantics true elegance is more than anything an inner mood and spirit, skeptical people sometimes associate elegance with people who may be rather questionable in one respect or another but who are nevertheless aesthetically impeccable. Elegance can perhaps be defined as a distillate of style, equilibrium, sublime simplicity, and, maybe, a bit of boredom.

(*Alberto Lattuada*)

Elegances Parisiennes Official journal of the French fashion industry published between April 1916 and February 1924, along with the following supplements: Tailleur de Paris,

Elegance, Alberto Lattuada, 1999. Unpublished sketch for the *Fashion Dictionary*, Baldini Castoldi Dalai Publishing.

Elegances Parisiennes: evening dress, 1922 (Prints Collection A. Bertarelli, Milan).

Blouse, and Elegance du Soir. Its name and columns are taken from a monthly that was published between 1867 and 1871 and devoted to "contemporary fashions, litterature, fine arts, and the theater."

Elegante Welt (Die) German fashion magazine published in Stuttgart between 1912 and 1969. At first a fortnightly, and later a monthly, after World War II the magazine dealt with the themes of beauty, elegance, and luxury. From the time of its début and all through the 1930s it was edited by F.W. Koeber who, in 1949, also became publisher.

Elementi Moda Consulting business started in Milan in 1979 by Ornella Bignami. It works on stylistic creativity, market research, product analysis, and fashion trends for important international textile and clothing companies. It participates on the panels devoted to future trends at Pitti Immagine Filati and Interstoff. Ornella Bignami is president of Intercolor and a member of working committees at the principal textile trade fairs such as Première Vision, Moda In, and Expofil.

❑ 2001, Spring. The executive committee of Interstoff Asia is made up of Ornella Bignami for Italy, Nelly Rodi for Paris fashion, Sachiko Inoue of Tokyo, and the New York agency Here and There. The international textile fair, held in Hong Kong, sees big names such as Levis and Donna Karan, and 9,000 buyers from 60 countries. There is a seminar organized by Elementi Moda on marketing and design.
❑ Elementi Moda works with the Knitwear Service Center on a *Notebook of Knitwear Fashion Trends*, which the Center distributes to its members. The 170 pages of this seasonal book include updates and photos of the latest trends.
❑ Ornella Bignami is a member of the Trend Concertation which establishes operating guidelines for Première Vision, in particular for linen production.

Eley & Kishimoto English brand created in 1992 by Mark Eley, from Wales (1968), and his wife Wakako Kishimoto, born in Sapporo, Japan (1965). He graduated from the Polytechnic in Brighton in 1990 with a course of study in fashion and weaving. She completed her studies at the Central Saint Martin's in 1992. Each of them a specialist in printing on fabric, they started working with famous designers such as Chalayan, McQueen, and Caseley-Hayford. Their first Rainwear collection was made with PVC in fanciful patterns for raincoats, gloves, and umbrellas. The first official collection presentation occurred in London during Fashion Week for Autumn-Winter 2001. Even though production has increased considerably, and they have become a large company, Eley and Kishimoto prefer a calm management style, family-like, in a small workshop in South London where they are assisted by a small group of artisans. They are famous for their cheerful and lively fabrics printed in original and very colorful designs acquired from designers such as Saint-Laurent, Ribeiro, Jill Sander, and Louis Vuitton. In addition to clothing and accessories (gloves, sunglasses, underwear, and sneakers), the brand also includes various items for the home, including furniture, ceramics, and wallpaper.

❑ The brand wins the *Vidal Sasson Award*. Every year it gives £25,000 to the collections which distinguish themselves for the best cutting.
❑ 2002, Autumn. The new Eley & Kishimoto collection makes its début in 12 English shops in the New Look chain. The collection consists of cotton shirts and jersey tops in lavender, chocolate, transparent blue, and military green.
❑ At the London Fashion Week for Autumn-Winter 2003-2004, the designer-couple brings back, to great success, the classic Chanel-inspired tailored suit.

Elgort Arthur (1940). American photographer. After working in dance photography, for the New York City Ballet, he made his fashion début in 1975, when he began to work with Vogue. His photos place the fashion models and the styles in scenes from daily life.

Eliotex Revolutionary textile material with buoyant proprieties: 8 ounces keep almost 300 pounds afloat. It's not by accident that the textile entrepreneur Elio Cattan uses it to manufacture incredibly thin bathing suits. A square yard of Eliotex is 0.02 inches thick and weighs half an ounce.

Elise Topell German fashion house. It opened just a few months after the end of World War II and closed in the early 1970s. It was named after its founder, who was considered the Madame Vionnet of Germany. After working for various houses in Berlin, she opened her own atelier there in 1945, moving a few years later to Briebach Castle, near Wiesbaden, where her collections were presented.

Elite Model Management Model agency with offices in New York, Milan, Paris, Los Angeles, Chicago, Atlanta, Miami, Toronto, Barcelona, Seoul, Singapore, and Cape Town. It employs 500 models, including women and men. It was founded in 1971 in Paris by John Casablancas. Six years later, the headquarters was moved to New York. The agency is divided into several departments. There is one strictly connected to the world of fashion services, and one which is basically devoted to the superstars. There have been many models, some of them very famous, including Claudia Schiffer, Amber Valletta, Linda Evangelista, Isabella Rossellini, and Valeria Mazza. The agency also represents movie stars such as Natasha Kinski, Ornella Muti, and Brooke Shields. And it works at finding new faces and actors for advertising, TV, and the theater. In 1983, Casablancas launched Look of the Year, a sort of contest in which 75 entrants from 56 countries have participated.

❑ At the beginning of the new century, the agency launches the new names and faces of Natalia Semanova, Gisele Bündchen, Roberta Scotto, and Sarah Calogero.

Elizabeth Arden (1878-1966) pseudonym of Florence Nightingale Graham. Born in Canada, she moved to New York and went to work for a pharmaceutical company, which she left not long after, attracted by the cosmetics industry. In 1910, she adopted the "stage" name Elizabeth Arden and opened her first salon on Fifth Avenue. It was an exclusive beauty shop which offered its high society New York clientele treatments and massages for the body and face. The "total beauty" concept, followed from the beginning, would bring her good luck. Gifted with great intuition, in 1912 she developed a series of colored powders, a sort of precursor to blush. A few years later, returning from Europe, she introduced the first eye make-up in the American market, and a light non-oil face cream, called Venetian Cream Amoretta, that was revolutionary for its time. In 1915, with the launch of Arden Skin Tonic, she began to brand her products with her own name. It was a winning intuition which anticipated the age of beauty marketing and allowed her, along with other initiatives (see the creation of the first American joint stock company and cosmetics in small sizes suitable for travel), to build an empire. By the year of her death, the Elizabeth Arden group consisted of 17 companies and 40 beauty salons throughout the world. Thanks to constant investment in the field of research and image, the group today represents a classic of the avant-guard.

❑ 2000, November. Unilever sells the brand to the U.S. group FFI Fragrances for about $240 million, with $190 million in cash and $50 million in stock. Unilever had acquired Arden in 1989.
❑ FFI changes the group's corporate name to Elizabeth Arden Inc. The company employs 1,300 people and sells beauty products in more than 40,000 shops in the U.S. and 90 other countries.
❑ 2002. Catherine Zeta-Jones is featured in the Elizabeth Arden advertising campaign, which wins the Fifi Award, a prize given each year by the German Fragrance Producers Association to the best launch of a new line.

Elle Fashion monthly published in Italy by RCS and directed by Daniela Giussani. It is the Italian edition of Elle, the cult magazine founded in Paris in 1945 by Hélène Lazareff. The first issue came out on 17 September 1987. For the market in women's magazines, the moment was hot: the Italian edition of Marie Claire (the principal rival of Elle) had just been launched, and the new Rusconi weekly Eva was about to be published. Elle, directed by Carla Sozzani, aimed at a decidedly higher target, with sophisticated, refined graphics. It was conceived for a young, cultivated urban woman with a middle to high income who wanted a magazine to provide suggestions about fashion and beauty. The initial circulation was 300,000 copies and the first issue was a success. But success stopped there. By the second issue circulation already began to drop. Sozzani left, and the fifth issue, in January 1998, was edited by Lamberto Sechi, the editorial director at RCS. In March, Daniela Giussani was hired as co-editor. In July, she became sole editor and introduced small but specific changes: sections about news, travel, women's stories, and many columns made Elle a more approachable magazine, and things began to change, with circulation slowly rising to a steady 150,000 copies. Thanks to synergies with the 29 international editions, Elle became known for its capacity to anticipate fashions and trends on a world-wide basis.

❑ 2005, January. After 16 years, Daniela Giussani leaves the monthly to become editorial director at EDIF, which publishes Elle and Elle Décor. The new editor is Danda Santini, who arrives from Glamour.

Elle French weekly. A small revolution on glossy paper which deeply influenced the image of women in France and all over the world. Elle was founded right after World War II by Hélène Gordon-Lazareff, a highly charismatic figure and a symbol of the contemporary feminine press. She had her professional training in New York under the guidance of Carmel Snow and Diana Vreeland of Harper's Bazaar. On one of its first covers, for the 2 May 1949 issue, was a very blond and beautiful 16 year-old girl. It was the début of Brigitte Bardot. Inside were articles by Colette and Marcel Pagnol. First a monthly, and then a weekly, the magazine was from the start very innovative in concept. It acquired a wide and affectionate readership among the most modern, independent, and active members of the female universe. It soon became a very trendy magazine, with great influence on the major cultural debates of the time. Directed with authority by Lazareff, who for her working style would be nicknamed "the Czarina", it was ahead of its time, introducing an innovative journalistic slant and anticipating many of the arguments of feminism. It also published many of the great names in photography. The formula proved successful and the figures confirm it. From an initial 110,000 copies, within ten years the magazine would stabilize at around 800,000 copies, reaching the record figure of 1 million copies in the early 1960s. On its pages, the first generation of designers was launched, from Michèle Rosier and Sonia Rykiel to Emmanuelle Khanh and Paco Rabanne. But the main characteristic of the magazine, an editorial policy which is today still the secret of its success, is the great harmony between the themes of culture and business and the pages devoted to beauty and fashion. Acquired in 1980 by the Filippacchi Group, Elle is today directed by Anne-Marie Périer and published in 21 foreign editions.

❑ Besides more than twenty editions around the world, the magazine has in recent years started 16 web-sites, including those in India, Taiwan, China, and Brazil.

Ellen Tracy American company specialized in clothes for the working woman. Established in 1949 by Herbert Gallen, in the beginning it manufactured only shirts. In 1962, the company hired the designer Linda Allard. Two years later, she became head designer and diversified the lines. Department stores in the U.S. offer three different collections: Linda Allard for Ellen Tracy, Company by Ellen Tracy, and, for evening wear, Ellen Tracy Dresses. In the 1990s, the company tripled its turnover and signed commercial agreements for tights, eyeglasses, bags, and scarves.

❑ 1999. Herbert Gallen and Linda Allard, his wife and the company's very famous designer, celebrate the brand's 50th birthday, relying for the new promotional campaign on the face of the former top model Cindy Crawford.
❑ 2000. Stephanie Seymour, another icon of the 1990s, joins Cindy Crawford as the image of the *griffe*.

Ellesse Sportswear company established in Perugia in 1959 by Leonardo Servadio. The first products were ski trousers in elasticized fabric. Seven years later, demand caused the company to build a new headquarters and plant. In 1970 and '74, further success came from the revolutionary and patented jet pants (they would be shown at the 1979 exhibit which the Pompidou Center dedicated to Italian design) and from an innovative padded jacket, both for skiing. Later, the line grew to include tennis oufits, windsurf wear, swimwear, and leisure time clothes. Meanwhile, the company, which was the first in its field to put a brand label on the outside of its garments, carried out a massive sponsorship program. Over the years, it sponsored tennis champions such as Boris Becker, 10 national ski teams, various tennis opens, and the Italian soccer team that became world champion in 1982. In 1988 the brand sold licenses in the U.S. and Canada, and in 1989-1990 in Japan. In 1993, the Pentald Plc Group acquired 90% of the company. Between 1995 and '97 it acquired the rest and also took over the brand in the U.S. and Canada. Ellesse makes the Magic Air jacket and it made the racing outfit worn by Jean Luc Cretier, the French skier who in 1998 won the men's downhill at the Olympics in Nagano.

❑ 2001. The European turnover is €210 million, 85% of which comes from the U.K.
❑ 2002. An international reorganization of the company, owned by the British Pentland Group, is launched. The guidelines include the introduction of new management, a product restyling, and a reorganization of the sales network. The effort is led by Bill Sweeney, president of the Ellesse Division, and Christopher Lee, the creative director.

Ellis Perry (1940). American designer. After a long apprenticeship with two manufacturing firms, John Meyer of Norwick and Manhattan Industries, he designed a leather line in 1975 and went out on his own in 1978. He has remained successful thanks to his ability to revisit traditional styles and keep them youthful.

❑ The third millennium begins in the best possible way, with excellent results for the first six months of 2000.

Combined revenues are $150 million, an increase of 31.8% compared to the same period in 1999. Profits go from $4.5 million to $5.4 million.
❑ 2000, August. Agreement with CBD International for the distribution of activewear in Europe. A joint venture with Grand National Apparel for the Canadian market is considered.
❑ The designer receives the prestigious *Coty Fashion Award* for women's clothing. He is also recognized by the Council of Fashion Designers of America, of which he was the first president, for his men's wear.
❑ He establishes an award in his name which is to be given each year to promising young talents in men's wear, women's wear, and accessories.

Ellis Sean (1970). English photographer, born in Brighton. He went to work for The Face and quickly made a name for himself with an aggresive and rather ironic style inspired in equal measure by Helmut Newton and Guy Bourdin. He uses the term "fashion story" to describe his method, which consists in developing a theme with several images over many pages. He calls himself a storyteller doing fashion features.

Eloisa Alba (1977). Sicilian designer born in Catania. She was featured, together with Matilde Giuffrida (1965) and Alfonso Zappulla (1973), in a collective presentation of 30 garments during the High Fashion Week in Rome in January 2003. Eloisa has her own atelier in Catania and has distinguished herself for minimal-chic clothes enriched with embroidery and oriental details. Giuffrida, from Syracuse, has made good use of the intarsia techniques typical of the Sicilian baroque. Zappulla, who is also from Catania, has presented bridal dresses as well as clothes decorated with glass paste.

Elvis Jesus & Co Couture English brand of ready-to-wear created in 1997 by Kurt Levi Jones (1968) and Helen Littler (1969) after completing their course of study in fashion. The unusual name was inspired by Kinky Friedman's novel *Elvis Jesus and Coca-Cola*. The two designers meet in a club in Manchester in 1988 at the peak of the Acid House scene. Their style comes from the town's youth culture and its impressive Asian tradition. They produce limited series of clothes, using old saris, along with small dresses and brightly colored, witty tops. Their clientele consists of very young girls, including the latest pop stars.

❑ 2001. Known as the "sari brand" for the wide use of that traditional Indian garment in their collections, it changed direction completely, focusing more on women's clothing and on shirts and sweaters with the logo on them.
❑ 2002, August. The fashion week organized by International Enterprise Singapore along with the local federation of fashion and textiles is an excellent occasion for the designer Helen Littler to present the brand to the Far East market.

Elvstrom Line of sportswear created in 1975 by two friends with a passion for sailing, Beppe Croce and Paul Elvstrom. At first, the seal of quality for the products, which were rigorously hi-tech, was provided by the continuous sailing victories of the Danish Paul Elvstrom: 4 Olympic and 13 world titles. Then they enlarged the range of products, including navy-style casual sportswear, accessories, shoes, watches, and eyeglasses. All of this was meant for men with a passion for sailing. (*Sofia Camerana*)

Emanuel David and Elisabeth. English designers, both born in 1952. They created Lady Diana's wedding dress. It was 1981 and the couple, husband and wife, had designed their first collection only four years before, after graduating from the Royal College of Arts in London.

❑ 1990. They launch the David Emanuel Couture brand. The designer receives clients by appointment in his suite at the Lanesborough Hotel in Knightsbridge.
❑ The designer obtains experience as a set and costume designer. He creates the costumes for *Cinderella* at the London Palladium and for *Frankenstein* at Covent Garden, performed by the Royal Ballet. He also works with La Scala in Milan.
❑ The designer publishes his first book, *Style for all Seasons*.

Emanuel Schvili Shirt factory in Bologna established in 1968 by Emanuel and Giorgia Schvili. It opens its first single-brand boutique in Milan, followed by one in Bologna. Success arrives during the 1980s with embroidered shirts, first with traditional designs and later with cartoon characters from Warner Bros. (Bugs Bunny, etc.) and Walt Disney.

❑ At the beginning of the new century, production covers all age segments. Emanuel Schvili Baby is conceived for babies up to 24 months; the Junior line for kids goes up to 14 years; and the Emanule Schvili Donna line and the Sport line are for adults and leisure time. The latest creations are Linea Casa and the Donna Trend collection, which is for girls aged 2 to 10 years. Emanuel Schvili has about 15 points-of-sale in Italy, with a kiosk inside La Rinascente in Piazza Duomo in Milan.

Embossed Honeycomb fabric, also known as ashlar-worked, with relief effects alternating with grooves on its surface, and which on the whole gives the idea of a geometric pattern. With fabric, it is obtained through a special weave. With knitwear, it is necessary to use special stitches which hold some parts tightly and leave others more loose. This effect can also be achieved with elastic yarns that create a pattern similar to a honeycomb.

Emilia Bellini Historic *griffe* for underwear and linens. It was named after its founder. All through the 1970s, Emilia Bellini represented "the best" for underwear and linens that were "made in Florence." In Summer 1952, she participated in the first presentation of Italian fashion at the Sala Bianca in Palazzo Pitti. In 1963, she was a recipient of the French "Bon Goût" gold cup. Palazzo Strozzi dedicated an exhibit to her in which it was possible to admire pieces of the most valuable manufacture, unique in their extraordinary workmanship. The 15th century Florentine palace where her creations, admired throughout the world, were produced also displayed masterpieces from the past of inestimable value. These included blankets in white lacework that it had taken more than a generation to complete as well as a small handkerchief that had required more than a year of work. She wrote an encyclopedia dedicated to color in which she listed all the shades and tones of every single hue. Her daughters Evelina and Clara were her helpers and continued her tradition.

Eminence French company of men's underwear, established in 1944 through a partnership between Georges Jonathan, a sales representative, and Gilbert Sivel, a weaving technician. In 1947 they invented Kangaroo panties, the panties which give support, and marketed them in transparent packaging. The brand rapidly became a leader in the industry. Thirteen years later, the Athena line was launched, aimed at a lower-level consumer, and sold in department stores. In 1991, the company became part of the Swiss group Hesta, which already owned Schiesser and Ragno. In 1997, the turnover was 383 million French francs. The firm employs 670 people.

❑ 2001, August. The French company acquires the Italian brand Liabel from Sara Lee.
❑ 2002. The company ends the year with a turnover of about €120 million.
❑ 2003. The Société Industrielle de Lingerie (SIL) passes under the control of Eminence. A licensee for Christian Dior underwear, it had a deficit of €3 million at the end of 2002 and had been in receivership since November of the previous year.
❑ The French company obtains the Italian license for Cacharel underwear. SIL is to design and produce the underwear in France, but Liabel is to manage the distribution in Italy starting in January 2004.

Emmetex Italian factory making fabrics for clothing. Its premises are in Prato and it is directed by Mario Marcello Maselli. Creativity, flexibility, and quality have been the signposts on a journey which has made this company a leader in its field, with more than 3 million yards manufactured each year, 65% of which is exported. The company was established in 1979 to manufacture hi-tech fabrics for outerwear and sportswear. Rapid growth caused it to differentiate the product line into stretch, bistretch, velvets, and jacquards in different materials. The raw materials and finishings were also diversified, becoming very innovative in their technology and ecologically-minded in the manufacturing process. Each year the company invests about 5% of its turnover in research on trends and technology. Each seasonal collection is presented at Prato Expo and at Première Vision in Paris. It is divided into at least 150 different themes according to very specific criteria in terms of colors, weaves, patterns, and performance. At least 70% of each collection is innovative. The final product is manufactured by partner companies connected to the leading brand through a joint relationship. Quality and safety are guaranteed by technical controls, very careful monitoring, and strict tests of stability through successive washings and exposure to light. (*Giuliana Zabeo Ricca*)

❑ Emmetex offers four clothing lines: Basic for men and Basic for women, both for leisure time, and Sportswear and Glamour for younger women. Spring-Summer 2001 sees the launch of Platinum, a young collection meant for a higher-level market. Outfits made from high-quality fibers are integrated by special fabrics in catonic and ceramic polyester to protect the body from electromagnetic waves and UVA rays.

Empire Empire-style clothes are characterized by a very high waist just below the breasts, so that one speaks of an "Empire waist." This fashion dates to the first two decades of the 1800s and the court of Napoleon. It was launched by the Empress Josephine. The empire dress consisted of a tunic, usually white, with a tiny bodice fastened below the breasts by a ribbon or a belt. It had a very low neckline, short puff sleeves, and a skirt that fell loose and straight below the breasts. Madame Récamier would wear one to receive her guests in the famous salon at the Abbaye-aux-Bois. The unforgettable Audrey Hepburn wore one as Natasha in the film *War and Peace*. The style has been presented again and again throughout the 20th century by the great names of fashion, including Lanvin in the early 1900s, Rochas in the 1930s, Balenciaga, Dior, and Givenchy in the early 1960s, and Romeo Gigli's relaunch in the 1980s.

Eng Melinda (1953). Chinese designer. She became famous after a small appearance playing an underwear designer in the Woody Allen film *Celebrity*. In real life, she enjoys creating artistic evening dresses with fabrics that are lightly draped on the body. She avoids buttons, machine seams, and zippers in order to allow the fabric to fall naturally. Born in Hong Kong, as a very young girl she moved with her family to New York's Chinatown. She attended the Parsons School of Design. She showed her talent working at the English knitwear house Pringle as head designer for men's and women's knitwear. Convinced of the importance of simplicity combined with comfort, when she opened her atelier she designed garments that were cut very simply, in lightweight fabrics such as chiffon, crepe, and georgette.

(*Priscilla Daroda*)

❑ 2003. A "floral" year for the Chinese designer, who revisits her favorite fabric, silk chiffon, in flowered patterns.

Engel Hart Thomas (1972). American designer. He studied at the Fashion Institute of Technology and at the age of 25 went to try his chances in Paris. He went regularly to the Berçot studio and then became the assistant to André Walker and Veronique Leroy. His first collection, inspired by the Rock'n'Roll Dandies, combined different influences, while the second, for Winter 2002-2003, joined several urban themes and made use of luxury fabrics and important details. The Summer 2003 collection, presented with the help of the Andam association, won great appoval from buyers and the press.

(*Maddalena Fossati*)

English Eccentrics English brand of ready-to-wear created in 1982 by Helen David (1955), Judy Littman, and Clare Angel. The idea came from Helen, who specialized in fabric design after her artistic studies at St. Martin's. At first, the three friends manufactured only printed fabrics following artisanal procedures. They gradually increased their collection with pieces manufactured in their distinctive fabrics. Patterns were inspired by motifs and colors from art history, such as classic decorations and Renaissance frescoes. In 1992, Phaidon Press published a book about them.

❑ 2001, February. On the eve of a show

at the Museum of Natural History for London Fashion Week, an article was published in The Guardian about Helen David's experience in Mexico on the trail of the painter Frida Kahlo.
❑ Some models by the three business friends are kept at the Fashion and Textile Museum in London, in the area dedicated to *Notable British Fashion Designers*.

Enka World-wide leader in the manufacture of viscose thread. It is located in Germany and employs more than 2,000 people, with a European production of 25,000 tons of spun thread. It is a company that looks to the future, employing recyclable materials and modern techniques with complete respect for the environment. The raw material for Enka viscose is wood cellulose and through an elaborate production process it replicates the high quality of natural fiber. It is suitable for every kind of application in the textile industry, from fabrics to threads for knitwear and embroidery. Blended with other fibers such as polyamide and polyester, it acquires more body, adding volume and brilliance. An innovative and versatile material, it allows great creativity thanks to its range of wonderful colors and silky feel. Enka Sun is a thread perfected by Akzo Nobel, offering protection from damaging sun rays. Enka Moda also plays a role as a talent scout. Two years ago, in collaboration and with the sponsorship of the National Committee of Italian Fashion, an international research project called Enkamania was launched. It allows emerging young designers, selected by competition, to work with textiles and to use Enka viscose in their creations. Out of one hundred entrants, 21 are chosen as finalists, and 5 of them are offered the opportunity to present their first collection during Milano Collezioni Donna. At the end of the presentations, an award is given. In September 2002, the 5 finalists were Bless, Icarius, Ichiro Seta, Rohka, and Zac Posen. The jury was composed of Franca Sozzani (the president), Peter Lindbergh (a photographer), Jean-Paul Gaultier, Philip Treacy, Milla Yovovich, and Enrico Freidhof, with the participation of Donna Karan, Yamamoto, and Isabella Blow. The award, *ex aequo*, went to Ichiro Seta and Rohka.

(*Gabriella Gregorietti*)

Enriquez Rachele (1938). Journalist. From 1989 to 1995 she was editor-in-chief at Vogue Spain. She started her career in the 1960s as an editor at Annabella. She left in order to participate, as managing editor, in the adventure of the Milan weekly Il Milanese. The enterprise was a precarious one, despite the efforts and talents of a director such as Angelo Rozzoni, a main figure in the best years of Il Giorno. Lamberto Sechi hired her at Panorama where, as editor of culture and entertainment, she would work for 16 years, until she was offered the chance to manage Vogue Spain in Madrid. She returned to Italy as deputy manager of the monthly Carnet. Since 1998 she has been editorial consultant for Sette, the weekly magazine of Corriere della Sera, a position for which she was hired by Andrea Monti and in which she continues to work with Maria Luisa Agnese, the present director.

Entre-deux A strip of lace inserted between two pieces of cloth. A classic ornament in linens for the house, it is also used in dresses and blouses.

Enzo Italian high-fashion atelier opened in Milan in 1957 by Enzo Sguanci. After attending the Academy of Fine Arts at the Brera, he was a cutter in the atelier of Remo Gandini and designed for Jole Veneziani. Enzo was immediately noticed for a very precise, dry, and refined style that was accurate in the cutting and which emphasized extremely trendy geometric shapes. His tailored suits and coats were highly thought of.

E-Play Brand of casual clothing with a strong research component created by Livio Graziottin (1965), a graduate of the School of Art and Industrial Design in Venice. His work is produced by Gruppo Fashion Box (Replay). The brand was born in 1994, at the start of the internet phenomenon. The letter *E* in the name stands for electronic, as in e-business, e-mail, etc. Over time, the technologic and futuristic inspiration became more nuanced, going from revisited ethnic to retro, with influences from contemporary art and design, in a melting pot characterized by an extremely creative use of

Sketch by Enzo, 1960 (from *La Sala Bianca – La nascita della moda italiana*, by Guido Vergani, Electa, 1992). Giovanni Battista Giorgini Archive.

technology that was often experimental, on the level of both materials and processes.

(*Ruben Modigliani*)

Épure Brand created in 1997 by Gérald Rossi, a French designer educated at Esmod who emphasizes the technical aspect of materials and a sobriety of line. His designs tend toward an urban elegance with sweet nuances. There are blouses and large sweaters with hoods made of microfibers, wide skirts in dark colors made of nylon and other fibers, and, above all, tapering at the bottom.

❑ 2001. Opening of the first boutique in Paris.

Equipe 84 Italian clothing-store chain named after a well-known Italian rock group of the 1960s. The look of the brand's shops and its clothing were inspired by the music and tastes of the young counterculture that emerged around 1968. The line's signature pieces featured alternative materials not commonly found in clothing at the time, such as home-furnishing fabrics, tea towels combined with lacework and transparent veils. In a more familiar 1960s spirit, the store was also known for Nehru jackets in leather and batik, ponchos and boots. The company closed its doors in 1976.

Eram French shoe company that is among the most important in terms of production. It has 13 plants in France, Spain, and Portugal with daily production of about 50,000 pairs. The company has 780 points-of-sale and 450 franchise shops.

❑ 2002. The year ends with a turnover of €1 billion.
❑ Eram five brands, distributed in a total of 1,600 company-owned shops and 249 franchises in Luxembourg, Belgium, Germany, Poland, and Switzerland. The employs 10,500 people in 10 production plants located in the French regions of Maine and the Loire and in Portugal.

Erès French brand of bathing suits. Created in the mid 1960s by Irene Leroux, its success has steadily increased thanks to spontaneous testimonials from stars of show business and fashion who prefer Erès products because of their cut, quality manufacture, palette of colors, choice of fabrics (long-lasting treated cottons), and lack of attention that the designer gives to sensationalism. In 1997, Chanel acquired 100% of the company, but left total autonomy in the hands of the founder, who in 1998 launched an underwear line in muslin and taffeta.

❑ The approach taken to the American market is supported by the opening of two single-brand stores, one on Madison Avenue in New York, and one in Palm Beach.
❑ 2002, August. Erès bathing suits are featured in the fourth edition of *Vogue Takes the Hampton's Celebration*, a promotional event organized in East Hampton by Vogue America.

Eric Pseudonym of Carl Erickson (1891-1958), an American illustrator. His touch and his palette, in which one can see the heritage of the Expressionist painters and the Fauves, run counter to the precise and linear illustrative style of the 1920s. He was of Swedish origin. In 1914, after two years at the Academy of Art in Chicago, he moved to New York. He made his début in Vogue in

1916. He would become a pillar of the magazine for 30 years, along with René Bouet Willaumez and, later, René Bouché, working for a long time from Paris.

Erica Textile company established in the early 1900s under the name Cotonificio di Busto and then renamed, during the 1950s, Cotonificio Erica and then, in the late 1970s, Erica Industria Tessile. Its headquarters is in Legnano. Specializing in printed patterns for women's prêt-à-porter, it works closely with the best names in fashion, revisiting the ancient Como tradition and rejuvenating the product through research on new technologies, new fibers, new blends, new finishings, fresh inspiration, and the latest trends.

❑ 2003. About 50% of the production is exported to the Far East (Taiwan, Korea, Japan, Hong Kong), Spain, Germany, the U.S., Belgium, and France.

Erickson Beamon American brand of high-fashion costume jewellery. It was created in New York in 1983 based on an idea of Karen Erickson and Vicki Sarge (1954): to manufacture handcrafted costume jewellery of very high quality following the latest women's fashions. The two designers work with the greatest stylists, from Rifat Ozbeck to John Galliano. With a presence in London since 1985, they opened a boutique in Belgravia in 1994 and then one in Toronto, Canada.

❑ 2003, April. The brand celebrates its twentieth anniversary. Since Spring of 1983, when the two designers created their first crystal and beads necklace, they have dressed Nicole Kidman, Cher, and Milla Jovovich, and worked with John Galliano, Givenchy, Chanel, Donna Karan, and Emanuel Ungaro. Their showroom has become one of the most important New York places for fashion.
❑ Opening of the new boutique Outlet 7 on Seventh Street in New York.

Ermanno Scervino Brand created in 1997 through the merger of two names, Ermanno Daelli and Tony Scervino. The first brought creativity, the second entrepreneurial skills. Daelli joined the Tuscan house after various experiences: he lived in both Paris and London, and faced the challenge of the clothing market by opening a boutique in Florence and one in Cortina. Indeed, it was by observing the clients that he discovered, besides an ability to match colors, his vocation as a fashion designer. He worked with important companies and in 1985 he designed his first collection of women's accessories, within a short time conquering the world's shop windows. In 1990 he presented his women's collection in Milan and that same year designed a men's collection. Thus, prior to his meeting with Scervino, for whom he now designs exclusively, he became known for fashions with a well-tailored cut and line, a rigorous and cosmopolitan taste, and a re-use of ethnic influences. His research on materials is remarkable. The brand's power also lies in the high quality of its fabrics, which Daelli often designs personally, and in their technological innovation. The corporate strategy is based on direct selling: the collections, presented at every Moda Donna in Milan, are offered in the showroom on via Montenapoleone. *(Lucia Mari)*

Ermenegildo Zegna World leader in men's fine clothing. In the language of television, we can say that with its market share of 30% it has a large audience, especially among men who like elegance. This elegance can be informal, with unstructured lines and tailoring details combined in a comfortable style that doesn't forget to add a touch of irony. That's what Aldo Zegna, one of the sons of Ermenegildo, the founder, often says: "The man we dress is not stuck in the classic and traditional concept of the men's elegance. Those who wear Zegna follow new trends, but in a personal way, complying with the needs of a very functional wardrobe." It is fashion that is not imposed by decree, but that comes from an individual simplicity, a revisited suit filtered through the needs of a modern man and based on the quality of the fabric. Indeed, on the best fabric. And it was precisely with fabric that the history of the Zegna dynasty got its start, in 1910 in Trivero on the hills near Biella, when Ermenegildo established a factory to manufacture high quality fabric for men's clothing, the result of the direct selection of the best raw materials such as wool, mohair, cashmere, and alpaca.

With fine entrepreneurial intuition, a capacity for hard work, and pride in a name which is synonymous with trust, today the Group is a vital organization which anticipates changes in clothing and both interprets and experiences those changes as a major player in the fashion industry with an eye always focused on what is new. In fact, the Group has received awards for its production of the most precious wool and mohair, used in knit outerwear, casual wear and underwear, accessories, fabric, and men's clothing. Aldo Zegna and his brother Angelo took over from their father in the 1960s and realized that it is not enough to manufacture superb fabrics if the quality of the finished goods is left in other hands. The production cycle, from raw materials to processing, design, manufacturing, and distribution, was integrated, giving birth to a company in the men's clothing field which was then followed by others in knitwear, accessories, and sportswear. The expansion in production caused the Group to look for direct outlets in foreign markets, and to open branches in Spain, France, Germany, Austria, the U.S., Japan, Great Britain, Mexico, Turkey, Korea, and Singapore, as well as production plants in Spain and Switzerland. The Group's vertical integration was completed in the 1980s with the opening of the first single-brand boutiques in Paris and Milan. By 1998 the number of single-brand stores was 227 (41 directly owned, 32 franchises, and 154 kiosks). Each year, the *griffe* produces more than 2 million yards of fabric, 500,000 jackets and coats, 500,000 shirts, and 3 million ties. In 1998, the turnover was 902 billion liras (80% from clothing and accessories, 20% from textile products) with more than 80% from exports. The Group has 4,000 workers but still maintains the feel of a family business. The dynasty is now led by the third generation, Gildo, Paolo, Anna, Laura, and Benedetta. They are very active in a series of initiatives which could be summed up as Made in Zegna, the idea that a man should wear clothes made by Zegna at all times, from boardroom meetings to moments of leisure. As regards formal clothing, by 1977 there was already a Custom Made service to satisfy the needs of a refined consumer, one who loves to personalize his own suit in terms of style and fabric. In 1995 came the Idea Card. Those who carry it enjoy several special services, first of all the "check-up," which is no-charge mending of garments at the end of each season. For the very busy man, there is after-hours shopping, requested by just a phone call, and even the possibility of enjoying the Custom Made service by appointment at home or office. The Idea Card also allows clients to have a suit made for their children at 50% discount. The record year was 1999: the Group signed an agreement to acquire control of the Lanerie Agnona di Borgosesia and entered the field of luxury women's wear. In June, Zegna made its début in e-commerce, launching its internet site in the U.S. and becoming the first luxury brand of clothing to offer, along with corporate information, its products on the web. Zegna Sport soon followed, with a young and high-tech spirit, its first store opening in November on Rodeo Drive in Beverly Hills. Finally, the wardrobe of the Zegna man was enriched by small leather goods in precious materials. The Naples collection includes mainly bags for professional use, while the Traveler collection is very sturdy. The third generation is expanding, and with an ecological conscience. They are responsible for the creation of Zegna Oasis, a land in which the environment is protected and at the same time made accessible to visitors in order to promote, through direct experience, a knowledge of nature. This is something that the founder Ermenegildo had already cultivated along with his business activities, starting a reforestation project in order to give a new face to the mountainous land where his company is located. To remember this, there is now a panoramic road named after him.

(*Lucia Mari*)

❑ 2001. The Group has a turnover of €685.7 million, an increase of 8.4% compared to the previous year, and a gross profit of €61.3 million. The net assets are €334.5 million, triple the figure in 1996. Present in 64 countries, it has increased its competitive position in China by 30% and in Japan by 20%.
❑ 2002. The Ermenegildo Zegna group and the Salvatore Ferragamo group create ZeFer, a joint venture to develop the Ermenegildo Zegna brand in leather goods and shoes. Ferragamo's ability

and experience in leather support the diversification of the Zegna brand, which is a leader in men's clothing. The first shoe produced by the partnership is launched in 2003 and called Portofino.
❑ 2002. A year marked by difficulties and uncertainties in the principal world markets ends with a consolidated turnover of €660 million. The growth of sales in Asia by 15% and by a more modest 4% in Europe are among the reasons for the company's stable position. At the end of the year, there are 379 single-brand shops, of which 135 are company-owned.
❑ 2003. Zegna creates a joint venture in China, named ShaarMoon Ez, by acquiring 50% of ShaarMoon, a Chinese company run by the Chen brothers that is specialized in the manufacture of high-quality men's suits and jackets. The goal is to improve the brand's competitive position in China, where Zegna has 36 stores in 25 different cities and enjoys revenues of €33 million, 5% of the total. "The investment needed to bring our production to China is not yet finalized," said Ermenegildo and Paolo Zegna. "But the goal is to strengthen our presence in China, a country with an expected strong trend of growth."
(*Dario Golizia*)

Ermine High quality fur. Depicted in a medieval portrait at the National Library in Paris as the virginal ermine of Saint Catherine, and in the famous 1807 painting *The Consecration of Napoleon* by Jacques-Louis David in the Louvre as the imperial ermine, it stands for purity and royalty. These two concepts, so different and yet so similar, have probably always been associated with this type of fur. Due to its purity, it has deserved to be part of the most spiritual garments. Due to its preciousness and beauty, it decorated the robes that Venetian nobleman and judges of the 1200s wore during solemn ceremonies, was an essential element of the sumptuous elegance of the cloaks worn by the Doges in the 1400s, and was on a par with purple, silk, and gold in its use by royalty. A brave and aggressive animal of the forest, the ermine (*Mustela Erminea*) changes color with the seasons. In Summer it is reddish brown, with the belly part a whitish color. In Winter, with the exception of the tip of the tail, which remains black, it becomes completely white, dazzling on the snow, in which it camouflages itself to hide from enemies. Found mainly in the northern hemisphere, it lives in very different environments in Europe, Asia, and North America. The animal owes its name – as indicated by its Latin etymology, *armenius* – to the incorrect belief that Armenia was its original home. It appears more likely that Armenians were the first to trade the fur, or that Europeans found the fur in this region before the discovery of the New World. The ermine, which is most valuable with its white Winter coat, has strong fur but rather frail skin, which is why it is often preferred in white. Thus it has maintained, along with its extraordinary lightness, the aura of a rare, refined, and delicate fur, known most widely through Leonardo da Vinci's *Portrait of a Lady with an Ermine*, in which it symbolizes the virtues of moderation and kindness. Those which, after all, are its qualities as well.
(*Maria Rita Stiglich*)

Erotokritos Antoniadis (1967). Greek designer. He was born in Cyprus, where he still designs the largest part of his collections. The son of a winery owner and a manager of an art gallery, he studied art in San Francisco and fashion at the Studio Berçot in Paris. He worked as an apprentice with Thierry Mugler and later with Martine Sitbon. He launched his own brand in 1994, and two years later opened a boutique in Paris. Thanks to his casual-chic fashion, he has several stores all over the world.

Errebi Italian ready-to-wear company established in 1941 by Aldo Botticelli in Civitanova Marche. The jump in quality came in 1975, when the grandson of the founder, Roberto Botticelli, while maintaining the firm's artisanal tradition, optimized its technological resources and began to use designers such as Michel Perry and Gianni Barbato. Its men's and women's collections are today under the Roberto Botticelli brand, a *griffe* which is distributed all over the world, from New Zealand to the U.S. Single-brand boutiques in Rome and Riccione have been joined by new single-brand shops in

London and Madrid. In autumn 2000, the company launched a man-woman total look and a line called B-sport by Botticelli.

Erreuno Company established in 1970 by Ermanno and Graziella Ronchi, before they were married. The story starts in a basement on via Segantini in Milan, very far from the traditional streets of fashion. Ermanno was 23 and a clothing salesman. Graziella was younger, and a designer. In 1975, after constant visits to all the provincial boutiques, they began to enjoy larger revenues and were ready to become something larger than a simple family business. Their goal was a more creative line, and they called on the designer Gianmarco Venturi. The partnership would last 3 years. Graziella quit designing in order to be a common-sense creative filter, the person able to take a garment seen on a runway and turn it into a piece of clothing to be worn on the street in everyday life. She also played this role from 1980 to '88 when Giorgio Armani designed for Erreuno and established the house style: clothes that are believable whether worn by a model during a presentation or by a woman on the bus and at work. This remained Erreuno's credo even after the relationship with Armani: a style that is very classic, without useless frills or eccentricities. The company sells almost 50% of its production abroad, in the U.S., Germany, Japan, Belgium, and France, and has an alliance with a company in the Far East, adding two more lines, Donnaerre and Amamy, to the primary line.

❑ 2000, October. Ermanno Ronchi and the staff celebrate the company's 30th anniversary.
❑ 2001, April. The board of directors of the National Chamber of Fashion is elected for the period 2001-2003. Ermanno Ronchi is appointed vice-president.
❑ 2002, March. The first collection of Erreuno's new designer Marco Bignù, who replaced Gennaro Esposito. In this same year, the company produces the first collection of the designer Marella Ferrera.

Sketch by Erté (Victoria and Albert Museum, London).

Erté Pseudonym of Romain de Tirtoff (1892-1990), an illustrator and costume and set designer. He was born in St. Petersburg, Russia, and naturalized as a French citizen. He was 76 years old when a retrospective exhibit at the Metropolitan Museum of Art in New York caused him to be rediscovered by art dealers and collectors, improving the market for his work. This set him apart from the crowded group of illustrators, also masters of their trade, who devoted themselves to fashion and the smart set at the same time he did, the period between the two world wars and a short time before. In Russia, as a young boy, he studied in the atelier of Ilia Repin. In 1912, he decided to improve his talent at the Académie Julian in Paris and at the École Nationale des Beaux-Arts. Poiret discovered him and gave him his start, allowing him to earn a living by designing models for his collections, a trade that fascinated him. After all, according to legend, at the age of 6, young Romain created an evening outfit for his mother. From Paris, he sent drawings to Damsky Min, the most important fashion magazine in czarist Russia. Poiret opened the doors of the Gazette du Bon Ton to him.

Diaghilev asked him to design costumes and sets for his ballets. Erté's style, though influenced by the painting of the Pre-Raphaelites, and by floral and Art Deco patterns, had an original touch that was perhaps the result of pictures he saw in the library of his father, who was an admiral. These included 16th century Persian and Indian miniatures, from which he acquired certain precious decorative motifs, as well as a love for details and for gold and silver. Between 1916 and 1938 he designed innumerable covers for Harper's Bazaar. During the 1920s and 1930s he would work in both Paris and New York on the sets for the Folies Bergères (he designed several costumes for Joséphine Baker) and the Ziegfeld Follies. Hollywood also wanted him, and he created sets and costumes for *The Mystic* and *La Bohème*. He was very famous for his *Alphabet*, which used the shape of a woman to form each letter.

(*Angela Madesani*)

Sketch by Erté (Victoria and Albert Museum, London).

Erwitt Eliott (1928). American photographer, born in Paris of Russian descent. His given name is Elio Romano Erwitz. When he was two years old, the family moved to Milan. Ten years later, it moved to Los Angeles, where he would work in a photo lab and later open his own studio. At that time, he specialized in portraits. He moved to New York and came in contact with Robert Capa and the world of commercial photography. In 1953 Capa helped him join the Magnum photo agency, of which he would become president in 1969. An eclectic artist, able to go from portraiture to reportage without losing his sense of humor or ironic tone, Erwitt worked in fashion and advertising from time to time, providing photos for companies in the field.

(*Roberto Mutti*)

Escada German company of women's clothing. It was established in 1976 by Margaretha and Wolfgang Ley and named after a famous thoroughbred. The headquarters is in Munich. During the 1980s, new offices were opened in London, Milan, Canada, Japan, and France.

❑ 1999. The firm celebrates its 20th anniversary with a spectacular fashion show presented around the world and with the inauguration of an internet web-site.
❑ 2000, September. In collaboration with the Diamond Trading Company, which is part of the De Beers Group, and with the Pluczenik Group, the firm creates a diamond collection inspired in shape by the Escada heart. Also on sale are the Escada Accessories line of bags and shoes and a new fragrance, Sentiment.
❑ The owner of Escada, Wolfgang Ley, receives the Bambi, the most important German media award, previously given to Giorgio Armani and Jill Sander for the fashion sector.
❑ 2001. Escada Lingerie goes on sale, rounding out the accessory lines. In New York, a single-brand boutique opens on Fifth Avenue.
❑ 2002. There is a reduction in turnover of 8.7% to €772.9 million, and sales fall 3.7%, but profits grow.
❑ 2003, May. The firm negotiates the

acquisition of production plants in Slovenia as part of an ongoing strategy to become more competitive and reduce costs. With the closing at the end of 2002 of the last German production plant, the entire production of jackets, trousers, and shirts has been moved abroad.

❑ 2003. After opening a boutique in the Rappongi Hills neighborhood of Tokyo, Escada adds to its number of stores with an opening in Paris in July 2003 and one in Düsseldorf in August. In autumn, it is the turn of Moscow, St. Petersburg, Kuwait City, Glasgow, and Vancouver.

(*Pierangelo Mastantuono*)

Escargot American brand of sportswear, especially T-shirts, launched in 1986. It sells very simple T-shirts with carefully selected printed designs. All the symbols of American and Irish culture are available, as well as plants, flowers and dreamlike landscapes. The products are sold in 1,000 shops scattered across the U.S., Canada, Japan, and England. They can also be purchased on the internet.

❑ Created by Brenda and Jay Meinrich, the brand participates in 12 fashion events around the world each year.

Esclusa Manuel (1952). Catalan photographer. Learning the profession in his father's studio, he moved to Barcelona in 1975 and began to teach. In 1976, with Joan Fontcuberta and Tony Catany, he founded Gruppo Alabern, with the goal of helping to renew the language of photography. In the second half of the 1970s, he entered fashion photography, working almost exclusively for the magazine Ya Moda, before later devoting himself completely to artistic production.

Escoffier Marcel (1910). French costume designer for theater and cinema. The son of a very famous chef, he studied the decorative arts and made his début as an assistant to Christian Bérard. During the 1930s he was completely absorbed by the theater. In 1943 he worked in the cinema, designing the costumes for *Carmen*, a French-Italian film directed by Christian Jacques with Jean Marais and Viviane Romance. His working partnership with Jean Cocteau would be long and fruitful, resulting in costumes for *Ruy Blas* and *L'Aigle à deux Testes* in 1947, *Orphée* in 1949, *Nez-de-Cuir* in 1951, and *Princesse de Clèves* in 1961. He belongs to the historicist school, which in Italy is represented by Gino Sensani and which aims at an exact reconstruction of a period's costumes. He dressed Gina Lollobrigida and Gérard Philippe in *Fanfan la Tulipe*. In 1953, Visconti entrusted him with the complex costumes for *Senso* and he was assisted, in creating the military uniforms, by Piero Tosi. Almost 20 years later, still successful, he created the costumes for *Les Mariés de l'an II* and *Joan of Arc* directed by Fassini at La Fenice in Venice.

(*Angela Malesani*)

Eskimo Jacket that recalls the coat worn by Eskimos. It is an oversize sport jacket with a fur-trimmed hood, closed in front by a zipper or with frogs, in waterproof fabric. It was the uniform of '68.

Esma Started with the name Comis Tricot, it was the first trade fair in Milan dedicated to fashion. It focused on knitwear. By 1964, the Italian knitwear industry was already a leader on an international level in terms of exports. Entrepreneurs had business relationships with the most important buying offices, importers, wholesalers, and department stores in Germany and the U.S. The export program was put into effect at this international trade fair specialized in the field, at regular prices and for bulk orders. With the end of competition based on price and a decline in the role played by buying offices and wholesalers, during the 1990s Esma was renamed Modaprima-Esma. It was no longer open only to knitwear, but became an exhibition about global products and specialization in service: just-in-time, seasonal assortments, samples on request, counter-samples and references, scheduled production and personalization.

Esmod French school for fashion and design. Its graduates include designers such as Thierry Mugler, Hechter, José Lévy, and Mariot Chanet. Established in Paris in 1841, today this private school has about ten education centers all over France. It has an exchange program with the Fashion Institute of Technology in New York.

❑ 2002, June. A big party at the Unesco building in Paris to celebrate the school's 160th anniversary. For the occasion, the models created by the third year students are presented together with those of international guests.
❑ 2003. The Paris school has four branches in France, at Rennes, Lyon, Bordeaux, and Roubaix, two each in Germany, Japan, Syria, and Tunisia, and one each in Sao Paulo, Brazil, Indonesia, Korea, Lebanon, and Norway.

Espadrilles In the second half of the 1900s, women adopted a type of Summer shoe that was very comfortable and suitable for daily use from Mediterranean fishermen. These were espadrilles, a poor shoe of Spanish and Portuguese origin consisting of a sole made from twisted cord sewn on sturdy cloth. Available in many colors, both solid and in patterns, espadrilles are worn very often during Summertime.

Esposito Ernesto (1952). Shoe designer, born in Naples, where he lives and works. He left school in order to follow his passion for fashion, in particular for shoes, and worked at Russo di Casandrino, a tannery in the great tradition. His style is the antithesis of minimalism. His creative process starts with research into new contrasts and the combination of unusual precious materials, with an almost manic attention to even the smallest detail.

Esposito Marinella (1961). High fashion designer, born in Isola del Gransasso (Teramo). She presented her first collection in July 2000 in Rome, an autumn-Winter collection inspired by romanticism with lots of chantilly lace and macramé and bridal dresses embroidered with small pearls, strass, silk flowers, and passementeries. She has directed her own atelier for 15 years and participates in the Roma Sposa exhibition.

Esprit American brand of sportswear created in the 1970s by Susie Tomkins and her husband Douglas. Born in San Francisco in 1943, by the mid 1960s she was already designing mini-skirts and dresses and selling them from her van. In 1970, she invented Esprit de Corps, a collection with a strong casual feel. Its logo was created in 1979, and within a very short time the upside-down E traveled around the world. The photographer Oliviero Toscani was entrusted with the advertising campaign. New lines were created during the 1980s: one for children, Esprit Kids (1981), one for the household, and, in a joint venture with the German company Optyl, a line of eyeglasses. The 1990s were years devoted to ecology, with thorough research into recycled fabrics and materials. It was the beginning of what, in a play on words, would be called the E-collection, and which still characterizes the spirit of the company.

❑ 2001. Launch of the sportswear line Esprit Sports Women.
❑ 2002, April. The brand is reunified and now 100% controlled by Esprit Holdings, which takes over the shares owned by Esprit International. The new director, Ursula Buck, plans a return of the brand to the U.S. in grand style. For 2002, the brand is expected to be in 270 U.S. department stores, and a mega-store with all of the Esprit lines, including the new men's line, is planned. For the European market, the firm is considering the rapid opening of 18 shops one after the other.
❑ 2002, November. A franchise plan for the baby and children lines is in the works for the European market.
❑ 2002, December. The launch of Esprit Sports Men, a line of clothing for snowboarding, tennis, fitness, and running, in shops starting September 2003.
❑ 2003. The brand's restyling produces its first results, with an increase in turnover of 31% in the second half of 2002, with net profits of $555 million. Esprit distributes its products in 80 countries. One third of the global turnover comes from the German market. (*Pierangelo Mastantuono*)

Esse Tie factory established in 1991 as a joint venture between the Ratti Group of Como and the Ermenegildo Zegna Group of

Biella. In 1998, it acquired Diva, a producer of handmade ties. The company produces and distributes ties and accessories all over the world as a licensee of such brands as Lagerfeld, Valentino, Dupont, Balenciaga, and Cardin. The turnover for 1998 is about 20 billion liras, half of which comes from abroad. The production is about 500,000 pieces. The company employs 30 people.

❑ 1999. The firm acquires 67.5% of Cravatterie Nazionale, a company specialized in distribution. Next to the production plant in Guanzate (Como), the firm builds a second plant, with 100,000 square feet, for the organization and coordination of the clothing, accessories, ties, and furnishings divisions.
❑ 2002, June. Esse presents the Hugh Parsons collection, a recently-acquired English brand created in 1925, in Italy.
❑ The factory headquarters is in Oleggio, near Novara, where Diva ties are printed.

Estée Lauder Companies American cosmetics house, a leader in luxury products for facial treatments, perfumes, and make-up. It is named after the woman who founded it in 1946 with her husband Joseph. A woman of great intuition, with an innate sense of refinement and quality, she was often ahead of her time, introducing new theories and innovative beauty products. When her cosmetics appeared at Sacks in New York, she invented the idea of offering gift-samples to clients with each purchase. Then came the first seasonal make-up collections. In 1952, she launched a bath line inspired by the fragrance Youth Dew. Today, the group has production plants all over the world and about 10,000 employees. It is present in 127 countries with many different brands, some its own, and some acquired. Proprietary brands include Estée Lauder, Aramis, Clinique, Prescriptives, and Origins. The acquired brands include M.A.C, Bobby Brown, Essentials, Tommy Hilfiger, Kiton, Donna Karan, and Aveda.

(*Ginevra Falzoni*)

❑ 1999. Bobby Brown, a make-up company acquired some years earlier, is launched in Italy.
❑ 2003. The acquisition of Darphin, a company specialized in aroma-therapeutic crèmes, and of Michael Kors Perfumes, absorbed by the Aramis and Designer Fragrances division.
❑ 2005, April. Tom Ford, the former creative force at Gucci, returns to center stage, signing an agreement with Estée Lauder for the production and distribution of fragrances and a cosmetics line under his name.
❑ 2005, May. A license agreement with Missoni perfumes. The first woman's fragrance for 2006 is announced. The company signs a contract with Gwyneth Paltrow, who becomes the spokesperson for the *griffe*'s make-up and fragrances, among which is the historic perfume Pleasures.

Esterel Jacques. Business name of Charles Henri Martin (1917-1974). He made his début in fashion after being the president of a foundry in St. Etienne and the director of an import-export company. In 1950, in Cannes, he met Zizi and Louis Féraud and joined their *maison*. Their business relationship would last eight years, until Esterel opened his own business, setting up in a boutique on Rue Charron in Paris. He designed Brigitte Bardot's wedding dress, which guaranteed him the front page in the newspapers and citizenship in the official world of fashion. In 1963, he started a partnership with the billionaire Jean Baptiste Doumeng, and his position became more solid. The French Olympic Committee gave him the job of designing the women's uniforms for the games in 1964 and '68 in Tokyo and Mexico City. In the early 1970s, he was among the first to offer a unisex collection. After his death, the *maison* was directed by Benoit Bartherotte, Marion Lésage, and Janò. Today, Esterel is a company that sells by mail order.

(*Laura Asnaghi*)

Estevez Luis (1930). Cuban designer. He studied at the Traphagen School of Fashion in New York and began to work in the U.S. after an apprenticeship in Paris at the *maison* Patou. Since 1968, he has established himself working in Los Angeles and Hollywood, where he was successful with a collection entitled Eva Gabor.

Etamine Cloth fabric, in cotton or synthetic fibers. It is very light and transparent, but strong, and characterized by squared or rectangular vents. It is used as a reinforcement in tailoring, on curtains, and as a support for embroidery.

Ethnic Term first used in the 1960s when designers were looking for and experimented with new aesthetic approaches inspired by clothing from distant and unknown cultures. The clothes could be simple and comfortable, or, on the contrary, very skillfully worked and manufactured, but above all they were inspired by the clothes and costumes of people who were not part of the modernized West, and were often from South America, Africa, the Far East, and the islands of the Pacific. This is what allows them to be called ethnic pieces. This multicultural message has by now become deeply rooted in contemporary fashion.

Etienne Ozeki Brand of jeans, causal clothing and accessories. It is named after the line's creator, who lives and works in Hong Kong, where he is one of the four members of Purplepin Design. The distinctiveness of his products lies in the avant-garde production technology. Of French-Japanese origin, Ozeki, who is an expert in telecommunications technology and equipment, met the man who would become his business partner five years ago. Sukit, who grew up in Los Angeles and Italy, of Cambodian origin, is an expert in the restoration of ancient fabric. They combined their knowledge and skills in order to create the brand.

(*Sofia Camerana*)

Eton Crop A haircut worn by students at Eton, the boys' boarding school founded as a college by Henry VI in 1440. It is characterized by short, straight hair worn above the ears, and was copied in the 1920s and 1930s as a hairstyle for women. Some years later, a variation included a lock of hair falling on the cheek, the famous kiss-curl of the 1930s.

Etro A *griffe* and a company making fabrics and luxury prêt-à-porter. Its headquarters is at via Spartaco, 3 in Milan, in an elegant Art Nouveau building from the early 1900s. The *griffe* made its début in 1968 with the production of sophisticated fabrics for furniture. In the early 1980s, Gerolamo Etro, known as Gimmo (Milan, 1940), a keen collector of fashion, painting, and English antiques (helped by his wife Roberta, a woman of taste and intuition), and a passionate student of ancient history, reinterpreted the traditional Indian pattern known as paisley, offering it in new imaginative versions. This became the inspired calling card of the company, and was used on furniture fabrics, linens, rugs, quilts, sheets, and carpets, as well as scarves, shawls, and ties, and, through a special new process, on leather goods, including wallets, bags, and suitcases. The first boutique was opened in 1983 on via Bigli in Milan. It was followed by

Etro: Women's Autumn-Winter Collection 1999.

stores on via Montenapoleone, via Verri, and Vicolo Fiori (at the corner of via Pontaccio). In 1988, some rare perfumes (always with an oriental touch, inspired by the early original perfumes) were offered and presented in sophisticated boxes printed in paisley patterns. In a program of constant expansion, the Etro Homme Collection created an absolutely original style and gradually consolidated its position with the opening of more than 40 points-of-sale all over the world, including Tokyo, Singapore, Hong Kong, Paris (Faubourg Saint-Honoré in 1990 and Boulevard St. Germain in 1996), Rome, Madrid, New York (720 Madison Avenue, a prestigious older building, in 1996), London (Old Bond Street), and Berlin (1998). Toward the end of the 1980s, a new chapter was started with the arrival of the new generation, headed by one of the sons, Kean, who looks after men's and women's fashion. This was the beginning of the prêt-à-porter line. Kean became the firm's designer; Jacopo was put in charge of the textile division and imports of silk from China; Ippolito (a graduate of the University of London) became head of administration and finance. The youngest of the Etros, Veronica, who studied at the Saint Martin's School in London, became head of the style department. It is a well-defined and congenial arrangement for all of them, who form a close clan. But their father Gimmo remains the great head of the company, which has celebrated its 30th anniversary.

❑ Kean Etro renews the *griffe*, more conceptually than stylistically. For the men's presentation for Winter 2001-2002, he launches the "eco fashion" collection, produced with a "biologic" fabric and presented in a supermarket. The various models, divided into groups, are placed next to the different types of foods: like different flavors to be combined on a food trolley. For Summer 2003, he goes even further: not a presentation but a parade, a sort of country celebration on the streets in the center of Milan. He changes the script on the runway, "in search of a closer relationship with the public." Curious people who stop by indicate that they like the event and start to applaud the boys on wagons hauled by oxen, with the young men gaily dressed in tropical designs and patterns that resemble carnivorous plants. The season's best-seller is a jacket with many inside pockets, each with a label so that everything can be put in its place, including a portable phone, something that by now people cannot live without. For the Autumn-Winter 2003-2004 collection, there is another new idea: the presentation is on an old three-car steam train from the 1930s, with models as travelers. Thus he reaffirms the strong need to bring fashion to the final consumer. Garments are decorated with wrenches, bolts, gears, and rivets which seem to be the work of a crazy blacksmith. It is a reality show which receives the approval of the buyers, whose opinion is always the most important one. (*Lucia Mari*)

Etro: Women's Autumn-Winter Collection 1999-2000.

❑ 2001. A year to remember for its excellent economic results. The year ends with a consolidated turnover of €155 million, compared to €124 million the previous year. The clothing department contributes 52% of that, followed by accessories and leather goods with 25%, fabrics with 15%, perfumes with 5%, and the home collection with 3%. Results in the U.S. market are excellent, and the choice of Bergdorf Goodman as a selling partner proves to be a good decision.
❑ 2002. The company focuses on retailing. Over the course of the year it opens four new single-brand stores: in Moscow, facing Red Square, in the Petrovski Passage; the shopinshop at Villa Moda in Kuwait; in Bologna; and in Miami. The distribution strategy behind this calls for single-brand boutiques in Europe and the U.S. and franchise stores in Russia and Middle East.
❑ 2002. The year ends with a consolidated turnover of €170 million. Success is spread throughout all the markets: Italy is the most important, with 35% of the total, followed by the rest of Europe with 27%, North America with 19%, and Asia with 15%. The men's collection experiences constant growth, with €39 million, equal to 23% of the consolidated turnover, doubling the results for 2000 of €20 million.
❑ 2002. Etro Far East, the Japanese branch of Etro, has a turnover of Y5.2 billion in retailing, an increase of 12%. The main source of growth is women's clothing, with 47% of total sales. In Japan, Etro has 32 points-of-sale, including privately owned stores and licensees.

Etro Veronica. On becoming responsible for the women's line, she followed her brother's footsteps and for the Winter 2003-2004 collection she became a tour operator who uses clothes to create an exciting and nostalgic tourist brochure. The proposed destination is Venice, and the collection wants to be a synthesis that starts with Marco Polo and ends with the Third Millennium. It is a journey through memory, an "all-included" package with Casanova's damasked jackets, patchworks inspired by Harlequin, bodices with whalebones, a bag with Carnival masks, and the Golden Lion of the Film Festival transformed into a shoulder bag. (*Lucia Mari*)

Ettedgui Joseph (1937). Hairdresser and fashion entrepreneur. Born in Casablanca, he moved to London where, in addition to his regular trade, he worked as a scout for new designer talent in order to show their clothes in his salon. He had excellent intuition and was among the first to understand, purchase, and sell the clothes of Kenzo and of Martin Kidman, with whom he would create the Joseph Kidman brand. Over time he would multiply the number of his boutiques, which offered a large number of international *griffes*. His name was used for several points-of-sale: Joseph Café, Joseph pour la Maison, Joseph pour la Ville, and Joseph Bis.

E2 Behind this brand are the creative minds of Michèle and Olivier Chatenet, both of them French, work partners and life partners. After founding the Mariot Chalet brand together in the 1980s, they ended their working partnership, with Michèle hired by Comme des Garçons and Olivier by Azzedine Alaïa. Some time later, the two were hired by Hèrmes. In the year 2000, the brand E2 was born, a sparkling assembly of vintage clothing that was soon noticed by people in the trade. It was not an accident that Léonard, the French fashion house established in 1958, hired the couple as top designers. In 2002, their clothes were shown at the Musée de la Mode in Paris as part of the exhibit *Couturier Superstars*.
(*Maddalena Fossati*)

❑ 2003. Lèonard does not renew the contract of the two designers.

Etzdorf (von) Georgina (1955). Fabric designer, born in Lima, Peru. In 1981, she established, along with two business partners, Martin Simcock and Jonathan Docherty, a company under her own name, producing highly decorative fabrics for fashion, ready-to wear, high fashion, and accessories.

❑ 2003, February. Georgina works with

engineering students at Southampton University and with students at the Winchester School of Art to create scarves, bags and jewellery with luminescent materials such as phosphorus and light-emitting-diodes (LED). The collection, on which the English designer Anya Hindmarch also works, is called Nocturnalis and launched on the market.
❑ 2003. The designer, who lives in Salisbury, is among 40 names in English fashion invited to the Fashion Coterie, the annual New York event in the field.
❑ Etzdorf's clothing and accessories for fashion and the home are on sale at more than 300 points-of-sale in 20 countries and at the company's single-brand store in the Burlington Arcade in London.

Eula Joe. English illustrator and costume designer. During the 1950s, her drawings in the Herald Tribune accompanied articles by Eugénia Sheppard, a pseudonymous byline covering fashion. Later, she worked with the journalist Ernestine Carter of the Sunday Times. She also worked with Life, Vogue, and Harper's Bazaar. In the late 1960s, she worked for the New York City Ballet as a costume and set designer. She also worked with Diana Vreeland on exhibits dedicated to fashion at the Metropolitan Museum of Art in New York.

European Institute of Design School of design with locations in Milan, Turin, Rome, Cagliari, and Madrid. It was established in 1966 "to offer an education both theoretical and practical in the fields of design, fashion, the visual arts, and the communications arts." Among the various courses of study, there is one in Fashion Design that lasts three years. The various aspects of the fashion industry are studied, from drawing to the coordination of a collection and the organization of a show. The teaching methodology focuses on three areas: Creativity and Design, Image and Communication, and Marketing and Product. During the last year of study, every student has an internship at a fashion company. The institute also offers two master's degrees. The first, the Advanced Study program, requires 180 hours, from Thursday to Saturday. The courses include Costume Design, Fashion Editor Fashion Show, and Fashion Buyer. The second, the Research Study Program, is a full-time course that requires 1,000 hours, of which 600 are devoted to theory and 400 to practice. The aim is to prepare specialists for specific positions in the industry, such as Coordinator of Fashion Communication and Fashion Marketing Manager.

Evans Janson. Known as Travis (1968). Scottish photographer. He attended the course Combinet and Media Arts at Sheffield City Polytechnic. He made his début as an assistant to Nick Knight. From 1989 to 1992 he worked as a freelance stylist for i-D. His work has been published by i-D, Arena, Hommes Plus, and Purple Prose. He has worked for Levi's in the U.K.

Eve Boutique in Milan. The shop-sign, a small apple with a bite taken out, appeared for the first time in 1965. The brand offers a collection of bags, belts, shoes, wallets, and travel bags. Since then, the creations have been characterized by soft materials, unusual bulk, daring colors, and an artisanal accuracy in details. Over the years, the début brand has been joined by La Viaggeria and Midnight Express. The stores on via Solferino and via Mascheroni in Milan also offer a ready-to-wear collection with comfortable and practical garments. The designer is Guido Orsi.

Everest Timothy (1961). English tailor. Born in Southampton, he opened his men's tailoring shop in London in 1991, after working with Tommy Nutter and Malcolm Levine. A great supporter of the British tailoring tradition, he offered old fashioned hand-made suits, but personalized with modern and eccentric touches. This distinctive feature, and his moderate prices, guaranteed immediate success. The decision to locate his atelier in an 18th century house in the Huguenot heart of London, rather than on Saville Row, turned his atelier into a meeting place for the young people of the financial district, show business personalities, and politicians. Since 1998 he has dressed several ministers from the Labor Party who have been willing to appear fashionable but without deviating too much from tradition. In America his style developed a cult with the success of the movie

Mission Impossible, in which Tom Cruise was always impeccably dressed in the 007 style of the 1960s. In 1997, he launched a prêt-à-porter line for men, followed by one for women. He created the uniforms for the staff of the Cigar Lounge, an exclusive London club. (*Virginia Hill*)

❑ 1999, July. On the day of his wedding to the Spice Girl Victoria Adams, in the castle of Lutrellstown, near Dublin, David Beckham wears a crème and ivory suit made by Everest.
❑ 2000, March. Tom Cruise and Robin Williams wear Everest suits at the Oscars.
❑ 2000, June. He becomes creative consultant for the store chain Daks.
❑ 2000, October. A small diplomatic incident for the designer, creator of the very colorful uniforms of the British Olympic team at the Sydney games. During the final parade, British athletes wear tracksuits in colors that in Australia are symbols of homosexuality. The Japanese government says it is offended, to the point of omitting Everest's name from coverage of the event.

Everlast American brand of men's, women's, and children's sportswear. It was established in 1910 with the launch of boxing trunks that were the first to use an elastic waistband. The idea belonged to a Mr. Golomb, and the success was such that other products could be added. Since 1988, the brand has been produced and distributed in Italy by A. Moda, a company belonging to Alessandro Bastagli, who also has licenses for the Neil Pryde and Gold's Gym lines in Europe. In 1996, he created a company called Bavers in partnership with the Gianni Versace Group for licenses of leather accessories, children's wear, sport lines, and men's and women's underwear.

❑ 2002, October. The sports brand concludes an agreement with Tavil Associates of New York to produce a playtime line and a nighttime line for children and babies. The collection, launched in the middle of the following year, completes the clothing lines offered for the American market by the sports giant. BBC International obtains the license for casual shoes in the U.S. and Canada.
❑ 2003. The Sports Authority gives the Vendor of the Year award to George Horowitz, the president of Everlast, for the brand's excellent results in 2002.
❑ 2003. Despite the increased number of licenses, the company ends the first quarter with a decline of 11.7%, to $12.3 million. In the U.S. and Canada there are more than 20,000 Everlast points-of-sale. Everlast products are distributed throughout the world under 20 different licenses.
❑ 2003, June. A license agreement with Pac Paris, a world-class producer of perfumes, for the creation of a beauty line. Men's and women's fragrances, deodorants, and aftershaves are on the market by autumn.

Evins David (1917). English shoemaker. He worked in the U.S. after studying at the Pratt Institute in Brooklyn. During the 1970s, he launched the stretch boot in fabric. The use of leather, extraordinary skins, a modern classic style, and great accuracy in manufacture to the point of being almost "handmade" contributed to his fame and business success.

❑ 1997. At the age of 80, his creations were prominently featured in the book *A Century of Shoes: Icons of Style in the 20th Century* by Angela Pattison and Nigel Cawthorne.

Evisu Japanese line of jeanswear, created in 1988 from an idea by Hiehiko Yamane, a passionate student of original denim. With an American loom from the 1950s, restored to use in Osaka, Yamane manufactures selvedge denim: more than 40 yards a day, in a limited and very accurate production, with a hand-painted logo. In the early 1990s, the vintage phenomenon was very widespread and Evisu became a cult item extremely popular with music celebrities including Madonna, George Michael, the leaders of Oasis, and the Gallagher brothers. In 1997, production under license began in Italy, but always using Japanese denim. The Evisu jeans range from models that are widely available to precious ones of limited production, such as the one with jade buttons, an 18-carat gold embroidered logo, and pockets with Chinese silk inlays produced in 2000. In January 2002, the brand presented its collection in Florence during Pitti Immagine Uomo. In September of that same year, the women's collection made its début on the calendar of Milano Moda Donna.

Excelsior Modes Quarterly fashion magazine published in France between 1929 and 1939 as a supplement to the Excelsior newspaper, sent free to subscribers. Illustrated with large black-and-white photos, it was basically concerned with Paris fashions, beauty, aesthetics, lifestyles, and sports. A regular column was dedicated to the *Mariages des Personnalités*, with gossip and photo reportage about the jet set.

Executive The look of the career woman, the manager, the woman who has chosen a profession, and who wants to prove that she is capable of doing certain jobs that society reserves exclusively for men. It is the 1970s and this style becomes an integral part of women's fashion. It consists of suits, with pants or a skirt and a jacket, often chalk-striped, completed by a shirt in a man's cut or a blouse with a bowtie or a silk scarf tied around the neck. What was at first a casual jacket becomes a garment which can be worn both during the day and in the evening, not only as part of a tailored suit, but also combined with wide skirts and casual trousers.

Existentialism A philosophic system of thought which stresses individual responsibility, freedom of choice, and the authenticity of existence. Its country of choice: France. Official color: only and strictly black. It was a movement of narrow trousers, turtleneck sweaters, and severe blouses buttoned up to the neck for those who attended the Parisian "cellars" during the 1950s, fresh from lectures by Jean-Paul Sartre and Albert Camus. It was a dictatorship of color defied only by the use of certain typically (and thus authentically) French garments: the Brittany sailor's white sweater with blue stripes, the beret, and the white Alsation folk blouses worn by those who favored the bars in St. Germain de Prés. In some sense a precursor of minimalism, existentialism as an aesthetic form brought not only American jazz to center stage (in those years, Miles Davis had a "scandalous" love affair in Paris with Juliette Gréco), but non-representational painting and the non-narrative cinema of Jean Luc Godard as well. It was associated with the literary début of such themes as "nausea" (the title of Sartre's most famous novel) and "boredom" (the title of a novel by the Italian Alberto Moravia). A *tedium vitae*, or weariness with life, was expressed by dramatic make-up with heavy eyeshadow and a pale face for very slender young women, and by a neglected beard for men. Unique concessions to an appearance which cared little for decorum, frivolity, or a lively style. Apparently, exactly. (*Antonio Mancinelli*)

ExquisiteJ Brand created by Giancarlo Ferrari (Trento, 1964) and Francesco Bonamano (Milan, 1966). Ferrari studied at the Academy of Fine Arts in Florence, and Bonamano received a degree in architecture. Longtime friends with similar passions and tastes, at first they created jewellery and accessories for Marina Spadafora, Callaghan, Fiorucci, Phard, and Maska. They then expanded their activity to include bags and shoes, using unusual and original materials.

❑ The bags designed by Bonamano and Ferrari are successfully exported to France, Austria, Japan, and the U.S.
❑ Among the most successful models are the dog-shaped handbag in rabbit hair in black, pink, and white and the fish-shaped bag in soft metallic leather in sky blue, light blue, and fuchsia.

Extè Brand belonging to Ittierre of Isernia (from the Latin *ex tempore*). It was created "to experiment with trends, fabrics, and atmospheres." The first presentation, in January 1996, organized by a group led by Giancarlo Perna, was already set in a Blade Runner atmosphere in the former industrial area of the Bovisa gas tank on the outskirts of Milan. It featured knitwear combined with rubber, Lycra, and metal plates, carbon fibers, smearing, unpredictable finishings, and unexpected transparencies. In the collections that followed, this technologic research was refined using noble yarns such as cashmere contaminated by a thin steel thread which " adjusts perfectly, though, to bring back softness and sweetness." In Spring 1999, the brand offered garments in high-tech thread made from copper and steel, in order to fight stress, and clothes that sparkled, lit by strobe lights as in a disco. The Extè brand isn't limited to fashion, but also includes a home collection and accessories. The brand is present in these areas in some of the most important cities in Europe, Asia, and the U.S. In Italy, there are three single-brand boutiques, in Milan, Rome, and Capri.

❑ 2001. Antonio Berardi, already responsible for the women's collection, is appointed design director of Extè Uomo.
❑ 2001. Francesco Lampronti is the new general director of the *griffe*. With a degree in economics, he has had important positions at Calvin Klein and Emanuel Ungaro. Vincenzo Scognamiglio is the new brand manager.
❑ 2002. Extè promotes the Well-tech philosophy with a showroom exhibit of innovative products that combine high technology and design. These products show the need for a balance between style, harmony, well-being, and technology.
❑ 2004, September. The creative direction of the women's collection is put in the hands of Alessandro De Benedetti, a designer from Genoa. With this, the current designer, Sergio Ciucci, will devote himself exclusively to the men's collections.

Sketch, 1999.

F

Fabbri Cesare (1959). Italian designer. He lives and works in Florence. In 1981, he made his début in the world of fashion as buyer, art director, and designer for the Florentine brand Luisa Via Roma. From 1987 to '89 he designed the Zuccoli Donna collection for Gibò of Florence. He was given the task of managing the Oliver line for Valentino, for both men and women. From 1992 to '97 he was in charge of the Loewe women's collection. In March 1998 he started his own business and designed his first Autumn-Winter collection. By the third collection, his *griffe* was on sale throughout the world.

❑ 2002, September. For the first time, the Bloomingdales department store in New York dedicated all its windows on Lexington Avenue to him, on the occasion of the launch of his Spring-Summer 2003 collection.

Fabergé Peter Karl (1846-1920). Russian jeweler. He was a descendent of a Huguenot family and born Piccardie. In 1870, he was at the head of his father Gustave's goldsmith workshop in St. Petersburg after having traveled to Germany, France, England, and Italy in order to learn the secrets of the trade. In 1882, he won the Gold Medal at the Artisan and Industrial Exhibition of Moscow, drawing the attention of the Empress Maria Fiodorovna, who would commission jewellery from him in the ancient Greek style. Together with his brother Agafon, Peter Karl had, in fact, achieved fame thanks to the manufacture of copies of Greek jewellery found in the archaeological excavations at Kerc. Appointed supplier to the imperial court in 1885, together with jewellery manufacturing – essentially sets of jewellery based on stylized floral motifs and on gems with a cabochon cut – the young Fabergé promoted the manufacture of refined *objets d'art* which enjoyed great success among both the Russian and international public. Among his clients were the kings and queens of Europe, the court of Siam, and American industrialists such as John D. Rockfeller. In 1887, a Moscow branch was opened, with one in Odessa in 1900, in Kiev between 1905 and '10, and in London in 1903. The goldsmiths of the Fabergé house would visit the Hermitage to study and copy antique jewels from the time of Catherine II, applying an antique style to creations suitable to the taste of the late 1800s. The expansion of the business resulted in the opening of independent ateliers which worked exclusively for Fabergé. Afterwards, the best masters would come to the main workshop in St. Petersburg, in a building on the Bol'saja Morskaia. The entry of his children Eugène, Agafon, Alexandre, and Nicolas in the family firm brought new energy to the business. Guilloché enamels applied both to jewellery and objects were favored: boxes, cigarette cases, trays, clocks, frames, icons, and silverware. More than a hundred different colors were used to cover gold with iridescent reflections and enrich the colors of semi-precious stones, Fabergé's favorites, and of gems and pearls. In 1883 came the first orders from the imperial court for the famous Easter eggs, which would continue until 1916. Small masterpieces of technical ingenuity, they were inspired by important events of Romanov family life under the rule of Czars Alexander III and Nicolas II. There were sixty eggs in all, each in a different shape and of such extraordinary invention as to stir the admiration of the entire world. The jewellery, which continued to be characterized by references to the past and a taste for the East, acquired some Art Nouveau touches around 1910. After the fall of the Romanovs with the Russian Revolution, the house ceased operations, closing for good in 1918. (*Alessandra Quattordio*)

Fabi Italian shoe factory established in 1965 by Elisio and Enrico Fabi. It is renowned for the manufacture of men's and women's shoes and focuses on artisanal quality with production that is primarily hand-made and carried out entirely in Italy. The production plant is in Monte San Giusto, near Macerata, and has about 200 employees. A new plant was opened at the end of 2003, again near Macerata. The brand Telck by Fabi (men's and women's shoes for a younger market) and the Fuentes brand (men's classic and casual shoes) have been on sale for four seasons. The company closed 2002 with a total turnover of about €21 million, with Fabi contributing 60%, Telck 30%, and Fuentes 10%. In November 2003, the brand's seventh shop was opened, in Milan, following a shop in Moscow that was opened in October.

Fabiani Alberto (1910-1987). Italian tailor and designer, born in Rome. His talent was foretold, as he was the son of tailors from near Tivoli whose work was already famous in the early 1900s. He was educated in the use of scissors at a very young age. After his schooling, he went to Paris and various ateliers in order to learn about fashion. Once back in Italy, he opened his own atelier, first on via Frattina and then on via Condotti. His garments are unmistakable, especially the jackets, which Fabiani's tailoring skills endowed with great class. He was part of the by now historic group of designers (nine for high fashion and four for prêt-à-porter) who in February 1951 accepted the invitation of Bista Giorgini to present to American buyers Italian clothes that were free of the subjection of French fashion, and presented a collection in the sitting-room of his Florentine villa. Simonetta Colonna di Cesarò, who in 1952 became his wife and participated on that revolutionary day as an independent designer, says in her book *La Sala Bianca – Nascita della Moda Italiana* ('The Sala Bianca – The Birth of Italian Fashion'): "I convinced Alberto, I almost forced him. He was reluctant. Thanks to French fashions, he had acquired a rich and numerous clientele. It was understandable that he was doubtful, but my prodding made his fortune. He became the true, great figure of the Italian look. He was an extraordinary artisan, one of the rare designers who knew how to make his own models in cloth." Fabiani and Simonetta were among the first to leave Florence in favor of their own Roman ateliers. "One day we told each other that Rome was as good as Florence, that we could be in our own house, that everyone had a right to a stage for himself, instead of that group presentation. Individualism is a typical Italian weakness," remembers Simonetta. Some years later, Fabiani left Rome for Paris. He came back to Italy after 1970, and, as a consultant to several clothing manufacturers, he continued to work until his death. Among his collaborators were Forquet and, for men's fashion, Elio Costanzi. In 1960, his book *Stracci* ('Rags') was published.

Fabiano Anna (1962). Italian designer. She learned the profession watching her mother, who was a dressmaker. She designed her first creations for Fiorucci at the age of 25. From there, she was able to open her own shop in Porta Ticinese in Milan, where she presented a ready-to-wear line in which one could see a desire to create clothes with a high tailoring content and to personalize them with special details, sometimes on clients' requests. Her clients are professionals, creative people, students, and journalists. She accomodates their tastes and their preferences, either in basic refined styles or according to the latest trends.

(*Lucia Serlengo*)

Fabienne K French brand of ready-to-wear. During the 1970s it established itself with flexible clothes such as interlock (a very comfortable knitwear which broke away from the rigidity of classic materials) that could be worn all day.

Fabrice A brand named after a New York designer born in Haiti. He attained success in the 1980s thanks to evening shirts embroidered with glass beads, crystals, and strass in the Haitian style. Fabrice designs his collections in New York, but all the manufacturing takes place in Haiti.

Fabrikant Steve (1954). Brazilian designer. At the age of 14, he moved with his family to New York. He studied architecture in London, but ended up working for seven years in his family's factory. Knitwear was his first passion and it was in this field that he became famous. He started his knitwear designer activity in 1984 and within a few

Evening Dress by Alberto Fabiani (1950s) in a sketch by Brunetta (Biki Collection).

years he succeeded in selling his creations in department stores. In his lines, the Steve Fabricant Collections and Signature Lines, he combines wool and Lycra, and wool and leather, aiming for a modern look. But in the cashmere collection, his style is classic and traditional.

The Face British monthly magazine founded by Nick Logan in 1980. Because of its original and nonconformist approach to subjects such as fashion, music, the arts, design, film, and literature, it soon became a point of reference for the world of creatives. From 1981 to 1986, its art director Neville Brody designed a sophisticated layout, inspired by the artists of the Russian avant-garde of the 1920s. But already at the end of the 1980s a change became necessary and a new editorial team developed a graphic approach that was in decisive contrast with the glamour of the previous decade.

❑ 2004 May. The magazine folds after 24 years of irreverent journalism and style reporting.

Facis Historic brand of men's clothing, one of the symbols, in the post-war period, of the GFT group. established in 1953. It immediately became one of the main forces in the mass production of men's clothing in Italy and Europe. Since then it has perfected a complete and diversified wardrobe, developing, since the 1970s, through the study of body sizes, an ability to satisfy the multiple requirements of wearability, offering a wide range of lengths and sizes. A custom-made service completes the variety of services offered to important customers. It is a semi-structured product, available in a wide range of personalized sizes, shapes, and heights, offered in many fabrics and styles. Through the use of pre-measured clothes and computer support with the production plants, the availability of "custom made" models is guaranteed within six days, and delivery in Italy within ten days. The heart and brains of the production are in the historic plant in Settimo Torinese. In operation since 1961 in response to growing demand resulting from the consumer boom, Settimo since then has had the record as the largest Italian and European production plant. That is where the first mass production in the history of men's clothing got its start, with the manufacture of jackets and shirts. In Settimo Torinese, a thousand people are today employed. The Italian and foreign production is still planned there. Computer-designed models are created in this plant by a staff of 25 technicians who prepare 26 collections a year.

❑ 2002, November. License agreement with Luciano Soprani for the production and distribution of men's prêt-à-porter until 2010. Facis has 830 points-of-sale in Italy, and 320 abroad.
❑ 2003, February. The Turin group GFT (Financial Textile Group), controlled by the holding company HDP, closes for good, selling its brands Facis, Valentino, and Sahzà.
❑ 2003, April. After a long series of announcements and denials, 100% of Facis is sold to the Mediconf group of Palermo, owned by the Bucalo family, which is active in the production and distribution of men's clothing in the Bucalo chain of stores. In 2002 their turnover was €130 million.
❑ 2003. Relaunching of Facis at Pitti Uomo. The Autumn-Winter collection is by the Milanese designer Francesco Fiordelli (1963).

Faille Silk or synthetic fabric similar to taffeta (in Flemish "falie"), but with a more marked texture characterized by very evident diagonal ribs. In medium or heavy weight, it is rather stiff, sometimes rigid. It is used for evening clothes.

Fairchild Stephen (1961). American designer. He was born in New York, in a family well-known in fashion publishing. After college and studies in both America and Europe, he worked with the best designers, including Giorgio Armani, Ralph Lauren, Calvin Klein, and Valentino, all valuable experiences gained in the capitals of international fashion. After 17 years of apprenticeship and professional growth, he created his own *griffe* in 2001, establishing a joint venture with one of the most successful industrial groups, Mariella Burani. In the firm's Milan headquarters he created a women's sportswear collection complete with accessories and dedicated to a chic, sensual, and very modern woman.

(*Lucia Serlenga*)

Fairchild Publications "Our salvation depends on printing the news." This motto of Edmund W. Fairchild, the founder in the late 1800s of what would become an American publishing empire specialized in fashion magazines and newspapers, is still valid, even after more than a century. Indeed, it has become the credo of a publishing house which has distinguished itself for creating the most famous and influential publications for people in the field, such as DNR and WWD, which were followed in the 1960s by glossy monthlies for a sophisticated public. Owned today by ABC, the roots of Fairchild Publications go back to 1890 in Chicago when Edmund W. Fairchild, who had accumulated a considerable fortune selling soap, acquired the Chicago Herald Gazette, a newspaper focused on the men's fashion industry. Shortly after, his brother Louis joined the publishing venture and, on 29 March 1892, they began publication of the Daily Trade Record, a paper that was distributed to businessmen at the Chicago World's Fair. Success was such that Edmund decided to continue publication even after the fair. It was later renamed the Daily News Record, and then abbreviated as DNR. Today, it is published three times a week (Monday, Wednesday, Friday) with the latest news about the world of men's fashion, ranging from economics to the textile-clothing market and the latest trends. The women's equivalent wasn't late in arriving: the Fairchilds, who in the meantime had moved to New York, launched Women's Wear Daily on May 21, 1919. It was published first as a news page in the Saturday edition of the Daily Trade Record and became an independent journal (six days a week, later reduced to five) on July 13th of the same year. But the year which marks the beginning of the most important period in the history of the publishing house is 1960. If under the leadership of Louis Fairchild, the heir of Edmund, the number of publications increased considerably, it was with his young son, Louis John, that an interesting editorial shift took place. Already the head of the Paris branch, John was ambitious and farsighted. Creative, and endowed with brilliant writing skills, he decided to shorten the name Women's Wear Daily to the easier-to-say WWD and, while remaining focused on being the leading magazine in the field of economic and financial information for the fashion industry, he revitalized it by giving it international stature and a more sparkling and lively editorial approach enriched with scoops, reportage about society events and fashion collections, features about new trends, and profiles of designers who were for the first time treated as celebrities. Intuiting the growing importance of the star system, John invented and published, still in the 1960s, Los Angeles Magazine, the house's first monthly conceived for an upscale audience. A major feature of the magazine was the lively prose and a glossy look for "covering" events and the most celebrated personalities of the town, a symbol of cinema and show business. In 1972 came the start of W: twenty-six issues a year until 1993 when, with new graphics and an unusual oversized format, it was relaunched as an ultra chic and sophisticated monthly. The primary focus of W is fashion as an expression of lifestyle. The ideal and actual reader is a sophisticated woman interested in the latest news who is curious and cosmopolitan. The magazine, with features by the best photographers, reportage about the most international parties and most luxurious houses, pages filled with the latest news on fashion, beauty, and accessories, and exclusive interviews with stars and designers, was the perfect vehicle not just for describing the latest trends, but often for anticipating them. It was W that first referred to Jacqueline Kennedy Onassis as *Jackie O* and first used *hot pants* to define the micro-shorts that were in fashion during the 1970s. Even though John Fairchild retired in 1997, his sense of humor and brilliant style still have a place in W: under the pseudonym of Louise J. Esterhazy, an irresistible globetrotting countess, he writes a column that appears on the last page of the magazine. Today, Fairchild publishes, in addition to the already-mentioned magazines, a new monthly for teenagers, Jane, launched in 1997, and other niche titles such as Footwear News, Home Furnishings News, Children's Business, Supermarket News, Salon News, Golf Pro, Executive

Technology, and Brand Marketing. In 1999, the editorial group was acquired by Condé Nast. *(Grazia D'Annunzio)*

Fair Isle Sweater with multicolored geometric patterns made popular during the 1920s by the Prince of Wales, the future King Edward VIII, who later abdicated in order to marry Mrs. Simpson. He wore it when playing golf. It was named after a small island near the Shetlands and the Orkneys, north of Scotland between the North Sea and the Atlantic Ocean, that is especially renowned for its wool manufacturing. Besides the typical patterns, the sweater is characterized by a very wide crew-neck.

Fake London English brand of ready-to-wear created in 1995 by Desirèe Mejer, who was born near Cadiz, Spain, in 1968. After arriving in London in 1992, without any experience in the fashion field, she had the brilliant idea of recycling second-hand cashmere sweaters. Her creations are soft, eccentric patchworks of knitwear. By now, the model representing the Union Jack is famous. Since the line's launching in 1996, her particularly sophisticated ensembles have been worn by music and film stars.

❑ 2003, June. At the 63rd edition of Pitti Uomo, on the Puma stand, a new unisex sportswear collection is presented. It came from the union of three brands and their corresponding logos: Fake London (a stylized flower on cashmere), Puma (a cat), and the emerging Japanese Evisu (a Buddha).

Falchi Carlos. American designer of bags, shoes, and accessories. Born in Brazil, he lives and works in New York. He made his début in the early 1970s as a costume designer for very famous music stars such as Cher, Tina Turner, Barbra Streisand, and Madonna. At the same time, he launched his own brand under his name. He has always purchased 80% of the materials necessary for his work in Italy, and he produces his line of small leather goods and shoes there as well.

Falconetto Brand of fabric created in 1954 by Ken Scott with Jo Martin, an illustrator and the inventor of the house garden style, and Vittorio Fiorazzo (1923-1995), a financier and entrepreneur. Coming from an old style Padua family who were competitors of the Feltrinellis in the wood trade, Fiorazzo, after a trip to the U.S., convinced Scott and Martin, who already worked together and had attended the Parson's School of Design, to follow him to Italy. Falconetto fabrics (the brand was named after a Renaissance architect) were meant for home furnishings and fashion accessories. They were brightly colored, with floral patterns in a palette that was very daring but of great effect. The boutique was at first on via Gesù, in Milan, then on via Manzoni, and finally on via Corridoni.

Faliero Sarti Italian wool mill. The headquarters are in Campi Bisenzio, near Florence. In 1982, its founder, Faliero Sarti, was named a Cavaliere del Lavoro, an honor that recognized an innovative way of conceiving a product and a managerial philosophy which happily joined a family's entrepreneurship to a capable workforce. The firm, established in 1949, became a limited liability company in the late 1970s. The Group markets its products under the following brands: Faliero Sarti (fabrics for collections, in wool, cashmere, silk, alpaca), Sartimaglie (wool jersey, angora, viscose), Philos (linen, wool, cotton, silk), Philandia (weaving yearns produced by Filatura Tre Esse), and Tintoria del Sole (package and piece dyeing). A planning department carries out research on innovative fabrics with fashion content. The Group employs 260 people. In early 1998, the company obtained the *Certifex* imprimatur, an acknowledgment of high quality and organization.

❑ 2000. Monica Sarti, 30, the daughter of Roberto and grandchild of the founder, has recently joined the family business. After a year at FIT in New York and an apprenticeship at Anne Klein, she now works in a specific field, starting with yarns, continuing with fabrics, and arriving at scarves. Every season, she offers a small collection in some 15 different colors.

Fallaci Oriana (1930). Italian writer and journalist (*A Man*, *Inshallah*). Very young and talented, with an extraordinary eye, she received an assignment from the weekly magazine Epoca to cover the first collections in the Sala Bianca at Palazzo Pitti. It was the 22nd of July 1952. "In the kind of expectant silence found only in a court room, a convent, a classroom with students waiting for a test, and during the presentation of a collection, a model stepped out on the runway, tripping in a skirt that was too tight and with her eyes completely hidden by a cloche hat pulled down over her forehead. The girl was wearing a winter outfit and the temperature was 104°. The Murano lamps and the spot lights gave off an intense light that was hot and blinding, right on the 350 spectators in shirtsleeves and low-necked blouses who, reflected by the giant wall mirrors, seemed much more numerous than the crowd in St. Peter's during a Jubilee. Waiters moved silently, offering cold drinks and whisky on the rocks; in the background was the whistling of a fan. The girl made a pirouette and raised her fur collar as if she were very cold. Drops of sweat ran slowly down her perfect ochre-colored face, ruining her make-up. The 350 very hot spectators were buyers, and had arrived from Rome twenty-four hours before, on a special train, like presidents and kings, welcomed at the station by smiling hostesses with bunches of flowers. They came, for the most part, from Sweden, Holland, Norway, Germany, Switzerland, England, and, undoubtedly, from France.... Many were women... the vast majority ladies in their fifties, elegant and authoritative, wearing eyeglasses and jewellery. They were the kind of businesswomen who don't talk much, see everything, and don't smile in order not to show their gold teeth. They were strict women, used to big numbers and firm decisions, accustomed to leadership; important women, who, with the wink of an eye vainly lined with mascara, can change the course of a bank's business; women able to strike more fear and command more respect than a diplomat in top hat and striped pants. Before these inexorable judges, for five days, the world of Italian fashion presented its collections. On this occasion, it had the advantage of coming before the Paris collections: in the large ateliers on the Champs-Elysées, the winter models were still being sewn. Nine fashion houses presented their models: Antonelli, Capucci, Carosa, Ferdinandi, Giovanelli Sciarra, Poliboner, Marucelli, Vanna, and Veneziani. Sixteen companies presented sportswear and boutique styles, the kind of export items for which the Americans go crazy."

Fallai Aldo (1943). Italian photographer. He is the author of several advertising campaigns for Giorgio Armani. His style is clean and precise. He studied at the State Art Institute in Florence, where he was born, attending courses on advertising graphics and painting. After graduation, he taught for five years. In the early 1970s, he opened a graphic design and photography studio. In 1974, while working for various fashion catalogues, Fallai met Armani, who at the time was practically unknown. Since then, they have had a stylistic partnership which has given birth to several photographic campaigns, both for the Giorgio Armani line and Emporio Armani. Fallai introduced the portrait into fashion photography, with the clothing element seemingly secondary. He has worked with Condè Nast and with the magazines Max, G.Q., Grazie, Amica, Anna, Brutus, Esquire Japan, Mondo Uomo, and Emporio Armani Magazine. Designers such as Valentino, Ferré, Ferragamo, Cerruti, Calvin Klein, and Calugi and Giannelli have often entrusted the interpretation and documentation of their collections to him.

Famiglia 38 Fotografi Group of Italian photographers. An associated firm was established in Milan in 1989. Francesco Di Loreto, Paolo Mazzo, and Mino Visconti worked together to produce a type of photography based on the manipulation of any kind of visual support. Extremely creative, they organized exhibits with black-and-white hand-colored pictures inserted into fiberglass-reinforced plastic to decorate boutiques such as that of Hugo Boss, trade fairs such as Pitti Uomo, WP, and the advertising campaigns of Mariolo. They have worked with Dolce & Gabbana, Tod's, Valextra, Diesel, Allen Cox, Henry Lloyd, and others. Since 1998, they have published in D-La Repubblica delle Donne, Anna, Cosmopolitan, Marie Claire, Harper's Bazaar Italy, Vogue Gioiello, Moda, and Luna.

Fan An old Italian adage goes: "A San Simone, il ventaglio si ripone." The reference is to St. Simon's day, 28 October, and the idea is the consecration, through popular culture, of a highly useful objects, especially in the warmer seasons of the year. Varied in shape, it is usually semicircular, waved with the hand to create a breeze and ward off summer heat. It is made of a succession of light, thin laths of wood or sandalwood, ivory or mother-of-pearl, fastened together at one end, and across them is laid a strip of paper, fabric, or silk. The fan became popular in Europe after it was imported from the Far East, toward the end of the fifteenth century and the beginning of the sixteenth century. It attained its period of greatest popularity and elegance over the course of the eighteenth century, when it was used both by men and by women, and both during the day and in the evenings. Fans were refined, often valuable, and were hand-painted with mythological and Biblical scenes and figures, or else, more simply, with animals, flowers, and country scenes. It was also a tool for flirtation and gallant courtship. There is a language of love bound up with the fan. During the nineteenth century, printed fabrics replaced the hand-painted papers or fabrics and the use of fans in high society was restricted to evenings: this custom held firm for much of the twentieth century as well. Proust loved fans, and likewise, in the last years of the twentieth century, fashion designer Karl Lagerfeld loved fans. In the years leading up to the Second World War, the boxes of La Scala were still crowded with fluttering fans, and fans – to remain within the confines of Europe – still are seen during the great summer heat in Spain, used both by men and women. Beginning in the 1980s, there was a repeated attempt, with the growing popularity of the major Japanese fashion designers, to revive the fan in a minimalist version: rice paper, and sometimes round or triangular.

Fancy Flannel fabric, rough on both sides. The term also indicates a print pattern for fabrics characterized by small intertwined patterns. Fancy cord is a velvet with ribs of different widths, either wide and thin, open or closed.

Fanelli Giuseppe (1976). Italian designer. In 2001, after graduating from the Academy of Costume and Fashion in Rome, he participated in the Fashion Garden art exhibit organized by Maria Campitelli (Group '68) in Tigeste, and worked in the style department of Alberta Ferretti. In 2002, he worked as a freelancer on the Tuttocachemire knitwear line, and, for a short time with the product department of BVM Italy-les Copains. In that same year, he made a successful début with a mini collection at Alta Moda in Rome. In January 2003, he received the *Irene Brin* prize for fashion. Also in 2003, he worked in the style department of Antonio Marras.

(*Maria Vittoria Alfonsi*)

Fantasie d'Italia Fashion magazine published between the two world wars, edited by the journalist Lydia De Liguoro. In 1926, engaging in a polemic with the Paris monthly Foemina, the magazine organized some presentations of mixed Italian and French collections in Venice, in a precarious attempt to draw attention to Italian tailors. It was published from 1925 to 1932, when it changed its name to Domina.

Faraone Goldsmith's brand and jewellery boutique, opened in Milan in 1919. In 1961, the business was taken over by the Settepassi family. During the 16th century, in Florence, this family was already one of those very skillful goldsmith artisans who helped make the history of Italian jewellery. Its production is characterized by a very select choice of precious stones and pearls and by the very precise manufacture of jewellery through both innovative and traditional (plaster mould) techniques. In addition, Faraone offers a rich collection of antique English silver that is accompanied by small objects of contemporary manufacture suitable for gifts, and a designer line of jewellery characterized by a strong and youthful style, also in silver. Since 1989, Faraone has been the exclusive importer, in Italy, of Tiffany, the American brand that is among the greatest and most prestigious in the field, quoted on the New York Stock Exchange and known in every market all over the world. Beppe Modenese designs a jewellery line for Faraone.

Faret Daniel (1956). Son and grandson of textile entrepreneurs. After studying political science and working for two years as a

Geometric earrings with diamonds and black onyx by Faraone. Drawing by Brunetta (Biki Collection).

journalist, he decided to enter the family business and to create men's clothing. In 1983, his group acquired the *maison* Jacques Fath in order to relaunch the brand. Faret managed it from 1986 to 1991. He sold his shares in 1993, ready, the following year, to offer the Daniel Faret Collection, a new line of urban clothing for young people. It was for these collections that he received the *Oscar of Textiles* in the Designer category in 1997.

❑ 2003, January. He is asked to work on the launch of the new La Perla prêt-à-porter for the Spring-Summer 2004 collection.

Farhad Rahbarzadeh (1970). A designer of Persian origin, Farhad Rahbarzadeh signs his collection with his first name only. He was born in Frosinone, near Rome. He first presented at Alta Moda a Roma in July 1999. His clothes are worked with inlays and embroidery that combine different fabrics and materials such as raffia and silk as well as crystal and organza. A graduate of the School of Art, he studied architecture for four years at the University of La Sapienza in Rome. He started his career as a set and costume designer for the opera, working in Monaco, Tokyo, and Bilbao, and working with Franco Zeffirelli. He established himself with a prêt-à-porter collection that was presented in 1997. He presented at Milano Collezioni in February 2003.

(*Eleonora Attolico*)

Farhi Nicole (1949). French designer. She was trained at the Studio Berçot in Paris. After a time in the atelier of Pierre d'Alby, she moved to London. In 1983, she established her own company (which carries her name) together with Stephen Marks, for whom she had managed the fashion department at the French Connection department stores. In 1989, she launched a moderately-priced new brand called Diversion, as well as a men's line.

Farri Stanislao (1924). Italian photographer. He acquired a passion for photography in 1940. In 1955, after having worked as a printer, he decided to turn his passion into a profession. He opened a studio in his home town of Reggio Emilia and devoted himself to the reproduction of art work as well as industrial, advertising, and architectural photography. He published several books filled with his personal research on the area's civilization and culture and, alongside his professional work, did campaigns in both black-and-white and color, participating in various personal and collective exhibits. In 2003, Palazzo Magnani in Reggio Emilia mounted a large retrospective of his work, accompanied by a catalogue, *Memorie di Luce* ('Memories of Light'). He became interested in fashion photography and followed a non-systematic approach through commercial work carried out for clients such as Bormioli, Ferrari, and Max Mara.

(*Roberto Mutti*)

Farthingale A term of Spanish origin indicating the tail of a woman's jacket attached to the bodice at the waist and either cut on the bias or curled or pleated, dropping in an amphora-shape to the hips.

Fasano Italian jewellery shop. It was during the 1930s that a by now proverbial collection depicting animals, in particular the pheasant, made this family name part of the European panorama of the goldsmith's art. The story began in 1932. Mario Fasano opened a shop in Piazza Castello in Turin and, thanks to his wife Stella, it became a point of reference, and not only for people in the town. In 1952, a new boutique was opened in via Roma. In 1957, Mario's son Dario made his début and, in 1968, he took his father's place in the business. Today it is still a house with great tradition and style.

Fashion Italian fashion weekly. For 30 years it has been the leader of Italian specialized trade magazines. Created by Gianni Bertasso and now directed by Titti Matteoni, the magazine is known for investigations, articles, interviews, photo features, predictions, news, and columns useful a quick check of the textile-clothing business as a whole: covering fibers, yarns, fabric, children's wear, prêt-à-porter, high fashion, accessories, and jeans, all according to the rhythm of industry events and international trade fairs. The magazine has grown over the years, not just in content, but also in terms of parallel and complementary initiatives. These have included the Fashionguides, practical booklets rich in information about specific fields, updated periodically; the Fashioncalendars, distributed gratis during the collections with an appointment calendar, useful addresses, and other features; the Tabloids, with news published in real time during the prêt-à-porter presentations; and the internet website www.fashionmagazine.it with its corresponding free newsletter sent out every night via e-mail. In 2002, the magazine started Fashion Focus, a monthly with in-depth reports of 16 to 20 pages each on different aspects of the textile-clothing field. It started with men's clothing and went on to include such themes as fibers/yarns/fabrics, women's clothing, accessories, glasses/watches/perfumes, and distribution. Fashion has also organized seminars and round tables on current issues important to the industry.

Fashion The term is the direct translation of the French word *mode*, which, according to scholars from that country, appeared for the first time in 1482 to indicate a specific type of clothing. Little more than 70 years later there were references to new fashions and to the following of fashion. In Italy (R.L. Pisetzky) the word arrived in the mid-seventeenth century, when "fleetingness, variability, and novelty" were already considered to be essential characteristics of fashion. In the sixteenth century, the word costume was used to indicate a way of dressing that was longer lasting, more uniform, and slow to change. Although the original practice of covering the body and defending and assuring one's modesty was overtaken by the role of clothing as decoration, a sign of belonging, communication, and individual roles, the changing of garments, colors, and textiles became more complex over the course of centuries with the establishment of new powers, commercial exchanges, and the emergence of new social hierarchies. In Italy, an exporter of many important materials that differentiated specific fashions, from silk to lace, from gloves to embroidery, this new development was present in the towns, in arts and crafts guilds, and also in the aristocratic courts. The frequent changing of clothes was exclusively reserved for the upper classes, who had the means to personalize the image they presented. Although the new role of clothing had a strong influence in restricted circles, it did not enjoy the same degree of diffusion as at the French royal court. However, in different ways, clothing, and therefore fashion, was a means of affirming power: the lower orders struggled to follow it and the sumptuary laws – a mine of information, and which constituted a moralizing echo of the denouncements of saints and preachers – were, in the end, futile. Issued too frequently to be effective, they were unable to prevent the many obtaining access to the luxuries of the few, in order to demonstrate and affirm themselves socially, as well as demonstrate their financial means. Fashion is vanity and – with its mutations from one style to another, and its slavish pursuance of the ideals of beauty and seduction to attract the opposite sex – it promotes waste. But this is precisely the key

The fashion of 1922.

to its role as a bearer of riches: not only for those who take advantage of and follow it, but also for those who produce it. Fitelieu's condemnation (*La Contre Mode*, 1642) had a parallel in Colbert's revealing desire to procure Italian artisans who would reveal their skills to the lace makers of Limoges and Valencienne, prompted by the huge prices paid for that fashionable ornament, lace. Already, these phenomena, which have been a constant feature of fashion from the fourteenth century to the present, indicate the particular complexity of the competitive, social, and economic factors that underlie it. Hated, opposed or tolerated, fashion has provoked strong reactions in both men and women; it changes and becomes diffused, decays and becomes more complicated, seemingly with no master but itself, while benefiting from the development of new social groups, the progress of craft, art, and wars. It was only in the mid-seventeenth, and above all the eighteenth century, that people began to study fashion as a specific phenomenon, apart from the descriptions and advice on costume that can be found in works such as Baldassare Castiglione's *Il Cortegiano* (1528). Attention to fashion began with the tailors' books that, during the Renaissance, included sketches and pattern instructions for copying and, the following century, with the work of very careful observers such as Cesare Vecellio who, almost from an ethnographic point of view, recorded and drew the clothing of different populations, certainly without analyzing appearances in terms of fashion as such, but more to pinpoint the evolution of garments. These were the first works to suggest that fashions were initiated by princes and lords. However, taste is derived from a combination of aspects of life. In this respect, the parallel between architectural and clothing forms is important. The circle of the Roman toga echoed the unsupported arch. The severe Romanesque style was repeated in the fluid garments of the Middle Ages and, likewise, the Gothic style was reflected in the peaked cones of women's headwear and their pointed, elongated shoes. The closed, sixteenth-century schema was translated into magnificent gowns in the Baroque period, just as the fashion of the 1920s embodied many of the merits of Art Deco. It was in the mid-nineteenth century, with the increase in demand from the neo-romantic middle class, and in supply, through the birth of department stores and fashion magazines, that the term "fashion" took on its meaning of "a collective and passing enthusiasm for a type of clothing, design, or accessory." At the same time, it established the specificity of the industries and professions that made different types of clothing and accessories. During this period, authors (such as Balzac) began to focus their attention on fashion as a descriptive element in order to relate daily life at all social levels. At the beginning of the twentieth century, Proust evoked time lost in the elegances of

Silhouettes to illustrate 35 years of fashion (Prints Collection A. Bertarelli, Milan).

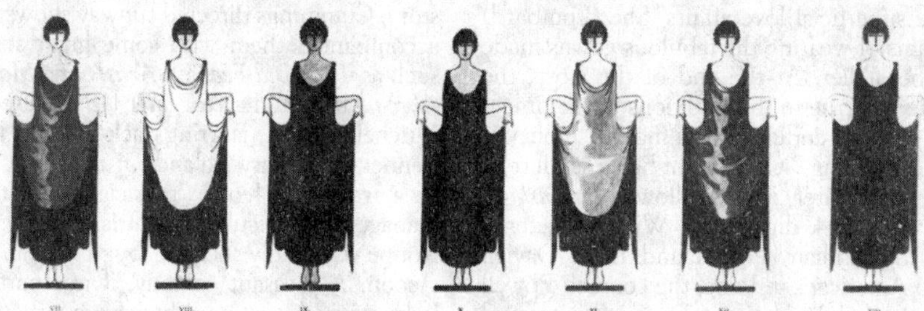

Intonation of black, *Encyclopaedia of Women's Clothing* by Piergiovanni, published by Unitas (Prints Collection A. Bertarelli, Milan).

Guermantes and in the dresses of Fortuny. At a theoretical level, scholars finally began to turn their attention to fashion, analyzing it as the result of a variety of instinctive and individual needs and, formulating a system of appearances (Flugel, Kroeber), they developed its sociological connections through the diffusion of designs in a process of class imitation. Lower social groups imitated those above them, always one step behind, as the clothing models continued so that the upper classes might distinguish themselves (Spencer, Veblen). In recent times, there have been more structural analyses of the fashion phenomenon, functionalist with regard to the individual, thereby drawing closer to the internal laws of the fashion system. Fashion is clothing, but it is also a way of being, of choosing objects, of determining the fortune of a particular form of transport or a tourist resort. After World War II, with a larger proportion of the population enjoying a more comfortable lifestyle, the expansion of the demand and supply of fashion reached new peaks, thanks to *prêt-à-porter* and runway shows in Italy and France, as was already the case in England, Spain, and the United States. Clothing became an aid to life and work, a way of belonging and communicating. The widely diffused, superficial view that fashion was futile and merely an indication of vanity, had by now been abandoned. Fashion is always strictly linked with its time. Often the half-hidden suggestions of change are very revealing: indicating the encounter between a desire and a particular need to break free, with the result that a new fashion is formed, once the economic climate is right. Sometimes the apparently bizarre nature of a new accessory, or a hairstyle that achieves wide popularity, blinds us to the disappearance of a garment that has been fashionable for years. The fashion for short garments (Courrèges, Mary Quant) during the 1960s was an expression of faith in progress, technology, and a modernity with an unlimited future. During the petrol wars and years of terrorism of the 1970s, feelings of nostalgia for retro and "poor" fashion were aroused. But short or long is one of the recurring extremes of the cyclical changes of fashion. The logical necessity of fashion sometimes takes advantage of that process of constant change necessary for its survival. Equally fundamental for the survival of fashion is the desire on the part of designers and industry to study the styles of the past, even though this type of research is becoming rarer. The irrefutable democratization of fashion has, little by little, halted the "trickle-down" effect, from elites, leaders and stars to consumers whose role is to diffuse and devalue it. In recent times, the creative role of street style has overturned such hierarchies. The jean phenomenon is typical of this reversal. (*Lucia Sollazzo*)

Fashion and Cinema Only about twenty successful movies focus specifically on fashion. Naturally, most of them were made in Hollywood though the Italian cinema was quick to follow. Curiously, only one such film has been made in France. The list begins with *Sinners in the Sun* (1932, directed by Alexander Hall, starring Carole Lombard, Chester Morris, and Cary Grant). An impoverished young couple, working at a fashion house, joins the rich members of an elegant area of California. Both partners have superficial love affairs. She (Lombard) dreams of wearing the fabulous gowns made in the atelier. At the end of the story, the comedy – true to the traditions of the time – has a happy ending with a moral: "money is not everything." Cary Grant had a small role. Two years later, it was followed by *Fashion of 1934* (1934, directed by William Dieterle, starring William Powell and Bette Davis). Two Americans in Paris, the conman Powell and the fashion designer Davis, plan to steal the patterns from a large atelier. He masquerades as a designer. They succeed in conquering the Parisian fashion world. A comedy with an impressive cast and splendid musical numbers (in particular *Spin a Little Web of Dreams*) by Busby Berkeley. Afterwards it was the turn of *Roberta* (1935, director William A. Seiter, starring Irene Dunne, Fred Astaire, Ginger Rogers, and Randolph Scott). Fleeing from the October Revolution, a Russian princess goes to Paris, becomes a fashion designer and her employer falls in love with her. Originally a theater musical, this romantic story in RKO style became famous for its songs (*I Won't Dance*, *Smoke Gets in Your Eyes*) and the exuberant dance numbers of Ginger Rogers and Fred Astaire, who were relegated to supporting roles. The first Italian film on the theme was *La contessa di Parma* (1937, director Alessandro Blasetti, starring Elisa Cegani, Antonio Centa, Maria Denis, Umberto Melnati, Osvaldo Valenti, and Nunzio Filogamo). An equivocal, ironic, and sophisticated story, with sequences filmed from real life in the world of *haute couture* in Turin. The strikers in the national football team fall in love with the model Marcella – nicknamed the Countess of Parma for her aristocratic bearing. According to Paolo Mereghetti's film dictionary, it is a "tasteful comedy, situated in the emerging high society of the period" (fashion rather than football) but which Blasetti defined as "the silliest film" he had ever made." During the same year, in Hollywood, *Vogues of 1938* was released (1937, director Irving Cummings, starring Joan Bennet, Warner Baxter, and Misha Auer). A minor musical in Technicolor, based on the rivalry between two fashion houses on Fifth Avenue. The whims of the wife of one of the owners causes a crisis for the business. A model with initiative is able to resolve the situation. More than a true story, Cummings directed runway shows and accompanied them with some great songs, such as *That Old Feeling*. *Artists and Models Abroad* appeared a year later (1938, director Mitchell Leisen, starring Jack Benny, Joan Bennet, and Mary Boland): it tells the story of a troupe of female musicians and their manager, in difficulties in Paris. Luckily, the troupe is kindly helped by a Texan oil tycoon. A pleasant comedy, if not particularly original, distinguished from others of the time by its emphasis on elegance and fashion. During the middle of the war, the *Lady in the Dark* was released in the USA (1944, director Mitchell Leisen, starring Ginger Rogers, Ray Milland, Warner Baxter, and Misha Auer). Fashion and psychoanalysis. Wooed by three suitors, the director of the magazine Allure (whose staff wear the most eccentric hats and garments) has problems with her subconscious. She goes to a psychoanalyst and has liberating dreams in Technicolor. In the end, not only does she gain self-assurance but also the right man. Based on a Broadway show, it was a typical romantic comedy of the 1940s: rich, stylized, often amusing. The music was by Kurt Weill and Ira Gershwin. *Laura* was also released during the war (1944, director Otto Preminger, starring Gene Tierney, Dana Andrews, Clifton Webb, and Vincent Price). It is an archetypal film noir, dense with ambiguity, mystery and necrophilia. While investigating a murder, a police officer falls in love with a portrait of the dead woman, Laura, the director of an advertising agency. The woman reappears in flesh and blood: it is discovered that the victim was actually an unknown model. It followed the best traditions of the genre, with Gene Tierney more beautiful and fascinating than ever in the elegant clothes of a (supposedly) femme fatale. At the same time, the French *Falbalas* was released (1944, director Jacques Becker, starring Micheline Presle, and Gabrielle Dorziat). It was the first film made by Becker after the Liberation, a rare example of a European comedy, both sentimental and ironic, set in the Parisian fashion world. It also contained personal memories linked with the director's adolescence, when his mother worked in *haute couture*. It was followed by a famous Italian film: *Cronaca di un amore* (1950, directed by Michelangelo

Antonioni, starring Lucia Bosé, Massimo Girotti, and Franco Fabrizi). Married to a rich industrialist, Paola meets Giulio, the love of her life. The two become lovers and plan to dispose of her husband. It was Antonioni's first full-length movie and introduced a (black) picture of Milanese bourgeoisie in the popular climate of Neo-realism. Bosé was splendid, both in the luxurious outfits designed by the very young Fausto Sarli and the immediately legendary undergarments. Some of the sequences were filmed in the salon of Noberasco's atelier, in Via Manzoni. From Hollywood came a remake, *Lovely to Look At* (1952, by Mervyn Le Roy, starring Red Skelton, Ann Miller, and Kathryn Grayson). Then came the second version, with important variations, of *Roberta*: three friends from Broadway go to Paris, where one of them has inherited a fashion house. After having discovered that it is riddled with debt, they rescue it with a gala runway show with a musical accompaniment (the fashion show sequences were directed by Vincent Minnelli). The famous songs of the original were used again, but this time Red Skelton took the lead role. That same year, *Le ragazze di Piazza di Spagna* was released in Italy (1952, by Luciano Emmer, with Lucia Bosé, Cosetta Greco, Liliana Bonfatti, Eduardo De Filippo, and Marcello Mastroianni). The story of three young seamstresses working in a Roman atelier, narrated by Emmer in an everyday style and veined with irony. In particular, one of them (Bosé) has the opportunity to become a model but gives it up to marry a worker. The three stories in the film – one of the prototypes of the so-called "pink Neo-realism" – are "narrated" by the writer, Giorgio Bassani. Another Italian film, the winner of the Silver Lion at the Venice Film Festival, was *Le amiche* (1955, by Michelangelo Antonioni, with Eleonora Rossi Drago, Valentina Cortese, Yvonne Fourneaux, Gabriele Ferzetti, Franco Fabrizi, Madeleine Fisher, and Ettore Manni). Taken from the story by Cesare Pavese, *Tre donne sole*, Clelia, the director of a fashion house, arrives in Turin to open a boutique. She associates with rich members of the bourgeoisie, models, and intellectuals; one of the group is a girl who attempts to commit suicide. With a screenplay by women (Suso Cecchi D'Amico and Alba de Cèspedes), the film is a bitter drama where the clothes (from the atelier of the Fontana sisters) contribute to the psychological make-up of the characters. *Funny Face* dates from 1957 (by Stanley Donen, with Audrey Hepburn, and Fred Astaire). A mature photographer discovers a young model with an unusual face and graceful bearing. He launches her on the world of fashion, falls in love, and she returns his feelings. A musical of great delicacy, elegance and style set in all the typical Parisian locations. Richard Avedon, who at the time worked for *Vogue* and *Harper's Bazaar*, supervised the images: the result is one of the most faithful films ever made on the world of *haute couture*. Dressed by Givenchy, Audrey Hepburn combined sophisticated grace with a natural sympathy in an unforgettable performance. Another Italian film is *Sei donne per l'assassino* (1964, by Mario Bava, starring Eva Bartok, and Cameron Mitchell). It is a film ahead of its time: the story of a serial killer set in the fashion world (see later *Sotto il vestito niente* and its successors). The proprietor and director of an elegant atelier kill a model in order to cover up a previous crime. This sets off a series of other murders. Baroque and sadistic, the film was condemned as immoral at the time. *Prêt-à-porter* (1994, by Robert Altman, with Julia Roberts, Sofia Loren, Marcello Mastroianni, Kim Basinger, Anouk Aimée, Lauren Bacall, and Rupert Everett). During the *prêt-à-porter* week, Paris is teeming with fashion designers, models, journalists, photographers, and VIPs. In the middle of it all, there is a murder. Critical as ever, Altman uses fashion as a metaphor for a society of appearances, where beautiful clothes hide a void. The designer Aimée makes a stand against consumerism by organizing a show with nude models. A small army of stars appeared in the film for the American director, among them the former models Kim Basinger and Lauren Bacall, as well as real designers (Ferré, Trussardi, Gaultier) playing themselves. *Unzipped* (1995, by Douglas Keeve, with Isaac Mizrahi, Cindy Crawford, and Linda Evangelista). This was an American documentary on the runway shows of the designer Isaac Mizrahi. Mixing film and video, color and black-and-white, the director alternates official runway footage with shots of the models behind stage. Some of the most famous models appeared as themselves – Cindy Crawford, Naomi Campbell, Kate Moss, Linda Evangelista – complaining of their sore feet and voicing their whims. In the 1990s, the soap opera *Beautiful* appeared, first in the United States and then across Europe. Numerous love intrigues are played out against the background of two competing fashion houses.

(*Roberto Nepoti*)

Fashion & Textile Museum (FTM). A London museum dedicated entirely to fashion, fabrics, and fashion's major figures. It opened in May 2003. In shape it is a kind of colored prism, designed by the Mexican architect Ricardo Legorreta. It is located in the Bermondsey neighborhood, in an area south of the Thames, the ideal stage set for a series of events completely devoted to fashion, including exhibits, summits, and workshops. For its opening, the museum organized *My Favourite Dress*, an exhibit for which 70 famous designers lent their favorite dresses. Some dresses were even donated to the museum, for example by Christian Lacroix and John Galliano. Zandra Rhodes donated 3,000 of her original models, and these became part of the museum's permanent collection. The collection can be viewed by appointment only, or else through the digital archives which will soon be available in the museum library.

(*Edoardo Ponzoni*)

Fashion Book The first databank for young European professional designers. It is promoted by the Chamber of Commerce of Prato and by the Committee for the Promotion of Young Fashion Designers, led by Annamaria Luminari Moretti. The idea came from the collections presented at Fashion & Technology, an event within Pitti Immagine dedicated to young designers. The databank operates by recommending young designers who have gained experience and competence in the clothing-textile field to business who may have need of them. It is a service focused especially on small and medium-sized companies, included those run by Chinese entrepreneurs. The databank is constantly updated and provides a way to balance supply and demand for this highly skilled labor. (*Gianluca Cantaro*)

Fashion Box Italian clothing company with headquarters in Asolo (Treviso). The business is directed by Claudio Buziol. In 2002, the turnover was €251 million, roughly even with the previous year. Some 70% of that came from exports. In September 2003, a maxi-space was opened on Corso Venezia in Milan for the sale of all the brands belonging to the group: Replay, Replay & Sons, E-Play, and Coca Cola Jeans Wear. A new line, We-R-Replay, made its début at Pitti Immagine Uomo in June 2003. It was a more modern casual collection for young men and women, with a goal of 100,000 pieces for the first Spring-Summer 2004 collection, launched on an international level. The production was artisanal in quality for shirts, T-shirts, and trousers, with prints and embroidery inspired by the world of motorbikes. There were also fancy patterns in an '80s style with Hawaiian, floral, palm, iguana, and butterfly prints. The new collection was a substitute for E-Play, which in the meantime had been moved to the prêt-à-porter division and thus fell under the management of Knit Box of Carpi. The distribution system includes 4,000 traditional points-of-sale, supported by 200 single-brand boutiques that present the company's image in all the fashion capitals of the world. Fashion Box is also interested in Brazil. In autumn 2003, the company opened a single-brand shop named Replay in San Paulo where a subsidiary, Fashion Box Brazil, had already been operating for a short time, making sweat-shirts, T-shirts, and jeans. The new company was created to serve South America, but it could also serve Europe. At the moment, the Fashion Box collections are produced by third parties in Italy, Eastern Europe, the Mediterranean area, and in the Far East. Another attractive market for the company is Japan. Following an agreement with the Japanese firm Hero International, a single-brand Replay store was opened in Tokyo, to be followed by three more.

❑ 2005. In January, Claudio Buziol, the founder, dies prematurely. The new company structure will have 90% of the shares in the hands of his wife and two children, with the remaining 10% going to the two general managers, Marco Bortoletti and Attilio Biancardi, the vice-president.

Fashion China International trade fair for clothing and accessories which takes place every September during the Intex of Shanghai. It has 120,000 square feet for 150 exhibitors, including about 30 Italian companies. The event was started in 2000 and, in addition to companies from Europe, there are exhibitors from the People's Republic of China, Hong Kong, and Taiwan. Italy was the partner of the September 2002 fair, on the initiative of the Igedo company, in collaboration with the China Garment Association and CCPIT-Tex. There is strong interest in a market which is growing more than 7% a year.

Fashion Coterie An event dedicated to clothing and accessories held every September in New York. It is organized in combination with Sole Commerce, which is dedicated to shoes. It is the most important fashion event on the East Coast, both for U.S. and foreign companies. In September 2002, there were 27 Italian companies present, in the Made in Italy section organized by the Italian Fashion Institute in collaboration with ICE. The exhibitors included Aida Barni, Carlo Pignatelli, Liolà, and Oroblù, as well as the Florentine designer Angela Caputi with her original costume jewellery, Giuggiù.

Fashion Factory Italian brand of ready-to-wear aimed at young women. Very innovative, it was created in 1998 by a knitwear factory which had been active near Milan since the 1980s.

Fashion Institute Burgo Established by the publisher Fernando Burgo, after 40 years of experience in the industry. The school is located in the Milan quadrilateral, at number 5 Piazza San Babila, right next to the church. Among the courses offered are stylism, fashion design, and model-making techniques. There are also various specialized and continuing education courses. Every July, the Institute organizes an individual summer course, a complete immersion in sketches, fabrics, and trends. The school works with famous companies, ateliers, and designers such as Armani, Krizia, D&G, Gucci, and Ferré.

Fashion Institute of Technology New York. It was established in 1944 in a few rooms on the first floor of the High School for Needle Trades. The idea came from a group of textile entrepreneurs, many of whom emigrated to America during the war and worried about the future of their traditional techniques. The first director of the Institute was Mortimer C. Ritter. He offered two courses, one on design and one on scientific management, for a hundred students, at no charge. In 1951, the Institute became part of the State University of New York and initiated a registration fee. In 1959 it moved to Seventh Avenue, in the heart of New York's fashion industry. During the 1970s it became a college and transformed itself into a campus with eight buildings. There are 11,200 students, both full and part-time, who take 30 specialized courses. Well-financed by New York State, New York City, and private donors, the school takes advantage of the most sophisticated technology and one of the most important fashion museums in the world. There is constant contact with people in the industry. Presentations are organized for the students and famous designers are often invited to speak; these have included Givenchy, Cardin, Versace, and Ferré. Former students include Calvin Klein, Norma Kamali, and Michael Kors.

Fashionist A term that derives from the French "façoniste." Manufacturing "à façon" refers to clothing made in series starting from a base model. Today, a fashionist is a manufacturing company that produces clothes for third parties, generally starting from a semi-worked material (i.e. from a previously cut fabric). Fashionists – who often work with one or more brands at the same time – sell to boutiques and fashion stores, but especially to the large distribution chains which apply their own labels to the garments, under their own brand, when "à façon" manufacturing hasn't already been requested by the famous names who aren't able to manufacture their models in great quantities.

The Fashion Liner On 20 February 1956, eight very beautiful members of the Italian aristocracy disembarked from the liner the *Cristoforo Colombo* in New York to become models for Italian designers: Lorian Gaetani

Lovatelli for Antonelli, Maria Teresa Siciliana di Rende for Schuberth, Consuelo Crespi for Fabiani, Diamante Capponi Cornaggia Medici for Veneziani, Mita Corti Colonna di Cesarò for Carosa, Kiki Brandolini d'Adda for Marucelli, Barbara Biscareti di Ruffia for Capucci, and Jacqueline Borgia for Simonetta. The idea came to Bista Giorgini, the promoter of the nascent Italian fashion industry and the organizer of the exhibitions at the Pitti Palace in Florence. He arranged a social whirl that involved Salvador Dalí, Marilyn Monroe, and Elsa Maxwell, the chronicler of the Hollywood's gossip, plus a succession of TV shows: the Dave Garroway Show (audience of 23 millions), Home (11 millions), the Jack Parr Show (10 millions) and the Igor Cassini Show (14 millions). The advertising results were huge and the success overwhelming. The fashion manager of NBC regretted not having a "French version of Giorgini" for the programs dedicated to the Paris fashion exhibitions, and Diana Vreeland, the famous fashion editor of *Vogue*, wrote that she had been fascinated by the clothes and hats. The creations of Italian milliners were also appraised, though these were the last glory days of the hat as a necessary article of elegance. It was another victory for the Florentine strategist, who was well aware how the success of the fashion industry in Italy could also benefit from a degree of snobbery, something to which Americans were then particularly sensitive. Giorgini had already "used" duchesses and marquises for photo services, and inundated buyers with noble titles and diadems during the Florentine parties. When Betty Bullock, the NBC fashion editor, proposed a second TV tour across the USA, the result was another aristocratic cruise of Italian fashion.

Fashion Model Management An Italian modeling agency. The pioneer in Milan, it was created in 1967. Lorenzo Pedrini is the president and one of three partners, together with Giorgio Santambrogio and Paolo Roberti, the founder. It has a staff of 50 people and belongs to the Next network, with branches in New York, Paris, Los Angeles, Miami, London, San Paulo, and Montreal.

Fashion-Plate A drawing that illustrates clothes, underwear, or any other garment, and which shows the particular shape and details of a garment, serving as a model for dressmakers and tailors and as a "base" for selection by clients. The expression "to look like a fashion-plate" meant to dress in a very fashionable way, with particular refinement.

Fashion Shoes and Leather Goods An exhibit of shoes and leather goods organized by Bologna Fiere in collaboration with ANCI, held for the fifth time in January 2003, with around 190 participating companies. In order to increase attendance by buyers and the public, the event begins after the final day of Expo Riva Schuh, a trade fair held around the same time at Lake Garda.

Fashion Victim A fashion victim is someone who understands nothing about fashion and passively and calmly follows the taste and instructions of his favorite designer, and is the victim of every branded product. Condemned by every self-respecting person in the fashion industry, it is a clear example of how not to use fashion.

Fashion Work Library A library and bookshop in Milan specializing in fashion. Opened by Diego Valisi in July 2000 at via Vigevano 35, it has about 14,000 titles between magazines and trendy books in about 2,000 square feet. A subscription, which costs €58 a year for students and €115 for people working in the industry, allows one to access a rich video library about the collections in Milan, Paris and New York from 1985 up to today. In a reading room with 20 seats it is possible to consult about forty collections of periodicals, for the most part complete: duplicate issues of magazines are on sale at collectors' prices. A large bookstore supplements the space dedicated to borrowing and reference. In the bookstore, which in June 2003 was moved to a space that is separate but still connected to the library, it is possible to reserve monographs on individual designers as well as picture collages of made-to-measure clothing. The space on via Vigevano is periodically used for photo exhibits, debates, book launches, and fashion presentations.

(*Pierangelo Mastantuono*)

Fath Jacques (1912-1954). French designer and creator of the fashion house bearing his

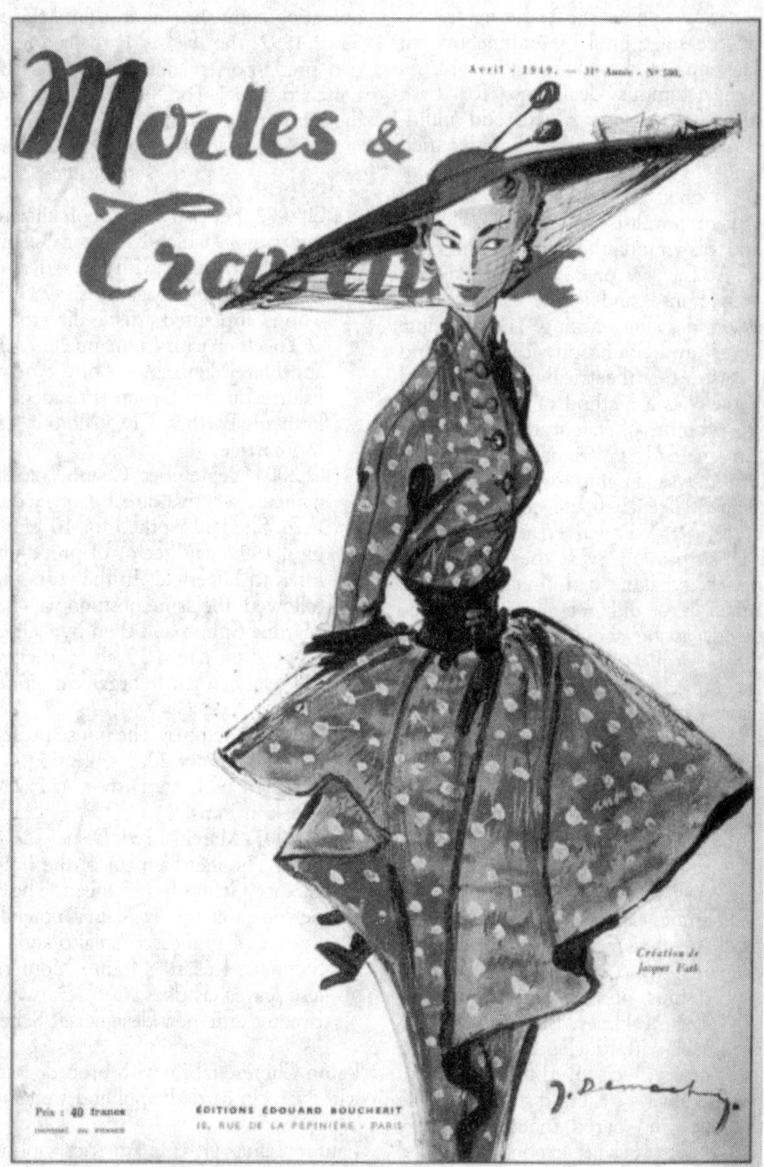

Dress by Jacques Fath on a cover of *Modes et Travaux* (1949).

name. He had a multifaceted personality that complemented his collections. After a first launch in 1937, they became successful with an international clientele only after World War II due to a strongly forward-looking style that was able anticipate future trends. He held the stage until his untimely death from leukemia at the young age of 42. As with other famous designers, for Fath fashion would provide a safe and multi-faceted refuge after a youth rich with varied experiences. He was born into a family of artists: his great-grandparents, in the mid 1800s, were novelists and fashion illustrators, and his grandfather was a landscape painter. At the age of 22 he worked in a publishing house, and in the evening took courses on drawing, cutting, and dancing. He was very aware of his physical beauty and of his taste for theatricality. He would exploit them as a method of advertising in order to promote his talent and the *maison* which, by the early 1950s, had a staff of 600 people and was an important part of the panorama of French haute couture. Fath's characteristic rapidity in creation, and his speed in surpassing, with the spur of his imagination, what he had already achieved with other lines, did not allow him to be considered, as he should have been, the inventor, before 1940, of what would later in 1947 be defined with Dior as the New Look. But Dior would have the intuition, very useful to the industrialist Boussac, to use, after the shortages of war and the Nazi occupation, yards and yards of cloth, almost in a return to a femininity once again forced into corsets. Nevertheless, Fath distinguished himself for the asymmetry of the different parts of a dress, the return to a figure sometimes caressed by extended and sinuous shapes but more often accentuated by them, with a wasp waist, a very large skirt, pronounced hips, and an ample bust softened by deep necklines. But his style also expressed itself with touches of imagination, accents of color which loved to clash with a line that was always clear and structured. He was the one who dared to combine very luminous colors such as lemon yellow and orange, to furnish very feminine dresses with details stolen from the male wardrobe, so that his preference for short hair went together with his thrilling collection of stockings decorated with lace. After his death, although his wife Geneviève took over the *maison* it nevertheless stopped presenting its collections in the spring of 1957, despite the fact that the family would maintain majority ownership of the various operating companies almost until the 1980s. Since 1992, the *maison* Fath has presented two prêt-à-porter collections a year by the Dutch designer Tom Van Lingen. In 1997 the *maison* was acquired by Group Emmanuelle Khanh, led by François Barthes.

(*Lucia Sollazzo*)

❑ 2002, February. The reorganization of the *maison*, which had been "silent" since 1998, starts with the arrival of a young English designer, Lizzy Disney, who is appointed artistic director.
❑ Together with Emmanuelle Khanh and Harel, Fath is part of the new France Luxury Group (President François Barthes, CEO Mounir Moufarrige).
❑ 2003, September. Céline Toledano is named executive director of Jacques Fath. She had worked for 10 years, up until 1993, as director of prêt-à-porter for Karl Lagerfeld. In the years that followed, the same position was held by Martine Sitbon and then by Céline. Now, at the age of 39, she participates in the relaunch and reorganization of the Fath.
❑ 2002, October. The house presents its Spring-Summer 2003 collection, designed by Lizzy Disney, at Fashion Week in Paris.
❑ 2003, March. Lizzy Disney leaves Fath. The management of the France Luxury Group has changed. The new person in charge is Alain Dumenil (owner of Francesco Smalto and Stéphane Kélian). Mounir Moufarrige also leaves, as does Ritu Beri, who becomes the new designer at Scherrer.

Faton Chinese fabric with brocade patterns, with warp in carded wool and weft in silk.

Faurer Louis (1916). American photographer. After working as a sign painter, he dedicated himself to photo reportage on social issues. In the 1940s, he moved from Philadelphia to New York and started a career as a fashion photographer. He worked with Alexey Brodovich at Harper's Bazaar. There he met Robert Frank, with whom he shared a style that was reduced to its essentials as well as a scarcity of means. In the 1950s and 1960s his interests shifted again, this time towards street photography and the avant-garde cinema.

Fausti Marina (1951). Journalist and editor of Donna. She was born in Gallarate, near Varese. She began her career in 1972 while still quite young, as a coordinator and assistant for the Fashion Committee of Clothing Entrepreneurs in Milan. Immediately, the following year, she was discovered by Condé Nast and hired as an editor at Vogue Italy, a position very much sought after by all young reporters, in a place where all the women journalists were known for being particularly attractive, elegant, blonde, and beautiful. She remained at Condé Nast until 1978 when she was hired to do special features at Linea Italiana (Mondadori), where she would stay until 1983. She is one of the few journalists who has had an interesting professional path, both in specialized magazines and in television, where she hosted a fashion program, Pianeta Moda (Planet Fashion) on Telemontecarlo. From 1983 to '88 she worked at RAI as an anchorwoman and journalist on the TV program Moda (Fashion). From 1990 to '95 she was a writer and fashion consultant for programs and special events broadcast by RAI 1. In the same period she was deputy editor of the magazine Moda, published by ERI-RAI. In 1995 she was hired by Vera Montanari, editor of Gioia, first as deputy editor for fashion and then as co-editor.

Fay Brand of clothing created in 1960 as a small fashion house for outerwear. The company was established by a certain Mr. Fay to satisfy the working needs of fishermen in the state of Maine. The only garment in production was a work jacket with four hooks. The Della Valle Group took over the brand in 1986, giving the company its own style and strategy, resulting in an immediate increase in production and sales. During the 1990s, the classic four-hook jacket was accompanied by the Travel jacket, the Motor jacket, the Double coat, and the Manhattan jacket. Today, the company, which is considered "the Italian Burberry," produces jackets inspired by those of New York's firemen, trousers and jackets for men, and women's clothing and bags, always with an emphasis on functionality and practicality, and always in an elegant style. In mid November 2002 the first Fay boutique was opened on via della Spiga in Milan. It was designed by the American architect Philip Johnson. (*Pierangelo Mastantuono*)

Fayolle Denise (1923-1995). French consultant for fashion and advertising. She received a degree in philosophy and practiced figure skating. She began her career as a journalist in 1951 at Votre Beauté. In 1953, she went to Sapac-Prisunic as director for style-fashion and advertising. Her ideas anticipated by a decade what would be a real revolution in clothing during the 1960s. Fayolle turned Prisunic upside down and gave it a new style with the help of some 60 assistants. The guiding policy: even what is cheap can be beautiful, as long as it is redesigned in a consistent, simple way. Her meeting with Maimé Arnodin, even though accidental (due to an article about Fayolle published in 1956 in Jardin des Modes), would be decisive. They became business partners in 1968 and established Mafia (Maimé Arnodin Fayolle Internationale Associés). It would have very important clients (Dupont de Nemours, Aborba, Les 3 Suisses, Yves Saint-Laurent Parfums) and act as a design department for entrepreneurs in the field and as a talent scout. After Mafia was sold to the advertising group BDDP in 1987, they established a new consulting and advertising agency called Nomad (Nouvelle Organisation Maimé and Denise).

(*Gabriella Gregorietti*)

Feathers The head of Mistinguette, heroine of the Folies Bergères, who had legs so magical as to inspire the autobiographical song *J'ai des jolies jambettes*, was like a pin head above the cloud of her ostrich feather cape, that she opened from time to time (as our forebears remembered with shivers of lasting excitement) to give the audience a glimpse of her gleaming sequinned breasts. When was this? Just before World War I, around 1910, the years when the dressmaker Paul Poiret, by reputation heir to the legendary fashion company Worth, decorated chiffon evening dresses with little pink

Ostrich feather boa and hat with osprey feather, for Consuelo Van der Bilt (Prints Collection A. Bertarelli, Milan).

and peach-colored swan's feathers and created turbans knotted around aigrette plumes. Mistinguette and Caroline Otero, known as "La Bella," were submerged in their stage plumage, as they performed their seductive songs and dances "inside" a cloud of ostrich, heron or swan's feathers, just as stars of the stage and silent screen like Sarah Bernhardt, Gabrielle Réjan, Lina Cavalieri, Gea della Garisenda (who sung *Tripoli, bel suol d'amore* wrapped in the Italian flag as if it were a marabou cape), Gloria Swanson, and Francesca Bertini sported exaggerated white boas, and the rather less lovely Italia Almirante Manzini and Dina Galli, who did not dare frame their faces with an overly showy boa, could not resist loading their hats with curled plumage and stiff feathers called *couteaux* because they cut the air like a knife. It was the Belle Époque, which started in the final decade of the 1800s and went on until 1914 when the massacres in the trenches began and the good times fizzled out. Research into the golden age of plumage in women's wardrobes (but also men's), and the use of feathers plucked from swans, ostriches, herons, peacocks, marabou, capercaillies, birds of paradise, and others, should start from this epoch and from the scenes of the "grands revues," the Moulin Rouge, the Folies Bergères, the theatrical stages and silent film sets. The exhibitionist divas from those years at the turn of the century exaggerated fashions rather than invented them. Milliners created immense constructions topped with ostrich boas, heron, and osprey feathers, and feather-trimmed clothes and shoes proliferated in the pages of D'Annunzio's novels *Il Piacere* and *L'Innocente*, the drawing rooms of the Proustian Guermantes family, the photographs of Count Premoli in Roman society, Toulouse Lautrec's posters for the fashion fortnightly *Revue Blanche*, in snapshots from the stands and enclosures of European racecourses, and in Dudovich's and Metlicovitz's advertisements. It was the prevailing fashion (in London in 1906, 18 kilos of plumage were sold at an exclusive auction for dressmakers and milliners) and the American Ornithologist's Union protested in vain against the annual slaughter of 5 million ostriches and other birds in Burma, Malaysia, Australia, and Indonesia to satisfy the vanity of "Western women." However feathers and plumage were not just for women. Sovereigns and soldiers went crazy for feathers in berets, kepis, helmets, cocked hats, and the various forms of headwear worn as part of a uniform. The Italian King Umberto I wore a cascade of white plumage when he received the German Emperor Wilhelm II in 1888, and the cascade was joined by a stiff plume when he welcomed Menelik's envoy Ras Makkonen to the Palazzo Quirinale, hoping to get a piece of Ethiopia for Italy. The plume, however, brought bad luck. Umberto had to give it up following the Italian defeat at Adua. Another osprey feather brought back luck to Italy: the one worn at parades by Benito Mussolini, who gave his nation an empire "avenging the shame of Adua," but reduced the country to ruins. The Duce was also fond of feathered cocked hats. Power feathered itself, and so did the garçonnes of the 1920s, and the Art Deco women of the 1930s went crazy for ostrich, marabou, and capercaillie. Futurism, with its theories of movement and speed so far removed from the languor of the boa, could not manage to oust the fashion for plumage; neither could the drama of the Great War, or the difficult, restless postwar period. In Paris in 1925 the craze for "negro" culture brought more feather embellishments. If her very pert behind and jiggling belly were not covered by the banana skirt fixed in the collective memory and erotic symbology of three or four generations, Josephine Baker would cheekily cover her modesty with ostrich feather fans and flared skirts of plumage. A few years later, at the beginning of the 1930s, a swan coat catapulted the painter Tamara Lempicka into the fashion spotlight, and in Hollywood the costumier Travis Banton, who was responsible for the all the Paramount stars' outfits, enveloped Mae West in pale blue ostrich feathers for *I'm No Angel* and accentuated Marlene Dietrich's bewitching virtues and sex appeal with furs and plumage in films by Josef von Sternberg. Ernest Lubitsch, the director of *Angel* (1937), created a cylindrical hat overflowing with feathers for Marlene, and following that Balmain made her an ostrich feather and white fox fur cloak. Jean Harlow, Ginger Rogers, and Carol Lombard often wore feathered boas, sleeves and hems, as did the Italian starlet Wanda Osiris: her

Hat with osprey feather, 1911 (Prints Collection A. Bertarelli, Milan).

body rouged to make her look more like a Creole, and adorned with *Coty*'s perfumed roses and an abundance of egret and osprey feathers. The seductive garments worn in exclusive brothels were trimmed with marabou (like the pale blue and pink slippers popular between the wars), heron, and ostrich feathers. Plumage was a continual theme in women's dress and their desire to please, which not even World War II could stop. It may no longer have been the golden age for plumage, but the theme was continually and diligently revisited by creations such as Jacques Fath's white-plumed hat in 1951, Wallis Simpson's ostrich fan, the swan cloak designed by Chino Bert (now a Franciscan monk) for Mila Schön, the colorful boas that complemented the revolutionary Biba styles at the end of the 1960s, Cardin's feather sleeves and scarves, Krizia's swan feather skirts in their Fall-Winter 1991 collection, Romeo Gigli's coats trimmed with bird of paradise feathers, and Stephan Janson's ostrich trimmed coats.

(*Eleonora Attolico*)

Fede Alexandra (1963). Fashion designer. After studying in Oxford and London, she moved to Sidney and then to Singapore, where she had her first experiences in the world of fashion. But it was in Rome, in 1992, that her career really started, when she designed an entire collection of men's ties and accessories for Fausto Sarli. In 1993, she began to do research on new technologies as applied to natural fibers, and in 1996, in collaboration with DuPont, she manufactured button-neck shirts and T-shirts in anti-stain silk and cotton under the brand AX Alexandra Fede. Also in 1996, she moved her atelier to Piazza di Spagna. She devotes herself to high fashion, manufactured with anti-crease fabrics, that are shrink-free in the washing machine. In 1998, she launched Stressless, a yarn containing trilobate carbon, used for total protection from electromagnetic waves and to facilitate the dissipation of electromagnetic fields from the body through a complex process of ionization. Also in 1998, in July, at Alta Moda for the Autumn-Winter 1998-1999 season, she presented her Gold Dress. It was manufactured using Mitsubishi technology that came from the space program, and is in the Guinness Book of World Records. In January 1999, at Pitti Immagine Uomo, she presented her Anti-Violence Collection, made with bullet-proof fabric. In 2001, she received a degree in the Technology of Advanced Fibers in St. Louis, Missouri, and helped further the historic preservation of more than 6,000 costumes from La Scala. In 2002, DuPont asked her to create the BodySculptor collection, for which she used fibers such as Lycra and Tactel, cut in innovative ways. In November 2003, in Paris, she organized the Wear Hi-Tech Fashion Show, an event dedicated to "intelligent" clothing.

(*Valeria Vantaggi*)

Feder Joe. American photographer. He opened a studio in New York sometime around 1910 and created an extraordinary archive for the designer Lucille (Lady Duff-Gordon). He would place his models in front of a white sheet, a common practice at that time.

Federtessile An abbreviation for the Federation of the Associations of the Textile and Clothing Industries. Established in 1975, it addresses common problems on behalf of the entire industry on national and international levels in its relationships with institutions, governments, unions, and various economic, political, social, and cultural organizations. Its task is to protect and promote the interests of the textile and clothing industry in its various components through all the different steps of the production cycle.

Fedora Traditional men's hat made of soft felt with a deep center crease and two side creases, often with a grosgrain ribbon banding the crown. Worn mostly in the early 20th century, the fedora got its name from the play *Fédora* by Victorien Sardou, written in 1882. In popular culture, including film, television shows and comic strips, fedoras were often worn by crime-fighting detectives and newspapermen.

Feet Queen Victoria of Britain would never refer to them, and anyway, at that time they were always carefully hidden under voluminous skirts. By contrast, in recent times a young red-headed bride who had only just fled from a palace of the very same royal court, reminded us of the eroticism of the foot, one of the most enduring fetishes. Chateaubriand's refined, cultured and elegant friend Madame Récamier was shown lying languidly on a sofa wearing a diaphanous white dress, with bare feet. In the 1800s, a slightly bored and very mischievous young lady, wearing one of those house dresses in which she could receive friends, could, while lying in that same position, create an erotic charge by kicking first one and then the other slipper into the air, catching them mid-flight and slipping them back on to start the game over again. This seductive technique, which was recommended by the manuals for the art of pleasure of the time, would never have caught on with Chinese women, who until not so long ago would neither have wished nor been able to carry it out: their feet were tightly bound by bandages so that they would remain tiny and pretty to look at, but they remained hidden and never bared. Men and women agree on the appeal of the small foot, made even tinier by tightly fitting ankle boots, for most of the 1900s, with perhaps the only exception being the fascination for the large feet of Greta Garbo. This standard disappeared with the flat, masochistic shoes worn by the strapping young women at the end of the century: they must have bigger feet now than even the men had at the time of the crinoline. But, these days, deprived of all that blushing18th century interest, bare feet are not even revealed by sandals (the latest fashions has them worn with socks), or gym shoes, or the Chinese slippers that are popular during summer months.

(*Lucia Sollazzo*)

Feith Tracy (1964). American designer. A native of Texas, he belongs to the group of designers of the New Underground Fashion in New York. He studied at an art school in Texas. In 1994, he moved to New York, where he presented his first collection. His work is based on the colors of Latin American ethnic textiles and the combination of precious silks with less valuable fabrics. His clothes, meant for a public from 20 to 40 years old, are on sale all over the world and in his showroom in Nolita ("North of Little Italy") in New York, which opened in late 1998.

Félix A group of photographers whose pictures regularly appeared in fashion magazines during the first decade of the 20th century, especially in Les Modes and The Ladies Field. Their style was very close to that of the Paris studio Reutlinger.

Fella Brand of ready-to-wear by the designer Samia Ben Khalifa, called "the Tunisian Coco Chanel." She created it in 1967 and, two years later, presented her first collection at the Hilton Hotel in Istanbul. She looks at traditions and renews them, using handwoven fabrics. Some 800 artisans work for her. She has a boutique in Tunis and one in Hammamet.

Felt A fabric that is a non-fabric, obtained not through the intertwining of threads, but through the compacting of fibers by various methods. The most common felts are made from wool, in order to exploit its tendency, under special conditions, to become matted. Used for clothing and accessories, felt gave its name to a classic hat, worn by men and women, with an upturned brim and a crown decorated with a grosgrain ribbon. It was a basic accessory from the 1920s on, until hats fell out of favor in the 1970s.

Fémina Historic magazine in the panorama of French women's publications. Created in 1901 as a bimonthly, it later turned into a monthly. From its début, the magazine addressed the issue of the professional emancipation of women, aiming to increase it. It was not by accident that in 1905 the magazine established the *Prix Fémina* for the best book by a female novelist. In the letters section, the magazine urged women to take a stand on social and political issues. Among its contributors were Colette, Man Ray, the illustrators Domergue, Boutet de Movel, and Lepape, and the photographers Gullot, O'Doyé, D'Ora, and Lipnitzki. It ceased publication in 1940, but appeared again, sporadically, in 1945. In 1956, it was relaunched under the name Le Nouveau Fémina, but wouldn't last for long.

(*Mino Colao*)

Femme French monthly. The first issue was published in 1971. It was a glossy review of high fashion. It tried to undermine Vogue's dominance in the field, but failed. The publisher Edilio Rusconi took it over in 1982 and transformed it into a quarterly, expanding the contents to include news and beauty. The graphic design was entrusted to Peter Knapp. Two years later, Rusconi gave up. Group F Magazine took over from him, and Femme returned to being a monthly.

Femme Actuelle French women's large-circulation weekly. By 1990, six years after its launch by the publishing group Prisma Presse, it was already a leader on the European market with a circulation of almost 2 million copies. Its readership consists of women of the low-middle class, and it offers easy-to-read content, practical suggestions, short articles, and fashions that are always practical and not too sophisticated.

Femme d'Aujourd'hui Belgian women's weekly. It was published for the first time in 1933. After World War II, it began to be distributed in France, with increasing success. Its formula is simple: practical columns, cooking, embroidery, and picture stories. In 1977, it absorbed L'Echo de la Mode.

Femme Moquette Italian brand created by two young Sicilian designers, Teresa Litrico, 31, and Annalisa Costa, 30. They met during a presentation in 1997. Their atelier is in Catania. They presented for the first time in Rome, at Palazzo Barberini, during Roma Fashion in January 2003. It was a collection that revealed their passion for artisanal skills, tailoring ability, in-house production, and close contact with dressmakers and embroiderers. The bright, Mediterranean colors of their island, the light and shining fabrics, and the jewellery-like details typical of the goldsmith's tradition in Sicily characterize a basic, consistent style that still knows how to be daring. Every collection features a new material. In 2003, it was georgette with a metal weft; the previous year, cork inlays, and, before that, innovative materials such as copper and rope.

Fendi Italian house of furs and leather goods. The double F was one of the very first brands of the Made in Italy movement to become world famous. The company was established in 1925, in Rome, as a small shop for bags and furs with a workshop next door, on via del Plebiscito. The founders, Edoardo and Adele Fendi, would develop and strengthen their business during the 1930s, but it was the second generation, represented by five sisters, Paola, Anna, Franca, Carla, and Alda, that brought new energy and ideas during the boom years. It was 1964 when Fendi opened its historic boutique in the heart of Rome on via Borgognona. The following year saw the beginning of its collaboration with Lagerfeld, who succeeded Bert and Cruz. It also saw the birth of the double F brand. Interpreting the suggestions of the five sisters, Lagerfeld started the long and laborious process that would lead to a transformation of the very concept of fur. In this way he reinterpreted, redesigned, molded, de-structured, and reinvented a garment that had traditionally been considered pompous, elegant, precious, bulky, and not always easy to wear. Fur was made less dramatic and it acquired softness, self-assurance, wearability, and reversibility. At the same time, the search continued for new materials, treatments, experimental techniques, tanning and dyeing processes, inlays, weaves, stitchings, shearings, and geometric manufacturing as well as the rediscovery of and use of forgotten and overlooked furs, even those considered "poor." In the Fendi interpretation, even the bag, though costly, lost its image of status-symbol and became more functional. Leather was printed, dyed, and woven. The double FFs, in black and brown and immediately recognizable, were combined with stripes and squared patterns. In the 1970s came the *granapaglia*, a type of calfskin worked in a special way with scratches. The *Giano*, *Astrologia*, *Pasta* and *Selleria* lines, all completely handmade and in limited numbers, were created. By 1987, it was the moment of the third generation, which launched the Fendissime line of furs, sportswear, and accessories for a young market. Two years later, the first company-owned store in the U.S. was opened, in New York on Fifth Avenue. After a line of fragrances, the Fendi men's line was created. Meanwhile, the empire of the five sisters enriched itself with numerous licenses, including knitwear, bathing suits, jeans, umbrellas, watches, eyeglasses, ceramics, furnishings, and linens. In total, about twenty licenses, besides furs and leather goods. About 80% of the production is exported. In Italy and abroad there are about a hundred boutiques and 600 points-of-sale, with a turnover of about 600 billion liras, which puts Fendi in fourth place among the brands of Italian prêt-à-porter. Fendi has created theatrical furs for both stage and screen, notably for *Gruppo di Famiglia in un interno* (1974) and *The Innocent* (1976) by Visconti, *La vera storia della Dama delle Camelie* (1980) by Bolognini, *La Traviata* (1983) by Zeffirelli, *Interno Berlinese* (1985) by Liliana Cavani, *Carmen* (1986), *The Age of Innocence* (1993) by Scorsese, and *Evita* (1996) by Parker. In October 1999, after many rumors, the house came under the control of Prada and

Fur coat by Fendi, 1969-1970 Collection.

Bernard Arnault. The management and direction remain in the hands of the Fendi family. In late 1999 Fendi was the target of several would-be acquirers.

(*Laura Laurenzi*)

❑ The third generation is represented by Silvia Venturini Fendi who, supported by Karl Lagerfeld, is responsible for the women's collection, which season after season becomes more and more innovative, always based on research, especially regarding furs, which are the key product of the house, now owned by the LVMH group. For Autumn-Winter 2003-2004, one must remember, for example, the Persian lamb described as "vacuum-sealed" in PVC bubble-wrap, like a package, producing an ice-cold effect that was at the same time radiant ("shining" in the proposal opened to men). Or other very colored furs, worked in a "basket weave." The notebook of inventions includes a fox skin cut in stripes and reassembled using small rubber bands, jackets with hair tufts, and sheared ermines varnished with oil. In addition, a "stuffed," ventilated, and heated fur; inflated, polished shirt-jackets and coats: a playful and transforming luxury that walks in snow boots, by now a part of everyday urban life. Special attention is always paid to accessories: the stars of Summer 2003 were sandals with heels illuminated by blinking lights, like a Christmas tree, together with a large bag inspired by ancient Rome and decorated with silver rostra, called the "Biga Bag."

(*Lucia Mari*)

❑ 2000, July. LVMH, in a joint venture with Prada (LVP Holding), acquires 51% of the business of the Fendi family.
❑ 2001, January. A joint venture with Aoi, for 30 years the distributor of the brand in Japan. The new company, Fendi Japan K:K:, will make its début with the Spring-Summer 2001 collection.
❑ 2001, June. A new Fendi boutique opens in the London neighborhood of Knightsbridge, at 20-22 Sloane Street. It has a raw iron floor, black panels, and brown tables.
❑ Prada sells the shares acquired in July 2000 to LVMH.
❑ 2001, December. The year ends with a loss of €20 million.
❑ 2002, January. The Fendi sisters begin to sell shares to LVMH.
❑ 2002, June. Fendi Uomo, the Spring-Summer 2003 collection, will be produced for the next five years by Ma.co, a factory in Soragna (Parma).
❑ 2003, May. The 67% stake owned by LVMH increases to 84%. Of the five Fendi sisters, the only one with a significant number of shares is Carla.
❑ 2003, May. The exhibit Goddess, at the Costume Institute of the Metropolitan Museum of Art, one of the most prestigious events in New York that spring, displays two dresses donated by the Fendi Archive.
❑ 2005, April. In Rome, the 18th-century palazzo Boncompagni Ludovisi becomes Palazzo Fendi. With its opening, the house celebrates its 80th anniversary.

(*Gabriella Gregorietti*)

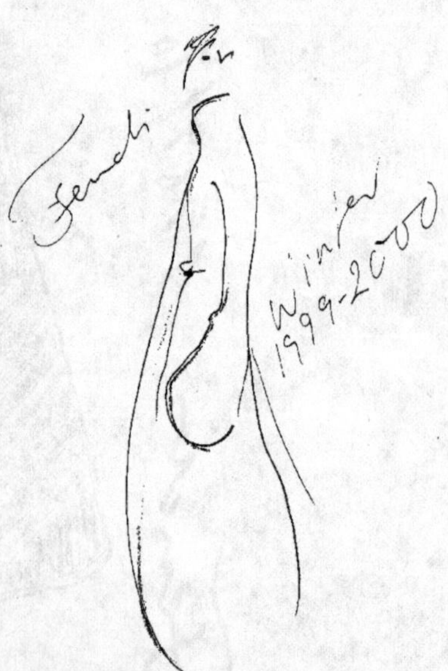

A sketch by Karl Lagerfeld for Fendi. Autumn-Winter 1999-2000 Collection.

Feng Han. Chinese designer born in Hangzou. She works in New York, where she arrived in 1986 without speaking a word of English. Her first job was as a shop assistant in Bloomingdale's. Later, she worked in a textile factory. It was there that she began to create scarves, from remnants of fabric. She sold them to friends and eventually to Barneys and Bergdorf Goodman. One of the buyers sensed her talent and placed an order for a line of shirts. She was launched. In 1993, she presented her first prêt-à-porter collection for women who, like her, live frenetic lives and often don't have a chance to change their clothes for different occasions. She uses strong colors, but simple cuts. Her organza dresses, the layering of fabrics, and the use of silk remind one of Gigli and Miyake. She is a regular at Fashion Week in Manhattan.

❑ 2002, October. She is one of eleven Italian, French and American designers invited to be part of The Fur Show Beijing 2002, organized by Saga Furs of Scandinavia and the International Fur Trade Federation. In the presentation at the Shangri-La Hotel in Beijing she has about 10 furs.

Fenouil Xavier (1978). French designer. Born in Istre, near Marseilles, he moved to Paris after high school in order to pursue his dream of working in the world of fashion. After working with John Galliano, Givenchy, and Christian Lacroix, he decided to create his own men's wear collection. He won an award at Hyères in 1999 and shortly after that his name appeared on the official calendar of Paris Fashion Week. His style is clean, basic, and modern.

Fenzi Andrea. Brand of knitwear. The company was established in Montecchio Maggiore, near Vicenza, by Giuseppe Fenzi. At first, it specialized in men's wear. In winter 1985-86 it made its début with its first women's line. The men's wear designer is Piera Boggiano, while the women's collection is designed by Isabella Francese.

Féraud Louis Eduard (1920-2000). French designer. In 1949, together with his wife Zizi, he opened a boutique in Cannes. It benefited from the attention focused on the Cannes Film Festival. Among his first clients was Brigitte Bardot. Buoyed by his success, he moved to Faubourg Saint-Honoré in Paris in 1960, creating his own line of prêt-à-porter. He often worked for the theatre as a costume designer. In 1978 and 1984 he received the *Dé d'Or*.

❑ 2000, June. The Féraud *griffe* presents its new models during the Paris High Fashion Week. The collection is by the new designer Yvan Mispelaere, a former assistant to Valentino and Miuccia Prada.
❑ 2002, June. Financial crisis; the presentation for July 2002 is canceled. A joint venture with Seccon-Groupe, Escada, and Michael Rover of the Kemper company.
❑ 2002, July. The brand is ready for its relaunch with haute couture and prêt-à-porter collections created by a new designer, Jean-Paul Knott, a Belgian (1966), who is under contract for three years. This young designer had already worked for Saint-Laurent and Krizia before launching his own line.
❑ 2003. The prêt-à-porter, presented the previous year, is replaced by two new lines: Louis Féraud (ready-to-wear) and Féraud Club (sportswear). Féraud GmbH, whose headquarters is in Germany, controls the brand internationally, and has a turnover of €44 million.
❑ 2003, March. Jean-Paul Knott leaves the *maison* before the contract is up, and the Belgian Matthias Heitzler becomes the new designer.

Fercioni Giovanni (1886-1961). Italian tailor and owner of a famous high fashion tailoring shop in Milan. The son of an employee of the Royal House of Savoy at the estate in San Rossore, he had cultivated his style of dress ever since childhood, when he had become fascinated by the elegant yet casual clothes that the Royal family and its guests would wear when hunting. He applied his first stitches to the red jackets worn by the princes during the hunt. By 1906, he was in Milan working in a men's tailoring shop and he became an expert in the manufacture of tailcoats and tuxedos. In 1910 he opened his first atelier. Among his clients were famous personalities of journalism and show business, from Renato Simoni to Nicola Zingarelli and Adolfo Cotronei. It was Simoni, the theater critic of the Corriere della Sera, who convinced him to devote himself to women's fashion, sending him his first clients. He started with tailored suits, went on to evening dresses embroidered with crepe georgette, and then to the great evening and wedding dresses that would become his specialty. Maria Pezzi, in her autobiography *Una vita dentro la moda* ('A Life Inside Fashion') says, "It was 1924. I was 16. At the time, a very romantic comedy was all the rage: *L'alba, il giorno e la notte*, with Dario Niccodemi. With three acts and just two characters, it was performed by Vera Vergani and Luigi Cimara. Vera would wear a Fercioni dress, a very short sleeveless *fourreau* in white *marocain* with a very deep V-neck in front and back, with a short flared robe on the hips and everything framed by an edging of silver straw. It was so beautiful, so fantastic." He dressed actresses such as Marta Abba, Elsa Merlini (he created her costumes for the film *La segretaria privata*, 1931), and Isa Miranda, both on stage and off. His extraordinary talent was documented in drawings by Dudovich in 1910, Sacchetti in 1920, Ester Sormani in 1930, Grau and Pallavicini in 1949 (for Bellezza magazine), and, in the 1950s, by Maria Pezzi. It is a history of style told by the best fashion illustrators. In 1952, he was invited, with the tailors and designers of the new generation, to represent the emerging Italian fashion industry in New York. His model was Luciana Angiolillo. Elsa Martinelli also wore his clothes in the 1950s. In 1960, Fercioni celebrated 60 years in business with a great party. After his death, his sons Aldo and Ruggero continued their father's work and moved the firm's headquarters from Corso Matteotti to via Santo Spirito, near Palazzo Bagatti Valsecchi. They closed the firm in 1973. Fercioni's grandson, Gian Maurizio Fercioni, is a theater costume designer.

Fernandez Kina. Spanish designer, born in Galicia. She arrived in Paris at a very young age and her curiosity pushed her towards the world of fashion.After she completed her professional education, she returned to Spain and decided to settle in La Coruña, where she began to design and manufacture her collections. In 1979, she established a clothing manufacturing company which caused her to look for new technologies as a way to add more style and quality to the collections. To help reach this goal, she chose a team of extremely skilled and qualified people.

Cocktail dress from the Kina Fernandez Collection.

Ferragamo Fiamma (1941-1998). The daughter of Salvatore, the great shoe designer, Fiamma di San Giuliano Ferragamo started working alongside her father at a very young age. For several years after his death, she was the designer of the firm. She was the oldest of six children. Kind, generous, and always available to others,, she was a great lady in a fashion world that in its customary self-involvement resembled her not at all. She was until the last moment a fundamental point of reference for everything that had to do with taste, selection, and the national and international relationships of Ferragamo. Just by meeting her one understood how intensely she identified herself with the goal of promoting the brand name of the family, which found in her the perfect and spontaneous symbol of a discreet and serene elegance that was beyond the merely fashionable.

Ferragamo Salvatore (1898-1960). Italian shoemaker, the most famous in the world. The 11th of 14 children, he was born in Bonito, a small village about 160 miles from Naples, from which emigration to America was often a necessity. Already at the age of 9, in just one night, little Salvatore, who left school in the third grade, created his first pair of shoes (with white cardboard) for a sister's first Holy Communion. He had clear ideas and wanted to become a shoemaker. His parents, despite their poverty, were not happy with his choice: in southern Italy a shoemaker is one of the humblest professions. But Salvatore, at 11, was an apprentice in Luigi Festa's workshop in Bonito and by the age of 13 he had his own shop where he began to create women's shoes. It was a workshop located at home in a space between the front door and the kitchen, with the shop window facing a church, and five workers of whom the oldest was 18. Then, in 1914, came the big leap: the ship *Stampalia*, emigration, and the United States. His brothers were already there: Girolamo was a tailor, Secondino a carpenter, and Alfonso ironed clothes in the tailor's shop of the American Film Company in Santa Barbara. But in Boston, his brother-in-law Joseph Covelli had already found him a job at the Queen Quality Shoes Company: thousands of shoes a day, soles and heels in half a second, one minute for sewing. Anyone else would have thanked God for such a job, but not the very young Salvatore, who had a more noble idea of the shoemaker's profession. He really couldn't stand those machines. They made shoes that were "heavy, clumsy, and squat, with a toe shaped like a potato and a leaden heel." He left the factory, joined his brothers in Santa Barbara, and convinced them to pool their small savings and invest in a shoe repair shop. As told in his autobiography *Il calzolaio dei sogni* ('The Shoemaker of Dreams,' Sansoni), which has a portrait of him painted by Piero Annigoni on the cover, Salvatore immediately understood that California, with its fast-growing film industry, would be the Promised Land. In fact, he wouldn't just repair shoes. The property man at the American Film Company would complain about the boots worn in the westerns: if they were easy to wear, the styling was no good; if the style was attractive, they hurt the feet of the actors. Ferragamo offered his services and produced some boots. The director Cecil B. De Mille would say: "We would have won the West sooner if we had had your boots." It was the definitive consecration. The biggest stars visited his boutique. The very first was Mary Pickford. The first original Ferragamo model was created for her in brown kidskin, "with two ears standing up in front." All of a sudden it seemed that the stars of the pioneering years of cinema in Santa Barbara, and of the Hollywood boom (Ferragamo had followed the studios when, for fiscal reasons, they moved to Hollywood, opening a boutique between Hollywood Boulevard and Las Palmas Boulevard), would feel like stars only if they were wearing shoes made by "the Italian shoemaker," "the shoemaker to the stars." It was 1923, and in Hollywood the future of this giant of what would later be called the Made in Italy movement was being decided. He created pale lavender sandals for Jean Harlow, cork-shaped heels for Gloria Swanson, slippers in multicolored satin for Lillian Gish, and loafers for both Douglas Fairbanks and Rudolf Valentino. He would use the strangest materials, including crystal, embroidery, feathers, kangaroo, antelope, sea leopard, and fish skins. He was a success also due to the comfort of his shoes. He studied the anatomy of the foot and patented a system of putting thin

A Ferragamo model in crocodile.

layers of steel in the sole of the shoe in order to provide arch support. His fame grew and with it his ambition. He returned to Italy, to Florence, in search of good artisans and opened his first workshop there in 1927, with 60 workers. Then came the financial crisis of 1929 and bankruptcy. But Ferragamo didn't despair, and made a comeback. Maria José walked to the altar wearing his shoes. Mussolini, who suffered from corns and chilblains, wore his boots. The Maharani of Cooch Behar came and ordered 100 pair. From New York, Paris, and London came the ladies who wear Chanel and Schiaparelli. The national policy of self-sufficiency, known as the Autarchy, and the scarcity of materials, fed his talent for new inventions. For evening sandals, he invented an upper in transparent paper. Steel for arch supports was by now of poor quality, so he created the most extraordinary, mythic shoe of the century, an orthopedic model which was a platform shoe, with a cork heel, that filled in the entire space formed by the arch of the foot. The model was a success, sold everywhere, was copied, and then was copied again. It marked a new era and immediately became a symbol of the times and of that style. In 1938, in installments, he acquired the Palazzo Spini Feroni on via Tornabuoni, which is today still the headquarters of the company. In that same year, he acquired the Michelangelo-style villa Il Palagio in Fiesole. Salvatore was now ready for the big step: in 1940 he married Wanda Miletti, a 20 year-old girl from his hometown who was the daughter of the local doctor and mayor. She would be the mother of his six children: Fiamma (died in 1998), Ferruccio, Giovanna, Fulvia, Leonardo, and Massimo, all of whom worked in important positions in the company after the premature death of their father in 1960. Salvatore left behind a company which was the symbol of creative and productive Italy: 20,000 models and 350 patents. An infinite number of models mark different epochs, times, and fashions: shoes that bewitched Greta Garbo, the Duke and Duchess of Windsor, Sophia Loren, Anna Magnani, Audrey Hepburn, and Marilyn Monroe, as well as many aristocrats and heads of state; the French toe, the platform heel, the stage toe, the Roman sandal, the shell model, the invisible nylon model, and the sculpted heel, shaped like the prow of a battleship. Salvatore left a business that his heirs have carried forward, always remaining faithful to his professional standards and not just defending the status quo. During the 1970s, thanks to the initiative and preparation of Wanda (the president of the company), the brand went

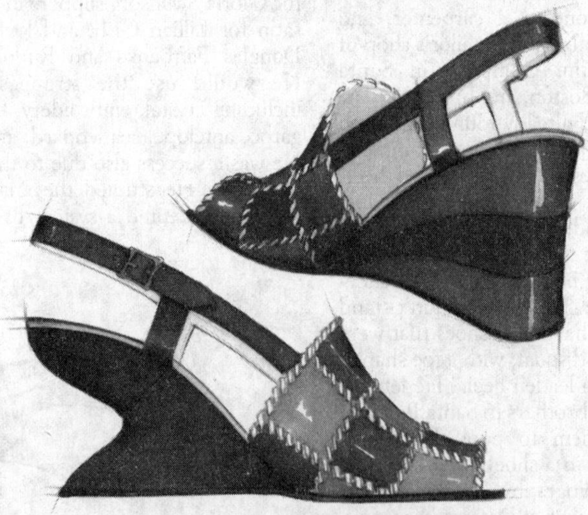

Platform sandals by Ferragamo (1940s).

from offering only shoes to the presentation of a total look, with fashion collections, men's lines, perfumes, and eyeglasses, all of which gradually conquered the market. In July 1996, Ferragamo acquired Emanuel Ungaro. In 1998, the turnover was 850 billion liras, most of which came from 38 different countries, from Europe to the U.S., the Far East, Africa, and Oceania. Ferragamo has 40 privately owned boutiques plus several exclusive points-of-sale. Besides Salvatore's children, several grandchildren also work in the company. Following the birth of the Salvatore Ferragamo Museum (in Palazzo Spini Feroni), the company has committed itself to art exhibits and cultural activities, and not just as a sponsor or patron. (*Eva Desiderio*)

❑ 1999. The French designer Marc Audibet creates the new Autumn-Winter 2000-2001 collection.
❑ The collection for Winter 2003-2004, to which the designer Graeme Black has contributed, experiments with shapes, volumes, and combinations. It interprets with common sense colors and references inspired by the Russia of St. Petersburg, recalling Constructivist art and a certain nostalgia for decadent opulence and taste reinterpreted in a very modern way. There were precious fabrics and ornaments, brocades, inlays with strong visual impact, and irreverent combinations such as a crocodile jacket with jeans. The accessories included cartoon-like floral and mother-of-pearl-covered platform shoes (they would have pleased even Salvatore, the founder) as well as incredible bags made of snake-skin decorated with small silver coins. (*Lucia Mari*)

❑ 2001, May. Leonardo Ferragamo becomes president of Altagamma, an association founded in 1992 with 43 prestigious Italian companies as members.
❑ A new store opens in Korea, in a prestigious commercial area of Seoul. The store occupies a four-storey building with a garden-terrace on the roof. It is part of the company's world-wide expansion plans which include the renovation of various sales points in a more sophisticated architectural style by the end of 2002, and new stores in New York, Tokyo, and London in 2003.
❑ 2002, June. A joint venture with Ermenegildo Zegna for the launch of the new brand ZeFer.
❑ 2002, October. Wanda Ferragamo, the president of the company, is named "Woman Entrepreneur of the Year" by the "Committee of 200," an organization that each year recognizes the top women managers and entrepreneurs all over the world. The ceremony takes place in New York. The citation: "For success in the transformation of a shoe factory into an international luxury concern, in which the family maintains total control of its own flourishing business..."
❑ 2002. Ferragamo is acknowledged as the best brand of the year in China. Asia is the continent where the *griffe* sells the most. Of the consolidated revenues of €641.1 million for 2001, about 46% comes from the Far East.
❑ 2002, December. In the historic center of Vienna, near the Hofburg castle, the brand opens a new store and continues its world-wide expansion program. In the course of 2003, new stores will be opened in Paris, on Avenue Montaigne; in New York, on Fifth Avenue; in Amsterdam; and in Tokyo, in the Ginza Chou Dori. Other boutiques will also be opened, or restyled, for a total of 100. The plans are all by the architect Michael Gabellini.
❑ Sales in Japan increase. Ferragamo has 20% of its turnover there. A new flagship is opened in the heart of one of Tokyo's most fashionable neighborhoods.
❑ 2003, May. Their name is Maharani and they are inspired by the celebrated jewelled-sandal created in far off 1938 for the Maharani of Cooch Behar: they are Ferragamo's very latest sunglasses. (*Gabriella Gregorietti*)

❑ 2004. Wanda Ferragamo is named Knight of the Big Cross by the president of Italy. The Salvatore Ferragamo group ends the year with a consolidated turnover of €549 million, an increase of 5% compared to 2003. The distribution network has 16 new points-of-sale, among which are important new boutiques in Osaka and Hong Kong (Pacific Place). Stores in Shanghai Center (China), Paris (Avenue Montaigne), and Milan (via Montenapoleone) are re-opened with a new concept.

❑ 2005, May. As part of the Fashion Project of the Province of Florence, with attendance by a large international public, Palazzo Strozzi hosts the fashion show of the historic *maison* Ferragamo, in a memorable evening organized by Beppe Modenese.

❑ 2005, June. A long-term agreement is signed between the Porsche Design group and Ferragamo Finanziaria. It foresees the production and distribution of shoes, bags, and leather accessories.

❑ 2006. The new symbol print of the season is GRIFFE, used in the entire range of products: silk shawls and scarves, small evening bags, and gloves' hems. Used in precious materials for shoes and bags, it plays a main role in the jewellery collection as well.

(*Maria Vittoria Alfonsi*)

Ferrante Aldo (1928). Fashion entrepreneur and talent scout. He started his career in the 1950s, selling corsets and bras, later working as a tie salesman and then for Magnaghi knitwear. His big chance came in 1960 after a meeting with Mariuccia Mandelli, who put him in charge of the agency for Krizia in south Italy. In 1967, together with Gigi Monti and Franco Tositti, he established FTM, a new sales method which concentrated in one prestigious showroom on via della Spiga in Milan all the most beautiful and current *griffes*, including Missoni, Montedoro, De Parisini, Caumont, Cerruti, and Callaghan, as well as some French houses. In 1970, the decision was made to coordinate, under the name of the young Walter Albini, the collections of some of the *griffes* in his portfolio. The collective presentation (Basile, Misterfox, Callaghan, Escargot, Diamand's), which was innovative and sensational, and held at the Circolo del Giardino in Milan, confirmed Albini's genius and Ferrante's intuition. Three years later, Albini started his own business. Ferrante then called on other young designers, including Muriel Grateau for Basile (which he owned) and a very young Gianni Versace for Callaghan. These were exciting years in which Italian prêt-à-porter was taking its first steps with Ferrante holding it by the hand. A path which he continued to walk with great care, collecting prestigious brands and always paying attention to changes in costume and the market.

Ferrari Madina. Italian entrepreneur. After her study of art and ten years spent in the theater as an assistant director, she married her second husband Dario Ferrari, the owner of Intercos, a company that manufactured cosmetics for large multinational corporations. Her own business was the result of a challenge, almost in fun. She decided to have her own business in order to be in "competition" with her husband, and thus created a new line of cosmetics. Success was immediate and today the Madina Milano brand has three stores: one in New York, in the heart of Soho; one in Tokyo; and, of course, one in Milan. The next store will be in Paris. The line has more than 1,800 products, including eye shadows, glosses, powders, lipsticks, and brushes, with three or four new ones added every month.

(*Gabriella Gregorietti*)

Ferrari Marina (1951). Italian designer of American origin. The brother of her father Igor was Oleg Cassini, one of the most famous tailors in the history of American fashion. Love brought her to Milan, where she married. In 1968, along with her husband and her father, she took over a manufacturing company and produced clothes under the Oleg Cassini brand. Eight years later, she separated from her family and the name Cassini, creating her own collection and presenting it in Milan.

Ferrario Haute-couture atelier in Milan, active between the two world wars and immediately after. As to reputation and quality, it was one of the great names, immediately after Fercioni and Gandini and alongside Moro and Giunta (a real Milanese dressmaker, very traditional: she served the solid, reserved bourgeoisie with everything from trousseaus to wedding dresses and tailored suits to evening gowns. It was of French inspiration, as one said in those days, and would purchase patterns and samples directly from the celebrated Parisian *maisons* or from the so-called model makers and then reproduce them many times and in different fabrics, adjusting the garment to the taste or the size of this or that lady. The atelier was on via Montenapoleone. It had a large clientele, probably not from the nobility, but rich. After the death of the owner, his daughter continued the business for some time.

Ferraro Franco (1940). Italian designer, born in Vercelli. After several years working with important fashion houses such as Agnona, Givenchy, and Dior, he established his own company in Serravalle Sesia in 1975, and named it Child. He also launched two lines (the second one in 1985) for men and women. He exports 95% of his production, especially to Japan, where in 1997 he signed a license agreement for his men's collection with the Fukusuke group.

Ferré Gianfranco (1944). Italian designer. An "Architect of Fashion" is what he has been called, and that is what he actually is, not only in the academic sense, because he graduated from the Polytechnic of Milan in 1969, but also for having worked out, as did Krizia, Missoni, and Armani, that style so close to industrial design and planning which is a characteristic of Italian prêt-à-porter. "I'm very proud of my education as an architect, of the analytic and logical method which teaches one how to be creative, but I also try not to fall into the trap of the overly-structured or of abstract simplification," he says. He has always been proud of his provincial and middle-class origins. Born in Legnano, a small town in hard-working Lombardy, to a family of small industrialists, he has never cut himself off from his roots: when he's not traveling around the world, he returns every night to his father's house, a small villa from the early 1900s. It is the mirror of his life and personality, and the place where he stores his memories and collections, including paintings of contemporary art and singular objects found during his travels, often in local antique markets, such as tie pins, which have become his trade mark. He has also been called the "Gran Lombardo," or "the Big Man from Lombardy," due to his powerful physique, and he is flattered by this because it expresses his perseverance, his capacity for work, and also his pleasure in daily routines and his taste for the things that he turns into fashion. These materials are the source of his best intuitions, such as the white shirt, a basic element of a man's wardrobe, that was transformed into an instrument of seduction, female power, and pleasure. It is also seen in his choice of fabrics, in the different cuts (floating like a sail in the wind, shaped to the body, or even in a stretch and wafer-thin fabric), and in his invitation to a richer and more sophisticated expressiveness in the design of cuffs and collars. His attention to refined, cultivated and often opulent details began long ago, with his first work experiences and his stays

Gianfranco Ferré. Collection 1999-2000.

in India, which were fundamental to his education. He started his career designing belts and jewellery and worked with Albini in the early 1970s. At that time, he began life as a commuter, and this was the rhythm of his university years, with a continued back-and-forth between Legnano and Milan. He would leave at dawn for Genoa by train, in order to design, starting in 1972, for the raincoat company Sangiorgio. This taught him the rules of industrial manufacturing. On the train, he would meet the two people most important to him in his career: Rita Airaghi, from Legnano, a distant cousin with a degree in Italian literature and medieval Latin, who would become his alter ego; and Franco Mattioli, a clothing entrepreneur from Bologna who would be his business partner for 25 years, from 1974 to 1999. In 1978, together with Mattioli, he established Gianfranco Ferré S.p.a. That year he also presented his first women's prêt-à-porter collection under his own name, at the Grand Hotel Principe di Savoia in Milan (he made his début with a men's collection in 1982). It was an international success and the start of a brilliant career. "Ferré has kept astonishing us for 20 years," the American journalist Dawn Mello wrote in Vogue Italy in October 1998. "His début collection showed the first minimalist style: clean, simple lines for a refined sportswear. As Dior's couturier, he developed a rich and voluptuous style that was admired for its elegance and spectacular nature. Today he enters the new millennium with a strong and specific vision that is deeply connected to his architectural education." Much discussed, especially in chauvinistic terms, was his selection in 1989 by Bernard Arnault, the leader of the LVMH group, to take the place of Marc Bohan as artistic director of Dior. By 1986, Ferré had made his début on the Italian high fashion runways in Rome, showing his tailoring ability through the cut and in the line of his clothes, in a dream-like vision of dressing and the wise use of materials, even unusual ones, borrowed from design, like straw from Vienna. "The Paris experience was really unique and was intended to restore haute couture and the house of Dior to their proper roles," the designer said in a 1997 interview with Panorama, speaking about his consensual divorce from the French *maison*. "After

Gianfranco Ferré. Autumn-Winter 1981-82.

eight years it was time to devote myself to my own company, also because I felt a growing sense of expectation on the part of the public that likes my style. Through this adventure, I have realized that certain things belong just to me. Because, after all, I did create some milestones in fashion, for example the use of the nude in 1988, nylon, and see-throughs." Once back at his company full time, in his studio on via della Spiga in Milan, Ferré followed from up close the work on his new headquarters in the former Gondrand building on via Pontaccio, near the Brera. It was 78,000 square feet and opened in October 1998, showing the new face of the Ferré brand, with eight lines of clothing and accessories. The turnover in 1997 was 1,400 billion liras, of which 75% was exported. Of that, 40% went to the U.S. and Japan. The firm has more than 400 stores for fashions and accessories, including proprietary shops and franchises. There is a license for perfumes with Diana de Silva. In 1997, the designer strengthened his relationship with his manufacturing partners, including Itierre from Isernia, a producer and distributor of jeans and sportswear, and the Marzotto group. He had been working with Marzotto since 1987, designing the G.F. Studio and GFF men's and women's collections. Since 1987, he has designed fur collections produced and distributed by Mondialpelli. Furs and leather are among the materials that interest him the most. In 1995, Ferré was the subject of a biography written by the journalist Edgarda Ferri and published by Longanesi.

(*Maria Vittoria Carloni*)

❑ Gianfranco Ferré, or the excellence of style. Again, forever, and more. His skill is sublime: cultivated and refined, he continues to create clothes for cultivated and refined women. The common denominator of every collection, which can be seen again and again, is that magic variety of interventions and alchemies performed on matter, of unusual assonances: the attention is focused on research, cutting, and structure, on the wise use of fabrics, especially on their manufacture. The bustier with small bone inlays sewn with raffia became a cult fashion; as did silk that wrapped the figure and became a sort of asymmetric tunic, a light cloth with soft draping; and cloth cut in small superimposed rectangles for unique models which seemed to take off. Unforgettable and incredible was the weaving motif shown in Winter 2002-2003: ermine, chinchilla, cashmere, even organza and taffetas, all knitted using ancient methods of sock manufacture. He is inspired by the world of emotions, sensations for a look that is enlivened by the exchange of different and far off cultures: an explorer of a very wide cultural and costume heritage, and then his willingness – a sophisticated divertissement – to pick an era to dress. This is how, for Winter 2003-2004, he proposed the Bonaparte "citizen": dresses which look like columns, with very uplifted breasts that emphasize the neckline à la Pauline Borghese, alternating with very luxurious superstar punk stud jackets, in a waterfall of small chains and delicate cameos. An ancient and at the same time modern preciousness, which matches precise forms and eccentric designs, even in accessories: the bags, in pony skin and snake skin, have a scepter-shaped handle made of real silver. For men, Ferré prefers the more classic typologies of urban dressing, with the ease of a casual spirit: his *griffe* is at the center of global plans to offer a new, complete identity, worked out in the Milan headquarters with great attention to the different production and distribution needs of It Holding.

(*Lucia Mari*)

❑ 2000, June. The donation of more than 32 models chosen from among the most representative of this career to the Costume Gallery of Palazzo Pitti.
❑ 2000. The new GF line for children, produced by Valtib.
❑ 2001, October. He arrives in Miami and chooses to open his boutique in the prestigious neighborhood of Bal Harbour Shops, on the other side of Miami Beach. Opened in 1965, this architectural complex has the most famous haute couture boutiques.
❑ 2002, March. It Holding, a company owned by the Molise entrepreneur Tonino Perna, acquires 90% of Gianfranco Ferré S.p.a. The transaction is to be completed within the month of June for a sum of €161.7 million. Ferré has 10% of the shares and the position of President.
❑ 2002, May. "Look to the future," this is the motto of the new GF Ferré collection for young people. It takes the place of the GFF and Ferré Jeans brands, and makes its début at Milano Moda Uomo in June 2002. Inspired by urban life, it is completed with a line of accessories (bags, eyeglasses, shoes, and beachwear). The clothing is manufactured by Itierre, the accessories by other firms belonging to the It Holding group owned by Tonino Perna.
❑ 2002, May. Design by Ferré's and technology by Allison: Pure Magnesium is the name for a new model of eyeglasses made from 92% pure magnesium. Very light, non-allergic, and resistant to atmospheric agents, it is produced in four versions.
❑ 2002, November. Ferré and It Holding agree to bring all licenses within the group. This decision should raise the turnover by 50%. Ferré produced only the first line in house, the others were manufactured on license. At the expiration of the contracts, the lines produced by Marzotto (men's and women's clothing) go to ITC (Bologna),

the eyewear to Allison (Padua), the perfumes to ITF (Lodi), the shoes, bags, and leather accessories to PAF (a new company near Florence which for the men's line at first relies on Mantelassi), and Jeans Couture to Itierre (Isernia). For men's clothing, in cooperation with Saint Andrew's (Cantarelli Group) the "custom made" program is relaunched.
❑ 2003, January. With the new year, an intense 2-year program of new shops and the renovation of already-existing shops is put into effect. The first is in Paris, at Avenue Montaigne 51, and celebrated by the presentation of a collection at the Galerie Nationale du Jeu de Paume.
❑ 2003, February. The most important shop, the one in Milan on via Sant'Andrea, is reopened, completely renovated. The architect Ferré personally follows the work. Enlarged to 5,000 square feet on two levels, it has men's and women's collections in two symmetrical areas near the entrance to the building, which was once the site of Biki's atelier. On the left is the men's space, on the right the women's, linked by a common hall. The real novelty is the creation, together with E'Spa, of another attraction: the refined Spa at Gianfranco Ferré, an oasis of relaxation dedicated to fitness and well-being.
❑ 2003, April. The design of eyeglasses continues: after magnesium, it is now the turn of 18 carat gold, combined and fused with titanium. A high-tech essential, with daylight lenses, and very precious.
❑ 2004, July. He presents the new young fragrances GF Ferré Lei and GF Ferré Lui in Paris.
❑ 2004, September. He receives a career award, the "Chi è Chi del Giornalismo e della Moda" ('Who's Who of Journalism and Fashion'), and an acknowledgment from the Region of Lombardy as the "fashion creator who has developed a style similar to design and industrial planning, turning personal talent into an entrepreneurial reality."
❑ 2005, February. During a gala at La Scala in Milan, he is given the "Longobard Seal," conferred on people from Lombardy who "in their respective fields have contributed to enrich the cultural, civil, and artistic heritage of the region."
❑ 2005, March. He designs new uniforms for Korean Air. They are presented in Seoul: blue for pilots and black for ground personnel, made lighter with beige and sea-blue green and light blue *celadon*.
❑ 2005, July. At the request of Fashion in Motion, he presents 60 pieces during a show at the Victoria and Albert Museum in London.

(*Maria Vittoria Alfonsi*)

Ferrer Josep (1929). Spanish designer (and brand of prêt-à-porter). He continued a family tradition, as his mother had a corsetry shop. A leader and supporter of many innovations in fashion during the 1960s, he started his own business in 1959, opening a boutique in Barcelona. Ferrer would give free rein to his inventiveness, above all in his numerous variations on the pantsuit. In 1970, in Florence, he successfully presented his collection at Pitti Moda. During the 1980s, the lessening of his creative spirit led to the brand's decline.

Ferrera Marella (1960). Italian designer. She attended the Academy of Fashion and Costume in Rome, but began her work in Catania, in the atelier that her parents opened in 1958. Since 1992 she has been part of the National Chamber of Italian Fashion, and her haute couture début took place in Rome in 1993. Although her clothes are very dressy, her style is characterized by used materials, including lava stones, shells, gold and rock crystal, papyrus, and terracotta. Known for her sumptuous formal clothes, including wedding dresses, since 1999 she has also produced a beachwear line. (*Laura Salza*)

Ferretti Alberta (1950). Italian designer, born in Romagna. In her mother's large dressmaker's shop, at a very young age, she refined her taste for precious fabrics, sophisticated color combinations, and accurate manufacturing, which are today still her trademarks. Animated by an innate aesthetic sense, an indisputable talent for fashion, and great initiative and determination, at the age of 18 she opened a boutique in Cattolica. It was an experience that allowed her to understand the varied universe of women and consumer trends. In 1974 she decided to design and produce her first collection. It was a success. But six years would pass – she's a woman of great imagination, but very practical, especially in business – before she decided to establish Aeffe, which she named using her initials (A.F. – A – effe, in Italian). The following year, in 1981, she presented her collection for the first time in Milan. Little by little, the company expanded and began to produce collections for some of the top names in prêt-à-porter: Moschino in 1983, Ozbek in 1988, Gualtier in 1994, and Rodriguez in 1997. The designer, who by 1984 had already diversified her offerings with Philosophy by Alberta Ferretti, a line aimed at a younger public, then left the financial management and distribution to her brother Massimo. She devoted herself to tasks more strictly linked to the creative process, producing work more and more characterized by clean, basic lines, and precious but light decorations and embroidery: a tribute to femininity, from clothes to accessories. Sensitive and attentive to the cultural phenomena of contemporary society, which she expresses and transforms through fashion, she is also a passionate expert on the historical and artistic heritage of Italy. In 1994, in fact, with several other companies, she promoted the restoration of the medieval village of Montegridolfo, which is now a tourist resort, a tiny oasis of relaxation between the Marche and Romagna. Aeffe had 580 employees and a turnover of 227 billion liras in 1998. In November 1999 it acquired Moonshadow, a company that controls the Moschino brand, whose production, since its début in 1983, has always been carried out by the company from Romagna. (*Anna Gloria Forti*)

❑ 2003, April. Alberta Ferretti is invited by Pier Luigi Calzolari, the rector of the University of Bologna, to give a master class on "Production and Culture of Fashion."

Ferri Edgarda (1934). Journalist and writer. She is the author of the book *Ferré* published by Longanesi in 1995. A news reporter who also covered crime stories, she was a war correspondent as well. During the 1970s and 1980s she followed fashion for Il Corriere d'Informazione and other newspapers, witnessing the birth of Armani, Versace, and Ferré, whose biography she would later write. With Rizzoli, she published *Contro il padre* (1983), *La tentazione di credere* (1985), and *Il perdono e la memoria* (1988); with Mondadori, *Maria Teresa* (1994), *Giovanna la Pazza* (1996), *Io, Caterina* (1997) and *Per Amore* (1998). Other books include *L'ebrea errante* (2000), *Piero della Francesca* (2001), *La gran contessa* (2002), and *Letizia Bonaparte* (2003).

Ferri Fabrizio (1952). Italian photographer. A student of the classics and a lover of music, he was born into a family of intellectuals that belonged to the historic Roman Left. At the age of 19 he became interested in photography almost by chance, with the portrait of a father and daughter taken during a public demonstration and published as a kind of photo-icon by the newspaper Paese Sera. The experience fascinated him. After working as a reporter on culture and politics for L'Epresso, Il Messaggero, and L'Unità, he turned to fashion photography and immediately began to work with major Italian newspapers, Linea Italiana, Vogue, and Mondo Uomo. His fashion photos are neither affected nor artificial: they are true portraits of women whose souls it seems he wants to uncover, and for whom clothing is seen as a complement to the personality. These photos are different from those in fashion during the 1980s: they attract for their mixture of sensuality, simplicity, and intensity, and they allowed him to make a name for himself as one of the most interesting and requested Italian photographers of the new generation. Open, curious, indefatigable, enthusiastic, and a leader, in the wake of his sudden success he became an entrepreneur, musician, writer, and director. In 1984, with Flavio Lucchini, he transformed a group of sheds that were part of a warehouse at the railway station at Porta Genova in Milan into Superstudio, with 70,000 square feet the largest photographic studio complex in Europe, and an important point of reference for fashion photography. In 1988, the company split into Superstudio 13 and Industria Studio. In the years that followed, additional initiatives were launched, including Industria Superstudio Overseas, with 50,000 square feet of studios in Greenwich Village, New York, a clothing line called Industria, and a school, the University of the Image, concerned multi-sensory perception. Fabrizio Ferri loves to astonish: he composes soundtracks for movies and TV screenplays. He wrote a short story – *Discrete avventure di Vito Zuccheretti, uomo comune* – and makes TV commercials and videos. One of these was the short film *Prelude*, entered at the Venice Film Festival in 1998 and later part of a trilogy with *Aria* and *Carmen* which won the *RAI Star Digital Show* award in 2001. He promotes campaigns that are always dominated by his minimalist style, such as the one for Blunauta in 2002. He has published several photographic books, including *Aria* (1997), the first book completely produced with a digital camera, dedicated to his partner in life, the ballet star Alessandra Ferri. Other include *Open Eyes*, *Acqua* and, in 2000, *Forma*. He lives between New York, Milan, and the island of Pantelleria.

Ferronière Women's jewellery worn on the forehead. In fashion during the 15th century, the precious stone, shaped like a teardrop, could be supported by a thin silk cord or mounted on a thin ring of gold or silver. The painting *Lady with an Ermine* by Leonardo da Vinci has a wonderful example of this.

Feruch Gilbert (1924). Parisian tailor, born in Oran, Algeria. Starting in the 1950s he dressed painters and artists such as Arman, Klein, and Fautrier. He was the first to launch a collar à la Mao Ze Dong in a tailored version.

Feurer Hans (1930). Swiss photographer. During the 1950s, before making his début as an illustrator, commercial artist, and shop window decorator, he attended a school for graphic arts in Zurich. From 1963 to '66 he lived in London and worked as a creative director for several advertising agencies and for the magazine Telegraph. Between 1966 and '67 he was in Africa. On his return, he began to work as a fashion photographer, first in London and then, starting in 1972, in Paris. He worked with Nova, Twen, Elle, Vogue (England, France, Italy, U.S), and Marie Claire. In 1977, he did the Pirelli calendar.

Fez Hat in the shape of a truncated cone, in the center of which at the top a long cord with a tassel on the end is attached. The name comes from Fez, a city in Morocco where it was manufactured and from which it was exported. It is worn especially in the Middle East. Similar to the fez is the Turkish tarbush, dark red and cylindrical in shape. Decorated with tassels and cords, Muslim Turks wear it instead of the traditional skullcap.

Fezza Andrew (1955). American designer. Even though he started his career in the late 1970s designing women's wear, he is considered especially a creator of men's fashion. With a very personal style, in which the soft silhouette of every garment is combined with an experiment in unusual materials, he also shows the influence of Armani.

Fiber A material that can be spun into yarn in different ways. In the clothing-textile field, fibers can be of animal origin (wool, silk, hair), vegetable origin (hemp, jute, linen, cotton), or artificial. Some artificial fibers, known as proteinics, are made from cellulose pulp (viscose, rayon, cuprum) or from casein. Those made from the spinning of fused glass and from chemical processes are known as synthetics, polymers treated in various ways through polyaddiction and polycondensation reactions. The categories are: polyamides, polyesters, polyurethanes, polyurics, polyephinics, polyacrylonitrilics, polyvynilics, polystyrenes, polyvynildenilics, and polytetrafluoroethilenics. They are malleable, resistant, durable, easy to wash, and easy to maintain. New developments in the industry have allowed only some of the categories to survive. Today, the term fiber refers almost always to synthetics.

Fichu Small triangular shawl, worn on the shoulders or around the neck and knotted or held with a brooch in front. Very fashionable in the 18th century, when they were used to decorate fashionably deep *décolleté*. Usually white or ecru, fichus were generally made of silk, lace or batiste. Fichus enjoyed a mini-renaissance in the 1980s when designer Christian Lacroix freely interpreted them in dresses inspired by his native Provence.

Field Patricia (1965). American designer. She is famous for designing the costumes for Carrie and her friends on the TV series *Sex and the City*. She has also been a costume designer for films: *The Hour of Violence* (U.S., 1996) and *Promises and Compromises* (U.S., 1995). Her brand is called House of Field. She has two stores in New York. One has her name on the front, in the West Village, and the other is at the Hotel Venus in Soho. Her style is very distinctive, at times dark and Gothic and at others quite funny and eccentric. She uses materials such as PVC, transparent vinyl, rubber, wet fabrics, and lots of denim. For more than twenty years her look has been the magnet for an intelligent and avant-garde style, loved by designers, stylists, and celebrities. Vinyl trousers and skirts, mini-skirts and long dresses in strictly stretch fabrics alongside maribu jackets, boas, and ostrich hats, Moulin Rouge-style satin corsets, and sequin dresses. And a series of eclectic accessories: bags printed with fruit-patterns or with very long fringes or made of knitted fabric; open-toed shoes in various colors with extremely high heels, sandals and boots in transparent vinyl. There are also gems and jewellery, as extravagant and eccentric as one can imagine: butterflies, skulls, cherries, letters of the alphabet hanging from the ears, crosses as pendants on necklaces, miniature ties, anchors, and arrows, in gilded silver and enamel as well as gold and diamonds.

Fielden David (1951). English designer. After twenty years on the British runways, he arrived in Milan with his Autumn-Winter 1999-2000 prêt-à-porter collection. He studied at the Birmingham College of Art. A former dancer and choreographer at the Rambert Ballet and a costume designer for the theater, he made his fashion début selling second-hand clothes on King's Road. In 1977, he opened a space of his own and launched a *griffe* that very much played on theatricality. Among his clients are Julia Roberts and Elizabeth Hurley.

Fifi Chachnil Brand of prêt-à-porter created by the designer Delphine Veron (1959). Heir of a family of Lyon weavers, she took courses on graphic art from Met de Penninghen and attended the Esmod School. After a trip to Egypt, which influenced her taste and creativity, she returned to France and recorded a CD singing in Arab under the pseudonym which she would later use as a brand name for her products: jewellery, clothes, and Barbie-style outfits. In 1986, she opened a boutique in Paris. In 1996, she launched a line of underwear. Her products are on sale at Barneys in New York, Agent Provocateur in London, and Kashiama in Paris.

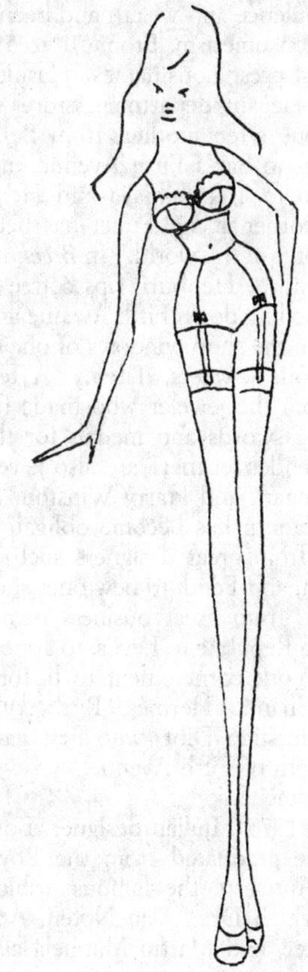

Fifi Chachnil. Summer model, 1999.

Fifth Avenue Historic shopping street in New York, for the elegant fashions of times past and for more current and trendy fashions today. Since the early 1900s, it has symbolized opulence and wealth and been a synonym for consumerism. From 50th to 59th Street, the most prestigious names in fashion and the most elegant department stores in town follow one after another, from Bergdorf Goodman to Sak's Fifth Avenue, and from Felissimo to Takashimaya and Henri Bendel. The corner at 57th Street has been called "the center of the world." In *Breakfast at Tiffany's*, Audrey Hepburn sips coffee at dawn while strolling down Fifth Avenue and stops to admire the shop windows of one of the most famous jewelers, Tiffany. A few steps away from the jeweler who made his fortune forging swords and medals for the War of Independence, there are also jewels by Cartier, Bulgari, and Harry Winston. In the last ten years, it has become obligatory for everyone, from great designers such as Versace, Prada, and Fendi to new ones such as Paul Smith, from great business names such as Banana Republic to Levi's, to appear on this New York corner, next to historic brands like Chanel, Hermès, Burberry's, Gucci, and Christian Dior, who first gave birth to the myth of Fifth Avenue.

Figus Angelo (1975). Italian designer. Born in Sardinia, he graduated from the Royal Academy in Antwerp, the famous fashion school from which Dries Van Noten, Ann Deumelemeester, and Martin Margiela also graduated, creating a genuine tradition known, indeed, as "the Antwerp school." The young designer, thanks to the sponsorship of Dries Van Noten, presented his first men's collection at the Café de la Dance in Paris, during the haute couture Fashion Week in July 1999. In 2000, he designed the costumes for a play by Ugo Rondinone in Ghent, Belgium, and those for *Rêves d'un Marco Polo* by Claude Vivier at the Opera House in Amsterdam. But Figus is interested mainly in women's prêt-à-porter. After the creation of a collection for Marks & Spencer, he transferred the dramatic and poetic style used in his men's wear collections to a women's line presented under his own name in Paris for Autumn-Winter 2000-2001. It was a mix of clothing and interior design, romantic souvenirs of his birthplace, Sardinia, set next to a contemporary universe. In 2002, he continued his activity as a costume designer, again with the Amsterdam Opera House, for a production of Wagner's *Lohengrin* staged by Pierre Audi. (*Gabriella Gregorietti*)

The Fila Group logo.

Fila Italian company specialized in sportswear, specifically clothing and shoes. It is a world leader with a turnover of 893 billion liras in 1998. The company's history began in 1926 when it was established by the Fila brothers in Biella, one of the foremost textile-clothing areas in Italy. It manufactured men's and women's knitted underwear. Almost fifty years later, in 1973, the company expanded the range of its products to include clothing for active sports. It started with tennis, with T-shirts and shorts which immediately distinguished themselves in their shape and color from the traditional ones that were always white. The Fila tennis clothes were worn by Adriano Panatta, Bjorn Borg, and Guillermo Vilas. From tennis to skiing to track and field, and to all the other sports as well: over time, Fila would dress champions such as Ingmar Stenmark, Alberto Tomba, Boris Becker, Monica Seles, Deborah Compagnoni, Grant Hill, Fiona May, Paul Tergat, and Mike Powell. In 1984, the company began a second diversification: the manufacture of sports shoes which, since the 1990s, has been its most important business in terms of revenue. A key to Fila's success is constant attention to costs, although not to the detriment of quality. In 1992, the Donna and Bambino lines were created and distributed. The group has 3,135 employees and operates all over the world with several brands, including Fila, Ciesse Piumini, Dorotennis, and Enyce. There are also numerous licensees who directly look after the design, production, and distribution of the Fila accessory lines for those categories of product that require specific knowledge and skills, such as eyewear (De Rigo), helmets (Piaggio), golf articles (Renaissance), and in-line skates (MGM). In recent years, the investment in new points-of-sale has been very consistent, with the opening of a new series of single-brand stores and corner shops.

❑ 2001, May. The opening in Milan, in Piazzetta Liberty, of the big Fila Sport Life Store on four floors.
❑ 2001, June. A partnership with Ferrari. The agreement for the Ferrari Collection brand is to last four years, with a renewal clause for four more.
❑ 2002, January. The start of the "never-ending story" of Fila's sale by HDP, with general managers taking turns and negotiations which involved, among others, Vanity Fair, Parker USA Continental, Golden Gate, and Nike.
❑ 2002, December. A partnership with Ducati Corse for the sponsorship of Superbike and the Desmosedici Grand Prix. A two-year exclusive license (2003-2005) for the use of the Ducati Corse brand on Fila clothing, shoes, and accessories. For Autumn-Winter 2003-2004, two distinct sportswear collections inspired by motorbike racing.
❑ A new line: Fila underwear.
❑ Fila has 200 points-of-sale in Korea (since 1990), and 16 in Italy, plus 8 stores.
❑ 2003, April. A return to the "historic" Fila-Fisi partnership (started during the 1990s). Beginning with the 2003-2004 season, it is to last four years and anticipates the development and supply of high-tech clothing for winter sports to 750 athletes. The opening of 13 points-of-sale in Italy, including Rome, Bari, Turin, and Cosenza.
❑ 2003, June. The conclusion of the sale of Fila. The RCS Media Group (formerly HDP) sells Fila Holding (brands: Fila Nederland, Ciesse Piumini, Fila Sport, and Fila USA) to Sport Brands International (SBI), which is controlled by Cerberus, a private American investment fund. It pays $351 million inclusive of Fila's financial debt from 1 January 2003. Fila confirms its intention to invest the remaining funds ($30 to $35 million) in the communication's sector.
❑ 2003, July. The baseball star Barry Bonds signs with Fila for a new pair of cross training shoes, the Bonds XT. The launch is in Chicago, at the All Star Game. The item is available in all 41 Foot-action stores all over the world.
❑ 2003, September. The birth of the Fingerwatch, ideal for those who practice running at every level. It is available in three sizes and four colors.
❑ 2003, October. The launch of a new project which sees the collaboration with Ducati for the creation of two new shoe models with a modern and aggressive design: the first to wear them are Loris Capirossi and Troy Bayliss during the MotoGp 2003 Race Championship. Agreement between Fila and FISI (Italian Winter Sports Association), thanks to which the company returns to the world of skiing, right at a moment of great attention to this sport. In Italy, the skiing program is rich and looks forward to the finals competitions for the World Cup 2004 in Sestrière, the World Championship in Bormio and Turin 2005, the Winter Olympics in 2006, and the Universal Games in 2007. Thanks to this agreement, the company will dress 750 athletes.
❑ 2004, February. A change at the top for SBI, with the appointment as president and CEO of the 51 year-old Steve Wynne.

Fil-à-Fil This pattern is obtained by symmetrically alternating two yarns, one dark and one light, both in weft and warp. In poplin or percale, it is a classic for the manufacture of shirts. More rare is a fil-à-fil of strong, thick wool that creates a diagonal zigzag effect, usually in tones of grey.

Filanto Italian shoe factory. Its headquarters is in Casarano, Apulia, near Lecce. Michele Zonno is the general director. It manufactures both a men's and a women's collection through two brands: Filanto and Bkt. In 2001, the turnover was €240 million, of which 85% was for export, through sales to 80 countries.

Filati di Ziche Wool mill. The entrepreneurial history of the Ziche family began in the second half of the 1700s with Francesco Ziche, "landowner and shop owner," and his wife Anna Maria Brunale, "a dealer in wool." But its real tradition in the wool industry started during the first decades of the 1800s in Thiene, thanks to Leonardo Ziche, the son of Francesco, who in 1822 became a dyer of textile fibers, passing the trade on to his son Valentino and his grandson Leonardo. It was Leonardo, in 1902, who started a small factory "for the grinding of rags" made of cotton and wool, near Zugliano. Some time later, the five grinding machines, which represented all of the factory's machinery, were moved to Thiene, where new warehouses for semi-worked products and raw materials were built. In 1926, on the initiative of Leonardo's sons Giuseppe, Giovanni Battista, and Alvise, a spinning operation was started in Thiene. Under their guidance, the company thrived. In the late 1950s, Franco and Valentino, the sons of Giovanni Battista, joined the business, and went in a new direction: that was the beginning of knitwear production. After a few years, Franco devoted himself exclusively to this field, starting a business of his own, while Valentino joined his uncle Alvise and focused on the spinning operation, opening a new plant in Zané in 1963 with a thousand spindles of carded yarn and some twenty workers. The factory grew fast: during the 1960s, it had a capacity of two thousand spindles with forty workers, and made its début in the fashion market refining its production. In the 1970s, Alvise retired and the company was managed entirely by Valentino, who focused exclusively on knitwear yarns. The introduction of advanced technology became a winning strategy. During the 1980s, Ziche acquired the Tintoria Industriale Tessile in Breda di Piave, near Treviso, and the plants in Zané were expanded. In 1997, a new production unit was opened: output went from 3,000 lbs. of spun yarn a day in 1986 to 15,000 lbs. a day at the end of the 1990s. The capacity grew constantly, reaching 15,000 spindles. Ziche Manifattura Lane has three plants in Italy and one in Croatia. It sells on every continent. Its turnover is more than €37 million. The use of wools such as merino, cashmere, alpaca, mohair, and angora, the introduction of new technologies, and the firm's flexibility and careful attention to changes in fashion have all served to guarantee the success of the company, which is by now known mostly through its brand: Filati di Ziche. The president and general manager is still Valentino Ziche, assisted by his son Francesco, who joined the business in 1999 and has been general manager since 2001.

Filatura and Tessitura di Tollegno Spinning and weaving mill established around 1900 on the initiative of some families in Biella. It boasts 100 years of being in business. The brand name Lana Gatto goes back to 1908. A new plant was built near Turin in 1910. It was moved to Tollegno in 1925. The number of employees reached 1,700, and increased to almost 2,500 after the acquisition of Lanificio Agostinetti and Ferrua. The important historic heritage of the company through the years is an important part of its identity, in which tradition and hyper-technology live together. Next to the old weaving room with its stone columns is a 150,000 square foot shed with more than 120 ultra-modern looms. The group's production includes yarns for knit outerwear, sewing threads, and weaving. To underline the company's international character, the Italian plants are accompanied by operations in other countries: a spinning mill in Poland, a commercial headquarters in Hong Kong, and the branch office Tollegno 1900 USA Inc. in New York. (*Silvia Martinenghi*)

Filatura di Chiavazza Company specialized in the manufacture of precious yarns made from noble fibers, mostly cashmere. Established in 1927 in Vagliano Biellese by Giacomo Borsetti, it started as a complete cycle carded spinning mill. The current production includes both very refined and ultra thin pure Pashmina yarns, and mixed yarns composed of camel, angora, mohair, silk, and baby merino. These spun yarns, either raw or stock dyed, are meant for knitwear, woven goods, and jersey. The structure of the company also allows for some items to be shipped from stock. Today, the company is led by the founder's grandchildren, Alberto and Piergiacomo Borsetti.

Filatura di Grignasco Spinning mill established toward the end of the 1800s on the initiative of some weaving mills in Valsesera. After rapidly becoming known in the field of spun yarn for fabrics, the firm has more and more specialized in the manufacture of yarns for underwear, a field in which it is now a world leader. The acquisition, about fifteen years ago, of the spinning mill in Gavardo, in the area of Brescia, allowed the firm to enter the field of yarns for knit outerwear, which today represents 50% of the Group's production. Today, the company has two plants, one in Grignasco (Novara) and one in Bostone (Brescia), that operate with very advanced technology – it was the first spinning mill to obtain an ISO quality certification – and it employs about 950 people. In the late 1990s the turnover was around 170 billion liras, of which 40% came from abroad.

Filatura di Pollone Spinning mill established in 1953 thanks to the entrepreneurial intuition of Attilio Botto, from Biella. It is a national and international leader in classic carded yarns, combed and open-end, in wool, natural, artificial and synthetic fibers, both for clothing and interior décor. The company's Carded Ultrafine is a registered brand for an exclusive and original product. The company has concentrated especially on the technology for open-end spinning, a technique born in 1968 and in the beginning used only in cotton spinning and then later applied to other fibers. During the 1970s and 1980s, the increase in production caused the firm to separate its activity by sector: weaving, hosiery, and knitwear. In the early 1990s, with the opening of markets in eastern Europe, production expanded again. The plant in Pollone, in the area of Biella, was joined by two more abroad, one in Poland in 1992 and one in Hungary in 1997. There are 240 employees. In order to face a general crisis in the industry, which caused even the mill in Pollone to suffer a 14% drop in revenues in 2002 (€21.2 million), the company focuses on the development of new products for 2003.

Fil d'Or Award created by the Bureau International du Lin for the best creation manufactured in pure linen. It has been given to, among others, the Dutch designers Puck Kroon & Hans Keminck. Someone who is awarded the Fil d'Or several times also receives the L d'Or (L stands for linen). Among the Italian designers, this has happened with Ferré, Montana, Coveri, Soprani, and Biagiotti. In 1983, in Monaco, it happened with Cinzia Ruggieri. Among non-Italians, it happened with the French Anne Marie Beretta, the German Jil Sander and, in 1987, the Belgian Nina Meert.

Fili Monthly magazine with models, drawings, and how-to instructions for sewing, knitting, embroidery, and crochet. It was first published in January 1934 in Milan by the publishing house Domus, owned by Gianni Mazzocchi. Emilia Rosselli Kuster was the editor until racial laws enacted by the Fascist government no longer allowed it. It was created to "free the Italian woman from the influences of foreign fashion." Alina and Maria Luisa di Ricaldona, Pia di Valmarana, Wenter Marini, Sandra Zelaski Gui, and Giuseppina Perti Baragiola all worked on it. Among the supplements issued by the magazine were Fili-Moda, which in January 1942 became a monthly of practical fashion edited by Paola Moroni Fumagalli, and the biannual of children's fashion Fili-Bimbi edited by Emma Robutti. When the government required tailors to make clothes inspired by regional costumes, Fili-Moda adapted, asking Maria Pezzi to create captions and sketches for a series of double-page spreads devoted to the styles and colors of costumes from Sardinia and Liguria. "The editor," says Maria Pezzi, "was

Cover of the monthly Fili-Moda, second issue, Summer 1941.

a very intelligent woman. Publishing a fashion magazine in that period was not easy. In addition to folk-inspired themes, I suggested features on how to re-style an old cloak and how to recycle old clothes, and suggested dresses, jackets, skirts, and sun dresses created by me." (*Stefano Grassi*)

Filmer Naomi (1969). English jewellery designer, born in London. She specialized in the goldsmith's art at the Royal College of Art (1993). Since 1994 she has worked regularly with Hussein Chalayan, creating unique pieces for his collections. She also designs for Tristan Webber and Julien MacDonald. Her conceptual style, which explores the space around the body instead of decorating it in a traditional way, is seen in her rings that are worn between the fingers. She uses negative space in an innovative and intellectual way.

Filo Event held twice a year, in April and November, at Villa Erba in Cernobbio, on Lake Como. It is dedicated to yarns, fibers, textile designs, and the ennobling of orthogonal and circular weaving. There are about 1,500 participants from all over the world, including non-European countries like Japan and New Zealand. At the 19th edition, in April 2003, TexClubTec also participated. It is an association of companies committed to research and the development of high-tech textiles.

Filodoro A hosiery company making stockings and tights. It was established in 1982 in Casalmoro, Mantua for manufacture with Lycra, and produces an average of 100 million pieces a year. It has 13% of the Italian market. It offers 7 collections for different market segments. The Omero line consists of graduated compression tights.

❑ 1994. The company is acquired by the American giant Sara Lee (Playtex and Lovable) which produces and distributes 6 lines through three selling channels.
❑ 2000, June. The fiscal year ends with a turnover of $100 million, a 13.5% increase.
❑ 2001. The existing brands (Filodoro, Filoverde, Omero, and Philippe Matignon) are joined by the English lingerie brand Gossard and Berlei.
❑ 2002, September. The company joins the world of *griffes*: agreements with Max Mara for Max Mara Hosiery, which since March 2003 has been distributed direct to 150 shops and 200 boutiques, and to franchises, with a special interest in the Russian market. A three-year license with Benetton to strengthen the teenage market in Italy, Greece, and Russia.

Filpucci Italian company and world-wide leader in the manufacture of creative and innovative threads in precious weaves and blends. Its headquarters is in the textile district of Prato, in Capalle. It made its name in the late 1960s with threads that were innovative and rather revolutionary for the time due to their technical content and imagination. During two decades of great expansion by the fashion industry, from the early 1970s to the late 1980s, Filpucci distinguished itself for a capacity to invent leading-edge products, often starting new trends. It introduced viscose thread in knitwear and manufactured the first cotton braid. Planning and developing non-traditional systems for the creation of special threads, Filpucci anticipated the era of light-weight thread with its Soffili series in the late 1980s. Led by Leandro Gualtieri, an entrepreneurial figure who has distinguished himself in the Italian textile industry, the company has pursued a consistent policy of change and progress, strengthening its own structure with an ISO 9001 quality certificate obtained in 1998. In 1998, the turnover was 83 billion liras, an increase of 10% over the previous year. The latest news in terms of creative, avant-garde technological innovation is the introduction in the Spring-Summer 2000 collection of a thread obtained from casein, which seems to promise excellent performance.

(*Silvia Martinenghi*)

❑ 2002, July. The turnover is about €55 million. The company's development is focused on the U.S. and the Far East. It is also on schedule with the opening of branch offices in Shanghai and Seoul.

Fingen Apparel An industrial holding company in Florence established by the brothers Marcello and Corrado Fratini. Their father Fiorenzo (who died in April 2001 at the age of 81) and their uncle Giulio created the first Italian jeans under the brand name Rifle in the 1950s. By the second generation, the Confezioni Fratini firm split and two different stories began. The cousins Cristina and Sandro, the children of Giulio (who passed away in 1996) remain linked to Rifle, which they transform into Super Rifle and Pacific Trail. Marcello and Corrado establish Fingen Apparel, each with 50% of the shares, and acquire the American brand Cotton Belt. The holding company adds an office for licenses which, in 1995, is awarded Calvin Klein Jeans, in 1996 Calvin Klein Asia and Europe, and in 1997 Guess Europe. For a short time, the two brothers have 20% of van Cleef and Arpels. Fingen Apparel groups together the companies CK Jeanswear Europe, Maco Apparel, and Euro Cormar. These produce and distribute on license, respectively, the brands Calvin Klein Jeans, for Europe and Asia, and Guess Jeans, for Europe, in addition to the proprietary Cotton Belt brand. Euro Retail manages the retail network of the three brands. A three-year plan anticipates growth in the licence business through new acquisitions of young and alternative brands, the relaunch of the Cotton Belt brand, and a new children's division. The long-term forecast expects to increase the current turnover of €234.8 million by 45%. In January 2003, Fingen acquired Sicem, a knitwear company in Soliera (Modena) which has the knitwear licenses of Armani Uomo, Krizia, and Roccobarocco, in addition to the proprietary brand Codice. Sicem employs 500 people in Italy and Romania, and has a turnover of about €70 million. Within the continuously evolving company, a new children's project has been started: the Kids division, in June 2003. The line of Calvin Klein Jeans for those under 16 (and perhaps, in the future, also for babies), which was presented at Pitti Immagine Bimbo in June 2003, was launched with the Spring-Summer 2004 collection. The goal for 2005 was to increase the turnover by €5 to €7.5 million euros, which is the norm for a children's *griffe*. As to Guess, which is divided into Guess Collection, Guess Jeans (belonging to Maco Apparel), G-Brand, Kids, and Baby, here, too, the idea is a relaunch. The entire *griffe*, including eyeglasses, shoes, watches, and underwear, moved into a new headquarters with 6,000 square feet on via Lambro in Milan. The goal is to reach young people between 20 and 30 years of age who are more and more fashionable in their style and tastes. For years, Guess has been produced on license by Focus Europe in Crevalcore (Bologna), part of the Focus Pull group. On the international level, in the first quarter of 2003, the turnover of Guess Inc. was €83.7 million. Fingen Apparel has a network of 32 proprietary stores in Europe displaying the three brands, plus Indigo Blu, the most recent. In April 2003, the group sold Sima Fashion to Fuzzi. For the future, within 2004, the firm at that time expected to open new single-brand and franchise stores for Calvin Klein (at present 350 in Italy and 250 more abroad) and for Guess. As a real estate holding company (Fingen Real Estate), the firm created a joint venture with McArthurGlen (after the one in Serravalle Scrivia) for a Designer Factory Outlet 15 miles from Rome along the Via Pontina in Castel Romano. The expected cost: €70 million.

(*Gabriella Gregorietti*)

Finollo Italian workshop for custom made shirts, opened in 1899 in Genoa by Emanuele Finollo. In the ever smaller European world of artisanal shirts, this boutique is an obligatory destination. To manufacture a shirt at Finollo takes nine hours of work, against eight minutes for a mass production garment. First a cloth model is made to test the fit, then there are three more steps to get the finished product. The collar, known because of its distinctive characteriestics as a Finollo collar, has a special cut which allows it to stand up perfectly without starch. There are custom made ties matched to the colors and fabrics of the shirts and, by request, hand-embroidered motifs, coats of arms, and monograms of all types. Today, the workshop is still on the street, via Roma, where it opened a century ago. It is directed by Roberto Linke with his wife Daniela Finollo and their two children Andrea and Francesca.

Fin.Part Holding company that is a major participant in the Made in Italy movement, quoted on the Milan Stock Exchange. The group owns the brands Cerruti 1881, Cerruti Jeans, Henry Cotton's, Marina Yachting, Frette, Moncler, Maska, and Boggi. It ended 2002 with a turnover of €458.2 million, an increase of 8.3% over the previous year. The operating income was €2.6 million, while the group's net result was a loss of €64.2 million, compared to a loss of €37 million in 2001. This negative performance was caused by a very bad net financial position (minus €402.3 million), which attracted the attention of Consob, the oversight body for companies listed on the Stock Exchange. Fin.Part paid the price for having formed a group using mainly external sources of financing at the start of the macroeconomic crisis of the early 2000s, which involved the clothing industry as well. Within a few years, Fin.Part had been transformed from a company involved in hotel management (up until 2000 the core business of the group was in the hotel industry: the Bonaparte Hotel Group) into a multi-brand group for luxury goods. It was the result of an acquisition campaign which accumulated debt to the detriment of profitability. Faced with this situation, Gianluigi Facchini, the president and general manager of the group, resigned. His place was taken by Ubaldo Livolsi, a financial consultant and former manager of Fininvest. He now leads the group's turnaround. The business plan, approved by the banks, foresees a concentration on men's and women's prêt-à-porter and sportswear, the sale of the remaining real estate and non-strategic businesses, and, finally, an increase in capital. The first two months of 2003 saw an increase in revenue of 7.9%. (*Dario Golizia*)

Finsler Hans (1891-1972). Swiss photographer. After the study of architecture and art history in his hometown of Zurich, he devoted himself to photography as a teacher and as a fashion photographer, with a style that was at the time considered particularly innovative and modern.

Fio Nadia (1960). Designer of Croatian origin, she has lived in Milan since 1993 and is completely self-taught in fashion. She learned knitting and crochet from her mother. Her creativity has led her to create unique pieces, always with these two techniques. Her first collection of hats and bathing suits was presented in Milan in 1999 in the Flying Dutch showroom.

Fiorentina Silvia (1926). Italian-American shoe designer, born in New York. Sometime in the 1950s, thinking about her passion for shoes, she decided to design a collection for American women but with Italian taste. Success was almost immediate, specifically in 1957, when she opened her first boutique at 789 Madison Avenue. Still manufactured at plants in Vigevano and Bologna, her shoes are today on sale in the most exclusive American department stores, including Bergdorf Goodman.

Fiorucci Elio (1935). Italian fashion entrepreneur and a strategist of style. It was 1967. Fiorucci had gained experience working in the shops where his father sold slippers on via Torino, via Eustachi, and a side street near Corso Buenos Aires, all in Milan. As a merchant ("I've always been a merchant. I don't like the role of designer. I'm a merchant who has had the humility to pay attention to life and the way people behave."), he came from a family of tradesmen, but he was far removed from the narrow-minded conservatism of a shopkeeper. He had been trying to get a sense of the times ever since a 1965 trip to England, in the period of Swinging London, and his discovery of Biba, King's Road, and Carnaby Street hit him like a thunderbolt. He would later say: "That chaos moved me. Saying it now can cause laughter in someone who doesn't remember the starched traditionalism and conformity of fashion in those days, the clothing stores either completely in the style of the old English aristocracy or else dominated by Parisian chic. That chaos was evidence of a new, open attitude about how to dress and how to be elegant. Fashion no longer came from above, like the Holy Spirit, but was generated from below, driven by a dizzying evolution in clothing. I have just one merit: that I understood it. The history of Fiorucci starts with the act of paying attention." One day, the son of the man who sold slippers had an idea for very colorful plastic galoshes. Galoshes were very old-fashioned and no longer worn very much,

A Fiorucci dress as seen by Maria Pezzi.

but bright colors and plastic relaunched them. It was an incredible success, and a shock to the somewhat dusty traditions of the Fiorucci shops. Something new was about to arrive in consumer goods, with new needs and a change of taste. It was 1967. A somewhat confused new generation anxious for rebellion was knocking on the doors of Italian fashion. It was happening elsewhere, but also in Italy, on a more elitist level. At Santa Tecla in Milan, and at the Piper in Rome, rock-and-roll was over, and it was the era yé-yé. The flower children were "blossoming" and hippies would chain themselves to traffic lights in the name of peace. It was the eve of '68 and its ideological mess. Feminism was growing stronger. It was a generation of consumers, according to one survey in Italy, that spent 540 billion liras a year on entertainment and luxury goods. It was a fertile and very new market. Fiorucci didn't miss the opportunity, becoming the ambassador and the Italian interpreter of that alternative fashion he had found in London. It was a rag shop, a total mixture of styles, "screaming" colors, provocations, and transgressions on Corso Vittorio Emanuele in the center of a commercial district which, from the point of view of clothing, was completely orthodox and devoted to bourgeois elegance. It was like the prayer of a pagan sect in the middle of a solemn Mass in Latin. But that sect had an endless army of potential converts. Success was immediate, and it wasn't short-lived. Two years later, there was already talk of "Fioruccism," a wide-spread phenomenon in the face of events and radical ideologies that should have crushed and suffocated something so ephemeral and devoted only to clothing. But "Fioruccism" wasn't a style connected to the creativity of a single person. It was the style of seeing things and reshuffling them through a culture that had lost its taboos. Fiorucci was able to observe and to choose, and to coordinate talented people who in turn were able to observe, even if they were slightly mad. Elio and his team traveled around the world, sniffing things out, buying, piling up hundreds of proposals and discoveries, things which they would mix and reinvent. They were the first to work with jeans, giving them a cut that made them very wearable and giving them an appeal which would exalt the female buttocks. They were the first to revolutionize the color palette of fabrics, inspired by Andy Warhol and the colors seen on television. They were the first to codify the fact that fashion could be anarchy, either in a genuine way or in a calculated way giving each person space for his own creativity, at the same time knocking down social barriers and the idea that elegance can be fit into categories. It was 1967. Since then, and for almost two decades, Fioruccism was an avalanche of mini-skirts in tulle, jeans that made the buttocks into an erotic magnet, T-shirts with mice and little angels, Hawaiian shirts, endless little rags, decorated tank tops, multi-shaped prototypes of femininity (the doll-woman, the pop art-woman, the shabby, the martial, the plastic woman), outfits, lace, flowers, and monokinis (1975), with two thin straps that drew even more attention to the bare breasts of the bra burners. Started as a transfer to Italy of what was happening in London, of what Biba was doing, as a kind of plagiarism, Fioruccism – carrying the lesson to an extreme – outlasted its models. The imitative provincial outpost became the center of an empire that was able to colonize even the United States, through a financial partnership with Montedison that in 1974 invested the capital necessary for growth. Later on, Fiorucci had brief alliances with Benetton and with the Italian-Iranian Massimo Nuhi. "We were a Milanese and Italian phenomenon. My company sold four, maybe five billion liras. Our fame was inversely proportional to our economic power. We became an international event, arriving in London and in the U.S., where the Made in Italy movement was represented only by Gucci and Ferragamo. We had 10,000 square feet on 59th Street in New York and a movie theater that was transformed into a store in Los Angeles. We had 2,500 points-of-sale in 32 countries." Italian stylism was still far away, Armani was just making his début, and Missoni and Krizia, the longtime representatives of fashion from Italy, were only starting to become known in department stores. Throughout the 1980s, Fiorucci, although seeing a decline in its image and the start of a crisis, managed to stay on top with record turnovers of around 200 billion liras, as in 1988. The 1990s were years of restructuring centered around the

store on Corso Vittorio Emanuele, which is still a winner for Elio Fiorucci and his brand.
(*Guido Vergani*)

❑ 2001, October. Fiorucci is on the Internet with a cheerful web-site enlivened by a big red heart on a pink background.
❑ 2001, June. In addition to the store on 59th Street, a second New York is opened on Broadway in Noho (the area "north of Houston"), in a less aggressive style than that of the late 1970s. With a severe look and neon lights, it cost around $10 million.
❑ 2002, February. Fiorucci gives Big Time a license to manufacture and distribute the jeans line in Europe, starting with the women's and children's Spring-Summer collections, with the men's collection to be added later.
❑ 2003, March. The closing of the historic store on Corso Vittorio Emanuele is announced, 36 years after its opening on 31 May 1967. It takes place in July, to make way for Hennes & Mauritz, a large Swedish clothing chain.
❑ 2003, May. Fiorucci tests itself with one of the symbols of our time: the automobile. It is a new challenge, combining the technology and practicality of Citroën with the creativity, love, and taste for color of Fiorucci in order to personalize a car for the year 2000. It is the birth, in a limited series of only 500, of the New Berlino Loved by Elio Fiorucci automobile, presented at the Bologna Motor Show in 2002.
❑ 2003, May. Fiorucci surprises once again. He closes the store on Corso Vittorio Emanuele but opens a new one with 10,000 square feet in the very nearby Corso Europa. The new store is opened in autumn. The ambience and the selection of merchandise is exactly in line with the Fiorucci spirit. The intention is to revive the old Fiorucci brand that was acquired by the Edwin group in 1992. A major relaunch of a wide range of products in perfect Fiorucci style is anticipated. The image of the new store, which occupies the space of the former Koivu, is certainly innovative but, as Fiorucci says: "it is different from that of luxury boutiques in which the architecture dominates everything... a rather Spartan store which is alive with real things. In other words, with little furniture and lots of substance..." (*Gabriella Gregorietti*)

The Fiorucci logo.

❑ 2003, October. The Internet adventure continues and Elio makes his début on www.yoox.com with his Love Therapy, based, according to tradition, on the concept of joy, happiness, and anti-sadness therapy. The site's content ranges from news to suggestions for the store. On the site it is also possible to purchase many items that are available in the new single-brand store on via Europa. Under construction is a multi-functional space dedicated to young people. A consulting company named Cucù, in collaboration with Oliviero Toscani, is being established.
❑ 2003, November. The Italian Fashion company is given the task of producing and distributing the women's line, mainly focused on denim, in Europe.
❑ 2004, July. The opening of a store in Japan, which is to be followed by others in Korea and China, dedicated to a clientele of young girls. In Hong Kong and the surrounding areas, points-of-sale for shoes, bags, and accessories are opened. In the same period, the Bologna children's wear company Grant, led by Mauro Serafini, signs an agreement with

Elio Fiorucci for the kid's and junior lines called Love Therapy by Elio Fiorucci.
❑ 2005, April. He designs a limited Summer collection for H&M called H&M Poolside. It is a line dedicated to men, women and children on sale in worldwide H&M single-brand stores. He signs an exclusive agreement with NK Home, and the famous angel, small hearts, and pin-up patterns reappear on a line of household linens.
❑ 2005, June. The new eyewear collection Funglasses designed by Fiorucci (and owned by the Japanese firm Edwin & Co.) is presented. It has 18 eyeglass models and 16 for sunglasses. After the launch in Asia, it will be available also in Europe.

Fisac (Italian Factories of Silk and Similar Fibers) A company making silk and velvet established in Milan in 1906. The acronym Fisac was adopted in 1932. The new company inherited weaving mills in Cermenate, Menaggio, Como, and Camerlata from its predecessor, Fabbriche Italiane di Seterie Clerici Braghenti & Co, which went bankrupt. It specializes in the manufacture of plain dyed and diapered fabrics for women's clothing. Several professional men from the Como area acquired substantial blocks of shares, and Alberto Clerici became president, general manager, and general director. During the 1920s, thanks to support from various Italian banks such as Credito Italiano, Fisac began a strategy of diversification of production and gradually acquired textile plants (in Monte Olimpino), velvet factories (in Como), printing works (in Luisago and Grandate), and a dye works (in Como). In 1931, Alberto Clerici left the company, and his place was taken by the new president, Furio Cicogna, who was also a manager of Châtillion. In the first half of the 1930s, the IRI obtained several seats on the board of directors and appointed Luigi Morandotti as president. The weaving mill in Monte Olimpino was closed in 1953, and the Como plants that produced velvet were closed in 1955 and '56. At around the same time, a new weaving mill was opened in Camerlata, on the outskirts of Como, thanks to investments by the Marshall Plan. In the late 1960s, Fisac joined the Montedison group, to be later absorbed by GIMI (Vicenza) in 1990. *(Pierangelo Mastantuono)*

Fischer Eileen (1950). American designer. Simplicity plus a natural and comfortable look are her guiding principles. She has never followed fashions or trends. Her goal has been to design a broad line of trousers, skirts, jackets, and shirts which would never look dated and would always be wearable and practical. Her outfits, mostly in linen, cotton, and wool, are suitable for any occasion. She began in 1984 and within a few years was able to win a very large clientele. She is in all the big department stores and owns 15 shops in the U.S. *(Priscilla Daroda)*

Fisico Italian brand of ready-to-wear beachwear. It was launched by Cristina Ferrari in 1989 with a collection presented in Milan. In 1997, she made her début at Milano Collezioni. In 1998, she offered the pubis-bikini which, because of its very small size, caused a scandal. The collection is produced in Bergamo and distributed in Italy, France, and Spain. It will soon be in England and the U.S. In the last three years, the turnover has had an annual increase of 40%.

Fissore Cristiano (1950). Italian designer of knitwear. Born in Rapallo, he began to work in his family's clothing stores at a young age. In 1977, he established his own company, called Cristiano Fissore, which manufactured cashmere sweaters in classic designs and refined colors. The company's headquarters is in an 18th century villa which overlooks the Rapallo harbor.

❑ The Fissore women's collection has always been designed by Lucia Bosisio, who creates cashmere garments with very precise details, sometimes precious, through continuous research on new and unusual threads.
❑ 1999. The birth of the Maison collection, which is presented once a year at *Maison et Objet* in Paris. Every collection is characterized by a single color, developed in numerous shades and tones. Entirely handmade, either knitted or crocheted, it is made even more precious through stitching,

embroidery, and decorations which, combined with unusual colors, result in modern garments that have an antique flavor.
❑ 2000. The men's collection undergoes a big change, from a classic collection to a new one in which research is the main feature, with unusual treatments, washings, and blends. The collection, directly coordinated by Cristiano Fissore, is immediately joined by the new Cristiano Fissore Genoa. More casual, it is completed with garments in different fabrics and in leather, such as buffalo skin and shearling. Inspired by the sea, in the beginning it is only in blue. Later it is enriched with new colors, inspired by hunting, fishing, and other elite sports.
❑ 2001. A commercial showroom opens at via Savona 97 in Milan. It is a large restyled industrial loft.

Fitzpatrick Joel (1967). American designer. A graduate of the Cal Arts School of Theater, he started his career as a lamp designer, and then turned to fashion. Together with John Chase, he opened the Pleasure Swell, specializing in T-shirts. A win in Las Vegas helped him open his boutique in West Hollywood, the Swell Store. More than a store, it is a meeting place for the promotion of artistic and fashion events, same as the one opened later in New York.

Fks2 Italian brand of jewellery. It is also the pseudonym of Franklin Santana, former top model, globetrotter, and collector of crosses, which he acquires during his travels. He presented his creations for the first time in November 2002 at the Art Café in Rome, although he had been working on them for seven years. Jewels are matched in the Metaphone women's prêt-à-porter and the Richmond men's collection. He offers crosses of all shapes, in gold and silver, with colored feathers, for necklaces and refined rings, applied on belts, short necklaces and long ones, with heart-shaped pendants and geometric-patterned bangles. His artisanal manufacturing is extremely accurate and performed in the goldsmith workshops of Arezzo.

Flabotin French term for colored flannels.

Flair Italian monthly magazine for women published by Mondadori. The first issue came out on 18 January 2003, with a circulation of 370,000 and the expectation that it would reach a steady 170,000 to 180,000 copies per month. Flair is edited by Valeria Corbetta, and aims to fill the void left among the Mondadori periodicals after the loss of Marie Claire (now published by Hachette), addressing a woman of middle to high culture who is sophisticated, open to new trends, has a career, but is also a mother and wife. Five hundred glossy pages on culture, fashion, cooking, news, curiosity, style, reportage, and beauty. Contributing to it are, among others, the novelist Margaret Mazzantini, the screenplay writer and author Marcello Fois, and the philosopher Roberta De Monticelli. (*Daniela Bolognetti*)

Flambé The term slubbing refers to an irregular torpedo-shaped thickening or twisting of a thread resulting from a technical defect in the spun yarn. Exploiting this defect in an *ad hoc* way, it is possible to produce slubby yarns which present a thickening at fixed intervals and with which fabrics like shantung or patterned knitwear can be produced. The term is also used for those fabrics that show "buttons" and lively colored strips, especially with very evident thickenings.

Flanders Fashion Institute A center for the promotion of Belgian fashion, opened in 2002 in Antwerp. It was conceived by Linda Loppa, the director of the fashion department at the local Academy of Fine Arts. It has more than just a didactic purpose: it is a place which provides a meeting place, the exchange of ideas, and support for young designers. The institute, a non-profit association, also operates as a museum. It collects archives concerning fashion, mounts theme exhibits, and organizes specific workshops for the study and recovery of local textile arts which are at risk of being lost. The project is completely supported by the town, which has donated the building which houses the institute.

Flanders Flax Fabric made from very precious linen fiber, coming specifically from

Flanders, but also manufactured in cotton. The surface is characterized by irregular gatherings. Manufactured on jacquard looms, in classic geometric and floral patterns, it was originally used only for table and bath linens. Today, this fabric is also used in clothing. It was used by Ken Scott in the late 1960s in lively and brilliant colors such as apple green, shocking pink, and porcelain blue for men's shirts and wide ties.

Flannel A combed or carded woolen fabric. It is warm and soft. The heaviest type is incorrectly called vicuna. Grey flannel trousers, worn by both men and women, are a timeless classic. Cotton flannel, very similar to plush, has a hairy surface and is used for shirts, nightgowns, pajamas, and bed sheets.

Flannel Bay A line of classic men's clothing produced by Clan, a company in Naples established by Antonio Deodato Laezza. The Laezza family's *griffe* is rooted in the tailoring technique of Naples, with the sobriety and elegance that flow from the attention to detail, such as the open buttonhole and the stitching, of the "sgarzillo." The suits are manufactured in five different lines with Australian merino wool from Carlo Barbera, fabrics from Ermenegildo Zegna's, and the "Superissimo" of the Cerruti Brothers. It ranges from the Tailor's Classic to the Outdoor line, and includes the Collection line, which is the most informal, and Soft, which is the most casual. City Wear is the overcoat collection. The showroom in Naples is at Porta Capuana, in via Colletta. (*Pierangelo Mastantuono*)

Flett John (1963-1991). English designer. He was a wild talent who could not completely find himself. He graduated from the Saint Martin's School in 1985. His first collections, with a cut that was elaborate, theatrical, and ultra-sexy, were purchased by Joseph in London and Bergdorf Goodman in New York. In 1988, he presented his first collection together with Galliano, Jasper Conran, and Betty Jackson. But his financial resources were almost depleted and, the following year, he reinvented himself as an assistant to Montana in Paris and, later, to Enrico Coveri in Florence. Just before signing a contract with Zuccoli for the design of a raincoat line, he died in Florence of a heart attack, on 18 January 1991.
(*Mara Accettura*)

Flip-flops Flat plastic sandal with short strips between the big toe and the toe next to it that hold the foot. Copied from the Japanese version, called *zori*, worn with white, black, or blue *tabi* cotton socks, specially made to fit around the thong. In origin this sandal was made of rubber and was used only at the beach or swimming-pool. After becoming a trendy shoe, it's now manufactured in more expensive materials and can also be a platform shoe to wear in town.

Fliselina Non-fabric fabric, one without the traditional elements of weft and warp, created by means of artificial and synthetic fibers. Similar to felt, but much thinner and lighter, it can have be rather rigid. During the 1950s, it was used as a stiff underskirt, like a crinoline, to support flared skirts. Fliselina is actually the brand name of a product made by the German company Freudenberg, although the name has by now been applied to all fabrics with the same characteristics. There is also a thermo-adhesive version, used as a reinforcing element in clothing.

Floeter Hubertus, known as Hubs (1910-1976). German photographer, born in Cologne. After his studies at the Bayerische Staatsfehranstalt in Munich, he worked during the 1930s in Cologne and Berlin. Only in 1938 did he open, with his future wife Ilse Reyer, his own studio in the Berlin. After 1945, he had a successful career as a fashion photographer in Stuttgart, Berlin, and Munich, enjoying a certain international fame.

Flou Large, soft, loose garments, often made in light and transparent fabric, sometimes in more than one layer.

Flow Scapa A brand created in 1967 in Antwerp on the initiative of the designer Brian Redding and his wife Arlette. From the beginning, they manufactured knitwear, and their tweeds immediately became famous for their quality and style. They are among the main players in the big success of Shetland sweaters. The company is organized in a men's, women's, and children's collection, as well as a Scapa Sport and a Scapa Originals collection, which is composed of vintage garments. In 2003, there were 35 points-of sales in Europe, including 2 in Paris. The turnover is about €30.5 million a year.

Flügel John-Carl (1884-1955). English essayist. He was the first in history to treat, from a psychoanalytic point of view, the experience of dressing oneself, relating the shapes and materials of clothes to the spirit of the time. A professor of psychology at London University, in 1930 he published *The Psychology of Clothes*, in which he offered a sociological interpretation of fashion, stressing three elementary functions of clothing: the selection of clothes, modesty, and protection. From there began the analysis of the clothing: when and why it is used to hide oneself, when and why it is used to show oneself off.

Foale Marion (1939). English designer. Her name is linked to that of Sally Tuffin (1938), with whom, in 1961, she launched the brand Foale & Tuffin, for youthful clothes in strong colors. The partnership lasted until 1972, when Sally decided to specialize in children's clothing while Marion, the author of *Marion Foale's Classic Knitwear* (Pelham Books, London, 1985), continued to design along the same lines, but focused especially on knitwear.

Fogal Swiss company making women's hosiery, established in Zurich in the 1920s by Léon Fogal. In 1969, he sold the company (including six stores in Switzerland) to the banker Walter Meler, who appointed his own son to manage the company. Thirty years later, that family is still at the head of this very fortunate brand, with 68 shops and several franchises in the most prestigious locations of the world. Three fourths of the production is in Switzerland, where the standard of quality is very high. Classic stockings are now accompanied by fashionable and casual lines, and by a line of underwear and a sports line. The range of colors, in 82 different shades, remains a strong point of the collection. For several years, Meler has had famous artists design the packaging for his shops. Some of the designs have been collected by various museums.

Fogarty Anne (1919-1981). American designer. Born in Pittsburg, she was among the first to design bikinis. She became famous especially for her paper doll: a model characterized by a bustier with gathered running stitches, a very deep neckline and an extremely rich and carefully worked skirt. Her first job as a designer was in 1948 at the Youth Guild Inc., where she specialized in clothing for teenagers. But it was in 1957 that Saks Fifth Avenue in New York presented the collection that gave her her first real success.

Folkies Lifestyle and style of clothing, started in the U.S. in the years of the Great Depression and lasting until the early 1960s. There wouldn't be much to distinguish Folkies from Beats, generically understood, if it weren't for the genuinely rural life of the former in contrast to the urban preferences of the latter. In both cases, clothing is intentionally of only marginal importance. And with that word "intentionally" we open up the possibility of an entire aesthetic based on the removal of any kind of gaudy decoration. Even in such different phenomena as the casual style and the complicated circumstances of the hippies, it is possible to trace back the influence of both an ethics and an aesthetics of the Folkies, who were capable of continuing up until the era of Grunge and the New Age Travelers of the 1990s.

Foncel Lucien. House of ready-to-wear men's fashion established in 1979 by the French designer Lucien Foncel, a former assistant to Cardin who was responsible for the men's and women's collections at Korrigan and, for nine years, at Cerruti.

Fonssagrives Lisa (1911-1992). Swedish model. A classic dancer, she moved to Paris during the 1930s. Her first husband was the dancer Fernand Fonssagrives. He pushed her towards a modeling career, showing her photos to Vogue. She posed for Horst and, one by one, for all the great photographers of the 1930s and 1940s. Elegant and sophisticated, but with strong facial features, she represented the ideal of femininity in that period. During the 1950s, she left Paris for New York, met Irving Penn, and married him. She was the trendiest model of her generation and, it seems, the best paid.

Font Josep (1965). Spanish designer of women's ready-to-wear. Born in Barcelona, he studied drawing at the Institute Feli. In 1986, he presented his collection at the Salon Gaudì. He was twice, in 1988 and in '89, a finalist for the Balenciaga award. He launched the Jfld line, which was very successful in Europe and later came to the U.S. Since 1990, his creativity has been at the service of a brand carrying his own name, produced by Prolam Asociados. In 1991, he established a company called Gabriella. He owns boutiques in Barcelona and Bilbao. Since 1993, he has also designed bags. In 1997, he signed a contract with the multinational company Itokin, which anticipated the opening of 35 single-brand points-of-sale in Japan and Southeast Asia. Two years later, he started a second line.

Fontana Leather goods company, among the largest and oldest in Italy. It was established by the Massa family in 1915 in Milan, where one of the company's two plants is still located; the other is in Florence. Besides its own women's line of bags, belts, and small leather goods, all of which combine tradition, a high level of artisanal craftsmanship, and modernity of style, the company produces accessories for Celine, Dolce & Gabbana, Cartier, Tod's, Anteprima, John Galliano, and Bulgari. For the Spring-Summer 2000 collection, Fontana also presented foulards, sabots, and hats.

Fontana Franco (1933). Italian photographer. He became interested in photography in 1961 as an amateur, and from the start had a preference for landscapes in color. After some early success due to an exhibition in which he participated in 1968, he began a rather varied professional career which can be synthesized by the several books he published: *Terre da leggere* (1974), *Skyline* (1978), *Paesaggio urbano* (1980), *Presentassenza* (1982), *Fullcolor* (1983), *Piscina* (1984), *Kaleidoscope* (1990), and *Sorpresi dalla luce Americana* (1999). He won several prizes, including, in 1992, the prestigious Photographer Award of the Photographic Society of Japan on occasion of the 150th anniversary of photography, when Mario Giacomelli had been chosen to represent Italy. As to his relationship with the world of fashion, everything started in 1986 when he published *I dogi della moda*, which was dedicated to Venetian designers. The book was noticed by Alexander Lieberman, the famous art director of Vogue, who suggested that he work with Vogue America. The collaboration would last for four years, until Fontana decided to decline a contract which would have required him to move to New York. He made several campaigns for Maria Grazia Severi, Loretta Di Lorenzo, Mondrian, Versace, and Valentino, who included him, along with 120 of his photos, in the monograph which featured the best photographers with whom he had ever worked.

(*Roberto Mutti*)

Fontana Lucio (1899-1968). Italian artist. In 1961, he designed three dresses that were manufactured in the atelier of Bruna Bini and Giuseppe Telese in Milan. They were sheath dresses, typical of the 1970s, on which Fontana put his unmistakable mark: a vertical cut on the yellow dress, a horizontal line of holes at waist height on the silver one, and six vents arranged in two rows for the black one. He later repeated the experience in partnership with Mila Schön. The inspired inventor of "Spatialism," and without doubt a major figure on the international art scene in the 20th century (he was born in Rosario de Santa Fé, Argentina, but lived and worked in Milan), he overcame the barriers that separated different art forms. He succeeded in creating tension between the cut of a garment and the holes that he designed in it, and gave life to the expressivity of material things, even in works that were small in size, such as some of his jewellery, in particular the unique pieces. Between 1957 and 1967, Fontana designed many pieces of jewellery, including rings, bracelets, and brooches, all with cuts, holes, and precious stones. Two unique pieces created in 1962 were a gold ring with a cut and a brooch in a horizontal cut with two blue crystals. In 1967, he worked with the goldsmiths at Gem Montebello, creating Ellisse, a bracelet with a silver cut, skillfully lacquered, and produced in 150 copies signed and numbered and 200 copies not signed. (*Cloe Piccoli*)

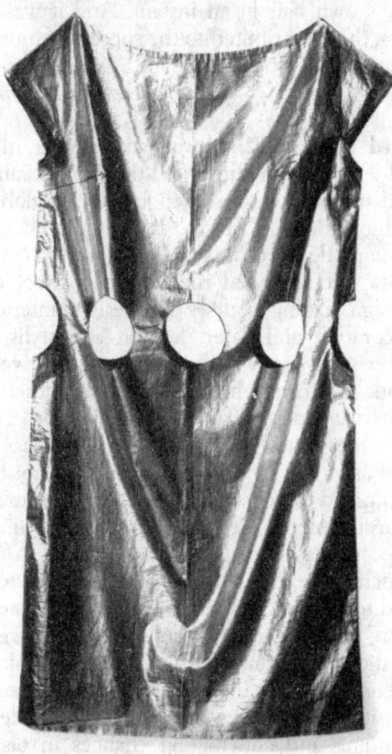

Lucio Fontana. Dress for Bini-Telese, 1961.

Fonticoli Nazareno (1906-1981). Men's tailor and Italian entrepreneur, born in Penne (Abruzzi). As a boy, while still in elementary school, he had to work in one of the many small tailoring shops in the village in order to help his family, producing one pair of pants per day. At the age of 14, with excellent experience as a tailor, he began to work as a professional, first in Milan and later in Rome. For years, although he was very good in his work, he remained in the background. After the liberation of Rome in the summer of 1944, he met Gaetano Savini. They both worked at Satos, a tailor's shop on via del Corso. Fonticoli was a master-cutter, Savini looked after sales and relationships with the customers. They found some rooms on via Barberini and, in 1945, started workshop for haute couture which they named Brioni, after the Dalmatian island which had been so fashionable between the two world wars. Their success was almost immediate. In 1948, Fonticoli was one of the founding members of the National Academy of Tailors. Starting in the winter of 1952, the workshop participated in the high fashion and prêt-à-porter presentations in Florence. By 1960, Fonticoli understood that it was necessary to expand the business on an industrial scale and to get ready for a new era in fashion, one based on a style of prêt-à-porter which, with the founding of the Brioni Roman Style production plant in Penne, he wanted to balance between high artisanal craftsmanship and mass production. From 40 employees in the early years, the company expanded to the 1,000 of today, and now supplies, beside its own shops, about 500 boutiques and department stores all over the world. By the time Fonticoli died, at the age of 75, the economy of his hometown was already based on the achievements of that son who, when a child, would cut and sew one pair of pants a day.

The Fool Group of British fashion designers including Simon Posthuma, Marijkekoger, Barrie Finch and Johie Leeger. They came together as a working group in London in the late 1960s and early 1970s. In the wake of the hippy movement they decided to offer haute couture for aristocratic freaks. They took their inspiration from the style of the Flower Children: ethnic outfits of second-hand clothes, home-dyed, embroidered, and decorated. They said that they did it for love, not money. They designed and made clothes for the jet set and for bands like the Beatles, who had just returned from their trip to India.

Fope Goldsmiths. In 1929, Umberto Cazzola opened an artisanal goldsmith's shop in Vicenza, in Contrà Sant'Ambrogio. After World War II, his son Odino, who was very keen on the goldsmith's art and also an expert on music, expanded the family business from an artisanal scale to an industrial one. This was the beginning of the Cazzola (Ficm) company, and its well-timed adoption of advanced technology for the production of extendible metal watch straps. With the entry of the third generation, Odino's children Umberto and Ines, in the family business, came the 1961 launch of the Fope brand (standing for Fabbrica Oreficeria Preziosi Esportazioni, or Goldsmith Factory and Jewellery Exports). As the name says, Fope focused its energy especially on the export of gold cases and straps for watches, strengthening its contacts with Switzerland, where the company had, among its clients, several firms that produced luxury watches. The 1980s saw the company confirm its leadership in the industry, becoming well-known as a producer of jewellery. In particular, its tubular mesh was highly appreciated for its synthesis of quality design and technical perfection. The introduction of a woman's watch came at the end of the 1990s. At present, Fope has more than 1,000 points-of-sale in Italy and abroad, with a branch office in New York directed by Giulia Cazzola. The turnover in 2002 was €17 million, of which 67% came from Italy, 17% from the rest of Europe, and 16% from the U.S. (*Alessandra Quattordio*)

Forall Company making men's ready-to-wear. It was established near Vicenza in 1970 by Gianfranco Batizza and Aronne Miola, the president and the managing director. Their passion, their managerial ability, and their professional background (each had experience in the industry) combined to make Forall one of the world's leaders in men's prêt-à-porter. They market several brands, including Pal Zileri, Pull. and a line specialized in custom made clothes and sold on the Internet.

❑ 2001, November. The Forall group, which is already a licensee of Krizia and Trussardi (for export), signs a four-year licensing agreement with Moschino. It is to produce men's clothing, both formal and casual, consisting of suits, coats, trousers, and shirts.
❑ 2002. The Group's turnover is €115 million.

Forbes Simon (1950). English hairdresser. One of the most creative hairstylists, in addition to being the owner of the famous London salon Antenna, he became famous in the early 1980s thanks to the mastery with which he used electric razors and small machines to create sculpture-haircuts of great impact. But his fame was linked in particular to hair extensions, a technique inspired by the hair styles of the Rastafarians in Jamaica. It was based on the grafting of synthetic hair and allowed one to lengthen one's own hair in an instant. And it was a look that contributed to the success of music stars such as Boy George and Annie Lennox. (*Ginevra Falzoni*)

Ford Tom (1962). American designer, the golden boy who reinvented the Gucci brand and turned it into a phenomenon of global fashion. Born in Austin, Texas, he grew up in Santa Fé, New Mexico. He moved to New York and attended the Parsons School of Design, taking courses on design, interior decoration and, later, fashion and stylism. After studying in Paris, he returned to New York and began his collaboration with the American designer Cathy Hardwick. He then moved to Perry Ellis, where he became first assistant. In 1990 came the big leap: he was asked to be part of the new style team at Gucci, responsible for the women's line. Success was immediate: the historic *griffe*, which suffered from an image that was too tied to its past, was completely updated and won, from the very first collection, the praise of the most influential international fashion magazines. Since then, his creative talent and sensitivity have been at center stage, understanding and anticipating changes in taste with lines, materials, colors, and suggestions that quickly set trends. In 1994, he was appointed creative director for all the Gucci lines, from clothing for men and women to accessories, objects for the home, and perfumes. He lives and works in London, Paris, Florence, and Milan, and is today the leader of a team of designers from all over the world. (*Cristina Lucchini*)

❑ 2001, July. Time magazine calls Tom Ford the best American designer. In an interview, Tom says: "Fashion isn't limited by clothes. Fashion is everything. Art, music, design, graphics, make-up, hairstyling, architecture, cars...."
❑ 2001, August. He designs a ring in the shape of a gold band, with the Gucci logo, two Gs upside down, impressed on it. Available in three sizes, it glittered, was simple and linear, and quickly became a cult object.
❑ 2001, October. The Saint-Laurent

collection is inspired by a modern version of the goddess Diana, the huntress: short, straight skirts in jaguar, leopard, and panther skin, all spotted, and light Safari jackets and tight pants in leopard.

❑ 2002, January. In Paris, Tom Ford returns to formality. For Gucci, an elegance inspired by the 1930s, a look at the past but revisited in an atmosphere of absolute relaxation.

❑ 2002, January. Milano Moda Uomo. For the Gucci men's collection, Tom Ford presents a very refined man, an F. Scott Fitzgerald hero. The Great Gatsby lives again, on a runway, in light-colored suits with pant cuffs 3 inches high and shirts with pointed collars. For evening, only black, Ford's favorite color, for sophisticated velvet tuxedos and tails, worn with precious overcoats lined with mink.

❑ 2002, July. After designing clothing and perfume for Saint-Laurent, he turns to watches. The collection is called Rive Gauche and has 35 models, in three sizes, for men and women.

❑ 2002, October. During a gala at Radio City Music Hall in New York, he receives the *Vogue Fashion Award* as best designer of the year.

❑ He launches an advertising campaign for a perfume, using the image of a completely naked man with long hair wearing eyeglasses. It recalls the 1971 photo of Yves Saint-Laurent, who had himself portrayed nude for his own male perfume.

❑ 2002. YSL, alias Tom Ford, presents his collection at the Rodin Museum in Paris. This time, he is inspired by Surrealism: a woman in tight sheath dresses, short, tiny jackets, and satin blouses. The last act of folly: nipples with make-up on them, seen through tank tops and transparent dresses. There are also mesh bathing suits and clogs with very high heels.

❑ 2002, December. The new jewellery collection contains fifty pieces in gold and precious stones expressly designed by Tom Ford for the opening of the Gucci boutique on via Condotti in Rome, the first one dedicated only to jewels and watches.

❑ 2003, March. The new YSL collection is inspired by the one created in the 1970s by Saint-Laurent. With an eye to the 1940s, it features a provocative and sexy woman in a girdle, with mesh stockings and a lace bra visible under an extremely low-cut dress; definitely seductive in the choice of materials (lace, rustling silks, stretch velvets), and in the very tight fit, with very high-heel shoes in bright colors.

❑ 2003, November. News of the lack of an agreement between PPR and the Ford-De Sole team, which was responsible for the worldwide relaunch of Gucci. The Texan designer is to stay with Gucci until April 30, 2004 and will present two collections, a men's and a women's. The missed renewal of the contract also means the end of the collaboration with Yves Saint-Laurent, a brand that also belongs to the group, of which the designer was creative director.

❑ 2004, November. The book *Tom Ford: Ten Years* is published by Rizzoli International. It is the story of 10 years during which the designer conquered the fashion world in Europe and America.

❑ 2005, April. After one year of "rest" and thousands of rumors about possible coups de theatre in the star system, an agreement is announced with the cosmetics giant Estée Lauder. The designer is to be in charge of a sort of restyling, focusing on a softer sensuality, different from the strong tones of his time at Gucci and Saint-Laurent. The products of the designer's work will have the label *Tom Ford for Estée Lauder*.

❑ 2005, May. An agreement is announced with Marcolin for the creation of an eyewear line under the brand Tom Ford. It will be Accessories, then, and not clothing, as a way to return to the world of prêt-à-porter. The official launch is expected during Silmo in October 2005.

(*Gabriella Gregorietti*)

Ford Models American model agency. In 1947, Jerry and Eileen Ford began to discover talent in New York. Today, they lead this legendary model agency which has contributed to the history of the fashion system. They launched Lauren Hutton, Kim Basinger, Melanie Griffith, and Sharon Stone, who passed from glossy magazines to the world of celluloid. Among the famous models represented by Ford have been top models such as Christie Birkley, Jean Shrimpton, and Jerry Hall. Today, the agency has branch offices all over the U.S. and in Argentina, Brazil, and Canada.

(*Alessandra Scifo*)

Formenti Egidio. A dealer in high quality fabrics. Born in Milan, for some years he worked as an agent for textile companies in Lombardy. In 1917-18 he opened his first shop at via Tornabuoni 89 in Florence. By 1924 he already owned six shops in the most important streets of the major Italian cities. He specialized in wool fabrics that he purchased in neutral colors and year after year he dyed them according to the demands of the market. At the start of World War II, he temporarily closed the business in order to devote himself to the working of straw, a typically Tuscan artisanal product.

Fornarina Shoe brand owned by the Fornari company from Civitecchia Marche. The first collections date back to 1947, but constant change over the years has allowed Fornarina to consider itself one of the leading Italian brands for young fashion. The firm has two brands on the international market: Fornarina and Fornarina Kids. There are branch offices and agencies, established in the 1990s, in Los Angeles, London, Munich, Hong Kong, and Nice. In the rest of Europe, there is a strong network of agents and distributors in order to make sure of supplies, which in Italy turns out to be particularly complicated. The marketing of the Sneaker Up!, which added a feminine touch to tennis shoes with glamourous and trendy inserts, dates to 1996. The market reception was good and this first model was followed by the Dune, One, Contest, and Pool lines. Today, Fornarina offers not only shoes, but also eyewear (produced by the Marcolin company from Belluno, a leader in the field), women's clothing, and bags.

(*Pierangelo Mastantuono*)

❑ 2004, March. The firm is acquired by Franco Romagnoli Spa, a manufacturer of children's shoes.

❑ 2004, April. The launch of the project Fornarina Vibe, a successful attempt to combine fashion and art. Every two seasons there will be a new collaboration with an emerging artist for the creation of a clothing line, the planning of the most important points-of-sale for the house, and the organization of special events. The first designer is Miss Van. She is French, 30 years old, an exponent of the graffiti movement, and someone who everyone remembers for the sexy dolls painted in acrylic on the walls of Paris, Brussels, London, Barcelona, and Madrid.

❑ 2005, February. Principe, a top company in the field of leather goods, signs an agreement with the Fornari group to launch the first Fornarina bag collection.

❑ 2005, June. In collaboration with the DJ, producer, and artist Howie B., a clothing line for men and women called Hvana is launched, using the most precious fabrics such as cashmere and denim. The distribution starts in the best boutiques of London, Tokyo, Paris, Milan, and New York.

Forquet Federico (1931). Italian designer. He was born to a family of French origin that fled the Revolution in 1789 and settled in Naples. One of his ancestors was a minister to Ferdinand IV of Bourbon. He grew up near Vesuvius, a member of society, attending the good salons. Music was his passion. At the age of 6, he began to study piano at the Conservatory. Then, at the age of 20, came the turning point. One of his hobbies was drawing. His works were just sketches, but Balenciaga, introduced to him in Ischia by a friend, liked them. It was 1955. The great tailor invited him to Paris for an apprenticeship in his atelier, where the young Ungaro and Courrèges were already finding their way. Thus, once having abandoned the university, he worked side by side with the master who, at the time, represented the peak of haute couture. After two seasons, he returned to Italy and settled in Rome in order to continue his apprenticeship with Fabiani and, later, to work in the dressmaker's shop of Irene Galitzine. In 1962, he felt he was ready for his début, which occurred on the runway of the Sala Bianca of Palazzo Pitti. It was a triumph: he presented both bon ton and chic, a very personal chic, a tribute to woman in order to make her seductive. In a phrase, the style of elegance. Irene Brin wrote: "Fourquet is the Italian Dior." Since that début, two important trends began to be seen: in some cases, people began to think that clothes and fine dressing were just too much trouble, especially that subtle refinement that came from expert cutting; and people began to like to dress in a simple, linear style, just when some of his colleagues were favoring a more baroque taste. But his clients stayed with him, and they were the best: kings and queens, princes and princesses, billionaires, divas, and first ladies. Outside Italy, he was by now a star, the English press calling him "Frederick the Great." He designed the first hot pants, and his nude look anticipated Saint-Laurent's. A very young Ira Fürstenberg, an exceptional model, looked as if she were wearing colored air; transparent skirts and trousers matched tops made simply of necklaces. Years passed, prêt-à-porter loomed on the horizon, arrived, and was successful. Fourquet, a fashion soloist, closed his atelier in 1972. "Since the beginning," he explained, "I've always done everything on my own. I have never had an assistant, or a designer, not only for my models, but also for accessories and fabrics. It would have been unthinkable, for me, to go into partnership with a manufacturer. My experience in this was limited to a small line sold in the Elizabeth Arden beauty salons, but just for a short time. Business for its own sake is not for me." There was a period during which he designed fabrics for interior decor, and then his stays in Rome became intermittent: he preferred to be in a beautiful house that he had near Siena, where he discovered another stimulating vocation: gardening. He designed his own, a harmony of green stippled by the colors of the changing seasons. So he became a garden designer, for his friends and the friends of his friends. This is how he lives today, this professional of elegance. But two clients have also remained friends: Marella Agnelli, whom he considers the inspiration of his fashion, and Allegra Caracciolo, who worked with him for some time. He has no regrets, except perhaps the desire to relive the emotions of the past: in his keepsake drawer he has a newspaper clipping in which Armani talks about him with gratifying words, praising his "clean style, and intelligent seduction," qualities found in them both. (*Lucia Mari*)

Forte Gabriella (1949). A top-tier manager and president, since 1994, of Calvin Klein Inc. She was able to globalize the company by emphasizing the strategic development of the brand and focusing on the expansion of the different lines of products in North America, Europe, and Asia. She signed important license agreements for eyewear, perfumes, and leather goods. Under her management, the turnover almost doubled, going from $2.1 billion in 1994 to $5.3 billion in 1998. Born in Formia, she graduated from Hunter College with a thesis on the conflict between the USSR and China. She then worked in the luxury goods field, starting and managing a consulting company. She also worked for Condé Nast Italy and as a market analyst at the Italian Institute of Foreign Commerce in New York. Before Calvin Klein, she worked from 1979 to 1994 for Giorgio Armani Inc., where she directed world-wide sales development, public relations, and international communications, in addition to all the operations in the U.S. Her amazing career is the result of an excellent combination of a sharp eye for fashion and a practical business sense. (*Eleonora Attolico*)

❑ 2002, February. She leaves Calvin Klein in order to become president of Dolce&Gabbana USA and director for accessories and licenses at Dolce&Gabbana S.p.A. Her arrival, at the beginning of February, coincides with the record boom of the D&G *griffe* and with the subsequent need to strengthen and expand the management.

Fortuny Mariano (1871-1949). Fabric and clothing designer. Fortuny's name is forever linked to the famous pleated fabric he invented and patented in 1909, the forerunner of the new permanent pleating techniques used by designers such as Issey Miyake. Fortuny was the original embodiment of the fashion designer as artist, a painter himself and born into a family of artists (his father, Mariano y Marsal was a celebrated Spanish painter). He was born in Granada, Spain, and lived for a while in Paris, but in 1889 he moved to Venice, where he developed his multiple interests as a painter, photographer and designer of flamboyantly creative sets for the theater and the opera. Early on he began creating his own fabrics, painting them and exploring techniques of diffused light. In his art and his designs he was inspired by Venetian art of the 15th and 16th centuries and Arabic cultures. His first steps in fashion were through the designs he created for the theater, beginning with a simple scarf, the Knossos scarf, which was printed with geometric patterns inspired by Cycladic art. In time he developed a dress to go with the scarf, a pleated silk cylinder that could be belted around the waist called the Delphi dress. All his dresses and original fabrics were made by hand in his studio. In Fortuny's lifetime, he dressed some of the world's most flamboyant personalities, who donned his clothes both in life and on the stage: Isabella Duncan, Eleonora Duse, Sarah Bernhardt, Peggy Guggenheim, and Emma and Irma Gramatica. Proust, in *Remembrance of Things Past,* dressed Mme. de Guermantes in "garments made by Fortuny," and wrote, "is it their historical character, or is it rather that each one of them is unique, that gives them so special a significance?" The Fortuny Museum at Palazzo Orfei, in Venice, houses a number of his works, clothes and furniture, and fashion museums throughout the world collect his designs.

Fossati Textile company that was already a participant at the Voltiana Exhibition which took place in Como in 1899, where it presented its production of diapered fabrics for ties and a cloth panel showing a panoramic view of the lakeside town. Ambrogio Fossati, the founder, had already established a business in 1856 in Binago, and later moved it first to Como, then to Ossuccio, and finally to Gravedona. In 1922, he established Sas Fossati & Co., which included Ambrogio's children Enrico, Angelo, Carlo, Fermo, Giuseppina, and Angelina. The company, with premises in Como, began in the second half of the 1930s to produce elasticized fabrics for girdles and bathing suits, in addition to silk fabrics for scarves, ties, pajamas, and dressing gowns. In 1954, the company split in two. One part, known as Del Vecchio-Fossati, continued to manufacture latex fabrics in Gravedona. The other, Fermo Fossati of Como, was registered in the name of one of Ambrogio's children. In 1990, the company was sold, and Ottaviano Mantero Scheuten and Filippo Saldanna established Fermo Fossati 1871, which in 1993 acquired the Tessitura Serica Carlo Riva, a firm in Galbiate, near Lecco, that manufactures shirt fabrics.

(*Pierangelo Mastantuono*)

Fossati Marina (1924-1994). Jewellery designer. She belonged to the artisanal world of Lissone, where she was born. Her father was a carpenter at La Scala. For her entire life, she was never ashamed of being called an artisan. On the contrary, she considered it praiseworthy and was proud of it. She arrived in Milan in the early 1960s, during the economic boom, and she carved out a space for herself thanks to perseverance in her work, an extraordinary technical ability, and the ambition to do new and original things. She started with the presentations at Palazzo Pitti, working for designers who would later become great names but were, at the moment, making their début. Her designs – rings, earrings, brooches, necklaces, and bracelets – displayed taste and imagination. She used relatively modest materials such as crystal, pearls, coral, ivory, and semi-precious stones. She deserves the credit for establishing Sharra Pagano on via della Spiga in 1970 in partnership with Lino Raggio. Marina liked working on an artisanal level and had no desire for a large business. After just three years, she split with Raggio and opened her own space at via del Gesù 15. In the late 1980s, she left the company to her associate Anna Tarabelloni, who maintained the offices and continued the Marina Fossati brand. She was a frequent visitor in the artistic circles of Bagutta, from which the first Italian literary prize was born.

(*Gabriella Gregorietti*)

Fosso Samuel (1962). Photographer from Cameroon. He started at the age of 13 and since then has worked continuously on the theme of the self-portrait. He was discovered by the French photographer Bernard Descamps, who presented him at the first African photography event in Bamako. He made a name for himself as one of the best African photographers, exhibiting his work in Paris, London, and New York. He works for Vogue France.

Foulard From the Provençal word *foulat*, in French *foulé*, to indicate a fabric in silk, silk and cotton, or wool that is extremely light and cut in the shape of a square with a fairly wide base. It is an accessory that is sometimes indispensable, and never completely absent from the wardrobe, a small trifle in chiffon for a breast pocket, a big silk square to knot around the neck, large, in colors, rich in motifs woven on weft and warp, or printed in patterns, to be tied on a handbag or worn as a shawl around the shoulders. It is a very important item which adds to the prestige of even the most famous *griffe*. In France, those by Hermès, Dior, Saint-Laurent, Chanel, and Givenchy are famous. In Italy, the most prestigious ones are by Gucci, Ferragamo, and Roberta di Camerino, followed by all the great designers of ready-to-wear, from Mila Schön to Armani and Ferré. They are manufactured for the most part in Como, in workshops which also produce for themselves, according to designs created in-house, foulards that are admired for their very rich prints in floral, abstract, and geometric patterns that are obtained through a long process of many steps according to the number of colors selected.

Fouli Elia (1927). Photographer and art director, born in Alexandria, Egypt. After working in film, he moved to Paris. In 1952, he met Guy Bourdin. From 1958 to 1966, he worked for Elle as a fashion photographer, and then from 1970 to 1982 as artistic director, after three years spent in New York working for Condé Nast.

Fouquet Jean (1899-1984). French jeweller. His father and grandfather were also jewellers. The grandfather, the founder of the dynasty, was Alphonse. The father was Georges (1862-1957). The mythical boutique-workshop was in Rue Royale. Georges, who made his début in 1891, went quickly from a classically-inspired collection to a modern one, typically Art Nouveau, specializing in *plique-à-jour* enamels. Extraordinary theatrically-inspired pieces were made for Sarah Bernhardt on designs of the Czech artist Alphonse Mucha. Jean made a name for himself as soon as he joined his father's workshop. At the age of 26 he won an award at the Exposition of Decorative Arts in Paris. After World War II, he brought enamels back into vogue. (*Alessandra Quattordio*)

Fourreau Style Known also as Princess style, this look was very much in vogue during the 1930s, 1950s and 1960s, but always with dresses of different lengths. Tight around the waist, it was meant to emphasize a woman's height. The dresses have smooth lines and a tight fit, obtained through the expert use of seams and darts or a belt around the waist.

Fox A silver fox for the seductress Greta Garbo in *Wild Orchids* (1929), a white fox over a fatal chiffon dressing gown for the jewel thief Marlene Dietrich in *Desire* (1936), a red fox for the enchanting Loretta Young in *Second Honeymoon* (1937), and a stole made of two whole foxskins, with head, tail, and paws for Dorothy Lamour in *Swing High, Swing Low*, also from 1937. In the movies, a machine for the creation of dreams and escape during the poverty-stricken 1930s, the theatrical and multiform luxury of fox fur was triumphant. An animal that lives in the wild, a member of the family of the Canidae and present in a vast area that includes Asia, Europe and the Americas, the fox stands out precisely for the variety of its pelt, which changes in accordance with its environment and the climatic conditions in which it lives. The animal is at its ease both in the desert heat and in the chill of northern climes. The color of the fur distinguishes the silver fox (*Canis vulpes argenteus*) with its dark pelt with bright white points; the blue or Greenland fox (*Canis vulpes lagopus*), the white or Arctic fox (*Canis alopex lagopus*), whose long and delicate fur is the finest there is; the cross fox (*Canis vulpes cruciatus*), so called for the cross-shaped patch of dark fur extending across its shoulders and neck; the gray fox (*Urucyon cinereo argenteus*), the red fox (*Vulpes vulpes*), which is the most common variety, the finest specimens of which come from Alaska and

Kamchatka. History tells us that the fox was already well known in antiquity, since techniques for preparing it are found in the verses of the *Iliad*, and that in classical Athens the headgear known as the *alopex* was in all likelihood made of fox fur. In more modern times, in the sixteenth century, we have documentation of 800 very rare black fox pelts sent as tribute, along with 2,400 sables and 2,000 beavers to Ivan IV, also known as Ivan the Terrible. The reports, actually quite conflicting, about the beginning of fox-breeding in captivity take us back to 1890, in the United States, at the mouth of the St. Lawrence, with a program begun by two partners, Dalton and Oulton, and in Canada, in Prince Edward's Island, where in 1894 a couple of silver foxes reproduced in captivity. In Europe the first successful reproduction in captivity was the work of the enterprising Norwegians who, in 1914, imported Canadian silver foxes. Today, foxes for breeding, a technique that is not particularly difficut but which requires great precision, come from Canada and also from Scandinavia, and are every bit as fine as wild foxes, but with the richness of their array of colors, the result of cross-breeding and mutations, they renew the myth of seductive beauty – long age propagated on the silver screen – of this fur that is so soft and lovely to the touch.

(*Maria Rita Stiglich*)

Fox Frederick (1931). Australian milliner. Fox studied hat making in Sydney, but left his homeland in the late 1950s to launch his career in London. He has collaborated with a number of prominent British designers, including Hardy Amies, and has become widely known for the hats he designs for Queen Elizabeth.

Fox Skin This term is used to describe fox fur, with its long, dense, soft hair. There is red, black, white, and beige fox fur, as well as fox furs dyed in artificial colors. But the fox skin par excellence is the silver or blue fox, the most chic, though it has now passed a little from fashion, even though we can remember full length fox fur capes draped over the shoulders of the divas of Hollywood, symbols of the luxury of the 1930s. There was also the entire fox, embalmed, with head, tail, paws, and glass eyes, worn around the collar of suits between the World Wars.

Fraise French term meaning a ruff, a rounded and completely pleated collar. In vogue throughout the 1500s and 1600s, it was made of muslin or linen, rigid with starch and, when large enough, supported by a light wire framework. Worn with both men's and women's clothes, after a century of success it became softer and lay on the shoulders. Its origin is uncertain. Some sources say that Caterina De' Medici brought it to France from Italy, others that it came directly from Spain. From time to time it is revived and reinvented by the designers of the day.

Francer Istvan (1956). Serbian designer, born in Subotica, on the border with Hungary. He studied at the Academy of Applied Arts in Belgrade and completed his education at the Parsons School of Design in New York. His career has included work in addition to fashion. For example, he has been the picture editor of books dedicated to Simone de Beauvoir and to the Paris of the 1930s and 1940s, and he has designed sets and costumes for the theater. His fame in the fashion world is especially linked to the Donna Karan brand, for which he worked from 1987 to early 2000 (men's and women's collection for the main line and the Signature Collection). For three seasons, starting with the Spring-Summer collection in 2001, he was chief designer and creative director of Maska Group. Since the Spring-Summer 2001 season he has designed a line under his own name produced by Fin.Part.

(*Mariacristina Righi*)

❑ 2002, June. He is chosen to coordinate the team for Cerruti's first lines in collaboration with Samantha Sung (formerly with Ralph Lauren) for women's wear and Adrien Smith (formerly of Gucci and Ferré) for men's wear.
❑ 2004, May. He is back at Donna Karan, after a first experience that lasted 14 years.
❑ 2004, July. He is appointed head director of DKNY men's wear.

Francesca Trezzi Milanese designer and brand name. She was born in 1974. At the age of 18 she began to produce handmade bags and accessories for friends and acquaintances. After obtaining a law degree from the State University of Milan in 1999, she chose the world of fashion and obtained a Master's in Fashion Brand Management from the Marangoni Institute. After a period with Ferré and experience as a production manager with Gilli, thanks to which she was able to deepen her knowledge of products and materials, Francesca decided to bet on her passion for accessories and on her creativity. In June 2002, she established her own company. She made her début presenting her first accessories collection for Spring-Summer 2003. (*Dario Golizia*)

Francesco Biasia Manufacturer and brand of bags. The company was established in Povolaro, near Vicenza, by Francesco and Carlo Biasia in 1977. The factory constantly reinvents a tradition of five centuries of working in leather in the Veneto, in the light of modern techniques and taste. Bags and accessories are distributed in more than 2,500 points-of-sale all over the world, and through single-brand boutiques in Rome, Milan, Paris, Prague, and Dubai. The most recent was opened in October 2002, a flagship boutique with 700 square feet on via della Vigna Nuova in Florence. At Mipel 2002, Francesco Biasia received the Goya *Big Bag* award. The company presents its collections at the most important industry trade fairs, including Madrid's Showroom and Modelform in Offenbach and Munich. The year 2002 ended with a turnover of €33 million and a gross profit of €2.7 million. In June 2003, Mariella Burani Fashion Group announced the acquisition of 60% of the company, for €10.2 million in shares of Antichi Pellettieri, without any cash payment. The other 40% remains in the hands of the founding family.

(*Pierangelo Mastantuono*)

Francesco Fino Brand name and designer who made his début in 1997 with a small collection of wedding dresses and formal clothes. In 1998, after a long collaboration with Marzotto and Zegna, he designed high fashion clothes and presented them in Rome during the fashion week dedicated to Italian couture. In July 1999 his creations were on the runways of Sposa Italia in Milan, and in September he made his début in prêt-à-porter at Milano Collezioni.

Francevramant French *maison* established in 1935 by Madeleine Vramant and the American France Obré. They had met in Mainbocher, where Vramant worked as a designer and Obré as a sales assistant. The partnership didn't last long, and each started a separate business. They retired almost simultaneously in the mid 1950s.

Francis Armet (1945). Jamaican photographer. He has lived in London since 1955. In the late 1960s he began to work in the fields of fashion, advertising, and reportage. He devoted himself to the photography of black people in Africa and presented the pictures in an exhibition at the Photographers Gallery in London in 1984. He is also a poet and a painter.

Franco Bassi Italian tie factory. It is named after the man who founded it in Como in 1973. It employs 20 people. The production is distributed in Italy (50%), Europe (15%), and the U.S. and Japan (35%). Each season, the collection is presented at Pitti Immagine Uomo and at the Cologne Fair.

François Villon French shoe brand launched in 1960 by François Villon de Benveniste. Princess Grace of Monaco, Farah Diba, Maria Callas, Rita Hayworth, Chanel, Jackie Onassis, Marlene Dietrich, Liz Taylor, Audrey Hepburn, Lauren Bacall, Catherine Deneuve, Jane Fonda, Mia Farrow, and Faye Dunaway (the list could continue) were all literally seduced by him. After obtaining a law degree, F.V.d.B. initially worked in the family's perfume business in Grasse. Called by Perugia, a famous name in shoe manufacturing, he became acquainted what a type of production that was clearly handmade and discovered a real inclination for this kind of accessory. In 1960, he started his own business at number 27 Faubourg Saint Honoré. His specific intent was to apply the principles of the custom made shoe to large scale production. His creations, all manufactured in Italy, distinguish themselves for their refinement of line, the quality of their materials, and the preciousness of details.

Very soon, Villon's shoes made their appearance on runways accompanying the collections of Hermès, Féraud, Chanel, Ted Lapidus, Patou, Nina Ricci, and Lanvin, and were soon distributed in boutiques all over the world. His boots for daytime, evening, and riding became famous, as did his urban cowboy boots, his flats, and his sabots. (*Giuliana Parabiago*)

Franco Ziche Knitwear factory established in 1960 by Franco Ziche, descended from a well-known family of entrepreneurs and the heir to a tradition going back to the 18th century. The plant in Thiene (Vicenza) produces men's and women's knitwear. Strengthened by the experience of his predecessors, Ziche was able to create a leading industrial group, Due Golfi, operating in the fields of real estate and finance. In 1975, the constant development of the group was confirmed by the founding of Giottotex for dyeing and finishing operations and later by the purchase of shares in a manufacturer of wool fabrics. Ziche's three children have worked in the company for a long time. Alvise is general manager of the group, Alessandro takes care of administration, and Francesca is in charge of private label activities. In 2003, Alvise hired the designer Maurizio Bonas as creative director. He was already the head designer for the Franco Ziche men's and women's lines. Alvise also hired Giuseppe Zanella, a great specialist in the design of trousers, as supervisor of a new team for the development of the Cleo&Pat line of men's and women's pants. In addition to a headquarters in Thiene and four manufacturing plants, the Group has since 1987 had an office in Munich for distribution and marketing in northern Europe. In 1995 a showroom was opened in Milan and in 1999 a commercial office was opened in New York for the U.S. and Canada. (*Maria Vittoria Alfonsi*)

Frani Paola (1962). At the young age of 20, she established Scrupoli, her first clothing line, along with Davide Fusaroli. But her real début came in 1986, with the collection Paola Frani, presented at Pitti Trend. That same year, she started a collaborative relationship with the Coin group. Later, she worked with Les Copains, Aeffe, Crimson, and Casadei Calzature. In 1991, her brand made its début at Milano Collezioni and the following year she opened a showroom in Milan.

❑ 1999-2002. The opening of six boutiques, in Milan, Sardinia, Paris, and Japan.
❑ 2001. The company has a turnover of 26 billion liras.
❑ 2003, February. On the Milan runways, the new collection is inspired by the 1960s and 1980s, with blacks, transparencies, inlays, exaggerated shoulders, mini-skirts, and mini-pants. The decorations have a punk style inspired by the idea of barbed wire.

Spring-Summer model 1998 by Paola Frani.

Frank Robert (1924). American photographer, born in Switzerland. After short apprenticeships in the early 1940s in Zurich and Basel, he moved to the U.S and worked as a fashion photographer for Life, Look, Fortune, and Harper's Bazaar, where he collaborated with the art director Alexey Brodovitch and the photographer Louis Faurer. Irresistibly attracted by photo reportage and the work of Eugene Smith, and by the writers of the Beat Generation, he traveled throughout the U.S thanks to a scholarship from the Guggenheim Foundation. The result was a photo book which which has had a lasting impact. It was first published in France by Robert Delpire as *Les Américains* and then a year later in the

U.S. as *The Americans,* with a preface by Jack Kerouac. As an artist Frank was close to the avant-garde, fascinated by the theater and underground poetry, although he never completely abandoned professional photography, continuing to produce fashion photos, catalogues, and very personal photo features. (*Roberto Mutti*)

Frankie B American brand of casual clothing. Created by the California designer Daniella Clarke, it is "half hippie and half rock and roll," as she defines herself. Married to the guitarist Gilby Clarke of *Gun's N' Roses*, by which she is inspired, she lives in Los Angeles and her collection is one of the most important on the West Coast. Loved by the film world, she has fans such as Jennifer Lopez, Rosanna Arquette, and Pamela Anderson Lee. For her unconventional and dangerously sexy designs for trousers, jackets, shirts, and T-shirts, she is inspired by the 1960s and 1970s and by rock and roll.

Frankie Morello Brand created in 1996 thanks to a partnership between Maurizio Modica, who worked in the theater and then in design with Alessi, and Pierfrancesco Gigliotti, a designer who studied in Stockholm, New York, and Japan, after leaving his native Naples. They presented for the first time in 1998, a men's collection with a macho-vintage look. Since then, they have offered men's and women's prêt-à-porter, with particular attention to fabrics, the use of unusual materials, asymmetries, colors, as well as ironic and theatrical details.
(*Silvia Paoli*)

Franzi Leather goods factory. In 1864, Felice Franzi established a leather goods factory in Milan and named it after himself. It was the first in Europe to produce a well-known, very strong leather tanned with vegetable products. With the best part of this leather, on which a particular grain called *Franzi* was stamped, trunks, suitcases, and handbags of great elegance were produced, in addition to a wide variety of small leather goods in both classic and modern colors. After five generations, the house is now managed by Oreste Franzi. Besides the historic headquarters on via Manzoni, the firm has opened a boutique on via Palermo, both in Milan.

Frarica Manufacturing company with production plants in Carpi and Este. Its product is famous thanks to the advertising slogan "The Shirt with a Moustache," launched by spokespersons such as Maurizio Costanzo and the actor Andrea Roncato. Actually, the shirt is manufactured with a very sophisticated technology, using computerized systems that allow a fit that is "extremely adjustable to the shape of the person wearing it." Established in 1947 in Carpi by the brothers Clodo and Cleomede Righi, today the factory has 280 employees, wholesale distribution for the Frarica line, and retail distribution for the Dino Erre line. In 1999, the turnover was 50 billion liras, with exports providing 15%.

❑ 2002, March. In Milan, at Corso Venezia 8, the first single-brand boutique for Dino Erre is opened. That is the brand of men's shirts for the company, of which Rino Righi is the general director.

Frassa Gherardo (1943). An organizer and curator of exhibitions, a profession that he began in order to "provide a stage" for the collection of jeans and ties that he created in his first business (he would later become an antiques dealer) as a seller of secondhand trousers, shirts, and suits at Surplus, the first shop of its kind, which opened in Milan in 1974, on Corso Garibaldi. He brought a fashion for secondhand clothes into the everyday dressing of young people and of some older snobs who liked elegantly faded and torn jackets. This job turned him into an archeologist of fashion, rummaging through old trunks, in the "bundles" of secondhand clothes that arrived at Resina (near Naples) from America, and in attics. An archeologist and, through his passion, a collector. Thanks to this precious collecting, he organized three exhibitions: *The Jeans Century* at La Rinascente in Milan in 1982; *Dreaming Some Ties* at Surplus in 1983, with one thousand American ties from the 1930s to the 1970s; and *A Tie at the Museum* at Spazio Inghirami in Palazzo Acerbi in Milan. Since that time, Frassa has specialized in the organization of exhibitions, closing his first business and selling the shop. Among the exhibitions for which he has designed the sets are: *Valentina at Modit* (Milan, 1985), *Forattini's Republic* (traveling, 1987-88), *The Clothes of Adventure*, *Anglo-Florentines: A Love Story*, *Art Nouveau Fabrics*, *Fred Astaire*, *Gabriele D'Annunzio's Wardrobe*, *The Whimsical Rule* (Pitti Immagine Uomo, 1986-1996), *The Eighty Years of the Corrierino* (Milan, 1989), *The Futurist Revolution of Clothing* (traveling, 1986), *Bulgari, A Monograph* (traveling, 1995-99), *Cut Out* (Milan, San Vittore Prison, 1998), *A Mirror of Europe* (2001-2003) and *Absolute Covers* (the most beautiful covers of LP records, the Museums of Porta Romana, Milan, 2002).

(*Fulvio Bertasso*)

Fratelli Rossetti Historic shoe factory in Parabiago, near Milan. It manufactures more than 400,000 pairs of shoes a year, with a turnover that in the late 1990s was about 70 billion liras. Some 50% of the production is sold in Italy and the rest is exported. Each year about 10% goes to the U.S., where the company has been active for more than twenty years and where, in June 1999, it opened a large showroom on Madison Avenue in New York. The company was established in 1955 by the brothers Renzo and Renato Rossetti, who were born in Sanguinetto, near Verona. Renzo began working at the age of 13, and was a typographer, mechanical draftsman, and artisanal producer of shoes for cyclists. Success came through the artisanal perfection ("We have always worked as if we had to personally answer to the custumer for every pair of shoes we sell him.") and innovation applied to a classic style. In the book *I Mass-Moda. Fatti e Personaggi dell'Italian Look* (Spinelli Publishers, 1979), Adriana Mulassano says, "Men, poor things, as to shoes, were really in a bad way. The market wouldn't offer anything other than laced shoes with fringes and 'derbies,' in black or brown calfskin. There were no new seasonal styles and no imagination. And so they started: the banning of laces, the promotion of loafers, the launch of the first very soft unlined shoes to be worn in summer without socks, the marketing of boots, higher heels, and the introduction of colors through an ageing process that would

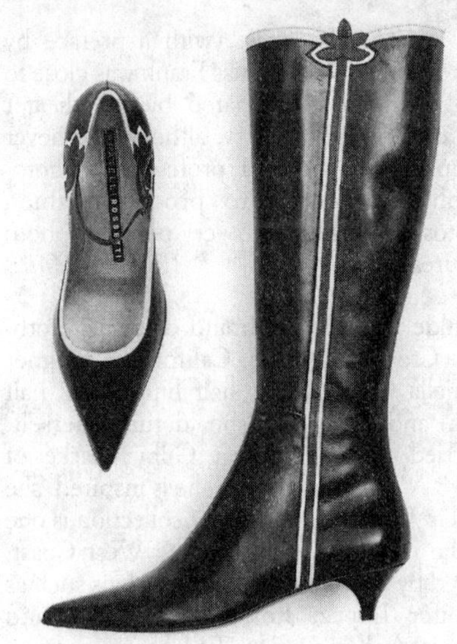

Two models by the shoe company Fratelli Rossetti.

make them more acceptable. Success was such that in 1966 the Rossetti brothers were forced to expand and build a very modern production plant." The first women's line was created in 1973. Single-brand boutiques followed one after another in Genoa, Venice, Milan (at via Matteotti-via Montenapoleone), Bari, Rome, Paris, and Chicago. In 1978, the Rossettis were pioneers in the launch of New York's Madison Avenue as a shopping district. In 1999, they reorganized "the store." Almost half a century of success and growth. They recently created the Flexa shoe: 18 pieces hand-assembled which adjust to the foot's movement thanks to unusual flexibility and a removable foot-strap.

(*Marcella Gabbiano*)

❑ 2002, May. The Flexa Sailing model is created at the explicit request of *Mascalzone Latino* (*Latin Scoundrel*), the Italian boat competing in the America's Cup. It has all the characteristics requested by the team members. The first prototypes are tested by the crew during training at Elba and in Auckland. The model goes on sale in July 2002 in two versions: the Flexa Sailing Professional, with the same technical standards as the shoe worn by the crew in the America's Cup, and Flexa Sailing, less high-tech, for fans of sailing in general. The shoe is available in red and blue, the colors of *Mascalzone Latino*, and in a sand color.

❑ 2002, November. Shoes, ankle boots, and desert boots in the brightest colors: red, green, and yellow; flats and heels, for singing and dancing. In the same style as the costumes by Elisa Savi, these shoes have been designed by the Rossetti brothers for the American musical *Fiddler on the Roof*, which received three Oscars in its film version and had more than 3,000 performances on Broadway in New York, in London, and in Japan. On the Italian stage, the show was revised in a Yiddish interpretation by Moni Ovadia, on tour in Italy from November 2002 to Spring 2003.

❑ 2003, February. Fratelli Rossetti opens its first outlet space in Foxtown, a large multi-brand store in Mendrisio, Switzerland.

❑ In early 2003, the company employs 260 workers, and is one of the most important in the field regarding turnover, number of employees, and international image. The entire ownership is still in the hands of the Rossetti family. The president of the group is Renzo Rossetti, who sets long-term strategy. His three sons have other operating functions: Diego, 46, in the company for more than twenty years, is the marketing and commercial director and coordinates all the communication activities in Italy and abroad; Dario, 44, in the company for more than ten years, follows coordination, planning, modeling, and purchases; Luca, 37, a graduate of the Bocconi University in Milan, is the general manager.

❑ The strategy chosen by Fratelli Rossetti at the beginning has not changed over the years and can be summed up in a concept that is still extremely effective even today: maximum harmony between technology and tradition, maximum equilibrium between quality and price.

❑ In Italy, there are 13 boutiques. Abroad, the company's main locations are in New York, Paris, London, Brussels, and Hong Kong.

❑ A rich collection of ethnic and period shoes accumulated over a period of 50 years by Renzo Rossetti finally has its own museum in Parabiago. He began the collection at an early age, before World War II, and very much desired to see it have its own space. The museum can be visited by appointment. It has 3,000 pairs of shoes that are perfectly maintained.

❑ 2005. After the opening of a third boutique in Paris, on Rue de Grenelle, comes the début of a new franchise store in Dubai. The company has a turnover of €55 million in 2004.

Fratelli Tallia di Delfino Factory specialized in pure wool, cashmere, alpaca, mohair, and silk fabrics for clothes, jackets, and coats. It was established in 1903 in Strona (Biella) by Delfino Tallia to manufacture drapery and clothes for the most refined tailor's workshops. Around 1933, the company reconsidered its original philosophy and oriented itself toward the market for mass production, which at present absorbs 75% of its output. Some 70% of the more than 900,000 yards of fabric produced yearly is exported.

Fratini Gina (1931). Pseudonym of Georgina Carolina Butler, a British designer born in Kobe, Japan of English parents. She spent her childhood in Canada, Myanmar, and India. She was educated in England and studied fashion under Madge Garland at the Royal College of Art from 1950 to 1953. She spent two years as a costume designer for the Katherine Dunham Dance Company, after which she worked as a freelance designer and costume maker. In 1964, she launcheed her own line. Influenced by her nomadic life and by the hippie trends of the moment, she offered a fashion that was ethnic in its cut and proportions. Over the years, she developed a more and more romantic style with reminiscenses of the past. In 1971, at the peak of her success, she was chosen by Princess Ann (on the suggestion of the court photographer Norman Parkinson) to design the dress for her 21st birthday. She thus developed a network of very high class clients, including Princess Diana, who she continued to dress even after closing her business. She returned to being a consultant, designing, among other things, collections for Norman Hartnell and underwear with Ossie Clark.

Fratteggiani Florentine shoe factory also famous for its leather accessories. Established in the early 1900s, it continued its activity until 1962. The company's great moment came in 1947, when the American magazine Harper's Bazaar published its filigree sculpted heels, and also emphasized the house's ability to invent interchangeable models. The two Fratteggiani brothers, Eduardo and Alfredo, succeeded in creating shoe–sculptures in ceramic, silver, strass, and even porcelain.

Fratti Giuliano (1906-1992). Creator of accessories and jewellery. Born in Milan, he was nicknamed "Mr. Button" and, as Maria Pezzi recalls, "the king of crazy jewels." His atelier was at via Montenapoleone 29, in the fashion building. That's what Fratti would call it, because in the same building both Rina Modelli and the milliner Projetti had their headquarters. Twice a year, owners and representatives of tailoring shops would arrive from all over Italy to purchase Fratti's belts, buckles, buttons, decorations, and jewellery. Active already in the 1940s, he had learned to use the most varied materials, matching rich ones with humble ones and creating original solutions. In 1947, the famous illustrator and designer Federico Pallavicini designed a jewellery line, to be manufactured in passementerie with feathers and raffia, for him. The painter Filippo De Pisis, a great name in the 20th century, designed, in one single night, an entire collection of accessories for him. He boasted clients such as the famous tailoring shops of Nicola Zecca, Carosa, the Sorelle Fontana, Gattinoni of Rome, Bonanno of Naples, Fercioni, Tizzoni, Venesiani, and Rina Modelli of Milan. He also had private clients such as Mistinguette, Isa Miranda, and Valentina Cortese. He closed his business in 1972, in order not to see, as he put it, the agony of haute couture.

(*Bonizza Giordani Aragno*)

Frattini Gabriella. Knitwear designer. The company was established in Fano in 1979. The management was entrusted to the Frattini siblings Gabriella, Nigia, and Roberto, while the style department could count on the creativity of four teams working on three different lines: Gabriella Frattini Donna, Sport Project, and Setball.

Fred Jewellery *maison* established in 1936 in Paris by Samuel Fred. Its name is linked to the sale of diamonds of exceptional quality and carat, such as the Soleil d'Or and the Blue Moon. An official supplier to the Princes of Monaco, and to stars and the international jet set, Fred, whose boutique is on Place Vendôme, has always paid great attention to the artistic appearance of a jewel, promoting collaborations with famous painters and sculptors – Picasso, Braque, Chagall – and urging new, young talents to contribute to the stylistic renovation of the collections. From this incessant commitment flow pieces of extreme inventive originality, making a diamond a very refined instrument, particularly suitable for the expression of the most advanced trends in research on contemporary jewelry.

(*Alessandra Quattordio*)

Freddy Italian brand of fitness and gym clothing and shoes. It is produced by a company in Liguria led by Carlo and Roberta Freddi, from Chiavari, who have been joined by Luca Sordi, the general manager. The firm produces about 1 million pieces every year and in 1999 had a turnover of 22 billion liras, 20% of which came from exports. Starting with Spring-Summer 2000, there are two lines: Music to Wear, streetwear geared to the music world, and Organi Geniali, which continues the tradition of clothing for sports activities. Sponsored by the Italian Gymnastic Federation, it avails itself of the collaboration of gymnast Yuri Chechi and dancers Rossella Brescia and Antonio Baldes, who design *ad hoc* lines. In recent years, the brand has invested a great deal in communication and advertising through the media, especially television. The positive effects of these investments can be seen in the firm's constant economic growth. The turnover, 90% of which comes from Italy, was expected to be €37 million for 2003, an increase of 71% over the €21.7 million of 2002. The distribution network has more than 1,500 points-of-sale.

❑ 2005, June. During Pitti Uomo, the

line designed *ad hoc* for the entire dance company of La Scala is presented, dedicated to the everyday life of dancers.

Frederics John (1906-1964). German designer. He worked in America and emerged during the 1930s as an exponent of the avant-garde. In 1939, he designed hats for Scarlet O'Hara, played by Vivien Leigh, in *Gone With The Wind*. Appreciated for his taste for picturesque and spectacular shapes, and for a palette of unusual and daring colors, he would create hats for many of the most elegant American women and for Hollywood stars such as Rosalind Russell.

Fred Perry Brand of casual clothing and accessories named after the first English tennis player to win the men's singles at Wimbledon in 1934. Perry repeated the exercise in 1935 and '36. This record of three consecutive wins remained unequalled for forty years. In the late 1940s, Perry was contacted by Tibby Wegner, a former Austrian soccer player, who suggested that they market a wrist band with his name on it. The two began a business partnership. Fred succeeded in convincing the greatest tennis players of the time to wear the Fred Perry wrist band during tournaments. It was a totally new promotional method for that time. The two partners immediately started to wonder what logo they could embroider on their new product. Perry suggested a pipe, as he liked to smoke, but Wegner objected, saying that women wouldn't like such a logo. They agreed on the laurel crown, a symbol with a great tradition in sports, and, furthermore, the trophy given to the winner of Wimbledon. The laurel crown "branded" and gave a recognizable identity to a line of jerseys which soon became famous and worn by everyone. A few years later, the cotton piquet men's jerseys were joined by other products, resulting in the creation of a true collection. A women's line and a children's line were launched later, always in the area of sportswear and leisure time. (*Valeria Vantaggi*)

French John (1907-1966). English photographer and illustrator. He was famous for his prints of whites on whites, very difficult to reproduce in magazines. He studied painting in Paris with Georges Braque. Once back in London, in 1937, he found a job with the photo agency Carlton Artist. He was a war reporter and, after the war, a fashion photographer. In 1948, he opened his own studio, from which would come some of the most important figures in English fashion photography, including Bailey, Donovan, and Dormer. During his career, he worked as an illustrator for the Daily Express and as a photographer for daily newspapers and magazines, including Harper's Bazaar. (*Angela Madesani*)

French Connection English group founded in 1969 by Stephen Marks, a leader of minimalist style and clothing in England, and by the *griffe* Nicole Farhi. It expanded its women's clothing lines to include men's and children's. In England, it has 60 points-of-sale, besides the large store on Oxford Street in London. Famous and successful all over the world, the group has opened 150 single-brand shops in 23 countries. In 2002, it had a turnover of £225 million, equal to €337 million. In June 2003, it was present at Pitti Immagine with the allusive brand Fcuk (acronym of French Connection and United Kingdom) and at Milano Moda Uomo (Superstudio) with the youth line by Nicole Farhi.

French Knickers Large underpants with lacework at the hems, created for the first time in the 1960s by Janet Reger, who was inspired by historic models. It is to be combined with a camisole.

Frentzos Angelos (1972). Greek designer, among the most innovative of recent years. He distinguishes himself for a very personal style which emphasizes the female silhouette and which makes a man both rigorous and extremely modern. He made his dèbut with a women's and men's collection that found a place in the most prestigious boutiques in the world. From 2001 to 2003, he was art director of the historic luxury label Alma. (*Sofia Catalano*)

Frette Historic brand of household linen. The history of Frette began in Grenoble, France in 1860, thanks to the entrepreneurship of Edmond Frette who, five years later, moved to Monza, near Milan. In 1878, he opened his first store in Milan. Two Italian partners, Giuseppe Maggi and Carlo Antonietti, joined the firm. In 1881, the company became a supplier to the Royal House of Savoy. After a time, it also supplied the Vatican and the big hotels such as the George V and the Ritz in Paris, the Savoy in London, the Cipriani in Venice, and the Mayfair Regent in New York. It has 40 points-of-sale in Italy as well as boutiques in the most important cities of the world.

❑ 2002. Frette (which became a brand controlled by the holding company Fin.Part), has 60 privately-owned shops in the most important Italian and American cities.
❑ 2002, July. Fin.Part floats the possibility of selling Frette, for a price "around €160 to €190 million." In order to stabilize its financial situation, it had earlier, in April, decided to sell only the sportswear branch, with Best Company going to Cisalfa and Moncler to Equinox.
❑ 2003, May. In the event there is no sale, due to a lack of interesting offers, Fin.Part says that a possible solution for Frette would be a spin-off and a listing on the stock exchange.

Freud Bella (1961). English designer, born in London. She is the great granddaughter of Sigmund Freud. She studied in Italy and did an apprenticeship at Caraceni. She discovered fashion through Vivienne Westwood. She made her début in 1990 designing her first collection. In 1993 she presented her clothes at the London Fashion Week. In her collections she is inspired by England and its past. She says, in fact: "You can take a Victorian silhouette and play with its forms without hiding its origins, making it sexy." Her style is elegantly eccentric and simple. She defines her creations as a "luxurious irreverence."

❑ 2002, July. Balmain, after its separation from the designer Gilles Dufour, would like to entrust her with the women's prêt-à-porter line and the supervision of the knitwear line.

Frey Silk factory in Como established in 1899 on the initiative of Adolfo Frey and various investors such as Giuseppe Stoffel and the Milanese company Roesti & Co. Frey distinguished itself at the "Esposizione Voltiana" in 1899 for the quality of its manufacture, for the silk it used, and for low price of its umbrellas and parasols. The factory's catalogue also included fabrics for ties. In 1926, Corrado Frey joined the company and between 1934 and the end of World War II he obtained control of the company's shares. In 1947, Corrado's son Corrado Jr., obtained the agency of the company and, in the two years 1960 to '61, became a general partner, sharing his father's shares with his sister Lucia. Today, the production is no longer focused only on ties, but also includes other accessories for men as well as bags and shoes for women. After being managed by the third generation of Freys during the 1970s, the company changed ownership in 1982 and the brand merged with Tessitura Orsenigo, located in Figino Serenza, near Como.

(*Pierangelo Mastantuono*)

Friday Look Or, how to dress on Friday in even the most formal businesses: velvet or cotton pants (according to the season), a button-down shirt, a pullover, and comfortable shoes. This look has been popular in the U.S. for a long while, but its first Italian victims are only just starting to appear among the desks and editorial offices of the Made in Italy movement.

Frisé A French term meaning curled or creased and referring to a fabric totally or partly manufactured with a patterned yarn of the same name and characterized by a consistent gathering and a swelling similar to that of a sponge. It looks like bouclé and is used in sportswear.

Frisoni Bruno (1960). French designer. He is of Italian background but was born and grew up in France. He started at a young age, working in the ateliers of Trussardi, Lanvin, and Yves Saint-Laurent before understanding that his real world would be that of shoes. In 1999, he created the brand named after himself and its success with people in the industry was amazing. Models such as Kate Moss immediately wanted to wear his special décolletée shoes. The designer continues to use unusual materials and to apply unexpected geometries that give an original touch to a heel or that make a line unique. The success is also commercial and the Bruno Frisoni brand has about 700 points-of-sale around the world.

(*Maddalena Fossati*)

Frissel Tony (1907-1988). American photographer, born in New York. She was among the first to remove the academic and glossy tone from the fashion pictures in Vogue and Harper's Bazaar, using girls with a casual and not too solemn look instead. She was also the first woman to join the staff of Sports Illustrated and to take photos of boxing matches, races, and champions. She would take photos with a small format camera, thus breaking the tradition, and the obligation, imposed by Condé Nast in favor of the large format. After World War II, she gradually lost interest in fashion, and would eventually abandon it completely to devote herself to portraits and photo-reportage.

Frith Paul (1960). English designer. After seven years in the Royal Marines, he decided to devote himself to fashion. He studied at the St. Martin's School in London (1989). He launched his brand in 1993-94 and immediately started to present his collections during the London Fashion Week. At first he concentrated on evening wear, selling his creations in the most elegant department stores in Europe and America. He has for several years also been designing prêt-à-porter, always remaining faithful to his sexy, modern style. He defines himself a "modernist junkie." He designs a line for the chain British Home Stores.

Friulane In order to avoid slipping on the lacquered surface of their gondolas, almost all Venetian gondoliers today still wear a pair of velvet slippers with a sole made from old bicycle tires. At one time these slippers were sold by women from the countryside who would go about carrying large baskets on their shoulders. Today, the ones made by Gianni Dittura at Dorsoduro 871 in Venice are famous and original. The slipper shape in colored velvet has since been used and ennobled by famous designers and brands, sharing a sort of common territory with the aristocratic English slipper bearing a coat of arms.

Frockcoat A type of Prince Albert coat which made its appearance in several collections during the 1998-99 season as a "basic" for pantsuits.

Frogs Particular type of fastener made of twisted silk threads or solid passementerie bent to form a loose buttonhole for a button usually made of wood and shaped like an olive or a bamboo reed. They are military origin in origin. They were used on women's robes for a long time during the 1800s and also on duffel coats in the period after World War II. Every now and then, they are revived: for decorative reasons, or to stress a military trend as in the Anna Karenina coats of the 1970s, or any time a designer prefers not to cut a particular fabric or fur for a buttonhole. (*Lucia Sollazzo*)

Frost French English fashion brand created by Jemima French, a designer, and Sadie Frost, an actress, who were friends since high school. In 1999 they launched an underwear line sold only by mail order. They then expanded the business, creating true prêt-à-porter collections. They offer a sweet and feminine style that is also sexy: the kind of fashion that appeals to them and their friends, and wives, mothers, and workers. They use only fabrics that are designed and printed exclusively for them.

Frou-Frou Term used to describe all those decorations (flounces, frills, laces, ruches, ribbons, etc.) which make a garment frivolous and mannered. It is an onomatopoeic term, sounding like the rustling of skirts and underskirts caused by fabrics such as heavy silk and taffeta. The evening dresses of the late 1800s were frou-frou, with their large crumpled skirts that made a small sound with every movement, and so were the Can Can costumes from the golden age of the Moulin Rouge. The pleats and draperies of Eleonora Duse's stage costumes would rustle, and so did the oriental dresses designed by Poiret for Sarah Bernhardt at the turn of the century.

Fruit of the Loom The white T-shirts with the Fruit of the Loom label arrived in Europe with the American armies that landed in Salerno, Anzio, and Normandy. They conquered Europe, withstanding even the fashion for decorated and painted T-shirts and without losing their leadership position in the U.S. Legend has it that the brand was created by the daughter of a fabric dealer in Rhode Island who used her watercolors to paint a fruit basket on the edge of some fabric. That was 1851. But it is known for sure that in 1906 James Goldfarb, a Polish immigrant, began to produce and sell T-shirts with that logo.

❑ 1999. On the edge of bankruptcy, the company enters receivership.
❑ 2001. It loses $157.8 million on total sales of $1.3 billion, of which $163 million comes from Europe.
❑ 2002, January. The firm is rescued and acquired by Berkshire Hathaway, a holding company in Omaha, Nebraska run by Warren Buffet, one of the richest men in the world. Among the most important and successful investors and analysts in the history of the stock market, Buffet is president of Berkshire Hathaway.
❑ 2002, November. The launch of a men's underwear collection for 2003. The Chicago company has been producing underwear for more than 60 years and, up to now, has had 32% of the U.S. market. Fruit of the Loom employs 3,000 people in Europe, and has its main plants in Ireland and Morocco.

Fruit of the Loom logo.

Fubu (For Us By Us) Brand of youth clothing created in the U.S. at the end of the 1990s. It was created by four designers making their début: John Daymond, Alexander Martin, Carl Brown, and Keith Parrin. Within a few years, they conquered the teenage market, and not only in the U.S., with astronomic sales (in 1999 about $400 million). Fashion made for young people by young people, it is appreciated by everyone without regard to social standing. The collections include sweaters, T-shirts, watches, caps, high-tech shoes, and Bermuda shorts. They expanded to other products, including bags, perfumes, and household objects. Films and video clips which display the line are also on sale. Within ten years, this favorite brand of U.S. rappers, has arrived in every corner of the world, with 56 single-brand stores and sales of $500 million. Particularly famous in Australia, Mexico, and Japan, in 2000 the American Basketball Association asked the four designers to manufacture the official uniforms for the 29 teams competing for the championship. In 2000, the brand arrived in Italy exclusively with Wage in more than 60 points-of-sale. A first men's street style collection was presented for Spring-Summer, followed for Autumn by women's and children's collections. In 2004, a single-brand store was opened in Milan, with four more in 2005 and five more in 2006.

Fujii Hideki (1934). Japanese photographer. He became interested in photography as a student. After an initial period in which he was self-taught, he became an assistant to Shotato Akiyama. He began his career as a fashion photographer for a company in Tokyo and for various magazines, in particular Fuzuko. Since 1967, he has diversified his interests, working for the Nikon Design Center in Tokyo and carrying out personal research on traditional printing techniques and on the relationship between painting and photography. He continues to work as a freelancer in the field of fashion, working in particular with Max Factor on a famous TV series with the model Hiromi Oka.

Fujiwara Giuliano (1947). Japanese designer. Fujiwara has long been based in Italy, although he is originally from Japan: he was born in Osaka and studied Oriental literature before attending the Bunka College of Fashion of Tokyo. He began his career designing menswear for Van Jacket in Japan, and moved to Italy in the 1970s where he became the menswear designer of Barbas. He launched his eponymous collection in 1986 and a women's line two years later. Fujiwara has often cited a formal and classic Japanese style, and the Ivy League style, as two of the inspirations for his rigorous designs.

❑ 2002, June. His collection at Milano Moda Uomo displays rigor and a formal minimalism in a perfect, almost ascetic, Japanese style. His style is simple and linear, without excessive decoration, and lean in shape. It stresses the quality of the fabric, its comfort and wearability, and clean, precise colors. The only transgressions are the colored stitches, the dots and stripes, and the hooded jackets, plus a distinctive "apron" worn tight around the waist and various creased garments.
❑ 2003, June. Once again a return to the rigorous and formal look which has made the Japanese designer famous, but with some amusing and ironic touches. He is inspired by the English fashions of the 1960s, and by the uniforms of boarding school students, revisited with the indisputable nonconformism of someone who rebels against the rules and allows himself some small eccentricities. He maintains a perfect tailoring cut in suits, jackets, shirts, and trousers, though they are made more joyful with colored bands and stripes which run along the hems of jackets and vests. There are in addition many varieties of pins to decorate and complete vests and ties.

Full&Fifty Italian mall, unique of its kind, because it combines the sale of new products with the outlet concept. It is located in Meda, near Milan and opened in April 2003. It is the first shopping center of this type. A renovated complex of 55,000 square feet, the first floor has stores that offer seasonal products, while the second floor is reserved for outlet stores with prices reduced 30% or more. A space called Play Placet is set aside for children. The fifty-fifty concept was invented by the Freeland-Capfin company, which since 1995 has been interested in this kind of distribution and was the first to introduce outlet stores in Italy.

Funk Glamour and fine dressing have always been central to black culture. One need only think about the Harlem Renaissance of the 1920s photographed and described by Carl Van Vechten. The direct heirs to that tradition included Little Richard, who was excessive and outrageous during the 1950s with his hair in a pompadour, satin suits, and showy make-up, and Sly Stone, who appeared at Woodstock in a leather outfit with very long fringes. They contributed to the spread of a style that was already sufficiently sensational. But what seemed to come out of the ghettos in a visual way in the 1970s was totally new. Tom Walke gave us a lively account of it in his 1974 essay *Funk But Chic*, describing a new generation of Beau Brummels and Gentlemen of Leisure in Pyramid two-tone shoes with four-inch heels worn with swaying Art Deco bell-bottoms and enormous eyeglasses. In the late 1960s, funk style could consist, for example, of the frequent use of suede-fringed vests and shell necklaces instead of a shirt, or the combination of a blouse draped in a 1940s style with 15 pieces of leather held together by knots in order to make a pair of pants. In the first half of the 1970s, the outrageous costumes worn by Patti Labelle and Nona Hendryx and by the Parliament-Funkadelic group seemed to come from another planet. The Labelle girls, dressed by Larry Le Gaspi, embodied the ideal of futurist amazons. The Parliament-Funkadelic group displayed sci-fantasy gear revisited in a glam key. Both were perfectly in sync with the parallel phenomenon of glitter rock.

(*Maurizio Vetrugno*)

Furbelow A flounce or a cloth hem, pleated or curled, applied at the bottom of a skirt or dress. It is also a decoration made of fabric, lace, or other material, in ribbons, bows, or fringes, curled and sewn along the neckline of a dress or blouse.

Furla Italian leather company. Established in Bologna in the 1930s by the Furlanetto family, it initially dealt in the distribution of clothing accessories. Later, it turned into a company for the manufacture of bags, shoes, and leather accessories. For 20 years it has been led by the siblings Carlo and Giovanna Furlanetto. The company, with sales of about €40 million, has distribution all over the world, with 56 single-brand boutiques in Italy and 24 abroad.

❑ 2000, February. The opening of the French market increases sales by 35% compared to 1999.
❑ 2002, February. Furla enters the teenage market. It is the birth of Furlina, a teenage comic strip character who appears on bags, accessories, and watches.
❑ 2003, May. Growth in the domestic market has always been the goal of Giovannna Furlanetto. The corporate strategy for achieving it includes a program that will open two boutiques in Sardinia, in Fort Village and Cagliari, and two in Sicily, in Syracuse and Taormina.

Fürst Peter H. (1939). Austrian photographer. His models, dressed only in underwear and placed in rarefied surroundings that remind one of a boudoir, and on specially arranged sets, have contributed to his fame as "the prince of underwear." In 1960, he opened a studio in Cologne, the city where he lives and works.

Fürstenberg (von) Diane (1946). Designer of Belgian origin, she is famous for her short jersey wrap dresses. After studying economics in Spain, France, and Switzerland, in 1968 she married the Austrian-Italian Prince Egon von Fürstenberg and in 1969 moved to the U.S. During the 1970s she showed her designs to the buyers at the big New York department stores, who showed great interest in her styles and in her aristocratic name. In the late 1990s, Vogue America dedicated an article to her short jersey wrap dresses which were back in style, especially among the well-off girls of Manhattan.

Fürstenberg (von) Egon (1944-2004). Italian designer. He is called the designer-prince and he plays along with it. After all, it was pure passion that caused Egon, the son of Tassilo and Clara Agnelli, to design clothes instead of following the more regular career of a banker with Chase Manhattan after his degree in economics in Geneva. His début was in 1975, with a collection of men's pullovers and shirts meant for large-scale distribution in America. It was a success. The big leap, which came in 1984, was the result of a request received from Lubiam to design a coat and jacket line, one which is still produced under the Prince Egon name. Some years later, it was time for the over-size collections designed for various Italian department stores. In 1990, he made his high fashion début on the runways in Rome with wedding dresses and formal clothes. His business has about thirty licenses, including cosmetics, sunglasses, interior décor fabrics, period-piece couches, ties, and small leather goods.

(*Minnie Gastel*)

Fusco Angelo (1956). Born in Rocca Monfina, near Caserta. He is a designer of ties, something which he did first as a hobby and then as a second trade in order to fill the free time afforded by his main occupation, plastic surgery. It is a medical specialty for which he qualified after receiving a degree in medicine in Milan and perfecting his skills through several courses in the U.S. and Brazil. Fusco has always been a "gourmet" of elegance, paying particular attention to "the detail which makes the difference." And the "difference," or, if you prefer, the punctuation, in men's clothing is, as is well known, the tie, especially the tie that is made in Naples. He became more and more careful in his choices and so demanding as to be unsatisfied with what the market offered him. So he decided to turn to the old artisans of Naples, asking them to manufacture for his personal use only small numbers of unique ties with very precise characteristics: no prints, worked only in jacquard, seven folds only, lined in silk same as the tie itself. Just two styles for each pattern and color variation. He gave them as gifts for selected friends. The word-of-mouth prompted requests from the friends of his friends who were charmed by these exclusive ties manufactured with the best fabrics and accompanied by a certificate reporting the date of manufacture and the code number of the silk archive, for later tidying up. Doc-ties closed in an envelope and sealed in wax with a logo. In short, the hobby became very pleasant work, and a way to relax, after hours spent in surgery. In December 2002, he opened a boutique on via Montenapoleone in Milan. It was expanded in January 2003. (*Lucia Mari*)

Fusco Antonio (1942). Italian designer. He exalted the great tradition of Neapolitan tailoring with his refined and precious hand-worked offerings. Part of a family that was a dealer in fabrics for interior décor, at first he attended design school, and then he enrolled in specialized courses in New York, Montreal, and Paris. In Istanbul, for the Cerruti group, he created and managed a clothing line. In 1976 he decided to return to Italy and settle in Milan. He opened a factory, which was a kind of source for ideas, and which allowed him to introduce his ideal of artisanal manufacture to the industry. He grew in the world of fashion, but often went against the stream: to the frenzies of prêt-à-porter he responded with a certain discretion and a manic attention to his work. Since 1979 he has been supported by his wife Patrizia. A major part of his line is the men's jacket, made lighter, thinner, and unstructured, but maintaining the construction of the shoulder for which Neapolitan tailoring is famous. Fusco, who brought to women's clothing the aplomb of the male wardrobe, invented the Milano jacket, the Portofino tailored suit, and the Montecarlo and Vienna coats. In 1999, he signed an agreement with the Inghirami Group, which is among the leaders in Italian clothing and textiles, and which, since the Spring-Summer 2000 collection, has managed the world-wide entire production cycle of the new Antonio Fusco Gold Signature line. (*Laura Asnaghi*)

❑ 2000, November. Antonio Fusco and GFT mutually decide to end their license agreement starting with the Autumn-Winter 2001 season. They have differences on strategy: the Neapolitan designer wants to "take back" the direct management of the production and distribution of the women's line, while GFT is geared more to a partnership relationship than a license.

❑ 2002, June. The Fusco men's collection is to be produced and distributed world-wide by Tombolini, a holding company from Urbisaglia in The Marche. Besides the clothing brands Tombolini and Regent (acquired in

A design by Antonio Fusco. Asteroid Collection, Autumn-Winter 1999-2000.

2001), it produces and distributes Mugler, Givenchy, and, more recently, Romeo Gigli. The license agreement between Fusco and Tombolini is to last three years starting with the Spring-Summer collection 2003. More than a license, it is a partnership, as president and general manager Fiorella Tombolini emphasizes, given the continued collaboration with Fusco, who still retains control of the stylistic part. The agreement envisions new distribution strategies: Italy will remain an important market, but the company wants to also develop markets in Europe, the U.S., and Japan. It also sees a parallel expansion into eastern Europe and Russia. Single-brand stores are also planned, starting with Paris.
❑ 2002. Tombolini ends the year sales of €60 million, Fusco with €15 million.

Fusco Giancarlo (1915-1984). Italian journalist, and extraordinary witness to his time. Born in La Spezia, he was sent to Florence by the weekly L'Europeo to write a portrait of Giovanni Battisti Giorgini, the inventor of the Made in Italy movement and of the fashion events in the Sala Bianca of Palazzo Pitti. The author of *Quando l'Italia tollerava* and *Le rose del ventennio* wrote: "Under the white hair, rather thin on the nape of the neck, his profile reminds one of certain knights found in paintings by the old masters, with a falcon on the arm."

Fuseau Trousers with a spindle shape (in Italian "fuso," used to spin threads), almost always in elasticized fabric, often with a stirrup. In 1960, Emilio Pucci launched the Viva trousers, manufactured in silk shantung lined with helanca and with stirrups. Worn in films by Audrey Hepburn, fuseau pants later became a necessary and comfortable garment for leisure time. At first worn under jeans and ski pants, they later became an alternative to elasticized leotards for dancing. In heavier weights, they are worn with boots in the coldest months. In printed, laminated and ornamented fabrics, they are often worn in the evening.

(*Maria Vittoria Alfonsi*)

Fustian A term that derives from El Fustat, a suburb of Cairo, where this fabric originated. Made of very resistant and compact cotton, with a velvety and slightly hairy surface, it is similar to suede. There are several varieties, of different weights. Used especially for jackets, skirts, and trousers, it was in vogue during the 1970s.

Futurism Futurism and fashion are not antithetical entries, at least for the following reason: Filippo Tommaso Marinetti, the founder of the movement, never lamented the unbearable frivolity of fashion, as poets and intellectuals often do, but actually adopted fashion as a code of ideal behavior for those artists destined to greatness, those peremptorily invited to update their work with every new season just as the French couturiers offer their new designs. At that time, of course, Italian stylism was still in the future. If this was the movement's ideology, then one shouldn't be surprised by the fact that right in their clothing designs futurists provided – thanks especially to Balla, Depero, Prampolini, Thayaht, and many others – some valuable information about everyday clothes in the 20th century. First of all, with the thousands of prophetic intuitions that can be traced to the two manifestos considered, on this subject, to be fundamental. The first, by Balla, was *Le Vêtement Masculin Futuriste*, 1914, of which there was also an Italian version, titled *Il vestito antineutrale* ('Anti-neutral clothing'). The second was *Ricostruzione Futurista dell'Universo*, 1915 signed by Balla and Depero. In *Ricostruzione Futurista*, clothing isn't actually discussed in a specific sense, except in a hint about "transformable clothing," from the point of view of a refounding of the world which takes into account new productive and social rhythms. But here also one has the feeling that the usual Futurist terminology – including velocity and dynamism – can't but be directly reflected in fashion and in the fashions of a season that is more and more marked by dramatic and uncontrollable events. So the *anti-neutral clothing* foreseen by the manifest of the same name – right at the dawn of World War I – can't be but pro-war, colored, phosphorescent, agile, hygienic, joyful, anti-Germany and so on. In short, it fostered a more comfortable and functional clothing (also suitable in peace time) which abandoned black, grey and dark half-colors – forbidding them even to grave-diggers, if necessary – in order to bring the Futurist rush into the streets, the salons, and the theaters. And it wouldn't be a surprise, after all, if some of the most convincing tests of such a mode of dressing were to be found in the theater. And it was true, on the other hand, that the followers of Marinetti, who were inflexible advocates of a closer relationship between art and life, were unable to limit themselves to a purely ideological proposal. They had to put it into practice. And they did, although sometimes only in sketches or in some discussions at the café, emphasizing even on this battleground the use of "bad taste" – made of unbalances and asymmetries – as a unique but still efficient antidote to the mediocre "good taste" of the bourgeoisie. And so on, with very gaudy waistcoats cut in unusual shapes; metallic ties and light bulbs transformed into ties; evening jackets with one sleeve rounded and the other squared; hats of every shape and size; overalls in all the colors of the rainbow with lozenge and cone-shaped cutouts made from different fabrics put one next to the other; not to mention the mismatched shoes that were also in different colors and an unspeakable number of accessories – the famous "modifiers" – which were sufficient to apply here and there with special "inflatable buttons" according to the taste of the person wearing them, in order to change in a flash (and thus extremely fast) the very structure of the garment. It is hardly necessary to add that such a concept of clothing – destined to be reverberate all through the 1950s thanks to the last Futurists, by then aged 90 – aimed in particular at the liberation of men, being that women's fashion was already "more or less futurist," as one could read in a winning if somewhat pandering manifest from 1920 in which, it is clear, the son of Futurism carefully offered (in quite an Italian style) a tribute to his mother. But that experience has not been lost, in spite of the unfortunate fact that futurist clothes were almost always

Giacomo Balla. A study for a waistcoat, 1930.

worn by their creators or by their patient companions. And it certainly stirs a certain tenderness to see again today the religiously kept pajama-overalls (what else to call them?) in which the old Giacomo Balla would stroll around his house in Rome, forced to paint portraits of ladies in order to support his family, although not yet tamed, or desperate. As if he already knew that one day the best Italian designers – those more open to the world in which they live – would have preserved his style for the future. Or, at least, a spark of it. (*Emilio Isgrò*)

Futuro Brand of knit support garments belonging to the Beiersdorf company, which was established in Hamburg in 1882. It offers several knitwear lines, as well as underwear and hosiery, developed through careful scientific research in order to preserve the health of the customer. The materials used are strong and flexible, with natural fabrics for comfort. Since 2001, it has been much more attentive to fashion trends, producing, for example, sleepwear tights with lace bodices in a large variety of styles and colors. It is the best-selling brand of curative clothing in the U.S.

Fuzzi Knitwear company established in 1954 by Adele Bacchiani Fuzzi in San Giovanni in Marignano, near Cattolica. At first, the collections were created by the founder, manufactured on hand looms, and distributed on the domestic market through three agents. In the early 1970s, after graduating her degree, the founder's daughter Anna Maria Fuzzi joined the company and created a staff of designers, opening the doors to the foreign market. Since then, the company has had continued success on an international level. One of the most important moments for the company was in 1983 when the first Jean-Paul Gaultier collection was created. In 1989 there was a partnership with Joop! And in 1993 one with Hugo Boss. In 2000, the company opened a production plant in Baragiano (Basilicata). In that same year it had sales of 89 billion liras. In 2002 it ended the year with sales of €70 million, a gross operating margin of more than €6 million, or 8.5% of sales, and a profit before tax of €5 million, or 7% of sales. The company employs 160 people. In 2003, it launched a new brand, Garbino, a line of men's knitwear for the high end of the market. It also acquired Sima Fashion, a company that owns several knitwear brands including Nani Bon, Fiume, Sevres, and Portobellos. Today, Fuzzi exports 95% of its production, including 80% to Europe. The best markets are France, Germany, and England, as well as the U.S. and Japan.

(*Daniela Bolognetti*)

G

Gabardine Wool or cotton diagonal fabric. Also refers to an overcoat made with this fabric. In 1902, Thomas Burberry registered the name as a brand and since then, along with the Burberry brand, it is practically synonymous with raincoat.

Gabber Youth movement of the 1990s, in the milieu of rave parties, in Holland. Groups of gabbers have also formed in Italy, especially in the north, where they have chosen their cult locations: the former Dylan in Coccaglio (Brescia) and the Gheodrome in Rimini. There are estimated to be around 20,000 members and, considering the many Internet sites dedicated to this "culture," the figure is believable. The average age is between 13 and 23, and, like many other youth movements, the members can be distinguished by their adopted uniform: Lonsdale button-neck jerseys, Nike shoes, tight jeans or Australian tracksuits, leather jackets, and baseball caps, in addition to the indispensable T-shirts of their favorite artists (Rotterdam Terror Corps or DJ Paul). Number one in their interests is, of course, music, especially the frenzied and deafening rhythms of hardcore and techno. Boys have shaved heads. The girls wear their hair long on top and very short below. The hard core members of the movement are called warriors and are recognizable by their colored tufts of hair and numerous piercings. (*Valeria Vantaggi*)

Gabriella Bellenghi High fashion atelier opened in Florence in 1933 and closed in 1964. Gabriella, the dressmaker who gave her name to the atelier, was famous for modeling the dress directly on the body and would use the most valuable and sought-after materials. Her evening dresses were often inspired by ancient costumes.

Gadda Odda (1910-2001). Prominent member of the high bourgeoisie in Milan. A relative of the writer Carlo Emilio Gadda, she was a woman with extraordinary vitality and zest for life. In the early 1950s, for economic reasons, she set herself up as a dressmaker. Her only prior experience was the making of a few simple dresses for herself just for fun. After that, for forty years, she dressed, with taste, genius, and imagination, the girls, the jeunes filles, and the ladies of Milanese society, for openings at La Scala, debutant balls, weddings, and cocktails. She never had assistants. All by herself, she cut, sewed by hand, embroidered, and applied sequins and decorations.

Gainsborough A rather showy hat that first appeared in England at the end of the 1700s. It had a very large brim and a rather high cylindrical top in black velvet or taffeta, with a ribbon and ostrich feathers. It also became popular in France, where it was named after a popular song of the time, the *Chanson de Malborough*. Now and then it comes back in fashion.

Galanos James (1924). American designer of Greek origin, born in Philadelphia. His place in fashion is due to his tailoring ability and the classic nature of his cocktail and evening dresses, which are very low-necked, especially in the back. After studying at the Traphagen School of Fashion in New York, he worked at Piguet in Paris in 1947. He made his début in Los Angeles in 1954. His clothes, often handmade, are in lace, chiffon, silk muslin, pearl embroidery, velvet, and brocade. In April 1997, the Los Angeles County Museum of Art documented his career in a retrospective film. He retired without making a fuss over it to his house in Palm Springs.

Galante Maurizio (1963). Italian designer. Born in Latina, he studied at the Academy of Costume and Fashion in Rome. His master was Capucci, with whom he worked when he was young, developing a particular interest in volume and the play of surfaces.

His first Collection came out in 1983. Starting in 1989 – the year in which he received, for the second time in a row, the *Occhiolino d'oro* award as best emerging young designer, and the *Fil d'Argent* at the International Festival of Linen in Montecarlo – Galante's activity became more and more intense. In 1990, his *griffe* was presented at Milano Collezioni, and he signed an agreement with Takashiyama Co. Ltd. Tokyo for the exclusive distribution of his Collection in Asia. In 1991, he began to present his prêt-à-porter Collections in Paris. The Autumn-Winter 1992-93 Collection was called "one of the most poetic and beautiful ever seen in Paris" by the New York Times. He has participated in haute couture presentations since 1993. In 1997, he created a partnership with the Felissimo Corporation and established a new company, Maurizio Galante SA, in Paris, where he moved. After consulting on the creation of Filati Bertrand, which presented at Pitti Filati, he was appointed professor at the European Institute for Design in Rome and Milan, and at the Domus Academy. He then designed the accessories for the Nokia portable phone. As artistic director, he curated the exhibition *Design 21 – Continuous Connection* that was organized by Unesco in New York in 2001 and in Paris in 2002. In July 2002, the designer's high fashion Collection offered sexy clothes with lots of see-throughs and low-necklines, a spectacular style for a woman covered in feathers, worked with fringes and frills, even on jeans and on jackets in denim and open-work lace. It is all a play of decorations and inlays, in jersey, in patchwork, and in crochet, on which 10,000 feathers are tied, even on a fur coat with interlaced feathers and ribbons, sometimes with gold or silver embroidery. In June 2003, at Palazzo Pitti in Florence, Galante celebrated his 20th anniversary in business, presenting his first men's Collection in the Giardino della Meridiana (Garden of the Sundial) and donating three dresses, designed some years before, to the Galleria del Costume.

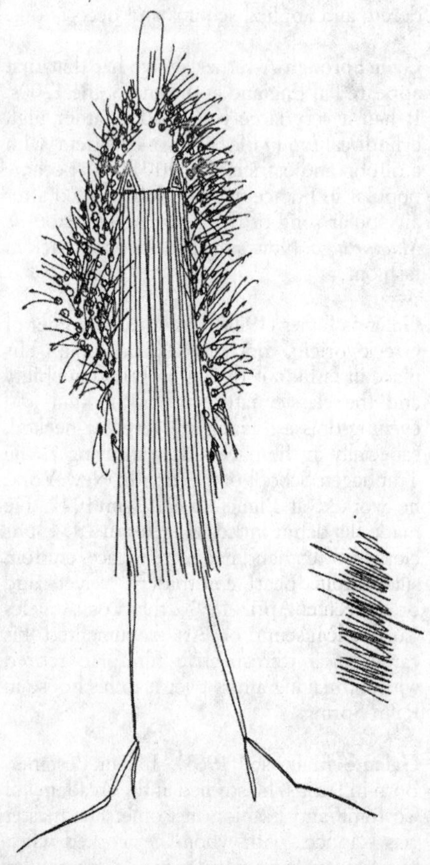

Evening dress by Maurizio Galante.

Galasso Angelo (1959). Italian designer, born in Francavilla Fontana, near Brindisi. He began his career in Rome, with a first boutique in the heart of the Parioli neighborhood. In 1998, he moved to London, where he opened a boutique in the center of the city, next to Harrods. He became famous immediately, bringing new and somewhat unconventional ideas to the British capital. Among his fans are Roger Moore, the actor and former 007, the soccer player David Beckham, an icon of male elegance, Michael Caine, Simon Le Bon, and, not least, Paul McCartney who, as a committed animal rights activist, asked Galasso for shoes made of cloth instead of leather. His men's Collections continue to be manufactured for the most part in Italy. In Autumn 2002, in a photomontage for the monthly GQ, the British Prime Minister, Tony Blair, was dressed for different moments of the day by various designers, just for fun. The Galasso shirt worn by Blair, called Corleone–Interno 8, a name clearly inspired by the Mafia, was white with blue buttonholes and a three-button neck. It had enormous success with Londoners. In just a few days, 800,000 pieces were sold. It was worn even by Mr. Blair, who received one sent as a gift. In 2003, Paul McCartney took 14 Interno 8 shirts on his European tour.

Galeotti Sergio (1945-1985). Fashion manager, business partner, and "companion-in-arms" of Giorgio Armani. Born in Tuscany, he was intelligent, brilliant, sharp, and ironic, gifted with a rare and contagious good humor. He had a light-hearted generosity and a desire to face life boldly, and with joy. He was one of the forerunners of the success of Italian prêt-à-porter. It was his doing that Armani, who designed for Hitman and third parties, decided to create his own Collection. Sergio saw his talent, but also understood that the times were propitious. Galeotti and Armani, 50/50 business partners, united in a perfect and iron-clad partnership of ideas and aspirations. They prepared themselves and dared to launch, even if with rather limited means, an ambitious creative project that would develop into Giorgio Armani SpA, in a really extraordinary series of successes. Galeotti would take care of the marketing, finance, and development, but also keep a careful and critical eye on the Collections. Armani followed the design and the study of what would become the famous Armani style. Galeotti, with an innate intuition for changes in clothing, developed brilliant projects for expansion, among which was the concept of Emporio Armani, well in advance of the era of second lines. At the moment of the firm's definitive success in all the foreign markets, and at the peak of his own success, Galeotti died, at the very young age of 40. Armani keeps the memory of his friend and business partner alive and is working to create a foundation in his name.

(*Cristina Brigidini*)

Galeries Lafayette French department store. It was established in Paris in 1912 by Alphonse Khan and Théophile Bader who, after a little while, acquired his partner's shares. It owed its immediate success to fashion and to clothing that was affordable by everyone. The corporate strategy and the advertising campaigns would always focus on this idea: chic at affordable prices. Ever since 1935, with branches that had meanwhile been opened all over France, the department store has emphasized the idea that it is a fashion emporium. In 1969, it opened a new location dedicated to men's clothing. Starting in 1980, the Festival de la Mode, organized by Galeries Lafayette, became an important event during fashion week. In 1989, the Lafayette Collection brand was created, followed by the Avant-Première, Biefing, and Jodhpur lines. In the 1990s, the Galeries Lafayette group (which includes Monoprix and Nouvelles Galeries) arrived in New York and Berlin. The figures for 1992 already give an idea of the turnover: the group employs 35,000 people and has 115 store chains, of which 392 are privately owned and 115 are franchises. In 1995, Galeries Lafayette opened an Internet Bistrot, hosting society events in music, art, and fashion.

(*Olivella Pianetti*)

❑ 2003, March. Galeries Lafayette sues Marks & Spencer for damages of €60 million. In 2001, the British company had decided to abandon the French market, closing 18 stores and dismissing 1,500 people. Galeries Lafayette took over the points-of-sales, offering the personnel either a job or a severance payment, as negotiated by Alan Julliet, who at the time was president of M&S France. According to Galeries Lafayette, the final figures set by Julliet were much higher than those agreed at the outset. The severance pay, between €15,000 and €23,000, was accepted by almost 90% of the workers, at serious cost to Galeries Lafayette. A spokesman for M&S declared: "We are certain that we complied with the terms of the agreement; that is why we are contesting this legal action." For his part, Philippe Lemoine, the co-president of Galeries Lafayette, expressed a desire to reach a solution before arriving in court.

Galimberti Maurizio (1957). Italian photographer. Deeply influenced by his study of the historic avant-gardes, he became interested in photography and joined the Gruppo Abrecal directed by Nino Migliori. He began to work with Polaroid instant film and soon became an expert, offering himself, still just a fan, as a brilliant interpreter with it. After becoming a professional, he distinguished himself with work that appeared in several magazines in the field, including Fotografare and Fotopratica. Before long, in 1992, he won the prestigious Grand Prix Kodak for Italian advertising. The creator of the Polaroid Collection Italy, he became a spokesman for the company and produced important exhibits of large format 20 x 24" portraits for the Venice Film Festival in 1996 and 1998 and for the Sanremo Festival in 1997 and 1998. In more recent times, he worked with Fuji Instant Film on several workshops and conferences. He has published in Time Magazine, Class, Max, Vogue, Vanity Fair, Cartier Magazine, and Kult, and with Giorgio Mondadori Publishers. He has had many one-man shows all over the world, accompanied by important catalogues, including *Polaroid and Roundabouts*, *A Journey Through Italy*, *Pro-Art*, *A Re-Composed World*, and *Luigi Veronesi Instantaneous*. In 2003 he contributed a series of unpublished photos to the book *Il fotografo, mestiere d'arte* by Giuliana Scimé, published by Il Saggiatore. In May 2000, Immagini magazine dedicated an entire issue to him. He works in advertising, architecture, and fashion. His work is carried out through both panoramic photos, taken with a Widelux camera, and through the famous mosaic compositions in which he photographs landscapes and composes portraits of important people in the world of culture, art, and fashion.

Galitzine Irene (1916). Italian designer. She has been called "the princess of fashion" and, in fact, she is a princess. She arrived in Rome as a child, fleeing Russia with her family. By 1943, she was a young woman of great charm and culture who studied art history and spoke several languages. She did not fail to be noticed by the Fontana sisters who became very famous in liberated Rome and saw in her the ideal ambassador for their clothes. Her first Collection was in 1959. She designed it in collaboration with Federico Forquet. In his tailor's shop Maria Carloni was also present; she had just left the *maison* Ventura. In 1960 came the launch of that *palazzo pigiama* (palazzo-pajama) which spread from the Sala Bianca of Palazzo Pitti all over the world, photographed and distributed by all the media. It was worn by Diana Vreeland, the most important American historian of fashion and the priestess of Vogue. The name for the new creation came from her. Galitzine immediately found herself famous. In fact, in that wide, precious, and very elegant evening outfit, her vision had already been expressed: very feminine trousers for a modern woman, or a large, swaying skirt; strong colors, which can make even a raincoat feminin; the end of black for evening in favor of tiny flaming dresses and silk tailored suits. After Fourquet, she worked with Elias Zabaleta, a Spanish designer. In 1988, she returned to Russia for the first time, invited to present her new Collection at the Rossija Theatre in Moscow in front of 2,500 people. Since 1990, the brand has belonged to the Xines company, owned by Giada Ruspoli. The designer has continued to supervise the product, starting with the creative phase. In 1996, Longanesi published her autobiography, *Dalla Russia alla Russia* ('From Russia To Russia'). (*Lucia Sollazzo*)

❑ 2002, October. The new Irene Galitzine haute couture Collection is presented at the Art Café in Rome. It is designed by Massimo Stefanini, who is from Orvieto, in Umbria. He has a degree in architecture and worked as a costume designer for the theater. The Collection contains very important pieces in silk velvet and precious lace embroidered in gold or embellished with fringes. The colors are very strong, with lots of black, dark red, and brown, as well as a softer ecru and powder pink. It is completed by mink busbies and very precious jewellery, all handmade.
❑ 2004, January. The brand participates in an exhibit on Italian fashion held at the embassy in Bern. Other events are held at the Bardo Museum in Tunis, the Le Corbusier in Algiers, the Borges Cultural Center in Buenos Aires, and the National Art Gallery in Kuala Lumpur.
❑ 2004, July. *Alta Roma* pays tribute to the company with a show in which the famous palazzo pajamas are presented, revisited with originality and brilliance by the designer Gentucca Bini. There are 12 models in jersey, linen, and silk, in

Evening dress by Irene Galitzine, in a sketch by Brunetta.

shades of white, beige, and ecru, combined with original flower-shaped hats.

❑ 2005. Galitzine exhibits and shows continue all over the world: Rio de Janeiro, Sao Paulo, Bogotá, Seoul, and Tokyo. From May to August some of its most important creations are shown as part of the exhibit organized at the National Museum in Minsk, Belarus. From July to September, some distinctive palazzo pajamas are shown at the Museum of the Mondragone Foundation in Naples, as a tribute to their originality.

❑ 2005. The Galitzine brand is active in several areas, such as clothing, accessories, and household items, including a complete line of furniture and interior décor objects.

(*Maria Vittoria Alfonsi*)

Gallenga Monaci Maria (1880-1944). Painter and designer of textiles and clothes. Her fame is linked to the invention of a technique for printing textiles with which she made clothes and furnishings that were very famous in Europe and the U.S. between 1915 and 1935. Born in Rome to one of the most cultivated families of the time, she grew up surrounded by scholars, poets, philosophers, and scientists. In 1903, she married Pietro Gallenga, one of the first doctors to specialize in oncology. She began to paint while still very young, fascinated by Renaissance painting. Fabrics depicted by the painters she loved, combined with her admiration for the work of Mariano Fortuny, stirred her interest in the textile arts and directed her artistic choices. Starting in 1915, there are records of her participation in important exhibits such as the Roman Secession, in which she presented panels and cushions printed in velvet, and the San Francisco Exhibition, in which she presented clothes that she designed and printed. She enjoyed great success at each. The early models and the first printing proofs recall, in their shape and choice of themes, those of Fortuny. But the artistic criteria that were the basis for her international success soon proved to be totally original. Sensitive and engaged in the cultural debates of her time, which asked questions about the role of the decorative arts, the search for a style that was at the same time both modern and national, and the qualities which distinguish an art product, an artisanal product, and a product of small industry from one other. She provided concrete answers which she pursued with intelligence and awareness. In the garment, which had in itself, as something that was used, the concreteness of life, she saw the possibility of a synthesis between the pictorial arts (in the decorations) and the plastic arts (in the cut of the tailoring). The garment represented, moreover, the most eloquent way to spread the new aesthetic ideas. Such an ambitious program could not be followed all on her own. Gallenga always worked in collaboration with the most famous artists of her time, who provided the patterns for her printed fabrics. The collaboration with Vittorio Zecchin was already in place by the time of the San Francisco Exhibition of 1915, and it was renewed for the exhibitions of Amsterdam in 1922 and Paris in 1925. She worked with Antonio Maraini for the Venice Bienniale in 1924. The sketches for the curtain she created for the Quirino Theater in Rome in 1925 were made by Marcello Piacentini. Her partnerships with artists also saw collaborations with Galileo Chini, Gino Sensani, Romano Romanelli, Carlo and Fides Testi, and Emanuele Cito di Filomarino. She participated with them on the programs of the National Institute for Artisanal Crafts and Light Industry established in 1925 to spread and strengthen the image of Italian products. She was awarded the silver medal at the Monza exhibition in 1923. In 1928, together with the other women entrepreneurs Bice Pittoni and Carla Visconti di Modrone, she opened the Boutique Italienne in Paris. Located on Rue Miromesnil, it was active until 1934 as a window on modern Italian taste. Apart from her first models, which remind one of Fortuny, Gallenga's clothes took current fashion trends into account. The recognition of her role was also confirmed by the French, who admired her pavilion at the Expo of 1925 and invited her, the only one in Italy, to participate in a high fashion presentation organized at the Lido in Venice by the magazine Fémina. Every garment, every interior décor object that she produced was unique: even though the style might be repeated, the fabric and the pattern were always different. The printing of the textiles was always carried out by hand with wooden blocks on the pieces of fabric before the garment was manufactured, so that the pattern could be adjusted to the shape and cut of the material. It was sometimes also done on partially finished pieces, so that the patterns would not print on the seams. The large patterns were sectioned off and composed of several moulds, obtaining ever changing compositions. This printing technique, which she patented, involved the use of metallic pigments, mostly gold and silver. Very typical was the technique of shading one color into another, producing a shadow effect. The fabrics used most were velvet and crepes of different weight, such as chiffon, georgette, and *marocain*. The patterns chosen were inspired by publications on art fabrics which had started to appear in those years, with a clear preference for fabrics made in Lucca in the 1300s. Starting in the mid 1920s, the modern artists in the group linked to her became dominant. Through the manufacture of these kinds of garments, Gallenga meant to answer the problem of how to create a style of fashion according to Italian taste that wouldn't be just an artistic product but could also, without losing its artistic content, pay attention to the necessities of production and marketing. Printing by hand, as reinvented by her, guaranteed aesthetic quality in the design, and, due to its rather fast execution, allowed pieces to be produced in multiples but without any decline in quality due to repetition. This opened new commercial horizons and transformed the artist into a manufacturing artisan. The patent and 7,000 wooden moulds, some hand carved and some drilled, now belong to the Collection of the theatrical tailor Umberto Tirelli.

(*Roberta Orsi Landini*)

Gallery of English Costume Platt Hall, Manchester, England. The original Collection was put together by two doctors, Willett and Cunnington, who were very keen on the history of fashion and among the first scholars to publish essays and books in the field. The Collection was acquired by the Manchester Corporation and put on display in an 18th century house. In 1947, it was organized as a museum. Even with the first curator, Anne Buck, the museum functioned at a high level. The Collection is composed of about 20,000 pieces from the 17th century up to today. The focus is more sociological than aesthetic. For example, it is interested in everything that concerns crafts and trade, especially if it is at risk of disappearing. There is a section devoted to the contemporary fashion industry. The storage areas and archives can be visited on appointment. The library is always open.

(*Virginia Hill*)

Gallia & Peter Millinery. Mariuccia Gallia, the daughter of a milliner of Turin, established Gallia & Peter at via Montenapoleone 3 in Milan in 1930. During the 1950s she worked with the most important dressmakers, such as Jole Veneziani, Biki, and Gandini. Her models, both inspired by Parisian designs and of her own creation, "dressed" the most beautiful and richest heads in Milan. In 1980, after the death of Mariuccia and her daughter Cornelia, the firm passed to the granddaughter, Laura Marelli. Today, hats are manufactured in the same premises and some of the models, from 1880 to 1960, have been published in the book *Il Cappello da donna* (Be Ma Publishing). Gallia & Peter creations have been shown in several exhibitions, including one in 1986 at the Domus Center in Milan dedicated to hats inspired by Futurist paintings, and one in 1992 at the atelier on via Montenapoleone dedicated to the most famous bridal hairdos. (*Marilea Somaré*)

Galliano John (1960). English designer. "Simplicity is a such a bore! Sometimes the real fun is in bad taste!" This is the provocation, in the best tradition of British eccentricity, of the designer born in Gibraltar in a Spanish family who learned the art and technique of tailoring in London in that mine of talent which is the Central Saint Martin's School. Very interested in folklore and the history of costume, and a true subversive spirit, he loved to dress as an Elizabethan pirate and to design theme Collections: from his final exam at Saint Martin's in 1983 entitled *Les Incroyables* to his first Collection in 1984 called *Afghanistan Repudiates Western Ideals* and those created for Christian Dior starting in January 1997. In one of those paradoxes of late 20th century fashion, that *maison* had become a coveted prey of high finance, and when the eccentric Englishman arrived in Paris in the mid 1990s in search of fortune and patrons, he was spotted by the emperor of luxury goods Bernard Arnault who, through the LVMH group, was in control of Dior. Succeeding Ferré, Galliano became artistic director. Neither the archives on Avenue Montaigne nor the clothes of the 25 Collections designed by the creator of the New Look starting 1947 held any secrets from this avid consumer of history. He was charmed by Dior's muse Germaine Bricard, known as Mitzah, and by the world that cosmopolitan lady evoked, the first years of the 20th century and the folly of the years before the catastrophe of World War I. Thus, from January 1997, every Dior Collection was a performance characterized by the historical reconstruction of an ambience or an event, with exotic references to far off lands and cultures. The *leit motif* was always the seduction of clothes cut on the bias, and fabrics that swayed gently, of drapery that wasn't used for interiors but hinted at the mystery of the female body. A *leit motif* which led the designer to perfection in his prêt-à-porter Collections: less pyrotechnic but probably more loved by women who are truly elegant. (*Maria Vittoria Carloni*)

❑ 2002, December. On the occasion of his 41st birthday, he is received at Buckingham Palace by Queen Elisabeth, who confers the decoration of Commander of the British Empire on him for his achievements in the world of fashion.
❑ 2003, March. In Paris, he presents a Collection with his own personal name, a brand which belongs to the LVMH group, same as Dior. The principal motif is, once again, flare, in all its possible interpretations. His new skirt moves, dances, and sways at even the slightest movement. It is either cut on the bias or flared, in panels or deep tight pleats that open like a wheel thanks to the insertion of light diagonal strips of fabric. The rhythm is boogie-woogie, the atmosphere that of the period after World War I, revisited in an ironic and somewhat comic strip key: herringbone tweed for tailored suits combined with muslin, knitwear decorated with ribbons and pompoms, flesh-colored lingerie, high platform shoes of the 1940s, and tiny silk dresses with cherry prints. A play on zippers stresses the flare of the white maxi-trench lined with fox. Galliano closes the presentation in a theatrical way wrapped in loose-fitting fox stoles.
❑ 2003, May. He opens his first single-brand boutique at Rue Saint Honoré 384 in Paris, where he has lived since 1991. The architect is Jean-Michel Wilmotte. Galliano boutiques are also planned for New York and Tokyo.
❑ 2003, July. The designer launches his first men's Collection, at the men's fashion presentations in Paris for Autumn-Winter 2003-2004. It is produced by Gibò, a compamy led by Franco Pené.

Gallo Italian company making men's, women's, and children's hosiery. It was established in Desenzano del Garda in the early 1900s. Almost a century later, led by the general manager Giuseppe Colombo, it has sales of 10 billion liras a year, with exports amounting to 20% of that. It is a factory, but the production philosophy is artisanal, setting rigorous criteria for controlled growth in order to safeguard the quality of the product. The eighty workers are mostly relatives of those who helped to establish and develop the company. Every pair of socks is submitted to nine quality tests. Only pure yarns are used, from extra fine merino wools to Scotia thread cotton, linen, cashmere, and 100% pure silk, of which 6 miles of thread are needed for each pair of men's socks. An in-house design department offers, for every Collection, 70 different patterns.

❑ 2003, May. The company acquires 25% of the historic hosiery brand Doré Doré, which was founded in Fontaine-Les-Grès, France. Giuseppe Colombo, the general manager of Gallo, personally acquires the remaining 65% of the shares of the new company, called Doré Doré 1819, of which he becomes the president. The goal is to relaunch a brand that was born in the early 1800s in a small family-run atelier, quickly grew to become a leader in the field of women's hosiery, and suffered a marked decline in recent years due to strong competition, with a turnover of €20 million.

Galtrucco Historic brand name of Italian shops specialized in fabrics. It is a small empire that started with a single cart that was at first pushed by hand and then, over time, pulled by a donkey and then by a horse. It was created by the Piedmont-born Lorenzo Galtrucco (1850-1912). An assistant, at the age of 8, to a travelling salesman who would beat him, then adopted by a greengrocer, he managed to save 270 liras out of the pay he received during his military service. He used the money to purchase fustians, knitwear, and cottons, and began to go from market to market in the area of Canavese and Lomellina. At the age of 35 he opened his first shop, in Robbio, near Pavia. When he died, he also had some "small shops" in Novara. To his 11 children, he said: "Don't let yourselves be led by a desire for easy and quick earnings, don't try to expand the business by associating with strangers. Go one step a time, helping each other: you will accomplish any goal." His heirs, guided, gradually, by Severino, Domenico, and Giuseppe, put this advice into practice (the company is still in the hands of the family) and almost all their goals were achieved. In 1913, a shop was opened in Turin; in 1919, on via San Gregorio in Milan, a warehouse was opened in order to sell wholesale and to serve as a headquarters; in 1923, a store was opened under the Southern Arcades of Piazza Duomo in Milan which would become the symbol of Galtrucco and later, after being destroyed by bombs during World War II, be rebuilt in 1949 according to plans by Guglielmo Ulrich; and in 1926 and in 1936 there were new shop windows in Trieste and Rome. At the beginning of the new century, the company, led by the third generation (Lorenzo, Domenico, Giancarlo, and Marisa Galtrucco) sold the shop in Piazza Duomo, Milan.

Gama Nuno (1966). Portuguese designer. He is one of the most important names in Portuguese fashion which, in recent years, has reached the European stage. He graduated in design from Citex (Portuguese Institute of Fashion) and after working with some Spanish brands, Gama opened his own atelier in Porto in 1991 in partnership with Pedro P. da Silva. In 1992 he won the *Sete de Ouro* award. He exports his *griffe* to the U.S. as well.

Gambina Maria (1969). An emerging name in Portuguese fashion. Her passion for design came out during a course on painting she took at the age of 20 at the Escola Superior de Belas Artes in Porto. Her first Collection was in 1992, presented at the end of a course at Citex. This performance opened the doors of Portuguese fashion to her. She twice won first prize at the *Sangue Novo* contest for young designers organized by the Associação Moda Lisboa. She then presented on the international stage in Stockholm, which was her début, and especially at the Workshop of Paris, where she was the first Portuguese to make a presentation. She offered her Autumn-Winter 1999-2000 Collection to the Japanese market. In November 1999 she was in San Paulo, Brazil, invited by Portugal Fashion International. The opening of her first boutique in Porto was followed by two openings in Lisbon. Her definitive international recognition came in March 2000 when her name was entered on the official calendar of Paris Fashion Week, which, along with the usual appointments, featured *Portuguese Designers*, an event dedicated to Portuguese fashion at the Carousel du Louvre. Despite her young age, Maria Gambina is today one of the most important designers of her country, able to reinterpret in a personal key the most current trends in streetwear. (*Pierangelo Mastantuono*)

Gamine Literally, a girl who hangs out on the streets. Also known as "rascal" style. Truffaut launched it in his film *Jules et Jim* (1962): a long cardigan, knickerbockers, a large scarf, and a flat beret. The haircut of Zizi Jeanmarie and that of Audrey Hepburn in *Roman Holiday* were also gamine.

Gammler Look A shabby and anonymous way of dressing in fashion from 1967 to 1973: second-hand clothes, creased blue jeans in poor condition, oversize pullovers and shirts, and oriental-style jewellery.

Gandini Remo (1893-1965). Italian haute couture tailor. The French considered him to be the best of the Italian tailors after the decline of the house of Ventura. He arrived in Milan from Fontanellato di Parma at the young age of 14 and worked at the Roveri fashion company. By the age of 17, he was head cutter. After four years of war, from 1915 to '18, and another period as an employee, in 1922 he went out on his own. At first he was on via San Paolo, then on Corso Monforte, and then, in the early 1930s, at via Senato 29, with a second entrance on via della Spiga, the street that, half a century later, would become the world's crossroads of fashion. He would choose the models in Paris and then recreate them for his private clients and for other Italian tailors. But he also designed his own models, according to a classic taste and with great rigor of line. His tailored suits were very famous, true status symbols indicating membership in high society. Until the last years of his life, he wanted to cut the cloth. He had a very bad temper and established with the clients that he chose (not everyone was welcome) a relationship based on a brusque tyranny, but also one of real friendship. His son, Giovanni Gandini, is the founder of Linus.

Logo of the Gandini Tailor's Workshop in Milan.

Gandoma A loose-fitting cloak in white or black wool in which Tuaregs wrap themselves for protection against desert sand storms.

Gant Brand created by Bernard Gant, an emigrant from Ukraine who landed in Manhattan in 1914 and began to sew shirt collars in a workshop where his future wife took care of buttons and buttonholes. Together, in addition to two children, they created a small business in New Haven, Connecticut where they manufactured shirts for themselves and for big brands such as Brooks Brothers. That was in 1941. In 1949, when the two children joined the company, the first sportswear Collection came out, along with the famous button-down shirt that was sold in the best shops. The company, number two in the world for the manufacture of shirts, was sold in 1969 to the Phillips Van Heusen Corporation. In the early 1980s, a group of young Swedes obtained, through the licensing of the brand, full creative independence. A European Collection, more appealing than the American one, was created. In 1999, a majority of the shares in Gant were acquired by the Swedish firm Pyramid Sportswear (the other partners are Phillips Van Heusen and the French group LVMH), which began to plan the company's future. (*Lucia Serlenga*)

❑ 2003, July. Van Heusen, an American company specialized in men's shirts which recently acquired Calvin Klein, agrees to sell its minority shareholding in the Swedish firm Gant. The company is acquired for about $19 million by a new group owned by LV Capital, a company financed by LVMH, the three companies that founded Gant, and the privately held company 3i Group.

Gap American company offering casual clothing. It is the number two U.S. company in clothing and today has more than 1,200 points-of-sale throughout the world, led by the multi-floor showroom on Fifth Avenue in New York. It produces and sells, at very reasonable prices, sportswear articles such as T-shirts, blue jeans, socks, and sweaters. Gap is also synonymous with backpacks, shoes, and all kinds of accessories. The idea for the Gap came in 1969 to a real estate agent in San Francisco, Donald G. Fisher. One day, needing to exchange a pair of jeans for a different size, he was shocked by the disorder and confusion in the store. Together with his wife Doris, he opened, in August of that year, a shop with well-organized shelves that were carefully subdivided according to the size of the pants. The store's name was inspired by the "generation gap." It was a success, first in California, and then all over the U.S. In 1974, a Gap line was launched, to be sold alongside the blue jeans of the most famous brands. In 1991, the trend became stronger, to the point that the other brands were no longer put on sale, developing the Gap line more and more. In 1983, the company acquired the Banana Republic chain of stores. In 1986, Gap Kids was launched. In 1990, it was the turn of Baby Gap, for newborns. In 1994 came the Old Navy Clothing Co., an ultra-casual line for the entire family at reasonable prices. Head designer for all the lines is Lisa Schultz (1955), who had been in the top ranks at Ralph Lauren. She is supported by 85 designers.

❑ 2000, August. Gap decides to focus only on the teenage market, overlooking the very important category of those in their twenties. As a result, Gap shares lose 21% on the New York Stock Exchange, erasing $7 million in market value in little more than a year.
❑ 2000, September. A decline in sales of 14% in the month of August. This was caused particularly by the poor performance of Old Navy, which lost 20%, and Banana Republic. Gap has a total of 3,348 points-of-sale. Millard Drexler, the president and general manager of the company, admits some strategic mistakes, among them reduced advertising in the media, which he says will soon be resumed. Marcia Aaron, an analyst at Deutsche Bank, says that it will take at least a year to restore the Gap's financial position. An article in WWD attributes the slump in sales not only to mistakes in the communication strategy but to a lack of strategy in general.
❑ 2001, June. The company, a leader in casual fashion, continues to accumulate losses. The competition from new chains such as Zara and H&M, which in fact were inspired by the Gap's business model, are literally bringing the Gap to its knees. The general manager, Millard Drexler, resigns. From the minute Drexler arrived to lead the Gap in 1983, there had been a real leap in quality on a world-wide level: 4,600 single-brand stores were opened, expanding the Collections for men, women, children, and expectant mothers. From a surplus of $757 million in 1999, the company went to a loss of $8 million in 2001, figures which caused a change in management and strategy.
❑ 2003, May. A positive first quarter, up 16% from the $2.47 billion in sales in the same period of 2002 to $2.86 billion at the end of March 2003. The best selling brand is Old Navy, with $1.2 billion, up 27.3%, followed Gap U.S. with $1.02 billion, up 20%, while Gap International posts its best performance ever, with $352 million, up 29.1%. Last is Banana Republic, holding at $351.3 million, up only 3.3%. For the group, growth has been steady for three quarters, while on the distribution front a policy of expansion has been moving forward. There are now 4,241 points-of-sale, with a reduction in Gap U.S. and growth in Gap International. No changes in Banana Republic or Old Navy.
❑ 2003, June. For a new Gap TV commercial, two queens of American pop music, Madonna and Missy Elliott, join together in a special kind of video. Madonna will perform *Hollywood*, a song from her latest album, *American Life*, while Missy Elliott will offer her version of *Into The Groove*, a big success from long ago 1984.

Gap-Groupe Avant Première French monthly review published from 1969 to 1990. Its goal was to inform people in the industry about the textile market and changes in the demand for fashion. Every season it would ask a panel of journalists to select some thirty models out of 350 or 400 that had been pre-selected. Their ranking of the garments would set fashion trends and was documented not by photographers but by a group of artists and illustrators. The magazine generated a series of specialized reviews such as Les Collections, Gap Sport, Hyper Gap, Gap Italy, and Gap Japan. Only Gap Sport survives.

Garbo Greta (1905-1990). Swedish actress. Cecil Beaton, a sharp observer of the costumes and customs of his time, wrote, "Perhaps nobody else has had such influence on the outward appearance of an entire generation." The image created for Garbo by the cinema – as also happened with Joan Crawford, another great trend-setter – is linked to the costume designer Adrian. He began to design her clothes in Hollywood in 1928 on the set of *Mysterious Lady* and continued until her retirement. From that first movie, Garbo established herself as an icon to be imitated by thousands of women. Among her costumes is a trenchcoat lined in wool with a Scottish pattern that appeared in Women's Wear Daily and was reproduced in thousands of copies. Greta Louis Gustafsson began her film career in Sweden in 1922. In 1924, she became famous after being chosen by Mauritz Stiller for the film *Gösta Berlings Saga*. She was noticed by Pabst, who offered her a role in *Die Freudlose Gasse* (1925). It was an international success and resulted in a contract with Metro Goldwyn Mayer and a move to Hollywood. That's where Garbo found not only Adrian as one of the creators of her image, but also the film star hairdresser Sydney Guilaroff. He invented the pageboy haircut for her. In an age devoted to haircuts *à la garçonne*, it was easily able to impose a vogue for half-lengths. As part of the Garbo image there are also some hats, such as the turban in which she appeared in *The Painted Veil* (1934) and the beret worn in *Ninotchka* (1939). (*Sofia Leoncina Gnoli*)

Garbo Rosy (1950). Italian designer of high fashion. She loves sharp colors and precious fabrics. She experiments with innovative combinations, such as fabric with Murano glass. While still very young, she opened an atelier in Padua, and during the 1980s she worked in Paris in various ateliers. She presented her Collection in Rome in 1996. She has dressed some of the main characters on the TV program *Secrets and Lies*.

❑ 2002, July. The presentation of the high fashion Autumn-Winter 2002-2003 Collection takes place to the rhythms of classic dance. Her silhouette is always respectful of tradition, elegant, and refined, with asymmetric cuts and floral decorations from the 1700s in Venice. There are wool tops, white satin pants with sequins, leaf-shaped embroideries in Autumn colors, satin and velvet trains, denim with lace patchwork, and green chiffon and black tulle, ending with the ritual of the bridal Collection.

Garcia Purification (1952). Spanish designer and brand of prêt-à-porter. After a long apprenticeship in Uruguay dedicated to knitwear and accessories design, she presented her first Collection in Barcelona in 1981, distinguishing herself especially with evening wear.

Garland Madge (1910 ca.). Teacher and director of the Fashion Department at the Royal College of Art in London. Born in Australia, she moved to England as a girl. She began her career with fashion magazines and reached the highest position in the field: director of the English edition of Vogue. She left journalism in 1948, when the Royal College gave her the task of starting a new fashion course, with the goal of educating high fashion designers who would be ready to challenge the supremacy of French fashion. She was chosen because of her wide knowledge and practical approach. In fact, instead of inviting theorists to teach her students, she invited people who worked in the field, and had them involve the students in the industry in various ways. These included manufacturers, artisans, designers, and tailors, among them Hartnell, Amies, and Stiebel. She urged students to go to fashion events, ateliers, and department stores in addition to museums. The Fashion Department has its own location in an elegant mansion in South Kensington; not really a school, it is more like an atelier. In 1952, Madge Garland married Sir Leigh Ashton, at the time the director of the Victoria and Albert Museum. In 1956, she left teaching. Among her students were Gina Fratini, Gerald McCann, and Bernard Nevill.

Garment District A neighborhood in New York that is the local equivalent of the quadrilateral in Milan and the center of the most important economic activity in the city.

The Collections of almost all the American designers are created and manufactured between 34th and 42nd Streets and between Sixth and Eighth Avenues. Seventh Avenue is better known as Fashion Avenue, and right there are the headquarters the Parsons School of Design, the American university of fashion. There are hundreds of shops selling fabrics, men and women hurrying on the sidewalks with sample cases, and trucks unloading bundles of clothes. Only here can one find the outlet stores where the great designers sell at reduced prices the Collections of past seasons.

Garofolo Tiziana (1969). Designer. She became well known in Summer 1999 when her name was mentioned as one of three finalists for the Infil Award, a prize given to young designers of underwear. Born in Nettuno, she graduated from the Koefia Academy in Rome in 1991. She worked for a time at the Maska company in Scandiano (Reggio Emilia), side by side with those responsible for the products. She then worked at 31 Tessile in Velletri, designing the Velvet Collection, at Euromoda in Cassino, at Hiam Ricci Couture in Rome on Collections destined for the United Arab Emirates, and at the Elvira Gramano and Storm Country firms in Rome.

Garrard British jewellery house, established in London in 1792. The heirs of Robert Garrard, who was the pioneer and first director, remained the owners up until 1946. Garrard later merged with the Goldsmiths and Silversmiths Company, and in 1988 became part of the Asprey Group. Since 1842, it has been an official supplier to the British Crown. Queen Victoria, along with many European sovereigns and rulers in the Middle East, commissioned many extraordinary pieces from Garrard. The firm created the jewels given to Princess Alexandra of England in 1863 on the occasion of her wedding to the Prince of Wales, as well as those created in the 20th century for Queen Elizabeth II. The stones used have in many cases been truly exceptional, for example the famous Koh-I-Noor diamond. Today, in its prestigious boutique on Regent Street, the firm continues to serve a clientele that is sensitive to classic taste, of which its pieces are a perfect synthesis, and to the very high quality of the gems used in them.

(*Alessandra Quattordio*)

Garren American hairdresser. Glamorous but also very outrageous (see the first haircuts inspired by the punk look of the early 1980s), throughout his career he has created several successful images. These include the platinum-dyed boyish hair of Andy Warhol and the chameleon transformations of Linda Evangelista. His extreme style, both in the pages of fashion magazines and on the runways of Marc Jacobs and Anna Sui, is softened when he works in the salon, in order to create styles that are more wearable, in tune with the personality of each woman.

Garretto Paolo (1903-1989). Commercial artist and designer, born in Naples. His family moved north when he was still quite young and he spent almost all his life between Paris and London and between New York and Italy. Paolo Garretto, wrote Giordano Bruno Guerri, "is by now a historic character, because the role he played in the graphic arts and the history of Italy (and not just Italy) from the period after World War I up to today was itself historic....He gave the graphic arts and design a totally new and revolutionary imprint, which was rooted directly in Futurism." His career went from Becco Giallo, an anti-Fascist satiric paper of the 1920s to L'Espresso, for which he illustrated several covers. His relationship with fashion was essentially based on work he did with the major magazines of the time, including Vogue and Vanity Fair. But right after World War II fashion became of more pressing interest to him when he founded and edited *Rivista* and *Per voi signore* ('Review' and 'For You, Ladies'). This was for the great illustrator an opportunity to deeply explore the world of fashion and female beauty, which he reinvented with his essential and revelatory sketches, showing the female readers of the day some possible models for a lifestyle and clothing style suitable for an Italy which was standing on its feet again.

Garter Underwear accessory used to hold up the stockings. It derives from the French *jarretière*, and it indicates both an ancient symbol of devotion to an institution or a noble family and the most modern and shocking element of women's erotic underwear. You only have to think about the popular tradition of the red garter that women wear on New Year's Eve and then give away as a gift. It belongs both to the male and female wardrobe. Today, it is almost exclusively worn by women. There are very, very few gentlemen who wear garters any more. The accessory consists of a band which holds up the stockings, worn on the upper part of each leg or under the knee, depending on the stocking's length. The term first appears in the 800s in the writings of Eginard. While describing the clothing of Charlemagne, he speaks about "garters" that hold up the monarch's stockings. It has been present in men's clothing since about 1200. In the mid 1300s, after an incident at a court ball hosted by the Countess of Salisbury, Edward III of England designated the garter as the symbol of the most prestigious honor given by the British Crown, the *Order of the Garter*, at the same time uttering the famous motto that is still present on the royal coat of arms: "Honni soit qui mal y pense." Used in the following centuries to hold up both men's and women's stockings, the garter began to decline in use at the end of the 1800s. This was due at first to the advent of women's suspender belts, then the popularity of tights and support stockings.

(*Gianluca Bauzano*)

Garçon Nathalie (1959). French designer and brand of prêt-à-porter. She studied fine arts in Paris and took the fashion courses at Studio Berçot. In 1981, she was hired by Cacharel as assistant to the artistic director Corinne Sarrut. In 1988 she launched her personal brand and presented her first Collection, which emphasized classic lines.

Garçonne A style which, starting in Spring 1924 in Paris, definitively revolutionized contemporary and future fashions. The

Garçonne, 1928 (Prints Collection A. Bertarelli, Milan).

Garçonne, 1927 (Prints Collection A. Bertarelli, Milan).

inventor of this simple and natural new look was Chanel. She created it for women after World War I who were engaged in an active life on several fronts. Loose blouses and pleated skirts hid unshapely bodies and revealed legs in flesh-colored stockings. The style required short and flat haircuts which over time took on a more and more masculine shape and ended up identifying the garçonne with a woman enclosed in a man's suit with shirt and tie, little make-up, and flat shoes. This was the clothing style of the emancipated and sexually free protagonist of a novel by Victor Margueritte titled *La garçonne* (1922). It was read avidly by ladies who were shocked by the situations in which a girl studying at the Sorbonne found herself. She adopted not only men's jackets, shirts, and ties, but also their habits. That book title gave its name to the signature style of those crazy years. (*Lucia Sollazzo*)

Gas Italian brand of prêt-à-porter produced by the Grotto company, established near Vicenza in 1986. Denim and sportswear are the main lines, with more than 6 million pieces produced each year and a total of 3,000 points-of-sale. It has a strong market in Europe, and is growing in Canada and the Far East. Milan is the brand's display city. After the opening of a showroom on via Tortona in April 2003, a two-floor GasStore was opened on Corso di Porta Ticinese. There are several lines: the Blue Jeans Basic, which is the core business; the Urban, with pieces for everyday city life; the most sophisticated, which is Blue Label; and the high-tech Active, which includes underwear and accessories. (*Valeria Vantaggi*)

Gaspari Pierantonio (1965). Italian designer. He took his first steps in the world of textiles in his father's company in Forlì. But by the age of 30, he felt the need to develop a style of his own, one that was minimalist and rigorous. He was a great success, to the point that he presents a Collection every season in Milan and Paris, and has a distribution network with 450 points-of-sale in Italy and all over the world. His style is characterized by a fusion of fabric and knitwear, in a continuous play of combinations and arrangements.

Gastel Giovanni (1955). Italian photographer. He is a fashion photographer, according to his official biography. But, in fact, in his fashion photos and still life photos, Giovanni Gastel – born in Milan to a noble family, the nephew of the director Luchino Visconti, a pleasant and refined man with a passion for theater and poetry – often pushes his research and interpretations beyond the level of a pure and simple trade. He began, at a young age, as a photographer for the auction house Christie's and as a shoe photographer for Mipel. His fortunate meeting, in 1982, with Flavio Lucchini and Gisella Borioli, the editor and director of Mondo Uomo and Donna, allowed him to carry forward, as chief photographer for those magazines, his work with very sophisticated and modern photos. On the other hand, he distinguished himself during the 1980s with his elegant studio work, working just with light. His unmistakable photographic style uses equal measures of irony and poetry. He works "in the old way," with a rare and precious Deardorf optical bench and only Polaroid or large format plates (20x25). A great experimenter, his manipulations and combinations result in new creations far removed from the original photo, through "old-mix" techniques, crossovers, pictorial re-workings, uncouplings, and stratifications. He has worked for the most prestigious magazines in the world, including Vogue Gioielli, for which he made the famous still life photos with jewels superimposed on fashion portraits. The jewels were positioned to create unusual and curious figures in the shape of a woman's body with the face given the abstract and precious shapes of brooches and mounted pearls. It was then photographed on a flat surface producing a very effective *trompe-l'oeil* effect. Among his clients are Dior, Versace, Tod's, Krizia, Trussardi, Guerlain, Fratelli Rossetti, Mandarina Duck, Hogan, Fragrances, and Pasquale Brun. The exhibits dedicated to him include *Fashion in Still Life* at Galleria Diaframma in Milan (1986); *Trussardi and Gastel* at the National Museum of Science and Technology in Milan (1987) and Palermo (1991); *Gastel per Donna* on Via della Spiga in Milan (1991); *Jewellery of Fantasy* at the Theater Museum of La Scala in Milan (1992); and his big one-man show *Gastel* at the Triennial of Milan (1998), which was desired by the art critic Germano Celant. He is a permanent member of the Polaroid Museum of Chicago and president of AFIP (Association of Italian Professional Photographers).

Gaster Owen (1970). English designer. He is considered one of the main figures in the rebirth of British fashion. A graduate of the Epsom College of Art & Design in 1992, he made his début on the runways in 1994 with a Collection that reinvented glamour in a rock-and-roll key. In fact, he counts among his clients famous rock stars such as Mick Jagger, the Spice Girls, and Janet Jackson. He mixes influences of different types, from reggae to Pop Art and from naturalism to technology, creating clothes that are feminine, modern, and sexy.

Gatsby A style based on the title character in the novel *The Great Gatsby* by F. Scott Fitzgerald, which was made into a movie with Robert Redford in 1973. Since that time, and throughout the 1980s, Gatsby meant a style of men's clothing inspired by the 1930s with loose-fitting, comfortable jackets, pleated trousers, shirts with white collars in thin stripes and in colors, two-tone shoes, and large-brimmed hats.

Gatti Juan (1950). Argentine photographer and art director. He graduated with a degree in the visual arts from the University of Buenos Aires. He opened a studio as an art director first in Buenos Aires and later in Madrid, where he moved in 1985. He works with important photographers such as Bruce Weber and Peter Lindbergh. More recently, he worked with the Spanish director Pedro Almodóvar, for whom he designs sets and takes set photos. Among his clients are Cacharel, Dior, Paloma Picasso, Loewe, Sibille, and Jesus Del Pozo. His photos appear in the French edition of Glamour, in the American edition of Elle and in the Italian, Russian, Spanish, and American editions of Vogue.

Gattinoni Italian house of high fashion established by Fernanda Gattinoni (1907-2002), who was born in Cocquio Trevisago (Varese). At a young age she was an assistant in the London branch of the French *maison* Molyneux, where she learned about formal fashions. Then she went to Paris, where she learned to venerate the client. On her return to Italy she was hired by the Ventura dressmaker's shop in Milan. She spent a short time there and then moved to Rome. World War II swept away everything, and she had to start over. In 1947, she opened her atelier on via Marche, taking with her part of the staff of Ventura's Roman atelier and those who remained from the office in Milan. Thanks to her old clientele, she built a new image that was still rooted in tradition. She moved to Viale Toscana 1, still the current premises of the atelier, not far from via Veneto. The atelier, adjacent to the U.S. Embassy, had Claire Both Luce as one of its usual customers. Famous personalities went in and out of the nearby Hotel Excelsior, including the mythical Eva Perón who, one day, also visited the atelier of Fernanda Gattinoni. Rome lived out its years as Hollywood on the Tiber, and actresses were fascinated by Italian fashion. Ingrid Bergman wore Gattinoni both on screen and in real life. Anna Magnani was an affectionate client. Audrey Hepburn had her costumes for the film *War and Peace* designed by

Cocktail dress by Gattinoni.

Maria de Matteis as well as the simple clothes for her holiday in Capri. Silvana Pampanini favored embroidered garments. The next generation opened new horizons. Fernanda was joined by her son Raniero (1953-1993), who received a strict education in the business from his mother but preferred literature to trade. Raniero wanted Stefano Dominella, a friend from school, to work with him as coordinator. The two successfully planned the *griffe*'s reorganization. They brought new ideas and avant-guard methods, reinventing and reproposing, in the full swing of the 1980s, the high fashion of *Maison* Gattinoni. Fernanda stepped aside, but continued to maintain her relationships with the clients and the workshop. In 1993, Raniero died. Stefano Dominella became president of Gattinoni, while Guillermo Mariotto, born in Caracas and already a designer for Raniero, became artistic director. In close contact with Fernanda, he successfully continued the union of artisanal handwork with research in new technologies. In 1996, a new prêt-à-porter line was created. It was presented in Milan and joined the other licenses of the firm, which include Gattinoni Boutique, Pret d'Immagine, Tempo, and Gattinoni Basic. The lines include sportswear, jeans, knitwear, and leather goods. In 1997 the Gattinoni fragrance made its début, along with a line of cosmetic products.

❑ 2001, May. A pair of jeans for one million dollars. Designed by Mariotto with the collaboration of the jeweller Roberto Zancan, these are denim pants completely decorated with precious stones, including 175 carats of diamonds, 188 of zephyrs and more than 4 pounds of gold. Even the Gattinoni label is made in white gold and diamonds. Presented with the last Collections, it was worn by Milly Carlucci during the charity event Pavarotti & Friends.

❑ 2001, October. The *maison* opens its third single-brand boutique in Verona, in collaboration with the Italstyle company of Gianluca Adometti.

❑ 2001, December. Fernanda Gattinoni celebrates her birthday receiving a prestigious acknowledgment from the municipality of Rome. The *La Lupa* award is conferred on her by deputy mayor Enrico Gasbarra in the Piccola Promoteca of the Campidoglio.

❑ 2002, July. The new Collection is presented at the Museum of Modern and Contemporary Art in Rome (on the site of the former Peroni brewery). This time, the designer treats a difficult theme. He is inspired by the famous Rembrandt painting *Anatomy Lesson of Doctor Tulpe* and creates a Collection whose motif is the human body. He interprets muscles, tendons, ligaments, the nervous system, the circulation system, and blood cells as embroideries, applications, prints, stitchings, and inlays, all in perfect correspondence with a skilled tailoring which redesigns shapes and the simulates the anatomy of the human body. The painting, admired during a trip to Amsterdam, had already inspired a previous Collection.

❑ 2002, September. Gattinoni will design new uniforms for the Italian army, the first time that this job goes to a high fashion atelier. The idea is to update the khaki Safari jacket look. The colors will be the grey and green adopted before World War I and used for 40 years after 1908.

❑ 2002, September. The ambassador of Italian fashion in China, Gattinoni presents its creations at the Dalian Fashion Festival, which brings together all the most important oriental *griffes*. It is the festival's 14th edition, held at the Congress Center Fumara, which has a capacity of 1,200 people. The exhibit displays are designed by the set designer of the Opera House in Beijing.

❑ 2002, November. Fernanda Gattinoni, the dressmaker-designer and founder of the maison, dies. The funeral is held in the Campidoglio.

❑ 2003, February. Mariotto wants to design for curvaceous women. Gattinoni Softwear is the new knitwear line created by the designer for "plus" sizes. He is inspired by the Anita Ekberg of *La Dolce Vita* and *Boccaccio '70*, an unusual figure for a fashion industry which favors slender women. Gattinoni Softwear will be distributed all over the world and manufactured on license by Koas Boss, a leading knitwear company.

❑ 2003, March. A five-year license agreement for the entire accessories Collection with the Sergiolin company of Emilia Romagna. Gattinoni ends 2002 with sales of €43 million. For 2003, new boutiques are planned for Miami and New York. In Italy, there are two single-brand franchise boutiques, one in Rome and one in Verona.
❑ 2003, June. Gattinoni makes its début in underwear. The Fragile Collection, presented on a test basis, goes into production. Innovative in its use of latex, it meets the needs of the market.
❑ 2003, June. Guillermo Mariotto's Collection for Rome Alta Moda is based on twelve famous women chosen by the designer for the mark they left on history. Joan of Arc wears a suit of armor and small macramé tunics. Shakespeare's Juliet wears an ethereal white dress embroidered with gold threads, Queen Isabella of Castille a grey bustier. Mary Stuart is in shiny-opaque black, Catherine of Russia in denim and gazar with a seductive girdle. Then, in chronological order, come Marie Antoinette; Maria Waleska; the Countess Castiglioni; Bernardette, in poor sackcloth clothes; Madame Curie, severe and masculine in black and white; Ella Fitzgerald, covered with sparkling sequins; and finally, Marilyn Monroe sprinkled with stars.

Evening model by Gattinoni.

Gatto Legendary shoemaker in Rome, famous among dandies for its custom made shoes. It was established in 1912 by Angelo Gatto, a Sicilian artisan from Noto, who learned the job at a young age and emigrated to England and France in order to deepen his knowledge of the craft. Since that time, Gatto shoes have distinguished themselves for their tapered and proportionate line, the quality of the skins (calfskin from France and Germany, leather from Italy) and the perfection of the stitching. In 1934 the workshop added to its resume the honor of being a supplier to the Royal House. Right after World War II, Gatto was joined by his grandson Giuseppe. The brand continued to be successful. When Angelo died in 1974, Giuseppe started a partnership with Gaetano Vastola, an assistant artisan who had been hired in 1953. In 1993, when Giuseppe died, his position was taken by his son Enzo who, together with Vastola, maintained the high reputation of the brand. They have about one thousand clients all over the world. Gatto has served, or serves, among others, the Savoy family, Constantine of Greece, Boris of Bulgaria, Faruk of Egypt, Tyrone Power, Alain Delon, Piero Sanjust, Gianni Agnelli, and Marco Tronchetti Provera.

Gaucho Gaucho pants are inspired by those worn by the cowboys who herd cattle on the vast pampas in Argentina. During the 1960s, Saint-Laurent made this look popular with boots, a shirt, and a wide belt with a big silver buckle either engraved in silver or embossed.

Gaultier Jean-Paul (1952). French designer. The *enfant terrible* of fashion, as he likes to call himself. He is considered the most direct follower of Vivienne Westwood, the eccentric and intellectual star of English fashion, in the space between the past and the avant-garde, between the best cutting and eccentricity. A mixer of different ways of dressing, an amused creator of impossible but desirable combinations of very different styles, always aiming to break the barrier between male and female through shocking variations on the theme, he has been able, ever since his first Collection, to make every presentation into an event, in the name of a multiform aesthetic and the most provoking inventions. And every season he is number one in sales. A careful manager of his own success through a wide range of media events – from cinema (with set costumes) to television (with his *Eurotrash* program for British TV) – he continues to surprise and to involve others in his customary yet always unpredictable challenges to the rules of dressing, rehabilitating them and at the same time upsetting them. A very important influence on Gaultier, who was not a very studious adolescent, was his grandmother, who had a beauty salon in Arcueil. There he saw his first fashion images, between haircuts, photos, and women's magazines, and he began to draw models and make sketches using those images as a visual storehouse of ideas. At the age of 18, he sent his sketches to Pierre Cardin, who hired him, and – after a short period that the restless young designer spent with Esterel, Patou, and Tarlazzi – in 1974 took him back, sending him to the Philippines in order to design some Collections meant expressly for the American market. Just two years later, he presented his first women's Collection for Spring-Summer 1977. His taste for amazing combinations, the appeals to kitsch, and the subversive accents on the runways drew attention to him. Since 1981, the Kashiyama group has been his financial partner for the annual prêt-à-porter Collections which are manufactured in Italy and always have great impact due to the topicality of the themes on which they are based, from London streetwear to the distraught memories of the '60s. His first prêt-à-porter men's Collection for Spring-Summer 1984 (emblematic title: *The Object-Man*) offered new opportunities for irony, disguise, and the mixing up of men's erogenous zones (such as a low neckline on the back), transposed from the women's wardrobe which he had in the previous Winter made fun of with very serious trench coats and raincoats. Later would come the men in skirts and even in "princess" dresses. His favorite theme, a direct attack on the clichés concerning the wardrobe of the two sexes, touched on something important in the models for Summer 1985. A revealing title: *A Wardrobe for Two*, an exploration of the androgynous appearance, contradicted, caricatured through gag-clothes, like the whale-bone corset under a tuxedo for women, and draped chiffon and lace over a

Sketch by Jean-Paul Gaultier.

men's formal shirt worn with boxer shorts. His spectacular presentations, superb in their choreographies and continuous surprises, became the *clou* of several rounds of Parisian prêt-à-porter, expected, commented upon, and certainly highlighted, by the daily press. He brought to the runway a Greek model with a very big nose, an old lady with white hair, and a solemn gait that was as quiet as it was incongruous in a daring dress. There was also a couple tied together by a single garment which started from her, extended to him, and offered, while it unwound like a horizontal bandage, new role inversions between the sexes. Another of his characteristics is a showy and intelligent mix of past and present in cutting and materials. Among his famous inventions (also in the Junior line, created with Elio Fiorucci in 1988) are sweaters with lace and satin, multiple torn T-shirts in superimposed layers that reveal the shoulders and part of the arms, aluminum can jewellery, stiletto heels line an upside-down Eiffel Tower, and, on top of everything, the concept of a corset, sometimes inspired by the taste of the 1800s, that would charm Madonna. She asked him to create the stage costumes for her 1990 world tour, and after that it became a fetish piece for the designer. The bottle for his first perfume would be shaped like a woman's bust enclosed in a corset, although contained not in a box, but – as a tribute to the new *High-Tech* Collection of 1993 – in a tin can. He likes to name his Collections in ways that are unusual for the fashion industry: *Tribute to the Jewish People*, *The Tattoos*, *Latin Lover of the '40s*, *The Punk Parisian*, *Cyberbaba*, *The House of Pleasure*, *Flowers Powers and Skin Heads,* and, for the men's Autumn-Winter 1998-99 Collection, *Italian Style*. In 1998 he created a junior line. He also designs furniture. He has published a photographic autobiography, a sort of picture story: *A nous deux la mode*. In Summer 1999, Hermès acquired 35% of the *maison*, investing about 45 billion liras.

(*Lucia Sollazzo*)

❑ 2000. He designs a line for Wolford. It includes a leotard and tights in tight-fitting and seamless knitwear on which are woven, in black and grey, striped stockings, garter belts, panties, and bras. The garments have neither hooks nor elastic bands.

❑ 2002, May. Jean-Paul Gaultier arrives in the U.S. to open a boutique on Madison Avenue in New York. The interior décor is by Philippe Starck. The same design will be used in about twenty more Gaultier boutiques all over the world.

❑ 2002, July. He closes the Paris Fashion Week with a Collection inspired by the Austro-Hungarian Empire of Franz Joseph. At the Palais de la Mutualité (formerly the House of the People), at Rue Saint Martin 325, which is now the new headquarters of the *maison*, a sort of court salon with stuccos and big lamps has been created, covering the spaces still under construction with decorated lengths of white cloth. To the sound of a Viennese waltze, a model strolls on the runway, flaunting her femininity, but not disdaining male clothing. Fifty-eight creations, from a baseball jacket embroidered like a kimono to evening dresses in the style of the Austrian court, for example a long garnet dress and one in Prussian blue velvet trimmed with ermine. To finish, accompanied by the Radetzky March, a bride with white feathers in her hair and a train more than ten yards long.

❑ 2002, October. During Paris Fashion Week, Jean-Paul Gaultier makes Calder's "holes" soft by means of large draperies with holes on which, thanks to ropes and swings, rather round acrobats go back and forth. Their "curves" reinforce the image of softness, which is the theme of the Collection. "Calder's works are rigid; in this context they become as sweet as Dalí's. What really interested me, this time, was the transformation of the garments, the jacket that becomes a skirt, the shirt worn as a shawl. Everything is almost liquid and loose on the body." Thus Gaultier describes his Collection made of small jackets with tails, very tight pants that are worn very low around the waist, even to the buttocks, extra large overalls, all accompanied by very high laced boots, large hats, embroidered stockings, and tiny boleros. There are contrasts in volume, from the very tight to the extra large, for example in dresses of silk jersey. There is a creative mix consisting of stockings worn with bikinis and pieces of cloth held together by small chains: caprice, for sure, but also attention to very precise products, from the satin nightgown embroidered like a kimono to skirts in white and green *toile-de-jouy* to platform sandals with a transparent band.

❑ 2002, October. The opening of a large new boutique on Avenue George V in Paris.

❑ 2003, May. He is appointed the new artistic director of Hermès. The début is to be with the women's prêt-à-porter line for Autumn-Winter 2004-2005. Gaultier will continue to design the lines of his *griffe* (of which Hermès owns 35%). He replaces Martin Margiela, who had worked for Hermès since 1997 and will now devote himself only to his own brand, which is controlled by Renzo Rosso, the owner of Diesel.

❑ 2003, June. As assistant to Jean-Paul Gaultier, the new artistic director of Hermès, the firm hires Boli Barret, a young emerging designer with an urban style who will be entrusted with the silk scarf line.

❑ 2004, June. The exhibit *Pain Couture* by Jean-Paul Gaultier opens at the Cartier Foundation in Paris. The space on Boulevard Raspail is transformed into a kind of bakery where the clothes are made with flour and water instead of fabrics. Master bakers work to put into effect the ideas of the British artist Souhed Nemlaghi.

❑ November. The designer begins an adventure of selling by mail order, working with La Redoute, a company that is part of the Pinault-Printemps-Redoute group. It is a mini-Collection of six historic pieces by the company, reinterpreted in JPG's style.

(*Gabriella Gregorietti*)

Gauze A light fabric in cotton, silk, or wool originating in Gaza, Syria. It is thin and transparent, irregular and soft, with an open and thin weft.

Gavello Brand of jewelry created in Milan in 1980 by Rinaldo Gavello, a designer of jewellery in a sculptural style, in which technique is skillfully allied to a wise study of human anatomy. Inspired by the world of design, in particular auto design, Gavello distinguishes himself for being an experimenter, both in the field of materials – he likes stones with the largest color spectrum, from semi-precious to brown and black diamonds – and at the same time as an *ante litteram* innovator, because in the 1980s he anticipated some creative ideas which would later reveal themselves as the result of avant-garde research at the turn of the new millennium. He has boutiques on via Montenapoleone in Milan, in Athens, and on Mykonos, and corner shops in London at Harvey Nichols. (*Alessandra Quattordio*)

Gay Grazia (1933). Public relations expert. Born in Turin, she studied in England. After 14 years with Banca Nazionale del Lavoro and a British oil company, she opened a public relations office in Milan in 1973, specializing in the fashion industry. Among her clients were Alberta Ferretti, Luciano Soprani, and Les Copains. At the end of 1998 she closed her office and began to work asa consultant to large fashion and textile companies.

Gazette du Bon Ton, La The leading fashion magazine in Paris in the pre- and post-World War I years, *La Gazette du Bon Ton* was founded by Lucien Vogel and published by the Librairie Centrale des Beaux-Arts from 1912 to 1925. Innovative in both its artwork and writing, the Gazette featured stunning color fashion illustrations obtained by the *pochoir* technique, a precursor to silk screening. Artists such as Leon Bakst, Georges Barbier, and André Marty were behind the stunning Art Deco fashion illustrations, many of which are currently in the hands of collectors and art museums, while its writers included Marcel Astruc, Tristan Bernard, Raymond Radiguet and Jean Cocteau. In 1925 Condé Nast purchased the magazine and merged it with *Vogue*.

Gazzarini Piero. Italian designer of men's clothing. He made his début in the mid 1990s. With his tenth Collection he finally obtained the consecration of the Milan runways, presenting his designs for the Spring-Summer 2000 season. His fashion is young and dynamic, characterized by a minimalist taste, with careful attention to details.

Gazzoni Concetta. Italian dressmaker, born in Rome. In the late 1800s she had an intuition which, almost a century later, has given birth to shops and fashion trends: the idea of second-hand clothes. She would buy used garments from the great ladies of the Roman aristocracy, renovate them, and finally sell them to the ladies of the lower and middle bourgeoisie. These garments were only called second-hand: for the great ladies of Roman society, who at the time were crazy for the young D'Annunzio, for "il Duca minimo," it would have been unthinkable to wear and show off an important dress more than once, perhaps twice, whether it were an evening gown or a fox hunting outfit. The dressmaker and her two nieces, Assunta and Giovanna, had a good business, but the change of wardrobe of their suppliers was faster than the speed with which they could sell to their middle-class ladies and the clothes would pile up. Concetta skimmed wardrobes from 1890 to 1946, filling five apartments with garments of the great fashion designers from Worth to Balenciaga. Some 60% of the Collection of original clothes, about 20,000 pieces, belonging to the theater costume designer Umberto Tirelli, including some items from the wardrobe of the Savoy queens – Margherita, Elena, and Maria José – came from that storehouse, in which Tirelli dug like an archaeologist of fashion.

G.B. Pedrini Brand of ready-to-wear. It began with the opening of a first store in Varese in 1986. The entrepreneurial idea, based on a complete range of products sold at reasonable prices, was such an immediate success that in the same year 20 more stores were opened in Italy, some owned by the company but most of them franchises. It was precisely through franchising that the brand developed. The firm was acquired by Gruppo Incom in 1994. At present there are 200 points-of-sale in Italy. The company is active in Europe and in Southeast Asia.

Geiger Collections Austrian fashion house. Established in 1907 in Tyrol, it made its name on an international level thanks to Walk, a light and soft knitwear fulled with water and heat which withstands even the hottest temperatures. The Super-Light Walk is the outstanding example: a square yard of this natural material weighs less than ten ounces and is made in more than 50 variations. Geiger, a worldwide leader in the production of women's Walk fashion, has sales of €34 million. It has 360 employees and exports 88% of the production, reaching about 2,000 shops in 39 countries. The headquarters is in Vamp, Austria.

Tyrolese outfit revisited by Geiger.

Gemelli Clothing store in Milan. It opened in 1930 as a shop for hosiery and gloves on Corso Vercelli, which at the time was a street on the outskirts of the city. The owner, Attilio Gemelli, immediately revealed his talent for what would later be defined as marketing: his clear and simple ideas, which he himself called "from the countryside," were an immediate success with consumers. After World War II, thanks to the commitment of the current president, Sergio Gramelli, the store took center stage and became a sophisticated boutique. It was one of the first to import, during the 1960s, the new prêt-à-porter from Paris. In the late 1970s, the business consolidated its position, becoming outstanding for the style of its offerings, a balance between classic items and novelties, and the range of its cashmere garments.

Genny Italian brand of ready-to-wear. It made its début in 1961. At the beginning, it offered skirts and blouses, the basic elements of a wardrobe, which Arnaldo Girombelli would produce under the Genny brand as a complement to the Collections on sale in his boutique in Ancona. It was artisanal production, greatly appreciated by his clients, so that in 1976 he hired a very young Donatella Ronchi as style coordinator: she would become his wife and, on his death in 1980, take over his position as head of the company. A forerunner of the Made in Italy movement and of its winning formula – a wise mix of fashion, industry, and attention to the public taste – in 1968 Girombelli opened his first plant for the production of quality tailoring. The staff consisted of one hundred people. In 1973 he began to work with Gianni Versace, an emerging designer who arrived first in Florence, and then in Milan, from his native Reggio Calabria. It was a partnership which would last until the 1990s. Besides Genny, Versace would at his début also design the youth line Byblos and the Complice Collection, started in 1975. The cooperation with designers and the openness to emerging talents, with their differences in origin and vocation – including Claude Montana, Keith Varty, Alan Cleaver, Dolce & Gabbana, Christian Lacroix, Rebecca Moses, John Bartlett, Richard Tyler, and Josephus Thimister – was the winning card for the firm, which in 1987 becames

Evening dress by Genny, Spring-Summer 1994.

financial holding company, emphasizing its international orientation. Since her husband's passing, Donatella Girombelli has been the soul of the group: in addition to corporate strategies (she is president of the holding company), she decides the style choices, especially for the Genny Collections, in tune with the transformations of society and changes in the role of women. After the strong and super-feminine style of the 1980s, after a more conceptual fashion in the 1990s, it was the moment to search for an equilibrium between luxury and simplicity. "Purist-modernist, classic and bright, and very Italian," is how Donatella (now assisted by her son Leonardo) loves to define the Genny of the year 2000. (*Maria Vittoria Carloni*)

❑ 2001, June. Preliminary agreement for the acquisition of Genny by Prada, which guarantees the present level of employment. Donatella Girombelli, president of Genny since 1980, says about the decision: "It was the best choice for our Group. The worldwide competition in the luxury sector today requires larger size in order to compete at a high level. The company's future will certainly be a better one, thanks to the combination with an important and fast-growing group such as Prada." Donatella Girombelli and her son Leonardo are to keep their positions in the new company.
❑ 2002, September. The début of Francisco Rosaf, age 37, the new designer of Genny. He revitalizes the tradition of lacework, which has always been important in the brand's history, and which returns in the form of a printed pattern on fabrics together with colored flowers.
❑ 2003, March. The three-year plan for the brand's relaunch, planned by Prada Holding after the company's acquisition in 2001, is on schedule. Genny closes 2002 with sales of €20 million, of which €2 million come from the men's line. The company aims for a selection at retail, while continuing to focus the economic effort on product quality.
❑ 2004, May. Prada Holding, the owner of the brand, decides to suspend production. The last season is Autumn-Winter 2004-2005.

Genoni Rosa (1867-1954). Italian dressmaker. Already called, in 1907, "the inventor of Italian fashion" by the most influential newspapers of the time, she was certainly one of the most important personalities in Italian fashion in the early 1900s. She was born in the province of Sondrio. After long apprenticeships in Milan, Nice, and Paris, she returned to Milan with the sought-after qualification of a première. In 1895, she found a job with the atelier H. Haardt et Fils, one of the most prestigious fashion houses in Milan, with branch offices in San Remo, Lucerne, and St. Moritz. From the beginning of her career, she was committed to the cause of social protest against the exploitation of women, taking part, together with Anna Maria Mozzoni, in the International Congress of Zurich in 1893 and actively participating in the Socialist Women's Movement that was headed by Abigaille Zanetta. She soon entered the circle of Anna Kuliscioff, the companion of Andrea Costa and later of Filippo Turati. She and Anna became friends and Anna would wear her modern and simple tailored suits, helping to promote them. In 1903, she became director of Casa Haardt, but soon rebelled against the established custom of copying French models for the rich bourgeoisie, the aristocracy of Lombardy, and decided to promote a clothing line in "pure Italian style." Starting in 1905, she taught History of Costume at the Professional Women's School of the Humanitarian Society of Milan, where she soon became director of the dressmaking department. On the prestigious pages of Marzocco, Vita d'Arte, and Vita Femminile, she wrote that the process of emancipation requires at the same time better education of the workers, the rationalization and simplification of the women's wardrobe, and its formal freedom from French models. At the Milan International Exposition of 1906, she proposed a group of models inspired by the work of famous Italian Renaissance artists, showing how it is possible to obtain numerous ideas from the great national artistic heritage. Two of these great designs, the celebrated dancing dress inspired by Botticelli's *Primavera* and the court mantle inspired by a drawing by Pisanello, are kept in the Costume Gallery in Florence. This experiment allowed her to win the Grand Prix awarded by the jury in the Decorative Arts section of the Exposition. Through her study of the sculpture and painting of classical antiquity, the Middle Ages, and the 1400s and 1500s, she revolutionized the field of clothing decoration, introducing three-dimensional naturalistic embroidery never experimented with in fashion before. In June 1908, she presented her Italian fashion solutions in the theater with the help of Lyda Borelli, an enthusiast supporter who wore some of her "revisitations" of antique designs. In that same year, in Rome, she participated in the first Congress of Italian Women, and gave a report about the relationships between fashion and the decorative arts. Due to her work, the first organizing committee for

Fashion of Pure Italian Art, led by Giuseppe Visconti di Modrone and supported by Franca Florio, was created in 1909. The following year, in the pages of Vita d'Arte, she promoted the National Contest for a Woman's Evening Dress, which aimed to establish and support the independent creativity of Italian dressmaking shops. Her success was at its peak between 1908 and 1912, years in which the New York Herald also popularized her designs. During World War I, she intensified her humanitarian activity to the detriment of her fashion business, even though she decided to publish *Storia della Moda attraverso i secoli* ('A History of Fashion Through the Centuries') in three volumes, of which only the first was published, in 1925. In 1928 she was forced to abandon her profession because of her open anti-Fascist beliefs. She died in Milan in 1954. (*Aurora Fiorentini*)

Genthe Arnold (1869-1942). German photographer, naturalized American citizen. He arrived in the U.S. in 1895 and opened a studio in San Francisco. In 1911, he moved to New York, where he would live and work until his death. He became interested in fashion and worked with Vogue and Vanity Fair.

Gentryportofino Italian brand of knitwear. In 1974, Camillo Bertelli, the owner of several boutiques on the Italian Riviera, decided to challenge the British predominance in high quality knitwear and updated the traditional English artisanal models with an Italian taste. The success of the line was immediate and within a short time the business reached levels of production that required a change in organization. So in 1978 Bertelli began a partnership with Armando Poggio, the owner of a company in Genoa, the Manifattura Ligure Maglierie, which was specialized in knitwear manufacture through the cutting technique.

❑ 2000, December. The Ligurian *griffe*, now part of It Holding, chooses a new creative director: after the long collaboration with Stefano Palatella (interrupted in Summer), the new Collections will be designed by Kim Dosa, a Korean with long experience in knitwear. The first line designed by her makes its début on the Milan prêt-à-porter runways in March 2001.

❑ 2001, September. The new public face of Gentryportofino is Juliette Binoche, photographed by Peter Lindbergh. The knitwear line which made the brand famous is joined by a new clothing line, and is distributed in 380 points-of-sale all over the world.

Genty Roy (1964). Artistic director. He studied art and philosophy in Paris. Between 1985 and 1990 he worked as a film director. In 1989 he began working as a freelancer with Issey Miyake. In that same period he was also artistic assistant at Zucca, Final Home, Marithe, and Kosuke Tsumura. In 1992 he joined the Issey Miyake Company as technical director and artistic assistant. Appointed art director in 1999, the following year he also became the director of *isseymiyake.com*. Together with designer Naoki Takizawa, he introduced a new way of creating a fashion presentation, with theatrical effects and a poetic mood capable of providing a total view of the Collection. (*Valeria Vantaggi*)

Georges Rech French prêt-à-porter house. It was named after its founder who, in 1960, in Paris, understood that consumer trends would put haute couture, with all its rituals linked to the purchase of exclusive designs on paper patterns and their reproduction by dressmakers, into permanent decline, opening the market and the creativity of designers to prêt-à-porter.

Georgette Renal Haute couture *maison* active from 1946 to 1966. The atelier was on Avenue du Président Roosevelt, later moving to Avenue Pierre 1er de Serbie, near the Champs Elysées.

Georgi Sonja (1915-1957). German photographer. She served her apprenticeship as a photographer with her mother Helga Walther and at the Institute of Photography Lette Verein in Berlin. In 1936 she married Heinz and opened a studio where, up until 1943, she established herself as a portrait photographer for the stars of fashion and film. In 1945 she moved to Sylt and then to Hamburg, always working for the textile industry and in fashion.

Geox Shoe and clothing brand. It belongs to the Nottington Italia company, established in 1989. Its headquarters is in Biadene di Montebelluna. The brand is famous for its worldwide patent of an extremely "breathable" porous sole. The clothing lines are also planned with the principle of "breathability" kept in mind. The brand is based on this. The annual production of shoes comes to 3.5 million pairs, of which one half are sold in Italy. At the end of the 1900s, there were 250 employees, plus another 3,000 outside workers. The turnover was 280 billion liras, of which 130 billion were in Italy. The brand is distributed in 59 countries.

❑ 2002, October. The company plans to double its points-of-sale within 2003, putting into place a commercial network of 300 single-brand stores, more than 30% of them directly owned, the others franchised. It has just opened the fifth shop in Berlin and plans, in the following months, to open 140 more all over the world. Geox, which started its retail project in 2000, has already opened 130 single-brand stores. The company has ended the 2001 with sales of 286 billion liras, 26% of which comes from export. By the end of 2002 the firm expects to reach €180 million.
❑ 2002, November. Mario Moretti Polegato, the founder and president of Geox, is 2002 winner of the *Entrepreneur of the Year* award, promoted by Ernst & Young, the Italian Stock Exchange, and Il Sole 24 Ore. In the citation, the company is recognized as "one of the best examples of entrepreneurial success in recent decades and one of the most interesting worldclass businesses." Polegato, for his part, has insisted that it is important for the industry to commit itself to technologic and scientific research in order to relaunch the Made in Italy movement. That is what happened at Geox, and it is the reason that its new idea, "the breathing shoe," protected by an international patent, has been able to conquer the market, resulting, according to Mediobanca, in the second best performance in Italy in 2001.
❑ 2003, January. The company ends 2002 with an increase of 22.1%, from €147.6 million to €180.3 million. Profits more than double, to €19.4 million from €7.3 million in 2001. Shoes represent about 96% of the turnover, with 4.7 million pairs sold. The remaining 4% comes from clothing. About 75% of the sales are in Italy, with 25% in the other European countries. During 2002, Geox developed a single-brand distribution network, opening new stores in the most important European cities.

Gerani Paolo (1963). Italian designer. He grew up in the family business, Gilmar (1960), which produces seven lines of men's and women's wear. He has been in charge of the design work for Iceberg Uomo since the brand got started, a position which he still has. Photographers such as Patrick Demarchelier, Albert Watson, Michel Comte, and Steven Meisel have worked on the brand's recent advertising campaigns.

Gérard Darel French brand and boutique of women's prêt-à-porter created in 1971 by Danielle and Gérard Darel. Their success can be seen in their many boutiques in France, about forty by the end of the 1990s. In 1999, the turnover was about 150 billion liras. In 1996, Darel scored a real advertising coup, winning at a Sotheby's auction in New York the black pearl necklace which belonged to Jackie Kennedy, reproducing it as costume jewellery and attracting great media interest to his brand.

Geriaux Paul. French photographer, active in the early 1900s. At a time when fashion photography was carried out in a studio using actresses as models, he distinguished himself by taking pictures outside the studio and instead of professional models using ladies from polite society. His photos were not published in women's magazines, but in several Paris newspapers.

Gerini Daniela (1950). Italian designer. She followed her mother Adriana who, starting in 1963, had one of the most beautiful boutiques in Milan on via della Spiga. She made her début in the 1980s, producing her own Collection with BVM (Les Copains). In 1999, she opened her own atelier in very prestigious premises, the former workshop of Biki, where she creates a special kind of fashion with very few designs, reflecting her taste for art and her passion for color.

Germanisches Nationalmuseum Nuremberg. Museum established by the Duke of Aufsess in 1852 in order to document the history and the culture of the German countries. Its clothing and fabric Collection is the largest in Germany.

Gernreich Rudi (1922-1985). American designer. He anticipated the era of the nude look, presenting, in 1964, a topless bathing suit. It caused a scandal. But just a few years later, all the beaches in the western world, despite fines and injunctions, were crowded with bare nipples. He was also famous for a series of daring designs of bras that glorified the breasts, and for dresses made of knit and stretch fabrics that adhered closely to the body, emphasizing it but not sheathing it. In 1951, he entered the world of fashion by way of ballet, in which he had worked as a dancer and as a costume designer, a job more consistent with the experience he had gained as a student at the Los Angeles Art School during the 1940s. Born in Austria, he left Vienna with his mother in 1938, emigrating to the U.S. after Hitler's Anschluss.

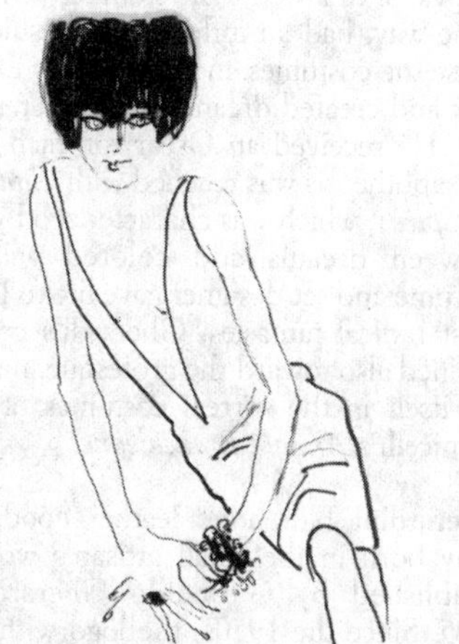

Rudi Gernreich, a model "seen" by Brunetta (Biki Collection).

Gervais Nathalie. Canadian designer from Quebec. She studied at the Fashion Institute of Technology in New York and at the Esmod in Paris. She started her career designing for brands such as Saks and Neiman Marcus, and later for Gucci. Valentino appointed her director of the Diffusione line. In 1998, she designed her first Collection for Nina Ricci.

G.F.S. Fabric Italian clothing company. It produces and distributes the SubDued brand, a descendent of the earlier Absolute brand which during the 1990s had been a true cult object for the trendiest teenagers in Rome and Milan. The company's philosophy, which is always and exclusively aimed at a young public, is based on interpreting the most significant contemporary trends, although without exacerbating them, anticipating the needs of young people. A strong point is the sobriety of the colors and fabrics, with precise cutting and great wearability. In May 2000, two new stores were opened for children from 0 to 12 years, in the heart of the Parioli neighborhood in Rome and in the Magenta area in Milan.

GFT Gruppo Finanziario Tessile (Textile Financial Group) It operates in the clothing field. It was established in 1930 from the merger of two companies, Donato Levi & Sons and the Unites wool factory of Biella. In 1954, it was taken over by the brothers Franco, Silvio, and Piergiorgio Rivetti, who relaunched the men's manufacturing plant FACIS (Fabbrica Abbigliamento Confezioni In Serie, or Mass Production Clothing Factory). They relied on an image strategy that was based on an effective advertising campaign and, above all, on a revolution in style that was no longer theoretical but calibrated on 25,000 male samples. During the 1960s, the number of lines grew to include lines for women: the most well-known is Cori (Confezioni Rivetti), designed by Biki. In 1971, Marco Rivetti became head of the company and began an upgrading of the factory and of the products. Subsequent agreements would attract prestigious designers to the *griffe*, including Ungaro, Armani (for women and men, and the Mani line, 1978), Valentino (Valentino Boutique and Miss V), Louis Féraud, Massimo Osti, Chiara Boni, and Claude Montana. The group introduced new industrial methods in order to guarantee a high stylistic content. In 1977, the firm established GFT USA, which also covered Canada and Mexico. The 1980s were a time of great success for the Group, with 35 subsidiaries, of which 18 were abroad (each with independent management), and the opening of new markets in Japan, China, Hong Kong, and Korea. In the mid 1990s, GFT entered the North American market, and then the Far East markets, which at that time were going through recessions. The market grew weak, and the burden of royalties became unsustainable. In 1997, the group was absorbed by the holding company HDP.

❑ 2001. The group acquires the American brand Joseph Abboud and all its license agreements. Little known in Europe, it is very famous in the U.S, Great Britain, and Japan, with a line of classic men's clothing, sportswear, and golfwear. The entire operation cost about 130 billion liras.
❑ 2002, February. After selling Sahzà to the Mariella Burani group in October 2001, it is now the turn of the Revedi companies, which manage commercial space in Italy and Switzerland. All of the companies are acquired at a cost of €3.7 million. Calvin Klein Inc. ends its license agreement with GFT ahead of time because it wishes to bring all its licenses back under its direct control. GFT's collaboration with Calvin Klein on the men's line goes back to 1992. The American license was due in June 2002, while those for Europe, the Middle East, and Asia were to last until 2006.
❑ 2002, November. Revenues at GFT have gone down 50%, from €99.5 million to €48.3 million. The reduction is in large part due to the loss of the Calvin Klein licenses and to supply interruptions with Valentino and Facis. The operating results, although negative, have gone from a loss of €5.5 million to a smaller loss of €3.7 million.
❑ 2003, February. At the end of the month, GFT closes for good, with the dismissal of the entire staff, 149 employees and 187 workers, some of whom should be hired by the Piedmont manufacturing company Codis. In March, the accounts are rendered. Although it ends 2002 with a loss, the company has reduced the loss from €79.6 million in 2001 to €12.1 million in 2002. This is thanks to the good performance, with revenues of about €80 million, of Joseph Abboud, the only brand still belonging to GFT.

Gharani Strok English brand created in 1995 by the Iranian Nargess Gharani and the Croatian Vanja Strok. Childhood friends who grew up in London, they decided to open an atelier after completing their fashion studies. Within a few seasons the brand became famous for their petticoat dresses and eclectic style. They regularly participate in the London fashion events and, since 1998, in Paris as well. Among their clients are singers and actresses such as Patsy Kensit.

Gherardi Piero (1909-1971). A costume and set designer expert in "spellbound" atmospheres, he was perfectly in tune with the films of Federico Fellini. An architect and interior decorator, he became interested in cinema with Mario Soldati (*Eugenia Grandet*, *Daniele Cortis*). He later worked on the colossal *War and Peace* by King Vidor. His first collaboration with Fellini was on *Nights of Cabiria*, where his unrealistic and creative genius was clearly expressed. After Pontecorvo's film *Kapò*, he dressed Fellini's universe and his actresses with unforgettable shapes and articles of clothing which, in some way, had an influence on fashion. He chose the costumes and the sets for *La Dolce Vita* and created dreamy atmospheres for *8-1/2*. He received an Oscar for each movie. The apotheosis was reached with *Giulietta of the Spirits*, which was characterized by color: between dreams and colored veils, the costume and set designer gave life to Fellini's most radical fantasies. Gherardi's creativity inclined also toward the grotesque, manifesting itself in the surreal costumes of Mario Monicelli's *Armata Brancaleone*.

Gherardini Florentine leather goods company born in the small artisan's workshop established by Garibaldo Gherardini in 1885. Since the 1950s, the logo with the G of Gherardini has characterized not only bags, suitcases, and wallets, but also raincoats, umbrellas, ties, scarves, and a prêt-à-porter line. Although it maintains its most classic models unchanged, the company has constantly diversified its product line. Since 1980, it has been led by Maria Gherardini.

Gherardini, 1980. Sketch by Maria Pezzi.

❑ 2000. The company, which in the early 1990s was acquired by a Japanese group, returns to Italian hands, those of Dadorosa (Group Danilo Dolci).
❑ 2001, August. Gherardini reorganizes its historic boutique on via della Spiga in Milan. The brand, acquired the previous November by Danilo Dolci, is scheduled for a big relaunch, both in Italy and abroad, especially in Japan. A new plant for the production of more than 300,000 pieces a year is to be built near Florence in the area of Scandicci, while design will be carried out in Ancona, at the Dolci factory. After a corner at the Osaka Hilton and a boutique opening in Milan, it is time for a restyling in Rome and Florence, and for new openings in London and New York.
❑ 2002, November. The reopening of the renovated boutique on via della Vigna Nuova in Florence. The opening of the first boutique in Seoul, South Korea. At the end of 2002, the turnover is €16 million, an increase of 20%. For the following year, the forecast is around €20 million.
❑ 2003, June. The Florentine *griffe* makes its début in the shoe world thanks to an agreement with Brain Management that is more a partnership than a license. The company from the Veneto will produce and distribute the new brand, while the Dolci group will finance and coordinate the project. The launch of Gherardini Shoes is expected for Spring-Summer 2004 and will focus on a middle-high target of women between 25 and 40. It will look not only to Italy and Japan, where Gherardini has had a consistent presence, but also to the rest of Europe, especially Spain and the Benelux countries. The goal is to reach a target of 450 stores in Italy. In anticipation of the advertising launch in 2004, Gherardini's sales increase 15%, bringing the Dadorosa turnover to €20 million, with an expected net profit of €2 million.

Ghergo Arturo (1900-1958). Italian photographer. After years spent in his hometown of Macerata, where he learned the basics of technique in his brother's photo lab, he moved to Rome. In 1929, he opened a studio on the very central via Condotti. His extreme attention to lights, which he never used in a naturalistic way, and to the graphic equilibrium of his compositions, and his accuracy with a pose accentuated by the use of a large format –Ghergo favored the 18x24 – all contributed to make him within a very short time the most requested photographer in town. He was the portraitist of film stars, ever since the season of the "white telephones" (Alida Valli and Isa Miranda, then Valentina Cortese and Rossella Falk), and of the aristocracy. He also took portraits of Pope Pius XII and King Hussein of Jordan. In fact, his style was influenced in equal measure by Art Deco culture and by the tradition of the 19th century bourgeois portrait, emphasized by skilled retouching. One result of this style was his work in the fashion world, which he approached with great precision in the photographic narrative of the clothing, which in his photos always had more importance than the models themselves, and in an immobility which is both a sign of his refinement and the taste of the times.

Ghesquière Nicolas (1971). French designer, born in Commines, in Touraine. He displayed precocious talent. By the age of 11 he had already filled notebooks with fashion sketches. In high school, he spent holidays with Agnès B. staging presentations. After working side by side with Jean-Paul Gaultier, in 1998 he was hired by Balenciaga which, since 2001, has been owned by the Gucci Group. The Collections he presents in New York are the most sought-after event of Fashion Week. The English-language press has called him – playing with "christology" and the aura of perfection that surrounds Balenciaga – the "messiah" of new fashion. "I design real clothes for real women, as Cristóbal would do," Ghesquière loves to repeat. Even if his thin silhouettes, often with large off-center shapes on the upper part of the body (shoulders as in the 1980s, embroidery and applique on the bust, worn with tight pants or skin-tight leotards) might require a femininity "designed" with regimens and massages. In 2001, he won the *International Award* at the Fashion Awards in New York, the equivalent of the Oscars for fashion. His style mixes romanticism and minimalism, technology and the techniques of the atelier. Thanks to him, the name of Balenciaga has returned to the top in the field of perfumes, particularly Ho Hang, Cristobal, and Le Dix, a name which Gesquière has also chosen for Balenciaga's "easy" line. (*Antonio Mancinelli*)

Ghini Gianni (1923). Milanese, and the right arm of Giovanni Battista Giorgini in the organization of 26 fashion events in the Sala Bianca of Palazzo Pitti in Florence from July 1952 to January 1965, when the inventor of those events and the promoter of an authentically Italian fashion, the father of the Made in Italy movement, resigned. Leaving in a drawer his degree in Agricultural Sciences, Ghini, in 1952, became a buying agent in the export sales office opened by Giorgini in the years between World War I and World War II. He became Giorgini's business partner in 1970 and, after his death, directed the firm until 1991.

Ghirardi Ugo, known as Ugone. An assistant during the presentation of Collections, from casting the models to consulting on accessories and the scheduling of the various entrances on the runway. He worked for several designers, starting with Krizia. Born in Milan, he worked as a hairdresser and make-up artist during fashion events. His taste and intelligence directed him to styling. Fashion people considered him to be very skilled. He died at a young age in the early 1990s.

Ghost English brand of ready-to-wear. It was launched in 1984 in London by Tanya Sarne (1940). A graduate in history and psychology, after joining the world of fashion as a model, she imported alpaca sweaters from Peru. She had already been successful with a sportswear *griffe* called Miz. She has been nominated more than once to be British Designer of the Year and in 1992 her brand received the British Apparel Export Award. Her Collections are all manufactured with original fabrics (including a particular type of viscose) and with the yarn-dyeing technique.

Giacchetta Massimo (1977). Italian designer of bags and accessories, born in Ancona. He studied at the Institute of Art in Macerata and, in 1998-99, worked on the bag Collections for Coccinelle. Since Spring-Summer 1999 he has created the bag Collections for the Fontana di Trebbia brand. His "signature" is a taste for color, in personal references of the past and in luxury that is never excessive.

Giacobbe Andrea (1968). Italian photographer. He moved to England, where he graduated from the Art & Design College in Bournemouth. Since 1992 he has been living and working in Paris. He made his reputation as a photographer, and also as a director of short films and videos.

Giacobini Silvana (1939). Journalist. She edited the magazine Gioia for twenty years. After working at RAI (the Italian State TV), she came to print journalism in the 1970s to be the director of Eva Express, published by Edilio Rusconi. In 1974, she went to Gioia, which she led until 1994. Under her editorship, supplements such as Salute & Bellezza

(Health & Beauty) and Gioia Casa (Gioia Houselhold) came out. In the meantime, she followed, as editorial director, the fates of Rakam and Spazio Casa. In 1994, she was called to Segrate by Ernesto Mauri, who at the time was editorial director of Mondadori periodicals, to launch Chi, a new weekly of news and the jet set, to immense success. In 1999, she published the book *Un bacio nel buio* (Mondadori) and in 2001 *Celebrità*.

Giacomoni Silvia (1938). Journalist and writer, she lives and works in Milan. A correspondent with La Repubblica since the newspaper's birth in 1976, she has often followed, alternating with Natalia Aspesi, the fashion events in Milan and Paris, and the men's fashion at Pitti Immagine. In 1984, she wrote *L'Italia della Moda* (with photos by Alfa Castaldi, Mazzotta Publishing), a journey to the center of the fashion system (stylism and industry) that was not blindly laudatory. It had interviews with foreign journalists such as Bernardine Morris of The New York Times and John Fairchild, the columnist and editor of Women's Wear Daily, and buyers such as Bruce Binder of Macy's and Dawn Mello of Bergdorf Goodman. She has published two novels, *La stanza vuota* (1989) and *Vieni qua, assassina* (Longanesi, 1993), and the essay-enquiries *Nobiltà della ricerca* (1979), *Designer italiani* (1984), and *Ecce coppia* (1990).

Giagnoni Carla (1932). Journalist. She was the editor of Brava Casa. In 1968, she was hired by Antonio Alberti at Amica. It was Alberti himself who wanted her with him at the Corriere d'Informazione in 1972, where she would remain as fashion editor until 1977, the year in which she returned to Amica as chief editor, staying until 1982. In 1984, she was hired by RCS to edit Brava Casa, a monthly that she led to an excellent level of circulation before leaving in 1994.

Giammetti Giancarlo. Fashion entrepreneur. During the 1960s he interrupted his architecture studies to become the business partner of the designer Valentino. He quickly made a reputation for himself as the creator of the brand's worldwide success, and also as an innovator in the fashion industry. He launched the concept of prêt-à-porter in Italy, promotes the use of license agreements for the distribution of branded products, understood the importance of an advertising strategy, and invited the great photographers to collaborate with fashion, inventing the advertising *groupage*. He was the first to understand the importance of communication and popularized Valentino's universe as the artistic expression of a great couturier and also as a well-developed network of creativity, affirming himself as a "designer in the shadow of another designer." In the 1990s he established, together with the designer, the Accademia Valentino. He also signed the first collaborative agreement between a government entity and the fashion industry, through an understanding with the municipality of Rome providing for events at the Accademia Valentino intended to relaunch the cultural prestige of the city. With Valentino, he also founded the association L.I.F.E. (Lottare, Informare, Formare, Educare, or Fight, Inform, Form, Educate) to help children with AIDS. Predicting the challenges of the 21st century and the difficulties that the large fashion houses would have in attempting to assure their continuity on their own, he strengthened the competitiveness of the Valentino brand in the world markets by signing, in 1998, the first agreement in Italy between fashion and finance, with the incorporation of the HDP Group (Holding di Partecipazioni Industriali, S.p.A., or Holding Company of Industrial Shares), with Maurizio Romiti as general manager. Through this operation, Valentino Garavani and Giancarlo Giammetti, with no direct heirs, guaranteed the creative continuity of the *griffe* they created.

Giancarlo Paoli Brand of shoes. It was created in 1988 on the initiative of two brothers who were very keen on fashion. Giancarlo is president of the board of directors and responsible for the fashion department, and Giampaolo Quadrini is the general manager. Every production operation is carried out on a regional level, in the Marche. The company's headquarters is in Porto S. Elpidio. The production is diversified in several different shoe lines: fashion, glamour, street, and sport.

Gianluca Gabrielli Brand name and Italian designer who made his début in 1989, winning the Occhiolino d'Oro, an award that the critics give to the best emerging fashion designer. Since the Spring-Summer 1998 Collection he has presented at Milano Collezioni.

Gianna Meliani Italian shoe designer and brand name created in 1971. The shoes are manufactured at the Gemini shoe factory owned by Bruno Meliani, Gianna's father. The factory headquarters is in Santa Maria a Monte, near Pistoia. The company also produces for Anne Klein and Yves Saint-Laurent. It has a showroom and office on Corso Venezia in Milan.

Gianni Binda & C. Textile mill making fabrics for accessories (ties, scarves, and foulards) and women's clothing. Established in 1945, the main offices are in Como. A branch office has been opened in New York and another will be opened in Paris. The firm, which sees the vertical organization of the production cycle, goes from raw material to finished product. The group employs more than 200 people and has a turnover of about 53 billion liras.

Gianni Bravo Brand of shoes. The brand's history starts with an urban design from Texas, developed with a very high heel made from precious materials such as snake-skin. In 1985, the shoe *griffe* was created in New York, and is by now well-established. Designer Gianni Bravo opened his first single-brand store and his headquarters in the U.S. But, after the American experience, the brand also arrived in Italy, from which it expanded into the Asian markets. In 2000, the first men's Collection was presented and, immediately after, the sports Collection. In 2003, in addition to points-of-sale in Riccione, Bari, and Naples, stores have opened in Milan (Galleria Vittorio Emanuele, Corso Matteotti, via Pontaccio), in Rome (via Condotti), and Bologna (via Ugo Bassi).

Gibb Bill (1943). Scottish designer. In 1970, Vogue called him the designer of the year for his work at Baccarat. His style is the result of serious study at the St. Martin's School of Arts and the Royal College of Arts. In 1975, he opened a boutique and designed a men's line. But, a few years later, he had to close due to financial difficulties. His designs, produced as a freelancer, have a bee as a logo.

Gibi Italian company of knitwear clothing. Its main offices are in Rome and it has been active since 1961, producing women's jersey dresses as well as skirts, pants, and outfits in cotton, precious wools, linen, and silk. It distributes 65% of its production in Europe, Japan, South Africa, Australia, Canada, Hong Kong, and the U.S.

Gibò Italian manufacturer. The company was established in 1962 by Carlo Zuccoli, and its first product was a printed organzine, along the lines of the "Emilio Pucci" style. Commercial success came immediately. In 1969, a production plant was opened in Tavernuzze, near Florence, and the company began to acquire a better and better reputation from a technological point of view. In 1970 came the meeting with Giorgio Armani, who designed two lines, Gibò and Gaia. In 1973, a third line was created, Bogy's, exclusively for raincoats. The Collection was designed in 16 days, immediately before Pitti Uomo. In 1975, Gibò produced the fabric for Armani's first women's Collection. Since 1976 it has linked its name to some of the most interesting designers of the time: Claude Montana, Jean-Paul Gaultier (first Collection, March 1981), Dirk Bikkembergs, and Sybilla. In 1988 the business was sold to Onward Kashiyama and the company focused on production (Helmut Lang, Paul Smith, Joseph, Jean Colonna). Since 1994, the company, guided by Franco Pené has further consolidated its role as a launching platform for new talents, such as Alexander McQueen, Hussein Chalayan, Victor & Rolf, and Antonio Berardi. For Spring-Summer 2003, the Gib line is back, designed by the artist-designer Julie Verhoeven.

(*Ruben Modigliani*)

❑ 2004, September. The Japanese designer Ichiroseta becomes creative director of the brand, replacing the artist and designer Julie Verhoeven.

Gibson Charles Dana (1867-1944). American illustrator. He is the "father" of the *Gibson Girl*, the independent, self-assured female who from the late 1880s up until the

Belle Époque was the symbol of the American woman and inspired both a song and a Ziegfield musical. He studied at the Art Students League of New York and worked for Harper's Bazaar, Collier's Weekly, and Harper's Monthly.

Gibson Elspeth (1963). English designer, born in Nottingham. She finished her fashion studies in 1984 and the following year found a job with Zandra Rhodes in London. After a short period as head designer at Monix, she launched her own brand in 1996. In 1998 she won the New Generation Designer of the Year award and opened her first single-brand boutique in Knightsbridge, London, the shopping area for the jet set and high society.

Gibus Men's hat also called a "chapeau claque," invented by Monsieur Gibus in 1823 to get around the problem of how to carry a top hat. It was a top hat which in the upper part contained a Spring mechanism which allowed it to be pressed down and made flat.

GIC Modyva Company of women's ready-to-wear. It was established in Empoli thanks to the intuition and skills of the entrepreneur Orfeo Ceccarelli, who transformed an idea into a large clothing company rooted in the culture of the Made in Italy movement and its pioneers. In 1975, the company reorganized itself as a group with a modern structure that allowed it to aim for new international markets, from Europe to Southeast Asia to the U.S, by means of effective marketing strategies. Modyva, Privilegio, and Deliaferrari are the names of the Collections through which the company maintains a dialogue with a female universe that is in constant evolution. It produces 350,000 pieces a year, including those under the Aigner brand, for which the group has a license. (*Lucia Serlenga*)

Giebierre Donna Italian company specialized in high quality prêt-à-porter. Established in 1986 by Tina Rossini, the director of the style office, and Cesare Garbati. The company has a total quality division which controls the details and finishing of every single garment; this has facilitated the entry into the Japanese, Chinese, and Korean markets, and the success of single-brand boutiques in Italy, Spain, and Monaco.

Giesswein Austrian company for Tyrolese clothing and accessories, especially those made from boiled wool, for men, women, children, and teenagers. It was created in 1954 by Elisabeth and Walter Giesswein. It worked for a small, private clientele using rudimentary systems (a home washing machine) to felt the wool. Ten years were sufficient to turn it into a technologically advanced business for wool hanging. Some 70% of the turnover comes from abroad, through 86 stores in Italy, 87 in Spain, 88 in the U.S. and 93 in France.

Gieves and Hawkes One of the oldest tailoring workshops in London. Its beginnings go back to 1785. Its historic headquarters is on Savile Row, the London street famous for its tailor's workshops. In 1809, the firm became an official supplier to the British royal family, a privilege it still maintains. The brand also includes a line of prêt-à-porter under the creative direction of James Whishaw that was started in 1999 and aims to reach a less formal clientele that is still interested in quality.

(*Sofia Camerana*)

Gigli Romeo (1949). Italian designer. When, during the 1980s, the entire fashion industry celebrated a strong woman with architectural silhouettes, an aggressive attitude, and large, reinforced shoulders like suits of armor, Gigli presented, with his intimate models, a concept of poetic and minimalist femininity that divided the world of fashion in two: on one side was the avant-garde press, which immediately understood the innovative content and the opening of a new approach; on the other side were those who remained very faithful to the idea of a woman who was showy and, in a term that was used at the time, aggressive. An unusual designer, Gigli was born in Castel Bolognese, near Ravenna, a province rich in history and culture. He was fed by the stimulation and fascination which he found in the very rich library of his parents, who were antiquarian bookdealers, and he was enriched by contacts with the different cultures that he came to know from up

Drawing by Romeo Gigli for the Winter 2004 Women's Collection.

close during the long stays in the Orient which kept him away from Italy for ten years. Every return was full of memories: objects, clothes, and jewellery to give as gifts, all of which unconsciously fed his passion and stimulated his interests, bringing him very close to the field of fashion. In 1979, he was in New York, working as an assistant in the atelier of Dimitri, where he learned the techniques of construction which would be the basis for his redesign of the female figure, which he would recreate in new proportions. In 1983, he presented his first Collection, produced by Zamasport, and began his collaboration with Callaghan. His début caused a small cultural shock: jersey dresses knotted around the body, tiny jackets, narrow and contoured shoulders that extolled a fragile and seductive anatomy, intense and undefined colors. All these required a new vocabulary, and immediately attracted the attention of journalists and buyers. In just a few years, he became a point of reference for Italian fashion. His Collections were presented in an old, bare garage on Corso Como in Milan and became the most exclusive and sought-after event. Later, he presented his Collection in Paris, as part of the French week of prêt-à-porter. A 20-minute standing ovation admitted him to the Olympus of the great. His clothes, remaining faithful to his first silhouette, over time became more precious, exclusive, and rich in artistic, historical, and cultural references. His creations reflect epochs and ethnicities, landscapes and poems, filtered through his complex and romantic personality. He believes in lightness; his fabrics are worked in a three-dimensional technique which make them airy, transparent, reflective, and changeable. The shapes hug the hips, the breasts, and the shoulders, in a way that is sensual but not carnal. His Collections, inspired by Venetian glass, the Empress Theodora, tribal Africa, the galaxies in space, Russian icons, and teenagers à la Lewis Carroll, follow an original aesthetic path, never part of a trend or a style that is common to others. He remains a fashion outsider, busy on a continuous journey inside himself. Besides the Romeo Gigli lines for men and women, he also designs G Gigli for a younger public, in addition to several other products and accessories, including leather goods, eyewear, and a perfume. He also designs household accessories: handmade carpets for Christopher Farr, lamps and mirrors for Ycami, glasses for Pauly in Venice, and mosaics for Bisazza.

(*Gisella Borioli*)

❑ 2000, September. In Milan, in a former toy factory from the 1950s on via Fumagalli in the Navigli area, Gigli opens his new space, Pangea.

❑ 2000, December. Plastic, futurist and very colored frames, metallic waves that support the lens: these are Gigli's offerings for Romeo Gigli Eyewear, produced by Allison for 2001.

❑ 2002, January. Until 2007, the Romeo Gigli and Gigli Collections, belonging to the group IT Holding, will be produced and distributed by Urbis Industrie Tombolini, the chief operating unit of Tombolini.

❑ 2003. A multi-ethnic Collection in Paris for Gigli. For the Spring-Summer 2003 he is especially inspired by deserts, by the Maghreb but also by deserts in India and China, from the pointed hoods of African barracans to printed fabrics with patterns inspired by ancient Chinese motifs, and to the warm colors of India, such as red, orange, and maroon. There are long and thin silhouettes, very constructed, but also very airy: polyester tulles with ruches at the bottom of a jersey mini-skirt, openwork corsets resembling lace, long and rustling skirts in waxed silk. Unusual materials worked according to modern techniques, precious materials such as gems, cashmere as light as shatush with a copper heart, embroidery in melted metal applied when hot, open-worked lace in fused polyester, slave bracelets, polished silver rings, raw minerals, belts with engraved copper plates applied to the leather.

❑ 2003. Some of the designer's most representative creations are exhibited at the MOMU in Antwerp, the Fashion & Textile Museum in London, and the Fashion Institute of Technology and the Metropolitan Museum of Art, both in New York.

❑ 2003, June. At the Fabrica del Vapore in Milan, the première of the new Gigli Uomo Collection for Spring-Summer

2004. In an underground atmosphere, as in a New York slum, an unconventional dandy is presented going against the mainstream, mixing different styles, cuts, and patterns. There are trousers tight at the ankles and striped with graffiti patterns, but also some that are flared with floral inlays, as well as khaki, red, and blue suits worn with patterned shirts and flowered ties in the style of the 1970s, and wide colored Bermuda shorts with mini Bomber jackets that fall to the waist. Gigli's man is self-assured, determined and eclectic, a world traveler.

❑ 2005, June. Luca Callegari is the new designer of the men's Collection, which makes its début with the Spring-Summer presentations. He had 12 years working side-by-side with Gianni Versace, was a designer of the men's Collections at Gianfranco Ferré (1998-99), worked at Anglomania on Vivienne Westwood men's and women's Collections (2000), and designed men's and women's Collections for Autumn-Winter 2002-03 at Just Cavalli

Gilardi Piero (1942). Italian artist. At the Beat Fashion Parade, organized on 13 May 1967 at the Piper Club in Turin, his hometown, he presented clothing and earrings in expanded polyurethane which artificially reproduced the forms of nature. He called it Vestiti Natura ('Nature's Clothing'). Ironic and polemical, he belongs to the field of Italian Pop Art. At the Piper Club, he presented a suit made of tree trunks of expanded polyurethane that covered the body from knees to shoulders, with a chain around the waist. For earrings he invented two *phytomorphous* outgrowths, dark green cabbages which tripled the size of the head. Before this came the Vestiti Stati d'Animo ('Mood Clothing') created in 1964. More traditional in comparison to Nature's Clothing, they reproduced the features of characters such as an explorer and a Woman in a mystic crisis. (*Cloe Piccoli*)

Gilbert Odile (1962). Hairdresser. She worked first in Paris with the famous Bruno Pittini, and then moved to New York where she worked with all the great names in hairdressing. She was on the most important fashion sets, and worked for great *maisons* such as Chanel and Dior, during fashion events. She defines herself as an artisan of hair and also invented a "chignon pin" which has been a great success with her admirers. (*Maddalena Fossati*)

Gill Leslie (1908-1958). American photographer. After studying painting, he devoted himself to photography during the golden age of fashion magazines in the late 1920s. Endowed with good composition skills and innovative taste, he published in Harper's Bazaar, of which he became art director, leaving a meaningful imprint on the magazine's style.

Gilmar Clothing company established in 1960 by the Gerani family. Owner of the brands Gerani and Iceberg, the company has the license to produce the Sui Anna Sui, Jeans de Christian Lacroix, and Victor Alfaro lines. Its advertising campaigns have been created by photographers such as Patrick Demarchelier, Albert Watson, Michel Comte, Steven Meisel, and Peter Lindbergh. A tie Collection, a line of bags and suitcases, and an eyewear line complete the Iceberg look. Since 1997, six fragrances have also been in production. A line of watches is planned, also for the same brand. The group is present in 50 countries with single-brand boutiques on Sloane Square in London and on Madison Avenue in New York, besides the one on via Montenapoleone in Milan. In 1998 the turnover was 320 billion liras, of which only 33% came from Italy. Silvano Gerani, Giuliana Marchini, and Paolo and Patrizia Gerani manage the administrative and creative departments of the company. (*Stefano Grassi*)

❑ 2003, June. Dun & Bradstreet gives Gilmar the D&B Rating 1, recognizing the ability of the company to stabilize its financial structure and its capacity to pay down debt with its own resources. Gilmar distinguishes itself not just in business, but also for the passion that its artistic director, Paolo Gerani, has for contemporary art. For the past year, some Iceberg boutiques, of which with future openings in Moscow and Rome there will be 11, have been showing the work of emerging talents.

❑ June. A long-term agreement with the Frankie Morello brand. The Gilmar group is to produce and distribute the men's and women's Collections and the accessories.
❑ October. Giambattista Valli begins working with the Gerani group and will launch a line under his own name.
❑ 2005, June. Agreement with the Alsatian company, Le Coq Sportif, to launch a special edition of shoes for the label Ice J Iceberg.

Gini Mimma (1938). Italian designer, born in Milan. She opened a shop at via Santa Croce 21 in 1991. She became known thanks to the fabrics she designs and has manufactured in India. By now her clothes have become cult objects. Of oriental inspiration, she offers only women's clothing with accessories such as bags and scarves, always rigorously made in fabric in a wide range of colors. Her creations are distributed in several boutiques all over Italy. On request, her shop offers a tailoring service for household accessories such as custom-made curtains, pillows, and bedcovers.

Gioia Italian women's weekly founded in 1937. It had 12 pages and cost 40 cents. In 1954 it was acquired by Edilio Rusconi. In 1955, he established Rusconi Publishing with Gente, Gioia, and Rakam. Within a few years the magazine was able to establish itself, giving more space to news. In 1974, after periods under Andreina Vanni and Giuseppe Pardieri, it was edited by Silvana Giacobini, who tried to emphasize a direct dialogue between the readers and the magazine. In January 1995, Vera Montanari became editor and updated the graphic layout, enriching the magazine with thematic supplements. As to the magazine's relationship with fashion, alongside the traditional features space was dedicated to the new offerings of Italian designers, in order to recommend a quiet prêt-à-porter that avoided excess and unnecessary sophistications.

Giò Guerrieri Brand designed and produced by the Milanese designer Elisabetta Guerrieri (1962). She became interested in fashion in her childhood, thanks to her grandmother Elide, who was a milliner and taught her sewing, and to her great aunt, Ines, who owned a dressmaker's shop. In the late 1970s, with the help of her mother Gianlorenza Abbiati (known as Giò), Elisabetta opened a boutique in the fashion quadrilateral. Already at the age of 18, the designer, a graduate of an art high school, created the first pieces for her shop, which was named Battaglia. She then sold it and began to work as a style and sales assistant at famous brands such as Iceberg, Armani, Chiara Boni, and others. Later, she returned to her passion and in 1988, along with her mother, opened a small atelier called "Giò Guerrieri" in her mother's honor. Nicknamed the "Queen of the Sheath Dress" for reintroducing this classic and elegant garment, reinventing it in a thousand ways, Guerrieri produces a women's prêt-à-porter line that is very appreciated for its tailoring cut. She also designs haute couture characterized by simple lines and precious fabrics. At present, Giò Guerrieri is distributed in more than 100 shops worldwide.
(*Sara Tieni*)

Gio Moretti Trendy Milanese boutique. It opened in 1970 taking the name of its founder, Giovina Moretti. In the middle of the famous fashion quadrilateral, on via della Spiga, it is organized as an open space distributed on three levels. Initially, it offered only clothing and accessories. Now it is possible to also find flowers, CDs, books, and furnishings. Everything has a particular international taste. Giovina Moretti is also a talent scout. Her boutique is in the Milanese tradition that looks for new designers. Among the brands on sale are Jean-Paul Gaultier, Roberto Cavalli, Blumarine, Jil Sander, Donna Karan, Chloé, Ermanno Scervino, Emanuel Ungaro, and Ann Demeulemeester.

Giordani Aragno Bonizza. Historian of costume and contemporary fashion. A curator and fashion consultant at the Museum Boncompagni Ludovisi, scientific director of the Micol Fontana foundation, and chief editor of Audrey magazine, Bonizza Giordani has also been a member of the National Commission for the Politics of Protection and Development of the Decorative Arts of Fashion and Costume. For the office of TV School Education, in 1982 she produced

History of Fashion and in 1990, for RAI 1, *The Great Exhibitions – Valentino –Thirty Years of Magic.* For the Center of Studies and Communication Archive (CSAC) of the University of Parma she organized the donated archives of the Fontana sisters, Federico Schuberth, Irene Galitzine, Centinaro, Walter Albini, and the Farani tailor's workshop. In addition, from 1982 up to today, she has conceived and organized exhibits and catalogues in Italy and abroad, including *The Design of Italian High Fashion 1940-70* (Rome), *Italian Fashion 1920-1980* (Tokyo, Osaka, and Kyoto), *40 Years of Italian Fashion 1940-1980* (New York), *Fifty Years of Fashion* (Rome, Castel Sant'Angelo), and *Artejeans* (Paris). In 2002, the exhibits included *Sarli – Fifty Years of Italian Style – 1952-2002* (Naples, Castel dell'Ovo), *The Worn Clothing. From Futurism to Abstractionism* (Rome, Museo del Corso), and *Women Between Thrills and Emotions* (Rome, Auditorium and Museum Boncompagni Ludovisi). In 2002, Bonizza Giordani contributed *High Fashion: When Did It All Start?* to the International Conference on Italian Fashion: Identities, Transformation, Production that was held in New York. (*Maria Vittoria Alfonsi*)

Giordano Basso Italian silk factory. It is named after its founder, who established it in 1927 in Breganze (Vicenza). Basso had no particular background. He worked in finance. He was simply motivated by a strong passion for silkworm breeding. He began production with a single old loom in the basement of his house. His clients were soon the most important ateliers of the time. During the 1960s the leadership of his son Gilberto introduced the company to foreign markets, including Japan, Europe, the Arab countries, and North America. The 1990s saw the début of high-tech fabrics, causing serious difficulties for small factories such as Giordano Basso which still worked the fiber with traditional methods. It was time for a management reorganization, by the third generation. New investments were necessary in order to satisfy the needs of every single customer, putting into effect a niche policy: fabrics in pure silk, blends of silk and wool, jacquards, and soft silk velvets which combined an extreme lightness with the greatest consistency.

Giorgetti Silvia (1957). Designer, born in Milan. She has a degree in the History of Art and has worked with one of the most prestigious firms in fabric decoration in New York. She considers herself an artisan who knows all the techniques, which allows her to manufacture fabrics that she turns into stoles, scarves, and, since 2002, articles of clothing. Her Collections always consist of just a few pieces which are almost one of a kind.

Giorgini Giovanni Battista (1899-1971). He is the father of Italian fashion and the strategist of the first Florentine fashion show on February 12, 1951, which represents the birthday of the Italian style in fashion, an independent style compared with the secular submission of Paris. "Under the white hair, slightly thin at the nape of the neck, the profile is reminiscent of certain knights that can be found in the paintings of the old Tuscan masters, with a falcon on the shoulder," wrote Giancarlo Fusco, important journalist and remarkable observer of his own time. Giorgini was a gentleman in style, blood, and smiles: "A gentleman," according to *Grazia* in August 1951. "He is well mannered and courteous, even when doing so must cost him considerable effort – behind his gentle appearance, there is a grip of steel, a first-class organizational intelligence, and a knowledge of the American market and of the psychology of buyers which, alone, explain the success of his undertaking far beyond the wildest expectation." His knowledge of the American market was the product of almost thirty years of work as a middleman for American department stores – searching and singling out skilled and affordable Italian craftsmen (especially in the sectors of ceramics, glass, straw, leather goods, household linen, known as "tovagliati"), the selection and the purchasing, shipping back to the American department stores. He was a bloodhound of the beautiful and refined, a buyer working on order – that was his profession. In 1921, just twenty-two and in search of a job, he came to Florence from Forte dei Marmi, close to Carrara, where his family owned a few marble quarries and a small factory that manufactured equipment for marble cutting. Giorgini's family was very patriotic, aristocratic, and Florentine in origin. "In 1918, when he came back from the front where he had fought as a volunteer, my father had to quit his studies. The head of the family had died, and the business had to be carried on. Bista, as he was known in the family, took on the responsibility, but he was not cut out for that sort of work. He wanted to be a diplomat. There was just not enough money to go back to school, however. My dad thought of a replacement for that. In Florence, a cousin of his opened an export office. He was dealing in ceramics. Export, in the mind of a young man, meant traveling around the world, seeing distant lands, just like a diplomat. That was where he began his profession. Two years later, he set up an office of his own."

It was 1923, and the young Giorgini fell in love with his work – finding the most beautiful objects, visiting the workshops of craftsmen, discovering a world that combined technical skill, artistic creativity, and manual dexterity. Giorgini understood that this profession could be more than just a commercial occupation, if he set himself the goal of discovering and familiarizing the rest of the world with the finest creations of Italian craftsmanship, a testimonial to the sensibilities. the tradition. and the culture of a people. He traveled around Italy to assemble a line of samples, with the finest examples of glassware, embroidery, and ceramics, and then he went off to America, speaking practically no English at all. It was, as he was often to remember later on, a humiliating experience: closed doors and countless refusals. He came back after "enchanting" only one important customer: Wallace C. Speers, the owner of the James McCutcheon & Co. of New York, where the finest home linen was sold. Speers was interested in the magnificent linen produced by Jesurum of Venice and by Olga Asta.

Giorgini took intensive courses in English and he traveled between Florence and the United States. After every trip, he had a few more clients in his portfolio, another department store or other that had named him as their exclusive agent in Italy. Those trips and his acute skills of observation made him particularly knowledgeable about the development of the American market. He knew how to predict the most successful products, and when he came back to Italy he was able to direct the craftsmen with whom he was in contact, helping them to improve or adapt their production to the lifestyle and requirements of the new clients from across the

Il N. H. e la N. D.
Giovanni Battista e Nella Giorgini
hanno il piacere di invitare la S. V.
ad un Ballo che daranno in casa loro
la sera del 14 Febbraio 1951.

Lo scopo della serata è di valorizzare la nostra Moda. Le Signore sono perciò vivamente pregate di indossare abiti di pura ispirazione italiana.

Alle ore 21,30 avrà inizio una presentazione di Abiti da sera di alcune fra le migliori Case di Moda Italiane.

R. S. V. P.
Via Serragli, 144

The invitation to the first Italian fashion event (Florence, February 1951) read: 'The purpose of this evening is to divulge our fashion. Ladies are then heartily invited to don clothes of pure Italian inspiration' (Giovanni Battista Giorgini Archive).

Collections of 1954 presented in the Sala Bianca, Pitti Palace, Florence. 'Who was there' by Brunetta (Giovanni Battista Giorgini Archive).

ocean. After those first years, good luck seemed on Giorgini's side. He had developed a selected network of artisans and a good circle of solid clients.

The clients were solid until the Wall Street Crash when he suffered by the crisis of 1929. In America it was no longer the time for embroidered table and bed linen and Italian leather goods. He had to start again, but business was slow. It was this event that led to his idea of reversing the flow of trade. He imported clothing from America and opened, downstairs from his office along Lungarno Guicciardini, a store selling ready-to-wear clothes, toys, gifts, and furniture objects from the USA. The store was called 'Le Tre Stanze' (The Three Rooms) and the sales girls were the Antinori sisters, Paola and Mimmi. For its opening Giorgini invited a native Indian-American princess, who had long braids and was very beautiful in a white buckskin dress, embroidered with beads and decorated with colored ribbons; she held a 'recital of Indian songs. The store was successful, but only for its gifts and furniture. The ready-to-wear was too ahead of its time for Italian tastes. Giorgini agreed to work in Spain as a buyer of artisan's objects and table linen for the James McCutcheon & Co. chain. The Three Rooms slowly declined. Along came the Second World War, the call to arms, his return to Florence under German occupation on September 8, the liberation of Florence, and his opening of an Allied Forces Gift Shop. In order to execute the shop, he found a space in Via Calzaioli, where Coin now stands – there was a long balcony and, all around it, a great many small rooms shaped like horseshoes. In every room was a craftsman. The success was so great that, at the end of the war, he was asked by the Allies to open two more shops, one in Milan and one in Trieste. Transport was almost nonexistent. He purchased an old Renault and did everything himself: loading and driving. The Italy that Giorgini drove through from the centre to the north was a devastated land.

It was in those years in that Italy that he started to think about the idea that he would carry out five years later. The idea of creating an Italian high fashion – which was an impossibility in the eyes of the foreign buyers and of the Italians themselves until Giorgini succeeded in envisioning it, bringing it to life and establishing it on the world

Journalists Misia Armani, Anna Vanner, and Bebe Kuster in a sketch by Brunetta (Giovanni Battista Giorgini Archive).

A sketch by the Sisters Fontana, 1951-52 (Giovanni Battista Giorgini Archive).

stage – began to develop in his mind in 1946, in that terribly difficult postwar period. It might well have seemed like overambitious madness. And yet, this intuition, which was apparently paradoxical – how could a product implicitly bound up with wealth and wellbeing be identified with a country in ruins? – proved to be a very powerful vitamin, as it were, capable of reinforcing and strengthening Italy's manufacturing and commercial situation in the space of just a few years, and outstripping even the most optimistic expectations by a huge margin. In 1949 and 1950 he experienced difficulties. B. Altman, a name of extreme importance among the major luxury department stores in New York, turned him down unceremoniously when he suggested that they sponsor a presentation of Italian fashion at the Brooklyn Museum.

The event would have required 25,000 to 35,000 dollars and B. Altman considered it to be an enormous sum of money, especially if spent blindly, 'without seeing the Collections first'. On 11 October 1950 the department store's management wrote to Giorgini: 'It would be fatal for us to present clothing that was derivative of French fashion'. No support for the presentation in the States, and, perhaps to mitigate the drastic nature of the rejection, the expression of interest in something of the sort in Italy, in order to allow the buyer, Miss Meison, to "visit the market," to see things directly and to buy those objects that she might consider wise and appropriate. Rather than just an expression of a wish, this was a clear operative suggestion – it softened the rejection, but at the same time it stimulated Giorgini not to give up. It was necessary to organize in Italy something that could demonstrate, directly in the field, the creation of a true, authentic Italian fashion, or at least, that could mark the beginning of a independent trend in Italian clothing production. Twenty-five years of experience as a purchasing agent for the United States, as the eye of the department stores on Italian craftsmanship, as an emissary of the beautiful, the refined, and the "hand-made" gave Giorgini extremely sensitive antennae with which to sense the needs of the American market, the trends of consumption, the waves of taste, an eye for what would work in America. It was not as if the United States

Sala Bianca, Florence 1956 (Giovanni Battista Giorgini Archive).

had shut off Italy's export of crafts goods, at the time a minuscule amount of business. In 1947 an operation that Giorgini had carried off had been extremely successful – an exhibition of furniture, fabrics for interior decoration, Murano glass, ceramics, leather goods, on the premises of Watson and Boaler, in Chicago. Designed by the interior designer Hag Mayer, an old friend of Bista, that minimal "expo" of Italian craftsmanship had opened a breach to the point that it persuaded the director of the Museum of Modern Art in Chicago, Meyric Rogers, to organize, in conjunction with Giorgini, a traveling exhibition that, under the name *Italy at Work*, opened in a number of American museums. But museums are not the same thing as the market, nor do they influence the market more than a certain amount.

On the whole, high-quality Italian craftsmanship was having a hard time. In America, what was working was the perennial, eternal Italy of Chianti bottles, mandolins, and spaghetti, and an extremely low-quality, cheap sort of export was beginning to gain ground. In order to invert this tendency or, at the very least, to create a small space for a more qualified *Made in Italy*, a powerful idea was needed, a product image capable of attracting the interest, the attention of the press, and to conquer the first pages in the news. An engine was needed to change and transmit speed to the noble train of the Italian artisan trade. The extraordinary intuition of Giorgini was in his understanding that this engine could be fashion: an Italian fashion invented from next to nothing because it was nothing compared to the success of the French haute couture. Giorgini had his work cut out for him, in terms of claiming lineage from the Etruscan "wardrobe," the Italian elegance of Catherine de' Medici, from eighteenth-century Venice, and the more credible and widely recognized excellence of Italian fabric manufacturers, Italian embroidery, Italian skill with needle and thread, a skill typical of a poor country, of a society in which clothing was made at home, where a mother might restitch a dress to be worn by her daughters. There was no such thing as Italian fashion. It had only given its first cry during the years when Mussolini imposed that the Italian ateliers designed independently, without drawing inspiration from Paris or copying, at least 50% of Collections.

Paris was *The Fashion*, in a totalizing and monopolizing way, apparently invulnerable to any possible assault, as very rooted myths are, furthermore alimented, year after year, by new talents and by an extraordinary capacity of self-promoting that has always been a French ability. While Giorgini was dreaming of an elegance designed in Italy, Italian fashion "houses" and Italian dressmakers were spending thousands of francs in Paris to buy exclusive patterns from Dior, Balenciaga, Fath, Patou, in order to quench the thirst for French elegance of their very Italian customers, voracious, after the years of war-enforced fashion diets, for French fashion, for "fashion-fashion," as people said in those years, on the model of "coffee-coffee," to distinguish it from the ersatz coffee available during rationing. So what reason was there to think, in the beginning of the 1950s, with the country still heaving and wounded from five years of war, that Giorgini should succeed in bending the power of that granite monopoly, if not to reverse, to alter a centuries-old trend? Well, perhaps because the ground had been broken by those early efforts. And certainly because, in this case, the idea of inciting dressmakers and aspiring designers to launch themselves in a creative autonomy, without senses of inferiority, the idea of organizing them and giving them a shared strategy was not an idea conceived with a view to the domestic market, too elitist and too snobbish, conditioned by the French tradition, but rather with a view to America, which was also, in the area of high fashion, reverent toward the French, but still capable of commercial pragmatism.

Sala Bianca, Florence 1956 (Giovanni Battista Giorgini Archive).

Among Giorgini's most important clients were I. Magnin of San Francisco, Bergdorf Goodman and B. Altman's in New York, the best of the department stores of the United States, the best which, in order to stay at the top in the field of high fashion, could look nowhere but to Paris, and could buy from no one but the ateliers of Patou, Dior, Balenciaga, the compact platoon of acclaimed masters of elegance. America was, therefore, also subjugated by French fashion. But Giorgini was sensitive to things in the Florentine air, both by tradition and as a citizen of his town, and so the "case Pucci" made him understand just how much the American market needed products that were not staid and academic, but was looking for a less stiff and formal way of dressing, freer and more colorful, and less formal.

In 1947, Pucci succeeded in making his way onto the decisive and miracle-working pages of *Harper's Bazaar*, where the story was told of how he had created a skiing wardrobe in

Saint Moritz for a friend of his who had lost her luggage. Those pages told the story and illustrated that story with a photograph that sparked the interest and commercial instincts of Lord & Taylor's, a department store on Fifth Avenue. The request to mass produce those "mises" was the first event in the adventure of Pucci, the first impulse in a long and clamorous success.

When, at the end of the 1940s, Giorgini began to develop the idea of an "Italian look" to be invented, reinforced, and offered to America as a way of regenerating the image of a discredited Italian craftsmanship, the "caso Pucci," if it had not exploded, was certainly bubbling away in the United States. It was the first signal of a market mechanism that could be exploited. "This was not the only indicator," recalls Elisa Massai. "Giorgini knew how to understand things," and he did. Between 1949 and 1950 Italian knitwear – helped along by the first yarns in cotton and wool, which the American assistance plans UNRRA and ERP were unloading in Italian ports – began to sell slowly at first in England and in the United States. This was the first bridgehead in an invasion that Giorgini's brilliant strategy was to render triumphant. "Dorville House," in London was discovering Laura Aponte, Marisa Arditi, Lea Galliani, and the Maglificio Mariangelo. In June of 1950 Henriette Tedesco, buyer for I. Magnin, opened the golden gates of America to Olga di Gresy and her label "Mirsa." This was an elite export, involving small numbers, but it was also a signal of the sharp reversal of a trend. Almost at the same time, Bettina Ballard, director of *Vogue*, and her rival, Carmel Snow, director of *Harper's Bazaar*, were going wild over the "rags" designed by Pucci in daring turquoise and shocking pink and, in Capri, they were discovering Simonetta Visconti Colonna di Cesarò and Tessitrice dell'Isola, who was actually known as Clarette Gallotti; the former was a duchess and the latter a baroness. This aristocracy was not swimming in money after the war, and fashion was an antidote to their financial problems, perhaps also to the boredom of having been for centuries without nothing to do.

The war had shaken up life considerably. For the great names of nobility, and for women in general, working was no longer taboo. On the contrary. It was a fascinating new idea. Simonetta Visconti was working, and she was designing a handsome fashion, by quite simply reproducing that which she herself, a woman of taste and determination, wore or would be willing to wear. This was the obvious secret as well of Lola Giovannelli Sciarra and of Stefanella, a duo working in the "Boutique" style, and of Giovanna Caracciolo, the mastermind of Casa Carosa. In 1949 the buyers of Bergdorf Goodman and Marshall Field, in search of novelties, had arrived in Milan to take a look at the models by Noberasco, Vanna, Fercioni, and Tizzoni. In Rome they had purchased Simonetta's models. Something was really changing. Zoe, Micol, and Giovanna Fontana, the three sisters from Trasteverolo, from the heart of Emilia, had come to Rome before the war to work as seamstresses. They had already made clothing for Mirna Loy, and in their atelier in Via Liguria, they were suddenly illuminated by the spotlights of Hollywood for the wedding dress that they had created for Linda Christian, for the five meters of white train that shone in the

Sala Bianca, Florence 1956, a model by Veneziani (Giovanni Battista Giorgini Archive).

Bettina Ballard of Vogue America portrayed by Brunetta (Giovanni Battista Giorgini Archive).

Basilica di Santa Francesca Romana, under the flashbulbs of dozens of elbowing paparazzi, the first newsreel wedding of the postwar period. It was 27 January 1949. There was, then, a thin opening. It had to be built on and the only way to do that was by convincing tailors and dressmakers to take what could be defined the Italian way to fashion; and, once achieved this goal, put in contact the several Italian *maisons*, tailors, dressmakers and designers with the buyers of American and Canadian department stores. Giorgini tried it, with considerable emphasis. The refusal of "B. Altman's" to sponsor an Italian runway presentation at the Brooklyn Museum left only one alternative open – that of luring the buyers across the Atlantic to a presentation of Italian apparel in Italy. An extremely difficult task, full of obstacles that would have seemed insurmountable to anyone who was less courageous. The real obstacle was the fear of arousing Parisian wrath. Giorgini must have realized this early and, in many cases, he was unable to overcome that fear. The psychosis over Paris had two aspects – the fear of being cut off from the circuit of French ateliers, of being barred from drinking at the well of ideas, patterns, and outfits, of clothing to be purchased on an exclusive basis and to be multiplied in a number of different versions, with variants of fabric and cut; and the sensation, practically a received idea, that their customers were so conditioned by the automatic link between elegance and Paris that they were often reluctant to entertain even the hypothesis of a "chic" (an ever-present word back then) that could exist anywhere but in the sacred precincts of Paris. Never had the *maisons* allied to present together their creations.

They had always presented many weeks after the Collections of Paris, so as to have the time required to translate and develop the indications and lines that the capital of fashion was imposing. That phrase, "immediately following," which was indispensable if there was to be any hope of persuading the buyers to extend their European stay, and to come from Paris to Florence, was also a way of ensuring that Italian high fashion would not be just a photocopy of the French "dernier cri" – perhaps it would be less than sublime, but certainly there was no risk that the buyers would see the same thing in Florence that they had just seen in Paris. Three revolutions in one – a few too many for Giorgini's idea to trigger immediate enthusiasm among those who saw, in the routine of buying and copying, a solid market, and reliable profits.

Giorgini entered into contact with the most important brands receiving only denials. His proposal seemed to terrify them. Then, what would he show to buyers who, only out of friendship, solidarity of profession, had accepted to change their program and come to Florence? Giorgini didn't give up. He simply turned to those whom, today, we would call the emerging talents. And he scored. Bluffing. On 27 November the invitations were also sent out (more than anything else, an announcement of intent) to Bergdorf-Goodman, Escobosa of I. Magnin in San Francisco, for Henry Morgan of Montreal. Giorgini's intentions were quite real, but they were based on a void, a void into which he had leapt, on faith, without a parachute. The rejections from the leading fashion houses had dramatically accelerated the speed of his fall. There was practically no time left to find a solution. On 28 December 1951, just over a month prior to the possible dates of the runway presentations, Giorgini wrote the minor houses, the up-and-coming or newly established designers.

"I have been working regularly with the North American market since 1923, and I represent many of the finest companies that

import Italian artistic and crafts products. No consideration has ever been given to fashion in any practical sense, since Paris is the world center as far as they are concerned. Italian fashion accessories have always been considered quite highly, however; among them, purses, scarves, gloves, umbrellas, shoes, jewelry, and so on. Since the United States is now quite well disposed toward Italy, it seems to me that the time has come to attempt to establish Italian fashion on that market. And, in order to achieve that purpose, since in Paris the Collections are presented to American buyers during the first week of February and of August, we must organize a presentation of our own Collections during the same period of time. Since I have already received confirmations of participation from many of the finest fashion houses, I would suggest that we work as follows:
Date: second week in February and August of each year. Venue: Florence. Procedure: Each High Fashion House will present a minimum of twenty outfits (morning, afternoon, cocktail, evening) worn by one, or if possible, two of its own models. Each House will pay for the expenses indicated above and will pay 25,000 Lire to the Ufficio Giorgini for our expenses involved in organizing the event and greeting the guests. Sales: these will be negotiated directly between the Houses and foreign buyers. In the interests of the Houses themselves, it is an explicit requirement that the outfits which will be presented be of exclusive and original Italian design. For this first presentation to be held next February, it is unlikely that many American buyers will be attending, because they believe that Italian Fashion is merely derivative of Parisian fashion, and, therefore, their interest is quite limited. On the other hand, we have often seen Italian clothing in *Vogue* and *Harper's Bazaar* under American and French names. It all depends, therefore, on our determination to show that Italy, which has demonstrated her mastery in the field of fashion over the centuries, has preserved her genius and can still create style with a wholly genuine spirit.
"The first presentation will take place in Casa Giorgini on 12 and 14 February 1951 – as per enclosed invitation. I would request that you respond with the greatest possible rapidity if your House is interested in participating." Italian fashion, with its trade volume of billions, with its vast armies of professionals in the industries of knitwear and apparel, the spectacular phenomenon of designer clothing which exploded in the middle of the Seventies, its beneficial and

Sala Bianca, Florence 1956 (Giovanni Battista Giorgini Archive).

Vera Rossi Lodomez, journalist and speaker of the Florentine exhibitions. Sketch by Brunetta (Giovanni Battista Giorgini Archive).

"curative" effects on the chronically ailing Italian trade balance – it all started with this letter of exhortation with a tone that is at times naive and dated, but which brims over with Italian pride and which, in order to trigger commercial interest, makes use of a little white lie.

It was not true at all that Giorgini "had already received confirmations of participation from many of the finest fashion houses." If the reCollections of Simonetta Colonna di Cesarò are at all accurate, he may have received a few positive responses before sending out the letters. But very few and far between. "I received a visit from Giovan Battista Giorgini," recalls Simonetta (professionally, she used only her given name). "Florence at the time was a major center for exports of crafts' products, lingerie, leather, and straw. He outlined his plan to me, a plan that was ambitious, difficult, and in some ways, revolutionary – to launch an Italian fashion on the worldwide market. Today that may not seem so revolutionary. But, at the time, fashion was a monopoly of French designers. Their word was law. All of the European houses, including the majority of Italian dressmakers, went to Paris twice a year to buy and to copy – and at times to copy without buying – the ideas of Balenciaga, Fath, and the other heavy hitters. The plan that Giorgini had in mind broke with tradition. It was potentially a boomerang. I accepted without thinking twice, without asking for time to decide. But I was not taking much a risk, because I was already designing original fashion, and I did not copy the French; I had a clientele of my own, which did not display withdrawal symptoms if they did not wear clothing in line with the commandments of Paris. I formed part of the sparse group of alternative Italian fashion, along with Schubert, the Fontana sisters, Pucci, and Germana Marucelli. For me, Giorgini's project was not a risk. It was a lifesaver. It was even more than that. It was a rocket ship. Without Giorgini, nothing would have happened. He had the courage to do things. He spoke little and he acted." Perhaps, when he wrote his incitement to "show that Italy has preserved her genius and can still create style with a wholly genuine spirit," Giorgini has already received the reassurance of one "yes', that of Simonetta. Perhaps he knew that Marucelli, the terrible Tuscan, a former apprentice seamstress who wore her hair in a bun and who established alliances with artists, was waiting for nothing better. Micol, Zoe, and Giovanna, the Fontana sisters, had also always been very well disposed toward Giorgini. "He had come to see us," recalls Micol. "He had said to us – 'You three do nice work. Very nice work. You can tell from the attention you receive. I am inviting buyers from various American department stores. You can present your Collection, as long as you agree not to copy French style. Let's see what happens.' We were already creating a bit of Italian fashion. Just a little because, it was obligatory that, in the Collections, most of the apparel be French or of French inspiration. But we had begun to notice that those few outfits which were entirely designed by us were successful. Actresses, who were the treasure of Casa Fontana, tended to choose the outfits that we had designed. Therefore, we were relatively immune to the fear of breaking away from Paris. And yet, it was not an easy decision. Turning our backs on Paris meant giving up a mechanism that we knew worked. Certainly, in the wake of the excitement over the wedding dress for Linda Christian, we had made a name for ourselves in Hollywood. On the runway of the Beverly Hills Hotel, with an audience made up of legends of the movies such as Frank Sinatra,

Rita Hayworth, Katharine Hepburn, Spencer Tracy, and Clark Gable, our outfits were greeted with applause and orders. We had that success to encourage us. And yet it took a great deal of courage to take Giorgini up on his offer. It meant that we would no longer be able to keep one foot in two shoes: with French fashion and a few Italian outfits. I remember that we had long family discussions. 'You're doing fine as it is. What else are you looking for?' our relatives would say to us. In the end, Zoe and I, the two eldest, won out. In life, you cannot stay in one place. You have to move forward."

At the end of December 1950, just two months from the final date, Giorgini had convinced one or two theoretical agreements to participate and several maybes. It was that letter that definitively anointed the thirteen apostles of Italian fashion, converting them to the credo of a possible "red, white, and green" style. There were nine names in the field of high fashion – Simonetta, Fabiani, Fontana, Schuber, and Carosa, from Rome; Marucelli, Veneziani, Noberasco, and Vanna, from Milan. There were four in the area of "boutique fashion": Emilio Pucci, who agreed to participate, though he held his presentation in his own Florentine palazzo, Avolio, Bertoli, and "Tessitrice dell'Isola." And they were converted in a hurry, because the times were truly ripe for an "1848" of Italian fashion, a younger fashion, against the occupying and oppressive foreign fashion, for a war of independence against the French. The letter of exhortation was dated 28 December 1950. On 3 January 1951, Simonetta replied that she "accepted with enthusiasm" and, on the same date, Casa Fontana replied: "We will participate with pleasure in your praiseworthy undertaking. We have taken careful note of the program in the certainty that the common effort will be crowned by the much sought after recognition of Italian creative capacity."

The timing involved some second thoughts for the Fontana sisters. On 13 January, they announced that the invitation "has been considered with great attention by our House and the Houses of Schubert and Carosa." They gave a tentative agreement, for themselves and for the "other Houses mentioned," and asked for an assurance that "there would be at least seven or eight representatives of American department stores, willing and ready to buy."

That was a guarantee that Giorgini could not provide. He had only obtained some vague promises from buyers who were preparing for their trip to France to attend the runway presentations in Paris – it was almost a "yes," but strictly as a favor for a friend. The announcement of Italian fashion did not arouse their curiosity. They were sceptical. Everything hovered in uncertainty. On 24 May 1951, Noberasco announced: "We will participate with four morning outfits, four afternoon outfits, six mid-evening outfits, four gala outfits, and two models." But the organizer was still on the phone, to ensure that the buyers would not jilt him, and that they really would make that "detour" to Florence. "I remember long phone calls," says Matilde Giorgini. "I remember one phrase perfectly. 'Be my doctors. Come to take my temperature, by all means come.'" Altman himself had some doubts, and he would not give permission to his buyer Gertrude Ziminsky, who wanted to make her friend Giorgini happy. No one would confirm their participation. "I convinced them to participate fraudulently," Giorgini admitted to Oriana Fallaci in 1959. "I assured each one that their direct rival would be present." All of the rest was ready and planned out, according to a program that cunningly joined work with socializing in a setting that would tickle the snobbish weaknesses of the American guests. On 12 February, day wear, sportswear, boutique fashion, and accessories would be presented; the 13th would be a day of relaxation and leisure; and the 14th, between a cocktail party and a grand ball, the evening wear would be presented. Giorgini had invited to the ball, along with his guests the buyers, and the fashion journalists, all of the Florentine aristocracy. In the invitation, the following phrase appeared: "The purpose of the evening is to promote Italian fashion. The ladies are therefore sincerely requested to wear clothing of pure Italian inspiration."

In the first week of that February, Giorgini intensified his phone calls to the buyers who were in Paris, spending their last dollars on orders from Patou, Dior, Molineux, Fath. He was practically begging them. In the end, they arrived. They were Stella Hanania for

"I. Magnin" of San Francisco; Gertrude Ziminsky of "B. Altman & Co.," of New York; Ethel Francau, Jessica Daves, and Julia Trissel of "Bergdorf-Goodman" of New York; John Nixon of "Henry Morgan," of Montreal – only a few persons, but extremely important ones.
If they had a negative opinion, it would have destroyed the undertaking immediately, constituting a precedent that would have taken years to erase. They arrived in Florence on the evening of 11 February. "Practically making fun of me and emphasizing how much of a favor they had done by coming to Florence," as Giorgini was to say. They were skeptical and their budgets had been sucked dry by their purchases of Parisian fashion. Along with the group that was coming to Casa Giorgini the next day, to attend the first (and in their minds, they probably expected it to be the last) Italian fashion show, there were a few uninvited guests – Hannah Troy, a famous designer from Seventh Avenue, in New York, Martin Cole of Leto Cohn-Lo, Balbo and Ann Roberts, importers who just happened to be in Florence.
There was no catwalk in the neoclassical salon of Villa Torrigiani in Via Serragli. The Italian fashion came to life at parquet level (but it was the same in Parisian ateliers), following a short path among chairs and armchairs. It was a domestic exhibition, rigorous, very well organized, but forcefully primitive: the library had been turned into a studio for the last-minute dressmakers' touches, and the guests' bedroom into a storeroom for accessories, shoes, hats, and bijoux. There was a piano and a pianist. The library also served as make-up room and locker room for the models. The buyers arrived all together. There was no crowd of journalists, partly because at the time there were only a few fashion magazines and also because Giorgini had limited the invitations. It was a test. And if the test had failed, it would have been better to avoid the media outcry. It already seemed risky that *Women's Wear Daily*, *Daily New Record* and *Retailing Daily*, all belonging to the Fairchild group, had announced in small paragraphs, the Florentine debut. Only five journalists were invited to the occasion: Elisa Massai, Elsa Robiola, director of *Bellezza* and correspondent for the weekly *Tempo* with the illustrator Gemma Vitti of *Corriere Lombardo*, Vera Rossi of *Novità*, Misia Armani of the periodical *I Tessuti Nuovi* and Sandra Bartolomei Corsi of the *Secolo XIX*. Except for the final ball, the event had been organized as a serious work conference and a low profile was expressly maintained in order to prevent any Italian newspaper printing something about the exhibition. On the other hand, Giorgini had certainly not given up directing the event. The sequence and contents of the shows had been carefully studied as to obtain the maximum result. "All the stakes had to be played immediately, at the first blow, on 12 February," wrote Roberta Orsi Landini, a scholar of the Italian fashion phenomenon. "No surprises had to be postponed to the 14th to the presentation of evening gears and to the grand ball. The buyers' interest had to be stirred immediately, on the first day, so that the in-between break turned into a curious waiting and not time for second thoughts or tedious expectation. What they had to see and learn immediately was the difference from Paris – the fact that it was a totally different fashion. On February 12 before the presentation of the morning dresses, the boutique styles and the sport and leisurewear were exhibited. This was a kind of Collection that Paris did not have and did not appear in the sophisticated fashion magazines of the French capital. The garments were unexpected, fresh, young, and wearable. It was a triumph of colors. The quality was surprising, the prices incredibly interesting. The buyers understood that it was going to open a market of wide perspectives. They immediately intuited that business was to come and kept their eyes open also in front of high fashion creations, in which the alternative features and the rebellion against the old submission to Paris were less evident." That *coup de theater* was the result of a deep, multi-decennial knowledge of the American market. "Giorgini," wrote Roberta Orsi Landini, "had intuited those that would become the winning characteristics of a possible Italian fashion: clothes, lines and trends careful to the changes of a world quickly in progress." "Nowadays it can seem a poor thing," said Elisa Massai, a direct observer of the debut, "but, for those times, the idea to open the exhibition with that apparently minor,

informal fashion was a brave and intelligent idea. Bringing under the spotlights, the knitwear, the beachwear, the fashion-boutique was like desecrating the tradition, the rite of high fashion. Giorgini did it and this was a sign of talent and intuition. He knew that those proposals were in line with the taste and costume, with the lifestyle of Americans. In May 1950 I had wrote an article about Olga di Gresy, the patron director of Mirsia, a knitwear company that already had a staff of 100 workers. I had been introduced to her by Bebe Kuster, director of *Novità*, and had drawn an article for *Women's Wear Daily*. Bista read it and immediately called me to know more about it. There result was under our eyes during that first exhibition. But, under the lights, there were also Franco Bertoli, Clarette Gallotti, Avolio and, in the rooms of Villa Torrigiani, even accessories had their fame: the bijoux by Giuliano Fratti, hats by Projetti, Gallia & Peter, the creative intuitions of Luciana Reutern, Romagnoli and Canessa, of the Florentine Biancalani. On the show menu, the not-exactly academic fashion was much more than a stimulating appetizer." There was great interest in the Fontana sisters, Jole Veneziani, Simonetta, Fabiani, Marucelli, Noberasco, Carosa, Schuberth, and Vanna, who the journalists of elegance defined as "creative designers." It was the first example of multiple alliances in a rather whimsical world, all presenting their designs together. Every brand, every studio, every personality had his own story, his own little glory in his past and everyone has risked something. In the library in Giorgini's residence, among small workshops awkwardly created for the nine ateliers, diverse stories, lives, characters, experiences, births endured together the anguish of the challenge; the aristocratic fiery nature of Simonetta and Giovanna Caracciolo together with the determination, the country people's intelligence of Zoe and Micol Fontana, the popular touch of Germana Marucelli, and the bourgeois character of Jole Veneziani; the irony and detachment of Fabiani mixed with the gold, the foundation cream, and the toupee of Schuberth. The anguish was as high as the stakes, aswell as the terrifying certainty of having the Parisian house as new enemies. "Loredana Taparelli, Yan Sprague, Franchina Novati,

Carmen Snow of Harper's Bazaar «seen» by Brunetta (Giovanni Battista Giorgini Archive).

the models, came back and forth in a short tour of the exhibition," recalled Matilde Giorgini. "There was an absolute and indecipherable silence. Was it seriousness, attention or embarrassment? Not a word, nor an applause or a nod of approbation or boredom. Nothing could be said of the scarce movements, of the impassive faces of the guests. My father was standing near the door of the library-locker room. Mom occupied another strategic position. They disoriented. They couldn't understand how things were going on." After the last model left the applause came. But it still wasn't evident. It could have been an applause of esteem, as it happens in theater when an excellent actor has a bad evening. Giorgini approached the buyers: "Does it work? Which is your impression?" Stella Hanania, the buyer for I. Magnin said: "Paris didn't move us like this." Gertrude Ziminsky of B. Altman: "It was worth coming." Designers, dressmakers, ironers, dressers, they all looked radiantly at the exhibition. The Italian fashion was born.

(*Guido Vergani*)

Giorgio Grati Label of women's knitwear Collection created in 1970 in Ancona. Originally called Giorgio Grati Tricot, it was not the first business established by the synonymous entrepreneur. On this occasion, however, Grati's name was at stake and it was an ambitious challenge. The new ready-to-wear line, of impeccable manufacturing and high-profile tailoring proved successful, and developed especially during the 1980s. The firm became a shareholder company. It entered the market sectors of shirts, coats, and jackets and gained excellent results, even in export. In 1989 entrepreneurial success led Giorgio Grati to the presidency of the Small and Medium Companies in Confindustria. In 1991 he obtained the honor of the Labor Knighthood.

(*Lucia Serlenga*)

Giorgio Visconti Brand of Italian jewelry. Originality of design determined its success since its début in 1945 at the peak of creativity, not only in the area of Valenza, but also at national and international level. Giorgio, with his sons Fabrizio and Andrea, brought the company to high quality standards, synthesizing artisan's traditions with a technological know-how, to which the family dedicates much of their entrepreneurial commitment. The essential shapes, taking note of fashion trends, often preceded a new taste and are provocatively innovative. These first stones proved revolutionary. One of the most significant is the snake-shaped pendant because of its graphic and decorative appeal.

(*Alessandra Quattordio*)

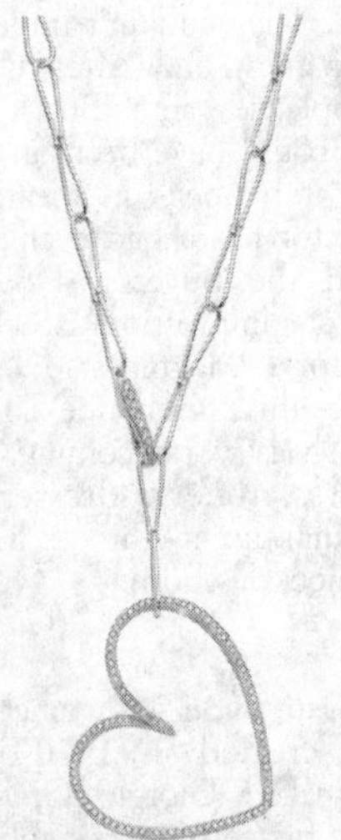

Necklace with a heart-shaped pendant by Giorgio Visconti.

Girbaud François and Marithé. French designers of ready-to-wear. A married couple in life and business, François Girbaud (1945) and Marithé Bachellerie (1942) have made a notable impact on the world of jeans, casual and sportswear. In 1965 they launched their first jeans called Stonewash Denim. They opened their first boutique in 1969 and became famous for their initial alterations to classic American jeans with leather or lace inlays, variation in cut (flaring or baggy jeans), and treatment and ageing of the material. This was rapidly followed with a complete line of clothing and knitwear. The couple proposed 14 lines, which included: *Compagnie des Montagnes et des Forêts* for leather, *Closed* for jeans, *Momento Due* for men, and *Dessine-moi une femme* for women. They define their latest designs as high-tech creations due to the use of ultrasound, lasers and adhesive heat.

❑ 2002, June. At the 68th edition of Pitti Immagine Uomo, forty years of creativity from the French duo were celebrated with an exhibition entitled *The Other Jeans: Il faut laver le jean des ses idées*. From the first washing experiments to the last creations. From the invention of the stone wash to the last Blue Eternal, a denim which perfectly maintains its color even after a very frequent washing.

Girdle Extreme interpretation of the multiform family of bustier. It has resisted the ostracism dedicated to ancient armors especially by Poiret, with the intention to tighten the waist in homage to the wasp waist. The name comes from the French *guêpière*. Generally in lace, it sheaths the breasts and slims the waist, without prolonging more than suspenders. It functions with two garters. It returned to fashion thanks to Dior's New Look (1947), extolled by Cinecittà's divas and starlets in the 1950s. In more recent times it has reappeared among leotards and tights, as seduction for revival dresses or on special occasions, preferably in black, but also violet, dark red, bottle green, and fuchsia.

Giudicelli Tan (1934). French designer. Born in Indochina with a Corsican father and a Vietnamese mother, he collected and

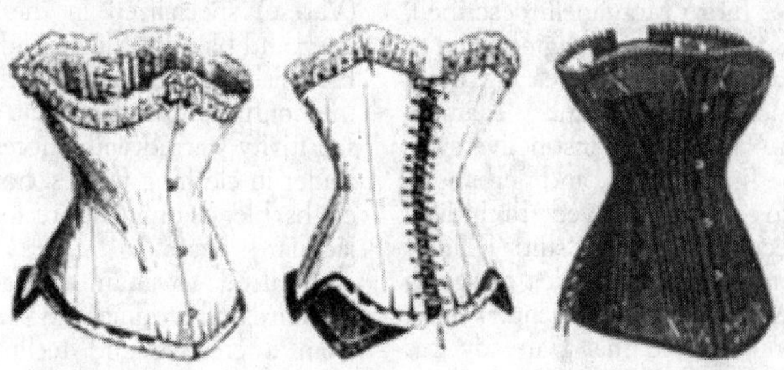

Girdles (from *Mode e Modi*, by Gillo Dorfles, Mazzotta Publishing, 1990).

summarized for himself the tastes of West and East, synthesizing them in his work. He created his first designs when he was still in school in Vietnam, all the time dreaming about Paris. In 1956 he arrived in Paris where he found a job at Dior. He later worked with the designer, Jules François Crahay in the fashion house, followed by Jacques Heim. In 1972 after being the designer for Mic Mac for a long period of time, he presented his own Collection characterized by a strong oriental inspiration. From a managerial point of view, his path was rather uneven. He always worked for third parties, designing, for example, some Hermès Collections with Claude Brouet. In recent years, he has proposed a new perfume for *Le Club des Créateurs de Beauté of Paris*.

Giuliani Aldo (1979). Italian photographer. Native of Grosseto, he first moves to Bologna, where he studies at the Dams, then to Milan where he graduates for the European Institute of Design before becoming Gianpaolo Barbieri's assistant. His photos appears on several publications, among which GQ, Max, Uomo Vogue, Maxim, Glamour, and creates advertising campaigns for Alessi, N.O.D., Chiara Boni and in 2003 for the IperCoop of Sesto San Giovanni.

Giuliano Ciro (1894-1978). Italian tailor. He followed in the art of his grandfather and father as they had a small tailor's workshop in Caprecotta. The review *GQ, Gentlemen's Quarterly,* has defined him as the "Bible of male elegance." It is fair to consider him together with the ancestors of Caraceni to be an absolute maestro. At the age of 15 he moved to Rome to improve his skills at Mattina and Cassisi, a good tailoring firm in the capital. By the time he was 20 he was already a cutter with Holding by Tritone, an English style tailor's workshop where Caraceni had also been. A few years later he opened his own workshop in Corso Italia, 32. The secret to his success were fabrics – always of extraordinary quality – and his ability to soften and 'italianize' his cutting. Lightness and flexibility are the qualities praised by Luigi Barzini Jr. when commenting on Giuliano's suits: "... he would lay the jacket on the client's shoulders as they were, without stuffing or rigid cloths or anything, so it would hang with gravity, loosely and naturally. The most traditional tailors used to lay the jacket on fake shoulders made with absorbent cotton, supports and various objects." His most faithful client was the actor Gary Cooper. In Italy Cooper became acquainted with Dorothy di Frasso, who was in love with him. She taught him the first lessons of Italian style by taking him to Giuliano. "He was a man slightly shorter than the average, wonderfully but quietly dressed, with curved shoulders, and a peaceful and melancholic face under thick, straight and slightly silver hair [...] And the cut of the suit, the aristocratic profile determined by a aquiline nose, the confidentiality and suavity of his manners made me think of a diplomat of the old school, or one of those 'Uncles' Earls' of the good society, who can allow themselves familiarity towards men and women without fear of being misunderstood." Thus, in a portrait of

Busti al Pincio, Indro Montanelli described, that due to his fame, he had imagined him to be "tall, authoritative and overbearing, more inclined to act with arrogance, than to receive orders." Out of an instinctive sympathy after the first meeting, and perhaps as a reaction to that disproved prejudice, Montanelli decided to order a suit: 'I didn't need one, but I enjoyed the idea of seeing him again and to become his friend. With a certain stupor I realized that I already was his friend. He came to me with the tape measure hanging from his right shoulder and a half-cigarette of a national brand in his mouth. "Oh," he said, as if he had been waiting for me until then. "You came! Give me a kiss," and he kissed me on both cheeks. "Shall we make a suit?" he added, looking at me with his quiet, melancholic eyes. "Let's make it," I answered. "How do you want it?" "What do you suggest?" Ciro leafed through a catalogue of samples, stopped at one, and showed it to me with an questioning look. "Eh!," I exclaimed. "Eh!," he answered. And I felt as I had just found Othello, the tailor of my childhood in the country who, despite his melodramatic name, was simply a farmer's son, and manufactured clothes in a way that, at a certain moment, they could be adjusted to fit our younger brothers and cousins, according to the rules of the frugal domestic economics of our old Tuscan families. It was the most beautiful suit I had ever had until then, but Ciro made me wear it, with the same lack of liturgical solemnity which Othello used to put me on his baggy jackets...'.

Giulini Vittorio (1940). President of Sistema Moda Italia. Born to an old Milanese family involved in the textile industry since 1800. He was a graduate in Chemistry from the University of Pavia with a Masters in Economics. He managed Liolà, a firm specialized in women's ready-to-wear. His commitment to the institutions connected with Sistema Moda is characterized by an intelligent passion, a great entrepreneurial preparation and a clear vision of globalization. He is President of Efima, the institute that instigates and manages the trade fairs dedicated to the clothing industry. He is also Vice-President of Pitti Immagine.

Giuseppe Bellora Factory of Fagnano Olona (Varese) specialized in the production of linen and blends of linen and cotton fabrics. Established in 1883, the factory's history is the confirmation of a great entrepreneurial sensitivity starred with success. It is market leader in clothing fabrics, house linen, linen cloths, blends of linen, precious cotton, from jacquard bases to *ratière*. It is strongly committed to maintaining high quality standards of product and service, especially from a creative and technological standpoint, as well as in the study of unusual blends and careful finishings. This has led to solid collaborations with the most significant Italian and international ready-to-wear firms. The company, so far focused only on the Spring-Summer season, has an agreement with a firm from Biella to soon distribute a wool, wool-linen and wool-cotton Collection.

Giussani Daniela (1943). Journalist and director of the monthly magazine *Elle*. She has followed a career just in women's magazines. In 1973 she joined the staff of *Annabella* (Rizzoli) as fashion editor. In 1983 she moved to Mondadori as chief editor of *Cento Cose*. Two years later she was called to *Donna* (Rusconi) where she became Vice-Director in 1987. Her return to Rizzoli took place in 1988 as director of *Elle*. Under her management, the monthly achieved excellent circulation, around 150,000 copies, which is a very high level for a monthly publication.

❑ 2005, January. After 16 years she became editorial director in Edif, which publishes both *Elle* and *Elle Décor*.

Givenchy (de) Hubert (1927). French designer. A rare combination in the history of fashion of formal simplicity and rigorous grace that focuses on the details, from fabrics to accessories, and the creator, a man with evergreen elegance, a composite culture, and an innate taste. In the second post-war period, he arrived in Paris from Beauvais. In a portrait for *Donna*, Maria Pezzi wrote, 'He had fought a tough fight with his bourgeois, Protestant family, which could not have regard for a son caught up in the fashion octopus. He soon found a place in the atelier of Jacques Fath, the youngest, most extrovert, and enthralling tailor of the moment. He would tell me, "There was a

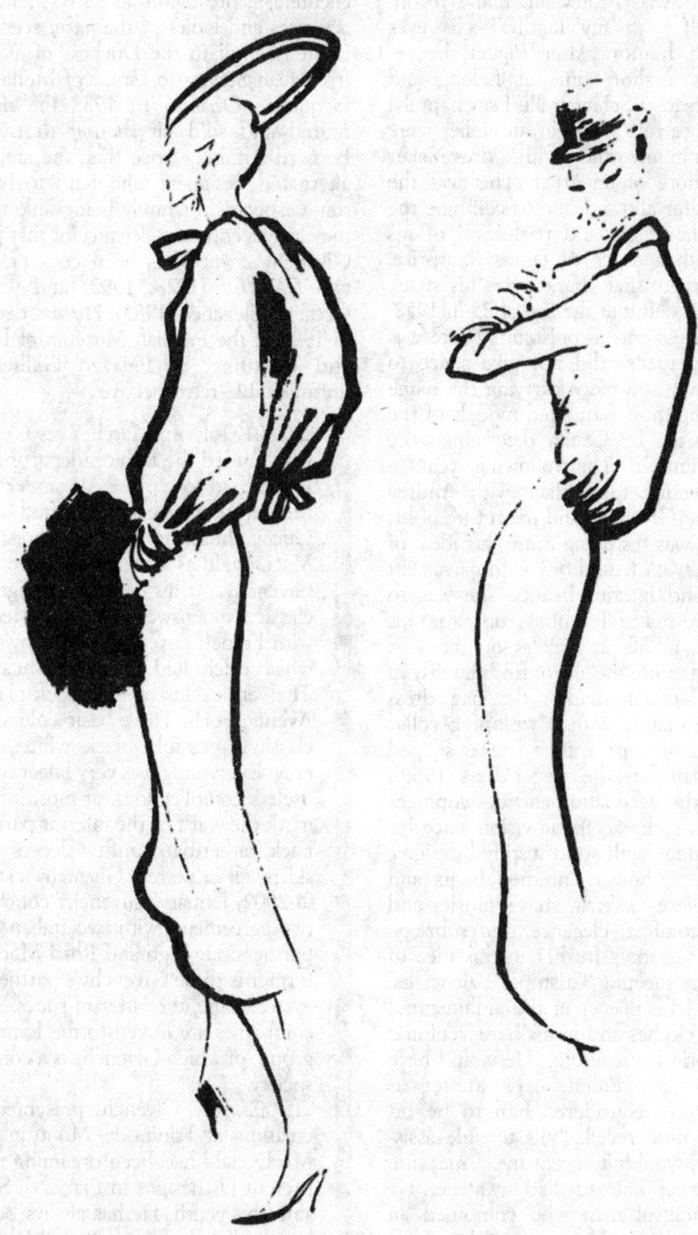

Givenchy's «blousant» backs, 1957 (from Bellezza).

mundane atmosphere, very perfumed, sensual, and dangerous. Only when I moved to Robert Piguet, who was more classic and, above all, a Swiss Protestant, that I reconciled myself with my family." His eyes shined with humor. After Piguet, he remained for a short time at Lelong and happily arrived at Schiaparelli. I say happily, because those four years in an atelier were different from any other, with a dressmaker who was more of an artist. This was the basis that later allowed him to combine the elegance, classicism, and perfection of his creation with a touch of fantasy, surprise, and eccentricity that characterize his style'. He made his debut at the age of 25 in 1952, and his success was astonishing. There was no newspaper that did not give space to Bettina's blouse, a piece carrying the name of one of the most requested models of the time. A sketch by Gruau determined the blouse's triumph. The following year, a decisive meeting took place with Audrey Hepburn for Givenchy and the future of his atelier. She was his living musé, his ideal of female beauty. A fresh body with naïve self-assurance and interior beauty, she was to become the natural ambassador for his classic cuts, in life as well as on the sets. His creations were the ally of fresh fantasy in joyful and tender shades: the bag dress (1953), the mantle with a wrapping collar (1958), and the one with a shelter-shaped collar, the ball skirt, the bustier dress (1969). There was the declination and development of Givenchy's characteristic vision since his first Collections with sport-inspired designs, apron dresses, flower-patterned pants and his masterpiece *tailleurs*, shirt's fabrics and forms for comfort, elegance, and sobriety. He placed his roots further in this idea of fashion after meeting Cristóbal Balenciaga: he recognized a master in the architectural creation of clothes and in his bare, sculpted vitality. Maria Pezzi wrote, 'He would have wanted to join Balenciaga's atelier as apprentice. He considered him to be his God. He would recall, "His terrible assistant, Renée, wouldn't accept me. I met him years later when I already had my atelier. He was a wonderful man who combined an amazing creativity with terrific technique. I learned from him that in life and in the profession you must never cheat: a five-hole button is useless when four are enough. Vionnet and he were the most innovative"'. When the Spanish tailor retired from high fashion in 1968, Givenchy inherited his clientele, as prestigious as his own, including actresses and ladies of the jetset scene from Lauren Bacall to the Duchess of Windsor, from Jean Seberg to Grace of Monaco and Jacqueline Onassis. In 1988 the designer retired and sold his *maison* to Lvhm of Bernard Arnault. Since then the atelier has alternated designers who tend to broaden some aspects, but rarely being able to keep the elusive, constant elegance of that period. Givenchy's work has been consecrated by two *Dé d'Or* (1978, 1992) and with the Oscar of Elegance (1985). He was dedicated in 1991 at the Parisian Museum of Fashion and Costume, at Palazzo Galliera, an unforgettable retrospective.

❑ 2001, July. In March Yves Carcelle, who guided the fashion department of Lvmh, had to replace Alexander McQueen, who has been hired by Gucci, chose the Welsh designer Julian MacDonald as artistic director of Givenchy. At his debut he designed a classic womenswear line, in perfect tune with French taste and Givenchy's style, which celebrated 50 years of business. The very exclusive show took place in Avenue Foch. Three basic colors, as classic as possible: black, white, and grey. Everything was very linear, without useless complications, at most a bow to mark the waist or the inferior part of the back, rather bare, puffed sleeves, corolla skirts, all in perfect Givenchy's style.
❑ 2002, January. Givenchy concluded two agreements with two Italian partners: De Rigo and Rossi Moda. The former is to be Givenchy's partner in an eyewear line, the latter in shoes. Both companies are linked to the Lvmh group, of which Givenchy is a controlled society.
❑ 2002, July. Givenchy presented its creations at Trinità dei Monti in Rome. MacDonald had been dreaming to present his designs in Piazza di Spagna since his youth. He has always been in love with Italy (Florence and Portofino in particular) and with its women.
❑ 2003, December. Ozwald Boateng was appointed creative director of the

men's line of the *maison*. He declares the challenge will be to reinvent the French gentleman.
❑ 2004. MacDonald left Givenchy. From Autumn 2005, the Collection is to be designed by Riccardo Tisci.
❑ 2005, March. Riccardo Tisci is appointed creative director of the Maison Givenchy. He will oversee the haute couture, prêt-à-porter, and accessories Collections.

Giwas Knitwear company. Established in Arre (Padua) in 1978 as a small artisan's workshop for the manufacturing of clothes for some big names of the Italian fashion scene. Towards the end of the 1980s it started to propose a Collection of its own for the medium-high segment of the market. In the years that followed, sales continued to grow and the distribution network was consolidated. The Wood brand best characterizes the company.

Glamour According to the Oxford and Webster's dictionaries, the term glamour means charm, prestige, thus a "glamorous" person is fascinating, enchanting, and attractive. The word derives from the Scottish term *gramarye*, which means magic. Nowadays it is the synonym for style and seduction, it is reminiscent of someone who shines from his own light without excesses. Beauty helps, but an 'ugly' person can also have glamour. Above all it is a matter of personality. Obviously the eye and culture of who's looking and judging never gives a unique response. Marilyn Monroe was, for some, sexy but not glamorous. For others, she matched both 'virtues'. Just a few divas meet everyone's agreement. For example, Gene Tierney. Looking at the 20th century, some writers and artists can be considered rather glamorous, for example Francis Scott Fitzgerald, Man Ray, and André Breton. In the 1950s and 1960s Françoise Sagan and Georges Simenon, in the 1980s Andy Warhol and Richard Avedon. If glamour accompanies elegance, then the following can be added to the group: Marlene Dietrich, Louise Brooks, Wallis Simpson, Jackie Kennedy Onassis, Ali Khan, Paloma Picasso, Lady Diana, and Gianni Agnelli. Many Hollywood personalities, especially from some films that are now part of history, belong to the 'glamorous' category: Ingrid Bergman and Humphrey Bogart in *Casablanca* (1942), Marlon Brando in *A Streetcar Named Desire* (1951), Ava Gardner in *The Barefoot Countess* (1954), Grace Kelly in *A Perfect Murder* (1954), Elizabeth Taylor and Paul Newman in *Cat on the Tin Roof* (1958), Marilyn Manson in *Let's Make Love* (1960), and Audrey Hepburn in *Breakfast At Tiffany's* (1961). The following European performers should be mentioned: Brigitte Bardot in *Et Dieu créa la femme* (1956), Jean-Paul Belmondo in *A bout de soufflé* (1960), Alain Delon in *Gattopardo* (1963). Characters can also be glamorous off the set, such as Jack Nicholson, Sean Connery, Marcello Mastroianni, Robert Redford, Harrison Ford, and George Clooney. For the females: Catherine Deneuve, Claudia Cardinale, Sharon Stone, Gwyneth Paltrow, and Nicole Kidman. Some top models have glamour, such as Naomi Campbell, Elle MacPherson, Linda Evangelista, and Carla Bruni. Finally, some sport personalities can be added to this curious list: Tazio Nuvolari, Michel Platini, Vitas Gerulaitis, John McEnroe, Michael Jordan, and Zinedine Zidane.

(*Eleonora Attolico*)

Glamour Women's monthly magazine for fashion and health published by Condé Nast. It is the "grandchild" of the *Glamour of Hollywood* magazine founded in 1939. It is managed by Dada Santini, whose took over from Valeria Corbetta. Its readership is characterized by young females. The recently introduced compact format has been successful because the magazine fits into any bag.

❑ 2005, May. Paola Centomo, former Vice-Director, became the new Director, after Danda Santini's move to the direction of *Elle*.

Glans-Magnani Brand of boutique-fashion created in Parma between the two wars by Carlo Magnani, son of Girolamo, Verdi's set designer. Very keen on horses, Magnani frequented the English world of horse-riding. These occasions converted him to the fashion of London gentlemen so much so that, besides wearing it, he also became an agent in Italy for Church's shoes,

Burberry's raincoats and Munrospun's sweaters. This spell as an agent convinced him to open his own business. He started with shirts, opening a workshop in his childhood house in Borgo San Vitale in Parma, buying in fabrics from London. He named his designs Glans, also applying a motto to the brand: *Ipse sua melior fama* (Better than its own Fame). His son Luigi (19141994) joined him and together they expanded the production to include a casual, sport line, entrusting the advertising to the painter Giorgio Tabet. Glans-Magnani was among the first fashion houses to be invited by Giorgini to the exhibition in the White Room of the Pitti Palace in Florence and to Capri Beach Fashion. The company's success led to the opening of a factory in the suburbs of Parma. Luigi headed up the business until 1975. Later he worked only as agent for the English brands, a business that is still continued by his family.

Gloves Originally in use by the Egyptians and in some areas of Asia, gloves arrived from there in Greece and Rome. They were first used rarely as an elegant accessory, rather like a symbolic instrument, full of messages during ceremonies, especially following their diffusion after the Barbarian invasions. In the Middle Ages, the glove was part of the rite of the feudal investiture, a sign of trust in the woman to whom it was given or of scorn if thrown away. The first women's gloves appeared in the 9th century in silk or wool, closed at the wrist by three small buttons, or with a large cuff and often lined with fur. They were often worn in leather for falcon hunting. Roger II, crowned King of Sicily, donned gloves similar to those of ancient Greece, decorated with thin embroidery in gold leaf of an angel between two pheasants. For dignitaries, gloves were worn in white leather. In 1200, Italy was already renowned for its particularly decorated gloves, the skin tanned with perfumed essences. It was suspected that the skin was sometimes tanned with poison. In 1300, gloves became commonly used. Pompous leather gloves, woven with golden threads, marked the first century of Renaissance, also for their precious stones. Scarlet, violet, and green would distinguish the church hierarchy: the Pope's glove is white with pearls. There were also cloth gloves, called *cirotheque*. In 1500, instead of applying gems on gloves, cuts were made on them to let cabochon rings appear on fingers. Women's gloves, almost entirely in golden yarn, were expensive and rich that sumptuary laws ruled their possession. It was forbidden to own more than 32 pairs of gloves. In 1600 there was a large variety, in satin, velvet, and cloth, enriched by laceworks, fringes, and embroideries. In 1700 utility was the primary consideration, with-

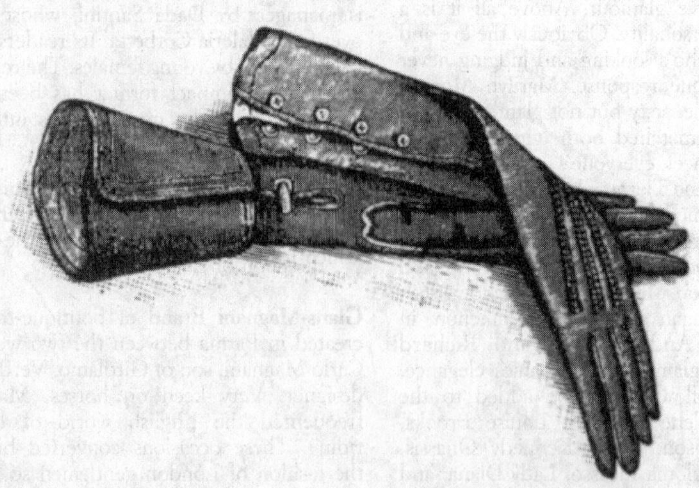

Evening gloves (from *Mode e Modi*, by Gillo Dorfles. Mazzotta Publishing, 1990).

out forgetting elegance. Feather linen gloves were very diffused, but, generally speaking, gloves were almost always held in hands. Ice-colored, shiny, glace-kid gloves cost double of those in kid. If they were in beaver skin, it was better to rely on the glove maker to wash them without causing damage. Women owned an extraordinary number of gloves, even 72 pairs with a huge range of styles. They would reduce or lengthen in inverse proportion to the length of the dresses' sleeves. Tight and long, that was how they were appreciated by the Directory's fashion, to veil bare arms when donning evening dresses. For men, who wore only one, just one color persisted, white. In the first 30 years of 1800, with the return to an elitist clothing, gloves became part of a researched style and were chosen to match the acid colors of clothes, such as bergamot peal, boreal blue, or flesh-color, while thin ribs, woven tulle inlays, and silver embroideries indicating their Neapolitan origins. Naples has become the main supplier of this elegant accessory, not only in Europe, but also in the United States. In this period half-gloves in fishnet has become very fashioned. In the mid 1800s, an elegant lady would never be seen without gloves, short, mostly closed by two small buttons, sometimes exceptionally long, decorated around the wrists by small flower, lace, or ermine garlands. Gloves were present in the home, often half-gloves in wool, rarely in velvet. The alternative to Scotland's thread gloves were leather yellow gloves (they has become a synonym of the gentleman and unsuspicious thief) for the day, white for the evening. At the end of the 1800s, gloves were no longer an absolutely necessary symbol of elegance or an instrument to protect from cold, they on the role of protecting the hands from skin contact as a sign of distinction and detachment. Several handbooks about good manners started listing the rules about shaking hands with a bare hand. After the fashion revolution of the 1920s of the 20th century, which saw the return of very long gloves, falling loosely on the forearms, gloves started following the taste's evolutions. They became more complicated with musketeer cuffs, colored inlays, made of crocodile skin, boar skin, they have a straw palm, a leathered back, meeting the needs of driving. They disappeared from daily use in the Winter, and reappeared again in fishnet and in silk for Summer. There was success with woollen gloves among young people, after having being forgotten for years they were back to underline a casual or military look. The last gloves in our memory are sexy and necessary: Rita Hayworth's in *Gilda*, very long and flaming. (*Lucia Sollazzo*)

Gn Andrew (1967). Designer from Singapore. He studied in England and enrolled at St. Martin's School of Art in London. During this time he won the French Connection Award, which was created for promising young designers of the English-French style. This acknowledgement allowed him to attend the Parson's School of Design. In 1990 he moved to Milan to attend the Domus Academy where he studied under instructors of great calibre, such as Romeo Gigli, Gianfranco Ferré, and Anna Piaggi. Two years later he moved to Paris to collaborate with the couturier at the Ungaro fashion house. In 1996 he decided to launch his own womenswear line, which is now sold in the most prestigious shops in the world. Since 2002 he has been present every year at the ready-to-wear week in Paris.

(*Maddalena Fossati*)

Gnoli Sofia. Academic specializing in the history of costume and fashion. She is professor at the European Institute of Design of Rome and collaborates with the faculty of sociology of the University of Urbino. She is the author of the volumes *Cento anni di stile sul grande schermo* (Zephiro, 1995) and *La donna, l'eleganza e il fascino* (Edizioni Del Prisma, 2000), a study based on archived documents, magazines of the period and living testimonies, which focuses on the birth of Italian fashion between the two World Wars.

Goalen Barbara. 1950s model. She was the favorite model of Coffin and was photographed almost exclusively by Henry Clarke. She was probably too aware of her beauty and skills: she would arrive on the set in a Rolls-Royce with a driver. She was the first British model to be sent to the Paris shows by British Vogue in order to create photos to document the lines and trends. She only worked for five years before retiring despite being very much requested.

Gobelin Manufactured fabric similar to hand-made tapestries, whose name derives from an ancient French factory that made arras and tapestries. It reproduces paintings and flower subjects through the different warps and wefts that give life to multiple effects and colors. Gobelins are industrially manufactured by jacquard looms and are used in clothing and accessories, especially bags and suitcases. The most common yarn used is cotton.

Godart Nikita (1955). French designer. He was convinced by the designer Michel Schreiber that fashion was to be his profession. He was a student of Schreiber's at the École Camondo, where Godart was studying interior design. His first exhibition took place in Autumn 1983. During the 1990s, his clothing was distributed by the Japanese group Daiya. In 1992 the French department store, Monoprix, commissioned an exclusive Collection.

Godely Georgina (1955). British designer. Her creativity has often been shaped by the study of human anatomy, by paying attention to the body and gestures. This study was not used to create a linear and minimalist fashion, but in order to achieve new inventions and not abstract fantasy. Her eclectic background includes studying in Wimbledon and at Brighton College in painting, sculpture, fashion and 3-dimensional drawing. She collaborated with Scott Crolla, with whom in 1981 she opened a cult shop, Crolla, inspired by neo-romantic tastes. In 1986 she launched her first women's Collection: sophisticated clothing of sculptural quality that glorified the female body, exaggerating its dimensions. Her maternity dress with its stuffed belly and the wedding dress with slashes around the breasts have attained their place in fashion history.

Godet Flared cutting of skirts, dresses or coats created by inserting one or more triangular pieces of material and fabrics cut on the bias in order to increase the width and volume of the fabric.

Goldberg Nathaniel (1970). French photographer. In 1996 he won the prestigious prize dedicated for young fashion photographers at Hyères. His photos are published in *Harper's Bazaar USA*, *W Magazine*, *Numèro*, *The Face*, and *Vogue France*. He lives in Paris and New York.

Golden Lady Company specialising in tights established by Nerino Grassi in 1967. Originated in the 1980s with massive investments in communications, which culminated with the choice of Kim Basinger as the face of the company. It has offices in Lyon, Nottingham, and Frankfurt. The group has acquired two established brands in hosiery and women's swimsuits, Omsa and Si-Si.

Goldin Nan (1953). American photographer and artist. She studied at the School of the Museum of Modern Art in Boston. In 1978 she moved to New York, where she lives and works. Since a young age, she has been using photography as a personal diary. She has proposed a visual path where fantasy merges with reality and everyday life with its excesses, in which she is protagonist with her friends and life partners. All of this features in a book published in 1986 entitled *The Ballard of Sexual Dependency*, which accompanied an exhibition of the same name. Since then she has published *Cookie Muller* (1991), *The Other Side* (1992), *Ten years After: Naples 1986-1996* (1998), and *Couplet and Loneliness* (1999). In 1996 she directed the movie *I'll Be Your Mirror*. Her style has influenced a whole generation of fashion photographers who, as she does herself, prefer the raw reality to formal cleanness.

Goma Michel (1932). French designer from Montpellier. He is a master in omitting the superfluous. He studied at the Academy of Fine Arts in Montpellier. In 1952 he was hired by Jeanne Lafaurie, where he remained for 10 years through the ups and downs of the Parisian house. In 1962 he moved to Patou, which proved to be an excellent training ground for Lagerfeld, as it turned out to be for Goma and his assistants, Tarlazzi and Gaultier. In 1973 he founded his own company. In the late 1980s, he became the creative director of Balenciaga's ready-to-wear line.

Gomez Jorge (1967). Spanish designer. Born in Las Palmas in Gran Canaria, he is the son of a famous interior designer, and he started working in the world of design from a very young age. He studied at several institutions before launching his synonymous brand in 1990 in Santa Cruz in Tenerife. In 1992 he opened a studio in Madrid. Two years later, he opened his first boutique in the Spanish capital. In 1998 he inaugurated a second boutique in Santa Cruz in Tenerife and, in 2002, he opened a new workshop in the Salamanca neighborhood of Madrid. His fame has grown due to his participation in international exhibitions, but largely thanks to export. (*Mariacristina Righi*)

Gommatex Jersey Textile company in Prato, Tuscany. At the outset it was a division of the large Gommatex S.p.a. which needed to independently produce a cloth support for its polyurethane coating. A creative intuition and a constant desire for innovation transpired in a jersey line in 1982, which had immediate success. This rapid achievement resulted in Gommatex Jersey, associated with a Group with a turnover of more than 200 billion, 75 employees, and production of more than 2.5 million of trendy fashion fabrics per year. The company has a very high level of technology. It is also strongly orientated towards creativity, research, quality, and novelty. International designers are

A model by the designer Jorge Gomez.

among its customers. It has been rewarded by an avant-garde production structure, a complete cycle at 80%.

Gomme Clothing brand created by the Japanese designer Hiroshige Maki. He graduated from the Fashion College of Nagoya, then he worked for ten years with an expert, Yohji Yamamoto. In 1986 he conquered the Japanese market with great success. He handles silk, plissé and other materials that model the body with absolute skill.

Goncharova Natalia (1881-1962). Painter and protagonist of the artistic Russian avant-garde. In 1913 she signed the manifesto of *Raggismo*. Her production was originally focused on theater costumes for Diaghilev's ballets. From 1913 to 1949 she became interested in the world of fashion, designing clothing for a Paris atelier where she combined Russian folklore and traditional elements with modern geometric decorations.

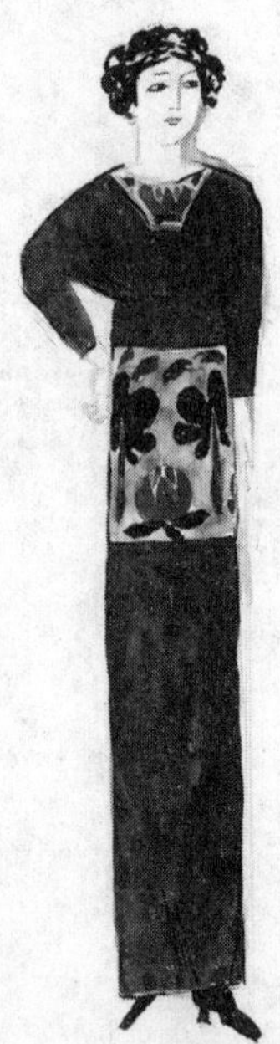

Natalia Goncharova: study for a dress, ca. 1910 (from *Art Fashion*, Biennial of Florence, Skira, 1996).

Gonnet Agathe (1952). French designer. She has theorized and manufactured transformable clothes. After a long apprenticeship selling her sketches to stylists' agencies such as Promostyl and Woolmark, and working for Kenzo and Montana, she started her own brand and in 1992 she presented her models during an exhibition.

Goran y Pejkosky (1975). Macedonian designer. A graduate of the University of Utrecht, he lives and works in Paris. His debut was in January 2000 during the high fashion shows, when he presented a highly geometric line characterized by folklore evocations from his homeland. He regularly superimposes fabrics and works on them with lasers.

Gore-Tex Fabric brand manufactured by W.L. Gore & associates, one of the 200 largest US private corporations. Its success in several fields – among which shoe designing and fabric lamination – has been obtained through innovation and research aiming at the setting of avant-garde techniques. For 45 years this was the company's commitment, whose business started in 1958 when Bill Gore and his wife, Vieve gave birth to W.L. Gore & Associates Inc. in their house's basement. Bill and Vieve's efforts were joined by those of their son, Bob who was a chemical engineering student at the time. The first patent concerned a solution set by Bob for a new isolated cable in Pfte, which gave origin to a material called Gore-Tex, a membrane of expanded polytetrafluoethylene (porous Teflon), with characteristics of absolute impermeability, air-conditioning, windproofing, excellent transpiration characteristics, and elevated comfort propriety. This was followed by new electronic products, thanks to which the company began to expand. A few years later, this expansion was made through the use of pharmaceutical products. In the late 1960s, the company's plants were located in Delaware, Arizona, Scotland, Germany, and Japan. Gore intervened in space technology that took the Americans to the moon, in high-performance techniques used all over the world, and in computer technologies. The exclusive textile technologies created by Gore must be attributed to the revolutionary membranes that the company invented: thin, light, and time resistant. The company's brands are Gore, Gore-Tex, Preclude, Hemobahn, Excluder, Glide, and Windstopper. The Italian headquarters is in Cavaion, near Verona. The main headquarters is in Newark, Delaware.

(*Maria Vittoria Alfonsi*)

❑ 2001, July. For the fans of mountain and trekking, Duratherm's technology guaranteed warmth and comfort even at the lowest temperatures. Gore-Tex applied it to the shoes presented at Ispo in Munich.
❑ 2002, May. Gore-Tex launched the new Paclite of 'third generation', which had undergone several improvements after the first model proposed in 1998 and its successive evolution in 2000. For climbers, for lovers of long and difficult travels, the new Paclite applications offered a minor overall dimension in luggage. It used a protective layer made by a substance oleophobic in carbon on the membrane, which allows steam to transpire and does not let anything in. The system, besides maintaining the membrane for a longer period, does not require an internal linen. Compared to the previous laminated, it is 15% lighter, more compressible and resistant, while transpiration and waterproofing are increased by 40%. Clothing manufactured in Gore-Tex Paclite are softer and more comfortable, more versatile, and sophisticated. Besides the classic mountain clothing, this material is also perfect for casual and sport garments. Thanks to the new adopted methodologies, the price has diminished by 25%. Gore-Tex, with its 114 research laboratories, launched a product that covered every need in the world of sport.
❑ 2002, July. Notwithstanding the difficult market conditions, Gore-Tex was not affected by the crisis. The diversification of products, not only highly technical in content, but also enlarged to include sportswear and city fashion, led to the brand in collaboration with Prada Sport. Two new products have also been launched: Airvantage, which exploited the principle of double glasses through inflatable interspaces, and Xcr Stretch Fabric which reduced transpiration.
❑ 2003, March. Gore-Tex, after years of research focused on technological perfection for extreme and dangerous sports, tried to reach the city and outdoor market with a new product, Gore-Tex Xcr. The newly created membrane of the American company reduced its thickness (0.6 mm) and growth in transpiration (+50%).

Gori Sisters A dressmaker's workshop active in Turin from the 1920s to after World War II. From 1931, four years before the Ente Nazionale della Moda was set up with its dictatorial regulations, the Gori sisters – with the dressmakers Palmer (in Milan) and Lamma (in Turin) – emulated fashions from Paris, by purchasing designs and fabrics from the French houses. In 1931, the Gori sisters presented their first evening dress completely of their own invention. Six years later, on the occasion of a ball organized by the mayor of Turin at the Palazzo Madama in honor of international fashion, they won the cup for the most Italian design. It was, recounts Natalia Aspesi in her book *Il lusso e l'autarchia* (Luxury and Self-Sufficiency, published by Rizzoli, 1982) an evening of black tulle and great swathes of black haircloth.

Gorman Greg (1949). American photographer. He took a course in news photography at the University of Kansas from 1967 to 1969, followed by a Masters in Fine Arts and Cinema at the University of Southern California in 1972. His career began in 1968 when, using a camera borrowed from a friend, he photographed Jimi Hendrix's concert in Kansas City and, immediately afterwards, The Doors. These first successes urged him to continue to portray situations which he recreates both in studios and outdoors. The photographs portraying David Bowie, Frank Zappa, Elton John, Joe Cocker and many others that are also used on record covers were produced in this way. The images of the following actors were also shot in the same way: Kevin Costner, Kim Basinger, Tom Cruise, and Robert De Niro. He also creates advertising campaigns with his famous nudes, and does work for clients such as Reebok, Rolex, Shisheido, and AT&T. His photos appear in *GQ*, *Vogue*, *L'Uomo Vogue*, *Vogue Homme*, *Amica*, *Tempo*, *Life*, *Esquire*, *Rolling Stone* as well as in the Italian, French, and German editions of *Max*. In 1990 and 1992 he published his photographs in *Volume 1* and *Volume 2*, his explicit male nudes in *As I See It* (2000) and in *Just Between Us* (2001), while his most recent anthologies are *Inside Life* in 2000 and *Prospectives* in 2001. He has co-directed the video *Love on Top of Love* with the singer Grace Jones.

Goths/Gothics Musical movement and young people's style. Following the fragmentation of style implied by Punk and after the split-up of the Sex Pistols (1978), it was possible to witness how various contemporary trends could give birth to very often antithetic styles. The beginning of the gothic tribe (known in Italy as *dark*) was due to the growing interest for a deeper and more suffocating musical style after the former punk adrenaline. John Lydon, on leave from Sex Pistols, inaugurated a season of New Spleen with P.i.l. and Siouxsie & the Banshees, the very first punks. Then Joy Division, Killing Joke and Bauhaus catalyzed the diffused need for introspection, giving life to a musical gender which was increasingly developing the connotations of Gothic. The Bat Cave Club was the renowned meeting point of new acolytes. From a clothing point of view, the New Romantic season, coming after punk, had opened the way to a zapping of clothing codes (with a wide catalogue ranging from Lord Fauntleroy to Morticia Addams). The gothic style had decided to paint everything in black. With this grim, sullen vision of glamour, it is vital to pay attention to the difference between the Gothics, in accurate historical reconstructions of 19th century clothes, and the Goths, who generally limited themselves to wear in black, with corsets, black laces, and gloomy make-up. (*Maurizio Vetrugno*)

Gottex Swimwear Brand of swimsuits. The swimsuits are the favorites of Madonna. Sophisticated materials and trendy colors are used for one pieces and bikinis. The original name of the company was Gottex of Israel, whose main offices have been in Israel since the 1950s when the Hungarian owners Lia Gottlieb and Armin Ruzow were forced to move out. In the 1960s, their daughter, Miriam Ruzow, decided to expand the business into the United States and to open a branch office in New York. The brand has a high fashion content. In the late 1990s the company was acquired by the billionaire Lev Leviev who, being an ultra-orthodox Jew, decided to forbid access to the exhibitions for men.

Goutal Annick (1946-1999). Perfume creator. She was a prodigy of the pianoforte, being awarded in a contest at the Conservatory of Paris at the age of 16. In order to be economically independent from her family (her father had a pastry shop), she helped the older owners of an hand-made homeopathic laboratory of perfumes, creams, and cosmetics. Her presence was fundamental in preventing the laboratory's decline. Through his experience, she discovered her real vocation, to be a "nose," as it is said in the jargon of the field of fragrances, colognes, and perfumes. In Grasse, in the laboratories of the Robertet fashion house, she created her first perfume, Folavril. She went on to create Sables, L'Eau de Camille, Passion and, with a lemon base, Eau d'Adrien that guaranteed her fame, not only in France. Her brand has four stores in Paris and exports all over the world through 450 sales points. In 1985 she arranged a partnership with the Groupe du Louvre, controlled by the Taittinger family, the great Champagne name. The brand's turnover amounts to 21 billion. In 1999, Annick passed away after 20 years' struggle against cancer. The company continues.

G. Petochi Roman jewelry. Located in Piazza di Spagna. Jewels, icons, high artisan's craft silverware or ancient English, American, French, Italian and, in particular, Roman silver jewels, jades, and mosaics. Tiny ancient mosaics mounted on silver boxes, necklaces, broaches, bangles in their original frames. The passion for this minor form of art brought Domenico Petochi, one of the heirs of the brothers Giuseppe and Domenico, who in 1884 had opened their workshop in Via dei Pontefici, to deepen his research in order to publish a book entitled *I mosaici minuti romani* (Roman Tiny Mosaics). The art with very small colored tesseras has been typical of Rome since the mid 1700s until the end of 1800s, and drew its origins from the studio of the Reverenda Fabbrica of St. Peter. The subjects represented sites of remains, landscapes of the Roman countryside inspired to ancient prints, to paintings and still lives or flowers, birds and butterflies, in which the artist could express himself more freely. Most of the Petochi's Collection is exhibited in the Vatican City. In the small *palazzo* in Piazza di Spagna, on the left of the stairs of Trinità dei Monti, where it has been since 1942, the jewel's boutique continues its business along the path traced out in 1928, when from a simple artisan's laboratory it turned into an atelier of jewels.

GQ American men's monthly. It was originally a quarterly publication as its acronym indicates, *Gentlemen's Quarterly*. Launched in 1957 by the American publisher Condé Nast, it is now a magazine focused on the man's world: from fashion to beauty, from suggestions about the modern life to clothes and travels. It is published in several countries. In 1988 the English edition was published with the same name, while the German *Man Vogue* (*Manner Vogue*) became *GQ* in 1997. There are also Spanish, Taiwanese, Australian, Japanese, Italian (first published in 1999, directed by Andrea Monti), and South African editions (from 1999). Every twelve months a monothematic issue is published, dedicated to the men of the year. Monti has been taken over by Paolo Bonanni.

Grace Pear Pseudonym and brand of Graziella Pera (1950). Italian designer of high fashion. She worked as costume designer at the *Bagaglino* cabaret show in Rome, but also for many films such as *Ricomincio da Tre* and *Fantozzi*. A graduate in architecture, she made her fashion début in 1992. Her clothes present fluid lines, but they drape at the same time. She also created the costumes for the TV program, *Carramba che sorpresa*.

❑ 2002, July. The designer and costume designer of *Bagaglino* opened her show with the female singing group, Finger Prints, presenting their new single, *When I Fall in Love*. Angelo Melillo was on the runway with a rose-embroidered corset on a black skirt, and Pamela Prati, who closed the presentation, donned a transparent red dress with gold embroideries.

Grachvogel Maria (1969). Designer living and working in London, but with Polish-Irish origins. She was very keen on fashion from a young age and, at the age of 14, she has learned cutting and manufacturing clothes all by herself. At 16 she was ready to sell her creations. However, she decided to accept a good suggestion to study business and marketing. At 17 she was the youngest person ever to pass the exams to work as stockbroker in the City. She started a brilliant career in high finance, interrupting it twice to try her chances in the world of fashion but with scarce success. In 1988 she found a business partner and finally, in the early 1990s, she launched her own brand. Faithful to her glamour-chic style, she proposed refined yet sexy evening dresses, much loved by movie stars. She invited her friend, Victoria Beckham to the runway for her brand. She designed a line of evening dresses for the department store, Debenhams, branded "G." Liberty allowed her the exclusive use of one of its flower patterns for her Spring-Summer 1997 Collection. In 2003 she opened a single brand store in Sloane Street, where a service of *demi-couture* is available as well as computers to check the Stock Exchange in real time.

(*Virginia Hill*)

Gramano Elvira. Wedding designer. She started her career in Naples, transforming a silk parachute, found in the countryside in the immediate post-war period, into a fairy-tale bridal dress. It is a brand that reaches as far as Beijing and Shanghai, where Chinese models don western-style bridal dresses for the first time. Her accuracy to detail and traditional manufacturing characterize her designs.

❑ 2002, April. To celebrate 50 years of activity, the Elvira Gramano atelier opened a new boutique in Rome inside the mall of Cinecittà Due, where the new boutique and ready-to-wear lines were proposed. The Gramano *griffe* is now managed by Elvira's son, Giuseppe, who also proposes the high fashion Collection in the atelier in Via XX Settembre. For a long time, the dressmaker's workshop has been employing a staff of designers selected through scholarships offered to the best students of the specialized schools around the world.

Grande Anton Giulio (1973). Italian designer of high fashion. He has a declared passion for laces and embroideries, but he does not dislike materials such as raffia and latex. He presented his creations at Palazzo Grimaldi in Monaco during the ball of the Red Cross. He is also exhibited in the Roman fashion events. He has participated in *Donna sotto le Stelle* (Woman under the Stars) with, as a background, the stairs of Trinità dei Monti in Rome.

Grantham Victoria (1968). British designer. She started working in the world of fashion at the age of 18. After studying at the best design colleges in London and after winning the most prestigious English fashion award, she moved to New York where she worked on the Donna Karan's menswear Collections. In 1997 she was called to Paris by the Lvmh Group to design the Louis Vuitton men's ready-to-wear Collection as head designer. In 1999 she decided to leave Vuitton in order to devote time to her own menswear line. At the same time, she designed the Spring-Summer Collection for Valentino Uomo. Since September 1999 she has been artistic director of New York Industry owned by the Staff International Group. (*Valeria Sico*)

Grasso Pino (1931). Milanese embroider. He started his career in 1958, working as an apprentice at the Milanese firm, Carriero. In the mid 1960s he opened a workshop in Via Donizetti, working for the emerging names in early Italian fashion. He researched increasingly sophisticated effects with hems, sleeves, and decorations, using the most developed techniques. His long list of clients includes Schuberth, Veneziani, Fabiani, the Fontana sisters, Marucelli, Mila Schön, Valentino, Armani, and Versace.

Grateau Muriel (1949). French designer. She has often worked in Italy: in 1969 for Basile and later for Complice and Mario Valentino. She is one of the founders of Promostyl, a firm offering promotional services and news about the latest trends for the textile industry and designers. From 1974 to 1981 she presented her Collections during the Paris fashion shows. Following this, she designed for third parties, especially in Italy, as well as working in interior design. Her interior design products are sold in her own store in Palais Royal area.

Grawe Tilmann. German designer. He studied in Frankfurt and then moved to Paris to continue his fashion studies. Initially he worked as Louis Féraud's assistant and later he became Paco Rabanne's right arm. He learnt the accuracy of forms and the pure elegance of style from Rabanne. He presented his first Collection in 2000, having researched the selection of materials, particularly leather and Plexiglas. The following year, Suzy Menkes, a big name of the *International Herald Tribune*, named him as one of the most interesting German designers of the fashion world. He presented his Collections during the ready-to-wear week in Paris. For the 2003 Collection he selected the German actress Alexandra Kemp to be among his models.
(*Maddalena Fossati*)

Grazia Women's weekly published by Mondadori, directed by Carla Vanni. Published for the first time in 1938 after the transformation of *Sovrana*, a successful periodical for bourgeois ladies of the Fascist little Italy, into an exclusive women's weekly. It was decidedly new, aggressive, and popular. Raul Radice guided this transformation, but he was later taken over by several directors, among whom was Giorgio Mondadori, until the 1960s. However, the modern periodical that had for many years maintained its leadership position for many years in the women's magazines sector (as well as the established competitors *Amica* and *Anna*, Rizzoli and *Gioia*, Rusconi), only developed in the course of the 1960s and 1970s under the direction of Renato Olivieri and Pier Boselli. These were the years of the big editorial successes and large circulation figures. In February 1978, with the arrival of Carla Vanni as the magazine's director, a new restyling season started. The quick and continuous mood changes of the female world and of the traditional reference target, in particular, prompt to a manic attention to the magazine's look and contents. In practice, there's no year without some small adjustments, small «make-up» operations, graphic innovations, entry of new columns and exit of old ones in an indefatigable research of harmony with the public. The magazines acquires new pages, the news conquers the first pages, new dossiers and reportages make their appearance as well as spaces and suggestions concerning health and look. Until February 1997, when the umpteenth revolution (the last one in the order of times) changes again the content and look of Grazia, introducing a new graphic and changing it format and technical characteristics.

Greasers Youth bands who introduced street style, a clothing style. La Honda, California, 1965: the meeting between Ginsberg, Ken Kesy and his Merry Pranksters with Sonny Barger, head of the Hell's Angels, is remembered as one of the most productive intersections in the history of counter-culture. On that occasion, bikers took acid for the first time during a party that lasted two days and concluded with alliances. The Grateful Dead, presented in a embryo formation among the Merry Pranksters, would always employ the Hell's Angels as their bodyguards in the future. Janis Joplin officially inherited them often wondering why and the Stones, on the advice of Jerry Garcia, successfully used the English contingent for the concert dedicated to Brian Jones in Hyde Park in 1969. They tried again, some months after the conclusion of the American tour, and the result was the Altamont mess. When the Angels arrived in La Honda they were already very different from the Bikers triumphantly embodied by Brando: Kenneth Anger, in Scorpio Rising, had already given a more updated version. Their style became decidedly baroque with chains, fringes, and studs. On the leather jackets, whose sleeves were sometimes cruelly removed, there were an enormous number of badges and signs that were very often ideologically worrying. Besides the Hell's Angels, other bands included the Satan's Slaver, Diablos, and Road Rats. All of them had a ostensibly demoniac behavior and they repeated their famous motto, "Better your sister in a brothel, than your brother riding a Japanese" (meaning a bike, of course!), while riding their Harley, Norton or Guzzi bikes. (*Maurizio Vetrugno*)

Great China Wall Vintage clothing brand founded by Alfredo Settimio, who moved from Italy in 1989 to start a new professional life in Los Angeles. Ten years later he put his idea into practice of transforming second-hand clothes into unique pieces using prints, embroideries, and decorations. His first clients are his closest friends, who prompt Alfredo to continue his inexhaustible research of interesting garments in American and world small markets and shops. The name of his brand derives from the first adjustments made with sequins and crystal small beads on a souvenir T-shirt of the Great China Wall. In May 2001, he opened his store in Melrose Avenue. There were approximately 50,000 unique pieces, hand-manufactured by a family of Mexicans working for Settimio. They could also be purchased through orders by fax or in person in the other stores in Los Angeles, Milan, Paris, and by Henry Bendel in New York. Settimio's jackets and pants are the favorite whim of divas such as Nicole Kidman. (*Pierangelo Mastantuono*)

Greenaway Kate (1864-1903). English illustrator. Her drawings for fairytales and children's books not only imposed themselves on fashion styles in the collective imagery of the Victorian society, but also inspired the fashion of the late 19th century. The capped bonnets, large décolleté blouses, and Empire-style dresses with wide collars and big swaying sleeves were distinctive elements of her style.

Greene Milton H. (1922-1985). American photographer. He started working at the very young age of 14. He immediately aligned himself with the world of fashion photography characterized by refinery and former rigor, which has points of reference in *Vogue* and *Harper's Bazaar*. He was assistant to Maurice Baumann, Eliot Elisofon, and, most importantly, Louise Dahl-Wolfe from whom he learnt his almost manic attention to atmosphere and to the use of delicate color in warm shades. His portraits are also famous, in particular those of Marilyn Monroe.

Greer Howard (1886-1974). Stylist and costume designer. He dressed Ingrid Berman (*Spellbound*), Katherine Hepburn, Ginger Rogers, and Sylvia Sidney on screen and Shirley Temple on her wedding day. An eclectic creator, he was born in Nebraska and started his career at the fashion house, Lucille. After moving to Europe, he became a theater costume designer. In Paris he worked for Molyneux and Poiret. In the early 1920s he became director of the costume department at Famous Players-Lasky (formerly Paramount Pictures), where he designed costumes for the stars Pola Negri and Nita Baldi in *The Ten Commandments* (1923). The work with Paramount Pictures made him very famous and convinced him to open a Hollywood fashion house in 1927. Greer continued his work in cinema collaborating with several studios at the same time.

Gregis Daniela (1959). Italian designer. Born in Fobbio, near Bergamo. In 1988 she collaborated with Naj Oleari Tomahawk and Team Ribbon. The following year she created the monograph and the coordinated image for the Radici Group. In 1992 she made the first double-face bags. In 1997 she presented a clothing Collection of her own, featuring the D'Ambrosio's inn. In December of the same year she invented the Advent Skirt 1999 (which was followed by those of 2000, 2001, and 2002). She always availed herself from her collaboration of figurative artists, drawing inspiration from the various arts.

Gregoire Lucille. Canadian milliner. She has been working in Marseilles since 1991, after graduating from the School of Fine Arts of Montreal and a long apprenticeship in large and small ateliers. She opened her own boutique and has created her own niche without giving in to the desire to astonish. She has perfected the art of intertwined straw, marine knots, and the use of leaves and flowers.

Gregoriana Roman atelier of high fashion that was highly trendy in the 1960s and 1970s. Located in Via Gregoriana 46, a few steps away from Piazza di Spagna, the atelier closed down a long time ago. It was established by Silvana Cerza who decided to open her own atelier after working for years as cutter and workshop director for Simonetta Visconti. She was also successful abroad, presenting her models in Germany, Austria, and the United States. Critics remember her robes-manteaux in red and blue shantung.

Gregory Pat. French company of women's ready-to-wear. It was established in Brest (Brittany) in the early 1960s by Jacques Jestin. In 1999 its turnover amounted to 23.5 billion liras, with a net profit of 1.6 billion and 100 employees. The styles are designed by the founder-owner's daughter, Maria Josée Jestin.

Grenadine Double-ply silk yarn, similar to organzine. The fabric obtained is light and transparent, particularly suitable for Summer clothing.

Grenson English shoe company. Established in 1866 by William Green who, after much experience in the shoe sector, decided to start his own company at the age of 31. He managed every aspect of production and the commercial side of the business. In 1874 William built the first factory in Rushed, where he lived with his family, and called it Greensyard. In 1885 his son, Charles, joined him in the management of the firm. At that time another plant was built that replaced the previous factory, and indeed increased its output in the following years. This new plant remained the company's main headquarters. William died in 1901 and Charles took over the direction of Green & Sons. In 1913 a new plant was opened in Irchester and Charles invented the Grenson brand, one of the first to be legally registered in London. In that period Grenson started to export up to half of its production to Commonwealth countries. In 1929 Charles' son, Sidney, became President of Grenson Shoes Ltd. In 1972 he was taken over by Heyden Green, whose contribution was significant in furthering exports to Italy and Japan. Today these exports still represent 50% of the company's turnover. In 1982 Terry Purlow joined the company, becoming its President in 1990. Grenson Shoes was and continues to be the pioneer of English shoe production.

(*Valeria Vantaggi*)

Gres Yarn in soft and velvet viscose, naturally shiny and silky to the touch.

Grès Pseudonym of Germaine Krebs (1903-1993). French designer. Her mastership in draping is unmatched, a real bearing structure of clothes entirely based on concentric pleating, degenerating spirals, intertwined, winding, or sculpted on the figure as by a geometrizing wind. Born in Paris, precious art studies, forced to quit sculpture, she transported the expressive sculpting into the models of a high fashion proudly rigorous and characterized by a sophisticated intelligence for women with classic tastes, allergic to the simple external appearance. Her favorite fabrics included jersey, thin wools, voluptuous silks, raw materials for evening dresses with their draping continuously reinvented, a result of an unmatched ambiguity, and a stubborn patience. Her coats had extraordinary asymmetry and she used intense oblique cutting. She started her career in 1933, making a partnership with Julie Barton and opening the fashion house, Alix. In 1941 the partnership split and she carried on alone, anagramming, for the boutique's sign, Grès, her husband's name, the painter Serge Cezrefkov. In 1960 she closed the boutique. An unusual personality in the world of the French couture, reserved but polemical, retreated in her look of exquisite elegance, bare but very elaborate, her designs brought international fame to her *maison*. She often attended the official manifestations of the *Chambre Syndicale du prêt-à-porter des couturiers et des createurs de mode*, wearing her characteristic turtledove turban, of which she was President from 1972 to 1991 and later honorary President.

(*Lucia Sollazzo*)

❑ 2003. The fashion house was reopened by the Japanese designer Koji Tatsuno.
❑ 2004, June. In Bourgoin-Jallien, France, an important retrospective dedicated to the work of Madame Gres by the Textile Museum.

A Grès dress as seen by Brunetta.

Grevi Mode Hat company. Established in 1875 the Grevi family has been operating in the sectors of straw and millinery for four generations. From the period of the weaving women, from whose hands came weaving as delicate a lace, from the Florence straw hats of the late 1800s, it gradually brought about more sophisticated and functional models both for men and women. From the soft panamas of D'Annunzio's style to the rigid straw hats of showmen like Spadaro or Maurice Chevalier. After the crisis of 1929, which inflicted a tough blow to export, the company turned to the domestic market. This activity was guided with ability and creativity for decades by Silvano and Alda Grevi, overcoming the difficult period of the war. Those were the years of *melousine* and satin felt hats, of exotic straws such as *parabuntal*, and of fabrics such as organza, velvet and straw *laizes*. During the 1960s, the company launched a hat in Tuscany lamb skin all over the world, without distracting from its traditional lines, which remained vital and precious. In the early 1980s, the Grevi Mode brand was launched, acquiring increased value in a reorganized company, both in the image and in the social structure, with the entry of the fourth generation.

(*Stefano Grassi*)

Griffe Jacques (1909-1996). French designer. The best student, the dauphin, the spiritual heir of Madeleine Vionnet, the queen of fluid oblique cutting and draping. She was already his mentor when he started his apprenticeship in the *maison* Mira of Toulouse, specialized in the reproduction of haute couture models. In 1935 he decided to move to Paris and he found a job beside Vionnet. He remained there until the closing of the atelier in 1939. The great dressmaker was at his side when, in 1948, he opened his own *maison* in Rue du Faubourg St. Honoré when, accepting Molyneux's heritage, he continued his business. Theirs was an extraordinary example of friendship and professional partnership. A super mastership in the oblique cutting, taste and inexhaustible fantasy in draping, tested on a wooden dummy, a gift by Mme Vionnet, before turning the fabrics into clothes, coats, and evening dresses. The designer, who retired in 1974, was also considered a master of colors.

Griffin Jeff (1967). British designer. After studied at St. Martin's School of Art in London, he completed apprenticeships with Gian Marco Venturi, Valentino, and Ferré. He started looking for a business partner before making his debut, and found Nick Hart. His fashion reinvents military uniforms and work clothes. In 1993 he launched the Griffin Laundry brand, later simplified to Griffin. He has been among the first to abandon the traditional runway show and to use the Internet. He has collaborated with Hugo Boss and Mandarina Duck. In 2001 he opens a store with a many windowed front sin West London.

Grima Andrew (1920). Jeweler. He interprets abstract expressionism in jewelry. Born in Rome and now an adopted Londoner. During the 1960s he started an avant-garde production combining gold and precious stones in tourmalines, opals, baroque pearls, raw quartzes, and exotic shells. In 1966 he opened a store in Jermyn Street. In 1970 he was bestowed with the *Royal Warrant* to the art.

Grimaldi-Giardina Roman high fashion house. Established in 1996 by Antonio Grimaldi (1970) and Silvio Giardina (1968). The two young designers have presented their Collections three times in Rome at different times of the year than the other fashion houses, starting in January 1999. Their designs inspire lightness and elasticity in their lines, while the colors are reminiscent of the transparency of water and never ostentatious.

Grisaille Combed fabric in light wool, usually utilised in the manufacturing of men's suits, but also used in womenswear. Its typical pattern is obtained with white and black threads which, all together, produce a grey effect. Indeed, the fabric's name comes from the French word *gris*.

Grosgrain A coarse-grained fabric with cords more marked than that of poplin, usually with a warp made of silk, rayon or synthetic fibers and a cotton weft. Can be woven in full or ribbon widths and used as decoration and trimmings on clothing and hats.

Groult Nicole (1887-1967). French dressmaker. She became devoted to the profession because of her illustrious family relationship: she was Paul Poiret's sister. However, she was an excellent designer and autonomous in her style, helped by the artistic talent of her husband, André Groult. Her business lasted longer than that of her brother due to her cautiousness and thriftiness. She closed her fashion house in the early 1960s.

Groupe Saint Liévin The group began from the merging of four textile industries, controlled since 1986 by the Holding Texinvest: the Saint Liévin spinning mill (1921), Ets M. Caultiez & Delaoutre (1879), Ets Paul Bonte (1910), and Sté Nouvelle Textile Saint Maclon (1946). The Saint Liévin spinning mill produced fantasy spun threads for knitwear, but also for weaving. Its structure was a continuous cycle starting with preparation, carding, and combing of the fiber. This large group (617 workers in 1999) originally dates back to wool weaving, but over the course of time it has transformed and expanded to include the development of new fibers, with continual investments in new machinery in the fantasy threads sector. Export has increased by about 40% with the production of 5.5 million kilograms.

Groves Andrew (1968). British designer. Born in Maidstone, Kent. He worked as Alexander McQueen's assistant before completing his fashion studies at St. Martin's School of Art in London in 1997. During the end of the course's exhibition he distinguished himself for his irreverent and, for many people, impudent models. He immediately opened his atelier and, within a few seasons, had earned himself the title of new enfant terrible of London fashion. His aggressive and sexy style follows into the steps of the maestro, McQueen.

Gruau René (1909). French-Italian illustrator. Born in Rimini, son of the Earl, Alessandro Zovagli Ricciardelli delle Caminate and Maria Gruau. He chose his mother's name as his pseudonym. The youngest child of a large family and becoming an orphan at the young age of 15, he quit high school to find a job that would allow him to be independent. His talent at drawing allowed him to earn his living. In 1926 he met Vera Rossi Lodomez, director of the magazine *Lidel*, with which he collaborated until 1930. Problems at the magazine urged him to move to Paris, where he began to collaborate with *Fémina*. From 1937 to 1938 he worked as a designer in Holland, England, and France. The magazine *Marie Claire* hired him during the Second World War. For Gruau this was the occasion to gain experience in illustrations for fashion, *feuilleton* (supplements), and short tales. After the Liberation, *Fémina*, *Vogue*, *L'Officiel de la Couture*, and *Harper's Bazaar* requested his collaboration. His style was successful, characterized by a surprising minimalism. The obvious reason was to simplify the printing process. He designed large surfaces of one single color with a nervous yet precise line and recurrent photographic themes, such as horizontal and vertical stripes and squares. Gruau particularly went along with the play of Chinese shadows: He attained the peak of his career in the period of the New Look. He illustrated the famous book *Cucina cucita a mano* (Hand-sewn Kitchen) for Dior. He designed for Jacques Fath and Balmain. In Italy, he collaborated with *Novità* and with the official magazine of the textile sector (*Trasformazione Tessile*, translated as Textile Transformation). He gradually abandoned fashion illustration to dedicate himself to advertising. He worked on the promotion of a perfume launched by Dior, and did the same for perfumes by Balmain, Griffe, Fath, and Elizabeth Arden. He also worked for cosmetic houses (Pajor, Rouge-Baiser, and Peggy Sage), fabric manufacturers (Dormeuil, Rodier, and Fred), fashion accessories (Bally, Perrin gloves, and Montezin hats), house linen (Scandale, Lejaby, and Valisère), and ready-to-wear (Blizzard and M. Griffon). With his posters for the Lido and Moulin Rouge created after 1956, he began to invade Paris. In Italy, his most celebrated advertising campaigns remain those created for Bemberg's fabrics and the *Schu-Schu* perfume by Schuberth. He created Laura Biagiotti's logo and matching images. He also created the image of the Academy of Costume and Fashion in Rome where, as professor, he held annual seminars for

Drawing by René Gruau (Prints Collection A. Bertarelli, Milan).

fashion and advertising graphics students. His drawings have become part of fashion's cultural heritage. Many books have been dedicated to him. (*René Gruau* by Joëlle Chariau; *Gruau*, Hercher 1989, and the monograph published by Franco Maria Ricci). There have been numerous important photographic exhibitions dedicated to his work, organized in museums and galleries across the entire world. Maria Pezzi, in her biographic book *Una vita dentro la moda* (A Life Inside Fashion), recalls, "I found a shy, reserved, and lonely person in his studio in Rue Jean Goujon with Liberty windows. On tables and scattered on the floor, there were numberless drawings with his monogram G, surmounted by a star. A sort of poetic brand. He told me that one day a small stain of ink had fallen on his signature and he had camouflaged it turning the stain into a star. His work was genial."

(*Bonizza Giordani Aragno*)

Drawing by René Gruau (Prints Collection A. Bertarelli, Milan).

Grumbach Didier (1937). President of the Union Federation of French Fashion. His career started in 1963 when he took on the responsibility of his family's company, Cerf Mandés-France, operating in the field of manufacturing established by his grandfather. He decided to shift the company's direction towards ready-to-wear high fashion, especially in partnership with Saint-Laurent. Later, as strategist for the company Créateurs & Industriels, established in 1971, he encouraged young designers, such as Ossie Clark, Jean Charles de Castelbajac, and Emmanuelle Khahn. In 1978 he became President of the company, Thierry Mugler. As both industrialist and in his institutional role, he has always been very attentive to the emerging names of fashion. In 1993 he published *Histoires de la Mode* (Editions du Seuil). Since 1989 he has been Director of Courses at the French Institute of Fashion.

Grunge Spontaneous youth movement and style, which made its debut with the Autumn 1991 Collection by Perry Ellis, in the official language of fashion: flannel shirts, secondhand Levi's, sweaters, and unkempt T-shirts. It comprises the typical wardrobe that a bohemian affected by recession and a student away from home have donned for years, which suddenly became fashionable. The reason why lies in the commercial success of music bands, such as Nirvana, Breeders, and Smashing Pumpkins who, in the rock scene, removed the glam metal wave of the headbanger groups, such as Poison and Guns'n'Roses, exactly as the Ramones had done with all the glitter bands 15 years before. Generally speaking, the rock'n'roll attitude had been focused on the identification with the male prototype of the black rebel for decades. From the pervasive influence of blues in the 1960s to the punks who would identify themselves with the reggae of Rastatarians, Grunge does not escape the trend. The generation of teens who had grown up in the shadow of suburban malls in the outskirts of town fervently imitates the psychopathic cool of the gangsta rap. As a phenomenon, Grunge brought to light a generation of defeatists whose main desire was to survive in society's hollow spaces. Disillusion was the new motto. A generation attracted to secondhand objects and to a matching geniality proclaimed dressing down to be a new, interesting code. From the female perspective, the style attitude of new anti-stars, such as Courtney Love and Kathleen Hanna, were immediately taken up by fashion designers, first of all by Anna Sui and Marc Jacob. They both translated the impulses into ready-to-wear, making large use of knitwear, patchwork, and satin mini dresses/petticoats. These designs were re-proposed in thousands of versions by many designers for the following three years.

(*Maurizio Vetrugno*)

Gruppo Botto Wool manufacturer. Established in 1876, the wool factory Botto Giuseppe e Figli of Biella is one of the most significant Italian wool companies. It forms part of the Botto Group with 1,200 employees and a turnover of 300 billion liras. The wool factory alone employs about 600 people with a turnover of about 160 billion and production of 5 million meters per year. The primary manufactured textile products are wool, silk, and cashmere blends, containing microfibers introduced to add some innovation to these already refined fabrics. From the most classic styles to jerseys, 60% of Botto's fabrics are manufactured for the womenswear sector with the remaining 40% made for the menswear sector. The companies Boglietti, Cascami Seta, and Botto Paola all belong to the Botto Group.

Gruppo Carma One of the historical conglomerate of the knitwear district of Carpi, established in 1946 by Maria Martinelli, a figurehead of local business. The start of mechanization of manufacturing processed is credited to Martinelli. Her factory was among the first to introduce electronics and to make an investment in technological innovation. After producing knitwear for several brands and companies, in 1975 the Group created its own brand, I Maschi, for men's sportswear and casual clothing. Shortly afterwards a line was created in collaboration with Jean-Charles de Castelbajac, which was a total look in men and women's clothing. More recently a brand was launched, aiming at a young and trendy clientele, named Simultaneous. The various companies of the Group are located in an area within 322 miles from the Carpi's headquarters. They produce about 500,000 pieces a year for a total turnover of more than 40 billion liras. 77% of the turnover is generated from export to Japan, USA, Europe, and Korea.

Gruppo Colombo Silk company with two offices in the Como area. It is a integrated organization, active in the various production phases, such as weaving, dyeing, and finishing. Its technology is typical of a silk factory, creating products such as silk, viscose, acetate, polyesters, nylon, Lycra blended with wool, cotton, linen (plain, dyed, and jacquard) with manifold possibilites of product personalization, both at weaving and finishing levels. The production presents a wide line of articles in an optic of a complete look and can be used in various sectors of the clothing market such as shirts, jackets, and pants with a large variety of matching coordinates.

Gruppo Conti The Italian market leader in knitwear. The Group produces 12,000 jerseys a day with the brands Bramante, Francesca, and Royal Wool Company, controlled by the Compagnia Finaziaria Conti (Co.Fin.Co.) of Sansepolcro. The company was created by Angela Carlotto (1919), from Belluno, who first moved to Milan to work in a spinning mill and, on the eve of the Second World War, at the age of 19 to Eritrea in Asmara, where she started her work with a single knitwear machine. In 1950 she returned to Italy with her husband and business partner, Elio Conti and their children Renzo and Cesare. They settled in Sansepolcro and started the business again from nothing, made determined only from her experience and her passion for the work. The Conti Group has an average annual turnover of 100 billion liras.

Gruppo Dondi Leading company in the production of knitwear fabrics. It started out as Dondi Jersey in the early 1970s in Fossoli, Modena because of the intuition and passion for knitwear of Edda and Lauro Dondi. They are now supported by their children Lorella, with her husband Guido Capelli, and Stefano Dondi. The company transformed into the Dondi Group in the 1980s. The Group distinguishes itself in excellent and unique creativity, a result of deep experience together with research and experimentation with avant-garde technologies. The entire productive cycle takes place within the company from design to distribution, according to a philosophy of superior global quality that involves every department, from the styling office to the employees and sales. There are four lines: Dondi

Jersey, Punto Tessile, All Over, and the recent addition, Tecno&Logico for high performance of comfort and functionality. The company is in close contact with the greatest Italian and international designers. Its Collections, visible also in the Milanese showroom in Foro Bonaparte, are presented at the principal fairs such as Première Vision, Moda In, and Ideacomo.

(*Silvia Martinenghi*)

Gruppo Lineapiù It is a world leader in the manufacturing of knitwear yarns. Established in 1975 in Capalle di Prato, the Group's success is thanks to a wide range of innovative products manufactured with precious and highly technological raw materials. The Group has created a yarn called Relax in carbon fiber, which is capable of blocking electromagnetic waves. The spinning combines the experience of wool with that of cotton. The Group consists of 15 factories in Italy with more than 1,000 employees. It has an annual turnover of more than 150 million Euro, which is equal to 10 million kilograms of yarn, divided into the four product lines: Lineapiù, Filoré, Filclass, and Cotonificio R. Ferrari. The latter line enlarged the production to include also weaving. In 1998 the Group acquired further plants – a knitwear company and a manufacturing factory, which designs and produces Collections under the name of Lineapiù System. In this sector, the debut was in partnership with Samsonite. In July 1999 at Pitti Filati the Group presented hyper-technologic fabrics, Cork (the wool weighs 30% less that the traditional yarn), Lac (a lacquered yarn), Bobol (Winter cotton with silver highlights), Jewel (yarn with Swarovski crystals). Giuliano Coppini is the President of the Group.

Gruppo Nadini – Maglificio di Vignola This knitwear group began about 50 years ago in Vignola, near Modena. In the 1970s the expansion of technical capability from solely knitwear to manufacturing determined the development of the Mondrian brand, which won the contract to manufacture Alitalia's female staff uniforms in the late 1990s. In the early 1980s the collaboration began with Gianfranco Ferré, in the form of a world license for the production and distribution of his knitwear and sportswear for men and women. Since 1993 the company has been entirely under the control of Giacomo Bizzini and his wife, Mirella Solignani Bizzini. In 1996 the Group's corporate name became Group Nadini. During the 1990s important license agreements were signed with Fendi and the American designer, Richard Tyler. The Nadini brand also has its own women's knitwear line. The turnover currently amounts to 67 million Euro for about 800,000 manufactured garments, three-quarters of which are exported. The company has 230 employees and about 1,200 employees in associated industries.

Gruppo Sicem The group is formed from four companies: Sima Fashion, Marchese Coccapani, Iteco, and Les Griffes Abbigliamento. It employs over 400 workers. The group specializes in the production of outer knitwear and in knitwear manufacturing and weaving. Established in 1971 in Soliera, Modena by Gianfedele and Silvana Ferrari who still manage the group together with their son Giorgio. In the early 1990s, the group acquired the brands Codice, Nani Bon, Giunco, and Sevres. Besides its own production, the group also sells to the large distribution chains as well as supplying to other Italian and international manufacturers.

Gruppo Sixty Italian group of brands concentrated on young fashion. Established and directed by Wicky Hassan, the group currently comprises Sixty and Sixty Active Spa with 12 branch offices worldwide and partnerships with other companies. In 1983 Hassan opened a clothing store called Energie in Via del Corso in Rome, which proposed a strong image connected to the expressive culture of that time (the dawn of street style and graffiti). After a few seasons the brand became an innovative jeanswear Collection distributed all over Italy. In 1989 Sixty Spa was established. A year later, Energie was accompanied by a new line, Sixty, and immediately afterwards the first exclusively women's line was launched, Miss Sixty. In 1992 the first branch office, Sixty USA, was opened. In 1993 the brand Murphy & Nye was bought and Sixty Active Spa. was created. In 1999 the Sixth flagship store was inaugurated in Covent Garden in London. It was the first in a long series of which there were more than 100 single brand sales points worldwide in 2003.

(*Ruben Modigliani*)

❑ 2003, September. Miss Sixty opened in Via Montenapoleone, Milan. The brand's expansion continues after consistently increasing its turnover, going from 490 million Euros in 2001 to 570 million Euros in 2002. The target in the near future is penetration of the US market. Soon three new stores were planned in Los Angeles (two Energie and one Miss Sixty) and one in San Francesco.
❑ 2003, October. The fourth American Miss Sixty store was opened in San Francesco. It is the 65th in the world.
❑ 2003, December. Turnover of 650 million Euros and net profit amounting to 5% of that. 35 million Euros in investments, 65% production in Italy and 35% abroad. Two new branch offices have opened, Sixty Brazil and Sixty South America. The style division is guided by Wicky Hassan, who follows the brands Energie, Sixty, Miss Sixty, Murphy & Nye, Killah, Dake9, Ayor, and Decauville.
❑ 2004, January. Continuation of the expansion strategy in South America with the opening of a flagship store in Buenos Aires. This opening follows the ones in Santiago del Chile, Ride de Janeiro, Sao Paulo, and Santa Fé.
❑ 2004, March. Killah, the young brand of the group, inaugurated a flagship store in Porta Ticinese, Milan.
❑ 2004, October. The group signed a license agreement with American Coty Inc. for the launch of a series of perfumes branded Miss Sixty.
❑ 2004, November. The group launched the new lines Energie and Miss Sixty Junior, clothing and accessories Collections for a very young target, 4-14 years. Continuation of the strategy already started with the brand juniors of Murphy & Nye, Refrigiwear, and Decauville.
❑ 2004, December. Markus Capone, co-founder and general manager of Miss Sixty Germany, became the new general manager of the business in Asia. In Germany he was taken over by Joerg Korfhage.
❑ 2004, December. The group attained a turnover of 640 million Euros with production of 22,000,000 pieces.
❑ 2005, February. Coccinelle and Miss Sixty signed a three-year license agreement for the production and distribution of bags branded Miss Sixty, designed by Giampiero Cartia.
❑ 2005, February. The group acquired the American brand Refrigiwear for the European and Japanese markets. In America, the brand continues to be produced by Refrigiwear Inc.
❑ 2005, April. Debut of the women's line Waxy, a Collection targeted at 20-35 years. It is in a lower market segment than the group's other lines, presenting mini-Collections with four issues per year.
❑ 2005, July. Renewal of the license agreement between Marcolin and the Sixty Group until December 2009 for the global design, production, and distribution of glasses and sunglasses for Miss Sixty Glasses line. (*Dario Golizia*)

Gruppo Zegna Baruffa A famous name worldwide whose origins are deeply rooted in the Biella area, by now a secular tradition. The great turning point occurred in 1974 when Giorgio and Giulio Zegna Baruffa created Zblb, incorporating the prestigious Lane Borgosesia established in 1850. In the 1980s, the product symbolic of the company is called Cashwool, a very pure wool as soft as cashmere and as shiny as silk. There isn't a knitwear factory that has not heard of the group and every spinning mill tries to imitate its yarns. Expansion occurred in 1990, according to a precise strategy of producing fantasy and classic yarns for outer knitwear. Research and innovation continue to characterize the Collections. A new course of business started during the 2000-2001 season with the introduction of three different lines (Baruffa, B Active, and B Exclusive) and direct branch offices in Hong Kong, New York, and Tokyo. In the latter part of the 20th century, production was around 10 million kilograms, using about 90% of extra-fine merino wools and, for the remaining part, noble fibers. The export quota touched

60%. Zblb is a family company guided using managerial criteria. It has seven productive plants.

G-Star Raw Denim Brand and streetwear company based in Amsterdam. The military inspiration pants of the company were introduced in the American market in 1998. They are characterized by a particular manufacturing technique that sees the use of torn cotton. In January 2003 the company was among the exhibitors at the 64th edition of Pitti Immagine. G-Star now has a branch office in New York and a showroom in Los Angeles. Penetration has also been strong in the Far East and in Germany, where there are five showrooms in total. G-Star Italy has its head office in Genoa.

Gtr Established in 1993 in the industrial area of Isernia (Molise) by Remo Perna, brother of Tonino Perna, founder of the Itierre holding. It owns the brands Soviet (Sportswear) and Jois & Jo (women's ready-to-wear). It is very active in the licensed production of casual and sportswear for a medium-high segment, distributed all over the world. For example, Helmut Lang Jeans, Anglomania by Vivienne Westwood, and Krizia World. In 1998 the group's turnover amounted to 120 billion Lira, with 200 employees and 4,000 workers in related industries.

Guabello Wool factory established in 1815 in Mongrando di Biella. It belongs to the Marzotto group. It has about 200 employees, achieves a turnover in excess of more than 24 million Euros, and produces more than 1 million meters of precious fabrics every year. In the last few years, modern machinery has been accompanied by the continuing use of artisans' techniques. Royal flannels are passed manually twice through giant 18th century fulling stocks. Recently the company has attained international leadership in the sectors of Saxony, combed flannels, cashmeres, and supers 100, 120, and 150s up to the exclusive super 180s, weighing only 200 g per linear meter, obtained from a yarn count of 2-150,000. A young technical and creative staff tests unusual solutions such as the cashmere-yak blend, created from cashmere and New Zealand wool of 17 microns. Among the precious materials, recent introductions have been vicuna and guanaco, Cites certified, which guarantees legal shearing that does not harm the animals.

(*Emanuela Fontana*)

Gualtieri Anna (1921). Journalist. She has managed *Arianna*, *Arbiter*, and *Rakam*. She started her journalist career at *Oggi* in the immediate post-war period. In 1954 the former director, Edilio Rusconi, temporarily became the editor and director of *Gente*, called her to the direction of *Gioia*. In 13 years, she increased the circulation from 60,000 to 600,000 copies. In 1968 she worked for Mondadori where she invented and directed *Duepiù*, before taking on the direction of *Arianna*. In 1970 she was managing editor of *Fabbri* and in 1980 she returned to Rusconi as director of the men's magazines *Arbiter* and *Gioielli/Griff*. In 1987 she was called to rescue *Rakam*, where she brought back the former circulation standards. In 1998 she was appointed to the editorial direction of Rusconi periodicals' sector.

Guanaco Wool and fur of a species of camel native to Patagonia. Its hair is brown-reddish, less precious than llama's. It was also commercialized as alpaca, with which it shares several characteristics, but it does have the same nobility levels.

Guariento Daniela (1973). Italian fashion designer. Born in Milan. In 1999 she was awarded the Infil Award, the prize for young underwear designers that created by Sponso for Infil, an Italian company leader of the sector. The award consists a scholarship for 5 million liras and an exhibition of the winning Collections at the International Conference for Parisian Lingerie in January 2000. In 1994 she graduated from the Marangoni Institute of Milan and started a long apprenticeship. After collaborating with two style consultancy firms, she worked as model maker in the artisan dressmaker's workshop of Angela Piatti Zardin. From 1995 to the end of 1997, she was at the Reality of Gigi Monti-Basile (designer, graphic, fabric selector, sample controller, and casting agent for advertising campaigns). In February 1998 she worked as a freelancer (for the positioning of embroideries and materials on garments, her resume says) at Prada for the women's Autumn-Winter Collection.

Gucci Italian company that originally specialized in handcrafted leather goods. It was established in 1921 by Guccio Gucci (1881-1953), son of a straw manufacturer who moved first to Paris and then to London at a very young age. During his time in London he worked as an elevator boy at the Savoy Hotel and gained his taste for beauty and elegance. On his return to Florence, after working for the firm Franzi of Milan, he opened his first small workshop in Via della Vigna 7 and Via del Parione 11, creating traveling and saddlery articles. In 1932 he moved to the larger rooms of Via della Vigna Nuova 11. Five years later he produced bags, suitcases, and sport items in his own artisan's productive plant along Lungarno Guicciardini. The first successes were linked to horse-riding items. Soon afterwards, the stirrup and bit became the symbols of the Florentine house. Sales were high enough for the company to open a new store outside of its hometown. In 1938, Gucci arrived in Rome with a store in Via Condotti. In those difficult years of autarchy, fantasy contrasted with the lack of raw materials, with the introduction of materials such as hemp, linen, jute, and the famous bamboo, which were less expensive than the usual skins and added to the *griffe*'s originality. In 1939, the passage from a one-man company to a limited responsibility company marked the official entry of Guccio's four children, Aldo, Vasco, Ugo, and Rodolfo to the business. In 1951, the boutique was opened in Via Montenapoleone 5 in Milan. The 1950s represented an important time in the life of the company. The old Florentine artisan workshop of Lungarno Guicciardini was moved to the rooms of Palazzo Settimanni, in Via delle Caldaie, today a very modern showroom. The distinctive feature of the brand became a ribbon inspired by the saddle's girth, in different sizes, in wool or cotton, in green-red-green colors for natural leather articles and in blue-red-blue for the colored skins. In the same year, it was decided that the company, which had by then achieved European recognition, would locate in a more steady way abroad and became one of the figureheads of Made in

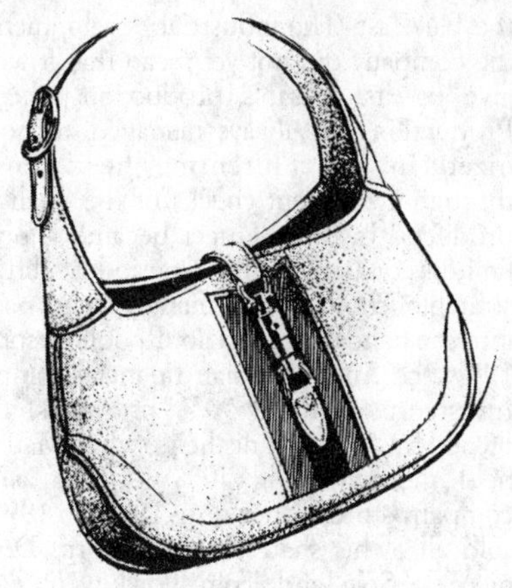

Gucci. A classic bag model.

Italy in the United States. Aldo Gucci opened the first American sale point in 58th Street in New York. In the meantime, the products destined to become classics were consolidated: the first bag with the bamboo handle (1947), the loafers with clamp (1952-53), the *Flora* scarf (1967) created by Rodolfo Gucci, and *Accornero* for Grace Kelly. Women with an unmatched style, such as Audrey Hepburn, Jackie Kennedy, Maria Callas, the Duchess of Windsor, chose Gucci. These are the years in which the company decided to adopt the logo GG to indicate the initials of the founder, as a decoration motif of a cotton fabric, called GG Canvas, with which bags, small leather goods, cases, objects, and the first clothing articles were realized. Thanks to the opening of new sales points in London (1961), Palm Beach (1961), Paris (1963), and Beverly Hills (1968), and to the creativity of production, the brand obtains meaningful consents in the most important world markets. After the great flood of 1966 in Florence, Gucci left the rooms of Via della Vigna and moved to Via Tornabuoni. The production potential developed with the opening, in 1971, of a new plant in Scandicci, near Florence. This allowed a further expansion of the direct network of shops during the 1970s – Chicago (1971), Tokyo (1972), and Hong Kong (1974) – and marked the beginning of a larger presence in the Far East. The industrial development of the company did not yet mean that it would give up its artisan's production schemes. Production was always managed and organized in the Florentine headquarters through a stringent checks of the quality of products. In 1982 Gucci became a public limited company. After a period of difficult strategic choices, the management passed into the hands of Maurizio, Rodolfo's son. In 1989, the Anglo-Arabian financial company Investcorp acquired 50% of shares, once owned by Aldo and his heirs, while Maurizio held the remaining 50% as well as the company's presidency until 1993. In 1993 he sold all of his shares to Investcorp. Domenico de Sole and Tom Ford were called upon to manage the relaunch of the brand. In 1995 Domenico De Sole, already responsible for Gucci America since 1984, was appointed President and Chief Executive Officer of Gucci Group N.V. In 1990 the American designer, Tom Ford, was made Creative Director for all production, the redesign of the brand's identity. Thanks to this remix of classic and modern, of tradition and innovation, the new style of the Florentine house conquered the world market. The brand returned as a leader in the sector of leather goods. The management also took a risk by launching men and women's clothing Collections, which immediately achieved great success with the critics and the general public. Between 1995 and 1996, Gucci became the first true Italian public company with the selling of the entire capital stock in the stock exchanges of New York and Amsterdam. In early 1999, Bernard Arnault with Lvmh conquered 34.4% of the capital, buying up shares in the financial market and acquiring the stock parcel owned by Prada and other investors, for a total investment of 1.5 million dollars. At this attempt to enter into the company's management, Gucci's supervisory board opposed, entrusting the management defense to the general manager Domenico De Sole. After the adoption of a new share plan for the employees, which granted them an option to buy Gucci's shares as owned by Lvmh, a new strategic alliance was approved in March 1999 with the French group Pinault-Printemps-Redoute (Ppr) for the creation of a multibrand hub in the world industry of luxury. In change of a quota of 40%, Ppr has invested 2.9 billion dollars in Gucci to finance the group's growth through acquisitions. The first opportunity came along in July 1999 with the acquisition of Sanofi Beauté, a company that controls Yves Saint-Laurent and an empire of perfumes, from Roger&Gallet to those of Krizia, Fendi, and Oscar de la Renta. While Lmvh continues its legal battle, independent shareholders gathered in an assembly have approved Domenico De Sole as the new partner, not only as general manager. Gucci closed the first semester of 1999 with a net profit of 225 billion Liras, a growth of 68% compared to the first six months of 1998.

(*Aurora Fiorentini*)

❑ In the marathon of Milano Moda Donna, a meeting with Gucci is not to be missed. When you say Gucci one immediately thinks of Tom Ford, the designer with an unquestionable charisma and undeniable personal charm, of which he is completely aware. He continues to proceed along itineraries of style very congenial for him. A master of uncontrolled seduction, his Collections should be read as a refined Kamasutra also for men's fashion trends. His Collections created for the Summer of 2003 were memorable because of this, with an eroticism pushed to the limit, which he himself defined as "vaguely pornographic" with explicit sex messages written even on the slippers. Pretty man or rock star, he is without a doubt a man who cannot go unnoticed, even when he wants to be as classic as *The Great Gatsby*. For women, the game is even easier and more explicit. A lady moved by naughty ideas, donning intriguing clothes that capture the public, especially in black, a color loved for its arrogant authenticity.

(*Lucia Mari*)

❑ 1999, November. Gucci group acquired 70% of the Calzaturificio Sergio Rossi, a women's shoe brand of the high segment of the market, for a value of 96 million dollars. The remaining 30% is still in the hands of the Rossi family. Sergio Rossi continues to play the role of Creative Director, while Massimo Braglia, a Gucci manager, is to be the Chief Executive Officer.

❑ 1999. The company closes the year 1999 with a turnover of 1,236 million dollars with a growth of 19% as to 1998. The net profit amounts to 330 millions, +69.4%.

❑ 2000, January. Tom Ford is appointed Creative Director of Yves Saint-Laurent Couture, a role that adds to the previous ones he has in Gucci. His role is to define the image and market's positioning of the YSL brand, plus all the communications' activities. In February, Yves Saint-Laurent Couture acquired 66% of Mendes. The acquisition allowed the direct control of aspects concerning the development, production, and distribution of YSL Women's ready-to-wear.

❑ 2000, May. Month full of operations for the Group owned by Ppr. First of all, it reaches an agreement with Schweizerhall Holding AG to acquire Boucheron International, historical house of jewelry and watches, whose turnover amounts to about 85 million dollars. Secondly, it announced a new joint venture, 65% controlled, with FJ Benjamin Holdings Ltd., for the exclusive distribution of Gucci, Yves Saint-Laurent Couture, and Sergio Rossi Products in Singapore, Malaysia, and Australia. This allows a superior direct control of the brands. FJ Benjamin had been Gucci's franchisee for 20 years, giving a fundamental contribution to develop the presence and fame of the group's brands in these markets.

❑ 2000, December. The group signed an agreement to develop the Alexander McQueen brand, which involved the acquisition of 51% of the business. Alexander McQueen continued to have complete creative independence.

❑ 2000, December. Gucci reached an agreement to acquire 85% of Bedat & Co., a Swiss company that operates in the sector of watches, established in 1996 in Geneva. Simone Bédat is the company's President, while her son Christian continues to be Chief Executive and Shareholder. In 2000 Bédat made a turnover of 20 million Francs, about 25 billion Liras.

❑ 2001, February. Gucci acquired Bottega Veneta, a luxury leather goods company located in Vicenza. Vittorio Moltedo remains general manager, Laura Moltedo creative director. The Venetian company had 32 single brand stores. Gucci acquired 66.67% through a capital stock's increase of 96.2 million dollars and the acquisition of preexistent shares for 60.6 million. The capital stock's increase is to be used to accelerate the brand's development.

❑ 2001, March. Reached an agreement to acquire 100% of Di Modolo Associates and Di Modolo, two Swiss companies specialized in watch design.

❑ 2001, April. Signed an agreement to develop the brand focused on the women's segment, clothing and accessories. The new business is owned both by Stella McCartney and Gucci Group. Stella McCartney is the creative director for the new company.

❑ 2001, June. YSL Beauté guarantees itself the license of perfumes and cosmetics branded Alexander McQueen. The agreement is to last ten years and controls the global development, production, and distribution. It guaranteed the world license to develop, produce, and distribute the new perfume, Ermenegildo Zegna, whose launch was expected for Spring 2000. In the year 2000, YSL Beauté registered a turnover of 536 billion dollars.

❑ 2001, July. Acquired 91% of Balenciaga. Nicolas Ghesquière, who holds the remaining 9%, continues to be the creative director. Through this operation, the Gucci group intended to accelerate the brand's development, focusing the strategies in the sectors of women's ready-to-wear, accessories, and fragrances. It acquired the full control of Australian JV through the acquisition of the remaining 35%, previously held by the partner FJ Benjamin Holdings Ltd.

❑ 2001, August. Signed an agreement to acquire 70% of the Calzaturificio Regain

Spa, a Marche's company producing 70,000 pairs of men's shoes annually. The company employed 50 people.
❑ 2001, October. YSL Beauté, the cosmetic division of the group, guaranteed the license to develop, produce, and distribute the perfumes and cosmetics branded Stella McCartney.
❑ 2001, November. Opening of the new Gucci flagship store in Moscow in Tretyakovsky Proyezd 1.
❑ 2002, January. The group is to no longer import skins from India as a form of protest for the lack of respect of Indians towards animals. This decision was probably influenced by Stella McCartney, supporter of animal rights and new designer for Gucci. The same decision had been taken by Timberland, Gap, Nike, and Reebok.
❑ 2002, March. Lvmh was in crisis after a drop in profits of about 1.56 billion Euros in 2001 and sold its shareholdings of its competitor Gucci.
❑ 2002, May. The group restored the control of activities in Taiwan by acquiring the quote held by the local partner Tasa Meng Corporation. Furthermore, it opened a three-floor space with a jewelry department in Taipei. Its look was decided, as always, by Tom Ford. Domenico De Sole declared that in 2002 he would invest 200 million Euros in new stores, 35 of which in Asia.
❑ 2002, July. In an interview in *Corriere Economia*, Domenico De Sole, Gucci's general manager, declared that notwithstanding the expected difficulties for 2002, the multibrand strategy, adopted in full agreement with Tom Ford, works. An improvement is foreseen for the second half of the year.
❑ 2002, July. Relaunching of Boucheron, the historical brand of jewelry. In 2005, Boucheron's boutiques are to increase from the current 10 stores to 60 worldwide. Until now Boucheron's turnover had been based more on fragrances than on jewelry and watches which, from 2002, on the contrary, were to represent 50% of the proceedings. The designer for the new Collection was Solange Azagury Partridge, born in Morocco, who has an successful boutique-workshop in London. Among the most precious jewels, there was a snakeskin set with 1,970 brilliants and browned gold jewels.
❑ 2002, September. The Milanese exhibition stressed legs with so tiny miniskirts that they could hardly be seen under the jackets, tight and fitted around the waist, or white silk jackets. Chinese-shaped minidresses, in pleated or embroidered silk, Kimono-shapes for strong colored jackets, and shorts or black lace underpants, worn in a ultra sexy way over bare breasts. The bamboo-handle bag is back, a Gucci must since the 1950s, but expressly big and sandal-décolleté in silver leather.
❑ 2002, October. Tom Ford, artistic director of Gucci, inaugurates boutiques all over the world. After Moscow, it was the turn of Manhattan, Paris, and Milan, all designed by him and the architect, Bill Sofield. The turnover registered a decline of 6.9% determined in particular by the crisis of leather goods. In early September the boutique of Madison Avenue was opened and, shortly afterwards, the third Paris boutique at number 60 of Avenue Montaigne, after those in Faubourg Saint Honoré and Rue Saint Honoré.
❑ 2002, November. Gucci, in collaboration with Sàfilo, launched two new lines of sunglasses, designed by Stella McCartney and Bottega Veneta. The unisex Collection by Bottega Veneta is designed by the Austrian designer, Tomas Maier. Stella McCartney proposed six models in different shapes and colors.
❑ 2002, November. Gucci's new megastore is in Via Montenapoleone, Milan. The old store, completely reorganized, at number 5, was enlarged with the new space acquired at number 7: four floors with four shop-windows and three entrances. In the basement, the women's Collections, at the first floor accessories and jewelry, while the two superior floors are dedicated to menswear.
❑ 2002, December. The third quarter of 2001 registered a drop in profits and

proceedings. The Gucci group, quoted at the stock exchange of Amsterdam and New York, registered proceedings amounting to 566.2 million dollars (-7.9% compared to 615 in 2000), an operative profit before amortizations of 80.9 (against 133) and a net profit of 56.3 (against 114.2). Proceedings are substantially steady (+11% with 1,660 against 1,642), while the net profit diminishes all the same (from 241.7 millions to 195.1). This decline has concerned especially the sales in markets based on tourism, such as New York, Hawaii, West Coast, and some European towns.

❑ 2002, December. Opening in Via Condotti, Rome, of the first store exclusively dedicated to jewelry and watches.

❑ 2003, March. Pinault-Printemps-Redoute (Ppr) has increased its shareholding in the Gucci capital from 59.6% to 61.06%, which it has been controlling since 2001. Serge Weinberg, President of Ppr, declared that he intended to raise the percentage to 70% by the end of 2003. Thanks to the acquisition agreement of 2001, the Parisian group committed to takeover the entire Gucci's capital stock at the prize of 101.5 million dollars by March 2004.

❑ 2003, March. The fiscal year 2002 closed with a drop of profits to 226.8 million Euros, against 312.5 of the previous year. Steady, on the contrary, proceedings at 2,544.3 millions against 2,565.1 in 2002.

❑ 2003, April. In the most elegant headquarters of Tokyo, Ginza, Gucci intended to create its Japanese headquarters and open a super luxury boutique. In Japan, where it owns seven sales points and 37 shop-in-shops, Gucci registered in 2002 proceedings amounting to 500 million Euros, about 20% of the total proceedings of the group.

❑ 2003, May. At the question: "How are you facing the crisis?," Domenico De Sole answered without hesitations, "Shaving costs. In 2001 and 2002 we invested 300 millions per year, more than two-thirds in new stores or to reorganize those we already had. This year capital costs are to be considerably reduced and the trend is to continue in the next two years, with a big benefit to the cash flow."

❑ 2003, June. The group acquired the total control of the join venture Gucci Singapore and Gucci Malaysia. De Sole comments, "Southeast Asia is a very important region and Singapore and Malaysia are more and more attractive. The total acquisition of our assets in those areas witness our commitment to further develop the Gucci brand in markets which we deem to have, in future, a good growth potential."

❑ 2003, July. In the first quarter of 2003, finished on April 30, the Gucci group registered proceedings amounting to 567.1 million Euros (compared to 607.6 millions of the same quarter of the previous year), while under the operative profile the first three months of the ongoing year marked a loss of 24.4 million Euros (against a profit of 20.4 millions). The only good performances, in terms of turnover, come from Bottega Veneta, Alexander McQueen, and Stella McCartney, with a countertendency leap of the turnover of 21.3% corresponding to 81.5 Euros. A good trend also for Japanese and Asian sales, besides Saint-Laurent. "For us," Domenico De Sole, President and general manager of the Gucci Group, commented "this has been the most difficult quarter we ever gone through."

❑ 2003, September. Claudio Paulich is the new general manager of the shoe's brand, Sergio Rossi. He replaced Massimo Braglia on the management since 1999.

❑ 2003, September. The French Group Pinault-Printemps-Redoute increased its shareholding in the Gucci group to 67.34%, getting closer to the target of 70% expected within the end of the year.

❑ 2003, October. Boucheron, in collaboration with Sàfilo, launched a new Collection of sunglasses. Designed by the creative director Solange, it was composed by four prestigious and exclusive models.

❑ 2003, November. The group

announced that Domenico De Sole, President and general manager of the Gucci group, and Tom Ford, creative director of Gucci group and of the brands Gucci and Yves Saint Laurent, did not intend to prolong their contracts beyond their agreed expiry date of 2004. Domenico De Sole said, "Gucci has been one of the great loves of my life, and the years spent here have been a fantastic journey. I want to thank Tom, whose creative genius has made possible our successes, as well as all the extraordinary colleagues all over the world. Thanks to their skills and devotion, we have been able to transform a small company in a bad financial conditions when I arrived in 1984 into a world power of luxury, thus creating more value for all our stakeholders." Tom Ford: "It is with a lot of sadness that I look at my future without Gucci. In the last 13 years this company was my life. We are leaving one of the most powerful teams of the sector and I'll do my best for the remaining time I'll spend here for the future success of the group. I couldn't be prouder of our work in Gucci or of the exceptional team of colleagues who have contributed with much more than just tough work: they put their heart in our research of excellence. I'm grateful for having the opportunity to share the joy of success with such a fantastic group of people. I would like to thank Domenico for his extraordinary leadership, his constant support, and friendship."

❑ 2003, November. Gucci acquired 70% of the shoe's factory Pigini Srl, a company that already collaborated with Gucci, manufacturing classic and sport women's shoes.

❑ 2003, December. The group obtained a financing of 460 million Euros from a pool of 15 banks, coordinated by Citigroup, Royal Bank of Scotland, and Unicredito.

❑ 2004, February. The Group PPR announced that it would launch a bid for the acquisition of the Gucci group's shares not yet in its possession. The bid was to be launched at the pre-fixed price of 85.52 dollars for share.

❑ 2004, March. Alessandra Facchinetti was made the new creative director of the women's clothing line. Born in Bergamo in 1972 and a graduate of the Marangoni Institute of Milan, Alessandra made her debut as designer for the Prada brand, soon becoming artistic coordinator of the Miu Miu line. She arrived at Gucci in October 2000 as style director of the women's division. She immediately showed exceptional qualities. John Ray was made the new creative director of the men's line. Born in Scotland, he decided to change his career and move to London where he studied fashion design at the legendary St. Martin's School of Art. On completion of his studies in 1992, he joined the stylistic team of Katherine Hamnett as assistant designer of the men's clothing line. In a short time, he became the director of the men's Collections. In 1996 Tom Ford called him into Gucci as style consultant for the men's line and, after a short time, he began working full-time at Gucci. Frida Giannini was the new creative director of the accessories line. Born in Rome in 1972, she studied at the Academy of Costume and Fashion. In September 2002 she became style director of Gucci's Leather Collection and contributed meaningfully to the success of the brand's leather Collections.

❑ 2004, March. The new financial director of the Gucci Group N.V. was Alexis Babeau, who replaced Robert Singer, in charge since 1995.

❑ 2004, March. The brothers Sergio and Franco Rossi, founders of the eponymous house, who had sold 79% of their company for 92 million Euros to the Gucci group four years before, sold the remaining 30%. They were to hold the usufruct with voting rights until 31st January 2007.

❑ 2004, March. Jean Christophe Bedos was made Boucheron's new general manager. He replaced Brian Blake.

❑ 2004, April. The bid launched on Gucci by the French Pinault-Printemps-Redoute, who owned 67% of the capital, is declared finished. The bid was launched at the price of 85.52 dollars per share, on the basis of the agreements of 2001 between Gucci, Lvmh, and PPR.

❑ 2004, April. Crédit Agricole sold 8.5% of its Gucci group's capital to PPR, which now controls 76.1% of the company.

❑ 2004, April. Robert Polet was announced as the President and general manager of the Gucci group, succeeding Domenico De Sole. Born in Holland in 1948, Polet arrived at Gucci after 26 years at Unilever, where he was President of the global division, Ice Cream and Frozen Foods. Polet declared: "I'm honored and proud to have been appointed to the management of Gucci. The different brands belonging to the group are world icons of fashion and luxury, and I consider this to be a unique opportunity. It will be a challenge taking Domenico De Sole's place and I can't wait to work with all the enormously talented people who belong to Gucci and write another chapter of its brilliant history."

❑ 2004, May. Toshiaki Tashiro, President of Gucci Japan, resigned from his charge. He joined the list of other managers who left the group: Robert Singer, financial director, Lisa Schiek and Tomaso Galli, communication directors, and Brian Blake, director of Boucheron's watches' division.

❑ 2004, May. Other managers leave the group: the independent members of the supervisory board resign.

❑ 2004, May. Diego Dolcini, GG shoe's designer, left his position.

❑ 2004, June. The group PPR, which owns £99.3 of the Gucci group, cashed a dividend of 50 million Euros. However, this amount covered over 25% of the financial burdens. In fact, the French giant disbursed a total of 7 billion Euros to gain control of the Florentine house, 2.6 of which was disbursed for the last bid. It had 380 millions of negative interests of debt.

❑ 2004, July. Shinichi Tanaka replaced Toshiaki Tashiro as President of Gucci Group Japan.

❑ 2004, July. In the prestigious Gallery Vittorio Emanuele in Milan, Gucci opened a store entirely dedicated to accessories. The store also featured a bar.

❑ 2004, September. Gucci established the Blutonic tannery in Tuscany, of which it controls 51.5%.

❑ 2004, October. Mark Lee is the President and general director of the Gucci Division. James McArthur is the new President and general director of Yves Saint Laurent.

❑ 2004, October. Robert Polet took over Giacomo Santucci as President and general manager of the Gucci Division.

❑ 2004, November. Marco Bizzarri, 42, is the new general manager of Stella McCartney. She commented, "I was immediately enthused by Marco's personality and sensitivity towards the creation of value of a brand in strong growth."

❑ 2004, November. Mark Lee delineated the future strategies of the group. "Gucci will continue to grow, but in a more consistent way with its image and tradition. Decentralization? No, I confirm the intention to continue the production in Italy, because the brand's strength is in the Made in Italy and, in particular, in the Made in Tuscany as to leather goods."

❑ 2004, December. Edmundo Castillo, Porto Rican designer, 37, winner of the 2001 CFDA Perry Ellis Award for the best accessories, is announced as Sergio Rossi's new art director.

❑ 2004, December. The group closed 2004 with a profit of 940.6 million Euros, a growth of 45.9% as to 2003. The operative profit has grown to 1.4 billion, 1.2 billion more than the previous year. To such a result the luxury division contributed with 394 million (against 237 of 2003), the distribution division with 754 million.

❑ 2005, January. Valérie Hermann, 41, is announced as the new general manager of Yves Saint Laurent. She was previously the ready-to-wear director of Christian Dior's women's line. Robert Polet said, "With Valèrie Hermann in quality of CEO and Stefano Pilati as creative director, we can count on a

really competitive managerial and stylistic team who will allow the brand to reach new important results."
❑ 2005, January. Isabelle Guichot is made the new Director of Business Development of Gucci group.
❑ 2005, January. Robert Polet explains Gucci's future strategies. "Gucci will continue to drive the entire group's growth. Our target is to double the turnover in the next seven years, also thanks to the good perspectives in the luxury market, which should grow between 4 and 7%. But we also bet on Bottega Veneta, which will start to make profit in 2006, and on YSL." Like his predecessor, Polet is convinced that China is to become one of the five most important regions for the group. Gucci had already been present there since 1997 with 8 boutiques.
❑ 2005, March. Isabelle Guichot was appointed Sergio Rossi's general manager.
❑ 2005, March. Frida Giannini is made the new creative director of the womenswear, a charge that adds to her present responsibility with Gucci's accessories line. She replaced Alessandra Facchinetti. John Ray maintained his role of creative director for men's clothing.
❑ 2005, March. The PPR group closed the first quarter with a turnover of 4.1 billion, a growth of 2.2% compared to the previous year. The luxury sector has registered a growth in sales of 10% reaching 711.5 million Euros. The brand Gucci that represents 60% of PPR's luxury sector, has totaled a turnover of 429 million, a growth of 19.3%. Bottega Veneta, whose proceedings valued 32.6 million Euros, registered a growth of 54.2%. Yves Saint-Laurent, 39 millions, registered a decline of 3.7%.
❑ 2005, April. A number of the managers left Gucci before the contract's expiry date are 38. The latest was Marco Semeghini, merchandising director for men. He is taken over by Gabriele Maggio, who keeps his position as sales manager.
❑ 2005, April. Mimma Viglezio is announced as the new communication director of Gucci group.
❑ 2005, May. Debut of the new line La Pelle Guccissima.
❑ 2005, July. Raphaelle Hanley replaces Simonetta Ciampi as YSL's accessories director. She is to work in collaboration with the creative director Stefano Pilati.
❑ 2005, July. Mark Lee is appointed general manager. (*Dario Golizia*)

Guerlain French brand of perfumes and cosmetics created in 1828. Its creator, Pierre-François-Pascal Guerlain, was a young chemist who, guessing the potential at the time of dawning beauty industry, decided to apply his knowledge to cosmetics and to the formulation of products for cosmetic use. Success arrived due to the idea of personalizing fragrances, dedicating them either to a single person (*Eau Imperiale* created in 1853 for the Empress Eugenia, still a bestseller) or to a special occasion (the eau de toilette commissioned by Balzac before writing *César Birotteau*). In almost two centuries, Guerlain has launched more than 260 perfumes. Some of the fragrances marked an age: from *Jicky* (1889), the first modern fragrance in which oils were synthesised, to *Mitsouko* (1919) that perfumed the collective infatuation for Japan; from *Shalimar* (1925), quintessence of beautiful and wicked years to *Vétiver* (1959) and *Chamade* (1969), olfactory translation of the liberty to which the youth of that period aspired. Guerlain has also been the only fragrance house in the world, whose 'noses' came essentially from the family. The opening of the Chartres' plant in 1973 brought about the creation of famous cosmetic lines, such as Issima and Evolution, and of famous make-up products as *Météorites*, *Terracotta*, *L'Or de Guerlain*, *Perfect Light*. In 1994 through a share swap between the family Guerlain and Bernard Arnault, the house joined the Group Lvmh.

(*Ginevra Falzoni*)

❑ 2002, January. At the age of 65, Jean-Paul Guerlain, the famous creator of cosmetics and fragrances, left the fashion stage. He remained in the company as the counselor of the President (to follow trends and raw materials). After the dismissal of Thibauld Ponroy, as Guerlain's Chief Executive Officer, Renato Semerari,

former marketing director of the international fragrances department of Christian Dior, was appointed to the role.
❑ 2005, May. The *maison* Guerlain was reopened at number 68 of the Champs-Elysées in Paris. The space, distributed on two levels, with a beauty institute on the first floor, was designed by the architects Andrée Putnam and Maxime d'Angeac. It also included a VIP room for the creation of custom-made fragrances.

Guerriero Stefano (1966). Italian designer. Born in Naples (his father was Neapolitan aswell, his mother is Danish), he was attracted by fashion during his Summers spent in Capri. In 1984, after graduating from high school, he decided to leave Naples to go to Milan. He worked as a model for Giorgio Armani and attended fashion designing courses. He joined Gianni Versace's atelier. He began with a position in the Versace factory in Novara, then as part of the staff in Via del Gesù. In 1991 he became consultant of Alberta Ferretti and, later, of Donatella Girombelli for the brand Genny. In 1998 he made his debut with his own Collection, exhibiting it during Moda/Milan.

❑ 1999. He was called to design the brand Les Copains.
❑ 2002, September. The designer called his Collection's exhibition, Holiday Couture, and he created a setting with a father, a mother, and a child on holiday in a meadow by a colored van. Stefano Guerriero's woman, with a long Jamaican hairdo, is relaxed and tranquil, appreciated luxury and elegance, but without ostentatiousness: leather jackets to wear over soft and large cotton pants, embroidered T-shirts and flowered track suits, and silk skirts with pop patterns.
❑ 2003, September. He replaced Simon Kneen at the artistic direction of Maska, a high fashion line inspired to the 'working woman'.
❑ 2004, February. Guerriero's production joined the East. In Japan he signed a three-year distribution contract with Misaki that foresaw the opening, within 2007, of a Guerriero single brand store in Tokyo.
❑ 2004, May. Debut of Guerriero's bags with a line of his own for the Spring-Summer 2004-2005.
❑ 2005, February. He reacquired 40% of his brand from BVM Italy.
❑ 2005, June. In Taormina, the designer received an award during La Kore, the fashion Oscars. In the course of the event other protagonists were awarded by the international fashion system.

Guess American company established in 1981 as a jeans producer by the brothers Maurice, Paul, and Armand Marciano. Today it produces and distributes women's, men's and children's clothing Collections, accessories (shoes, glasses, and watches), and household articles. Already operating in America, Asia, and the Middle East, the firm made its European debut in 1997 in Milan. Since April 1998 there was been a megastore in Piazza San Babila. Its style is young, casual Californian with a sexy touch.

❑ 2000, August. A record semester for Guess, a market leader in the denim sector, quoted at the Stock Exchange of New York. In the first semester of 2000, the net proceedings had increased to 48.6%, passing to 177.7 million dollars, compared to 119.6 registered in the same period of the previous year. The net turnover had increased to 47.7%, reaching 366.5 million dollars compared to 248.6 in 1999. Paul Marciano, founder, joint general manager, and co-President of Guess, had declared that he was "being extremely satisfied and optimistic for the *griffe*'s future."
❑ 2003, April. Relaunch of Guess in Italy and Europe with new offices, new management, and a better image. The Milanese headquarters were also new, 501.67 square yards in Via Lambro. The group's four lines are Guess Collection, Guess jeans, G-Brand, and children's wear divided into Kids and Baby (in Europe), as well as glasses, shoes, watches, and underwear. However, the contexts are different. Guess jeans are produced and distributed on license, for Europe, by Maco Apparel, which belongs to Fingen Apparel of the brothers Corrado and Marcello Fratini. Their purpose was to improve the image

and the fashion content for 20 and 30 year olds, and to increase the number of single brand shops. The purpose for the Guess Collection was similar, even if the content is different. For years the line had been produced on license by Focus Europe from Crevalcore (Bologna), belonging to the Focus Pull group (for Italy, Spain, France, Portugal, Greece, Denmark, Belgium, and also starting out in Saudi Arabia). The target was to promote the brand in a more incisive way on sale in the Guess shops and in the high level multibrand stores. In the first quarter of 2003, the turnover of Guess Inc. reached 83.7 million Euros (up 5.9% compared to the same period in 2002), but a decline of 1.7% compared to the same distribution network. The US company, with dropping results in the last three years, finished 2002 with a net loss of 11.2 million dollars (compared to a profit of 6.2 million Euros in the previous year). ❑ 2003, June. With the Spring-Summer 2004 Collection, the Guess Men's Collection and Guess Women's Collection lines were combined in a unique brand called Guess by Marciano. The intent was to give stronger identification to the brand.

Guia Ioannis (1963). Greek designer. He has been living in France since 1991, where he attended l'École des Hautes Études, graduating with a final thesis entitled *The Sexual Function of Men and Women's Clothing*. He studied fashion for three years at the Esmod-Veloudakis. He made his debut presenting his creations in Greece. In 1999 he presented his creations in Paris. He creates on the models' bodies, assembling and disassembling clothes so as they loosely follow articulations and they are not rigid structures.

Guida John (1897-1956). Fashion illustrator. He is one of the most interesting in the Italian panorama. Born in Naples by an English mother and Italian father, from Naples as well, he made his debut in 1914 as a model sketcher at the Circle of Artists with Sergio Tofano, Bruno Angoletta, and Aristide Sartorio. Between 1914 and 1943 he collaborated with the department stores S by P. Coen & C. in Via Tritone, Rome, for which he also created designs that featured in the Paris and London fashion exhibitions. He also buying sketches by Lucile, Patou, Vionnet, and Lanvin. For the 11 shopwindows he designed models in cardboard 70x100 with watercolor technique, which were renovated twice a week. Eclectic and curious, he gave model sketching lessons. He conceived the magazine *Le Mode in Fiore* (Blossoming Fashions), inspired by the French magazines. He collaborated with *La Donna*, illustrating and writing about trends from Paris. His good luck ended with the advent of the racial laws, which caused the closing of the Coen business. In the post-war period he worked for the fabrics' company Galtrucco and for Schuberth, Antonelli, and Centinaro. His unmistakable style witnessed an important moment in fashion, when, between the 1930s and 1940s during the domination of the French style, an Italian creativity was trying to come out. He died in Rome, poor, helped only by few friends.

(*Bonizza Giordani Aragno*)

Guidi Giovanni Cesare (1908-1995). Italian tailor. Born near Faenza, he began his career as a model sketcher and cutter in Florence. After learning the first rules about sewing from his brother, a man's tailor, he spent an apprenticeship period at the Florentine tailor's workshop, Italia Bernardini, from 1937 to 1939. During the war years, he was in Paris where he met Dior in 1946, and worked as a model's sketcher in the Fantechi atelier America, famous at the time for being the wardrobe supplier of Evita Peron. Once back in Italy, he opened his first tailor's workshop in Borgo Ognissanti 37, where he remained until 1950 when he decided to move into the more luxurious rooms of the Palazzo Feroni-Spini in Via Tornabuoni 2, next to Ferragamo. This is where he stayed until the end of his career. As fashion creator, he proposed his models with the name of Cesare Guidi-Florence. He occasionally illustrated fashion for the *La Nazione* newspaper. He dressed many divas of Cinecittà during the Hollywood years in the Eternal City. He participated in the first exhibition of Italian high fashion in the White Room of the Pitti Palace in July 1952), and worked in close collaboration with, at the time the famous millinery, Gigi of Florence. Invited to all the most important events at the time, Guidi was particularly appreciated for the quality of his jackets and coats and his *tailleurs* with their impeccable and essential lines, as well as the originality of the materials, a result of a far-sighted alliance with the wool factory, Faliero Sarti of Prato. His clientele included some renowned names of the jetset scene and cinema: the Princesses of the House of Savoy and Susan Strasberg, the daughter of the founder of the Actor's Studio of New York and actress in *Kapò* and *The Diary of Anne Frank*. From the early 1960s, the tailor added a successful boutique line to his high fashion line. In 1965 he also opened a young and innovative ready-to-wear Collection, making his debut with pioneering leather and suede garments blended with showy colored fabrics. Despite being very severely damaged by the flood of 1966, he continued his business with determination until 1976, when he retired for health reasons. In 1985 he donated a Collection of his creations and sketches to the Costume Gallery of Florence.

(*Aurora Fiorentini*)

An evening mantle by Giovanni Cesare Guidi, 1952.

Guidi Piero (1949). Italian leather goods' artisan. Bags, suitcases, briefcases, belts, jackets, scarves, ties, and shoes: all articles are branded with his logo of two embracing angels. During the 1960s, Guidi studied sculpture and bas-relief at the State School of Arts in Urbino. He started his business as a designer and entrepreneur with the Lineabold brand. His bags, in particular, have a strong personality: cloth and leather with steel and rubber finishings. He later created the following lines: Magic Circus (colored bags), Angeli (mixed leather goods), and Day Time (classic clothing). The painter Mario Schifano has posed for his advertising campaign.

Guild Shirin (1946). Designer of Iranian origin. He designs women's fashion in his London atelier. Without a professional education, he followed his instincts. In 1991 he launched his women's ready-to-wear line. His fashion has strong ethnic roots – he continually makes reference to the Iranian traditional men's clothing – and maintains a clean and refined line. Oversized and squared cuts are recurrent elements that immediately attracted a peculiar and faithful clientele all over the world.

Guillemin Olivier (1961). French designer with a taste for science fiction and space look. He works with plastic, paper, and metal. In 1987 he made his debut with his own Collection after working as an assistant for Alaïa, Mugler, and De Luca, designing men's models for Montana. From 1991 to 1993, he collaborated with Rabanne.

Guinness Lulu (1960). English designer of bags. She studied art for one year, then started a career as a video producer. In 1989 she changed direction again and began her own business in fashion. She designs and produces briefcases in an artisan style. After a few seasons, she launched a line of evening bags. She has been highly successful. Her eccentric style is best represented by her cult bag shaped like a violet vase. (A copy is kept in the fashion Collection of the Victoria & Albert Museum, London). Since 1990 she has been presenting her models during the London Fashion Week and working as consultant for great names, such as Norman Hartnell, Caroline Charles, Tomasz Starzewski, Colette Dinnigan, Mark Whitaker, Clements Ribeiro, and Lucien Pellat-Finet. She has created a line of evening bags at affordable prices for the department store, Debenhams. She opened her first boutique with the journalist-designer Selina Blow in 1995. The following year she opened a shop-atelier in Ledbury Road in the trendy area of Portobello. Three years later, she opened her most important sale point near Sloane Street, where she wanted to create a type of club for her most affectionate clients, such as the actresses Elizabeth Hurley, Judi Dench, and Madonna.

Guipure Big lacework in relief, manufactured using a spindle, a lace pillow, or a needle. It is manufactured using interwoven cotton small cords covered in silk.

Gulp Milanese boutique. It opened in April 1964 in Via Santo Spirito, and became a point of reference for the youth of the 1960s. The owner-designer Gabriella De Marco (her business partner is the sculptor Amalia Del Ponte, who decided the interior decor of the boutique using psychedelic lights, walls painted with undulating colored stripes, cardboard boxes as closets, a juke-box, and a bar) became the speaker of new trends, creating immediately successful designs in a small artisan dressmaker's workshop. "Miniskirts," wrote Maria Pezzi in a article for *Donna*, "the most audacious of these are worn when dancing the yé-yé, which has started to be popular, mariner pants that later appeared in high fashion, and jeanswear as bell-bottom trousers; skins, the first anti-classic leather that triumphed at Les Copains with Sylvie Vartan and Johnny Hallyday; blouses and handmade figurative or geometric T-shirts." In 1966 some models were dressed with mini dresses for the first time at La Scala's theater opening night, which caused a scandal. Gulp is also the favorite fashion of stars in showbusiness, from Caterina Caselli to Mina, from Ornella Vanoni to Carla Fracci. Still today this name is a synonym of personal style independent from fashion. Her most important and meaningful pieces are blouses, often inspired by artistic avant-gardes. (*Lucia Serlenga*)

Gum French brand of women's ready-to-wear fashion, created in Paris in 1996 thanks to the stylistic partnership between Yannick Flageul 81971) and Vincent Millet, who have attended the École Duperré. The former has worked in the advertising. He has also been the assistant of the designer Peter O'Brien and has worked for the *maison* Rochas. Also Millet has collaborated with Rochas designing jewels. In '98 he became artistic director of the *maison* Christoph Rouxel. To define Gum's style, the two creators speak of «ascetic baroque».

Models of the Milanese boutique Gulp, in a sketch by Maria Pezzi, 1960s.

Gunnung Anne. English model in the 1950s. One of the top models, she worked with the greatest photographers for the most important magazines. Recognizable for her boyish looks with short hair and an Audrey Hepburn style fringe. Sophisticated and elegant, she lived the high life, married to the Earl of Rutland.

Guru JackeT-shirt that became trendy in the western world during the 1970s after the West fell in love with the East. It was inspired by religious guides and Indian politicians. Pandit Nehru always wore one in white cotton. In the USA, it is called the Nehru look. Straight and long to the knees, very tight and closed by a thick line of buttons, it is manufactured in light cloth with a mandarin collar and long sleeves.

Guru Italian brand of clothing for young people. Matteo Cambi of Parma was the mastermind of this project which began with a Collection of twenty T-shirts for men and women and reached sales volume of nearly 70 million Euros after just a few years. In 1999, Cambi had the idea of creating a line of T-shirts and leisure wear inspired by the world of surfing with a short, punchy, easy-to-remember logo. It was not until 2000 that he had the idea that would bring real success to the small Parma-based company that had been founded in the meanwhile, Jam Session. This was the famous daisy which would become the Guru logo and would sell, that first Summer, 200,000 T-shirts. The only "failure" of the original projects was that, in reality, Cambi had hoped to create an alternative to a conformist style of dress. Something to wear everyday, without becoming a label. But in reality the numbers obtained and the wishes of the young man could not be reconciled. While in 2001 he sold 200,000 T-shirts, in 2003 the numbers rose to well over three million, making, in 2004, more than 70 million Euros of turnover. After winning a place in nearly all the European markets in 2005 Japan, the U.S., Russia, and Great Britain began to show an interest in Guru. China and India are the targets for 2006. In 2003 Guru Gang was founded, the line for little people, from the ages of 4 to 14, covering 15 percent of the overall volume. In 2005, during Pitti Bimbo, the baby line debuted, from 0 to 36 monts. In the same year, the company debuted GxG, a project for high-level denim produced in Japan and Italy. It included a complete look line and was presented in January at the Bread and Butter fair, and will be distributed in just 1,000 select shops. The Guru universe includes a name-brand license with Fabio Briatore: the Billionaire Collection which bears the logo of the famous club of Porto Cervo. Sponsorships have helped to spread brand-awareness. The first sponsorship was of the Parma soccer team, followed in 2004 by Formula One, with sponsorship of the Renault team and in particular the racer Fernando Alonso.

(*Gianluca Cantaro*)

Gypsy Jules-François Crahay launched a gypsy style Collection in 1959. In the early 1970s Thea Porter and Caroline Charles created a series of clothes and a two-piece suit, taking inspiration from the traditional gypsy costumes. It is a style characterized by particularly large skirts, which allow a quick swaying, and by blouses, often elasticized, which leave the shoulders bare, usually manufactured in light fabrics of brilliant colors. The main characteristic of the gypsy style is the presence of a scarf knotted around the neck or the hips.

H

Haageschool Voor de Kunsten. Dutch fashion school. It has two headquarters: Arnhem and Utrecht. It runs four-year courses with a compulsory entrance exam. It offers one of the best cultural beginnings for aspiring designers.

Habutaj Japanese term meaning soft, hairy, and gauzy. It refers to silk fabrics manufactured with short fiber threads that have been twisted slightly.

Hackett English brand of men's clothing and accessories. In 1983 Jeremy Hackett and Ashley Lloyd-Jennings met at the Portobello market where they were both looking for secondhand clothes. They decided to open a store in New Kings Road, London where they sold selected secondhand garments. This store became famous in a short space of time. From this success the idea was born to produce a line with traditionally English images. In 1991, with seven stores in London and good export, the majority share of the company was acquired by Dunhill Holdings. In 1994 Dunhill Holdings merged into the Vendôme Luxury Group (Cartier, Baume & Mercier).

Haerter Elsa (1909-1995). German photographer. She worked especially in Italy. She was the first to set fashion in exotic places. Born in Rottwell, Germany, she attended the Academy of Fine Arts and studied graphics with Willy Baumeister, a follower of the Bauhaus. At the age of 20, selling sketches to a costume company, she moved to Paris and earned her living by selling fashion articles and sketches to German magazines. In 1941 she moved to Italy where she started a long collaboration with the weekly *Grazia*, writing about fashion and photographing it with a style, which aimed to describe clothing beyond the setting of the image.

(*Luca Selvi*)

Hakaraia Lyall. English jewelry creator as well as a successful accessory and clothing designer. He sold his first creations to Whistles, Harrods, and Pelicano. It was the praise from department stores that convinced him to continue to experiment leatherwear adorned with precious stones. In 1998 he opened Bordello. The collaboration with Whitaker and Malem, who have worked for Prada, Valentino, and Gucci, allowed him to refine his cutting and manufacturing techniques. He designs knitwear, sportswear, gloves, bags, hats, belts, jackets, blouses, couture, and ready-to-wear. He also created Marilyn Manson's wardrobe for the singer's world tour, Cher's dress for the American Music Awards, and the corsets worn in a video by Skin, formerly part of Skunk Anansie.

Hall Chadwick (1926). American photographer. He was theatre critic and editor of *The Nation*, but the job offered to him by *Esquire* to photograph the famous and fashion changed his life. In 1965 he moved to London, where he still lives, and started to collaborate with *Elle*, *Harper's Bazaar*, *Vogue*, and *Queen*. He specialized in the production of advertising shorts and documentaries, among which the most famous in 1969 about the German photographer Leni Riefenstahl, Hitler's favorite director who created, *The Triumph of Will* (1935) and *Olympia* (1936).

Hall Duncan Nancy. Academic and critic of fashion photography, a field in which she specialized when she was assistant curator at the International Museum of Photo of the George Eastmen House. Those studies were merged into her book *Storia della fotografia di moda* (translated as History of Fashion Photography), which was published in 1978 and also reprinted also in French with a preface by Yves Saint-Laurent. The work analyzes the trends and the changes in the art of photography through 100 years of cover pictures.

Hall Jerry (1962). American model. She is married to the rockstar, Mick Jagger, with whom she has three children. Her talent scout was the illustrator, Antonio Lopez, who chose her as model and pin-up girl. In the early 1980s, not yet 18, she made her debut on the European runways and in front of the cameras of Norman Parkinson and Helmut Newton.

Halley Erik. British creator of jewels and accessories. He sets and assembles these eccentricities on clothes and shoes. Above all else, he invents dream scenarios with feathers, twisting and boiling them before spraying them with lacquer and coloring them. His feathers from peacocks, kingfishers, and birds of paradise are appreciated by Lagerfeld, Chanel, Jeremy Scott, and Hussein Chalayan.

❑ 1999, July. The designer who brought feathered decorations back into fashion' presented his first personal Collection during the Parisian haute coutere exhibitions.
❑ The exhibition of *La Beauté* in Avignon was among the shows that hosted the designer's works before the millennium.
❑ 2003, January. A parade of unique models by Micra (created by 11 designers among whom were Erik Halley, Yves Saint-Laurent, John Galliano, Van Cleef, and Arples) was presented along Parisian streets on the occasion of the Micrawards. The prototype design for this event by the designer was black covered with red Swarovski crystals.
❑ Halley's inventions are on sale in approximately fifty boutiques worldwide in the USA, Australia, Russia, Saudi Arabia, Hong Kong, Spain, and Italy. They are created in his workshop with a staff of four. (*Pierangelo Mastantuono*)

Halsman Philippe (1906-1979). Latvian photographer who became an American citizen in 1949. After moving first to Germany and then to Paris, he opened a firm specialized in portraiture and fashion photography for *Vogue*, *Vu*, and *Voilà*. In 1940 he moved to the USA where he portrayed famous personalities (Einstein, Churchill, and Marilyn Monroe) and worked as a freelancer for *Time* and *Life*, for which he created more than 100 covers, and other magazines. He collaborated with famous artists such as Salvador Dalí, by whose surrealism he was openly inspired and to whom he supplied photos that were used by the Spanish painter in several projects. His most renowned book is *Famous Jumps*, a compliation of the images of celebrated people who had jumped in front of his camera.

Halston Frowick Roy (1932-1990). American designer. Born Roy Halston Frowick in Des Moines Iowa, Halston emerged as the quintessential American designer of the 1970s, anticipating a modern ease with his use of fluid matte jerseys, and creating a slinky, luxurious opulence that would, 30 years later, inspire a generation of new designers, including Tom Ford at Gucci. Halston gave a clean new look to American fashion in the 1970s, with his palette of solid neutrals, fluid bias-cut silhouettes and emphasis on classic American design archetypes, such as turtlenecks, twin sets and blazers. He experimented with fabrics such as double-faced wools and Ultrasuede, Halston studied at the University of Indiana and the Art Institute of Chicago, where he began his career in Chicago as a milliner and window dresser, but in 1957 he moved to New York to work at Lily Daché and later Bergdorf Goodman. He founded his own company to design both hats and clothing in 1962; as a milliner he was most known for the pillbox design that Jacqueline Kennedy made famous in her White House years. In 1973 he sold his business to Norton Simon for 12 million dollars, and the company continued to expand into a plurality of licensing and production deals in everything from perfumes to household linens. It was sold several times again before his death in 1990. In 1983 he designed a Collection for the chain store J.C. Penney, and from then till his death in 1990 his company and its various licenses changed hands several times. In his later years Halston was photographed almost nightly at Studio 54, impeccably dressed in black and surrounded by women dressed in his designs.

Hamaui Daniela (1954). Journalist. She was

the first woman in Italy to manage a news magazine. From March 2002, she has been in charge of *L'Espresso*, an established magazine about news, politics, and economics. In May 1996 she conceived and directed *D-la Repubblica delle Donne*, the women's weekly supplement to *la Repubblica*. Her entire career has been spent in the field of women's magazines. In 1979 she started at *Annabella*. In 1980 she was hired by *Bella*, where she stayed until 1986, when she moved to the Mondadori publication, *Centro Cose Energy*. She moved up the editorial hierarchy until 1995 when she became the manager.

Hamilton Abe (1962). British designer. Born in Manchester, UK. After several jobs, including as a chef, he decided to study fashion in London, opening his first atelier in 1990. His clientele is enviable, with names such as Madonna, Imam, Yasmin Le Bon, and Helena Christensen. In 1993 he presented his Collection for the first time at London Fashion Week and won the New Generation Designer of the Year award. His romantic and refined style is evocative of the cinema divas of the 1930s. His dresses in latex and real flowers stirred a real clamor.

> ❑ 2001. He designed a nightwear line produced and manufactured by Caprice for the department store chain, Debenhams. The Collection was launched in 60 British department stores.

Hamnett Katherine (1948). British designer. She studied at St. Martin's School of Art in London. In 1979 she created her own lines. Elegance and functionality are the primary aims of her fashion, characterized by luxury and extravagance. Inspired by the styles of the 1950s yet interpreted with a contemporary touch, her Collections have always referred to the present day. Her ecological, animal rights, and pacifist T-shirts are particularly famous. She has been presenting her Collections in Paris and Milan since 1989. *(Marta Citacov)*

> ❑ 2001. The effects of September 11 badly hit London Fashion Week. Among the subdued exhibitions with the resonant rhythm of metal detectors, Katherine Hamnett, Burberry, Paul Smith, Clements Ribeiro, and Nicole Farhi withdrew from the proceedings.
> ❑ 2002, July. Hamnett announced a restyling that was functional to her return to the big names of fashion. The relaunch program saw the renewal of licenses and a reorganization of distribution and commercialization criteria.

H&M (Hennes & Mauritz). Swedish company of young, trendy clothing. In 2002 its turnover amounted to 6 billion Euros (5.037 Euros in 2001) with a profit before taxation of 840 million Euros. It employs 34,000 people with 850 stores in 14 countries worldwide. The President and majority shareholder is Stefan Persson, son of the company's founder. The general manager is Rolf Eriksen. The entrepreneurial rationale of the group is based on selling products at affordable prices with a high fashion content and an extremely high rotation of sales in dedicated brand stores. The company has focused on two different segmentation strategies. For the American market, where there are 45 sales points (20 more added in 2003), its target is young and trendy females. In Europe, it targets the whole family with both trendy and traditional products. The average prize of a garment is very competitive, around 17 Euros. Consequently, H&M's business is characterized by continual attention to costs, which carries through into the corporate side. The use of taxis is forbidden, cell phone use is limited, and the managers travel in economy class. It is also important for a company that sells 550 millions Euros of products to minimize stock in warehouses. The excellent performance of the Swedish company with its high market quota and elevated profitability is guaranteed by the designers' ability to detect trends in advance. The style department, located in Stockholm, is comprised of 95 people who are not allowed to copy from other designers. Speed is a fundamental requisite of the group's strategy; it only takes 20 days from the product's conception to its arrival in the store. Manufacturing has been decentralized overseas due to cheaper costs with about 900 mini-factories in Bangladesh, China, and Turkey. The company is careful with communications, investing 4% of its proceedings in its image. (The model Imam was the face of H&M in 2003.) The chain arrived in New York with the opening of a three-floor space on Fifth Avenue. In Autumn 2003, it made its debut in Milan in a strategic position (where Fiorucci's store used to be), just a few meters away from its competitors, Zara and Benetton. The first quarter of 2003 registered a turnover of 1.22 billion Euros, proceedings of 183.3 million Euros with a growth of 43% compared with the same period for 2002. In 2003 H&M opened 110 more stores in Germany, USA, France, Spain, and England. As well as entry into the Italian market, 2003 saw H&M become the main player in three new markets: Czech Republic, Poland, and Portugal. *(Dario Golizia)*

❑ 2004, November. The new line Karl Lagerfeld for H&M was launched. The German designer designed clothes and accessories for men and women as well as a unisex perfume, which were on sale in all 20 of H&M's markets. The collaboration stopped after just one season due to misunderstandings between the designer and the company.
❑ 2005, April. Elio Fiorucci returned to his store in Piazza San Babila with a beachwear line called H&M Poolside. Highly colored and designed for the Summer season, it was distributed in all stores from June onwards.
❑ 2005, May. There was another excellent collaboration for autumn 2005-2006. Stella McCartney designed a women's Collection of 40 pieces, produced and distributed with the brand Stella McCartney for H&M from November onwards.

H & M. Rayne English shoe brand. Roger Vivier was among its collaborators who manufactured shoes for Dior and Marks & Spencer. Edward Rayne took the firm, which he inherited from his parents, to the top of the British and American markets. Established in 1889 by his grandfathers for the production of theater shoes, the brand was linked to Delman for a short period. It was then acquired by the most important English distribution chains.

Hanes American group of men's underwear and men and women's hosiery. It is world leader in the T-shirt sector together with Fruit of the Loom. Established in 1901 thanks to the business partnership between Pleasant and John Wesley Hanes, who left the tobacco business to start in the fabric industry. They had extraordinary intuition because the idea yielded money through Hanes' two companies (one for the manufacturing of underpants and T-shirts, the second to manufacture and sell hosiery), which operate independently. The two businesses eventually merged in 1965 when they floated on the stock exchange. Thirteen years later, the group was acquired by Sarah Lee.

❑ 2000. Hanes designed uniforms for the 35,000 volunteers who accompanied and attended the handicapped athletes participating in the Special Olympics in North Carolina.
❑ 2003. 25 years after the group's acquisition by the Sarah Lee corporation, Hanes remains one of the top brands in the group. From its headquarters in Chicago, the corporation also controls Playtex, Wonderbra, and the underwear lines by DKNY and Ralph Lauren.

Hanro Swiss manufacture of men and women's underwear. Established in 1884 it was named after the two founders, Handschin and Ronus. The very pure cotton is worked to feel like silk, which is the guaranteed trademark of this company. The manufacturing process is slow and expensive. The business results have been witnessed by the success attained not only in Europe, but also in Asia and America.

❑ 2001, February. The brand is licensed by the German *griffe* Joop! for the manufacturing of underwear.
❑ 2002, August. Huber Holding, owner of Hanro Nova and the Hanro AG subsidiary since 1993 decided to close the production plant in the Tessin Canton for economic reasons. The Hanro Nova business was moved to Santa Maria de Feira, Portugal.
❑ 2003, May. The collaboration with Escada came to its conclusion. The Swiss company had been producing underwear since January 2001.

❑ 2003. From autumn the men's underwear for Joop! was also manufactured by Hanro.

Hans Rieger Austrian brand of ready-to-wear fashion that took its name from its creator. Hans Rieger launched the brand in 1992 after studying marketing and working as a fashion designer for several Austrian clothing industries.

❑ The designer's Collections are on sale by Rieger Fashion, the Salzburg's boutique in Munzgasse.

Harari Guido (1952). Italian photographer. After working simultaneously as a music critic and photographer, he devoted himself exclusively to photography in the 1980s, creating album covers for some of the biggest international pop musicians (from Bob Dylan to Paul McCartney, from Lou Reed to Frank Zappa, from Vasco Rossi to BB King). He organized personal exhibitions in Italy and abroad, and made photographic books about Claudio Baglioni, Paolo Rossi, and, in 2001, Fabrizio De André. He is considered to be a portrayer of great value. He is also devoted to social reportage (the one about fashion families was particularly famous), publishing in *Time*, *The Sunday Times Magazine*, *Sportweek*, *Amica*, *Stern*, as well as the fashion and advertising photography.

Hardwick Cathy (1933). Korean designer. Born in Seoul. She was not immediately interested in fashion as she started her studying with music. In the 1960s she opened her own boutique shortly after moving to San Francisco. She continued her business in New York, where she has had her own business since 1972. She distinguished herself for her original style. Among her most important creations was the Summer Collection in 1987, when she presented long jeans skirts buttoned along the sides, with long deep vents.

❑ She collaborated with Tom Ford and with some American houses of ready-to-wear, such as Joan and David, for which she created line that distinguished itself for the refinery of woven fabrics in light colors.

Hardy Pierre (1956). French shoe designer. He studied plastic arts in Paris. He was Camille Unglick's assistant and from 1987 to 1988 he designed Harel's Collections, one of the most famous shoe brands in France. From 1987 to 1992 he was the shoe sector manager for Dior. During the 1990s, he worked as an illustrator as well as teaching at the École Supérieure des Arts Appliquées Duperre and at the Institute Français de la Mode. From 1997 he was the creator of Hermès' shoe Collection. In October 1998 he started his own business and launched his women's shoe line.

❑ 2002. During the five years at Hermès, he also created a jewelry line.

Harel Shoe design house and manufacturer. Pierre Harel started to design shoes in 1922, creating décolleté with Louis XV style heels and stiletto boots. He strengthened the relationship between fashion and accessories. In 1935 the business was taken over by his second son, Armand. From this point onwards, several important collaborations began with Coco Chanel, Elsa Schiaparelli, Nina Ricci that continued in the post-war period with Dior and Balmain. Today Harel has three boutiques in Paris (Avenue Montaigne, Rue François, and Rue de Tourvion). Harel continues its tradition of exclusivity through the high quality of the brand's skins. For every shoe the artisan chooses an ad-hoc skin. The artisan treats many different skins with the same self-assurance, such as alligators from the Mississippi river (available in 33 different shades), iguana from Mali (44 shades), and Indonesian pythons and ostriches (33 shades), each of which has its own extremely restricted fan club. Even rarer animals such as the phosaurus (a subspecies of crocodile), the tejus, shark, or frog are used in the production of Harel's shoes. The manufacturing procedure, comprised of about 150 different operations, reveals the complexity of precise mechanics. The skins are treated in an unusual way; each one is adapted to fit just one foot. They are cut in 10-15 pieces before being joined together, glued, folded, and assembled. Once the basic work has been completed, they are left to dry for a long period.

(*Stefano Grassi*)

❑ 2002. Harel, with other brands such

as Scherrer, Emmanuelle Khahn International, and Jacques Fath, is acquired by the France Luxury Group, a company that has been established at the beginning of the year by Moufarrige and François Barthes.

❑ 2003, Summer. The women's shoe *griffe* Emeraude was relaunched. It has been created in 1922 by Pierre Harel. Hasley revitalized the eighty-year-old brand. Twenty styles were launched on the market, which rejuvenated the original shoe manufacturing with noble materials such as iguana, kid, and golden lamb.

Haring Keith (1958-1990). American painter. He is best-known as the designer of a series of Swatch watches, highly sought-after collectors' pieces. He attended the Manhattan School of Visual Arts for two years. He experimented with several unconventional artistic techniques. In December 1980 he started to design small groups of white stylized figures on advertising bills in the Ney York subway and on its walls. His success was immediate.

Harken Sailing Wear Brand of technical clothing for sailors. It was created in 2001 by a license agreement between the American Harken (specialists in boating equipment and established in 1967 by the brothers Peter and Olaf Harken) and the Italian Philteen, a clothing company in Bolzano Vicentino. Suggestions from professional sailors and research in technical materials characterize a line that also includes jerseys, sweaters, pants, jackets (designed by Massimo Piva), and shoes designed by Billy Carlesso. In 2002 Harken Sailing Gear was created with the launch of sailing accessories, gloves, 6 new shoe models, and sunglasses. (*Silvia Paoli*)

Harlow Daniel (1943). French hairdresser. His birth name is François Guérard. In 1962 he began as the assistant and student at the famous French salon, Alexandre. At Alexandre he experienced his first contact with a refined clientele, with the world of cinema, and fashion exhibitions. He quit Alexandre to open his own business called Harlow. Initially it was a tiny space – only 35.11 square yards. His success was immediate. Articles and photos were published in *Madame Express*, *Vogue*, and *Marie Claire* to announce the creativity of this young talent. He delighted in provocative slogans such as 'Harlow: for those who don't like hairdressers', a sentence that certainly didn't earn him the sympathy of colleagues. It stirred a protest instead. In 1978 he opened a new salon in the center of the Halles. His style focuses particularly on cutting. In the total punk age he cut hair along the streaks to add volume. During the 1980s and 1990s he owned 12 salons with 160 employees.

Harp Holly (1939). American designer. After graduating in Texas, she moved to Los Angeles where she opened her own boutique. In 1972 she created her own Collection, which was distributed by the department store Bendel of New York. The Collection was moderately successful immediately. Her talent lies in the soft and harmonious lines of her drawing. It is for this reason that she uses special fabrics such as painted silk and opaque jersey.

❑ 2002, November. Holly Harp with Oscar de la Renta, Balenciaga, Givenchy, Pauline Tingere, and about forty more designers present a selection of 'perfect clothes for Summer parties' at the Holiday Clothing Show. During the event at the Metropolitan Pavilion of New York, the Texan designer presented her partywear Collection and evening bags.

Harper's Bazaar American fashion monthly. It is the competitor of *Vogue*, from which it has often stolen away the best talents such as the photographer, De Meyer, and the journalist Carmel Snow. She coined the phrase New Look for Dior's first Collection in 1946. In 1932 Snow became the top name and innovator of the magazine. The monthly was established in 1867 by Fletcher Harper. Initially it was a weekly magazine and remained that way until 1901, when sales problems advised its transformation into a monthly. This did not help the magazine because it was acquired 1913 by William Randolph Hearst, already a highly successful publisher. He immediately set up the magazine as Vogue's competitor thanks to strategist hirings, exclusives (a ten-year

A cover of *Harper's Bazaar* dedicated to Emilio Pucci, December 1963.

contract with the illustrator, Erté), and big names. In 1929, Hearst added a second 'a' to the word Bazar. From that moment on, the review took off. A few years later, the magazine's success was helped by the revolution of graphics studied by Alexey Brodovitch and his discoveries of talented photographers (from Man Ray to Martin Munkacsi and Richard Avedon). His artistic tastes led him to collaborate with Couteau, Dalí, and Chagall as well as many other artists. The monthly has helped many people to grow professionally, such as Diana Vreeland (on the editorial staff from 1936 and made director of Vogue in 1962) and photographers such as Bob Richardson and Irving Penn. The last great director was Liz Tiberis, who passed away in 1999. The magazine has many foreign editions.

❑ 2001, May. Glenda Bailey became Editor-in-Chief of the magazine. She came from rich experience in Italy as a designer and has worked for American edition of *Marie Claire*, which has become the bestselling American fashion magazine in just five years: a record in the quickest increase in circulation.
❑ 2002, June. Stephen Gan, collaborator of Harper's Bazaar, received the fashion award in the Creative Visionary category. This 40th edition of the CFDA's award maintained a low profile. It was held in the New York Public Library where it began.
❑ 2003. The magazine is published in 18 countries, among which Singapore, Taiwan, Turkey, Hong Kong, and the Czech Republic.

Harriet Hubbard Ayer American cosmetics company. Established in 1877 by Harriet Hubbard Ayer. At the start of her career she was Elizabeth Arden's business partner. She then became a fierce competitor to Arden and Helena Rubinstein. The company's headquarters in rue du Faubourg Saint Honoré was a hotel in the 1700s, furnished by the architect, Jean Pascaud. At the death of Harriet, the company was taken over by Liliane Dodge. During the 1940s she created two perfumes that remained her only unique creations, Je Chante and Malgré Tout. In 1950 Unilever USA acquired the company, and moved the headquarters a few blocks away to large premises once occupied by Worth. From 1955 to 1975 the best names of the international jetset gathered in these premises, from the Duchess of Windsor to Brigitte Bardot. Ayer's products have been diffused in more than 70 countries. In 1978 the company was sold to a German distributor.

Harrison Géo. French tailor of the early 20th century. He had a men's atelier at number 18 of the Boulevard Montmartre. He founded the quarterly magazine, *L'Homme Elégant*.

Harrods London department store, established in 1849 by Henry Charles. Destroyed by a fire in 1883, it reopened in the Knightsbridge area. In 1898 the first lift was inaugurated. It has always followed fashion very closely. In 1985 the House of Fraser group sold it to the Egyptian brothers, Al Fayed.

❑ 1999, June. Harrods, famous for its strong dress code of 'No jeans, no shorts, no leggings', bowed for the first time in 150 years, to allow a rock concert by Aerosmith, who were in London to promote a new record.
❑ 2003, April. The most precious shoes ever manufactured were put on sale. Harrods displayed a pair of shoes worth 1 million pounds worth in the store windows. They were created by Stuart Weitzman with 642 round and oval rubies and platinum, inspired by Dorothy's slippers in *The Wizard of Oz.*

Harrow School School of design and communications located in Harrow, outside of London. The big names in fashion lecture there, such as Vivienne Westwood or John Galliano. The fashion section is the most renowned and it has existed for 150 years. It covers every type of course, from production to sales, from publicity to the history of fashion. Several designers have begun their careers at Harrow because Ralph Lauren and Gucci hire several new graduates every year.

Hartford Brand of swimwear, sweaters, T-shirts, and sports knitwear created in the mid 1980s by Yves Shareton. After studying a subject far removed from fashion in America (oil), the French designer returned home and opens the brand's headquarters in Paris. The production, which was initially focused on the plants in Normandy, was moved to the former colonies. The opening of the Casablanca plant was followed in 2002 by one in Marrakech. Hartford made its debut at Pitti Immagine in the 1990s, simultaneous with its debut in the American market. Today the Collections enjoy a reserved space at the New York Collective and at Le Dôme, a Parisian autumn event. In Italy the products are on sale at Pupi Solari, Milan, Capri, and by Vela in Portofino. The company has recently opened a Parisian boutique in Places des Victoires, which takes the place of Coveri.

(*Pierangelo Mastantuono*)

Hartnell Norman (1901-1979). Fashion designer of English style and designer for the Royal family. He was still a student at Cambridge when he had already designed clothes for the magazine *Footlights*. In 1923 he opened an atelier in Burton Street with his sister and became the preferred tailor of the British aristocracy. In 1935 he designed the bridal dress of the Duchess of Gloucester and for the nobles invited to the wedding, including the Queen. In 1947 he designed the bridal dress for Elizabeth and in 1953 he designed the dress worn at her coronation. He was later entrusted with the creation of army and police uniforms, and he became interested in costume design. His style was rather conservative, in deference to the rigid protocol imposed by the Royal family. Lengths were under the knee for the daytime and hats were not to have overly large brims so as not to hide the face. In 1977 he was appointed a knighthood. After his death, the fashion house was initially guided by Manny Silverman and, later, by Marc Bohan. However, times were no longer suitable to the style of Hartnell and the company closed down in 1992.

(*Anna Gloria Forti*)

Harvey Nichols English department store. Opened in 1813 by Benjamin Harvey. In 1820 it extended its product range to sell linen, fabrics, and oriental carpets. Acquired by Debenhams in 1919, it gave a large sales space to fashion. In 1985 it was taken over by the Burton group and, six years later, by Dickson Concepts. Today it sells most of the European brands.

Hasegawa Yutaka (1946). Japanese designer working in Germany. After attending the Bunka Fashion College of Tokyo, he began his career as a designer for women's Collections for the Japanese brand Itokin. He moved to Hamburg and started his own company by opening a boutique and a fashion atelier in the space of three years from 1975 to 1978.

❑ 2000. He collaborated with the design of technological products for the multinational company Sony. He designed a monitor in two versions, 15 and 17 inches, for Good Design, the international contest organized by the Museum of Architecture and Design in Chicago.

Haseltine Loanna (1975). American designer. Born in Oregon, she has lived in Alaska, but from 1995 she has been living and working in Paris. After studying textile and fashion design at the Bassist College of Portland (USA), she followed the courses at the Chambre Syndicale de la Couture Parisienne, which allowed Loanna to make her debut in 1998, with her first women's Collection characterized by an avant-garde style after collaborating with John Galliano and Ocimar Versolato.

Haten Fause (1967). Brazilian designer. Born in San Paolo, he grew up in contact with fashion thanks to his father's manufacturing business. Self taught, he soon began to create his first designs, selling them to private clients. In 1987 he launched his first brand, der Haten. He perfected his skills at the Parisian house, Torrente. In 1997 ha started his ready-to-wear Collection. In 1999 he designed clothes for Giorgio Beverly Hills. In 2000 he presented his designs in New York and the Brazilian textile industry awarded him with the Abit Fashion Brazil award as Designer of the Year. He combines architectural design with technological materials, without giving up or ruining femininity. From 2001 he designed Haten F, an easy line for the shop chain Riachuelo.

(*Laura Lazzaroni*)

Haute Womenswear brand. It is almost in limited edition, characterized by hand dyeing and handmade inlays of lace and old wools. The clothes are unique pieces, made according to a modern concept of artisan original haute couture. The clothes are designed by Vincenzo de Cotiis (1958), who graduated in architecture from the Polytechnic of Milan. He has also been a interior designer (he designed the interior at his hotel, Saint Raph di Milano). In the end he became a fashion designer. His passion for malleable materials, the recycling of fabrics, objects from the past, and unusual assembly emerges in each of his works. He is at his eight season in fashion.

(*Silvia Paoli*)

Havelock Men's sleeved coat with a pelerine long to the hips. Created in the mid 1800s, it became famous when it was worn by Franck Havelock as an evening coat. It became a sleeved sports coat from the 1970s onwards.

Hawaiian It is impossible not to recognize the Hawaiian style at first sight. American tourists returning from these islands interpret the style best. They wear oversized printed shirts, often in very ostentatious colors, with fruit, flower, exotic birds, or dancing girls patterns.

Hawes Elisabeth (1903-1971). American designer. She was a modern and anticonformist thinker. She created pants for women, having strongly stressed that pants were the most practical and comfortable piece of clothing in which to work and practise sport. She believed that young women were becoming increasingly involved in these two fields. Among other things, she constantly appealed for America's independence from the European style rules, in particular from the tyranny of French fashion. (*Roberta Giordano*)

Haye Ji (1968). Korean designer. A star in her homeland, she was adopted years ago by the Paris fashion scene. Her first haute couture exhibition was in July 1999, but it was her second Collection that stirred a clamor as the young designer sold half of her Collection to one of the richest ladies of the planet. Notwithstanding her success, she works with only two assistants in an atelier of few squared yards.

Hayford-Casely Joe (1956). English 'rocker' designer. He has dressed groups such as The Clash, U2, Brand New Heavies, and Betty Boo. He studied at the Tailor and Cutter Academy and at the St. Martin's School of Art in London. He is renowned with the general public for his coarse cloth clothes (the fabric used to make military tents). In the last few years he has abandoned street fashion to propose a more feminine and refined fashion.

❑ 1999, September. At the headquarters of the Honorable Artillery Company among sergeants in uniform, he presented his new Collections characterized by corsets in colors inspired by the artist Toulouse-Lautrec: charcoal, amber, black, and white. The sleeves were bell-shaped and elasticized.
❑ 2001. For the autumn-Winter season, he contrasted the 'dark-lady woman', wearing aggressive shoes and the 'good-boy man', who wore anti-rain *cabans* and high neck sweaters.
❑ 2003. Hayford-Casely, who grew up in Savile Row, continued to dress stars such as Lou Reed. He experimented with well-shaped knitwear and jackets through embroideries, pleats, and skins. His women's clothing is on sale in New York at Takashimaya as well as in small independent stores in Italy and Japan. His menswear can be found in Selfridges and Duffer in London.

H.B. (High Bulk). Extremely bulky yarns made up of stabilized fibers and retrieving fibers. They contract because of water or steam and force the normal fibers to arch, undulating or inflating all the yarn.

Hdp Holding of Industrial Shareholdings. Established 6 March 1997 by the partial division of Gemina. It took over 100% of the editorial group RCS, the majority parcel of Gft Net (a fashion group), and Fila. The group's president is Guido Roberto Vitale, the vice-president Paolo Mieli, and the general manager Maurizio Romiti. On 1 May 2003, 44.883% of the ordinary stock became controlled by a syndicate agreement represented by eleven shareholders (Fiat, Mediobanca, Gemina, Italmobiliare, Generali, Pirelli, IntesaBci, Sinpar, Smeg, Edison, and Mittel). Initially the holding consisted of two prevailing businesses: publishing with the Group Rizzoli-Corriere della Sera, and fashion, which was a sector that the company entered into in 1988, acquiring the majority (53.2%) of Fila, a company owned by Biella competing in activewear. This first experience in fashion was amplified in 1995, when the Milanese holding was joined by the Gruppo Finanziario Tessile of Turin (Gft). In March 1998 (in the meantime, Gemina has become part of Hdp) the acquisition of the Valentino fashion house, next to Fila and Gft, preluded an entry into the Italian luxury sector, which has never really taken off. In the three-year period 1998-2000, the Milanese holding had very bad financial results, influenced by the negative trend of fashion companies. It was a loss calculated around 843 billions of old Liras. The negative results of the previous three years continued in 2001. The net consolidated proceedings amounted to 3,357.2 million Euros in line with the 3,357.7 of 2000, but this was resulting from contrasting trends. The rise of 14.9% registered by RCS was in contrast with a decline in the proceedings of Fila (-2.4%) and Gft Net (-39.7%) guided by Valentino. The operational result was negative with 33 million Euros, while the net result for the year was -232.1 million Euros. However the real Achilles' heel for the group was the financial net debt of 594.4 million Euros. The negative results of the controlled companies in the fashion-clothing sector have heavily influenced Hdp's accounts. Within Gft Net, which closed with a loss of 79.6 million Euros, Valentino, despite increasing its turnover of 12%, had a negative operational profit of 16.8 million Euros (against 14.8 in 2000) and a net loss of 28.5 million (against 25.6). The financial debt at the end of 2001 amounted to 281.7 million Euros. For Fila, the operational results amounted to -45.1 million Euros, while the net result was -139.7 million Euros, double compared with the previous year. These results forced the board of directors to examine 'the complex procedure of negotiations towards selling Fila and Valentino' and to focus on the group's involvement solely in the publishing and communications sectors. In March 2002 Hdp announced that the controlled Gft Net had sold Valentino to the Marzotto group. The agreement concluded with the vision to transfer 100% of Valentino's capital against a sum, inclusive of all financial debt, of 240 million Euros. In 2001 Valentino's turnover was 132.5 million Euros, with a loss of 28.5 million Euros. The debts for the Hdp group (155 million Euros) were to be reimbursed in full at the closing. This operation was an important step in establishing Hdp's strategy of removing the group from business in the fashion sector and a focus on the publishing and communications sectors. For this purpose, Hdp had already sold some branches belonging to Gft Net (Sahzà, Revedi, Bosconero's factory, and its license with Calvin Klein) in 2001 and in the first few months of 2002. In July 2002, Gft Net sold Facis SpA. (an established brand of Italian menswear) and 96.3% of Svik's production plant to Mediconf for a sum of 6.2 million Euros, excluding financial debts. In order to close completely the group's activity in the clothing sector, only the sale of Fila remained. On 10 June 2003, Fila Holding was sold to Sport Brands International, controlled by the private American fund Cerberus. Cerberus' own operational shareholdings included Fila Nederland BV, Fila Sport SpA., Ciesse Piumini Srl., and Fila USA Inc. The luxury adventure was over. The corporate name changed accordingly from Hdp to RCS MediaGroup on 1 May 2003. RCS MediaGroup controls RCS Quotidiani, RCS Periodici, RCS Libri, RCS Pubblicità, RCS Diffusione, and RCS Broadcast, which are all active in the sectors of publishing and communications.

(*Dario Golizia*)

Head Edith (1907-1981). American costume designer. She was a legend in her business. After working on hundreds of films, in which she achieved 8 Oscars and 33 nominations, she died while working on the film *Dead Men Don't Wear Plaid*. Excellent in all styles and eras, she was capable of adjusting the costume to suit the varied temperaments of different characters. She dressed practically all the great women's actresses from Marlene Dietrich to Bette

Davis, from Liz Taylor (*A Place in the Sun*) to Audrey Hepburn, from Barbara Stanwyck (*Double Indemnity*) to the blonde and icy Hitchcock heroines Grace Kelly (*Rear Window*) and Tippi Hedren (*Birds*). However she always said to prefer men's costumes "It's much easier to work with men. All they want is to be finished quickly." Her name was linked to several westerns (*Shane*). She made her debut as designer at Paramount Pictures, where she remained for 29 years, eventually becoming the head of the costume department. She then moved to Universal, where she worked for the rest of her life. Her life was spent on sets, but her creations were copied all over the world, influencing fashion far beyond her world in cinema. (*Roberto Nepoti*)

Headbangers Generic term used, in absence of a better one, to describe heavy metal fans. It is a musical style that grew rapidly from the crossover between the hippy culture and 'hardness' of the rockers. The fashion of Heavy Metal unexpectedly merged a certain shabbiness (typical of hippies with denim and long hair) with the brilliance inherited first from psychedelics and later from glam (Spandex jeans, snakeskin and leopard print, and metal accessories), and also with leather clothing and a passion for badges that was typical of Greasers.

Heavy Metal Kids Youth movement and natural fashion. Born in the late 1970s from the merging of hard rock and heavy rock fans. Thirty years on, the Heavy Metal Kids donned the original rockers' clothing with leather or suede jackets, and welcomed the aesthetics of drawings and symbols (badges) characteristic of horror movies. They were peaceful and quiet notwithstanding their look, and in contradiction to other fashion movements they did not introduce a subculture. Their unique originality consisted in having very long hair like neo-hippies and their minimalist dancing style called idiot dancing (a simplified version of the headbanging of the Californian Hell's Angels), during which they rhymed the music of their groups. Ten years later, in the late 1980s, a more incisive and politically engaged current (the Trash) was born within the movement. It was created after the birth of the anarchic violence of punks. Trash did not modify its costume or clothing; it only became more theatrical and baroque.

(*Gabriella Gregorietti*)

Hecht Laetitia (1968). French designer. Daughter of a master upholsterer, she became a sales assistant of haute coutere at Jean Louis Scherrer at the age of 16. She became Lolita Lempicka's assistant at the age of 20, and later became assistant to Sophie Sitbon. In 1995 she created her own line with her husband Philippe, which experienced good success. He big occasion occurred in 2001 when Jean-Jacques Wegnez, President of Guy La Roche, offered her a five-year contract; Hecht became artistic director of the women's Collections. In March 2002 she presented her first autumn-Winter Collection in Paris. In the same year she received the *Kore*, the Oscar of Italian fashion, in Agrigento, Sicily.

(*Maddalena Fossati*)

Hechter Daniel (1938). French designer. He can be credited as one of the activists of sportswear clothing to be worn also in cities.

A creation by Daniel Hechter. Winter 1998-99.

Son of textile entrepreneur, he made his debut with his first womenswear Collection in 1962. This was followed by a childrenswear Collection in 1965 and a menswear Collection in 1968. Sylvie Vartan, Anouk Aimée, and Johnny Hallyday are just some of his clients. In 1971 he began to design clothing for individual sports (tennis and skiing). In 1976 he made his debut in accessories (belts, small leather goods, and eyewear). In 1997 he decided to give *carte blanche* for his lines to a young German designer, Grit Seymour.

❑ 1999. The company was acquired by the German group, Miltenberger Otto Aulbach, which took over the sales network and the brand's development. The company works through a system of differentiated licenses for clothing, underwear, shoes, swimwear, and household linen lines.
❑ 2003. The men, women, and sportswear Collections for autumn-Winter 2004 were presented in the new showroom opened at Düsseldorf's harbor in Germany.

Hee Lee Houng. Korean designer. She is the most renowned couturier of *hanbōk*, a traditional garment that she creates using very light silks. In 1977 she opened her first store. Four years later, she made her debut with a private exhibition at the Shila Hotel of Seoul, one of the most luxurious establishments in town. She is actively involved in the development of relationships between the North and South Korea. In 1991 she received an acknowledgment for her work from the Minister of Culture. In 1992 she participated in the ready-to-wear week at Paris for the first time. In 1997 she opened her headquarters in Paris and continues to present her Collections in the French capital.
(*Maddalena Fossati*)

Heel "I don't know who invented high heels, but all women owe him a lot," Marilyn Monroe once said. Certainly, the heel, with the toe, constitutes the most decisive component of all models of shoes. It draws attention, it determines the gait, it is an irresistible creative space for any fashion designer: the heel is, despite its location, especially looked at and admired. The most common forms are: bell-shaped or tapered, when its form is reminiscent of an hourglass, with lesser or greater degrees of accentuation; Louis XV, when the heel is high and the rear section is especially concave. The stiletto heel is an exaggerated version of it, and it has a highly pointed shape and a tiny base. The cone-shaped heel has an upside-down version of the geometric shape, while the Cuban heel is covered with leather. The stacks or wedge-heeled shoes joins the sole, becoming an integral part of it. Manolo Blhanik and René Caovilla feature ever-changing, creative heels, showing that it is still possible to invent things in this field. Famous heels? The globe heel of the Fontana Sisters (1940), the brass-cage heel of the Calipso sandal that Salvatore Ferragamo presented in London in 1955, on the occasion of an exhibition at the Tea Centre in London, and il tacco a campana designato per l'opera *The Golden Shoe Bob in* 1956 da Andy Warhol. (*Giuliana Parabiago*)

Heim Jacques (1899-1967). French designer. He was the couturier of Mme De Gaulle. His father Isidore was of Polish origin and in 1898 he opened a small fur shop in a Parisian apartment with his wife Jeanne. In the day it was a workshop and during the night it became their house. Isidore's skills and courage were awarded. The first rich and important clients arrived, headed by Victoria Eugenia, the Queen of Spain, and the wife of the composer, Claude Debussy. Inbetween the two wars, he invented a 'poor' fur manufactured with rabbit skins. Coco Chanel, a loyal client, was crazy about it. The firm's success was aided by Jacques' entry into the business, who had higher ambitions. In 1925 Jacques created coats and clothing with fabrics designed by Sonia Delaunay for the Exposition of Decorative Arts. In 1930 he gave his name to the atelier, dedicated to haute couture, with a clothing section also for young girls. He became famous by designing a series of swimming costumes and beach pajamas. In the second post-war period he anticipated the bikini with a two-piece model called Atomo. In 1934 the balance sheets allowed the business to expand with the opening of branch offices on the Côte d'Azur, in Rio de Janeiro, and in London. After the German occupation of France, Heim attempted to escape the racial prosecutions by travelling to England through Spain and Portugal. However he was arrested in Spain and imprisoned in a refugee camp. He returned to Paris in 1945 and continued his business by creating perfumes (the most renowned is Shandoah). In 1950 he established the company, Marie Carine, which was a precursor of ready-to-wear. In 1958 he was appointed President of the Chambre Syndicale de la Haute Couture. In 1966 he created a men's line. After his death, the business was survived by his son Philippe.

❑ 1969. The business closed down two years after Heim's death.

Heiman Max (1919). Dutch tailor. In 1984 he presented his Collection at the Haagse Gemeentemuseum of La Hague, which was to host a permanent Museum of Fashion one year later.

Heisel Sylvia (1963). American designer. Her creations are characterized by a sophisticated elegance. She constantly tries to combine practicality with refinery. After launching her first overcoat Collection in New York for Henry Bendel and an exclusive women's line, in 1987 she presented her first independent Collection for Spring 1988 for the department store Barney. She also designs bijoux and creates costumes for the theater and cinema.

❑ 1999. She opened a flagship store in Thompson Street, Soho, London.
❑ 2003. Her lines are on sale in more than 50 American stores.

Helanca Trademark belonging to the Swiss company Heberlein & Co. for a crimp elasticized yarn with continuous filaments, usually made of nylon, and mostly used for hosiery and knit undergarments.

Helen Morley Brand and English designer working in the USA. Her fixed idea is femininity, which is demonstrated in her bridal dresses. They are very tight with elaborated corsets and skirts in very light fabrics that model the body. After studying in Oxford and at the London College of Fashion, she moved to New York in the early 1990s. While working for other designers, she discovered her passion for bridal dresses. She has introduced romantic and sexy evening dresses into her line for the last few seasons.

Helena Rohmer. Jewelry designer and brand name. Born in Madrid, where she now lives. After studying political science in London, she returned to Spain to cultivate her family's artistic inclination. She has a sober and minimalist style and, in a short space of time, her jewels became appreciated not only by women, but also by men for her simplicity. Renowned also outside of Spain, she has created jewels for Paul Smith and Donna Karan.

Hellmuth Marc (1970). French designer. Born in Clermond Ferrand, he is a graduate of the École Supérieure des Arts Appliquèes Duperre in Paris. He began his career working for Dior, Thierry Mugler, and Yves Saint-Laurent. He was worked as the artistic director at Mila Schön since the Spring-Summer 2003 Collection. He has designed a final, coherent line of cultivated quotations and with loyalty to Schön's inclination for tailoring through filtering Schön's history and emphasizing the couture imprint of the brand. Memorable are his wonderful taffeta blouses decorated with jabot-origami.

(*Lucia Mari*)

Helly Hansen Norwegian clothing company of sportswear practised in extreme climates. The company was established in 1877 when the Navy Captain Helly Juell Hansen patented the first waterproof fabric made of bleached cloth and linseed oil. Since then the technical aspect of the clothing has increased at the same pace of experimentation. The situations that climbers can meet on mountains or sailors can encounter at sea (temperature, humidity, effects of salty or cold environments) are recreated in a laboratory. The company, which was the first to adopt three-layered clothing (technical underwear, intermediate isolation, and external protection) studied and manufactured competitive clothing for the Young America crew for the America's Cup held in New Zealand (October 1999 to January 2000).

❑ 2001. More than 500 Helly Hansen

product lines are distributed in twenty countries for men, women, and childrenswear.

Helvin Marie. Model. Her mother is Japanese and her father is American. She married the photographer, Bailey. As the friend of another top model, Jerry Hall, she was on Mick Jagger's list as the one of the cast members under contract for Jagger's expectation of a future as a director-producer (which never came true). In her autobiography *Catwalk, the Art of Modern Style*, she recounts her physical and moral efforts to become famous in an entertaining way.

Hemingway Wayne (1961). Son of a Canadian Native Indian chief. In 1982 he created the brand Red or Dead with Gerardine, selling secondhand personalized clothes and shoes at affordable prices at Camden Market. The brand is now present in 120 sales points and has five exclusive stores in Great Britain. His street fashion, designed to be shortlived because of changes in trends, is dedicated to a young, individual, and working clientele. Red or Dead was one of the first to commercialize Dr. Martens shoes, transforming them into necessary fashion accessories for a punk rock clientele and, in particular, for girls to whom these yellow-seamed heavy boots have changed the foot silhouette. Red or Dead has been presenting its Collections since 1988.

❑ 2000-2001. The two designers take a break to reflect and 'hibernate' the brand.
❑ 2002. Red or Dead published *The Good, the Bad, and the Ugly*, a chronicle of twenty years of the brand, written by Tamsin Kingswell and published by Thames & Hudson.
❑ 2003. Using messiah-like tones, the Hemingways announced their return to the business.

Hemp Textile fiber from the hemp plant (*cannabis sativa*) extracted by a retting and threshing process. The plant's origins are in central Asia, but today it is cultivated in several regions with a temperate climate, such as Europe, particularly Italy. It is a resistant yarn that creates a rough-looking and strong fabric with an irregular surface.

Hennin A modern version of the legendary witches' hat. Cone-shaped, very tall, and tapered, in cardboard or starched cloth that is covered with fabric. A long transparent veil hangs down from the top and it can also cover the face and body. Chantal Thomass presented it in a very showy way worn over a silver girdle with white, transparent stockings. It has attained its place in the history of costume. Originally from Flanders, it was widespread all over France and England during the 14th and 15th centuries.

Henri à la pensée French house of fashion objects. Halfway between a department store and a boutique of unconventional articles, it placed accessories and elegant clothes next to gifts for more than a century from the 1800s to the 1960s. It was situated in a prestigious location – Faubourg Saint-Honoré – with a rich clientele that included Ingrid Bergman and Françoise Dorléac. Sportswear was positioned next to embroidered boleros, pure silk blouses, and sophisticated knitwear. There are other stores in Biarritz, Cannes, Deauville, and Tunis.

Henry Guillaume (1978). French designer. After a short period working for the magazine *Citizen K*, then studying a little mathematics, followed by studies at the École Supérieure des Beaux Arts et Arts Appliqués at Troyes, he designed his first Collection in 2001 with Henry Achkoyan's assistance for the shoe Collection. He was selected for the Swiss Textile Award in Gwand and the following year he presented his second Collection at the Who's Next exhibition in Paris, a launching platform for young creators. His fashion is colorful and composed of unpredictable forms such as shorts that finish surprisingly as tulle dresses. From September 2002, as well as continuing with his own businees, he worked as Julian McDonald's assistant at Givenchy.

(*Maddalena Fossati*)

Henry Jack. American designer. He studied at the Esmod Institute and, immediately after graduating, he left for Japan. This experience was to influence all his creativity. In 1995 he launched his own line, which was sophisticated and street fashion at the same time. He first designed a women's Collection and followed that with menswear. In 2002 he presented his designs in Paris with the support of the third arrondissement, the Marais neighborhood, where he has located his men's clothing boutique. He has also a boutique just for women's clothing.

Henry Cotton's Brand of ready-to-wear fashion. Established in 1978 and acquired in 1993 by Pepper Industries-Trebaseleghe of Padua, today it is owned by the Fin.part group. The first Collections were composed of just a few leather garments. Over the course of time, the Collection have grown to create a total look for city life and leisure for casual men and women. The line focuses on the quality of materials and the researched sobriety of lines.

Henry Lloyd English company of clothing for sailing established in July 1963. In the early 1960s, the Englishman Henry Strzolecki, who was very keen on sailing, wanted to exploit the new possibilities that the new hydro-repellent and waterproof technical materials could offer in the sailing market. He led the sector's research into the most technical innovations for forty years. The main clothing lines are Atm (Advanced marina technology), which focuses essentially on sailing and offshore, and the fashion line for men, women, and children, which also includes more casual clothing. During the 1970s the company equipped Sir Ranulph Fiennes' Transglobe Expedition, the first circumpolar journey around the world that lasted for three years. In 1987 it supplied the clothing for the crew of Stars and Stripes of the America's Cup and was awarded with the Queen's Export Award.

Henry W. Bendel A legend in the American women's fashion sector. In 1896 Henry W. Bendel, who combined creativity with a talent for business, opened a store influenced by European tastes in New York. Its interior was French in design and in its clothing proposals. Bendel became so famous that he was hired as one of the permanent collaborators for *Harper's Bazaar*. Every season he designed a Collection of his own as well as importing the most current fashions from Paris. After the Second World War, he even converted his American colleagues into designers. Since 1991 the boutique has been located in Fifth Avenue in an old building of the 1920-30s, with Art Deco windows.

Henshall Scott (1976). English designer. He launched his own brand after completing his fashion studies in the late 1990s. After his initial success, he incurred financial problems and lost the brand. In 2002, thanks to a new Japanese sponsor, he was successful in buying back his brand and in starting the business again. He maintains his former passion for knitwear. His very short and sexy cobweb dress was worn by the actress Jodie Kidd at the English première of the film, *Spiderman*. His most recent line is a combination of British style and a sense of humor. He has 15 single brand stores in Japan and his fashions are sold in many department stores and boutiques around the world.

Hepburn Audrey (1929-1993). American actress. Born in Brussels, her real name was Hedda van Heemstra Hepburn-Ruston. Thin with big fawn eyes and a long neck, she possessed a juvenile passion for dancing and made an unmistakable black silhouette on the cinema posters. Hepburn's beauty was simply unusual for the 1950s when she triumphed as the pin-up model. From her very first appearances, she imposed herself as an unquestionable icon of taste. Her first successful film, *Roman Holiday* (1953), besides giving her an Oscar as Best Actress, made an impact on the fashion world. The white blouses worn with large skirts with elastic bands at the waist and a scarf around the neck became popular. Hepburn had arrived at Hollywood from Broadway where she had been the protagonist – expressly chosen by the author, Colette – of the theater production of the novel *Gigi*. Two more of her films, *Funny Face* and *Arianna*, launched other fashions, such as tight pants to the ankles, colored tights, black pants that were ancestors of the future stirrup-pants, and ultra-flat shoes. *Breakfast at Tiffany's* (1960) marked the triumph of the black sheath dress and oversized sunglasses. Notwithstanding the fact that Hepburn often wore creations by Valentino, Saint-Laurent, Emilio Pucci, Ralph Lauren, and André Laug, and accessories by Gucci, Hermès, Louis Vuitton, and Ferragamo, her name is linked particularly strongly with Hubert de Givenchy. The two met on the set of *Sabrina* (1954), when the director Billy Wilder entrusted the French couturier, on Hepburn's suggestion, to help Edith Head in the creation of costumes for the protagonist. Thanks to that movie, a lifetime connection was born between the actress and the designer. From that time, Givenchy designed most of Hepburn's outfits both on the set and in her private life. Hepburn said on many occasions: "I need Givenchy as American women need a psychoanalyst".

Hepburn Katharine (1907-2003). American actress. Tall, thin, with an aristocratic attitude, she wore her signature outfit from very young: pants and an oversize sweater. Born in a well-off family of the New England's bourgeoisie, she was the youngest of six children. She started her acting career in spite of not having the backing of her father. When she arrived in Hollywood, George Cukor – who was to direct her in her cinema debut, *A Bill of Divorcement* (1932) – took her under his protection, enlisting her in elegance courses with the young heiress, Laura Harding. At the same time, her production studio, Rko, urged her to dress in a more feminine way. However, Hepburn refused to abandon her own style, apparently shabby and rebellious. She convinced the costume designers first, and then the producers, to comply with her. The multitude of her roles during her long and happy career, marked by four Oscars, was unhindered by her inimitable look and personal taste. The severe pantsuits, the pied-de-poule outfits worn in *The Woman of the Year* (1942), the sophisticated clothes created by Adrian for *The Philadelphia Story* (1940) are now part of the history of fashion. In 1940 the actress' name appeared in the list of the best dressed women of New York. After the death of Spencer Tracy, the great love of her life, in 1967, she made her wardrobe even more vital, composed of 20 pairs of pants, an infinite number of white T-shirts, cardigans, and high neck sweaters. In 1985 she received the Council of Fashion Designers of America award, simply wearing a T-shirt, black silk pants, and a white silk scarf. On that occasion, Calvin Klein defined her as: "The incarnation of the modern style". (*Sofia Leoncina Gnoli*)

Herchcovith Alexandre (1971). Brazilian designer of Romanian and Polish origins. He studied at the Santa Marcelina College of Arts, where he enrolled because he had been designing clothes for himself and his mother since the age of 10. His mother and close friends were later to wear some of his first designs. As a teenager, he divided himself between the sub-culture of San Paolo and an orthodox Jewish education. This was how he discovered ironic unconventionality and an experimental taste for contradictions that now characterize his work. His debut was in 1993. He considers his job as a parallel with visual arts and is often induced to experiment. He draws inspiration from Brazilian culture and folklore. He arrived in Europe to present his creations at the London Fashion Week in 1999 and afterwards in Paris.

Herman Daniel (1972). Swiss designer. He graduated from the Central St. Martin College of Art and Design in 1998. Two years later he won the Swiss Textiles Award of Lucerne. In 2001 he presented his designs twice in London and in Gwand, Switzerland. He has distinguished himself for his light clothes manufactured with superimposed cloth, cut with laser, and for the thin latex used for shirts and lingerie. He has also worked with John Galliano.

Hermann Gerson German fashion house in business from 1835-1938, when Gerson's successor, Freudenberg, was forced to close the business due to racial oppression. He had transformed a fabric shop into the atelier that dictated the fashion rules in Berlin. The boutique was in Werderstrasse. The atelier's balance sheet had been extremely positive in the early 20th century.

❑ Notwithstanding the fact that the business had been closed for 65 years, the Fashion Bazaar Gerson & Comp. is considered among the pioneers of the modern department store. It was capable of making fashion through its rudimentary dressing rooms, lit by candles, not only in Berlin, but throughout Europe. The Tzar of Russia was among Gerson's loyal clients.

Hermès French brand of leather articles,

bags, cases, haute couture (until 1956), ready-to-wear, furniture, table sets, jewels, perfumes, horse-riding and golfing wardrobes, and particularly scarves and ties. It is a great name for luxury items. The story began in 1837, when a saddler, Thierry Hermès, opened a store selling horse tackle in Paris. Forty years later, at the dawn of the Third Republic, the second generation of Hermès moved to Faubourg Saint-Honoré, to the location that was to become part of history. It still is the brand's headquarters and its commercial showroom. In the 1920s Thierry's nephew, Emile-Maurice, started to create suede garments after acquiring his brother Adolphe's quota. In 1927 he launched a bijoux line with a logo from the horse-riding world. In 1929 the first Collection was designed by Lola Prusac. Some accessories date back to the 1930s marking not only the history of Hermès, but also that of fashion, such as the belt inspired by the dog's collar and the bag inspired by saddle bags, launched for the first time in 1935. It was reduced in size and became famous in the post-war period thanks to Grace Kelly who showed it on a cover of *Life* in 1956. From that moment on, the bag was called Kelly. In 1949, Hermès anticipated ready-to-wear fashion through the ready-made system, a sort of custom made ready-to-wear. A flagship of this innovation is the woman's dress *Hermeselle* in printed cotton. In 1951 on the death of Emile-Maurice, the company passed to his sons-in-law Robert Dumas and Jean Guerrand. Hermès' business and boutiques multiplied. Today there are 55 Hermès owned boutiques and about a hundred licensees worldwide. In the 1960s, the company made its debut in the perfume sector. The company is still managed by Jean Louis Dumas, grand-nephew of the founder and part of the fifth generation of Hermès. The family still owns 86% of the capital stock. Hermès distinguishes itself for the handmade manufacturing of small leather goods. Its philosophy is 'innovating while continuing with tradition'. It is with this reference to tradition that, more than a century after the opening of the first shop, the brand remains connected to what was its original vocation – the world of horses. In the early 1990s the company, which towards the end of the century had a turnover amounting to about 800 billion, started to buy acquisitions, especially in the field of textile companies. Catherine de Karolyi, Nicole de Versian with young Lacroix, Bergère, Bally, Myrène de Prémoville, Giudicelli, and Audibet have all worked for Hermès' ready-to-wear. In 1999 Hermès took over 35% of Jean-Paul Gaultier.

❑ 2001. The group's turnover amounted to 1.227 billion Euros, up 8.2% compared to 2000, which was an excellent year from the standpoint of economic results. All of the markets grew, particularly the Japanese market had distinguished itself with a substantial 23% increase.
❑ 2001. Opening of new sales points in Tokyo, Lisbon, Berlin, Paris, Miami, Chicago, Pusan, and Singapore, and a new branch office in Shanghai.
❑ 2002, March. Debut of Hermès' e-commerce, exclusively for the American market. Accessories are on sale through the site.
❑ 2002. The French company Hermès International SA achieved a turnover of 1.242 billion Euros, up 1.3% compared to 2001. In the European market, proceedings increased by 1%, while in the United States the growth was 4%.
❑ 2002. Opening of Hermès in Tokyo. The project was attended to by Renzo Piano and Rena Dumas, wife of the President and creative director Jean Louis Dumas Hermès, who follows the interior design of all Hermès' boutiques.
❑ 2003, May. The collaboration with Martin Margiela comes to a end after six years. From the autumn-Winter Collection 2004-05 the new designer was to be Jean Paul Gaultier. This new role did not change his role with his own brand, of which Hermès has a shareholding of 35%. *(Dario Golizia)*

Herno Italian raincoat company. Established in 1948 by Giuseppe Marenzi in Lesa, on Lake Maggiore, it converted from artisan production to industrial methods in 1969. In 1992 it employed more than 600 people. It has both men's and women's lines.

❑ 2002, March. Claudio Marenzi, heir of the company, becomes Vice-President of the Classico Italia, the Italian group of men's high fashion that joins together

companies for a global turnover of 350 million Euros a year. Luca Mantellassi, President of the Chamber of Fashion of Florence and Vice-President of Pitti Immagine, had been President of Classico Italia until 2004.
❑ 2002, June. Barbara Gast became the new project manager of the men's and women's lines, starting with the Spring-Summer 2003 Collection.

Herrenjournal German men's fashion magazine. It was published for half a century from 1931 to '81 by the Deutscher Fachverlag of Frankfurt. It became *Der Modedirektor – das Blatt des Eleganten Hernns.*

Herrera Carolina (1938). Venezuelan designer. Before becoming interested into fashion, she was simply considered as one of the ten most elegant women in the world. In 1981 she launched her own line in New York, based on jackets, *tailleurs*, and cocktail dresses. The clothes were sober, essential, but above all, very feminine. Her grandmother and great-grandmother used to buy their wardrobes from the great Parisian tailors based in New York. For this reason, the rigorous cutting and the sculptural structure of her dresses have often evoked Poiret and Balenciaga. Born in Caracas, she married the landowner Reinaldo Herrera. Nancy Reagan, Kathleen Turner, and Caroline Kennedy are among her most famous clients.

❑ The section dedicated to the Spanish designers of the Smithsonian National Museum at the Behring Center exhibits one of the dresses created by the designer.

Herrera y Ollero Spanish brand. Established in Madrid in 1945 by Rafael Herrera (1925) and Enrique Ollero (1926), they were very skilled in artisan business as they were both sons of tailors. Their fashion intelligently drew inspiration from France, filtering its trends and adjusting them to the costume of Madrid society.

Herzigova Eva (1973). Model. Born in Litvinon in the Czech Republic. She started her career at the age of 16, when she won a model contest organized by the Madison Agency in Prague. Her fame is due to the unforgettable advertising campaign of the WonderBra, which made her the model of men's dreams. She vaguely looked like Marilyn Monroe, candid, and curvaceous. She appeared in the 1997-98 editions of *Sport Illustrated* dedicated to swimwear. Thanks to a health regime, she lost enough weight and rounded off her curves, so as to continue modeling and appearances in advertising campaigns as those of Spring 2003 by Louis Vuitton, Burberry, and more. She had a role in the film by Vincenzo Salemme, *L'amico del cuore*. She married Tico Torres, the drummer from Bon Jovi in 1996. (*Silvia Paoli*)

❑ 2003, October. The model presented a beachwear line with her name in Paris. It was to be manufactured in Milan. The line consisted of original swimming costumes in lively colors that turn into miniskirts and beach robes with dotted patterns in microfiber and tulle. During the commercial shot in the French capital, the traffic blocked the city because of the model's beauty.

Heskia Samantha (1967). English designer of bags. Born in London of Persian origin. She finished her interior design studies in 1988. After several working experiences, she put together a group of artisans specialized in the working of small beads in 1995. This was how she began her production of bags. She introduces new materials into every Collection. In 1999 she used bone, mother-of-pearl, and plastic. Every creation is a highly refined unique piece.

❑ The production of bags is accompanied by that of shoes, scarves, belts and silken nightwear.
❑ 1999. Birth of the Collection Samantha Heskia for Debenhams, for whose label the designer created two accessories' Collections. The business collaboration came to an end in 2001. The designer's creations are exported to five countries – Hong Kong, Spain, Belgium, Japan, and the USA. In the USA, Heskia's lines are on sale by Language and Verve, and in London by Harrods.

Hettabretz Italian company specialized in

the manufacturing of women's leather, cloth, and fur clothes. It has been active in Bologna since 1960. The brand derives its name from the founder's name, Enrichetta Bertuzzi. In 1987 she opened a showroom in Milan in Palazzo Borromeo in Via Manzoni. In 1993 she began production of menswear, inspired by luxurious fabrics and finishings. The company still belongs to the Bertuzzi family and it is now guided by the third generation. In 1998 the firm renovated its style to regain its market position.

❑ 2001. In the Winter Collection, among the traditional leather pieces, knitwear and cloth made their appearance, still matched with fur. In the same year, Hettabretz introduced a ready-to-wear line.
❑ 2003. A green chinchilla blanket and an ostrich blouse with a pekan collar were are the contributions of the Bolognese firm to Luxury & Yachts, the first Italian conference of luxury products held in Verona. The highlights of the conference were sunglasses studded with Lancaster diamonds and rifles by the Brothers Piotti made-to-measure as if they were dresses. Hettabretz collaborated with the Roman school of marketing development, Ateneo Impresa, setting a communication project for the aspiring managers to diffuse the brand's visibility through the process from production to the market.

Hettemarks Italiana Clothing company. Established in Bari in 1959 by the Swedish family, Hettemarks. The company was one of the most important in this sector in the 1960s. In the mid 1980s it employed about 800 people, mostly women. It manufactured the brands Mammi, Sprint, Linea 4, and Harrison's, as well as a women's line designed by Enrica Massei. The company was in receivership since 1976, although it was rescued for a short time thanks to the intervention of Gepi, it later closed.

Heuwagen Madeline (1971). French designer of German origin. Born in Saarbrucken, Germany. She studied fashion at the Esmod Institute in Paris in 1994 and fashion management at the Institute Français de la

Hettemarks models. Sketch by Maria Pezzi.

Mode of Paris in 1998. As a student she worked with several Parisian designers and created her own brand in 1994 with the help of a Philip Morris award. Initially she sold her designs in France and Japan. She defines her style as "classic with humor".

❑ Heuwagen's creations are often on display in Thébaïde's windows, a Parisian boutique with a homely feeling owned by Eléonore Dubrule, who welcomes and helps young designers in search of a stage such as Christophe Guillarme, Ralph Kemp, and Jack Henry.

Heuzey Léon. French fashion historian. In his essays *Recherches sur les figures de la femme voilée* (1873) and, above all, in *Histoire du costume antique d'après les etudes sur le modèle vivant* (1922), he studied draperies and plissés of Greek and Roman tunics, which are significant details of a simple fashion inspired by a traditional palette of colors.

Heylen Anne. Belgian designer. She studied at the Antwerp Academy. In 2001 she presented her Collection in Paris with doll-like puppets that moved along the runway through a mechanic system of moving cables. *Satellites of Love*, as the Collection was called, toured worldwide and the objects became collectors' objects.

Heyraud French brand of high fashion shoes. Established in Limoges in the 1950s, it imposed itself on the market thanks to production attentive to fashion and a precious custom-made line for both men and women.

❑ 1995. Bata sold the brand to the Eram group, which controlled several French companies in the shoe sector, among which Tbs, Buggy, Bocage, Gémo, and France Arno.
❑ Bertrand Heyraud published *Shoes*, a book that is his personal tribute to the fashion sector to which he devoted his life.
❑ 2003. Heyraud's shoes are on sale in about fifty single brand stores in France; three stores in the Côte d'Azur, two in Nice and one in Cannes, plus the boutique along the Champs-Elysées.

Hickey-Freeman Established American brand of men's clothing. It represents classic American elegance. The brand has just celebrated its centenary. Jeremiah Hickey and Jacob Freeman, the founders, started in 1899 with a modest clothing factory. They overcame the years of wars and the Depression. They were the official suppliers of uniforms for the American army. The brand has brilliantly resisted the invasion of the Made in Italy, maintaining its loyalty to a rigorous and classic style. Its golfing clothing line, *Bobby Jones*, is one of the bestselling ranges in the USA. Today the company is managed by Duffy Hickey, a grandson who has modernized the cutting and adopted lighter fabrics to meet the needs of the new Wall Street generation.

❑ In the last years of the 20th century, the company passes under the control of Hartmarx, which controls 12 clothing brands among which Perry Ellis, Burberry, Tommy Hilfiger, and Pierre Cardin.
❑ 2001, July. Bobby Jones, the sportswear division of Hickey-Freeman, is distributed in Europe by Lyle & Scott. The golfing clothing brand is on sale in the Far East and in the United States.

Hidalgo (de) Luis. Spanish designer. He went to Italy following his sister Elvira, a famous soprano, who had Maria Callas among her students when she became a singing teacher. He worked for Biki and opened an atelier in via Visconti di Modrone in Milan with Manolo Borromeo and Alma Filippini for a few years. He worked as a buyer for La Rinascente. The journalist Maria Pezzi recalls that he was a man of extraordinary sympathy and vitality as the talent scout for Missoni.

Hiett Steve (1940). English photographer. He studied graphics at the Royal College of Art in London in the early 1960s, and only became interested in fashion photography later on. He alternated the work as a photographer with that of musician and graphic designer, living between London and Paris. At the end of the 1960 he worked for *Vogue*, *Marie Claire*, and *Lui* as well as directing TV commercials. In 1999 he published the book *Vogue's Glittering World*, a catalogue from an exhibition with the same title, which focused on his past work. Since 2000 he has followed advertising campaigns for Trussardi.

Hi-Fashion Japanese magazine. First published in 1960 in the years of the diffusion of Western fashion in Japan. It was initially a bi-monthly and then became a monthly. *Hi-Fashion* distinguished itself from its rival periodicals born in those years because it was the only one that specialized in Paris fashion. It is considered, on an international level, to be the most representative magazine of Japanese fashion and the first one to promote ready-to-wear in Japan.

Hilfiger Tommy (1952). American designer of men's fashion. His turnover is well over 1,500 billion Liras. Son of a jeweler and a nurse, he grew up with cereals and Catholicism. At the age of 17 he had already proved his fashion intuition. He opened People's Place in his hometown, Elmira (New York State), a store with ebony walls and incense-perfumed candles on sale, bell-bottom pants, and patchwork jackets. In 1978 the store

Luis de Hidalgo (seated), Manolo Borromeo and Alma Filippini, in a sketch by Brunetta, 1950s.

became bankrupt, which was Hilfiger's first and last failure. He married Susan Cirona, who he had met through his business. They designed clothing for various jeans firms, including Jordache, Tattoo, and Pepe for 6 years (even during their honeymoon in Bombay). In 1984 he received an offer from Calvin Klein, but he did not take up the offer because Zvia, a Los Angeles clairvoyant, stopped him: "Wait, something better is coming". The following day, he met Mohan Murjani, king of Indian textiles and former supporter of the fashion experience of Gloria Vanderbitt, who decided to give the financial support to his line. There was a test to the head-spinning ascent of Hilfiger, Murjani was replaced by Silas Chou, the king of Hong Kong textile. A fortunate look? He said, "The classics, which I re-elaborate, chino pants, blue blazers, button-down shirts, loafers, are my backbone". However, the uniform which earned him the media's visibility is streetwear, that is T-shirts, jeans, parkas, underpants, baseball berets, padded jackets, and sneakers. These clothes are all tattooed with an enormous logo. The writing Tommy Hilfiger, plus a white, red, and blue flag of nautical inspiration (a family passion). Since then, one night in 1994, the rapper Snoop Doggy Dog went on TV with an extra large Hilfiger's blouse, becoming the totem of the African-American teenagers. "Other designers have never accepted the power of the Black Urban Youth. I have, instead, cuddled them because at the end they are the real trend carriers, those imitated by the white teenagers". Contradictory to others, he does not believe that streetwear is a fickle niche: "My model client is a total loyal fan: logo, singers, athletes, and soft drinks. We live in the era of big brands, which are absolute drugs". While he enflames the crowds, critics detest him. Amy Spindler of the *New York Times* dismissed him just by saying: "His big artistic dilemma is to decide where to put his logo". The long-gone Liz Tiberis, when she was director of *Harper's Bazaar America*, was more conciliatory: "Come on, someone has to dress America". But it is Hilfiger himself who earns 25 billion dollars a year with his wages and bonuses who does not consider himself as an orthodox designer: "I am a creative director, I supervise marketing, advertising, the brand's image with the public. Even if I design several products, I don't consider myself a total innovator like John Galliano who creates what did not exist before". The unorthodox designer created the uniforms of the Ferrari's technical teams.

(*Benedetta Pignatelli*)

❑ 2001, July. The company acquired the license for Europe, Tommy Europe, for a value of 200 million dollars.

❑ 2001, November. A four-floor store opened in the Soho area of New York.

❑ 2001. The company had 145 direct stores, 15 of which in Europe (there were 90 in 2000). In Italy, the distribution network of the American brand included three direct stores (Turin, Catania, and Pesaro) and 125 sales points in department stores and specialized shops.

❑ 2001. Tommy Hilfiger Inc.'s turnover amounts to 1.880 billion dollars, up 4.9% compared to 2000. The net profit amounted to 131 million dollars, up 24%.

❑ 2003, February. Tommy Hilfiger Corporation appointed Joel Horowitz, the former general manager, as President. He replaces the designer himself.

❑ 2003, March. The American company focused on the Indian market and reached an agreement with the group Arvind Brands, which was to sell Tommy Hilfiger's clothing through a distribution network of exclusive sales points and department stores.

❑ 2003, June. The fiscal year closed with a turnover of 1.89 billion dollars, a small increase compared to 1.88 billion of 2003. The net profit, on the contrary, diminished to 126.7 million dollars, against 134.5 million of the previous year. For the fiscal year 2004 the company expected a decline in proceedings of 7-9%.

❑ 2004. Opening of a new store in Amsterdam (the second in the Netherlands), in which the men and women's sportswear Collections are on sale, plus the denim line. A space is also dedicated to fragrances, body cosmetics, watches, hosiery, bags, underwear, and

shoes. The store was also to become the point of reference for the Tommy Hilfiger's childrenwear Collection.
❑ Thanks to a third contract renewal of the Tommy Hilfiger Corporate Foundation All-American Golf Classic, more than 1,600,000 dollars were collected, which the company gives to ADL (Anti-Defamation League), an organization that fights against anti-Semitism. The event was organized at the Montammy Golf Club and Alpine Country Club. The rich program concluded with a live performance by Cindy Lauper.
❑ The Tommy Hilfiger Corporate Foundation announced its commitment towards the Washington DC Luther King Jr. National Memorial Project Foundation, thanks to a money contribution of 5 million dollars to be provided in the space of 3 years.
❑ Tommy Hilfiger and Tommy Jeans were launched in Australia. The event was celebrated on a yacht moored in Sydney Harbour with VIPs and stars who enjoyed the first show of the new Collections.
❑ Another big event (almost 1,000 guests) to welcome the new flagship store in Seoul.
❑ New sunglasses for the American brand. The captivating Jackie-O line: it drew its inspiration from the extra-large shapes of the 1960s. The glasses were manufactured in a variety of materials ranging from plastic to metal and also come with polarized lens.
❑ The True Star line was launched, which included perfume, body lotion, and shower gel.
❑ With the slogan *Personalize Your Denim Tour*, the company reached the young generation and all those who wanted to distinguish themselves. The initiative took place in more than 18 flagship stores in 9 countries, involving young fashion designers and fashion students. Jam sessions with famous DJs were part of the event. The result was a unique jeans model with writing, patches, prints, and drawings. A serial number is applied to stress its originality.
❑ In December, Tommy Hilfiger Corporation acquired the Karl Lagerfeld brand with the purpose of relaunching the Lagerfeld Gallery Collection and other lines on a world level by the German designer.
❑ 2005. The American brand with premises in Hong Kong took over the rights to distribute the brand in Italy from Fincom.
❑ A large space was opened in Piazza Oberdan in Milan. It hosted the showroom, the offices, and a new store.
(*Dario Golizia*)

Hill Virginia (1967). Designer and fashion academic. She specialized in History of Clothing at the Courtauld Institute of London (1993), after following a course in restoration of ancient fabrics in Florence and a degree in History of Art from East Anglia University (1989). She has worked in museums and as a theater costume designer. Since 1994 she has been living in Milan where she started working in the fashion sector, manufacturing garments using artisan techniques acquired during her travels in Africa and the East. In 1998 she was invited to present her designs in Kobe Japan as an emerging, young talent.

Hilton Line of ready-to-wear fashion from Vestimenta group. Established in 1962 in Mattarello (Trento), it is now composed of 10 operational units, 2 commercial head-quarters, 3 direct sales points in Japan, 800 employees, and a turnover that amounted 220 billion Liras in 1998, 70% of which was attained through exports. The Hilton line, which was accompanied by a women's Collection towards the end of the 1980s, is distributed in Europe, America, Canada, the Far East, and Japan.

❑ 2001. The company split and gave origin to Borgo 21, of which Armani holds 60% of the shares, the remaining 40% is owned by the Mosterts family. Hilton is still owned completely by Mosterts.
❑ 2002. The year closed with a consolidate turnover of 51 million Euros and a total production of 414,000 pieces, 45% of which were sold the company's label. The number of employees was 520.

❑ 2002. In addition to the headquarters in Mattarello (Trento), production was enriched by 5 new production units, each specialized in different operations. Jackets and coats are manufactured in Vicenza, menswear is made in Trebaseleghe, fluorescent fabrics in Gallarate, men and women's pants in Padua, and Ungaro's womenswear is produced in Vaprio d'Adda.
❑ 2003. An agreement was signed at the beginning of the year for the global production and distribution of Trussardi Uomo and CK One men and womenswear.
❑ 2003. The company decentralized the technical clothing production and CK's knitwear to Hong Kong. "These are small productions that are carried out in laboratories and factories of suitable dimensions", claimed Roberto Zanetto, general manager.

Hindmarch Anya (1968). English designer of bags. Born in Burnham-on-Crouch. Completely self-taught, she started designing in London in 1987. Six years later she opened her first boutique in the exclusive Walton Street. In 1995 she opened a store in Hong Kong, and in 1997 a second boutique in London. She has a high level clientele that appreciates quality.

❑ 2001, February. The designer received a prize from the British Fashion Council as Accessory Designer of the Year. The award of Designer of the Year was awarded to Alexander McQueen, while the Best Designer of the New Generation was given to Stella McCartney. In the same year Hindmarch also received the Award for Excellence by Luxury Briefing.
❑ She opened six new international stores. For the autumn-Winter Collection 2002 she launched her first line of women's shoes and boots.

Hip-Hop Urban fashion born in the Afro-American ghettos of New York in the wake of the musical and artistic movement. The first expression manifested itself at the end of the 1970s in the South Bronx, along with four other components of the hip-hop culture: graffiti, rap, breakdance, and DJing. In principle, it did not present itself as a new trend, but as the manifestation of a new point of view opposed to disco music and its myths. It was an alternative to gang culture, a positive way to stay in contact with the street, and the community and the day-to-day spirit of Afro-Americans. The fundamental elements of fashion were unlaced Puma sneakers, Kangol berets, heavy gold jewels, and oversized clothes. The brilliant colors of the clothing reflected the chromatic elements of graffiti that appeared all over the walls in the entire city. Oversized pants and unlaced shoes were perfect for the acrobatics of breakdance. International fame was later conquered by rappers who contributed in introducing this style to the masses. It was at this point that the fashion industry began to see a possibility of making some profit. Niche companies, such as Cross Color and Karl Kani, experienced an unprecedented success. Tommy Hilfiger, although distant from the spirit of hip-hop, rode the wave of its success in becoming the most important designer-divulger of this fashion. Among the most important brands there are Fubu, Pelle Pelle, Avirex, Rocawear, J.Lo, Ecko Red, and Mecca. (*Francesca Gentile*)

Hip Huggers Very tight pants and skirts that show the belly in the hippy style.

Hippy One of the most important movements of the 20th century for its fans and social contribution. It touched not only the world of fashion, but also those of culture, music, and art, and society in its complexity. Its roots could lie in the beatnik ideology. The birth of the hippy movement can be placed between 1966 and 1967 in San Francisco. In the Bohemian neighborhood of the Haight Ashbury, the first group of Flower Children, the so-called representatives of the hippy people, came to light. The flower was chosen as symbol of freedom and innocence, while the hippy expression seemed to come from 'hip' or 'free' 'in the wind' (the etymology is controversial). In the late 1960s, the hippy movement became politicized. In the USA it was connected with the protest movement against the war in Vietnam, while in France in May 1968 it animated students' protests. In the 1970s it increasingly transformed at political-ideological level, developing the idea of giving life to a society parallel to that of the bourgeoisie in which to live following one's desires and inspirations, without taboos and sexual inhibition, with a full behavioral freedom. The hippies' commandments influenced young kids in a lingering way, who, in the full blossoming of the movement, were still children. It was through them that the hippy philosophy surfaced in the 1980s, which generated the New Age, one of the fashion's trends of the 1990s. If pop music and underground display the roots of the hippy universe in music and art, the elements that characterize fashion for the hippy movement are long hair and the basic clothes, an answer to the bourgeois clothing style. Jeans, simple tunics in natural cotton, bare feet, no make-up on women's faces, sandals, low-waisted and loose skirts and pants (hipster) are some of the most evident elements of this period's fashion, born, above all, from the desecration of wardrobe. This non-dressing led to a total diffusion of jeans. All of these elements returned in the fashion of the 1970s, with a triumph in patchwork. They were to have a new moment of glory in the Collections on the eve of the new Millennium. The fashions were created by the most famous international designers, who offered an extremely decontextualized interpretation on a political level, seen as an extreme freedom in behavior, dressing, and showing oneself. (*Gianluca Bauzano*)

Hipster Low waist pants, which are tight around the hips leaving out the belly. In vogue during the 1960s, but the fashion was more demure then as hipsters were worn with blouses and T-shirts that cover the bare skin, often accompanied by a high leather belt. They returned impetuously back in fashion forty years later. Following the rules of the nude look, these pants leave hips and belly completely bare both in Summer and in Winter. They are worn with minimal tanks, T-shirts, or very short jackets in the new wake of glamour that takes its revenge on minimalism. If referred to skirts, long, mini, or micro, this clothing takes the name of hip skirt.

Hipsters & Hipcats There had never been a Bohemian age as sophisticated as that of boppers, whose particular jargon is called hip. From 1944 onwards, the be-bop made its appearance in the jazz clubs of New York. Onomatopoeically, the name described perfectly the syncopation, speed, and coolness expressed by the new musical style. Jazz had entered into its adult period, it had matured, and was in search of rehabilitation. Hipsters were its protagonists. It was a rehabilitation, despite being necessarily contained in its boundaries. With the massive recruitment of African-American people during the Second World War, the daily cases of racism were less and less tolerated. This was not an isolated incident. Symbolically Hipsters would react with scorn even by the extravagant costumes of performers, of African-American singers, and jazzmen on the stage a decade earlier. The zoot-suiters, such as Cab Calloway, of the age of swing, Louis «Satchmo» Armstrong were removed as Uncle Toms for white people's entertainment. A certain clothing exuberance did actually remain, but it wanted to be more intimate, more culturally black, and to be acknowledged as more authentic. In place of the showy zoot-suits, the rule was replaced with a sober and more linear taste with the following adjustments: goatees, leather berets, the omnipresent dark glasses with the heavy turtle frame, such as Dizzy Gillespie, or the scarf around the neck on a double-breast white striped suit, such as Thelonious Monk. It was a bohemian and intellectual style, the beginning of visible Black pride, and the anticipator and inspiration for the existentialist vogue that was to be successful also on the other side of the Atlantic.

(*Maurizio Vetrugno*)

Hirata Akio (1925). Japanese milliner. His hats were sculptures that framed the head and shoulders. After studying at the Bunka College and his debut in Tokyo, he decided to further his creativity and technique in France by working for Jean Barthet for three years. In 1965 he opened his own atelier and boutique, the Salon Coco in Hiroo. His hats were all handmade. He collaborated with Japanese designers, such as Yamamoto, Comme des Garçons, and Mori, and also European designers, such as Balmain and Nina Ricci. Hirata's hats have toured the world on the heads of Japanese first ladies.

❑ 2003. Close to the age of 80, the

Japanese master was remembered for his contribution to Parisian haute couture. To celebrate his art, periodical exhibitions such as the one held at the Palais Galliéra, in which the designer's hats were shown next to shoes of Japanese inspiration created by the Belgian, Martin Margiela, and next to bottles of Opium perfume by Yves Saint-Laurent, which imitate the bottles of the traditional Japanese tradition.

Hirayama Keiko (1941). Japanese journalist. She graduated in literature from the Nikon Women's University. After working in the advertising department of Shiseido, she became chief editor of the Japanese magazine, *Hanatsubaki*. In 1976 she asked various important French designers, from Thierry Mugler to Claude Montana and Jean-Charles de Castelbajac to Tokyo's fashion exhibitions for the first time. Since 1992 she has been organizing exhibitions connected to the world of fashion in art gallery spaces, sponsored by Shiseido: Punk Fashion on the fashion of the 1970s and, in 1994, an exhibition dedicated to Stephen Jones' hats. At present she works as freelancer for several magazines.

Hiro Pseudonym of Yasuhiro Wakabayashi (1930). A Chinese photographer, born in Shanghai. In 1946 he moved to Japan with his family. He studied in Tokyo. In 1954 he moved to New York where he studied photography at the School of Modern Photography. After a series of apprenticeships with several photographers, he became the assistant to Richard Avedon. In 1956 he attended the courses of Alexey Brodovitch at the New School for Social Research of New York. From 1958 he started to work for several magazines, including *Harper's Bazaar*, with which he collaborated exclusively from 1966 to 1974. After sharing a studio with Avedon for a long time, he finally opened his own in 1971. In 1969 the American Society of Magazine Photographers nominated him as Photographer of the Year. Hiro's photos are characterized by strong visual impact, typical of an advertising approach with very bright colors and close-ups.

(*Luca Selvi*)

Hishinuma Yoshiki (1958). Japanese designer. After being Miyake's assistant, he made his debut in 1984 with a line of his own. Eight years later, he faced the judgment of the critics that follow Paris' exhibitions. They signaled him for his architectonic touch at the service of a very futuristic fashion, characterized by corsets with a metal structure.

❑ 1996. He received the Mainichi award for fashion for his capacity to use the most innovative technology in the reinterpretation of the Japanese tailoring tradition.
❑ 1999. Holland celebrated Hishinuma's talent with an exhibition at the Gemeentemuseum Den Haag. The event was a panoramic look at ten years of designing.
❑ 1999, March. The designer's new Collection stirred a general consent, with his fringed hems and cut-through wool dresses. *Vogue*'s co-editor Isabella Blow adopted enthusiast tones in her comment to the show: "The best is still to come for Hishinuma".
❑ 2000. He designed the costumes for the ballet *Arcimboldo 2000* by the Dutch Dance Theater.
❑ 2001. Publication of the book *100 Flowers, 100 Butterflies*, in which the designer and one of the most important Japanese photographers, Nobuyoshi Araki, pay a tribute to the energy of Tokyo's women.
❑ 2003, May. The World Company Ltd announced that it was to take care of Hishinuma's Collections from the autumn onwards.

Hitman Italian company of men's clothing established by Nino Cerruti in 1956, when the heir of the Lanificio Fratelli Cerruti of Biella decided to join the world of manufacturing. The production plants are located in Corsico and Gaggiano, near Milan, employing 350 people. Annually it produces 120,000 pieces, collaborating continually with a network of ten other Italian companies specialized in coats, pants, and jackets. The heritage of Hitman is intrinsic to the engineering technique of the various phases of tailoring manufacturing, based on typical industrial timing and standards. Since its debut the company, which works exclusively for the brands of Cerruti, has been producing the line Flying Cross. The line was born from the idea of the founder and tailor-designer Osvaldo Testa. It was a trendy brand, but with time it adopted an Anglo-Naples style, a fusion of rigorous Neapolitan tailoring ability and an English taste in fabrics. Since the early 1990s, the line's designer has been Maurizio Zuccotti. New politics in distribution have increased the number of clients by 30%.

❑ 2001, May. The company, in collaboration with the department store chain, Coin, decided to develop the Ishtar project to experiment with new technologies in the production and selling of custom-made clothing. The experiment, which began in the Coin department store at Piazza Cinque Giornate in Milan, and foresaw the use of the Internet. It has Portuguese, French, and German partners among others.

Hlam Brand of ready-to-wear fashion launched in 1997 by Gunn Johansson and Pierangelo D'Agostin. It is a total look line for men and women in a minimalist style, which is defined as being elegant, comfortable, and multifunctional. It is rich in detail, fabrics, and in its technical inspiration in manufacturing. The line is suitable for every occasion, being fluid and reversible.

❑ 2001, Autumn-Winter. The line drew its inspiration straight from the 1940s, dating back, in particular, to the beginning of women's pants.

Hochschule der Kunste Berlin Established in 1975, it is an art school that covers several disciplines with more than 4,500 students per year. A four-year course helps designers specialized in textile and in fashion in general.

Hoechst German group leader in fiber manufacturing. It is ranked second in the world, especially for the production of polyester fibers. After selling to Courtaulds in 1993, the company focused on acrylic and viscose. 60% of the business is dedicated to technical application. The turnover is divided as: 34% in Europe, 43% in Northern America (Hoechst Celanese), 12% in Latin America, and 11% from Africa and Asia. The group's president is Wolfgang Hilger.

Hogeschool voor de Kunsten Dutch school. It runs a four-year course for those who want to become fashion designers. There is a compulsory admission test. The two campuses are in Utrecht and Arnehm, and it is dependent on the Dutch Academy of Fine Arts.

Holding Bonotto Wool factory established in 1978 in Molvena, Vicenza. It manufactures fabrics that are continually researched and evolving, intended for women, but now also for men, in fibers that have now amplified from wools to include natural and artificial materials. The company, a family business, is already at the third generation. It privileges research, but also focuses on traditional quality, aesthetics, and creativity with links to art and culture. The company produces 2 million meters of fabric every year, which are produced in the various plants of the group with its 200 employees and a turnover of 50 billion Euros (60% comes from export).

❑ Its clientele includes: Marella, Liz Claiborne, Max Mara, Ellen Tracy, Ittierre, World Itochu, and Byblos, for which the company produces wool, viscose, silk, linen, cottons, and quality alpaca.
❑ Lorenzo Bonotto belongs to the association of Young Entrepreneurs of the Sistema Moda Italia with 37 more entrepreneurs of the textile sector.

Holleis Sylvia (1968). French designer of Austrian origin. After graduating in economics at the Sorbonne, she attended design and fashion courses at the Studio Berçot in Paris (1993). She worked with Lagerfeld, Guy Laroche, and Jean Colonna. In 1995 she launched her first brand, Bauhaus. She produces silk-screen printed T-shirts, which sell in France, Japan, and the United Kingdom. The artistic printing remains the starting point of her Collections for women's fashion. Since 1996, the brands have been Sissi Holleis and Sissi Shirt.

❑ 2000, October. She opened her first Parisian boutique in Rue de Nemours.

Homespun Handmade fabric similar to bouclé, which is heavy and knotted, but very warm to wear. It is used for sport jackets and coats.

Honey Magazine that is regarded as documentation of the fashion and customs of the young people in the 1960s. It was published in London (1959-86) by the International Publishing Corporation. Its style included simple, confident graphics and language. The magazine, often riding against the current, was the stepping stone for young and emerging creators and designers. At the time, this included the inventor of the miniskirt, Mary Quant.

Hong Miwha (1955). Korean designer. She graduated from the Bunka School, the most prestigious Japanese fashion school, and worked as designer in Japan. In 1989 she established her own fashion house and presented her Collections locally, mainly in Seoul. In 1993 she arrived in Paris. S made her debut in New York in 2001. She regularly participates at the Paris fashion shows. Her motto is to introduce femininity to masculine garments.

Hood Headgear of conical shape attached to the back of a jacket or the neck of a coat. It can be sewn on, attached by buttons, or a zip in order to remove it when necessary. It is used particularly for protection from rain, snow, or wind in sportswear, raincoats, and jackets, but also for furs and Winter coats. Hoods are deemed necessary for anoraks and parkas. From the 1980s the hood was also incorporated into clothing with sweaters and pullovers. Here it serves as a sort of neckline, scarf, or foulard. If cut on the bias and very large, it forms a soft draping on the back or in the front. A particular type of hood is the *cagoule*, similar to a balaclava, tighter around the head and neck, often closed by a coulisse or attached to a scarf.

Hope Emma. Shoe designer. She belongs to the generation who graduated from the Cordwainers College of London in the mid 1980s, along with Christine Albrens, Patrick Cox, Paul Harnden, John Moore, and Elizabeth Stuart-Smith. Very simple and elegant, her shoes use the most refined soft leathers, silk velvets, grosgrains, and embroideries. They are all manufactured in Florence. The brand is now famous internationally, which has led to her collaborations with Anna Sui, Mulberry, and Paul Smith.

- ❑ 2000, Spring. She opened her third London store in Notting Hill.
- ❑ Her brand is on sale in Italy, Norway, Saudi Arabia, Japan, Hong Kong, USA, and Australia.
- ❑ 2002, December. Her year ended with a significant exhibition dedicated to Indian manufactured shawls from 1800 to the present day. The event 'On The Fringe: Indian Shawls in Chicago' remained open until July 2003. Among the masterpieces, there were handmade pieces from Kashmir and a 2.74 yd. shawl manufactured in 1870.

Hope B. McConnick Costume Center Collection of clothes and accessories at the Chicago Historic Center. It retains more than 50,000 pieces that date from the 18th century to the present day, all of which were manufactured in the local areas. In the men, women, and children's sections, there is a variety of clothing: ceremony outfits, uniforms, working clothes, casual clothing, and sporting uniforms. Among the high couture pieces, there are pieces from the great European couturiers such as Poiret, Schiaparelli, and Dior.

Hoppé Emil Otto (1878-1972). German photographer, who was British naturalized. His photographs of Diaghilev's Russian Ballets were defined as 'the essence of movement'. He collaborated with *Vogue* and *Vanity Fair* from 1916 onwards.

Horowits Ryszard (1939). Polish photographer. Imprisoned as a child in the concentration camp of Auschwitz, he was one of the youngest survivors along with the director, Roman Polanski. After studying at the Superior School of Fine Arts and the Academy of Fine Arts, he left Krakow for the USA, where he studied graphics, painting, and photography at the Pratt Institute of New York, following the seminars of Alexey Brodovitch. He started a career as art director for several agencies. He left this in 1967 to open a fashion and advertising studio for photography. He collaborated *Harper's Bazaar*, *Sports Illustrated*, *New York Magazine*, and *Town & Country* as well as devising campaigns for AT&T, Toshiba, Chanel, and Saks Fifth Avenue. He also had several personal exhibitions. Extremely fanciful and with heavy impact, both from a chromatic standpoint and for the audaciousness of shots, his photos were often made with digital techniques, which Horowitz was among the first to invent.

(*Roberto Mutti*)

Horst Paul. Pseudonym of Bohrmann Horst (1909-1999). German photographer, naturalized American. His photography has a strong theatrical component. Influenced by Steichen, they evoke the purest spirit of the 1930s. At the age of 23, he became assistant to the photographer, George Hoyningen-Huene, for whom he had previously posed. In 1932 he started collaborating with Condé Nast. In 1935 he took over from his master at *Harper's Bazaar*. His vision of women is full of grace and sensitivity. Still-life scenes of interiors and advertising writings often feature in his fashion photography. He was comforted by the intellectual everyday life of Paris in the years between the two wars, he was friends with Coco Chanel, Cocteau, and the very young Luchino Visconti. After the war, in which he fought on the American side, he became the favorite photographer of Diana Vreeland. He was a great portrayer and a formidable travel reporter. He worked for *House & Garden* for a long time. He had several exhibitions in the USA and Europe. Among his books, *Photographs of a Decade*, his autobiography salutes the 1930s. In 1991, the German publishing house, Schirmer-Mosel, published the volume *Horst, Six Decades of Photography*.

(*Angela Madesani*)

Horvat Frank (1928). Italian photographer naturalized French. Born in Abbazia (a town that now belongs to Croatia), he moved to Milan when he was very young. There he studied drawing at the Brera Academy and worked as a graphic designer for an advertising agency. In 1951 he encountered photography through reportage of a pilgrimage in Southern Italy. He then moved to Paris where he met Robert Capa and Henry Cartier–Bresson, who encouraged him to continue with photography. After selling his first work sold to Epoca, he traveled as a photo-reporter through India, Europe, and the USA, publishing his work in *Paris Match*, *Picture Post*, and *Life*. In the second half of the 1950s, he became interested in the world of fashion. He approached it with a fresh and dynamic style, deliberately contaminating the static reportage style, which characterized fashion photography up until that point. His black and white pictures featured refined backgrounds, in which elegance dominated with a light touch. Jacques Moutin, artistic director of *Jardin des Modes*, offered him a collaboration. Since then Horvat has also been published in *Glamour*, *Elle*, *Harper's Bazaar*, *Esquire*, and *Vogue*. Starting in the 1970s, he became interested in digital techniques with which he constructed highly fanciful images (from the fairytale Puss in Boots to Virtual Beast where he set exotic animals in the urban background of Paris) as expressly 'disconnected from the time-space relationship'. He lives and works in France. (*Roberto Mutti*)

Hotel German brand of women's clothing. Established in 2000 by the designers Ingken Benesch and Kai Duenhoelter. A great passion for modern aesthetics and materials stimulate their Collections. The clothes are sensual, which discreetly cover and uncover the body, thanks to particular geometrics. It is a style that tends to veer away from the seasonality of Collections.

Hot-pants Their first appearance dates back to 1970. They belong to the generation of trash-fashion and to the gipsy, hippy, and later punk style, the label of the protest movement born in England and widespread in Italy. The angry air existent in the rhythms of the Rolling Stones and the desire for freedom resulted in unisex, low-waisted bell-bottom pants, which were consecrated by Raffaella Carrà on Italian television of the time. Dressing like a Blob with a miniskirt alongside a maxi and, as a tribute to legs, hot-pants that were irreverent and provocative worn with with tops, tanks, and micro-sweaters. Advertising profited and the bottom with the most fans in Italy was covered by very tight blue denim shorts. 'Who loves me, follows me,' was the slogan for a brand of jeans in a campaign directed by Oliviero

Missoni's hot-pants and miniskirt, in a drawing by Brunetta (from *Missonologia*, Electa, 1994).

Toscani. A seductive item not only in Summer, but which became increasingly shorter from season to season. From runways to the high street, girls (and not just girls) went in search of this ironic hot-pants. They sent out an image of an irresistible expression of youth, appearing beneath long coats and worn with serious blazers that swallowed up the hem. Unrevived during the 1980s, they reappeared just before the Millennium. This time they were interpreted more aggressively. Most designers featured them in their Collections. On occasion hotpants represented their entire Collection. The reinvented hot-pants proposed a new hot-fashion, which saw Lolitas on shockingly high platform shoes. These girls were the pin-ups of the late 1990s a la Vargas, a great illustrator who secretly dreamed up femininity in the 1950s. These were hot-pants that resembled underpants: soft or tight, trimmed or fringed, they were cut audaciously, becoming a spicy proposal for the evening, in glossy and elasticized satin, so tiny to drive one to distraction. They were 'the missing shorts' and a very hot trend. Reckless hot-pants created in transparent plastic, or spotted with sequins, or in black leather with candid or optical-effect T-shirts. These hot-pants paid tribute to the 1970s and disco music. Aggressive hot-pants worn with stockings invoked sin for femininity stressed by bare legs, a type of high-voltage seduction, which is an explicit declaration of the right to eroticism. (*Lucia Mari*)

Houbigant French fragrance company. Established in 1775 by Jean-François Houbigant in Rue du Faubourg Saint-Honoré. The first shop's sign had the indicative name: *A la corbeille des fleurs*, and it seems that Marie Antoinette visited it personally. Since then the company has always served the royal families. It created the Windsor soap in tuberose-scented almond paste and an ox-marrow cream for Queen Victoria. In 1829 it expanded to an international level. In 1870 the company served Napoleon III. In 1880 it changed its location to Neully. Fougère Royale was the favorite essence of Maupassant. The company's fragrances were also famous in Russia at the Czar's court. Several essence were invented for Alexander III from the Cologne Impériale Russe to the Bouquet de la Tsarina. At the Universal Exposition of Paris in 1900, the firm had huge success with the Parfum Idéal. During the 1920s, a branch was opened in New York and two more boutiques in Paris. During the Second World War, it refused to use substitutes for natural products and, as a result, its production was limited. In the 1970s, laboratories and offices were also opened in the USA in New Jersey. New fragrances were created, such as the famous Rose is a Rose and Quelques Fleurs. Today the firm still ranks as number 40 in the world.

House of Jazz English fashion brand. After studying at Middlesex University and spending time as Matthew Williamson's assistant, Hazel Robinson met Pablo Flack, the manager of the renowned 333 Club in London, a colorful character with an entrepreneurial spirit who abandoned his studies at the London School of Economics to rent a pub in Shoreditch, transforming it into a meeting point for designers. Robinson designed a sponge headband as a promotional freebie for the club's clients. The success was immediate and Robinson and Flack launched a Collection together in 2000. Their knowledge of what the cult object for the next season would be as well as their ability to not take themselves or fashion too seriously made them irresistible. The super-stylist Katie Grand is their creative consultant. They won financial awards to sponsor their exhibitions for two consecutive years. Their list of clients mirrors a rare capacity to create trends – one of their main clients is Browns in London. (*Virginia Hill*)

Howell Margaret (1946). English designer. She graduated in fine arts from Goldsmith's College in London in 1970. The following year she started to sell shoes to several shops. In 1972 she added women and menswear to her catalogue. She reinvented the white shirt of English businessmen, rendering it softer. Her style is English, sophisticated, educated, and traditional. It is quintessentially preppie with a few variations on the theme: cardigans, pleated skirts, and pullovers in traditional fabrics, such as tweed and cashmere. She has presented her Collections at exhibitions since 1995.

❑ 2001, Autumn-Winter. The new Collection was presented through the photography of Bruce Weber, who first collaborated with Howell in the 1980s.
❑ 2002, Spring. Opening of the new London flagship in Wigmore Street.

Hoyningen-Huene George (1900-1968). Russian photographer born in St. Petersburg, later naturalized American. In the 1920s he moved to Paris where he studied painting. He distinguished himself as a movie extra and for his friendships in the artistic world with personalities, such as the director Jean Renoir and the model Kiki de Montparnasse, the muse of Man Ray. After achieving success as a fashion designer, he was published in *Harper's Bazaar*, *Fairchild's* magazine and, from 1925, in *Vogue*. He studied photography at the same time. From 1926 to 1936 he became one of the top authors for *Vogue*, for which his work was characterized by aesthetics that were influenced equally by Ancient Greece and surrealism. The characteristic diffused light and the dedicated care to composition were so great that photos that were always shot in a studio seemed to be taken in the open air. After meeting Horst, who would pose for him as a model and introduced him to photography, he left his place at *Vogue* and, in 1936, moved to New York and to *Harper's Bazaar*. Ten years later he arrived in Hollywood, where he made his name as celebrity photographer. He published *Hellas*, *Egypt*, and the monograph *The Elegance of the Thirties*.

Hubert Brand of ties. Launched in 1968 by a family that had been active in the tie sector for two generations; from the knotted ribbons of the early twentieth century to the most evolved forms today. A new tie Collection is designed twice a year, based on the rationale of the pleasure of wearing a tie, rather than the obligation. In 1992 the Huberteam line was launched, which was a more discreet line to join the most extravagant. The style department is part of the company. The brand is distributed in Italy, Europe, and the Far East.

(*Sofia Camerana*)

Hubert René (1899-1966). American costume designer of Swiss origin. His rapport with Gloria Swanson, who he dressed both for movies and for her private life, made him one of the most renowned costume designers in Hollywood. He started working at Paramount Pictures, then at Metro (where he designed costumes for Norma Shearer and Joan Crawford), and to Fox, where he worked on all of the most important productions of the 1940s and 1950s, including dramas, comedies, historical films, and westerns. He designed outfits for Marlene Dietrich, Joan Fontaine, Jennifer Jones, Marilyn Monroe, Maureen O'Hara, and Ingrid Bergman (Anastasia). He also contributed in a particular way to the success of Linda Darnell for whom he designed costumes for *Forever Amber* and *My Darling Clementine*, among other films.

Hubertus Traditional unisex hunting jacket. According to the classic English design, it is bright red, tightly fitted, with a collar and pockets in black velvet.

Hucke German clothing company. It is one of the sector's leading companies. Established in the late 1940s, the company began with women's ready-to-wear. Following this success, it developed menswear lines and very successful children's lines. It exports 30% of its production to 24 countries – its first markets were in Benelux, Switzerland, United Kingdom, and France. There are 30 branch offices worldwide.

❑ 60% of Hucke's production is exported into 20 countries, including the Ukraine, Scandinavia, and Hong Kong. Hucke Italy is located in Genoa.

Hugo Boss German company of men's ready-to-wear. There are 8 plants operating in 6 countries with 2,000 employees. The company was established in 1923 in Metzingen, near Stuttgart, by the commercial agent Hugo Boss. Before the war the firm supplied clothing to the army and police. It later became the most significant German company of men's clothing, thanks to the careful management of Uwe and Jocken Holy, the founder's grandchildren. International success occured in the 1980s, with the appearance of yuppies and white collared males, for whom Boss is a status symbol. In the 1990s the company created two more brands:

Baldessarini, the more refined, and Hugo, a line targeting a young and casual public. The company was acquired by the Italian group Marzotto in 1991.

❑ 2000, October. Boss joined the womenswear sector, targeted to exploit new segments of the international market. The initial total investment amounted to 75 million German marks.
❑ 2001, December. After consolidating the Boss brand in the Italian market, the group focused on the Baldessarini and Hugo brands. Hugo was strong in Germany, Northern Europe, and the UK. However its quota in the Italian turnover of Hugo Boss was marginal, as well as that of Baldessarini, the leading brand of the group. This line is characterized by a high tailoring content and is manufactured completely in Italy. It is distributed through ten multibrand boutiques.
❑ 2001. The Collection Boss Woman, launched in late 2000, had a turnover of 48 million Euros, incurring a loss of 28 million Euros compared to the projected 14 million. The group admitted that the line was not to break-even in 2002. This was a big problem for Boss Woman.
❑ 2001. The total turnover amounted to 1.095 billion Euros, up by 195 compared to 2000. The net profit amounted to 107 million Euros, a growth of 8% compared to the 99 million of the previous year, but below the growth expected by the company. The Boss brand recorded a 16% growth, Hugo 48%, and Baldessarini 52%.
❑ 2002, March. Following the negative trend of Hugo Boss Woman, the mother company brought the style and development back to Metzingen to the group's headquarters to regain direct control of the line. Cristina Salvador was replaced by Lothar Reiff as the designer of the woman's Collection. Reiff is the creative director of all of Boss' Collections.
❑ 2002. The German group closed the year with a turnover of 1.093 billion Euros in line with 2001 results of 1.095 billion. The turnover only grew by 1.3% due to the exchange effect. Profits amounted to 74.7 million Euros, a clear decline if compared to 117.6 million of 2001.
❑ 2003, May. The turnover of the first quarter closed with a decline in sales of 5%, arriving at 340 million Euros. Estimates concerning 2003 foresaw a stable situation compared to the previous year. Not taking into account the impact due to the strengthening of the Euro, the turnover remained unchanged compared to the same period of 2002. The net profit of the period diminished to 44 million Euros, from 53 of the first quarter of 2002 at comparable exchange rates.

(*Dario Golizia*)

Hugony Boutique of perfumes, ready-to-wear women's fashion, and gift articles in Palermo. It was established in 1818 in the middle of the Restoration period after Napoleon's troubles, as the first fragrance shop in Italy. It was opened by Jacques Auguste Hugony, at 204, Corso Vittorio Emanuele. The boutique was named Articles from Paris, and it became well-known throughout Europe for its creams, powders (at that time it was rice powder), and essences; everything was sold in collectable containers. In 1920 Agostino Hugony moved the store to Piazza Verdi and later, in 1935, to Via Ruggero Settimo to amplify the fashion side of the business. This commercial strategy was also followed by his son Enzo and, after his death in 1985, by his daughters Elena and Jole.

(*Antonella Romano*)

Humbert Pascal (1966). French designer. He attended painting courses at the School of Fine Arts in Mulhouse. At the age of 19 he created the first clothing Collection for his boutique. From 1989 to 1991 he lived in London, where he designed clothes and theater costumes. He later moved to Paris to collaborate with Barbara Bui. Since 1999 he has been designing high fashion.

❑ 2000, April. In Singapore he participated in the French Fashion Furor, an event organized by the French Embassy and the Institute of Tourism of Singapore. Among the French designers presenting their Spring-Summer

> Collection there were Jerome Dreyfuss, Dominique Siroup for haute couture, and Christina Dior, Tom Van Lingen, and Eric Bergere for ready-to-wear.

Hunter Joe (1967). English designer. Alongside Adam Thorpe, he made his name in the late 1990s with clothes that could be defined as war material because he guaranteed their manufacturing with bomb-proof hi-tech materials. Pins, decorations, and badges all became necessary fashion details. It was a style comprising military coats, oversized pullovers, camouflage pants, and uniforms for guards of honor and camps. The bestselling jacket was also purchased – it seems – by Michael Jackson, with an air filter in the collar.

Huntsman Famous tailoring workshop at 11 Savile Row in London. Here the manufacturing of a suit requires a two-year wait. The workshop was made famous thanks to the excellence of its fox-hunting and horse-riding gears. Established in 1849 by Henry Huntsman, it specialized in sports clothing and suspenders. It later adopted a classic style, earning itself the first Royal Warrant, a certificate of suppliers to the Royal Family, in 1865. In 1919 it moved from the West End to its present address. Today 70% of the manufacturing is done by hand by a group of tailors skilled in just one element of suit manufacturing (shoulders, sleeves, back, and pants). From 1932 it was no longer under the control of the founder's family.

Hush Puppies Comfortable, waterproof shoes in leather or suede, often in bright colors, manufactured by the American firm Wolverine. They are the favorites of Martin Scorsese.

> ❑ 2003. From the Rockford headquarters, the company distributed its shoes, clothing, and family accessories in 80 countries.

Husky The most copied hunting jacket worldwide. It was created more than thirty years ago by Steve Gulyas, a retired American aviator, and his wife Edna. After settling in Tostok (New England), they specialized in clothing for cold temperatures, particularly for hunting and fishing. (Husky is the name of a famous polar dog.) The quilted nylon jacket with a hairline velvet collar has always been the favorite of the English Royal Family, who wear it when riding. From 1999 the brand became a total look line. It is produced and commercialized by Giuseppe Veronesi, who introduced Ralph Lauren, Timberland, Clarks, and Allen Edmond's to Italy.

Hutchings Roger (1952). British photographer. He graduated in land management, and then studied documentary photography at Newport College of Art. After working as a freelance photo-reporter, he was hired by *The Observer* in 1982. He traveled around the world – from India to Sudan, from Sri Lanka to Bangladesh – documenting crisis and war. His most renowned works became traveling exhibitions with accompanying books: Bosnia (1994), Ataturk Children (1997) About Kurds, Berlin (1999), and Thatcher Years (1999), a severe analysis on the England of Margaret Thatcher's government. Since 1990 he has been the official photographer for London Fashion Week. In 2001 he created Armani Backstage, an important reportage of backstage at the opening of the Armani Theater in Milan and published in a volume. He works for newspapers such as the *Independent*, *Stern*, *Der Spiegel*, *The Sunday Times*, alternating with photo-reportages for fashion sessions.

Huth Walde (1923). German photographer. She attended the State School of Applied Arts in Weimar where she became interested in photography. This interest was concreted when she started to work at Agfa. After which she became a portrait photographer. In 1953 she opened a photography studio for fashion and advertising in her hometown. She collaborated with the *Frankfurter Illustrierte Zeitung*, a magazine to which she remains faithful. She refused a contract proposed to her by *Vogue*, joining the fashion photography circuit, particularly in Florence and Paris. Her pictures are characterized by open air backgrounds and a balanced relationship with architecture. Since 1986, she closed her studio and devoted herself essentially to personal research. (*Roberto Mutti*)

Hutton Lauren. American model and actress. Born in Charleston, South Carolina, and grew up in Florida. Her charm and her toothy smile guaranteed her a long contract with Dior in the 1960s. She was *Vogue*'s cover girl on 25 occasions. She was the face of Revlon from 1973 to 1983. In 1992 she became the first modeling millionaire, opening up the way for her colleagues with big advertisement campaigns. In 1990 she returned to the runway. She launched a new concept of beauty, no longer connected to the stereotypes of age and size. She acted in several movies – the most famous being *American Gigolo* with Richard Gere.

Huybens Ann (1962). Belgian designer. Born in Leuven, she found fashion after following an unusual path. Initially she was a dancer, then a costume designer, followed by a period as an apprentice in a dressmaking workshop. In 1990 she opened her first shop in Gent. She uses silk muslin, wool, mohair, and leather and reinvents them with dried flowers, fishbones, jelly, and feathers. She prefers round shapes, which follow a silhouette, or gothic and unstructured lines. Her inspiration lies in nature, the do-it-yourself of her childhood. Her exhibitions are real events, a cross between art and the environment. Together with the landscape architect Patrick T'Hooft, she forms the creative team of the early Fleming, because "designers share one nest".

(*Laura Lazzaroni*)

Hyde Nina (1934-1990). American journalist. A graduate of Smith College, she wrote the fashion column at the *Washington Post* from 1972 onwards. She was renowned for her analytic approach to fashion as a mirror of the contemporary society. She was awarded with the Council of Fashion Designers of America award and nominated as a knight of arts and literature.

Hyères International festival of new fashion talents. Since 1986 the ancient thermal resort of the Côte d'Azur has been the location of this important annual event, the Festival of Art and Fashion. Young photographers and newly graduated designers enjoy the first and most important occasion to encounter the professional world of fashion. The central moments of the festival are the exhibitions that a jury, usually composed of great fashion designers, oversee in order to assign awards to promising talent. In 1999 the names awarded were: Alexandre Matthieu, Stéphane Courdet, and Christof Beaufays, a young Belgian designer about whom Gaultier said: "He offers the vision of the man of the third millennium".

❑ 2002. The Grand Prix of the fashion section was equally assigned to Félipé Oliveira Batista and to Rivière de Sade.
❑ 2003, April. The event, sponsored for the fifth consecutive year by the Group Lvmh, awarded the Italian-Belgian designer Sandrina Fasoli for women's fashion and the Austrian Ute Ploier for the menswear. Fasoli also won the 1,2,3 award with the French Laurent Edmond.

Hympendhal Beatrice (1940). German designer. She works in Duesseldorf. Since her first original creations in 1978, she earned the fame of being an avant-garde fan. Her brand became the symbol against mainstream fashion.

Hyper Hyper Covered London market of fanciful clothing for young people. It is a point of reference for small factories that produce clothes and accessories. It is in Kensington High Street. Since 1983, when it was invented by Lauren Gordon, it has been a mine of new talents. Hyper Hyper supports only emerging designers and producers, not only offering them a stage, but also organizing collective stands during the most important events dedicated to ready-to-wear and during the London Designer Shows.

A sketch by the Belgian designer Ann Huybens.

I

Iaf International Apparel Federation. Established in 1976 by a group of clothing entrepreneurs in the USA, Europe, and Japan with the purpose of promoting the common interests of its members and support their global activity. It was the world's first federal representative institution for the sector. The federation gathers once a year in the autumn in London at its headquarters at 5 Portland Place. The president remains in charge for a year and every member sits on the board of representatives.

Ian & Marcel Brand of ready-to-wear. Both Canadians, Ian H. Cooper (1946-1992) and Marcel B. Aucoin (1951-1991) met in Toronto in 1976. The former studied fashion design at the Ryerson Polytechnic Institute, and the latter studied furniture and fabric design at the Sheridan School of Design in Canada. They moved to London where Ian graduated with a Masters in fashion at St. Martin's School of Art. In 1979 they established their own company, creating Fortuny-style evening dresses in pleated silk, and developing liquid latex and silk-based technique, which allowed them to decorate fabrics as well as welding them without the use of seams.

Icap Italian knitwear company. Established in 1961, its headquarters are in Santa Maria degli Angeli (Perugia). With the brands Pitti, Spirito, John Ashpool, Escargot, and Golf Club, it exports about 30% of its production in western Europe as well as in northern America and Japan. It holds the license for men and women's knitwear of Giorgio Armani, Emporio Armani, and Giorgio Armani Underwear.

Icarius (1975). Brazilian designer. Born in Curitibal, he studied fashion design at the School of Santa Marcelina in San Paulo. His talent was noted for the first time during one of the many exhibitions organized by the school, when he presented the provocatively titled collection, My Mother's Cancer. His debut on the international runways coincided with the Spring-Summer 2001 collection presented in Paris. He proposed mystical images of new saint women with sophisticated and sensual lines, as a reflection of Senohora Aparecida do Brasil. In March 2002 he won Enkamania, an international research project for new fashion designers promoted by Enka, a world leader in yarn production, in collaboration with the National Chamber of Italian Fashion. In April 2003 he was chosen as the new creative director for all the lines of the Roman company Lancetti, after the resignation of Enzo Fusco. (*Sara Tieni*)

❑ 2005, May. The collaboration of Curitibal with the company came to an end. The artistic division was entrusted to an in-house team.

I.c.a.s. Acronym of the Cappelli A. Sorbatti industry. The Sorbatti family from Motappone, near Ascoli Piceno, has been producing and selling hats and berets since the 1920s. From its artisan roots, the company has transformed into a modern industry, rooted in the entrepreneurial tradition of the Marches. Price, quality, design and the wide range of classic, sports, casual and promotional hats for men, women, children, and babies are all elements on which the hat factory relies. It employs 24 people and has a production plant of 1,050 square yards. It can manufacture up to 2,500 hats a day.

Iceberg Clothing brand. In 1974 Giuliana Gerani, already the founder of the Gilmar group in the 1960s created a new brand. It is a synthesis of comfort and elegance in casual clothing with avant-garde and state-of-the-art technical innovation in the manufacturing and materials. Iceberg made its debut on the Milanese runways in 1995. The brand is sold all over the world with single brand boutiques in Milan, Rome, Paris, Beverly

Iceberg Woman, Autumn-Winter 1999-2000.

Hills, Capri, and Amsterdam. The diffusion of Iceberg's collections has been made possible thanks to a selling network that is revealed in its own showrooms in Milan, Rome, New York, Paris, London, Düsseldorf, and Antwerpen. Today Iceberg offers a young total look for men and women. As well as clothing, there are complete lines of accessories made on license: perfumes, glasses, leather goods, shoes, porcelains, ties, and watches. A new collection has been recently added called the Ice Ice Bay for little boys and girls from 4 to 12 years. In 2002 a new concept was started with the reopening of the restyled boutique in Riccione called the H-Art Store Iceberg (H stands for house and Art for contemporary art). Therefore, fashion art furniture can be all found in the boutique art gallery re-created in the warm and welcoming atmosphere of a chic New York apartment that contains a pop reference. This reference is to Pop Art of which Paolo Gerani, son of Silvano Gerani and Giuliana Marchini, founders of Gilmar and owners of Gerani and Iceberg, currently vice-president and creative director of the company, is an enthusiast collector.

❑ 2003. The photographer David La Chapelle drew inspiration from the film *Scarface* and directed the Iceberg's Spring-Summer 2003 commercial campaign.

❑ 2005, June. An agreement was made with the Alsatian company Le Coq Sportif to launch a special edition of shoes for the brand Ice J Iceberg.

i-D British magazine founded in 1980 by Terry Jones, the graphic and artistic director of the British edition of *Vogue*. It was initially launched with a low circulation as a quarterly, but in 1983 it became a bi-monthly, a point of reference for style rather than for traditional fashion. Its purpose was to document street fashion, new ideas, and looks, mixing content written in an unconventional tone and emphasizing the visuals as well as text. It registered and documented the most stimulating expressions of the pop culture during those years through emerging talents, from designers to photographers, film directors, journalists, and advertising agents. It made its name due to the selection of its creative photographers and its editorials about society and avant-garde fashion. More than a fashion magazine, it has become the expression of a generation and the symbol of an age. Thanks to an irreverent approach in illustrations (one of the most famous photographs was of Roy George dressed as a nun) and a clear and neat typographical image, the magazine was also an artistic expression. Every issue is dedicated to a specific theme. As well as clothing, it also features music, places, and trendy clubs. Notwithstanding its success, it fell into financial difficulties and in 1984 it had to ask for the support of a co-editor, Tony Elliot of *Timeout*. In 1987 it took on the look of a hardcover magazine and was published at the same time as the first edition of the i-D Bible, with an extent of 164 pages, once a year, dedicated to night clubs, music, fashion, and hairstyle. For its 20th anniversary, Terry Jones published a book that provided a photographic path of the magazine's history, presenting a page from every issue until December 2000. It was like a visual novel, which illustrated the last twenty years of the 20th century, in a kaleidoscope of colored pictures, changes, and trends. In 2003 *Fashion Now* was published and edited by Terry Jones and Avril Mair for Taschen editions. It contains a selection from the i-D magazine, which presents the work of the 150 most important names of fashion to the young emerging talents. Biographies and direct and exclusive interviews made it a fundamental document for contemporary fashion design. (*Gabriella Gregorietti*)

Idc (International Design Creation) French glasses manufacturing company. Established in 1980 by the optician Jean François Rey, son of the glasses' maker from Jura. It has 8,000 sales points and a boutique in Rue Saint-Etienne in Paris. Linear or extravagant, his glasses followed fashion throughout the 1980s. The second line is called Sous le soleil.

Ideabiella The Ideabiella Association was founded in 1979 on the initiative of a group of textile entrepreneurs from Biella, manufacturers of high quality draping fabrics, in order to create meeting opportunities with the major international buyers. This exclusive event stirred great enthusiasm for unique and precious textile products, which were made exclusively in Italy. The first event saw the participation of 44 companies. Today there was 61 Italian exhibitors. It is held twice a year, in March and September, at the Exposition Center of Villa Erba in Cernobbio.

Ideacomo Created in 1975 by Beppe Mantero and a group of silk entrepreneurs from the Como area. This niche fair currently gathers together an elite of about 70 companies manufacturing high quality, innovative, and refined fabrics. It distinguishes itself for its club philosophy. It is different from the other international events of much larger dimensions through its ambition to confirm itself as being an unusual fair, which provides selected and homogenous meetings. Ideacomo takes place twice a year, at the end of March and October, in the splendid glass pavilion designed by the architect Mario Bellini in the park of Villa Erba, Cernobbio, on Lake Como, where the director Luchino Visconti used to play when he was small.

Iff (International Fashion Fair) Organized by Senken Shimbun Co., it is held in Tokyo, every six months, at the Pacifico Yokohama Exhibition Hall. In July 2003 it celebrated the 8th edition. Apart from women, men, and children's wear, it displays furs, leather clothing, bags, shoes, and accessories. In 2003, 21 countries participated in the event for a total of 534 exhibitors.

Igan Ussaro Artistic name and anagram of the designer Ugo Massari (1956). Born in Salsomaggiore. His menswear and womenswear is produced by the company Mina of Fidenza and is characterized by the originality and the use of unusual materials, such as shells, leaves, wood, and metal. In 1995 he proposed his real idea: designs in recycled plastic called Eco Fast Dress 2000. It was produced by the Sacplast factory in Pavia: swimming costumes, bridal dresses, shoes, T-shirts, and skirts. Everything was vacuum-packed and pocket use-and-throw-away packages.

Igea Textile manufacturer established in Prato in 1964. It employs 100 people and has an annual production of about 2 kilos yarn, with a turnover of 56 billion Liras in 1998, equally distributed between Italy and overseas. There are currently three lines on the global market – the company sells its products in more than 20 countries – Igea (fanciful yarns in precious fibers), Azimut (classic yarn in pure merino wools and total easycare wool-viscose), and Filigea (collection of stock service yarns).

Igedo Company German exhibition organising company. Its president is Manfred Kronen. The company organizes several fairs and international events. The most significant event is Cpd woman.man. Held in Duesseldorf twice a year, in February and August, it is the largest and most complete European event about fashion. At the beginning, the event was created to only support womenswear. In 2002 it expanded to include menswear, swimwear, and underwear (previously hosted in a separate location). After which there was also an area for jeans and streetwear and another for the fabrics of the following season. In January 2003 Revolutions, a window for trendy young fashion with emerging or cult brands, was born. In September 2003 an exhibition was scheduled in Moscow called Collections Premieren Moscow, which would replace the Moda Moscow. In 1989 Igedo Company created the European Fashion Diamond award given to companies and personalities, which had distinguished themselves in management and performance. On August 3, 2002, the award was given to Umberto Angeloni for the Roman men's tailor boutique Brioni, renowned for its tailoring garments, which had been enjoying a tradition of high artisan's skill for half a century.

Ihram The piece of pure cotton in which men wrap themselves to reach Mecca. Ihram means 'condition of purity', which is necessary to enter the Ka'ba.

Ike Behar American brand of shirtswear. Named after the designer of Cuban origin who arrived in New York at the age of 20 with tailoring experience from his family's workshop. After successfully designing for Ralph Lauren and other big names, he decided to launch his own brand in 1982. The American press immediately defined him 'the wizard of shirtswear'. He pays an almost maniac attention to every detail. His shirts are the result of 52 production steps. Refined cotton, finished seams, refined collars and buttons are the brand's strong points, which are manufactured in several workshops and sold in the brand's own stores in the USA. (*Priscilla Daroda*)

Iki Italian brand of ready-to-wear fashion. Created in 1992 by Giovanna Buglioni, manager of Fpo, a company located in Osimo (Ancona) that manufactures elasticized and raw-cut knitwear pieces. Iki means 'the charm of the geisha' according to the definition of the Japanese philosopher Kuki Shuzo. Production witnesses the alliance between research and artisan's traditions. Products are distributed in Italy and overseas. From 1998 the brand had a showroom in Milan, in Via Montenapoleone, and two single brand boutiques in Dallas and New York.

Il Cavaliere Azzurro Archive composed of 750 volumes and 420 textile samples of ties, clothing, and interior decor. Its name was thought up by Stefania Farné with reference to the artistic movement founded in 1912 by Kandinskij and Marc. Farné put together the collection, searching through old catalogues, collections, and private libraries as well as among the rags of the textile industry stores, which took her to Como, the home of silk and ties. The archive, which starts from 1800 up until the end of the 1900s, is also a working laboratory to which designers and producers turn for research.

Image Fashion & Communication School of fashion styling and journalism. It offers a full time two-year course of study. Established in 1989 in Via Forcella in Milan. It was the product of the collaboration of several professional journalists. In 1997 it enlarged the structure of its programs with the purpose of a even superior specialization, changing from a one-year to a two-year course with daily lessons. The course includes show direction, production of fashion events, food styling, beauty styling, and interior design. The school's aim is the professional introduction of all of its students in the worlds of fashion and journalism.

I. Magnin American department store chain on the west coast of the USA. Established by Mary Ann Magnin, who emigrated to San Francisco to London with her family in 1870. In order to sustain her eight children, she sewed clothes that her husband Isaac tried to sell from door to door. This proved successful as Mary Ann was able to open a store in San Francisco six years after their arrival. In 1893 a store was opened in Los Angeles, followed by stores in San Diego and Palm Desert. I. Magnin remained in the hands of the family until 1943. In 1994 the business failed and some of its buildings now host another great chain, Macy's.

Iman (1956). Top model. Launched by the photographer Peter Beard. Iman Abdul Majid Haywood, a Somali student of the Nairobi University, initially modeled for Yves Saint-Laurent. She then modeled for all of the big names of fashion, becoming the star of that generation of models. In 1979 Otto Preminger gave her the role of Sarah in *Human Factor*, his last film based on the novel by Graham Green. In 1992 she married the rock star David Bowie.

Imec Women's underwear company. Established in the 1930s, Imec was the first Italian company to introduce innovative fibers and techniques in the 1950s. It made its name internationally by imposing itself with collective imagery thanks to a revolutionary campaign in the early 1960s. The campaign was designed by the three twin daughters of the company's owner. Today the Imec brand targets a traditional female clientele, who have a wide range of medium and high level proposals: underwear, corsetry, pajamas, nightgowns, lingerie, swimsuits, and beachwear. Established in 1936 in Paderno d'Adda by Nino and Jone Colnaghi, Imec is now a limited responsibility company, producing a million pieces a year with a turnover of 45 billion Liras (1998). Its brands include Peach Tree, for girls and young women, John Khol, medium-level brand for men, and Silvia Mantegna, medium-high level brand for modern and emancipated women.

Imitation of Christ American brand of men and womenswear founded by the actress Tara Subkoff and the artist Matt Damhave. The movie star and style icon Chloe Sevigny is the artistic director and promoter. IoC made its debut in 2000 during New York fashion week. Creating an event and stirring scandal characterizes the group's work. In 2001 it attracted media attention by setting a show in a funeral house in East Village, Manhattan. The two founders and designers prefer to define themselves as 'social engineers' and create vintage fashion enriched by the personal touch. Each garment is a unique piece on sale in selected boutiques in the USA. (*Francesca Gentile*)

Imprimé Any printed fabric. The most famous *imprimé* are in silk or chiffon.

Imta Desii Mode Italian wool factory. Its headquarters are in Montemurlo, near Prato. Established in 1950 to manufacture blankets and plaids. For its first 15 years it was a medium-sized factory managed by two business partners. In 1965 a third partner joined the factory, Renzo Desii, who was strong in management experience in Prato's industries. His entry marked the beginning of a speedy growth in the quantity of production. In 1981, Desii's son, Luca, substituted one of the partners from outside of the family. This was the time of rational organization and management readjustment. The company's quotas were shared between Gualtiero Gualchierani, his son-in-law Renzo Desii, and Luca. Luca Desii later became (and is still today) the owner of the firm with his sisters Annalisa and Cristina. Through the years, the differentiation of typologies and the growth towards increasingly new markets have led to company towards global production of textiles for clothing, with a particular attention for luxury export. The raw material is cashmere. Germany and Japan are the most profitable markets for the firm. The company often promotes charities and sponsors the restoration of art.

Incanuti Alberto (1962). Fashion expert. Born in Borgosesia. Self-taught, he has been a consultant for Marzotto, the Vestebene group, Ekafil, Maska, Blumarine Uomo, and David Valls for many years. He also devotes himself to the collection of customized vintage clothing, which are obtained by the recycling and assembling of old fabrics (or clothing pieces) found in small second-hand clothing markets around the world.

Incom Italian clothing company. Established in 1959 by Vasco Nencini in Pieve a Nievole, near Pistoia. It produces ready-to-wear fashion for men and women and raincoats for its own brands Incom Uomo, Incom Raincoat, Carol, Gimoda, and, with a worldwide license, Katherine Hamnett of London. It also works for some of the most important private labels: Dutch Mexx, German Esprit de Corp, American Tommy Hilfiger and CasualCorner, and British Marks & Spencer), carrying out the research of materials and the creation and development of designs. In 1990 it began to buy out companies, such as Vranco Spa, a Romanian state clothing company, GB Pedrini, the Tunisian Sabricom, and Bianchi of Subbiaco (Arezzo). In 1995 it opened Euroconf Industria in Romania for the manufacturing of men and women's clothes.

❑ 2002. The turnover of 100 million Euros registered a light decline compared to the previous year (-2.5%). The casual clothing line, Ernest Hemingway, displayed financial growth, which is produced and distributed all over the world (excluding Japan) thanks to a 12-year agreement with the Hemingway Foundation. The brand's development expectations were good. This year Hemingway has produced a retail turnover of 1.5 million dollars.

Incotex Brand of the Italian company Industrie Confezioni Tessili. It manufactures pants for the high segment of the market. Established in 1951 by Carlo Compagno in Venice. At the beginning of the 1980s, the company was transformed into an industrial reality with the entry of Compagno's sons, Marzio and Roberto to the family business. Pants for Burberry, Façonable, and Ermenegildo Zegna were manufactured on license. The company's own lines, Incotex and Rem, were distributed in Italy through 400 sales points. Seventy per cent of the turnover was acquired through export, especially in Japan and the USA, where a subsidiary company called Incotex USA was created.

❑ 2001. The year closed with a turnover of 37.7 million Euros (+25.9%), while the profit before tax had diminished to 2.32 million compared to the previous 2.58 million. The net profit amounts to 775,000 Euros. The export quota was still high at 50%.
❑ 2002. The company acquired 80% of Montedoro of Castellanza, a manufacturer of raincoats and casual jackets in Varese. The operation, which was worth 1.3 million Euros in total, represented the first step of the diversification process started by the Venetian company. This diversification was to be concluded by 2004 in order to complete the offer with products of the same market segment, creating distribution synergies. Montedoro's turnover amounted to about 3 million Euros in 2001. In the past, it had experienced golden times by collaborating with designers such as Walter Albini and Giorgio Armani. After which it had been sold and acquired more than once.
❑ 2002. The year closed with 35 million Euros, 39 million including Montedoro.
❑ 2002. Alberto Biani became the creative director of the new women's division that had been created at the beginning of the year.
❑ 2003. Incotex's production increasingly took on total look characteristics. After Montedoro, the Venetian company acquired 70% of the wool factory Zanone, a company from the Biella's area, whose turnover had amounted to 5 million Euros in 2002. Alberto Zanone, founder of the factory carrying his own name, remained as the manager of the company.

Incroyables Definition of eccentric menswear of English inspiration in vogue during the French Directory (1795-1799). Jackets, with long tailcoats at the back, very tight and double-breasted, had sleeves with very high cuffs. The high-waisted trousers were buttoned under the knees and fastened by ribbons. A piece of fabric was wrapped around the neck several times with a bowtie pinned onto it. The outfit was completed by redingote decorated by enormous frogs, colored stockings, and high boots. It was the style of the young men of that period, who protested against the expressly shabby garments of the old revolutionary.

(*Gabriella Gregorietti*)

Indreco Devanlay French giant of the clothing and textile sectors with almost 8,000 employees and a global turnover of more than 500 million Euros. It was established as a result of the alliance of manufacturing (Indreco) and knitwear (Devanlay) in 1975. It was an alliance that encouraged autonomy. The group's president and owner is Léon Cligman of Indreco (passed down by his family), while Devanlay is quoted on the stock exchange. Indreco produces complete clothing lines and ready-to-wear for Yves Saint-Laurent and Lacroix. Devanlay produces the same for Jil, Timwear, Scandale, Bombon, and Lacoste.

(*Fiorella Marino*)

Industria Brand of men and women's clothing created in 1992 by the photographer Fabrizio Ferri. He founded the firm after failing to find a black T-shirt with long sleeves, comfortable enough to look good outside the pants, but excessively large and encumbering when tucked inside. Ferri asked himself how many other pieces of the modern wardrobe were not available in the fashion market. After conducting a survey among his friends, he compiled a list of 300 pieces, which included the so-called Sardinian jacket, a garment of rustic elegance worn by Sardinian hunters. A complete line was created, which had considerable success on its debut: from 0 to 300 sales points in two seasons. When the production agreement with Paolo Bizzini expired, the collection was no longer marketed.

(*Daniela Fedi*)

Industrie Confezioni Tessili Established in 1951 by Carlo Compagno. The Venetian based company began with a small artisan's factory, creating pants and uniforms. During the 1970s it was dedicated to the exclusive production of pants. In the early 1980s, the brothers Marzio and Roberto Compagno took over their father's role in the company, and launched the Incotex brand. They decided to start a direct retail distribution. Today the company is specialized in the production of high-quality pants for men and women. It is the market leader with an annual production of about 600,000 pieces and a turnover of 35 million Euros in 2002 with an export quota of 48% in the USA, Japan, and Europe. In 2001 the company started growth by focusing on complementary products, similar in taste and with strong brand identity linked to a single product. The first step was the acquisition of Montedoro, an established firm in the Varese area, specialists in raincoats and casual jackets. In 2002 Alberto Biani was appointed creative director of the new woman's division created at the beginning of the year. In 2003 it acquired the wool factory Zanone, a prestigious company in the Biella area, specialists in high quality products.

Induyco Spanish clothing industry. It has large and successful businesses in other sectors: hi-tech and communications, pharmaceuticals, and cosmetics. The brands of Induyco Industrias y Confecciones, which produces 6 million pieces annually, are distributed in Spain and Portugal by the partner El Corte Inglès, a chain of department stores.

❑ 2002, July. It launched the new Sfera brand in the Iberian market to compete with the rival Inditex with the Zara brand. In the mid-term, the company intends to export Sfera in other markets. It opened six new stores in Spain, in the spaces once occupied by Marks & Spencer's department stores.

Infil Men, women and children's underwear company. Established in 1946 in Novara by the Provera family who had been operative in the sector since 1920. In 1997 it had produced about 7 million pieces, offering a range of more than 20 basic fabrics, from wool blends and double-facing to the more precious wool-silk, wool-cashmere, cottons, Scottish thread, and Microform-Lys, a microfiber patented by the company that is thinner than silk and cashmere and is used with wool. From 1990 to 1997 the company's turnover had more than doubled, achieving 44 billion Lira.

Infiore Brand of underwear, corsetry, and swimwear manufactured by Emmeci, a leading company of Vedano al Lambro with 40 years of business and a turnover of 40 million Euros at the end of 2002. The best of its collections have been presented on Milan's runways. Among the new creations for Spring-Summer were the Double Bra, which can be worn as either a seductive push-up or, by removing the padding, a refined bra in transparent tulle. The seamless underwear line was designed for practical and sport use. This was accompanied by a swimwear line, a teenager's underwear collection, and a men's underwear line. Infiore's single brand stores were opened in 1999 and are in constant growth. In 2003 the number of stores was 90 (10 of which were solely in Milan) with a target of reaching 220 by 2006.

Ingeo New revolutionary fiber from the American company Cargill Dow Llc (Minnesota), specialized in the fibers and polymers sectors, with a turnover of 65 billion dollars. Launched in January 2003, Ingeo underwent 14 years of testing with an investment of 750 million dollars. The fiber is manufactured on license by leading companies worldwide (14 at the beginning). Thanks to an agreement with Far- Eastern Textiles of Taiwan, which belongs to the Far-Eastern Group, clothing articles with the Ingeo brand were to be manufactured and sold in summer 2004. It was the world's first synthetic fiber derived from 100% natural resources (one of which is wheat), yearly renewable and offering the same performances of synthetic fibers derived from oil. The company has the only technology capable of combining economic development and social and environmental responsibility through a fermentation process. Vegetable sugars (currently taken from wheat and later to be taken from other waste materials such as grass and newspapers) are transformed into lactic acid and then are polymerized to obtain a fiber. Its name derives from the Greek meaning natural ingredients of the earth. Ingeo's production process uses the carbon that plants take from the air through photosynthesis, thus avoiding the waste of carbon taken from limited reserves of oil. In April 2003 Cargill Dow signed an agreement with Toray Industries, an international leader of fibers and fabrics that operates in 19 countries. Toray is to have the technology license, a supply of raw materials, the Ingeo brand, and the products to sell in several countries, including Japan and Europe. Another agreement was signed in May with the Italian Radici Group, which began business with interior design fabrics in 1946. It is a multinational company active in more than 15 countries, with a turnover of 1,530 million Euros, 7,000 employees, and 60 plants. The agreement allows Radici to manufacture continuous threads, both raw and dyed, branded Ingeo.

(*Gabriella Gregorietti*)

Inghirami Italian clothing group. It is among the four most important conglomerates in Italy. It controls more than 40 companies in Italy and overseas, with a total turnover of about 700 billion Lira. Within its structure, it counts some of the most prestigious names of the textile sector (Reggiani, Cantoni, Duca Visconti di Modrone, Multifibre, Lanificio di Carignano, and Textiloses et Textiles) and some of the most renowned manufacturing brands such as Sanremo, Ingram, Fabio Inghirami, Reporter, and Pancaldi, as well as licenses with important brands from Laura Biagiotti to Guy Laroche. It was established in 1949 in San Sepolcro as a shirtswear factory by Fabio Inghirami. Its success allowed the company to increase the production to a total look: jackets and suits of classic and traditional inspiration, reinterpreted with modernity, and always open to study and research. The company's development took place between 1970 and 1990, through acquisitions of specialized companies in their own sectors with traditional background. The group's main characteristic is its vertical organization. From yarns to fabrics to clothes manufacturing, the one element that favors synergy between the various companies is an elevated know-how. The product knowledge and the introduction into old and new markets is a real strength. In the last few years, important investments were made in Spain, Hungary, Bulgaria, France, and China, where a joint venture was created for the production and selling in the Chinese and Asian markets. The group has branch offices in New York, Barcelona, Paris, Budapest, and San Paulo. Among the group's latest news was a custom-made project, which allows the client to purchase custom-made clothes at affordable prices with the guarantee of quality, speed, and the alliance with the designer Fusco for a new line.

❑ 2002, January. Among the most curious items displayed at Pitti Immagine Uomo was the revolutionary 'use and throw-away' shirt *One Day*, manufactured in a fabric non fabric, which is to cost about 20 Euros.
❑ 2002, May. 'Now by Pancaldi' is the new collection with which the group relaunched the Pancaldi brand, the group's only womenswear line. It was targeted at a 25 to 30 year-old age group and made its debut in July.
❑ 2002, June. The Pitti Immagine Uomo award was presented to Giovanni Inghirami, the president of the group, during the opening ceremony of Pitti Immagine Uomo (62nd edition), which was held, as usual, in the Cinquecento room in the Palazzo Vecchio (city hall), Florence. Giovanni's father, Fabio Inghirami, was remembered on this occasion. The president of the Florence Center for Italian Fashion, Alfredo Canessa, justified the award: "In two generations and starting from one of the Tuscan poles of fashion, the one in the area of Arezzo, the Inghirami group

imposed itself as one of the most meaningful European realities in the clothing and textile sector".
❑ 2002, July. The group organized an international contest for young designers. The judging panel was chaired by Beppe Modenese, and composed of Laura Biagiotti, Daniela Giussani (Elle Italy), Richard Buckley (Vogue Homme International), Franca Sozzani (Vogue Italy), and Alfredo Canessa. Its job was to evaluate the creations of emerging designers who had studied architecture or at fashion schools. A sketch of a new design for men or women together with a written report was to be entered by the emerging designers. The prize was 25,000 Euros.
❑ 2002, December. The Inghirami group with the Duca Visconti di Modrone, Reggiani, Fabio Inghirami, Ingram, Reporter, Pancaldi and Sanremo brands arranged a joint venture in China. A market where it expected to open 60 to 70 new stores in three years and where it had been present at production level since the mid 1990s. The new spaces in the coastal areas of the south and southwest were to be managed by the Sanremo Shanghai Garment company with an agreement with the Sanremo Shanghai Garment group Imp & Exp Corp. owned by the State. At the end of 2002 a turnover of 7 million Euros was expected for the new company, of which the Italian Group holds 65%. In the meantime Inghirami was exploring other markets in order to increase its single brand stores from 40 to at least 210 in two years. Inghirami, which produces its lines in Italy, China, France, Hungary, and Bulgaria achieved a turnover of 250 million Euros in 2001.
❑ 2003, January. For Pitti Immagine Uomo, the Inghirami award was awarded to Isabel Fernandez, aged 25, from Madrid, and to Caroline Barulis, aged 22, from England. The theme to develop was 'ecology as a must for evolution'. Fernandez introduced pieces of landscape to her designs in a new vision of the body-environment relationship. Barulis gave life to multifunctional garments, drawing inspiration from the unusual cutting of Japanese designers.
❑ 2003, May. An agreement was signed with the designer Chiara Boni, who had left the Textile Financial group in July 2002, an organization founded in 1985. Inghirami was to manufacture the designer's menswear collection, which was exhibited at Milano Moda Uomo (June 2003). 50% of Chiara Boni's brand passed to the control of the San Sepolcro group. (*Gabriella Gregorietti*)

Inghirami Fabio (1920-1996). Born in San Sepolcro (Arezzo), he graduated in law, but abandoned the profession after only three years to launch himself into the world of textile entrepreneurship, where he became a protagonist. In 1977 he joined the National Association of Clothing Industrialists, of which he immediately became the president (a charge that he held until 1983). During those years he promoted an unusual agreement between the sector's associations and the Florence Center for Italian Fashion, which had been distant until then. He reorganized the exhibition (men and children in Florence and women in Milan). His role in institutions was very relevant and he was regarded as mediatory balance whilst having the willingness to do and to risk that had characterized his industrial path. At the guide of Efima, the institution that oversees the fairs dedicated to knitwear and clothing, he was among the promoters of Modit and the Uomo Moda event in New York. The merger of Modit and Milano Vendemoda is credited to him. In the last years of his life he was president of the Ente Moda Italia, whose task was the promotion of Made in Italy through the organization of manifestations and exhibtions.

(*Emanuela Fontana*)

Innocente Variazione Italian ready-to-wear brand. Designed by Pino Innocente for linearity and essentialness. The company has a showroom in Milan and made its debut at Milano Collezioni in 1997.

Institut de la Mode de Marseille Established in 1988, this center, together with the Museum of Fashion and other professional bodies, is located in the Espace Mode Méditerranée and coordinates formative courses, events, and corporate consultancies.

Institute Carlo Secoli Fashion school established in 1934 in Treviso. It moved to Milan in 1945. The school runs two-year courses with five branch headquarters in Italy. It is renowned for the seriousness of its courses in industrial model making and in product and process assistance, which prepares the student for the different aspects of work in industry. Famous overseas, the school also organizes special courses in Japan. It also offers lesson updates for the staff of those companies wishing to keep up-to-speed with technical and stylistic news.

Institute Ida Ferri Established in 1927, it is located in Piazza Cairoli 2 in Rome. It is one of the most prestigious schools in the capital. In November 2002 for the 75th anniversary of high fashion, Ida Ferri, who experienced the events of almost a century of fashion, was celebrated at the Art Café with a exhibition of 300 creations, the most meaningful show of the last 4 years. The collection was particularly inspired by the circus with mini clothes for acrobats or multicolored striped asymmetric garments for clowns. During the high fashion shows in 2002, in the traditional show dedicated to the graduates of the various schools, the protagonists were once again the designs by Ida Ferri. Inspired by the Parisian *fin de siècle* and by the Belle Époque, it was one of the most applauded and original collections ever presented in the Roman Auditorium.

Institute Marangoni It was the first school specialized in fashion in Milan. Established in 1935, it has graduated three generations of professionals including Franco Moschino, Domenico Dolce, and Donatella Girombelli. Every year, about 500 students – 40% of whom come from abroad – access a complete program of courses, which features fashion design, computer design, model making analysis, history of art and costume, fibers and threads, and marketing. Each study plan lasts for a few years, with the possibility to do work experience placements at some of the most important companies in the fashion sector and in style agencies. The institute's aim is to introduce 100% of its graduates to the world of work. It also runs a specialization Masters, lasting for a year at full time.

❑ 2003, October. The second headquarters of the institute opened in Fashion Street, London.
❑ 2004. The number of enrolled students is 1,500 from 71 countries.
❑ 2005. Institute Marangoni celebrated 70 years of business. It has trained three generations of professionals, more than 30,000 people.
❑ 2005. The school moved to the central Via Verri in the fashion quadrilateral.
❑ 2005. The educational offer expanded. Apart from traditional courses in fashion, the following courses were added: design, styling, accessories, business, promotion, and buying. New courses began in design: product, interior, communications, brand, and living design.

Institut Français de la Mode Established in 1986 in Paris and directed by Pierre Bergé. The study of fabrics, the management of new technologies, and the management training in fashion are the key courses at the school. IFM was created on the initiative of the Ministry of Industry. It runs seminars and multidiscipline teaching that addresses, in particular, the industries producing fashion.

Interbrand Italian company specialized in brand evaluation. It was a pioneer in the sector, using advanced techniques. The criteria used in brand evaluation are: the influence on the market in its category; the goals achieved or what it wants to achieve; the attained targets according to age and consumer type; the degree of knowledge reached among the client base. According to Interbrand, the top ten fashion brands in the world are: Levi's, Nike, Adidas, Reebok, Chanel, Benetton, Armani, Lycra, Wrangler, and Hugo Boss.

Interlock Crossed cotton fabric. It is a variation of jersey, but it is easier to cut because it is less elasticized.

Interstoff Asia spring exhibition of fibers,

yarns, and fabrics. Held in Hong Kong every six months, it has more than 300 exhibitors and more than 10,000 visitors. Since March 2002 an ad-hoc pavilion has been dedicated to the latest novelty materials for underwear, nightwear, and beachwear.

Intertextile Beijing Exhibition of fibers, threads, and fabrics. It is organized by Messe Frankfurt with Chinese partners in Beijing. In March 2002 it occupied 8,361 square yards in the Chinese World Trade Center with 250 exhibitors and 18,000 visitors. In October 2002 it moved to Shanghai with 700 companies in 25,083 square yards at the Shanghai New International Expo Center.

Intesa Moda An association created between Milan and Florence in January 2001 on the initiative of Italy Fashion System and the Florence Center for Italian Fashion, which both control the most important exhibition centers in Italian fashion: Florence for menswear and Milan for womenswear. The target of the new organization, chaired by Leandro Gualtieri, a textile entrepreneur from the General Council of the Florence Center, is the elaboration of new strategies to strengthen the promotion of the Italian fashion system and a better spending of resources. It is a wide strategy which, according to the president's vision, must consolidate the Italian exhibitions in the clothing and textile sectors internationally, intensifying the partnership with public institutes, while respecting the autonomies of the two centers. *(Lucia Serlenga)*

Intreco Italian company of children's fashion. Established by the Comunello family in Ponzano Veneto (Treviso) in 1978 and managed by Piero Comunello and his brother Adriano. It owns the brands Papermoon and Cacao and the Reporter Junior license for the Inghirami group. In January 2003 Intreco was acquired by the Danieli family (Roberto Danieli and his 30-year-old son Marco) who, after selling Diadora and Stonefly, have maintained a quota in Lotto and are co-owners of Gitexpoint, which distributes Spalding, K2, and Spider.

Intscher Maria (1974). Canadian designer. After moving to London, she graduated from St. Martin's School of Art in 1997. Since then she has collaborated with Alexander McQueen, Dirk Bikkembergs, and Strenesse. In 2000 she made her debut with her own line of sensual clothes, which cover and uncover the bosy discreetly due to particular geometries. Her style tends to keep the designer away from the narrow seasonality of collections.

(Gianluca Cantaro)

Invicta Established brand in sports accessories for mountain climbing. It was launched in 1921 in Turin by Cesare Mattalia, who acquired a British brand (1906) and linked it to the company's trend for trekking. In 1960 Giovanni, Mario, and Vincenzo Garrino took over the company as sport became a mass phenomenon. From 1970s to '90s there was the birth of the school backpack, investments in advertising grew, and the range of Invicta's products expanded to include clothing, shoes, and leather goods. *(Giampiero Remondini)*

❑ 1999. The merging of Invicta, brand linked to the outdoor, with Diadora, specialist in sports articles, brought about the birth of a new group, Diadora-Invicta, located in Caerano San Marco, near Treviso. Diadora was sold to Invicta by the Danieli family.
❑ 2000, September. The new Ricksac collection 2001 was launched. It was inspired by minerals and rocks. The technicality of mountain backpacks was combined with solid shapes, natural colors, and soft lines. It was matched with a super-technical clothing line, which guaranteed maximum comfort in the most adverse atmospheric conditions.
❑ 2000, October. Opening of a Diadora Store in Florence in an innovative concept, not just a shop but also a meeting point. In an old building in the historical center, two steps away from the cathedral, it was a three-floor space with the Invicta and Diadora collection on the first floor. There was also an area dedicated to young people with free Internet access and videogames. In the basement there was a museum

documenting the constant presence of the two brands in the history of sports and adventure.
❑ 2001. Invicta's new Spring-Summer collections were based on light fabrics, fresh colors, and a particular attention to detail. Everything could be matched with shoes, creating a total look. The Daypack collection presented the lines B2B, U.R.Ban, and Half Time.
❑ 2001-2002. New strategies contribute to a turnover growth of 5% with a total amount of 300 million Euros. The target was the reorganization of distribution and the separation of the image of the two brands.
❑ 2003, April. The reorganization occurred in the last two years determined a return to a net profit of 500,000 Euros in 2002 and a profit before tax in growth of 75%.

Io Donna Women's weekly with *Corriere della Sera*. Directed by Fiorenza Vallino, it made its debut on March 23, 1996, born from the transformation of *Donna Oggi*. The editorial staff was composed of 38 journalists and excellent collaborators including Lucia Annunziata, Lilli Gruber, and Beppe Severgnini. "This magazine's big innovation", explained Vallino, "is in the fact that it is sold with a newspaper that has a very masculine publication. We had to break away from schemes, trying to capture an unisex public. Frequent research has more than once focused and confirmed our target. The education level is high; 65% of our public is composed by women, 35% by men, for a total of 1,800,000 readers a week." As well as fashion and beauty, there are columns with a high-reading rate: 'Banana Peel' by Giusi Ferré, 'From Trend to Trend' by Cinzia Leone, 'Americana' by Ennio Caretto, and 'Hearts&Spades' by Maria Latella. There is a page completely dedicated to classic music and opera. The news section, which often contains editorials written by *Corriere della Sera*'s special reporters, promotes campaigns and interventions of high civil content. The fashion section, whose vice-director is Bruna Rossi, is consistent. The use of immediate and easily readable photographs clearly transmits the season's trends. Photography is often carried out overseas, and one or two pages describe where the location where the service was shot. Sometimes photos are structured using collage effects or photomontages, creating an unusual picture for the Italian editorial panorama. The layout was revised in September 2003.

Ionesco Irina (1935). French photographer. After studying in Romania, she returned to Paris, where she still lives, in 1946. A famous dancer, she was forced to cut short her career after an accident. She became interested in painting, first of void spaces and then, after meeting Anouk, of figures. In 1965, she became interested in photography after receiving a reflex Nikon as a gift. Self-taught, she shot charming black and white portraiture in atmospheres influenced by her cultural roots: the surrealism of her friend Breton, symbolist painting, symbols of decadence, and theatricality of false lust. Among her favorite models, always photographed in a studio of baroque taste where mirrors were omnipresent, there was her daughter Eva, who appears in many of her works. Through remaining in contact with the artistic world, she worked in the field of fashion publishing from 1978 for the magazine *Mode International*.

(*Roberto Mutti*)

I Pinco Pallino Brand of children's clothing. Managed by Imelde and Stefano Cavalleri (1950), partners in both life and work. They were able to create a winning business in the province of Bergamo through constant expansion and with a particular loading of joy that makes the world of I Pinco Pallino completely exclusive. The company has a classic, casual, and baby line, each accompanied by accessories. The brand has several single brand stores throughout the world and is on sale in the most significant department stores. This global success was rewarded with the prestigious Column One award from the *Wall Street Journal* in 2000. It certainly wasn't an easy path, one that started in 1982 at Pitti Bimbo, which marks its first success. Twenty years later, the company's turnover amounted to 19 million Euros. This is fashion in small measures for little boys and girls, and, curiously for redheads: this is how Imelde and Stefano imagine them and how the public sees them in advertising and in the sales points. A 360°

couple, united in the social field. They have always collaborated with humanitarian organizations and charities, both in Italy and abroad, promoting and supporting cultural initiatives. Their involvement was acknowledged in 2001 at an institutional level by the Province of Milan, in the presence of the former Cardinal, Carlo Maria Martini. They collaborate with WWF, Fai, Unicef, and Anlaids. They also support the venture of Italian Association of Libraries and the Italian Association of Pediatricians, which promotes reading for children.

(*Lucia Mari*)

❑ 2001. The company made a turnover of 18.6 million Euros from clothing and shoes for children, up by 15% compared to 2000.
❑ 2002. Opening of the first single brand boutique in Rome, in Via del Babbuino.
❑ 2002. Despite a difficult year for the clothing and textiles sectors, the company registered a turnover of 19 million Euros, up 5% compared to the previous year. 50% of the production is exported.
❑ 2002-2003. The company focused on distribution. A sales point was opened in the Wafi Wall department store in Dubai, the first in the United Arab Emirates. The brand's presence was also consolidated in the Far East with four boutiques in Japan, eight in Taiwan (opened in partnership with the company Why and 1/2). A second store was opened in Milan, which focused exclusively on clothing for babies.
❑ 2003. The brand was distributed in more than 400 boutiques in Italy and abroad.
❑ 2003. An agreement was signed with the company Ma Mere to expand in the Japanese market. The target was the opening of 15 sales points and to attain an annual turnover of 12.4 million Euros. There were three sales points in Japan, plus another one with Ma Mere, in Tokyo and Osaka, making an annual turnover of about ¥200 million, 1.65 million Euros.

Iraci Daniela (1969). Italian photographer. After studying fashion as a model, she devoted herself to photography, first as an assistant and then by working in advertising and graphics. In 1996 she began to work exclusively in photography. She soon started to exhibit her work in personal and collective shows. In her research, she was particularly attentive to the elaboration of techniques and color. Professionally she was dedicated to still-life, advertising, portraiture, and fashion. On the fashion side, she has published her photos in Italian magazines such as *Vogue Pelle*, *Vogue Gioiello*, *Caffelatte*, *Io Donna*, *Urban*, *Mood*, and foreign magazines such as *Paper* (New York), *Adidiot Magazine*, *Marie Claire* (Belgium), *Boulevard* (Holland), and *Biz* (Turkey). She has also carried out campaigns for clients such as Swatch Place Vendôme, Swatch Square, Nintendo, and Actelios.

Iribe Paul. Pseudonym of Paul Iribarnegaray (1883-1935). French illustrator. He was praised for his formal audaciousness and iconographic originality, a precursor of the Art Déco. In 1908 he created a catalogue for Poiret entitled *Les Robes de Paul Poiret racontées par Paul Iribe*. In 1913 he designed for the Lanvin brand. His illustrations were published in the French edition of *Vogue* and *Fémina*. He designed advertising pages for Paquin, Callot, and Bianchini-Férier. After a happy experience as costume designer and set designer in Hollywood (among the others, the film *The Ten Commandments* by Cecil B. De Mille in 1923), from 1920 to '26, he returned to France and collaborated with Chanel as a jewelry designer.

Irié French brand of ready-to-wear. Created in 1987 by the Japanese Sueo Irie (1946). She graduated from the Osaka College of Design, and worked for Hiroko Koshino and, in Paris, for Kenzo. After these experiences, she began her own brand. In the late 1980s, her tiny stretch jackets and big patterned silk blouses were very successful.

Ironside Janey (1917). Director of the fashion department at the Royal College of Art in London. Born in England, she studied costume at St. Martin's School of Art. After her graduation, she opened her own dressmaking workshop. When the department

Paul Iribe was invited by Paul Poiret to witness his fashion in a volume of illustrations.

opened, she worked as the assistant to the director Madge Garland. In 1956 she took over as director. A this point she closed her tailoring business. She modernized the teaching methods. She understood the new necessities of the fashion industry – designers were capable of working in a market much larger than that of high fashion ateliers. She encouraged individual creativity and experimentation. David Sassoon, Marion Foale, Sally Tuffin, Ossie Clark, Anthony Price, and Janice Wainwright were among her students. In 1962 she published *Fashion as a Career*. She was very active in the research for funds for the department. In 1964 she launched a course in menswear. She resigned in 1967 after a clash with the authorities who denied university status to the fashion department alone. She is married to the painter Christopher Ironside.

Isaia Neapolitan fashion house established in the 1920 and '30s of the last century as a fabric store. It was one of the pioneers of the Neapolitan tradition with Mariano Rubinacci, Kiton, and Borrelli. Established in Casalnuovo at the end of the Second World War, Isaia was already at the third family generation. Very closely linked to the city, it began its ascent by creating business relationships with the most important fashion houses of Naples. In 1957 Enrico, Corrado, and Rosario Isaia opened their first workshop-factory. In the late 1960s the company's production reached 200 pieces a day. The characteristic that distinguishes every suit is its tailoring and artisan's finishing. These virtues launched the company to the conquest of foreign markets. In many of Isaia's shops, a tailor takes the client's measures and manufactures a custom-made suit. The company is directed by Gianluca Isaia, who hired Douglas Anderson from Dior to design an eponymous collection, and Sonia Rykiel. The international presentation of the new collection occurred at the New York headquarters of the company on Fifth Avenue. Isaia was among the promoters of a quality hub under construction near Marcianise, in the area of Caserta, where 160 small and medium-sized companies operating in the territory were to gather. Since September 2003 the firm has been active in running a course of traditional tailoring for about twenty young people. (*Daniela Bolognetti*)

Isetan Japanese company of department stores. In fashion it follows the market politics of focusing on young people with the brands Moschino, Donna Karan, Cerruti, and Montana. Since 1991 it has also had the C'est Magnifique line. Established in 1886 in Tokyo as a kimono boutique, it developed in the 1930s. In 1989 it arrived in the USA thanks to a joint venture with Barney's. It has 15 branch stores all over the world.

❑ 2001. Agreements were signed to sell the Isetan brands in Ado stores, including the popular women's line, New's Square Casual.
❑ 2002, February. It absorbed Iwataya, a group leader in the department stores of Kyushu, and relaunched the chain.
❑ 2002, March. Isetan amplified the Ado projects. The bag collection New's Square Handbag, presented in August 2001 with sales for ¥2.5 billion, was introduced into Ado stores.

Isham Ashley. British designer, born in Singapore. He moved to London where he studied at the London College of Fashion, St. Martin's School of Art, and Middlesex University. In 2001 he launched his own brand. He draws inspiration from rich, jetsetting women, creating luxurious but practical clothes. Embroideries, inlays, and drapings make his style essentially glamorous but not vulgar. In 2003 he won a sponsorship to participate in London Fashion Week.

Isogawa Akira. Japanese designer. From 1987 he has lived and worked in Sydney, Australia. As an emerging creator of the late millennium, he started to design T-shirts. *Harper's Bazaar* wrote that his clothes are "the best vision for the eyes". In 1999 his creations caused real hysteria episodes at Browns in London. His style has the delicacy of origami, of hand-painted silks, but not to the detriment of modernity. Some of his creations are showing at the Powerhouse, the Museum of Design in Sydney.

Issermann Dominique (1947). French photographer. She started as a complete beginner when she studied literature in Paris. After working as a set photographer in cinema and as photo reporter and portrait photographer of divas for the magazine *Zoom*, she came to fashion photography in 1974 due to a competition. The following year she turned professional. She started to collaborate with the magazine *Vingt Ans*, before moving on to the magazines of the Condé Nast group: *Elle* and *Mirabella*. She devised the advertising campaigns for Sonia Rykiel (with whom she had collaborated since 1979), Maud Frizon (since 1983), Nina Ricci, Saint-Laurent, Dior, and Kookai. In 1987 she exhibited her photos at *Rencontres Internationales de la Photographie* in Arles and won the Oscar for fashion photography. Her images are recognizable for their stylized touch and sophisticated atmospheres. (*Roberto Mutti*)

Istituto Superiore della Moda Fashion school in Naples. Its three-year courses are for aspiring designers, and aim to develop the students' handworked skills and creativity. Every year the students are sent to companies and ateliers for industrial experience.

Italian Fashion School Courses organized in Milan by the Chamber of Fashion, aimed at educating professionals 'with basic skills and a specific knowledge to cover, above all, the new necessities of the sector'. In 2001 a new course was started for Art Director Corporate Image next to the already existing Fashion Buyer, Project Maker and Responsible Research, and Multimedia Development. The basic subjects are marketing, communication, English, commodity economics, and information technology. The courses are free, financed by the European Social Fund and the Lombardy region. They last for 8 months, three of which are spent at the companies associated with the Chamber of Fashion. An admission test is obligatory for high school and college graduates because the number of places is limited to 18.

Italian Fashion Service Established in December 1951 from the alliance between the Fashion Institute of Turin and the Fashion Center of Milan, which was made to promote Turin as a possible crossroads of Italian fashion. Eleven months before, on February 12, 1952, Florence – through the first show organized by Giorgini – had proposed itself as a candidate for the as engine of Made in Italy. Turin and Milan took the blow and were united in the attempt to win it back. The Italian Fashion Service claimed the right to coordinate and discipline the fashion movement. In winter 1952, an article in *Popolo* entitled *Lights and Shadows of the Dominium of All Vanities* accused the Italian Fashion Service of having formed a division that stole away eight tailors and designers from the White Room of the Florentine Pitti Palace. Simonetta, Fabiani, Schuberth, Lola Giovannelli, the Fontana sisters, Ferdinandi, Mingolini-Heim, and Garnet.

Italian Institute of Fashion Not-for-profit company established in 1983 on the initiative of the Industrial Fashion Association and the Center for Italian Fashion in Florence. Its aims were to co-organize some of the Pitti Immagine events and to promote and improve the image of Made in Italy abroad. Besides organizing the participation of qualified Italian companies in the most important international events and contributing to the development of commercial opportunities in new emerging markets, IIF manages (with the support of the Ministry and Institute of Foreign Commerce) six-month exhibitions specialized in Italian fashion in New York (*Made in Italy at The Collective* for men's fashion, and *Made in Italy at Fashion Coterie*, women's fashion), in Hong Kong (*Europe Selection* in collaboration with Igedo of Düsseldorf), in Moscow (*Alta Moda Italia* at Moda Moscow), and in Tokyo (*Ginza Collections*). The president of IIF was Umberto Angeloni. Marco Mayer acts as its managing director.

❑ 2000. The new millennium starts with Piero Costa as the president and Raffaello Napoleone as vice-president.
❑ 2002, March. The Italian Institute of Fashion organized the international event Children's Club, dedicated to children's wear. The Italian brands invited were Farò da grande, Katherine Hamnett Junior, Lastrucci, and Q come Quore.
❑ IIF's administrative and legal headquarters are in Florence, the commercial one is on Milan.

Italo Cremona Company of sunglasses and frames for corrective lens. It was named after its founder who established it in 1920 in Gazzada, near Varese, working with plastics in order to obtain toilette articles, combs, toys, and glasses. Through time, the optic division (250 workers out of a total of 350) increasingly became the core business of the company, with more than 2 million pieces a year and distribution into 60 countries: 20% in Italy, 18% in Europe, 21% in the USA and Canada, 26% in the Far East, and the remaining between Australia and the Middle East. The Diablo-Made in Hell brand proposed a catalogue of 30 models. The company also produces for third parties: the first glasses designed by Valentino and Krizia, and now the Versace and/or Versus lines.

❑ 1999. The president of the company became the founder's son, Nando Cremona. The corporate name is I.C. Optics Spa. It has five brands under license (Gai Mattiolo, Cesare Paciotti, Shimano, Gianni Versace, and Versus) and two of its own (Diablo and Starring). From 1991 to 2003 the creative collaborator for Versus and Versace was Leonardo Balbi.
❑ 2002. The new collections bet on hyper-technological materials, from polycarbonate to thermoplastics with anti-scratching system. Futuristic lenses, wrapping and super protective masks and a panoramic vision with the introduction of lenses also in the arms.
❑ 2003, January. The Luxottica Group Spa acquired the production and distribution of IC Optics, which belongs jointly to Italo Cremona Spa and Gianni Versace Spa. Following the acquisition, Luxottica signed a ten-year contract (renewable for 10 more years) with the brands Versace, Versus and Versace Sport for the design, production, and distribution of sunglasses and eyewear globally. Its expected turnover was of 90 million Euros.

IT Holding In April 2000 Molise Ittierre Holding, guided by the President Tonino Perna (1948) and by the general manager Giancarlo Di Risio (1956) changed its corporate name to IT Holding Spa. It is not a simple name change, but an effective operation of 'strategy corporate naming'. The group intended to give itself a new image in the light of several launching operations of its own brands and the acquisition of other brands and licenses which, having been carried out in the last year, transformed the group into an protagonist of Made in Italy, concentrated on luxury. "The change", says Perna, "is necessary to confer to the company a more coherent connotation with the present role of the Holding and the Group, which is active non only in the clothing sector, but also in that of accessories and similar items, with diversified shareholdings". The targets declared to the financial community for 2000-2002 are explicit: "An average growth of 30% in the selling of our own brands, and a target turnover for 2002 of more than 500 million Euros". Ittierre did not disappear. It remained as a company within the group that followed the young lines of Versace, Dolce & Gabbana, Gianfranco Ferré, and Roberto Cavalli, as well as its own brands, such as Exté, Romeo Gigli, and Husky. At the end of 2000 the group scored again. Gianfranco Ferré chose the group as his new industrial and financial partner. At the end of the operation, the Perna group has 90% of the capital stock of Gianfranco Ferré, while the designer maintained a quota of 10%, as well as the role of President and total creative autonomy. The targets declared by Ferré are the strengthening of the clothing and existing accessories lines, and the creation of new lines including a high couture line. The operation brought about the birth of an entirely Italian luxury extreme, not only in terms of share control, but above all as the cultural profile and the reference values. 2000 closed with a turnover of 838 billion Liras (compared with 717 billions in 1999) and a gross operative margin of 84.5 billion Liras. The group, located in Prettoranello di Isernia in Molise, started in 1982 on the initiative of Perna as a company focused on licenses and capable of providing a high quality service to its partners. It continually created its own brands, such as Exté and Gentry Portofino, and has production and distribution licenses with brands, such as Versus, Versace Jeans Couture, D&G, D&G Jeans, D&G Sport, Gianfranco Ferré Jeans, and Sport. It became world leader with 65% of the market in the branded youth clothing segment. 1999 can be considered a year of conquests. Ittierre acquired the Mac Malo group, a world leader in the cashmere sector. The value of the operation was 100 billion liras. It guaranteed a twenty-year exclusive of the brands owned by Romeo Gigli, while the Tonino Perna group, which controlled 85% of Diners Club Italy, absorbed the publishing house Franco Maria Ricci, the pick in the strategy of development and qualified initiatives, which were complementary and synergic to the group. It also joined the eyewear business, acquiring two companies. It took over Allison Spa for 11.2 billion Liras, which had acquired Optiproject Srl for 7.1 billion Liras. A five-year contract and a world exclusive with Roberto Cavalli, for the creation and development of a clothing line dedicated to the fashion of the new generation, strengthened the area of licenses, an established business of the group. In 1999 it acquired the license of the English brand Husky for 16 years. After these acquisitions, the holding reorganized itself. It created two divisions to manage licenses and brands separately. The group is managed by a highly powerful computer system with a uniquely computerized warehouse, which is a limited responsibility company with capital stock. The group employs 1,000 workers directly, plus 600 working in external production units. In 1998 the turnover amounted to 651.5 billion (up 7.2% compared to 1997) with an export quota of 68.3%. The supplying-distribution structure, the links between production and logistics, the stocking of millions of pieces in the warehouses, the delivery system of 80,000 pieces a day are innovative thanks to the optimization strategies set by interdisciplinary groups of the Polytechnic of Milan. Ittierre also has a vocation for research. Its laboratories have produced super-technological and exclusive fabrics, which are highly praised by Exté, the label that mixes past and future with the present. Cult fashion are the small transparent jackets with electronically welded feather linen, which inflate to increase warmth; the blouses in carbon fiber; the knitwear worked with rubber, plastic with jersey; the Kevlar, a fabric cut with laser used in space missions, combined with viscose; glass fiber, neoprene for divers' equipment, and vinyl. Everything is created in a continued triumph of contradictions, as these materials, smeared, polished, and painted, match with noble fibers such as linen, cotton, wool, also in the precious cashmere version.

(Dario Golizia)

Itokin Japanese clothing company. It has 5 production plants and 13 stores for wholesale selling. It manages about a hundred brands, its own and western brands. Since 1989 the company also began to design furniture and accessories such as artificial flowers and decorations for interior decor. Established in 1950 by Kingo Tsujimura, it is currently managed by his son Koiki. It has branch offices in New York, Milan, and in the most important towns of the Far East.

❑ 2000-2002. The Japanese company focused its interest on new brands at reasonable prices. This strategy determined a noteworthy increase in sales. As well as the new lines, there was also the license for Jokomoda, deriving from a contract with the Spanish Sybilla. This license determined a raise of 30% in 2001. The line was renamed Jokomoda de Sybilla to strengthen the identification with the renowned Spanish brand.

ITS International contest for new designers. Established in 2001 on the initiative of the Trieste agency Eve, it was directed by Barbara Franchin. Its (International Talent Support) addresses the students enrolled in the last year in the most important fashion schools in the world. The contest, which takes place in Trieste in the July, is supported by a number of sponsors and aims to be a meeting platform for students and avant-garde companies in fashion and communications (among them, Diesel and PlayStation). Interface of Its One is a capillary network that is in constant expansion, to which 400 fashion schools participate from 60 countries, including the Academy of Antwerp or the Royal College of Art of London. *(Sara Tieni)*

❑ 2005, July. With the 4th edition of Its, Its Photo began, which is dedicated to emerging photographers. This covers not only fashion images, but also experimentation and research for the 17 young people in competition. The first edition was won by Danielle Mourning.

IULM Free University of Languages and Communications with premises in Milan and Feltre. Since 2002 it has run a short-study degree in communication in fashion and design. There also courses in marketing, management, consumer sociology, sociology of communications, semiotics, history of design and fashion, quality management, language of audio-visual instruments, and digital planning. The courses last two or three years. It is necessary to have a high school dialoma or equivalent. At the end of 2002, the annual cost was 6,200 Euros.

Ivan et Martia French brand of ready-to-wear. Established in 1964 by two students (from Casablanca and Milan) in fine arts who met in Paris. After a short time, they were very successful in relaunching the trend of spotted fabrics. In 1974 they opened their first boutique at the Halles of Paris. In 1997, they opened a second boutique in Paris called Leopard Legend.

Ivanez Laetitia (1968). Designer for the Les Prairies de Paris brand, whiose clients include the stars Andie MacDowell, Kate Moss, and Emmanuelle Béart. Nicknamed Mowgli (after the protagonist of *Jungle Book*), Ivanez found herself in the world of fashion partly by chance and partly against her will. She had a short period of time to take over her father's business because of his sudden and serious illness. She started to become interested in clothes, developing a passion for fashion. Her collection always drew inspiration from studying and considering the everyday life of women. She created particular garments that are always supported by a logic of their own. From her experience of her son Paolo's birth in 2001, Laetitia decided to create a line for new mums and a newborn line called Bonne Mère. (*Mariacristina Righi*)

Ivy League Style of clothing associated with a conservative American undergraduate dress code, named after a group of prestigious American East Coast colleges including Harvard, Princeton and Yale. Ivy League is more commonly used to speak of men's fashions than women's; the women's equivalent is more commonly called "preppy." The boys' look features button-down white shirts and narrow striped ties (typically from Brooks Brothers, the New York haberdasher), worn with grey flannel suits, casual khaki trousers, and Oxford shoes. When applied to women's fashions, the style usually indicates pearl necklaces and cashmere twin-sets, navy wool or camel hair coats and navy low-heeled pumps.

IWS The International Wool Secretariat is an organization established in 1937 by the sheep breeders of New Zealand, South Africa, and Uruguay (80% of the world production) to promote the use of pure virgin wool. The headquarters are in London with offices in Great Britain and in 34 countries around the world. It intervenes in the modalities of wool use with technical and trend research. It follows communications on the product and promotes massive advertising.

J

Jabot Lace decoration or a decoration in the same fabric of the blouse. Due to its softness it is often similar to a ribbon or a bib. It enriched the front of ladies' refined night-gowns of the 1800s with tiny ribs or very thin pleats. In the same period the jabot decorated men's shirts in very fine linen, initially for daywear, then only on evening outfits. In men's fashion, the disappearance of the jabot caused the birth of the tie in a size that has remained almost unvaried until today. In women's fashion, the jabot survived the division into two pendant ribbons from the collar or the plissé vest, equally mobile, on low-necked blouses, or as a cascade of Valencian lace, as in more recent times beneath an ultra masculine *tailleur*.

Jacassi Franco (1949). Italian collector from Piedmont. His taste for research and adventure caused him to travel from a very young age. After studying sociology at the University of Trento, he devoted himself to the study of pictorial avant-gardes. In the early 1970s he opened a modern art gallery and started to collect reviews, ancient books, prints, patterns, and fashion photographs. In Vercelli he opened the Dialoghi bookshop, which put him into contact with the most famous entrepreneurs of the textile sector, therefore entering the world of fashion. For Loro Piana he organized a significant patterns Collection and a book entitled *The Elegance of Style*. The research and re-evaluation of refined and precious materials, sought after with curiosity, stubbornness, and a deep-rooted passion, caused him to visit second-hand markets, old fabric shops, artisans, rescuing ancient buttons, buckles, ribbons, precious fabrics, embroidered tuile, silk flowers from destruction; all of which would have been impossible to reproduce. His task was to collect new things that belonged to another era from around the world. Everything was accurately selected, giving way to an extraordinary Collection of ancient materials from late 1800s to the 1970s. In his atelier in Milan, the Collection is available for use by tailors, designers, and producers, all wishing to draw inspiration for their Collections. Anything can be found there: magazines, photos, patterns, ancient books, original sketches by Dudovich, Guida, Lopez, Boccasile, as well as prints and posters. There are also ancient fabrics from high fashion, tuile or jais embroideries, sequins, passementeries, and all sorts of accessories: French and American bijoux, buckles in Bakelite or mother-of-pearl, haute couture clothes by the most famous tailors, and even an exceptional Collection of buttons from 1500 to 1900. The Collection includes millions of pieces in more than 50,000 models from Liberty to the 1970s. Jacassi's business does not stop here: he provides new ideas for books on fashion and costume, does technical consultancy for the designing of corporate libraries, organizes theme exhibitions about fashion within various events, from Milano Collezioni to Modit, from Pitti Immagine to the Fashion Vintage Show at the Castello di Belgioioso.

(*Gabriella Gregorietti*)

Jackson Betty (1960). British designer. She created her first womenswear Collection in 1981 in London. She is particularly famous for the use of Timney Fowler printed fabrics. A graduate from the Birmingham College of Art, she was an assistant in the studio of Wendy Dagworthy. After which, she became head of the style department of the Radley Cooper Quorum group. In 1985 she won the award for Best English Designer of the Year. The fashion designer Antonio Berardi says: "She has modernized knitwear". Since 1986 she had also designed a men's line.

❑ 2001. The designer, already awarded with the Royal Designer for Industry, celebrated 20 years in the world of fashion at London Fashion Week, presenting the 44th Collection of her career. Her production, even if it isn't the youngest and hippest of the London scene, continues to represent "the wilder side of conservativism".

Jackytex Italian textile company. Its headquarters are in Terranova Bracciolini (Arezzo) Established in 1972, it has always been characterized for its research and strong innovative spirit: the use of viscose when it was used only for lining; the different choices in the quantity of use. These entrepreneurial virtues caused quick growth up until the international successes in the late 1970s: meeting with stylistic ready-to-wear and successes on the runway. It then experienced further developments through the introduction of electronic machines and the use of new fibers for the six-color gobelin, the unusual elasticity in Lycra, the new knitwear products, and exclusivity for designers. The monocentric, familiar management of those years was replaced by diversification of production cycles. It established an associated company, the Knitting, for the weaving of plain dyed fabrics. In 1997 the group employed 70 workers, produced more than 1.5 million precious fibers, and had a turnover of 43 billion, 40% of which came from export. The end of the millennium projected the company into advanced methods, techniques, and weaving mills creating inlayed velvets and new fibers.

❑ At the beginning of the new century, Jackytex's products were distributed all over Europe (Germany, France, Benelux, UK, and Spain), the Americas (USA, Brazil), and in the Far East (Japan, Korea, and Hong Kong).
❑ 2003, February. The company presented a new fabric called Ingeo at the Salon du Textile in Paris, obtained from 100% recycled fibers from ecological materials such as wheat, and manufactured on behalf of the American company Cargill Dow.

Jacob Mary Phelps (Caresse Crosby). American dressmaker. In 1914 she invented a very light bra without straps and whalebone supports. Its purpose was not to extol the breast, but to flatten it. Her idea was a product of the *garçonne* fashion of the 1920s, the crisis woman. The bra was successful throughout the decade, guaranteeing the dressmaker with a place in fashion and female costume history.

A sketch by Marc Jacobs, 1997 (The Museum at the Fashion Institute of Technology, New York).

Jacobs Marc (1963). American designer. Born in New York City. After graduating from the High School of Art and Design in 1981, he attended Parson's School of Design where he graduated in 1984 with the best grades, obtaining three awards. At the same time, he designed his first handmade knitwear Collection, presented with his own label for Ruben Thomas Inc. In the same year he established a company with Robert Duffy, the Jacobs Duffy Design. In 1986 Jacobs designed the first ready-to-wear Collection for Kathiyama USA, always with his label. Two years later, he made a quality impact with a show in a huge parking lot in New York. In 1989 Jacobs and Duffy united with Perry Ellis. Duffy was appointed president and Jacobs vice-president of womenswear design. In Autumn 1993 he established the Marc Jacobs International Company. In 1994 he signed his first license for Renown Look and Mitsubishi for distribution in Japan. Shortly after, he signed a license for men and women's shoe Collection with Iris, which has its plant near Venice. In January 1997, Jacobs was appointed artistic director and Duffy studio director for Louis Vuitton.

(*Maria Vittoria Alfonsi*)

❑ 2001. Jacobs and Duffy presented a second line Marc by Marc Jacobs, which included shoes, bags, and accessories. Men and women's shoes are the result of an agreement signed with the shoe factory Rossi Moda Spa.
❑ 2001, September. The designer launched his first fragrance, Marc Jacobs Perfume.
❑ 2003, December. Debut of a household Collection composed above all by furniture.
❑ 2004, March. He signed an agreement with Imaginex Holding Ltd (already distributor of Lane Crawford and Joyce) to cover the Hong Kong market and a large part of China.
❑ 2004. The Italian Sàfilo Spa started the production of an eyewear Collection, which was to be put on sale from Spring of the following year.
❑ 2004, July. Opening of the first multibrand store in the USA, in Newbury Street, Boston. This was followed by another important event: the third woman's fragrance, Blush, was launched thanks to an alliance with the established Lancaster group.
❑ 2004, August. Thanks to the new agreement with Imaginex, new stores are opened in Shanghai, Beijing, and Chengdu.
❑ 2004, September. Jacobs signed a license agreement with Fossil, American company specialized in watches. This foresaw the production and distribution of men and women's watches branded Marc Jacobs and Marc by Marc Jacobs. The launch was expected for Autumn 2005 and 2006.
❑ 2005, March. Opening of many sales points: two in Los Angeles (at 8400 Melrose Place) and one in Florida, in Bal Harbour.
❑ 2005, June. Marc Jacobs received the Fashion Designer of America award for womenswear.

Jacomo French perfume house. Established in 1970 with Gérard Courtinne as its founder. His certainly modern fragrances are nonetheless classic for the bottles that reproduce the sculptures to which they inspire. Aimed at a young, demanding, and sophisticated public, the company launched a women's line (*Chicane*, *Silence*, *Coeur de parfum*, and *Anthracite*) as well as a men's line (*Eau cendrée*, *Jacomo de Jacomo*, and *Anthracite pour homme*). In 1983 Courtinne opened a workshop in Deauville, and five years later he added a line of accessories. The company's ownership passed on to Martell, then to Jean d'Avèze, and finally, in 1987, to Balmain.

Jacquard Knitwear fabric. A system based on perforated cardboards, applied to machines that work jersey, drives several threads into forming a pattern. Highly elaborated fabrics for interior decor are jacquards: damasks, brocades, and gobelins.

Jaeger English clothing brand. Established around 1880 by Lewin Tomalin, with clothes that were manufactured following a method proposed by the German doctor Gustav Jaeger. He generally considered animal fibers, particularly wool, to be ideal for human

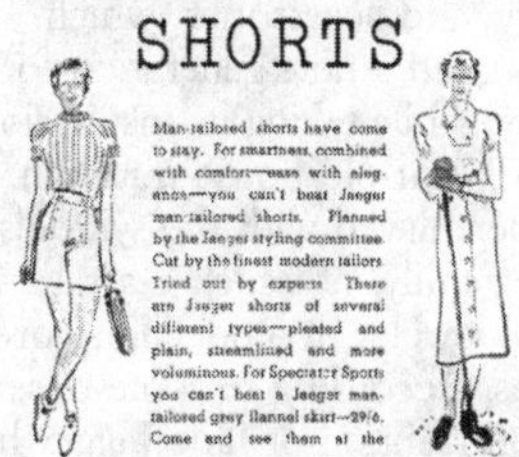

Advertising of the English house Jaeger.

clothing. Oscar Wilde and George Bernard Shaw were among his clients. Since the 1930s, the brand has produced a knitwear and clothing line in high quality natural fibers for men and women.

Jael Brand of men's knitwear. Designed by Jens Kaumle (Stuttgart, 1968) and manufactured in Italy. She made her debut with the Spring-Summer 2000 Collection. The designer lives between London, Paris, and Milan. She studied stylistics at the Royal College of Arts in London, while she started to work in Paris and Milan: first for Moschino, then for Tommy Hilfiger, and for Levi's Germany.

Jagger Jade (1971). Jewelry designer. She is the daughter of Mick Jagger. She works between London and Ibiza. Very trendy, she is a protagonist of a new swinging London. She models for Vivienne Westwood and collaborates with the young designer Matthew Williamson. She has been often seen at public occasions with the grandson of Harold Macmillan, Conservative Prime Minister from 1957 to '63. Her jewels are considered to be New Age. She designs and manufactures *debardeurs* with beads using the Venetian system called 'mille fiori' (a thousand flowers).

❑ 2000, September. She signed a contract with Garrard & Asprey.
❑ Her first Collections, for Spike and Graffiti brands, were aimed at a young public open to new fashion trends. She became creative director at Garrard. Jade Jagger and her staff of four created a very personal style of watches, silver jewelry, and accessories, which represented a new generation for jewelry, while taking its inspiration from the 270-year-old house tradition. The designer played with the symbols of the Royal Family, of which Garrard was official jeweler, remodeling swords and crowns. According to some observers, the contribution of Jade Jagger has brought about a rebirth for Garrard.

Jaguar Very rare and expensive fur, brown with full black or ring-shaped spots, with smaller spots inside.

Jais A polished and black stone (also called Gages' stone, a village in Licia) obtained by the working of a variety of very hard lignite originating from Minor Asia. In addition to black jais the «bijoux de deuil» were manufactured, the jewels of mourning that Queen Victoria imposed on her courtesans on the death of her husband Albert, and now antique objects. Jais was used for the whole century in different applications and decorations, in the form of beads or small shining cylinders applied on evening dresses in chiffon, crepe, or satin, to make fantasy buttons, to decorate bags and dresses' fringes.

James Charles (1906-1978). British designer. He was nicknamed the "architect of fashion" for his wise cut and his evening dresses of sculpted shapes. A man with a difficult temper, he was, according to Balenciaga, one of the greatest world couturiers. Friend of Cecil Beaton and Gertrude Stein, he drew inspiration from painting, using the drawings of famous artists to create his models. His famous plissé blouse was inspired by Matisse and the matelassé white jacket was taken from a drawing by Cocteau. Born in Sandhurst, England, he studied at Harrow. He emigrated to Chicago where, towards the end of the 1920s, he made his debut as a milliner, but the business failed. In 1928 he moved to Long Island. A manicurist wore his hats and they were noticed. He opened a showroom in New York. In 1929 he started designing clothes and, in the same year, he presented his first Collection in London. Throughout the 1930s, he commuted between London, New York, and Paris. He was among the first to introduce the spiral zip fastening and the divided skirt. He became one of the favorite tailors of Marlene Dietrich and Gertrude Lawrence and, in 1940, he settled in New York. Four years later he designed clothes for the salon of Elizabeth Arden. In 1947 he returned for a short time to Paris to present a Collection that was very successful. Once he had returned to New York, his business experienced some ups and downs, which caused him to retire in 1958. He continued to teach couture until the 1970s. In 1980 a retrospective was dedicated to him at the Brooklyn Museum. (*Eleonora Attolico*)

James Richard (1953). English tailor. After studying photography at Brighton College (1978), he moved to London where he worked for several years at Browns, the famous boutique in South Molton Street. He started as shop assistant until becoming a buyer of menswear. He has clear ideas about the necessity of modernizing the English tailoring tradition, just as his inspirer, Paul Smith. He thinks that tailoring should be made more accessible to a larger clientele. His style proposes traditional fabrics and cuts matched with unthinkable colors, such as emerald green, cherry red, and wisteria. He opened his first tailor's shop in Savile Row in 1992 and a second boutique in New York in 1997. His client base are young, creative professionals. He is also appreciated by stars such as Elton John, Madonna, Liam and Noel Gallagher, and designers such as Christian Lacroix and Isaac Mizrahi.

❑ 2001. The British Fashion Council appointed James as Menswear Designer of the Year on the occasion of the annual British Fashion Awards.
❑ For the Spring-Summer 2003 Collection, the designer launched three different lines: the most classic, Savile Row, and Myfair and Savile Sport for leisure time.

James Lock & Co. The world's most famous milliners. Established in 1676 in London, the shop is still where he opened more than 300 years ago at 6, St. James Street. Its fame is linked with bowler hats, both city and horse-riding versions, and to the formal, grey, and black top hats. It is also renowned for its country, sporting hats, for which drier, harder, and more durable felts are used than those adopted by the Italian tradition of the soft Borsalinos. Lock served the Admiral Nelson, the Duke of Wellington, Oscar Wilde, Charlie Chaplin, the Duke of Windsor, and Cecil Beaton. He was able, however, to keep updated with changing fashions without abandoning his secular production. He also introduced women's millinery designed by Sylvia Fletcher.

Jamin Puech Accessories brand. Created by the designers Benoît Jamin and Isabelle Puech who won the first prize at the Hyères festival for young designers in 1991. Their production is in excess of 20,000 bags a year. At the beginning, they used ancient fabrics found at Parisian flea market, pearls, buttons, all discovered at secondhand markets, and various materials from the Marché Saint Pierre, a bazaar of fabrics and accessories. The range of their creative universe expanded to include sequins, knitwear, and ribbons. They design accessories Collections for the American department store Bergdorf Goodman, for Lagerfeld, Chloé, and Adam & Roppe.

Jan & Carlos Brand of the American designers Jan Pottorf and Carlos Baker. They work in Italy and presented their Collection during the Autumn-Winter 1996-97 shows at Milano Collezioni. They want to design, in their words, "clothing pieces free from conventions that transcend seasons".

Jan & Marcel British brand. Its designers have tested an unusual use of fluid latex as a decoration and seam. They presented in London their first fashion Collection in Spring 1979, composed above all of evening dresses in pleated hand-painted silk. They both passed away in the early 1990s.

Jane Blanchot French millinery company. It carries the name of its founder, who was a sculptor and continued to devote herself to her vocation, while also following a career as milliner, which began in 1910 with the opening of an atelier in Paris. Until the 1960s, she designed hats, exploring particular forms and structures. Her passion for sculpture urged her to also create jewelry. After the war, as honorary President of the Chambre Syndicale de la Couture, she struggled to safeguard perfectionism and artisan's ability of the profession.

Jäneke Brand of accessories and bags of German origin, with premises and a factory in Veduggio, in the area of Brianza. The company, still managed by the family, took its name from the founder, Giorgio Jäneke, who left Hamburg for Milan in 1830, where he established a factory of turtle and ivory combs and accessories. He was the first to manufacture them mechanically in Italy. In the early 1900s, his sons moved the business to Veduggio. In the second post-war period, machines were introduced for the manufacturing of combs from plastic layers and to injection molding. The modernization and technological innovation processes are still the characteristic feature of this brand, which also produces suitcases and traveling bags that are exported all over the world. (*Laura Lazzaroni*)

Janson Stephan (1957). French designer. He works in Italy. His shows have always had the atmosphere of an out-of-the-moment event, fantastic and mundane. He creates designs without following trends, but reelaborating the seasonal themes in a new and original fashion and sometimes even against the mainstream. Born in France, Janson's neighbor in Paris is Yves Saint-Laurent, in Rue Spontini. Although he has never met him in person, he visits his atelier, observing, chatting with his premières, and watching the rehearsals. He is fascinated by couture. Some basic elements of his fashion were probably inspired by Laurent: the oblique cut, the frills falling down in a certain way, his love for geometric patterns. In Paris he studied at Saint Roch's School of the Chambre Syndicale de la Haute Couture. He then worked for some French clothing brands and, for some time, for Kenzo. In 1980 he moved to New York, invited by Diane Fürstenberg, who entrusted him with the direction of all the licenses of her clothing line and, later, of her couture Collection. Janson retained the memory of the taste for comfortable and practical clothes from this experience, which always plays down his highly tailored Collections. In 1986 he opened his own atelier in Milan and, in 1988, he creates his distribution company, Apolide. He collaborates, as style consultant, with some Italian clothing companies. In 1998 he was hired to design Pucci's Collections, which turned out to be a short experience. (*Minnie Gastel*)

❑ 2003, July. The designer creates a women's larger sizes line for Marzotto, which he calls Stephan.

A sketch by Stephan Janson.

Jantzen American knitwear company. Established in Portland (Oregon) in 1910 by John and Roy Zehntbauer, sons of a cooper from Missouri, and by the Canadian Carl Jantzen. The factory, with the name of Portland Knitting Company, would have continued to manufacture knitwear if the local rowing team had not requested some special wool swimming costumes to protect athletes from cold in 1913. In 1928 the company, which had changed its corporate name to Jantzen, became famous outside of the USA, in Europe, South America, and Australia, not only for its swimming costumes but also for sportswear. Another goal was scored in 1923, when Jantzen chose a new design for his garments: a picture of a girl diver (the first real pin-up) that drove truck drivers crazy. A future movie star, the protagonist of Tarzan, contributed in the brand's launch: Johnny Weissmuller, 5 times Olympic swimming champion, chose Jantzen during his competitions. Since then, the Jantzen brand has always been synonymous with swimwear. Esther Williams wore Jantzen during her aquatic movies. In 1947, Norma Jean Baker, a completely unknown, was chosen to launch the first Jantzen swimming costume in elasticized fabric, called Double Dare,

Logo of Jantzen' swimming costumes.

because it extolled the chest. This girl became famous with her new name: Marilyn Monroe. In 1954 the corporate name was changed to Jantzen Inc. Sales and proceedings attained its historical best in 1973. the company had 4,500 workers.

❑ 2002. Jantzen was bought out for 25 million dollars by Perry Ellis International, one of the biggest swimwear brands, whose products are distributed in the USA and in 30 countries worldwide. The growth of Perry Ellis' proceedings, which indicated a 7.9% increase in royalties at the end of the year, was meaningfully attributed to the acquisition of Jantzen. From its headquarters in Portland. Jantzen produces and sells Southpoint and Trademarks articles, of which it has the licenses, as well as of Nike and Tommy Hilfiger.

Japan Fashion Association Established in 1989 as a organization whose purpose was to promotion fashion and international exchanges. In 1990 it transformed into the Association of Japanese Fashion under the management of Goto Noboru, President of the Chamber of Commerce and Industry. It organizes cultural activities and prestigious events all over the world.

Jardin des Modes Fashion monthly. In 1992 the Musée des Arts Décoratifs of Paris dedicated a historical exhibition to the publication for its 70th anniversary. Founded in 1922 as a supplement to the periodical *L'Illustration des Modes*. One year later, Condé Nast bought the magazine and changed its name to *Le Jardin des Modes*. In 1933 the first cover by Hoyningen-Huene opened the era of durable collaborations with significant photographers. After the interruption of publication during the war, it was issued fragmentally until 1947. In 1952, with a new layout and fewer articles, *Jardin des Modes* was the mouthpiece for ready-to-wear, which was still dawning. In 1954, Hachette took it over. In 1961, it was revived with a new logo and the collaboration of Helmut Newton, who imitated other great photographers (Sieff, Knapp, Horvat). In 1971 the publication was in financail difficulties. The magazine closed down, notwithstanding the efforts of Hélène Lazareff and the France Edition group. The Editions du Henin relaunched it in 1977. In 1979 Boulainvillier International Publication became its new owner and changed the editorial politics with a large format (the new layout was by Milton Glaser) and much news under the direction of Ginette Sainderichin and Alice Morgaine.

(*Olivella Pianetti*)

Jardin des Modes (from *Anni Venti – La nascita dell'abito moderno*, Centro Di, Florence, 1991, catalogue for the exhibition held at the Galleria del Costume).

Jardini Rossella. She started her career in fashion in 1974 by opening a small shop called Il Pomeriggio (The Afternoon), in which she sold designer clothes, such as Issey Miyake, Ter & Bantine, and other famous names. In 1986 she worked with Nicola Trussardi to develop clothing and accessory lines. In 1978 she created, with two designing friends, the Alveare line. In 1981 she met Franco Moschino and collaborated with him on the Cadette Collections. After a period at Bottega Veneta, she returned to Moschino in 1984. She worked as first assistant for the Moschino Couture line and the accessories, then for all the lines. In 1994 she became the heir as creative director for the company's production and image. (*Silvia Paoli*)

Jarvis Michelle (1965). British designer. She has been working in Italy since 1991. She creates waistcoats, bags, oversized shirts, nightrobes, and pajamas using the waste rags of Como's silk industries, composing patchworks.

Jasiak Daniel (1965). French designer of Polish origins. He studied fine arts in Tourcoing and Decorative Arts in Paris. He carried out his apprenticeship at Lidewig Edelkoor. Later he worked as an independent consultant for six years. In 1992 he opened his first atelier. He is "lonesome". He did not want alliances with the industry and created custom-made unique pieces for his clients who never knew what the final result would be. He says: "What I do is work, not fashion". To allow himself the luxury of such small production in France, he has a connection with the Japanese ready-to-wear industry, but only and exclusively with that country. He is the only designer to accept the cut and sewing of the 'flesh clothes' of Jana Sterback, which stirred a scandal in London during a show of Winter 1997-98.

❑ Jasiak's technique contemplated the assembly of the varied fabrics, from kimonos to dust rags, in a patchwork that he later cut and composed to create very light shirts. Wool sweaters and scarves are handmade manufactured by his mother Maria.
❑ In 2000 he was among the inventors of Egostyle, a triumph of custom-made clothing, which privileges the personalization of the look compared with ready-to-wear. The original production, a reaction against the uniformity of the industrial fashion, was put on sale in his Parisian boutique in Rue Cassette and in Brussels.
❑ 2001, August. He created the clothes for the wedding of the former pop group Eurythmics, Dave Stewart with Anoushka Fisz.

Jaspée Fantasy three-thread yarn, each in a different color. The fabric obtained with it, mainly in wool, is worked to obtain a variegated effect. It looks like straight ribbed gabardine.

Jault Olivier (1971). Designer of shoes and sandals for Ines de la Fressange, Myma, Holland & Holland, Kookai, and Maud Frizon. Designer and model-maker, Jault is capable of designing but also of manufacturing a shoe from heel to upper. He studied at the Institute Duperré, and then completed an apprenticeship at Charls Kammer. After which he went to the Bureau-de-Style Oascal Mai and, later, to design shoes for Givenchy, under the eye of Monsieur Hubert, and also for Yves Saint-Laurent.

Javits Eric (1956). American milliner. His hats, devoid of useless decoration, tend to look like sober sculptures for the head and frames for the face. Among his various designs, which promoted women to regain a taste for hats, an accessory out of fashion, the most distinguished hats were for the day and the cocktail hour. He designed hats, other than for the Collections of several designers, also for theater and TV shows, for the serials *Dallas* and *Dynasty*.

❑ 2000. He launched the Squishee line with ostentatiously bare hats and bags.
❑ 2001. Britney Spears wore a Javits' creation during her exhibition at the MTV Music Awards, the show that awards the singer of the year. In 2003, Pink, another emerging teen idol, wore the hats of the American milliner.

JB Martin French shoe brand. Established in Fougères in 1921, it developed according to a classic style, focusing on production efficiency and the acquisition of new plants. The range expanded to include men's shoes and comfort shoes. In 1985 the management passed from the hands of the Martin family to Jean-Claude Duriand, who acquired 33% of Palladium and the licenses of Chevignon and Kenzo Man.

A Louis XV model by JB Martin, Spring-Summer 1999 Collection.

J.C.M. Company of ready-to-wear fashion. Established in Bologna on the initiative of Francesco Rocca and Vito Monti. Men's clothing are manufactured with the Jey Cole Man brand are manufactured: suits, jackets, pants, shirts, and accessories. Under the direction of the new designer, Giuseppe Belli, the production shifted towards nomadic aesthetics, characterized by washed fabrics, damask linen, and cottons, which accompanied the original, informal elegance of the company. Some openings in franchising are under preparation, and these shops are in addition to the stores in Riccione and Bologna, in order to consolidate the Italian market and to prepare for the international adventure.

Jean Baptiste Rautureau Men's shoe line. Established in 1995 by the French shoe factory Freelance and characterized by a sophisticated image and a research stylistic content. The line was named after the owners' grandfather, Guy and Yvon Rautureau. In 1870 their ancestor opened a shoe workshop in La Gaubretière, where the offices and the plant of the group are still located.

Jean Marie Farina French perfume brand. Established in 1800 by Jean Marie Farina (1785-1864), who is regarded as the main individual responsible for the success of eau de Cologne. Born in Piedmont, he arrived in Paris from Germany (where his parents had emigrated) at the age of 30, bringing with him the recipe of a new type of water distilled in Cologne, based on orange flowers, lemon, bergamot, rosemary, and lavender. He opened a laboratory in Rue Saint-Honoré, and named the fragrance *Extra Vieille*. Today it is said that Napoleon was the fragrance's testimonial: he used liter after liter. In 1840, once Farina – who had enriched his catalogue with more types of eau de Cologne and some cosmetics – had reached the pinnacle of fame, he sold his business to the Collas family. The business remained with the Collas family until 1862, when two cousins took it over, Roger and Gallet. Still today, two famous eau de Cologne struggle for the title of direct descendant from Farina's formula: the *Extra-Vieille* by Roger & Gallet and the *4711 Kölnische Wasser* by Mülhens.

Jeans Pants that marked the aesthetic culture of the second half of the 20th century. In addition to their practicality, they represented and continue to represent a symbol (although changeable over history) from workers' uniform or the uniform of youth protests, from rebel to pop, to passé partout without age or role limits. They can be basic or interpreted according to a style, in traditional indigo or colored, faded, marbled, stone-washed, torn, or starched. Every decade creates its favorite list, preferring a certain type of finishing, color, or style. Worn with a blue blazer is the informal uniform of businessmen, whereas a baggy version is the favorite garment of the rap rebellion. The fabric is similar to denim (from Nîmes) – it actually has the same Levantine structure (diagonal lines, front different from the back) – but it is lighter. Created in Genoa. It is a highly resistant, light fustian, from Genoa, actually called jean or jeane. It was present in the market since the Middle Ages, but its transformation into working trousers dates back to the 1800s, when it was used by longshoremen. It was only from 1850 that the term jeans was used to identify not the fabric but a model. In San Francisco, Levi Strauss, with his partner Jacob David Youphes, launched a model of resistant trousers with five pockets for the gold-diggers. After approximately a century, from the 1840s to 1900s, jeans became a trendy garment, first in the USA and then in Europe. In the late 1960s, during the outbreak of the hippy movement, they were the common denominator of rebellion. With the passing of time, jeans have changed models and their manufacturing techniques, following the temporary rules of designers' fantasy rather than political ideologies. As well as the historical Levi's, two other jeans manufacturing companies represent the identification between a clothing piece and a brand: Lee and Wrangler.

Jemenez Elisa (1965). American designer. Daughter of two sculptors and an art graduate from the University of Arizona, she started her career as sculptor and joined the world of fashion by creating designs for her sculptures. She was discovered by the gallery owner Holly Solomon, protagonist of the New York art scene, and designed her first Collection in 1996. Her imagination is boundless, with holes, rips, hems refinished with candle flame, burnt fabrics, and cloths washed in tea and spices that follows the lines of the body and the fantasy of the wearer. Every garment is a unique piece, a game without an obvious balance of geometric forms and colors created with precious and non-precious fabrics. Within three years, Jemenez conquered the fashion world and Hollywood. Her garments, which can be purchased only through the Solomon Gallery (as works of art) or at her Manhattan showroom, have been worn by the biggest stars of cinema and music.

(*Manuela Parrino*)

Jens Kaeumle (1967). German designer. Born in Stuttgart. After graduating from Armgartstr (Hamburg) and obtaining a masters from the Royal College of Arts in London, he made his debut with Moschino. After which he collaborated with Tommy Hilfiger to create a 'capsule Collection'. He then went to Levi Strauss in Germany. In 1999 he established the design studio Jael in London, where he attracted clients such as Bree and Jasper Conran. In March 2000 he became head designer for Emanuel Ungaro Homme, while he began working on his own brand Jens. His Collections, intended for men, don't rule out women with certain garments. For the Autumn-Winter 2003-2004 he proposed, for a first time, a line of bags with many pockets, exactly like the new Eskimos, velvet jeans, and nylon anoraks.

Jérôme French fashion house. Established in 1920 at 104, Faubourg Saint-Honoré by Jérôme Feldstein. Its immediate success prompted the couturier to also open a Summer store in Aix-les-Bains. However, the German occupation of the 1940s forced him to close the business.

Jérôme L'Huillier French brand. Established in 1989. In 1996 an important contract was signed for the import and distribution with Japan. This determined a huge growth of its turnover and sales points. Its design is characterized by a feminine and refined style. In 1999 it presented three-quarter length overcoats in leather and stretch dresses long to the feet.

Jerphanion (de) Dauphine (1960). French designer. She attended courses at Studio Berçot. She started out as assistant at De Luca and she continued to work in the role of co-assistant for both Lagerfeld and Chloé. She has been director for Japanese licenses and responsible for accessories. She was also mannequin vedette for Mugler. She has never started her own business. In 1993, Lagerfeld appointed her as director of his ready-to-wear division.

Jersey Towards the end of the 20th century, it was a heavy knitwear fabric worn by the fishermen of Jersey. The actress Lily Langtry first adopted as her clothing in the 1920s on the set and in her private life. Made light, soft, and naturally elastic, it adjusted to the several changes in looks during those years. It is a sheared, simple fabric. Research, fashion, and technology have assisted the evolution of the jersey-system, which is now protagonist of a large, elegant segment of the textile market.

Jesurum Establihed lacework manufacturer and a boutique in Venice. If Michelangelo Jesurum had not established a school in 1868 to guarantee himself the necessary workforce to start the business he had in mind (1870), the profession of lacework would have been finished. In 1800 the tradition of Venice and Burano, which had conquered Europe from the 1500s and from which all the great schools of France and Flanders had been born, had declined to the point of being almost forgotten. Jesurum found the last women trained in the art and asked them to teach it. The initiative was enough to allow a quality production to start again. In 1878, tablecloths, sheets, shawls, and bridal veils branded by Jesurum won the gold medal of the Universal Expo of Paris. Marguerite, the Queen of Italy and wife of Umberto I, commissioned a tablecloth in Venetian stitch, which took ten years of work. Two samples were made: one of which can be seen in the Venetian showroom by arrangement. In the 1920s, the business was sold to the Levi Morenos family.

Jet Set Swiss brand of casual clothing. On June 13 1969 in St. Moritz, some friends opened an improvised store selling faded jeans, secondhand Hawaiian shirts, and Chinese working pants. In 1975 they presented their first clothing Collection for their brand and opened a boutique in Zurich. In 1980 they created a ski Collection. Five years later, a denim line was launched by Blue System. The essentially casual image has a strong fashion content: a mix that determined the brand's success in the 1980s.

Jill French magazine of fashion and costume. Published between June 1983 and February 1987 by the Ag Presse group. It was a sophisticated magazine for an elite public, paying attention to the latest fashion trends. It made a refined use of black and white, and only rarely alternated with color. Since 1984, all articles have been translated into English. Born as quarterly, now it is a bimonthly.

Jiménez Joan (1961). Spanish designer. Born in Mataró (Barcelona). He graduated from the Instituto Internacional Feli Arte y Técnica del Vestir, and started his career by creating fabric patterns. At the same time he self-produced a first knitwear Collection, which was an immediate success. In 1990 he started collaborating with some Spanish clothing companies, creating women's Collections. In the Autumn-Winter season 1991-'92 he made his debut with his first own Collection. His creations are characterized by constant research, which goes through different means of expression.

Jimmy 58 French shoe factory. Established in 1936 in Marseilles. The designs were extremely classic up until 1960, when fashion was already blowing an innovative and rebellious wind and Marie-Rose Sinanian took over the management of the family business. All of a sudden, they were overthrown by fantasy and eccentricity with a unisex heel. The only thing that resisted the change, which attracted a new, trendy clientele, was the artisan perfection of the manufacturing.

Jinteok (1938). Korean designer. Her first store, opened in Seoul in 1965, was a point of reference for Korean fashion, thanks also to her involvement with the foundation of Seoul Fashion Designers Association. Her creations have always made reference to the traditions of Korean clothing mediated by a typically western taste. Representations of nature are the defining characteristic of her style.

JM Weston Established brand in men's shoes. Established in 1881 in Limoges, France, where Eduard Blanchard started manufacturing handmade shoes of high quality. The company resisted the advent of the mechanization of production of the 1930s, without deviating from its artisan traditions. In 1976 it was acquired by E.P.I. Corporation, owned by the Descours family.

Joan and David American ready-to-wear brand. Joan and David Helpern established the company in the late 1960s, immediately proposing whole Collections of clothes, shoes, and accessories. The first store was opened in 1985 in Madison Avenue, New York. The success was so great that the brand was known outside of the USA in just a few months. Joan is the designer, while

David is the management. Now there are six boutiques in New York and 61 worldwide in Brazil, Japan, Spain, the UK, and the USA.

Jodhpurs Horse-riding pants for ladies, inflated on the thighs and tight along the calves. They were created in the early 1900s, taking their name from the town in Rajastan, India, where they worn by the locals on an everyday basis. They were brought to Europe by the British because they were worn by the British cavalry at the time of their rule. In 1970 they returned to fashion Collections, reproposed, reinterpreted, and modified by the various designers.

Jogging The principal physical activity during the second half of the 20th century. From the President of the United States to beginners at the weekend, everyone has practised jogging at some point. It is defined as light running, possibly in close contact with nature. The most indicative clothing for this kind of activity is, undoubtedly, the tracksuit. Composed of two pieces, it can be made in warm cotton or in synthetic material with elasticized pants around the waist and the ankles. The upper part has long sleeves and elasticized cuffs. During the 1970s, jogging clothing became fashion and the tracksuit experienced popularity, especially among women.

Johnny Lambs Italian ready-to-wear brand. It has the interesting translation into English of the name Gianni Agnelli. Initially it proposed only swimming boxers. The company was established in 1978 by its president, Giorgio Tocchi, the inventor of the casual Friday, which is ironically casual clothing fit for traditionally formal occasions. It is the casual style for Friday, usually the day when the working rules would impose a wardrobe as formal as in the rest of the week, but the closeness to the weekend allows some transgressions. In 1980 it launched the men's total look. In 1983 it started franchising politics, launching women and children's Collections. In 1999 the brand had 300 sales points around the world, 8 of which are single brand stores in Italy and 6 in South Korea.

(*Valeria Vantaggi*)

❑ At the beginning of the new century, the brand was acquired by Fin.Part.
❑ 2002, Autumn. Fin.Part sold the Johnny Lambs brand to an entrepreneurial group in northeastern Italy. The 1.5 million sale implied the moving of the company's premises to Brescia.

John P. John (1906-1993). American milliner of German origin. Born in Munich. He learned the profession from his mother while he was still very young. He made his debut in 1928 with the name of John Fredericks, which was turned into Mr. John in 1948. In 1939 he designed the hats for Scarlett O'Hara, alias Vivien Leigh, in *Gone With The Wind*. Appreciated for his passion for picturesque and spectacular forms, for the plasticity of his ladies' hats, real sculptures, and for a palette of unusual and audacious colors, he created hats for many of the most elegant women of America and for Hollywood's divas, such as Rosalind Russell.

John Sean Clothing line. Established by the king of rap Sean "Puff Daddy Combs". Born in Harlem, the African-American neighborhood of New York, Combs, also known as "P. Diddy", quits college studies to enter into the world of music. His talent and personal style soon took him to the top of the A&R. Only 24, he established the Bad Boy Entertainment, the first music label exclusively dedicated to hip hop. The success of artists such as Craig Mack, Biggie Smalls, and Notorious B.I.G. launched the company in the international music market, promoting an unusual kind of music and a new urban language. In 1998 Combs started the clothing brand John Sean, presenting 32 men's suits for a target between 12 and 40 years, built to his own image and similarities. The Collection attracted the public's curiosity obtaining, for three years in a row, a nomination to the award yearly assigned in New York by the Council of Fashion Designers of America. Combs, to meet the taste of a larger clientele, as well as progressively abandoning the overly restrictive rules of the hip hop aesthetics, later decided to also launch a womenswear line, adding urban chic to his creations.

(*Francesca Gentile*)

John Smedley English knitwear brand. The Smedley family, active in the sector of yarns for more than 300 years, still manages the factory established in 1784 by John Smedley and Peter Nightingale. The two entrepreneurs, prompted by the technological innovations of Sir Richard Arkwright, started their business in the middle of the Industrial Revolution in the northern England. They started with a spinning mill for the cotton imported from India and Egypt, having the garments knitted outside of the factory. Their vision of modernity and efficiency foresaw the complete automation of the production chain under a single roof. They achieved it fifteen years later. Being enlightened industrialists, they offered good working conditions. Furthermore they invested in charities, among which the Smedley's Hydro, a center for water cures. In 1893 the factory became a limited company. The business expanded and new machinery were purchased, making them capable of producing a large variety of knitwear products. Already in the first decades of the 20th century, the company offered a large range of articles, from underwear to swimwear to jerseys for golfers. It specializes in the manufacturing of precious yarns, such as the Australian merino lambswool and sea island cotton, for which the company is still renowned. The premises – amplified and modernized – are still the same as those in 1784. (*Virginia Hill*)

❑ In the last 40 years of the 20th century, the company attained its maximum expansion with four lines: Voyage, Luxury Range, Men's Wool and Cotton, and Ladies' Wool and Cotton, becoming the symbol of British style in the world.
❑ 1998. The launch of a new line of products in merino wool from New Zealand, obtained from sheep exclusively reared for John Smedley, was announced at the 58th edition of Pitti Immagine Uomo.
❑ The company manufactures all of its garments in national plants through 35 steps of hand-finished manufacturing, which includes the immersion of knitwear in selected English waters to guarantee its softness. The brand was distributed in 30 countries and exported 70% of its production.

Johnson Betsey (1942). American designer of clothing for disco music. Born in Connecticut, she studied at Pratt Institute of Brooklyn and in 1964 she graduated with the best grades from Syracuse University. Her creativity earned her a collaboration as guest editor with the magazine *Mademoiselle*, where she was contacted by Paul Young, in search of new talent to launch his boutique chain Paraphernalia. In 1969 she opened her own showroom in the Upper East Side in Manhattan. She called it Betsey Bunki and Nini. During the 1970s-80s she collaborated with various American ready-to-wear brand, including Alley Cat. It was through these experiences that she developed an eccentric, young, humorous, and sexy style, mixing vinyl and sequins. It was essentially a disco fashion, influenced, according to Johnson herself, by her dancing studies. In 1979 she finally made her debut with her own label.

(*Anna Gloria Forti*)

❑ After the launch of the Betsey Johnson Label, the designer opened a series of stores in the USA, including one in New York in Soho. Anticipating the trend that would transform the street in the core of shopping, a store was opened in Melrose Avenue, Los Angeles. In 1998 a store was opened in London. The following year, another store opened in Vancouver, Canada.
❑ 2002. On the occasion of her 60th birthday, the designer presented the models of her Spring Collections in her house in East Hampton.
❑ 2003. The designer joined the Fashion Walk of Fame in New York. She was honored for her contribution to American fashion. An original sketch of hers and a short biography are placed in the pavement of Seventh Avenue, covered by a bronze and granite plate with her name.
❑ 2003. There are more than 40 stores in the world and more than 1,000 specialty stores in the USA and in Europe.

Johnson Beverly (1953). American model. She was the first black model to appear on the cover of *Vogue*, photographed by Scavullo in

1974. Her unexpected success was important for the introduction of African-American women to the world of fashion.

Johnson & Marié French tailoring workshop. The company was located in Rue des Pyramides, Paris. It had famous clients such as the General De Gaulle, the industrialist Marcel Boussac, and the writer Michel Leiris, who wrote about it in his *Journal*. It closed in 1970.

John Wanamaker American department store. Opened in 1861 in Philadelphia. Its founder, John Wanamaker, was a pioneer of the home delivery service and of the mail selling system. He is also remembered for starting an education program for his employees and a pension scheme.

Jones Kim. English designer. She studied fashion at St. Martin's School of Art. In 2001 she launched her own brand with a line of menswear. In 2003 she added a women's line. Her style is relaxed, comprised of American-style sweaters, T-shirts, and comfortable pants, worn by trendy personalities such as John Galliano.

Jones Stephen (1957). British milliner. Born in Kirby, Liverpool. He studied fashion at St. Martin's School of Art from 1976 to 1979 before deciding to specialize in millinery. He opened his first salon in a fashion boutique in Covent Garden in 1980. He became one of the most famous personalities in New Romantic London. A frantic participant in the capital's nightlife, he made friendships in the worlds of music, art, and fashion. Everybody was wearing his hats. Steve Strange and Boy George (he was also invited to appear in Culture Club's video of the cult song Do You Really Want to Hurt Me? in 1983), Spandau Ballet, and Grace Jones were among his initial fans. Throughout the 1980s and 1990s he maintained and increased his status as the king of hats, dressing the heads of all the most famous personalities in music, theater, and cinema as well as models and actresses for publicity. His creativity seemed boundless and independent to fashion trends. At the age of 20, his capacity to capture and interpret the inspiration of others led him to collaborate with the big names of high fashion and ready-to-wear including Gaultier, Mugler,

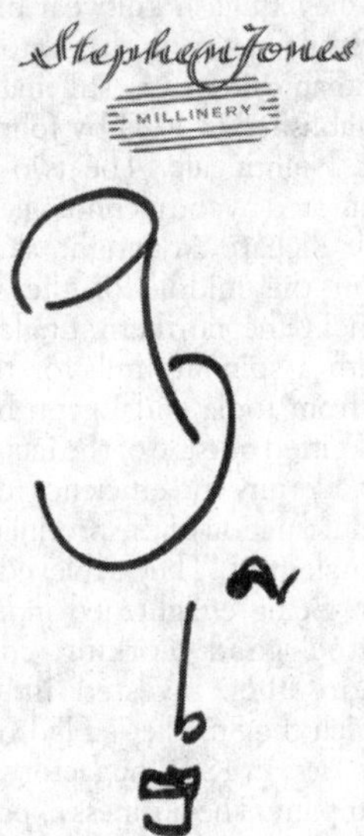

Drawing and brand of the milliner Stephen Jones.

Comme des Garçons, who saw his talent in 1984 and brought him to Paris to create their Collections. In 1990 he launched Miss Jones and Jonesboy, lines of great diffusion. In Japan, where he has lots of fans, he has accessories lines under license. He is the artistic consultant of the cosmetic house Shiseido. His hats are in the fashion Collections of the Victoria and Albert Museum in London, Brooklyn Museum in New York, Kyoto Art Museum in Japan, and the Australian National Gallery in Canberra. They have been included in important exhibitions such as *Addressing the Century* at the Hayward Gallery, London, and *Art and Fashion* at the Museum of Modern Art in San Francisco.

❑ During the collaboration with Shiseido, he created colors for more than 200 beauty parlors and took on the role of art director for the fragrance division. During the last few years he has been in charge of the color selection for Fsp, a cosmetics brand created for teenagers.
❑ 2003, Spring-Summer. He designed hats for the Collections of ten designers, among those were Brioni, Christian

Dior, John Galliano, and Emanuel Ungaro. Jones produced an accessories range exclusively for the Japanese market, which featured sunglasses, bags, scarves to match hats, and Japanese hats created by Alps Kuwamura.
❑ His brand is distributed all over the world in 19 Italian cities and in 100 cities in the Far East.

Jones Terry (1945). British graphic designer. After graduating in 1966 in graphics from the West of England Art College and working as a freelance, he was appointed artistic director of Vogue at the age of 27, where he remained until 1978. His technique, condensed in the book *Not Another Punk*, can be considered linked to the faraway dadaism and to the closer punk movement. His style uses very different techniques from collage to photocopying. He is the theorist of the design that is defined in Italy as *di getto* (instantaneous), and which he himself defined as 'instantaneous, automatic' in the title of the volume *Instant Design. A Manual of Graphic Design*, published in 1990.

Jonvelle Jean-François (1943-2001). French photographer. From Cavaillon, in southern France. His career began very quickly after moving to Paris. At the young age of 20, he was hired as an assistant by Richard Avedon. Enthusiastic about the female universe and women and their charm, he dedicated exhibitions and books to females, such as *Balcons* in 1998 and *Fou d'Elles*, always using the magic of black and white. He frequently worked for *Marie Claire* in the fashion, advertising, and portraiture sectors. (*Roberto Mutti*)

Joop! German ready-to-wear brand. Created in 1978 by Wolfgang Joop (1944), who had started out as a freelance designer for international fashion houses in the 1970s. In 1978 he launched a synonymous Collection of furs. From 1981 he presented a ready-to-wear Collection with the brand name Joop! (with the exclamation mark). Professor of the Superior Institute of Fine Arts in Berlin, he has obtained several prizes including the Fil d'Or and the Goldene Spinrad. In 1985 he launched his first menswear Collection and an accessories line. He also opened a restaurant chain. Two years later was the time for cosmetics and of the perfume *Joop!*, which conquered the American market. Later he started eyewear and jeans lines. In 1988 in Hamburg, he established the company Joop! Fashion GmbH. He is famous for eccentric fashion, extremely amplified, in which many elements are superimposed on different layers. His ever-trendy Collection extolled the body and its femininity. He often draws inspiration from artistic movements that have appeared in the course of centuries. For example, his 1987-88 Collection was inspired by the Italian Renaissance.

Jorando Italian fashion house established abroad by the brothers Nicolò and Francesca Jorando. Francesca, 35 years old, was keen on fashion and design. After high school she worked for Baghera, a trendy Roman boutique, while her brother concluded his studies in business and management in New York. In 1980, after a journey to Indonesia, they decided to launch their first shoe Collection. Through the years, they expanded their production to include accessories and clothes. The inspiration for their creations comes from their travels all over the world. Multi-ethnic colors and forms pay particular attention to cultural differences. Today Jorando is a brand in the shoes, accessories, and bags sectors, with export to 19 countries worldwide.
(*Daniela Bolognetti*)

A sketch by Francesca Jorando.

Joseph English fashion brand. Joseph Ettedgui – the mind and soul of a brand that revolutionized English taste – was born in Casablanca by Moroccan parents. In the late 1950s he arrived in London with the dream of becoming a hairdresser. He lived in the era of Swinging London and opened his hairdressing salon – Salon 33 – in 1971 in the mythical King's Road. A 360° creator, he could not resist the temptation to exhibit the fashion pieces of his young fashion designer friends in his shop. He preferred one above all: Kenzo, the young Japanese designer in love with Paris. The French capital also offered Joseph his greatest inspiration; he was very skilled in picking up the clean, refined style of Parisian girls and in interpreting it for the less sophisticated girls across the Channel. In 1984 he launched Joseph Tricot to great success. In the same year he opened Joe's Café in London. He was one of the first designers to apply a total concept in his company. From graphic to store design, everything was studied and coordinated to promote a lifestyle besides selling clothes. In 1985 he creates his perfume *Joseph parfum de jour*. In the 1980s and 1990s he opened several single brand stores in the UK, New York, and Paris. His Collections were put on sale in the most famous department stores around the world. His capacity of recognizing talent rendered his boutiques, where he showed other designers' Collections as well as his own, fascinating for their avant-garde vision, suitable to Joseph's philosophy. His Joseph Tricot Collections have received several awards from 1990 up until today.
(*Virginia Hill*)

Jouny Cyd (1968). French shoe designer. In 1993 she made her debut, winning the prize for accessories design at the Salon des Jeunes Créateurs in Hyères. The following year, Adidas entrusted her with the creation of a prototype for a new soccer shoe. From 1994 to '98, she collaborated with the shows of Loris Azzaro, Missoni, Sophie Sitbon, Mugler, Grès Couture, and Castelbajac. In 1999 he designed a Collection of shoes and matching bags in a limited and numbered series, handmade, for Anna GV, an Italian company.

Jourdan Charles. French shoemaker. Born in Romans. In 1921, at the age of 38, he started his own business. In Paris he opened an atelier at the 1, Boulevard Voltaire and hired 30 artisans, who were able to manufacture 40 pairs of shoes everyday. In the second post-war period, his three sons, René, Charles, and Roland improved production, achieving 900 pairs a day. They also transformed the Collection into a symbol for high fashion. In 1957, numbered tickets were distributed at the opening of the company's first boutique in Paris in order to control the incredible flow of clients. Women queued diligently. In the late 1960s, Dior entrusted his business to Jourdan to manufacture and distribute Dior's shoes all over the world. Single brand boutiques opened all over the world. In the 1980s a menswear Collection was launched. The brand has always focused its energies on avant-garde choices, such as those of the surrealist photographer Bourdin for advertising campaigns or the idea of dressing models as characters from famous paintings. Favorite pieces and evergreen, the models Maxime, a flat décolleté with a butterfly-shaped ribbon, and Madly, varnished flat platform shoes with square heels. (*Giuliana Parabiago*)

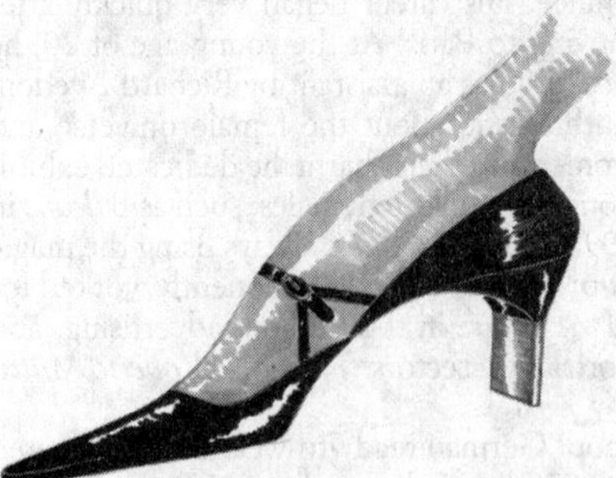

A model by Charles Jourdan.

Journal des Dames et des Modes, Le One of the most important French fashion periodicals from the early 20th century, and now highly collectible. Writers such as Jean Cocteau were often featured in its pages. Published between 1912 and 1914, each issue contained unbound art deco-style fashion illustrations by artists including Georges Barbier.

Journal du Textile French weekly. Established in 1963 by Hennessen. It is uniquely dedicated to the professionals and operators of the textile and clothing sector. It has a large format, published on paper in black and white. Articles are accompanied by photographs. It is the pulse of the French and European markets, informing about fashion trends, distribution, selling and management techniques, and about the calendar of events, shows, and salons. It periodically publishes dossier about men and women's fashion, accessories, or fabrics, or about a particular subject, chosen from time to time. It hosts fixed columns as *L'Air du Temps*, in which fashion journalists and style studios report the actual trends, or as *Le baromètre du marché*, which offers a statistics of sales in the largest towns. Furthermore, it regularly proposes a sort of bulletin with the quotations of various designers, their popularity, and the level of their sales in France.

(*Gabriella Gregorietti*)

Jouy Cloth of printed cotton, usually reddish or light blue on a ecru-colored background, with patterns showing country scenes. Called Toile de Jouy, from the name of the manufacturing company in Jouy-en-Josas, where Christophe-Philippe Oberkampf established the first cloth printing mill in 1759.

Joyce Bimonthly magazine. Published by Alsojoy Diffusion since 1987. From an aesthetic point of view, it differentiates from its competitors for the graphic use of drawings instead of photographs, even on the cover. Most of the publication is naturally reserved to fashion, accompanied by columns about the jetset, news, music, cinema, theater, and beauty. Its founders, Florence Lafargue, chief editor, and Michle Hauville, director, maintain its high level as a prestigious review through presenting only luxury products, while keeping its price at a competitive level.

Joyce Multinational company selling luxury products. It started with a boutiques in Hong Kong and Kowloon, which took their name from their founder Joyce Ma. Opened in 1971, they represent the nucleus of the present Joyce Boutique Holding composed by about 30 stores. It has mass distribution of luxury clothes that are never perfectly imitated. Clothing and accessories for men and clothes in the various sales points of high fashion and avant-garde, which Joyce purchases exclusively in Europe, the USA, and Japan. They can be purchased in stores with Joyce signs, but also in franchised stores (Emporio Armani, Prada, Missoni, Donna Karan, Jil Sander, Thierry Mugler, and Sonia Rykiel) or in multibrand boutiques (Michel Klein, Issey Miyake, Yohji Yamamoto, Comme des Garçons, Martin Margiela, Ann Demeulemeester, and Dolce & Gabbana). Joyce also owned a magazine distributed in Asia, a restaurant (Joyce Café), and a flower shop (Joyce Flowers), where Christian Tortu's creations are on sale. Elected, in the late 1990s, as one of the most elegant women in the world, Joyce Ma has opened new stores in Taiwan, Bangkok, and China. In January 1999, the Italian group Hdp joined the capital stock of the multinational.

Juicy American brand of casual and sportswear. In 1996 Gela Nash-Taylor established Juicy Couture with Pamela Skaist-Levy. Nash-Taylor was born in Corning, New York. She spent her childhood in a dozen states including: Ohio, Colorado, Michigan, Pennsylvania, California, and Iowa. Her experience in adjusting to different environments helped her to start her first career: acting. She studied dramatic art at the prestigious Carnegie Mellon University in Pittsburgh, obtaining a B.F.A. After some time in Broadway, she decided to move to Los Angeles to start a career in television. During her first pregnancy she realized that she was unable to find pregnancy dresses. Willing to have her own business, she looked for someone who could help her to create the clothes that she herself would wear herself. She found Pamela Skaist-Levy. Fascinated by fashion since her childhood, Skaist-Levy studied at the Fashion Institute of Design and Merchandising in Los Angeles. Although she excelled in several sectors, she decided to focus on design. She drew inspiration from architecture in designing a line of hats called helmet. Fred Segal, Bloomingdale's, and Barney's sell her accessories. These innovative creations were incredibly successful with the press. The Travis Jeans Inc. was established in 1990, which revolutionized the world of pregnancy clothing, proving that women wish to dress well also during those nine months. In six years, Travis Jeans was so successful that the two partners chose to sell the company and invest in a new activity, Juice Couture. This brand is appreciated by women with different lifestyles and also by celebrities. Madonna, Cameron Diaz, Gwyneth Paltrow, Kate Beckinsale, Britney Spears, Nelly Furtado, Dido, Jennifer Lopez, and Julia Roberts are regular clients.

Jules French chain of non-expensive men's clothing. Created in 2000 from the restyling of Camieu Homme. There are 132 single brand stores with a turnover of more than 236 billions Liras in 1999. Jules is the new name for an old, solid commercial organization. In 2000, the chain has opened 20 more sales points.

Julian Alexander (1948). American designer. Born in Chapel Hill, in North Carolina. He started to work in his father's menswear store while still very young. "My father", he loves to remember, "taught me to take care of business as well as of aesthetics." In 1975 he moved to New York. Two years later, at the age of 29, he won the first of five Coty Awards in the category of Outstanding Menswear, which were to mark his career. Few years later, he became the youngest designer to be welcomed into the Coty Fashion Hall of Fame. His brand produced accessories, eyewear, bags, jeans, and shoes, but Julian has also created a line of interior décor articles. During his career, the designer also invented the car colors and uniforms of Paul Newman's Indianapolis racing team. The NBA team Charlotte Hornets also entrusted Julian with the restyling of their uniforms.

(*Pierangelo Mastantuono*)

Julian & Sophie Brand of young fashion, ready-to-wear, and casualwear. Founded by the designers Julian MacDonald and Sophie Cheung, also life partners. Julian made his debut in September 1998, sending out invitations to the press and sector's operators for his London show, which was never to take place, about his clothing line *Nothing Nothing*. After the diffusion of another fake invitation card in February 1999, the first real show took place with the Spring Collection 2000. For the Autumn-Winter 2000, the two presented their creations during London Fashion Week, winning the BFC New Generation Award. The brand also won the prize reserved for young talent in English fashion in the following year. From that moment on, *Nothing Nothing* exhibited six times during London Fashion Week, and 14 times worldwide from Hong Kong to Iceland. They also revived interest with their Autumn-Winter 2002 and Spring-Summer 2003 Collections. Their clothes, inspired by interior decor patterns, Julian's complicated cuts, and the abstract drawings of Sophie's embroideries stirred further interest. On February 14, 2003, another sensational event took place. Rejecting the invitation to present their models on the runway, the two designers locked themselves in a room at the Great Eastern Hotel in London and, imitating John Lennon and Yoko Ono, spent three days in bed to protest against the war in Iraq.

(*Pierangelo Mastantuono*)

Julien Faure French silk factory. Established in 1864 in Saint-Etienne by Henry Faure, and moved to Saint-Just-Saint Rambert in 1992. Every year the Collections change in their choice of colors, the contrasting materials, and the tests on new weaves. Silks, always up-to-date, are highly researched by designers such as Gaultier, Ralph Lauren, Stephane Kelian, Ungaro, Valentino, and Charles Jourdan. 60% of the turnover comes from export, with 150 patterns for silk fabrics and 100 exclusive ribbons each year.

Juliet Romantic fishnet skullcap embroidered with pearls. Named because it was worn by Norma Shearer, who was 35 at the time, in the movie *Romeo and Juliet* directed by George Cukor in 1936.

Jumper Jersey dropping down to the hips with a loose line and straight cut. They are often V-shaped and low-necked, worn with a mid-length, pleated skirt. This outfit was launched by Chanel in the 1920s, but it is continuously re-proposed. The jumper, in its sport version, was the typical garment of mariners and fishermen to protect them from the cold. In the late 1800s, jumpers were named sweaters initially in England and then in the rest of Europe and the USA, used in sport and leisure time.

Jumpsuit Bell-bottom pants used during the day and for walking in the first half of 1800s, starting from around 1822. In the romantic period, pants were an element of menswear. Long trousers became diffused after the partial disappearance of culottes, whose use remained solely in ceremony uniforms. Tight at the malleolus, they shape the legs and have stirrups to keep the pants tight and stretched. They were adopted for dancing and walking with the difference that, for the latter, the bell-bottom leg was still in use, or even more favored, the shape kept large around the waist to accentuate the width of the hips. In the early 20th century, the jumpsuit was also a very tight leotard that covered the whole body, arms, and legs like a second skin, with a zip fastening under the chin. It was manufactured in different types of fabrics, from knitwear to silk, always mixed with other elastic or stretch materials. In the early 1900s, it became clothing used by sportsmen.

June, July, August Japanese ready-to-wear brand. Established in 1989. The name and Collection were created by June Inoué who had been Jean-Paul Gaultier's assistant since 1982. The brand is characterized by researched and sophisticated clothes, which are perfectly finished with a tailoring cut.

Jungle Book Style that became trendy in the early 1990s, inspired by the military (camouflage garments, printed clothing resonant with the patterns and colors of the tropical forest). It drew its inspiration from the spontaneous fashion of the Rastafarian movement, which appeared in Europe from Jamaica in the late 1970s. It was revived by several designers such as Vivienne Westwood in the 1980s.

Jungle Jap Parisian boutique. Before becoming famous with his ready-to-wear line, Kenzo Takada opened this boutique in Galérie Vivienne in 1970. The clamorous success attributed to the boutique in the small world of fashion in those years brought about the creation of the Kenzo brand.

Jute Textile fiber obtained from the jute plant through a process of stalk maceration and beating. It is used in clothing blended with silk and wool.

K

Kahng Gemma (1954). American designer. Born in Korea, now a naturalized American, she creates clothes mainly for a woman engaged in work. Her models are practical and comfortable without surrendering to a touch of sensuality. Her purpose is to combine classic elements with unexpected eccentric details, all without compromising the garments' wearability.

Kaiserman Bill (1942). American designer. Born and grew up in New York. He established the Raphael company in the multicultural climate of Brooklyn in 1970. In the course of a decade the company has sold the value of more than 30 million dollars through Collections of women and men's wear and sportswear. The business has found space to expand. The Bill Kaiserman label became a licensee of international brands such as Van Gils in the Netherlands. His talent has been acknowledged with various awards, among which are three Coty Awards and the Best Designers of America. In the 1980s he arrived in Milan and, while his brand's fame grew in Europe, Asia, and the USA, he developed his business with international companies such as Mitsuie and Kashiyama. Italy honored him with a knighthood. In the early 1990s he returned to the United States where he developed new licenses with companies such as Hartz&Co, Format, and Mondo. He also designed new Collections for Avirex and created a revolutionary fabric covering. Furthermore he launched Skins, a new street style clothing line for men and women.

(Lucia Serlenga)

Kaliano French brand of ready-to-wear fashion. Created in 1993 by Joelle Grossi, a designer from Aix-en-Provence in France. She learned the profession in her parents' boutique and by working for Lacoste. She designed a romantic fashion in the simplicity imposed by the ritual wardrobe of men.

Kallisté Trendy shoes and Made in Italy fashion for a high level target. Present in the market since 1952 when Giacomo Rossi, founder of the company, opened a production plant in Alseno, between Parma and Piacenza. Today as well as the trendy Kallisté Collection and the young line Key-té, it produces Etro and Daniela Jasoni. It has single brand boutiques in Paris and Milan.

Kalloch Robert (1893-1953). American designer and costume designer. Fashion designer for Lucille Ltd., he had several actresses among his clients and thus entered the world of cinema. In 1933 the President of the Columbia, Harry Cohn, entrusted him with the costume department of the movie company, with the precise task of better characterizing his stars. Kalloch carried out this task perfectly, designing elegant costumes for Barbara Stanwyck (*The Bitter Tea of General Yen*), Claudette Colbert (*It Happened One Night*), and Irene Dunne. A decade later, he quit Columbia for MGM, where he dressed Judy Garland and Hedy Lamarr. His last movie was in 1948 with Mirna Loy in *The House of Dreams*.

Kamali Norma (1945). The brand was created in New York in 1977, but its creator, Norma Arraez, was already a renowned professional. After graduating from the Fashion Institute of Technology in 1964, she opened a boutique with her husband in 1968. She sold unusual fashion purchased in London as well as her own designs. In 1974 in Madison Avenue she proposed a small Collection of her own. In 1977 she divorced and established Omo Norma Kamali (On My Own) and made her own name as one of the most fanciful American fashion designers. She created coats with parachute cloth, elegant evening dresses in jersey, and tight skirts and pants in plush. During the 1980s her swimming costumes characterized by Hollywood style become the distinguishing mark of a golden decade.

❑ 1989. She received the American Success Award of the Fashion Institute of Technology from George Bush Snr. during a ceremony held in the Rose Garden of the White House.
❑ 1992. The first eyewear line was launched and the swimsuit Collection was diffused worldwide. The sports Collection, Omo Gym for woman, and Norma Kamali Beauty, a cosmetic line and face products were launched in quick succession.
❑ 1996. She launched her Internet site: www.omo-norma-kamali.com, which was one of the first examples of search engines online for images of fashion Collections. The following year direct marketing arrived on her web site. Thanks to the service 'Shop like a celebrity', the client receives clothes directly at home, chooses, pays within 48 hours for those which she has chosen, and the rest is sent back by courier.
❑ 2001. The Metropolitan Museum of Art in New York displays shows her patented sneakers, which inspired many other designers.
❑ 2002. The New York's Fashion Walk of Fame welcomed Norma Kamali. Her bronze and granite plate is laid in her honor in the Seventh Avenue area between 34th West and 41st Street.
(*Pierangelo Mastantuono*)

Kammer Charles (1949). French designer. His creativity led to the origination of the eponymous line in 1983, which was refined and elegant. His other line Sacha was launched in 1974 and was younger and self-assured, named in honor of the singer, Sacha Distel. Born in Paris, he started working in his father's factory for men's shoes. In the 1970s he took a totally different direction and worked on the concept of total look, proposing a clothing Collection linked to shoes. He collaborated with designers such as Montana, Mugler, Marithé, and François Girbaud. He represents a meaningful creative and market reality.

Kanebo It plays a lead role in the Japanese textile sector. It was a launching platform for world leadership in the production of wool, silk, cotton, polyester, nylon, and acrylic.

Charles Kammer, Spring-Summer Collection 1998.

The group is also active in the drugs and cosmetics' sectors. It is the second largest Japanese producer of cosmetics.

Kangol 'K' stands for silk, 'ang' for angora, and 'ol' for wool, which are the three materials that the French milliner Jacques Spreiregen proposed to use in the manufacturing of berets when he started his business in 1938 in Cleator, in the northeast of England. Initially his hats were worn the area's students, but with the outbreak of the Second World War, Kangol became one of the official suppliers to the army. Kangol is particularly renowned for contributing to the image of the General Marshal Montgomery with his proverbial beret, still in the Collection and familiarly called "Monty". In the post-war period, the company diversified the production, specializing in golf hats, felt hats, and women's hats. It entered the fashion market thanks to the artistic director, Graham Smith, who conquered the interest of Liz Taylor, Joan Collins, and Princess Margaret. In the 1960s Kangol created a line for Mary Quant. Kangol also obtained the rights to commercialize some models with the writing "Beatles," naturally in swinging London style. In the following decade, rappers chose it spontaneously, turning it into a symbol of belonging. It was in the 1980s that the brand began a international ascent, licensing Collections of shoes, bags, watches, sunglasses, and stationery. The company, which in the mid

1990s employed 1,000 workers, has branches in England, the USA, South Africa, and China.

Kaplan Jacques (1924). French designer. In the late 1950s he was renowned for using fur, dyeing it in showy colors, and applying prints to make it less solemn. Born in Paris, his first work experience was in New York at the branch office of his father's company established in 1889. He was among the first to propose synthetic furs. He retired in 1971.

Karan Donna (1948). American designer. Born as Donna Faske in Forest Hills, Long Island. She decided to become a designer when very young, having been surrounded by the world of fashion from childhood (her mother, father, and uncle all worked in the industry). After high school, she attended the Parson's School of Design in New York. She spent the Summer of her second year, working for Anne Klein & Co. She was later hired as their assistant designer. In 1974 Anne Klein died suddenly and Karan became the stylistic director at the age of 25. In 1982 she created the diffusion line Anne Klein II, which already bore her hallmark clean and modern style. Two years later these qualities were distinguished in her eponymous Collection, Donna Karan, which was the surname of her first husband who she married in 1973 and divorced immediately after. The launch of her own brand was made possible by Takiyho Inc., Japanese company owner of Anne Klein & Co. The Collection, dynamic and essential in style, introduced her concept of the seven easy pieces. She proposed an intelligent wardrobe composed by few interchangeable pieces, perfect to wear in every moment of the day for a working woman, to whom she looks with particular attention. The color black is still the basis of her Collections today, a non-color that she regards as a canvas ready for painting. She reintroduced the leotard, proposing it in new, tight modeling stretch fabric to wear as clothing with a jacket for the office, and with a necklace for the evening. The versatility and simplicity of the leotard had a huge impact on the dressing style of the second half of the 1980s, when there was a renewed interest in physical fitness and the leotard was capable of embracing this. Karan's wrapping forms are typical of her style to accentuate the feminine lines and hide its defects. She uses cashmere, preferably in black, to stimulate the senses. Since the start of brand, new lines

1964: the Beatles wearing Kangol berets.

have been launched and new stores have opened every year. The most successful line is DKNY (through record of sales). It is medium expensive with a target young, active, urban clientele who appreciates a casual elegance. Several agreements have concluded on license, one of the most important is the one with Estée Lauder for a line of cosmetics in 1997. The Donna Karan empire now includes: women's, men's, and children's wear, with lines ranging from elegant to casual, as well as accessories, cosmetics, and interior decor lines. Her second husband, Stephan Weiss, who she married in 1977, manages the company. It is a business that employes 2,000 workers and is quoted on the New York stock exchange. During the 1990s, Karan embraced the New Age philosophy in an attempt to find an existential balance in her frenetic life. She said: "Everything I do is a matter of heart, body, and soul". Her personal and economic involvement is very important to her on the social front. She participated in two committees for the struggle against AIDS and in a charity for the research on ovarian cancer. She has won the Council of Fashion Designers of America award on several occasions, as well as the Coty American Fashion Critics award and other awards in the course of her career. Her old college honored her with an *ad honorem* degree in 1987. She lectures regularly at the Parson's School of Design and she is on the committee of directors. Several books have been written about her, her style, and her ascent to designer of international fame.

(*Virginia Hill*)

❑ 2001, April. The designer announced the sale of Donna Karan International for the sum of 250 million dollars. The purchaser is the French group Lvmh, which had already acquired Donna Karan's holding company. The total sale amounts to 643 million dollars. The brand's headquarters remain in New York. Lvmh's intention is to ferry the company towards a luxury market.

❑ 2003, May. Donna Karan International announced that it would not produce a men's Collection for the first time since 1992.

Karina Harvat Austrian clothing brand, specializing in knitwear. It was created in Vienna in 1993 by the eponymous designer, who had just graduated from the Institute Marangoni of Milan. She also has a market in Italy and in the USA with her very simple elegance.

Karnak A very precious Egyptian cotton, which is not grown at the moment. The term karnak is now used to define any very fine and light cotton fabric.

Karyn Gauger French ready-to-wear brand. It took its name from the designer who created it in 1986. After her studies at Esmod School, Karyn designed for Synonime of Georges Rech. From 1983 to 1986 she worked for Peclers Paris, the consulting style agency of Dominique Peclers. During her time here she participated in the creation of several ready-to-wear Collections (Initial, La Redoute, and Valisière). Through continuing her collaboration with Peclers, she established her own company in 1986. She created a functional clothing with pantsuits or apron dresses, inspired to an essentially casual line.

Karzai Hamid (1955). Political premier of Afghanistan. After the liberation of Kabul from the Taliban regime in 2001, he became the head of the new government. He has appeared in articles about everyday events because the designer Tom Ford defined him as the "most elegant man on the planet, very elegant and very proud". A charismatic leader of the Pashtun ethnics, he made wool mantles trendy (from which the Pashtun people take their name). Even Prince Charles wears them. Karzai also launched the use of pakol, the mujaheddin beret in wool or fur. Cultivated, refined, and a polyglot, he is married without children with seven brothers and a sister. He describes himself as a "moderate Muslim". He is flattered by the attentions dedicated to him by the Western world. (*Antonio Mancinelli*)

Kasha Hairy fabric manufactured with wool and fur.

Kashiyama Japanese manufacturing industry established in 1927. It has been among the leaders of luxury clothing since the 1970s when it began manufacturing on license for

Ralph Lauren, Saint-Laurent, Calvin Klein, Sonia Rykiel, and Cerruti. It has branch offices in Paris, Rome, and New York. It owns the plants of Gibo in Italy. In Paris the industry has made a partnership with Gaultier. In a boutique in St. Germain, young unknown talents of fashion are welcomed.

Kasper Herbert (1926). American designer. Often considered the American Pierre Cardin, Kasper is primarily known for moderate and bridge sportswear lines sold in department stores. Born in New York, he studied at New York University and the Parson's School of Design, before completing his early training in Paris, first at the École de la Chambre Syndicale de la Haute Couture and later in apprenticeships at Jacques Fath and Rochas. He returned to New York and joined Leslie Fay in 1964, where he has remained for the most part of his career, first as designer and later as vice-president.

Kassuri Japanese technique of weaving and printing very similar to Ikat, in which the threads are printed first to form patterns on the fabric. Kassuri patterns were taken up by Kenzo in 1972 for shirts and summer pants.

Kasuko Yoneda (1955). Japanese designer who arrived in Paris in 1973 to attend the famous Studio Berçot. After her degree, she worked as an assistant to Guy Paulin and Christian Aujard, before moving to Tiktiner to design their Collection. She made her début with her own Collection in 1987, financed by the Japanese group Itokin.

Katayone Adeli (1967). Designer of Iranian origin. She has been living in the United States since the age of 10. She grew up in Los Angeles and, while still a teenager, started designing clothes for herself and her friends. In the early 1990s, she worked as a designer for the group Parallel and, in 1996, decided to quit that company to launch a line with her name. When it seemed that Stella McCartney was not going to renew her contract with the fashion house Chloé, Katayone Adeli was in the list of the possible successors. In 1999 she was included in the small group of new talents for the Perry Ellis Award by the Council of Fashion Designers of America. In September of the same year, she opened her first store in Bond Street, New York. Her clothes are nowadays on sale in the best stores in London, Paris, and Tokyo. (*Manuela Parrino*)

Kata Zone An artisan's technique of Japanese printing created with small wooden molds. It was very successful in the West in the late nineteenth century and was reproposed by designers such as Kenzo and Kawakubo.

Katherine Pradeu French brand of ready-to-wear women's fashion created in 1997 by the designer Katherine Pradeu in Paris. After attending the courses of the Studio Berçot, she started her career in charge of knitwear for Peggy Roche and Jean Rycher. She worked four years for. Lolita Lempicka, receiving a good apprenticeship before opening her own business. Her fashion is very open to new, technological materials and is sold by Henri Bendel in New York and Absynthe in Paris.

Katsura Yumi. Japanese designer of high-quality fashions. She presented a Collection in Rome in 1999. She started her career as a designer of bridal dresses in 1963. In 1988 she officially opened the Museum of the Bride in Kobe which has 55 of her dresses, representating 25 years of activity. In 1994 she opened the Yumi Katsura Bridal House in New York. In 1998 she publicized herself with a celebration in the Palace of the Bride in Tokyo, with a Victorian style chapel on the sixth floor. Her creations are on sale at Saks, Bergdorf Goodman, and Neiman Marcus. Brooke Shields and Yoko Shimada have modeled for her. In addition to the New York bridal house, she has 7 more stores in the US.

Kawakubo Rei (1942). Japanese designer. She is Madame Comme des Garçons, a *griffe* established in 1969. She was born in Tokyo, where she began her career in fashion working in a textile company. In 1981 her first Paris Collection upset the *prêt-à-porter* scene with an emphasis on pauperism that seemed to propose rags rather than dresses. The models were pale, uncombed girls, wrapped in layers of fabrics that had nothing to do with elegance. In addition, everything was stressed by black, a sort of color-philosophy which creates anguish and anxiety. Her shows seem to boast decadence, shabbiness: actually, it is a style made of subtle references, of clothes which break rules, create the unexpected. She herself says: "A fundamental element of my career was the fact of living it as a means of being exposed to the reaction of the public." Cultivated and always closer to art than to the concept of products for the clothing market, she is the priestess of minimalism, in the past as well as in the present, the avant-garde of poor stylism. Her fashion is the expression of her coherence. She detests decorations and is indifferent to seasonal trends: she is not influenced by the ideas of others, but starts every time from the beginning. The facts say she is in the right: she has fans all over the world, even men, for whom she can get away with designing suits featuring female patterns. She says: "Masculinity can be expressed with flowers, you just have to work around it." She sees fashion as an escape from daily chores, a desire for freedom, especially within oneself. Western and Eastern elements, tailoring volumes and researching materials are her favorite ingredients: she is a voice outside the choir, representing free inventions that sometimes let themselves be seduced by "the complete opposite," but a he-she mix, in which the tailcoat is enriched with ruches and the blouse's frills stress the rigor of the tie. This is an exception which is not a rule: if one looks at the steps she has taken, it is evident how her ideas have always been ahead of the field, and have become current concepts. She is far from the mass, a little mysterious, charming but enigmatic. The designer has influenced fashion by sweeping away stereotyped images and setting a completely different look. More than describing her models, you breathe the atmosphere, one that has affected the younger generations and stirred criticism by those traditionalists unable to see in her Collections a boundless creativity, both in fabrics and in colors. Her proposals are always subdued in tone, in particular in her knitwear: turtlenecks with checked longuettes, alternative yet simple and refined sportswear. Or plaid patterns for Empire-style midi-dresses, swaying skirts matched with pale blouses. And a sort of do-it-yourself style, with rolled-up jersey panels tied around the body. A continuous discovery in the name of the poor: it is here that Rei Kawakubo expresses her power. She creates a brave and revolutionary fashion design, an anarchy that destroys the old rules and creates new ones. (*Lucia Mari*)

❑ For the Fall-Winter Collection 2001-2002, presented in the Wagram salon of Paris, the designer launched the "erotic woman" by Comme des Garçons. To the music of *Je t'aime, moi non plus* by Serge Gainsbourg, models displayed lingerie-dresses shaped as petticoats, with bras worn over the jackets.
❑ 2003. She experimented with collaborations with dance groups and big names in international photography.

Kebaya Tight bolero in lace or batik, worn on sarongs by Indonesian and Malaysian women.

Kefiah The fashionable connotation of this scarf, which represents the struggles of the Palestinian people (but also the participation in demonstrations by protesters and students), is connected to the long wave of multiethnic chic. Even though it does not represent a real triumph, its recurrent appearance on the catwalk attests the intention to ennoble the external look (read: fashion) with something more profound, updating an old piece of Eskimo philosophy with a touch of frivolity.

(*Stefano Bucci*)

Keïta Seydou (1921-2001). African photographer from Mali. Born to a large family, at the age of 14 he received a Kodak Brownie camera and became interested in photography. He was also taught to print in black-and-white by a photographer in Bamako, the town where he lived and worked as a carpenter. In 1948 he opened his own portrait studio and in 1962 was appointed the official photographer of Mali. That same year his fame moved beyond Mali's borders, first at the joint exhibition "African Explores" at the Center for African Arts in New York, then in 1994 at the Fondation Cartier in Paris, and two years later with the retrospective at the Smithsonian Institution in Washington. His black-and-white portraits have an extraordinary elegance: men and, above all, women wrapped in their very beautiful drapings become a tribute to the art of being and looking, because, as the photographer himself says, the best poses are those chosen by the subjects, and "when we say '*I ka nyé tan*' many translate it as 'you look good here', but the real meaning is 'you are beautiful just the way you are.'" His subjects stand out against very colored backgrounds in his studio and are defined by the objects, accessories, cars, radios, medals, and hats that describe their taste. From this point of view, Keïta, who escaped the destiny of most African photographers of ending up as a photo-journalist, is an author that, through his portraits, talks about fashion and the way of being a member of his people. (*Roberto Mutti*)

Kékeikian Jacques. French shoemaker. Of Armenian origin, he arrived in Marseilles in 1922 and started working with his brother, also a shoemaker. His sandals, which were loosely inspired by Greek-Roman models, were immediately noticed on the Côte d'Azur. Manufactured in thick leather and finished with a saddler stitch, the Tropéziennes model had a thong style that enchanted Colette. But it was in the 1950s that he achieved greatest success, when his sandals were discovered by Brigitte Bardot, Michèle Morgan, and Queen Fabiola. He increased the number of models he produced and named them after the mythical locations of the Mediterranean, such as Capri and Corfu. During the 1970s, his sandals were chosen by designers such as Jean Charles de Castelbajac, Kenzo, Michel Klein, and Helmut Lang. His three sons continue the business, and they round out the Collection with models for other seasons than summer.

Kelly A bag created last century, at the same time as the maison Hermès was founded, as a saddle-bag for horse-riders during hunting. But it was only in 1930 that the Parisian house decided to make it a woman's bag by making it substantially smaller. During the 1950s this large bag, characterized by its unmistakable "lock" fastener, was one of the maison's great successes. In 1955 it was publicized by the woman whose name made it famous: Grace Kelly, Princess of Monaco, who was pregnant with her first daughter, Caroline, used this bag to hide her pregnancy from photographers. Splashed across every magazine, from that moment on the bag became the "Kelly." Made traditionally in black, brown, blue and bordeaux, during the 1980s the Kelly bag started to be manufactured in brighter colors, such as yellow, red, emerald green and zephyr blue. Nowadays it is available in three models – hard, soft and very soft – and in different skins, and can be requested with or without a strap. (*Minnie Gastel*)

Kelly Grace (1929-1982). American actress. Cool and impeccable, the perfect example of American upper-class style, she represented the other face of the explicit sensuality of the 1950s. She arrived in Hollywood from the Academy of Drama in New York. She came from Philadelphia, from a rich family of Irish origin. She won her first important role in 1952, when Fred Zimmermann wanted her at the side of Gary Cooper in *High Noon*. But confirmation of her star status was made with Alfred Hitchcock who, between 1954 and 1955, made her the lead character in three films: *Dial "M" for Murder* (1954), *Rear Window* (1954) and *To Catch A Thief* (1955). In *Rear Window* her wardrobe was entirely created by Edith Head, the most renowned costume designer in the history of cinema. In the movie, dresses follow one another as though it were a fashion show translated onto the big screen: from the sophisticated corolla skirt in perfect New Look style, to a more casual look made of cigarette pants and loafers that the actress wears in the last scene. Symbolic of her style, and more and more popular in the fashion of the time, she wore pearls, a silk scarf knotted under her chin and carried the famous Kelly bag created by Hermès. She had a short but brilliant career, from 1952 to 1956 when, in order to marry Prince Albert Rainier of Monaco, she abandoned the world of celluloid for good. (*Sofia Leoncina Gnoli*)

Kelly Patrick (1952-1990). American designer. His brief career started and ended in Paris. He made his début at the age of 22 when he opened a small shop in Atlanta. He tried New York but, notwithstanding a scholarship to the Parson's School, he had no success. He arrived in Paris in 1979 and, to earn his living, sold his creations in streets and squares. The magazine *Elle* discovered him, which was enough to find a place for him on the *prêt-à-porter* stage in 1985. Two years later, a partnership with the Group Warnaco allowed him to open a space in America. He was talented, and had a taste for fantasy and borrowing elements. He designed for Benetton, but only two years after becoming the first American in history to be admitted to the Chambre Syndicale du *Prêt-à-porter* des Couturiers et des Créateurs de Mode, he died.

Kemp Ralph (1965). French designer. He studied at the Parisian Esmod School. In 1985 he was hired by big maisons. He worked for Chantal Thomass, then for Marithé & François Girbaud; then for Dorothér Bis and the Bureau de Style Peclers Paris. For a while he was employed by Kenzo Homme. In 1993 he created his own brand and imposed his model of a strong woman. Two years later he opened his Parisian boutiques and his creations were presented for the first time during the Paris week of *prêt-à-porter* in 2002.

(*Maddalena Fossati*)

Kennedy Onassis Jacqueline (1929-1994). As wife of President John Kennedy, her first role was as the "First Lady" of the United States, and her second marriage made her the wife of the richest Greek shipbuilder of the second half of the century. She was born Jacqueline Lee Bouvier in East Hampton (New York). Her neat and rigorous style deeply influenced fashion for at least two decades. She married John Fitzgerald Kennedy in 1953; in 1960 her husband was elected President of the United States and, while in the White House, Jacqueline appointed Oleg Cassini as her official designer. This marked the start of unforgettable bon-ton tailleurs with bag-shaped jackets and three-quarter sleeves, however, it was Roy Halston who created her celebrated pill-box hats that are nowadays synonymous with the Jackie style. It became a style immortalized by the press on the covers of worldwide magazines. She was even called "Her Elegance" by the magazine *Women's Wear Daily*. But it was not only Oleg Cassini behind Jackie: there was also Givenchy and, at the time of her wedding with Onassis, Valentino too, who in 1967 dedicated her an entire Collection and, in 1968, created the bridal dress for her second wedding ceremony. In her last years she often wore clothes by the designer Caroline Herrera. Several accessories were also linked to her name: from the strap bag with the classic H-shaped buckle designed by Hermès, to the Capri sandals she had manufactured by the dozen by Canfora, a renowned Capri shoemaker, and the big oval sunglasses and backcombed hairstyle.

Kenneth Cole American brand that initiated with shoes but developed into clothing and accessories. The founder's history can be filed under the heading "entrepreneurship made in the USA." In the mid-1970s he collaborated with his father in the family business, the El Greco Shoe Company. His début occurred in 1982, when, during a shoe fair in New York, he sold his first women's shoe Collection from a truck parked in front of the Hilton Hotel. That marked the beginning of Kenneth Cole Productions Inc. Quoted on the Stock Exchange since 1994, *Forbes* put it in the list of the 200 World's Best Small Companies. Nowadays it is also present at international level with shoes, womens- and menswear, and accessories under the brands Kenneth Cole NY, Reaction and Unlisted, and with more than thirty lines of products under license. Cole's urban and contemporary fashion matches his social engagement, as witnessed by his often controversial advertising campaigns. He is the son-in-law of Mario Cuomo, former Governor of the State of New York.

(*Laura Lazzaroni*)

Kenneth D. King Brand and name of an American milliner. Extremely precise and careful about details, he designs fanciful creations that "decorate" the head. Elton John is among his most enthusiastic admirers.

Kent State University Museum This museum, founded in Cleveland in 1985, covers many fields: it ranges from fashion to design, including the machinery and utensils used in high tailoring techniques. Clothes, fabrics, accessories, but also glass objects and accessories chosen by the Rodgers & Silverman School of Fashion Design and Merchandising. In addition to a huge Collection

Kent State University Museum, Ohio: a sketch by Shannon Rodgers, published in *Vogue America* in October 1947.

of European and American clothes of the 18th and 19th centuries, the museum's Collection also contains clothes by Blass, De La Renta, Chanel, and Dior.

(*Anna Santini*)

Kenzo French *griffe* of *prêt-à-porter* created in 1970. It takes its name from its founder, the Japanese designer Kenzo Takada (Hyogo, 1939). The fifth of seven children, he would have liked to study styling, but his parents enrolled him in the English Literature courses at university. He stayed just 3 months at Gaibo College in Kobe, before leaving for Tokyo in 1958 where he entered the Bunka Gakuen, the prestigious school of fashion design. In the third year of studying he won first prize. After a period of work for a chain of department stores, he left Japan for Paris. He arrived in France in 1965, saw the shows of the great names of fashion, like Cardin, Dior, and Chanel, and sold some sketches to Louis Feraud and others. He worked for Bon Magique and Jardin des Modes. He restyled and painted (creating a décor of canes) his first boutique: this was the start of the Jungle Jap boutique in Galérie Vivienne in 1970. Clothes – and knitwear – revolutionized the style of that moment: shapes, materials and Japan's traditional drawings were harmoniously mixed with European styles. Ten years later the company born from the Kenzo brand was chaired by François Beaufumé, who remained in place until 1993, the year in which the Arnault Group took control. But already in 1976 Kenzo's boutiques were in all the largest cities of the world, selling different lines: menswear, womenswear, childrenswear, jeans, accessories, home linen, perfumes for men and women, bath products, and even writing pens. An eclectic talent, Kenzo has created theater costumes, in particular for the *Course du Temps* by Stockhausen (1979), and directed a movie, *Rêve après Rêve* (1980). He has exhibited at several shows and retrospectives and has won numerous prizes. When he turned 65, Kenzo Takada announced his retirement from fashion and his *maison*, "to give a new direction" to his life. This occurred after the show on 7 October 1999.

(*Anna Gloria Forti*)

❑ 2002, May. Kenzo made a surprising return with a line of *prêt-à-porter*, accessories, and house linen named Yume that in Japanese means "dream." The Collection was produced as a joint venture with the LVMH Fashion Group, which in 1999 absorbed the Kenzo maison. At the same time, the designer realized a dream he had long had, the creation of a line of ready-to-wear fashion to sell through mail-order. This unique Collection was reserved to the catalogue of La Redoute, part of the PPR group (Pinault Printemps Redoute), a rival to LVMH in the struggle for world leadership in the luxury sector.

❑ 2003, March. After the departure of Roy Krejberg, the designer of the men's

Kenzo: sketch for Woman's Fall-Winter Collection 1998-1999.

line, the maison announced that it would not present a Collection during the Paris fashion week of *prêt-à-porter*. The official explanation (they preferred to focus on the opening of the new flagship store, which was to be built in the former Samaritaine Sport building) seemed to hide another coup-de-théatre: that Kenzo Takada may have been contacted by LVMH to return to his *griffe*. (*Pierangelo Mastantuono*)

Keogh Lainey (1957). Irish designer. She founded her knitwear company in 1984. Her garments are sexy and voluptuous, created using innovative yarns and unconventional materials such as latex and metal wire. She presented her Collection for the first time during London Fashion Week in 1994.

Keogh Tom. American illustrator. In the years 1947-51, he was the star of *Vogue France* since the first cover he designed for the issue of Christmas 1947. Following his early death, his style remained unique and very personal, characterized by vivid touches that framed areas of uniform colors, and by the surrealist backgrounds in which he set his fashion.

Képi Military hat worn by the French Light Infantry in Africa. Tall and rigid, covered with cloth, featuring a peak, a chinstrap, and a trailing neck cover behind. The fashion of the 1930s adopted it from the Foreign Legion: Gary Cooper acted a legionnaire in *Morocco* (1930), co-starring Marlene Dietrich, and in *Beau Geste* (1939).

Kerrigan Daryl (1964). American designer of Irish origin. After studying fashion in Dublin, she moved to New York in 1986 where she launched her own brand. Young and casual clothing: jeans are at the center of every Collection. Since February 2000 she has designed the women's lines for Hilfiger.

Kertész André (1894-1985). Hungarian photographer. Born in Budapest, after his studies at the Superior Institute of Commerce and his first job at the Stock Exchange, he became interested in photography as an amateur with an Ica camera but, following a fire which destroyed his first films, he gave it up. After moving to Paris in 1925, first he sold photographs for 25 francs each to earn a living, then he started collaborating with magazines such as *Berliner Illustrierte*, *La Nazione*, *Frankfurter Illustrierte*, *Time* and important reviews such as *Bifur* and *Vu*. This is the period to which the photographs of the famous series *Distortions* and his first volume *Enfants* (1933) belong. From 1936 he was in New York where he first worked for Keystone and for fashion magazines that did not publish his works because his style was too removed from American taste. In 1949 he started a long and fruitful career with *Harper's Bazaar*, *Collier's*, *Coronet* and *Vogue America*. In 1963 he canceled all his contracts to dedicate his time to personal work. Among several recognitions, he has received a honoris causa degree from the Royal College of Art, and the Légion d'Honneur.

Keupr/Van Bentm Brand of a couple of Dutch avant-garde designers: Michiel Keuper (1970) and Francisco van Benthum (1972). Their creations are the result of a surreal and ironic vision of reality. Their models, which are always one-off pieces, are on the border between installations and *haute couture*. The Dutch couple studied at the Arnhem Institute of Fashion and won the Grand Prix Hyères in 1998. Their clothes are often presented in exhibitions of contemporary art. (*Gianluca Cantaro*)

Kevin Krier & Associates Company that organizes fashion events: they select the location, music, lighting, casting, technical direction, choice of flowers, invitation cards to sponsors, and the press releases. For more than 15 years, it has been important in the fashion world, organizing spectacular shows for Gucci at the American Fashion Awards, and the shows at Madison Square Garden for Tommy Hilfiger. Among their clients are: Yves Saint Laurent, Dolce & Gabbana, Stella McCartney, Tiffany & Co., Badgley Mischka, Ellen Tracy, Hugo Boss, Carolina Herrera, Kenneth Cole, Anne Klein, and Bottega Veneta. The company produced legendary events for the Aids Project in Los Angeles, for the fiftieth anniversary of the *New York Times* (New York, 1993), the relaunch of *Elle*, and for the Hachette Group (New York, August 1993). "I have a big passion for what I do," says Kevin Krier, President and founder of the company. "Our job requires special attention to cultural and behavioral trends: just by anticipating what is going to happen, it's possible to draw attention and be successful." The company has branch offices almost everywhere (Milan, Florence, Paris, London, Tokyo, Seattle, Chicago, Las Vegas, Washington, and San Francisco), but has chosen New York as his headquarters.

Kevlar Aramidic synthetic fiber, available under the form of staple or continuous filament yarn. It is resistant to fire, cutting and abrasions. Kevlar is a DuPont brandname. It is used to manufactured sails. In 1992 Murphy&Nye was commissioned to produce the outfits of the "Moro di Venezia" sailing team in the America's Cup. It was the first to use Kevlar fabrics to create light but at the same time thermal and waterproof garments.

Khanh Emmanuelle (1937). French designer. An example of female eclecticism who turned from a model into a designer, and became one of the pioneers of *prêt-à-porter* during the 1960s. Her style was unmistakably young and crisp, well in tune with the fashions of that time. Famous details were the long collars on her coats, the rounded ones on jackets and blouses, the low-waist skirts and the minis with frills, lace decorations on linen fabrics and embroideries, transparent umbrellas, skiing outfits,

A sketch by Dominique Barrau for Emmanuelle Khanh, Summer 1999. Evening dress.

and inexpensive furs. Everything started in the Balenciaga atelier, where she was working in 1956. For a while she modeled for great tailors like Givenchy and had no idea that manufacturing her own dresses would make her fortune. She got good reviews and became the leading character in a photographic service for *Elle*. Her approach was a new and alternative way to make fashion compared to *haute couture*, and was rewarded with the opportunity to design for some Parisian *griffes*. She started with Dorothée Bis and, from 1962 to 1967, for Cacharel, but also for Missoni, Krizia, and Max Mara. In 1972 she launched her own label, signing a contract with the company Troisa for production and commercialization. However, this contract was cancelled legally after a decade. In 1987 she got back possession of her company and production of her line and started over, establishing Emmanuelle Khanh International to develop the business and license contracts.

(*Lucia Serlenga*)

❑ At the beginning of 2000, Emmanuelle Khanh International and other brands, such as Scherrer and Jacques Fath, were acquired by France Luxury Group, a company established in 2002 by Moufarrige and François Barthes.
❑ The label massively shifted its attention towards eyewear, with a special attention paid to children's glasses.

Khansa Jamil (1968). Lebanese designer. Born and raised in Beirut, he graduated in Fashion Design. In 1994 he moved to the United States and in Los Angeles deepened his background training. His talent for *haute couture* opened the doors to success: from Africa to America, the Middle East to Europe, the list of his international clients lengthens every year. His high fashion shows all over the world (in January 2003 he presented a Collection during AltaModaRoma) make him one of the most interesting international and avant-garde style-setters.

Kiam Omar, artistic name of Alexander Kiam (1894-1954). Mexican designer. Born in Monterey, he designed for a department store in Texas, then he worked as a freelancer in New York before leaving to study in Paris. He designed for theater on Broadway, then the cinema. In 1933 he was appointed costume director of Samuel Goldwyn Productions and United Artists, where he created models for Janet Gaynor (*A Star Is Born*), Miriam Hopkins, and Merle Oberon. He then moved on to work with the producers David Selznick and Hal Roach. He worked once more with Merle Oberon in *Wuthering Heights* (1938), co-starring Lawrence Olivier, which was also his last movie.

Kidman Martin. English knitwear designer. After studying fashion at Central Saint Martin's College (1985) he started working for Joseph Tricot in London. The following year, one of his pullovers – hand-worked with cherubs and rococo decorations – was a big success with buyers and fashion critics. The inspiration, he said, came from studying an old porcelain dish. He worked for Joseph until 1994, then launched his own line.

Kid Mohair An expression used to indicate a smooth, bright and soft wool, obtained from angora kid.

Kieffer Antoine (1933). French graphic artist. He worked for *Fémina*, *Illustration*, and *Elle*, supervised by Peter Knapp. Twice he has been artistic director of *Vogue France*: from 1964 to 1966 and from 1990 to 1993. He was more involved with fashion when working in the artistic direction of the style agency Mafia, with which he then created a new agency, Kieffer Haberland Associés.

Kiehl's Since 1851 An American brand of cosmetics dating back to 1851. It is synonymous with spontaneity and simplicity, and a real status symbol with New Yorkers. The store is a former drugstore and its 300 varieties of creams, by now sold all over the world, are still prepared there. The business is managed by the Heidegger family, now in the fourth generation, which tries to keep the original recipes intact, adjusting the products to the new needs of the market.

Kiener Franz. German writer, his book on philosophic anthropology, *Kleidung, Mode und Mensch* (1956), brought together fashion and architectural styles, which he considers to be influenced by the same Zeitgeist.

According to Kiener, clothes are the direct expression of the individual ego and their characteristics are an amplification of our self-awareness.

Kieselstein-Cord Barry (1948). Creator of jewelry or, as he calls them, "body sculptures." His ambition is to free jewelry from fashion trends, and to combine evocations of the past with suggestions of modern art. An example are his buckles inspired by the old West, like the *Winchester*, created in 1976 and still in production. Some of his creations are displayed at the Metropolitan Museum of Art in New York. (*Roberta Giordano*)

Kilgour, French & Stanbury (now Weatherhill, Kilgour, French & Stanbury). English tailor at 8, Savile Row. For some dandies this boutique is simply worth a trip to London. In the late 1980s, the boutique associated with Weatherhill, which specializes in hunting outfits. It is the last tailor to manufacture walking breeches, similar to riding breeches.

Kilt Scottish skirt. It is a symbol of Scotland and its clans, which are represented by the tartan patterns with which it is manufactured. It was turned into a status symbol in 1800 when Queen Victoria and her husband Albert wore them on their holidays at Balmoral Castle. As a toga form of drape to cover the shoulders, the kilt was already in existence before the Middle Ages. Since 1600 it has been a symbol of Scotland, and entered women's contemporary wardrobes in the 1940s. Modernized around the 1970s, it also began to be worn by Ivy League girls.

Kim Bernardin (1963). Korean designer. She studied at the MGM (school of plastic arts) in Korea. For her women's *prêt-à-porter* Collections in fabric and knitwear, she draws inspiration from the world of nature.

Kim Cristina. Korean designer. She was raised in the United States but she works between Los Angeles, London, Milan, and New York. She designs for the brand Dosa. She often draws inspiration from art. A shawl she created reproduces the thoughts of Cy Twombly. "My work," she says, "starts from materials, fabrics, from the knowledge of their origins and history." She explains her minimalism, taking inspiration from the

Kilt for man and woman, in a sketch of 1992 (Prints Collection A. Bertarelli, Milan).

Buddhist concept of purity. She has turned her back on holding shows because she does not like to "throw my creations in people's faces." In partnership with the designer Pippa Smail, she designed jewelry and showed them in December 2002 at the Nine Dering Street Gallery in London, of which she has become curator.

Kimijima Ichiro (1929). Japanese tailor. He has presented his Collections in Shanghai and Beijing to great success. The son of a pianist and an architecture graduate, he started his career as an architect and only in 1976 turned to making clothes, becoming famous for his refined, soft and elegant garments.

Kimono Traditional Japanese garment. It is still used, especially during official ceremonies. Soft and loose, with characteristically large sleeves, it is fastened around the waist by a broad sash (*obi*), measuring 76.2 inches in height and 3.66 yards in length, often in richly embroidered silk. The several ways to knot it around the waist take on different meanings, a secret which is transmitted from mother to daughter. Splendid examples from Japanese history are seen in costume museums around the world. Kimonos appeared for the first time in the 12th century, worn by members of the aristocracy, who would don several colors, one on top of the other. In the centuries that followed, their extraordinary embroideries became rich elements of decoration. A rule of the Samurai class in 1600 forbade colors and decorations, so in that period the kimono became almost a monkish garment, just black or white, no longer made from silk, just simple cotton. Following the influence on European art and fashion of Japanese prints, in the late 1800s and early 1900s the kimono was portrayed by painters, such as Toulouse-Lautrec, who also wore it as a night robe; and by Mucha and Gustav Klimt. At the same time the kimono became, for the Western woman, an elegant afternoon or house-party dress, and reappeared as a night robe. The term "kimono cutting" indicates the style in which the sleeve is cut in the same size as the armhole. The *obi* and its large but flat bow has long been a feature of fashion. Fortuny dedicated the same attention to the kimono that he did to other ethnic garments; Ferré took it up in some models when he was more influenced by fluid colors, which he assimilated during his travels to the East. In the 20th century the most renowned creator of kimonos was Itchibu Kuboto (1971), who exhibited in museums around the world. He is a specialist in the *tsujigahana* art, a method of dyeing that was used at the end of the sixteenth century. (*Lucia Sollazzo*)

King Arthur (1921-1991). American jeweler. Interpreter of a goldsmithery style inspired by informal art which spread during the 1950s and 1960s. He began producing jewelry in New York in a naturalistic taste, which started a trend in the USA and in Europe. His first experiences in the working of metals date back to the years of his youth, to the time he was working in the Merchant Navy. He sets raw stones in modeled metallic frames. He opened his first boutique on 59th Street, then, in 1962, on Madison Avenue. Over the next two decades, he opened 18 stores in the US and several sales points in Europe. The brand died with him. (*Alessandra Quattordio*)

King Bill. American photographer. At a very young age he cultivated a passion for painting, but then turned to photography, inventing an immediate and simple style. After moving to Europe, he settled in Paris and, from 1965 to 1971, he lived in London, where he made his name publishing in the English edition of *Harper's Bazaar* and then also in *Cosmopolitan* and *Elle*, working for Ferré, Laura Biagiotti, Armani, Valentino, Diesel, and others.

King's Road A street in London. This road is a perfect example of how London can change, while still remaining original and attractive. The name of this long urban street, which runs soutwest from Sloane Square, comes King Charles II, who had it built, according to the popular legend, to reach his lover Nell Gwynne more quickly (though more likely there was a shorter route through Hampton Court). The street remained closed to traffic until 1830, when it was opened to the public. The current fame of King's Road dates back to the 1960s, when it became the stage for new trends. Swinging London exhibited new clothes and haircuts there, as well as new musical tastes and a degree of daring summed up by the miniskirt designed by Mary Quant. In the mid-1970s, Vivienne Westwood and her former boyfriend Malcom Mclaren opened the shop Sex (at number 430), where they prepared the advent of punk (the shop is still there: now it is called World's End after the name of the surrounding area, and has a clock that runs backwards). Nowadays you can still find punks there with a sense for making money from the foreign tourists, from whom they ask a pound to be photographed. On Saturday afternoons in particular, it is easy to step into past fashions and trends, which makes King's Road a place of extraordinary interest for the history of recent fashions. Although its economy is generated by shopping, the street has never given itself up to the vulgarity suffered by another icon of the 1960s: Carnaby Street. Nowadays King's Road has shops, antiques and lots of coffeehouses, some outdoor, indicating the further Mediterranean transformation of London. For this reason the street remains popular with both habitués and occasional visitors. To distinguish the former from the latter it is sufficient to take note of a linguistic whim: only the locals use the article "the": *the* King's Road.

(*Beppe Severgnini*)

Kippah The skullcap worn by Jewish worshippers. Jewish children also wear it in the synagogue during prayers. Orthodox Jewish wear it under their large black cap.

Kirat (1958). Indian model. Her beauty and wish for independence took her away, during the 1970s, from a certain future as a maharani. She should have married the maharajah of Khandu when, in Paris, she was discovered by Cardin. An amazing career opened up in front of her. She was among the favorite models of Saint-Laurent and a constant presence in Valentino's and Versace's first shows.

Kirkland Douglas (1935). Canadian photographer. In 1956 he was Irving Penn's assistant in New York, the city where he got his professional education and which he left in the 1970s to move to Los Angeles. In 1960 he was hired by *Look* magazine and started portraying the stars of cinema and fashion. He became world famous for his shots of Marilyn Monroe wrapped in her bed sheets, which he completely recreated in the studio. For *Life* he made several reportages around the world. He was set photographer for movies such as *2001: A Space Odyssey*, *Out Of Africa*, and *Titanic*.

Kisson Asif (1974). English designer of accessories. He comes from a Jamaican family. He follows courses of applied arts learning almost anything, from ceramics to batik. After his degree, he chose to follow his passion for fashion, focusing on feathers, which he works in several ways to create very original hairdos. He produces unique handmade pieces that have stirred the interest of sophisticated movie stars. In 2003 Harrods launched an exclusive line of his cocktails and dedicated an entire window to his creations.

(*Virginia Hill*)

Kiton Industrial tailor's workshop. Established in 1968 in Arzano, near Naples, by Ciro Paone and Antonio Carola, it counts at present 250 tailors. The refinement of its fabrics and handmade stitching limit their annual production to only a few thousand pieces. The artisans no longer work in the studio, but in an avant-garde structure in which personal skill and experience merge in the groups' synergy, thus creating rigorously handmade suits equal to the best of Naples' tailoring school, and always faithful to the rules of traditional elegance. Much care is also given to ties. Taking a silk square to start with, only two ties are manufactured, using a folding pattern taken from local traditions. A tiny hem finishes the tie to give it thickness. The chosen patterns are only micro-geometric patterns or plain dyed backgrounds that are purely in the classic tradition. Kiton distributes its products in the most prestigious clothing shops in the world.

(*Stefano Grassi*)

❑ 1998, March. Kiton won a Sotheby's auction for the clothing Collection of the Duke of Windsor. The wardrobe was exhibited at the Excelsior Hotel in Florence.

❑ 1999. The President of Italy, Carlo Azeglio Ciampi, nominated Ciro Paone a "Cavaliere di Lavoro", a high honor for people in industry.

❑ 2000. The launch of the sporting line Kiton Outdoor; opening of the second factory in Arzano and of the branch office in Via Sant'Andrea.

❑ 2003. The company employed more than 300 workers and its suits are distributed in 21 countries, with sales points in ten cities in Japan, two in Russia (Moscow and Cellabinsk), in Mexico, Syria and Israel.

Kitten Heels Woman's heel of medium height and curve. It is known as "Sabrina's heel" because Audrey Hepburn wore this kind of shoe in Billy Wilder's movie *Sabrina* in 1954.

Klavers Niels (1970). Young Dutch designer. Together with Alexander van Slobbe, Viktor & Rolf, Saskia van Drimmelen, Keupr/van Bentm, Oscar Suleyman, Melanie Rozema, and Jeroen Teunissen, he represents the new generation of designers in the Netherlands. He designs clothes, but also shoes and bags. He is better known in his own country than abroad (though he has already shown his *prêt-à-porter* Collections in Paris), also because the Centraal Museum of Utrecht has hosted an exhibition with his creations and those of other young designers. (*Giulia Crivelli*)

Klein Bernat (1922). Painter and designer of Yugoslavian origins, educated in Israel and in England. He took his knowledge of paint colors as inspiration for textile design. After some experience in English cotton and wool mills, in 1951 he opened a firm which follows textile design.

Klein Calvin. American designer. He founded the *prêt-à-porter* company carrying his name in 1968. John Fairchild, the celebrated and feared editor of the only fashion newspaper (*Womens Wear Daily*) that can extol or pan a designer, speaks of him as one of the world's best designers, as a real rarity in the panorama of American styling, which is characterized by an excellent cutting ability but little imagination. Not bad for the son of a drugstore owner in the Bronx. At school he made sketches of models in his math book and at home, after homework, he would practice sewing. Thus, having won over his parents' resistance, he studied for a degree from the Fashion Institute of Technology in New York in 1962. With Barry Schwartz, a schoolmate, who, like Calvin Klein and Ralph Lauren, was born in the Bronx, the designer has built a fashion and perfume empire. Whereas Lauren spent his days showing around his tie catalogue to department store buyers, Klein carried his sketches in a small case. After five years of apprenticeship in various companies, he started his own business, specializing for a few years in the design of suits and neatly cut overcoats. In his exhibitions there's no sense of show business. Young, tall, attractive, and impeccably dressed, he is always present where it matters, capable of partying hard at the weekends but of turning into a very precise manager on Monday mornings, his personal image is a strong feature of his success. Not only does he have creative talent but also advertising wisdom, for example, the incorporation of a strong eroticism in the campaign for the famous K jeans, for which he chose a very young Brooke Shields in 1971. This was the year he introduced perfectly cut sportswear garments and practical coordinates into his Collections, such as sailors' jackets, wraps in soft rustic fabric and with a fur collar, shirts in crepe-de-Chine, striped silken blouses, sweaters, and velvet suits. His style is always very simple. He likes shades that match overlaid garments. Season after season, his designs continue to pick the still unexpressed wishes of a clientele that contributes faithfully to the growing success of the brand. He balances simplicity and precious touches in a sophisticated game of harmonies. His clothes focus on practicality: no useless decorations, no frills, but an elegance that always brings a second look. A new clothing line, CK, and an underwear line are sold through a huge distribution network, supported by advertising campaigns built around the daring photographs by Bruce Weber. He is an eternal boy but also a star, though in constant danger because of his private difficulties, and thus his meeting with Kelly was very important. Having left Ralph Lauren's atelier, she became his wife, and brought order to his life, while collaborating on the more sophisticated and feminine aspects of his second creative period around the end of the 1970s. Not just increasing the presence of evening dresses, but also introducing a greater degree of gracefulness in the day clothes. In addition, very linear jackets with squared shoulders and tight at the hips; snug blazers and very studied, simple blouses; but without giving up the sober image stressed by the restrained use of expensive fabrics. Klein owes the loyalty of his customers to his careful research, the lack of complicated decorations and accessories, making his clothes – cut in a way to allow the maximum wearability – ready for mass production. It is also due to the incomparable taste of his jeans, garments that for so long were considered extraneous to the fashion world. He was the first designer to receive the awards for the men's and women's Collections from the Council Of Fashion Designers of America in the same year (1993). In 1973 he won the Coty Award which had never been presented to such a young designer. From 1997 a joint venture has linked the CK line with the Stefanel line of shops, which produces and distributes upon license in Europe and in the Middle East. Recently, it has launched a new children's line in the European market, mixing American and European styles: basic jeans, denim jackets in different shades, and the permanently present T-shirts with the CK logo for little boys; and low-necked blouses or breathtaking shorts for little girls. The erotic advertising campaign that accompanied it stirred a scandal and the banning of the posters, with the accusation of being on the edge of pedophilia. In the Calvin Klein empire, the perfumes represent 34% of the group's total turnover.

❑ Marketing of a limited edition of the unisex perfume cK One. The three bottles were designed by three urban artists: Delta, from Holland, who created a futurist line, the graffiti artist Espo, with his long-necked women, and Futura, from New York, with the mysteries of shadows.

❑ 2002, December. Calvin Klein Inc. was acquired by the clothing giant Phillips-Van Heusen for 430 million dollars cash and shares. The potential royalties, which could be between 200 and 300 million dollars, were to be deferred over the course of the years. Klein and his partner Barry Schwartz had already tried to sell the company in 2000, but were unsuccessful. Klein remains the design inspirer of the 12 different products, for the lines Calvin Klein Collection, Ck and Ck Calvin Klein, which as a whole have a turnover of 3 billion dollars a year. One of the first effects of the sales is the creation of a partnership with the company Vestimenta from Trento in Italy, which from 2004 has been responsible for the distribution of the women and men's *prêt-à-porter* lines, the first not produced inside the company. Under license, Vestimenta already manufactures Emmanuel Ungaro's women's *prêt-à-porter* and Trussardi's men's *prêt-à-porter*, and has a joint venture with Giorgio Armani.

❑ 2003, April. The designer admitted in public to abuse of drugs and alcohol and declared he wanted to seek a cure. In 1988 he had been hospitalized for drug problems.

❑ 2003, June. Certain terms of the license linking the Calvin Klein company (already acquired by Phillips-Van Heusen) to the Warnaco group were modified, and an agreement was signed for the beachwear line, which was to become effective from the beginning of 2004. At the same time, Fingen Apparel, a licensee of Calvin Klein Jeans, created an under-16 division designed by the stylist. The designer, 60, announced that he was no longer to follow the Collections closely, but that he was to have a consultancy role (in style/administration), in collaboration with Bruce Klatsky, President and CEO of Phillips-Van Heusen.

❑ 2003, October. Sara Dennis left her post as Senior Vice-President of the jeans, underwear, and swimwear sector of Calvin Klein to move to Liz Claiborne, a New York company quoted on the Stock Exchange. It was also announced that Phillips-Van Heusen intended to relaunch the clothing line cK Calvin Klein in Asia in 2004, following its suspension in the United States, Europe, and the Middle East because of poor results. A fundamental element in this operation was the long-term license with cK 21 Hidungs Pte. Ltd for the men's and women's sportswear, menswear, men's and women's shoes, bags and small leather goods. This also favored the opening of stores and shops-in-shops in Singapore, Malaysia, Thailand, Hong Kong, and China, while franchised sales points were to be opened in Korea, Taiwan, and China.

❑ 2003, December. The first American Calvin Klein Underwear Store was opened in Prince Street, New York: a large space for men's and women's underwear and fragrances.

❑ 2004, January. A contract was signed with the Swatch Group for the worldwide launch of a Collection of bijoux and jewels.

❑ 2004, March. Robert Mazzoli became

Warnaco's Chief Creative Officer and was to follow the underwear Collections bearing the Calvin Klein brandname.
❑ 2004, July. A new swimwear line for young girls was launched, called Choice Calvin Klein by Warnaco Swimwear, a division of the Warnaco Group.
❑ 2004, September. Launch of the new high-level line for men and women called Ck39 from the name of New York street where Calvin Klein's headquarters and graphic studio are situated. It covers trousers, jean jackets, knitwear garments, and vintage style T-shirts.
❑ 2004, November. Calvin Klein Inc. elected Giuseppe Rossi as General Manager and General Director of Calvin Klein Europe. In Rome, the first Italian Calvin Klein Collection store was opened. On three floors, the interior décor was by RetailDesign and the architect Paolo Lucchetta, who took inspiration from the work of John Pawson for the flagship stores of New York and Paris.
❑ 2005, February. The Italian shoe factory Rodolfo Zengarini from Montegranaro obtained the license for the production and distribution of the women's shoe Collection. Zengarini, already licensee of the men's line, replaced Rossimoda.
❑ 2005, April. A month of openings: the first was the store in Dubai's Wafi Mall, in partnership with Belbadi Fashion, where every article manufactured by the Calvin Klein empire can be bought. The own-brand store Calvin Klein Collection was opened in Italy, on Corso Matteotti on the corner with Via S. Pietro all'Orto in Milan.
❑ 2005, May. Calvin Klein concluded an agreement with Finger for the opening of 50 freestanding ck Calvin Klein stores in Europe and the Middle East, and with Warnaco for the women's swimwear.
❑ 2005, June. Kevin Carrigan was appointed Creative Director and was to have responsibility for the look of the men's and women's retail and wholesale activities, and of the design supervision for coats, jackets, hosiery, knitwear, handkerchiefs, ties, and umbrellas.

(*Edoardo Ponzoni*)

Klein Michel (1957). French designer and brand of *prêt-à-porter*. He started working very young: at 15, he was selling drawings of fabrics to the Saint Laurent maison; at 17 he worked with Maud Frizon and Dorothée Bis. When just 18 the Group Créateurs & Industriels financed his boutique Toiles in Paris and sponsored his first *prêt-à-porter* Collection, bringing immediate success. At the age of 20, he designed the costumes for two theater shows by Bob Wilson: *Death, Destruction and Detroit* and *Edison*. The 1980s saw the definitive launch of the brand, with new shops and an important licensing contract in Japan. In the 1990s four minor lines were created (Klein d'oeil, Klein Quand, Indigo and Toiles). In 1994 he was employed by Guy Laroche to design its *haute couture* Collection.

❑ 1997. He left Guy Laroche to join the American designer Alber Elbaz. Klein was credited with taking Guy Laroche away from *haute couture* more in the direction of *prêt-à-porter*. Michel then opened a new space at 330, Rue Saint-Honoré. It is a store-apartment in a typical Parisian building, which can also be used for exhibitions of art, design, photos, and sculpture.
❑ 2003. Michel Klein's production is characterized by small pieces (bustiers, shirts, boleros) inspired by the South America of the 1950s. Issue of a new women's perfume for the Club des Créateurs de Beauté. Other than the Espace Michel Klein in Rue Saint-Honoré, there are almost 20 sales points in France, 2 in the US (Brooklyn and Melrose Place, Los Angeles), plus 10 stores in Europe, half of which are in Italy.

Klein Naomi (1970). Canadian designer. She is the author of *No Logo*, the bible of the people of Seattle. The book opens with a analysis of the social and economic role which brands have played in the last 30 years. Nike, Shell, and McDonald's are three logos taken as examples. This is her background: "My grandfather organized the first strike at Walt Disney, my father and mother were Leftist radicals." Klein's next book was published in 2003, *Fences and Windows*, which assembled two years of interventions and comments written about demonstrations and meetings. She writes for *The Guardian*, *Newsweek International*, *New York Times* and *The Village Voice*.

Klein Roland (1938). French designer. Though originally from Rouen, Klein has been called the 'grandfather' of British fashion, given his four-decades long career in London. After studying at the Ecole de la Chambre Syndicale de Couture de Paris in 1955-1957, Klein worked at both Dior, then for two years as Karl Lagerfeld's assistant at Patou, before moving to London in the swinging 1960s. He joined Marcel Fenez, then a top ready-to-wear line, and eventually became general manager. He launched his own line in 1973, and his own shop in Chelsea in 1979. He is known for his understated eveningwear, and his designs were often worn by Princess Diana. He designed the uniforms worn by British Airways stewardesses from 1985 to 1992.

Klein Steven (1963). American photographer. Born in Providence, Rhode Island. He graduated from the Rhode Island School of Design with a thesis on painting. Since 1990 he has regularly worked for the magazines of the Condé Nast group, offering an aggressive style but clearly defined pictures.

Klein William (1928). Photographer, painter, and American film director. Born in New York to a family of Hungarian origin, he grew up in the mean streets of Manhattan. A self-taught photographer, he likes to experiment with the use of the flash and rather exaggerated zooms to create particularly innovative new visions. In 1954, after 6 years in Paris, he attended the atelier of Fernand Léger, later spent some time in Milan where he created murals for Italian architects, and then returned to New York, where he worked for *Vogue America*. During this period, his book *Life Is Good & Good For You in New York* (Nadar Prize 1956) was published in Paris rather than New York, where he had not been forgiven for the aggressiveness of his graphics and his political commitment. After seeing the book, Fellini invited Klein to work with him, which allowed the American to get to know Rome very well, and to which he later dedicated a book. His photos stand out from those of other photographers for the use of weird locations, unexpected characters (such as dwarfs and wax statues), very ironic installations, and for the thin but evident understanding between the photographer and his model. In 1965 he gradually abandoned photography to devote himself to cinema, co-directing an important film (*Away From Vietnam*, 1965) with the directors Alain Resnais and Jean-Luc Godard, and documentaries on the Black Panthers (*Mister Freedom*, 1965), the boxer Cassius Clay-Mohammed Alì (*Cassius the Great*, 1974), fashion (*Fashion in France*, 1985), the famous French dancer Babilée (1985), and once more about fashion with *In & Out of Fashion* (1993). In 2002 he published a remasterized anthology of his best 20 films on DVD with the title *Messiah*. In 1978, he returned to photography. In 1980 the Museum of Modern Art in New York, and in 1983 the Centre Pompidou in Paris dedicated two broad retrospectives to his work. In 1994 he published the volume *Mode In and Out*. And in 2002 the volume *Paris + Klein* ideally concluded his work on cities that, since 1954, has touched on New York, Rome, Moscow, and Tokyo.

(*Roberto Mutti*)

Klein Anne (1921-1974). American designer. Born Hannah Golofski in New York, she was considered a pioneer and champion of women's sportswear. She began working on 7th Avenue selling her sketches while still in her teens, and in 1937 joined Varden Petites as designer of the children's line. In 1938 she married Ben Klein with whom she founded Junior Sophisticates. She founded Anne Klein & Co. in 1968, which was sold to the Japanese firm Takihyo in 1973. The brand quickly achieved a reputation in the 1970s for smart career clothes for the college-educated women then entering the job market in droves. At her death in 1974 the artistic direction of the label passed into the hands of Donna Karan and Louis Dell'Olio, who designed the line to great acclaim until Karan left to found her own company in 1985, and then by Dell'Olio on his own until 1993. Currently designed by Charles Nolan, Anne Klein remains a commercially powerful brand with a venerable history based on its founder's original belief that many women wanted a smartly tailored and well-made Collection of separates not modeled on a man's wardrobe, but as powerfully simple as one.

Klimt Gustav (1862-1918). Artist, among the founders of the Vienna Secession. Interested in industrial design, he created a practical, modern fashion, simplifying the lines of clothes, preferring straight cuts, and focusing on bag dresses softened by sophisticated details typical of the Secession's taste. The tailor's workshop of his friend Flöge manufactured his jackets and clothing for homewear, distribution of which was limited to his friends. In 1911, at the International Exposition in Rome, the Parisian designer Poiret was particularly struck by the artist's creations, and henceforth involved many artists in fabric design.

Klossowski Harumi (1975). Jewelry designer. She is the daughter of the painter Balthus and the Japanese painter Setsuko. Self-taught, she started mixing and assembling old Chinese buttons with semi-precious stones. She works with Galliano. In 1999 she exhibited her creations at Sotheby's.

Knapp Peter (1931). Swiss photographer and graphic artist. He attended the Kunstgewerbeschule in Zurich where he became interested in photography. He moved to Paris in 1951 to attend a painting course at the École des Beaux-Arts and at the Julian Academy. At the same time, he opened a photographic studio. In 1955 he was made art director of the magazine *Nouveau Fémina* and, in 1959, of *Elle*, for which he made his first photographs and where he remained until 1966. From 1968 he was art director at Rencontre and a photographer for *Vogue*, *Stern*, *Time*, *Elle*, the *Sunday Times* and the ateliers Courrèges and Ungaro. From 1974 to 1977 he worked for *Elle* as art director. During the 1980s he was responsible for the design and layout of a series of books published by the Centre Georges Pompidou. From 1986 to 1990 he worked for the publishers Hachette-Filipacchi as art director for *Decoration International* and *Femme*. He taught at the Ecole Supérieure des Arts Graphiques in Paris. (*Luca Selvi*)

Knee-high Stockings Nylon stockings that end at the knee in a wide elastic band, made to be worn with pants.

Knickerbockers Large pants tucked in below the knees. Their name derives from Dietrich Knickerbocker, a pseudonym with which the writer Washington Irving wrote his *History of New York* in 1889. The book was illustrated with drawings of Dutch immigrants wearing this type of pants. During the 18th century, they were taken up by women who practice sports. Yves Saint Laurent relaunched their use during the 1960s and 1970s.

Knight Nick (1958). English photographer. After his studies in England, he worked from 1986 to 1990 for Yamamoto, under the artistic direction of Marc Ascoli. Then on numerous magazines belonging to the Condé Nast group. Knight also contributes to the newspapers *Libération*, *The Independent*, and the *Sunday Times*. He photographed the girls for the Pirelli Calendar 2004.

Knitwear From the end of the nineteenth century up until the eve of World War II, knitwear consumption was monopolized, as the journalist and historian Elisa Massai wrote, by "British and Swiss supremacy in classic designs and French for boutique models." During the second half of the nineteenth century, particularly in Lombardy and Piedmont, dozens of hosiery and knitwear production companies were formed. But although the market for vests and socks was strong, there was little demand for outer knitwear, given that consumers in search of a high quality cardigan or sweater looked to Scottish designs. This Anglophile trend damaged the market, and not without reason, throughout the first half of the twentieth century. The only exception to this was the success of high quality local consumption during the two wars, represented by the Perugian designer Luisa Spagnoli, who produced angora knitwear for women, and the Milanese Avon Celli, who made designs for men, both of whom were also pioneers of the export trade. The small outer knitwear companies, based on a decentralized production where the work was done by hand

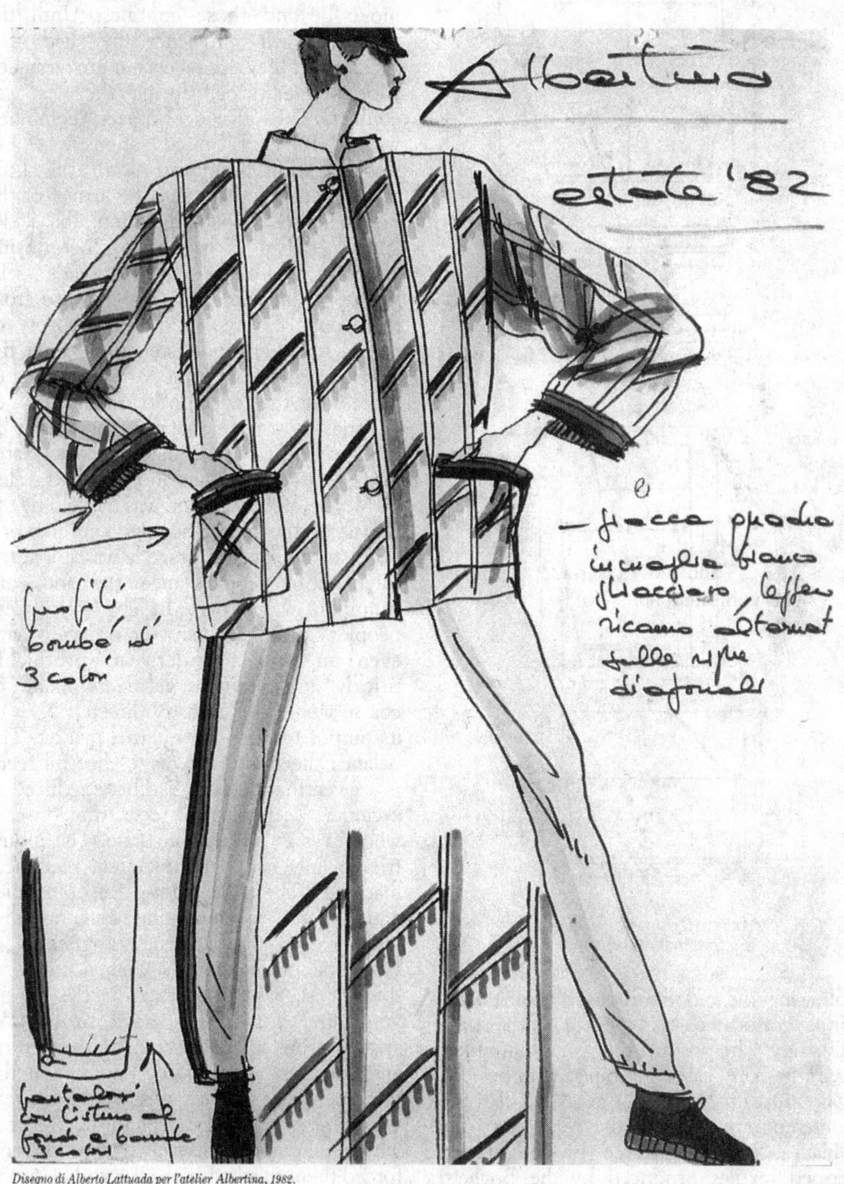

Disegno di Alberto Lattuada per l'atelier Albertina, 1982.

Knitted jacket designed by Alberto Lattuada for the Albertina Collection 1982.

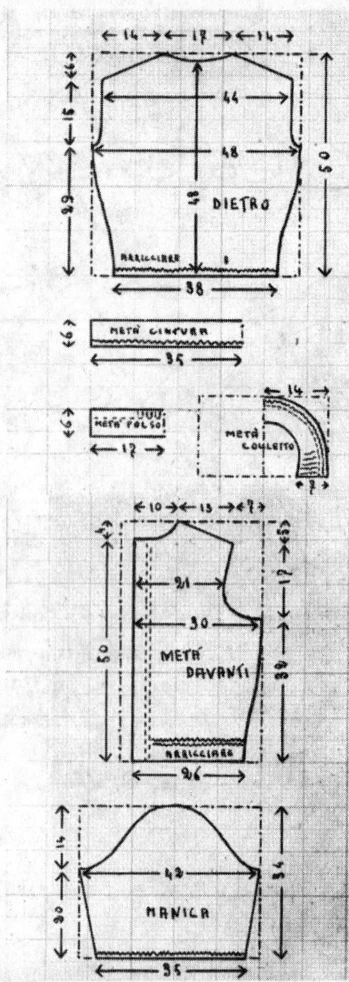

Knitting instructions for a small summer shirt (from *Fili Moda*, Summer 1941).

following the old traditions of home knitting, continued to operate with some difficulty. The production of knitted underwear, in many cases combined with hosiery, was more fortunate. According to the contemporary press, at the 1881 Expo the Milanese were captivated by the knitted striped textiles produced by the Boglietti Guglielminotti firm from Biella, by Volpato's long-sleeved vests, by undervests, corsetry, woollen underpants, tights, and scarves. Although local products made little impression on the wardrobes of Italians, who preferred foreign pullovers, round-necked sweaters, cashmere and lambswool, at least they were more widely diffused in the underwear sector, without managing to move beyond those confines. Until the period of self sufficiency they had little success and life became even more wretched shortly afterwards, during the years of conflict. The advent of peace, combined with UNRRA aid (United Nations Relief and Rehabilitation Administration), the European Recovery Plan and the arrival of the first bales of wool and cotton, the widespread arrival of synthetic fibers using viscose, acetate and nylon threads (self-sufficiency at least served a purpose from this point of view), and the discovery of acrylic fibers and polyester: these were the developments that marked the beginning of success for the Italian knitwear industry, of victories in a sector that was considered by other countries to be mature, if not saturated. Italy was in ruins and people traveled by bicycle, but the period was marked by the arrival of the motor scooter and the first domestic appliances. Tragedy was still at the forefront of people's memories and consumption was down. In an Italy where people knitted at home in order to save even on woolen underwear (producing prickly and scratchy garments made of coarse wool), the industry directed 97% of its output towards the internal market. The balance sheets did not make cheerful reading, given that demand had been reduced to a cinder. Technological reconstruction as a whole was in a desperate state. The industries mainly had hand-operated, rectilinear machines. The most avant-garde companies added motors to hand looms, a solution that did not even approach the automatic type. Domestic production by women still predominated, while "knitting circles" were very rare, with a dispersed production system using women based in the central and southern areas of the country on the increase. Some of the most active knitters were the women of Carpi, near Modena, where the crisis of the straw hat production forced them to take up needles and learn the craft of knitting pullovers. And so the Carpi phenomenon was born, then spreading across Emilia, Tuscany, Umbria, the Veneto, Piedmont, Lombardy and to the south, along the Adriatic coast, down to Bari,

Putignano, and Barletta. It was the phenomenon of decentralised production that moved from knitting needles to cotton looms, to "knitting circles," to Variantex and transformed country houses, utility rooms in apartments, barns, cupboards under stairs, stables, and into workshops. The vertical business model was abandoned, forming a geography of production that Elisa Massai and Paolo Lombardi described in their historical overview of the sector ("L'industria della maglieria nell'alta moda e nella moda pronta dal 1950 al 1980," in *La moda Italiana*, Electa, 1987). They relate how "the vertical company was substituted by the combined presence, within a short distance, of all the production processes: spinning, dyeing, knitting, sewing up, pressing, machinery factories, maintenance workshops." It was the beginning of the 1950s. Italian prosperity had yet to arrive, and with it the desire for a more relaxed wardrobe, suitable for leisure time. The success of Italian knitwear could only be achieved by increasing the export market. The first signs of this came in 1951: 1,341 tons of goods sold abroad (in order of quantity: socks, outer knitwear, knitted gloves, knitted underwear), in England, Germany, France, and the United States, for a value of 5 billion lire, equal to 31 million dollars. Most of the exports were fashion products, by Laura Aponte and Marisa Arditi from Rome, by Lea Galleani from Milan, by the knitwear factory Mariangelo, by Mirsa and Luisa di Gresy. The clients were Dorville House in London and the Magnin stores in San Francisco and Los Angeles. It was a luxury export, the type that would make the Avagolf label famous a few years later. A very elitist outlet, which was expanded by companies in Carpi, which offered the rest of Europe sweaters, pullovers, and large jumpers with creative designs, the opposite of a standardized production, perhaps lacking a high level of finishing and technical aspects but unbeatable in terms of price and fashionable content. It was no coincidence that the Made in Italy project of Giovanni Battista Giorgini's Florentine fashion house was launched in 1951: a show of Italian fashions in front of a small group of American buyers. For the first time, Italian designers realized their own potential and presented themselves to the rest of the world. Success was immediate and, on the American markets, it also acted as a showcase and a propeller for unsigned Italian products. This success reverberated across all the phases of knitwear production and throughout the entire sector, which began, suitcase in hand, to follow the export road far and wide. That first leap of 1951, was followed by an immediate hike. It initiated a growth at accelerated rhythms, which only began to slow twenty years later, in 1972. Two decades of constant growth and, at the end of it, the figures testify to a 60% increase in exports compared with the start of the period. However, not everything during that time was rosy, or easily achieved. Increases in production costs created problems, as did competition with countries from the developing world. But the flexibility of the structure, elasticity of management, entrepreneurial intelligence, and market intuition overcame these difficulties. In the mid 1960s, Asian competition crossed the path of Italian knitwear on the American

Knitted skiing outfit designed by Alberto Lattuada for Albertina, 1973.

market, which alone absorbed 28% of the country's exports. It was an enormous conquest, but the loss of competitiveness forced Italy to retreat noticeably. In 1971, the US quota of global exports had dropped to 6% and was made up almost entirely of high quality products, because Tawain, Korea, and Hong Kong were by then unbeatable at producing low-cost goods. More than a retreat, it was almost a total failure, but softened by a parallel increase in European sales. After taking a beating across the ocean, the Italian industry launched a counter-attack in the countries of the Common Market, increasing the fashion content of the products and, in order to bring down costs, speeding up decentralization, even extending to zones that were "still characterized by the availability of unemployed labor." It was no coincidence that an industrial census of 1971 revealed that unemployment at national level had doubled over the previous ten years, and that the geography of knitwear production had significantly changed, with a drop in Piedmont and Lombardy, contrasted by increases in Emilia-Romagna (18% of the national workforce), the Veneto (15%), Tuscany (8%), and Apulia (4.6%). Despite the American crisis, the export market grew 260% between 1966 and 1972, with peaks of 14% in Germany and 5% in France and Benelux. The "miracle" continued, helped by the increasing fashion for casual, informal wear, encouraged by the political events of 1968, and the growing importance of leisure time. However, success began to fade. Asian products began to swamp the European markets as well. The petrol crisis and the subsequent wave of inflation suffocated consumption. A tough period followed but fortunately it did not last too long. The two years 1973-74 registered a significant drop. In Europe people began to speak of a saturated sector that needed to be broken up. The European Community was to put embargoes on imports from low-cost countries. But it was neither luck nor these embargoes that the entire clothing and textile sector needed to move onwards. The very Italian weapon of decentralization provided the key to maintain and relaunch the country's presence in the field. Unlike other countries, which were hindered by slow, more elephantine entrepreneurial structures, Italy was able to resurrect its knitwear industry precisely because its production was decentralized and its organization was pliable enough to permit a counter-attack. It could defend itself, study its opponents, size up the field and embark on a come-back in a short period as soon as opportunities presented themselves. The adversary was competition in the medium-low and low cost sectors. Knitwear was an instinctive market, made up of quick changes, that little by little was being reduced by dominance of designers who anticipated new tendencies and dictated broad styles of dress. In order to escape the crisis, knitwear raised its aim and increased its fashion content (Missoni, Krizia, Valentino, Albertina, Avagolf, Noni Sport, Alma, Milena Mosele, Naka, Pier Luigi Tricò and, shortly afterwards, Armani, Antonella Tricot, Biagiotti, Malo Tricò, Blumarine, Napoleone Erba, Tricò Cinque), personalizing the product with a strong image and brand politics and refining the "counter-attack" strategy. The companies' structures were closely positioned to the point of consumption. Benetton is the exemplary case: it changed its commercial relationship with its own sales network, moving directly to retail, and installed tills with computers, so that details of sales and changes in demand could be transferred directly to the company. Thus it was possible to calibrate quantities and assortments of new stock rapidly and also, given the link between management and production lines, to intervene in mid-season to alter the color palette according to information arriving from the sales points. The "counter-attack" was successful. From 1974 to 1984, knitwear experienced growth comparable to that in the 1960s, despite the less favorable economic world climate: production increased by 32%; exports by 66%; employment (roughly 153,000 employees) did not suffer significant cutbacks even in the face of increasingly sophisticated technology. During the same period and in the same sector in other European countries, production and employment dropped by 18% and 24% respectively. This positive trend continued in 1985-86. In the first of those years production volumes increased by 7.3% and exports by 14%. In 1986, production increased by 14.6% and exports by 17.2% but – a danger signal – imports increased significantly (25.9%), a phenomenon that grew over the next few years. In the following decade, with the exception of 1992, the trend was negative: 1998 closed with a drop in production and exports of approximately 15% compared with 1986, the final year of growth. In contrast, knitwear imports went through the roof: roughly 1000% more compared with 1986. Despite this, at the end of the twentieth century, the commercial balance of the Italian knitwear sector (2.7 billion dollars) remained positive.

(*Guido Vergani*)

Knots Sportwears Company of casualwear and sportswear founded in 1991. It designs and produces clothing and accessories for sailing, sports, and leisure time. In 1992 it clothed the judges of the Kenwood Cup, and in following years was the technical sponsor of Trieste Generali, the winning boat in the Sailing Tour of Italy. It provided the equipment to the judges at the Admiral's Cup.

Knott Jean-Paul (1966). Belgian designer. He studied fashion at FIT (Fashion Institute of Technology) in New York. From 1988 to 1999 he worked for Yves Saint Laurent in Paris, collaborating with the couturier himself. In Brussels in 1999, he set up the Jean-Paul Knott brand and the following year created his first Collection. After a short period with Krizia, he settled in Paris and in 2002 designed the *prêt-à-porter* for the brand Louis Feraud. He continues to present his own Collection. (*Maddalena Fossati*)

Kobe Fashion Museum This is the first Japanese museum entirely dedicated to fashion. The Western clothing industry came into being with the arrival of the first foreign ships when Kobe's harbor was opened in 1868. This met with the demands of European and American traders, but also with the Japanese themselves, who were looking towards modernity. In constant growth during the twentieth century, Kobe was nominated the Japanese Fashion City in 1973. The purpose of the museum is to record the development of this local industry. The museum's Research Center offers help to designers and operators through courses, access to sophisticated computers, and a library. The center systematically collects examples of the local textile production. The museum's main Collections include European clothes and accessories from the 18th century to the present day, ceremonial costumes made using traditional manufacturing techniques, sailing clothes, jacquard and fabrics, and American and European prints. There's a large audiovisual department and a Collection of original fashion photos. Officially opened in 1997, this very modern museum hosts permanent and temporary exhibitions.

(*Virginia Hill*)

Koefia Academy Founded in Rome in 1951, the International Academy of High Fashion and the Art of Costume Design had its first premises in Piazza Cavour, then moved to Via Cola di Rienzo. Fashion, costume, graphic design, and modeling courses are held there. Students can enrol after an admission test; fashion design is a three-year course.

❑ 2001. Fifteen former students presented their luxury *prêt-à-porter* Collections manufactured using a combination of silk, plastic, metals, and knitwear.

❑ AltaRomaAltaModa 2002 opened with a two-day event entirely dedicated to fashion schools. Koefia presented the Empire-style clothes already seen during the Academy's show that concluded the school year.

❑ 2002, September. Nadja Juri, a young designer at the Koefia Academy, was among the five finalists in the second Moët & Chandon Young Fashion Award.

Kogan Serge (1910). French tailor. After an apprenticeship in his father's tailoring workshop, and a short period as a designer and model maker with Robert Piguet, he was hired by Jacques Heim where he stayed until 1945. He worked for three years with Dior and Balmain, then with Lucien Lelong and Heim, before leaving in 1948 to go to the United States. After returning to Paris, he opened his tailor's workshop in 1951. His own business lasted until 1953.

Kohler Delphine. French designer and stylist

for the shoe brand Facteur Céleste. Her passion for "*zoris*," – Japanese thong sandals, which in Céleste's Collections are available in hundreds of versions, fabrics and models – originates from a visit to the Shoe Museum in Hiroshima, Japan, in 1994. Tetsuo Ushioda, the museum's curator, told her the history of these traditional shoes and Delphine returned to France with *zoris* on her feet (she wears them all year round) with the idea of developing a Collection starting from a single type of slipper. Every Facteur Céleste thong sandal represents the safeguarding of now disappearing craftsmen's traditions, as is the case for the manufacturer of *espadrilla* soles, and damask fabric dyers. In China she has set up a factory to produce special socks to wear with the slippers.

(*Mariacristina Righi*)

Koike Kazuko. Fashion expert and Japanese writer. Her training started in Paris, where she studied at the École de la Chambre Syndicale de Couture. Once back in Japan, she soon became an eminent authority on the history of fashion and costume, with several publications in this field. She teaches at the famous Bunka Fukuso Gakue school, where her courses are always packed, and it is considered an honor to be one of her students. She has created a fashion museum of her own, of which she is the curator. A consultant to the department stores Seibu, she has collaborated with Issey Miyake and Rei Kawakubo.

Kokosalaki Sophia (1972). Greek designer. Born in Athens, she received a Masters in the Art of Fashion at Central Saint Martin's College in London and immediately after made her début with her women's Collection, in which excesses as well as banality were equally banned. Later she designed a Collection for Joseph. Mandarina Duck sponsored her second show.

❑ 2001. She was entrusted with the artistic direction of the Ruffo project for two seasons, Spring-Summer 2001 and Fall-Winter 2002-2003.
❑ 2004, July. She designed the uniforms that the athletes were to wear during the opening and closing ceremonies at the Olympic Games in Athens 2004.

Kollar François (1904-1979). Hungarian photographer naturalized French. In exile in Paris in 1924, during the Horthy regime he first worked as a worker at Renault, then as a photographer for several agencies, eventually getting published in *L'Illustration*. He mixed reportages (including a famous one commissioned to him by *Horizons de France* on the world of labor) with advertising photography (Dunhill), portrait photography (Coco Chanel, Edith Piaf), and fashion photography, for which he used the avant-garde techniques of that time: solarization, exaggerated perspectives, and overexposure. During the 1930s, he photographed the great Collections by Fath, Balenciaga, Lanvin, and Balmain for *Harper's Bazaar*, *Le Figaro illustré*, *Les Modes*, *L'officiel de la Couture*, *L'Art et La Mode*, and *Die Dame*. In 1934 he published the book *25 Photos de Kollar*. The 1989 retrospective at the Palais de Tokyo in Paris allowed the public at large to rediscover his art. In 1987 his archives were donated to the French State.

Kolodrovat Lidija (1962). Bosnian designer. She first studied cinema, then at the Superior School of Textile Design and Fashion in Zagreb. She moved to Portugal in 1990. She alternates fashion with costume design for the theater. She opened the space Pedro y el lobo in Lisbon.

König René. German sociologist. He teaches at the University of Cologne. In his essay *Sociology of Fashion* (1967) he claims that fashion is among the engines of social dynamics and a foundation of modern mass society.

Konishi Yoshiyuki. Japanese designer, known for the originality of his color-rich sweaters, often inspired by kilim rugs.

Kookaï French brand of *prêt-à-porter*, created in 1983 by Philippe de Hesdin, Jean-Louis Tepper and Jacques Nataf, three Parisian packaging dealers. The idea was to offer girls an economic and sexy line of ready-to-wear clothes: two basic seasonal Collections, updated each month with spur-of-the-moment new creations. It proved successful: there are now 400 Kookaï stores in Europe.

Korda Alberto (1928-2001). Cuban photographer whose real name was Diaz Gutièrrez. Very famous for being the official photographer of Fidel Castro since 1959, as well as for taking the most celebrated picture of Che Guevara and being the main correspondent of the newspaper *Revolucion*. Korda started his career in 1956 opening a studio of commercial, fashion and advertising photography in Havana, in which his work was dominated by the American style. His activity as a photographic reporter was always accompanied by commercial works for Cuba Export, Contex, and Cuba Moda.

Kors Michael (1961). American designer. Born and raised on Long Island, near New York City, he attended the Fashion Institute of Technology. His mother was a model. He started his professional career at the age of 19, designing a Collection for the Lothar boutique in New York, for which he started to work as sales assistant. His success with the industry was such that he was urged to start his own business. In 1981 the Michael Kors label made its début and the first Collection, based on perfectly structured luxury sportswear, was presented. It was distributed, among the others, by Bergdorf Goodman, and Saks Fifth Avenue. In 1995 he launched the line Kors Michael Kors manufactured by Onward Kashiyama USA, the brand factory of Onward Kashiyama Japan. In November 1997 he presented his first line of men's *prêt-à-porter* and, at the same time, was appointed the designer for Céline, of which he was made artistic director in 1999. He is considered a pioneer of the minimalist style. He lives in Paris and New York.

❑ 1999. Kors sold his share of his company to LVMH, also the owner of Céline.
❑ 2000. Launch of the first perfume produced and distributed by Parfums Givenchy. He opened two sales points in Madison Avenue, New York. For the Spring-Summer 2001, he brought the "pilot woman" by Céline onto the catwalk; they wore camouflage sweaters and bomber jackets.
❑ 2002. Opening of the boutique in Soho and the flagship store in Tokyo.
❑ 2003, March. The designer announced that when his contract with Céline ended, he would leave the maison. The Fall-Winter Collection 2003-2004 was the last he designed for them. The announcement came like lightning in a clear sky: only a few weeks before, at the renewal of his annual contract with LVMH, Kors had let understand that his collaboration with the group was to continue for a long time.

Korvin Kathy, Fashion designer. In 1997 Cacharel commissioned her to create a line of jewelry. After this and other experiences in the field of bijoux, she launched her own clothing *griffe*.

Koshino Hiroko (1938). Japanese designer. Sister of Junko and Michiko, also designers, all of whom are daughters of a dressmaker from Osaka. Koshino has a thriving and diversified business operating primarily in Japan. Many of her most striking women's designs innovatively interpret traditional Japanese kimonos, playing on both scale and pattern. One of many Japanese designers to first attract international attention by showing in Paris in the 1980s.

Koshino Junko (1941). Japanese designer. The second of the Koshino sisters, she attended the famous Bunka Fakuso Gakuen school and won the So-En prize for the most promising designer on the course. In 1965 she opened an *haute couture* atelier in Tokyo and in 1977 she presented her creations in Paris, where she moved in 1989.

Koshino Michiko (1950). Japanese designer. The youngest of the Koshino sisters, after a period of apprenticeship in her mother's store, she opened a shop in London in 1973. She was the first to use neoprene and to get inspiration from the dawning New Age. She is also the only designer to have allowed her brandname to be used to sponsor a line of condoms.

Kostümforschungsinstitut von Parish German research institute on fashion. Its headquarters are in Munich and it has been open to the public since 1970. It takes its origin from the Collection of Hermine von Parish and includes monographs, periodicals, books, and documents which describe fashion from the beginning of the 1900s to the present day.

Kostumhaus Maison of ready-to-wear fashion established in Berlin in 1990 by Jane Garber in partnership with other young designers who, later, were to abandon the venture. Before German reunification, Jane worked in East Germany designing costumes for the theater and some music bands. In 1995 she presented the first Kostumhaus Collection in Paris and Düsseldorf, a brand that in 1999 became fully hers. Her training as a textile designer induced her to give great importance to fabrics during the design process. She often combines traditional and high-tech materials. Her palette is based on very few colors.

Krahn Julia (1978). German photographer. After attending a school of graphics and photography in Freiburg, she started studying medicine, but interrupted this to devote herself to photography. In 2001 she moved to Milan to work for magazines such as *Mood*, *Arts*, *Vintage*, and *Glamour* and working, through the agency Griangraf, for advertising campaigns.

Krejberg Roy (1961). Danish designer. He graduated from the DKTS (Denmark Academy of Fashion and Design) in 1981. In 1995 he started working with Kenzo, became his dauphin and from January 2000, after taking up the *sukado* (baton) he has been Kenzo's official successor for the men's line. His belief: "Adjusting and adding, evolving without looking for a useless perfection, which is a sort of de-personalization and no longer suitable to the times." Ethnic elements, a mix of styles and materials, oriental precision, a natural attitude and a love for colors are his kingdom. He has always distinguished himself for his rigorous but also fanciful and elegant Collections.

Krieger Bob (1936). Italian photographer. Born in Alexandria in Egypt. His mother is of Sicilian origin, his father is Prussian. From a very young age he was fascinated by the world of art, in which he became interested thanks to his great-grandfather, Giuseppe Cammarano, painter of the Neoclassical pictures in the royal palace at Caserta, Italy. Although he started photographing at the age of 11 (he can still remember the first shot he took, a portrait of his mother), it was only in 1962 that he entered a studio as assistant "because I was broke." After moving to Milan in 1967, where he still lives and works, he started his own business immediately publishing in *Harper's Bazaar* and *Vogue* and documenting the birth of the Italian *prêt-à-porter*. From 1970 to 1975 he was art director of *Bazaar Italy*, then he returned to his camera working for the most famous designers (Krizia, Versace, Valentino, Biki, Romeo Gigli, Bulgari) and publishing in magazines such as *N.Y. Times Magazine*, *Vogue*, *Esquire*, and *Harper's Bazaar*, but also making his name in the advertising field and getting three covers for *Time*, among which, in 1982, the one dedicated to Giorgio Armani. Though linked to fashion, he puts some distance between himself and this sector in his personal artistic research on nudes – he published two very beautiful books, *Metamorfosi*, in black and white, in 1990, and *Anima nuda* in color, in 1998 – and on portrait photography. In the last years, La Versiliana in Pietrasanta and Spazio Krizia in Milan have given two exhibitions of his work. *(Roberto Mutti)*

❑ 2002. An exhibition of his portraits was organized in non-traditional spaces such as the International Airport of Malpensa.

Kristina Ti Italian brand of *prêt-à-porter*. Created in 1987 thanks to the common passion for fashion by the Turin siblings Cristina (1966) and Marco (1964) Tardito. Their launch platform was the family business, Tamigi Spa, a company manufacturing swimming costumes. This was to achieve their present style: beachwear based on sophisticated materials, first, and a revolutionary style in clothing which opened the doors to them of Contemporary in Milan, Le Group in Paris, and Première Collection in New York. Their first own-brand boutique was opened in 1987 in Porto Cervo. The brand, to which a line for little girls from 4 to 12 has recently been added, is on sale in 300 shops around the world. The Collection has been presented at Milano Collezioni since the Spring 2000. *(Laura Salza)*

Krizia Brand and artistic name of Mariuccia Mandelli. Italian designer. In Spring 1999, New York University opened the doors of its Gray Art Gallery for the first time to a fashion designer, hosting the exhibition that celebrated 40 years of Krizia's work – the exhibition that had been mounted at the Triennale in Milan in 1995. The exhibition was a cross-section of Krizia's most representative clothes, which were hung on headless dummies-sculptures invented by the costume designer Gabriella Pescucci. Also included were the animals-symbols that have always characterized Mariuccia Mandelli's Collections and the special effects and lights and mirrors designed by set designer Dante Ferretti. Born in the city of Bergamo Alta, she decided as a young girl to launch herself into the world of fashion with a friend, Flora Dolci. A table and a sewing machine, a première and 5-6 workers in a Milan apartment offered by the musician Lelio Luttazzi were the background to her first creations. These were simple articles, characterized by a rigorous linearity when compared to the elaborate clothes of that time: dresses, skirts, and blouses that the young and strong-willed Mariuccia, shy but determined, crammed into her cases to start a pilgrimage through the boutiques of half Italy. She was even taken for a detergent seller. She sold her first skirt (she still remembers this) to a store in Corso Vercelli in Milan. She also managed to sell the first tailleurs bearing the label K, nowadays worn by millions of women, men, and children all over the world, that generated a turnover in 1998 of 500 million dollars. Krizia's official début occurred in 1957 at the Samia in Turin, where her malleable style met with the favor of the buyers. At the same time Elsa Haerter, of the magazine *Grazia*, and Henri Bendel, of the small but prestigious department store in New York, discovered her talent. The first photographs in the newspapers propelled her on the path to fame and fortune. As her collaborators she wanted two Italian designers who were later to become famous: first, Walter Albini, and second, Karl Lagerfeld. But she was always the one who supervised and made the designs, using the same technique of squared figures which then were turned into clothes. Krizia was the first to change the look of traditional fashion. During the 1960s, when

Krizia: Fall-Winter 1981 Collection.

twin-sets were trendy, she invented knitted pullovers and, with a mix of yarns, sweaters with which she immediately changed the traditional schemes of dressing. At Palazzo Pitti, cradle of the Italian *prêt-à-porter* in the mythical White Room, she made her début in 1964 with a black and white Collection of plissé dresses (one of her recurrent themes) to be worn with mini cardigans. This Collection allowed her to win the "Critica della moda" award, attributed before only to Emilio Pucci. Her passion for knitwear urged her to start the label Krizia Maglia in 1967. This was the year she met Aldo Pinto, who became her husband and working partner. New, ironic lucky charm animals were created, to form an extraordinary and propitiatory menagerie. The first was a jacquard sheep in 1968, followed by a cat, bear, and fox, then a series of more dangerous animals, such as a leopard, tiger, and a panther (her symbol) stylized in 1920s fashion.

However, handcrafting her clothes was too limiting and her company soon became industrial, with a factory on the outskirts of Milan. Here she could study and elaborate her inventions, with the machinery ready at hand to make the first sample. She tested innovative and technological materials,such as anaconda skin, and metallized silver, bronze,and gold. She used high-quality materials for sporting clothes, for which in America she was called Crazy Krizia. And she continued her stylistic path always with the aim of dressing a truly, feminine woman with an uninhibited spirit. She paid close attention to modern and contemporary art, with some of her clothes being inspired by Kandinsky, pop art, Klimt, Burri, and Calder. There were also historical references, for example, to Gengis Khan and the warriors of Xian. But above any creation, it is her neat and precise touch that stands out: it is extolled in coats and jackets, each one different from the other, some shoulders rounded, some pointed. Brave, enthusiastic and capable of strategic intuitions, she was, with Albini and Missoni, among the first designers to leave Florence for Milan, where she had been presenting her models since the early 1970s. It was the move that began the fashion miracle in Milan. In 1984 she opened her business headquarters in the historical Palazzo Melzi d'Eril in Via Manin

Krizia: Fall-Winter 1999-2000 Collection.

and dedicated a particular space as the meeting point for cultural activities, whether exhibitions, concerts, debates, or visits from writers from all over the world. In 1985 she became an associate of the publishing company La Tartaruga. After more than 40 years of success, Mariuccia is still faithful to her beliefs and doing the job that she loves as much as she did on the first day. She is demanding and strict, above all with herself: meticulous, precise, a perfectionist, but also attracted by breaking the rules. On the eve of 2000 she designed 32 annual clothing Collections, included those produced in America, Japan, and China. She has several licenses, from perfumes to bags, glasses, ties, watches, and even sparkling wine. She counts 53 own-brand boutiques around the world, 202 in Japan and more than 600 sales points. She has even designed an exclusive, refined hotel, the K Club, on the island of Barbuda in the Antilles.

(*Laura Dubini*)

❑ Faithful to her belief, Krizia continues to make fashion for a woman free from prejudice. Her designs are an anthem to contradictions, for instance, her fabrics match cashmere and leather, leather and chiffon, chiffon and knitwear: a continuous assemblage of different characteristics which the eclectic designer translates into clothes and accessories. They often have touches of softness for garments that sway around the body: in short, an easy way to dress, with irony, like the giant *pied-de-poule* for her incredible, seamless handkerchief skirts, and an unerasable imprint on bags that were all the rage in the 2001-2002 season. Krizia and the game of opposites, which continued the following winter: this time the game was played on volumes, now big, now tiny, while in 2003-2004 her woman was a sort of angel-demon. Chaste and scandalous: contrasts in perfect balance. Her shows are always characterized by her fetish animals, especially her beloved printed panther. And her men's Collection follows this relaxed philosophy: her men are both tender and strong, whimsical in a formal suit with a flowered lining.

(*Lucia Mari*)

❑ 2001. The Museum of Contemporary Art of Tokyo displayed Krizia's work in an exhibition entitled *Krizia Moving Shapes*. She was the first foreign designer to receive such an honor from the museum.

❑ 2002. A separation took place at the beginning of the year between her and the Belgian designer Jean-Paul Knott. The Fall 2003 Collection marked the début of Krizia's new creative talent, the 34 year old Harrish Marrow, owner of one of the most important London brands.

❑ A special Collection was prepared for oversize women, with a joint venture between Krizia and the group Miroglio. The *Per Te Aktive, by Krizia* line is the natural evolution of *Per Te, by Krizia*, which Vestebene-Miroglio has been producing and distributing for many years now. These are young-looking jeans and other garments dedicated to more curvaceous girls.

❑ The year 2002 closed with a decrease of 2%, on a total turnover of €220 million. The result was accepted positively by the company's top management, considering the state of the world's economy.

❑ 2003, February. Krizia was among the guests of honor at the Fashion Institute of Technology in New York. The occasion was the event "Fashion, Italian Style", dedicated to the output of the greatest Italian designers. The Milan boutique in Via della Spiga was reopened, having been restyled by the architect Piero Pinto.

Kroeker Alfred Louis (1876-1960). American anthropologist. He tried to find cycles in the trends and variations in women's fashions. To do that he examined prints, drawings and photographs of evening models from 1787 to 1936. His thesis was that changes are never dictated by economic reasons, but by the wish for change, and that these changes undergo fluxes and repetitions following a certain pattern.

Kroeker Mark (1969). American designer. Born in Peura, Illinois. He studied at the Parson's School of Art in New York. Before launching his women's Collection for

Spring-Summer 2000, he worked as an interior decorator. The keyword in all his creations is instinct, while interest in alternative materials is a constant theme.

Kroner Rob (1943). Dutch designer. He created an exclusive line of *prêt-à-porter* for the Liberty department store in London. After an apprenticeship of 13 years, during which he worked for Dick Holthaus, Frans Molenaar and Frank Govers, he created a *griffe* of his own of practical and comfortable clothes in knitwear and leather, easy to wear and not expensive.

Krüger Serge (1942). French designer, former photographer and founder of the photographic agency Photoka. He made his début in 1976 with Triple Force, a type of cloth pants. Similar to jeans, but with a chic look, he presented them at the Parisian men's fashion event *Sehm*, where they won resounding success. The following year he launched *Slooghy*, also a model of men's pants, which were produced in a single size and with a single seam on the inside leg. They were made from polyurethane and polyamide to imitate human skin. In 1979 he opened a boutique at Les Halles and launched *Charnel*, a clothing line for men and women in cloth, skai, and flannel. He broke off his career in fashion to work as an entertainment organizer in his night clubs, Le Tango and Le Moloko in Paris.

(*Michele Ciavarella*)

K-Swiss Line of shoes and sportswear created in 1966 thanks to an idea by the brothers Art and Ernest Brunner, Swiss Olympic skiers who moved to California and became tennis players. The first product (later reproposed, was the Classic, the company's best-selling article) was a tennis shoe made entirely in leather, originally in white. It had an external rubber sole, a strengthened toe and five leather straps on the sides. In 1999 the brothers set up a clothing line. K-Swiss also produces two other shoe lines: laceless Royal Elastics, and National Geographic, under license from the National Geographic Society.

Kult Italian monthly about fashion, art and design or "creative avant-gardes" as the line under the title says. Established in Milan in 1998, it is published by Pem. Its articles treat several themes, stressing the new trends in cinema, theater, and visual arts, with particular attention to the influences between the different art forms. The emphasis is on fashion, with beautiful pictures by innovative and often young photographers. They layout is very captivating and strong, but it is not superficial and never redundant.

Kumagai Tokio (1947-1990). Shoe designer. In 1970 he graduated from the Bunka Fakuso Gakuen and moved to France, where he worked for Castelbajac. He also worked for Fiorucci in Italy, before opening his own boutique in Paris, where he sold his own hand-painted shoes, inspired by surrealism, Kandinsky and Pollock. He died young.

Kunert German hosiery company, the European market leader. It produces the brands Hudson, Kunert, and Silkona. In 1990 it started an acquisition strategy, beginning with Burlington. The group also owns a jeans line. It employs 4,000 people.

Kutoglu Atil (1968). Turkish designer. After completing high school in Istanbul where he was born, he moved to Vienna to specialize in business and administration. While still a student, he collaborated with Vakko and Beymen, which are Turkish companies in the fashion field. In 1991 he presented his first Collection thanks to the sponsorship of the mayor of Vienna, Helmut Zilk. In 1994 he won the Diva-Woolmark award as the best Austrian designer. Later he met with success in Milan, Paris, and New York. In 1997 he was awarded the Salzburg Prize. In 2000 his clothes were shown at the exhibition "Klimt und die Frauen" at the Belvedere Palace in Vienna. His international dealings have not prevented Kutoglu from remaining linked to his Turkish roots, and the influence of the East is present in all his Collections. His favorite materials are leather, organza, and velvet. His most important clients are members of the European aristocracy, such as Francesca von Habsburg and Pilar Goess. He conquered the American market through the help of a compatriot, Ahmet Ertegun, founder of the music label Atlantic Records.

(*Francesca Gentile*)

K-Way Short raincoat in nylon invented in 1961 in Pas-de-Calais, France. Though a registered name, today the name K-Way is used to identify all those small hooded raincoats based on the original model. During the 1980s, all youngsters had a K-Way. Small in size, it is slipped on over the head. It can be folded into a sort of pocket and fastened around the waist with an elastic strap. For the K-Way company, the designer Philippe Starck has recently designed a rainproof jacket with peculiar zip fastenings in plain but changing colors that "respect the urban landscape."

Kyoto Costume Institute Japanese museum dedicated to Western women's fashions in clothes, accessories, and underwear from the 17th-20th centuries. Founded in 1978, it is an open window on the metamorphosis that has taken place in the Japanese wardrobe, which has passed from very rooted local traditions to Western styles. The promoter and curator of the Kyoto Costume Institute is Akiko Fukai, a journalist, writer and promoter of exhibitions on the history of Western fashions. An important exhibition was "Revolution in Fashion 1715-1815", presented in Kyoto in 1989, and a year later at the Fashion Institute of Technology in New York, and the Musée des Arts de la Mode in Paris. (*Anna Santini*)

Kyuso Brand created by two Belgian designers. When Egidio Fauzia, the son of an Italian miner, married Joke, his Belgian wife, they opened a store of eccentric clothes in Maasmechelen in Belgium. They soon started to put together a *prêt-à-porter* line that takes its name from a sign they saw in a shop-window in Sicily. They present their *haute couture* Collection in Paris.

L

La Bagagerie French brand of bags. When Jean Marlaix opened his first tiny sales point on the Champs-Elysées in Paris in 1954, the bags on the market were all stiff and had a short handle. His models immediately broke with the past and offered a younger-looking, colored accessory with a sporty cut, in tune with the trends of the *prêt-à-porter*. Nowadays, every six months the heir Frederic Marlaix renews the same irreverent spirit with fashion. The company's success has gone beyond the French borders as La Bagagerie has two shops in New York (on Madison Avenue and West Broadway), a corner in the Galeries Lafayette in the Trump Tower (also in New York), and distribution in Japan since 1974, through the Shiseido group. Other outlets have been opened in Asia and Australia.

(*Giuliana Parabiago*)

La Belle Jardinière A department store in Paris, opened in 1824 by Pierre Parissot on the Quai aux Fleurs. Thirty years later it occupied 25 buildings in the Ile de la Cité. In 1864 the municipality of Paris decided to appropriate the site to build the hospital Hotel-de-Dieu. In 1866, La B.J. reopened on the other side of the Seine, in Rue du Pont Neuf, where it closed down 104 years later.

La Bottega di Brunella Italian brand of clothing. Established in 1965 in Positano by Vito (designer) and his wife Brunella (dressmaker). They started out with careful research into fabrics which they created on special Neapolitan looms, and used to manufacture the first garments. Almost 40 years later, the company has maintained its craftmen's charm and family management, which now includes the three children: Cristina is in the general manager, Annamaria is in administration, and Antonio follows production. The womenswear is now accompanied by a men's and a children's line. The tailoring style is based on continual research into materials and fabrics: from the cotton gauze for light Summer and neo-romantic dresses to the hand-embroidered delavé jeans, from bemberg for a little retro Thirties-style pieces to the black-and-white optical number, to the stretch jersey and bi-elastic Lycra. And, above all, linen, matched with chenille or wool, also used in ethnic-style accessories (bags, shoes, belts, and scarves), combined with leather and cork, straw or wood. The Spring-Summer 2003 collection follows the rules of the season, interpreting them with extreme originality. Ethnic models inspired by the magic of the Orient and Indian atmospheres, long dresses-cum-caftans made from cuprum and silk, light baggy pants, and soft swaying chiffon garments in warm, sunny colors, from orange to bright yellow to tobacco brown. (*Gabriella Gregorietti*)

Lace From a technical point of view there are two types of lace: the kind made using a needle (a development of embroidery) and pillow lace (derived from passementerie). Lace was made completely by hand for three centuries until the first machinery appeared in Nottingham, England at the beginning of the 19th century, invented by John Heathcoat, and later by Leavers, who dreamed up the name "Calais lace." Lace appeared on the textile scene relatively late, in the second half of the 16th century. To start with, the two centers for lace-making were Venice, for needlework lace, and Flanders for pillow lace. Before then, to achieve the transparent effect (in lace due to the delicate structure with tiny holes and spaces), a scallop-edged piece of linen was embroidered, then cut and the threads pulled. Then somebody had the brilliant idea of reversing the process: instead of destroying the fabric, they created a mesh to embroider over. Lace was also used by men until the 18th century for jabots and frilled cuffs that appeared from beneath their jackets. From the beginning of the 19th century it was used exclusively for women's clothing, for dresses, jackets, veils, umbrellas, shawls, and to decorate underwear and accessories. The art of lace-making quickly spread from Venice and Flanders, first to France, and then to England, Spain, and Switzerland. It was probably imported to Asia and South America by missionaries. Some of the most famous types of needlework lace are those from Alençon and Argentan in Normandy, and for pillow lace Chantilly, Valenciennes, and Burano or Venetian lace. The art of handmade lace is still taught in some specialized schools. Museums throughout the world have collections of antique lace. One of the most famous lacemakers is Riechers-Marescot in Calais, France, where lace is produced for the world's greatest couturiers.

Laced Shoe with a Fringe Low-heel or medium-heel shoe, rather high-necked, with a fringed toe cap, almost always with three holes.

La Chapelle David (1963). American photographer, originally from Canada. He arrived in New York in 1978 and worked as a doorkeeper at Studio 54. In that mythical night club he met Andy Warhol, who introduced him to the editorial staff of *Interview*. But his real chance to shine as a photographer was offered him by the magazine *Details*, which gave him a commission. From that moment, whenever his camera was on the fashion business, he created an alternative vision made up of colors and joyful sensuality, born from a combination of the pop, cyber, and rock cultures. Like a brand, his pictures are almost always recognizable. He exaggerates without scruple, mixes reality with invention, uses the computer wisely, and describes a reality that exists only in his imagination.

❑ His work has been published in *Interview*, *Vanity Fair*, the *New York Times* magazines, and *The Face* and has made campaigns for Diesel, Mal, Levi's, Estée Lauder, and Iceberg. He has made a promo for Giorgio Armani, the brand that launched him in 1991, using a black-and-white picture of the face of an angel on a full page in the most important Italian newspapers. Very few know that the original color picture appeared in 1992 in *L'invincibile ripreso*, a joint exhibition on the theme of angels in Milan, which was his first European exhibition. He has had various solo exhibitions around the world, but was still unknown to the public at large in Italy until he was given a solo exhibition at the Museum Ken Damy in Brescia in 1993. He has published two books so far. Like their author they are unusual in size and original in composition: *LaChapelle Land* (1996) and *Hotel LaChapelle* (1999).

Lachasse Typical English high-quality tailor established in 1928, with headquarters in London.

La Cloche Spanish jewelry company highly appreciated for its creations in gold, platinum, and precious stones, with a characteristic style, first, in Art Deco, and then in the taste of the 1940s and 1950s. Established by the Lacloche brothers in Madrid in 1875, it opened branches in San Sebastián, Biarritz, and Paris. In 1920 the maison took over the Fabergé boutique in London. It had a moment of fame in the mid-1900s, but closed in the 1960s.

Lacoste Brand of casual and sportswear. The crocodile logo, the origin of which has several hypotheses, is attributed to René Lacoste (1904-1996) during his tennis career: at that time he had a small crocodile embroidered on the pocket of his jacket. In 1933 he retired from tennis, designed and decided to produce a button-neck short-sleeve sweater in white piqué cotton, with a small green crocodile embroidered on the left side of the chest. The garment was immediately successful as sports clothing, especially in tennis and golf, thanks to having a longer back than front, so as to remain well tucked inside the pants even after large or brisk movements. Success and diffusion arrived during the 1960s when sporting fashion came out of its restricted world and became simply informal. In 1963 Lacoste jerseys were manufactured in 4 colors, in 1967 in 21, and were equally suited to men, women and children. The company has for years struggled against imitation, and the brand is now seen on a wide range of clothing, shoes and accessories. (*Ruben Modigliani*)

❑ 2000. The new creative director was Christophe Lemaire, a "student" of Christian Lacroix. He had the task of introducing the brand towards modernity, though remaining linked to its sport roots. He took over from Gilles Rosier, who had widened the crocodile's horizon of sportswear.
❑ An agreement was signed with Samsonite for the manufacture and distribution of leather goods. The diversification is transverse compared to the other three areas of business: actiwear, which represents 20%, sportswear with 60% and Club clothing.
❑ 2001. Consolidated turnover was €850 million, +8% compared to 2000: 75% was represented by clothing.
❑ 2002, May. Lacoste eyewear aimed at the Brazilian market. The Group L'Amy, which produces and distributes the crocodile's glasses, signed a distribution and production license agreement with Technol Group, a South-American eyewear producer.
❑ 2002. 600,000 pieces of leather goods were sold, generating a turnover of €10 million. The brand is distributed in 120 countries and has 718 own-brand boutiques, 433 in Europe, 156 in Asia and 129 in America, most of them franchised. 65% of Lacoste is in the hands of the Lacoste family, now in the second generation; the remaining 35% is owned by the French company Devanlay, which also produces and distributes clothing. In the last ten years, the annual growth rate has been constant around 8-12%, transforming a single-manufactured brand, the shirt, into a lifestyle. The shirt, however, is the best selling item and is still produced as it was originally, using 38.63 miles of Egyptian or Peruvian cotton and mother-of-pearl buttons. The Italian market ranks third for importance, with about €70 million of turnover.
❑ 2003, January. Lacoste opened a store on Fifth Avenue, New York.

(*Dario Golizia*)

Lacroix Christian (1951). French designer. Lacroix burst onto the scene in the early 1980s with a brand new silhouette – the pouf skirt – and new source of inspiration, his hometown of Arles, in the Provence region of southern France, whose colors and design traditions continue to infuse his creations today. He studied art history at the University of Montpellier and moved to Paris in 1973, where he initially began studies to become a museum curator. He started designing fashions instead, encouraged by long-time business partner and friend Jean-Jacques Picart, and worked as an assistant both at Hermès and to designer Guy Paulin. In 1981 he was hired by the somewhat flailing couture house of Patou, and revived their couture business almost overnight with a show that turned him into a fashion star, and introduced the world to his bold mix of pattern, Provencal inspirations and joyful approach to color. He set up his own couture house in 1987, and in 1988 designed a ready-to-wear collection produced by Genny, the Ancona-based firm. Since then he has launched a number of secondary lines, including Bazar, a jeans line, a wedding division, perfumes and home accessories. He won the prestigious French design award, the *Dé d'Or,* in 1986 and 1988. He has also developed a long and much acclaimed career designing costumes for theater and the opera. A lover of flamboyancy and theatricality, Lacroix brings a unique sensuality, joy and opulence to the couture and all his designs.

❑ 2001. His fashion house is acquired by the French group LVMH.
❑ 2002, April. Lacroix is named artistic director of Emilio Pucci.
❑ 2002, June. Bazar Enfant, a line for children, is launched.
❑ 2002, October. He participates in *The Fur Show Beijing 2002*, presenting a line of fanciful furs.
❑ 2003, April. He signs an agreement with the French company Sil for the production and distribution of the first Lacroix underwear line, launched in Summer 2004.
❑ 2003, May. Lacroix takes part in the *My Favorite Dress* exhibition to celebrate the opening of the Fashion & Textile Museum of London.
❑ 2003, June. Lacroix makes his menswear début.

Christian Lacroix, *Haute couture*, 1988 Collection.

La Donna Italian magazine founded in 1905 in Turin and moved, fifteen years later, to Rome. In the capital it started to bring together the initiatives and interests of the emerging Italian bourgeoisie. It had articles about fashion services, specially about France, accompanied by the subjects that were about to become the staple of women's magazines: beauty, interior décor, news and culture, with a particular focus on the female universe. A wider cultural perspective was also made possible by the constant use of big names in literature, criticism, and journalism. It ceased publication in 1968.

Lady Di (Princess Diana) (1961-1997). Diana Spencer. Daughter of the Earl John Spencer and Frances Shand Kidd. She married Charles Windsor, Prince of Wales, on 29 July 1981, the heir to the throne of England. Before her wedding, she was no style icon, being tall and a little clumsy, with a preference for small flowered patterned dresses, so much loved by English women. The day of her wedding she chose a romantic dress, vaguely nineteenth-century in style, designed by the English creators David and Elizabeth Emanuel. It was a triumph. On the day following the ceremony, celebrated live on TV in front of millions of spectators, Diana's dress, replicated in thousands of copies, became the symbol of the bridal dress of the 1980s. In the years that followed the wedding, though abandoning her flowery patterns, she was unable to distance herself from the courtly elegance made up of ruches, frills, and hats. Only after the divorce from Charles did she detach herself from court etiquette and started to dress to flatter her slender body. Then, though continuing to use English designers like Catherine Walker, she began turning to Valentino, Lacroix, Lagerfeld (Chanel), Galliano (Dior) and, finally, Gianni Versace, a great friend and the designer of the Princess's wardrobe on several occasions. In a few years, thanks to her tall, slender beauty, the result of hours of working out, Princess Diana was increasingly imitated, from her haircut to the shade of the tights she wore. Diego Della Valle named one of his creations the D-bag. (*Sofia Leoncina Gnoli*)

Lady's riding-costume Outfit used in the nineteenth century by women to ride side-saddle. It comprises a tight bodice often

From *La Donna*, 1930. Coat manufactured by the dressmaker's workshop Ventura for Maria José of Savoy.

accompanied by a waistcoat, and a very large and long skirt to hide the legs, though sometimes the skirt concealed a pair of trousers. At the end of the century, the lady's riding-habit – a prototype of women's sportswear – was adopted to practice the sporting activity of the moment: riding a bicycle.

La Falaise Loulou (de). Collaborator and very close friend of Yves Saint-Laurent, also a personal support during the designer's several difficult periods. Born in Sussex, she had an androgynous figure and a Marlene Dietrich face. Her father, Oswald Birley, was the official painter to the English court; her mother, Maxime de la Falaise, modeled for Schiaparelli. She started her career as a model for *Vogue* and for Saint-Laurent in 1972; eventually becoming the director of the accessories section. Thirty years after her first job, and about one year after Saint-Laurent retired from fashion, Loulou opened a boutique in Rue de Bourgogne in Paris in February 2003 where she made her début in stylism with her own collection of clothes and jewels.

Lafaurie Jeanne, baroness Loppin de Gémaux (1897). French designer. She made her début in 1925. Her career suffered frequent highs and lows: in the 1950s she enjoyed her greatest success (Courrèges was the designer) but also her first defeat, when she was declared bankrupt in 1954. She bounced back into business through a company formed by her richest and most faithful clientele, and entrusted the collection's design to Michel Goma. She retired in the 1960s.

La Femme Chic French monthly dedicated to *haute couture*, with drawings and (later) full page photos. Publication began in 1911, at the fading of the Belle Époque, and lasted until 1971 when *haute couture* was about to be supplanted by the *prêt-à-porter*.

Laferrière French dressmaker's workshop established by Madame Laferrière (1847-1912). At her début, she owed her success to a single client: the Empress Eugènie, wife of Napoleon III. Her creations were worn by actresses, noblewomen and in the courts of England, Russia, and Norway. During the Universal Exposition of 1900, the maison was offered a stand.

Cover of *La Femme Chic*, 1942.

La Fressange Inès (de) (1957). French model, whose real and rather imposing name is Inès Marie Laetitia Eglantine de Seignard de La Fressange. Discovered and launched by the magazine *Elle*, she modeled for Kenzo and Mugler. In 1984 she signed an exclusive contract with Chanel, the maison guided by Lagerfeld. She has a natural aristocratic elegance and her face has been chosen to portray France on coins. In the 1990s she left Chanel to become a designer of clothing and house linen. She opened her first boutique in Avenue Montaigne in Paris. More followed in Japan and Europe. She married the Italian Luigi D'Urso.

❑ 2000, July. The designer was fired by the majority shareholder, François Louis Vuitton, from the maison Vuitton. She was accused of having designed a line of soaps without the authorization of the majority shareholder. The court ruled the action unjustified, condemning Vuitton to pay damages. The sum fixed by the court was still rather low for a case of this nature, about 260,000 dollars.

❑ 2001, October. She returned to the catwalk for Moschino, Eric Bergère,

Jean Paul Gaultier and to fashion photographic services for *Elle* and *Marie Claire*.

Laganà Barbara (1970). Designer. In 1999 she was one of the final trio of designers competing for the Infil Award, a prize for the young creators of underwear. She was born in Somma Lombardo (Varese). In 1992 she graduated from the European Institute of Design in Milan, where she studied fashion. She worked as a shop assistant in several of Milan's boutiques, and as collaborator in showrooms on the presentation of collections. She designs sport jackets and since 1998 she has worked in the Filippo Mori style studio.

Lagerfeld Karl Otto (1938). German designer. His nickname is Kaiser, the emperor of fashion, due to his German background: he comes from a family of rich industrialists in Hamburg. From a very young age, he showed an extraordinary passion and talent for the arts. When he arrived in Paris in the 1950s, not yet fifteen, to finish his secondary studies, he still did not know which art he wished to follow: with an omnivorous and voracious intellectual curiosity, he had a growing passion for the eclecticism and cosmopolitanism of the Grand Siècle. His innate taste for the futile and ephemeral, and his drawing skills directed him towards fashion: at the age of 16 he won first prize, ex aequo with Yves Saint Laurent, in the contest organized by the International Secretariat of Wool, and he was invited by Pierre Balmain to work in his *haute couture* atelier. In 1958 he moved to the maison Patou to complete his experience in the field of *haute couture*. But the group of important ateliers was not enough for his uneasy and free spirit: in France and in Italy *prêt-à-porter* was dawning and Lagerfeld became an independent designer collaborating with, among others, Charles Jourdan, Krizia, Ballantyne, Cadette, and Mario Valentino. The first major turning point of his career arrived in 1965: the meeting and the beginning of a collaboration with the Fendi sisters, an alliance which still continues and which, in 1985, was celebrated at the National Gallery of Modern Art in Rome with the exhibition "A working path – Fendi-Karl Lagerfeld". For the Roman maison, the designer created

Karl Lagerfeld, drawing for the exhibition *Art Fashion*, Biennial of Florence, Skira, 1996.

collections of revolutionary furs, which transformed a bourgeois status symbol into an avant-garde dressing style. In 1977 he created the first clothing line, and in 1983 came the second turning point: Chanel appointed him artistic director of the maison, entrusting him with the design of the *haute-couture* collections, *prêt-à-porter*, and accessories. Lagerfeld was able to interpret the spirit of Mademoiselle Coco, renovating it through his personal inspiration, though retaining the unmistakable style of the brand. Less fortunate was the path of the *griffe* KL, which he founded in 1984 and which has a fan as its symbol. In 1998 he wound up the company, partly because his time was very much taken up by his activity as fashion photographer for the major international fashion magazines and other designers. Lagerfeld is also a costume and set designer (he has worked for the Burgtheater in Vienna, La Scala in Milan, and the Comunale in Florence) and an original illustrator of drawings that accompany the press files of his collections, and his working notes. In 1986 Longanesi published *Un diario di moda Anna Chronique*, written with his friend, the Milanese journalist Ana Piaggi: it tells the story of the daily and extraordinary life of two aesthetes. In one of his rare interviews, he made fun of the myth of the designer: "There's an anecdote about Diaghilev. When, before the start of a ballet, he was told that the costumes were not ready, he answered: 'Do not worry, they are just rags.' Bursting into tears, crying on taffeta, is ridiculous. Fashion must be joy: the lady that purchases a dress does not need know how much you suffered to create it. With a dress of that nature and at such a price, the whole thing has to be simply a happy game."

(*Maria Vittoria Carloni*)

❑ 2003. As a photographer, he published the volume *Waterdance/ Bodywave*. In 1995 he had published his *Off the Record*.
❑ 2004, November. The stylist designed a complete collection for the Swedish giant H&M, named *Karl Lagerfeld for H&M*, which was put on sale in all 20 H&M markets. The collaboration came to an end after only one season due to misunderstandings between the company and the designer.
❑ 2004, December. Tommy Hilfiger Corporation acquired the brand Karl Lagerfeld. The goals were to develop distribution of the collections in the USA, the geographic expansion of the brand, and the creation of new growth opportunities through the broadening of Karl Lagerfeld's range of articles.
❑ 2005, May. Bernard Arnault, President of LVMH, renewed the collaboration with Karl Lagerfeld for at least five more years. For the next two years, the maison hopes to break even with a turnover which should touch on 500 million euros.
❑ 2005, June. For Winter 2006 the launch is expected of Lagerfeld's new line by the Tommy Hilfiger Corporation. A quality jeans collection for young men and women at lower prices than the *prêt-à-porter*. In fact, it should cost 50% less.

Laguna Hannibal (1967). Venezuelan designer. In 1982 he moved to Spain, settling in Madrid in 1998. He started an alliance with the brand Bellocotton, which specializes in the manufacture of cotton knitwear. In 1986 he opened his first sales point of *prêt-à-porter* and four years later his own maison. He also designed a line of jewels and accessories besides a line of bridal dresses with Pronovias. Very close to the world of art, he has taken part in a hundred exhibitions. He is particularly appreciated for his very personal creations, which eliminate the barriers between day and night, creating a modern version of luxury and elegance.

(*Estefania Ruilope Ruiz*)

Lahrer Félix (1971). French photographer. He started his career during a stay in London from 1994 to 1997, collaborating with magazines such as *Wad*, *Vogue*, *Jalouse*, *Parso*, *Town and Spoon*, *Tetu* and *Vogue France*. He became interested in cinema and directs films dominated by ironic atmospheres such as *Claudia's Dream* in 2001 (where he imagines Claudia Shiffer flirting with giant puppets of King Kong and the Pink Panther) and *Barbie Killer in Playland* in 2002. He has also had two solo exhibitions. He lives and works in London and Paris.

Lalique René Jules (1860-1945). French jeweler. The most versatile and productive creator of Art Nouveau jewelry. In 1885 he set up a company in Paris where he started designing and producing for himself and other jewelers (Boucheron and Cartier). The pieces and sets he created for Sarah Bernhardt

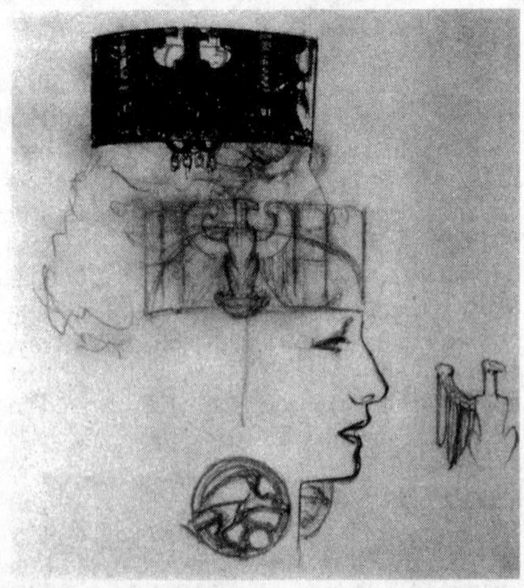

Tiara and jewels of Lalique for Sarah Bernhardt.

are particularly famous. His fame was confirmed at the Universal Exposition in Paris in 1900. His interest in non-precious materials induced him to experiment with glass, horn, ivory, mother-of-pearl, and unusual stones for that age, such as opal and tourmaline. Nature and women, in particular, were his primary sources of inspiration.

Lalonde Alain (1913-1974). Textile entrepreneur in Paris. He took over the family company in 1958. He reorganized it and started alliances with new, young designers whom he discovered and maintained with his money, for example, Emmanuelle Khanh, Christiane Bailly, and Daniel Hechter in 1965. The company closed on the death of the owner.

L'Altra Moda Company of womenswear. It has been operating since 1991 when it was founded to impose quality scheduling on the delivery times of *prêt-à-porter*. The brand, which produces a second line called Compagnia Italiana, is distributed internationally through own-brand stores, franchises, shops-in-shops, and multibrand shops. The annual turnover in 1998-1999 was over 30 million dollars.

❑ 2002. Product value totalled €45,768,061, an increase of 4.5%, with a profit of €1,484,637 made outside Italy.

Lama Concept Dutch brand of fabrics for fashion and interior décor, created in 1998 by Yvonne Laurysen (1972) and Erik Mantel (1965). They both graduated from the Design Academy of Amsterdam and were both apprenticed by Milan designers. Starting from the method used to draw metals, they set up a system to obtain expanded materials which they named Furore and which they presented at Première Vision in March 1999.

La Matta Company in the Veneto area specialized in the manufacture of leather garments. Established by Piergiorgio Asola in 1975 in Trissino, near Vicenza, the brand combines the leather tradition of Veneto and northeast Italy with the fabrics and accessories from Biella and Como, and with the tanned calfskin of the south. La Matta does not only get its raw materials from Italy: the soft leather for gloves, colored with aniline to guarantee non-deformability and softness, and the double-face sheepskin are from Spain; and suede comes directly from North America. During the 1980s the company created the lines La Matta Uomo and La Matta Donna, which have won market share through international multibrand stores. Besides its own *griffe*, it produces the leather collections of designers like Armani, Polo Ralph Lauren, Corneliani and Max Mara. It provides leather garments to Gianfranco Ferré, with whom the company has been collaborating for more than two decades. At international level the major partners are American – Neuman Marcus, Bergdorf Goodman, Barney's in New York, Louis of Boston – and Japanese, such as Isetan and Swank Shop. The consolidated turnover of the company, at present guided by Lorenzo Asola, amounts to about €20 million.

Lambert Eleanor (1903). American journalist and public relations manager. She has devoted her life to supporting American fashion. Born in Crawfordsville in Indiana, after studying at the Chicago Art Institute she moved to New York. In 1936 she married the journalist Seymour Berkson, who died in 1959 leaving her alone with a baby, William, who is now a successful art critic. In 1942 she became the promoter of the Fashion Press Week, an initiative meant to illustrate American fashion to the international press, concentrating all shows in one week. She helped launch designers like Charles James, Bill Blass, and De La Renta. The American government awarded her several honors, but she herself has been the promoter of numerous organizations, such as the Council of Fashion Designers of American, which gave her two awards, one for her career (1988), and one for her particular contribution to the development of fashion (1993). She has also been awarded a degree *honoris causa* from the Parson's School of Design. She instituted the international award Best Dressed Poll.

Lamberto Losani This brand, now in its third generation, is represented by cashmere knitwear on sale in the best stores around the world. Nowadays, Paola Losani follows the development of the product, while Valentina manages the commercial side. The story began in 1939 when Giovanni Losani started a small business producing wool hosiery and knitwear garments. At that time he used angora, which came from local rabbit fur. After World War II, it was his son Lamberto who decided to change the company's direction: a factory was built, with emphasis on the constant investment in better technology. Emphasis was then placed on cashmere knitwear, resulting in a success that has not diminished.

Lambertson Truex (LT) American company and brand, a manufacturer of bags, established in 1998 and conceived by the American designers Richard Lambertson and John Truex. For the line of accessories, the pair collaborate with Geoffrey Beene, Calvin Klein, Gucci, Barney's, Bergdorf, and Goodman. In 1999 the brand received the Perry Ellis Award for the accessory category and, in 2000, the prize awarded by the Council of Fashion Designers of America. The basic idea consisted in creating a bag which, "boundless" and "timeless," combines comfort and style. Classic shapes, the creative use of skins, and the same forms and colors form the maison's rules. Lately, following the same criteria, Truex and Lambertson have produced a classic line of shoes. In Italy their products are distributed in Milan, Venice, Padua, and Capri. (*Daniela Bolognetti*)

Lambrugo Silk factory founded by Alberto Giulio Lambrugo in 1918, with the acquisition of a hand weaving mill in Gironico (Como). The company produces silks for ties for the company Roscasco and to create menswear. In the 1920s and 1930s, it purchased mechanical looms that continued the production of silk linen. In 1959, Alberto Giulio Lambrugo split from his brothers to found the company A.G. Lambrugo with his son Gianni in Montano Lucino (Como). In 1962, when Alberto Giulio died, the company changed its name (A.G. Lambrugo of Giovanni Lambrugo) and became a one-man business. The business now focuses on the production of dyed bemberg linings and, since 1978, on the manufacture of women's clothes which quickly almost completely supplanted the silk production. In 1990 the corporate name changed again to A.G. Lambrugo & Sons.(*Pierangelo Mastantuono*)

Lambswool Wool from the first shearing of the lamb. Under a microscope it is seen to have an end as sharp as that of a needle, and is not cut in same way as other shearings. Of fine quality, it is particularly soft and is often blended with cashmere. The highest quality lambswool is Geelong.

Lamden Sherald (1960). English designer. After working as the designer for *Ghost*, he started his own business under the brand Seraph and made his début at London Fashion Week in Fall 1997. His style, which has been called innovative by the press, reveals strong oriental influences.

Lamé Fabrics manufactured with the introduction of threads; these were once metallic but are now very bright and resistant synthetic and flat laminates. Traditionally in gold and silver, and used for brocades, bouclé etc., lamés are mostly used in the manufacture of women's evening dresses, but there are also examples, mixed with more traditional threads, used in menswear.

La Merveilleuse Famous manufacturing house founded by Giuseppe Tortonese in 1912, after the big exhibition at Valentine's Park, in which fashion pavilions exhibited the best products from Turin's ateliers. The company quickly achieved success thanks to its famous blouses, which were popular throughout Italy. Annual production was 30,000 pieces, and the company was obliged to open a second store in Turin and a shop in Via Condotti in Rome. With its many ateliers and manufacturing companies, Turin was considered the capital of fashion. In the second post-war period, the company, always in the avant-garde, started a *prêt-à-porter* line characterized by its sobriety and practical elegance. But with the organization of the Italian fashion world under the leadership of Palazzo Pitti, taste was changing, leaving La Merveilleuse out of date. After a series of alternating fortunes, the company closed at the end of the 1960s.

Lami Alma Maria. Italian dressmaker. She was typical of Florentine fashion in the years preceding the Italian fashion shows in Florence. From a long-established family, which boasts among its ancestors Vincenzo Lami, whose portrait is kept in the Uffizi, she took

Classical studies in Florence before deciding to turn to *haute couture*. In Florence she studied the basic concepts of cutting and sewing at one of the several dressmaker's workshops in town. She later moved to Paris, where she collaborated with Elsa Schiaparelli. Once back in Florence, in the late 1930s she opened a small workshop inside her house in Via dei Corsi, on the corner of Via Tornabuoni, where she mostly manufactured garments for the Florentine aristocracy based on models she saw in the Paris collections. On 21 May 1950, the Lami workshop participated in the Florentine Fashion Evening at the La Pergola Theater with other Florentine workshops like Chioffi, Aiazzi Fantechi, and Magnani, and craftsmen's companies that manufactured accessories, such as Salvatore Ferragamo. This was one of the initiatives held in those years in Florence to demonstrate the need to organize the fashion industry in Italy. Fabrics were of excellent quality, and the decorative elements were typical of the Italian artisan's craft, like embroidery and passementerie. The garments made, however, were rarely original but based on French models copied from paper patterns. The Lami workshop was not involved in the birth of Italian fashion in the White Room at Palazzo Pitti, but it continued its activity at full speed until the mid-1970s. (*Stefania Ricci*)

Laminate Inorganic synthetic fibers. In the manufacture of fabrics, steel, copper, argent, zinc, titanium and gold are woven and used in a blend with other fibers for their anti-stress and chromatic virtues, and for their resistance and quality. The threads are reduced to micro-dimensions by being passed through a draw-plate, or into long and thin lamellas through beating or pressing machines.

Lamsweerde (von) Ines e Vinoodh Matadin The most famous Dutch couple of the moment was born in the *Vogue* academy of fashion in Amsterdam. The photographer and his make-up artist and partner started working together in 1990, making photographs which, with the use of digital touching up, were provocative and endowed with a sense of theatrical violence. The couple produced advertising campaigns for Joop!, Patrick Cox, and Thierry Mugler, and their work is seen in several international magazines.

Lancel French leather goods' company. Its motto is "accessible and intelligent luxury." In 1876, Alphonse and Angèle Lancel opened a boutique for smokers in Paris, at 17 Boulevard Poissonnière. It was visited by Georges Sand, Andrée Vally, and Eugène Sue. In a short time, the couple opened three new outlets in the capital and other French towns, and became well known for the sale of decorations and gift articles. In 1901 Albert Lancel took over management of the company. The leather line was created in the 1920s; perfumes and cosmetics ten years later. At the end of World War II, Lancel specialized in bags, cases and small leather goods. In 1956 the company created the famous Kangaron, a case with external pockets. In 1976 Edgar and Jean Zorbibe took over the business and started an international development program and further promotion of the brand. By the 1980s, the Lancel Sogedi Group had 20 companies and branches, 1,000 sales points and was the third largest leather goods' company in France, but it also sells watches, ties, and ashtrays. (*Marilena Bergamaschi*)

Lancel's Advertisement: "Modern Luggage." *L'Illustration*, 1929.

❑ 2001. Turnover totaled 120 million dollars, 70% of which originated in Italy. The prestigious French company, with premises on the Champs-Elysées, numbered 110 own-brand shops and 800 licensees. In Italy it has 70 shops and 1 own-brand boutique in Milan.

Lancetti Pino (1932). Italian designer. His constant reference to the world of art has resulted in his becoming recognized as a tailor-painter. Drawing inspiration from Modigliani, Kandinsky, Picasso, Vasarely, Klimt, Sonia Delaunay, and, above all, Matisse, he was able to create models and fabrics of great chromatic impact both in *haute couture* and in *prêt-à-porter*. Born in Umbria, he started as a painter and ceramics decorator but, once he had completed his studies at the San Bernardino Academy in Betto di Perugia, he moved to Rome where, in 1954, he opened his first atelier in Via Margutta. During this period, he worked closely with Carosa, Simonetta Fabiani, De Luca, Schuberth, Antonelli, and the big names of the dawning Italian fashion world. The journalist Irene Brin and the director of the Gallery of Modern Art in Rome, Palma Bucarelli, were among the first to believe in him and to encourage him to establish his own maison. In 1961 he made his début at Palazzo Pitti, Florence, but his greatest success came in 1963, when he presented a collection inspired by military styles. Actresses like Ginger Rogers, Silvana Mangano, and Annie Girardot became his clients, as well as Salima Aga Khan, Anna Bonomi, and Princess Soraya. At the end of the 1960s and early 1970s, he presented collections inspired by the great masters of art, then shifted his interest to folk style, emphasizing soft, falling lines. His clothes were presented in settings like the Villa Medici, Palazzo Doria Pamphilj, and, in 1996, the Casino dell'Aurora in Palazzo Pallavicini. In 1999 Lancetti was bought up by the Compafin group directed by Ugo Paci, who made his own name in the industrial field by managing the cosmetics group Veruska & Joel. In January 2003 Paci died and his wife Luisa took over the reins. She gave responsibility for the company's artistic direction to Icarius, a young Brazilian designer who had already presented his models in Paris.

(*Eleonora Attolico*)

❑ 2005, May. The relationship between the maison and the young Brazilian designer was broken off.

Lancôme French cosmetics company founded in 1935 by Armand Petitjean. Perfumes, make-up, and treatment lines have always been the basis of Lancôme's product ranges. The company very quickly reached international status. Always ahead in the research and creation of successful fragrances, the brand went through a difficult period around 1960, which finished with the selling of the company to L'Oréal. After conquering the American and Asiatic markets, the new Lancôme restyled its image, betting on testimonials that embodied an accessible beauty, removed from any stereotype. Famous faces representing the company have been those of Isabella Rossellini (for ten years), now those of Juliette Binoche (for the perfume *Poème*), Inès Sastre (for the perfume *Trésor*), and Cristiana Reali for make-up and treatments.

Land's End International leader in mail-order selling, thanks to an excellent quality/price ratio. In 2001 turnover totalled 1.6 billion dollars, 20% of which arrived via Internet sales, a channel the company took up in 1995. The company distributes 269 million catalogues annually. In 2001 it launched the new service of custom made pants and jeans, on the base of the information provided by the customer.

Landshoff Herman (1905-1986). German photographer. The son of a renowned musicologist, he studied drawing to become a cartoonist, but in that the creative laboratory of the Bauhaus he encountered photography. The rise to power of National Socialism, which closed the school and promulgated racial laws, forced him to emigrate to Paris in 1933, where he worked for the French edition of *Vogue* and *Fémina*. In 1941 he reached New York and continued to work in the world of fashion publishing on *Vogue* and, in the post-war period, on *Junior*, *Harper's Bazaar* and *Mademoiselle*. His style – which impressed and influenced the young Richard Avedon – had a fresh, dynamic vision that did not seem to resemble fashion photography, which at that time was rather static. Land-

Pino Lancetti, sketch for the Collection 1981.

shoff preferred to work on external sets and often asks models to move on skates, to jump as if in a moment of happiness, or to ride a bicycle in front of his camera. Landshoff also made a good name for himself as an architectural and portrait photographer. He made a series of portraits of famous photographers, among whom Weegee, Ansel Adams, Irving Penn, and Richard Avedon, and of personalities such as Einstein and Oppenheimer. In 2002 the Fashion Institute of Technology of New York dedicated him a big solo exhibition of his most important black-and-white works of the 1940s and 1950s.

Lane Kenneth J. (1932). American jeweler. Exoticism and eccentricity in his fancy bijoux were the creative characteristics of this designer who, after working in advertising and being an apprentice in the shoe firm of the designer Vivier, devoted himself to goldsmithery in 1963, designing jewels in strass, glass and golden metal, matched with buttons and evening shoes. His work was much appreciated by the Duchess of Windsor, Jackie Kennedy, and Diana Vreeland.

Lanerossi Italian wool factory established in Schio and Piovene Rocchette, near Vicenza, between 1849 and 1869, by Alessandro Rossi (1819-1898) on the preexisting industrial structures of the wool mill established by his father Francesco. At the start of the 20th century, the Lanificio Rossi was the most important wool factory in Italy. It had more than 5,000 workers and dozens of plants in the Vicenza area. In 1962, having taken the corporate name of Lanerossi, the company passed under the control of the Italian energy group, Eni. In the 1960s the Lanerossi brand indissolubly linked its image to the Italian industrial boom. In the late 1970s it entered a period of crisis resulting in the liquidation of the company. In 1987, it was incorporated into Marzotto, becoming a division in its textiles sector. Recently the famous logo, formed by concentric white curves on a red background, has undergone a delicate restyling. The Lanerossi is at present specialized in the production and sale of pure wool knitwear and yarns, and in the production of blends for different industrial uses (raw articles and fabrics). At the end of 1998 the company had 741 workers and a turnover of 90 million dollars. Production was 9,780 tons, with an export quota of 46% in 40 countries.

- ❑ 2001, April. For the Fall-Winter 2002-2003 yarn collection, Lanerossi worked with the Style Institute Peclers Paris, one of the most important world observatories of consumer trends. After a study conducted with Ornella Bignami, who determined the evolution of the collections of the last 10 years, the company decided to take a different path in the research of new yarns and colors. The goal is to pick up the macro-trends in the evolution of demand, singling out the materials that better interpret consumer needs.
- ❑ 2002. Lanerossi no longer existed as a company, but only as a presence within the Marzotto group's textile sector.

Lang Helmut (1956). Austrian designer, born in Vienna. His fashion is as understated as he is. He designed his first clothes at a very young age. In 1977 he opened a boutique in Vienna of custom-made clothing. His designs contain the spirit of the avant-garde artistic and cultural movement to which he belongs, the Wiener Moderne. In 1986 he made his Paris début with a *prêt-à-porter* line. The following year, his first men's collection was very successful. He regularly designed more lines: shoes (1990), jeans (1994), accessories (1995), shirts (1997), and ties (1998). The opening of his boutiques have marked the steps of his success: Monaco (1995), Milan (1996), New York (1997), and Hong Kong and London (1998). Listed among the so-called minimalist designers, he is able to give his simplistic creations an artistic touch: the red of a huge stripe that characterizes a simple sweater; the raw cut tunic in tulle that covers the dress. The use and unusual matching of materials (silk and plastic, for example) support his apparent minimalism. His shows, to which only a few selected names are invited, have no fuss or spectacle: no catwalks, and his models are almost without make-up and walk quickly on low heels. In the late 1990s, his *griffe* was acquired by Prada.

(*Paola Pollo*)

❑ 2002. The Prada Group purchased 51% of Helmut Lang. Turnover reached €41.8 million.
❑ 2004, October. Prada bought out the entire company.
❑ 2005, May. An announcement was made that the brand would be suspended while waiting for an offer to buy it.

Lang Jack (1939). French socialist politician. He has always believed in the importance of fashion as an art in itself. He was responsible for the setting of shows in the Carré du Louvre. He was Minister of Culture during the Mitterand presidency and, in the late 1990s Jospin appointed him Minister of National Education. Eccentric and extravagant, in 1984 he shocked the National Assembly by wearing a Mandarin neck suit created by Thierry Mugler.

Lanificio dell'Olivo Italian yarn company. Founded in 1880 by the Querci brothers, who were the founding members of the Organization of Industrialists in Prato. Starting in 1947, it oriented its production towards the manufacture of special yarns. In 1958 the introduction of new gauzing techniques marked the company's decision to produce fantasy yarns. Currently, the strong point of the wool factory lies in continuous yarns, in particular viscose and nylon, which are made both for knitwear companies and the textile sector. Other than in the working of artificial fibers, the company has long and acknowledged experience in the transformation of alpaca.

Lanificio Egidio Ferla Established in 1927 in Ponzone Biellese, it follows the tradition of the industrial district of Biella and manufactures exclusive fabrics. The company is renowned for the creativity and refinery of its products, fibers and colors. The production capacity is of about 400,000 meters of fabrics a year for both men's and women's clothing, 60% of which is exported. It is the market leader in the production of fabrics in baby alpaca (Peruvian and first shearing, produced in limited quantity, approximately 1.5% of the total alpaca production). Among the company's other products are sport fabrics in Woolair and very fine lambswool, Summer super-fine in wool-linen, wool-silk, and Suri-linen-cotton (Suri belongs to the alpaca family).

❑ 2002. Turnover was €5,324 million, almost 50% of which derived from exports. The company employed 50 staff.

Lanificio Fratelli Cerruti Established in August 1881 by Stefano, Antonio and Quirino Cerruti. In the early 1900s, production amounted to 10,000 rolls of fine-combed fabrics. The company began to export its products, especially towards America. During World War I, the wool mill delivered gray-green cloth to the army: 17,000 meters in 1917. Silvio, Antonio's son, studied at the Textile School in Aache, Germany, and in 1944 became the sole owner on his father's death. In 1945, the company employed 700 workers, had 140 looms and more than 7,000 spindles. Silvio reorganized the company, aiming at producing only very high quality fabrics. On his death in 1951, management was taken over his son Nino, who in 1956 established the manufacturing company Hitman and, in 1965, Cerruti 1881. The wool factory has offices in Hong Kong, from which it controls the Far East. Nino's brothers, Attilio, Alberto and Fabrizio, also help run the company.

Lanificio Fratelli Fila Producer of combed and carded fabrics in wool and high-quality fibers, such as mohair and camelhair, for menswear and womenswear. Established in 1911 in Coggiola, it is one of the oldest in the Biella area. In 1997 the company was acquired by the Viana family.

Lanificio Luigi Colombo Based in Borgosesia, near Vercelli. It started production in the late 1960s: though this has been a short period, it has been sufficient to bring the wool factory – which is still named after the founder – to second place in the world ranking of pure cashmere production. Luigi Colombo became an orphan at the age of 10, and grew up with his aunts and uncles who, at the time, were among the big names in the wool industry and themselves owned a plant in Prativero. This environment meant Luigi would follow a sure path: he studied at the

Institute Quintino Sella of Biella, and spent part of each day working his uncles' plant. At the end of his studies, he ran this plant for twenty years with a cousin. With this background, he started his own business, choosing the niche of the products of highest quality but greatest difficulty. On presentation of his double-face product, it was immediately adopted by the biggest names in fashion. During the 1970s Luigi was supported by his three sons: Giancarlo, in charge of production; Roberto, marketing; and Paolo, who has experience in a large accounting company. The entry into the top management of the second generation did not alter the company's original intentions. Strategies, style and intense financial efforts (15 million euros of investments from 1999 to 2002) make it one of the most advanced in the sector. The company's successes with fabrics stimulate it to enter the knitwear sector, and from early 1994 its label is available in the most prestigious boutiques of the world. In 1997 the wool company opened a branch office in Osaka and another in New York. In 2000, turnover reached 50 million euros (a real boom which required new staff, bringing the personnel to a total of 320 workers), while the export quota remained at 60%. In 2001 the turnover reached 70 millions. The year 2002 represented the return to "normality." A large part of the fabrics and knitwear is made with material from Inner Mongolia (350 tons in 2001), on which capillary checks are conducted by Colombo HK Ltd, with branch offices in Beijing. International acknowledgment of the company has been made official with its entry into the Club Europés 500. *(Maria Vittoria Alfonsi)*

Lanificio Policarpo Company established in 1945 by Policarpo Cerruti and Daniele Gerometta along the perimeter of old and crumbling Austrian barracks, in Vittorio Veneto. The original philosophy of producing products of exclusive quality in different colors, patterns and weaves has brought the company success (it has 240 workers) and win market share in foreign markets. At present it considers itself a complete cycle wool factory which produces combed and carded draping fabrics for menswear, in pure wool and exclusive fibers.

Lanificio Raffaello It has its headquarters in Massalengo, near Lodi. Established in 1968 on the foundations of the Lanificio Cremonesi-Varesi & C., which was created in 1888 and was for those years absolutely futuristic: 50 mechanical and 46 hand-operated looms for the manufacture of shawls and flannels, and a workforce of about 220 people. By 1909, the year that a fire destroyed the plants, the number had grown to 1,000. In 1913, the Cremonesi-Varesi wool factory changed its name to Varesi Lombardo. Racked by problems in the early 1920s, it underwent reorganization. In 1968 it was bought up by the Lanificio Raffaello, whose majority shareholder is Sigfrido Battaini. In 1987 the company was acquired by the Michele Solbiati Sasil company. Its average turnover between 1996 and 1998 was around 5.3 million dollars. Since 1993 it has been working exclusively for third parties: dyeing, twisting and winding yarns, dyeing and finishing fabrics. To commercialize its products, in 1992 it created the Raffaello Industrie Tessili, whose turnover (about 5 million dollars in 1998) mostly comes from exports.

Lanital Proteinic fiber obtained from casein, the protein in milk, which was discovered in 1935. It was the year of the sanctions imposed by the Fascist autarchy which encouraged Italy to be self-sufficient. Manufactured by Snia Viscosa in 1937, it partially replaced wool, achieving a total output of 1,200 tons. Independent research by American Atlantic Research Associates Inc. concluded that the ideal formula was that of Arlac: in 1943 Snia Viscosa produced more than 5,000 tons. The formula repeats the molecular structure of wool with convincing results in terms of warmth and softness. It is resistant to moths.

Lannoo Marc (1963). Young Belgian designer, who belongs to the new wave of stylists from the Netherlands. His models are Dries Van Noten, AF Vandervost and Dirk Bikkembergs. His creations won the attention of the public at large in February 2002 at the Silhouette Fashion Show, a space in Düsseldorf's Cpd reserved for young European talents. The following month he made an appearance on the margin of the Paris Week, a show replicated in the Fall-Winter 2002-2003.

Lanvin French fashion house, one of the most ancient in *haute couture* which, despite highs and lows, is still going. It was opened in 1885 in Paris by Jeanne Lanvin (1867-1946) who had completed an apprenticeship in the atelier of Madame Félix, a milliner. When, 13 years later, she married the Italian Emilio di Pietro, she was already well known. Her daughter was Marguerite Marie-Blanche and since her birth the dressmaker created paired outfits for mother and daughter. During the 1920s the success of the maison Lanvin was extraordinary. It employed 1,200 workers, and had 7 branch boutiques in the French holiday locations and in capitals such as Madrid and Buenos Aires. Her clothes were moderate in their volumes, but rich in the old-style embroideries that made them unique. The founder, a woman of exquisite taste and in tune with her time, liked to work with artists. Paul Iribe designed the silhouette of a mother bent over her daughter, which is still today associated with the very successful perfume *Arpège* (launched in 1927), and the black bottle was designed by Armand Rateau, the creator of the Pavilion of Elegance at the famous Exhibition of Decorative Arts (1925), of which Madame Lanvin was the President. Lanvin dressed actresses, singers, and movie stars, from the Dolly Sisters to Yvonne Printemps, to Arletty for the film *Les Enfants du Paradis* (1945). On Jeanne's death, her daughter took over the reins of the maison: the choice of Castillo as fashion designer (his stylistic direction lasted from 1950 to 1963) introduced a period of success that achieved its height when Maryll, the wife of Yves Saint-Laurent and niece of the great Jeanne, invited the Belgian François Crahay (at Lanvin from 1968 to 1984) to replace Castillo. Crahay produced colorful collections that, for three years, were awarded the Dé d'Or. And when Montana (1990-1992) replaced Crahay, his collections too won the same award. Since 1976 the *griffe* has produced a line of *prêt-à-porter* clothes that has been run by Dominique Morlotti since 1992.

Jeanne Lanvin, sketch for "Tunisienne" afternoon dress, 1928.

❑ 1999. The brand was bought by the giant L'Oréal.
❑ 2000. The brand registered a growth in turnover, representing 4% of the consolidated sales of the L'Oréal Group.
❑ 2001. Alber Elbaz became the maison's new designer.

❑ 2001. The maison returned to independence, after being sold by L'Oréal.
❑ 2002. Jérôme Picion wrote Jeanne Lanvin's biography.
❑ 2003. Christophe Blondin, for two years the creative director of Lanvin Homme, left the maison and was replaced by Martin Krutzky.

(*Adele Melzi*)

A sketch by Brunetta for Lanvin (Biki Collection).

La Perla Italian world leader in women's underwear. In 1954 Ada Masotti, a corset maker from Bologna, set up a production company, Not having elastic fibers available, she focused on tailoring handmade pieces. She chose the company name. Nowadays the company is managed by the second generation, with Alberto Masotti, the founder's son, as President. He is responsible for the company's huge growth up to the present levels, with more than 20 brands. Strong points are their Leawers lacework (named after an English loom, of which only 1,200 examples remain in the world), Cornelly embroidery, macramé (embroidery on a fabric which is later destroyed), *soutache* (an ornamental braid applied by hand usually in fancy pattern); the *frastaglio* (traditional Florentine flat stitch working). La Perla has exclusive worlwide rights to the production of the extremely elastic Lycra crépe-de-chine.

❑ 2001, September. The brand linked to underwear and beachwear lines made its début at Milano Moda Donna. In the previous four years the company had offered a limited range of women's clothing. To achieve its sales targets, the group created a new styling department and allocated investments in marketing and distribution. Shops were opened in Monaco, Moscow, and Chicago.
Creative Coordination was entrusted to Sigurd Steinunn, 35, from Iceland, who had worked with Calvin Klein and Tom Ford. Steinunn was supported by six designers and by Anna Masotti who, after graduating from Dams, was made Fashion Coordinator.
❑ 2001. Consolidated turnover of €235 million, 48% in the Italian market, 52% abroad. The company had 54 own-brand shopes, 38 of which were abroad, and the workforce totalled 1,400 people, plus as many in the associated company. Début of the new boutiques in Japan (Fukuoka) and US (Costa Mesa, Chicago) and of the web boutique, www.laperla.com.
❑ 2002, April. Grigioperla Touch is the new men's *prêt-à-porter* of La Perla, which made its début at Milano Moda Uomo.
❑ 2002, September. Alliance between technology and fashion, and with Nylstar, a giant in technological innovation in the field of fibers and yarns. In addition to product innovation, the distribution network was further expanded through new own-brand shops, in addition to the 15 in Italy and 24 abroad. After the début in Madrid, La Perla also opened in Soho, New York.
❑ 2002, December. Alessandro Dell'Acqua moved to La Perla. The designer from Naples became the new

Creative Director of the *prêt-à-porter* lines. The year closed with a turnover of €250 million.
❑ 2004, November. The company celebrated 50 years of business with an exhibition dedicated to the Bologna painter, Elisabetta Sirani (1638-1665). The choice was dictated by the desire to pay tribute to female creativity.

Lapidus Rosette (1936). French designer. Sister of Ted Lapidus and wife of Jean Mett, an industrialist, she started her own business in 1961, after working for six years with her brother. She opened a boutique in the heart of Paris and, in 1969, a *prêt-à-porter* line that she named Torrente, to avoid confusion with the family names already known in the fashion world.

Lapidus Ted. Brand of Edmond Lapidus (1929). French tailor, born in Paris (his father was a tailor who emigrated from Russia to France), he discovered avant-garde technologies in Japan that allowed him to make possible his requirement for high quality with industrial production. During the 1950s, he returned to Paris and, after a short apprenticeship at Dior, he opened his own *haute couture* atelier. Paradoxically, immediate success in *haute couture* allowed him to present himself as one of the anticipators of the movement that, in the 1960s and 1970s, was to revolutionize fashion. His *prêt-à-porter* line was unisex, and featured the military look and safari style. The safari jacket, one of his biggest successes, sold millions. He also introduced jeans into *haute couture*, and he referred to himself as a street tailor. His popularity and the ownership of several licenses guaranteed a good performance in the *prêt-à-porter* line until the mid 1980s. From 1986 to 1990, the brand looked for a new stimulus, and ownership of the company changed frequently before ending up in the hands of a branch office of the Crédit Lyonnais in 1993. Ted's son, Olivier, tried hard to follow in his father's footsteps, but his father prevented him from using the family name for commercial purposes. Olivier decided to work in Japan under the pseudonym Olivier Montagut. In 1984 he patented a solar energy garment but he soon abandoned his brand, and, in 1991, after reconciling with his father, he took over leadership of Ted Lapidus' *haute couture*. Olivier is much more revolutionary than his father, to the point that his style is known in the fashion sector as the "chaos theory." He goes to extremes and in 1997 proposed hologram-effect fabrics and fibers obtained from plants and fruits, mixed with powder from rubies and emeralds. (*Olivella Pianetti*)

Lapin French term to define a very soft, warm fur, with sheared hair. Originally only gray or white were possible but ater pastel and bright colors became trendy. Traditionally considered a "poor" fur, it was re-evaluated by the fashion of the 1970s, during the period of political protests, and used as a substitute for rarer and more precious furs.

La Pinuccia Italian model. This is how she was referred to in Milan; the article "La" before her real name is a connotation of affection. She was the first-ranked of the models in the Ventura dressmaker's. She was not beautiful, but had a splendid figure, and was sexy, generous, flirtatious, animated, friendly, and diplomatic. She was the lover of a famous ageing industrialist. She had plenty of jewelry because her taste was extremely refined, but she was also romantic. An indication of her romanticism is that when she fell in love with a young sailor, she took him to Milan where she had opened a small, elegant boutique selling hats and accessories. However, a female Pygmalion was not the style in the 1950s. Pinuccia wanted her sailor to study, but the young man did not believe in studying to achieve success in life: the result was that her jewels and boutique disappeared. But Pinuccia was always supported by her rich customers, and all had become her friends.

(*Maria Pezzi*)

Lardini Company producing classic clothing for men and women. Established in 1978 by the Lardini brothers in Filottrano, Marche, it has 200 workers. The original production (jackets, coats and trousers) was exclusively for men. The first Lardini collection was held in 1993. The cut was inspired by Italian tailoring traditions and is enriched by the use of cashmere, mixes of wools and cashmere, camelhair, alpaca, and lama. It purchases raw materials from the most refined wool producers: Loro Piana, Ermenegildo Zegna, Carlo Barbera, Cerruti, the English Hield Brothers, Alexanders of Scotland, Jerome Fabrics, Martin and Sons, Johnstons, and Robert Noble. Cottons are submitted to finishing procedures to give them a *worn* look. Pretty much at the same time as the début of the company's first women's collection (Fall-Winter 2003-2004), Lardini opened a showroom in Via della Spiga, Milan.

La Redoute This is the name of a street in Roubaix where the wool industrialist Charles Pollet built his spinning mill. He began a mail-order company in 1922 and advertised the sale of knitting wool in the Journal de Roubaix. Seventy years later La Redoute's catalogue, which is mainly based on knitwear, has 1,200 pages and is mailed to 8 million families. In 1998 the company's turnover amounted to approximately 1,600 million dollars, and its staff totalled almost 7,000 people.

❑ 2002. La Redoute is the main brand of Redcats, which belongs to the Ppr Group. It is mail-order leader in France and the third largest in the world. Its dominance is maintained by a database containing 16 million addresses (8 million of which are active), and by an efficient logistical service. It also has an Internet site which allows customers to order more than 55,000 articles in complete security: lines are textiles, interior decor, and technical products for leisure time.
❑ 2004, September. Emanuel Ungaro was called on to design the men's line. He made his début with the Fall-Winter 2005-2006 collection.

La Rinascente Italian department store. It was opened in Milan next to the Cathedral by Senator Borletti on 7 December 1918. Its opening was a sign of trust in the future of a country that had just come out of a long war, economically shattered, but on the winning side. It was opened on the site of the former drugstore Aux Villes d'Italie, started by Ferdinando Bocconi in 1865. Gabriele d'Annunzio, of whom Borletti was a patron, named the store La Rinascente. On Christmas Eve, just 18 days after it was opened, a fire caught light in the department store. It reopened almost immediately, keeping faith with the its purpose to "bring fashion to everyone." Even in those early years, La Rinascente represented modernity. In a documentary made by the Italian TV about the 1930s, of which the department store was taken as a symbol, Gaetano Afeltra, from the Corriere della Sera, said that in Amalfi, his hometown along the Salerno coast, people anxiously waited for the monthly catalogue of the Milanese store and would leaf through it as if it opened a window on fashion and the world. Until the 1950s-60s, when clothing shops were rare and not yet of high level, and the big chains offered medium-low quality products, the store was extremely popular during the Christmas period with the female public. La Rinascente was rebuilt from the ruins of World War II. It represented fashion, and was the stage for the Italian postwar boom. A forerunner of clothing stores offering *prêt-à-porter*, in 1963 it created a scandal by offering a corner to the clothes of Pierre Cardin: for the first time fashion designed by a great couturier was presented at affordable prices. Cardin was followed by other designers, for example, Lanvin with collections dedicated to men. A priority of the company was to offer customers a complete service of clothes and accessories, making use of internal and external consultants (among others, Biki's designer Louis de Hidalgo, Alma Filippini, owner of the *griffe* Alma, Adriana Botti, and a very young Giorgio Armani), and the store has always maintained its reputation for offering fashionable items just as trends come through. It has mounted large events, such as the market-exhibition about Mexico, and *Silk+Silk* in Winter 1985-86, in which fashion was combined with culture, tradition, and distant ethnic groups. In the city of the Trienniale, it was also a test-bed for graphics, furniture, and interior décor, and invited important names in industrial design and architecture to collaborate with it, such as Gio Ponti, Bruno Munari, Max Huber, Tomàs Maldonado, Roberto Sambonet, and Albe Steiner. La Rinascente has constantly increased the number of its sales outlets, created stores of a lower level (Upim, since 1928), invented a chain of food markets (Sma, 1961) and supermarkets (Città Mer-

A poster by Marcello Dudovic for La Rinascente, 1926.

cato, 1972), Do-it-Yourself stores (Bricocenter, 1983) and conducted a policy of acquisitions. But, though gaining from 70.5% of the group's total turnover from food sales, it continues to be the stage of the great names of ready *haute couture*, from Valentino to Zegna, from Ralph Lauren to Versace and Dolce & Gabbana.

(*Maria Vittoria Alfonsi*)

❑ 2000. The group, quoted on the Milan Stock Exchange and controlled by Eurofind (which holds 53% of the share capital) closed the year with a turnover of more than 6,000 million dollars.
❑ 2001. The year closed with a consolidated turnover of €5,749.7 million (+3.7% compared to 2000) and a consolidated net result of €59.1 million (+6%).
❑ 2002, May. The Group focused its resources on the relaunch of the Upim division, which specializes in clothing and household accessories. €150 million were allocated over the next four years to reorganize the distribution network, to restyle old stores, and to open new ones. The chain counts 150 stores directly managed, plus 220 branch stores. Upim's turnover for 2001 totalled €538 million.
❑ 2002. Turnover increased again, reaching €6,145.6 million, while the net consolidated result decreased (€50.8 million) because of tax pressure. The net financial position, however, improved €+18.5 millions, against debts of 77 millions in 2001. (*Dario Golizia*)

Larionov Michail (1881-1964). Painter, choreographer and costume designer, a leading figure in the Russian avant-garde. At the Moscow school of painting, sculpting and architecture he met Natalia Gontcharova, whom he married and with whom he formed the group The Blue Rose and magazine The Golden Fleece. He was the inventor of a primitivist style and the Futurist simultaneism. In 1913 he moved to Paris where he worked with Diaghilev's Ballets Russes, designing costumes that, notwithstanding their extreme avant-garde nature, influenced French fashions. He wrote the manifesto *Why we paint our faces* in which he theorized the possibility to integrating art and life through painting the body.

Larizzi Sidonie (1942). French designer of women's shoes. She was renowned for her high heels and the showy imprint of her creations. She collaborated with the most prestigious names in fashion: Ungaro, Patou, Chloé, Chantal Thomass, Balmain, Oscar de la Renta, and Lacroix. After different experiences in artistic and commercial fields, in 1978 she launched a line carrying her name and at the same time opened a boutique in Rue Marignan in Paris. She easily passed from classic materials (crocodile, lizard, ostrich) to the more unusual (cork, straw, gauze and wood), making creations that were all very personal.

La Robi Italian brand of *prêt-à-porter*. It made its début in 1998 in Milan. The designer is Roberta Mazzega. Production is farmed out to a network of workshops. Present in selected outlets in Italy and some European countries, the last collection sold 8,000 pieces of cashmere knitwear.

Laroche Guy (1921-1989). French couturier. Born in La Rochelle. He started very young as the assistant to Jean Dessés. In 1955 he moved to the United States to study the new working techniques of the *prêt-à-porter*. In 1957 he opened his own maison in Paris, and his first 60 designs included several innovative ideas, such as the relaunch of colors such as coral, turquoise, and topaz, and the use of rich *broderie*. He was acclaimed by the press and success had arrived. In 1961 he moved his atelier to Avenue Montaigne and launched his first *prêt-à-porter* collection. During the 1970s, besides opening a menswear boutique, he created the perfumes *Fidji*, *Eau Folle*, *Drakkar*, and *J'ai osé*, followed by *Drakkar Noir*, *Clandestine* and *Horizon* in the 1980s. On his death, he left the artistic direction to Angelo Tarlazzi whose position was taken by Michel Klein in 1993. In 1997 the American designer Alber Elbaz was the new artistic director, but not for long. In 1999 he was replaced by Saint-Laurent.

(*Olivella Pianetti*)

❑ 2004, September. Hervé L. Leorux, known as Hervé Leger, was made the *griffe*'s new artistic director.

Guy Laroche, *prêt-à-porter* design by Ronald Van der Kemp.

Larrainzar Javier (1969). Spanish designer, born in Madrid. He is one of the leading names in Iberian fashion. He studied drawing at the Institute Marangoni in Milan and attended a Master's course at the Domus Academy. In 1989 he moved to New York to work with Oscar de la Renta, where he remained for three years. Once back in Madrid, he opened his own *haute couture* boutique and in 1993 made his début on the Pasarela Cibeles. He considers fashion as something functional and wants his clothes to be practical and easy to wear. His style is sober and elegant, his clothes last years and do not go out of fashion. Black-and-white are his favorite colors and trousers his best selling article. (*Estefania Ruilope Ruiz*)

Lars Byron (1965). American designer. He made his début in 1991, but his official investiture as designer occurred with the fall collection of 1992, inspired by the legendary aviator Amelia Earhart. He draws his inspiration from baseball as well as from aviation, with curious ideas like the bags that resemble mess-tins. Influenced by the fashion of the 1940s, Lars adjusts the shirts and men's articles to female fashion, but he is always careful to extol the sensuality of the transposition.

Larsen Gunnar (1930-1990). Danish photographer. He became interested in photography in 1946, which he studied in depth in the early 1950s. He bought his first professional camera – a Rolleiflex 6x6 – and began working as a travel photographer in black-and-white for Danish magazines and newspapers. He started working in the fashion field in 1956 and 4 years later moved to Paris where he made his name as portrait photographer (Brigitte Bardot, Roger Vadim, Catherine Deneuve) and as an interpreter of the best fashion shows of the time: Courrèges, Dior, Yves Saint Laurent, Paco Rabanne. Hos photographs were published in *Stern*, *Elle*, *Harper's Bazaar*, *Marie Claire*, and *Vogue*; they were very personal images, sometimes harsh and rich in contrasts, like his black-and-white prints. In the late 1960s he worked with the most important models of the time, such as Twiggy and Carol St. John. One of his pictures of the latter became famous, when she was seen in a miniskirt surrounded by a crowd of curious people in front of a building in Moscow. In 1971 he helped John Casablanca to open his model agency and from 1973 to 1977 collaborated with International Fashions. He created his own magazines, like *Gunnar's Coiffure* and *Mode Avantgarde*. In the 1980s he took up set decoration and choreography to great effect.

L'Art et La Mode French magazine founded in 1880 with the subtitle "Magazine of elegance," but which closed in 1967. This periodical was the first to publish an advertising fashion image. During the 1920s the subtitle was changed to: "Magazine of jet set life." With black-and-white illustrations and colored drawings, the monthly discussed and illustrated the latest fashion trends, followed cultural life in Paris, reported on social events, literature and theater. From the late 1940s, it became the official voice of French *haute couture*.

Lartigue Jacques-Henry (1894-1986). French photographer. Born to a well-off family, he received the first of his numberless cameras at the age of 6. He very soon started "collecting" the most important moments of his youth in photographs: beautiful women at the Bois de Boulogne, the first planes, his father's car, racing cars, his childhood games, etc. Fascinated by speed, he photographed sport events using cameras with fast shutter speeds and filled large albums with his pictures. Jacques-Henry was also a professional painter who studied at the Julian Academy, painted still-lifes and sports events, presenting his work in solo exhibitions. He dedicated himself to photography with the passion of a beginner, and his work was exhibited at the Galerie d'Orsay in Paris next to photographers like Brassai, Man Ray, and Doisneau. A very religious man, he sold his pictures to Catholic magazines, while continuing to take beautiful fashion photos that remained unknown for years. During a trip to New York, he showed his photos to John Szakowski, director of the photography department at the Museum of Modern Art, who recognized Lartigue's genius and immediately organized a large solo exhibition. At the age of almost 70, Lartigue was discovered as the great photographer he always had been. To mark this exhibition, *Life* dedicated him a 10-page spread. The issue received wide circulation because it was published immediately after the assassination of President Kennedy. From that time one he published books, the first being: *The Photographs of J-H Lartigue: A Family Album of the Belle Époque* (1966), *Diary of a Century* (1970) with Richard Avedon, and *Lartigue and Women* (1973). He was given solo exhibitions all over the world and in 1974 took the official portrait of the President of the French Republic, Valérie Giscard d'Estaing. In the 1980s he devoted himself to fashion photography, though either with a strong sense of irony, as seen in his pictures taken at Versailles, or with that elegant taste seen in his autochromes of the 1920s and seen again, 60 years later, in his sensual portraits of contemporary women in the Bois de Boulogne. It might be said that Lartigue always shot his models as if he were photographing a fashion reportage. This is supported by the fact that Cecil Beaton designed the costumes of the film *My Fair Lady* after drawing inspiration from one of Lartgue's photographs without even having met him. The archive the photographer donated to France in 1979 is managed by the Association des Amis de Lartigue of Paris. (*Roberto Mutti*)

La Samaritaine Big department store in Paris with 16 million customers every year. In 1870 Ernest Cognacq opened a small shop near the Pont Neuf. Nowadays it occupies a building that has a surface area of 50,000 square meters and is a jewel of Art Nouveau architecture designed by the Franzt Jourdain. It is also present in three other giant shopping malls in the French capital. The chain was taken over by the family Renand in 1951.

Lastex The material most commonly used to manufacture corsets and girdles in the early 20th century, as well as other pieces of underwear. Its name is a registered trademark belonging to an American company which patented a thread of elastic rubber combined with silk, cotton or rayon.

Lategan Barry (1936). South African photographer. At the age of 25 he moved to London (1961) and, after having several jobs, turned his hobby of photography into a profession. He became famous in the 1960s, having launched the model Twiggy and set the trend of tall, slender girls. He has also worked for Ferré, Basile, Versace, Coveri, Giorgio Armani, Capucci, and Krizia.

Lattuada Alberto (1926). Italian designer born in Caronno Pertusella (Varese). His career began in 1955 with drawings for the daily *Womens Wear Daily*, even though he had been working for some years with *Mamme e Bimbi* directed by Silvana Bernasconi. He worked for several women's periodicals (such as *Novità*, *Bellezza*, *Annabella*, and *Marie Claire*) and for a long time dedicated his time to the International Wool Secretariat. Known for his sense of irony, corrosive jokes, coyness and introversion, he became renowned for his avant-garde collections of clothes, knitwear, furs, shoes, and sportswear. ("What I prefer is sport at a very high level. And I think I have been one of the first to use this type of clothing in eveningwear."). From 1973 to 1990 he created albums and colors for Pitti Filati and the Avia factory (then Zegna-Baruffa). Always faithful to his personality and style, he still creates up-to-date collections. He teaches at the Polimoda in Florence.

❑ 2003, July. The exhibition "Alberto Lattuada: a Master at Polimoda" was held at the Costume Gallery in Palazzo Pitti. The exhibition was split into: "rural country western," "Manhattan Rhapsody," and the wonderful "Victorian eccentrics." The event stressed the success and extraordinary career of this illustrator-designer, a leading figure in Italian fashion for 50 years. Alberto Lattuada is well recognizable for the incisiveness of his work, and the cultivated and refined style with which he has described, with subtle irony, the birth and the evolution of the Italian fashion industry.

Lauffenmühler German textile group. A leader in Europe, it employs about 450 people. The company, was founded in 1835 by Johannes Müller from Lauchringen, in the region of high Renania. Its production department is organized vertically, from the production of thread to that of fashion fabrics, high performance fabrics for technical and protective use, elasticized materials, and shirt fabrics. Its products are known internationally. They are essentially based on cotton: yarns and fabrics worked in the Lauchringen plant are submitted to high precision quality controls, while dyeing, finishing and surface treatments are carried out in the plants at Wiese in Lörrach-Brombach. The company achieved DIN EN ISO 9001 certification in 1992.

Laug André (1931-1984). French designer. After working as a military trainer and in an import company, he decided to abandon the north of France and moved to Paris. Here he made his fashion début, designing for the fashion house Raphael in its early days, and at the same time learning everything about the organization and the creative system in an *haute couture* maison. After three years he gave this up to work for Nina Ricci as the assistant to Monsieur Creay on the maison's first collection for the American market. As a freelancer he also worked for Philippe Venet and Courrèges. Maria Antonelli invited him to Rome in 1961 and it turned out to be a successful relationship. He designed nine *haute-couture* collections for her and six *prêt-à-porter* during a partnership that lasted five years. In 1968 he opened his own atelier in Piazza di Spagna. His style was characterized by great care attached to the fabrics, and the almost austere elegance in his skilfully finished clothes. He died in Rome. Since then his *griffe* has continued under the management of Olivier.

A design by André Laug.

Laugesen Jens (1967). Danish designer. He moved to Paris in 1987 to study *Haute couture* at the Chambre Syndicale de la Mode, from which he graduated in 1991. Once back in Denmark, he became a fashion journalist working as a freelancer for several Scandinavian magazines. In 1994 he returned to Paris to gain a Master's degree in Fashion Management at the Institute Français de la Mode. Then for six years he worked as a designer at several Parisian maisons. In 2000 he studied for another Master's degree, this time in Fashion Design, at London's Central St. Martin's College. His show at the end of the course was very successful and the Maria Luisa boutique in Paris dedicated its shop windows to his clothes during the Paris *haute couture* week. His headquarters are now in London where, at the end of 2002, he launched his own brand of women's clothing.

(*Virginia Hill*)

Laura Ashley English brand of fabrics and clothing since 1954. It was created by the genius and business intuition of Laura Mountney (1925-1985) and her husband Bernard Ashley. They lived for seven years in London. In 1961 they moved to Wales and everything changed. The rural and romantic atmosphere which surrounded them gave Laura her first ideas for an article of clothing: a short-sleeved cotton top inspired by a gardener's shirt. Since that time floral patterns were always found on her designs: from pinafore dresses to Edwardian style dresses with frills, tight bodices, and puffed sleeves. Other than clothing, she became famous all over the world for launching a country-chic style that took in wallpaper, bed linen, and interior décor fabrics. Today the brand has stores all over the world and a mail-order catalogue.

(*Eleonora Platania*)

❑ 2002, May. The year closed with a growth in turnover of 7% to €448.4 million but a fall in before-tax profits of 9%.
❑ 2002, May. Laura Ashley suffered again from the decline in clothes sales. It core business – interior décor – is the one the company decided to bet on, and reorganized the distribution network.
❑ 2003, January. The British brand announced the closure of 35 stores in Europe, meaning it gave up on the German market and underwent reorganization in Holland, Belgium, and France.
❑ 2003, May. In the fiscal year ending 25 January, the British company registered a before-tax loss of £4.9 million (€8.7 million), against a net profit of 9.3 millions the previous year. Turnover rose 5.5% to £292 million pounds, with sales growing 6% (at constant exchange rates) in the United Kingdom, but declined 9% in the rest of Europe.

Lauren Ralph (1939). American designer, born Ralph Lipschitz in Bronx, New York. A self-taught fashion designer, he learned the profession working between 1956 and 1966 as a shop assistant, buyer, and agent in several department stores in New York, including the Alexander stores, Allied stores, Bloomingdale's, Brooks Brothers, and Rivetz in Boston. He took evening courses in business management at City College in New York. In 1967 he designed a handmade tie collection branded Polo for Beau Brummel. Its huge success took him, a year later, to establish the independent brand, Polo by Ralph Lauren, which made its début with a tailored menswear collection. Since starting out, his style has interpreted the past with a touch of romanticism, blending the traditions of the English aristocracy, above all, the impeccable Duke of Windsor, with the stars of old Hollywood, such as Cary Grant and Fred Astaire. He then designs bearing in mind such things as sports, African safaris, and vacations in New England. He says: "My purpose in fashion is to achieve the dream of dreams: the most beautiful reality that one can imagine." In this manner he has created a style that is by now recognized as typically American. He designs for Wasps (White Anglo-Saxon Protestants), but his style is appreciated all over the world by those looking for a slice of the American Dream. In 1971 he launched his first womenswear collection and introduced the famous logo of the polo player into knitwear. That same year Lauren opened his first boutique in Beverly Hills, and a corner space in Bloomingdale's, New York. The first international store opened in London in 1981 and now there are more than 100 around the world. The New York showroom in the former Rhinelander mansion in Madison Avenue opened in 1986; it mirrors his way of thinking about fashion and life, proposing an eternal elegance and a very high, timeless quality. There are now about 20 clothing lines for men, women, teenagers and children. His several fragrances and the line of household items are also successful. Several lines of accessories are produced under license. He has also designed several costumes for the cinema. In 1973 he clothed Robert Redford in the movie version of F. Scott Fitzgerald's *The Great Gatsby*. In 1977 he launched a new fashion when he dressed Diane Keaton in men's clothes in Woody Allen's *Annie Hall*: jackets and pants in soft tweeds, shirt and tie, waistcoat and felt hats, everything assembled in a totally new ironic and sensual way. The list of prizes and awards he has won is extremely long, including an ad honorem degree in Classical Literature from Brandeis University in 1996. Some of his creations are in the permanent collection of New York's Fashion Institute. In 1983 a retrospective of his work was held in the Denver Art Museum in Colorado. He has made significant donations to humanitarian causes, for example, research into cancer and Aids. In 1998 he offered 13 million dollars for the restoration of the first American flag, the original star-spangled banner. The company was quoted on the New York Stock Exchange in 1997. Two years later it was bought by Club Monaco, Canadian traders in retail fashion, for 52.5 million dollars, making its own name as one of the international powers in the field of *prêt-à-porter*.

❑ 2000, January. The American company bought the licensee company for Europe, Poloco of Paris, for 200 million dollars.

❑ 2001, August. Lillian Wang von Stauffenberg and Lauren DuPont were the new designers for the women's collection.

❑ 2001, September. In the first half of the year the company had a turnover of \$898.3 million, +3.8% on 2000; net profits amounted to \$125.1 million. The multinational had 231 stores worldwide. In the United States sales represented 78.1% of the total; in Japan and Europe, respectively, 10% and 7.3%. The clothes and shoes bearing the Ralph Lauren brandname were mostly manufactured in Italy.

❑ 2001. Global sales reached a level of 2.6 billion dollars.

❑ 2002, February. For the first time the group presented its men's collection in Milan, in its headquarters at 27 Via San Barnaba (designed by the architect Mino Fiocchi). It is an exact reproduction of the designer's house.

❑ 2002, December. 25 years after signing a license agreement with Seibu, Ralph Lauren took back control in Japan, acquiring 50% of the company operating under the general license. The total investment amounted to \$70 million.

❑ 2003, January. Lauren chose Via

Montenapoleone for his first own-brand boutique in Milan. The store was expected to open in 2004.
❑ 2004, March. With more than 20 collections, 265 stores all over the world and a retail value of 8 billion euros, Polo Ralph Lauren aims at reaching, in the next five years, a turnover of 1 billion dollars in the European continent alone.
❑ 2004, September. The American maison opened its flagship store in Via Montenapoleone, Milan, though it already has 12 others already in Europe.
❑ 2005. Sales grew around 38%.
❑ 2005, February. Notable increase in profits, especially in the third and the last quarter of 2004. And the new year begins with an increase of receipts, rising to 74.8 million dollars, over the 35.4 million of the year before. Increasing sales, with a rise of 38 percent.

(*Dario Golizia*)

Lavallière Muslin tie with a soft, swaying effect. It was named after Louise de la Vallière, the favorite of Louis XIV. Used also by men, especially in the nineteenth century, and an accessory of the woman's tuxedo.

An English dandy and his valet trying to knot a Lavallière tie, 1838 (from *188 Tie Knots*, by D. Mosconi and R. Villorosa, Overseas, 1984).

Laver Jacques (1899-1970). English scholar of costumes and curator of the Fashion Fund at the Victoria and Albert Museum. His studies of dress styles in Europe through the centuries have highlighted the close relationship that exists between appearance and psychological mood: "We wear our spirit, not our body." According to Laver, through their wardrobe, men tend to set a hierarchy, whereas women use theirs to attract. Among his books: *Costume in Antiquity Clothes* (1952) and *Modesty In Dress* (1969).

La Viola Claudio (1948). Italian designer of fashion and interior décor. Born in Milan, he started his career in the 1970s/80s with a men's boutique, where he offered classic garments, though with new cuts and proportions. At present he is mainly involved with the design of articles of interior décor and accessories.

Lazareff Hélène (1909-1988). French journalist. A symbol of the contemporary female press. She was hired at Paris-Soir in 1938 but her real apprenticeship took place in New York, under the guidance of Carmel Snow and Diana Vreeland at *Harper's Bazaar*. Once back in Paris, she opened the monthly *Elle*, which she then turned into a weekly. The "Czarina" (from the title of a biography of her) was ahead of the times: she introduced an innovative form of journalism, anticipating many aspects of feminism and working with the big names in photography. In 1965 she received the Neiman Marcus Award.

Lazzaroni Nuccio (1938). Italian designer and fashion illustrator. An anti-character par excellence, reserved, more similar in appearance to a professor or a businessman than a fashion designer. After starting his design career very young for important fashion houses (Carosa, Antonelli), boutique collections (Gibò, Valditevere), and national and international magazines, and after working as a consultant for department stores (La Rinascente, Coin), he designed all the collections presented by Wanda Roveda at Palazzo Pitti and in Milan. He began to specialize in the creation of bridal dresses, and works with the most prestigious names in this sector in the international markets.

❑ 2002. He created the bridal collections for one of the most important Japanese multinationals.

Lds Italian textile company in Montemurlo di Prato. It manufactures three brands: Leathertex, Lds, and Lineaesse, each with different types of product, created by the businessmen Francesco Favini and Renzo Bini, whose credo it is to manufacture using new technologies. Leathertex was the first to be created, in 1970, and produced flocked fabrics, something that was completely new for Prato. Six years later came Lds, with coagulated and smeared materials, and perfect, very soft imitation skins. By the time their children were working in the family business, the third brand, Lineaesse, was launched: this has the same innovative philosophy concerning the fabrics and is closer to local tradition, but was conceived with different criteria. Lds now uses three plants for its manufacturing, producing 4 million meters of fabrics a year. It emphasizes high quality technology and research, and attention to ecological matters through the use of sophisticated procedures and the purification of working environments. In 1981 Franco Bini (Renzo's son) and Vieri Favini (Francesco's son) took over the company. The Group is undergoing increasing expansion. The separate but complementary activities of the three companies cover the markets from shoes to leather goods, interior décor, clothing for the young, and synthetic furs.

Leacril Synthetic fiber produced in Italy. It has several advantages: it is resistant, soft, light and elastic.

Leather Animal skin, usually from cows, that is tanned to prevent decay and improve suppleness and strength. It can be finished in various ways, including glazed, colored and sueded. Many designers from the 1960s on have included leather clothing in their upscale ready-to-wear collections, including Yves Saint Laurent, Versace and Armani.

Leathertex Italian textile company located in Montemurlo. Established in 1976. It produces smeared, coagulated, polyurethane fabrics, reinvented finishings, imitation skins and synthetic furs. It employs 120 people. The production cycle respects strict ecological rules. The company's top products are higly resistant flocks in nylon, velvets, quilted damasks, reproduction skins, including stretch versions, and the X-Type line for sportswear and streetwear.

Lebedev Tatiana. Russian designer and costume designer. She studied art at the Academy of Fine Arts in Moscow (1982) and set and costume design at the Theater School of Moscow (1989). She worked as a costume designer until 1992, when she moved to Paris to attend the fashion course at the École de la Chambre Syndicale de la Mode. She gained experience in the theatrical field and with Parisian designers such as Chantal Thomass. In 1995 she created her first collection of womenswear. The following year she created the brand FuturWareLab. Her collections are always forward-looking and typified by technological research. Contemporaneously, she continues her career as a costume designer.

Le Bihan Marc (1967). French designer, born in Paris. From 1982 to 1986 he was an apprentice at the very famous Manifacture des Gobelins, and collaborated with the artists Telemaque, Burraglio, and Ribberzani. From 1990 to 1993 he attended the ENSAD school and, immediately after, courses at Central Saint Martin's College in London. He won an award at the Hyères festival dedicated to young artists in 1993. The following year he created his own *griffe* and presented his designs in Paris in 1995. Two years later he launched a unisex line. In March 1998 he participated at the exhibition *Createurs de Passions* at the Carousel du Louvre, which features 22 young French designers during Paris fashion week. The exhibition later moves around Europe, America and the Far East.

Leblon Sege (1964). Belgian photographer. He studied in Brussels at INSAS and became interested in photography while reporting on the war in Lebanon. He then moved on to fashion photography, and was immediately published in several magazines – *The Face*, *Dazed and Confused*, *Big*, *Jalousie*, *i-D*, *Self Service*, *Purple*, *Doing Bird*. He worked with brands, such as Cacharel, and with young designers, like Tsumori

Chisuto. He was also involved in exhibitions in Brussels, New York, and Tokyo. In 2000 the publishing company Basel published a monograph of his.

Lebole Long existent brand of the Marzotto Group. Created as a clothing company during Italy's economic boom, Lebole clothed generations of the lower-middle and middle classes. In the mid-1980s, together with Lanerossi, it was taken over by Marzotto. Though losing much of the prestige it had enjoyed during the roaring 1960s, Lebole continued to maintain its leadership in Italy in the sale of jackets and coats (about 4.1% market share), with a turnover in 1998 of about $50 million. In 1998 the brand began a radical restyling, adding shirts, knitwear, and accessories to its range of suits. It expanded its collection and opened dozens of corners in the most important Italian department stores.

Lebon Mark (1957). English photographer. He studied at the West Surrey College of Art & Design and specialized in Communication Design at the North East London Polytechnic. Until the early 1980s he was a fashion photographer for magazines like *i-D*, *The Face*, *Arena*, *Blitz*, *Vogue*, *Harper's Bazaar*, and *Queen*. He worked with the designers Rifat Ozbeck, John Galliano, Jean Paul Gaultier, Vivienne Westwood, and Bodynap. He lives and works in London.

Le Bon Marché This is the oldest of the Paris department stores. Founded in 1852 by Aristide Boucicaut, 25 years later it had become the largest retail store in the world. Its characteristics of free entrance, fixed and marked prices, and a continuous supply of goods were once innovative but are now common. It was originally called Au Bon Marché and inspired Zola to write his book *Au Bonheur des Dames*. When it was bought and relaunched by the Group Agaghe in 1987, it turned the *Au* into *Le*.

Lebourg Christophe (1962). French designer. After graduating from the Parisian school de la Chambre Syndicale de la Confection et de la Couture, he received training with Andrevie, Montana and Yamamoto. These are excellent credentials and the Textile Financial Group hired him to design a minor collection. He made his début in 1984, almost hiding behind the pseudonym of Christophe Dimitrios. Success, though, convinced him to reveal his identity in the second show. Despite working for third parties – Callaghan, three years of artistic direction at Cacharel from 1986 to 1988, Tarlazzi and Lanvin – he did not give up working on his own collections. This is why his *griffe* goes missing for long periods, but always reappears on the catwalks eventually.

Le Cachemirien The Paris shop (Rue de Tournon) belonging to clothes designer Rosenda Arcioni Meer, an Italian from Fabriano, married to an Indian. Born to a family of horse-breeders, at the age of 18 she moved to Hamburg to study. After her degree she arrived in New York to follow the course of the Fashion Institute of Technology. She returned to Italy to work as a designer at Byblos, but understood there was more she wanted to learn. In Paris she studied Vionnet's oblique cutting and the art of draping at Madame Grès. She met and married an Indian, and then discovered his country and its fabrics. Since then she has not designed an item of clothing that is not made with Indian fabrics: embroidered organza from Kerala, muslin from Bengala, "brocart" from Benarès, cashmere. She opened a crafts shop in Kerala and the Paris shop in 1995.

L'Eclaireur Parisian boutique. The creators of this famous boutique are Martine and Armand Halida, who offer typically French brands to their predominantly Arab clientele. The shop, which opened in the Avenue des Champs-Elysées in January 1980, only measured 23.4 square yards but immediately became a reference point for fashion and the first boutique in town to sell Timberland shoes. In 1990 the shop moved to Rue des Rosiers, in the heart of the fashion neighborhood of Marais. They not only sold clothing, but also accessories, design objects, and furniture, and in 2000 opened a space dedicated to menswear. In January 2003 Hadida launched the felt sculptures of the young artist Cyprien Chabert in a new space at the Palais Royal, which he had inaugurated with the erotic drawings of Piero Fornasetti. At present the Hadida family is

engaged in new projects which include exhibitions and events linked to gastronomy.
(*Maddalena Fossati*)

Lecoanet Hemant French fashion house. In 1994 the maison won the *Dé d'Or*, the Oscar of Parisian shows. It was born from the business partnership between Didie Lecoanet (1955), a young designer who had just graduated from the Roederer Academy and completed an apprenticeship by Lanvin, and Sagar Hemant (1957) who, born in New Delhi, studied fashion management in Germany. They started with a boutique in Faubourg Saint-Honoré. In 1984 the maison presented its designs. The following year, the pair became a foursome with the arrival of Roy Gonzales, who had worked with Cardin and Patou, and Juliette Cambursano, who formerly worked at Balenciaga.

Leddi Colomba (1963). Milanese designer. She attended the Conservatory Giuseppe Verdi and graduated from the Marangoni Institute. In the early 1980s she started working with several designers, one of whom was Nanni Strada. In 1992 she joined the "Frammenti" group founded by Ada Lusena (a designer who worked with Walter Albini and Romeo Gigli). After four years she opened her own atelier in the yard of an old building in Via Rovere. Her collections are independent of any trends or fashion; they are based on forms and materials inspired by different epochs and cultures that she reinterprets. It is a new way to consider the tailoring profession: starting from a predefined base, there are several variables that determine the choice of fabrics and colors to suit a customer's taste and needs. Her creations are often one-off pieces manufactured following traditional methods. She follows her own ideas, mixing traditional patterns with an oriental inspiration, creating caftans and embroidered jackets with contrasting linens. She uses details such as high-quality embroidery wisely. She is very careful in the materials she uses: cotton gauzes, Indian silks, linen, and cotton for the Summer, velvet, coarse Scottish wools, and jacquard fabrics for the Winter. In March 2002 Colomba Leddi's Fall-Winter 2002 collections were presented at the seventeenth Parisian Workshop, together with ten other up-and-coming names in Italian fashion. In October 2003 she was at White Milano, the event organized by Superstudiopiù that focuses on womenswear and accessories.

Le Drezen Christian (1968). French designer. Self-taught, he started as Kenzo's assistant and then passed to the womenswear style office at Christian Dior. His first women's collection was presented in 1998. He also designs theater costumes and handmade bijoux.

Lee Brand of jeans ranked second in the world after Levi's. They were first manufactured in 1889 for the cattle-breeders of Kansas by David Lee. Also by Lee was the ancestor of the overall, the Lee Union-All, which was launched in early 1890, while the first zip-fastening jeans appeared during the 1920s. In 1969 the brand was bought by the giant Vanity Fair Corporation, which also owns another important jeans label, Wrangler.

Lee Jeong Woo (1957). Korean designer. Daughter of Lee Young Hee, one of the most esteemed couturiers in her home country. She studied at Ewha University in Seoul and in 1992 attended the Esmod fashion school. The following year she became her mother's assistant. In 2001 she presented her designs at the Paris *prêt-à-porter* week, and the same year she launched the fragrance *Sa Fille*. She is also present at Seoul's Fashion Week.

Lee Jimin (1967). Korean designer who grew up in the Philippines, studied in New York and Paris, and then moved to Hong Kong in 1994. There for 6 years she worked for Joyce Ma, designing the maison's luxury line. She then went back to New York, where she opened her first boutique and in 2001 a second in Seoul. She has an open smile and a curiosity about the world. Her fashion is a mix of East and West, customs and traditions, rituals and atmospheres blended with daily life, free inventions inspired by the martial arts and Buddhist monks. A favorite theme of her style is the mixture of fragments of ethnic traditions with mysticism, plus a dose of male-female, simple-sophisticated contrasts. (*Lucia Mari*)

Lee Young Hee Fashion brand launched in Paris by the designer Lee Young Hee to alternating fortunes in French fashion. In 1997 she started to prepare her succession, leaving the maison's direction to her young daughter (Lee Jeong Woo), with whom she created a collection. Her style makes use of Asiatic traditions in a mix of shiny jerseys, glazed leather and transparent veils.

Le Fay Morgane Brand of Zen-style ready-to-wear-fashion: very light and large fabrics; veils over veils of different shades, so as to create movement. The designers are Liliana and Carlos Casabal. From Argentina, where they opened their first boutique in 1972, they moved to New York in 1982, and opened a small atelier. Working at first alone, they now have more than 100 collaborators, and very elegant boutiques in Manhattan and California.

Leflesh Brand created in 2001 by Edward Buchanan, an English designer, and Manuela Morin, an Italian stylist. He studied at the Parson's School of Design, while she graduated from FIT (Fashion Institute of Technology) in New York. After some working experiences at Michael Kors, Gap and Giorgio Armani, Edward arrived at Bottega Veneta in 1996 where he became the designer of the men and women's *prêt-à-porter*. Here he met Manuela, who had already worked for the Group as a consultant, then as the designer of their shoes and accessories. In 2001 they resigned, she to work for Anna Molinari, he with Iceberg. In the same year they presented their own brand Milan's *prêt-à-porter* week.

(*Maddalena Fossati*)

Le Franc Bérengère (1969). French designer of *prêt-à-porter*. She arrived in fashion after seven years of TV journalism. In 1997 she decided to attend the Esmod courses in Paris, and started her fashion career as a clothesmaker for Pao Mao. She made her début during a collective show in September 1999. Her fashion aims at, as she herself claims, "redistributing the body's proportions." Her style is minimalist, but she uses volumes. For the Spring-Summer 2000 collection, she used technological materials and laser cutting.

Léger Hervé (1957). French designer. He started as the assistant of Tan Giudicelli and later Karl Lagerfeld, working on Fendi furs and Chanel collections. In 1985, he launched his own label, which underwent some ups and downs, but found funding of 50% from the Seagram Group in 1992. Léger is a self-taught designer and trained originally as a hairstylist.

(*Valeria Vantaggi*)

Léger Michel (1947). Self-taught French designer. He started as a window-dresser, then, in 1974, presented a collection of sweaters for the Italian company Beutler. In 1976 he opened a boutique selling clothes he designed himself. He has often drawn inspiration from the style and technique of Fortuny. In 1983 he moved to Japan, where he still lives and works successfully. In 1990 he started a menswear line.

Leggings The idea of covering the ankle and the lower part of the leg was common in the Middle Ages as a means of keeping warm. The area covered can range from the foot up to the hip, to the thigh or simply up to the knee. Leggings are often fastened around the top of the foot. The practice of dressing legs was used for children and teenagers in the early 1900s, when spats were all the rage. During the 1980s, leggings returned to fashion, especially with leg warmers inspired by the world of ballet. Black was the prevalent color, but they also came in paler shades and different patterns.

Legler Italian cotton mill in Ponte San Pietro, near Bergamo, established in the second half of the 1800s by the Swiss Legler family. In 1972 the Leglers joined a group which, headed by the State institute Gepi, rescued a famous Italian cotton mill, the one built near Capriate d'Adda in 1878 by Cristoforo Crespi (his brother Benigno founded the newspaper Corriere della Sera with Luigi Torelli Viollier), and in 1976 the Legler family took complete control. The mill (spinning, weaving and dyeing) is famous above all for its enlightened form of neo-capitalism of the founder, who built a workers village around the factory that featured houses, a school, a kindergarten, a church, and social centers. The village is a still an example of excellent industrial architecture and has been renamed Crespi d'Adda. Following a crisis, around 1930 the ownership of the company passed to Banca Commerciale Italiana, which merged the cotton mill with two other companies to create Stabilimenti Tessili Italiani (S.t.i.). In 1935 the bank sold its ownership, and the company, which manufactures raw yarns and finished spun yarns for knitwear and hosiery factories, was first directed by Bruno Canto, later by Michele Bagnarelli. It eventually merged with the company Manifattura Rossari & Varzi. In 1971, the mill went into liquidation and, the following year, the Legler family heard its story. They succeeded in relaunching it to produce denim and widening the production to include cotton based Flat and Cord fabrics. During the 1980s, the Legler family sold their ownership to the Polli group, which is at present supported in its management of the mill by the Indian Group Piramal.

❑ 2001. Turnover was €228.9 million, +13% on 2000, with a gross operating margin above €25 million. Over the previous two years, the annual production of denim passed from 17 to 28 million meters. The times of crisis of mid-1990s had long since passed: at that time debts amounted to 400 million dollars.
❑ 2002, January. In order to support its investments, the company raised some capital, taking it from €33.5 to 44 million. It also asked for a bank loan of €24 million.
❑ 2002. Turnover of €266.6 million, 55% of which from exports. The company employed 776 workers.

Le Gouès Thierry (1964). French photographer. Since 1986 he has worked for important international magazines such as *Vogue*, *Glamour*, *Arena*, *Harper's Bazaar*, *Interview*, and *W Magazine*. He lives and works in Paris and New York.

Le Grand Lionel. French glove maker. Active from the 1930s to the 1970s. He was the inventor of the velvet-calfskin, a very soft material. He has often worked with the great Paris designers creating gloves for shows to match the various collections. He also exported French brands into the United States brands through license agreements. Hermès, Fath and Dior owe him their introduction to the US.

Legroux Soeurs French maison of *haute couture* established in Roubaix in 1913 and moved to Paris in 1917. Of the two sisters who founded and guided it well after the 1950s, the history of fashion especially remembers Germaine for her discreet creative talent and commercial ability, which prompted her to take frequent trips around Europe to test the market.

Legs The so-called "zones of respect" of the human body, almost always belonging to women, have never ceased to play a defining role in the alternation of fashions, and in the continual seesaw of concealment and display. The taboo which for centuries surrounded the sight of women's legs has now been done away with – for a very long time women and fashion had no legs – but it still stirs old emotions that have not been diminished one iota by the extraordinary shortening of the skirt for which Mary Quant was responsible in the 1960s. Among the most meaningful pictures to illustrate the Belle Époque is the one of the lady who, getting on a streetcar and lifting her dress, offers her ankle and part of the calf to the avid glances of the ticket collector and an elegant gentleman with a straw hat. Such a sight was a rarity, and an occasion not to be missed. More intense, but essentially identical, is the glance of the young man in a recent TV advertisement that follows the movements of the long legs of a girl wearing fishnet tights as she gets into a car. Of course our eyes are more accustomed to this kind of view than those of the gentlemen of the early 1900s, but as a song of the period between the two images says: "Black eyes are very beautiful, blue eyes even more, but I like legs further and further more." Legs are liked better because they were the last to be freed from the obsessive taboo imposed on them – a steady and silent taboo, as always occurs with things considered "evil" by the rule of an outdated Catholic Church. After all, legs were not even mentioned in any sumptuary laws, in fact legs were not talked about, full stop. But in 1553 a voice was raised to reproach the sinful audaciousness of women who had shortened their dresses, supposedly to prevent themselves from falling over in the mud, but also to show their velvet slippers and colorful stockings. This voice belonged to the legislators of Ascoli. What they referred to, in fact, was ankles, anticipating the fetishism, typical of the nineteenth century, that surrounded the sight of a foot revealed for an instant by an uplifted skirt. However, it is obvious that reference to a portion alludes also to the whole. But it was in the early days of World War I (1915) that ankles came into sight and, later, legs up to the knees. This was the moment that the association began between short skirts and war, or at least between short skirts and times of trouble. This was the result of women having to replace men at work, the need for them to move without hindrance, the need to save on clothing materials, and because, as the war was killing off the country's youth, it was beneficial to arouse men's desire in order to balance the demographic gap. All true. But the *garçonne* who hid her curves but, with her androgynous cunning, showed her legs, was simply copying a tiny slice of the sexual freedom of her male counterpart. Studies on changes in taste, skirt volumes, and the relative heights of hemlines show that over the span of a century there were minimum alterations in the amount of visible leg. In the 1930s, there were variations of only a few centimeters of leg left visible above the ankles. It is known that Dior's famous New Look – a reaction to the privations and humiliations of the war – was quickly rebuffed by women for its rejection of the corset and their lost freedom to show their calves. But in the long-term, in the late 1950s and early 1960s, the image of the tape measure on the front pages of newspapers indicating the length or shortness of a skirt, was all the rage in the battle of the hemline. Then came the revolutionary miniskirt which revealed women's thighs. It was an extraordinary shock. It is true that the sight of women's legs signalled the disappearance of favorite seduction accessories such as bras and garters, yet men's euphoria at the advent of the miniskirt remained for years after its passing, even when women's fashion, which originated in the streets and was copied by designers, offered the unflattering maxiskirt, and boots and trousers started hiding what had previously been left visible. But among the many revivals of the 1980s, miniskirts made a comeback, though they were somewhat altered. Women's legs no longer shot out from beneath a tight piece of cloth in a healthy, athletic manner, but they deliberately and provocatively extended from petal-shaped skirts or very indiscreet hot pants. Since then, variations in the length of hemlines have coexisted, and often long skirts simply make use of very long slits to show a flash of legs inside. Thus, it might be said that, at the start of the 21st century, legs have lost that pre-eminence that was so long denied them and which was then thrust limitlessly upon them. Once again, generous necklines and the use of transparent materials distributed over all parts of the female body have returned to the spotlight those divine parts of the female body that are the favorite target of censure and the glory of the curvaceous women of the 1950s.

(*Lucia Sollazzo*)

Lehl Jurgen (1944). Japanese designer. Although he was born in Poland and lived for a long time in Germany, he is deeply attached to the oriental lifestyle and philosophy. He is a big innovator in the field of techniques: for example, laser cutting, computerized information of details sent to knitwear machines, and extreme care taken in the choice of materials and new technological fabrics. He is a fan of the purity of the kimono and the simplicity of lines, because it leaves him free to focus on fabrics and colors. He designed an underwear and a household line for Tint. His *prêt-à-porter* line was created in 1972 after he had worked in a Japanese textile industry.

Lei Monthly magazine of the group Condé Nast Italy. Founded and directed by Flavio Lucchini, its target market is girls who already have an independent life or who would like to. Compared to the traditional glossy magazines produced by the publisher, this magazine is daring in its graphics. The models are taken from the streets, and the fashion illustrated is decidedly wearable, even if it slightly anti-conformist. The periodical was initially received enthusiastically by the public but after two years sales declined. The editor tried to change the magazine's profile, calling in Franca Sozzani to edit it in 1981. The graphics and content were altered, and the public and new advertisers seemed to support this change in direction. But decline loomed. In 1989 Donatella Sartorio was given the task of halting the slide in sales and Neville Broday was in charge of the graphics. Nonetheless, sales continued to decline. In 1991 further changes were made: Giovanna Calvenzi, formerly of Rizzoli (photo-editor of *Amica* and chief-editor of *Max*) was appointed as the new director, but the crisis continued and the magazine closed.

(*Stefano Grassi*)

Leiber Judith (1921). American designer. She established the leather goods and accessories' brand carrying her name. Born in Budapest, Judith Peto (who married Gerson Leiber in 1946) received her training in the Hungarian Bag Association. In 1947 she moved to the United States where she earned her living designing for the manufacturers on Seventh Avenue. In 1963 she decided to start her own business. Her day and night bags, hand-cut and sewn with meticulous craftsmanship, and manufactured in crocodile, silk and metal, and often studded with precious stones, have been very successful and are collectors' items.

(*Eleonora Attolico*)

Leibovitz Annie (1949). American photographer. Famous for her portraits, Leibovitz has always been particularly interested in letting a person's true nature reveal itself. She took the photos for Krizia's catalogue in 1993, and took the opportunity to photograph Mariuccia Mandelli. In 1969 she started studying art and photography at the San Francisco Art Institute, and the same year registered her first success as a photographer with a portfolio presented to Robert Ingsbury, art director of *Rolling Stone* magazine. Jan Wenner, its editor-director, asked the young photographer to accompany him to New York to photograph John Lennon during an interview. One of these portraits was published on the cover. In 1973 Annie Leibovitz was made the magazine's photographer-in-chief, a position she retained until 1983, when she joined *Vanity Fair*. About her working style, she says: "It's a real joy to be photographed by me. Sometimes I ask people to pose in mud or I have them hanging from the ceiling." Her portraits of people from showbiz and the art world are fascinating for her settings, the rejection of any hagiography or embellishment. Consecrating the sitter is not part of her style; on the contrary, she always introduces a touch of humor or irony in her pictures. She lives and works in New York.

(*Luca Selvi*)

❑ As strange as it can seem, her initial inspiration came from the photographs by Cartier-Bresson and those made by her father for the family album, which, when she has a solo exhibition, she displays in order to explain the origins of her visual taste. But they also explain the direct relationship that exists between the image and direct knowledge of people: she argues that, when she wants to photograph someone, in fact what is happening is that she wants to know that person. She has had exhibitions all over the world and published several books, one of which, *On Women*, was made with Susan Sontag in 2000. That same year, she took the extremely elegant photos of the girls for the Pirelli Calendar.

Leigh Dorian (1920). American model. She associated with the jet set and represented an ideal of style that harmonized with the New Look during the 1940s-50s. The muse of Richard Avedon and Irving Penn, her real name is Elizabeth Parker. Her sister Susy was also a very famous model. Brought up in a strict and very well-off family, Elizabeth did not try her fortune in Hollywood, notwithstanding Diana Vreeland's insistence, but inspired Truman Capote to write *Breakfast at Tiffany's*. In the 1960s she opened a modeling agency.

Leiter Saul (1923). American photographer, born in Pittsburgh. In Cleveland he attended a theological college, but quits in 1946 to move to New York to start working as a painter. Thanks to his friendship with Richard Pousette-Dart, he became interested in photography. An autodidact, his work started to be associated with that of the photographers of the New York School: William Klein, Helen Lewitt, and Robert Frank. In 1954 he opened his own studio. From 1958 he worked for Henry Wolf at *Harper's Bazaar*. In 1959 he moved to London for four years and worked for *Esquire*, *Elle*, *Snow*, *Queen*, *Vogue*, and *Nova*. He lives in New York.

Lella Chic Boutique located in Sesto San Giovanni, a small suburban town squeezed between the city of Milan and the city of Monza. Jolanda Cavaggion attempted to make the town more liveable in 1957 by opening a small, discreet shop that expanded during the 1980s, thanks to the taste and passion of Jolanda's daughter Lella. The small shop became a large, sophisticated boutique furnished with antiques. For more than 30 years, Lella Cavaggion won and maintained the esteem of the great names in international fashion by making her boutique a trendy point of reference. In addition to running the shop, Lella also worked as a fashion consultant and fashion coordinator for some of the largest clothing companies until the mid-1990s when, after a long and happy collaboration with Missoni, she decided to leave the world of fashion.

Lellasport A store in the heart of Milan and, later, a factory that made female sportswear. This brand has been worn by Milanese women for more than 30 years. It was established in the mid-1950s by Domenico Lella, a ski champion, with his wife Valeria Carema and sister Francesca (nicknamed Cicci), who made the decisions on style. These were Lellasport's business steps: a first store in San Pietro all'Orto and a workshop in Corsico; then a factory that produced windcheaters, tailleurs, trousers and pullovers, men's colored shirts, swimming costumes and horse-riding outfits. For many years the store also enjoyed the exclusiveness of Marinita's skirts; produced in very limited runs, they were very sought after. Nowadays Lellasport no longer has a store or a factory: its garments are made by others, which it sells in Italy, Switzerland, Germany, the United States, and Japan.

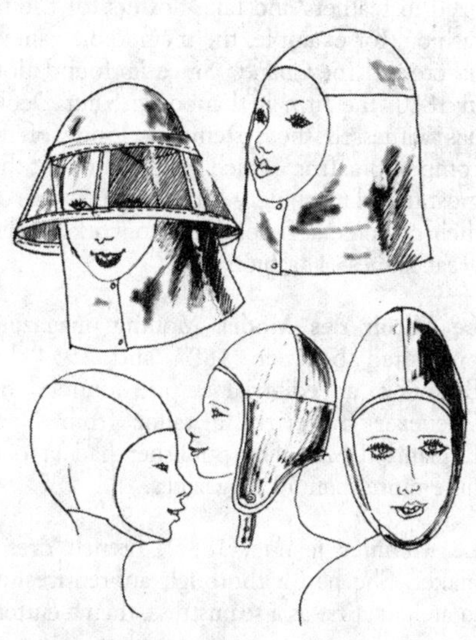

Casquettes and cagoules by Lellasport designed by Brunetta (Biki Collection).

Lelong Lucien (1889-1952). French tailor, founder of the maison which carries his name, one of those – like Molyneux, Patou, Schiaparelli, and Chanel – who created the prestige of French fashion after World War II, thanks to the closely linked relationship between stylism and culture: fabrics designed by Dalí and bijoux created by Cocteau. Lucien learned his trade with his father, Arthur, the founder of a fabric factory (1896), and his mother Eléanore, a good dressmaker. He discovered his vocation in the family business which, as soon as the World War I was over, he expanded by creating his own fashion house. With a workforce of 1,200 people, he became immediately famous for the neat tailoring of his designs, and his skill in choosing and manufacturing fabrics. He was assisted in this by his very beautiful wife Natalie Paléy, the daughter of the Grand Duke Paul of Russia. He later hired the most promising designers of the moment to design his collections: such names as Christian Dior, Pierre Balmain, and Hubert Givenchy. An enlightened manager, after a journey to the United States to learn the working methods in the mass production of clothes, he created a line of *prêt-à-porter* branded L.L. Edition. From 1937 till the end of World War II, he was President of the Chambre Syndicale de la Couture Parisienne, in which role he was able hinder the transfer of Parisian fashion houses to Berlin during the German occupation. But many of them had shut down, refusing to work so as not to be forced to sell their designs to the Germans. The maisons that continued to work were unable, one peace returned, to regain the status they had before the war – with one exception: Chanel.

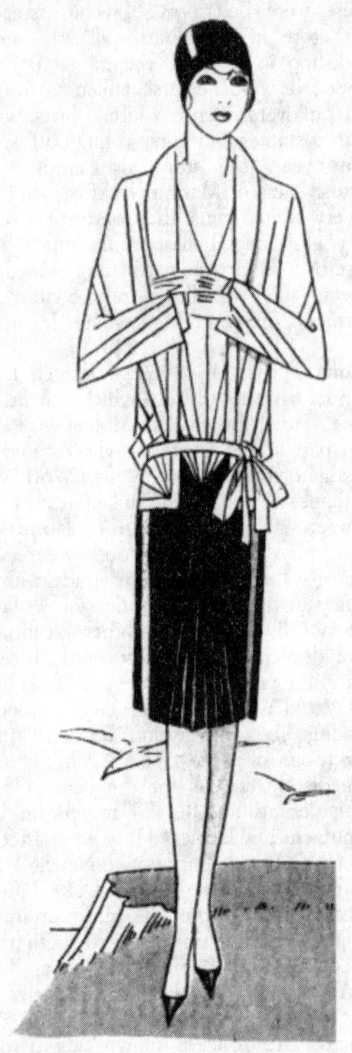

Lucien Lelong, Day's Outfit, 1928 (from *Anni Venti - La nascita dell'abito moderno*, Centro Di, Florence, 1991, catalogue for the Galleria del Costume).

LeMaire Charles (1897-1985). American designer and costume designer. He won three Oscars (*Eve against Eve* with Edith Head, *The Tunic* and *Love is a Many Splendored Thing*). He is part of cinema history, in particular for clothing Marilyn Monroe in her most important films: the red dress in *Niagara* or the flimsy pleated white dress lifted by the rushing air of the subway in *The Seven Year Itch*. Originally an actor, his real career started with Broadway shows, like *The Ziegfield Follies*. After moving to the world of cinema, he became head costume designer at Fox and participated in several productions, often working with other designers. He also worked in other kinds of films, thrillers included, such as *The Kiss of Death*. Without giving up the cinema, he opened his own atelier, designing clothes for the females stars in their private life. In 1962 he retired to devote himself to his favorite activities: reading and painting.

Lemaire Christophe (1965). French designer. He began his career working with Mugler, but got his apprenticeship with Yves Saint Laurent. He worked for Michel Klein but Klein quit in 1986 to work for Jean Patou, where Lacroix was head designer of *haute couture*. When Lacroix created his own atelier the following year, he took the 22-year-old Lemaire with him to head the *prêt-à-porter* department. In 1991 Lemaire created his first collection and in 1999 opened his first boutique in Rue de Sevigné, Paris.

Lemarié André. French house that specialized in feathers and fake flowers for use in fashion, for example, the memorable camellia created for Chanel. Since its foundation in 1880, the firm in Faubourg Saint Denis has witnessed the systematic closing of its competitors, from which the firm bought the most useful machinery and inherited some of their customers. It continues to work for the great names of fashion.

Le Miroir des Modes Monthly magazine published between 1887 and 1934 by Butterick, an editorial empire founded by Ebenezer Butterick, a tailor from New England (USA). The publisher had at one time more than 30 magazines.

Le Monnier Jeanne (1887). French dressmaker. She had a thorough apprenticeship in ateliers: first as a seamstress, then a cutter, and finally a première for ten year at Lewis. She started her own business during the 1920s and won fame in the Paris fashion world in the season between the two wars. After retiring (the date of her death is uncertain), Bernard Devaux took her place.

Lempereur French manufacturer established in 1929 and successfully directed by Albert Lempereur (1904), the grandson of a craftsman in the Parisian neighborhood of Marais, where the vast majority of clothing craftsmen and manufacturers are based. The term *prêt-à-porter* was coined by him as a literal translation of ready-to-wear, an expression he had discovered on a study trip to the United States after the war.

Lenci Light and compact cloth in various colors. It takes its name from Helenchen Konig-Scavini (1886-1974), nicknamed Lenci, the founder of the company that first manufactured it in Turin in 1919. With this particular fabric, which was perfected by her brother Bubine using the felt of Borsalino hats, she manufactured the famous dolls designed by the artists of that time: Riva, Chessa, Sturani, Quaglino, and Dudovich. Under the direction of Pilade Garella at the end of the 1920s, Lenci experienced international success. The company started to produce flowers and bouquets and, later, ceramic sculptures created by artists like Tosalli, Grande, and Vacchetti. They were exhibited during the 1930 Triennale at Monza. Today the factory is run by the Garel family.

Lenglen Suzanne (1899-1938). Tennis player, winner of the Wimbledon tournament. Patou designed her tennis outfits. She was born in Paris and spent her life between Paris, a country house in Marest-sur-Matz (Compiègne), Nice, and Paris again, where she died of malignant anemia. "More admired than Sarah Bernhardt, most desired than Josephine Baker, more elegant than Anna Pavlova," wrote her only biographer, Gianni Clerici (*La Diva du Tennis*, Rochevignes Ed., 1984. Paris), with a degree of exaggeration. European champion at the age of 15 in 1914, Susanne won her first Wimbledon after World War I in 1919. She continued to win there every time she entered the competition until 1925, with the exception of a single absence in 1924. In 1926, as the world number 1 (men included), she turned professional, making her début at Madison Square Garden, and earning 100,000 dollars for a four-month tour throughout the United States. She was the first tennis-player to abandon wearing a corset and to play in light clothes, a pleated, knee-length skirt, and stockings held by elastics bands around her thighs. She introduced the trend of wearing a silk turban, as well as that of the cardigan she wore during the warm-up (which always matched the turban). She asked Patou to design tennis garments which she both wore and sponsored, though this of course went against the rules of the amateur game.

Lenthéric Small perfume manufacturer founded in Paris by Guillaume Lenthéric in 1885. Not well-known abroad, but appreciated in France for its creativity, during *Les Années Folles* it commissioned Lalique and Baccarat to create stylish bottles (*A Bientôt*, *Coeur de Paris*, *Confetti* and, above all, *Le Parfum de la Dame en Noir*) that are now very rare collector's objects. Taken over by Dunhill in 1967, after a short time the maison closed down.

Leo Van (1921-2002). Real name Boyadijan Turkish, Van Leo was a photographer of Armenian origin who became a naturalized Egyptian. He arrived in Egypt with his family in 1924 and in 1927 moved to Cairo where he became a great portrait photographer in his studio in Avenue Fouad. Over 57 years of work, he photographed thousands of people, using a style reminiscent of the one used to portray Hollywood stars. For this reason, he is considered to have been one of the masters of "glamour" photography.

Léonard Maison producing *prêt-à-porter* and accessories, established in 1958 by Jacques Léonard. Daniel Triboullaird was the artistic spirit behind the company. In 1960 he patented a system of knitwear printing and raw manufacturing. During the 1970s he designed collections of silken jerseys, ties, and scarves. In 1984 he dared to create kimonos for the Japanese market, which sold with success. The Léonard boutiques (more than 130 in Japan and mainland Asia alone) offer men's *prêt-à-porter* collections, interior décor fabrics and bijoux.

Leonovitch Ekatarina. Russian designer, born in Moscow, where she graduated from the Textile Academy. Member of the Russian Association of Painters and Designers of the International Federation of Painters and Graphics of UNESCO. She loves extreme modernity in clothing and has always prompted young designers to follow their creative inclination, even risking severe criticism. Eclectic, with a strong personality, she designs clothes, paints, and fabrics, and illustrates books. She is a point of reference for those wishing to join the fashion business. (*Lucia Mari*)

Leopard Spotted animal fur, very rare and expensive. Characterized by small black spots on a white or golden brown background.

Leo Pizzo Goldsmith company established in Valenza (Italy) in 1971 by Leonzio Pizzo who, with his entrepreneurial spirit, hinted at the potential of industry in Valenza and focused especially on the export market, adopting artisan and semi-artisan's craft methods. The company, which reached high quality standards technically and for the use of expensive materials – for example, diamonds, precious colored stones, corals and turquoise in the Summer collections – has a totally in-house production cycle. Pizzo has been supported by his wife Rosaria Di Giorgio since 1988. He directs the creative team, developing traditional themes alongside those suggested by research, plus others of naturalist or *animalier* subjects, and in particular the image of the anchor, which has become one of the company's symbols. The brand is distributed in Europe, the USA and Asia in retail or bulk, as well as in Italy. (*Alessandra Quattordio*)

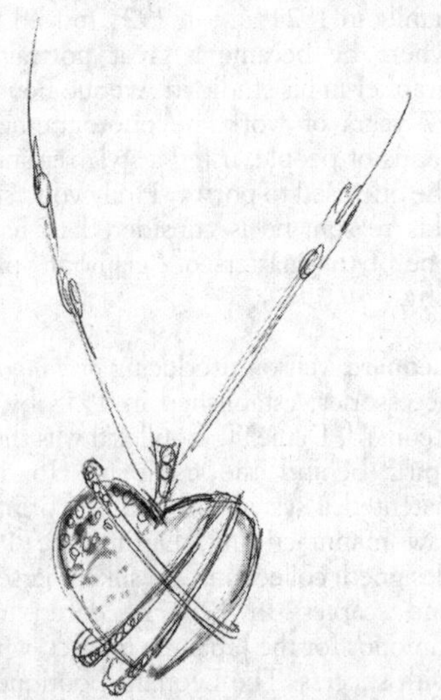
Heart-shaped pendant by Leo Pizzo.

Léotard The celebrated French trapeze artist Jules Léotard introduced this garment in 1800, since which time it has carried his name. During the 1950s it was used by dancers and gymnasts, though only in black. In the 1970s it became the traditional outfit of disco dancers. In 1965, the French designers Courrèges and Heim designed synthetic, elastic leotards in various fabrics and patterns, also in a leopardskin pattern. Manufactured in several materials, leotards are produced with different lengths of sleeve and necklines. They are a constant feature of athletes' and dancers' clothing, and as an item of general underwear.

Lepage Jean-François (1960). French photographer. He started his activity in the 1980s, working for the magazines of Condé Nast, but, after a decade, he quit the fashion world to devote himself to painting and artistic photography.

Lepage Serge (1936). French designer. He took over the artistic direction of Schiaparelli to promote its image, in accordance with the desire of the new owners. At the time, the news that a dress he created, embroidered with more than 500 diamonds, had to be escorted by the police created a sensation. While Serge Lepage worked for Schiaparelli, his own maison, which had been operating for fourteen years, remained closed. It reopened in 1979.

Lepape Georges (1887-1971). French illustrator. The women he drew had turned their backs on Decadentism, the frills of Art Nouveau and the Belle Époque, and started the age of the femme-*garçonne*. They were not *femmes fatales*, but they had a very jaunty, carefree look. In his two-dimensional photos, the color was distributed in blocks, like in oriental prints, by which Lepape was fascinated. In 1911 he designed the catalogue *Les Choses de Paul Poiret*, then went to work for Lanvin. His easily recognizable touch dominated various magazines for years, for example, *Gazette du Bon Ton*, *Fémina*, *Harper's Bazaar*, *Modes et Manières d'Aujourd'hui*, *Vanity Fair*, and *Vogue*. During the 1920s he held classes in New York and his drawings were imitated by young illustrators. His last cover drawing was 1938 but he later worked on book illustrations.

Lepel Corsetry company in Carpi (Italy). Since its foundation (1957), it has achieved and consolidated real leadership in the sector. Managed by the brothers Stefano and Massimo Leporati, the company has three plants – at Carpi, Poggio Rusco, and Colli del Tronto – which in 1998-99 produced a turnover of about 35 million dollars.

Le Petit Echo de la Mode Historical magazine in French women's publishing. Founded in 1880 by Monsieur de Penanster, at first it was a monthly with just four black-and-white pages. The magazine then went through a restyling, with the inclusion of a "detachable" novel, for a target audience of middle-class women. Success brought the magazine a very long life, even continuing to be published during the two World Wars. In 1955 it was renamed *L'Echo de la Mode*, and on 4 July 1977 it was absorbed into *Femme d'Aujourd'hui*.

Le Puy Capital of the French department Haute Loire. It is especially renowned for the traditional lacework that bears its name. Le Puy lace has a peculiar weave whose origin dates back to a young girl, Isabelle Mamour, who in 1407 is supposed to have created a dress for the Black Virgin to celebrate the famous statue's jubilee that year. Lace-making rapidly spread through the region and in the middle of the 17th century, after conquering Paris and the royal court, laces began to be exported to South America thanks to a missionary, François-Régis, who was later canonized and made the patron saint of lace workers. The first mechanical loom was introduced in 1893, which led to a huge expansion in output. The region counted 120 lace factories and 120,000 lace workers. From 1925, the Laurence family practically had the monopoly on lace products manufactured in Le Puy, enabling it to get through (though not without difficulty) the crises brought by the Wall Street Crash in 1929, World War II and the social upheavals of 1968, when part of women's protest rejected embroidered brands and underwear. In the late 1980s, George Laurence (from the family's fourth generation) introduced the mechanical spindle and won back prestigious customers (Lacroix, Balmain, Chanel, Chloé, and also Petit Bateau and La Perla), as well as conquering several foreign markets. Today Dentelles Laurence employs 25 people working 75 looms, but, since the fall of the Berlin wall, the countries of Eastern Europe have invaded the market with goods at very cheap prices, once again endangering the survival of Le Puy's lacemakers.

(*Mino Colao*)

Leroy Veronique (1965). Belgian designer. A young talent. She studied at the Studio Berçot in Paris. Later she became the assistant of Didier Renard, Alaïa, and Martine Sitbon. She opened her own atelier in the Parisian neighborhood of La Bastille. She defines her style "ultra sexy normal," and typical elements of it are humor, Barbie-style hairdos, fake cowboy boots, and very strident synthetic colors. She made her début in 1991. More than once she has been awarded the *Canette d'Or*, *Courtelle*, and *Venus de la Mode* for Le Futur Grand Créateur.

Lesage Albert (1888-1947). Founder of the famous Lesage embroidery maison established in 1924. But its story began earlier, when at the end of World War I, Albert, freed following four years of imprisonment in Germany, emigrated to the United States and found a job in Marshall Field's department store. At the time this was an important "practice ground" for him in learning how to cut made-to-measure clothes. Nostalgic for France, he returned to Paris in 1922, and set up in partnership with the embroiderer Michonnet who, since 1858, had been working for the great tailors, and two years later, took over the Marie-Louise Favot company and changed its name to his own. Besides becoming his wife,

Mademoiselle Favot was of major importance to the new company because she worked as a designer at Vionnet and opened this door to Lesage. He wanted to earn the dressmaker's esteem, therefore he invented shadowed embroidery and embroidery techniques suitable for oblique cutting. He became the favorite embroiderer of Maison Worth, Paquin, Lelong, and Molyneux, and, from 1934, of Elsa Schiaparelli, whom he assisted in conceiving and manufacturing highly decorated clothes based on sketches by Cocteau and other artists. After World War II, while his son François (born 1929) opens a branch office in Los Angeles, he created a Silk Department with Jean Barrioz. The following year, in 1947, Albert died. His son successfully took over the business, testing new materials and creating new professional alliances with Dior, Balmain, Balenciaga and, later, Givenchy, Saint-Laurent and the up-and-coming designers of the 1980s, such as Lagerfeld, Calvin Klein, Blass, and Hanae Mori. For every *haute couture* collection, Lesage offers couturiers from 100 to 120 embroidery samples: each sample requires between 20 and 30 hours of work. The maison's archives contain 60,000 samples. The chasuble and mitre worn by John Paul II on World Youth Day in 1997 were embroidered by Lesage. The Fashion Institute of Technology in New York, the Galliera Museum in Paris, the Fashion Foundation in Tokyo and the Los Angeles County Museum of Art have dedicated several exhibitions to the company's work. In 1987 the maison launched an accessory line, especially bags, designed by Gérard Trémolet. (*Valeria Vantaggi*)

Lesage Marion (1958). French designer. Her father is François Lesage, owner of the famous embroidery maison; her mother has designed for Griffe and Cardin. After high school, she attended Studio Berçot in Paris and in 1979 was hired as a designer by Benoît Bartherotte for the maison Estérel. In 1985 she created a line of jewelry of her own. In 1988, at the age of 30, she set up her own maison in partnership with Bartherotte and designed her first collection. Management problems forced her to close in 1992, but the company Jacques Garella immediately invested in a new brand of hers called Indies. In 1999 she opened a boutique in Rue du Près Au Clair, Paris, where her articles are inspired by travel.

Les Copains Italian clothing brand, synonymous with fashion for the young. Created in the 1950s, it took its name from the title of a successful French radio program entitled *Salut les Copains*. This was the start of the career of Mario Bandiera, who was otherwise fated to work in the antique business, like his father. He immediately captured the industry's attention with a beautiful knitwear collection. Knitwear became a style associated with freedom, and was to be at the center of the company's industrial development, which, in the 1960s, was based on what can be defined as Les Copains' historical creation: the mini-pull. Sufficiently tight to excite a young imagination, it was tested by the young girls working on Gianni Boncompagni's TV team. The company achieved one success after another, and was even praised by *The New York Times*, when in 1973 it praised the company's new women's *prêt-à-porter* line. There was no lack of imagination, or humor. In the 1980s, sweaters and T-shirts that ridiculed politicians became very popular. Winterwear was characterized by very tight striped T-shirts worn under wool jackets. Les Copains' styles for young girls consisted of tops, low-waist pants, tiny pullovers, tunics and blouses, made in constantly new technologically invented materials. Everything is of course sewn together using quality thread, the one currently used is made of cashmere. The company has acquired its renown as a result of two forward-looking steps in the Mario Bandiera's development strategy: the acquisition of 50% of the Maglificio di Marsciano (a company that manufactures cashmere knitwear), and the auction acquisition of the manufacturer Associata di Ponte Felcino 1862, which specializes in cashmere yarns and threads. The group places great importance on the continual updating of machinery. Exports total about 300,000 pieces a year, representing about 30% of overall global production. Les Copains also designs accessories, glasses, tiles, and perfumes. (*Lucia Mari*)

❑ 2001, April. Les Copains wanted to open a small building in Ginza to give a

new image, a total look, to Japanese consumers. Since 2000, the Japanese turnover has risen, partly due to the opening of new sales points. There are 15, 4 of which are own-brand shops, while the remaining 11 are shop-in-shop.
❑ 2002, April. License agreements signed with Drops for the rainwear collection of Fall-Winter 2002-2003 and with Unionseta to launch a men's and women's beachwear collection. Unionseta has a turnover of 8.5 million euros.
❑ 2002, May. The BVM Group, controlled by the Bandiera family, is headed by Les Copains. This month it acquired the majority shareholding in Lothar's. In 2001 BVM's turnover amounted to 140 million euros. In addition to Les Copains, BVM produces and distributes the brands Antonio Marras, Stefano Guerriero, and Victor Bellaish.
❑ 2003. The group's most recent line is called 86.62.88. Its contemporary identity is immediately revealed by the label's name. The numbers refer the body measurements of the new generation of young women. The brand has extended its presence in the world through 25 own-brand shops and 99 corners. Particular attention is paid to the evolution of Far Eastern markets, Arabian countries and the USA.
❑ 2003, July. A joint venture was set up with La Commerciale, a company owned by Gaetano Navarra and Marcello Casazza, which produces and distributes the Gaetano Navarra label. Gaetano Navarra's turnover is to be expanded using Les Copains' Japanese and American distribution channels. Production was to continue in La Commerciale's plants in Bologna. The result of this joint venture was to be Gaetano Navarra's men's collection.
❑ 2004, April. Les Copains signed an agreement with the Redwall Group, which would produce and distribute bags branded Les Copains and Blue Les Copains.
❑ 2004, September. Rodolfo Zengarini joined the maison as a partner for the production and distribution of Les Copains shoes.
❑ 2005, April. Antonio Berardi took over the creative direction of the brand Trend Les Copains. Besides following the top collection, the designer also creates the Les Copains line.

Leser Tina (1910-1996). American designer. She was considered an innovator for the originality of her swimming costumes, beachwear, and orientally inspired silk dresses. Born in Philadelphia, she studied at the Philadelphia Academy of Fine Arts and at the Sorbonne. She opened a boutique in Honolulu (Hawaii) in which she sold Chinese brocades, cotton dresses, sailing clothes, and printed silk garments. After moving to New York in the 1940s, she succeeded in selling her creations to Sacks Fifth Avenue, then established her own *prêt-à-porter* company in 1953. In addition to swimming costumes and beachwear, she designed pyjamas, matador pants, and cashmere dresses.

Les Folies d'Elodie Name of one of the two boutiques (the other is called Les Nuits d'Elodie) opened in Paris in 1972 by the sisters Annie Socquet-Clerc and Catherine Pepiot, creators of a handmade *prêt-à-porter* (two annual collections of 40 pieces each), and of accessories, from bags to jewels, and of an "airy" lingerie characterized by a palette of 50 colors.

Les Gars Roman maison created in 1992 by the alliance of Alessandro Pischedda and Ennio Terlizzi. The two designers are the inventors of glamorous sheath-skirts with a very tight waistline. Their eveningwear is based on geometric designs in black and white. Pischedda, of Swiss-Italian origin, has worked with Versus by Versace, while Terlizzi has worked in various bridal dress ateliers in Rome. In the early years the two designers focused their efforts on bridal dresses. Their first show was held in January 1999, followed by a second in July 2000. The *griffe* aims at the creation and diffusion of a simply cut *prêt-à-porter* line.

(*Eleonora Attolico*)

Les Grands Magasins du Louvre Department store opened in Rue Marengo, near the Louvre by Alfred Chauchard (after making a lot of money, he became a very famous art collector) in Paris in 1855, at the time of the Second Universal Exhibition. For the epoch the department store was ahead of its time, with an automated system of goods distribution from the warehouses to the sales counters to the despatch department, and it remained such for many decades through the 20th century, until the site was taken by the Louvre des Antiquaires, a sort of modern bazaar of antiques.

Leshommes Brand of ready-to-wear fashion created by two Belgian designers, Tom Notte and Bart Vandebosch. Both are graduates from the Royale Académie of Antwerp. Their style has been very popular with both the public and the industry. Their first Paris show was held in July 2002 during the men's week. The brand's success found it an immediate market in Italy, Hong Kong, Germany, and Belgium.

(*Maddalena Fossati*)

Le Silla Brand of shoes with the courage of its ideas. They are created by Ennio Silla, the designer and owner of the company Sicap, which also produces the lines Le Silla Project and Sillasport. Jennifer Lopez, Paola Barale, and Martina Colombari sometimes provide the company with testimonials. The brand's success is confirmed by its showroom in Via Montenapoleone, and the own-brand boutiques in Corso Vercelli in Milan, Via Rome in Florence, and in Moscow, plus it has its own window in the prestigious Crocus City Mall. Next opening: London.

(*Giuliana Parabiago*)

Les Mauvais Garçons French theater costume workshop, managed by Laurent Rozenkorf and Argi Aluet. Perhaps following the example of Umberto Tirelli, who, to assist Luchino Visconti and the costume designer Piero Tosi in the philology of costume, provided his tailoring company in Rome with 20,000 authentic garments from between the years 1600 and 1900, Les Mauvais Garçons has collected and rents out 15,000 garments and accessories from the 20th century.

Les Modes French big format fashion monthly. From its foundation in 1901 by the Group Goupil-Cie to its closure in 1937, it was the forerunner of all the innovative content and presentation decisions taken by the fashion press. To start with, the glossy paper it used, the high-quality color photographs shot by famous professionals, the use of stars and jet-setters as models, detailed descriptions, name-dropping, and columns dedicated to news, medicine, art, and men's fashion.

Les Tropeziennes Brand of luxury and high-quality fashion shoes, created in Italy by Tania Ercoli who, with Massimo Palazzo, founded Sosolla, a company that currently manufactures the brand and distributes about 64,000 pairs per year. Production in Civitanova Marche is the work of expert craftsmen, with the support of technologically advanced machines. Besides shoes, the brand makes bags and bijoux made of silver and precious stones. The spirit typified by the products is eccentric but precise.

(*Giuliana Parabiago*)

Le Tanneur French brand of bags and leather accessories. Created in 1898, it was famous for the quality of its leather and the refinery of the details. It was acquired in 1987 by the company Andrelux.

Levi Pisetzky Rosita (1898-1985). Scholar of clothing. An intellectual of the upper Milanese bourgeoisie, she was defined "the lady of Italian costume" by Guido Lopez in an article written after her death in 1985. A self-taught historian, her life was spent studying archives, literary texts, and iconographic sources in order to publish treaties on the history of costume in Italy. Her first studies were published between 1937 and 1938 in various women's magazines and reviews. They are still noteworthy for their accuracy on the history of lace of that period. Between 1954 and 1962, she wrote on the history of costume through the various ages for *Storia di Milano* (History of Milan), published by Treccani in 16 volumes. These articles were expanded and reprinted in a five-volume work by the Italian Editorial Institute with the title *Storia del costume in Italia dal 1964 al 1968* (History of Costume in Italy, 1964-68). In 1978 Einaudi published *Il costume e la moda nella società italiana* (Costume and Fashion in Italian Society), which represented an updated description of her findings. She was the first to treat the subject seriously, studying costume as a means of communication and social document. At an advanced age she donated her own specialized library to the Bertarelli Print Collection in Milan and her collection of clothing to the Civic Collections of Applied Art in Milan, both of which are located in the Castello Sforzesco and open to the public. After her death, her wardrobe was donated by her family to the Bertarelli Collection. It is an interesting collection of handmade Milanese garments from the 1950s and 1960s.

(*Virginia Hill*)

Levi Strauss The most famous five-pocket jeans in the world. A legendary brand, with almost 150 years of history, became one of the most representative symbols of costume evolution in the 20th century. Levi Strauss, from Bavaria, moved to New York in 1847. Three years later he left for the West with the intention of selling packaging cloth to gold miners. However, he was the one who discovered a gold mine, by using that same cloth to make cheap, resistant trousers for the men who went seeking their own fortunes. Levi Strauss & Co. was established in San Francisco, where its founder lived until his death in 1902. The company passed to his grandchildren, who expanded the business. But the crisis of 1929 brought about a huge transformation in the company's clientele, and new social groups decided the universal success of Levi's as leisure garments, not simply as working pants. The boom in jeans has never ceased since the 1950s-60s: the young during the era of protest elected the mythical 501's as the uniform that signified opposition to conservative bourgeois respectability; jeans – the unisex garment par excellence – has overcome generational, social, and cultural barriers to conquer the planet. Levi Strauss & Co. is still the world's leading manufacturer of jeanswear and the strongest and most recognized jeans brand internationally.

(*Cristina Lucchini*)

❑ 2000. The reorganization strategy of the brand continued, with the year closing with a turnover of 4.6 billion dollars. In order to face the crisis, the San Francisco group cut the workforce and closed plants. Robert Hanson, President of Levi's Europe, said: "At world level we have been able to stop the decline in sales, which have diminished 9.6% compared to the 13.7% of 1999."

❑ 2001, November. The shoe business was strengthened with the introduction of a new line, Original Levi's.

❑ 2001. The year closed with a turnover of 4.26 billion dollars, a decline of 8.3% on the year 2000. The fall was greater in the American market. Net profits of 151 million dollars crashed 32.4%.

❑ 2002, April. The company announced a jobs cutting exercise of 3,300 places and the closure of six plants in the USA. Jeans production was decentralized to external factories, while the remaining plants produced other clothing lines.

❑ 2002. Turnover of 4.13 billion dollars represented a fall of 3%, while net profits of 25 million dollars were a crash of 84%. The sharp decline in profits was the result of reorganization costs, without which net profits would have diminished only 24%. The company's debts fell to 100 million dollars. The company numbered 12,000 workers.

❑ 2003, March. The first quarter closed

FOR SOLID COMFORT...
it's always been
LEVI'S
AMERICA'S FINEST OVERALL
SINCE 1850

Advertising bill of Levi's in the 1950s (from *Jeans*, by Ugo Volli, Lupetti).

in the red, with profits of 24 million dollars against 42 millions in the same period a year before.

❑ 2003, June. Levi's celebrated 150 years of activity with a strategy of attack. First, the women's sector: the first Levi's store dedicated exclusively to women is opened in Paris in July. Then, production and distribution. "In the last five years," explained Joe Middleton, the European President of the group, "the market of denim has witnessed a boom. For us this meant a decline in sales. Jeans had become trendy, fashion, everyone has produced low quality garments, embroidered and strange jeans, and lots of new companies have joined the business." The American company made the mistake of sitting on a successful formula that had lasted 150 years and stopped updating its product. (*Dario Golizia*)

Levy José (1963). French designer who studied at the ESMOD and mades his début in 1990 with a men's *prêt-à-porter* collection. Since then his designs have focused on wearability and included allusions to children's wear.

❑ 2004, September. He was invited to design Emanuel Ungaro's men's line. His début occurred with the Fall-Winter 2005-2006 collection.

Lévy Sophie (1969). French jewelry designer and, since 1994, also of furniture. She draws inspiration from fashion, nature, and visual culture to create objects of great beauty, in which colors and light are the essential elements.

Levy Vanessa (1973). French designer: she has created a hyper-feminine fashion based on micro garments: skirts, tops, and very tiny dresses that seem expressly created in small sizes. Her clothes are aimed at creating a femme-enfant, however, her collections are filled with energy, and characterized by a desire to break the rules and to let one's fantasy loose. (*Lucia Mari*)

Lewis French fashion house established in 1890 in Rue Royal in Paris. The address was prestigious and the start excellent. In the 1920s, the maison employed 300 people and had three ateliers in Nice, Biarritz, and Monaco.

Leyendecker Joseph (1874-1951). American illustrator. Through the advertising for the shirtswear company Arrow he expressed the image of the typical young American man. Leyendecker was born in Germany, but emigrated to the United States, where he designed several covers for the *Saturday Evening Post* and *Collier's Weekly* in the early years of the 20th century.

L'Huillier Jérôme (1958). French designer. After working for Balmain, Givenchy, Shimada, and Lapidus, in 1990 he presented his own *griffe*. In 1992 he designed a make-up line for Shiseido and in 1993-94 he was responsible for the Unanyme line by Georges Rech.

Liabel Company leader in underwear, originally founded with the name Maglificio Bellia. The founder was Bernardo Bellia, an innkeeper from Pettinengo, a little village in the area of Biella, who, in 1851, was charged to provide the Savoy army with woolen jerseys. The reunification of Italy in 1860 opened the national market up to Bellia, resulting in unstoppable expansion that, from the 1930s, promoted the company to the top ranks of knitwear production, a leadership that it was to maintain after World War II. Between 1993 and the early months of 1997, the multinational Sarah Lee Corporation bought up Liabel 100%, relaunched the brand and reorganized management. In October 1999, Liabel acquired Dim and the distribution rights on Dim hosiery, tights and underwear, and the Rosy brand. Liabel Baby was created the same year; this line makes baby clothes manufactured with selected fabrics that have been tested in a pediatric hospital before production is started. In September 2001, the year Liabel celebrated 150 years of history, the company (turnover: 35 million euros) joined the group Eminence, a French company that specializes in underwear, and is the owner of the brands Eminence and Athena. In March 2003 the company signed an agreement with Cacharel. From 2004 the company from Biella has been responsible for the distribution in Italy of the knitwear produced by the

Parisian maison. The underwear is manufactured in France by Sil, a factory also belonging to the Eminence group.

Liberman Alexander (1912-1999). Russian art director, photographer and sculptor naturalized American. In 1943 he became art director of *Vogue*. In this role he distinguished himself for discovering and training new photographers, for opening the magazine up to include literary articles, and for following the dramatic events of those years. He was made editorial director of the Group Condé Nast in 1962: in addition to *Vogue*, he controlled *Mademoiselle*, *Glamour*, *House and Garden*, *Traveller*, *Details*, *Allure* and *Vanity Fair*. He remained in charge until 1982. Liberman had studied mathematics, philosophy and architecture in Moscow, London, and Paris where, in 1930, he graduated from the School of Fine Arts. Before emigrating to New York and being hired by *Vogue* as assistant to the art director Agha, he had worked in the atelier of the poster illustrator Cassandre and on the editorial staff of *Vu*. His editorial engagements never diverted him from his passion for sculpture and photography. In 1959 his works were presented at the Museum of Modern Art in New York and, in 1961, at the Museum of Decorative Arts in Paris. In 1960 he published the book *The Artist in His Studio* and in 1995 *Then Photographs 1925-1995*.

Liberty London company and store opened in 1874 by Arthur Lasenby (1843-1917) in Regent Street. It sold oriental silks and porcelains, Indian and Japanese fabrics. But, while Art Nouveau and, in fashion, the so-called aesthetic movement were becoming more and more widespread, the store started proposing fabrics of its own production, the Liberty Art Fabrics collections, which met with huge success. In 1884 Lasenby launched a clothing line designed by the architect E.W. Godwin, a theorist of a new way of dressing. Ten years later, Godwin arrived in Paris. Through the decades Liberty fabrics fascinated the big names of French fashion, from Poiret to Saint-Laurent and Cacharel who, across the 1960s-80s, chose Liberty flowered printed cottons for *prêt-à-porter* though for a younger generation. (*Marta Citacov*)

Lidel Italian fashion magazine founded in 1919 whose name derives from the Italian initials of its five sectors of interest (Reading, Illustration, Drawing, Elegance and Works), and from the journalistic pseudonym of its founder and editor in chief, Lydia Dosio De Liguoro. At its start, Lidel stood behind the newly created Milanese Women's Fascist Association and their struggle against the temptations of luxury. Lidel worked to encourage the birth of Italian fashion, inviting its readers to purchase products made in Italy. In 1923 it promoted the first Italian Pattern Makers competition, which awarded winners with a show at the Milan Fair, an important prelude to the current shows of Milano Collezioni. But, in its initial support of Italian fashion, the magazine avoided being sectarian and sidestepped catering to provincialism. After Lydia De Liguoro's departure from the magazine, in 1927, she was replaced by Gino Valori. Under the artistic direction of Francesco Dal Pozzo, the visual and graphic qualities of the magazine flourished, showcasing the work of Rene Gruau and Brunetta, then at her début. Lidel ceased publication in the late 1930s. Its founder continued her career as editor of the magazine *Fantasie d'Italia,* collaborating on reports for the Italian Silk Institute and promoting fascist directives which, imposed by the National Institute of Fashion, set quotas for the "Italian content" in workshops, mandating that at least 50% of a collection be designed and manufactured in Italy.

Liechtenstein Roy (1923-1997). American artist and one of the masters of Pop Art. Consumer articles, advertising images, icons of mass culture, TV images, comics, and cinema were at the center of Liechtenstein's paintings. In 1979 he made a T-shirt entitled *Untitled Shirt*, in which he magnified the image's print screen, in the same way he did in his paintings.

Lieke Madsen Dutch brand of *prêt-à-porter* launched in 1997 by the designer Lieke Madsen, who graduated from Esmod and Studio Berçot in Paris (1980-82). From 1983 to 1988 she was Lagerfeld's assistant, and also worked on the Fendi and Chanel lines. She has successively worked at Dior, Electre, and Revillon. After starting her own business, she continued to design for other maisons, including Emmanuelle Khanh.

Light (wool) Fabric in natural fibers, especially combed wool. It is light, resistant and uncreasable, ideal for Summer garments.

Ligresti Giulia (1968). Entrepreneur and designer. She studied Economics at Bocconi University in Milan and Queen Mary College in London, became a journalist for local TV networks in Lombardy and a manager in various sectors of the SAI group. In July 1997 she was made President of Richard Ginori and sole general manager of the museum at the company Manifattura di Doccia. Her first goal was the restyling of the Richard Ginori stores, in accordance with the concept of global store – keeping faithful to tradition but introducing innovative marketing. Next came raising market share through the winning over of a new segment of the public, linked not only to the household environment but also to fashion. November 1997 marked the start of the Gilli line, a collection of bags and accessories handmade in Florence. The Gilli brand was chosen as a memory of a journey to Jordan, during which a tourist guide, unable to pronounce the name Giulia, called her by the initials on her backpack, GL. From Spring 2000, the Gilli line was distributed by the Zappieri Group, a leader in the fashion field for more than 40 years. It has 9 showrooms in Italy and 10 more around the world. Among Gilli's most famous pieces is the shiny, high-tech trolley in silver PVC, a unique piece offered, at the political summit in Florence in November 1999, to the leader's wives, among whom was Hillary Clinton. (*Gabriella Gregorietti*)

Linda Dresner Trendy boutique in Park Avenue, New York. It is named after its owner and offers articles by the most avant-garde designers. The favorites are Chloè, Narciso Rodriguez, and Jil Sander.

Lindberg Peter (1944). German photographer. After studying painting in Berlin and in Krefeld, he started working as a window dresser in Duisburg, then became an assistant photographer to Hans Lux and, finally, in 1971, he opened his own advertising photography studio in Düsseldorf. In 1978 he moved to Paris, where he still lives and works, and where he began to work in the field of fashion photography for *Stern*. During the 1980s he made his name being published in *Interview*, *Marie Claire*, and in the American, English, French and Italian editions of *Vogue*, before passing definitively, in 1992, to *Harper's Bazaar*. His campaigns for Armani, Prada, Jil Sander, Lagerfeld, Calvin Klein, Donna Karan, and Mizhari are famed, and in particular others for perfumes: *Trésor* by Lancôme, *Giò* by Armani, and *Eternity* by Klein. In 1992 he directed the documentary *Models*, a film starring Linda Evangelista, Cindy Crawford, Naomi Campbell, Tatjana Patiz and Stephanie Seymour. In 1996 he did the Pirelli Calendar. His style, characterized by an engrossing black-and-white, uses expressionist atmospheres to create images suffused by a dreamlike subtlety.

Line Term that indicates the cutting style chosen for a garment, but it takes on different meanings according to its qualifying adjective – straight, flared, wide, fluid, tubular, etc. – and the noun which translates the quality of a particular line into a precise image. Already in the mid-1800s the definition "Princess Dress" was circulating: this was a robe which, uncut around the waistline and with deep folds opening down to the hem, is closed in front with a row of small buttons. It was popular with princesses (from here the definition) and in the court of the French Empress Eugènie, and it often returns to fashion. The princess line is as constant as the "Corolla Line," which represents the extreme rebirth of crinoline, the skirt widening like an open corolla, and with a very squeezed waistline: this form of dress was reintroduced by Dior in 1947. The "Egg Line" was typical of skirts in the first decades of the 20th century: it swells as it rises from a narrow bottom, and the hem gathers up the material. The 1950s were characterized by lines developed over several phases, from the Bag Line (1950) and Tent Line (1951), both designed by Balenciaga, to the Trapeze Line (1958) by Yves Saint Laurent. Contrary to its name, the Bag Line has a rare balance of shapes, descending in a straight line from the shoulders to the hem, tightening at the knees and ignoring the waistline. The Tent Line originated as an overcoat, with tiny shoulders and a collar, then flaring open; its shape was taken and used in Summer dresses and light Summer coats. The Trapeze Line also flared from top to bottom, ending at knee level, the back soft and loose from shoulders to hem. In the 1950s certain lines were referred to by letters of the alphabet, for example, Dior's H (1954), with a high front, waistline low down on the hips, and marked by a horizontal band; Dior's L (1955), which gradually widened from the shoulders and waist to form the oblique sides of an imaginary triangle, the hem forming the third side; and Dior's Y (1955), these were very thin dresses, with the shoulders given large, open collars or, vice versa, if the Y is upside down, tunics with deep vents at hip height. In this sequence of alphabet letters, the most emblematic line of a particular period was the S line, which summed up, in the late 1800s, the condition of women as a whole: they were locked in a corset which, worn low around the chest, emphasized both the breasts and the bottom, and was further accentuated by large skirts that created the two curves of the figure.

Linea Italiana Fashion magazine. The first number, issued in the Spring-Summer of 1965, was published by Aracne of Milan. It was a six-monthly periodical directed by Marzio Simonetto. With issue no.°8 in the third year (Spring-Summer 1968), the magazine passed to the company Arnaldo Mondadori and was turned into a quarterly under the editorship of Anna Vanner. In Spring 1972, with Fabrizio Pasquero as editor, it became a bi-monthly and, a year later, a monthly magazine. During this period, reviews were the official form of periodical in Italian fashion. The difficulties suffered by women's publications, created by the contemporary launching of other women's magazines, even by Mondadori, brought the review to a close in 1985. However, through its photographic reviews, the magazine had helped document Italian fashion in a period of historical importance for the development of Italian design and its identity.

Lineapiù Italian yarn producer and world leader in its sector. The company is located in Capalle di Prato. Among its several products, it produces a yarn in carbon fiber called Relax, which was created in 1993 by transforming the chemical elements into a filament and then combining it with wool, cotton and viscose. It is a yarn that filters and screens up to 60% of electromagnetic fields. The company was established in 1975 to manufacture knitwear yarns. In just a few years, it had expanded to number 15 independent factories, each with a different and specific technology. The workforce totals 950 people, and the average annual production is 10 million kilograms of yarn in five lines of products. In 1998 turnover was over 170 million dollars. The group's strong point lies in its constant innovation on the basis of a deep knowledge of materials, in particular the most traditional: wool, silk, cashmere, alpaca, mohair, camelhair, angora, cotton, and viscose. The company took two decades to complete its research on raw materials. Its products are appreciated by designers all over the world. As yarn is a semi-worked article, it is difficult to get it generally liked. Lineapiù runs a complex program to create interest around its yarns: masters degrees, specialization courses for young graduates, and exhibitions like that on Azzedine Alaïa at Palazzo Corsini in Florence. At Pitti Filati, in 1999, the company presented a yarn studded with Swarovski crystals and the yarns Cork, Bobol and Loc, which create, in the fabric, particular optical effects by absorbing and reflecting light.

(*Giuliana Zabeo Ricca*)

❑ 2000. Acquired 50% of Julien Mac Donald.
❑ 2002. Registered a turnover of 150 million euros; 1,000 workers in the company's 15 factories; 30 million sweaters manufactured every year. Giuliano Coppini is the group's President, supported by his daughter Lola.
❑ 2003, February. Shalon is the company's new product. It is a tri-dimensional viscose yarn, capable of adhering to the body in a sensual way.

Linen One of the most ancient vegetal fibers, known since the first lakeside civilizations dating back to 6000 B.C. From central and western Asia it spread into India and Egypt, where it was used to clothe royalty and the priesthood. For centuries it was associated with divine rituals. Pharaoh's mummies were wrapped in bands of very pure linen, and the Turin Shroud is the same material. The plant *Linum usitatissimum* (from the *linaceae* family that numbers more than 200 species) produces fibers that are used in spinning and weaving, and oily grains that are useful in industry and medicine. The yarn obtained is long, resistant, smooth and shiny. Depending on its thickness, it can be used to manufacture rough fabrics or soft, very light ones. In relation to weight and weave, the yarn is used to manufacture household linen, underwear or outer garments. A Summer fiber par excellence, linen is appreciated for its freshness, transpirability, insulating power, anti-allergic characteristics, and dyeing resistance; until the years between the wars, it was a constant and central presence in the Summer wardrobe. During the 1950s and 1960s it suffered a severe crisis, but *prêt-à-porter*'s rediscovery of the fashions of the 1930s has returned it to use.

(*Cristina Lucchini*)

Ling Carla (1939). She is the coordinator of the calendars arranged each season for the Milan fashion shows. Ling is the surname of her husband, who is a member of the long-established Chinese colony in Milan. She started her career at the age of 21 when she was hired by Beppe Modenese, whose assistant she became. When he was was entrusted with organization of the schedule of the Milan shows in 1979, Carla supported him in this very delicate and difficult task, though continuing to run the studio at the same time.

Linguiti Mariarosaria. Dressmaker from Naples. She started her activity in 1959 almost for fun, following her creative instinct and presenting, in an apartment-atelier in Via Filangieri, a collection that alternated designs of her own with others inspired by designs by Yves Saint Laurent and Ungaro. Since then she has never stopped and continues to be so successful that she cannot meet all the requests for made-to-measure clothes she receives. She has never been tempted to move into *prêt-à-porter*, and has customers all over Italy; for this reason she's never been interested in either expansion or the marketplace.

Linificio e Canapaficio Castellini This company was founded in 1850 in Paderno Dugnano, near Milan. It manufactured jute bags for the Italian Postal Service and the cloths used to cover deckchairs on the beach, including that of the Hotel Excelsior in Venice. Later, with the support of an industrial plant in the Varese area, it started manufacturing linen, hemp, jute articles, even bedsheets and house linen. In 1997 Emanuele Castellini, the company's owner and general manager, entered into an association with his cousin Piero Castellini, an architect and man of refined taste, to open C&C, a sophisticated boutique in Via della Spiga in Milan. Combining their professional worlds and passions, they have created a sort of atelier for the house: from garden furniture to cashmere, linen and silk fabrics for interior décor, unisex pyjamas, night robes, slippers and accessories. C&C's offerings are also on sale in exclusive stores in Turin, Portofino, London, Paris, and Monaco.

❑ With 12 workers, the company belongs to the families of Piero Castellini Baldissera (33.3%) and Emanuele Castellini (33.3%), and to Sobiati Sasil weaving mill (33.3%). Emanuele Castellini is general manager. There are 5 own-brand stores, 3 of which are direct. There are 263 multibrand stores.

Li-Ning Clothing brand created in 1990 by Li-Ning (1964), Chinese Olympic champion (3 gold medals at the Los Angeles Olympics in 1984). It has a catalogue of one thousand products distributed through multibrand stores and exclusive sales points. In Europe his products are already on sale in Spain, Bulgaria, Greece, Russia, and the Czech Republic.

Links of London English brand of jewelry and accessories. The company was created in 1990 by the couple Annoushka Ducas and John Ayton, and is located in Guildford, near London. The name "links" comes from cufflinks. These were Annoushka's first creation: for her mother's customers (her mother owns some fishing boats in the Northern Sea), she had created a pair of cufflinks with a small silver pendant fish as a gift. These cufflinks became a best-selling article, as did some sweetie bracelets, which look like colored candies, and other pendants and accessories. She uses precious and semi-precious stones, lapislazuli, rose quartz, mother-of-pearl and onyx set with gold and silver. Lots of jewels are hand-finished using ancient and traditional manufacturing techniques. The most heavily used material is silver, as a result of which which Annoushka was awarded the Oscar as best silver designer in the United Kingdom Jewelry Awards. In addition, the company was awarded the Best Retail Image Award. Links of London has 100 workers and a turnover of about 17 million euros. In London the brand is distributed in 9 shops and the large department stores, abroad in 9 own-brand boutiques and in 300 sales points, among which Hong Kong, Tokyo, Dubai, Paris, Toronto, and Singapore.

(*Gabriella Gregorietti*)

Linters Very short fibers which stick to the cotton seeds after ginning. They are used to manufacture artificial fibers.

Liolà Long established firm in the Italian textile and clothing industry. Founded in 1800, it has always belonged to the Giulini family, whose entrepreneurial tradition has now reached the fourth generation and who still direct the company, though supported by a managerial team. Created as a weaving and spinning mill, it began manufacturing in 1958. Diversification was further strengthened through the acquisition in 1965 of a knitwear plant and through the creation of a dyeing-printing mill in 1975. There are 3 plants (Legnano, and Borgomanero and Dormelletto near Novara) which provide a complete textile cycle, from yarn dyeing to printing, knitting and manufacturing. There are 130 franchised stores in Europe, Asia and America. Every year from 4 to 8 collections are presented for a complete range of sizes. Liolà is a niche product for sweater technology. Exports represent 50% of total production.

❑ 2002. The general manager was Vittorio Giulini, President of the Italia Fashion system. The company's motto is: "The Jersey Collection, 100% Made in Italy." There are 3 production plants for producing 25 types of product from yarn to finished products; there are 4 annual collections: Spring (day and nightwear); Summer (day and formal clothing), Winter (daywear) and elegant (fall and Christmas); finally, 160 own-brand shops around the world.

Lipperheidescher Kostumbibliothek German library that specializes in fashion. Set up in 1877 by Franz von Lipperheide, editor of the magazine *Die Modewelt*, it has a collection of 32,000 books, magazines, lithographies, photographs, and original sketches.

Liseuse Knitted jacket in light wool with long sleeves, to wear over a night gown or pyjamas. Since the 1950s it has been considered the classic type of shawl. So called because it was used when reading in bed (from the French "*lire*", meaning to read).

Liso Susanna (1955). Italian clothes and costume designer, a member of the Tailors and Dressmakers Association of Rome. She graduated in applied arts (specifically in fabrics) in 1973, then studied History of Art at university and began her career as a theater costume designer collaborating with various companies and set designers. In 1977 she created the Tartarughe (Turtles) manufacturing and commercializing fabric and knitwear collections. In 1989 she opened a second sales outlet for a complete line of accessories. In 2000 she renovated the company image by moving into a larger space, and opening another store, in 2003, in the center of Rome. She has presented her lines at Pitti Trend in Florence, Contemporary in Milan, and at AltaRomaAltaModa, though continuing her activity as a costume designer for dance and art video shows. She is married to the artist Claudio Adami, who does the graphics of the publications that present her collections like "vernissages".

Litrico Roman tailor's workshop opened in the 1950s. It was established by Angelo Litrico, from Catania, who became the owner of the former Atelier Marinelli, where he did his apprenticeship, and then changed its name to his own. One of the peculiarities of his creations is a marked eccentricity created through the use of fabrics, decora-

Angelo Litrico, sketch of a jacket, 1962.

tions, and colors he borrows from women's fashion. In the 1970s, Litrico also launched a women's line distributed by Biagiotti Export. Nowadays the atelier is directed by the siblings Angelo, Giusi, and Franco Litrico.

Liviana Conti Knitwear company and brand established in 1976 by Liviana Conti and her husband: she is the designer and creative mind, he is the company's general manager. At the beginning, Liviana Troffei used to design a knitwear line for children called Lamelamatura, but in 1982 she decided to launch into women's knitwear. Soon the brand Liviana Conti became synonymous with simple, unadorned collections, a good use of materials, and sophisticated production techniques. Since 1999 the company, which manufactures 100,000 pieces a year, has created a men's knitwear line called Dual.

❑ 2002. Registered turnover of 7.5 million euros, 45% of which was from exports. The company employs 45 people and has 500 sales outlets worldwide. The designer's versatility has resulted in the development of new lines of products and accessories, such as shoes and a collection of household accessories. The men's line Dual is no longer produced.

Livoli Lea (1912-1987). Fashion creator and milliner. She started her career in her hometown of Florence, in an embroidery school directed by her mother, manufacturing household linen and underwear. She married Renato Livoli and, after World War II, she opened a fur atelier in Via Castel Morrone, Milan, and later in Via Piave. After moving to Via Montenapoleone 14, she exhibited her Mirsa and Naka *haute couture* knitwear creations in the boutique under the atelier. In the 1960s she designed a ready-to-wear fashion collection, perfumes, stockings, and scarves. In the 1970s she moved her atelier, which had become famous for its bridal collection, to Via del Gesù 4 and showed hat and clothing collections in Rome and Florence. In 1974 Gheddafi ordered an exclusive line from her. In 1978 her daughter Giulia took over her place and the business continued until 1993.
(*Marilea Somaré*)

Llama A wool fiber that gets its name from a member of the camel family that lives at high altitudes in the Andes. Llamas are bred by the Inca population. Only the females can be sheared each year. Every animal can provide 4 kg of bright, warm, pale red wool.

Loafer Flat shoe with fringes, of Norwegian origin. Traditionally worn by men, it is also worn by women wanting comfortable footwear.

Lobb John Famous shoe store at 9 St. James's Street in London: custom-made shoes manufactured by a series of craftsmen, each responsible for a different manufacturing phase. John Lobb (1829-1895), the founder, was born in Tyardreath, Cornwell, and at the age of 20 emigrated to Australia, where he started making shoes for gold diggers and had a successful shop. When he returned to London, he first opened a shop in Regent's Street and then in St. James's, its present premises. John Lobb, now in the fifth generation, has shod the rich and famous. The company the official shoe supplier of the Court of England. Lobb has been granted three Royal Warranties, the supply certificates issued by the Royal House: by Queen Elizabeth, by her husband the Prince of Edinburgh, and by Prince Charles. A pair of Lobb shoes can cost up to 2,500 euros and the waiting list is one year. (*Mara Accettura*)

Locking Shocking Spanish brand of *prêt-à-porter*. the first Locking Shocking collection was presented in 1996 at the Mediterranean Jeans section of the Salon Gaudí in Barcelona. In 2001 Locking Stocking collections were presented in the most important specialized salons, and from 2002 they have been shown on Spanish catwalks, for example, Circuit, Barcelona, and the Pasarela Cibeles in Madrid, where the brand's Spring-Summer 2003 collection won the L'Oréal-Paris prize for the best collection of the season. (*Mariacristina Righi*)

Loden Mantle coat of Tyrolese origin, manufactured, as Anna Canonica Sawina writes in her technical Dictionary of Fashion (Sugarco 1994), in "carded wool fabric, heavy and coarse, gauzed and strongly milled, with the characteristic hair front, made waterproof by special treatments." Its "death," as one would say using using the language of gastronomy, is its bottle-green color. It has a traditional shape, with sleeves open at the armhole, a collar without lapels, an oblique pocket, and a long vent in the back. There are 405 different models. It was worn by the Austrian emperor Franz Josef and the Duke of Windsor. It is still worn by plenty of Milanese males, not all of them nostalgic for Maria Theresa of Austria, nor all "mittel-European," but they are all aware of its sober, almost camouflaging elegance and comfort. The word *loden* seems to derive from an ancient German word meaning hair.

Loewe Spanish brand of leather goods. In 1846, Heinrich Loewe Rossberg, a skin and leather craftsman from Germany, established a high-quality output of leather goods in Madrid and enjoyed success until the late 1930s. Later, under the direction of Enrique Loewe Knappe, the founder's grandson, the company shifted its focus in towards a complete range of accessories, including scarves, umbrellas, and bijoux. In 1965 Loewe launched a *prêt-à-porter* line and, shortly after, a men's line. Nowadays the

A model from the Locking Shocking Collection.

company is guided by the fourth generation of the Loewe family and has about 50 shops around the world.

❑ The famous Spanish brand was bought by LVMH in 1985 and changed its designer from Narciso Rodriguez to José Enrique Ona Selfa. Loewe still has a Spanish heart, but its appeal is international. It has 100 stores and thinks about the future starting from its headquarters, which is located in a historic building, the Miraflores, in Madrid.

L'Officiel de la Couture et de la Mode de Paris A sophisticated French monthly founded in 1921 in Paris by Max Brunhes, that used the best photographers of the time to present the *haute couture* collections in its pages. The magazine's main photographer from 1934 was Philippe Portier: he was the first to take photographs of clothes in the street, historical buildings, castles, or luxury hotels. At the start of the war and the Nazi occupation, the magazine interrupted publication until 1941, when it restarted with the collaboration of the couturier Lucien Lelong. In the 1950s, it added a column dedicated to fabrics and to the trends being followed by the great maisons, from Rodier and Ducharne to Bianchini Férrier, and sections were introduced dedicated to beauty, a horoscope, and news items. Since 1971 the magazine has been edited by a company: l'Officiel de la Couture.

Hat by Jean Blanchot, published by l'Officiel in 1934 (from *Histoire de la mode ou XX siècle*, by Y. Deslandres and F. Müller, Somogy, 1986).

Lognon Gérard. A master of plissé. Under Napoleon III, his great-grandmother Emilie was a lingerie embroiderer and a specialist in ironing pleated shirtfronts. His grandfather George opened a shop which used cardboard molds to pleat fabrics. Among his customers were Maison Fortuny, Chanel, Paquin, Fath, Dior, Balenciaga, and Hermès. Grandson Gérard continues the tradition. His atelier is in Rue Danielle Casanov in Paris. Galliano owes to him the perfection of the plissé in the "parka" presented in his Summer 2002 collection.

Lohse Remie. Danish photographer. He worked in Paris, becoming interested in fashion in 1933. He was defined by *Vogue* as the master of candid-camera. His photographs of models moving through the streets of Paris was initially considered a little unorthodox to document fashion. His photographic taste was close to Martin Munkacsi's.

Lola Millinery American brand of women's hats. Its name derives from Lola, a traditional milliner. Born in Holland in 1947, she grew up in Paris but moved to New York in 1974. She creates real compositions for her customers, mini works of art using showy accessories. She studied the art of millinery in London and specialized at the Fashion Institute of Technology in New York.

Lolita Lempicka French brand of *prêt-à-porter*. It takes its name from the founder who, after attending the Studio Berçot, started her career in 1984 when she opened a boutique in the Parisian neighborhood of Marais. This was followed by her first show, which the press received warmly. Lempicka likes to mix elements, for example, a touch of nostalgia with modernity. The mother of three children, and helped by her eldest, Elisa, she designs what she loves to wear. The common factors in her collections are precision, attention to details, the use of high-quality materials, and a constant search for perfection. In 1995 she opened a showroom called Les Mariées de Lolita dedicated to brides. Very keen on the cinema, she has designed the costumes for several films.

(*Ilaria Boero*)

Lolita Pompadour French jewelry brand, created in 1996 by Virginie Epron in Paris. After working in the field of fashion bijoux, she studied art and graduated in 1993. She calls herself the "princess of kitsch" and finds inspiration in the junk markets of Paris.

Lombardi Marisa. Fashion entrepreneur. Born in Milan, she opened her first boutique in 1965 in Corso Vercelli, Milan. In 1970 she opened one of the first own-brand stores, Pucci, first in Via Montenapoleone, then in Via Cino del Duca. Her chain of own-brand stores was followed by Missoni in 1976, Armani in 1983, and Comme des Garçons in 1989, all of them in Via Sant'Andrea. Today Marisa has three shops in Milan, one of which is in Via della Spiga. She is the Miyake's ambassadress to Milan. A lover of modern and contemporary art, she's also a collector.

London College of Fashion Originally named the Barrett Street Trade School (Technical School of Dressmaking), it was established in 1915. It changed to become the LCF after the war and, between 1952 and 1972, was the only state school entirely dedicated to fashion. It has always manifested a practical rather an artistic approach, educating the technicians of fashion, such as model-makers and cutters. It is divided into two sections: the School of Fashion Design and Technology, which offers courses of 2, 3 or 4 years in stylism, model making, fabrics, knitwear, embroidery, and millinery; and the School of Fashion Promotion, with courses of journalism and fashion management. It has more than 1,000 students.

London Institute Established in 1986, it represents a group of five London art academies: Camberwell College of Art, Central Saint Martin's College of Art and Design, Chelsea College of Art and Design, London College of Fashion, and London College of Printing. The Institute was conceived with the intention of creating a unified managerial system and, at the same time, with the hope of strengthening the image and the productivity of the fashion colleges, though each still remains independent in its management, course structure, selection of teachers, and students. Since 1993 they have all been certified as universities. Among their most famous graduates there are: John Galliano, Rifat Ozbek, Stella McCartney, Bruce Oldfield, Katharine Hamnett, Hussein Chalayan, and Alexander McQueen.

Longchamp Historical brand of leather goods founded between the two wars by the Frenchman, Jean Cassegrain, who had a small shop of articles for smokers. One of his products was a pipe called Lonchamp; one day in 1948 he had the idea to wrap it in leather, and this was the start of his entry in the leather goods' trade. About ten years later, his success allowed him to set up a real factory in Segré (Maine-et-Loire), which still manufactures kidskin cases and, since 1970, a luggage line in nylon and leather. In 1993 the company launched the bag Le Pliage, made of washable nylon, with leather handles and a large choice of colors. Over a period of ten years, the company sold 5 million pieces. The founder was succeeded by his son Philippe, whose daughter Sophie and Isabelle Guyon are the designers. The company employs 1,200 people and exports to 70 countries.

Longhi Company manufacturing leather clothing, established in Parma during the 1930s of the past century. After making a turnover, in 2001, of about 14 million euros, it has passed under the control of Ermenegildo Zegna. In thee early 2002, Zegna absorbed also the majority of the Group Guida, owner of Longhi: the President Enrico Pennacchi has been confirmed in his charge. Nowadays Longhi represents one of the most important brands of Zegna's luxury leather sector.

Longo Luisa (1959). Designer-artisan specialized in hand-painted fabrics. Born in Bologna. She uses liquid colors to create a shaded effect and by means of a particular technique she can treat silk, satin, chiffon, organza, velvet, and damask. In January 2003 she participated in Rome's fashion week, presenting an installation of clothes moved by a fan. She attended the École du Louvre and did an apprenticeship in an artisan's workshop where she learned the techniques of color composition. She manufactures carves, stoles, dresses, skirts, and blouses, but also paintings using cloth panels, bedcovers and screens.

(*Eleonora Attolico*)

Longuette Any female garment that reaches to mid-calf level. In vogue during the 1960s, it was taken up again a decade later with the name of midi, a term no longer used.

Look A less elegant term for "style," a word that well defined people such as Jacqueline Kennedy, Marcello Mastroianni, the Duke and Duchess of Windsor, and even Mother Teresa of Calcutta. If style is connected to the body and soul of an individual, one's look represents a person without taking into account his or her mind or personality. Bleached hair or violet streaks give a punk look, Morticia's make-up tells us she is a vamp, a pantsuit identifies a manageress on the upward path, a cigar in the mouth suggests a man "who never asks." The important thing is that appearance (even better if branded) prevails over substance. The look is an invention of the 1960s and, at least in origin, indicates a "sense of belonging": to a social class or a political group, to a caste or a gang. Consequently, almost by chance, generations of cloned androids began to appear in the pages of fashion magazines and weeklies. Dozens of professionals with their watch fastened on top of their shirt cuff, industrial quantities of socialites toting a Kelly (the first to do so was Princess Grace) or a branded backpack (in this case the model was Madonna, another person whose image is based purely on looks rather than style), thousands of young men wearing Blues Brothers sunglasses, hundreds of children looking as though they are fresh from a wedding at Buckingham Palace: all of them imitators of someone else. "Look" is certainly a hateful term when used in this way: it has only one acceptable meaning, when it is connected to an individual's personality or mind. Otherwise it would do better to disappear from the dictionary. (*Stefano Bucci*)

Lopez Fatima (1965). Portuguese designer. Born in Madeira, she started to make her own name in the world of fashion in 1992 when she presented her collections in Portugal in shows open to 2,000 people. In 1999 she found some space at the Paris salon of the *prêt-à-porter* and in the following years continued to launch new lines of clothing, accessories, and jewelry, and to open boutiques. Her creations are very successful in the United States, Japan, France, and Italy. There was much talk about her for her creation of the "most expensive" bikini in the world which, made for Ezziddeen with 60 De Beers' diamonds and 1.7 kg of gold, required 150 hours of work. Price. 1 million euros.

Lopez Marc (1960). French trendy hairdresser, who has worked for *Vogue*, *Elle*, *i-D* and *The Face*. He has style the hair of many models in the Paris shows, in particular for Yamamoto and Westwood. Born in Paris, he was discovered at the age of 25 by the English photographer Nick Knight and the artistic director Marc Ascoli.

Lopez Rafael (1974). Designer born in Aguilas, Spain, now working in London. He graduated from the fashion Academy of Murcia, took a first Master's degree at the Marangoni Institute in Milan, and then a second at the Central Saint Martin's College in London. He worked as designer for several ateliers such as Oscar Suleyman in Paris, and Les Copains in Italy. He launched his own brand in 2000 in London, immediately winning awards and getting sponsorships for his shows from important brands, such as Mario Boselli for fabrics and Saga Furs for furs. He presented an almost couture style for an elegant woman who does not turn her nose up at a luxury fur coat. His clothes are on sale in department stores and fashion boutiques in Europe, Japan, and USA. (*Virginia Hill*)

Lora & Festa Knitwear yarn company. Established in Borgosesia as a wool mill in 1885, in 1926 it developed into a complete cycle spinning mill, offering combed yarn with on-site dyeing. Specialized in the working of natural and exclusive fibers of very high quality, it is highly thought of in its sector. Its products are reserved for leading knitwear factories or big names in the fashion world. Their combed yarns with a very *haute couture* content are produced to meet the requirements of the world markets and 50% go to export markets. Product quality is based by careful research and selection of blends and colors, and the use of avant-garde techniques.

❑ 2003. Turnover in 2002 amounted to 23 million euros, 48% of which was from exports. The company employs 160 workers. The company is owned by the Loro Lamia and Festa Bianchet families.

Lord and Taylor Chain of American department stores acquired by the group May Department Stores Co. in 1986. Their foundation dates back to 1826 (America's oldest store), when Samuel Lord and George W. Taylor opened their first drugstore in New York. This became a point of reference for the New York fashion world, specially in the years that Dorothy Shaver was the company's president (1949-59). In constant expansion, it now has 62 sales points in 17 states.

L'Oréal French cosmetic group, the world's largest. Established in 1907 by the chemist Eugène Schueller, the brand made its début in the hair products sector for professional use. Over the years, the group expanded its activity to cover all market segments (perfumes, treatments, make-up). As a partial result of large acquisitions that foster research and new products, the group today offers a unique combination of over 500 brands, ranging from the highest quality to the mass distribution brands, making a total of 80,000 products and about 200 new articles launched every year. Almost 5% of turnover is allocated to research. In Italy, L'Oréal has four companies: L'Oréal Saipo, Parfums et Beauté, Helena Rubinstein, and Cosmétique Active. The majority shareholder is still the Bettencourt Gesparal family, descendants of the founder.

(*Ginevra Falzoni*)

❑ 1999. Turnover grew 12%.
❑ 2000, March. The French giant announced the acquisition of the American group Carson (turnover: 380 million dollars), which specializes in ethnic cosmetics and the African markets, in which it makes 25% of its turnover. The purpose of the acquisition was to give L'Oréal better penetration of these markets.
❑ 2000. Acquisition of two companies: Scandinavian Respons and 35% of the Japanese Shu Uemura.
❑ 2001. L'Oréal Italy, the group's Italian holding, closed 2001 with a turnover of 878.3 million euros, +6.3% on 2000.
❑ 2002. The balance sheet had a consolidated turnover of 14.3 billion euros, +8.9 millions compared to 2001. The group has more than 48,000 collaborators and sells in 150 countries. These results are greatly due to the sales boom in China (+61%), where the distribution network was strengthened and, above all, a new production plant was under construction. Active since 1908, L'Oréal Italy is the third largest cosmetics company in Europe and the fourth largest in the world. A new production center is to be built in Milan, which will support the long established Turin plant.
❑ 2005, April. The actress Eva Longoria signed a contract with L'Oréal Paris to become the brand's new "face".
❑ 2005, May. The group announced the acquisition of Texan SkinCeuticals, a company which distributes its cosmetic products to dermatologists, plastic surgeons, and high level spas. The group's target is to integrate the company into its cosmeceutics division.

Loredana Clothing company for little girls and teenagers from 1 to 16 years (medium-high segment). Established in 1956 in Putignano, near Bari, it has become an important point of reference in the children's clothing sector. The acknowledged prestige and success of its collections come from a long family tradition in the field of children's manufacturing. Since Angela and Giovanni Leogrande opened their first small workshop, they have always placed great attention on details, the quality of the fabrics, and the various clothing lines. At present the company, named after the couple's daughter, continues to be guided by the family, though it uses a team of internal and external collaborators. The company's philosophy is to manufacture everything with the greatest care: from creation and production to delivery, from the relationship with suppliers to that with clients and consumers. After World War II, the number of customers grew slowly, and also the interest and will of the family to create fashion for young people. In 1953 the number of workers had grown to 5 and the business was run in two small rooms; in 1965 the company started distributing across Italy through a personal distribution network. The birth of the line *Dolci Tentazioni* dates back to 1970 (target: 1-7 years) and to 1977 the arrival in the company of Loredana, the founders' daughter, as a young designer. The Marina line for babies made its debut in 1980, and in 1990 the company participated for the first time at Pitti Immagine Bimbo. In 1996 an agreement with the American company C&C allowed Loredana to export to the USA. From 1997 to 2002 the company diversified its products, creating new lines: in 1997 the *Le bellissime di Loredana* line of formal clothing appeared; in 1998 it was the turn of *Loredana le bimbe*, for children from 1 to 8 years, and *Loredana le scarpe*. Finally, in 2002, the LEJ line was created for girls from 8 to 16. The company has thus built a complete product portfolio for girls from birth to adolescence. Each line has its own character, colors, and design. What they have in common is taste, their image, and the high quality of the fabrics and manufacturing. The products are made in about 20 external workshops in Putignano. The company has 35 workers. The Loredana Store in Xiamen, China was opened in 2004. (*Dario Golizia*)

Lorenzi Gianmarco, real name of Gianni Renzi (1956). Shoe designer. He designed his first shoe at the age of six: Dad Antonio and Mom Italia, owners of a small shoe factory in The Marches, promptly manufactured it, thus deciding his fate. His name is linked to luxury accessories, his market is international, and his fame is connected to his genius in creating heeled shoes of unusual shape, made with exclusive leathers.

Lorenzini Italian company of high-quality shirts, men's underwear and women's *prêt-à-porter*. It was founded by Antonio Lorenzini in 1920 in Merate, where it still has its production plants, to which a new workshop was added near Bergamo in the 1980s. In the 1960s, the third family generation took over the reins and decided to bet on a niche product that would allow the quality of the fabrics and the artisanal qualities of the manufacturing to be stressed. In the 1980s, the company also started a women's *prêt-à-porter* line and adopted a strategy that combined the rules of handmade manufacturing with modern technology throughout the entire production process. Giancarlo and Antonia Lorenzini, the owners, make the styling decisions with the assistance of external consultancies: in the past, these have been Moschino and Guido Pellegrini.

Lorenzo Banfi Brand of a shoe company established in 1978 by Renzo Banfi. Its headquarters is in Parabiago, near Milan. Since 1985 it has also produced leather goods. It exports to 25 countries, including Japan, USA, and Germany. In 1997 turnover reached 13 million dollars. It has patented an ecological sole all over the world.

Loretta Di Lorenzo Clothing company established in 1970 in Carpi with products designed for a young clientele in the medium-high sector of the market. The founder and designer is now supported by her daughter Sabrina in the creation of the two lines: Sabrina Di Lorenzo and Zooi, which are distributed in Italy, Europe, and the Far East.

Lorgnette Glasses with one or two lenses held up to the eyes by hand. They were in fashion in the early 20th century when no lady, however shortsighted, would have dared to wear glasses, which was the prerogative of a few emancipated men.

Loris Story Manufacturer of socks for children, men, and women, and babies' accessories, founded in 1946. It bears the name of its founder, who substituted an exotic "y" at the end of her name in the hope of achieving an international dimension to the firm, which is something that has indeed happened; a large part of their production is now exported. The firm is currently managed by three out of five of Loris Stori's children.

Loro Piana & C. Italian wool factory with headquarters in Quarona, Valsesia. The world of clothing owes Tasmanian fabric to this company. Loro Piana decided to launch a fabric of its own to be used in priests' clothing, based on wools from Tasmania. That's how the Tasmanian, an exclusive brand of the company, was born. The word Tasmanian was introduced into the Zingarelli Italian Dictionary in 1998. From 1812 the Loro Piana family worked with textile fibers in the valleys of Biella. In Quarona, Pietro opened a wool mill in 1924, naming it after himself and profession: Ing. Loro Piana & C. ("Ing" signifies engineer). Pietro was succeeded by his son Franco and, in the 1970s, by his grandchildren Sergio and Pier Luigi. All three generations have been united by a passion for textile quality and perfectionism. The most refined wools, the Tasmanian, cashmere, and vicuna are the group most exclusive products. In 1994 Peru granted the company a quota of vicuna, when the wool was put back on the market after 40 years of prohibition. This step had been taken to prevent the extinction of the animal. At the auctions in Geelong, Australia, in December 1997, the group successfully bid for the most refined batch of wool ever produced: 119 kg of wool that had a record thinness of just 13.4 microns. Australian wool averages 24 microns and the threshold of 14 microns had very rarely been achieved. Since the 1980s Loro Piana has been buying the Top-Line1PP: the batches of the best wool taken from the 5 million bales on the market. The company has plants in Quarona, Borgosesia, Roccapietra, Ghemme, and production units in Dalina (China) and Stafford Springs (Connecticut), as well as its own supply units in Beijing and Mongolia. It has branch offices in London, New York, Singapore, Seoul, Tokyo, and Hong Kong. In 1996 the consolidated turnover was 190 million dollars. In addition to fabrics, the company also produces men's and women's clothing lines, accessories, and a household collection. It has opened a showroom in Via Montenapoleone, Milan.

(*Giuliana Zabeo Ricca*)

❑ 1999. Turnover of 225 million dollars, +12% on the previous year. New store openings in Capri, Ischia, Santa Margherita, Forte dei Marmi and Porto Cervo, which joined the existing sales points in Milan, Malpensa Airport, Rome, Florence, Udine, and Venice, where it has recently opened a second space dedicated to menswear. Overall, in 1999 the company had 11 stores in Italy. In the United States, shops were opened on Madison Avenue (New York) and in Aspen.

❑ 1999. The transformation of Loro Piana continued from a high quality textile company to a group producing clothing, furs, cashmere accessories, and household collections.

❑ 2000, March. In Sydney, Loro Piana bought the most refined batch of wool ever produced. It was a batch weighing 99 kg, and with a thinness of 12.9 microns. It was produced by the Ash Windradeen farm in Pyramul. The exceptional thinness of the Australian batch is even more noteworthy because the sheep – says the Italian company – had been bred following a traditional method, in an open paddock, and not according to the "sharlea" method, in which the same result in terms of thinness would have been less significant.

❑ 2000. The company's expansion continued: it closed the year with a turnover of 288 million dollars, +28% compared to 1999. The gross operating margin was 61 million dollars. It opened 28 new shops.

❑ 2001, March. The Portofino boutique was opened. The Italian group focused its efforts on Germany, Switzerland, France, Japan, and the United States.

❑ 2001, April. The company's target was to diversify its products into segments consistent with a philosophy of timeless luxury. The first target of this diversification was Sail and Walk, a brand of sailing shoes. For fall and Winter, a women's sports jacket, New Icer, and the men's cashmere or suede cult piece, Piumo Cortina, were launched.

❑ 2001, November. Opening of the first own-brand store in Seoul, Korea.

❑ 2001. Turnover amounted to 263 million euros, +10% on 2000.

❑ 2002, September. The company sponsored the New Zealand team at the America's Cup. Garments were manufactured using the Zelander light

frame storm system, a very light and resistant fabric made 70% from New Zealand merino wool and 30% nylon.
❑ 2002. The group's consolidated turnover for the year 2002 totalled 259 million euros, compared to 261 the previous year (-1%). "We are in line with the results of 2001. Without the dollar effect, we would have grown 4%," stated Sergio Loro Piana. "For us the dollar area represents about 38% of total proceedings. In America we have 3 fabric production plants and 9 stores. It was a good year for the finished goods department. The increase in proceedings would have reached 15% at constant exchange rates." The excellent performance of the finished goods business was determined by the own-brand stores which from 2002 have represented 60% of sales. With the 14 new openings in 2002, Loro Piana reached a total of 59: the last début was in Rue Montaigne, Paris. The own-brand stores development was begun in 1999 and cost 49 million euros.
❑ 2003, April. Inauguration of the Tokyo store in the neighborhood of Rappongi Hills. The new opening followed the company's development plan for the Far Eastern market where, since 1999, it had opened 13 corner shops and shops-in-shops in Japan. Over the previous 6 years, the Loro Piana turnover in Japan tripled. In 2003 it represented 10% of global turnover. The company had 60 sales outlets.
(*Dario Golizia*)

Los Angeles County Museum of Art California, USA. The section dedicated to textile and clothing numbers more than 50,000 pieces, ranging from fragments of medieval fabrics to creations by contemporary Japanese designers. Within the museum, the Doris Stein Research Center collects materials concerning fashion, books, sketches, photographs, and prints.

Lotto Italian brand of sports shoes and clothing. In 1973 it launched its first line of tennis shoes, then entered the soccer boot market. Since the 1980s it has developed its own products with the collaboration of various famous athletes to study and test the performance of their products: John Newcombe, Boris Becker, Martina Navratilova, Ruud Gullit, Andreas Muster, Demetri Albertini, Ivan Zamorano and Andriy Shevchenko. Lotto combines technological research with sports design. Besides sponsoring teams, it is also a partner of important tennis tournaments, such as Wimbledon and others on the ATP circuit. In 2002, it registered a turnover of about 245 million euros (+13.2% compared to 2001). The current President is Andrea Tomat. Today Lotto's products are distributed in 80 countries.
(*Daniela Bolognetti*)

Louboutin Christian (1964). French shoe designer. Unusual materials (he created boots using palm tree bark for a show in Pigalle) and sculptured heels characterize the shoes of this Parisian designer. After studying figurative arts at the Roederer Academy, he did an apprenticeship at Charles Jourdan, then worked for Frizon and Chanel until he entered the long and meaningful collaboration with Roger Vivier. His first collection was presented in 1991, then he opened a boutique in Rue Rousseau in Paris which counts among its usual clients Caroline of Monaco, Madonna, Nicole Kidman, Cher, and Carolyn Bessette-Kennedy. In 1998 he received the Fashion Footwear Association of New York Award for the best shoe designer of the year.

An evening shoe by Christian Louboutin.

Louis Jean Professional name of Jean-Louis Berthault (1907-1997), a French clothes and costume designer. he designed the famous sleeveless evening dress worn by Rita Hayworth in the key scene in the film *Gilda* (1946). He was renowned in particular for clothing the femmes fatales of cinema, like Rita Hayworth, Joan Crawford, and Marlene Dietrich. He worked for 17 years at Columbia as head of costume design, before moving to Universal. His career started with fashion. Originally a designer at Drecoll, he was hired by the Hattie Carnegie House, and some of the most famous women of the time among his clients, including Wallis Simpson, the Duchess of Windsor. He was introduced around Hollywood by one of them, Mrs. Cohn, the wife of the Columbia president. In 1954 he made Judy Garland's costumes in *A Star Is Born* and was nominated for an Oscar. From 1961 he designed his personal line of *prêt-à-porter* and devoted himself to his personal atelier, continuing to collaborate with the world of cinema as a freelancer. Marilyn Monroe wore one of his sequin-studded creations when she sang Happy Birthday to President Kennedy at Madison Square Gardens. Nancy Reagan was wearing one of his dresses when her husband was sworn in as President. (*Roberto Nepoti*)

Louis Vuitton French company that manufactures fashion and leather goods. In 1835 Louis Vuitton (1821-1892) left his home region of Jura for Paris where he specialized in the manufacture of cases for rich people. Seventeen years later he was invited to design the luggage for Empress Eugenia of Montijo. This experience made him understand the imminent decline in old trunks, which were no longer suitable for ship or train journeys. In 1854 he opened his first leather goods store in Rue Neuve des Capucines in Paris, where he offered very light trunks in poplar wood and baggage more suitable for the new means of transport. In 1896 his son Georges created the "Monogram," a small piece of cloth printed with the initials LV that guaranteed the originality of the product; he also patented waxed cloth bags, like the "steamer bag". Louis Vuitton's grandson, Gaston, worked for the company, but he also collected travel items and old luggage dating as far back as the 16th century; these are now part of the collections of the Musée des Arts Décoratifs de Paris. Members of the aristocracy and royalty never traveled without their own expressly commissioned trunks and cases, for example, the Prince of Egypt Youssouf Kemal, and the Sultan Ismaïl Pacha. For Luigi Barzini and Scipione Borghese who, in 1907, organized the Beijing-Paris car race, the maison designed rainproof cases. The trunk of the explorer Savorgnan de Brazza could even contain a camp bed, and the one made for the opera singer Lily Pons could hold 36 pairs of shoes. The trunk designed for the orchestra conductor Léopold Stokowski contained a little desk with a small table and shelves for books and music. Even today the company will make luggage to meet the requests of its clientele. Since 1959 production has expanded to include a line of bags, small leather goods, and accessories. In 1998 Louis Vuitton joined the world of *prêt-à-porter*, with the American designer Marc Jacobs responsible for the men's and women's collections. He has since been appointed artistic director of the maison. In 2003 Louis Vuitton sold its goods in 50 countries exclusively through more than 300 boutiques of its own property. In 1989 Louis Vuitton was bought up by LVMH, a world leader in luxury goods, whose president is Bernard Arnault. (*Giuliana Parabiago*)

❑ 2001. Registered turnover of 3,612 million euros and operating results of 1,270 millions.
❑ 2002. Registered a turnover of 4,194 million euros and operating results of 1,297 millions. All markets grew: Europe (+8%), USA (+12%), Japan (+15%). At the end of the year there were 299 own-brand shops. Of these, 7 were new: 1 each in Tokyo, Kobe, Osaka, Moscow, Amsterdam, Macao, and Germany, the restyled and reorganized stores numbered about 30. Yves Carcelle became the company's new President in December 2002.
❑ 2003, April. Louis Vuitton opened its first shop in New Delhi, India.
❑ 2004, September. The Shanghai store, the largest store in the Asia-Pacific area, was restyled. Louis Vuitton had 13 shops in China.
❑ 2005, January. The first store in Japan was opened in 1978 (it now has about

50), in Hong Kong in 1979, in South Korea in 1996 (now 16), in China in 1992; now Louis Vuitton is arriving in South Africa and India. "The future markets are India and South Africa," says Serge Brunschwig. "We are preparing big marketing operations and the opening of stores. In this way we create an emotional impact and start to introduce the Louis Vuitton universe into the luxury niches of new consumer markets." Overall, the brand has 335 own-brand, own property stores all over the world. "To mark the company's 150 years, we have accelerated the expansion project with 21 new openings, from the New York Building on the Fifth Avenue in Manhattan, to Osaka and Shanghai."
❑ 2005, March. The actress Uma Thurman became Louis Vuitton's new testimonial.
❑ 2005, July. The diversification process of the French brand continued. After a line of jewelry was launched, Louis Vuitton eyewear (sunglasses) made their appearance. Zeiss is the chosen partner to produce high protection lenses.
(*Dario Golizia*)

Lovable Italian company making corsetry and women's underwear. It is mainly renowned for its "heart bras," thus called because of the little heart sewn between the cups. From 1989 it was owned by the Felli family from Bergamo but in 1996 it was taken over by the American multinational Sarah Lee of Chicago, the owner of Playtex, Liabel, Filodoro, Dim hosiery, Badedas, Glisolid, and Aqua Velva. Before being acquired by the American company, Lovable had broken in on the big commercial success of Playtex's Wonderbra with the creation of a push-up model called Love Up, to which La Perla answered with the Sculpture version.

❑ 2002, July. Lovable celebrated 40 years of business and became a division of Sara Lee Intimates Italy, a satellite of the American giant, Sara Lee Corporation. The corporation is active in various production sectors such as food, household products, and cosmetics, but particularly underwear, which represents 44% of its total turnover. At world level it has a turnover of 17.7 billion dollars, 32% of which originates in Central and Western Europe.

Lowe-Holder Michelle. Canadian designer, working in London. After studying in her own country, in 1998 she arrived in London to obtain a second degree from the Central Saint Martin's College. She started her career designing knitwear collections and leather garments. In 2003, her *griffe* had become a total look, with a complete womenswear line and a household collection. She has always been interested in the recycling of materials and research into new working techniques. Her designs are on sale at Barney's in New York and other trendy stores. (*Virginia Hill*)

Lubiam Italian menswear company. "Service is a strategy" is the motto of this company established in Mantua in 1911 by Luigi Bianchi. The company focuses on the combination of craftsmen's skills with the benefits of industrial production, to make high-quality suits available to a wider public. The construction of a tailor-made suit is part of the tradition of Italian fashion: it is part of the culture of perfect wearability. Today, research and constant innovation enable Lubiam to reduce the number of production processes. Programmed production gives constant and uniform quality in each of the 120 working steps, using wools with particular twisting and finishing, linen with silk, and light but very bright cottons. There are four lines: classic and formal, the tailor-made line, the soft line, and the new line. The company is directed by Giuliano Bianchi. In 1998 it had a turnover of 52 million dollars. It exports about 35% of its products to the USA, Great Britain, Benelux, and Scandinavia.
(*Stefano Grassi*)

❑ 2001. Registered turnover 40 million euros, a steady value compared to the previous year. The company had 700 workers, 450 in Mantua and 250 in Tunisia.
❑ 2002, January. Début of Eddy & Bros, a new line for a market aged 25-35. The launch was in three steps: Italy first, then the rest of Europe, and last the USA, where Lubiam has had a

showroom in New York since 1968. The American market represents 40% of foreign turnover.

Lubin French brand of perfumes created by Pierre-François Lubin in 1798. This was the year that the famous fragrance *Eau de Lubin* was created. After rapidly becoming supplier to the French, Russian and English courts, the maison's founder was the first to try his fortune in the southern states of the USA. When he died in 1829, the brand was taken over by the Prot family until 1960, when it was bought by the German group Mühlens. In addition to the overwhelming success they received at the Exposition des Arts Décoratifs in 1925 in Paris, Lubin perfumes were also remembered for the originality and fantasy of their bottles. Among the most famous: *Kismet*, *L'Océan Bleu*, *Lune de Miel*, *Ouvrez-moi* (enclosed in a bag) and *Fumée* (a tromp-l'oeil depicting a cigarette box), *Nuit de Longschamp*, *Gin Fizz*, and *L'Eau Neuve*.

Luca Luca Brand of women's fashion founded in 1991 by the Milanese designer Luca Orlandi. His family has been in the textile business for generations. He moved to New York where he started an apprenticeship with the company Hero Group which produces for Oscar de la Renta, Bill Blass, and Oleg Cassini. He decided to start his own business and in 1992 opened his first boutique in Madison Avenue, Manhattan, now the address also of the company's headquarters. He also opened other boutiques in Chicago, Palm Beach, Dallas, and Bal Harbour. In 2001 he became a member of the Council of Fashion Designers of America. His collection, which is distributed in the United States and abroad, has expanded to include a sports line, shoes, and accessories. The symbol of Luca Luca's style is the sophisticated *femme fatale* dressed in chiffon and leather.

(*Francesca Gentile*)

Lucas Otto (1903-1971). English milliner, born in Germany. He left Germany just before the advent of Hitler and settled in London where his talents were almost immediately recognized. He was offered a platform to operate from, a market, and the credentials to conquer America too.

Lucchesi Florentine tailor. Its premises were in Via dell'Oriolo. In the early 1900s, it was one of the most prestigious tailor's workshops in Florence. It was founded by Gioacchino Lucchesi in 1830 though no official document states his activity. But it seems that the artisan's dynasty dates back to 1600 and has its roots in the town of Lucca. His son Gustavo, and Gustavo's heir Felice served Florence's aristocracy and upper middle classes. And the fourth generation, represented by Marino Lucchesi, continued the old profession, selling to important clients like Luigi Dalla Piccola and Luciano Berio, who visited Florence during the Music Festival in May. The workshop closed in 1987.

Lucchini Fabrics company established in 1831. It specializes in the manufacture of fabrics for *haute couture* and collaborates with the most important Italian *griffes*, among which Valentino, Versace, Gattinoni, Curiel, and Balestra. Since 1939 Lucchini's premises have been in Via Sant'Andrea, Milan.

Lucchini Flavio (1928). Journalist and publisher, born in Curtatone Montanara. Lucchini has contributed to the success of Italian fashion through the magazines he edited. In 1950 he founded and edited *Fantasia*, a fashion monthly. His name was connected with the launch of the weekly *Amica*, the magazine that assisted the Corriere della Sera group to respond to the stranglehold the publishers Mondadori and Rizzoli had in the women's magazines sector. *Amica* was conceived by Franco Sartori, with Enrico Gramigna responsible for the graphics and the editorial launch. Three years later Lucchini took over direction of *Novità* which, for Condé Nast, he transformed into *Vogue*. In 1977 he created *Lei*, a monthly for young girls. Compared to Condé Nast's traditional glossy publications, this magazine was rather an upstart. It began well but sales fell off. With Gisella Borioli, his wife, in 1980 he founded the monthlies *Donna* and *Mondo Uomo* under his own company, Edimoda. Though in direct competition with the Condé Nast periodicals, the two enjoyed a long success. *Donna* launched the careers of great Italian photographers like Fabrizio Ferri and Giovanni Gastel. For *Eri*, the Italian State television's publishing house, he designed the layout of the monthly *Moda*. Not content to sit on his laurels, in 1983 Lucchini started an ambitious and very difficult project (the Italian market was packed with women's magazines): the launch of a new weekly called *Eva*, under the editorial command of Francesco Cevasco. The idea was innovative: the first issue was published at the end of September and sold more than 150,000 copies, but within a few months the circulation declined and the project failed. Following the death of Franco Sartori, the general manager of *Vogue Italy*, in 1990 Lucchini was called back to Condé Nast to take Franco's place as director of the Italian office. Internal problems resulted in Lucchini selling 30% of his company Edimoda (publisher of *Donna* and *Mondo Uomo*) to his publishing partner Edilio Rusconi, starting a slow detachment from the world of publishing. In 1993 he accepted a position in Condé Nast Italy as a consultant, though his mind was moving slowly towards art. Nowadays Lucchini pairs his management of the Superstudio group (photographic studios, spaces and services for fashion communications and design), with his activity as a sculptor, inspiration for which comes exclusively from the world of fashion that he helped to create.

Luchford Glen (1970). Photographer. He started his professional career working as the assistant to Eamon McCabe and Norman Watson, and his first published pictures appeared in 1989 on the pop group the Stone Roses and in *The Face*. Since then he has confirmed his position as a fashion photographer in *Arena*, *i-D*, *Interview*, *Rolling Stone*, *Harper's Bazaar*, *Vogue Homme International*, and in the English and French editions of *Vogue*. He collaborates with several brands, such as D&AD, in 1995 with Jenny Surille and in the period 1997-98 with Prada. He also works in the cinema: his movie *From Here to Where* got a special mention at the Edinburgh Film Festival in 2000.

Luciano Barbera Brand of men's and women's ready-to-wear fashion designed by Luciano Barbera and made using the high quality fabrics produced by Carlo Barbera & C. from Biella. It offers classic designs and accessories distributed by Grilux Spa. In 1975 another line was created, the Linea Club of belts, shoes, and golf bags. The brand has two showrooms: in Via Montenapoleone, Milan, and at 730 Fifth Avenue, New York. In 1998 turnover amounted to 13 million dollars, with exports representing 85%.

❑ 2000. The consolidated turnover totalled 15 million euros.
❑ 2001. In a year of crisis for the sector, the company from Biella increased its turnover to 19 million euros.
❑ 2002. Turnover was 17 million euros, 65% of which was derived from the USA. Luciano Barbera's five children work in the company. Production is decentralized to third parties. The company planned to strengthen its distribution network and expand its competitive position in Russia, where it has opened an own-brand boutique.
❑ 2003, April. With the crisis that dramatically hit the textile-clothing sector over the previous two years, several textile companies decentralized their production to countries where labor costs are cheaper. The strategy adopted by Lanificio Barbera is different: "The development strategy relies on inverted decentralization. Tradition, specialization and the thinness of the wools are the weapons with which our company intends to fight the competition from China and Eastern Europe which will never be able to equal the quality of Italian products, despite their competitive labor and production costs."

Lucile Professional name of Lucy Sutherland (1863-1935), London's *haute couture* designer famous in the first two decades of the twentieth century. She had an atelier with offices in London, Paris, Chicago, and New York. She numbered movie stars and actresses like Sarah Bernhardt among her customers. She designed the costumes for the theater production *The Merry Widow* and for Broadway's *Ziegfield Follies*.

Lucio Costa Italian brand of ready-to-wear fashion. It takes its name from the designer who created it and made its début on the Milan catwalks with the Fall-Winter Collection 1987-88, all focused on knitwear.

Lucky Professional name of top model Lucie Daouphans (1922-1963). She died very young after founding a retirement fund for models. She worked ten years for Dior (1950-60).

Lud Russian model and cover-girl of the 1930s-40s. She is especially remembered for the extreme versatility she was able to give to her photographic image and for the theatricality she expressed when modeling for Hermès and Fath. Lud abandoned her career to marry a lion-tamer.

Ludwig Reiter Austrian shoe factory founded in 1885. Shortly after being opened by Reiter, his workshop received the order to manufacture the boots for the imperial police of Vienna. Reiter's son, also called Ludwig, opened the company's first factory, where the brands Fox and Piccadilly were made. These boots were given a special and more resistant sole invented by Charles Goodyear. In the mid-1990s, an expressly retro line was created with the launch of Cricket, a shoe similar to the model adopted by the Austrian army in the 1970s, but more comfortable. 2003 saw the launch of the Anna Reiter shoe for women; this is a flat shoe with an extremely soft sole made with horse hair. Another original design was the Tiger Sandal. The company is now run by the family's fourth generation.

Luigi Borrelli Shirt factory in Naples, set up in 1957 by Luigi Borrelli. The company benefits from the great tailoring tradition in Naples. In the early 1980s, the company Luigi Borrelli Spa was founded, which expanded its range of products to include ties, pyjamas and men's night robes. The company grew and, in 2000, created a line of coats and jackets (Profilo), knitwear (Btr), and trousers (Class 99). Borrelli has opened stores in New York, Palm Beach, Melbourne, as well as Naples and Rome.

Luigi Taroni Company of textile products established in 1911 by the brothers Ettore and Pietro who maintained the weaving mill founded in the Como area by their father in 1869. The company's products were made using mechanical looms in the weaving mill and hand-looms in private households. The lines were composed of clothing and linen for ladies and gentlemen, silk velvets, umbrellas, church garments, and fabrics for ties. The Taroni company ceased production in 1934. The Como plant was bought by Tessitura Serica Clerici Taroni & Co. (1935), established by Pietro Taroni's heirs, Alberto Clerici, Luigi Carlo Clerici, Paolo Lucca, and Emilio Greco.

Luisa Spagnoli Manufacturing company established in the early 1930s by the Italian entrepreneur Luisa Spagnoli. At the beginning it produced only outer knitwear with the brand Angora Luisa Spagnoli. After twenty years of success, in 1952 the brand-name was changed to its current form, while production was expanded to include women's clothing and a younger line created in the early 1990s by Nicoletta Spagnoli, the great-grand-daughter of the founder. Luis Spagnoli's genius and organizational skills were not originally applied to the fashion industry, but to chocolates and candies. Before breeding angora rabbits in the garden of her villa in Umbria, she had started her brilliant career in 1919 launching one of the most important brands of Italian chocolates, Perugina. But the success of the famous *Bacio* (Kiss) was not enough. Taking angora wool as her starting point, she tried a career in fashion. In a short time her designs became very popular in Italian shops. When she died in 1935, her brand was already very famous in the USA and the company, now in the hands of her son Mario, and then Lino Spagnoli, had already made the big leap. Since the opening of the first shop in Perugia in 1940, the company set a record for direct stores in Italy, which numbered 140 by the year 2000. Mario Spagnoli's daughter had her grandmother's name and renewed her fame, but in a completely different field. A writer, journalist and leading member of the socialite and intellectual life of the Rome of the 1960s and 1970s, she is the author of *La Lunga Vita di Giorgio De Chirico*, published by Longanesi, a delicious and graciously irreverent book about the private life of Giorgio De Chirico. (*Ilaria Ciuti*)

❑ Turnover of 106 million dollars

(+9.4%) and a net profit of 6.6 millions. The chain of shops consisted of 145 sales points in Italy's largest cities. The company employs 700 people, 550 of whom work in the shops.

❑ 2001, May. The company reorganized itself to reach a younger audience. Nicoletta Spagnoli, general manager and great-grand-daughter of Luisa Spagnoli, the company's founder, said: "In the beginning we had some difficulties about changing our products which have always been designed for a traditional public. Then, we started to implement a gradual renewal and the younger public got our message."

❑ 2001, June. "Changing under the banner of tradition," is the Spagnoli motto: no acquisitions, no Stock Exchange, no new managers. From some viewpoints, this makes it an unusual case in the modern fashion business in Italy. Début of a perfume and the opening of a shop in New York.

❑ 2001. Knitwear continued to be the company's flagship, to which have been added coordinated accessories. The company's transformation also involved the restyling of 145 sales points.

Luis Trenker Clothing brand created in Alto Adige (northeast Italy) in 1995, through a joint venture between the brothers Hansjorg and Michi Klemera, and a Bavarian partner. The brand takes its name from Luis Trenker, a legend in his homeland, who was an actor, director, writer and mountain climber (35 films, among which *Love Letters from Engadine*, in which he also acted in 1938; 31 novels; and an intensely lived life spent between the peaks of the Dolomites and New York). And Trenker's spirit, charm and spontaneity are the inspiration for the slightly bucolic, but also elegant, simple, and amusing collections. The brand is distributed from Alto Adige to the rest of the world. Luis Trenker clothes are worn by Arnold Schwarzenegger, Jutta Spiedel, and Kastelruther Sparzen.

(*Maria Vittoria Alfonsi*)

Lumberjack Shoe brand distributed by La 3A Antonini, a company established in Verona in 1945 as an craft activity by Ivo Antonini and his cousins Alvaro and Ezio. In the mid-1950s, 3A Antonini was already an avant-garde industrial company in the shoe sector. Over a span of 59 years the product has changed more than once, complying with the evolution in customs and market demand, transformations that have been made possible by the use of advanced technologies. Between 1965 and 1975 the company was very successful in the children's shoes sector; and in the 1980s with the launch of the Lumberjack shoe. The company is now managed by the third generation and was one of the first to believe in the importance of the advertising message. The most important choices made have concerned production and marketing. First, through a decentralization strategy over several stages: first in the Verona area, then in southern Italy, and later abroad. The second step concerned changes made to the distribution network to meet the demands of the marketplace. The Lumberjack brand is now distributed to a network of retailers rather than wholesalers. The new brand's philosophy is focused on constant updating, shifting from the traditional outdoor nature of the brand towards a more fashionable and casual style. Acer, a production plant near Brasciov in Romania, was opened at the end of 2000. It employs 200 people. The company's goal is the direct production of shoes in an area that has now become an object of interest to other companies. The entire production process occurs under the supervision of Italian technicians specialized in quality control, in order to keep production standards to the levels requested by ISO 9002 certification. In 2002 Antonini's turnover was 56 million euros, 18.44% from exports. The company has 1,480 multibrand sales points, 6 own-brand stores, of which 2 are owned by the company and 4 are franchises.

(*Dario Golizia*)

L'Uomo Vogue Italian men's fashion magazine founded in 1967 to accompany *Vogue Italy*, and from the second issue already an independent magazine, first bi-monthly then monthly. Under the direction of Franco Sartori (until 1976), Flavio Lucchini (1976-79), Cristina Brigidini (1979-92), Aldo Premoli (1992-2000), Franca Sozzani and now Anna Dello Russo, the magazine has followed and sponsored men's *prêt-à-porter*. At the beginning its approach was in contrast with the traditional elegance of the 1950s-60s, then, during the 1980s, it documented the birth and the ascent of the emerging *griffes* and later became the speaker of the new need for design and essentiality. The magazine has always employed very important photographers: among others, Ugo Mulas, Oliviero Toscani (who started to work for the magazine very young), Bruce Weber, Carlo Orsi, Norman Parkinson, Horst, Helmut Newton, and Lord Snowdon.

Lupfer Markus (1969). German designer working in London. Lupger interrupted his studies in Tier to finish them in England, at Westminster University (1997), graduating with top grades. His final year collection was immediately displayed in the shop windows of Koh Samui, a very trendy London boutique. His style is sophisticated and modern; he favors the newest of fabrics and pays great attention to details. His creations were presented for the first time during London Fashion Week in 1998. That same year he found a powerful Japanese agent who launched him in the Asiatic and American markets. Since 2000 he has worked for Top Shop, a large chain.

(*Virginia Hill*)

Lupi Italo (1934). Architect, designer and graphic artist. For Pitti Immagine he worked on the organization of the exhibitions *Latin Lover/A sud della passione* (1996), *Il motore della moda* (1998) and *Volare* (1999). Since 1991 he has directed the monthly magazine *Abitare* which, in 2003, celebrated 40 years of publication. He graduated from Milan Polytechnic, has worked with Pier Giacomo Castiglioni, and has been graphic consultant for La Rinascente and art director of *Domus*.

Lurex Trademark for a metallic yarn invented by Dow in the 1940s. It can be produced in a range of colors and incorporated into a variety of woven and knitted fabrics to create shimmering light effects. Designers such as Gianni Versace who aim for evening glamour often use Lurex in their designs.

Lutens Serge (1942). Photographer and make-up artist. He's considered to have been one of the most brilliant make-up artists, famous for his dreamy, conceptual and very refined creations, as well as for the innovative audaciousness of the colors he uses. His made his début in 1963 on the pages of *Vogue France*, with a series of avant-garde maquillages. In 1968 he was appointed artistic director of Christian Dior Beauté. He started shooting his first studio photographs. From 1980, the year he left Dior, he was head director of Shiseido make-up collections and image, for which he also dreamed up advertising campaigns.

(*Ginevra Falzoni*)

Lutz German designer. He came to the notice of the business operators after posing in 1992 for a reportage on sexuality by Wolfgang Tillman for *i-D*. He moved to London where he studied at Central Saint Martin's and graduated in 1995. After a three-year period at the atelier of Martin Margiela in Paris, he returned to London to teach at Saint Martin's. In 2000 he created his own *griffe*, which was first presented in Paris during *prêt-à-porter* week. He takes vintage clothes, disassembles them, cuts them anew and assembles them again in new shapes. (*Maddalena Fossati*)

❑ 2004, November. During the Gwand Swiss Textiles Award Festival he was awarded the Ackermann *Prêt-à-porter* Prize.

Luxardo Elio (1908-1969). Italian photographer. With a masterly use of light, he created a statuesque and refined photographic style. Born in Brazil to an Italian family, he arrived in Rome in 1932 where he made his name as an interior, fashion, and advertising photographer. But his real success depended on his ability to make innovative portraits with a skilful use of light. Very keen on cinema (he regularly attended movie theaters, considering them an important stimulus for his ideas) and very interested in the use of lights made by the great Hollywood photographers, he employed reflectors used on movie sets to characterize his style. Thus he became the photographer of the stars of Cinecittà, from the times of the "white phones" until the 1960s. Though rather rigid in style, his photography was current for its romantic and very accentuated composition, even during the post-war period when Luxardo started diversifying into other fields. He began photographing for the advertising business, both Italian fashion products and others such as those made by Motta and Ferrania. In the portrait field, his fame remained undimmed: one of the prizes received by Miss Italia was the possibility of making a book of black-and-white photographs with him.

Luxottica World leader in the design, production and marketing of sunglasses and spectacle frames for the medium-high segment of the market. The company has been quoted on the New York Stock Exchange since 1990 and in Milan since 2000. It was established in 1961 by Leonardo Del Vecchio who, after a brief experience as a medal engraver and printer, decided to start his own business in the sector of metallic items for the spectacles business. Luxottica's premises are in Agordo, near Belluno, a district that makes almost all Italian glasses. The small factory (only 10 people) used to specialize in the making of products for third parties. It was in 1967 that the big strategic intuition arrived: though continuing to manufacture semi-worked products for third parties, the company started producing complete glasses, marketing them with the brand Luxottica. This was a highly successful decision and, after only four years, it dropped its work for third parties and devoted itself exclusively to the production and sale of its own brand. It presented its first collection in 1971 at Mido, the International Fair of Optical Items. "We had an innovative product. Basically the company had been founded as a third party supplier, specialized in the manufacture of all components. The day we assembled all of them we were able to sell the finished products at prices lower than anybody else. Thus, we prepared a catalogue with such competitive prices that retailers came to us en masse," recalls Leonardo Del Vecchio. The small workshop expanded. Production efficiency, research, vertical organization, internationalization, corporate culture, marketing strategies and wise investments: these are the reasons for the company's success. For Luxottica efficiency and research are essential to gain and maintain an advantage over its competitors. Continuous research into efficiency has led to the centralization of all production steps, thus allowing a quality check on the finished product and the holding onto its customers. This circle also permits lower costs and greater investment in research. At present the company can manufacture 125,000 glasses a day in 6 plants. To keep market leadership, though, management has realized that it is not enough to be good producers: one also has to know the market. This was the cue for the brilliant idea to integrate wholesalers into the final part of the process in order to understand and meet the needs of consumers. The first distribution company, Scarrone, was bought in 1974. Thanks to its efficiency, productive specialization and vertical integration, Luxottica has had the means to conquer world markets since the early 1980s. The management also understands the need to create a commercial structure abroad. Thus, in 1981, with the creation of its first associated company in Germany, the strategy began of expansion abroad, which has been continued sometimes with partners and, in other cases, through joint ventures. At present the company has 29 branch offices and 100 independent distributors in 120 countries. This is the winning formula: centralized production in a few privately owned plants that are capable of meeting the needs of the market rapidly, which are constantly monitored through the distribution network. Finally, the marketing strategy of partnership with world famous designers and the acquisition of famous brands. The first collaboration with the world of fashion dates to 1998, with a license agreement with Giorgio Armani, which was followed by contracts with other international designers. These branded lines have allowed Luxottica to capture the greatest market share and to promote the group's image. In the 1990s, the company began an acquisition campaign of prestigious brands. In this, the financial market has also played an important role. For a company which produces and sells all over the world, the opinion of financial markets can become an excellent business card. Notwithstanding the fact that the company has excellent economic-financial indicators, in 1990 the group decided to quote itself on Wall Street and in December 2000 on the Milan Stock Exchange. Three more strategic moves have allowed the glasses giant to reach its current size. First, the acquisition in 1995 of the US Shoe Corporation, the owner of Lens Crafters, which, with more than 860 shops, is the largest glasses retail chain in North America. Second, diversification into sunglasses. In the late 1980s, 90% of Luxottica's output was reading and sight glasses, yet, the market was moving towards sunglasses, an item that follows the whims of fashion and is therefore subject to constant evolution. Luxottica then diversified its strategies through other acquisitions. After acquiring the Italian brands Vogue and Persol in 1990 and 1995, it made the big leap in 1999 when it took over the historic brand RayBan from Bausch & Lomb, which at the time was in a bad financial situation. After heavy investment, RayBan has finally made up lost ground. Finally, in March 2001, the group acquired Sunglass Hut International Inc., the world's largest sunglasses retail chain, with more than 1,600 sales points in North America and 250 in the rest of the world. The purpose of this operation was twofold: on one hand it has allowed it to consolidate the American market; on the other, it can now promote other lines in the same shops. The ten-year agreement signed in 2003 with Versace allows Luxottica to design, produce and distribute spectacles and sunglasses branded Versace, Versus and Versace Sport. Shortly before, in November 2002, the renewal of the license agreement with the group Armani had been announced. At present Luxottica manufactures about 2,450 models of frames and sunglasses. Production is almost entirely carried out in the six plants of Sedico, Pederobba, Turin, Agordo, Rovereto and Cencenighe. In addition, the company owns a plant in China for the manufacture of metal frames. The models are commercialized with its own name and licensed brands: RayBan, Vogue, Persol, Arnette, Killer Loop, Revo, Sferoflex, and T3 (owned); Chanel, Versace, Versus, Ferragamo, Bulgari, Byblos, Genny, Ungaro, Tacchini, Moschino, Web, Anne Klein, and Brooks Brothers (licensed). Luxottica products are sold in 120 countries and on all 5 continents. It has a commercial network of 1,000 agents, 29 branch companies, and 100 independent distributors, who reach 200,000 sales points all over the world. In 2002 the turnover was 3.13 billion euros (+2.2%), with operating profits of 601.5 millions (+18.1%) and a net profit of 372.1 million euros (+17.6%). The net turnover of the group in the first quarter of 2003 amounted to 704.5 million euros, the operating profit 111.4 millions, and net profit 65.6 millions. (*Dario Golizia*)

❑ 2003, June. Leonardo Del Vecchio joined the board of directors of Gianni Versace Spa.

❑ 2003, June. Giorgio Armani, a group shareholder with 5.02% of the capital, quit the Luxottica board.

❑ 2003, August. The group acquired 74% of the capital and therefore control of the Australian optical chain OPSM, which has 481 sales points.

❑ 2003, December. The group registered a turnover of 3 billion euros, profits of 370 millions and has branch offices in 30 countries.

❑ 2003, December. Leonardo Del Vecchio planned his succession: "The company will pass on to the management and the family will play only the role of shareholder. We are working on this. I have five children, three adults and two little ones... But Luxottica has a good management, and the company counts on it."

❑ 2004, January. Fortified by the strength of the euro, Luxottica signed an agreement to buy Cole National, the second largest glasses distributor in the American market, for 401 million dollars. The operation has a strategic importance because it allows the group to widen its offer in the American market with products complementary to those distributed by Lens Crafters and Sunglass Hut, which are also owned by Luxottica.

❑ 2004, February. The license contract with Chanel was renewed until 2008.

❑ 2004, May. The partnership between Versace and Luxottica was a success. In the first year, a turnover of 90 million euros was achieved.

❑ 2004, June. A five-year agreement with Donna Karan was signed to design, produce and distribute Donna Karan and DKNY sunglasses throughout the world.

❑ 2004, July. Cole National Corporation approved the merger with Luxottica (price per share 27.50 dollars).
❑ 2004, September. The new board of Luxottica directors was under preparation. At the shareholders' meeting, the number of directors was increased from 9 to 12, and a new general manager, Andrea Guerra, was appointed.
❑ 2004, October. A new five-year agreement with Dolce & Gabbana was signed to design, produce and distribute Dolce & Gabbana and D&G Dolce & Gabbana sunglasses worldwide.
❑ 2004, December. Excellent economic results for the group: turnover (3.2 billion euros) grew 14.1%; and profits (286.9 millions) by 7.3%.
❑ 2005, January. Luxottica sold its shareholding of 21% in Pearle Europe to Hal Investments.
❑ 2005, March. The first quarter of 2005 closed with a turnover of 1.037 billion euros (+34.8%), an operating profit of 136.4 millions (+13.6%), and a net profit of 76.3 millions (+7.3%).
❑ 2005, July. The group's acquisitions continued with the purchase of Chinese Xueling Optical. (*Dario Golizia*)

LVMH Giant French group selling luxury goods. The acronym stands for "Louis Vuitton-Moët-Hennessy" and identifies a group associated with high quality products, subdivided into four categories: fashion (Dior, Kenzo, Céline, Lacroix, Vuitton, Givenchy, Loewe, Berluti, and strong holdings in Gucci, and Fendi); wines and champagne (Moët Chandon, Veuve Cliquot, Pommery, Mercier, Chateau d'Yquem, and Hennessy); perfumes and cosmetics (Guerlain, and the essences belonging to the various fashion maisons). In 1998 total turnover was 6.9 billion euros. The workforce numbers 33,000 people. The president of the group, holding 31% of the shares, is Bernard Arnault who, in partnership with the Irish company Guinness, has won control of the group, and strengthened it by bringing in Dior, Lacroix, Céline and the healthy remains of the Agaghe Willot textile empire, which he resuscitated in 1980 with a large investment by the French government.

❑ 1999. Attained a turnover of 10 billion dollars (+23% on 1998) and a net profit of 818 million dollars (+160%).
❑ 2000, August. The group bought 67% of Pucci. According to the terms of the agreement, the remaining 33% remains in the hands of the Pucci family. Laudomia Pucci di Barsento, daughter of Emilio, remained as president. In the same month, the group acquired the American giant Art&Auction, established in 1979 and dedicated to the world of art.
❑ 2000, October. LVMH received the award for the best balance sheet of the year. Best not only in terms of results, with growing turnover and profits, but in terms of clarity and readability. The honor was awarded by the French Financial Analysts Association and by the Journal des Finances.
❑ 2000, November. The group acquired a shareholding of 3.5% in Tod's, the company belonging to the Della Valle family. This investment is the ideal continuation of the development of the excellent relationship between the two groups. The French giant expanded its empire in the field of distribution with the acquisition of La Samaritaine, one of Paris's oldest department stores. Cost of the operation: 275 million dollars, of which 180 millions were financed by raising capital. LVMH also decided to join Rossi's capital stock; Bernard Arnault made the announcement specifying that he had also decided to enlarge his partnership with the prestigious Italian shoe brand by also involving the Givenchy and Emilio Pucci collections.
❑ 2000. The following acquisitions were made during the year: Miami Cruiseline Services, world leader in luxury duty-free goods on cruise ships; the control of the fourth largest cosmetic company in the United States, Urban Decay; the periodical Connaissance des Arts; Omas, an Italian company that specializes in the production of high quality pens; a majority shareholding of the US cosmetics company Fresh.
❑ 2000. The year closed with a 35% rise in turnover and the year 2001 opens with an investment for the group in

Italy: a global store on three floors in Via Montenapoleone, designed by the American architect Peter Marino.

❑ 2001, January. The group Arnault and De Beers, the world's largest diamond producer, concluded an equal joint venture for the sale of diamonds and jewelry.

❑ 2001, April. The operation was finalized through which LVMH acquired the American *griffe* Donna Karan for a counter value of 243 million dollars. This followed the operation of December 2000, when the luxury giant bought out Gabrielle Studio, the company which owned the Donna brand.

❑ 2001, May. The general assembly of the Fendi group approved the balance sheet for the year 2000, which registered proceedings for 332 million dollars, double 1999. Such growth was made possible by the company's reorganization by Prada-LVMH, which now controls 51% of the *griffe*.

❑ 2001, October. LVMH acquired 45% of Rossimoda, an Italian company that specializes in shows for the high segment of the market.

❑ 2001, November. The acquisition campaign of the French group continued. Now it was the turn of Casor (67% of its capital), a former producer of clothing collections branded Emilio Pucci.

❑ 2001, November. The Group LVMH and Prada concluded an agreement with the intent, on the French side, to acquire all the shares in Fendi held by Prada, i.e., 25.5% of the total. After the operation, the luxury giant owned 51% of Fendi, while the Roman maison retained 49%. The line Fendissime, created in 1987 for a young market, was withdrawn from the market. Fendi has 83 privately owned stores. LVMH also acquired the Italian company Acqua di Parma.

❑ 2001, December. LVMH sold its Gucci shares to Crédit Lyonnais (11,565,648 shares with a value of 1.15 billion euros). The war between Arnault's group and PPR (the François Pinault group) was over for the possession of Gucci.

❑ 2001. The year closed with a turnover of 12.2 billion euros (+6% on 2000) and a massive decline in net profit, only 10 million euros against the 722 millions of 2000. The reason for this decline was the distribution department, which represented losses of 194 million euros. In 2002 Arnault was to focus on internal growth, profitability and cash flow. This program included the development of Fendi and Donna Karan, two *griffes* controlled since the end of 2001, which the group considered rich in potential.

❑ 2002, March. Acquisition of 20% of Corrado Maretto, the former licensee of Louis Vuitton shoes and specialized in women's shoes for the high segment of the market. 80% of the company remained under the control of the Maretto family.

❑ 2002, April. Christian Lacroix was appointed the new artistic director of the Italian *griffe* Emilio Pucci.

❑ 2002, May. Kenzo Takada returned to LVMH and the group acquired a minority shareholding, 17%, of Kenzo Takada Inc.

❑ 2002, October. Louis Vuitton aims for the conquest of Paris. The maison built an unprecedented commercial empire in the heart of Paris. LVMH purchased the department stores next to La Samaritaine in Rue de Rivoli, and planned to convert them into shops to sell its luxury products.

❑ 2002, November. Début in Piazza Strozzi, Florence, of the first Fendi boutique. The Roman maison has 84 direct sales points and 450 indirect.

❑ 2002. LVMH closed the year with a consolidated turnover of 12.7 billion euros (+4% on 2001), an operating profit of 2 billion euros and a net profit of 556 millions. The secret of this success consisted in focusing on the most profitable brands or on those with a higher potential. Particularly positive were the performances of Wines & Spirits (+2%), Fashion & Leather (+16%), Perfumes & Cosmetics (+5%); negative the Retailing Division (-4%). Growth in all reference markets was good, in particular in Japan (+15%), thanks to the new 10-floor megastore opened in Tokyo. And Christian Dior did wonders, with a turnover of 492 million euros, which represented a growth of 41% and an operating profit of 33 million euros: this performance was due to the success of the collections designed by John Galliano. Louis Vuitton registered a growth in sales in Europe and the United States.

❑ 2003, April. Louis Vuitton opened its first boutiques in Moscow and New Delhi. With these new openings, Louis Vuitton now has 298 stores, and a presence in 51 countries. The Asiatic market, Japan not included, represents 15% of the 4.12 billion euros turnover of LVMH's fashion and leather goods business: this was a growth of 1% on the previous year.

❑ 2003, April. The group acquired almost total control (97%) of Rossi Moda. The company, leader of the Veneto shoe district, produces and distributes several brands, among which Givenchy, Pucci, Lacroix, and Jacobs.

❑ 2003, May. The shareholding in Fendi was increased to 84.1% after the acquisition of the quotas belonging to Alda, Anna and Paola Fendi. Silvia Venturini Fendi maintained the role of Creative Director.

❑ 2003. LVMH sold 36% of the brand Michael Kors for 13.9 million euros.

❑ 2003, May. Pucci designed the first technical shoe for the Vivara line. It was to be produced by Sabelt and distributed by Rossi Moda. The collection was inspired by a famous printed pattern found in the archives of the Florentine maison.

❑ 2003, June. The license rights for the perfumes Marc Jacobs and Kenneth Cole were sold.

❑ 2003, August. Acqua di Parma, after the OK from the Anti-Trust, is entirely controlled by the French group, which had already owned 50% of the capital since September 2001.

❑ 2003, September. Fendi opened a boutique in Tokyo on two floors. In Japan Fendi had 38 own-brand boutiques and 96 around the world.

❑ 2003, September. Antonio Marras, a Sardinian designer, was made Kenzo's new artistic director.

❑ 2003, September. Emilio Pucci opened a new store in London. The sales point was designed by the architects Vudafieri Partners & Deux L.

❑ 2003, October. The group sold the champagne brand Canard-Duchene.

❑ 2003, December. Concetta Lanciaux, Bernard Arnault's right arm, presented the group's strategies. "We are in the luxury business, rather than in the fashion business, with strong brands such as Dom Pérignon, Hennessy, Moët & Chandon, Dior, Louis Vuitton, and smaller but strongly developing brands such as Kenzo, Givenchy and Marc Jacobs, and brands which are to be relaunched such as Donna Karan and Fendi. What we want is to make these brands managerially independent."

❑ 2003, December. Ozwald Boateng was made the new creative director of Givenchy's men's collections.

❑ 2004, January. In the controversy with Morgan Stanley, which had been accused of issuing negative ratings on the LVMH group, the court decided in favor of the French group. The investment bank was condemned to pay 30 million euros damages.

❑ 2004, February. Morgan Stanley appealed against the verdict.

❑ 2004, March. Opening of the first Pucci boutique in Venice.

❑ 2004, April. Roberto Menichetti was made the new creative director of Céline womenswear, replacing Michael Kors. Céline's president, Jean-Marc Loubier, stated that "it may seem a paradox, but this is a meeting between a brand and a personality. Roberto is a world citizen, and Céline's identity is that of a sophisticated, delicate Parisian woman at her ease everywhere, in New York as well as in Shanghai." Céline closed 2003 with double-digit growth in its turnover. It had about 100 own-brand boutiques.

❑ 2004, June. Veuve Clicquot and Emilio Pucci "marry."

❑ 2004, July. Dior opened a shop in Rue Royale, Paris. It's the company's fifth boutique in the French capital and the 168th worldwide.

❑ 2004, July. A second Pucci boutique was opened in New York.

❑ 2004, July. Louis Vuitton opened a new boutique in Sloane Street, London.

❑ 2004. Emilio Pucci signed an agreement with Wolford to launch an exclusive line of tights and leotards.
❑ 2004. Since the Pucci brand was bought by the French group, turnover has increased by 400%.
❑ 2004. Raphaele Canot was appointed the new artistic director of De Beers.
❑ 2004. Nicholas Knightly appointed to direct the design team for Louis Vuitton leather goods.
❑ 2004, October. Dior opened a megastore in Tokyo, built on seven floors: five for sales, two to the Dior Museum. It is the largest store in the Far East.
❑ 2004, December. Two famous brands, Emilio Pucci and Rossignol, signed a five-year license agreement for the production of ski clothing, technical knitwear, and accessories, presented in two annual collections – Summer and Winter.
❑ 2004, December. Excellent economic-financial results for the group. The total turnover, 12.62 billion euros, grew 6% (+11% at equal exchange rates and area). The operating profit, 2.42 billions, represented an increase of 11%. The group's net profit for the first time exceeds 1 billion euros, 1.01 billion, registering a sensational growth of 40%. Finally, debts had been reduced from 5 to 4.6 billions. The leading division was Wines & Spirits (+8%), followed by Fashion & Leather (+5%). A decline of 1% was represented by perfumes, watches and jewelry. In particular, the brand Louis Vuitton registered a record year. The other brands, Céline, Marc Jacobs, Pucci and Berluti continue to grow, especially in Asia. Fendi and Donna Karan, on the other hand, still suffered difficulties.
❑ 2004, December. The Christian Dior group had a turnover of 13.2 billion euros, a growth of 6% on 2003. Net profit, at 464 millions, also enjoyed strong growth at +53%.
❑ 2005, January. Christian Lacroix was sold to the American group Falic.
❑ 2005, March. Riccardo Tisci was appointed the new designer for Givenchy. He is the third Italian designer working for LVMH, with Antonio Marras, at Kenzo, and Roberto Menichetti, at Céline.
❑ 2005, March. Carole Kerner returned to the leadership of Donna Karan New York.
❑ 2005, March. Partnership with the Spanish group El Corte Ingles, to develop the controlled company Sephora.
❑ 2005, March. LVMH created an ad hoc division, New Perfumes, guided by Laurent Houel, whose purpose is to group the fragrances and give life to two new lines: Fendi and Pucci. The Rome label's perfume was being produced by LVMH's biggest competitor, PPR, through a license contract due in July. Pucci, on the contrary, made its début in the world of perfumes.
❑ 2005, March. In the first quarter of 2005, turnover was 3 billion euros at constant exchange rates, representing an increase of 11%. In particular, the division Wines & Spirits grew 13%, and Watches & Jewelry 21%.
❑ 2005, April. The controversy with Morgan Stanley continued. The French group asked 183 million euros extra for moral damages from the American investment bank.
❑ 2005, May. After only two seasons the collaboration with Menichetti came to an end. The divorce was consensual and the Umbrian designer decided to devote himself to his own collection.
❑ 2005, June. The controversy ended over use of the name Kenzo between the designer himself and LVMH, the brand's owner for 12 years. Before the official decision of the court, the parties reached an agreement in which "the terms are to be maintained confidential."
❑ 2005, June. Bernard Arnault, owner and president of LVMH, with assets of 14.3 billion euros, is the richest man of France. *(Dario Golizia)*

Lycra Brand of synthetic fiber that has been on the market since 1959, one of the most famous products made by DuPont. It is a segmented polyurethane belonging to the group of elastam synthetic fibers mixed with other fibers. It allows linen fibers to be stretched to seven times their original length. It is extremely thin and the fibers are white and opaque. Having undergone technical improvement over the years, its degree of elasticity has been increased. It is used in underwear and since the 1990s has also been used in stretch and elasticized fabrics.

Lyle and Scott Long-established brand of English knitwear. Its name has been linked to golf champions. The company was established in Hawick, Scotland, in 1874 by two partners, William Lyle and Walter Scott. Golfing champions such as Ian Baker-Finch and Greg Norman won the English Open Championship wearing Lyle and Scott clothes: every hand-worked garment is made from 10% cashmere, merino wool and natural fibers, and has an average content of 2.4 km of thread. The company's traditional cardigans, waistcoats, and pullovers have been added to since 2002 with a younger line that incorporates the company's established motifs: in particular, the gray, lemon and white outfit worn by Norman when he won the Open in 1986. In November 2000, the company opened a sales point in Tokyo; in January it was present at Pitti Uomo and later at the Golf Fair in Monaco. In July the same year, the brand reacheed an agreement with Hartmarx to distribute Bobby Jones clothing (the sports division of the American company Hickey-Freeman) in Europe. From September 2002 it has designed the official pullovers of the Scottish rugby team.

(*Pierangelo Mastantuono*)

Lynes George Platt (1907-1955). American photographer. At first attracted by literature, he tried to write a novel, but in 1925 moved to Paris and made the acquaintance of several members of the artistic avant-garde. He continued to move back and forth between Europe and New York, where he opened a bookshop (that he later moved to New Jersey) and the publishing company Stable Publications. His authors included Gertrude Stein, René Crevel, and Ernest Hemingway. Having been given a camera, under the guidance of a professional photographer he took up photography. Renowned for his portraits of famous personalities and friends such as Gertrude Stein and Jean Cocteau, he exhibited them in personal exhibitions, but he also produced theater photographs and amazing male nudes of intense sensuality. In 1932 he opened a studio in New York and began publishing his photos in *Town and Country* and *Harper's Bazaar*, which were characterized by clear references to Surrealism. From 1946 to 1948 he directed the Vogue studios in Hollywood, but on his return to New York he was so overwhelmed by debts that in 1951 his archive and studio were seized and put up for auction. Thus, only 600 photos, which were purchased by Alfred Kinsey to illustrate homosexual eroticism in his Institute's collection, escaped the destruction Lynes himself perpetrated on his works for fear that they could damage his reputation.

Lynx Light, gauzy fur, with thick, long hair. Almost white background with gray-brown-yellow streakings. Often used to decorate cuffs and collars.

M

Mabitex Founded in 1963, it produced men's trousers "with a tailored and sporting feel" and later women's trousers, which were becoming increasingly popular in contemporary fashion. Currently, the company produces about 1,000 pairs a day. In 1973 it opened a factory at Roreto di Cherasco. Although trousers remain its core product, since 1986 it has broadened its outlook with the brands Nick Name and Vestium Officina, designed by Luca Rejnero, who changed the logo to V-o for the Fall-Winter 1999-2000 Collection. The company has 1200 shops globally.

Mabkhout Wahb (1964). Moroccan photographer. After studying science at high school in Morocco, he now lives and works in Paris, London, and Milan. He studied for a diploma in styling and modeling at the Marangoni Institute. In 1998 he began his career as a model, branching out into fashion photography at the beginning of the 1990s. His most important clients are Dolce & Gabbana, Gianfranco Ferré, Sergio Rossi, and Exté. He works for *Cosmopolitan America*, the German edition of *Amica*, *Vogue Italy*, *Marie Claire*, and *Max*. He also published a book, *Fashion Tribes*, in June 1999. (*Valeria Sico*)

Mabro Male Clothing company founded in 1957 by Manlio Brozzi, the heir to a longstanding family tailoring tradition. New factories were opened in 1970 that brought together the different production phases of suits and coats made of Tasmanian wool, cashmere and silk, without neglecting made-to-measure tailoring, which continued alongside industrial production. During the 1990s, the group produced garments for prestigious labels, such as Pierre Cardin, Berry of London, and Maxim's of Paris. A production crisis at the beginning of the new century led to redundancy pay-offs for a large number of the 400 employees at the Tuscan plant.

Mabrun Italian leather clothing company. Founded in 1936 at Bassano del Grappa as an artisanal workshop producing leather accessories and sporting garments. Today, it specializes in ready-made leather fashions for men and women. Recently Mabrun has launched a sportswear line called Martin Eden, which is aimed particularly at a youthful clientele. The company's collections are sold in 1,100 shops around the world. Mabrun is also available in more than 30 department stores.

Mac & Maggie A brand of ready-made clothing and the name of about forty Dutch boutiques. It constitutes a small empire in Holland, Belgium, Germany, and England and developed out of a distribution company – Peek and Kloppenburg – in 1976 as a result of an intelligent strategy, that of targeting the youth market even at the cost of exaggerating the designs.

> ❑ 2003. The entire production was amalgamated under the two brands Peek & Cloppenburg and Mac & Maggie.

MacDonald Julien (1972). British designer. Julien MacDonald was born in the town of Merthyr Tydfil but, as his first name suggests, he has French origins through his maternal grandmother. As a boy he studied fine art and did not consider a career in fashion until he discovered it when taking a course of textile design. Consequently, he enrolled at Brighton University and later at the Royal College of Art, where he obtained a Master's degree in 1997. In the same year, he created his first collection of glamorous creations and elegant knitwear and became known in London with his own-name label at the age of only 28. He is called "the wizard of knitwear" for his designs that, inspired by a fairy-tale world, mix unusual materials (for example, silicone, crystals, ermine tails, sequins) in an ostentatious display. His first collection so impressed Lagerfeld that MacDonald was immediately invited to do an apprenticeship as a knitwear designer for Chanel. He has collaborated with McQueen, Berardi, and Koji Tatsuno. On 14 March 2001 he was appointed artistic director of Givenchy women's collections (*haute couture* and *prêt-à-porter* accessories). In July of the same year he presented his first collection for Givenchy.

❑ 2003, January. MacDonald designed the uniforms for British Airways air hostesses. He replaced skirts with trousers for the first time in 30 years though retained the airline's traditional colors: red, silver, and blue. They were worn by 100 hostesses for a five month trial period and were definitively adopted in 2004. The hats, designed in collaboration with Stephen Jones, are in the style of the 1950s. For the stewards he designed pinstriped suits.
❑ 2003, February. MacDonald presented a collection at London Fashion Week presented at a sparkling evening. He designed mini dresses encrusted with Swarovski crystals and sequins, and crocheted ponchoes showed alongside fitted biker outfits in soft leather, fox-fur and rabbit jackets, which provoked the fury of animal rights demonstrators.
❑ 2003, March. On the Paris catwalks, for Givenchy Julien MacDonald mixed Parisian and London styles. He created a very black collection, full of leather and knitwear, often combined with furs. Small dresses in shiny jersey with gold or sequined hems, and which highlighted the silhouette, napa leather jackets with high knitted waists fitting closely around the hips, suits in jersey decorated with zips, high leather boots that fit like a glove, textiles and knitwear in black-and-white checks.
❑ 2004, March. He designed his last Givenchy collection for Fall-Winter 2004/2005.

Macfarland Pond Toby (1968). English photographer, published in *Vogue France* and *The Face* with fashion shoots for Yamamoto, Nike, Hermès, and Cartier.

Mackenzie Andrew (1954). British stylist. Born in Wales, graduated from the Dyfed College of Art and Design, later specializing at the London College of Fashion Technology. He has lived and worked in New York, Paris, and South Africa. Since 1980 he has lived in Italy and has designed a collection of jeans and menswear under the label Amk-Andrew Mackenzie, launched in Spring-Summer 1998. At his first catwalk show in Moscow in October 2002, he provoked and fascinated with his "electroclashers," later shown in Stockholm and Rotterdam. Mackenzie has also successfully participated at AltaRomaAltaModa.

❑ 2002, June. At the Milano Moda Uoma, men's catwalk shows, Mackenzie presented a collection that combined a revival of 1970s American designs with Andy Warhol's Pop Art and Bowie-style decadence, with punk and psychedelia, using chains, studs, unexpected juxtapositions, zips, metal decorations, and long laces strung around the wrists.
❑ 2002, June. For their Italian summer tour, including their appearance at Festivalbar and the Heineken Jammin Festival, the Turin-based band Subsonica, founded in 1996, wore clothes created exclusively for them by Mackenzie.
❑ 2002, October. Mackenzie presented his Spring-Summer 2003 collection in Moscow, comprising men's and women's clothing as well as the Flash Uomo line.
❑ 2003, January. At the Fantasy exhibition held in the Palazzo delle Esposizioni at AltaRomaAltaModa, Mackenzie exhibited a unique garment created for the occasion, inspired by the surreal and imaginary. A few days later, he showed his designs in the Auditorium with a performance that once again payed homage to the 1970s and the icons of that period, from Warhol and Iggy Pop to Bowie, reliving the spirit of the glory years of Pop Art.
❑ 2003, June. Less extreme and dark compared with previous years, the new Uomo collection, drawing on digital and technological stimuli, was as fresh and irreverent as the youthful spirit it sought to embody. Mackenzie's models were

accompanied by laser projections and water displays, representing street culture as a form of life philosophy. The garments themselves were associated with various aspects of streetwear, from the very sporty to the most elegant.

Mackie Bob (1940). Californian stylist, born in Los Angeles. A great enthusiast of feathers and sequins, he has worked a great deal for the television and theater. Among his actress muses are Carol Burnett and Cher, who attended the 1986 Oscars wearing one of his dresses: covered with sequins and cut away at the stomach. In 1979 he published a book titled *Dressing For Glamour* and launched a pret-à-porter range in 1982.

Mackintosh (also Macintosh). A waterproof overcoat, which appeared on the market towards the middle of the nineteenth century. It took its name from Charles Macintosh (1766-1843), a Scottish chemist, who invented a waterproofing method that he patented in 1823, in which two layers of woolen fiber are joined together by rubber dissolved in coal-tar naphtha. In 1830 he founded Macintosh & Co with Thomas Hancock, previously one of his competitors. In 1851 Joseph Mandleburg found a solution to the smell of rubber in waterproofed textiles, producing the first odorless overcoat. Although waterproof Macs were originally full-length, voluminous garments, during the course of the twentieth century they began to reflect the influence of changing fashions and contemporary styles.

Maclaren Norrie (1948). Scottish photographer and art director for various fashion magazines. He belonged to a creative group of individuals who published two independent magazines, *Deluxe* and *Boulevard*, during the late 1970s. In 1975 he was an assistant to Stanley Kubrick on the film *Barry Lyndon* and later in 1980, on *The Shining*.

Macramé A form of very heavy and uniform lacework, made of a series of knots and plaits. Both the name and technique are of Arab origin. Used for applied decoration or for evening dresses.

Macy's An American chain of department stores. It was declared bankrupt at the beginning of the 1990s but was acquired by Federated Department Stores Inc. in 1994. Its oldest and most famous store is located on 34th Street in Manhattan, where it takes up an entire block and is considered one of the most important shopping emporiums in the world. Founded in 1858 by R.W. Macy, ever since 1924 the New York store has organized a grand parade through the streets of Manhattan on Thanksgiving Day, in order to mark the beginning of the Christmas shopping period. Macy's has also recently inaugurated a Benefit Shopping Day, held in Fall, when a percentage of the day's takings are donated to about sixty charitable organizations.

❑ 1998. Macy's by Mail Catalog was created to enable mail-order shopping.
❑ 2000. The first Macy's store outside North America was opened in San Juan, Puerto Rico.
❑ 2003, August. The San Francisco store presented Oscar De La Renta's new collection of household accessories inspired by the decor of his three houses: one with exotic interiors in the Dominican Republic, one in urban New York and the third in the countryside of Connecticut.

Madame A monthly German fashion magazine published in Munich by Magazinpresse Verlag. It was founded in 1952 out of the merger between the two magazines *Figaro* (1950-52) and *Die Elegante Welt*. With features on couture and ready-to-wear fashions, as well as interior design, lifestyle, travel, art and culture, it maintains a steady distribution. Figures from the first half of 2003 show that the magazine sold about 96,000 copies of which over 20,000 are subscribers.

Madame Figaro French weekly magazine for the readers of *Figaro*. Founded in 1980 as a monthly supplement to the daily newspaper, it began to be issued fortnightly from January 1983 and then weekly from September 1984. It averages 120 pages and covers food, shopping, fashion, celebrities, cinema, and literature, in line with the traditional model of women's magazines. In

1980 it employed 5 journalists but by 1997 the team comprised almost 100 people. From its inception, it has been run by Marie Claire Pauwels. Its subtitle is "The weekly with sound values." Thanks to its formula and intelligent journalism it has achieved popularity beyond France with various international editions: in Portugal (1988), Japan (1990), England (1993), Korea (1994) and Greece (1994). In 1996 it generated a new supplement entitled *Maison Madame Figaro*. After 20 years in charge, Marie Claire Pauwels is assisted by an editorial director, Anne Gilet. However, the management of the bi-monthly *Maison Madame Figaro* remains firmly in Pauwels' control.

Madame Margé American designer who achieved fame during the 1930s. Also known as Marguerite, she achieved an international reputation for her batiks and Indian designs.

Madame Suzy French milliners. In 1941, Bergdorf Goodman, the refined New York department store, began to stock the firm's hats but their immediate success did not persuade the owner-designer to move to the United States. The Parisian atelier turned her into one of the most prominent designers during the post-war period.

Madapolam Cotton cloth originating from the Indian city, Madapolam. Lightweight and fine, it is well suited for use as underwear and bed linen. It is generally produced in white or pastel shades.

Mad Carpentier French tailoring house founded in 1940. After the closure of Madame Vionnet's Parisian fashion house, Madeleine Maltézos and the sales director, Suzanne Carpentier, opened their own atelier in the city. It shut in 1950, after ten years in business.

Madeleine et Madeleine-Anna French tailoring house. La Maison Madeleine opened in 1921 on the Champs-Elysées, run by Count Hubert de Montagu, and also stocked furniture and items for the home. In 1924 it joined forces with the atelier Anna, changing its name to Madeleine et Madeleine-Anna. In 1926, the label became famous for its invention of the first women's smoking jacket in gold lamé.

Madison Avenue In Manhattan, New York. It is considered "the" fashion street. It has also been nicknamed the "Italian mile" for its high concentration of Italian shops and designers, in particular between 57th and 79th streets, where brands like Armani, Valentino, Prada, Moschino, Etro, Ferré, Dolce & Gabbana and Versace occupy prestigious shop spaces. What once used to be a quietly elegant street has now become a meeting point of designers from all over the world, who use masters of interior decor to present and exalt their image. One of these is Peter Marino, who has worked on important projects on Madison Avenue, from the nine-storied Barney's on 61st Street, which cost 267 million dollars in 1993, to the minimalist temple on four floors dedicated to Armani, which dominates the whole of 65th Street. Nothing is left to chance when designing a new store on Madison Avenue: the shop windows and furniture are studied in minute detail by professionals in order to transmit opulence and luxury. The race for shop space is still underway. As the space between 57th and 72nd is entirely occupied, it continues to the north, where it is still possible to acquire something from the last fruit-seller in the area. However, it has only been during the last decade that Madison Avenue has become synonymous with wealth and luxury. For years it lived in the shadow of the nearby Fifth Avenue, where Tiffany and Saks has always represented American glamour. At Madison it is now possible to breathe a sense of "European flavor." Old, low-rise buildings with boutiques, bistros and small restaurants copy their European counterparts. This is most evident beyond 86th Street, by Carnegie Hill, currently the most sought-after residential area. This is tranquil and elegant, like a European neighborhood with shops run by their owners, which is nowadays a rarity. As well as fashion, Madison Avenue also has a separate business side. For years, the midtown area of Madison, between 30th and 40th Streets, was the center of the publishing world (now partly relocated to the Flatiron district). Later on, with the construction of the Sony (previously the AT&T) and IBM (1993-94) skyscrapers, Madison Avenue's business center has moved to 55th Street. Neighborhood life revolves around bars, galleries and the internal courtyards of the two buildings. The cultural aspects of Madison Avenue are not to be overlooked, with real treasures – such as the Pierpont Morgan Library on 36th Street, once the residence of J. Pierpont Morgan, with its rich collection of drawings and manuscripts – and the imposing Whitney Museum on 74th Street, the symbol of contemporary American art, as well as the very elegant uptown galleries. (*Priscilla Daroda*)

Madonna Born Maria Louise Veronica Ciccone (1959). American pop star and actress, who also became a fashion inspiration for her young fans. In 1984 she capitalised on this by founding Madonna Wanna-Be, a clothing company aimed mainly at teenagers. Her look was unique, constantly pursuing a type of sexy sensationalism. She wore underwear as outerwear, with basques and cone-shaped brassieres. Typical features included high heels, a bare midriff, tight mini-skirts and lace tops with rigid cups. Of Italian origin, she has relatives in Pacentro, in the province of L'Aquila. Born in Detroit (Michigan), she abandoned her university studies to move to New York, where she worked as a model before becoming a singer. Among her most famous records are *Madonna* (1982), *Like A Virgin* (1985), which sold more than 5 million copies, *Who's That Girl* (1987) and the soundtrack of the film *Evita* (1996). Her acting career began in 1985 with the film *Desperately Seeking Susan* and she married the actor Sean Pean, from whom she divorced in 1989. In 1990 she acted alongside Warren Beatty in *Dick Tracy* (the soundtrack is also hers). In 1996 she was nominated for an Oscar for *Evita*. Her daughter Maria Lourdes was born the same year. The father was her personal trainer, Carlos Leon. (*Lorenzo Leonarduzzi*)

Madras Cotton textile woven with large multi-colored checks, typically in bright, vivacious colors. Orginally from the Indian city of the same name where, at the end of the nineteenth century, it was handwoven and dyed exclusively with vegetable dyes. Today, the term refers solely to the design, regardless of the type of fabric used. It is mainly used for summer clothing, particularly shirts and trousers, as well as 1950s revival jackets. Avant-garde designers (such as Moschino, Westwood, Kawakubo) have often used madras for entire garments. The menswear collection of Comme des Garçons from Fall-Winter 1997-98 used it in a double version. (*Cristina Lucchini*)

Mafia French fashion and advertising consultancy. Mafia (Maïmé Arnodin Fayolle International Associés) was founded in 1968. In 1985 it was sold to the BDDP advertising group. The founders, Maïmé Arnodin and Denise Fayolle launched Nomad (Nouvelle Organisation Maïmé And Denise) two years later.

Magic Marketplace A large exhibition of men's, women's and children's clothing and accessories, held in Los Angeles twice a year in February and August, for a period of 4 days, bringing together over 3,000 vendors from all over the world. The fair is split between the Las Vegas Convention Center and the Sands Expo Convention Center. The different companies are divided into four areas, according to each different sector: Magic for men's clothing and accessories, WWDMagic for women, Magic Kids for children and The Edge for Avant garde brands. Many Italian companies participate under the banner of Ice (in collaboration with the Italian Fashion Agency).

Magli Bruno. Italian shoemaker. A Bolognese family firm: Bruno and Maria began making shoes by hand in the 1920s. In 1936 they headed a small company and, after an enforced gap during the war, work got underway again in 1947 in a new hangar. During the 1960s, the company's high heeled sling-backs and pointed shoes made headlines. They opened a series of shops in Bologna, Genoa, Milan, Rome, Venice, and Turin. After the deaths of Bruno and Maria, their children, Mauro, Sandro and Morris, continued to run the business, creating a "total look" that included a men's range, a series of overcoats, bags, and accessories. The company exports 80% of its production.

❑ 2001, June. Match Race is the new shoe created by Magli Sport for the sailors on Mr Geko in the Wally Cup.
❑ 2001, December. Opera (an investment group involved in luxury

goods companies with a capital of approximately 225 million euros, owned 50% by Bulgari) completes the acquisition of Bruno Magli Plc. With this 150 million euro operation, Opera becomes the proprietor of Bruno Magli companies in Italy and abroad, the American license, and sales outlets. Opera is actively involved in the corporate management of Bruno Magli in the United States. Other shareholders participating in the take-over are the Japanese Mitsui, which currently holds 2% of the package, and the pension fund Verizon, with 19%.

❑ 2002, March. The new stylistic director of Bruno Magli is Ernesto Esposito, who exhibits the Fall-Winter 2002-2003 collection in the Via Bigli showroom in Milan. Esposito collaborated with Louis Vuitton and Sergio Rossi. In 2001 Bruno Magli sales production totaled 89.1 million euros compared with 91.3 million in 2000. Exports make up 80% of turnover. Their retail outlets consist of 65 own-brand shops, 25 of which are in Italy.

❑ 2002, November. The six companies belonging to the Magli family acquired by Opera now make up a single group headed by Bruno Magli Plc. As well as the reorganization of the companies, the objectives of the brand relaunch include increasing the number of retail outlets, investing in the accessories sector, and focusing on the Japanese market.

❑ 2002, December. A new Bruno Magli store opened on Via Roma in Florence. Exports represent 72% of turnover.

❑ 2003, March. Bruno Magli Japan was created, a joint venture with Itochu and Kanematzu-Ginza (a leader in footwear and leather retailing). The aim of the new company, with headquarters in Ginza, is to develop the brand and reach a total of 35 own-brand stores and corner outlets, creating a turnover of over 35 million euros by 2005 (compared with the current 8 millions) in Japan alone. Overall, the own-brand stores increased from 66 to 77 by the end of 2003 in order to reach a quota of 100 by 2005. The Fox Town outlet in Mendrisio was opened, followed in April by the Via Condotti store in Rome. The United States market was also strong, representing approximately 38% of turnover. Currently, Magli has six own-brand stores in America and a network of 50 corners in department stores (Neiman Marcus, Barneys and Bloomingdales). In 2002, Magli registered a turnover of 73 million euros with a production of 500,000 pairs of shoes per year.

❑ 2003, June. New stores opened in Moscow and Kuwait City, plus a second boutique in New York.

❑ 2004. Michele Alberti was made the company's new commercial director. A new strategy was launched to try and bring the label's accounts back on track, focusing on a reappraisal of the distribution network. The first six months of the year demonstrated a 63% increase in the United States for the menswear collections and a 25% increase for womenswear, with similar growth in the Japanese market as well.

❑ 2005. The company, which is 94% controlled by Opera (the investment association that includes the Bulgari Group) closed 2004 with a turnover of 52 million euros, 40% of which was made in the USA.

(*Gabriella Gregorietti*)

Maglierie Daisy Knitwear company based in Florence that originally only produced women's garments. Founded by the Piccini family in 1957 and taken over by Mario Zetti in 1961. Its creations are exported to various department stores in the United States, Germany and Great Britain. It is also sold in Australia, Canada, and Japan, while approximately 20% of its designs are sold on the Italian market.

(*Giampiero Remondini*)

❑ 2003. The company launched a range of men's knitwear created by a team divided between management, design, marketing, sales, and administration. America has been the most receptive foreign market, absorbing 55% of goods for export, followed by England at 35%. In addition to the roughly 150 commercial designs, the company also produces personalized garments, both in terms of design and weave, to order.

Maglificio Emmevizeta Knitwear company founded in 1959 by Sergio Monti, specializing in cotton and woolen garments. In 1968 the quality of its products was improved by the acquisition of automatic knitting machines. Over the following decade the company doubled in size. From 1971 onwards it produced designs in cashmere, mohair, and silk and initiated a collaboration with Pierre Cardin. During the mid-1960s, designers such as Ungaro, Ferré, and Valentino worked in its sample studio and the company began to supply the Gruppo Finanziario Tessile. The next generation of the Monti family joined the firm, which improved its equipment technology, the range of looms and formed new alliances with designers. In the 1980s they worked for Gucci, Ferragamo, Westwood, and Donna Karan. In the 1990s, the company targeted Japan, produced all the ranges for Staff International, acquired the Demetra brand, became the licensee of J. Mishra, began a working relationship with Hilfiger, Calvin Klein, and Escada Sport, and researched and applied ecological dyes in collaboration with the Centro Botanico in Milan. In 1998, this led to an entirely natural collection, down to the buttons, packaging and labels, consisting of vegetable and mineral dyes. The company has a production capacity of 140,000 garments per year.

Magnano Angelo (1897-1973). Tailor, academic, researcher and fashion writer. Born in Licata (Agrigento). After working in Padua, he moved to Verona and bought out Mangioni, the historic Calabrian tailoring atelier. In addition to tailoring, he was passionate about, and made a particular study of, dress history. He collaborated with numerous magazines, including *Lingua Nostra*, and wrote *Il taglio degli abiti attraverso la moda e il costume, e la storia delle sue basi fondamentali* (bequeathed to the Maestrelli Foundation in Milan) and *L'arte dei sartori in Verona*, a history of tailoring in the city from 1290. Extending his research to include numerous national and international libraries (the Library of Congress in Washington, the British Museum, the Bodleian Library in Oxford, and libraries in Dresden, Leipzig, Amsterdam, and Berlin), he obtained access to very valuable material. He donated his research to the public library in Verona, where there is now an exceptional collection of documents on the history of dress held in the Magnano archive. His sons, Luigi and Cesare, worked alongside him but the family ceased their tailoring activities in 1993.

Magnaschi Pierluigi (1941). Journalist and director of *Milano Finanza Fashion*, the first Italian daily newspaper dedicated to the world of fashion, first published on 10 December 1997 by Class Editore owned by Paolo Panerai. He also directed *Mf*, *Italia Oggi*, and the weekly magazines of two daily newspapers for the same editorial group. At the end of July 1999, Magnaschi became the director of the news agency, Ansa. Originally from Piacenza, Magnaschi began his career at *L'Avvenire*. In 1977 he took over the Christian Democrat weekly, *Discussione*. Later he became assistant editor of *Il Giorno* and the editor of the Sunday edition of the *Corriere della Sera*. He continues to be the director of Ansa.

Magnoni Paula Clelia (1959). Jewelry designer. Born in Buenos Aires to Italian parents, with three children, a well-seasoned traveler, attracted from an early age by the magical fascination of precious stones, antique ornaments and jewelry as symbols rather than merely forms of ostentation. For years she has collected rare and curious pieces, which she succeeds in endowing with a new vitality. Mah-jong counters, lucky animals, such as salamanders and frogs, old ivory buttons, dagger handles, precious coral tortoises, buckles and African amulets, shells, glass and stones all contribute to make up a surprising and curious collection. Her designs, created in workshops in Milan and Rome, are slowly coming to notice. A necklace in ebony and red coral, a ring in Italian quartz with a superb ivory Buddha and another necklace made of amber, ebony and gold, all possess a rare beauty. Paula Clelia Magnoni uses materials such as stream pearls, aquamarine stones, amethysts, yellow quartzes, coral, ivory, ebony, jade from Japan, Brazil, India, Tibet, Thailand and the Dominican Republic. In March 1999 she held her first exhibition, at the Spazio Bigli in Milan, and later in Rome and Bologna. In

December of the same year she exhibited in New York at Henri Bendel.

(*Marilea Somaré*)

Mago the pseudonym of Max Goldstein (1926). One of the most talented Swedish costume designers, he worked for the cinema and theater. In the 1950s he produced designs for Ingmar Bergman's films (*Sawdust and Tinsel*, *Smiles of a Summer Night*) in a style that combined grace and functionality with a light irony. From an Israeli family, he was born in Berlin and moved to Sweden at the age of 13. A few years later he was hired as a designer on the daily newspaper, the *Stoccolma Expressen*. In 1949 he began to design for theater magazines, creating elegant, frivolous and imaginative clothes, working later in films. After Bergman, he frequently collaborated with the director Arne Mattson.

Magrath Sportswear Brand that specializes in golf products. It belongs to Nautica, the company founded in 1983 by David Chu, later renamed Nautica Enterprises Inc. after it was acquired by State-o-Maine. E. Magrath Apparel Company produces two collections, one under its own name, the other called Byron Nelson: sweaters, shirts, pants, shorts, jackets. After the closure of the German branch, Nautica Europe, during the second half of 2004, it no longer has a European headquarters. As part of this strategy to reduce financial investments and to increase diffusion throughout Europe, the European section – that made up no more than 2% of annual sales – was to be run entirely by Nautica Apparel in New York.

(*Pierangelo Mastantuono*)

Magrini Gitte. Italian costume designer. Born in Milan, died in Rome in 1976. Some of her ideas, such as the camel coat worn by Marlon Brando in *Last Tango in Paris*, became cinematic icons. Assistant costume designer for *Eclisse*, she began to work autonomously for *Deserto Rosso* and collaborated on various other films by Antonioni. She designed costumes for Bertolucci (*Il conformista*) and for Truffaut (*Les deux anglais et le continent*).

Mahdavi Ali (1974). Iranian photographer, who moved to Paris, where he studied at the École Nationale Supérieure des Beaux Arts. He brings his own highly personal style to the world of fashion, and won the Polaroid prize for young creative photographers in 1996.

Mahfouz Abed. Lebanese designer. With a degree in electronic engineering, in 1995 he took over his mother's and sister's small but busy tailor's workshop in Beirut, expanding it and transforming it into a sophisticated atelier. It was immediately successful. By 2003, Mahfouz was running a style office with more than ten designers. In July 2003 he presented collections on the catwalks of Rome during the *haute couture* fashion week, with designs inspired by strong Arab traditions, using chiffons, sequins, and multicolored organzas.

Maïmé Arnodin (1916-2003). French consultant stylist and journalist. Married with three children, after gaining a diploma at the École Centrale des Arts et Manufactures, in 1951 she started as a journalist for *Jardin des Modes*, becoming editorial director five years later. During these years, she supported up-and-coming designers (like Emmanuelle Khan, Gérard Pipart, Christiane Bailly), and acted as a consultant to the clothing production companies, working with Albert Lempereur (owner of a making up factory, who coined the phrase "*prêt-à-porter*"). She left the newspaper in 1958 in order to work on promotional sales and publicity at the department store Printemps. But her ambition was to form her own style and fashion company, which she did in 1960. She advised various industrial fashion and textile firms on products and promotional sales and produced a publication entitled *Colori Maïmé Arnodin*. Eight years after the partnership with Denise Fayolle and the launch of Mafia (Maïmé Arnodin Fayolle International Associés) she became a talent scout for emerging designers and worked as a style and image consultant for various important clients, such as Dupont de Nemours, Absorba, Les 3 Suisses, and Yves Saint Laurent Parfums. Mafia was sold in 1985 to the advertising group BDDP. In 1987 Arnodin went on to found another advertising and communications agency with

Denise Fayolle, entitled Nomad, Nouvelle Organisation Maïmé and Denise.

(*Gabriella Gregorietti*)

Mainbocher (1891-1976). American designer, who achieved great fame in Paris between the two world wars. For American women his name was a hallmark of good taste, innovative materials, and elegance without complications. Born in Chicago, he studied at the Academy of Fine Arts and the Art Student League in New York. Between 1911 and 1917 he lived between Monaco, Paris, and London. After World War I he decided to stay in Paris to attempt an operatic career, which he was forced to abandon due to problems with his vocal chords. Instead, he began to collaborate as a designer on *Harper's Bazaar* and moved to *Vogue*, where he was taken on as an editor, later becoming responsible for the French edition. He remained there till 1929 and the following year he began to work as a designer, becoming the first American couturier with a Parisian atelier on Avenue Georges V. He became instantly known for his close-fitting gowns, sweaters lined with fur and his very simple black dresses, suitable for any occasion. His models appeared on the catwalk wearing white gloves, pearl necklaces and with bows in their hair. He designed Wallis Simpson's wedding dress, which brought him press attention from around the world. In 1940, with France already at war, he decided to return to New York, where he continued to run an atelier until 1971.

(*Eleonora Attolico*)

Maki Akira (1949) American designer of Japanese origin, known for creating a balance between creativity and industrial necessity in ready-to-wear fashion.

Malandrino Catherine. French designer, born in Grenoble. After a diploma at the Parisian institute Esmod, a spell at the *haute couture* atelier of Louis Féraud, followed by the artistic directorship of Et Vous, she moved to New York in 1996. Diane von Furstenberg employed her to work on her collections. At the same time she opened L'Espace Catherine, her own boutique, in the fashion district of Soho. As well as the collections signed by Catherine, the boutique also stocked other little treasures made in France, from Michel Perry shoes to real ballet shoes by Repetto, from Foundation Maeght books to sugared violets. Even in New York, Catherine's style remains "so very French" (as they say in America). Her collections reinterpret all the American myths and traditions but are viewed with a critical French gaze. Her cult product is a vest with the Stars and Stripes flag, created before September 11, 2001, and worn by many stars, including Madonna and Sharon Stone, and even the designer John Galliano.

(*Mariacristina Righi*)

Malatesta Italian brand of New York fashion. Created in 1997, when two Italian stylists decided to transport the colors, silks and cashmeres of India, modified in accordance with Mediterranean tastes, to America's fashion capital. Malatesta accessories (shawls, sarongs, and bags), designs by Cristina Gitti are now on sale in some of the most prestigious shops and department stores around the world, including Bergdorf Goodman in New York, Harvey Nichols in London, and Joyce in Taipei.

Malerba Italian hosiery company, founded in 1926 by the Malerba family originally from Castiglione delle Stiviere. It produces articles for men, women, and children. It has two factories (in Varese and Castelnuovo Valsugana) and a warehouse in Galliate Lombardo. The company has a strong presence in Germany and Spain. At the end of the 1990s, it formed an agreement with Walt Disney to produce socks with designs inspired by the characters Mickey Mouse and Donald Duck.

(*Giampiero Remondini*)

❑ 2002, June. The Malerba group acquired Brigatti, the historic Milanese brand of clothing and accessories, relaunching it in the summer of 2003. Guido Scalfi, the president and main shareholder (at 51%, the rest being owned by the Malerba family) explains that the aim is to revive the Brigatti tradition. One of the fundamental aspects of the relaunch is improved distribution, based on a select number of outlet spaces as well as own-brand boutiques. The aim is to increase the

Brigatti turnover to over 7.5 million euros over a three year period from 2002-2005, with a third of this in Italy and the rest abroad, mainly in the Far East and the United States. Turnover in 2001 totaled 50 million euros (50% made in Italy and the rest abroad). As well as Brigatti, the group includes Malerba hosiery and underwear and the license for Verri Sport men. However, the partnership with Missoni Sport was terminated.
❑ 2003, May. After beginning a new development cycle in 2001 and reaching a profit (1 million euros on a turnover of 40 millions) in 2002, Malerba intended to increase its own-brand shops. To the existing 5 in Italy, and the 1 in Barcelona, it added another in Galliate Lombardo (Varese). It currently has 2,000 retail sales outlets, 1,500 corner spaces in department stores in Italy, and a further 6,000 in the rest of Europe.

Malevich Kasimir (1878-1935). Russian painter. His work reflected a constant attempt to reconcile artistic creation and social commitment. In 1918, with the Socialist revolution almost complete, he developed a form of work clothing comprising a gray uniform, identical for all professional categories. The following year, with the help of his architecture students, he designed fabrics with small geometric motifs against white and gold backgrounds, which were displayed at the Laboratory of Applied Arts at the Museum of Fine Art in Moscow. After 1920, considering different parts of the body as geometric forms, he created accessories and garments with asymmetric lines based on stylized cubes and spheres. These were all bespoke pieces, created almost entirely for friends and relatives. During the same period, he made clothing, fans, sweaters, and scarves with black-and-white geometric motifs, which complemented his Suprematist paintings.

Malhas Rushdi (1965). Saudi Arabian designer, born in Jeddah. From an early age he traveled around the world with his family. Fascinated by fashion, Arab textiles and western designs, at high school he studied the history of his favorite designers: Chanel, Dior, and Balenciaga. After school he studied architecture at university. In 1995 he founded Malhas, with its headquarters in Milan. In 1996 he presented his first collection with a show at Milan's Central Station. In 1998 he opened his own brand store in Via Santo Spirito in Milan. Malhas currently employs 20 members of staff.

❑ 2001. Malhas launched its first line of accessories.

Malhomme Julien (1980). French designer. Studied art before moving into fashion. After attending the École Duperré, he collaborated with various prestigious fashion houses and became the assistant to designers David and Ellie Medeiros. His first menswear collection, created on completing his studies and presented in 2003, was very well-received and awarded with the *Grand Prix Homme* at the Dinard Festival. He proposed a dynamic male figure and dispensed with shirts in favor of vests and wide silk pants.

(*Maddalena Fossati*)

Maliparmi Paduan clothing brand with an ethnic feel: long African-style dresses, bags, studded belts decorated with medallions in a South-American style, sandals, shirts. The team of designers at the Paduan fashion house aim to reinterpret the atmosphere of streets and cities around the world to produce garments that are not simply folkloristic or exotic in appearance but which also revitalize historic craft techniques in the light of new technology. In 2002, the Italian-Danish chromatic artist, Marine Baris, collaborated on the collection.

❑ 2003, February. In the exhibition *Una borsa a regola d'arte*, held in the thirteenth-century granaries of Lispida Castle at Monselice (Padua), 15 artists and photographers (including Giovanni Gastel) reinterpreted the Marrakech bag.

Maljana Italian knitwear company based in Milan. It was in business from 1959 to 1984, producing cut and sewn outer knitwear for women. The designer was Adriano Beccarelli. Its creations were sold in Europe, North America, and Japan. The Italian market absorbed 50% of its products.

Malo One of the brands of the group

Manifatture Associate Cashmere, founded in 1972, by the entrepreneurial brothers Giacomo and Alfredo Canessa. In the 1970s and 1980s it established a growing presence, particularly in Italy. From 1990 onwards, the company sought to increase its export trade by opening commercial branches in strategic markets (New York, Düsseldorf, Paris, Tokyo). At the same time, the company began to open a series of flagship stores aimed at promoting the brand's image: currently it has 17 commercial outlets in cities and holiday destinations in Europe and the United States. In 1999, the company, one of the global leaders in cashmere knitwear, was purchased by Itierre, a group from Molise.

❑ 2002, December. The company, which joined It Holding in 1999, had two factories in Florence and Piacenza and a network of 26 own-brand stores.
❑ 2003, May. Malo designed a line of sunglasses (two models, for men and women) at Mido. It was produced by Allison, also part of the It Holding group. An essentially classic design, the sunglasses have spherical pivots and inner frames in laminated gold. Each one is numbered and can be personalized with the owner's initials.
❑ 2003, June. The stylist Gianni Bugli, who had previously collaborated with Lacroix, Kenzo, and Versace, joined the knitwear group.
❑ 2005. From Fall-Winter 2005/2006, Fabio Pinas, after five years experience with Brioni, became the company's new creative director.

Malossi Giannino (1954). Expert and author in the interdisciplinary fields of fashion, show business, communications and design. He began working with Elio Fiorucci in the 1970s. He has curated exhibitions and written publications that develop his research. These include *Il senso della moda* (XIV Milan Triennale, 1979), *Tipologie dei comportamenti* (Venice Biennale – Special Projects, 1980), *Ricerca sul Decoro* (Centro Domus, Milan 1981), and the volumes *Liberi tutti, vent'anni di moda spettacolo* (Mondadori, 1987), *This was tomorrow. Pop design da stile a revival* (Electa, 1987), and *La regola estrosa, cent'anni di eleganza italiana* (Electa, 1993). From 1996 he has directed the Fashion Engineering Unit at Pitti Immagine, a center researching the economic value of creativity. He has curated exhibitions and written publications for this project, including *Il motore della moda* (The Monacelli Press, New York, 1998), *Volare, l'icona italiana nella cultura globale* (The Monacelli Press, 1999) and *Uomo Oggetto* (Abrams, New York 2000).

Malouf Colette (1963). American designer of hair accessories in leather, plastic, resin, crystal, diamonds, and gold. She has been described in the American press as "a genius in the art of decorating hair." After having made jewelry in recycled materials, selling them to her university friends, Malouf began her professional career in 1987 designing a hair band that sold out at Bergdorf Goodman in two weeks. From the mid-1990s her products have also been distributed in Europe and Japan. In 1998 she won a prize for the best accessories designer from Fashion Group International. Her accessories feature in Michael Kors fashion shows, often stealing the Long Island designer's limelight. Colette is the only hair accessories designer who is a member of the Council of Fashion.

❑ 2003. The spring accessories collection was called French Riviera.

Malta Silvano (1949). Italian designer, born in Cesena. His designs have a theatrical and ironic tone. His career began in Rome as a costume designer, collaborating with the theatrical tailor Umberto Tirelli and costume designer, Pierluigi Pizzi. He took over from André Laug at Antonelli tailors, to whom he was introduced by Beppe Modenese. He designed clothes for high society from 1968 to 1975, at the same time working on the boutique collections for Marina Lante della Rovere (1970-74), Trells, Pims (1970-82), Paola Signorini and the knitwear company Milena Mosele. From 1982 to 1989, he established contacts in Japan in order to produce and distribute his own clothing line, Renown, and opened 60 boutiques in Osaka, Tokyo and Kyoto. During the 1990s, he preferred working on short-term collaborations, with Pianoforte by Max Mara, with Basile, with the Milanese tailor Mosè and Calvin Klein lingerie.

❑ 2003. *Dannati e intoccabili* was the title of Malta's novel on the world of fashion. A mix of fiction and reality, the stylist painted a dark picture of the fashion industry.

Ma Mère The group is a leader in the distribution of children's fashion in Japan, Italian designs in particular. In 2001 it had a turnover of 1.5 billion yen. The multi-brand store Ma Mère Collections opened in Fall-Winter 2002 at Seibu in Tokyo, stocking sportswear for children with collections by Simonetta Jeans, 1950 I Pinco Pallino, Replay & Sons, Agatha Ruiz de la Prada and Cacharel. In contrast, the four Ma Mère boutiques (2 in Tokyo, 1 in Osaka, and the other in Nagoya) have a more elegant style, carrying lines by Pinco Pallino and Simonetta. D&G Junior is sold at both types of outlet.

Mammina Armando (1959). Organizer of fashion exhibitions and product events. He is at the helm of the Expo Cts fairs: Milanovendemoda and Sposa Italia. Born in Palermo, after graduating in law and taking a Master's degree in strategic marketing, at the end of the 1990s he became the director of Momi. He concentrated on breathing new life into the large Milanese clothing fair, diversifying and updating the products offered. After his time at Momi ended, he was given another important opportunity as the director of Milanovendemoda. For the fair season of 2002, he established O-Zone, a section dedicated to some of the most interesting new names from around the world. Here he introduced Claudia Rosa Lukas, Psst, Katty Xiomara and Hartman Nordenholz to the public in Milan.

Mammini Italian tailoring house specializing in equestrian wear, situated in Via del Corso in Rome. It was founded in the mid-nineteenth century by Attilio Mammini, who was tailor to Giuseppe Mazzini. During this period, tailoring ateliers did not yet produce clothing suitable for horse riding. The change came about in the late nineteenth and early twentieth centuries, when a new way of mounting horses was adopted and the stirrups shortened. As a result the leg was more bent in the saddle and pants needed to be fuller. Pericle Mammini, Attilio's son, decided to redesign riding trousers to improve the rider's bearing. Taking the advice of Prince Odescalchi, in 1929 the family opened another atelier in Rome, close to Piazza Santi Apostoli. Up until the 1940s, it was popular with cavalry officials and also supplied the House of Savoy. Mammini's fame was based on his tailoring expertise and his choice of luxury textiles. Baggy pants were made with cover-coat and cavalry twill for winter, and cotton and suede fustian for the summer, a procedure that continues to this day although demand is much reduced. Gary Cooper, passing through Rome, ordered pants made of French leather and several jackets. Marlon Brando and Elizabeth Taylor were also esteemed clients, as was the Iranian Empress Soraya, who ordered Amazonian outfits. The atelier served champions and gentlemen riders, such as the brothers Piero and Raimondo D'Inzeo and Graziano Mancinelli. To this day, it is one of the few workshops able to make bespoke jackets for equestrian competitions and fox hunting.

Mandarina Duck Italian brand of bags, luggage and clothing. Seven is the company Finduck's lucky number: it launched its first Mandarina Duck bag in 1977 and its first collection of clothing in 1997 under the same label. The brand embodies the style known as urban chic. It combines parchment-like textiles with opaque nylon. Md20, the successful youth line from 1989, employed mitrix, an exclusive textile made of 50% nylon and 50% polyester. Their production covers bags, suitcases, and rucksacks, and jackets and pants. Some pieces are on display at the Museum of Decorative Arts in Berlin.

❑ 2000, September. Twenty-two artists were chosen for the Mandarina Duck Award by a jury of six. The initiative was featured in the magazine *Search for Art*, run by a non-profit committee promoting forms of art outside the traditional channels. The project attracted thousands of artists.

❑ 2001, May. 2000 was a positive year for the Finduck group, the holding that controls the Mandarina Duck, Lamarthe and Tibaldi brands. It had a turnover of 102 million dollars, which represented a 15% growth.
❑ 2002, February. Turnover in 2001 reached 122 million dollars (20% growth) and profits doubled to 15 millions. Record sales in December. For 2002 the focus was on the new collection of jewelry, on sale since the previous fall, and watches, in partnership with Seiko.
❑ 2002, May. A polyhedral, multifunctional bag was designed exclusively for Ford Focus. It can be attached to the rear seat of the car and holds equipment for the office, such as floppy disks and cds, as well as drinks, clothing, and other objects. Removed from the seat, it can be carried around the neck or on wheels like a trolley.
❑ 2002, September. The *prêt-à-porter* Spring-Summer 2003 collection was presented at the Place Vendôme in Paris. Production was by Mondrian in Vignola (Modena), while the design and distribution remained with Finduck. The collection was designed by George Gottle in harmony with the style of the bags: elegant sportswear based on technical materials. The turnover for 2001 closed at 103 million euros (a 20% increase on the previous year).
❑ 2002, September. The new London store opened in Conduit Street, designed by the Dutch Marcel Wanders, who had already collaborated on the collection of Murano bags.
❑ 2002, October. At the International Exhibition of Architecture in Venice, Mandarina Duck and Droog Design received a prize for their collaborative project. Droog Design also designed the Mandarina Duck Paris store.
❑ 2003, February. The Finduck Group closed 2002 with a turnover of 110 million euros, an increase of 10% on 2001. It expanded its partnerships. It collaborated with Visibilia for glasses and with the Spanish company Idesa (Idea Parfums) for a collection of perfumes and cosmetics. Following the partnership with the Japanese company Seiko for watches (50 thousand sold in 7 months), 15 million euros of investments in cosmetics were planned by 2006.
❑ 2004, October. The Mandarina Duck Group ceded the Lamarthe brand to Mario Gardini, president and general director of the brand since 2000.

(*Gabriella Gregorietti*)

Manfield French footwear brand. Although by now totally autonomous, even down to its horse logo, it was originally a branch of an English shoe company founded in 1844 by James Manfield, with a vast and undifferentiated range of products. Launched in France (the Paris store was opened on the Boulevard des Capucines in 1898) and Belgium, the company aimed its products at high-level consumers. Under the Thierry family, the French branch made its mark on the quality footwear market, offering a vast range of male and female designs, the latter produced in Italy, in about fifteen stores. Their most typical products are riding boots, low-heeled moccasins in nap leather with a buckle, and patent '*nus-pieds*' sandals.

Manganaro Robertina (1958). Born in Calabria, the transsexual designer is the promoter of superb and refined fashions. For the summer, she uses silk and organza and for the winter cashmere and furs. Her evening gowns have flowing lines and hand embroideries. In 2000 she showed in Milan at Piazza San Carlo and in Rome during the Official Fashion Week.

Mango High street female fashion brand launched in 1984 by the Andic brothers, who opened their first store on the Paseo de Gracia in Barcelona. From the first, its growth has been unstoppable. In 1985 there were just 5 retail outlets, but by 2002 the number had reached 655. The chain operates in 69 countries across the five continents. Outside Spain, the brand functions with a franchising system and, over the last 7 years, has used specialized teams of collaborators. These teams fill a large number of requirements, from implementing image information systems to supervision and graphic design. Mango employees are, on the whole, youthful, and women make up 75% of the personnel. The infrastructure is constantly growing, overseen entirely by its headquarters in Barcelona. Today, Mango is the second largest Spanish exporter in the textile sector after Inditex (Zara, Massimo Dutti), with an international turnover of roughly 1000 million euros. The secret of its success lies in its ability to adapt to the tastes and culture of the countries to which it exports. Although it follows current fashions, it also offers a traditional collection that evolves at its own pace, independent of broader fashion cycles.

(*Estefania Ruilope Ruiz*)

❑ 2002, May. The aim was to open 895 stores, 660 of which are to be located abroad, by 2005. Mango closed 2001 with a 17% increase on the previous year, registering a turnover of 841.4 million euros (over 266 made in Spain and approximately 575 abroad).
❑ 2002, October. Over a brief period of time, the company planned to open stores in Russia, in Moscow, Rostov, Krasnodar, Saint Petersburg, Kaliningrad, Voronezh, Ekatrinburg, Nizhniy Novgorod, Chelyabinsk, and Volgograd. The expansion of Mango into Eastern Europe began a few years previously with its own-brand stores opening in Hungary, Latvia, the Ukraine, Slovenia, Slovakia, Lithuania, Romania, Poland, Macedonia, and the Czech Republic.
❑ 2003, February. An investment plan comprising over 13 million euros to open 100 new retail outlets by the end of 2003. The expansion was to take place mainly in Asia and Europe.
❑ 2003, February. The first Mango store opened in Rome, in Via Cola di Rienza.
❑ 2003, March. Two new openings in Italy: in Turin and Bologna. Mango now owned 10 stores in Italy.
❑ 2003, March. Mango continued to enjoy strong growth. In 2002, store turnover had reached 950 million euros (up 13%) and the group's consolidated turnover 745 million euros (up 11%). 72% of the total comes from abroad.
❑ 2003, April. To the 4 existing stores in China, another was added in Shanghai. Seven more followed. The inauguration of the first store in Milan was announced in August, located in the former VIP cinema in Via Torino. The Mango distributing network now totaled approximately 700 own-brand stores in 70 countries.
❑ 2003, July. Plans to launch in the United States in 2005, starting in New York and subsequently covering the most important American cities. The location in Manhattan was yet to be established: possibly Fifth Avenue, to be followed by a second opening in Greenwich Village.

Manguin Lucille (1905). French tailor who continued to work, although not always in the front line, from 1930 to 1956. Daughter of the painter, Henri Manguin, she was drawn to fashion by Poiret, who frequented her father's studio in Paris. She began to work for friends in a small apartment and went on to open an atelier in 1938.

Maniero Emanuele (1968). Stylist, born in Padua. With a diploma from the New Academy of Fine Art in Milan, he gained experience in the family firm, which produces leather clothing. Later he worked for Trussardi. In 1994-95 he spent time in India. The leather clothing in his first women's collection for Spring-Summer 2000, which was the result of vast research into materials, are more design than fashion products in the strict sense of the word.

Manifattura di Ferno e Borgomanero Italian textile company founded in Ferno (Varese) in 1913 by Piero Broglio, producing cotton fabrics for men's shirts and cotton-linen mixes for shirts and coats for both men and women. Carlo Schapira, a member of the fourth generation of the family, led the company until 2002 as CEO. Carlo Schapira is one of the founding members of the Busto Arsizio Textile Exhibition, together with a group of industrialists, bankers, and members of parliament.

❑ 2002. Schapira was killed in a car accident.

Manifatture Associate Cachemire A leader in the production of cashmere knitwear, the group was founded in 1972 on the initiative of Giacomo and Alfredo Canessa. Between the 1970s and 1980s, it gained ground with the Malo brand, opening factories in Campi Bisenzio (Florence) and Borgonovo Val Tidone (Piacenza), followed by another in Genoa. From 1993 onwards it opened sales outlets across Europe and the United States. It produces 500,000 garments a year and had a turnover of 61 million dollars in 1998.

❑ 1999. Mac-Malo joined the It Holding group, bringing with it the Florence and Piacenza factories and its 26 own-brand stores.
❑ 2002, Fall. The owner of the company, Alfredo Canessa, was made president of Ballantyne, the top brand of Dawson International, a leading company in the creation of cashmere clothing.
❑ 2003, May. Malo eyewear by Allison is founded, a line of sun and eye glasses with gilt interior fittings. A preview of Allison's collection was held at Mido in Milan. It joined the existing lines of clothing, accessories, and interior design objects.
❑ 2003, June. The stylist Gianni Bugli joined the creative team at Malo. Bugli, who previously collaborated with Lacroix, Kenzo, and Versace, took over the knitwear range.

Mann Judy (1951). Chinese designer, working in Hong Kong, creating *prêt-à-porter* clothing.

❑ 2002, April. The stylist sat on the jury for the Footwear Design Competition, held annually in Hong Kong.

Mannequin From the French, where the word is also used to refer to the models themselves, originally derived from the Dutch word *mannaken*, diminutive of the German, *man*, to signify a little man, in other words a puppet or doll. Indeed, in its first incarnation in the eighteenth century, it was a doll, dressed in a miniature version of contemporary fashions. These mannequins, which in Venice were called "*piavole di Franza*," were sent in elegant boxes from Paris to the different European capitals, even as far as the Russian court. The true mannequin, namely a support used to make clothing, originated in the nineteenth century. Initially made out of willow reeds, it was later stuffed in order to simulate the female bust and the male torso. Fixed on a tripod of black wood, it was present for a long time in every tailor's atelier until it began to be replaced, though not everywhere, by mass production or more precise cutting techniques. The term mannequin also refers to shop dummies, made of solid wax, equipped with a head, arms, and legs rather than just a torso, used in window displays. Originally expressionless and decidedly unnatural, they now possess an unsettling "hyper-realism," so much so that they act as a "*trompe l'oeil*" next to posed models in "life" presentations. Mannequins, often from Japan, that are made to fit historic costumes provide an interesting indication of changes in stature and the human body over the course of the centuries. (*Lucia Sollazzo*)

Manoelli Roberto (1936). Manager and organizer of fashion product events. Originally from Milan, after completing his studies at the textile university in Biella, Manoelli began a career in the distribution of clothing and textiles in Italy and abroad, discovering and promoting the importation of French and English designers. He opened a series of Italian fashion stores along the Côte d'Azur and opened the first fashion outlet store in Milan. In 1969 he created Assomoda, the first association of fashion agents, followed by Milanovendemoda, a *prêt-à-porter* salon, which was amalgamated with Modit into Momi, the abbreviation of "Moda a Milano". He headed Momi for 14 years, promoting "Made in Italy" fashions. He founded the Franchising Salon and was involved in marketing and communications, as well as editorial and television productions.

Manolo and Arnaldo Ferrara The ready-made fashion brand of costume designers, set designers, and interior decorators. Manolo Alfonso and Arnaldo Ferrara live and work in New York. Alfonso was born in Cuba. Arnaldo, who moved to the United States in 1978 and first came to attention as a sculptor, was born in Venezuela to Italian parents. Together they designed *prêt-à-porter* collections, including Manolo Ready Couture and a line of wedding dresses called Original Bride Couture by Manolo. They designed the interior of the New York bar

Silencio. They took part in the Milan Triennale in 1994 as designers, in the Maggio Danza in Florence in 1995 as costume designers and in the Florence Biennale in 1996. With about thirty other creators of different forms of art, including Calvin Klein, Gucci, Missoni and David Bowie, the designers were invited by Pitti Immagine to take part in the project New Person-New Universe. The exhibition, held at Leopolda Station in Florence, took inspiration from the discovery of new planets made possible by the Hubble telescope.

Man Ray Pseudonym of Emanuel Radnitsky (1890-1976). Artist and photographer. Line, color, texture and above all sex-appeal: all these factors contributed to the secret of his profoundly innovative fashion photography, influenced by his artistic work (Dadaism and Rayography). He began his professional career in Paris, where he arrived in 1921 from New York and where Gabrielle, the wife of the artist Francis Picabia, introduced him to the fashion designer Poiret, who invited him to photograph his models and introduced him to Worth, Lanvin, Boulanger, Mainbocher, Premet and Redfern. In 1925 his work was published in the first French edition of *Vogue*, for whom he worked until 1930. It was a series of photographs taken in the Pavilion de l'Élégance at the Grand Palais. The garments were hung on wooden mannequins, lending the shoot a surrealist feel. From 1930 he began a collaboration with *La Femme de France*, *Fémina*, and *Beauté*. In 1934, he was invited by Alexey Brodovitch to work with *Harper's Bazaar*. Among his most famous images are the series of African over-garments from 1937, which was inspired by an idea of Nusch Eluard, the wife of the poet. After the war, Man Ray completely abandoned fashion photography in order to concentrate on his artistic research. (*Angela Madesani*)

Mantero Italian silk company based in Como and founded by Riccardo Mantero in 1902. Riccardo, who emigrated from Novi Ligure on a bicycle, and wearing his entire wardrobe, began his career as a salesman for the weaving firm Camozzi-Rosasco and later for Bosisio-Camani-Cattaneo. At the same time he learnt the trade of "coventer," acting as the "umbilical cord" between clients and industry, between demand and supply and becoming an interpreter of demand. By liaising with clients he discovered how their needs diverged from the range of designs offered by the large firms (such as a brighter color or a smaller design) and then sourced silk weavers who could meet their requests. In 1902 he began working on his own with a stock of fabric pieces on the third floor of Via Mentana 12, with the help of his wife and sister-in-law. He had a natural talent for commerce. By 1923 he was able to set up a showroom in Via Volta, where Mantero still has offices. In 1927, after purchasing some looms and installing them in an existing silk factory, he founded the Fabbrica Seterie Riccardo Mantero. In 1940, he acquired the weaving firm of Menaggio and began industrial production, while still retaining a strong commercial bent. This he transmitted to one of his sons, Beppe, who spent nine months of the year traveling for work with a suitcase full of samples, just as Riccardo, the first of his eight heirs, would do after him. Beppe greatly increased the fortunes of the family firm. When his father died in 1951 he began to expand it by first acquiring Alitess (making textiles designed for *haute couture*) and the historical Como silk factory Cugnasca, in 1956. Like the Crespo 180 silk during the 1940s, a particular type of silk called Favola enjoyed widespread popularity during the 1950s: it was a matelassé characterized by a relief effect. It was, above all, the success of Favola that financed the opening of a new factory in Grandate (where weaving production was later supplemented by dyeing and print works) in 1960. Mantero undertook heavy financial investments just at a time when many middle-class Italian entrepreneurs chose to take their money to Switzerland, worried by the first signs of the clash between the Christian Democrats and the Socialists for control of the centre-left. The factory at Grandate began operating in 1964. In time, various firms linked to the Mantero brand flourished: Interseta Ltd, which produced ties (1972), Mantero of America Inc (1976) and Mantero France (1978). Beppe died in November 1982, to be succeeded by five of his eight children: Riccardo, Federico, Cristian, Michele and Moritz. On 27 December 1989, all the family's businesses were merged to form Mantero plc, which was renamed Gruppo Tessile Serico the following year, becoming the holding company for the Mantero group and devolving all the administrative activities to Mantero Seta plc. This produced a colossus that was unprecedented in the silk sector. At the beginning of the 1990s, this was the structure of the group: 11 billion lire of investments, all self-financed, in the renewal of machinery and new technology, net revenues of almost 274.5 billion lire; profits of 13 billions; fixed assets of 85 billion, 24 billions of which were in machinery alone; 956 employees with a total increase of 20% since 1980; two factories (Grandate for weaving, dyeing, printing, with a daily palette of 15,000 colors and 3,000 silk designs, and a finishing works at Sant'Abbondio for the pre-dyed, jacquard-woven ties); 5 lines of figured and printed textiles for ties; 4 lines of textiles for women's medium-high range *prêt-à-porter*; and its own collection of scarves. During the last decade of the twentieth century, Mantero – run by Riccardo, Cristian, Michele, Federico and Moritz: the last two were respectively president and CEO when the group celebrated its hundredth anniversary in 2002 – expanded into the wool sector and synthetic fibers, giving rise to a joint venture with two Japanese firms in order to create and sell high-quality polyester fabrics. In 1995, the group had an annual turnover of about 445 billion lire, 68% derived from exports, representing an increase of 11.5% compared with the previous year, thus doubling net profits. In 1996, the turnover was 440 billions, reflecting a general downturn in the market. However, in 1998 the group's net profits again reached 29 billions. From then, up until the first two years of the twenty-first century, various changes and wide-ranging strategic decisions were necessary in order to maximise the level of service offered to clients, in order to meet the opportunities afforded even during a period of financial difficulty.

(*Pierangelo Mastantuono*)

❑ 2002. The company celebrated its hundredth anniversary with the publication *Mantero 100 anni di storia e di seta*, edited by Massimo Pacifico, text by Guido Vergani and published by Fos.
❑ 2002, June. At Pitti Immagine Uomo, Mantero revealed that it had signed a license contract for the production and global distribution of Emilio Pucci ties.
❑ 2003. The year closed with a 7% drop in turnover (in 2002 it was equal to 122 million euros).
❑ 2003, November. The silk company's three year restructuring plan was negotiated. 6 million euros were allocated to production, logistics, innovation, and human resources. The company would continue to focus on high-quality products.
❑ 2004, March. "La tessitura" (Weave) is the name of the company's new concept store; 1,000 square meters in the center of Como, in an industrial building dating from 1887 where the company's looms have been in operation for over a hundred years. The store stocks fashion accessories and household furnishing items. 2.5 million euros were invested in the project.

Manuel Henri (1874-1947). French photographer, who began working in the fashion sector in 1905, initially for Worth. Up until 1939 he collaborated with *Vogue*, *Les Elégances de Paris*, *Le Miroir de Modes*, *Monsieur*, *La Femme de France*, *Les Modes*, and *The Ladies Field*. The anti-Semitism that pervaded France immediately following Nazi occupation forced him to abandon his work. As a consequence 300,000 fashion plates were lost.

Manuel Jacques (1897-1968). French costume designer. During the 1930s and 1940s, he dressed most of the female stars of French cinema, from Annabella to Edwige Feuillière. He began working for films as an assistant to Marcel L'Herbier and went on to become his costume designer for the film *L'argent*. He taught the art of costume design at Idhec, the cinema school in Paris.

Manuel Alves & Jose Manuel Gonçalves A Portuguese brand named for its two founders, who opened a boutique in Bairro Alto in Lisbon in 1981. The two designers also produce theatre costumes and collaborate with the brands Carlo Giotto, Mauritius, and Quazar.

❑ 1995, the move and subsequent theatrical debut with the costumes for Pirandello's *I giganti della montagna*.
❑ 1998. They created their first *prêt-à-porter* line, named after the two designers. In the same year they won the *Globo de Ouro* and the *Look Elite* for the best collection of the year, going on to win it again in 1999. After theater, they had their first taste of cinema, designing the costumes for João Botelho's film *Trafico*.
❑ 2000. At the opening of Lisbon's fashion museum, the two designers' work was represented with garments symbolising their creativity.

Manuel Canovas French fashion house specializing in the creation of *haute couture* interior décor textiles, beachwear and lingerie. It bears the name of its founder who launched it in 1963 in Paris. After training at the Fine Art Academies in Paris and Rome, where he studied architecture, painting, design, and archaeology, Canovas decided to found his own firm of household fabrics. From his first collection, Canovas achieved a reputation for his design talents, his creative use of color, his knowledge of design techniques, taking inspiration from nature and American folklore. He created a collection of beachwear in perfect harmony with the firm's other lines, in terms of the sense of color and the elegant prints. The line was enriched with accessories such as bags and shoes and underwear was added to the beachwear. The Maison Manuel Canovas is now part of the Colefax and Fowler group.
(*Mariacristina Righi*)

Manufacture d'essai Italian brand of footwear launched in 1990. The line is characterized by a high-tech style and the combination of advanced, technological materials with traditional ones.

❑ 2003, January. The brand makes its first appearance at Pitti Uomo at the Fortezza da Basso, alongside 60 other "new entries."

Mao Name of a form of shirt or jacket, an obvious reference to the clothing always worn by the Chinese communist leader Mao Zedong (1893-1975). It can also refer to a whole outfit: a closed jacket, with a stand-up collar fastened with a button, with two front pockets and loose pants. It is usually made of black, dark blue or khaki green cotton. During the early 1960s, the fashion for the Mao suit spread throughout London, in particular for women, thus becoming a unisex style, a form of ideological uniform, and adopted as such especially by left-leaning artists, intellectuals, and radical-chic women. However, the Mao shirt-jacket (also known as "Korean-style") still remains a constant in contemporary fashion.

Mapplethorpe Robert (1946-1989). American photographer born in New York. Mapplethorpe had a passion for the saxophone, which he studied and played with some talent, but later decided to enroll at the Pratt Institute, from which he graduated in 1970 with a diploma in photography. His first images were influenced by his collaboration with the singer and poet Patti Smith, one of his fellow students and, at that time, his muse. After starting with a Polaroid camera, he then progressed to a Hasselblad, which he used solely on a tripod. He remained faithful both to black-and-white images and the square format, which he considered particularly harmonious. His relationship with fashion was not a direct one, even though it was intense: before dedicating himself entirely to research (portraits, nudes, and his shocking flower photographs), he produced the volume *Lady* in 1983 with images of the model and bodybuilder Lisa Lyon wearing designs by Armani, Ferré, Carolina Herrera, Montana, Krizia, Saint Laurent, and others.

Marabou A bird belonging to the stork family, with soft gray feathers along the body, becoming particularly light, pale and frothy at the tips of the wings. Marabou feathers were often used in the large, composed hats of the early twentieth century to balance the elongated line of riding-jackets. They were also employed around the hems of the opulent evening dresses of the period, as an alternative to ostrich feathers, or in boas and muffs.

Marais Stephen (1960). French make-up artist. Originally from Saint-Malo, he studied economics in Paris. Early on, he realised that tables and graphs were not his passion and so he enrolled at Christian Chauveaux's school of make-up. He began his first collaborations with famous designers, such as Jean Paul Gaultier, Comme des Garçons, Givenchy, Hermès, Prada, and Genny. He was asked to work on some of the most famous shoots in the world, with talented photographers such as Peter Lindberg and Richard Avedon. For the make-up artist, a face reflects personality and his aim is to give women the possibility to see a previously unknown part of themselves. In 2002, he opened his first own-brand boutique in Paris in the rue Saint-Honoré with a line of make-up embodying glamour and originality.

Maramon y Posadillo Gregorio (1888-1960 c.). Spanish doctor who dedicated himself to fashion research. In his volume, *The Psychology of Gesture and Clothing*, he argued that the three functions of clothing were hierarchy, sexuality and protection against the cold. However, he owed his fame to endocrinology, as a European pioneer in the field.

Marani Angelo (1953). Fashion creator, specializing in printed textiles. In 1969, he helped found the Marex group. The printing, weaving and dye-works at the Coreggio factory were Marani's true creative laboratories. The women's line, which bears his name, is diffused throughout Italy and has been particularly successful in the Middle and Far East and South Africa. In September 2002, after 30 years of work, Marani presented his first female collection at Milano Moda. It included clothes made of fabrics that had undergone ageing techniques, sometimes involving three or four different procedures, before being sewn together. These fabrics were produced to order in France.

❑ 2003, February. Marani's catwalk show at Milano Moda Donna began with a hippy spirit and ended with a refined elegance. The collection was very colourful, imaginative and slightly rock-chick. It started with a series of leggings, a symbol of the 1980s, which he reinterpreted in different textiles, colors, laminated, shiny or with florals, worn instead of tights under mini-dresses, tunics with medieval patterns, evening sheath dresses. Jackets with animal-style prints were worn over cargo pants.

Marant Isabelle (1967). French designer, following a family tradition in the sector. Her mother, Christa Fiedler, is a fashion designer. She began by collaborating with Michel Klein and Yorke and Cole. She was an assistant to Marc Ascoli in his work for Yohji Yamamoto and Martine Sitbon. Her first collection, in 1989, comprised jewelry and accessories. In 1990 she launched the Twen knitwear line and in 1995 she presented a catwalk show under her own name. In 1997 she received the Howard Prize for the best creator of the year. In 1998 she opened her first boutique in Paris and designed a collection for the department stores Monoprix and Prisunic.

❑ 2003, January. The executive committee of the Fédération de la Couture nominated two new members of the association: Isabelle Marant and Agnès B joined Christian Dior, Chanel and Sonia Rykiel in the pantheon of French fashion.

❑ Hooded parkas, Rumanian shirts: the new Marant collection was entitled Ligne Étoile. It was Isabelle's second *prêt-à-porter* collection, and was more accessible, pushing the boundaries of city and casual wear.

Marcasiano Mary Jane (1955). American designer, specializing in knitwear. She launched her company in 1980, making highly wearable designs, aiming to combine textile, color, and luminosity in a harmonious way. She often experiments by combining and exploiting the contrast between traditional weaves and textiles and Lycra. She has influenced many very young fashion designers.

❑ 2000, April. Together with about 30 other "eco-aware" designers, Marcasiano collaborated on the fourth Wellman's Annual Master Apprentice Collection, an event organized by Pepsi Cola. On 22 April, Earth Day, a range of clothing made entirely from fibers obtained from recycled bottles and made working side-by-side with students from eight different colleges, went on display in the atrium of the Citicorp Center in New York.

Marc Cain German women's knitwear brand. The three lines, Marc Cain Collections, Sports and Gala, are strongly linked to the Italian tradition, updated with a rather severe style that is typically German. Its debut in Italy took place in 2002 at Milanofreestyle. In March 2003, Marc Cain was among the German firms taking part at Fashion China Partner Mission, an event held at the Kunlun Hotel in Peking, organized by Igedo Company in collaboration with the firm Shanghai Jasmine Consulting. The collection for Spring-Summer 2003, however, moved in three different directions: Ritz has a sporting and casual feel in grays, blacks and whites, blues and greens; Riviera, characterized by whites, vanillas, and cane sugar tones, is informally casual; Provence is ethnic with military touches, from sky blue to dust gray.

March Charlotte (1930). German photographer. After studying art she dedicated herself to teaching and in 1956 she joined the Fashion College in Hamburg. She opened a photography studio in 1961, working in Germany, France, and England in the fields of advertising and fashion. She has an uninhibited and relaxed style, like her models who are often posed looking directly towards the viewer. In 1977, she published the volume *Man oh Man! A Project for the Emancipation of the Attractive Male*, featuring provocative male nudes.

Marchioro Egidio (1932). Italian tailor born in the province of Verona. He spent time in workshops from a very early age, learning the rudiments of the trade, until he joined the studio of Giuseppe Cometti, who was considered at the time to be a true master. In 1960, at the age of 28, he opened his own tailor's atelier. A member of the Academy of Tailors, he is a witness and example of tailoring talent united with Italian style.

(*Maria Vittoria Alfonsi*)

Marcolin Spectacles manufacturing firm with an international market, quoted on the Milan Stock Exchange since July 1999. It was founded by Giovanni Marcolin Coffen at Vallesella di Cadore in 1961 as an "Artisan Factory." Its headquarters are at Longarone. It is run by twin brothers, Cirillo and Maurizio. During the years it has grown and been transformed, increasing its human resources, research, and quality standards, and expanding its factories, until the 1990s when its glasses were recognised across the world as cult objects. In little more than 40 years, the small workshop, which originated with the idea of making metal rather than plastic frames for glasses, grew into a group comprising 1,200 employees, 4 factories and 15 branches across the world, with 6 million frames produced in 2002 from about 400 different models. The brands include: Replay, Miss Sixty, Fornarina Vision, Up!, Mossimo Vision, Essence Eyewear, Unionbay Eyewear, Bob Mackie, Cover Girl, NBA Eyewear, The North Face, and Cébé (ski masks and ski sunglasses). The licensed brands are Dolce & Gabbana, D&G, Roberto Cavalli, Costume National, Chloé, and Montblanc. In February 2001, the group continued to expand on the international market and acquired 100% of Creative Optics Inc., a leading American firm in the distribution of eyeglasses. The aim of the operation, valued at about 16.5 million dollars, was to double the company's presence on the American market. The 2001 balance recorded an increase in turnover of 7.4%. The net profits increased to 5.1 million euros (more than 3.5%). The 2002 balance also closed with an increase: the turnover rose to 71.8 million euros (more than 28%).

❑ 2003, January. The Montblanc Eyewear line is launched, comprising 18 models of spectacles and sunglasses for men and women. The Montblanc line is distributed in 2,600 retail outlets, including 400 in Italy and 200 in the United States.
❑ 2003, October. A four year license contract is signed with Timberland for the production and global distribution of eyeglass frames and sunglasses.
❑ 2003, November. The group did not renew the license for the production and distribution of Fornarina Vision Up glasses.
❑ 2004. The group's business activities totaled 98.4 million euros, up 15% on

2003. Gross profits were therefore 1.7 million euros, against a loss of 6.1 millions in 2003. The consolidated turnover is certified at 173.2 million euros (up 10% compared with 2003) giving a net result of 1.2 million euros.
❑ 2004, October. The company signs a three year license with Kenneth Cole Productions for the production and distribution in the United States of spectacles and sunglasses with the label Kenneth Cole New York and Reaction Kenneth Cole.
❑ 2004, November. Diego and Andrea della Valle each acquire 12.184% of the joint stock of Marcolin. Together, the members of the Marcolin family own 29.248%.
❑ 2005, March. During the first quarter, the company has a turnover of 42.7 million euros, 6.2 millions fewer than the same period the previous year. The gross operating margin has also dropped considerably, from 6.3 millions to 3.9 millions.
❑ 2005, April. Stefano Dolce and Domenico Gabbana sell their share of 4.99% of the company to Diego and Andrea della Valle, who control approximately 40% of Marcolin, making them the largest shareholders. A five-year license agreement is signed with the Tom Ford Company: "We are witnessing an unprecedented phenomenon: the launch of a completely new brand that is already famous. Not because it concerns an actor or a rockstar, instead it involves the leading figure in fashion," commented Maurizio Marcolin.
❑ 2005, May. The license is obtained for the production and global distribution of Ferrari spectacle frames and sunglasses. The first collection was to be presented at the beginning of 2006.

(*Dario Golizia*)

Marelli Giuliano (1942). Designer specializing in knitwear. He began his career in the 1970s as a designer for the Coats Italia group and head of Centro Orientamento Moda for the creation and development of handcrafts, through the national and international women's press in collaboration with the Italian Design Center. He designed the knitwear collections for Gft. From the 1980s he was a designer and responsible for the company image of the Grignasco Group, with particular attention to industrial knitwear. Each season he studied and implemented the new trends in fibers, colors, stitches and lines, pinpointing new products to meet the needs of the market. He also designed and produced two collections of knitwear for Pitti Yarns, in which Grignasco yarns were interpreted and proposed in key trends. He researched, again for the knitwear sector, yarns, color boards and models worked into designs, going on to create 400 exclusive prototypes, achieving notoriety in the press as a promoter of products in this sector. From 1982 to 1988, he was a consultant to the committee of stylists for Pitti Immagine Yarns, researching fashion trends in Italian and foreign knitwear and organizing joint catwalk shows with Armani, Ferré, Versace, Missoni, and Krizia. He collaborated with Lanvin, Yves Saint Laurent, Anne Claire and, at the request of the Irish government, created a new line of knitwear produced in Ireland by a pool of knitting factories in Donegal. He has wide editorial experience, including the publication *Cento nuovi punti a maglia* and *Cento jacquard da tutto il mondo* (Edizioni Paoline). He was the creator of the newspaper Benissimo Trend, available in Italy, Germany, and the United States, for the production of knitting yarns by Filature di Grignasco. He has produced two encyclopedic works, comprising more than 100 pamphlets for the RCS Group and is the director of Moda Bimbo, published by Publicom. Since 2001, he has taught at the Metaprogetto laboratory, part of the architecture faculty at Milan Polytechnic.

(*Sara Tieni*)

Marelli Giuseppe, known as Pinotto (1931). A manager in the Italian clothing industry and one of the contributors to the international fortunes of the sector. While he was still a student he undertook work experience at Rovelli-Marelli, the textiles factory owned by one of his uncles. In 1953, he joined De Angeli-Frua, which was at the time a colossus in the production of printed textiles for womenswear, in order to work at Tessinoni, which produced very successful hand-printed fabrics. His clients included Emilio Pucci. In 1964 he was the financial director of Hitman, a clothing firm that was part of the Cerruti group, which was under construction at the time. For eight years he collaborated with Giorgio Armani, who was, along with Nino Cerruti, head of style and who left Hitman in 1972 to set up on his own. In 1968 Marelli became director-general of the company and, in 1970, CEO. Three years later he became vice-president of Holding Cerruti 1881, while continuing to run Hitman. In practice, he oversaw all the finished products of the Cerruti 1881 brand, greatly increasing the turnover of the firm (650 employees) and bringing their exports up to 65% of the total production. In 1996, he left the job. Soon afterwards he joined Veneto Abbigliamento and since then has been working on the relaunch of Basile.

Mare Moda Capri In 1961 the newspaper contest Moda e Turismo in Italia – instigated by municipal corporations, businesses, and regional associations – proposed holding a series of fashion events in some of the most picturesque areas of Italy, such as Capri. The suggestion was well-received and the first edition of what was to become an exemplary event took place in September 1967 with the support of two famous citizens of Capri by adoption, Emilio Pucci and Livio de Simone. It was organized by Rudi Crespi and Giorgio Pavone, assisted by Franco Savorelli di Lauriano. Angelo Sacchetti was later to liaise with the press and take care of public relations. Pasquale Acampora, the general secretary of Sergio Capece Minutolo, was elected as the president of Mare Moda Capri. Exhibitions, conferences, debates, ad hoc presentations of new books, competitions, "International Fashion Encounters" (dedicated to one or two different countries, with catwalk shows) were all satellite events to the main shows, held at the Certosa, Marina Piccola, Anacapri and in the Quisisina theatre. The catwalk show was accompanied by a jury-awarded prize, called the Tiberio (made of gold and silver), that has been awarded in the past to, among others, Pucci, Geinrech, Cardin, Rabanne, Gucci, Valentino, De la Renta, Givenchy, Gianni Bulgari, Cerruti, Lanerie, Agnona, Sarli, De Simone, Mila Schön, Missoni, Krizia and Roberta di Camerino. Extravagance, true creativity, corals and turquoises, chains and straw, topless and beachwear, absolute elegance and some of the first examples of street fashion, are alternated in an extraordinary mix. The event continued until 1978. *(Maria Vittoria Alfonsi)*

Margaine-Lacroix Parisian tailors, famous during the Belle Époque and Art Nouveau periods, partly for having patented two designs, the Brassière-sylphide and the Robe-sylphide, which were very suited to the style of the time. Jeanne Victorine Margaine Lacroix (1868-1930) founded the atelier on the Boulevard Haussman in Paris.

Margiela Martin (1957). Belgian designer. Margiela studied at the Fine Art Academy in Antwerp. He began a course in graphic design and then moved into fashion, presenting his first designs in a collective with five other finishing students at the Academy. He worked in Milan in the early 1980s, afterwards returning to Antwerp, where he was employed as a designer by various department stores. In 1984 he created his first collection of ready-made womenswear. In the same year he became Gaultier's assistant, where he remained until 1987. In Paris he collaborated with Jenny Maeirens and in October 1989 he launched a *prêt-à-porter* collection. His designs had an immediately recognizable style: great creativity in the use of techniques and ideas, with elements taken from many different cultures, ethnic motifs, used and recycled materials. In 1989 the Musée Galliera in Paris dedicated an exhibition to his work. He was the first designer, in 1990, to break with tradition and hold a catwalk show outside the Cour Carrée of the Louvre: from then onwards he has always selected atmospheric places to hold his shows, such as railway tunnels or abandoned garages. He continues to be highly experimental and his collections are always a melting pot of ideas. In 1997 he was nominated artistic director for Hermès *prêt-à-porter*. *(Marilena Bergamaschi)*

❑ 2002, June. After Tokyo and Brussels, the Maison Margiela opened for the first time in Paris, in a historic building at 25 bis Rue du Montpensier.
❑ 2002, July. Renzo Rosso, president of the Diesel Group, acquires the Maison Martin Margiela. The Belgian designer,

who works for Hermès and has a boutique in Paris, needed a strong business partner in order to expand. Rosso became the main shareholder and president of the Neuf Group, the proprietor company of the Margiela brand, which followed its management. Mitsubishi Corporation also joined the group as a minor shareholder. Martin Margiela and Jenny Maeirens, with whom he founded the fashion house in 1988 in Paris, still remain as shareholders. In 2002 Margiela was sold in 260 multi-brand stores across the world and had a turnover of over 18 million euros.
❑ 2002, August. The Summer-Spring 2003 collection was presented one day in advance of the Paris *prêt-à-porter* shows. Like other Margiela collections, it is characterized by a "no name" label and held in an unknown location. The Belgian designer runs his career outside the normal conventions.
❑ 2003, March. For the Paris catwalk show (as usual ahead of the official calendar) another original location and captivating set design was used: a large hangar along the Ourcq canal, at La Villette, with a cultural and cinematic exhibition held at the same time in the neighboring streets. Each model appeared on the darkened runway illuminated by two light panels held up by boys with sandwich boards. Sober and sophisticated as ever but with great irony and imagination, Margiela's women wear jackets fastened with transparent plastic belts, to emphasize the waist, with many waistcoats, a recurring motif for the following season in several other collections. Severe colors, such as beige, sand, black, and mustard, and distinctive features in pure Margiela style were combined with a hint of vintage. At the conclusion of the show, the large balloons on the roof were burst to release a shower of colored confetti.

Margon Ready-made fashion firm (clothing and accessories), founded in 1965 by Gianfranco and Fiorella Maronati. Originally producing only skirts, during the 1970s the firm expanded to create an entire *prêt-à-porter* collection, even exporting to Japan, as a result of working with fashion designers like Walter Albini, Miguel Cruz, and Gianmarco Venturi. Margon has a factory in Magenta and 98% of the 40,000 garments it produces annually are for export. The turnover was about 12 million dollars with an annual increase of approximately 15%. Davide and Katia, the children of the founders, are also employed in the firm.

❑ 2002, December. License contract with Lancetti Creazioni for the production and distribution of the women's *prêt-à-porter* line. After the Compafin Group bought Lancetti in 1999, the relaunch of the brand was based mainly on the acquisition of new licenses. Margon, with show rooms in Via Canova in Milan, was one of their objectives.

Mari Lucia (1932). Journalist. From 1961 to 1987 she was a fashion correspondent for *Stasera*, followed by *Paese Sera*. Afterwards, she moved to the newspaper *Il Giorno* where, as a full-time commentator, she followed the catwalk shows and wrote a weekly column entitled "Agenda Donna" until 1997. At the same time she wrote for *Gente*. In 1969 she had the idea of "dressing" the songs for the FestivalBar competition, approaching such designers as Enzo, De Barentzen, Sarli, Zanolli, Litrico, and Biki, who won with the dress designed for *Acqua azzurra, acqua chiara* sung by Lucio Battisti. In 1981 Lucia Mari received an award from the Italian National Chamber of *Haute couture* for her articles for *Paese Sera*. She wrote the entries on Italian and French fashions from 1900 to 1960 in the Modern Encyclopedic Dictionary published by Labor. For her humanitarian activities she received the UN prize Civiltà senza frontiere in 1992. From 1999 onwards she began a very intensive television career, including work as a fashion critic for Sky TV channels. She has also written for the Russian daily newspaper, *Izvestia*.

Maria Di Ripabianca Brand of the knitwear company La Perugina, which produces two lines, Maria Di Ripabianca Cashmere for men and Maria Di Ripabianca Cashmere for women. It was founded in 1964 by Vitaliano

Quagliarini and his wife, Maria Bianconi. Originally the company produced knitwear made of wool and other yarns under the brand Niki Line. Then in 1990 it added collections using cashmere and high-quality yarns such as extra-fine merino wool, cashmere-silk, cotton, and linen. Maria Bianconi is the designer and the company has a presence in the main foreign markets: Europe, America and Japan. During the last few years, an interior décor line has been added to the company's cashmere products.

❑ 2003. In July the company attended the New York Collective: the event provided a showcase for the Spring-Summer 2004 collections of 53 Italian brands.

Maria Luisa The name of four trend-setting boutiques in Paris opened since 1988 by the Venezuelan Maria Luisa Poumaillou. Her French husband, Daniel, takes care of their administration, while their twenty-seven year old daughter, Alexandra, assists with the buying. The first boutique sells a range of clothing in Rue Cambon, while the other three specialize in shoes, menswear, and a mix of male and female *prêt-à-porter*. The store windows often preview the work of promising young designers, such as Rick Owens, Stéphanie Parmentier, and Sofia Kokosalaki.

Marie Claire French monthly fashion magazine. The gamble taken by Jean Prouvost, who founded the weekly newspaper *Marie Claire* in 1937, dedicated to a female public, amply paid off with the success of a continually evolving formula, which nevertheless remains true to its aim to provide its readers with new copy, sophisticated images at an accessible price, innovative graphics and varied proposals, with a colorful and optimistic cover featuring a fresh-faced, youthful woman. Moving to Lyon during the war, the newspaper continued until 1944. It reappeared a decade later as a monthly magazine, with greater attention to its contents and the needs of its readers, 75% of whom came from the provinces. For women who needed practical advice but also entertainment, the news stories by Louise de Vilmorin from Venice, Moscow, and Montecarlo became legendary. In 1960 the

Cover of *Marie Claire*.

supplement "101 ideas for happiness" became "101 ideas, fantastic fashion opportunities." The magazine did not merely perceive women as managers of the household but also as a force for social change. In their interests, important battles were fought by Marcelle Auclair, at the avant-garde of contemporary female and social problems. Rechristened "The couple's magazine" in 1968, it took a leading role in the campaign for birth-control and supported militant feminism, without losing sight of the evolution of clothing. Indeed, in 1974, the editor-in-chief, Claude Brouet, ran a feature on male fashion. Ever changing, the monthly magazine was reacquired by Evelyne Prouvost in 1976, who became director. In 1977 the L'Oréal group took over 40%. Although fashion continued to be at the top of its agenda, *Marie Claire* maintained its guiding role, with features on law, testimonials and health, with particular attention paid to relationship issues. During the 1980s, with Catherine Lardeur as editor-in-chief, the magazine launched regional issues, with ten different editions. In 1982 an even bigger development took place, in the form of international editions, firstly in Japan and subsequently in many European countries, as well as overseas. The Italian *Marie Claire*, after the weekly version in the 1960s under Palazzi, was issued in a monthly edition by Mondadori in October 1987 under the direction of Vera Montanari, who was succeeded in 1994 by Chicca Menoni. The Italian formula remained faithful to the French original: a publication rich in information and emotion, dedicated to women who live, love, and work. In 2003 control of the magazine passed to the Hachette Rusconi group, with the return of Vera Montanari.

> ❑ 2002. Russian, Polish, and Chinese editions were launched. Currently there are 24 national editions of the magazine. Seven are published by the Marie Claire Group, including *Marie Claire Maison*, *Marie France*, and *Cosmopolitan*.

Mariella Burani Multi-brand and multi-product fashion group with headquarters at Cavriago, in the province of Reggio Emilia. Selene, the first nucleus of the firm founded in 1960 by Walter and Mariella Burani, still features on the façade of the factory. At the time, Mariella produced and distributed children's clothing. The company, still administrated, developed, and guided by the Burani couple (they respectively hold the roles of president and creative director), has strategically evolved to take a leading position in the sector. After a decade concentrating on the production of women's *prêt-à-porter* clothing, at the end of the 1980s it began to concentrate on licenses. The group was joined by famous brands such as Valentino, with the Carisma and Carisma Rouge collections (1993), Gai Mattiolo *prêt-à-porter* and ready-made (1996), Gai Mattiolo Fashion Jeans (1997), and Calvin Klein Collectionline (1999). But the main development that allowed the group to attain its current stature was its policy of acquisitions. In 1999, it purchased the longstanding brand Mila Schön, the knitwear company Dimensione Moda and the internet provider Sedoc-Trading. In 2000, this strategy continued, with the acquisition of 60% of Gabriella Frattini, a leader in luxury knitwear. But 2000 was an important year for three other reasons: first of all, the company was quoted on the Stock Market, secondly it diversified into the sector of leather goods, by acquiring two companies, Bracciallini and Dei Mutti and, finally, because it launched fashionweb.net, the official website of the Italian National Chamber of Fashion. 2001 was an even busier year, bringing a new look to the Group, as it chose to concentrate on its new leather goods production. A new brand, Antichi Pellettieri, was launched by merging four firms – Baldinini, Mario Cerruti, Mafra (luxury footwear) and Enrico Mandelli – which created leather garments. The year closed with the acquisition of Moda Trading, for a long time the license owner of Mariella Burani's jeans and sportswear lines; the formation of a joint venture with Stephen Fairchild, for the production and distribution of the men's and women's clothing lines; and, finally, with the important acquisition of a branch of Gft, which includes the Sahza brand and 13 spaces in the most prestigious international department stores. These acquisitions allowed the Group to close 2001, a dreadful year for fashion companies, with a turnover of 221.7 million euros (up 40%). In February 2002, Mariella Burani Fashion Group took over another part of Gft, absorbing Revedi Plc and Revedi Sa, which has 18 outlets in Italy and Switzerland representing a value of 3.7 million euros. A month later Itm, a firm in Como producing silk and jersey textiles, came under Burani's control. The cost was 12.3 million euros. The year concluded with the acquisition in December of 50% of the Germany company René Lezard Mode, a manufacturer of luxury clothing for men and women. This policy paid off. The year closed with a turnover of 273.9 million euros (up 23.5% on 2001) with a net result of 11 million euros (up 96%). In mid-2003 the Group signed an agreement with Sector for the production and distribution of Burani watches, bringing to 18 the number of its active licenses. The partnership was to last five years, with the possibility of renewal. The launch on the market was fixed for Spring 2004. Subsequently the Burani Group acquired 60% of the Vicenza firm, Francesco Biasia, for 10.2 million euros. In June 2003, Interbanca bought a share of 33% of Burani Designer Holding Bv, a company set up under Dutch law belonging to the designer's family. The merchant bank's participation as a minority group encouraged new investments, in order to maximize medium-sized "made in Italy" companies.

> ❑ 2003, September. 30% of the capital of Antichi Pellettieri S.p.A is sold to L

Capital, a fund that reports to LVMH SA, for a value of 25 million euros. Antichi Pellettieri, created in 2001 to bring together the group's leather business, controls the Baldinini, Sebastian, Braccialini, Biasia, Mandelli, and Cerutti brands. In 2002, it had revenues of 75 million euros and a gross operating margin of 9.5 millions.

❑ 2004, February. Hopa, the company that reports to Emilio Gnutti, increased its quota in the Mariella Burani Fashion Group to 5%.

❑ 2004, June. The group launched the collection Amuleti J, aimed at young, fashionable women.

❑ 2004, July. A four-year license agreement is signed with Braccialini for the production and distribution of the line of accessories signed Mariella Burani.

❑ 2004, November. Braccialini, the women's accessories firm, opened its first flagship store in the UK, in London. There are 14 own-brand Braccialini stores, of which 8 are in Italy and 6 abroad. The group buys out Don Gil, an Austrian luxury clothing distribution chain. The group had a turnover of 428.9 million euros, up 19.6% on 2003 and a gross operating margin of 53.3 millions, up 22.6%.

❑ 2005, February. The group focuses strongly on a youthful public with the line "Amuleti J" designed by Gabriele Colangelo. The brand is presented on the runway on 25 February, together with big names like Gianfranco Ferré, Etro, Roberto Cavalli, Trussardi, Moschino, and Dell'Acqua. The designer commented, "For me it is like taking an exam, an important challenge that I tackle with great emotion mixed with a touch of apprehension." The same month, the Emilian firm diversified into the sector of natural products of herbal origin for cosmetic and alimentary use, acquiring 80% of Bioera. The remaining 20% of the firm, which had a turnover of 36 million euros and a gross operating margin of 6.5 millions, remained in the hands of its managers.

❑ 2005, March. The first quarter of the year concluded with a turnover of 117.6 million euros (+11.5%) and a gross operating margin of 14.5 millions (+12.8%). The Braccialini brand, which closed 2004 with a turnover of 23 million euros, up 30% on 2003, focused decisively on Eastern markets and announced the opening of 6 new stores, of which 5 were franchises and one self-owned.

❑ 2005, April. Mariella Burani Fashion Group acquired 100% of Bernie's AG, the leading distributor of luxury goods in Switzerland, with 16 exclusive stores, for a value of 2.2 million euros. Bernie Lehrer, founder and president of the company, remains at its head. A five-year contract was also signed with Sover for the distribution of glasses in Italy and abroad.

❑ 2005, May. The group "dresses" the MilleMiglia. It supplies clothing and accessories to the pilots and the entire staff. On the opening day, 19 May in Brescia, it presented a preview of the Spring-Summer 2006 collection. Walter and Andrea Burani, president and CEO of the group, took part in the competition behind the wheel of a Ferrari 750 Monza.

❑ 2005, June. The Oscar for a Career in Fashion 2005 is awarded jointly to Mariella Burani and Yamamoto. During the same month the LVMH group acquires 7% of Burani. Massimo Gatti signed an industrial and financial contract with Mariella Burani Fashion Group. The agreement allows the company to expand in the leather goods sector. *(Dario Golizia)*

Marie-Louise Bruyère French fashion house. After an apprenticeship with the Callot sisters, Marie-Louise Bruyère worked as a pattern maker for Jeanne Lanvin between 1920 and 1928, the year she launched her own label with Besançon de Wagner, first based in Rue Mondivu and later (1937) in Place Vendôme.

Marie Marine Parisian boutique. It was one of the first, in 1952, to sell luxury *prêt-à-porter*, following the lead of some of the famous tailors, such as Fath. The boutique was opened by the cousins Fred and Marcel Salem. It had an immediate and long-lasting success. In 1966 they opened another Marie

Marine boutique in Deauville. Subsequently, during the height of the ready-made clothing boom, the boutique abandoned its policy of selling a variety of high-quality styles in order to stock exclusively Escada.

(*Fiorella Marino*)

Marie Mercié The brand and store named after the milliner who since the late 1980s has had a boutique in Rue Saint Sulpice in Paris with highly theatrical window displays. A trend-setter capable of reviving the popularity of the small hat, she previously studied art and archaeology, successfully worked as an artist and directed the magazine *Latitude*. She presents collections twice a year, which are also distributed through department stores such as Printemps in Paris and Barney's in New York.

Marilyn French model agency founded in 1986 by Marilyn Gauthier. The agency has its headquarters in Paris and employs about 30 people. Two other offices are situated in New York and San Paolo. In addition to the traditional sectors of male and female models, in 1995 the agency opened a Celebrity Division, with various famous figures. As well as Kate Moss and Carla Bruni, the agency employs models chosen more for their personality than for their beauty. The founder explains: "I do not like canonical beauties, such as the blondes with blue eyes you see in catalogs. Instead I prefer an ugly nose, if it is coupled with a beautiful gaze."

Marimekko Finnish textile company founded by the designer Ratia Armi in 1951. It produces fabrics for clothing and interior decors, mainly made of cotton, and places strong emphasis on design and creativity. The company's success allowed the designer to create clothing collections as well, primarily in cotton and jersey. However, for the last twenty years, the strongest lines have been those for household purposes.

❑ 2000. The company had 25 stores nationally, a branch in Sweden, and more than 700 across the world.
❑ 2002, December. The Helsinki stock exchange included Marimekko in its main index.
❑ 2003. The net sales for 2002 totaled 49.3 million euros with 27% from the export market. A partnership was established between Marimekko and Iittala, a household design company, which had already produced a candelabra for the Helsinki firm.
❑ 2003, November. The Bard Graduate Center for Studies in the Decorative Arts, Design and Culture in New York, in collaboration with the Museum of Art and Design in Helsinki, staged the first American retrospective of Marimekko's products from 1951 to the present.

Marina Aliverti From 1998 a fashion consultancy firm, working for shops and companies. From 1990 to 1998, it was a female clothing brand. The Marina Aliverti Plc. Collection included silk clothing, evening dresses and knitwear, and supplied markets, including Japan, France, and Germany. The offices of the current firm are in Via Montenapoleone in Milan.

Marina B Jewelry brand, launched by Marina Bulgari (Rome, 1930), daughter of Costantino and granddaughter of Sotirio. Marina began working in the family firm and in 1979 opened her own atelier in Geneva, creating the Marina B brand. Her very original, personal style quickly brought her an international following, also thanks to the opening of a series of stores in New York, Milan, Jeddah, Riyadh, and London. In 1987, Marina introduced a universal joint that linked small spheres of coloured stone. In 1996 Sheikh Ahmed Fitaihi, owner of a

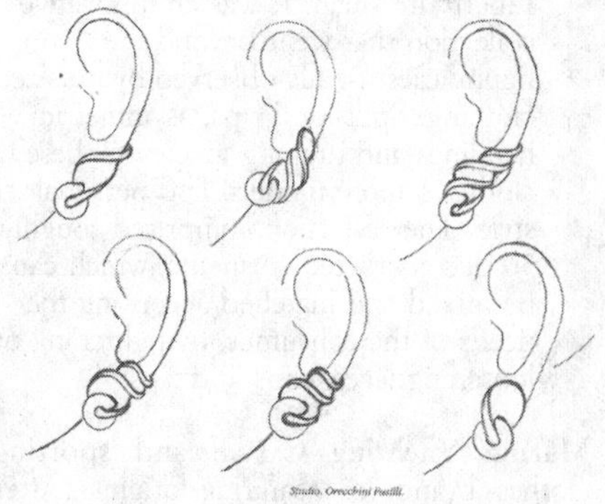

Study by Marina Bulgari for her "*fusilli*" earrings.

chain of luxury boutiques in Saudi Arabia, acquired the brand. The collections, still designed by Marina Bulgari, even after the change of ownership, were enriched with new creative twists. For example, details such as the Marina B Cut were developed in order to obtain triangular, heart-shaped stones. A love of architectural effects and a curiosity regarding the technical construction of jewelry led to the use of ever more innovative processes, using clasps and springs in very inventive ways, allowing stones or other materials to move or be substituted to create new or interchangeable pieces. In 1998 Marina created the Spring necklace, made from a series of clasps. At the end of the 1990s, a line of women's watches appeared. In the twenty-first century, Marina B has produced highly wearable pieces of jewelry, returning to her favorite themes, such as animal motifs, or introducing new ones inspired, for example, by the Chinese horoscope.

Marina Rinaldi Outsized clothing brand, founded in 1980 as part of the Max-Mara Fashion Group, aimed at women wearing size 46 and upwards. To flank the main collection, the Persona line was launched in 1985, followed by Marina Sport in 1986 and Marina Rinaldi Basic in 1994. From 1984, the collections have been available internationally, with outlets in Paris, London, New York, Tokyo, Moscow, Düsseldorf, and Los Angeles.

❑ 2003, February. The MR line was launched for Fall-Winter 2003-2004, presented in a showroom in Piazza Liberty in Milan. It was an innovative collection that went beyond the boundaries usually observed by outsized clothing. Splits and rips, asymmetric hemlines and draping give even these clothes a more modern and personal style. The collection comprised roughly 50 deconstructed garments, which can be mixed and matched according the needs of the consumer, by tightening or loosening laces, clips and zips.

Marina Yachting Casual and sporting clothes brand, of seafaring origins. After twenty years as a sailor, Nicolò Gavino set up base in Genoa. There, in 1887, he opened a notions store. Two generations later it was a thriving commercial success. In 1965, the firm presented its first collection at the Nautical Fair in Genoa but the brand was not launched until 1972. Today, 30 employees are based at the modern headquarters at Carasco, which has an area of 8,000 square meters, and more than 750 shops across Italy distribute the different lines of Marina Yachting (classic), My Marina Yachting (for women), M Y sport (for young people) and Waterline for the beach, with towels and matching swimwear.

❑ 2002, September. Marina Yachting celebrated its 30th anniversary at the Sardinia Cup regatta. To coincide with the anniversary, in May *Le parole del mare* was published, an anthology of 70 pieces, chosen and edited by Valiera Serra, a reporter on sailing events. Published by Baldini&Castoldi, it celebrated the history of the brand and its passion for the sea, sailing and sport, the focus of its research from both a stylist and technical perspective. Marina Yachting was acquired by the Fin.part Group in 1996. (*Valeria Vantaggi*)

The Marina Yachting logo.

Marinella Neapolitan store and brand of ties, clothing and "English goods." The original shop sign read: "Marinella E. Marinella-Shirtmaker and Outfitter." Opened by Eugenio Marinella, on 26 June 1914 at 287 Riviera di Chiai, it is still owned by the family. Inherited by Eugenio's son, Gino, who led the company until the mid-1990s, for a long time the store continued to look like an artisanal workshop of a very exclusive kind, selling English garments and creating ties, shirts, scarves and selling very British textiles. The firm, currently run by Gino's son, Maurizio, has specialized in ties over the last twenty years (producing roughly 120 a day), both ready-made and made-to-measure and with seven folds. The consistency of the latter model derives from the many layers of fabric, rather than the shape. In 1998, Marinella had a turnover of roughly 4 billion lire, with 25 employees. The history of Marinella began about a month before the outbreak of World War I and is intertwined with elegant Neapolitan society. The journalist and writer Matilde Serao celebrated its inauguration in the daily Neapolitan newspaper, *Il Giorno*, in her famous column "Mosconi". The workshop of English goods – which fills 20 square meters on the ground floor of the fifteenth century Palazzo Satriano – was furnished by don Eugenio, following the anglophile tastes of Neapolitan gentlemen. The Villa Reale (now belonging to the council), which stands opposite the store, was still – in the early twentieth century – visited by Neapolitan aristocrats and members of high society. According to Serao's article, Marinella offered violets to women and Floris English cologne to men. *Floris* and *Penhaligon* scents, Look hats, Acquascutum raincoats and Kent luxury textiles were the products imported to Italy for the first time by Eugenio Marinella for a refined clientele, which included the Agnelli family, members of the House of Savoy, and the Neapolitan Royal House of Bourbon. Everything in the store apparently remains unchanged: the stucco on the crossed vault hung with an antique brass lamp, the small table with the cash till and the display cabinet in glass and mahogany. The processes of hand making, the system for importing textiles from the county of Kent and the sale of Marinella products have also all remained unchanged. The head of the company still designs the patterns for the ties and travels to England to choose the textiles: the so-called "square," a piece of silk measuring one meter by 20 centimeters, sufficient for 4 to 8 ties. From the end of the 1970s, however, the production of made-to-measure shirts was abandoned, in order to focus on ties, whose width, according to the Marinella family, should range from 8.5 to 9.5 centimeters at the widest point. As for the color (to contrast with the suit and shirt) and the fabrics (jacquard for the regimental style, light silk for printed textiles and wool for winter outfits) the main principal was tradition. A fundamental rule was to always choose one's tie and, above all, never to wear a matching tie and handkerchief.

(*Stefano Grassi*)

❑ 2002, September. Marinella opened a second atelier in Milan. Like the Neapolitan headquarters in Palazzo Satriano, the Milanese store is located in a historic building: an eighteenth-century ex-convent at 5 Via Santa Maria alla Porta. For the first time the firm opened a store separate from the workshop-salon in Naples. In addition to ties, the shop sells perfumes, knitwear, leather goods for men and women, watches, and hand-made sunglasses (in titanium and pure acetate) created by Optical City. In 2002, Marinella's turnover totaled 8.3 million euros.

❑ 2002, November. Marinella and Valextra, two historic companies, together produce a line of ties entitled Marinella for Valextra in silk jacquard twill in various colors, both plain and with a figured design.

❑ 2003, May. The *Wall Street Journal* prints a long interview with Maurizio Marinella (1955), the latest heir to the dynasty, on its front page under the headline: *The Ultimate Necktie*.

❑ 31 March, 2004. The first "Italian Tie Gala" is held with Seri.co. The event celebrated the accessory that symbolizes masculine elegance, and benefited a worthy cause at the same time.

❑ 2004, April. Marinella took part in the conference organized by the Quality Committee in collaboration with Class Editori-Milano Fashion Global Summit. It provided an occasion to relaunch Naples as the fourth Italian fashion capital, after Milan, Florence, and Rome.

❑ 2004, May. Maurizio Marinella bought out the Savoy bootmakers, Arturo Ballini's historic shop on Via Vincenzo Monti in Milan. The Neapolitan company's aim is to continue to create a niche product in the equestrian sector.

Marinetti Filippo Tommaso (1876-1944). Founder of the Futurist movement. On 5 March 1933, Marinetti wrote the *The*

Futurist Manifesto of the Italian Hat, which he signed with Monarchi, Prampolini, and Somenzi. The manifesto was published in the Rome weekly newspaper, *Futurismo*, and proposed a competition that was to run in conjunction with an exhibition at the Galleria Pesaro in Milan. It featured hats made by different firms, including the *aerodynamic hat* made in 1934 by Borsalino.

Marinotti Franco (1891-1966). Italian entrepreneur, Cavaliere del Lavoro. In 1956 he founded the International Center for Arts and Costume in the Palazzo Grassi in Venice, which organized themed fashion exhibitions, primarily aimed to inspire designers to use fabrics produced by the company Snia Viscosa (such as rayon, merinova, lilion, and rilsan), of which Marinotti was president. For the first time anywhere, the relationship between fashion and art was studied, giving rise to runway shows as showbiz. Marinotti made the fortunes of Snia Viscosa, a forerunner of commercial relations between Italy and the Soviet Union after the 1917 revolution. He learnt his professional know-how by joining Cascami Seta when he was very young age, and at the age of 22 ran a textile factory for the company in Russia. In 1929, he became director of Snia Viscosa, which was in difficulties, turning it around and running it until his death.

Marioboselli Italian textile company, the only one in Europe to oversee the entire silk manufacturing process: spinning, twisting, weaving, dyeing the thread as well as the finished fabric, printing, and packaging. It was founded in Garbagnate Monastero, at the same time as the arrival of silk, 400 years ago. The headquarters are still located there though the firm now has 7 factories. Marioboselli Jersey became known internationally when it created its interlock jerseys for designs by Emilio Pucci. Marioboselli Yarns was founded to produce twisted silks for weaving and currently but it also creates yarns and knitted fabrics in viscose, crêpe, and stretch. On average, the Group has a turnover of 115 billion lire comprised of 56% yarns and 44% textiles. It is made up of Marioboselli Yarns (two factories for air texturized twisted yarns, artificial and synthetic yarns and fibers), Nobiltez (twisted yarns for technical, industrial use), Silk 2000 (special silk yarns, both pure and mixed: crêpe, figured and chiné), and Cofrika Silk (yarn and fabric dyed and printed, made of silk and artificial and synthetic silk-type fibers). At the beginning of 1999, a group venture was launched with the firm Chemlon of the Nylstar Group, with an operating base in Eastern Europe. The project was called Twista and the factories in Hummené in Slovakia replicate the products of the Italian brands represented by Marioboselli.

❑ 2002, July. Mario Boselli, president of the National Chamber of Fashion, was awarded the Legion of Honour.

Marioni Female footwear brand of international standing. It was founded in 1947 by Natale Marioni at Fratta Polesine, in the province of Rovigo. The move from craft to industrial production occurred in 1961, with the arrival of Natale's son, Lino, who concentrated on a medium-high quality production in order to obtain an output of 150-180 pairs of shoes a day. In 1985, Maurizio Marioni, the grandson of the founder, joined the firm, consolidating the brand with a simple, classic, quality style.

Mario Petris One of the leading Milanese hairdressers, originally from Friuli. He had a studio on a mezzanine floor in Via Montenapoleone with his sister Mary. They created hairstyles for the girls from the generation of Gulp, Cose, Nuccia Fattori's boutique, the flower children and their very bourgeois mothers. He retired in 1999.

Mario Portolano Italian glove company. It was launched in 1895 in Naples as a family-run enterprise, and is now into its fourth generation. The company, which has its own high-quality brand and various lines in conjunction with different designers, *haute couture* and *prêt-à-porter* fashion houses, oversees all phases of the production cycle: from treating and dyeing the leather to the final stitching of the gloves. Skilled craftsmanship is combined with the quality of the materials and creativity of design. The two heirs, Aldo and Ivo Portolano, opened a branch in Baguio and named it Adriste Philippines Inc.

❑ For Fall-Winter 2003, a new licensed collection of gloves is created for Avirex. ❑ Now a branch of Adriste Philippines serves the Hong Kong market with Itasco of Tokyo for Japan.

Mariot Chanet French brand with an emphasis on creativity and technical innovations. For example, the use of clips and metal poppers instead of traditional sewn seams. The company was created in 1987 by two designers, Michel Meunier (1956) and Olivier Chatenet (1960), both professionally trained in *haute couture* ateliers and with a shared desire to get ahead. From 1989, they produced a knitwear line and from 1994 they collaborated with Hermès on women's *prêt-à-porter*. In 1997 the brand closed, a victim of the recession in the French market, but at the end of the 1990s, the duo reformed the company, specializing in bespoke production for private clients. In 2000 this new role gathered greater momentum. The designers focused on reconstructing second-hand garments, in particular vintage and ethnic ones. They began to show on the Parisian runways again.

Mariotto Guillermo (1963). Venezuelan designer and artistic director of the Maison Gattinoni. Born in Caracas, he took a degree at the California College of Arts and Crafts in San Francisco. After moving to Paris and later to London, he arrived in Milan at the age of 21. A collaboration with an interior design studio opened the doors to the world of fashion and, for two years, he worked on women's *prêt-à-porter* for Basile. In 1988 he designed the first *haute couture* line for Gattinoni. After the death of Raniero Gattinoni, he was appointed artistic director. In 1994, he created a scandal by sending a nude model down the catwalk, intended as a biblical reference to Eve. The following year he presented a Mona Lisa, swathed in white organza with her face veiled in lace. The Fragile collection appeared in 2001: the Israeli model Moran Athias appeared arm-in-arm with a Palestinian model. In 2002, a pregnant Nina Moric modeled, crowning a summer of features on the covers of Italian magazines. In July 2003, Guillermo paid homage to the 700th anniversary of La Sapienza University in Rome and to the first year of the Science of Fashion course, with a lecture to the students, covering the important developments in twentieth-century fashion, and with an exhibition of 32 garments from the new winter collection at the university's museum.

(*Pierangelo Mastantuono*)

Mark Ecko Brand of casual clothing, including jeans and male and female accessories. Founded in New Jersey in 1993, it bears the name of its owner. It began with a series of T-shirts hand-decorated with graffiti, which were instantly adopted by various important celebrities from American show-business, including the director Spike Lee. Success was instant, allowing the company to expand to produce a line of "urban-street style" for the youth market. Today the company also makes a line of cosmetics, as well as publishing the monthly, *Complex Magazine*. A children's clothing line has been available since Fall-Winter 2003.

Marks & Spencer One of the most important British retail groups. "Don't ask the price, it's all for a penny," was the slogan of the Lithuanian immigrant Michael Marks, who invited the public to buy from his market stall in Leeds in 1882. Twelve years later he entered into partnership with Tom Spencer. From the market to the department store: from the beginning of the twentieth century the firm developed rapidly. In 1907, there were already 60 shops. The balance sheet was also improved by the arrival of Marks' son, Simon, who became director in 1911 and presided over the group, with Israel Sieff, until 1964. The firm was quoted on the London Stock Exchange in 1926 and today the chain has branches in the United States and South East Asia. All its products are sold under the Saint Michael brand.

❑ 2002, May. Marks & Spencer profits were up 30.7%, closing at 646.7 million pounds (1.03 billion euros). Turnover increased (7.6 billion pounds, up 8%), thanks to the clothing range. Marks & Spencer benefited from restructuring, which eliminated external firms from the core-business, the closure of stores in continental Europe and the sale of the Brooks Brothers brand to the Del Vecchio Group for 225 million dollars. A number of stores were renovated at a

cost of 140 million pounds, while another 100 were due to be overhauled by 2003. After three years of crisis there was a turnaround, partly aided by an improvement in the clothing lines.
❑ 2002, June. The View From brand of sportswear was acquired from Nova International, with a subsequent contribution of 100 million pounds to the company's turnover. The line, created by the former Olympic champion, Brendan Foster (currently CEO of Nova International), was available at the beginning of September in 110 stores. The acquisition formed part of a policy of diversification, with the intention of integrating the Marks & Spencer brand with other lines, given the success of the Per Una collection and the menswear collection, Blue Harbour.
❑ 2002, July. The company registered an increase of 14.8% in the clothing, shoes and gift sectors, while United Kingdom sales increased as a whole by 9.1%. The strongest growth took place in the womenswear sector.
❑ 2002, December. Vittorio Radice, 45, chief executive of Selfridges for 7 years, joined Marks & Spencer. He has been credited with the transformation of Selfridges, with the modernisation of the London headquarters at a cost of 100 million pounds and improved retail sales in other English cities.
❑ 2003, July. An increase in turnover in Great Britain of 5.4%, mainly due to the food sector (up 8.1%). Sales of clothing and gifts were also up (3.9%), while household goods were down by 1.4%.

Marks Handbags American brand of colorful bags in several models. It was named after the founder and owner, Lana Marks, who is considered a queen of leather and has become famous also for the friendship which linked her to Princess Diana. Crocodile, alligator and lizard are her favorite skins and she uses them to manufacture the 150 models of bags she makes. The dyes the leather in a wide variety of colors, from yellow to fuchsia, to light green, whatever the trends are demanding. The very simple and rigorous lines mirror her English origins. She moved to the United States to open a leather accessory company in 1987. She owns shops in New York, Palm Beach, and Aspen.

Marlboro Classics Brand of casual clothes for the young, created and distributed globally by the Marzotto Group. Founded in 1984, with headquarters at Valdagno in the Veneto region, its production has developed progressively: from the first collections of sportswear. The focus has changed to casual garments, more recently in a western style. Double-breasted, faded trench coats, "Made in Mexico" boots, python skin belts, Texan hats, and Madras cotton checked shirts epitomize the Marlboro style. There are three different lines: Western Classics, the core of the collection, American Classics, specializing in urban sportswear in natural colors; and Utility, a line of jackets and sweaters, with a look distilled from the wardrobes of members of the military, carpenters and firemen. The most recent addition is Leather, a line of large jackets in waxed calfskin, oiled suede and treated nap leather. Today Marlboro Classics is more similar to a brand owned by the Marzotto Group than merely a license, given the opening of a Marlboro Classics Division at the Valdagno plant and the length of time of the agreement, which expires in 2019 but the possibility of renewal is strong. The collection is distributed in 41 countries, across a network of 180 own-brand shops, almost 350 shops-in-shops and 1,800 retail points across the world, from the Arab Emirates to the People's Republic of China.
(*Pierangelo Mastantuono*)

❑ 2001, June. At the Marzotto showroom in Milan, an exhibition of the most important images from Marlboro Classics advertising campaigns over the previous ten years. It was curated by the photographer René Salle, the creator of 30 of the images on display, and reflected the space and freedom of the Far West, the leitmotif of the Marlboro campaigns. The event was dedicated to 50 Years of Italian Fashion and sixty years of Pitti Immagine Uomo. As a result, the exhibition afterwards moved to Florence to the Teatrino Lorenese in the Fortezza del Basso, during the

period of the Pitti event. In 2000 Marlboro had a turnover of 240 billion lire.
❑ 2001, December. A new store opened in Paris in Saint-Germain-des-Près. The distributing network comprised 145 own-brand stores, 290 shops-in-shops and 1,800 retail points in 36 countries. The turnover in 2000 was 124 million euros on the sale of about 4 million items.
❑ 2002, May. An agreement was signed with Philip Morris to extend the global license of Marlboro Classics to Spain and open stores in the country's three main cities before the end of the year. It is not possible to expand into the United States, as the country's laws forbid the sale of goods linked with tobacco. Expansion into Spain opens up the South American markets. In 2001, Marlboro Classics had a turnover of 131 million euros with an operating revenue of 12%. During the last decade, the brand enjoyed an average annual growth of over 20% and boasted 473 retail points across the world.
❑ 2003, April. A new Marlboro Classics shop was opened in Milan on Corso Venezia. In 2002, the Marzotto brand announced profits of 146.9 million euros (compared with 132.5 in 2001) with an increase of 10.9% and an operating result of 17.2 million euros (13 in 2001). The growth is due to the strong development of women's clothing lines (up 20%), to success in the Spanish market, the opening of 42 new own-brand franchise stores and the two individually run stores in Paris. 84% of turnover is gained from menswear sales. In total, the brand had 517 stores.

Marly's Italian ready-made women's fashions company, founded at Arzignano in the province of Vicenza, in 1996 by the Lagnerini family. During the 1970s, designers such as Soprani, Venturi, and Albani collaborated with the firm. During the 1990s, own-brand stores were opened in Venice (1990), Arzignano (1992), and Tokyo (1994). In 1998, a group of managers, including Paolo Bastianello and Antonio Pisanello, with the support of three English merchant banks, acquired control of the company. The Marly's Group, which had a turnover of 25 billion lire in 1999, 30% of which was made in Japan, employed 110 people. It has four different brands: Marly's, Marly's 1981, Marly's News and, most recently, Marly's Couture designed by Tomaso Stefanelli.

❑ 2003, March. An exclusive contract was signed with Carlo Pignatelli for the production and distribution of his *prêt-à-porter*. Initially the agreement, which was to last five years with the possibility of renewal, only covered womenswear. It excluded the two lines Sposa Carlo Pignatelli Couture and Fiorinda by Carlo Pignatelli, which continued to be produced internally, along with the menswear collections.

Marni Line of clothing and furs, designed since 1991 by Consuelo Castiglioni, a Swiss designer who transformed fur coats from status symbols for older ladies to fashionable garments for young women with an interest in new styles. Over the last few years, the collection has been enlarged to include textiles garments as well as a line of bags and accessories. Furs still feature though Consuelo Castiglioni, a confirmed vegetarian, only uses the skins of animals raised especially, treating and transforming them with her very personal style. Adored by the American press, Marni counts Madonna, Elle MacPherson, and Stella Tennant among its faithful customers. (*Daniela Fedi*)

❑ 2002, January. Following the London and Milan boutiques, a store was opened on Avenue Montaigne in Paris, in conjunction with Fashion Week.
❑ 2002, September. The Marni woman, as designed by Consuelo Castiglioni, is both romantic and rebellious. Light and feminine, almost childlike, garments are mixed with flowered blouses, the leitmotif of the brand, with hard biker jackets with buckles and locks or gold chains. The leather, silk and cotton cargo pants, in both plain and printed versions, are combined with little shirts in hand-made French lace and waistcoats lined with fox-fur. Again, romantic flowers are everywhere: they were printed or embroidered, even on biker jackets.

❑ 2003, March. The collection was suited to an elegant, discreet and moderate woman, with printed and twill textiles, very low waists with belts emphasizing the hips. An occasional reference was made to the 1980s, with large, broad-shouldered jackets. The coats and dresses caress the body.
❑ 2005, January. The menswear collection was previewed in Milan. The essential style and discreet elegance of the female line was translated into menswear, which had already featured occasionally as part of the women's runway shows. Marni Sneakers are launched in June, a line of gym shoes by Marni and Kamei Proact Corporation, the Japanese company that owns the license for the Patrick brand, which has followed all the technological aspects of production. The style is a vintage look that combines nature and technology.

Marongiu Marcel (1963). French designer, who spent the first 19 years of his life in Stockholm. He began to work in Paris and in 1982 became the assistant to France Andrevie. He launched his first line of clothing, Creatis, in Stockholm. However, he presented the first garments under his own name in Paris. His is a purist style, as he likes to define it, occasionally influenced by classical influences (he studied, and is passionate about, Ancient Greek), with tunics and clean lines. There is nothing "de trop" in his clothing. What is his aim? To create collections for young women who are not necessarily particularly wealthy. His first own-brand store opened in Paris in 1998 at 203 rue Saint-Honoré.

❑ 2003. A sake tableware collection featured cobra-shaped vases, elliptical bowls, oriental-inspired coffee cups and salads bowls with very asymmetrical lines. The Saturne and Sten collections, designed for Artoria Limoges, one of the most important French porcelain manufacturers, could only be by Marongiu.

Marpessa Mannequin and top model, who left her hometown of Amsterdam at the age of 16. She moved to Milan to make her dream of becoming a model come true. She soon had her first photo shoots and found fame and friends. Later she went to France and the United States, where she worked on the runway for Chanel, Lagerfeld, and Alaïa, and appeared on the covers of *Vogue*, *Elle*, *Madame Figaro*, *Cosmopolitan*, *Marie Claire*, *Photo*, and *Harpers & Queen*. In 1987, the photographer Ferdinando Scianna chose her for the first Dolce & Gabbana catalog. She struck up a friendship with the two designers, which resulted in a publication, *Marpessa, un racconto*, in 1993. Marpessa has worked for photographers such as Weber, Newton, and Ritts and received a fashion Oscar for the best runway model in 1988. In 1994 she gave up full-time modeling but fashioned remained her passion. In 1996 she appeared in a television advertisement for *D*, the weekly women's supplement of the Italian newspaper *La Repubblica*. In the same year, *Vogue Germany* dedicated a monograph to her.

Marras Antonio (1961). Italian designer, born in Alghero. He first worked with the Piano Piano Dolce Carlotta brand, afterwards he designed for Tre Vaghissime Donne and a successful line of shirts for Sanstire. In 1996, he debuted in *haute couture* at the runway shows in Rome. In 1999, he presented his first *prêt-à-porter* collection at Milan Fashion Week. His designs sometimes evoke the colors and richness of Sardinian costumes.

❑ 2001, December. A book on Antonio Marras, written by Cristina Morozzi with photographs by Berengo Gardin and published by Sardust, was presented at the Cappellini showroom in Milan.
❑ 2002, June. The menswear line was presented at the 62nd Pitti Immagine Uomo. The spectacular debut took place in the suggestive Torre del Gallo, an extraordinary building constructed at the beginning of the twentieth century for the antiquarian Stefano Bardini. It was built on the ruins of an ancient castle thought to have belonged to one of the Ghibelline families. The tower, which can be seen on the hills from Florence, had been closed to the public for over 50 years.
❑ 2002, June. Shortly before the presentation of the menswear collection

at Pitti Uomo, a striking exhibition opened in Via dei Banchi Vecchi in Rome, at the A.A.M (Architecture and Modern Art) gallery. Some of the simple, male inhabitants of Lodine, a small Sardinian village in the middle of the countryside, met with Antonio Marras and agreed to take part in his project. They became models for a day and Marras, together with the photographer Salvatore Ligios, revolutionized the traditional rules and stereotypes of virility with images of 20 Sardinian men. Circolo Marras was born, a project combining art and fashion, where the designer's clothing is interpreted by everyday people, captured by Ligios's photographs and text by Flavio Soriga.

❑ 2003, January. Antonio Gramsci (like Che Guevara) becomes icon-as-decoration for Antonio Marras's T-shirts and shirts (in black on white shirts or in fuchsia on baggy sweatshirts). At the start of the runway show, the designer read from one of the *Letters from Prison*. It ended with a shower of letters raining over the spectators like subversive flyers. The invitation included Gramsci's phrase "I hate the indifferent" (taken from *La città futura*).

❑ 2003, March. The Fall-Winter 2003-2004 collection presented at Milan Fashion Week was inspired by Eleonora d'Arborea (1340-1402), the last Sardinian queen, famous for having created the "Carta de Logu," a form of ante litteram constitutional map. The focus was on black, with a few red touches in the kilt worn over baggy pants with large boots. Gauze, silk, velvet, embroideries, soft jackets, and voluminous skirts, all decorated with different chains in metal and folk-style bijoux.

❑ 2003, May. At Masedu, the museum of contemporary art in Sassari, Massari presented *Il racconto della forma*, a stylistic journey through clothing, with designs, photographs, videos and installations.

❑ 2003, June. The collection for Milan Moda Uomo was dedicated to the sea. It was inspired by the film *Fitzcarraldo* and the book *Sea and Sardinia* by D.H. Lawrence. The set design for the runway show was the ocean liner, the *Conte Biancamano*, in the Museum of Science and Technology in Milan.

❑ 2003, September. The French group LVMH entrusts Marras with the artistic direction of Kenzo's women's line. His combination of nomadic intellect and sense of his own roots, which he shares with the Japanese designer, meant he was well-equipped for the role. Like Kenzo's creations, his own designs are born from a double sense of belonging, between inheritance, history and diverse traditions. Even though he was forced to travel for his career, he has decided not to leave Alghero, where he lives in a large house-workshop, on a hilltop looking over the sea, surrounded by members of his family, who participate actively in his creative work.

❑ 2005, July. Inauguration in Alghero of the exhibition *Minyonies* (curated by Giuliana Altea and Maria Luisa Frisia); the name of the show comes from the word in Alghero dialect that means 'childhood.' Thirteen artists of the most recent generation presented their work, focusing on the home setting and family emotions.

❑ 2006, January. In collaboration with Pitti Immagine, a monographic work is published, devoted to the designed and published by Marsilio.

Marshall Francis (1901-1980). English illustrator, involved in fashion from 1925 onwards. He succeeded in uniting his graceful style with the need to describe. In 1928 he began a collaboration with the English edition of *Vogue*, covering fashion and social events. After the war, he worked freelance.

Marshall Field & Co American department store founded in 1901 by Marshall Field, who began his career by purchasing a share of the luxury emporium that Potter Palmer had opened in Chicago at the end of the nineteenth century. It was the ability to provide customers with a fully rounded service that set Field apart. It guaranteed the repair and conservation of all the goods it sold, it refunded unsatisfied customers and took back used products, even clothing.

Service and quality have been the recipe for the constant commercial success of this store for over a century.

> ❑ 1990, June. The chain passed under the control of Dayton Hudson Corporation, known today as the Target Corporation.
> ❑ 2001. Marshall Fields took over two important American chain stores: Dayton of Minneapolis and Hudson of Michigan, which then changed their names. As a result of the merger, Marshall Field had 64 department stores in 8 American states.

Marsupial Influenced by the kangaroo's pouch for holding their young, this term is used to refer to a large pocket, with two side openings, used on the front of sweatshirts and other sportswear. It has become the name of a garment (marsupial jacket or sweatshirt, etc). It is also a small, oval bag, fastened with a zip and attached around the waist, sometimes called a bum bag.

Martha New York boutique famed for the promotion and sale of French fashions. It was opened in 1934 by Martha Philipps and, after World War II, enjoyed great success. Later, suffering from competition from department stores, Philipps and her daughter, Lynne Manulis, attempted to promote new designers during the 1980s. However, in 1993 the woman referred to by the *Wall Street Journal* as "The grand dame of Manhattan couture," was forced to close her store.

Martial and Armand Franco-English fashion house. It is a rare example of an international style alliance. It was in business from 1905 to 1951 in Place Vendôme, Rue de la Paix in Paris and Albermarle Street in London. The company was made up of Jules Renou, Elie Dupui, Marie Vallet, Walter Shyeer and Milton Abelson.

Martin Charles (1848-1934). French illustrator who worked in the world of fashion from 1912, when he was already relatively old and famous for his close collaboration with the satirical journals, *Le Rire*, *Le Sourire* and *La Vie Parisienne*. It was *La Gazette du Bon Ton* that offered him the opportunity to illustrate fashion. From then on he also worked for the *Journal des Dames*, *Fémina*, *Vogue* and *Vanity Fair*.

Martin Richard. American fashion historian, who was curator of the Costume Institute of the Metropolitan Museum of New York. He taught History of Art at the Fashion Institute of Technology and was a fellow of the Art and Archaeology Faculty of Columbia University and New York University. In 1997 he edited *The Saint James Fashion Encyclopedia: a survey of style from 1945 to the present*, a summary of the most creative fashions since World War II in America, Australia, Canada, China, Japan, and Europe. He wrote widely on leading designers, from Albini to Kansai Yamamoto, from Balenciaga to Versace, from Halston to Vionnet. Among his most important publications are *Fashion and Surrealism* and *The New Urban Landscape*. He received an award from the Council of Fashion Designers of America in 1996 for "having promoted fashion as art and culture."

Martinelli Annalia (1956). Journalist, editor of *Consigli Pratici*. After a few years as a theater critic for *L'Ordine* of Como, *L'Avvenire* and *Famiglia Cristiana*, she became the editor of *Eva Express* in 1985. Following a short spell as a correspondent for *La Notte*, in 1995 she joined the Quadratum Group as the assistant editor of *Intimità*. In 1997, she took over as editor of *Consigli Pratici*, a monthly magazine launched in 1968 by the publishing house Cino del Duca and acquired by Quadratum Editors in 1995. Martinelli redesigned the look of the magazine, turning it into an even more rounded women's publication, where practical advice on fashion, the home, sewing, embroidery and make-up sat alongside features covering a wide range of subjects and opportunities for dialogue with its female readers.

> ❑ 2000. At the end of her time at *Consigli Pratici*, she became vice-director of the SE company, which specializes in art publications and editorial magazine projects on fashion, health and interior design.

Martinelli Elsa. Italian model and actress, born in Grosseto. She began to appear on the runways at the beginning of the 1950s and was much in demand as a cover girl. At about the same time she was discovered by Hollywood cinema. In 1954, she acted in the film *The Indian Fighter.* Among her other films were: *Donatella* (1956), *Pelle viva* (1963), *Garofano Rosso* (1975).

Martini Alviero (1951). Italian designer, who created the Prima Classe brand. His *prêt-à-porter* is characterized by clothing suited to a dynamic lifestyle. His leather goods are "marked" with geographic maps. The brand debuted in 1989 and now boasts 1,000 sales outlets and 15 own-brand stores.

❑ 2001, November. The New York store opened on Madison Avenue.
❑ 2001, December. Land Rover, the famous British off-road vehicle, chose Martini to design the interiors of the Freelander, their most unconventional model.
❑ 2002, December. The year closed with a turnover of 20 million euros (up 5%), thanks in part to the strong performance of the new line of footwear. Other new ventures include a Scarabeo 200 Aprilia signed by Aliviero Martini – all in black with seats and bags made with the famous leather printed with maps.
❑ 2003, January. The first store in Rome opened in Via Borgognona, to coincide with the *haute couture* shows.
❑ 2003, February. Mission to Mars is the new destination of Alviero Martini, who has always linked his collections with voyages. Sneja, the Bulgarian dancer and acrobat from the Orpheus circus, opens the Milan runway show with a display of her skills. Martini's Martian woman relived the 1960s of Pierre Cardin. On this occasion, Martini presented Aprilia's Scarabeo scooter, upholstered in the famous Geo-print.
❑ 2003, November. The company was sold to Final, owned by the entrepreneur Luisa Angelini, already a partner. The designer, Alviero Martini, no longer the majority shareholder, still remained as the fashion house's creative leader.

Martini Coveri Francesco (1974). Italian designer, nephew of Enrico Coveri, son of Silvana Coveri, who took over the brand after her brother's death. Francesco joined the fashion house at 22, signing the You Young Coveri collection. From Alessia Mertz's Poppea-style bath to garments personalized with emails to the latest candy girls, his runway shows have always been full of innovation. He is the artistic director of the Enrico Coveri Man and Woman line, which has been presented at Milan Moda Donna since the Spring-Summer 2002 collection. He received the Ago d'oro award in 1998 and the Donne Circe and Arte e Immagine nel mondo in 2002.

Martini Sportline Italian brand of sports and casual wear, founded in 1978 with headquarters in Turin. Its style embodies a knowing balance between tradition and innovation.

Martins Osvaldo (1972). Portuguese designer who studied design at Citex. He won the fourth edition of the Sangue Novo competition, enabling him to gain work experience at the fashionable Peclers studio in Paris. He has shown his *prêt-à-porter* creations in the New Lab salon in the French capital. His collections reflect his very positive spirit and strong vitality. He loves to mix colors and to distance himself from the sobriety of black.

Marty André-Edouard (1882-1974). French illustrator, set and costume designer. He designed the first posters for Diaghilev's Ballets Russes in 1910, ensuring him a certain fame among those in the business. However, he already featured on the pages of the *Gazette du Bon Ton* with fashion drawings that were never calligraphic. He only considered it a job, but he did it with talent, collaborating with *Vogue*, *Fémina*, *Jardin*, and *Harper's Bazaar*. One of the many books he illustrated was *Modes et manières d'aujourd'hui* by Tristan Bernard.

Marucelli Germana (1905-1983). Designer and tailor, predating the period when Italian fashion broke free from the French idiom. Growing up, like Elsa Schiaparelli, surrounded by Florence's history of art, she was one of the few designers and seamstresses to understand the importance of the relationship between fashion and art. Her name featured large among the group of designers invited to the first "made in Italy" runway show organized by Bista Giorgini in Florence during the winter of 1951. As a participant, Marucelli already had a long and successful tailoring experience behind her. Her Milanese atelier was famous, even more so because she had transformed it into an artistic and literary salon that was attended on Thursdays by poets such as Quasimodo and Montale, and the best intellects of the time: for instance, versatile and brilliant architects such as Gio Ponti, and the artists Savinio, Casorati, Gentilini, and Campigli. The latter painted her portrait in 1950. It shows a woman with a warrior's profile, her hair in a large, severe bun, just as she was in real life, convinced of her own ideas and impervious to the changing currents of fashion as spectacle. She continued a family tradition: her mother was a tailor at Settignano and her aunt Failla was a famous tailor in Florence. Germana frequented the workshops of both relatives. Later she became a pattern maker: she purchased patterns and fabrics from Paris to sell them on to Italian tailors' workshops. She had a formidable eye and memory, so that she was able to half-buy, half-copy. Maria Pezzi, in her autobiography *Una vita dentro la moda*, written with Guido Vergani, related that, "one day, Germana visited her most important client, the Milanese tailor Ventura, to offer him some French designs. Madame Hannà, the fearsome director of the salon, took one out of the case, counted the small plissé pleats, and asked: 'But did you buy this or copy it? This dress is already one of our exclusive models.' She confessed that she had copied it from memory. Hannà thundered: 'I would tell the police, if you were not so good. It's a perfect copy'." She moved to Milan in 1938, after having run the Gastaldi workshop in Genoa, where she opened a small atelier in Via Borgospesso, but she had to leave it during the war because of the bombing. She returned in 1945 and established further her personal vision of clothing (she considered it to be a form of architecture, a hand-created space, a form of painting for its color and of sculpture for its form) in harmony with the female form. In 1947, with perfect intuition, she anticipated the New Look, which Fath and Dior were developing and, later, with the Pannocchia line, the Parisian sack. Helped by the businessman, Franco Marinotti, the founder of Snia Viscosa, she purchased the building (in Corso Venezia) and archive of the historic Ventura house. During this period she collaborated with various artists, such as the abstract artist Capogrossi, Piero Zuffi, and Getulio Alviani, whose cine-visual experiments inspired her to design clothes integrating breast-plates and shields made of light aluminum, ahead of Paco Rabanne's inventions. These were working alliances as well as inspirational ones: producing textile designs and garment prototypes. Every collection embodied elements from Renaissance and avant-garde art: the Impero line (1951) looked to Botticelli, Fraticello was inspired by Fra Angelico's delicate color palette; in 1968 Manzù inspired the Vescovo line, while the designs and line of the Astratta collection were reminiscent of Picasso and Mirò. Few designers had her ability to create following a single inspiration that intertwined thought with an aesthetic message, set in a climate of intellectual research. During the 1970s, when Milan became the capital of *prêt-à-porter*, her ever unique creativity possessed a solitary elitism even though she enjoyed

Marucelli, black riding coat with fox fur trim.

fame on both sides of the Atlantic. Her inspiration was too pure for the ever-changing rhythm of the runways and broader consumption. However, she continued to produce work following her own vision up until her death. (*Lucia Sollazzo*)

Characteristic shell pleats by Germana Marucelli.

Maruyama Keita (1965). Japanese designer, who began as a costume designer for the theater and cinema. She presented her first collection in Tokyo, appearing on the international stage in Paris in 1997. Her collections, sought after for their elegance and femininity, reflect some of the characteristics of the typical Japanese woman and are enriched with rigorously hand-crafted embroideries on knitwear. In order to popularize the use of traditional clothing among the young, in Fall 1999 she designed a collection of kimonos.

Mary Matté *Haute couture* Turin tailoring atelier, taking its name from its founder. During the 1930s, '40s and '50s, it dressed Piedmont high society. The atelier on Via Roma was a reference point for all elegant women of that era. Matté mixed her creations with French patterns, which she bought in Paris or from the importers Rina Modelli and Sorelle Guidi, adapting them to the tastes and measurements of her clients. In 1937, she obeyed the decree of the Fascist government to create a specifically Italian fashion independent of French influences, and participated in the Self-Sufficient Exhibition in Turin, together with Binello, Gambino, Gori, Sacerdoti, San Lorenzo, Trinelli, Tortonese, and the furriers Rivella and Viscardi. Lucio Ridenti sang their praises in the magazine *Lidel*: "Now we are our own bosses in the field of fashion. (...) We just needed to believe in our own abilities, take off that blindfold with the embroidery of appearances made, unfortunately, of commercial interests, which the industrialists and, above all, the French tailors placed over the eyes of our own naïve tailors and our even more ingenuous clients for too long."

Marzotto Industrial textile and clothing group. The inheritance left by Gaetano Marzotto at his death in 1972 was not solely made up of portfolios, industries, balances, brands, and markets. He also left his children, who took over the administration of the group, a far larger company than he had received from his father Vittorio Emanuele. But above all he left a legacy of entrepreneurial pride and industrial culture that was not crushed by the administrative fear of reality, even during periods of financial hardship, years of crisis, and economic storms. In a sort of spiritual will, Gaetano wrote, "I did not run the company as if it were a portfolio of shares in a safe, instead I spent and assumed risks in order to created remunerated work." His philosophy was one of development and expansion, as soon as the economic climate allowed it. This was his cultural inheritance, which was passed on to the fifth generation of the Marzotto family when he was succeeded in 1972, just when the textile production industry was in crisis. In 1975, the group announced losses of around 6 billion lire. Eighteen years later, in 1993, the operating profits totalled more than 128 billion, on a turnover of 2,000 billion. In 1984, the turnover was 402 billion, in 1997 more than 2400, three quarters of which was earned abroad, with an average annual growth of

Seal and stamp released for the 50th anniversary of the Marzotto industry. Virginio Barison's design shows the first four generations of the entrepreneurial family from Valdagno.

14.73%. At Gaetano Marzotto's death, the products and markets that accounted for most of the turnover at the end of the twentieth century did not even exist. The group now had works in seven countries (Italy, France, Germany, Switzerland, the United States, Tunisia, and the Czech Republic), a commercial presence in 90 others, a position in the front row, often as leader (in the case of yarn and pure wool textiles, long fiber linen yarns and classic menswear) among the big clothing and textile producers across the globe, and a growing presence in the sportswear and womenswear sectors. The company's figures and achievements testify to an extraordinary, victorious turnaround. Within three decades, the more than a century old Valdagno firm changed its appearance without betraying its original, historic direction, profiting from the culture of expansion and constantly updating its own aims despite the highs and lows of the general economic climate. It embodied an entrepreneurial strategy that, before being put into action, had to draw on new blood through a phase of overhauls (1972-83), significant restructuring, and adaptation of machinery. One of their main priorities was to be able to respond to a multi-faceted market and to different needs, and as a consequence their restructuring strategy, they placed an emphasis on exports. Meanwhile, many European clothing and textile firms froze investments, considering the crisis to be irreversible, thereby opening up opportunities to Italian goods, and the creative virtues, taste and intelligence of Italian industry. The objective during that decade was achieved: exports rose from 12-13% to 40%. As soon as restructuring was complete, Marzotto remained faithful to its deep-seated cultural background. It continued expanding, a necessity in order to establish dimensions and structures in line with the multiform diversifications of the international market and in order to reinforce the key elements of the Valdagno company, namely a horizontally and vertically integrated group that oversaw the entire production cycle, from the raw materials to the finished garment. Marzotto looked to acquire large companies in difficulty. Bassetti, one of the most important Italian textile groups but by this period large and failing, was taken over by Marzotti in 1985. Marzotto split the company, ceding the household linens division to Zucchi (in 1991 it sold the cotton works to Olcese) in order to concentrate on the National Linen and Flax Works, thus assuring its world leadership in the linen yarn sector. It was a great financial and administrative undertaking. However, during the course of a single year, it was so well assimilated that, in 1987, the Group was able to continue expanding, acquiring the state-owned Lanerossi Group, founded over a century before and a pioneer in the textile industry. The annexing of Bassetti and Lanerossi, regenerated by an administrative expert, put Marzotto in a strong enough financial position to expand abroad with, however, a change in their philosophy: no longer to pinpoint companies that were struggling. In 1989, Marzotto took over the linen works Le Blan, a leading player in France, thereby consolidating its world leadership in the sector of linen manufacture. At the end of 1991, after the acquisition of the wool factory Guabello of Biella, they continued their policy of expansion with the conquest of the German arm of Hugo Boss, which had been purchased in 1989 by a Japanese group for a very large sum, mismanaged, and therefore put on the market again at a much lower price. It was a great entrepreneurial coup. Hugo Boss was an 850 billion lire business. In the 1993 balance sheet, the Boss acquisition brought Marzotto's turnover very close to 2 thousand billion lire and sealed the international character of the Group (63% of their sales were made outside Italy). With the need to continuously relocate production abroad in order to maintain competitivity, Marzotto soon opened a linen factory with local partners in Tunisia. During summer 1994, it acquired the wool factory Mosilana in Brno in the Czech Republic in order to focus on combed textiles in pure wool and to build a bridge with Eastern markets. The group has 9,300 employees. After having overseen the renewal and expansion of the company, in June 1998 Pietro Marzotto handed over its presidency to Jean de Jaegher, remaining a member of the executive committee alongside his brother Paolo and Andrea Donà dalle Rose. (*Guido Vergani*)

❑ 2001, November. The quarterly figures for the Hugo Boss holding led to an increase in net profits of over 14%.
❑ 2002, February. At Arezzo, the workers' union lobbied local entrepreneurs to reacquire the Lebole brand from Marzotto and bring it back to its historic base in Tuscany. No official offer was made to Marzotto who, in any case, decided to close the Florentine works. The regulated National Linen and Flax works was also in difficulties due to strong competition from outside Europe. The total turnover was reduced by 20%.
❑ 2002, March. Marzotto ended 2001 with a net profit of 118 million euros (down 10.8% on 2000). Turnover, which reached 1,757 million euros, grew by 9.3% (18% in Italy and 82% in other markets). The increase was due to the development of the German Hugo Boss (up 19%) and Marzotto clothing (up 7%). The textile sector experienced a strong downturn with a drop of 10.8% to 379.9 million euros.
❑ 2002, May. After receiving authorization from the anti-trust committee, the Marzotto Group took over Valentino Plc 100% from HDP. Marzotto agreed to pay HDP 240 million euros (35.6 millions for the capital and 204.4 millions for the financial debt). The managerial committee nominated Antonio Favrin as President, Michele Norsa as CEO, and Fabio Giombini as Managing Director. During 2001, even though its business volumes reached 132 million euros, Valentino made a loss of 28.5 millions.
❑ 2002, May. Michele Norsa was appointed to relaunch Valentino, which is now part of the clothing devision of Marzotto, alongside the Hugo Boss and Marlboro Classics brands.
❑ 2002, May. The global turnover in 2001 registered 1,756.6 million euros, an increase of 9.3%. 15.7% of this came from the clothing sector. Revenues,

Advert for Marzotto textiles during the 1940s.

however, decreased – with the group's net profits stable at 118 million euros (down 10.8%).

❑ 2002, November. A drop in turnover and profits. Marzotto closed the first nine months of the year with a net turnover of 1,389 million euros, down 3.2% on same period in 2001. Profits were also down, from 206 million euros to 140 millions (-31.9%). Figures for the third quarter also showed a decrease. The comprehensive net profit for minority shares was 52 million euros, compared with 81 millions during the same period in 2001, while shareholders' net revenues were 25 million euros, almost half the 47 millions from the same period in 2001.

❑ 2003, January. Marzotto sold their non-strategic shares. 20% of the capital from a real estate company, sold to Pirelli&C. Real Estate, brought a net gain of 28 million euros. Similarly, it gave up its hydro-electric palnts to the Eusebio Group, resulting in a net gain of 15.7 million euros. The aim was to reach a total of 44 million euros during the course of 2003.

❑ 2003, January. Matteo Marzotto, 36, joined Valentino's board of directors. From 1992 onwards, he had held various roles within the family firm, becoming CEO of Marzotto Distribution in June 2002. From 1994 to 1999, he was on the board of directors of the Young Entrepreneurs Group of Confindustria.

❑ 2003, February. Stefano Festa Marzotto, vice-president of the company, is entrusted with the development of the brands Belfe and Post Card in the markets of the Far East.

❑ 2003, February. Marzotto closed 2002 with profits down by 25% at 75 million euros (compared with 118 millions in 2001) and an increase in turnover at 1,788 millions (up 1.8% on 2001). The growth in business (up to 1,789 million euros from 1,757 millions in 2001) was attributed to the consolidation of Valentino, which compensated for a drop in the wool textile sector. Marzotto clothing and Hugo Boss remained stable. Operating profits totaled 125 million euros (7% of turnover), a drop of 32.2% compared with the 185 millions of 2001. The net shareholder profits dropped to 42 million euros, from 56 millions in 2001. Extraordinary proceeds increased to 28 million euros (8 millions in 2001), thanks to the sales of the real estate company and hydroelectric plants. Net debts increased from 419 to 638 million euros, due mainly to the acquisition of Valentino and its concurrent debts (234 million).

❑ 2003, May. UBS reduced its participation in Marzotto to 2%. Some members of the Marzotto and Donà dalle Rose families – but not Pietro Marzotto – agreed on a syndicated pact for the control of the company, which would transform the group into a holding partnership of the brands Hugo Boss, Linen Works, Marlboro Classics, Zignago and Valentino industries.

❑ 2003, May. Giovanni Gajo is the new President of the Marzotto Group, taking over from Innocenzo Cipolletta. Antonio Favrin remained as CEO, also taking over the role of Vice-President from Jean de Jaegher. The board of directors (serving three years from 2003-2005) consisted of Ferdinando Businaro, Luca Corabi, Andrea Donà dalle Rose, Sergio Erede, Gaetano Marzotto, Nicolò Marzotto, Pietro Marzotto, Umberto Marzotto, Luigi Amato Molinari, Roberto Notarbartolo di Villarosa, Paolo Opromolla, Dario Federico Segre and Giuseppe Vita. During the first quarter of 2003, thanks to the consolidation of Valentino and the recovery of the textile sector (up 13%), the turnover totalled 544.2 millions (up 3.5% compared with the 525.7 million of the same period in 2002), despite the drop (-5%) in the clothing sector, due primarily to a drop in revenues at Hugo Boss. The drop in net profits, however, was quite significant, the overall profits of minor shareholders went from 49.8 million in the first quarter of 2002 to 36.8 millions (down 26.1 points), while the accrued profits of the holding company dropped from 22.5 millions to 15.5 (a drop of 31.1%).

❑ 2003, July. A three-year license agreement was signed between Stephan

Janson and Marzotto for the new line Stephan (substituting Ferré Forma, which had come to an end) dedicated to larger women. The license is renewable for three further years, following the Marzotto tradition: the company has never signed an agreement with a designer for less than ten years. The collection (for sizes 44 to 60) was to be launched in Spring-Summer 2004. It would be produced and distributed by Marzotto in 80 multi-brand stores and some corner spaces abroad. Sales were to focus first on Italy and then the United States, Spain, Japan, England, and Russia, with the aim of taking over 40 million euros in retail turnover by the end of three years. The outsize market demonstrates significant growth rates, approximately double that of the standard collection. 24% of European women wear larger sized clothing.

(*Gabriella Gregorietti*)

❑ 2003, October. The contract between Valentino Garavani, Giancarlo Giammetti, and the Marzotto Group was renewed for a further three years. Damiano Biella joined the creative department: his previous experience was at Gucci and as design director of Celine.

❑ 2003, December. The consolidated net turnover for 2003 rose to 1,743 million euros, with a decrease of 2.5% on 2002 with the exchange rate unchanged. The group's operating profit was 133 millions (7.6% of the turnover), an increase of 5.7% on 2002.

❑ 2004, June. Pietro Marzotto sold his share of the group (17.42%) to his brother, Paolo, the financier Canova and to Antonio Favrin, the group's CEO. He continues to own 10.5% of Zignago.

❑ 2005, December. In 2004, Hugo Boss had a turnover of 1.2 billion euros (compared with 1 billion in 2003) and a net profit of 88.2 millions euro (+7%). The group from Valdagno announced its intention to separate its clothing and textile sectors in order to re-evaluate their distinctive roles and to promote their development.

❑ In the same month, Valentino, the label owned by the Marzotto Group, bought the majority shareholding in the Valentino boutique, Japan. "It is the second biggest luxury market after the United States and during the last few months it has shown positive signs of growth. It is also an important point of reference for the development of the other Eastern markets and we plan to spend 10 million euros during the next three years to relaunch distribution," declared CEO Michele Norsa.

❑ Consolidated turnover for the year totaled 1.824 billion euros, +5% on 2003; consolidated net profits totaled 82 million euros (+41%). In particular, the clothing sector, with a profit of 1.5 billion euros, increased 5% at the current exchange rate; while the textile sector, with a turnover of 302 millions, confirmed the figures of the previous year. Overall, the percentage of foreign turnover was 83%.

❑ 2005, March. Valentino signed a license contract with the Spanish company Pronovias, for the production and exclusive global distribution rights to a collection of wedding dresses. The own-brand Missoni store opened in Catania. The first quarter closed with a turnover of 572 million euros (+8% on 2004), and an operating profit of 89 millions (+16%), and a consolidated net profit of 56 millions (+27%).

❑ 2005, May. A contract was signed between Marzotto and Verzoletto to launch a joint venture in the woolen yarn sector for pure wool, acrylic mix and carded knitwear. The joint venture – with a consolidated turnover (2004) of 122 million euros, 69 millions of which made were by Marzotto and 53 by Verzoletto, and an annual total production of 15 million kg – becomes the European leader in terms of volume.

❑ 2005, June. Marzotto SpA and Valentino Fashion Group SpA separate. In the same month, Hugo Boss announced the launch of Boss Orange, a line of men's sportswear to debut in Summer 2006. (*Dario Golizia*)

Marzotto Gaetano (1952). Textile and clothing entrepreneur, President of Pitti Immagine. He studied at Morosini Naval College in Venice and took a degree in

Business Economics at Bocconi Institute in Milan. After a period of work experience at Olivetti in the Department of Planning, Programming and Information Systems Control, he began to work for Necchi as a "controller" and assistant to the managing and financial director. In 1980 he joined the Marzotto Group, starting in the Textile and Central Services Acquisitions Division. He directly oversaw the acquisition of Bassetti in 1985, the partnership with Zucchi in 1986 and the merger with Lanerossi in 1987. From 1989 to 1994 he directed the Marlboro Division and managed the relaunch of the new line Marlboro Classics. From 1991 to 1997, as the Group's Vice-President, he headed the restructuring of the clothing sector, in particular Ferré and Missoni menswear and strategic relations with Hugo Boss. From 1997 to 1999, he was director of the Development of Foreign Markets and the Development of New Markets (China, Russia, America). He was a partner of Hirsch & Co. Management & Consulting Milan.

Marzotto Marta (1931). Italian designer. Explosive, unstoppable, and a veritable volcano of ideas, Marta Marzotto is a society queen, much talked about, loved and envied. She is brilliant at self-promotion, aided by her straightforward and willing approach. Intelligent and shrewd, she is the kind of person who never gives up, the result of her Emilian blood and peasant roots. Her charm is endowed with a streak of madness, something she turns into a positive quality, and it was no coincidence that she named her clothing collection *Marta da legare* (which perhaps might be rendered very loosely as *Crazy Marta*). Marta entered fashion on an industrial scale in 1991 when she signed a contract with the Standa chains of supermarkets to design their line of womenswear. Paraphrasing Standa's own slogan, she christened the operation "Marta of the Italians": the clothes were a sell-out, proving her right. She diversified the collections. The secret of their popularity was based on their interchangeable nature: just three garments made it possible to change outfits up to six times. The association continued until 1996. Work amuses her: for example, before the Standa contract, she had designed and financed a small collection, which was immediately made into 3,500 garments and sold to a famous boutique on Rodeo Drive in Los Angeles. Once the collaboration with Standa ended, her brands continued to appear at Milano Collezioni, where each season's *prêt-à-porter* is presented. Marta Marzotto is an inspired eclectic: in a single collection it is possible to find Javan textiles, Turkish kaftans, Persian motifs, echoes of Morocco, or flowers wafted by an Oriental breeze for gauzy beach dresses in the style of Gauguin. The runway show of March 1998 was particularly memorable, a meeting point of delightful follies, with ostrich feathers and Viking hats. Above all, fashion for Marta is like a first love that is never forgotten: her point of reference following from her career as a model during the years of the Dolce Vita. She gave up the profession to become a wife, a leading member of Rome's high society and a muse for Renato Guttuso.

(*Lucia Mari*)

Masana Josep (1894-1979). Catalan photographer. His specialties were portraits and publicity campaigns for the worlds of fashion and showbusiness. In 1920 he opened his first studio in Barcelona, and, in 1935, inspired by his experience of the historic avant-garde and cinematic expressionism in particular, he opened the Savoy Cinema. He used various recognizable motifs in his own work, such as photomontage and repeated images reminiscent of Futurism.

Masatomo Rynshu (1951). Japanese designer who studied graphics and design at the Tama Art College. In 1985 he founded the design studio Ma-Ji Creation. Seven years later he launched the Masatomo Inc. brand, debuting at the Paris menswear Fall-Winter shows. In 1996, he opened his Paris store in the Marais district. The following year he clothed Mick Jagger for the Rolling Stones' world tour. It was only in 2001 that the designer changed his name from Masatomo Yamaji to Rynshu Hashimoto. In subsequent years his collections have appeared under his new name.

(*Maddalena Fossati*)

Masenza Italian jewelers, in business in Rome from the beginning of the twentieth century (with shops first in Piazza di Spagna and later in Via del Corso). During the 1950s, Masenza invited artists such as Guttuso, Fazzini, the Basaldella brothers, Cagli, Capogrossi, and Emilio Greco to design jewelry. During the long post-war period it was a point of reference for the stars of Cinecittà and the international jet set.

Mash The principal brand of the firm Acon (Ambrosini Confezioni), founded in 1973 with the production of the first pairs of pants with five pockets. From the start it specialized in jeanswear and casualwear for men, women, and children. Managed by Giuliano and Federico Ambrosini and Stefano Ambrosini, in 2000 the company had a turnover of over 100 billion lire, 15% of which was made on the foreign markets. It produces about 3 million garments per year. The works at San Martino Buon Albergo (Verona) employ about 150 people, 1,500 more are employed elsewhere by the firm. In Italy, the brand is stocked in about 500 retail outlets, including in-store spaces.

Maska Italian womenswear *prêt-à-porter* firm, founded in 1968 in Scandiano (Reggio Emilia). It distributes four clothing lines, including M.K. for a youthful customer base. It has opened showrooms in London and Düsseldorf and exports to Japan. The brand has experienced highs and lows in its search for a lost style, but this has been rediscovered with Simon Kneen who has designed the company's collections since Spring-Summer 2003. The look has been revised and corrected, without abandoning the tailored over garments that have always been the company's specialty: severe trouser suits that almost became tail-coats for winter 2003-2004. But the jackets could also be teamed with tiny slips that fluttered around the waist. Kneen's signature often has a sharp edge: 360° restyling in order to rejuvenate the new brand in the Fin.part stable. (*Lucia Mari*)

❑ 2002, June. Simon Kneen, from Liverpool, was made creative director at Maska. He had already worked for the company in the past, as well as the GFT Group, Belfe, Simint, Laura Biagiotti, Les Copains, Trussardi, Pierre Balmain, and Adrienne Vittadini. Furthermore, he has designed a line that has been distributed in own-brand stores bearing his own name. He replaced Istvan Francer who moved on within the Fin.part Group to manage the principal Cerruti lines, collaborating with Samantha Sung (who came from Ralph Lauren) for women's collections and Adrien Smith (with experience at Gucci and Ferré) for the men's.

❑ 2003, February. Simon Kneen's second collection showed in Milan with a new interpretation of Maska's classic garment, the perfectly tailored jacket. Within the Fin.part Group, Maska, which closed 2002 with a turnover of 65 million euros, is increasingly considered to be a high quality product.

❑ 2003, June. Fin.part sold all its shares in Maska for 26.1 million euros. 85% of the shares were purchased by Go & Create Investment, a Luxemburg company of an industrial group coordinated by Luigi Francesconi, while the remaining 15% went to Gianni Trevison, CEO of Maska. The deal was intended to reduce a net financial debt of about 20 million euros.

Maskrey Brand of body jewelry. After years of experience as a make-up artist in the fashion business, Maskrey invented a type of jewelry applied to the skin that looks like a tattoo. Refined, elegant, and above all temporary, it is very popular among singers, dancers and stage performers. He negotiated with Estée Lauder and Givenchy for the production and distribution of the product. Various kinds of accessories, from bags to belts, as well as some types of garment are added to each new season's collection. His clients include Browns Focus, Harrods and Barney's N.Y.

Massai Elisa (1918-2003). Italian journalist. Her father, Mario Massai, was a pilot and a celebrated aviation reporter for *Corriere della Sera*: he died on a job in the skies above French Morocco during the opening flight of the new Rome-Rio de Janeiro line. Elisa Massai was among the most important chroniclers of fashion, and closely followed the economic aspects of the sector. For a long period she was a correspondent for

Womens Wear Daily and other Fairchild titles and, as such, was among the five journalists invited by Bista Giorgini to the baptism of Italian fashion in February 1951 in Florence. The others were Elsa Robiola, Misia Armani, Vera Rossi, and Sandra Bartolomei Corsi. She started to work in fashion by chance. She related: "In October 1949, I worked for the financial daily newspaper *24 Ore*. One of my colleagues, Antonio Giordano, was a correspondent for the American Fairchild editorial group. Every now and then he sent in news and articles on financial and industrial issues. That day in October, he telephoned the director's office of *WWD*: 'We know that some American buyers are in Milan to buy dress patterns. It seems they are interested in Noberasco, Vanna, Fercioni, and Tizzoni.' They wanted a feature describing what they had bought, what type of garments, and for how much. Giordano did not know where to start, he knew nothing about the world of fashion. He begged me to help him out. In fact, to take over the article myself. I toured the tailor's ateliers and wrote the piece, which was printed on the front page. Immediately afterwards, Giorgini got in touch with me. She was already trying to get her project underway and the news that foreign buyers were hunting for new ideas in Italy suggested that the idea had some substance to it: the American market was ready to open up to fashions that provided an alternative, also in terms of price, to French dominance." Together with Paolo Lombardi, Massai wrote a lengthy article on "The ready-made and *haute couture* knitwear industry from 1950 to 1980" for the volume *La Moda Italiana* (Electa 1987) edited by Grazietta Butazzi and Alessandra Mottola Molfino.

Massaro Historic French brand of shoes, traditionally linked with fashion and the famous French ateliers. It started out at the end of the nineteenth with a cobbler who moved to Paris in 1894 to seek his fortune and set up in the Opera district, beginning a collaboration with Madeleine Vionnet. His son, Raymond Massaro (1929) consolidated his early success through professional collaborations with Grés and Chanel. He invented the first ballerina shoes. One of his most famous bespoke clients was Marlene Dietrich. The shop is still located near the Opéra in rue de la Paix. At the turn of the century, Raymond, who was by then over 70 years of age, still coordinated all the production for Karl Lagerfeld, Thierry Mugler, and John Galliano, as well as his personal collections.

❑ 2001, October. The Musée International de la Chaussure in Romans dedicated a retrospective to 10 years of Massaro at the court of Chanel. The 25 pairs of shoes in the exhibition cover the period from 1990 to 2000. They include footwear in crocodile skin, sandals with gilt and silver-gilt finishings, and Louis XV and Charles IX style shoes, from the personal collection of Mouna Ayoub.
❑ 2003, March. On the Milanese runways, 33 pieces produced by Raymond Massaro, Michel, Francois Lesage, Desrues, and André Lemarié are shown, all small businesses progressively acquired by Chanel, but maintained in an independent fashion. The title of the show is, fittingly, Satellite Love.

Massei Enrica (1947). Italian designer. From her studies in art, she retained her taste and search for a harmonious, unusual color palette, even at a time when black predominated, together with a faithfulness to geometric minimalism, particularly in the style of Kasimir Malevich. During her first years of apprenticeship in Paris, as assistant to Lagerfeld at Chloé, she learnt the daring inventiveness of fashion. Her *prêt-à-porter* collection (1978) was innovative in its use of unusual textiles and new materials (for example, plastics with a mother-of-pearl sheen), the new cuts she introduced with linear forms, and her technical expertise in the combination of pure and neutral colors in both a decorative and structural sense. She worked at Sanlorenzo in Turin, her family's tailoring atelier, and presented two *haute couture* collections in Rome, but moved to Milan when she began producing *prêt-à-porter*. She also collaborated with big firms, such as Hettermarks and Vestebene. These experiences enriched her designs for ready-made clothing, which were intended for active women who choose functional

Design by Enrica Massei, Fall-Winter Collection 1982-83.

clothing for their own comfort, but who wish to be in harmony with the rational grace of design. (*Lucia Sollazzo*)

Massimo Rebecchi Italian ready-made clothing brand, bringing together the lines Alpha, T.d.m., and Viamaggio. The group grew out of a collaboration between the stylist Massimo Rebecchi, the Florentine businessman Franco Rossi, and Orfeo Grossi. The brand combines knitwear and overgarments, shirts and leather garments and places an emphasis on tailored details.

❑ 2003, February. Rebecchi presented the Alpha by Massimo Rebecchi collection to the *prêt-à-porter* salon Fashion Coterie in New York.

Master Loom Italian textile industry, with headquarters at Montale in Pistoia. It was founded in 1988 following the development of two wool factories by Sivano Gori who, right from his entrepreneurial debut, has concentrated on innovation and research. Today the company has two partners: Michele Alaura and Enzo Casanova. It produces two lines: Master Loom and Laboratorio. The first is strongly directed towards innovative research into materials, finishings and image; the second focuses on a mid-range consumer, producing casual fashions. Master Loom produces 2 million meters of yarn annually, with a turnover of 15 million euros, 65% from exports. It has 35 employees. The firm's main success stories are its indigo jeans; its innovative washed silk, ahead of the rest of the market, which resulted in a notable increase in turnover; and washed linen from the early 1990s, which still constitutes a staple of their summer production. Ongoing research into healthy fibers has led to carbon that protects against magnetic fields and to kevlar, an anti-bacterial synthetic. However, natural fibers, such as linen, flax, cotton, silk and wool, remain the staple of their collections. By Fall 2000, the firm had passed under the control of Ermenegildo Zegna, bringing to a close for Zegna an intense three-year period of investments at a cost of about 140 million euros.

Matelassé or quilted Doubled or stuffed textile, over sewn with horizontal, vertical or lozenge motifs. The technique is used for practical or sporting garments, such as Husky jackets. Matelassé is also a fabric in silk, cotton, rayon, or other synthetic fibers, with padded relief surfaces and damask-like designs, used to make elegant garments. The effect is obtained on double fabrics using different, perhaps intertwining, weaves.

Mateldi Filiberto (1885-1942). Painter, caricaturist and illustrator. After a brief period as an actor in Rome, where he was born, from the beginning of the 1920s he drew for about 30 different periodicals, including *Il giornalino della Domenica*, *Lidel*, *Il Balilla*, and *Il Secolo XX*. He also illustrated about 40 books with an elaborate and vigorously elegant style. With Gustavino he was the author of the drawings for the 14 volumes of *La Scala d'Oro*, a series of books for children from the 1930s, and of the unsettling illustrations for *The Golden Ass* by Apuleius. As a fashion illustrator, he worked for *Illustrazione Italiana* in 1933. His images of curvy women bordered on caricatures. He was married to the famous illustrator Brunetta.

Matievi Nikolina (1979). Croatian designer, born in Dubrovnik. She studied at the University of Fashion Design. After studying in Atlanta for one year and in London for three, she returned to Dubrovnik, where she opened an atelier in 1999. Despite her youth, she has already gained a great deal of experience: in May 1999, immediately following her degree, she organized an exhibition of her designs in London, and that same year dressed the finalists in the Best Model in Croatia competition. This was followed by further exhibitions in Dubrovnik. Typical features of her designs are natural and unusual materials, creations inspired by the sea, sails, and the past mixed with the present.

Matsuda Misuhiro (1934). Japanese designer, whose label is called Nicole, a name chosen as a tribute to a French model. He has the ability to marry the purity of Oriental minimalism with Western decoration. Born in Tokyo, he studied at the University of Waseda and in 1964 took a diploma at the local fashion institute, Bunka College. After spending six months in Paris to perfect his knowledge, he opened his own firm in Tokyo in 1967. It met with great success, to such an extent that during the 1970s it continued to create new lines and open boutiques for men and women all over Japan. In the 1980s the Matsuda label was launched on foreign markets. Matsuda, whose headquarters are located in the Shibuya district, is a member of the Council of Fashion Designers of Tokyo. He designed the costumes for *Baldios*, a Japanese cartoon that had little success in Europe.

Matsushima Masakï (1963). Designer, born in Nagoya-shi (Japan), who later moved to Paris. In 1988 he presented his first collection for Tokyo Kumagai Accessoires and, in 1992, founded his own company. Two years later he produced his first line of women's clothing. His garments are always immediately recognizable for their long, fitted silhouettes and the use of special materials.

❑ 2000, February. The museum at Kent State University in Ohio celebrated Japan fashion with the large exhibition Japanese by Design, dedicated to the creations of Issey Miyake and Masaki Matsushima.

❑ 2002, April. He was a member of the Jury for the tenth Brother Cup China, a competition organized by Brother Industries of Hong Kong, open to young fashion creators from 25 different countries.

Matti Milanese furriers founded in 1847. Under the name Matti-Crivelli it became a favorite of the aristocracy, who went there to order clothes to wear at the opening night of La Scala. Its clients included the Duke of Genoa, thereby justifying the use of the title "Suppliers to the Royal Household." In 1979, the company began an association with the designer Moschino and presented on the *prêt-à-porter* Milan runways until 1993. The atelier is currently run by Gianluca and Mimma Matti, the fifth generation of the family.

Mattioli Franco (1927). Italian clothing entrepreneur. As a manager, he played an important role in the success of Gianfranco Ferré. At 14 he was a porter in a textile store, a textile salesman at 17 and later a store director. In 1958 he founded Dei Mattioli in Bologna, a clothing company. After a while he began to produce a second line, Baila, which he entrusted to a newly graduated architect-designer from Legnano. The first runway show was in 1974 and was particularly popular in the United States. 1978 was a turning point with the arrival of Gianfranco Ferré as a 49% partner. In 1999, Mattioli announced his intention to sell his shares.

Mattiolo Gai (1968). Italian designer. When he was only 19, he presented his first collection at Modit in Milan, with the help of his father. Against the wishes of his entire family, who wanted him to become a lawyer, his father lent him 50 million lire in order to attempt a career in fashion. After high school, he opened a small atelier in the heart of Rome, his home city, and began creating patterns under the close guidance of a tailor and pattern maker. The very small venture nevertheless began to have results:

his garments, which combined classicism and creativity with small details that made them unique, were immediately popular. The details were of prime importance for Mattiolo, who is a perfectionist, and tenacious and passionate about his work. He dedicates an almost maniacal attention to buttons: they are jewelry, small masterpieces, in some cases loving works of art. They are made of pure gold or precious stones, personally sourced by Mattiolo, and are micro-sculptures rather than simply fashion accessories. There is always a great variety of buttons in his collections: in the shape of fir trees on the dress he sent to the First Lady, Hillary Clinton; and lucky-charms for the Fall-Winter 1999-2000 collection, with the inscription: "Gai Mattiolo wishes you a happy new millennium." He has become a commercial and runway success, also thanks to his alter ego, Attilio Vaccari. Today Gai Mattiolo is an international industry. His creations are present in many countries, thanks to a fine distribution network. It has expanded over the years to include Gai Mattiolo Maglia, Schoking Gai for larger sizes, Gai Mattiolo Couture Textiles, and footwear, hats, bijoux and all forms of accessories, including perfume. From the runways of Milan and Paris, his clothes appeal to many celebrities, who also have the chance to choose from the Gai Mattiolo Royale line, a limited edition of bespoke garments, only distributed in 25 retail outlets across the world. Mattiolo's fashion often borrows from the past but is reinterpreted with an acute eye on the future. It is a memorial that emphasizes the feminine, dusting off past eras and fashions. From 2000, Mattiolo has remained faithful to his style commandments: a woman should be a "siren of seduction," every collection "the synthesis of a philosophy," fashion "a song of glamour": an ever-present, well defined glamour in every garment, where even the smallest detail becomes a jewel. Indeed, jewelry – along with his heart signature – are the symbols of his runway shows: for his debut he used Swarovski crystals for a pair of jeweled handcuffs, in 1999 he made a suit fastened with three priceless rubies and completely cut away at the back. The next logical step, the following season, was to present dresses made of platinum threads. Very close to his sister Giada, who works with him and is a spectator at every runway show, Gai still retains a boyish spirit: mild and reserved. He prefers soft tones and manners even when taking drastic decisions. As a result, when he decided to stop showing on the runway in Rome, he organized an event with Jack Nicholson in order not to deprive his native home and followers of his much-awaited show. The definitive step from *haute couture* to *prêt-à-porter* came with the show on the Castel Sant'Angelo bridge, which saw the birth of "prêt-à-couture," a term which summed up his new challenge: to find "a contemporary balance between an easier luxury and a more artisanal industry." His successes are many and memorable, but for him personally, the most important recognition was making four chasubles for Pope John Paul II.

(*Maria Vittoria Alfonsi*)

❑ 2003, February. An exceptional guest attended the Milano Moda Donna runway show for Fall-Winter 2003-2004. In the front row, dressed in a very elegant sari of black-and-white gauze was Tara Gandhi, grand-daughter of the Mahatma. Mattiolo dedicated the collection to her, while a voice in the background diffused Gandhi's famous phrase: "Violence is the only thing the atomic bomb cannot destroy."

❑ 2003, July. The production of Gai Mattiolo Couture was to be carried out internally and no longer by the Mariella Burani Group, starting with the Spring-Summer 2004 collection. The Emilian Group still holds the license for jeans, which dates back to 1998. In February, after closing the boutiques in Rome in Via Borgognona and in Milan in Via della Spiga, Mattiolo announced that he would open a new store in Via Mario dei Fiori in Rome in September.

❑ 2003, July. Mattiolo returned in grand style to AltaRomaAltaModa: he reacquired the licenses for his brand and returned to own couture production. He opened the new boutique in Rome and launched his eighth perfume, *Man's*. The runway show was held at the Fori Imperiali in front of the Temple of Saturn. It began with a dancer performing inside a 3-meter crystal ball and concluded with 20 dancers in white tights, representing modern gladiators. (*Pierangelo Mastantuono*)

❑ 2004, September. A contract was signed with Rodolfo Zengarini, the shoe factory, for the production of the line of men's shoes. The label also grants the license for scarves and ties to the Achille Pinto company.

Mattli Giuseppe (1907-1982). Swiss designer, famous for being the creator of many collections for Chanel. He was born at Locarno. After a period in London in order to learn English, he moved to Paris where he worked for the *haute couture* house Premet. In 1934 he returned to Great Britain and opened his own atelier, making both *haute couture* and ready-made garments. In 1955, he abandoned *haute couture*, creating ready-made collections until the early 1970s, notable mainly for his imaginative cocktail and theater gowns.

Mattout Pierre-Henry. French designer. At 17, he moved from the provinces to Paris and immediately began working for Cacharel with the Japanese designer Atsuro Tayama. This was followed by three years at Maison Dior. He moved to New York and offered his collection of men's shirts to Barney's. In 1999, he joined the official calendar of French fashion.

Mauboussin French jewelers, opened by Georges Mauboussin in 1923, in rue de Choisel in Paris, after a period of apprenticeship in the workshop of his uncle, Jean Baptiste Noury. He designed, worked metal, and cut and set stones. He enjoyed instant international success: firstly, with his participation at the French Exhibition held in New York in 1924, and afterwards at the Exhibition of Decorative Arts in Paris in 1925, where he was awarded a gold medal. This was consolidated with his own Paris atelier. The little room on the floor above the showroom, where he presented and sold his creations, was the scene of three memorable themed exhibitions between 1928 and 1931 dedicated, respectively, to emeralds, rubies, and diamonds. For his Art Deco jewelry, with their extraordinary range of colors, he loved to combine stones of great value with semi-precious materials, such as rock crystal, coral, onyx, and jade. During the recession, his cousin Marcel Goulet joined the firm and contributed to its commercial revival. In 1942, Marcel's son, Jean Goulet, also joined the company, which moved to 20 Place Vendôme. Arab princes and Hollywood stars became frequent visitors to the atelier, including the Maharajah of Indore, Queen Nazli of Egypt, Marlene Dietrich, and Greta Garbo. Floral and animal-shaped jewelry was typical of Mauboussin's production and many of his designs had a strong Oriental influence. During the 1970s, his sons, Alain and Patrick Goulet-Mauboussin, took over the reins of the company, maintaining the high level of its international fame linked, more than ever, with the exceptional quality of the stones. (*Alessandra Quattordio*)

Maud et Nano French fashion house, founded in 1942, during the middle of the German occupation, by two former employees of the atelier Suzy. At Suzy, Maud was in charge of sales and Nano was a pattern maker. They joined forces, rented a prestigious showroom in Faubourg Saint-Honoré and met with success. Nano left in 1955, while Maud remained until 1964.

Maud Frizon Footwear brand founded by the French mannequin and favorite model of the designer Courrèges (Nadine is her real name). At the end of the 1960s, she designed a collection of footwear, which was produced by an Italian company, and with her husband Gigi De Marco opened a store in Rue des Saints Pères, on the corner of Rue de Grenelle. One of her main designs was a high boot without a zip, which was worn by Brigitte Bardot and Catherine Deneuve. By 1973, the husband and wife team owned two companies with about 300 employees. To the women's collection, whose cone-shaped heels became famous, were added men's and children's ranges, a line of scarves, and knitwear. Designers such as Alaïa, Missoni, Montana, Mugler, and Rykiel collaborated with the fashion house. In 1992 the brand was sold.

❑ 1999. The brand was bought by Beauty Group, a holding with headquarters in Hong Kong.

❑ 2002. As part of a project to diversify from the traditional product, a line of perfumes was launched.

Mauri Rossella (1952). From 1970, when she was just twenty, she has been the hyperactive, supportive and ever-present shadow of Mariuccia Mandelli, known as Krizia. Over time she has filled all roles: secretary, supplier relations, organizing runway shows, and collection sales. She is head of the press office.

Mauro Krieger Classic menswear brand, formed in 2000 in a commercial agreement with Ma. Co., owned by the Caruso family. The line mixes traditional Italian tailoring techniques with a modern twist, using Anglo-Saxon fabrics and modern, comfortable textiles. The Krieger brand has five showrooms in Italy, as well as the Emilian base in Soragna. It has a presence on two international markets: distribution in Japan is coordinated at the Milanese headquarters in Via San Pietro all'Orto and it has a store in Paris in Avenue Basquet.

(*Pierangelo Mastantuono*)

Mavi Jeans Brand produced by the Turkish company Erak (3,000 employees and an annual turnover of 250 million dollars). It was launched in 1999. Three years later it was exporting 2 million pairs of jeans to the United States a year. The success of the company lies in the strong design and its studied wearability, being adapted to the different male and female physiognomies of the 32 countries where the brand is available. The company was founded by Sait Akarlilar (1940), who began as a worker and, in 1959, set up a workshop making jackets and pants. His sons, Elif, Ersin, and Seyan, are also employed in the firm. The factory at Cerkezkoy makes 11 million pairs of jeans a year (150 kilometers from Istanbul).

Ma Walter (1951). Hong Kong designer. Often inspired by the cultures and ethnic clothing of Australia and Southeast Asia, where he enjoys a strong following.

Max Factor Cosmetics firm founded in Los Angeles in 1909, famous for its links with the cinema. Originally from Poland, Max Factor, a theatrical hairstylist and make-up artist, decided to move to Hollywood, predicting the rapid development of the cinema industry. Here he created his first cosmetic products, which he made specifically for the big screen. He was responsible for the successful image of many great stars (Mae West, Jean Harlow, Greta Garbo, Joan Crawford, Lana Turner, and Elizabeth Taylor) who inspired entire generations of women. In 1918, he launched Colour Harmony, the first line of cosmetics with blusher, foundation, lipstick and eye shadows in matching colors. In 1928, it was the turn of Panchromatic Make-up. Designed for use on Technicolor films, it won an Academy Award. After that came make-up for television. Max Factor's winning strategy, adopted in the 1920s and maintained to this day, was to offer women the make-up of the stars. Acquired by Procter & Gamble in 1991, the brand is now distributed in more than 120 countries.

Maxfield Parrish London fashion house launched in 1974 by the designer Nigel Preston (1946). He owes his success primarily to the stage clothes he creates for famous pop stars. He often uses suede and leather to make entire garments, with an overall classic feel and soft, very wearable lines.

Maxime Claude (1945-1992). French hairdresser, very famous during the 1960s, above all for his professional skill and dyeing techniques. His rise, which began with the opening of the first Parisian salon in 1965, was swift. Three years later, his success required him to open a second salon. His fame increased hand in hand with the inauguration of further salons: 7 in Paris, 5 in the provinces and 2 abroad.

Maxi-mini Throughout the 1960s, the two different lengths contrasted and coexisted. Mini skirts and dresses, launched by Mary Quant and Courrèges, were worn under maxi-coats so long that they skimmed the ground. The mini was nearly always worn with boots that went over the knee and sometimes even to the top of the thigh. Both lengths have remained in fashion and survived into the third millennium.

Max Mara Italian company, a leader in the creation, production and sale of women's clothing characterized by elegant design and an excellent price-quality relationship. When Achille Maramotti (1927) founded the company in Reggio Emilia in 1951, continuing a family passion (his great-grandmother was a tailor and his mother directed cutting and sewing schools in Europe), was he anticipating the idea of *prêt-à-porter* in a period when fashion was still tailored and took its inspiration directly from Paris. During 50 years of activity, the history of the company has been intertwined with the history of dress, translating the vibrations and tendencies of the elite into consumer products. With great intuition and a pervading innovative spirit, Maramotti commissioned young designers of obvious talent as well as big names, while keeping their role hidden from the public, to create the Max Mara style, made up of simple, contemporary silhouettes, beautiful textiles and perfect cuts. Names such as Emmanuelle Khanh, Lagerfeld, Soprani, Guy Paulin, De Castelbajac, Dolce & Gabbana, and Anne Marie Beretta enabled the company's products to reflect fashionable tendencies in harmony with the needs of the market. A strong focus was also placed on the definition of the company's image, the advertising campaigns, presentations and runway shows (of Max Mara and Sportmax), which always employ the most famous creative and photographers, such as Sarah Moon, Paolo Roversi, Fabrizio Ferri, Arthur Elgort, Albert Watson, Gianpaolo Barbieri, Peter Lindberg, Steven Meisel, and Richard Avedon. In addition, Max Mara publishes a biannual magazine containing news and fashion. Its international expansion policy is worth noting: on the eve of the millennium there were more than 1,000 Max Mara stores in 90 countries, divided into 6 distribution chains: Max Mara, Sportmax, Marina Rinaldi, Max & Co., Marella and Pennyblack. At the start of the century, turnover exceeded 1,600 billion lire a year, and the company employed almost 3,000 staff. Now that the founder (made a Cavaliere del Lavoro in 1983), dedicates himself above all to finance, with different roles in various credit institutes, his three children, Maria Ludovica, Luigi, and Ignazio, run the company.

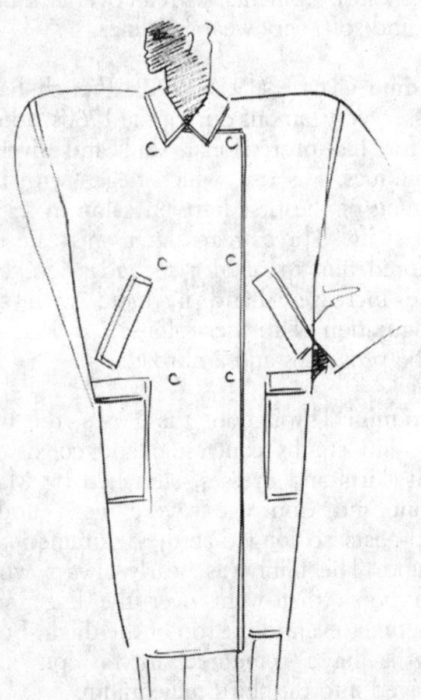

Max Mara Fall-Winter 1985-86 Collection, coat designed by Anna Maria Beretta.

❑ 2001, April. For the first time, Max Mara linked its name with another firm. Together with Lycra, a registered brand of DuPont, it concluded a co-marketing operation, in the interests of quality. Max Mara used its store windows across the world to publicize the link between its Spring-Summer 2001 collection and DuPont's revolutionary fiber.

❑ 2002, March. Max & Co., the youthful brand in the Max Mara Fashion Group, opens its fifth store in Milan with five windows, on Corso XXII Marzo. It joins the company's more than 200 own-brand stores already in Italy.

❑ 2002, May. From Fall-Winter 2002, Max Mara, in collaboration with DuPont Textiles & Interiors, launches a line of hosiery. This project, run by the new company Max Mara Hosiery, is expected to make a turnover of 25 million euros within a few years. Max Mara tights are characterised by high-quality materials and production. They are situated in a medium-high price range.

❑ 2002, May. 40% growth in the Chinese market, with the opening of two new Max Mara stores and one Max &

Co. Although it has had stores in China since the mid-1990s, Max Mara has intensified its presence. As part of a joint venture with Fairton, a Hong Kong company, the Maramotti family brand is now present in Canton, Shenzen, Shanghai, Dalian, and Shenyang, with two Marina Rinaldi stores in Peking and Shanghai. With another Chinese partner, three franchise stores have been opened in Beijing, one in Xian and another in Chengdu, a highly populated city in the province of Sichuan. In 2001, the Max Mara Group had a turnover of over a billion euros and the Chinese market alone is worth about 10 million dollars. In 2001, the growth in China was 25% and the Spring-Summer 2002 sales were up by 40%.

❑ 2002, September. The collection presented at Milano Moda Donna was defined by Laura Lusuardi, fashion director of Max Mara, as "a covered transparency." In other words, aggressive but not provocative. The 2001 turnover was 1.065 billion euros.

❑ 2002, October. Max Mara entered the world of perfumes and cosmetics for the first time, in partnership with Cosmopolitan Cosmetics (51%), a company that is part of the Wella Group. Quoted on the Frankfurt stock exchange, Wella has managed brands such as Gucci, Rochas, Montblanc, and Dunhill.

❑ 2003, March. At the Milano Moda Donna runway shows, the new collection played with forms and chromatic graphics, reinterpreted with a futuristic eye.

❑ 2003, April. Hanging Around was the title of the exhibition arranged at the Corso Vittorio Emanuele store in Milan. It was created in conjunction with students from the Istituto Marangoni, who produced new interpretations of the simple coat hanger for Max Mara. The exhibition at Max & Co. linked up with the Hanger Art Exhibition, organized in October 2002 in the Omotesando boutique (Tokyo) with creations by Japanese artists.

❑ 2004, May. The first Max Mara perfume was presented at the Corso Vittorio Emanuele store in Milan.

Sportmax 1976 designed by Castelbajac.

❑ 2005, January. In Reggio Emilia, following a long illness, the founder of the label Achille Maramotti passed away. He left the administration of the company in the hands of his three children, Maria Ludovica, Luigi, and Ignazio.

❑ 2005, March. Max Mara took part in the Universal Expo 2005 in Aichi, Japan, an event that brought together 125 countries and a million visitors. Max Mara contributed to the Italian pavilion with its staff uniforms.

Maxwell Vera (1903). American tailor. She made her debut at the relatively late age of 44, having spent a long period in the ballet corps at the Metropolitan in New York and having learnt her trade by working with Adler & Adler, a prestigious American tailoring firm. She was known for her choice of textiles that were not normally used by ateliers and for having been a pioneer of suede skirts and jackets in the United States.

Maywald Wilhelm, known as Willy (1907-1985). German photographer. He completed his art studies at Krefeld in Cologne and, during the period 1928-1931, the High

School of Figurative Arts in Berlin, working at the same time as an assistant in a cinema studio. In 1931, he was in Paris where he first worked at Harry Meerson's studio and later opened his own, specializing in portraits, architecture, reportage and fashion. He collaborated with *Fémina*, *Harper's Bazaar*, *Vogue*, *Réalités*, *Picture Post*, *Life*, *Elegante Welt*, and *Photo Prisma*. In 1942, he began a series of portraits of people from the worlds of theater, literature and art, such as Marc Chagall, Le Corbusier, Pablo Picasso, and Jean Costeau, in the volume *Artists at Home*, published in 1949. From 1946, in his new Paris studio, he started to work in fashion again, becoming the official photographer for the Maison Christian Dior.

Mazzei Gabriella (1965). Born in Lamezia Terme, she attended the European Institute of Design in Rome, taking a course in public relations. She moved to Milan at the beginning of the 1990s and began a collaboration with Sergio Salerni (E20), organizing events and runway shows. She became a partner in 1997. She set up her own company, Without, in 1999 with her husband Andrea Leonardi. This is an agency specializing in the production of runway shows, concepts, location searches, lay-out, managing suppliers, casting, fittings and show callings.

Mazzei Margherita (1967). Neapolitan designer. She began her career in fashion very early on as an atelier model. While taking her high school diploma, she worked in *prêt-à-porter*, assisting with important representative clothing studies. Early on, however, she began to feel the need to express herself in a more creative and personal way. In 1995, she met the man who was later to become her husband and with him founded Made, a company that has been making underwear since 1996 and that has now become an important player in the field of corsetry and beachwear. Her designs are characterized by their perfect wearability and attention to the female form. Currently the collections, two a year for underwear and one for swimming costumes, are distributed in 500 shops across Europe, in four franchising stores in Italy and through the Victoria's Secret shops in the United States. The designs are produced at the factory in Melito (Naples), currently employing about 30 members of staff.

Mazzetti Giovanna (1933). Journalist. She became editor of *Amica*, a women's weekly, which she joined in 1969 as a trainee, after having worked briefly for the Gruppo Finanziario Tessile, where she was in charge of marketing for the Marus stores. The editor of *Amica* at the time, Antonio Alberti, asked her to come and work on fashion. She gradually moved up the internal career ladder at Rizzoli, the publisher, and took over the helm from 1990 to spring 1999.

Mazzini Brand of bags and footwear founded in 1962 by Enzo Mazzini, who started the business after taking his diploma at the Tuscan Leather School. A few tools and a quantity of leather was enough to start the company and he was shortly joined by his brother Gastone. During the 1960s the company took off and their products were distributed across the whole of Italy, participating at all the most important fairs. They created an "office" collection in black leather with nickel accessories and a new line of footwear. Now Mazzini Moda is quoted on the stock market and serves an international market. (*Giuliana Parabiago*)

Mbc The young and trendy brand of the Milanese holding Multimoda Network, founded in 1999 by Clemente Signoroni and Gianfranco Bertoli. Multimoda also owns Simultaneous and Castelbajac. Its products are designed for a public aged between 15 and 35 years of age, while the Serial Kids line caters for children up to 13. A compilation of instrumental lounge music entitled *Mbc-Ws 1 One* was released at the beginning of the twenty-first century, the first collaboration between a clothing brand and the Twilight Music label, which specializes in disco music. At Christmas 2001, the brand of T-shirts, sweatshirts, hats, and bags encountered cell phones: a new bag designed for fitness and free time was created for the Wind Style project, the purpose of which was to increase use of Wind's service among the public.

Mbc Italy Casual clothing and sportswear company for young people, men, women, and children. It was founded in 1996 by Paolo and Giulia Muccifora. Its headquarters are in Formello (Rome). Its brands are Mbc-Ws, Waterfear, Tea4Two, Mbc Zoo Friend, Audace Boxe and Audace Nuove Leve. It is marketed through a network of their own stores located in the main Italian cities, through franchise stores and about 1,500 multi-brand retail outlets across the country. The president is Gianluca Cedro and the company has recently joined the Gava Group, an important player in the retail sector both in Italy and abroad, which includes the Ventaglio Group among its shareholders. *(Lucia Serlenga)*

McCardell Claire (1905-1958). American designer from Maryland. She was one of the most vivacious representatives of American fashion. A student at the Parson's School, in 1929 she began to work with Richard Turk, the designer of Townley Frocks, a brand of women's and children's clothing that also produced monks' habits. In 1938 she created her Frock: a predecessor to Saint-Laurent's Trapeze collection, it was wide, expanding towards the bottom, and did not emphasize the waistline. After that, she worked as part of Townley, producing her own brand. She designed for working women and used details to mark his own style: striking overstitching, large cuffs, appliquéd pockets, metal rivets and hooks, and shoelaces instead of buttons. In 1942, she created a loose, unstructured gown (*popover*); in 1944, she had Capezio produce his *pumps* (patent ballerina shoes), inspired by those worn by classical dancers. She then revived the Empire style, the *dirndl* (Tyrolean-style skirts), short socks and backless dresses. *(Laura Salza)*

McCartney Stella (1971). English designer, the daughter of Paul and Linda McCartney. Interested in fashion from an early age, she did work experience in Lacroix's atelier in Paris at the age of 15. After high school she went to work for Betty Jackson for a brief period and later for English *Vogue*. She took a degree at Saint Martin's and while she was there did further work experience with Edward Sexton, a Savile Row tailor. She gained notoriety at her graduation fashion show in 1995 by inviting her friends, including Naomi Campbell, to model for her. The paparazzi, who were already out in force because of her famous parents, went wild. Immediately afterwards, she opened her own atelier in the fashionable area of Notting Hill Gate. In 1996, she was chosen by the CEO of Chloé, Mounir Moufarrige, to take over from Lagerfeld as stylistic director of the French fashion house. Lagerfeld, indignant, apparently commented: "Chloé wanted a big name and it got one. In music not in fashion." The move, for whatever reason, had the desired effect: that of relaunching the brand at the same time as other Paris firms who had taken on very young English designers. It suffused the collections with novelty and freshness. McCartney's style for Chloé looked to the past for pretty laces and embroideries, reinterpreted in a decidedly sexy, 1970s Pretty Baby look, with eyes firmly focused on the 1990s.

❑ 2002, January. After launching her own company in April 2001 and joining the Gucci Group at the same time, Stella opened her first store, investing roughly 1.5 million euros in a deconsecrated church in West London, near Portobello Road.
❑ 2002, August. Adidas employed Stella McCartney to redesign some historic models. McCartney gave her signature to the Adidas Monza, designed for Formula 1 pilots, and the Boxe Champ Speed. The two styles, made in blue, pink, yellow, orange, and beige, with the three Adidas stripes, carry the Snm brand of all Stella McCartney's products. The designer, who was soon to be married to the editor of *Wallpaper*, Alasdhair Willis, sold her house in Notting Hill for 1.5 million pounds and moved to the more elegant area of Belgravia.
❑ 2003, May. Inauguration of the new New York store, in Bruton Street, four storeys of an entirely renovated Edwardian building, previously an art gallery. McCartney joined the Absolut Vodka project with her Absolut Stella, as part of the Absolut Fashion collections (Versace, Gucci, Gaultier).
❑ 2003, July. Alongside Seamus Heaney, Nobel prize for literature, she received an honorary degree from the

University of Dundee in Scotland. The ceremony was held at the Estorick Gallery in North London.
❑ 2003, March. Although her father was not present, Stella dedicated her runway show to him and her siblings. The show began with a remixed version of a song from Mary Poppins. It was an easy to wear and light collection in terms of colors and textiles. Blouses made of ribbons, floaty skirts and tapered, fitted pants. The only eccentric touch was the use of large zips as decoration and inside-out clothes worn back-to-front. Nothing extravagant for the evening, instead simple jersey dresses with some crystal baguette decorations.
❑ 2004, September. The collaboration between McCartney and Adidas continued. A women's collection called Adidas by Stella McCartney is launched in New York. From February 2005 it has been available in selected stores in Japan, the United States, and Europe.
❑ 2005, May. The collaboration between the English designer and the Swedish giant Hennes & Mauritz is announced. McCartney follows the partnership established between H&M and Karl Lagerfeld. The collection will be called Stella McCartney for H&M and will be made up of 40 pieces for Fall-Winter 2005-6.

McConnell Gareth (1979). Irish photographer. After studying at the Northern Ireland School, he moved to England, where he attended the West Surrey College of Art and Design and the Royal College of Art in London. In 1999 he became a professional photographer, publishing in *Dazed & Confused*, *i-D*, *Exit*, *Sleaze Nation*, *Life*, *The Observer*, *Tank*, and *Source*. He also works in the music field, for Universal Music and Island Records.

McCord Museum of Canadian History Montreal, Québec. A museum dedicated to the history of Montreal and Québec. The clothing and textile department holds about 16,000 pieces. It collects men's, women's and children's clothing and accessories produced locally. Most of the garments date back to the late nineteenth and early twentieth centuries. The oldest object is a hand-painted silk wedding dress from the nineteenth century. The textile collection includes the oldest American patchwork quilt (1726) and the oldest Canadian embroidery (1764).

McDean Craig (1970). English photographer and filmmaker. He began his studies at the Mit Cheshire College in London and at Blackpool College. He gained experience as an assistant to Nick Knight. He made a name for himself publishing in *i-D* and *The Face*, carrying out photo shoots for important clients such as Levi's and working in the music business with Bjork and Iggy Pop. He later moved to New York and established himself definitively with his campaigns for Yamamoto, Givenchy, Calvin Klein. He was published in *W Magazine*, *Harper's Bazaar* and the Italian edition of *Vogue*. In 1999 he published *I Love Fast Cons*.

McDowell Colin. English journalist and writer. Passionate about the world of fashion and an expert in all its secrets. He was once a designer himself for 8 years in Italy, with Pino Lancetti and Laura Biagiotti. He teaches at the Central Saint Martin's College of Arts in London and writes for various magazines and newspapers, including *The Guardian*. Among the books he has written, *100 Years of Royal Style* is dedicated to the queens of England, their taste and style in clothes from the Victorian period to the present. *Everywoman's Guide to Looking Good* is, instead, a collection of suggestions on how to look truly elegant. His *Directory of Twentieth Century Fashion*, a more serious and complex work, published in 1984, elaborated his theories on certain phenomena in the history of fashion. In his view, each change brought about with a new generation is the fruit of political and social conflicts, which McDowell even defines as "anarchical and subversive."

McFadden Mary (1938). American designer with an ethnic influence. She has made great use of African and Chinese textiles, in quilted jackets and pleated silk tunics in the style of Fortuny. Born in New York, she spent her childhood on a cotton plantation near Memphis, Tennessee. With a degree in sociology from Columbia University, from 1962 to 1964 she worked in public relations for Dior in New York. In 1965, she moved to South Africa, where she worked as a fashion editor for *Vogue*. In 1968, she married in Zimbabwe and opened an atelier for young African sculptors. She returned to New York and in 1976 launched a company designing evening gowns made of bright and vivacious fabrics. She received the Coty Award in 1978 and is now part of the Council of Fashion Designers of America. Her list of honors increased with a second Coty Award, a Neiman Marcus Award and a recognition from the Rhode Island School of Design. McFadden is now present in two American Halls of Fame: at Coty Hall and in the Best-Dressed List Hall of Fame.

❑ 2002, March. At South Beach she received the Fashion Week of the Americas career award, as "an American fashion legend and an international innovator." For the first time since it was launched in 1999, the prize was awarded to a non-Hispanic designer.

McGrath Pat (1966). English make-up artist, famous for unusual make-up and her very personal use of color to emphasize different facial features. She is considered one of the leading make-up artists at an international level. Beauty editor of the magazine *i-D*, she often collaborates with the hairdresser Eugene Souleiman, for important designers, such as Prada and Dolce & Gabbana, and for photo shoots as well as backstage at runway shows. In 1999 a contract was announced with Giorgio Armani to create a line of make-up. With hindsight, this ensured an impressive launch for the company's cosmetics sector. For Spring 2003 at John Galliano, McGrath's make-up was inspired by Indian culture. Recurring colors were cobalt blue and marigold yellow. Her make-up for Galliano's Christian Dior collection has a very different tone, making use of kabuki colors: whites, blues and pinks.

McInnes Malcolm. Scottish designer, who took a degree in fashion at Saint Martin's College. After working with Rifat Ozbek and John Galliano, in 2000 he debuted on the runway with his own collection, which was already characterized by a strongly personal style. Sweaters in wool, cashmere, mixed yarns, mohair and jersey decorated with graphics and geometric forms, reminiscent of primitive designs and tribal tattoos. McInnes's colors are orange, acid green, brick red often combined with black weave, with sometimes naïf results.

McKnight Sam (1959). English hairstylist, known for the elegant appeal of his creations, often with a touch of nonchalance. Among other things, he was responsible for Princess Diana's new look. His creations are characteristically easy to wear and he works with an extreme care for details. He often likes to say: "Hair is like clothing. Every women needs to have a hairstyle that makes her feel at ease. This is what makes it sexy and seductive."

❑ 1999, August. A famous brand of gin launched a cocktail using the name of the hairdresser to the stars. The Sam McKnight Fever is made of blueberry juice, gin and lemon.
❑ 2001, September. McKnight made curly hair fashionable again on the runway.
❑ 2003. The hairstylist continued to feature on magazine covers. He was responsible for Nicole Kidman appearing in a black wig on the cover of *Another Magazine*.

McLaren Malcolm (1943). English entrepreneur, musician, talent scout. He gave a voice to and dressed the punk movement during the 1970s. In 1971, he opened a shop selling second-hand clothing on the King's Road in London with his partner Vivienne Westwood. Originally called Let it Rock, it was later renamed Too Fast to Live, Too Young to Die, Sex, and Seditionaries. It sold clothing in PVC, leather and rubber and fetishist and sadomasochistic accessories. Their T-shirts carried obscene or rebellious slogans, such as "Anarchy in the UK," and "God Save the Queen and the Fascist Regime," which cost the couple several denouncements for obscenity. Later on, McClaren became the manager of the Sex Pistols, whose single *God Save the Queen* (1977) became number one just when Queen Elizabeth II was celebrating her Silver Jubilee, despite being banned from the radio and TV.

❑ 1986, January. The legal dispute

between the Sex Pistols and the impresario finished after eight years of polemics, to the detriment of the latter. The companies, Glitterbest and Matrixbest, which controlled the activities and takings of the band under Malcolm McLaren, came under the control of the Sex Pistols.
❑ 1989. A new trend hit discos across the world: *Vogue*. It was McLaren again who, his punk outfits set aside, launched *Waltz darling* (released by Epic). The single – the most commercial offering ever from the ex-manager of the Sex Pistols – with Jeff Beck playing sitar – was likened to "a new way of dressing and moving on the dance floor." It is danced with slow, balanced movements, held for a few seconds in very elegant poses, in imitation of cover images on fashion magazines (with *Vogue*, of course, in pole position). In order to have an idea of the "official" choreography, it was necessary to wait for Madonna's single *Vogue*, publicized with a high patina video in black-and-white, in which the singer goes through the appropriate moves flanked by male and female dancers in very luxurious dress.
❑ Summer 2003, the Sex Pistols announce a new American tour, returning for the first time to the original line-up before the arrival of Sid Vicious. The announcement of his desire to hold one of the concerts in Baghdad is typical of McLaren.

(*Pierangelo Mastantuono*)

McLaren Norrie (1948). English photographer, born in Glasgow. He moved to London and, after an apprenticeship as an assistant at the Whitecross Studios on the King's Road, he became immediately known in the 1960s for his eclecticism: a director and writer for television and cinema productions as well as a photographer for independent, famous magazines during the 1960s and 1970s, such as *Deluxe* and *Boulevard*. In 1975 and 1980 he was assistant to Stanley Kubrick on *Barry Lyndon* and *The Shining*. Since then he has continued to work between London and Scotland in the fields of photography and television.

McLaughlin-Gill Frances (1919). American photographer. After receiving a prize from *Vogue* during the second half of the 1940s, she joined the staff at Condé Nast as assistant to Tony Frissel. She mainly did shoots with small cameras in outdoor settings.

McQueen Alexander (1969 ca). English designer. In 1997, before he was even thirty, he was appointed, not without some opposition, as artistic director of Givenchy, the French fashion house that dressed Audrey Hepburn, one of the most elegant women in the world. This young and controversial talent, awarded the title Designer of the Year in 1996, has had a respectable career. At 16 he decided to leave school and went knocking at the door of Anderson and Sheppard, tailors in Savile Row. Later he worked with the theatrical costume designers, Bermans and Nathan, gaining a good grounding in cutting methods. Afterwards he collaborated with the Japanese designer Koji Tatsuno and with the Italian Romeo Gigli. He returned to London in 1992 to complete his training at Saint Martin's College of Art. Here he presented the collection that paved his way to worldwide acclaim. The Birds, The Highland Rape, The Hunger, Dante are some of his most recent lines.

❑ 2001, McQueen became a designer at the Gucci Group, which acquires 51% of his own brand. Domenico De Sole, enthusiastic about the new acquisition, has great faith in the investment's ability to compete with arch-rival LVMH.
❑ 2001, October. At the Paris runway show, McQueen's collection was based on Spain and two different aspects of the bullfight, with a female toreador dressed in a black, closely fitting outfit and a woman-bull dressed in blood-colored flounced clothing, pierced with a javelin.
❑ 2002, March. A new line of men's clothing is created in collaboration with H. Huntsman and Sons, a famous tailors founded in 1849 and based at 11 Savile Row. For McQueen, it represents a return to his origins, as his career began in Savile Row. The bespoke collection unites the geniality and sensitivity of

McQueen's style and the handcrafted skills of one of the most classic tailors in London. It is made up of 12 designs, requiring between 4 and 6 fittings and 5 months of work. It is sold exclusively at McQueen's boutiques.

❑ 2002, July. The English designer opened his first New York boutique, on West 14th Street.

❑ 2002, October. Part pirate daughter and filibuster queen, part youthful Amazonian: this is the woman sent down the Paris runway by McQueen. In the background, a giant digital screen (20x10 meters) projected images in keeping with the theme, and created by the designer with the director John Maybury. The music was by Earth, Wind and Fire. The show began with pirates wearing scrunched and ripped chiffon garments, blouses with puffed sleeves, tight pants tucked into high boots, small brocaded jackets. After a nocturne intermezzo and dimmed lighting, the scene turned to fifteenth-century England, with rich ruffs and ruched jackets, black Counter-Reformation silhouettes, pierced python skin and embroidered ivory silk. The final section took up the colors of the tropics, 26 bright hues, green, orange, turquoise, blue, chiffon and rainbow-colored organza, flame-colored feathers everywhere, fitted, gold jackets, and tight skirts printed with brilliant rays like a burning sun.

❑ 2003, January. At the British Museum before a select group of journalists, the designer presented his first perfume, *Kingdom*. The launch of a line of cosmetics was announced for September.

❑ 2003, March. The *prêt-à-porter* Fall-Winter 2003 collection was presented on the Paris runways. It was inspired by Tibet, Russia, and the Orient, with suggestions of the Kamasutra. The show ended with the presentation of a one-off piece, a kimono with an embroidery of a man being seduced by ten women; it was worn open by a semi-naked model wearing only briefs and laced sandals.

❑ 2003, March. The designer (34) opened a new own-brand store in London at 4-5 Old Bond Street.

❑ 2003, June. The designer was awarded a CBE (Commander of the Most Excellent Order of the British Empire) by Queen Elizabeth II, for his "important contribution to the excellence of English fashion." Receiving the same award immediately before him were Sting, Anish Kapoor and Dave Gilmour, the guitarist from Pink Floyd.

❑ 2003, June. At a ceremony held at the New York Public Library, the Council of Fashion Designers of America (CFDA) gave out prizes to the best American and non-American designers of 2003. From more than 450 designers, the Fashion Design Award for the best international designer was given to Alexander McQueen. His predecessor in 2002 was Hedi Slimane.

❑ 2003, July. Alexander McQueen opened his first own-brand store in Italy, at 8 Via Verri, Milan. The store was previously occupied by Yves Saint Laurent, who moved into Via Montenapoleone, in the former-Gucci space.

❑ 2004, June. The designer debuted in Milan with his first menswear collection. In reality, it is the second, because the first was presented the previous season but without great publicity. His tailoring experience, acquired on Savile Row, is immediately apparent; the designs succeed in combining the transgressive streak that has made him famous with his bespoke tailoring skills.

❑ 2005, May. From Spring-Summer 2005/6 the collection of sports shoes made by Puma in collaboration with McQueen was made available across the world. The collection was presented in September 2004 at women's fashion week in London.

Meano Cesare (1899-1957). Writer, journalist, organizer of cultural events, with many interests. He was born in Turin. His *Dizionario commento della moda* was published in 1938. It was commissioned by the Italian Fashion Agency and contains an interesting collection of pieces taken from works by ancient and modern authors. The publication represented a move to Italianize fashion terminology, right in the middle of the period of self-sufficiency when French terms and not just French fashions were proudly ostracized. He wrote for all the major daily newspapers, in particular the *Corriere della Sera*, was assistant editor of the magazine *Scenario*, wrote the libretto for the opera *Ghedini e Alfano* and was one of the first playwriters for radio. He gained success from his theater writings (18 plays), beginning with *Nascita di Salomè* (1937), which were translated into 15 languages and performed in Europe and South America.

(*Lucia Sollazzo*)

Meatpacking District An area in New York, situated on the West Side of Manhattan, between the 17th and 12th Streets, behind Chelsea. Once it was a commercial meatpacking district, but today only about 30 of the original 127 meatpackers have survived. The rest of the area, mainly made up of lofts and exhibition spaces, is occupied by designers, art galleries and fashionable bars, as part of the transformation of the area into one of the most vibrant and trendy parts of New York. Alexander McQueen was the first star in the fashion firmament to open a store in what many people consider to be the "new Soho." The next to follow in his footsteps were Stella McCartney, Rubin Chapelle, the French-Moroccan designer Yigal Azrouel, the Brazilian Carlos Miele, the clothing and accessories shops Dernier Cri and Scoop, the jewelers Laura Mady's and the French household goods shop Bodum.

(*Francesca Gentile*)

Medeiros Elli. Accessories designer. She was a model, the leader of a punk rock group in the 1970s and queen of French pop in the 1980s. She has acted for some of the most interesting French directors, including Olivier Assayas and Tonie Marshall. She is an eclectic artist, born in Montevideo in Uruguay. Her mother had theatrical aspirations and as a result she made her debut on television in her home country at a very early age. She arrived in Paris at 14. After an experience with the pioneers of French punk and playing with the Clash and the Sex Pistols, she made her name with the massive hit *Toi mon toit* in 1986. In December 2002, she modeled for the designer Hugues Ferrière at his graduate fashion show at Saint Martin's College of Art. She designed bags and jewelry for the heroine of Brian De Palma's film, *Femme Fatale*. The gold and diamond serpent, which covers the naked body of Veronica in the film, was produced by Chopard jewelers in Geneva. Her line of swimming costumes (for men and women) is stocked by Chez Martin in Paris.

Mediterranea Italian brand of ready-made men's fashion. It was launched in 1993 as part of a collaboration between the designer Fabrizio Fabbri and Elio Cravero, owned of Elfra, a Turin based clothing company. It debuted at Altro Uomo in Florence. In 1994 the collection was enriched with several items of knitwear and was presented in New York and Cologne, resulting in a doubling of turnover. In 1996, it debuted at Milano Collezioni Uomo. Today the brand is distributed throughout Europe, the United States, Japan, Taiwan, and Hong Kong.

Meerson Harry Ossip (1911-1991). French photographer of Polish origins. His images are unusual for their depiction of figures against a white background, without perspective. He began in the world of cinema and continued to borrow its tools, he worked for the magazines *Plaisir de France*, *Fémina*, *Die Dame*, *Votre Beauté*, and *Harper's Bazaar*. During the 1960s, he documented the creations of Carita. In 1978, he became editor-in-chief and artistic director of the magazine *Mode Internationale*.

Meert Nina. Belgian designer. She opened her tailoring workshop in Brussels in 1970. International success arrived in 1984, when she opened a store in Paris. In Belgium, she is considered an *enfant prodige* of fashion. She repopularized romantic clothing, with lace and embroidered linen and silk dresses. Her poetic and imaginative wedding dresses, made with great sartorial skills, are equally famous. In 1987, she received the Fil d'Or for her linen creations.

Meisel Steven (1954). American photographer, born in New York. He began to work at a very early age as an illustrator for *Womens Wear Daily* and as a design teacher at the Parsons School of Design before he became interested in photography. His fashion images published in *Lei* in 1982 opened his path to a world that greatly appreciated the transgressive look of his images and his decision to abolish half-tones and careful compositions. He has been responsible for many advertising campaigns for Dolce & Gabbana and has an exclusive contract with Condé Nast. In 2003, for his Valentino campaign inspired by the 1970s, Meisel reaffirmed his standing, using the new model Natasha Vojnovic, made-up to resemble Donna Jordan, the muse of Helmut Newton, Toscani and above all Andy Warhol, who made her the protagonist of his film *L'Amour* in 1973. He discovered both the Italo-American model Linda Evangelista and the Scottish Stella Tennant. He has worked for, among others, Coeri, Gaultier, Jil Sanders, Laura Biagiotti, Dolce & Gabbana, Valentino, and Versace. He is also known for his photographs of Madonna (to whom he dedicated a successful book), Nicole Kidman, and Uma Thurman.

Mélange Indicates a mixture of colors, in yarns and textiles. It can be either in similar tones that blend into one another or in strongly contrasting colors.

Méléard Benoit (1972). Footwear designer. Born and raised in Paris, where today he presents spectacular shows of his visionary shoes for women, which are practically forms of architecture for the feet. A former ice-hockey player, after he took a diploma as an ad-illustrator at the École Supérieure des Arts Modernes, he was one of 12 students out of more than 2,000 to be selected for further study at AFPIC (Association pour la Formation des Profession des Métiers de l'Industrie du Cuir) in 1994. After work experience with Robert Clergerie, in 1996 he began designing shoes for Charles Jourdan and the "alternative" designer Jean Colonna. In 1997, he debuted on his own and encountered the creator Jeremy Scott, for whom he designed delirious shoes (in gilt leather, with unequal heels, one a high stiletto and the other a low, square heel) for the Rich White Women runway show. Today he continues to produce his own line as well as collaborations with very high profile brands such as Loewe and Diesel. Obsessed with shapes and geometry, and with a fetishist love for women's feet, for the Tip Toe collection of 1998 he created little boots and open-toed shoes with very high arches but no heel, forcing the models to walk on tiptoes. "A cruel collection, just as every fashion diktat is cruel," he commented. The Spring-Summer 2000 line was inspired by Minnie Mouse at the court of Versailles, with high eighteenth-century style shoes surmounted by enormous circles or squares placed vertically on the upper. Méléard himself admits to being "attracted by extremes that border on the ridiculous but not interested in futuristic materials. I believe in leather, the real kind."

(*Antonio Mancinelli*)

Melik Elena (1919). Italian journalist with a pioneering interest in cosmetics and beauty. Born in Saint Petersburg to an Italian father and Armenian mother, she moved to Italy and began to work in 1947 as a secretary at the magazine *Confidenze*, published by Mondadori. The following year, while still in the same job, she edited a page of letters on beauty, the first of its kind, with advice and replies for the female readers. Later she moved to Grazia and in 1953 she began to write a proper column on cosmetics with suggestions and photographs by the editorial staff. During the course of her lengthy career, which continued until the end of the twentieth century, she received many recognitions for her work and she is rightly considered to be the queen of beauty editors. She was particularly appreciated for her honesty and straight-talking, with a capacity for criticism where necessary.

(*Ginevra Falzoni*)

Melloni Roman furriers. In business from the 1930s, the company closed in the mid-1970s. It was one of the most important ateliers and its black breischwantz cloaks with white ermine hoods were famous. It played a big role in the development of the fur industry, introducing the intarsia technique. Other typical products were the striped Chinese goat coats and, at the beginning of the 1970s, cloaks made of monkey fur.

Meltin' Pot A line of jeans created in 1993 by Augusto Romano in order to breath new life into the family textile firm located in Salento from 1967. Romano was one of the first to bring streetwear to Italy, adapting the

American Hip-Hop culture to the Italian casual clothing tradition. In 2002, the business made almost 20 million euros, with a sale of almost a million garments through 700 Italian retail outlets and 400 shops in continental Europe. The company, whose turnover reached 40 million euros, also owns the brands Evo Basic, Go-Go Style, B-side and Get Real.

Menchari Leila. Window dresser for Hermès Paris. Since 1978, she has decorated the shop front in Faubourg Saint-Honoré four times each year. She studied at the Academy of Fine Arts in Paris. The writer Michel Tournier has described her as the "queen magician." Her latest invention was to display the collection of Hermès jewelry on blue sand. She has said, " I am not a creator, I do not imagine anything, I observe and interpret nature."

Mendès French clothing production company, founded in 1902 by the tailor Cerf Mendès, who made himself famous cutting and sewing coats and suits. From 1950, it joined the *prêt-à-porter* company Maria Carine, which was launched by the great couturier Jacques Heim. In 1957, however, the two firms, which had previously been complementary allies, became competitors and ten years later Mendès absorbed Carine. It was the result of a consolidated success story, above all as the exclusive producer of the Carven, Madeleine de Rauch and Grès collections. Later, it became the industrial ally of nearly all the first rank fashion houses, from Givenchy to YSL (becoming partners with the Saint-Laurent Rive Gauche), from Dessès to Ungaro, from Laroche to Patou.

Mendez Mariana (1974). Venezuelan designer, born in Caracas. She took a diploma in Fashion Design at the Domus Academy in Milan. Her first collection of bags was presented in Milan in 1997; based on the textile tradition of the South American Indians, it used innovative materials such as elastic vegetable fiber and printed latex, as well as natural colors and textiles. She focuses strongly on highly technological methods in order to obtain special effects.

(*Mariacristina Righi*)

Meneses Antonio (1932). Spanish designer, born in Barcelona. He debuted in 1958, after having studied design at the School of Fine Arts in the Catalan capital and practiced as a tailor in a *haute couture* atelier. He is famous for having launched the fashion for maxi-coats in Spain in the 1970s.

Menichetti Roberto (1966). Italian designer, born in Buffalo, America, but brought up in Gubbio, where he lived and worked in the family firm producing the most exclusive garments for the collections of Jil Sander and Helmut Lang. He was taken on as Claude Montana's assistant in 1990 and three years later moved to Jil Sander. The German designer appointed him as creative director of the womenswear lines and project manager of the men's line. In 1998, the young Umbrian designer was assigned the task of relaunching the Burberry brand and developing the global style of the English company. Burberry is now controlled by Great Universal Stores (GUS), a large Anglo-Saxon chain that had a turnover of about 3.4 billion pounds in 1998. The first step was Burberry's Prorsum: a fashionable line produced in Gubbio and presented with success in July 1999 in Florence at the 52nd Pitti Uomo.

(*Daniela Fedi*)

❑ 2001. Menichetti left the artistic guidance of Burberry's Prorsum in the hands of the English Christopher Bailey.
❑ 2002. Menichetti's first collection for Cerruti arrived on the runways. Although he had already ceded 100% of the firm to Fin.part, Nino Cerruti expressed a positive opinion of the young designer. But in March, after only one season, the association came to an end.
❑ The family firm was to produce Menichetti's first personal collection. His menswear line was presented at Milano Moda Uomo in January 2004, a month before his womenswear. Both collections were completed with a series of accessories.
❑ 2004, October. He debuted in Paris as the creative head of Cèline. Menichetti took over the artistic director of the historic French fashion house from the American Michael Kors.
❑ 2005, May. After only two seasons,

the collaboration between Menichetti and Cèline came to an end. The decision was mutual and Menichetti continues to design his own collections.

Menkes Suzy (1942). English fashion journalist with the International Herald Tribune. She was born in Beaconsfield in England. She is capable of harsh judgments: she has had "disputes" with various designers and big companies in the sector, who have then excluded her from the presentation of subsequent collections. But she has never renounced her right to criticize. Certainly, her approval favors the fortunes of runway shows, which never begin until she has arrived. She always sits in the front row: she often begins to write her article on her laptop and is even capable of finishing it on the backseat of the taxi taking her back to her hotel. She has an unmistakable presence, emphasized by her beloved vintage jackets and above all her curious hairstyle: a sort of turned back quiff, the kind of "banana" that used to be fashionable for children, years ago. Her incorruptible nature is legendary and it is said that she only accepts flowers and chocolates from the large fashion houses, returning gifts that are too expensive to their senders. "I alternate positive and negative opinions, everything depends on the collection," she has always said about her articles. She is the personal friend of many designers, but she does not allow herself to be influenced or intimidated by any of them. Christian Lacroix once said of her, "Sometimes I can tell that she is being extra harsh on me precisely because we are friends." Her dry writing style has had success because it is based on the link between fashion and political-cultural events and costume. Her vision is not just the result of her personality, but also of her degree in History and English Literature from the University of Cambridge (1963-1966), where she took a Bachelor of Arts degree followed by a Masters. She was the editor of *Varsity*, the Cambridge student newspaper. She has an excellent knowledge of different styles, having also studied in Paris at the École Guerre La Vigne, which later became the Chambre Syndicale de la Couture. Here she learnt to sketch designs and make toiles. The "coup de foudre" came when she had an opportunity to attend a runway show by Nina Ricci and was fascinated by it. She began her career in journalism in London. She was a "junior reporter" on *The Times* from 1966 to 1969. Afterwards she became fashion editor at the *Evening Standard* (1966-1977), at the *Daily Express* (1977-1979) and again at *The Times* as Fashion Editor-in-Chief (1979-1987). She then briefly moved to *The Independent* (1987-1988). She joined the *Herald Tribune*, succeeding two legends, Hebe Dorsey and Eugenia Sheppard. Stakanova-like, it is said that she sees 600 collections a year. For her frankness she has been nick-named "Samurai Suzy." She is the widow of the foreign correspondent, David Spanier, has three children and divides her time between London, Paris, and her house in the Ardèche. She wrote and published *The Windsor Style*, a tribute to Edward VIII and his wife, Wallis Simpson. For more than 200 pages, the reader is given the opportunity to inspect the wardrobes of the celebrated couple and the jewelry cases that were a genuine weakness of the Duchess.

Menoni Kicca (1956). Italian journalist. From 2002, she has been the editor of *D-la Repubblica delle Donne*. Originally from Milan, with a degree in architecture from the Polytechnic and a specialism in urban planning from the University of Venice, she began her career on the editorial team of *Casabella*, a longstanding magazine covering architecture and design, under the editorship of Alessandro Mendini. In 1974 she took over the direction of *Vogue Bambini* and worked for *Lei*,published by Condé Nast Italia. Pragmatic and modern in her view of fashion and interested in a different way of living, she joined Mondadori in 1980 with the task of transforming the magazine *Cento Cose* from a DIY monthly to a fashion and costume publication, for a young, evolving readership. In 1985, Mondadori also assigned her the responsibility of *Linea Italiana* and *Linea Uomo*, both very demanding monthlies given that they were in direct competition with those published by Condé Nast. In 1990, she relaunched *Cento Cose*, renaming it *Cento Cose Energy*, dedicated to beauty, sport and fitness. Since 1994, she has directed *Marie Claire*.

Men's hats During the 1920s Italy annually exported about 12.5 million men's felt hats and more than 11 million straw or chip hats. In total there were more than 1,000 hat manufacturers in Italy, employing roughly 20,000 workers. From the mid-1950s, un unstoppable decline set in: hats, which until that moment had been an essential item of mens' wardrobe, went out of fashion. Little by little the old hat manufacturers gave up. Long-established shops disappeared. The light, foldable *plume* models, enormous cowboy hats, classic trilbies, and the various shapes that fashion has created over the years – sometimes by changing the size, or enlarging or reducing the brim, or raising or lowering the top – no longer had a place in the concept of elegance, except in the minds of the few, obstinate traditionalists. The most important centers of production were deserted. Felt hats were manufactured in dozens of small factories and shops scattered all around Italy: from Alessandria to Monza, from Biella to Intra, from Voghera to Sagliano Micca, from Spinetta Marengo to Alzano Maggiore, from Montappone to Montevarchi and Prato, from Maglie to Cremona. Pretty much everywhere there were small companies that manufactured high-quality products. Even in the mid-1930s, Monza was still flooding the Western world with Verdi-style homburgs, exporting 80% of what it produced. Now, there are only about 20 or so hat factories in all of Italy, and they produce mainly for women. In Italy, the market leader has always been Borsalino. Giuseppe Borsalino, the founder of the family, emigrated to France around 1840. In Paris he specialized in the art of hat making and, after various problems, he returned to Italy in 1857. In Alessandria, he opened his first workshop-store. The company flourished and soon the brand became known all over the world. Giovanni Giolitti only wore Borsalino hats, and John Dillinger had a gray Borsalino on his head when he was shot down by American police in 1934. At moments of his greatest renown, Al Capone expressly ordered hats for himself and his most faithful lieutenants from the Piedmont factory. He wanted the felt to be manufactured with beaver hair blended with fibers from wild rabbits. The name Borsalino was even taken as the title of a film starring Jean-Paul Belmondo. A fundamental characteristic of a prestigious hat is the leather strip that rings the inside; it must always be made of kid leather and come from Liège in Belgium. The hat is completed by the ribbon, invariably in satin, and silk lining. The few companies that still make these chic items manufacture them using the techniques of a century ago, and using the same ancient instruments: the wooden moulds, cast iron grips, spring-operated vaporizers, and cherry-wood counters. Sure, the craftsmen's skills, handed on from one generation to the next inside the workshops, are slowly disappearing, at the same rhythm with which ancient instruments are gradually substituted with new machines. Sure, rabbit skins are no longer used, and pretreated hair from Argentina or Australia is used instead; but the more than forty phases of production, from blowing to packaging, which in a period of 7-8 weeks give birth to a felt hat, are still there. Only in this way does the highest quality hare or wild rabbit fur become a real hat, and merit the name of prestigious brands such as Borsalino, Rossi, Barbisio, and Bagnara di Cardanello.

(*Stefano Grassi*)

Menta Giuseppe (1937). Designer, student of color techniques, creator of textiles. Born in Cremona, from 1950 he began to work in a print works, following evening courses in design. At the age of 30, he was taken on by Bordogna as a textile designer and began to create exclusive designs for *prêt-à-porter* firms and *haute couture* tailors. In 1974 he founded his own company focusing on research into textiles with the aim of producing environmentally friendly, naturally dyed fabrics. He launched the ecological brand Menta Veste Natura in 1992. After teaching at the Royal College of London and at the Ripamonti Institute in Como, he now runs a laboratory of graphic design at the design faculty of the Polytechnic of Milan.

Menudier Rodolphe. Footwear designer. He was born in Bordeaux and works in Paris. He studied at AFPC (Formation Professionnelle des Industries de la Chaussure) and, in 1987, he began his career, collaborating with Michel Perry and with French and Italian firms. He was discovered by Karl Lagerfeld who gave him the opportunity of designing a collection of shoes for Chloé in 1992. Two years later he launched his own brand. He has a world-wide market. In 2000 he began to supply Christian Dior. The store on Rue de Castiglione is still a point of reference for quality Parisian footwear. The original interior, made of walls covered with white crocodile skin and metal cupboards was designed by Cristophe Pillet, one of the most imaginative French interior designers.

Menuge Francis (1954-1990). French manager. Gaultier owes his success to Menuge's administrative abilities. From his first runway show in 1976 to the license contracts with Japan in 1981, to the birth of the Gaultier firm in 1982, Menuge guided the company, succeeding in maintaining the fragile balance between the rigorous running of the brand, an innovative communications strategy and the imaginative creative vein of the French designer.

Mephisto Shoe company founded in Bolzano in 1965. It is one of the most important in the world, producing 11,000 pairs of shoes a day, with 1,700 employees, 220 "concept stores" in Europe, Asia, the United States and Canada, 12,000 retailers, and a turnover of 300 billion lire in 1997, of which 80% came from exports across 40 different countries. Quality (a choice of leathers treated with natural methods, a careful selection process even down to the laces) and comfort (special padding in specific areas, a heel with a double softening effect, an air-jet system for air circulation) are the secrets to the company's long-lasting success. Together with some of the most famous reflexologists in the world, the firm has invented the Mobil Reflex with special "partitions," comprising a system of small, soft pads, which continuously massage the reflex points of the foot in order to improve blood circulation and stimulate the back muscles.

Merce Roser (1947). Spanish designer. Born in Barcelona, where he attended the School of Fine Arts, specialising in painting. In 1971, after the success of his first appearance with a *prêt-à-porter* women's collection, he opened an atelier. Since 1985, he has also designed menswear. He uses a very bold palette, which he inherited from his love of painting.

Mercier Laurent (1966). Swiss designer. Previously working for Jean Paul Gaultier and Escada, he soon became the couturier to stars such as the singer Lenny Kravitz and the German punk-inspired Nina Hagen. He worked for Oscar de la Renta for a few seasons. In 2001 he launched his own line and, after a few months, he was offered a position as a designer for the Maison Balmain. He shows on the Paris runways.

❑ 2002, November. Laurent Mercier, who joined Maison Balmain in 2001 after designing two *prêt-à-porter* collections for the company, was officially made artistic director of the couture collections and successor to Oscar de La Renta. His first *haute couture* collection was shown on the runway in January. To coincide with the Paris shows of the previous July, Oscar de La Renta announced his early retirement for health reasons (he still had one year to complete of his contract).
❑ 2003, June. After only 7 months, Mercier left the French house. Balmain did not present the Fall-Winter 2003-2004 couture collection in July, returning in January with the Summer 2004 collection.

Merino A breed of Spanish goat, the most diffused and famous for its very fine, sought-after wool. It is also used to refer to a light fabric, with a herringbone pattern, made of fine quality wool.

Merloz Robert (1965). French designer. After being the assistant to Yves Saint-Laurent for many years, he founded his own fashion house. After debuting on the runway in 1993, the company became so successful that it opened two stores in Paris and Japan. In 1997, he presented a collection entirely in "Dalmatian style," in other words covered in black-and-white spots.

Merola Artisanal firm producing gloves, founded in Naples by Leopoldo and Giuseppe Merola in 1878. After their initial success, the brothers decided in 1885 to open a store in Rome at 143Via del Corso. Up until the end of the 1920s the company, which owns a factory and a tanning works, enjoyed a period of great prosperity. After the difficulties due to the period of self-sufficiency and the war, the company experienced a new phasc of great expansion after World War II.

Today, the grandson of Leopoldo, Alberto, continues to run the family firm. Audrey Hepburn in *Vacanze Romane* (1953) and Kate Winslet in *Titanic* (1997) both wore Merola gloves. Examples of the 20,000 pairs produced every year have found their way into the wardrobes of all the European royal families. They are sold at Harrods in London, Bergdorf Goodman in New York, in Brioni shops around the world and in Magli stores in Italy. Merola made gloves for the films *The Patriot*, with Mel Gibson, *Gangs of New York* by Scorsese, and those worn by Nicole Kidman in *Cold Mountain*.

Mersojapova Zelja. Russian designer, with a diploma from the Institute of Technology at Omsk, an important centre north of Kazakhstan. She makes fashionable clothing, with faint constructivist echoes, not only in the choice of materials, but above all in the desire to transmit an absolute creative freedom. Her clothes convey messages that mix past and future, suggestive, emotional clothing, with daring and unusual combinations. Her creations are contemporary but, in some cases, embody the same theatricality that characterizes the art of her native country.

Merù Italian jewelers. The Merù family, Sardinians living in Milan, began with a watch shop in the 1960s in Via del Lauro but in 1967 moved to 3 Via Solferino. The Merù family began to create their own micro-jewelry, using gold, silver and cheaper materials. Their rings and earrings became instantly recognizable: with fishing wire and enameled mosaics. Merù was discovered by the journalist Camilla Cederna and the designer Brunetta, who gave them publicity in the column *Il lato debole* of the weekly magazine, *L'Espresso*.

Earrings and necklace carrying messages by Merù in a drawing by Maria Pezzi.

Merveilleuse A very light tunic, fastened at the shoulders and with a generous décolleté, in perfect Neoclassical style. The French revolution radically changed women's fashions. Crinolines, busts, padded "faux-cul" and large skirts, full of frills and flounces, were put to one side and clothes became essential and very simple. Inspired by the clothing of the Greek democracy, the tunic became women's ideal dress. It later became known as "La merveilleuse." The muslin used to make it was so transparent and light that it revealed the body beneath in revolutionary nudity. The shirt-dress was fastened underneath the breast with a ribbon that highlighted the décolleté. This line then developed into the Empire style, which was less eccentric and audacious. In 1795, it was the role of Madame Tallien to dictate the vagaries of fashion. The lover of the Count of Barras and the secretary of the Municipal Council in Paris, she challenged the prevailing climate of the city, wrapped in an evanescent "robe en chemise" of cream colored tulle, protected only with an equally light shawl. Her hair was carelessly tied back, imitating the style of Roman matrons, her eyelids shone with mother-of-pearl eye shadow, precious rings decorated her feet encased in flat sandals fastened with long laces, tied around the ankle. The "merveilleuse" was revived on many occasions during the twentieth century.

(*Gabriella Gregorietti*)

Messori Italian menswear clothing brand. Launched in 1984, it proposed a total look for young men. It is designed by Germana Martinelli, who owns the brand and oversees its distribution with her husband, Lanfranco Messori. In 1990, it debuted in New York.

❑ 1999, February. The first shop opened in London.

❑ 2002, July. The brand featured in the exhibition, The Collective, in New York organized by Enk International.
❑ 2003. MJ, the Messori line of jeans, was launched: informal clothing for a younger market.

Messori Gianmarco (1976). The son of Lanfranco Messori and Germana Martinelli, owners of the Messori company, has a successful career in the footwear industry. He debuted with a Spring-Summer 2000 collection with a sporting, high-tech image. He makes many references to other cultures, the result of his passion for traveling.

Metradamo Italian brand of ready-made women and menswear. It was founded in Milan in 1979 by Elio Zadra. It emphasizes high quality, prestigious textiles, attention to detail, wearability, and a focus on innovation.

❑ 2003, May. Metradamo launched a menswear line for Spring-Summer 2004. The collection was presented in the showroom at 8 Via Rugabella in Milan, and sold in the same outlets where they have sold women's clothing for years: San Carlo in Turin, Cicchi Ginepri in Milan and Tiziana Fausti in Bergamo. Like the womenswear, the men's range is high quality and until now has sold out 90%, a measure of its success. Metradamo continues to concentrate on distribution in Italy, which accounts for 60% of its sales. Abroad, its most important market is Japan.

Metzner Sheila. American photographer. Since 1970 she has worked for Chanel, Fendi, Ralph Lauren, Victoria's Secret, and Comme des Garçons. Her work has been published in *Arena*, *i-D* and, above all, the Italian and English editions of *Vogue*. She had a privileged relationship with *Vogue* from 1978 to 1990, when the art director Alexander Liberman broke off the relationship with the famous phrase, "My dear, you are a great artist but *Vogue* does not need art." She has a timeless style that recalls the pictorialism of Steichen and the photography of the past: her women are fascinating, appearing in all their beauty thanks to the softness of their forms and their languid gestures. In 2000, she published the volume *Form and Fashion*.

Meunier Sébastien (1974). French designer. At only 21, he won a design competition initiated by the American company Mattel, a games manufacturer, which awarded first and second prizes to his new look Barbie, which was produced commercially in the United States the following year. In 1997, he obtained the Esmod diploma and received the Buste d'Or award as a designer and pattern-maker for menswear. The following year he was selected for the salon Who's Next in Paris and won the Prix Homme at the Hyères festival. During the same period, he also presented his first collection but his first runway show at the Paris menswear fashion week did not come until 1999.

(*Maddalena Fossati*)

Mexx Clothing brand, whose garments and accessories are distributed in more than 40 countries across Europe, the United States and Asia. Founded in 1980, it employs more than 1,500 people. Its headquarters are in Voorschoten in the Netherlands, in a nineteenth-century factory that has been refurbished by the American architect Robert Stern. It produces many different lines for men, women, and children. The latest to be launched (1999) was MiniMexx Studio, a line of smart children's wear, offering clothing for parties and first communions. The products for children include garments from 0 to 6 months. The brand also creates perfumes, shoes, lingerie, bags, watches, glasses, and socks. The group has 400 own-brand stores across the world, with 5,000 other stores distributing the brand. The executive director is Rattan Chadha.

❑ 2003, January. Mexx's plans for further expansion included the opening of 50 new shops in Europe before the end of 2003. The new stores were to be located in Great Britain, Germany, France, Belgium, Holland, and Luxemburg. The other area of development was to be in the "ready-made" sector, in the form of the Mexx Flash collection, namely a collection of clothing that can be delivered to stores within 7 days.

Meyer Adolph de (1869-1946). French photographer. An unusual and bizarre character: even the date of his birth is uncertain. Of noble origin, he was a baron of German descent and was related to the English king Edward VII. He lived with his wife in a refined and exclusive environment during the last years of the Belle Époque before it was all swept aside suddenly and tragically by World War I. It was the beginning of the war and the hostilities between France and Germany that made him feel like a stranger in his own country, so he decided to emigrate to the United States. His photographs were characterized by a delicacy of tone and spectacular compositions, gaining him popularity in both the artistic and commercial worlds, as demonstrated by the 21 photographs printed between 1908 and 1912 in the magazine *Camera Work* directed by Alfred Stieglitz. Adolph de Meyer was one of the first great photographers in the world to focus on fashion with dedication and continuity: he introduced his pictorial style into images of *haute couture*, creating vague and suggestive atmospheres with delicate and sparkling light effects that tended to disintegrate forms, thereby creating an intense emotional tension. A meeting with the editor of Condé Nast in New York led to an close collaboration with *Vogue America* that lasted 10 years. Betraying the faith of his possessive editor, he moved to the competitor *Harper's Bazaar*, where he worked until 1934. The "flou" effect, obtained by placing a gauze in front of his Pinkerton-Smith lens on a low flash, the sepia prints and the clever use of mirrors, which created interesting lighting effects, served to create a romantic atmosphere and had a strong influence on all fashion photography of that period. However, they were also the techniques that immediately dated Meyer's production, which was slowly put to one side: at his death, the successful photographer was poor and forgotten by the world that had once exalted his refined images.

(*Roberto Mutti*)

Meyer David. French footwear designer, made famous to the wider public by his wedding shoes, presented at the Exercices de Style competition in September 1998. The following year he received a positive response at Midec Imagine, the international footwear fair in Paris, and in 2000 he won the Glass Slipper Award, reserved for new designers. At the Paris Expo fair in March 2003, Midec nominated him as a symbol of creativity in the sector.

Meyer Gene (1955). American designer, with a passion for color. His original and anti-conformist menswear uses strong tones, particularly for the accessories. He was born in New York and after brilliant results at the Parson's School, he began to work in 1977 as Anne Klein's assistant designer. Afterwards he moved to Geoffrey Beene, before moving to the Italian group Mondo Inc. in 1994. This development led the designer to move from women's clothing to men's. In 1997, he received the Perry Ellis Award for the best menswear designer. His line, in demand at the best American stores as well as in Europe, is aimed at a youthful man in search of a free and creative style. The collection is produced solely in Italy.

(*Silvia Martinenghi*)

❑ 2003, April. An example of Meyer's woven bedcovers, using the unusual cut-and-paste method that had been a favourite of Henri Matisse, is displayed the Cooper Hewitt Museum of Design in New York. The covers designed by Meyer are produced by M&M Design International.

Mézard Edith. French designer. At the end of the 1980s, she founded and gave her name to a brand of underwear, perfume and clothing for the home, designed using modern shapes, natural materials and the most sophisticated traditional techniques. The "house specialty" is hand embroidery, enriching linens for the bed, bathroom and dining room. The laboratory-boutique based in the stables at the Château de l'Ange at Lumières in Provence also produces soaps and fragrances for the body and the house, including old recipes for aromatic waters for perfuming underwear. (*Ruben Modigliani*)

Mf Fashion A fashion insert that appears four times a week in the daily paper, *Milano Finanza*, founded and directed by Paolo Panerai. It is the first daily Italian newspaper devoted to the world of fashion, and considers the industry primarily from an economic perspective. Launched in December 1997, today the paper has a maximum circulation of about 210,200, and an average of almost 118,600 copies. In October 2001, the first edition of its offshoot, *Magazine for Fashion*, appeared at the newsagents, a publication also directed by Panerai with the co-direction of Nicoletta Ferrari. The editorial is currently coordinated by Simona Melegari and Mara Gaudenzi, with the assistance of about a dozen collaborators. This was another landmark, being the first trade magazine intended for people working in the sector. It takes the form of a monograph and is issued twice a month. It sometimes spotlights men's and women's collections recently shown on the runways, or jewelry or design. After the first ten issues, the magazine had circulation figures that equaled the daily paper. During the last few years, Panerai has given up his role as sole administrator of the Class Editori Group, taking on the position of president and maintaining direction of the titles. A good strategist and careful observer of the dynamics of the world of fashion, nowadays Panerai often speaks at conferences on the fashion system.

❑ 2002, October. *The Best Will Survive* was the title of the first Milan Fashion Global Summit, a conference organised by the director of the magazine, Paolo Panerai, and Frederick Kempe of the Wall Street Journal. The two-day conference was intended to set aside current trends and to look to the future, beyond the current economic crisis. The speakers brought their experience from the clothing and textile sectors across the world, from Kuwait to Russia.

Mh Way Italian leather goods company. Founded in 1982, with headquarters in Fizzonasco, in the province of Milan. It began by producing objects and folders in cardboard, intended for use by architects and designers. The following year it launched the Puma line, a project that revolutionized the traditional briefcase, turning it into a rigid, square, semi-transparent container in corrugated polypropylene that was imitated all over the world. In 1985, it presented Impronta, an innovative line, both technically and in terms of its design, made in seamless fabric. From then onwards the success of the brand allowed the company to open stores in Milan and Paris, in addition to franchising shops and retail spaces elsewhere. It also expanded its production to include various lines of bags and accessories, for work, travel, and free time. More recently, the Tenore line, a collection in natural colored leather, and the Pronto line, unisex colored or bicolored bags in nylon intertwined with silver threads, fitted pockets, hidden straps, zips, and pull-out openings. Mh Way's products are all designed by the Japanese architect, Makio Hasuike, who also oversees the company's image, from its packaging to marketing. Today, Mh Way objects have become cult articles across the world, and have received awards at the Triennale, Macef, Smau, Design Plus, and Compasso d'Oro. The Zoom telescope and the Impronta rucksack are on display at the Museum of Modern Art in New York, the Pompidou Centre in Paris, the Permanent Exhibition in Vienna and at the Triennale in Milan. To mark its 20th anniversary in May 2002, Mh Way produced a limited edition of the Impronta line, with eight new products.

Mialy Miki (1960). Japanese designer, born in Fukuoka. He studied at the Gakuen fashion school in Osaka (1981). During the rest of the 1980s, he worked as a freelance designer first in Osaka, and in Paris from 1989. In Paris, he launched his own brand in 1992. In 1995, he opened a boutique at the Forum des Halles, followed by another in Tokyo in 1999. In the same year, he won the Mac prize in Japan, where his line is very successful.

❑ 2003, January. Mialy's first runway show of the year was shown at the Paris Expo.
❑ 2003. In Spring, his creations were displayed in an exhibition at the Atmosphère d'Hiver salon at the Jardin des Tuileries.

Miani Guglielmo (1905-1987). Italian tailor and clothing entrepreneur. At 18, he emigrated from Apulia to Milan and found work in a tailoring workshop on Corso Vittorio Emanuele. After a while, he set up on his own with an atelier in Via Manzoni, on the ground floor of Palazzo Borromeo. Here he also opened one of his first Larus stores, selling made-to-measure clothes and raincoats, and accessories. In the 1950s, he opened another shop in the Galleria (he always campaigned for it to be returned to its role as a metropolitan salon and he restored the legendary Camparino-Zucca bar) and, later on, a third in Via Montenapoleone. He was passionate about theater and musicals. He was a great friend of Totò and dressed half of the Milanese journalistic community. Orio Vergani invented a slogan for his ties: "Cravatta Club annoda l'amicizia" (Club ties knot friendships). Queen Elizabeth II awarded him an MBE for "the importation, development and commercialisation of the most prestigious English textiles and clothing." The shop sign changed from Larus to Larusmiani and a fourth shop in Corso Vittorio Emanuele sealed the extraordinary success of his lengthy career. Today, Larusmiani is a more diversified company. It is heavily involved with textiles, especially finished cottons and other natural fibers. It is run by Riccardo Miani (1935), Guglielmo's heir, assisted by his son Willy, hence the line of 100% cashmere men's, women's, and children's wear entitled Willy Maini and sold in the stores in Via Manzoni and Via Bagutta.

Mib Manifattura Italiana del Brembo, launched in 1969 and known all over the world, sometimes only by its initials. The Italian tanning factory produces skins for fur garments at Pontirolo Nuovo in the province of Bergamo. It is owned by the Carminati family and directed by Roberto Scarpella. Right from the start, the company has combined avant-garde techniques with a respect for the strictest ecological regulations. The factory, which covers an area of 25,000 square meters and employs 230 members of staff, is located in a hundred year-old building. All steps that make it possible to work in harmony with nature have been taken: water and air purification systems and the filtering of all emissions are kept under constant control. Members of staff work in a healthy and pleasant environment. In conjunction with its sister company Htp (High Tech Processings), machines and high-tech procedures using computers have been implemented. At the same time, handcraft skills have been conserved, an invaluable complement to the unending research in the world of fashion, which has given rise to a series of innovations and dramatically affected the preparation of skins. The company has introduced many inventions that often distinguished by specific names; their worth is underlined by the fact that they continue to be used, sometimes under different forms, and either modified or combined. Year after year, the Mib factory has created nap leathers, prints, mixes, the "Thousand lights" coloring, photo-sculpture, eco-compatible dyes that are natural and safe, and the "Top Line," which subverts tanning traditions; then there is the company's reversible, non-leather leather, lined with very different materials and worked on the outside in a variety of ways: plucked, dyed, sheared, printed, frosted, shaded, and bleached; and, in addition, the Stone-Dyed effect, which produces an unusual mixture of tones, as on textiles, and the Dual Band effect, which plays on the contrast between background and foreground colors. Mib also works with shaved effects, velvets, cashmere, and even silks (sometimes so fine they measure zero millimeters!), along with natural fading techniques. Other effects are Stone-Printing and "leather impression" techniques, that fulfill the continuous demand for reversible garments. There has also been a return in demand for batik combined with Stone-Dyes, and for curled effects on depilated leather, sometimes combined with shaved and highlighted motifs. And, most importantly, the "new tanning," which makes reference to the historic Top Line and identifies a certified article according to the UniIcec norms. The furs are accompanied by a label with the wording "low environmental impact fur," "certified quality fur," "fur created in Italy." The company focuses on skill, quality, and environmentalism. Its headquarters are characterized by rational modernity combined with antique elegance. They house the Mib Design Center, which is opened to researchers from across the world.

(*Maria Rita Stiglich*)

Micam-Shoevent The most important international footwear exhibition in the world. It is held every six months in Milan and Bologna and is an opportunity to present the new collections by world leaders in the sector. Its importance can be summed up statistically: on average there are 1,100 participants, including the most representative Italian and foreign (about 100) firms (the Visitor space is reserved for the most fashionable foreign designers). There are 20,000 Italian buyers and 8,000 from the rest of Europe, the United States and the Far East.

❑ 2002, September. Almost 34,000 visitors, of whom 20,206 were Italian and 13,648 foreigners, representing an increase of 4% on September 2001. From this year on Micam was to be held at the Milan Fair space. It was a record event, with 1,229 footwear manufacturers, of whom 180 were from abroad. It was a positive sign in a very difficult year: the figures for 2002 were the worst in the previous ten years. The commercial balance equaled 4,295 billion (down 11% in value and down 33% in quantity, compared with the previous year). Exports dropped 8.4% in quantity and 5.7% in value. 303 million pairs of shoes were sold abroad (28 million fewer than 2001). Imports rose alarmingly, with a total of 208.6 million pairs: up 9.9% in quantity and 7.4% in value.
❑ 2003, March. 1,254 companies participated, including 203 foreigners (in the Visitor area alone, the number of exhibitors rose from 30 to 50). There were 31,523 visitors. The presence of foreigners was particularly encouraging: 12,030 buyers (5.8% more than in March 2002), in particular from France, Germany, Switzerland, the United Kingdom, Spain, Belgium, and Holland. The participation of the USA and Russia remained unchanged, together with Eastern European countries. The numbers from the Far East were disappointing and, unsurprisingly, there was a strong drop in the Far Eastern presence, due to the outbreak of SARS. Micam was the first fair to be held after the announcement of the war in Iraq, coming at an already difficult time with a drop in production of 4.4% in quantity and 1.5% in value.

Michael of Carlos Place London atelier founded in 1953 by the Irish designer, Michael Donellan, who trained at the Maison Lachasse. Nick-named the "Balenciaga of London" for his theatrical creativity, he was a fashion consultant for Marks & Spencer and for Bradley's line of furs. The atelier closed in 1971.

Michel Vivien (1963). French footwear designer. He began to work at Tony Carel's when he was only 20 and remained there for two years, collaborating with designers such as Martine Sitbon and Thierry Mugler. In 1990, he signed a contract with the footwear brand Michel Perry, which continued for five years. Afterwards he collaborated with Casadei, Sergio Rossi, Charles Jourdan, Givenchy, Lanvin, and Dior. In 1999 he launched his first collection.

Michelotti Elio (1948). Journalist. Director of *Rakam*, a "monthly magazine on female crafts," founded by Edilio Rusconi. He joined the magazine as art director in 1974. As the years passed, he mastered the secrets, from embroidery techniques to the science of decoration, to become one of the greatest experts in Italy. After six different editors, when Anna Gaultieri moved to editorial direction in 1997, Michelotti was appointed head of the magazine.

Michel Schreiber French men's tailor. From the mid-1970s, he designed the clothes worn by François Mitterrand. The atelier takes the name of its proprietor, who trained with the men's tailor, Paul Portes. In 1960, he began an association with Patrick Hollington and together they formed a brand that was also distributed in department stores, such as Printemps and Prisunic. In France, he was one of the first to break with the conformity and uniformity of men's fashion through his use of form and color.

❑ 2000, April. The Musée Galliera de la Ville de Paris organized an exhibition on 40 years of fashion, from 1960 to 2000. Schreiber's clothes were presented as an example of developments in construction.

MicMac French brand with two eminent godfathers: the German playboy (one-time fiancé of Brigitte Bardot) Gunther Sachs, who wanted to invest in the fashion world, and the writer Françoise Sagan, who invented the brand's name. The designer is Tan Guidicelli (formerly of Dior, Ricci, Heim, and Chloé), who combines French chic and American informality. MicMac offered a style that is popular with a sophisticated international clientele in search of jeans, cardigans, T-shirts, and shirts for men and women, a little different from the rest. At the end of the 1970s (in 1974, Guidicelli began to work on his own) the brand disappeared.

Design by Brunetta for MicMac.

Micro fiber A polyester or viscose fiber, initially used for knitwear. Now micro fiber textiles are often used for raincoats, windcheaters, and for sportswear. They are soft and light, velvety to the touch, ideal for the outer layer of fur-lined garments.

Midali Martino (1952). Italian designer. His collections are modern, essential, almost minimalist. Born in Modena, he began to be known at the beginning of the 1980s with a series of T-shirts inspired by Pop Art. As well as his first women's line of clothing, he produced one for men and one entitled "Midali Milano," for a lower range of the market. The company has a few own-brand stores in Italy, has opened two retail outlets in New York and foresees a franchising network.

❑ 2001, December. The new Marghera space was opened in Milan.
❑ 2002, April. Midali presented the Fall-Winter 2002-2003 collection in the showroom on Via Bronzetti. It included three lines of clothing for different types of women: unstructured garments for the first line, playing on interesting cuts and essential forms, with a particular emphasis on artificially aged fabrics; thick and hardwearing woven clothes in the second line; and tapestry textiles with baroque and unusual prints for the third. The collections are typified by unusual combinations of textiles: Prince of Wales checks with fur collars, velvet flower decorations, pin-stripe inserts. The youthful line is fresh and slightly 1970s, and features unusual combinations of textiles, prints and colors.
❑ 2002, September. A unique presentation for the Milano Moda Donna runway shows, at the showroom in Via Bronzetti, featuring only T-shirts.
❑ 2002, October. The company presented works by Fabio Tita, known as Fabius, made especially for Midali on Via Ponte Vetero in Milan. The pieces are zoomorphic "inspirations," made out of rough materials, mainly iron. Midali is particularly interested in the relationship between art and fashion: his previous runway show included highly original hat-sculptures.

Martino Midali outfit, 1999.

Midi A mid-length for skirts and dresses that, as a consequence, has struggled to make a mark. At the end of the 1960s, the midi appeared with its message of restoration: almost twice as long as the mini and only a little shorter than the maxi, it was often worn with knee-high boots. But attempts to establish this fashion met with little success. Only a decade later, with the recession that occurred in the 1970s – in the West skirt lengths are an economic barometer – did skirts lengthen again and the midi resurfaced, although without a precise role. Now it is often simply referred to by the French word, *longuette*, and every now and then it plays a part in designers' collections.

Midinette A French term that combines "midi" (midday) and "dinette" (a baby's meal). It has been used in France for a long time to refer to young apprentices working in fashion houses and tailors' workshops. Before they could turn their hands to making clothes and hats, they were often given a variety of jobs, from sales to home deliveries. Soon the term began to take on a pejorative meaning, signifying bold and free young women, with questionable morals. During the early twentieth century, a number of plays and operettas immortalized this type as a classic combination of seamstress and student, at a time when fashion and its environment were regarded with some suspicion.

Mido The most important trade event for glasses. It is held at the Milan Fair during the first half of May. For a few years, it has also been a showcase for fashion design applied to glasses. A cross between status symbol and fashion accessory, spectacles and sunglasses have become an essential element of an individual's look. Every year, Mido features new brands, generally hailing directly from the fashion world, such as Prada, Gattinoni, and Vivienne Westwood in 1999. The Italian glasses industry had a turnover of 2400 billion lire in 1998, 70% of which came from exports. It accounts for 24% of the world market, and is second only to Germany.

❑ 2002, May. The exhibition, in its 32nd show, featured 1,200 companies from all over the world. The most important sectors included Mido Trend, with the most avant-garde models, and Mido Tech, dedicated to technology and innovation. Two zones were reserved for foreign buyers: Foreign Club and the exclusive Mido Club. In collaboration with the Milan Triennale, Mido sponsored the exhibition, *Gli occhiali presi sul serio* (*Glasses Taken Seriously*). ❑ 2003, May. Visitor figures dropped by 33.4% due to the SARS epidemic and the Easter holidays. In particular, the Italian presence decreased (by 48.8%) more than foreign companies (down 20.9%). There were 1,118 exhibitors.

Miele Carlos (1964). Brazilian stylist born in Sao Paulo. His basic line, M Office, has about a hundred retail outlets across Brazil and a turnover of roughly 60 million dollars. The originality of his creations is due to the intelligent mixture of the aesthetics of indigenous cultures (for example the use of feathers and shells) with a metropolitan style (reflected in materials like fiber-optics and Teflon). In 2000 he began a partnership with Coopa-Roca, a female cooperative based in Rocinha, one of the largest slums in Rio, in order to produce textiles made from cheap materials recycled from the city streets. In 2003, he opened a store in New York (the first one outside Brazil) in the Meatpacking District of Manhattan. The shop was designed by the architecture studio, Asymptote. (*Francesca Gentile*)

Mifur International leather and fur fair founded in 1995. It is held in the pavilions of Milan Fair in March, contemporaneously with two other important fairs, Mipel (leather) and Micam (footwear). Mifur represents the main Italian showcase for fur, leather clothing, raw materials, accessories, and machinery. For five days Milan becomes the capital of leather and fur.

❑ 2001, March. Mifur, which also has a vintage section from the 1950s and 1960s, concluded with a joint runway show by the most important companies in the sector. Characteristics were exoticism and craftsmanship, luxury and comfort in designs from all around the world, and a very wide range of skins,

techniques, and designs. Such rarities as toad and sea wolf were seen, as well as woven techniques that treat furs like textiles.
❑ 2002, March. The seventh Mifur ended with positive results: 250 exhibitors and roughly 12,000 buyers and specialist participators. In particular, 6,113 companies took part for the first time (2,389 foreign ones and 3,715 Italian) compared with the 4,888 registered in 2001 (1,742 foreigners and 3,146 from Italy). There was a strong contingent from the United States (122 companies compared with 109 in 2001) and Russia (260 compared with 148). Furthermore, there was a greater presence from Turkey, Korea, France, Germany, and Azerbaijan. There are also encouraging signs from the market: the turnover from the fur sector in 2001 was 2.3 billion euros, an increase of 1.9% on the previous year. The export trade accounted for 15% of the total. The fair was broadened with a series of events: in particular a runway show, Sense of Winter, and an evening on the theme, The Mirror of Fashion – A Fur Photo-Shoot, organized by the Italian Fur Association and Saga Furs, the association of Scandinavian fur producers.
❑ 2003, March. In 2002, the fur sector enjoyed its best performance in ten years, with a turnover of 2.56 billion euros and an increase of 11.3% on 2001 (the lowest results were registered in 1999, with 1.64 billion). For the third year running, Italian exports increased: in 2002, they totaled 265 million euros (up 18.1% on 2001). Imports also rose (up 11.7%) by 289 million euros. The sector employs 46,100 people. The eighth Mifur had 270 exhibitors and 12,000 buyers. The year's novelty, introduced by AIP (the Italian Fur Association), was to label each fur as a response to accusations regarding the abuse of protected species and even domestic animals. The label on every fur contains the scientific, Latin name of the animal used, cleaning instructions and the name of the producer.

Miglio Nando (1939). Italian artistic director and director of runway shows. Born in Venice, he began his career in fashion at an early age, first as a photographer in London and then as an assistant in the press and public relations office of the Rinascente department store in Milan. Afterwards, he became art director and fashion editor for *Harper's Bazaar* in Italy. During the 1980s, his consulting studio organized the direction and background music for the runway shows of some of the most famous Italian and foreign designers: Valentino, Versace, Armani, Fendi, Gft, Dior, and Chanel. He directed advertising campaigns, working with photographers such as Penn, Newton, Avedon, and Krieger. In 1984, he "staged" the Genny runway show at the White House for Ronald and Nancy Reagan. From 1983 to 1987 he was in charge of the press office and global image of Gucci. Currently, he oversees communications strategies for Hugo Boss, Canali, and Pal Zileri. He likes to dress in white all year round.

❑ 2001, December. During the annual Visual Awards ceremony, the magazine *Visual Trend* praised Nando Miglio for his "professional engagement in visual marketing" throughout his lengthy career. The prize he received was significantly titled Ars et Labor.

Miglionico Michele (1965). Designer, born in Milan. He opened an atelier in Potenza in 1989. He considers himself self-taught, even though he learnt a great deal from his father, a tailor at Caraceni in Milan. He debuted outside the official calendar of *haute couture* runway shows in Rome in January 2000. His fashion is inspired by Courrèges and early Yves Saint Laurent. His favorite textiles include crêpe doublé, georgette and mousseline.

❑ 2002, November. After years of showing on the Rome runways, Michele Miglionico decided to open an atelier in Via Veneto in Rome.
❑ 2003, July. On the AltaRomaAltamoda runway, he paid homage to Diana Vreeland, the director of *Vogue America*, watched by her son, Frederick Vreeland, and his wife, Vanessa. The designer created seventeen gowns, in red and black, as well as

prune, green and pearl gray. His full, red ball-gown was made using more than 22 meters of hand embroidered silk gazar.

Mikimoto Kokichi Mikimoto, a diligent, friendly Japanese man, was the first person to produce a cultivated pearl, after years of experiments in 1893 in Mar. He became the official supplier to the Japanese royal family, beginning a tradition of high-quality production that continues to be prestigious. Mikimoto Quality and Mikimoto Top Quality are considered the most authoritative parameters in the classification of cultivated pearls, which are regulated by five internationally recognised evaluation criteria: color, form, brilliancy, pearly surface, and dimensions. The opening of the first Tokyo store dates to 1908. From 1920 onwards, others were opened in London, Paris, New York, and Los Angeles. The firm, of which Tohiohiko Mikimoto is the president, named a collection of pearl jewelry after Princess Grace of Monaco and initiated a collaboration with the Princess Grace Foundation – USA, an organization that supports young artists from around the world. Mikimoto Milano Collection is a line of jewelry made from gold, cultivated pearls, precious stones, and diamonds, which are designed and created in Italy by Giovanna Broggian. This collection, which is linked with the face of Catherine Deneuve, uses avant-garde techniques in the settings that respect the integrity of the pearl and emphasize its aesthetic qualities.

(*Alessandra Quattordio*)

Maison Mikimoto Jewel.

Mikli Alain (1955). Armenian designer and entrepreneur. He has allied style and fashion with the glasses industry. He studied at the École d'Optique in Paris. In 1978, he opened a small studio where he created his first designs, which were extravagant and richly inventive. He has been invited to collaborate with some of the most famous designers, including Montana, Lagerfeld, Chanel, Gaultier, and Donna Karan. He owns the license to produce glasses for Philippe Starck and Jil Sander. He has created lines for Bausch&Lomb, Opto-Inter, and the Italian group, Persol.

❑ 2003, April. Mikli's 25th year of production. The turnover of the last few years has grown continuously: in 2000 it reached 30 million euros (up 20% on the previous year), in 2001 it was 35 millions, and in 2002 40 millions. The collections designed by Alain Mikli include the brands Mikli, Alain Mikli, Starck Eyes, and Issey Miyake. They are produced entirely in the Jura region of France and in China. The growth of turnover is due to the Asian market (excluding Japan), representing 2.9 million euros in 2002. During the 1980s, he collaborated with Chantal Thomass, Guy Paulin, Anne Marie Beretta, Claude Montana, and designed the Onyx line for RayBan and the Izzard line for the Japanese firm Sun Reeve. It was his idea to eliminate screws from glasses and substitute them with a type of zip, the "biolink." Every piece is unique. His favorite material is acetate with inserts in wood and cotton. In 2001 his dragonfly glasses debuted all over the world. He collaborated with Philippe Starck for the Starck Eyes collection. Together with Issey Miyake, he launched folding glasses. During the 1990s, Wim Wenders asked him to create eight pairs of glasses for the film, *Until the End of the World*; Bono, the singer of U2, launched "miklivision," camera-glasses that leave your hands free.

❑ 2003, April. The new line of glasses by the Armenian designer was made exclusively in titanium, a resistant but extremely light material. In its raw state it is gray, but Mikli's shell mounts are very colorful: red, blue, chocolate brown, khaki, plum, and black. Every year, the brand sells 450,000 pairs of glasses and has 220 collaborators. In 2003, turnover had reached 24.5 million euros.

❑ 2003, June. Alain Mikli glasses opened a new shop in Helsinki. The French group had ten own-brand stores around the world. Like all the others, this one was designed by Philippe Starck.

Milano A smooth, compact knitted textile that produces a very traditional jersey look. Used for jackets, suits, and overcoats, it does not "open" easily and is therefore notably hardwearing.

Milanovendemoda Exhibition launched in 1969 by agents and commercial representatives in the clothing sector, all members of the Assomoda association. The aim was to open a direct dialogue with buyers in the city of Milan, the base for an increasing number of designers and where the fashion business enjoyed great vitality. From year to year, the exhibition, which was held at the Jolly Hotel in Milano Due, attracted a growing number of fashion houses and firms. In 1982, Milanovendemoda was absorbed by Expo Cts, the company that organizes fairs for the Commercial Union in Milan. The following year, the exhibition was integrated into the fashion system at Milan Fair through an agreement with Efima and Modit. This alliance was consolidated in 1990 with a unique event: Momi-Modamilano, run together by Modit and Milanovendemoda, in parallel with the two seasonal appointments of the Milan runway shows.

❑ 2003, February. At the end of the Momi-Modamilano joint venture, which combined Efima and Expo Cts, Modit and Milanovendemoda went their separate ways again. In the pavilions of Milan Fair, there were 335 exhibitors, more than those at Momi 2002 (290 exhibitors). The two commercial areas were called Trend and Luxury; Bridal Preview is the area reserved for new collections, plus the Accessories space. The most innovative sectors are The Closet and Light (already featured in previous shows) and the new display, O-Zone, which features emerging designers and new brands, from Claudia Rosa Lukas to Katty Xiomara, from Anu Leinonen to Psst to Pierre Braganza. In collaboration with the Francesca Kaufman gallery, MVM also hosts the collection of Susan Cianciolo, a 35-year-old New Yorker, whose one-off pieces are considered true works of art. The exhibition includes Seven, an avant-garde showroom-art gallery from New York, which introduced new creators and brands to Milan, such as Asfour, Bernard Wilhelm Boudicca, Marjan Pejoski, Preen, United Bamboo, and Cosmic Wonder. There were more than 11,000 visitors, of which 31.3% were foreigners. The traditional foreign clients (Germany, Great Britain, and France) only represented 11%, having been overtaken by Greece (16%) and Spain (13.2%). The Eastern presence was notable, with Russia and Japan and, of course, the United States.

Milena Mosele The brand of an Italian company producing *haute couture* knitwear, founded in 1956 in Bologna. The turnover is made up almost equally of sales in Italy and abroad. It absorbed the Antonelli di Roma atelier, a protagonist of the first runway shows in the Sala Bianca at Palazzo Pitti in Florence. The company's internal staff of Milena Mosele, Gelsomina Zuppiroli, and Roberta Salomone design the collections, but have often been assisted by Silvano Malta and Roberto Quaranta.

Miles Italian outer-knitwear company. Founded in 1962 by Sivia Stein Bocchese, it has collaborated with YSL and Celine. It works with Alaïa, Sonia Rykiel, Armani, and Dolce & Gabbana. Since 1977, it has produced a collection of throws, cushions, and womenswear named Miles Home, made of knitwear. They are high quality products, of which 70% is exported.

❑ 2003, June. Following the decision to concentrate more closely on high-quality knitwear for important fashion houses such as Armani, Valentino Boutique, and Louis Vuitton, the Abitificio brand was licensed out. The company that accepted the challenge was Confezioni

Peserico. Its task is to strengthen the womenswear brand, and to improve the supply and market strategies.

Milizia Giuseppe (1947). Italian jewelry designer. Originally from the Apulia region, he took a degree in architecture and, after a period of work experience in Paris, moved to Rome where he continues to live and work. He uses avant-garde materials and techniques, natural colors, and unusual combinations of high-tech materials and precious stones with fragments of wood and Murano glass. In August 2002, he presented his jewelry collection in Toronto, where it enjoyed great success.

Miller Lee (1970-1977). American photographer, born in New York. She studied drama in Paris, became a model for great photographers and moved to Florence, where she studied art. She was the favorite model, assistant and muse to Man Ray. In 1931 she published her first fashion shoot in *Vogue*, featuring sports clothes. The following year she left Man Ray and returned to New York. She began traveling again and moved to Egypt with her second husband. Afterwards she returned to Europe with the photographer Roland Penrose, whom she later married. She continued to be part of the international artistic community and, alongside her photographic research, she carried on working for *Vogue*. As well as her fashion shoots for the magazine, she contributed reportage features and real photographic stories. Her activities as a photographer and chronicler continued in collaboration with her husband Penrose (who was awarded a knighthood in 1966) until her death.

Miller Nicole (1952). American designer born in Lenox, Massachusetts. Her studies at the Parisian *haute couture* schools taught her the importance of dress construction. Convinced that few women have perfect bodies, she aimed to flatter them as much as possible and to disguised any defects. Her taste for colors was inspired by her frequent travels to Brazil and her interest in the world of performance, in particular Broadway musicals. During the second half of the 1990s, she was one of the first American designers to send actresses down the runway instead of models: Minnie Driver, Jill Hennessy, and Gretchen Mol all accepted her invitation.

❑ 2002. Miller celebrated 20 years of business as one of the great American designers. Her first "hip smock dress" was presented in 1982.
❑ 2003, July. She launched a special silk tie to mark the inauguration of the National Constitution Center of Philadelphia, the first American museum dedicated entirely to the constitution. There were 30 Nicole Miller boutiques in the United States.

Miller Nolan (1935). American designer. The popularity of the famous television series, *Dynasty*, was partly thanks to Miller, who created the often extravagant clothes worn by the female cast. Capable of creating the 25 to 30 garments a week necessary for each episode, his designs were sometimes knowingly ostentatious, with strong echoes of Joan Crawford from the 1940s. *Dynasty* was not the only program associated with the designer, who became one of the most influential figures in the 1980s for the tastes and fashions of Americans: he also produced some of the clothing for *Charlie's Angels*, *Love Boat* and *Hotel*. After his work in cinema and TV ended, Miller continued to design for Nolan Miller Couture, and became a member of the council of the Fashion Institute of Design & Merchandising. His collaboration with the multi-national toy firm, Mattel, produced two very elegant limited edition Barbie dolls: the Illusion Barbie (1998) and the Evening Illusion (1999).

Milliner This term is used to refer in general to professionals who create, construct or decorate hats for women, in the most varied forms and textiles, in particular styles, felt or straw. Almost till the end of the eighteenth century, the term was generic and included not only the true milliner but also people who worked with any sort of material related to clothing and those involved in its sale, from mercers to makers of ribbons, lace, and buttons and bows. It was not until the end of that century, with the rediscovery of the hat and the end of the fashion for very high, powdered wigs, that an appropriate statute

Designs for small hats at the beginning of the 1940s. From the monthly magazine *Fili Moda*.

ratified the corporation of milliners in France (1776), their right to make, as well as to dye and decorate with artificial flowers, women's hats. This was the premise for creative hat fashions that swiftly changed to match hairstyles, adapting their size to suit curls, fringes, and bandeaux. Hats have had moments of obscurity and also euphoria, often definitively characterizing particular periods in fashion: the very large hats of the early twentieth century, laden with fruit and flowers, so important that women used to wear them indoors or at the theater in the afternoon, to the caps drawn down over the eyes of the female stars of the 1930s, to the cloches of Greta Garbo. The milliner began to work closely with *haute couture*. Some of the most famous designers began as milliners, such as Coco Chanel and Jeanne Lanvin. In more recent times, as fashion has become an increasingly powerful phenomenon, the hat has not always enjoyed parallel fortunes, apart from the return of the fur hat or the men's felt hat in the 1970s. This changed in the 1980s, when various revivals used hats to complete a particular look.

Milner Deborah (1964). English designer. Born in Surrey, she opened her atelier in London after studying at the Central Saint Martin's College of Art (1987) and the Royal College of Art (1990). She is loved by the English aristocracy, especially for her wedding dresses. In 1993, she took part in London Fashion Week for the first time. She designs clothing for the television and adverts. An expert in cutting, her style is based on the search for new silhouettes and materials. She created the clothing for the milliner Philip Treacy's Fall-Winter 1997 runway show. In 1998-99, her clothing-sculptures in stainless steel featured in the exhibition *Addressing the Century – 100 years of art and fashion* at the Hayward Gallery in London. Her first *prêt-à-porter* collection debuted in 1999.

❑ 2001, October. Deborah Milner's innovative garments, produced in collaboration with the English Laser Centre, which promotes partnerships using laser technology in the textile field, were displayed at Grand Central Station in Manhattan.

Milona Lambros (1969). Designer of Greek origins, born in New York. His highly rigorous, almost architectural style is the fruit of collaborative experiences with the illustrator Joe Eula, the fashion house Adolfo, and the Halston studio. From 1990 onwards, he worked in Europe for the Maison Balmain, Lanvin, Balenciaga, Raffaella Curiel, and Siari Fabrics. In 1995, he debuted his brand produced by the Alma

Group. In 1998-99, he was responsible for the style of the Bagutta collections.

(*Lorenza Branzi*)

❑ 2002, Summer. In an interview in 2001, Milona declared, "Some designers want to create wedding dresses. I want to create clothing for people getting divorced." Perhaps in memory of this phrase, Princess Lilly Sayn Wittgenstein Berleburg asked him to design her wardrobe immediately after her separation from Prince Alessandro Schaumburg Lippe.

Mimmina Ready-made women's clothing company. Founded in the 1960s in Arezzo by Mimmina Rachini, it employs roughly 100 members of staff. It has own-brand stores in Milan, Forte dei Marmi, Paris, Geneva, Japan, and Mexico. It produces 5 lines, characterized by an elegant wearability and aimed at different consumer brackets. It is distributed across the world. The firm is run by Enrico Risaliti.

❑ 1998, Spring. The two Risaliti brothers took their designs to Havana. The runway show at the Hotel National was intended to cross the bridge between the Caribbean and Central American markets, which are decidedly more receptive to imports. In March, the Impresa Italia Presenta took place, the first celebration of Made in Italy products in Cuba.

Minagawa Makiko. Japanese designer, primarily known for his textiles printed with designs of woods, flowers, and landscapes. Born in Tokyo, he studied at the Kyoto City University of Arts. He specialized in yarns, colors, and textiles. He is the director of Issey Miyake's textile department.

Minaudière A small, metal evening bag, first created by Cartier in 1900. Today it is sometimes decorated with diamantés and hard stones and worn over the shoulder, with or without a chain.

Mingolini-Guggenheim Italian fashion atelier, bearing the name of its two partners. Its headquarters were in Piazza di Spagna in Rome. It served a young, bourgeois clientele, who wanted a well-made, carefree style. Mingolini was proud of his approach to fashion, which was still linked to the practice of constructing clothing on a tailor's dummy, studying proportions, and without the help of a pattern. The success of the atelier ended with Mingolini's untimely death.

❑ 1986, July. Rome celebrated the relationship between art and fashion, and therefore also the creations of the Piazza di Spagna atelier, with the event entitled *Marmi. 40 anni di Moda per 40 anni di sport*, held among the statues in the Foro Italico.

Minimalism A minimum cannot exist without a maximum: this is the key to interpreting the minimalist phenomenon (simplify, clean, reduce) that characterized the early 1990s, in contrast with the early 1980s, which were full of color, consumerism, and goods. Everything was abundant, overloaded and rich in the 1980s, purified and cerebral in the 1990s (the colors were gray, khaki, beige, black, and white, and there was no make-up, jewelry, or high heels). The contrast was similar to a comparison between the philosophies of two architectural giants, Mies van der Rohe ("Less is more") and Le Corbusier. Minimalism said Yes to everything that was poor, bare, and rough. It appeared in the design of interiors and exteriors, which were suddenly reduced to bare essentials, and in literature, with writers such as McInerney, Leavitt, and Easton Ellis. In fashion, minimalism had a flag-bearer in Zoran (and also Calvin Klein) and a muse in Miuccia Prada (and Jil Sander), who was able to pare down her taste to a minimum, building an empire of millions on this look. The official death of the movement in fashion can be dated to Tom Ford's menswear runway show of Spring-Summer 1999 for Gucci: he displayed an explosion of feathers, sequins, printed textiles, and vivid colors. It was the end of Jansenism and a return to luxury.

(*Laura Salza*)

Mink A fur that will live on, in the history of costume, as a symbol of the economic recovery of the roaring 1950s, as the tangible sign of social climbing, and as the precious object of every woman's dreams. From the silver screen, Hollywood invited women to dream with Elizabeth Taylor in *Butterfield 8*

(1960), and with Doris Day in *That Touch of Mink* (1962). In the real word, mink was worn by stars and celebrities like Clare Booth Luce, the United States ambassador to Rome, Queen Elizabeth II of Great Britain, Maria Callas, and Brigitte Bardot (before she became an animal rights activist), and even, in the version of a full-length, Spanish-style black cape, Salvador Dalí. It was and it continued to be the fur par excellence, the unrivalled dominatrix, the all-powerful queen. Just as the king of lakes and rivers is the mink itself, distinguished by its two Latin names of *Mustela vison* (the American mink) and *Mustela lutreola* (the European mink), and found throughout North America and northern Europe and Asia. The animal has a thick, soft, glistening pelt, and its hide is flexible and strong. The classical mink has a dark-brown fur, called "standard" or "wild," or even, more poetically and in a clear reference to the North American mink, "of the Great Lakes." It can be raised in any country with a cold, humid, water-rich environment, because each of the animals requires from 200 to 400 liters of water annually. Today, most minks are raised in captivity; the first experiments in doing so were carried out by American breeders around 1850, while in Europe mink-breeding was begun by the Scandinavians during the great worldwide depression of the 1930s. This led to the countless mutations in the pelt, and varieties of color that were rigorously natural and differenti from the standard pelt, ranging from white to black, and for which each label – American Legend, Blackglama (only black), American Ultra, Canada Majestic, NAFA, Black NAFA – has trade names of its own. Minks offer a magnificent range of options for the creativity of fashion designers working in fur, and in recent years, with the assistance of revolutionary developments in the tanning industry, they have dyed mink, made it reversible, shave it, plucked it, trimmed, napped, sueded, and brined it. Docile and majestic, the mink has always complied, certain that it will conserve its regal sovereignty.

Mipel International Fur Market held at Milan Fair twice a year, during the runway show seasons. It is reserved for producers and shop owners, prior to consumer distribution. Sponsored by AIMPES, the international category association, it was launched in 1962. In the first show, 68 companies participated, with 1,760 Italian buyers and 230 from foreign countries. The results were immediately telling. During the first months of 1962, compared with the same period of the previous year, exports increased 57% in quantity and 51% in value. From then onwards, there has always been a direct correlation between the number of foreign buyers at Mipel and the growth of exports, which reached a little more than 20 billion lire in 1962, but which had risen to almost 60 billion ten years later. In 1982, the total had increased to 734 billion lire and to 1,671 billions in 1990. The promoters of the fairs were Guido Angelo Guidetti, Gino Borelli, Oberdan Cavari, Enrico Frender, Umberto Locati, Guido Pieracci, Amato Santi, and Romeo Siletti.

❑ 2001, September. The 80th Mipel, with 369 exhibitors (279 Italians and 90 foreigners). Seven themed sectors: Accessories, Travel and Business, Glamour, Overseas, Domani (Tomorrow), Galleria (Gallery), Saloni Fornitori (Suppliers Salon).

❑ 2002, March. The interior of Mipel was completely redesigned by the architect, Denis Santachiara, to create a clear, elegant, and functional pathway through the exhibition, with wide, completely white spaces, highlighting the objects displayed by 400 companies (including 108 foreign businesses). In 2002 year, scarves, umbrellas, and belts were included. There were more than 16,000 visitors in March 2001 though the economic climate was not favorable. During the first quarter of 2002, Italian exports of bags, suitcases, and other articles registered a drop in sales of 5.6% compared with the same period in 2001.

❑ 2003, March. There were 16,082 visitors, a decrease of 2% on Spring 2002, though there was a strong foreign presence (up 17%). There was a total of almost 400 exhibitors, with almost 150,000 new products. There were fewer Japanese and Russians and, above all, Americans (down 11%) and Germans (down 18%).

Mir Carmen (1903-1986). Spanish tailor. she opened her own atelier in Barcelona in 1940, after moving from Balsaren, where she was born and her parents owned a textile factory. Her style was popular in the 1960s and 1970s for her unusual take on garments that originated mainly from England: the mini-skirt and the Barbarella fashion. In 1977, Carmen handed the business over to her daughter-in-law, Elisa Lacambra, by which point it had developed into a traditional Spanish tailoring brand.

Mirabella American fashion magazine, defining itself as "an antidote to trends," founded in 1989 by Grace Mirabella and published by the Hachette Filipacchi group. Born in 1930, the journalist Grace Mirabella began her career at *Vogue* with Diana Vreeland. In 1971, when the legendary Vreeland left the Condé Nast monthly, she took over the helm for the following 17 years. During this period she improved distribution figures, making the magazine less scholarly and cerebral and directing it towards the needs and problems of women of the time. In publishing, Mirabella is the only example of a director whose name has become a magazine title.

Mirman Simone (1920). French milliner. Even at the height of her success, her passion for craft was her creative weapon. She was born Simone Parmentier, in Paris. She trained at the atelier of Rose Valois. She moved to London in 1937 and began to work for Elsa Schiaparelli. Ten years later, she formed her own fashion business and attracted very high profile clients, such as Princess Margaret of England. Dior, Saint-Laurent, and Hartnell all asked her to collaborate with them on their runway shows.

Mirò Women's clothing and accessories company. It was founded in 1983 by Emi Vincenzini, who was the favorite model and collaborator of Walter Albini and Alessandra Tilche. It produces roughly 15,000 accessories a year: bags in soft leather, papyrus and textile, and above all 60 different models of hats. The turnover in 1997 was roughly a billion lire, aided by the lines of unstructured garments.

Emi Vincenzini model for Mirò.

Miro Antoni (1947). Spanish designer born in Barcelona. His family was in the fashion business and he learnt the trade in his father's tailoring workshop. He set up on his own when he was 19, opening a boutique called Groc, which became a point of reference for people who did not want to dress like Franco's functionaries. In 1967, he launched a brand of ready-made clothing under his own name. It was so successful that he opened various own-brand stores in Europe and the United States but, after a few years, they fell victim to the failure of the business that produced his garments and he was forced to down-size, focusing on his store in Barcelona. He survived the difficult economic climate, investing a great deal of his talent in his menswear collection, designing for Zegna as well as receiving the Premio Balenciaga.

Miroglio Italian textile company. The group from Piedmont has been one of the most important in establishing the leadership of

Italian-made fashion products. Founded in Alba in 1947, it began as a warehouse for textiles in bulk. Today, the company is still firmly in the hands of the same family (at the end of 1998, Franco Miroglio handed over the reigns to his children, Edoardo and Nicoletta), which, from one generation to the next, has extended its production base to include clothing. The group is split into two divisions: Miroglio Textiles and, since 1955, Vestebene (*prêt-à-porter* for men and women). It has global exports and roughly 40 factories spread across Italy, France, Greece, Tunisia, Egypt, and countries in the East. Above all, it produces viscose and cupro fabrics, and artificial discontinuous fibers similar to cotton fibers. The staple of Miroglio's synthetic fabrics is continuous fiber polyester, made of uninterrupted threads, cut and used like a carded textile. Defined as an intelligent fiber, when mixed with others it has a positive effect on all forms of manufacture. It can be machine washed, it has stable dimensions and can be produced without pollution. Chemically safe, it is also used to make water bottles. It requires special, automatic machinery to dye it. It is also used for drainage under asphalt on motorways. In 1989, the group began to acquire other textile and clothing companies in France, Germany, Spain, and Great Britain. This development increased Miroglio's turnover to 1.4 trillion lire in 1997.

❑ 2001, November. Motivi, Mirogli's youth line, debuted on TV, with an advert created by the Emanuele Pirella agency.
❑ 2002, September. Miroglio Espana's business was worth roughly 30 million euros.
❑ 2002, November. Opening of the London store. Currently, there are 140 across Europe.
❑ 2002, March. The Miroglio Group and Mariuccia Mandelli sign an agreement for the creation of the Per te Aktive brand, by Krizia, for oversized young women. It is the natural extension of the Per te by Krizia line designed by Mariuccia Mandelli and produced and distributed by Vestebene-Miroglio for more than 14 years. The launch was planned for Spring-Summer 2003. The use of "k" in the brand name underlines Miroglio and the designer's focus on women who weigh several kilos extra.
❑ 2002, October. A few days before his 80th birthday, Carlo Miroglio, president of the group, was award the honor Cavaliere di Gran Croce. The head of the froup since 1954, he has been active in the company for over 60 years, together with his brother, Franco. Now into the third generation of the family, in 2001 the company had a turnover of 824 million euros and employs more than 6,900 staff.
❑ 2003, February. The Miroglio Group's results increased: 2002 closed with a turnover of 882 million euros (6.6% higher than the previous year) and a gross operating margin of 99.6 million euros (up 33.7%). Exports were stable at 18% of the business's total. For the first time, clothing takes the lead over textiles with 471 million euros (up 10.8%). In 2002, 115 new stores were opened for the four clothing brands, Motivi, Oltre, Elena Mirò, and Caractère, making a total of 556.
❑ 2003, June. Continuing growth of Elena Mirò, the Vestebene-Miroglio brand for oversized women. By the end of 2002 the number of shops in Europe had risen to 143.

Mirsa Italian women's knitwear firm, founded at Galliate (Novara) by Olga di Gresy who, immediately after World War - II, focused on fashion and, taking up the offer of Giovanni Battista Giorgini, showed her designs at the runway show of 12 February 1951 in Florence: an event that marked the beginning of "Made in Italy." Mirsa – who always remained very faithful to the Pitti Palace – is an important name in the knitwear sector. Even before Giorgini invited American buyers to a runway show of Italian designs, Mirsa, with the help of Odette Tedesco, the buyer for the I. Magni department stores, had a presence in America. In 1950 the company had 80 employees, a number that had increased to 650 by 1973. At the end of the 1950s, exports accounted for 80% of production, due in part to the collaboration with the designer G.B. Vannozzi (1970-75). Following changes in the industry and market, Mirsa closed down in 1984.

(*Lucia Sollazzo*)

Designs by Mirsa (second from the left), Sanlorenzo, Nanisport, and Lesi.

Mirtillo Children's clothing brand produced by the Barbara knitwear factory in Busto Arsizio. The brand was founded in 1976 by the brothers Bruno and Sergio Magni who, in collaboration with the designer Giovanna Andreoli, continued the business first started by their parents, Giovanni and Carmela. To the initial Mirtillo line, they added Mirtillino in 1990, a line dedicated to babies from zero to two years old, and X-Tension for children and adolescents. Afterwards, in 1998, the company made its production even more specialized, launching Mirtillo Intimo (underwear) and Mirtillo Notte (nightwear). With these lines, each year the knitwear factory offered a complete collection for very small children, made up on average of 600 garments. In 2002, the business made about 15 million euros, producing about 1 million garments. It is present in Italy in 800 multi-brand retail outlets that specialize in children's clothing and the brand is distributed abroad in almost 700 stores.

(*Sara Tieni*)

❑ 2003. For Pitti Immagine Bimbo, Mirtillo presented a collection of footwear produced under license by Lanza Bimbo, which also oversees its distribution. For new-borns, babies and children, it is currently only distributed abroad in Spain and Portugal. The retail expansion continued with corners and Mirtillo own-brand stores, including one in Milan in Via Pontaccio and one in Barcelona, in addition to new openings in various Italian provinces.

Misani Ivo (1938-1993). Creator of unusual jewelry, both in terms of shapes and materials. He debuted in Milan in the 1960s, but made a name for himself as the creator of cult objects in the 1980s, when wearing a Misani creation became an irrefutable badge of style for women and teenagers who were sensitive to the dictates of fashion. His need to experiment led him to use stones, leather, and crystals, and to introduce surprising stones such as baddelite – of natural origins but treated artificially in order to obtain unusual colors and dimensions – or Plexiglas, combining it with yellow gold and precious or semi-precious stones in revolutionary compositions. He was intellectually open to avant-garde innovation and an attentive observer of trends in art and fashion. He was attracted to informal, neo-tribal and primitivist tastes. Drawn towards the sculptural dimension of jewelry, he gave life to forms that were sometimes full of Baroque exuberance, sometimes vigorously essential. After his death, production was continued thanks to the help of his wife Susan Mirsani. Mirsani collections, made by Orosette, are distributed all across Europe, the United States, and Japan.

(*Alessandra Quattordio*)

Misia Founded in September 2002 in Milan, the salon is reserved for entirely innovative designers and brands. It embodies a new concept, that of juxtaposing fashion and interior décor. It is entirely dedicated to accessories (bags, shoes, bijoux, belts, scarves, gloves, glasses, and hats), but also to a selection of other objects for the interior. It is held twice a year, in the Spring and Fall, and is aimed at specialized boutiques and multi-brand clothing stores, as well as interior design and decoration shops.

Mispelaere Yvan (1967). French designer. He attended the Studio Berçot and in 1989 was in charge of *haute couture* at the Maison Lanvin. He had further experience with Claude Montana. In 1994 he went to work with Valentino in Rome, where he stayed for four years, until he moved to Prada in Milan. In 2000, he returned to Paris to work at Louis Féraud and, after a three year absence, he debuted on the Paris runways in 2003 with his own label.

Miss Maggie Brand of jeans and casual women's clothing produced and distributed by Italian Fashion, a textile manufacturing company from Urbania (Pesaro). Miss Maggie jeans owe their success to careful research into different treatments and washes that achieve a worn effect. Even though the first collection was produced simply to finish off remnants in the warehouse, by 2002 Miss Maggie had registered a 12.5 million euro turnover. Its financial success, despite the unfavorable economic climate, was due to a strategy of expanding the lines to include new creations in colored fabrics, brightly colored skirts, military pants and easy-to-wear evening dresses.

(*Eleonora Attolico*)

Missolin Benoit (1973). French designer born in Avignon. He studied at the Chambre Syndicale de la Couture Parisienne before joining the Studio Berçot. He worked as an apprentice in various famous fashion houses, such as Thierry Mugler, Jean Colonna, and Christian Lacroix. In 1997, he presented his first collection and debuted in 2001 with his first Paris runway show in the Paul Ricard space, with his first lines of menswear and accessories. In 2002 he took part in the *prêt-à-porter* fashion week. He also won the Swiss Textiles Award at the Gwand 2002 fashion event. (*Maddalena Fossati*)

Missoni A brand leader in world style, especially in the knitwear sector, which it has revolutionised with its unusual, unmistakable, vibrant sense of color. With Missoni, knitwear has become fashion and, at the same time, applied art. The company was founded by Ottavio (Tai) Missoni (1921) and his wife Rosita Jelmini (1931) in 1953, the year of their marriage. They met in London during the 1948 Olympics: the handsome Ottavio, the Italian 400-meter running champion in 1938 and world student champion in Vienna, was a finalist in the 400 meter hurdles. He also had a small firm in Trieste that produced tracksuits. The tiny Rosita, who was very young but already very determined, came with fashion experience gained with her family's firm, which produced shawls and linens for the home. They began with a small workshop in the basement of their home in Gallarate. Their first client was the Biki boutique in Milan and then, in 1958, La Rinascente. Anna Piaggi was the first person to cite them in the press (*Arianna*, 1965), which also gave them their first cover in 1967. The first runway show, a collaboration with Emmanuelle Khanh, came in 1966. In 1967, they debuted at the Palazzo Pitti in Florence, with a preview of the nude look. In 1969, they built the factory at Sumirago, with their house attached. Although it was still a "house and workshop," their success was by then worldwide. In 1970, Bloomingdale's opened a Missoni corner in their New York headquarters. The same year marked the invasion

Missoni outfit in a design by Maria Pezzi (from *Missonologia*, Electa, 1994).

of the "put-together" look, a free and only apparently casual mixture and juxtaposition of stitches and designs, which was to become the distinctive feature of the Missoni style, together with patchwork, colored stripes and the black-and-white and rainbow "flame motif." These were followed by Greek key motifs, grids, Scottish checks, folklore designs and especially abstract "African" designs. Materials included knitwear-furs, felts, tweeds, and elasticized fabrics. The variable thickness of the yarns and textures, graphic and technical inventions, thoughtful color combinations, links to abstract and informal art, decorative elements taken from Anglo-Saxon applied art, a careful evolution of forms, and above all freedom and joyful creativity: these are the elements that have turned Missoni into a way of life rather than simply a fashion, making their garments much-loved objects, flattering in their shape, color and substance. In 1972, *The New York Times* wrote that Missoni "makes the best knitwear in the world and, according to some people, the most beautiful fashions in the world." *Womens Wear Daily* listed them among their top 20 Fashion Powers, and *Vogue America* among the top 10 European designers with the greatest influence on international clothing trends. In 1973, Missoni was awarded the Neiman Marcus Award. It was the first in a long series of recognitions: the Tony Award in 1976; the Premio Italia in 1986; and the Pitti Immagine in 1994. Rosita received the International Design Award in New York; Ottavio was made a Cavaliere del Lavoro in 1993, received the Pitti Immagine award in 1994, followed by the Honorary Royal Designer for Industry honor in 1997 in London. Towards the mid-1970s, they added furnishing fabrics and household linen to their collections of knitwear, accessories and jewelry. Ottavio began to display his tapestries in art galleries, first in Venice and then throughout the rest of the world. In 1976, the first Missoni boutique was opened in Milan: 5 more followed in Italy, 2 in Paris, 3 in Germany, 3 in Japan, another 5 in the Far East, and 1 in New York. Ottavio, who always wears a sweater, is listed among the ten most elegant men in the world. A flower and a star were named after Rosita. 25 years of their work was celebrated, in 1978, at the Rotanda della Besana in Milan, with a retrospective that moved to the Whitney Museum of American Art in New York two years later. In 1994, in Florence and later in Milan, the Missoni world was described in the exhibition, *Missonologia*. In 1995, Gallarate celebrated with the exhibition, *The Ottavio and Rosita Story*. In 1996, there were two exhibitions in Japan: at the Sazon Museum of Art and at the Nagoya City Museum. Missoni creations feature in the permanent collections of the MoMA in New York, the Dallas Museum of Art, and the Museum of Costume in Bath. The Missoni pair have also designed costumes for the opera (*Lucia di Lammermoor* at La Scala in Milan, 1983) and for ballet (*David Parsons Dance Company*, 1994). In 1997, the first all-fabric Missoni collection was created, produced and distributed by Staff International. In 1998, Missoni M was presented for men and women, in collaboration with the Marzotto Group. In the same year, the Missoni company acquired a new headquarters, a 6-storey building in Via Durini, Milan. Rosita and Tai moved there with their children, to whom they passed on the firm in 1997, at the peak of a series of new successes, feted by the press and consumers for their exemplary faithfulness to their own style. Angela (1958) became art director, responsible for style; Vittorio (1954) commercial director; and Luca (1954) technical director. Nine grandchildren make up the Missoni tribe, guaranteeing the future of the firm. And so the tradition continues, with strong family connotations and an artistic-artisanal character, which, despite its vast expansion and international success, has made the name of Missoni so loved, and not just in the worlds of fashion and culture.

(*Isa Tutino Vercelloni*)

❑ 2000. Luca Missoni presented his first menswear collection for winter 2001-2002. Knitwear is reinterpreted with superimposed graphics, strips, zigzags that look like brushstrokes, and flame motifs. It was the fruit of continual research into textiles, stitches, weaves, and patterns that has always been a part of the history of Missoni and of fashion itself. The collection played on the contrast between dry, plain fabrics, soft silks and brilliant, luminous knits. For Spring-Summer 2002, faded colors, pierced cotton piquet, very light cashmeres.

❑ 2001, December. The Missoni Sport shoe collection was to be produced and distributed by Big Time. The license is worth more than 13 million euros. As for the rest of the production, Missoni announced, "We will not create any more licenses. From 2002, we will produce and distribute the Missoni Sport line ourselves." Powerful investments were made in a 2,500 square-meter space near Samirago, dedicated entirely to the Sport line. The shops and own-brand corner spaces were also restructured. Within the brand, the search for new types of fabric and knitting techniques continued. The white, beige and gray flame motif remained popular.

❑ 2003, January. After approximately 20 years of collaboration with Seibu, Missoni changed its Japanese distributor for its primary line. It signed a five-year

Design by Brunetta for the Missoni collection. Runway show at Palazzo Pitti, Florence, 1970.

distribution agreement with Kashiyama Onward, one of the largest textile industrials. Japan represents a market worth roughly 15 million euros and 25% of the brand's business. The Missoni company closed 2002 with a turnover of about 130 million euros (over 62 millions of which were made from its primary line). Also new for 2003, celebrations for the company's fiftieth anniversary, marked by two exhibitions, one in Milan and the other in Tokyo, and the opening of a new 70 square-meter boutique inside Harrods in London.

❑ 2003, April. The new Missoni showroom was opened in Via Solferino in Milan: the building was an umbrella factory in the late nineteenth century, it is situated at the end of a courtyard in the historic center. Vittorio Missoni explained that the location is perfect, not just to present the different lines but also for shows, exhibitions, and other types of event. The former-factory belonged to distant relatives of Rosita's grandparents.

❑ 2003, May. Missoni celebrated 50 years in business with a large runway show in the Town Hall square in Vienna, for the opening of the 11th Life Ball, a traditional charity evening held to raise funds to combat HIV/Aids.

❑ 2003, June. The menswear collection, which represents roughly a third of the company's turnover, was relaunched, focusing primarily on the development of accessories. In 2002, Missoni made 51 million euros on direct sales, compared with 48 millions the previous year. Exports (main markets Japan, USA, and Germany) accounted for more than 85% of the entire business. Alongside multi-brand stores, the company owns 12 directly controlled own-brand boutiques and about one hundred franchises.

❑ 2003, June. At Milano Moda Uomo, Luca Missoni presented his collection: knitwear with a thousand colors mixed together, tight, micro polo necks in cotton crêpes printed with lozenges, sweaters in viscose and tulle, cardigans with large, ostentatious zigzags, very light vests in linen thread, in a small net weave, or interspersed with lurex threads, transparent tops that simulate tattoos, sweater-shirts in silk and lamé for evening wear.

❑ 2003, July. Fashion and design for the Japanese car Mazda, the sponsor of the AltaRoma runway shows. After the series of MX-5 sports cars, with exclusive interiors in numbered series, Missoni created the colors and interiors of the latest MX-5, made as a one-off and sold in an online auction to raise funds for AISM (Italian Multiple Sclerosis Association). The fashion house celebrated its first half century.

❑ 2003, November. The celebrations continued and where better to stage them than in Tokyo, at the Yoyogi National Stadium, where the new Spring-Summer 2004 collection was presented. In addition, Tai and Rosita displayed more than a hundred outfits from the retrospective held in Milan the previous month, including the very famous blue tracksuit marked "Italia," by Ottavio for the national athletics team in 1948, and the first gold Lurex suit from a far-off 1958. Japan (which represents a fifth of the company's turnover) loves the Italian style and the event attracted 3,000 people.

❑ 2004, January. A contract was signed between Missoni and Pagnossin, the head of the Richard Ginori 1735 group. It created the license for a line of tableware and household objects designed by Rosita, part of the Missoni Home project.

❑ 2004, April. The third Golden Dame Award is held at the Poldi Pezzoli museum in Milan. "The people who make Milan great" include Ottavio and Rosita Missoni.

❑ 2004, June. The license for the production and distribution of the spectacles and sunglasses lines was agreed with Silvio Vecellio Reane (Allison, It. Holding Group), for a five year period.

❑ 2004, September. The license linking Missoni and the Marzotto Group was renewed until 2010. The launch of a women's perfume signed by Estée Lauder was announced for Spring 2006.

❑ 2005, February. The Universal Expo

2005 is held in Aichi, Japan, and Tai was invited to represent the Friuli Venezia Giulia region. The stand includes the installation "Harmony from Diversity." The work consists of mannequins "dressed" completely in patchwork knitwear and was the result of collaboration between Ottavio and Luca Missoni (Tai and Rosita's second son) and the designer Angelo Figus.

❑ 2005, March. The first Missoni shop in Catania was opened.

❑ 2005, May. The Aramis and Designer Fragrances division of Estée Lauder and Missoni create a license that enables the beauty colossus to produce and distribute the Missoni perfume line.

Missoni Angela (1958). Italian designer. She worked in her family's company for 17 years, learning different methods of production, organization and sales, before she created her own collection. Currently, she is the artistic and creative director of Missoni, responsible for communications, the image and style of the company. At the presentation of the Spring-Summer 1998 collection, she appeared on her own on the runway to receive the spectators' applause, officially underlining the generational change within the fashion house. For Winter 2001-2002, she presented a collection on the runway dedicated to her father Ottavio's 80th birthday: one-off pieces, with the tabloid-patchwork that heralded the success of the brand. The designer was inspired by Picasso's iconography for the Summer 2002 collection and, for the following winter, she evoked the Danube, Transylvania, the Secession, and the fable of Hansel and Gretel.

❑ 2002, October. For Milano Moda Donna, Angela Missoni proposed a light and seductive collection of stripes, geometric motifs, and patterns typical of the Missoni style, with the addition of various extra touches. Light scarves draped around the neck, floating ribbon-strings completed the garments like jewelry. Bustier-dresses with small Greek key motifs in contrasting knit and rayon, mini kimono-blouses in silk crepon printed with small geometric flowers, with appliquéd patchwork, short skirts that seem like patterned scarves.

❑ 2003, March. The colors were even more sensual and romantic. Wave designs on knitted shorts, draped blouses in silk crêpe, mini-dresses that looked like seamless sweaters or with necklines decorated and fastened with long rows of buttons. Missoni also brightened up furs, with knitted fabric linings with wave motifs.

Miss Sixty Youth fashion brand belonging to the Sixty Group, founded at Chieti in 1989 by Vicky Assan and Renato Rossi. A trendy line with a casual and "provocative" look: elasticized shirts and T-shirts, 1960s style skirts and pants. Underground collections, whose trademark is stretch fabric that hugs the body. Among the fans of Miss Sixty are Angelina Jolie and Jennifer Lopez; Emma Bunton (former Spice Girl), Destiny's Child, and Anastacia: all of whom are figures who undoubtedly help the brand to maintain its fashionable reputation. Launched with a great advertising fanfare in 2002, just like the Group's other brands (including the famous jeans line, Energie), it aims to become a total look, with glasses, bags, underwear, different kinds of accessories, and a line of perfumes and cosmetics. These are all products that have been successful for Assan and Rossi's other brands. The company, which, in 2001, registered a turnover of 490 million euros with a growth of 25% on the previous year, relied on the US market for a significant slice of its takings and was not even affected by the general crisis that struck the fashion world after 11 September. (*Daniela Bolognetti*)

❑ 2003, October. The fourth US store of the Italian brand was opened at 45 Grant Avenue in San Francisco. It is the first where the line is joined by Energie, directed towards a male public. The Miss Sixty Californian flagship store covers approximately 800 square meters. It is the 65th store globally.

❑ 2004, January. Expansion in South America continues. The brand opened a flagship store in the Alto Palermo shopping center in Buenos Aires.

❑ 2004, October. A global license

agreement was signed with the New York firm Coty Inc. for the launch of a series of Miss Sixty perfumes.
❑ 2005, January. The two lines Energie and Miss Sixty Junior were presented at Pitti Bimbo, dedicated to children aged between 4 and 14.
❑ 2005, April. A new female line, Waxy, was announced for a target public aged between 20 and 35. It has a lower price range and a diversified distribution network, with the aim of supplying a continuous and rapid service that reacts quickly to the latest trends.

Mister Freedom English *prêt-à-porter* brand. It is the name of a shop opened on the King's Road in 1969 by Tommy Roberts (1942), after an unsuccessful foray into children's clothing and interior design. The deciding factor in its success was the arrival of fashion designer Pamela Motown, who won the seal of approval of the hippy generation with her vaguely exotic clothing interspersed with garments inspired by cartoon characters. It was a winning formula but not a long-lived one. In brief, the label was discontinued, to reappear at the beginning of the 1990s, with a line of T-shirts. (*Valentina Crepax*)

Mitsukoshi A Japanese chain of department stores. In 1673 it was already the name of a store that applied concepts of modern mass commerce: highly visible prices and goods that could be handled. It was opened by Takatoshi Mitsui. At the end of the nineteenth century, the emporium sought to establish contacts with French tailors, an initiative that was extended to include Italian fashion as well and is successful to this day. It is the first Japanese department store to have its headquarters and a shop front in Paris. The cultural policy launched by the store chain from 1914 onwards found a naturally fertile terrain in France. The success of the art exhibitions organized in Japan led the company to plan similar ventures in Europe. Mitsukoshi set up a headquarters in Paris in a restored and restructured building from the era of Napoleon III. The inaugural exhibition was dedicated to 58 of the most important Japanese ceramicists. (*Eleonora Platania*)

Mittelmoda International competition for young designers. It had a modest launch in 1993, with only twelve participants, based on an idea of the Fairs Association of Gorizia, in collaboration with the National Chamber of Italian Fashion and the Italian Textile Association. Today, Mittelmoda selects young designers and students from 367 different fashion schools across 56 countries. Each year the participants have to present their collections and portfolios by May. The 36 winning designers receive financial awards and the opportunity of work experience with some of the most important Italian companies. The competition aims to promote freedom of creativity among the young and to give them the chance to enter the reality and needs of the fashion system. (*Sara Tieni*)

❑ 2002, September. Mittelmoda celebrated its tenth anniversary and changed its name to The Fashion Award. To mark the anniversary it organized three exhibitions and a workshop, in addition to the usual runway shows. Mittelmoda: 10 Years, Other Fashion, and Lace in Costume and Fashion were held contemporaneously in a single large hall in the fair building in Gorizia. The first show, 10 Years, comprised a gallery of large-scale photographs of previous winners. The second, Other Fashion, was an atelier of sculptures wearing original and creative garments: for example, the Spanish designer Suzy Gomez's metallic dress, the dress made of plastic bottles by Enrica Borghi, the chessboard with T-shirt and ties by Laura Ambrosi, the clothes-climbing furniture by the American David Byrne, the photos by Luisa Raffaelli and Misha Klien, Fritz Kok's mermaids, and erotic figures by Roy Stuart. The third exhibition, Lace in Costume and Fashion, marked a return to the past with Chantilly lace and clothing from the late nineteenth century from the collection of Marianne Stang. The workshop was based on the theme of the relationship between fashion and ethnocultural roots. The winner of Mittelmoda in 2002 was a young Australian, Ramon Martin, from the

University of Technology in Sydney. His collection was chosen from a group of 36 designers by a jury led by Beppe Modenese. The second prize went to Dimitri Ouvarov from the Moscow State Textile University.

Mitten A type of glove with one pocket for the four fingers, and one for the thumb. Used often by children and for skiing, due to its usefulness in keeping the fingers warmer than the classic five-fingered glove.

Miyake Issey (1938). Japanese designer, born in Hiroshima. His mother died of radiation poisoning years after the atomic bomb was dropped on the city. He is a designer with a rare loyalty to the purity of his own vision: an encounter between elements of the East and the audacity of, and search for, the West. Right from his first Paris runway show (1973), the aestheticism of his linear, geometric shapes developed into austere metamorphoses, accompanied by the stratification of the fabrics and his moving drapery, sometimes inspired by ancient Japanese costumes and at others by futuristic forms of delicate armour. After completing his degree at Tama University (1964), the following year he was already in Paris for a fashion apprenticeship with Laroche (1966) and Givenchy (1968), which he completed with two years in New York at Geoffrey Beene: all significant names in contributing to the cut, taste and distinctiveness of the young Miyake, whose first name means "a life" and surname "three houses." After his runway debut in New York (1971) he felt ready to return to Paris. His Japanese stylism – already admired at the beginning of the 1970s in the Parisian *prêt-à-porter* environment alongside the colorfulness of Yamamoto and the enchantment of Kenzo's extraordinary little white shirts – was characterized by a rarefied elegance evident in his every runway show. The attention he pays to textiles, which are often produced exclusively for each collection, to their weave and muted colors, in indefinable variations of white, gray and strong tones rendered in somber hues, makes his collections unique and always unusual. They follow a consistent path, yet at the same time are sensitive to changes. After almost 30 years, he is an irreplaceable presence in *prêt-à-porter* fashion across the world. Miyake sells approximately 200,000 garments every year and more than 100 factories in Japan work for him. In Fall 1998, the Cartier Foundation in Paris dedicated a large exhibition to him in a space designed by the architect Jean Nouvel. Miyake himself chose the title: *Making Things*. On this occasion, Philippe Trétiack wrote for *Elle* magazine: "He has never cease to search, interrogate, scrutinize his materials and he has drawn various replies and signs in order to design what might be the clothing of the future. A tailor of the wind, a poet of delicacy, an architect of a feather-light armor for the next millennium, Miyake, year after year, is becoming the master, the guru of the most fluid modernity." For the Spring-Summer 2000 collection, significantly called *A-Poc* (*A Piece of Cloth*), a single piece of cloth became a long or short skirt, a T-shirt, bikini, socks, and gloves.

(*Lucia Sollazzo*)

Mizrahi Isaac (1961). American designer, working in New York. After a decade of successes, in 1988, the year of his first collection, he received the Perry Ellis Award from the Council of Fashion Designers of America, and a year later another for the best designer of the year. He was then obliged to downsize drastically, to the point of giving up the New York runway show of Fall 1998. With a diploma from the Parson's School, he learnt his trade at Ellis, Banks and Calvin Klein.

❑ 1998, October. The official announcement of the brand's closure, after ten years in business. Partly for financial reasons, but also a growing involvement in the world of TV, off-Broadway theater, and the writing of novels and strip cartoons. There are talks with Dreamworks to turn the character of *Sandee the Supermodel* into a film.
❑ 2003. The *Isaac Mizrahi* television show meets with success. Its formula is part game-show, part special guest appearances of his celebrity friends. As for his fashion production, he continues to produce lines of jackets, shoes, and jewelry.

Mizuno A world sportswear colossus. The company was born in 1906, the idea of Rihachi Mizuno and his brother, Rizo, who opened a shop selling sportswear articles in Osaka to fund their great passion for baseball. From 1911, they organized various tournaments that became the most important in the country. After opening a branch in Tokyo, Mizuno also began to produce golf and ski accessories. The thirtieth anniversary of the company, known as Mizuno Sporting Goods Company, was celebrated with the production of a series of gliders. In 1943, a new factory was opened in Yoro. But the definitive success of the firm was not sealed until after World War II, when it supplied some of the best American athletes with sportswear for the Olympic Games and with the invention of the "compressed" golf club. The 1960s were marked by a continuous expansion in the golf sector and an agreement with Speedo for the production of swimwear. The decade closed with the arrival of Mizuno America in Los Angeles. Expansion at a global level was completed with the agreement with the French Olympic Giyu company and the Italian Colmar for the skiing sector. The mid-1970s brought a prestigious partnership with the Carly Bates company. By this time, Mizuno was spread across the world, a leader in baseball clothing, also thanks to the collaboration with the American Major League. With an increase in its distribution and turnover, it negotiated higher profile celebrity endorsements: Carl Lewis signed a contract in 1987 and in 1990 it was the turn of Ivan Lendl. The last decade of the century focused on environmentally friendly methods of production. The Crew 21 project was launched, an acronym for Conservation of Resources and Environment Wave. This new direction led to the manufacture of running shoes made from recycled plastic bottles, and golf bags and walking shoes made from used rags. In 2000, the line of Speedo Fast Skin swimming costumes was launched, with low resistance to water friction.

(*Pierangelo Mastantuono*)

Mocafico Guido (1962). Swiss photographer, who publishes in the American edition of *Harper's Bazaar*, *The Face* and *Dazed & Confused*. He has created advertising campaigns for Gucci, Christian Dior, Armani, and Hermès, among others.

Moccasin Style of shoe. Over time, it is the model that has enjoyed the most abiding success. It was first used by the Native Indians of North America as an extremely flexible leather sole that was raised at the sides, laterally binding the foot. It was, and still is, the most comfortable shoe to wear. The shape is made with stitching around the heel, the front section is made with a piece of leather called a vamp, or insert. The moccasin is constructed in the opposite way to other shoes, in which the upper covers the toes, instep and heel, then comes down to the sole, where it is fixed. There is also an assembled model, or "fake moccasin," made in the normal way with upper attached to the insole. The tubular model, on the other hand, can be made without an outer sole, without an inner sole, or without both: the sole is made of an upper and lining joined together, or perhaps by an upper alone. This type is for summer wear, without socks, and for this reason is sometimes referred to as "Capri style." The history of this type of footwear is also linked to its popularity with students: during the 1920s, it was almost the emblem of American university students. During the 1960s, Italian youths only wore college blue and burgundy on their feet, often with a penny inserted in the toe cap. In contrast, moccasins in beaten leather, with a more robust feel, were popular with yuppies during the 1980s. Long established moccasin brands include Quintè of Milan, and Gucci, who launched the gilt version. In the 1990s, Tod's revived the driving moccasin, with rubber caps on the sole.

(*Giuliana Parabiago*)

Moda Monthly magazine on fashion and "everything about costume, performance, culture," as described by the subtitle, an important feature of the publication set up by Flavio Lucchini in 1983 and edited by Vittorio Corona until the early 1990s. It is published by Nuova Eri, which is owned by the RAI. The new magazine, launched with a great fanfare of publicity, attracted strong interest. Aimed at a young and emancipated female readership, it gained popularity for its style of graphics, its strong use of photography, and its ability to pinpoint themes that were of interest to new generations. The fortunes of the magazine began to decline at the end of the 1980s, mainly due to editorial problems. For a while, the magazine was trapped in a crisis of concept and readership, which led to a lengthy dispute between editors and publisher. In 1993 Nuova Eri gave up the magazine, which closed shortly afterwards.

Moda Seasonal periodical dedicated to fashion news and women's clothing, founded in Turin in 1959 by Anna Vanner, who edited it until its closure in 1967. Brilliant photos, a birds-eye view into the VIP world, and with features directed at a female readership, the magazine included permanent sections on hairstyles, make-up, hats, accessories, textiles, knitwear, ready-made and *haute couture* fashions.

Moda del Sol Spanish association. In 1963, as the *prêt-à-porter* phenomenon became more diffused across France and Italy, it assembled various textile and clothing industries in order to bring Spanish fashions up to date with trends in other countries. The concept was that strength came through numbers. This alliance of textile industries and clothing industrialists was entrusted to a single designer, José Maria Fillol, who had much experience in Paris. In the 1960s and 1970s the experiment was successful. The Moda del Sol collections were shown at the *prêt-à-porter* salon in Paris and even crossed the ocean. From 1981, the association produced a publication with the season's fashions so that the members could have a window on the international creative world and fashion design.

Moda in Tessuto & Accessori Exhibition Event dedicated to textiles and accessories. It was launched in 1964 and is held twice a year, in the spring and fall. The spring exhibition, held in February, is less important and attracts fewer visitors. Organized by Sitex, the Agency for the Development of the Textile Image (Max Dubini is the president) the event is continuously evolving.

❑ 2001, February. With 595 exhibitors, 450 Italians and 62 new firms (40 Italian), the 35th event closed very positively. As confirmed by the number of visitors (24,866), the event had increased in size: +9% compared with the previous edition, almost equaling the numbers of the Fall event.

❑ 2003, February. The 39th show drew 19,642 trade members (16,072 Italians and 3,570 foreigners). German and French attendees decreased, while the United States presence grew (+35.6%) and the Japanese presence quadrupled.

Modal Artificial cellulose fiber. Viscose modified to obtain a high level of tenacity and stability. It is soft to the touch and has a shiny surface. Water resistant, it is used in sportswear. Modal and Promodal are Lenzing brands.

Moda Parma Event launched in 1956 to promote the producers of furs, clothing, knitwear, and buttons based in the area around Parma. The idea was initiated by the Chamber of Commerce, which organized the event with Maria Pezzi, Alberto Lattuada and Beppe Modenese. Each year 25 industrialists were selected and presented with suggestions for the next fashionable colors (a table of three colors) and lines. The individuals in charge of the event oversaw, step by step, the collections created for the three days of runway shows, which were held in historic and artistic sites in Parma. The event lasted for about a decade.

Modaprima International exhibition of knitwear and clothing organized by Efima and promoted by Moda Industria, the Italian association of clothing and knitwear industrialists. The event, which is traditionally held at Milan Fair, takes place in December and June to present the Fall-Winter and Spring-Summer collections. One of the features of the event, aimed at mass markets, is to enable the quick introduction of new stock, thanks to the pre-programming of orders.

❑ 2002, June. The Fashion Store Service was introduced, a pavilion dedicated to interior décor and visual merchandising. For this edition, the 52nd, there was a growth in foreign visitors (+51%) and exhibitors from China (10 in total). The event was organized for the first time by Luigi Ciocca, the new president. It was announced that the event intended to focus increasingly on small-scale dealers. Models For a Day was the novelty of the Fall edition. A photographic set was arranged for visitors aged 18 to 25. The resulting photographs were used to select the face for the advertising campaign of Modaprima 2003. The visitor numbers increased, particularly those from Asia, Denmark and Austria. ❑ 2003, June. For the summer edition, the conference space hosted a workshop entitled Visual merchandising and purchases: a winning partnership. The drop in visitor numbers, especially from the Far East, was attributed by the organizers to the outbreak of SARS.

Modaprima-Esma Event for *prêt-à-porter*, knitwear, "private label" professionals, and ready-to-deliver flash fashion specialists. It is a "business-to-business" occasion, revolving around the most innovative methods: rearranging seasons, creating specific samples and, above all, product-service packages, which is one of Modaprima-Esma's main objectives. The salon is divided into four sections, corresponding to the different specializations: Private Label, Fashion Prepared for the GDO, Ready-to-Wear, and Production Districts. Visitors arrive from 50 countries as well as retail buyers, wholesale dealers, importers and specialists in organizing sales by correspondence. A typical feature of the event is the competitive pricing of standard quality Italian products.

Model Lisette (1906-1983). Austrian, naturalized American, photographer, whose full name was Elise Felic Amélie Seybert Model. After taking studies in classical music and painting, she moved to Paris in 1926, where she married the painter Evsa Model. In 1933, she embarked on photography, beginning with the portraits of unusual people that were to make her famous. Five years later, in New York she met Paul Strand, Berenice Abbott, and the art director Alexey Brodovitch, and collaborated with *Harper's Bazaar*. Her research centered around visual games, such as splitting images in the Reflexions series, the part-social, part-sociological analysis of her series of Running Legs, with the legs and feet of passers-by photographed from a grate at pavement height. Her work as a photography teacher at the New School for Social Research in New York was very important: the students strongly influenced by her work include Bruce Weber, Robert Mapplethorpe, and Diane Arbus.

Modelli Naka Italian women's knitwear company, in business from 1951 to 1978, which worked with the designer Ezio Casalino. It exported 50% of its production.

Model Maker The forerunner of the designer, a contemporary of the fashion sketcher, this term defines the person who designed clothes for fashion magazines, the theater, cinema, TV shows (though in these last cases he or she is more commonly known as the costume designer). Necessary to this profession are creativity, good taste, understanding of how the body moves, and knowledge of fabrics and the history of fashion and costume.

(*Maria Vittoria Alfonsi*)

Modenese Giuseppe, "Beppe" (1929). Public relations expert, communicator, organizer of fashion events, strategist for the global image of Made in Italy and, as a passion, the creator of a signature collection of jewelry for Faraone. He applied lessons learnt from Giovanni Battista Giorgini in Florence (Sala Bianca at Palazzo Pitti) to the needs of the designers who were appearing in strength in Milan in the second half of the 1970s, namely a single centre for runway shows so that buyers and journalists would avoid the arduous grind of moving from one area of the city to another. Most importantly, he was convinced that a combined event, though the runways were still individual and not collective, would reinforce the image of Italian *prêt-à-porter*. In alliance with the Clothing Industrialists Association, he fought for this idea. The result was the birth in a pavilion at Milan Fair of Modit and the Runway Show Centre, afterwards renamed Milano Collezioni. During the 1990s it was organized by the Chamber of Fashion, with Modenese as the president from 1998 onwards. It was a winning solution. Later it was copied by the French with the Carrousel du Louvre, just at the time when, little by little, the major Italian brands began to desert the runways at the Milan Fair in favor of other backgrounds, creating small theaters and locations in houses. Modenese assisted many emerging designers, particularly ones who were focusing on the US market. Many of them publicly recognise his role in their success. His career began in 1952 when, arriving in Milan from Alba, he found work with Ridotto. Ridotto was a very unusual shop, opened by Giorgini and Olga di Gresy, the founder of the knitwear company Mirsa, in Via Montenapoleone, a sort of proscenium for the most refined selection of Italian craft production. Its management was entrusted to Modenese and the beautiful Neapolitan, Paola Carola. Almost at the same time, he was offered a program on fashion and interior design on television, which was still in an experimental phase. The program continued for ten years. In the 1960s, he was in charge of image and communications for a colossus, Dupont de Nemours, and for the Commission for the Safeguard of Linen. From 1976, he was responsible for public relations and the press office of Idea Como, from 1977 of Mipel (International Fur Market), and from 1979 of Ideabiella. He was a consultant for the Rinascente department store and for the Milan Fair. In addition to Modit and the Milan Collections, he contributed, with the Clothing Industrialists Association, to the creation and organization of Anteprima, Ideamaglia and (1986-90) Contemporary.

❑ 1998. The start of his collaboration with Expo Cts for the Milan International Antiques Fair.
❑ 1999. The Sitex Association entrusted him with consultancy and the running of the press office for the international trade fair Moda In.
❑ 2001. He was made President of *MittelModa Premio*.
❑ 2002, July. Italy's First Lady, Franca Ciampi, awarded him the honor The Capitoline Wolf. In December 1994, he received the Gold Ambrogino and, in 1999, The Camun Rose, the highest honor awarded by the region of Lombardy.
❑ 2003. He began working with Expo Cts for all fashion events.
❑ 2003, May. Alba, his home town, awarded him the Gold Medal of the City.
❑ 2003, June. The Apulia region honored his career with the Gold Seal of Frederick II.

Modes et Travaux Parisian fortnightly founded in November 1919 by Edouard Boucherit (who died at the age of 102), who edited and directed the magazine until its last edition, number 457, in 1939. It was printed at Clichy, at the graphic arts press of Paul Dupont. It covered everything to do with the world of women, from basic clothes making to household chores, knitting and sewing to the arts of the hostess. It broadly reiterated the main features of *Broderie Moderne*, one of the first and most diffused illustrated fashion and women's work weeklies, issued in Paris between 1905 and 1914. After the war, transformed into a monthly and directed by André Belanger, it returned to the press and, at the end of the 1960s its readership reached a peak, with the sale of over 2 million copies. From 1981, the title was owned by Édition Mondiales. From then onwards, Hélène Tokay and Carine Newejons took over the editorial direction.

Modesto Bertotto Italian wool factory, founded in 1889 at Sandigliano di Biella. Up until 1997, it remained in the hands of the family whose name it bears. Afterwards, it was acquired by the San Biagio Group, a company specializing in yarns, becoming its textile division. Taking advantage of the research done by the group in the yarn sector, the wool factory updated its range of textiles, using new mixes of natural fibers and special finishings. The turnover, from 1996 to 1998, was a steady 12 billion lire per year.

❑ 2003, April. It opened a store in the new shopping center Full&Fifty, opened by Freeland-Capfin in Meda, a town in Brianza. The shop, measuring 5,500 square meters on two floors, stocks full-price clothing from the current season's collection as well as goods discounted from 30%. The service, Amisuraduomo, has recently been launched. Offered by the San Biagio group, it provides customers with a home tailoring facility, for jackets, shirts and pants.

Modit Italian *prêt-à-porter* event, founded at the same time as the Runway Centre at Milan Collections. It gave a further impulse to the plan to turn Milan into the fashion capital of Italy. It was launched in March 1978, following the initiative and investments of the Clothing Industrialists Association (president Fabio Inghirami; director Armando Branchini) and Maglieria (president Giorgio Malerba; director Alfredo Ciampini), with Beppe Modenese as consultant. Modit and the runway shows of the Milan Collections were held at the same time, in neighboring pavilions in Milan Fair, but it was ensured that their contents were markedly different. The event, which changed its name to Momi-Modamilano at the beginning of the 1990s, acted as an engine, tow-rope and catalyst within the relationship between designers and industry: a relationship and alliance that represent the focal point of the success of Italian fashion and the role played by Milan in this sector.

Mods Youth movement of modernists (hence the abbreviation), born in England at the end of the 1950s as a reaction to the Rockers (or Teddy Boys). Described by sociologists as the "rubbish of the United Kingdom," they wore their hair in a bob, often with a middle parting. The sexes differentiated themselves: twin-sets, skirts below the knee, very little make-up, big socks and flat shoes for the girls; houndstooth check hipster pants for the boys, short boots with a heel or Clarks desert boots, printed velvet jackets, shiny waistcoats, pink checked shirts with a round collar for the boys. They bought their clothes at John Stephen and Michael Ingram at Carnaby Street, which was later to become the heart of trendy London. It was a movement that opposed the system but at the same time took advantage of it (working and saving to buy records, clothes, and above all a Vespa or a Lambretta to decorated with numerous horns and mirrors), the icons of the Mods were The Who and The Beatles, and the television program *Ready Steady Go!*, which launched the new London fashion, first in England and later across much of Europe and North America. In 1979, the movement, which came to an end even before the Beatles split up, had a brief comeback in Europe, re-named New Mods in reaction, this time round, to the punk movement. It was aided by the film *Quadrophenia* (by Frank Roddam, music by The Who) and songs by The Jam. The writers favored by the New Mods were J.D. Salinger (*Catcher in the Rye*), Colin Macinnes (*Absolute Beginners*), and Nick Cohn, author of the book that inspired the film *Saturday Night Fever*. (*Laura Salza*)

Mod's Hair A salon founded in Paris in 1974 by two hairdressers, Frédéric and Guillaume, who came from the world of fashion magazines. Today, Mod's Hair runs a hairstyling agency for photo shoots and has a chain of 250 franchises around the world.

Moessmer Wool factory in Brunico (Bolzano) in Val Pusteria. It specializes in the production of fabrics made of felt, loden, alpaca, cashmere, and tweed. It was founded in 1870 by Josef Beikircher who shortly afterwards became a partner with the Viennese Josef Moessmer. At the beginning of the twentieth century, it had 40 employees. During the 1930s, production totaled 60 thousand meters of fabric per year. There were three key men in the history of the firm: from the end of World War I, the director and co-proprietor Franz Luis Walter; from 1947, the director Hermann Larisch, and finally, the CEO Anton Walker, who directed the wool factory from 1984, once it had become a public company. Moessmer employed 160 people, produced about 850 thousand meters of textile per year, and owned 4 stores in Brunico, Bolzano, Cortina, and Ortisei.

Moffitt Peggy. American model. With a brown bob, she learned how to align herself with the artistic and cinematic images of the 1960s. She became the muse and favorite model of the tailor, Rudi Gernreich. Peggy, the photographer William Claxton (her husband), and Gernreich formed a solid, creative threesome that was a first for the fashion world.

Mohair The hair of the Angora goat raised in Anatolia, South Africa, Texas, and

Mexico. It is fine, soft, long and shiny, even after dyeing. Because the hair is quite thin, it can be spun at 36 microns. Kid mohair, from the baby goat, drops to 24-25 microns. It makes light clothing with good insulating properties. Its light weight means it is also used for summer garments.

Moiré Monotone textile in silk, cotton, rayon, or acetate with a wavy surface effect, like the veins and striations of marble. It is pressed between two metal cylinders, which flatten some threads while leaving others intact. This results in an optical reflection of chiaroscuro that changes with the light. It is used mainly for blouses, skirts, and evening gowns.

Molco Willy (1943-2002). Italian journalist, born in Cairo. He studied in Milan and Paris, taking a degree in Law. After having run the weekly magazines *Novella 2000* and *Oggi*, he edited the women's title *Anna* from 1986 to 1989 and the monthly *Moda* from 1992 to 1995. At *Anna*, he greatly improved the quality of its fashion images, employing the best photographers on the European and American markets and using some of the most famous models. He also began the process of turning Anna into a service magazine, a task that was taken over by Mirella Pallotti, the editor who followed him. At *Moda*, he emphasized the main feature of the magazine, that of anticipating fashions by closely monitoring youth trends and keeping a watchful eye on the United States: lifestyles, street fashions, cinema, music, literature. During his career, Molco was also responsible for *Sette* and *Radiocorriere*. From 1997, he acted as an assistant to the news directors of the television channel Raiuno, first Marcello Sorgi and from July 1998, Giulio Borrelli. For Raiuno, he produced the special *Versace-Lagerfeld, Parallel Lives*, shown in Summer 1994.

Molenaar Frans (1941). Dutch tailor, the most famous in Amsterdam, so much so that in December 1986 the Municipal Museum of The Hague dedicated a monographic exhibition to his work. As well as *haute couture* collections, he created *prêt-à-porter* for men (he designed the Herzberger, Muller, and Kollem lines) and women (Jasmin's, Milo, Pisa, Van Schuppen). He studied at the Technical School of Fashion and Clothing in Amsterdam and attended the famous Rundschaueursus in Munich-Gladbach. He began working with the only Dutch couturier established in Paris, Charles Montaigne, and at the beginning of the 1960s he collaborated with Nina Ricci and Guy Laroche. He opened his own fashion house in 1967.

Molénac Fréderic. French designer. In 1996, he designed the Grès collection for the first time, giving it a very individual allure, with high neoprene boots and luminous T-shirts, rubber gabardine and boiled nylon pants. All in black, gray and white.

❑ 2001, July. With the presentation of his Fall-Winter creations, he joined the official calendar of Paris Fashion Week. With the Russians Seredin and Vassiliev, and the Frenchman, Fred Sathal, he was one of a group of new faces. The collection of hats for Spring-Summer 2002 brings Molénac fame beyond the borders of France.

❑ 2003, January. At the same time as Versace opted to present his *haute couture* by appointment, Fréderic disappeared from the official calendar, choosing to hold his show on the margins of the Paris week.

Molho Renata (1951). Journalist and author. Dress and fashion critic for the *Sole 24 Ore* financial newspaper. She has written for their Sunday supplement since 1991. She contributes to many Condé Nast titles (*Vogue Italia*, *L'Uomo Vogue*, *Casa Vogue*, *GQ*) and to the monthly magazine *Abitare*. She teaches various journalism courses (at IULM, IED, Urbino University). She is the author of many introductory books and is one of the first Italian journalists to have approached fashion as a socio-cultural phenomenon.

Molinard Historic brand of French perfume, also famous for its jewel-like bottles: true works of art created by René Lalique and Baccarat. It was launched in Grasse in 1849, as a small workshop of "eaux parfumées." Afterwards the house opened its own distillery and shops in the Provencal style, attracting the rich Russian and English clientele holidaying along the Côte d'Azur. It then turned to Paris, where it reached the height of its success in the 1920s and 1930s with perfumes such as *Habanita*, Molinard's bestseller, and *Le Baiser du Faune*, which won the prize for the most beautiful perfume bottle in the world at the international exhibition in New York in 1939.

Molinari Anna (1958). Italian designer. Her parents were textile industrialists who produced textiles in Carpi, where the young Anna grew up. In 1977, with her husband Gianpaolo Tarabini she launched the Blumarine label to sell knitwear and *prêt-à-porter* that had an instant success, so much so that the designer debuted at Modit in 1980, where she was recognized and awarded a prize for the best designer of the year. From Modit to Milan Women's Collections in 1981. The 1980s were a period of great creativity for her: to her first line (that widened the brand to include perfumes, bags, and numerous other products) she added the Miss Blumarine collection. In 1990, she opened her first own-brand store in Milan. In short, success was continuous and also a family affair, as the firm (Blufin at Carpi) includes her daughter Rossella Tarabini (responsible for the Anna Molinari line, launched in 1995) and her brother Gianguido, who has followed the menswear line since 1996. In late 1999 the company had more than 700 retail outlets in Europe, the United States, Japan, and Korea. Anna Molinari also has an ironic and humorous side, as shown by the time she appeared on the runway in a pram, pushed by the top model Carla Bruni, dressed as a nanny. Molinari's style is typically feminine, often with high potential: a femme-fatale or a femme-enfant, capable of arousing exciting and prohibited fantasies. *Divertissement stilistico by Anna Molinari* is the name of a label launched in 1978. It presented girls dressed in flowers in an enchanted wood. She repeated this characteristic for the Winter 2003-2004 collection, dedicated to her granddaughter Elisabetta, with metropolitan fairies wearing clothes that were clouds of light. Rose petals (flowers that Molinari says are part of her DNA) appear season after season; she offers a fairytale wardrobe that is always accompanied by the whimsical hats of the English milliner, Philip Treacy. (*Lucia Mari*)

Sketch by Anna Molinari for Bluemarine, Fall-Winter 1999-2000.

❑ 2001, September. New, own-brand boutique in Kottodori in Tokyo.
❑ 2002, April. The Blufin Group (Blumarine, Anna Molinari and Blugirl) ended 2001 with sales totalling 70.8 million euros (+30% on 2000).
❑ 2002, September. Debut on the runway for Blugirl, the Blumarine line dedicated to a younger market.
❑ 2002, December. The Carpi company, Blufin, which manages the brands Blumarine, Anna Molinari and, more recently, Blugirl, forecast year end sales of approximately 80 million euros (an increase of 9%).
❑ 2003, January. Spazio Blu is launched: a company that exclusively produces the lines Miss Blumarine, Miss Blumarine Jeans and Blumarine Baby. With these three collections, Molinari covers the female market aged 0-16. The three brands are owned by Blufin (together with Blumarine and Anna Molinari). The new company was created by

Spazio Sei Fashion Group, the licensed producer and distributor of the small size collections by Anna Molinari.
❑ 2003, February. For the Fall-Winter 2003-2004 collection at Milano Moda Donna, Blugirl, the very young collection by Blumarine, was presented in a green meadow against an English countryside backdrop with horses, a castle and a collector's red Ferrari in the distance.
❑ 2003, February. At Milano Moda Donna, Rossella Tarabini, who designed the brand created by her mother, announced, "Anna Molinari's pretty baby has decided to set foot in a poetic and perverse brothel." Appearing on the runway are dresses and short skirts with flounces, cut-off lamé vests, ballet shoes with a heel, Charleston style short dresses in tulle with woollen fringes. Severe black or pastel colors, from lilac to pale blue.
❑ 2003, July. The Kore prize, the fashion Oscar for the most fashionable collection of the year is awarded to Anna Molinari in Taormina. After the recent opening of boutiques in Marbella and Shanghai, another appeared in Rome at 24 Via Bocca di Leone, a new own-brand Blumarine-Anna Molinari franchise. The Carpi Group closed 2002 with a turnover of 80 million euros (an increase of 9%) and net profits of 3 million euros (up 25%). There were approximately a thousand non-exclusive retail outlets and 30 own-brand stores.
❑ 2004, April. A new line of Blumarine watches is launched, licensed out to the Bari company Global Watch. It was presented at the Swiss salon Baselworld. Plans continued to expand internationally, after the own-brand store of Saint Tropez, a boutique was opened in the Emirates Tower in Dubai, the store is part of the Fashion Villa Moda complex.
❑ 2004, May. As part of the Premio Valore Donna Città di Milano event, established by the local authority for Municipal Social and Female Policies, Anna Molinari is one of the ten women singled out for her social commitment.
❑ 2005, April. Anna Molinari was awarded an honorary degree in Educational Sciences at the University of Urbino.

Molleton Textile covered with gauze on either side, finished with a long pile. Made with soft, thick carded threads, it resembles a light blanket, like those used on airplanes and in hospitals. It is generally characterized by basic weaves, such as cloth, twill, or corduroy and is, on the whole, made of cotton or wool. The theatrical tailor Umberto Tirelli and the costume designer Piero Tosi used it for *Medea*, directed by Pier Paolo Pasolini.

Mollino Carlo (1905-1973). Italian designer, architect and photographer. He designed public and private buildings, furniture, and prototypes of cars and planes. He referred to himself as an eclectic figure who used photography as the common element where all his projects converged. From the 1930s till the end of the 1950s, he produced portraits and figures that clearly alluded to a fashion dominated by essential lines and a surreally delicate atmosphere.

Molyneux Edward (1894-1974). London designer from Ireland, still active in France in the late 1970s, nicknamed "the Captain" because of his official rank in World War I. When he was still very young he studied art (he was an artist and continued to paint now and then: some of his pictures are owned by the National Gallery of Art in Washington) and made a living by drawing for advertisements and magazines. He won his first prize in a competition at the age of 17, organized by the English branch of Lucille, the fashion house. It changed his life. He learnt the tailoring trade and became the assistant of the founder, Lady Duff Gordon. He opened his own *haute couture* atelier in Paris in 1919. Success was immediate, partly due to his classic designs with a perfect timeless cut, and partly owing to his sparkling social presence, his parties, and his activities as a costume designer, such as the clothes created for the play *The Barrets of Wimpole Street*, which revived the use of crinoline in 1922. Like many other fashion houses, he closed during the German occupation of France in 1940, to reopen again at the end of the war, roughly at the time as the more

Sketch by Molyneux, 1946.

brilliant Chanel. A decline in his fortunes forced Molyneux to retire in 1954, giving up the atelier to Jacques Griffe. His return to fashion after a 10-year absence caused a sensation, in a world that no longer resembled the aristocratic grace of his outfits, for example, his little black dresses that were so loved during the 1930s by the stars of the cinema and high society ladies.

Momi-Modamilano Launched in 1990 as a result of the merger between Modit, the fair that touted *prêt-à-porter*, and clothing and knitwear companies organized through Efima, and Milanovendemoda, an exhibition that started out as Assomoda and was later acquired by Expo Cts for the Commercial Union of Milan. Together with Milan Women's Collections it is, with approximately 350 fashion houses exhibiting, the focal point of Milan women's fashion week, which is held twice a year at the end of September and February. Momi-Modamilano comprises several sectors: Fashion Accessories, Boutique, Contemporary, Complementary-Bijoux, New Design-Borsino Stilisti, and Studio. The event attracts roughly 21,000 visitors from 95 countries.

❑ 2002, October. The *prêt-à-porter* salon closed on a positive note with a visitor increase of 9.4%. Business was very good for the 300 exhibiting companies: 68.4% were Italian and there was a strong increase in the foreign presence, with France doubling, Spain up 40.4%, Greece 58.2%, Russia up 30.7% and Japan up 54%. Among the innovations at MomiArteEvents were three artistic performances: i-Dress-undress with giant photographs and videos by Matt Jones on a striptease theme, Leeta Harding: Photographs with 60 fashion photos, portraits of New York life and WelcomeTothe Future PlanetofStyle, with eclectic and futuristic creations by the group of artists AsFour.
❑ 2003, February. Momi officially closed and its stylistic inheritance was taken over by Milanovendemoda and Modit. A press release announced the closure for the following reason: "Strategic differences between Expo Cts and Efima, the two partner firms in Promozione Moda Italia (Pmi) (the owner of the Momi-Modamilano brand), has announced the liquidation of Pmi and the consequent division of the *prêt-à-porter* event into two separate events, Milanovendemoda and Modit."

Moncalvo Riccardo (1915). Italian photographer. He continued a family tradition: his father was the owner of an industrial artistic photography studio in Turin. Their early interest in photographic research resulted in their images being included in a large number of exhibitions. Riccardo inherited his father's studio in 1935 and made a mark with his eclectic professional activities. He worked for important clients, including Fiat

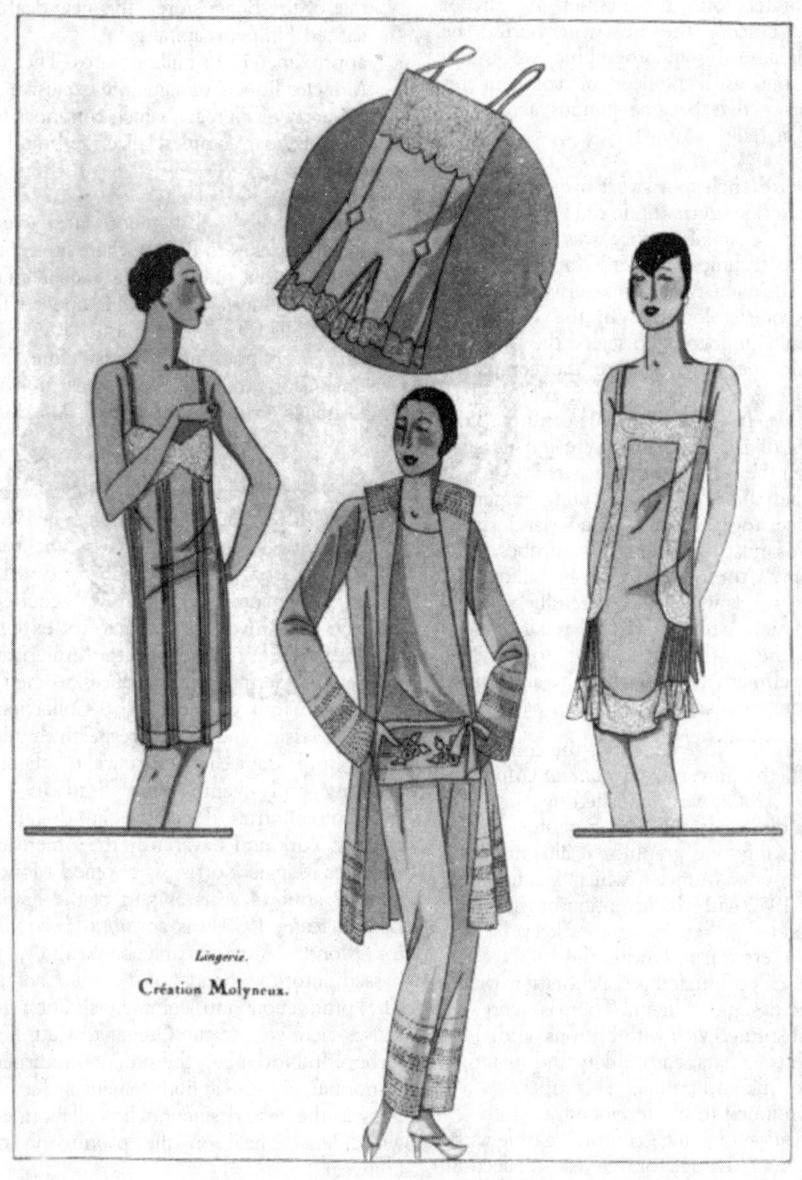

Sketches by Molyneux: slip, pyjamas, dressing gown (from *Anni Venti – La nascita dell'abito moderno*, Centro Di, Florence, 1991, catalogue for the Galleria del Costume).

and Pininfarina, and was Carlo Mollino's preferred printer. He took portrait shots of theater and cinema actors and closely collaborated with the Fashion Agency of Turin. During the post-war period he consolidated his photographic work and stood out as a pioneer of color in his laboratory that became famous across the whole of Italy.

Moncler French sportswear firm. In 1952, at Monestier de Clermont, in the French region of Isère, a small factory was founded to produce technical clothing for the mountains. The name Moncler is derived from the initials of the location. In the 1950s, the mountain climbers who scaled the Karakorum and the Makalu wore the company's "duvet." A few years later it relocated to Grenoble. In Italy, the 1980s confirmed the success of the brand that created its style through the use of puffer jackets in cities. It appealed above all to a younger market. Moncler, together with Timberland shoes, were a must in preppy wardrobes. The company's turnover exceed 40 billion lire, thanks to a wide and carefully selected distribution network (1,650 retail outlets) across the world. In addition to Italy, its principal markets are in Europe and Japan. The company has joined the Fin-part stable.

❑ 2002, November. For the company's fiftieth anniversary, *Now and...Moncler 1952-2002*, was published by Baldini&Castoldi. Using photos, drawings and graphics, it illustrated the history of Moncler, which was founded in 1952 with the invention of the first padded jacket designed to keep factory workers warm. During the 1980s, Moncler initiated a collaboration with the designer Chantal Thomas, who substituted zips with buttons, added fur trims, collars, embroidery and materials like silk and ermine. This aspect continued to be developed, until the creation of some "couture" garments by Férnand Lasage for this year's collection.
❑ 2003, February. Fin.part sells Moncler for 30 million euros. The brand was bought by a newly created company, owned 51% by the brand's designer Remo Ruffini, 24% by Vela Financial Holding Group (Gruppo Bucherer) and 25% by Pepper Industries owned by Fin.part. Further to the 3.4 million euros gained from the sale of the Boggi stores, this new deal earned Fin.part capital gains of approximately 16 million euros. The Moncler license remains the exclusive property of Fin.part, which continues to produce and commercialize the brand's products.

Mondati Donato. Italian tailor. He moved from The Marches to Rome, where he learnt his trade in an old tailoring atelier that supplied the House of Savoy. He opened an atelier in Via Po during the 1950s. His clothing is very traditional, and is defined by Cristina Giorgetti and Enzo Colarullo as Anglo-Italian in the volume *Moda Maschile dal 1600 al 1990* (Octavo Editore).

Mondi German ready-made womenswear company. It was founded in Munich in 1967 with a knitwear line designed by the trio Margaretha Ley, Herwing Zahm, and Otto Bruestle. The company, which was acquired in 1993 by Investcorp, aims to export European luxury goods to the American market. In Germany, it produces women's clothing in four different lines: Collection, Sport, Classic, and Gala, respectively divided into daywear, sportswear, classic clothing and eveningwear. Sold in 65 different countries, the clothes are designed in New York and Bavaria by the American designer Maggie Norris, who joined Mondi in 1998 after 14 years as part of the Ralph Lauren team. 1999 was an *annus horribilis* for Mondi. After risking bankruptcy, it passed into the hands of Fehmi Chama. The production and commercialisation licenses were sold to the Gilmar di Cattolica Group. In November, the situation returned to normal with the announcement of Jeetoh Peng as the head designer, who collaborated with Vera Schaal on the production of knitwear.

❑ 2000, March. The partnership between Gilmar and Mondi came to an end. In August the first collection of sportswear was presented. Fehmi Chama entrusted the Fall-Winter 2001-

2002 line to two of the team's designers. Annette Vogt took over *prêt-à-porter* and Michaela Burger knitwear.
❑ 2001, May. Imaginex of Hong Kong acquired the distribution rights for menswear for the Asian market. The aim was to increase the menswear own-brand Mondi Uomo stores to 50 by 2004, with particular focus on Italy, where the line is produced by Imaginex.

Mondialpelli Wholesale fur and fur clothing production firm, founded in Milan in 1955 by Alberto Ravizza, and Fernanda and Enzo Picciocchi. In the era of the classic fur coat, they created a different style based on a high quality, *prêt-à-porter* production. The firm developed out of family links, through the marriage of Alberto and Giovanna, the sister of Fernanda, and evolved rapidly due to the decision to produce and distribute the Pikenz collection wholesale. At the beginning of the 1970s, it began to export, above all to the United States, Japan and Germany, and for many years distributed the *haute couture* line Melegari and Costa. The second generation of the family entered the firm, with Umberto Picciocchi in 1972 and Roberto Ravizza in 1981, who were President and CEO respectively. They led a young team that each year made 140 garments for the Pikenz collection and 140 for Gianfranco Ferré. The contract with Ferré dates back to 1987 with an agreement that was launched with the *haute couture* designs for July in Rome. The first Gianfranco Ferré Fourrures collection in March 1988 revolutionised fur: natural, almost wild, with splits in front, behind and at the sides, right up to the back. At the end of 1997, the headquarters in Via Fieno were opened, a few streets away from their historic base in Piazza Diaz. A thousand square meters, equipped with software, digitizers, the most modern machinery and decorated in the most elegantly rational way (180 drawers of buttons were used in a single collection). The Pikenz and Gianfranco Ferré lines are created and displayed here. The Ferré line has changed its name from Fourrures to Furs. (*Maria Rita Stiglich*)

Mondino Jean Baptiste (1949). French photographer and director, from an Italian family. An eclectic author, he has used some highly diverse methods in order to communicate his art: in 1977 he opened the Studio de l'Air where he created rock records following his interests as a musician and composer. The following year he turned to photography, producing black-and-white portraits and fashion images. During the 1980s, he became established by working not only as a photographer but also a graphic designer, art director, and the author of adverts and videos for Bjork, Madonna, and other pop singers. He has published in the most important magazines in the sector and worked for YSL, Jean Paul Gaultier, Alaïa, Calvin Klein, Adidas, and Printemps. He combines innovative techniques with a real talent for images and compositions, creating sophisticated photographs that breathe life into a fantastical and unreal world, dominated by luxury and glamour, but also a hint of transgression. His style is typified by his artfully ugly rendition of the model Kate Moss and his image of a spectator in front of Courbet's *The Origins of the World*, which plays with the perspective to give the impression that the figure's head is entering the genitalia depicted in the painting. In 1999, he published the volume *Déja vu* and in 2003 *Two Much*, whose title refers to the excesses of contemporary society as well as the fact that it was the second volume. Also in 2003, he produced highly creative images for the Lavazza Calendar and presented his only personal collection at Carla Sozzani's premises in Milan. It was called On Sale as a reminder that his products are commercial works rather than pieces of art.

Mondo di Marco A "total look" brand of menswear. Produced in Italy with Italian textiles, its distribution is coordinated by Mondo Inc. of New York, with headquarters in the Crown Building. It was created in 1984 by Marco Wächter, but following the death of its founder, Mondo di Marco is now run by his family, led by Pina Fattorini Wächter. Its distribution is concentrated mainly in the USA and Canada. The menswear brands Gene Meyer and Pronto Uomo are also owned by the company and, more recently, the women's knitwear line, MdM. At the end of 2000, the brand came under the control of the holding company Perry Ellis International, an American giant specializing in casual wear.

Monge Ines (1964). Spanish designer born in Bilbao. She works in a team with Elisa Amann, also from Bilbao. They are based in Barcelona and have twice been featured on the cover of *Vogue Spain*. Their creations are made of humble materials: left-over fabrics, rags, fringes, braid and samples, in order to reveal the contradictions inherent in what they describe as "the false splendor of fashion."

Mongolian Wool Fleece from the wether, or lamb from Mongolia with a very thick, long, and curly hair. Originally only white and beige, it is now dyed in all colors to produce a showy and extravagant garment. Very fashionable during the 1970s.

Monoprix A chain of French department stores that sells a little of everything: food, accessories, menswear, and clothing for women and children made using technological fabrics (micro fiber, Gore-Tex) and sophisticated ones (cashmere) at very affordable prices. In the clothing sector, its philosophy is the "democratization of fashion." In 1998, Monoprix had 360 stores. Founded in 1932 by the Lafayette Group, seven years later the chain already had 56 outlets. In 1997, it took over its legendary competitor, Prisunic.

❑ 2002. Turnover grew by 1.7%. An even higher increase than that registered by its owner, Galeries Lafayette.
❑ 2003. The first three months of 2003 registered an increase of 4.7% compared with the same period in 2002.

Monroe Marilyn (1926-1962). American actress. With an innocent and slightly sulky expression, she was a blonde who inspired a series of imitators in Hollywood, her voluptuous body often wrapped in shiny, red or flesh-colored lamé covered in diamantés. Norma Jean Baker Monterson progressed from an unhappy childhood, marked by orphanages and adoptive families, to a brief period as a model in which she caused more interest than the clothes she wore, up until the famous advertising calendar where she posed naked: this was the path that led to the cinema. Already blonde and adorned in tight-fitting clothing, she appeared in her first roles: *All About Eve* (1950) and *The Asphalt Jungle* (1950). Shortly afterwards, she wore the legendary gold lamé dress with the low-cut back in *Gentlemen Prefer Blondes* (1953), which was immediately reproduced in a flurry of copies. It was created by William Travilla, the actress's favorite designer. It was again Travilla who chose what has become possibly the most famous dress in the history of cinema, for *The Seven Year Itch* (1955). The white dress was lifted by a draft from the grate above the metro to reveal Monroe's "intimates," the term her character used to describe her undergarments. Immediately following her early death, Monroe became an immortal icon of style. She contributed to the popularity of vertiginous high heels, naked effect sandals with very thin laces, boat-neck tops and Chanel No. 5 perfume, which, she often said, was the only thing she wore in bed at night. As for those clothes that hugged her like a second skin, it is hard to forget the one made for her in May 1962 by the French designer Jean Louis to celebrate President John Kennedy's birthday party: it was made from flesh-colored silk with an almost transparent effect, and shone with tiny diamantés like little drops of water. It became an inspiration for more than one fashion designer. (*Sofia Leoncina Gnoli*)

Monsieur French magazine covering "fashion, etiquette and everything a man is interested in," launched in 1914. Between 1920 and 1924, it became a monthly. It was the first magazine dedicated solely to the masculine world, to men who wished to be elegant without excessive frivolity, ready to accept advice on comportment and not just clothing, for all occasions. English, American, and Italian fashion, society and culture columns, reportage on the latest novelties and theater and sporting news. Its graphics and illustrations, both drawings and photographs, were of a very high standard.

Monsieur Gilles Very flighty, Belgian hat maker. He aided the professional development of De Barentzen and Rocco, whom he discovered in Ischia and with whom he launched Marchio Barocco, which later became the Maison Rocco Barocco. Despite his great creativity as a milliner, he has always preferred to stay out of the limelight. At the end of 2000, the most important boutiques in Rome on Via Borgognona displayed some of the creations of Gilles Stenglé, alias Monsieur Gilles, including examples from the private collection of Rocco Barocco, whose career was launched in part due to the assistance of the French milliner. Red hats with roosters' feathers and felt hats decorated with marabou feathers: regardless of whether the designs were from the 1960s or the present, the whole collection is imbued with a surprising freshness and modernity.

Montaigne Charles (1900-1989). French designer, born in Holland. His real name was Charles Meuwese. During the 1950s, he attempted to anticipate the future of ready-made clothing by producing paper patterns of his garments, accompanied with a book of photos of the made-up items and labels to sew onto the finished model. It was a disaster. Nevertheless, his fashion house survived the blow and only closed in 1973 due to his advanced age. Even though he was the grandson of a textile industrialist, or even because of this, he was 12 when he went to a tailor's atelier for the first time. At almost 22, he was experienced enough to be taken on as a cutter by Madame Vionnet. Jacques Griffe worked under him. In 1939, when Vionnet closed for the war, he was brave enough to set up on his own with his wife Sonia, the star of the atelier's models, and the première Madame Catherine. His style was directly influenced by that of the great Madeleine.

Montana Claude (1949). French designer. Both during his initial, more aggressive phase and after he developed a more sophisticated, sculpted, structural simplicity, he was one of the creators who shaped *prêt-à-porter* during the 1970s, in France and the rest of the world. His mixed origins (a Catalonian father and German mother) are reflected in his minute physique, as slender as a flamenco dancer, and his upright, perfect bearing. His vision of the female form possesses great energy and is entrusted more and more to different tones of his single, chosen color, Yves Klein blue, in clothing modulated like weightless armor, cloaks projected into space with careening scarves or spiraling collars. He was 20 years old when he debuted on the runway in 1978. But he already had a noteworthy and varied apprenticeship behind him: creating jewelry in London, then in Paris, an illustrator for fashion magazines and, finally, as assistant to the Swedish fashion designer, Jean Voight, who specialized in leather clothing. During the early 1970s, leather was his favorite material, which he frequently combined with knitwear. Even though his first show was attacked by the American press who detected in it a unsettling form of severe Germanic military style (it featured models in black leather waistcoats and shorts covered in metal chains), the look became a uniform for young women. During the 1980s (he received the fashion Oscar for his Spring-Summer 1986 collection) his models were vaguely space-age, austere women, wide-shouldered but fragile, with geometric, aerial hairstyles, whom he presented in theatrical runway shows, with illusionistic lighting and extremely measured movements and gestures. From winter 1990 until 1992, he was responsible for *haute couture* at the relaunched Maison Lanvin and two consecutive collections (July 1990 – January 1991) won the Dé d'Or. (*Lucia Sollazzo*)

❑ 2002, April. The Maison Claude Montana announced that it would entrust the production of its menswear line (leather garments, knitwear, and overcoats) from Summer 2003 to different Italian partners. Montana, who returned to the Paris runway shows, remained only as the brand's external consultant. In July 2000, the businessman Jean-Jacques Layani became the owner of the Montana Création company and appointed Béatrice Bongibault as general director. A specialist in the luxury goods sector, she already had held the same post at Chanel, Dior, Valentino, and Escada. Creation was entrusted to an internal style department, with a series of freelance designers, under the direction of his son, Laurent Layani. The collection, made under license, including *prêt-à-porter* women's clothing, was entrusted to Multimoda and produced

by Fiba. The footwear and bags were made respectively by Franco Paolucci and Cip. The license for the production of glasses is owned by the French firm Bourgeois, and the jewelry by Apm.
❑ 2002, September. Stéphane Parmentier was made the new creative director. His first collection debuted in October, at the Carrousel du Louvre in Paris. Previously, he had worked for Lanvin, Lagerfeld, and Givenchy. He also produced his own signature line.
❑ 2003, May. An agreement is reached with ECCE (Entreprise de Confection et de Commercialisation Européenne), a company specializing in menswear, for the production and distribution of men's *prêt-à-porter*. The partnership with Montana joined the other licenses owned by ECCE, a company that has a turnover of 100 million euros a year and that has, for a long time, been responsible for Givenchy, Gant, Scherrer, Courrèges, Rochas, Eden, Park, and Arrow.

Montanari Vera (1950). Journalist. Editor of *Gioia*, a women's weekly published by Rusconi Editore. She was born in Milan. Very knowledgeable in current affairs, social and civil issues, as a young woman who experienced the events of 1968 and worked at Radio Popolare. She began to collaborate with *L'Uomo Vogue* in 1980. Precisely because of her diverse experiences in the news field, she was immediately taken on full-time and soon became the head of news coverage at the magazine. After a few years, she became editor-in-chief at *Per Lui*, a young men's title with a new focus, also published by Condé Nast. She moved to Mondadori in 1984 to relaunch the weekly magazine *Bolero*. Afterwards, she moved on to become the editor of *Dolly*, a mini-magazine that was very popular with adolescents; finally, in 1987, she launched the Italian version of the French magazine, *Marie Claire*. She established a good position for the magazine within the sector and ensured an excellent image for it, with a truly vivacious contemporary spirit. In 1995, Rusconi offered her a "silver platter," the editorship of the weekly *Gioia*, one of the most-read women's publications, which was in need of restyling. She took on this new challenge with great resolve and once again demonstrated her journalist talents, developing a magazine that was rich with useful ideas and subjects, intended for a very wide public with specific demands. Since 1998, she has also been the editorial director of *Donna*, also owned Rusconi, which was purchased by the French Group Hachette in 1999. (*Cristina Brigidini*)

❑ 2003. After *Marie Claire* passed from Mondadori to Hachette Rusconi, Montanari returned as the editor-in-chief of the title.

Montebello Giancarlo (1941). Italian jeweler. After attending the Castle Art School in Milan during the second half of the 1950s, he became acquainted with some of the leading figures in the world of design and architecture, such as Dino Gavina, Carlo Scarpa, and Achille and Pier Giacomo Castiglioni. He became interested in jewelry design and in 1967 opened a workshop with Teresa Pomodoro dealing with precious metals. Under the brand-name Gem, he launched a line of jewelry designed by artists, such as César, Sonia Delaunay, Piero Dorazio, Lucio Fontana, Hans Richter, Larry Rivers, Niki de Saint Phalle, Jesus Soto, and Alex Katz. The photographer Ugo Mulas played a fundamental part, producing a series of fascinating pictures in black-and-white of the avant-garde creations of the

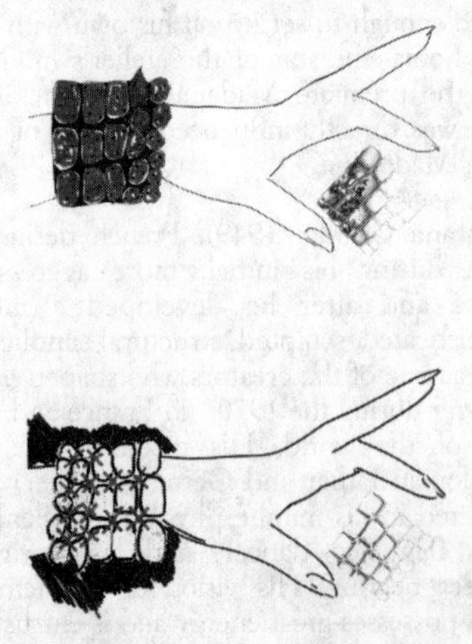

Giancarlo Montebello, bracelets 1997-1998.

Montebello atelier. Montebello's work as the "editor" of artistic jewelry continued until 1978 when he took up its design, culminating in the collaboration begun in 1983, with the jeweler Trizio di Bari. In 1987, he began to create jewelry and art objects for the Sociéte des Amis du Musée National d'Art Moderne – Centre d'Art et Culture Georges Pompidou. During the 1990s, he finished the cycle of *Ornamenti per Bradamante* using stainless steel chains: jewelry to wear like clothing. Today, he researches forms and materials, developing the concept of different components following the potential of what he describes as "*ars combinatoria*," always placing the relationship between body and jewelry at the centre of his work.
(*Alessandra Quattordio*)

Montedoro Italian ready-made clothing firm founded in Castellanza (province of Varese) in 1958 to produce raincoats, overcoats and sportswear. During the 1970s, it made use of the stylistic collaboration of Walter Albini and Giorgio Armani, resulting in great visibility on the runway and the market for a time. During the 1990s, the brand was relaunched. The company has its own showrooms in Milan, New York, Düsseldorf, Paris, and Tokyo.

❑ 2002. 80% of Montedoro of Castellana was acquired by Textile Production Industries. The operation, worth 1.3 million euros, represented the first stage in a diversification process that took place between 2001 and 2004. The purposes of the diversification were to expand the brand's range of products and to create distribution synergies. In 2001, Montedoro had a turnover of approximately 3 million euros.
❑ 2003, June. Launch of the company Slowear to bring together the administration of the brands Incotex, Montedoro and Zanone.

Montefibre One of the main companies producing acrylic fibers (the Leacril brand) at a global level and polyester fibers (the Terital brand) at a European level. It closed the first six months of 2002 with net profits of 4.3 million euros, compared with 0.1 million during the same period the previous year.

Montenapoleone (Via). The backbone of the Milanese fashion retail circuit. As Guido Lopez and Silvestro Severgnini relate in *Milano in mano* (published by Mursia), the street "runs along the ditch that still survives underground, which surrounded the Roman walls. Some traces of it still remain here and there in the cellars of the odd-numbered side of the street." The fashion bulldozer has transformed what Van Wood once defined in a song as "the living room of Milan" into an obsessive parade of shoes, miniskirts, suits, bolero jackets, blouses, cashmere, outfits for professional men and women, bags, jewelry, and watches. It was natural and predictable that Italian *prêt-à-porter*, Milan's great success story, would need a stage to promote its image, buying into streets that the banks had deprived of life. But there have always been strong protests about the transformation of the street that, after World War II, definitively replaced the Vittorio Emanuele Gallery as a meeting point, a central axis for walking and a place to "do lengths," as going up and down Via Montenapoleone came to be known in 1950s slang. Indeed, it was in 1950 that a great Milanese author, Raffaele Calzini, began to complain: "In about 1920, it was a tranquil and noble street that attracted, at most, aristocrats and the solitary wealthy from Via Borgospesso, Via Santo Spirito, Via Gesù, and Via Sant'Andrea. For some inexplicable urban phenomenon, at first timidly, then more bravely, finally boldly, and afterwards even insolently, Via Montenapoleone competed with other elegant Italian streets: with the Florentine Via Tornabuoni, the Roman Via Condotti, Quattro Canti in Palermo, Via Chiai in Naples." The criticisms, grumblings and regrets multiplied directly in relation to the fashion invasion. Tears were shed in newsprint when, during the 1970s and 1980s, the drug store Parini, a sort of Milanese Fauchon in the field of spices and sauces, and the fruitsellers Moretti, whose goods sold at phenomenal prices, ceded to the opening of Valentino and the hosiery firm Fogal. The tears were even more heartfelt when Versace ousted Ricordi, the record store that had cradled, in the listening booths with headphones, the first loves of two generations, and when Salumaio, the gastronomic centre of Via Montenapoleone, accepted, comforted by a very large sum, to move into an inner courtyard to make space for the store front of Corneliani. But nobody, during the 1920s and 1930s, lamented when Bottega della Poesia, a bookshop-cum-art gallery founded by Enrico Somaré, Emanuele Castelbarco, and Walter Toscanini, was forced to close, to be replaced by Marco, a fabric shop. The truth is, that long before the designer boom and the birth of Milan as the *prêt-à-porter* capital, Via Montenapoleone was, in terms of the relative number of shops, a fashion street. The metamorphosis was, above all, a slow one, with a gradual growth of designers, a development that followed an internal logic.

Montesinos Alama Francis (1950). Spanish designer born in Valencia. She began her training at the Escuela de Artes y Oficios with a specialization in Interior Design, partly to convince her parents to transform the family firm into an interior architecture studio. Her artistic activity was strongly influenced by the world surrounding the Beatles and the birth of the Ibiza phenomenon. During the 1960s, she opened a shop in Valencia and in 1978 she presented her first *prêt-à-porter* collection on the runway in Barcelona. She took part in numerous specialized fairs in Spain and abroad. During the 1980s, she opened other own-brand boutiques across Spain and began to show in Madrid, with the inauguration of the Pasarela Cibeles. During the 1990s, she extended her production beyond *prêt-à-porter* to include jewelry, household linens, theatrical costumes, and even cars. Her fashion work continues alongside collaborations with the theater and performing world. At the end of the 1990s, she won the Nova Prize and presented collections on the runway at the Portuguese Expo, at Pasarela del Carmen in Valencia and even at the Picasset penitentiary centre. (*Mariacristina Righi*)

❑ 2000. She created the costumes for the world preview of *Swan Lake*, performed by the National Ballet of Cuba and for the prima ballerina Maria Jimenez, in the show *Blanco y Negro*. She designed the Summer 2002 swimwear line for Dolores Cortes, which was presented on the runway in Madrid.
❑ 2003, April. She described her career, techniques, and tricks of the trade to the students on the spring course at the Università Internazionale Mendez Pelayo in Tenerife. The course, lasting a week, was titled "Creation and Artistic Imagination in Theatrical Design and Fashion".

Montgomery (Duffle coat). Large woolen jacket with a hood, reaching down to the thighs or the knee, fastened with frogging made of olive-shaped braid pulled through buttonholes made of loops of braid or leather. In its most classic version, it is made of camel skin, in different colors, or some other heavy fabric. It was originally worn by members of the British military marines. It owes its name, Montgomery, to the English general Bernard Law Montgomery, winner of the battle of El Alamein, who used to wear one during World War II over his military uniform. Its success continued into peacetime, when the left-over models were sold to the public and the Montgomery became an essential (but above all comfortable) garment in the wardrobe of both men and women, worn in particular by generations of high school and university students in the late 1940s and 1950s. Forty years later, it returned but the colors were new: burgundy, wood green, navy blue.

Montgomery David. American photographer born in Brooklyn, New York. He arrived in Great Britain in 1960. After working as an assistant at Laster Bookbinder, he joined the staff of *Queen* in 1962. During the 1970s, he worked for *Vogue* and *Harper's Bazaar*. He lives in London.

Monti Gigi (1934). Clothing industrialist. From the age of 21, Monti was involved in fashion as a production consultant for numerous companies. Creative and concrete, his job was to link the needs of the designer with those of the market. With two partners, Ferrante and Tositti, in 1967 he bought the Basile luxury *prêt-à-porter* company, became its president in 1969 and transformed it into one of the most significant Italian fashion brands. He left the company in 1995.

Monti Tedeschi Antonia (1905). Italian journalist. Reserved, with a strong character, precise and strict at work in both words and

Evening gown designed by Alama Montesinos.

clothing, she was the editor of *Annabella*, *Marie Claire* and *La Donna*. She also edited *Il nuovissimo cucchiaio d'argento* (1972).

Montone Sheepskin coats and jackets, either smooth or suede on the outside, shaved on the inside. This characteristic means that the garment can be reversed. Although in the past it was heavy to wear, improved production techniques have reduced its weight considerably.

Montorsi Italian tailors. Giovanni Montorsi founded the atelier in Rome in 1920. He was 37 at the time and had trained as a cutter at Tanfani and Bertarelli, a company making ecclesiastical garments. His first atelier, in Piazza della Pietra, produced men's garments. For 12 years, Montorsi was the trusted tailor of Umberto of Savoy. His wife encouraged him to branch out into women's clothing. In 1929, he bought a building at Via Condotti 65 and rented out the windows to Salvatore Ferragamo. The rest of it he filled with assistants and cutters. During the Fascist period, the atelier attracted the wives and lovers of members of the regime. The famous wedding dress of Edda Mussolini, wife of Galeazzo Ciano, was described in the papers: "It was a creation made of satin, with a garland of pearls and orange blossom on her head and long, white leather gloves." The atelier was organized like a French fashion house, with a series of workshops with a very high level of craftsmanship, producing clothes, furs, sporting outfits, and women's underwear. There were more than 100 members of staff, including workers, premières, models, and porters. The salon included a tea room, a milliner's room, and a corner set aside for gloves and shawls. After the death of the owner, the business continued under Montorsi's two daughters, Adriana and Donatella. In 1957, the building was sold and the atelier moved to Via Sistina. It closed at the end of the 1970s.

(*Bonizza Giordani Aragno*)

Mood Fortnightly magazine. In September 2000 the first edition of a new magazine was published. It was innovative compared with the contemporary panorama of Italian publishing and selective in its contents, graphics, and images: *Mood*, the spirit of things, is a refined and cultured publication, edited by the founder Gianni Bertasso. It aims to illustrate current social trends, filtering the messages that arrive not just through fashion but also design, art, and cookery. In other words, all forms of expression capable of reflecting changes in taste. Respected journalists in the fields of news reporting, art and design collaborate with the bilingual English-Italian magazine. It is characterized by a strong spirit of research and experimentation, particularly from the point of view of iconography and contents. *Mood* has a strong distribution network within the trade in Italy and abroad through the most important fair events, and is aimed at all those who work in the fashion, design, and art sectors: designers, PR, journalists, architects, art galleries, show rooms, retail outlets, companies, agencies and institutions, schools and professional colleges. However, it is also aimed at a wider public following the development of trends, who subscribe to the magazine or purchase it from news kiosks, specialized shops, and retail outlets.

Moon Sarah (1941). French photographer. Her real name is Marielle Hadengue. Until the early 1970s, she was known for her very personal style, consisting of combinations of lights and shadows, grainy images, intense sepia exposures that recall the Impressionists, as well as spontaneous visions (a rotating peacock, a girl dressed as Little Red Riding Hood in front of a mysterious backdrop set up on the road), and strong echoes of Surrealism. In this context, her settings are of interest, which allude to fashion rather than describing it directly, and her alternating use of black-and-white and color. She took up photography in 1968 when she packed in modeling. First she worked for Cacharel and Condé Nast, and than as a freelance producing her own images using a soft-focus technique. Her work has appeared in *Vogue*, *Time*, *Life*, *Harper's Bazaar*, *Elle*, *Stern*, *Votre Beauté*, *Graphics*, *Marie Claire*, and *Nova*. She has had numerous exhibitions across the world and received important prizes such as the Dada Award in 1972 for fashion photography and the Grand Prix de Cannes in 1979 for the Cacharel advertising campaign. Her many books include *Coincidences* (2001). She has also made about fifty advertising films (she is currently working on a film project based on the life of her friend Lillian Bassman, the 82-year-old photographer and art director of *Harper's Bazaar*) and photographed the Pirelli calendar for 1972. She lives with her husband, Robert Del Pire, a critic and editor, in Paris.

Moonboots Voluminous, unwieldy snow boots, very cozy due to their thick foam-rubber lining. The exterior made of a synthetic material, shiny or matt, which can be brightly colored or more typically, white or navy. Fur versions are also available. Worn for après-ski, they first emerged in the early 1970s, after the world had seen them on the feet of the American astronauts who first set foot on the moon.

Moore James (1935). American photographer. Studied with Brodovich and assistant to Avedon and to still-life photographers Rouben Samberg and Laster Bookbinder. In 1960 he opened his studio and started working on fashion photography. Two years later he joined the team at *Harper's Bazaar*, where his first work, *The Fair Foot*, caught the imagination of both public and publishers with its sense of mystery. The teachings and practices of Brodovich ("You have a blank piece of paper in front of you on which you can write or draw anything. What do you do?") guided Moore's activity. In the second half of the 1970s, he abandoned photography, which he found too constrictive, in favor of TV advertisements.

Moorehouse Marion. American model. She worked in the 1920s and 1930s, the years of the flapper style. She was the first of the top models, known in those days as *mannequin volanti*. Discovered by the photographer Steichen, and often signed up by Horst and Hoyningen-Huene, her success was so great that it ennobled her profession and turned models into superstars. Her slim and slender figure was perfect for the ideals of elegance of the period.

Morabito French fashion house specializing in fur and jewelry. In 1905, Jean-Baptiste Morabito moved to Nice as a jeweler and case-maker, after an apprenticeship in Naples at his father's studio. He opened his first shop in Paris in the Rue Saint-Honoré in 1921. The development and evolution of this commercial enterprise was entrusted to his son, Armand. In 1947 the perfume *Morabito No. 7* was launched, its bottle designed by Lalique. The founder's grandson, Pascal Morabito, contributed to the continuing prestige of the brand with the opening of a new shop in Place Vendôme in 1982, followed by others in New York, Geneva, Hong Kong, and Tokyo. 1998 saw the launch of the perfume *Passion Mediterranée* and a range of cosmetics.

Pascal Morabito *Diamant libre.*

❑ 1999. The year of jewelry. Commissions were requested by Piper Heidsieck, Royal Côteau, Prince d'Orléans, and Cattier. The organizers of the Deauville American Film Festival commissioned the trophy from the company.

❑ 2001. Creation of a futurist sculpture *Tête a 360°*. For the film world, another statuette was commissioned for the winner of the Deauville Asian Film Festival – a further honor bestowed by the organizers of the Deauville American Film Festival. Morabito was also behind the article brought out to announce the launch of the new Paris-to-Marseille high-speed train line.

Moral Jean (1906-1999). French photographer. Studied with Remie Lohse, from whom he acquired a light-hearted and anti-conformist style. His pictures, often taken in the streets of Paris, have been published in *Harper's Bazaar*.

Moran Gertrude. Known as Gussy, or even Gorgeous Gussy. A few centimeters of lace appliquéd to her knickers at Wimbledon in 1949 caused a stir among photographers and tabloid editors, the expulsion of their creator, Ted Tinling, by the tournament's master of ceremonies, and even prompted a question in Parliament.

Morawetz and Moncourtois The creative team behind Chanel make-up. A former lecturer in make-up at two academies of cinema and theater, Dominique Moncourtois has worked for Chanel since 1969. Heidi Morawetz, a well-known freelance make-up artist, joined her in 1980.

> ❑ 2002. The pair, who now traditionally create four new ranges annually for Chanel, ended the year with Les Perles de Chanel.

Mordoré A very fashionable hue in the 1930s, now rarely seen. A warm brown with a hint of gold flecks, perfect for faille or taffeta fabrics.

Morellato Brand of jewelry made by the watch-strap company of the same name. Founded in Bologna in 1930, twenty years later Morellato had become the European and world leaders in their field. A careful marketing strategy ensured a diversification of products, and led to the introduction of jewelry boxes produced under the Arca Astucci brand in 1986, and in 2000 to a jewelry range that synthesized high-fashion and wearability. The *prêt-à-porter* collection, which proposed straps in steel, and in leather embellished with gold and precious stones, served to please even the most varied tastes, and met the desired levels of flexibility with interchangeable straps and components. The rapid success of the jewelry line led to franchises at Fortunoff in New York and in the Japanese department store Marui. The Morellato Group, based in the region of Padua, has subsidiaries in Germany, Spain, and France. In 2002, under the guidance of Massimo Carraro, the group's co-owner and administrator, Morellato made sales of 60 million euros.

> ❑ 2005. The first six months of the year registered an increase in revenues of 40%. The group aimed to close the year with an overall turnover of almost 100 million euros: 25% more than the previous year.

Morelli Paul (1949). American jewelry maker. His recurring theme is nature: flowers, butterflies, and nuts all feature frequently in his creations, where they are cast into fine, well-chosen settings. His creative spirit is the fruit of an upbringing in a family of artists. His parents were theater costume designers, and engendered in their son a taste for the ornamentation of clothing. In his teenage years, he discovered that his real passion was for jewelry, and above all for pearls. He started to design and to sell in the early 1970s, in New York's famous art galleries. By the 1980s he was working on a more commercial level, and selling in department stores such as Bergdorf Goodman in New York.

> ❑ 2002, October. To celebrate twenty years of sales of his jewelry at Bergdorf Goodman, the president of the chain organized a retrospective of Morelli's work, which included the diamond necklace designed to celebrate the occasion by Morelli's wife, Darci Kistler.

Moreni Popi (1947). Italian designer, trained in France. In her youth, after studying fashion and costume in Turin, she went to Paris and entered the design studio of Maïmé Arnodin. In 1967, at the age of just 17, she was taken on by Promostyle to oversee its womenswear. In 1973 she set up her own consultancy service for textile makers and the prêt-a-porter industry. Three years later she started her career as a designer with her own boutique at Les Halles. In 1979 she presented a complete collection which earned her a contract with the mail-order company 3 Suisses, designing clothes for men, women, and children. In 1988 her career flourished further when she was taken on by the mail-order giant, La Redoute.

> ❑ 1997. Moreni won the Cosmetique News Prize for best perfume, her eponymous fragrance having been launched the previous year.

Moretti Luca (1967). Italian designer. Moretti was first noted on the Milan runways in summer 2001 with a collection which thoughtfully combined fabrics such as Lycra, organza, silk, and elasticised satins. In March

2003 he showed at Milano Moda Donna. His work aims to elaborate on contemporary fashion using sophisticated means.

Morgano Knitwear manufacturer. Founded in 1969 by Giovanni Bessegato in Badoere di Morgano in the Italian province of Treviso, the company specialises in the production of men's and women's knitwear, made from merino wool, and dyed once assembled. In the 1980s Bessegato's sons, Alessandro and Andrea, joined the firm. A line of children's clothing was launched, and meanwhile cashmere became a staple of the menswear and womenswear ranges. More than a million items are produced every year for the three ranges, Morgano, Morgano Junior and Lineamidas. 25% of production is bought by the Italian market, the remainder being distributed in North and South America, Europe, Australia, and the Far East. The company employs 84 staff and yearly sales average around 18 million euros.

❑ 2002. Morgano launched itself in Eastern Europe with the first stores opening in Poznan and Bratislava.

Morganti Walter (1922). Tailor for Catagneto Carducci, specializing in hunting wear, heavy *casentino* wool coats, and gentlemen's countrywear. He hails from a dynasty which included Gioacchino Morganti (known as "Ventunpelo") and his uncle Antonio, and which is rooted in the tradition of the tailors of Maremma so praised by the young Giosuè Carducci: Domenico Raffaelli, Giosuè Mati, Ferdinando Ambrogi, Francesco Borsi, and Pietro Fazzini. In 1911 Antonio opened a workshop that doubled as a tailor's and barber's shop, calling it "Arte e Moda. Fratelli Morganti." The barber's shop did not survive, but Walter measured, cut and sewed in the same shop which saw the passing through of the Italian elite, such as Della Gherardesca, Antinori, Incisa, and some of the great names in entertainment, including Marcello Mastroianni. In 1996 Walter, while remaining involved in the tailoring business, handed over management of the firm to Czech Florin Cristea.

Mori Hanae (1926). Japanese designer known for her butterfly emblem. Born in Shimane in Japan, after studying at the Catholic university in Tokyo, she turned to the creation of fashion. At the end of the war she married fabric manufacturer Ken Mori, who joined forces with his wife to open a small shop in Tokyo in 1955. In this period she specialized in film costumes, working with famous directors such as Ozu, Kurosawa, and Oshima. In the early 1960s she met Coco Chanel, and then decided to concentrate on *haute couture*. She presented her first collection in 1968 in New York, where she also opened a boutique. Nine years later she opened her *haute couture* house in Paris and became the first Japanese designer to become a member of the Chambre Syndicale of Paris fashion. In Tokyo, one of the other capitals in her empire, she and her two children looked after the running of the Mori Group, which expanded from clothing to include accessories, and household accessories. Her style is a mixture of Japanese traditionalism and European tailoring: most famous are her evening dresses which are often made from exclusive silks and reinterpret the traditional form of the kimono.

(*Anna Gloria Forti*)

❑ 2003. The Hanae Mori Studio range became the responsibility of Mori's daughter-in-law, Pamela Mori. Hanae still looks after the financial management of the four billion dollar empire, based in Omotesando.

Mori Ilario. Italian designer. The son of a tailor, he has designed ready-to-wear clothing for men since 1995. Having lived for some time in London at the height of the Punk era, the use of vinyl and plastic in his clothes belies a degree of influence from this period, without taking it to extremes. He now has an important base in Paris, with a showroom in Rue de la Roquette.

Morin-Blossier French tailoring workshop, active in the late-nineteenth and early-twentieth centuries, the creations of which may be found in numerous museums today. The founders Victoire Morin and Marie Blossier moved to Paris from Vienna some time after 1878, and were at the height of their success between 1885 and 1905. They specialized in the clothing of the court, which was heavily influenced by the fashions of Middle Europe, and became tailors to

Queen Maud of Norway, Queen Alexandra of England, Queen Margherita of Italy, Queen Alexandra of Denmark, and the Russian Tsarinas. The workshop closed down after World War I.

Morlotti Dominique (1950). French designer. Born in Paris, he entered the world of fashion after studying Classics at university. In 1975 he trained with Ted Lapidus before moving to work as assistant to Popy Moreni. In the 1980s he was in charge of menswear at both Balmain and Dior. In 1990 he set up on his own, and two years later Lanvin took him on as Artistic Director. Since 1996, he has been principly occupied with men's *prêt-à-porter*. An eclectic creator, he has even composed some of the music for Lanvin's runway shows.

❑ 2001. Morlotti left Lanvin menswear, having ceased to work on their womenswear collections six years earlier. He continued to work independently. The eclectic designer composed soundtracks for his own runway shows. He also worked on costumes for the film *3/O* with Gérard Lanvin and Samuel le Bihan.
❑ 2003, June. He deserted the Paris runways for the Spring-Summer 2004 shows, opting instead, like many of his colleagues, for a private show.

Morra Anna (1962). Italian designer born in Milan. Before starting as a designer, she worked as a model, fashion editor, fashion scout, and freelance stylist. From 1988 to 1993 she lived by the Nile, and the fruits of all her fashion experience were revealed in her womenswear and accessories collection which she designed during this period in Egypt. In 1998 she brought out a range of swimwear, characterized by high-quality materials and without fastenings, for maximum comfort.

Morris Lee Robert (1947). American jeweler of German origin. He was the founder of the Artwear Gallery in New York, which he ran from 1977 to 1993. His first works were exhibited in the Sculpture to Wear gallery, which opened in New York in 1972 and specialized in art jewelry. His first creations, very modern in both style and form, were based on primitive motifs. Fascinated by the symbols of magic and ritual, he created artworks on a grand scale. Later he became involved in the fashion world, with jewelry collections for famous designers such as Donna Karan.

Morrow Hamish (1968). English designer born in South Africa. Having enrolled for Central Saint Martin's in 1989, he was unable to finish his course due to the need to find work. He only returned to his studies in 1996, at the Royal College of Art. After his Masters, he joined the creative team at the Italian fashion house Byblos, under English designer John Bartlett. He returned to London in 2000 to set up his own business. He continued to work as a fashion consultant, including among his clients Louis Feraud, Top Shop, and Kangol. His women's *prêt-à-porter* collection demonstrated strong links with contemporary British art and he gained important recognition on the London runways. Loved by the Radical Chic scene in America, the F.I.T. has displayed his clothes, and New York store Henri Bendel organized displays in the shop, dedicating entire windows on Fifth Avenue to his work. His clothes are sold world-wide and are popular with the most fashionable actresses.

Mortensen Erik (1926). Danish designer. He began his career with Holher Blom, who was tailor to the Danish royal family. He worked with Pierre Balmain from 1948 and became his number two in 1960. When the French designer died in 1982, Mortensen became chief designer at the maison, winning two Dé d'Or in 1983 and 1987. In 1992 he became Artistic Director at Scherrer.

Morton Digby (1906-1983). Irish designer, active from 1928 to 1957. At the age of 22, having just completed his studies in art and architecture, he was taken on by Lachasse. He stayed there only till 1933, when he decided to open his own workshop which, after the war, produced mainly for the ready-made clothing industry. His skill was to transform the traditional cuts of tailoring, making them softer, adapting them to his styles, and using unusual materials.

Moscheni Francesca (1963). Italian photographer. Graduated in stage design at Milan's Accademia di Brera, with a thesis on the photographer Gianni Berengo Gardin. In 1985 she became a professional photographer, working at *Harper's Bazaar*, *Bazaar Uomo*, and *West*, providing reportage and portraits. She continued to work in these areas while extending her portfolio to still-lifes and interiors. In 1989 she returned to work more directly with fashion, researching the images for the exhibition *Uomini Made*, fashion images for *Uomo Vogue* and *Per Lui*, and producing fashion reports, catalogues, and advertising campaigns. She works for various agencies and titles. She specializes in projects that allow her to produce exhibitions on her own and collaboratively, and their accompanying catalogues.

Moschino Franco (1950-1994). He was the enfant terrible of Italian fashion, and lived on after his death from Aids following 10 years of success with his label. An iconoclastic designer who never wanted to be known as such, he arrived at the top by overturning all the rules: of good taste, style, advertising, presentations, and runway shows. Franco Moschino studied Fine Arts at the Accademia di Brera in Milan. He planned to be a painter, but his role as an illustrator for Versace in 1971 set him on the fashion road. In 1977 he was fashion designer for the historic Italian label Cadette, where he honed his skills and developed his own precise stylistic language. In 1983 he started up his own label, with an explosive mix of paradoxes, challenges, and elegance which criticized and mocked the excesses of the fashion system and the paroxysmal society which was the image of the 1980s. His style was ironic, surreal, ingenious, and perverse. It declared "Stop the fashion system," but its success was of course thanks to that system. A theorist of freedom and improvisation, he claimed not to be an inventor, but a "restaurant trying to provide those well-cooked traditional dishes which were invented by unknown cooks." His work did indeed revisit all the aesthetics of the century, adopting and reworking them with a hybrid injection of humor. He replaced the buttons of Chanel-style suits with windmills, and embroidered black sheath dresses with their price. He made

Moschino: drawing for the exhibition *L'abito oltre la moda*, Palazzo Fortuny, Venice 1991.

skirts out of ties, jackets with fried eggs on the pockets, T-shirts emblazoned "Moschifo" (*schifo* means "disgusting" in Italian), dressed printed with the words "no dress no stress," tops with *trompe-l'oeil* breasts, shirts with multiple sleeves, multicolored blazers, waistcoats printed with cartoons, suits with appliquéd symbols of geese, Andalusian skirts made out of tartan, and toreador-style evening jackets. His personal style, despite

Moschino, Fall-Winter Collection 1987-1988.

being unpredictable and striking, was in fact based on classic, well-made shapes, perfectly cut and with seductive details which proved attractive to all markets. The first line to be launched was Moschino Couture, and soon after came Cheap & Chic, Donna and Uomo, Moschino Jeans, lingerie, swimwear, bags, scarves, jewelry, perfume, all of which broke with fashion clichés. Publications, advertisements, and runway shows were similarly full of surprises: He would send pairs of knickers to actresses instead of invitations, he made his models go down the runway on their knees, he appeared in his own adverts in disguise, and created a fake Cardinal to promote his range of jeans. He created a scent for men with a two-headed bottle, and his women's fragrance was provided with a drinking straw. He published Dadaist catalogues and created every kind of provocative entertainment imaginable, saying "There is no creativity without chaos. The Moschino concept is based on complete freedom of choice. There are no rules. You wear whatever color you want, and if you still like what you were wearing last year, you can wear it this year, and next year if you want." All of this of course rang a strange note in a period where *prêt-à-porter* ruled, and labels dictated fashion. Late 1993 saw the retrospective *Ten Years of Chaos* at the Permanente di Milano. The show was a journey through thousands of Moschino's creative anomalies, culminating in an exhibition of paintings where the designer revealed to the public for the first time his original persona, that of painter. The exhibition was held at the end of 10 years of the life and work of this *enfant terrible* of Italian fashion, who in this short period had left an indelible mark on the world which he so wanted to challenge, becoming himself a cult figure, and obtaining cult status for his clothes. He died in September 1994. His staff, under the leadership of his closest collaborator, Rossella Jardini, have continued his work and succeeded in the miracle of consolidating the success of the Moschino brand. In Fall 1999, the label was taken over by the Ferretti group. (*Gisella Borioli*)

Prêt-à-jouer will always be the way for Moschino. The range continues to produce the thousand anomalies which continue, as in the past, to turn some items into genuine status symbols. Irony and unbridled fantasy go hand-in-hand, particularly in the Cheap & Chic diffusion line. One style, many styles, for those with more enthusiasm than money. Fashion as the art of putting an outfit together in total freedom. Blazers with no buttons which fasten with a safety-pin, or sprinkles of sequins on patched pants. 2002 saw the memorable "On the road" men's collection, combining vintage pieces with sports and formalwear. This was a paradoxical look, covering every possibility, whilst contradicting everything with which we were familiar – an ingeniously invented and delightful disorder. The same approach was taken for the womenswear collections: The cheeky winter 2003-2004 show saw a complete mechanic's overall decorated with frills, and a necklace made out of a metal spring-catch. (*Lucia Mari*)

❑ 2002, May. In a joint venture with Bluebell Far East (49.9%), Moschino (50.1%) created Moschino Far East, to aid distribution in the Far Eastern market, including Japan. Sales of 70 million euros were envisaged by 2006. This is an agreement that seals the long collaboration between these two businesses: Bluebell has been distributor for Moschino in the East since 1989, apart from in Japan, where distribution has been managed until now by Sanki Shoji.
❑ 2002, July. Licensing contract with Sector to produce a collection of watches under the name of Moschino. The Sector Group (with 15 production partners world wide) had 150 employees and sales of around 90 million euros in 2001. It was responsible for around 14% of watch-making in Italy.
❑ 2003. The Moschino label celebrated its 20th birthday. The first Parisian store (with seven windows) was opened at 32 Rue de Grenelle, in the 7th arrondissement, and a shop was opened in central Moscow, in the Petrovsky Passage Mall. The Moschino brand has a distribution network of 24 dedicated stores, and 31 franchises in department stores. Shares in Moschino Spa are held

70% by Aeffe and 30% by Sportswear International, and in 2001 sales equaled 285 million euros.

❑ 2003, July. Launch in the Rome store of the new Moschino watches, the heart-shaped "Time 4 love" and "Time 4 Peace." Each has charms representing symbols of peace, love, a lucky horn, and the initial "M" of the late designer. "I love 4 ways" has a linked chain, inspired by old pocket watches. "I love Moschino" has a leather strap, and "My name is Moschino" a traditional metal strap.

❑ 2004, October. Vincent Darré, head of creation and development of the Moschino collection from 2001 to 2004 left the label to become artistic director at Emanuel Ungaro, taking over the post of Giambattista Valli.

Moses Rebecca (1956). American designer, born in New Jersey. Having graduated in New York from the Fashion Institute of Technology, she began her career as a designer with a sportswear collection launched at dedicated runway shows. In 1993 she moved to Italy and signed a contract with Genny, designing for Genny Collection and Genny Platinum. In 1996 she launched her own first line of *prêt-à-porter* clothes and accessories, concentrating on simple sophisticated knitwear made from the highest quality materials. Cashmere became the key element of her collections, created for every season, and in 36 shades. Since 1998 she has dedicated herself exclusively to her own range. She is one of the directors of the Council of Fashion Designers of America and a member of the Italian National Chamber of Fashion. (*Silvia Martinenghi*)

❑ 2002, November. Rebecca Moses canceled her Spring-Summer 2003 collection due to disagreement with Herno Marenzi. Differing opinions on how to conduct a growth strategy for the brand threatened to damage the image of the Rebecca Moses name, which at that point was looking for new partners.

❑ 2002, November. Rebecca Moses was appointed Creative Director at Pineider and redesigned the entire range of products. The Tuscan company, which became part of the Hopa Group in 2000, has undertaken a big re-branding exercise, which began with the re-styling of the historic Florence store in Piazza Signoria. In addition to the visiting cards, writing paper and invitations traditionally produced by the business, now there are sophisticated objects from the designer's collection. She has studied various ranges produced by the house, which was loved by Stendhal and Byron, and reinterpreted them with simplicity and elegance. The range now includes products for children and babies, for the home (tableware and linen, pieces of furniture, tartans, vases, perfumes and essences, candles, picture frames), and for travel (leatherwear, handbags, totes, weekend bags, and even bags for laptops and wicker baskets for picnics).

Moshammer Rudolph (1945). German tailor. Began at 22, working only on men's clothing and opening a shop in Munich. Three years later, he started to work also on womenswear. He is difficult to categorize among the traditionalists, and precisely for this reason, he has earned a certain reputation.

❑ 1995. He published his autobiography *Mama und Ich*. On the cover, the mother of the designer is seen with an electric blue head of hair.

❑ 2003, December. Moshammer created a diamond swimsuit in honour of the 60th birthday of *Holiday on Ice*. The famous German ice spectacular asked the designer to create the bejewelled outfits to be worn by the female cast members of the show from December 25th.

Moss Kate (1974). Supermodel. Born in England in Croydon, Surrey. Hazelnut eyes, light brown hair, 1 metre 69 centimetres tall. She was discovered at the age of 14 in New York's JFK airport by Sarah Doukas from Storm model agency. Her first job was for the cover for of the English monthly magazine, *The Face*, where she appeared topless. Her minute frame (some wondered if she were even anorexic) and her childlike face made her one of the iconic models of the 1990s (she was Fashion Personality of the Year in 1995). She was continuously photographed, not just for the her own fashion sense, which mixed *haute couture* with her own individuality, but also because of her romance with American actor Johnny Depp, and stories of drug-taking and alcoholism. In September 2002 she had a daughter, Lola, with her partner Jefferson Hack, a publisher. She has done runway shows and advertising campaigns for the biggest fashion names, and her image is particularly linked with the perfumes of Calvin Klein. (*Silvia Paoli*)

Mossant French producers of men's hats. Founded in Bourg-de-Péage in 1833, the company is now more than a century and a half old. Starting life as a small workshop, it became, thanks to Charles and Casimir Mossant, the sons of its founder, a factory with enough partners and money to make new investments and increase the range of products. In the 1930s, the Mossant name was almost as famous as that as the Italian Borsalino. The level of production bears witness to this: 2000 felt hats a day were absorbed by the French, American, Spanish, and Soviet markets. Well into the post-war period, as use and fashion for head-gear declined, Mossant filled the gap in its income by beginning to make mass-produced clothing.

Mother-of-pearl The inner surface of some types of shell. Iridescent with tints of pink, blue, and gray, it is most commonly used to make buttons but also some accessories. It can be ground down and used in make-up, particularly eye-shadows and lipsticks.

Mottola Molfino Alessandra (1939). Art scholar and fashion historian. Particularly known for her research since 1967, first as curator, and then director of the Poldi Pezzoli museum in Milan. She was responsible for the organization, installation, and catalogues of various exhibitions. These include: *I pizzi: moda e simbolo* (1977); *1922-1943: vent'anni di moda italiana* (1980); and *Gioielli. Moda. Magia. Sentimento* (1986). From 1979 to 1989 she was also in charge of the scientific cataloguing of the museum's collections, during which she personally documented the collections of woven fabrics, lace, and embroidery. Her research into textiles led to her founding, with other academics, the Centro italiano per lo Studio della Storia del Tessuto (Cisst), of which she became the first president. She collaborated with the municipality of Venice in 1980 to set up the Lace Museum on the island of Burano. Six years later she was one of a group of organizers of the exhibition on the history of dress at Munich's Stadtmuseum, *Anziehungskrafte. Varieté de la Mode 1786-1986*. In 1987 she was one of the writers of the two-volume *La Moda Italiana*, published by Electa. She also participated in the review *Gianni Versace: l'abito per pensare* in 1989. With Grazietta Butazzi she produced the nine-volume series *Idee di Moda* published by De Agostini in 1991 and 1992. She planned and organized the new fashion documentation centre, Moda Documentata in Milan. In 1995 she became part of the Milanese cultural commission for the care and valuation of decorative arts. She now is one of the directors of Milan Municipality's Culture and Museums section, collaborating with Claudio Salsi, the Director of Civic Collections of Decorative Arts, in the creation of new textiles and fashion spaces at the Castello Sforzesco. (*Franco Belli*)

Mouclier Jacques. President, since 1991, of the Chambre Syndicale de la Couture, of which he had previously been Acting President for 20 years. Before him this role was bestowed solely on couturiers. Since the end of the 1970s, he has been equally involved in fashion and table arts. He organises the *Journées de la mode*, and was involved in the planning of the Maison de la mode which was established in 1993. He is also the founding President of the Centre International des Arts de la Table and Vice President of the Union Français des Arts du Costume.

Mouflon or muflone. A fabric used mostly for coats. It is has a long pile, and is very dense, warm and soft. Its name comes from that of the wild sheep, similar to a goat, which lives in remote areas of southern Europe.

Moukhina Vera (1889-1953). Russian sculptress and costumier. She worked in partnership with the designer Nadejda Pétrovna Lamanova at Moscow's Atelier of Modern Dress. Here she presented individual and original creations: hats and scarves of geometric design, sculptural dresses made out of plastic. The sketches of her clothes were published in the fashion magazines *Krasnaia*, *Niva*, and *Atelier*. In the mid-1920s, Moukhina frequented institutions where experimental modern Russian dress was being produced, such as the fashion atelier and the dress section of the Academy of Fine Arts in Moscow. The printed and embroidered fabrics produced from her designs reflected the new aesthetic criteria which gave preference to the dynamic use of geometric figures. Her creations were presented in Paris at the Exposition des Arts Décoratifs in 1925. In 1933 she became a member of the artistic committee of Moscow's fashion chamber.

Moura Alexandra (1973). Portuguese designer. Born in Lisbon, she completed her studies at IADEM, (Instituto de artes visuales, diseño y marketing). She collaborated actively with Ana Salazar and José Antonio Tenente. In 2000 she was invited to attend Optimum, a forum for new cultural trends and Portuguese fashion. She returned there the following year, presenting her Fall-Winter 2001-2002 collection. From October 2001, she began to promote her work through Loja Modalisboa-design. Her outfits are striking for their refined urban style, based on traditional methods, and on the use of simple materials.

(*Estefania Ruilope Ruiz*)

Mouret Roland (1961). French designer. Born in Lourdes, he started his career in France, as an artistic director, model, and stylist. In the 1980s he moved to London, working in the fields of music and art. At this same time he created the label People Corporation and opened the Freedom Café in Soho. In February 1998 he presented his first collection at London Fashion Week. He won the British Designer of the Year prize at the Elle Style Awards 2002, and the Vidal Sassoon Cutting Edge Award. His style is one of the major exponents of what might be described as semi-couture: a fashion comprised of unique pieces, with highly-worked details and an emphasis on drapery, cut, silhouette, and the putting together of the fabrics. In 2003, in addition to his primary range, he also designed jeans, knitwear, leatherwear and accessories. He also launched Rm Rough, a jewelry collection with uncut diamonds. His workshop is on the famous Kings Road.

Mozzillo Angelo (1965). Italian designer and entrepreneur. Born in Caserta into a family of textile producers, he studied Fashion Design Management at the Domus Academy in Milan. In 1995 he founded his company in his hometown, where he produced and distributed women's *prêt-à-porter* clothing. His products were produced by high-quality businesses and traditional workshops, and distributed through shops and department stores, such as Bergdorf Goodman in the USA, Walter Gross in Zurich, and Veneto in Cannes. In 1998 he opened a showroom in Milan in Via Montenapoleone. He also designs *haute couture* fashion which he shows in Rome.

❑ 2003, January. For his début at AltaModaRoma, he presented a hybrid woman – half bird and half fish. Her clothing adorned with studs, she represented a living contrast between punk and hedonism.

❑ 2003, July. Mozzillo presented his new collection entitled *Tacchi metropolitani* (Metropolitan heels) at Hadrian's Temple. Against a minimal backdrop of a single tree with crystal branches, and a suspended sculpture, he showed 21 outfits inspired by 1970s punk. 32 workshops had worked to produce these 21 outfits, and the single *haute couture* pieces were produced in limited editions of between 1 and 15 items. With sales of around 5 million euros, and a distribution network of 120 sales points (12 of which are in Italy), Mozzillo is now aiming mostly for *prêt-à-porter* sales abroad, particularly in the USA and Japan.

Mr. Alzie Pseudonym and label of the black American milliner. It was in the middle of his career that his creations were at their most varied, from models of sober elegance, to those of a more audacious and innovative form. His creations are included in the collections of the Black Fashion Museum in New York, and the Philadelphia Museum of Art.

Mr. Fish Label of the English designer Michael Fish. Born in London, he began his career modestly as an errand boy for a haberdasher's. He then became an apprentice with New and Linwood who provided the shirts for Eton College. In the early 1960s, he was taken on as a designer at Jermyn Street shirt-makers Turnbull and Asser, and brought a wave of modernity into this very traditional world. These were the years of Pop Art and psychedelic art, and he designed shirts in gaudy colors and striking designs. His shirts with fish-shaped ties in matching fabrics were a huge success among the more audacious London gentlemen. He opened his own boutique in 1966 with the help of Barry Sainsbury. He chose an address close to Savile Row, remaining in the right part of town to keep close to his loyal customers. The show was soon being visited by all of "Swinging London," from the Duke of Bedford and Lord Sainsbury to David Bailey and Mick Jagger, who wore one of his mini-shirts performing at a Rolling Stones concert in Hyde Park. He dressed the actor Terence Stamp exclusively in Liberty prints for the cult film *Modesty Blaise*. In 1967 and 1968 his clothing, like all fashion in that period, took on a more ethnic, hippy look. He worked with shot silks, organza, embroidery, and pearls. In 1969 he published a sartorial treatise entitled *Doing your own thing*, in which he argued against the rigid rules of English sartorial tradition, and in favor of a new individuality. He continued however to swing between the old England and the new, with his modern clothing of the very highest quality. (*Virginia Hill*)

Mr. Pearl Ready-to-wear fashion label named after a South African designer who moved to London's East End in the 1980s to work at the Royal Opera House as costume designer. Mr Pearl created corsets for Mugler, Dior, Ferré, and Galliano. These literally took one's breath away, and were inspired by those belonging to his great grandmother, who was a dressmaker during the Belle Époque. Designed after rigorous study of anatomy and the history of dress, the refined and theatrical corsets of Mr Pearl are real works of art. He declared "I am trying to capture a dream; to create a beauty so strong as to seem unbelievable. My corsets are nothing to do with the real world, they are other-worldly." The designer, who likes to wear his own corsets, has worked in recent years for John Galliano, Alexander McQueen, Thierry Mugler, Antonio Berardi, and Christian Lacroix. He reached pop celebrity status when he created the corset worn by Spice Girl Victoria Adams for her marriage to footballer David Beckham.

Muehling Ted (1953). American jewelry maker. His works are worn as sculptures on the body, and it is their form which is their most striking aspect. He graduated in industrial design at the Pratt Institute in Brooklyn. He specializes in copper- and bronzework. Known in particular for his gilded pod-shaped earrings of 1981, he has worked for the Artwear Gallery with Robert Lee Morris.

Mugler Thierry (1948). French tailor. Having worked in 1965-1966 for the Opera de Rhin in his native Strasbourg, he moved from dance to fashion in 1967. In 1970 he designed the collection "Café de Paris," and by 1974, his boutique Gudule had become the most fashionable in Paris. He founded a fashion house in his own name, and became its owner in 1986. Since 1990 he has also created perfumes. Eclectic and curious, he finds his influences in history, automobile bodies (particularly American cars of the 1970s), and cinema (the Hollywood of Busby Berkeley and Edith Head). He creates corsets for Madonna and mini-dresses for Sharon Stone. Celebrated for his ironic and post-modern style, he is also a photographer, and is well-known for his shots of his own clothes in the baroque heart of Prague. In 1988 he published a book, *Thierry Mugler Photograph*, in which fashion experts underline his explosive glamour. His clothes have a defined structure, despite some theatrical and deliberate "body conscious" exaggerations of proportion (wide shoulders, slim waist). He was tailor to Daniel Mitterand. (*Laura Salza*)

❑ 2000. Thierry Mugler decided to abandon his work as a fashion designer and devoted himself completely to the creation of perfumes, among the most famous of which is *Angel*. Created in

1992 in collaboration with Clarins, it fought for pole position with the mythical *Chanel No. 5*.
❑ 2002, December. The Clarins Group was on the point of giving up Mugler's *prêt-à-porter* and *haute couture* ranges, the company having registered losses of 476,000 euros in the first half of the year. The perfume sector, however, remained safe.
❑ 2003, June. Thierry Mugler Couture closes down. Clarins confirmed that the Maison Balmain has taken over 4 of the 7 boutiques, as well as the factory in Saint Barthélemy d'Anjou, near Angers. Clarins maintained ownership of the Mugler label and of perfume production.
❑ 2003, July. The Clarins Group stated that the factory in Saint-Denis La Plaine had ceased production, but that Thierry Mugler Couture, and Mugler leather goods, glasses, and jewelry would continued to be produced under license. The 5-year license for menswear with Tombolini was renewed, while a decision on the license of *prêt-à-porter* womenswear was still awaited. Tombolini planed to take over the Paris store Thierry Mugler Homme and the two in-store shops at Galeries Lafayette and Madelios.

Muir Jean (1928-1995). English designer. She was known for her fluid and feminine silhouettes, and a preference for jersey and suede which took traditional workmanship to the next level. Born in London, she rose through the ranks and learned her trade on the job. She was taken on by Liberty in 1950 as a warehouse assistant, promoted to store cashier, and finally to designer. She was then taken on by Jaeger, where she remained from 1956 to 1961, the year in which she set up her own label, Jane & Jane. She founded her business in 1966, by which time her pure, classic style had already been established. Her clothes were known for their carefully worked detail, and striking, almost always uniform color. Her sense of elegance combined with a guaranteed comfort ensured that her collections appealed to the most refined ladies. In 1980 Leeds City Art Gallery published the monograph *Jean Muir*.

Muji Japanese chain of shops, gradually spreading in Europe and America. It produces its own brand which includes stationery, bags, and clothing, all of which is characterised by a very Japanese minimalist style. In Japanese, Mujirushi Ryohin means "no brand, good quality." In Japan there are now more than 200 shops. In the UK, there are 7 in London, 1 in Manchester (opened 1998), and 1 in Kent (opened 1999). Muji can also be found in France and North America. Since 2003, 5 more shops have opened in Europe.

❑ 2003, February. Controlled by the Ryohin Keikaku group, Muji planned to sell a range of clothing designed by Yohji Yamamoto. A range of furniture and household goods, designed by famous names, was planned for the future. In a new plan of retail expansion, a further 15 new stores were planned to open in Japan, in addition to the 270 existing retail points.
❑ 2004, December. The first Italian store of the Japanese chain opened in Milan at 36 Corso Buenos Aires. It follows Great Britain, France, Ireland, and Sweden, where Muji has been present for several years.

Mulas Ugo (1928-1973). Born in Pozzolengo near Brescia, Italy. He died in Milan where he had lived and worked. He was one of the icons of Italian post-war photography. He was a man blessed with a strong classical education, and high and humane intelligence. He began to take photographs while he was still a law student, but soon abandoned his studies in favor of a course at the Accademia di Belle Arti. He spent much time around the Brera area, and at the Bar Giamaica, above which he rented a room with his friend Mario Dondero, who would later become a well-known reporter in Paris. Mulas' first photographic report covered the 1954 Venice Biennale (he would continue to report on it until 1972). His interest in art, important to him not least because it led to his friendships with the likes of Lucio Fontana and Alberto Giacometti, was equalled by his interest in reportage, photographing the suburbs and rebuilt areas of post-war Milan in an expressive black-and-white. In his studio, he worked on advertising, documentaries and also in the theater, working with Giorgio Strehler and Piccolo on various shows, the most symbolic of which was, in 1964, Brecht's *La vita di Galileo.* He traveled memorably to Russia and around Europe for *L'Illustrazione Italiana*, *Settimo Giorno*, *Rivista Pirelli*, and also for New York publications, between 1964 and 1967, where he came into contact with soon-to-be famous artists such as Andy Warhol, Frank Stella, Christo, and Robert Rauschemberg. Everybody was struck by the intuitive capability which allowed Mulas to photograph the works of these artists in a way that conveyed their spirit. He brought the same manner to the world of fashion. His first job was with Mila Schön, who was enchanted by Mulas' ability to interpret her designs with a creativity combined with very careful composition. Mulas, whose work was published in *Vogue* and *Novità* (working for Krizia, Valentino, Biki, Tricò, Forquet, and La Rinascente) often made artistic references in his work, placing models and clothes among the sculptures of Moore and Cascella, or using jewelry designed by Arnaldo Pomodoro or Jean Cocteau, in addition to work with artists and designers, such as Mila Schön and Lucio Fontana. In the last two years of his life, he dedicated himself to the creation of *Verifiche*, a conceptual work focusing on the language and the essence of photography.

Mulassano Adriana (1939). Journalist. She started her career on the editorial team of *Amica* in 1961. In 1968 she moved to the *Corriere della Sera* newspaper, where she remained until 1986, when she took over the editorship of *Linea Capital*. Here she told the story of Italian fashion, helped new designers make their names, and promoted the Milan fashion shows, contrasting them with those in Paris. Her articles, written with a language free of the clichés so often used by those in the fashion industry, were imbued with a great mastery of the industry, and an ability to pick out the real "next big thing" as soon as it had appeared. Anyone wishing to find a complete account of the history of Italian fashion need only turn to her writing at the height of her career. In 1979 she published *I Mass Moda / Storia e personaggi dell'italian look* (published by Spinelli), which told the stories of the protagonists of Italian fashion, from Albini to Fiorucci, from Armani to Miguel Cruz, Quirino Conti and Ferragamo, all accompanied by photos by Alfa Castaldi. At the end of the 1980s, after returning to the *Corriere della Sera*, she gave up journalism to work in the Armani Press Office, eventually concentrating solely on the fashion house's major events.

Mulberry Accessories brand founded in 1971 by Roger Saul. The optimism of his 21 years, some help from his mother, and a small saving of five hundred pounds was enough to get him started. Under the symbol of the shady foliage of the Mulberry tree, Mulberry was among the first companies to establish an authentic British outdoor style. The happy combination of both high-quality and high-resistance fabrics helped to establish the brand world-wide. Having started with a range of belts, and especially bags, aimed at lovers of the outdoors, from 1975 the range of products was extended to clothing and household furnishings.

❑ 2000. The investment company Singapore Challice Ltd (Ong Beng Seng and his wife Christina Ong), which also owns Singapore's Club 21, and the franchises for Armani in England and Armani Exchange in the United States, bought 41.5% of Mulberry.
❑ 2001. Pre-tax losses of 1.7 million pounds (2.7 million euros). Challice invested 7.6 million pounds to re-launch the brand, including the reopening of the Bond Street store in London.
❑ 2002, December. In the first half of 2002 the gross loss was 1.05 million pounds, despite an increase in sales to 13.3 millions, a 10% increase on 2001.

Mule Style of shoe where the heel is left uncovered, this being its only similarity to a bedroom slipper. Mules have always been decorative footwear: brocade and velvet in the 17th century, babouche-style in the 18th, and satin in the 19th. In the 20th century they became virtually ubiquitous: high-heeled goddess fashions in the 1950s, ethnic in the 1980s, and in the 1990s, spangled with glass-beads, seed-pearls and sequins. Since summer 2002 they have once again become *haute couture*.

Munich Fabric Start Fabric fair which opened in Munich in February 2003. The show incorporated the Euroruch exhibition, which had previously taken place in Cologne, and was a key reference point for clothing manufacturers in Germany and Eastern Europe. Seven hundred collections were shown by manufacturers (75%) and their agents (25%), from Italy, France, Switzerland, England, Scotland, and naturally, Germany. Also a wide range of accessories and yarns in the Munich Yarn Show. On the inaugural day of the fair, a forum was held on current trends, hosted by the styling agency Peclers Paris.

Munich Fashion Fair Fair held in Munich, Bavaria, specializing in high-quality menswear and aimed at German buyers. After the great success of its opening in 2003, it has moved to the new venue the "Carrea." Held twice a year, in January and July, at the second fair in July 2003 the number of collections presented doubled from 80 to 150. Scheduled immediately after the Pitti Immagine Uomo tradeshow, it represents the first opportunity to present men's fashions to the German market.

Munkacsi Martin. Pseudonym of Martin Marmorstein (1896-1963). Hungarian photographer. Worked mostly in the United States. Always took photographs from a completely original angle, for example, outside, in the water, or from a vehicle at high speed, all of which made him a master and were imitated by many photographers of subsequent generations, from Avedon to Horvat. His style took the name of "realism in movement." He began his career in Hungary as a journalist for the sporting journal *AZ Est*, for which he produced such innovative and dynamic photographs that he soon became considered the top Hungarian sports photojournalist. This explains very well the bold perspectives and the dynamic style that he then applied to his fashion photography. He lived for some time in Berlin, but with the rise of the Nazis, moved to New York in 1934. It was here that he caused a sensation with his first fashion shoot, which was published in 1933 in *Harper's Bazaar*, a magazine with which he went on to have a long relationship. The photo shows a young woman, healthy and fit, running down a beach in a bathing suit. He also published pictures in the *Berliner Illustrierte Zeitung* (whilst living in Berlin), *Ladies Home Journal*, *Life*, and *Town and Country*. Munkacsi's originality made him a much-followed master, both by artists dedicated to fashion, such as Richard Avedon, and by photojournalists like Henri Cartier-Bresson. In "his" New York, both the Museum of Modern Art, in 1975, and the International Center of Photography, in 1978, held important retrospectives of his work, and in 1996 the Magyar Fotografiai museum in Budapest held the exhibition Munkacsi Munkacsi. (*Angela Madesani*)

Murakami Takashi (1962). Japanese artist and designer. Born in Tokyo, he lives and works between Paris and Japan. His artistic début was in the world of "manga" (Japanese comics) and of "anime" (cartoons). He began his career with a well-known animation studio, but immediately decided to return to university to study Nihonga, a traditional form of Japanese painting from the 19th century. In 1991 he obtained a doctorate at TODAI (the prestigious National College of Fine Arts and Music at Tokyo University) and continued by pursuing contemporary art, soon becoming a guru of the Japanese New Wave, and a high profile figure in Neo Pop. His first exhibition was called Takashi, Tamiya. In 1992 he produced his virtual image: This is the famous *Mr Dob*, a blue puppet resembling Mickey Mouse, with a huge head and eyes popping out of their sockets. The character, despite his demonic appearance, could also be good, and brought to mind the old "manga" characters of the 1970s. *Mr Dob* (an abbreviation of "dobojite," which means "because") lived in his own world, completely divorced from reality, and according to Murakami was meant as an emblem of the anti-consumerist movement. The character then became the trademark with which Murakami branded his products, from T-shirts to watches. In 1994 a bursary took him to New York, where he was invited by the Rockerfeller Foundation Asian Cultural Council to take part in their International

Student Program. The next year, he returned to Japan where in 1996 he founded Hiropon Factory, a clear homage to Warhol and a production studio for his own works, and those of young up-and-coming artists (painters, musicians, and photographers). In 1998 he was invited to teach in Los Angeles at the UCLA Art Department. In 2001 in Tokyo and California he presented the exhibition Superflat – a compendium of his artistic creations. In the essay *A Theory of Superflat Japanese Art*, he argued that the formal characteristics of classical Japanese art may be found in contemporary cartoon art, and he highlighted the continuity between traditional art and the Abstract Expressionism of Pollock or the Pop Art of Andy Warhol. His works, shown in museums and galleries worldwide, play on the opposition between East and West, past and present, classical culture and pop culture. His style may be described in pop terms by the world of "otaku" (initially defined by the acronym poku: pop + otaku), and is known as "superflat" (a term first used by the art historian Tsuji Nobuo to characterize the lack of depth and spatial representation in the work of Hokusai and in oriental painting in general). After his success in the United States, Murakami's art arrived in Europe. In 2002 his touring exhibition KaiKai Kiki opened in Paris at the Fondation Carrier, before transferring in January 2003 to London's Serpentine Gallery. In the Coloriage section, Murakami exhibited creations which revealed the same provocative ambiguities as the work of Warhol, hovering between classification as commercial or artistic products. The transition from the world of art to that of fashion was the result of the exhibition's success in Paris: Marc Jacobs, Artistic Director of Vuitton, met him and decided, not without a degree of risk, to have him collaborate in the new summer collection of 2003. And so another new look was created for Vuitton bags to follow the success of Stephen Sprouse's graffiti, and the fairytale patchwork of English designer Julie Verhoeven. Presented in 2002 at Spring-Summer 2003 womenswear runway show, at the Parc-Citroën, the new collection of handbags and totes reflected the highly colored, ironic, and childlike spirit of the Japanese artist, who re-launched the celebrated Vuitton logo in three different versions: a multicolored monogram, pink peach blossom or red cherry blossom (for the classic cylindrical Papillon bag), and, Murakami's favorite subject, his "floating" eyeballs, with their multicolored lashes and pupils, which for Vuitton become "Eye Love." (*Gabriella Gregorietti*)

Murkudis Kostas (1959). Greek designer. Lives and works in Munich. Born in Dresden and brought up in Berlin, he kept his parents' nationality. Enrolled in the Chemistry faculty of Berlin University, he studied "Design applied to fashion." For some years he worked for Helmut Lang. In 1996, he set up his own business, débuting in 1997 with his Spring-Summer womenswear collection. In the same year he also launched his first menswear collection on the Paris runways.

❑ 2000, September. Kostas Murkudis was appointed Creative Director of New York Industries, a casual clothing line produced by Diesel International. As well as designing menswear and womenswear collections, he was responsible for their advertising campaigns. The designer appeared on the cover of *W.*, monthly magazine of *Womens Wear Daily*, the American fashion and luxury newspaper.

Murnt Delphine. French designer. Attended Studio Berçot from 1995 to 1997 and immediately after graduating collaborated with major fashion houses. First with Alexander McQueen at Givenchy, then with Martine Sitbon and Thierry Mugler for *haute couture*. In 1999 she was offered an interior design project in Lisbon, where she moved for a period. But fashion was her passion, and in 2000 she returned to Paris and worked on her first runway show for the women's *prêt-à-porter* fashion week. More shows followed, resulting in the recognition of Delphine as a young talent to watch.

Murphy&Nye American fashion company producing sportswear and casual wear. Founded in 1933 in Chicago as producers of sails for yachts, launches, and ice-breakers. The sails proved to be winners in the MacKinac Race regatta and the Star world championships in 1936. This success allowed the company to extend production to include crew uniforms and Newport pants, the latter named by the company's founders, Jim Murphy and Harry Nye, in honor of the America's Cup, which was held in Newport, Rhode Island. Since 1992 the brand has been part of the company Sixty, and produces four *prêt-à-porter* ranges, popular with sailors, skiers, snowboarders, and lovers of casual dress in general.

❑ 2002. The year ended with excellent returns for all brands of the Sixty Group.
❑ 2003, June. At the opening of Pitti Uomo, the Sixty Group had their best wares on display: at the Fortezza da Basso they showed Murphy&Nye, Dake 9, and preview the new range, Decauville.

Musée Christian Dior The house where Christian Dior was born in Granville, Normandy, has been transformed into a museum in which themed exhibitions of the designer's work are held. The first, which opened on January 22, 1988, was dedicated to *La femme mise en scène*. Fifty outfits, accompanied by photographs and designs, revealed the relationships of the great designer with some of his famous clients, such as Olivia de Havilland, Ava Gardner, and, above all, Marlene Dietrich. Dior was very fond of the house in his childhood. The Villa des Rhums is situated in a marvelous position, surrounded by flower gardens on a cliff top looking towards the Channel Islands, and not far from the Mont-Saint-Michel.

Musée de la Chemiserie et de l'Elegance Masculine This museum in Argenton-sur-Creuse specializes in men's clothes and accessories. Founded in the 1980s, its highlight is a collection of men's shirts dating from the 18th century onwards. The brainchild of clothing industrialist J.R. Graveneaux, its exhibitions, which have been officially open to the public since 1993, have been enriched by further items of clothing and examples of the tools of the fashion trade, thanks to donations from private collections and local businesses.

Musée de la Mode de Marseille Opened in 1993 in the Espace Mode Méditerranée, the collections of this museum number 5,000 items of clothing, through which it is possible to trace the history of fashion and the most important couturiers from 1945 to the present day. A rich collection, it is generally presented to the public through themed exhibitions, reflecting the evolution and revolutions of style and taste in the last fifty years. Monographic shows are also held, curated by illustrious art-directors and dedicated to fashion houses such as Balmain, Cardin, Courrèges, Dior, Lanvin, Chanel, and Lacroix. The museum curators continually ensure its collections are up-to-date, and season after season they comb the ateliers of designers such as Alaïa, Gaultier, and Lagerfeld, in search of the fashion items that best represent contemporary trends. In 1997 a new gallery was opened in which to house rotating displays of the museum's extraordinary permanent collection.

Musée de la Mode et du Textile Established in 1977 in the Rohan wing of the Louvre, the museum of fashion and textiles brings together one of the most important fashion collections in the world. Since 1999 a central hall has housed the permanent collection, which is comprised of eighty-one thousand items, including clothes (dating from the 17th century to the present day), fashion accessories, textile samples, even books, drawings and original prints. Ninety percent of these collections originate from personal donations, including those of great designers such as Vionnet, Schiaparelli, Poiret, Dior, Chanel, and Ricci. In 1997 and 1998, while renovations to the main gallery were underway, the museum constructed a temporary two-floor structure housing two "theaters." The display in the first of these examined the geometry of the body, tailoring, and decorative motifs. The second, curated by Ezio Frigerio, comprised 250 outfits, from the 16th to the 20th centuries, and a selection of accessories and jewelry, demonstrating the presence of exoticism throughout the history of Western fashion.

Musée de l'Impression sur Étoffe Mulhouse, France. Museum dedicated to the local printed fabrics industry. Machinery and materials used in production demonstrate the printing process, whilst a collection of printed fabrics from throughout the world offer a historic and ethnographic interpretation.

Musée des Beaux Arts et de la Dentelle Hand- and machine-made pieces form the basis of the collections of this museum, which was founded in Calais in 1930. Formerly independent, it is now part of the Musée des Beaux Arts. It offers periodic displays on the role of lace in the history of fashion.

Musée du Costume Avalon, France. The museum has a collection of more than 2,000 pieces based on the collections made by the Carton sisters, who were passionate and meticulous collectors of fashion throughout their lives. Today the museum is housed in the hunting lodge of the Condé Princes. The display takes the visitor on a historical journey, made up of period sets constructed with minute attention to detail. There is a themed exhibition once a year.

Musée du Textile Cholet, France. Textile museum on the banks of the river Sauvageau, in a former factory founded in 1881, which provided a textile weaving and bleaching service to local businesses. The chronological displays are dedicated to spinning, weaving and trimmings.

Musée du Textile et des Costumes de Haute-Alsace Husseren-Wesserling, France. Museum dedicated to the textile arts of the region, housed in the former printing works of the city of Wesserling. Displays include traditional dress, textiles manufactured by Boussac (active until 1978) and technical materials.

Musée Galliera 10, Avenue Pierre de Serbie, Paris. The Galliera Palace was built at the end of the 19th century, in the Italian Renaissance Style, to house the private collection of the Duchess of Galliera. The Duchess however gave her collections to the city of Genoa, leaving the palace and its gardens to Paris. The palace remained closed until 1977, when it reopened under the name of the Museum of Fashion of the City of Paris. The museum's collections would grow to include *haute couture* and luxury *prêt-à-porter* from the 19th and 20th centuries, displayed in continuous temporary exhibitions. Among the most important of these were shows dedicated to individual designers – Poiret, Schiaparelli, Balmain, Givenchy, and Fath – other shows included an examination of fashion in the 1930s, the new fashion of jeans, and in 1998 *Cachemires parisiens – A l'école de l'Asie – 1810-1880.* This exhibition was dedicated to the cashmere shawls, inspired by Arab, Egyptian and Chinese motifs, which were highly fashionable last century, and which are coming back into fashion today in the creation of dresses, jackets, and coats. (*Elena Guicciardini*)

Musée Historique des Tissus Lyon, France. Founded in 1890 with the support of the local Chamber of Commerce, and coordinated by its president Edouard Aynard. Since the mid-19th century, there had been plans for a permanent collection both for educational purposes and to bring together a historical collection representing the local industry. This project was finally realized with donations from local manufacturers of samples which had been shown in the Exposition Universelle in Paris in 1889. In the following decade, the museum purchased the prestigious private collections of Spitzer (in 1893) and Goncart (in 1897). The collection is divided into Eastern and Western textiles, covering all principle types. The museum includes a conservation studio which has been active since 1985, and a Textiles Centre founded in 1988. Themed exhibitions are frequently held.

Musée International de la Chaussure Romans, France. Shoe museum housed in a former monastery. The display in chronological order includes examples of footwear from all over the world, from antiquity to the present day. Machinery and various tools demonstrate manufacturing techniques.

Musée National des Arts et Traditions Populaires Founded in Paris in 1936. Collections are based on dress, textiles, and household linens, and the collection of traditional costume which since 1884 had been held at the ethnographic museum at Trocadero. Today the collection comprises more than 10,000 articles.

Musée Saint-Laurent 11, Rue de Cambrai, Paris. The collection has 5,000 examples of *haute couture* and *prêt-à-porter* dating from 1962, 2,000 pairs of shoes, 15,000 accessories, thousands of hats, film and theater costumes (*Belle de jour*, *Aigle à deux têtes*), and more than 120,000 archive documents (written, visual, and audio). The museum is open to scholars and researchers. The curator is Hector Pascual, the director is Philippe Pons. Temporary exhibitions are planned for the future.

Musée Vuitton This nineteenth-century building in Asnières was both the home of Louis Vuitton (founder of the fashion house) and the first home of the business. The two principle rooms house the full range of suitcases, alongside posters and photos which recount in an unadorned display the 150 years of craftsmanship. The establishment, which is still used in the production of certain items, is a living testimony to this tale of entrepreneurship. Visits by appointment.

Museo Boncompagni Ludovisi Rome. In addition to the departments of painting, sculpture, and graphic art, this museum has a section dedicated to the decorative arts, architectural ornamentation, fashion, dress and design, for the historical period corresponding to that covered by existing departments, i.e., from the late 18th to the end of the 20th century. The opening of this section, and the related documentation centre, was the outcome of the testamentary wishes of Princess Blanceflor Boncompagni Ludovisi de Bilt, who left her estate to the Italian State. The villa housing the museum is an unusual example of eclectic architecture, devised in 1901 by the architect Giovan Battista Giovenale (1849-1934). It is located in the residential area built close to Rome's Aurelian city walls, between Porta Pinciana and Porta Salaria, following the division into lots of the park of the Villa Ludovisi. Restored by the Environmental and Architectural Office of Lazio, and then by the City of Rome's equivalent office, the museum houses a permanent display of the furnishings left by the Princess, and rotating displays of her collection of decorative art, dating from 1900-1980. This includes objects by Basile, Cadorin, Chini, Cambellotto, Casorati, and Leoncillo, and is a testimony to the variety in the applied arts in Italy from the Liberation to proto-rationalism. The fashion collection – managed by Bonizza Gordani Aragno – is a selection of clothes by the Fontana sisters, Gattinono, Sarli, Valentino, and Molineaux since the beginning of the 20th century, and other donations from the tailoring house Paradisi di Roma, and from the collections of Palma Bucarelli and Maria Vittoria Alfonsi. Fashions from 1900 to the modern day are presented, enhanced by videos and storyboards.

Museo della Calzatura di Vigevano A homage to what has for years been the prime industry of the Lombard city of Vigevano. The museum was opened at the end of 1958 and was named after its inventor, Pietro Bertolini, a pioneer of the shoe industry and collector himself of historical and modern shoes from all over the world. The museum is at present located in one of the large galleries in Palazzo Crespi, which is also home to the civic library, but a transfer of the collections to the Palazzo Sforzesco in Milan is currently being planned. Of the more than 2,000 pieces which were displayed when the museum was first opened, 500 have been preserved, of which 200 are on permanent display (the remaining 300 are in storage due to lack of display space). The creation of the museum was very well publicized, and many businesses, collectors, tourists, businessmen, and even missionary organizations donated very interesting and valuable items to the collections. Among these were shoes that had belonged to Benito Mussolini and Pope Pius XI, and those worn by Pope Giovanni XXIII during the Conclave during which he was elected Pope. Another pair, found at the castle in Vigevano, was said to have belonged to Beatrice d'Este. There are also military boots from various periods, Indian and Persian slippers, the curious Chinese shoes used for the binding women's feet, sandals from Nigerian tribes, moccasins from the Cheyenne and Shoshone native American tribes, cowboy boots, and Inuit snow boots. There are also reconstructions of shoes from the past, including those worn by Charlemagne. (*Denis Artioli*)

Museo dell'Arte del Cappello Founded in Ghiffa (province of Verbania, Italy) after the closure of the historic hat manufacturing firm Capellificio Panizza. The museum

A poster by the illustrator Codognato (Museo dell'Arte del Cappello, Ghiffa).

documents the hat-making process from the stage known as "*feltrazione*" right up to the finishing touches. *Feltrazione* refers to the creation of a manufactured product, made not with woven fabric, but fibers from the pelt of animals such as the beaver, hare, and rabbit. When these fibers are placed in a warm, damp atmosphere, they meld together and form a felt which is, so to speak, a non-woven fabric. It may also be considered as a "fur" that has been reconstructed without the natural support of the skin. It is porous and therefore breathable; it is malleable, and can therefore be modeled into various shapes, and can be easily steamed. Soft and warm, it can be trimmed, glazed, given a suede or velvet effect, and also dyed various colors. In the second section of the museum, which is dedicated to finish, a selection of sewing machines is displayed along one wall. These were used in the company's trimming department, and for the printing of linings and Moroccan leather. There is a large collection of Panizzi hats, as well as those produced by American manufacturers, also on display are advertising posters from various periods, advertising cards for shop windows, and labels.

Museo dello Scarpone e della Calzatura Sportiva Montebelluna (near Treviso, Italy). Founded in 1984, this museum is situated in the sixteenth-century Villa Zuccareda Binetti. Since 1992 it has been managed by a foundation made up of the principal local producers of sporting footwear as well as confederations of artisans. The collections comprise more than 2,000 pieces and tell the story of the most important local industry; the production of sports shoes and boots. Amongst the material that has been collected are patent archives, prototypes, catalogues, photographs and magazines.

Museo del Merletto Burano (Venice). Founded in 1978, the lace museum on the island of Burano was the result of an undertaking by the Venetian authorities to re-launch the local lace industry. The Consortium for Burano Lace was set up at the same time as the Fondazione Adriana Marcello. The foundation had been named after the Venetian Countess who, keen to uphold the tradition, had in 1872 sponsored the School of Lace, which closed down in the 1950s. The Consortium fitted out a museum containing hundreds of pieces in the old school building. Professional training courses were also run until 1995, when the consortium was disbanded. Now the museum is one of the Civic Museums of Venice.

Museo del Tessuto Italiano Established in Prato (Tuscany) in May 2003, in the former factory of textile manufacturers Cimatoria Campolmi Leopoldo. The building is a fine example of late nineteenth-century architecture now completely restored, and the only such building still standing inside the fourth-century city walls. The exhibition occupies one of the halls of the factory, which was purchased by Prato Municipality for more than 20 million euros, and which will become, when it is completely opened in 2007, a very important cultural centre and library. The museum was originally founded in 1975 at the Istituto Tecnico Statale Tullio Buzzi, which had in turn been set up in 1897 to provide training for the wool trade. Prato has been chosen as a fitting home for the first specialised textile museum because of the rich textile tradition in Tuscany, which has produced and exported wool and materials world-wide since medieval times. Today in Prato, 40,000 people work for around 8,000 businesses and exporters specializing in yarn, fabrics and their related machinery. The museum has a collection of more than 6,000 pieces, dating from the early Christian era until today. It is among the first 10 museums of its kind in Europe, containing rare pieces such as fragments of textiles from the pre-Columbian epoch, or the red canvas used for the shirts of Garibaldi's soldiers. One section is dedicated to innovative and high-tech materials. As well as a large collection of textiles, the displays include historical dress, machinery used in the production of textiles, and the materials used in the dying and design of fabrics. For the opening of the museum, as well as the permanent displays, an exhibition was held entitled "Prato veste il cinema: il mito attraverso I costumi della collezione Tirelli." This included a selection of more than 40 outfits and costumes created for films, most of which had been made out of fabrics produced in Prato, such as the lace and silk worn by Winona Ryder in Martin Scorsese's *The Age of Innocence*, Sean Connery's habit in Jean-Jacques Arnaud's *The Name of the Rose*, and the costumes of Fellini's *Canova* and Zeffirelli's *Tea with Mussolini.*

❑ 2001, May. A themed exhibition was held in the old seat of the museum, illustrating the roots of contemporary design. The show consisted of 12 examples of women's outfits from the 1960s, all from the private collection of Osanna Vannucci, accompanied by a selection of fabric samples. These run through the most significant stages of this revolutionary period in the history of fashion: from Mary Quant's miniskirt, to the concept of the "total look," to textile innovations including synthetic and artificial fibres which were experimented for the first time by great tailors such as Valentino, Balestra, Ken Scott, and Emilio Pucci.

Museo di Palazzo Fortuny The museum is housed in Venice in the fifteenth-century Palazzo Pesaro degli Orfei, the palace which became, at the beginning of the last century, the house of the wealthy Spanish intellectual Mariano Fortuny y Madrazo (1871-1949). He was a painter, set-designer, costume-designer, fashion designer, photographer, and above all, a collector. He amassed printed fabrics, furnishing fabrics, his own fashion and costume creations, 10,000 photographic plates, 2,000 photographic prints and 4,000 books. His widow donated the building to the City of Venice, having first transformed the interiors into display spaces for a museum. Palazzo Fortuny has been closed for restoration since 1996.

Museo Ferragamo Palazzo Feroni, Via dei Tornabuoni, Florence. Established in May 1995. The 12,000 examples of shoes by Salvatore Ferragamo, which belong to the Ferragamo business and the family archive, are shown in rotating displays, 200 pairs at a time. The displays tell the story of the extraordinary creativity, craftsmanship and style of the great maestro of shoemaking, from the 1920s until his death in 1960. The museum also shows and organizes various exhibitions: 'Bruce Weber' during the Florence Biennale in 1996, 'Cenerentola', curated by Stefania Ricci, Michael Howells and Jenny Beavan for the 1998 Biennale, and 'Audrey Hepburn' in Spring 1999.

Museum at the FIT New York. The museum at the Fashion Institute of Technology was founded in 1967 as a collection to support the courses run by the institute. Today it boasts the biggest collection of costumes and textiles in the world. Open to the public as well as to scholars, the museum holds temporary exhibitions, houses research archives and displays that aid in the teaching the history of fashion. The collection contains clothing from the 18th century through to the particularly rich selection of twentieth-century labels. There are also examples of men's and childrenswear, sportswear, and uniforms. There are more than 20,000 accessories. The textiles collection is equally important, comprising around 30,000 examples, dating from the 17th century to today, and of every type and origin. 250,000 fabric samples are catalogued, and these can be lent to institute members for short periods. There is also an innovative textile archive, including pieces of fabric from which visitors may cut small pieces, and a vast collection of historical documents and important fashion photography.

Museum fur Kunst und Gewerbe Hamburg, Germany. The dress and textile collection originated with the founding of the museum in 1877. Originally it was an archive that documented local art and handicrafts. Today there are around 22,000 examples of costume, accessories, and textiles. Apart from some a few finds dating to the 16th century, the collection ranges from the 18th century to the present day. Since the 1970s the collection of fashion has become one of the museum's priorities.

Museum of Costume Bath, Great Britain. Housed in the Assembly Rooms, the Georgian architectural jewel made famous by the novels of Jane Austen. The museum was founded in 1963 with the donation of the collection that belonged to dress historian Doris Langley. It now holds more than 20,000 items and accessories for men, women, and children. The oldest pieces date from 1500. The collections have always reflected leading fashion trends, both historic and contemporary. Every year the museum sends a fashion expert to choose the outfit which they feel best represents new fashions. The Fashion Research Centre is part of the museum, but housed outside the Assembly Rooms in a nearby house. It is open to scholars and the public, and includes a specialist library, collections of magazines, photographs, albums, and a collection of dress, accessories and textiles dating from the 18th to the 20th centuries, all of which are available for consultation.

(*Virginia Hill*)

Museum of Fine Arts Founded in Boston in 1870, the collection of examples of textiles and costume began immediately. There are notable collections of Andean fabrics, textiles from the Spanish colonial period, Indonesian batiks, and textiles from the Aegean region. The dress collection is based mainly on the McCormick and Lehman donations of European clothing from the 16th to 19th centuries. Donors from Boston also provided examples of locally made embroidery, as well as a large collection of items by Worth from the end of the 19th century. The D.W. Ross and W.S. Bigelow collections also contain pieces from the late 18th century through the first decades of the 19th.

Museum of the City of New York Houses one of the three most important collections of fashion in America, containing more than 25,000 items of clothing and accessories. The clothes date from the mid-18th century to the present day, and represent both local manufacturing and the most important fashions of this great cosmopolitan city. Among the items of greatest historical significance are the ball gowns worn at the inauguration of George Washington as President in 1789. Also notable are the collection of wedding dresses dating from between 1754 and 1997, and that of dresses by the Maison Worth created in Paris for high-society New York clients. Acquisitions of clothes continue to be made from the city's current designers. The collection is enhanced by an archive of photographs and fashion magazines.

Museum of Welsh Life Costume gallery in Cardiff, Great Britain. Opened in 1975, the museum was recently renovated. The collection includes costumes and accessories of Welsh manufacture and origin, dating from 1700 to the present day. There is a working eighteenth-century loom, which helps tell the story of local weaving. One room is fitted out as a 1950's tailor's shop, complete with all the original material. Other areas are dedicated to national Welsh costume.

Museu Nacional do Traje Lisbon. The idea of a Portuguese costume museum was suggested in 1974, after an important costume exhibition. The museum opened in 1977 in the Angeja-Palmela palace, in Lisbon's botanical gardens. The basis of the collection was around 7,000 pieces from the wardrobes of Portugal's faded royal dynasty, and has grown thanks to many donations. For the most part, womenswear is represented. There are also significant collections of Court clothing and folk dress. A large gallery is given over to textile technology. The displays are changed every two years. A specialist library is open to the public.

Museu Textil i d'Indumentaria Barcelona. The museum of textiles and fashion came into being only in 1982 when various collections were brought together. It is housed since 1969 in the old palace of the Marquis of Llio, which now belongs to the city. The collection was established in 1883 by the council, but the first museum was not founded until 1964. Successive donations and important acquisitions enlarged the collections. The textile section is very broad, with examples from the 4th to 20th centuries. Among the oldest articles are Coptic tunics from the 7th and 9th centuries, holy vestments from the 15th and 16th centuries, and thirteenth-century Hispano-Moorish tapestries. Various types of embroidery and lace are well represented, as well as the materials used in their production. A fundamental part of the twentieth-century fashion collection is the Balenciaga gift, which includes examples of the designer's work before he went to Paris. These, as well as other outfits by Spanish designers, document Spanish and Catalan styles. Recently the museum has bought clothes by Spanish *prêt-à-porter* labels such as Sybilla, and international labels including Ungaro and Alaïa.

Muslin Very fine textile, light and transparent, although its cloth is not particularly soft, due to its finely twisted weave. Originated in the city of Mossul, Iraq, from where it takes its name, it can be made from cotton, wool, and silk. It is the silk version to which the French term "mousseline" refers particularly. Light cotton muslin was worn by Marie-Antoinette at the Trianon; her unforgettable *fichus*, light as a feather, were made of the fabric. Silk muslin gave life to clothes, particularly to skirts, and in the 19th century, blouses. The artist-tailors of the Belle Époque and the early 20th century printed wool muslin with contemporary and oriental designs for dresses and shawls. In all its variations, muslin has continued to be an essential for the ever-important accessory, the foulard.

Musso Roberto (1960). Italian designer. Born in Vigevano, he started out in spring 1995 with a collection characterized by the influence of oriental culture and traditions. This has remained his signature look, but it is represented through simple, unadorned, linear clothing in muted colors. He is constantly on the look-out for new materials. Based in Milan, his creations have become known all over America, being sold at the New York department store Barney's.

❑ 2003, February. On the runways of Milano Moda Donna, Musso's new collection was inspired by travel and distant, exotic countries: Clean lines and essential, tailored cuts; bright textiles borrowed from antique saris; bouclé weaves and tulle ribbons. Skirts in boiled wool inspired by origami, which, being cut on the bias, take on the appearance of handkerchiefs. Light, colorful knitwear, capes and cloaks, and skirts in drifting satins. Also from the Far East were the valuable antique edgings of Musso's coats, which are available in limited editions.

Mustang German clothing manufacturer. Established by Luise Hermann in 1931, the firm produced work uniforms and overalls which were used early on by the Wehrmacht. However, by the time war broke out in 1939, these were no longer in use and the company closed. It reopened with difficulty and opinions differed about its role. The result was the continuation of the production of work wear, but also shirts and suits. Albert Sefranek, a new partner in the firm, guessed that jeans, copied from those worn by the occupying American forces, could work miracles for the company. He was right, they were a huge success. By 1958, the jeans label of Mustang had been created. Thirteen years later, although jeans still made up 60% of exports, the business widened its range of products to encompass a total look. Mustang had cornered the market in Germany. In the 1990s, Hermann's heirs handed over control of the business to those of Sefranek, who, while continuing to produce jeans, applied a new strategy: fashion aimed at the very young "rock chick." The company found an ally in this new enterprise with Joop, another successful German brand. Under a youthful banner, Mustang financed Walter Van Beirendonk for the W< (Wild and Lethal Trash) range, which the Belgian designer had initially designed for Heaven. W< for Mustang was presented in Paris in 1994.

❑ 2000. License obtained by Mustang for the production of Bogner jeans.

Myma French shoe business. Founded in 1934 by entrepreneur Bertrand Lozes, who concentrated production on children's shoes, but began to produce women's footwear in 1948. The company became famous for a high quality of workmanship combined with *haute couture*, all at a reasonable price. The collection was sold through the department store Printemps and around 30 smaller shops around France, and became a firm favorite with French women, young and old.

❑ 2003. After a crisis in which the company reached the brink of bankruptcy in 2001-2002, the doors are still open at Rue Louis-Vigne.

Myrvold Pia (1960). Norwegian designer and artist. Self-taught in art and fashion, she started to pursue a creative career at the end of the 1970s. Her range of work spans from painting to performance art. In 1983, she became in involved in textiles and ready-to-wear fashion (which she called "wearable art") with a collection of clothes designed to look as if they had been modeled in a mud bath. In 1994 she showed at Paris Fashion Week. In 1998 she designed her first men's collection. The same year she created an outfit for Cartier on the occasion of the presentation of their new jewelry range Paris Identity. For Winter 1998-1999 Myrvold presented a series of interactive dresses at Paris Fashion Week. This, her ninth, collection (called Post Machine) incorporated electric switches into the fabric, allowing the models to activate sounds and images generated by old radios, telephones, and recycled gramophones. Dream Sequence was the designer's visiting card for the new millennium. It is an idealistic range inspired, she says, by the great dreamers of the modern epoch, who, with small acts of civil disobedience, reinforce their non-violent efforts to create a better world.

N

Nadar (1820-1910). Pseudonym of the French photographer Gaspar-Felix Tournachon. Born in Paris to a family of printers, he studied medicine and worked for various newspapers, both as a writer and a caricaturist, for which he adopted the name Nadar, and which he continued to use as a photographer. Closely involved with the progressive circles of the socialist and positivist movements, he was a pioneer of medical photography, aerostatic photography (taken from a hot-air balloon) and reportage, although he became famous for his extraordinarily refined portraits. Among the many activities that took place in the famous studio at 35 Boulevard des Capucines was Nadar's experiments in fashion photography.

Naf Naf French ready-made clothing company. Originally it was called Naphtaline, a boutique opened in Paris in 1973 by the brothers Gérard and Patrick Pariente. Success came five years later when the pair (born in Tunisia in 1950 and 1955 respectively) presented their first Naf Naf collection. From then on, they enjoyed increasing fortunes in the fashion world, thanks to their choices of fabric and the collections' excellent value for money. For its 25th anniversary, Naf Naf took a new direction, abandoning the playful image of the first years, and pensioning off the original piglet logo in favor of a more adult look. The brothers changed the interior décor of their retail stores, as well as their target market, paying greater attention to the female public aged between 18 and 25 years. In 1995, two megastores were opened on the Champs-Elysées and at Les Halles. Soon after, it was the turn of Nice and, in 1997, Moscow. The products made by the Paris company are available in 27 countries, 20 of which are European. There are 138 megastores in France.

❑ 2002 was a good year for the group, which also owns Chevignon, Chevignon Kids and Naf Naf Enfant, with a turnover that reached 245.5 million euros (30% of which is made in Spain, Italy, Greece, and Russia). Their net profits were approximately 14 million euros, an increase of 22% compared with the previous year.

Nagasawa Yoichi (1957). Japanese designer. He studied for a diploma in 1980 at the Mode Fashion Academy. He became the indispensable assistant to Tokyo Kumagai until 1987. He launched his first collection in 1992 and won the Mainichi Fashion Award, given to young designers. Five years later, he debuted in Paris during Fashion Week. He designed the uniforms for Japan Asia Airlines. For Fall-Winter 2003-2004, his runway designs were patterned asymmetrically: pants with white lozenges under black jackets, suits with zigzag motifs, and muslin-spotted tops. Particular care was dedicated to accessories, such as long leather gloves, sometimes decorated with buttons that extended high up the forearms.

Najar Jean-Paul (1948). Fashion creator from 1985 to 1987, art collector, photographer, pianist. He was born in Buenos Aires and studied Economics in Paris. In 1978, he met and married Denise Sarrault, a famous model from the 1950s and 1960s, who was particularly used by Givenchy. For her, and with her, he designed a hat collection in 1985, which was mentioned in *Womens Wear Daily*; in 1986, he designed a line of hats for Emmanuelle Khanh and an *haute couture* collection called Denise Sarrault that was shown at the Hotel Plaza in Paris. In 1988, the couple opened a boutique, but it was short-lived.

Naj-Oleari Italian textile company founded in 1916 by Riccardo Naj-Oleari. Up until the 1970s, it mainly produced coarse textiles for ecclesiastical wear, but under the management of the third generation of the family – the brothers Angelo, Riccardo and Giancarlo – it began to manufacture printed textiles and waterproof fabrics for umbrellas. The first store opened in Milan in 1975. During those years, in parallel with Laura Ashley, the company took advantage of the fashion for textiles with small designs. In 1996, it was acquired by the Biella group Modafil. Currently, it produces printed cotton textiles, children's clothing and a line of objects, bags, and stationery. It employs 50 members of staff, and has four own-brand stores in Italy. The product ranges have been extended to include perfumes, beauty products, sunglasses, umbrellas, and even a specially designed ergonomic chair.

Nakano Hiromichi (1942). Japanese designer, son of a Shinto priest, artist with a multifaceted personality. He moved from Tokyo to Paris, intending to buy antique toys, and stayed to work as a cinema critic. Soon he also began to develop his passion for fashion and became famous in his own country as a designer for TV and music stars. In 1991, he created his first collection of *prêt-à-porter*, which reflected his fantastical, almost playful, style. He showed on the runway in Paris for the first time in 1998. He is one of a group of fashion designers, which includes Pierre Cardin, Yves Saint Laurent and Fiorucci, who were employed to create clothing for the dolls of the Takara Company Ltd, a real cult in Japan. During the course of the ten-year collaboration with Takara, Nagana designed seven Barbie models, which have become collectors' pieces. After the end of the license contract with Mattel, he continued to make clothing and accessories for Jenny, the oriental "cousin" of the American doll.

Nakayama Iwata (1895-1949). Japanese photographer. Having completed his studies at the School of Fine Art in Tokyo, he left with a scholarship for the United States in 1918 and, in 1921, opened a studio in New York. Five years later he moved to Paris, to a new atelier, where he worked in fashion photography. He became part of the art scene and met Man Ray, whose research profoundly influenced Nakayama's style, which was first linked to pictorialism, and afterwards to photomontage and off-camera images. In 1927, he returned to Japan and became a point of reference for avant-garde photography in his own country.

Nannini Italian leather goods company, launched in Florence in 1945 by Virgilio Nannini, who directed it for more than 20 years. In 1966, his sons Ubaldo, Giorgio, and Paolo took over and still run the business today. In 1992 they were joined by the third Nannini generation (Silvia, Paolo, Luca, and Sandro). The original line of bags was extended to include accessories, from shoes to glasses, watches, scarves, and gloves. The first own-brand store in Florence has been joined by shops in Rome, Paris, Brussels, Hong Kong, Tokyo, Osaka, Seoul, Aruba in the Caribbean, and Jakarta in Indonesia. After the showrooms in Florence, Paris, and Brussels, a further one was opened in Milan in Via Lovanio in February 2002. The company's turnover increased greatly with the Oriental expansion initiated in 1998. The opening up of markets in Japan, Korea, Hong Kong (a trampoline to enter the Chinese market) increased turnover from 15 billion lire in 1997 to 23 million euros in 2002 (an increase of 200%).

Naoki Takizawa (1960). Japanese designer, born in Tokyo. He took a degree at the Kuwusawa Design School. From 1981, he entered the Miyake Design Studio, where he was responsible for the Plantation line. From 1993, he was responsible for the Issey Miyake men's collection. In 1998, he received the Mainichi Fashion Prize, which the Japanese daily newspaper *Mainichi* awards every year to figures who have distinguished themselves in the fashion sector. Before him, Miyake himself and Kawakubo had received it.

❑ 2001. To mark twenty years of collaboration with the Miyake studio, Naoki began his runway show at the Carrousel du Louvre for Fall-Winter 2001-2002 with a howling wind.
❑ 2001, April. The collaboration between the Japanese designer and Alain Mikli resulted in the Libellula glasses range, the result of three years work divided between France and Japan. The frames were launched in six different models, for spectacles and sunglasses. The concept is that of an

insect that adapts to the needs of technology: special materials, such as titanium, acetate, grilamide, and stainless steel make it possible to bend the frames so that they can be placed in the transparent cocoon-case designed by Takizawa.

Napa leather High quality leather, made of sheep, kid or lamb skins, and occasionally also cow. It is particularly soft and is well suited to special treatments, such as weaving and folding.

Napapijri Sports and mountain wear line made by the company Green Sport Monte Bianco from Aosta, founded at the beginning of the twentieth century by the Rosset family. In the middle of that decade, Giuliana Rosset initiated the Napapijri (Finnish for the Arctic Circle) project, adding clothing to the firm's existing line of technological rucksacks. Right from the first collections the brand with the Norwegian flag met with success, with ski and after-ski clothing that was tested during exploratory expeditions and under extreme conditions. In the course of a few years, the Aosta headquarters were flanked by new production units and numerous joint ventures with technologically advanced companies, allowing the brand to maintain its high production standards. Today Giuliana Rosset is the CEO of a public company. Thanks to investments on the international market, it is predicted that by 2004 half of Napapijri's turnover will come from abroad. Napapijri has a wide distribution network with approximately 600 multi-brand stores in Italy and partnerships across the world, controlled by 3 branches run from the USA, France, and Germany. The recent opening of the own-brand store in Milan followed others in Chamonix and Paris, while the Tokyo store, in the Shibuya area, is the first step on the way to expansion in the East, a priority for the company. From 2000, the Napapijri Geographic company, of sportswear, accessories, and shoes for men and women, has been joined by Napapijri Kids, a collection of about 80 unisex garments for children from 2 to 16 years old.

(*Pierangelo Mastantuono*)

Napoleone Raffaello (1954). From 1989 general director and from 1995 CEO of Pitti Immagine, the agency that organizes Florentine fashion shows. He has made significant organizational improvements and has strengthened it from the point of view of creativity, image, and international communications, under the presidencies of Marco Rivetti, Mario Boselli, and Gaetano Morzotto. With a degree in law, he was head of personnel at Salvatore Ferragamo. Previously, he worked in Florence as secretary general at a pharmaceutical company, linked to the first private group in France, and in Rome for a company building sailing and cruise boats (where he was a shareholder).

❑ 2005. From 2004 onwards, he has been a member of the board of directors of Yoox, the online store selling luxury goods and the global e-commerce partner of the most important international brands in the fashion sector.

Nars François. French photographer and make-up artist. He has proved his talents working with Lagerfeld, Valentino, Versace, and the photographers Avedon, Ritts, Newton, and Desmarchelier. He moved into photography in 1994, making a name for himself at *Vogue*, *Harper's Bazaar*, and *Elle* with his images of top models taken in natural light with a large format 8x10 camera. The pictures were later published in *X-Ray*.

Nast William Condé (1873-1942). American publisher. Even though he acquired the title from Arthur B. Turnure seventeen years after it was first launched, he was the real father of *Vogue*, which was, until his very intelligent editorial intervention, a magazine on clothing and society with a distribution of about 10-15,000 copies. A New Yorker by origin, Condé Nast was brought up in St Louis in Missouri. He studied at Georgetown University and found work with the publishers of *Collier's Weekly*, becoming responsible for promotions. He stayed there for ten years, long enough to learn the trade and save some money, and then decided to set up on his own, buying the monthly magazine that no-one would have bet a dollar on. Twenty years later, *Vogue* sold 150,000 copies and was the second-ranking magazine in the United States in terms of advertising power. The turnaround was the result of his talent, distribution strategies, ability to attract the best illustrators and photographers, and professional partnership with the talented journalist Edna Woolman Chase. The revenues from *Vogue* enabled him to produce *House and Garden*, *Dress* and *Vanity Fair*, as well as conquer Europe with editions of *Vogue* in England (1916), Spain (1918), and France (1920).

National Chamber of Italian Fashion Established in 1958, this is a nonprofit association which disciplines, coordinates, protects, and promotes the image and development of the Italian fashion industry. A reorganization of its structure has recently caused a clean division between the nonprofit activities, which continue to be coordinated by the association, and the service activities for associates and non-associates, which are managed by the new Fashion Chamber. The Chamber has 160 associates among the various segments of the textile and clothing sectors, and has two offices. The one in Milan covers the organization of events and the calendar for presentation of the collections. The office in Rome looks after relationships with the various institutions and organizes the Fashion Week in Rome. The Chamber organizes four annual *prêt-à-porter* events: Milano Collezioni Donna (February-March and September-October), and Milano Collezioni Uomo (January and June-July). The two events held in Rome are instead linked to *haute couture*. Currently, Mario Boselli is President, and Beppe Modenese Honorary President.

❑ 2002, April. The calendar and rules of the presentation of the collections were laid down to avoid the delays and problems that resulted during previous presentations. It is essential that all those brands that do not have their own location show in Milan Fair (though, in the future, they will be moved to the City of Fashion which is due to be built in the Garibaldi-Varesine district). The timetable (9.30am-7.30pm) and the daily number of shows (10 shows a day for 10 days,but for 9 days from the second semester 2003) have been fixed. The Chamber (usually) decides to keep a fixed schedule and to give preference to the requests of those maisons that are associate members.

National Institute of Fashion Established by the Fascist government on October 31, 1935, as a result of the economic sanctions placed against Italy by the League of Nations following its abortive colonial war in Abyssinia. The purpose of the foundation of the Institute was to promote self-sufficiency in clothes production. It was created on the basis of the Independent Institute of the Permanent Fashion Exhibition, which, founded in Turin in 1932, had the task to prompt fabric manufacturers, ateliers, and accessory manufacturers to Italianize the national wardrobe. The decree that created the Institute forced Italian fashion operators to declare what they were doing and making, in a sort of self-census, and in exchange they were given a sort of brand confirming the "Italian nature of the fabric used and inspiration injected" of at least 50% of their designs, of which they had to submit copies. The need for designers to provide copies of their creations was too complicated, so the Institute agreed to make do with a photo or a sketch. The Institute also had the right to schedule the calendar of the presentation of the collections, which it arranged several months in advance of the French collections, to limit the Italian dependence on Paris designers. In 1937, a special corps of vigilantes was created to search through the storerooms of the ateliers and to fine those who maintained an association with French designs up to 2,000 lire. In 1939 a golden badge was created to be assigned to the most deserving (i.e., "Italian") collections based on the criteria of the "nobility of manufacturing and technical and artistic qualities." During the war, the Institute invited the Italian clothes-makers to base their creations on national customs. Its activity was not completely in vain, in particular for those people who made lace, straw articles, and passementerie by hand. But it was also capable of complete nonsense, for example, when in 1937 in a campaign was undertaken that proclaimed that sometimes fashion "distracts women from their domestic life, from their fundamental purposes: this happens because of the fashion for imported designs (...), which intends to transform a woman into a young and desirable beauty, rather than a mother." Presidents of the Institute were Thaon di Revel, and Earl Giriodi Panissera di Monastero. Director general was Vladimiro Rossini.

National Institute of Fashion Technology New Delhi, India. State school of fashion founded in 1986 under the guidance of the Indian Textile Minister. It offers various courses, such as fashion design, technical training, and management studies. The courses last from one to three years depending on the specialty. Following the school's success, others have been founded, such as the F.I.T. of Mumbai.

National Museum of Applied Art Oslo. Includes a fashion collection dating back to 1876. Most of the clothes in the collection, dating from 1700 to the present day, are locally made, apart from a few examples of international labels. The collection of court dress from 1905 to the 1990s forms an important nucleus. A smaller section contains traditional European and Asian dress. In addition to the dress collections there is also a collection of sketches by Norwegian designers.

National Museum of Ireland Dublin, Ireland. The museum owns a collection of clothing, covering local production from the 18th to the end of the 20th century as well as a collection of locally made textiles, ranging from archaeological finds dating from 750 BC to contemporary fabrics. Weaving is represented in all its variants, from Coptic linens to nineteenth century industrial silks. It also possesses an important collection of Irish and European lace and embroidery from the 15th century onwards.

National Museum of Scotland Edinburgh. In 1985, a single costume collection was formed from the collections of the National Museum of Antiquities of Scotland, the Royal Scottish Museum, and the Charles Stewart Collection. It numbers more than 15,000 pieces, dating from the 18th century onwards. The emphasis is on local products, work and everyday clothing, rather than *haute couture*. Nevertheless, the museum owns examples from all the main English and continental fashion houses of the 20th century. Its library collects books and documents relating to fashion.

Nativo Filippo (1913-1987). Italian men's tailor. He was very well known for his ability to calculate measurements by eye. A mayor of New York wanted a copy made of a double-breasted jacket that was a perfect fit and hung beautifully. For Nativo, it was enough to see him once in the middle of a crowd. A Sicilian, carrying on a family tradition (his father had a small workshop at Santa Croce in Camerina, near Ragusa), between the two wars he lived in Tunisia working in the building trade. In 1945 he returned to Italy, this time to the north, and went to work in the tailoring atelier of Ristori in Florence. He set up on his own, experimenting with new materials. He attracted clients like Bista Giorgini, who launched the runway shows at Palazzo Pitti, and was one of the most important figures in the new Italian fashion industry. It was for Nativo that a very young Enrico Coveri appeared on the runway wearing an outfit that could be changed with a system of zips. After his death, his son took over the atelier.

Natori Josie (1947). American designer of ultra glamorous underwear, her creations can be worn both under and over other clothes. Her most famous pieces are little slips and bras exclusively embroidered in the Philippines. Some while ago she also launched a men's line. With a degree in economics, she began her career as a consultant and currency trader on Wall Street. However, in 1977, after nine years in high finance, she created her own company selling luxury underwear. She owns two important stores, one in New York and the other in Manila. President Clinton invited her to take part in the Small Business Trade Council. During the 1990s, she launched the perfume *Natori*, with substantial success. She has been awarded the prestigious Ellis Island Medal of Honor. In collaboration with the Asia Society of America and the Fashion Institute of Technology, she runs a course on traditional Philippine tailoring, where she teaches the use of fabrics such as pina (a fiber taken from pineapples) and abaca (obtained from bananas). The best pieces of work by her students are displayed as part of "Philippine Style 2000."

❑ 2002. The publication *Josie Natori*, written by Victoria Fung, celebrated 25 years of the designer's career.

Nattier Italian textile company run by Vittorio Azzario and located Trivero (Biella). Before it closed, it was a determining factor in the success of Italian fashion. It was one of, if not the first, to produce the double-face textiles that made the fortune of Mila Schön. It was a providential ally of all the great designers of the 1960s, starting with Paco Rabanne.

Nautica American brand of casual and sporting *prêt-à-porter*, founded by David Chu in 1983, with a menswear collection inspired primarily by the military, athletic look. The Taiwanese Chu, who has a notable talent for design, first studied architecture and planning. He debuted with six sporty and functional pieces that brought him immediate success. Subsequently the brand has expanded to include a vast line of accessories and a perfume. In 1997, Chu created the first collection of swimming costumes and clothing for women, which was very well received. As a consequence, he extended his work to include household furnishings and children's wear. The brand, whose logo is a boat with its sails blown by the wind, has 100 shops around the world. Nautica Jeans Company and a new fragrance, *Latitude Longitude*, were launched to coincide with the new millennium.

❑ 2001, Spring. The New York store opened on Rockefeller Plaza.
❑ 2001, May. Nautica took control of Earl Jeans Inc., for 45 million dollars. The company already owned the brands John Varvatos, E. Magrath and Byron Nelson. The acquisition led to the launch in October of a line of leather belts, military and desert boots, and clogs.
❑ 2002 closed with a tiny increase in net sales from 692 million dollars to almost 694 millions. Warnaco Group became the new license holder of Nautica Apparel, the swimwear department. Presented in July 2003, the new women's and children's beachwear collection is entirely produced, distributed and commercialized by the swimwear giant.
❑ 2003. David Chu celebrated 20 years of the seaside collection with a runway show in Milan.

Navarra Gaetano (1970). Italian designer. Of Spanish origin, he was born in Bologna where he gained experience in his family's knitwear factory as he grew up. He has combined a technical background with his innovative personal taste to create a dynamic image for contemporary life. With a shaved head and arms decorated with tribal tattoos, Navarra himself reflects the spirit of a free man and the "rock soul" embodied in his

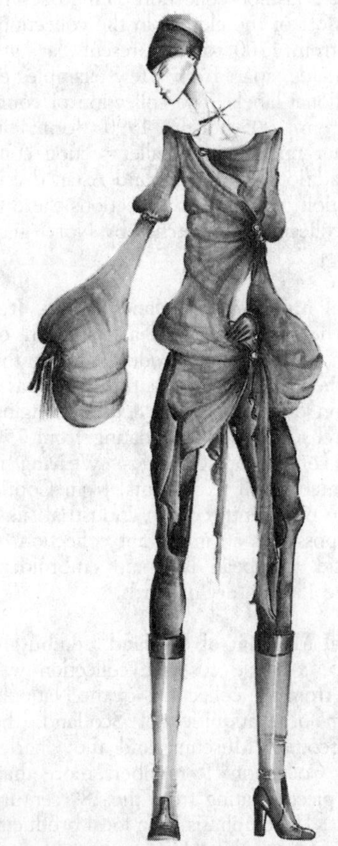

Gaetano Navarra, shirt in Scottish silk and riding pants in black fustian.

collections, which manifest a taste for provocation blended with an extreme femininity. Since his first line of *prêt-à-porter* knitwear, which debuted in Milan in 1986, his success has increased continuously, as is confirmed by his presence at RomaAltaModa. The company has its headquarters in Bologna and produces garments that are sold in 500 stores in Italy, France, Germany, Great Britain, and across the Atlantic. In 2003, his brand expanded to include a line of menswear. The company has showrooms in Milan and Rome and is stocked in 300 retail points in Italy and abroad. The jewel in its crown is the boutique on Sunset Boulevard, Los Angeles.

Navarro Noella (1976). Spanish designer, born in Canals. As a young girl she moved with her family to Valencia. After a diploma in Applied Arts specializing in Fashion Design, she completed her training with a further diploma in Patronaje Industrial. In 1997, she took part in the first Pasarela Jove, organized in Valencia. In the event's second year, she won a prize for her work, marking a real turning point in her career. In 1998, she opened her own atelier in Valencia, where she prepares all her collections. In 2000, she participated in Pasarela Gaudi, the Barcelona runway show, with her Fall-Winter 2000-2001 collection. In 2003, she presented her creations in Madrid at the Pasarela Cibeles for the first time and launched her Nona brand.

(*Mariacristina Righi*)

Navel New erogenous zone (or supposedly so), joining the other most celebrated parts of the female body. It has been celebrated by the mostly young fashions of the early 2000s: midriff-revealing shirts and T-shirts, low-waisted pants and skirts, and evening dresses that show off the navel in a more subtle and elegant way. The dancing maids depicted in the 4 A.D. mosaic in the Roman villa in Piazza Armerina sport a forerunner of the modern bikini, offering a rare sight in ancient art of a navel. Increasingly anthropological interpretations of fashion and costume history point to the navel as a vital symbol that represents both separation from and dependence on the maternal figure, a constant reminder of her power. In India, Shakti, the female energy force, is believed to be held in the navel. As we wait for cosmetics and plastic surgery to deal with this important part of the woman's body, jewelers across the world have already had the idea of embellishing it with diamond and ruby settings.

Nazareno Gabrielli Italian leather goods company founded in 1907, when an expert bookbinder and leather decorator opened a craft workshop in Tolentino, in the Marches, ornamenting objects with chasing, repoussé, and burnishing techniques and, afterwards, with more sophisticated processes such as engraving, photo-engraving, and xylography. By 1922, the activity was a flourishing business, employing more than 70 members of staff, manufacturing articles of clothing and furnishings, small leather items, bags, and gloves. In 1928, Fiat selected the company to supply the decorated leathers

Nazareno Gabrielli, Fall-Winter 1999-2000.

intended for the corridors and seat panels of the first royal train to be built in Italy. From the postwar period onwards, the prestige of the brand continued to grow, based partly on the use of modern and innovative production systems, and partly on contributions by well-known artists and designers. In Summer 1999, David Passino, the CEO and main shareholder, had to acknowledge the crisis and sell Gabrielli to the holding company of Angelo Corona, which made it a part of the Pineider firm.

❑ 2001. The company was acquired by Lediberg, which guaranteed the survival of the historic brand. N.G. Diaries were launched. The N.G. label continues to symbolize quality leather goods.

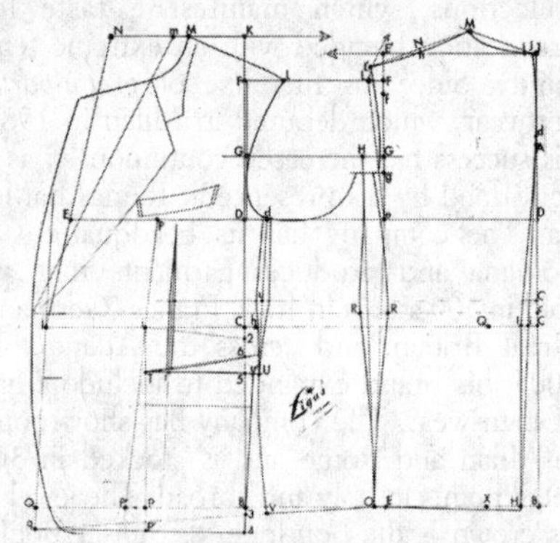

Technical and scientific pattern for the cut of a male jacket, 1930s.

Neapolitan tailoring The cult of elegance has its own sanctuary in Naples. In the 1930s, Naples wa one of the most elegant cities in Italy. Serafini, De Nicola, Morziello, Gallo, Blasi, Rubinacci, Balbi, and Piemontese are the names of some of the famous tailors. To be dressed by Renato De Nicola, loitering through the endless fittings in his studio in Piazza Dei Martiri, in the years after World War I, was a rite of passage for anyone wanting to enter what Camilla Cederna called "society." Jackets made by Angelo Blasi and Gennaro Rubinacci were a sign that you had made it socially in the decade preceding World War II. They were worn not only by the descendants of an aristocracy that had outlived itself, for whom knowing how to dress was form of self-defense, but by members of the new industrial and intellectual elite. Count Roberto Gaetani di Laurenzana claimed that he had suits fitted sitting down to make sure the material hung properly in that position. Before being swallowed up by Fascist conformity, fashionable poets and painters, song writers and journalists, comedians and actors, and young captains of manufacturing and transport industries were the shining protagonists of a golden era. They were the ones who brought into the limelight and introduced to an ever widening public a male fashion that was completely liberated from the worn out 19th-century stylistic traditions and which looked above all to other European styles, in particular British understatement. In the 1920s and 1930s, riding the wave of English fashion, jackets were also shortened in Naples. Lines softened. Materials, including the really heavy ones used in the British tradition, were treated with such mastery that they became more wearable. This rapid development resulted from the very high level of craftsmanship of the emerging names. Above all, it was the fineness and elegance of the cut that made the Neapolitan school of tailoring famous. Salvatore Morziello was renowned as one of its founding fathers; from the beginning of the century, he ran the most important men's tailor's shop in Naples with his business partner Giovanni Serafini. The lawyer Porzio, the future first president of the Italian Republic De Nicola, Edoardo Scarfoglio, Ernesto Murolo and Salvatore Di Giacomo were all dressed here. At the time suits were still rigid and wooden, with padding and shoulder pads, but Morziello introduced more flattering lines. Don Salvatore did not use a tape measure, but took his measurements by eye, feeling the client's shape with his hands and fingers. Incredibly the suits that came out of his workshop fitted perfectly. All the future great tailors, up until Attolini, Blasi and Rubinacci, who made their fortunes in the period from the 1930s to 1960s, boasted that they rose through ranks of the workshops of Antonio Gallo, Salvatore Morziello, or Renato De Nicola. It is thanks to the magical art of cutting to measure, a major development of enormous dexterity – the result, in turn, of a tradition of artisan excellence – that Gennaro Rubinacci created the Neapolitan jacket in the early 1930s, the true forerunner of the modern male jacket.

Necchi Italian make of sewing machines. Immediately after the end of World War I, sewing machines were only imported from abroad. In 1919, the entrepreneur Vittorio Necchi (years later he was made a Cavaliere del Lavoro) sensed the potential for a business and built the first Italian sewing machine in his laboratory in Pavia. It was dated 1920 and was called *Iri*, taken from the name of the firm (Industrie Riunite) that produced it. In 1927, Necchi launched the first domestic bobbin sewing-machine. From 1955, Necchi machines did zigzag stitch. By 1947, the Lombard company had started to export its products, starting with America. In the 1970s, the first electronic machines were made, which combined high technology with design aesthetics, earning themselves a place in the most prestigious museums across the world.

(*Pierangela Fiorani*)

Neck bag Small bag created by Tom Ford for Gucci, with long handles: it is worn around the neck.

Neck holder Dress or top with large braces that, starting from the chest, run around the neck to form a neckline that leaves the shoulders and neck bare. Also known as freeback or flyback.

Nederlands Kostuummuseum The Hague. Municipal museum dedicated to fashion. It was opened in 1952 to bring together three existing collections: that of the Museum of Applied Arts, the foundation of the Dutch Museum of Fashion, and the collection of the actor Cruys Voorberg, which was acquired by the city in 1951. It owns more than 40,000 pieces dating from the 17th to the 20th centuries. French *haute couture* designers are well represented. From 1967 onwards, it has collected contemporary Dutch clothing.

Negrini Fencing Line Italian company making clothing and equipment for the sport of

Umberto Boccioni, *Seamstress*, 1903. Oil on canvas (Volonteri Collection, Savona).

fencing. Founded in Verona in 1897, it played a fundamental part in establishing the sport and art of fencing by becoming the official supplier, first to the Royal Army and Royal Navy, and later also to the Italian Armed Forces. After World War II, thanks partly to the arrival of Angelo Negrini, it also began to gain a name for itself abroad. It is directed by Anna Maria Negrini, who runs the tailoring atelier, and her sons, Paolo and Michele, who interpret the growing needs of a global market. The company supplies Olympic athletes, including Valentina Vezzali, Giovanna Trillini, and Alfredo Rota, with clothing and equipment.

(*Maria Vittoria Alfonsi*)

Nehrdich Rolf-Werner (1910-1970). German photographer. Between 1935 and 1943 he ran a fashion photography studio in Berlin, working in a field that was still very marginal at the time and enjoyed little importance at an international level. After 1945, he directed the Institute of Modern Photographic Art at Kassel and, during the 1950s, he transferred his activity as a fashion photographer first to Düsseldorf and later to Hamburg.

Neiman Marcus Chain of American department stores. Along with other famous stores, such as Bergdorf Goodman, it is part of the Neiman Marcus Group. Today it has approximately 30 stores and over 7,000 employees. It was founded in 1907 by Herbert Marcus, Carrie Marcus Neiman and A.L. Neiman. It has become an institution, thanks partly to the Christmas catalogue which proposes the impossible. The group has always offered a very personalized customer service. From 1938, it instituted the Neiman Marcus Award, which is given to designers and other professionals in the fashion industry. Previous recipients include

Poster dedicated to Italian fashion at the Neiman Marcus department store (from *La Sala Bianca – La nascita della moda italiana*, by Guido Vergani, Electa, 1992).

Chanel, Salvatore Ferragamo (1947), Roberta di Camerino (1956), and Missoni (1973). Neiman Marcus was the first store to import Italian knitwear, starting with Mirsa.

Nelissen Robert (1946). Dutch designer. A great admirer of YSL and Armani, his style is measured, moderate, and very feminine. He created his *prêt-à-porter* luxury brand in 1977. Previously, he had worked for Balmain, Cardin, and Dorothée Bis. He designed the uniforms for the Air France stewardesses. When the company Kashiyama acquired the Japanese license for Rochas, he was called to take over its artistic direction. In 1989, he designed Lanvin's *prêt-à-porter* line.

Nelly Rodi Style bureau bearing the name of the person who founded it in Paris in 1985, after 30 years of experience in the world of fashion and the textile and clothing industries. It employs 25 people (designers, sociologists, and stylists), who provide a concrete analysis of the continuous changes taking place in the sectors covered by the agency: clothing, beauty, and the home. As well as publishing seasonal booklets on current trends for each sector, the agency offers consultancy to assist with the creation of collections, distribution advice, promotional strategies, catalog text, press releases, and public relations services.

Nepo Arik. Russian photographer who trained in France. After studying to become a cinema technician, in 1937 he began to work for the French edition of *Vogue* and, a year later, the English one. After active service in World War II, he surrounded himself with the staff of *Vogue France*. He died in 1961.

Nervesa Firm producing men's clothing, outer garments (jackets, suits, overcoats), and pants. It was founded by Giuliano Caponi in 1961 at Nervesa della Battaglia, a village that has come to symbolize the Italian defense along the River Piave during World War I. The outer garments, entirely produced within the company, are of a traditional type: all linings are stitched in place rather than being fused. The company's vocation for tailoring is underlined by its "bespoke" service, which provides personalized garments very quickly. In 1997, it was awarded the Marco Polo Prize by the Foreign Center of the Union of the Chambers of Commerce of the Veneto Region, for its success in terms of image and commercial value. It employs 306 staff, including those working freelance, and had a turnover in 1998 of 45 billion lire, 50% of which came from exports. Its principal markets are in the European Union, Switzerland, Eastern Europe, where the company owns three shops, the Far East, Canada, Australia, Japan, and China. It has 750 Italian clients. The signing of the license for menswear, linking Borsalino and Nervesa Moda Uomo, was a prestigious event.

❑ 2002, July. The company participated in Made in Italy at the Collective, a New York salon reserved for buyers, together with 58 menswear companies, whose displays are organized by the Italian Fashion Agency. The Collective is held every year on the piers of the Hudson River and includes approximately 400 exhibitors.

Nessler Charles. German hairdresser who invented the permanent wave, which he advertised in 1906 in the *Hairdresser's Weekly Journal* in London where he lived and worked. The advert described an artificial wave that outlasted washes. The system, based on ammonia, did not gain many converts. This did not change even after Nessler, who moved to Paris in 1909 (changing his name to the French Nestlé), perfected it with the use of rollers. It was not until the 1920s that the perm became popular.

Neuber Shop selling corsets and basques, opened in 1886 on Via Tornabuoni, Florence, by the Swiss-German Helen Neuber. From 1919, after the store moved to Via Strozzi, it also stocked menswear, with garments in a sober and elegant, traditional style.

Neulander Simon Else, better known as Eva (1900-1942). German photographer. In 1925, she ran a photographic studio in Berlin, initially collaborating with Heinz Hajek-Halke and later working on her own. She took portraits and fashion photographs, publishing in *Die Dame*, *Elegante Welt*, and *Konfektionaer*. Young talents passed through her studio, such as Helmut Newton, who became very influenced by her style. In 1934, she married the dealer Alfred Simon. Shortly after the troubles began, as a Jew she was forced to hand the studio over to her friend Charlotte Weider. In 1938, she was prohibited from practicing her profession and, four years later all trace was lost of her in the concentration camp at Majdanek-Lubin. (*Roberta Mutti*)

New Age A combination of theories and philosophical doctrines based around the advent of the so-called Age of Aquarius (or the New Age). What was initially solely a spiritual doctrine evolved into a wide-scale success, as new age themes created or relaunched authentic styles of life and thought, marked by a relaxed vision of existence and its characteristics. New Age music describes in comforting notes the relationship between nature and humankind. During the last few years, many designers have presented collections inspired by soft colors, the most natural materials possible and the unambiguous simplicity inherent in New Age beliefs, in distinct contrast with the noisy and jostling styles of other collections and fashions. Based on a classification of time that takes its origins from the position of the sun amongst the constellations, it was precisely the arrival of the sun in the constellation of Aquarius (in the mid-1970s) that globally launched the complex doctrine that spiritualists had known and practiced for very many years. New Age was diffused throughout the world through music, writings of spiritual philosophers (in particular the world best-seller by James Redfield, *The Celestine Prophecy*) and above all the birth of thousands of groups of thought and philosophy that drew on this life theory in a direct or indirect way. The philosophy seeks to expand as far as possible the individual's spirituality, it is opposed to the Christian religion (and is in turn bitterly opposed), widening the concept of God to the single individual and all individuals, it professes to believe in reincarnation and pays great attention to the Oriental philosophers. A principal characteristic of New Age is that the search for knowledge is replaced by the search for wisdom, which is obtained through all disciplines of human activity, from the economy (with the massive relaunch of environmental issues and the search for a different relationship between man and the environment), to politics (emphasizing cooperation between individuals), to medicine (privileging the use of natural remedies). Psychology is fundamental, strongly underlining values that transcend the individual and allow room for so-called paranormal phenomena.

(*Antonio Dipollina*)

New Balance American footwear company. Founded in 1906 at Belmont (Massachusetts) it produced sports shoes. It was the first to introduce orthopedic models on the market for sporting disciplines and sole supports. In 1976, it launched the 320 model, which enjoyed wide success among Americans. In 1979, it was launched on the European market and set up headquarters in England, near Manchester. It is the only company in the world to produce shoes of different widths.

New Boxer Clothing manufacturer with headquarters in Bangkok, Thailand. Founded in 1988, with an initial capital of 2 million dollars, it manufactures clothing for men, women, and children of different brands, including lines of accessories (bags, umbrellas, belts) and jeans. It has different headquarters in Europe and Brazil.

New Design A new section, dedicated to young designers, at the Momi-ModaMilano event. Launched on March 28, 1998, it is directed towards young talents who have already produced a collection. The guests at the event are able to present their own lines in an exhibition space that is differentiated from that of Milan Collections.

New Edwardians (Teds). English youth movement, with a strong focus on clothing and fashion. It began in the early 1950s, as a popular revival of the opulent Edwardian period (1901-1910), with an additional touch of American Western inspiration. The members of the movement were known as Teddy Boys. The unisex look was based on knee-length riding coats (black, bright mauve, red, yellow or green), with padded shoulders and narrow waists, buttoned up high with velvet revers. They were very similar to the famous American "zootsuits." They were worn with precious embroidered waistcoats, frilly shirts, and fastened at the neck with strings or thin ties, cowboy style. Their pants were straight and tight, and so referred to as "drainpipes," and they were sometimes highlighted with a band of silk along the sides. Hair was normally worn long, swept back in a high quiff, with exaggerated sideburns. Though the luxurious, rich, and sophisticated Edwardian period lasted less than a decade (it came to an end with the death of Edward VII in 1910), this fashion went on for little longer. However, it represented a post-war period of carefree youth, amusement and a return to pleasure, almost an attempt to rediscover the lost madness of that English aristocracy. Although limited, the New Edwardians movement had its importance, above all in men's fashions and the development of street style. *(Mariella Gardella)*

Newhouse Samuel Irving (1928). American publisher known above all by the initials of his name. S.I.E. was at the helm of the Condé Nast editions in the United States, both the group's books and magazines, such as *Vogue*, *G.Q.*, *Glamour*, *Vanity Fair*, *Details*, and *Allure*. In 1985 he bought the very refined magazine *The New Yorker*. He has also worked on gastronomic and interior decoration magazines.

❑ 2002, October. His son, Jonathan Newhouse, the current president of Condé Nast International, announced the launch of the Portuguese edition of the magazine *Vogue*. It is the fourteenth in the world.

New Look An ultra-feminine style of clothing that accents the silhouette: a wasp waist, modeled bust, high chest, round hips, wide and fluid skirts that hang to 20-30 centimeters above the ground. Already before World War II it had attracted the interest of great creators such as Balenciaga, Fath, and Balmain. But the term was invented by Carmel Snow, American editor of *Harper's Bazaar*, to describe the first, revolutionary collection by Christian Dior on February 12, 1947. Indeed, the figure of Dior's woman could not have been more innovative, as it

1946-48. The period of the New Look launched by Christian Dior.

did away with the square shoulders, orthopedic heels, and tight skirts of wartime dress. Dior's reaction to the dark years was a return to the past, both for its sculpted beauty and also for its use of rigid underwear that had previously been abandoned, such as basques, whale-boning and corsets, not to mention the rigid tulle organza linings used to underpin meters and meters of fabric in the long pleated skirts, so that they rustled and moved. The New Look had a great following but also provoked countless polemics. The most active women considered the style to be reactionary, even offensive, almost an invitation to return to nineteenth-century roles. The textile producers were happy, the tailors a little less so, as they had to acquire Dior's patterns. But the clamor resulted in free publicity and the style continued, until the mid-1950s, when the H line, the antithesis of flowing dress, was followed by the A and Y lines, liberating the waist and hips. *(Lucia Sollazzo)*

Newman French brand of sportswear. "Life is too short to dress in a sad way," was the philosophy that aided its initial success. Born in 1966, it first produced solely jeans, until its founder Jacques Jaunet decided to follow the fashion for casual wear for both sexes, with a particular emphasis on sports clothing. Its great early success, thanks partly to the characteristic metal triangle used in place of a label, later ran into difficulties in the face of competition, forcing Newman to downsize and partly orient its production towards a more classic style.

Newman Byron (1948). English photographer. He studied art and design at Leicester College of Printing. In 1977, he was the art director for Deluxe. He moved to Paris, where he is responsible for photography at Mode International. He has collaborated with *Friends*, *Time Out*, *Rolling Stone*, *Cream*, *Lui*, and *Playboy*.

New Republic American menswear brand, founded in 1981 by Thomas Oatman. The style of his clothes is consciously backward looking, with a predilection for cuts, textiles and jacket lengths that recall the Edwardian period.

New Romantics Youth movement and spontaneous fashion. It originated in London at the start of the 1980s as a reaction to Punk, and slowly diffused across the Western world. The clothing looked to the past, through evocations, juxtapositions, and combinations: lace, scarves, cloaks, and velvets breathed life into a neo-dandy fashion, represented by designers such as Vivienne Westwood and Stephen Jones. The ideological contribution of contemporary music was important, with groups such as Spandau Ballet, Duran Duran, and Depeche Mode, and singers such as Steve Strange and Boy George.

Newton Helmut (1920-2004). German photographer, naturalized Australian. He has influenced fashion photography more than any once else in modern times. He was born in Berlin where, after his studies at the American School, he began his career as assistant to the fashion photographer Else Simon, better known as Eva. He turned his back on Nazi Germany, passing through Singapore, where he stayed for a year, then emigrating to Australia, whose citizenship he later obtained. He fought in the Australian army during World War II, after which he returned to photography and worked as a freelance for *Vogue Australia*. In 1958, he moved to London and then to Paris, beginning collaborations with *Nova*, *Marie Claire*, *Elle*, *Queen* and, from 1961, he helped to radically revise the image of *Jardin des Modes*. His unmistakable and aggressive style, with strong undertones of sensuality and sexuality, led him to collaborate during the 1960s with *Playboy*, *Stern* and *Life*, while his association with the American, Italian, English and French editions of *Vogue* became more established. He gained a pivotal role within *Vogue France*, alongside Guy Bourdin, during the 1970s. After 1971, a heart attack made him strongly reconsider his very frénetic work schedule and decide to pursue more selective choices. A highly sensitive creator, he always imposed his own vision with authentic determination: almost shy with regard to personal matters, he became a celebrity solely through his images, which were always produced with extraordinary technical skill, alternating a very precise and almost calligraphic color with an extremely refined black-and-white, which contained cultural echoes of Expressionism and the style favored by aggressive photoreporters, to whom he sometimes declared his debt. His use of Polaroids, on the other hand, was consciously direct and slightly "dirty," as if he had made the images for himself. He created advertising campaigns for the most famous brands across the world and each time not only transmitted his vision of a very decisive, autonomous, independent woman, but also his consciously voyeuristic style, sometimes containing eccentric fetishistic references, which were appreciated by many but violently opposed by others, who considered them chauvinistic. His approach provoked continuous debate with certain fringes of the feminist movement. But Helmut Newton, who lived in Montecarlo until 1981, always responded with innovative, succinct phrases ("The sexiest part of a woman's body? Her ankle"), a good dose of auto-irony ("I am a salon communist"), and original initiatives such as *Newton Illustrated*, the large format magazines dedicated entirely to his photos, or the book *Sumo*, published in 1999: 480 pages, 50x70cm format, 30 kg weight at a price of $1500. His photographs are included in numerous publications (*White Women*, *Helmut Newton Portraits*, *Pola-women*, *A World Without Men*, *Us and Them* and the recent *Yellow Pages*, inspired by a murder trail that took place in Monaco, which Newton documented in 2002 as a correspondent for *Paris Match*) and displayed in exhibitions across the world. His professional collaborations with his wife June (also a photographer and known by the pseudonym Alice Springs, after the Australian town), were also important. He died in Los Angeles in a car accident in 1984. (*Roberto Mutti*)

New York Industrie Italian brand of ready-made clothing for men and women. New York Industrie, the company, was launched in 1977 in Noventa Vicentina in the province of Vicenza and became part of Staff International in 1984. It has a continuous presence at the runway shows in Milan, Paris, and New York. It uses various textiles, natural and technological. The garments are distributed all over the world and can be found in Italy in own-brand stores (Reggio Emilia, Modena, Riccione, and Rome). The Beirut pants are one of the company's most famous creations: a male design updated for women, fitted at the bottom with small splits at the sides. Staff International also produces and distributes Bella Freud, G-Y'm and other brands, on a contract license basis. The group has given industrial support to the innovative creations of Martin Margiela and Vivienne Westwood. Kostas Murkudis is the artistic director of the fashion house. Helped by designers of international repute, the German designer of Greek origin has transformed the direction of the company, starting with the Fall-Winter 2001 collection. Shapes, cuts and textile treatments have undergone a restyling to direct the product towards a younger market.

❑ 2002, March. The company opened an own-brand store in Paris in the Marais district, and the department store Lafayette began to stock New York Industrie.
❑ 2003, Spring. Staff International sold the license for New York Industrie to McAdams, another firm from the Vicenza region. Since the Spring-Summer 2004 collection, McAdams has controlled the design, production, and distribution of the brand.

Next Chain of English stores, "places for shopping, places for living," says their slogan. In 1981, Hepworths, the inheritor of a tailoring dynasty, acquired the chain Kendalls to add women's clothing retail spaces to it. By the following year, there were 70 Next stores. In 1984, 52 menswear shops were opened, followed by ones that stocked childrenswear and household objects. They launched an innovative concept: the mini-department stores included coffee shops, florists, and newsagents, in addition to the clothing spaces. In 1986, J. Hepworth & Son changed its name to Next and its products were diffused widely thanks through their mail-order catalog. Since 1994, it has opened 300 retail points across 16 different countries. Each garment is created individually by an internal team of designers. Internet sales of Next products were launched in 1999, with the publication of their entire catalog, which totaled 833 pages in Spring-Summer 2002. From 2000 the "Next day delivery" service was activated which offered home delivery the following day for orders placed on the internet before 5pm. There is an archive of Next collections from 1982 to the present, held at the Department of Museums, Art and Music at Leicester County Council. It can be consulted on appointment. There are approximately 330 Next stores in Great Britain and roughly 50 more across the Channel.

Next G+U. R.+U Now German *prêt-à-porter* brand. At the start, the founders Uta Riechers and Martin Wuttke, who work in Berlin, proposed recycled, modified, and reassembled clothing. Then they changed direction to clothing designed for the techno music community. From 1995 onwards, they have won various fashion design prizes and presented their collections on runways in Düsseldorf, Paris, and London. Now they have own-brand stores in Berlin and cities across Germany. They also work freelance for various Japanese fashion houses. Both are involved in an important social project: involving individuals with mental disabilities in their production process. What does the long and complicated brand name stand for? Next Generation You Are You Now. Their motto is Urban mutation couture. (*Valeria Vantaggi*)

Nichanian Veronique (1957). Parisian designer, who trained at the École de la Chambre Syndicale de la Couture and then debuted with Nino Cerruti in 1976. During her ten-year collaboration with the fashion designer from Biella, Veronique created the menswear collection and oversaw the foreign market licenses. In January 1988, she moved to Hermès, where she was artistic director of menswear. The collections, aimed at young men between 19 and 25, made of light textiles, gently caught in tapering lines, with neutral colors such as burnt earth, bark brown and stucco, were intended to "purify" the Hermès style. However, some people accused Nichanian of having strayed too far from the fashion house's traditions. At the end of the same year, she received the Grand Prix du Jeune Créateur from the City of Paris. Today, in her office on the Faubourg Saint-Honoré, 15 years on from the start of her collaboration with the house founded in 1837, Veronique continues to create clothing in light, undulating cottons, such as muslin, using gentle tones, above all yellow, light gray and tobacco brown.

(*Sara Tieni*)

Nichols Rozae (1960). American designer. She was born in Los Angeles and studied at the Art Center College of Design in Pasadena, California. She collaborated with Surplus, Harriet Selling, Freego and Bensimon, before creating her own collection of womenswear under her own name. Her style is characterized by an unusual use of materials: costly fabrics used as cheap ones and vice versa.

Nicholson Ivy (1934). American model. In the 1950s and 1960s, she was a star on the runways of Paris, Florence, and Rome, and on the covers of *Elle*, *Vogue* and *Harper's Bazaar*. For Andy Warhol, she appeared in the film *Couch*, and took part in the projects of the Factory, the group of creators surrounding the master of pop art. She married a Roman aristocrat, whom she later divorced. She remarried in New York and had two children, Gunther and Penelope, with an eighteen-year-old member of the Factory. From the mid-1970s, Ivy, who had already experienced some emotional difficulties, disappeared entirely. Many years later, in 1987, the photographer Eric Luse from the *San Francisco Chronicle* photographed a "bag lady" on the streets of San Francisco with very singular movements and bearing, and a face that revealed a ruined beauty. He took a few photos and showed them to an old fashion correspondent, who immediately recognized the individual as Ivy Nicholson. Two journalists ran to find her in Market Street and in the areas frequented by homeless people. Furio Colombo related the incident in an article for *Panorama* in May 1987: "They found her seated on the ground next to a bonfire of rubbish, together with two older women, Brigitte, an alcoholic who read the fortunes of passers-by, and Dondy, who always pushed a shopping trolley full of old newspapers. On the wet pavement the younger woman opened a black plastic folder of the kind used by aspiring models as they go from one photographic agency to another: 'Look, do look, feast your eyes,' ordered Brigitte, when she saw the journalist spying on the group from behind. They were all fashion photographs. A splendid woman, aged eighteen, twenty, thirty (...) languid, feline, aggressive, innocent, distracted, she looked out with large dark eyes, sometimes intent, almost sulky, sometimes with a beautiful smile. Inside a milk carton there was a roll of film. 'This is the film,' explained the woman. She coughed and scratched her hands opening the rusty lid. She tried to show the stills to her friends, holding them up against the light of the fire. (...) She continued to cough but refused the blanket one of the journalists offered her: 'Too new, my boy, I see you have no experience of life on the streets. Here they'd steal it straight away.' They told her that Andy Warhol was dead. 'I know, I know he's dead. People throw away newspapers, they get blown by the wind, you just need to sit here and the pages arrive.' The three women laughed. One of the famous ex-model's teeth is missing, a premolar, and with a childlike gesture she covered her mouth."

(*Fulvio Bertasso*)

Nicky Term used for a type of chenille and the pullovers made from it, which were fashionable during the 1950s and 1960s. It occasionally resurfaces, with different uses.

Nicoletta Ruggiero The name of the most refined and elegant line produced by the Ma.Ni Group that was founded in Ferrara in 1989 to produce and distribute women's *prêt-à-porter*. The Group's other line is called Miss NR and is more youthful and trendy.

Both productions are characteristically made using craft techniques and exclusive materials.

Niebuhr Lili (1903-1997). German photographer. She worked for years as an apprentice, assistant, and retoucher for many studios in Hamburg and Berlin before acquiring the studio of the Jewish photographer Bruno Winterfeld in 1935, during the so-called "Aryanisation" of photographic studios. Specialized in fashion photography, in 1943 she fled Berlin and later dedicated herself to plant photography.

NIFT National Institute of Fashion Technology of New Delhi. It was founded in 1987, by the Indian Textile Minister in collaboration with the Institute of Technology of New York. India exports many millions of garments annually to the United States, Europe, and Japan. The institute operates with schools in seven cities providing professional and academic training for young people wishing to study the most advanced fashion technologies and their relative management. (*Pier Giorgio Mora*)

Nigo Japanese designer. An eclectic and rather mysterious character, designer, journalist, and musician. Very little is known regarding his true name, age, or training. A friend of Jun Takahashi, whom he met in 1988 at the Bunka Fashion College, the two collaborated on the series of Nowhere T-shirts and the Undercover line. In 1993, with a limited series of T-shirts freely inspired by the film *The Planet of the Apes*, he launched the brand A Bathing Ape, often abbreviated to Bape, which soon became famous and was snatched up by the youth of Tokyo and New York. The line, at the beginning only comprising clothing and accessories, was extended to cover various other elements, from interior design to furniture, to games. His fashion is orientated towards comfort, practicality, and simplicity. It is very much focused towards the world of youth, its legends and its metamorphoses.

Nihommatsu Koji (1965). Japanese designer. He studied at the prestigious fashion school, the Bunka Fashion College in Tokyo, and immediately afterwards moved to Paris. He began to work for Kenzo and later became the artistic director of the Epoca brand, which is part of the Sanyo group. In 1995, he launched his first collection, revisiting European fashion classics with highly technological fabrics and finishings. (*Maddalena Fossati*)

Nike American brand of trainer shoes. It has played a vital role in making trainers the footwear of choice for everyday use, in its many styles, colors, and technologies. It boasts Michael Jordan, the star of the Chicago Bulls and one of the greatest basketball players of all time, as a celebrity endorser. It was launched in Oregon, at the beginning of the 1960s, by Phil Knight and Bill Bowerman (who died in 1999). In Greek mythology, Nike was the goddess of victory and represented success in war and athletic competition. The same success was achieved at the Olympic Games in Barcelona in 1992 by the American basketball team (the famous Dream Team, made up of the NBA professionals) wearing Nike shoes. It was a great publicity coup for Nike. It was the first brand to offer, at the beginning of the 1980s, shoes specifically designed for every sporting discipline: jogging, aerobics, body building, running. Nike's coup over the competition was to insert pockets of air in the heel and sole (copying the technique from Dr Martin's), with the result that Nike Air monopolized the market. In the heart of Manhattan, the company has a highly modern showroom on two floors, organized according to each different sport. (*Lorenzo Leonarduzzi*)

❑ 2002, April. Nike and Philips announced their collaboration to develop electronic equipment designed for physical activities. It began in September with the launch of a CD player adapted to the needs of sporting individuals.
❑ 2002, June. The launch of the franchising operation of the European sector of the multinational. The Viennese store (350 square meters) was the first in a series of test spaces opened in Europe within the course of a few months. The multinational aimed to open 100 European stores by 2008. The birth of the Nike Presto line of casual clothing, following the success of rapid

use shoes without laces. The wider collection includes clothing, watches and bags.

❑ 2002, December. Inauguration of the Milan store, on two floors in Corso Buenos Aires. In the second quarter of 2002, the total sales in Europe, the Middle East, and Africa increased by 8%. On the American continent, however, sales decreased by 8% for the same period.

❑ 2003. The global launch of shoes for children aged between 1 and 6 years old, inspired by the Lego Bionicle series.

Nimei Jewelry brand owned by the Italian company Worldgem (province of Vicenza). Dynamic communication techniques, distribution, and sales have enabled the firm to rapidly establish its four brands on the national and foreign markets: Nimei, Yukiko, Miluna, and Kiara, which each serve a different market band. While Nimei and Yukiko are designed for a public with classic tastes, Miluna and Kiara satisfy the youth market, sensitive to changes in fashion. In particular, Nimei represents the feather in the firm's cap, with its many collections in which pearls, always accompanied by a guarantee of high quality, play an important role. Examples of different tones – white, lavender and peach – are combined to produced the refined and decorative effects of the La Perla collection. The Nimei La Perla strands are quoted in the financial newspaper, *Il Sole 24 Ore*, every second Tuesday of the month.

(*Alessandra Quattordio*)

Necklace chain and hearts by Miluna, a Nimei brand.

Nina Donis *Prêt-à-porter* brand created and launched in 1992 by two designers from Moscow, Nina Neretina (1968) and Donis Poupis (1969). Donis, born in Cyprus, moved to Moscow in 1989, a year of monumental changes (the fall of the Berlin wall) and significant developments in the Soviet Union. He met Nina at the Textile Academy, which they both attended from 1987 to 1992. Their style is influenced by European fashions, at that time by the English pop style of McQueen and Westwood. Their new collections, by now known and sold across the world and presented at London Fashion Week, continue to refer to the ideas that inspired them in the past, while always paying attention to the present.

Nina Ricci French fashion house, founded in 1932 by Maria Nielli Ricci, known as Nina (1883-1970), who was born in Turin but emigrated to Montecarlo as a young girl, where her father, a ribbon producer, aimed to expand his activity among the most effervescent female clientele of the late 19th century. The premature loss of her father significantly affected Maria's destiny. Noting her ability to sew clothes and, above all, hats for her dolls, her family found her employment in one of the city's ateliers. However, her talents and hard work must have been an extraordinary force, given that she was already a première in Paris by 18 and employed by Raffin, one of the most successful fashion houses of the time, by 25. Nina stayed there for twenty years and became a partner. The store's sign included her name and surname, that of Luigi Ricci, a jeweler of Italian origin and an unlucky meteor in her life. Their marriage was brief, although it produced a son, Robert (1905-1988), who was the true force behind the launch of Nina Ricci in 1932. Like many other Italian fashion houses in recent years (Fendi, Missoni, Versace), the family, a synergy of strength and aims from one generation to the next, has been the secret behind this world conquering brand, one of the most popular in Paris, that enjoyed particular periods of success during its long life, such as during the 1960s and the late 1980s. It was Robert who convinced his mother not to abandon fashion as she approached the age of fifty. Despite being only 27, he had a long-term vision and his advertising experience was invaluable. The unbeatable technical skills of Nina and her view of elegance that never overwhelmed a woman's personality did the rest. And so Nina Ricci was born and it was an immediate success: even though the fashion house dressed some famous actresses, such as Danielle Darrieux and Micheline Presle, it was primarily aimed at middle-class women, offering impeccable models that were destined to last, and at moderate prices. In a few years (1932-39), the 25 members of staff became 150 and the workshops grew from 4 to 12. Nina Ricci overtook all other houses in terms of client numbers. After World War II, the perfume, *L'air du temps*, launched by Roberto Ricci, who was by now owner of half Nina Ricci's capital, became one of the top five perfume successes in the world with its flowery overtones and its Lalique bottle designed by Christian Bérard. In the *haute couture* sector, with an absolute coup de grâce, Nina was succeeded by a young Belgian designer, Jules François Crahay, whose first collection (1959) gained the enthusiasm not only of the press but also of the female public: a hundred women wanted his Crocus suit. But Crahay went to join Lanvin (1963) and was replaced by Gérard Pipart, who was perhaps the designer most in tune with the aims of the founder: that of respecting the form and well-being of women, over and beyond contemporary trends. Pipart combined tailoring skills acquired from working with Balmain, Fath, and Givenchy, with a love of detail, a harmony of forms and colors. To this he added a sporting touch, the elegance and ease of ample and soft garments, coats and blouses, soft shoulders, prints, and wafts of chiffon. Pipart received the Dé d'Or in 1987 for the best collection. In 1994, Nina Ricci was a formidable group, present in 130 countries, with more than 100 *prêt-à-porter* lines, thanks to the foresighted introduction of new capital and the work of Roberto Ricci's son-in-law, Gilles Fuchs, hailing from a perfume company in Grasse and therefore well prepared to manage a company that, notwithstanding its successes in the fashion field, based 75% of its business on perfume. (*Lucia Sollazzo*)

❑ 2000. The new millennium was marked by the acquisition of Nina Ricci by Antonio Puig, a Spanish group specializing in cosmetics.
❑ 2002. The company took part with other French brands (including Cacharel and Christian Lacroix) in Lingerie Americas held at the Metropolitan Pavilion & Altman Building in New York.
❑ 2002, Spring. James Aguiar took over from Nathalie Gervais and Massimo Guissani, creators of womenswear. He designed the women's and men's *prêt-a-porter* and accessory lines. The first men's collection by Aguiar debuted in Summer 2003.
❑ 2003, April. Lars Nilsson left Bill Blass and returned to Paris to join Nina Ricci. The Danish designer, who had left the French capital in 1999 to move to New York, was to help relaunch the fashion house.

Nine West American footwear firm. In twenty years it has become a giant in the sector. It produces bags and shoes for Calvin Klein and is also behind brands such as Pied-à-terre, Enzo Angiolini, Easy Spirit, and Pappagallo. Founded in 1977, it was originally called Fisher Camuto after the names of the two partners, Jerôme Fisher and Vincent Camuto. From 1968 to 1977, the pair had worked for the Sumitomo Corporation of America, an importer of Japanese shoes that sought to explore and develop the Brazilian market. Not by chance, Fisher Camuto had its first headquarters in Brazil. Today it is based at White Plains in New York state. The Nine West Group, thanks to its fashionable style, reasonable prices and good quality, now operates on a global scale. It is present in 42 countries and has over 1,000 shops. After passing under the control of the American group Jones Apparel, Nine West began the new millennium in a phase of expansion.

❑ 2002, Spring. An agreement was signed with Esprit for the production and distribution of shoes, bags, and leather accessories for women. The five-year contract covered the commercialization of the lines in department stores and Nine West retail points in the USA and Puerto Rico.

Nippon Albert. American clothing entrepreneur. Albert Nippon was born in Philadelphia in 1927 and graduated from Temple University. In 1953, he married the designer Pearl Schluger, also born in Philadelphia in 1927. Beginning with a successful line of maternity clothing, Albert and Pearl developed an extensive fashion business sold largely through department stores. In 1973, the couple founded Albert Nippon Inc. to commercialize their growing sportswear brands. The company is well known for conservative, often ladylike, coats and sportswear pieces.

Nishijin Textile Museum Kyoto, Japan. A permanent exhibition in the Nishijin Textile Center, opened in 1976. It traces the story of a particular type of silk brocade that is typical of Nishijin, a neighborhood in Kyoto. The exhibition is chronologically presented, from the origins of the fabric in 500 AD, through Chinese and, later, European influences, with the arrival of Jacquard looms, up until the creation of a workers' association in 1883. Exhibitions, demonstrations and runway shows are organized to keep this important local tradition alive.

Nizzoli Marcello (1887-1969). Architect and industrial designer. In 1923 he won a competition held by the Piatti silk factory in Como for shawl designs with geometric motifs influenced by Art Deco. In 1925-26, he designed scarves whose patterns were heavily influenced by Futurist art. He was an exponent of the second wave of Futurism and the author of important architectural projects, including houses for the staff of Olivetti at Ivrea. As an industrial designer, he was responsible for the famous *Lettera 22* typewriter made by Olivetti.

NN Studio Italian brand of *prêt-a-porter* clothes, design and craft objects. It offers clothing (since 1991), furniture (since 1992), ceramics (since 1993), furnishings (since 1994), as well as printed textiles, and wallpapers. Every year, something new is added but it must conform to the principle of continuous research into lifestyles focusing on personalizing taste rather than fashions. It all started in a place that is now famous: 10 Corso Como in Milan, created by Carla Sozzani.

Noberasco Vita. Milanese tailor and a beautiful and highly intelligent woman. She was one of the nine *haute couture* professionals invited by Giorgini on February 11, 1951, to demonstrate the existence of an Italian style that was uninfluenced by French fashions. According to Maria Pezzi, she was, with Germana Marucelli, ahead of all others on the road to independence from Paris because she was more intelligent and less bourgeois than both her male and female colleagues. She had begun to create garments before the Florentine shows and also knew how to carry out research, for which she had a huge collection of fashion-related newspapers and magazines. At that time it was rare for someone in the trade to have such a forward-looking interest. Her library, once the atelier was closed, was acquired by the jeweler Giuliano Fratti and a very young Walter Albini.

Noki The pseudonym and brand of the British designer J.J. Hudson. He was born in Aberdeen, Scotland, in 1971. He shares his time between London and Brighton and is an icon in the gay community and beyond. Of his work as a designer, it is said "he bases himself more on philosophical concepts than on fashion and fashion marketing." In addition to designing T-shirts, sweatshirts, jeans and shoes, he also works as a multimedia artist. During London Fashion Week 2002, for example, an exhibition was held displaying some of creations. Noki works on imperfect, used or partly creased garments and adds details to them: inserts, designs, applications of various sorts. His garments are all, therefore, unique and are sold in some of the trendiest shops in London. He is passionate about Adidas trainers from the 1980s, and made a name for himself with a T-shirt with the logo of the German company, altered and partly covered but recognizable nevertheless. As a consequence,

Vita Noberasko ha ripreso in pieno la sua attività di modellista. Alcuni abiti da sera della sua collezione rivelano l'eccezionale qualità di saper creare con senso d'arte e mano da scultrice...

Vita Noberasco in her Milan atelier in a drawing by Brunetta for the magazine *Bellezza*.

Adidas invited him to design a limited edition of trainers for them.

(*Giulia Crivelli*)

Nolita An area of New York. Nolita, or rather "north of little Italy," is the new alternative neighbourhood in New York and is, above all, the centre of youth fashion in the city. Located alongside the shops and restaurants of a Little Italy that is slowly disappearing and was captured so masterfully in Francis Ford Coppola's *The Godfather*, are the boutiques of Tracey Feith and Christopher Totman, shops like Calypso and Language that stock the best of alternative and youth fashions, from America and abroad.

Nomination Italian jewelry company founded in 1983 at Sesto Fiorentino. In 1987, it created the modular bracelet Nomination, thanks to the combination of plaquettes in steel and gold decorated in relief or with enamels with letters of the alphabet and various symbols. The immediate success of this piece of jewelry allowed the company that produced it to develop other ideas, all utilizing different modular elements that express messages and references that are easily identifiable by a young public. Little by little, rings, bracelets, pendants, necklaces, and watches appeared. Many international celebrities – from Madonna to Tom Cruise, Julia Roberts to Jennifer Lopez – have worn Nomination designs at public events and have turned the pieces of jewelry into cult objects. In 2003, Nomination was selected by the Academy of Motion Picture Arts and Sciences to provide a modular bracelet that can be personalized for the highly desirable "Gift Basket," an exclusive gift given to the best Hollywood artists on Oscar night. Other successful pieces include Xte, the line of extendable bracelets in gold, diamonds and precious stones, with ornamental multi-colored motifs, and Rh Nomination, a collection of military inspired pendants and Croce, again made with linking steel plaquettes.

(*Alessandra Quattordio*)

Noni Sport Italian external knitwear company, founded in 1949 by Alina Allazetta and Adele Mariani Malacarne. It enjoyed success and attention throughout the 1950s and 1960s. It employed designers such as Alberto Lattuada and Toni Aboud. In 1970, it was taken over by Ragno who sold it nine years later.

Nonsolomoda Magazine program on fashion and the world of performance broadcast on the Mediaset network. Created by Fabrizio Pasquero, it was subtitled, "A weekly program on various vanities." It covers fashion in the widest sense of the word, namely everything that is trendy and related to the pleasures of life. The great innovation of Nonsolomoda is that every feature constitutes a short video for an anonymous sponsor. From 1995-96, the features, which previously were only accompanied by a voice-over narrative, were introduced by Roberta Capua, shot in close-up in the style invented by the Target, the program broadcast immediately before Nonsolomoda. The program's use of photography is also significant. With contributions from photographers including Hans Visser, Charles Rose, Fabio Gianchetti, and Luca Robecchi, it manages to be journalistic and therefore informative, while at the same time creating an extremely elegant image, which adds to the luxurious quality of each feature. It is this combination of true documentary and "setting" designed to enhance the advertising editorial accompanying each film. It is the only program dedicated to fashion to be broadcast for twenty years and has very many imitators. Silvia Toffanin has taken the place of Roberta Capua and presents the program, to whose title has been added "And contemporaneously," in order to underline the very up-to-date nature of its content.

Nordica Italian ski boot manufacturer. During the 1960s, after a new type of ski boot was invented in Austria that substituted metal clasps for laces, Nordica of Montebelluna (Treviso) was the first firm to adopt them in Italy. Founded in 1938 by the brothers Adriano and Oddone Vaccari, it began by manufacturing footwear intended for leisurewear but, after a pause the war when they furnished boots for the military, the company focused in particular on the production of ski boots. At the end of the 1960s came a great innovation: ski boots made entirely of polyurethane. In 1989, the company was bought by the Benetton group and in 1990 it launched a range of sportswear for winter and summer. Beating competition from Atomic and Head, the Tecnica group took over Nordica, which had been put up for sale by Benetton. The transfer became operative at the beginning of February 2003, at a cost of approximately 38 million euros. On the same date, Benetton purchased 10% of Tecnica.

Nordiska Museet Stockholm museum dedicated to Swedish daily life. The clothing collection has more than 43,000 pieces dating from 1520 to the present, that include traditional costumes, fashion items, textiles and materials used in textile production. It also owns an important collection of locally manufactured jewelry and an archive of documents related to fashion.

Nordstrom American chain of department stores stocking casual clothing. The first shop specialized in footwear and was opened in Seattle in 1901 by a young and penniless Swedish immigrant named John W. Nordstrom. During the 1960s, the company, which already held an important position in the footwear market, decided to extend its production to include clothing for women, men, and children. Today it owns 143 retail stores in 27 American states and has 23 international stores, mainly in Europe.

Norel Norman Pseudonym of Norman D. Levinson (1900-1972). American designer. During his long career he collected a series of firsts, for example, he was the first American couturier to win the consideration and respect of the great Parisian tailors, and the first to receive the Coty Award. He was born in Indiana. During the 1920s, he studied in New York but, contrary to popular belief, he never attended the prestigious Parson's School. Instead he studied for a diploma at the Pratt Institute. In 1922, he began to work with Paramount Pictures, designing costumes for Gloria Swanson, and Rudolph Valentino. From 1928 to 1940, he worked for Hattie Garnegie, a famous fashion house, where he matured the essence of his future style: adapting French chic – in vogue at the time – to American tastes. He created costumes for the Ziegfeld Follies and the Cotton Club, and he dressed stars such as Joan Crawford, Paulette Goddard, Katharine Hepburn and, later on, Lauren Bacall. In 1941, with an administrative partner, he founded the fashion house Traina-Norel. From 1960, Traina was removed from the label, which became known solely as Norman Norel. His style had a distinct identity and an unmistakable glamour that was apparent in his dress shirts and evening gowns, and in the baroque use of textiles and sequins. His women's smoking jacket was created ten years before Yves Saint Laurent's. He founded the Council of Fashion Designers of America. He was the first American designer to launch his own perfume. He is considered an icon of American fashion.

(*Anna Gloria Forti*)

Norfolk Unisex tweed jacket with applied pockets, box pleats and a half-belt attached at the back. Fashionable from 1880 and worn by country gentlemen, it was revived in the 1950s and is a sportswear classic.

Normand Robert (1969). French designer. He took a diploma at the Berçot studio at the age of 20 and immediately afterwards became an assistant to Adeline André. For a while he worked for Yoneda Kasuko and, for two years, he worked at Arnaud and Thierry Gillier, where he learnt the basics of the trade and all the details of production. In 1994 he was menswear designer at Dorothée Bis. The following year he joined Lanvin. In 2001, he created a company that bore his own name and became a consultant for the Pucci menswear collection in Florence. Today he produces a collection of men's and women's clothing under his own name.

(*Maddalena Fossati*)

Noronha Warren (1977). English designer. After a brief experience as the assistant of Antonio Berardi, he launched his own brand in 2002. His powerful and dramatic style was immediately appreciated within the world of performing arts and fashionable shops in Europe and the United States.

Northridge Laddie (died in 1959). American designer. Famous creator of bespoke hats on 57th Street in New York. He loved wide hat brims.

North Sails Italian sportswear brand. Since 1987 it has been produced and distributed by the company Tomasoni Topsail (the president is Leopoldo Poppi, the CEO Giuseppe Fedeli), which was founded in Rapallo in 1972, where it still has its headquarters. It made equipment for sailing boats. In 1983 it broadened its outlook to include sportswear, and distributed the Henri Lloyd brand. The North Sails collections (two per year with a total of 565 models) are distributed in 1,100 Italian retail stores and 550 in the rest of Europe. The turnover in 1998 was 50 billion lire, 30% of which was from exports.

Nova English fashion monthly published between 1965 and 1975. Founded by Harry Fieldhouse and Harry Peccinotti, it was published by Georges Newhes. It covered the iconoclastic fashions of the 1960s. The magazine was accompanied by the slogans of the women's liberation movement and provocatively and ironically uncovered the dynamics regarding the objectification of the female form, ridiculing the traditional images of *haute couture*. It attracted the best photographers of the time, from Terence Donovan to Helmut Newton and Sara Moon, and exploded with color, insolence and vivacity. However, it traveled at an unsustainable speed and the publication came to an end with the first signs of political and economic change.

(*Stefano Grassi*)

Novaceta Industrial producer of "naturally intelligent" acetate fibers. They are cellulose fibers of natural origins. They are comfortable, versatile and attractive to fashion designers. Novaceta is the first European group to enter the market for cellulose acetates and had a 300 billion lire turnover in the late 1990s, from an annual production of 30,000 tones of yarn. Their products include: Silfresh, Situssa (a close mix of cellulose acetate with polyamide: practical, machine washable, non-crease and very strong) and Silcolor, which is dyed before the yarn is spun, and is available in 59 basic colors with 7,000 variations.

Novalis Fibre French-Italian synthetic fiber company. It specializes solely in flakes of nylon polyamide, without a continuous thread. The product has a short fiber, like wool or cotton. It is used in carded yarns with top nylons, and in combed yarns with high quality wools. Technical innovations mean that it is now possible to use it with cottons. Used in the measure of 20% in knitwear, it adds greater resistance to mixes and increases the softness of micro fibers. Novalis is a joint venture undertaken by Snia Fibre and Rhône Poulenc.

Novità Italian women's magazine launched in 1950 by Emilia Kuster Rosselli, who was its editor until 1958. With a modest financial contribution from her family, an adaptable and very young editorial team, in a short time the magazine became very popular, becoming a point of reference for a vast female public at medium-high level, who, in the optimistic post-war years, looked for something more in their publications than fashion and so-called female skills. The intuition of the director, a woman with many interests and a great sensibility for new things, was precisely that of creating, at a time when women were discovering new roles and had new aspirations, "a practical magazine that did not yet exist, for a modern, intelligent, elegant, and curious woman, a magazine that gives her news and ideas when she lives at home and which reminds her of home when, out of necessity or desire, she lives away." A thoroughly Italian magazine, *Novità* focused on fashion, interior decor, art, antiques, social problems, literature, cooking, and gardening, delicately recording the cultural interests that had sprung up again after the turmoil of the war, and the new need for elegance in clothing and living. During those years it became a sort of prototype, providing ideas for a large number of other publications supported by stronger publishers. On the death of Emilia Kuster Rosselli, the directorship passed to Lidia Tabacchi, who had been her competent and faithful alter ego for many years. Novità was acquired by Condé Nast in 1962, thanks to the prestige that Emilia Kuster enjoyed in the international publishing world, and to her friendly relations with and esteem felt by the French section of the famous American group. In 1965 the title, after gradually moving towards a more international format, became *Vogue Italia*.

è di moda la moda italiana

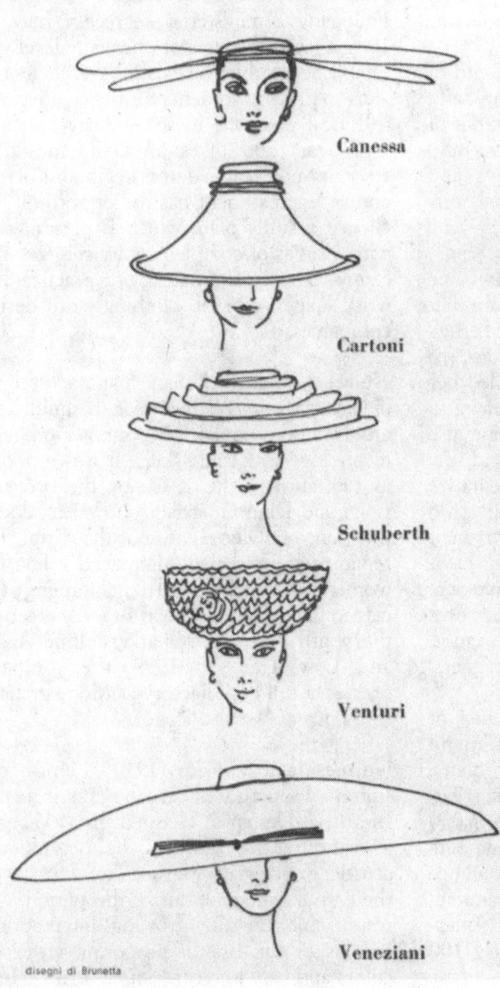

disegni di Brunetta

La moda italiana è, per gli stranieri di qualsiasi parte del mondo, soprattutto colore, colore e fantasia, ed è proprio questo che i compratori stranieri si attendono di trovare quando vengono a Firenze, per assistere alle sfilate della Sala Bianca a Palazzo Pitti. Tutto il mondo è a caccia di idee per questa moda sempre irrequieta e da qualche anno irrequietissima, e le idee italiane, possiamo convenirne senza modestia, fanno in questo momento, per dirla in termine di borsa, premio su tutte le altre. Forse perchè sono idee brillanti e spiritose, idee giovani e fresche, e forse anche perchè noi non montiamo in cattedra per dettare le fragili leggi della moda, ma le offriamo con molta semplicità come un bel mazzo di fiori del nostro paese, festoso di mille colori.

Quest'anno a Firenze l'incontro di queste richieste con le nostre offerte si è svolto con particolare felicità e l'XI^{a} Manifestazione Fiorentina ha segnato un netto progresso sulle precedenti. La giornata dedicata alle collezioni delle "boutiques" è stata addirittura esaltante, tanti i vari modellisti si sono presentati con collezioni spiritose e piene di inventiva. Un vero fuoco d'artificio di idee allegre, divertenti, di buon gusto o per lo meno per tutti i gusti, perchè alcune realizzazioni di colore troppo contrastate e non abbastanza raffinate, corrispondono meno al nostro modo di vedere l'originalità nell'abbigliamento. Ma gli stranieri si esaltano proprio a questa vivacità perfino violenta, che per loro è il simbolo stesso di questo nostro paese pieno di sole e di colore, sorridono beati alle mille trovatine della feconda genialità dei nostri modellisti e avremmo quindi torto a non rallegrarci con loro. Non tutta la "boutique", del resto, si abbandona senza ritegno alla fantasia e alcune case di maglieria, per esempio, hanno fatto sfilare in pedana creazioni di una signorilità, di una raffinatezza, di una misura davvero eccezionali. È qui, veramente, che la moda italiana può distinguersi dalle mode di tutto il mondo. Anche le giornate dell'Alta Moda, quest'anno, sono state di un livello nettamente superiore, con alcuni successi clamorosi che hanno sorretto successi non meno notevoli, anche se meno appariscenti.

Vera

(Continua a pag. 40)

A page from the monthly magazine *Novità* from March 1956 (from *La Moda Italiana – Le Origini dell'Alta Moda e la Maglieria*, Electa, 1987).

NRF National Retail Federation, founded in New York in 1990. It was created from the merger of the American Retail Federation, created in 1935, and the National Retail Merchants Association, founded in 1911 under the name of National Retail Dry Goods Association. It brought together 55,000 distributors of clothing and household furnishings, including chain department stores. It offers assistance, consultancy and a vast, widespread service, partly diffused through its in-house news bulletin.

Nude look It became popular at the end of the 1960s, when it was launched by Saint Laurent, since when it has never been out of fashion. It is characterized by light and transparent textiles, vertiginous splits and equally vertiginous décolletés and barely veiled posteriors.

Nuez Margarita (1940). Spanish tailor. She was born into a family tradition: her mother was a tailor at Foz de Calandra, near Teruel. Margarita moved at a very early age to Barcelona with her sisters but founded her own atelier in 1974. The queen and princesses of the House of Bourbon are her clients. Influenced by her husband, the painter Carlos Mensa, she is a representative of the cross-references between art and fashion. Designs by Nuez are on permanent display in the contemporary clothing pavilion at the Textile Museum in Barcelona, which exhibits approximately 100 garments by Cristobal Balenciaga, Pedro Rodriguez, Chanel, Pierre Cardin, and Italian designers.

Nukke-Ja Puku Museum A museum of clothing and dolls in Hatampaan Kertano in Finland. The collection of women's clothing and accessories, dating from 1770 to the present, contains more than 3,000 pieces. The menswear collection numbers 1,000, the children's 7,000. The provenance of the clothing is as varied as its manufacture, but is primarily European and American. The exhibition of approximately 100 pieces changes annually.

N° Un Biannual French menswear magazine, much sought after by bibliophiles for its graphics, paper, and photos. Published between 1957 and 1967 by the French Association for Male Elegance, it brought together the principal French producers of clothing for men, such as Armorial, Dial, Eminence, McDouglas, Mossant, and Noblet. Each issue was themed, from the car to city life to the various realities of the male world. Seasonal fashion innovations were illustrated with drawings, or high quality color photographs set against a white background.

Nuova Accademia di Belle Arti (Naba). Following a ministerial decree in Italy, in 1989 a fashion course at university level was established within the existing Accademia. It aims to prepare students for the creative and technical positions in the industry. It lasts four years and takes a maximum of 25 students per year. At the beginning of the course, each student has the opportunity to choose a study plan, which is personalised with a series of complementary subjects and exams. Theory alternates with practice and work experience at clothing and design companies.

Nuova Centauro Italian manufacturer of men's and women's footwear. Its guidelines are tradition mixed with innovation, and technology with craft skills. It was founded as Centauro in the 1940s by the brothers Luigi and Dino Guardiani. In 1972, Albert, the son of Dino, entered the firm. He renamed the company, launched a line for women and, while still maintaining the classic lines, launched two brands aimed at the youth and sports markets: Blue Again and Low Tide. In 1999, the company opened a full-cycle factory at Montegranaro (province of Ascoli Piceno).

Nurmesniemi Vuokko (1930). Finnish designer. He studied at the Institute of Industrial Design in Helsinki. In 1953, only a year after his diploma, he became the artistic director of Marimekko. He stayed there until 1960 and, during this period, was responsible for the growing international success of the brand, proposing vivacious colors and easy to wear, simple forms. He is part of a generation of Finnish designers, world pioneers of a clean and minimalist style. Issey Miyake professes to have been strongly influenced by his work. In 1964, he set up on his own, producing clothing and furnishing textiles under the name "Vuokko

Oy." He describes himself in the following terms: "I am a functionalist. A garment must be simple, indeed functional, but never boring." He also follows this spirit for the menswear line, defined as "the uniform of architects." He has received many recognitions and prizes. Many museums display his creations. In 1988, the Vuokko Oy company closed down. In 1990, the new Vuokko Nurmesniemi Oy was founded. Its name refers to the designer's previous experience and relaunched his designs.

❑ 2002, April. Nurmesniemi presented the Spring-Summer 2003 collection at the Design Museum in Helsinki. Alongside the designer were other Finnish labels, which had collaborated on seasonal fashion shows and events across Europe for ten years. They include Designer Shop by Iris Aalto, Positive Design by Pirjo Friedriksson and Nemaki by Tua Rahikainen.

Nuti Ilaria (1969). Italian designer and entrepreneur. Born in Vicenza, she represents the third generation of a family of leather manufacturers. In addition to her training in the family firm (Diana of Vicenza), she has had a great deal of work experience abroad, particularly in New York. Her creative style led her to design her own collection of handbags in different leathers in 2002. Her famous product is the Number One, which has been bought by Madonna and Queen Rania of Jordan. The designer has her own up-to-date and well-constructed website. It contains the designer's motto: "A handbag should be capable of holding a woman's most intimate emotions." (*Giulia Crivelli*)

Nuttal Sonja (1964). English designer born in Liverpool. She attended various fashion courses and work experience placements with designers such as Norman Hartnell and Gina Frattini. After her Masters degree at St. Martin's (1993), she worked as a consultant for various designers and department stores. In 1994, she launched her own line. She regularly takes part in London Fashion Week. Since 1995, she has taught design at different English colleges. She sums up her style with the phrase: "I want women who wear my clothes to feel desired." She preaches the art of understatement with modern and refined forms. The American journalist Suzy Menkes has described her as "the feminist designer."

Nutter Tommy (1943-1992). English tailor. He abandoned his architecture studies in order to join the workshop of G. Ward & Co., London tailors in Savile Row. In 1969, with the help of Cilla Black and Peter Brown of Apple (the Beatles' record company, which was also located in Savile Row), he opened a shop on the same street. Nutters, which in London slang means "crazy people," became the most trendy tailoring atelier of the Swinging Sixties. It dressed three of the Beatles for the *Abbey Road* album cover. From the start, Tommy Nutter was the favorite tailor of the music world and the international jet set. He created Mick and Bianca Jagger's wedding outfits for their marriage in St. Tropez in 1971. Both wore a men's suit typical of Nutter: a jacket with fitted shoulders and wide revers, a high buttoned waistcoat and flares. Everything was made of the finest materials and was made using traditional techniques. John Lennon and Yoko Ono wore similar outfits for their wedding. Nutter closed the shop in 1975 and the following year began to work for Kilgour French & Stoubury Tailors, a very traditional London tailoring firm. In 1982 he set up again on his own. Timothy Everest and John Galliano, as a student, both worked for him. The stars returned, including Elton John and Bill Wyman, and he made Jack Nicholson's outfits for his role as The Joker in the *Batman* film. Nutter definitively retired a few years later.

(*Virginia Hill*)

Nyl Italian *prêt-à-porter* brand. It was launched in January 2001, designed by Raimondo Ciofani and produced by the clothing production group Lamberti. Two years of preparation were required for the first Fall-Winter line, followed by a debut on the Milan runways in October 2002. Ciofani, who lives in Rome, was the designer and creator of Swish Jeans until 1998 when he moved to the Sixty Group. In Nyl he has created a youthful, dynamic and flexible fashion, perfect for every occasion. He abandoned the denim and transgressions that made him famous in the past and created a commercially safe collection "of substance." He used avant-garde textiles worked with lasers, water resistant silks and nylons, emery-treated stretch cottons for tight pants and tracksuits, and masculine fabrics for long skirts. Basic colors (just black and white), printed denim patchwork, leather, suede, and cotton for 1970s revival designs, transparent black for the evening, and fun details such as zips with small stones, necklaces on shoes, and silver chains hanging between the legs. Shirts were given a prime role, made of cotton jacquard and often worn underneath a bustier or with a tie. (*Gabriella Gregorietti*)

Nylon American fortnightly women's fashion and culture magazine launched in April 1999. It is based in Los Angeles. Its success is mainly due to its creative director, the former top model, Helena Christensen, who has passed over to the other side of the fence. Christensen also writes for the magazine and contributes photo shoots.

Nylon DuPont brand patented in 1935 and commercialized in 1938. Originally polyamide 66, the company's research into perpolyamides brought success. Versatile and resistant, it was successful during the 1940s, due to the shortage of raw materials following the war. The name nylon was given to all long chained polyamides and amides. An incorrect popular legend attributes the term to the Japanese defeat, supposedly taken from the initials of the phrase, "Now You've Lost Old Nippons."

Nylstar Synthetic fibers company specializing in continuous thread nylon micro fibers: super opaque and soft to the touch, classic and shiny, or almost natural. Nylstar produces the anti-stress comfort fiber, Meryl Souple, an updated version of Meryl: it is extremely absorbent with regard to humidity and body vapor and eliminates static electricity. It does not create sparks or discharge a magnetic field. The elastomere fiber Élite is by the same company: this provides the textile in which it is used with an elastic strength. Elastomere is like cold rubber, it is relatively heavy and stable. A mixture of between 3% and 30% of these fibers in a textile is sufficient to ensure elasticity.

Ocariz Miriam (1969). Spanish designer. Born in Bilbao. A Fine Arts graduate with a diploma in fashion design from Bilbao's International Lanca School, she belongs to the successful upcoming Spanish fashion scene. Her carefully crafted designs are admired all over the world. She makes "innocent" looking clothes, using floral or printed fabrics. In her work, she uses clothes as a form of expression and communication, perfectly balancing fabrics, shapes and in many cases, actual drawings. Her influences are German Expressionism and contemporary art. She is particularly fond of silk, linen, and knitted fabrics.

(*Estefania Ruilope Ruiz*)

Occhio di Pernice (Bird's Eye). Fabric with a small pattern, similar to that of an actual partridge's eye. This material has become a classic, used for men's jackets and coats since the 1940s. Its dark surface is covered with small lighter dots that create an irregular chromatic effect. The pattern is achieved using a "T cloth" weave, alternating two light threads with two dark ones. The final effect is that of very small, almost round, dots, with at their centre a light dot on dark background.

Ocelot A fur obtained from the ocelot, a South American wild cat. This valuable and rare fur has a yellow background covered with dark oblong patches.

Odalisque Inspired by Diaghilev's Ballets Russes, Paul Poiret is credited with having launched the odalisque fashion style during a theme party he gave in his garden called *One Thousand and One Nights*. The fashion featured light, smooth fabrics, strong and vivid colours, wide-legged pants fastened tight at the ankle, like the ones traditionally worn by the women in a harem, turbans and voluminous evening capes. The term odalisque is still used to refer to a style of wide-legged crinkled or pleated pants, gathered at the ankle by a tie or elastic.

Odicini Andrea. Women's couture dressmaker, inspired by the Parisian scene. He opened an atelier in 1981 in Palazzo Cambiaso in the centre of Genoa. Palazzo Cambiaso represented an important fashion inheritance for Odicini, since it had previously hosted a branch of the famous Milanese fashion houseVentura, and then Fina Trottman, who in 1945 took over the palazzo's outlet, archives, and clientele, reviving its fame until the end of the 1970s. Odicini also has a ready-to-wear line. His collections range from elegant suits to evening dresses. Odicini boasts an international clientele.

Odile Lançon French ready-to-wear label, created in 1984 by the eponymous fashion designer (1949). Lançon specializes in suits and very feminine coordinates, using pastel colours and natural fibres, such as linen and wool crêpe. Her path to success is impressive: she worked for four years in the creative department of Promostyl, and then moved to Max Mara to design the Sportmax Collections.

Oestergaard Heinz (1916). German fashion designer. He founded his own label in 1952, after working for labels like Shroder-Egger-inghaus. At the time he was considered the best German dressmaker and his feminine and seductive collections were inspired by the Parisian fashion scene. From 1979 to 1984 he taught at the Fachhoch-schule Für Gestaltung di Pforzheim (Institute of Decorative Arts). In 1967 he abandoned his teaching career and started working as a designer for Quelle, a mail order clothing company.

Ogden Jessica (1970). English fashion designer born in Jamaica to a large family. Her

father was a television director and her mother a Bounty model. She moved to London to study sculpture at the Byam Shaw School of Art. Although she is a self-taught fashion designer, she is considered a real artist in her genre. In 1993 she set up her own label. She had previously worked for the NoLoGo label, producing one-off pieces from old clothes with incredible flair. Her passion for vintage fabrics is an enduring aspect of her work, and she has become famous for her "patchwork" technique of incorporating old pieces of fabric into her clothes as appliqués and panels. The Design Museum, the Design Council and the Craft Council of London have all organized exhibitions of her work. Amongst her fans are many famous names from the hippy-pop scene, and she is also the darling of the fashion designer Jean Touitou, who often supports her work by sending her fabrics from his old collections. All Jessica's garments are characterized by a hand-made look. Hers is a street style that mirrors the everyday life of different people, whatever their looks, size, culture, or age. For this reason Jessica Ogden produces her garments in one size only, so that they never fit the body tightly, but adapt to different shapes.
(*Gabriella Gregorietti*)

Ognibene-Zendman Couture label, founded in Rome in 1965 by Sergio Ognibene (1929) and Peter Zendman. Zendman was the son of New York lace merchants, and in 1958 had already set up his own dressmaking business called Escalier. This fashion house has always been fond of simple, clean and slightly masculine creations using muted colours. They are also interested in the use of different materials, ranging from plastic to metal; for example, in 1966-67 they launched a short evening dress made of Mikado lamè, with a gold and silver check pattern and a skirt cut in an arched shape. Over the years the two designers have become "converted" to ready-to-wear. At present their collections are presented twice a year in 16 US cities, in prestigious stores such as Bergdorf Goodman, Saks Fifth Avenue, and Neiman Marcus.

Oh Justin (1965). English designer. He studied fashion at Central St. Martin's in 1987 and then at the Royal College of Art in 1991. In 1989 he designed his first ready-to-wear collection for Charles Jourdan in Paris. Once his studies were completed, he started working with Yohji Yamamoto, French Connection, and Marks & Spencer. In 1994 he launched his own label and since then he has regularly taken part in London Fashion Week. In 1997 he designed the strips for the Oxford and Cambridge rowing teams. In 1998 he produced his first collection for the American catalogue Spiegel. His individual style of dressmaking favours very feminine dresses, made from classic shirting cotton.

Ohya (1970). Japanese designer. She attendd the Bunka Fashion College until 1992 and in the same year she designed accessories for Issey Miyake. In 1996 she launched her own label called Ohya Design Zoo and took charge of Issey Miyake's Haat range. In 2002 she showed her first couture collection in Paris, using nonconformist presentation methods rather than the usual runways. She has becomes successful thanks to her "bookwear" creations, i.e., folding garments that resemble books.

Oilskins Long, airproof and waterproof jacket with fastenings in front and around the cuffs, with matching pants with the same characteristics. Necessary for those who sail or go out to sea, oilskins were until few years ago only yellow in color and made from a rather rigid and heavy waterproof material which hindered movements. Now the fabric has been modernized and more colors are available, from white to light blue. The most famous oilskins, almost considered a status symbol, have always been made by the Norwegian company Helly Hansen.

Olcese Alessandra (1960). Fashion show director. A law graduate, she moved to London where she studied for a diplomatic career. She stumbled across the fashion world by chance: "At the time I was doing odd jobs just to make a living," she recounted. Then, after running Giuliano Fujiwara's press office and working in Franca Soncini's PR office, in 1997 she founded a company called Random to organize fashion shows and events. The business was a success and her clients now include many important and well-established names such as Bluemarine, Max Mara, Sportmax, Alessandro Dell'Acqua, Antonio Berardi, Salvatore Ferragamo, and La Perla. She organizes a total of fifty fashion shows a year around the world. *(Valeria Vantaggi)*

Oldfield Bruce (1950). English designer. He dressed Diana, Princess of Wales. After obtaining a diploma in teaching at Sheffield City Polytechnic, he studied fashion design at St. Martin's School of Art. He began his career in fashion working in a Henri Bendel store in New York, which allowed him to hold his first fashion show in America as early as 1973. In 1975 he opened his own atelier in London, first with a ready-to-wear collection and then with couture. In 1984 he opened his own shop in London. His clientele includes several members of the Royal family and the aristocracy. His style pays constant homage to femininity: he is particularly admired for his slinky evening dresses, "directly draped over the body."

Bruce Oldfield: sketch for an overcoat, 1984.

Oldham Todd (1962). American fashion and interior designer. Originally from Texas, he became established by selling his creations to Neiman Marcus in Dallas. He then moved to New York and signed a contract with the Japanese distribution company Kashiyama to produce the Times Seven range, launched in 1990. A year later he created his first collection under his own name, followed shortly after by a range of jeans, sunglasses, shoes, and perfume. He has stores in New York, Miami South Beach, Los Angeles, and Tokyo. In 1998 he began producing a sportswear range for men. Admirers of his original, multiethnic, sexy, and colorful styles include Susan Sarandon and Cindy Crawford. In 1998 the excessive costs of fashion shows and advertising forced him to shut down his major range and go on the defensive: private clients, a cheaper range, a line of jeans, and a single boutique in Soho.

❑ Towards the end of the 1990s, Oldham intensified his collaboration with MTV, and after designing the interior of a bus sent by the music channel on tour around America to encourage young people to vote, he has worked on the interior design of the Tiffany Beach Hotel in Miami and some shopping malls in Las Vegas.

❑ 2001, September. The Target chain commissioned Oldham to create a range of home accessories. The Todd Oldham Dorm-room Collection was launched across 1019 Target stores in summer 2002.

Olimpias Italian textile group, based in Grumolo delle Abbadesse, near Vicenza. Founded in the 1980s, Olimpias brought together a group of textile manufacturers and related companies (yarns, fabrics, dyeing, and finishing) with the aim of offering a complete range of services in the textile field. This holding company, under the presidency of Armando Boccaletti, is linked to the Benetton Group and has consolidated annual sales of 600 billion lire, with an annual production of 20 million kg of yarn (cotton and wool) and 60 million meters of fabric (cotton, wool, and blends). The main affiliates of the group are: for yarns Galli Filati (carded wool and blends), Filma (combed wool and blends) and Goriziana (superior quality cotton); for fabrics Lanificio Follina (specialized in wool, polyester, traditional and modern blends), Tessuti Pordenone (cotton and stretch fabrics for casual wear) and Piobesi (cotton jersey and stretch fabrics for fashion and sportswear); for finishing processes Tex-control (labelling and processing), Stefani (dyeing), Maglificio Fontane (knitwear), Tiesse (preparation, dyeing and finishing of fabrics with avant-garde techniques), Essegigi (printing and finishing) and Color Service (dosage and mixture of fabric dyes, using high-precision software). In the short term the group aims to increase its potential by further expanding in foreign markets, given that 50% of its production is currently for Benetton.

❑ 2004. The Olimpias Division was launched at Première Vision, presenting Spring-Summer collections from Lanificio Follina, Tessuti Pordenone and Piobesi.
❑ In 2003, the Olimpias group, comprising 12 affiliate firms with about 2,000 employees, increased its presence at fashion fairs and events, attending Moda In in Milan, Pitti Immagine Filati, and Mod Amont in France.

Oliver André (1932-1993). French fashion designer, and Pierre Cardin's right hand man. He spent his whole career, except for a short spell producing his own creations in New York, bringing balance to Cardin's avant-garde creations with his moderation and classic taste. He studied at the École des Beaux Arts in Paris and then worked as Cardin's assistant, designing the men's collections and also taking an active part in the creation of the women's collections.

Olivieri Renato (1925). Journalist and writer. Former editor of *Grazia* magazine. He started off his career in the early 1950s in Turin working for *Popolo Nuovo*. But it was only in 1953 that he got involved in the fashion world, when Arnoldo Mondadori employed him in the editorial office of *Grazia*, the most important women's weekly magazine of the time. A few months later, the founder of *Grazia* promoted Olivieri to the role of editor, a position he was to keep for twenty years. Under his influence the magazine started dealing with national issues and topics of general interest, transforming itself from a women's magazine to a family one. After a brief spell at *Casaviva*, an interior design magazine which he founded and later went on to inspire similar magazines, Olivieri became editor of *Arianna*, which was merged with *Cosmopolitan* during his time there. By observing and studying the style of the American press, Olivieri brought new standards to his magazine, introducing a revolutionary way of presenting news and graphics. After three years as editor, he moved up to a managerial position on the board of the magazine.

Olivier Strelli Belgian ready-to-wear label. Nissim Israel (1946) left his native Zaire and moved to Brussels, where in 1975 he launched a fashion label called Olivier Strelli, taking his inspiration from traditional African fabrics. Starting off with a shirt collection, he later launched a complete menswear range, popular for its bright colors. Between 1983 and 1991 he opened three boutiques in Brussels and Paris, started out in women's and children's wear, and launched the Strelli perfume. In 1989 Sabena Airlines commissioned Strelli to design their flight attendants' uniforms. By 1999 the Strelli label had become so successful that was distributed all over Europe, the USA, and Asia, both through its own-brand shops and a franchising operation.

❑ Galerie Ravenstein of Brussels invited Strelli and 15 other couturiers to contribute to an exhibition called Fame On You, a tribute to the greatest pioneer of Pop Art, Andy Warhol, revisiting his themes through photographs and fashion drawings.
❑ Strelli's label is now present throughout Europe: it has showrooms in Belgium, France, Great Britain, Greece, and Scandinavia, and about 20 shops.

Oltolina Italian firm that specializes in extremely fine fabrics for men's and women's shirts. It was founded in 1888 in Asso, near Como. Oltolina produces the Assofil range which offers the finest poplin on the market. The firm is very well advanced in terms of engineering and technology, though it still keeps to its traditional values. Oltolina's products are made using the best twisted yarn in the world.

Omicini Luciana (1933). Journalist and editor of *Annabella* magazine from 1976 to 1982, when the feminist movement was at its most active. It was important for the editors of fashion magazines to create a rapport with the public during that turbulent time. This is exactly what Omicini did with *Annabella*. After leaving *Annabella*, Omicini became the editor of *Insieme* from 1984 to 1991, cleverly using photography to project a dreamy image of motherhood through the glossy pages of this women's family magazine.

Ona Selfa José Antonio (1976). Belgian designer of Spanish origin. He studied fashion design at the Brussels Chambre and has worked with Olivier Theyskens. He is the new star designer at Loewe (founded in Madrid in 1846, and part of the LVMH Group), designing their women's ready-to-wear collections since 2002. He loves the flamenco style, and tries to incorporate it in his creations. He is an expert in leather, and the cut of his skirts, pants, and shirts give them great movement. He has a passionate, imaginative, and perfectionist style that combines his Brussels academic training with the passion of his Spanish background.

(*Estefania Ruilope Ruiz*)

On Aura Tout Vu French workshop that designs and manufactures costume jewelry, buttons, and accessories. It started off in Paris as a small craftmen's workshop opened by Livia Stoianova, Yassen Samonilov, and André de Sa Péssoa. Three years later, after various successes, it became an established business. Alongside its own collections, the workshop designs for many ready-to-wear labels and couturiers like Dior, Rabanne, Lacroix, Galliano, Saint Laurent, and Ted Lapidus.

Ones Italian manufacturer of silk fabrics, from Como. In 1925 Angelo Onnis registered the label "Giovanni Ones di Angelo Onnis," continuing the wholesale silk production started by his father in 1872. In 1929 he began producing cloth for women's clothing, using home-based workers whom he provided with looms. In 1936 Ones moves his machinery to a factory in Maccio di Villa Guardia in Como, first renting, and later buying the premises. Since 1965 the company has concentrated on the production of a range of medium-weight fabrics for Italian and foreign ready-to-wear retailers rather than wholesale. Their exports increased around the time of the retirement of the last of Angelo's heirs: in 1984 75% of Ones' total sales came from exports, a figure that later settled at 50%. At the beginning of the 1990s the firm switched to more classic, less fashion-oriented products. They gave up manufacturing in 1996 to concentrate on acting as dealers.

(*Pierangelo Mastantuono*)

Ong Benny (1949). English designer of Asian origin, known for his very feminine evening dresses. Born in Singapore, he studied at the St. Martin's School of Art in London and started his own business in 1974 after working for different companies.

Onitsuka Tiger Sports shoes and young fashion clothing launched in 2000, inspired by 1960s and 1970s trends. The label was developed from an old range called "Tiger" made by the Japanese clothing company Asics, founded in Kobe in 1949 by the former black-market beer merchant Kihachiro Onitsuka, and now one of the world's biggest producers of sports shoes. They have updated old styles using high quality materials and technological innovations, adding references to Pop Art and 1960s teenage culture. (*Pierangelo Mastantuono*)

Onori Verre Couture Italian couture label, founded in Frosinone in 1985 by Mauro Onori e Fernanda Verre. They design minimalist, simply cut evening dresses, mostly in black-and-white. They have been holding runway shows in Rome since July 1997.

Onyx Italian designer label devoted entirely to teenage fashion. It has 21 stores in Italy, and is best known for its T-shirts and vest-tops. Onyx has recently developed a "total look" approach to the market, producing jeans, tracksuits, and sport shoes, and a range of beachwear which includes swimsuits, flip-flops, and sarongs. Onyx's philosophy is based on the freedom to experiment with clothes, thereby capturing young trends and appealing to the young's tastes. Onyx's accessories, shoes, and sunglasses and are very sought after by young people. At present Onyx has about ten flagship stores, a network of about 2,000 European customers, and a dynamic branch in Barcelona which always keeps its finger on the fashion pulse. There are two main collections: Onyx and Onyx Jeans, which is famous for adding a touch of vintage to its creations to appeal to the latest generations. Apart from its vast range of accessories (shoes, bags, belts, hats, scarves, and costume jewelry), Onyx also has a line of sunglasses produced by De Rigo. The revolutionary hi-tech Onyx stores are dynamic and entertaining, offering interactive spaces where people can read, listen to music, watch television, and surf the net, as well as shop.

Op Art 1960s art movement that had a great influence on the fashion of the time. Taking inspiration from Victor Vasarely's paintings, designers such as Cardin, Balenciaga, Castillo, Heim, and Lanvin created optical illusions playing on depth and relief and the relation between the background and foreground, using decorative black-and-white geometrical patterns (checks, waves, lozenges, stripes, and mosaics). When these "optical" designs reached the shops they were very popular. At the beginning of the 1990s Op Art underwent a brief revival.

Opelka Viennese tailor working in Paris from the 1930s to the 1960s. He had an atelier in Rue de la Boètie, with clients such as Jean Gabin, Prince Rainier of Monaco, and the Duke of Windsor. His label is still alive today, operating in Paris as Opelka Cumberland, after a merger with another company.

Orbace Traditional fabric made from thick coarse wool. Dense, compact, and very heavy, this material is originally from Sardinia and until recently was still made by the women of the island from the wool of their flocks. Spun and dyed with vegetable colors, usually black, but also red, the fabric was used for women's and men's local traditional costumes. The term "orbace" (Sardinian dialect for the old Italian word *albagio*, which comes from the Arabic *al baz*) is seen as a reminder of the Fascist era, as it was used to make the uniforms of high-ranking members of the regime, thus enjoying its "moment of fame." Orbace reappeared in the 1970s, used in a lighter version for the modish evening capes and coats that took the place of furs. At the end of the 1970s it was used again for men's outdoor wear.

(*Lucia Sollazzo*)

Orb Ron Label created by Ronald Pineau, a French designer originally from Nantes. He explored the fields of music and architecture before breaking into fashion. At the age of 20 he opened a boutique in Nantes called Avant Gard. In 1996 he launched a range of figure-hugging ergonomic clothes that allow maximum freedom of movement.

Orcel Gilbert. French milliner. Active on the fashion scene from 1938 to 1972, who retired when the concept of the hat as an essential item of dress died out. After the war he became established worldwide and won a Neiman Marcus Award, which is considered the equivalent of the Oscars in the fashion business. A few years after starting out he had four ateliers that produced a total of at least thirty hats a day.

Oreste Boggio Casero Manufacturer of fine and extra fine fabrics in pure wool, cashmere, silk, and linen. It was founded in 1972 in Cerreto Castello (Biella) by Oreste Boggio Casero, an experienced project manager for major wool industry manufacturers. Seventy percent of output is exported to the USA, the Middle East, and Europe.

❑ 2000. The Biella-based manufacturer created Mythos Super 180's, a 14.5 micron wool fabric, so fine as to be comparable to cashmere.

Orfi New York ready-to-wear label. Orfi stands for Organization for Returning Fashion Interest, which, contrary to how it sounds, is not a social organization, but a designer label run by three New York designers: Donald Hearn, Scott Kruger, and Ana Gonzales. Their philosophy is to create urban streetwear clothing. In 1995 Kruger and Hearn, both recent graduates in Architecture from the Rhode Island School of Design, decided to open a sort of experimental art studio on New York's 14th Street. Alongside their passion for art, the two designers cultivated an interest in fashion, acting as consultants to various fashion designers. In 1998 they were joined by Ana Gonzales, when the group stepped fulltime into fashion by founding Orfi. Their first men's collection mixed formal and streetwear. They later produced a women's range inspired by the same spirit.

(*Manuela Parrino*)

Organdy Fabric similar to voile, originally produced with silk organzine yarn, but now also made from cotton, rayon, and synthetic yarns. It is very sheer and treated with stiffener.

Organza (or Organdie) A fresh and crisp fabric, taking its name from the French *organdi.* A sheer but resistant thin cotton muslin, it was used in the 1800s to bind books. In the late 19th and early 20th centuries, it was still primarily made of cotton but had silk organzine thread in the warp, when it was used for evening and wedding dresses, and to make ruffles, sashes, and trimmings for skirts. After World War II synthetic and articicial fibres are added to the blend, and organza was used to make colorful cocktail dresses with geometrical, striped, and checked patterns, and naïve and sporty designs that contrasted with its new-found fluidity. Organza was revived in the 1960s in the romantic neutral and pale shades of the 1800s, to make petticoats for wear under full pleated skirts.

Organzine Light fabric, made using two more more twisted threads of organize silk yarn. It is similar to muslin, but is more compact and robust and not as soft. In the second half of the 1950s, Emilio Pucci, who was always ready to experiment with fabrics, launched a new silk organzine jersey to make colorful T-shirts and dresses, that were popular for their versatility, wearability, and resistance to creasing.

Oriani Mario (1926). Journalist, and editor. He began his career as a sports writer for *Il Corriere della Sera* and *Il Corriere dell'Informazione*. Il Corriere's publishing group appointed him as editor of *Amica* from 1972 to 1974, from where he moved on to become editor of *La Domenica del Corriere*, but he only lasted a year there. In 1975, together with Renato Minetto, he founded a publishing company called Segesta Eight, and brought out *Abitare* magazine. Later he founded another publishing company called Portoria, which specializes in nautical, sport, travel, and tourism magazines.

Orlando Massimo (1971). Designer born in Lecce. He is seen as an experimental designer for his sculptural dresses and unusual use of materials like copper, steel wool, zincified iron, and silicon, which he combines with silk, pearls, and shells. He held his first Rome couture fashion show in January 2000. He graduated from Rome's Academy of Fashion and Costume in 1993 and showed his first creations a few months later.

(*Eleonora Attolico*)

Orlane French cosmetics house founded by Guillame D'Ornano in 1947. After starting off in perfumery, D'Ornano sensed a growing interest in beauty treatments and between 1948 and 1950 he launched the very first products containing active ingredients (Crème Astrale, Crème à l'Orange, Crème Active), introducing a new concept: that our skin needs both a day and a night cream on a daily basis. At the same time Orlane used revolutionary advertising methods, showing the internal structure of our skin for the first time. Orlane's successful products, which are the result of scientific research and discoveries, include: Crème a la Gelèe Royale, Extrait Vital, Hydro-Climat, and B21 Bio-Energic. In 1970 Orlane was bought by Morton Norwich, then became part of Max Factor (while the founder's descendent Hubert D'Ornano created the Sisley cosmetics brand), and was finally acquired by the Italian Kelemata group in 1985. For the last few years the make-up artist Romualdo Priore has been artistic director of the cosmetics division.

Orlon Trade name for one of the first acrylic fibers, invented by Dupont in the 1950s and noted for its soft handle and lightweight warmth. Because of this, and because it is machine washable, it is often mixed or substituted for wool in knitwear.

Organza, Alberto Lattuada, 1999. Drawing commissioned by Baldini Castoldi Dalai for the 1999 edition of their *Fashion Dictionary*.

Oroblu Hosiery range created in 1987. Specialized in the production of support and anti-cellulite tights. Distributed throughout Europe, USA, South America, Japan, and South Africa.

> ❑ 2002. Oroblu attended the New York Fashion Coterie, the most important East Coast exhibition for up-and-coming labels on the American market. The Made in Italy section is managed by Ente Moda Italia in collaboration with the Institute of Overseas Commerce.
> ❑ 2003. The Oroblu division was the only success story in a bad year for its parent group CSP International, whose losses doubled at the end of 2002 despite a good year for the lingerie market. Sanpellegrino and Oroblu accounted for 29.2% of the group's total sales, an increase of 6.4% from 2001.

Oro-Incenso-Mirra Milanese ethnic and antique jewelry shop. Founded in 1995 by Giovanna Frossi, who had worked at the Milanese Jewelry mecca "Il Discanto" for thirty years, under the direction of Rosanna Giancola. Frossi has been assembling an impressive collection of necklaces, rings, and bracelets since 1968 as a result of various trips to India, Morocco, South America, and Thailand, attracting a discerning clientele to her shop in Via San Fermo. The jewelry is presented with flair and experience by Frossi, and comes with a certificate guaranteeing its authenticity. Continual trips abroad, and work with important museums like Geneva's Barbier-Mueller Museum, have brought new discoveries. Her collection has gradually has expanded to include clothing – mainly kimonos and accessories from the Far East – 19th century Asian jewelry, a fine selection of Victorian and traditional Mediterranean pieces, including coral jewelry, tortoiseshell ornaments and miniature mosaics. She has done some memorable work with designers like Romeo Gigli. *(Alessandra Quattordio)*

O'Rossen French couture-house founded in Place Vendôme, Paris, by the brothers Stanislav and Louis O'Rossen, and in business from 1913 to the 1940s. In 1933, Louis also opened an atelier in Rue du Faubourg Saint-Honoré, where he made suits and theatrical costumes. By 1947, the label was limited to perfumes, and was bought by Parfumes Jacques Griffe in 1952.

Orry-Kelly Business name of John Kelley (1897-1964), an American costume designer. He formed one of the most celebrated partnerships between a costume designer and screen star with Bette Davis (like Garbo-Adrian and Dietrich-Banton). His creations influenced American women's fashion for over 30 years: his dresses for Ingrid Bergman in *Casablanca* were copied by millions of women. Born in Australia, he arrived in Hollywood in 1932 and thanks to his friendship with Cary Grant he joined Warner Bros., where he worked as wardrobe director for eleven years. His most intriguing outfits for Bette Davis were those worn by the actress in *Jezebel* (1938). Famed for his lavish life style, his weakness for alcohol cost him his job at Warner. He then moved to Fox and from 1950 to 1964 he worked freelance for all the major American studios, though always making the costumes for Bette Davis. His formative Broadway experience proved essential for his work on the film musicals *An American in Paris* (1951) and *Les Girls* (1957), for which he won two Oscars. He won his third for *Some Like it Hot* (1959). *(Roberto Nepoti)*

Orsetto Warm mohair fur, made of 90% mohair and 10% polyamide.

Orsi Carlo (1941). Italian photographer. Born in Milan, he was already a member of the arty Brera scene at a very young age. His first job was as assistant to Ugo Mulas, from whom he learnt the art of picking out the artistic and cultural season's new faces. He was discovered by the journalist and writer Domenico Porzio, who got him started on reportages for weekly magazines like *Oggi*, *Panorama*, and *Il Mondo*. It was at this time that he started working in fashion. He was one of the first photographers to picture models and clothes in the street as part of everyday life. His work appeared in *Vogue*, *Linea Italiana*, *L'Uomo Vogue*, *Moda*, *Donna*, *Amica* and *Vogue Germany*. He has done many advertising campaigns for La Rinascente, La Perla, Borsalino, Trussardi, and Malerba. The writer Dino Buzzati wrote the preface to *Milano*, Orsi's photographic book about Milan in the 1960s, just after the opening of its first subway line.

❑ From the 1980s he has worked in advertising and taken portraits of celebrities and famous publishing and cultural personalities. He has published three books, based on the work of the sculptor Arnaldo Pomodoro.
❑ In 1997 be founded *Città*, a prestigious high-brow magazine with essays on and images of Milan.

Orta Lucy (1966). Textile designer. Born in Birmingham, England, she lives in Paris, where she has been producing loungewear since 1991, using high-tech fabrics printed with slogans, symbols, and signs taken from a personal archive assembled with her husband, the Argentine artist Jorge Orta. She creates constructions for the body, with easy to assemble light carbon-fiber frames that work with zips, Velcro, and pockets. Lucy was inspired to produce a mini "existential" collection by her involvement in a Staff International project with artists using clothes as a means of expression. She created "message-clothes" for her Spring-Summer 2000 Collection, printed with quotations from Martin Luther King and Aung San Sun Kyi (both Nobel Peace Prize winners), and the architect-philosopher Paul Virilio. (*Mariacristina Righi*)

Ortiz Cristina (1952). Spanish designer. After a diploma from the Paris École de la Chambre Syndicale de la Haute couture in 1986, she worked for the Spanish department store El Corte Inglés. Following this, she worked with Enrica Massei and San Lorenzo. In 1994 she arrived in Milan to begin her job as head designer for Prada's women's division. In November 1997 she becomes Maison Lanvin's official designer, creating elegant and minimal, but wearable collections.

❑ 2002, Summer. She left Maison Lanvin to be replaced by Albert Elbaz.

Ortiz Monasterio Pablo (1952). Mexican photographer. After studying economics in Mexico City and New York, he moved to London, where he worked as assistant to a fashion photographer while studying photography at Ealing Technical College and the London College of Printing. After several trips to Europe and Asia he returned to Mexico, where he concentrated on social documentary photography with an element of sophistication and beauty that derived from his past as a fashion photographer.

Oscar Suleyman Women's ready-to-wear label. Oscar Raajmakers and Suleyman Demir were both born in Holland in 1972 and they followed the same course at the Fashion Department of the Arnhem Arts Academy from 1992 to 1996. They started off working together for various designers, including Vivienne Westwood, Dice Kayek, and Veronique Leroy. After creating collections for Bijenkorf, an Amsterdam department store, and the Parisian boutique-cum-gallery L'Epicerie, they launched their first women's collection in 1996.

(*Mariacristina Righi*)

OshKosh B'Gosh American brand established over a century ago, best known for its *Bib Overall* dungarees designed for farmers and railroad workers, and recognised for their quality and durability. The name comes from the Wisconsin town Oshkosh where the company was founded in 1895, which in turn had been named after the chief of the Native American Fox tribe who had been buried there. Legend says that William E. Pollock, owner of OshKosh, heard the phrase "Osh-Kosh by gosh" during a theatrical show, and decided to use it for his company.

❑ In October 1999, the label broke into e-commerce, making it one of the first labels to sell its products online.
❑ OshKosh signed a licensing agreement with the Target chain to produce the Genuine Kids by OshKosh range for children up to the age of seven.
❑ Forbes included OshKosh in their 2002 list of the best 200 hundred small companies.
❑ The Wisconsin brand's clothing, including T-shirts, swimwear and children's wear, is distributed and sold in over 50 countries. OshKosh B'Gosh also distributes a variety of products such as car seats, hair accessories, pyjamas, bed-linen, shoes, and hosiery through licensing deals.

Osti Massimo (1944-2005). Italian designer. He was seen as a "designer of clothing-objects." He favoured comfort and practicality over fashion trends. His work was based on research: the combined use of different materials, special finishes, and dyeing and the waterproofing of different types of fabric. He used a new material devised by Japanese technological research for his summer 1991 collection to make a waterproof reflective jacket, which picked up even the weakest light sources through glass micro-spheres. As well as being sold in the shops, the Reflective Jacket is used for mountain and sailing expeditions, and in other situations where people need to be easily visible to rescuers in case of emergency. The use of this fabric, the result of research into natural materials, has revolutionized a traditionally conservative field.

❑ In 1999 the fashion magazine *Arena Homme Plus* nominated the Italian fashion designer, who created the Stone Island label, as the most influential fashion designer of the 1990s.
❑ Summer 2000, the launch of Levi's ICD+, the result of the an Osti-Levi's-Philips collaboration and the first credible example of technological clothing. A range of jackets with mobile phone and MP3 player incorporated into the pockets, the result of a long term Philip's project called Wearable Electronics. Every time that the phone rings, the MP3 player stops playing. The jackets are made of waterproof and washable fabric.
❑ 2005. The designer died in Bologna after a long illness. He left a wife and two sons, plus a daughter born from his relationship with the actress Isabella Ferrari.

Otter Short haired, sheared, and shining fur similar to a beaver's, but dark brown or black, and more precious.

Ottina Stefano (1934). Fashion designer and businessman who was born into a Milanese family working in textiles for generations. After graduating from Bocconi University, he founded a clothing company called Punch with Vittorio Solbiati in 1965, which became famous for the fitted "tapered body" cut of their shirts and made Punch's fortune. Ottina practically reinvented the shirt, using natural and mixed fibers and special weaving techniques for the fabrics. In 1975, New York's Madonna Store held a retrospective of Ottina's work, displaying the Punch shirts worn by Jack Nicholson, John Lennon, Elton John, Paul Getty Jr, John Travolta, Richard Gere, and Robert Rauschenberg. In 1994 Punch, which then had a turnover of about 3 billion lire, was bought by Fenicia, a historic Italian tailoring company. From then on Ottina devoted his time to design and research into the history of the textile field, putting together a collection of fabrics.

Otto Haas-Heye. German designer and dressmaker. During World War I he worked in Berlin for the atelier Alfred-Marie and later set up on his own, alternating teaching work (at Berlin's Decorative Arts School and Zurich's Fashion and Art School) with costume design, which he continued until 1958.

Otto Karla (1954). Expert in public relations, advertising campaigns, events and media relations in the fashion field. Born in Germany, she started her career in Italy, working for Fiorucci and setting up her own office in Milan in 1980. Milan has remained her base, though she has another office in Paris. Her stable of clients includes many big couture and ready-to-wear labels.

❑ In 2000 she widened her network of clients, and managed the opening of a boutique in Los Angeles' West Third Street and a shopping complex in Tokyo, in an area with over 200 shops and restaurants.
❑ In 2003, she continued to work on launches and re-launches from her Milanese headquarters in Via dell'Annunciata. Among her most recent successes, her work for Pucci, Marni, and Bally.

Ottoman Medium-weight, closely-woven fabric, with clearly visible horizontal threads. Can be made from silk, wool, cotton, or rayon, with different wefts.

Oudejans Anne Marie (1964). Dutch designer. Her Tocca label produces very limited edition garments with a fresh and young style. She has been blessed by free publicity from supermodels like Claudia Schiffer, Helena Christensen, and Naomi Campbell, who often use her clothes for everyday wear. Oudejans lives and works in New York. In 1999 she presented a range of couture evening dresses called Loch-Ness in the studio of painter Julian Schnabel.

❑ In 2002 she launched a range of accessories with suede, leather, and woolen bags.
❑ Her 2003 Tocca Collections were characterized by a mixture of "Belle Époque," late 1960s, and masked ball themes.
❑ Her creations are distributed all over the USA and in 16 other countries.

Ouka Lele (1957). Spanish photographer and artist. Her real name is Barbara Allende. She was involved with the 1980s art scene in Madrid, which signalled a renaissance for the whole of Spain. She takes portraits, and black-and-white prints which she then paints over, and she also makes backdrops which she uses for both fashion and advertising photography.

Outerbridge Paul (1896-1958). Photographer from New York. He studied anatomy and aesthetics at the Art Student League, photography at the Clarence White School, and sculpture with Alexander Archipenko. At the same time he worked as an illustrator, painter, and set designer. In 1925 he moved to Paris where he opened his own photographic studio, joining Man Ray and Hoyningen Huene's artistic circle. He moved to Berlin and then London, but in 1929 he returns to New York, where he workd for various important fashion magazines such as *Vogue* and *Harper's Bazaar*. In 1943 he moved to California where he developed an interest in portraiture and reportage. Although he only held one exhibition and published one book in his lifetime, his work was rediscovered and re-evaluated in the 1980s with numerous exhibitions (including one in San Francisco and one at the Photokina in Cologne) and two monographs.

Outlet Big trading spaces selling designer remainders, samples, unsold or excess stock, and previous seasons' collections at reduced prices, with reductions from 20% to 70%. Outlets originated and spread rapidly in the USA (there are over 300), and are now slowly multiplying across Europe (there are currently 70, but its likely that the number will double over the next few years). The concept is "cheap and chic," allowing the public to dress in designer labels without spending a fortune. The first Italian outlets usually only sold single labels at factory outlets in city suburbs (Aspesi in Legnano, Fratelli Rossetti in Parabiago, Lario 1898 in Cirimido, Samsonite in Corsico, Tacchini in Caltignaga near Novara, Superga and Siport in Segrate, Fila in Biella, Prada in Tuscany, Antonio Fusco in Corsico). Others such as Coccinelle, Fenegrò, Etro, and Larusmiani are sold at stores in city centres, similar to the label's boutiques, but at cheaper prices. In the 1990s, they began following the American and French model, with big multi-store outlets bringing together different well-known designer labels, ranging from menswear, womenswear and children's fashion to sportswear, footwear, bags and luggage, lingerie, swimwear, and sunglasses. The first southern European outlet opened in Mendrisio, Canton Ticino on November 4, 1995. Foxtown has very modern architecture, with various buildings spread over different levels; it includes a casino and has expanded from 9 to 130 shops selling a total of 200 labels. It is very popular, with 50% of its profits made at weekends. The American company McArthurGlen opened the Serravalle Scrivia Designer Outlet just a few kilometers from the Milan-Genoa motorway exit on September 7, 2000. It is in the middle of the countryside and is laid out like a small village with boutiques and cafés lining the streets. Luca De Ambrosis Ortigara is McArthurGlen's managing director for Italy. Baa McArthurGlen and Fingen are continuously expanding their trading activities, going from 60 to 120 outlets and planning the opening of 15 more. They opened another designer outlet along the Via Pontina in Castelromano in October 2003, with 20,000 square meters selling 95 prestigious labels. They aim to repeat the success of Serravalle, which brought in 118 million euros and had 7 million visitors in

2002. In 2004 they opened a third outlet near Florence and in 2005 another near Padua. Outlets have become the new distribution channel of the third millennium, using industrial trading strategies to sell designer labels at lower prices whilst maintaining their prestigious image. In an interview with *Corriere della Sera* (12 May 2003), Luca Bastagli, managing director of the most important outlet group, says of the four new outlets to be opened in Santhià, Modena, Rome, and Molfetta in Puglia: "They will be proper life-centers like the American ones, with restaurants, and spaces for leisure and entertainment." (*Gabriella Gregorietti*)

Outrage Italian ready-to-wear label, founded in 1983 by the journalist Sergio Vismara and his wife Ornella Benedetta. The label, named after a famous American boat, first became known for its sweatshirts, making them for the America's Cup in the 1980s. They later expanded their range to include urban sportswear and other sports items. Fabric research has played a central role in the company, particularly for their range of waterproof garments. In May 1999, Outrage was bought by Tomasoni Topsail, present for the last 25 years on the Italian and European markets and also owner of the Henry Lloyd label.

❑ Tomasoni has begun a range of skiwear.
❑ Outrage is one of the strongest of Tomasoni's five labels, giving the best results, with North Sails. In 2001, Outrage brought in 20% of the group's total income.

Overalls Futurism launched them, more than as an outfit, as a subversive and liberatory value, a way of escaping fixed schemes and prejudices. On the occasion of the exhibition *Venti anni della Galleria del Costume 1983-2003*, the futurist overalls, invented in 1919 by Florentine Thayaht with his brother Ram, were part of the heritage of the collection of Palazzo Pitti. Thayaht considered it a "universal outfit," a do-it-yourself solution, creative but inexpensive, seven buttons, a belt, a straight-line cut, and little stitching. Even the Italian name was invented by Thayaht: the model was a "T," cut from a single piece of fabric, in cotton or African canvas, utilized completely without wasting any fabric. Established in the name of a protest against the bourgeois taste that characterized apparel in the years immediately following the war, it was a forerunner of a comparable Russin Constructivist creation, developed four years later, in 1923, with the name "Varst" by Rodchenko and his wife Stepanova, who saw the factory worker's overall as the revolutionary clothing of the new man. Until recently considered little more than cheap kitsch, at most tolerated as sportswear or worn only at home, nowadays the overall moves out into the streets, and is worn with nonchalance, even on elegant occasions, by the divas and popstars of the moment. Madonna wore one to the theatrical opening in London, with sneakers studded with Swarovski crystals, but the former Spice Girl Geri Halliwell, or Britney Spears and Jennifer Lopez wear them with elegant high-heeled shoes. From Manhattan to Los Angeles, from London to Paris, the imperative is: everyone wearing sport overalls. The best loved overalls are from the Californian label Juicy Couture: made of chenille, low-waisted pants, a tight-fitting blouse with a hood, created successfully by two friends, Gela Nash Taylor and Pamela Skaits-Levy, who in 1996 including in their brand Juicy Couture a series of glamorous and sexy overalls: they sold like hotcakes. Dolce & Gabbana designed for Madonna a tuxedo-overall. On the runways, the overall is a star. White like the overalls worn by aviators at the turn of the century, for Cerruti, modeled with 1940s curves for Donna Karan or "working class" dark blue for Yamamoto.

Overknee Old fashioned over-the-knee socks, made of thick opaque black cotton, like the ones worn by Egon Schiele's women and by Silvana Mangano in the film *Riso Amaro*. They are back in fashion, particularly amongst long-legged, skinny girls.

Oversize This term describes any loose, comfortable, bigger than average garment. This 1980s look was revisited in the late 1990s by many designers, including Jean Paul Gaultier.

Owen Gaster (1959). Designer, born in Lebanon to English parents. He studied at

Epsom College of Art and Design. He creates avant-garde but wearable pieces. He presented his first Collection for Fall-Winter 1994, when he immediately caught the attention of important clients like the international group Joseph and Galéries Lafayette in Paris.

❑ From 30 April to 6 June 2002, Owen displayed his designs at the British Council's Window Gallery in Prague, together with other British and Czech artists who have been regular guests of the gallery for ten years. Amongst the designers showing with Owen: Richard Dewhurst, Vexed Generation, Tord Broontje, and Jessica Ogden.

Owen Kirsten (1969). Canadian model. Born in Montreal, she moved to Paris in the mid-1980s and was hired immediately by the Zoom agency, run by Gaby Wagner. She was recognised more for her sense of style than her beauty. Photographed by Peter Lindbergh and Paolo Roversi, she was one of Jean Paul Gaultier's preferred models, but above all, she was the perfect face for Kawabuko's Comme des Garçons designs.

Owens Rick (1961). American designer born in Ponteville, California. He studied painting at Otis Parsons for a brief period and later took a course in pattern cutting for mass produced garments. He had his debut in New York in 2002. His creations take inspiration from the slums of Los Angeles, rather than the exclusive hill areas.

❑ 2005, July. The Los Angeles designer launched his new "Lilies" Collection, a second range which developed the jersey tops and skirts from his main collection.

Own Label founded in Brussels by Thierry Rondenet (1965) and Hervé Yvrenogeau (1966), to develop fashion, home furnishing, and graphic design projects. They both took diplomas in screen printing and the printed image at La Chambre in Brussels. In January 1999 they presented their first men's collection, called Winner Takes All. It included pyjamas worn under a biker jacket, and nylon dressing gowns worn as raincoats. Later that year in July they showed a men's themed collection in Paris and Tokyo with DIY decorated jeans and T-shirts. Their speciality is the layering of different pieces. Each season, Own acts as a patron to young designers and provides a showcase for their creations, starting with Sandrine Rombaux and Pascal Gautrand.

(*Giampiero Remondini*)

❑ 2001. Rondenet and Yvrenogeau won the 300,000 Belgian franc Modo Bruxellae Prize in an annual competition that brings together the best young Belgian designers who have produced fewer than ten collections.
❑ The label sold 70% of its production in Japan, with the rest distributed in Belgium, London, Paris, Los Angeles, and Moscow.

Oxbow French label founded in 1985. It specializes in sportswear and accessories for windsurfing, snowboarding, mountain biking, and racing. This impressively large range of clothes and accessories, in a wide range of colors, fabrics, sizes, and personalized prints, is sold exclusively in specialist sports shops, although recently you can also find some of their clothes in standard clothes shops.

❑ 2003, Summer. Oxbow launched a range for kids aged 6 months to 4 years, producing their jeans, T-shirts, shorts, and beach wear in small sizes.

Oxford Closely woven, soft, pure cotton fabric, sometimes with a slight sheen, used mostly for men's shirts. Woven from white thread alternated with another color, so as to create a barely discernable characteristic pattern of tiny squares.

Oxford Bags Very wide-legged pants, flared from the knee down, worn long so as to rest on top of the shoes. They used to have a very high turn-up. Their name comes from the Oxford University students who first wore them in the 1920s. The Duke of Windsor wrote: "While I was at Oxford, these very wide-legged pants were fashionable, transforming the students of the oldest and most renowned university in the British Isles into so many little elephants. I had a pair myself, but my tailor made a big scene about them." The style has had various revivals in the 1970s and again in the 1990s. They were once more very popular with teenage boys and girls, particularly in high-tec fabrics. Equally famous were Oxford Kilties, lace-up shoes with leather fringes and laces.

Oxford Clothes American menswear label founded in 1916. In the USA, this label represents the *non plus ultra* of men's suits, using some of the finest fabrics and designs in the world. Their clothes are produced in their Chicago factory, using tailors from all over the world. Crittenden Rawlings is president of the company. It takes 20 working hours to make one of their suits, with a record 1,125 hand-sewn stitches for its lining alone. Their prices are very high, and one can pay up to $8,000 for a silk suit. Their fabrics are one of the company's trump cards: particularly the wool, which comes from England, Scotland, Italy, and New Zealand. They have recently added a pure silk suit to their range, copying styles worn by Edward, Duke of Windsor, which they bought at an auction. Lately they have introduced a more casual, lower cost range to attract a younger clientele.

(*Priscilla Daroda*)

Oxford Industries Inc. Big American ready-to-wear manufacturer based in Atlanta, Georgia, that produces clothes and accessories for men and teenage boys (70%) and women (30%), distributing them through their own brands (Oxford Shirt, Oxford Slacks, and Oxford Dresses) and under license for Oscar De La Renta, Polo, Jane Barnes, and Arcade. The company has nearly 40 factories in the southern USA, Central America, and Europe.

❑ 1999, November. Phillips-Van Heusen closed a deal for the sale of all Izod Club Golf's trading activities to the Atlanta group. The Izod ranges for men, women and children continue to be distributed in the same specialist shops.
❑ Oxford Industries acquired the license to produce and distribute DKNY Kids, a Donna Karan's range for children and babies, previously produced by Esprit de Corp in San Francisco. In December 2000 Tommy Hilfiger entrusted the production of its women's golf collection range to Oxford. Their 2002 financial results were not positive, reporting a 16.6% decrease in sales and a 31.1% drop in profits, though they showed signs of recovery in the latter part of the year.
❑ Oxford Industries completed the acquisition of Viewpoint International, owner of the Tommy Bahama brand, which produces sportswear, men's and women's swimwear and home furnishings. The final deal, announced in April 2003, amounted to 325 million dollars in cash and shares.

Oxus Italian brand of designer bags, conceived by Raphael Mamet and made using the experience of master leather craftsmen from Gru.P. Italia, a company specialized in producing fine leather goods for famous brands. Oxus is one of the main companies operating in the field, with a head office in Milan and a factory in Salzano. Oxus designs are small, strong pouches with a sculptural quality, that take the shape of their content.

Ozbek Rifat (1953). Turkish designer, who worked in Italy with Walter Albini at the beginning of his career. He went to England in the 1970s to study architecture, which he interrupted to enrol at the St Martin's School of Art. His first creations, commissioned by a chain of department stores, were inspired by Oriental themes. He launched his first collection in 1984. He became internationally established from the late 1980s, with a rich, imaginative, multi-ethnic style. His collections often take inspiration from art, but also from folk traditions: amongst his most famous themes are existensialism, orientalism, Capri of the 1950s, Martha Graham's ballets, various books and films, but also ideas borrowed from street style and the "disco" look, adapted for a ready-to-wear style. In 1987 he launched the Future Ozbek range. He started working with Aeffe in 1988, which produced and distributed his designs, since when Ozbek has consolidated his popularity. He approached the 1990s with a new vision: an all-white collection inspired by the New Age, which made him one of the world champions of avant-garde fashion. He then began to experiment with video as a means of presenting his collections. In 1991 he debuted on the Milanese fashion scene; in 1994 he held a fashion show in Paris; in 1996 he designed the costumes for the opening ceremony of the Olympic Games in Atlanta, launched the perfume Ozbek, launched a range of rugs and kilims, and took part in the Biennale fashion exibition in Florence. In 1997 he made his debut in New York.

(*Anna Gloria Forti*)

❑ Ozbek's most recent creations have been based on media, films, books, and English youth culture. In 1998 he acted in the film *Love is the Devil*, based on the life of the painter Francis Bacon.

❑ During Winter 2002 Ozbek "went Elvis," working in London on clothes inspired by the King, on the occasion of the release his *Greatest Hits*. Creations by Rifat, Julien Macdonald, Ben de Lisi, Ghost, and many others were auctioned by Sotheby's on 5 December to raise funds in support of the Prince's Fashion Initiative.

❑ 2003. Ozbek worked with Christopher Farr, a London-based rug-maker, and he also launched a range of perfumes for women called Ozbek by Rifat Ozbek. Was named creative director of the Pollini ready-to-wear woman collection.

Rifat Ozbek, sketch for Summer 1998 Collection.

P

Pablo et Delia English ready-to-wear label from 1971 to 1979, designed by Pablo Meshedjian (1937-86) and Delia Cancela (1940), who both trained at Buenos Aires Fine Arts school. At the beginning of the 1980s they worked on fashions for the catalogues of the mail-order company 3 Suisse.

Paciotti Cesare (1956). Shoe designer. In the 1980s his men's line, with its nonconformist designs and outrageous advertising campaigns, stood out in what was a traditional and conservative field. The brand's story started in 1948 with Giuseppe Paciotti's classic and very high quality range of shoes. After his artistic studies, Cesare inherited the business from his father in 1980. Innovation and high quality are combined with strong geometric shapes and the prolific use of metallic accessories. At the same time he started working with Versace and Gigli. At the beginning of the 1990s he launched a women's collection, followed a few seasons later by a range of handbags, cases, backpacks, hatboxes, and overnight bags. In 1998 he launched a range of eyewear.

❑ 2001. The year closed with a turnover of 49 million euros, an increase of 13 million from the previous year.
❑ 2002. Launch of the new collection "Paciotti 4Us." The brand was one of the 40 Italian exhibitors participating in WSA International in Las Vegas, one of the most important fairs for the US shoe market. Launch of a handkerchief shaped bag called Hebe, like the "servant" of the gods charged with pouring out ambrosia at banquets.
❑ 2003, February. The New York Fashion Institute of Technology Museum celebrated Cesare Paciotti's shoes, along with Gucci handbags, and hundreds of other designer pieces, in the exhibition *Italy, in the Life Styles.* From May to August Cesare Paciotti's more classic footwear was featured at the Metropolitan Museum of Art in New York in *Goddess*, an exhibition exploring and underlining the influence of Classical dress on the fashion of the last three centuries, through a collection of hundreds of garments, prints, and photographs from 1800 to the present day.

Padded down jacket Originally worn for sporting activities, then – as happened with the Parker and Husky jackets – adopted for everyday use, especially but not only by young people. Very warm, it is padded with goose down. In fact its success both as protection against the cold and as a fashion garment is down to the use of natural fibers in place of synthetic or vegetable fibers for the padding. Black or brightly colored, in the form of a jacket or calf-length coat, in times when animal rights and ecology are respected, it is preferred by young women to wearing furs. With its characteristic striped or lozenge-shaped padding, sewn into waterproof silk, this garment has been seen during many seasons, and looks likely to become a timeless classic.

Paisley A pattern originating in Asia, often used for shawls from the 19th century onwards. Like many fashion terms, it became known by the name of a city: in this case Paisley, a Scottish town famous for the production of a type of combed wool perfect for square shawls or dressing gowns, decorated with purple and brown patterns copied from precious Indian cashmere shawls from the turn of the 18th and 19th centuries. Paisleys were adopted straightaway by the most elegant women, starting with Josephine Beauharnais who was given a splendid one by Napoleon. The paisley or cashmere pattern has never really been shelved. Every so often it reappears on the fashion scene: like in the 1980s when it had yet another revival as the emblem of the

Italian fashion house Etro, appearing on shawls, dresses, skirts, necklaces, bags, and even furnishings.

Paisley Museum Museum of the paisley shawl, named after the town. In Paisley in the 1800s shawls were woven to imitate those imported from Kashmir from the end of the 1700s (with multicolored furled leaf patterns), but using less prized wool for a less exclusive market. The museum was instituted in 1871 when this fashion was already declining. It has over 1,000 examples which are shown in rotation. The museum is equipped with a weaving workshop where old techniques are taught. The Study Centre allows for close analysis of the shawls and other paisley-related materials.

Pakerson Men's shoe company founded in Cerreto Guidi (Florence) in 1923 by Giulio Brotini, who was descended from a family of craftsmen that had worked for the court of the Grand Duke of Tuscany in the 19th century. From 1946 it was managed by his son Luciano. It soon developed into a small business, but without abandoning its craftsmen's traditions. It took the present name of Pakerson in 1958. In 1964 it won the Oscar for the best footwear for export. The family continuity of the company is ensured by Antonio and Andrea Brotini, trusty custodians of an exclusive, high-quality craft.

❑ 2003. Announcement of the opening of two shops in Russia, in Moscow and St Petersburg. Contract for a line of footwear with the designer Valentin Yudashkin. Having been one of the biggest promoters of the expansion of Italian footwear in Eastern Europe, Antonio Brotini quit the presidency of ANCI, the Italian association of shoemakers, to take up the top position at the equivalent European association.
❑ 2003, September. Given the excellent results from the Russian market, two more flagship stores were opened in Almati, Kazakstan and in Kiev, Ukraine. The collaboration with Yudashkin continued with a complete line of footwear, handbags, and women's accessories for Summer 2004.

Palacio & Lemoniez Miguel Palacio (born in 1962 in Bilbao, Spain) and Fernando Lemoniez (born in 1964 in San Sebastiàn, Spain) started designing and producing their collections together in 1983, the same year that they opened a shop in San Sebastiàn. In 1990 they moved to Madrid, where they gradually consolidated their business, presenting elegant clothes that are always in step with the fashion of the moment. From 1991 (when they won the first of two T de Oro awards, for the best young designers) they started showing their collections on the Madrid runways and in 1992 they won a prize from the Spanish magazine *Telva* as the best Spanish designers. In 1993 they showed their Winter collection in Frankfurt and in 1994 started their overseas expansion. In 1995 they moved to Paris and presented themselves at Fashion Week. In 1999 they were still based in Paris, with a show room in Rue de l'Université.

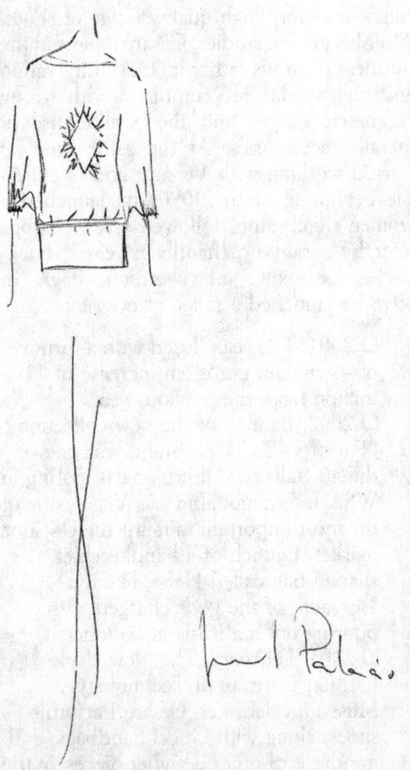

Sketch by Miguel Palacio.

In 1999 the partnership broke up and both designers went back to making their own creations. Fernando Lemoniez showed his new collection on the Cibeles runway.
For Fall-Winter 2002-2003 Palacio showed a collection inspired by the trends of the 1970s: with very high-waisted gabardine flared pants. The colors were black, brown, and sky-blue.

Palatella Saverio (1958). Italian designer. After dabbling in T-shirts he designed for Gentryportofino, who from 1988 to 1992 produced his line, and he collaborated with several yarn manufacturers. This experience in knitwear and spinning enabled him to specialize in the fine knitwear sector. In 1993 his brand formed a productive alliance with the Gruppo Manifatture Associate. In 1998 Palatella chose to pursue research. In 2000 he temporarily suspended his collection in order to link his name with the Gentryportofino brand. In 2001 he returned to the market with his Saverio Palatella women's collection. This is a ready-to-wear collection with some added couture pieces, which has attracted numerous artists including the American jazz musician Jimmi Scott, who has played at his shows, the Malian singer Rokia Traore, and the multiethnic group Ekova. The Saverio Palatella men's collection debuted in Fall-Winter 2003-2004.

Palazzi Carlo. Men's fashion designer and entrepreneur from the 1960s to the 1980s. His success began in 1965, with his first shop and fashion-house in Via Borgogna in Rome. Three years later he had a shop on Fifth Avenue and in a short space of time in Japan (7 show rooms in Tokyo and Osaka), Canada, London (2 shops), and Palm Beach. Born in Urbino, he started off as an junior high schoolteacher, then moved to Rome after the war where he did a bit of everything to get by: searching for and identifying Americans fallen on the Italian battlefield, hotel barman, for 13 years shop assistant and then manager of a city-center shirt shop where he learned the trade that enabled him to set up on his own. In her book *Mass-Moda/Fatti e personaggi dell'italian look* (Mass-Fashion/Makers and events of the Italian look, published by Spinelli, 1979) Adriana Mulassano recounted: "He caught the right current straightaway: in men's fashion it was the time of revolt against gray and black. He saw some samples of embroidered silk shirts in Milan (even now in Brazil they call them 'Palizzis'), bought them up and sold them in a frenzy, meanwhile he changed the face of the tie, widening it from six to nine centimeters, using novel, gaily-colored floral fabrics (...) He invented the 'guru' shirt, with a high collar and a zip up the back. In 1970 at the Palazzo Braschi *haute-couture* show he presented shirts, jackets, and pants all made from the same tweed fabric (...). In 1971, he created another very successful piece for the "nonconformist evening": a velvet jacket over very sporty herringbone tweed pants and waistcoat."

Paley Natalie. Very famous model of the 1930s, partly because she was the daughter of the grand duke Paul of Russia. Her unmistakable style was linked to the house of her husband Lucien Lelong. Her polished beauty, much admired at a time when Slav looks and high cheekbones were held in high regard, had a great influence over women of the era. She retired in 1952.

Palladium French brand of footwear. Very well known for the *Pallabrousse* model created for the army in 1947. This robust canvas shoe with a vulcanized rubber sole has since been adopted by boy scouts, hunters, fishermen and lovers of the outdoor life in general. In the 1980s it became popular with young people, with uppers in different colors and fabrics.

Pallini Adriano (1897-1955). Italian tailor. Born in Teramo. He belonged to the Abruzzese school of tailoring. After moving to Milan in the 1930s, he opened his first atelier in Via dell'Orso, specializing in men's fashion. He made frequent trips to London to source special and unusual fabrics. His style was sober and classic, with characteristic wide lapels. A passionate art collector, he dressed Giorgio De Chirico, Massimo Campigli, Arturo Martini, Piero Marussig, Lucio Fontana, and many others. One of his clients after the war was Giovanni Gronchi, who then went on to become President of the Republic. He also created women's suits of which Claretta Petacci was a fan.

Pallotti Mirella (1946). Journalist. She was editor of *Anna* magazine. She was one of the main protagonists of women's magazine publishing in the 1970s and 1980s. She worked on *Europeo* and *Tempo*, and in 1971 joined *Panorama*. After a stint in the Fiat press office she was employed by *Grazia* in 1973, where she stayed until 1978, when Pietroni asks her to join the new weekly *Insieme*, of which she was editor from 1980 to 1984. This is when her career really began as an editor specialized in restyling and revamping troubled titles. In 1984 she transformed *Duepiù* into *Donnapiù*, and in 1987 *Bella* into *Più Bella*. In 1990 she relaunched *Annabella* as *Anna*, of which she remained editor until 1997.

Palmer Marta. Milanese dressmaker. She headed an established fashion house in the 1930s, during the Fascist regime, and she was very successful because she designed her own styles, rather than copying (or buying in) from Paris as others did at the time. In today's fashion scene she would be one of the top designers. Milanese society ladies loved her, and her shop in Corso Vittorio Emanuele became a meeting point and kind of salon for them. The luckiest were invited to her villa in the Lombardy countryside, where they may have met Paola Borboni, Palmer's friend and client. Many dresses from her collections were shown in women's magazines of the time, especially *Lidel*, an esteemed title that patriotically campaigned for Italian fashion, free from Parisian diktats.

Pal Zileri The Pal Zileri brand represents the pinnacle of the Forall Group: on average it produces about 1,100 formal jackets, 500 casual jackets, 1,800 pairs of pants and 1,400 sports items a day. Forall Confezioni S.p.A. was founded in 1970 in Quinto Vicentino (Vicenza) by some industrialists from the textile sector, producing classic men's fashion using hi-tech fabrics for suits, sportswear, jackets, and shirts. From 1981 to 1998 the group had over 1,000 employees and about 300 outside workers, and their exports increased from 20% of their output in 1988 to 54% in 1996. Pal Zileri is just one of their ranges (the youngest), which also include labels such as Pal Zileri Pull and Pal Zileri Sport. In the last few years they have also added the High Generation range and www.Sartoriale.it, which is particularly refined in its use of fabrics. The Pal Zileri label (the name comes from Palazzo Zileri) also offers a made-to-measure service.

❑ 2001, June. After closing deals for Krizia and the export license for Trussardi, the Forall group also acquired the right to manufacture Moschino menswear. The four-year partnership included overcoats, suits, pants, and shirts, and presented to the Milan Collections at the Moschino Uomo runway shows.
❑ 2001, October. The Milanese shop reopened in Via Verri.
❑ 2002. The year closed with a turnover of 116 million euros, 60% of which was from exports.
❑ 2003, January. At the Pitti Uomo fair the label presented a formal jacket with inside padding, adding practicality to a formal piece. At Milano Moda they showed the "tramp" collection in bouclé and loose knit wool. Before the end of the year the Forall Group had planned to add another ten or so brand-stores, through franchising or partnerships, to its 60 already present on the world market. In Italy they are planning expansion in the South, with the opening of three new stores.

Pambianco Strategie di Impresa Consultancy for strategy and internationalisation of Italian companies, with offices in Paris, Düsseldorf, New York, Tokyo, and Beijing. Set up in 1972 by Carlo Pambianco, after 12 years experience working with important Groups including Grignasco, Gft, and Ermenegildo Zegna. The services they offer cover market research for companies revising their strategies, foreign market development projects, headhunting at director level, corporate public relations, sourcing brand licenses, and the sale and acquisition of companies. The present staff is made up of 25 consultants. Pambianco currently represents an important point of reference for businessmen in the clothing industry and the economic press. Pambianco organizes many initiatives specifically for the fashion sector: conferences, round tables, market reports, manager salary surveys, account analyses and reviews of brands up for license and merger

& acquisition operations. Pambianco's services are shown on their website www.pambianco.com. Since 2001 their website www.pambianconews.com has also been active, giving daily news reports on economic and financial events in the fashion sector. In June 2003 the site had 18,000 registered users, 60,000 monthly readers and 600 pages online. The monthly increase in registered users is currently at 5%.

(*Dario Golizia*)

Pam Hogg English ready-to-wear label. Created in 1983 by the designer of the same name, one of the most original in England at the time. After a course in fabric printing at the Glasgow School, Pam attended the Royal College of Art, specializing in printed fabrics. From her first collection she showed an unorthodox talent that predicted future trends. Her retro patchworks have been a source of inspiration for many designers, echoing the hippy trends of the 1970s. She opened a store in Newberg Street, in London's West Soho. Her collections are characterised by an unexpected eclecticism: rangning from sexy dresses that recall turn of the century corsets, to ultramodern body-hugging stretch dresses cut with transparent panels to reveal the body, to glamorous and extravagant evening wear with fetishist echoes. Some of her pieces are unisex.

Pamplemousse Ready-to-wear brand. Limited editions and tailored cuts designed by Angela Moles, a minimalist inspired by Japanese dressmakers, who made her debut in 1981 with Giuliano Galletti in Bologna. Two years later she opened the Universal Market division. She designed Zucchero's outfits for his *Miserere* video.

Panama Men's Summer hat made from plaited straw with a broad brim and a dented crown. It took this name in 1906, the year in which the American president Theodore Roosevelt sported one whilst on an official visit to the Panama Canal. Its shape is similar to that of a felt hat, but it has the advantage that it can be rolled up and unrolled again without losing its shape. It is made from straw from the leaves of the *Carloduvica palmata*, a plant that grows in Ecuador. It is the ideal hat for hot climates. Very elegant, with a price to match, it is often used by wardrobe designers for movies set in the first half of the 20th century. Worn by Dirk Bogarde when playing the character Gustav von Ashenbach in Visconti's *Death in Venice.*

Pancaldi Italian shoe manufacturer based in Molinella (Bologna). From 1998 it has produced a men's collection. This high-quality brand has been made famous by its close relationship with *haute couture*, manufacturing for Escada, Gigli, Alaïa, and Coveri. The company was founded by Natale Pancaldi in 1888 and is now in the hands of the third generation of the family, who have a prized collection of hand-made shoes from the 1930s to the present day: a small museum in its own right.

Pancaldi & B. Shirt-makers founded in 1949 by the Bolognese Albertina Bottazzi Pancaldi. Over the years the company's range of products has expanded from men's and women's clothing (Pancaldi classico, Regent, Via Vivaio, Now) to include a younger range and a leather collection.

Panepinto Giampiero (1963). Italian designer. Born in Palermo, he lives and works in Milan, where he took his degree in Architecture. However, like some of his other illustrious colleagues he quit the profession in favour of knitwear and fabric creations. In 2001 he produced his first collection, after years of experience in the fashion sector. His passion for the Far East and its way of life means that he values comfort and simplicity as essential elements of contemporary dress. These qualities, with a taste for finding novel and apparently casual combinations for outfits, can be found in his men's and women's collections, which were joined in Spring-Summer 2003 by a children's mini-collection, producing miniature versions of his "grown-up" shirts. For his shows he uses an experienced team and focuses on a contemporary style that harks back to distant eras, borrowing the best details and techniques from the past. His "Knit & Cake" women's Fall-Winter 2003-2004 collection combined fabrics and colors to create a "greedy" look that reached its apex with glass beads in the shape of little cakes and tarts.

A sketch by Laura D'Ancona for the Panepinto Spring-Summer 2004 Collection.

Paninari Italian youth movement: a fashion and lifestyle phenomenon that filled the Italian news programs for a good part of the 1980s. Born around a bar in the centre of Milan (Il Panino, from which the name comes) they were middle-class young men aged between 15 and 25, typified by their style of dress, party-loving, and totally noncommittal attitude. Their Roman counterparts were rough types from a lower social class, also dedicated to the way they dressed, but with less attention to detail. The Milanese Paninari had a real uniform: a Moncler puffa jacket, Armani jeans, Timberland boots, and the classic Burlington colored check socks. With hindsight, they were the pure incarnation of the show-off spirit of the 1980s. They traveled around on fancy motorbikes, and had a slang all of their own, but their most distinctive trait was that of hanging around in groups in the city center. They usually gathered outside fast food joints and the trendiest clubs where they listened to their preferred dance music. The media became enamoured of them, especially in 1984, and the phenomenon was subjected to a thorough analysis – especially the clothes – as the trend caught on with young people all over Italy. They had their own official publications, their own comics, and hundreds of pages dedicated to them in mass-distributed magazines. They found a solid point of reference in the emerging TV network Fininvest (particularly the channel Italia 1 with its afternoon light-entertainment programmes). The phenomenon was already on the decline after a few years: in 1987 there was no longer any trace of the true Paninari, but the movement's founding philosophies found favour with a very wide range of young people.

Pantofola d'oro Sports shoe company. It is said that it was John Charles, a center-forward for Juventus in the 1950s, who referred to a handmade sports shoe as a *pantofolo d'oro*: "It's not a shoe, it's a slipper... a golden slipper." About ten years earlier, in his small shoemakers' workshop in Ascoli Piceno, which had belonged to his father and before that to his grandfather since 1886, Emidio Lazzarini had invented a shoe that perfectly fitted the sportsman's foot. First used by wrestlers, then by the local football team Ascoli Calcio, the secret of the Pantofola d'oro was its calf-leather sole, so supple that it could be bent in half with the lightest of pressure. They were ideal for the feet of the Brazilian Garrincha, who suffered from a congenital deformity, but

who, thanks to a pair of Pantofola d'oro, was able to play for his country in the 1958 World Cup. Also, the Russian giant Yascin, who wore a size 47. Their true consecration came in the 1970s and 1980s, thanks to champions like the footballer Johann Cruyff and cyclist Francesco Moser. The expansion of the footwear industry and of big international brands present a company of craftsmen like that of Lazzarini with a challenge to which they can only respond by offering the highest quality. These days Pantofola d'oro make luxury sports shoes for football, five-a-side, and free time, still using the patented sole made from 18 different components, and the upper, which is shaped for at least two days. Their products are sold through about 200 shops in 40 countries worldwide, with the main outlets being in France and England. They have distributors in Australia, the United Arab Emirates, and Iceland.
(*Pierangelo Mastantuono*)

Paolo Cecchi Italian wool mill, based in Calenzano, Prato. Its defining moment came in the middle of the 1960s when it started producing double-face fabrics for stylish coats made from very fine combed wool. It started in 1928 as a semi-artisanal company offering a complete production process: spinning, warping, weaving, dyeing, and finishing. It became a textile manufacturer in 1957. In the following years it abandoned carded wool in favor of more masculine combed wools, and kept in step with the changing market by updating its facilities. The decision has been costly in terms of investment and research. The company found its crucial asset in the early 1990s: continuous production and very quality standards. Running the company is Nicola Cecchi, son of the founder Paolo. It has 200 employees. For years an outright rejection of advertising limited them to Italian clients only, but the company's recent adoption of carefully targeted advertising has brought satisfying and lasting relationships with international clients. (*Giuliana Zabeo Ricca*)

Paolo da Ponte Italian manufacturer of ties, belts, and silk accessories, based in Bassano del Grappa. Active since 1923, it reached its current size in 1972 when it opened a new factory. It exports 40% of its produce to over 30 countries. It has always been owned and run by the Baggio family.

Paper Denim & Cloth Limited edition jeans. This was the brainchild, in November 1999, of Scott Morrison, a New York designer and manufacturer whose creations are now on sale in the biggest American department stores. Jeans, jackets, and T-shirts made from specially selected denims and cotton jersey that come directly from American, Italian, and Japanese manufacturers. Each hand-finished pair of jeans is labeled with its own number, starting from zero at the beginning of each season. There is a different label design for each batch of 50,000 jeans. The reinforced waistband of the women's styles and the flat stitching with frayed edges are details that have been kept from the original design. To honor the entrepreneur Richard Gilbert, who supported the project from the beginning, Morrison decided to create the "2rsgxx" style: the cut of the jeans was achieved by copying the silhouette of a model dressed as a cowboy. On the label's orders, only 12 pairs were produced each week to be sold in 16 shops around the world.

Pappa e Ciccia Children's clothing label founded in Busto Arsizio in 1984, when its first collection, with its characteristic logo showing two bunnies, was presented at the Pitti Bimbo fair in Florence. In 1997 it opened its first own-brand store in central Milan, and in 1999 its first corner in the Italian department store La Rinascente. The company realized its market potential in 2000, increasing communication with the end-customer and opening points of sale in strategic locations such as airports. At present the Pappa e Ciccia collections are distributed in 450 sale points in Italy and abroad. There are 5 own-brand stores, and 25 corners and shops-in-shops. The label current has three lines: Pappa e Ciccia Baby, Kids, and Classic.

Paquin French fashion house that opened at the end of the 19th century (1891), and enjoyed its heyday in the first 20 years of the 20th century, though it remained in business, with various changes in its artistic direction, until 1956. The founder and dressmaker of

Suits by Paquin, Lanvin, and Doeuillet, and a Paquin coat in a drawing by Valentine Gross for the *Gazette du Bon Ton*, 1915 (Prints Collection A. Bertarelli, Milan).

the fashion house was Jeanne Beckers (1869-1936), the first woman, a century on from the renowned Rose Bertin, to achieve success in French fashion on the same level as great dressmakers like Worth. Her Parisian atelier in Rue de la Paix was called Paquin, the nickname of her husband and adviser Isadore Jacobs, who was an expert businessman. A woman of rare elegance, Jeanne used techniques learnt from her time at Maison Rouff, and from the start – with her meticulous attention to detail, careful choice, matching of fabrics, and refined use of lace overlays – she expressed a bold, grandiose style embodied by use of the celebrated Paquin shade of red. Ahead of her time in her approach to both advertising and promotion, she organized fashion shows in theaters and sent groups of models dressed in her clothes to elite events. After five years of business Maison Paquin took some English partners and moved to London, keeping a Parisian base in Rue de la Paix. It came as no great surprise when Jeanne Paquin was made president of the fashion area of the Paris Universal International Exhibition in 1900: by then she was famous for her dazzling gold and silver evening dresses and blue twill suits. Not only did she show her creations at the Exhibition, but also herself, in the form of a mannekin inlaid with silver, shown sitting at her desk. Although well aware of her success and the great respect she was afforded, she did not stop in her search for self-improvement, joining forces with artists like Léon Bakst, the costume designer for Diaghilev's Ballets Russes, and George Lepape and Paul Iribe, for whom she drew some wonderful fashion-plates. Her rich and modern collections were inspired by memories of distant lands and a passion for Japanese objects; in 1907 she launched the Impero range, creating a kimono-style cape and re-inventing the suit with a pleated skirt that made it practical to wear even when traveling by subway. When she opened a branch of the fashion house in New York, it specialized in furs, adding yet another string to her bow. As her branches multiplied across the world, from Spain to Argentina, she invented the fashion cruise, taking her creations to the main cities of Latin America. All this did not stop her from also presiding over the Chambre Syndicale de la Haute couture from 1917 to 1919. At the age of 50 she unexpectedly retired. The fashion house was run by different designers over the years that followed: Madeleine Wallis, a specialist in furs; the Spaniard Ana de Pombo (1936) whose Velasquez style dresses were much admired; another Spaniard Antonio Canovas de Castillo (1942) and Colette Massignac. The fashion house was relaunched by a young Basque, Lou Claverie, in 1949, but despite this, and the incorporation of the house of Worth, in 1956 the house of Paquin ceased business and closed its doors for good.

(*Lucia Sollazzo*)

Paquin dress from the beginning of the 1900s.

Paraboot French range of footwear created in 1919 in Iseaux. The idea for it came to Rémy Richard-Pontvert during a trip to the USA, when he discovered the famous Boots and the novel use of India rubber to protect shoes. On his return he created a particularly robust men's style called Michael, with a sole made from hevea, a rubber obtained from the caoutchouc tree, and an upper with double stiching over a band of leather which made it waterproof. These days as well as the Michael style, Paraboot produces a complete collection of women's and men's shoes, with a range specifically for sailing and golf and a range of suitcases.

Parah Swimwear and underwear brand (one of the leaders in Italy). Its story began in Gallarate in 1950: Edda Paracchini made items of underwear at home and her husband Giovanni Piazzalunga, a banker by profession, sold them at weekend markets. Success has meant that now the group has three companies (one, the Gruppo Tessile Associato, produces 160,000 items of knitwear, women's clothing, and men's casualwear a year) belonging to the Piazzalunga family, with a total of almost 120 employees. Their average turnover over the last few years has been 31 million euros.

Parasol Parasols, or umbrellas designed primarily to protect women from the sun, were an important female fashion accessory from the 16th to the 19th centuries. Over the years their shape and decoration became highly elaborate, and they were often made of silks and satins, embroidered and fringed. Ivory inlays and other decorative touches were used to accent handles. Parasols were still highly important in the late 19th century, but were generally abandoned in the early 20th century as women sought greater freedom in their clothing in general.

Pareo A traditional Polynesian garment: a rectangle of flowered fabric that the natives (both men and women) tie around their hips. Depending on how you tie it, it can be worn either as a skirt or a dress: in Hawaii there are many manuals on sale that demonstrate the different ways. Made famous in the cinema in 1937 by Dorothy Lamour, who played the part of a South Seas woman in the movie *Hurricane*, its fame spread in the 1950s and 1960s thanks to the "exotic" (and aquatic) musicals of Ester Williams and Elvis Presley. In fashion the term is now used to describe any kind of skirt that is tied at the side, around the hips or above the chest.

Pareto Spinola Ileana (1935). Fashion manager. In 1963 she started working for the exclusive boutique Billy Ballo in Santa Margherita Ligure. As manager and buyer, she focused on Livio de Simone and Falconetto, designed by Ken Scott. She created the Billy Ballo range with the owner Giorgio Balbi, putting Walter Albini in charge of the design. The collection was well-received at Samia di Torino and, in 1965,on the Pitti runway in Florence. In 1967 she became involved in the organization of Mare Moda Capri with Anne Sophia Benazzo. From 1968 to 1987 she was an agent for Ter et Bantine, Chantal Thomas, and Kansai Yamamoto. In 1969 she set up Assomoda (an association of the main representatives of the fashion industry) with Roberto Manoelli and others, and Milanovendemoda, the first international ready-to-wear exhibition held in Milan. She is currently working with Promozione Moda Italia (an organization that brings together Efima and Expo Cts), looking after relationships with existing exhibitors and looking for new ones. She is also one of Gianfranco Ferré's talent scouts. (*Fulvio Bertasso*)

Paris Joyce French fortnightly magazine simply called *Joyce*: since 1978 – the year it was founded by Michel Hauville and Florence Lafargue – it has been considered the showcase for French luxury. It also covers society and cultural events. Its covers go against the stream, using designers and illustrators rather than being photographic.

Parka An Eskimo garment from the Aleutine Islands. Similar to an anorak, the parka is made from a waterproof fabric, often padded, with a front zip fastening. It ends at mid-thigh level and can have a hood, sometimes trimmed with fur. Originally designed for skiing and mountaineering, it has now become a item of casual-wear.

Parker Suzy (1932-2003). American model and actress. She was often featured in the pages of the main fashion magazines in the 1940s and 1950s, with her sister Dorian Leigh. Her sophisticated beauty and supple figure were celebrated by the photographer Henry Clarke. She modeled clothes as if she were acting a role. She was one of the first (1953) to wear the famous Chanel tweed suit on the runway, and she was the first to sign an exclusive contract with the American cosmetics firm Revlon.

Parkinson Norman. Pseudonym of Ronald William Parkinson Smith (1913-1990). English photographer. The term realism in movement, first coined for Martin Munkacsi, whose work influenced Parkinson at the end of the 1930s, can also be applied to Parkinson's work. He used decidedly British rural settings for his fashion shoots for *Harper's Bazaar*, but from 1949 when he started working for *Vogue* in New York, his pictures were dominated by urban environments of skyscrapers and traffic-filled streets. He became the official British court photographer in 1981. That same year the National Portrait Gallery in London held an exhibition showing half a century of his work in fashion. He was also an airborne photographer during World War II.

Parks Gordon (1912). American photographer. He worked mostly in the field of social documentary photography, but occasionally also in fashion. He did a feature on the model Bettina in Paris at the end of the 1940s which appeared in *Life* magazine. In 1962 *Life* published his reportage about fashion in Hollywood.

Parnis Mollie (1905-1992). American dressmaker. After studying at Wadleigh High School in New York, she worked as an apprentice for a shirt-maker and for the clothing company David Westheim. She married a fabric designer in 1930 and together they opened a luxury ready-to-wear business aimed mostly at the older woman. It was a well-chosen target market which ensured lasting, quiet success.

Parson's School of Design The first American higher education institution to open a branch in Paris in the 1920s. Amongst its most famous alumni are the painters Jasper Johns and Edward Hopper, director Joel Schumacher, fashion photographer Stephen Meisel and designers Marc Jacobs, Donna Karan and Isaac Mizrahi, the latter two now working there as tutors. Founded in 1896 in New York as the Chase School by the painter William Merrit Chase, it was renamed in 1904 in honor of the designer Frank Alvah Parson, who was its director for twenty six years. He is credited with sensing the strong link between fashion, art, and industry that was then evolving, and exploiting this synergy in courses on fashion design, pattern cutting, fabrics, accessories, graphic design, advertising, and communication. Parsons offers 2-4 year courses resulting in diplomas, degrees, and specialist qualifications, giving its students the possibility to learn the fashion trade "hands on" through internships with important clothing companies like Reebok or prestigious European fashion houses like Chanel.

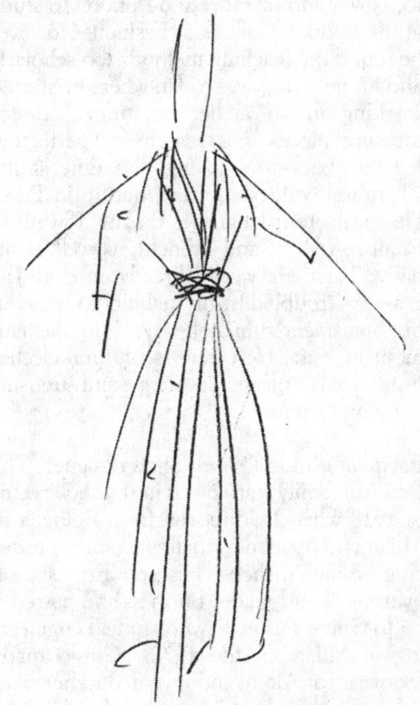

Sketch by Claire Mc Cardell from the Parson's School of Design Archive.

Parure French term indicating a matching set of jewelry, such as earrings, necklace and ring, particularly used to describe important or expensive pieces. When applied to underwear the term refers to a coordinated French lingerie set, often custom-made or of embroidered silk or fine cambric, which in the early part of the 20th century was deemed an essential part of an elegant wedding trousseau.

Pashai Morteza (1962). Iranian designer. Born in Mechbed, he toured the capitals of Europe to perfect his innate talent for fashion. After fleeing Iran during the Khomeini revolution at the age of 23, his first stop was Sweden, where his brother was already living, and he attended a fashion design course there. He learned the language and started studying medicine, but soon his passion for pattern cutting and sewing (which he started at the age of 14 in Iran) took over and he moved to London to study at the London College of Fashion. However he found the teaching methods too scholarly and his next stop was Milan where he started working in an atelier creating made-to-measure pieces. His search for perfection led him back to studying, this time at the Chambre Syndicale de la Couture in Paris. He speaks four languages fluently (Swedish, English, Italian, and French), as well as his native Farsi. He works directly on cloth (he is always troubled by his inability to draw) in his apartment-cum-atelier in Rue Bachaumont in Paris. He creates sculptural clothes using folds, pleats, layering, and unusual structural solutions.

Pasquali Guido (1946). Shoe designer. The Pasquali family started out in the shoe sector in 1918 when Italo moved from Bologna to Milan and opened a small workshop producing women's shoes. His son Ermes took over the "hand-made" business and passed it on to Guido Pasquali, who studied engineering in Milan, in the 1970s. Guido made footwear for Albini and invented a shoe with colored stitching: a high-heeled shoe stitched with a matelassé pattern in seven different colors. He works with Armani, Missoni, Ferré, Valentino, Tarlazzi and Mugler.

❑ 2003, Summer. Guido Pasquali joined Baldinini, Cesare Paciotti, and Bruno Magli in following the trend for ancient Roman style sandals, sometimes made from gold leather.

Pasquero Fabrizio (1938). Graphic designer, art director and journalist, born in Sanremo. Pasquero is an authoritative figure in the fashion world. He was editor of *Linea Italiana* and he created the television programme *Nonsolomoda*. His career has always been divided between fashion and publishing, marking the strong link between the two sectors. As head of Mondadori's *Linea Italiana* in the 1980s he adopted an aggressive approach to the specialist market, making the Segrate-based publisher a leader in that sector. After leaving Mondadori, he moved into television, conceiving and producing the programme *Nonsolomoda* for the Mediaset network, bringing all his energy and experience to the project. He has many and varied interests: he is an expert and collector of classic cars and motorbikes, a keen gardener, an ecologist and lover of nature, a slow-food enthusiast and a wine connoisseur. A man of great intellectual curiosity, he is always open to new things and to subjects as diverse as architecture, contemporary art, design, and fasion.

Passementerie Tassels, ribbons, cords, tapes, bows, braids etc., used as trimming and decoration for clothes. Chanel uses them as an accessory to trim the skirts and jackets of its suits. In *Gone with the Wind,* Scarlett O'Hara makes herself a dress and hat from green velvet curtains decorated with passementerie in order to impress Rhett and make him think she is a fine lady when in fact she is struggling with her finances.

Patafisic Knitwear label that started out in Florence in 1996 with a system of tubular knits using fine yarns like angora, viscose, cotton, and mohair to make "wearable wrappings" that show off the body. They experimented with craft techniques to achieve a smooth line with minimal stitching.

Patagonia Label founded in Ventura, California in 1975. It has always specialized in sportswear, producing items for fishing, yoga, surfing, skiing, free climbing, and mountain biking. It has 1,000 employees with an average age of 35, thirty own-brand shops across the world including 4 in Europe (in Chamonix from 1987, Munich from 1990, Dublin from 1991 and Milan from 2002). It pays great attention to the use of ecologically correct materials, and donates 1% of its sales to groups working to protect the environment. In line with this policy it focuses on pieces made of PCR, a fabric made from recycled plastic. The company explains that "making 150 garments from PCR saves on a barrel of petroleum and avoids the emission into the atmosphere of half a ton of toxic substances." Their website www.patagonia.com gives updates on their ranges for men, women, and children, as well as information about their research.

Pataugas French brand of canvas or leather boots with rubber soles designed for fishing, hunting, and outdoor work, founded in 1950. Pataugas (from the French *patauger*, meaning to splash around) has become a generic term used for thick soled canvas ankle boots or higher boots. Pataugas was taken over by the André group, and later marketed colored styles of its boots.

Patchwork A method of assembling scraps of fabric, mixing different patterns and pieces to create real works of art. The American quilts from the early 1800s are particularly beautiful, often with naïf or romantic designs. In the 1940s knitted patchworks also became popular, although they were never as interesting as the fabric designs. In the 1960s the concept of patchwork spread to ethnic-inspired, knitted or fabric garments, like Missoni's "put together" clothes.

Patellani Federico (1911-1977). Italian photographer. A pioneer of photo-journalism. He photographed fashion with the same approach he used for news subjects. He made clever use of light, capturing all the details possible within the picture frame. After studying law, he took his first pictures in East Africa in 1935, during Italy's war in Ethiopia. In 1939 he created the first photo-essays for the new magazine *Tempo*. After working as a war photographer for several years, in 1946 Arturo Tofanelli, the editor of *Tempo*, employed him on to work for the magazine on a freelance basis. He covered news, current affairs, celebrity subjects, and fashion. His fashion photographs had an autonomy that contrasted with the pictorial style of Arturo Ghergo and Elio Luxardo. During the same period he was also working for the magazines *L'Illustrazione Italiana*, *Le Ore*, *Marie Claire* and *Bellezza*. From 1956 to his death he no longer worked in fashion, but took long trips during which he made extraordinary and prestigious photo stories.

(*Angela Madesani*)

Patou Jean (1880-1936). French designer. Founder of one of the great French fashion houses between the two World Wars. Patou was one of the precursors of the designer label concept, and the first house to monogram its creations and extensively propagate its perfumes and other lines derived from the couture. Born in Normandy to an important family of leather tanners, Patou began his career as an assistant to an uncle who was a fur dealer. He opened a small dressmaking shop called Maison Parry in Paris in 1912.

Evening dress by Jean Patou, 1931 (Patou Archive).

The following year an important American buyer bought his entire collection, but the war interrupted his business. He served as a captain in the Zouave corps until 1918 when he reopened his couture workshop. His earliest collections employed the new jerseys made by Rodier in special shades of beige, green and *bleu Patou*, even before Chanel famously employed them in her collections. From 1922 he defined the style that would make him famous, emphasizing a casual and modern elegance that found particular expression in chic sportswear pieces like pleated kilts and cardigans. He dressed the actresses Constance Bennet and Louise Brooks, Josephine Baker and the Dolly Sisters, and aristocrats from all over Europe including the grand duchess Maria Pavlovna. Early on he understood the nature of commercializing his new designs, and opened stores in Monte Carlo, Biarritz, Deauville and Venice. These chic watering holes provided him with sales points from which to dress the most watched women of the period: his sweaters, including some famous Cubist-inspired styles, his early bathing costumes and his elegant embroidered and beaded "princess line" evening dresses, often worn with magnificent fur-trimmed capes, all defined luxury in the period. In 1925 he launched his first perfumes: his legendary fragrance *Joy*, which up till the end of the 20th century was still one of the century's most expensive and best selling perfumes, was created in 1930. Like many other companies, Patou suffered the consequences of the Wall Street crash, but his business was on the way to recovery at the time of his death in 1936. The management of the house was passed on to his brother-in-law Raymond Barbas. Over the years many designers have tried their hands at reviving Patou, with greater or lesser success, including Marc Bohan and Christian Lacroix.

❑ Under the guidance of Jean de Mouy, assumed in 1980, the high standards of quality for all Jean Patou products - fragrance and Haute Couture fashion - have been strictly mantained. Along with Chanel and Guerlain, Patou is nowadays among the only three houses that create their perfumes by themselves. Each month the Nose provides Jean Patou's managers with 10-20 new formulas from which new fragrances are selected.

❑ 2002. Chiara Mastroianni is chosen as new face of Jean Patou perfumes, featuring in the international advertising campaign photographed by Peter Lindbergh.

❑ Created along the same lines as Patou's Haute Couture with the same care and attention, *Joy* is nowadays the most expensive perfume in the world. *Eau de Patou 1000* is the most recent fragrance launched by the "perfume designer" Jean Kerleo.

Knitwear designs by Jean Patou, 1928 (from *Anni Venti - La nascita dell'abito moderno*, Centro Di, Florence, 1991, catalogue for the Galleria del Costume).

Patrizia Pepe Label conceived in 1993 by Claudio Orrea and Patrizia Bambi, and produced by Tessilform in Capalle (Florence). It has a young, modern, dynamic, ready-to-wear style that is presented with a refined image, with a market presence through several own-brand shops. In 2003 12 new stores opened in Europe. The 2002 operating profit was around 5 million euros. Designer Gaia Leonori is the creative director.

❑ 2004. The Florentine company's success continued. Eleven years after its conception, turnover had risen from 3 million euros in 1994 to 66 million euros in 2004, an excellent result at a time when the market was in crisis.
❑ 2005. A men's collection was launched.

Pattern maker In the clothing sector, this term is used to describe the person who designs and oversees the production of clothing, hats, underwear, shoes, and other accessories in general. Alternatively, it can refer to the worker who prepares the prototype and makes the patterns. It has also come to refer to an employee in a workshop who produces clothing and who, often using innovative technology, prepares and tests paper patterns by making collection prototypes, enabling them to be reproduced in multiple "copies." Immediately after the *haute couture* runway shows in Paris, for example, designs by the big brand companies are presented to tailors and seamstresses by distributors, who have selected them exclusively for their country. The tailors touch and examine the garments placed on mannequins and choose the ones they consider to be most suitable for their clientele. They then purchase the paper patterns, which serve as a basis (especially for the cut) in order to create several garments. The paper patterns are not sold exclusively. At the after-show presentations several tailors from a single city are often present and they sometimes buy the same designs. In addition to the paper patterns, which are reproduced by pattern makers, tailors can also obtain the exact information for the other details, such as buttons and embroideries. However, these references represent an extra cost. Some seamstresses, after having attended the necessary schools, are specialized in the creation of paper models, so that they can produce their own, exclusive designs, taking inspiration from current trends, modifying and personalizing them according to their clients' wishes. Some of the most famous representatives of this profession are Rina Pedrini, Rivella, Zenobia and Naide of Turin, and the Guidi sisters.

Paul & Joe The label took its name from the sons of its French creator, Sophie Albou. Literally born into fashion (both her parents were designers), at the age of 20 she joined the house of Azzedine Alaïa as a general assistant. This valuable experience led her to work for 8 years on Garage, a line of men's shirts. In 1995 she launched her first men's collection. Colorful and irreverent, it broke with the classic traditions of dark colors and classic cuts for men's fashion and met with great success. In 2001 she opened her first London shop, and in 2003 she launched a line of cosmetics. (*Maddalena Fossati*)

Paul & Shark Company that specializes in sailing wear, and which has a shark as its logo. Founded as Dama S.p.A. in 1921, it took its present name in 1957. Its clothing is sold in 200 stores around the world, through a franchising operation and shops-in-shops. The total look (pants, Bermuda shorts, swimsuits, and also jackets, blazers, socks, shoes, and umbrellas) includes knitwear, using a hi-tech machine washable wool called superwash, and more recently a "total easy care" yarn that dries in a domestic spin-drier. The most recent new lines have been for golf, yachting, and items for divers to wear before and after diving. There has been a women's range since 1999.

(*Laura Salza*)

Paulette Parisian hat company founded in 1929 by Pauline Adam Marchand: its success lasted nearly half a century. Her famous draped turban, created during the war, always featured in her collections. Paulette gained international fame through cinema and theater. Audrey Hepburn wore her hats in *My Fair Lady*. She opened branches in London, New York, and Buenos Aires. The jet set's preferred milliner, she also worked for Piguet, Chanel, Féraud, Mori, Scherrer, Ungaro, and the then up-and-coming Montana and Mugler. She was head of the Chambre Syndicale de la Mode from 1957 to 1961. She received the Légion d'Honneur in 1974 and died in 1984.

Paul Harnden Scottish brand of footwear,

distributed throughout the world. Founded by Paul Harnden at the end of the 1980s in a remote corner of the Highlands. They make shoes inspired by old designs using "aged" leather.

Paulin Guy (1945-1990). French designer. Born in Lorena, he started working for the Printemps stores in Paris, first as a lift attendant, then as a buyer, which led him on to fashion design. In 1968 he moved to New York, where he worked with the American chain of boutiques Paraphernalia during the same years as Emmanuelle Khanh and Mary Quant. He returned to Paris in 1970 and joined forces with Georges Edelmann for a new collection. His work also took him to Italy where he signed a contract with the Girombelli Group in 1979. He designed for MicMac, Sportmax and others, until he presented his own women's collection in 1980. For the period 1983-85 Chloé appointed him as artistic director, having just lost Karl Lagerfeld. In 1986 he started working for himself again and continued to do so until 1990, the year of his final collection and his death. Paulin is remembered mainly for his knitwear.

Paulo Cravo Eponymous label of the Portuguese designer, in partnership with the fashion designer Nuno Baltasar. Together they offer clients a personalised service, even when working on industrial-level projects. Their collections are exquisitely feminine, using very high quality materials and a simplicity of cut for their various pieces, without ever losing sight of a strong commercial edge.

Paunovic Dusan (1968). Serbian designer. He has been living in Milan for 15 years. After attending Belgrade's Fine Arts Academy he enroled at the Istituto Marangoni. He worked for the Yugoslavian designer Zoran for six years. In 1999 he launched his own line of womenswear. He started out in a very small space in Via Agnello, then expanded into a house and atelier in Via Vincenzo Monti. He does not draw his creations, but models the fabric directly around the body, like the great couturiers. His favors reversible and hand-made fabrics, silks from Taron and Clerici, and cashmere from Loro Piana. He is an outsider: no publicity or PR, no shows or showroom. He does everything himself with the help of two assistants and three small workshops. He handles his sales directly and every season he takes his collection to the USA to sell it without the use of intermediaries. He has limited distribution, with a single exclusive shop in each city.

Pavesi Emanuela. Fashion photographer. Immersed in the fashion world, fashion was not just her occupation, but an all-consuming passion. From the beginning of the 1960s she started wearing Saint Laurent, and putting together a rich collection of vintage clothes with pieces by YSL Rive Gauche and Couture, Chanel (couture only), Balenciaga and Courrèges, with a few precious pieces from the 1920s. In 1972 she won a *Vogue Italy* contest and became the fashion editor. In 1973 she completed a degree in Philosophy and Psychology. She has worked with all the great photographers, including Helmut Newton, David Bailey, Gianpaolo Barbieri, Peter Lindbergh, and Sarah Moon. She has followed Prada's image from its conception, working on its first ready-to-wear show, and in 1978 producing the book *Prada a Milano* with the photographer Albert Watson. She left *Vogue* in 1992 and started working as a photographer. Her work is published in *Allure*, *Vogue France*, *Vogue Japan*, *Uomo Vogue*, *Glamour*, *Mademoiselle* (American edition) and in the *New York Times* supplement. (*Valeria Vantaggi*)

Pavone Giorgio. A public relations man, he worked with Rudy Crespi. They organized events including the Summer shows of Mare Moda Capri. His first marriage was to the Italian model Loredana Tapparelli, who dominated the Italian runways in the 1950s with Luciana Angiolillo, Genny Genestretti, and Franchina Novati.

Peacock John (1943). English illustrator. He works for the BBC and is the author of a *Chronicle of Western Costume*, which tells the history in sketches of 4 millennia of fashion, styles, modes of dress, and recurrent trends. It is not so much an academic study as a personal journey, which stops at 1990.

Pearce Fionda English fashion label founded in 1994 by Reynold Pearce (1967) and Andrew Fionda (1967). The two met during a fashion course at Trent Polytechnic in 1985. They both did a Masters in fashion, one at Central Saint Martin's and the other at the Royal College of Art. They gained experience independently working with designers like Galliano and Roland Klein. Their first runway show was held in the London department store Liberty's in 1995. They are amongst the most talented of the English New Generation of designers, and they get lots of media attention. They are admired for their talent for modern and minimalist tailoring. Their clients include Nicole Kidman and Helena Bonham-Carter. They have designed a range called Pearce II Fionda for the English department store Debenhams since 1997.

Pecci Italian wool manufacturer, based in Capalle (Florence). One episode from the company's history demonstrates its capacity. In 1951 the US army based in Germany ordered 1,800,000 blankets to be parachuted to its troops in Korea in three months time. Pecci coordinated a team of manufacturers to produce the blankets under the strict quality controls of the Societé de Surveillance de Genève. They were delivered 2 days early. E. Pecci & C. was founded in 1902 by Luigi Pecci, grandson of Giustino Pecci, whose signature can be seen on an 1884 invoice which is the first official document of the family wool business. Luigi was succeeded by Enrico in 1936. At the end of the 1960s his son Luigi took the helm, followed by his brother Alberto after Luigi's premature death in 1973 (the family have founded a museum of contemporary art in Prato in his name). The company acquired Priverno in 1976 and then Pontoglio in 1986. Further acquisitions have made the Pecci Group manufacturers of fabrics and hangings, combed and carded wool, knitwear yarns, jersey and ready-made garments. In 1998, with Ceritex, Cisq and Iqnet, they were awarded certifications for the high quality of their products and their elevated operating levels. (*Giuliana Zabeo Ricca*)

Peccinotti Harri. American photographer of Italian origin. He has been the artistic and design director for numerous magazines including *Vogue*, *Town* and *Elle*. His fashion photography has an ethnic and social slant, with particular attention paid to the backgrounds for his subjects. He took pictures for the Pirelli calendars in 1968 and 1969.

Pecler's French design and image consultancy created in 1970 by Dominique Peclers, a graduate in Political Sciences who was passionate about fashion and who had been director of the design office of a department store. The consultancy has 50 employees and is represented in 18 countries by 11 textile industry professionals. Their aim is to create a bridge between creativity and industry in all sectors of the textile, cosmetics and furnishing fields, predicting trends and future consumer needs, providing market reports and advising on strategy. The consultancy has over 60 clients throughout the world including Carrefour France, Du Pont de Nemours, Lancôme, Pinault, Printemps, and Unitika Japon.

Pecora Paolo (1961). Milanese designer. He started off as a buyer for a group of Milanese stores. He set up his own business in 1988, presenting a women's collection of masculine shirts in a wide range of fabrics and colors. From 1990 he started producing knitwear in jersey and coordinating fabrics, and in 1995 he presented a men's collection which brought about collaborations with several leading Japanese shirt manufacturers. His style is characterized by distinguished but modern lines, with a constant use of color. His women's range is currently produced by Miles of Vicenza, while his men's range is produced by Crespi of Gallarate.

Pecoraro Maurizio (1962). Italian designer. Born in Palermo, he took an interest in fashion from an early age. He moves to Paris when still very young, working there with Thierry Mugler. Once back in Italy he joined Gianni Versace's creative team, and in 1989 he took on the creative direction of the Alma range. He launched his label in September 1998 with a collection of timeless elegance and skilled tailoring. In January 2003 he presented one of his collections at the AltaRomaAlta Moda fashion week, and received the award from the city's mayor as the best young Italian designer, with a talent for reinventing *haute couture* in a modern way. (*Eleonora Attolico*)

❑ 2002, September. The Sicilian designer's Spring-Summer collection paid homage to the art of the 1960s.
❑ Pecoraro masterminded the relaunch of Vionnet, the designer label belonging to the Watelin de Lummen family and founded in 1912. The designer signed a two-year contract. Vionnet was shown on the runways of the Parisian *haute couture* fashion week and was sponsored by Villa Moda, the Kuwaiti luxury fashion emporium opened by the Sheik Majed al Sabah.

Pedro Garcia Famous Spanish brand of footwear, founded in 1968 by Pedro Garcia Vidal, well-known for making shoes for the Queen of Spain, and also for having sold many pairs of his shoes to one of the temples of classic English footwear, Russell & Bromley. The founder's son Pedro Jr. is in charge of the brand with his wife Dale, and his sister Mila is marketing director. Together they design the shoe collections (there are two ranges, one more luxurious, and the other more informal) where style and comfort are perfectly combined.

Peek A Boo A pierced earring with extra pieces to decorate the edge of the ear as well as the ear-lobe.

Peek & Cloppenburg Dutch department store. They have expanded into Belgium with their P&C label. Their motto "La mode, c'est belge" is justified by the fact that they buy in many articles from Belgian companies. Peek & Cloppenburg was started by Dutch pioneers in Amsterdam in 1869, producing men's clothing. In 1961 its production increased after a merger with Lampe, who produced women's and teenage clothing.

Pejoski Marian. Designer. The Macedonian thirty-something designer moved to Great Britain in 1987. There she started designing her collection which she sold at the London boutique Kokon to Zai, along with other little-known but imaginative designers (Noki, Russell Sage, Emma Cook, Adam Entwisle). The shop gained cult status after a short time: in fact it was there that her clothes were discovered by Björk, the Icelandic singer famous for her eccentric outfits, for whom Pejoski designed the famous "Chinese lantern" dress which she wore to the Cannes 2000 premiére of *Dancer in the Dark* (which went on to win the Palme D'Or), and the swan-shaped dress that she wore to the Oscars. This launched Pejoski on the international scene: her trashy-chic comic strip creations – think Betty Boop and Daisy Mae – enjoy great success.

(*Antonio Mancinelli*)

Peleponnesian Folklore Foundation In Nafplion, Greece. This collection of regional Greek costumes created by Ionna Papantoniou is well-known for its rare and historically important examples. Over the years she has also added a collection of fashion garments and accessories, mostly of French and English manufacture, which have been donated by rich Greek families. She also received an important donation of clothes and working material by the Greek designer Yiannis Tseklenis, who was famous in the 1960s and 1970s. The collection also includes photographs, periodicals and sketches.

Pellat-Finet Lucien. French designer, called the king of cashmere. As a boy he was struck by the vision of a sweater in a boutique in the South of France. In 1994 he designed and launched his first collection of luxury streetwear, and two years later came his men's collection. In 1997 he showed in Paris for the first time, and his clothes were sold in the Parisian concept store Colette, the event which "made" him. In 1998 he designed a children's cashmere range and opened a boutique in Saint-Germain. He was courted by the American market and his clothes are sold at Barney's New York. In 2001 he initiated contacts with Japan which led to collaborations with architects and artists like Takashi Murakami, and the opening of a store in Aoyama, the most fashionable area of Tokyo. In 2003 he launched a range of jeans colored with organic dyes.

(*Maddalena Fossati*)

Pellegrina Cape worn by both men and women, fashionable in the 1800s, but in use from the Middle Ages. It was worn as a simple "pilgrim" style cape or collar in Holland in the 1600s. Characterized by a wide collar covering the shoulders and going

Women of Corfù, from the Peloponnesian Folklore Foundation's collection of regional costumes.

down to the elbows, or sometimes the wrists. Applied to a dress or cloak, the "pellegrina" was longer at the front, reaching the waist at the back. It was famous for the style worn by Sherlock Holmes for his investigations. Made from heavy wool for the Winter, the women's Summer version was made from ruched lace. The style was revisited in the 1900s.

Pellegrini Guido (1945). Designer. A creator of fur and leather fashions from the years of the Dolce Vita until he became established between 1960 and 1970. He favored Persian lambskin in black-and-white, evoking Andy Warhol's pop art, or in beige and brown zebra or tiger patterns. He infected his unisex jumpsuits and leopard-print creations with a kind of African fever. He interpreted the hippy style with ethnic folk creations such as a long breitswanz redingote with self-colored panels, a provocative and seductive garment more suited to a starlet than a flower child. (*Lucia Mari*)

Pellegrino Renaud (1946). French leather accessories designer. His first notorious success was a bag in the shape of a cardinal's mitre. His Parisian boutique, which overlooks the courtyards of Faubourg Saint-Honoré, is a must for those in search of luxury accessories. Crammed with bags, wallets, and briefcases of every shape and form: big and tiny, rigid and soft. Born in Nice, he trained in a craftsmen's workshop and then in the shoe industry, arriving in Paris in 1969 where he started his career making bags for Maria Carita's boutique, and then later for Saint Laurent, until in 1983 he decided to produce his own range.

❑ As well as bags, he designs a range of luxury footwear, including some outstanding black leather slippers with mink panels.

PellicceModa Specialized Italian magazine that covers mainly furs and fashion. It was founded by Enzo Lancellotti and his daughter-in-law Anna Maria Sapelli Lancellotti, who became its editor following the death of Enzo, and who continued working on the magazine with her husband Alberto for another thirty years. In 1990 it became part of the Motta Publishing Group, and after a brief period under the direction of Francesca Scopelliti from 1994-5, it was put under the charge of Cristina Navarrete Motta. To the already existing seven annual bilingual Italian-English issues and the exclusively Italian issue aimed at the general public during the fall fur sales season, she added a Chinese edition in 1998 and a Russian edition in 2001. Special editions (in Italian, English, Spanish, Russian, and Chinese) covering important international events are published under the magazine's title, and they also publish the *PelliceModa In Shop* annual guide, which gives an up-to-date overview of the world's fur companies. The guide can be found at all ready-to-wear fashion fairs and is a valuable tool for those working in the sector. Over its long history, PellicceModa has reported on the latest styles with previews and articles using the best illustrators (like Brunetta Mateldi) and photographers, often discovering and then showcasing their talents.

(*Maria Rita Stiglich*)

Pellini Emma (1900-1966). Costume jewelry designer. She started in Milan in 1947 producing Venetian glass jewelry for French and Italian *haute couture*. In 1951 she took part in the Italian fashion showcase organized by Bista Giorgini. From then on, the American market took great interest in her creations. In 1952 she took part at the New York Fair of Italian Manufacturers. Her first Milanese boutique opened in 1962, following the initiative of her daughter Carla (1925). In 1972 the founder's grandchildren Donatella and Ernesto joined the company, dealing respectively with the creative and administrative sides of the business. Donatella Pellini has been responsible for the most lively phase in the company's history, collaborating with young ready-to-wear labels like Mugler, Lacroix, Gigli, and Fendi. These days they produce ethnic, very individual styles using glass and resin, with the addition of natural materials like herbs, flowers, and mineral powders. Pellini jewelry is distributed throughout the world, and is particularly popular in Japan.

❑ In the last few years Donatella's work has been celebrated in exhibitions of her

designs and sketches at the Milan Triennale and the Victoria and Albert Museum in London.
❑ Since 2000, Pellini has started producing bags, belts, and hats as well as costume jewelry. A boutique has been opened in Rue Jacob, Paris.

Donatella Pellini, colored glass earrings.

Peluche Warm synthetic or natural fabric with a furry surface that is similar to fleece and velour, but with much longer hairs. Used for jackets, coats, hats, and cuddly toys.

Penn Irving (1917). American photographer. He started off working as a graphic designer after studying design with Alexey Brodovitch at the Philadelphia School of Industrial Art, then moved to New York in 1938. In 1943 he became assistant to the editor of *Vogue*, Alexander Liberman, who gave him the job of organizing the staff photographers. Penn was snubbed by big names like Cecil Beaton and De Meyer, who were little inclined to deal with, and even less to obey, a young unknown. They complained to Liberman who decided to entrust Penn to an assistant to show him the secrets of the large format camera and transform him into a photographer. Liberman himself commissioned Penn's first *Vogue* cover for the October 1943 issue: it is not a portrait or figure, but a still-life composed of fashion accessories against a sheet of paper held in place by a hat pin embellished with a pearl, on which are written the cover lines. It is an idea that could only have come to somebody trained as a graphic designer. Penn had an excellent knowledge of all the photographic processes and his images stand out for the simplicity of their composition, which seems thought out to bring into greater relief the shape and elegance of his ever-graceful figures and the abstract play on lines and dimensions. It is hard to distinguish between Penn's fashion photography, where he gives a lot of space to the model's personality, and his studio portraits: in the latter Penn plays around with space using moveable panels that recall those of August Sander, concentrating the gaze on his subjects so as to corner them (in the case of Truman Capote), or play with them, as with Duchamp. An incredibly eclectic artist, he passed from the figure to the nude, from the elegance of sepia-toned black-and-white to the delicacy of color used in all possible shades. His memorable and classic images include still-lives inspired by Caravaggio's school of painting, slightly wilted flowers, ready-made compositions of cigarette butts or abandoned objects, elegantly formal headless nudes, and often disturbing and provocative creations on the theme of food. Held in high regard by collectors, he has held retrospectives all over the world and has published various books including *Moment Preserved*, *World in a Small Room*, *Flowers*, *Irving Penn* (a catalogue of the 1987 exhibition at the Museum of Modern Art in New York), *Passage* in 1991 and *Still Life* in 2001. (*Roberto Mutti*)

Percale A medium weight plain weave cotton fabric similar to madapolam, but with a finer yarn and a closer weave, used for chemises and blouses, but also for undergarments and bed-linen.

Peretti Elsa (1940). Jewelry designer. Famous for her perfectly anatomical *Bone* bracelet, and *Diamond by the Yard*, gold and diamond chains sold by the meter. She worked as a model in London and New York and studied interior design in Rome, then in 1969 she began making silver jewelry, which was displayed in a Bloomingdales boutique. The designers Halston and Sant'Angelo, whom she had modeled for in the past, asked her to collaborate on their runway shows. In 1974 she joined the team of designers working for Tiffany New York, producing decorative ornaments of formal simplicity, with a decidedly sculptural edge. She takes inspiration from nature to create her biomorphic jewelry made from silver, gold, precious stones, horn, ebony, and ivory. Her designs are now some of Tiffany's biggest sellers.

Perfecto American brand of jacket: a legendary black leather blouson style created in Oakland by John D. Perfecto, the son of an Italian emigrant, who was inspired by the jackets worn by US pilots during World War II. It became the symbol of the Hell's Angels, and, as worn by James Dean in Nicholas Ray's movie *Rebel Without a Cause*, the emblem of a whole generation. In 1954 Perfecto sold the design to the Schott brothers, who produced it for Harley Davidson.

Perint Palmer Gladys (1947). Hungarian illustrator. She belongs to the great tradition of Constatin Guys, Renato Gruau, and Brunetta of using sketches, drawings, and watercolors to document runway shows and fashion. Using subtle exaggerations and a comic-strip interpretation of reality, she takes an ironic and shrewd look at the world of the runway, the clothes, the models, and the audience.

Perlon A German manufactured synthetic fiber, superior to nylon for its elasticity.

Pernas Antonio (1944). Spanish designer born in La Coruña. After studying engineering at university, he began producing clothes and textiles with his wife María Freire. His first women's ready-to-wear collection was shown at the major international showrooms, in Paris and Düsseldorf. He showed on the Madrid Cibeles runway from 1991 to 1999. He subsequently showed as part of a collective with other founding members of the Asociación de Creadores de Moda de España: Jesus del Pozo, Angel Schlesser, Roberto Verino, and Modesto Lomba. In 1997 he won the T award as best Spanish designer from the magazine Telva. In 2002 he went back to showing his collection independently at Cibeles. His collections have won other important awards over the years such as the Vidal Sassoon, the Kapital and the Colección Màs Creativa.

Sketch by Antonio Pernas.

Perraudine Séverine (1963). French designer. She produced her first small collection for Spring-Summer 1985 after apprenticeships with Agnès B and Michel Klein. However her true entry into the world of Parisian ready-to-wear came a year later, when the press was full of her apron dresses and her crossover sweaters draped at the shoulders. She was not yet 30 when she designed the Relacher collection in Japan and worked alongside the Missoni family.

Perret Dorothée (1972). French designer. Born in Lyons. Straight after her diploma at Studio Berçot in Paris she started working with Martine Sitbon and Guy Laroche. She launched her first womenswear collection for Fall-Winter 1998-99, which found coverage and praise in the trend magazine *Spoon*. Her work was immediately noticed (and bought) by stores like Onward in Paris, Purple in Tokyo, and Penelope in Brescia. A year later she founded the company bearing her name and distributed her clothes around the world. At present 80% of her production is sold outside of France. Every garment she creates is unique, made with hand-painted and numbered fabrics.

Perrin French textile group, and the leading French silk manufacturer. It was formed around Eugéne Perrin's business in 1992. Its companies include Verel de Belval, whose fabrics are used by many French designers, Tissages Perrin, Alpasoie, Henry Chagny, and Siegl.

Perris Bernard (1942). French designer. His mother was a dressmaker, which is why at the age of 17 Bernard left to enrol at a fashion school in Paris. By 1962 he was already Guy Laroche's first assistant, then moving on from Valentino to Heim and Dior. He set up his label in 1969 and applied his own experience of *haute couture* to ready-to-wear. He has worked in cinema.

❑ The opening of a shop in Madison Avenue, New York, led Perris to work with some internationally recognised French names, like Gilles Mendel and Jean Louis Scherrer.
❑ Perris' clothes played a major part in Nagisa Oshima's movie *Max mon amour*, in which Charlotte Rampling wears a different outfit for every scene.
❑ The garden as a garment. The garden at Perris' Provencal retreat was photographed by Claire de Virieu for her title *Fashion Designers Gardens*. Other gardens featured were Giorgio Armani's at his house in Pantelleria, Yves Saint Laurent's in Marrakech, and Valentino's in Tuscany.

Perry Michel (1949). Shoe designer, whose father was a craftsman in the same field. He is considered one of the most inspired contemporary shoe designers. He launched his first collection in 1987 after studying Fine Arts in Belgium and Paris, and then working with Philippe Model from 1983 to 1985. He produces 20,000 pairs of shoes each season which are distributed to 150 shops as well as being sold in his Paris boutique in Rue des Petits-Pères. His styles break with tradition, inventing new lines and details, and he has a clear preference for longer shapes and high heels.

❑ He opened his first New York store in Park Avenue at the beginning of the year. Americans soon caught on to his very feminine "not just for walk" shoes, with their pointed toes, narrow heels and rich colors. Previously just a few of his styles had been available at Bergdorf Goodman and Saks Fifth Avenue, and for the first time New Yorkers were given access to his complete collection at this shop rather like a Salvador Dali painting.
❑ For his Spring-Summer 2004 collection, Perry designed some "scarf" shoes with colored fabric that wraps around the foot and ties at the calf.

Evening sandal by Michel Perry.

Persol Brand of eyewear with a long history. It started with Giuseppe Ratti's optical business in Turin in 1917 and now belongs to the Luxottica Group. Amongst its many successes are the invention in 1939 of flexible arms made of Meflecto acetate, the arrow hinge and the 649 model from 1957, which was worn by Marcello Mastroianni in the movie *Divorzio all'Italiana*, by Tom Cruise in *Cocktail*, and by Jack Nicholson in *Blood & Wine*. Persol's defining feature is their polarized, anti-reflective, photosensitive lenses made from very pure silicon based crystal. Their styles are always very carefully designed, with teardrop, square, rectangular, oval, and pointed shapes.

Personalità Italian TV show for women covering fashion, culture, home decoration, and current affairs. In 1960 female viewers would switch on once a week in the afternoon, not to watch the latest soap, but to see *Personalità*, directed and presented by Milan Contini, who was previously editor of *Marie Claire* and before that *Grazie* during its first years in the 1940s. Part of the show was dedicated to fashion, with the latest styles presented, described and commented on by an off-screen man's voice: the warm persuasive tones of Beppe Modenese who – apart from his voice – was known only for his hands which would occasionally appear on screen to point out a certain fabric, cut or detail. There was also a section covering children's clothes, recommending items – not forgetting clothes for "special occasions" – that should be practical, natural and created with the child's wellbeing rather than the mother's ambitions in mind. It was produced by Maria Vittoria Alfonsi, who had strong experience from working on *Marie Claire* and Silvana Bernasconi's *Mamme e Bimbi*, it also dealt with subjects like children's nutrition, health, games, and practical childcare advice. The programme (which today would be called a "format") stopped in June 1964. It was preceded by *Vetrine*, which ran from 1954 to 1959 and was produced by Elda Lanza: a very young Beppe Modenese worked on the show presenting home furnishings and decorations.

Personality Manufacturer of handmade ties, founded in 1977 and based in Milan. Their ties can be personalised at the customer's request. Fifty percent of their production is exported to the rest of Europe, Japan, and the USA. The company is directed by Giuseppe Ruggirenti.

Persoon Jurgi (1969). Belgian designer. He graduated from the Académie Royal in Antwerp in 1992, and two years later started working with Walter Van Beirendonck. He started out with a women's collection in Paris in 1996. He favors craftsmanlike tailoring and reinvents traditional English men's clothes. He has a "dark" style, and he presents his collections with particular care, aiming to stun the audience, for example, with models imprisoned in cages on the quays of the River Seine or laid out like insect specimens on an entomologist's bench. In 2002 he chose to show his collection at the Palais Galliera, which houses a famous fashion museum.

Pertegaz Manuel (1918). Spanish designer, born in Aragona. He started as a tailor's apprentice at the age of 12, specializing in the cutting of men's suits. He opened a Barcelona showroom in the 1940s and he showed his first collection in the USA in 1945. He moved to Madrid in 1968. It was written of him that "He took a steadfastly traditional approach to Spanish theatricality."

Perugia André (1893-1977). French shoemaker of Italian origins. One of the first stars of European footwear. He started working in his father's shop at a very young age, and was noticed at once for his striking creativity. The owner of Nice's best known hotel, the Negresco, introduced him into high society and brought about his initial success. He moved to Paris in 1920 and opened an atelier in Faubourg Saint-Honoré, working with the most famous dressmakers of the time, particularly Poiret. He is renowned for his high heels and his ability in coupling different materials like chamois and kid, leather and silk. He designed styles inspired by Picasso and Braque for Charles Jourdan. In the 1950s he abandoned made-to-measure shoemaking and moved into mass production with the Perugia Boutique label in partnership with François Villon. Sadly, the project soon ended in failure.

Per Voi Signora Women's monthly. Launched in 1932 with the title *Per voi signora, per i vostri ricami e la vostra casa* (For you madam, your embroideries and your home), it was edited by Angelo Vergani. It presented drawings, photographs, and patterns for knitting, crochet, and embroidery designs for the house, bed-linen and clothing. It changed its title to *Rivista di moda, ricamo e lavori femminili* (Fashion, embroidery and feminine crafts magazine) in 1935 under the editorship of Mario Soresina, championing exclusively home-produced Italian fashion. Its last issues were published in 1947.

Peschini Antonio (1938). Roman *haute couture* dressmaker, nicknamed Trottolino. Originally from Pescara, he came from the Abruzzo tradition of dressmaking. At the age of 25 he was employed by the Senes Stop atelier in Rome's Via Veneto. He worked there until 1985, becoming a head of department. He decided to set up on his own, and opened a dressmaker's in Via Tevere. He cut and sewed his own creations as well as styles copied from paper patterns and toiles bought from the big Parisian fashion houses that he then adapted to the sizes and tastes of his clients.

Pescucci Gabriella (1943). Italian costume designer. She won an Oscar in 1994 for her costumes for Martin Scorsese's movie *The Age of Innocence*, and she designed 2,000 costumes for Gilliam's *The Adventures of Baron Munchausen.* Together with Milena Canonero and Franca Squarciapino she is the most in-demand Italian costume designer in international cinema. She studied at Florence's Fine Arts Academy, and took an apprenticeship at the dressmaker's Tirelli (she says of herself, "I grew up amongst the clothes from *Death in Venice*"), where she is now one of the partners, and was assistant to Piero Tosi and Pierluigi Pizzi. During her career she has worked on both arthouse movies and studio blockbusters: Fellini's *Orchestra Rehearsal* and *City of Women*, Ettore Scola's *Passion of Love*, *La Nuit de Varennes*, and *What Time is It?*, Sergio Leone's *Once Upon a Time in America*, and big productions like *The Name of the Rose* and *The Scarlet Letter.* Her versatility enables her to move between different periods with ease, dressing Mary and Joseph in *For Love, Only for Love* and designing the 18th century costumes for *The Night and the Moment.* She alternates her work in cinema with theater, for example in 1972 she worked on *Norma* at La Scala with the director Bolognini, and in 1992 she worked on *La Traviata* with the director Liliana Cavani. (*Roberto Nepoti*)

❑ 2000, September. The town of Siena asked Pescucci to redesign the 360 costumes for the players and city factions taking part in the historical procession to commemorate the special millennium Palio (a horse race in Siena's main square). The designer took a cue from the sketches inspired by the historic period from the late 1400s and early 1500s that had already been used by Olla, Manichelli, and Pollai as patterns for their costumes for the previous special Palio in 1981.
❑ 2003, May. The brown moleskin cloak worn by Michelle Pfeiffer in *The Age of Innocence* was shown as part of the exhibition dedicated to the Sartoria Teatrale Tirelli's work for cinema, held at Prato's Textile Museum.

Pessina Company dealing in silk products, founded on Gaetano Pessina's initiative in 1903. The assets of the Pessina family (Gaetano, Ambrogio, and Aurelio's children), the Pagani brothers and Salvatore Dell'Oca were all put into the Como dye works founded in 1904. In 1912 the family opened a factory in Tavernola (Bergamo) for the dyeing and loading of silk cloth. A department for the printing of the cloth was opened at the Como dye works in the 1930s. The experimental company Esercizio della Tintoria Ambrogio Pessina (Ambrogio Pessina Dyeing Firm), which rented the dye works with the workers made into stakeholders, came to an end in the second half of the 1940s. At the end of that decade Ambrogio stood down as director of the business, which continued with its dyeing and printing business for third parties until its closure in 1984.

Pessina Bruno. Founder of the Como silk business of the same name. The Pessinas are a family of textile entrepreneurs. Bruno, brother of Ambrogio, registered the company Sas Tintoria Italiana Bruno Pessina & Co. in 1925. The business was engaged in the dyeing, dressing, and printing of yarns and cloth, and the sale of dyes and other chemical products. On Bruno's death, his wife Giuseppina Carughi took up the management of the business until 1939. After a period of transition the company was acquired by the Solbiati family and the headquarters moved from Como to Milan (1943). In the 1950s they decided to invest in modernising the production machinery. The company experienced steady losses throughout the 1960s and in 1976 Pessina ceased trading. (*Pierangelo Mastantuono*)

PET Polyethylene terephthalate, more commonly known as polyester, used for the production of textiles from the second half of the 1940s, and then in 1977 first used in the USA to make bottles. Fifteen years later the use of PET became more widespread, to the extent that PET bottles were recycled. The resulting polyester polymers are then reused for textiles, through a process of fusion and spinning which produces a good quality fiber that is easily incorporated into yarns for woven cloth, knitwear, and fleeces. (*Silvia Martinenghi*)

Peter Shop Milanese milliner's. Founded by Mario Peter, born in Biella, who opened a milliner's shop at 4 Via Bigli in 1910, specializing in the wholesale supply of women's hats. His daughter Luciana joined the company in 1948 and continued the business with Peter Mode, which specialized in wedding headgear of their own production and imported from France. Peter's granddaughter Paola Battistoni joined the firm in 1996 and launched the Peter Shop brand. The business expanded into accessories, gloves, scarves, and costume jewelry, and offers a hire service for special occasions.

Petit Bateau French company and brand of children's clothing. In the 1990s it started producing for youngsters aged from 12 to 18. It all started from a white cotton "petite culotte" invented by Pierre Vaton de Troyes in 1893 when he took his scissors to the encumbering underwear worn by his 13 children. An empire was born which reigned until the 1970s, when it begins to suffer at the hands of the competition, but was saved from bankruptcy by the Breton cosmetics group Yves Rocher. After a disastrous year they re-launched the brand in 1988 with an advertising and communications strategy devised to rid it of its dated image (with adverts by Sarah Moon). In 1994 Lagerfeld sent his models, led by Claudia Schiffer, down the runway in tight Petit Bateau T-shirts. From that moment, mothers also started wearing the T-shirts designed for 12, 16, and 18 year olds. The company's new and increased success can be seen in the following figures: 1,800 employees; 100 own-brand shops around the world; 25 million T-shirts, briefs, and other cotton garments made in France (2 factories), Turkey, and Morocco.

❑ 2001. The year ended with a turnover of 165.9 million euros, an increase of 13 per cent. Net profits soared by more than 31% to 13.1 million euros.
❑ 2002. Petit Bateau Italia recorded a turnover of over 22 million euros. The tenth own-brand store opened in June, adding to the 900 points of sale and 50 in-store outlets already present in the country.
❑ There are about 5,000 Petit Bateau retailers around the world, and 103 stores in France alone. 2002 ended with the company another step ahead, with about 37 million garments produced, giving a turnover of 228.4 million euros.

Petit Gris Fur produced from the thick soft coat of the Siberian squirrel. Naturally gray, it is often dyed other colors and was very fashionable in the 1940s, also used for linings. The common squirrel has a less prized coat in various shades of brown.

Petit Patapon French children's fashion label. In 1985 Noelle Tutenuit, a young biologist and mother of 5 children, started channeling her creative energies into making simple knitted and fabric clothes for her children, using carefully chosen colors and materials to create a unique and original style. She was encouraged by friends and family to start producing on a larger scale, taking advantage of the support and know-how of her family's textile business Distese

S.A., which was run by her husband François Gros. In this way the Petit Patapon project came into being in 1987, producing personalised clothes and accessories that take into account the individuality of every child. There are two collections a year, divided into four age groups: Petit Patapon newborn; Petit Patapon first steps (6 months – 4 years) with ranges that follow the latest trends; Petit Patapon Pixie et Cie, fine clothes for special occasions for children aged 4 to 14; and Petit Patapon P.K. Kids, trendy "rough and tumble" clothes for children aged 4 to 12. There are 70 flagship stores around the world, with ten own-brand stores in Italy. *(Sara Tieni)*

Petteni Mirella. Italian model born in Bergamo and famous in the 1960s. She was favored by Ugo Mulas and Giampaolo Barbieri for her classic profile and aristocratic elegance. Consuelo Crespi pointed her out to Diana Vreeland who then suggested her to Helmut Newton, who launched Petteni in the USA (he called her "countess"). Married twice, with two children, she is a supporter of the designer Zoran, and she still does the occasional modeling job. In 1997 she featured in a Mila Schön advertising campaign alongside Benedetta Barzini, shot by Martina Vergani. In 1998 she modeled for Carlo Tivoli's catalogue. She is one of the presenters of the Capalbio short film festival.

Petticoat At the end of the nineteenth century the petticoat was a garment that caught men's imagination and sent shivers down the spines of the young (and not so young), but by the start of the 20th century it had begun to transform slowly into a lightweight veil. Of differing degrees of transparency, it now reveals even more of the body in a game of "now you see me, now you don't," emphasizing a woman's curves. Petticoats can be made of flannel, madapolam, lawn linen or cotton, fine muslin, taffeta, lace, pure silk, or rustling satin. It is naturally hand embroidered with insertions, openwork, satin stitch, sheaf stitch, and all sorts of fashionable stitches of the moment. In the first decade of the 20th century, the petticoat remained relatively unchanged. The first real revolution occurred in the 1920s when Paul Poiret replaced muslin and flannel petticoats with versions in cotton, batiste, and much finer muslin to be worn under short linear dresses or under "handkerchief'or "dancing" skirts divided into segments. Increasingly alluring, petticoats triumphed in real life, literature and on the screen: they were associated with the heroines of F. Scott Fitzgerald, Gloria Swanson, Jean Harlow, Joan Crawford, Doris Duranti, vamps and femmes fatales. During World War II, petticoats underwent a "lull'; when central heating faded to just a memory, petticoats were often made from thick cotton or even wool. Silk ones were looked after with great care and kept for special occasions. But once the war was over, women were taken by an irrepressible desire to dress up, both on top and underneath. Ultra-feminine, lightweight sets of underwear became popular, with matching petticoats, panties and bras, that nearly always matched a nightdress, and often a dressing gown too. In 1947, Marcel Rochas began his Fall-Winter fashion show with a model wearing a little white satin skirt with a black lace body: it was a sign of what would become known as the underwear revolution. Petticoats increasingly followed the line of the dress. The French look and the New Look took over, which, both emphasizing the bust, meant that petticoats were cut like a bra at the top, and had pleats on the hips for dresses with very wide skirts, while the straight models were very tight-fitting. To create a tight "wasp" waist, a lace *guêpière* was sometimes worn over the petticoat, if it was not part of the dress itself (above all in the evening with bare shoulders). The following year, after the *guêpière*, Rochas created the *bustier-guêpière* with a little petticoat that was still in white satin, but covered in lace. An example of this type of petticoat was the *jupon* designed by Lilian (one of the leading lingerie designers of the time) made of lightly starched white batiste or sumptuous and rustling stiff taffeta. It was known as the musical jupon, because "every step is accompanied by a little rustle that will make our men dream like they used to fifty years ago," according to the press at the time. The classic petticoat returned to being mainly white, made from in lawn cotton or linen, with pastel colors to follow, though the elegant versions were still in black or ecru lace. Next, the petticoat reappeared in satin, pure silk, crepe silk, satin crepe, lace, bias cut, embroidered, scalloped and decorated with lace trims, flounces, frills and inserts; it was sometimes even open at the side and was closed like a dressing gown with a knot. With the arrival of nylon and other synthetic fibers – popular due to their transparency, their crease-free nature (which eliminated the need for ironing), and the huge variety in which they were available – a large section of the young was won over. In the evening, sparks really flew when a woman took off these garments, and she felt a sort of shock that was at first worrying, but research put an end to static electricity. Without striking a blow, the petticoat won the battle against the large bloomers/underskirt presented by Vionnet in the 1950s, but it had some formidable rivals: cami-knickers (a descendant of the *combinaison* that was so popular during the Roaring Twenties), which were then replaced by the slip (made of special transparent material cut to show off the body) and then the three-piece (bra, knickers, and petticoat) were all extraordinarily successful. But petticoats did not give up the struggle and they returned to the big screen with Cybil Sheppard, Julia Roberts, and Jennifer Lopez. Fashion, in a game of endless revivals, has created petticoats increasingly similar to dresses while dresses have become increasingly similar to petticoats. Shoulder pads, which were once part of the petticoat, have now become a classic piece of clothing. Cadolle, which has provided lingerie to the most fashionable women of Paris since 1800, presents petticoats which are recognizably updated versions of styles popular in earlier eras. Harking back to the *Emmanuelle* years of the 1970s, the story of the petticoat as part of a woman's wardrobe continues.

(*Maria Vittoria Alfonsi*)

Pezzani Gianni (1951). Italian photographer. Despite graduating in Agricultural Science in 1979, his true passion for photography, inherited from his father, soon emerged. He is skilled in the dark room, where he achieves the selective tones that characterize the body of his professional and personal work. He began exhibiting his work at the end of the 1970s, and has had retrospectives in Milan, Modena, Arles, and China. He started working with Condé Nast magazines in 1983, a collaboration that still continues. The following year he moved to Japan to work for Mamiya Cameras and for Japanese fashion clients like Zygos, Barbice, Bigi Company, and Stockman Company. He traveled to New Zealand, Australia, India, China, Malaysia, Thailand, Bhutan, Russia, and Indonesia to take photographs that are always in tune with the local culture. In 1993 he returned to Milan, where he works for the leading fashion advertising agencies and publishers.

Pezzi Maria (1908). Italian journalist. She started out at *Fili Moda*. After the war she worked for the newspapers *Corriere d'Informazione* and *Il Giorno*, and for the monthly *Donna* during its final years. An out and out Milanese, she has lived in the same solid, bourgeois house opposite Foro Bonaparte since birth. Pezzi's house is her anchor: she is a very active curious woman who has contemplated all the new experiences of the century she has lived through with levity, grace and insight. She has observed the century through its fashion and style – points of reference which were once thought fatuous but are now seen as crucial. She can certainly be defined as a fashion journalist, although this definition is too limiting for a woman who, with Irene Brin, invented the role, as somebody who could sense and comprehend the spirit and the highs and lows of an era. She has always modestly described herself as a reporter when recounting the career that she started by chance in Paris, encouraged by her friend, the illustrator René Gruau, who admired her skill and competence at drawing. They were the years of the absolute, uncontested predominance of French fashion: Italian dressmakers would go on pilgrimages to Paris to buy styles by Chanel, Lelong, Vionnet, Grès, Lanvin, Molyneux, and Schiaparelli, which were then recreated in Milan by Ventura, Tizzoni, Ferrario, and many others: for them it was enough to enjoy the glory reflected by the French designers. And then when the Italian dressmakers gradually decided to risk their own designs, Maria Pezzi was there record the debuts of Gigliola, Curiel, Marucelli, and Veneziani. From then on, thanks to Giorgini's inspired idea of holding runway shows at the Palazzo Pitti's Sala Bianca in Florence, there was no stopping Italian fashion, nor Maria for that matter. She was always in the front row, armed with a notebook and her extraordinary intuition in understanding that names like Cappucci, Valentino, Basile, Caumont, Cadette, Ken Scott, Walter Albini, Krizia, and Missoni would come to be the greats of Italian style. On her ninetieth birthday Missoni presented her with her biography *Maria Pezzi, a life in fashion*, written by Guido Vergani and published by Skira. The volume includes twelve of her articles, dedicated to *Men, women and objects in fashion.* *(Isabella Mazzitelli)*

Portrait of Maria Pezzi by Brunetta.

Pfister Andrea (1942). Italian shoe designer. His creations have adorned the feet of many celebrities: Ursula Andress, Claudia Cardinale, Candice Bergen, Jacqueline Bisset, Cher, Valentina Cortese, Madonna, and Liza Minelli. He has worked with companies like Krizia, and he has collaborated with most important tanneries to produce collections of leathers, with a level of creativity and imagination usually reserved for textiles. He was born in Pesaro and spent his childhood in Switzerland. He studied Fine Arts at the University of Paris and in Amsterdam in 1963 he won first prize in the International Competition for best footwear designer, heralding the start of a perfectly successful career. In 1964 he settled in Paris where he designed for Lanvin and Patou. In 1965 he presented his first private collection, and two years later opened his first boutique in Paris and met his future business partner, Jean Pierre Dupré. In 1974 he opened a company in Vigevano, near Pavia, and launched a range of bags, scarves, and belts. In 1987 he opened a boutique in Milan in Via Sant'Andrea, which later moved to Via Montenapoleone. He has a fascinating collection of historical footwear at his holiday home in Positano, with styles from the 1700s, works by sculptors like Biraben, and a shoe designed by Dalí for his wife Gala.

(Giuliana Parabiago)

❑ 2001, March. The Fin.part Group announced their acquisition of the brand and its manufacturing and trading activities. They also acquired the shop in Via Montenapoleone, the atelier in Vigevano and, most importantly from a creative point of view, the label's archive of designs, for a total of about 3.5 million euros. The deal also provided for a 5-year extension of current designers' contracts.
❑ 2002, July. An own-brand store selling shoes and accessories opened in Rodeo Drive, Los Angeles.

Pfleger Caren (1945). German designer. She created her label – Caren Pfleger Design – after studying at the New York Fashion Institute of Technology, and gaining useful work experience with two Parisian houses, Givenchy and De Castelbajac, from 1977 to 1982. She has won praise for her wool and leather creations and her accessory collections, which have won three Fil d'Or awards.

Phildar French textile company. For a long period starting in 1943 it was a leading manufacturer of knitting yarns and sewing thread. Their products were distributed in France and Europe through a network of over 2,000 stores, which were crucial to the group's transformation when women working at home starting casting their knitting aside, and the company's output was halved. They avoided collapse by diversifying their production to include knitwear and underwear. But what really turned the business around was the decision to transform it into a distribution company which is now one of the leaders in the clothing sector in France. The capital is held by the Mulliez family.

Philippe Sandrine (1970). French designer working in Paris. She is at the beginning of her career, after apprenticeships at Popi Moreni and Courrèges. She took part in the

Salone Workshop in 1996. In 1999 she was sent to display her designs at the Coulisses de la Mode exhibition in Tokyo, which was the final event of La France au Japon.

Philippe Adec Fashion house known for its very modern and trendy women's suits. It takes its name from the Parisian designer who started the business with his wife Irene in 1976, designing a typically 1980s style of stonewashed jeans cut like jodhpurs. From that moment on the house has always been at the forefront of success, with a range of day wear and evening wear. Its elegantly casual pants still remain its strong point.

Philippe et Gaston French dressmaker's founded by Philippe Hecht and Gaston Kauffmann in 1922. They became successful above all for their beaded evening dresses. Following the failure of the business in 1937, and then the traumas of the war, only the name of Gaston remained. The company was then acquired by the textile manufacturer Boussac. The new owner attempted to re-launch the business and tried in vain to employ the young Dior, whom he soon after sponsored to set up on his own.

Design by Philippe et Gaston.

Philippe Model Label and name of the milliner most loved by designers. Born in Sens, France in 1956. After graduating he learnt to make hats and leather accessories using scraps from his family's tannery. He was later taught by Denise Frère, a pattern maker for Maison Riva Marchesi and he was apprenticed to the celebrated Madame Paulette. He launched his designer label in 1981 despite the declining trend for hats, and he found enthusiastic allies in designers like Gaultier, Mugler, Miyake, and Montana. At the same time he launched a range of gloves, bags, and shoes. He opened his own boutique in Paris in 1984.

Philo Phoebe (1973). French designer. She gained experience with Pamela Blundell, and studied at Central Saint Martin's in London where she met Stella McCartney. The pair became inseparable, to the extent that when McCartney was employed by Chloé, Philo followed her to Paris. Stella left Chloé in 2001 to start her own label, and Phoebe took her place as head designer.

Phoenix Art Museum Arizona, USA. Recently renovated and renamed the Fashion Design Collection, it has 4,000-5,000 pieces either received from local donors, or acquired by the Arizona Costume Institute. The oldest examples date from the end of the 1700s. The curators have concentrated on documenting the work of American 20th century designers, but they also buy pieces from big European names like Balenciaga, Dior, and YSL. Within the museum, the Astaire Library of Costumes has a collection of fashion-related prints, books, and periodicals.

Piacenza Historic Pollone wool mill, in the province of Biella, specialized in the manufacture of sophisticated fabrics using fine fibers. The business has been run by more than ten generations of the Piacenza family since 1773: one of the more recent ancestors was Felice Piacenza, a businessman with a passion for botany (hence the Parco Felice Piacenza in Burcina), a promoter of the Industrial Union at the beginning of the 1900s and founder of the Wool Mill School for the training of qualified workers. In recent years the company, under the direction of Riccardo Piacenza, his son Vittorio, and his grandsons Enzo and Carlo, has concentrated on the production of cashmere, leading them to open a branch in Beijing in 1993 for the quality control of the raw materials. In 1990 they launched a range of pure cashmere sweaters and accessories for the international market.

❑ 2000. Piacenza produced a blanket designed by Gianni Carpo made from a bend of Italian and Spanish wools to commemorate the new millennium.
❑ 2001. The year ended with a turnover of nearly 40 million euros, an increase of 12.8%.
❑ Piacenza is a member of the prestigious club *Les Hénokiens*, an international association open only to 29 family businesses with over 200 years' history behind them. The company was accepted as a member only after a very rigorous selection process involving the assessment of their management and financial stability.

Piaggi Anna (1931). Emblematic figure of the fashion world, with a taste for intellectual and irreverent provocation, a natural bent for aesthetics, and an editorial background. Also a passionate and dedicated collector of vintage clothing, books, objects, music, and "things" that she freely interprets with a precise aim: to capture the beauty of "the contemporary moment." She has a rare talent for picking up special pieces and rare objects (sometimes just words) during her travels around the world, always with an eye for that special something. Throughout this life-long mission, she has had two illustrious mentors: her husband Alfa Castaldi (whom she married in New York in 1962), a photographer with a wide-ranging and eclectic knowledge of culture, and Vern Lambert, an English eccentric and collector of vintage clothes. Following her subtle and imaginative sense of humor, her modern and ironic approach to enjoyment and her irrational logic on a very personal "ego trip," Piaggi has brought her carefully catalogued collection of clothes out of the wardrobe and gradually assimilated them into her daily life. They are clothes to be worn on an imaginary, abstract stage, acting out an imaginary, whimsical part, with the fashion world as the only point of reference and with the aim of provoking a reaction. Piaggi finds different ways of matching and combining outfits, mixing in different creative media (take for example her famous presentations of Missoni's collections). Armed with her cultivated talent, her rare sensibility, her creativity, and able to interpret different styles, trends, eras, music, and objects, Anna Piaggi revels in creating ostentatiously irreverent "mixes" with supreme intelligent indifference and total control over the desired effect. A Milanese with a traditional education, Piaggi started off as a translator at Mondadori, she then became a fashion journalist in the 1960s when Mondadori brought her in as the fashion editor for a new fashion monthly called *Arianna*. She introduced a modern and innovative edge to the magazine, working with her husband Alfa Castaldi (who was later to become one of the most intelligent and respected Italian photographers), and the editor Anna Riva. In the 1970s Anna worked as an "editor at large" for Condé Nast and introduced, with her special reportages, great photographers such as Chris von Wangenheim, Giampaolo Barbieri, and of course Castaldi. From 1981 to 1984 she planned and edited *Vanity* (Condé Nast), an interesting and sophisticated experiment seeking a new means of expression in collaboration with the great American artist Antonio Lopez. However, the extraordinary drawings and accompanying text presented topics that were perhaps too sophisticated and difficult at a time where consumerism was having a boom. In 1988 Piaggi started a column (which later achieved cult status) for *Vogue Italia* called "D.P. Doppie Pagine di Anna Piaggi," which still continues, and resulted in publication of the book *Fashion Algebra* (Leonardo Arte, 1999) ten years later. The book is packed with characters, hints, cross references, and quotations, all recounted in a very personal, unique, and original style of writing, very well-informed and always avant-garde. This vibrant and receptive journalist-aesthete, sophisticated writer, attentive observer of deeds, misdeeds, events, objects, and famous, up-and-coming or unknown characters, has an international resonance and appeal. She combines a mass of visual stimuli with her sparkling writing in a provocative and lively approach to a variety of arguments covering modern cul-

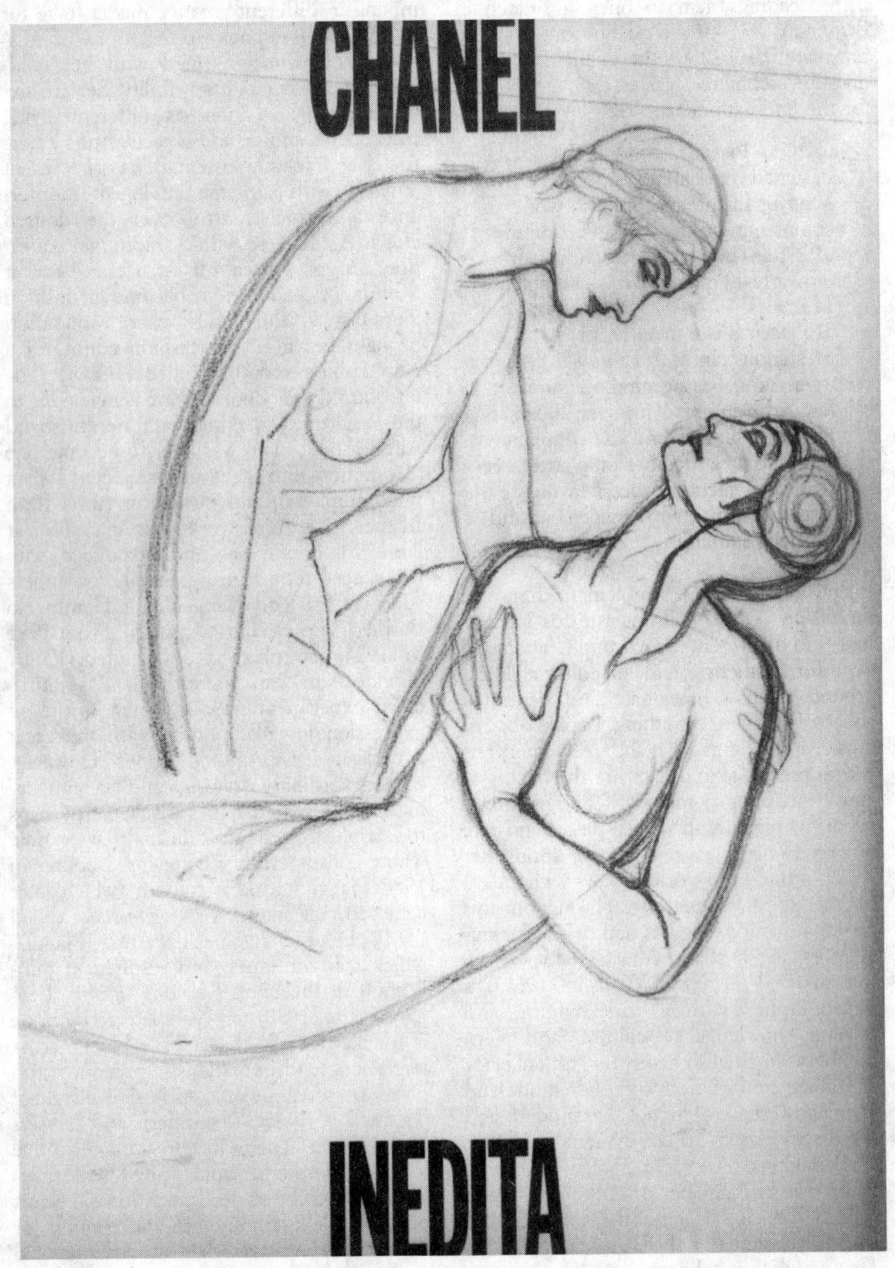

Chanel depicted as Marianne of France by Paul Iribe. From "Doppie Pagine" by Anna Piaggi for Vogue Italia (*Fashion Algebra*, Leonardo, 1998).

Chanel in a drawing by Paul Iribe. From "Doppie Pagine" by Anna Piaggi for Vogue Italia (*Fashion Algebra*, Leonardo, 1998).

ture and current customs. She was a fashion and society columnist for *Panorama* for several years (1993-97) and she has also worked on various international editions of *Vogue*. She wrote a fashion and lifestyle column for *L'Espresso Piú* from 1987 to 1989. The famous fashion designer Karl Lagerfeld (Chloé, Chanel, Fendi) chose her as his muse and he also named a book after her, called *Anna-chronique* (Longanesi 1986), in which Piaggi is the heroine, featuring in Lagerfeld's drawings of extraordinary dreamlike events: Piaggi herself wrote the text and Vern Lambert did the research. The book was also published by Thames & Hudson, with the title *A Fashion Journal*. (*Cristina Brigidini*)

Pianegonda Italian company that produces polished rhodium-plated sterling silver jewelry, without the addition of chemical substances. Founded by Franco Pianegonda in Camisano Vicentino in 1994. Their collections immediately found a market thanks to their original sculptural designs, with reflective surfaces sometimes embellished with precious or colored stones, often inspired by 1970s styles. At the beginning of the new millennium the return to fashion of retro styles (generously sized plate-like pendants hung on ribbons or plaited threads and linked or organically shaped rings) was enthusiastically received and followed by the Venetian company. The resulting creations were very positively received by the public and led to the rapid escalation of the brand, and the opening of their own stores throughout Italy, Spain, and Greece. Their designs are distributed by Saks Fifth Avenue in the USA, and by Fortnum & Mason in London. (*Alessandra Quattordio*)

Pianforini Pietro (1943). Italian designer, born in Parma. He presented his first complete ready-to-wear collection in the early 1980s. His simple, rather minimalist clothes gained exposure abroad as well as in Italy, particularly his knitwear. He has a show room in Milan.

Piano Piano Dolce Carlotta Ready-to-wear label born in 1987 from a collaboration between the designer Antonio Marras and the businessman Edoardo Marini. They produce co-ordinating separates, dresses, sweaters, and accessories, with a light, feminine, romantic, flowing, ironic and elegant style. They use very carefully selected Italian-made fabrics, nearly always lightweight and with exclusive prints. The label is exported all over the world. They have been showing at Milano Collezioni Donna since 1995.

❑ 1998. The Sanstitre collection was launched, consisting of dozens of different styles of white shirts.
❑ 2003, February. Marras displayed his creations at the New York Fashion Institute of Technology as part of the Fashion Italian Style exhibition.

Piattelli Bruno (1927). Designer from Rome. After studying law, he began working at his father's tailoring shop which until then had been aimed at a private international clientele. In the 1960s he started designing for big manufacturers, winning contracts with Ellesse, Lebole, and Lanerossi. In 1969 the first Piattelli sales points were opened in department stores like Barney's in New York and Takashiyama in Tokyo, and Alitalia commissioned him to design the uniforms for their ground staff. He did a lot of work for cinema and theater. He designed the white linen suit worn by Marcello Mastroianni in the musical *Ciao Rudy*, and he made nearly all the star's costumes during his long career. He also made clothes for Manfredi, Tognazzi, and Nero, and he has had many foreign clients like Michael Caine and Orson Welles. He also designed women's fashion and dressed the actresses Virna Lisi, Mireille Darc, and Gina Lollobrigida. He produced a range of bed-linen and furnishing fabrics in the 1970s. He was one of the advisors to Francesco Rutelli, mayor of Rome, from 1993 to 2001. (*Eleonora Attolico*)

Piatti Independent company producing plain and embroidered silk shawls, small rugs, cushions, scarves, handkerchiefs, fine lingerie and head scarves for wholesale and export, founded in Como in 1912. In 1925 the owner Carlo Piatti moved the manufacturing business to a factory in Brescia that specialized in the production of fringes, embroideries, and all the other types of accessories they had in their catalogue at the time. The same year the company sponsored a national competition for the design of cross and satin stitch embroidered silk shawls. The business risked failure in 1930, but kept going until the early 1950s. Carlo Piatti is remembered for the national prize he established in 1925 and for the innovations he introduced to the silk industry together with other Como businessmen.

(*Pierangelo Mastantuono*)

Piazza Sempione Womenswear company. Founded in 1990, it takes its name from a square in Milan. Their very wearable pieces are designed by Marisa Guerrizio. With an annual production of 250,000 garments, and over 540 sale points throughout the world, the company has a steady annual growth of 20%. In 2004 Piazza Sempione had a turnover of 34 million euros, an increase of 13% on the previous year, and their gross operating margins increased by 11%, improving company profitability. Some great photographers have worked on the label's advertising campaigns, amongst whom Michael O'Brien, Sarah Moon, Armin Linke, and Patricia Peacock.

Picasso Paloma (1949). Daughter of Pablo Picasso and Françoise Gilot, she started off as a theatrical costume designer, but immediately showed a marked preference for jewelry. She designed necklaces using sequins from the Folies Bergères bikinis, and when she showed her first creations to Yves Saint Laurent he immediately gave her the task of designing a collection of jewelry for his next runway show. She designed for the Greek brand Zolotas in 1972-73, and started working with Tiffany in 1980, creating numerous one-off pieces, including boxes inlaid with precious stones, insect brooches, and necklaces set with some of the largest and most precious examples of colored stones. Chicago's Natural History Museum, The Field, has one of her bracelets on display, made of 408.63 carat moonstone. In addition to her jewelry, she has launched a perfume and a red lipstick called Paloma, a range of scarves, and a range of bags and accessories.

Piccinino Bianca Maria (1924). Journalist, and female presenter for Italian State television fashion programmes from the 1950s until 1994. After graduating in Sociology, she started off in television as a newsreader and writer and presenter for science programmes. She was then given the job of fashion correspondent; she attended all the ready-to-wear runway shows in Florence, Rome, and Paris (at the time they could only broadcast images of the shows three months after the event so as not to reveal the clothes before their "release date"), and interviewed all the greatest Italian and foreign dressmakers. She was the first woman to present the afternoon news, and after the reforms, the News at 1.30pm. At the same time she was studying the fashion phenomenon in relation to the evolution of society and the great events that shape it (fashion and costume, fashion as communication, fashion as a symbol of power), and she gave seminars on the subject at the Universities of Madrid, Florence, and Bologna. On leaving Italian State television, she continued her teaching work at Rome's fashion academies, while also giving Masters seminars to young designers. She has written two books, one of which (*What shall I wear?*, published by Gremese) was particularly successful.

(*Maria Vittoria Alfonsi*)

Pichat-Chaléard French silk company, based in Lyons. Set up by Jean Pichat and Pierre Chaléard in 1921, who then acquired a factory four years later and expanded to London in 1927 and New York in 1937. In 1961 the company was the biggest exporter in the French silk industry, winning an award for its export activities. Pierre's son Jacque Chaléard has been running the business for the last twenty years or so, and through his efforts the company has formed strong alliances with French designers and has widened its production to include synthetic fibers.

Pickwick Brand of sportswear for children and teenagers. The company was founded in 1996 by two very young business partners who still hold all the capital: Diego Barbaresi, the designer, and Marco Nicolini, the managing director. Over the years the company has taken the name Global Industry. At present it has licensed its brand to three different firms: the Pickwick Junior range of clothing to Supergin in Bologna; its range of shoes to the footwear manufacturer Elisabet di Monte Urano (in Ascoli Piceno) and its range of stationery to Cartorama of Verona. They are mainly distributed nationally, with 750 customers, 10 franchise stores, and 6 of their own stores, including one in Corso Como in Milan and one in Via Tomacelli in Rome. They have increased their production to include men's and women's ranges, accessories, sweatshirts, T-shirts, backpacks, key-holders, belts and hats, bringing in a turnover of 30 million euros in 2002. In 2003 they planned to expand to the Spanish and French markets.

Picone Giuseppe (1934). Neapolitan textile and fashion designer. He started out in Naples producing cotton hand-printed clothes for women; the profile of an altar boy is a recurrent theme in various shapes and colors in his patterns, and it became his design signature. He moved to Rome in 1958 and with time opened a show room in Via Gregoriana and a boutique in Via Sistina. He also had sales outlets in Tokyo and Osaka. The altar boy, almost a logo, also appeared on his ceramics that he exhibited at the Milan Triennale.

Pied de Poule Fabric where the different colored weft and warp yarns create a short of chessboard pattern. The name refers to the effect obtained, which looks like a chicken's footprints. Made from carded or combed wool and used for men's and women's casual and outdoor wear. Originally just black-and-white, it was later produced in shades of gray, brown and blue.

Piel Dennis (1944). Australian photographer. After studying architecture, he worked at a printing company and then decided to become a professional photographer. Encouraged by Alexander Libermann, he found success as both an advertising and fashion photographer in 1979, working steadily for *Vogue* in close collaboration with Irving Penn, Richard Avedon, and Hiro.

Piercing Metal ring or small object, usually made of steel, used particularly at the end of the 1990s to decorate and embellish various parts of the body: a sort of extreme evolution of the use of earrings. However the practice of piercing is more than just a matter of decoration; it is part of a real current of thinking above all amongst adolescents, but also young adults. The philosophy behind it is to communicate one's unease and disapproval of society, in part by referring back to primitive and tribal customs. In this way the body becomes a means of communication, and piercings give out different messages depending on their size, shape and where they are on the body, in the same way as an item of clothing. The practice of piercing can be included in the series of body modifications defined as technomutations. These include tattoos, scarification, and branding (the latest development being people branding their name or a number onto their arm.) Technomutations as a whole represent the search for a unique personality outside the norms proposed and imposed by society. They are a violent response to plastic surgery and body building, which aim to sculpt the body to perfection and erase all defects. By "disfiguring" themselves with these technomutations, people want to present an unpolished, imperfect type of identity, where beauty comes from diversity. Added to this, particularly for piercing, is the desire to awaken an untamed sexuality able to unite the masculine and feminine sides found in each individual: in fact it is no longer just the ears, eyebrows, lips, navel, and nipples that are pierced (they are considered as purely fashion phenomena belonging to the initial phase of the piercing trend), but also the most sensitive parts of both men's and women's genitalia: from rings through the clitoris, vulva or outer lips, to scrotal piercings and the Prince Albert, a piercing through the man's urethra which tradition claims was used in Victorian England to hold the penis between the legs so as to avoid showing any bulges in one's pants. The many different types of piercing have been documented in a book about technomutations which has now become a cult object: *Manual to make of yourself what you wish*, by Bodhipat A-rà. It includes oddities like the fact that the nose, lips and eyebrows are the parts of the body preferred for piercing by young people aged 18 to 25. The tongue, nipple, navel and genitalia on the other hand are favored by adults aged 25 to 40, who are motivated by sexual gratification rather than aesthetics. Genital piercing is very common within the US gay community and amongst heterosexuals, mostly women, in Italy.

(*Gianluca Bauzano*)

Pierlot Claudie. French designer. Her simple, modern, and wearable styles brought her immediate recognition and exposure. After finishing her studies, she started working for a small knitwear business in Montpellier. She arrived in Paris in 1972, and was employed by Jacqueline Jacobson. She set up her own designer label in 1984 and within five years she had two Parisian boutiques and her clothes were distributed in French and American department stores.

Pierluigi Tricot Pseudonym of Pierluigi Scazzola (1927). Italian designer, born in Rome. He attended a boarding school and then studied law at university. In 1958 he made some blouses from fabric he had hand dyed. His first client was La Rinascente department store, who commissioned him to make some headscarves. He started working with knitted fabrics, using tailoring techniques to produce luxury knitwear. He launched his first collection in 1961 with a runway show at Rome's Modern Art Gallery, which was greatly admired by Irene Brin. Giorgini chose 20 of Tricot's designs to include in the Palazzo Pitti shows in Florence, in which Tricot participated until 1977. He showed his "*scudo*" range made of lurex and wool jacquard at Mare Moda Capri in 1967. He was invited to New York where he was well received by the press and Irene Brin urged him to go to Paris. His first important clients were Jacqueline Kennedy, Lauren Bacall, Rudy Crespi, Claudia Cardinale, Allegra Agnelli, and Bona Frescobaldi. He produced a more commercial range, Tricot Sport, from 1970 to 1975. He produced clothes for his boutique in Via delle Carrozze, which he closed together with the rest of his business in 1997.

Piero Gazzarrini Italian ready-to-wear label, taking the name of its founder who started it in Empoli in 1982. It employs 137 people both directly and as freelance workers. It has produced over ten menswear collections, holding its first runway show at Milano Collezioni Uomo in 1999. The designer is Cristian Arni. Seventy percent of its production is distributed in Italy through 150 points of sale and an own-brand store in Milan. The rest of its production is exported throughout the world, and it is particularly strong in Southeast Asia.

Piero Milano Jewelry company founded in Milan in 1953 by Piero Milano and Luigi Benzi. They favored "special pieces" made to high technical and creative standards. Their two Piedmont workshops in Valenza and San Salvatore Monferrato have demonstrated their versatility and imagination producing pieces in different styles, from romantic to minimalist, going from figurative to geometric designs for both luxury and everyday pieces, using diamonds and precious and semi-precious stones. The Milan-based company's designs are sold all over the world, and they have a showroom in Via della Spiga. The business has been run for some time by Rosella and Piero Benzi and Andrea Milano.
(*Alessandra Quattordio*)

Pieroni Patrizia (1954). Italian designer. Born in Via dei Banchi Vecchi in Rome, she has an atelier called Arsenale which has become a barometer for the city's trends: you can find everything there, from clothes to ethnic accessories. Her styles are inspired by "everything that is not fashion; by poetry and art in general," and she is convinced that fashion is culture and should be seen as such, experimenting with unusual materials to produce "niche" creations. She showed her collection at AltaRomaAltaModa for the second time in 2003.

Evening dress by Patrizia Pieroni.

Pierre D'Alby French ready-to-wear label founded by Zyga Pianko in 1951. He came to Paris from Teheran as a textile trader, and set up a clothing business called Piantex, which evolved with time into the more French and aristocratic sounding Pierre D'Alby. He employed a group of creative young designers who contributed to the company's success. He sold the business in 1992 and joined forces with Irene Gregory, one of the designers he worked with from the beginning of his fashion venture.

Pierre et Gilles This couple of French artists have been on the scene since 1977. They first met at a party in Paris and they become inseparable in both life and work to the extent that their names have created a brand of two connected elements, the world of the photographer Pierre, and that of the painter Gilles. Theirs is a naïve paradise, withut any sense of guilt whatsoever: their kitsch aesthetic is intentional, emphasized and theatrical to the extreme without ever being vulgar, while the expressions of the subjects portrayed (women transformed into goddesses, singers astride improbable theme park swans, crying Red Army officers) are intentionally conventional. Their images have been published in *Marie Claire*, *Façade*, *Actuel*, *Playboy* and *Samurai*, but they have also worked for the record industry creating album covers, and they are especially in demand for their portraits, which have transformed people like Madonna, Björk, Catherine Deneuve, and Johnny Halliday into colorful icons. Pierre et Gilles' skill lies in creating images with universal appeal, almost like sophisticated versions of the tacky little scented calendars that you used to find in barber's shops: you feel that they want to tinge reality with a cheap perfume. Their "danger" lies not in their message, but in the way they communicate it: they jump freely from one subject to another without making any statement, so that the viewers feel like indulgent uncles or aunts faced with two dissolute nephews. Among their most important exhibitions was the wide-ranging retrospective held at the Maison de la Photographie in Paris in 1999.

(*Roberto Mutti*)

Pierre Mantoux Italian brand of women's hosiery. An importer of German hosiery, Ottorino Giangrossi founded the Milanese hosiery production company Ilcat (Industria Lombarda Calze a Telaio) in 1932 in partnership with his sister-in-law. His son Remo took over the running of the business with his wife Velia in the 1960s: they launched the Pierre Mantoux brand and passed from wholesale to retail distribution. With their 56 different shades in the 1970s, their polka-dot style in 1976, and their Scala-lace style in 1982, they conquered the international market (30% of sales) and won the attention of *haute couture* and ready-to-wear companies. In the 1990s the brand launched its first cashmere blend tights following two years of research. Velia Giangrossi has brought a totally female management structure to the company with her daughters Fulvia and Patrizia (respectively the managing director and general manager), and her granddaughters Chiara and Costanza. (*Giampiero Remondini*)

❑ The Fall-Winter 2002-2003 collection was dominated by their Felce tights, with a big opaque leaf pattern against a black background, and their Tattoo tights with a tribal pattern.
❑ 2003, June. They launched a range of swimwear designed by Patrizia Giangrossi and presented at the Moda Mare runway shows in Positano.
❑ For Winter 2003-2004 they presented the Mimesis tights, reminiscent of men's tie designs, and the very sheer Lycra floral-patterned Flower Power tights.

Pietroni Paolo (1940). Journalist. Twice editor of *Amica*, from 1974 to 1979 and from 1982 to 1988. He spent a large part of his career with the Rizzoli publishing house, where he soon became established for his innovative ideas. With his first experience at *Anna*, guessing the market, he created a magazine that was highly sensitive to the wave of feminism during that period, then when he took up the reigns of the magazine again at the start of the 1980s, he revolutionised its content and target, taking the magazine in a completely different direction. He explained in an interview that the woman it addressed "feels unique in the world, and if she meets a woman wearing the same designer dress as her, she feels that hers is different because she is wearing it."

In 1985 he launched *Max*, a monthly style magazine published by RCS, aimed at men with high aesthetic aspirations. It features fashion personalities, legendary entertainment celebrities (more from cinema than TV), exclusive and aggressive photos, veering towards a sexuality that is very free, and often too ambiguous for its readers. The result: between 80,000 and 100,000 copies distributed in the first few years with sales in France, Germany, and Greece. He created another revolutionary concept in 1987, when he invented *Sette*, the weekly supplement to *Corriere della Sera*, conceived as a means of promoting and recycling information from Rizzoli's titles with the addition of big illustrated articles that knew how to best catch the attention of the most varied readers. It was the trump card that allows the *Corriere* to get the better of its rival *La Repubblica*, which then hastily released its own supplement *Il Venerdì* a few weeks later. After his experience editing *Lo Specchio*, the weekly supplement to *La Stampa*, Pietroni was called in to take up the position of editorial director for Class Editore's periodicals.

Pignatelli Carlo (1944). Italian designer. Born in Brindisi, but made Turin his home. He is best known for his bridal and occasion wear. He opened his first atelier in 1970, working for private clients. He held his first runway shows in 1980. He first showed at the Milano Collezioni in 1993 and in 1995 he was made official designer for Juventus football club and the Italian Football Federation.

❑ 2002, September. Carlo Pignatelli Donna is present, along with other Italian labels, at the New York Fashion Coterie, the most important East Coast fashion event.
❑ 2002. The year ends on an up, with over 70,000 garments sold and an increase in turnover of 15 percent from the previous year. The Carlo Pignatelli Ceremonia does particularly well, bringing in 70 percent of the total annual sales. Export sales are also up on 2001, representing 30 percent of the total income.
❑ 2003, March. Announcement of a 5 year deal with the Marly's group in Vicenza to produce and distribute the women's ready-to-wear collection.

Pignatelli Luciana (1935). Italian designer known in the 1960s for her ready-to-wear collection branded Princess Luciana, characterized by miniskirts and fanciful prints. She had a showroom in Piazza dell'Orologio in Rome and she sold to American department stores. She produced a Westernised version of the kaftan in flannel. *Life* magazine did a story on her, her sister-in-law Consuela Crespi, and her sons Fabrizio and Diego Pignatelli. She decided to abandon her business in 1967-68 to work with the cosmetics company Eve of Rome, which was later sold to the Gilette Corporation. She now lives in London and designs jewelry for Lotus, for a Southeast Asian market that includes Bangkok, Singapore, Malaysia, and New Delhi.

❑ She is the author of *The Beautiful People's Beauty Book*, full of beauty tips from somebody who created and represented beauty in the 1960s and 1970s.

Pigott Marcus & Alas Mert English photographers. They are considered two of the most interesting and in-demand up-and-coming photographers. They have been working together since 1997 and divide their time between London, Paris, and New York. Their images have been published in *Visionaire*, *i-D* and *V* magazines and they have worked on advertising campaigns for Missoni, Gucci, Levi's, Hugo Boss, Yves Saint Laurent, and Fendi.

Piguet Robert (1901-1953). French designer. An unsuccessful banker, in 1918 he moved to Paris from his native Yverdon, a small Swiss town on the shores of Lake Neuchâtel. He brought nothing but his brief experience as a shoe designer for Bally, and a few sketches of his batik print designs. He dared to show these to Maison Lanvin, which rejected them. Unshaken and undeterred, in 1920 he opened his own dressmaker's with the support of his lawyer brother, but it did not work out. He worked for Poiret and then for Redfern, who produced the first women's uniform for the Red Cross.

He looked to his family for support again and set up a new fashion house in 1933. This was managed by his second brother Georges, and was followed by a branch in London in 1936. He alternated sober day-wear with sensational evening dresses that evoked the finery of the 1800s. He is still renowned for his pleated crinoline supported by a stiffened band, and romantic long, full-skirted dresses with contrasting fitted bodices, as modeled for the fashion magazines by his wife Mathilde. He launched the perfumes *Bandit* and *Fracas* in 1944. He stayed in business until 1951, when he retired for health reasons. His clients included many stars of French cinema and theater such as Arletty and Edwige Feuillère. (*Lucia Mari*)

Pikenz Italian furrier. Founded by Enzo Picciocchi in 1951, it had its first headquarters on the corner of Via Mazzini and Via Torini on Piazza Duomo in Milan. The company moved to Corso Matteotti in September 2000. The company started off with *haute couture* furs, recently adding a younger and less formal range, and expanding to include knitwear and accessories: overcoats and raincoats with fur lining and trimmings, cashmere sweaters, crocodile and ostrich skin handbags. They are the exclusive distributor of the Gianfranco Ferré Fourrures range of furs.

Pilati Stefano (1965). Italian designer. He was chosen by Tom Ford to work on the Yves Saint Laurent women's ready-to-wear collection in March 2000. He started off in 1984 working for Nino Cerruti, and then as a contributor to *Uomo Vogue*. He worked on Armani's men's collection in 1993. He became Miuccia Prada's assistant for her Miu Miu range, after being employed as a fabric sourcer in 1994. In June 2002 he succeeded Tom Ford as creative director of the Yves Saint Laurent ready-to-wear range, including accessories and luggage. The house's style took a marked change of course, with the Texan's indulgent sensuality giving way to a more classic, discreet, bourgeois French elegance.

Pile Very warm and soft, thermal and water resistant synthetic fabric. Due to these qualities it was initially used mainly for tracksuits and other items of sportswear, but it is now also used for pyjamas, T-shirts, and other garments and accessories including hats, gloves, and slippers.

Pillbox A small tambourine-shaped hat, made famous in the 1960s by Jacqueline Kennedy, who always wore one to match her outfit.

Pilotto Francesca (1963). Italian designer. She started her career in Sardinia in 1990, where she opened a shop in the center of Nuoro embroidering plain linear dresses. She has an atelier in Via Santa Barnaba in Milan. Her *haute couture* collection has been shown on the runways of AltaModa Roma since July 2001, under the new label Francesca Pilot-t. Her clothes are handmade from precious silks and textiles made from processed cork, marble and coral. She owns the patent for cork fabric. Her collections nearly always pay homage to Sardinia, with colors, techniques, pleating, and styles inspired by Sardinian costumes.

Piña Manuel (1944). Spanish designer. His ready-to-wear collections are characterized by knitwear and simple flowing fabrics. He started out in Barcelona in 1979.

Pinafore Sleeveless woman's dress, usually with a round neck, worn over a shirt or over a polo- or turtle-neck.

Pinault François (1936). French businessman and entrepreneur. He owns the PPR (Pinault-Printemps-Redoute) group, a distribution giant that has acquired Sanofi, the company that owns Yves Saint Laurent, and that blocked the acquisition of the Gucci Group by LVMH, the luxury goods company owned by Bernard Arnault, by increasing its own stake in Gucci. A self-taught and self-made man, he is one of the richest men in France. He was born in Brittany in Les Champs Geraux. He started dealing in the wood trade in 1963, becoming the European leader in this sector. His earnings enabled him to acquire big distribution companies in the 1980s and 1990s like Conforama (furniture and electrical goods), Printemps (a chain of department stores), Redoute (mail-order sales), and in 1994 Fnac (a chain of bookshops that also sells CDs and electronic gadgets). PPR's acquisition of Gucci shares preluded its attempt to form a luxury goods group to compete with Arnault's, and it turned out to be a winning move.

Pince-nez Spectacles without arms that rest on the bridge of the nose, held in place by a small Spring. They were fashionable at the turn of the 19th and 20th centuries, but then fell into disuse.

Pineau Ronald (1966). French shoe designer. Born in Nantes, he studied marketing. He opened three multi-label boutiques called The Avantgarde between 1984 and 1990. Following that he created shoe collections for Palladium and Kickers and formulated their stores' philosophy of stylish trading. He launched Ron Orb, his own range of shoes and bags, in 1995. He opened a showroom in Paris.

Pineider Manufacturer of fine paper, writing materials, and leather business accessories. The company has had the same shop in a historic building in Piazza della Signoria (Florence) on the corner of Via Calimaruzza since it was founded by Francesco Pineider in 1774. Another branch was opened in Via Tornabuoni in 1861. Pineider was acquired by Maurizio Gucci's company in 1989, and then two years later it passed into the hands of the Franco Cosimo Panini group. In 1997 it was bought outright for 5 billion lire by Angelo Corona. Corona then invested 15 billion in the business, opening 17 more shops and increasing the turnover from 15 to 60 billion lire. Pineider bought the leather goods business Nazareno Gabrielli in July 1999.

Pinet Brand of luxury women's footwear founded in 1885 and reputed to be one of the oldest and most prestigious in France. Its founder François Pinet trained in his father's workshop and then set himself up in Rue Paradis-Poissonnière in Paris in 1863. At the beginning of the 1900s his son opened shops in London and Paris, gaining recognition for the brand. Following that, the made-to-measure collection developed into a high-quality mass-produced range, designed for a period by Roger Vivier. At the end of the 1980s the brand became part of the André Group.

Pinko A range produced by Cris, a company founded in Fidenza by two young entrepreneurs, Pietro Negra and Cristina Rubini, in the mid-1970s. Pinko was originally developed as "instant fashion," a concept by which "flash" collections are released each week, to meet the demands of a continually evolving market. Towards the end of the 1980s, the company directed its strategy along new lines, introducing the concept of "semi-planned" fashion and a new distribution formula that saw the take-off of Pinko franchising. Creating a distinctive global image and ensuring distribution through multi-label sales channels are the keys to the strategy that established Pinko on the international market. Their turnover is steadily increasing and in 2002 it exceeded 50 million euros. (*Valeria Vantaggi*)

Pinocchietto Recent term used to refer to capri pants, very widespread in the 1950s not only on the island of Capri but in all the most fashionable holiday destinations. Brigitte Bardot often wore them in Saint-Tropez and was copied by all the young girls of the time. Short and fitted, they end just under the knee, with a slit at the hem. They became popular again at the end of the 1990s, in hi-tech and stretch fabrics. Prada launched a casual style which has been a resounding success.

Pintaldi Angela (1960). Jewelry designer. With an artist's soul, she can transform natural elements into precious wearable sculptures. She uses stones that recall her homeland of Sicily, and the southern countries where she has lived, Morocco, India, Mexico, and the Italian island of Pantelleria: her materials are as diverse as river pebbles and rock crystals, rough aquamarines and nuggets of gold, sea coral, amber and obsidian. Her jewelry is unique, because it keeps the original form of the materials used. When Palermo became too small for her she moved to Milan and Paris. An opportune meeting with Hélène de Rothschild and the American journalist Polly Mellen introduced her to a sophisticated international circle. She produces her pieces in limited numbers, true to the craftsmanly and artistic aspect of her work, which are sold in a few exclusive outlets around the world: her Milan showroom, Bergdorf Goodman in New York, and some Parisian art galleries. She has chosen not to communicate her work through advertising, but through books entrusted to famous photographers, where she herself models and acts as a spokeswoman for her jewelry. The Mexican photographer Leo Matiz dedicated a book to her where Angela, thanks to her extraordinary resemblance, brings Frida Kahlo back to life. (*Gisella Borioli*)

Pinto The Achille Pinto Tessitura Serica (silk mill) was founded when the Casnate (Como) factory that had hitherto been working for third parties, started producing its own "smooth and damask, patterned and original cloth." In the second half of the 1950s the company name changed to Tessitura Tintoria Stamperia Achille Pinto Foulard Sciarpe Cravatte (Achille Pinto mill, dye and printing works for foulard, scarves, and ties). Achille's children joined the company's management in 1963 and the business became a limited company, increasing its production capacity and investments. In the mid-1970s the company received some Japanese capital. From 1988 to 1992 the business was run by Achille's son-in-law, Matteo Uliassi, and his family still manages the company today.

Pinturier Jacques (c. 1930). French milliner. He learned the trade and its techniques from his uncle Gilbert Orcel, a designer and famous milliner in the postwar period. He stayed in the company from 1949 to 1963, then moved on to manage the hat department at the design studio of Antonio Canovas del Castillo. He opened his own atelier in 1968, working for private clients and for the runway shows of big fashion houses. He had a taste for experimenting with unusual materials for hats, such as aluminum.

Pipart Gérard (1932). French designer. He won the Dé d'Or in 1987. He learned the basics working for Pierre Balmain when he just sixteen. He then worked for Fath and Givenchy, where he stayed until 1953. He served as a soldier in Algeria in 1957, and experimented with military fabrics to find new tailoring techniques. On his return he started a permanent collaboration with Maimé Armodin for Jardin des Modes. He designed for Chloé for five years, but not exclusively, working freelance for other ready-to-wear labels. He returned to *haute couture* in 1964, working for Nina Ricci where he gave full vent to his passion for the richness of fabrics and shapes.

Piquadro Leather goods company founded in Bologna in 1987, by the then 22-year-old Marco Palmieri, who is still president and managing director of the company. In just three years he managed to transform the small craftsmen's business into a limited company. Piquadro started selling its products (trolley bags, weekend bags, diaries, wallets, and cases) to the general public online Via its website www.piquadro.com. It opened its first own-brand boutique in Via della Spiga in Milan in 2001. When the private equity fund Fineco Capital acquired a 25% stake in the business in February 2002, Piquadro was able to reinforce its presence in existing markets and expand into new ones. Over a few months in 2002 he opened a showroom in Corso Vittorio Emanuele in Milan and another three own-brand boutiques in Rome (Via Fratina), Florence (Via della Vigna Nuova), and Milan's Linate airport. They currently produce 500 items which are renewed annually in 6 ranges. The company turnover exceeded 13 million euros in 2002, a 25% increase on the previous year. They presented their new Piquadro Expansion System collection at Mipel in March 2003.

❑ 2005, June. The BNL Investire Impreso private equity fund, managed by BNL Gestioni bought into a new holding company that was to control Piquadro Design Factory, the operating company that heads the activities of the Bologna business Piquadro Spa. It amounted to 35%, equal to an investment of 8.4 million euros.

Piqué Textured cotton fabric, originally only white, but now also colored. The term comes from the French word *piquer*, meaning to pierce or perforate, because of the fabric's quilted appearance. It has two wefts (one thick and one fine) and two warps (one very loose): the very taut supplementary chain forms a hollow as it passes over the wefts. The underside of the fabric looks smooth, while the surface has a brocade, raised cord or honeycomb pattern. It is used for shirts, undergarments, bed linen, children's clothes, clothing in general, and furnishings.

Piras Fabio (1963). Designer. Born in Switzerland to Sardinian parents. He studied fashion at Central Saint Martin's College in London (1993) and opened his own atelier in London in 1994. His women's fashion is serious and sombre, while of his men's fashion he says: "I design for myself. It's autobiographical." He now teaches fashion at Saint Martin's.

❑ 2000. Piras started working with Brioni, designing the label's first women's collection.
❑ The designer's own label creations, which dismiss trivial details in favour of a return to minimalism, are sold at the Koh Samui boutique in London.
❑ 2005. Piras has been the new creative director at Malo since Fall-Winter 2005-2006.

Pirelli The pairing of Pirelli and clothing occurred in 1877, when Francesco Casassa joins the rubber manufacturing complex founded by G.B. Pirelli as a partner, and started up the production of haberdashery, medical supplies, overcoats, capes, heavy coats for travelers, coachmen's and military uniforms. The garments were well designed, well made, reliable and technical. With time Pirelli acquired an increasingly glamorous aura: first with its famous calendar, and in more recent years with a communications strategy using famous photographers and playing on irony and sex appeal (like Annie Leibowitz's 1994 image of the sprinter Carl Lewis in the start position wearing stilettos). At the end of the 1990s Pirelli's communications director Carlo Corti Galeazzi had the idea of producing a range of well-designed clothing and accessories that recalls the world of Pirelli (the tyre tread as a graphic motif, rubber as a signature material). The first ranges from the P-Zero label were presented in January 2002: men's and women's outerwear and footwear. A range of watches was launched in February 2003.
(*Ruben Modigliani*)

Pirovano Italian fashion house. A few years before World War II, after a few modest but lucky business ventures in the clothing sector, Emma Maria Bonfanti used her intelligent creativity to start producing designs from what was little more than a craftsmen's workshop, with the help of her sisters Iride and Anita. Despite the difficulties posed by the outbreak of the war, her dressmaking creations, combined with those of her husband Felice Pirovano, a renowned leather goods dealer, became immediately popular, and their two shops in Via Montenapoleone (leather goods at no. 1 and the dressmaker's at no. 8) were visited by Milan's best and most demanding clientele. Over 100 people were employed in their workshops. These days the atelier still pays great attention to detail and uses refined dressmaking skills to create styles in step with the times.

Piscinina Term in Milanese dialect used affectionately to refer to the young girls starting out at dressmakers and fashion ateliers: they would do a bit of sewing, tidy the rooms and deliver packages to customers. They wore aprons, smiled at the titillating gossip, and blushed under the gaze of the customers' husbands and lovers. Some went on to become premières and others, like Olga Villi, a star model and then actress.

Pisenti Celeste (1979). Italian designer. She has worked for Costume National and Moschino. She designs the Blugirl range for Blumarine: they are whimsical and romantic clothes with echoes of another era, short taffeta skirts worn over tight jeans, pale blue or pink satin evening dresses, frills and ruffles, appliquéd flowers and sequins, or a more Anglo-Saxon style consisting of riding jackets, tartan pants, and Argyle sweaters. At just 24 she showed her first personal collection, called Celeste All That Jazz, on the Milan runways: 22 hand-made pieces inspired by Brigitte Bardot, Amanda Lear, and the 1920s starlet Clara Bow. The following season she expanded and completed the collection with smoking jackets, oversized blouses with sequin logos, full ruffled skirts, silk palazzo pyjamas, fox fur muffs and hoods, low-cut court shoes with bows, and mini handbags, all in soft colors like pink and sky-blue. (*Gabriella Gregorietti*)

Pita Orlando (1962). Cuban hairdresser working in the USA. Loved by Americans and sought after by the fashion system, he established himself in the hairdressing world with his subversive style that rejects stereotypical beauty. Always in search of new effects, in Madonna he found the ideal muse for his creations as well as a very faithful and enthusiastic client. He takes an original approach to hair care, maintaining that hair should never be washed with water and shampoo, but should be "dry cleaned" using aromatic oils, like the ancient Egyptians did.

Pitti Immagine Nonprofit company with mixed public and private capital, which originated from the fashion business developed by Giovanni Battista Giorgini at the beginning of the 1950s in Florence, where he used the Palazzo Pitti's Sala Bianca to hold his runway shows. That experience – managed since 1954 by the Florence Center for Italian Fashion, now a holding company of Pitti Immagine (thus named since 1988) – kickstarted Italian fashion's successful venture on the international scene. The company's first president was Marco Rivetti, who gave an innovative boost to a modern vision of the market. He was followed by the textile manufacturer Mario Boselli. The managing director is Raffaello Napoleone. Pitti Immagine is an authoritative figure in the international field of fashion fairs and exhibitions. Pitti Immagine currently operates eight trade fairs for the high-quality textile and appareal industry: Pitti Immagine Uomo (menswear), Pitti Immagine Bimbo (childreswear), Filati e Fragranze (threads and yarns and perfumes, colognes, and scents), all in lorence; Pitti Immagine Living (home furnishings), and the trio of women's fashion (White, NeoZone, and Cloudnine), in Milan as well as important cultural initiatives, events, research, and communications, that bring together the most advanced Italian and international fashion industries with other sectors and other forms of expression for contemporary creativity. In the last fifteen years they have introduced vital changes to the character and organization of textile and clothing fairs. In fact Pitti Immagine can be credited with the invention of fashion culture: the combination of the traditional fair's platform for meeting and the exchange of information with a more general forum for discussing the various sociological, economic, and communication issues that continually arise from fashion products. This innovative format was conceived by Luigi Settembrini, who was called in 1985 to take up the role of communications consultant, which he stayed until 1995. It has spawned important exhibitions, events, runway shows, research, conferences, seminars, and publications in association with museums, institutions, and figures of international standing in fashion, art, and contemporary creative and scientific culture. These events have added a new dimension to the fairs, presenting new ideas, views, and interesting stimuli to fashion professionals and an informed public. Thanks to this and to the other advanced services on offer to exhibitors and visitors, the fairs currently organized by Pitti Immagine have achieved impressive results: they are followed by professionals, experts, and by the international press; they are considered an essential point of reference for the sectors they cover; and they represent fashion trends, creative and technical developments, and diversification processes in the fashion market at the highest level.

❑ 2001. Guggenheim Prize for Business & Culture.
❑ 2002, February. Gaetano Marzotto, first son of Vittorio, was elected by the Florence Center for Italian Fashion as the new president of Pitti Immagine, replacing Mario Boselli.

Pitti Immagine Discovery This Foundation is concerned with the exchange between the various types of visual media (art, fashion, architecture, design, photography, cinema), and through this the construction of an up-to-date fashion culture with its own analytical and representative tools, on a level comparable to contemporary culture. The Foundation has the task of autonomously promoting exhibitions and publishing projects, and of drawing attention to the most innovative artistic phenomena from which fashion takes its materials and for which fashion itself is increasingly often a reason for, and subject of, reflection and production. To succeed in uniting these different elements – culture, entertainment, groundbreaking research and the popularisation of artistic media – the Foundation adopts sophisticated strategies and different means (exhibitions, books, performances, installations, videos). While doing this, the Foundation must also maintain a vital and constant link with the economic realities of which it is originally an expression, and over the years consolidate its status as an institution in the field of contemporary culture. Pitti Immagine Discovery officially came into being on 9 April 1999. The challenge was to find a place in Florence where attention could be concentrated on the most stimulating research into contemporary media. In Spring 2002 Pitti Immagine and the Florence Center for Italian Fashion transformed the project into the Pitti Immagine Discovery Foundation, with the aim of bringing greater consistency and institutional standing to the Group's activities in the contemporary field. Alfredo Canessa is the Foundation's president, Lapo Cianchi is the general secretary and Francesco Bonami is the artistic director, fashion curator Maria Luisa Frisa.

Piver L.T. French brand of perfumes and beauty products. In 1774 Pierre-Guillaume Dissey opened a small perfume shop in Rue Saint-Martin in Paris. Success came in 1813 thanks to three new scents created by Louis-Toussant Piver: *Véritable Eau de Cologne*, *Triple Eau de Cologne*, and *Eau de Cologne de Princes.* It was the first perfume house to use amyl salicylate in the composition of its perfumes, producing the innovative bouquets of *Floramye* (1903), and *Pompeìa* (1907). Then came two versions of *Cuir de Russie* (1914 and 1939) that further strengthened Piver's reputation. The brand started to diversify its range, particularly with hair products, to counteract a moment of difficulty in the 1950s and 1960s. The company was acquired by Rhône-Poulenc in 1979.

Pizarro Octavio (1972). Chilean designer. He has been in charge of design at Maison Fath since 1998. He was born in Viña del Mar and studied Fine Arts in Santiago. He moved to Paris and started working in 1994. Three years later he became Bernard Perris' assistant at Maison Sherrer.

❑ He has worked on Jacques Fath's ready-to-wear range since Fall-Winter 1998. In 1997 Fath was acquired by the Emmanuelle Khanh Group.

Pizzi Pier Luigi (1930). Costume and set designer and theater director. He did an incredible job of displaying Emilio Pucci's work at the retrospective held at the first Florence Biennale (September–December 1996) and he set up the exhibition *La regola estrosa* for Pitti Immagine. Milanese, he started off in 1951 working for Genoa's Civic Theater. He had a happy and productive working relationship with Giorgio De Lullo and Romolo Valli's Compagnia dei Giovani (Company of Young People), creating the visuals for most of their shows. His work in opera has been prodigious, both in terms of quantity and quality. Amongst the operas he has worked on: twenty at La Scala, including Rossini's *Signor Bruschino* (1957), Gluck's *Armide* (1996), and Nino Rota's *Cappello di Paglia di Firenze* (1998); Gluck's *L'Alceste* for Maggio Musicale in Florence in 1966; Rossini's *Tancredi* (1982), *Mosè in Egitto* (1983), *Comte Ory* (1984), *Maometto II* (1985), and *William Tell* (1996) at the Spoleto Festival; and Berlioz's *I Troiani* for the opening of the Bastille Opéra in Paris. Umberto Tirelli, the theatrical dressmaker who has long worked with Pizzi, says of him: "He has a sixth sense that can guess what can be achieved with a material, he grasps ideas suggested to him by everyday life, by the latest fashions and the distant past. He picks up everything from a theatrical perspective. How often my dressmaker's has become his experimental laboratory: using an oxy-hydrogen flame instead of scissors; melted plastic poured into in plaster casts, singed to make it look old, then decorated with Christmas tree ornaments; three-ply nylon; thick flannel, his granny's duster; rubberized fabrics. Imagination, creativity, and boldness run riot, often influencing or predicting fashions."

❑ 2002, Venice. Pizzi held a set- and costume-design workshop at the University of Venice, studying the staging of the opera *Thaìs* by Jules Massenet for the Malibran Theater.
❑ 2003, January. Pizzi directed and designed the sets and costumes for *Der*

> *Rosenkaval* by Richard Strauss, conducted by Jeffrey Tate at La Scala's Arcimboldi-Teatro.

Plain One of the three basic weaves, along with satin and twill. It is the simplest weave because it involves a ratio of just two threads and two wefts. The front is identical to the back. Because it has the greatest number of points of knotting between thread and weft, plain weave fabrics are absolutely the strongest, but the surface tends to be grain and dull. In the field of cotton production, it is the most commonly used weave for linens, in the woolen field it is used for heavy cloths, cool wools, and light Scottish patterns.

Plassier Stéphane (1965). French designer and ready-to-wear label. Original and multi-talented, Plassier describes himself as a "dressmaker-decorator." His creativity has been unleashed in many different fields: fashion, graphic design, advertising, decoration, theater, and cinema. He held his first runway show in 1983 and had his second show with the Groupe des Halles in Fall the same year. His brides are always spectacularly nonconformist, appearing on the runway dressed in sugar and chocolate, in cage-dresses filled with fluttering birds, or dresses decorated with fresh flowers, shells, and fishes. He dressed the actress Bernadette Lafont in two movies by Jean Pierre Mocky in 1987 and 1988.

> ❑ 2002. Plassier created a range of chinaware for Raynaud. His plates and vases are sold in the house boutique.

Plastron Covers men's shirt fronts. Fixed or removable, it often has ruffles, lace, pleats, or embroidery. Worn with a tuxedo or evening suit. In women's clothing, a *plastron* is the same as a ruffle or jabot.

Plataform shoes Shoes with a very high wedge made of cork or covered in the same material as the upper: canvas, leather or suede. Particularly comfortable if the wedge is the same height from the toe to the heel. Fashionable in the 1970s, they enjoyed a brief revival in 2000.

Platinum Guild International International marketing organization set up in 1980 by the world's biggest platinum producer Angloplatinum, with the aim of promoting the manufacture and consumption of platinum jewelry. The London headquarters coordinates the activities of the operating organizations present in (in order of volume of consumption) China, Japan, USA, Italy, Germany, and India. It has had a branch in Italy since 1987, based in Milan and run by Françoise Izaute (managing director), and Milena Granata (market development manager). The branch's intensive promotional activities are aimed at jewelers, and its impressive public information and communications program have brought about an increase in the annual consumption of platinum jewelry in Italy from 20 to 1,800 kilograms.

Platon (1970). English photographer. He studied at Saint Martin's School of Art and then the Royal College of Art in London. He became established in 1992 when he won a special competition to work for the English *Vogue*. His work is also published in *The Face*, *Arena*, *The Sunday Times Magazine*, *The New York Times Magazine*, *Vanity Fair*, *George*, and *Newsweek*; he took a famous portrait of Bill Clinton that was published on the cover of the December 2000 issue of *Esquire*. He has worked on advertising campaigns for clients like Levi's, Moschino, Eyewear, and Issey Miyake. His work has held exhibitions in London, Tokyo, and Milan.

Platt Lynes George (1907-1955). American photographer. His unusual, vaguely surreal images of fashion have been compared to those by Cecil Beaton. He was self-taught. He started out in 1932, worked for *Harper's Bazaar* and ran *Vogue*'s photographic studio from 1946 to 1948.

Playtex Leading brand of lingerie. Its fortune's were greatly increased in the 1990s by the miraculous breast-boosting Wonderbra. Founded in the USA in 1932, the group renamed itself the International Playtex Corporation (IPC) in the 1960s and opened divisons and factories throughout Europe. Playtex is also known for its Criss Cross bra, and it launched its first range of men's underwear, Cacharel Homme, in 1994.

Plein Sud French ready-to-wear label.

Launched by the designer Amor Faycal in 1983. Born in Tangiers to a Moroccan dignitary and an artistic Russian mother, Faycal mixes Western style with elements inspired by the Far East. The label has its own factory in Chatellerault.

Plissé Any kind of pleated fabric. There is the 'plissé soleil' with pleats fanning out like the rays of the sun, the 'plissé lampion' pleated like a Venetian lantern, the 'accordion' with pleats like the bellows of an accordion, and the 'plissado' invented by Mariano Fortuny.

Plissé soleil Tightly pleated full skirt. The small, sharp pleats spread out from the waistband all the way down to the hem, creating a buoyant, swishing skirt. The term can also be used to describe a sleeve, train, or any other part of a garment characterized by the fan-like arrangement of its pleats. It comes from the French words *plisser* (to pleat) and *soleil* (sun).

Plumetis Very light cotton fabric embroidered with tiny raised polka dots. Plumetis is used to make romantic prom dresses or Summery dresses for country picnics.

Plunkett Roy (1910-1944). American chemist who worked at the DuPont research laboratories and who invented Teflon (polytetrafluoroethylene) in the 1930s, a material defined by Guinness as "the slipperiest in the world." First used as a non-stick coating for cooking utensils, it has also been successfully adopted in the clothing industry. Ideal for soft and comfortable sports socks that reduce rubbing between the foot and shoe.

Plush Cotton fabric of different weights, with a velvety, "furry" side (in French called *peluche*). It is used to make ski sweaters, jogging tops, tracksuits, and even T-shirts and pullovers. There was a wave, during the 1960s, of hooded athletics tops made from this material printed with the names of American colleges.

Pochette French term used in women's clothing to refer to a small and elegant bag without straps or handle, and in men's clothing a small handkerchief (preferably colorful and not overly pressed) to put in one's jacket pocket; also used in the 1970s to refer to a kind of leather clutch bag. The term originates from the 1700s, when pockets (in French *poches*) were not sewn into clothes but were replaced by little pouches that were hung around the waist and hidden under a jacket. The 1920s and 1930s were golden years for the pochette bag, but it stayed on the scene in different sizes and fabrics for the rest of the 20th century.

Poell Carol Christian (1966). Austrian designer. He developed his first men's collection in 1993 and founded the company C.c.p in 1994. His avant-garde styles are famous for the quality of their tailoring and carefully chosen fabrics. He has also produced a women's collection since Fall-Winter 1999-2000.

Point d'esprit Tulle fabric embroidered with tiny dots. Used for veils, frills or transparent sleeves, usually black.

Poiret Paul (1879-1944). The first creator of fashion in the modern sense of the word. Poiret "le Magnifique" was born in Paris, his father was a cloth trader. Destined to work in the family business, he soon showed a preference for dressmaking, and after gaining experience in various ateliers including Cheruit, in about 1898 he joined the dress-

Paul Poiret, a portrait by Cecil Beaton (Prints Collection A. Bertarelli, Milan).

Paul Poiret, evening dress influenced by Cubist art (from *Anni Venti - La nascita dell'abito moderno*, Centro Di, Florence, 1991, catalogue for the Galleria del Costume).

maker and patron of the arts Jacques Doucet, who passed on to Poiret his taste for collecting. This experience, acquired in a refined and elegant environment where Sarah Bernhardt and Gabrielle Rejane were habituées, formed a modern and original personality. He worked for Maison Worth in 1900 and 1901, where his prototypes for casual suits and a kimono-style cape did not meet with the approval of Jean Philippe Worth. He was forced to leave the maison due to differences in outlook, and in 1903 Poiret set up his first independent business at 5 Rue Auber. He immediately attracted attention for his daring business choices, for example, he built large windows so people could see his designs from the street, contrary to the *haute couture* practices of the time. He moved to a larger premises at 37 Rue Pasquier from 1906 to 1908, taking with him a high-ranking clientele snatched from his more traditionalist rivals. He immediately took to the simplification of the female silhouette, rejecting the corset and other constricting and anachronistic garments in favour of a sensual and flowing line inspired by the Neoclassical period and the Directoire. In 1909 he set up his home and studio in a very luxurious building in the grounds of a big park in Avenue d'Antin, where he held fashion shows, receptions, and parties (like the famed *La Mille et Deuxième Nuit* in 1911, the apotheosis of Orientalism) that were to make him famous all over the world. He showed himself to be ahead of the times once again when he published the first albums of sketches by the best-known illustrators of the time to publicise his designs: *Les Robes de Paul Poiret racontées par Paul Iribe* (1908) and *Les Choses de Paul Poiret vues par Georges Lepape* (1911). At the same time, he organized touring fashion shows to bring his collections to the public's attention all over Europe. Influenced by the decorative richness and the colors of Diaghilev's Ballets Russes, Poiret launched a collection with a strong Eastern influence in 1910 and 1911, with turbans, Turkish pants and veiled harem tunics that were to become distinctive of his style. His jupe-entravée and jupe-culotte, the first attempt at pants for women to wear at home, caused a great stir. After a visit to Vienna's Wiener Werkstätte he set up the Atelier Martine in Paris, dedicated to interior design, where he designed extraordinary patterned furnishing fabrics, rugs, furniture, and household ornaments in collaboration with celebrated artists like Raoul Dufy. He also demonstrated his entrepreneurial foresight in 1911 through his desire to establish himself in the field of perfumery and cosmetics with his *Rosine* range, characterized by very precious essences and rare silver and crystal bottles designed by Lalique. In 1913, when Etré joined the team, Poiret went to the USA where he signed deals and licenses for the mass production and distribution of clothes and accessories with his label, including bags, gloves, and hosiery. By this time he was also recognised as the King of Fashion on the other side of the Atlantic, and in 1917, not long before he was called up for the French army, he opened a branch in New York and created Poiret Incorporated for the distribution of a ready-to-wear collection that was ahead of its time. He took up business again in 1919, but by this time the period of the war had changed the world. Some badly chosen ventures put his finances at risk. He was bled dry by the opening of a covered dance-hall called *L'Oasis* that aimed to transform his garden in Avenue d'Antin into a society haunt, and by his excessive generosity in hosting sumptuous costume balls. Despite the fact that his designs were no longer as well-received as before the war, because they seemed too far removed from the less affluent present, Poiret decided to open new branches in La Baule in 1919, Cannes in 1921, and Deauville and Biarritz in 1924. With Chanel's garçonnes and Patou's casual fashions hot on his heels, during the 1920s Poiret periodically took refuge in theater and cinema costume design, a more suitable outlet for his creative exhuberance: he made some memorable clothes for Marcel L'Herbier's *L'Inhumaine* in 1924. He was soon forced to leave his historic residence for a more modest abode at 1 Rond Point des Champs Elysées, where he remained until 1929 while his atelier went into receivership. Undeterred, Poiret attempted one last costly venture for the 1925 Expo. He acquired three boats docked in the Seine and transformed them into floating luxury showcases: *Amore*, a salon dedicated to his range of perfumes; *Delizia*, a restaurant completely furnished with objects and fabrics from the Atelier Martine; and *Orgia*, a gallery for fashion shows decorated by 14 giant panels painted by Dufy. He incurred debts of one and a half million francs and was forced to auction off his valuable private art collection in November 1925 to cover his debts. The fashion house went into liquidation in 1926 and Poiret left the company he created, selling even the name. Totally ruined also because of the 1929 economic crisis, the following year Poiret wrote a touching biography entitled *En habillant l'époque.* In 1932 he tried to start afresh, setting up a small business in the Étoile area with the help of a subsidy from the Chambre Syndicale de la Couture. He christened it Passy 10-17, the telephone number of the fashion house. Comforted by the possibility of being able to regain possession of his label, he took on occasional work for the London department store Liberty's, and for Printemps in Paris in 1933, when he organized a special fashion show to commemorate the opening of the Pont d'Argent. But he soon sank into obscurity. Poiret died in poverty in 1944, shortly before his friend Jean Cocteau managed to complete a retrospective exhibition of his paintings. (*Aurora Fiorentini*)

Polac Juliette (1964). Jewelry designer. Born in Paris, she studied design there and learnt the art of cutting stones at the atelier of Gilles Royaux. She went to live in Crete at the age of 22, and began to work for a jeweler there, who was to become her husband. She opened her own atelier in 1990. In 1993 Naila de Monbrison held an exhibition of Polac's work at her gallery in Rue de Bourgogne in Paris. Polac currently lives in Athens. As well as in Greece, her jewelry is famous New York and Paris. Her pieces are made from pure gold or hammered silver, and decorated with shells that she has picked up in Morocco or India, or other natural elements that give them a slightly primitive, tribal feel. She has recently produced some silver pieces with sacred figures, inspired by votive offerings from Greek Orthodox churches.

Polacchino Leather or suede ankle boots done up with a zip or laces that tie through hooks or eyelets at the front.

Polaroid American brand of eyewear. The brainchild of Edwin Land (1909, Connecticut), an aspiring inventor with his own laboratory in Cambridge (Mass.), who received an order from Eastman Kodak for polarizing filters for cameras worth 10 million dollars in 1934. Land, working with his young assistant George Wheelwright, had in fact registered the patent for polarizing filters, obtained by the perfect vertical alignment of millions of miniscule needles of iodine. Land's wife Clarence Kennedy gave the product is name, Polaroid. The first press conference about Polaroid was held at Harvard on 30 January 1936: Land later told how the journalists attending were already wearing his glasses made with polarizing filters. The Polaroid Corporation was founded in 1937. Over a million pairs of "polarized" glasses were sold in 1939, and by 1940 Polaroid had 240 employees. In 1948 Polaroid started manufacturing cameras in addition to glasses and lenses. In the 1950s Land's glasses became a cult object in Europe as well, a status symbol for the new generation. The current manufacturing methods are still based on Land's principles: the original filters block the glaring horizontal light reflected by water, snow, ice, and wet roads. In addition to two polarizing filters the lenses are coated with two UV filters to protect against damaging rays, two "cushions" to make them shatter-resistant, and two hard resin layers to make them scratch-resistant. There are about 150 designs with 600 variations of shape, polarization, and lens color. The Xoor collection, created in 1997 with the slogan "fashion and function" is designed for maximum comfort and vision and is characterized by the most up-to-date Italian design. The Furore collection combines Polaroid's know-how with Italian design flair.

Polatti Dario (1952). Sociologist who studies fashion phenomena, and has taught at the University of Urbino. He led one of the Dams workshops and the Stars workshops at the Università Cattolica del Sacro Cuore in Brescia in 2001-2002, as part of the program of events called *The Arts profession*, which involved academics, journalists, and names from the music and entertainment industry. The following year he held a workshop on the *Organization of events in the fashion* *field*, a course where he shared his personal experience and expertise of fashion shows with his students.

Polhemus Ted (1947). Lecturer in anthropology based in London but born in Asbury Park, New Jersey. He is considered the guru of street style and spontaneous fashion. He became known in Italy for his exhibition *Street Style*, held in 1994 in collaboration with Pitti Immagine. The metropolitan tribes (Polhemus calls them "global tribes") of the 1970s had a great influence on world fashion, which seeks out and copies the styles of the people. He also maintains that London, the city he made his home in 1989, is the world center for inspiring contemporary Western taste. (*Laura Salza*)

Polignac (de) Ghislaine. Pioneer of ready-to-wear for her ideas, imagination, and sense of the possibilities that technology offered the clothing industry in the 1950s. A princess, and client and friend of many of the most important protagonists of Parisian *haute couture*, in 1952 she accepted a job as a style consultant working on the renewal of the clothing collections in the department store Galeries Lafayette. At that time their garments had little aesthetic appeal: the fabrics were chosen to appeal to customers for their resistance to wear and tear rather than their beauty, mimicking *haute couture* in overly traditional and drab colors. It was not an easy task to convince the management of Galeries Lafayette that the most efficient stylistic weapon was simplicity, aided by a more joyful palette and by fabrics with a lighter weave (the princess was also a pioneer in the discovery of the Italian textile industry). She won her battle by wearing her own creations, and getting even Wallis Simpson, the Duchess of Windsor, to wear them, and by using her title to attract the attention of the women's magazines. Her career lasted twenty years. She retired in 1972.

Polimoda Institute of further education for the study of fashion. Based at Villa Strozzi in Florence. Polimoda organises specialized training courses at university level for various fashion disciplines. It was set up by the Councils of Florence and Prato and associated organizations, following an agreement with New York State University's Fashion Insitute of Technology. An agreement with Florence University allows the Institute to hold integrated courses and to offer qualified students the opportunity to obtain a University Diploma in Costume and Fashion. Polimoda has also been a member of the International Foundation of Fashion Technology Institutes since 1998, an association of the world's leading fashion schools offering the highest level of training. The main disciplines covered by the Institute are women's and men's fashion, knitwear, footwear, accessory design, millinery, textile design and manufacture, fashion product management and marketing, as well as the International Fashion Design course, held in Florence and New York. The Institue has close links with the fashion industry.

Polkadot Term invented by the German designer Heinz Oestergaard to describe fabrics with a pattern of large dots, arranged in staggered rows.

Pollen Arabella (1961). English designer. Her creations can often be seen at England's highest society events: her colorful suits, worn by young, high-society women, stand out in the crowd at the Ascot races thanks to their impeccable cut and tailoring. In fact she started out as a dressmaker with a private clientele: then, as often happens in England, the royal family played an important role in promoting her fashion. Arabella's breakthrough came when she designed the wardrobe of the newly wed Diana, Princess of Wales.

Pollini Shoemakers based in San Mauro Pascoli (Forlì), founded in 1953 by Vittorio, Alberto, Lucia, and Lidia Pollini following in the tradition of their father Ettore. In the 1970s they launched a new concept of boot: they took a professional riding boot without fastenings and with minimal stitching, then modified it for city wear. In 1998 Pollini launched their own collection of men's and women's leatherwear.

❑ At the end of 2000 Pollini joined the Aeffe Group, controlled by Alberta and Massimo Ferretti. The parent company planned a restyle of the Pollini brand in order to relaunch it on the market within a year.

❑ 2001. Pollini's new collection of casual clothing consisted of about 60 women's pieces and 40 men's pieces, which were conceived by Massimo Ferretti as Aeffe's luxury sportswear range. They were made from the highest quality fabrics with a distinctive cut, and distributed in a hundred or so shops throughout Europe and the USA.
❑ 2002. Pollini represented 18% of the Aeffe Group's income with a turnover of 50.6 million euros, an increase of 4% compared to the previous management.
❑ 2003, March. Pollini pushed open the doors to the Far Eastern market, signing a three year export deal with the Japanese Itochu Corporation: the Pollini and Pollini Studio lines of men's and women's footwear and leather goods and ready-to-wear have been distributed from Fall-Winter 2003-2004. A five-year agreement was signed with Fairton Strategy Limited to distribute Pollini in Hong Kong, Taiwan, and China.
❑ 2003. The Turkish designer Rifat Ozbek took up the artistic direction of Pollini's line of women's clothing.

(*Pierangelo Mastantuono*)

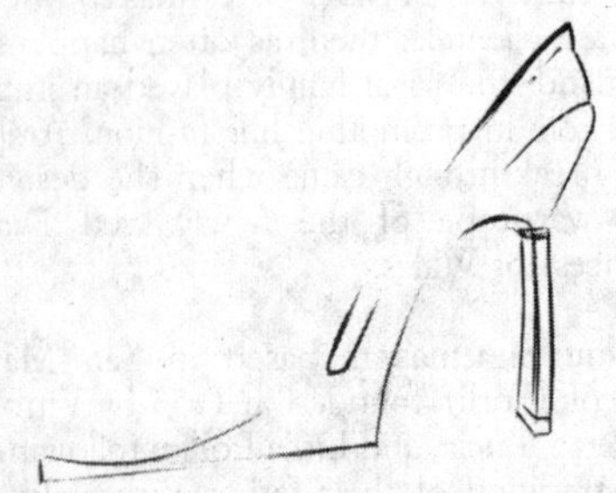

Stiletto court shoe by Pollini.

Pollock Alice. Owner of the Quorum boutique in Chelsea, which was very popular with London's youth in pop's golden years. She was responsible for the debut of Ozzie Clark in 1964, who designed his first clothes exclusively for Quorum.

Polonaise Relaunched by Saint Laurent at the end of the 1970s for sumptuous brocade evening redingotes with precious fur trimmings at the hem and sleeves, after the style of Anna Karenina or Lara in *Doctor Zhivago*. In the 1700s it was a three-quarter length redingote with a straight collar that was worn over crinolines. The dressmaker Charles Frederick Worth revisited the style in the second half of the 1800s.

(*Gabriella Gregorietti*)

Polo neck sweater Closed pullover with a high, roll-down neck. Very comfortable for Winter sports under the windcheater. Worn by Marcello Mastroianni in Fellini's movie *La Dolce Vita*, from which the Italian name of the sweater derives. It was also popular with Yves Montand.

Polo shirt Short-sleeved shirt designed to be worn on the world's polo fields. It went from being simple sportswear to a status symbol in 1927 when it was reinvented by René Lacoste, the tennis champion and businessman who transformed the way people dressed on the courts of Wimbledon and Roland Garros with his crocodile logo (until then they played in long pants, shirt and tie). His creation then made its way from the courts to a more public domain, and with time it became more of a classic item rather than a trendy one, satisfying the desire for an elegant piece of sportswear.

Polyester Synthetic fiber. Seventy percent of synthetic fibers are classified as either polyesters or polyamides. Winfield and Cickson of the Caloco Printer's Association introduced the first polyester fiber in 1941; in 1963 DuPont launched Dralon. Polyester fibers are crease resistant, quick drying and keep their shape. They are resistant to chemicals, solvents, and microorganisms and absorb little moisture. They add shine, strength, and drape to wool, silk and cotton. They just need special treatment to allow them to be dyed, and to make them breathable and moisture repellent.

Polyolephine Synthetic fiber. It has just two by-products: polyethylene and polypropylene, with textile characteristics that are not currently made use of, despite research that has proved its indisputable suitability for clothing and furnishing. It is a low cost fiber that does not need to be ironed, is resistant to wear and tear, and keeps its shape. It is used for some children's products for its water-repellent qualities.

Pom d'Api French make of children's footwear, which is the only one in France to cover all sectors of this niche market. The company exports 41% of its products. The brand was created in 1975 by the brothers Guy and Yvon Rautureau, who had joined their father's business five years earlier and modernised it. In 1980 they create the Free Lance range, aimed at teenagers and women. The range conquered the fashion scene and boosted the company's bank balance with imaginative designs like the Perfecto, with its diagonal zip fastening, worn by the singer Sting and copied all over the world, becoming a cult item for punk kids. They once again attracted youthful consumers in 1993 by raising the sole of the basketball boot by 5 centimetres: they sold 100,000 pairs in three months. In 1988 they acquired the Spring Court brand of tennis shoes. The company has two factories in France, but 40% of their production is with third parties in Tunisia and the Far East. They have 240 employees. In 1997 the Group produced 500,000 pairs of shoes, for a total turnover of 78 billion lire.

Pomellato Italian jewelers. The Milanese company was founded in 1948 and nearly twenty years later (1967) was transformed into a designer brand through the meeting of minds of Luigi Signori and Pino Rabolini. It takes its name from the dappled (*pomellato*) pony that was chosen as the brand's logo. In the 1970s they went from producing classic chains to pendants made of gold and precious stones like *The King* and *The Bear*, that were destined to become Pomellato's mascots. The company has had a shop in Via San Pietro in Milan since 1982, and started opening shops all over the world in the mid-1980s. They started producing silver pieces in 1982 and then watches in 1989. In the 1990s they started using diamonds and high-carat cabochon cut colored stones in impressive settings.

❑ 2002. Pomellato, a sponsor of WWF Italia, launched the *Earth can save Man* project in favor of safeguarding the 100 eco-environments most at risk in the world. Queen Rania of Jordan is the patron of the initiative. In the fall of the same year Pomellato launched Stress, a limited edition women's watch which is one of the brand's most recent successes. In 1994 Pomellato had already declared "an undertaking to protect our natural heritage," creating DoDo, a line of coordinating jewelry with the aim of telling a story and communicating universal messages. DoDo creations owe their name to the long-extint bird.

❑ 2002, July. Pomellato opened their third store in Japan, the second in Tokyo in the Ginza area. The enthusiastic response to the young DoDo brand led the management to test out their first flagship store in Via Filangieri, Naples.

❑ 2003. At the end of 2002 the company had a turnover of 67.3 million euros, representing an increase of 22.5 percent compared to 2001. The DoDo brand alone registered a 47% increase in sales, and overseas sales rose by 32%. The most successful market was Japan, which provided nearly a 50% rise in income.

❑ 2003, February. A Sotheby's exhibition marked the debut of Pomellato USA, which planned to open 60 new concessions and their first flagship store within two years, in addition to distributing their products in Bergdorf Goodman and Saks Fifth Avenue in New York, Greenwich, Boston, San Francisco, and Aspen.

❑ Following the good results of the Naples experiment, Pomellato opened more DoDo stores in Galeries Lafayette in Paris and Bloomingdales, New York.

(*Pierangelo Mastantuono*)

Pomodoro Arnaldo (1926). Italian sculptor. In 1951 he founded Studio 3P with his brother Giò and Giorgio Prefetti to produce jewelry and gold pieces. These unique pieces were displayed at the X Milan Triennale and also stole the limelight at the Venice Biennale in 1956. From the 1960s Pomodoro designed sculptural jewelry in the form of spheres, disks, and molten gold and silver surfaces made in Milan by Gem Montebello and photographed by Ugo Mulas. The artist created two extremely modern dresses for

Bruna Bini's collection in 1961. The first, called *The Astronaut's Secretary*, was made of fabric combined with rubber tubes which form the skirt. The second was called *Black Spring*, and was an impressive richly embroidered skirt teamed with black gloves and a sky-blue top.

Pomodoro Giò (1930-2002). Italian sculptor. He started working with his brother Arnaldo in Pesaro, in association with Giorgio Prefetti, who produced their first pieces of jewelry: buckles, brooches, necklaces, bracelets with a dense, sculptural texture that were displayed at the X Milan Triennale and the Venice Biennale in 1956. From the 1960s his jewelry was made by Gem Montebello. In 1967 he designed a white and yellow gold bracelet with rubies and diamonds (now part of the Gigliola Gagnoni Pomodoro collection) that echoes the themes of his sculptures.

Giò Pomodoro, design for a dress by Bini, 1961.

Pompea Underwear and hosiery company. The business was founded by Adriano Rodella in Medole (Mantua) in 1996. It became an industrial holding company in 2001, and developed into a market leader for hosiery and women's, men's and children's underwear in Italy and other European countries, particularly Spain. In 2002 the company's turnover was 172 million euros. Pompea has 450 employees in Italy and 435 abroad. In December 2002 it acquired the Roberta brand from the Ladyberg Group. Given the seasonal and fluctuating nature of the hosiery market, Pompea expanded into underwear, which now represents 30% of its turnover. Its hosiery and underwear is made from soft microfiber, produced using advanced circular weaving technology that guarantees maximum comfort and practicality. The simple seamless T-shirts, vests, panties, and shorts come in black-and-white, but also turquoise, coral, apple green, and batik prints. One of its latest launches was the Barbie range, for 3 to 5 year old girls.

❑ 2003, May. Having expanded into underwear, and increased the volume of its business by 22.4% in 2002 and by 15.9% in the first three months of 2003, Pompea turned its attention to the foreign market. By the end of 2003 the company aimed to achieve a turnover of more than 176 million euros, with 34% coming from foreign markets.

❑ 2003, June. The famous Roberta brand, acquired for 5 million euros in December 2002, was ready to be relaunched, and distributed in supermarkets and department stores. The range has a young, bright image, like its designer, the 23 year-old Serbian Naida Tarakcija, who has chosen pink, sky-blue, ruches, and sprigs of flowers for the Winter collection. Pompea has an annual turnover of 157 million euros, with 1,950 employees in Italy and abroad.

❑ 2004. In November a totally new brand called GYM dedicated to beachwear and free time was launched. The company invested two million euros to acquire a factory in Serbia with about 1,000 employees specialized in the manufacture of hosiery yarns.

Pompilio Elvis (1961). Belgian hat designer, who trained at the Lièges School of Plastic Arts. After his studies he worked in the advertising serigraphy sector for five years, during which time he developed a marked leaning towards hat design. His rather eccentric creations for men and women made of linen, straw, velvet, felt, and plastic soon caught the attention of personalities like Madonna and Harrison Ford. His Lièges apartment-atelier-showroom soon became too small to accommodate the growing orders coming in from designers like Valentino, Christian Dior, Thierry Mugler, and Anne Demeulemester. He opened his first shop in Brussels in 1990, and another in Antwerp soon after. He was awarded the Victor Prize and started showing his collections in Paris. A true "fashion star," Pompilio wears his own creations and models them himself on the runway, earning the respect of the fashion crowd. He represented Belgium at the Seville International Expo in June 1992. In September 2003 he started selling a children's range of hats. After the launch of the Hats International Group, that involved a team of about twenty collaborators, in 2000 Pompilio signed an agreement with Chanel, working on their *haute couture* and ready-to-wear collections. On 30 June 2002 he closed his Brussels boutique, and then in December his Parisian boutique, after presenting his Fall-Winter 2002-2003 collection. The reason was clear and simple: "I've been working 7 days a week for 15 years. In order to do this well I have to oversee everything. It's too much, really too much." He continues to create hats, but accepts clients only by appointment. Pompilio has been running his own school for milliners since September 2002.

Poncho A garment of South American origin, it is a square or rectangular woolen cape, with a hole in the center for the head, that falls softly over the shoulders. It is one of the simplest and most ancient of garments. At the beginning of the 1970s it was rediscovered and worn as part of the ethnic fashions of the time.

Pontoglio Italian company specialized in the manufacture of velvet fabrics. The business started out in Milan in 1883 as Sacconaghi & C., and changed to Manufattura Pontolgio in 1992. Over these hundred or so years the company structure has changed, from being run by a single family to becoming a holding company. In the 1960s, when Pontoglio had 500 employees, it was acquired by Snia Bpd. Despite the disruption, an effort was made to maintain the high-quality standards of its products. Pontoglio's fabrics are also used for car upholstery. At the beginning of the 1980s the company turnover was around 6 billion lire. In 1985 Pontoglio finally joined the Pecci Group. Widespread restructuring and technological innovation along with the positive trend for velvet in recent years have led to an increased turnover of about 22 million euros and an annual production of 2.5 million meters of fabric, which is destined for mid to high-level domestic and export men's and women's markets.

(*Silvia Martinenghi*)

❑ 2003, January. Pecci's stable of brands were displayed at the fourth I-TexStyle, the annual trade fair organized by the Italian Institute for Foreign Trade in New York.

Pontremoli Patrizia (1942). Journalist. Pontremoli, who married the publisher Giuseppe Della Schiava in 1963, was editor of *Cosmopolitan*, taking the place of Laura Bonaparte, who left in 1979 to join the Rizzoli group. She creates the women's astrology magazine *Astrodonna* with Adriana Cavedini in 1990. She continued as editor of *Cosmopolitan* until the magazine closed in 1997.

Poole Henry. The name that started the tradition of men's suits in Savile Row, London. Henry, son of the military tailor James Poole, inherited his father's tailoring business (founded in 1806 in Regent Street) in 1846, and, thanks to his talent and his expert public relations, the company became the arbiter of men's fashions of the time. The atelier has dressed Edward, Prince of Wales, Charles Dickens, Winston Churchill, and Charles de Gaulle. It is credited with the invention of the tuxedo. Today the company exports to the USA, Japan, and the Middle East, as well as the European market. Its tailors go on a tour of Europe and the USA twice a year to visit their clientele.

(*Mara Accettura*)

Pop Art Pop artists choose to see and represent the world through the eyes of the inhabitants of a big contemporary city. They do not feel that urgent need for nature – and natural energy – that inspired their predessors in action painting. The pop artists' world is an entirely artificial world, highly refined and shaped by technology. A world populated by figures produced by methods of mass communication (particularly visual ones like photography, cinema, the popular press, shows, and big rock concerts), by mass-produced goods, and of course by advertising. The world inhabited and represented by pop artists is crowded with machines: household appliances, subway trains, cars, airplanes, etc. Obviously fashion has also contributed in a big way to the creation of the contemporary figure that so fascinates and consumes pop artists. Warhol once said that the only current Italian artists were fashion designers. But in reality that which more or less exerts a direct influence on pop artists, because it is an integral part of their world, is perhaps street fashion. It is fashion created collectively, inspired by original little inventions whose authors are often unknown, and continually shaped by an infinite series of imitations, adjustments, emphases, modifications, and contradictions that spread at lightning speed across the natural network that unites the smallest and most sensitive minorities (including transvestites) with the most wide-spread conformist majority ready to accept every nonconformist suggestion. It is fashion with that constant original element of popularity – or even of intended virtual poverty – that immediately characterized the three fundamental garments that we could define as essential street fashion and as essentially pop: jeans, T-shirt and (leather or cloth) jacket. Street fashion is certainly an integral part of the world that inspired Pop Art. And it is certainly worth remembering that through fashion and Pop Art the image of the American world has ended up winning over, generation after generation, a large percentage of young people all over the globe. Perhaps never in history has a culture turned out to be so captivating and naturally irresistible for the masses. Even an instrument of conquest. *(Emilio Tadini)*

Poplin Originally a fine light woolen fabric made exclusively for the Pope and produced in the Papal city of Avignon. Now used to mean a fine, compact, plain weave fabric, characterized by a warp yarn that is finer that the weft yarn. The most common poplins are made from mercerized cotton with a twisted warp yarn with a higher thread count than the weft. It has a characteristic cross rib and a fine sheen. Commonly used for shirts, but also lightweight dresses and jackets.

Popova Lioubov (1889-1924). Russian painter. Futurism and Cubism (she traveled to Italy and studied with Metzinger in Paris) encouraged her to become part of her country's avant-garde artistic movement. From 1914 she turned away from painting to create clothes and textile designs, transferring the geometric compositions of her paintings onto fabrics. She started teaching at Svomas in 1918 and at Vkhutemas in 1921, whose ideological and practical intent was to bring art closer to industrial work. In 1922 she joined the Productivist group Inkhuk and worked on the publication of *Lef* magazine. In 1923 and 1924 she worked as a designer at the First State Textile Print Factory in Moscow. It was here that she invented new kinds of geometric patterns and abstract symbols in a range of pastel tones. They were designs for the nomenklatura rather than the masses. When it came to mass production she sacrificed niceties in favor of functionality and technology, with cuts and details in line with the technology of the machinery used by the clothing industry. *(Cloe Piccoli)*

Liubov Popova, "Summer," 1924 ((from *Art Fashion*, Biennial of Florence, Skira, 1996).

Porfin! Label created by Alejandro Sàez de la Torre, launched with the opening of the boutique-workshop Por Fin in 1991. The same year Alejandro attended the Marangoni Insitute in Milan. In 1992 he specialised in fashion and costumes for theater, cinema, and TV in Valencia. He moved to Paris in 1995, though from 1996 to 1999 he showed his collections at the Pasarela Gaudí in Barcelona and then at the Pasarela del Carmen. The Porfin! men's and women's ready to wear collections have been enthusiastically received at the Pasarela Cibeles in Madrid since 2002. (*Mariacristina Righi*)

Portable phone Mobile apparatus by which one makes phone calls, with a microphone and a receiver: available since 1983. The first glimpse of it for most people dated to three years later, in 1986, at the movies: Michael Douglas, playing Gordon Gekko – the money-minded tycoon in the film *Wall Street* – walks on the beach talking into the first Hollywood portable phone. The scene nowadays looks démodé because the phone was the size of a loaf of bread, yet the object immediately became a status symbol. Technology has progressed a long way since those first models, and from "status symbol" the

Sketches by Alejandro Sàez de la Torre for Porfin!

portable phone has turned into a "style symbol." The last example? The Xelibri model by Siemens. The ironic and vaguely Orwellian advertising looks almost like a teaser, a provocative commercial which sponsors something that has nothing or little to do with images. In fact, the Xelibri is a banal Gsm phone, but it can be hang around the neck like a pendant, and it is nice to look at, to touch, and to exhibit. The communication focus is the phone's design and its concept as a fashion item, so much so that strictly practical functions are not so important. The phone producers' idea is that of lines of portable phones should created according to a sort of Swatch philosophy: two collections a year with the intent of convincing buyers to buy two, perhaps three models to alternate and match with one's tie or shoes. (*Antonio Mancinelli*)

Porter Thea (1927). English designer born in Damascus, Syria, but she completed her studies at London University. At the beginning of the 1950s she returned to the Middle East where she started trading in textiles and carpets. She then moved the business to London at the end of the decade. She startd creating her own dresses from 1964. The Arabic and Middle Eastern influence is clearly visible in her designs and is accentuated by the use of exotic and fine fabrics. She often used chiffon, crêpe de chine, silk brocades, and embroidered velvets in particular for her sophisticated evening dresses. Her elegant caftans became instantly popular. In 1968 she opened a boutique in New York and in 1974 another shop in Paris. In the 1970s she was one of the promoters of the gypsy style, consisting of flounced dresses and oriental colors, low and very low-waisted pants, and teamed with fabric or suede tops decorated with strips of fur or rich silk and chiffon scarves. In the 1980s her clothes gained international recognition, especially from fans of the hipster fashion.

Porto Fashion Award Event started in 2000, which takes place every two years in Oporto in Portugal. It awards prizes to fashion personalities and organizes a competition for emerging young designers. The initiative, promoted by Icep Portugal (Portugal's Tourism and Trade Office) and by Cenestap (Portugal's Center of Applied Textile Studies), has the aim of creating cooperation between Portuguese entrepreneurs and recent graduates from European institutes. At the 2000 event, prizes were awarded to Zara, Caramelo, DuPont, Adolfo Dominguéz, and John Rocha. The young designers, who present their creations at a final runway show, are judged by an international panel that awards a representative from each country 5,000 euros (10,000 if they use Portuguese materials). First prize is 12,500 euros (which is doubled if Portuguese materials are used).

Posen Zac (1980). American designer. Born in New York of Bohemian origin, he grew up in Soho. Very precocious, he created clothes for his sister. He soon left the Brooklyn art school to go to Central Saint Martin's in London. Not yet twenty, he worked at The Metropolitan Museum of Art alongside Richard Martin, head of the Costume Design department: an ideal place to "live and breathe" fashion, and perceive all its stimuli. He started dressing a limited group of customers who are charmed by his talent and his Vionnet-inspired, sinuous, bias cut dresses that celebrate the body. He juxtaposes this soft, caressing style with another more structured one that creates a sort of moving sculpture for strong, practical women: a perfect synthesis of proportion and volume. His family – father, mother, and sister – contribute to the running of the fashion house he founded in 2001. After just two runway shows he won over the most demanding public and obtained flattering reviews from the specialist press. In February 2001 the *New York Times* "made" him with an article dedicated to his work. In 2002 he showed for the first time during Fashion Week and the celebrated Victoria and Albert Museum in London acquired one of his dresses for their collection. The German viscose manufacturer Enka also took notice of him and included him in the group of finalists for a presentation organized in Milan in September 2002.

(*Lucia Mari*)

Potter Clare (1892-1974). American designer. Responsive to the demands of a practical and dynamic kind of woman, she favored simple fluid lines. She was ahead of other designers in catching the transition from a lifestyle which requires rather formal clothes to one more suited to casual items, interpreting the change with sporty clothing also suited to city life.

Pottier Philippe (1905-1991). French photographer nicknamed the "Fashion Bible" for having been the official photographer for the Officiel de la Couture for 25 years. He had the great Nadar as a teacher. He started working for the French edition of *Vogue* in 1934 and was immediately hailed as a wizard with his use of lighting. He then worked for *Plaisir de France*, *Fémina* and in 1945 for *Elle*, which was his launch pad to the Officiel. He had a studio in Rue Verneuil. Pottier, who also loved color photography, took portraits of the most famous models of the time, including Bettina, Nicole de Lamargé, Simone D'Aillencourt, Capucine, and Odette Rousselet.

Pour Toi Knitwear collection designed by Luca Coelli, an art director with a degree in architecture and Sam Rey, an American artist. A solid couple in both life and work, in the early 1980s the two produced a collection of handmade knitted garments under the Yoko label, which was instantly popular with the Milanese fashion crowd. Deanni Ferretti, the owner of the knitwear factory 'Maglificio Miss Deanna di San Martino' in Rio (Carpi), immediately accepted the challenge of producing their creations industrially under a new label, Pour Toi, which was soon joined by a line of clothes to wear around the home called Pour Toi Ce Soir. The official launch took place in 1985, when the Camera Nazionale della Moda Italiana [National Chamber of Italian Fashion] sponsored a runway show of young designers' work called Le Proposte di Milano Collezioni [Offerings from Milan Collections], which also marked the debut of Dolce & Gabbana. For several seasons Pour Toi was one of the most interesting fashionable Italian collections. In 1988 the couple suffered a personal crisis, to the extent that a year later Miss Deanna was forced to entrust the artistic direction of the line to other desingers: first Cesare Fabbri, then Jan & Carlos. In 1991, following the early death of Luca Coelli, the production of the Pour Toi line ceased definitively. Sam Rey worked with Angela Missoni on the launch of her range for a few seasons. He currently lives in Australia where he creates small stitch tapestries and mosaics with the same appealing chromatic combinations that made Pour Toi so successful. (*Daniela Fedi*)

Poynter Phil (1973). English photographer. He first became known for his work for the magazine *Dazed and Confused*, of which he was the art director until 1994, but he has also worked for *Spin* and Atlantic Records. His characteristic style is to to construct often ironic stories with a big emotional impact. His clients include Diesel, David James, Givenchy, and The Verve.

Pozzi Milanese men's fashion store. Very famous from between the wars until the 1950s, it was situated opposite a legendary brothel. After working as a sales assistant at Bellini, Claudio Tridenti took over the men's classic clothing emporium "Pozzi" in the 1920s. He was the first in Italy to import Burberry designs, regimental ties and Church shoes. Known as a fine salesman, supplier to the royal family and the Milanese upper classes, he is remembered for having had 500 foulards printed with a speech by Mussolini which sold out. He invented a wallet-diary made of regimental fabric. The store closed towards the end of the 1970s.

PPR With a presence in 65 countries worldwide, the Pinault-Printemps-Redoute Group competes in two different strategic areas, business-to-business distribution, and, through Gucci, the luxury market. It was founded in 1963 by François Pinault (who started his career in the timber industry). By the middle of the 1990s, PPR had become one of the European leaders of business-to-business distribution. Its strategy is based on ownership of several brand leaders and on the multi-stranded distribution network of selling via mail-order, on the internet, and in department stores, to meet the different customer requirements. In 1988 Pinault SA, a specialist in the sales, distribution and processing of wood, was floated on the Paris Stock Market's Second Marché. Two years later the group acquired CFAO, a company specializing in the distribution of electric material and trade with Africa. In 1991 the group acquired Conforama and Printemps, and next was the turn of La Redoute. In

1994 the PPR Group was founded. In the same year they also took over Fnac. In 1995 the group was floated on the CAC 40 index on the Paris Stock Exchange. In 1996 the group acquired SCOA, the main distributor of pharmaceuticals in Africa, through its European affiliate Eurapharma. In addition to these came the women's underwear chain Orcanta, and Fnac Direct. In 1997 the group took control, through Redcats, of Ellos, the leader in the Scandinavian mail-order market. In 1998 it was the turn of Guilbert, a European leader in furniture distribution, and 49.9% of Brylane, the fourth largest home-shopping company in the USA. In 1999 the Group diversified towards the luxury market, acquiring 42% of the Gucci Group, which had itself that same year taken over Sergio Rossi and Yves Saint Laurent. In 2000 Conforama entered the Italian market, buying 60% of Emmezeta, while the Gucci Group acquired Surcouf, the largest distributor of computer accessories in Europe. Gucci's purchasing campaign continued, as they took over Boucheron, Bottega Veneta, and Balenciaga, and signed partnership agreements with Stella McCartney and Alexander McQueen. In September 2001 a legal battle with LVMH over Gucci ended with the withdrawal of the group's opponents following PPR's increase in Gucci's quota to 53.2% that year, and in 2002 to 54.4%. In 2002 the group focused its strategies on distribution and the luxury market, selling its non-strategic assets. It also concentrated on profitability, pursing a path of efficiency and cutting costs. Sales reached 27.4 billion euros, with gross profits of 1.82 billion and net profits of 1.58 billion.

❑ 2003, September. The French group PPR increased its shares in luxury Italian group Gucci to 67.34%, approaching its goal of 70% ownership by year's end.

❑ 2003, November. The group announced that Domenico De Sole, President and Managing Director of the Gucci Group, and Tom Ford, Creative Director of the Gucci Group and of the Gucci and Yves Saint Laurent labels, would not be extending their contracts when they expired in 2004. De Sole declared, "Gucci has been one of the great loves of my life, and the years I have spent with the company have been a fantastic journey. I would like to thank Tom, whose creative genius has made our success possible, and also our extraordinary colleagues across the world. Thanks to their skill and devotion, we have been able to transform the small business, in difficulties when I joined it in 1984, into a world power in the luxury goods market, and so have created something of value for all of our stakeholders." Tom Ford said, "It is with great sadness that I look forward to a future without the Gucci Group. For the last 13 years, this business has been my life. We are leaving one of the strongest teams in the sector, and I will do my best in the remaining time that I have with the company to assure the future success of the group. I could not be more proud of our work at Gucci, or the exceptional team of colleagues who have contributed with so much more than just their hard work: They have put their hearts into our quest for excellence. I am grateful to have been able to share my joy at the success of the group with such a fantastic group of people. I would like to thank Domenico for his extraordinary leadership, his constant support, and his friendship."

❑ Gucci acquired 70% of the shoe factory Pigini srl, the company which collaborated with Gucci as a supplier, producing women's classic and sports footwear.

❑ 2004, March. Alessandra Facchinetti was appointed as the new Creative Director of Womenswear. Born in Bergamo in 1972 and a graduate of the Istituto Maragoni in Milan, she started her careeer designing for Prada, soon becoming Artistic Coordinator for Miu Miu. She joined Gucci in October 2000 as Style Manager for Womenswear, and soon proved to be exceptionally talented. The new Creative Director of Menswear is John Ray. Born in Scotland, in 1986 he decided on a career change and moved to London to study design at the legendary Central St Martins. Having finished his studies, in 1992 he became part of Katherine Hamnett's design team as Assistant Menswear Designer. In a short time he took over management of menswear. In 1996 John was taken on by Tom Ford at Gucci as consultant designer for menswear, and soon began to work full-time for the company. Finally, the new Creative Director of Accessories is Frida Giannini. Born in Rome in 1972 she trained at the Accademia del Costume e della Moda. In September 2002 she became Style Manager for Pelletteria Gucci, and made a significant contribution to the success of the brand's leather goods. In April, Robert Polet was made the new President and Managing Director of the Gucci Group, replacing Domenico del Sole. Polet, who is Dutch, arrived at Gucci after 26 years with Unilever.

❑ PPR raised the stake held in the Gucci Group to 67%, with a unit price of 85.52 euros, as agreed in 2001 by Gucci, LVMH, and PPR.

❑ In November Jean-Paul Gaultier signed a partnership agreement with well-known French mail-order company La Redoute, for its Spring-Summer 2005 collection. Around 20 outfits and accessories will be produced under the label La Redoute by Gaultier.

❑ In December the French group sold Rexel, the world leader in the distribution of electronic goods. The sale made 3 billion euros for PPR, which will be spent on reducing the group's debts.

❑ 2004 ended with a profit of 940.6 billion euros – an increase of 45.9% on 2003. Gross profits increased to 1.4 billion, higher than the 1.2 billion of the previous year, and in line with analysts' forecasts. The luxury market contributed 394 millions (compared to 237 millions in 2003), and distribution contributed 754 millions.

❑ 2005: in addition to her role managing all of Gucci's accessories, Frida Giannini was made new Creative Director of womenswear, taking over from Alessandra Facchinetti. PPR finished the first quarter with a turnover of 4.1 billion euros, an increase of 2.2% on the previous year. Gucci, which represents 60% of PPR's luxury sector, had a turnover of 429 millions, an increase of 19.3%. Sales at Yves Saint Laurent for these first three months of 2005 amounted to 39 millions in comparison to 40.5 millions the previous year. *(Dario Golizia)*

Prada Mario Prada was born in Milan, and worked from 1913 as a craftsman. He had a shop in the Galleria Vittorio Emanuele II where an international clientele fought over his handbags and trunks, shoes and unique accessories in leather, crystal, and silver. His purpose was very clear: "To fill the gap in the market left by items which have had a brief moment of use but which are then no longer wanted, creating instead objects that are stylish, and stay that way, without going out of fashion in a season." Almost a century later, his niece, Miuccia Prada Bianchi inherited her grandfather's ideas and success. She is the former dutiful daughter of the *haute bourgeoisie*, a former revolutionary of 1968, and lover of the theater and mime. She enrolled at the Scuola del Piccolo Teatro and as a member of the UDI (Italian women's union) of the Communist Party. She was 20 when she was thrown into running the family business in 1978, along with her business partner and husband Patrizio Bertelli. She has transformed it into an international group in the luxury goods sector in competition with labels such as Louis Vuitton, Chanel, Hermès, and Gucci. A company with a very substantial industrial element, at the end of 1998 Prada – which is made up of 8 manufacturing bases with 1,200 employees, and has on-going partnerships with more than 300 Italian factories – has 60 Prada stores, 17 franchises (in countries where sales through a local company are obligatory), and 118 outlets in department stores, mostly in Japan and the USA, with total sales of 1.15 billion lire. Each step on the ascent to the top ranks of international fashion has been led by the carefully considered creative intuition of Miuccia and the aggressive business and communications strategy of Patrizio Bertelli. The early 1980s saw the invention of the famous bags and rucksacks in Pocono, a Prada-patented nylon with a silk effect, and of the Prada logo of the inverted metal triangle (inspired by the locks on Mario Prada's trunks), which immediately became cult items. In 1983 Prada's first shoe collection was launched, and in 1989 came the great leap into women's fashion. The most spectacularly hedonistic and consumerist decade of the century was still ongoing, but the young Milanese political sciences graduate, a stranger to the obscure world of fashion designers, began moving in a completely different fashion direction. Quickly labelled as "minimalism," Prada's fashion was in fact a conceptual elaboration, extracted from the aesthetic disorder of our times and completely unselfconscious. Prada *is* Miuccia: the shy, young middle-class girl who chose New York as her stage. She went out and about with bare legs even at 10 degrees below zero, or wore woolen socks with sandals; she liked to wear a long chiffon skirt over another in course tweed, and she invented the parka. Only after having gained recognition in the USA and with the British press did Prada and Bertelli take their collections back to the Milanese runways. There, those same Italian journalists who, before the move to America, had left empty rows at the shows on Via Melzi d'Eril, were now left outside the gates of the new base on Via Spartaco. A scandal broke out in the press, and accusations of censorship were rife, but once peace had been made, the name of Prada became popular well beyond the world of fashion and the runway shows. The Prada name also gained profile as the couple, who already had a mutual passion for contemporary art, turned from being mere collectors to patrons of the arts. Their first exhibition was held in 1993, showing work by Eliseo Mattiacci and Nino Franchina. In 1995 the Foundazione Prada was founded, a Milanese exhibition space which showed the work of Anish Kapoor, Michael Heizer, Louise Bourgeois, Dan Flavin, Laurie Anderson, Sam Taylor Wood, and Mariko Mori. In 1997, Patrizio Bertelli, an expert sailor, decided to sponsor and enter the 2000 America's Cup in New Zealand. This choice offered publicity for the new Prada Sport range, for which a research lab was set up to investigate the design and behaviour of new materials. This publicity also reflected positively on the other Prada lines, Prada Donna, and Prada Uomo (established in 1994), and on the Miu Miu line (1993). In June 1998 there was another coup-de-théatre when Prada became the primary shareholder in Gucci, with 9.5% of their capital. Bertelli assured the management of the Florentine group that this was not a hostile bid, but rather that he had in mind a fusion of the two organizations, resulting in the birth of an Italian luxury goods giant. In January 1999 however, French giants LVMH (Louis Vuitton Moët Hennessy) raised its stake in Gucci to 34.4%, and Prada sold its shares to Bernard Arnault, raising an intake in cash of 300 billion lire in a six-month period. A few months later this money was invested in the increasing international development of the brand, first with the acquisition of a majority of shares in Helmut Lang, then the taking over of De Rigo (glasses manufacturer) and a smaller acquisition of shares in Church's, the English shoemakers. Another great coup came with the purchase of Jil Sander (through 75% of ordinary shares, and 15% of those floated on the Stock Exchange). Eventually Prada became the majority shareholder in Church's, and signed an agreement with Bernard Arnault's company Lunch for possession of the Fendi label.

(*Maria Vittoria Carloni*)

❑ 2000, July. Joint venture with LVMH, establishing LVP Holding BV in order to acquire 51% of Fendi.
❑ 2000, October. 100% acquisition of Azzedine Alaïa.
❑ 2000. Début of the Prada Eyewear and Prada Beauty collections.
❑ 2000. Consolidated sales equal 3,177 billion lire, an increase of 56.5% on 1999. Gross profit margins increased by 49.8% to 1,908 billions but net profits fell to 184 billion lire. However this figure was influenced by the surplus value resulting from the sale of the Gucci shares to LVMH, net profits from which would have amounted to 134 billions. Debt levels remained high, not due to mismanagement, but rather due to the multiple acquisitions made in 1999 and 2000: Church's, Helmut Lang, Jil Sander, Fendi (joint venture with LVMH), and Azzedine Alaïa.
Significantly, the relationship between net debt and net assets for the group has improved from a discrepancy of 2.88 in 1999, to 1.61 in 2000, thanks to the increase in capital assets of Prada Holding to a value of 260 million euros. In particular, the Prada label enjoyed 2,301 billion lire's worth of business (an

increase of 31.4%), while Miu Miu made 246 billions (an increase of 39%). This created a total of 2,547 billion lire, an increase of 32.1% with net profits for the two brands of 384 billions (an increase of 12%).

❑ 2000. The balance sheets for Jil Sander, sales of which represent 10% of total turnover, show sales of 134.8 million euros. The label has a particularly strong presence in Germany and the USA. In Italy the company has a showroom in Piazza Castello.

❑ 2001, February. Acquisition of 70% of Santacroce.

❑ 2001, April. Acquisition of 51% of Car Shoe, a brand conceived and patented in 1962 by the Lombard craftsman Gianni Mostile, a maker of shoes for car enthusiasts. The value of this deal is not known.

❑ 2001, July. Acquisition of 70% of Genny. Rumours put costs at between 100 and 120 billion lire, a sum from which the substantial debt should be subtracted.

❑ 2001, November. Agreement with LVMH for the sale of 50% of Prada Group's investment in LVP Holding BV (which holds the shares in Fendi owned by LVMH and Prada) for an estimated value of 295 million euros (to be paid in 5 stages), a higher figure than the 275 millions spent on the 1999 acquisition. Prada and LVMH had bought 51% of Fendi in October 1999, paying 425 million dollars. This arrangement helped bring down the debts of the Italian group.

❑ 2001, December. Opening in New York of the first Prada flagship store, Studio OMA, designed by Rem Koolhaas.

❑ 2001. The much awaiting floatation on the Milan Stock Exchange is postponed due to an unfavorable economic climate. The large number of acquisitions made by Prada in previous years (Helmut Lang, Jil Sander, Church's, Byblos, Genny, and 51% of Fendi with LVMH), led to severe debt levels for the group, which as a result considered the issuing of a bond.

❑ 2001, December. Bond increased by 700 million euros in favor of Prada. Investor demand has been five times greater than availability. Of the 700 millions, 300 will be used to increase capital, and 400 will be put towards paying off debts.

❑ 2002, March. First Prada store opened in Moscow in Tretyakov Passage in the city center. The Group's partner in Russia is Mercury Distribution.

❑ 2002, June. Joint venture with the Puig Group for the production and distribution of Prada branded perfumes and cosmetics. With the acquisition of the remaining 25% of Jil Sander, Prada now has total control of the German label.

❑ 2002, August. Prada bought up the remaining 24.29% of Genny Spa. The Genny and Byblos labels, including Ozium, produce high-end *prêt-à-porter* as well as having licenses for the production of leatherwear, eye-glasses, and perfumes.

❑ 2002, September. Fabio Zambernardi was appointed Design Director of clothing, shoes and accessories for both Prada and Miu Miu.

❑ 2002. Launch of the limited edition sports watch, GTS Chrono-Automatic IWC for Prada.

❑ 2002. There were at total of 160 Prada and Miu Miu outlets. The group made 1.57 billion euros, compared to 1.62 in 2001. The geographical distribution of the business remained unchanged: 26% in Italy, 25% the rest of Europe, 23% North America and 26% Japan and the Asian Pacific. The historic labels of Prada and Miu Miu contributed 83% to turnover. Net profits equaled 27 million euros.

❑ 2003, January. Opening of the Miu Miu boutique in the Shibuya district of Tokyo.

❑ 2003, March. Prada and Avante-Garde Optics (Luxottica Group) put the finishing touches to an agreement for the distribution of Prada glasses in the USA, Canada, and Puerto Rico.

❑ 2003, March. Bertelli announced the Group's annual plan. Investments would be decreased from 130 million euros in 2002 to 100 millions in 2003, and concentrated on the re-launch of the younger brands. In 2002 debts were reduced by more than a billion to 770 million euros.

❑ 2003. Opening of the new flagship store in Tokyo, in the Ginza district, making three in all in Japan. To mark the occasion, Prada produced a limited edition line of 2,000 bags aimed exclusively at the Japanese market.

❑ 2003, June. Finalizing of an agreement between Prada and Aedes which would lead to the establishment of Real Estate International. The latter acquired Prada's real estate assets for an estimated value of around 100 million euros. The joint venture (80% Aedes and 20% Prada) aimed to develop Prada's estates for housing, offices, shops, and play areas.

❑ 2003, June. Opening of the new Prada Epicentro in Tokyo, designed by architects Herzog and de Meuron.

❑ 2003, July. Agreement for a 10-year license with the Luxottica Group, world leader in the eyewear sector, for the production and distribution of glasses and sunglasses with the Prada and Miu Miu labels. The agreement included the acquisition by Luxottica of all of the producers and distributors of glasses wholly owned by Prada, for a total value of 26.5 million euros.

❑ 2003, October. Three of the Prada group labels reach the top five in American weekly DNR's top ten menswear collections for Spring-Summer 2004. The Prada label tops the list, fourth is Helmut Lang, and fifth, Jil Sander.

❑ 2003, November. The group sold 55% of Church's to private equity investors Equinox. The remaining 45% continues to be held by Prada.

❑ 2003, December. Opening of the seventh store in the People's Republic of China, the first in the south of the country, in Guangzhou. The shop is located in the prestigious "Pearl" shopping center on Huanshi Road. It is two floors high and has a total floor space of 380 square metres.

❑ 2004, February. The new store for women's leatherwear, shoes, and accessories opened in Milan on Via della Spiga. The boutique has four windows on Via della Spiga, and two on Via S. Andrea. It replaced the much smaller shop which had been a few hundred meters away.

❑ 2004, June. At the New York Public Library, Miuccia Prada was named by the International Award of the Council of Fashion Designers of America, as best foreign designer of the year, by a jury made up of 450 stylists, designers and other members of the American fashion industry.

❑ 2004, July. Another "Epicentro" was opened, this time in Los Angeles, designed by Rem Koolhaas and Ole Scheeren. The shop is on Rodeo Drive, Beverley Hills. It is on three floors and has a floor space of 2,200 square meters, of which 1,400 are retail space. This follows the opening of the famous Epicentro Prada in Aoyama, Tokyo, in June 2003, and another on New York's Broadway in December 2001. Two new stores, one Prada and one Miu Miu, were also opened in Taipei, at the Taipei 101 shopping center. This brings the total number of Prada and Miu Miu stores in China (including Hong Kong and Taiwan) to 33, with 26 Prada and 7 Miu Miu outlets.

❑ 2004, October. Prada gained complete control of the Helmut Lang Group. The Prada Group had originally acquired 51% of Helmut Lang in August 1999, and now bought the remaining 49%. Helmut Lang himself continued to have a role in the company as Creative Director.

❑ 2004, November. The Prada Group announced a new organizational structure. Carlo Mazzi was co-opted onto the administrative board, Donatello Galli was made Director of Administration and Finance of the Prada Group, and Tomaso Galli, already Corporate Communications Manager for the Gucci Group, took on the role of Director of Communications and External Relations for the Prada Group as a whole.

❑ 2004, December. Overall turnover of 1.46 billion euros. The 2004 assessment was based on a period of 13 months, from 1 January 2004 – 31 January 2005. For the 12-month period comparable to the previous year, sales had increased by more than 6% on a like-for-like basis. Prada and Miu Miu represented around 85% of total sales. However despite the great success of the Prada and Miu Miu brands, the result has been tempered by losses and by the decrease in value of Jil Sander and Helmut Lang.

❑ 2005, January. The fashion house signed an agreement for the sale of three industrial real estate developments, which were bought jointly by Pirelli & C. Real Estate (25%) and Soros Real Estate Investors (75%).

❑ Helmut Lang, ending the creative directorship of his own label, comments "I would like to thank everyone, particularly my team, and all the Press and customers who have supported the business over the last five years."

❑ 2005, May. The exhibition "Miuccia Prada: Art and Creativity" was held in Shanghai, drawing on a vast collection of creations from 1988 to today.

(*Dario Golizia*)

Pradeau Katherine. French designer. She attended the Studio Berçot in Paris in the early 1990s. After finishing her studies she worked as an assistant for Lolita Lempicka, Philippe Adec, and Sonia Rykiel. She unveiled her debut collection to the French press in 1996, who hailed her as a rising star. She has presented her collections at the Parisian ready-to-wear shows since 2000.

Praline French model. Famous in the 1940s and 1950s, she began modeling during the war. She was launched by Balmain and Dior when they were assistants for Lelong. She died in a car crash just a few years after she was crowned Miss Cinémonde.

Prandoni At the beginning of the 1900s Giovan Battista Rosti took over a small men's tailoring business called Prandoni, that was founded in Milan at the turn of the 19th century. Rosti became famous for his suits, which he made for Giacomo Puccini (who was particularly fond of his overcoats with fur collars), Arturo Toscanini, the aristocracy, the Italian royal family, and the Duke of Bergamo. Rossi married twice. He had two sons, Angelo and Ugo, with his first wife, and two, Gianfranco Carlo and Fortunato, with his second wife. In the 1920s Angelo Rosti, who took charge of the business, counted Guglielmo Marconi and Gabriele D'Annunzio among his customers, though they often had problems settling his bills. By 1925 the business was so successful that their workforce grew from 20 tailors to 200, and from a typical family business it developed into a real company. The Milanese headquarters were in Piazza San Fedele, where the Banca Nazionale del Lavoro is today, and where the comic actor Virgilio Talli's Teatro Manzoni was destroyed by an air raid in August 1943. After the war Prandoni moved to Piazza Belgioioso. They made special individual tailoring dummies for their most important clients. Prandoni also had a branch in Genoa. They also distributed the famous English Yardley cologne. Prandoni's clothes had a particularly military and formal style, with square shoulders and a well-defined waist, especially their dramatic tightly-belted overcoats. The business closed in about 1960.

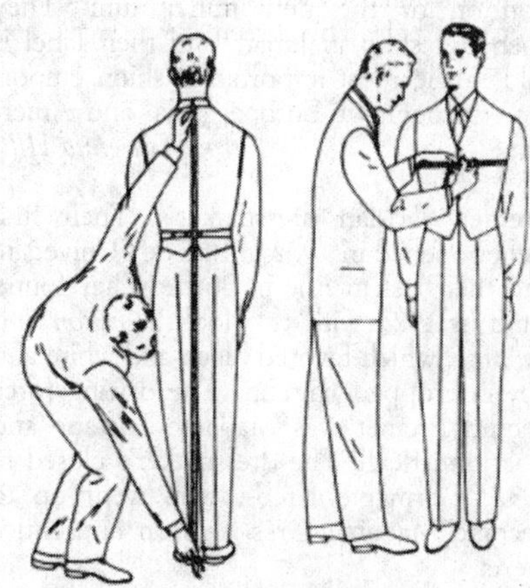

Technical sketches for men's tailoring.

Prato-Expo One of the key international textile fairs for men's, women's, and children's apparel. The first Expo was held in 1979, and there are two per year (at the end of February and in September) in Florence (Fortezza da Basso) where the best manufacturers from the Prato area present their fabrics to about 8,000 representatives from Europe, North America, and the Far East. The fairs are organized by the Consorzio Prato Trade, a division of the Unione Industriale Pratese (Prato Industrial Union), which has 140 carefully selected members from the textile industry. Prato Trade's president is Mario Maselli, and the director is Vincenzo Pagano.

Preen English ready-to-wear label founded in 1996 by Justin Thornton (1969) and Thea Bregazzi (1968), who met aged 18 when they were fashion students. Thornton has a fashion degree from Winchester School of Art and has worked on Helen Storey's collection of recycled clothes. Bregazzi graduated in fashion from the University of Lancashire and then became a stylist working for various magazines. They began by opening a boutique on the Portobello Road where they sold their slightly trashy, slightly Victoriana influenced collection which became an immediate hit. They were soon hailed by the press as pioneers of a post-punk, post-fashion style that heralded the London of the new millennium. They opened a shop in Japan, and their label is sold in the most important fashion emporiums throughout Europe, Asia, and America. (*Virginia Hill*)

Premet Parisian dressmaker's. Their first atelier opened in 1902 in Rue de l'Université and their last in Rue la Boétie. They found fame in 1923 with two looks, *Garçon* and *Gamine*, which favored black-and-white and boyish cropped haircuts. The driving force behind Premet was Madame Lafranc and Charlotte Révil. The dressmaker's closed in 1931. Germaine Krebs, who went on to become Madame Grés, was an apprentice there.

Premiata Footwear business and brand. The Mazza di Montegranaro family have been making classic hand-crafted men's shoes since 1885. Vincenzo Mazza opened a factory in 1946, and personally oversaw production until his son Graziano took over. The company name was changed to Premiata in 1994. A showroom was opened in Milan, a deal made with Magnum of Tokyo to distribute their shoes in Japan, and a collection of women's shoes was launched.

Première Position in a dressmaker's that makes made-to-measure clothes and *haute couture*. A premiére is a sort of interpreter, who translates the designer's sketches into toile samples which she fits to the atelier's house model (another symbolic and constant figure in the dressmaker's world) in order to select the right fabrics and work out the best cut. The premiére is an essential figure. Every good dressmaker's has at least five, each with his or her own specialisation. There are premiéres for suits, cocktail dresses, princess dresses and evening wear. There is also a premiére specialized in pleating and drapery. Men can also be premiéres, usually working on coats and more structured garments. Balenciaga was one of the few designers who could do without premiéres, because he was an excellent cutter and a born tailor.

Premiére Vision Biannual textile fair with a high international profile, which takes place at the Parc des Expositions de Villepinte near Paris. It was founded in 1973 by a group of 15 textile manufacturers from Lyons. Today the fair hosts hundreds of exhibitors from across Europe. At the October 1998 fair there were 833 exhibitors from 14 countries and 41,615 visitors. The fair is popular on an international level because it offers a wide range of high quality fabrics and the opportunity for fashion professionals to observe the latest trends.

Premoli Aldo (1954). Journalist. He was editor of *Vogue Uomo*. After starting out as a cultural contributor to magazines such as *Belfagor* and *Alfabeta*, he crosses over into fashion in 1982 when he started at Condé Nast. He worked on several titles there, becoming editor of *Vogue Pelle* and then *Vogue Uomo* in 1992. He sealed the magazine's reputation as a leader in the world of men's fashion, and created the additional *Vogue Tessuti* supplement which features the worlds main textile manufacturers.

Premonville (de) Myrene (1949). French designer. She has fashion in her blood because of her mother, a house model who often worked for Fath. Her fashion debut was precocious, she was just four when she appeared on the cover of *Elle* with her mother. She started out at Promostyle working as Popi Moreni's assistant, then worked for Fiorucci and Hermès, and set up her own business in partnership with Gilles Dewavrin in 1983. Three years later she closed the business and went on to produce collections under her own label, several of which took art as their inspiration (including Russian Constructivism for Fall-Winter 1991-92). She pays great attention to detail and her clothes are known for their femininity. She was one of the first people to design pants with stirrups. She has been showing her collections in Paris since 1990-91 and she opened two own-brand boutiques there in 1999.

Prénatal Brand of clothing and one of Europe's biggest chain of stores for mothers-to-be and children up to the age of eleven. Founded in 1961, the company is Italian and has its headquarters in Agate Brianza near Milan. The first store opened in 1963, and Prénatal now has branches in 7 countries with a total of 354 sale points that use the same marketing tactics across Europe. Prénatal supports several good causes: it sponsors scientific conferences, surveys, research, and sporting events for children. In 1997 Prénatal was bought by the Artsana-Chicco Group from Grandate near Como: an empire built by the self-made Piero Catelli.

Preppie (Preppy) An English word used to describe an American lifestyle and way of dressing. Preppy teenagers are very neat, and wear sensible fabrics and knitwear in a few well-matched colors. This manner of dressing ended up influencing their lifestyle. The look has not changed since it was typical of Ivy League students at the end of the 1970s. For men: corduroy pants, tweed jackets, Shetland sweaters in Winter, or madras pants and shirts and Indian cloth jackets in the Summer. For women: white blouses, tartan skirts and kilts, tweed dresses and blazers.

Preston John. English designer. He started working on his collection in 1992. He aims to add an element of originality to traditional fashions. He shows in Paris on a regular basis and has spaces both in the French capital and in Hong Kong.

Prêt-à-porter Création Founded in 1957 by Jacques Heim. An association of ready-to-wear dressmakers, which at the time was marginal to the *haute couture* business. The association organized collective fashion shows of the members' collections: Carvin, Grès, Laroche, Griffe, Dessés, Lanvin, Madeleine de Rauch, Maggy Rouff, Nina Ricci, and Heim himself. The initiative ended in 1962.

Prialpas Company producing vulcanized rubber soles. Founded in Sona (Verona), it had a turnover of 31 million euros in 2001. The company has two bases (one in Sona where the management is based, and one in Vigevano). They produce soles for 500,000 pairs of shoes every day, exporting to over 40 countries. The company had a new lease of life in 1968, a time of great change in fashion and culture, when it started producing vulcanized rubber shoe accessories, as well as pre-printed soles, in response to the new demands of the changing market. The president Giuseppe Parolini – with solid experience from his time as an Economics lecturer at the University of Verona – and his team are driving the company towards becoming the most innovative and creative rubber sole manufacturer in the world, rapidly responded to customer needs thanks to an aggressive growth strategy. Their ability to bring together technology and fashion can be seen in their new product ranges Tema, Casual, and Binamico, which are held in high regard in the medical-scientific field. (*Maria Vittoria Alfonsi*)

Primigi Italian brand of footwear. Founded in 1960, the brand is produced by Imac Spa Divisione Igi, which has been a leading children's shoe manufacturer for over 30 years. Other ranges produced by the group include Primigino, Primigi Più, Easy Op Confetti, and Igi. They also produce Action Man and Kappa sports shoes under license. They are distributed in 1,400 points of sale in Italy and 800 in Europe and the rest of the world. The company policy focuses on researching new shapes and on the quality of the raw materials, from the softest leather to vulcanized cloth. They have expanded the brand to include a range for teenagers.

Prince Albert Coat A long frock coat for men, usually black or grey, with pointed or rounded lapels, that is a precursor of the morning coat. Other variations on the design include redingotes.

Prince of Wales Fabric design. It became famous, and a must for suits in every fashionable man's wardrobe, after being worn by Edward, Prince of Wales, the future King Edward VIII of England, who abdicated so that he could marry the divorcee Wallis Simpson. It is made from Saxony, a woolen fabric that takes its name from the region where its raw materials come from. The Batavian weave (a diagonal design that regulates the interweaving of the weft and the warp) creates a soft reversible fabric with large squares containing alternating small check and pied-de- poule motifs. The Duke of Windsor made the fabric and pattern popular, but Prince of Wales fabric was already used from the time of Edward VII to make the suits of the heirs to the English throne, hence its name.

Princesse A very stylized range of women's clothes using vertical front and back seams to follow the body's shape without restricting it, thereby creating a natural silhouette. The style was launched in 1863 by Charles Frédéric Worth and revolutionised women's dress. His first designs were for the Empress Eugènie and Princess Alexandra of Wales. They were flowing and comfortable, without defined waists, which made them very different from the women's dresses of the time, which made use of corsets and full skirts. The Princesse style was taken up again at the beginning of the 20th century and in the 1930s. The designs always had a fitted bodice with several vertical panels flaring out from below the bust.

Principe Clothing store opened in Via Strozzi, Florence in 1935 by the Morandini family, and named in honor of Prince Umberto of Savoy. Specialized in men's tailoring, selling shirts, ties, and socks. In the 1950s the shop started selling garments imported from England. In 1967 it was renovated and started selling women's and children's clothing as well. It has a very successful branch in Forte dei Marmi.

Pringle of Scotland Scottish brand of luxury knitwear, in cashmere, lambswool, and Shetland wool, made by a company founded by Robert Pringle in 1815. It is now part of the Dawson International Group. In the 1950s Pringle's diamond-patterned twin-sets became a status symbol.

❑ 2000. Pringle was taken over by S.C. Fang & Sons, a leading knitwear manufacturer based in Hong Kong. It is run by chief executive Kim Winser, who was the first woman on the board of directors at UK retailer Marks & Spencer.
❑ 2001. Stuart Stockdale was appointed the new creative director. His collections have always maintained a strong link to the label's Scottish heritage whilst also introducing significant new designs that have transformed the fine knitwear label into an important name in luxury goods.
❑ 2005. The label founded by Robert Pringle celebrated its 190th birthday with 19 limited edition items, one for each of its decades.
❑ 2005, May. It was announced that Stockdale would quit as creative director.
❑ 2005, July. Claire Waight Keller is the new creative director. She will be in charge of menswear, womenswear, and accessories collections for the fall-Winter 2006 line. Her experience involves Calvin Klein, Ralph Lauren, and Gucci, alongisde Tom Ford.

Prini Textile company founded by Dante Prini in 1936. Prini started off producing damask ties first in rayon and then in synthetic materials, with a weaving mill opened in Villa Guardia near Como in 1956. In the early 1970s the business left Villa Guardia and based itself at a new mill in Lucino which also had printing facilities. In the 1980s the production was broken down into divisions: Kitex and Kiseta, opened in 1980, both dealt with the production of printed damask fabrics for ties, Kitex for synthetic fabrics, and Kiseta for silk. Lineaseta (1986) dealt only with natural fibers, making products aimed at the higher end of the market in Italy and abroad. The women's clothing division was divided into two sections: Kicomo (1981), producing medium-high quality items in synthetic fibers, and Kimoda (1987) aimed at the lower end of the market. In the 1990s the company's financial situation forced the board to "give Arca Marchant Spa the task of restructuring the company's debt with the banking system." But it was not enough, and the business closed. (*Pierangelo Mastantuono*)

Printemps Paris department store. Created in 1865 from the experience of Jules Jaluzot (former head of department with the Bon Marché chain) in partnership with Jean-Alfred Duclos. Despite being founded after its direct competitors Bon Marché and Galéries Lafayette, Printemps managed to catch up with them. After a fire in 1892, a bigger and better equipped store was created. At the beginning of the 1900s a furniture department was opened. Today the group also controls La Redoute, a mail-order clothes catalogue.

Prisunic Chain of French department stores founded by the Printemps group in 1931 following a revolutionary principle: to sell all items at a price of 10 francs or less. Obviously over the years the price limit has increased, but it has always remained at a low-medium level without sacrificing quality.

Prochownick Italian tie company. In 1880 Hermann Prochownick arrived in Milan from Leipzig to start producing ties, scarves, and foulards in silk and wool. In the 1930s his sons Carlo and Luigi italianised their surname to become Procovio (but they kept the original company name). They expanded the business and start exporting abroad. The factory is in Via Bandello in Milan. The company has 65 employees and about 1,700 clients and 70% of their Prochownick label products are destined for export. They do not manufacture for third parties.

Proietti Elisabetta (Betty) (1962). Italian designer and businesswoman. Born in Umbria, she returned there after many years of business in Milan and Rome, because it is there in her native hills that she can best express her creativity. In 1985 she graduated from the Academy of Costume and Fashion in Rome, where her thesis is still on display. From 1985 to 1988 she completed her training with Miguel Cruz, soon becoming his assistant and assimilating her teacher's clean shapes, linear solutions, and passion for knitwear. In 1988 and 1989 she worked as an assistant designer on Lancetti's *haute couture* and ready-to-wear collections. From 1988 to 2000 she designed the Gruppo Parah Spa's swimwear and clothing collections. In 1989 she founded Snc, a design consultancy serving the clothing industry. She has been a lecturer in design and fashion at the Academy of Costume and Fashion in Rome since 1995, where she coordinates and assists young designers for their Final shows. She also works for Madis and other labels. In 2002 she took up the challenge of setting up her own label, producing in Umbria a "total look" knitwear collection comprising twenty pieces that transfer the concept of fabric clothing to knitwear, including oversize cardigans cut like trench coats, pleated skirts with fringed belts, shawl sweaters, and low-waisted pinstripe pants with knitted fabric turn-ups.

(*Maria Vittoria Alfonsi*)

Sketch by Betty Proietti.

Projetti Milanese milliner, in business from between the wars until the beginning of the 1960s. She had an atelier in Via Montenapoleone, on the corner with Via Manzoni, in the same building as Rina Modelli (real name Enrichetta Pedrini), the most famous Italian pattern maker of the time, and Giuliano Fratti, the "king of crazy jewelry." Two generations of rich Milanese folk fought over her hats. The less wealthy bled themselves dry in order to possess them, and bought them by paying for them in instalments. Maria Pezzi remembers her like this: "Rather plain, charming and sexy. Not fat like most of the dressmakers and milliners who spent a good part of their lives sitting down. She was the lover of a very sporty engineer who loved mountains and climbing and would drag the very reluctant Projetti along with him: she would return three kilos lighter after each trip. Her energy and vitality were overwhelming and she was sincere to the point of being offensive. She would sometimes refuse royal clients and wives of dignitaries with the sharp retort 'you do not have the right face for my designs'. However she was in fact capable of making a hat that would suit even the devil: she would place it on the client's head, and with an artist's touch she would manipulate the felt, adjust the veil, and add a feather or two, framing their face to perfection."

Promod Distributor of women's clothing in Europe, founded by Francis Charles Pollet in 1975. It has an average annual turnover of 260 million euros, and 260 of its own stores in 8 European countries.

Promostyl International fashion observatory with offices in Paris, London, New York, and Tokyo. For more than 25 years Promostyl has been predicting changes and trends and helping businesses profit from such changes through its reports and tools like its Trend Books. Promostyl's studies are conducted on the basis of analyses which are then transformed into research and development in the textile and clothing fields.

Prontisti In fashion, the term has always been used to refer to those who produce clothing at a fairly fast rate, without following the classic seasonal programme. A term reserved for small businesses, whose size has allowed them to react quickly to current trends, setting themselves against bigger companies that work to longer timescales and plans, and often produce for third parties. In the light of the current upheaval of certain aspects of the market and the increasing speed of the turnover of fashions, even big business are investing in the the ability to quickly catch on to trends and include them in their production.

Pronuptia Brand belonging to one of the most important French producers of ready-to-wear bridal wear. Created by Henri Micmacher and distributed all over the world through a franchising operation. After a boom in the 1960s and 1970s, the brand had a moment of crisis caused by the diminishing number of marriages that affected the whole sector, but the intervention of a big financial group in 1986 meant that it soon overcame this. Henri Micmacher's wife, who initially designed the first pieces herself, now makes use of external collaborators, including Jean Paul Gaultier, Azzedine Alaia, and Thierry Mugler at the end of the 1980s. Pronuptia's signature style however remains romantic, with hints of retro.

Prouvost Jean (1885-1978). French textile manufacturer and publisher. He formed the first French textile group and the first world wool group by gradually taking over French and overseas competitors, managing brands like Stemm, Rodier, Lesur, and Les Laines du Pingouin. In 1954 he had a share in two ready-to-wear lines: Jacques Fath Université and Givenchy Université. Between 1924 and 1930 he acquired and successfully relaunched the newspapers *Paris-Midi* and *Paris-Soir*. He then founded the magazines *Marie Claire* (1937), *Paris-Match* (1949) and *Télé 7 Jours* (1956).

Provenzale (Provençal) Cotton fabric with a dark blue, red, brown, or black background and a white or colored floral print. The women of Provence wore dresses, skirts, and blouses made with this fabric.

Prusac Lola (1893-1985). French dressmaker born in Belgium. She was called Leontine, but chose Lola as her working name. She set up on her own in Paris in

Sketches, designs, for hats (from *Fili Moda*, Summer 1941).

1937, after being discovered by Hermès. Her creativity played on a taste for high-quality craftsmanship, fabrics, jewelry, and hand-embroidery, fuelled by research trips to India, Greece, and Egypt. She worked up to the age of 87. (*Fiorella Marino*)

Psychedelia (in England). Cultural, existential and spontaneous fashion movement. If we wanted to set a date to commemorate the rift between English and American psychedelia, April 1967 would be suitable, when Paul McCartney was returning to England after a visit to Haight Ashbury. *Sgt Pepper* had been finished on the 3rd of that month. After that Paul left and gave a brilliant technicolor account of his trip to San Francisco, talking of a free community living in perfect harmony. George Harrison went there in August and it was more or less like escaping from a nightmare. Even if the Beatles neither invented psychedelia or brought it to Great Britain, they certainly guaranteed its diffusion, particularly in visual terms. It's useful to remember that if in America psychedelia had above all folk, beatnik, and bohemian origins, in England it derived directly from Mod and Pop Art. In any case English psychedelia had more stylistic links with the New York scene where Pop Art reigned supreme; Warhol can be defined as psychedelic but only in an alternative, negative, and lunar sense, and fashion designers like Tiger Morse and Betsey Johnson were the equivalent of John Bates and Mary Quant in terms of modernism. It's simply that suddenly psychedelia and psychedelic seemed the right terms to define what was going on in Swinging London in 1966 and 1967. The New Renaissance was signalled by events like the 14 Hour Technicolor Dream (at Alexander Palace, the venue for the best music of the time), and the opening of clubs like UFO in Tottenham Court Road, a sounding board and home to experimental bands like the Third Ear Band, Soft Machine, and Pink Floyd. The opening of boutiques like Granny Takes a Trip, Mr. Freedom and Biba in London, and Betsey Johnson's Paraphernalia in New York was very important, in as much as they were autonomous bastions of taste reflecting or predicting the mood coming from the street. The Beatles too opened their own proto-mega-psychedelic store called Apple, with its own associated record label. Jimi Hendrix was the icon for all, if there ever was one. Underground magazines were set up, like *International Times* and the Australian Richard Neville's *OZ* with its brilliant graphics by John Goodchild. 1966 heralded the end of Flashy Pop and Mod Art, after which there was a retroactive trend stylistically speaking, as if Pop Art had been bewitched by Art Deco, then Art Nouveau and finally Victoriana. In terms of their style, psychedelic clothes were the expression of what John Bates designed for the TV series *The Avengers* (iridescent space-age fabrics, modernist lines, cut-aways), the colors were the acidic tones of screen prints, and access to second-hand and vintage clothes paved the way to the concept of pastiche uniforms, grandad spectacles, Victorian walking boots and much more, all in a sea of crushed velvet, the material that best connoted the new Chelsea dandies from 1966 to 1969. (*Maurizio Vetrugno*)

Psychedelia (in the United States). It's impossible to talk about psychedelia in the USA without going into the specifics of psychotropic substances, and its pointless to do so without underlining the huge mass distribution of psychoactive agents that until then had been available only to scientific researchers, shamans, and post-metaphysical philosophers. The fragmentation of reality, the ecstatic acceleration or standstill of time, and the brilliant vibration of colors remain the most easily translatable elements of this synethesia which is the mark of the psychedelic experience. Timothy Leary, already with a doctorate in psychology, found a way to get himself thrown out of Harvard for supplying his students with the drug psilocybin along with questionnaires about it. Ken Kesey, with his Merry Pranksters (amongst them the embryo of the future Grateful Dead), shook up the California scene by going round in an old multicolored bus and making converts. An account of that period can be found in *The Electric Kool-Aid Acid Test* by Tom Wolfe, where amongst other things he describes the meeting between Kesey, Ginsberg, and Sonny Barger, the leader of the Hell's Angels. It was only on 6 October 1966 that the production and consumption of LSD was made illegal.

It's a typical case of "too little too late." As the happenings multiplied (such as the memorable Human Be, held at the Fillmore Auditorium in San Francisco from 1963 to 1966) so did the admissions to rehabilitation clinics. In the meantime new venues were being opened. In San Francisco the Matrix and the Avalon Ballroom had the idea of using "psychedelic" posters designed by Rich Griffin to advertise their concerts, and on the scene Grace Slick and Janis Joplin aroused interest as style icons as well as performers. In Los Angeles venues like Ciro's and The Trip hosted groups like The Byrds, the very mysterious Love, and Jim Morrison's Doors. In New York there was Steve Paul and the Dom's Scene, an extension at the time of Warhol's Factory. It's worth underlining the importance of the use of lights in shows, along with projections (films, slides, gelatine) and strobe lights. Warhol designed the projections for the Velvet Underground's *Plastic Inevitable Show*, while the Grateful Dead could count on the distinguished Augustus Stanley Owsley III, who was also responsible for a very impressive sound system. For the record, the Blues Magoos were the first to have explicitly used the word psychedelic in the title of their album in 1966, and they boasted top notch collaborators: Diana Dew designed clothes for them that lit up on stage; Christopher Pluck, a famous Vidal Sassoon hairdresser, created the Magoo cut; and Bruno Contenotte was responsible for the magic of their light shows, making use of his experience gained from working for Walt Disney. Similarly Janis Joplin worked with Linda Gravenites to create her multicolored and multi-layered outfits. The fabrics usually had patterns that owe as much to Kashmir paisley as to Emilio Pucci.

Psychobilly Youthful and spontaneous fashion movement. Like all styles following the punk explosion of 1976, the psychobilly movement was a reformation of existing trends, a cocktail of previous fashion codes. Aspects typical of the punk look, such as the unrestricted combination of clothes, were applied to 1950s rockabilly fashions typical of the look which went with the early sounds of Sun Records by Sam Phillips. To this mix was added a psychotic interpretation of the visual and musical detritus of the earlier forms of rock: surf rock, and its variant "hot rod," psychedelia, and the punk of garage bands of the 1960s. All this resulted in a mutant form of rockabilly known as psychobilly. Musically speaking, this new aesthetic can be attributed to (among others) Poison Ivy Rosarch and Lux Interior of The Cramps. In the early 1980s The Cramps released a handful of very popular singles and an album *Songs the Lord taught us* (1980). Characteristic hairdos would come in a range of gravity-defying styles and lurid colors, particular favorites being pink, green, and electric blue. The designs that appeared on leather jackets and certain accessories were inspired by the Mississippi Wetlands, and reflected in the New Orleans look sported by Prince, La La, and Dr John. As well as these voodoo influences, further inspiration came from the vast repertory of Exotica, from Yma Sumac to Les Baxter.

(*Maurizio Vetrugno*)

Pucci Emilio (1914-1992). Italian designer. He invented a unique style, recognizable for its printed textiles (first stylized, then geometric), and for his incredible use of color, which brought together shades in unforeseen combinations. His prints were designed to be shown off at their best when seen in motion on Pucci's dynamically cut dresses. Pucci was born in Naples but his father, the Marquis Emilio Pucci di Barsento, was of Russian extraction. After studying social sciences at the University of Athens in Georgia, and then in Portland, Oregon, he signed up as an officer in the Italian Air Force in 1938. Having continued his studies with a degree in political sciences at Florence University, he fought courageously in World War II. His introduction to fashion came about quite by chance in 1947 amidst the snow of Zermatt, where he was training with the Olympic ski team. Toni Frissel, a well-known photographer for *Harper's Bazaar*, immortalized Pucci in a shot with a female friend for whom he had improvised a ski outfit. A year later Pucci's first collection of sportswear appeared on the cover of the same magazine. His outfits were bought up immediately by the department store Lord and Taylor, and were given the label "Emilio" in the USA. The American market

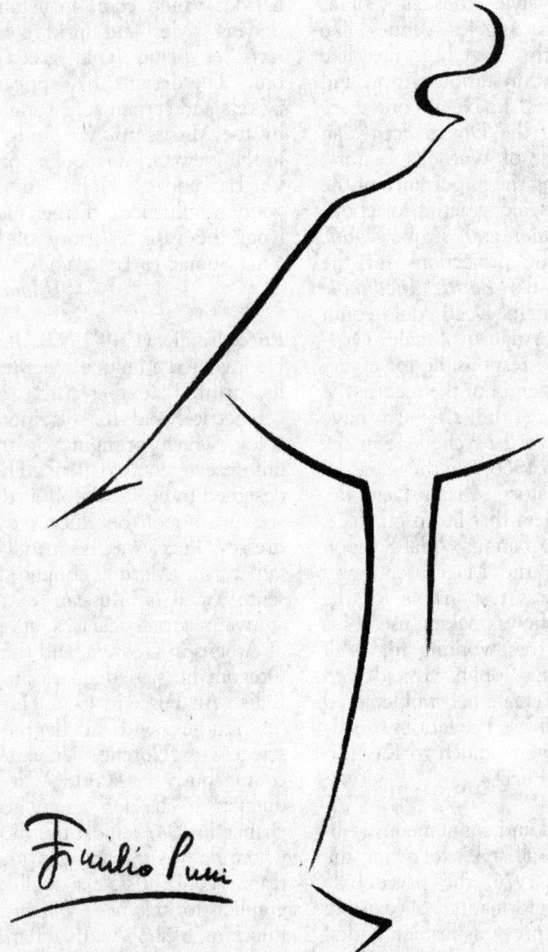

Sketch by Emilio Pucci.

welcomed Pucci's comfortable and practical fashion. In 1949, he launched his first beachwear collection in Capri, based on black-and-white prints created by Guido Ravasi of Como. So great was the collection's success that in 1950 Pucci decided to open a boutique on the Canzone del Mare at Marina Piccola. His clothes were cut and assembled in the family home in Florence, where he had set up a small workshop in order to cope with the influx of requests. In 1951 his designs appeared in his first Italian runway show, organized by Giovanni Battista Giorgini at Villa Torrigiani, on Via Serragli, Florence. The show was attended by America's most important buyers. From then on, Pucci would be present at every Florentine fashion show until 1967, the year in which he began to show in his own building on Via dei Pucci. In 1953, his palette of colors became suddenly more daring, printed on shirts, pants, scarves, and dresses in jersey, silk, and synthetic fibers. This range was big news on the international fashion stage, and won Pucci the 1954 Neiman Marcus Fashion Oscar for best designer of the year. Among his most famous were his Sicilian collection of 1956, inspired by the Sienese Palio in 1956, and his Botticelli collection of 1959. From the very beginning of his fashion career, Pucci was interested in experimenting with materials. In 1953, with Legler, he produced synthetic velvets for sports pants, and in the same year he worked with cotton producers Valle Susa to create printed *wally pliss.* In 1954 Pucci made famous a new jersey for the production of light-weight, crease-proof clothing. This was produced by Mabu of Solbiate and Boselli of Como, and made out of very fine silk organzine. In 1960 he patented a light, comfortable elastic fabric called *emilioform* composed of Helanca synthetic and shantung silk. From this Pucci produced his Viva ski-pants and his famous outer-space style Capsule. In 1962, having become increasingly influenced by the Orient, he produced his first *haute couture* collection. This was notable for its rich fabrics and the workmanship of the embroidery, which included Swarovski crystals attached by hand to the palazzo pants which were already so much in vogue by that time. In 1966 the first Pucci fragrance, *Vivara* was launched, followed by *Miss Zadig* in 1974 and *Pucci* in 1977. Meanwhile in 1968 he had become involved in the creation of menswear, having signed an agreement with Ermenegildo Zegna. Having invented the "total look" ahead of time, Pucci had signed licenses on all sorts of accessories and other items; from lingerie for Formit, to porcelain with Rosenthal; from rugs for Dandolo Argentini to Parker pens. In 1971 he even designed the emblem for NASA's Apollo 25 space mission. His clothes were sold in no fewer than 51 countries. In 1980, Pucci's daughter Laudomia joined his design team, and on the death of her father, she took over the business.

❑ Early 2000. The movie *Isn't She Great?* is released in which the famous American writer Jacqueline Susann, played by Bette Midler, is such a Pucci fanatic that she even has "Emilio" curtains in her pink study. She wears Pucci from head to toe, and even has a dog called Pucci Poo. The fashion world cannot ignore Puccimania. Katell Le Bourhis, adviser to Bernard Arnault and responsible for the dress collection at the Metropolitan Museum, visited the archives at Palazzo Pucci and was struck by the profound influence of "Emilio." In April, Cristina and Laudomia Pucci di Barsento – owners of the *prêt-à-porter* label Emilio Pucci, signed an agreement with LVMH, which acquired 67% of the business. Arnault had listened to Le Bourhis's advice. The Managing Director of LVMH was the young Catherine Vautrin, who had been on the board since 1998. Laudomia Pucci continues to co-ordinate design and brand policy, whilst the production side of the business is incorporated into the Fashion and Leather division of the Arnault Group, chaired by Yves Carcelle.

❑ 2002, April. Christian Lacroix was appointed Artistic Director of Emilio Pucci. Nobody, possibly, other than the "arlésien" with his Mediterranean spirit, could better take on the legacy of the "Prince of Prints." Thanks to Lacroix, the shades and combinations of colors of the fashion of an innovative and gifted artist live on. Pucci's exuberant, optimistic and at the same time highly glamorous vision of life was to be seen both in his ready-to-wear and beachwear collections. (*Maria Vittoria Alfonsi*)

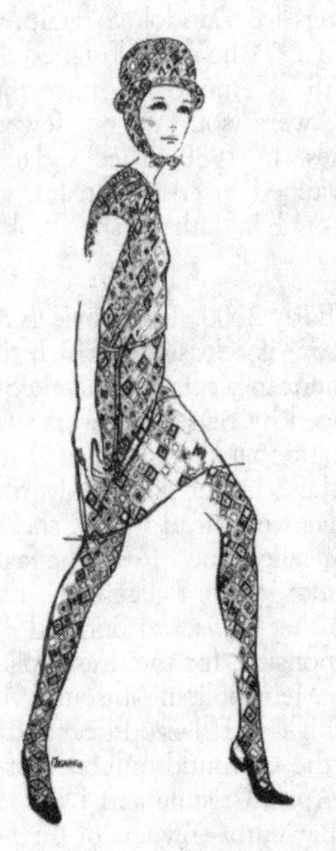

Emilio Pucci, outfit for Braniff, 1965 (from *Emilio Pucci*, Biennial of Florence, Skira, 1996).

Pucci Laudomia (1961). Italian fashion designer and entrepreneur. She took her Baccalauréat in France at 18 years of age, and graduated in Rome in political sciences at 23. She gained experience on a commercial level in major department stores and speciality stores in America and the Far East. For two years she was in charge of *prêt-à-porter* and accessories at Givenchy in Paris. In 1992, after the death of her father Emilio, she became President and Executive Director of Emilio Pucci Srl. After the April 2000 agreement with LVMH, she was made Artistic Director. She entered the world of fashion "by chance," following her extraordinary father who, in her first week working for Emilio Pucci, took her to Atlanta for fashion shows and exhibitions, of which she had been completely "starved." The young graduate loved her new line of work and was soon climbing the career ladder, albeit in an untraditional fashion. (*Maria Vittoria Alfonsi*)

Puck & Hans Dutch ready-to-wear label. Named after the designer and manager of the business, Puck Kroon and Hans Kemink. They began by opening an avant-guarde boutique (selling Westwood and early Gaultier) and soon afterwards launched their own range of clothing, which won them the Fil d'Or in 1987.

Puig Castellò Antonio. Founder in 1914 of the Spanish firm of the same name, specializing in the perfume and cosmetics sectors. Today the company owns the cosmetic lines of Nina Ricci, Carolina Herrera, Payot, and Paco Rabanne, and manages the licenses of the beauty ranges for Comme des Garçons and Hussein Chalayan. Their first product, Milady, was the first ever lipstick to be 100% "made in Spain." Their first big success came however in 1940, when the firm created a "self-sufficient" lavender water – made completely from Spanish essences at a time when there were no imports into the country. *Agua Lavanda Puig*, based on rosemary, lavender, and lemon, found immediate success and sent the company to the top of the market. This resulted two years later in its founder's having to move the factory and headquarters to Travessera de Gràcia, near Barcelona, where the main production center can still be found today. Puig's sons started to get involved in the running of the business, and new business strategies were undertaken as Antonio, Mariano, José Maria, and Enrique became the decision makers. This passing of control to the second generation soon bore fruit, and in the 1960s a new factory opened its gates at the Besos Industrial Park in this Catalan city. After the opening of a wing in the USA, in 1968 it was Paris's turn. Paco Rabanne was incorporated into the Group, while in America Carolina Herrera collaborated with them to produce a fragrance in her name. In 1995 the firm acquired Spanish brand Genesse, and a substantial part of Perfumeria Gal. New production facilities were bought at Vacarisses for the production of beauty products. The year afterwards Puig Beauty and Fashion Group was established, comprising cosmetics and fashion managed by Excom, the executive board run by three members of the family and an external member. In 1998 they took over the perfume and fashion label Nina Ricci, followed by the Spanish label Myrugia in 2000, and in 2001 the remaining part of Perfumeria Gal was acquired. In June 2002 Prada's top management announced a joint venture with Puig for the creation and distribution of perfumes and cosmetics.

Pulitzer Lilly (1932). Designer. Known in the USA for designing and producing a dress to wear around the house which, thanks to its comfort and bright colors, became a sort of domestic uniform for American women in the first half of the 1960s. The dress, known by its wearers as "the Lilly," helped fill the coffers of the business that Pulitzer had founded on Palm Beach in 1959. Soon there were sales points all over the USA, and these remained open until 1984.

Pullover Long-sleeved wool top, with a V-neck in its most classic form.

Puma German shoe and sportswear manufacturer. Worn by Pelé in the 1958 World Cup final, by Boris Becker on the grass courts of Wimbledon, and by Linford Christie when sprinting for Gold in the Olympics. Founded in Herzogenaruach in 1948 by Rudolf Dassler and his brother Adolf as part of a family business which had been going since 1924. Today it is an international company with more than 70 factories, and bases in another 57 countries. The Italian branch was opened in 1997.

❑ 2001. A record year for the German multinational, with a turnover of 598.1 million euros – an increase of 29% on 2000.

❑ Futurenet secured the five-year license for the production and distribution of a new line of casualwear. The company, based in Padua, near Venice, already managed the Puma Black Station brand, for which it produces the Nuala and Platinum ranges. The new line was available for distribution in the Spring in around 200 shops in Europe and the USA.

❑ 2002. For the Spring-Summer 2003 collection a unisex shoe was designed by Neil Barrett. This fashion shoe, made of a mixture of new leather, appliquéd canvas, and aged leather, is presented at Milano Moda Uomo and represented the first stage of what was to be an ongoing partnership.

❑ The year concluded with the launch of the Feline range, aimed at girls of 15 to 20 years old. The collection includes shirts, vest tops, T-shirts, shorts, and tracksuit pants stamped with the number 48, the year of foundation of the German fashion company.

❑ The future looked rosy at the end of 2002. Consolidated sales had reach 909.8 million euros, marking an increase of 52% and pre-tax profits of 124.4 million euros.

❑ 2003, January. Long-term partnership with Schiesser Lifestyle GmbH to produce the underwear line Puma bodywear Man & Woman from Fall-Winter 2003. Puma cosmetics and perfume are produced by Muelhens, eyewear by Licefa, watches by Iom and socks by Dobotex.

❑ Fashion industry Oscar for Puma. The Forum Award is presented annually by the German magazine Textil Wirtshchaft to the fashion houses that have excelled in the clothing sector.

❑ June represented a new phase in the Puma story. Monarchy Enterprises, a Dutch company that has been increasingly involved with Puma since 1996, puts its 40% share of the sports company up for sale. These had an estimated value of 580 million euros.

❑ Le Bonitas of Prato won production rights for underwear and swimwear for the Italian, French and English markets.

❑ The company's dominance of its markets seems to be proved by the sales for the first six months of the year, which jumped to 644 million euros. For the first time in the history of the business, sales of clothing exceeded those of footwear.

(*Pierangelo Mastantuono*)

Punk Spontaneous youth fashion movement. Their older brothers shouted "Make love not war," but at the end of the 1970s, their own motto was "No future." The punk movement was born in England but had soon gripped youth all over the West. The hippy styles of parkas, clogs and flowered skirts were overtaken by a very aggressive look: black, studs, chains, ripped tights, safety pins, and Doc Martins boots. Punk fashion preferred synthetic fibers (vinyl, fake leather, and plastic), and took to the extreme an ideology of dirty, ugly, ripped-up clothes. The great interpreters of punk ideology were groups such as the Sex Pistols and the Clash, whilst from a fashion point of view, Vivienne Westwood and Malcolm McLaren's shop Sex, on the Kings Road in London, was the only place to go. Thirty years later, Westwood's clothes have not changed style, but her prices are those of a couture designer. The remaining Sex Pistols (Sid Vicious died of a drug overdose in the 1980s) regrouped for a new album, provoking a wave of punk nostalgia. Meanwhile in the USA, punk has been kept alive thanks to William Gibson's literary cyberpunk movement – a provocative type of science fiction which has won the hearts and minds of a new generation.

(*Valentina Crepax*)

Pupi Solari Milanese shop, which for more than 30 years has not only sold fashion, but has "made it happen." Stamping ground of those wealthy clients who prefer not to shop at the high-profile boutiques of the individual designers. Pupi Solari (born Genoa, 1927) opened a small childrenswear shop in Milan in 1969. The store, on Via Alpini, sold labels such as Nouveau-Né, Valerie Goad, Chipie, and C.P. Company. Intelligence, business flair, and an innate attractiveness were rewarded, and 10 years later, the shop moved to Piazza Tommaseo and womenswear also became available. Safe classic fashions were soon followed by labels such as Fusco, Jil Sander, and the minimalist outfits of Zoran. The shop expanded to include a tea-room and wedding dress department (Pupi Solari "Il matrimonio"). In 1991 the menswear department opened, stocking Aspesi, Car-Shoe, Piombo, William Lockie, and the in-house range Host-Uomo, co-ordinated by Pupi's son Andrea Host-Ivessich. Since 1985 Pupi Solari has also been available in Genoa, with an outlet on Via Roma.

Puppa Daniela (1947). Architect and designer. Since 1979 she has been responsible for the accessories collections of Gianfranco Ferré, with whom she has been friends since their days as students. She also followed the designer in his years at Dior, where she mostly designed handbags, and the collaboration continued after Ferré left the fashion house. She graduated in 1970, and became an editor at *Casabella* from 1970 to 1976, and at *Modo* from 1977 to 1983. She also designs lamps, vases, and furniture for Cappellini, Alchimia, and Fontana Arte.

Purple Very ancient substance extracted from the secretions of the glands of gastropod molluscs and used to dye fabrics by the Phoenicians. Purple (actually a range of colors from purple to crimson) has always been synonymous with nobility or high ranking dignitaries. For Romans purple was the symbol of the senatorial and equestrian order, and for the Byzantines it was fit only for the king. Today it is the color of the cardinal authorities. The same color is now created using synthetic dyes.

Pustorino Historic menswear and tailor's shop at the Quattro Canti, Palermo, Sicily, specializing in typical "Englishman's fashions." It was opened more than a century ago by Pietro Putorino. The lettering on the old amaranthine sign is in italics. The coat of arms of the House of Savoy indicates that the shop has furnished the royal family. The original interior has remained intact, including Ducrot furniture, frescoed walls, and the wooden panels designed by Ernesto Basile. In the 1920s and 1930s, the inventor of Futurism, Filippo Tommaso Marinetti, asked Pustorino to make him a waistcoat with the outline of his hands drawn at the level of the pockets. This was maybe the only deviation from the rigorously classic ever made by the tailor, whose clients included King George V of England, King Alfonso of Portugal, the Duke of Aosta, the Florios (famous Sicilian entrepreneurs and industrialists), Raimondo Lanza di Trabia, and all of Sicilian aristocracy. Pusterlino's last descendent, Natale, died in 1996, leaving the shop to a favorite pupil, Gaetano Pizzo.

(*Antonella Romano*)

PVC Synthetic material, polyvinylchloride, invented around the 1930s or 1940s from the waste material of industrial processes. It became popular in fashion in the 1960s, a period which saw an explosion in the use of synthetic fabrics. Now used mostly in the production of fake leather for jackets and pants. Applied as a coating onto polyester jersey, 60% of PVC is produced in black, but it also comes in other colors, according to the season.

Pyjamas The term comes from the Hindi pyjama or paijama which literally means leg covering. National costume of the Hindus and Persians. In the 1920s Chanel launched them as elegant garments for the beaches of Biarritz or Baden Baden. Originally they were for nightwear only, used at the end of the 1800s by the English and by travellers to tropical countries. They arrived in Europe after the Great War, and were also worn by women instead of a nightdress. The American divas of the 1930s, from Greta Garbo to Joan Crawford, appeared on screen dressed in flowing satin wide-legged pyjamas: Claudette Colbert sported a more jaunty style in *It Happened One Night.* They came back into fashion in a big way in the 1960s in the form of palazzo pyjamas, created by Irene Galitzine in Rome. These had very wide plain or printed silk or chiffon flared pants, teamed with a long tunic top.

P Zero Pirelli's clothing and accessories label. The tyre manufacturer launched a line of technical sailing shoes using their "P Zero" rubber originally created for Ferrari for the sole. They were so successful that the following year a line of clothing and accessories was launched, with Allegri in charge of outerwear, Brighton Industries for luggage, and Sector for watches. The distribution was entrusted to multi-brand shops, but the opening of some P Zero shops is planned for the future. A children's range is on its way. The overseas markets for the label include France, England, Sweden, and Spain.

(*Silvia Paoli*)

Q

Quant Mary (1934). English designer. Part of the Swinging London scene, she shared with Courrèges the invention of the miniskirt. Born in London, she studied at the Goldsmith College of Art, where she met her future husband Alexander Plunker Greene (1933-1990). Soon after graduating in 1955 she opened her first shop, Bazaar, on the Kings Road with Greene and Archie McNair. Soon after, she started designing and making her own clothes, and found instant fame with her young and timely fashion which captured the spirit of 1960s London. She gave teenagers already rebelling against the wardrobes and habits of their mothers the possibility to dress in a daring and revolutionary way with respect to the bourgeois formality of the previous generation: thigh-skimming skirts, skinny ribs, splashes of color, patterned tights. She also used new materials: PVC for a line of rainwear. In 1961, her success meant the opening of a second shop in London, and two years later she embarked on the US market with Ginger Group. In 1966 she founded her cosmetics company (with its daisy logo) and was awarded an OBE. She designed collections for the American chain J.C. Penney and for the Puritan Group, and under her own brand she produced shoes, bed linen, carpets, wallpaper, and hosiery. From 1968 she rode on a new wave of success, but this died out in the 1970s, and her star as a designer faded. However the Group carrying her name continues to do good business, even away from the spotlight.
(*Renata Molho*)

Quintè Milanese shop selling made-to-measure shoes from the finest leathers. Adolfo Quintè, the founder of the brand, was born in Lodi (Italy) in 1883 and opened his first shop in Milan in 1929. In 1930 came a second shop in Via della Spiga which at that time did not yet feature on the fashion scene. Gabriele D'Annunzio was an admirer, and made this dedication: "To the great Quintè who with his immortal shoes allowed me to adopt Severo Severi's motto *insuetum iter.*" Shortly before the war he opened a shop in Via Dante and an atelier on the second floor of 2 Galleria del Corso. In the 1950s Adolfo's son Bassano joined the business, and his sense for the importance of the world of theater, opera, and cabaret brought collaborations with various companies. Quintè's clients included Frank Sinatra, Maria Callas, Josephine Baker, Wally Toscanini, Gino Cervi, Wanda Osiris, Gino Bramieri, Walter Chiari, and the poet Giuseppe Ungaretti. Quintè can still be found in Milan today, in Corso Venezia.
(*Giuliana Parabiago*)

The Quintè logo.

R

Rabanne Paco (1934). French designer. Born in San Sebastián in Spain. Endowed with an almost magical ability to see into the future, Francisco y Cuervo (his real name), the son of a republican general who was executed by a Francoist firing squad, used pliers instead of needle and thread and metal in place of cloth, creating futuristic fashions that unleashed furious controversies. The year was 1965. From her throne, Chanel launched scandalized cries of dismay: "This is not a couturier, this is a metallurgist." Young Paco preserved his sang-froid and continued with his daring and provocative experiments; in any case his work shook the foundations of the structure of haute couture, unmovable in its stubborn traditions. He engaged in a succession of innovative investigations into the world of materials. He used aluminum, one of his emblematic metals, for a panel-bedecked mini-dress that seemed to foreshadow the Space Age, and which was one of the most widely photographed fashion items of 1968. This was truly the precursor of a revolutionary concept, and Salvador Dalí said of him, in an opinion that sharply differed with Chanel's: "He is Spain's second-greatest genius, after me." Metal, but not only metal: the outfit that he created out of little plastic disks, and worn by Audrey Hepburn in a movie, wound up in the collection of the Metropolitan Museum in New York. He decided to devote his life to fashion after attending, in Paris (where he had arrived as a child, after leaving Barcelona to rejoin his mother, who had been forced to leave Spain as a refugee) the School of Fine Arts with plans to become an architect: a useful point of departure because it was here that he received an education that embraced the latest developments in all the artistic and intellectual disciplines of the period, the late Fifties and early Sixties, a period that was a testing ground for all sorts of different forms of new media of expression. Pop Art, new kinds of music, neon or wire sculpture, and plastic design began to exert their influence upon him. He supported himself during his studies by making accessories for the most important fashion ateliers: and this served him as a ticket into the world of fashion, a subject that was already familiar to him through his mother, chief seamstress for the great Balenciaga. In 1964, he made the leap and went into business for himself, presenting a collection that consecrated his courageous avant-garde approach. His new collection was greeted with admiration but also shock, because the presentation featured black fashion models, who had never before appeared in the history of haute couture. Aside from his beloved aluminum and plastic, he made use of pleated and silvery paper for a new phalanx of metropolitan Barbarellas. With the passing

Metal outfits by Paco Rabanne, 1990-91 (from *Le Costume, la haute couture 1945-1995*, Flammarion).

years, he ushered in other materials: fluorescent leather, metallic jersey and taffeta, outfits made of plexiglas and fiber-optics, and occasionally studded with reflective disks. By this point he was dressing princesses, actresses, and matrons whose names were best known in the stock exchanges of the world, happily decked out as Bond-girls. The Chambre Syndicale could no longer afford to ignore him and, after having forced him to linger in the waiting room for a number of years, finally inducted him with all due honors. The year was 1971. He was even inducted into the *Who's Who*, the prestigious listing of international celebrities, as well as the *Encyclopaedia Britannica*. With the passing years and with technological progress, the shaped and assembled sheets of metal, once rigid and weighty, became increasingly elastic and weightless: this led to the creation of aluminum jersey, which had the look and feel of real. It was the development of hi-tech that allowed incredible virtuoso accomplishments, capable for instance of transforming metals into exquisite pieces of lace. A dream factory that truly created thrilling excitement worthy of the end of the millennium: the restult was an amusing setting in which incredible materials shamelessly enveloped cyberwomen, brave warriors of the New Look. Unleashed fantasy: outfits made of tin, copper, and imitation leather. He knitted furs, and stitched the feathers on a cape with adhesive tape. He happily put together materials with irreverent whimsy: fine lace with plastic, lamé with chrome-plated steel mesh, paper, and tulle. He made wedding dresses that caressed the bride with rectangles of opalescent rhodoid, evening gowns that featured an explosion of extremely thin plastic tubes. Skimpy outfits were borrowed from the field of costume jewelry, featuring glass paste and sequins, sheaths made of semiprecious stones, carved strapless bras. And what about the hair? Plexiglas antennae, articulated metal helments, fountain sprays of aluminum, and iridescent paper turbans. The shoes, too, were raised on metal structures, with ballerinas dancing in an astral production of Giselle. Sirens from across the galaxy wearing looks far ahead of their times, silver and white, embellished with icy or iridescent hues. Every runway presentation was an authentic "space odyssey." Intriguingly worked surfaces refracted light and shot out cosmic sheens and glows. The 1991 metal-mesh bathing suit transformed Naomi Campbell into an android. Rabanne's fashion stimulated a consideration: this designer was the instigator of a concept of clothing that formed part of the artistic, technical, and sociological trends of an era. An era in which he chose to create in the present, taking inspiration from the future. He won a broad array of awards, including the *Dé d'Or*. He produced his first men's collection in 1976. Then he went on to create perfumes, naturally marketed in bottles made of recycled aluminum. He was constantly looking to the future, theorizing a simplified form a apparel that was more in keeping with humanity's nature's biorhythms. In so doing, he returned to his idea of moulded, biodegradable clothing. In 1986 his fashion house was purchased by the Spanish group, PVIG. During the Paris fashion week, in July 1999, he announced his retirement. In 1991, the French publisher Laffont brought out his book *Trajectoire d'une vie à l'autre*. (*Lucia Mari*)

❑ 1999. He published *Le Feu du Ciel*, a book that he had written with equal proportions of pessimism and optimism that added up to his vision of the world. He produced a brand new fragrance which he named *Ultraviolet* and which he marketed in a small, violet-colored, spherical bottle.

❑ 2000. His unisex line, Paco, ceased production, to keep with the general trend toward mainstream fashion of the house.

Racamier Henry (1912-2002). French businessman. He began his career working in the steel business, and enjoyed great success. At the age of 65 he sold his company and focused on the Louis Vuitton company which was entrusted to his direction by the owners, who were related to him through marriage. He transformed the company from a small, elite, artisanal operation (producing trunks, bags bags and valigie) into a universal status symbol *griffe*. In the 1990s, the rising influence of the new partner Bernard Arnault obliged him to leave the Vuitton company. But he did not retire. He created the Orcofi group, which would in time become a new player in the luxury business. It purchased Lanvin, Philippe Model, Daum, and Andrelux and introduced the Inés de La Fressange *griffe*.

❑ 2002. He died at the age of 90 of a heart attack, while traveling to Sardinia. He was survived by his wife and his twin daughters Caroline Bentz and Laurence Fontaine.

Radaelli Textile manufacturer with plants in the Lecco area. The founder was Alfredo Radaelli, who had studied at the school of silk manufacturing (Scuola di Setificio) in Como, and had deepened his experience working around Europe, in Germany and France. In 1893, in the plant located in Rancio, near Lecco, the Radaelli Finzi Perrier company began to manufacture velvets. In 1911, after opening a dyeing plant in Lecco, the company inaugurated a new plant in Mandello del Lario, equipped with looms and facilities for finishing fabrics. In the same years, the company expanded its line of production of velvets for items of women's apparel to include fabrics for furnishing and upholstery, supported by contracts for the Italian state railroad company. While 1919 was the year of "outstanding sales," 1927 was the first year that the company operated at a loss, a product of both the general crisis in the industry, and the increasingly ferocious internal competition. This phase of uncertainty extended into the 1930s, when the company began to encounter logistical difficulties in obtaining high quality raw material. In 1936, the company began to export products to the United States. In the 1950s, the company founded a throwing mill, and began to work on experimental basis with synthetic fibers. The 1960s witnessed a period of crisis due to problems with internal management. In 1976 the shares of TEPF, the holding company based around the throwing mill, were sold. The company entered the 1980s with a cautious trend toward revival, and that trend strengthened with the company's entry into the field of Parisian high fashion and the popularity of the catalogue of printed velvets for women's apparel. The last decade of the twentieth century began with the largest profit in the company's history, due largely to the sales of middle- to high-quality velvets for women's apparel and for home furnishings. (*Pierangelo Mastantuono*)

Raffaelli Lucia (1941-1999). Bolognese fashion model and journalist. In the 1960s she worked as a model for *Grazia*. After the birth of her first child, she began to work journalism. In September 1969 she was hired by the Condé Nast group as an editor, and before long she became a deputy editor. She worked there until 1992.

Raffia Plant fiber used in weaving, obtained by crushing and processing the leaves of a palm tree that grows in the tropics.

Raglan Method of cutting and stitching sleeves, which are joined to the body of a coat or outfit with a diagonal stitch from the base of the neck to the armpit. The name is taken from Lord Raglan (1788-1855), British commander in chief during the Crimean War.

Raincoat More than a clothing piece, an element of style, especially in the world of cinema. It identifies typologies of men, situations, and emotions. In the collective imagery, it's worn by action men: detective or gangsters. But it also appears on the arm

Advertisement for raincoats (from *Apparel Arts*, facsimile edition published in 1989 by GFT and Electa).

of British and American gentlemen. It is often used to shroud the silhouettes of secretaries and starlets who, during the film, turn into stars and heroines. Its simplicity and plain character means it does not distract from the face of its wearer, even if buttoned right up or the collar is turned up, for example, on Humphrey Bogart in *Casablanca* and Gene Kelly in *Singing in the Rain*. But also Michèle Morgan, Audrey Hepburn, and Marilyn Monroe, who created a different type of woman when wearing a raincoat. It is also standard wear an entire gallery of policemen, detectives, and police chiefs: from Maigret to Inspector Clouseau, Kojak and, ironically, Columbo. The raincoat, a garment present in men's and women's wardrobes, was born towards the end of the 19th century. Like all clothing items, it follows the rules of fashion, and, though keeping its basic characteristics, it varies in width, length, materials, and colors according to the moment. Through the years it has become identified with particular brands and styles: Barbour, Burberry, gabardine, the trench-coat, Mackintosh, Ciré and K-Way. (*Gianluca Bauzano*)

Rakam Monthly magazine published by Rusconi. The magazine was founded in 1930 as a publication focusing on embroidery, as its name suggests, evocative as it is of the arabesque and the fantastic. In the 1940s, the *Rakam* fell into line with the dominant ideology in Italy, and featured a "handsome, healthy, affectionate, desirable, Italian woman." In the years immediately following the war, it began to feature high fashion, but without any notable success. In 1954, Edilio Rusconi purchased the magazine and made it part of his publishing house, and restored it to its old approach. The magazine began once again to focus on how-to and useful tips, and the success was not long in coming: distribution soon rose to 400,000 copies. In 1986 it attempted to return to the field of fashion, but the discouraging results soon pushed it sharply back onto its original tracks. In the meanwhile, the editorship had been held, following the golden years under Elvira Frezza, by Anna Tuveri, Gabriella Brioschi, Susanna Barbaglia, and Anna Gualtieri. In 1998 the editorship was entrusted to Elio Michelotti, who had spent his entire working life at the magazine, where he had served a long apprenticeship, finally becoming art director.

❑ 2000. Beginning in the July issue, Rakam appeared on newsstands with a complete graphic redesign, but with the same contents and features that had made it famous. Alongside the "historic" features focusing on lace and cross-stitch, the readers could not also read about subjects ranging from furnishing to cooking, do-it-yourself, exercise and health, and beauty tips.

Rakocevic Verica (1948). Serbian high fashion designer. She was born in Belgrade. For her collections, she took inspiration from the traditions of her native land. She designed ethnic overcoats made of colored wool, jackets with distinctive embroideries, and skirts studded with pearls reminiscent of folk costumes. She studied engineering, and then opened an atelier of her own in Belgrade. She recently had a runway presentation in Los Angeles, with such eminent spokespersons as Sharon Stone and Kevin Costner. On more than one occasion, she took part in Alta Moda, or Haute Couture fashion week, in Rome. (*Eleonora Attolico*)

Rambaud René. French hairdresser. He was famous in the 1920s and 1930s for moving in the opposite direction from the short hairstyle and the flapper look; instead he emphasized Renaissance styles, or hairstyles from the seventeenth or nineteenth century, theorizing his approach in books like *La psychologie du coiffeur pour dames*.

Ramie A plant fiber used in weaving, obtained from plants of the Urticaceae family, which grow in China and in Japan.

Ran (1959). Korean fashion designer. She lives in Milan, where she studied at the Istituto Marangoni. She is known as Irene Hong, the label with which she sells her designs. She owns a refined boutique in the heart of the Milanese Cinque Vie section, in Via San Maurilio. Her collections join modern style and oriental atmospheres. The designer's favorite color is rose, sometimes paired with a pale, antique green, and in the winter, bordeau. In her boutique she

Due interessanti albums per il ricamo:

La Novità del Ricamo

Recentissimo album con disegni originali in grandezza naturale e atti al ricalco.

Vi sono anche tavole speciali per il ricalco con ferro da stiro caldo.

L'album ha un'artistica copertina a colori e una grande tavola interna pure a colori.

PREZZO L. **8.**—

Nuovi disegni per ricamo

Ricco album con disegni completamente inediti e in grandezza naturale.

PREZZO L. **8.**—

Sono due pubblicazioni che hanno avuto il più grande successo e che tutte le famiglie dovrebbero acquistare.

SOCIETÀ EDITRICE " UNITAS „ — MILANO

VIALE MONFORTE, 12

When *Rakam* was first published, there were many publications on embroidery. This advertisement was publicizing the publication of new issues (Prints Collection A. Bertarelli, Milan).

sells poetic, feminine evening and daytime wear, wedding dresses, patchwork stoles, strapless bras, but also bags, shoes, hats, and fabric flowers. Her materials are exquisite: inlaid chiffons, brocades, damasks, taffetas, and exquisite embroidered silks, French lace, cashmere and silk, and wools with the subtlest pinstriping.

(*Gabriella Gregorietti*)

Rankin (1966). Scottish photographer. He is a very representative figure in the new British wave of photography: aggressive, transgressive, and exceedingly rich in creativity, a creativity that contaminates all fields of endeavor and is willing to engage in irony; Rankin himself is now widely recognized for his highly personal style as one of the leading figures now working in the field of fashion photography. In 1991, he founded, with Jefferson Hack, *Dazed and Confused*, which immediately won acclaim as one of the most influential and unpredictable publications in the field, with such innovations as a layout that made it possible to leaf through the magazine in either of two directions. Alongside the individual pictures that were featured on the covers, Rankin also often did photography for shocking layouts (in one famous layout, a model wore an outfit that caught fire), but he also worked for such publications as *Rolling Stone*, *Interview*, *Spin*, *Big Issue*, *The Guardian*, *Harper's Bazaar*, *Independent on Sunday*, and *Snoozer*. In 1999 he opened with Alex Pround, a series of London galleries bearing the name, the publishing house Vision On, which debuted with his first book, *Nudes*, followed by others, such as *CeleBritation* (his best-known portraits), *Snog*, and *Sofasosexy* in 2002. With other publishingh houses, he published the retrospective collection, *Rankin Works*, in 2000 and, in 2002, *Work in Progress # 1*, *Breeding* (black and white studies of androgynous models), printed in a signed, limited edition of 1500 copies. In 2000, he introduced the fashion quarterly *Rank* and the magazine *Another* in which he continued his line of promotion of young creators. He has done many photographs for album covers: for U2, Spice Girls, Pulp, Salad, Morissey, and Maniac Street Preachers, though if the subject turns to portraits, then the most important one is the photograph he took of Queen Elizabeth II on the occasion of her Jubilee, along with the photographs of nine other selected photographers. The portrait was exhibited at Windsor Castle in February 2002 and then moved to the National Portrait Gallery in London. Recently Rankin has also begun to direct short films. He has had numerous shows in Europe and in the United States.

(*Roberto Mutti*)

Rap Youth protest movement that exploded, at the beginning of the 1980s, out of the run-down inner-city areas of the largest American metropolises. It has influenced the spheres of music (*rap* or *hip-hop*), painting (graffiti), and social lifestyle in general, with its powerful denunciation of the collapse of the large cities. More than being creative in artistic terms, rap adopts styles that have been developed previously, interpreting them and reinventing them in a system of "recycling" that also affected the aesthetics of clothing: rappers had short hair, trimmed above the ears, wore second-hand clothes, oversized Bermuda shorts, jogging outfits, bomber jackets, baseball hats, and jogging shoes.

Raphael Parisian fashion house founded in 1924 by Rafael Lopez Cebrian. At first it was in the Rue du Faubourg Saint-Honoré, later in the Avenue George V, it specialized in *tailleurs* and evening gowns. It ceased operation at the beginning of the 1950s.

Rapoport Debra. American artist and milliner. She lives and works in New York. Endowed with an unusual gift for manipulating objects and transforming them into something different from their original form and function, she makes use of that gift to create sculptural hats, dense with materials and new ideas. In 1985 she began work on a series of hats called *Hoop Hats*.

Rastafarians Youth movement, lifestyle and spontaneous fashion movement. It took root in Jamaica and invaded England at the beginning of the 1970s. It was linked to the spread of raggae music. The "rastas" generally wore camouflage uniforms, jeans, rough-weave wool caps in the colors of the Ethiopian flag (red, green, and gold) and wore their hair long, braided into the distinctive dreadlocks. This style, which in the 1980s also influenced such fashion designers come Vivienne Westwood, is not limited to clothing, but also has a genuine ideology that basically breaks down to a movement for the proud affermation of ethnic identity among the young Jamaicans, but which also calls for the existence of a great black nation and a messiah, identified in the person of the late emperor of Ethiopia Haile Selassie, the ideal leader of the struggle for the redemption of the black race and its return to the promised land of Ethiopia.

(*Ruben Modigliani*)

Ratti Italian silk manufacturer. It is based in Como. It is world famous for the high fashion content of the fabrics, its rarefied nobilitations of cloth, its many end-uses: apparel, upholstery, ties, and accessories. Antonio Ratti founded the company in 1945. Creativity and technology, avant-garde design, continuous cycle from design to production – these are its chief features. Every year, five thousand new designs are added to the 150,000 designs already in the archives, which can be consulted online and rapidly revised with the computer-assisted design system developed in collaboration with ENEA. A library of five thousand visual-arts books, continuously being updated and computerized, serves as the driving force behind the design office. The company has been listed on the Italian stock exchange, or Borsa, since 1989. It has annual revenues of a little less than 400 billion liras, with 1,100 employees. It has carried out a policy of judicious investments and acquisitions strategically oriented toward the development of the corporation. It is organized into manufacturing, distribution, financial corporations with a total of seventeen different product areas in the larger sectors of: technology, major names, furnishings, foulards and shawls, ties, and women's apparel. It sells in thirty-four countries around the world. It has branches in Paris, New York, Singapore, and Hong Kong and plants in Italy and France. In 1985, Ratti Foundation was set up to support endeavors, research, artistic, cultural, and technological studies both for textile production and for the safeguarding of cultural and artistic resources, as well as for the undertaking of initiatives, events, and shows. It possesses a major collection of antique fabrics. In 1999 the Ratti Foundation organized in Como the exhibition *Six Hundred Years of Silk and Color: The History of Cloth Dyeing Techniques*. Antonio Ratti, in 1996, donated to the Metropolitan Museum di New York a workshop for the restoration of textiles.

(*Giuliana Zabeo Ricca*)

❑ 2000. The year ended with revenues of 140.3 million Euros and a net loss of 3.8 million Euros.
❑ 2001, May. The group has concentrated for the past half century on silk prints, which still constitute 50 percent of the materials treated, and it began to harvest the fruit of the diversification that it undertook in 1998 with the production of blends and polyester. A new production line for beachwear and lingerie was offered through the Setamarina division. Overall, Ratti produces 5.6 million meters of fabric per year.
❑ 2001, August. The board of directors conferred full authority upon Donatella Ratti, president of the Group and the new managing director.
❑ 2001. Business results decline. The balance sheet featured a consolidated turnover of 131.5 million Euros, a 6.5 percent drop from 2000 and a loss of 10.4 million Euros. The decline reflected the difficult situation that characterized the textile-apparel sector, and especially the silk business. The chief company in the group, Ratti S.p.A., had turnover of 93 million Euros and a net negative balance 8.8 million Euros.
❑ 2002, January. The group continued its restructuring, with a view to returning to profitability through a greater degree of flexibility which should allow it to compete in an increasingly turbulent market.
❑ 2002, February. Antonio Ratti dies, founder and former president of the group.
❑ 2002, April. Donatella Ratti rules out any hypotheses of mergers with other corporations in the area in order to make it through the difficulties that are afflicting the group. According to her, the best possibilities are in the area of fabrics for women's apparel, which

constitute 60 percent of gross revenue, compared with the 45 percent of 1997. Accessories represent 14.4 percent of total turnover, a sector within which the importance of foulards is growing while the volume of ties declines.
❑ 2002. Another hard year for the Como-based group. The total revenue, equal to 118 million, drops by 10.2 percent. This drop affected all markets, but especially foreign markets, where Ratti achieved 64 percent of its total revenue. The Italian market, 36 percent, dropped by 7.2 percent. The business result was negative by 3.8 million Euros, an improvement over the 10.4 million of 2001. All the same, the restructuring, now under way, offers encouraging signals. The cash flow was in fact positive to the tune of 3.7 million Euros and made it possible to undertake new physical investments and to reduce the financial debt level to 15.7 million.
(*Dario Golizia*)

Ratti Foundation Como, Lungo Lago Trento, 9. Founded in 1985 by the silk entrepreneur Antonio Ratti who donated his collection of ancient fabrics to the Foundation: 2,870 specimens (most of them operated silks, but also Copt fabrics, cashmere shawls, women's "ties" and 1,551 catalogue-books). As the Foundation's purposes are to conserve historical clothing and textiles, and to enable study and research, spaces and containers have been specially designed to allow these activities. The Foundation promotes research, the advancement of technology for the study of ancient and modern fabrics, and, in a wider sense, the diffusion of a textile culture. Every year it holds a course in Visual Arts.

Raudnitz French fashion houses at the end of the nineteenth century and the turn of the twentieth century. One was called Raudnitz et Cie., the other was called Ernest Raudnitz. Both had headquarters in Paris. The owners denied that they were related, but in fact they appear to have been related, even though they presented their products separately at the Exposition Universelle of 1900, the high point of success for both companies. Special mention should be made of the tea outfits made by Ernest Raudnitz. In 1902, they went out of business.

Rauschenberg Robert (1925). American artist. A leading member of the New Dada and Pop Art movements, he featured in his work the influence of Dadaist collage and, in particular, the style of inserting actual objects into artworks. In 1974 he created a shirt printed with pieces of newspaper. His photographic studies, which date from the years 1948-1949 at Black Mountain College, were not entirely forgotten because, while Rauschenberg focused on painting, his style was syncretic and could be seen in both his combine paintings and in his silkscreens where we find photographs taken from the daily press, skillfully manipulated and overlapping. In this way, he represented a moment of critical consideration on the use of images in our society, as well as an attempt to shatter the barrier that divides art from life: it is in this context that we should view works such as *Bed* (1955), where a real, unmade bed was hung on a wall.

❑ 1997. At the end of the year, the Guggenheim Museum in New York dedicated a major retrospective to his work, exhibiting the works that made him famous in the 1960s.
❑ 1998, January. Christian Marinotti Edizioni published *Anagrams (A Pun)*, an introductory essay by Gillo Dorfles, devoted to the seventeen large paintings done expressly for the occasion of Rauschenberg's return to Italy, following a thirty-year absence.
❑ He currently lives and works in Florida.

Ravasi Guido (1877-1946). Industrialist in the silk business and designer. Following a period of apprenticeship in Austria, Germany, Czechoslovakia, Switzerland and France he founded a single-owner company, with weaving being done in San Mamette (near Como), thus updating and rejuventating the family-owned company and modernizing the style of its product line. He held less than 50 percent of the corporate capital in the company, allied with the Milan bank of Bellinzaghi and by a group of Milanese industrialists. He personally supervised the design of the fabrics. Production, which was done mostly in the weaving mill of Oltrona and in the two mills in Binago and Como, chiefly involved the manufacture of silk fabrics for ties, "artistic fabrics," handkerchiefs, and scarves. In the 1920s, it was the "art" line of production, marketed in a sort of museum-workshop in Como by SAR (Società Anonima Ravasi), that was critically acclaimed at various national and international expositions. The sector devoted to ties relied upon an extremely thorough and far-reaching network for distribution throughout Europe, the Middle East, Japan, Africa, America and Australia. From 1923 until the beginning of the 1930s, Ravasi was a member of the Consiglio Artistico (artistic board) of the Esposizione Internazionale delle Arti (international exposition of the arts) which, at the time, was held in Monza. In 1972, following the death of the founder, various shifts in ownership and changes in corporate identity and structure, the company finally became property of the Ratti company. That same year, the Seterie Ravasi ended their history.

(*Pierangelo Mastantuono*)

Ravers In times in which people subscribed to a system of exaggerated consumption, as the phenomenon of fashion-victims seems to indicate, the Ravers, though the label is quite generic, represented an important point of trend reversal. Between the winter of 1987 and the following summer, an intentionally anti-fashion style began to take root, in place of the elaborate styles that had been pursued up till then. Instead of a profusion of *griffes*, simple T-shirts, hairdos with rollers, and the timid beginning of piercing, which began with the frequent habit of chipping teeth. Contributing to the phenomenon was an explosion of such events as raver-parties (often illegal), in industrial warehouses at first and later in the open air, and the development of wave of so-called Balearic music (a mixture of Acid House, Techno, Afro and Funk) offered in such discotheques as Amnesia, Glory's, and the Space in Ibiza, at the time the peak of the Spanish *Movida*. It was inevitable that upon the return from the holidays there would be a desire to relive the atmosphere and the euphoria of that summer of 1988, generating a collective phenomenon that continues still, focused on both marathon dancing and apparel.

(*Maurizio Vetrugno*)

Ravizza It's the oldest gunshop in Italy. It was founded in Milan in 1871. Over the course of the years, it also became a full-fledged temple to sporting elegance with a complete assortment of products: from original loden coats and jackets made of hand-woven Austrian linen to the most up-to-date American jogging shoes. For the past ten years or so, there has been a apparel-making workshop in the shop at Via Hoepli 3, where, in three weeks, it can cut, assemble, and stitch an entire wardrobe for man and woman.

Rawlings John (1912-1970). American photographer. He became a member of the Condé Nast group in 1936, as the London director of the *Vogue* studio. In 1945 he opened a studio of his own in New York. In the years between 1936 and 1966, his photographs were featured on more than 200 covers for *Vogue* and *Glamour* as well, of course, as numerous photo shoots. The rediscovery of his archives, which had been left closed after his death, made it possible to make use of pictures that are emblematic of the style of the 1940s and 1950s. In 2001 the handsome and extensive monograph *John Rawlings: 30 Years in Vogue* was published, which summarizes his work at the magazine.

Ray-Ban Brand of eyeglasses developed out of a patent for a type of sunglasses, symbolic of the heroes of the Second World War because they were worn by General Douglas MacArthur, the supreme commander of Allied forces in the Pacific during the Second World War. From the years following WWII to the present day, they have become a sort of status symbol of Americanism in fashion and in aesthetics. *Time* magazine included them in a collection of icons of Americanism: Coca-Cola, Harley Davidson, and Heinz Tomato Ketchup. The patent was taken out on 7 May 1937 by the Bausch & Lomb company, an American optical products manufacturer that was founded in 1853 and has since become a worldwide colossus. The prototype, known as Anti-Glare, consisted of an extremely light frame – 150 grams – made of gold-plated metal with two green lenses made of mineral glass to filter out infrared and ultraviolet rays, was renamed Ray-Ban, for marketing reasons. The name came from the phrase Banish Rays. The story of Ray-Bans, however, began at the turn of the twentieth century with a request from a solitary long-distance balloon adventurer. In 1920, lieutenant John MacCready had crossed the Atlantic Ocean, and his eyes had been damaged by the sunlight because he had no suitable eye protection. Once he had finished the crossing, he contacted Bausch & Lomb to ask them to manufacture a highly protective pair of eyeglasses, both panoramic and elegant. This led to the prototype made in 1937. It was immediately adopted by the pilots of the Army Air Force and Bausch & Lomb became the army's sole supplier. When General MacArthur, Ray-Bans on his nose, landed in the Philippines, surrounded by photographers with flashbulvs and movie cameras, those sunglasses became mythical and it was to pay a debt of gratitude that in the 1950s, a model of sunglasses was dedicated to the general. After authentic heroes, it was the turn of movie heroes to become the more-or-less involuntary spokesmen for Ray-Ban: Marlon Brando and James Dean, Jack Nicholson in *Easy Rider*, John Belushi and Dan Aykroyd in *Blues Brothers*, Tom Cruise in *Top Gun*. Among the best known models are the Large Metals, the Wayfarers, the Shooters, and the Outdoorsman, the Baloramas, and the Olympias. Of the Large Metal Aviator glasses, there are 6 million sold worldwide every year. At the end of April 1999, the Ray-Bans, along with other brands in the sunglasses division of Bausch & Lomb, were purchased by the Italian company Luxottica, owned by Leonardo Del Vecchio, for about 1.2 billion dollars. The entire acquisition amounted to annual revenue of about 830 billion liras.

❑ 2003, June. The sunglasses worn by Cameron Diaz, Drew Barrymore and Lucy Liu, the stars of the second film in the *Charlie's Angels* series were created specially by Ray-Ban. For the movie, the designers created three different models, one per "angel." Ray-Ban introduced five new models for the historic collection of eyeglasses, which were added to already crowded array of 43 models. The first Junior collection of sunglasses debuted: their marketing claim was "My First Ray-Ban." Lorenzo Scaccini, a Milanese photographer who "specialized" in children's products – he also did the pictures for the campagns of Versace Young, Chicco, Pampers, Mister Baby, and Sony Playstation – was responsible for the image and opted for Saint-Tropez as a background.

(*Gianluca Bauzano*)

Rayne Edward (1922). English shoemaker. He joined the family company at a very young age. That company was HM Rayne, founded by his grandparents in 1889, and specializing in the production of shoes for the theater and, with the inauguration in the 1920s of a refined store in London's Bond Street, also in non-theatrical footwear. In 1951, following the death of his father, Edward Rayne became the director of the company. For a certain period of time, he formed an alliance with the Delman company of New York, but in 1961, he sold his company to Debenhams Ltd., one of Great Britain's leading marketing groups. Rayne shoes, of various styles, but invariably sophisticated, are world famous and have appeared in runway presentations along with collections by Dior.

Rayon A French name given at the turn of the twentieth century to the brand-new material viscose, following a disagreement with the silk manufacturers. An artificial fiber derived from chemically modified cellulose, which was marketed both as a silk-like continuous thread, and as a cotton-like tuft. The largest manufacturer of rayon in the world is Enka Viscose (AKZO), with an 11 percent share for continuous thread. It is currently very widely used both in fabrics (for apparel and linings) and in knitwear. The leading textile industry locations for consumption are the districts of Prato, Como, Carpi, and Varese.

Rébé A label that, along with the maison Lesage, was used for over a century for the most famous embroideries and laces in French high fashion. It takes its name from the double initials of René Begué whom Worth called "the artist," in recognition of his exceptional creative gifts. Much of the work done by Rébé is now on exhibit at the Musée des Arts Décoratifs in Paris, where it was donated by the artist. Begué worked for a very considerable number of fashion houses: we was 17 when he started as an illustrator for Paquin, in London; immediately thereafter he was hired by the embroidery house Vitet, where he soon created an impressive reputation for himself. He worked first for Doucet, Poiret, Doeuillet, and Schiaparelli; later Balenciaga, Fath, and Christian Dior asked for his work. His name is linked to the most spectacular runway presentations, the most celebrated maisons, and the most prestigious clients: suffice it to mention the wedding dress of the Empress Farah Diba. No one knows René Begué actual date of birth, but it is said that he died at over a hundred years of age, in 1980.

Reboux Caroline (1840-1927). French milliner noted for her veils in lively colors, her silks, and the braidwork on her hats. Born in Paris, she was first discovered by Princess Pauline von Metternich, wife of the Austrian ambassador to France. It was the princess who first began to wear Reboux's creations in high society, thus bringing her customers such as the Countess De Pourtalés, the Countess Virginia di Castiglione and the Empress Eugenia de Montijo. In 1870, she opened an atelier in the Rue de la Paix (in 1900, she had 100 employees), becoming the uncontested queen of Parisian millinery until the First World War. In the 1920s, by this point old and tired, she handed over the job of running the maison to Lucienne Rebaté, a former employee of Chanel. The heir decided to eliminate cloche hats, instead headdresses that tended to shade the face. Among her customers were also actresses such as Greta Garbo, Arletty and Marlene Dietrich who wore her creations in the movie *Knight Without Armour* (1937). The maison Reboux ceased operations in 1956. Three hundred creations by Madame Reboux are in the collections of the Musée de la Mode et du Textile in Paris.

Caroline Reboux, as depicted by René Gruau. Collection of the Union Française des Arts du Costume, Musée de la Mode et du Textile, Louvre, Paris.

Redaelli Italian garment manufacturer. In 1920, the Raffaele Redaelli company was founded in Capriano (Milan) and produced military uniforms as a subcontractor. The production of civilian clothing, which began in 1937, is nowadays distributed throughout Italy under the brand names of Redaelli and Redster by Redaelli. In 1956, the company, which had already moved to Verano Brianza, became a corporation. In 1970 and in 1975, new plants were built. In the 1980s the company began to work with the fashion designers Ted Lapidus, Maurizio Baldassari and Nicola Trussardi. Later, the company signed a production agreement with Ferré that lasted almost until the end of the 1990s. In 1989 it began to produce Gianmarco Venturi and in 1990 Fendi. More recently, contracts have been signed with Antonio Fusco, Luciano Soprani and Carlo Pignatelli. The company has a number of plants, 750 employees, and turnover of more than 100 billion lires. It has 400 shops in Italy and 500 more scattered throughout the world.

Rede Italian socks and stocking manufacturer that was founded in 1938 at Parabiago by Mario Re Depaolini. The company produces high-quality men's, women's, and children's socks. Beginning in 1964, it has been run by the founder's wife, Carla. Aside from the factory in Parabiago, it also possesses the throwing mill for synthetic fibers in Garabiolo and a packaging company. It produces 50,000 pairs of women's socks a day, and every year, one million pairs of cotton and Lycra panty hose.

Redfern British and French fashion house. It developed out of an idea of John Redfern's. Redfern (1853-1929), was a busy trader in woolen cloth from the middle of the nineteenth century, on the Isle of Wight. Encouraged by the developing tourist trade on the island, he opened a tailoring department for ladies. Later he opened a subsidiary in London. He achieved fame when he was commissioned to supply the trousseau for the Princess of Wales. In 1888, he opened more subsidiaries in New York, Chicago and Paris. In the French capital, the fashion house presented creations that combined Parisian elegance with British taste. In 1916, the International Red Cross commissioned the Redfern fashion house to design its new uniform. The fashion house ceased activity at the beginning of the 1930s.

(*Olivella Pianetti*)

Redingote This Italian term technically describes a frock coat. It has shifted in meaning like few other terms in the history of apparel. It is derived from the English term, "riding-coat," and was present in Italian sartorial terms in the mid-nineteenth century as the *redingotto*. It was a cape that became a jacket and, much refined, became a piece of everyday dress for men, then took on decided connotations of special occasions or ceremonies, and returned in a much more tapered version, like a *princesse*, but not buttoned, in women's capes. At first it was the large cape that men used to wear in the eighteenth century when traveling on horseback. At the end of the eighteenth century, women began to adopt the *redingote* as an outfit with a well-designed torso area, with one or more collars, and then transformed it, in the early years of the nineteenth century, into a cape, while in contrast, the *redingote* almost entirely replaced in menswear the long jackets of the previous period. The interplay between capes and suits continued for many years in women's fashion in the nineteenth century. Finally the *redingote* reappeared in its definitive form, which can be linked back to the modern-day meaning of the term, in 1874, as a cape that was close-fitting in the cut of the torso and the waist,

The Italian term "redingote" derives from the English term, 'riding coat', describing a coat worn on horseback.

belted, and usually flared out to the hem. The men's *redingote*, stabilized as an urban jacket, with single lapels, a true forerunner of the modern men's jacket, preserves its original appearance in the tailcoat.

(*Lucia Sollazzo*)

Red or Dead English label of ready-to-wear fashion. It was launched, in 1982, by Wayne and Geraldine Hemingway, both born in 1961 in England. They began with a pushcart at Camden Market, the little cult flea market held on Sundays in London. They featured the style of leftist youth and penniless students, capable of creating a look with very little. They reworked second-hand clothing, combining it with Doc. Marten's work boots. A rebel look made up of girls wearing colorful outfits worthy of Doris Day with heavy twelve-lace-hole work boots on their feet, and boys dressed like James Dean (used clothing generally came from America) with steel-toed boots. From their vendor's stall, the Hemingways rose to single-label stores, offering lines of clothing and shoes that invariably featured humor and casualness. Surrealistic prints, shoes with unexpected shapes and colors. They are capable of understanding a generation that is no longer exceedingly young, but that has not yet grown old, and is determined to be nonconformist and protest-oriented, if only in their clothing. Their success was recognized with the invitation to join the committee of the British Fashion Council. They have had and continue to have considerable influence on young British fashion.

❑ 1999. Wayne Hemingway, founder and director of the house, sold his share of the company for a sum that has never been revealed.
❑ 2003, April. The label returned to the spotlight following a two-year absence, with a line created by a hybrid of the New Renaissance (Harvey Bertram-Brown and Corlyn Corben) at the decision of The Pentland Group, the majority shareholder. (*Virginia Hill*)

Red Wing A manufacturer of work boots and work shoes, founded in the city of Red Wing, Minnesota by Charles H. Beckman in 1905. The real boom in production came with the arrival of the First World War, when the American army shipped out wearing Red Wing N. 16s. During the Second World War, the company was working at full capacity to make the 239 variants on the military combat boot, with various sizes and widths. Another important phase in the company's development came with the birth of the petroleum industy, between the 1960s and the 1970s, when the "hard work shoe" became familiar in Mexico, Canada, South America, Europe, and in the producing nations in the Middle East. The company produces thousands of pairs of shoes and boots every day through its four brand lines: Worx and Red Wing Shoes for work, Irish Setter for hunting and fishing, and Vasque for leisure.
(*Pierangelo Mastantuono*)

Reebok Trademark of a manufacturer of athletic shoes. In 1895, the English athlete Joseph William Foster conceived and began to produce a type of shoe with a hobnailed sole for faster running. In 1958, two of his grandchildren founded a second corporation which absorbed the J.W. Foster & Sons company, with the name Reebok, from the name of an African gazelle. In 1979, the company took a new direction through the efforts of Paul Fireman, a partner in a company that distributed outdoor sporting products: the launch of the Freestyle, the first aerobics shoe designed expressly for dance. Its success took the company to the forefront of the international athletic shoe market. In 1984, Fireman purchased the company from Joseph Foster and transformed it into a corporation. In 1998, Reebok launched The Pump, a shoe that automatically pumped itself up to fit the foot. Reebok was engaged in an intense activity of sponsorship and research in the areas of running, fitness, rugby, tennis, soccer, baseball, track and field, golf, and mountain climbing. (*Giuliana Parabiago*)

❑ 1999. In the field of sports apparel, the company introduced Hydromove, an exclusive technology based on thermoregulation and comfort. This innovative structure allows body heat to push sweat toward the outside of the fabric for faster evaporation. The athlete, therefore, remains dry and the body preserves a constant temperature, which slows the onset of exhaustion and helps to improve performance.
❑ 2000, December. The company signed a multiyear contract with Venus Williams, the famous tennis champion. In the same period, Reebok and the National Football League (NFL) announce a exclusive partnership that also serves the purpose of reorganizing and reinvigorating the business of NFL products. The ten-year contract calls for the NFL to hand over all production, distribution, and sales of the trademark for the 32 league football tems in the United States and for those in the World League (Europe). The license includes shoes, team uniforms, training apparel, aftergame wear, and a new line of apparel. The agreement ensures Reebok of exclusive rights to develop a new line of NFL-branded fitness equipment.
❑ 2001, April. The company launched in North America, in collaboration with Clearly Canadian Beverage Corporation, Reebok Fitness Water, an extremely sophisticated product: this is water enriched with essential vitamins, minerals, and electrolytes. Reebok Fitness Water satisfies the demands of sports consumers, who are attentive to and aware of health.
❑ 2001, August. The company signed another major ten-year contract for a strategic partnership with the NBA, the

National Basketball Association. Thanks to this agreement, Reebok acquired the rights to design, produce, and distribute all merchandise tied to the NBA, the Women's Basketball Association, and the National Basketball Development League.
❑ 2002. Paul Smith designs a pair of running shoes for Reebok – in a limited edition, at a 145 Euro retail price – with a vaguely 1980s look. The company has revenues of 3.1 billion dollars.
❑ 2003, June. A new entry in the phenomenon of fashion and rap: this is a long-term partnership between Reebok and 50 Cent, the rapper who is leading the ranking of biggest-selling music star on earth. The first fruit of their collaboration was the line of shoes called G-Unit Collection by RBK. This collection of shoes debuted, with a very limited distribution, in the fall, but the full-bore launch, in grand style, would take place in the first few months of 2004. This was not the first time that Reebok collaborated with a rap star: in fact, the brand launched, on 18 April 2003, the S Carter Collection by RBK, the product of a collaborative design process with the rapper Jay-Z, and it enjoyed enormous success in the United States. In a single weekend, in fact, 10,000 pairs of the first running shoes marketed were sold: the Shaun Carter, which cost 95 dollars.
❑ 2003, September. The new collection devoted to women's tenniswear was developed by the American fashion designer Diane von Fürstenberg.
❑ 2003. Reebok International Ltd. had approximately 6,000 employees worldwide.
❑ 2005 August. For 3.1 billion Euros, the company is published by the Germany group, Adidas, which paid 34 percent more than the price as quoted on the stock exchange.

(*Edoardo Ponzoni*)

Rees Dai (1961). British milliner. He was born in Wales and lives in London. He studied ceramic and glass design at the Central Saint Martin's College of Art (1992) and at the Royal College of Art (1994). He collaborated with avant-garde fashion designers, in particular Alexander McQueen, Julien Macdonald, Sonja Nuttall and Moschino, and he specializes in shop window and boutique design. His sculptural headgear, inventive and innovative in the use of materials, have been requested for a number of exhibitions, including, in 1998-99, *Addressing the Century - 100 Years of Art and Fashion* at the Hayward Gallery in London. The Victoria and Albert Museum purchased some of his work for its permanent collection. Dai Rees Millinery and Accessories has existed as a trademark since 1997, the year in which the fashion designer began to take part in the London Fashion Week with his own collection.

❑ 1999. Ail is the name of the womenswear collection at the turn of the new millennium.
❑ 2000. There is a common theme uniting the Spring-Summer 2000 Collection with the Fall-Winter 1999 collection. *Truit*, as it has been dubbed (tree, in Gaelic) takes its inspiration by the landscapes of Wales. The very geometric cuts of the patterns exalt the feminine silhouette and, as always, the fabrics are produced exclusively by English and Irish factories. The graphic motifs hark back to Celtic virtuosity and the embroideries hark back to the British tradition. The shoes that are paired with the collection are by Christian Louboutin and the jewelry was designed by the fashion designer himself, with Naomi Filmer.

Refrigiwear Apparel company that was founded in 1954 in New York. It specialized in the sector of work clothing: items endowed with unparalleled thermal insulation and equally noteworthy resistance to wear, practicality of use, and lightness, often innovative as well in their forms and wearability. The chief objective was to give each customer genuine professional tools that would never let the user down, even in the most extreme weather conditions. Thanks to its particular qualities, it became the most commonly used brand among technicians working in the Meat Market of New York. These outfits have become cult objects among young people. In Italy, where it has an alliance with the Sixty group for the production of coats, it sold about 100,000 items in 2002.

Reger Janet (1935). British fashion designer of women's underwear with a special emphasis on the sexy. She first gained general notice in the 1970s for her night shirts with side vents, her satin pajamas, and her outfits made of inlaid lace. Born in London, she graduated from the Leicester College of Art. She got her first job working for Fenwick department stores. In 1975, she opened her first boutique in Knightsbridge. Her company was purchased by Berlei in 1983, but already the following year Janet Reger had been asked to come back to take charge of the design sector. Her lingerie has been exported throughout Europe, to the United States, and to the Far East.

❑ 2002. The new version of the website janetreger.co.uk is launched online, designed to be an "online shop window." One month after the launch, sales have tripled over the old website.

Relang Regina (1906-1989). German photographer. Born in Stuttgart, where she studied at the Akademie für Bildende Kunst. From 1932 till 1939, she lived and worked in Paris: first as a painter and costume designer, later as a photographer for *Vogue*. After World War Two, she was frequently commissioned by the Roman ateliers to photograph their creations. In his essay on fashion photography in the 1950s in Italy for the book *La moda italiana* (Electa, 1987), Paolo Barbaro wrote: "...She appears to have been one of the photographers who was most keenly intent on bringing out the "Italianity" of the creations. In a number of photographic coverages for the Sorelle Fontana and for Carosa she had the models poses in archaeological sites in Rome and Pompeii or else in the Gardens of Bomarzo." Beginning in 1971, she abandoned fashion and devoted herself to artistic photography.

Rena Lange German high fashion and prêt-à-porter firm. It was established in 1963 by Peter Gunthert (1936), who began with a swimwear shop, a traditional item in the marketing continuum of the city of Munich. Six years later, after marrying Renate, a fashion designer who began her career in Berlin before becoming an apprentice cutter in Frankfurt, and who later became the label's fashion designer. Now the Munich-based fashion house has 120 employees, 18 boutiques around the world, and exports to 26 countries.

❑ 2003. She presented for the Spring-Summer 2003 season sensual outfits and suits with sharp lines and cuts. Stretch piqués, brightly colored bouclés, embroidered suede and silk georgette, all worked with innovative techniques, were offered in an extraordinary mix, but it was especially linen, with all the hues of fresh fruit, that was the most extensively used material. The collection stood out for the lightness of the fabrics and for the broad array of colors: from white to beige and blossom, from fuchsia to black. *Stern* outfits were presented with exclusive fabrics but also with humorous details: hearts, the fashion designer's logo, lightened in a humorous way the pinstriped suit. The distinctive and delicate floral designs were reinterpreted with lace, embroideries and jacquards.

Renata (1934). Professional name of Renata Baumeisten, a German fashion designer. After completing her studies at the School of Fine Arts in Dusseldorf, she went to Paris to work as a graphic designer for the fashion magazine *Elle*. It was only later that she began to design clothing: to develop her skills in this new art, she moved to New York for a year, where she learned about the developing prêt-à-porter market, becoming the chief designer for the label Prikene. In 1973 she launched a line of her own under the label Renata, which was distributed worldwide. In 1980 she opened a boutique in Paris, specializing in women's apparel, with natural fabrics and hand-embroideries. Her love of embroidery and linen led her to design collection of napkins, curtains, and pillows for the home, as well. This was so successful that in 1991 she opened a second boutique, also in Paris, in which she offered her line of home accessories. Her label by this point was well established and Renata apparel can be found around the world, from Barneys in New York to Shiseido The

Ginza, in Japan. She very recently launched a new line for a younger target more closely in tune with shifts in fashion.

Renato di Bosso Pseudonym of Renato Righetti (1905-1982). Italian artist. Born in Verona. "A man's character is revealed by the tie he wears," he wrote in the Futurist Manifesto on Italian Ties, signed along with Ignazio Scurto in 1933. A member of the Second Futurist Movement, he designed an anti-necktie, made of a very light, shiny, durable metal.

Renée Fashion model. She was an icon of the flapper, or *garçonne*, style. She was the preferred model of Poiret, in the 'Teens and Twenties, an institution of the maison, along with the couturier Christian and Reine, the sales director.

René Lézard German *griffe* of men's and women's prêt-à-porter. It was founded in 1978 by Thomas Schaeffer. In 2002 the Mariella Burani Fashion Group announced the acquisition of 50 percent of the company's capital. The cost of the purchase was nearly 12 million Euros. The remaining 50 percent of the company remained in the hands of Thomas Schaeffer. On 30 April 2002, the label brought in revenue of 71 million Euros and a net profit of some 1.4 million Euros. In September of that same year, with the slogan: *Relax – The Harmony of Contrasts* a new shop was inaugurated in Hamburg, in the newly renovated Heine-Haus in the Jungfernstieg quarter.

(*Edoardo Ponzoni*)

René Mancini Shoemaker founded in Paris in 1936 by the Italian shoemaker of that name who had emigrated to France. The house offered both shoes at accessible prices and more refined models. The latter models, which had come to the attention of Balmain's mother, allowed Mancini to win commissions from major fashion houses that in time became regular clients – among others, Givenchy, Balenciaga, Scherrer and Chanel. His famous Chanel sandal dates from the end of the 1950s. Over the course of a few years, the international *beau monde* came knocking at the door of his atelier: from Jackie Kennedy and Caroline of Monaco to Garbo and Callas. In the 1960s Mancini began a mass production of luxury shoes. Today, the company, under the leadership of his children Alain and Claire, distributes collections in France through more than 30 boutiques.

Renoma Apparel label introduced in Paris in 1959 by the brothers Michel and Maurice Renoma, who were continuing the family's tailoring business into the branch of ready-to-wear fashion. The hipster style became an international phenomenon in part due to their work. In 1963 they founded the Renoma Star company and opened a Parisian boutique in the Rue de la Pompe. In 1992 and 1996 they created the *griffes* U.P. and 400a.

❑ 2003, June. SADEV, the French corporation that produces and distributes Renoma, signs a licensing agreement with the French designer Christian Lacroix.

Renown Japanese apparel manufacturer. In the domestic market, it is the leader in the field of prêt-à-porter. It also produces underwear and intimatewear and women's hosiery. The group philosophy is growth, in part through the acquisition of leading labels. Among them, the best known is Acquascutum (the historic British raincoat maker) which became a Renown property in 1991.

❑ 2002. The company recorded its twelfth consolidated balance at a loss: it was down 1.5 billion yen. In order to halt the hemorrhaging of assets, the company liquidated the most unprofitable divisions, abandoned its old offices in Harajuku, and implemented mandatory retirement for some 380 employees and, finally, moved the most poorly performing divisions to the affiliated companies. The new Arnold Palmer collection was presented by the corporation as one of the key labels that would restore the brand to profitable balance sheets. In the days when his career was peaking, in the 1980s, Arnold Palmer would sell about 40-50 billion yen annually. Then the Arnold Palmer line experienced a severe decline. Even though the items were substantially updated, Renown wisely preserved the old logo, creating a vintage link with the original label. In a surprising move for an old-style apparel group like Renown, they also opened a series of shops that they ran directly, in order to create a presence for the label. In Harajuku, the Arnold Palmer Premium Store enjoyed sales to the tune of some 30 million yen in the first month, and the other stores produced an average volume of 10 million yen monthly.

Rep (French, *Reps*). A very strong fabric made of wool, cotton or silk, with diagonal or vertical ribbing, also known as *canneté*.

Replay Italian label of ready-to-wear fashion for men, women, and children, owned by the Gruppo Fashion Box. Replay was founded in 1978 by Claudio Buziol in Asolo. Over the course of five years of its life, from 1993 to 1998, the company watched its turnover skryocket from 90 to 360 billion liras, with 75 percent of that revenue coming from exports, with 4,000 sales outlets around the world and more than 200 single-label shops. Alone, Replay represents some 80 percent of the entire group production (with 500 employees) which has two other labels, Replay 6 Sons and E-Play, and offers a total look that covers all age groups. Production which, throughout the 1980s, included only jeans and shirts and was divided into basic collections, less subject to the changes of fashion, and fashion collections which have always stylistically underscored the Italian image of Fashion Box.

❑ 2002. The company ended the year with positive results: the turnover increased by 3.4 percent and profits were in line with 2001.
❑ 2003. Replay renewed its eyeglasses license with the Marcolin Group, with a renewal of the license for the Replay logo in the sectors of watches and perfume. The only investment scheduled was the development of a project in the the United States: in September the renovation of the New York store was completed. The main market for Replay is certainly Europe, followed by the Far East, Eastern Europe, and South America. Soon, investments will be focused on the United States and South America. In Russia, Replay is present with a direct sales outlet in St. Petersburg.

Reporter Clothing line. It takes its inspiration and its name from the 1974 Michelangelo Antonioni film with Jack Nicholson, *The Passenger* (the title in Italian was, in fact, *Professione: reporter*). The guiding concept of the line is the idea of an international man who often travels for work, and whose wardrobe ranges from sportswear to the sophisticated classic look, with special attention to the selection of fabrics and details, with a search for new solutions, especially in terms of the shaping of the shoulders and the interiors of the jackets, which are a continuous area of evolution. In 1994 the label was acquired by the Gruppo Inghirami Company. Today, single-label Reporter stores are present in many cities in Italy and throughout Europe – Milan, Florence, Brussels, Budapest – with advance distribution in the leading Asian department stores, beginning in Shanghai. In recent years, Reporter consolidated important athletic partnerships. (*Pierangelo Mastantuono*)

Repossi Costantino. Jeweler. Regular clients at the Monte Carlo shop, which was opened in the 1970s following the success of the Turin in the Via Lagrange, included international celebrities from the worlds of film, entertainment, and music, such as Liza Minelli, Frank Sinatra, and Ryan O'Neal. Even Maria Callas commissioned Repossi to set her famous jewels. The reputation of his creations even reached the Middle East, ranging from the courts of the Arab ruling houses to rich oil dealers like Adnana Kashoggi. Repossi's jewelry is timeless: refined yet simple design, gems set in "natural" settings, without decorative superstructures.

Resortwear An English term that, especially in France, in the 1920s and 1930s, became indicative of holiday wear, especially beachwear, in the brand new discovery of sunshine and life in the open air, in locations that were certain to become society watering holes: the first shorts, the wrap-around skirt for bicycling, tennis outfits, and beach pajamas.

Restivo Mary Ann (1940). American fashion designer who succeeded in combining elegance with the practical needs of the working woman. She studied at the Fashion Institute of Technology in New York. From 1962 to 1974, she put her name on a line of her own for the Genre label. After that, she founded a company of her own which, in 1988, was purchased by the Leslie Fay Corporation. In 1992, her label was discontinued. Since 1993 she has been freelancing as a consulting fashion designer.

Rétif Patrick (1958-1992). French jeweler. He created jewelry for the collections of Gaultier, De Castelbajac, Lagerfeld, and Girbaud, working with gold and silver but also glamorizing materials like plastic, plexiglas, and leather. He debuted in 1979. He always designed attention-getting creations with a distinctive element of research.

Reville and Rossiter British couture house. They made the outfit the queen wore in 1911 for the coronation of King George. Reville was the creative half of the partnership; Rossiter the commercial strategist. Thirty years after the company's foundation, it merged with Worth, the French couture house that had made clothing for all the courts of Europe.

Revillon French furrier. Louis-Victor Revillon (1806), who worked with fur as if it were a fabric, decided in 1839 to purchase the venerable Parisian maison of Givelet. His children entered the business as well, and between 1865 and 1875, the company expanded so considerably that it absorbed the furrier Pouchard and went on to open branch offices in London and New York. Revillon was responsible for creating the fashion of seal fur. In the twentieth century, the *griffe* prospered, launching perfumes and, in the years following the Second World War, diversifying its line of production with prêt-à-porter and accessories. Beginning in 1981, an alliance of capital and strategies with the Cora Group, a major distributor, served to further drive expansion, through the opening of exclusive boutiques around the world, among others steps.

❑ 2002. The French-based France Luxury Group and and the Swiss group Leman Capital were battling to take control of Revillon which, despite its impressive history, found itself being pushed out of the market (even though it continued to rely on a loyal clientele). According to *Le Monde*, the two groups "hope to take advantage of the opportunities for acquisition created in the luxury field by the depression that came in the wake of 11 September."

Revlon American manufacturer of cosmetics founded by the brothers Charles and Joseph Revson with their friend Charles Lachman (the L in Revlon). The debut on the market took place in 1932 with a series of nail polishes, created in a room on 44th Street in Manhattan: a hymn to color in order to react to the grey years of the Great Depression. Then came the debut of a line of color-coordinated lipsticks and nail polishes – the first in history – which also introduced another major novelty: the manufacturing date on the packaging. Always leading the pack in terms of research, Revlon boasted many firsts both in the fields of treatments and in the fields of make-up. During the years of the Second World War, it introduced a make-up collection that set trends in terms of bright and sexy colors (Fatal Apple, Ultra Violet, Sheer Dynamite). In 1951, it developed the first solid creamy foundation, and then offered for very young women a line that was oil-free. In 1958 it succeeded in creating the first stable emulsion in a foundation. In the 1960s, the name became synonymous with daring advertising and advanced marketing. Revlon developed The Wordly Young Innocents make-up: fresh and youthful hues that were represented by the childish beauty of Jean Shrimpton. This was also the period of the famous Blush-on, rouge with an applicator brush that made the use of this accessory for applying colors to the face much more common. Later, in 1972, the phenomenon of the perfume Charlie exploded, along with the invention of a stable and soluble form of collagen, which led to the development of a new generation of treatment products. In the 1980s, the cosmetics house took on the problem of light aging and developed the innovative Age-less. Present in more than 175 nations, Revlon today operates with 27 distribution structures, and is today among

Revillon furriers, the "ape woman," in a sketch by Brunetta for *Bellezza*, 1960 (Biki Collection).

the sector's world leaders. Among its latest successful creations, Colorstay Lipcolour, the first kiss-proof lipstick, the founding product in an entire line of smear-proof make-up, whose image was linked to the famous faces of Cindy Crawford, Melanie Griffith and Salma Hayek.

❑ 2001, July. The Brazilian Colorama company (the leader in Brazil in the nailpolish business) owned by Revlon was purchased by L'Oréal for 64 million Euros.
❑ 2001, October. Revlon debuted in the eyeglass business through a deal with the Filos Group – which now owned Revlon – and the German company, Metzler: this led to the holding company, European Eyewear, which develops and distributes eyeglasses worldwide for United Colors of Benetton, Sisley, Vivienne Westwood, Longines, Aigner, Krizia, Kappa, Paloma Picasso, and Marc O'Polo, as well. At SILMO, the eyewear trade fair in Paris, Filos presented the new Revlon Eyewear collection. With Revlon a worldwide production and distribution license was signed for women's sunglasses and eyeglasses, beginning with 25 new models. The worldwide revenue goal for the first year was to reach 20 million Euros and the project called for coordination of image between make-up and eyewear.
❑ 2001. Revlon ended the year with negative results of 28.3 million dollars, in contrast with the 51.3 million dollars with which it closed the same period of the previous year. (*Ginevra Falzoni*)

Rexlane Prato-based manufacturer that has been working since 1964 in the sector of fabrics for menswear and womenswear. The products are aimed at a medium to high-end market sector and are the product of production, often in blends, of both natural fibers (silk and linen) and technological fibers (lycra and nylon). The company's banner is innovation: from worsted fabrics in the 1970s to the double-face fabrics of the 1980s and all the way up to fabrics of the present day with high fashion content. In 1993, the company diversified with a line of accessoris: scarves and shawls.

❑ 2003. The company presented its womenswear collections at Première Vision and its menswear collections at Ideabiella. Aside from these two important events which are held twice yearly, Rexlane presents pre-collections to a limited number of clients, with the trends in fabrics and colors for the season, and a post-collection with the latest developments in terms of fantasies. Six annual meetings to maintain an ongoing conversation with its most important clients.

Reynaud Alain (1924-1982). French designer. He was the right-hand man of Jacques Fath. For him and for his wife Geneviève, he designed the allegorical costumes of the Dawn for the legendary ball held in Venice in 1951 by Charles de Bestegui. He was the director of the Maison Fath in New York. Later, he accepted the invitation of the Milanese fashion designer Biki to work with her in the creative direction of the maison; he then became – in the 1950s – the Pygmalion of the house's client Maria Callas, completely revolutionizing her style of dressing. Not only did he hand down a sort of Ten Commandments to La Callas (what she could and could not wear, and when), but giving a sense of structure to her wardrobe, cataloguing it and classifying in such a way that the renowned soprano would never have difficulties with selecting outfits and coordinating them with the right accessories. He created clothing for Jeanne Moreau for Antonioni's film *La Notte*. At the end of the 1960s, he launched the first joint venture in the field of fashion with Japan, founding Biki-Japan.

Rheims Bettina (1952). French photographer. After ending her career as a model, she opened with partners a gallery for contemporary art in Paris and, in 1978, she entered the field of photography, doing pictures for album covers, celebrity portraits, movie posters, and coverage for the Sygma agency. She then devoted herself to fashion photography, publishing her work in *Egoiste*, *Vogue*, *Marie Claire*, and *Globe*. Her creative work focused especially on female nudes: her women were young, cheerful, a little mysterious, and intentionally provocative. Among her creatons were *Female Trouble*

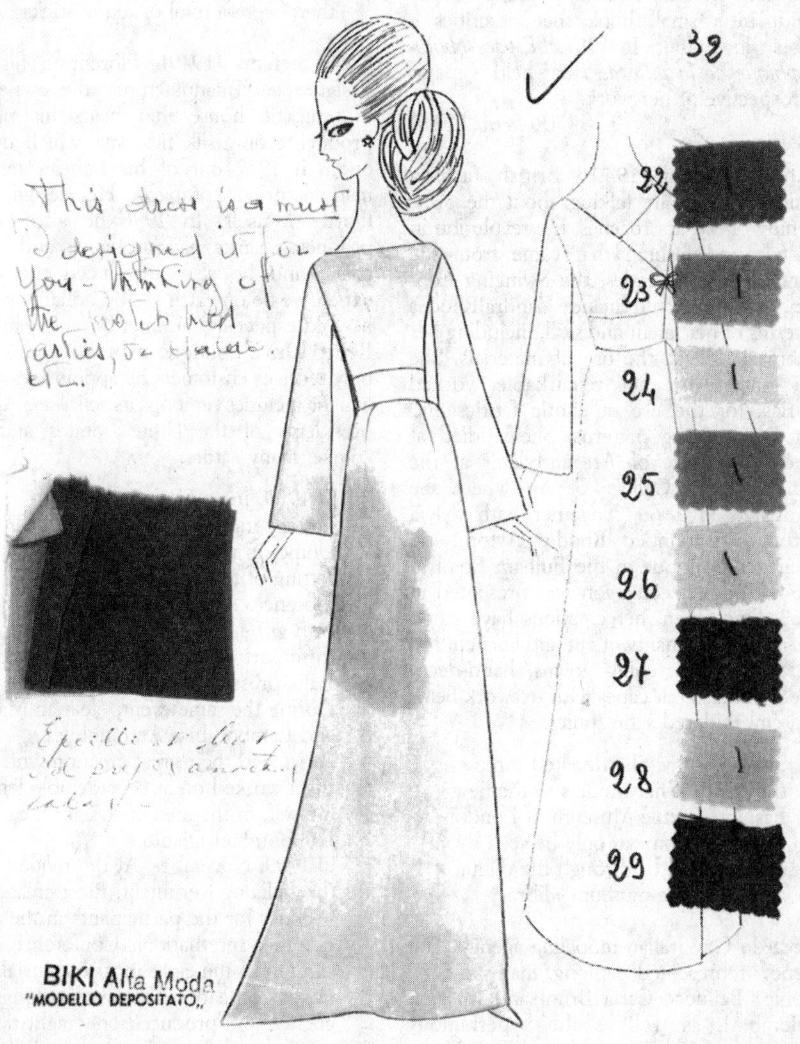

Alain Reynaud, outfit designed for Maria Callas. This sketch is in green. La Callas wrote on the sketch, "Excellent, but I prefer another color." She suggested a shade of orange.

(1991), a project in which it is imagined that the protagonist is a seductress who photographs in the nude the women that she conquers, *Femmes Fatales* (1999) and, more recently, in 2002, *Morceaux Choisis*, a project commissioned by the English fashion magazine *Delicae Vitae* and published by Steidt in a small book that describes a lesbian love affair. In 1987, *l'Espace photographique de la ville de Paris* held a major retrospective of her work.

(*Roberto Mutti*)

Rhodes Zandra (1940). British fashion designer. If we are talking about the overturning of old approaches, the revolution in lifestyle and fashion that came from the London of the Beatles, the Swinging London, then we should include Zandra Rhodes in terms of her talent and skill, including her technical skill in the use of materials. She was known for her remarkable worked fabrics, for the use of exotic fabrics and Art Deco zigzag patterns. She studied at Medway College of Art and later at the London Royal College of Art where she graduated in 1966. Together with Sylvia Ayton, she founded Rhodes Ayton, and opened a boutique in the Fulham Road in 1967. Her first collection was presented in 1969. Since then, her creations have stood out for the originality of cut and line: chiffon and light silk evening gowns, hand-decorated, but also felt capes with fretwork hems and embroidered satin tunics.

❑ 2003, May. She donated three thousand of her models to the new Fashion Textile Museum of London. The collection can only be seen by appointment or through the digital archive in the museum's library.

Riccardo Gay Italian modeling agency. The agency represented, among many others, Monica Bellucci, Carla Bruni and Martina Colombari, as well as the hyperfamous Naomi Cambpell, Carol Alt and Kate Moss. It began operations in the late 1960s. Today, aside from modeling proper, it also handles communications strategies and the organization of special events, beauty contests, photo shoots, calendars, and sponsorships. Among the most significant undertakings of 1998-99 we should mention the alliance with Italjet and with Chronostar for the production of the Torpedo scooter and the Mode watch, both labeled Riccardo Gay.

❑ 2003, April. The agency produced a line of fashion lipsticks. Included with the April issue of the magazine *Y-18*, there were a total of ten lipsticks.

Ricci Stefano (1949). Florentine fashion designer and manufacturer, the owner of the necktie house that bears his name, producing only silk ties, and which developed in 1972 out of his father's textiles manufacturing company. He designs the fabrics himself. In 1996 he also began producing shirts, jackets, suits, and overcoats, and he also introduced the most expensive tie on earth (1,500 dollars), which he sold especially in America, at Bijian, the Rodeo Drive boutique in Los Angeles that only receives customers by appointment and which includes among its clientele many presidents of the United States and, of course, many actors.

❑ 1999, June. He organized the participation of Classico Italia at Pitti Uomo, in the splendid and theatrical setting of the courtyard of the Uffizi in Florence. Alongside the creations of his own *griffe*, the other 23 maisons that form part of the Consorzio Classico Italia presented their own collections. During the same event, Neiman Marcus and Lamborghini Automobiles christened their great creation which Ricci worked on at considerable length himself, in the area of design: the Lamborghini Diablo.
❑ 1999, November. At the request of the Italian government, Ricci created neckties for the participants in the Florence International Conference, a summit of the eight most industrialized nations on earth. The fashion designer created and produced only eight ties, one for each leader, including: Bill Clinton, F. Enrique Cardoso, Tony Blair, Massimo D'Alema, Lionel Jospin and Gerhard Schröder.
❑ 2002, September. "Solo Una," the exquisite necktie created by the fashion designer with a value of 10,000 dollars (the most expensive necktie ever made)

was exhibited in the 18-meter display window of Brandimarte, a silversmith in Florence.

❑ 2003, January. After the boutiques in Monte Carlo and Beverly Hills (on Rodeo Drive), and the three shops in China in Shanghai, Dalian and Chengdu, the label of shirts, ties, and men's overcoats and coats opened a flagship store in Beijing, in the St. Regis Hotel.

Richard Edward Men's fashion label, behind which lurks the talent of two fashion designers: Richard Bengtsson, born in Sundsvall, Sweden in 1962, and Edward Pavlick, born in New Jersey in 1966. Arriving from different educational fields – Richard studied at the Stockholm school of art and design, while Edward studied industrial design – they pooled their creativity in 1993 launching a line of knitwear, the Holiday shirt line. Later, they created entire collections of apparel, with runway presentations in the chief fashion capitals, such as Paris and Milan. (*Daniela Bolognetti*)

Richardson Bob (1928). American photographer. He debuted as an illustrator fashion designer, taking interest only later on in photography, with spectacular results right from the beginning. In fact, his first layouts were published by *Harper's Bazaar*. The most fertile period was the 1960s, when he worked with the great art director Alexej Brodovitch. He lived in Paris, worked frequently for Valentino and published his photographs in the French, American, and Italian editions of *Vogue*. There is a clear influence in his work of the atmospheres of the most classic cinema, from John Ford to Luchino Visconti.

Richardson Terry (1967). American photographer, who was literally born into the profession. An unusual character even in the world of fashion (he dresses in jeans and a T-shirt, shows off his tattoos and a prominent moustache), loves non-conformist behavior, just like his father Bob in his day, whom he also imitates in the style of his work: at first he fought against the sarcasm that surrounded him because he didn't like complex sets or assistants, he never took test Polaroids and he never designed choreographies or lighting schemes. Quite simply, he would appear on the set with two compact Yashica/Contax cameras, and to those who questioned his approach he would offer little pills of wisdom ("You're not going to let machinery and technology be the basis of your creativity, are you?") or artfully targeted ironic phrases ("I'm nearsighted, I could never focus with bigger cameras"). The fact remains that he did famous photographic portraits of such famous personalities as Faye Dunaway and Catherine Deneuve along with his layouts in *The Face*, *Vogue France*, and *Harper's Bazaar*, as well as his exhibitions in Paris, London, and New York. His campaigns for H M, Anna Molinari, Evian, Supreme shops (for whom he shot a 2002 calendar) and, recently, Gucci, were famous; at the same time, he had a decidedly innovative long-term relationship with Sisley and with its creative director Nikko Amandonico that began in 1990. Here, in campaigns rich with a harsh and mysterious allure, catalogues that were sent out in brown-paper wrappings to keep them from falling into the hands of minors, there emerged a daring conception of the body and sex that has come to embody a way of seeing: photographs that are only apparently immediate, ironic gazes, composition of stunning efficacy, acceptance of such technical "errors" as the so-called red eyes, a subtle parody of erotic photography, implemented with the same stylistic methods. (*Roberto Mutti*)

Richmond John (1961). British fashion designer. He takes his inspiration from the 1950s, from body building and from hard rock. After taking his degree at Kingston Polytechnic, he began in 1982 to work as a consultant for other *griffes*. In 1985, he formed a partnership with Maria Cornejo. In 1987 he went into business on his own and, two years later, founded the label Destroy. In 1996 he debuted with a womenswear collection that was joined, a year later, by a menswear collection.

❑ 2002. He staged his runway presentations in a little church in Milan's Via Daverio. That is hardly a surprise since the fashion designer, for season after season, has used this delightful little "house of God" to present his

Sketch by John Richmond for the 2003-2004 Fall-Winter Menswear Collection.

collections to his colleagues. What was striking this year was the contrast between the frescoes on the walls and the especially powerful collection. This time Richmond really did provoke: a principal theme of his collection was in fact religion. There were T-shirts with appliquéd crosses, necklaces with glittering crosses, and jeans and T-shirts with appliquéd images of Jesus, and a white cape reminiscent of a priest's stole.

Richter Darja (1965). German fashion designer. She began working in France in 1993. She studied fine arts in Berlin. She reached the field of fashion via cinema: she designed the costumes for Peter Greenaway's film *The Pillow Book*. She prepared for her debut by working as Martine Sitbon's assistant. She uses the system of silkscreening on fabrics and loves to overlap different types of fabric. Beginning in 1998, she has been creating fabrics for Versace's prêt-à-porter.

Richter Uli (1926). German fashion designer. He launched his maison in 1959, after an experience as the fashion director for Horn, in Berlin. Over the years, he became known for his classical style. He presented his first prêt-à-porter collection in 1963. In 1981 he retired.

Rickus Laura (1967). American photographer. After studying fashion design in Boston and Paris, from 1987 till 1992 she worked in the world of fashion as a freelance illustrator for a number of American houses and, from 1991 to 1996, as a model. She then moved to the other side of the camera, behind the viewfinder, out of curiosity, and quickly decided to become a full-time photographer, working with publications like *You* and *Best Looking,* and doing calendars and campaigns. A considerable portion of her work is dedicated to research, with models as the actors, into an alluring vision that borders on the surreal: she has held personal and collective exhibitions. Her work has been published by *Photo* and *Immagini Foto*.

Ridenti Lucio (pseudonym of Ernesto Scialpi, 1895-1973). Theater critic and journalist. After abandoning his career as an actor because of a problem with his hearing, he founded in 1925, together with Pitigrilli, the theater magazine *Il Dramma,* and was the editor until 1968. Tall and thin, quite a dandy, he was an habitué of the renowned (but long-since closed) Milanese shirtmaker Truzzi. He was a devotee of the tuxedo, the tailcoat, and the monocle. In the 1930s he also worked as a society writer, assiduously frequenting high society and an observant fashion journalist. From the pages of the daily *La Gazzetta del Popolo* in Turin, he criticized Nazi women's style and the love of

French fashion, emphasizing the need for a truly Italian fashion. In *Il Dramma* there was a considerable flow of advertising for furriers and fashion houses, including the house of the master hosier Franceschi, the first in Italy to produce women's stocking with a line down the back. (*Marilea Somarè*)

Ridgers Derek (1950). British photographer. Born in London. He studied graphics and advertising design at the Earling School of Art, together with the future pop star Freddie Mercury. He graduated in 1971, and worked for ten years in the field of advertising as an art director, and then went on to become a full-time photographer. After his first successes – portraits of pop stars for the *New Musical Express* – he continued to work on portraits of young punkers and habitués of London night spots (working with a technique somewhere between comics graphics and Renaissance painting), identifying the innovative style of spontaneous fashion, a style that was frequently intentionally unpleasant, and straight from the street. He has had exhibitions in London, Dublin and Paris.

Rieger Hans. Austrian fashion designer. He maintained that fashion should be created while watching women walking down the street. He did not develop as a fashion designer but as a marketing expert, a subject that he studied at the University of Vienna. At the end of the 1980s he discovered his true calling: after working as a freelancer for various Austrian apparel manufacturers, in 1992 he presented the first collection with his own label.

Rijksmuseum Amsterdam, Netherlands. Since it opened in 1885, this museum has featured a section devoted to apparel and textiles, with an initial core collection consisting of clothing and accessories donated by the Dutch royal house. Today there are more than 10,000 items, subdivided into the following categories and periods: men's and women's clothing from 1720 to 1960, children's clothing from 1700 to 1950, accessories from 1500 to 1960, ceremonial garb from 1750 to 1930. The museum has always collected the possessions of the upper classes, and strictly focused on items manufactured locally.

Rilievi A Bolognese embroidery business. Over the course of the years, the business has developed the sector of accessories, designing buttons, zipper-pulls, and frogs to be used with fabric treatments. Based on a crafts tradition, since 1997 it has featured a collection of fabrics. The activity includes materials research, the study and development of prototypes, the preparation of items, and all the various techniques of embroidery, ranging looms with microcrochet or handwork and needlework, or mixed techniques such as embroidery by electronic machine, cornely or bernina, as well a painting techniques on fabrics and materials. The company has worked with Armani, DG, Ferré, Ferretti, BVN, La Perla, Dior, and Lacroix.

Rimbotti Vittorio Emanuele (1920-2001). Engineer and entrepreneur, he was from 1989 on the chairman of the Centro di Firenze per la Moda Italiana. His main input in the leadership of the CFMI took the form especially in the crafting of agreements for the management of fashion events in Milan and Florence and in the promotion of major international initiatives in the field of culture and fashion-related research, as well as the trade fairs in the sector. In particular, he was decisive in supporting the planning and implementation of the project of the Biennale di Firenze.

❑ 2001, October. He died just before the first board meeting of Intesa Moda, a body promoting oversight and cooperation for which he had fought, and whose existence marked the end of the diatribes between Florence and Milan.

Rimmel Eugène (1810-1887). Founder, in 1844, of the perfume maker of the same name and the inventor of the table of lampblack for eyelashes, with an attached little brush to dip in water, rub over the product and then onto the eyelashes. Spit took the place of water because it mixed better. That cosmetic will always be called "rimmel," at least in Italy and several other countries.

Rina Modelli The company founded by the pattern maker and dressmaker Enrichetta

Enrichetta Pedrini, Rina Modelli, in her Milanese atelier. Sketch by Brunetta for *Bellezza* (Biki Collection).

Pedrini (1889-1973). Twice a year, during the collections, Rina Modelli would go to Paris, purchase the original patterns and sketches and, one month later, transform the Milanese workshop into an atelier, clearing the long work tables, placing chairs along the walls of the three large rooms, opening the doors that led onto the long hallway, and have a runway presentation with models wearing items purchased from the great names of French haute couture: Lelong, Vionnet, Balenciaga, Schiaparelli, Dior, Balmain, Nina Ricci, Fath, Givenchy. For one week, this runway was besieged by the seamstresses and tailors of all Italy who, in turn, would buy patterns, sketches, and the right to reproduce them. In the company's account books, we see names like Zecca, Stop Senes, Velia Biagiotti, Carosa di Roma, Fercioni, Tizzoni, Montanari per Ventura, Gigliola Curiel and others from Milan, Bonanno and Maglio of Naples, Solaro, Longo and Camollo of Turin, and even the Sisters of the Piccole Operaie from Trani. Enrichetta Pedrini was born in San Martino near Ferrara and had begun her career as a dressmaker, a profession that in the years of autarky and the Second World War, she developed with a line of her own and then returned almost completely to the profession of pattern maker, with those two trips a year to Paris and the subsequent presentations to the Italian houses. Rina Modelli had three offices in Milan, in the Via Piatti, in the Via Rovello, and finally in the Via Montenapoleone, number 29. Maria Pezzi, in her autobiography, *Una vita dentro la moda*, recalls: "The Romagna-born Signora Pedrini, the powerful and impressive *Sciura Rina* resembled Colette, stout, lovely complexion, lively, made-up eyes, a loose work smock and a little chiffon choker always at her neck. At the runway presentations in Paris, the Italian couturiers and tailors and their colleagues the pattern makers, would keep an eye on her, watching to see what she chose because she had impeccable taste. When an outfit interested her, she would pretend to doze off, to nap for a little while to deceive the watchers. In all the ateliers, one vendeuse would keep an eye on her and her alone." Beppe Modenese remembers: "She would make her choices and the following morning, escorted by her daughter Dogle, she would come back to fine-tune her selections. The 'mannequin de cabine' would walk out showing off the outfits that she had selected. One day Enrichetta looked at one model with a particular intensity. She couldn't identify what was bothering. Then she said: "Oh, Dogle, quel li l'è el mè paltò." The model, in her haste, had put on the overcoat that Enrichetta had left in the 'cabine'." She would buy 250 models each season. She had married by proxy Amedeo Pedrini, who had emigrated to the United States and then become a factory worker for Breda and chief of cell in the Communist Party. From their stormy marriage two children were born: Maria, known as Dogle, and Danilo. The older girl, along with her husband, Attilio Faré, continued her mother's profession, and also opened in 1967 the first boutique of Saint Laurent Rive Gauche in Italy. Today the family tradition is being carried on by the grandchildren, owners of the Kalathea company, which distributes French luxury prêt-à-porter collections and paper patterns of high fashion models by Laroche, Ungaro and Saint-Laurent. (*Marilea Somarè*)

Ritts Herb (1952-2002). American photographer. Born in Los Angeles, he went to New York to study economics and art history, but then he returned to California to work for his father's furniture manufacturing business. Photography represented for him a passion refined by his own self-education but also an acute artistic sensibility: this led him to publish his first photographs in *Newsweek*. In 1978, he used a gas station in the desert as a set for pictures that he took of a friend of his, a still unknown young actor, Richard Gere, who would soon afterward become spectacularly famous. *Vogue USA* bought the photo session and commissioned Ritts to do a photo session on Brooke Shields, introducing him into a mechanism whereby he became the best-loved photographer of the star system, sought after by actors and top models. His style is characterized by sharply contrasting blacks and whites in which beauty and seduction dominate, but also a sensibility that is particularly attentive to the evolution of contemporary taste and aesthetics. He thus went on to do photographs of great sensuality, utilizing such natural elements as water, sand, and mud to create unprecedented body effects: this is a product of his self-educated approach and his perfect knowledge of the places in which he sets his photography, open spaces, desert, natural locations. Although he never wanted to be trapped in a single genre, Herb Ritts became famous for his portraits of actors and actresses, even in difficult situations, as revealed by his photograph of the late Christopher Reeve in his wheelchair, of the Dalai Lama and politicians such as Ronald Reagan, and for the videoclips of Madonna (for whom he also shot the covers of *Like a Prayer* and *True Blue*), Michael Jackson and Chris Isaak. He has published a number of books: *Men, Women* (1986), *Duo* (1991, with the subject of a gay bodybuilder couple) and *Africa* (1994), in which the protagonists were not only models, but also women and warriors of the Masai tribe. The transition to fashion was obligatory: layouts in *GQ*, *Vogue*, *Rolling Stone*, *Vanity Fair*, *Interview*, *Mademoiselle*, and *Esquire*. Among his clients are Giorgio Armani, Calvin Klein and Donna Karan. He photographed two refined Pirelli calendars: in 1994, setting color photographs of Karen Alexander, Melena Christensen, Cindy Crawford and Kate Moss in the Bahamas, and in 1999 by creating in the studio and ideal historic progression in black and white that began with the Belle Epoque, revisiting past decade by decade and culminating with a powerful image of a dark and shiny female nude that represents the future.

(*Roberto Mutti*)

Ritz Sadler Apparel label that was founded in 1946 in Bologna and launched by Giorgio Faccioli, who, along with his wife Raffaella, opened a shop in 1964 in Cortina. This was the beginning of the company's rise, with classic items of apparel for men and women, accompanied by accessories, the leather line, and the Ritzino line, for children. Ritz Sadler, at the end of the 1960s, arrived in Milan, in Via Manzoni, and in Bologna, in Via Farini. In 1969 Faccioli organized in Cortina, together with Giovanni Nuvoletti, one of the first "reviews" of made in Italy, Cortina-Moda, which was reprised the following year. Among the guests, the Missonis, Emilio Pucci, Mila Schön, and Achille Maramotti for Max Mara. Faccioli also brought to Cortina cultural events and exhibitions at the highest level, like the one dedicated to the work of the painting of the America of the New Deal, Norman Rockwell (1990). In August 1999, the Ritz Store was opened in Cortina, a newly renovated showroom in the Corso Italia.

(*Emanuela Fontana*)

Riva Anna (1935). Italian journalist. She has been a correspondent for *Vogue Germany* since 1981, an established and well-respected publication in that market. She was born in Reggio Emilia, and took a college degree in jurisprudence; she has been a journalist for more than thirty years. An immensely likable woman, gifted with humor, generosity, and communication skills, she has an extraordinary and apparently innate instinct for fashion. She began to work for Max Mara in 1958, and in 1962 she wound up at Mondadori, working for the monthly *Arianna* where, with Anna Piaggi (the pair established a long-lasting working relationship), she was able to implement her particular inclination for fashion, made up in part of curiosity and careful attention to every shift in lifestyle, collected and recorded with a rare sensibility and acuity. She later moved on to *Linea Italiana* (also published by Arnoldo Mondadori), the official mouthpiece of Italian fashion, where the new image, still in progress, was being created of what was known as the "Made in Italy": a perfect venue for all emerging talents. In 1975 she changed employers: she was hired by *Annabella* (now, *Anna*; Rizzoli Editore), thus coming into contact for the first time with the diverse and emerging audience of the large-circulation weekly. In 1980 she was offered the editorship of *Mondo Uomo*, a men's fashion magazine founded by Flavio Lucchini (Editoriale Rusconi), which was intended as a rival for the success of *L'Uomo Vogue*. Over the years, her sensibility for "the things and events of fashion," of which she always offered a personal and original view, led her to become an important personality, much loved by the fashion designers, who valued her entirely personal and at times intuitive interpretation.

Riva Heinz (1938). Swiss fashion designer. He was born into the profession: his moth had a fashion atelier. After studying in

Zurich, where he was born, he worked in Paris and London. In 1963, he arrived in Rome where he worked in the *maison* Irene Galitzine. In 1966, he went into business on his own, with runway presentations in the Roman high fashion shows.

Riva Lorenzo (1938). Italian fashion designer. After his first runway presentation, at the age of 18, he also opened his first atelier and the press was soon singing his praises. The year was 1958. In the 1970s he moved to Paris where he worked with the most famous couturiers. In 1974 he became the artistic director of the *maison* of Balenciaga, a fundamental experience for his professional training; in the 1980s he returned to Milan and presented a collection of wedding dresses. This was to become one of his "specialties." In 1991 he presented a collection of high fashion in Rome and then a prêt-à-porter collection, at Milan's Collezioni. In 1996 he presented his collection in New York, at the Cristinerose Gallery in SoHo.

❑ 2001, July. He held a runway presentation in Rome, during the high fashion week, or Settimana di Alta Moda. The clothing that appeared on the runway was dedicated to the great movie stars, from Greta Garbo in *Ninotchka* to Charlize Theron in *Badgers Vance*, by way of Frida Kahlo, the legendary Mexican painter.
❑ 2003, February. In the Fall-Winter 2003-2004 collection, exquisite passementerie imported from Kazakhstan, and delicate *ramage* and white wool fringes on hems and cuffs.

Riva Sofia. Italian photographer. After classical studies and courses in theatrical design at the Accademia di Brera, she was hired in the 1970s at *Vogue* as a fashion editor: this world became her passion and in the course of a few years, during which she carefully studied the photographers, like Barbieri and Toscani, who based their style on clean lines and composition and a spare essential approach, she became a photographer herself. She works for *Vogue* and many other magazines, specializing in a very challenging sector, fashion photography with children.

Rive Droite Fashion historians date the birth of Parisian haute couture to the creation in 1858, in the Rue de la Paix, of the *maison* of Charles Frederick Worth, the favorite couturier of the Empress Eugenie, of the most elegant women of the Belle Epoque, ranging from actresses to high-priced prostitutes. The popularity of the quarter, in the wealthy VIII arrondissement on the right bank, or Rive Droite, of the Seine, only grew during the years that led up to the period between the two world wars. Among those who were drawn there were Poiret, Chanel, Nina Ricci, Schiaparelli and the Spanish designer Balenciaga. In the two decades that followed World War Two, when new creators were proliferating there and, alongside the haute couture, luxury prêt-à-porter began to take root, the Rive Droite continued to be the world fashion crossroads. It all revolved around two streets there: the Rue du Faubourg Saint-Honoré and Avenue Montaigne. Overlooking the first of the two streets is the Elysée, but for the average tourist, any interest that the French presidential palace might hold was overshadowed by the adjoining shop windows of Cardin, Féraud, Lanvin, Azzaro, or Versace. Equally renowned is the Avenue Montaigne, where one sees the original house of Christian Dior, alongside those of Nina Ricci, Ungaro, and Scherrer. In the immediately surrounding area, you will also see Balmain and Balenciaga, in the Rue François I, and Carven at the Rond-Point des Champs Elysées. In the 1960s, haute couture however slid into a period of transition, which was only to be accelerated by the youth revolt of May 1968. The creation of the unisex style, and various social, economic, and technical evolutions, along with the general shift in lifestyles caused the sector to decline. Today, high fashion serves to encourage other, more lucrative activities, such as selling perfumes or name prêt-à-porter. Only 18 *maisons* still belong to the Syndicat de la Haute Couture.

Rive Gauche It took the crisis of haute couture, which had triumphed for a full century on the rive droite of the Seine, to encourage a number of its creators to cross the river and launch into a new adventure on the Left Bank. Here, the new center of gravity of fashion was situated between the

Place de Saint-Germain-des-Prés and the Place de Saint Sulpice, dominated by the church of Saint Sulpice which represented the most hide-bound nineteenth-century traditionalism (in Parisian slang, *sulpicien* is synonymous with bad taste). And yet it was here that, in 1966, the renowned Saint Laurent, already set up on the Avenue Georges V, on the Right Bank, decided to create the subsidiary, Saint Laurent-Rive Gauche. His undertaking won many followers: Féraud and Castelbajac opened their boutiques in Saint Sulpice, and Rykiel, Givenchy, Kenzo, and Rabanne did so in adjoining streets. But the most astonishing development came in 1997 with the simultaneous inauguration, on the Place de Saint-Germain-des-Prés, of a subsidiary of Christian Dior and an Armani shop. In vain a petition circulated by French intellectuals attempted to prevent the invasion of fashion in what had been from the 1940s to the 1960s the headquarters of Sartre and the most daring avant-garde writers and artists. The bottle was lost. There is a dense presence of Italians such as Versace or Romeo Gigli and Japanese designers such as Yamamoto, Kawabuko, and Miyake. In practical terms, fashion in Paris has long since abolished the old social boundary between *rive droite* and *rive gauche*.

(*Elena Guicciardi*)

Rivella Turinese furrier. Famous in the 1950s and 1960s. It was founded by Francesco Rivella, who was the owner of the Casino of Saint Vincent. He also founded a tannery, which allowed him to make profound innovations in the furrier's art, introducing a significant fashion content to his creations. He would present his collections at SAMIA, the apparel fair of Turin. He was the first to dye beaver skins in fashionable colors. He was also the first to make massive use of advertising, forcing his competitors to adopt this strategy. This gave a strong kickstart to the sector. When Francesco Rivella died, his employees continued to run the company, but not for long.

Rivetti Marco (1943-1996). Italian industrialist of the apparel sector. He was the chairman and managing director of the Gruppo Finanziario Tessile (GFT). He was born in Turin, and began to work at GFT in the early 1970s, reporting directly to his uncle Piergiorgio, the father and boss of the family-owned company, with whom Marco had always had an uneasy relationship. Those were the years of the energy crisis and apparel manufacturing, like nearly all the sectors in worldwide industry, was going through a difficult period. Even Facis, a leading label for menswear and the flower in the buttonhold of the Italian fashion industry, had suddenly seen its sales plummet. Marco Rivetti was the first industrialist in the Italian textiles sector to understand that something had changed profoundly and, together with his little staff of colleagues, he attempted to find a response to the changed tastes of the public. This led to his collaboration with Giorgio Armani and Sergio Galeotti, at the time practically unknown. The fact that he had brought together on a working basis what were then the very new ideas on apparel of Armani with the manufacturing and distributing power of a colossus like the Gruppo Finanziario Tessile, ushered in the ear of star designers and the Made in Italy on a worldwide scale. Rivetti, joking, years later, would say that in order to find new ideas and invent the contemporary Made in Italy, it had taken a protester from 1968, as he had in fact been. A knowledgable collector and lover of contemporary art (he had been a crucial figure in the creation of the Museo di Rivoli), a well read and insightful man, who made decisions and choices quickly, he was also one of the first to understand that fashion was not only big business but also a form of body design: it was more than just runway presentations but also a substantial section of contemporary culture. This understanding underlay many of the projects of Gruppo Finanziario Tessile, which began to undertake collaborations with such critics as Germano Celant, architects such as Arata Isozaki, Frank Gehry, and Aldo Rossi, artists like Oldenburg. The same philosophy, that is, to give space to the culture of fashion and to culture in general, was applied by Rivetti when, in 1985, he agreed to become president of what were at the time the languishing fairs of textiles and apparel in Florence, knocked to their knees by the great power of the fashion designers of Milan. In Florence, Franco Tancredi, then president of the Centro Moda, had recently hired a consultant (1984) named Luigi Settembrini, in order to attempt what seemed to be an unlikely revival of the fairs in the Fortezza da Basso. Settembrini, long a consultant of the Rivettis and GFT, convinced Marco to accept the position. This led to the birth of Pitti Immagine, which today not only organizes several of the most important fashion fairs on earth, but is also considered one of the most lively international workshops of the culture of fashion.

Rivière James. Label and working and professional name of Enzo Teora (1948). Italian jeweler. The son of a southern Italian farmer whose business was wiped out by a hailstorm, he emigrated to Milan where he attended courses in Industrial Training School and, subsequently, the Art School in the Castello Sforzesco of Milan, at one of the most exciting and fertile periods in cultural terms that the capital of Lombardy experienced, following the Second World War. A pupil of Giacomo Benevelli, he took his inspiration primarily from the work of such designers and artists as Bruno Munari and Luigi Veronesi, who were friends and fellow adventurers in the world of work. From the former, he adopted a subtly poetic vein of irony, especially in connection to research into the theories of perception; from the latter he borrowed a sensibility for geometric abstraction and chromatic interplay. He debuted in the late 1960s. From silver, thoroughly expored in all its expressive potential, he moved on around 1975 to gold, at first combining it especially with colorful stones: turquoise, malachite, lapis lazuli. A significant phase in his working career was represented by the introduction of titanium, featured in a broad range of chromatic variants, joined with gold and pearls. Over the course of the 1980s, he took inspiration from space (the brooch-pendant *Viaggiando nello spazio*, or 'Travelling Through Space') and the legend of Atlantis, expressed in creations veined with surrealism and magical accents. In 1995, he presented at the Galleria Vismara in Milan a personal show entitled *Emersioni*. Since then, he has been focusing his attention on the decorative and symbolic qualities of semiprecious stones, corals, ambers, and pearls, presenting one-offs or limited-edition pieces in the Milanese ateliers of Via Brera, which he opened in 1991, and Via Bigli which, inaugurated in the fall of 2002, also features silver sculptures and objets-d'art.

(*Alessandra Quattordio*)

Rivolta Milanese custom shoemaker. It was active from the 1940s to and throughout the 1960s. It was considered one of the finest shoemakers in Milan, along with Panicola. It had a display window in the Via Verri. It used the finest leather, German hides tanned with aniline, Russian leather tanned with chromium. There was a very long waiting list for a pair of shoes. The shop, with its eighteenth-century chairs, its awnings, its glass and mirrors, looked like something out of the first act of Der Rosen Kavalier. Greeting the customers was Rivolta's wife, a tiny, elderly, elegant, and ceremonious old lady. She would invite a customer to sit down and, unfailingly, with just a hint of a smile, she would whisper: "Signor Rivolta will be here directly." Then, through a glass door, a theatrical entrance made flesh, a living coup-de-théâtre, he would arrive, small, smiling, fast-moving, with tousled white hair. He wore a white smock, clean and ironed. He wore a dark-blue lavallière bow tie with white polka dots. Physically he was somewhere between Arturo Toscanini and Charlie Chaplin's Calvero, from *Limelight*. Rivolta's last produced shoes that gave every man's foot, even small, fat feet, an unrivaled slenderness.

Rizzo Alberto (1931). Italian photographer. In 1960 he moved to the United States, first to California and later to New York where he began to work with *Harper's Bazaar*. From that time on, he published in *Newsweek*, *Uomo Vogue*, *Mademoiselle*, *Domus* and for the French, Italian, and American editions of *Vogue*. His dynamic style, profoundly influenced by the technique of collage, and by the powerful colors and the Op Art of the 1960s, characterized his work, both in his original still-lifes and in his fashion layouts. He worked for Bulgari, Chanel, Seiko, Saks Fifth Avenue, Bloomingdale's, Max Factor, and Danskin. He showed his work in many exhibits, at the Metropolitan Museum in New York and at the Venice Biennale in 1981.

Robadin Dominique (1964). Creator of costume jewelry. Of Swiss and Italian descent. Born in Geneva, she studied art at the Ecole des Arts Décoratifs (1987). Among her various working experience in the field of fashion and jewelry, she worked for a certain period in Milan and for Bally in Switzerland where, in 1993, she launched her own linea di costume jewelry. She worked with Ungaro. Her ceramic jewelry coated in pure gold has won numerous prizes and has been distributed around the world. She works out of Geneva.

Robe di Kappa Italian casual apparel label: T-shirts, polo shirts, and sweaters. Founded at the end of the 1960s by the Maglificio Calzificio Torinese which the Vitale family had founded in 1916. It was created by the young Maurizio Vitale, in those years of sociocultural transformations, assisted in terms of style, image, advertising, and publicity, by enterprising young men like him, such as Oliviero Toscani, Castelbajac and Emanuele Pirella. Also in those years, Vitale established the jeans brand Jesus Jeans, which won widespread attention for its daring and taboo-breaking advertising campaigns. At the end of the following decade, the company moved decisively into the sector of sports apparel, signing a series of major sponsorship agreements: soccer teams, such as Juventus, Ajax, and the American national track-and-field team. Maurizio left the company in 1986 due to an illness from which he would die. In 1994, the company declared bankruptcy. A short while later, the Gruppo Basic, under the leadership of Marco Boglione, once a close colleague of Maurizio Vitale, purchased the label and reintroduced it. Since 1999, Robe di Kappa has been a sponsor of the Italian national soccer team. The company has a presence in 70 countries. The Gruppo Basic employs some 300 people.

❑ 2000, October. During the first day of SMAU 2000, the awards were assigned to the winners of the Prize for Italian Commercial Electronics. Among those receiving recognition was Basic.net, the website of the Basic Group with the following notation: "An effective example of an electronic platform for the integration of the processes of the production line, capable of capturing the opportunities deriving from globalization in order to increase competitivity on a worldwide level."

❑ 2001, April. The first Robe di Kappa shop is inaugurated in Portofino. The shop will serve as a model for future stores.

❑ 2002, February. The BasicNet Group signed its biggest yet agreement for European co-branding with Sony Entertainment Europe. This collaboration was a strategic move designed to "position" the Kappa trademark in the futuristic playworld of the Playstation2, *Wipeout Fusion*. The Kappa trademark would create and offer for sale on its own website Kappastore.com a clothing line devoted to *Wipeout Fusion*, consisting of eight T-shirts, two PlayStation2 carry bags, and two caps.

❑ 2002, July. BasicNet signed an agreement of partnership with Golsport Pty Ltd., a leading company in the distribution of athletic products in the soccer sector in Australia. Golsport Pty Ltd. thus became a licenser for apparel and footwear with the Kappa and Robe di Kappa logos, and became part of the network of Gruppo BasicNet, adopting the business system which currently includes 36 licensers in 71 countries.

❑ 2003, June. The inauguration of new single-label points of sale in the territories of the former Yugoslavia (Montenegro, Belgrade in Via Knez Mihajlova), Moscow and Prague.

(*Edoardo Ponzoni*)

Roberta di Camerino Label of the Italian fashion designer Giuliana Coen Camerino (1920) who combined her own surname with her daughter Roberta's first name to create a name for the bags she designed in velvet, with green, red, and dark-blue zones, embroidered with gold and heraldic crests, designed during her forced stay in Switzerland to escape the Fascist race laws. Those bags were so popular with international high society that, in the years following WWII, Giuliana had returned to Venice, her birthplace, where an important fashion journalist, Elsa Robiola, published them in *Bellezza*. Well before her popularity exploded, triggered by the Florentine runway presenta-

Roberta di Camerino: velvet bag and clothing in a sketch by Maria Pezzi from the late Sixties.

tions, the bomb of Made in Italy, the fashion designer, like Emilio Pucci, was already very popular in the United States. Maria Pezzi, in her memoir *Una vita dentro la moda*, written with Guido Vergani, recalls: "It was 1952. One September, in Venice. In the motorboat that was running from the Hotel Europa to the Lido, Elsa Maxwell, the journalist who had made society gossip her profession, was holding in her hands a handbag made of red and green velvet, a handsome little trunk that was called Bagonghi and had been made by Roberta di Camerino. At the embarcadero of the Danieli, the actress Eleonora Rossi Drago boarded the boat carrying the same bag and, as another motorboat went by, the Hollywood journalist saw with annoyance another Bagonghi in black and beige. I was not surprised. I had been the first journalist to write about Giuliana and her popularity in America. I knew her story: her wealthy and happy youth in Venice; fleeing with her husband from the Nazi round-ups, she was dressed as a nun, with her new-born son in her arms, while he was dressed as a priest and death was snapping at their heels; the first little bag that she made for herself, a bucket model, by taking apart another purse; the "could you make one of those for me?" from a woman from Lugano; the return home, and the founding of Roberta di Camerino, relying upon the remarkable craftsmanship of Venice, especially the craftsmen who made gondolas: for the snaps and the studs, the specialists in brass; for the velvet, the masters of upholstery. Giuliana became "la dogaressa." In 1956, she was given the Oscar of Fashion, the Neiman Marcus Award. She was invited, in January 1952, to the third edition of the runway presentations in Florence, as the designer of the fashion boutique, the fashion designer expanded her creativity to wardrobe, with a quest for simplicity and liveliness in outfits with linear forms, well suited to travel, light in the suitcase. In 1983, she signed an important agreement with the Mitsubishi Corporation: this led to the foundation of Roberta di Camerino Far East and was consolidated in the Japanese market. The year 1995 witnessed a revival on the Italian market with major licensing agreements. In the same year, Roberta di Camerino donated to the Galleria del Costume of Palazzo Pitti outfits and accessories from the 1960s and 1970s.

❑ 1999. Roberta di Camerino Brand Diffusion Venice was joined with the Brand Coordinator Lugano. The managing director of both lines was the Ligurian and Tuscan industrialist Francesco Pellati. The owner of the label, the fashion designer Giuliana di Camerino, was counting on the relaunch not only for the apparel sector – which she was personally overseeing with her grandchild Tessa Zanga – but also for the debut in two new manufacturing sectors: the sector of jewelry (there was already an agreement with Cozza Gioielli) and the home goods sector, for bath robes, towels, table cloths, and linen, which would be manufactured by Besana.
❑ 2000, September. The label is reintroduced, in Italy and worldwide, with only with a vast array of accessories but also with women's pret-à-porter, produced by Gibierre.
❑ 2003. Twenty single-label boutiques are opened in Korea, Thailand and China. (*Lucia Sollazzo*)

Robert Friedman This is a line of shirts for men and women, produced by the Fabry's company, founded in 1977. The style of the line is in keeping with the trademark, which focuses on fabric research, while the patterns are of high quality in terms of design and tailoring.

Roberts Julian (1972). British fashion designer. He studied at the Royal College of Art. He worked as an assistant to Jasper Conran. In 1998 he launched the label Nothing Nothing. The outfits in his first collection were exhibited in the display windows of Liberty. He debuted in the London Fashion Week in February 2000.

Roberts Michael. Writer, fashion designer, photographer, illustrator, director, art director. He is in charge of the fashion and designer section of the *New Yorker*, after working for the *Sunday Times* and for the magazine *The Tatler*. He makes intelligent fun of the stereotypical images of fashion with a childish illustration technique that conceals a profound and ironic understanding of fashion.

Roberts Patricia (1945). English designer of highly colored knitwear, cardigans, and sweaters. After graduating from Leicester College of Art, in 1967 she began to work in the knitwear department of IPC department stores in London. Five years later, she went into business on her own. The interest of *Vogue* opened her way into the boutiques where she would introduce herself, with a suitcase full of her handmade sweaters. The first store with her name on it opened in 1976. She opened two others in 1979 and 1982.

Robilant (di) Gabriella (1900-1999). Fashion designer. She opened, in 1936-37, an atelier-shop in Milan in the Via Santo Spirito and called it Gabriella Sport. In fact, she designed an athletic fashion or, as the slang term would emerge later, casual: pullovers, skirts, after-ski, and the loose women's trousers that were becoming popular in those years. Gabriella de Bosdari had been the wife of Andrea di Robilant and, with him, she had experienced, between Venice and Paris, an intense life of socializing and carefree pleasures, typical of high society of the time. After her divorce, she arrived in Milan, with her children, and began working, anticipating, perhaps out of necessity, the period of self-sufficient women, who raised their families and found "fulfillment." Gabriella Sport was successful, to the point that it outlived, along with its reputation, the difficult years of the second world war. When, in the years immediately following the war, in Rome (where she had moved to escape the bombing of Milan), she decided, with financing from a group of friends, to buy the Roman headquarters of the Sartoria Ventura in the Piazza di Spagna, she decided to keep the old name, even though she was working in high fashion now. She was assisted professionally by Madame Anna, who had been the intelligent, strong-willed director of the *maison* Ventura. The adventure was short-lived. In 1949, Gabriella remarried with the Sicilian prince Giardinelli. For a few years, she commuted between Palermo and Rome, while operating the couturier atelier, or *sartoria*. But at the turn of the 1950s, she retired. Later, she became the national chairwoman of the Soroptimists and wrote a book, *Una gran bella vita* (Mondadori). She lived to be nearly a hundred.

Gabriella di Robilant: a Gabriella Sport model (from *Fili Moda*, Summer 1941).

Robiola Elsa (1907-1988). Milanese journalist. She was a crucial figure in the history of fashion journalism. Together with Gio Ponti, the great Italian architect who edited *Domus*, she founded in 1941 the magazine *Bellezza* and edited it for more than two decades, managing to keep it going even during the harshest years of the Second World War, and in the 1950s, holding its head up in the face of competition from *Vogue* and *Harper's Bazaar*. In the postwar years, the monthly was published by Aldo Palazzi, who also published the weekly *Tempo*, where the journalist was special correspondent for fashion, and *Marie Claire*. *Bellezza* had taught Italian women in wartime to dress with leftovers and had urged dressmakers to inventive, and not to be content to offer the models, more or less disguised, but still copied wholesale from the French *griffes*.

This past tradition ensured that the magazine and its editor would line up entirely on the side of Giovanni Battista Giorgini in his attempt to present to American buyers an original and autonomous "Made in Italy" in the world of fashion. When, on 12 February 1951, the first Italian fashion shows were held in Giorgini's drawing room in Florence, Elsa Robiola was among the very few Italian journalists present, along with Elisa Massai, correspondent *Women's Wear Daily*, Gemma Vitti of the *Corriere Lombardo*, Vera Rossi of *Novità*, Misia Armani of the periodical *I Tessili Nuovi,* and Sandra Bartolomei Corsi of the *Secolo XIX*.

Rocha John (1953). Irish fashion designer of Chinese and Portuguese descent. He left his native Hong Kong to study fashion in London. He took his degree in 1977 and, the following year, presented with his first womenswear collection. Having fallen in love with Irish textile traditions, he moved to Dublin in 1979 and opened his firsts store in 1985. Between 1987 and 1989, he stayed in Milan to monitor the production of his line. The 1990s saw a rapid rise in his reputation. In 1993, he launched the menswear line and won the first of many awards: British Designer of the Year. In 1995, he inaugurated showrooms in Paris and Dublin and signed an agreement with the Waterford Wedgwood Group to design furnishing accessories. In 1996, John Rocha Jeans was founded. In 1997, he made an agreement with Itochu Fashion Systems, Japan, for Asian distribution. In 1998 he opened his London shop in Sloane Square. His style lies somewhere between the Asian and the celtic. He designed the uniforms of Virgin Atlantic Airlines. He has designed costumes for the movies. He owns the hotel, The Mirrison, in Dublin, which he furnished entirely.

❑ 2002, October. Conran-Octopus published *Texture, Form, Purity, Details* in which Rocha tells his story and illustrates his philosophy which has always tied him to the world of the image, The book is highly illustrated, with photographs and drawings.

(*Virginia Hill*)

Rochas Marcel (1902-1955). French tailor and fashion designer. He debuted in 1925, with an atelier in Paris in the Faubourg Saint-Honoré. Over the years, he gave increasing importance to shoulders, designed the Bali outfit, based on the costume of Balinese dancers, the *canadienne* jacket, kimono sleeves, and the guêpière or girdle. His style, young and modern, was often ahead of its time. He lived an intense life, in emotional terms – he married Hélène, his beautiful muse, a third marriage – and in economic terms, with the creation of many companies and the launch of successful perfumes: Avenue Matignon, Mouche, Moustache. His death caused a moment of crisis for the *maison* and the elimination of the high fashion department. Hélène took over the perfumes sector – in those years, Madame Rochas and Eau de Rochas were developed – but the process of transformation became unstoppable. In 1987, a new owner arrived, the German group Wella. In 1989, the widow Rochas left the company. The new management put a new perfume, Byzance, on the market and, in 1990, a line of women's prêt-à-porter, with the contribution of the Irish fashion designer, Peter O'Brian. The *griffe* also inaugurated a line of men's fashion.

❑ 1999. The fragrance Rochas Man was created by Daniela Candio.
❑ 2002. Launch of Aquawoman, created by Michel Almeiras (Robertel).
❑ 2002, November. Olivier Theyskens accepted the offer of Wella to relaunch the image of the maison beginning with the Fall-Winter 2003-2004 collection.

Rockabilly Blinding colors, tuft of hair on the forehead, shirts with leather laces and a silver bolo tie, pointed-toe boots, especially in snakeskin, even better still if studded with rivets, leather jackets, jeans that will live forever, skin-tight pants, big collrs. It was the fashion of the rock'n'roll boys of the 1950s, used both by music stars and the Teddy Boys of England. From the early 1980s, the look has reemerged, revised, led by the American band the Stray Cats. The success of the revised look lasted for the entire decade of the 1990s.

Rockers Youth tribe of the 1950s associated with a lifestyle, more than a fashion movement. It began to spread in London in May

1955 to the notes of *Rock Around the Clock* by Bill Haley and the Comets: theme song to the movie *The Blackboard Jungle*. The origins of this proletarian movement, a forerunner of the youth protest movement, dated back to postwar California. And specifically to Hollister, where in 1947 a group of hoodlums terrorized the village, riding in formation on powerful motorcycles through town and starting fights that resulted in the destruction of bars and restaurants. The choice of this sort of vehicle expressed a rejection of the automobile: the dream of the average American in those early postwar years. Likewise, every piece of clothing worn by these bands represented a challenge: the leather studded pilot jacket, worn by warriors of the skies, the provocatively exhibited and filthy motorcycle boots, propped up on the tables, the stained, torn work jeans, the pocket knife always close at hand and the neckerchief, always ready to cover the face, just like bandits from the Old West. With symptomatic simultaneity, these movements of rebellion were echoed in Europe by the movements of the Blouson Noirs in France, the Halbstarken in Germany, and the Teddy Boys in England. But the lowest common denominator, which in 1953 merged great protest energies in an international movement, was the movie, *The Wild One* directed by Laslo Benedek. The protagonist, Marlon Brando, leader of a gang that rapes and kills, immediately became the icon of a youth protest movement that attacked the establishment with behavior on the verge of delinquency. And if, in the United States it inspired the Hell's Angels, in England it encouraged the establishment of the first group of rockers. What unleashed them was nothing other than the film *Blackboard Jungle* with its mix of race, country, and hillbilly music, entitled *Rock Around the Clock*: the veritable music banner of the movement in symbiosis with the motorcycle. To the energetic rhythm of the song by Bill Haley that would remain on the charts for five months, selling 22 million records, the hordes of rockers gathered and multiplied, especially in the counties of the mining districts to the north of London, where, in a geographic and cultural coincidence, the motorcycle industries also prospered, first among them the BSA of Birmingham, which would be featured on the cover of the record by the Rolling Stones, *Rock'n'rolling*. When in the 1960s, rockers would arrive in the major cities, they would brawl with the Mods: a rival gang that dressed with great care and acted very daintily, even though both groups were of working class origins. The tensions rose, coming to a climax in 1964 with the fights in Claxton to the south of London. It was not so much because of the dynamics of these incidents, which ended with more than 90 arrests, as much as because of the advance of the modernist spirits of the Mods, consumers of the new 45 rpm records, admirers of Italian elegance, constantly moving on Vespas, the rockers at the end of the 1960s finally succumbed. Despite their own views, they became a classic of youth revolt, a reference for the punk movement of the 1970s, the heavy metal and hard rock movements of the 1980s. In the decade that followed, they inspired the menswear collection, Fall-Winter 1994-95, by Dolce & Gabbana dedicated to Marlon Brando and the Rebels. The rockers remained, in particular, the first historic example of how a youth rebellion could be transformed into an extraordinary source of profits, for an industry that was attempting to supply the protest consumptions of the new generations. (*Gianluca Lo Vetro*)

Rockport American manufacturer of shoes, casual apparel, and accessories, founded by father and son, Saul and Bruce Katz, in 1971. In the second half of the 1980s, the ProWalker jogging shoe was introduced to the market and the brand was purchased by Reebok International, which created Rockport Walking Institute to educate Americans about the health benefits of walking regularly. In 1987, Rockport appeared on the international market: in the space of less than a decade, Rockport production was being marketed in more than 30 countries around the world. Added to the sports shoes and the two lines of women's shoes Walking Pump and Soft Impressions, was the first collection of men's apparel. In the late 1990s, Rockport established a link with Jack Nicklaus, "golfer of the century," creating a high-quality shoes for the greens. Even though it was forced to deal with a sharp decline in revenues at the turn of the millennium, in the summer of 2002 Rockport established a licensing contract with the Gordon Ferguson company of New York, producing men's sports apparel beginning in the Fall-Winter season of 2003. It was the first American manufacturer of fitness shoes to receive the certification of quality from the APMA, the American Podiatric Medical Association, in 1985.

(*Pierangelo Mastantuono*)

Rodchenko Alexandre (1891-1956). Artist, protagonist of the Russian avant-garde. He was one of the theorists of Constructivism. With his wife, the artist Varvara Stepanova, and Lyubov Popova, he contributed to LEF, the Constructivist magazine that featured the contributions of various artists with the intention of creating a linkage between art and industrial production. The idea was to develop a comfortable and functional apparel, with straight-line cuts and geometric decorations reminiscent of the influence of Cubism. The overall, understood as work clothing, was certainly the item of apparel that best exemplified the concept of practicality and functionality as theorized by the artist and his wife, and it was in fact to overalls that the couple devoted their greatest creative attention. (*Cloe Piccoli*)

Rodeo Drive In Los Angeles, this is the golden street of luxury shopping: it climbs sharply, twisting along the slopes of Beverly Hills, far from the traffic jams and smog of downtown. In California, the rich have always fled any appearance of city to take refuge in the countryside, in the canyons or on the hills, creating unlikely oases in the desert. The name, Rodeo Drive, harks back to the dawn of the Yankee conquest of the Far West, when California was the homeland of *chicanos* and *vaqueros*. But the Americans don't seem to mind. In fact, they like the country reference that nowadays goes hand in hand with the most unrestrained exclusive luxury. The commercial section of Rodeo Drive is no more than a quarter mile long, barely 500 meters of high-density concentration of limousines in which the matrons of Beverly Hills have themselves driven around by chauffeurs to do their shopping. It was in Rodeo Drive that Julia Roberts, the star of *Pretty Woman*, goes shopping. The street begins with the shop of Bulgari, and ends with Tiffany's, and between the two leading jewelers, it assembles all the most important *griffes,* from Chanel and Saint-Laurent and Versace to Armani and Valentino and Fendi. Rodeo Drive is not just fashion shopping. All sorts of other luxury items have their display windows here. Whenever Ferrari brings out a new model, it is here that they put it on display for American buyers. There isn't much else here: a couple of monuments, including some very private ones, such as the O'Neill House, a home designed by Don Ramos, which makes clear reference to the Catalonian architect Gaudí, and the shopping center, the Anderton Court Building by the architect Frank Lloyd Wright, quite similar to the Guggenheim Museum in New York. (*Enrico Bonerandi*)

Rodier French label of ready-to-wear fashion. It relied upon its own chain of stores. It was founded in 1853 as a textiles manufacturer. It was founded by Eugène Rodier who invented the *Kasha*, made in wool from Kashmir, and revolutionized knitwear fabrics by creating jersey. It has long belonged to the Prouvost group.

❑ 2002. Two Rodier Woman shops were opened: one in Belgium, near Antwerp, and one in Cannes.
❑ 2003, April. It signed a long-term contract with Tibbett Britten France, which is part of the British group Tibbett Britten Group plc, the international colossus of logistics, specializing in the stocking and distribution of foods and, of course, clothing: among the clients we should mention: Dixons/PC City, Erès, Episode, Gap, MF Girbaud, Hermès, Hugo Boss, Hyparlo, Intermarché, Metro, Perrier and Système U. The company operated for the fashion house 21,000 square meters in Cambrai. Currently, Rodier owns 160 stores, 150 licensees in the leading French department stores, and is present in about 300 multilabel stores scattered throughout 35 countries worldwide.

Rodo An Italian leather goods manufacturer, founded in Florence by Romualdo Dori. Established in the 1950s, at first it produced bags that copied Dutch wicker baskets. It became a typical feature of the company to produce bags with special interweavings in the handles and straps as well. Today, the company's production includes shoes and belts.

❑ 2002, November. AOI, the most important distributor in the fashion sector in Japan, acquired the exclusive rights to import Rodo and manage the concessions.
❑ 2003, April. The company, by this point identified with high-end women's footwear, suffered from the declines felt in the leather goods and shoe sectors and identified by the trade associations of the sector. But the company was confident and decided to target the Middle East, where in Riyad and Dubai it planned to open franchising stores. The leading markets for the company remained, in any case, the U.S., Italy, and Japan. Rodo, which had 6 single-label shops worldwide and 12 corner shops in department store, in 2002 had turnover of 8.2 million Euros.

Rodriguez Narciso (1961). Cuban fashion designer. He lives and works in exile in New Jersey. He designed the wedding gown in which Carolyne Bessette, in 1996, married "John John" Kennedy. He studied at the Parsons School in New York. He served an apprenticeship with Anne Klein, in the years when Donna Karan and Calvin Klein worked there. He arrived in Europe in 1995, summoned by Nino Cerruti who made him the artistic director of his collections. He dressed Sigourney Weaver for her appearance at the Oscars. In 1997, the Italian textiles manufacturer Aeffe asked him to design its line of ready-to-wear fashion. He was very successful. But he accepted the invitation of the Spanish *maison* Loewe and, under their patronage, he presented his collection in Paris in March 1998.

❑ 2003. He won in New York, for the second consecutive year, the prize as best women's fashion designer, organized by the Council of Fashion Designers, and based on a survey of the work of more than 450 fashion designers.

Sketch by Narciso Rodriguez, 1999.

Rodriguez Pedro (1895-1990). Spanish fashion designer, professionally close to Balenciaga. Before his debut, he served a long apprenticeship as a tailor in Barcelona. In 1919 he opened his own *maison* with his wife Ana Maria, a professional dressmaker. Ten years later, he presented a collection at the International Expo of Barcelona and his fame was assured. The Spanish Civil War forced him to leave the country. He resumed work in 1937 in San Sebastián. Two years later, at the end of the war, he reopened his atelier in Barcelona and then moved to Madrid. In 1978, his success began to decline and he was forced out of business. But he did not retire: he continue to work for his most faithful clientele. His outfits, as simple as two pieces of cloth stitched together or a Baroque as his love of hems of precious stones, can be admired at the Museu Textile i d'Indumentaria in Barcelona which, after his death, dedicated a room to his work. (*Eleonora Platania*)

Roehm Carolyne (1951). American fashion designer. She went into business for herself in 1984, with a line targeting working women (functionality and, at the same time, great care in the patterns, fabrics, and details), and she retired in 1993. She learned her trade by studying fashion and costume at Washington University in Missouri and by working for ten years with Oscar De La Renta.

❑ She devoted herself to teaching about gardening and the art of flower arrangements. In 1997, she published *A Passion for Flowers* (HarperCollins) in which she applied to floral composition the lessons that she had learned in the fields of style and elegance: "I can't tell you how many times I have seen an outfit ruined because of bad accessorizing; the same thing is true for flowers: even the loveliest flowers 'don't work' if they are put in the wrong vase or set against an inappropriate background." Two years later, she appeared in bookstores again with *Winter Notebook* (again, HarperCollins).

Roelli Testu Label of men's ready-to-wear fashion. Founded in 1986, it folded in 1991, when the two fashion designers that created it, the Swiss Michael Roelli (1959) and the French Jean-Luc Testu (1960), decided to work on an exclusive basis for the men's prêt-à-porter line of Dupont. The two designers met at the Paris fashion school ESMOD, and served apprenticeships with Mugler and Alaïa; they then went into business together and, before debuting in France, they tried out for their ideas for two years in the Ivory Coast.

Roger Gallet French perfume house founded in 1862, renowned for having renewed the universe of fragrances and the art of toiletry. The founders, Armand Roger and Charles Gallet, were two cousins by marriage of the Collas family, to whom Jean-Marie Farina had sold the formula for his famous cologne, the Extra Vieille (still a best-seller for Roger Gallet, which kept the same name and the same original ingredients). Emphasizing research and creativity, both in the formulations and in the image, the *maison* succeeded in establishing itself quickly in the higher realms of the perfume business. In 1879 it created the first round bar of soap in history, with a violet scent, and wrapped in a refined silk plissé. Another fundamental step forward was the introduction at the turn of the twentieth century of the fragrances Narkiss, Cigalia, and Jade, whose exquisite little bottles were made upon commission by René Lalique. Among the most recent creations, let us mention the three bath lines Bouquet Impérial, Lavande Royale and Vetyver, created in conjuction with the scents of the colognes of those names (1991); the Doux Nature product line (1997); the perfume Eau pour Soi (1999). In 1975 the house was purchased by the Gruppo Sanofi.

❑ 2003, September. Il museum-bookshop of Bernay (Normandy) presented the exhibition *Roger Gallet, The Art of Toiletry from 1862 to Today*. A collection of more than 500 items from the Roger Gallet collection.

Rogosky Moritz (1966). German fashion designer. Since 1996 he has been on the official schedule of the runway presentations of Paris. He lived in New York as an adolescent. From 1985 to 1987 he attended the Studio Berçot. He debuted in 1990 with his own name.

Rohka A label created in 2000 by the professional union of the Colombian fashion designer Maria Restrepo and the Scottish fashion designer Ian Phin. After taking her degree in Colombia, Maria studied design at the ESMOD of Paris. Ian graduated in textile design at the Duncan of Jordanstone College of Art, and then continued his studies at London's Royal College of Art. After working together for Romeo Gigli and Versace (Maria also worked for Marni), they decided to found together the Rohka project. At first, only accessories, scarves, stoles, collars; later they went on to include womenswear and knitwear. All their work has always taken inspiration from various ethnic groups and from nomadism. A sort of voyage around the world of fashion. They opened an atelier in Milan where they produce their line, which is distributed in Italy and around the world through high fashion shops (such as Biffi and Banner). At their debut, they won (on equal standing with the Japanese Ichiro Seta) the international fashion designer competition Enkamania. They share a love for the material aspects of textiles, always quite original and subtle, and they devote research and specific travel to finding crafts traditions from distant lands (such as the circular weaving machines from the Shetlands). Lines with embroideries, block prints, marble effects, and sepia-toned nuances or painterly hues for the colors all contribute to make each item they create a unique creation.

(*Daniela Bolognetti*)

Romain Hippolyte (1947). French illustrator. Since 1980 he was contributed to *Libération*, *Rock and Folk*, and *L'Express*. More than documenting the fashion, he likes to satirize the world of fashion, the runway presentations, the flora and fauna. He has published the books *Simple mais couture*, *Les dessous de la mode* and La Couture épinglé, voyages au pays de la mode.

Romanò Marcella (1967). Italian designer. Born in Como, she has always lived in the world of fashion: her father runs a company in the Como region called Nephila, which "converts" fabrics to adapt them to the requirements of buyers. It was here that she served her apprenticeship as a creative and an entrepreneur. She was curious and sensitive to new trends, and she completed her studies with a degree from the Accademia di Brera. Then she began with a small collection of accessories, and finally took the leap into the world of prêt-à-porter, in 1998, with a complete womenswear line. Her collections are limited to a few items, in a unique mix of fabrics, embroideries, and prints, invariably original and personally conceived by her. For the summer of 2002, she designed an eclectic and colorful wardrobe, made up of white T-shirts with appliqués of shells, flowers, butterflies, sheath dresses in striped cotton or in silk, patchwork jeans, embroidered, with the denim mixed with other fabrics.

(*Gabriella Gregorietti*)

Romper suit First appeared in the first half of the 20th century as a children's garment, worn mostly in the summer. All-in-one, it has short puffed pants, gathered with elastic or a tie. The two-piece version has short pants with a bib attached with straps crossing over at the back. The term was later used to describe an elegant piece of lingerie, nearly always made of silk, with a top and knickers combined to make a comfortable and softly flowing garment.

Ronay Edina (1945). Hungarian fashion designer. She studied in London and worked as both an actress and a modell. Her reputation is based on her hand-made knitwear creations.

Ronis Willy (1910). French photographer. He learned his trade in his father's studio, devoting himself to landscape and reportage, work that he returned to after the war, in 1945, working for *Life*, *L'Illustration*, *Point de vue*, and *Le Monde Illustré*. He was a careful observer of his native Paris, and he did a sharp-eyed coverage of a working-class *arrondissement* that he published as a book in 1954 with the title *Bellevue-Ménilmontant*. Since then, he has done numerous books, personal and collective shows, and has received many prizes. He considers himself an eclectic artist, and he has devoted himself to all sorts of photography, including fashion photography, working with *Vogue France*.

Rosa Chà Trademark of a line of beach apparel. The Brazilian Amir Slama (1966), with his wife, founded it, at the beginning of the 1990s. Success was immediate, and the entire line, which consisted of swimsuits, wraps, shorts, and skirts, was covered extensively in fashion magazines, including *Vogue*, *Harper's Bazaar*, *Elle*, *W Magazine*, *Sports Illustrated,* and *Cosmopolitan*. It was the new material, the unusual stitching, and the embroideries that really determined the style, designed to emphasize femininity. There is nothing ordinary about these swimsuits, often destructured and braided. Total production, manufactured in Brazil, ran to 500,000 items per year, and was distributed through the 21 Rosa Chà single-label outlets and in specialty shops. In the United States, the products are sold in 250 high-end stores, such as Barneys New York, Bergdorf Goodman, Language, and Fred Segal. Rosa Chà is also present in Europe and in Japan. *(Valeria Vantaggi)*

Rosasco Textile manufacturer in the Como area. It grew out of the Camozzi Rosasco company, founded in 1899, and specializing in the production of linings and fabrics for the manufacturing of women's clothing. It developed as a single-owner company under Enrico Rosasco (1909). In 1919 his sons Eugenio and Mario joined the company, in the roles of partners and members of the board. In 1920 the company acquired the weaving mill of Appiano Gentile, operating alongside the one in Como. In 1925 they opened a throwing mill in Domaso. Rosasco expanded its line of operations to include ties, high fashion fabrics, damasks, and finally fabrics for raincoats. With the passing years, the original raw material, silk, was joined by cotton, wool, rayon, and other fibers. It became an incorporated company in 1960. When Eugenio Rosasco died (1961), son of the founder and long the chief of the company, a period of impasse began, as indicated by the steady decline in the annual balance sheets, culminating with the closing of the sector dedicated to neckties and with the concentration of production at Appiano Gentile. Beginning in 1970 the crisis became irreversible and the terminal corporate situation was resolved in the only way possible, with the sale of the Appiano Gentile plant and the warehouse. In 1978 Rosasco officially ceased operations. *(Pierangelo Mastantuono)*

Rose Idée French company that produced and marketed the jewelry *griffe,* Bijoux R. Woloch. The little costume jewelry atelier of Rose and Joseph Woloch had its Paris debut in 1939: wife at the cash register and supervising commercial operations, the husband at the workbench, tools in hand, and overseeing matters artistic. Shortly thereafter, one of their brooches, *Chien*, won the Drags prize which was, at the time, very important. The bracelet, *Rose,* which the jeweler designed for his wife pleased both the mass buying public at the Galeries Lafayette and Coco Chanel. In 1942, the grand *mademoiselle* asked him for a pair of earrings that "look like a pigeon's nest and allow one to imagine the straw and the egg." This was the birth of a classic accessory of the Maison Chanel: with an average of more than 4,000 items sold per year. In 1966, the R. Woloch company was renamed (Rose Idée), it modernized its production, and launched itself into the export business: a policy that allowed it to grow gradally, with a 45 percent leap in sales in 1982. In Europe, it commanded a leadership position with 600,000 items sold yearly: 90 percent of them exports.

Rose-Pulham Peter (1910-1956). British photographer. He began to devote himself to fashion photography at the beginning of the 1930s. His photographs with a Surrealist flavor, done on commission from Victor Stiebel, were published in 1931 and 1932 by *Harper's Bazaar* which sent him to Paris as a correspondent; it was there that he became influenced by the painting of the masters of Surrealism, with whom he developed close friendships. He worked with the fashion designer Charles James. He had a very distinctive working method. In fact, he would destroy all the negatives that he took with his large-format (6x6) Rolleiflex.

Rose Valois French fashion house, founded in 1927 by the dressmaker of the same name, who had worked in the atelier of Caroline Reboux. A great art lover, Rose often took inspiration for her creations from the Impressionists and the various avant-garde artists of the early twentieth century.

Rosier Gilles. French designer. After his studies at the Chambre Syndicale de la Couture, he began his apprenticeship working at the maisons of Balmain, Dior, and Guy Paulin. He became Gaultier chief assistant, then artistic director of Leonard. In 1992 he created the short-lived label Gr816. He continued to work as an independent consultant for Repetto, a renowned house for dance costumes. He began designing collections again in 1996 under his own name, and was very successful. He considered his fashion to be a "workshop experienced as a factory in motion."

❑ 1999. He replaced Kenzo Takada (who had completed thirty years of his brilliant career), working at the Louis Vuitton Moet Hennessy.

Rosier Michèle (1929). French designer. About her, the daughter of Hélène Gordon-Lazareff, the founder of the fashion magazine *Elle*, a journalist of the Herald Tribune wrote: "She did for prêt-à-porter what Courrèges did for high fashion." At first she seemed well on her way to a career in journalism, but she abandoned it to establish, with Emmanuelle Khanh, whom she met in 1959, and Christiane Bailly, a trio of fashion designers who were to shake the foundations of French fashion at the beginning of the 1960s. In 1962 she founded *V de V* (Vêtements des Vacances) and, after collaborating with various fashion designers, she helped to spread the use of sports apparel in everyday life and the use of unusual materials such as black paint and vinyl. The Americans dubbed her, for this reason, the "plastic queen." In 1974, she left fashion to work in the movies.

Rosselli Colette (1912-1996). Italian writer, painter, and journalist. Anyone who was a child in the 1940s will remember the book of Susanna, with which she debuted as a children's illustrator. The most faithful readers of the women's weekly *Grazia* will associate her name with the column of Donna Letizia, who answered readers' letters, dispensing practical advice but also ironic and pungent commentary on how to live, later published as a book. She was born in Lausanne and took a degree in French language and literature. She was also a talented painter. She wrote many children's books. Among them: *Per bimbi buoni and cattivi*, *Il cavaliere Dodipetto*, *I poemetti di Susanna*, and *Prime rime*. She also worked in the United States with *Harper's Bazaar*, *Mademoiselle* and *Vogue*. Educated, refined, with a special elegance all her own, made up of trousers and jackets, she loved to go for long walks in the mountains, but also to stay at home, in fact in any of her several homes, which she had furnished with great style, first of them all the one overlooking Rome's Piazza Navona, and which she had described in *Casa di randagia* (1989), one of her last books, along with *Ma non troppo* (1986) and *Nuovo saper vivere* (1991). Married to Indro Montanelli (second marriage), she died in Rome. (*Bonizza Giordani Aragno*)

Rosselli Kuster Emilia (1903-1958). Italian journalist. She was born in Livorno to a family of considerable civil engagement (she was a cousin of Carlo and Nello Rosselli), and already at a very young age she devoted her attention t the world of feminine pursuits by opening in her native city a school of embroidery. Encouraged by this experience, with the lucid, "courteous" determination that was so distinctive in her, in 1933 she persuaded the architect Gio Ponti to publish, as a free gift supplement to *Domus*, the bible of architecture and design between the two world wars, the magazine of embroidery and fashion *Fili* that, under her editorship, was beginning to catch the impressed attention of the Milanese artistic world of that time (Lucio Fontana, Fausto Melotti). She became such an authority in the sector that in 1940 the Milan Triennale hired her to organize, together with Fabrizio Clerici, an exhibition that was to remain a landmark in the history of the art of embroidery. Forced into clandestinity during the years of racial persecutions, she returned to journalism in 1950 and founded, with the financial support of her husband Roberto Kuster, *Novità*, a magazine that was vaguely inspired by prestigious American publications, such as *Vogue* and *Harper's Bazaar*. This magazine opened its interests, with an elegance and a spirit that were decidedly Italian, today we would say European, to the worlds of fashion, furnishing, and art, current events, social problems, cooking, and gardening. It was a magazine that, in its pleasant and well calibrated presentation, revealed in the context of the women's magainzes of the postwar period an innovative drive that we can scarcely imagine nowadays. A charismatic woman, spiritually elegant, possessed of numerous interests and considerable culture, Emilia Rosselli Kuster had a great admiration for French fashion of the 1950s, which she introduced to the wider audience in Italy, though at the same time she offered a great contribution to the launch of Italian fashion, giving a substantial assist to her friend Bista Giorgini, the inventor of the runway presentations of Palazzo Pitti in

Florence. She sensed very early the importance of the role that photographers played in the presentation of fashion, and encouraged their participation. She introduced the great Ugo Mulas, for instance, to the field of fashion photography. Her prestige and the respect that she enjoyed in non-Italian publishing circles (during the Paris collections, in the parterres of the Fashion Editors, she was seated between Hélène Lazareff, Eugenia Sheppard, Bettina Ballard, and Françoise Giroud) were the foundations for the successive developments of the magazine, after her death in 1958.

(*Marina Rovera*)

Rossetti Elsa (1915). Journalist, organizer of events and fashion runway presentations in Italy and around the world. Editor of the fashion department of *Stampa Sera* from 1960 till 1989 and of the *Radiocorriere* from 1965 till 1971, she coordinated for 21 years (beginning in 1955) and presented the runway presentations of SAMIA in Turin doing, for the same body – and for the first time – runway presentations to promoted Italian fashion in Dusseldorf, London, Belgrade and, for the Italian Trade Commission, in Tripoli (until the advent of Gheddafi), in San Salvador, Copenaghen, Dublin, and Reykjavik. She played this role, at the behest of Fiat, throughout the 1970s, with a focus on the winning combination of fashion and automobiles, in Saloniki, Athens, Rhodes, Voloz, Buenos Aires, and Stockholm: travel that was adventurous at the time, and for which she chose the best known top models. Later, she organized the Raincoat Week in Florence (at the behest of Beppe Modenese) and, in the 1970s and 1980s, for the Associazione Serica Comofoulard, the runway presentations and spectacle at the Auditorium of Bonn, at the Royal Albert Hall in London, and in Dusseldorf while, for the Associazioni Industriali of Padua and Milan, she took to Moscow, in 1984, the first Italian runway presentation of prêt-à-porter, high fashion, and footwear.

(*Maria Vittoria Alfonsi*)

Rossi Sergio (1935). Designer of footwear and leather entrepreneur. The experience from which he began his march toward a line of successes was the trade of his father, a craftsman who had always made shoes to measure. In the 1960s, he began his career at San Mauro Pascoli with a group of colleagues and a desire to create a style capable of rising above fashions and trends. He made his mark in the following decade with a line of women's shoes, handmade and innovative in design. Beginning in the 1980s, his business grew and diversified: this led to the creation of the lines Le Tinì by Sergio Rossi, Miss Rossi, the bags and the menswear collection and he also began his collaboration with Dolce & Gabbana and with Gianni Versace. The plant in San Mauro Pascoli now gives work to 400 employees. The company owns 12 boutiques and has 16 sales outlets in franchising around the world.

Sandal with stiletto heel, by Sergio Rossi.

❑ 2000, August. *The Wall Street Journal* devoted a long article to the acquisition (70 percent) by Gucci of the shoemaker. The Rossi family held on to a share of ownership.
❑ 2001. The turnover reached 24 million Euros.

Rossi Vittorio. Creator of costumes, set designer, director, writer, playwright, and professor at the University of Paris. He has received numerous international awards, including, in 1987, the Medaille de Vermeille from the City of Paris and, in 1996, the Légion d'Honneur, presented by France's president, Chirac. After studying architecture at the University of Rome, he began has career as a costume and set designer, working for major film production houses and such directors as William Pabst, Sergio Leone and Duccio Tessari. In the theater, he worked with Giorgio Albertazzi, Maurizio Scaparro, Virginio Puecher, and with La Scala in Milan, and the Teatro Olimpico in Vicenza. He worked intensely in the world of dance, ranging from the creation of sets and costumes for the *Racconto Siciliano*, conceived by Luchino Visconti, with music by Bucchi, a *Requiem per un destino* to music by Ennio Morricone (both produced with the Dutch dancer and choreographer Pieter Van der Sloot), to *Don Quixote* with Rudolph Nureyev and *Sleeping Beauty*, with Carla Fracci for the Arena in Verona, where he was a consultant for the set design for ten years, also creating unforgettable costumes for *Aida*, *Cavalleria Rusticana*, *I pagliacci*, *Turandot*, *Tosca*, and many other magnficent productions. He was acclaimed as a "man of the great spaces," "*sorcier*" (wizard), "*magique*" and "*magicienne*" (magical and a magician) by the French press, which hailed his direction, set design, and costumes in the *Aida* that inaugurated in 1984 the Palais Omnisport of Paris-Bercy. He worked on the inaugural performances for the Deutschlandhalle in Berlin, the Stadthalle in Vienna, the Westfallenhalle in Dortmund, the Hallenstadium in Zurich, the Palais des Congres in Strasbourg, and Earl's Court in London. He designed the sets for the *Aida* that was staged in Luxor for the 125th anniversary of the inauguration of the Suez Canal. He died in 2003.

(*Maria Vittoria Alfonsi*)

Costumes by Vittorio Rossi for the ballet *Sleeping Beauty*, starring Carla Fracci (Arena of Verona, 1978).

Rossi Lodomez Vera (1902-1988). Italian journalist. Elegant, educated, endowed with an autenthically Tuscan wit and a notable sense of humor, gifted with perfect fluency in a number of different languages, she played an important role working alongside Giovanni Battista Giorgini, collaborating on the great runway presentations of Palazzo Pitti. She was a friend of the great illustrator Gruau, and she traveled with him in the United States to visit the schools of fashion: at the time, an astonishing and memorable event. She worked for *Novità* and other women's periodicals. In particular, she is remembered for her column – with the byline Vera – *Annabella in Cucina* ('Annabella in the Kitchen'), the book with the same title (Rizzoli, 1955), and especially the first edition of the *Cucchiaio d'Argento* ('Silver Spoon,' *Domus*, 1950) and the *Nuovissimo cucchiaio d'argento* ('Brand New Silver Spoon,' 1972), on which she worked as coauthor. Her fashionable Christmas parties (like those held by Jole Veniceni) continue to be remembered.

Rostel Anett (1965). German fashion designer. She was born in Berlin, and studied Fashion Design at the Fachochschule für Wirtschaft und Technik. After graduation, she immediately debuted with a collection of women's apparel on the runways of the CPD Dusseldorf, Atmosphère and the Salon du prêt-à-porter in Paris. Her style takes its inspiration from Japan and from Asian culture in general.

Rota Titina (1898-1978). Italian costume designer. In the years following the Second World War she was the editor of the weekly *Grazia*. She was Milanese and was born into a family of musicians. Nino Rota, who won an Oscar for the soundtrack of *The Godfather*, was her cousin. She worked in theater for a number of directors, among them Guido Salvini (*La Locandiera*), Max Reinhardt (*A Midsummer Night's Dream* and *The Merchant of Venice*), and Renato Simoni. In the years following the war, she retired to Capri, devoting herself to painting.

Costume by Titina Rota for *Il favorito del re*, Milan 1932 (Ricordi archives).

Roth Christian. Designer of eyewear. Along with his partner Eric Domege he conceived sunglasses and eyeglasses with personal and innovative lines. Since 1998 the two designers have been working regularly with the CXD division of Charmant USA, a subsidiary of the Japanese corporation with the same name, which already represented the Christian Roth name. The collection, created for Michael Kors Eyewear, was on sale worldwide in 2001 following a runway presentation at the Vision Expo East. There are 13 models: 9 sunglasses and 4 eyeglasses. There is no logo on the arms. The designer's distinctive style is enough to identify them. The spokesperson chosen for this minimalist collection dominated by titanium frames was the rock singer Lenny Kravitz. The creative effort won Roth a prize for the category "sporty casual eyewear" at the International Optics Fair in Tokyo, in October 2002.

Rothschild Klàra. Hungarian dressmaker. Active from the 1930s to the 1970s, with the differences dictated by the changing historical circumstances. Before the war, she had an atelier in Budapest with 150 employees. In the postwar period, the Communist regime forced her to close down her business (1951) and to become a fashion designer for powerful state officials, with visas for seasonal trips to Paris to buy patterns and to gain inspiration from the haute couture runway presentations. Each year, the dressmaker would produce two collections of 130 outfits, with runway presentations held in the major hotels of the Hungarian capital.

Rouff Maggie (1896-1971). French fashion creator. Born in Vienna. Her parents ran the *maison* Drecoll. It was there that she learned the trade. In 1929, with her husband, Pierre Besançon de Wagner, she opened her own atelier in Paris and presented her first collection. Eight years later, she debuted in London as well. Over the course of her career, she wrote a number of literary works, collections of poetry, impressions, and aphorisms. In 1942 she published *The Philosophy of Elegance* (Paris, Edition Litteraires de France). She retired in Cannes in 1948. The following year, the *maison* was sold to the Mendel-Fourrures company, which entrusted the creative supervision to the countess of Dancourt, one of Maggie Rouff's two daughters. Neither she nor other fashion designers, such as Serge Matta, Michel Malard and Guy Douvier, succeeded in halting the decline of the *griffe,* which would vanish from the stage of haute couture in the mid-1960s.

Rouxel Christophe (1964). French designer. A former assistant of Yves Saint-Laurent and Chanel, he designed a type of extreme luxury that was a response to minimalist fashion. He begain with prêt-à-porter and in 1998 had a runway presentation in Paris of his first haute couture collection. In his tailoring techniques, the lines of an outfit spring from the belly, considered a symbol of femininity, and extended vertically to free up one's movements.

Roveda Wanda. She is the only designer of wedding dresses to have seen one of her

A New Jimmy model made of lace and ostrich plumes, by Maggie Rouff, in a sketch by Brunetta for the magazine *Bellezza*, edited by Elsa Robiola, 1961 (Biki Collection).

creations exhibited at the Guggenheim Museum in New York (1996). A tireless creator of wedding and non-wedding collections, she began her long career in the 1940s, when she decided to transform a simple pastime into a profession. In 1962 she presented, at the request of Bista Giorgini, a mothers-and-daughters collection in Florence, at the Sala Bianca. La Roveda and her Rovedine, as Irene Brin was to call them, became famous and much loved.

Wanda Roveda, wedding gowns in a sketch by Maria Pezzi, from the Seventies.

Roversi Paolo (1947). Italian photographer. After an initial period of interest in news photography, he opened a studio in his hometown of Ravenna, where he dedicated himself to still-life and portrait photography. He moved to Paris in 1973 and it was there, through Guy Bourdin, that he first encountered the world of fashion. A refined artist, he was capable of bringing out in the style of his images both explicit references to the culture of the beat generation and dreamy atmospheres of mystery and childhood memories. In order to achieve this, he made use of very special lights that were well suited to the substantial quality of large-format 20x25 cm. Polaroid film, and he was the first to use this film in the field of fashion. He worked for *Harper's Bazaar*, *Vogue*, *Uomo Vogue*, *Arena*, *i-D*, *Interview*, *Marie Claire*, *W*, *Elle* and did campaigns for Christian Dior, Cerruti, Valentino, Yves Saint-Laurent, Alberta Ferretti, Givenchy, and Kenzo. Among his book, which were companion pieces to his infrequent but magnificent exhibitions, *Nudi* (1999) assembled a series of female bodies endowed with a mysterious eroticism that appears as well in the book published the following year by Carla Sozzani. The introduction to *Libretto* (Editions Stromboli, 2000), a small book that contained color pictures with a mysterious allure, properly renders the spirit that animated Roversi: "This little book came into existence by chance, without any particular reason. You should take it as is, as you pick up a rock, the way you listen to a song or a bird whistling at the far end of the garden." (*Roberto Mutti*)

Rovira Pedro (1921-1978). A Spanish fashion designer who is considered almost a forerunner of minimalism. He studied medicine at the insistence of his family, but immediately after graduating he took an apprenticeship with a couturier in Barcelona, where he learned the profession and, in 1948, made his debut in high fashion. At the turn of the 1960s, he joined haute couture with a line of ready-to-wear fashion that survived him by a year.

Rowe Franklin. Black American fashion designer. Born in the Bronx in New York, at the age of ten he was already drawing sketches that he tried to sell in the neighborhood stores. He graduated from the Fiorello Laguardia High School of Music and Arts (the one in *Fame*) and, later, received a scholarship that allowed him to attend the prestigious Traphagen School of Fashion. In 1980 he moved to Santa Fe in New Mexico, where he began work as a designer, winning a clientele that was largely composed of people from the world of entertainment and sports. Three years later, he returned to New York and founded Franklin Rowe International. Mistrustful of "trends," he emphasized a classical and elegant style intended for a vast audience and public of men and women. He favored leather and silk. In 2003 he launched the Fifi line, intended for "larger" women and Frankee, a children's line.

Rowley Cynthia (1958). American fashion designer, from Illinois. She offered clothing that was designed to fit women's bodies, under the banner of femininity. She designed outfits that were classic in design, in line with the strictures of *bon ton*, winking an eye at modern, and in some cases avant-garde details. She taught at Parsons School of Design in 1992-93 and showed collections regularly during New York's Fashion Week. She began selling her first collection to the most important American stores. In the years that followed, she expanded her production to include menswear, accessories, and lingerie. In 1995 she received an award from the Council of Fashion Designers of America as a new talent in the field of fashion. In 1996, she was given the Michelangelo Shoe Award and in 1997 the Michael Award's Women's Wear Designer of the year. In spring of 2002, following an extremely successful launch in Japan, she presented in the United States her collection of cosmetics that was slated for a worldwide distribution program. She published *Swell: a Girl's Guide to the Good Life*, *Home Swell Home*, and *The Swell Dressed Party*.

Sketch by Cynthia Rowley.

Royal Ceremonial Dress Collection In London, Kensington Palace has permanent exhibit of ceremonial outfits belonging to the British Royal Family and the British court. The palace was rebuilt by Sir Christopher Wren at the end of the seventeenth century at the behest of King William III, who used it as the seat of his government. It then became a royal residence over the centuries that followed. Queen Victoria was born there, and Princess Diana lived there. In part, it is still used as a private residence. Queen Victoria opened part of the palace to the public in 1899. Some of the halls of the dress collection were recently modernized with a sophisticated technology in such a way that visitors can experience the courtly sartorial works in a virtual form. The rest of the exhibition is designed according to a chronological and thematic progression. Court outfits and uniforms dated from the eighteenth century onward. There is excellent documentation of the various men's and women's court dress from the eighteenth century to 1939, when the custom of court dress was abolished. The rules imposed by the court specified the outfit and the decorations to be worn in accordance with rank and with the occasion. Moreover, there are exhibits regarding the crafts that specialize in the production of this particular type of apparel. After the Second World War and with the development of London high fashion, it was popular couturiers who dressed the ladies in waiting and the queen herself. Among Queen Elizabeth II's favorite dressmakers: Norman Hartnell and Hardy Amies. Both are well represented in the collection.

(*Virginia Hill*)

Royal College of Art London. The fashion and fabrics section of this prestigious nineteenth-century academy of art dates back to the years immediately following World War II, the period of Dior's New Look which was indirectly responsible for its foundation. The idea of a professional school of fashion was introduced by the Ministry of Trade and Industry in order to contend with the reborn supremacy of Parisian fashion following the war. This led to the project of a school where the professionals of the present day could help to train the professionals of tomorrow. The executive committee included two industrialists, two fashion designers, and a journalist. The then editor-in-chief of *Vogue England,* Madge Garland, was summoned to supervise the course. At first looked upon by the industry with a degree of suspicion, good working relations were later developed that continue to the present day. Since 1969, the two-year course has been accredited as a university Master's degree. Enrollment is possible with a high-school diploma in fashion or fabrics. It is recognized as one of the best specialization schools in the world.

Rozanova Olga (1886-1919). Russian painter and poet. At the dawn of the Soviet revolution she was, with Rodchenko, a protagonist of productivist art and created avant-garde clothing, notable both in design and colors, with the utopian goal of changing the lifestyles of the inhabitants of the large cities. Before 1917, she had been a member of the Suprematist movement.

Rubartelli Franco (1937). Italian photographer. After an extensive array of highly eclectic studies (classical high school, Italian Naval Academy, department of political science), he began to do fashion photography, using his wife, a famous fashion model, as his subject. In the 1960s, improvisation combined with flair was a winning array, especially if the young photographer, who had decided to devote himself with great passion to shooting, "dared" to show his pictures to Consuelo Crespi, representative of *Vogue* in Italty. She in turn showed the photographs to the editor-in-chief of *Vogue America*, Diana Vreeland, who considered them to be very good and published them in an 18-page layout. From that point on he began to publish in magazines such as *Queen*, *Life,* and the Italian, French and British editions of *Vogue* and to work for Courrèges, thanks to his powerfully innovative style that made use of color in a daring and almost hypnotic manner. Rubartelli's work remained deeply linked to his relationship with the model Vera von Lehndorff, better known as Veruschka, with whom he also engaged in photographic performances whether there was a clear link to the field of body art. In 1968, the German publisher Bucher brought out an international edition of his book, *Veruschka*.

Rubecchini Liliana. Creator of women's underwear. She was born in Florence. In the 1970s and the 1980s and at the beginning of the 1990s, the name of Liliana Rubecchini was synonymous with night shirts, dressing gowns, camisoles, bodysuits and highly original "outfits" that were epitomes of femininity and extremely sexy. She was especially talented in matching colors and fabrics (lace with pure silk and satin, with various inserts) and at creating an unfailing new succession of models, with embroideries with love knots, little tassels, and intriguing slits.

Rubinacci Amina. Neapolitan dressmaker. She had an atelier in Via dei Mille. She began her business in 1967. She was a master of knitwear, which she interpreted with a very colorful palette and an extremely meticulous approach to execution, a sartorial perfectionism that runs in her blood. In fact, she was a daughter and a sister of the profession. Her father Gennaro, known as Bebè, was one of Italy's great men's tailors. He had dressed King Umberto di Savoia (Humbert of Savoy), as well as Vittorio De Sica, Eduardo De Filippo, Curzio Malaparte. Her brother Mariano nobly continued the family tradition.

Rubinacci Gennaro (1895-1961). Neapolitan tailor. The atelier of Gennaro Rubinacci, also known as Bebè, opened its doors in the 1920s in the Via Chiaia, and later moved to the Via Filangieri, where it stands today. It immediately established itself as one of the most elegant and exclusive shops in Naples. In contrast with most of his colleagues, Rubinacci was not born into the profession of the couturier. He had solidly established bourgeois traditions: his family, a century before, were silk-traders working with the Far East, and they ran a famous shop in the Via Medina, not far from the Castello Angioino (Angevin Castle). Bebè was a refined aesthete, a passionate collector of classical antiquities and antiques. He was skilled at choosing talented workers, and among them in particular the young Vincenzo Attolini, a pupil of the master tailor De Nicola. In the early 1930s, he designed what would go down in history as the Neapolitan jacket, a forerunner of the modern men's jacket. Rubinacci was the inspirer of a men's fashion that, while faithfully harking back to the dictates of English style, was softened in its lines and lightened in its fabrics. His suits stood out for the fluidity of line and their great wearability. His outfits had an elegant drop, adapting to various physical structures without ever losing their recognizability. The Rubinacci label enjoyed considerable popularity beginning in the 1960s. After the shops of Naples and Capri came the shops in Milan, Paris, London, and New York. The present owner of the company is Mariano Rubinacci, son of the founder Gennaro.

❑ 2001, July. Mariano Rubinacci opened a showroom-atelier in Via Montenapolene 18 in Milan. For the occasion and in conjunction with the Milan runway presentations of the Spring-Summer 2002 menswear collections, he hosted the exhibition *L'uomo and il mare - Percorsi dall'uniforme al blazer* ('Man and the Sea-Development from Uniform to Blazer'). It was based on a collection that reiterated the development of the men's jacket.
❑ 2002, October. He inaugurated in Rome a boutique with a private club. The fourth atelier, furnished in the label's distinctive colors, black and yellow, stands out from the others because of the addition of a private club, a sort of parlor enriched with art objects and silks of all sorts, in which to talk about fine clothing but also culture. For the inauguration of the Roman showroom, alongside his own fashion creations, he hosted the presentation of a book entitled *Diario di una giovane principessa* (1886-1897), by Adele Monroy di Pandolfina (Quiritta Edizioni). The hostess of the event was Alessandra Rubinacci, the first-born daughter of Mariano, and sole managing director of the company.

Rubin Chapelle A prêt-à-porter label created by the Austrian designer Sonja Rubin (1971), and Kid Chapelle (1970) from Ohio: they met at the Fashion Institute of Technology and, in 1995, decided to join creative forces. They had both previously worked for other fashion designers and had developed a taste of minimalism but wanted to further personalize it. Kid, a former engineer, considered clothing to be a field of construction and used visible stitching, strong colors, and geometric meshes. Sonja is very fanciful. Together, they love to dress free women, without preconceptions, and a little extravagant. They have already won a place for themselves in the department stores of America.

❑ 2003, March. In New York, on Fourteenth Street, they opened a futuristic store with semi-movable sectors, plasma screens, and other technological developments designed by the architect Annabel Selldorf. Rubin by this point had joined the sizable army of fashion designers who have just said "no" to furs.

Rubinstein Helena (1872-1965 Paris). Founder in 1902 of the line of cosmetics that bear her name. She moved from her native Poland at the age of 20 to Australia, where she opened her first beauty parlor, and then later moved to London, and then Paris, with stops and time spent in New York; she lived for nearly a century and through two world wars without ever tiring of telling woman that beauty is the fruit of patience and persistence, beginning with the cleansing of the skin as well as its nourshment and care.

Jean Cocteau called her the "empress of beauty" and she was certainly a pioneer in the beauty industry, as well as the leader of a company that created avant-garde products and an extensive network of beauty salons around the world. But Helena was never a great beauty, even if 27 great painters of her time, but Marie Laurencin and Dalí, Dufy and Van Dingen – Picasso left his painting of her unfinished – did her portrait over the course of fifty years, from when she was 38 to when she was 88 years old. All of those paintings captured her in different aspects of her personality: her imperiousness, the sensuality that was the foundation of her success in society, and her emotions. Those who met her in the last years of her life remember her as she appears in the portrait by Sutherland: still powerful at the age of 90, entirely covered with wrinkles, wearing one of those sets of jewelry that made her collections of pearls, emeralds, and diamonds so famous. Equally famous was her collections of opaline, paintings by renowned artists and African sculptures in her home at Quai de Bèthune in the Ile Saint-Louis. Among her products, suffice it to mention the first moisturizing cleanser (Skin Dew) and the first biological cream (Skin Life). She dedicated the creation (1953) of the Helena Rubinstein Foundation to women, endowing part of her fortune to education, medicine, law, and the welfare of women and children, in a vast array of nations, including the United States, France, Tunisia, and Israel. A major personality who gathered her ideas and her experience in a lucid autobiography, *My Life for Beauty*.

❑ 2003. The *maison* introduced Stellar Gloss, a new lipstick with an innovative formula that ensures the greatest possible sheen and glow for lips and a formulation that ensured constant moisturizing and nutrition. In the same line, Stellars Color was included, an ultradurable nail polish (the advertising campaign mentioned five days of perfect durability) in order to create a special "glass" effect. (*Lucia Sollazzo*)

Rucci Ralph Chado. American fashion designer, of Italian descent. He debuted about twenty years ago in New York where he has been doing his runway presentations ever since, with an occasional runway presentation in Paris. The trade publications compared his style with that of Oscar de la Renta. He studied at the Fashion Institute of Technology. His fashion is anti-spectacular by definition and is based especially on an incredible devotion to fabric research.

Ruching A pleated, fluted, or gathered strip of fabric used for trimming skirts, necklines, and cuffs. It is usually used on women's garments, but some men's shirts have small and discreet ruchings.

Rude Boys A fashion tied up with the musical phenomenon. Chris Blackwell, the founder of Island Records and the mastermind behind the worldwide success of Bob Marley and reggae, owed his initial success to the production of a hit single in 1964, *My Boy Lollipop*, sung by Millie, a young Jamaican girl of 14. Millie was thus responsible for the first worldwide success of Ska (or Blue-beat as it was known at the time), the source and origin of all the Jamaican musical styles that followed. Blue-beat is a cocktail of different styles, a mixture of Rhythm and Blues and Pop Tamba Motown propagated by American radio stations, and grafted onto the body of the local Caribbean rhythms of Jamaica. The spread of this Rock Steady/Blue-Beat/Rudie Blues style was entrusted to sound systems (mobile audio systems) that were popular at the time, just as they are today, and to the technical skills of DJs like Prince Buster, who were authentically creative in their mixes. The splendid garb of the Rude Boys owed a debt of gratitude to the sophisticated elegance of the New York jazz scene in the 1950s as well as to the Italian style that had been adopted almost simultaneously by the Mods of England. Leather jackets were worn with pipe-stem trousers. De rigueur were dark glasses, berets, and Pork-pie Hats. Typically Rude Boy and Jamaican is, instead, the style of trousers riding above the ankles, as well as the love of iridescent fabrics (two-tone). The end of the 1970s saw many of the protagonists of the original era, such as Desmond Dekker, coming back to popularity, thanks to the success that Ska groups, such as the Specials and Selecter, had in the market.

Ruff Rigid pleated or creased collar. Invented in Italy in the 16th century and made popular by Caterina de' Medici. It then reached exaggerated dimensions to the point of becoming a real wheel around the neck.

Ruffinelli Carla (1922-1998). Painter, illustrator, and fashion journalist. She was born in Turin. She studied at the Accademia Albertina, where she was a pupil of Felice Casorati. During the war, she worked on the creation of the first Italian animated cartoon feature, *Il ladro di Baghdad* (The Thief of Baghdad). She illustrated, for the San Paolo publishing house, many books for children and young people, including fairy tales by Andersen, Perrault, and the brothers Grimm. For nearly thirty years, in the magazine *family Cristiana*, she drew a page of fashion tips entitled, *Mi vesto così* ('This Is How I Dress').

Ruffo Leather garment manufacturer founded in 1966 in Milan by Ruffo Corsi and later run by his son Giacomo. It also produced the leather collections of Gianni Versace and Jil Sander. In 1997 it launched the line of bags and accessories, Origami Express, based on the ancient art of origami, and in 1998 the *griffe Ruffo Research Uomo & Donna*, put in the hand of young designers. It is committed to Antonio Berardi for the first two seasons, then to A. F. Vandevorst.

❑ 2000. The Greek fashion designer Sophia Kokosalaki, Athenian-born and 28 years old, who developed professionally in England after taking her masters the Central St Martin School in London, was appointed to design the *maison*'s Research collection for both men's and women's prêt-à-porter. The young fashion designer was put in charge of the Tuscan company's avant-garde label for two seasons, beginning with summer 2001; that label accounts for almost 20 of orders.
❑ 2003. The project Ruffo Research ends up with Haider Ackermann. Before him il duo Alexandre Matthieu worked at it.

Ruggeri Cinzia (1943). Designer, active in fashion as well. She lives and works in Milan. After attending the Brera Academy of Fine

Cinzia Ruggeri, clothing from the 1985 Spring-Summer Collection, published in *Donna*.

Arts, she spent two years as an apprentice with Carven in Paris. For over ten years (mid-1970s to late-1980s) she created and put her name on two of her own lines of prêt-à-porter, Bloom and Cinzia Ruggeri, distributed internationally and presented regularly during the Milanese collections. She has collaborated creatively with: the Centro Tutela Lino (Linen Protection Board), Castellini (underwear), Kim Top line (sportswear), Cotonificio Cantoni, Nino in Germany, Driade and Poltrona Frau (furniture), Glass (mirrors) and still works with Rapsel (fabrics, mirrors, objects). She has taught at the Palermo Polytechnic in the fashion and furnishings program and at the Polimoda of Florence for the Fashion Institute of Technology of New York. She has designed costumes for films and theater. Among her creations, forerunners of many of the themes and ideas that current fashion has later picked up on, sometimes many years later, we should mention the kinetic and behavioral outfits of 1981, the outfits of light and liquid crystals from 1982 (it was exhibited at the Milan Triennale), the "arci-moda," (1980-81), the decorations concealed at the bottom of the lining of pockets or pearls abandoned along the hem of an overcoat, the spiderweb-wedding dress, the holes and cuts in outfits for a body/exterior communication (1979), asymmetrical and diagonal outfits (1983-84), three-dimensional outfits, nature outfits like the one with its back covered with ivy, the low-wall outfit with flower pots for real flowers, the overalls with a real, growing lawn (1982), the ziggurat outfit, the tablecloth outfit, the utensil jewelry, the insect decoration. She has taken part in a great many collective exhibitions (Venice Biennale 1981; Milan Triennale 1983, 1985, and 1992; FIT, New York; Victoria and Albert Museum, London, 1987) and she has expressed in numerous personal exhibitions her multi-language of fashion, design, anthropology, ecology, and emotions: right up to the recent *Antoillogica*, held in the Spazio Krizia in 1998. Awards: *Fil d'Or* of Monte Carlo in 1983 and 1984, *Città di Milano* in 1985, *L d'Or* of Monte Carlo in 1986, anjd *Vivere sul velluto* in 1994 in Verona.

❑ 2003, October. At the Castello Belgioioso in the province of Pavia, she inaugurated a personal show entitled entitled *Psssssfttttt*, in which she exhibited outfits, accessories, small installations, and design objects.

(*Isa Tutino Vercelloni*)

Ruiz de la Prada Agatha (1960). Spanish fashion designer. She debuted as a painter in her birthplace, Madrid, and was influenced by the world of Pop Art and realism. She debuted in fashion at the age of 21, with runway presentations in Madrid in which she broke away from the traditional approach to Iberian couture, which was just then emerging from the straitlaced years of Francoism. She has a distinctive use of bright colors and spare, playful forms. Beginning in 1991 she worked on home furnishings, designing plates, tiles, refrigerators, washing machines, furniture, and watches, establishing temporary alliances with Swatch, Hierba Monesal and Absolut Vodka. In 1995 she produced a childrenswear collection, at first on an exclusive basis for the chain of department stores El Corte Inglés. In 2003 she launched her first, very non-conformist menswear collection: silk trousers with organdy overtrousers, suits made of corduroy and heavy canvas, in absolutely unorthodox colors: orange, yellow, fuchsia.

Ruohonen Anna (1967). Finnish menswear designer. She took a degree at the University of the Applied Arts in Helsinki and went on to take a master's in design at the French Insititute of Fashion in Paris. She has worked for Margiela, José Levy, and Olivier Desorges. In 1997, in Naples, she was a finalist in the Master of Linen competition for young designers, and in that context she presented her first collection, with the Leningrad Cowboys. Her creations are in the display windows of Absinthe in Paris, and Beam's and Paranoid in Tokyo.

Rykiel Sonia (1930). French designer. It was during her pregnancy, in 1962, that she made her first outfits: they were maternity clothes for herself. After a brief creative collaboration with her husband's company, in 1968 she opened her first boutique at the Galéries Lafayette. Eclectic, tireless, and

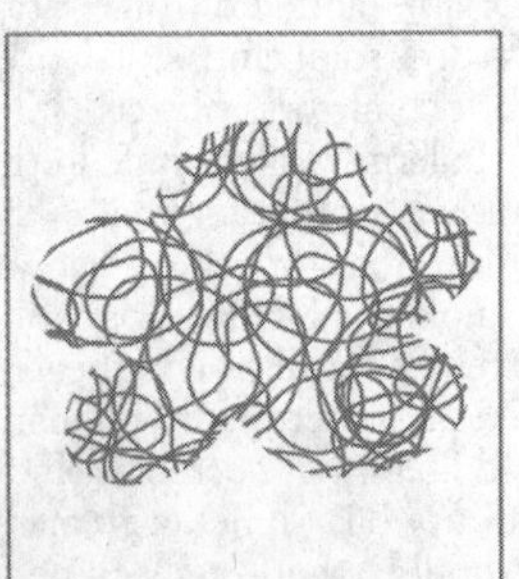
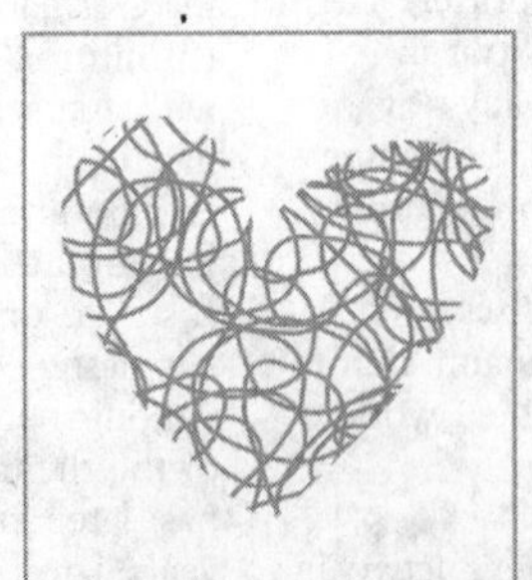

Sketches for tiles by the designer Agatha Ruiz de la Prada.

versatile, Sonia wrote books and fairytales, collaborated on the restoration of the Hotel Crillon, designed a collection for men and children, created lines of accessories, and a perfume that would be followed by a line of cosmetics. Her fashion, almost entirely created with remarkable wools, immediately captured the attention of the public with its simplicity and fluidity, daring and intuition: black, the fetishistic color of the first collections; extreme and provocative juxtapositions; pullovers – she designed more than six thousand of them, in tricot, sewn, torn, adorned, sequined – became a cult item, to the point that, for the celebration of her 30th year in business, the fashion designer designed the bottle for her latest line of perfume to look like a pullover. Known as the queen of tricot, it had been her flash of inspiration that put knitwear on the same plane of respect as silk and chiffon, transforming it and reinventing it with elegance. In 1985, she was awarded the Légion d'Honneur. A tireless experimenter, an ambassador of non-conformism, she produced clothing that also won over the new generation. Her talent for communication continues. In 1998, she said: "At the dawn of the year 2000, women give life to clothing. It should not be the other way around. The provocation is the woman, never the clothes that she wears." Indeed, it is no accident that "démode," the term that she coined in 1976 to describe making fashion in relation to one's own body, remains a highly topical concept and word.

(*Maria Vittoria Pozzi*)

❑ 1999. Twenty years after her first book, *Et je la voudrais nue...*, *Paris Sur le pas de Sonia Rykiel* was published. In the meanwhile, books commemorating 20 and 30 years in the fashion business and the collection of children's fairytales, *Tatiana Acacia*, named after her granddaughter, the daughter of her own daughter Nathalie.

❑ 2000. She created a new fragrance, Rykiel Rose, which took its place alongside *3ème Sense* (1978), *Le Parfum* (1993), Sonya Rykiel (1997), and Rykiel Homme (1999).

❑ 2001. She hands over control, but only in part, to her daughter, Nathalie, the blithe muse of the first outfits created by her mother while she was still pregnant with her. A former model, Nathalie is now the label's artistic director. Among her creations are the lines Sonia Rykiel Enfants and Modern Vintage Sonya Rykiel, to which we should add an entire series of scented candles, skin jewelry, candy, and even Euro converters.

❑ 2003. Nathalie, with her mother, opened "Woman," a sophisticated boutique of the senses located in the Parisian neighborhood of Saint Germain (4, Rue de Grenelle). If you go past the roomful of vibrators and stuffed animals (more voluptuous than childish), you will find a space reserved for hard-to-find hard toys, erotic playthings on display among the black and pink silks, sequins and lace: the bright red vibrator bunny, the clitoral stimulator shaped like a toy mouse, a pair of dice to use to determine the sequence of foreplay. "This is not a luxury sexy shop, rather it is a boutique intended for women who have an approach to pleasure that is free of any sense of guilt," says Nathalie Rykiel.

(*Edoardo Ponzoni*)

S

Saab Elie (1964). Lebanese designer. She studied in Paris but began her career in her home country, designing wedding and ceremonial dresses for Arab royal families (including Queen Rania of Jordan's outfit for her coronation) and for Middle Eastern high society. Her first fashion show was held in 1993. In 1998 she made her debut on the *haute couture* runways of Rome, presenting garments with very elaborate drapes and intricate embroidery done by hand by the 100 people dedicated to the task in her Beirut studio.

❑ Since 1998, Saab's collections have been produced exclusively in Milan.
❑ 2002, March. Gaining international fame, the Lebanese designer dressed winning actress Halle Berry for the Oscars award ceremony.

Sabbadini Italian jeweler. Four generations of the Sabbadini family have dealt in precious stones and jewelry. Everything is conceived and made in the family. The boutique designed by Renzo Mongiardino opened in Via Montenapoleone in Milan in October 1998. The showroom with attached workshop is on the third floor. Sabbadini's fame derives from the company's knowledge and use of precious stones of the highest quality. It is unique in the way it shows off the stones by using an invisible setting, so that, although the gold is there, you cannot see it. Invisible settings are also used for superb brooches, elegant rings, and sophisticated ear-rings. The symbol of the Sabbadini style is the bee-shaped brooch, which are made by hand in gold with semiprecious stones, or with emeralds, rubies, diamonds, and pink, blue or yellow sapphires. Sabbadini's creations are known throughout the world, from the showroom in New York to the exhibitions in Tokyo, St Moritz, Palm Beach, Beverly Hills, Southampton, and Crans-sur-Sierre. (*Marilea Somaré*)

Sabbah (1965). Moroccan designer born in Casablanca. He has been working in New York (with a showroom in Center Street) since 1997, making exclusive designs for a very thin slice of the public who have very personal ideas about how and why they dress as they do. He likes camouflage materials, which he searches out around the world. Before setting up on his own, he worked for a long time in Paris as assistant designer to Chantal Thomass and Jacques Esterel. As well as being involved in fashion, he takes part in film and media events, produces hip-hop music, and writes poetry.

Sabbia Rosa French women's lingerie boutique in the Rue des Saints Pères in Paris. It was opened in 1976 by Monette Moati. It sells *haute couture* lingerie in a choice of over 30 colors and a vast array of silk prints.

❑ 2003. The designer added a line of silk stockings in 25 colors which can be combined with matching underwear.

Sable The tsarina of furs. The Siberian people paid the *iassak*, the tax that ended up in the tsar's personal coffers, in sable. The Monomachus's crown, called a *chapka* and made of gold filigree over a gold base studded with precious stones and pearls, was trimmed with sable; sable also adorned the sumptuous jewel-encrusted cloak that the tsar wore for official ceremonies. Every possible eulogistic adjective or expression has been used to describe the magnificence of sable, and the French even compare it to a fluffy "mousse." It has even been suggested that the Golden Fleece sought by Jason and the Argonauts in Greek mythology, which was guarded by a dragon in the depths of a forest in Kolchis (today the country of Georgia), was in fact sable. Long before the discovery of oil, it was universally considered black gold. Despite the presence of sable in Asia, North America, and Europe, the history of the fur runs hand-in-hand with that of Siberia. In that unbounded empty land it played the same role as gold in the Gold Fever in Canada and Alaska. The poor animals were the object of such indiscriminate hunting that at the beginning of the 20th century it had disappeared from vast regions of the Russian empire and the Tsarist and then the Soviet governments had to take protective measures. Russian sable (*Martes zibellina*) has thick, shiny, silky fur in a myriad of hues from brown to light beige, to almost white. It is undisputed that the best is the Barguzinsky, named after the region of Barguin, near Lake Baikal. Breeding, which started in the Soviet Union in 1931, focuses on dark colors, but Nature has created the Royal sable, by transforming an anomaly into a virtue: in the Royal sable, a lack of pigmentation in the tips of the fur creates an incredible silvery sheen that brings an extraordinary beauty to its appearance. Sable is as precious today as it was in the past, when it was part of the Tsars' *Great Treasure*. When the Russian aristocracy fled the country, they took with them sable pelts, not money. (*Maria Rita Stiglich*)

Coat with sable collar and muff, 1912 (Prints Collection A. Bertarelli, Milan).

Sabot A type of clog with a wooden sole and leather upper enclosed at the front but which leaves the heel completely exposed at the back. It is similar to the Dutch clog but without the raised point at the front. In France, they were very commonly worn by the revolutionaries in the late 1700s. For the whole of the 19th century and early 20th century, they were worn by farming children at least until their first communion. In the 1978 Italian film by Olmi – *L'albero degli zoccoli* [The Tree of Wooden Clogs] – they become the poetic symbol of the events of a few peasant families in the southern Bergamo region. Nearly a century later, a new social class revived them as a new status symbol. At the end of the 1960s, as part of the youth-driven revolution, they were boldly worn by young people and hippies throughout the world, both in cities and in winter with thick colored wool stockings.

Sacchetti Angelo (1922-1997). Journalist, PR, press and advertising agent, and organizer of fashion events. After World War II, armed with a degree in literature, he turned to journalism writing for *Ciak*, *Costume* and other magazines. In 1950, he worked with Ezio Redaelli for the Miss Italia competition, becoming the cinematographic press agent. A chance meeting with Giansevero Fila in 1958 took him into the world of textiles and, in 1961, he became wholly involved with public relations and advertising for fashion houses, looking after their contacts with the press. He also organized some shows at the Festival of Men's Fashion at San Remo, of Moda-Mare Capri and Cortina Moda. Extrovert, friendly, and with immense vitality, he is remembered for example for the time when, for the launch of a product, he hired out the Castel Sant'Angelo, illuminating it with 900 torches. In his final years, he organized the Liguria Moda-Mare al Covo di Nord-Est and Cinema Festival del Mare in the gardens of Naxos.

Sacchetti Enrico (1877-1967). Italian illustrator and poster designer. For *Lidel* and French women's magazines, he recorded the fashions of the 1920s and 1930s in a non-calligraphic style and with an ability to capture the essence of a design. He worked for *La Nuova Antologia*, *Il Secolo XX*, and *L'Illustrazione Italiana*. In 1929-1930, he

Drawings by Enrico Sacchetti, 1930s.

designed the cover and plates of the novel by Orio Vergani *Io, povero negro* [Poor Negro] that has been translated into many languages.

Sachs Gloria. English designer. Having qualified in textile decoration, she studied in Fernand Léger's studio in Paris and collaborated with architects Gio Ponti and Franco Albini in Milan. She established her own brand having worked as a designer for Saks Fifth Avenue in New York. She carved herself a niche on the fashion scene with her passion for non-matching coordinates and her interpretation of very classical fabrics, such as tartan and spots that she creates by dyeing yarn in her mill in Scotland.

Sackman Laurence (1948). English photographer. He made his debut aged 18 by publishing a ten-page feature in *Nova*. By 1972 he had turned professional, and his photographs were published in *Marie Claire*, *Vogue Hommes* and *Harper's Bazaar*. In the 1980s, he gave up photography to concentrate on writing.

Safari jacket A type of jacket worn on safari, also called a bush jacket. Adopted in military and colonial circles, it is also the source of inspiration for sports jackets and is made in linen, cotton, waterproof fabrics, and corduroy. It usually has four bellows pockets and a belt around the waist. During the Fascist period, the safari jacket was worn in Italy as a uniform. The classic version is in twilled cotton, a very hard-wearing and long lasting fabric, and is typically used for military wear; it was adopted for the first time by the English for colonial uniforms. It can be either cream, khaki, or blue.

Sàfilo Italian eyewear manufacturers. Sàfilo makes and markets labels such as Gianfranco Ferré, Gucci, Polo Ralph Lauren, Pierre Cardin, Laura Biagiotti and Valentino. The brand was created in 1934 when the Tabacchi family bought the oldest Italian industrial plant producing lenses and frames (it was founded in 1878 in Calalzo di Cadore). Since then, it has gone from strength to strength, so much so, that in March 1987 Sàfilo shares were sold on the Stock Exchange in Milan. The company has a worldwide marketing operation and two factories outside Italy, in Austria and Slovenia.

❑ 2000. The new distribution center in Padua went into operation to improve logistics. The trading branch Sàfilo Portugal was launched.
❑ 2001. The Sàfilo Nordic, India, Hong Kong, and Singapore branches were opened. Productivity at the Longarone factory increased. The new contact lenses Carrera Contact were launched on the Italian market.
❑ 2001, July. Vittorio Tabacchi made a public purchase offer and became the majority shareholder of the group.
❑ 2001, December. The company withdrew from the Stock Exchange where it had been quoted since 1987.
❑ 2002, January. A new line was launched under the Yves Saint Laurent label, a division of the Gucci Group.
❑ 2002, April. The Group's profits increased substantially. In 2001, profits were up by 23% on 2000; operating profits were up by 28%, and net profits increased by 41%.

❑ 2002, June. Sàfilo bought the Salmoiraghi & Viganò chain of shops.
❑ 2002, September. A new showroom was opened at 142 Champs-Elysées in Paris.
❑ 2002, October. The Group opened a base in London. A deal was signed to market the collections of the labels Bottega Veneta and Stella McCartney, strengthening the already established relationship with the Gucci Group.
❑ 2002, December. The American fashion house Liz Claiborne puts its initials to an agreement with the Veneto firm for the launch of a new collection. The brand successfully completed the refinancing of the debt and, in association with the transaction, Credit Suisse First Boston Private Equity became a minority shareholder in the Group, with a holding of around 270 million euros.
❑ 2003, February. The Sàfilo Group and Armani Group announced a deal for the manufacturing and marketing of a collection of Giorgio Armani and Emporio Armani glasses.
❑ 2003, April. The group battled through the crisis and in 2002 increased both sales (+6%, the equivalent of 894 million euros) and operating profits (+12%).
❑ 2003, April. After his brother Vittorio sold off his share, Giuliano Tabacchi bought 50% of the Alberto Aspesi company belonging to Intek.
❑ 2003, June. Vittorio Tabacchi was made a Cavaliere del Lavoro.
❑ 2003, July. Sàfilo acquired Outlook Eyewear, the Denver (USA) based distributor of the eyewear brands Liz Claiborne and J. Lo by Jennifer Lopez. As a result of the agreement, Sàfilo added the license for the Liz Claiborne brand to its portfolio, including the lines Liz Claiborne, LizSport, Claiborne, Liz Claiborne Readers, Crazy Horse, First Issue, and Villager. Sàfilo also added J. Lo by Jennifer Lopez, and B.U.M Equipent to its range of sunglasses. All the brands acquired through Outlook were to be distributed exclusively in the USA and Canada.
❑ 2004, January. Vittorio Tabacchi, the owner of Sàfilo with about an 80% share in the company, decided to expand the business by distributing as well as manufacturing eyewear. The first step in this direction was taken in Spain. The Emporio Optical group, which controls about 70 shops in Spain, was acquired through a corporate chain with the Luxemburg based Angiolucci International at its head. The operation cost 18 million euros, plus 5 millions to acquire about 10 sales points in the Canary Islands from the Program Vision Group.
❑ 2004, March. Sàfilo celebrated 70 years of business by opening it's 27th office in China. The Sàfilo Group is currently present on the world market with its own brand collections Sàfilo, Carrera, Smith, Oxydo, Blue Bay, as well as the ranges produced under license for Bottega Veneta, Boucheron, Burberry, Diesel, Dior, Emporio Armani, Giorgio Armani, Gucci, Max Mara, Oliver, Pierre Cardin, Polo Ralph Lauren, Stella McCartney, Valentino, and Yves Saint Laurent. Sàfilo also distributes Fossil, Nine West, Kate Spade, and Saks Fifth Avenue for the American market. It has two specific collections for the sports sector, Carrera and Smith, and it has negotiated sponsorisation agreements and contracts with world famous athletes and teams for various sports.
❑ 2004, May. Sàfilo Group and Marc Jacobs International agreed on the launch of a new range of Marc Jacobs eyewear. They signed a seven-year license agreement for the production and distribution of the eyewear collection, and the agreement is then renewable for a further four years.
❑ 2004, December. The year closed with a consolidated turnover of 940 million euros, +8.5% at a constant exchange rate, and a net profit of 19.8 million euros, up 30.8% from 2003. The group achieved growth in all the main international markets, with particularly positive results in the Far East (+30% despite the negative effect of the exchange rate), North America (+10% with exchange rate parity), and Europe (+4.5%).
❑ The Sàfilo Group concentrated its technical and design know-how on the

The Sàfilo logo.

development of a new and exclusive collection of sunglasses, "IMATRA R.C., INC.," chosen by the motorcycle racing champion Valentino Rossi. Vittorio Tabacchi, President of the Group declared that "the collaboration between the Sàfilo Group, the 'IMATRA R.C., INC.' brand and Valentino Rossi guarantees the success of the new collection."
❑ 2005, April. The group finalised a partnership with Juicy Couture for a collection of sunglasses and spectacles planned for launch in March 2006, so adding to its portfolio of licenses that included Alexander McQueen, Boucheron, Bottega Veneta, Burberry, Diesel, Dior, Dior Homme, Emporio Armani, Giorgio Armani, Gucci, Marc Jacobs, MaxMara, Polo Ralph Lauren, Stella McCartney, Valentino and Yves Saint Laurent. Sàfilo also has various brands of its own: Carrera, Smith and Sàfilo Elasta. Sàfilo distributes the collections of Liz Claiborne, Fossil, Nine West, Kate Spade, and Saks Fifth Avenue under exclusive license.
❑ 2005, May. Rationalise so as not to delocalise. This was the manufacturing plan for 2005-2006. The group's Vice-President Giovannino Lorenzon, in charge of the manufacturing plan, explained that "We have chosen not to delocalise. It's a choice that we really believe in: our strength lies in tradition, and the accumulated abilities of those who have worked in the eyewear field for generations. But the competition from the Far East, which produces very low cost products, and the sales of counterfeits have forced us to rationalise our production."
❑ The "OXYDO SUNGLASSES" collection, designed by Enzo Sopracolle, produced and distributed by the Sàfilo Group, and aimed at a young and trendy target market, reinforced the group's link to music. The collection has been the subject of several television promotions featuring the model Fernanda Lessa during the Festivalbar music show. (*Adele Melzi*)

Sage Russell (1969). English designer. Before his successful entry into the fashion world (winning the New Generation prize in London Fashion Week in 2002), his career spanned both antiques and multimedia work. His interest in clothes led him, without any formal training in the field, to gain experience from the tailors in Savile Row and the shirtmakers of Jermyn Street in London. In 2003, he launched a line destined to reach a wide market. He caught on to the eccentric trend that mixes the sexy with the puritanical with great irony. He willingly uses old drapery with vintage materials. He is doing an interior design project with Hine Cognac and is creative consultant for Amnesty International.

Sahzà Brand of womenswear launched in 1994 by the GFT Womenswear Division Group. It was developed as a response to a potential gap in the market for American-style sportswear targeted essentially for 25 to 45 year olds with a moderately high price tag. The distribution and display strategies, together with a supply system organized along modular lines and in delivery groups, makes Sahzà a good example of advanced forms of franchising and retail selling.

❑ 2001. The brand was bought by the Mariella Burani Fashion Group.

Saia [Twill] Known as *serge* in French, with cloth and satin it is one of the fundamental weaves. The points where the weft and the threads meet are arranged diagonally so that parallel grooves and ribs form at 45-degree angles. Rarely used in drapery or woolen goods, except for gabardine, it is extensively used in cotton fabrics (jeans, drill, Levantine, etc.) or in light feminine fabrics such as silk, or silk and wool mixes. Batavia is a type of twill which is used to achieve colored or patterned effects, such as chequered fabrics, bird's eye, hound's tooth, Prince of Wales check, herringbone, grisaille.

Saint Laurent Yves (1936). French designer born in Oran in Algeria. He entered the fashion world officially in 1957, when, as the 21-year-old assistant to Christian Dior, he was asked to take over when the master died of an heart attack in a hotel in Italy. The Trapeze collection established the young designer as the child prodigy of French *haute couture*, despite only just having graduated from the École de la Chambre Syndicale de la Couture in Paris,. He distinguished himself from his predecessor by the decisiveness of his sartorial cuts and by the soft but quintessential lines, which bore witness to his complete independence from the rest of the French fashion scene and his supreme individuality. Saint Laurent worked at Maison Dior until 1960 when was called up to do military service in Algeria. It is there that he learned, from his friend and future associate Pierre Bergé, the sad news that Christian Dior had replaced him with a new designer, Marc Bohan. When he returned to Paris, he decided to set up on his own. With the help of Bergé and the financial backing of the American J. Mack Robinson, he officially opened his studio in the Rue Spontini on 20 January 1962, presenting his first signed collection. His success was immediate. His designs were snapped up by France's high society and by buyers from the American department stores, who appreciated the value of a line that was not overly elaborate but used well researched fabrics. Meanwhile the fashion press acclaimed the impeccable cut of his suits, which became the only true rivals to Chanel's style. The next collections drew inspiration from history, art, and literature, revealing the designer's passion for the cultural world and, in particular, for the theater, for which he often designed costumes. The work of Matisse (1981), the paintings of Picasso (1979), Pop Art (1966) and even the writings of Marcel Proust – which prompted the taffeta dresses of Winter 1971-72 – offered him continuous sources of inspiration. In 1965, minimalism and the geometrical works of Mondrian influenced one of his most successful collections, which is remembered for its rigorous lines, jersey dresses, and vinyl raincoats. The collection of Winter 1976, dedicated to the Ballets Russes, won international acclaim and was said by the *New York Times* to be "revolutionary, destined to change the course of fashion." His exotic origins and the years of training spent in direct contact with the Arab world permeated his style. The strength and unusual combination of colors, the opulence of the fabrics, the richness of the embroidery, the inventiveness of his prints and some ethnically inspired garments – such as the sahara jacket or djellaba – were the hallmarks of his style, all the while combined with great formal rigour. Nor should not be forgotten Saint Laurent's penchant, like that of Chanel before him, for putting tailored cuts and the main features of the male wardrobe into his womenswear collections. In 1966, he introduced a women's version of black tie for eveningwear, a simple black outfit comprising a jacket with satin lapels and a skirt or pants, to be worn as an alternative to the traditional long dress. In 1964 he created his women's fragrance *Y*, the first in a successful series, which included the bestsellers *YSL pour homme* (1971), *Rive Gauche* (1971), *Eau Libre* (1975), *Opium* (1977) and *Kouros* (1981). In 1978 he lent his name to a range of beauty products, which added cosmetics to the brand and, in 1992, he chose French actress Catherine Deneuve, a client of his since the 1960s, as a face for his advertising campaign. Saint Laurent and Bergé were among the first to introduce a marketing strategy into the world of *haute couture* that has now become commonplace, that of establishing the ready-to-wear line Yves Saint-Laurent Rive Gauche in 1966 to be sold in franchised boutiques. From the beginning it was never intended as a substitute for *haute couture*, but as a field of great creativity, releasing original and sought-after designs into the market. Production was entrusted to C. Mendès, a company manufacturing other ready-to-wear brands, such as Patou, Grès, and Chanel. The decision to enlist a single supplier to tailor the clothes, working exclusively for the brand, turned out to be a sign of great foresight, a move well ahead of its time. The success of 1970 made Yves Saint-Laurent Rive Gauche the leading exporter of luxury ready-to-wear womenswear. In December 1982, that side of the business expanded to create a second line, Variation, and sales increased as a result of granting licenses, which functioned in such a way to ensure that the Saint-Laurent colors,

Sketch by Yves Saint Laurent for his contribution to the *Visitors* exhibition in the Sala dei Gigli in the Palazzo Vecchio. Biennial of Florence, Skira, 1996.

design, and image were respected. The base at Rue Spontini became too small and Saint Laurent moved to 5 Avenue Marceau. Museums throughout the world – from the Metropolitan in New York (1983) to the Musée des Arts de la Mode in Paris (1986), to the Sezon Museum of Art in Tokyo (1990), to the Musée de la Mode in Marseilles (1994) – have dedicated retrospective exhibitions to the designer, celebrating his creativity and hailing him as one of the greatest ever contributors to the history of fashion. The Group was quoted on the Stock Exchange in Paris in 1989. Today the estate is owned by François Pinault as part of the holding group PPR.

(*Stefania Ricci*)

Proposals for a skirt and dress by Yves Saint Laurent in a drawing by Maria Pezzi, 1965.

❑ 1999. The company was bought by the Gucci Group.

❑ 2002, January. On the runway at the Centre Pompidou, Saint Laurent made his final exit from the fashion scene with an outstanding retrospective fashion show of 300 designs from the past and present: the atmosphere in the room was feverishly high, especially at the end when Catherine Deneuve sang for her lifelong friend *Ma plus belle histoire d'amour c'est vous* [You are my greatest love story]. Saint Laurent read out a long and personal farewell letter: "I believe I have never betrayed the boy who showed his sketches to Christian Dior with the greatest of trepidation... I have lived for this job, have always loved it and respected it to the very end. Fashion is not art, but needs an artist to exist. Clothes are certainly less important than music, architecture, or painting, but they are what I knew how to do and did, perhaps contributing to the transformations that have taken place during my lifetime. Today, we no longer strive only to make women look more beautiful but also to reassure them. Many people exorcise the ghosts of their ego through fashion, whereas I have always wanted to put myself at the service of women, serving their bodies, their movements, their very lives." About his life, the designer said, "I have known those false friends drugs and tranquilisers, and the prison of depression and clinics. I belong to what Marcel Proust called 'the magnificent and pitiful family of neurotics'."

❑ 2002, June. Stefano Pilati, already the probable successor to Tom Ford for the women's ready-to-wear, took over the complete creative direction of the house, including accessories and luggage. Pilato provided a completely new stylistic point of view; the excessive sensuality of his predecessor gave way to a more classic, discreet, and bourgeois elegance.

❑ 2002, December. With its 850 square meters of floor space, the new Yves Saint Laurent Rive Gauche store that opened in Milan became the famous French label's largest in Europe. The space at number 27 Via Montenapoleone (formerly Gucci) replaced the existing shop at number 8 Via Verri, which was in turn replaced by an Alexander McQueen boutique.

❑ 2002, December. Saint Laurent and his right-hand man Pierre Bergé gained public interest and recognition for their Foundation which occupies the building in Avenue Marceau. From this point on, the designer focused on the activities of the Foundation, which houses 5,000 dresses and 15 objects from the private collections of Saint Laurent and Bergé. The Foundation awards study bursaries and organizes fashion and contemporary art exhibitions. (*Adele Melzi*)

Saint Martin's School of Art or Central Saint Martin's College of Arts. English fashion school founded in 1854. It is considered the "Sorbonne of fashion," a hotbed of talent and the most prestigious school of fashion and design in the United Kingdom. Its slightly decadent classrooms opposite Charing Cross have seen the leading figures of the British new wave pass through: McQueen, the soul of Givenchy, Galliano, the revolutionary of Dior, Ozbek, Berardi, Oldfield, Hamnet, and Stella McCartney who is responsible for the Chloé collection. Courses last between 3 and 5 years. It costs £1,600 a year to study there for a member of the European Community, but £6,000 a year for everyone else. Having taken A-levels, students have to get through a very tough selection process to be admitted, which is based on an interview and an exam revolving around the candidate's book of drawings and sketches. Once awarded a place (150 chosen from on average 700 applications), the students can attend a wide range of classes in a variety of directions: menswear, womenswear, cut, and fabrics. There is intense competition among students and a highly stimulating atmosphere. At the end of each year only a group of students are allowed to show their work in the final exhibition: a personal collection who parade in front of an audience comprising buyers and designers who have been invited from around the world. (*Anna Santini*)

Sakina M'sa (1972). For those that live on the Camoro Islands, every object has a soul and its own life. When a loved one dies, an object is often buried with them to stay in contact with the deceased's soul. When her grandfather died, Sakina M'sa buried a piece of white cotton, which her dog later dug up. Sakina noticed that in the intervening period, it had changed color and appearance. She believes that even items of clothing have an identity that should be respected and a date of birth. Her collections therefore derive from fabrics that have been buried before being used.

Saks Fifth Avenue Big American department store which, since it first opened in 1924 in Fifth Avenue, has generated a business empire, with chains of stores across the United States. It was founded by Horface Saks and Bernard Gimbel and has survived on the back of the big labels to become a major attraction, aimed at the higher, more refined class of consumer interested in fashion. The chain has 12,000 employees. In the last 15 years, it has has changed hands twice: first to the British Group BAT Industries and then to Investcorp.

Sala Josep (1896-1962). Catalan photographer. He studied painting at Llotja and won recognition as a photographer in 1927. That year he was awarded the silver medal in the First Spanish Salon of Photography and began to work for the fashion magazine *D'Acì I D'Allà* where he became known for his use of oblique lighting and ability to create an atmospheric feeling both in fashion images and in elegant still-life compositions.

Sala Bianca When, on 22 July 1952, the doors of the Sala Bianca of the Pitti Palace were thrown open to welcome buyers and journalists for the first time to see the fashion shows in Florence, Italian fashion was not being officially baptized but entering its fourth incarnation. In just two years it had acquired, under the watchful eyes of international observers, unique special characteristics that made it a product, or rather a collection of products, of extreme interest. The date is recorded in the history books because from that point on the venue and the collections presented there were closely connected. Even today the Sala Bianca remains synonymous with Italian style. The following ingenious intuition was the key to its success: if fashion was only an image, it was essential that this image was constructed and presented in a form that was consistent with the values that it was meant to be representing. Creativity, originality, and the subtleties of Italian design – endorsed and mirrored in the organization of the shows – spread through the world from the Sala

Bianca in the heart of Florence. It paved the way for an economic phenomenon of far wider proportions and much greater consequence. It created an aura of prestige which spread from fashion to all goods that were made in Italy, making them famous and sought after across the world. It was a private individual, Giovanni Battista Giorgini, who started off this incredible story. In February 1951, he succeeded in organizing, with surprising ability and daring, a completely original fashion show for a few American buyers and their clients to whom were then presented all sorts of other products. It was not the first time that the creations of Italian dressmakers had been presented on official runways. However, it was absolutely the first time that a fashion show, presented as purely Italian, was staged exclusively for foreign buyers and journalists. There were only a few of them, but they were of great importance and their opinion could be either a death penalty or a life-line. Their approval opened the door to immediate success which grew from year to year under the management and direction of Giorgini. None of this overwhelming climb to success was left to chance or spontaneity, but was built up, show after show, with an amazing clarity of vision in the choice of how to reach such heights. The type of collections, the way they were presented, the production of the first show revealed a winning formula, which the following shows, organized by Giorgini until Spring 1965, went on to perfect. Starting with an initial concept, all the others followed from the same idea: the desire to establish a modern, efficient, and creative Italy. Perhaps because fashion was not his foremost interest, Giorgini knew how to extract from it a product/image whose full potential could be exploited, using it for ends that went way beyond the world of fashion itself. Fashion had always been, for everyone and everywhere, synonymous only with Paris. Setting out to vie with such competition was pure madness: the Italian fashion product distinguished itself by presenting different and original characteristics that could reach a new and much wider section of the market. It had to prove itself to potential buyers as something that was worth the risk of investment. As a result of the show's production and the type of designs that were first shown on that famous occasion

The first fashion show at the Sala Bianca in 1952 (from *La Sala Bianca – La nascita della moda italiana*, by Guido Vergani, Electa, 1992. Giovanni Battista Giorgini Archive).

(on 12 February 1951), it was immediately clear to the sceptical audience that a new and very different Italian fashion existed.
As there were only a few tailors and a few models, Giorgini decided to group them by type of clothing rather than the traditional way of grouping them by the name of the designer. This meant that their distinctiveness was confirmed and enhanced by the proximity of being shown in succession. He began by showing the outfits from the fashion boutiques, intended to be worn in people's free time, for sport and on informal occasions. This was a type of fashion that had not been presented in Paris and therefore comparisons could not be drawn with sophisticated French fashions. The clothes were upbeat, unexpected and youthful, the colors surprisingly jubilant, the quality impressive and the prices very attractive. In this environment, boutique wear was the winning card, clearly demonstrating the existence of an independent and original Italian fashion scene. The opening days of successive shows were always reserved for boutique wear. It had sold well until then and would continue to do so; however, if the Italian product/image was to take a leading role, it had to so in the world of *haute couture*, where creativity and novelty are combined with refined elegance.
The fashion houses that were invited to show at the Florentine runways were not chosen by chance, but rather for their unique qualities and ability to stand out from French fashion. Giorgini's ability to spot the type of features that would be seen as highly original and complete winners probably came from his knowledge of the American market. America was the mirror of the future that was awaiting Italy. Most women worked and were forced to spend the whole day from dawn until dusk away from home, using public transport, and as a result their fashion requirements were less demanding. They – and soon women from all over the world – needed clothes that were less sophisticated than those designed by the Paris tailors and more suited to an active lifestyle. It was therefore the moment to introduce an elegance that played on clean and quintessential lines, on cut, on top quality materials that could keep their perfect shape over time. These were the features of Italian design that stood out to the buyers right from the first show in February 1951. Presented by Giorgini, it was confirmed on their agenda that Italian collections, receiving international attention for the first time, translated the heritage of the Renaissance artistic tradition into line, cut, and wearability. Complete with all the elements on which the image of Italian fashion is methodically built up, the message was wholeheartedly and instantly assimilated by the buyers and circulated by the press in the intended way. The statement that Italian fashion was the fruit of its artistic tradition was far from a casual comment; it played a decisive role in constructing the image. It was not a verifiable fact, like cut or wearability; instead it was presented as the irrefutable truth, an axiom, a priority category, which enriched the actual features of the product with a significance and quite different quality. The statement became an incisive and efficient way of foregrounding the idea that creativity was a gift peculiar to the Italian spirit. Art had always been

Dress from the dressmakers Carosa (from *La Sala Bianca – La nascita della moda italiana*, by Guido Vergani, Electa, 1992. Giovanni Battista Giorgini Archive).

associated with generating the new and the beautiful, revealing the unexpected that had never been seen before. The custom of living in a city full of art, in direct contact with works of great value, without the museum acting as an intermediary, inevitably produces an aesthetic taste for refinement. All Florentines, particularly fashion designers, cannot help but be artists. In practice, it was being implied that Italian fashion was an art form of the most modern and topical type. Creativity was conveying a multifaceted message that resonated throughout the huge clothing industry, from *haute couture* to accessories. It justified an infinite diversity of products of both functional and aesthetic form in order to satisfy new and hidden market demands. In *haute couture* this was noticeable in the line and cut of the garments, in the beauty of the fabrics and in the type of decoration; in the less exacting field of boutique wear, it was noticeable in the unexpected and continuous innovation of function, form, decoration, and materials. The first and most loyal group of tailors that Giorgini had gathered was already demonstrating a varied and versatile creative ability: fresh refinement from Simonetta, spectacular design by Schuberth and formal rigour from Germana Marucelli. Good taste, moderation and a sense of proportion – part of the aesthetic heritage of the Renaissance – were soon recognized as the most important features of Italian dressmaking. Cleanliness of line, which came to represent the utmost elegance, was combined with very precise tailoring and perfect, but not excessively complicated, cuts. The simplicity of line helped to highlight the beauty of the embroidery and the materials, which were often the truly innovative part of the design. The quality of the dressmaking and the beauty of the materials pleased buyers from the most prestigious department stores, who had to satisfy the demanding tastes of their top clients who were used to the charms of Paris. The quintessential line, however, attracted a different category of buyer, dressmakers, who, having bought a prototype could copy and remake the design without too much difficulty. Even more openly than for *haute couture*, boutique and leisure wear – the real novelty of the Florentine runways of international acclaim – played the originality card by creating

A design by Vanna (from *La Sala Bianca – La nascita della moda italiana*, by Guido Vergani, Electa, 1992. Giovanni Battista Giorgini Archive).

surprising juxtapositions of ideas and by their use of materials. The variety of types of garments that were proposed as boutique wear matched the equally varied demands of the market and was already proof of a multitalented creativity. A less showy but very important area owed its success to its revolutionary combination of style and practicality. It was the answer to the problems of so many women who were busy at work all day and needed elegant clothes, which were nevertheless informal, crease-proof, and suitable for wearing for hours at a time without seeming ostentatious. Avolio's silk raincoats and the gorgeous Mirsa knitwear – which could be worn in an infinite number of ways at any time of day or on any occasion – were designed for just such women. The most explosive ideas that were most eagerly written about by the press were the outfits in boutique wear intended for

The audience in the Sala Bianca (from *La Sala Bianca – La nascita della moda italiana*, by Guido Vergani, Electa, 1992. Giovanni Battista Giorgini Archive).

leisure wear, as they were the most unpredictable and therefore the most keenly awaited. The fact that many of the clothes were designed to be worn at the weekend or on holiday provided limitless scope for invention. The postwar atmosphere was characterized by a need for fun and for asserting vitality and was therefore open to fashions that were playful, joyous, youthful, colourful, and energetic. Increasing affluence meant that the frequency of such events increased to cater for audiences from ever wider social classes, clearly indicating as early as the 1950s the future success of these types of clothes. Pucci astonished audiences with his revolutionary combinations of colors; Bertoli with his creations with ribbons, paillettes, and braids; the Tessitrice dell'Isola, Myricae, Valditevere, Scarabocchio, Baldini, Falconetto, and others with their woven, hand printed and hand painted fabrics. Weaving by hand meant that unusual threads and materials could be used, such as ribbons and paillettes, and the very famous printed patterns by designers such as Pucci, Roberta di Camerino, Falconetto, and Ken Scott were of outstanding and often exceptional quality. *Trompe-l'oeil* effects were sought after; the vast repertoire of folkloric traditions were employed; scales were transposed so that little botanical details were reproduced on a huge scale; and meanings were subverted so that everyday or decorative objects became decorative motifs. Handcrafted fabrics, embroidery, or appliqué using paillettes, semiprecious stones, and shells meant that Italian garments were often unable to be copied by foreign dressmakers and elevated them to a position where they were above competition, carving themselves a special niche somewhere between *haute couture* and mass-produced clothes. Besides, they demonstrated and extolled the incredible refinement of Italy's artisan abilities and broached the idea of artistic expression as a form of joyous creativity. These multiple features that were peculiar to boutique wear and dressmaking immediately became a reality from the very first Florentine runway shows. It was a good way of presenting them, but did not fulfil the initial aim of the shows that Giorgini had intended. The sum total of a number of different, even if very rich, single ideas, would not automatically have generated that key and fundamental concept of creativity as a special skill of the Italians, as their innate disposition from which burst continuous and multiple ideas and beautiful forms. On their own, they would not have been able to promote other types of production. It was necessary to create a single matrix which continually referred to that overarching concept of Italian-ness characterized by its historic and artistic traditions. A constant stream of intelligent promotional events was dedicated to achieving this task. It was also important that the dressmaking workshops always presented themselves exclusively as vital parts of a single body; this was a task for individuals, but also reliant on the way that the shows were presented and organized. All the key players of the Sala Bianca were called upon to help create this vision of a country made up of very rich and fertile soil, where the ability to create beauty and the outburst of vitality were not and would never be a

Dress by Marucelli (from *La Sala Bianca – La nascita della moda italiana*, by Guido Vergani, Electa, 1992. Giovanni Battista Giorgini Archive).

chance phenomenon. The framework and associated events that took place alongside the Florence fashion shows reflected and helped to reinforce the ideal of continuity between the artistic production of the past and of the present. The photographs that were circulated to the press to publish, and the filmed revivals were always historically oriented. Behind the models was a backdrop showing glimpses of Florentine views, statues, and monuments of Florence, the Boboli gardens, or the inside of centuries-old palaces. The very fact that the shows took place in the most beautiful hall of a famous palace, with its imposing but balanced proportions and its delicate stucco decoration, created an atmosphere that impressed the audience, creating a sense of expectation and gently encouraging people to make connections between the elegance of the past and that of today. The whole of the rest of the city served to reinforce the idea that art for the Italians is like the air that they breathe or the milk that has nourished them. In this sense, Florence was the perfect city to frame the events. Giorgini tended to organize the balls that ended the fashion shows in places of outstanding beauty that were little known to foreign guests, such as the Boboli gardens, the Torre del Gallo ad Arcetri, or the Belvedere Fort. From 1953, a second historic focal point for the fashion shows was created, as well as the Pitti Palace: the Strozzi Palace became the place where negotiations were held between buyers and dressmakers. Famous antique dealers furnished the most prized rooms for the occasion, creating an office/drawing room for all of the dressmakers in which they could do business with their clients, making them feel like guests in a stately and very elegant residence. Here clients could feel with their own hands the quality of the materials, see outfits that had not been part of the runway shows, agree prices, and delivery dates. A series of historical/promotional exhibitions was conceived in the early years to reinforce the idea that the roots of Italian fashion were steeped in a magnificent past. One of them was the ceremony that recalled the wedding of Eleonora de' Medici and Francesco Gonzaga, Prince of Mantua, which was performed by Florentine aristocrats in January 1953. Another was the exhibition of dresses and fashion sketches held at Palazzo Strozzi in January 1956. And yet another was the grand display of historical costumes which was the forerunner to the Italian fashion show at the Festival of Italy in Philadelphia in March 1961. In less than ten years, Italian fashion had managed to construct a self-image from all of these ideas that rivalled that of Paris fashion. The French were forced to admit, resentfully, that Florence was a new fashion capital. The prestige that had been created by Italian fashion spread to all Italian products from handcrafted objects to industrial design; it spread from fashion to everything that was designed and manufactured in Italy. The characteristics of Italian textiles celebrated in the outfits were the connecting link that made the transition possible: the artisan made his masterpieces by hand thanks to his raw material, fabric, which was by contrast an industrial product. Italian silks, wools, and cottons immediately became the most

Dress presented by Vanna (from *La Sala Bianca – La nascita della moda italiana*, by Guido Vergani, Electa, 1992. Giovanni Battista Giorgini Archive).

prized in the world and were publicised by various promotional events. They had the same aesthetic quality, novelty and originality that could be found in Italian clothes sold to markets abroad. They were often products that were new to the market in terms of their mixes, colors, and finishing. They knew how to be elegant, fun, or practical depending on the type of design or market. They were an eloquent testimony to technological knowledge and a modern entrepreneurial ability that fed off that same formula of a culture able to generate new works of art. By drawing on historical and artistic tradition and by combining the creativity of Italian dressmakers with that of the textile industries, Giorgini replaced the image of Italy as full of folklore and good will with an image of Italy as a nation of creative and brilliant people. More than just fashion, Giorgini had persuaded people to buy into the unlikely union of intelligence, refinement, and joie de vivre. His organization of the shows and, above all, his innovative formula aimed to provide concrete evidence of all of the key themes and qualities inherent in Italian fashion. The first fundamental concept was the common matrix of creativity, the idea that all dressmakers, each with his own distinctive style, was drawing inspiration from the same sublime artistic tradition. A symbol of this was the Sala Bianca as the only platform. Despite the practical demands of the buyers, for whom every minute mattered, Giorgini appreciated that gathering together a number of different dressmakers under a single roof would save the buyers' energy and time, making them better disposed towards Italian fashion. If novelty, practicality, and sharpness were the trademarks of Italian fashion, these should be reflected in the presentation of the designs as well. During a stay of just a few days in Florence, the buyers could get an overview of collections by dressmakers in various cities without the hassle of having to travel around visiting different locations. Instead they were offered a warm and personal welcome with parties and entertainments organized to provide a break from their heavy work schedule. It was a new formula for showing fashion to an international audience and was immediately greeted with approval. The fact that the Florentine runway was shared meant that it had to be selective; only the crème de la crème of those who were impervious to the French influence were invited and from their collections only a few items were shown and exposed to the public's judgement. The *haute couture* houses did not show more than sixty outfits, but as the boutiques were many more numerous they only got to show between 15 and 20 designs. For the dressmakers, these figures were feasible – especially when compared to the Paris runway shows and to those weighing up their creative abilities – but for the journalists, the numbers were still too high. They pointed out that there were generally fairly few innovative ideas in a collection and showing so many designs from the same house risked repeating them and making them seem boring. Besides in Palazzo Strozzi, the negotiating base, every dressmaker could show buyers as many variations as he wanted without taking anything away from the liveliness of the fashion show. The platform of the Sala Bianca, the emblem of a unique Italian fashion, should not, according to Giorgini, promote just a few dressmakers but should serve the interests of all dressmakers who should each be given equal space, opportunity, and means for making themselves stand out and be sufficiently appreciated. Unfortunately, not all of the houses understood the importance of maintaining a united front. The history of the Sala Bianca is punctuated by betrayals, defections, escapes, and regrets. Not only was the shared platform deeply unsatisfactory for some single-minded dressmakers, but it subjected everyone to a hotly contested and cruel comparison; and yet on the other hand it was a source of great stimulation. To be the first or last obviously had its disadvantages, particularly the last, as by then the buyers had already bought a lot from their competitors. A good rule seemed to be to rotate the combinations and juxtaposition of houses for each show. The overall organization of the event, which lasted on average four days, began with millinery displays and gained momentum, like a performance. Every detail and every moment was carefully planned, so that everything flowed smoothly along the tracks of elegance, class, and efficiency. No one show was allowed to repeat its predecessor; each one had to astound and get audiences talking about the people involved, the initiatives, and the unexpected ideas. The buyers had always to have something new to discover and purchase, and the journalists had to have something to write about: "Paris is the springboard for new lines, Florence for ideas." Presenting new young brands was an essential component and one of the most eagerly awaited. The most famous dressmaker discovered by Giorgini was definitely Capucci, but he certainly was not the only one. Many dressmaking workshops, some already flourishing, took that important leap forward of breaking into the international market having been invited to show at the Sala Bianca. Sarli, Enzo, Centinaro, Baratta, De Luca, De Barentzen, Mingolini-Guggenheim, Galitzine, Lancetti, Forquet, Balestra, Valentino, Mila Schön, Krizia and others made their decisive breakthrough on to the international arena in Florence. New brands were sometimes introduced in a particular way, either in a youth/veteran juxtaposition at the Sala Bianca or with a day dedicated just to them. Among the many different initiatives that were introduced into the fashion show calendar, great care was taken over those that presented branches of Italian production that the audience did not yet know about. Many products that were publicized in this way went on to become so important that they soon required their own specialist shows and buyers, with their own calendar and venue where they were presented. This was the case with fabrics, leather goods, shoes, knitwear, menswear, and children's wear. From the platform of the Sala Bianca, the following made their debut on to the markets: fabrics and menswear in 1952; children's wear in 1954 together with designs by Antonelli Sport; leather goods in 1955; mass-produced clothes in 1956; teenagers' fashions in 1962 with the romantic creations of Wanda Roveda; women's underwear in 1964 designed by Irene Galitzine. Together with new lines, such as the "*pannocchia*" (corn cob) line by Marucelli, the "*palloncino*" (balloon) collection by Simonetta, or new models for formal clothes, such as the palazzo pants by Galitzine, the continuous presentation of new areas of production served to reinforce the idea of Italian fashion as a source of perpetual creativity. Contemporaneous to the runway shows at the Pitti Palace, they set up exhibitions of the best of Italian production in accessories, jewelry, shoes and bags in the reception rooms of the Grand Hotel di Firenze. As these exhibitions were by no means of secondary importance in comparison with the main runway events, their opening was part of the official program and had the air of a society event. In fact it was an essential part of the itinerary for both the buyers and the press, who were guided towards pleasing discoveries, which translated into important purchases or articles in newspapers throughout the world. The ingenuity of these ideas meant that the prestige spread rapidly of an increasingly clear image of Italian fashion that had been won; this can be seen in the export figures. These soared vertiginously in the space of a few years, and included products that had never before been seen as particularly important, such as buttons and gloves. But the most important products to be launched into the international arena were obviously Italian fabrics, which is what Giorgini had intended as he saw the textile industry as the natural sponsor of fashion shows. Italian fabrics were the heart of promotional initiatives with their own formula, which anticipated the coupling of some fashion houses with important names in the textile industry, the most famous silk factories of Como, la Rivetti Lini and wools, the cotton mills Val di Susa and Legla, La Rhodiatoce and others. From 1952 until 1954, each display launched a particular type of Italian fabric. There was another important category of entrepreneurs, besides the textile industries, that Giorgini wanted to get involved with the Sala Bianca: those manufacturing ready-to-wear garments. Alongside the textile manufacturers, they were always invited to the Florentine evenings. Even if Giorgini had originally envisaged an image of Italian fashion in terms of *haute couture*, he had always known that the future lay with ready-to-wear. *Haute couture* was the means of opening the door, but its days were numbered. The improvements in the quality of design, cut and materials used in ready-to-wear were crucial to the development of this side of the industry and, consequently, for the textile industry too, which could certainly not survive on the sales they made to the big fashion houses. Ready-to-wear was obviously the product/fashion that had potential to develop but it was necessary to get their first, before the French. By the time in 1965 that Giorgini, tired and embittered from too many quarrels, abandoned his leadership of the Florentine runway shows, which continued until 1982, the new trends in production were already clearly defined. The magical aura of the Sala Bianca from then on slowly diminished. But that was not true of the image of Italian fashion that he had created, which continued along the path of success, strong and footsure, without needing the support of any father figure or guardian. (*Roberta Orsi Landini*)

Salazar Ana (1944). Designer born in Lisbon, where in 1972 she opened her first clothes shop selling only garments that she designed. Considered the pioneer of Portuguese fashion, she set up in Paris too in 1985 with a showroom. Four years later, she presented *Ana Salazar Parfum*, the first Portuguese perfume to be marketed worldwide. In 1997, the weekly Portuguese publication *Expresso*, in its special issue to mark its 25th birthday, referred to her as one of the most important people in the country.

Salemi Roselina (1955). Editor of *Anna*, the weekly women's magazine published by RCS Periodici. Born in Ancona, she studied philosophy at Catania University, then began her journalistic career by writing for the dailies *Il Diario* and *L'Eco di Padova*. In 1980 she joined *Il Giornale del Sud*, which was under the editorship of Giuseppe Fava at the time. From 1983, she was the Sicilian correspondent for *La Repubblica* as well as working for *L'Espresso* and the monthly *Pagina*. In 1985 she moved to Milan to work for *Domenica del Corriere* and in 1987 she moved on to *Il Corriere della Sera* editing national news. In 1990 Mirella Pallotti asked her to be deputy editor of *Anna*, an appointment which was confirmed by Edvige Bernasconi. She has been editor of Rizzoli's weekly women's magazine and its monthly sidekick *Salve* since February 2003. She has written *Sulla pelle delle donne* (1988), *I ragazzi di Palermo* (1993) and the novel *La fontana invisibile* (1995).

(*Sara Tieni*)

Salerni Sergio (1948). A film director who specialises in fashion. He began his career in 1978, visually documenting the collections of some of the top Italian labels, from Versace to Ferragamo, from Ferré to Gucci and Armani. At the same time, he produced advertising videos and films – among others for Valentino, Ferré jeans, and Versace perfumes. Many designers put him in charge of the direction, lighting, sound track, and staging of their runway shows. He has invented a way of doing things that he continually refines. He has also produced and directed television programs about fashion, such as *Stelle della Moda*, *Versace & Chanel*, and *Notte di Moda di Parigi*. He has been the technical and artistic coordinator of special events like *Fire & Ice Ball* in Los Angeles and *Diamonds are Forever* in Syon Park, London.

❑ To cope with the increase in his workload, Salerni divides his own company Solaris in two: Videogang specializes in video production and the new E20 manages events which often go beyond the narrow perimeters of fashion. E20 has also organized other types of events such as the Charity Ball in Syon Park in London, the Frock'n'Roll Charity Show in Spain, and concerts for stars like Lenny Kravitz, Iggy Pop, and Take That.

Salopette French word which is used to describe a pair of wide, comfortable pants that extend over the chest in a bib-like apron, which is held up with braces that cross behind the back. A work garment that was also worn by women during the two world wars, it became fashionable in the 1960s when popular forms of clothing were transposed into ready-to-wear. Made in denim, with small and large pockets, it was worn as leisure wear and on holiday, and also became a favorite garment for maternity wear – in light wool for winter or in cotton with little floral motifs for the warmer seasons. The version in silk is intriguing in its lively contradiction of a popular form and very fine fabric. In France, it is one of Adolphe Lafont's *pièces de résistance*.

Salvadori Giovanni (1892). Dressmaker and embroiderer. Born in Spesiano in the province of Treviso, he began his career designing decorative and ornamental motifs to be embroidered on dresses, cloaks, and accessories. Between 1922 and 1924 he moved with his family to Rome and opened his first dressmaking workshop in Via Giovanni Fattori. Here he made clothes embroidered using the French Cornely machine. Alongside his own work, the firm operated an embroidery division that supplied the most important Florentine dressmakers of the time and also received many foreign commissions. His creations ended up as a strange union of hand embroidery, finishing effects, little cord underlinings carried out mechanically, and glass beads applied by crochet hook. These techniques were also used by Salvadori in his finishes for astrakhan or breitschwanz coats. Following a fall-off in production in 1929 due to the economic depression, Salvadori set up his final base at 1 Via Lamberti, with the name "Modelli-Ricami-Confezioni-Salvadori Firenze." He remained active here until 1934/1935.

Salvini A brand of jewelry made by the Damiani group. A classic style brought up to date to fit with contemporary canons, in the 1970s the Salvini brand represented a combination of well-researched design and technical innovation that lay at the heart of the group's output. The creations, which used top quality precious stones, were first associated with famous models such as Melanie Rogers and René Simonsen and then, in the 1990s, with the actress Francesca Neri, who endorsed the brand. At the turn of the millennium, famous photographers such as Christophe Kutner, Daniela Federici, Brigitte Niedermair, and Gianpaolo Barbieri were used for the advertising campaigns. (*Alessandra Quattordio*)

Samet Janie (1931). French journalist. In 1987 she won a fashion Oscar as best journalist working for the French and foreign dailies. In 1994, she was awarded the Légion d'Honneur by the French Minister of Culture, Jacques Toubon. Having studied law at university, she went to work for *L'Aurore* in 1955. In 1979, she was made editor-in-chief of the women's column in *Le Figaro*. A sharp and attentive observer of what happens in Paris and the rest of the world, she knows how to analyze the ephemeral aspects of fashion with great lucidity, pointing out and highlighting its ups and downs. (*Gabriella Gregorietti*)

Samia Exhibition for the international clothing market, organized by Ente Italiano della Moda and various associations of dressmakers and fashion manufacturers. It was operative in Turin from 1954 until the mid-1960s. Its winning formula is to bring together and compare not only the creativity of stylists designing dresses, but also those designing accessories – shoes, hats, and jewelry – with firms making ready-to-wear (including San Lorenzo, Togno, and Carlo Tivioli) and particularly well-trained Turin tailoring (La Merveilleuse and Juvenilia). Samia was the meeting point, especially in the first four exhibitions, for names that would soon become important figures in ready-to-wear fashion, such as Krizia. But the extension of Giorgini's first Florence shows in the Sala Bianca gave dress and knitwear designers in Florence a new direction, by providing them with new possibilities in terms of order and exports. The subsequent *haute couture* diaspora in Florence and Rome, just before the base of fashion was handed back to the Milan fashion houses, ousted Samia, jeopardizing the importance of the exhibition that was the forerunner of what happened in Milan at the start of the 1970s.

Samsonite American world leader in the production of luggage items. The Italian division is run by the chairman and managing director Beppi Fremder. In May 1997, the Italian division bought Valextra from the French Andrelux (the Vuitton family). In association with Linea Più of Prato, it launched the Active Wear line of clothing.

❑ 2000. Samsonite Black Label, a new range of women's clothing, was launched. Structured and almost tailored, the line looks modern and technically comfortable. The style is essential, with no sense of excess. It was designed by 35-year-old Gigi Vezzola, who trained at the Marangoni Institute and learned from Krizia and Dolce & Gabbana.

❑ 2000. The designer Philippe Starck created a range of very light bags and suitcases in grays and browns.
❑ 2005. Quenint Mackay, previously accessories designer at Loewe, was made Samsonite's creative director.

Samsung Group Korean textile company. Today it is one of the world's leading business conglomerates. The Group operates in various sectors, among which, clothing textiles and machinery for the chemical, textile, and electronic industries. It also has businesses in the food, insurance, and hotel sectors. But its dominant vocation is textiles, where its activities range from manufacturing synthetic threads and fibers to combed wool fabrics, from menswear and womenswear to furnishing fabrics.

(*Marcella Gabbiano*)

Samugheo Chiara. The pseudonym of Chiara Paparella (1935). A photographer born in Bari (Italy), she started out in the 1950s. She was the first to use pictures as a form of journalism, with reportages on the south of Italy and fashion, socio-political surveys for Cinema Nuovo and above all for the weekly *Tempo* during the 25 years it was under the editorship of Arturo Tofanelli. She also produced reports on the stars and leading figures in cinema and entertainment with countless portrait covers. She photographed Gina Lollobrigida wearing Chanel and Valentino, Sofia Loren wearing Schuberth, Catherine Spaak wearing Capucci, and Rosanna Schiaffino wearing German Marucelli and Missoni. Samugheo (she changed her surname at the suggestion of Pasquale Prunas, journalist, art director, editor and lifelong partner) has shown at the Guggenheim Museum in New York, at the Venice Biennale (presented by Paolo Portoghesi), at the Cannes Festival, and at Cankarjev Dom in Ljubljana. Some of her publications are *Carnaval*, *Costumi di Sardegna*, *Al Cinema con le stelle*, *Lucca e la Lucchesia*, and *Il reale e l'effimero*.

Sanchez Fernando (1934). Spanish designer and one of the first to promote lingerie. His flowing shirts, pyjama-style pants and use of synthetic materials in garish colors have made him famous. Having studied at the Chambre Syndicale de la *Haute couture* in Paris, at the end of the 1950s he went to work for Dior and designed underwear, accessories, and knitwear. He then went to the furriers Revillon and stayed there for about ten years until 1973, the year he founded his own lingerie company in New York. Since 1983, he has launched a men's and women's ready-to-wear range which is famous for its use of stretch velvets and very elaborate brocades.

Sandal The most primitive form of shoe. Fashionable in the 1920s, the sandal was essential to any woman who wanted to look alluring and vaguely available. It was only after World War II that the sandal (as elegant as ever) was able to reveal everything that lies between the ankle and the tip of the big toe.

Sander Jil (1943). German fashion designer and entrepreneur. The most important representative of German fashion and one of the biggest names in international fashion, she has succeeded in creating a style that is intelligent, minimalist, and decidedly contemporary. "Strong and pure" are the adjectives that are often used to describe her designs. Considered the German Armani, her clothes are characterized by her use of neutral colors, purified lines, full-bodied materials, and cuts "made by the knife" – as she herself describes them – to create a femininity deprived of any frivolity, but not without a certain seductive austerity. Born in Wesselburen, near Hamburg, she is methodical and creative, reserved and determined, fragile and energetic, and has managed to build up an empire in just a few years that was quoted on the stock market in 1989. With a diploma in textile engineering from Germany she went to Los Angeles aged 19 where she completed her studies and had her first experience as a journalist in the editorial office of *McCalls*. Returning to Hamburg, she became fashion editor for *Costanze* and *Petra* and took on management responsibilities. As a freelance designer, she worked with a number of firms, among them, Callaghan. In 1968 she opened an avantgarde boutique in Hamburg, the first of its type, where she sold clothes that she designed alongside garments bought in Paris and Italy. Strengthened by this experience and with an ambitious project in mind, she

Jil Sander: men's suit Fall/Winter 1997/1998. Drawing by François Berthoud.

opened Jil Sander Moden and presented her first real collection in 1973, with all her pieces in varying tones of khaki. She had a difficult start as a fashion designer wanting to create top quality modern clothes, but of too great an elegance to be produced in Germany, where luxury ready-to-wear was still unheard of. It was only natural that she found the necessary materials, firms, and people in Italy. In 1975 she was in Paris where she presented two collections in successive seasons. Too purist for French taste, her runway shows were a flop. As a result she was forced to move to Milan, a city which is more austere and therefore more in tune with her own personality. The first Italian presentations were quiet affairs reserved for just a few people, but the important buyers took note and were soon fighting for an exclusive deal over her work. Her designs for intelligent, independent, business-like women were very popular: "The women who I think about when I am designing are very self-aware and full of self-respect," she says. Success came quickly and the purity of her designs, her constant research into materials, and her obsession with quality were all prized. In 1979 she launched *Woman Pure*, her first perfume, with an advertising campaign built around her own serene, fair and delicate features, ensuring herself instantaneous fame and creating a new stereotype for German women. Her international reputation was confirmed in the following years as her business activities developed and moved into cosmetics, eyewear, leatherwear, and menswear that she showed in Milan in 1996. She has received numerous awards and prizes for her fashions and perfumes. With a passionate interest in contemporary art, she is a discerning collector and a generous sponsor of exhibitions of leading German artists such as Georg Baselitz and Joseph Beuys. From Fall 1999, the Jil Sander label was part of the Prada Group. (*Gisella Borioli*)

❑ 2001, May. Record sales, with a 17% rise in profits. The number of own-brand shops throughout the world rose to 20.

❑ 2003, May. Jil Sander returned to the company she founded, which had been controlled by the Prada Group since 1999.

❑ 2005, July. The new creative director was Raf Simons. He would begin in January 2006 with the first menswear collection. The designer took over from Jil Sander after the umpteenth split with the Prada group, which owns the company.

Sanderson English manufacturer of wallpapers and fashion-oriented home furnishings. Arthur Sanderson, an importer of French luxury wallpapers, set up the business in 1860. From 1879 the first Arthur Sanderson & Sons wallpapers were made, at first with patterns printed by hand, and later by machine. After the founder's death in 1882, the business passed to his sons John, Arthur, and Harold. Under their leadership, Sanderson became the first company in England to produce materials printed to match the patterns of the wallpapers. In 1940 the company bought the machinery of Morris & Co., who had gone into liquidation. In 1955, the royal household awarded Sanderson the royal warrant, a symbol of quality. In Italy it was Giuseppe Palombella, a Tuscan company specializing in household linen for more than 40 years, that produced and distributed the ranges. The joint venture began with matching bed linen, and went on to develop tableware, and a bathroom range (dressing gowns, bathmats, and sponges). In June 2003, the runway presenting Vivienne Westwood's latest designs was decorated with Sanderson wallpaper with floral motifs, which started rumors of a possible collaboration between the two.

(*Pierangelo Mastantuono*)

Sandonnini Stefano (1969). Italian photographer. Trained at the European Institute of Design in Milan, he worked with Bob Krieger on major advertising campaigns and then, in the US, with Fabrizio Ferri. Torn between a passion for sport (in 2002 he published a book of athletes' portraits *Sport Passion*) and for photography, he is now committed to producing fashion reports which are published in *Cosmopolitan*, *Harper's Bazaar*, and *Esquire*.

Sang Seok Lee (1970). Korean photographer. Having studied creative literature at Kyong Won University in Seoul and followed this with a diploma, in 1992, from the Korean Academy of Photography of the Image, he began his photographic career by specializing in the field of fashion and fashion shows. He has produced catalogues for Pizza Hut Korea, C&L Music, L.G. Fashion (from 1998 to 2001), and Samsung Fashion (from 1999 to 2001), and has done campaigns for *Elle Korea, Korea Madame Figaro*, Seoul Collection and Lee Sang Bong Ready-to-wear. In 2001, he closed his Studio Fiction in Seoul and moved to Europe where he studied at the Italian Institute of Photography in Milan and took up work again.

Sangallo (broderie anglaise). Type of lacelike material, in cotton, linen or rayon for rather childish clothes – little summer skirts, retro style nightdresses, little shirts and trims. Originally from San Gallo, a Swiss canton.

Sanjust di Teulada Piero (1923-1966). One of the last great Italian dandies. Manager of Dalmine, managing director and chairman of Siderexport, and then Insurance Brokers Marsh and McLean Italian, he loved a little touch of disorder in the way people dressed, a sign of supreme snobbery. It was better if the suit had some small defect and so he always refused to have the third fitting with the tailor. He liked striped shirts in strong colors and used to buy fabric in Genoa from Crovetto. He had 200 pairs of shoes and loved those that were over 30 years old. He had them made to measure at Gatto's. He never wore a pullover under his jacket which he always wore open. Hats (he never left the house without one) he would crush on purpose. He often carried gloves, but rarely wore them, preferring to hold them in his hand. He never failed to wear a tie which he thought of as a state of mind. He liked the buttonhole on the lapel of his dinner jacket to be trimmed in red.
He was the one who started the fashion for wearing watches on the cuff, not as an affectation but out of necessity. He described the following to Luigi Settembrini and Chiara Boni in the book published by Mondadori *Vestiti, usciamo* [Get Dressed, We're Going Out]: "We were boys in Rome and Gianni [Agnelli] was a friend of ours and we saw him often. A number of us were short of money, including me, and I therefore could not afford to own more than four or five shirts. In order not to ruin the edge of the cuff by having it rub against the metal strap of my watch, I always wore my watch over my left cuff. Gianni liked it and copied me. Although there was no question of him not having enough shirts."
He had a nose for good tailors, even those that were still waiting to be discovered. He was the one who offered surety for Domenico Bombino's tailor's shop; he had met Bombino at the Bar Giamaica in Milan, the legendary café in Via Brera. He told the person interviewing him that he knew Bombino was talented as he had sewn a counter-buttonhole for a flower under his lapel. In addition to Bombino, his tailor was Donini-Augusto Caraceni. When dressing Sanjust, the tailor started with the shirt which laid out on the bed to be able to build around it the outfit for the day. In the same text, he also said: "To dig back into the

origins of my relationship with style, it is perhaps necessary to know that I was born as the sixth boy into a family of nine children and for years wore the clothes handed down from my older brothers.... I remember the first time that I wore a new suit was when I went to the Naval Academy and from that moment on a lust was unleashed."

(*Virginia Hill*)

Sanlorenzo Turin fashion house. It showed on the *haute couture* runways in Rome from 1968 to 1976. Founded by Teresa Sanlorenzo in 1945, the workshop originally only made French *haute couture* designs for private clients. Slowly it freed itself from this subjection. Daughters Enrica and Paola joined their mother in 1968 and from 1975 the company took part in the Milan shows with its ready-to-wear collections. In 1977, Enrica set up on her own as Enrica Massei, while Paola carried the family brand forward.

❑ 2002, November. Paola Sanlorenzo and Kristina Ti were the sponsors of *L'Eccellenza Italiana*, a show that was held in Palazzo Carignano in Turin.

Sanremo Italian brand of menswear. The company, launched by Sergio and Rino Comunello, expands substantially in the 1970s, producing goods for both the domestic and foreign markets. In the 1990s, it became part of the Inghirami Group.

Santa Eulalia A Spanish company producing fabrics and readymade clothes, founded by Domenec Taberner in Barcelona in the middle of the 19th century. In 1900 it began its made to measure service, but it was not until 1940 that it became a recognized *haute couture* house. From then on, the brand made not only fabrics and classic and elegant outfits, but also accessories and ready-to-wear dresses.

Sant'Andrea (Via). Street in Milan in which Ugo Foscolo lives. It is in the center of the so-called fashion rectangle (Via della Spiga, Via Manzoni, Via Montenapoleone and the stretch of Corso Venezia beyond the Cerchia dei Navigli). It is a slightly skewed rectangle because the streets of old Milan are not drawn with the rule and precision of a town planner and tend to curve and bend away from their axis. Whereas Montenapoleone was largely monopolized by fashion even before Milan became the capital of ready-to-wear, Sant'Andrea was a road full of antique dealers. Biki was the only tailor to have his own workshop there and it had no shop window. Fashion has since scorched the area. Largely flushed out by being given key money, the antique dealers such as Dino Franzin, Silva, Sacerdoti, Zecchini, Schieppati and La Bottega del Mago left the area. However, the invasion was not able to shift Il Baretto di Ermanno Taschera, who arrived in Sant'Andrea in 1963, and Sevigné, a glass and porcelain shop.

Sant'Angelo (di) Giorgio (1933-1989). Florentine designer. Having emigrated to the States in 1962, he began designing fabrics and jewelry. Diana Vreeland, then editor of *Vogue*, had complete faith in him. He was often inspired by ethnic clothes, and hippy and street fashions.

Santho (von) Imre (1900-1946). Hungarian illustrator and photographer. In 1929, he found himself in Berlin where he opened a painting studio and, six years later, a photography studio. Until 1938 he produced images that were exceptionally creative for the period, and which were published in, amongst others, the magazine *Die Dame*. In 1945, he was back in Budapest teaching fashion photography in a private school.

Santini Maria (1933). Journalist and editor of *Milleidee*. She began her career with *Il Giorno*, where she worked on the women's and children's supplements. She moved to *Grazia* where she wrote on fashion, and then to *Gioia*. In 1970 she became editor-in-chief of *Bella* and transformed it into a weekly magazine on the subjects of fashion and women's work. From this formula evolved *Milleidee* in 1975, a monthly magazine about crocheting and knitting, of which Santini was editor until 1995. At the same time, from 1990 to 1995, she was also editor of *Benissimo*. She then took over *Consigli Practici*, where she stayed until 1997.

Sarafpour Behnaz. Designer born in Iran. Before even finishing her diploma at the Parsons School of Design in New York, she had her first introduction to Anne Klein, with whom she began working. She collaborated with Narciso Rodriguez, Luis Dell'Olio, and Richard Tyler. In 1994 she moved to Isaac Mizhari and designed her first collection for Barney's in New York. Her debut on the runway came in Fall 2002 with a romantic collection using simple lines in white and black. Anna Wintour, editor of *Vogue America*, supported her, describing her as one of the most promising young designers. In the same year, she was nominated in the category of up-and-coming designers for the Perry Ellis prize.

(*Francesca Gentile*)

Sara Lee American textile and food group based in Chicago. Since the late 1980s it has been the world leader in underwear. Founded in 1939 by the Canadian entrepreneur Nathan Cummings, it took the name of Sara Lee Corporation in 1985. Thanks to a perpetual expansion strategy, it now markets globally. It sells hot dogs, furniture, tights, lingerie, T-shirts, and body products. In the underwear sector it has bought the Playtex brand, the French group Dim, and England's Pretty Polly, the leader in the field of tights and stockings.

❑ 2000. It bought Nestlé USA, the leading coffee company in Brazil, plus Cafè Pilao and La Sol y Oro, Argentina's leading underwear brand. The business therefore focuses mainly on food products, household goods, and underwear.
❑ 2001. As a result purely of acquisitions, the Sara Lee Bakery Group tripled its sales, which were already at $3.4 billion. The main fashion brands that Sara Lee owns are: Bali, Barely There, Champion, Dim, Hanes, Hanes Her Way, Just My Size, Playtex, Unno and Wonderbra.

Sarchi Wilma. Italian public relations manager. She began her career working as an editor/translator in a press agency. In 1975, she founded Studio 75 and, in the early 1980s, set up the Institute of Studies and Training in Public Relations with some colleagues. On behalf of the Associazione Industriale dell'Abbigliamento e Maglieria she managed the press offices of the fashion shows Anteprima, Ideamaglia, and Modit, and then extended her collaboration to the Pitti Palace in Florence. She has helped assert German fashion by collaborating with Igedo from Dusseldorf. A specialist in the field of luxury products or products with a high image content, she worked for several years with the Comité Colbert (a French association which brings together the 72 historical luxury brands from France) while in Italy she has helped establish historical jewelry labels such as Boucheron, Asprey, and Marina B. Since 1992, she has looked after Louis Vuitton in Italy. Since 1999, she has collaborated with the LVMH Fashion Group, managing not only their institutional communications, but also the Givenchy and Celine brands.

Sarda Andres. Spanish designer and fashion entrepreneur. He was born in Barcelona to a family that has worked in the textile industry since the 19th century. Immediately after finishing his degree in textile engineering, he worked in the family business, looking after the American market. In 1962, he founded the business named after himself, which produces underwear and beachwear for women. With a watchful eye on developments in the industry and the market, he was one of the first to use elasticized fabrics in his collections. The first to be launched on

Sketch by Andres Sarda (February 2003).

the market was Risk, which aimed to transform underwear into a fashion garment. 1980 saw the turn of Andrés Sardá, his first line, which uses very high quality materials and has a highly advanced and innovative design. Afterwards, Andrés, who now has his daughter Nuria working with him, launched the University line, which is much younger and cheaper than the other two.

Sardinia Adolfo (1933). American designer. Having escaped family pressure to become a lawyer, he was saved by following his aunt, Maria Lopez, from Cuba, where she comes from, to Paris. She presented him to the Maison Balenciaga where Adolfo got to know the world of fashion and tailoring. In 1948, he decided to leave Paris for New York, where he learnt the millinery trade. In 1962 he opened his first shop, accompanying his hats with a line of clothing. The garments were ready-to-wear, but could be adapted to fit and because of the quality of the cut and sewing were close to being *haute couture*. First Lady Nancy Reagan provided him with a spontaneous endorsement.

❑ 2002, April. He took part in the Latin American fashion show organized at the Fashion Institute of Technology in New York.

Sari Garment typically worn by Indian women, which consists of a rectangle of cotton or silk, without any sewing or cutting, that is wrapped around the body. It hangs to the ground, leaving one shoulder exposed, and is held in place by folding the fabric in a particular way.

Sarli Fausto (1927). Italian designer. He is considered the founder of the Roman school of *haute couture*. His creative and wearable style was typified by the care taken in the cut, the mastery of the fabrics and the attention paid to embroidery and inlay. He began his career as a draughtsman, winning a number of competitions as a fashion designer. In 1957, a jury comprising Schuberth, Capucci, Marucelli, Veneziani, and Simonetta gave him a prize for his young talent, which allowed him to show at the Pitti Palace. In 1961, he began working in television, designing costumes for Mina in the programme *Giardini d'Inverno*. In the 1970s he set out to conquer the Japanese market. He then launched a ready-to-wear line that gave rise to designs with careful studied details, cuts and lines, which were nevertheless wearable, casual, and accessible in terms of price. In 1989, he opened his Roman workshop in Via Gregoriana. For Sarli, the 1990s was a period of diversification with the launch of his perfume *Sarli*, and a menswear line of ties, waistcoats and accessories. Even if they were not signed by him, the costumes worn by Lucia Bosè in the Michelangelo Antonioni film *Cronaca di un amore* [Chronicle of a Love Affair] were designed by Sarli when he was only 23. The Giorgio Cini Foundation in Venice entrusted him with the restoration of Eleonora Duse's dresses.

❑ 1999-2000. The mayor of Rome, Franco Rutelli, awarded him a plaque commemorating 40 years of work. He is also awarded the Città di Milano prize for his 40 years in the world of *haute couture*.
❑ 2000, May. He remembered his 40 years of work with an exhibition in the Museo Barracco alongside the *haute couture* fashion shows in Rome.
❑ 2002. The exhibition *Fausto Sarli: 50 anni di stile italiano* [50 Years of Italian Style] was held at the Castel dell'Ovo in Naples, which went on to the Museo del Vittoriano. His half century of creativity was celebrated in Rome with a fashion show in the Piazza del Campidoglio.
❑ 2003. In the Fall/Winter collection 2003/2004, Sarli combined real clothes with real style, without slipping into vulgarity or ostentation but presenting short transparent skirts (alternated with very wide flapping skirts and dresses covered in embroidery and little flowers). The show closed with a powder gray wedding dress that took 350 hours to make.
❑ 2003, June. The Museo della Moda opened in Naples in the Mondragone Palace (in the Spanish district) and Sarli gave 50 important dresses to its permanent collection.

Sarmi Ferdinando (1912-1982). Italian fashion creator. He left an important job in the Vatican for a brief appearance in the world

Fausto Sarli: sketch for the Spring-Summer Collection 1998.

of cinema (in 1950, he was one of the three main actors – with Lucia Bosé and Massimo Girotti – in Antonioni's *Cronaca di un amore*) and then concentrated on fashion at the insistent request of Elizabeth Arden, who by chance, having met him at a reception, heard him talking about clothes, accessories, and make-up. He began in New York. His name is associated with "the most beautiful evening dresses in the world," as Diana Vreeland wrote. He won the Neiman Marcus prize.

Sarne Tanya (1940). English designer. She started as a model and in 1984 created the brand Ghost. She pays great attention to technological fabrics for clothes that, for example, can be put in the washing machine and then worn without needing to be ironed. For a period, Tanya worked in New York, but she is now a permanent fixture on the London runways.

Sarong Traditional garment worn by men and women in Malaysia and Indonesia. It is a piece of cotton or silk that is wrapped around the body and fastened at one side, either at the waist or at chest height and is usually full length. It is very similar to the Polynesian pareo. It is worn with a tight-fitting bolero called a *kebaya*. In 1985, Ungaro, Versace and Armani made wrap-around sarong skirts, with a folded border wrapped around the waist.

Sarouel Trousers that are wide like a skirt to the knee and then become narrower lower down, either by wrapping them or buttoning them round the leg. They are inspired by Middle Eastern pants.

Sarrault Denise. French model. She belongs to the Capucine, Suzy Parker and Dorian Leigh type of model: blonde, stately, polished and a fine lady. She was one of Givenchy's favorites. She has posed for the most famous photographers, including Helmut Newton and Bert Stern. She married the art collector Jean-Paul Najar, has helped to organize the ready-to-wear runway shows in Paris, and has designed hats and, in 1987, an *haute couture* collection. She lives between Barcelona and the Côte d'Azur.

Sarrut Corinne (1945). Born in Paris, she is the artistic director of Cacharel. As early as 1965, after studying fine arts, she became a designer for Cacharel, thanks to her brother-in-law Jean Bousquet who founded the brand. About twenty years later in 1986, Corinne set up her own brand, but without leaving Cacharel, where her role is to advise, guide, and define basic trends. Her clothes are sold in boutiques bearing her own name (in Paris, Lyons, and Tours) and in the Cacharel shops in Milan and Marseilles. She has a large showroom in Tokyo.

(*Giulio Alberoni*)

Sarti Faliero (1916-1985). Italian entrepreneur. In 1949, he set up a wool mill in Prato, and from then on devoted his time to the textile industry: perfecting the quality of the fabric and at the same time creating new mixes. In the 1950s and 1960s, the "Made in Italy" phenomenon began in his workshops. His work with upmarket fibers – cashmere, alpaca, linen, and silk – which he experimented with at first in the textile district of Prato, soon won him clients from the world of *haute couture*: from Capucci to the Fontana sisters, from Schuberth to Sarli to Irene Galitzine, and from Chanel to Cardin. His commitment to research and experimentation without ever forgetting about the purity and linearity of the fabric won him and the Group (still in family hands) the trust of designers from the 1970s onwards, such as Valentino, Ferré, Donna Karan, Dior, Ungaro, Montana and Gaultier. In 1982, he was made a Cavaliere del Lavoro.

(*Ilaria Ciuti*)

Sartor Luca (1968). Italian designer born in Montebelluna. He has a diploma in fashion design from the Professional Institute of Treviso and another diploma from the Accademia di Belli Arti, specializing in industrial cutting. He began his career in fashion as a textile consultant for Italian and foreign firms, such as Simint, Sima, Itac, Agenco Trading, Belfe, and Lotto, working in marketing, research, and production. In Fall/Winter 2000/2001, he started his own line called ri(Edizioni), based on customised vintage clothes made from the very best materials and in an original style.

Sartori Franco (1929-1987). Italian journalist and editor. Son of a *Corriere della Sera* manager, he too worked for the newspaper company and, having been marketing manager, was given the task of researching a weekly women's magazine with an innovative feel. This saw the birth of *Amica* an avantgarde monthly magazine with Enrico Gramigna as editor and Flavio Lucchini as artistic director. In 1964 Sartori moved to Condé Nast Italia where, having taken over *Novità*, he founded *Vogue Italia* and remained its editor for the rest of his life. He also became managing director of Condé Nast Italia and helped expand with *Casa Vogue*, *Uomo Vogue* (begun in 1967 as a supplement of *Vogue Italia*), *Vogue Sposa*, *Vogue Bambino*, and *Vogue Gioiello*. He was a man of elegant looks; austere and inseparable from his Tuscan cigars, he inspired a certain awe and was blessed with an excellent eye for choosing journalists and collaborators for his magazines. Many of the best journalists specialized in fashion, beauty, and home decoration were trained at Condé Nast. Under his direction, the publishing house placed new emphasis on fashion images, photography, and graphics, creating a sophisticated and refined means of expression that would influence other publications in the field in the years to come. Others learnt from the Condé Nast look, with *Vogue Italia* and *Uomo Vogue* considered the bibles of luxury and the latest styles, something that was continually asserted by the talent of Italian designers. At the height of his success, and while still young, Sartori died in New York after a heart transplant. His associate manager was Attilio Fontanesi who contributed to the extraordinary advertising and financial success of the magazines, thinking up innovative advertising strategies, such as the famous *groupage*.

Sash Long strip of clothing worn knotted around the waist or low on the hips, often fringed. A sash can be worn as part of an outfit to create a fitted silhouette, or emphasize a slim silhouette; they were often featured on early 20th century blouses or dresses.

Sassoon Vidal (1928). English hairdresser. His style of cutting and his mainly geometric hairstyles was, during the 1950s and 1960s, one of the springboards of the aesthetic revolution which accompanied the liberalization and change in fashion in the era of Swinging London, the Beatles and flower power. He opened salons and shops in Europe, Canada, the United States, and Singapore (a total of 10 in the mid-1990s) and created hair products. Passionate about his job, he founded a school of hairdressing in 1969 and an academy in 1973.

Sateen (in Italian, *Rasatello*) A cotton fabric in a satin weave, with a diminished sheen.

Sathal Fred (1966). French designer. She came on the scene in 1994 with her first collection entitled A Ma Zone Urbaine. The next collection was called Etoile de Vie Filante. Raised on the spectacular coastline near Marseilles, she wanted to be a volcanologist. However, a meeting with a theatrical costume designer set her future along a different path. Having just set up in Paris, she dressed singer Bjork with her first poetic designs. She financed her own creation of 300 garments for the season, with the help of 3 assistants. In 1998, she designed the costumes for the musical *Notre Dame de Paris* (music by Riccardo Cocciante) and its success persuaded her to focus on the theater.

❑ In collaboration with Enki Bilal she designed the costumes for a production of Romeo and Juliet.
❑ 2000-2001. For Winter/Fall, she presented dresses which mixed elements of Charleston and North African costumes: pantaloon-style pants from *Arabian Nights* and silk and taffeta dresses with dominant frills.

Satin (in Italian, *Raso*). Name of the third fundamental weave, alongside plain and twill (with its derivative, "Batavia"). The word satin is used to describe all fabrics that make use of this weave and which have a smooth, flat appearance, shaven, as the Italian word *raso* indicates, and with a silken sheen. If all other conditions are identical, a satin weave will be shinier than a twill or plain weave, because it has longer bridles, which are better at reflecting the light. This weave involves ligature stitches reduced to minimum, which therefore do not produce the distinctive grain effects that are typical of the other two weaves. Fabrics made with a satin weave are therefore more fragile and less durable. They can be made with any textile fiber.

Satin Generic term for any cotton or silk material that is particularly shiny and smooth. It was originally produced in the Chinese city of Zaitum. Many different types of satin are now available. Chinese satin is smooth and glossy; decoupé satin is similar to velvet; ottoman satin has flat ribs; and then there is satin that appears to change color because it has warped threads and wefts of different colors.

Saucony Originals Brand of sports shoes. In 1998 a hundred or so pairs of running shoes were left during the night in metro stations in New York, Los Angeles, Philadelphia, Detroit, and Chicago. The following morning, thy were all gone. People, youngsters especially, started asking for them in the shops. This is how the myth of Saucony was born. By 2001, they had sold two million pairs in the USA. In Italy, they are distributed by Sportlab.

(*Gianluca Cantaro*)

Sautoir Very long necklace that hangs down as far as the waist. They are nearly always made of pearls (either real or cultivated) and shortened by knotting them. Movie stars wore them in the 1930s when they were an essential part of any Charleston outfit; there was a fashion for twirling them when dancing.

Savoia Milanese boot factory. It began in 1925 when Giuseppe Ballini took over the workshop from a succession of former owners who had been chief shoemakers to the cavalry regiments since 1870 in the traditional base in Via Vincenzo Monti. It was Ballini who changed the name to Stivaleria Savoia. It mainly made boots both for military wear and specialist boots for riding and hunting. Some members of the royal family were regular customers and even Mussolini had pairs of boots made there (one pair is kept in the remembrance reliquary in the family tomb in Predappio). After the war, the clientele changed and the customers were mainly civilian as the army slowly phased out the use of boots. Production of riding boots and men's boots that were made by hand to measure therefore decreased. Now production is 80% shoes. The surviving handmade models are made under the Ballini-Savoia name. The business has been a constant success. The shop is currently managed by Giuseppe's son Arturo, who has run and worked in the shop since 1970. In the adjacent workshop, some craftsmen still make riding boots to measure, for polo and other equestrian sports: every customer has a model of his own foot made in wood, from which his shoes are made. These wooden models are catalogued and kept. Sales of shoes have increased as, on top of handmade products, they have also introduced lines of men's and women's ready-to-wear shoes. The shop also sells shoes by Church's and Edward Green. The shop sells saddlery – particularly for polo – as well as clothes from some of the important English manufacturers, such as Burberry, Smedley and Tanner Krolle, and the famous Husky that was first imported by Ballini in 1974. (*Marilea Somaré*)

Savorelli di Lauriano Franco (1932). A marketing and PR expert who helped establish Italian fashion exports from its outset, for which Pitti Immagine Uomo rewarded him with a prize in 1996. Born in Milan, he studied economics in Genoa, took a Masters degree in business management and then, in 1958, began his collaboration with Helena Rubinstein, the American cosmetics giant, which lasted until 1997. For forty years, his career has been a series of successes: the extraordinary parties organized with Roberta di Camerino on San Giorgio island in Venice; the association he set up with Sergio Galeotti for Giorgio Armani from 1974 to 1980; his twenty-year working relationship and friendship with Mario Valentino; his collaboration with the Fendi sisters and designer Karl Lagerfeld; and promotion of the fashion shows held in the Sala Bianca in the Pitti Palace that led to the birth of the Italian ready-to-wear fashion industry. But Savorelli has not only been the *éminence grise* of famous fashion houses. In association with Beppe Modenese, he set up two prestigious international fairs in the 1970s: Idea Como and Idea Biella for drapery. In 1969, he established the fashion show Mare Moda Capri with Rudy Crespi, and the first Pitti Uomo in 1971, with the then president Franco Tancredi.

Sawatari Hajime (1940). Japanese photographer. He studied at Nihon University in Tokyo with Kishin Shinoyama and from 1963 to 1966 worked with the Design Center in Tokyo as a freelance photographer specializing in the fields of cinema, reportage, and fashion. In 1979, he was Japanese photographer of the year.

SB Studio Design studio and fashion consultancy founded by Silvana Belli, a Milanese designer. It was set up in the early 1960s at the height of Swinging London (minidresses, ankle-length frock-coats and colored PVC jackets), working for women's weekly magazines and above all for Pipermarket, a commercial offshoot of Piper di Roma, the forerunner of Italian nightclubs. But the studio's strength was knitwear, with its research into stitches, natural yarns, synthetic fibers, colors and technical compositions, machinery and working processes. Silvani Belli worked for various textile and chemical industries, such as Filature di Prato and Monsanto USA. She designed for Schiaparelli Tricot and Moreau de Limoges, and showed at the Pitti Palace for Albertina, Celli, and Nardini. In the mid-1970s, she was summoned to Carpi by the local knitwear mills and took part in the conception and setting up of CITER (the region's textile information center). With Loredana Ligabue, who became the first director, she set up training courses for knitwear makers of all ages, offered lessons in fashion design, and seminars for small and medium-sized industries. At the beginning of the 1990s, the studio closed, but its archives are conserved at CITER.

Scaasi Arnold (1931). Canadian designer. His clothes are *haute couture*, with elegant, low-cut necks and sometimes decorated with feathers or fur. His real name is Arnold Isaacs, but since he was young he has preferred to spell his surname backwards. Having studied in Montreal, he moved to Paris where he completed his studies at the Chambre Syndicale de la Haute Couture. He then went to New York where he worked for Charles James from 1951 to 1953, learning various tailoring techniques. In 1957 he opened his own ready-to-wear fashion house in a townhouse in New York but, from 1963, he began to focus exclusively on *haute couture*. His most famous clients have been Barbra Streisand, Claudette Colbert, Elizabeth Taylor, Margot Fonteyn, Aretha Franklin and former First Lady Barbara Bush.

Scacchi Factory producing silk goods that was founded in the aftermath of World War II by Giuseppe Scacchi. From 1949, the factories in Solbiate Comasco have made silk, rayon and mixed fabrics. In 1954, the company began producing printed fabrics destined for the upper end of the market, both for its own goods and for other manufacturers. The following year, the firm was quoted as being among "the Italian makers of *haute couture*" in the pages of the magazine *I tessili nuovi*. In 1967, the private company was transformed into Giuseppe Scacchi Fabbrica Seterie SpA, shortly before Giuseppe Scacchi's death. His sons take over the company until 1972 and in 1973 Jacob Brunner, a relative of Scacchi's widow, took charge. In 1989, the firm changed its name to La Scacchi 1930 but went into liquidation in 1995.

(*Pierangelo Mastantuono*)

Scaioni Egidio (1894-1966). Italian photographer. He worked in Paris. Around 1920, he had the idea of using different European countries as settings for his fashion photographs. The dramatic lighting of his images, in which the figures were sometimes masked in cellophane, won him the reputation of being considered Steichen's best follower in Europe. In 1929, he went into business with John de Forest Thompson, with whom he opened a studio in London, but this was destroyed during a bombing raid in 1940. His black-and-white photographs, heavily retouched and art deco in style, were largely inspired by Steichen and Baron de Meyer. His photographs were published by *Time* and *Fortune* magazines.

(*Angela Madesani*)

Scarabocchio Brand of ready-to-wear fashion that used to be based in Florence. During the 1960s, it was shown at the Sala Bianca in the Pitti Palace. Its collections had a maritime theme, inspired by Biarritz and Deauville, with endless blue and white stripes; it was a young look with a sporty feel and, consequently, included a lot of knitwear.

Scarfato Alain (1957). French hairdresser. His father Jean was born in France in 1926 to a family of Italian immigrants. He became a famous hairstylist and successfully fought for hairdressers to be granted union rights and for professional training schools. Alain took over his father's salon but only after a long breaking-in period with L'Oréal, Patrick Alès, and Vidal Sassoon. From 1993, he became artistic director of the group that has brought together eleven *haute couture* hairdressing practices in France.

Scavia Italian jeweler. The history of this family, which is now on its third generation of jewelers, began after World War I when Domenico Scavia opened his workshop in Milan on Corso XXII Marzo. The business was continued by his daughter Sara, who in the 1970s opened a shop on Via della Spiga, and then by the grandson Fulvio Maria, who became famous for the value and quality of the precious stones that he uses in his settings, but above all for the originality of his creations.

❑ 1999. The brand won the Tahitian Pearl Trophy with the Quinees jewelry set.
❑ 2000. Winner of the Dia for the millennium ring.
❑ 2002. The company began production of accessories, with ranges of bags, eyewear, wallets, leather goods, perfumes, scarves, and umbrellas.

Scavullo Francesco (1929-2004). Italian-born American photographer. He is famous for his technique of using diffused lighting and his portraits of subjects who were rarely posed with solemn expressions, as was typical of the time. He started working for *Vogue* when he was very young. He then worked in the studio with the great Horst P. Horst. In 1948, he was taken on by the new magazine for teenagers, *Seventeen*. Over the years, his photographs were published in *The Ladies Home Journal*, *Harper's Bazaar* and, above all, in *Cosmopolitan* which often his used his work on the cover. Scavullo published many books including *Scavullo on Beauty*, *Scavullo Men* and *Scavullo Women*.

Schall Roger (1904). French photographer. His portraits of Chanel are famous. He was introduced to the world of journalism by Lucian Vogel, through whom, in 1932, he worked with *Vu* and *Jardin des Modes*. Between 1933 to the beginning of World War II, his images were published in *Vogue*, and he worked for *Marie Claire* between 1940 and 1944. From 1945 he worked purely in the fields of advertising and fashion, but immediately after the war he published a collection of photographs taken in the streets of Paris during the German occupation, in a volume entitled *Paris under the Boots of the Nazis*. He passed on the business and his archive to his son Jean-Frédéric in the beginning of the 1970s.

Schatzberg Jerry (1935). American photographer. Although he is generally known for his contributions as a fashion photographer to *Vogue*, he began his career working for *Glamour* in 1956. Two years later Liberman invited him to work on *Vogue France*, which he left in 1962 to join *Vogue America*. His pictures are often taken out of doors, with a vibrant and dynamic city as a backdrop, against which the beautiful, smiling, ethereal models stand out. He made his mark as a film director with two films: *Puzzle of a Downfall Child* with Faye Dunaway in 1970 and *Panic in Needle Park* in 1971.

Scheichenbauer Franco (1933). Italian photographer. His models, often shot with a wide-angle lens or in very glamourous close-ups, were typical of fashion photography in the 1960s and 1970s. His photographs are enhanced by the intentional display of the grain of the film and chromatic processes. In the 1980s, Scheichenbaur left Italy to settle in Cuba where he lives and works.

Schella Kan Austrian brand of ready-to-wear fashion. It was founded in Vienna in 1984 by two schoolfriends, Anita Aigner and Arnauld Hans. They took part in a collective fashion show in Paris and their clothes are sold in Belgium, Germany, France, and Austria.

Scherrer Jean Louis (1936). French designer born in Lyons. His style is simple. His luxury ready-to-wear is known for its prized velvets, and overcoats with leather and suede finishes. His designs are inspired by the Orient and in the 1980s he produced Mongolian and Chinese style cloaks and coats. He chose fashion as an alternative to ballet, which he was forced to give up following an accident. Dior took him on a year before the master died, following which Scherrer worked with Dior's successor, Yves Saint Laurent. After three years with Féraud, he created his own label in 1962. His talent scout was Julia Trissel, the buyer for Bergdof Goodman. His brand was relaunched in 1976 and four years later won the Dé d'Or, which brought a further decade of success. His journey has been one of highs and lows as a result of the continual changes in ownership of the company of which he is director. In 1992, he had to hand it over to the Japanese group Seibu who entrusted the brand, first to Erik Mortensen, then to Bernard Perrys. In 1997, the house was bought by the French company EK Finance, which choses Stéphane Rolland as its designer.

❑ 2002. Mouffarige and François Barthes founded the France Luxury Group that bought Scherrer, along with other labels.
❑ 2002. Stéphane Rolland launched a menswear line and focused on the *haute couture* side of the business.
❑ 2002. Ritu Beri was chosen by the France Luxury Group to design ready-to-wear for Scherrer.
❑ 2003. Ritu Beri left the group.

Schettini Filippo (1900-1990). Milanese furrier. Famous for his eclecticism, he was simultaneously a furrier, an editor, and an art dealer. When, during the 1950s, the economic boom worked miracles for his workshop on Via Filodrammatici in Milan, he opened an art gallery in New York selling pictures by Lucio Fontana, Max Ernst, and Fernand Léger, then one in Milan. As well as being a dealer for Fontana, he sold the paintings of Dova, Crippa, Veronesi, Baj, and Tancredi. A handsome and elegant man, it seems that he used to give his furs to the wives and partners of painters in return for their artworks. He died, however, in disgrace in Milan and only two of the artists that he loved came to his funeral.

Schettino Shop in Capri that sells hand-made sandals. Giovanni Schettino started it up in Anacapri at the end of the 1920s, when he was just 15 years old. Since then it has produced made-to-measure, leather, monk-style sandals, but also criss-cross strappy sandals. It is also famous for its Capri model with three little strips across the front and one behind to hold the heel. In 1955, Giovanni Schettino moved down to Capri to 53 Via Roma, where even today his daughter Lidia continues. The brand is also renowned for its women's sandals decorated with beads, and its moccasins, some with and some without a sole. Its most famous customers have included Jacqueline Kennedy Onassis, Marcello Mastroianni, and Johnny Weissmuller.

Schhoerner Nobert (1966). German photographer who started out at the age of 21. His work is published by *Details*, *The Face*, *Arena* and *The New York Times* and he has done advertising campaigns for Levi's, Nike, and Prada.

Schiano Marina. Model and jewelry designer born in Bacoli (Naples). Thin, very tall, with oriental features and an irrepressible Neapolitan vitality, she began by modeling for Livio De Simone in Naples. She moved to Milan and posed for photographer Giampaolo Barbieri. Next came New York, where, through the agent Eileen Ford, she worked extensively with Avedon and Hiro. She became an inseparable friend of Andy Warhol. In the 1970s, Saint Laurent asked her to manage his office in New York and be responsible for the company's dealings in North America. After spending time as a designer for Calvin Klein and collaborating with the magazine *Vanity Fair*, she began designing jewelry.

Schiaparelli Elsa (1890-1973). An example of the finest creative genius, Elsa Schiaparelli was one of the most important fashion designers of the 1930s. Born in Rome in Palazzo Corsini into a family of intellectuals, she had a cultured and comfortable adolescence. In 1914 she met Count William de

Wendt de Kerlor in London, married him, and together they moved to New York. By the age of 25, she was already separated with a daughter. She had no full-time job but collaborated with antique dealers trying to earn money through dealing in art objects so that she could return to Europe. She is eventually able to do so in 1924 where, having arrived in Paris, she met Paul Poiret who encouraged her to concentrate on fashion. Having tried, without any luck, to get a job in Maggy Rouff's workshop, she began designing black pullovers with white *trompe-l'oeil* designs for herself in a small flat on the Rue de Seine. Her designs were well received, with even the American store Strauss interested in her work. The volume of orders she received forced her to set up a workshop in 4 Rue de la Paix. Tattooed sweaters, X-ray pullovers with the human skeleton traced on them, simple jersey swimming costumes, and innovative accessories were the first articles she designed under the label *Schiaparelli pour le sport*. Extravagant and anticonformist, she soon surprised people with her powerfully original designs often linked to the art world. Colors, materials, processes and patterns were always the result of long research and experimentation, where borrowings from the work of others were combined successfully with a sense of irony. Riding the wave of her growing success, Schiaparelli opened a branch in London in 1933 (at 36 Upper Grosvenor Street) and in 1935 moved her studio to 21 Place Vendôme. This was designed by Jean Michel Frank and Diego Giacometti who conceived the entrance as an enormous golden bamboo cage. By the late 1930s, more than 400 tailors were working for her, and with extreme farsightedness in the Parisian world of *haute couture*, she set up a boutique section selling ready-to-wear clothes. She was a pioneer in introducing materials such as tweed, embossed fabric resembling tree bark (*écorce d'arbre*) and artificial fibers in the traditional repertoire of evening dresses. In Summer 1936 she designed a cape made from transparent rhodophane, a type of plastic, which she called "glass cape." Her collaboration with Schlumberger proved profitable; together they worked on jewelry and buttons in unusual shapes and in association with the French firm Colcombet, in around

Elsa Schiaparelli, suit, 1937.

1936, they produced a material like perforated patisserie paper, which they used for highly original suits. Instinctively revolutionary, Schiaparelli was the first to produce a collection around a single theme, opening the series with her *Stop, Look and Listen*, which was followed by *Neoclassica* (Winter 1936/37), *Butterflies* (Spring 1937), *Seabed* (Spring 1938), *Circus* (Summer 1938) entirely embroidered by Lesage, *Pagan* (Fall 1938), *Cosmic* (Winter 1938/39), *Commedia dell'arte* (Spring 1939) and *Tournures* (Summer 1939). In 1936 and 1937, she increased her experiments with surrealism; a collaboration with Salvador Dalí, for example, led to the design of are balldresses with lobsters painted on organza, velvet bags in the shape of telephones, a suit studded with gaudy red lip patchwork, and hats in the shape of an inkpot, a hen's nest, or a ram's leg. At the same time, Jean Cocteau designed delicate women's outlines for her that were

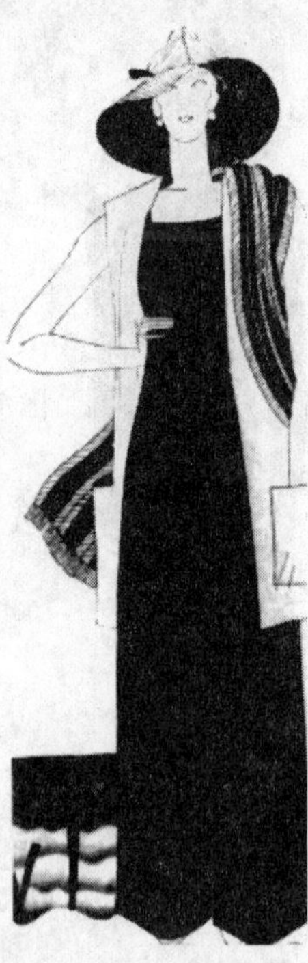

Beach pants by Schiaparelli, published in Vogue, July 1929.

then embroidered by Lesage with superb precision (1937), or winking faces illusionistically confused with the silhouettes of neoclassical columns and vases that she used to decorate very fine ensembles. While Elsa Triolet and Louis Aragon created necklaces for her inspired by aspirins, Jean Clement and Jean Hugo dreamed up jewel-like buttons which soon become the emblem of the house. Maracel Vertés designed the advertisement for the perfume *Shocking* (1937), for which the sculptress Leonor Fini based the shape of the bottle on Mae West's curvaceous body. *Shocking* was followed by *Sleeping* in 1938, and the male fragrance *Snuff* in 1939. Still inspired by surrealism, in 1937, Schiaparelli designed the famous suit with drawers for pockets based on Dalí's famous *Venus of Milo with Drawers* from 1936. At the same time she developed zips in colored plastic as a decorative rather than functional element of the dress, overturning the classical canons of dressmaking by imposing her own version of them. Like Lanvin, she created her own particular chromatic tonality – shocking pink, probably inspired by one of the pinks stirred up by Bérard, which became a dominant theme of many collections and of famous garments like the Phoebus dress in the *Cosmica* collection. World War II disrupted her work, so she moved to New York and served in the International Red Cross. It was only after the war that she opened an atelier in New York (1949) and, having returned to Paris, she gathered as members of her team some of the most promising young talents in fashion design, including Hubert de Givenchy, Pierre Cardin, and Philippe Venet. The female silhouette that she created – square and quintessential with padded well-defined shoulders – influenced international fashion until the dawn of Dior's new look. Before closing her studio, she gathered her memories in a brilliant autobiography called *Shocking Life*, published in 1954.

(*Aurora Fiorentini*)

Schiesser International Leading German knitwear group based in Baden Würtenberg. They have also won themselves a prime position in the men's and women's underwear market. For a few years now, the brand has sought an international dimension on the European market. The first step was to buy the French brand Eminence, producers of pants and underwear for men.

Schiffer Claudia (1970). Born in Rheinberg, Germany, she has blue eyes, blond hair and is 1.8 metres tall. She was discovered aged 17 (celebrating a friend's birthday) in a disco in Düsseldorf by Michel Levaton from the Metropolitan agency. She abandoned her plans to become a lawyer (like her father) and moved to Paris, where, having been on the cover of *Elle*, she was offered the Guess campaign in 1989. Claudia is a modern-day Barbie, the new Brigitte Bardot. She modeled for Chanel (Lagerfeld loves her), Valentino, and Versace. She became a regular face on magazine covers and was offered deals worth millions. With a group of other supermodels, she set up the Fashion Café, publishes fitness videos, and has written her memoirs. She has also tried some film work, but with little success. When she went with the American illusionist

David Copperfield, it caused a great stir. In 2002, she had a little boy, Caspar, by her husband, the producer Matthew Vaughn.
(*Silvia Paoli*)

Schlesser Angel (1958). Spanish designer. He entered the fashion world in 1983 as a result of his collaboration with the designer Juan Rufete. His first menswear ready-to-wear collection was produced for Fall-Winter 1984-1985 and in 1988 he presents his womenswear ready-to-wear collection for Spring-Summer 1989 on the Cibeles runways. In the years that followed, he alternated showing his designs in Barcelona and Madrid. He won a number of prizes (among them, the Vidal Sassoon, the Lancia Vanidad and several times over the magazine Telva's T for best Spanish designer). He also designs clothes for films and international events like the Barcelona Olympics in 1992. With Amaya Arzuaga in 2001, he accompanied the country's president José Maria Aznar on an official trip to Mexico, where they presented their collections at a fashion show.
(*Mariacristina Righi*)

Sketch by Angel Schlesser.

Schlumberger Jean (1907). French jeweler. He is considered to have been one of the 20th century's finest goldsmiths. He arrived on the American scene in the late 1940s after numerous successes in Europe designing jewelry for Elsa Schiaparelli and high society. In 1956, he started working with Tiffany and soon after became Vice-Chairman. His favorite sources of inspiration were flowers, leaves, animals, objects found in the sea, and mythological creatures. His most famous pieces were the magnificent *Trophy* he made for Diana Vreeland, the sinuous *Iguana* for Elizabeth Taylor, and the *Little Bird on the Big Rock*, a brooch made with gold, diamonds and a yellow 218-carat diamond known as the *Big Rock*.(*Giuliana Parabiago*)

Schneider Stephan (1969). German designer who lives and works in Antwerp. Born in Duisburg, he studied at the Royal Academy in Antwerp from where he graduated with the top diploma of the year, allowing him the opportunity to show his designs in Paris – although not on the runways – at the Fashion Week. He creates both menswear and womenswear. From 1996, he has had a boutique in Antwerp and another in Tokyo since 2001.

Schnurer Carolyn (1908-1956). American designer. In New York, she was one of the pioneers of the casual look that broke the influence of European fashions on the US in the interwar years. She traveled extensively in search of inspiration – to the Andes, Turkey, South Africa, and Japan – making Western-style clothes with an unmistakable exotic touch. Graduating from the Traphagen School of Fashion in New York (1939-40), she designed for her husband's company, Burt Schnurer Inc. In 1946, she gave the brand her own name. She knews how to get the best out of linen, cotton, cashmere and alpaca, but also chintz, jersey and velvet. She left the business in 1950 to become a textile consultant to J.P. Stevens.

Schoenberger Dirk (1967). German designer. Originally from Cologne, he moved to Antwerp to work as a creative assistant to Dirk Bikkembergs. In 1996, he launched his first menswear collection in Paris, which has a typically English tailoring but mixes in the occasional casual touch, such as the use of faded material. The garments are handmade in Belgium in small batches, and sold in exclusive shops in Europe, America, and Japan. In January 2002, he presented his first womenswear collection, with organzas, silks, and great tailoring. *(Silvia Paoli)*

Schön Mila (1919). Italian designer. Maria Carmen Nutrizio Schön was the sister of the journalist Nino Nutrizio who founded and was editor for many years of the Milanese daily newspaper *La Notte*, which was published in the afternoon. She was born in Traù in Dalmatia. For years, she chose and bought clothes for her own wardrobe from Parisian couturiers ("I like wearing Balenciaga during the day and Dessés for the evening.") Having moved to Milan, she became a designer when her marriage ended. In 1958, she opened a little studio in Via San Pietro dell'Orto. In 1965, at Giorgini's invitation, she presented her *haute couture* collection in Florence which stirred enthusiasm and appreciation from the press and the US buyers – it was her linings that were a real hit. She says: "The uncompromising way in which I give as much attention to the inside as to the outside of a garment is my signature. Reversibility gives me a sense of order and cleanness of style, which I seek above all in the invisible parts of an outfit." In 1966, she presented her creations in Dallas and Houston and received a Neimann Marcus Award for color, fashion's equivalent to the Oscars. In the same year in New York, her designs were worn by the women who won first and third places in the *Womens Wear Daily* poll of the world's most elegant women. Always on the up, she then moved her studio to its current base in Via Montenapoleone. In 1972, she produced her first menswear and womenswear ready-to-wear collections, which were accompanied by a complete line of accessories: bags, shoes, scarves, and perfumes. Schön also designed the air hostesses uniforms for some international airlines. Hers was the first Italian label to be imported into Japan. In 1986, the Japanese multinational corporation Itochu invested in the registered stock of the company and in 1993 bought its entire parcel of shares. Despite this, Itochu's role has always been only financial, with the creative and managerial side of the business in the hands of its founder. As early as 1995, the house decided to give up on *haute couture* and concentrate exclusively on ready-to-wear. She was asked to design collections for Anna Domenici, Mariuccia Mandelli's long-time right-hand woman, which she did for two years. In 1998, the label adopted a new strategy and handed over its lines to a style studio founded by eight young creators, who were all bred and trained in-house at Central St Martin's and the Royal College of Art in London: Cristina Barreto, Lisa Cameron, Stefano Citron, Greg Myler, Federico Piaggi, Darryl Rodriguez, Paolo Trillini and Steven Verno. Each designer has his or her own specialization: one is an expert in knitwear processes, another in constructing the clothes, and another in color. Their underlying aim, which has proved to be a winning formula, is to remain faithful to the philosophy of the company, but to keep an eye on the future. Schön style, characterized by graphic purity and linearity, has always stood out for the

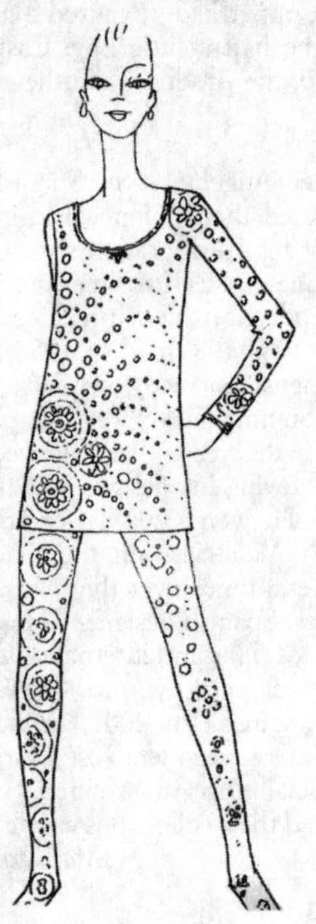

Tunic and pants in embroidered chiffon. Sketch by Chino Bert for Mila Schön, 1969.

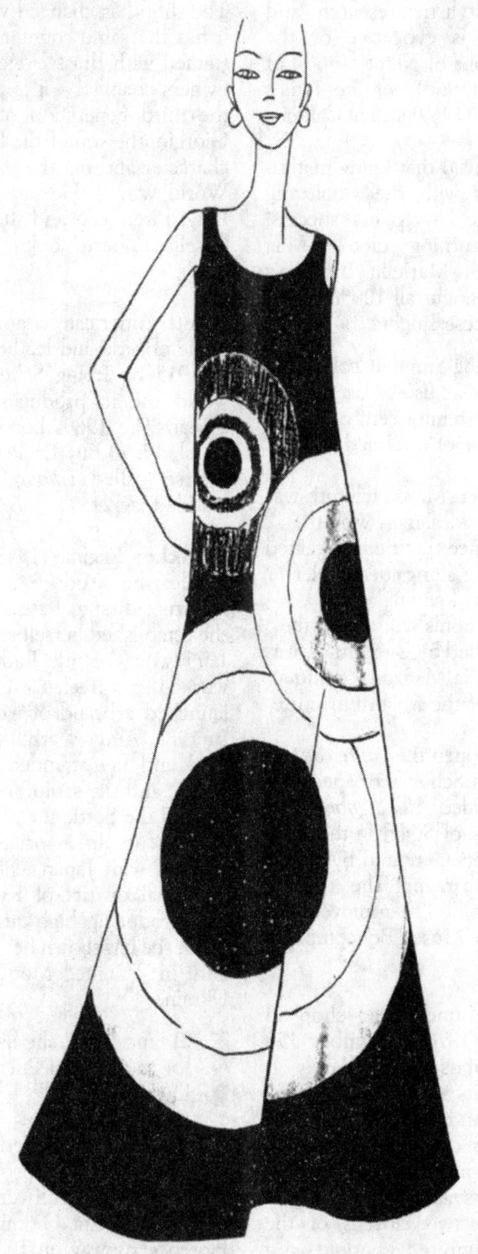

Mila Schön, Spring-Summer Collection 1996.

rigour of its cut, and for the constant interplay between stylistic research and future planning. It is evocative of the geometrical abstractions of Klimt (1966), of Bauhaus sculpture (1968), of Fontana's experiments with cuts (1969) and of Calder's mobiles.
Schön has never archived that lining material, created in 1960s with the wool mill Agnona, that was the key to her success. October 1999 was a turning point for Mila Schön Investment as Mariella Buranai's Group from Emilia bought all 100% of the shares from the Japanese Itochu.

❑ 2001. The Spring-Summer collection was distinctive for its use of laser-cut perforated leather reminiscent of lace – it created an image of a refined and elegant woman.
❑ 2002, September. Marc Helmuth was chosen as the new designer, with the wealth of experience that he had gained in France, working alongside Mugler, Saint Laurent, and Lanvin.
❑ 2003, April. Schön's work from the 1960s, photographed by Ugo Mulas, was exhibited in the Via Manzoni boutique on the occasion of the Milan Furniture Show.
❑ 2003, July. To open the *haute couture* season in Rome, a Schön retrospective was mounted entitled *Alla Signora dello Stile* [To the Lady of Style] in the Auditorium di Roma, curated by Bonizza Giordani Aragno. The anthological exhibition then moved to three rooms in the Museo Boncompagni Ludovisi.

Schostal Memorable underwear shop in Rome. It opened in 1870 at number 158 Via del Corso. Almost immediately it became famous for its stockings, bodices, nightcaps, ties, and hand embroidered shirts made from shirting or cambric. Today, it is mainly known for its men's underwear and the quality of its vests and socks. Schostal was the surname of two citizens of the Austro-Hungarian Empire, Leopold and Guglielmo, who owned the firm in Vienna. It after set up branches in Rome, Naples, and Palermo, but its success in Italy was due to Lazaro Bloch from Turin, who, with three employees from the head branch, founded a company and took over the Italian branches. The shop has changed very little since then; it has the same counters and shopwindows framed with brass ledges. Neither have the owners changed – it is now in the hands of the third generation of the Bloch family. Giorgio, the son of the founder, was a great character and ran the shop before and after World War II. He was a personal friend of Luigi Pirandello and the composer Alfredo Casella. Roberto took over from him.

(*Eleonora Attolico*)

Schott American brand of sports jacket made of hide and leather that was founded in 1915 by Irving Schott. It is one of the world leaders, producing 450,000 garments a year. The 1960s boom in leather fashion enabled it to buy La Perfecto, producers of the so called *chiodo*, the black leather studded jacket.

Schrecker Regina (1948). Italian designer. While she studied art, languages, and literature, first at Lausanne and then Milan, she established herself as a top model and in 1971 won the title Lady Universo. Having worked as a freelance fashion designer, she launched a brand of womenswear in 1980. In 1983, Andy Warhol painted her in New York and then attended her fashion shows in Milan, and the sculptor Arnaldo Pomodoro created the bottle for her perfume. In 1990, she set up an association of cultural exchanges with Japan, collaborating with the industrial district of Kyoto on researching and producing high-quality brocade. Since 1993, she has shown her collections in Russia and in Prague, Mongolia, Beijing, and Ukraine.

❑ Since 2002 she has created costumes for the Festival Pucciniano in Torre del Lago.

Schuberth Emilio Federico (1904-1972). Italian dressmaker born in Naples. He was one of the magnificent nine who were invited by Bista Giorgini to show on the Florence runway on 12 February 1951, the event that served to establish and legitimise Italian fashions. He owed his notoriety to an innate sense of performance, communication and dressmaking skills that he learnt from the Neapolitan school. In the early 1930s, he

worked in the Montorsi studio, where he was in charge of the underwear section with its delicate combinations of silk and lace. In 1938 he opened a milliner's shop with his young wife in Via Frattina. He received so many commissions from his customers that in 1940 he decided to set up an *haute couture* studio in Via Lazio, moving, a year later, to Via XX Settembre.
His style was unique; he loved luxurious fabrics and embroidery and had an innate ability to mix techniques and materials. He dressed the classic but romantic woman: small waist, sizeable bust, and round shoulders. His sumptuous style mixed elements from the 19th century with Hollywood. Loved by queens and stars of the cinema, his clients included Soraya, who had fled Persia with the shah, for whom he designed, in a single night, a wardrobe that was worthy of a true empress. King Farouk of Egypt was a regular customer, who used to have Schuberth dress his wives and lovers. Maria Pia of Savoy commissioned him to make part of her wedding trousseau. He also dressed Brigitte Bardot and Martine Carol. The soubrettes loved him, and he created dresses for the grand finale of musical shows. He made the most of the dresses worn by Wanda Osiris, Elena Giusti, Silvana Pampanini, Valentina Cortese, Lucia Bosé, Silvana Mangano and Lorella de Luca in the film *Poveri ma belli* [Poor but Beautiful]. Sofia Loren and Gina Lollobrigida were also loyal clients. In 1949 he showed at the Palazzo Grassi during the Venice Festival. His studio used to be visited by various dress and costume designers, for example, Jon Guida, Costanzi, Pascali, Pellizzoni, Balestra, De Barentzen, Lancetti, Guido Cozzolino (known as Gog), Ata De Angelis, Folco, and Miguel Cruz. In the 1951 film by Metz and Marchesi *Era lui sì, sì*, he plays himself as he does a dress fitting for Sofia Loren who is just starting out on her career. He used to turn up to society events accompanied by twelve exquisitely dressed and made-up models. He liked to flaunt jewelry, not to show off but to attract the media's attention. He took part in the popular television programme *Il Musichiere* both as a costume designer and participant, singing *Donna, cosa si fa per te*. In 1957, he signed a deal with Delia Biagiotti, the mother of the fashion designer Laura, to export her ready-to-wear line to the American and German markets. He launched the perfume *Schu-Schu* with a publicity campaign endorsed by René Gruau. His archive of designs has been given by his daughter Gretel to the University of Parma to the department directed by Arturo Carlo Quintavalle. (*Bonizza Giordani Aragno*)

Portrait of Emilio Schuberth by Fulvio Bianconi.

Schuessler Karena (1963). German shoe designer, who studied in Germany and Italy. In 1988, she moved to Paris to attend the Chambre Syndicale de la Haute couture. While she was following the 3-year fashion design and pattern-making course, she worked for Sidonie Larizzie and Dior. She is passionate about shoes. In 1991, she was taken on by Stephan Kelian as a designer and designed collections for Maud Frizon, later also taking responsibility for the Esprit Europe line. She set up on her own in Summer 1996. Two years later, she diversified into men's shoes and bags, and in 1998 opened her first boutique in Paris.

Schulze Heinz (1907-1985). German designer. She dressed some of the most famous stars of stage and screen, working as a costume designer for UFA, the most important film company during the Nazi years. Her style did not follow other trends in fashion, but was highly personal, paying great attention to the cut and sartorial composition of the garments. After the war, she moved to Monaco and opened her Heinz Schulze-Varell studio.

Scianna Ferdinando (1943). Italian photographer. He was studying literature and philosophy at the University of Palermo at the time of his decisive meeting in 1963 with the writer Leonardo Sciascia, with whom he struck up a long and deep friendship. It was Sciascia who wrote the long introductory essay to *Feste religiose di Sicilia* (Religious Festivals in Sicily) in 1965, the book which won him the Nadar Prize with which the young Scianna was then able to enter the photography world. Even when he was little, he used to take photographs of people in his town, but it was not until many years later, in 2002, that he gathered these images together (with portraits of Jorge Luis Borges, Alberto Sordi, Maurizio Calvesi, Alberto Lattuada, Alfonso Gatto, and Henri Cartier-Bresson, all taken when they were visiting Sicily) in a book that accompanied an exhibition *Quelli di Bagheria*. Feeling encouraged by *Feste religiose di Sicilia*, he moved to Milan. In 1967, he was taken on at *L'Europeo* as a photo-reporter, then as a special correspondent, and, from 1974, as the magazine's Paris correspondent. He stayed in Paris for 10 years, deepening his friendship with Henri Cartier-Bresson, who introduced him to Magnum where he became an associate member in 1987 and then a permanent member two years later. He continued his reportage work, publishing various books of which the most important were *Les Siciliens* and *La villa dei mostri* (The Villa of Monsters) in 1977, *Kami* (1988) – a documentary about the reality of life in a Bolivian village – and the monograph *Le forme del Caos* (Forms of Chaos). He got into fashion photography in 1987, at the suggestion of Dolce & Gabbana, for whom he did a few advertising campaigns, the first of which involved going behind the scenes of a runway show. He has been published in *Grazia*, *Stern*, *Marie Claire*, *Vogue* and *Moda*. In 1989 he produced *Maglia* (Knitwear), a volume about the Italian knitwear industry with texts by Guido Vergani.
His approach mixes fashion photography with elements of reportage, in a manner reminiscent of the early work of his friend Frank Horvath. Scianna, however, knows how to introduce new elements, by juxtaposing distant realities, like the ancient ways of his native Sicily, with the fashion world that is regenerating and branding the place. Fashion uses the everyday people of Sicily for its backdrops, setting up shoots in the shade of barbers' shops, in bars where bead curtains keep out the heat, in markets and the streets. These are all elements, highlighted by his usual decisive, refined black-and-white photographs, that are found in his *Marpessa, un racconto* (Marpessa, a Tale, 1993) and above all in *Altrove, reportage di moda* (Elsewhere, Fashion Reportage, 1995). Between 1989 and 1999, his monographs on Leonardo Sciascia, Ignazio Buttitta, and Jorge Luis Borges were edited and published by Sciardelli. In 2001, he gathered together his writings published in various French and Italian titles in a volume called *Obiettivo ambiguo* (Ambiguous Lens).

(*Roberto Mutti*)

Sclavi Fabrizio (1947). Journalist and editor of *Amica*. Having studied at the Accademia di Brera, he worked for a year in Japan for an Italian fashion company. In 1972, he started working for *Uomo Vogue*. In 1981, after a period spend with *Vogue* in the US, he returned to Milan to take over as deputy editor for the new monthly magazine *Mondo Uomo*, becoming editor in 1983. In 1988, he moves to *Maenner Vogue* in Germany, first as a special correspondent, then as fashion editor. In 1991, he was summoned to the fashion company Etro to look after its image and PR. In 1993, he was made editor of *Donna*, but after a few months he accepted Condé Nast's offer to return to Germany and transform *Maenner Vogue* into the Italian edition of *GQ*. He remained editor of this title until 1998, when he took over *Amica* with co-editor Giusi Ferré. Both left in 2002 and the reins were passed to Luisa Rodotà, with Emanuela Testori taking over the fashion pages.

Scognamiglio Francesco (1975). Designer born in Pompeii. He made his debut in July 2000 in Rome out of season in the salons of Palazzo Barberini. His first collection was inspired by the 1980s and the New York club The Circle. He studied at the European Institute of Design and collaborated briefly with Versace. He opened his own studio in Pompeii in 1998, seeking to continue the Neapolitan tradition of dressmaking.

Scott Ken (1919-1991). George Kenneth Scott, known as Ken Scott, invented a world made of spectacular flowers, interlaced leaves, animal prints, and exotic fruits. He was the spokesman of a fashion that was quintessential and simple in terms of form, but extremely detailed in terms of prints and colors. An American born in Indiana, his father was a photographer. His enthusiasm for painting leds him to enrol at the age of 18, first at the Parsons School of Design in New York, and immediately afterwards at the highly selective Moses Soyer. He was soon spending time in William Hayter's studio where he mets artists such as Matta and Chagall, who remained his lifelong friends. It was at this time that he had the opportunity to meet Peggy Guggenheim, the famous art collector who in 1944 organized a solo show for him.
In 1946 he settles definitively in Europe, starting off in France. To begin with he led a bohemian life, sharing his time between Paris and Eze, a spot on the Côte d'Azur where he rented a house that remained his refuge for the rest of his life. Still in France, he makes his debut in textile design with Joe Martin, another designer from the US, creating floral patterns for famous French textile producers. Ken Scott drew the famous sketch entitled *Rose à longue tigue* that was printed by Abraham and chosen by Christian Dior for his *haute couture* collection for Spring-Summer 1954. This provided the touchstone for success that spurred him to strive for new goals and experiment in new markets. Having traveled throughout Italy, he settled in Milan in 1955 and opened a studio in Via Sant'Andrea. Here he founded Falconetto with Vittorio Fiorazzo, a company specializing in printed furnishing materials. Producing designer fabrics revolutionized the tastes of the period, which had favored, for interior design and fashion, fabrics that did not wander too far from traditional uniform colors in muffled tones. In addition to his stylized floral designs, it was his use of bright colors and their unexpected combinations that was most surprising. His designs were soon adopted by many Italian fashion companies, such as Veneziani, Biki, De Barentzen. and various luxury Milanese ready-to-wear brands from the 1950s.
Scott was the first to print floral motifs on wool to be used in clothing. From collections of fabrics, followed by collections of foulards and scarfs, he quickly crossed over into the world of clothing. From 1962, he begans designing clothes and accessories in his own name. Dahlias, hydrangeas, convolvuli in shantung silk,· twill, crepe and taffeta were typical of his early shows. However, it was the use of non-crease, practical, innovative synthetic fabrics, such as Ban Lon jersey and Qiana Dupont jersey, that brought him renown as the designer of modernity and color. Even the subdued atmosphere of the Sala Bianca in the 1960s was shaken up by the presence of a colorful cowboy surrounded by even more colorful, elasticated floral dresses that did not lose their shape. He liked to put on runway shows in unexpected venues, like a big-top circus on the Via Appia Antica, and the busy city streets, causing a stir by making his models dance to music. He also designed all the accessories for these performances – shoes, hats, bags, jewelry, and even eyewear – giving rise to the idea of the total look, a concept of which he was a forerunner. In the 1970s he offered lovely cotton, wool, or synthetic blouses with fanciful stitching and buttons bearing his initials, and even evening dress-petticoats and beach-pyjamas with clear gypsy overtones. Others sought to copy the joyful luxuriance of his floral designs and colors, but never achieving the same effect. Ken Scott's style remained inimitable, partly due to his use of a twelve-color technique of printing, which was far more complex than that used by most textile businesses and printers of the time, who usually were only able to print in six colors. His invitations, brochures, press releases, posters, and publicity photographs, together with the venues and themes of his shows, also document his unbridled creativity. In 1968, dressed as a lion-tamer, he made his models move like cats, dressed in cloaks, all-in-ones, and leopard and zebra maxi-dresses, while in 1972 at the Piper Club he showed his famous Findus collection, which began the trend for pop-art in Italian fashion. Enlarged watermelons, courgettes, fried eggs, peas, chicken legs, aspar-

Ken Scott, tunic skirt and dress with shawls, in a drawing by Maria Pezzi.

agus and strawberries abounded in daywear and evening dresses made in the most eclectic range of materials, among which Bandura, a very new nylon crepe produced by Bancroft. It was at this time that he opened his restaurant called Eat and Drink in Milan in Via Corridoni, in which touches of surrealism were most evident in his pasta necklaces, fantasy materials in the shapes of salami and sausages, and his porcelain buttons in the shape of plates laden with spaghetti. In his Lovers (1967), Circus (1968), Gypsy Caravan (1969) and Sport collections (1969), his first show dedicated to menswear (1970), and his Unisex (1970) and Kimonomania collections (1971-72), Ken Scott traveled through the history of international costume like an *enfant terrible*. He died in 1991, but his business is continued by the foundation bearing his name which he himself set up in 1989, and which owns his archive, his various brands, and the Studio Ken Scott.

(*Aurora Fiorentini*)

❑ 1998. The exhibition *Il Giardiniere della moda* (The Gardener of Fashion) was held in Modena.
❑ 2001-2003. Scott's designs were widely represented in the exhibitions *Moda Italiana 1950-1970* in Salzburg, *Vestire Italiano* in Carthage (Tunisia), and *Gran Sera* in Berlin.
❑ 2003, April. A permanent exhibition of Ken Scott's most memorable garments, accessories, and décor was opened in one of the rooms of the Mu-Mo near the Castello di Sartirana (Pavia).

Scuola di Costume e Moda (School of Costume and Fashion) University of Urbino, Italy. It was set up in 1998 within the Training Science faculty. The fashion design course teaches students cultural, artistic, and communications skills and places great emphasis on preparing them to face the realities of the industry. The course lasts three years and attendance is compulsory; there are places for 25 students who have a secondary school diploma.

Scuola Pubblica per la Moda (Public School for Fashion) Set up in 1999 by the Lombardy Region with the collaboration of the National Chamber of Fashion and Fashion Industry, it offers various courses designed to equip students with the range of skills required to deal with the reality of the whole of the fashion industry. The main courses, which involve doing work experience with firms in the sector, are the two-year Fashion Design and Production/Styling courses. Textile Design, which focuses on textile designing, and Pattern-Making, for those hoping to get into the technical side of making clothes, are one-year courses.

Seal Fur made from seal skins, which are dyed and finished like a beaver or bear fur. Thick, resistant and bright, seal fur was launched for the first time in fashion by the Parisian fur maker Revillon at the beginning of 1900s, though already in the second half of the 19th century the demand for this skin had seriously decimated the seal population.

Seamstress Once upon a time, seamstresses were a mainstay of society, at least of women's life, alongside hairdressers, beauticians, clairvoyants, and doctors. Every woman had a seamstress and was often unwillingly to pass on her details in case the preparation of her own clothes got delayed or held up. Those who were lucky had their seamstress come to the house, not only for fittings, but to work under supervision for a certain number of hours cutting and sewing but also altering, taking in, lengthening and turning up the whole family's clothes. Other women went to some address in the neighborhood or perhaps a bit further afield to find their seamstress bent over her pedal-operated Singer. Seamstresses were of varying ages, with a measuring tape dangling around their neck, scissors tied to a ribbon that hung from a belt, and pins everywhere, stuck into a little pin cushion attached to the bib of their apron, and some would even hold pins between their teeth during fittings. On the floor there was always a tangle of threads and off-cuts of material and every seat was laden with fabrics and work that was yet to be done. Music would be playing from a radio that was permanently switched on and smells of food would waft through from the kitchen. Seamstresses were supposedly women of easy virtue, but this is more a myth than a reality. They were known as seamstresses to distinguish them from proper dressmakers who had their own workshop and employees. Humble, modest, ready to hand and cheap, seamstresses made the more simple clothes, including alterations and children's clothes. Dressmakers, on the other hand were haughty, commanding, obsequious and expensive; they made the important outfits, for weddings, special occasions and evenings out. Women who were more thrifty used to get everything made by their seamstress and would even boast about it. Pushed out by mass-produced clothes and ready-to-wear, both seamstresses and dressmakers have disappeared as have all the material shops and haberdasheries, where once dressmakers and seamstresses would flock to buy lining material, buttons, zips, ribbons, press studs, hooks, and grosgrain. The nostalgia of seamstresses remains but there is also still a need for them. Who do you go to now when you have fine cotton from Egypt, silks from India or China, or remnants from the market? Who is able to take things in, let things out, shorten them or let them down? Who do you go to now to copy that tempting design smiling from the pages of a fashion magazine? For some time now, in the larger cities, little shops have cropped up run by Indians, Sri Lankans, or Chinese where for relatively little money and fairly quickly, any dress can be copied or adjusted. But it is a far cry from the real thing. The only trace left of seamstresses now is references in the occasional out of date play or novel. (*Isabella Bossi Fedrigotti*)

Searle American make of coats. For the great American public, Searle is the classic coat; they make the same model every year, but with minor variations. Behind this label is a family business with 200 employees, which in just 5 years has grown considerably and now has more than five shops in New York alone. Its success is linked to its owner Steve Blatt, who in 1980 designed the *Itî coat* with wide shoulders and a slightly flared cut. Since 1997, with the arrival of Heike Jarick, Searle has updated its style, making it younger, reaching out to a less traditional audience and diversifying into clothing and accessories for women.

Sears Roebuck & Co American mail-order group. It is a worldwide distribution giant. It was founded in 1893 by Richard Warren Sears and Alvah Curtis Roebuck. Their catalogs advertize work clothes, denim and fabrics sold by the meter, but also goods for farming: agricultural machinery, saddles, guitars, plus materials and plans to construct a house. Since 1990, the group has focused on womenswear.

Sebago American brand of shoe founded in 1946 by Daniel Wellahan and John Marshall in Portland, Maine. Together, they decided to commercialize the local tradition of hand-sewn moccasins, which is a typical Indian craft. The name "Sebago" means "large expanse of water" in the local Indian language. Moccasins, like boating or rain shoes, continue to be made by hand and require more than 100 different stages of production. Special stitching, internal support and waterproofed leather makes them practically indestructible. The firm employs more than 1,000 people and is run by Daniel Wellahan Jr. It produces four lines: Classic, Docksides, Campsides, and Drysides.

Sednaoui Stéphane (1963). French photographer. After packing in modeling, Sednaoui became a professional photographer in 1986 starting out by doing publicity campaigns for Jean Paul Gaultier. He is considered one of the most interesting of the new generation of photographers, as is confirmed by his pictures seen in *Details*, *The Face*, *Vogue Homme International* and *Vogue America*. In 1991, he moved to New York, where he lives and works. He is known for his celebrity portraits.

Séeberger Family of French photographers with German roots. At the beginning of the 20th century, the three brothers Julius (1872-1923), Louis (1874-1946) and Henri (1876-1956) photographed models out of doors for the magazine *Mode Pratique*. From 1911, they contributed regularly to *Jardin des Modes*, *Fémina* and *Harper's Bazaar*, which, through their photographs, introduced French fashion to the Americans. The studio passed to Louis's sons Jean (1910–79) and Albert (1914) in around 1935 but it closed down in 1977 having sold 37,000 fashion photographs to France's Bibliothèque Nationale.

Segre Simona (1955). Cultural anthropologist. Her *Mode in Italy* was published by Guerini scientifica. She analyses business strategies, marketing techniques, and stylistic intuitions which sometimes anticipate real revolutions in what people wear. She teaches marketing and fashion communication at IULM in Milan.

Seibu A chain of Japanese department stores. There are about thirty of them, but the first one opened in Tokyo in 1940. Controlled by Seibu Department Stores, the company, in the early 1960s, introduced a new policy offering exclusive distribution of international labels. It was the first Japanese chain to focus on fashion and has 20,000 employees.

Seidner David (1957-1999). American photographer. He started his career at just 14 and had his first front cover published aged 19. He immediately became known for the quality of his black-and-white photographs, his daring framing, and his fondness for photomontage, which is unusual in fashion photography. Having turned professional, he lived between Paris and New York and in the 1980s spends two years working exclusively for Yves Saint Laurent. He then worked mainly as a freelance, with his work published in *Queen*, *Harper's Bazaar*, and *Vogue*. In 1986 he published *Momenti di moda*, an original account of the birth of the Paris-based Musée des Arts de la Mode et du Textile at the Louvre. He had many solo exhibitions throughout the world.

Seiligmann Salomon (1961-1939). French clothing entrepreneur. He begins by making flannel shirts in his little studio in Vaucouleurs in Lorraine. As a result of his very aggressive business and industrial strategies, the firm grew in the 1940s to have a turnover of 120 million francs and employ 8,000 people. But it was unable to keep up with developments in the market and was bought by the Indreco Group in 1968.

Select Modeling agency based in London. It opened in 1978 and has been run by Clare Castagnetti, Chrissie Castagnetti, and Tandy Anderson since 1999. Besides having famous male and female models on their books, they also have a lot of new faces still unknown by the public.

Selene Italian ready-to-wear company founded by Walter Burani in 1960 in Reggio Emilia to produce and distribute outdoor clothes for little girls. Having achieved 1,000 sales points, the company launched a line for older girls, while investments allowed them to modernize and expand their production plants. In the mid-1970s the business expanded to include women's clothes. In 1988, it set up the company Mariella Burani, which has its own set of stores and works with licensing agencies. In 1996 Selene USA was created. The Italian company currently has more than 40 own brand stores and franchised shops around the world, all designed by Antonio Citterio. 1998 closed with direct sales (excluding licenses) of 180 billion lire, an increase of 29% on the previous year. Exports accounted for 55% of the sales. Sub-licenses were granted through the Mariella Burani Fashion Group to 18 firms making knitwear, ties, cosmetics, leather goods, eyewear, and accessories. Selene has five of its own brands and produces the Carisma and Carisma Rouge lines for Valentino, under a licensing agreement that dates back to 1993. Since 1996, Selene is the exclusive distributor of Gai Mattiolo ready-to-wear and the Shockingai by Mattiolo line. In March 1999, it signed an agreement to produce the Calvin Klein Donna line starting in Spring-Summer 2000. The following November, the company bought 100% of Mila Schön Investment.

Selfridges Eight-floor London department store in Oxford Street opened by Harry Gordon Selfridge on 15 March 1909. For the first time shopping became an all-round experience: under a single roof you could buy everything from the useful to the ephemeral, from bargains to luxury goods in a single open space that was not divided by partitions. Customers could leave their children in a playgroup, while they shopped and perhaps make use of the credit system. Today Selfridges, which has also opened a store in Manchester, offers an enormous choice of goods in four main fields – fashion, furnishings, beauty, and food – and also offers a personal shopping service. Vittorio Radice has been Chief Executive since 1996.

❑ Vittorio Radice noticeably developed the Food Hall to include a huge selection of first-rate wines and 17 restaurants, bars, and cafés. The department store is one of the founding sponsors of London's new Tate Modern at Bankside.
❑ 2002, September. The second Selfridges opened in Manchester.
❑ 2003, May. The Canadian food magnate Galen Weston, who already owned the luxury supermarket Fortnum & Mason, wished to buy the Selfridges Group for around 900 million euros.

Self-sufficiency in fashion At the end of October 1935, the Fascist regime launched the National Agency of Fashion, which sought to Italianize female wardrobes and to promote their self-sufficiency. The war in Ethiopia had just broken out. Mussolini declared from his balcony, "We have been patient for forty years, it is time to stop," and the troops of the quadrumvirate Emilio de Bono boldly set off to liberate Adua, Axum, and Macallè: but their boldness was soon frustrated by the resistance of the Ethiopians. In Geneva, the League of Nations, the first version of the United Nations, declared Italy to be an "aggressor state" and considered economic sanctions and an embargo on certain products. Rome replied with the ideology of self-sufficiency: "we are enough for ourselves." The Italian population had to "consume Italy" and happily wear wool made using milk protein, "lanital," and cotton made from broom. Textiles began to be manufactured independently and fashion, too, had to become independent. Similarly, certain words adopted from English and French had to be given an Italian equivalent: *amoretto* instead of flirt, *arzente* instead of cognac. It was the duty of tailors to create an elegant national style, but they were not enthusiastic. Mussolini was a strong proponent of this venture, even before sanctions made it necessary for Italy to support herself. Flexing his famous jaw on a podium at the Sforza Castle in Milan in May 1930, Mussolini proclaimed, "An Italian fashion in furniture, decorations, and

From *Fili Moda*, Winter 1941.

clothing does not yet exist. It is possible, and necessary, to create one." And immediately "fashion draft-ups" were launched. In April 1933 Turin, elected the capital of elegance, organized exhibitions and runway shows in a search for "Italian-ness" and Mussolini sent a telegraph: "If the beginning is good, the sequel will be even better: we have to have faith." Faith was supplemented with decrees from on high. *Lidel*, one of the most enthusiastic magazines to follow the order to create an Italian style, recommended "a slender form rather than a thin one," and illustrated fashion models with strong arms, pronounced hips and small, rounded breasts. The endocrinologist, Nicola Pende, prescribed the perfect measurements for models to the Agency of Fashion: 156-160 centimeters in height, weighing 55–60 kilos. To "healthy" women who were blessed with that "soft grace that we have been proud of for so many centuries and have only begun to deny in the last decade," should be given

SE AVETE DEL CRESPO O DELLA MAGLIA DI SETA, POTRETE FARE VOI STESSE
QUESTI SEMPLICI TURBANTI. OSSERVATE LE DOPPIE INCROCIATURE SUL DA-
VANTI E SUL DIETRO CHE VI DANNO LA POSSIBILITÀ DI MODELLARE LA STOF-
FA SUL VOSTRO CAPO CON UNA FORMA MORBIDA, ADERENTE E SOLIDA

Self-sufficient fashion, the magazine *Fili* shows how to put on a turban (from *Fili Moda*, Summer 1941).

the national dress, following the orders of Mussolini. But the tailors complained because their clients wanted Parisian models, or at least something that resembled them. Only Marta Palmer and the Lamma tailoring atelier in Bologna zealously followed the directives, even putting a stop to the ritual of the twice yearly trip to Paris. The Agency of Fashion then invented the stamp of authentication given only to patterns that were "of Italian invention and production." In each collection, at least 50% of the garments had to gain this seal of approval or risk a fine of between 500 and 2,000 lire. Once fashion houses had obtained it, they often concealed it from their customers, otherwise their clothes would languish unsold in their store rooms. This deception could merit a fine of between 1,000 and 5,000 lire fine (a very hard blow at that time, as revealed by the lyrics of a contemporary song: "If only I could have a thousand lire a month"), but it was worth the risk if it saved a collection. The mania for elegance, and the conditioned reflex that chic could only be Parisian, therefore appeared to be immune to these laws and the proclamations of Mussolini, even though, during the years of self-sufficiency and "the Italian marching proletariat," he was at the height of his popularity. In 1937, the magazine *Per Voi Signora*, as Natalia Aspesi pointed out in her lengthy and important volume *Il lusso e l'autarchia* (Rizzoli, 1982), had every right to be indignant: "After fifteen years of Fascism, two years after the founding of the Agency of Fashion, when the memory of nine months of sanctions was still strong, some Italian tailors continued to base their collections entirely on Parisian models and considered the garments bearing the Agency's stamp to be unimportant, artistically inferior, so that they did not in any way represent the essence of their work. In fact, their existence was to be shrouded in absolute silence. Their true collections were made up of French patterns." This was not stubbornness on the part of professionals or a form of embryonic resistance to the regime. Tailors had to follow the wishes of their customers and this, complained *La Gazzetta del Popolo*, "showed that they greeted Italian dress with personal sacrifice and they put up with it as if they had to put up with a monk's tunic, purely for the spirit of the discipline, while all their dreams of elegant exoticism followed the direction to the French border, where those doors were well closed." Some seeds, however, took root. The runways at the Villa d'Este (a show held in Spring 1938 on the wishes of Mario Allamel and organized by Carlo Rossi), and at Campione, Mirafiori hippodrome, the ateliers of Milan, Turin and Rome, and the designers Ventura, Battilocchi, Ferrario, Gori, Gandini, Zecca, Fercioni, Luigi Bigi, Biki, Vanna, Fumach-Medaglia, Biancalani, Rovescalli, Ayazzi-Fantecchi, Cerri, and Tizzoni squeezed many drops of Italian talent from their partial obedience to the order to "create and dress in Italian style." "They were beginnings," remembered Biki, "attempts that were based mainly on the use of Italian textiles, local passementerie, laces, embroideries made by our highly skilled artisans. But, despite these efforts, there was a lack of competency and united purpose. There was no cohesive strategy and it was easier to buy French cloths from Pedrini, which he bought in Paris and sold in Italy at a great profit." Those attempts did not please consumers with unlimited means. Rich aristocratic women did not renounce their designs by Chanel, Molineux, Lanvin, Patou, Vionnet, Lelong, and Schiaparelli. But by now war was in the air: Paris began to distance itself and, a little later, ravaged by Nazi boots, it became the buying monopoly of the sisters of Eva Braun, the wives, companions, friends, and fiancées of the Third Reich. At the Agency of Fashion it seemed to be the right moment for the definitive effort, "in the light of the new tasks that Italy will most certainly have to accomplish in the fashion sector, in the new

1937, the rediscovery of the bicycle. From *Il lusso & l'autarchia* by Natalia Aspesi, published by Rizzoli. Design by Brunetta.

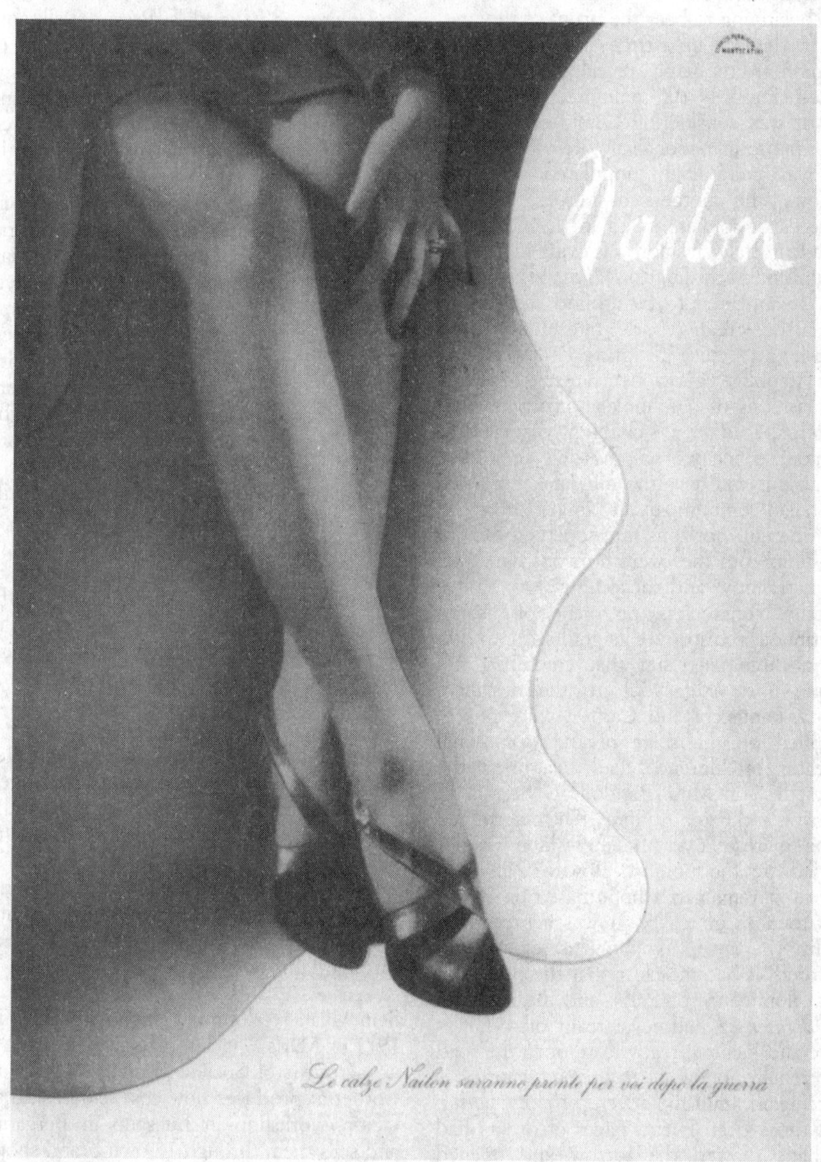

Nailon
Le calze Nailon saranno pronte per voi dopo la guerra

Self-sufficient fashion. With this poster from 1943, Montecatini announced that "nylon tights will be ready for you after the war."

European order that will be created by the Axis powers." On the eve of the conflict, there was a congress on the theme of "clothing and self-sufficiency." When Italy was beginning to bear the brunt of the first, bitter defeats in Africa, the Agency of Fashion triumphantly revealed that it had issued almost 14,000 guarantee patents and that it was considering a gold seal for the most patriotic, nationalistic dress. The country was increasingly populated with war widows, the mothers of heroes, and the fiancées of soldiers killed in the field. But "Made in Italy" fashion was living months of optimism. According to *L'Illustrazione Italiana*, it appeared to be around the corner, after the great parade of self-sufficient clothing in Venice in Spring 1941. The aim was "to oblige capricious women ... to follow the fashions of our homeland: our textiles, patterns, ready-made clothing, an exclusive fashion, which we will be able to export because it will have the unmistakable mark of Italian commitment and imagination. (...) All foreign horizons are opening up to clothing." But they were horizons darkened with tragedy and becoming ever more gloomy. Nonetheless, the Agency of Fashion continued to distribute its gold seals: to Biki for a three-piece suit that combined silk crêpe, linen and wool, to the designers Ayazzi-Fantecchi and Ciottoli who, photographed on the stage of the Communal Theater of Florence, had beautified the hairstyles of Mita Pandolfini, Simonetta Corsini, and Paola Antinori. The determined hope to create a very Italian fashion was not buried by the bombs. However, in substance, it remained a hope based on only a few touches of reality. It was a precarious reality because, as soon as peace was restored, it became clear that the psychological dominance of Paris, and the need for the *dernier cri*, had never really died. It was alive and kicking, ready to re-open the road to French monopoly, to enslave wardrobes once again, until the advent of *prêt-à-porter*. But those decrees and pages of orders had perhaps plowed the furrow and opened people's minds to the idea that it was possible to attempt an Italian approach to fashion. As the journalist Elisa Massai recounted, "Self-sufficiency at least had the merit of obliging the fashion houses in part to turn their backs on the very easy solution of purchasing in Paris, then reproducing and selling in Italy. The result was that everyone bought the same things. Certainly, there were two or three designers who used Paris and recreated its models: Pascali, Pellizzoni and Elio Costanzi. But nobody thought of stealing from the great French designers any more. Otherwise, they would risk losing their customers. Casa Ventura even boasted a French female tailor, born and trained in one of those legendary ateliers and captured during the 1930s. Setting extremes to one side, the nationalistic idea of an Italian form of dress was not totally senseless. Italian artisans were of the first order, its ateliers were highly skilled and its men's tailors some of the best in the world. Often the textiles, sold as English, were actually Italian, with the exception of some cashmeres that were not produced in Italy until the 1950s. The idea of a specific Italian style, which did not pay tribute to France, was not in fact a strange one. Indeed, it was planted in fertile soil, with a favorable background. This was demonstrated by the first runway show of Italian *prêt-à-porter*, held in Florence in February 1951. The period of self-sufficiency during the war set something in motion: "badly copied patterns that nevertheless had something original about them."

(*Franco Belli*)

Selling Harriet. German designer. Her ready-to-wear is produced in Italy by Target. She was born in Hamburg and studied at the Kunstschule before arriving in Milan in 1979. Here she designed her first clothes in a style that still makes her stand out: coquettish, sexy, seductive clothes, with provocative necklines and daring, see-through fabrics.

Sem Milanese clothing company founded in 1971 by Maria Angela Corbetta. The name is an acronym of Società Esercizi Magazzini. Corbetta produces low-cost clothes in a factory/workshop in Luzzano in Bergamo and sells them through 15 own-brand shops in the leading cities of north and central Italy. She produces a hundred or so examples of every model, taking care to keep things simple and rigorous, partly to keep production costs down. In 1997, she produced Sunmoon, an underwear collec-

Sem designs in a drawing by Maria Pezzi.

tion. Her Milanese customers have renamed the shop in Corso Vittorio Emanuele "Sem Laurent."

Senard Catherine (1958). French designer. She had a brief and meteoric career lasting just eight years. She was born in Rouen and studied history and archaeology at the Sorbonne, but chose fashion as a career. In 1984 Biba displayed one of her dresses reminiscent of Venus di Milo's drapery. In 1986, she set up her own brand but two years later the people producing her clothes went bankrupt and she missed a lot of her delivery dates. She survived for another four years, but her image had suffered a blow. She then gave up on fashion and, on the strength of her degree, concentrated on teaching. *(Mino Colao)*

Senneville (de) Elisabeth (1946). French designer. Her strength is her ability to move seamlessly from one experience to the next, from a commercial career to a creative one. From being the director in 1964 of the Parisian Miss Dior boutique, in the 1980s she began printing ancient works of art on her clothes inspired by the reworkings of the masters of pop art such as Roy Lichtenstein and Andy Warhol. Having designed for various firms, sometimes putting her name to collections and sometimes not, she set up on her own in 1975. Her innovations include hyper-geometric cuts, bright colors, and the use of Velcro to replace buttons during her Chinese-inspired period. She also produces ranges of clothing for babies and children.

❑ 1999. She opened a boutique in Rue d'Assas and used bright fabrics and optic fibers.
❑ 2000. Her line for the home was launched in microtransparent neoprene. The designer turned her attention to anti-magnetic materials.
❑ 2001. Senneville introduced anti-pollutants and products made from active carbon for clothes to be used about the house, swimming costumes, and women's dresses.

Sensani Gino Carlo (1888-1947). Italian costume designer, painter, and set designer who greatly influenced Italian fashion until after World War I. He was one of the most sought after costume designers in theater and was asked to collaborate with the biggest Italian directors of the period: Camerini (*Il cappello a tre punte*, *Il signor Max*), Blasetti (*La corona di ferro*, *La cena delle beffe*), Alessandrini (*Cavalleria*), and Poggioli (*Addio giovinezza*, *Le sorelle Materassi*), but also with French film directors like Chenal (*Il fu Mattia Pascal*, which Sensani handled in the style of Toulouse-Lautrec) and Christian Jacque (*The Charterhouse of Parma*, which was released posthumously in 1948). In Poggioli's films, he also worked on the sets, claiming that they too were part of his responsibilities as costume designer. Working closely with the teaching director Luigi Chiarini, he taught at the Experimental Center for Cinematography creating many Italian costumes for the new recruits. The theatrical dressmaker Umberto Tirelli recounts, in his autobiography *Vestire i sogni*, "A travel companion for Soffici, Palazzeschi and De Pisis, Senzani did not stick to simply updating the costume tradition. He turned it upside down, by prising open its history and its precise reconstruction of cuts, materials, techniques, and linings. His renaissance was a true renaissance, with stays and iron corsets for women, justicoats and quartered shields for men. His interpretation of the 19th century did not draw on art deco and was not bastardised by influences and elements from the period in which Sensani was working. He was a great philologist of fashion."

Sentier District of Paris in the 2nd arrondissement. In the 1980s, it was the center of ready-to-wear in Paris with more than 1,000 little textile and clothing businesses concentrated in the area. You find wholesalers there, as well as those producing young fashion (like Naf Naf), plus cutting and sewing workshops. Many of the big names in the clothing industry have their head offices in Sentier.

Sequin Bright metallic or synthetic small chip manufactured in a wide variety of colors. It has a small central hole, often filled by a small bead, where the needle goes through when it is sewn on a fabric. The term is also used to indicate small beads used in embroideries and decorations.

Serapian Stefano Memorable brand of leather goods, founded by Stefano and Gina Serapian immediately after World War II. On the Milanese fashion scene at least, the women's bags made by this Armenian-born couple for a long time rivaled those produced by Gucci and Pirovano in terms of quality and reputation. Next came small leather goods and, most recently, men's briefcases and travel bags. The firm has now passed to the next generation and today is run by their son Ardavast. It has two factories in Milan and another one in Varese, which is the largest and most modern and produces goods to be exported mainly to the Japanese, English, and American markets. The export side of the business is very strong and accounts for 90% of the annual production. The goods are distributed directly to shops through agents who represent them in different territories. They have been involved in numerous collaborations with big fashion houses, producing and distributing lines of leather goods for them. Ardavast is president of the Fondazione Stefano Serapian, which since 1997 has awarded an annual prize at Bologna University for the promotion of Armenian history, literature, music, and cinema studies.

Seredin & Vasiliev A label that is the result of the collaborative partnership between Vladimir Seredin (1969) and Serghei Vasiliev (1972), who studied together at the Academy of Fashion in Moscow in the 1980s. At the end of the decade (1989), they set up their label and studio. To begin with, they worked mainly in theater, opera, and cinema, but in 1999 presented their first *haute couture* fashion show at the Ritz in Paris. Their talent caused a real stir, particularly their use of extravagant materials, sense of humor, and emphasis on femininity. In 2001, they presented their first ready-to-wear collection, again in Paris. (*Sofia Catalano*)

Serge Matta *Haute couture* French fashion house. Active from 1959 until 1961, it was set up, with little success, by the brother of the more famous Roberto Echaurren Matta, the Chilean painter. For the designer who had gained experience working with Fath and Schiaparelli, it was not creative talent that was lacking but administrative skills. The house shut down and Serge went to work with Maggy Rouff.

Sergio Tacchini Brand formed in the 1960s by Sergio Tacchini, who became an entrepreneur after a career as an international tennis player. Today, besides tennis, he designs clothing for skiing, golf, the gym, swimming, and leisurewear. His annual sales exceed 150 million euros, he has 6,000 shops throughout the world and he is the head of Sandys Spa, the company run by Alessandro Tacchini, his son.

❑ 2000. Sergio Tacchini sponsored the French skipper Karine Fauconnier, thereby entering the world of sailing. The huge trimaran that bore the brand's name was also launched.
❑ 2003. Sergio Tacchini sponsored the Spanish tennis player Juan Carlos Ferrero, who reached number 1 in the ATP rankings after his victory at Roland Garros and reaching the US finals.

Serica Lombarda Company producing silk fabrics, founded in 1926 by Serafino Lonati, Luigi Berra, and Carlo Pozzi. Two years later, they started making fabrics for ties in Cavallasca in the province of Como. In the second half of the 1930s, other shareholders underwrote the company's capital, among them Marco Canepa, Ambrogio Pessina, and his son Gaetano, who owned the dye-house of the same name. From the end of World War II until 1966, Serica Lombarda was run by Marco Canepa's sons, Giovanni and Franco. With their father as chairman, Giovanni oversaw the technical and creative side of the business and Franco looked after the administrative side. In 1966, Giovanni left to set up his own firm Tessitura Serica Giovanni Canepa. Franco, however, stayed with the company until his death in 1968, when it was passed on to other members of the family. It was the heirs who orchestrated the move to Gironico, also in Como, in the early 1990s, and changed the name of the company to Serica Lombarda-Lambrugo.

(*Pierangelo Mastantuono*)

Serikos Italian firm producing artisan-made fabrics set up in 1984 in Lurate Caccivio in the province of Como. It has four lines of products: Serikos, a classic ready-to-wear line made using the traditional processes of the Como silk industry in natural bases, dyed threads, and Jacquard; Laboratorio Tessile which uses innovative materials for a more casual look; Serikos Sport, which specializes in working with the new generation of fibers, such as Tactel, Lycra, Strata, Diablo, acetates, polyesters, and viscose, with particular finishes such as waxing, oiling, fly-trap and other effects; and Neck-wear, which produces fabrics for ties.

Serra Gianni (1970). *Haute couture* designer. Born in Alghero, he uses techniques and textiles from men's tailoring. He went to the Istituto Marangoni in Milan and in 1991 moved to Rome where he worked as a costume designer for the theater. In 1998, he went into business with Gianluca Misiti, son of Antonio Misiti who is a men's tailor in Rome. Their first fashion show was in July 2000 as part of the official Rome *haute couture* show and they presented day dresses in alpaca, tweed, chalk-stripe, and Prince of Wales check. For evening wear, their experimental dresses combined voile with stiff card.

Setaichiro The label of Ichiro Seta, the young Japanese designer who was discovered at the Milano Moda Donna show for Winter 2003-2004. His CV includes working with Jean Paul Gaultier and Yamamoto. In Milan he won an award in the Enkamania competition for young designers. On the back of this international acclaim, he presented a collection on the runway for the first time. He mixed charm with a rainbow of bright colors on flared silk and viscose skirts. It is a comfortable look with a fondness for artisan-style knitwear and incredible cotton padding that complements the see-through patchwork to great effect. He loves research and experimentation: he cuts chiffon into little bits, then frays and curls them to make small masterpieces. He has 30 sales points in Italy.

Seterie Cugnasca The company was founded in Como in 1920 by Giuseppe Cugnasca. Between the wars, its customers included some of the biggest names in French *haute couture*. In 1956, it was bought by Manero, one of the major textile groups that operates at international level. For many years, Cugnasca traded under its own name, asserting its excellent production reputation which established it as one of the most important textile businesses in Como. Managed by Cristiano Mantero, the Seterie Cugnasca proved to be one of group's best assets. Towards the end of the 1980s, in the process of reorganizing the business, Seterie Cugnasca was completely bought up by Mantero. However, even today the name Cugnasca is associated with a top-quality collection of textiles for women's clothing that reflects avantgarde research into new mixes of threads, color studies, and the application of new finishing techniques.

(*Hélène Blignaut*)

Settembrini Luigi (1937). Settembrini was born in Milan to Neapolitan parents, whose families had played a part in the political and artistic history of Naples. Luigi is considered one of the best Italian experts in communications and image creation. Recently, he has focused on relaunching the exhibition possibilities for Florentine clothing textiles, on thinking up and realizing marketing plans for the city's textile industry, on promoting fashion as an essential component of contemporary culture, and on promoting the cross-over between present-day communication and artistic strategies. He has organized nearly all the city's major fashion events, for example, the *Nascita della Moda* (Birth of Fashion) exhibition with Luca Ronconi and Gae Aulenti (Palazzo Strozzi 1992 and Musée du Louvre 1993); the fashion section of the exhibition *The Italian Metamorphosis 1943-1968* (Guggenheim Museum, 1994); the *GA Story* event under the direction of Bob Wilson, produced by Pitti Immagine on the occasion of the European Summit in Florence (Stazione Leopolda 1996); and the planning of the Florence Biennale, as, together with Germano Celant and Ingrid Sischy, he curated the first one that opened on 21 September 1996. (*Guido Vergani*)

❑ 2000, June. He was appointed director of the Valencia Biennale – The New World, which first took place in June 2001. Settembrini was responsible for the communications and marketing strategies. These included his relaunching of exhibitions of clothing textiles in Florence, the Florence Biennale, and the exhibition *Stanze e Segreti* (Rooms and Secrets) at the Rotonda della Besana in Milan.
❑ 2003, June. Second Valencia Biennale.

Settepassi Old jewelers that has been trading on the Ponte Vecchio in Florence since 1850. After merging in 1961 with the Milanese firm Faraone, the Settepassi-Faraone workshop has continued to represent, both in Via Tornabuoni in Florence and in Via Montenapoleone in Milan, a cardinal point on the international map of goldsmith creativity. Known for the quality of its pearls and its vast array of diamonds and other precious stones, Settepassi is constantly at the forefront of the field thanks to its entirely handmade production processes, handcrafted style, and unique inventiveness. Since 1989, it has been the exclusive distributor of Tiffany jewelry in Italy. (*Ilaria Ciuti*)

Seven Jeans "Mysterious" brand of jeans set up by Jennifer Scruby at the beginning of 2002. According to some observers, the underplayed launch of this line of pants, T-shirts, jackets, and miniskirts was a well thought out strategy to attract public attention. There was no publicity, no non-commercial references on the internet, and only a few front covers of fashion magazines and a fleeting appearance in an episode of *Will and Grace*, with Debra Messing and Matt Damon.

Sewing machine A humble tailor from Saint-Étienne, France, invented the sewing machine but it was greeted with great hostility. Soon after it had been patented on 17 July 1830 a workshop was opened in Paris with 80 machines to sew military uniforms. A small, angry crowd of tailors working from home attacked the workshop, seeing it as a threat to their livelihoods. The inventor was beaten and chased away but rather than giving up he went on to improve his creation. Between 1830 and 1845, the sewing machine conquered the Western world. In France, England, and America alone, roughly thirty patents were issued for a variety of innovations: over the course of a century these became about a hundred. Although it was a European invention, the sewing machine became most widespread in America. In Philadelphia in 1856, Isaac M. Singer built the first pedal sewing machine and, 30 years later, the first electric one. At the end of the twentieth century, Italy was producing about 200,000 machines per year. The Necchi brand is the most famous. (*Pierangela Fiorani*)

Poster for Müller sewing machines.

Seydoux Fornier De Clausonne Jerome (1936). Chairman of Chargeurs, which since 1981 has been the leading group for marketing and teasing wool on the international market. Seydoux belongs to the generation of textile managers that only took over the reins of the family business after gaining experience in other fields. They adopt aggressive investment, research, and development strategies in order to keep up with competition in the sector.

Seznec Marie. French model. Her hair having turned gray at a very young age, she displayed it on the runway; it was part of her allure and her way of attracting attention and turning heads. She was Lacroix's favorite model. She ended her career in 1990.

Shadowed A term used to describe any speckled or streaked fabric. It was fashionable during the 1930s and 1940s. The term also refers to knitwear threads with two or more colors.

Shafran Nigel (1964). English photographer. He was an assistant to various still-life photographers in London and New York between 1982 and 1986. He went on to work with *Vogue*, *I-D*, *Harper's Bazaar, Harpers & Queen*, the *Independent on Sunday Review*, and *Vanity Fair*. He has also worked for Levi's and Wrangler.

Shahtoosh Very fine and soft wool produced by the coat of a Himalayan goat. The animal is now protected, making it illegal to market the wool. It can be twisted several times so that it becomes so fine that it can fit through a ring.

Shamask Ronaldus (1945). Dutch-born designer who took Australian nationality. His architectural training led him to create two and three dimensional clothes, working with cut and form. Having worked as a window dresser in Melbourne (1963-1966), as a fashion designer in London (1971-1977), and opened a store on Madison Avenue in New York (1979-1986), he was the subject of much speculation in 1981 when, as part of a Fall-Winter collection, he presented a spiral coat whose construction was much prized. Shamask was also one of the first to get interested in Japan, launching his *Hakima* pants. From 1985, he focused on men's fashion, employing unusual colors and fabrics.

❑ 2003, May. He was invited by the Fashion Institute of New York to exhibit drawings, sketches and garments in the exhibition *Goddess*.

Shantung Originating from the Chinese province of Chan-Toung, a silk fabric made from coarse irregular threads, which produce a rough surface, with knots, lumps and an iridescent finish.

Sharra Pagano Italian jewelry house founded in 1969 by Lino Raggio. It produces jewelry designed by Raggio himself and Gianfranco Signori. Owing to the excellent quality and originality of the designs, the pieces – made in metal with special glazes, in glass and in synthetic resins – are often commissioned by big name designers who use them to complement their own creations on fashion show runways, among them, Albini, Armani, Dior, Valentino, Versace, and Moschino. In the early 1980s, they opened a shop on Via Spiga in Milan. Improving production and boosted by proposals for trend-based leather goods, in May 1999, Lino Raggio opened a new shop in Corso Garibaldi in Milan, while retaining the original point of sale in Turin on Via Monte di Pietà.

Shaw Benitez Women's clothing line designed by the Americans Jan Shaw and Carlos Benitez that is produced and distributed by the Nadini Group: sales in 1998 reached 70 million dollars and 800,000 garments were produced. In 1999-2000, they showed in Milan for the first time. The knitwear collection was characterized by its lack of sewing and its tubular appearance, while jersey and innovative materials were used for elegant and very feminine dresses as a result of exclusive experimental research. Previously, the pair chose to call themselves Jan Carlos, making their debut in 1996-1997 in Milan under the auspices of the firm Creazioni di Matelica.

❑ 2001, September. The two designers joined Giuliano Coppini's Lineapiù

System Group in an agreement that covers the production and distribution of the brand.
❑ 2002, February. The Jan & Carlos brand presented an elegantly primitive woman on the Milan runways. Her dress featured leather boots with strategic openings around the ankle, brown clothes, asymmetrical cloth and velvet kilts, ponchos, masculine pants with turn-ups, shoulderless cloaks, and dresses made from net or torn mesh, dressed up with playful bridles and reins, made in leather or satin.
❑ 2002. The designers ended the arrangement with Lineapiù.

Shawl Squares or rectangles of cloth worn draped over the shoulders. Shawls were initially brought back by English and French soldiers returning from India, and showcased that country's rich fabric designs and patterns. Shawls mostly fell out of use after the second half of the twentieth century, though there was a revival in the 1960s when a rustic macramé version came back into fashion. They are often today replaced by scarves, often of silk and in every possible pattern, and highly collected when produced by fashion houses including Fendi, Gucci and Hermes, in both lightweight wools and silks.

Sheath Dress Especially famous was the classic black tapered sheath dress, introduced by Chanel and called the *petit noir*, an emblem of the 1920s. With straight lines, sleeveless, the sheath dress became a protagonist again in the early 1960s, indispensable for afternoon wear or for dinner invitations, but also as an all-purpose outfit for various occasions. Often worn with a coordinate jacket.

Sheeler Charles (1883-1965). American photographer. In 1923, he started working in *Vogue*'s New York office, alternating between fashion photographs and other topics, such as urban architecture and industrial plants (the photographs that Ford commissioned from him in the late 1920s are famous). His images displayed a painterly quality influenced by the work of Steichen and Stieglitz: he also painted, approaching it like commercial photography in a rigorous highly photographic style.

Shelabarger Patty (1980). Young Italian-American designer. It is her witty and extravagant intuition that stands out. Her trademark characteristics are street fashion, "Tokyo-girl" influences, headgear inspired by Lego figures, and green and yellow floral lace and embroidery that appears to come straight from a Barbie house. This girl, who sports an eye-catching head of pink hair, has created a cartoon alter ego called Anna Barger, an imaginary model halfway between Naomi Campbell and Betty Boop, who appears in animations on the internet, wearing pink-heeled boots, fishing pants, and a yellow eco-friendly fur. Besides an early line of chairs, Patty has created little outfits for dogs and babies. The pop star Madonna commissioned her to make her daughter Lourdes Marie's wardrobe and some mini furniture for her room. She is sold in shops and exclusive department stores in London, New York, and Chicago.
(*Pierangelo Mastantuono*)

❑ 2000. Patrizia Shelabarger developed the character of Anna Barger, a former editor and model, who has become the designer's muse.
❑ 2001. The brand was bought by Fashion Management of Vicenza.
❑ 2003, June. Her collection for little girls between the ages of 4 and 14 was presented at Pitti Immagine Bimbo and made available in Italian shops from Spring-Summer 2004. Patty Shelabarger, who no longer has anything to do with the group, was replaced by the English designer Louise Palmer.

Sheppard Eugenia (1911-1984). American journalist who was one of the first to develop a critical and objective approach to fashion. She was present at the very first fashion shows that Bista Giorgini organized in the Sala Bianca in the Pitti Palace in Florence, the shows which led to the birth of Italian fashion. Having started at the *Dispatch* in Columbus, Ohio, she worked on *Womens Wear Daily* and the *Herald Tribune* from

1932 to 1966. The following year she moved to the *New York Post*, where she wrote the daily Inside Fashion column.

Sherman Cindy (1954). American photographer and artist. She studied at Buffalo University and graduated in photography in 1976. She started making self-portraits, underlining the need to rediscover feminist themes, not as a war cry, but by poignant observations on the role of the woman as seen through a consciously stereotyped image that makes her more fragile. She switched from her original choice of black-and-white – reminiscent of 1950s cinema – to color in the 1980s to mock the role of the pin-up, and in 1983 to mock the fashion system in a long piece of work that she did for *Interview*. Grotesque, violently and absurdly composed figures inhabit her images that slide increasingly towards the decomposition of the body, by using bits off mannequins and masks. Cindy Sherman's photographs have influenced the new generation of fashion photographers.

Shetland Wool provided by sheep from the Shetland Islands off the north of Scotland. The wool is prized, as it is soft and delicate, but looks hairy and glossy. Carded or combed, the fabric made out of it is medium weight with herring-bone or diagonal patterns.

Shiatzy Chen Chinese ready-to-wear label. The name means literally "styles for Chinese." Its creator is a small, timid woman who is always dressed in dark colors. In Asia she is a star. She is inspired by everything that catches her interest, from an architectural detail, to an old dress, to a film. She uses Chinese, French, and Italian textiles. She has had a boutique in the Rue Saint-Honoré in Paris since 1990.

❑ 2001. The brand opened another store in Paris. The firm has grown as a result of the special attention that is spent on making sure its Chinese designers are cutting edge; they are sent to Paris every year to study the latest trends in fashion and design.

Shilling David (1953). English milliner. He has reintroduced girls to hats, with his over-the-top style that is often in tune with club fashion. At the age of 12, he used to make his mother hats to wear to Ascot. On behalf of the United Nations, he has undertaken to revive traditional craftsmanship from Africa, Asia, and Latin America.

❑ He joined the advisory board of the Royal Academy School. Recently, he has applied his creativity to the services of institutions who deal with humanitarian problems, creating logos for them. Most recently, he has been working with metal to create flexible and delicate steel sculptures reminiscent of his famous hats.
❑ 2003, July. He was commissioned to make an installation for Henley Festival of Music and Arts, which comprises two layers of steel which stretch for 60m along the banks of the River Thames.

Shimada Junko (1961). Japanese designer who grew up in Paris from a very young age. Before setting up on her own in 1981, she gained experience in the design office of the department store Printemps, then with Mafia and Cacharel. One line bears her name; the other, which is cheaper, is called Part 2.

❑ A menswear line was added to the women's collection.
❑ 2002. The designer took part in the initiative set up by the Michelin Group to personalise their famous mascot; the result is a handbag.

Shine Name of a trendy French boutique. It brings exposure to small brands that are not widely available in Paris. It was opened in 2000 by the Italian Vinci d'Elya, who has married the owner of the Ernest Le Gamin brand. The shop is in Rue de Charonne, in the Bastille area.

Shinoyama Kishin (1930). Japanese photographer. The son of a Buddhist monk, he studied photography at the University of Nihon in Tokyo from 1961 to 1963, then published his first images in *Camera Mainichi*. He worked for the Light House agency and in 1966 won the prize awarded by the Association of Japanese Critics for the best young artist. From 1968 he worked freelance for fashion and advertising magazines and two years later was voted Japanese photographer of the year. Specializing in nudes, his photographs were very sculptural and almost abstract, dominated by surreal and highly theatrical atmospheres created using artificial lights and very wide angle lenses. His first successes in Europe – with a famous exhibition at the Photokina in Cologne in the 1970s – allowed him to introduce Japanese photography to an outside world. This is how he presented his series on the tattoo parlour in Yokohama and the series on the bodies of naked dancers; the photographs were taken with a camera that was especially set up to take multiple exposures and published in a book *Shinorama* in 1985. In 1990, he ventured into using large format images in his *Tokyo Nude*.

Shirt While in the opera, Lola had a blouse "of milk" (Cavalleria Rusticana), the "chanteuse" of the "café chantant" was always urged to take off her camisole, in the most exciting unveilings (noone talked about strip-tease yet...). In any case, inevitably, it was a shirt or a blouse that was being discussed: that is, the article of clothing made of various types of cloth (a linen cambric or a silk cotton, from flannel to organdy, from madapollam to lace, from Dutch cloth to taffeta and batiste and so on) that once, long ago, women wore directly over their skin, beneath layers of clothing (one well known type of blouse was the one worn by Isabella d'Este, also known as Isabeau, the wife of Charles VI king of France, the ancestor of our "blouse"). Over time, the shirt "that dear friend that resolves all situations, strange, absurd, accomodating, lending itself to help us when the wardrobe betrays us" while having, at the same time, "many styles and cuts, running from the neck to the waist and even further down," worn inside or outside of the skirt or the trousers, loose or with a belt, with sleeves and necks that – alongside the motifs before or behin – determines its style. So important that it is used in a wide array of sayings (I'd give my shirt, born in a silk shirt, to gamble away one's shirt, to be left in shirtsleeves), or it has risen to the level of a symbol: in the nineteenth century, Red Shirts for Garibaldi's volunteers, in the twentieth century, light blue for the Italian nationalists after the First World War, black shirts for the followers of Fascism, brown shirts for the adherents of National Socialism; and in some languages, such as Italian, the word for "straitjacket" is shirt, i.e., *camicia di forza*. For that matter, in 1945 the linen blouse with very short sleeves with dark hems (the same shade as her pants) worn by Babe Paley, known at the time as Mrs. Stanley Mortimer – the world's best dressed woman – began a trend, and in September of 1946 these articles of apparel actually began a feminine "school." "Three Hundred Blouses at the Luxembourg," as the headlines of the time put it to describe the secretaries, interpreters, typists, stenographers, and taxi drivers from all over the world who had accompanied the delegates to the conference of Paris: the blouses worn by these young women were for the most part "men's shirts," worn with a tie. Years in which women's magazines suggested "make yourself a blouse" (with a pattern produced by the Marangoni pattern-making school), even though there are still shirt-makers and custom shirt tailors who are willing to make perfect ones, especially for men, with spare collars and double cuffs (with cuff links): classical shirts, in solid color or pinstripes for daytime, white (very rare the colored variants) for ceremonial or for evening wear: from models with the greatest level of opulence, with lace, ruffles, and jabots, to the more sober models, with little pleats and ribbings. Because we must remember that the shirt has "always" enjoyed a role of special importance in men's wardrobes: suffice it to recall how much fashion was influenced by "Robespierre" collars! Collars that in the twentieth century became soft, unlined, with long pointed tips (George Frazier, columnist of the Boston Globe, in an article on shirts claims that "the shape of the collar is the most important thing"), while its said that John Brooks once, while in England, noticed at a polo match that the players had their collars fastened down by buttons to keep the tips, while galloping, from slapping their faces. Brooks, after returning to New York, had the first shirt made of Oxford cloth with a "polo" collar, the now famous "button-down shirt." And it was in the United States that we first those flowered "Hawaiian shirts," which arrived in Europe with the first American tourists, who caused considerable numbers of ironic comments and indulgent smiles, even though the men of the United States like to wear oversized shirts with strips, check, plaids, which however exert a great influence on the women in the audience, to the point that Elizabeth Taylor used the style, with allure and seductivity, in *Cat On a Hot Tin Roof*. And it was precisely this type of shirt, a few inches longer, made of flannel or other comfortable cloths, became the "practical companion for the night," unisex, in one of those many revivals of fashions that recall paintings, illustrations, and films that recall bygone eras. And, speaking of films, it is not possible to overlook a number of scenes in which a youthful Lana Turner, followed by the far more "pneumatic" Jayne Mansfield and Jane Russell, imposed their look with their tight and partially unbuttoned shirts... And the magnificent Mexican shirts, and the Brazilian shirts, all flounces and furbelows, worn by Carmen Miranda (the older readers will certainly recall *That Night in Rio*), or films, in more recent times, with Brigitte Bardot and Jeanne Moreau in *Viva Maria!* A completely different style were, instead, the extremely simple shirts, almost always worn with classical pants or jeans, by the three symbols of style and elegance: Grace Kelly, Jacqueline Bouvier (Kennedy Onassis), and Audrey Hepburn, much like the shirts worn by another Hepburn, the great Katharine, who almost made it into her uniform. Years in which this item of clothing was created, and indicated, specifically for various occasions: that is, for the morning, the afternoon, the early evening, evening, for the city, country, mountains, beach, excursions, cruise ship, travel. Among the many variations on the theme, we can mention the "vareuse" (the name comes from the Breton word "varer"): a shirt made of rough canvas used by fishermen or, if made in a heavy cloth, and item of clothing worn in the army; and, in contrast, the little fronts made of lace, velvet, piquet, worn with cocktail outfits, and the many "tops" preceded by "body stockings." Shirts, or blouses, with square, round, or oval necklines, pointed, "American-style," polo-neck sweaters, capes, various stitches (like the cuffs), in white piquet (in the Crawford style) or from which long thin Modigliani neck emerge; besides there are also shirts with "glove" sleeves, adeherent, balloon sleeves, ham sleeves, puffy sleeves, long, short, and very short sleeves; with pleats, micropleats, macropleats, drapery, ruffs, jabots-simple, double, or triple; with flounces of crumpled lace; with interplays of buttons in various sizes and all sorts, on the front, the back, the sides; with "Lavalliere," or "Verdi" ribbons, and ribbons in velvet or stain, popular in white, but to be worn "according to the mood of the day, and in any case always coordinating the color with the color of the outfit." And in menswear, in the Fifties (Capri docet!) we see shirts with small white and red checks, to be worn without a tie, unbuttoned, with black linen trousers, and following those, the first pink shirts (a color that was previously considered to be only for women), which aroused just as much irony and smiles – and polemics! – as the "Hawaiian" shirts. In the meanwhile, women's shirtmakers went absolutely wild, seizing often with both hands (from every style), borrowing from the peoples of the Andes, the Magyards, the Africans and Tyroleans, even though the "lovely" white or black shirt still continued to represent the basic item, with trousers, skirts, and cocktail outfits, along with the unisex sporty shirt in light-blue denims, grey, if not – in the more "value-added" styles – with the names of major designers, in cotton or white linen with tiny gold buttons with "monograms." In 1947 it was written that "the blouse was meant to signify in a certain sense 'novelty,' while in fact it is nothing more than a continuous return of inspirations, styles, and outfits." In effect, we could also repeat this in first years of the third millennium: since we see, for the summer of 2003, alongside classic shirts with stripes or checks of every size, a number of men's shirts made of white cambric, sweater neck and shirtsleeve made for applied starched collar and doubled cuffs (which waiters used to use, for practical purposes, showing that they were always impeccable; or the mad pianist of the sitcom, whose shirts always used to "fly" in every direction); and for women, in the game of "dessus-dessous," an elegantly named game of upside down, here we have the *déshabillé* blouse in black chiffon nero, fragile lace, very soft, very light crêpe chiffon "like a cloud," a dust-colored muslin:

translucent, fluffy, sexy, in the tradition of the greatest femininity.

(*Maria Vittoria Alfonsi*)

Shirtology Clothing label. It is all about the "*esthéthique de la pornographie*," an underlying concept clearly articulated by its creators Jacky Rzenno and Marc Schils, who are inspired by the erotic iconography of Quaintance, Peter Berlin, and Ken Duncan. The two designers, who have a base in Paris, have an atypical style and, according to many, an extreme outlook on fashion. They use sexy transparencies, Turkish bikinis, veiled pants, and reinforced tops decorated with plastic feathers. Everything is worn by models with pumped up muscles, whom they select in the street or from visiting bodybuilding gyms, rather than following the traditional path of going to modeling agencies. The area around Rue Portefoin is in keeping with Shirtology's character and the entrance is presented like an ancient Egyptian museum.

(*Pierangelo Mastantuono*)

Shiseido Leading Japanese luxury cosmetics house. Founded in 1872 in Tokyo by the doctor and chemist Yushin Fukuhara, Shiseido's success depends on its deep integration of art and science. One such example was its creation in 1897 of Eudermine, an innovative face cream both in terms of its image and formula. A few years later, Fukuhara converted his pharmacy into an American-style drugstore and sent his son Shinzo to study at Columbia University. A chemist by training and an artist by vocation, in 1915, Shinzo took over the running of the company and decided to concentrate more on cosmetics than pharmaceutical products. He surrounded himself with artists who created the design department while he worked on the branding and logo for Shiseido – the famous camellia which became the emblem of the house. The leading line focuses on how to combat the effects of ageing skin; Shiseido has always given and continues to give particular attention to its research activities in this area. The Yokahama laboratories, which are among the most modern in the world, employ more than 1,000 dermatologists, biologists, and researchers, who develop avantgarde formulas and treatments every year. Remaining faithful to its roots, the house continues to value the artistic and cultural dimension of communication, and attaches great importance to the contributions to the company's image of artists and photographers of international fame. Today, the company has 9 production bases in Japan and 11 in the rest of the world, and covers markets in more than 50 countries.

❑ 2000, November. The Research into the Science of Life laboratory was set up.
❑ 2001. Shiseido set up 10 factories abroad: 3 in the Americas, 2 in France and 5 spread across Asia and Oceania.
❑ 2001-2002. The group's sales were largely based on cosmetics, which account for 76.3% of total sales.
❑ 2001. It introduced the highly successful innovation Fine Rice, which is a type of hypoallergenic rice used in all the major Japanese hospitals. Another important development was Shiseido's introduction of technologies in the chemical sector, in particular, chromatherapy and the creation of pigments containing photochromatic titanium dioxide which is widely used for paints in the car industry.
❑ 2002, October. The company announced consolidated profits of 90 million euros for the first half of 2002, which was 20% up on forecasts. The figure was particularly surprising when one considers that during the same period the previous year Shiseido had lost 15 million euros. The success was due partly to the launch of a new line of treatments and make-up, and partly to favorable conditions in the European and Middle Eastern markets.
❑ 2003, March. With Milan Municipality, the group backed the *Segnali d'arte, segnali di moda* (Signals in Art, Signals in Fashion) competition set up by *Grazia* which awards prizes to young designers during ready-to-wear week.
❑ 2005. Shiseido's facial product Bio-Performance Super Lifting Formula, created using innovative biotechnology, won the 2005 Skincare Prix d'Excellence.

Shoes The twentieth century was a period of great change in women's footwear. The unexpected changes in lifestyle with women's emancipation, the development of new technologies, and research into new materials all led to new shapes, new styles of heel, and different thicknesses of sole. During the first half of the 20th century, women's legs were increasingly revealed to sight, consequently giving greater emphasis to the shoe, of which the most extreme examples were the low-cut shoes and little buttoned boots worn for the Charleston. In Italy the 1940s were marked by a sense of economic self-sufficiency and the scarcity of leather, leading to substitutes such as cork and wooden wedges. The *dolce vita* bought with it not only flared skirts but also stiletto heels. In the 1950s, people started talking about specialist shoe designers like Ferragamo, René Caovilla, and Mario Valentino. Renato Guttuso's sketch for the brand Alexandria is from 1951. The 1960s combined ballet shoes (for example, Audrey Hepburn) with models inspired by Yves Saint Laurent's *haute couture*, Pierre Cardin's homage to space travel, and Capri sandals. Mary Quant and her miniskirts brought shoes decisively into the open. The political 1970s saw the return of the clunky clog, platform shoes, and saw the introduction of folkloric and ethnic influences.
The 1980s was the crowning decade for shoe designers, bringing with it huge expansion in ready-to-wear footwear, and the liberalisation of fashion away from a single style. It was a highly creative period of "cohabitation" when everything was juxtaposed with its opposite. The trend continued into the 1990s, the decade of fashion revivals, in which the 1940s, 1970s and ethnic fashion were all exploited again. At the end of the decade, snakeskin, jewelry, cut-glass decorations, the inclusion of lace and transparent material, and studded denim were all seen on high street shoes: the shoe had become embellished and worn like a dress, with the same intention of winning admiration.

Shon Julie (1966). Korean designer. As a child, she moved to New York and stayed there to study at Parsons School of Design. She continued her studies in Paris, where she moved in 1987, graduating the following year. Her first collaborations were with the New York designer Anne Kleine and the French style agency Pecler's. In 1988, she moved to Barcelona and started work with Purificación García (1988-1991) and David Valls (1991-1993). In 1993, she launched a ready-to-wear collection under her own name that is sold in the US and Japan as well as in Europe. These days, Julie Shon's collections are not only shown in Spain, alternating between the Gaudí runway in Barcelona and Cibeles in Madrid, but are also shown in leading European specialist salons. (*Mariacristina Righi*)

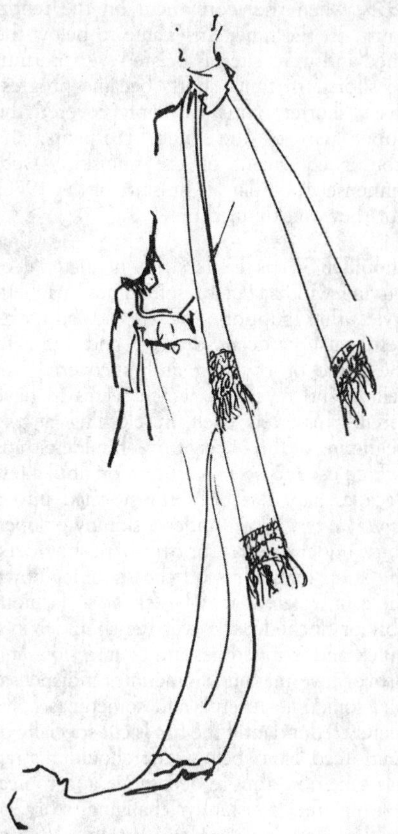

Drawing by Julie Shon.

Shorts Thigh-length women's pants that come in different fabrics and materials. They were first introduced as sportwear in the 1930s. The first woman to wear shorts was the American tennis player Alice Marble in

1933, when she wore them on the tennis court. At the time, they came to below the knee and were later associated with Bermuda shorts. In time, shorts became progressively shorter, until they only covered the upper part of the thigh. Hotpants, the trouser equivalent of the miniskirt, were immensely popular at the start of the 1970s but they quickly died out.

Shoulder Straps Little strips of material of varying widths, flat or sometimes spaghetti style, that support (or should support) petticoats, petticoat dresses, and bras. In the game of covering and uncovering, of veiling and revealing, which seems to have forcibly asserted itself in clothing at the beginning of the 21st century, shoulder straps (which used to be a secret fashion until a few decades ago) has been transformed into a *mode de vie*. Worn under a skimpy or open shirt, under a jacket, or over bare shoulders, the strap often slips off the shoulder down the arm, where it may be left to sit fashionably or hitched back over the shoulder in a quick and irritated gesture or in a slow and provocative manner. Sometimes indispensable, sometimes useful, and sometimes completely redundant if the bra is cut specially or reinforced from below, the shoulder strap has taken on a more decorative and topical role in the constantly changing story of fashion. (*Maria Vittoria Alfonso*)

Shrimpton Jean. English model. 1.75m tall and with green eyes, she was known by her nickname "Shrimp." In the 1960s she was considered the most beautiful woman in the world, and the one most in tune with the fashions and lifestyle of Swinging London. She married David Bailey, who photographed her for *Vogue*, thus launching her career. A second marriage to the actor Terence Stamp inspired the plot of Michelangelo Antonioni's film *Blow-Up* (1966). After having had a child, she withdrew from fashion and opened a hotel in Cornwall.

Shu Uemura (1928). Cosmetics brand and Japanese make-up artist. The name "shu" means excellence. Born in Tokyo, Shu Uemura started out in Hollywood in 1955. He was the official make-up artist for actors like Shirley McLaine, Edward G. Robinson, and Yves Montand. He returned to Japan and set up Japan Make Up Inc. in 1967 which introduced a series of highly original handcrafted make-up products to the market. In 1982, the company became Shu Uemura Cosmetics, selling aromatherapy-based treatments for the body and face, as well as all sorts of make-up accessories. Shu Uemura is a real pioneer of cosmetics in Japan, where until the 1960s make-up was only used on stage. He is considered an authority in the art of make-up and organized training for new recruits: around 10,000 make-up experts have been trained at his beauty college. For him, make-up should not be a form of disguise, but should bring out and make the most of what he calls "everyday beauty."

Sicons Italian clothing company. Founded in 1963, it no longer operates, but had its heyday in the mid-1980s. Its main base was in Valdagno (Vicenza). The factories in Valdagno, Treviso (leather clothing) and Gambellara (textile clothing) had the capacity to produce 500,000 garments a year and employed around 600 people. For a long time, they worked with Giorgio Armani. Alongside their own goods, they manufactured clothes for brands such as Emporio Armani, Trench Coat, Leather Coat, Virtus Palestre, Gucci, and Oliver "V."

Sieff Jean Loup (1933-2000). French photographer born to a Polish family. He studied photography (at the École de Vevey in Switzerland, which has recently dedicated a room to him) and also literature and journalism for a short time. He began his career as a reporter for *Elle* in 1955 and for Magnum for a two year period in 1958 and 1959, collaborating with *Réalités* and *Jardin des Modes*. He moved to New York and, from 1961 to 1966, was published in *Harper's Bazaar*, *Vogue, Queen, Twin, Look, Esquire, Match* and *Glamour*. In 1966 he returned to Paris and worked with *Nova, Femme*, and *Vogue France*. He never wanted to be known specifically as a fashion photographer – an activity which he gave up on in the 1970s to concentrate on research and the nude – to the extent that he claimed that "fashion photography does not exist." His subjects – the models as much as the clothes – were taken both in black-and-white and color with wide angle lenses that not only increased the depth of the field but served to introduce the external surroundings or elements of the internal setting, so that they are not seen as mere backdrops. The results were sometimes permeated by a strong erotic charge. Sieff surrounded his beautiful and mysterious women with unmade beds, mirrors, and veils, and lingered on the curves of their bodies, paying particular attention to their legs. He had many exhibitions in both France and abroad and published numerous books. Among the most famous are *Portraits de dames assises, de paysages tristes et de nus mollement las* (1982), *Vers les cieux d'or* (inspired by Guy de Maupassant's travel diary of Sicily) in 1984, the hotly debated and ironic *Hommage à 93 derrières choisis pour leur qualités plastiques, intellectuelles ou morales*, which comprised almost a hundred female bottoms, *Jeanloup Sieff: 40 Years of Photography* and *Faites come si je n'étais pas là* in 1999. (*Roberto Mutti*)

Sigerson Morrison American shoe label. Founded in 1991, when Kari Sigerson and Miranda Morrison realize that they are the only two adults enrolled in the design course for shoe designers at the Fashion Institute of Technology in New York. The London of the Sixties, where Miranda grew up, and motorcycle trips in Nebraska, which are part of Kari's past, are two of the chief influences that can be perceived in their collections. They are aimed at a woman who does not allow herself to be easily won over by passing fads. Their innovative style won them the CFDA prize for accessories in 1997. In 1996 they were among the pioneers of Nolita, a trendy Manhattan neighborhood, and in 2000 they inaugurated their first flagship store there. In 2002, they opened another one in Los Angeles and in 2003 a store in Tokyo. They were successful with their line of purses and small leather accessories, which accompanied their highly popular shoe collections. Among their best sellers were flip-flops with a low heel: thousands of pairs in a few days. In September of 2003 they present their line Belle, at a more accessible price, which won the Footwear News Award as the best new product of the year.

Sign of the Times London shop in Kensington, opened by Fiona Cartledge at the end of the 1980s. It sells the work of some of the most experimental and innovative designers around.

Silano Bill (1938). American photographer. He studies with Alexey Brodovitch, art director of *Harper's Bazaar*, and became a fashion photographer in the 1950s. Moving to Europe, he worked in France for *Marie Claire* and in England for the English edition of *Vogue*, capturing the changing world defined by the fashions of Mary Quant and the music of The Beatles and The Rolling Stones. In 1965, he returned to New York and began working again with *Harper's Bazaar*, mixing fashion shoots with portraits and still-lifes of accessories and jewelry. He also published in *Vogue*, *Vanity Fair*, *Tatler*, and *Woman's Own*.

Silfresh Antibacterial fiber used by the underwear companies Cotonella, Julipet, Garda, Argentovivo, Baci Rubati, Perofil, and Grigio Perla. Silfresh is not only resistant to bacteria, but can survive being washed many times and at very high temperatures.

Silk Natural fiber. An ancient Chinese proverb describes silk as "the material to wear to reach God." It has always been synonymous with nobility, elegance, and luxury. Its magnificence originates as the silk filament with which silkworms spin their cocoons. Sericulture began in China about 2600 BC, and even today the country accounts for two-thirds of the world's production of raw silk thread. Its history spans millennia and is interwoven with the history of the relationship between the East and West. The golden age of silk weaving in Europe was undoubtedly the 16th century: sumptuous damasks, brocades, and velvets were produced in Venice, Florence, and Lyons for courts throughout the world. Silk fabrics divide into four groups: cloth or taffeta, twill or diagonal, satin, and jacquard. The quality of the material depends on the name or fineness of thread and the grade of the twist. The type of fiber, on the other hand, determines its resistance: organzine, which is made from long twisted fibers is much more resistant than *bourrette*, which comes from silk waste. The most famous types of silk are shantung, characterized by knots that project out of the fabric; ottoman with a spooled effect; organzas; and all the silks that are printed either in part or all over, which are the speciality of many of the silk firms in Como. Silk production used to be a common industry in northern Lombardy, but it died out many years ago. As a result, the countryside looks different as the mulberry trees have disappeared.

(*Cristina Lucchini*)

Simmos Raf (1968). Belgian photographer. He publishes photographs of Fortuny in a unique style inspired by English boarding schools and 1970s cinema.

Simon (1973). Italian photographer. Having studied languages at school, she got a diploma from the Istituto Europeo di Design in Milan where she was taught by the photographer Edward Rozzo and Marriuccia Casadio, the art consultant of the Condé Nast Group. It was through Casadio that she got to do her first advertising campaign for CP Company Uomo in 1996. She is a multifaceted creator whose clients include Sixty, Baci Rubati, Diesel, Sony, Universal, Mescal, and Virgin. Her work has been published in *i-D*, *Mix Mag*, *D-La Repubblica delle Donne*, *Marie Claire*, *Gulliver*, *Surface*, *Carnet*, *Stile*, and *Caffelatte*. She also photographs the human figure and the urban landscape in color – as seen published in *Zoom* and *Immagini FOTOpratica* – in a style that is typically immediate, linear and quintessential.

Simon Taryn (1970). American photographer who graduates from Brown University in Providence and enters the photographic world, publishing for *The New York Times Magazine*, *Visionaire*, *Harper's Bazaar*, *Vogue France*, and *Vanity Fair*. In 2001 he was awarded a study bursary by the Guggenheim Foundation. He lives in New York.

Simone Pérèl Women's underwear firm that takes its name from its founder, who in 1948, had a small shop selling corsets in Paris and just 8 years later built two factories in France and one in Tunisia. It has 500 employees. Since 1985, the group has been run by the second generation: Philippe Grodner and Catherine Pérèl. They have three lines of products.

Simonetta Fashion house founded in 1946 at 5 Via Gregoriana in Rome by Simonetta Colonna Cesarò (1922). She married Gaio Visconti di Modrone by whom she had a daughter named Verde. Her first collection comprised 14 designs made from the only fabrics that were available immediately after the war: dishcloths, gardening aprons, butlers' uniforms, laces, and ribbons. In 1947 *Vogue America* sent a journalist and photographer to Italy to do a feature on the most beautiful women in Rome. This was when Simonetta was discovered by *Vogue* which devoted 2 pages to her. The big American department stores Bergdorf Goodman and Marshall Fields were the first to buy her designs. Simonetta was the first *haute couture* Italian fashion house to be invited to New York by Bergdorf Goodman to take part in celebrating their fiftieth birthday in November 1951. Simonetta dressed Doris Duke, Clare Booth Luce, Norma Shearer, Dorothy McGuire, Zsa Zsa Gabor, Lauren Bacall, Dinah Shore, Merle Oberon, Chid Charisse, the Duchess of Windsor, Marlene Dietrich, and Jacqueline Kennedy. She also won a number of prizes, including the Davidson Parkson Award from R.H. Macy & Company, the Philadelphia Fashion Group Award, and Filene's Dressing Talent Award. She was also a member of the New York Dress Institute's Hall of Fame. Her second marriage was to Alberto Fabiani, also a couturier, and together they had a son named Bardo, who is now a famous and respected photographer. Fabiani and Simonetta kept their two brands quite separate, but decided – on the back of successes at Florence's Italian *haute couture* seasons and on the advice of Farchild – to leave Rome in 1962 and move to Paris. They wanted to be the pioneers of an international concept of fashion, but were ahead of their time. Fabiani returned to Rome in 1964 and Simonetta remained in Paris until 1972 when she went to India to do philanthropic work. She now spends her time between Rome and Paris. Her designs are on display in the Galleria del Costume in the Pitti Palace in Florence, the Victoria and Albert Museum in London, the Musée Galliera in Paris, the Mode Museum Munchen, the Kunstgewerbe Museum in Berlin, the Mode

Simonetta, lace ball-gown presented at the first Italian fashion show, 12 February 1951, in the Florentine house of Giovanni Battista Giorgini (Giovanni Battista Giorgini Archive).

Museum in Cologne, the Metropolitan Museum in New York, and the Brooklyn Museum of Fine Arts also in New York.

Simonetta Italian brand and firm that makes children's clothes. In 1950, Maria Bianca Mazzarini Stronati decided to open a small dressmaking shop in Jesi catering to babies and small children. With the help of her three children, Roberto, Simonetta, and Valeria, the business grew and in 1981 became an industrial enterprise. Much attention is spent on researching materials and the details. Today, with the involvement of the third generation, Simonetta has become a leading firm in the field of high-quality baby clothes. The continued emphasis on new ideas and new technologies is the driving force behind the company's success. It produces nearly 500,000 garments a year that are sold in boutiques and department stores in 27 countries. The main factory, in Jesi, has nearly 100 employees and an entourage of a further 200 people. As well as the first line, the firm has branched out with Simonetta jeans, Simonetta tiny, and Simonetta shoes, and is also licensed to produce Cavalli Angels, Cavalli Devils, and Cavalli Junior, designed by Roberto Cavalli.

(*Sara Tieni*)

Simonetta Rina (1895-1986). Journalist and writer. Born in Milan, she followed fashion for a long time without ever slipping into the trap of adopting fashion jargon, and always maintaining a critical distance. She worked with Italian State television on radio reviews and entertainment programs. Her son Umberto is one of the most interesting writers of the generation that came to light in the 1950s and 1960s.

Simons Raf (1968). Belgian designer who grew up on the Belgian-Dutch border and studied industrial design in Genk. Walter Van Beirendorck taught him the basics of the trade, and his meeting with Linda Loppa, director of the Royal Académie des Arts, changed his life. With Linda's father, who is a well-known dressmaker in Belgium, he produced his first signed collection.

❑ 2003, January. With Francesco Bonami, Simons curated the exhibition *Il Quarto Sesso* (The Fourth Sex) about the excesses of adolescence. It was presented as part of the Pitti Immagine Discovery programme.
❑ 2005, June. Simons celebrated ten years in business with a runway event, the video installation *Repeat* and the monograph *Raf Simons Redux* at the 68th Pitti Immagine Uomo in Florence.
❑ 2005, June. The designer presents his new second line, Raf by Raf Simons. With this collection, the designer returns to the distinctive traits of his style in a new and modern key. A sort of basic at lower prices than his first line.
❑ 2005, July. Simons was appointed creative director of Jil Sander and planned to make his debut in January 2006 with his first menswear collection. He took over from Jil Sander after the umpteenth falling out between the designer and the Prada Group, who own the company.

Simpson Adele (1903-1995). A New York designer who was one of the first to design clothes for the working woman. She knew how to "take cotton out of the kitchen," to quote a 1940s expression, using the fabric for her clothes. Her garments are designed and made with wearability and functionality in mind, so that you can take something off to make the garment more suitable for either the day or evening, for work, for cocktails or for a society event. Having studied at the Pratt Institute of Design in Brooklyn she worked for Ben Gershel (1923-26) and then moved to Mary Lee Fashions where she signed a collection. In 1949 she set up her own company, Adele Simpson Inc. Her clothes are displayed in many museums, including the Metropolitan Museum of New York. Besides Margot Fonteyn, who was one of the first to appreciate her, her most devoted clients included the wives of four American presidents: Eisenhower, Johnson, Nixon, and Carter.

Sims David (1966). English photographer. He got into fashion photography in 1990 working as the assistant to Enrique Badulescu and Norman Weston. Three years later he produced his first advertising campaign for Calvin Klein Jeans and worked with the designer Melanine Ward and the model Kate Moss, doing features and covers for

Harper's Bazaar, *W Magazine*, *The Face*, *Arena*, *i-D*, *Vogue Uomo*, and *Dazed and Confused*. In 1994 he won a prize as the best young fashion photographer. He did campaigns for Calvin Klein, Gap, Prada, Yamamoto, Levi's, Jil Sander, Hugo Boss, and Louis Vuitton. His style aims to reproduce reality, either by using natural light or by capturing his models in unconventional poses.

Simultaneous Total look ready-to-wear fashion brand for men and women. It is produced by Carma from Carpi. To begin with, at the end of the 1980s, the company put its name to a knitwear collection designed in minimalist style by Kristopher Millar and Lois Swandele. The brand has its own shop in Milan.

❑ 2002. Having been bought in 1999 by Multimoda Network, the brand has enjoyed a considerable increase in sales.

Sinclair Company producing leather and sheepskin garments. Stationed near Marostica (Vicenza) where its factories are based, it was founded in 1978. It was set up as a family business, which has made considerable advances in the market. Its goods are typically Italian, both in terms of the care with which the materials are chosen and the production processes, which combine artisan skills with modern technologies. The company sells to Europe, Canada, USA, Russia, South America, and the Far East.

Sinclair Susanna (1963). Italian photographer. With a Roman father and Scottish mother, she has lived for a long time in England, Argentina, and the US, and now divides her time between Milan and London. She works as a fashion reporter and dedicates a lot of time to her own personal research which led her to show at *Whatever Love Means* in Milan and London in 2002. The following year she took part in *Fashion Show*, a photographic performance involving 12 self-timer images, with her wearing a different dress by the designer Patrizia Brenner in each one, suggesting that the female body is both a victim and hostage to fashion.

Sindacato Italiano Alta Moda It is founded in 1953 in opposition to Bista Giorgini's Florentine fashion shows by the dissenting Roman faction: Fabiani, Simonetta, Lola Giovanelli, Schuberth, the Fontana sisters, Ferdinandi, Mingolini-Heim, and Garnet. The union's constitution forbade the members from taking part in the shows at the Sala Bianca in the Pitti Palace and laid down that they should present their own collections, each in their own studio, two days before the shows took place in Florence. It was an outright declaration of war. Rome raised the flag, asserting its right to do things on its own and the dressmakers justified this decision by complaining about the cost of traveling to Florence.
In reality, the schism arose because they were annoyed at the promiscuity of the runway, which mixed everything together (*haute couture*, boutique wear and ready-to-wear), and at being limited to showing only 18 dresses over the three days of the Pitti Palace shows. Simonetta Visconti, who with Fabiani was one of the first to walk out, recounts, "One day, we told ourselves that Rome was just as good as Florence and that every place had the right to its own exclusive revolution. Individualism is a typically Italian weakness." The press sided with Florence. Even the journalist Irene Brin, despite being Roman and friends with a number of the dissenting faction, waved the Florentine flag: "We are deeply loyal to Giorgini's idea, in terms of the unity it creates, the time it saves and the choice of work. If we have to balance this with something for Rome, it is as a consolation: we can offer lots of sales, a lot of praise and lots of promises. But if we have to prepare a future, we will have to avoid the many errors that have been made and side, once again, with Giorgini." Drop by drop, the future led instead to other diasporas.

Sing Gurvinder (1975). Designer of Indian origin who works in London. He studied at Central St Martin's College. He specialises in embroidery and, as such, collaborates on collections for Alexander McQueen, Julien McDonald, and Christian Lacroix. In 1999, he set up his own label Guvinda. In February 2000 he showed on the London Fashion Week runway.

Sinibaldi Bennati Marina (1958). Jeweler born in Modena. Passionate about art and painting (she studied fine art), she started out by making unique pieces for fashion shows. Next, she made clothes that she herself hand paints. She has won herself space in boutiques all over the world, but is still closely tied to the true artisan dimension of her work.

Sinibaldi Debora (1956). Florentine by birth and Milanese by adoption, she is the daughter of a couple of hippy artists (her father is devoted to painting and restoration, her mother to wrought iron). She grew up in an atmosphere of great openness, turmoil, and stimuli. She is a traveler and has always moved between the US and Europe. After the Accademia di Belle Arti in Florence, she moved to New York and became a knitwear designer. Having returned to Italy, she joined Gianfranco Ferré's design team and collaborated with him for many years. Her next step was Celine (in 1993) which allows her to refine and develop her creative talents. During the same period, Debora Sinibaldi experimented in the field of design and, with a friend, created a new collection of knitwear and luxury accessories for the home, NJAL. In the meantime, Marco Calcinai joined the company, starting off by looking after its management. At the start of 2000, Debora Sinaldi designed a collection of knitwear under her own name. The strong teamwork with Marco Calcinai created Debora Sinibaldi Srl, which is a completely self-financing company. Currently, the designer is responsible for all of Celine's knitwear and works on her deboraSinaldi line, a collection of clothing and accessories sold in international boutiques and department stores.

Siniscalchi Vittorio (1926) Milanese shirtmaker. He discovered his passion in life very early on when he studied at a cutting school. After his first shop, which he opened in Milan in Via Cerva in 1945, he moved to Via Santo Spirito, then Via Montenapoleone, and, from 1975 to 1989, to Via del Gesù. He has made shirts for Luchino Visconti, Paolo Stoppa, Moratti, Piero Pinto, Beppe Modenese, and Cesare Romiti. He kept a personal paper pattern for every client. His particular way of making the shirts involved a first fabric pattern, which after various fittings and alterations, served as a prototype for the true shirts that were made in 650 varieties from pre-washed fabrics. The house believes in: sleeves pressed by hand, darts in the shoulders, internal stitching, finishes and buttonholes by hand, and open necks. His son Alessandro joined him in running the new shop in Via Carlo Porta in 1989.

(*Marilea Somaré*)

SINV A holding company set up on 1 January 2000. It controls the clothing company Sportswear International SpA in Carrè (Vicenza), which is a leader in designer casual wear, producing and distributing Moschino Jeans, Krizia Jeans, and Byblos Blue worldwide. Sportswear International was founded when Ambrogio Dalla Rovere met Adriano and Rossella Goldschmied in 1975. Daily Blue was their first line of jeans, aimed at the middle to high end of the market alongside competitors like Fiorucci, Jesus Jeans, and Americanino. Next came lines that also targeted the male market with brands called Daily Man and Freezer. Differences between the founders led to the Goldschmieds leaving the business and a complete restructuring of the company. 1985 was the turnaround year. The company signed a licensing agreement with Krizia to produce and distribute its Krizia Jeans line worldwide. The company changed its strategic direction. Its goal was no longer to create its own lines of jeans, but to concentrate on building long-term collaborations with prestigious and emerging labels, which would be able to contribute positively to the success and development of Sportswear International. The idea of a network forms the basis of its operational philosophy and is the link that joins the fashion designer's creativity to the market. After Krizia, other important collaborations were set up between 1985 and 1994, including one with Byblos that led to the creation of Byblos Blu. In 1994, another licensing agreement was signed for the production and international distribution of Moschino Jeans. SINV became a first-rate player in the field of brand licenses and continued to expand commercially to the extent that today it has a presence in 60 countries. In 2000, the newly established SINV Holding made two purchases: it bought 30% of Moschino (a company made up of Aeffe at the time of the purchase of Moon Shadow, who hold the trademark) and 100% of Sartorie Riunite, headed by Victor Vittoria. Alongside Sportswear International, the companies that make up SINV are: Daka, a company buying raw materials; Geo, providing production and logistic services; and Modex, a modeling and prototype business. The growth of the Veneto holding company is amazing: 250 billion lire of sales in 2000 grew to 273 in 2002 (141 million euros). Their recipe for success? "It requires an ever tighter rapport between the manufacturer, which is us, and the fashion house and 3,000 points of sale that are the clients on the other." Those who claimed that the idea of licensing was dead are keeping very quiet. SINV has licenses to make Krizia Jeans, Voyage, See by Chloé, Jean Paul Gaultier jeans, as well as those owned by Victor Vittoria and Moschino Jeans. In 2003, SINV Terminal was opened in Milan: it is a 5,000 square-meter area that houses all of the showrooms. Expansion of production facilities has allowed the three million garments made in 2002 to rise to five million in 2004. The company has two-fold aims for the future, most importantly, to buy minority shares in the houses. Ambrogio Dalla Rovere says: "The aim is for proper full licenses to account for 50% of our sales and to get the other half from licenses in brands in which we only have a minority share."

(Dario Golizia)

Sisley Italian brand of casual clothing that today is part of the Benetton Group. In the 1960s and 1970s, at the height of the jeans boom, the brand was highly successful and dozens of shops opened throughout Italy. However, with the increase in competition and changes in fashion, they lacked the financial resources to keep ahead in the market. These resources have since been provided by Benetton.

❑ 2003. Production of a new collection of Sisley watches was entrusted to the Sector Group.
❑ 2003, May. The expansion of Benetton and Sisley continued in the main cities in Russia, with plans to open more than a hundred shops before the end of 2004.
❑ 2004, June. With the United Color of Benetton jewelry and Sisley jewelry brands, the group entered the jewelry sector. The Gruppo Songa looks after manufacturing and distribution. However, both lines are distributed in Italy by Mabina srl.

Sistema Moda This is the name of the courses relating to the fashion business set up by the Scuola Direzione Aziendale of Bocconi University in Milan. In 1991, a group of experts offered companies throughout the fashion sector (textiles, clothing, shoes, leather goods, jewelry) the possibility to develop their own human resources through customized courses and workshops held in the companies themselves. The teaching method mixed traditional lectures with a special system called the "management model" which integrates training and research. The courses were mainly directed at top level managers.

Sisto Maddalena (1951-2000). Designer and illustrator. Her sketches included all types of women. She had a particular style: an intelligent and poignant irony and an eye for capturing the essence of things, be it a dress, a movement, a physical look, or a lifelong habit. She could be compared to Brunetta Mateldi in terms of her talent, her ability to create illustrative harmony, and the grace of her palette. She worked for *Glamour*, *Elle Décor*, *Marie Claire*, *Elle Germany* and *Sette*, illustrating Lina Sotis's column. Lina has written about her: "She was the perfect example of professional flexibility. She was always there, but she never weighed you down. Maddalena was so tiny and light that she seemed like one of her women, as if she had just walked off the page. She belonged to that group of women who are the most elegant and least showy, charming you with their grace." She did campaigns for Fiat, Peter Stuyvesant, Bulgari, Fiorucci, Coin, Absolut Vodka, and Lavazza. Her exhibitions include: *139 Signorine*, Studio Grazia Fava, Milan, 1984; *Un tè alla moda* (A Fashionable Tea), Galleria Lu Austoni, Milan, 1985; *Anomalie* (Anomalies), Palazzo Cuttica, Alessandria, 1987; *Maddalenas italianische Kunst*, Galleria Grosse Bleichen, Hamburg, 1998; *Maddalena Sisto – 70 signorine di fine millennio – Addowaii* (70 Ladies from the End of the Millennium), Villa Pignatelli, Naples, 2001;

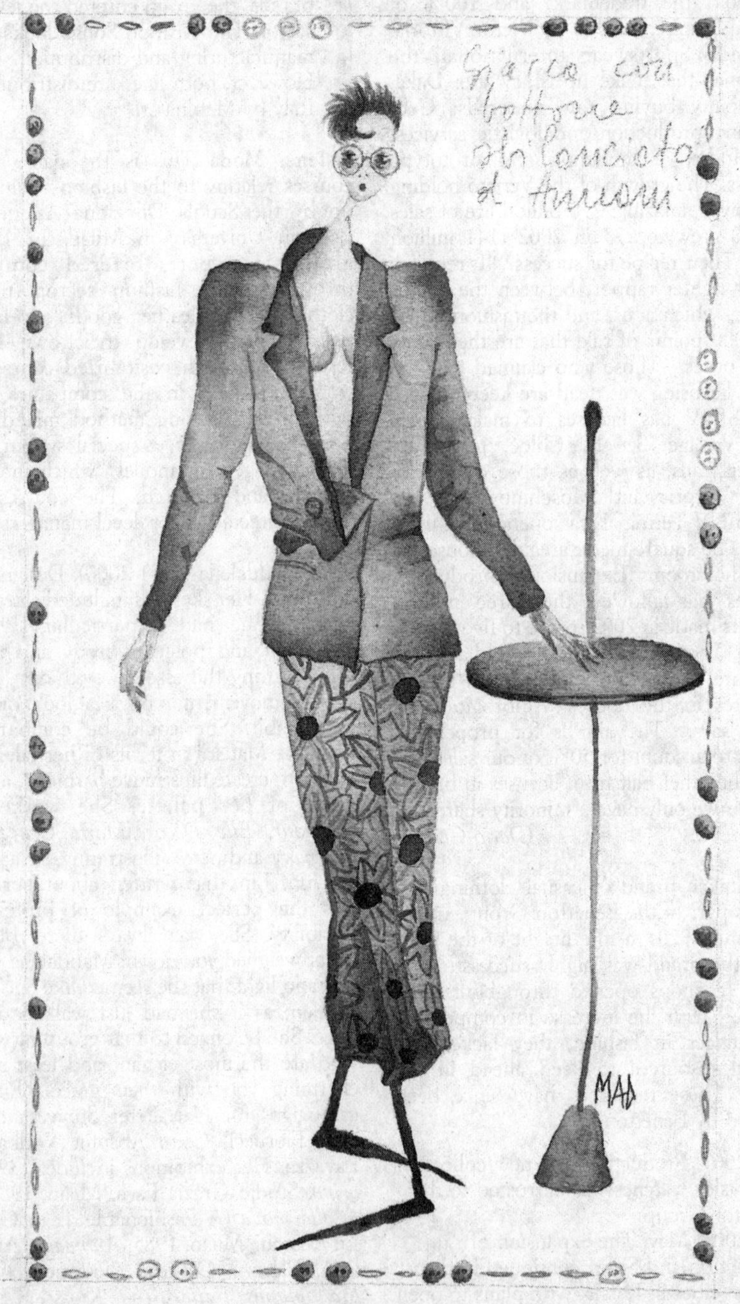

Giorgio Armani jacket, as seen by Maddalena Sisto.

Drawing by Maddalena Sisto.

and *Il mondo di Mad-Maddalena Sisto torna ad Alessandria* (The World of Mad-Maddalena Sisto Returns to Alessandria), Galleria di Palazzo Guasco, Alessandria, 2002. In *Il Bloc Notes di Mad*, the catalogue of the exhibition that took place in Lucca from 14 October to 12 November 2000, she presented her vision of the fashion world through 69 illustrations.

(*Valeria Vantaggi*)

❑ 2004, February. *Il mondo di Mad* was shown at the Milan Triennale. Fashion, design, and costume were combined in one exhibition, which not only represented some of her signed drawings, but also a sort of voyage, through women's fashion, over the last thirty years. Maddalena Sisto had an incisive and distinct outlook; her work revealed an uncontainable desire to capture and describe the present.

Sitborn Martine (1951). French designer. English music from the 1960s and 1970s has always provided excellent background music for her fashion shows. Born in Casablanca, she arrived in Paris aged 10. She is known for her fluid masculine/feminine style and perfect cuts. After graduating from the Studio Berçot, she worked with various American, Asian, Italian, and French ready-to-wear firms, one of which was a lengthy relationship with the Maison Chloé for whom she designed nine collections. Her own label, launched in 1985, has benefited from the invaluable support of Marc Ascoli in terms of artistic direction and from famous photographers such as Vallhonrat and Knight for its images.

Skarland Julie (1960). Scandinavian designer who lives and works in Paris. She produced her first collection in 1991. At first she openly declared her attachment to her Scandinavian roots and cultural heritage, with a line that evoked northern forests, snow-covered landscapes, fairies, witches, and tales from the North. In the years that followed, her sources of inspiration have been more varied, as a result of her extensive travels throughout the world: geishas and oriental empresses in Summer 1995 gave way, in Fall-Winter of the same year, to the shiny waterproofs worn in the foggy ports of northern France. 1996 marked her encounter with Native Americans; then came the lights and colors of the desert inspired by a trip to Morocco and the Egyptian pyramids. Next she returned to Norway and launched a new material, Twool, in Paris. Her next collection was a homage to St Moritz and winter sports. A "rising" brand, her designs are now sold in small, elitist Paris shops such as Absinthe in Rue Rousseau, near Les Halles.

❑ 1996. Le Musée de la Mode in Paris welcomed her as part of the *Japonisme et Mode* exhibition.
❑ 1998, March. Some of her creations officially entered the permanent collection of the Musée de la Mode et du Textile in Paris.
❑ 1999, April. She exhibited in Cologne at *New Scandinavia: aktualles design aus dem Norden.*
❑ 2001, January. She showed in *Jouer la lumière* near the Musée de la Mode et du Textile in the Louvre.

Skinhead Youth movement characterized by a high level of aggression: shaven heads, bomber jackets decorated with images of skullsand threatening writing, and big boots often reinforced with steel toe caps. The movement originated as a reaction to the middle-class hippy movement in England in the mid-1970s. Socially, its reference point is the working classes in industrial cities, but it took only a few years for the political extreme right in England to exploit thousands of young people whose only point of social and cultural reference is the skinhead movement. The phenomenon spread throughout Europe, including Eastern Europe. In Germany, skinheads have been completely taken over by the neo-Nazis. In other countries, Italy among them, odd groups of skinheads remain who refuse to associate with the far right and adhere instead to the original cultural and social references of the movement. In some cases, they adopt the stylistic urgency of the original movement, especially in music, which was that of a counter-culture and had nothing to do with the right, with, for example, black Jamaican music or English ska. (*Antonio Dipollina*)

Skinny rib It was a term used in the 1960s, when little tight-fitting sweaters with narrow ribs were all the rage. They came back into fashion in the 1990s when the look was minimal.

Skrebneski Victor (1929). Polish photographer. Born of a Russian mother and a Polish father, the family moved to the US when Victor was 7. He studied photography at the Art Institute of Chicago and then at the Moholy-Nagy Institute of Design. In 1952, he opens a studio in Chicago and from 1963 began working for Estée Lauder. He also did photographic campaigns for Valentino and Nikos, for *Vogue Italia*, *Town & Country* and *Interview*. Through photography, he continually explored images of the human body, creating elegant and provocative nude compositions that have a surrealist influence.

> ❑ 1999, September. *Skrebneski: The First Fifty Years* was published by Edition Stemmle on the occasion of a retrospective of his work at the Museum of Contemporary Photography in Chicago. The book recounted the first fifty years of his career in the world of beauty and fashion. His work can be seen in the permanent collections of the Museum of Contemporary Photography in Chicago, the Los Angeles County Museum of Art, and the Museum of Modern Art in New York.

Slacks In the world of fashion, slacks have becomes synonymous with wide pants, particularly when cut for women. They are an ultra classic model that were worn as early as the 1920s.

Sleeve In 1800 it was observed that "fashion can be particularly recognized by its sleeves." In the mid-twentieth century, it was reiterated that "the clothing revolution starts with sleeves." This "part of male and female garments that covers the arm," long, short, three-quarter length, fitted, full, raglan, kimono, bell-shaped, round, puffed, ruffled – whose "insertion" has always represented a challenge and a delight for tailors – has, without doubt, played a very important role in the history of clothing. Its most ungenerous reincarnation was the half-length variety, or rather the type of cloth sleeve that covered only the upper arm. The sleeve has inspired popular sayings such as "roll up your sleeves" or "an ace up your sleeve." It went through particularly glorious periods in previous centuries, especially in male fashions. For example, consider the opulence, luxury, and originality of the sleeves of the various Henri and Louis (kings and emperors) to confirm its importance. However, with the end of the Napoleonic empire, men's fashions – following the more sober and elegant English style and later adopting the straight cut jacket – became simpler. In fact, there have been very few "revolutions" or variations in coat and jacket sleeves (mostly round or raglan) during the twentieth century, with the exception of a few evening shirts, with simple or double cuffs, sometimes pleated or with lace, another example of returning fashions. In women's fashions, sleeves have been made of fabric or fur, decorated with lace, embroidery, stones, or pearls, and enjoyed periods of particular prominence, for example when they were worn in the style of the Amadis, the Venetians, Louis XIII, nuns, priests, sailors, Turks, Bedouins, Persians, gardeners or shepherdess style (the "petite bergère"), in the Sévigné and Du Barry style, puff sleeves or ruffled sleeves, as seen in the portraits of girls and women at the coronation of Napoleon or the Empress Eugènie with her ladies-in-waiting, or women painted by Boldini. And they resurfaced in some collections, especially *haute couture* ones, in evening clothes or garments for all occasions, from the start of the twentieth century until today. At the end of the 1940s, for example, sleeves were long and close-fitting, with a high, turned back, double cuff or, "handkerchief" sleeves, particularly at the elbow, for Christian Dior; bell-shaped to the elbow, over long sleeves edged with fur for Balmain; with high lace cuffs for Fath; round and "falling" with a small double cuff for Rochas; draped from the shoulders and completed with small cuffs embroidered with stones for Grés; very full, puffed, with a ruffled cuff for Schiaparelli; and very large, cloak sleeves, cut in a single piece together with the bodice for the great Balenciaga. Subsequent generations of designers created sleeves that were attached down to the waistline, three-quarter length with incrustations of lace or velvet, with small buttons up to the elbow, with little cuffs with triple bands of ruffled lace or embroidered using the English stitch. These were sleeves that became more and more essential, apart from when they were omitted altogether or substituted by little shoulder straps, even when the arms revealed beneath were not always suitable.

(*Maria Vittoria Alfonsi*)

Slimane Hedi (1968). Lebanese designer who lives and works in Paris. He was thrust into the limelight when he took on the task of designing the Yves Saint Laurent Rive Gauche Homme line in 1996, which was greeted with immediate success. He has never studied fashion. Having attended courses in art history at the École du Louvre, José Levy employed him as artistic director in 1990. He then moved to Jean-Jacques Picart where he spent three years working as an assistant while attending the Hipokhagne, one of the highest level university faculties in the French system, preparing for admission to political sciences. He finally joined YSL at the invitation of his mentor Pierre Bergé. When the Gucci Group bought the YSL label, Slimane was paid to launch the men's Black Tie collection under his own name. "He is so talented that he deserves his own brand. I am a great admirer of his," said Tom Ford, artistic director of Gucci. However, in July 2000 Slimane chose to work for LVMH as artistic director of the men's Dior collections. In September 2001, the monthly American magazine *GQ* heralded him as the man of the year in the category of emerging talent. Stylistically, he belongs to the new wave of young couturiers who give new life to tailoring by employing contemporary forms and lines. Elements of street style are mixed with tailoring alchemy. Thin jackets with thin belts that knot around the waist, Slimline motorcycling outfits like a streak of black ink, and handmade stretch tulle shirts are examples of an androgynous and sexy male fashion which often uses materials that are typically feminine. At Pitti Immagine Uomo in June 2002, Slimane created a large installation called *Intermission* at the Stazione Leopolda in Florence: 34 6-meter tall monoliths provided a new interpretation of the Hall of Mirrors in Versailles and 400 neon lights in metallic structures recreated the mazes in the gardens. The palace's chandeliers were replaced by simple ventilators that gave off a modulated sound. There were no clothes, but instead it represented the designer's interpretation of Frenchness. The event was curated by Francesco Bonami, the co-ordinator of artistic projects for the Pitti event, and Jérôme Sans, director of the Palais de Tokyo in Paris.

(*Antonio Mancinelli*)

❑ 2003. The designer's second photographic book, entitled *Berlin*, was published by 7L/Steidl.

❑ 2004. Slimane launched the first male eau de Cologne since 1947 for Dior Homme. There are three essences: eau noir, cologne blanche, and bois d'argent, the result of three years in the studio that involved returning to the rules of the great men's perfumeries and the tradition of Avenue Montaigne. In June, *stage*, Slimane's third photographic book, was published by 7L/Steidl with music and pop groups as its leitmotifs. In September, he presented a collection of furniture for Comme des Garçon's new shop Dover Street Market in London. The project was called F System.

❑ 2005, July. His book "London, birth of a cult" came out, about the new music scene in Great Britain and America.

Slit Look One of the fashions from the early 1970s. Hot pants or miniskirts were worn with very high boots under open maxi skirts or under unbuttoned full-length coats.

Sloane Ranger In 1979, the magazine *Harpers & Queen* coined the term to define its targeted readers: well-to-do, upper middle-class or even aristocrats that chose to live in the area around Sloane Street and Sloane Square at the start of the Kings Road in London. The female Sloane Ranger – wearing a Laura Ashley blouse, a pleated skirt, flat shoes and a pearl necklace – was epitomized by Lady Diana Spencer, who later married Charles, Prince of Wales. The men opt for tweed blazers, Shetland pullovers, green Wellington boots, and the ubiquitous Husky. Who was their icon? The young Prince Andrew before he married Fergie. The Sloane Rangers represented the respectable – but not necessarily less aggressive – alternative to London's punk rockers, who were unashamedly ugly, dirty, and bad. Sloanes, by contrast, were young, rich, and sensible, and typically worked as landscape architects, financial brokers, lawyers, or in PR. Could they make a comeback? Yes, would seem to be the answer according to London's *Daily Telegraph*, the most right-wing of the English broadsheets. At the most recent Countryside Alliance march in London (Sloane Rangers like the countryside), there were whole armies of young people wearing Gucci moccasins who had never seen a clod of earth in their life.

(*Antonio Mancinelli*)

Sloggi German brand of underwear. It is a leader in the women's lingerie market. Its track record reads as follows: half a billion items sold in Europe between 1979, when it was set up, and 1997, of which 50 millions were sold during the final year of that period. Right from the beginning, it used a new material: cotton with a lycra base.

Sloppy Joe Baggy woolen sweater that was very fashionable in the 1940s and 1950s. In the period between the end of World War II and the birth of the New Look, as a controversial response to excessive elegance and the luxury of *haute couture*, two versions of this wide and enormously long sweater were worn: as a round or V-neck. An informal garment, its extreme measurements and softness provided a good contrast with the extremely tight-fitting pants with which it was worn.

Slouch hat Hat with a little soft brim launched by Greta Garbo in the 1930s. A crocheted version came back into fashion in the 1970s and at the start of the 1990s it was worn as a hip hop accessory. It is often made of velvet and highly eccentric in style.

Small Geoffrey B. (1960). American designer. He is a pioneer of avantgarde creators in the US. He began his career in 1979 in Boston in his parents' loft with a Singer sewing machine. He twice (1979 and 1980) won the Oscar for fashion creator of the future, with Calvin Klein and the journalist Bernardine Morris on the jury. In 1994 he became the third American to be signed up as part of the official calendar of the French Chambre de la Mode. In 1998, he also signed an eyewear collection. His headquarters is in Boston at 115 Kingstone Street. His total annual sales are valued at $2.5 million. His clothes are distributed in 11 countries in the Far East, Europe, and America. With an eye on prices and street fashion, he aims to be the leading brand for young people in the 21st century.

(*Fulvio Bertasso*)

Smalto Francesco (1927). Italian dressmaker. He worked in Paris where, at the beginning of the 1980s, he opened his own studio in Rue La Boétie, putting to good use the skills he learnt as a boy in Italy and then working at Cristiani and Camps.

Smith Graham (1938). English milliner. He started out in 1967, having studied at the Royal College of Art, working for Lanvin in Paris. Despite the decline in popularity of women's hats (though not so much in England), they are still considered an essential accessory for emphasizing one's silhouette and height. He has used his creative imagination to design hats for both Princess Diana and the Duchess of York (he claims that the English royal family are the salvation of the milliner's profession). He is considered a master of restraint and elegance.

Smith Paul (1946). English tailor and designer. The first item that he sold was a Union Jack handkerchief for the breast pocket. Today, his shops sell all sorts of things, from robots to ties. However, he has always been anti-conventional. He has transformed tailoring into an explosion of colors, inventiveness, and fashionable trends mixed with the most traditional qualities of material. He still has the spirit of a twenty-something, cutting-edge designer, which is why he continues to ride the crest of the wave. His clothes are like his personality: amusing and serious at the same time, eccentric but wearable. He opened a multi-brand shop in Nottingham in 1970, and nine years later opened his first proper shop, revolutionising the concept of selling space, which from then on was no longer just the space used for the display of goods, but a meeting point for anyone interested in style. In 1994 he launched a womenswear line that mirrored the cuts and stylistic concept of his menswear. His first menswear fashion show was in 1976 in Paris. From that point on the label has grown from strength to strength. Today the British designer has about 7 large own-brand stores in Great Britain, 50 or so in the Far East, 1 in New York and 1 in Paris. He has also been asked to be a dress consultant to the Prime Minister Tony Blair.

(*Marta Citacov*)

❑ 2001, February. In the Queen's birthday honors list, Paul Smith was recognized for his contribution to British fashions.

❑ 2001, November. *You can find inspiration in everything (but if you can't, look again!)* went on sale. It is neither a fashion monograph, nor a catalogue of his clothes, but a collection of images in which the designer is shown in the most disparate situations. The 288-page volume was edited by Alan Aboud who had worked alongside Paul Smith for over ten years as art director. The project was also signed by Jonathan Ive (designer of the iMac). The same year Smith opened another shop in London, near the Royal Exchange.

❑ 2002, March. He opened his first own-brand shop in Italy, in Via Manzoni in Milan, designed by Sophie Hick. He then opened his first men's shoe shop in Paris.

❑ 2002, April. Collaborating with Cappellini, he launched his interior design collection called Mondo at the Salone del Mobile in Milan. During the same period, the designer organized *Great Brits*, an exhibition that pays homage to the greatest British designers. The exhibition was held in his own studio in Milan at Viale Umbria 95. The designer chose four young names: D. Mathias Bengtsson, Tord Boontje, Daniel Brown, and Sam Buxton.

❑ 2003, March. After the enormous success of their first collaboration, Reebok asked Smith to design a new collection of 1980s-style men's and women's shoes. They were titled Paul Smith – Reebok 2. The materials used are mainly nylon (in orange and blue) and real leather (red and blue).

❑ As a world exclusive, it was possible to buy David Bowie's first book *Moonage Daydream: the Truth behind Ziggy* for the fashionable sum of £250 only in Paul Smith shops (there are about 250 of them throughout the world). Each of the 2500 editions are numbered and signed.

❑ 2005. In February he opened his first shop for the Pink line in the Daikanyama district of Tokyo. The flagship store measures 120 square meters and is entirely for womenswear and accessories. It is called Paul Smith Pink+. In March he released the Black collection (following an earlier Blue version), the second official women's line to be found in department stores such as Harvey Nichols, Harrods, and Selfridges. (*Pierangelo Mastantuono*)

Smith Willi (1948-1987). American designer. With a wealth of talent and sensitivity, he was heralded at the time of his death as the most successful black designer in the history of fashion. It is, in particular, his summer clothing and sportswear that stand out among all his collections. In 1976 he founded the Willi Wear Company with Laurie Hallet. He also used his creative talents to design collections for men and anticipated many of the elements that later came to characterize the American casual look of the 1980s and 1990s.

Smith Wynn (1967). American designer born in San Francisco. To break her in, she spent two periods in Geoffrey Beene's studios in New York and Paris in 1989 and 1990. Her fashion (she began in 1995 by giving her name to a brand that was changed to Wink in 1997) is typified by excellent cuts, fastidious attention to detail, an eye on the masters such as Courrèges, Armani and Kawakubo, and a sense of transgression. She shows in New York.

The Smiths Eveningwear label designed by Tony Smith, a New Yorker who gave his creations an almost geometric look. Very light fabrics, minimal stitching, and jackets that seemed like cardigan: these were some of the distinctive elements. In 1985 he opened a shop in SoHo where he sold imported clothing as well as a menswear and womenswear collection designed by him. Beginning in 1996 he launched the line called Thesmiths, which sold throughout the United States and in Japan.

Smock At some time during their childhood, all little girls wear a smock dress for a smart occasion. This type of stitching holds together lots of little folds, forming embroidered honeycomb stitching on a square section or on the whole of the front of the body of the dress.

Sneakers Originally, they were American two-tone college shoes, made of linen and plastic. Today sneakers, which were formerly gymnastics shoes, have changed their look and are worn by everyone given their undisputed comfortableness. Some styles are more popular with the young, while others are more elegant and better reflect one's own personal style. Classic, neutral and with branding that is not too obvious, Tod's and Hogans always win first place. The most "in" however are Adidas by Yamamoto, Converse All Stars and Nike PanAm Moores. Neil Barrett has designed a new sneaker for Puma. Completely black, Sergio Rossi sneakers are ultra sophisticated whereas Chanel's are more fun and trendy.

SNIA Historic Italian firm specializing in the production of artificial and synthetic fibers (until a few years ago it was called SNIA Viscosa). Relaunched between the wars thanks to the entrepreneurial and innovative talents of Franco Marinotti, the company soon conquered the market to become the European leader. Its products range from rayon to polyamide fibers to acetate. During the period of economic self-sufficiency imposed by the Fascist regime in 1935, it provided one of the most successful and important examples of industrial autonomy. In 1937 in Rome, the Mostra del Tessile (Textile Exhibition) provided an opportunity to create links between the production of synthetic fibers and materials used in fashion. The big fashion houses, designers and the main players in the world of clothing textiles, both in Italy and abroad, all use materials woven from SNIA Viscosa fibers and threads. Over the years, they have never compromised on quality or efficiency to the extent that today the Italian chemical group has all the necessary guarantees in place to regulate the fibers sector (it has an agreement with Rhone Poulenc), as well as the specialist chemistry and bioengineering sectors, through the two main companies in the Sorin Caffaro Group.

Snow Carmel (1888-1961). American journalist. She was born in Dublin, Ireland, and moved as a young emigrant to the US where her mother opened a dressmaker's. She started working for *Vogue* in 1921 where, thanks to her excellent ability to predict fashion, she soon rose to vertiginous heights. After 10 years she moved to *Harper's Bazaar*, turning it into a magazine that seriously rivalled *Vogue*. Condé Nast, the owners of *Vogue*, and Edna Woolman Chase, editor-in-chief, considered her a traitor for the rest of her life. At the fashion shows in Paris and Florence (she was one of the first to appreciate the birth of Italian fashion), she seemed barely to follow the models on the runway; at times, it appeared that she had even fallen asleep. But this was only a guise because her intuition led her always to choose the best of every collection for the photographs. She commissioned Dalì and Chagall to illustrate *Harper's Bazaar* and, with Alexey Brodovitch, the magazine's artistic director, she was one of the main supporters of the photographic talent of Dahl-Wolfe, Horst, Munkacsi, Penn and Avedon. (*Adalberto Cremonese*).

Soeurs Callot French fashion house. In 1895, the four sisters Callot – Marie Gerber, Marthe Bertrand, Regina Tennyson-Chantrell, and Joséphine Crimont, the daughters of a painter and a lace maker – opened a workshop in Paris at 24 Rue Taitbout, putting their family's experience and Marie's successful embroidery shop to good use. Their creations, based on a wide variety of colors and a daring matching of laces, in particular won a large American clientele. The four sisters were quite happy to experiment by mixing laces, fabrics and furs together, almost creating clothes influenced by the Orient in the early years of the twentieth century. During one of the premières at their dressmaker's shop, the famous *couturière* Madeleine Vionnet said about them: "The Callot sisters dress women, but do not decorate them: they are real dressmakers." From 1927, the maison was managed by Marie's sons, Pierre and Paul, and was later bought by Marie-Louise Calvet. It closed in 1954.

(*Eleonora Platania*)

Soho District of New York. Not to be confused with a London district of the same name, this area in south Manhattan (the name means "south of Houston," which is the avenue that forms its northern boundary) was transformed from being the artistic center of New York to Big Apple's fashion center in just a few years. Next to the most fashionable art galleries and restaurants in the city, one finds boutiques and shops of designers from all over the world. It is here that Louis Vuitton, Prada, Helmut Lang, Comme des Garçons, Agnes B., Yoshii Yamamoto, and new designers like Dosa, Vivienne Tam, Atsuro Tayama, and Marc Jacobs have decided to open their shops.

Sokolsky Melvin (1935). American photographer. In 1959 when barely 21 years old, he joined the staff of *Harper's Bazaar* where he was confronted with the clean, linear images of the magazine's big names. He invented a style that was closely tied to surrealist imagery, creating complex choreographies where elegant models, secured in a series of straps or inserted into giant transparent plastic bubbles, are released into the air as though in a fairy tale. He was influenced by great painters like Van Eyck, Hieronymus Bosch, Salvador Dalì, and Balthus. One of his fashion images for *Harper's Bazaar* includes a mirror that portrays the photographer as he is taking the shot, just like in Velazquez's *Las Maninas*. Particularly careful about the quality of his images, he is famous for his choice of film – a fine granular black-and-white and a Kodachrome 25 slide of very fine grain that enables him to obtain really saturated colors. These constitute his recognizably 1960s style that lies halfway between the classicism of Avedon and the inventiveness of Hiro. He is published in *McCall's*, *Esquire*, *Newsweek*, *The New York Times Magazine*, and *Ladies Home Journal* and has produced various fashion campaigns using models such as Twiggy, Julie Christie, Ali McGraw, and Mia Farrow. In 2002, he published a monograph called *Seeing Fashion*. He lives in New York.

Solbiati Italian textile manufacturer of high-quality linens though it is only in recent decades that the company has focused on research into and the production of linen, becoming a world leader in the field. It was founded in 1874 in Busto Arsizio by Michele Solbiati to produce cotton, velvet, and fustian fabrics. Later, it moved to Lonate Pozzolo (Varese), sticking to the same production formula even when Leopoldo and Carlo, the founder'sons, took over the company. It was the next generation in the 1930s and 1940s – Enrico and Peppino – who introduced artificial fibers, particularly viscose. The current fourth generation – Andrea and Vittorio – entrusted the future of the company to linen, which is an extraordinary success. At the end of the 20th century, the business averaged sales of 80 billion lire a year. It produces 5 million meters of fabric a year, exporting 65% (as well as linen, it also produces cotton, wool, viscose, and viscose linen). The business carries out important research, especially into the manufacturing of overtwisted and crinkled linen threads; it uses techniques for ageing fabrics and special discoloring processes. In 1984, it patented Sasil di Erbacina, a vegetal fiber. The Lanificio Tessilclub di

Prato and the Brasilian Brasperola Group are both important associated firms. Vittorio Solbiati, the current chairman, tells an anecdote: during one of his first trips to America in the 1970s, he was nicknamed John Linnen partly as a pun on his textile speciality but partly because of his physical resemblance to John Lennon. Solbiati linens were used by Bruno Munari to decorate one of his rooms in the 1988 Venice Biennale and by Luca Ronconi for the scenery of Spontini's *Vestale* at La Scala.

(*Giuliana Zabeo Ricca*)

Sollazzo Lucia (1922-2000). Journalist and writer who lived and worked in Turin. An astute observer of fashion and costumes, she followed fashion shows and *haute couture* and ready-to-wear events for twenty years for *La Stampa*. She watched and wrote about the industry with a deep and specialist knowledge, and a great narrative ability. She entered journalism working for the *Gazzetta del Popolo*. In 1996, Longanesi edited her *Tutti in Vetrina. Il romanzo della moda italiana*. Journalism, however, never distracted her from her true passion: literature. She published collections of poetry titled *Unico Nord* (1973), *Le nevi dell'Eden* (1988), *Vestiaro* (1990), *Ombra futura* (Archinto, 1977) and *Noctua* (Manni, 1998), and the novels *La morte dei Cabraz* (1953, Soroptimist Prize) and *Juke Box* (1964).

Solo-matine Brand of clothing launched in 1994 by Swiss designer Natalia Solomatine. She studied in Moscow at the end of the 1980s, then got a diploma and a fashion design certificate in Geneva in 1990. In 1994, she worked in Ernst Walden's studio in Zurich. After a few appearances in Switzerland, she moved to Paris. She has contributed to various editions of *Who's Next* in the French capital. In 2003, she showed in the official fashion calendar as part of Paris ready-to-wear week.

(*Maddalena Fossati*)

Sombrero Hat, with a cone-shaped crown, that provides shade (*sombra* in Spanish) thanks to its wide stiff brim. It is typically worn in hot, sunny countries, like Spain, Latin America, and above all Mexico. Pedro Armendariz always used to wear one on screen.

Soncini Franca. Expert in external relations and communication strategies for brands and designers. She has been active in the field since 1977, the year in which she opened her Milan office. Today her clients include Issey Miyake's Pleats Please and A-Poc lines, Alberto Aspesi, Bi's & Curious, Guerriero, Bless, Hilton, Martin Margiela, Jan & Carlos, New York Industries, Nicola Del Verme, Patrizia Pepe, and Setaichiro. This range of clients, for many of whom Soncini also takes care of advertising campaigns and press relations, describe her as a simple "PR person," but also a true cultivator of cultural crosscurrents. She is known for her collaborations with photographers of international repute, such as Robert Frank for Aspesi, or with avantgarde artists (Tomato, the London group of graphic artists), which whom she works on shows and advertising. She began with Fiorucci in the 1970s, but even earlier had performed as a drummer with a rock group. She says about herself that she likes "intellectual and ethical honesty, something which I learnt from the Japanese." In fact, she was Rei Kawakubo's only Italian PR agent at Comme des Garçons. This collaboration was then followed by an alliance with Miyake which confirmed her place, once and for all, among the narrow group of intellectuals working for and in fashion. (*Antonio Mancinelli*)

Sonia Russian model. The elegance of her movements and the grace of her appearance helped her become Vionnet's favorite model in the 1930s. Her poses for the photographer Hoyningen-Huene are part of *Vogue*'s great history. When Vionnet retired in 1939, Sonia, who in the meantime had married the French couturier Charles Montaigne, also retired from photographic shoots and fashion shows.

Soprani Luciano (1946-1999). Italian designer. He is considered to have invented the androgynous look. Born in Reggiolo, the last of six brothers, at 18 he was an agricultural expert with a diploma from Lo Zanelli in Reggio Emilia. "But," he used to say, "I always continued drawing dresses, skirts, bolero jackets, risking noisy slappings and poorly hidden anger from the family." Fashion was his passion. At 19, he was taken on as a fashion designer by Max Mara, one

Jacket and sports outfit by Luciano Soprani in a drawing by Maria Pezzi.

of the leading Italian fashion companies. "It was a tremendous training for me. Achille Maramotti, the boss, wanted me to understand sewing and to realise what constructing a design involved, the transition from the scribble on the paper, from the inspiration, to the final dress." After two years, he was already responsible for 7 collections. In 1974, he left the provinces and arrived in Milan, which at that time was establishing itself as the capital of readymade *haute couture*. He designed for Basile and GFT. In 1982, he made his debut on the runways of Milan with a line that still carries his name today: garments made with great ability and sartorial technique, under the banner of comfort and functionality. Since then, a number of recognizable constants have defined his style, such as his use of non-colors, the quality of the materials and the combination of masculine fabrics with very feminine lines, even if they are always somewhat austere. In 1986, he was the first Italian to join the Japanese distribution company, Kashiyama. He conquered the Far East market but his association with them did not last more than 5 years. At the end of the 1990s, Soprano conceived and produced four men and women's clothing collections, and designed about 20 lines under license, from textiles to every type of accessory. He puts his name to 7 fragrances for men and women. His last fashion show – on 24 September 1999, a month before he died – finished, as always, with him appearing on the runway with his models.

(*Minnie Gastel*)

❑ The person who took over from Soprani was called Dilio Ortigoza, a Venezuelan, but his overthrowing of the stylistic canons meant that he had to be replaced by Alessandro Turci, a 43-year-old Italian, as creative director, who restored the sober style of measured good taste that is so important to the house's clients (with an eye also on the demands of their daughters). He began with a womenswear collection for Spring-Summer 2003. At the wishes of Satinine, the company that bought the brand in 2001, he also produced menswear collections, home collections, accessories, and also perfumes. Turci boasts a solid background. Besides a degree in law, in 2002 the California fashion magazine *Flaunt* picked him out as one of the people shaping the fashion scene in Milan.

❑ 2002, February. A first step for the relaunch of the label. A 5-year agreement was signed between the Studio Soprani and AFC to produce and distribute the first Luciano Soprani ready-to-wear womenswear line worldwide, begining with the Fall-Winter collection 2002-2003.

❑ 2002, November. An alliance was formed between Luciano Soprani and FACIS, a company with 830 points of sale in Italy and 320 abroad, to produce and distribute a menswear line for 7 years both in Italy and abroad.

Sorbier Franck (1961). French designer. He presented his first collection in 1987, having gained experience with Esmod. He immediately grabbed the attention of the press and the industry with the very personal cut of his tight-fitting jackets, which redefine the silhouette. After two seasons away from the runways, during which he worked with some fur labels, he returned in Fall 1998 with a line of ready-to-wear clothes. His choice of theme was Impressionist art.

❑ 2002. Sorbier showed at the Opéra Comique during Paris Fashion Week. He was accompanied on the piano by Michel Runtz, who composed music specifically for the event. The show included the stunning Adriana Sklenarikova Karembeu.

Sorbo Mario (1968). German designer born in Italy but moved to Düsseldorf when he was very young where he finished his secondary schooling. In 1990, he graduated from the Academy of Applied Arts in Vienna, following courses with De Castelbajac and Vivienne Westwood. In 1991, he was awarded a Fashion Master's degree at the Domus Academy in Milan, with Romeo Gigli as his tutor. He designed an experimental womenswear collection and in 1997 showed his first menswear collection in Paris. This was then distributed in Paris, London, New York, Los Angeles, and Tokyo.

Sorelle Fontana (Fontana Sisters) Italian dressmakers and label. Zoe (1911-1979), Micol (1913), and Giovanna Fontana (1915) were born in Traversetolo in the province of Parma. As young girls, they learned the trade in their mother's dressmaker's workshop. Zoe, the eldest, after brief stays in Milan and Paris, arrived in Rome in 1936 (where she was soon joined by her sisters) and after a short while began working for the dressmaker Zecca. Her sister Micol was an apprentice at the dressmaker Battilocchi, while Giovanna sewed dresses at home. In 1943, the three set up on their own, opening a dressmaker's shop in Via Liguria where they began dressing some of the biggest names among the Roman aristocracy. Elisa Massai, a pioneer of the fashion press, remembers, "They had the knowledge and skill of true craftsmen and the intuition of those who have risen through the ranks. They used and caught on to other people's designs. Not everything came completely from their own ideas, but they were among the first to create an embryonic type of Italian fashion." A big break came in 1949 when they designed Linda Christian's wedding dress for her marriage to Tyrone Power in Rome: it was a front page story and and from that point on they had strong links with the jet-set circles. In 1951 they showed at the first fashion show in Florence organized by Giorgini in front of an audience of international buyers. In 1957, they moved their workshop to a bigger premises at 6 Via San Sebastianello, and the following year they were invited to the White House to represent Italy at the Fashion in the World conference. The *haute couture* creations of the Fontana sisters stood out, not only for the quality of the dressmaking, but as a result of their 19th-century romantic lines, which they embellished with embroidery and appliquéd strass, pearls, and lace. Their first memorable chief-dressmaker was Armena Carloni, the sister of Maria Carloni, another great dressmaker who worked for Ventura and Irene Galitzine. During the 1950s and 1960s, their clients included Marella Agnelli, Jackie Kennedy, Princess Soraya, Liz Taylor, and movie stars. In 1952, their workshop served as the backdrop to Luciano Emmer's film *Le ragazze di Piazza di Spagna* (The Girls from Piazza di Spagna). A short while afterwards, they designed Ava Gardner's dresses for *La contessa scalza* (The Barefooted Countess) (1954), *Il sole sorgerà ancora* (The Sun Will Rise Again) (1957) and *L'ultima spiaggia* (The Beach) (1959). Again for Gardner, in 1956 they designed one of their most famous dresses – *il pretino* (the little priest), with its cassock-like shape that was later copied by the costume designer Danilo Donati for Anita Ekberg in a scene in Federico Fellini's *Dolce Vita* (1960). In 1960 at the request of US buyers, they launched a ready-to-wear line and later added lines of leather goods, umbrellas, scarves, jewelry, and bath and table linen; the perfume *Micol* was launched in 1991. In 1972, the Fontana sisters retired from the official *haute couture* shows, but continued to produce both *haute couture* and ready-to-wear garments. Their collaborators included: Balestra, de Barentzen, Giulio Coltellacci, Pistolese and Alain Reynaud. In 1992, the company and the Sorelle Fontana label are taken over by an Italian finance group. Micol is still involved in fashion through the Micol Fontana Foundation, set up in 1944, which promotes creativity on the part of young Italian artists by running competitions and awarding bursaries.

(*Paola Pisa*)

Sorelle Ramonda The name of a clothes empire. Today in Alte Ceccato in Vicenza, the company has an 18,000 square-meter emporium with 30 concessions for the most prestigious fashion labels. A further 25 points of sale are scattered in Treviso, Rome, Trento, Gallarate, Cremona, Bassano, Rosà, Milan, Belluno, Montebello della Battaglia, and Palazzolo in Brescia. The company was set up by the mother Amelia who, during the 1930s and 1940s, used to sell off-cuts by cycling between the various markets of her native Rosà in Vicenza, where she lived with her 8 children.

Having moved to Alte in 1954, the Ramonda family opened a shop selling fabrics and off-cuts for tailors in 1958. In 1965, another clothes shop was set up, and in 1975 they opened their new headquarters. The Ramonda phenomenon is based on "quality products and reasonable prices." The chairman is Giuseppe (known as Beppe) Ramonda, Maria Ramonda (the first to have followed in her mother's footsteps), and Ginetta Ramonda (both of whom are always there at the cash desk and during purchas-

Fontana Sisters (Zoe, Micol and Giovanna), cocktail dress, 1958 (from *La Sala Bianca – La nascita della moda italiana*, by Guido Vergani, Electa, 1992. Giovanni Battista Giorgini Archive).

ing). The support team is provided by Beppe's wife Carla, and a team of nephews and nieces.

Sorrenti Davide (1974-1997). Italian photographer. He moved from Naples with his family to the US where he began photography at the age of 18. In 1995, he turned professional and was published in *Interview*, *Dazed & Confused*, *Paper*, and *Raygun*, but he died very young.

Sorrenti Mario (1971). Italian photographer. From Naples, at the age of 10, he moved with his family, first to Washington and then New York, where he now lives and works. After studying at the School of Visual Art, which he attended while working as a designer at his mother's graphic agency, he discovered photography at the age of 17. He entered the fashion world in 1989 as a model and three years later began his photographic career with Calvin Klein who commissioned him to do a campaign for perfume and fashion. His work is published in *i-D*, *The Face*, *Arena*, *Interview*, *Harper's Bazaar* (with whom he signed a year-long contract in 1992) and the French, Italian, and English editions of *Vogue*. He has also done campaigns for important designers, such as Joop, Dolce & Gabbana, Iceberg, GAP, and CK Obsession, and he continues to collaborate with Calvin Klein. He caused a stir when one of his photographs for a 2002 Ungaro advertisement showed a white dog sensuously licking the foot of a blonde model. He has shown in various exhibitions in New York, Paris, and London. In 2002 Steidt published his book *The Machine*, which he dedicated to his photographer brother Davide (see above entry) who, as a sufferer of thalassemia, was often linked up to medical machinery.

❑ 2001. He contributed to the world of music doing video-clips for PJ Harvey, Delamitri and Desirée, and record covers for Maxwell.
❑ 2002-2003. For the third year running, he took part in the traveling initiative *Elle Décor's Dining by Design*, presented by Taittinger Champagne.

Sorrenti Vanina (1973). Italian photographer. She moved to the US with her family and then to Paris, where she now lives. She turned professional in 1998, and is considered one of the most interesting photographers of the new generation. She is published in international fashion magazines, such as *i-D* and *Surface*, and has made a short film on the designer Susan Cianciolo.

Sotostich Trendy brand of male fashion founded in Berlin in 1998 by Marcos Soto and Markus Stich. It presents itself to the world as an alternative name in German fashion, with a style that values quality without compromising on design. Its collections are inspired by Berlin as a center of contemporary music and modern art, and they have a sure, masculine and mature style. There are plans for a line of made-to-measure clothing and also to expand into the Milan and New York markets.

Souleiado French company specializing in Provençal fabrics made using the traditional technique known as *de l'indiennage* because it derives from India. In 1938, Charles Demery inherited a factory in Tarascon (founded in 1760) where he found 40,000 old prints. He decided to relaunch the artisan production processes, focusing on fashion and furnishings, and preserving a dying profession. The company is still in the hands of the family and is run by the grandson Jean-Pierre.

Souleiman Eugene (1961). English hairdresser. Fascinated by the idea of being able to manipulate and shape hair as if it were a raw material, he is an non-conformist in the world of hairdressing. He loves experimenting but always creates casual effects that look very natural. Alongside make-up artist Pat McGrath, he is a permanent presence behind the scenes at Prada and Dolce & Gabbana fashion shows, for whom he has created many successful looks. Since 1998 he has worked as a session stylist with Tony & Guy.

Sozzani Franca (1950). Italian journalist and editor of *Vogue Italia*. At a very young age and with a degree in literature and philosophy, she entered Condé Nast as an editor for *Vogue Bambini*. She then moves on to *Lei* (Italian version of the American *Glamour*) of which she became editor in 1979. In 1982, she founded *Per Lui*, a men's version of *Lei*, and in 1988 was appointed editor of *Vogue*. As a reference point for everyone in the fashion industry, from the major names in design to those just starting out, she innovatively created a new image for the magazine. From the pages of *Vogue*, she has launched the careers of those that have gone on to become the leading names in fashion and fashion communications. Despite her delicate and fragile appearance, she has a will of steel and is blessed with a special gift and interest in discovering new talent and research, combined with a rare ability to make decisions and bring ideas together. She has come, quite rightly, to be considered the most influential and important person in the international fashion journalism scene. The pages of her magazine, which are highly influential, often provide previews of emerging fashions and extreme trends as they are finding their feet and taking shape. In 1994, she was made editorial director of all the Condé Nast titles in Italy.

❑ 2002, July. An exhibition of covers of *Vogue Italia* opened in Rome in the Musei Capitolani. Entitled *The Covers: Vogue Italia 1988-2002*, it was curated by Franca Sozzani.

Spada Valerio (1972). Italian photographer. After secondary school, he enrolled for two years at the Istituto Italiano di Fotografia in Milan in 1994-1995 but, restless and curious, he did not attend the lectures on a regular basis and made trips abroad. In this way he visits Athens, Monaco, London, and Madrid, combining dreams, plans, and cheap boarding houses as he gravitated towards the fashion world in the hope of being able to enter it on a permanent basis. In 1995 he was given the opportunity to produce his first editorial by *Down Town Magazine*. In 1996, he did advertising campaigns for Renault Twingo, Telecom Italia, Levi's, Lycia, Collistar, and Deborah, and he produced fashion editorials for the magazine *Max*, for which he also created a calendar. He became involved with the music scene and in particular with the singer Vinicio Capossela, whom he accompanied on tour in 2001, creating an interesting black-and-white reportage and the record cover for *Canzoni a manovella*. Also in 2001, with Luca Martire and Fabrizio Montana he founded the fashion and visual culture magazine *Stile*; he took artistic and editorial control and published many reports in it. In 2003, he became editor of the latest title, *Cross*. A young photographer with a rigorous and very distinctive style, Spada uses light in a highly selective way. He pays great attention to the composition, switching between showing the whole body and just details (an eye, the softness of the face, a gesture of the hand), and uses color to underline the attraction of a sensual atmosphere. As one of the most interesting photographers of his generation, he tends not to get stuck in any one particular style, but is always open to new ideas, and has thus become, in his activities also as an art director, a point of reference for other photographers.

Spadafora Marina (1959). Italian designer born in Bolzano. Avantgarde by vocation and with knitwear as the family tradition, she chose a New Age philosophy of life. As the creative spirit of the family wool mill, she studied at the Fashion Institute of Los Angeles and worked as a costume designer in Hollywood, where she met her first husband Sean Ferrer, son of the actress Audrey Hepburn and the actor/director Mel Ferrer. After the Hollywood experience, she returned to Italy and made her debut in Milan in 1987 with her first collection of knitwear. She soon moved on to full ready-to-wear outfits and a menswear line. Her fashion is the result of research into stylized forms and materials which experiment with new techniques to create a personal and non-traditional style. Both spiritual and with an eye on the future, her fashion shows reflect her personal understanding of life: in 1993 she invited the Lama Gangchen Rinpoche onto the runway; in 1994, ignoring differences between the sexes, she dressed young girls and effeminate men in very feminine clothes; in 1998, eschewing the excessive nature of fashion shows, she presented just 16 models referring to the four seasons for women. Her second marriage, involving a Buddhist ceremony in Tibet, was to the director and producer Jordan Stone. They have three children. In her free time she teaches meditation at the Università della Terza Età in Milan.

(*Gisella Borioli*)

Marina Spadafora, 1999 collection.

❑ 2001. Savignano sul Rubicone was the location for *Angels and Demons*, a group exhibition in which the designer showed her creations alongside Denis Curti.
❑ 2001, September. A New Age feel for the Spring-Summer 2001 Milan fashion show. Live soundtrack by Rino Capitanata, who is not only a composer, but also the managing director of the company. After 11 September, the designer originally wanted silence. However, instead of the usual disco tracks, she chose live music which is both serene and solemn, out of respect for the victims of the tragedy. A zen bell announced the end of the fashion show.

Spade Kate. American handbag designer. Her bags are really popular with girls for their clean but stylish lines. As a journalist, she covered accessories for the magazine *Mademoiselle* but in 1993 decided to launch a line of nylon bags in lots of different colors, signed with a little white label. Just two years later, she won a best accessory designer prize. She subsequently went on to use different fabrics, designs, and colors, but always keeping the same simple, modern, functional style. From sporty and practical bags, she has diversified to produce leather goods, travel accessories, and stationery.

(*Priscilla Daroda*)

❑ 1999. She launched a range of shoes.
❑ 2001. Start of her eyewear collection and simultaneously Estée Lauder presented a range of beauty products with her signature. Next she launched her eau de parfum *Kate Spade*, which smells of the designer's favorite flowers: gardenias, jasmine and lilies of the valley.
❑ 2002. Aid to Artisans, an international nonprofit organization promoting and creating economic opportunities in the field of fashion, invited Kate Spade to curate a course in Cambodia. She immediately accepted with enthusiasm, recognizing the social and economic importance of such an initiative in the country. Walid Halabi, a member of the fashion house's development department, spent three weeks teaching various artisans basic tailoring techniques. Kate is keen to work on future initiatives organized by Aid to Artisans.
❑ 2003, June. She opened the American Boutique Week in the historic district of Georgetown (Washington, D.C.) with bags, shoes, eyewear, beauty products and accessories, next to a collection of men's accessories created by Jack Spade, Kate's business partner and lifelong companion. The layout was designed by the architect Roger Marvel who came up with the concept of dividing it into three clearly defined sections to underline the basic ideas that the designer wishes to communicate: timelessness, distinctiveness, and the unexpected.

(*Edoardo Ponzoni*)

Spagnoli Nicoletta (1957). Clothing industry entrepreneur. Having graduated in chemistry, she went on to do a graduate course at the University of San Diego in California, and is the author of articles published in

Chemical Research and other specialist magazines. A member of the board of directors for the Industrial Association of Perugia, Nicoletta Spagnoli is the managing director of Luisa Spagnoli SpA and SIS (Società Immobiliare Spagnoli). Nicoletta belongs to the fourth generation of Spagnoli: all four generations have the same entrepreneurial style, based on a passionate engagement with the culture of development and a pride in managing a firm that continues to play an important role in the economic and civic growth of Perugia.

Spagnolo Saverio (1909). Men's fashions designer and journalist. He was born in Campi Salentina (Lecce) and graduated in law. For some time he follows a forensic career, but then gave it up to concentrate on fashion. In 1937, he set up the magazine *Abbigliamento Italiano*. He later drew and wrote for *Arbiter*, *Petronio*, and *Esquire & Derby* as he improved his knowledge of fashion and costume, collecting documents and putting together an archive. The result was *Adamo allo specchio* (Adam in front of the Mirror), a volume which, with technical accuracy and an observer's knowledge, recounts half a century of the Italian male's wardrobe, set against the social and cultural events of the time.

Spalding & Bros Manufacturer of sports clothing and accessories. In 1876, Albert Goodwill Spalding (1850-1915) made the first baseball for the American Major Leagues. An entrepreneur and player, Spalding played for the Boston Red Sox setting some records and standing out for his integrity during a period of ethical crisis in the National Professional Association. Having retired from the playing field, he opened a shop in Chicago with his brother J. Walter, investing $800 of capital. In 1885, he opened his first shop in New York and the company was named after the premises on Fifth Avenue: A.G. Spalding & Bros, 520 Fifth Avenue, New York. President McKinley nominated him to represent the United States at the Paris Olympic Games in 1900. After opening 14 Spalding & Bros shops, including some transatlantic branches, Albert handed over management of the company in the early 1900s, but continued to play a supervisory role. In September 1915, he died at the age of 65 at Point Loma, near San Diego, leaving behind a company destined for international success in the clothing and sports accessories markets. In the 1930s, when Spalding was already a leading supplier of footballs, the company launched its leather headgear with little wings to protect the ears: the new FH5 model cost $10. Throughout the 20th century, the firm continued both to employ sportsmen and women and to lend its staff to sport: Richard Law is a recent example; he became vice president of the American Soccer League, having managed the Spanish and Mexican branches of Spalding for 8 years. Golf and basketball may be the two most important sectors of the business, but Spalding has branched out into all different types of sport and even produces stationery. Its catalogues do not just feature pens, but leather goods, diaries, watches, eyewear, and gift items. In April 2003, it was announced that the whole of Spalding Sports Worldwide Inc (except for the golf sector) was being bought by the Russell Corporation. The historic company, which today has its headquarters in Chicopee in Massachusetts, exchanged hands for $65 million.

(*Pierangelo Mastantuono*)

Spastor Label founded in 1995 by an alliance between Sergio Spastor and Ismael Alcaina Guerrero, respectively from Girona and Barcelona, who were both born in 1976. They have presented their own collections on the Gaudì runway and in the Paris ready-to-wear shows. In 2001, Spastor received the L'Oréal prize for the best collection on the Cibeles runway. Last year they launched a mini collection of shoes in collaboration with Kollflex. They stand out for their avantgarde and decidedly feminine creations. Their main objective is to prove that men and women can wear the same clothes without losing their own intimacy.

(*Estefania Ruilope Ruiz*)

Spats Leather or cloth stockings worn over the shoes and tied by a strap under the sole. They were fastened at the side by a line of small buttons. Originally used to ward off the cold, they reached up to the knee or even the thigh, and were worn in winter by small children and older girls. In 1800 and in the first decades of 1900 they were in vogue short, just above the ankles and made from beige or light gray cloth. They were worn by elegant men and women and were often knitted. They reappeared in the 1980s as a fashion accessory.

Spazio Sei Italian children's clothing company founded in Carpi in 1992. Spazio Sei Fashion Group controls five of its own brands – Ki6?, Parrot, Le Parrotined, MPD and Lu-Ma – and licenses for the Byblos baby range and Ice Ice Baby by Iceberg. In 2002, ten years of history and growth achieved sales worth 20.4 million euros, a 67% increase on the preceding year. Exports have been another success story, up 35% in countries like the United Arab Emirates, the former Soviet Union, and Australia. The launch of Ice Ice Baby and the chic baby sportwear by Ki6? were both positive, while Byblos 616, presented in June 2001, confirmed the promising statistics of the year before. The only flaw in an otherwise excellent year was the dead end that the group encountered in the Far East. In China, Spazio Sei got caught up in problems with the licensing group Good Baby Group, the local giant in the baby field. The Miss Bluemarine line for Spring-Summer 2004 is the work of designer Anna Molinari and harks back to the 1940s: stripey sailor tops, embroidered stockings and flounced skirts.

(*Pierangelo Mastantuono*)

Spectator American two-tone shoe: black-and-white or brown-and-white. Demonstrating extreme elegance in terms of color, this shoe was originally part of the sporting wardrobe. It is also known as a correspondent shoe. They were first worn in the 1920s and stayed in fashion until the end of the 1930s, later enjoying a revival in the 1960s. Spectators were worn by literary figures, such as the *Great Gatsby*, and by the stars of the silver screen such as Douglas Fairbanks and William Powell. The journalist Eugenio Scalfari, founder of the Italian newspaper *La Repubblica*, loves them.

Speliopoulos Peter. American designer born in Springfield, Massachusetts, into a family of Greek immigrants. He studied at the Parsons School of Design in New York. His first major job was in 1982 when he became assistant stylist to Laura Biagiotti. He then worked for Christian Dior, Gloria Sacks, Carolyne Roehm, and Joseph Aboud. Between 1993 and 1997 he was creative director at Donna Karan and from 1997 till 2002 he was at Cerruti. He has designed costumes for numerous theatrical productions in Greece, the UK, and the US. He is currently creative director for Donna Karan and LVMH. (*Giulia Crivelli*)

Spencer Men's jacket, short at the waist, that originated in England at the end of the 18th century. It is an example of an item of clothing that takes its name from the person who first wore it, in this case, Lord Spencer (1758-1834). It could be either single or double breasted with lapels. At the turn of the 19th century it entered women's wardrobes to cover the bust. During the course of the 19th century, it was very fashionable for men. From 1815, the year of the Vienna Congress, the Spencer was embellished with big braided loops and this model was known as the Hungarian or Hussar Spencer.

Sperry Make of shoe. Paul Sperry, a passionate seaman from New England, focused on making boat shoes from the end of the 1930s. In 1935 he invented and made his famous non-slip sole, using a bit of rubber on which he made little cuts in the shape of a fish's backbone. He adapted it to a pair of canvas shoes, giving rise to the Sperry Top Sider. From 1939, Sperry became an official supplier to the American army. The Canvas, produced in numerous versions, including leather, was a very fashionable accessory in the 1960s and even John Kennedy wore a pair. In the 1980s and 1990s, Sperry supplied sailing teams and regattas such as the Whitbread Round the World Race.

Spoerri Daniel (1930). Rumanian Nouveau Realisme artist whose work immortalizes objects as emblems of consumerism in a reflection of contemporary society. Famous for his paintings of tables laid out with plates, glasses, cigarette butts, and leftovers, he produced garments using objects as symbols of those that wore them. The sweater *La chemise du chasseur d'oiseaux/ Hommage to John Cage* from 1976 is covered in little whistles and strange instruments that reproduce the songs of different birds. Spoerri also designed models for the Fontana sisters.

❑ 2000. After three years, he finished his reconstruction of the hotel room where he lived and worked for a few years in Paris and published his memoirs in *Chambre n. 13 de l'Hôtel Carcassonne, Paris, 1959-65*.
❑ 2000, November. In collaboration with the Associazione degli Istituti Culturali Europei in Milan and in honor of the start of the new millennium, la Galleria del Credito Vatellinese presented a retrospective of the artist entitled *La catena genetica del mercato delle pulci* (The Genetic Chain of the Flea Market). It comprises 25 rough wooden tables, on which the artist assembled a notable quantity of objects gathered over 20 years spent roaming flea markets stalls.
❑ 2003. He exhibited his works in the Galerie Ernst Hilger in Vienna, the Kunsthaus in Vienna, the Brno House of Arts, Villa Pavoni in Switzerland, and in the Stadt Galerie Klagenfurt. He lives and works at the Giardino di Daniel Spoerri, a park situated in the Seggiano area on Monte Amiata. The Giardino houses a collection of sculptures and contemporary art installations by a variety of artists.

Spook Per (1939). Norwegian designer who works in France. Having attended the School of Fine Arts in Oslo, where he was born, he moved to Paris to work first with Dior, then Saint Laurent, then Féraud. In 1977, he set up his own house, designing warm and comfortable clothes made with natural materials. In 1981, with the support of an international group, he opened a shop on the Avenue Georges V, before moving in 1992 to Avenue Montaigne, but in 1994 it closed.

Sportswear A word of American origin that refers to sports clothing, including shoes. Over time, it has also come to describe, more generically, a casual look comprising combined separates, creating a way of dressing that contrasts with the more formal office look worn in the city. Sportswear first infiltrated fashion at the beginning of the 1960s with jeans and all their denim derivatives (from jackets to skirts), and in the following decade when Lacoste, Fred Perry, and Fila ventured into making everyday clothes. The advent of street style has allowed city dwellers to wear puffer jackets and sailing shoes or trainers. It was not until the 1990s, however, that sportswear became *haute couture*: for example, the volumes and shapes by Helmut Lang, Prada's experiments with new materials, and Costume National's couture lines, which are played down by the use of zips.
(*Maria Vittoria Pozzi*)

Sportwear Company Italian clothing brand originally known as Chester Perry. In 1975 it became C.P. Company: a company that set out to change our concept of casual wear, and to experiment with new materials, lines and functionality. In 1982, a second brand was set up: Stone Island. It is created by chance during some trial dyeing of a typically industrial fabric – lorry tarpaulin. C.P. Company was taken over in the mid-1980s by the Gruppo GFT (Gruppo Finanziario Tessile from Turin) and Trabaldo Togna. In September 1993 the firm is bought by Carlo and Cristina Rivetti and renamed Sportswear Company. Carlo Rivetti (born in Lausanne in 1956 and an economics graduate) became chairman. Sportswear Company now has more than 120 direct employees and produces more than a million garments a year. (*Gianluca Cantaro*)

Sposaitalia Show organized in Milan every year by Expo CTS and Efima which presents a preview of the clothing and accessories collections dedicated to brides and weddings. More than a hundred firms, who are leaders in the sector on an international scale, take part. Visitors come from more than 50 countries. Since 1998, Sposaitalia has been held in July. The exhibition, which is the hub of a highly creative but also industrial sector, also offers image-based events, plus relevant and innovative services, such as areas dedicated to trends in fashion, studio meetings, market analysis, and displays of costumes and fashion culture.

❑ 2001. Sposaitalia changed its image and logo to reflect the special role the event has on the international stage. As confirmation of the show's success, the number of participating firms rose 7% in July 2000. Sposa Trend Designer is devoted to luxury bridal wear and is given its own space.

Spring Court First brand of tennis shoe made in France in 1936. In 1988, the owner Theodore Grimmeisen handed the company over to brothers Guy and Yvon Rautureau, the son and grandson of shoemakers, who have relaunched the brand. As well as their success on the tennis court, Spring Courts were adopted by young people in the 1970s and became an essential part of the way they dressed. The Vulcalux factory in the Dordogne makes 1,300 pairs of these shoes a day.

Springs Alice (1923). Pseudonym of Australian photographer June Brown. She met and married Helmut Newton when she was working as a model. At the beginning of the 1960s, when the couple settled in Paris, she taught herself photography and once stood in for her husband when he was ill. From then on she focused on fashion photography (she was published in *Elle*, *Marie Claire*, *Vogue* and *Vogue Homme*) and, from 1976, on portraits of artists and celebrities, whom she photographed in their own environment. She took these portraits for magazines such as *Egoïste*, *Vanity Fair*, *Stern*, and *Interview*, and they were often accompanied by specially made video stills. She often collaborated with Helmut Newton: together they created the touring exhibition *Us and Them*.

Springs Industries American industrial group from South Carolina, and one of the biggest textile producers in the US. Specialists in cotton fabrics used in clothing, the home and industry, the company controls 44 factories scattered throughout the US, Great Britain, and Belgium, which manufacture the following brands: Springmaid, Wansutta, Ultrasuede, Skinner, Pacific Graber, Performance, Fashion Pleat, Customs Design, and Pacific Silver Cloth.

Sprouse Stephen (1953). American designer famous for being inspired by rock'n'roll. He has a techno-punk style and was one of the first to use futuristic materials. He also played around with bright colors, using them to contrast with the simplicity of black. Having started his career as an assistant to Halston, he has been designing his own collections since 1984. Many artists have worn his clothes, including Mick Jagger, Courtney Love, David Bowie, and Iggy Pop. He was curator of the Rock Museum in Cleveland and edited the Andy Warhol Foundation catalog in 1996.

❑ 2000. To celebrate the new millennium, Sprouse organized an unusual event. The theme was the landing on Mars of the Mars Pathfinder Rover, which had taken place the year before. He showed garments with three-dimensional prints taken from NASA photographs for which the public had to wear special visors. For the grand finale, men were dressed in clothes made entirely from plastic and women wore garments that reacted to the light of the reflectors.
❑ 2001. Louis Vuitton asked Sprouse to create graffiti for his winter collection of bags.
❑ 2003. The artist's most representative material was exhibited at the Florentine show *Il quarto sesso* (The Fourth Sex).

Squarciapino Franca (1940). Costume designer who won an Oscar in 1991 for the film *Cyrano de Bergerac*. She was introduced to the profession from the stage as she used to be an actress. She created her first collections in 1972 with the set designer Ezio Frigerio. The play was *King Lear*, directed by Giorgio Strehler at the Piccolo Teatro in Milan. For Strehler she has also designed costumes for Strindberg's *The Storm* (1980), *The Marriage of Figaro* (1981), *Don Giovanni* (1987), *Fidelio* (1990), and *Così Fan Tutte* (1998), the latter a posthumous production by Strehler. Among others, she has also worked with Ronconi, Pasqual, Liliana Cavani, Bob Wilson, and Werner Herzog. She is precise in her philological reconstruction of historical costumes and often uses unusual materials made possible by the latest developments in the textile industry.

❑ 2000. The Friends of La Scala dedicated an exhibition to her in the theater's Museo Teatrale.

❑ 2000-2001. She designed the costumes for Ambroise Thomas's *Hamlet*.
❑ 2002. The actors in *Romeo and Juliet* wore her costumes at the Bolshoi Theater in Moscow.

Squicciarino Nicola (1948). Essayist and researcher. He teaches at Florence University. In 1986, he wrote *Il vestito parla* (Clothes Talk), an essay which examines the symbolic value of clothing as a form of visual language from both a personal and social point of view. By highlighting the anthropological, psycho-sociological, and cultural benefits of fashion, Squicciarino widened our understanding of clothing, freeing it from its limited role as a feature of consumerism.

Stadtmuseum Set up after the fall of the Berlin Wall, this museum brings together the Berlin Museum and the Markisches Museum. It boasts a collection of some 10,000 garments and accessories, nearly all of which were produced dressmakers or manufacturers in East and West Berlin in the 20th century. Its collection is an invaluable source when trying to reconstruct the history of German *haute couture* and ready-to-wear since the war. Its archive constitutes a rare collection of information and documents the communist fashion system, from design to production to distribution, during the period 1952 to1990.

Starching Technique used to perfect the appearance of a fabric. The starching proceeding can be mechanical or chemical. In the first case the cloth is driven into a machine, which makes the fabric brighter, shinier, and softer. Using the chemical process, the garment becomes airproof, waterproof, crease-resistant and stands wear and tear, especially in the case of cotton and viscose. When using oily materials, starching gives fabrics a more brilliant and waxed look, and makes it fire-resistant: it does not stretch or shrink. (*Gabriella Gregorietti*)

Starck Philippe (1949). French designer. For Wolford, he created the six-combination tight fitting dress; for K-Way the waterproof jacket Wet Duke Starck; and, using Technogel, he created polyurethane soles covered in a three-dimensional material for the shoemaker Otto Block. He was born in Paris and is the son of an aeronautical manufacturer. At the age of 20, he became artistic director for Pierre Cardin. He traveled the world and settled for a while in the US, but then returned to France in 1976. He designed Les Bains Douches, a famous nightclub, and in 1984 the Café Coste next to the Beaubourg, later the Balmain and Dorothée Bis showrooms, and François Mitterand's Elysée Palace apartment. He has designed innumerable objects, including a lemon squeezer for Alessi, toothbrushes for Fluocaril, a motorbike for Aprilia, and the Ford Ka.

❑ 2001, April. He designed a series of watches for Fossil. Eurostar, the high-speed train, appoints Philippe Starck as its artistic director, spending at least 115 billion lire on its redesign.
❑ 2002, May. He designed a line of bags, rucksacks, and briefcases for Samsonite.

Starkey Hannah (1971). British photographer born in Belfast. She studied photography at Napier University in Edinburgh and at the Royal College of Art in London, where she graduated in 1997. Her style, like so many young British creators, reflects a strong artistic background, thanks to which she has established herself with surprising speed, in 1998 winning the John Kobal Portrait, and *The Sunday Times* and Condé Nast prizes. This enabled her to publish a ten-page feature in *Vogue Hommes Internazional* on her research into a night-club in London. Taking reportage as a starting point, her interpretation goes beyond reality, imbuing it with a subliminal quality. Her photographs are held in some public collections.

Starzewski Tomasz (1962). English designer born in London. He opened his first workshop in Fulham after he finished studying fashion at Central St Martin's. He made a name for himself through his evening dresses and opened a boutique in South Kensington in 1990. Two years later, he designed a line of daywear. In 1996, he opened a big shop on Sloane Street selling all his lines: ready-to-wear, evening wear, and bridal. In 1998, he began to sell his *haute couture* line in the US. His style meets the demands of his young, rich clients who are more interested in elegance than the minimalist and conceptual fashions that hit London in the 1990s.

❑ 2000, October. He showed at the Royal Castle in Warsaw, with Polish supermodels Magdalena Mielcarz and Renata Gabryelska on the runway.

Staub Christian (1918). Swiss photographer. Passionate about research in the fields of both photography (his first image was taken with a pinhole camera) and the arts, he got into Surrealist and Cubist painting during a stay in Paris from 1938 to 1940. After returning to Switzerland, he studied at the School of Applied Arts in Zurich and became a professional photographer. From 1943 to 1946 he worked freelance for a number of magazines, including *Du* and *Annabelle*. After meeting Willi Mayward, Dior's favorite photographer, he focused more intensely on fashion and society photography. After his first trip to New York in 1956, he decided to take up teaching photography at the Advanced School of Design in Ulm, the National Design Institute in Ahmadabad (India), Berkeley University in California, and Washington University in Seattle. His more recent work reflected his interest in experimentation: he also liked using a panoramic camera with a rotating lens.

Stavropoulos George (1920-1990). Greek designer known in the world of *haute couture* for his classical-style pleated togas which were sometimes asymmetric across the shoulders. Having turned down a job with Dior in Paris in 1952, he decided to move to New York in 1961 where he opened a workshop creating kimono jackets, and employing his sartorial skills to work with taffeta, lace, and lamé. He remained faithful to ideals of softness and practicality in his designs. He often used to say, "I do not want to crush a woman in a dress."

Stecking Adrienne (1930). American designer. She studied at Washington University and at the Parson's School of Design in New York. She gained her first professional experience with the wholesale firm B.H. Wragge and then with Fogarty. In 1972, she began to produce her own line of dresses and accessories, focusing on functionality. Her underlying aim was to mix garments rather than limiting the customer to wearing outfits designed to be worn as a unit.

Steel Lawrence (1963). American designer working in Milan. He began designing in a minimalist vein but then focused on a simplicity that aims to inspire sensuality. He designs for a decidedly sexy, but never vulgar, woman because his philosophy is to play with the simplicity of garments, crafting them by using cuts that hug the body, and fabrics that glide over curves and natural colors. Steel was born in Hampton, Virginia, and graduated from the Art Institute of Chicago in 1985. From 1985 until 1990 he worked as a designer for Moschino in Milan and between 1990 and 1993, he was on the staff of Prada working on their women's ready-to-wear line. In 1994, the firm Casor di Bologna signed to manufacture his label.
(*Paola Pollo*)

Lawrence Steel, evening dress, Spring-Summer Collection 1999.

Steele Valerie. American fashion historian. In 1997, she became curator of the Fashion Institute of Technology Museum in New York where, having graduated from Yale in 1983, she had taught from 1985 until 1996. She has produced a series of books on the history of fashion, its social impact, erotic value, and iconic proliferation, including *Fetish: Fashion, Sex and Power* (Oxford University Press, 1996) and *Fifty Years of Fashion: New Look to Now* (Yale University Press, 1997). For the Fashion Institute she has curated the exhibitions *Claire McCardell and the American Look*, *Shoes: A Lexicon of Style* and *East Meets West*. According to the *Washington Post*, she is "one of the most cerebral women on the fashion planet," while the *New York Times* describes her as "a historian in stilettos."

Stefanel Italian textile group. With a turnover in 1999 of more than 600 billion lire, it produces and distributes 11 brands, has more than 5,000 points of sale throughout the world, employs 1,300 people, and has been quoted on the Stock Exchange since 1987. The company's history began in 1959 when Carlo Stefanel (1925-1987) set up the Maglificio Piave at Ponte di Piave in the province of Treviso. In 1966, his children Giuseppe and Giovanna joined the company, and on the death of their father took charge, Giuseppe as chairman and managing director, and Giovanna as designer of the collections. In the mid-1970s, the Maglificio Piave had its first commercial turning point, creating the Sigma brand and choosing to retail its products through its own network of representatives. In 1980, the first franchise opened in Siena with the new Stefanel brand, and was launched abroad, in Paris, two years later. Between 1982 and 1984, the name Stefanel completely replaced the original name of Maglificio Piave. Between 1984 and 1988, the company increased its sales and number of shops almost fourfold. Through acquisitions and international agreements, by the end of the 1980s Stefanel had turned into a large industrial group and diversified into sportswear, jeans, and ready-to-wear. Thanks to a joint venture set up in December 1995, Stefanel has manufactured the CK lines for Calvin Klein since 1987. It now owns the following brands: Peter Hadley (men's and women's collections in an Anglo-Bostonian style); Be and SPQR City, resulting from the collaboration with the French designers Marithé and François Girbaud; Museum, a sophisticated outdoor look; and New England and Rebecca Allison, who are shirt specialists. It has three factories to produce its own collections (Ponte di Piave, Salgareda, and Bucharest in Romania) and three other factories for the other brands.

❑ 2000. It bought 95% of Hallhuber, the German company that owned 44 points of sale in Germany, with sales in 1999 of 92 billion lire. The deal was worth 35 billion lire.
❑ 2002, May. The financial year ended with profits of 1.1 million euros, compared with a loss of 9.7 millions in the previous 12 months. The Ponte di Piave group had sales worth 267.1 million euros.
❑ 2003, April. It handed the control of Interpool (women's classic and sports clothing) over to Acon, a clothing company with the Mash brand, for a price of 4.73 million euros.

Stefanelli Tommaso (1962). Italian designer born in Casarano near Lecce. He started out in 1993, showing at the Milano Collezioni with a label produced by the Alessandra di Casale sul Sile knitwear mill near Treviso.

❑ 2003. For the Winter collection, he decided on "total white," with optic white cashmeres, to open the show. He finished with black, combining delicate and lightweight materials with thicker, heavier ones. He relaunched the nude look, but with a different slant.

Stefano Bi Shoe manufacturer from Ferrara. Founded in 1991, by 2000 it had average annual sales of 7 billion lire. In 1996 it was bought by Bernard Arnault of the LVMH Group.

Steichen Edward (1879-1973). American photographer. We are indebted to him for early color fashion photographs and the first color photographic front cover (*Vogue America*, 1931). His family emigrated from Luxembourg to the States, where Edward studied art at the Milwaukee Art Students League and then moved to Paris in 1900.

Alongside painting he starts practising photography. In 1902, he co-founded Alfred Stieglitz's Photosecession movement in New York. During World War I, he was a navy and aviation photographer, which greatly influenced his photographic style. Having settled in New York, he gave up painting to concentrate on photography and, in 1923, became the first photographer for Condé Nast's publications, particularly *Vanity Fair* and *Vogue*. His fashion photographs and portraits were the most expensive of the period. He worked a lot with Marion Morehouse, his favorite model. In 1947, he left Condé Nast to become director of the photographic department at the Museum of Modern Art in New York.

(*Luca Selvi*)

Steiger Walter (1942). Swiss shoe designer. He worked with Lagerfeld and Montana and, when very young in the 1960s, he designed some models for Mary Quant. He started out with Bally for which he launched a very extravagant line named Bally Bis made of paper and plastic. The press declared it a success and opened his first boutique in 1973 in Paris. Since then he has become famous for his ability to change the usual proportions of shoes, his desire to revolutionize standard designs, and his use of aerodynamic heels reminiscent of airplane cockpits.

Stella Cadente Brand of readymade fashion and jewelry founded in 1991 by designer Stanislassia Klein (1967), who graduated from the Studio Berçot, then worked as a color specialist in the cosmetics industry. In 1984, she was assistant to Christophe Lebourg of Cacharel, Montana, and Corinne Cobson. She designed clothing collections for Poles (1989-1990), Paule Ka, and Irene Van Ryb (1995), and jewelry for fashion shows by Chloé, Fath, Daniel Swarovski, Lagerfeld, Mugler, and Agnes B. Stella Cadente began with glass and crystal jewelry, followed by a line of knitwear in 1995. 1998 saw the label's first runway show and the following year, it made it on to the Carrousel du Louvre for the Fall-Winter Fashion Week.

Stella Cirquelar Set up in 2000 by Alessia Parenti (1968), this label perhaps has closer ties to art than to fashion. The clothes, which are unique items, are all modular: "They can be dismantled," explains the artist-designer. "The same garment offers various possibilities. It can be worn as a jacket and then, once the sleeves have been taken off, it becomes a skirt. I start with shapes. I choose, for example, a circle and start elaborating it, adapting it to my body." All the garments, mainly made in elasticated materials, have painted applications, with handmade decorative details.

Stepanova Varvara (1884-1958). Russian painter. In 1923, she theorized the Constructivist dress seen in the pages of *Lef* magazine. Intended to be worn at work, it was a garment that prioritizes social functions over aesthetics. All decorative elements were banished in favor of the dress's comfort and functionality. Married to the painter Rodchenko, from 1920 she was the publicity designer for Inchuk (Institute of Artistic Culture) and in 1924 and 1925 she taught in the textile design faculty of Vhutemas (Workshop for Advanced Technical and Artistic Studies). With Ljoubov Popova, she was one of the forerunners of developments in Russian textile printing. In the 1920s, they worked together for Cindel, the large fabric factory. It drew on traditional Russian clothes to create a simple wardrobe of uniforms, sports kits, and overalls for all types of professions.

Stéphane Kélian French brand of shoes, bags and accessories, famous for its elaborate and prized interlaced workmanship. Today it is one of the most famous and important brands of shoe in the world, selling 250,000 pairs of shoes a year to 27 countries. The name of its founder and creative spirit is Stéphane Kéloglanian (1942), an Armenian immigrant. In the 1970s, at the height of the crisis in the shoe industry, he decided to bet his money on creativity and fashion, transforming the little artisan factory producing men's shoes, founded in Romains by his brothers Georges (1929) and Gérard (1932). In 1977, he presented a collection of women's shoes and the following year opened his first shop in Paris on the Rue des Saint-Pères. He has bought the Mosquitos and Miss Maud brands and the line of women's shoes signed by Kenzo.

❑ 2001, December. Kemos, a French finance company bought the business through Alain Duménil. Kemos already held the majority share of France Luxury Group, who own the Jean-Louis Scherrer and Francesco Smalto brands. ❑ 2003. Alain Tondowski became the new art director.

Stephen Stephen American brand of jewelry. It takes its name from the New York designer who earned his reputation in the 1980s, first in fashion with Geoffrey Beene and Donna Karan, and then in the world of accessories and jewelry. Silver and highly colored stones lie at the heart of his creations. Their irregular cut is reminiscent of antique jewelry. The cameo is a recurrent model that he makes with a variety of stones: bakelite, coral, turquoise, and jade. He makes one-off pieces which are also on display in the Costume Institute of the Metropolitan Museum in New York.

Sterlé Pierre (1905-1978). French jeweler. The jewelry made by this goldsmith is a faithful reflection of 1950s taste; he inherited a passion for the job and also a shop in Rue de Castiglione from his uncle. Having set up his business in 1934 in the Rue Sainte-Anne, working for jewelers like Boucheron, Chaumet, and Puifocart, he opened a workshop in Avenue de l'Opéra in 1945. He established a close working relationship with the dressmaker Jacques Fath and surrounded himself with cultural and artistic figures, such as Colette, Cocteau, Dalì, and Léonor Fini. Gold thread, arrow brooches, with diamonds and rubies set in platinum, and floral and animal designs are all typical of his output.

Sterling Dietmar (1945). German designer. Produced by the company Mendès, his clothes appeared on the market in 1982; loose-fitting and comfortable, simple and not in the least extravagant, the style is loosely Japanese. Sterling studied at the Academy of Fine Arts in Munich. Having worked in Berlin and Munich, he moved to Paris, where he also designed for Jacque Gilles and Tomwear.

Stern Bert (1929) American photographer. Born in Brooklyn, he began his career as an assistant to H. Bramson, art director of *Look* and, when he was barely 20, he became interested in photography, particularly cinematographic shoots during his military service. From 1953, he worked in fashion and advertising. He was the first to introduce color advertising inserts which, because of the quality of the images, were difficult to distinguish from the editorial pages. He was also known as a talented portraitist with a glamorous and romantic style, for which he was commissioned to produce the Pirelli calendar in 1985. His pictures of Marilyn Monroe – taken for *Vogue* in 1962, showing her in happy surroundings without realizing that it would be the actress's last shoot – are famous.

❑ 2000, April. *Marilyn Monroe: The Complete Last Sitting* was presented in Rome at the Galleria Minima Peliti Associati, in the courtyard of the Palazzo Borghese, as part of the exhibition *Marilyn Monroe – l'ultimo set*. In 1962, it was Stern's idea to ask Marilyn Monroe to pose for *Vogue*. 23 photographs taken six weeks before the actress's death were exhibited. During the three days posing at the Bel-Air Hotel, 2,700 photographs were taken as fashion shots, portraits, and nudes. Destiny would have it that the 20 photographs that were chosen were published when Marilyn was already dead (August 1962). It therefore became a memorial tribute, *Vogue*'s homage to Marilyn Monroe.

Stevenson Edward (1906-1968). American fashion and costume designer. His name is linked to two masterpieces: *Citizen Kane* (1941) and *The Magnificent Ambersons* (1942), two films by Orson Welles. Having arrived in Hollywood in the 1920s, he began working for MGM in 1925; in 1927 he was assistant costume designer to Fox; and in 1928, he became head of First National's costume department. He then opened his own fashion company, which kept him away

from cinema for some time. He returned to work for the screen in the mid-1930s, creating the dresses for *Roberta* (1935). Having undertaken to work for eleven years with RKO, he designed the costumes for famous horror films like *Murder, My Sweet* (1944) and *Out of the Past* (1947). He dressed women stars such as Joan Fontaine, Susan Hayward, Dorothy McGuire, Irene Dunne, and Donna Reed. In the last 15 years of his career – and life – he worked almost exclusively for Lucille Ball, creating designs for her popular television shows (*I Love Lucy*) and films. It was one of her films, *The Facts of Life* (1960), that won him an Oscar.
(*Roberto Nepoti*)

Stevovic Tajana (1973). Serbian designer. Having graduated from the Academy of Applied Arts in Belgrade, she embarked in 1997 on a Master's degree in fashion design at the Domus Academy in Milan. In collaboration with Carla Sozzani (10 Corso Como) she worked on the lines O-Zen and NN Studio during 1998 and 1999. In 2002, her first collection was presented in Milan. Thirty or so combinable garments are indicative of the style that the designer likes to develop: a half-way house between tradition and avant-garde, linked to her own roots but mediated through Italian culture. Layerings and contrasts, light and quintessential lines, exclusive but not excessive materials, which are all based on the central shape of the apron in its varied forms and uses.

Stiebel Victor (1907-1976). South African designer. He worked in London and at the age of 17 moved to Durban. A forerunner of the casual but well-cut look, he opened his own fashion house in 1932. English *Vogue* immediately noticed his Greek-inspired evening dresses in pastel colors. Despite the regime of austerity, the postwar period was his most creative moment, featuring his intuitive nude-look and suits with clean lines. In 1955, at the peak of his success, he signed a rather bizarre agreement with three other very famous English designers, a sort of gentleman's agreement in which each would take part in the others' fashion shows, with the aim of launching English fashion in the rest of the world. His fashion house no longer exists.

Stieglitz Alfred (1864-1946). American photographer. After studying in Berlin, he returned to New York in 1890 and devoted himself to photography, deepening his understanding of technical matters and expressive qualities related to light. He was very interested in composition and research and briefly acknowledged abstraction. With Edward Steichen and Alvin Langdon Coburn, in 1902 he founded the Photosecession movement and the excellent magazine *Camera Work*, which published the work of the great artists of the time up until 1917, when it shut down. Stieglitz was also known as a gallery-owner having opened the 291 on Fifth Avenue in 1906 and An American Place in 1929. They showed the work of photographers and artists who were able to influence public taste, for example, Picasso and Matisse, but were also a meeting point and a forum for debates on photographic aesthetics.

Stile Quarterly Italian magazine founded in 2001 around an idea by Luca Martire, Fabrizio Montana, and the photographer Valerio Spada, to whom the management and artistic creation is entrusted. It is a quality publication which dedicates considerable space to fashion editorials with a few digressions into graphics and design. Its characteristics are every photographer's dream: well written but spare texts, well-printed photographs, features that are each 8-10 pages long, a sensual feel that is never vulgar, an intelligent layout, and top-quality graphic design by the talented Dutch Punch Drunk Studio. Nearly all the artists that are published are young and up-and-coming. Names that should be mentioned are Heidi Niemala for her delicate colors, Caroline Delmotte for her surrealist touches, Daniel Hill for the way he uses cuts of light, Emmanuel Thibault for the originality of his compositions, Bruna Rotunno for her sensuality, Cricchi Ferrante for delicate atmospheres, and Simon's sense of spatiality. Spada also publishes his own excellent features in the magazine.

Stivaleria Impero Prestigious artisan workshop in Rome specializing in made to measure riding boots. It was founded in 1936 by Giovanni Mongiu, a craftsman originally from Sardinia who had trained ever since he was a boy at the Stivaleria Ferrini. He used to make boots for the police in the Italian colonies in Africa, particularly for the cavalry stationed in Libya, Somalia, and Ethiopia. They had a canvas leg with a leather border and laces at the front. The founder of the company died in 1958, but his son, with the same name, decided to continue his father's business. From 1965 until 1975, he worked mainly for the horseback police, then moved on to the army, for whom he is still the official supplier. Army boots extend up above the knee and are made of glossy lined leather. Memorable clients of the Stivaleria Impero include the d'Inzeo brothers, Prince Alessandro Torlonia, Graziano Mancinelli, Michel Robert, and Frédéric Cottier. The bootmakers still accept orders by correspondence; the client has to fill in a form with foot, leg and calf measurements. Besides the classic riding boot, Mongiu also offers a polo boot with a zip at the front, the Field boot, and the cowherd model in thick leather with leather laces.

Stizzoli Ready-to-wear company based in Ronco all'Adige in Veronese. For 25 years it has produced women's knitwear garments: jackets, coats and suits known for their wearability and comfort. They have a showroom in Via Montenapoleone in Milan.

Stockings Created to keep the cold at bay, they have undergone several transformations through the centuries. A rather vague concept of the stocking dates back to the 7th century B.C. when the Shiites used to wear a sort of cloth legging with a leather sole. From the year 1000, stockings were worn throughout all the Middle East and Europe. Initially they were made of cloth, but then became knitted. Only in the 16th century, when William Lee invented the knitting machine in England, did the real era of stockings begin. The most refined version was made of silk, whereas the coarsest was made of wool. The use of culottes until the French Revolution made them a very visible men's garment, but the advent of pants in the early 1800s hid them from sight and they lost importance.
Their evolution in womenswear was quite different. From the year 1700 they developed into different forms, sometimes colored, embroidered with hem stitches, or decorated with lace inserts. With the shortening of skirts at the start of the 1900s, stockings became increasingly visible. They were transformed into an important item of formalwear, and made very thin in natural or artificial silk (but they often laddered and women would try to hide it by wiping the ladder with a damp finger). The introduction of nylon after World War I brought

Advertisement of "Duofil Germani" Stockings in Marie Claire (September 1957).

about a revolution: in 1937 the American W.H. Canothers, the inventor of the of the nylon thread, patented the material, leading to the replacement of the more expensive silk stockings with nylon ones. Industrial manufacture of nylon stockings began toward the end of the 1940s. They made their début in Europe with the arrival of the American forces at the end of the war. The first stockings were a natural flesh-color, and made in different thicknesses classified by *denier* (a unit of measure still used today to define the weight of silk and nylon). They had a seam that ran down the back of the leg but advances in technology have eliminated the seam, leaving a one-piece stretch stocking. With the arrival of the more practical tights in the 1960s, stockings and their associated garments – the girdle, suspenders and the garter – were practically done away with. However, the revival of the miniskirt in the 1980s returned stockings to the market as a symbol of femininity. They were also available in a self-supporting elasticated version, with trimmed or laced hems. Next came patterned tights and stockings, which added to the range of heavy cotton, chine and microfiber tights, plus those with golden or silver textures, or the classic white tights worn by nurses. More recently we have been offered very light and transparent retro models, often decorated with a single black line, baguette patterns, monograms or logos, such as Chanel's double C on a plain background. Other types are lace tights and fishnet tights, sometimes tightly woven, but also so large as to resemble a fisherman's net. Another modern revival is the return to the stockings of the 1960s, in bright or fluorescent colors, or in patterns like multicolor horizontal stripes, classic Argyle lozenges, or Scottish tartan. However, the one type of stocking or tight that has never gone out of fashion is the very veiled, transparent stocking that is almost invisible. In addition to the brands Pierre Mantoux and Philippe Matignon, famous names include Pompea, New York, Wolford, Oroblù, SiSi, and Omsa. (*Gabriella Gregorietti*)

Stole In the 1960s, it was very fashionable to wear a large fur scarf that was either straight or slightly shaped so that it curved around the back over evening dresses or elegant afternoon suits. Today the word has taken on a wider meaning to include a long cashmere or wool scarf that is wrapped around the shoulders.

Stonefly Company founded in 1993 that makes shoes mainly for the city and leisurewear. It succeeds in combining design, Italian style, and complete comfort. Technological research has allowed them to develop two unique patents: Shock Air, which allows the foot to sweat, and Blu Soft, which absorbs shocks. Stonefly shoes are sold in 30 countries. Annual sales of 24 million euros in 1997 had risen to around 88 millions in 2003.

Stone Island Brand of clothing founded in 1982. From the beginning, it was the result of advanced research into fibers and fabrics that had never been used before in the clothing industry. Paul Harvey, the designer, uses natural fibers together with innovative materials produced by the latest technology: intelligent fibers, carbon fibers and glass, ceramic or aluminium fibers. Instead of being standardized, each item of clothing becomes an unrepeatable garment. In Summer 2001, Stone Island Series 100 was launched as an experiment in making women's clothes out of a single material. Nylon thread alone was used to develop a series of shouldered garments and extremely sexy jerseys. (*Gianluca Cantaro*)

Stonewashed Any fabric that, like denim, has undergone special dyeing treatments in order to look discolored and faded on the front, as though faded by the sun.

Stonewood + Bryce Brand of men's fashion that is sporty but luxurious, with street style and military details. It was created in 1998 by two Australian designers, Theo Vaderzalm and Peter Mikic. Having met at RMIT (the Royal Melbourne Institute of Technology), where they studied fabrics and fashion, the two of them had different experiences, as a designer and as a stylist for pop singers, before meeting again in London to set up this line that has already won favor with celebrities such as David Beckham and Robbie Williams. It is sold in famous stores in London, New York, and Tokyo. They have plans for a women's line and their own brand shops. (*Silvia Paoli*)

Stoppi Isa. She was a photographic model in the 1960s who was discovered and launched by Giampaolo Barbieri. She is married ("1968 was an important year for everyone") with two children and has retired, but occasionally agrees to do a fashion show. She is nicknamed "the Italian Monroe" because of her blonde hair and blue eyes, but her face is very sculpted, very Italian. Because of a brief love affair with the playboy Gigi Rizzi (former Mr Bardot), she is cited in Giangiacomo Schiavi's book *Ho ammazzato Gigi Rizzi* (I Killed Gigi Rizzi). She is preparing a book on *Ragazze degli anni 60* (Girls from the 1960s) (e.g., Mirella Petteni, Benedetta Barzini, Marina Schiano, and Elsa Martinelli) who in that era took an image of the Italy of the economic boom to the US.

Stop Senes Roman dressmaker's in the Via Veneto that was popular above all in the 1950s. It bought patterns and materials in Paris from Dior, Givenchy, and later Saint Laurent, in order to copy them in even bolder cuts. The workshop was frequented by Roman high society who chose its clothes for official and society functions, such as opera premières. It was managed by the famous Madame Anna.

Storey Helen (1959). English designer. She began as an assistant to Valentino and then to Lancetti in Rome. In 1990, she created her own label. She has a store on the King's Road and has enlisted some of the most important department stores as her clients. In 1992, she created a second brand, called Second Life, inspired by ecological issues. She has also launched a casual line of clothing called Real Classics.

Storm English modeling agency set up in 1987 in London. It was Sarah Doukas's idea, but was made possible by the financial support of Richard Branson, who owns the other 50% of the business. Two years later, Storm also took male models on its books. Its success enabled it to open branches in Germany (1990), Spain (1993), and Cape Town (1997). Slowly over the years, the agency has diversified into sectors other than fashion: with film and celebrity divisions, sports personalities, and artist management. Sarah Doukas discovered the then unknown Kate Moss at JFK Airport in New York and persuaded her to work in the world of fashion and advertising.

Storm Jim (1943). Actor and American designer. Born in Highland Park (Illinois), he has since lived in England and California. At 18, his passion for acting led him to set up a theatrical company in San Diego, which made its debut at the Shakespeare Festival with *Henry VIII*. After numerous performances on stage and screen including some serials (in Europe he is best known for having played the role of the rich and powerful editor Bill Spencer in the soap *Beautiful*) and without completely abandoning the world of acting, he decided to follow in the footsteps of his family who make clothing in California. He entered the fashion world as an entrepreneur and creator. In 1994 he went to Italy and, after eight months presented Jim Storm the Actor's Collection with jackets, suits, jeans, and shirts made entirely of leather for Fall-Winter 1995-1996.

(*Maria Vittoria Alfonsi*)

Strada Nanni (1941). Italian designer known since the 1960s for her research into the modularity of clothing. Born in Milan, she studied fashion design, and created her first collection for Cadette in 1967, then accessories for Fiorucci, bathing costumes for La Perla, jerseys for Missoni, and Avon Celli in 1969, and for Sportmax in 1970. In 1974 she had the brainwave of producing knitwear without any sewing, using hosiery machines. When this technique was applied to clothing, she won the coveted design award, the Compasso d'oro, in 1979 for a seamless dress. At the same time, she produces her first mountain, cold-weather, puffer jacket for Dolomite and the Sottosport collection for Zegna. In the 1980s, she designed mainly for the Far East and China. From 1984, her production expanded and she opened a series of shops in Portugal and in Japan. In 1985 she opened the Nanni Strada Design Studio in Milan where she launched her famous *torchon*, the pleated travel dress that was reinterpreted a few years later by Issey Miyake. In 1994, she produced *Il manto e la pelle*, a film presented at the Triennale di Milano and, in 1998, she published her autobiography *Moda Design*, which also

Styles by the designer Nanni Strada in a drawing by Maria Pezzi, 1976.

provides the reader with an interesting insight into the close rapport between design and fashion as seen from an insider's point of view. (*Laura Salza*)

❑ 2003, April. The Milan Triennale devoted the exhibition *Abitare l'abito* to Nanni Strada's design work; it was curated by Raimonda Riccini and designed by Italo Lupi.

Strand Clare (1973). English photographer, born in Sussex. She finished her studies at Brighton University in 1995 and made a name for herself as a photographer while still at the Royal College of Art in London: she showed in some group exhibitions, sold her first pictures to public and private collectors, and was published in *Dazed and Confused*, *The Face*, *The Independent Magazine*, *Creative Camera*, and *Attitude*. Her most famous studies are on teenagers, whom she photographs in color in the style of classical portraiture.

Strapless Bra Bra without shoulder straps, reinforced under the cups or on the sides with plastic or iron whalebones, in order to emphasize or accentuate the breast. The first dress with this kind of neckline, created by the designer Mainbocher, dates back to the 1930s: since then it has been reinterpreted in many ways, usually to be sexy and provocative.

Strass Crystal, which is very rich in lead and imitates the splendor of diamonds and precious stones. Its strong refraction makes it very sparkly. It is used to decorate suits, shirts, cuffs, necklines, shoes, and evening bags.

Straw hat A round hat with a hard flat crown and a stiff brim, banded by a broad ribbon. Straw hats, along with fedoras and other men's dress styles, came prominently into fashion in the late 1800s and early 1900s, and were one of the hat styles most favored by Gabriele D'Annunzio, as seen in many photographs. They also became a show business staple, adopted with flair by Maurice Chevalier, Odoardo Spadaro and Nino Taranto. Straw hats became the symbol of the "interventionists", who demonstrated in favor of Italy's intervention in World War I. Also known as a "boater" because it was part of the summer rowing uniform, along with a striped blazer and flannel trousers. In Lombardy it is called a "magiostrina".

A 1930s advertisement for Dobbs, New York showing a straw hat and a panama.

Strenesse German brand of women's clothing designed by Gabriele Strehle. The label takes its name from the Strehle couple who set up a firm selling coats and clothes in a very classic style in 1949 in Noerdingen. The end of the 1960s marked the first big turning point for the brand. To the root of the family's surname – Stre – they add "nesse," intending, explained Gerd, the heir to the firm, to create a French-sounding brand that immediately conjures images of fashion. Gabriele, Gerd's wife, took charge of the stylistic changes. Having entered the firm in the 1970s with a diploma from Munich Fashion College, Gabriele changed the feel of the collection, which led indirectly to a restructuring of the firm. The new client that Strenesse was addressing was a contemporary woman that combines aesthetics with functionality in a quintessential style: she keeps up with the times but does not acknowledge the excesses of fashion. It is this new breed of more mature customer that they wished to target. In 1993, the line Strenesse Blue was created to integrate a selection of informal clothes with the formal designs of the first collection. And a broadening of the label's distribution network on an international scale was implemented at the same time. Italy was chosen as the springboard for this international launch. Strenesse showed for the first time in Milan in 1995. Coinciding with its runway debut, Strenesse Group Italia was launched, a subsidiary that operates independently from its German parent company. In 1996, the German company signed its first licensing contract for making shoes and in 1997 an agreement for bags. In early 1998, Strenesse had 370 employees, producing 800,000 garments a year for 350 clients in Germany and 450 abroad. It sales for the year were worth 130 million marks. 1998 and 1999 brought new turning points: Gabriele was still the company's force for change and is described by her husband Gerd as "the company's fortune." In 1998, she signed her first collection in her own name, thereby creating a new identity for the company.

❑ 1999. The licensed Gabriele Strehle Jeans brand was launched.
❑ 2000. Strehle GmbH & Co became Strenesse AG. Strenesse USA Inc. was founded in New York. Simultaneously, Strenesse Italia SpA was set up in Milan, dedicated to men's clothing.
❑ 2001. The first line of Strenesse Gabriele Strehle perfumes was launched.
❑ 2002. Strenesse launched a website at www.strenesse.com and *The Limitless Luxury Collection*, a CD with music from the collection.
❑ 2002, March. A flagship store was opened in Tokyo.
❑ 2004, May. Boris Becker (three times Wimbledon tennis champion) signed a contract to advertise Strenesse AG. It was the result of the sportsman's fondness and interest in fashion and style, and because he has been nominated as the best dressed man in Germany on several occasions.

Strenesse, Fall-Winter Collection, 1999-2000.

Stretch Yarn A term used to describe all elasticated fabrics. After appearing in the Paris collections in the 1960s, stretch fabric played an important role in the production of underwear and swimming costumes in the 1970s. The first fashion designer to use it and extol its virtues was the Tunisian Alaïa, who is famous for his sinuous lines and tight-fitting minidresses. (*Maria Vittoria Pozzi*)

Stromilli Textile firm manufacturing silk products. After a long apprentice period in Guido Ravasi's companies (1918 to 1928) and Gualdo Porro's workshop (1928 to 1931), Umberto Stromilli opened his own studio producing technical drawings for textiles in 1932. During World War II, Stromilli set up a small mill in Villa Guardia (Como) that specialized in the production of English-style gauze. In 1967, his son Sergio joined the firm. A change was made in the company name (Tessitura Stromilli SAS) after a non-family partner joined in 1997.

Stucchi Company set up in 1939 when Alberto Ambrosini and Adriano Stucchi joined forces to trade in silk, wool, and rayon fabrics, mainly for women's clothing. The following year saw a shake up in the company, with the departure of Ambrosini and a host of new shareholders, resulting in a change of name to SASA, an acronym of Sa Stucchi Adriano. To begin, their output was mainly destined for the Italian women's clothing market, but in the second half of the 1970s, the factories produced goods of medium-fine quality that were sold to companies that made up clothes rather than to retailers, thus creating openings on the international markets. The early 1980s saw an expansion into the sector of furnishing textiles but the company was wound up in the mid-1990s. (*Pierangelo Mastantuono*)

Stucchi Silk mill founded in 1870 by Edoardo Stucchi that expanded when a factory was built in Lurate-Caccivio in 1893. The excellent quality of its silks meant that they were exported across the world and that the company won the Grand Prize at the Universal Exhibition in 1900. Stucchi had more than 1,000 employees in 1934 when the company was at the peak of its success. For the majority of the 20th century, Stucchi represented the prestige of the Como silk industry, which focused on the spinneret, the wealth of its silk worms, and the value of the silk mill. Then, due to a change in the market, decline set in for the industry. The Tessile Operati agency intervened, taking over a part of the old building that housed all the looms, and eventually bought the brand itself. Today Tessile Operati is known for its production of raw silk, which is sold in the Como region.

Studio Berçot Private French fashion school founded by the painter and illustrator Suzanne Berçot in the late 1940s. From these artistic origins, the school focused on creative development and the individuality of the student. Besides artistic and aesthetic subjects, there is also a technical and management program to enable students to work in the fashion industry. Since 1970 the course, which lasts two years, plus a year spent in industry, has been formally recognized. Students are accepted at the age of 18, when they have taken their secondary school exams. There is a permanent teaching staff, but people working in industry are occasionally invited to teach. Former pupils include Nicole Farhi, Martine Sitbon, and Ocimar Versolato. The school is directed by Marie Ruck.

Studio Edelkoort Consultancy firm founded in Paris at the end of the 1980s by Dutchman Lidewij Edelkoort. Through the work of the Trend Union team, he predicts trends, colors, and materials in fashion, cosmetics, and furnishings by analysing developments in society and consumer trends. He publishes books of trends and perfects his predictions by tailoring them to suit the requirements of each client. He also responds to enquiries deep into the future: looking 3 to 10 years ahead. In 1987, he predicted the fashion for cycling shorts in the female wardrobe, which happened in 1990, when the English designer Liza Bruce launched them. The Studio has a publishing house which prints the weekly *View of Color* and *Interior View*.

Studio Mayer et Pierson Leopold Ernest Mayer and Pierre-Louis Pierson were two French photographers who had a portrait studio in Paris in the second half of the 19th century. In 1860 it was visited by Napoleon

III. Almost by chance, the studio entered the fashion history books when, in 1853-1857, it created an album with portraits of the Countess of Castiglione in all her countless outfits (today it is kept at the Metropolitan Museum of Art in New York). The studio closed at the beginning of the 20th century.

Studio Reutlinger (1850-1937). Photographic workshop founded by Frenchman Charles Reutlinger (1816-1880). He was a forerunner of the *haute couture* photographer because he used to take portraits of fashionable women before the modeling profession existed. The studio, which was taken over by his brother Emile and son Léopold, worked for many magazines (*Les Modes*, *Coming Modes*, and *The Ladies Field*) and for designers such as Doucet and Lanvin. When Léopold died in 1937, the business closed.

Studio Talbot Taking just one of the names of Henry Fox Talbot – one of the inventors of the photographic process known as calotypes – the less famous Studio Talbot specialized in the 1910s in fashion images produced by making albumen prints that were then hand colored with aniline dyes. The studio's images were printed as heliographs in Paris's *Les Modes*, one of the first periodicals to publish fashion photographs from 1901.

Sture Lars (1961). Norwegian jewelry designer. He was born in Nordfjord in Norway and studied the goldsmith's art at the National College of Art in Oslo (1992). He moved to London and attended a further course at Central St Martin's before starting up his own business in 1993. He began with a reasonably low-priced commercial line (his little sea-urchin-shaped earrings are typical of his work) before launching a collection of more special pieces in 1995. He works with various designers, including Sonja Nuttall, Joe Casley-Hayford, Owen Gaster and Fabio Piras.

Stüssy Clothing label set up in 1980 as a result of Shawn Stüssy's passion for surfing. To begin with the young sportsman patented surfboards and then moved to T-shirts, casual wear, and street clothing. He was so successful that he opened his first showroom in New York in 1986, becoming a point of reference for hiphop culture. His breakthrough came in 1996 when Paul Mittleman becomes the label's artistic director and expanded the brand to produce proper men's and women's collections, accessories, shoes, and eyewear. All the Stüssy lines are closely based on streetwear.

(*Maddalena Fossati*)

Stylist The English word does not mean a fashion designer or creator, but the person responsible for the style of photographs, in other words, the person who creates a particular look for an advertising image, or who chooses the appropriate clothes to communicate a particular type of fashion. Stylists can be consultants to fashion designers, or those who make suggestions at the moment of creativity or on the eve of fashion shows and during runway rehearsals. They are the ones who thin down the collections by throwing out some designs and changing the order of presentation. They are the ones who are horrified by a particular accessory or rave about a hairstyle. There is a small army of them. Carla Sozzani advises Krizia, the almighty André Leon Talley from *Vogue America* advised everyone, Carine Roitfeld is Tom Ford's right hand, and Alex White is at Miuccia Prada's side. Alexander McQueen trusts Katy England's judgement, just as Narciso Rodriguez trusts Lori Goldestein, while Calvin Klein and Helmut Lang rely on Melanie Ward.

Sui Anna (1955). American designer and the daughter of Chinese immigrants. She is considered the queen of extravagance. Born in Michigan, she grew up in Detroit and moved to New York to attend the Parson's School of Design. She founded her company in 1980, having made a name for herself as a designer thanks to photographer Stephen Meisel's feature on her in *Lei*. She is strongly influenced by the New York punk scene and her style focuses on rock music. In 1991, she presented her creations in New York and her friends Naomi Campbell, Linda Evangelista, and Christy Turlington model for her for free. At the beginning of her 1990s, her antennae, predicting almost everything, picked up on grunge fashion in the street. On the runway of the 1999 New York fashion shows, she presented black-and-

Sketch for a dress by Anna Sui.

white and patchwork designs and ponchos inspired by Bob Dylan's songs. She has two showrooms: one in New York and the other in Los Angeles. (*Eleonora Attolico*)

❑ 2000, February. As part of *Fashion in Motion*, the Victoria and Albert Museum in London hosted a small fashion show by the designer. The season included exhibitions of designs by Alexander McQueen, Vivienne Tam, Christian Lacroix, and Philip Treacy.
❑ 2000. Launch of her online boutique at www.annasuibeauty.com and promotion of her second fragrance *Sui Dreams* on a worldwide scale.
❑ 2001. She made a short film during a private party. The material, directed by Zoe Cassavettes and Noah Bogen, was then used as a backdrop to present her next winter collection. The film was reminiscent of the spirit of the pop period and Andy Warhol's parties. Actors/guests include: Vincent Gallo, James Iha, Maggie Rizer, Duncan Sheik, Carmen Cass, Rufus Wainright, Verushka, Marc Jacobs, Karen Elson, and George Condo.
❑ 2002. Two dresses from Sui's Spring 1997 collection were shown in the exhibition Men in Skirts at the Victoria and Albert Museum.

Suleyman Oscar. Women's fashion label created by Oscar Raaijmakers and Süleyman Demir in 1996. They both studied at and graduated from the Fashion Institute of Arnhem in the Netherlands, which was where the other more famous Dutch fashion duo, Viktor & Rolf, also graduated from. Raajmakers collaborates with Veronique Leroy, while Demir, who is Turkish-born and arrived in the Netherlands at the age of 15, works with Dice Hayak and Vivienne Westwood. Their clothes, photographed by a number of avantgarde magazines, reflect a notion of fashion and women that is extremely conceptual and never boring. Both born in 1970, they claim to be working "on the constant redefinition of clichés of beauty, elegance, femininity, and good and bad taste. But we are young and this can be a problem." It is a problem that they tackled with their most famous collection, Paper Cut-Out Dolls, inspired by paper dolls that led to cut-away designs. On the runway, they presented black suits, leather jackets, tailored pants which sprout little white cotton fins, like those that stick out to form the paper fold from the silhouette of paper dolls. The press loved them.

(*Antonio Mancinelli*)

Sulka American men's ready-to-wear fashion house. It was As Sulka, a businessman, and Léon Wormser, a shirtmaker, who set it up in 1895 in New York. Dismissive of scissors, they cut their shirts by knife, and soon stood out for the high quality of their materials and their sartorial knowledge. At the beginning, they produced firemen's and policemen's uniforms. Slowly they caught the attention of Wall Street bankers, politicians, and artists. Success enabled them to expand abroad, to

Paris in 1911 and to London in 1920. In 1989, Sulka was bought by the Vendôme Group.

Sundsbø Sølve (1970). Norwegian photographer. He publishes in *The Face*, *Harper's Bazaar*, *Numéro*, and *Big* and does campaigns for Ungaro, Bally, Patrick Cox, and Levi's. His campaign image for Yves Saint Laurent's *M7* perfume showing a male nude was surprising in its evocation of the photograph taken in 1971 by Jean Loup Sieff for Saint Laurent's first men's fragrance. (*Roberto Mutti*)

Superga Brand of tennis and sport shoe. The tennis model (the 2750) is universally known in the basic version: white canvas. But it has been reproduced in countless different variations – in cashmere, Oxford cotton, fleece, sponge, and linen. Superga's history began as a company that produced articles in rubber, particularly shoes (for sport and leisure from the start of the 20th century). After a long period of being owned by Pirelli, it was bought in 1993 by So.Pa.F, an investment group, which named Franco Bosisio – the man who planned the rampant success of Swatch watches in Italy – as managing director. In addition to the abundant lines of shoes and boots, Superga produces women's, men's, and children's collections of clothing (with the children's collection produced by Altana). It also creates a line of eyewear (produced by Italiana Occhiali) and stationery (by Pesenti Pigna). (*Giuliana Parabiago*)

Surah Soft medium-weight lustrous fabric of silk or rayon, characterized by fine twill lines, originally made in Surat in India.

Surfers Youth movement and a spontaneous fashion. Whereas surfers might be considered protohippies (a return to nature, nomadism, minimal attention paid to clothes, and a Californian origin), it is also true that a sport has rarely been so radically identified with a way of life: in the words of Nik Cohn, "Never has a more peacock-like sport been invented." Surfing has always relied on its mythology, origins, heroes, and mythic stories, but it was at the beginning of the 1960s that it became accessible to a generation of barely adolescent Californians. From a certain point of view, surf style represented the epitome of the era's hedonism: riding the waves, beach parties, Beach Boys and girls, car races. Their clothing fashions evolved from an initial phase in which the relaxed summer preppy look met the exotic fascination of Hawaii, then developed towards an increasingly relaxed style. Aside from performing on the waves, the image of relaxation became increasingly dominant: baggy pants and shorts, sweatshirts (with and without hoods), T-shirts with slogans, and sandals. Many specialist firms started up in the 1970s, for example, Billabong, Quiksilver, and Rip Curl, which also provided technical garments like neoprene wetsuits and accessories – and then there were funkier companies like Komodo and Mambo. It is interesting that surfing has its equivalents in the mountains (snowboarding) and in the city (skateboarding). Originally these evolved as a substitute for the real thing (waves), but they later developed their own language. Notable innovations have developed in surfing technology and clothing as a result of the interaction between these different disciplines.

(*Maurizio Vetrugno*)

Suspenders Men's clothing accessory used to hold up a man's pants, but used sporadically also by women and children. Manufactured in the 18th century from string or a couple of simple leather strips, in the 19th century they were made from cotton, velvet, and even rubber, until the intertwining of different yarns with rubber threads established the most recurrent model of the last 100 years. They are adjustable in length, thanks to the use of buckles, and are attached to buttons sewn on the front and back of the inside of the pants: the buttons can be eliminated if the suspenders have steel fasteners attached at either end. Suspenders went out of fashion in the 1950s to be replaced by the leather belt, thus they went from being an essential accessory to an eccentric fashion item, sometimes also used to bring a touch of color to trekking clothes, or, as in some 19th century revivals, made of black elasticated fabric to demythicize dinner jackets and tuxedos. During the 1970s suspenders briefly came back during the fashion for unisex garments, though women's models were more feminine and decorated with passementerie and embroideries.

Sutherland Lucy Christiana (1862-1935). English dressmaker. Lucy Sutherland was a survivor of the Titanic. She used to cut and sew dresses for her sister, the writer Elinor Glyn, and, when she was forced to enter into an uncertain marriage, she decided to go against the grain and take up dressmaking. In her work she looked back to the elegance of the 18th century, and became successful, partly because her already famous sister introduced members of high society to her workshop in Old Burlington Street. She also designed costumes for the theater. At the beginning of the 20th century she moved to Hanover Square and called her fashion house Lucille. In 1910, she set up shop in New York, in 1912 in Paris, and in 1915 in Chicago. Between 1916 and 1920, Ziegfeld had her make the magnificent costumes for his musicals. But, immediately after World War I tastes changed. In the space of just a few years, Lucille's glory waned and her company went bankrupt in 1923. She, however, remarried and became Lady Duff Gordon. Her autobiography was entitled *Discretions and Indiscretions*.

Sutor Mantellassi Artisan firm making shoes: *sutor* is Latin for shoemaker. Mantelassi is the surname of brothers Ettore and Enea, who were shoemakers in Florence. The company was founded in 1912 and it has remained in the family ever since. Today it is run by the new generations of Mantelassi who remain faithful to the artisan tradition. This loyalty is indicative of the house's style, whose tour-de-force is a slightly square-shaped shoe whose origins date back to the fashions of the 17th century. This attachment to tradition can also be found in the important collection of shoes in the company archive; in addition to its own models, it holds many historical shoes from all over the world. Sutor Mantellassi has also developed a series of accessories, small leather goods, and suitcases made using the same materials and manufacturing processes as their shoes.

❑ 2002, January. The Florentine house celebrated its 90th birthday with a limited edition shoe that was made to measure by sculpting the upper rather than cutting it.

Suture English fashion brand founded in 1995 by Tom Adams (Belfast, 1961) and Philip Delamore (Welwyn Garden City, 1968). Adams studied art at Loughborough University and the Royal Academy, and then embarked on a career as a costume designer. Delamore studied fashion and textiles at Cheltenham & Gloucester College of Higher Education. Their look is clean and modern. Their printed fabrics are interesting from a technological point of view.

Suzanne et Roger Label on Madison Avenue in New York that unites two French fashion companies that left Paris during the Occupation in 1941: those formed by Suzanne Remy, forewoman to the milliner Agnès, and Roger Vivier, a great shoe designer. Their professional alliance and their workshop has operated since the end of World War II.

Suzanne Talbot French *haute couture* house set up in 1917 by a dressmaker of the same name. Her name will always be associated with the original geometric creations that introduced Art Déco into fashion and used unexpected materials, such as chains. She was considered one of the greatest talents in *haute couture* between the wars and remained on the scene until 1957.

Suzuya Japanese label which, founded in 1951, enjoyed considerable success in the West from the early 1970s. They opened a shop in Paris on the Champs-Elysées but the label no longer exists.

Svend Brand belonging to Svend Gravensen, a French milliner in the 1940s and 1950s, who worked with Fath, Balmain, and Heim. In 1950, he decided to set up on his own and opened his own house. But it was a short-lived burst of independence and he soon returned to his role as the sidekick of the great designers.

Swarovski Founded by the Bohemian Daniel Swarovski in 1895, the Austrian company is still the world leader as a producer of cut crystal. The company uses high precision electronic tools invented by Daniel Swarovski himself, that have been perfected with the passing of time to reach their excellent current standards. Crystals that resemble precious and semi-precious stones, strass and even natural stones are the main areas of production. In the fields of jewelry, accessories, and furnishings, they have continually found new ways of applying their skills, bringing on board designers and stylists of international fame. 1976 marked the birth of the Swarovski Silver Crystal, the first line of finished products that the firm offered to the market: candleholders, paperweights, and other gift items. In 1987, the Swarovski Collectors Society was formed, which proposed limited edition articles designed by architects and artists of international repute, such as Ettore Sottsass and Alessandro Mendini. In 1989, the company launched a collection of *haute couture* accessories, which can today be bought in boutiques and certain department stores together with Swarovski Jeweller's Collection. In 1992 a new series of vases, goblets, and watches was launched, signed by designers such as Giampiero Maria Bodino and Borek Sipek. Thanks to its in-house style team, the Austrian firm has established a clearly defined image for itself, particularly after it set up a trend book in 1999 aimed at the world of fashion and jewelry.

❑ 2003, February. The launch of Crystal, a super luminous material creating lunar effects. This innovation was presented in New York during the fashion show of the child prodigy Zac Posen, who uses the material in some of his creations.

Swatch Swiss watch manufacturer founded in 1982.The name comes from the contraction of "Swiss watch." The first Swatch was designed to combat the Japanese digital invasion of the watch market. In the early years of the Japanese attack, the Swiss watch industry was literally overwhelmed by the competition from the East, which replaced traditional watch mechanisms with an electronic quartz crystal – the reliability was excellent and the prices unbelievably low. Switzerland's watch production (96 million watches in 1974) made by more than 1,600 manufacturers rapidly halved. In 1981 the Swiss watch's dominance of the world stage dropped from 30% to 9%. Owing to the imminent crisis in the industry, the political, industrial, and financial forces of the country entrusted 900 million Swiss francs to Nicolas Hayek, an expert in rebuilding industries, and Ernest Thomke, to launch a counter-offensive. Under the direction of Hayek, the two biggest firms in the country, SSIH and Asuag, founded the Société Suisse de Microéléctronique et d'Horologerie (SMH). Hayek relied on two engineers – Elmar Mock and Jacques Muller – who have an in-depth knowledge of electronics and plastic materials. The Swatch phenomenon happened very quickly, starting with a collection of 300,000 pieces in 1982. The number of components in the company's watches is reduced from 90 to 51; the casing is plastic, and the whole thing is enclosed in anti-scratch glass. The result is a shock-resistant, waterproof watch that is cheap to produce, and whose accuracy is guaranteed by a quartz crystal. Above all it is industrially interchangeable in the sense that simply changing the color of the plastic and the design of the face is enough to create a new model. In 1984, Swatch production reached a million pieces and they have now sold more than 150 million watches throughout the world. The fashion for plastic watches has become popular because it is a trend that manages to adapt to changes in people's lifestyles. The queues in front of Swatch shops and the immensely high prices bid by collectors for the very rare models are a phenomenon of the times. For example, a Kiki Picasso model, of which only 140 were made, was sold at a Zurich auction for 26,000 euros. Since 1992, Swatch has no longer been synonymous with just watches: it has already launched itself into the markets for telephones, answerphones, faxes, lights that you can switch off and on with your watch, personal beepers, and mobile phones. In fact even a small Swatch car has come on the market: it is small, so ideal for parking, and has a hybrid engine, thanks to a joint venture with Mercedes.

(*Luigi Chiavarone*)

❑ 2002. The Diaphane One was produced in translucent plastic and aluminum with a diamond embedded at

the 12 o'clock position. It is the most expensive model that the Swiss company has made.
❑ 2003, April. Following the public and critical success of the exhibition Melting Pop, curated by Gianluca Marziani, Swatch Italia made the special Melting Pop model in a limited edition of 120 to mark the occasion.
❑ 2003. In Basel, the new Winter collection inspired by the Dada movement was announced at the world exhibition of jewelry and clocks.

Swimming Costume For women it can be a single piece, a twin piece (the bikini), or simply the bottom half (the thong). For men it's composed by a single-piece in the form of shorts, however small or tight. Swimming costumes made their appearance in the second half of the 19th century, when, rather than the traditional country holiday, people started heading to the seaside. At that time people were still covered: women wore little low-necked tunics with leggings that reached the ankles, and men wore tight, sleeveless, thin-striped leotards that reached the knee. They were all made from in wool, as this material was considered more suitable for absorbing humidity. During the 1920s swimming costumes continued to be very demure, but everything changed in the 1930s when "sunbathing" came into fashion as being something very healthy. Women wore a light cotton sundress over shorts to play badminton on the beaches of Deauville and Biarritz. It was a Frenchman, Louis Réard, who was invented the bikini, and presented it in his collection of July 1946. It was given the name bikini (after an atoll in the Pacific Ocean where the first hydrogen bomb tests were being conducted at the time) as it was considered as explosive as the bomb. In the mid-1960s the mono-kini appeared, a tiny "swimming costume": just a tiny triangle in front and back, with a string through the bottom. It was the originator of the thong, which first appeared in Brazil. (*Gabriella Gregorietti*)

Swinger International Italian firm of ready-to-wear fashion. It was founded in Verona in the early 1970s by the Facchini family. It mainly produces and markets denim and casual wear for men and women. The company caught the attention of the public and fashion world with its own Swinger brand when it was the first to create Denim Fashion. Since the mid-1980s, it has combined its know-how, industrial capabilities, and the quality and talents of the company's own tailors with the creativity of important designers. It is in this vein that the first collaboration was signed in 1988 with Rocco Barocco, and continued with Fendi, Ungaro, Laura Biagiotti, Mila Schön, and Vivienne Westwood. The constant development of the company was given a new boost in September 2001, when it moved to new premises in Bussolengo (Verona). In April 2002, Swinger took over Byblos. The company's chairman is Dino Facchini, who was joined a few years ago by his son as managing director. (*Maria Vittoria Alfonsi*)

Swinging London The term Swinging London dates to April 16, 1966. The American weekly *Time* quoted the adjective used by the editor of the London monthly *Encounter*, Melvin Lasky, who was trying to describe what had been happening for some time in the city. In the parlance of the day, the word "swinging" connoted excitement and pleasure. And this is what London had become since 1963, the year which marked the end of the very long British aftermath of the war. A series of developments sparked a revolution in attitudes that extended to clothing, sexual practices, music, politics, society, and language. Swinging London introduced words like "trendy," "cool" and "square." The ideas behind Swinging London and the Swinging Sixties were fun, informality, and youth – revolutionary ideas in a society as hierarchical as England's. The whole period can be traced back to these values (or lack of values, as the older generation claimed). Consider the primary instigators of the changes: Mary Quant, a student at Goldsmith's College, created the minidress and helped launch the careers of models that only a few years earlier would have been considered inconceivable, such as the skeletal Twiggy. Scotsman John Stephen, in a narrow road in central London called Carnaby Street, sold clothes that were cheap and slightly shabby that could be thrown away without remorse a week later. The hairdresser Vidal Sassoon introduced cuts that would only stay fashionable for a short time (with one exception – long hair for men). The Beatles, The Rolling Stones, and The Who marked a dramatic break from the music of the past and became role models. Mick Jagger's arrest for possession of drugs and the Beatles' overshadowing of the royal family at the Prince of Wales Theater were episodes that did not go unnoticed. All of this was accompanied by a political and social earthquake. In 1963, the Profumo affair, which saw a British government minister caught up in a sex scandal, demolished the credibility of the establishment. In 1964, Harold Wilson's Labour government took power for the first time in 13 years and accelerated the demise of the Empire. In 1965 Winston Churchill died. The road was now open for new heroes, who were changing forever the face of London, Great Britain and – no exaggeration – the whole of Western society.

(*Beppe Severgnini*)

Swish Jeans Italian make of jeans. The brand was created at the end of 1994 by Marcello Mastrantuono who predicted the end of the unisex phase of jeans and focused instead on jeans which are highly feminine. His first collection, presented at the Milano Collezioni in 1995, was designed for a young, sexy, daring, ironic woman. He immediate won himself notoriety thanks to a series of strong slogans and publicity campaigns using famous top models such as Naomi Campbell, Carla Bruni, and Claudia Schiffer. It was the first brand of jeanswear to enter the Milano Collezioni calendar.

Sy Oumou (1952). Senegalese designer with five children and a series of three husbands. She is an innovative designer and a woman of grand ideals who has succeeded in melding the glittering lights of fashion with strong social issues, such as the emancipation of African women. Her dressmaking workshop in the medina in Dakar hosts students to whom she teaches the artistic techniques of African costume. Her project provides training for young people, not just in terms of craftsmanship, but in appreciating and valuing their own artistic talents, encouraging them to persist in pursuing those talents, giving them a sense of freedom and equipping them with the tools they will need to establish themselves in the West. To cope with so many demands, she has set up LEYDI, a workshop for design and for training in the arts, the traditional and modern techniques of costume, and African and Western influences. Pupils come from Senegal and other African countries, but even as far away as Europe and America.
Haute couture and ready-to-wear, however, remain her chosen field, but she also collaborates with the world of theater and performance and teaches fine arts in Dakar and abroad. Oumou Sy designed and presented, in Dakar and Geneva, the performance *La Vie a des Longues Jambes* (Life has Long Legs); she "invented" the Dakar Carnival; and she opened Metissacana – the first cyber café in Western Africa – in the Senegalese capital. In 1998, she was awarded first prize by the Prince Claus Foundation (Royal Palace in Amsterdam). In 2000, she represented African fashion at the Universal Exhibition in Hanover and the Prince Claus Foundation voted her an Urban Hero. In 2001, she received the FRI Net Africa award (Yaounde). In the last ten years, she has shown in Dakar, Milan, Berlin, Paris, London, New York, Geneva, Venice, Lille, Brussels, Catania and many other cities. The Wereldmuseum in Rotterdam and the Kindermuseum in Amsterdam both house some of her creations, as does the Galerie Ifa in Stuttgart and the Kunsthalle in Vienna. (*Maria Vittoria Alfonsi*)

Sybilla (1963). Designer who is symbolic of the Spanish movement in the 1980s. It is her decomposition of form, overlaying of fabrics, and use of non-gaudy colors that are her characteristics. Born in New York to an Argentine father and a Polish mother, after a brief period as an apprentice at Saint Laurent in Paris, she presented her first collection in Madrid at the age of just 20. Her second défilé, in 1985 at the Gaudí show in Barcelona, brought her general recognition. From 1987 until 1992, she linked up with Gibò, an Italian textile group, and in 1988 showed at Milano Collezioni. The Itokin group manufactures and distributes her label in Japan. In 1993/1994, she launched a young line, calling it Jocomomola, and in 1996, she designed a rucksack for Vuitton.

❑ 2001. Jocomomola, a licensed line arising from Itokin's contract with the Spanish group, recorded an increase of 30%. The new women's line was therefore renamed Jocomomola de Sybilla to reinforce the identity of the Spanish brand and appeal to its existing clients.
❑ 2003, July. Capucci presented evening wear designed by the Spanish designer in Paris.
❑ 2003. For Fall-Winter 2003-2004, the new line was produced under a license by Pier di Mogliano Veneto (Treviso) and distributed internationally by Daniele Ghiselli's Milan studio.

Sylvie Fleury (1961). Swiss artist. In *Untitled* (1992) she put together a pink carpet, a striped couch and several pairs of new shoes, mostly by Stéphane Kélian. In other assemblies, the artist has presented hanging clothes, and toilettes with make-up and mirrors. She considers fashion one of the most important aspects of our consumerist age, as the need to define a contemporary identity is so deeply rooted in us.

Symonds Anthony (1964). English designer born in London. Before finishing his studies at Central St Martin's School, he was already working with John Galliano and won the designer of the year award at Graduate Fashion Week. After graduating in 1994, he worked for Krizia, Moschino, English Eccentrics, and Vivienne Westwood, until he decided to create a women's line bearing his own name in 1998. He begins each collection by studying the fabrics; and though the designs may seem relatively simple, their construction is complex and technologically advanced.

Szczotarska Katarzyna. Polish designer. She left Poland to move to London and study fashion, first at Middlesex University and then at the London College of Fashion. For two years she worked as an assistant to Martin Margiela in Paris and then as a designer for the Arcadia group in England. From 2002, she appeared on the official calendar of the London fashion shows and immediately won the New Generation award. Her style is full of elegance – couture contrasted with postmodern elements.

T

Tabacchi Lidia (1933-1980). Italian journalist. From the foundation of the magazine *Novità* she was the alter ego of the founder Emilia, also known as Bebe, Rosselli Kuster, and finally took over her position in 1958. Under her guidance, the magazine, purchased in 1962 from Condé Nast editions, was gradually transformed until it became Vogue Italia. Receptive, open to new developments, emblematic of a crucial period in fashion and design, it represented a link between two eras. Her background was firmly grounded in work at other women's magazines, and she was an expert in the fields of knitwear, embroideries, elegantly set and designed dining tables, she expressed her innate aesthetic sense in all the aspects of fine living. She belonged to the group of editors of women's magazines who established themselves in part with their personal image and their charm. She was chic when this word, not yet exploited by the industry of trends, contained a variety of nuances and meanings. (*Marilea Somaré*)

Tabak Italian furrier, founded in Milan by Maximillian Tabak, in 1946. At first, the company would purchase hides and furs from around the world to supply them to apparel manufacturers. It was only occasionally that it would produce items of its own. In 1981, things changed. Massimo Tabak, the grandson of Maximillian, took over management of the company and decided to open a shop in the Via Bigli, in Milan, and to offer his own production of furs in tune with current fashions. Those were the years in which Tabak was riding the wave of the market, with advertising campaigns entrusted to major photographers. In 1995 the furrier moved to Corso Venezia. Here the shop remained until 1997, when it moved to the Via Bixio, transforming the label as well to Tabak by Deltafurs, with a dual production of sheepskin jackets and leather items, in prêt-à-porter and in high fashion. Tabak established an alliance with Cesare Manzini, setting aside for itself the role fashion designer and artistic director. The distribution of the product was very thorough in Italy and overseas, with special attention to the market of the former Soviet Union.

Tabard This term is used by Boccaccio, as well (*"Io ti lascerò pegno questo mio tabarro,"* literally, 'I will leave this tabard with you as a sign of my love'). It describes a long and ample men's cape and in certain areas in the north of Italy, the term is still used. In particular in Venice, in the eighteenth century, the term described the broad cape with a double mantle on the shoulders, worn both by noblemen and noblewomen. It was very common during the 1960s, but the tabard traces its roots back to the Middle Ages, when it was worn as a military or ceremonial uniform.

Tabard Maurice (1897-1984). French photographer. The son of silkmakers, he debuted in fashion designing fabrics, and then in 1914, following his father, he moved to the United States, where he attended the New York Institute of Photography and became such an established portraitist that he photographed the president of the U.S., Coolidge. In 1927 he returned to Paris, where he began his career as a fashion photographer, publishing in *L'Album de Figáro*, *Vu*, *Jardin des Modes*, and later in *Bifur*, *Silhouette*, *Vogue*, and *Marie Claire* where he also directed the studios. He met Brodovich (who was the choreographer in photographer of the Ballets Russes and the art director of the department stores Trois Quartiers) and worked in advertising. His experimental work, influenced by the solarizing and the photograms of Man Ray and the Surrealist movement, was published in *Die Form, Modern Photography, Photo Graphie*. From 1946 to 1949 he returned to New York where he worked for *Vogue* and *Harper's Bazaar* and, upon his return to

Europe, he emphasized his experimental work and devoted himself to exhibits and shows.

Tabarrificio Veneto Label of the Artigiana Sartoria Veneta (Venetian Artisanal Clothing Makers) which, in 1968, was founded in Mirano, near Venice, and which, through the Barena label as well ('barena' is a local term used to describe the lands that emerge from the waters of the lagoon at low tide), revitalized various distinctively Venetian or lagoon-based models of clothing as: rain capes, dustcoats, working overalls, fisherman's breeches. The most representative item, along with the Venetian shawl with long, hand-knotted fringes, is the *tabarro* (or tabard), an ample men's cape, a winter garment widely used in the Venetian area from the seventeenth century to the beginning of the twentieth century. A sort of archaeology of clothing underlies these repechages. Some of the model are based on items that are in the collections of local museums. (*Ruben Modigliani*)

Taffeta From the Persian, "taftah." One of the loveliest silk fabrics, with a tight, almost rigid structure, a brilliant and luminous appearance, rustling at every slightest movement. The iridescent luminous sheen of taffeta is a result of warp and weft in different colors. It is also made with artificial and synthetic fibers.

Tahari (1952). Israeli fashion designer. He works in New York. He is the standard-bearer of stretch fabrics. He loves the modern, comfortable, and sexy look. He grew up in Israel where he began his studies in electronic engineering, abandoning them as soon as he arrived in London. He discovered fashion while working as a courier for an apparel company. But his true dream was New York where he managed to arrive in 1971, during the boom in night life. He found work as an electrician in the Garment District, and there he learned sewing techniques and, by night, plunged into the New York bacchanal. He took his inspiration from the wild youth of the New York nightlife to design and create his first adherent top, ideal for the nights of wild celebrations of the period. It made him a millionaire in just a few months. In 1974, he opened his showroom and designed modern cocktail suits, low-maintenance and inexpensive, that were immediately popular, especially in the period when girls would go to work with polyster printed outfits. He designed his first women's jacket, which remained a must for many years. He always succeeded in being ahead of the trends. He did it recently as well, with the introduction of his new line Theory, based entirely on stretch materials: dresses, trousers, and shirts for women but, in a year's time, he also introduced stretch garments for men as well. (*Priscilla Daroda*)

Taiana Weaving mill founded in 1933 by Virgilio Taiana in Olgiate Comasco, in the industrial district of Como. It is currently run by his son, Claudio Taiana. It specializes in the production of classical menswear and womenswear fabrics but also dynamic and trendy fabrics, intended for apparel, shirts, swimsuits. The weaving mill has developed a vast array of technical fabrics for sportswear that are in great demand. With a turnover 25 billion liras yearly – that was in 1999 – and an extensive sales network, the company also has a presence in international markets.

Tailcoat (Tails) Men's evening and ceremonial suit. In French it is known as a *queue de morue* (swallow tail) and there is a slightly different version called a *queue de pie* (magpie). The jacket is always black, with a silk collar and lapels, short and open in the front to show the white, low-necked piquet waistcoat. The shirt has a starched shirtfront and collar, double cuffs, and is worn with a white bowtie. The matching pants have satin stripes down the sides of the legs. The outfit is often worn by orchestra conductors during performances. Its origin dates back to the late 1700s when it was still part of the military costume. It was Lord Brummel that, in the early 1800s, made it into a dandyish garment worn in everyday life. Towards the middle of the 20th century, its function changed and it is now used only as a ceremonial suit. In 1840, *Mode et Costume* wrote: "The tailcoat, a symbol of modern civilization, is the uniform which a man of culture must wear in society and during ceremonies. It's seen wherever life and pleasure are taken seriously, it's worn by beggars, godfathers, men in mourning, ball-goers, the ardent admirer of an actress, and by the bored man drinking his evening cup of tea. It's the external manifestation of a mystery and, though fashion can influence its form, it remains unchanged." From *Vestiti che usciamo*, by Luigi Settembrini and Chiara Boni: "If you want to learn how to wear a tailcoat, watch any of Fred Astaire's old movies. His elegance has never been matched." Like the tuxedo, the tailcoat has frequently returned to fashion in a female version since the 1920s, reinterpreted according to the tailor's or designer's fantasy.

Tailleur This is a French term, describing a woman's tailored costume or suit, and it brooks no discussion. It is a timeless pairing of a jacket and a skirt, or else a jacket and pants, elegant and refined, as well as sober and sporty: in any case the term always conveys a connotation of tailoring. There was a time that the *tailleur*, given the specific details of its rigorous cut, could only be made by a men's taior, in French, of course, a *tailleur*. It was the great English tailor John Redfern who made the first *tailleur* in 1885 for the Princess of Wales. At first, it was reserved for informal occasions, especially in the morning, and the *tailleur* gradually affirmed itself, simple, without frills, emphasized by masculine accessories, from the waistcoat to the cravat, in the last decade of the nineteenth century, as a distinctive expression of a desire for an active life, a need for liberty that verged on feminism. This was fashion's first step in the direction of women's emancipation. All the same, the *tailleur* of the time, although it did represent an escape from the impediment of traditional dress, was anything but convenient for women: the tailor transferred into the new item of clothing the heavy fabrics, the horsehair paddedstructure, and the padded shoulders of the men's outfit and it was not until the First World War that the skirt would be shortened, to be met by high boots, at the height of a hand's-breadth below the knee. It would be necessary to wait for the revolutionary intuition of Giorgio Armani, in the 1970s, once again marked by an upsurge of feminism, before the *tailleur* for women could include a destructured jacket, light fabrics with a solid framework, and the absence of all structure. A noteworthy forerunner of a complete break in the clothing of the new women was the revisitation of the *tailleur* by Chanel: during wartime, she had only jersey to work with and it was with this knitwear fabric, structured, light and yielding to the iron, that Coco created her *tailleur,* soft, rigorous, but absolutely feminine in its relaxed loosen-ess, later reworked, during the 1920s and beyond, into the famous tweed suits, the jacket adorned with braidwork and golden buttons. Never forgotten and often on the crest of various fashion waves, the *tailleur* became a provocative disguise and taboo-breaker for many of the divas of the passt. Marlene Dietrich loved to wear a jacket and trousers, the first woman to dare to do so in public, a forerunner of what would become the timeless woman's pantsuit. Joan Crawford, on the other hand, preferred the skirt, concentrating her attention on the jacket (created for her by the Hollywood costume designer Adrian): a handsome jacket with broad padded shoulders with a view to slimming the hips, a model that was copied again and again, somewhat stern, preferably dark, embellished with embroideries and passementerie. The *tailleur* is timeless. Fashions come and go, but the *tailleur* remains. It clings to the body as if it were a cardigan, it is illuminated with sherbet hues and costume jewelry, it can be sexy or stern, often it turns a page and looks back, it reappropriates the 1930s and 1940s silhouette, it rereads with a contemporary eye the teachings of Patou, Schiaparelli, Chanel. At times it narrows the torso and lengthens the hem; it becomes austere, but also mysterious and seductive. Androgynous and reserved. And even intriguing, when the skirt plays at being thrifty and shrinks to a microskirt, under jackets that allow glimpses of nudity. The conventions shatter, and new ones are attempted, invented matches: a hint of a bolero jacket, a vague reference to ski pants, a comfortable jacket with a sliding belt at the waist, accompanied by cigarette pants. And then there are hemmed tube pants, joined with a very trim and tapered tailcoat-jacket. Underneath, shiny blouses, colorful little pullovers, or else nothing at all, worn over bare skin. The ways of the *tailleur* are infinite. It respects the severity of a jacket, shirt, and skirt, or else it breaks the rules and gives way to countless other combinations. The *tailleur*

Tailleur by Jeanne Lanvin. Illustration by Pierre Brissaud for the *Gazette du Bon Ton*, 1920.

had established its own unique presence by the 1980s, a veritable gymnasium of stylistic exercises for the best known names in fashion: the extraordinary allure of Saint-Laurent, the magnificent shoulders of Valentino, the simplicity of Mila Schön, the grace of Krizia, the audacity of Versace, the geometries of Ferré have all separately given an unmistakable look to the jacket and carried out new cuts and innovations on the multiform skirt, bringing as well, to the *tailleur,* whether black or in various exquisite colors, the elegance of the tuxedo.

Takahashi Jun (1969). Japanese designer. He studied at the Burka Fashion College in Tokyo and, together with Nigo, who now designs the line, A Bathing Ape, he debuted at the lowest level of production with a line of T-shirts that he named *Nowhere*. In 1994, he created his label, Undercover, for women, men, and children. His fashion is multi-layered, eclectic in choice of colors, and highly wearable. His success in Japan was so considerable that in a very short time he had opened 17 boutiques. He was soon noticed by Rei Kawakubo, the women behind Comme des Garçons, and he designed a minicollection for her. After his experience, Undercover began to be sold in the Comme des Garçons stores in Tokyo and in shops like Corso Como 10 in Milan.

Takashi Yamai (1964). Japanese designer. He has always worked with his wife Yoriko, and in fact the couple is in sharp contrast with the cliché of the traditional Japanese couple. He graduated from the Bunka Fukuso fashion school, and worked for other *maisons* such as Bigi Co. Ltd, Tokyo Kumagai and in particular for the Japanese fashion designer Zucca. The year was 1995 when he launched his first prêt-à-porter collection based on the concepts of lightness and freshness in the selection of fabrics. He offered for everyday wear easy outfits, made principally out of silk, cotton poplin, knit-wear, and linen. (*Maddalena Fossati*)

Takizawa Naoki (1960). Japanese designer. He graduated from the Kuwasawa Design School in 1981, and then joined, the following year, the Miyake Design Studio. At first he was in charge of the Plantation line, but in 1989 he began to work on the womenswear Collection and, in 1992, he became an associate designer. In 1993 he was given full responsibility for the men-swear line that bears his name: Issey Miyake Men by Naoki Takizawa. In September 1998, he received the Mainichi Fashion Grandprix, a recognition that the Mainichi newspaper, one of the leading Japanese dailies, awards each year to professionals who have distinguished themselves in the field of fashion.

❑ 2001, January. For Milan Moda Uomo, the new Fall-Winter Collection of Takizawa for Issey Miyake was a genuine poetic performance, divided into three phases, for three different methods of dressing. Three imaginary worlds recreated on the runway, the worlds of shadow, ice, and light. In a stylistic and chromatic equilibrium, the man in the shadows wears short jackets, or long ones stretching to the knee, vests and sweaters with soft and destructured lines, in indefinite tones of "non-color," or in earth tones, in wool, velvet, and suede. The man on ice prefers orientalizing lines, jackets and shirts with Korean-style collars, long scarves worn like shawls over the jackets, flashy woolen boas around the neck, and fur-lined hats, all in dark-blue and black. Then color and fantasy patterns burst forth: the man in the sunlight wears shirts and sweaters with colorful stripes, ecru vests with orange designs, and is surrounded by the brightest colors, orange, green, and red. And the runway presentation culminates in a burst of enthusiasm, an erupting wave of joy: the models dance, leap, hurtle into the air, stepping on jackets and shirts, scarves and berets.

❑ 2001, March. It was a cherry-blossom festival, the petals that fall in the winter and cover the heads of the models and the runway in showers. The outfits were printed with black and white patterns, the skirts and tunics were very colorful, orange and brown, dark blue, red, and green.

❑ 2001, April. Libellula, the new hi-tech eyewear, designed by Naoki Takizawa and Alain Mikli. Conceived in France but manufactured in Japan, after three years of design, they have the lightness and colors of the dragonfly (in Italian, "libellula" means dragonfly), thanks to the use of such materials as titanium, acetate and grilamid. The glasses fold away into an egg-shaped case.

❑ 2002, April. On the runways of Paris the woman of Issey Miyake, designed by Naoki Takizawa, was enveloped in long ribbons of cloth, stitched in a sartorial manner. She was wrapped in luminous silk like a silkworm in a cocoon. Long, almost monastic clothing moves in subtle interplays of plissé, jackets and blazers mimic the motions of a waves lapping at the shore, long scarves undulated around necks, everything is shifting and iridescent. References to nature in the accessories as well, shiny and silky. Handbags that open and close

like mussels, backpacks like scarab beetles, and little shell-shaped bags on belts.
❑ 2002, June. For the Summer menswear Collection, the ideas were colorful. Stripes, both broad and thin, in various combinations of color, a patchwork that cheers up the metropolitan style. Long, baggy Bermuda shorts, complete with short, straight jackets, smocks, flowered or in double-face.
❑ 2003, January. In a runway presentation dedicated to travelers, the most appropriate outwear, according to Miyake's protégé, is the poncho. A traditional piece of outerwear that is redesigned: "It helps to protect travelers, it frees them from constriction. Jack London would have liked it."
(*Gabriella Gregorietti*)

Talk American monthly magazine founded by the film production house Miramax and edited by Tina Brown. Aside from culture and entertainment, it focused great attention on fashion. The first issue, which cost more than 50 million dollars to launch, was published in September 1999. Among the bylines were illustrious names in American journalism, politics, the movies, and fashion. "The idea," explained Tina Brown, "was to create a product in the style of the old American magazines, when an article by Truman Capote would appear next to an interview with Doris Day or a recipe. A sort of sophisticated rotogravure, one of those magazines that you can roll up and slip into a bag or into the pocket of your jacket and read anywhere." The mastermind of *Talk* was Tina Brown (1957), a British journalist who began her career at the age of 25 as an editor at *The Tatler*. At the end of the 1980s she arrived in New York to run the magazine *Vanity Fair* and then she took over *The New Yorker*, the most educated and snobbish weekly in America. In both cases, the "mistress of journalism" revolutionized the content and the style of the magazines, transforming them into products of spectacular image but elite readership, a pair of cult magazines.

Tam Vivienne. Chinese fashion designer. Born in Canton in China, she moved to Hong Kong at the age of three. The dual cultural exposure can be clearly detected in her work, an expression of an original encounter between the Oriental and the Occidental. Immediately after taking her undergraduate degree at the Hong Kong Polytechnic, she went to New York where, in 1994 she launched her *griffe* and staged a runway presentation of her first oriental-style Collection. In 1995 came her Collection inspired by Mao, and 1997 another Collection dedicated to Buddha. The impact was so original and modern that it won over celebrities and fan around the world. Some of her creations became so famous that they were included in the permanent archives of various museums, from the Andy Warhol Museum in Pittsburgh to the Metropolitan and FIT in New York, and finally the Victoria and Albert in London.
(*Lucia Serlenga*)

Tamaruyama Keita (1966). Born in Tokyo. Japanese designer. He studied at the Bunka Fashion College. He worked as a designer for Japanese companies. He created custom adverstiing videoclips. In 1997, he debuted on the runways of Paris with a womenswear Collection that was dominated by color and which combined oriental delicacy and sensibility with the western spirit.

Tanadori Yokoo (1936). Japanese illustrator known around the world as a psychedelic graphic artist. In 1999, he exhibited his latest creations on the theme of angels at the Ginza Pocket Park in Tokyo. In 1995 he was recognized in Tijuana as the best digital artist during the CyberFest. From 1960 to 1964, he studied at the Nishiwaki High School and at the Japan Design Center. Between 1976 and 1977, he worked on the Collections of Issey Miyake. He did the set design for Maurice Béjart's ballet, *Dyonisos* (1984). Beginning in 1982, his paintings are on display at the Metropolitan Museum of Art in New York.

Tancredi Franco (1922-1989). President of the Centro di Firenze per la Moda Italiana from 1967 till 1987, he was one of the chief masterminds behind the initial development of the international fashion fairs that are held in Florence. In 1967 he contributed to the planning and organization of the first Italian women's prêt-à-porter event (Pitti Donna). In the years that followed, he encouraged the creation of such other events as Pitti Uomo (1972), Pitti Bimbo (1975), Pitti Filati (1977) and Pitti Casa (1978). With the Associazione Industriali dell'Abbigliamento and with the Magliecalze association he reached in 1983 an agreement for cooperation that led to the creation of EMI-Ente Moda Italia (he chaired it until 1989) for the promotion of Italian fashion overseas and the organization of specialized events in conjunction with the Pitti events. Tancredi also played a decisive role in the critical phase that the Florentine fashion events traversed in the first half of the 1980s, that is, before taking on in 1988 the name of Pitti Immagine and inaugurating a new season of international successes and broad approval from the leading protagonists of the Italian fashion industry. (*Roberto Rosati*)

Tang David (1954). A Chinese creative, a fashion designer who reinvented outfits and lifestyles of the most nostalgic and kitsch Shanghai, the Shanghai before Mao Tse-tung, still colonial in its atmospheres. Thus, the old city lives again in the creations of Tang (who in the meantime has been designing boutiques in London and New York): the red glass lanterns inspired by the library of the China Club to the outfits for a Nympha Egeria called Gong Li. Elegant products intended for wealthy Asians but designed with an eye to the western markets as well.

Tani Barbara (1978). Italian designer. Born in Florence, after graduating from arts high school, she went on to study photography and graphics at the Istituto d'Arte. But her true love was fashion, and so she began to work on trends, colors, and fabrics with the Comitato Moda Italiano and with Promotrade. She then went on to work for New York Industries, Belfe and I Blues. In 2000, she created a line of her own. Her Collections are built around a continuous investigation of materials and colors, while the models have linear, simple, and essential forms.

Tappé Herman Patrick. American fashion designer and milliner. Active from 1910 till 1940. He designed the wedding dress in which Mary Pickford, "America's sweetheart," was married to Douglas Fairbanks. He had designed it for the daughter of the publisher Conde Nast, for a photo layout to be published in *Vogue*. It was simple, bare-shouldered, with lace trim, accompanied by a silk and tulle veil. The actress saw it and decided to wear it to the altar. His style can be described as romantic and feminine. He is also known for his hat design.

Tapscott Ruth Daphne also known as Billie (1903-1970). Tennis player. She shocked the audience at Wimbledon in 1927, by appearing on court with bare legs. "It's how we play at home," she explained. Her example probably inspired Joan Austin Lycett, who was the first to appear on Centre Court, in 1931, without even wearing knee socks.

Tarabini Rossella (1967). Italian designer, daughter of the profession: her mother is Anna Molinari. After attending DAMS in Bologna, she continued to study art in London. After returning to Italy, she joined the family company, working as an assistant to the art director for advertising deisgn and for the runway presentations of Blumarine. In 1995, she designed her first Collection for Anna Molinari.

❑ 2002, February. For the Spring-Summer Collection, Anna Molinari designed slightly retro-style outfits, slightly reminiscent of the 1920s. An elegance that keeps its distance from minimalism, in order to gain a new appreciation for a nonconventional and nonconformist femininity.
❑ 2002, September. In clear contrast with the prevailing trends, the legs are covered and black is adopted: this time, no veils, no translucence, no miniskirts, but still very seductive outfits, in order to be at one's ease at all times. *Bon ton*, even in the discotheque, shorts with flesh-colored pantyhose, fur jackets and glitter rowing shirts to be worn over silvery miniskirts.
❑ 2003, February. Rossella Tarabini takes Anna Molinari's "pretty baby" to a "poetic and perverse bordello." On the runway, the label presented suits and flounce skirts, ribbed shirts, dancer's shoes with heels, in the Charleston style,

little tulle outfits with wool fringes. Absolute black of pastel colors, from lilac to pale blue.

Tarantino Tarina (1973). American creator of costume jewelry. This young designer has been dubbed "the queen of sparkle." She is the daughter of artists, and she grew up in an exciting setting and in a city that is just as exciting–Hollywood. She lives in a house that once belonged to a silent-film star, Fatty Arbuckle. She began her career almost as a game, harking back to her favorite pastime as a child. She took inspiration from a small Collection of jewelry with colorful stones that her grandmother owned in the 1970s. She began by mixing terracotta pendants with vintage and glass beads that she found in the flea markets. She loves to match Swarovski crystals (her favorite) with surprising materials, such as wood or resin, and "blends" a surprising array of materials. This leads to dashing, versatile costume jewelry. Bracelets, rings, earrings, necklaces and brooches, flower-shaped or heart-shaped, etched roses, butterflies in filigree and stones, little Buddhas, antique-style chokers. These little objects have attracted the attention of stylists and fashion journalists, and in just a few years they became an essential must for movie stars, and even appeared in such cult television serials as *Friends*.

(*Gabriella Gregorietti*)

Tarlazzi Angelo (1945). Italian fashion designer. He was born in Ascoli Piceno. He established his reputation in prêt-à-porter, but his past was in haute couture after working with Jean Patou, first as an assistant and later as a creative director, from 1972 till 1976. He arrived in Paris in 1965 with not much money, plenty of enthusiasm, and a portfolio full of sketches. Behind him was an apprenticeship with Carosa, a legendary name in the Roma of *La Dolce Vita* (he was only 19 when he went to work instead of studying political science as his parents had hoped) and lots of copies he had done of the illustrations of Brunetta "one, ten, a hundred, to develop the skill." At first Paris was pretty hostile to him, and he had plenty of disappointments, until he decided to try the atelier of Patou, in fact, where his confident new style won interest. And he was hired. He made his presence felt right away. A first shock to the slightly old-fashioned image of the *maison* came with the idea of presenting the Collections with beautiful cover-girls, rather than entrusting them to chilly, reserved mannequins. Then came the nude-look "which is seduction, not sexy," a word that he rejected entirely. He would say, in this connection: "While I like a jacket worn over skin, the vampish sheath dress is horrible." His secret was to uncover and discover women without rendering them vulgar. And he added: "It is not the clothing itself that should enchant us, but the woman who wears it." History records that he made a brief return to Italy, where he worked with Laura Biagiotti and Basile: but working under a boss wasn't his style, and so he returned to France to attempt the great adventure of setting up shop on his own. The year was 1977. At this point, he also showed good business instrincts. Just five years went by and he was the president of the company that controlled his women-swear lines (Angelo Tarlazzi and the distribution Tarlazzi Due) and, subsequently, menswear as well. In 1986 he developed the Bataclan label, intended for the very young consumers, and in 1989 he succeeded to the very prestigious throne of Guy Laroche, who had died that year. He considered his creations to be nothing more than tools that he loved to play with: a soft dress without a cinch at the waist and normal length, can be worn in different ways, either gauzy and so short that it becomes a mini; or draped asymmetrically or blouson style at the hips. He sought unconventional combinations: he know how to slip a strict blazer over a gypsy skirt; he liked to set the stage for an active, mobile woman who was also seductive, caressed by the nuances of Paris and the bright colors of Italy. His most memorable qualities were the clean cuts, the natural volumes, the elegant, youthful silhouette, and especially comfortable, qualities that contributed to the success of the *griffe,* which clearly intended to transmit an undeniable love of liberty. An intelligent fashion that was always in step with the times, which focused importance on accessories, considered absolute co-stars of elegance: "If a woman has imagination," he said, "with a few well-chosen accessories, she can create a personal style all her own." Among the folk styles that we should

Angelo Tarlazzi, design for Carosa, 1969 (from *La Moda italiana. Le origini dell'alta moda e la maglieria*, Electa 1987).

mention, he converted peasant dress into haute couture: in linen embroidered with raffia; or else gringo outfits, double-breasted spencer jacket over tight pants or wrap-around skirts, fastened with big leather belts. And then there were the shantung safari jackets, worn over pleated chiffon skirts. Everyday luxury, then, entrusted to lengthy cardigans that underscored the refinement and simplicity of his style.

(*Lucia Mari*)

Taroni, Industria Serica The production of fine silk fabrics – single colors and worked, especially for women's apparel – under the label Sa Industria Serica Taroni, was begun in 1921 by Amedeo Taroni with Ernesto Bossi, Edoardo Rapuzzi, Martino Mazucchelli and Giulio Verga. In the plants located in Como and Maslianico, fabrics were processed that were intended both for the Italian and the international markets. Between the first and the second half of the

1920s, there was an expansion in the number of shareholders, with a consequential increase of corporate capital. A silk spinning mill located in Arcellasco (near Como) was purchased in 1926; a decade later Agrippino Porlezza, the son-in-law of Amedeo Taroni, took Agrippino's place at the head of the company. In 1963 the company closed the weaving mill in Maslianico and the production of apparel for luxury women's clothing was concentrated in Como. In 1999, the heir Giampaolo Porlezza sold the business to Michele Canepa. Now Taroni exports to 70 countries and, aside from the fabrics for garments used by all the major international *griffes*, it also produces flags (including the Vatican flag), sacred paraments, and outfits for cardinals. (*Pierangelo Mastantuono*)

Tarquini Luigi. Italian painting, fashion illustrator, dress designer. Born in Rome, after studying fine arts, he worked in the 1950s for *Arbiter* and for *Esquire* documenting everything that was happening in fashion. But he created fashion as well, designing shoes for Genesco and patterns for Brioni (1956), Sanremo and other apparel manufacturers.

Tartan What the business card or the family coat-of-arms is for us, tartan is for the Scots. The use of tartan dates back to the traditions of the Middle Ages. Every clan, every family possesses a tartan of its own and, despite the deceptive appearance, each one is slightly, but absolutely different from all the others. After the Second World War, skirts and kilts became very popular. In the 1980s, a number of fashion designers featured tartan trousers and a number of Winters Collections focused on the distinctive and traditional tartan structure.

Tarulli Marche-based hat company founded in 1990 by Roberto Tarulli in a continuation of his family's traditional occupation. Today the company offers a vast array of high fashion models for men and women, manufactured with quality materials, characterized by a very high-quality artisanal workmanship. The company entered the headwear market with special attention to the fashion sector, in an attempt to make the hat an essential accessory for any look and men's dress and lifestyle, as in the old days.

Tasmania Island to the south of Australia that produces especially fine wools, used to make high-quality worsted, wrinkle-proof and very light, perfect for Spring-Summer.

Tassel Gustave (1926). American fashion designer noted for his sense of proportion, the simplicity of line, the finishing of every detail, the sculptural forms, either tapered or bell-shaped. Jackie Kennedy Onassis often wore Tassel's "black dinner dress." After studying at the Fine Arts Academy in Philadelphia, he decided to leave for Paris where he worked for a certain period as an illustrator for Geneviève Fath. He became friends with James Galanos, who helped him in 1956 to open his own atelier in Los Angeles. In 1972, when Norman Norrel died, Tassel continued to lead the *maison*, renaming it the House of Norrel, Gustave Tassel. An experience that lasted four years. In 1976, he resumed independent work.

Tassi Karim (1966). Moroccan fashion designer. He has lived and worked in Paris since 1988. He studied at the International Institute of Design and in Casablanca, and learned the business by working for tailors making tunics, for the children's apparel label Totoche and then, later, opened a boutique of his own. Once he arrived in Paris, he attended the school of the Chambre Syndicale. After graduating, he established the Fashion Department at the University of Quito, in Ecuador, and then returned to France where he began to present his own Collections in 1999.

Tata-Naka Women's fashion label founded in London in 2000 by Tamara and Natasha Surguladze, two identical twins. They left Russia to come to London in 1996 to study fashion at the Central Saint Martin's school. After graduating, they immediately presented a Collection of their own. Their runway presentations, always broken down into two phases, reflect two philosophies and two styles that are in perfect harmony. They move from the Old Russian style to hypermodern cuts, with fluidity and modernity. Their client list features many American actresses but also the finest fashion shops in Europe, the U.S., and the Far East. They design a line for the Top Shop house in England.

Tati French department store. It sells everything. From pantyhose, suits, and tuxedoes to jewelry, candy, and Christmas tree ornaments. The history of Tati is a long one, that began in 1948, with the opening of the first retail outlet, in Paris. In 1975, an updated, more striking store sign: dark blue letters against a pink background. This was the the critical moment for expansion, with a slogan that blared out from the rooftops: "*Tati les plus bas prix*" (Tati, the Lowest Prices!). That year, two other stores were opened, again in Paris, in Rue de Rennes and in Place de la République. In 1984, instead, the first store in the provinces, in Nancy, was opened. It was followed by stores in Lille (1985), Rouen (1988), Montpellier (1989), and Le Havre (1991). In 1992, aside from a new retail outlet in Bordeaux, the first house line was introduced: *La Route est à nous*, designed by Andrée Putman. In 1994, the chain inaugurated spaces devoted to jewelry and, that same year, the perfume was presented. In 1995, the group began to move abroad: a department store in Strasbourg, another in South Africa, and then on to Switzerland, Germany, Israel, and Lebanon. In 1998, they began an eyewear line.

Tatlin Pseudonym of Vladimir Levgrafovitch (1885-1953). Russian artist. Born in Moscow. A Soviet militant, he was, with Rodchenko, one of the founders of the Constructivist Movement. A forerunner of industrial design, he also created his own furniture and designed outfits with a view primarily to functionality. He created and work overcoats and jackets with removable flannel linings for the intermediate seasons, and fur for the winter. He also invented outfits with elements that could be replaced when they were worn out.

Tatsos Maria (1966). Journalist. Editor of *Top Girl*. Born to a Greek family, she began her career at *La Provincia di Como* and the *Giornale del Popolo* of Ticino. In 1991 she was hired at *Vera*, where, at first, she reported on business and law. She was moved to the head office and quality control, where she gained management experience that led her, in 1998, to the editor's job at *Top Girl*, a young-target monthly newly founded by Gruner-Jahr-Mondadori, with an audience of girls 13-19.

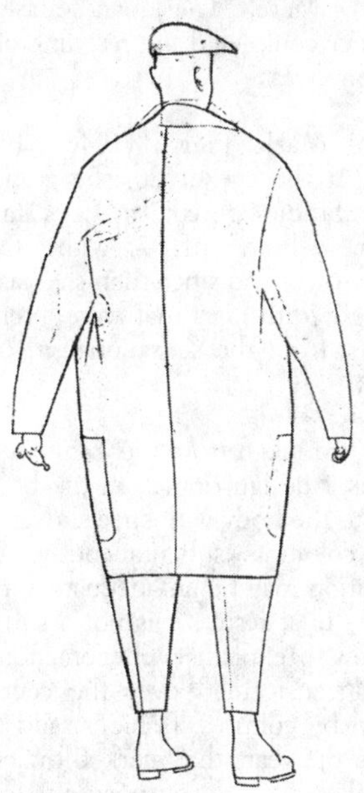

Tatlin, sketch for men's outfit 1923-1924 (from *Art Fashion*, Biennial of Florence, Skira, 1996).

Tatsuno Koji (1964). Japanese designer. He moved to London at the age of 18, where he gained attention with his shirts made from old kimonos. In 1983, he founded his company, Culture Shock, and opened a boutique making custom suits, made out of antique Japanese fabrics. In March 1990 he had his first runway presentation in Paris and, having achieved notice and with the support of Franca Sozzani, editor of *Vogue Italy*, he enjoyed success.

❑ 1997, March. Tatsuno was tapped by Joyce Ma, founder and chief executive of the Joyce boutiques of Paris, for a show in the new space that she had just opened for young talents. The title of the exhibition was *Koji Tatsuno An elegy to the body and clothes*.

❑ 2003, March. The Japanese fashion designer completed the restyling of the Maison Grès.

Tattarachi Marie Pierre (1946). French designer. At the age of 26, she graduated from the Studio Berçot, a Paris fashion school. She debuted in 1975 with a Collection of her own, and since then she has held the spotlight with lines that were intentionally distant from the sensationalism of the runway.

Tattoo Word taken from the Tahitian term, *tatou*. It is a design drawn on the body by cutting into the body with special dyes or by injecting colorants subcutaneously. While this definition may be an adequate explanation of the final result, it is not a sufficient explanation to explain a phenomenon that has been transformed over the centuries, influenced by cultures, fashions, and social history. In the years that marked the end of the last millennium, the tattoo was essentially an expression of art and fashion that merged into that remarkable form of expression that we call Body Art, including the variant of Body Painting. Previously theorized by the architect Adolf Loos ("The impulse to decorate one's own body underlies the origin of figurative art," he wrote), Body Art attained planetary notoriety at the end of the 1970s, when Keith Haring (1958-90) transferred his Graffiti Art from the walls of the New York subway onto human bodies. In 1979, the French-born artist of Italian descent, Gina Pane (1939), signed the official manifesto of tattooing as art: "the body is no longer representation but transformation." Among the chief contemporary practitioners of Body Art is Shirine Neshat, an Iranian artist who uses her own skin to denounce the condition of women in her homeland, forced into silence. Alongside this artistic phenomenon, fashion, with such practitioners as Gaultier, Gigli, Galliano and Versace, has taken ownership of tattooing to give outfits the allure of the geographic variable of desire. While many entertainment figures have adopted the decoration used by Berber women with henna, giving meaning to an elaborate form of maquillage commonly described as Body Painting. No one knows exactly when tattooing was first invented, nor where. The clay dolls found in Egypt and dating back four thousand years were tattooed, while the earliest documentation on a human body came from the discovery, in the 1920s, of the mummy of a completely tattooed Scythian warrior dating from the fifth century B.C. There is also a tattoo on the shoulder of the mummy of Similaun, the body of a wayfarer who died 5,300 years ago, frozen to death and discovered in the Alps less than ten years ago. In the west, the word tattoo arrived, in the eighteenth century, with Captain James Cook when he returned from one of his trips to the great South Sea. The British explorer brought to old Europe what is perhaps the loveliest expression of the art of tattooing, the polychromatic Polynesian form, which is distinct from the Japanese art (which uses the *irezumi* technique: the color is inserted with tiny needles under the skin), from that used by the populations of sub-equatorial Africa (which practices scarification: cutting into the skin in order to obtain raised scars) and that used by North African peoples (who dye their

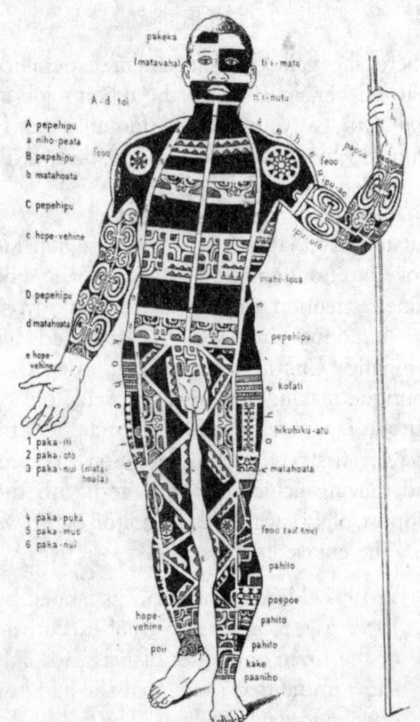

Chart of Tahitian tattoos (from "Lo Specchio," supplement to *La Stampa*, no. 10, 1998).

skin with henna). Looked upon with hostility in the Christian west, tattooing at first became an expression of certain marginalized social classes, such as sailors, convicts, and prostitutes, and later become a distinctive mark of a few youth avant-gardes, such as the Punks, finally culminating in piercing. (*Michele Ciavarella*)

Tayama Atsuro (1955). Japanese designer. He arrived in Paris with his diploma from the Bunka College in his pocket, and in 1974 he became the head assistant to Yohji Yamamoto. From 1974 to 1982 he worked as the chief director of Yamamoto Europe. Already the owner of his own company in Japan, he opened his first boutique of men's prêt-à-porter in 1990 in Paris, in the Marais neighborhood, and second boutique in 1997, in Saint-Germain-des-Près. His Collections are currently on sale at the Espace Colette, one of the best known and trendiest Parisian shops.

Taylor Rebecca (1969). New Zealand-born fashion designer. At the age of 22, just after taking her degree from the Massey University Design School, she left her country to move to New York. She entered the world of fashion through the tradesmen's entrance, preparing, as her biography tells the story, "three hundred tuna-fish sandwiches for the guests at Cynthia Rowley's runway presentation." She worked intensely for five years and finally met Elizabeth Bugdaycay, with whom she decided to establish her own womenswear label. She debuted in 1999 during the New York Fashion Week. Success came immediately. She offered a style that emphasized femininity, blending vintage details from the 1960s and 1970s. Her pink cashmere cardigan with a leopard-spot print, to be worn either with jeans or with an evening gown, became an emblem of her aesthetic. Other distinctive features were the use of bright colors (black was entirely eliminated) and a preference for natural fabrics. In 2000 she was awarded the prestigious Perry Ellis prize for a young designer of women's clothing. Among her clients are the actresses Cameron Diaz, Jennifer Lopez and Courtney Love. She designed many of the outfits worn by the stars of the television series *Sex and the City*.

Tcherassi Silvia (1966). Colombian fashion designer. She is a beautiful blonde, somewhere between Grace Kelly and Deborah Kerr. Born in Barranquilla, an industrial and port city overlooking the Caribbean Sea. She is married and has two children. She debuted at Milan's Moda Donna with a Winter 2003-2004 Collection, after runway presentations in Paris, Dusseldorf, Washington, Los Angeles, and Miami, where she was chosen "New Star in Fashion." On the occasion of Bogotá Fashion, the magazine *Vogue* gave her an award for her professional career. She began with interior design, but her quest for new forms of expression and a stay in Europe were enough to make her head in a new direction, and so she became a fashion designer. Certainly, she loves contrasts: her women may have the delicacy of a ballerina on tiptoe or the aggressivity of a rock star. A pluralistic style that brings together extremes where fabrics are concerned: evanescent or "crunchy," such as taffeta with crocodile-skin reliefs. She was chosen "woman of the year" in 1998, while in 1999 she received a special award from her government as an influential figure in the contemporary history of Colombia. Among her well-known clients, Hillary and Chelsea Clinton. (*Lucia Mari*)

Tchicaya Patrice Félix (1960). French photographer of Congolese descent. At a very young age he left his family to move to London where he entered the world of fashion. His work is marked by his ironic view and his skill at conferring allure and mystery on even the most ordinary clothing.

TCN Label specializing in women's underwear: pajamas, corsets, and swimsuits. Created in 1984 by Totón Comella (1968), a woman from Barcelona whose family is a name in the world of textiles. In 1991 she debuted on the Pasarela Gaudí in Barcelona and hers was one of the most highly acclaimed runway presentations. In 2001, she ventured into designing a streetwear Collection. The key to her success lay in her intelligent use of fabrics. She worked perfectly with velvet, lycra, cotton, silk, and distressed leather. She employed many technological methods for the finishings (distressed, fused, and metallized fabrics). Each of her Collections was characterized by inspiration of a specific theme: the 1920s, the mountains, or other themes, with very precise details. (*Estefania Ruilope Ruiz*)

Techno The mass explosion of the phenomenon of rave-parties, beginning in 1988, had the effect of rendering visible to many the ironic use of the fetish of technology and the obsession with the oppressive decibel level, so typical of the new music generically described as Techno. The most radical frequenters of this scene, garbed in radiation-proof overalls and camouflage commando fabrics, seem to be refugees from a science-fiction disaster movie. In terms of style, it is easy to see the influence of the fascination of the post-atomic scenario from a previous time. Anthropologically it is interesting to notice the return in a ritual form of noise, in a civilization (specifically, the English civilization) that is increasingly moving away from the industrial dimension. (*Maurizio Vetrugno*)

Técla French jewelers, in the Rue de la Paix in Paris. The first Técla Collection of cultured pearls was created in 1912 by Jo Goldman. Even now, the decor of the boutique remains unchanged, the creation of Jansen, inspired by the Far East. A Técla bracelet, made of gold and small pearls, was on Brigitte Bardot's arm in Roger Vadim's film *Et Dieu crea la femme* (1956) and helped to spread the reputation of the jeweler among the mass public. For forty years, the store and the label were managed by Pierette Scali Thétys. *Les Marines, Les Océanes* are the name of a few of the current Collections, and pearls are always at the heart of them.

Tecnica Italian shoe manufacturer. It was founded in 1960 and at first it produced only work shoes, in keeping with the production already established by Oreste Zanatta. His sons, Giancarlo and Ambrosiano, shifted production in the early 1970s toward the sports sector. And it was in 1970 that Tecnica presented its first Moon Boot: it became a synonym for after-ski and sold over 300 million pairs around the world. Today, the company produces ski boots, after-ski footwear, trekking boots, outdoor shoes, in-line skates, apparel and accessories. Through a series of purchases, mergers, and marketing agreements, the group also operates the labels Think Pink (sports apparel, acquired in 1992), Lowa (German company, market leader in trekking footwear, purchased in 1993), Dolomite (acquired in 1998), Marker (ski fasteners, snowboards) and Volk (skiing).

❑ 2002, March. Giancarlo Zanatta, president and managing director of the Gruppo Tecnica (the Tecnica, Dolomite, Nitro, Lowa, Think Pink and Marker labels, as well as distributor of the products of Volkl and Elan), was appointed chairman of Assosport, national association of manufacturers of sporting goods.
❑ 2002, April. Agreement signed for the acquisition of the last 15 percent of the shares of Marker International, a German ski-fastener manufacturer, of which it had owned 85 percent since 1999 through the holding company CT Holding. From turnover of 59 million Euros in 1999, Marker International rose to 64 million in 2001. The Gruppo Tecnica ended 2002 with a turnover of 294 million Euros, a 4 percent increase over the year before, which had already enjoyed an increase of 16.7 percent.
❑ 2003, January. Agreement signed between Benetton and Tecnica for the purchase of the Nordica label. The Montebelluna-based company won out over the competition of several sector leaders, including Atomic and Head. Benetton received a 10 percent share of Tecnica's capital.
❑ 2003, April. Tecnica purchases Rollerblade as well. (*Valeria Vantaggi*)

Teddy Boys British youth movement and ensuing fashion. In 1950 the British edition of *Vogue* stated that "there is a new formality, verging on the Edwardian, in men's dress in London, which recalls the years before 1914." That had been a glorious period for British high society, a period that many certainly wished to bring back. The young snobs of the London fashion district decided to go ahead and do it. The new Edwardians adopted as their apparel-uniform pipestem trousers, stiff, high white collars, and damask vests. Beginning in 1954, however, their style was adopted with a provocative and satirical intent, reworked in a less expensive version by the young proletarians of the outlying areas of London, the so-called Teddy Boys. And Teddy was the working-class modification of the Edwardian expression. The Teds were accused of all sorts of criminal acts, from racist assaults to thefts. And their clothing was transformed into a synonym of their vandalism. They also wore drape-suits, turned-up or buttoned collars, drain-pipe trousers, bootlace ties, thick-soloed suede shoes and they pomaded their long hair with brilliantine, combing them into quiffs. The movement vanished toward the end of the 1950s. Every so often it reappears as a lifestyle phenomenon. In the 1980s it was linked to the rockabilly revival in a slightly cartoonish and cinematic version, in the American-graffiti style. (*Gianluca Bauzano*)

Teerobe Negligee/outfit created in 1864 by Worth. It was revived at the end of the twentieth century as an elegant and spectacular housecoat, with princesse cut, in double fabric, with ample sleeves, a neckline decorated with ribbons and strips or cloth, or other passementerie.

Tegon Sergio (1940). Italian entrepreneur. He was born in Mirano, in the province of Venice, and he entered the field of fashion at the age of 16, working as a shop clerk at the Coin department store in Mestre. At the age of 30 he founded the Seventy label for an industrial production of men's and women's apparel. In 1975, in the wake of Seventy's success, he launched Pepper Industries and began to produce sportswear, especially jeans. Between 1977 and 1981, he added new labels to the company: Lemon (young people's apparel) and Pepperino (childrens). Over the years, he developed Pepper Industries on an international scale, acquiring such prestigious labels as Henry Cotton's, Moncler, Balajò (knitwear) and Cerruti Jeans (production on license), and bringing the overall revenue to about 200 billion liras. In June 1998 he radically shifted his approach: he sold Pepper Industries with the subsidiary companies and, through the Cà Dà Mosto company, he produced and distributed the Seventy lines, with a staff of 35 people and a turnover of some 40 billion liras.

❑ 2003, January. The turnover was steadily rising: in 2002 it reached 35 million Euros with a 17 percent increase. The womenswear line occupied 60 percent of gross revenue, while the menswear Collection accounted for 40 percent.

Teisner Kirsten. Designer. Assisted by a group of fashion designers, she supervised the two Danish prêt-à-porter lines In Wear (for women) and Matinique (for men): actually, these were practically unisex items. The Collections have a casual-sporty look, meant especially for young consumers.

Teller Jurgen (1964). German photographer. He studied at the Bayerische Staatslehranstalt Photographie in Munich (now the State Academy for Photography and Design) from 1984 to 1986. He collaborated with numerous magazines including *i-D*, *Arena*, *The Face*, *Homme Plus*, *Dazed & Confused*, *Details*, *Art Forum*, *Vibe*, *Stern*, *AbeSea*, *Index*, *W Magazine*, *Interview* and the English, French, Italian, and American editions of *Vogue*. He worked for clients such as Miu Miu, Comme des Garçons, Katherine Hamnett, Calvin Klein, Alessandro Dell'Acqua, Anna Molinari, Hugo Boss, and Louis Vuitton. He is considered to be the first figure in a new wave in photography as a result of his way of doing direct portraits with a cold, raw light. He also worked in the musical field with covers for Bjork, Dave Stewart, Elastica, Elton John, Simply Red, Sinead O'Connor. Pitti Immagine Discover organized a personal show of his work in the Summer of 1998. He published the books *Jurgen Teller by Jurgen Teller* (1999) and *Go See* (2000), where he did portraits of non-professional models as they crossed the threshold of his studio. He has done personal shows in Tokyo, London, and Florence. He lives and works in London.

Temperley Alice (1975). British fashion designer. She graduated in textile design from Central St. Martin's and then went on to take a master's in textile printing and technology at the Royal College of Art. She began to sell her single items which she was still a student, but before launching her own label she spent a period at Ratti in Italy as a stylistic consultant. In 2000, she inaugurated

Temperley London, a line of women's apparel. Her experience in the textile business led her to create her own prints and to supervise down to the tiniest details the decorations and crafts embroideries done in the Far East. She sells in department stores and exclusive boutiques around the world. (*Virginia Hill*)

Temple St. Clair Carr Trademark of a goldsmith and jeweler. It takes its name from its designer who, born in a small town in Virginia, developed a passion for antique objects, of which she became a collector. She adored ancient history and art and spent many years studying in Italy. In 1987, she introduced her first line of jewelry and immediately won a following among the American public. Her most famous creations are in the Byzantine style, and form part of the archeological Collection. In her work, we can also sense a passion for the artisanal work that she continues to study in the workshops of Florence.

Templier Raymond (1891-1968). French jeweler. He was a practitioner of the geometric Art Deco style, and was one of the founders of the Union des Artistes Modernes. Heir to a solid family tradition of goldsmithery, but also linked by intellettual affinities to the artistic avant-garde, he expressed in the form of jewelry a purism that took its inspiration from the early years of industrial design, utilizing by preference the white metals (platinum and silver), together with diamonds and onyx.

Tenente José Antonio (1966). Portuguese fashion designer. After a brief excursion into the world of architecture, he went on to study Fashion Design at CITEX. In 1986 he presented his first two Collections. In 1988 he did runway presentations in France and Italy. In 1990 he opened a shop in Lisbon. He is considered one of the finest Portuguese fashion designers and his prestige has spread to an international level, allowing him to win major prizes in various countries around the world. He expresses himself with a sober and rigorous spirit, conveying the image of the eternal romantic. Aside from designing fashion Collections, he also designed costumes for a number of theaters and dance companies and he has been the personal fashion designer for many public figures in Portugal.

(*Estefania Ruilope Ruiz*)

Tennis (*The wardrobe of tennis*). The earliest followers Major Walter Clopton Wingfield, who in 1873, in Great Britain, invented the rules of the sport derived from the "jeu de paume," the ancient French game of lawn tennis, would wear simple, bright white flannels: long belted, narrow-waisted trousers and shirts with collars and cuffs. To tell the truth, the only clear regulation that can be found in the announcment for the first matches of Wimbledon, published on 9 June 1877 in the newspaper, *The Field*, refers to the shoes, which had to be heel-less. At any rate, this was, for many years, the classic outfit for tennis, with the concession of rolling up one's sleeves in order to be freer to move, as Spencer W. Gore had done, the first winner on grass of the All England Croquet and Lawn Tennis Club, and with very few variants, documented by the prints and photographs of the last decades of the nineteenth century: the knickerbockers or plus-fours and the shirt with horizontal stripes that seem to have been the clothing worn by the stronger of the Renshaw twins, Willie, seven-time winners in singles at Wimbledon. Less concerned with etiquette, the Americans, who were soon won over the new English pastime, resolved the problem by donning the usual outfit worn for strolling or for baseball, including the colorful hat with a bill. Women, whether in the old continent or the new world, stoically gripped their rackets dressed in flowing skirts, with crinolines, corsets, heavy underwear, heels, and little caps, even after 1884, when they were permitted to take part in the London competition. Reacting to all this elaborate nineteenth-century elegance was Maud Watson, along with her sister Lillian. Maud was an unbeaten champion, from 1881 to 1886, in 55 matches. She chose to opt for a certain simplicity, carrying out a bland revolution by dressing exclusively in white and eliminating from her silk shirt the stiff closed collar with a bowtie or a tie. Italian female tennis players were given a few interesting suggestions, though they were vague concerning style, in the magazine *Margherita* dated 15 September 1891: "For tennis, an amusement that has become universally popular, costumes are being created that are lovely and appropriate, and woolen fabrics with balls, sticks, and triangular, either painted or woven, are the ones that are most popular." Added to these, the following years, were striped fabrics, considered "proper for tennis outfits." It would take until the new century before the skirt became a few inches shorter and the sleeves were shortened to half length, thanks to the American female tennis player May Sutton, who, in 1905, was the first foreigner to write her name in the golden album at Wimbledon. About fifteen years of gradual, yet daring conquests in the emancipation of the clothing took place and behold, at the beginning of the 1920s, the "Divine" Suzanne Lenglen showed her calves, while in her inimitable style she floated lightly through the air, showing off the creations signed by no less a designer than Jean Patou, and turbans made of dyed tulle, matching the cardigans fastened with a long line of buttons. Tennis fashion had reached a level of refinement made up of lovely sweaters and soft pleated skirts, increasingly likely to rise above the knee. It was the elegance as well of Helen Wills, the "Queen" (8 victories at Wimbledon between 1927 and 1938), that gave it a further touch of light elegance with the small white visor that she invented herself. The decade of the 1930s showed that the time had come for short pants. If, at the end of the 1920s, the Spanish player Lilli de Alvarez had worn (tulle) shorts beneath her skirt, in 1933 Helen Jacobs won the women's championship of the United States dressed in daring shorts "that were a full hand's breadth above the knee!" In men's tennis as well there were those who felt that the austere and burdensome city trousers were obsolete, and cut them down to shorts. The innovator was Bunny Austin, a student at Cambridge "who always had his nose stuck in his damned book of Shakespeare" and an ace at tennis; in 1933 with Fred Perry he took the Davis Cup from the renowned "French Musketeers." Even though Austin no longer suffered from the cramps that he had suffered when he was playing "in full regalia," among the gentlement long pants resisted the change for many years still to come. But as we know full well, short pants wound up prevailing, and gradually abandoning the comical form of loose underwear, and they found the ideal companion for their tennis existence: the piqué polo shirt, invented by René Lacoste, the "Crocodile," and destined to worldwide fame and longevity. With respect to the measurements of the clothing worn on court, the ladies were every bit as aggressive. Shorts and skirts (short and often extremely short) became their variegated uniform, and on that uniform they happily applied all of the seductions of fashion. Their standard-bearers could be considered, between the end of the 1940s and the beginning of the 1950s, Gussy Moran, who was, rightly enough, rebaptized Gorgeous Gussy and whose lace-trimmed panties and especially black shorts, in lamé or leopard-skin are still remembered and, for the 1960s, the Brazilian player Maria Ester Bueno, whose salmon-pink outfit with its teardrop neckline and fourteen rows of lace under the skirt caused shock and scandalized the twelve Elders of the Board of Directors of the All-England Lawn Tennis Club. Wimbledon remained for many years a citadel of austere clothing and was the last to surrender to the spirit of 1968: a revolutionary wind howled through the realms of lawn tennis as well, which became "open," that is, accessible to professionals as well, and among the various things consumed in the bonfire of traditions, tennis whites were included. The 1970s were colorful, extremely colorful; cheerfully colorful with all the hues of the rainbow, even the most unusual ones, and garish with surprising patterns, such as the American-flag tennis outfit worn by the American player Rosemary Casals. At the same time other phenomena were beginning to develop and would not cease, such as a heightened research into an ever-changing array of fabrics and materials, increasingly technical, as well as the growing use of sports apparel in everyday life, and the triumph of Italian style in the world of tennis as well. "The list of tennis pros who wear Italian style on the court – wrote a specialized French magazine in 1980 – is astonishing: among the top fifty in the ATP ranking, twenty-nine." They were Borg, McEnroe, Gerulaitis, Tanner, and Vilas, to whom we should add, to mention just one representative of the gentler sex, a champion as elegant in her bearing as Chris Evert. It was a splendid period in terms of sports competition, but also a remarkable period for tennis fashion, which, with the 1980s, recovered all its inborn refinement. The apparel was often created by famous Italian fashion designers (Valentino at the lead), unrivaled in making the clothing comfortable, free, and white (without abandoning color entirely), essential and yet rich in creativity. From then on, we have sort of lost some of the style of that fashion which, referring in particular to the early years of the twentieth century, Gianni Versace considered "very refined in terms of the image of white, with these stripes, these polo shirts, these short pleated skirts." The times had turned to non-conformism, indifference to rules, an absolute and much-heralded freedom, a time of "I'll wear what I happen to have or whatever I feel like wearing," and it spread to the tennis court as well. Even the polo shirt was forced on some occasions to modify itself in order to keep up with the times. Provocative necklines and mini-minis were the preferred outfits of Serena and Venus Williams, the sisters who often played against one another in the finals of a Grand Slam. The elegance of a distant time was forgotten. (*Maria Rita Stiglich*)

Ter et Bantine Italian *griffe* of ready-to-wear fashion. Manuela and Gianni Gherardi, husband and wife, worked on the project together. He supervised the field of management, while she was in charge of the creative sector, and in 1989, they presented their first Collection. Their debut on the runways came a few years later: in 1993, in Milan. The style of the clothing, tending toward the minimalistic, found markets from Hong Kong to Switzerland. The label had already actually been used, with no link to the present label, between 1967 and 1973, by the French fashion designer Chantal Thomass.

❑ 2003, February. An acquisition of 51 percent of the label was made by the Società Mafra (Mariella Burani group).

Terragni Manufacturing company producing silk and velvet fabrics. The Terragni Co. was founded in 1925, but it grew out of a partnership with the same name already working in Como at the turn of the century. The company was run by Alessandro Terragni who, in collaboration with his brother Antonio and his nephew Giuseppe, had established his "base" in Como. In 1932 the second generation of the Terragni family took over. At the beginning of the 1940s, there was a substantial increase in production and turnover. Most of that increase came from the "house specialties": silks for apparel, religious paraments, and material for flags and banner, but also fabrics for women's apparel, at a less exclusive level. In 1949, a printing facility was added to the weaving mills, which made it possible to move into the sector of women's "fashion" apparel. In 1962, the Terragni company became an S.p.A., a corporation held in shares, and then folded entirely in 1974.

(*Pierangelo Mastantuono*)

Terragni Sandro (1908-1978). Como-born industrialist in the silk sector. He was one of the most innovative and creative manufacturers, and an extraordinary ally of Italian fashion designers between the 1950s and the 1970s, the period in which the Made in Italy was born and matured. The eldest of five siblings, he graduated from the Scuola Serica (Silk School) of Como and started work in the weaving mill that his paternal uncle Alessandro had founded in 1920. After a few years of apprenticeship, he purchased the company, along with his brother Mario who would work alongside him as the administrator of the company. During the Second World War, the company also manufactured parachutes. In the years after the war, the plant was moved from Via Indipendenza (where it stood next to the house of Giuseppe Terragni, the great Rationalist architect who, however, was not related) to Via Viganò, increasing the number of looms to 120 and opening a printing facility at Montano Lucino. He combined an admirable technical skill and a great degree of creativity. In the weaving mill, his innovations had to do with the first blended threads for fine fabrics such as satins and *marocains*, the first blends of wool and viscose acetates. He worked with the fashion designers Irene Galitzine, Heinz Riva, the Fontana Sisters, Dior, Balenciaga, and Saint-Laurent. After his death, the company became little more than a "converter" and was run by his son Giorgio and his nephew Paolo.

The Terrible Three Trio of British photographers, consisting of David Bailey, Terence Donovan and Brian Duffy. They worked in London in the 1960s. The poses of their models were clearly inspired by the attitudes of young London hoodlums. All three came from the working class and stood out for their radical choices in the climate of Swinging London: choices that deeply marked their work as fashion photographers. They worked primarily for the British edition of *Vogue*.

Terzoli Laura (1952). Journalist. Editor of *Cento Cose*. Immediately following high school, she joined Condé Nast as a fashion and current events editor at *l'Uomo Vogue* and *Vogue Bambini*. In the meanwhile, she was also an editor of the underground magazine *Cannibale*. In 1984 she moved over to Mondadori, as managing editor of *Cento Cose*. She made a brief layover at Rusconi's *Eva* in 1987, and then she returned to *Cento Cose*, where in 1996 she became editor-in-chief. She also wrote a novel, *Melania dei sortilegi*, set in the Middle Ages.

Teso Giuliana (1948). Italian designer of furs and ready-to-wear fashion. Born in Bergamo. In 1978, she joined the new furrier business founded by her husband Riccardo, the Papillon company of Vancimuglio near Vicenza. Two years later, in order to personalize her fashion production, she presented her first Collection. In 1983, she participated in the Pelzmesse in Frankfurt, the international fur fair, and in 1984, she took part in the highly selective American Legend event, with reversible crocodile-stamped minks and furs for evening wear adorned with pearls and costume jewelry. In 1987 she was invited to Contemporary, in the context of Milan Collezioni. The American department stores Bergdorf Goodman and Neiman Marcus dedicated display windows and corner shops to her work.

❑ She continued her stylistic development, establishing her presence in American, Far Eastern, and European markets. Philip Hockey – located in London, in the heart of the City – selected her creations to offer his demanding clientele the elegance and quality of Italian Style. A Teso corner shop is in the Fashion and Novelty Department of the London department store Harrods. She opened single-label shops in Moscow and St. Petersburg. Currently, she is also presenting a vast Collection of overcoats with fur trimming, made with the attention and craftsmanship used in the making of the furs, along with a new line of leather, suede, and fabric. The balanced merger of roles between Riccardo Teso – the entrepreneurial soul of the company – and his wife Giuliana – the creative spirit – represents the driving force and winning cards of this company.

Sketch by Giuliana Teso for the 2003-2004 Fall-Winter Collection.

Tessilstrona A Piedmontese woolen mill founded in 1966 in Cossato, in the province of Biella, by Francesco Mello Rella in partnership with his brother-in-law Franco Grosso. The company's plants are capable of implementing the entire manufacturing cycle: from the purchase of the wools, directly in Australia, to their transformation in the internal spinning, warping, weaving, and finishing departments. With its 150 employees, it produces approximately 25,000 square meters of fine patterned fabrics in pure virgin wool and fine fibers. The turnover is between 20 and 30 billion liras. It exports roughly 60 percent of the product, especially in Canada, Japan, Germany, Hong Kong, China and the United States. Also involved in running the company are the founder's children, Corrado, Grazia and Maurizio.

Tessitrice dell'Isola Label that the Baroness Clarette Gallotti used for the outfits and the hand-woven fabrics that she created. Together with Pucci, Avolio, and Franco Bertoli, she was a member of the little quartet summoned by Bista Giorgini on 12 February 1951 to do a presentation for the American buyers for the so-called boutique fashion, which proved to be the trump card of the Made in Italy and which helped to seal the success of that debut, ensuring also the triumph of the nine couturiers of high fashion. Clarette lived and worked on the island of Capri. She was a handsome woman, a blonde who dressed almost exclusively in peplums and tunics: the fashion that she created was very colorful and distinctly Mediterranean.

Tessitura di Novara Woolen mill specializing in superfine worsteds in silk wool, pure silk blended with pure cashmere, silk cashmere, pure silk and in waterproofed treated fabrics. It was founded in 1932 by Luigi Baldi in Pernate (Novara). The quality of the product is the identity that joined the various generations that took over the management of the corporation. The Baldis were joined, in the 1960s, by the Pasquino family. Together they survived the crisis of the 1970s thanks to a very well calibrated positioning on the market and the feature of high quality.

Tessitura Serica Molinelli Manufacturer of silk fabrics for ties. It was founded in 1934, and is headquartered in Como, with a plant in Appiano Gentile. It is family owned and run. It has 80 employees, with a manufacturing capacity of 130,000 meters monthly. It is present in all the world markets, with 60 percent share of exports.

Testa A venerable Italian men's tailor shop. It was founded in Rome in 1918 by Orazio, father of the present-day owners Osvaldo and Oliviero. The first atelier was in the Via del Corso but as early as 1936 it had been moved to the Via Frattina, where one of the three Testa shops still stands. Orazio was a pupil of Mattina (the tailor to King Victo Emmanuel) and he was immediately successful, due to his skill as a tailor and his refined taste. The true turning point came when his sons joined the tailoring business in the 1960s, helping to update the image of men's clothing, in clear opposition to the traditional man in gray. They were the first to offer long jackets, vents, accordion pockets, and large buttons on the jackets, shirts with large French collars, jacquard fabrics, patterned velvets, jersey and patchwork. In the 1960s and 1970s, the label finally established itself thanks to its collaboration with Cerruti on the Flying Cross line and with such other major fashion manufacturers as Lebole, Lanerossi, Fila, and Lubiam. In 1973, along with the tailors Datti, Palazzi and Piattelli, Testa founded the Gruppo dei Quattro, and took part in the first Pitti Uomo in Florence. He did a great deal of work with the movies and television. Actors such as Giannini, Franco Nero, Montesano and Alessandro Gassman appeared on the set dressed in clothing by Testa. In the 1990s, the family tradition continued with Orazio's grandchildren, Odoardo and Federico.

Testa Michelangelo (1913-1980). Publisher and editor-in-chief of the magazine *Arbiter* from 1946 on, and from 1951, the mastermind, organizer, and manager of the Festival della Moda Maschile in San Remo. In 1971 he was named by an English jury as one of the 100 most elegant men in the world. He began his career in the field of cultural and literary journalism: he chanced to become acquainted with the owner of *Arbiter* who insisted on hiring him as an editor. He grew to love it so that he purchased the publishing house, L'Editore, which published many magazines besides *Arbiter*, including some on sports. It was under the aegis of *Arbiter*, which employed major names in journalism and graphics, that a conference was held in 1951 with textiles and apparel manufacturers, major figures in the press and advertising, in order to explore the possibility of an initiative that appeared odd, if not provocative at the time: a Collection of men's fashion that many considered both radical and useless. The project was submitted to a number of tourist boards, which all responded with a sharp "no"; in San Remo, on the other hand – thanks to the insistance of the Commissioner of Tourism Adriano Morosetti – the idea was accepted (though reluctantly). Even if many looked upon the idea of a men's tailored fashion event with irony, and even though there were no professional male models and the ideas were still quite unclear, the events were very popular with both the public and the press. Spontaneous, human, and authentic, the Festival of San Remo brought on stage genuine wizards of scissors and needle and thread, from all over Italy and in some cases from outside of Italy, joined by their love and passion for their work. It was the right setting for a great school of couture that had its high points in Naples, Abruzzo, Rome and Milan. After Testa's death, there were some who tried, with high points and low points (mostly low points), to keep the event going. But their charismatic leader was gone. It all ended. *Arbiter* was sold to Rusconi Editore: but shortly thereafter, the magazine ceased publication, and was replaced by *Il Piacere*. (*Maria Vittoria Alfonsi*)

Testino Mario (1954). Peruvian photographer of Italian, Irish, and Spanish descent. After graduating from the American School of Lima, he studied economics at the University of the Pacific and law at the Catholic University before moving to California, where he studied international affairs in San Diego. In 1976 he moved to London where he studied photography in a private school. His first published photograph appeared in 1981 in British *Vogue*, even though he remembers with some irony that it was about the size of a postage stamp. Then, he was obliged to be patient while waiting for success: it finally happened in the 1990s when his photographs of models wearing apparel by Trussardi, Versace, Saint-Laurent and, especially, Gucci were published by *Vogue*, *The Face*, *Visionaire*, *W Magazine*, and *Vanity Fair*. His most recent campaigns were in 2002 for Roberto Cavalli and in 2003 for Prada. Thanks to his immediate style, inspired by everyday life, though often characterized by bright colors and a search for feigned tones of provocation, he established himself as a world-class photographer, capable of doing memorable portraits, such as the one he did of Lady Diana, published in *Vanity Fair* in 1997. He continued his portrait work with photographs of Gwyneth Paltrow, Meg Ryan, Julia Roberts, Jane Birkin, and Madonna. His work has been featured in various exhibitions around the world. He published, in 1998, the book *Any Objections*, in 1999 he published *Front Row/Backstage*, in 2000, *Party* and in 2001, *Portraits*. In 2001 he did the photography for the Pirelli Calendar, in a high-glamour style. (*Roberto Mutti*)

Testoni Footwear manufacturer. Founded in Bologna in 1929, it produced only shoes for men. It then expanded its line of product to include women's footwear and luxury leather goods, with systems still based on the old artisanal approach. The company is family-owned and -run. Guiding the company is the third generation: the daughter of the founder Amedeo Testoni, Marisa, with her husband Enzo Fini. The company, which boasts an elite clientele, has a showroom in Via Montenapoleone in Milan, another in Via Condotti in Rome and 50 single-label boutiques.

❑ 2000, October. The Bologna-based footwear manufacturer acquired 30 percent of Futurnet, a Padua-based company, under the leadership of Stefano Martinetto, which holds the Puma license for the Puma Black Station Collection (Nuala and Platinum lines). Futurnet, founded in 1998 as a importing company for the labels Evisu and Fake London, achieved a 2001 turnover of 11 million Euros.

❑ 2002, June. Futurnet signed a five-year licensing agreement with the

German company Puma for the production and worldwide distribution of a new line of casual apparel.

Testu Jean-Luc (1960). French designer. He received his training at the ESMOD design school in Paris and finished his apprenticeship with Thierry Mugler and Azzedine Alaia. In 1986 he created, together with Michael Roelli, the Roelli Testu label, a *griffe* dedicated to prêt-à-porter menswear, and it enjoyed an immediate success. In 1991, the pair was appointed to design the menswear Collection of the *maison* S.T. Dupont. But the true leap forward came five years later when Jean-Luc Testu left the *maison* to become the creative director for menswear for Thierry Mugler. In the meanwhile, he designed the Testu line, which he presented under his own name in 2001 in Paris. He continues to have regular runway presentations in Paris. (*Maddalena Fossati*)

Tête à Tête French millinery label, founded in 1985 by Josette Desnus, after a lengthy apprenticeship with Paulette, the master hatmaker. As well as selling to private buyers, the *maison* creates items for the runway presentations of major *griffes*.

Textielmuseum Vrieselhof Belgium. A textile museum with a special interest for lace: more than a thousand items in the Collection, dating back to 1600. The Collection of outfits dates from the nineteenth century and the early twentieth century. The acquisitions are designed especially to focus on contemporary Belgian fashion. The library has, aside from specialty books, an archive of fashion publications.

Textilbibliothek Textile-sector library in Sankt Gallen (San Gallo, or St. Gallen) in Switzerland, founded by the city's Executive Commercial Board in 1878. From 1886 to 1991 it was located in the city's Industrial and Artisanal Museum. Then it was moved to the Foundation of the Chamber of Commerce and Industry, the body responsible for its operation. The library has a wide variety of material related to all the sectors of the textiles industry, especially concerning creative aspects (fashion photography, illustrations, prints) and local production (there is a huge Collection of lace produced in St.

Textielmuseum Vrieselhof, Antwerp. Sketch for the Maison Valens, Brussels, ca. 1950.

Gallen). Through its sophisticated computerized cataloguing system, it is possible to access the Collection online as well. The library also produces educational and scholarly publications.

Textile Conservation Studio Hampton Court Palace, Surrey, England. This restoration center is located inside Hampton Court Palace, residence of Henry VIII. It was founded in order to meet the challenge or textile restorations within the network of British royal palaces. In order to clean and conserve enormous tapestries and carpets, special structures were conceived and built that are unique. The center offers technical consulting services (research, analysis, cleaning, restoration, installation) to public bodies and private clients. It can work on any sort of fabric, from archaeological finds to antique clothing. Until 1999, the center included the school of textile restoration of the University of London (Courtauld Institute of Art), now located elsewhere.

Textile Paper Fiber obtained from cellulose, the chemically treated yarn of which gives a papery and starched hand.

Textil Mitteilungen German weekly specializing in fashion and textiles: interviews, coverage, and analysis of the various fashion sectors. It was founded in 1948 and is published by Branche Business editions, Dusseldorf. It is distributed through subscriptions.

Textil Wirtschaft German weekly specializing in fashion and textiles (news, fashion, industry and business), published by Deutscher Fachverlag editions in Frankfurt. Present circulation of the magazine (50,000 copies) mostly focuses on the German European markets. Deutscher Fachverlag publishes a total of 80 titles, many of them in the fashion sector. Alongside the magazines that are published in Germany there are magazines published in Italy (Fashion), Austria, Poland, Czechoslovakia, Hungary, and Turkey. These publications are completely independent of headquarters in terms of contents and approach. The publishing group has joint ventures in the U.S., China, and France. (*Silvia Martinenghi*)

Thaarup Aage (1907). Danish milliner. Born in Copenaghen. He served an apprenticeship in a hat-making workshop in a department store in his native city. He traveled around Europe as a hat-salesman for others. He emigrated to India where his women's hats made the community of colonial women swoon. In 1932 he moved to London and opened his hat-making shop in Berkeley Street. It was Beaton who first sensed his talent and introduced him into the pages of *Vogue*. That was enough to bring aristocratic high society pouring into his atelier, led by the princesses of the royal house, as well as the jet set. One of his clients was Vivien Leigh. Particularly popular her his daring inventions that used diaper pins, knitting needles, artificial vegetables, and recycled headwear from such regional traditions as berets from Brittany and Basque Country. In the years following WWII, he expanded his objectives and created mass-produced public for the larger public, such as the Teen and Twenty, without ever abandoning his elite clientele. Many of the most incredible hats of the young Queen Elizabeth were his creations.

Thaher Chemirik French jewelry trademark, named for the Algerian designer who also created fashion and interior décor, as well as costumes. He studied architecture in Algiers and took courses in decorative arts and set design in Paris. He was discovered by Karl Lagerfeld, who hired him to design the costume jewelry for a runway presentation. Chemirik recalls that he was so excited that he ran to call his father from a public telephone, forgetting that his father was dead. He designed items for the boutique of the Musée des Arts Décoratifs and showed his Collections at Naila de Montbrison, a Parisian crossroads for contemporary creativity in the field of jewelry.

Thatchers German apparel label. It featured clothing in a sexy and cosmopolitan style: a symbiosis between streetwear and couture. It was founded in 1994 by Ralf Hensellek and Thomas Mrozek, with two different young-people's lines, expanding to four in 1998, with Couture Jeans and Existentials. The guiding concept was that fashion is a system of communications and it was through communications that the two fashion designers worked: with exhibitions on computers, CD-Roms and Internet. The titles of their Collections already tell the story of their style: Beware of Killer Capitalism (Fall-Winter 1996-97), Pure Inferno (Summer 1997), Style Thriller (Fall-Winter 1997-98), Homestory 1998 (Summer 1998), She-Dog (Fall-Winter 1998-99).

❑ 2001. The fashion creators opened Thatchers The Shop, a space where they could test their ideas before manufacturing products. Later they presented their complet Collection there. (*Valeria Vantaggi*)

Thayaht Pseudonym of Ernesto Michaelles (1893-1959). Italian painter and sculptor. He shifted his artistic aesthetic into the field of fashion. He discovered couture in 1918, when he met Madeleine Vionnet in Paris; he designed for her outfits with rich geometric combinations and daring color assortments: furs, eveningwear, sports apparel, and swimsuits. At almost the same time as the Soviet Constructivits, he designed a sort of overalls with many pockets as an everyday outfit. The 20 July 1920 edition of La Nazione documents it: it is a men's overall, T-shaped, with a belted waist and four pockets. This is not a work uniform, but a handy, modern item of clothing, for everyday wear. In 1929, he made contact, through Marinetti, with the Second Futurism and Aeropittura. In 1932 he wrote the *Manifesto per la trasformazione dell'abbigliamento maschile* (Manifesto for the Transformation of Men's Clothing) with his brother Ruggero, who called himself Ram. He conceived a spare wardrobe that lacked pockets and buttons in order to lower production costs. Stimulated by Aeropittura, he invented such new items as the aeroshoe, comfortable and very light.

Ernest Thayaht, sketch for a pair of overalls, 1920 (from *Art Fashion*, Biennial of Florence, Skira, 1996).

Théâtre de la Mode Promotional French high fashion event organized at the end of 1945 to reaffirm, after the wartime hiatus, the French monopoly which as, at the time, worldwide and unquestioned. Maria Pezzi described it: "Two hundred wire dolls, descendants of the mannequin-dolls of the seventeenth and eighteenth centuries, the 'piavole de Franza' as the noblewomen of Venice used to call them, told the world that the haute couture of Paris was still alive. They stood 70 centimeters tall. The Catalonian sculptor Joan Rebull had shaped their heads. The great couturiers, from Lelong, Patou, Piguet and Schiaparelli to Vionnet, Balenciaga, and Fath had dressed them. Cartier and Van Cleef Arpels bejeweled them. Christian Bérard, Cocteau, and Boris Kochno designed little stage sets. The dolls debuted at the Pavillon Marsan of the Louvre. It was the Théâtre de la Mode. In the first year of peace, it went on tour: London, Barcelona, Stockholm, New York." It was rediscovered in the archives of an American museum, and was restored and, in 1990, exhibited in Paris, New York, and Tokyo. (*Luigi Chiavarone*)

Theatrical Wardrobe Until the 1930s, the wardrobe considered necessary for a prose actor of a leading theatrical company in Italy was generally represented by six suits for Summer, winter and half-seasons; formal wear (tails, redingote, dinner jacket); three or four pants and casual jackets (white flannel, gray flannel, white cloth, and khaki cloth); three dressing gowns (one in camelhair, two in silk); six scarves, wool or silk; at least 24 ties for the day, and 12 for the evening; walking shoes (black, yellow, light brown, two-tone, patent leather with small gray spats); sports shoes; beach shoes; riding, hunting and marsh boots; overshoes; a hunting suit (optional); walking hats for summer and winter; black or gray or beige bowler hat for the races; straw hats (panama or chip hats for Tuscan-style gentlemen); a yachting beret; and an opera hat. In addition, five or six coats in blue, brown-gray, or black; two overcoats for the mid-seasons; three raincoats, six sports sweaters, with and without sleeves; two umbrellas; four walking sticks; and twelve pairs of gloves. For the onstage wardrobe, the assortment varied according to the actor's possibilities and the credit he had with his shirt manufacturer. It was necessary, though, to have three pairs of cuff links, shirtfront buttons made from precious metals or beads, enamels, or diamonds. Also necessary was a good set of pipes and cigarette holders, stage wallets made from Russian leather, crocodile or black satin, a black ribbon to be worn on a hat or the arm in case of mourning, handkerchiefs of very refined batiste, scarves, white silk or patterned cache-col, an evening astrakhan fur, a young bear fur with a mink or otter fur collar, a hunting fur with a fox collar, an evening coat with a white satin mantle for very mundane comedies, a dustcoat, a beret and driving glasses. A large part of the cost involved was paid through installments, which was deducted by the management from the actor's wages. The wardrobe of very elegant actors, like Luigi Cimara and Lucio Ridenti, was five times greater than this minimum list, to which had to be added a golden cigarette case and a platinum watch to be used when wearing tails.

Theory American label of ready-to-wear fashion for women and men. The New York-based company produces for a clientele seeking practical and comfortable outfits. It focuses on simple lines and traditional fabrics, such as cotton and wool, mixed with lycra and spandex. The colors range from safari to olive green and white. The sports Collection includes cargo pants and is inspired by the essential look of yoga clothing. The label is sold through major department stores in the United States.

(*Francesca Gentile*)

The Three Group of British photographers composed of Nyholm, Lincoln and Phillips. They worked for advertising and fashion in the 1930s. Their pictures are warm in tone and elegant.

Theyskens Olivier (1977). Belgian fashion designer, considered one of the rising new talents of recent years. He was born in Brussels. His romantic avant-garde style consists of constructed crinolines, bodices, strips of veil overlapping in a careful study of the body. He makes no secret of his aspiration to imitate the fashion of Christian Dior and Cristobal Balenciaga. He studied, from 1995 to 1997, at the Ecole Nationale Supérieure des Arts Visuels in Le Cambre. Although he never graduated, Theyskens already presented his first Collections at the end of 1997 in Amsterdam and Ostend (August 1997). He debuted in Paris in March 1998 with his own prêt-à-porter line, with a Fall-Winter Collection that was both spiritual Gothic: black leather corsets, purple T-shirts and long skirts with trains. He was 21. He refused to sell anything, saying: "I believe that these clothes are hard to reproduce without losing in quality. I really prefer to start next season." Madonna wore his outfits during the Festival of San Remo in 1998 and in two of her videos *Ray of Light* and *Frozen*. His creations appear regularly in *The Face*, *Harper's Bazaar* and *Vogue Italia*. Beginning in January 2003, he became the creative director of Rochas. His debut Collection for this *maison* was presented in Paris, during the week of Fall-Winter prêt-à-porter, and won critical acclaim. Theyskens did a runway presentation of an elegant and very well constructed Collection with clear 1950s inspiration. He paid homage, with respect and savoir-faire, to the fashion of Marcel Rochas, re-interpreting it with modern girdles, crinolines, capes, and taffeta sheaths with large flounces.

(*Eleonora Attolico*)

Thigh Highs Very sexy stockings that do not use a suspender. They arrive at the thigh where they remain thanks to a band of silicon applied to the inside. Thigh Highs are very often embroidered or decorated with lace.

Thimister Josephus Melchior (1962). Belgian fashion designer. Together with Martin Margiela and Ann Demeulemeester he belonged to the Antwerp group that revealed to the fashion world the existence of a pool of Belgian creativity. Born in Maastricht, he moved to Paris. For five years he was in charge of the Balenciaga Collections. In 1997, he launched a line of his own. He explored the realm of understatement, a word that he emphasizes and that he puts into practice with clothing distinguished by an almost monastic rigor.

Thinking Small This is the label of the creations of Geoffrey B. Small, an American fashion designer (1959). Known for his work on recycled clothing, the line is distributed by select boutiques around the world. Small began his career at the age of twenty with an old sewing machine, and by 1993 he was the first fashion designer in Boston to have a runway presentation in Paris. Six years later, he moved to Italy by virtue of a working contract with the manufacturing group CPA. In 2001, he ended this corporate experience and returned to his world of hand-made creations.

Think Pink Label of sportswear and casual fashion. It was founded at the beginning of the 1980s, inspired by the free life of California and immediately entered into a synergyt with free climbing, the great sports phenomenon of those years. It was distributed in all the leading world markets, from Europe to the Far East. Under its banner, moreover, licensing of a children's apparel line, eyeglasses, and perfumes developed. The label belongs to G.B. International, a company that has been part of Gruppo Tecnica since 1989, one of the largest industrial groups on earth in the sector of sports. The group has turnover of 400 billion liras (1998), employs some 1,100 persons, and is present in the leading world markets with direct subscidiaries (USA, France, Germany, Switzerland, Austria, Japan) or else with distribution agreements.

31 Février Brand of purses, created in 1987 by Hélène Népomiatzi and Marc Gourmelen. The line is noted for the originality and the irony of the creations. More than actual purses for daily use, these are surprising accessories. The pair debuted as designers for Lagerfeld and continued work with the leitmotiv of unpredictability. They also have a a seconda line called Jour Férié and a show room in Paris in the Rue du Faubourg Saint-Honoré.

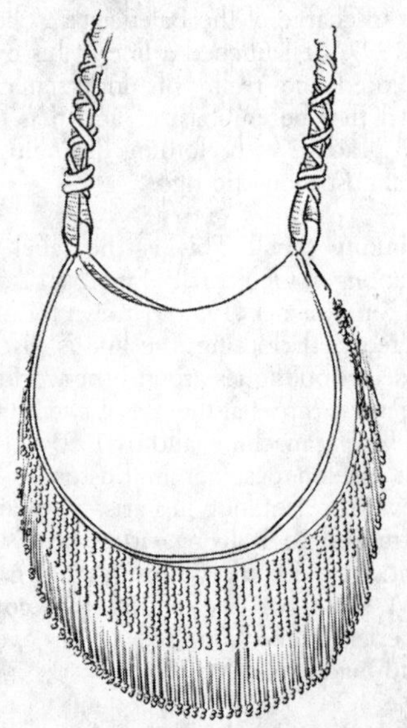

31 Février, purse.

Thomas Pink English chain of shirt shops, with headquarters in Chelsea since 1984. It takes its name for the legendary tailor of Mayfair who lived in the eighteenth century and who made the finest hunting jackets that money could buy. Handmade shirts, generally classical in design though the line includes bright colors and modern patterns. Since 1985 the label also has a women's line. Among the clients, Hugh Grant, Anna Wintour, Christie Brinkley, Stella Tennant.

❑ 1999, September. The LVMH Group, worldwide leader in the luxury market, announced a majority holding of the label.
❑ 2001. The single-label sales outlets, aside from the "historic" ones in London and New York, were now also in Brussels, Paris, Boston, San Francisco.

Thomass Chantal (1947). French designer. She was known especially as the queen of ultrasexy lingerie: guêpière or girdle, garter-belts, and sophisticated pantyhose. She began to take a profound interest in fashion as a child. She debuted as a fashion designer in the late 1960s, when she began to work with her husband Bruce, who painted scarves that Chantal then transformed into clothing, launching a fashion in Saint Tropez that even infected Brigitte Bardot. After working with Castelbajac and Kenzo, in 1976 she launched a line under her own name.

❑ 1995. She was licensed by the Chantal Thomass company and could no longer use her own label. To protect her own creations, she donated to the Fashion Museum of Marseille 40 silhouettes from the years 1986 to 1995, complete with accessories.
❑ 1998. She regained control of her label.
❑ She published for Flammarion the book *Trouvez votre style* in which she gave advice on what not to do and on a basic wardrobe, suitable for all occasions, holidays, weekends, and eveningwear.
❑ 1999, June. She scandalized Paris and provoked a general state of shock by the exhibitionism with which she presented

her new Collection with living mannequins, in the display windows of the Galeries Lafayette.
❑ She established an alliance with Sarah Lee, worldwide leader in the field of lingerie. Previously she had worked for such huge firms as Walford and World.
❑ 2001, July. Retrospective at the Fashion Museum of Marseille for her thirtieth anniversary in business. *Plaisirs des femmes, Chantal Thomass, 30 ans de création* was the title of the exhibition, which extended over two stories of the museum. On the second floor was the lingerie (more than 100 items), the accessories (50), furniture and decorative objects. Many written and visual documents (drawings, sketches, archival photographs, videos) illustrate Chantal's artistic development and work. On the third floor were the prêt-à-porter creations: twenty articles with the *griffe* Ter et Bantyne, including two one-offs in painted silk from 1967, others under the name of Chantal Thomass, from the 1970s up till 1975. In all, some eighty creations presented alone or highly accessorized, documenting the debut of an unmistakable style. At the same time as the retrospective show, a film festival was held that focused on the history of underwear and the female nude. Chantal herself selected some of the movies that were shown, from Truffaut and Godard to Preminger, Vadim, and Lubitsch.
❑ 2002, June. New retrospective show at the Musée des Beaux Arts et de la Dentelle in Calais. More than 200 items, in an installation designed by Bob Verhesit, entirely pink (Chantal's favorite color).
❑ Numerous sales outlets in France, including the showroom in the Rue du Cherche Midi on the Rive Gauche, and the large single-label shop in the Place du Palais Royal.
❑ She designed supersexy swimsuits, almost always sold at the Galeries Lafayette.
❑ 2003, April. She received the Flacons d'Or 2003 prize.

(*Gabriella Gregorietti*)

Thompson Jim. American entrepreneur. He vanished mysteriously during an expedition in Africa in 1970. In the middle of Bangkok his large store still stands, the product of the merger of little boutiques that he had created previously. He landed in Thailand during the Second World War, and never left. He loved Thai techniques in silk working, improved on them, and made artisanal processes industrializable, without distorting their tradition. He added soft cottons to the silk fabrics, in an extraordinary range of colors, alongside a prêt-à-porter line, household, pillows and other furnishing items.

(*Marilea Somaré*)

Thong Bathing suit that consists of two tiny dots that cover the nipples and a strap that makes it possible to reduce the shape of the panties as much as possible. Legend has it that it was invented in Ipanema, the beachfront of Rio de Janeiro, on a midsummer's day in 1972. Officially the maternity of this skimpy bathing suit is attributed to Rose di Primo, a Brazilian woman of Italian descent who, in order to attract attention at a party on the beach, supposedly chopped down her swimsuit. A few years later, sorry for what she had done, Rose supposedly entered a convent of the Presbyterian church, while her invention, a sledgehammer blow to the sense of common decency, continued to spread (and continued to to shrink) to all the beaches on earth. A men's thong (obviously without a top) was presented by Tom Ford for Gucci in 1995. The point of focus: the G at the center of the straps that meet above the cleft in the buttcheeks.

(*Laura Salza*)

Thorimbert Toni (1957). Italian photographer. After taking a degree in photography at the Centro di Formazione Professionale Bauer in Milan, he distinguished himself with a famous layout on young people in a Milanese neighborhood that was published in *Abitare*. Beginning in the 1980s, he worked for such Italian periodicals as *Max*, *Amica*, *Capital*, *Sette* and then worked up to such international venues as *Details*, *Mademoiselles*, *GQ*, *Wallpaper*, *Tatler*, *Brutus*, *Gulliver*, *Das Magazine*, *Du*. He has had many personal and collective shows.

Tiburzi Alberta. Italian photographer. Her career in fashion began when she became a famous top model often photographed by Richard Avedon, Newton and Hiro. It was Hiro who gave her a Minolta reflex camera and asked her, after he saw her first photographs, "Why don't you became a photographer?" Alberta accepted the suggestion that she become a fashion photographer and moved behind the lens, just as Sarah Moon and Deborah Turberville had done, publishing in *L'Espresso*, *Vogue*, *Harper's Bazaar*, *Lui*, *Amica* and establishing herself immediately with her powerful personality. She admired the style of Guy Bourdin, and captured his vivid colors and his preference for outdoor settings. She is known for her meticulous research and her careful use of lighting, which she often prefers indirect, using mirrors of all sizes, which convey an intense luminosity and sharp angles. She lives and works in Rome.

Tie A mandarin of imperial China, returning from a journey in the West, told his friends: "Europeans all look alike, in their clothes and physical appearance. If it were not for the tie they wear around the neck, it would be impossible to tell them apart." For centuries cravats and ties have been a permanent feature of the male wardrobe (though the late 1990s was a difficult period for manufacturers). The first men's accessory that resembled a tie dates to the 3rd century B.C: in what is now China, Huang-Ti, the sovereign of the Celestial Empire, used to wear fabric hung around his neck. Augustus, the emperor of Rome, would often wear a sort of wool tie (known as a focal) for warmth and when he was sick, though only in private because, as Quintillion wrote, Roman men were not allowed to show signs of physical weakness. It was in fact almost a scarf, which was useful in combating tonsillitis or a sore throat. Augustus never wore it in public, because "only bad health can justify wraps for the legs, a neck scarf, and earflaps." Focals were also worn by orators to protect their vocal strings. The bare neck was a sign of virility and power in ancient Rome for hundreds of years. It is necessary to move forward several centuries to find something similar to the focal, but as an article of clothing in the name of elegance rather than functionality or to protect the health. In the middle of the 17th century, the advent of the fashion for long, curly wigs rendered unnecessary the large collars previously worn by the Court and aristocrats, therefore, something else became necessary to give shirts a finishing touch. The Sun King understood this, and it is said that he spent a lot of money on lace ties, but at that time they were not yet known as *cravattes*. The pioneers of the tie as we know it were the officers and foot soldiers of a regiment of light cavalry that arrived in France as mercenaries around 1660 during the Thirty Years War. The regiment was composed of Croats who had been recruited in Bosnia. An item of their uniform was a string made of muslin, silk, or raw fabric that was knotted around the neck to indicate their rank. The ends hung loose on the chest and finished in a ribbon, a tassel, or a rosette. This colorful item knotted around the neck was known as a "croatta", which developed into *cravatte* in French, and *cravatta* in Italian. Louis XV even created the post of the Cravatte-Bearer. Towards the end of the 17th century, the fashion of the lace cravat (a sort of embroidered napkin that dropped onto the chest) went into decline, in part because the Bosnian soldiers' string was being taken up, and in part because sumptuary laws, which attempted to curb the display of luxury, forbade expensive necklaces and pendants. The successor to the Bosnian croatta was the Steinkerque tie: this was wound twice around the neck, then the deliberately rather shabby ends were tucked into the first buttonhole of the shirt. The effect created was one of refinement. A century later in France, it was still the military that dictated fashion, though they were quickly followed by the rising bourgeoisie. The trend this time was the black cravat, which was also wrapped twice around the neck and fixed with a simple knot on the chest. It became customary to wear a black cravat during parties at the Court, and as part of the military's parade uniforms. But this did not last long because the Revolution was at hand and social change of course brought changes in fashion. Only the dour, dry Robespierre resisted the changes and continued to wear clothes typical of the old regime. The Revolution brought into being the napkin-shaped cravat with flapping ends, which was worn by Camille Desmoulins and became a distinctive sign of the Danton's Jacobins, and

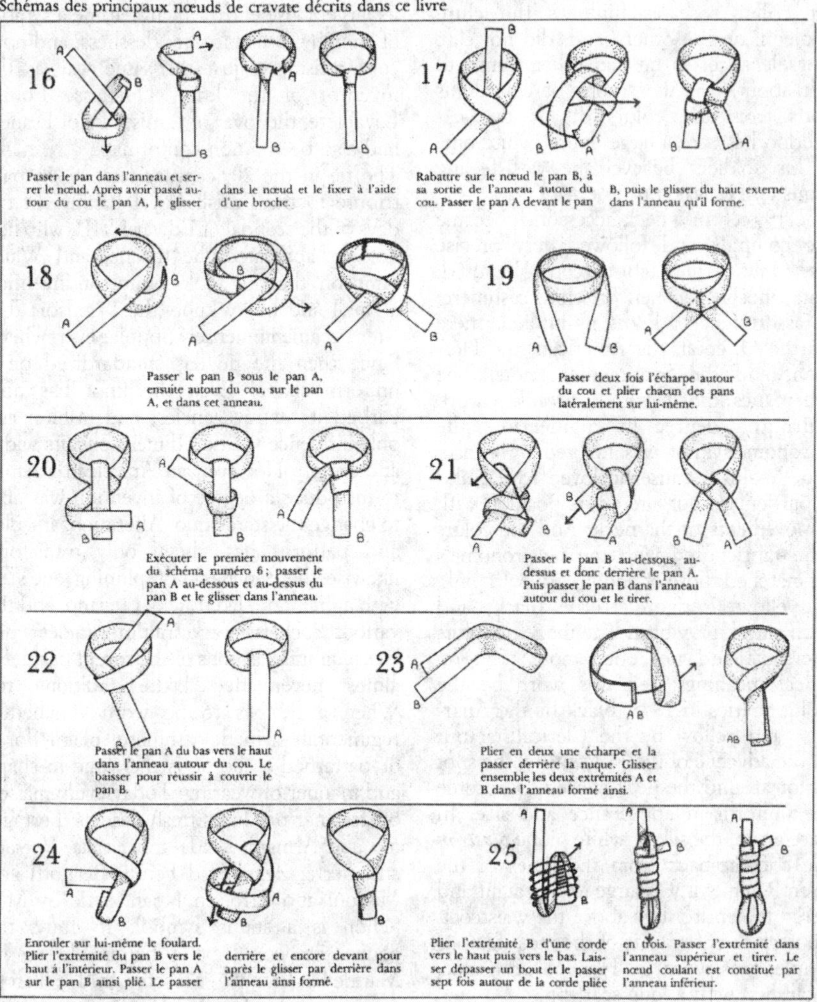

Schémas des principaux nœuds de cravate décrits dans ce livre
16
Passer le pan dans l'anneau et serrer le nœud. Après avoir passé autour du cou le pan A, le glisser
dans le nœud et le fixer à l'aide d'une broche.
17
Rabattre sur le nœud le pan B, à sa sortie de l'anneau autour du cou. Passer le pan A devant le pan
B, puis le glisser du haut externe dans l'anneau qu'il forme.
18
Passer le pan B sous le pan A, ensuite autour du cou, sur le pan A, et dans cet anneau.
19
Passer deux fois l'écharpe autour du cou et plier chacun des pans latéralement sur lui-même.
20
Exécuter le premier mouvement du schéma numéro 6; passer le pan A au-dessous et au-dessus du pan B et le glisser dans l'anneau.
21
Passer le pan B au-dessous, au-dessus et donc derrière le pan A. Puis passer le pan B dans l'anneau autour du cou et le tirer.
22
Passer le pan A du bas vers le haut dans l'anneau autour du cou. Le baisser pour réussir à couvrir le pan B.
23
Plier en deux une écharpe et la passer derrière la nuque. Glisser ensemble les deux extrémités A et B dans l'anneau formé ainsi.
24
Enrouler sur lui-même le foulard. Plier l'extrémité du pan B vers le haut à l'intérieur. Passer le pan A sur le pan B ainsi plié. Le passer
derrière et encore devant pour après le glisser par derrière dans l'anneau ainsi formé.
25
Plier l'extrémité B d'une corde vers le haut puis vers le bas. Laisser dépasser un bout et le passer sept fois autour de la corde pliée
en trois. Passer l'extrémité dans l'anneau supérieur et tirer. Le nœud coulant est constitué par l'anneau inférieur.

Different ways to knot a tie (From *188 Ways to Knot a Tie* by Davide Mosconi and Riccardo Villarosa, Overseas, 1984).

therefore a political symbol. And the cravat became even more political when, with the guillotining of Robespierre and the passing of The Terror, the Counter-Revolutionaries wore a white cravat on a waistcoat decorated with lilies (another political symbol). And a small red ribbon worn around the neck (a direct reference to the guillotine) also became popular, substituting the lace jabot cravats worn by bourgeois women.

Fortunately, the political earthquake passed in France and fashion naturally moved on as a result: but the concept of the cravat/tie remained and entered the Romantic age in triumph. A treatise on how to knot a cravat was even written by H. Le Blanc in 1828, titled *The Art of Knotting a Cravat*. The dandy of the century, Beau Brummel, claimed: "A man and his tie are one and the same," and invented his own knot. No more loose folds of the muslin cravat, but precise knots of a fabric almost made rigid by starch: the result was a sort of plastering of the neck because the tie was circled

around the neck three or four times and the shirt collar rose as high as the chin. Napoleon, on the other hand, did not care about elegance, as he had other things to think about, but the troops perceived his moods from the colors of his ties. At Waterloo he wore a large, loose, white one, and his soldiers believed he was feeling optimistic. He was: but in error.
In the 19th century, neck accessories became more complex and followed very precise rules. Only certain fabrics could be used: batista, muslin, jaconet, or white cashmere. The assortment of knots multiplied: there were the Oriental, the American, the Herculean, and the Sentimental knots. The Mathematics knot was full of folds, a work requiring a degree in engineering; the Gastronome's knot was favored by Gioacchino Rossini because he loved to eat and this particular knot altered its position with the movements of the neck. And the colors of the fabric used with the Gastronome's knot matched those of good food: ham pink, pâté yellow, Perigord truffle black, and pigeon's neck gray-blue. The range of colors for cravats and ties once more took on political meanings: red was worn by the Revolutionaries in 1848, black by the Anarchists, and yellow by the Clericalists: but with the advance of the 19th century, the spot of color around the neck started to become more uniform in appearance and size. In France again, the silk or white piqué *plastron* made a come-back from the times of the Ancien Régime: it was large and straight and covered the entire shirt above the waistcoat, from neck to chest. One of the most famous examples was worn by Honoré de Balzac, embellished with a long scarf-pin.
During the more contained social customs of the Victorian Age, ties were put on sale with a pre-made knot, both the classic form and bow ties, and with either a skimpy knot or an enormous one, according to taste. Even Gabriele D'Annunzio, who, when just 20 years old, was at the center of the salons of Rome in the late 19th century, perennially made use of the pre-made knot. It took the English king, Edward VII, to rebel against this trend. In the early 1900s he invented the "Free" knot, the forerunner of all the present-day models, of which he was prouder even than for his second invention: turn-ups on pants. The Free knot was popular at the same time as the lavallière neck-tie, with its large, loose ends, which became a symbol of anarchy, brilliance, recklessness, and non-conformism, in just the same way as the inventor of the knot, Duchesse Louise Lavallière, the lover of Louis XIV of France, had also been a non-conformist.
The tie in the 20th century once again paid tribute to the British Royal Family. In the days of the scandal of Edward VIII, who had not yet abdicated the throne, and Wallis Simpson, the king took comfort in inventing a small and bulky knot (the Windsor) that later became immensely popular everywhere. Since then the tie has standardized on a uniform shape. Even the knot has now curbed its extravagancies, and fashion can only influence the tie's dimensions: its width and length. Not even an American attempt to introduce a degree of invention was able to change the status quo. Alterations in color and patterns have been only transitory, likewise the penchant for pinning one's tie with a diamond, like Lucky Luciano, and the various Polynesian and Californian ties worn by Gauguin. Fashions of the recent past have almost never affected the traditional tie. When a tie has to be worn – whether regimental, striped, cashmere, plain, floral, or patterned – the tie is the same in shape and manner of wearing. Today every maison or designer produces fresh designs: Ferragamo and Armani, Prada and Krizia, Versace and Ferré, Zegna and Fendi, Biagiotti and Missoni and Etro. In Japan, a tie by Mila Schön is a status symbol. In Italy, the equivalent would be a handmade tie by Marinella. In 1984 Mosconi and Villarosa published a book called *188 Ways to Knot a Tie*. (*Virginia Hill*)

Tiel Vicky (1943). American fashion designer. Born in Washington, she studied at the Pratt Institute and at Parsons School in New York and Paris. In 1964 she joined forces with Mia Fonsagrives with whom she had already worked on the costumes for *What's New, Pussy Cat?* Together, they created a line with the logo Mia et Vicky. In the heart of St. Germain in Paris, in the courtyard of a lovely *hôtel particulier*, after Mia married Louis Féraud, Vicky continued to work alone. Her prêt-à-porter line, begun in 1973, was based especially on important outfits, for evening wear and for cocktail wear.

Tiffany American jeweler. Charles Lewis Tiffany (1812-1902) opened in New York in 1837, in partnership with his friend John B. Young, the shop of Tiffany Young, specializing in stationery and decorative objects, for the most part from the Far East. A few years later, in 1841, success allowed the partners to expand the range of products offered for sale. They began to import from Europe German costume jewelry and Parisian glass paste objects. It is difficult to imagine that from such modest origins the house would climb to the importance that it claims nowadays in the field of jewelry. The purchase and the subsequent sale by Tiffany of the famous gold-and-diamond belt of Marie Antoinette marked, in the mid-nineteenth century, a significant momento that made it clear, on the one hand, that the European tradition might well constitute a creative resource of considerable scope, and on the other hand just how interesting jewelry could be for the U.S. market. In those years, Tiffany opened its Paris office and began in the United States a vast and diversified production of not only jewelry, but also silver, in collaboration with the silversmith John C. Moore and his son Edward. Tiffany also drew freely on the youthful American tradition, developing its history and culture (that of the Indians, for instance). One of the company's greatest boasts was, during the years of the Civil War, the sale to President Lincoln of a pearl necklace for his wife. Tiffany & Co.was present at all the most important international expositions, and it became famous also for the quality of its gems, precious and semiprecious stones (sapphires from Montana, fire opals from Mexico, tourmalines from Maine). One of the company's most popular inventions was the six-clip setting for diamond solitaires. Louis Comfort Tiffany (1844-1933), who replaced his father at the turn of the twentieth century, had a fine artistic sensibility and a great enthusiasm for the ideas of William Morris, the painter and decorator; Tiffany modeled his production on the Liberty, or Art Nouveau, style that had become established in Europe. He successfully introduced the use of enamels

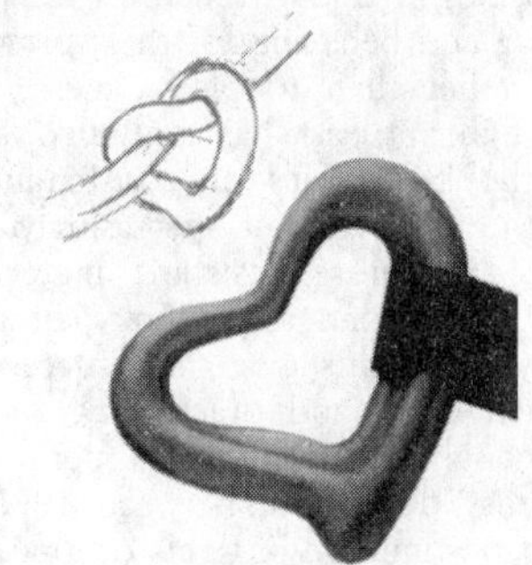

Tiffany, heart, by Elsa Peretti.

and began the production of items of furnishing that were to make history: first and foremost, lamps. In 1907, Tiffany opened its shop on Fifth Avenue. Aristocrats, titans of industry, and Hollywood stars became faithful customers. When, in the 1950s, the house was no longer controlled by the Tiffany family, it became necessary to establish working relationships with new designers. At first, the house worked with Jean Schlumberger and then, in the 1960s, Donald Claflin and Angela Cummings. In the 1970s, it was the turn of Elsa Peretti and Paloma Picasso who continue today to work for the house of Tiffany. Tiffanys is quoted on the New York Stock Exchange.

(*Alessandra Quattordio*)

Tiger-skin Very expensive and rare fur, with short thick yellow hair and black stripes.

Tight This is an Italian term, commonly but mistakenly translated as "morning coat" in English, though that is actually the "*abito da giorno.*" It Italian this is a suit worn for daytime ceremonies and occasions of considerable importance. Tight grey or black jacket, single-breasted, cutaway, round tails that hang to calf-length, grey pin-striped trousers. The waistcoat is pearl grey, the shirt is worn with a tie or ascot.

Tights (see also Stockings). The classic definition of tights is a women's leotard up to the waist, however, this simple description does not do justice to their social and technological importance. They have even been referred to as "the invention of the twentieth century." The evolution of silk and nylon stockings helped women on the path to dressing and behaving for their personal comfort rather than to please men. This trend, in tights at least, has continued, even beyond the boundaries of post-feminism, due to the discovery of increasingly less apparent and more resistant materials. However garish, patterned, slinky, or invisible they are, tights owe their success to their functionality and practicality. In the 1990s, though, they entered a period of crisis: across the world, between 1991 to 2000 the consumption of tights dropped by 30%. (*Stefano Bucci*)

Tiktiner Dina (1918). French designer. She was known for a look that the experts called "Côte d'Azur" or "Riviera." She inaugurated her first atelier in Nice, her home town, in 1948. She is considered to have been a pioneer of the total look, and she specialized in summer wear with simple lines and bright colors. Helped by her husband Henri Viterbo and her daughters Vivienne and Micaela, she opened numerous boutiques Paris, London and in the United States. After selling the label in 1989, the family recently reacquired it.

Tilberis Liz (1948-1999). American journalist, editor of *Harper's Bazaar*. Born in England, she began her career in fashion magazines in 1974, when she joined *Vogue England*, where she moved up the editorial chain until she became editor-in-chief. In 1991 she was hired to manage Condé Nast. She became the editor of *Harper's Bazaar* in 1992, on the day that Hearst Magazines celebrated its 125th anniversary in publishing. She expanded the horizons of the New York-based magazine, introducing artistic themes journalism at the highest levels. She was diagnosed with cancer in 1992, and spent the last years of her life working vigorously on behalf of the Ovarian Cancer Research Fund, while also editing her magazine till the day she died. She told the story of her disease and the fight against cancer in her book *No Time to Die* (Little, Brown Co, 1998).

Tilley Kaat (1961). Belgian fashion designer. She specializes in wedding outfits. Her Collection in any case is highly original: nothing is ever obvious or banal. She is famous for her delicate and romantic pastel colors. After studying at the Academy of Fashion in Antwerp, she went into business for herself in 1984 in Louvain with the *griffe* Mina Krystallos, but a year later she began to use her own name.

Tilmans Wolfgang (1968). German photographer. He immediately aroused great interest by photographing ordinary people in their everyday space, without special treatment. He studied at the Bournemouth College of Art and Design. His photography hwas been called crude and realistic. He has published in *i-D*, *Interview*, *Spex*, *Tempo*, *Vibe*, *Brutus*, *Ray Gun* and *Switch*.

Timberland Label linked indissolubly to the concept of the outdoors, which has developed from footwear to apparel (men's, women's, and children's wear) and a vast line of accessories. Its history began in 1918, when Nathan Swartz moved from Russia to New England and opened a crafts shoemaking shop. He was successful and, along with his sons Herman and Sidney, he purchased half the shares of the Abington Shoe Company. Production was characterized by injection form-molding, a technology that makes it possible to attach the sole to the uppers without stitching, thus ensuring that the footwear will be totally waterproof. In 1973, the Swartzes created the Timberland label. The logo depicts an oak tree. In 1979, they launched the first boat shoe and entered the Italian market. Since 1991, Timberland has been quoted on the New York Stock Exchange. Present in 88 countries, with 132 retail outlets, in 1998 it had net profits of 38.4 million dollars, up from the 29.8 million dollars of 1997.

❑ 2002. In order to present the Fall 2002 Collection of work clothing, Timberland hired exceptional models. The protagonists of the first Timberland "Working Man's Fashion Show" were the construction workers rebuilding the historic Soldier Field Stadium in Chicago. High technology in the manufacture of this clothing, which is water resistant, and uses hi-tech materials offering freedom of movement. These were the distinguishing features of this new

Collection, with items such as waterproof overalls or fur overcoat with hood for arctic temperatures. On this occasion, Timberland also presented a number of outfits and shoes for the Spring 2003 Collection.
❑ 2003, April. In the first quarter, turnover increased by 20 percent (271 million dollars) and net profits increased by 39 percent (19.3 million dollars). The increases were a result of exports, which accounted for 49.5 percent of total volume. Even though footwear is the company's driving component, the best performances were produced by apparel and accessories.
❑ 2003, June. Hodges Boo was the new fashion designer for the womenswear line: she debuted with the Spring-Summer 2004 Collection. He had worked for Paul Smith and joined Timberland in November 2002. The objective was to "renew" the Timberland items in a more glamorous and feminine mode, with more adherent, sexy items. The goal was to expand and reinforce the image of the womenswear line, which currently represented 10 percent of Timberland's revenue. Timberland is present in the Italian market with 108 franchising stores, and it had recently and considerably increased its turnover in Italy. In 2002 the figure was 72 million Euros (a 30 percent increase) with predictions for the end of 2003 of 84 million Euros (a 17 percent increase).

Tinling Teddy Cuthbert Collingwood known as Teddy (1910-1990). Born in Eastbourne (Great Britain), he was famous as a fashion designer for women tennis players. In 1949, he became *persona non grata* at Wimbledon, when he designed for the American player Gertrude "Gussy" Moran a pair of underwear-shorts (later known as hot pants) which caused a scandal. From that time on, Tinling's creations were worn for years by the best female tennis players, both on the field and in private life: Conolly, Bueno, King, Court, Goolagong, and less well known and more beautiful champions, such as the Italian Lea Pericoli, known as "La Divina," who wore shorts with lace and feathers.

Tino Cosma Tie manufacturer. It was founded by Vittorio Cosma in Venetia in 1946. At first, it was an artisanal workshop. Vittorio's oldest son, Tino, reorganized the company in 1968, putting his own name on the first Collection of ties and opening a marketing office in Milan. In the 1970s, the company grew sharply. Dating from this period was the construction of the factory in Motta di Livenza, with 140 master tie-makers. In 1983 Tino Cosma Inc. was founded, with offices in New York and a shop on Fifth Avenue.

❑ 2002. Aside from the Milan showroom in the Magenta area (Via Alberto da Giussano) and the New York showroom, Cosma ties were sold in the U.S., Canada, Hong Kong, and in the sales outlets of Barcelona, Lisbon, Stockholm, Greece and Switzerland.

Tirelli Umberto (1928-1992). Costume maker and designer, historian of costume, collector. The son of a merchant who sold wine and grains, he was born in Gualtieri, a town in Emilia near river Po. He discovered that he had a love of clothing by frequenting the moe of Luigi Bigi, a tailor and the ambassador of French fashion in Milan in the 1930s and a fellow townsman. In 1952, Giorgio Sarassi who, with Bigi's help, had made his fortune in the business of fabrics for high fashion, found Tirelli a job in Milan: a delivery boy and display designer for Marco, a fabric shop in the Via Montenapoleone. Almost directly across the street was the boutique of Mirsa where Beppe Modenese worked with Paola Carola. In order to save money, in order "to survive because our pay was minimal," Tirelli recalled in his autobiography, *Vestire i sogni* (written with Guido Vergani for the Feltrinelli publishing house), they decided to rent a place together. In 1953, he met Pia Rame and Carlo Mezzadri who had just purchased the theatrical costume maker Finzi. They offered him a chance to try out. It was the beginning of a spectacular career: the costumes for Lila De Nobili in *Come le foglie*; some of the costumes, also for De Nobili, for the legendary *La Traviata* staged at La Scala in 1955, directed by Luchino Visconti; the move to Rome to work in the Sartoria Safas for the sisters Emma and Gita

Maggioni; the costumes for *The Leopard*; and he set up in business for himself in 1964. From that time on, Tirelli was on a tireless quest for impossible materials, an inventor of solutions. From then on, he became much more than simply a costume maker. He was a profound scholar of fashion over the centuries, he was the ally, the supporter of costume makers in the design phase as well, and not merely in the process of bringing a costume to fruition from the cocoon of a sketch. He worked with the biggest names of theater costumes in the second half of the twentieth century, from De Nobili, Piero Tosi, Pierluigi Pizzi, Luciano Damiani, and Danilo Donati to Gabriella Pescucci, Vera Marzot, Gitt Magrini, Ezio Frigerio, Milena Canonero, Marcel Escoffier, and Maurizio Monteverde. His contribution was essential to them in terms of culture, philology of fashion, the recovery of age-old techniques, the quest for authentic outfits (he had a Collection of 20,000 items, dating from the seventeenth century to the days of Chanel and Dior) in almost archaeological excavations in attics, lofts, abandoned armoires, among the rags of the flea markets. In 1986, Tirelli donated 100 authentic outfits and 100 theatrical costumes to the Galleria del Costume of Palazzo Pitti in Florence. Since his death, his *sartoria* has been run by Dino Trappetti, Gabriella Pescucci and Giorgio D'Alberti. (*Giampiero Remondini*)

Tivioli Carlo (1935). Italian furrier. He was born in Brescia, and spent his youth in Turin, frequenting the intellectual and artistic milieu of the 1960s. He learned the furrier's art in the workshop of a brother-in-law and, at the end of the decade, he opened a small atelier in Milan. In 1971, his creations were presented for the first time on a runway, during the week of high fashion in Rome: the next day, the press was enthusiastically acclaiming his Red and Blue Collection, with skirts and blouses made of Persian lamb, overcoats made of kangaroo hide, tunics in zebra skin, mink loden coats, and sable raincoats. The fashion designer captured the spotlight with the nonconformism of his creations, always executed with artisanal mastery. The wealthy 1980s allowed him to show off a great deal of luxury accompanied by an extraordinary lightness of construction, a constant feature of his technical skill. Several of his best known creations have gone down in furrier history, such as his mink piqué, inspired by kinetic art, the colored mosaics inspired by Vasarely, his honeycomb, his goffré, his diamond-point chiaroscuros. For the last few years, Tivioli has been putting his expertise to a good cause, helping the young men and women working in the furrier workshop for the community of San Patrignano.

Carlo Tivioli, sable jacket with gold embroideries, 1999.

❑ 2001-2002. Luxury and elegance for the Fall-Winter Collection. But also wearable and versatile items, alongside the more classic models. Fur treated as a fabric, pastel shades along with the more traditional black and beige, for a 1950s style, tight- and high-waisted, with the bell-shaped flare bottom. More sporty and youth-oriented heavy jackets, in a military camouflage, in some cases worn over Bermuda shorts. Lots of accessories and, for the clothing, brocades and sequins for eveningwear.
❑ 2003-2004. This was the year of the bit revival of furs, in all runway presentations. Tivioli interpreted fur in an original and surprising way. There

were fringed furs harking back to the era of jazz and the Charleston, with ultraluxurious furs alongside less extravagant ones, but the big role was played by color. There were reds, turquoises, pinks, dark blues; the furs were very light, floor length, adorned with numerous tails, an exalting look for modern and transgressive women.

(*Minnie Gastel*)

Tizzoni Giuseppina (1889-1979). Italian dressmaker. She was one of the protagonists of the first attempt in the 1930s to create an autonomous Italian fashion, freed from its subjugation to Parisian fashion. There was an attempt to impose such a fashion by decree of the Ente Nazionale della Moda, established by the Fascist regime on 31 October 1935, in the period of autarky that was a response to the sanctions imposed by

Carlo Tivioli, sketches for furs and heavy jackets in chinchilla and sable, 1999.

G. Tizzoni
ABITI - MANTELLI - PELLICCE
VIA S. SPIRITO, 26 - VIA SPIGA, 25
20121 MILANO
TELEF. 701-311

Trademark of the Tizzoni tailoring shop.

the League of Nations for Italy's aggression against Ethiopia. The Ente required dressmakers to produce Collections that were 50 percent "of Italian design and production," monitored the Collections through sketches or photograph, and awarded a certificate, a label warranting "Italianicity of fabric and design." Giuseppina Pagani, who had been a "piscinina" (the term used in Milan for beginning seamstresses) and then a junior seamstress at Fumach, set up shop in 1920 with the name of her husband, Tizzoni: an atelier in Milan's Via della Spiga, at the corner with the Via Santo Spirito. Even before the autarky diktat, her Collections, like those of the best-known dressmakers in Milan and Rome, were mixed, original outfits and outfits of French fashion, purchased from pattern makers and revised in two or three versions or inspired by the creations of the big Parisian names, often just pirated and plagiarized. About her Maria Pezzi wrote: "A typical dressmaker, short, fat, countrified, with a consummate professional skill and an infallible eye." During the war, the G. Tizzoni company evacuated and did its presentations in Como. At the end of 1944, while northern Italy was experiencing the nightmare of Nazi and Fascist occupation and civil war, the magazine *Bellezza* wrote: "Despite the heavy downpours of a rainy autumn day, the trains of the Ferrovie Nord bring from Milan a considerable number of spectators and the lake ferries bring members of the audience from distant banks." Times were dark, but the ladies found "a memorable Tizzoni cape, black, for afternoon wear, trimmed with mink." For several years, Giuseppina had been working in partnership with her daughter Carla Tizzoni (1915-1986) who helped her, while holding in reserve her degree in chemistry and pharmaceuticals. At the end of the war, they reopened together the shop in the Via della Spiga and, in 1959, the *sartoria* took the name of mother and daughter. In the 1960s, the Tizzonis employed about a hundred people and enjoyed notoriety at the peak of the high fashion heap, especially for their gala evening wear and wedding dresses. At the beginning of the 1970s, Carla designed a boutique line, a forerunner of prêt-à-porter.

Tocca American label (headquarters in New York) for apparel and accessories, beauty products, and underwear. It is much beloved of Hollywood's stars. The style is simple and feminine. The Tocca Casa Collection was launched in 1997 while the most recent line (2000) was intimatewear. The first shop (Tokyo) was opened in 1997, while the following year the enormous New York space was inaugurated and, in 1999, the London boutique. The Collections are sold in the United States, Europe, Australia, Japan and Asia, as well as by Internet.

(*Mariacristina Righi*)

Todd Duncan Scottish company, specializing in the cashmere yarns sector. It belongs to the Dawson International Group and has offices in Kinross in Scotland. It employs 350 person. Since June 2003, the director for all markets, except the United Kingdom, with the title of sales director, is the Italian Stefano Finotti, who previously worked at an Italian spinning mill.

Tod's SpA Operative holding group quoted on the Milan Borsa from November 2000 on, which controls that labels Tod's, Hogan, and Fay. The chairman, managing director, and majority shareholder is Diego Della Valle; the vice president is his brother Andrea Della Valle. The origins of the company date back to the turn of the twentieth century, when Filippo Della Valle, Diego's grandfather, founded a small shoe manufacturer. "My family has always had leather as a ruling force," recalls the chairman. "My grandfather Filippo was a shoemaker, who worked in his kitchen at home, at first helped by my grandmother and then by the six children as they grew up. Twice a week my dad (Dorino), who was in charge of production, and uncle Pasquale, in charge of marketing, would travel by night (on bi-

Tizzoni, Empire-style outfit in a sketch by Brunetta. The outfit was worn by Adriana Botti for an inaugural soirée at La Scala. From the Fifties.

cycles or in freight trains, to save money) to Pescara, Forlì and Bologna, to sell our products to wholesalers who serviced the market stalls." At the end of the 1960s, poppa Dorino set business on his own, with the help of his wife. This was the beginning of Calzaturificio Della Valle di Sant'Elpidio a Mare, a small town in the Marche. "My mother, Maria Micucci," Diego Della Valle continues, "would stitch together soles and uppers, letting be sleep in the baskets of shoes to keep an eye on me." In that period the kitchen was transformed into a little factory. Diego began working for the company in the 1970s, after an attempt at university studies. He took just four exams in two years, in the department of law. "In effect, the lack of a desire to study has always been a family disease. So I went back home and started working with my father." As time went by, he took on greater responsibilities within the structure of the footwear manufacturer that was producing, at the time, only women's shoes. In 1979 he became the boss. At the turn of the 1980s, he introduced the first Tod's loafers, featuring an unusual sole that had 133 little raised rubber circles: in order to make one pair of loafers required 100 manufacturing steps, many of which involved hand labor. The strong point of the Tod's line was also the selection of fine American leathers and British hides, all rigorously water-repellent and produced by quality, small-scale tanneries. In 1986 Diego Della Valle became the sold administrator of the company, which in the meanwhile had been renamed Tod's S.p.A. New concepts in terms of product lines, marketing plans, and corporate strategy transformed the primordial family workshop into one of the leading players in the production and marketing of luxury footwear and leather goods. The three labels, Tod's, Hogan, and Fay, each had its own brand identity, but they all partook of the same philosophy, a well-balanced mix of tradition and innovation, quality and creativity. In particular, the Tod's label ws synonymous with luxury footwear and leather goods. A number of models, the Driving Shoe and the D Bag, have become cult products, expressions of a new concept of elegance, for men and for women. Hogan, a label that was introduced in the 1980s, stood out for its high design content: the basic model, inspired by English cricket shoes from the 1930s, was made with a double overlapping upper in order to make the shoe more durable, with a foam rubber padding of the edges and the insole, and a sole with an undulating design to ensure maximum flexibility. Initially focused on the production of footwear (for women, men, and children), Hogan recently diversified into leather goods. The Traditional and Interactive models were the "best sold," real successes in sales in the line of Fay products, an apparel label that dates from the end of the 1980s, and characterized by functionality and wearability. The line, which focuses on menswear but is also intended for women and children, consists of basic items, updated, and new proposals. Excellence in quality is an absolute must for the entire group, and it is guaranteed by the high proportion of craftsmanship in the manufacturing process and a strict control of the raw materials and all the phases of the production process. Production is primarily carried out in nine fully owned plants (7 for footwear and 2 for leather goods) and, in part, outsourced to a few specialized workshops, with which the company has established stable and long-lasting working relationships. Diego Della Valle has always rejected the policies of expansion through acquisitions that have been implemented by some of the players in the luxury market. "I don't see the advantages of controlling an entire sector for the sake of size. Each of my labels has its own research and product offices, they run independent advertising campaigns, and the same is true of the single-brand shops. In short, whatever synergies there may be are limited to manufacturing and logistics. Because of the risk that if you purchase without having organizational structures and good management to apply to everything that you have purchased, then in the end you no longer control anything." And the results would seem to prove him right. In the year 2000 the company had a consolidated turnover of 487.2 billion liras (251.6 million Euros), an increase of 14.5 percent over 1999, and a gross operating margin (or EBITDA, that is, Earnings Before Interest, Taxes, Depreciation, and Amortization) of 118.7 billion liras (61.3 million Euros), a 7.7 percent increase. In 2001, the rise in economic indicators was still in double figures: turnover increased by 26.6 percent while the EBITDA registered a leap upward of 31.5 percent. In 2002, a year of crisis for the luxury sector, the manufacturer had a repeat year. Net revenues amounted to 358.2 million Euros, a 12.5 percent increase, the EBITDA was 91.8 million Euros, a 13.9 percent increase. That same year, investments in non-physical immobilization of capital, amounted to 28.6 million Euros, most of which was due to the expansion of the network of direct distribution and sales, which grew by another 21 new shops. The capital locked up in material investments amounted to 15.8 million Euros, of which 38 percent was allocated for the construction of a new manufacturing plant adjoining the headquarters of Sant'Elpidio a Mare. All the investments were self-financed, given that the financial situation was in the black to the tune of 46.7 million Euros. For the future, Diego Della Valle is optimistic: "We have an easy road ahead of us, we really can't do anything but grow: our investments have been for the most part 'self-supporting,' and now all we need to do is gather the fruits of our work. When this phase of uncertain consumption patterns subsides, the growth of Tod's will be double-digit, but 'heavy' double-digit." Revenues and the gross operating margin of the first quarter of 2003 have increased (at constant rates of exchange), compared with the same period in 2002, by 3 percent and 17 percent, respectively. The label Tod's, accounting for 57.2 percent of total sales, continues to bring in the lion's share. During the same period, we acquired 4.6 percent of Italy's Banca Nazionale del Lavoro, so that Della Valle is now the third-largest shareholder, after the Basque group BBVA and Le Generali. "The objectives of this investment," explained the 'patron' of Tod's, "is to help, along with the other primary partners, to reinforce the stability of the bank. I am an industrialist, not a financier. I decided to buy into BNL on the basis of an industrial project, and I am in for the long term." At the end of 2002, the distribution network included 71 directly operated sales outlets and 37 franchised stores. The ownership structure is as follows: Della Valle family (63.1 percent), Lazard/SOFIDIV (3.5 percent), State of New Jersey Common Pension Fund (3.3 percent).

(*Dario Golizia*)

Togno Rita (1913). Italian fur designer. She was born in Asti. Responding to an early ambition, as soon as she finished an exclusive course in dressmaking, she moved on to Milan where she continued her apprenticeship in a strict school for future furriers. Her first items, made in a small Turinese workshop, were greeted in the years following WWII with an unexpected popularity because of their impeccable cut and rigorous execution. Within a few years Togno had become a well-known name, alongside names like Tivioli, Viscardi and Naldoni. They were responsible for the importance that Turin won in the furrier trade. She collaborated, with high fashion items, on the Roman runway presentations of Mila Schön and Irene Galitzine, thus increased her reputation even further with the novelty of her creations: colored, intarsiaed furs, reversible in other futs or fabrics, sculpted, transparent *breitschwanz* shawls and geometrically intarsiaed chincilla, dazzling in its elegance.

Toi Zang (1961). American fashion designer. Born in Malaysia, he established himself at the beginning of the 1990s with an exceptional color sensibility. In 1992 he launched the line, Z. In his wardrobe, exotic origins and passions found an excellent synthesis with a measured pragmatism.

Toledo Isabel (1961). Cuban fashion designer, who moved to the United States. From her debut in 1980, she has been featured in *Vogue* and *Harper's Bazaar*. She calls herself a dressmaker because, she says, it is necessary to know fashion from the interior. Her creations, for which she often uses denim and flannel, are aimed at women who are "profoundly feminine and creative."

Tolentino Gianni (1947). Italian fashion designer. The phases of his career run from the Accademia di Brera, his collaboration with Dior and Mila Schön, his hiring as a fashion designer in Pucci's atelier. Milanese by birth and education, Gianni Tolentino, who still lives and works in the capital of Lombardy, creates high fashion womenswear, prêt-à-porter, and wedding dresses. For costumes, he works as a consultant with opera houses and film production houses.

Tolo Crespi Pseudonym of Bartomeu Carbonell Crespì, fashion designer for Palma of Mallorca. At the end of the 1980s, he graduated from the Escuela Balear de Diseño with specialties in tailoring and *patronaje industrial*. His first collaboration (from 1989 till 1991) was with Victorio y Lucchino. In 1991, he collaborated with Hermes Govantes and created costumes for a number of theatrical productions. From 1991 till 1995 he worked with Pepe Rubio for the creation of costumes for a number of television programs and with the Lunelon company, designing a number of Collections. In 1996 he launched the first Collection Crespi y Romero, which he presented at the Espacio Gaudí in Barcelona, dedicated to young creatives. In 1997 Bartomeu Carbonell Crespí presented his first Tolo Crespi Collection. In 1998 he was at the Pasarela Gaudí, while the next year he presented also at the Salon du prêt-à-porter in Paris. In 2000, he took part in an event in Tokyo, Japan, dedicated to young fashion designers, and the Workshop salon in New York. In 2001 his Tolo Crespi Collection was presented for the first time at the Pasarela Cibeles in Madrid.

(*Mariacristina Righi*)

Tom & Linda Platt Label of a pair and couple of American fashion designers who have lived and worked together for the past 25 years, creating outfits that reflect a spirit of modern youth and which are a hymn to color and combinations of different fabrics. High technology is their strong point: everything is computer-designed with sophisticated techniques. They seek out fabrics, traveling around the world. Their clothing is especially featured in major American department stores.

Tombolini Eugenio (1933-1987). Italian couturier. He debuted in 1964 in Urbisaglia, near Macerata, and in the course of a few years he created the menswear line Urbis. In 1980, management of the company was taken over by his daughtger Fiorella. Beginning in 1990, in less than a decade, the company tripled its sales, producing men's and women's ready-to-wear fashion and couture Collections.

❑ 2001. It acquired the label Regent.
❑ 2002, January. Five-year agreement with IT Holding to produce and distribute the Collections Romeo Gigli and Gigli.
❑ 2002, June. Agreement with Antonio Fusco, for which Tombolini produces and distributes worldwide the menswear Collection of the Milanese *maison*. This is a three-year agreement that began with the Spring-Summer 2003 Collection. The total volume expected, by the end of the three-year period, was some 10 million Euros. Fiorella Tombolini, chairman and managing director, stated that in reality this is a partnership, given the long-term working relationship with Fusco, which in any case maintains design control. The company's turnover, at the end of 2002, was 60 million Euros.
❑ 2003, June. Confermation of rumors of negotiations underway for a possible licensing agreement with Maurizio Galante. The license is for both men's and women's prêt-à-porter.

Tom Tailor Apparel manufacturer. Behind the English name, there is a solid Hamburg-based company with more than thirty years of experience in the production of sportswear, from shirts to pullovers, from overcoats to swimsuits, accessories included. The company has an international marketing structure with a special focus on exports, especially to the Far East. Shirts represent 33 percent of the turnover and in the German market alone, the company sells about 1.5 million shirts annually.

Tomè Joao. Portuguese fashion designer. He attended courses in fashion design at the IADE in Lisbon, and created in 1989 a collective label with Francisco Pontes, a fellow university student. Their creations were a combination of various styles: from casual and sporty to urban and grunge and streewear, all the way up to high fashion. Their passion for the world of fashion made them famous in the homeland so that they were asked to design clothes for celebrities from the worlds of dance and television, as well as to create costumes for several ballets. (*Estefania Ruilope Ruiz*)

Tondowsky Alain (1969). French footwear designer. Polish by name and descent, he moved to Paris, where he attended the courses of the Studio Berçot. He has always taken inspiration for his creations from the actresses in Hitchcock films from the 1950s and the refined elegance of Romy Schneider in the 1970s. Even though he changed and modified each season his models and his details, the style of his creations reflected and remained bound up with the sort of ideal women, but at the same time with a mixture of opposites, the superabundance of the 1950s with Japanese minimalism. Beginning in 1989 he designed the Collection of Stéphane Kelian for a year and, in the years that followed until 1994, he worked with Gianfranco Ferré for Dior. He also worked for the theater. After working as a consultant for the purchase of accessories for the department stores of Printemps, in 1997 he set up in business on his own and put his own name on his womenswear line. Beginning in 2001, he added a menswear line, which was especially successful in the United States. The line featured broad, comfortable shoes with thick soles, reminiscent of traditional British men's shoes. The new womenswear Collection was called Pure Instinct and was conceived for various types of women, which he called "*les poseuses.*" High, stiletto heels, pointed narrow toes, each shoe had an ideal model. It might be Bianca Jagger, Iman, or Gerry Hall. Each model bore the name of the woman for whom it had been designed. Tondowsky loves white shoes even in the winter and little straps that wind around the ankle many times, a jagged revealing edge and a high heel, stout equestrian boots. Aside from the single-label shops in Paris, he is distributed in 60 sales outlets around the world, including two in Milan, the Vetrina di Beryl and Viverre. (*Gabriella Gregorietti*)

Toni Gard German prêt-à-porter *griffe*. It exports to the rest of Europe about 40 percent of what it produces. The company was founded in 1965 by Toni Lirsch (1941), who trained in the *maison* Detlef Albers in Berlin. Between 1965 and 1970, it opened its first two men's and women's boutiques in Dusseldorf, in the context of a style that is rooted in the aesthetic of contrasts: the new and the traditional, the classical and restrained extravagance.

❑ 2001. Licensing agreement with Gabriella Frattini, the fashion company based in Cavriago (Reggio Emilia) and owned by the Mariella Burani Fashion Group. The contract covers the production and distribution of the Toni Gard men's knitwear line in cashmere and wool on the international market, beginning in the Spring-Summer 2002 season. The agreement is for two years, with an option to renew for another five years.

Tony and Guy An English company, a leader in the hairstyling market, with a separate division for cosmetic products. The masterminds, owners, and founders are four Italian brothers: Toni, Guy, Bruno and Anthony Mascolo, influenced by their parents, who were both talented hairdressers. They were born in Scafati, in the province of Naples. The four brothers opened a hair salon in London in 1963. In 1970, having been very successful, they opened a second shop in Mayfair, and began to work in the field of advertising photography. Bruno and Anthony began to work with *Vogue*. The strong suit was a feminine and versatile style, for all ages and faces. The 1970s and 1980s confirmed and increased the success of the Mascolo family which, with their unmistakable style, were sought after worldwide. In the mid-1980s, the shops of Tony and Guy in London grew to three. They began a plan of international expansion that would lead them in 2002 to some 350 salons worldwide and 15 academies. During this period of growth, the Tigi Haircare and Tigi Cosmetics products were developed. In the new millennium, they developed the furniture division, Innovia. In 2002, innovation continued with an internal satellite channel: the Tony Guy Channel, for training and communicating with the company's staff. After finishing their studies, the third generation of the Mascolo family also chose the family profession, launching a youth line of products and cosmetics called

Essentials. Sacha Mascolo received a prize in 2002 as the best hairdresser of the year.
(*Sofia Catalano*)

Top An English term used around the world, describing various items of clothing, especially women's apparel, to be worn with a skirt, pants, trousers. Generally, a top is a very shirt knitwear item or else a bikini bra. In the United States, on the other, top means men's shirts.

Top-Girl Monthly for teenage girls from Gruner-Jahr-Mondadori, founded in 1998, with Maria Tatstos as editor-in-chief. *Top-Girl*, explained the managing director of the publishing house, Philippe Guesdon, "is designed to please a very difficult target, which over the course of six years contains three different age groups with differing wishes and needs." A true novelty for Italy, it mirrors its German counterpart, *Young Miss*, which is in its turn a version of the U.S. publication *YM*. It is rich in fashion, columns that establish a direct relationship with its readers on subjects such as love and couples, and many stars from the fields of music, entertainment, and sports.

Top Hat Men's formal hat created by English tailors before 1789. With a high and cylindrical top and a small brim, it can be in bright silk or black felt, sometimes also gray. The top hat was the symbol of Romanticism and Belle Époque.

Topless A term, used in many languages besides English to refer to a swimsuit missing the top part. The topless, designed in California by Gernreich, is basically nothing more than a high-waisted pair of shorts from which two slender straps run up, crossing over the breast and back. In the midst of the popularity of the miniskirt, at the dawn of the era of unisex fashion, the topless was a protest garment, often stigmatized or forbidden. But it soon exhausted its value, making way for extremely daring bikinis. Playing on the false dual bikini, the next development was in the 1970s, the creation of the young and impetuous manager of Robe di Kappa, Maurizio Vitale: the monokini, which even though it was presented as offering the possibility of buying different sizes of tops and bottoms, also meant that it was possible to do without a top.

Toque Popular in the 1920s and 1930s, this is a little woman's hat with a flat top, stiff sides, and no brim. In the late nineteenth century, fur toques were very common. It reappeared in the 1930s in felt, with a veil, or in jersey or draped wool and with a jewer or a feather in the center.

Toray Industries Japanese group that is a world leader in the production of synthetic fibers and fabrics, with plants in Asia, Europe and United States. It has 25,000 employees. Its entry into the European market (it acquired Soficar) and in America is intended to conquer it a leading role in the production of carbon fibers.

❑ 2003, April. Agreement with Cargill Dow, American company that owns rights to the brand new fiber, Ingeo. The two groups share the determination to reconcile the creation of new products with respect for the environment. On the one hand Ingeo is the first synthetic fiber derived from natural resources, and on the other the program Project New Toray 21 is based on principles of safety, health, and respect for the environment. With the newly signed agreement, Toray will hold the rights to license the technology, the name, and the supply of raw materials for the production and distribution of the fiber and associated products, in various countries around the world, including Japan and Europe.
❑ 2003, May. The fiscal year ended with turnover of 1.03 trillion yen and a 1.6 percent increase, but the net profits dropped sharply, by 52.3 percent, at a level of 5.8 billion yen.

Torcato Julio (1957). Portuguese fashion designer. In 1988 he was a finalist in the Young Designers competition of Portex, after attending design school at the Cooperative of Arvore (Porto) and fashion design courses at the Fashion Academy. The following year, he won the first Portex prize. He has shown at all the SEHM shows in Paris. Since 1990 he has been design director for the apparel manufacturer Ricon.

Torello Viera Biella-based woolen mill, founded at the turn of the twentieth century by Albino and Giovanni Torello Viera. It is currently based in Strona. As early as the end of the 1970s, the company distinguished itself for its creativity (the designer was Franco Bernascone) and research, blending in its fabrics natural fibers manmade fibers and focusing on innovative finishings. Success came with its close working relationship with Giorgio Armani, to whom the Torello Viera woolen mill supplied most of the fabrics for his menswear and womenswear Collections.

Tornade Bill A label that was founded at the turn of the 1980s in France by Francis and José Ronez. It immediately expanded into a series of men's, women's, and children's prêt-à-porter and enjoyed an immediate success, and enjoyed a rapid growth in popularity in Scandinavia, Japan, and the United States, ultimately opening a single-label retail outlet in New York in 2002. The label is also sold at Entre Nous, a Parisian boutique, the menswear counterpart of L'Eclaireur.

Torrente French high fashion house founded by Rose Torrente-Mett in 1968 in Paris. This fashion designer, with her green eyes and mop of red hair a la Shirley MacLaine, had the determination and energy of a Madeleine Vionnet or a Coco Chanel. Of Russian descent, the daughter of a tailor and the sister of Ted Lapidus (she was born Rosette Lapidus in 1936), worked for her brother in the second half of the 1950s. At the tender age of 23 she decided to go into business on her own: "I am like a jet plane, my engine is revving, I have to take off," she confessed to her brother. She opened her atelier in Avenue Matignon at the corner of the Rue du Faubourg Saint-Honoré. She excelled in designing highly structured tailleurs and overcoats, simple and essential, and her style was so new that it attracted and immediately seduced sophisticated and demanding clients like Marlene Dietrich, Romy Schneider, Natalie Wood, Marina Vlady, Raquel Welch, Paulette Goddard, Catherine Deneuve, Brigitte Bardot, Claudia Cardinale, and Ursula Andress. Since she could not use her brother's surname, nor the surname of her husband Jean Mett who owned an apparel-manufacturing company, she invented Torrente as a name for herself, a name that she chose because it "evoked music and water." In 1971 she made her official entry into the world of haute couture and joined the Chambre Syndicale de la Haute Couture. Quite soon she had a number of licensing contracts in France and worldwide, and she launched a prêt-à-porter line, Miss Torrente (which was at first manufactured by her husband, until he joined the *maison* as administrator in 1974). In 1971, she launched with Vestra the Torrente Uomo menswear line and a line of accessories, eyeglasses, foulards, and leather goods. With her brother she began a project that she would carry on alone, a Maison de la Mode, at 9, Rue du Faubourg Saint-Honoré. In 1988 she moved to the Rond-Point des Champs Elysées, in a *hôtel particulier* that once housed the atelier of Paul Poiret. In 1992 she was named a Chevalier de la Légion d'Honneur. She added jewelry to her prêt-à-porter lines (especially Tahitian pearls) and, in 2002, Torrente Maison, an elegant line of home underwear (bed and bath). Also in 2002 she won the Marionnaud prize for the launch of the perfume L'Or de Torrente, a potpourri of flowers, fruits, and vegetables captured in an egg-shaped bottle decorated with iridescent opaline leaves in relief. She began a policy of opening new sales outlets. In Paris a boutique on the Avenue Victor Hugo, then others in various points around France. In January 2003, she launched her first Collection of men's and women's shoes and, after a few seasons' absence, she resumed her menswear Collection for Spring 2003 and 2004. She was the managing director, the president, and the artistic director of the *maison*. Since 1985 she had been delivering lectures at the school for higher commercial studies and she was deputy chairman of the Institut Français de la Mode. In February 2003, after 34 years as a creator of fashion, she decided to retire (to spend more time with her family, according to the press release), left the stage, and sold her shares in the Torrente Group to the Chammas Group which, as a

shareholder since 1985, in fact controlled the *maison* since March 2002.
(*Gabriella Gregorietti*)

Torretta Roberto. Argentine fashion designer. He lives and works in Spain where he moved from Buenos Aires in 1972. He established himself in Madrid and entered the world of fashion through the Trip Diffusion company in Barcelona. In 1981 he founded Snif, an apparel manufacturing company. He specialized in the production of cotton sportswear, but his creations became progressively richer and more complex. The first Collection designed by Roberto Torretta that had a runway presentation (in Madrid) was the Spring-Summer 1984 Collection. In 1988, he opened his own proprio showroom and his Collections began to be sold in the finest Spanish boutiques. In 1996 his items were presented for the first time in the Pasarela Cibeles in Madrid. In 2002 he was awarded two prizes in recognition of his brilliant career in the world of fashion. These were the Alfiler de Oro, assigned by Fermoda and the Pasarela Costa del Sol. (*Mariacristina Righi*)

Torricelli Raffaello (1910). A lawyer, he was also the president of the Centro Moda di Firenze from 1962 until 1965 and of the Chamber of Tourism (Azienda di Turismo) from 1961 till 1970. In that capacity, he supported the fruitless struggles of Giovanni Battista Giorgini to endow Florence with a Palazzo della Moda (Palace of Fashion) and an urbanistic complex, at the Cascine, that would include much needed fair and congress structures as well as a hotel, conference rooms, a movie theater, workshops of the craftspeople of the sector, a costume museum, and an archives. With a surprisingly farsighted approach, Torricelli always considered fashion to be a fundamental component of contemporary culture. In the decade that he spent at the helm of the Azienda di Turismo, he was the chief promotor of the construction of the Palazzo dei Congressi, he set up the Mostre Mercato d'Arte Contemporanea at Palazzo Strozzi and the Biennali d'Architettura which involved the participation of Alvar Aalto and Frank Lloyd Wright. In 1983, he founded, and remained president for 10 years, the Associazione Amici della Galleria del Costume di Palazzo Pitti, which was absolutely decisive in the development of that museum.

Tortu Christian. Set designer, decorator, fashion designer. Originally and in the first place, a florist who revolutionized his profession, shaping it in accordance with his own creativity. Born in the 1950s in France, in Maine-et-Loire, to a family of florists for many generations, at the age of 22 he left Saumor to work in various French provinces, arriving in Paris in 1977. In the French capital, he opened a number of stores, the last of which at 6, Carrefour de l'Odeon, which rapidly became a sort of "islet of nature" in the heart of the city. In the 1980s, he founded a label that took inspiration from floral compositions for scented candles in natural wax, incense, soaps, lines of plates and cups decorated rigorously with natural motifs. The motto, still valid, was "XXth century will be vegetal, or not be." Following the New York opening of the shop on Fifth Avenue, Tortu began to work as a set designer for the installation of exhibits in museums, for the runway presentations of the leading fashion designers (Valentino, Dior, Chanel), for the Festival of Cannes. His staff consists of 13 people, he opened boutiques in New York, Tokyo and in the Latin Quarter of Paris. Giorgio Armani turned to him to create the floral corner shop of the Milanese shop in the Via Manzoni.
(*Pierangelo Mastantuono*)

Torun Vivianna (1927). Swedish jewelry artist, who worked especially in silver. One of her "pieces," *Assymetrical Necklace*, 1959, has been called "a milestone in modern jewelry" (Barbara Cartlidge in *Twentieth Century Jewellery*). In 1948 she opened her first workshop in Malmø. She traveled. In Paris, she became a friend of Picasso, Braque and Brancusi. She was very beautiful and was photographed by such renowned photographers as Gilles Ehrmann. Among her best known creations, a double-vortex brooch and bracelet-wristwatch for a show that she held at the Musée des Arts Décoratifs in Paris. She lives in Jakarta, in Indonesia.

Toscani Oliviero (1942). Italian photographer who had brilliant intuitions and a provocative stance. He attained worldwide notoriety through shocking photographs, but also through social messages with a universal language. He was born in Milan, and grew up on photography, a presence in his family from when he was small. He was an apprentice with his father, a famous reporter of *Il Corriere della Sera*, but that was not enough. From 1961 till 1965 he studied graphic design and photography in Zurich, in one of the most respected schools in Europe. He was hired by Flavio Lucchini, art director of the newly founded Italian edition of *Vogue*, and worked for this magazine where his direct, spare style was successful – midway between the realism of photojournalism and the fiction of fashion photography. Right from the beginning, he worked with all the leading international fashion magazines. His contribution was crucial to the success of *L'Uomo Vogue*, the first magazine dedicated to men's fashion, where he was the main photographer from the magazine's founding, in 1967, until the beginning of the 1980s. But other successful magazines in the 1970s and 1980 looked up to him as the mastermind, the protagonist of their most precise images: from the weekly *Elle*, to *Lei*, *Donna*, *Moda*, and *Mondo Uomo*. He was also the creative power behind many of the most innovative advertising campaigns of the fashion industry, since the 1970s. He did a famous picture of a woman's derriere as the symbol of Jesus jeans, as well as a series of invariably provocative pictures created for Prénatal, Fiorucci, and Esprit. In 1982 he began his professional partnership with Luciano Benetton. He was responsible for changing the label from Benetton to United Colors of Benetton. In the company he had total liberty in the field of image and communications and handled large advertising budgets which he used to manage a communications campaign with strong social contents: he scandalized the bourgeoisie but he won acclaim prestigious prices, including the Grand Prix d'Affichage and the UNESCO Grand Prix. From the very beginning, his campaigns focused on controversial themes with shocking images: from racism to AIDS, from Mafia to war, from religion to pollution, from a newborn baby still linked to an umbilical cord to the handicapped. He founded the bimonthly *Colors*, distributed worldwide through the thousands of Benetton stores, an unconventional publication that examined the hypocrisies and absurdities of the life of modern consumerism. Again, with the sponsorship of Benetton and in a monastic seventeenth-century villa renovated by the Japanese architect Tadao Ando in the countryside around Treviso, he founded Fabrica, an arts workshop, a school and laboratory in which to develop young creative talents found around the world. In his maturity, Toscani is much more than a photographer: he is a great communicator, an art director, a director. His work has been studied in debates, exhibitions, international expositions such as the Venice Biennale, the Biennale d'Arte e della Moda of Florence (1986, 1998). He won the highest award assigned by the Advertising Festival of Cannes for a television spot, many prizes and international recognition. Three wives and six children. He lives half the time in a large farm in Tuscany, where he raises Apaloosa horses.

❑ 2001. The relationship with Benetton was broken off. Toscani began working as a freelancer, with the name Oliviero Toscani Energie. (*Gisella Borioli*)

Tosi Piero (1927). Italian costume designer. He studied Fine Arts with Ottone Rosai, in his native city, Florence. It was against the backdrop of Boboli that he began his long working artistic partnership with Visconti, who introduced him into the movie business by assigning him to design the costumes of *Bellissima*. He would collaborate on all of Visconti's greatest films, adopting as the occasion called for it an everyday attention to realism (*Rocco and His Brothers*) or the magnificent reconstruction of a period piece (*Senso*, *Il Gattopardo*), a job for which his profound artistic culture made him especially well suited. In films such as *La caduta degli dei* (*The Damned*), *Death in Venice*, and *Ludwig*, the selection of fabrics, the cut of the outfits, and the furnishings all contributed in decisive manner to the narrative of the film and the intentions of Visconti. He also had an intense period of collaboration with Mauro Bolognini (*Il bell'Antonio*, *Metello*, *La viaccia*, *Senilità*), all adaptations of literary works whose atmosphere Tosi's costumes spectacularly evoked, and with Liliana Cavani (*The Night Porter*, *Beyond Good and Evil*). His work with Fellini was more infrequent (the episode of *Toby Dammit*), as with Pasolini (*Medea*), De Sica, Comencini, Castellani. He theorized that it was impossible for a costume designer to become a fashion designer and viceversa. He won numerous Nastro d'Argento awards.

(*Roberto Nepoti*)

Tositti Gianni (1934). Entrepreneur in the field of prêt-à-porter. At the age of 24, he entered the world of fashion, working as a representative for Krizia and traveling around Italy with his fashion samples. In 1962, he did the same work for the Missonis. In 1969, he founded, with Aldo Ferrante and Gigi Monti, FTM, inaugurating in the Via della Spiga in Milan a new method of marketing: a collective showroom for all the fashion designers in their "stable." The following year, the three businessmen purchased Basile. In 1972 they hired Walter Albini to design five Collections and had runway presentations at the Circolo del Giardino in Milan. It was the first signal of what would soon be happening in Milan, with the decision by Krizia and Missoni to abandon the Sala Bianca in Florence and to have their presentations in Milan. He worked on the labels Genny and Complice at the beginning and on Callaghan, Issey Miyake, and Soprani. He was the first to import the Ralph Lauren label to Europe. He is a style consultant for the Turkish Beymen group.

Total Look Every fashion designer, especially over the course of the 1980s, imposed his or her own concept of elegance and won a number of faithful consumers willing to pledge allegiance to her or her style. With the result that a *griffe* tended to dress all the spaces and demands of an individual, who would then accept in unreserved manner all of ideas and proposals, which would monopolize his or her individual wardrobe, from head to foot. This led to the creation and spread of the expression of *total look* to describe the complete production of a name, from lines of clothing to accessories.

Totman Christopher (1967). American fashion designer. He loves the colors and fabrics of South America, especially those from Peru, so much so that all the sweaters that he designed were handmade by a cooperative of Peruvian women. He is considered to be one of the most interesting fashion designers of the fashion underground of New Nork. After presenting his Collections for two years in his showroom-loft in SoHo, he opened a shop in NoLita (North of Little Italy). Even though his outfits with their linear cut and geometric contrasts and colors were very popular in London, Tokyo, and Los Angeles, he continued to prefer a limited production. The Fall-Winter 1999 Collection for instance contained only 14 items: "For a mass production, I would need a team of assistants and I still can't afford that."

Tourdjman Georges (1935). French photographer. After working in the movie business for a number of years, in 1963 he moved to New York to learn photography. Beginning that year, he worked with Ike Weegler and became a pupil of Brodovitch, who was to influence profoundly his way of composing and shooting. In 1964, he returned to Paris where he set up a studio and worked for L'Oréal, Hermès, Dior, Chanel, Dim, Lanvin, and Rabanne. *Queen*, *Marie France* and other women's magazines often used his work for cover shots.

Tournafol Christian (1968). French designer. His creations are evocative of Brittany, his birthplace, along with the traditions of the maritime world and the Celtic culture of that region. He took a degree in clothing manufacturing at Brest, at the School of Fine Arts in Nancy and at the Lycée de la Mode of Cholet. He debuted professionally working in the ateliers Chantal Thomass, Jerome L'Huillier and Michel Klein. In 1996 he presented his first Collection, inspired by the traditional costume of the Bigouden region, rich in colors and embroideries. In 1997 he had the brainstorm of assembling in an unusual way a fisherman's sweater and a long skirt, thus creating the sweater-suit, which became a key item of his Collections. He also designed the Busnel and Busnel Marine lines, specializing in knitwear. (*Alessandra Scifo*)

Christian Tournafol, 1999-2000 Fall-Winter Collection.

Tournure A French word that is practically untranslatable, also known as *faux cul*. It is an elastic bulge, form or bustle, to be worn under a skirt. Very fashionable at the end of the nineteenth century, when the volume of the fabric was entirely gathered in the back, to form an exaggeratedly arched silhouette. It reappeared sporadically throughout the entire twentieth century, especially for evening wear. In the 1940s Balenciaga used the *tournure*, and at the end of the 1980s, Chanel, Balmain and Lacroix rediscovered it. For the 1993-94 season, it was used by Yohji Yamamoto and Vivienne Westwood.

Toyofuku Tomonori (1925). Japanese sculptor. He created small items of jewelry and major monuments: among other things, a 1,650-metric ton granite fountain in Kurume, in 1983, and an iron sculpture in the port of Fukuoka, in 1996, both on the island of Kyushu, where he was born. He lived in Italy, in Milan, beginning in 1960. He was a kamikaze flier, and he eluded death on the last day of the war (15 August 1945), a student of Zen philosophy, and he was also a member of an avant-garde group called Shinseisaku. His first exhibition was at the Tokyo Gallery, in 1960; he had a hall at the Venice Biennale in 1962. He is an abstract artist who prefers mahogany and stone, which he carves out and drills in accordance with an unmistakable code. His wife, Kazuko, is a painter; his daughter Nazuko designs jewelry made with modest materials. *(Mario Pancera)*

Traeger Ronald (1937-1968). American photographer. He studied at the San Francisco Art Institute. He arrived in London in 1963, where he worked for *Elle* and *Vogue France*.

Tramontano Italian leather goods label. Since 1865, in its historic offices in Naples, Tramontano has designed and produced for generations: bags, luggage and accessories in leather, in keeping with the techniques of the finest Neapolitan crafts tradition. Tramontano leather is tanned with natural methods. The workshops also make custom items. It has a "bridgehead" in Milan, in the courtyard of Palazzo Borromeo, in Via Manzoni 41. One of its most attractive items is the T-bag, designed by the American designer Timothy Greenfield-Sanders, in a limited, numbered edition (750 items). It is reminiscent of the little trunks used in the stagecoach era, made of leather and canvas with bamboo laths and visible pockets. The Fall-Winter 2003-2004 Collection, with its vaguely retro flavor, takes us back to the 1960s-1970s: handmade bags, suitcases, and studded handbags, made of leather and bamboo or with inlays of ponyskin, models taken from the historic archives with large ring handles, and the more modern organizer bags or the shopping bags shaped like haversacks, super equipped with handy accessories, nécessaires and internal pockets. The winter versions of the summer bags are made of wool and leather or ponyskin and leather the backpacks are light and very soft. The Fiordo line, totally white, is made with an exclusive waterproof Scandinavian leather: tanned by an age-old method that makes it resistant to wear and again, that was used by Nordic fishermen. For men, light travel bags with wheels, or unlined so that it can be rolled up, with a snap-hook fastening for yachtsmen. *(Gabriella Gregorietti)*

Tran Hélène (1954). French illustrator. Born

in Paris. He studied at the Ecole Supérieure d'Art Graphique. In her design and composition she had a theatrical and spectacular taste. *Vogue*, in its American and British editions, often made use of her work which, many thought, was evocative of the painter-illustrator Marcel Vertès in its view of society in runway presentations and ateliers.

Tran Hin Phu (1975). Swiss fashion designer. His beginnings were linked to architecture in a firm in Berne. It was not until 1997 that he began a career in fashion that led him to work for the couture pages of the *Sunday Times* and to work as an intern with a number of London *maisons*. In 2001, he won the Swiss Textiles Award in the context of Gwand 2001 and presented Collections in Lucerne. That same year, he founded the label that bore his name. After major international awards, he presented for the first time in Paris in 2002 during the women's prêt-à-porter fashion week.

Trastornados *Griffe* created by José Enrique Garcia and Paco Navarro, who brought together their training in architecture and philology and their studies in music and art. They began to work in the in the world of fashion by producing a number of one-off items, the product of the manipulation of fabric, painting, and graphics. The first complete Collection was shown in 2002 at the Semana Internacional de la Moda in Madrid and at the Gaudí Salon in Barcelona. Later, they were selected to present a Collection (the Fall-Winter 2002-2003 Collection) in the space dedicated to the new talents of fashion within the context of the CPD Salon in Dusseldorf in Germany, while with the Collection for Fall-Winter 2003-2004 they presented in Madrid at the Pasarela Cibeles.

Treacy Philip (1967). Irish milliner and fashion designer. Born in County Galway. He moved to London to study for a masters at the Royal College of Art (1990). He was considered the *enfant prodige* of hats, and when he was just a student he began to collaborate with such famous fashion designers as John Galliano and Rifat Ozbek. In 1991 he opened his own atelier and launched his own prêt-à-porter line, as well as beginning a successful and ongoing collaboration with Karl Lagerfeld and Chanel. He won the British Accessory Designer of the Year award and began to take part in the London Fashion Week. He signed a contract with Debenhams department stores for a mass distributed line. His brilliant and extravagant creations were shown in various exhibitions: 1996, La Biennale di Firenze; 1997, the Cutting Edge show at the Victoria and Albert Museum in London; 1998, *Addressing the Century: 100 Years of Art and Fashion* at the Hayward Gallery in London. He creates apparel for television and in 1998 he was in charge of the advertising campaign for Max Factor International. In 1999 he worked with the Maison Givenchy in Paris.

❑ 1992, 1993, 1996, 1997. He won the British Accessory Designer of the Year award, as he had done in 1991.
❑ From 1999 to 2003, he expanded his collaborations with major names: his creations were worn with items by Versace, Valentino, Alexander McQueen, and Thierry Mugler. He also designed accessories for men.
❑ 2002, July. The English hatter, purveyor to the Royal House, was present in Rome, a guest of the event Donna sotto le stelle, the runway presentation held on the Spanish Steps, (Scalinata di Trinità dei Monti).
❑ 2003, June. For high fashion week in Paris, the "mad hatter" presented an ironic homage to Andy Warhol's Pop Art. Naomi strode down the runway with a can of Campbell's soup on her head, the other models balanced on their hair either banana peels or pictures, in pure Warholian style, of Marilyn Monroe, Liza Minnelli, or Tina Chow. The unusual hairdress accompanied outfits by Calvin Klein, Kate Moss, David Beckham, Joan Collins. Not everything however was a Warhol tribute. There were also creations by Treacy, light and evanescent, brilliant and luminous, as always vivid and imaginative, wobbling like mobiles by Calder. (*Virginia Hill*)

Tree Dorothy, known as Dolly (1906). A costume designer, English by birth, who worked in America. She was well known for

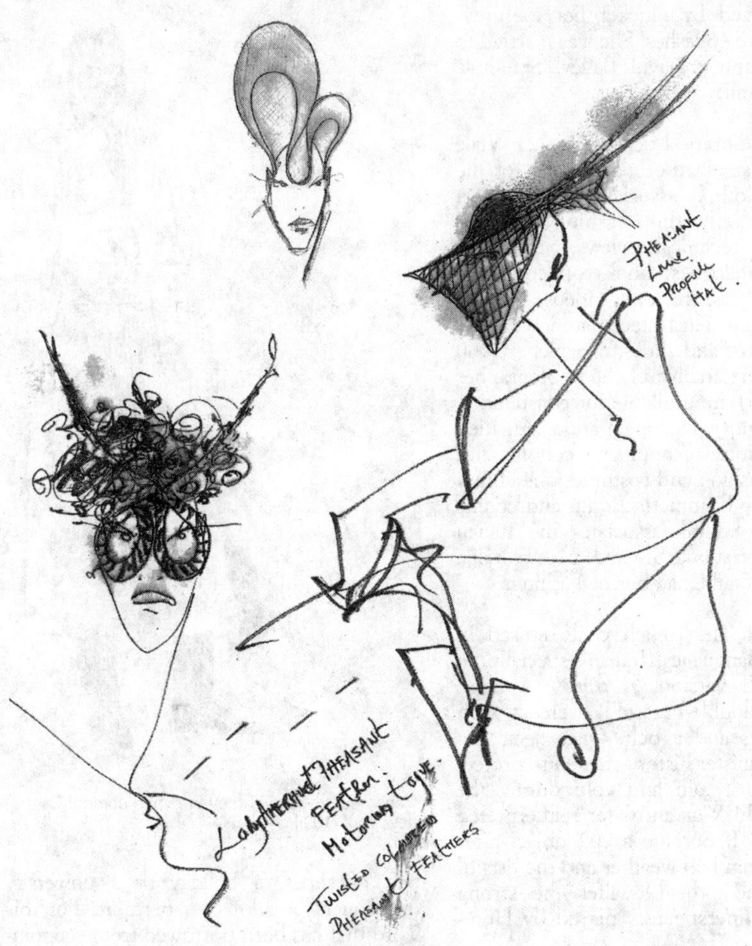

Philip Treacy, hats designed for his involvement in the exhibition *Visitors*, curated by Luigi Settembrini and Franca Sozzani (Biennial of Florence, Skira, 1996).

her elegant creations in Victorian style. She debuted on Broadway in the 1920s, designing costumes for musical comedies and, in particular, for Mae West. She was hired as a costume designer by Twentieth Century Fox, and three years later she moved on to MGM, where she stayed for a decade. Her creations were worn by Judy Garland, Lana Turner, and Jean Harlow (*Saratoga*, 1937) and by the sophisticated Myrna Loy in *The Thin Man* (1934). Her finest creations had to do with period pictures, in which Dolly's costumes contributed in decisive manner to the creation of the atmosphere. For instance *Little Women* (1933) and *David Copperfield* (1934).

Tree Penelope. British fashion model. She was considered the symbol of the fashion of the 1970s. The propensity of fashion designers for androgyny began with her very skinny figure. She belonged to a family of the British upper classes, and debuted on the runways at the age of thirteen, a discovery of the photographer Diane Arbus. Another element of her allure were large eyes, which she emphasized by plucker her eyebrows and using fake eyelashes. She was married to the photographer David Bailey. She now lives in Australia.

Tremelloni Library Located at 223 Viale Sarca in Milan, in the headquarters of the textile and clothing associations. Its subject is predominantly the "fashion system." Monographs, technical reviews, periodicals, designers' catalogues, books on costume's exhibitions, press reviews, videos,. graduation theses, and illustrated materials (about 100,000 photos and slides, of which 30,000 come from the archive of the photographer Elsa Haertter) are available for consultation by all and sundry. Documentation is divided in three sections: technology, economy and marketing, fashion and costume. The library is directed by Fiammetta Roditi and counts among its founding associates the Italian Textile Association, Sistema Moda Italia, and the National Chamber of Fashion.

Trench Coat The trench coat is used in many other languages, Italian especially, in its shortened version, *il trench*: a light, waterproof double-breasted overcoat with raglan sleeves and a belt. Once again, an item with a sinister history created to protect soldiers against rain and cold during the Second World War and later reinterpreted by Burberry. It became a cult object after protecting from bad weather and the fists of gangsters and other lowlifes the strong shoulders of investigators played by Humphrey Bogart.

Trench coat by the Hickey Freeman company, New York, 1934.

Trend Technical term borrowed from economics where it is commonly used to identify the development or growth of a certain sector. From the stock exchange and economic markets, it has been shifted to defined more general concepts of progression, orientation, and direction, until it finally was adopted for fashion (widely used, for instance, is the adjective 'trendy,' or fashionable). It has unfortunately been overused, in part because of the success of the fashion industry (for instance, 'the trend of the latest runway presentations'). So that by this point, at least according to publications and opinion makers, everything or nearly everything can be considered in terms of trends (more or less positive): a haircut or a pair of shoes, a holiday or a university department, a color or a perfume. For this word that has been borrowed from economic analysts, the inevitable fate that has already befallen the word "look" seems to lie in wait: it will eventually come to mean nothing. (*Stefano Bucci*)

Trend The term dates from the nineteenth century. If defines a set of signs capable of expressing with a certain degree of accuracy the future. Focusing the evolution of style means drawing a number of trends. More than theories on the origins of processes – imitation, distinction, identification, differentiation, and conformism – this is a matter of constructing flows of orientations that determine fashions. Each link in the production chain involves specialists and industrialists in the textile and apparal manufacturing process, working hard to reduce the risks of error. For each transition, then, devices are activated to identify trends developed through concerted actions, periodical consultations with experts of various countries, members of *bureaux de style* of the *comité de mode*. From these exchanges, the *cahiers de tendences* are developed, which contain illustrations of materials, forms, and colors of the new orientations, more or less accurate, checked totally or partially by the manufacturers of fibers, fabrics, threads, and apparel, with advantage of putting one's products in line with general trends, and launching trend-setting lines.

(*Lucia Serlenga*)

Trend Union Label of a consortium in Paris that produces the ideas of 11 fashion designers, each specializing in a particular sector of clothing, from intimatewear to casualwear, from men's fashion to women's fashion, and each of them agreeable to a creative alliance. The initiative, which dates back to 1987, was the brainchild of Li Edelkoort, a Dutch fashion designer, who took her degree at the School of Fine Arts in Arnhem.

Tricker's British shoe manufacturer founded by master shoemaker Joseph Tricker in 1829, in Northampton. The production of the classic models in calfskin, with treated oak bark soles, is still solidly in the hands of the family heirs, now in the fifth generation. In the London shop in St. James' the custom department is still at work. More recently opened points of sale are the second London shop in Newgate Street and the shop in Pickering, North Yorkshire.

Tricot Pierluigi. Pseudonym of Pierluigi Scazzola (1927). Italian fashion designer. He studied at the Convitto Nazionale in Rome, the city where he was born, and went on to study law at the university. In 1958, he began hand-dying fabrics and made blouses. La Rinascente, his first client, commissioned him to make foulards. He began to work on knitwear, cutting it as if it were a tailored cloth. He focused on luxury knitwear. In 1961, he presented his first Collection at the Galleria d'Arte Moderna, to the enthusiasm of Irene Brin. Giorgini selected 20 creations to show in Florence on the runway of Palazzo Pitti, where he was to be present until 1977. He took part in Mare Moda Capri in 1967 con his "scudo" line, in lurex and jacquard wool. He was invited to New York where he was acclaimed by the press and Irene Brin urged him to go to Paris. His first important clients were Rudy Crespi, Jacqueline Kennedy, Claudia Cardinale, Lauren Bacall, and Allegra Agnelli. From 1970, he founded a more commercial line, Tricot Sport, which ceased operations in 1982. He continued to work for his own boutique in Rome's Via Delle Carrozze. In 1997, he retired entirely.

Tricot 5 Label of an Italian company

Trends in women's fashion between 1925 and 1931 (from *Fashion and Antifashion*, by Ted Polhemus and Lynn Procter, Thames and Hudson, 1978).

producing high-quality men's knit outerwear (sweater, cardigans, and other varieties). It was founded in 1952 with the label Peter Brown. In 1998, with the arrival of new partners, it extended production to women's fashion and established a new label, Passadore.

Tricotage Zimmerli Swiss manufacturer of women's underwear and corsetry, founded in 1890. Toward the 1920s del, the company had four factories in Friburg and Aarburg (Germany), and at Montebeliard and St Quentin (France), with a total of 1,250 employees. It had stores of its own in New York, London, Paris, and Buenos Aires. It survived its owner, (name of Zimmerli), who died in 1928.

Trifari American jewelers. The descendant of a Neapolitan family of jewelers who emigrated to the United States in the early twentieth century, Augusto Trifari began in 1909 a production of costume jewelry. The company won a place for itself in the U.S. market, beginning in 1930s, with the arrival of the designer Alfred Philippe. Made famous in the 1950s by the first lady Mamie Eisenhower, who wore them at balls in the White House, Trifari costume jewelry became very popular throughout the 1960s and 1970s. Today they are much sought after by collectors of vintage costume jewelry.

Trigère Pauline (1912). French dressmaker. More than a designer of women's outfits, she was a true craftswoman. She was born in Paris, moved to New York in 1937, after completing her studies and working in her father's dressmaking boutique and in Armand's dressmaking boutique. In the United States, she worked for Ben Gersel, Travis Banton and the Hattie Carnegie Fashion House. She founded the House of Trigère in 1942. She was famous for her little outfits with slim silhouettes, skirt just down to the knee. She was also renowned for her choice of fabrics, which she always merged into a singular, pioneering mix, and for her outfits in tulle with appliqués of embroidered flowers.

Trisci Riccardo (1974). Italian fashion designer. Born in Como from a family originally from Puglia. He took a degree at the Istituto d'Arte in Cantù and began to work, designing fabrics for respected fashion designers. He moved to London and worked with the *maison* of Antonio Berardi, before enrolling in the Central St. Martin School. At the end of the course, his graduation Collection was purchased by a company in Tokyo, thus officially marking Riccardo's entry into the world of fashion as an independent fashion designer. His creations were published in prestigious international periodicals, and he was popular with entertainment stars. In 2003, he was appointed artistic and creative director of Puma Rudolf Dasseler Schufabrik and Coccapani.

(*Sofia Catalano*)

Trish McEvoy An American brand of basic make-up products, created by the make-up artist of that name, the most popular among American models and actresses. She had been working in this field for some 25 years, even though she learned the trade when she was very young and was helping her grandmother out in her perfume shop. She moved to the United States where she found her first job with Esthée Lauder and was successful enough to launch herself in business for herself. In order to meet her clients' demands, she created and marketed a line or her own. But it was with her husband, the famous dermatologist Ronald Sherman, that her real success began. Together, they opened a beauty center where they sold their new cosmetics line, designed for the greatest protection of the cutomers' skins. Their products, famous as well for being easy to use, are sold in more than 300 shops around the world.

Tritapepe Pasquale (1890-1951). Italian tailor. As a master tailor, he belonged to the great tailoring school of Abruzzo that boasted such names as Domenico Caraceni, Ciro Giuliano, Nicola Amazzalorso, Nazzareno Fonticoli, Costante Zopito, De Fulgentiis, Di Tecco, Ferrari, Camillo Modesti, Luigi Fagnese, Dante D'Indino, Donato Pavone, Tobia Agresti, Vincenzo Di Donato, and Luigi D'Alessandro. He was born in Atri. At the age of twelve he ran away from home and from an authoritarian father, winding up in Rome where he found work in a tailor's shop. Life was harsh. In order to make ends meet, after work, he would do minor repairs to firemen's uniforms. At the age of 17, he managed to open his own first tailor's shop in Porto d'Anzio and later in Rome itself, where he met the chief tailor of Second Royal Piedmontese, a battalion that was much beloved by King Victor Emmanuel III. The chief tailor fell ill and named him as his substitute. And so, deeply idealistic republican though he was, he happened to cut and sew a little, tiny uniform. He understood that it was for "sciaboletta," the king of Italy. Years later, he told his son Nino, who carried on with strict perfectionism his heritage as a tailor: "I moved me so deeply that I came close to questioning my republican loyalty." The uniform was so perfect that it made his reputation among the aristocracy. He would have been well advised to sink his roots in Rome. But a love affair led him to leave, going first to Castellammare di Pescara, and then to Pescara, a city where he worked, for a clientele that was largely Roman, until he died. Just before he died, he told his son: "The minute you realize that you don't know how to practice this profession, go right ahead. Modesty can only help you."

Triumph International A manufacturing group specializing in women's underwear, corsetry and swimsuits. It was founded in 1886 in Germany. It has a presence in the markets of 120 nations in Europe, North America, Australia, Asia, and Latin America, with production of more than 200 million items yearly, made in the factories of 15 different countries. The total work force is about 35,000 employees. The sales volume is more than 2 trillion liras. In 1986, the group purchased the French compny HOM (intimatewear, leisure wear, and beach wear), a label that joined Triumph, Sloggi (especially underwear for men and women: 12 million items yearly), and Gaja (lingerie). Since 1994, the group's products have met environmental standards both in terms of materials used and in terms of manufacturing process. In 1996, it launched a revolutionary men's underwear with a horizontal slot-opening. Three years later, it launched Aqualife Body Float, a bathing suit that, thanks to its unique cellular structure, helps you to float.

❑ 2000. Italian turnover was 160 billion liras, with 419 employees.
❑ 2002, January. After the boycotting campaign against the multinational, it closed its plant, Myanmar Triumph International, in Rangoon, Myanmar (Burma). The accusations, from the International Labour Organization, among others, were exploitation of child labor and economically encouraging the military regime of Rangoon. The advertising campaign featured an iron bra with the slogan 'Support breasts not dictators.' A thousand workers lost their jobs.
❑ 2002. Added to the existing brands were Valisère and BeeDees. At year's end, the volume of investment was 50.5 million Swiss francs, the employees were 37,273, and turnover had declined from the year before by 4.6 percent.
❑ 2003, June. Opening of the new outlet (the first one is in Trescore Balnerario, where Triumph has its Italian headquarters), inside the Fidenza Village in the province of Parma.

Trope Donna. American photographer. She worked for *Vogue Beauty*, *Dazed & Confused*, *Citizen K*, *L'Officiel*. Her portraits have been shown at the Victoria and Albert Museum in London and at the Venice Biennale.

Trottmann Italian dressmaking house. Fina Trottmann purchased in 1945 the Genoa branch of the renowned Sartoria Ventura of Milan: a separate branch where she had worked for many years. She immediately established a reputation as the trusted dressmaker of the most important families of Genoa and Milan. Thirty years later, in 1976, when it went out of business, the company had 120 employees, furrier and millinery departments, and an archive of 3,000 entirely original patterns, purchased in Paris. The dressmaking house was the sole agent in Italy for Louis Vuitton, Hermès and Chanel accessories, until they opened stores of their own. When it went out of business in 1976, the premises in the Palazzo Cambiaso were taken over by another dressmaker of Genoa's high society, Andrea Odicini.

Trousse French term for evening bag. From the Belle Epoque on, women never went out in the evenings without a *trousse*. Rigid, shaped like a round or rectangular box, with a built-in internal mirror, it contained the needful make-up, from powdered rouge to lipstick. Made in tortoise shell, ivory, crocodile skin, Chinese lacquer, precious metals such as silver or gold, decorated with enamels and precious stones. In the 1950s the *trousse* was supplanted by the *pochette*.

Troy Hannah. American fashion designer. In reality, more than a creator of fashion, we should describe her as a fashion entrepreneur, because she used the services of designers such as George Samen (1950s) and Murray Neiman (1960s) and purchased French and Italian patterns and modified them. She preferred Italian *griffes* and, for that reason, she was awarded in 1954 the Italian *Ordine al Merito della Repubblica*. She debuted in 1937, but did not enter the limelight until the 1950s. She was petite, and she specialized in outfits for women shorter than 160 cm, suited both for daytime wear and evening wear.

Trussardi Nicola (1942-1999). Fashion designer and entrepreneur. When gloves were indispensable accessories for elegant man or woman, Dante Trussardi founded, in 1910, his glove business, in Bergamo. Sixty years later, his grandson, Nicola, a young manager with a degree in economics, took over the management of the family business, following the tragic death of his father and his older brother. He understood that the destiny of gloves were by this point sealed and that, without a decisive change in direction, the company was destined to decline and fall. He studied leather, processes, market, and the new trends that were reinforcing Italian style around the world. In 1973, he added to the glove line a complete new line of accessories with a functional design and made of soft and refined leather materials. This led to the label with the greyhound logo, selected as a symbol of modernity, agility, and speed. Thanks to bags, luggage, and small leather items, the Trussardi name became a worldwide emblem. The next step was almost natural, with the presentation of the first Collection of prêt-à-porter. These were the years between

Trussardi model.

the late 1970s and the early 1980s. An expert in marketing, he immediately focused on the world of the media with spectacular operations that, in Milan, brought his runway presentations into exciting new spaces: Teatro alla Scala, the Piazza del Duomo, the Pinacoteca di Brera, the Stazione Centrale, the Borsa, the racetrack, or Ippodromo, and the Palatrussardi, an immense tensostructure built to house concerts and major events. He surrounded himself with intellectuals and artists, who gave their contributions to the *griffe*: from the painter Renato Guttuso from whose drawings he derived a sunflower print, to directors and costume designers invited to collaborate on the staging of the runway presentations. The entrepreneur and fashion designer, with the close collaboration of his wife Maria Luisa, offered a prêt-à-porter with contemporary and dynamic lines; he favored the use of leather reinvented by new technologies of processing and other modern and precious materials, such as neoprene and microfibres. But he did not stop at fashion: he was one of the first to grasp the unstoppable value of *griffes*: he put his name on bicycles, tiles, perfumes, automobiles, interiors of airliners, helicopters, home furnishings, underwear for the home. He became a sponsor of cultural events intended to develop Italian creativity around the world. He designed costumes for theater, dance, opera, cinema, and sports. He played himself in the movie *Prêt-à-porter* (*Ready to Wear*) by Robert Altman. In 1995, he opened in Milan, in the renovated building of an old hotel, the Marino alla Scala, his suo showroom with cafeteria, shop, and spaces for shows. On average, in the later years, the turnover stabilized at 750 billion liras per year. In 1998, he founded a school for future fashion professionals, photographers and communicators. He died at the age of 57, in a car crash, on an April night in 1999. The group continues to be run by the family.

❑ After the death of their father, it was the children Beatrice and Francesco who took over the management of the *griffe*. The "touch" of the two young people became immediately apparent. Theirs was a younger fashion. The runway presentation for Winter 2003 ranged from the vaguely British style, with minor references to India in the form of damasked fabrics, and sporty suits. British style: knit pullovers with leather inserts, velvet suits, regimental stripes printed on the suede blazers. On the occasion of that runway presentation, the maison announced a licensing agreement with Vestimenta, for formalwear and for men's sportswear, beginning in Spring-Summer 2004. A season that Francesco Trussardi would not live to see: in January 2003, he died at the age of 29 in a car crash, by a tragic fate, just as his father had died. Beatrice remained alone to run the corportation. Determined to carry on the work that her brother had begun, for Winter 2004, she presented one of the finest runway presentations in the history of the *griffe*. A way of being, more than just a fashion. The desire to please, rather than to astonish. A wardrobe intentionally for daytime wear, intentionally outside of any trends, and therefore easy to wear. Interchangeable items in bright and complementary colors. Add, remove, add again: the fun of creating a personal style. Leather remained a fundamental element for the house, from suede to pony skin, from water buffalo to nubuck. A separate story should be told about the fabrics (extraordinary silks, embroidered cottons for ponchos), the knitwear, in lamé as well for informal items and accessories, the pride of the label: bags, purses, shoulder bags with color patchwork. (*Lucia Mari*)

❑ 2002. Three new boutiques opened: in Saudi Arabia, China and Korea. The maison signed an agreement for licensing, manufacturing, and worldwide distribution for men's and women's shoes. The contract was signed with Le Mazza, company owned by the Premiata, specializing in the production of footwear, with offices in Civitanova Marche. The agreement ran for three years, from 1 January 2003.

❑ 2002. The year ended with turnover of 125 million Euros (a 3 percent increase) and gross operating profit of 9.95 million, about half of what came in in 2001 because of the reorganization of the Group and the IPO of Rotondi

Trussardi, leather evening gown, 1998.

Evolution. Some 55 percent of revenue came from Italy, 45 from the rest of the world.
❑ 2002, July. An IPO was launched on Rotondi, a company that has been quoted on the Italian Borsa since the 1930s, for a price of 12.7 million Euros.
❑ 2003. Commercial contract with the Japanese multinational Mitsui, which replaced the Tejin company. The agreement for the production and distribution of clothing and accessories in Japan was valid for five years and called for an increase in sales from 39 million Euros in 2002 to 46 million Euros in 2005. Among the objectives, modernizing the distribution network with a network of single-label stores and closing the two stores in Tokyo that had been run by Tejin.
❑ 2003, January. Francesco Trussardi died at the age of 29, in a car crash like his father.
❑ 2003, January. Signature of a five-year agreement with Vestimenta, a Trent-based manufacturer of the Hilton label, a partner with Giorgio Armani in a joint venture established in 2001. Vestimenta would produce and distribute the first line of Trussardi men's clothing. Special concentration on leather accessories, with which Trussardi first established its name, expanding to clothing only in the 1970s. The concentration upon the leather sector should lead as early as 2003 to a 50 percent increase in sales.
❑ 2003, March. Beatrice Trussardi, 32, took over the leadership of the company, with the title of president. "Our company, which has been in operation for a century, is family run and will continue to be family run." Matteo Felli, formerly general manager, became the new managing director.
❑ 2003, April. The company's strategy was to concentrate resources on the leather goods business, licensing the other lines of production to others. The production of women's apparel, considered to be the accessory of the accessory, was still linked with the company. (*Gisella Borioli*)

Truzzi Milanese shirtmakers. Founded in 1890 by Luigia Truzzi with a shop in the Via Broletto, it was purchased in 1924 by Tina and Ferruccio Ballini. In 1948, they opened a Truzzi shop in the Corso Matteotti. The sign remained beneath those porticoes until 1993, when the son Luigi moved the shop and workshop to the Via Santa Eufemia and, in 1997, changed the name to Luigi Ballini, while continuing the great tradition of quality and style. Members of the Italian royal house wore Truzzi shirts. Truzzi made for Hitler wool pajamas with a fabric made specially in Biella, which was carefully weighed by officials of the Gestapo, both before and after cutting and stitching, to ensure there was no wastage. Among the illustrious clients, Von Karajan, Horowitz, Benedetti Michelangeli, the Falcks, the Pirellis, Enrico Cuccia (who only bought white shirts; when he was away, his wife would order them), Cardinal Montini, Gaetano Afeltra, considered the most difficult client, the race car drivers Varzi and Chiron and, among the women, Giannalisa Feltrinelli. For each individual client, a paper and cardboard pattern would be prepared, upon which the shirts would be cut in the preferred fabrics, including voile, linen, and poplin, while special care was devoted not only to the stitching, but also to the pressing, done by modern pressing machines. (*Marilea Somaré*)

Tse Manfucturer of knitwear for men, women, children, and home use. It was one of the first to use cashmere not only in the traditional sweaters, but also in everyday clothing. The cashmere used by Tse was of excellent quality even if it required no special treatment and could be machine washed. In 1998 the Tse New York line, more contemporary, was launched: it included not only knitwear but also casual clothing. Five single-label boutiques in the United States, two in Hong Kong and eight in Japan. This is the identity card of Tse, founded in 1989 as a development of the label of the Cashmere House of Augustine Tse. The main office is in Santa Ana, in California. Since 1998, Hussein Chalayan has been the style consultant.

T-shirt Is there anyone on earth who doesn't have a T-shirt in their dresser, the classical and unmistakable cotton shirt with a round neck, short sleeves, and straight cut? It was the item of clothing worn by American soldiers and sailors beneath their uniforms during the First World War. Then it was adopted by manual laborers and farmhands. Beginning in the 1960s, the T-shirt increasingly became a billboard on which to place slogans, jokes, famous sayings, illustrations, famous paintings, humor, social or political commentary, company logos, and commercial names.

Tuffin Sally (1938). British fashion designer. She founded in 1962 with Marion Foale a boutique near Carnaby Street. Their outfits in particular featured a great variety of printed motifs and vivid use of colors. In 1972 the company shut down and Sally Tuffin devoted her efforts to the creation of children's outfits.

Tuleh New York prêt-à-porter label, founded by Bryan Bradley, a former fashion designer for Calvin Klein, and Josh Partner, fashion journalist. The first Collection was presented to the press in 1997 and received glowing reviews. Young movie stars of Hollywood, from Cameron Diaz to Jennifer Lopez, adored the vintage and retro style created by these two fashion designers, both originally from the Midwest. The real success arrived in June of 1999 with the awarding of the Perry Ellis prize, assigned each year by the Council of Fashion Designers of America to the best new fashion designers of womenswear lines. "Behind the creation of each Collection," say Bradley and Partner, "there is always a single, unique idea: forcing women to dress more carefully and to undress more slowly."
(*Manuela Parrino*)

Tulle Whether in gauze or silk, a very light, very fine fabric, with a loose weave and subtle mesh. A classic material for debutante balls or for wedding dresses or elegant evening gowns. It is very vaporous and is overlaid in multiple layers, whole, often in pleated flounces, or in petal shapes. Often used in trim and hair styles, especially the *point d'esprit* tulle.

Turban A long scarf made of cotton, silk or wool, to be wrapped around the head in a number of different shapes. Typical of Indians and Muslims, Taking inspiration from Diaghilev Ballets Russes, Poiret introduced it as an accessory for harem pants, and for exotic, eastern-style tunics. Very popular in the first twenty years of the twentieth century, it often returns to fashion, both for evening and daytime wear.

Turbeville Deborah (1937). American photographer. She came into contact with the world of fashion as a model in the 1950s and, once her career ended, she attended seminars taught by Richard Avedon and Marvin Israel and worked as a design assistant for Claire McCardell, as a contributor to *The Ladies Home Journal* in the early 1960s, and as a fashion editor for *Harper's Bazaar* (1962-65) and *Mademoiselle* (1965-71). She was discovered as a photographer by Diana Vreeland, art director of *Vogue*, and in the 1970s she began her professional career working for the Italian and French editions of *Vogue*, for *Marie Claire* and for *Nova*. Features of her photography were blurring and monochromy, creamy soft colors, but also atmospheres charged with mystery in which the protagonists were alluring, sensual women, sometimes shameless, who seem to ignore the gazes of observers. One image was a group of models in a public bathroom, printed to great scandal by *Vogue America* in May 1975. She had many exhibitions in the United States and in Europe as well as many books: *Maquillage* in 1975, *Wallflower* in 1978, *Unseen Versailles* in 1981, *Les amoureuses des temps passé* in 1985.

Turcato Giulio (1912-1995). Italian painter. He designed jewelry. Among the abstract painters of the postwar period, he joined, in 1947, the Gruppo Forma L and, later, he was a member of the Gruppo degli Otto. In 1965, he made the brooch entitled *Fantasioso* with Gherardi in Rome. It has abstract forms and arabesques in gold, with 13 diamonds and 4 emeralds. That same year, he made a number of bracelets entitled Schiava. Until the 1980s, Turcato created gold and silver abstract jewelry.

Turlington Christy (1969). Top model. Born in Oakland, California. Green eyes, brown hair. Half American and half Salvadoran, she represented the most refined and elegant look of the 1990s. She was 13 when she was discovered by the photographer Dennie Cody who saw her riding on horseback and sent photographs of her to a modeling agency. After a contract with a San Francisco agency, she signed with Ford but did not become a professional model until finishing high school, at the age of 18. In 1993 she was named the face of the year. Her image was linked on an exclusive basis to Maybelline cosmetics, Calvin Klein perfumes, and the Strenesse label. She did runway presentations for the biggest names in fashion. In 1999, she took a B.A. in Comparative Religion and Philosophy and, after leaving the runways, devoted herself full time to yoga, which she has been practicing for 15 years. She wrote a book entitled *Living Yoga* and oversaw the Nuala line, devoted to yoga, from Puma. She also has a line of Ayurvedic cosmetics called Sundari. In 2002 she married Ed Burns. In her career she was on the covers of a thousand international magazines, the last of them was *Vogue America*, October 2002.

(*Silvia Paoli*)

Turnbull Asser A brand of shirts created by Reginald Turnbull and Ernest Asser in 1885. The store of the same name is located at 71 Jermyn Street, in the heart of London's St. James. T & A was purveyor of shirts Winston Churchill and still is to Prince Charles who assigned it in 1980 a Royal Warrant, but its custom-made shirts with mother-of-pearl buttons have always been worn by stars of politics and entertainment, such as Ronald Reagan, Michael Caine, Al Pacino, and Donald Sutherland.

Turra Lavinia (1961). Fashion designer. She was a biologist and researcher who moved into the field of fashion in 1988 with a line of event outfits, for ceremonies, with tailored details and cuts. She called it *Nous sommes Hysteriques*. She debuted in the prêt-à-porter section of Milan Collezioni in February 2000. She has a youthful, essential style, with special attention to details.

(*Laura Salza*)

Turtle-neck Sweater Men and women's sweater, manufactured in various fabrics, characterized by a tight neck that rises halfway up the neck. Unlike high-necked sweaters, the neck is not doubled over.

Tussor A fabric made of tussah silk, a wild silk produced in China and India. It is a very shiny and irregular fiber, which comes from silkworms grown in a state of nature. Often has colored stripes.

Tutino Vercelloni Isa (1934). Journalist. She was the editor of *Casa Vogue* for 24 years, from the foundation of the monthly in 1968 until 1992. She joined the profession working at *Marie Claire* and at the weekly *Tempo* under Arturo Tofanelli, at the beginning of the 1960s. In the middle of that decade, she moved to Condé Nast. She worked for many years with *Vogue*, *l'Espresso*, and *il Corriere della Sera*. An expert in art and design, she always kept a close eye on fashion, with a critical sensibility, cultural depth, and a journalist's attention, considering fashion to be one of the sensitive indices of those that mark the development of taste and style. In the field of fashion, she published the books *Milano Fashion* (Edizioni Condé Nast, 1975) on the beginnings of the prêt-à-porter industry, *Missonologia* (Electa, 1994), *Krizia. Una Storia* (Skira, 1995) and, in collaboration with Carla Sozzani, *Krizia* (Leonardo Arte, 1995).

Tuxedo (or dinner jacket) A form of men's eveningwear, and the most elegant formal clothing in a man's wardrobe. Also worn on formal occasions, the tux exists today in a multitude of different cuts, colors and fabrics, which often border on bad taste. The most classic version is in light black cloth and comprises straight-legged pants with a satin strip down the side, a single-breasted jacket with one or two buttons and satin lapels, a white shirt with a shirt front and cufflinks, a bow tie, a cummerbund and black patent shoes. It was first worn in the casinos of Montecarlo in 1880 and immediately became the modern alternative to the white tie.

Tweed The name is thought to have derived from a mispronunciation of twill (or *tweel*, as filtered through the Scottish accent), which describes a fabric with a diagonal weave, whose irregular appearance derived from the weaving of two or three weft threads instead of just one. Since this method was used in the major textile centers that stood in the nineteenth century along the river Tweed,

Female version of a dinner suit, 1926 (from *Anni Venti – La nascita dell'abito moderno*, Centro Di, Florence, 1991, catalogue for the Galleria del Costume).

which separates Scotland from England, and which would help to explain the confusion. Tweed is world-famous for its robust construction, which ensures its great durability and long life. At first, grey and black threads were used, and the classic motif was herringbone. Today it is produced in many colors and patterns. Harris tweed is a special variety made famous by the Dowager Countess of Dunmore who encouraged it among the manufacturers of tweed on the islands of Harris, Lewis, Uist and Barr, in the Outer Hebrides. The label Harris Tweed guaranteed that the cloth was made from pure virgin wool, carded, woven, spun, and hand-dyed with plant dyes by the inhabitants of those islands. Nowadays it is no longer an artisanal fabric; instead it is produced in some 600 mills, in a quantity of nearly three million meters per year. Excellent in quality, with its distinctive light-dark pattern, especially in herring-bone, and in a vast array of colors, it differs from normal tweed because it is rougher. Harris Tweed became a registered trademark in 1909 and the logo, a globe, is taken from the Dunmore family crest. Donegal (or Irish tweed) is another type of tweed, originating from County Donegal in Ireland. Linton tweed, produced by the English Linton company, founded in 1919 by William Linton, was used in haute couture by such fashion designers as Chanel and Schiaparelli, as well as Dior, Balenciaga, Courrèges, Balmain and Saint-Laurent.

(*Gabriella Gregorietti*)

Twiggy (1949). English fashion model. Born Lesley Hornby to a lower-class British family, she became the symbol of a generation: the generation of the 1960s, young people who dressed like the Beatles, the Rolling Stones and the way that Mary Quant said to dress. She was working as a shampooist at a hairdresser's shop in London, at the age of 16, when she found in the photographer Justin De Villeneuve her Pygmalion, who created her as a celebrity when she was just 18, a character who was the talk of the press and who imposed her own style as well as her own make-up: emphasized freckles and black eyebrow pencil to highlight her brows. Her friends, because of her skinny, supple physique, nicknamed her Twiggy, and that was the name under which she was named by the Daily Express as the "face of '66." A forerunner of the anorexic look, she was photographed by such great photographers as Avedon and Penn. Paul McCartney wrote *Back in the USSR*, a song that was meant to be used in the soundtrack of *Twiggy in Russia*, a film that was never even put into production. Ken Russell cast her in the movie *The Boyfriend*. In 1974-75, she played in a television series as the main character and, that same year, she recorded a single, *Here I Go Again*, and an LP, *Twiggy*. In 1997, at the age of 48, when she had already been married for years to the theatrical actor Leigh Lawson, she published *Twiggy in Black and White*, her biography.

(*Laura Salza*)

Twill A silk fabric with light diagonal ridges, used for making ties, foulards, and summer blouses. The same fabric, but in cotton, is used for very fine, light shirts.

TwinCinc Label of men's ready-to-wear fashion owned by the French company Cinc, founded on 1 January 2000 by Christophe

Cottin (1971) and Christophe Contentin (1970), both graduates of the ESMOD school and, respectively a fashion designer and a pattern cutter. This partnership grew out of their desire to create a top-quality line of menswear, which would combine in an optimal manner forms and fabrics, an alternative to the classical suit. Its price policy has always been moderate and, after seven menswear Collections, from Winter 2003-2004, the trademark has also been enriched with a womenswear line. It is distributed in France, Italy, Switzerland, Spain and Japan. (*Maddalena Fossati*)

Twin Set An English term used to indicate, since the 1930s, two knitwear items, coordinated in both color and yarn. The first was usually a sleeveless sweater shirt, the second a little over sweater, with buttons and buttonholes. The twin set marked a development toward the elegance of knitwear; it also appeared in the role of complementary item, in thin combed wools, worked in satin knit, and later in cashmere, always in natural shades. It returned to fashion in the 1960s, now in colors, usually pastels, with ornamental knits and jacquard patterns, especially in the outer sweater. Especially renowned were the pure cashmere twin sets of Marella Agnelli.

Twist In Italian, the word is "ritorto." It is a worsted fabric made from highly twisted wools, with an elastic and springy finish, which does not wrinkle.

2Link The name of a chain of trend-setting boutiques. Behind it is the aesthetic and commercial supervision of Alberto Bellotti. In 1998, the first retail outlet was founded in Cantù (near Como), with a line of products that was a mix of home furnishings and design (80 percent) and fashion. Two years later, the company set up its first franchised store in Siena and the store in Milan in the Largo La Foppa, marking a decided shift in the product mix toward the fashion sector. In 2001, 2Link opened a store in Como in the Via Olginati and Bellotti's product mix moved almost entirely away from design and toward finding new designers and fashion trends in the segment of medium-high to upscale fashion. In 2003, he opened another Milanese store in Via Solferino 45. In brief, a strong period of growth in the context of a "strong consumer abandonment of certain types of products, especially in the fashion sector," as Bellotti recalled. "Ready-to-wear fashion was created to bring fashion to an increasingly broad market share, and it had rapidly risen to price points that were 'not suitable' for that purpose. It completely abandoned the real needs of the end consumer. Manufacturers and marketers have never really become 'acquainted' and have never learned to created the powerful synergies that are necessary in a period of 'lean times.'" In the rapid consumer abandonment of fashion as fashion, a major role was also played by the social phenomenon of 'vintage' clothing, of 'unhemmed' items, of the 'false poverty' look which makes it unacceptable to show up at a party or a dinner 'dressed in brand-new outfits.' Only a few really 'strong' labels, with appropriate marketing and sales network, will survive, and there will be more room for small labels with a correct price-to-quality ratio." The 2Link stores were designed by the architect Pillet.

Tyen (1953). Vietnamese photographer and specialist in cosmetics. Born in Hanoi. He moved to Paris while still very young, where he attended the Ecole des Beaux Arts, attending courses in interior decoration. But before he could finish his studies, he was summoned by Max Factor to work on the creation of the colors of stage make-up for the Paris Opéra. It was there that Tyen learned the importance of lighting and of the use of make-up. Working in the theater, he also met many photographers, who introduced him into the world of fashion publishing. He worked with *Vogue France* and *Vogue America*. Since 1980, he has been the creative director of cosmetic products of Maison Dior. Since 1985 he has been devoting himself chiefly to photography, doing campaigns for Versace, Lacroix, Montana, Valentino, Ferré.

Tyler Richard (1948). Australian-born fashion designer who now lives in Los Angeles. Born in Sunshine near Melbourne, at the age of 16 he left school and began to work for a dressmaker. At 18, with the help of his mother, a dressmaker, he opened his first shop in Melbourne. The shop was successful. In 1978 he moved to Los Angeles. There

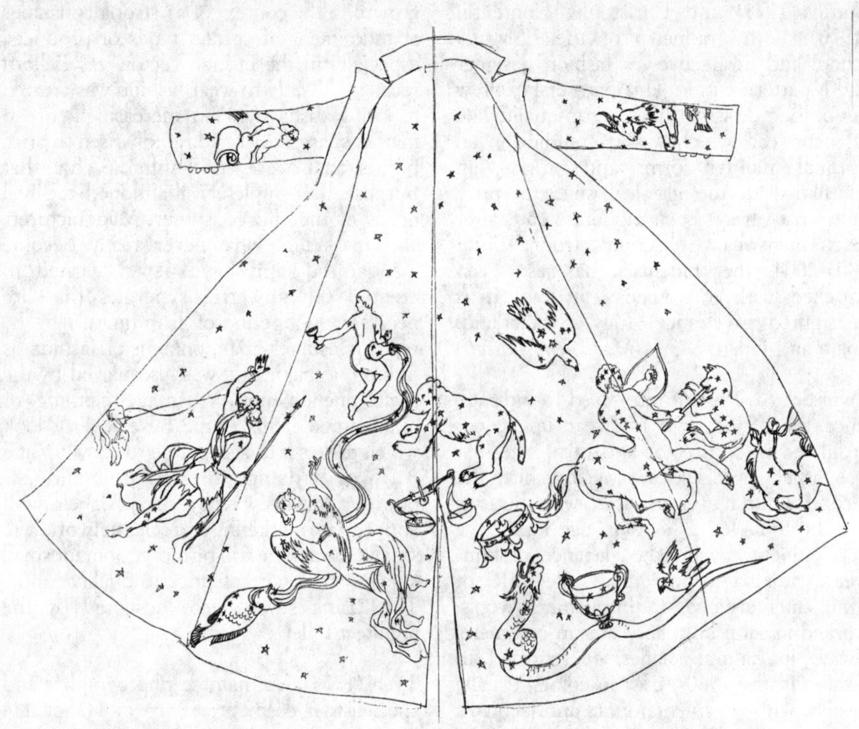

Richard Tyler, sketch designed for his involvement in the exhibition *Visitors*, installation by Gae Aulenti (Biennial of Florence, Skira, 1996).

the career ran into difficulties. In 1987, when he was broke and about to return to Australia, he met the actress and businesswoman Lisa Trafficante, who became his second wife. Together, they opened a showroom. Skilled in the selection of fabrics and in details, all handmade, he became famous thanks to clients such as Julia Roberts, Janet Jackson, Sigourney Weaver and Oprah Winfrey. In New York, he debuted in 1993. For a number of years, he designed the Anne Klein Collection.

U

Uco Leading Belgian textile group that produces, amongst other things, fabrics for clothing. The labels Pierre Balmain, Prélude, and Robert le Héros are some of the many that have found a profitable partnership with the group.

UFAC (Union Française des Arts du Costume). Association founded in 1948 by François Boucher, a curator from the Carnavelet Museum, and textile and clothing manufacturers. UFAC's collections belong to the Musée des Arts de la Mode and the Musée des Arts Décoratifs, both in the Louvre. Through donations, Boucher and then Yvonne Delandres put together this important collection of clothes, accessories, and costume jewelry from the 1700s to the present day. UFAC's aim is to add to this collection with new acquisitions, including documents such as drawings, advertising materials, catalogues, and photographs. They periodically organize exhibitions in museums all over the world.

Journal des Demoiselles, 1901, print (Collection of the Union Française des Arts du Costume).

Uféras Gérard (1962). French photographer born in Paris (where he lives and works). He has worked closely with the newspaper *Libération* as a photo-journalist since 1984, as well as *Time*, *L'Express*, *The Independent Magazine*, *The New York Times* and *Le Monde*. Alongside this he has also developed fashion and advertising work that has been published in *Beaux-Arts*, *Jardin des Modes*, *Das Magazin*, the Italian and French *Marie Claire*, the women's supplement of *La Repubblica*, *Madame Figaro*, *Io Donna*, and *The Fashion*. He has received numerous awards and held several exhibitions of his work.

UISTA Unione Italiana Stampa Tessile e dell'Abbigliamento (Italian Textile and Clothing Press Association). From its base at the Circolo della Stampa (Press Club) in Milan, in the 1960s the association organized meetings, debates, awards, and visits to the major textile and clothing factories. The journalist Giuseppe Rasi was president, and Mila Contini, Elsa Robiola, and Mariapia Chiodini Beltrami were on its board. Its permanent members included Barbara Vitti, Silvana Bernasconi, Elisa Massai, Lucia Mari, Vera Rossi Lodomez, Rina Simonetta, Graziella Vigo, and Maria Vittoria Alfonsi. Its honorable members included Giovan Battista Giorgini, Ferruccio Lanfranchi, Franco Rivetti, Gian Sandro Bassetti, Aldo Zegna, Ferruccio Ducrey Giordano, Paolo Faina, Emanuele Nasi, and Tommaso Notarangeli. The association broke up after a few years following the premature death of its founder and soul, Giuseppe Rasi.

Ulster Museum In Belfast, Northern Ireland. Its first collection was destroyed by a fire bomb in 1976, which was a year of intense conflict between Protestants and Catholics. After that, the museum worked hard to rebuild a collection of historic *haute couture* and general fashion. Each season the museum acquires a piece by an international designer, an Irish designer, and a department store so as to best represent fashion trends at every level. The museum has more than 4,000 pieces of clothing, accessories, and fabrics, dating from the end of the 17th century to the present day.

(*Virginia Hill*)

Ultramarin Shop founded in 1996 in Kollwitplatz Berlin, an area of bars, restaurants and trendy boutiques. It showcases young Berliner designers. Specialized in women's clothing, it also offers street-styles for men. However, the boutique's real speciality is wedding dresses that it cuts and sews to order, offering a small sample collection of "necessary madness."

Umberto Severi Label and name of the founder of the Tesam Group, protagonist of the prestigious and perhaps most unique entrepreneurial story of the Carpi knitwear district. In the 1970s the group went from being the biggest exporter of clothing to the biggest importer thanks to the first Italian joint ventures with nascent groups from the Far and Middle East and Mauritius. A total of 12 companies – representing spinning mills, dye-works, knitwear factories and support industries – with over 2,000 employees, a design research team, a studio-lab monitoring fashion trends, and constant technological innovations in their production processes, all built up over thirty years or so, has become the jewel in the crown of the multitalented businessmen of Carpi. This is particularly due to the personality of Umberto Severi, an astute businessman but also a passionate art collector: he has works ranging from the 15th to 20th centuries, statues by Pomodoro, and Lalique crystalware, collected under the banner of the Severi Foundation. When the Tesam Group's spinning mills, knitwear factories, and dyeworks closed down at the beginning of the 1990s, many works of art and Umberto Severi's residence, the Palazzo Foresti, had already been donated to the municipality of Carpi.

Umbrella The umbrella's original purpose was to protect us from the sun (parasol); in French there is still a semantic difference between *ombrelle* (provider of shade) and *parapluie* (shield against the rain). Invented by the Egyptians to protect pharaohs and high priests during religious ceremonies, the umbrella first appeared in its modern form at the end of the 1500s with Caterina de' Medici. At the beginning of the 1800s the parasol, which until then had been an accessory used only by the aristocracy, became a universal, practical, and essential object in many shapes and forms, including such extravagant designs as the umbrella-fan or the umbrella-hat, which left the hands free. In the 1920s it was always co-ordinated with a dress or suit, handkerchief, or bag. Usually made from 8 segments, there was a Japanese style that had 12 to18 segments made from waxed paper or floral cretonne which then disappeared from the fashion scene, except for the odd appearance in runway shows of designers like Jean Paul Gaultier. It is still used for special occasions or in certain Asian countries where it is part of the local costume. The umbrella, on the other hand, was only used to shield the rich against rain by servants between coaches and door entrances. In 1700 an English aristocrat called Jones Hanway was mocked for using an umbrella himself. In the 1800s the umbrella became much lighter (350 grams, as opposed to the 1.5 kilograms of the older styles) thanks to metal fixtures invented by Fox and Deschamps. There was greater use of handles made from precious materials such as silver, ivory, and tortoiseshell that were often carved or engraved. In the 1960s umbrellas made of colored and transparent plastic and synthetic materials began appearing, including famous designs by Courrèges and Emmanuelle Khanh. The golfing umbrella has multicolored segments, and Jean Paul Gaultier produced a style with a luminous handle. The folding umbrella, designed to fit in bags and sometimes even pockets, was invented in 1928 by a German engineer, and at only 22 centimetres it was marketed with the brand-name Knirps (meaning pygmy). The most historic umbrella shops are Swayne Brigg which has been in business since 1750 in Piccadilly,

London, and Madeleine Gèly in Paris, which has an important collection of vintage umbrellas. (*Gabriella Gregorietti*)

Underpants In the 1970s and 1980s, not that long ago, the man who wore traditional underpants was, in the eyes of young women, an unfashionable grand-daddy figure. Underpants eliminated the possibility of romantic encounters and snuffed out any possible passion with ironic looks and embarrassed giggles. At this time, briefs were the more popular – indeed essential – choice, available in every imaginable color and pattern. Then arrived the boxer short, the modern-day cross between underpants and shorts. They came striped, checked, tartan, in a range of colors, and coordinating, or deliberately clashing, with shirts and socks. Even though football star David Beckham's g-string got us talking in 2003, boxer shorts have endured. They have had enormous success in replacing briefs, and have even been worn on top of tights by women, or shown off peeping above pants, the waists of which have, for both men and women, descended ever-further below the navel. For women, knickers have been replaced, first by slips and then thongs. Recently styles have been reminiscent of the 1930s, in black satin and transparent lace, also provocative in red satin, romantic pastel colors, or for Winter even in wool (if not pure cashmere) embroidered with flowers, fruit, and sparkling moons and suns. They have been revealed above jeans, shown off or glimpsed through transparent muslin or even slits in skirts, alternatively they have been worn as hot pants with high boots. They have acquired a new, almost brazen value, being no longer only a means of secret seduction, but an item of clothing to be seen, or partially seen. They have had a recent opportunity for revival thanks to some more "avant-garde" designers, influenced by the British, who have turned underwear into "outerwear," although this trend has its roots, as always in the world of fashion, in historical dress. (*Maria Vittoria Alfonsi*)

Underskirt A skirt realised in stiff and reinforced material, usually in tulle, to wear under a skirt in order to give it form and volume. It was fashionable in the 1950s and 1960s as a modern development of the crinoline.

Underwood Patricia (1947). American milliner. Trained at the New York Fashion Institute of Technology in 1972. She received an award from the Council of Fashion Designers of America in 1984. She started off creating hats for Lipp Homfeld from 1973 to 1975 (Hats by Lipp) but decided to open her own atelier in New York in 1976. Admired by the big American designers, she has worked for Ellis, Caroline Roehm, Donna Karan, De La Renta, Klein, and Bass. She achieved a reputation for her Twenties-style cloche hats and a very fine straw cowboy hat shown in 1991. She favors neutral colors and in 1994 presented a collection inspired by Modigliani. Her hats are sold at over 100 different outlets in the USA. (*Sandra Cecchi*)

❑ The designer's 25-year career has been studded with various trade awards, some of the most important being a Coty Award, an award from the CFDA for the American Accessories Achievement category, and a nomination from Fashion Group International as entrepreneur of the year.
❑ Her hats, made and finished by hand, are created with carefully selected materials and special techniques: for example, she uses horsehair, a plaited yarn once made from real horse hair but which is now produced synthetically in Switzerland, or Milan straw, a plait of natural straw originally supplied directly by Milan manufacturers and that now comes from the Far East.
❑ The 2003 collections confirmed Patricia Underwood's style, with Winter pieces in Italian calf leather and Summer pieces in ultra-light transparent fibers.

Ungaro Emanuel (1933). French designer born in Aix-en-Provence, the son of a tailor from Puglia who fled from the Fascist regime. He learned the trade from his father Cosimo "an exceptional man, who taught me intellectual rigor and honesty." In 1955 he left the south of France for Paris in pursuit of his ambition to become a fashion designer. He worked at a dressmaker's shop,

Emanuel Ungaro, creations from the 1977 collection in a sketch by Maria Pezzi.

then was fortunate enough to spend six years with Balenciaga, "my teacher." Despite already having some experience he agreed to start out at the house as a beginner, in other words, somebody who sews linings and passes pins. At Balenciaga's school he learnt that "a good couturier must be an architect in the design, a sculptor in the form, a painter in the color, and a musician in the harmony and philosophy." Strengthened by this experience, he decided to set out on his own and with the help of Sonja Knapp, a textile designer and at that time his partner, he rented his first atelier in Avenue MacMahon. They raised the three months advance on the rent by selling Sonja's Porsche. It was 1965 and Ungaro had already decided on his aesthetic philosophy: a baroque and sensual melange that appealed to great actresses like Catherine Deneuve and Anouk Aimée. In 1967 he moved into his base in Avenue Montaigne and found famous customers in Jackie Kennedy, Lee Radzwill, the Duchess of Windsor, Lauren Bacall, and Ira Fürstenberg. The appeal of his clothes was found in the use of color and mix of printed fabrics. He is the most painterly of the great designers, using the brightest range of colors. In 1971 he signed an important contract with GFT, the Italian clothing giant from Turin. Strict with himself and with others, and with a determined personality, he creates his clothes while listening to classical music and opera, preferring Rossini. Before each runway show he follows an almost superstitious rite. He asks the women of the family to prepare him a plate of meatballs in sauce, a typical dish from Puglia that reminds him of his childhood. He is married to the Italian Laura Bernabei. In 1996 Maison Ungaro joined the Ferragamo group. *(Laura Asnaghi)*

❑ In 1999 the house won the top Spanish award *La Aguja de Oro*. In 2000 they launched a line of eyewear for men and women with Luxottica; a new line of swimwear called Ungaro Sun, a range of accessories called *I love Ungaro* and the new perfume *Desnuda*. In 2002 Ungaro received the T de Telva award. In 2003 he created Diane Kury's costumes for the film *Je Reste*. His labels are currently Emanuel Ungaro Couture, Emanuel Ungaro Paris (ready-to-wear), Ungaro Fuchsia, and Ungaro Feve. The designers says of his recent work: "I love everything that sings. I love Débussy and Free Jazz, Paolo Uccello and Motherwell, Proust and Peter Handke, colors, Impressionism; I love the warmth of the South and the cold of the North. The couturier is born to be always one step ahead, to guess at desires. I should never speak out. My clothes speak for themselves." *(Maria Vittoria Alfonsi)*

❑ Summer 2001. Ungaro denied the rumours of him being close to retirement and signed for another four years with Salvatore Ferragamo, the group that owns his fashion house.
❑ Ungaro participated in High Fashion Week Moscow, which hosted various high-calibre international designers.
❑ 2002 was the year that he opened showrooms in the East: Moscow, Beijing, Shenzen Taipai, and Singapore now all have their own Ungaro boutiques.
❑ The Pugliese company Mafra acquired the license to produce and distribute Ungaro's babywear ranges from Spring-Summer 2003. The company's baby collection is dedicated to 0-2 year olds and 60% of the production is for girls.
❑ 2003, February. Agreement with the Tuscan company Le Bonitas for the launch of two new collections: Ungaro Sun (women's swimwear and beachwear) and Ungaro Moon (underwear, corsetry, and sportswear).
❑ 2004, September. Emanuel Ungaro signed an agreement with the English group Marchpole to develop his menswear, and they appointed José Levi as artistic director of the men's collection.
❑ 2004, October. After seven years, Giambattista Valli quit as the house's artistic director to dedicate himself to his own range, produced by Gilmar.
❑ 2004, November. The new creative director is Vincent Darré. He arrived from Moschino where he was in charge of the creation and development of the top line.
❑ 2005, January. Emanuel Ungaro

returned to *haute couture* with a collection of about thirty outfits designed by Darré, which were supervised by Ungaro himself.
❑ 2005, March. Darré's first ready-to-wear collection made its debut on the runway. It stood out for the lack of floral patterns that have characterized the Ungaro style over the years, which were replaced by new more geometric designs.

Uniform Ready-to-wear label, the brainchild of Roger Lee and Lesley Sealey, both born in 1972. Roger graduated in fashion design from Kingston University and went on to specialize in women's clothing through a Master's degree at the Royal College of Art in London. Lesley took a degree in textile design at Nottingham University and a diploma in multimedia textiles at the Royal College of Art. Previously, Roger had worked with Karl Lagerfeld and Lesley in India. They created their label Uniform with a women's collection for Fall-Winter 1998-99, and for two seasons they received the British Fashion Council's New Generation sponsorship. Their collections stand out for their use of traditional materials treated in an unusual way. (*Mariacristina Righi*)

Union pour le Vêtement Creative alliance and enterprise for egalitarian fashion in terms of wearability and quality. The result of the meeting of designer Didier Vervaeren, screen print artist Hervé Yureogeau, and graphic designer Thierry Rondenet at the Hyères Festival for young talent in 1994, where they all found success. All three come from Brussels and have studied the work of Soviet Constructivists in fashion.

Unisex A clothes style suitable both for women and men, based above all on the standard styles of pants (particularly jeans) that became a real fashion in the 1960s and 1970s – a kind of play on role reversals using shirts, waistcoats, blazers, and oversize sweaters. It opened up the possibility (and created the desire) for men to wear floral or patterned fabrics and strong colors that until then were only used by women.

United Bamboo Ready-to-wear label created by the Vietnamese Thuy Quang Pham (1968) with his partner Miho. who deals with research into textiles and production processes. Thuy studied at Cooper Union in New York where he graduated in architecture. Straight after his degree he joined the artists' group Bernardette Corporation. The United Bamboo range was launched in Fall-Winter 1999-2000.

Unitika The third biggest Japanese industrial textile group after Kanebo and Toyobo. It has over 5,000 employees, and covers all sectors of the textile industry. In a joint venture with the French group DMC in 1991, it built a large polyester factory called Inoseta in the Isère region. The aim is to become the leader in the medium and high-quality microfiber sector.

Unwerth (von) Ellen (1954). German photographer. Born in Frankfurt, she left home at an early age to go and live with a group of friends. She completed high school and worked first in Munich at the Roncalli Circus, and then as a model in Paris from 1975. Ten years later she moved over to the other side of the camera and started working mainly for various national editions of *Vogue*, as well as *Interview*, *George*, and *Vanity Fair*. She is greatly admired for her expressionist inspired images which are both captivating and aggressive. She has conceived numerous advertising campaigns for Chanel, Adidas, and Diesel and has worked with the designers Valentino, Dolce & Gabbana, Moschino, and Gucci. Recently she has turned her hand to cinema, with several shorts and a feature called *Inferno*. There have been many exhibitions of her work and four books: *Snaps*, *Couples*, *Wicked*, and the most recent, *Revenge*, which was published in 2003 with a print run of 5000 copies, 200 of which were signed by the author. She divides her time between New York and Paris.

U(p)m Museum of Decorative Arts in Prague, Czech Republic. It has been collecting textiles and clothing since it was opened in 1885. It has 20,000 pieces, including Coptic fragments, embroideries, tapestries, silks, and textiles from every period, including some contemporary Czech pieces. The clothes date from 1750 to the present day, and are mostly locally made.

Urbinati Laura (1961). Italian designer. She defines her collections as "a cultural mix of old Europe and intellectual California." In 1986 she moved from Rome to Los Angeles where she designed her first collection of swimwear, and five years later opened a showroom on Sunset Boulevard. In 1996 she opened a shop for clothing and accessories in Milan.

❑ The brand's Milanese boutique in Piazza Sant'Eustorgio, sold 5,000 of its turquoise polka-dot hot pants. They became one of the cult items of the Summer, along with Antik Batik's voile beach shirts, and Gucci's plastic handbags.
❑ The Spring-Summer 2003 collection, inspired by bikinis from the 1970s, was shown together with another 125 labels from around the world at Lingerie Americas, the sector's first international show, which was held from 4-6 August 2002 at the Metropolitan Pavilion & Altman Building in New York.

Urbini Alfonso (1910). Italian men's tailor. From the region of Abruzzo, he started in the trade at the age of 12, working in the Bacchetta brothers' workshop in Roseto. In 1924 he joined the Pescara tailor Pasquale Tritapepe as an apprentice, and went on to become his favorite pupil. In 1934 he followed a course in pattern cutting in Rome directed by Giovanni d'Adamo. A year later, he opened his own atelier in Pescara. In 1954 the magazine *Arbiter* named him as the best tailor. He retired in 1980.

Utopia A brand belonging to Gemmindustria, a company founded in Milan in 1943 that operates in the production and distribution of precious stones and pearls in the jewelry business. The brand found immediate success in the market at the beginning of 1996 thanks to a well-planned marketing operation and an effective international advertising campaign. The jewelry stands out for the very high quality of its South Sea pearls, which are presented in many different compositions, often playing on the contrast between colors: white, gold, silver blue, etc. Among the various types of pearls used, Keshi pearls hold a special position: they are seedless pearls that form spontaneously inside the *Pinctada maxima* pearl oyster and are characterized by unique semi-baroque drop or button shapes. The Batik collection is typical of the technical skill and precious materials of the brand, with natural stones, diamonds and South Sea pearls combined in intricate settings. Utopia's products are available in Europe and the USA in jewelry shops equipped with instruments capable of certifying the quality of the pearls. (*Alessandra Quattordio*)

Necklace with pearls by Utopia.

V

Valditevere A fabric manufacturer and later, a company running fashion boutiques, founded in 1952 by three women from Italian high society and aristocracy, Donina Gnecchi, Vittorina Pacini and Piretta Rocco di Torre Padula. The idea at first was to preserve a tradition of the upper Tiber valley, San Sepolcro, Città di Castello: hand weaving. "Donina and I were good designers. Vittorina and I knew lots of peasant women who had stopped doing hand weaving and we persuaded them to return to their looms. That's how we got started," recalled Piretta Rocco. The fabrics (cotton, wool and, later, linen) inspired the desire to create fashion: highly colored after-ski skirts, ponchos, outfits with a great and youthful imagination. Valditevere was a pioneer of the runway presentations in Florence, where it was based and still is, with a boutique in the Via dei Rondinelli. It is run by Donatella Martelli, the daughter of Piretta Rocco, who has established alongside the old company Valditevere Donna (all of the partners are women), focused on exports.

Invitation postcard from the Valditevere boutique (from *La Sala Bianca – La nascita della moda italiana*, Pitti Immagine-Electa, 1992).

Valente Sergio (1941). Roman hairdresser. He has also been called the coiffeur of fashion designers because he has worked since the 1970s for the runway presentations of great names. In 1971, he opened his salon in the Via Condotti. Two books have been written about him: *Ricci and Capricci* (1985) in which Pia Soli described him as one of the most creative minds in the sector, the second one, *Idee per la testa* (1995), containing ten years of hairstyles. He was invited by the Chinese government to teach haute coiffure lessons on television.

Valentina Professional name of Valentina Nicholaevna Sanina (1904). Russian costume designer and fashion designer, she worked in the United States. She designed clothes, to be worn on the set and in private life, for the most elegant female stars: Greta Garbo, Gloria Swanson, and Katharine Hepburn. She was born in Kiev, went to Paris as a refugee, and then moved to America and founded there, in 1928, her own fashion house. Her outfits were rigorous and sober, and were designed with a view to the body that would be wearing them. In 1957 she closed her atelier and retired. Maria Pezzi wrote: "In New York, in 1961, I was invited to a cocktail party by the Russian architect Barmasch, in his incredible house, with an entirely plastic hanging garden illuminated by an artificial sun. Among the varied invitees I noticed an elderly women who vaguely resembled Greta Garbo. She was dressed absolutely out of fashion but she was very elegant. They said to me: "Don't you know Valentina? Until three years ago, she was the most original dressmaker working for the stars of Hollywood and she is an overwhelming personality." I asked to be introduced; she looked sternly at my beautiful flowered blouse and said, without moving her lips: "You should never wear a print fabric near your face, because it alters the personality of your features. Prints are only good to wear from the waist down." They told me that in the golden years, when Hollywood was a magnificent big super-luxurious corporation, full of incredible flashy vulgarity, she created the same sort of revolution that Isadora Duncan caused in the world of dance. She trimmed away all the unnecessary superstructure and returned to a classical simplicity, in which all the counted was the cut and the drop and the feel and the quality of the fabric. In fact, her guidìng rule was: elegance is not the simplicity of luxury, but the luxury of simplicity."

Valentine About French fashion house that specialized in hats. It was founded by the daughter of Edmond About, a writer and member of the French Academy, who founded it, naming it after herself and managing it herself. The year was 1909. The Belle Epoque was drawing to an end. Valentine was a little more sparing in feathers and tufts than the exaggerated fashions of those years.

Valentinitsch Ines (1972). Austrian fashion designer. She was born in Graz. She studied with Helmut Lang in Vienna and at the Domus Academy in Milan. She has carried out major collaborations in Italy and elsewhere. She has worked with many apparel manufacturers and producers of knitwear, haute couture and accessories, not to mention her experiences with consortiums such as lace producers such as Austrian Embroideries, or Swiss Textil. For them since 1993 Ines has designed entire lines or individual items, while continuing the collection that bears her name, which debuted at the end of February 1999, during Milan Collezioni, and which since then has been presented in various occasions on the runways of Europe. (*Mariacristina Righi*)

❑ 1999. She designed the FusCo per Angelo Fusco collection.
❑ 2001, March. She sent down the runways models with beer cans and (fake) joints in their hands. There are countless parallels with Vivienne Westwood.
❑ 2001, October. The urban jungle, a savage and yet metropolitcan panorama, was the setting for Valentinitsch's Spring-Summer 2002 collection, with women wrapped in braided lianas enveloping their bodies. Fabrics and accessories were evocative of the world of apes. At the door, journalists were given little voodoo dolls, completed with pins.
❑ 2002, September. On the occasion of her first appearance at "White," the section of Momi-Modamilano dedicated to the most innovative names in prêt-à-porter, the Austrian designer presented outfits with concave 1980s shoulders, white balaclavas, and modernist ski overalls.
❑ 2002, April. Thanks to the agreement with the Japanese group Itochu, the Austrian designer launches Ini, the youth line intended at first only for the Japanese market.

Valentino He was born Valentino Garavani (1933). Italian fashion designer. Ever since he was small, he clearly showed that he had a idea of style and elegance. It was an aspect that would clearly emerge in the first outfit that he created for his aunt Rosa, the owner of a passementerie shop in Voghera, in the Via Turin, where he loved to spend his afternoons playing with bolts of cloth. Even then he especially loved red: a color that, in later years, would become his good-luck charm and the strong suit of his palette. He understood this when, during his apprenticeship with Jean Dessès in Paris, he went to the Opera in Barcelona and was overwhelmed by the entirely red stage costumes: "It was at that moment that I understood that, after white and black, there is no color more beautiful." Valentino Clemente Ludovico Garavani was seventeent when he left Voghera to learn the fashion business in Paris. His speed at sketching models immediately won him a job with Dessès, where he worked until 1955, and then moved to a position with Guy Laroche. His transalpine apprenticeship lasted until 1957. That was the year in which he returned to Italy, where he opened, with his father's help, an atelier in Rome in the Via Condotti. From a young apprentice designing the shadows for major atelier, he was now the owner of his own business. His debut took place in Rome, and was understated. It was, in fact, a fiasco, and he failed to sell even a single item. In those years, he became acquainted with Giancarlo

Giammetti, a student of architecture who would become his manager and his administrator, as well as his communications director. In 1962 in Florence, Valentino was the last to present his collection in Palazzo Pitti. The hall overwhelmed his with a deafening roar of applause. "My mother said to me: 'You hear them? They want you, because you've done it, you've won.' Less than an hour later, I had sold my entire collection and I was swamped with orders." Since then, his successes have followed one upon the heels of the other, punctually, season after season. "The Americans love this Italian who has become the king of fashion in just a short while," wrote Woman's Wear Daily in 1968, after a dazzling runway presentation all in white, studded with capes and lightly draped outfits. "Creativity," said Valentino, "is difficult to explain, it is like an internal force, an enthusiasm that never wanes and which gives me the strength to continue working in new ways. As I look at things and people in the street, my imagination continues to march and my ideas take shape through my pencil." His volcanic flow of new ideas – for women and refined elegance – left its indelible mark in the jet set. Farah Diba fled from her crumbling empire wearing a Valentino suit. Liz Taylor met Richard Burton while wearing Valentino. Jackie Kennedy married Onassis in a Valentino outfit of ivory lace that, for years, women copied around the world. The list of celebrities that have worn Valentino is endless: da Sophia Loren and Nancy Reagan to Brooke Shields and Sharon Stone. There are few who have been able to resist the allure of his outfits, a synthesis of luxury and grace modulated with modernity. He reinvented bows, transforming them into a symbol of femininity: one of his first outfits embellished with this detail won a legendary burst of applause that lasted for ten full minutes. He is an absolute master of his profession, of technique, and he has transformed this artisanal ability into a compass by which he charts the ongoing continuity of his line, even when in 1978, through a manufacturing agreement with the Gruppo Finanziario Tessile, he launched his first line (over time, the number of lines has grown to eight, including menswear and womenswear) of ready-to-wear fashion. Since

Valentino, evening gown, 1979.

1968, he has presented his collections of prêt-à-porter on the runways of Paris, as he has also done since 1989 with his haute couture creations. His success has never known declines, it seems immune to flops and comebacks. But Valentino is especially proud of having created the Life Foundation to raise funds to help children afflicted with AIDS. A reality that came into existence in 1990, the same year in which the fashion designer celebrated in Rome and Milan his thirtieth year in business, with an exhibition at the Accademia Valentino, a space designed and equipped for exhibitions and cultural events. In January 1998, the "Rolls Royce of fashion designers," as the Americans call him, sold his *griffe* for 500 billion liras (the annual turnover of the *maison* was 1.2 trillion liras) amidst much weeping, and maintaining a place for himself as the creative director, to HDP, the holding company run by Maurizio Romiti. He said: "I have seen too many of my colleagues being ushered out of their ateliers through the tradesman's entrance, in order to make way for new creatives who have then undermined the originale style of the *maison*..." Valentino is a private man, but he also knows how to engage in polemics with stylish irony. When the American journalist, Suzy Menkes, the terror of fashion designers, decreed in 1990 that the end of the phenomenon of top models had arrived, and criticized those who continued to use them, Valentino replied by purchasing a full-page advertisement in the *International Herald Tribune*: "Suzy, you've got it all wrong. Love from Valentino and the top models" was the slogan beneath a photograph of Claudia Schiffer, Nadya Auermann, and Elle McPherson. He lives and works in Rome, Capri, London, New York and Paris. He purchased an eighteenth-century castle just an hour away from the French capital, which he considers as his refuge. He refuses to allow it to be photographed. The only pictures that have been taken show Valentino as he strolls in the immense park with his pet pugs. There is a vast forest, which he minimizes, describing it as: "Big enough to go horseback riding in it."

❑ In 2001, Valentino – much loved by the stars of Hollywood – chose to celebrate his fortieth years in business in Los Angeles. The party, a benefit (it was a fundraiser for Child Priority) was organized with Steven Spielberg and Kate Capshaw, Tom Hanks and Rita Wilson. During the evening, there was a book presentation of *Il libro rosso di Valentino* which – edited by Franca Sozzani – contains pictures of 40 women (including Ashley Judd, Ines Sastre, Isabella Rossellini, Kate Moss, Mila Jovovich) dressed in "Valentino red" and depicted by the most important photographers of the time. That same year, in March, Julia Roberts received her Oscar wearing "vintage" Valentino and gleaming in black silk in the mass media of the world, helping to launch what would become one of the most significant trends of fashion in recent years: vintage.

❑ 2002, February. He represented Italy, with its historic and rare capacity to blend creativity and craftsmanship with taste and superior elegance, during the culiminating ceremonies of the Winter Olympics in Salt Lake City, broadcast around the world.

❑ 2002, March. After months of negotiations and rumors, HDP sold the Roman *griffe* to the Marzotto Group. The deal is done for 240 million Euros, including the financial debts accumulated over recent years, which on 31 December 2001 amounted to 204.4 million Euros.

❑ Valentino Intimate and Valentino Sand were the first creations of the new management. With a three-year licensing agreement, the Como-based company Albisetti took over production and distribution rights worldwide for the intimatewear and men's and women's swimwear collections. The new lines debuted at Lingerie Americas, the first event in the sector held in the United States, which from 4 to 6 August 2002 featured 22 Italian underwear labels at the Pavillion Altman Building in New York. There were more than 125 manufacturers invited from around the world.

❑ 2003. In the first two months of the year, Marzotto had 1.8 percent increase in turnover, to be attributed for the most part to the consolidation of Valentino.

❑ 2003, May. Valentino, with a series of his "cult" outfits, took part in the exhibition My Favorite Dress at the Fashion Textile Museum, a London fashion museum built at the behest of the fashion designer Zandra Rhodes in the neighborhood of Bermondsey, south of the Thames.

❑ 2003. He launched the Valentino Timeless watches and the youth line Valentino R.E.D. (Roman Eccentric Dressing), which reinterpreted his unmistakable timeless modules such as jeans, but also his more classic items such as the short "Jackie" overcoats or the "V Logo" of 1968, by now part of fashion history. (*Antonella Amapane*)

Sketches by Valentino published in the Skira catalogue for the exhibition *Visitors*, Biennial of Florence, 1996.

Valentino Mario (1928-1991). Fashion designer of footwear and leather prêt-à-porter. He made his mark with his idea of lightening and coloring in unusual shades suede and working it as a yarn, after reducing it to strips. His first shoes with a decolleté and with stiletto heels were made of pink leather, when he set up his own little shop in Naples, continuing his father's business (1953). A coral flower adorned one of his sandal models the next years. Now, at the Museum of Footwear in Paris, these creations are exhibited as an example of pioneering femininization. When his impulse to experiment led to the application of leather for blouses, jackets, trousers, and blazers, the results were immediately viewed as astonishing. Designed by Muriel Grateau in pastels, in cobalt, green, strawberry, and beaver, the runway presentations in Milan (1977) featured long capes in contrasting silks, barbaric and sumptuous, they revealed both stylistic innovation and artisanal flair. The next challenge was to employ leather for every possible use as a fabric. While fashion designers like Armani, Montana, Versace and Lagerfeld came to work for Mario Valentino, subtle colors were applied to leathers that were as soft and iridescent as silk, embossing simulating the wales of corduroy or the stripes of piqué, handfretwork evoking the lace of Sangallo, leather cut into the thinnest strips imaginable and then woven on a loom, to produce Prince of Wales weave effects, along with herringbone and tweed in avant-garde creations.

(*Lucia Sollazzo*)

Valextra A manufacturer of high-quality leather goods, included in Stanley Marcus's famous book *Quest for the Best*. The label was a product of a merger of the terms Valigeria (luggage) and Extra. It began operations in 1938 under the leadership of Giovanni Fontana, who opened a shop in the Piazza San Babila, in Milan, and with an adjoining workshop. A decade later, production moved to the factory in the Via Bono Cairoli, also in Milan, and extended to include smaller leather goods as well, with the creation of one of the first attaché cases which, in 1954, received the Compasso d'Oro (Golden Compass) award. In the 1990s, the headquarters was moved to the Via Orobia.

❑ 2001. Emanuele Carminati Molina, a developmer and the owner of a tannery working with furriers, became the sole owner of the label. As early as April 2000, Carminati had purchased 81 percent. His new management focused on the label's crafts tradition. In the Winter of that year, the Marinella for Valextra line of ties was marketed. Distribution took the form of personalized production, only in Valextra boutiques, in Milan, Rome Fiumicino, Verona, Padua, Lugano and Saint Moritz.

Valle Giorgio (1941). Journalist. He was editor-in-chief of *Amica* and *Mondo Uomo*. He has worked in the world of publishing since 1971, first at Rusconi, then at Mondadori, where he became the managing editor of *Grazia*. In 1986 Paolo Pietroni hired him as deputy editor of *Amica*, where the next year he became editor-in-chief. In 1990 he moved to Condé Nast, where he was the editor first of all of *Myster*, then over to Rusconi to be editor of *Donna* and finally *Mondo Uomo*, a men's fashion monthly founded in 1981 by Flavio Lucchini.

Valles J. Arlington (1885-1970). He was the only Hollywood costume designer to dress only male stars. He won an Oscar in 1960 for his costumes for Stanley Kubrick's *Spartacus*. He worked especially for MGM actors, such as Fred Astaire (*Easter Parade*, 1948) and William Powell. His period costumes for *Portrait of Dorian Gray* (1945), *Madame Bovary* (1949 version), and *The Forsyte Saga* (1949) with Errol Flynn, were especially acclaimed.

Valleverde Italian footwear manufacturer. Armando Arcangeli, 58, is the founder and president of the footwear manufacturer based in Coriano in the province of Rimini, and he was appointed a Cavaliere del Lavoro in June 2002. In November 2001, he was awarded the Entrepreneur of the Year award, in an event hosted by Ernst & Young with the support of the Italian Borsa. The prize, now present in 20 different nations, is in its fifth year. In the United States it dates back to 1883. The company manufactures 2 million shoes and, in 2001, it had a turnover of approximately 300 billion old liras (220

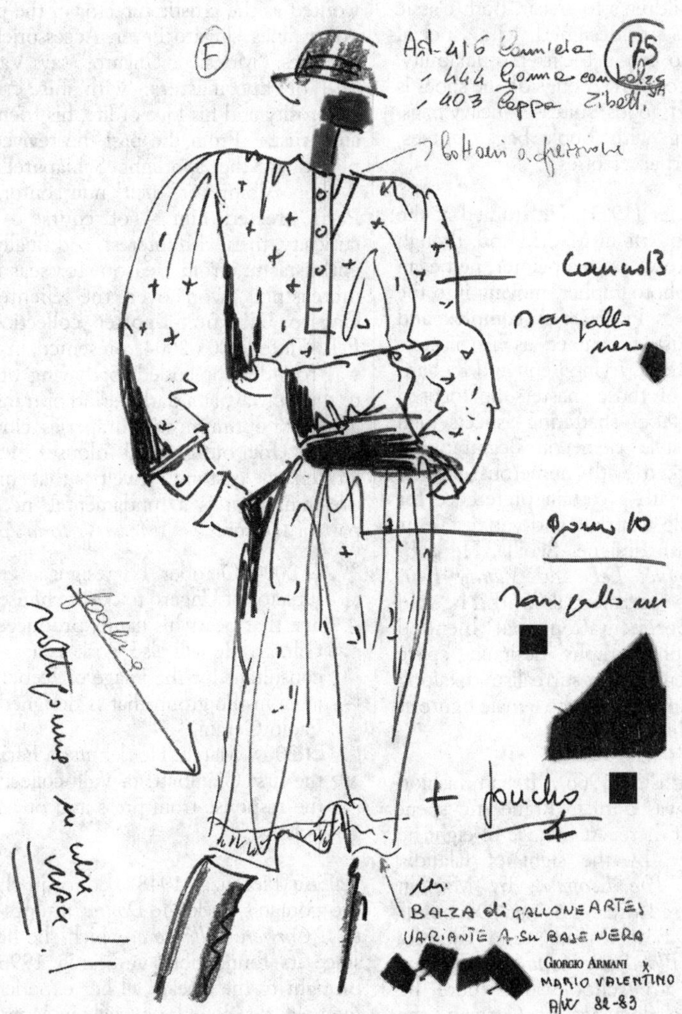

Sketch by Giorgio Armani for Mario Valentino, 1982-1983 Fall-Winter Collection.

billion was earned by Valleverde, the rest by the other label, Sanagens). There are excellent commercial relations with the most important shopping centers in China. In 2002 a retail outlet was opened in Shangai, to be followed by one in Beijing. The shoes, which cover the three sectors of women's, men's, and children's footwear, both classic and athletic, are designed with special technologies to produce extreme flexibility, softness, and comfort. Alongside the shoes is a line of leather goods: suitcases, heavy bags, trolleys, along with book bags, purses, backpacks, and accessories.

Vallhonrat Javier (1953). He studied at the School of Fine Arts in Madrid and, though he continued to work as a painter, he began to work as a photographer, moving into the fashion business in 1978. A complex and fascinating artist, he named as his masters Hoyningen-Huene, Irving Penn and Richard Avedon, but of those masters he focused more on the taboo-shattering aspects than the classical style elements. Beginning in 1980 he worked with numerous fashion personalities, with a certain preference for the Italian Aldo Coppola and young talents like the Spanish designer Sybilla. He published in *Vogue*, *Lei*, and *Vanity Fair*. Alongside his commercial work, he did personal experimentation that blended painting and photography, designing space with clear references to surrealism, exalting chromatisms and placing the female figure at the center of his interest.

Valli Giambattista (1966). Italian fashion designer. He was born in Rome and spent his early youth there. At the age of eight he was captivated by the sight of Claudia Cardinale in *The Leopard*, by Marilyn Monroe in a red dress singing "Diamonds Are a Girl's Best Friend," and by Rita Hayworth in *Blood and Sand*. In 1980 he attended an art school, and there he discovered the drawings of Cocteau, the illustrations of Gruau for Dior, the watercolors of Saint-Laurent, and went on to imitate them, copy them, and ultimately "consume" them. In 1986 he attended the fashion school at the Istituto Europeo di Design, and the following years a course in illustration at the Saint Martin's School of Art. In 1988, he met Roberto Cappucci. Then he worked for Fendi in 1990 as the senior designer for the Fendissime line, in 1995 for Krizia, again as senior designer for the women's prêt-à-porter line. In 1997, Emanuel Ungaro appointed him director of the creative office for couture and prêt-à-porter, and beginning in 2001 he has also worked as the artistic director of the prêt-à-porter lines Ungaro Fever, Accessories, and Licenses. "Monsieur Ungaro," says Valli, "is one of my masters: with his creative generosity and his love of life, his friendship and trust.." From the past, he revived and placed in the spotlight Schiaparelli and Walter Albini for their non-conformism. Paris greeted him – of course – with curiosity, then with interest, and finally with enthusiasm: from season to season he increasingly won over the clientele of Ungaro. His prêt-à-porter collection for Fall-Winter 2003-2004, presented in Paris, was roundly applauded for having brought to the runway, at a dark period of transition, a burst of optimism with draperies, clouds of chiffon for outfits and blouses, legends written in costume jewelry: that hint of dreaming that is a fundamental, necessary part of fashion. (*Maria Vittoria Alfonsi*)

❑ 2004, October. He resigns as creative director of Ungaro to devote himself to a line that bears his name, produced by Gilmar. He will also work as a consultant for the image of Iceberg, a label in the group that is designed by Paolo Gerani.
❑ 2005, March. He debuts in Paris with the first Giambattista Valli collection; the response from press and buyers is positive.

Vallino Fiorenza (1948). Editor-in-chief of the woman's weekly *Io Donna,* a supplement to *Il Corriere della Sera*, which she has run since its foundation, in March 1996. She brought to the weekly all her experience in the field, developed especially in Mondadori where she worked for *Donna Moderna* and *Confidenze*, where she was editor-in-chief from 1993 to 1995. She is very focused on current topics and a growing awareness of the universe of women, and has ensured that her work has always been marked by a moderate but unflagging engagement. An effort that has won her, as her greatest recognition, the UNESCO prize for work against the violence and abuse to which the women of the world fall vicitims. In 1998 she received the special Marisa Belisario award for journalism.

Valls David. Spanish fashion designer. He was born in Igualada (Catalonia). In 1984 he launched a menswear collection. He presented many times at the Paserela Gaudí. The London 1960s exerted a major influence on his creativity. Timid and introverted, he saw his womenswear collections win a place of honor. He designed a fashion that was practical and straightforward. He likes to focus on small details.
(*Estefania Ruilope Ruiz*)

Valsecchi Antonella (1968). Milanese fashion designer. After specializing at the Istituto Marangoni and serving an internship at the Saga Design Center in Copenhagen, she took a job in her family's fur business. She remained in the sector but, in the Fall-Winter 1999-2000 season, she presented her line of women's leather and fur accessories and also a few items of apparel, in the same materials, adding to her love of design her own artisanal experience from the workshop.

Van Beirendock Walter (1957). Belgian fashion designer. Since 1982 he has been the director of his own prêt-à-porter maison which debuted with an evocation of the eroticism of the canvases of Allen Jones. In 1985, he launched a menswear collection. He showed repeatedly at the British Designer Show of London and in 1991 founded a second line, Wild and Lethal Trash.

Van Cleef & Arpels French jeweler. The creations of the Parisian maison – founded in 1906 by Alfred Van Cleef (1873-1938) and his cousins Charles, Julien and Louis Arpels, experts in precious stones – genuinely wrote history. The headquarters was in the Place Vendôme, but within just a few years, they were joined by the shops in Nice, Deauville, Vichy, and Cannes. In the early 1920s jewelry from Van Cleef & Arpels was timely in its interpretation of the oriental and neo-Egyptian styles that were popular in the salons of France. Art Deco was at the gates. In 1929 the company opened its New York store, and in 1935 it opened the Monte Carlo store. In the 1930s, the house style was defined, proposing totally innovative creations by adopting a type of setting that had never been used before: the invisible *serti*. This technical device, which made it possible to present the gems without seeing the metal beneath, led to a production that focused on models with a floral inspiration – roses, camelias, crysanthemums, ivy leaves – and an animal inspiration. Dating back to the same period is the invention of the Ludo Hexagone bracelet, constructed with geometric mesh in a honeycomb shape. Also highly considered were the clips, including the famous *Passe-partout* (1938), to be worn separately on the lapels of the jacket or mounted on "*colliers chaîne-serpent*." It was especially to the credit of Louis Arpels, with his numerous contacts in the world of the jet set, that the *maison* enjoyed such success around the world. Perceptive in identifying trends and developments, the *maison* launched various innovative creations such as the zip necklace (or "fermeture éclairé"), inspired by the zipper, and the "*collier coriphée*," composed of a close-knit line of golden ballerinas with diamond tutus. In the 1950s, the company triumphed with its

Van Cleef & Arpels, sketch for a ruby and diamond necklace with platinum settings, for Wally Simpson, Duchess of Windsor.

lacework production of braided metal wire, twisted and knurled. Then came the snow-crystal clips. The company made history in the field of precious accessories. The *minaudières* of the 1920s, little evening bags disguised as golden cases studded with gems, are still famous. The company, which rose to international renown with jewelry, perfumes, and watches (and remarkable expansion in Asian markets), is currently under the management of the third generation of Arpels who preserved 20 percent of the ownership, while in 1999 60 percent ownership was purchased by Cartier.

(*Alessandra Quattordio*)

Van den Akker Koos (1930). Designer of Dutch descent, he is the creator of patchwork outfits, decorated with overlapping fabrics, inserts and variegated motifs. After studying at the Academy of the The Hague, where he was born, he moved to Paris where he was hired by the house of Dior. When he returned to Holland, he opened a boutique but decided to try his luck in America. It was 1968. His embroidered fabrics were so popular that he quickly succeeded in opening a number of shops in Manhattan and creating a prêt-à-porter label. The immense personality of his creations, in particular his collage outfits, lay the foundation for his success. In recent years, he has downsized his operations considerably, but he still has a boutique of his own in Greenwich Village.

Vanderbilt Gloria (1924). Heir to one of the largest family fortunes in the United States, she lent her name, face, and body to a line of jeans from Murjani International, "the jeans that hug your bottom." From the beginning of the 1980s, Vanderbilt were the fastest selling jeans in America. The surname, which belongs to the entrepreneurial history of the United States is found on dolls, greeting cards, soy bean sprout desserts and luggage and furniture.

(*Lorenzo Leonarduzzi*)

Van Der Kemp Ronald (1966). Dutch fashion designer. He graduated from the Gerrit Rietveld Academy of Art and Design in Amsterdam. After a very short apprenticeship, he designed Bill Blass prêt-à-porter collection, the womenswear collections of the major department store, Barneys of New York and, in 1999, he was named artistic director of the *maison* Laroche.

❑ At the turn of the new millennium, the fashion designer abandoned the position of designer of the department store chain Barneys, making way for Benhaz Sarafpour.

Van Der Straeten Hervé (1965). French jeweler. A creator of costume jewelry, he founded the company in 1985, at the age of 20. Creators of fashion like Saint-Laurent, Balmain, Lagerfeld, Lanvin, Rifat Ozbek, Martine Sitbon and Lacroix commissioned him to create costume jewelry per runway presentations. The materials that he loves best are bronze and brass, hammered and gilded. His subjects, often anthropomorphic, partake of the folk saga and the fairytale dream, and occasionally are spectacular in size. With an international presence (Europe, United States, Japan, Arab nations), the maison also produces decorative objects for the home.

❑ 2002. The line of porcelain designed for Bernardaud, an historic Limoges firm, went on the market.

Van De Velde Henry (1863-1957). Belgian painter and designer. Protagonist of the Art Nouveau movement. He designed and made, with his wife Maria Séte, avant-garde outfits decorated with syntethic linear motifs in a "dynamic graphic style." In 1900, he published *Die Kunstlerische Hebung der Frauentracht*, a text in which he declared his intention to rationalize women's fashion with the elimination of frivolous and superfluous details in favor, instead, of an essential linear cut that would be in line with Art Nouveau architecture, art and design. Put into production from 1897 on, Van De Velde's outfits were almost immediately exhibited at the museum of Krefeld.

Van Gorp Lieve. Belgian fashion designer. She was first a student and later a teacher at the Royal Academy of Fine Arts in Antwerp and has designed for Scapa of Scotland. She began to create on her own a collection of accessories. In 1995, she opened a shop in Antwerp. At the same time she presented in Paris her first prêt-à-porter, inspired by rock stars such as Madonna and conceived in three dimensions for a woman who is strong and at the same time sensual, with a decided emphasis on bosom and waist. Beginning in 1997, he also designed a menswear collection of simple and classical items.

Vanina De War French apparel house. It was established by Vanina Buston (1915) in 1935, in Paris. It specialized in knit clothing, and the maison shut its doors in 1951.

Vanity Case More commonly known as a beauty case. A travel bag that contains toiletry items. Such an object has existed since the nineteenth century, when it was very voluminous, with internal compartments that contained crystal and silver bottles, brushes and combs, manicure utensils, also in such valuable materials as ivory, tortoise shell, and silver. The exterior was in leather, skin, or parchment, but there were other more luxurious versions, such as those made by Van Cleef & Arpels in the 1930s, in gold, laquer, and enamels, genuine pieces of traveling jewelry.

Van Lamsweerde Inez (1963). Dutch artist. She began working as a fashion photographer, and worked and continues to work for trendy magazines like *The Face*. In 1993 in New York, where she lives, she began to bring into the field of art ideas from the field of fashion. In that year, for the Vivienne Westwood show at the Stelling Gallery in London, she did a number of portraits of fashion designers. From then on, her photographs have been decontextualizzing aspects of the Fashion System and inserting them into artistic situations. This is work that helps to reflect on identity through fashion, as the artist explains: "If you're wearing a fur, you're saying something different from someone who is wearing a bathing suit or a pair of jeans. A very tight white gogo boot immediately directs you to a certain type of imagination."

❑ 2001. The photographer and her collaborator and companion Vinoodh Matadin direct the Icelandic singer Bjork in the video of *Hidden Place*. She worked on the runway presentations of Balenciaga and Yamamoto.
❑ 2001, June. Pitti Immagine Discovery promotes in the Stazione Leopolda in Florence an exhibition on the work of Inez and Vinoodh. The show was held to celebrate the first 50 years of Italian fashion. It was called The Final Fantasy, the series of portraits of three-year-old girls upon whom the two artists superimposed the lips of young adults.
❑ 2003, March. She was invited to the exhibition Melting Pop which, in the Palazzo delle Papesse in Siena, presented a series of combinations of visual arts and other creative languages.

Van Lingen Tom (1962). Dutch fashion designer. As a boy he lived in Arabia and in England. In 1984 he graduated from the school of the Chambre Syndicale de la Haute Couture, after studying at the Charles Montaigne Academy of Fashion in Amsterdam, and studying set and costume design at the Royal Academy of Fine Arts in Antwerp. He designed for Cardin from 1984 to 1988, and subsequently worked as an assistant for Bernard Perris and, from 1992 to 1997, he was the artistic director for the Maison Fath. He debuted with his own name in 1999.

❑ His first personal collection, presented in March 1999 at the Yvon Lambert Gallery in Paris, gravitated around the concept of "pleasurewear" and was emphasized by the continually changing light of 7 luminous balloons, which provided the only lighting in the room.
❑ 2002. Tom took on the challenge of creating a "capsule collection" on an exclusive basis for Colette.
❑ For the shows of 2002, Van Lingen adopted the gimmick of "mechanical marionettes": models in white outfits decorated with yellow checks and wreaths of flowers around their necks, whose gait was punctuated and interrupted suddenly by a voice-over: "1, 2, 3... Stop!"

Vanna A dressmaking shop founded in the 1930s by two matrons of the Milanese bourgeoisie, Anna Carmeli and Manette Valente. The offices were in the Corso di Porta Nuova. It operated through World War Two. In an article done for the magazine *Fili* about Milanese society events held during wartime, Brunetta, among others, described Donina Gnecchi "in Vanna trousers with dark-blue and red stripes, loose on the hips and supported at the shoulders by Tyrolean suspenders." Natalia Aspesi in her book, *Il lusso & l'autarchia* (Rizzoli 1982), recalls a number of her creations from 1942, under the heading of jury-rigging and improvisation: "The choker necklaces made of wood chips, the little cluster of cherries to worn perched atop a hair-do, the butterfly knots of waxed percale to be worn next to one's ears, the nets that hold back one's curls on the small of the neck." Vanna was among the true pioneers of Italian fashion in the runway presentation of 12 February 1951 in Florence, held in the parlor of Bista Giorgini in the Villa Torrigiani, and in the subsequent runway presentation held in the Hotel Excelsior and in the Sala Bianca of Palazzo Pitti.

Jacket-overcoat by Vanna, 1957.

Vanni Carla. Italian journalist. The editor-in-chief of *Grazia*, a historic women's weekly published by Mondadori. Born in Livorno, she took a degree in law, married, with two children: the boy became a lawyer, the girl an architect. She began working at *Grazia* in 1959 as a young editor and, through hard work and great dedication, she became managing editor and, in 1978, editor-in-chief, replacing Renato Olivieri. A woman of wide-ranging interests, she was especially attentive to all the cultural and lifestlye phenomena and issues of modern living; she noted them, expanded upon them, and commented upon them in *Grazia*, which was considered one of the most respected and closely read women's weeklies in Italy, in terms of quality, accuracy, reliability, and elegance of graphics and image, in continuous evolution. In over twenty years as editor-in-chief, she succeeded in allowing the magazine to evolve without revolutionary changes, in a contemporary and highly qualified context, both personal and highly distinctive. She became the editorial director of women's publications for Mondadori in 1987, and she worked hard to ensure the success of other publications as well.

Van Noten Dries (1958). Belgian fashion designer. The son of a tailor and a seamstress, he graduated from the Royal Academy of Arts in Antwerp. He is one of the founding fathers of the stylistic *nouvelle vague* that that school engendered and the leader of the so-called "Sextet of Antwerp." While he was still a student, he caught the notice of buyers from the New York department store Barneys and from the store Whistles; they purchased his entire first sample-collection. In 1985, he created a small outpost in Antwerp, a boutique, and in 1986, he debuted on the runways of London, with a menswear collection. In Spring of 1987 he presented his prêt-à-porter womenswear collection. Five years later, he arrived in Paris. An eccentric, but a restrained one, he chooses classical forms and fabrics and then diversifies and develops them with original ideas and with great sartorial skill. His collections are always experimental, but they also respond to a shrewd commercial policy. He has three single-label shops and is present in 500 sales outlets around the world.

❑ 1999, September. The book *Dries Van Noten: shape, print and fabric*, is published, a tribute by Andrew Tucker to the creative processes of the Belgian fashion designer, more than to the production itself.
❑ For the Fall-Winter 1999-2000 season, the fashion designer brought to the runway the monastic-mediaeval style of outfits in clinging wool. While the felt jackets are very reminiscent of Balenciaga, the velvet skirts and the tops with gilded embroideries are typical of Van Noten.
❑ The catalogue of products by the Belgian fashion designer is one of the most interesting in the Fall-Winter 2003 season, after the ones put out by Blumarine and Roberto Cavalli. This was the response from the survey conducted by Fashion magazine among the 70 most prominent retailers in Italy. Dolce & Gabbana stand out in the categories of sell out and creativity.

Van Ommeslaeghe Patrick (1967). Belgian fashion designer. He was born in Oudenaarde. In 1985, he discovered his true calling and quit medical school to enroll at the Royal Academy of Fine Arts in Antwerp. Two years after graduating, he moved to Paris and worked for Balenciaga, Gaultier and Adeline André. His first collection of women's apparel was presented in 1999. It was rife with cultural references and citations, as were the collections that followed.

Van Rooy Willy. Dutch fashion model and fashion designer. He did not wait to leave the runway or for this or that photographer to stop asking him to pose. He decided to begin a career as a creator of fashion right away. He took a diploma in 1966 at the Academy of Fine Arts of Totterdam, and pursued both professions at the same time or in alternation. He began to do runway presentations in Japan and then wound up being photographed by Newton and Bailey and on the runway of Saint-Laurent. In the meanwhile, in New York, he designed leather outfits for Jimi Hendrix and invented a sort of monk's habit that impressed Diane Vreeland. In 1982, he abandoned the modeling profession and moved to Spain where, with some success, he designed shoes. Since 1994 he has lived and worked in Los Angeles.

Vans American manufacturer of sports shoes, founded by Paul Van Doren. At first it specialized in surf shoes and skateboarding shoes, he opened his first single-label shop in 1966 in California. Over the course of the 1980s, he launched lines intended for other types of sports such as baseball, basketball, and football. In 1988, the company was sold to the McCown DeLeeuw Co., creating a powerful distribution network to market these shoes internationally.

(*Giulio Alberoni*)

Van Saene Dirk (1959). Belgian fashion designer. Born in Leuven. He studied, from 1977 to 1981, at the Royal Academy of Fine Arts in Antwerp and, in the early 1980s, he began to design outfits for a number of department stores in Belgium. In 1983 he won a series of prizes, including the Golden Spindle and the Price of the Press. The following year, he debuted in London, along with the so-called Group of Six, the fashion designers Dries Van Noten, Ann Demeulemster, Walter Van Beirendonck, Dirk Bikkembergs and Marina Yee who, along with him, brought an unexpected wave of Belgian creativity onto the center state of worldwide fashion. Again with the other five, he presented in Paris as well, where however he also presented alone in 1991. Between 1992 and 1994 he became the fashion designer in charge of the Scapa of Scotland collection (Renown-Look), in Japan. He has a boutique in Paris.

❑ He opened a boutique in Antwerp in the Nationalestraat, the road that concentrates in a few meters the most important fashion designers of Belgium, the Group of Six.
❑ He was creative director of the fashion magazine *N°A*.

(*Valeria Vantaggi*)

Van Slobbe Alexander. Dutch fashion

designer. He create the label So, in 1989, finding two excellent colleagues and administrators in Marteen Wentholt and Cristoph Mollet. In 1994, he won the Theo Limperg Prize for the best and most original design. In 1998 he launched a new line, So Genes, as well as a special collection entitled "A Composition with Red and Yellow," created for the Mondrian Exhibition at the Musée de la Mode in Marseilles. He lives and worlks in Amsterdam and teaches at the Academy of Arnhem. In men's fashion, which he designs with eliminating feminine motifs, he is considered a master of minimalism. His palette is limited to black and grey.

❑ 2000, September. An exhibition at the Centraal Museum in Utrecht celebrated the leading figures in Dutch fashion at the turn of the millennium, including Van Slobbe and Viktor Rolf.
❑ 2000. The creative repeated the experience of collaboration with Claudy Jongstra, which had been so successful three years before. Alexander worked on the fashion design of the collection, Claudy on the textile design.
❑ 2003. From February to April, the fashion designer participated in the exhibition entitled *Reality Machines*, dedicated to some thirty contemporary Dutch photographers, architects, and designers. The initiative was held in the main hall of the Nederlands Architect Institute.

Vargas-Ochagavia A company, owned by Jesus Vargas (Ciudad Rezal, 1913) and Emilio Ochagavia (Pamplona, 1922-1997), that has lasted a lifetime. The two Spanish fashion designers joined forces in 1943 and opened in Madrid their *maison;* in 1947 they presented their first collection. Over the years they have presented outfits that over time attained distinction in high fashion, copying the cuts and decorations of Iberian popular clothing. The business closed after Ochagavia's death.

Varty Keith (1952). British fashion designer. Born in Darlington. He worked in Paris for Dorothée Bis and found success in Italy working with many companies such as Complice and Byblos.

Vass Joan (1925). American fashion designer, especially of knitwear. Her best known creations are made of chenille, alpaca and angora. After working for ten years as the curator of the department of prints at the Metropolitan Museum in New York, she decided in 1977 to change her way of life, founding a non-profit organization to help knitters to improve their products and to become better known. And so she began to design for her associates sweaters, hats, and scarves which they would make and then sell. The New York department store Henri Bendel purchased the collection as a whole. From then on, she was on easy street. In the 1980s she presented three lines for men and women.

Vázquez Jorge. Spanish fashion designer. Afer a very brief experience with the Inditex Group (producer of the Zara collections), at the age of 18 he began to study design, first in Madrid and later in the United States. Subsequently he went to work for Antonio Pernas and Angel Schlesser. He worked with the Fedón Group where he oversaw the design department, before moving on to the accessories sector of the FunBasic company. During the same period he launched his first collection of women's prêt-à-porter. In his first runway presentation at the Pasarela Cibeles he also presented a menswear collection.

(*Mariacristina Righi*)

V de V French label of ready-to-wear fashion. Almost an acronym because it stands for *Vêtements de Vacance*. The company, created by Michèle Rosier, daughter of the owner of *Elle* and, at the time, a journalist, was founded in Paris in 1963. The first collections, thanks to the idea of creating quick-drying swimsuits that were made with nylon plume, were a great success. Fashion designers such as De Castelbajac, Kenzo, and Agnès B. worked for the *griffe*. In 1990, Sergio Tacchini purchased the *griffe*, thus acquiring the impetus to win new markets. Eight years later, the Parisian company became Italian and presented for the last Summer of the Summer of the millennium a new line: Sport Active, neoprene items with removable waterproof pockets.

Veil (Italian variant, *veletta*, is derived from veil, but is a feminine diminutive that accurately conveys the delicacy of what English can only attempt to identify as a "hat-veil." The Italian term almost equals in grace the evanescent, brief span of fabric – tulle, lace – that was used to cover the face or only the eyes of women in the nineteenth century.) Simple, almost always black, the *veletta,* or veil, embellished by delicate reliefs, by tiny vague embroideries, enveloped the face between chin and cap, dangling from a cunning small hat, knotted around the back of the neck, more as an homage to seduction, captured so frequently by Boldini in his portraits of ladies, than to modesty. At the end of the nineteenth century and the beginning of the twentieth century, dangling from hats, the veil barely covered the eyes, accentuating the gaze with its mystery. The fashion of the *tailleur*, along with boaters and straw hats, would relegate it among the many ornaments of a forgotten style; but the *veletta* would still have a chance to transform itself from a weapon of seduction into a useful defensive tool, a veritable curtain against the dust of the road during the early trips by automobile: worn over the hat and fastened to the back of the neck with fluttering knots, it evoked the old loosely worn veils that were standard fasteners for hats in the French First Empire style. In more recent years, during the cyclical revivals, the veil has reemerged, a short, taut mask over the eyes, dangling from tiny little hats, almost as if to emphasize, with ironic nostalgia, a fashion that was more feminized than feminine. Wally Toscanini, the daughter of the great conductor, always wore a veil, and did so extraordinarily well, and not only to cover the effects of the passing years. (*Lucia Sollazzo*)

Veil, 1919 (A. Bertarelli collection of prints and drawings, Milan).

Velcro A two-part adhesive strip, based on a system patented by the Swiss company Mistral. At first, it was designed for home furnishings and household use (curtains, pillow or sofa cases), it is now widely used in fashion as well in place of buttons or zippers. It is often used on windbreakers, hoods, or down jackets.

Velia A millinery shop and workshop opened in Rome by Velia Lisi in the Via Firenze 26, in 1922. Between the 1950s and the 1960s, it made hats for Rome's high society. After the death of Velia Lisi, the shop was inherited by her niece Anna Vanoncini who, along with her daughter Paola, not only continued to make hats for the same clientele, but also began in the 1990s a collaboration with Gattinoni.

Velvet A technique that originated in the East and which was brought in the Middle Ages to Italy, to Venice, Lucca, Florence and Genoa, before arriving in Tours and Lyons in France. Velvet features a dense pile surface, smooth, compact, and brilliant. This result is obtained with either of two weaving systems. The loveliest, softest, and most luminous velvets are made of silk, but these are also the most fragile and the costliest. Nowadays, the same effect can be obtained with viscose, rayon, and synthetic fibers. Cotton velvet is a classic, and is always in fashion. For sports, corduroy is used, with wales of varying thickness and density. Velour, on the other hand, is a fabric similar to velvet, with a short, dense pile. It is soft and very warm, and it is normally used for overcoats or heavy jackets.

(*Gabriella Gregorietti*)

Venet Philippe (1931). French designer. Born in Lyons, he began to work early as an apprentice to a local tailor, Pierre Court. He moved to Paris, in 1951, where he worked as a tailor and cutter for, first, Fath, and then Schiaparelli and later Givenchy. In 1962, he opened his own maison of high fashion and, the following year, he converted to prêt-à-porter. His outfits, "with nothing superfluous," as he likes to say, had a simple and well-tailored line. In 1985, he won the Dé d'Or. The maison ceased operation in 1994.

Veneziani Jole (1901-1988). Italian fashion designer and furrier. She had her *atelier* at number 8 in Milan's Via Montenapoleone and from the courtyard a strong scent of caramel would always waft up, a pleasant gift from the Caffè Pasticceria Cova whose kitchens faced that courtyard. There was a large eighteenth-century hall, all grey and gold: painted panels; dressing rooms with large wall mirrors and heavy curtains to muffle the voices and preserve absolute discretion on the choices of the clients, all jealous, all rivals. She, the Milanese Jole, would be seated on her throne: dressed in a light pastel blue, her white hair still cut like a child's, her pink, mother-of-pearl complexion, her courteous smile. Before she had a cataract operation and "miraculously" regained her sight, she wore a pair of important-looking, ostentatious, aggressive, glittering eyeglasses that she had designed for herself. Her hands were pudgy, adorned with precious red pearls and sapphires; those "very special" hands for which, in all the countless articles written about her, she was always dubbed "velvet paws." I myself coined this term for her, because of my astonishment at seeing those hands as they palpated, caressed, rubbed against the grain

"A character out of a painting by Piero della Francesca closely examines the Veneziani line," Brunetta, 1958.

those magnificent pelts of sable, not only with unrivaled competence, but almost with a sensual pleasure. In terms of her knowledge and familiarity with furs, her creative fantasy, her quest for new ideas, her courage – a great courage – Jole Veneziani was a pioneer, perhaps without parallels. In contrast with many fashion designers, there was no early predestination underlying her decision on a profession, no foreshadowings of her later success. She was born in Taranto into a cultural and artistic milieu, her father was a lawyer and a writer, her mother was a great classical music lover, her brother Carlo was an acclaimed playwright. And it was with him, in Milan, that this little, lively, fanciful, and generous-spirited young girl tried acting, and then journalism. After the death of her father and the sudden change in the family's fortunes, she revealed her exceptional strength of character, a combination of determination, practicality, imagination, and willingness to run risks. She became an administrator in a major French company that dealth in furs and she immediately discovered her true passion. While the bombs that would cause destruction in Milan were falling, she opened her first *atelier* in the Via Nirone: "When I decide to do something, I do it right away. I don't know the word tomorrow." There was something different about her furs, and so they were sought after by the major dressmakers to be worn by their models in the runway presentations. From this first contact with high fashion another *atelier* was immediately established, where she herself would create the fashion from then on, with astrakhan, chincilla, seal, and mink. The war came to an end, Italian fashion made its first appearance, and she immediately became an international celebrity: covers of *Life*, *Harper's Bazaar*, *Vogue* with headlines reading: *Italy evening bravura of Veneziani*; *C'est la dernière folie européenne, la plus belle* (NB: European, not just Italian), and there was a hail of prizes and awards. She was a courageous gambler, and on the international markets she always managed to secure the most exclusive shipments of furs, leaving American and French giants empty-handed; after she signed a contract for an especially remarkable group of sables, the Soviets insisted on giving her a diamond brooch. And in turn, she gave it to Anna Bonomi,

Outfit by Jole Veneziani, sketch by Brunetta, 1952 (from *La Sala Bianca – La nascita della moda italiana*, Pitti Immagine-Electa, 1992).

who had purchased the coat that she had made from those sables. She was the queen of the Frankfurt fur fairs, the most important international fur marketplace. I witnessed one of those fairs, massive, ostentatiously rich in the German way, with more than ten nations presenting their products. At the Veneziani runway presentation, not included in the official program, the applause filled the room, as frenzied as at a rock concert, until, when the last white and black minks left the runway, the room erupted in a cry of "Viva l'Italia!" In the years from 1955 to 1968, J. V. was not only a great fashion designer, not only did she create furs worthy of a museum for the most important women in the world and entire dynasties, not only was she a pioneer of color, of tweed techniques and processes to take pounds and pounds off the weight of these fur coats, not only was she the first to create an industrial collection for Eurofur, with two-tone sports jackets, and not only was she the consultant who changed the dark colors of the Alfa Romeo to other, bright, more feminine colors, as well as an adviser to many other textile manufacturers. She was all this, but, in her work and in her social life, she was the true representative, the true interpreter of the years of the Italian economic miracle, that boom that may have been reckless but which was also vital and magical in its vigorous rude creativity. Her right hand-woman was Sandra Boghossian, a former fashion model, helped by Giuliana Cova Radius. When I dragged him to Pitti in 1963, Dino Buzzati wrote in the *Corriere della Sera*: "Jole Veneziani unfurled the banner, especially the banner so beloved by women everywhere, and she did not wait for the finale; from the very first notes she waved the fatal flag, the objective of a thousand dreams, the classic emblem of social triumph, of economic security, of luxury, of the Dolce Vita, his majesty, the mink." And he added: "There was a little festival on the runways of Pitti of the economic miracle, so open and amusing that it could hardly scandalize anyone." The scandal would only come later, in 1968, when the rotten eggs and lurid tomatoes would splatter against those furs at the opening of La Scala on the inaugural evening of 7 December. That marked the end of a Milanese era and the beginning of the decline of the star of Jole.

(*Maria Pezzi*)

Ventilo A French prêt-à-porter label. It debuted in 1972: shirts and skirts. The creative force was Armando Ventilo. His brother Jacques was in charge of business, he was the manager. The company's initial success allowed it to venture onto the runways during the official Paris fashion weeks. Armando was identified as one of the ten fashion designers of the moment. But, after four runway presentations, he prefers more direct approach that also allowed him to work in home furnishings. In 1986 he inaugurated a three-story shop in the Rue du Louvre in Paris: clothing for various levels of market and age, lingerie, objects for the home. His fashion (four lines: Armando Ventilo, La Colline, Chemise Blanche and Home Wear) is a skillful mélange of styles and materials, with a view to being wearable and timeless. The inspiration came from the Orient (there is a zen flavor to his 25 boutiques in France, Belgium, Italy, the United States, and Japan), Provence, and America. Since 1998, Armando has designed the Maison line for La Redoute, a major name in catalogue sales.

Ventura Milanese fashion house founded in 1815 by Domenico Ventura. It immediately became famous for its skill at reproducing or recreating French outfits and models. It won a vast clientele, after Italian unification, in the international markets as well. In 1869 the company opened a subsidiary in Geneva; it counted among its clients the Austrian royal family. In the same years, the headquarters in Milan was regularly patronized by other royals, in particular by the queen of Italy, Margherita, who lived part time in the Villa di Monza. There developed a certain interest for an Italian fashion that might be less

Evening gown by the Sartoria Ventura, published in the magazine *Moda*, 1931.

obsequious to and respectful of Paris: even the queen and her ladies-in-waiting clearly approved of this tendency. The Ventura company was appointed a Purveyor to the Royal House of Italy. At the end of the First World War, the Milanese *sartoria* became intensely busy, especially with runway presentations but also with participations in international events, such as the Fiera Campionaria (1920), which saw the involvement of other well-known names in Italian fashion, such as Ferrario, Radice, Fumach-Galli, Marta Palmer, Montorsi, all of them competing with the *ateliers* of Paris. In 1923, Ventura opened a subsidiary in Rome in the Piazza di Spagna, at the corner of Via della Croce. Among the 300 employees there was a valet in livery who operated the elevator. There were two stories of workshops, with embroiderers, seamstresses working "light" and seamstresses working "heavy." On the second story was the main reception room, with adjoining dressing rooms to try on clothing. For many years, the *atelier* in Rome was run by Madame Hannà, a much feared Dutch *première*. Counting all the various offices, the company now had 800 employees. The owner of the company, Vittorio Alberto Montana, was appointed chairman of the union of Italian high fashion. Among the company's clients were movie and theater actresses, such as Clara Calamai and Isa Miranda, and members of the nobility, such as the princesses Colonna, Barberini and Odescalchi, and the wealthy bourgeoisie. Among the most famous outfits of the Casa Ventura, there was the wedding gown of Maria Josè of Belgium, created in 1930 to sketches by the prince and heir Umberto. The royal wedding was an event that involved the entire city, and the wedding dress, in an illustration by John Guida, was published in all the newspapers and magazines of the time. "It was a gown with lace glove sleeves so narrow that," as Fernanda Gattinoni, then première at Ventura, recalled, "it was necessary to cut them with scissors, thus launching a new fashion." At the beginning of the 1940s, the company shut down. The Milan offices were taken over by Germana Marucelli. The Roman branch continued without great changes until 1942, when the Contessa Gabriella di Robilant (known as Gaby) took over, renaming it Gabriella Sport, but maintaining the structures and part of the staff, in order to produce a line of sporty apparel. A sector of the archives and the rest of the staff were taken over by Fernanda Gattinoni for her *atelier*." (*Bonizza Giordani Aragno*)

Venturi Gian Marco (1946). Italian fashion designer. He graduated from the Istituto Tessile in Prato. He took a degree in economics in Florence. But he chose to go into fashion and designed a line of women's prêt-à-porter for Domitilla (1974). Then came numerous projects with Lebole, Sander for leather, Marko's Alexander, Biba for knitwear and, in 1979, with Erreuno, a Milanese house that hired him to do their collections for six seasons. In 1981, he went into business on his own with the name GMV: there were menswear and womenswear lines, and beginning in 1987, also Sport, Underwear and men's and women's Jeans. His style: rigor and refinement, color and personality for men.

❑ He entered the millennium with three boutiques in Japan, more than ten franchised sales outlets open in New York and offices in Rome, Milan and Florence. (*Lucia Serlenga*)

Venturi Maria (1933). Journalist and author. She was the editor of *Annabella*. Previously the editor-in-chief of *Novella 2000*, in 1983 she took over as editor of *Annabella*. Under her leadership, the Rizzoli weekly underwent an adjustment of content that moved it toward a larger audience, while still maintaining the traditional target composed of women aged 25 to 44. After she left *Annabella*, she became an author of romance novels, genuine bestsellers. The most recent one was *La donna per legare il sole* (Rizzoli, 1999).

Vénus et Neptune French millinery house founded in Paris at the end of the 1970s by the fashion journalist France Ann Bennett. For 18 years, the milliner, who created directly on her clients' heads and used discontinued industrial materials, survived the decline of the fashion of the 'little hat.'

Verband die Mode Designer German association of fashion professionals: designer and textile and apparel technicians. It was founded in 1986 in Munich.

Verbeke Annemie. Belgian fashion designer. In 1987 she created hew own collection of knitwear, very simple and classical, but with vivid and original details. She is a member of the board of the Association professionelle des producteurs belges de tricots, for whom she designed the trendy lines.

Verde Veronica Trademark of ready-to-wear fashion. It was created in 1983, based on an idea by Rosanna Ansaloni, who was, in those years, a fashion designer and model: to create a new way of interpreting the concept of lingerie, "correcting" the traditional items made of cambric and lace, until they had become full-fledged evening gowns. The line debuted with a new men's-style pajama: a double-breasted silk number for the night, made in various colors and combinations. The model attained instant popularity: from Italy, it very quickly became known around the world, and was worn by Lady Diana and Caroline of Monaco as well. For the first ten years, the label specialized in intimatewear and then, from the mid-1990s on, it produced two new lines: corsetry and beachwear, which, in keeping with the rest of the production, was characterized by elegance and femininity.

Verdura (Duke of) Fulco (1898-1978). Italian jeweler. He was Chanel's favorite. Palermo-born, in 1927, hoping to become a fashion designer and creator of jewelry, he moved to Paris and then, ten or so years later, he moved on to New York. There he worked as a designer for the jeweler Flato who put him in charge of the California subsidiary. In 1939 he founded his own company in New York, on Fifth Avenue. He designed the neo-Byzantine style bracelets worn on more than one occasion by Madame Chanel: his bizarre and surreal style enchanted her, with the freshness of his inventions and the unusual chromatic combinations. He loved to mix precious and semi-precious stones, gold and platinum, nature and history, fiction and reality. He was famous for his pearl chokers and his creations based on the theme of seashells. Today, production – overseen by the designer Maria Kelleher Williams, a faithful interpreter of the Verdura style – continues under the supervision of Ward Landrigan, who purchased the company in in 1984. The showrooms are at 745 Fifth Avenue in New York.

Verga Factory of silk products, at first located in Bregnano, and founded in 1940 by Luigi Verga. In 1945 the production facilities were moved to Bulgorello di Cadorago, in the province of Como. In 1961 a printing department was set up alongside the weaving mill, with a resulting change in company name to Tessitura Serica e Stamperia Luigi Verga. At the beginning of the 1970s, the company also began to do its own industrial trasformation of raw treated silk into manufactured products; in 1973 a textile finishing department was set up.

Vergottini Family of hairdressers – at first, the brothers Cele, Lina, Bruno – which dictated fashion in hairdos, especially in Milan in 1960s and which is still well known and influential, with its geometric cuts. It was called the *Casco d'oro*, like the pop singer Caterina Caselli with her long blonde bangs that covered her eyebrows and the fade cut high up on the back of the neck: a creation that brought the name of Vergottini and their salon in the Via Montenapoleone to the front pages of the daily press. This led to the creation of the "vergottinata" look, either with long or short hair but always with an unmistakable, squared-off cut. From the United States, Paris, and London they would flock to the Via Montenapoleone, legendary journalists like Diana Vreeland, photographers like Bailey, Newton, Avedon, Clarke, and models like Veruschka, Fiona von Thyssen, Isa Stoppi, as well as movie stars (Monica Vitti) or television stars (Raffaella Carrà). Even the protagonist of the sophisticated graphic novel by Guido Crepax, *Valentina*, is a "vergottinata." But alongside the smooth, squared-off hair in the *Casco d'oro* style, other lines and other cuts soon developed. Quite popular was the savage cut, created for the theater of Giorgio Strehler with Goldoni's *Il Campiello*: a permanent with the hair dried naturally and distributed around the face in an unkempt manner.

Verhoeven Julie (1969). Artist and designer whose talent ranges from fashion to design and art direction. After an early experience as assistant to John Galliano in London, she was a design consultant for Martine Sitbon. Later, for the Spring-Summer 2002 season, Marc Jacobs put her in charge of designing a collection of bags for Louis Vuitton: bags that became cult objects, so that in just a few days the surging demand made them an international success. Julie has exhibited her work at the Mobile Gallery in London and at Colette in Paris and works with the magazines *Dazed & Confused*, *Self Service*, *The Face*, *Numero* and for the website http://www.showstudio.com. She was involved in directing a promo for Sugababes and recently produced an animated film for the artists Fisherspooner. She has also worked as teacher at the Central St. Martins. Gibo by Julie Verhoeven is her first fashion collection. (*Gianluca Cantaro*)

❑ 2004, September. She steps down as creative director of Gibò. She is replaced by the Japanese designer Ichiro Seta.

Verino Roberto (1945). Spanish fashion designer. He was born in Verín in Ourense, where his parents owned a company that manufactured articles of leather goods. After finishing his business studies, he decided to move to Paris to follow his dream of attending the Academy of Fine Arts. In 1967 he returned to Spain to run the family company. In 1982 he presented his first collection of prêt-à-porter womenswear with his own name, and later took part in various specialty salons (Milan, Paris, Monte Carlo). In these years he also opened his own showroom and his first boutique in Paris. In 1984, his collections were presented first in Barcelona and then in Madrid, at the Pasarela Cibeles. His Fall-Winter 1990-91 collection was also presented at the CPD in Dusseldorf, Germany and, that same year (1990), Verino was appointed president of the Asociación Española de Prêt-à-Porter Femenino. In 1991 he received the Bailey's prize for the best Spring-Summer 1992 collection presented at the Pasarela Cibeles and the renowned T assigned by the magazine *Telva*, which he went on to win again in later seasons. In 1992 he opened his first boutique in Madrid and also received the prestigious Aguja de oro (Golden Needle) award. In 1999 he founded the Asociación de Creadores de Mode de España together with Jesus del Pozo, Angel Schlesser, Antonio Pernas and Modesto Lomba. In 2000 he launched his prêt-à-porter menswear line and began distribution of his collections in prestigious sales outlets such as Harrods in London, Saks and Bergdorf Goodman in New York. He now has 53 boutiques in Spain while there are 46 more inside the department stores of the El Corte Inglés chain. (*Mariacristina Righi*)

Sketch by Roberto Verino.

Veronese Ettore. Biella-born fashion designer who has worked with many prestigious sportswear manufacturers and couture houses for collections of menswear and womenswear. Currently he is working on his "reworking" project, which will entail stitching antique elements of all sorts into outfits in order to make original creations. *Papier de chine* is the name of the line of prêt-à-couture devised by Veronese. Pure linens obtained from old sheets, bleached and redyed, canvases taken from antique mattresses, cottons and lacework, Sangallo laces, silks embroidered with early twentieth century passementerie. The creation of the items begins with the recovery of old materials, the redying of the fabrics, and then the assemblaged of items with stitching directly upon dressmaker's dummies, and then finally the seamstresses put together the final creations, with certification labels to document the provenance of the clothing.

(*Daniela Bolognetti*)

Veronese Nietta (1933). Fashion journalist. In the 1950s she debuted as the editor-in-chief of the magazine *Fortuna*, and then moved on to *Grazia*, *Annabella* and *L'Illustrazione Italiana*. But it was for the weekly *Gente* that she dedicated herself completely to reporting on the fashion industry. Aside from journalism, she worked for many years in public relations, always, inevitably, in the context of the textiles industry. First for Rhodiatoce, then, for three decades, she oversaw the image of the Belfe company.

Veronesi Italian jeweler. It has existed for over a century. In 1896, Giulio Veronesi opened his first shop in Bologna in the Via Orefici. In 1920 he moved to the Palazzo Ronzani and, shortly thereafter, he handed over the business to his two older sons, Raffaello and Galileo. The jeweler's attained considerable renown in the late 1940s. In 1964, their Gemini ring received the Diamonds International Award in New York as the finest piece of jewelry of the year. In the 1970s, the family opened a second shop in Bologna and the Galleria in Cortina, where auctions of international importance were frequently held. Currently, the Veronesi jewelry company owns a private collection of jewelry that once belonged to the Duchess of Windsor, Greta Garbo, and Andy Warhol. It continues its production to exclusive designs of one-off items, unique in terms of style and gem quality, all of the stones being of extreme perfection, from the diamonds and rubies to the yellow or pink sapphires.

(*Gabriella Gregorietti*)

Veronesi Luigi (1908-1998). Italian artist, graphic designer, and photographer. He had already established a reputation in the 1930s for his artistic choices that led him in the direction of abstract art, and he spent long periods working in Paris where he sensed an atmosphere different from that of Fascist Italy; he entered into contact with Leger and Kandinsky, and designed for textile companies. In the area of photography, he experimented with solarization and off-camera images, obtaining results – abstract photographs – that were similar to those created by Man Ray and Laszlo Moholy-Nagy, whom he had not yet met. In the postwar period, he worked as a graphic designer for such important magazines as *Ferrania*, *Campo Grafico*, *Domus*, and *Casabella*, but he also continued to work on set design, painting, and photography, doing fashion layouts as well, featuring such experiments as double exposure and solarization.

Versace Donatella (1955). Italian designer. After taking a degree in languages at the University of Florence, with the support and the encouragement of her brother Gianni, she soon asserted her iron will and her modern intelligence. From the very beginning of Gianni Versace's debut as a fashion designer, she was his closest colleague and his inspiration and muse. A real woman, who rendered concrete the volcanic and oneiric genius of her brother, unfailingly influencing his creative decisions. Through contacts and friendships with rock stars such as Madonna, Sting, Elton John, Jon Bon Jovi, Courtney Love, Prince and Jennifer Lopez, Donatella helped to transform the Versace label into a trademark with an international success. She joined the company as the director of photographic campaigns and later supervised the style of all the accessories and licensing lines, debuting as a complete fashion designer in 1993, when she designed her first Versus line. In 1997, following the murder of her brother, she

Sketch by Donatella Versace, gala evening gown.

took on the role of artistic director of the *maison* and, together with her brother Santo, she took over the direction of one of the largest luxury groups in the world. The Gianni Versace S.p.A. is one of the few *griffes* that control the entire production cycle of fashion products, from conception and design to production, marketing, and final sale, through boutiques that they run themselves and others in franchising. "Everything that I know about fashion I learned from Gianni. In particular, I can say that I learned from him always to try and seek out new things, even at considerable risk, and never to be afraid of criticism. The Versace style is constantly on a quest for what fashion is lacking," says Donatella who, with her collections, has added her own modern and personal touch to the Versace style, attaining significant development in areas not strictly linked to apparel: the expansion of the Home Collection line, the new cosmetics lines, the creation of the Atelier line. If Gianni was a pioneer in the use of image in advertising campaigns, Donatella certainly continued his tradition.

❑ 2002. Donatella confirmed her status as the favorite designer of the Asian market by winning the International Designer of the Year during the MTV Asia Awards. During the evening's events, in Singapore, Donatella won over candidates of the caliber of John Galliano, Stella McCartney, Marc Jacobs, Miuccia Prada.
❑ 2003. "This is the right time to make changes," said Donatella. And so in the two Parisian haute couture events, no runway, only presentation.
❑ After Britney Spears, the singer Christina Aguilera was the new spokesperson for the lines designed by the fashion designer. The new campaign saw the popstar dressed in leather pants and biker jackets, brown wool or white leather trench coats.

(*Maria Vittoria Alfonsi*)

Versace Gianni (1946-1997). "I am profound in my superficiality." That is how Versace used to describe himself, when he felt like analyzing himself, paraphrasing Friedrich Nietzsche, and openly declaring: "I like to read and I like to look, and I use those ideas and those stimuli freely in order to transform them into fashion." He was unrestrained in his quotations of others, in the way he freely mingled and contaminated genres and his use of history, even personal history; that is how this fashion designer succeeded, with an uncommon gift for synthesis and rigor in his excess, in becoming unique and recognizable. Among other things, in the invention of his label, a Medusa's head, a reference to Magna Graecia. "In Reggio Calabria, across from our house, there were relics of Graeco-Roman mosaics depicting the Gorgon, and we children would always go and play there. When the time came to select a symbol, I thought back to this ancient myth: those who fall in love with the Medusa cannot escape. And so why not suggest that those who are conquered by Versace cannot turn back? It is the seduction that never ends." The adventure of the young Calabrian, little interested in studies and who became his mother's main assistant in her dressmaker's shop and apparel store, began on 5 February 1972 with a trip to Milan: summoned by Ezio Nicosia and Salvatore Chiodini, he designed a collection for Florentine Flowers, and was immediately successful. His name began to circulate among the various apparel manufacturers who were turning into fashion houses: that same year the fashion designer worked for De Parisini in Santa Margherita and, beginning in 1973, he moved definitively to Milan to work with Callaghan, Genny and Alma. In 1976, the great leap forward: Santo Versace, his older brother and the student in the family (he had a degree in business from the university of Messina and had a studio in Reggio Calabria), came to Milan to lay the foundations of a company that would bear Gianni's name. The first collection to bear the fashion designer's name was presented on the runway of the Palazzo della Permanente in Milan in March 1978; in September, in the showroom in the Via della Spiga, the first menswear collection was presented. In twenty-five years of development, the *griffe* was transformed from a family-owned company (along with the two brothers, the little sister, Donatella Versace) into a successful national group. The image and the communications became absolute strong points for the Gianni Versace corporation: in 1979, not

Gianni Versace, 1992-1993 Fall-Winter Collection.

Gianni Versace, evening gown, 1992-1993.

even a year after his debut, he began working with the American photographer Richard Avedon, who immediately put his imprint on the advertising campaigns. The fashion of this designer stood out for the daring experimentation acompanied by the emphasis on the beauty of the models, who were less and less mannequins (i.e., just dummies wearing outfits), and increasingly models to admire and imitate (Linda Evangelista, Christy Turlington, Claudia Schiffer, Naomi Campbell). Versace began to communicate his image through a series of books: the first one was *Versace teatro* (1987) published by Franco Maria Ricci, the last one, published posthumously in December 1997, was *The Art of Being You* (Leonardo Arte, the publishing house of Leonardo Mondadori). From collection to collection, the fashion designer never placed limitations on his inspirations: leather treated and colored as fabric, presented in October 1981; outfits in metal mesh in Fall-Winter 1982-83; colorful silks, printed geometric motifs in 1989; leather and metal pins on the dizzying nudes of the early 1990s, causing an outcry of scandal over a supposed bondage (sado-maso) fashion in the mass media in America. That same press that, with a cover story in *Time* magazine, in April 1995, would hail him as the man of the moment and the champion of a new classicism: "He transmits signals of elegance without ever forgetting his distinctive note, eroticism." Once again there was a shift in his style, as he foreshadowed in an interview in September 1994, during a personal show at the Kunstgewerbe-museum in Berlin (one of a long series of shows which, beginning in September 1981, were to punctuate his career): "I try to use a light touch. Lightness is one of the most important things in life and also in culture, and I mean culture with a capital C. When you lack lightness, you slip into vulgarity. I like to think that what comes out of my head is a feather." The fashion designer had begun to give a sample of his lightness with his more experimental line, Atelier, a workship for the creation of high fashion models, presented for the first time, in January 1990 at the Hotel Ritz in Paris. In the meanwhile, on 6 July 1989, in Milan the Versus line was born, dedicated to young people, an alternative to the conventional way of dressing, and in 1991 Signature, a collection of Versace classics, followed, in 1993, by Home Signature, porcelains, underwear, tiles, and objects, which reflected the taste of the fashion designer for home furnishings. An eclectic taste, which was found in the interiors of his various homes, palazzi, and villas, in Italy and in the United States: from the former Palazzo Rizzoli in Via del Gesù, in Milan, redesigned by Renzo Mongiardino, to Villa Fontanelle at Moltrasio on Lake Como; from the town house in New York, furnished with the contributon of his various artist friends (Julian Schnabel and Roy Lichtenstein, Philip Taaffe, Francesco Clemente, and

Frank Moore) to Casa Casuarina in Miami's South Beach, where, on the front steps, Gianni Versace was murdered early on the morning of 15 July 1997. Twenty days before, on 25 June, he had presented in the Boboli Gardens in Florence, produced by Pitti Immagine, the last work that the fashion designer did for theater, in collaboration with Maurice Béjart: the ballet entitled *Barocco Bel Canto*. His career as a costume designer had begun on 19 March 1982 at the Teatro alla Scala in Milan Richard Strauss's *Josephslegende*, with the choreography of Joseph Russillo. In 1984, he first met Béjart and the beginning of a great friendship; but Versace would also work with Robert Wilson, Roland Petit, John Cox, William Forsythe, and Twyla Tharp."

❑ 2001. The year ended with production value of 521.59 million Euros, a 14.3 percent increase over 2000. The increase in profits, however, was limited, just 8.8 percent, because the company received "other income and revenue" equivalent to 29.56 million Euros. The gross operating margin, 47.97 million, dropped 6.9 percent, while operating profit, 18.54 million, dropped by 28.6.
❑ 2002. The consolidated turnover was 482.8 million Euros, registering a drop from 2001 of 5.4 percent; the gross operating margin, 39.8 million, dropped by 17.1 percent, while the operating profit, 13.4 million, dropped by 27.6 percent. The financial liabilities also grew worse, from 100.6 million to 129.9. "It has been a difficult year for the entire fashion and apparel sector," commented Santo Versace, "which was further hurt by the rise of the Euro against the dollar and the yen. All the same, we are convinced that our restructuring and revitalization plan will allow us to capture market opportunities."
❑ 2002, October. The major personal show that the Victoria and Albert Museum of London dedicated to the fashion designer was called *Gianni Versace at the V&A*. The show was curated by Claire Wilcox, author of the book *The Art and Craft of Gianni Versace*. On the occasion of the inauguration of the retrospective, his brother Santo said: "It has taken us two years to recover from his death. But Gianni is not really dead, he is just as powerful now as when he was alive."
❑ Ittierre, a company in the IT Holding group, would hold until Fall-Winter 2007-2008 the license of the apparel lines Versus, Versace Jeans Couture and Versace Jeans Signature. The collaboration between the holding and the label of the Medusa began in 1988.
❑ 2003, January. A ten-year agreement was signed with Luxottica for the design, the production and the marketing worldwide of Versace, Versus and Versace Sport eyewear. The licence, which can be renewed for another ten years, came after the acquisition of IC Optics, which since 1999 has been managing Versace's eyewear.

(*Maria Vittoria Carloni*)

Versolato Ocimar (1961). Brazilian fashion designer. He studied in Paris. After designing collections for Paloma Picasso and Lanvin, he had a label of his own for a clean and sensual fashion in a basically dark palette.

❑ The fashion designer, who had done a number of excellent collections for Jaguar, Tiffany and Vicuña, as well as his partnership with Lanvin, created three main product lines: OV Ocimar Versolato, Ocimar Versolato Luxo and OV Spor, as well as lingerie and perfumes O Boticario, on the market from 2002 on.

Vertès Marcel (1895-1961). Painter, illustrator. He worked for *Vogue*, illustrating the world of fashion and ateliers. Born in Budapest. He studied under Zala, the favorite sculptor of the emperor Franz Josef. In 1919, he moved to Vienna where he was successful as a billboard artist. But he considered it an expedient and little more. In 1925, he abandoned that successful career and left Vienna, traveling to Paris where he devoted himself to lithography: illustrations for numbered editions of Colette, Zola, and especially Pierre Louys and collaborations for fashion magazines.

Veruschka She was the tallest fashion model

– 1 meter 85 cm. – ever to tread the boards of the fashion runways. Angular, legs that reach to the sky, she was Richard Avedon's favorite model and the ideal subject for the body-painting launched by Holger Trukzsch in the 1970s. A symbol of the fatal and transgressive beauty of the 1960s, she played herself in *Blow-Up* (1966, Antonioni) and in a documentary by the photographer Franco Rubartelli presented at the Venice Film Festival in 1967. She was a countess, born Vera Gottliebe von Lehndorff (her father was one of the mutinous generals who organized the unsuccessful attempt to assassinate Hitler in 1944), and long ago she abandoned public life. (*Laura Salza*)

Vesperini Vannina (1974). Russian fashion designer. She has been in business for a number of years in Paris, she specializes in the concept of mix-lingerie, because the "top" is designed but so is the "bottom." Since 2003, she has had a Paris boutique in the Rue des Saints-Pères. She especially designs outfits made of silk, ispired by "pajamas," baby dolls, and corsetry, boxers and *bustiers*.

Vestra Major men's apparel manufacturer. It is over a century old, and was founded in 1894 in Alsace, where its headquarters are still located, in Bischwiller. Aside from its own label, it also produces for *griffes* such as Pierre Cardin, Cacharel and Ted Lapidus. It has 3,500 employees and a dozen plants in France and in Tunisia. It launched its "custom-made" program, in a week, for the same cost as a prêt-à-porter suit.

Vetrina di Beryl (La) Milanese shoe shop. Opened in March 1986, in the Via Statuto, it quickly established itself as a must for the more fashionable consumers. Unfailingly trendy, it offered footwear from Costume National, Free Lance and Ernesto Esposito and often reinterpreted the style of the most famous designers on an exclusive basis, in some cases modifying materials and colors. In 1996, it also launched an apparel collection, in line with its core philosophy that was always slightly avant-garde.
(*Valeria Vantaggi*)

VEV-Prouvost A French industrial group active in various sectors of the textile industry: it produces fibers to be used by the apparel industry, threads, cottons, and wools destined for retail sale (among the many, the best known is the Pingouin label) and cotton fabrics for the shirts designed by Pierre Clarence, Dior and Cardin. Created through a series of mergers, it had nearly 17,000 employees in 1987, and then just a little over 5,000 employees at the beginning of the 1990s, after restructuring and sales.

Vezzoli Francesco (1971). Fashion designer, an expert on embroidery and *arte povera*. He was a pupil of Alighiero Boetti. The techniques of *petit-point* embroidery and the art of pillow lace were the foundations of his artistic research. A revival, in a high fashion version, of the age-old techniques of embroidery that today survive in Italy only in Burano and in small towns in the center and south of the country. Vezzoli featured his creations in ironic videoperformances that involved legendary protagonists such as Audrey Hepburn, Veruschka, Silvana Mangano and Valentina Cortese. These techniques led to the creation of one-off or personalized items, occasionally through simple details or accessories such as handmade handbags, to be worn with designer evening gowns. (*Daniela Bolognetti*)

VF Corporation American textiles group. It is headquartered in Wyomissing, Pennsylvania. It controls 27 percent of the denim jeans market. It was founded in 1889, and the complete name is the *Vanity Fair* Corporation. After taking over the Wrangler and Lee jeans brands, it owns Jantzen (swimsuits and leotards), the Jansport backpack line, and the Spanish Vivesa company, reinforcing its control of the lingerie sector. Today, the group employs some 63,000 people.

❑ 1999. The company celebrated the centennial of its foundation by absorbing six new brands: Brittania, Bestform, Lily of France, Fibrotek, Penn State Textile and Horace Small.
❑ 2000. Acquisition of the brands Eastpack, Gitano, Chic Jeans, North Face and His.
❑ 2001. VF Corporation launched its new internal lines of knitwear and swimwear. At the same time, the

company took measures to reduce costs, which should result in savings of 115 million dollars a year.

❑ At the end of 2002 the company became profitable again, with a 6 percent increase in sales over the same period of the year before. As for the annual balance sheet, the net loss remained 154.5 million dollars, but the top management predicted a slight improvement in sales volume for the end of 2003, thanks especially to the sectors of outdoor wear, jeanswear and intimate wear. It was for these three sectors that further acquisitions were expected during the year.

❑ The label that did best in the European market in 2002 was Lee. It brought in double-digit growth and opened a London flagship store. Wrangler focused on the Asian market instead, with openings in China and Russia.

❑ 2003, May. The first London and European shop of The North Face, brand in the VF universe, opened. The opening of the eighth retail outlet of the sports label crowned a clearly positive year, which saw sales in Europe, in the first quarter of 2003, rise by 73 percent compared with the same period in the previous year.

VGrantham Uomo A menswear line designed by Victoria Grantham, an English fashion designer who lives and works in Milan. The debut of the collection: Fall-Winter 2001. In 2002 she had a new licensing contract for manufacturing and distribution, with the GILD in Coriano (Rimini), which offered new opportunities for advancement to the menswear of Victoria Grantham. She was an assistant to Donna Karan and Marc Jacobs and even before that, the winner of a scholarship for the section Classical Men's Apparel by Alfred Dunhill. The fashion designer reconsidered each season the techniques and tradition of Savile Row, merging them with the trends of the moment. For this reason, as well, in the Fall-Winter 2003 collection – dedicated to a hero somewhere between punk and military – she inserted a flash of outfits made to measure. (*Antonio Mancinelli*)

Via de' Calzaiuoli This is the heart of the historical center of di Florence: it runs from Piazza della Signoria to Piazza Duomo. The name comes from the *calzolai*, the artisan and merchants of the canvas footwear with soles that were so popular among the fashionable young people in Florence from the fourteenth to the sixteenth centuries. But already in the Middle Ages, the street was the center of the city business district. Overlooking this street were monuments of the importance of Orsanmichele, the thirteenth-century grain silo that was later transformed into a church, the most Florentine monument in Florence, as it has been called, because of its mixed character, both civil and religious. Over the centuries, the street, made into a pedestrian thoroughfare and closed off to cars, has preserved its original quality as a shopping center, becoming an obligatory passage for city shopping and tourism, in a cheerful but also chaotic melting pot of styles that range from youthful trend shops to souvenir shops and deluxe jewelers.

Vicini A pool of companies that includes a footwear manufacturer, an embroidery plant, and a heel plant. Total employees, approximately 400. It not only produces the collection of shoes with its name, but also the line by Roberto Cavalli, DSquared and Giuseppe Zanotti Design, respected for its unique creations; especially famous is the denim boot, tattered and distressed, invented for Britney Spears.

Victoire Chain of boutiques (four in Paris, four in the rest of France and one in Tokyo) and label of ready-to-wear fashion distributed also in Italy. The first store was opened by Alain Lalonde in Paris, in the Place des Victoires. The fashion designer on an exclusive basis at the time was Catherine Chaillet, who designed the fabrics, and selected and offered accessories. In 1965 Lalonde monopolized the square with another retail outlet of only men's prêt-à-porter. Two years later, he sold it all to Antoine Riboud, who hired Françoise Chassagnac to manage it. The Victoire line has been characterized over the years, as a classical fashion with minimalist sytle. The men's and women's outfits are always made of natural fabrics (linen, cotton, cashmere and wool) and the colors, never garish, tend to oscillate between black, dark blue, hemp, and white. The knitwear (this statistic is from 1999) constitutes 40 percent of production.

❑ Under the management of Gilles Riboud, the family-owned company expanded, with 11 shops for menswear, womenswear, and accessories in French territory. The most recently opened shop is the one in Saint Tropez, in the Boulevard Louis Blanc.

Victor Sally (1905-1977). A particularly innovative American milliner, she made hats shaped like Chinese lanterns, accordions, and even inspired by the architecture of Frank Lloyd Wright. Born in Scranton, Pennsylvania, after studying painting in Paris, she began her career very young at Macys department stores. After marrying Sergiu Victor in 1927, the managing director of Serge, a manufacturer of hats, she became the company's first fashion designer. But the real turning point came in 1934 when she founded her own company. She was the one who launched the little sailor hat in the 1930s, contributing to the creation of a women's style that was both saucy and easy-going. Her creations met with the favor of Mamie Eisenhower, Eleanor Roosevelt, Queen Elizabeth II, and Judy Garland. She retired in 1968 at just the right time, that is, when American fashion was beginning to tend toward casual wear, making hats an increasingly marginal accessory.

(*Eleonora Attolico*)

Victoria and Albert Museum Founded by Queen Victoria as an expression of the tastes and trends that developed during her reign, this museum, inaugurated in 1840 with the specific intent of assembling a collection of fine fabrics and to design new materials for high couture and tailoring, came to focus over time on fashion. It now contains the world's most important collection (80,000 items) in the areas of fabrics, outfits and costumes. Since 1971, it has chosen to focus its attention on the creatives of the twentieth century. Among the most popular rooms, is the one prepared by Cecil Beaton for the permanent exhibition entitled *400 Years of Fashion*. Over time the museum has expanded its interests to include other sectors of arts and crafts. (*Anna Santini*)

The Victoria and Albert Museum in London has the world's most important collection of fashion. From its archives, a sketch by Victor Stiebel.

Victoria's Secret American brand of women's underwear. Founded in San Francisco at the beginning of the 1970s, it was purchased in 1982 by The Limited Inc. From that moment on, it began its great expansion, with the opening of 790 shops throughout the United States. The growth of the company, which is headquartered in Ohio, has been progressive, to the point that nowadays there are over a thousand sales outlets, most of which are located in major shopping centers. Each year, at least 370 million copies of the catalogue are mailed out to every corner of the United States. By mail and by Internet. The company's national and international reputation has also been enchanced by the linking of its image to important top models, such as Laetitia Casta, Gisele Bundchen and Tyra Banks. Some feminist groups have repeatedly protested the company's policies and operations.

❑ At the beginning of the new century, from its headquarters in Columbus, Ohio, Victoria's Secret distributes its production of lingerie, pajamas and

knitwear to more than 1,000 stores in the United States. Recently created is Victoria's Secret Beauty, a line of cosmetics.
❑ 2003, September. It was among the 100 exhibitors invited to the first Salon of Intimatewear organized by Expo CTS. After the closure of the Bologna event, Intimate, the event held at the Milan Fiera is the only initiative in the sector in Italy. (*Francesca Gentile*)

Victor Victoria Italian ready-to-wear fashion label. It was owned by the Sartorie Riunite. It was founded in the late 1980s. The company, founded by Giovanni and Paola Gamba, was located in Molina di Malo, Vicenza. In Milan, it had its showroom. In 1992 Giambattista Gamba, with a degree from the University of California in Berkeley, joined the company as director in charge of corporate strategies, stylistic and product decisions. Victor Victoria, a style that emphasized the alternation of masculine and feminine elements, capturing and emphasizing contemporary aspects of dress, produces and distributes 200,000 items through over 500 sales outlets in Italy and around the world.

Victor Victoria, outfit from the 1999-2000 Fall-Winter Collection.

❑ 2000. The brand was fully absorbed by SINV, a Vicenza-based company that holds a considerable share of Moschino and the licenses for the production of brands such as R.e.d. Valentino and DKNY Jeans by Donna Karan.
❑ 2002. The company took part for the first time in Pitti Immagine Uomo. The line presented, Victor Victoria Uomo, found "hospitality" in pavilion devoted to brands with a strong tendency to develop new ideas.
❑ 2002. For Winter, Victor Victoria sent a collection onto the runway that took its inspiration from the Middle and Far East.
❑ 2003. For the Fall-Winter collection, Victor Victoria chose once again to focus on ethnic heritage. In the season when Vivienne Westwood put men with false breasts on the runways, the maison of Giovanni and Paola Gamba made use of the clothing tradition of the Amish people. (*Silvia Martinenghi*)

Vicuña A fine wool. It is the warmest and especially the rarest wool, described as the "fiber of the gods." It is taken from a member of the Camelidae family of the Andean steppes. It was used by Inca emperors. In 1960, the vicuñas had dropped in number from over a million in 1400 to fewer than 5,000 head. Six years later, marketing of vicuña was forbidden, in order to allow repopulation under close monitoring. In 1976, the Convention of Washington listed vicuñas as an endangered species. In 1987, Peru asked the Convention if it could shear and market the wool of a small percentage of vicuñas. The shares of wool, however small, were purchased by the Italian manufacturers Loro Piana, Agnona and Condor Tips (Peruvian), companies considered to be among the most reliable on earth. Vicuña can only be threaded to a fineness of 12 microns, compared with the 15 microns minimum of cashmere. Vicuña is long and silky, a wheat color or a bright tawny hue. Every adult animal produces 250 grams of wool every two years, very little in comparison with the still invaluable merino sheep (3-4 kilos yearly), and little enough compares with an exceedingly rare cashmere she-goat (300-500 grams yearly). A vicuña overcoat requires the fleece of 25-30 Camelidae.
(*Giuliana Zabeo Ricca*)

Vidotto Giovanni. Illustrator and dress designer. Endowed with great taste and skill, he has worked for Ferré, Genny, Ferragamo. He is one of those assistants, one of those *coéquipiers* who work in the shadows but are often decisive to the outcome of a collection.

Vieira Miguel (1966). Portuguese fashion designer. Born on the island of Madeira, he studied art and design and took a course in textile quality-control in Oporto. He has worked in the world of fashion since 1988. In 1989 he began to design his own collection, which was characterized by an elevated level of elegance and personality. Beginning in 1991 he debuted on the runways of Portugal. In recent years, he has expanded his line, including a number of items of sportswear and an array of accessories that range from shoes to bags in all shapes and sizes. Of particular note is his collaboration on the design of Guess! shoes.
(*Estefania Ruilope Ruiz*)

Vigna Giorgio (1955). Sculptor, creator of design objects, set designer, costume designer, and creator of decorations for stage and fashion, he has already produced a rich line of jewelry, sometimes conceived as one-offs, at other times as limited editions. He was born in Verona. He has staked his reputation on glass, which he "developed" into various forms of expression. He is a teacher at the Istituto Europeo di Design, and he has often taken inspiration from the natural, geological, and mineral world, shaping glass and resins into plastic forms, to which metal is added with purely structural functions. In other cases, however, he has used gold as a material on its own, rich in symbolic values. In 1999 he created sculptural jewels in Murano glass dedicated to the four elements: Water, Earth, Fire, and Air. He has made vass – Sasso, Fonte, Stilla, Fuochi d'acqua – and ornaments – the Talismans – for Venini, where since 2003 he has been the artistic director for the Progetto Gioielli ('jewels project'). He serves in the same position for the Gruppo Italian

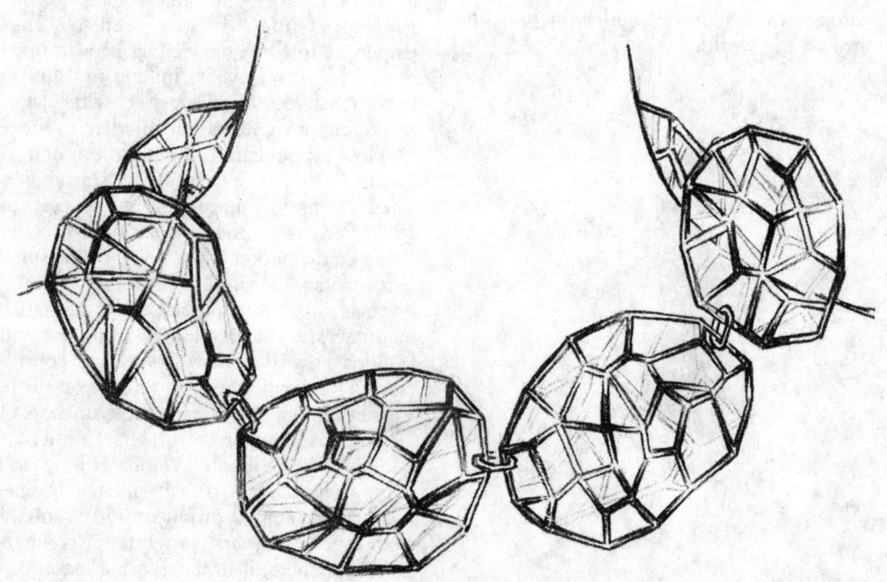

Preliminary sketch for a bracelet, by Giorgio Armani.

Luxury Industrie, which is also affiliated with the Murano glassmaker. His creations are on display at the Studio Giorgio Vigna in Milan, the Galerie Naila de Mombrison in Paris and the Studio Miscetti in Rome. In 2003, he had persona shows at the Museo Correr in Venice and at the Museo Villa Pignatelli in Naples.

(*Alessandra Quattordio*)

Vigneau André (1892-1968). French photographer. He studied painting in Bordeaux and Paris and opened a studio in Lausanne and then returned to Paris in 1920 where he did advertising illustrations to live and continued to paint and sculpt. The mannequins that he created for the Siégel company were immortalized by Man Ray. In 1930 he opened a major studio for advertising photography (among the clients were Bugatti, Vuitton, Kodak, Dunhill, Sandoz, Grand Maison de Blanc) where, in 1931, Robert Doisneau began working as a young assistant. He was interested in the mixture of various languages, and he began to travel in Europe, Russia and the United States. He then moved from 1940 to 1949 to Cairo where he directed the Egyptian film studios. He later returned to Paris as the director of production for French television.

Vignelli Lella (1931) and Massimo (1931). Architects and designers. They designed unisex outfits with strict, spare lines, vaguely based on Maoist uniforms. They did so in the United States, in New York, where they have run a highly successful studio since 1971 which, among other things, designed all the signage for the subway system. After their studies (Lella in Venice and at the Massachusetts Institute of Technology; Massimo in Milan and in Venice), they worked in Chicago and Milan. In 1981, the Padiglione d'Arte Contemporanea in Milan held an anthological show of their projects.

Vigolo Mario (1899-1978). Italian illustrator and designer. The brother of Giorgio Vigolo (a well known musicologist, who won the Bagutta prize in 1961 with his book *Le notti romane,* and a critic for the Italian newsweekly *Il Mondo*), after graduating from the Academy of Fine Arts he immediately began to design fashion outfits and fabrics. In the 1930s, his creations were shown in the display windows of Piperno, on the Corso in Rome. He was one of the official illustrators invited to Paris for the diffusion and importation of French fashion to Italy. He worked with the Sartoria Zecca, the Sorelle Botti, Rina Pedrini and many other major names. He illustrated and commented on fashion in such specialty magazines as *Moda*, *Fantasie d'Italia*, *Lidel* and *La Donna*. In the postwar period as well, he collaborated with many high fashion houses, such as Veniceni, Schuberth, Carosa, Antonelli, Sorelle Fontana and Albertina. The magazine that made the greatest use of his illustrations was *Costume*.

Viktor & Rolf Label of the Dutch fashion designers Viktor Horsting and Rolf Snoeren, both born in 1969 in the southern Netherlands, the same Holland that produced so many "subversive" cultural movements that contributed to the creative expressions of the present day. For them, too, it is possible to speak of an alliance between couture and conceptual art. The pair met while they were still students in the fashion section of the Academy of Arnhem, where they graduated in 1992. The following year, they created their first collection, Viktor & Rolf, due to a "decision that was artistic, not practical," and they won the competition of the Festival International Créateurs d'Hyères. From then on, they have taken prize after prize in a series of creations that rejects all compromises with commercial reality. In contrast with many of their "official" colleagues, they prefer to be present, with the outfits-qua-installations ("fashion must be able to be everything except useful," the duo sings out in unison, criticized as being anti-feminists and anti-modern), in galleries of art and only later in runway presentations. After a first attempt in France, with the Fall-Winter 1998-1999 collection, based on overcoats and outfits made out of genuine vintage Puccis and Diors, they continued to debut in Paris with their couture collection for Summer 1999. The model Maggie Rizer was covered by them, in a happening that was ten outfits long, with overlapping creations, one worn over the other, increasingly embroidered and bulky, until the model was wearing seventy kilos of clothing and embroideries for a womanly figure that was no longer even slightly human: only a dream, an icon, a secularly chic

Madonna. Much discussed for their vision of clothing so old-fashioned that it is transgressive and avant-garde, they are beloved by magazines like *Visionaire*. They are working on a sort of meta-fashion: a fashion that is that reflects itself and its systems of communications and allure. On the one hand, the duo operates with painstaking care of outfits that are virtually sculptures with proportions that are all wrong (necks that are "too high," accumulations of ornaments with necklaces made of Christmas decorations, abnormal dresses that prevent movement, exaggeratedly voluminous sleeves, excessive skirts, and jabots afflicted with giantism) but executed with absolutely exquisite tailoring. On the other hand, they work on the example of Duchamp and his "ready mades," creating in 1996 a "virtual" perfume that only exists as an (empty) bottle, which is in turn a parody of the bottle of the legendary Chanel N. 5. They sold hundreds. The result? A genuine prêt-à-porter collection for Summer 2000, presented in New York, which destabilized the American Dream with tailored suits and jackets in exuberant stars-and-stripes prints; the commission for the uniforms of the staff of the Central Museum of Utrecht (soberly made of hand-stitched denim); and the definitive consecration in Paris of their couture line, which was included on the official calendar. In January 2003, the men's line was launched.

(*Antonio Mancinelli*)

❑ 2003, October. The Dutch duo celebrates its first ten years of activity in Paris, with an exhibition entitled *Viktor&Rolf par Viktor&Rolf*, which reviews all their stylistic innovations in the field of high fashion, where they started, all the way down to their latest prêt-à-porter collection. With the exhibition for the tenth anniversary show, the presences in the museums rise to more than thirty, almost a record for young designers.

❑ 2004, October. On the occasion of the spectacular runway presentation for the Spring/Summer 2005 collection, the first perfume, Flowerbomb, produced by Oréal, is introduced, with a bottle that is a cross between a giant gem and a grenade. On the runway, two types of women: the first, in total black, wearing motorcycle helmets, the second, after the coup-de-theatre, completely dressed in ribbons in all shades of pink.

❑ 2005, April. In Milan, their first single-label boutique is inaugurated. Seventy square meters with upside-down interiors, so that you walk on the ceiling and the fireplace, throw rugs, and chairs are on the ceiling and the lamps are hanging upwards from the ceiling on the floor.

Village There are many fashion designers who have taken their inspiration from this neighborhood in New York, or better, from the multiracial population that circulates there day and night, innovating their collections, beginning from the street, from spontaneous fashion. Some, like Gianni Versace and Donna Karan, have admitted this publicly, others have not. But it is in any case here, between Washington Square and Bleeker Street, that the creativity of the American melting pot is at its best, The young people of the Village often have no money for clothes: and so they recycle old clothing and old fashions, they invent new combinations and solutions that then they will find, reworked and refined, the following season in the chic display windows of Fifth or Sixth Avenue. Merchants have long since sensed the possibilities of selling used clothing, and so they palm off at absurd prices vintage rags upon Japanese tourists or the scions of New York's well-to-do families. The stretch of Broadway, which cuts through the Village, between Eighth Street and Twenty-Third Street, is packed with this sort of vintage clothing shops, and it is an odd coincidence because it was precisely on this stretch of Broadway, at the end of the nineteenth century, that Ladies' Mile extended, the most fashionable shopping area. For that matter, the Village is also filled with little T-shirt shops and large chain stores like the Gap or Banana Republic. In the West Village, around Christopher Street, gay fashion is concentrated – often only to be coopted by the heterosexuals as well – while in the East Village it is still possible to find bars and restaurants where the passage of major figures in American culture, such as Allen Ginsberg and Bob Dylan, does not yet seem to be shrouded in the mists of the past. In the Village, in any case, it is still possible to breathe the air of freedom, outside of constricted rules, and in a costant state of evolution, despite the fact that long ago artists and intellectuals abandoned the Village in a quest for new areas in New York, such as TriBeCa or Harlem.

(*Enrico Bonerandi*)

Villi Olga (professional name of Olga Villani, 1922-1989). Theater actress. She won fame as a fashion model, on the eve of the Second World War. She was a peasant born in the countryside around Mantua, and then moved to Milan for work, becoming a "piscinina," or go-fer, doing all lines of work, from stitching to deliveries, in a dressmaker's studio. She was tall, beautiful, remarkable in appearance and very determined in learning posture and gait, just as she was later to learn, with the same determination, diction and recitation. She was noticed by Biki who tested her as a mannequin. Olga enjoyed immediate success and soon was working alternately on runway presentations and in roles as a soubrette with Macario and Nino Taranto. In 1945, Luchino Visconti signed her up for a small part in Hemingway's *The Fifth Column*. She remained a theatrical actress for the rest of her career.

20/100 Vincent Dumas A label of men's ready-to-wear fashion. It debuted in 1993. Clearly, the *20/100* name is a French pun: "vingt-cent" sounds like "Vincent." The French designer Dumas designed clothing that attempted to escape from the rigid strictures of men's apparel. He named two of his runway presentations *Afrique* and *Paris Jazz*.

Vinogradova Victoria. Russian fashion designer and set designer. After graduating from the Academy of Applied Arts in Moscow, she immediately began her career. She designed an avant-garde prêt-à-porter, in some cases it could even be called aggressive, with working and finishing that enriched each fabric as well as an on-going process of research, especially on materials. Her women were 'bad girls' with a romantic spirit and, on the other hand, a rocker style with plenty of embroideries and ribbons. In general, her collections were message of total escape, contradictory sensations greeted with enthusiasm by her young audience. She is already very popular in Russia. She participated successfully in the collective show of Russian fashion designers in March 1996, at the Milan Fiera.

(*Lucia Mari*)

Vintage A cultural phenomenon. A sentimental concept. A transverse trend. Which, instead of wearing the clothing of novelty, prefers to wear memories. In fashion, vintage is the rehabilitation of the cult of the "poor" look of the 1970s, which for wearing only used clothing as a way to reject a political and social system intended to promote – according to the "revolutionary" thinking of the time – induced needs for capitalistic consumer goods. From the 1990s on, 'used' clothing played a new and unprecedented role, that of custodian of memories. It is no accident that the etymology of the term descends directly from the language of the oenologist, and from an Anglo-French phoneme: "vintage" originally refers to the year of a grape harvest, and therefore to a fine old wine. Equally ripened were the outfits revived in this move "back to the future," revived from second-hand stores to new life in specialty clothing boutiques that featured previously worn clothing (in Milan Cavalli and Nastri and Franco Jacassi, in Lugo di Romagna A.N.G.E.L.O., in Paris Didier Ludot, Catherine Arrigoni, Les Trois Marchés and Le Bonheur de Sophie, in London the vendors of Portobello Road and Notting Hill, in New York Little O and Resurrection, in Los Angeles Paper Bag Princess). In Italy, a central location of vintage fashion is the second-hand fair that is held at the Castello di Belgioioso, in the province of Pavia. But this is not the end of its allure, in the retro flavor of accessories and outfits that have been "recycled" from intense periods of fashion creativity: the 1950s, the 1960s, and the 1970s. In a certain sense, even the great affirmation of ethnic style can be interpreted as Vintage. Which in any case responds to a two-fold demand of contemporary aesthetics. On the one hand, the requirement of satisfying the unprecedented demand of assembling in total mental freedom outfits that come from different eras and styles, thus appointing vintage as a true exemplar of the Postmodern Wardarobe. Protagonist: the free-form recovery of items and accessories subject to reinterpretations (sweatclothes that lose their sleeves and become skirts, shirts that are transformed into bags, trenchcoats recut into evening wear). On the other hand, it corresponds to more deep-seated motivations: the desire for stability, security, reliability. Which, in uncertain times like the ones we live in, become inevitable and crucial requirements. The perennial confusion of the debate over everyone's everyday life, increasingly invasive technology, the disorder of conflicting socio-cultural signals all trigger a yearning for a genuinity "*d'antan*" which has a great deal to do with Romanticism and tradition. This helps to explain why, over recent years, many fashion houses have worked directly upon used clothing (the first to do so was the Belgian designer Martin Margiela, followed by the American Susan Cianciolo and the Italian Antonio Marras) or else have created specialty lines in simil-vintage fashion. Or else brand-new outfits that seem old, from ripped and restitched jeans all the way down to the patchwork of antique fabrics for mass production. The principal antidote to the "most deep-rooted syndrome of our contemporary age, an addiction to the new and the future, rendering obsolete anything that is not brand spanking new" (James Hillmann), the "old" – whether real or merely apparent – will save this world, too crazed with a thirst for the new.

(*Antonio Mancinelli*)

Viola Sandro (1931). Italian journalist and major writer in the panorama of Italian publishing over the last half century. Born in Taranto, at an early age he was already reporting, in January 1958, on the fifteenth edition of Italian High Fashion, the runway presentations in the Sala Bianca, for *L'Illustrazione Italiana*. He was the first journalist to "focus" on an essential component of the "color" of the runway presentations: the fashion journalists. From then on, as a feature reporter, he was sent to cover the fashion events in Florence, as well as Paris, Milan, New York, and London, where he focused on the "specialists." Viola noted: "Dressed in fatigues, assailed by haste, the fashion journalists present at the Sala Bianca suggested, with the sheer power of their disenchantment, their skepticism, and the depth of their boredom, the image of the veteran boxing reporter, an image that the American cinema created through the wonderful acting of Humphrey Bogart, who made that role the very emblem of disillusionment." He worked at *L'Espresso*, he was a correspondent for *La Stampa*, and he was one of the founders of *La Repubblica* where he was an editorialist and for which paper he traveled as an international correspondent, as a political analyst, but with the love of things seen and tasted that is more typical of the literary correspondents of another era. In journalism, and not only in journalism, he is one of the last, elegant dandies.

Vionnet Madeleine (1876-1975). French dressmaker. She sublimated the bias cut and brought many innovations into Parisian fashion between the two World Wars. She revolutionized dressmaking technique to the degree that she was compared, in the world of haute couture, to the protagonists of the avant-gardes painting in the twentieth century. Often, she would cut her creations in a single piece, sleeve included. She was especially interested in the perfect drop and drape of her outfits. In 1973, the Metropolitan Museum of New York held a

Outfit by Madeleine Vionnet in a sketch by Thayaht, published in the *Gazette du Bon Ton*, 1923.

major retrospective show of her work while she was still alive. In 1990, Editions du Regard published a biography: *Vionnet* by Jacqueline Demornex. She learned the trade in a little shop in the banlieue of Paris. At the age of 21, after a more-refined apprenticeship in a boutique of women's underwear in the Rue de la Paix, a divorce, and the tragedy of a daughter's death, she moved to London where she began working for the dressmaker Kate Reilly. When, in 1901, she returned to France she had sufficient credentials to be hired as a première by Madame Gerber, the fashion designer for the Callot sisters. In 1907 she went to work for Doucet and stayed there for five years, creating outfits that were moving against the grain, in contrast with the waning style of Art Nouveau. Her creations were light and airy, and they were modeled without corsets or busts (Poiret too had eliminated) and also creating shoes. In 1912 she opened her *maison*. Two years later, she was forced to suspend operations because the First World War had broken out. At the end of the war, her bias cut, her lavish drapery, which she tried and tried again on a dressmaker's dummy 80 cm tall, and with a lavish use of fabric that made cost no object, ensured her a place in the spotlight. In 1922 the *maison* took offices at 50, Avenue Montaigne. Some ten years later, her success was documented by the existence of 20 ateliers on five stories and more than 1,000 employees, including premières, directors, sellers, tailors, seamstresses, administrative clerks, shop clerks, and delivery boys. The fashion designer had her alter ego in the dressmaker Marcelle Chapsal. She began working with her in 1912 and made her a partner, splitting the fashion house into two divisions. Her creations (almost always in crêpe, crêpe de chine, gabardine and satin) were so distinctive, destructured and draped, that often her clients required lessons in order to learn how to put them on. She was a trendsetter and was widely imitated, even when, in 1935, she shifted to Romanticism, with taffeta ribbons. She had closed up shop in 1914, at the outbreak of the First World War. She closed her business definitively in 1939 and retired for good, at the outbreak of the Second World War. She was 63 years old. She died 36 years later, just months short of turning 100 years old. (*Renata Molho*)

Outfit by Muguette for the Maison Vionnet, from the Twenties (from *Histoire de la mode au XX siècle*, by Y. Deslandres and F. Müller, Sornogy, 1986).

Viscardi Italian furrier house, founded by Giuseppe Viscardi, in 1904. It was especially popular in the first few decades of the twentieth century and in the effervescent Turin, a center for arts and fashion. It opened a subsidiary in Rome (which would continue to operate until the 1950s) and, in the 1930s, it moved its Turin store to the newly renovated Via Roma. Following the death of the founder, his son Luigi took over the company, expanding the made-to-order high-market furrier business into a more industrial production. The best years coincided with the postwar period and the so-called Italian economic miracle which led to a booming market for furs as status symbols. He organized the furriers of the city into an association, and was its chairman for many years. He also opened a shop in Milan. His early death led to the decline of the *maison* which was unable to withstand the animal-rights movement, and the new fashion that had long been allergic to fine furs, and it ceased operations in the early 1990s.

Viscose and Rayon Fibers. They were the

product of the process of cellulose spinning discovered in 1891 by da C.F. Cross and E.J. Bevan, two chemists who patented the process in 1892. It was only many years later that Courtaulds Ltd. began to market rayon in America as well with the label The American Viscose Co. Used during the Second World War, viscose and rayon immediately caught the attention of international business: Du Pont de Nemours Co., Industrial Rayon Corporation, American Enka Co., SNIA Viscosa, Glanzstoff, and Toyo. Viscose and rayon are the most common materials used to make imitation silk. The continuing research into viscose has made it irreplaceable because of its remarkable versatility. It is used either pure or in a blend with other natural or synthetic materials that exalt its image and intrinsic value.

Visibilia Italian eyewear manufacturer. It exports to about 70 countries with its own sales organization in Austria, Germany, Denmark, Switzerland and Spain. It has production of more than 1.5 million items annually. Among its lines are Anne Marie Perris and Chagall, with a very broad range, in metal, plastic, and combined materials.

❑ 2000, May. On the occasion of MIDO in Milan, Visibilia announced that signing of an agreement with Stefanel for the production of a line of eyewear for the Treviso-based company.
❑ 2002. Mandarina Duck, part of the Finduck group, signed a licensing agreement with Visibilia. The new collection of sunglasses was presented in March.

Visionaire American quarterly of fashion and art. It has circulation of just 2,000 copies but it is more influential than any other magazine in the United States. Each issue is monothematic. It was founded and is run by Stephen Gan, fashion editor of the monthly *Details*, the model Cecilia Dean and James Kaliardo, make-up artist and hairdresser. They call it an "album of inspiration." The first issue, which came out in 1991, cost 10 dollars at the newsstand and 10,000 dollars to produce. The twenty-fourth issue, for which Tom Ford, fashion designer at Gucci, agreed to become an art director, sold for 425 dollars and all included, the entire edition cost 1.5 billion liras to produce. It is practically hand-made, and it has continuous and financially burdensome inventions of packaging. Its attitude toward fashion is one of detached irony. It attacks, without fatally wounding, the protagonists of the *griffes*. Humor is, in any case, the key to the success of this publication, which continues to operate without advertising.

Vitale Barberis Canonico Manufacturer of menswear fabrics in wool, mohair, cashmere. It was founded in Prativero di Biella in 1936 and is still owned by the same family. Turnover, which in 1993 amounted to 72 billion liras reached, in 1998, 111 billion liras. It produces more than 4.5 million meters of fabric, against the 3.5 million of 1993.

Vittadini Adrienne (1944). American fashion designer of Hungarian descent. The mass media have called her "the queen of knitwear." From Budapest, her birthplace, Adrienne Toth (Vittadini by marriage) emigrated to the United States in 1956. After working for various knitwear companies, in 1972 she opened her own company. For her collections she drew inspiration from Calder, Picasso and Miró, as well as from the Dick Tracy comic strips. She created original fabrics using Italian threads. Her lines are practical and modern, but very feminine. She renewed the knitwear industry by developing new computerized techniques.

Vitti Angelo (1958). Italian fashion designer. He presented for the first time "off the calendar" in Rome in January 2000. He was noted for his painted outfits and for those embroidered with modern solutions. He graduated from the Liceo Artistico in the Via di Ripetta in Rome and the Accademia di Belle Arti, and entered the world of fashion when he was 20.

Vitti Barbara (1939). Italian public relations consultant. She was born in Milan, and began to breathe the air of fashion as a little girl, attending runway presentations with her mother Gemma, a fashion journalist, and helping her in her work. She became a fashion editor, but she was almost immediately invited to work at SNIA-Viscosa in public relations. She was in charge of image for Armani (1980), then for Valentino (1986) and the Inghirami Group (1992). Now she is in charge of various social events and communications, often for major houses.

Vitti Gemma (1902-1992). Fashion journalist. She began her career, however, as an an illustrator for the Galtrucco shop in Milan. She moved on to journalism when she was hired by the Milanese afternoon daily *Il Corriere Lombardo* to write a woman's column. In that period, the postwar period and the 1950s, she also worked for other magazines such as *Beauté* and *Lei*. But her real rise to a higher level came when the weekly *Alba* put her in charge of all the magazines fashion pages, and she invented a new way of presenting the runway presentations. She called it "subject coverage": she would write a plot and have the models act it out, making use of set designers and artists.

Vivier Roger (1907-1998). French designer of footwear. "The secret," he once said, "is to discover the age-old forms and then reinterpret them in the light of the present-day, with the improvements required by our more frantic gait, a less formal custom of using exquisite models, a time reserved only for those rare ceremonial occasions." A fairly simple definition, but one which describes the heart of his creations. A sculptor of shoes, a tireless inventor, a fanciful experimenter, in his long career he has written an important chapter in the history of fashion and accessories. Virgola, Cancan, Pulcinella, Guignol are just a few of the names that he gave to his prestigious creations now in the collection of the Victoria and Albert Museum in London, the Metropolitan Museum in New York, the Musée des Arts et de la Mode in Paris. Born in Paris, he studied at the Ecole des Beaux Arts, discovering the world of shoemaking almost by accident, urged by a few friends to design an extravagant collection. This led to the beginning of a long career which led him to work with Pinet and Bally in France, Rayne and Turner in Great Britain, and Miller and Delman in the United States. And it was an orthopaedic shoe that he designed for Delman and which was rejected, but later made by Elsa Schiaparelli, that launched in the 1940s the fashion of stacks, or wedge-heeled shoes. He stayed in the United States during the Second World War, and he opened with Suzanne Remi, in Madison Avenue, a millinery shop that soon proved to a meeting place for all those who followed fashion. In 1947, upon his return to Paris, he met Christian Dior, who appointed him to supervise the styling of his shoes. From "custom shoes," Vivier shifted, widely imitated, to a prêt-à-porter line. His partnerships with the Maison Dior lasted for ten years. In 1957, he started his own business.

(*Giuliana Parabiago*)

❑ 2000. The brand is purchased by the Della Valle Group.
❑ 2001, March. Roger Vivier is licensed on an exclusive basis to Tod's.
❑ 2002. The revival of the brand begins with a collaboration with the shoe designer Bruno Frisoni and a profound research into the archives of the footwear couturier in order to rediscover its entire past and repropose it in a modern context.

Viyella Trade name given in 1894 to an English-made fabric, light and gauzy, in a twill weave, in a 55 percent wool and 45 percent cotton blend. Soft and warm, it was originally used for making night shirts and men's underwear, it is now used for men's and women's daytime shirts.

Vogel Lucien (1886-1954). French illustrator, journalist, publisher. He was the artistic director di Fémina. Together with Michel de Brunhoff, he founded, in 1912, *La Gazette du Bon Ton*. It is to his credit that fashion periodicals began to use artists such as Barbier, Drian, Lepape, and Martin to document outfits and trends. He was the founder of the magazine *Jardin des Modes*, which was later acquired by Condé Nast and which he edited, even after the Second World War. He was the the editor, in the 1920s, of the French edition of *Vogue*.

(*Luigi Chiavarone*)

Vogt Christian (1946). Swiss photographer. After studying at the School of Decorative Arts in Basel, he traveled extensively, worked as an assistant in Munich for Will McBride and, since 1970, has run a studio of his own in Basel, where he lives. He is well known for his refined work on artistic nudes, and he is successful in fashion and advertising, working with the magazines *Du*, *Camera*, *Photo*, and *Life* and holding many personal and collective shows.

Vogue American fashion magazine, founded in 1892 by Arthur B. Turnure. When Condé William Nast, the son of a renowned American cartoonist, purchased the magazine in 1909, it became the most respected fashion magazine in the world. Thanks to the untiring energy and the extraordinary acumen of the journalist Edna Woolman Chase, who worked for *Vogue* from 1895 until 1957, Nast, a skilled "dream merchant," succeeded in hiring the best known illustrators of the period, such as Lepape, Vertés and Benito, and the most respected writers. But it was photography that became his obsession, and in fact he was one of the first to consider it as an authentic art form. Nast persuaded Cecil Beaton, who had joined *Vogue* as an illustrator, to venture into photography, much as he had convinced Edward Steichen to give up painting in order to become the great photographer that he ultimately proved to be. The relationships between Condé Nast and his workers were very possessive, and when one of his employees went over to the competition, he would be quite upset. This was what happened with Adolphe de Mayer, one of the first great photographers of the 1920s, when he was hired by *Harper's Bazaar*, the rival magazine, published by Randolph Hearst. But the biggest heartbreak for Condé Nast was linked to Carmel Snow, his exceptional editor, who dared to become the editor-in-chief of the rival publication. The best photographers on earth published their work in the pages of *Vogue*: Man Ray, George Hoyningen-Huene, Horst, and Jacques-Henri Lartigue. This was a characteristic that lived on, even after the earthquake in ownership caused by the crisis of 1929 and after the death of Nast himself in 1942, with the transition to ownership by the Newhouse family. Nowadays *Vogue* has eleven editions in eleven countries (the Italian edition was founded in 1965, with the absorption of the magazine *Novità* and, since 1988, is has been edited by Franca Sozzani). The magazine's level of quality and prestige has always remained impeccable, just as during the life of Condé Nast. Thanks to this extraordinary continuity it is possible, as Alexander Liberman, the long-time art director of the monthly, once said, to reconstruct through *Vogue* an unparalleled visual history of the fashion and elegance of an entire century.

❑ 2001. Prince Charles of England posed as a model for the Peruvian photographer Mario Testino. The four poses, shot in the full relaxation of the estate of Highgrove, were published in mid- January in the English edition. Two more photographs from the shoot were displayed at the National Portrait Gallery in London in February.
❑ One year exactly after the attack on the Twin Towers, *Vogue* and the CFDA (Council of Fashion Designers of America) marketed a T-shirt with the signatures of 241 American fashion designers, to gather money for the Twin Towers Fund.
❑ Fourteen years of *Vogue Italia* on exhibit at the Musei Capitolini. The exhibition 'The Covers of *Vogue Italia* 1988-2002' features 160 covers from the Italian edition, edited by Franca Sozzani.
❑ 2002, October. Tom Ford, fashion designer of the year, Karolina Kurkova best top model, Alexander McQueen "revolutionary" designer: these were the decisions of the *Vogue* Fashion Awards, the annual ceremony that is held at New York's Radio City Music Hall.
❑ 2003, May. At Pitti Immagine, 'the Children of *Vogue*,' a photography exhibition at Palazzo Strozzi in Florence. The 150 portraits done by the great artists of photography are a tribute to the 30 years of *Vogue Bambini*.

(*Adalberto Cremonese*)

Voile A semitransparent fabric, very light, made of silk, cotton, wool or artificial fibers. Used from the nineteenth century on, it was relaunched by the nude look.

Voinquel Raymond (1912-1994). French photographer. In the course of a decidedly versatile career, he worked primarily in the movies as a screenwriter, set photographer, and director of photography in contact with the most important directors of the period

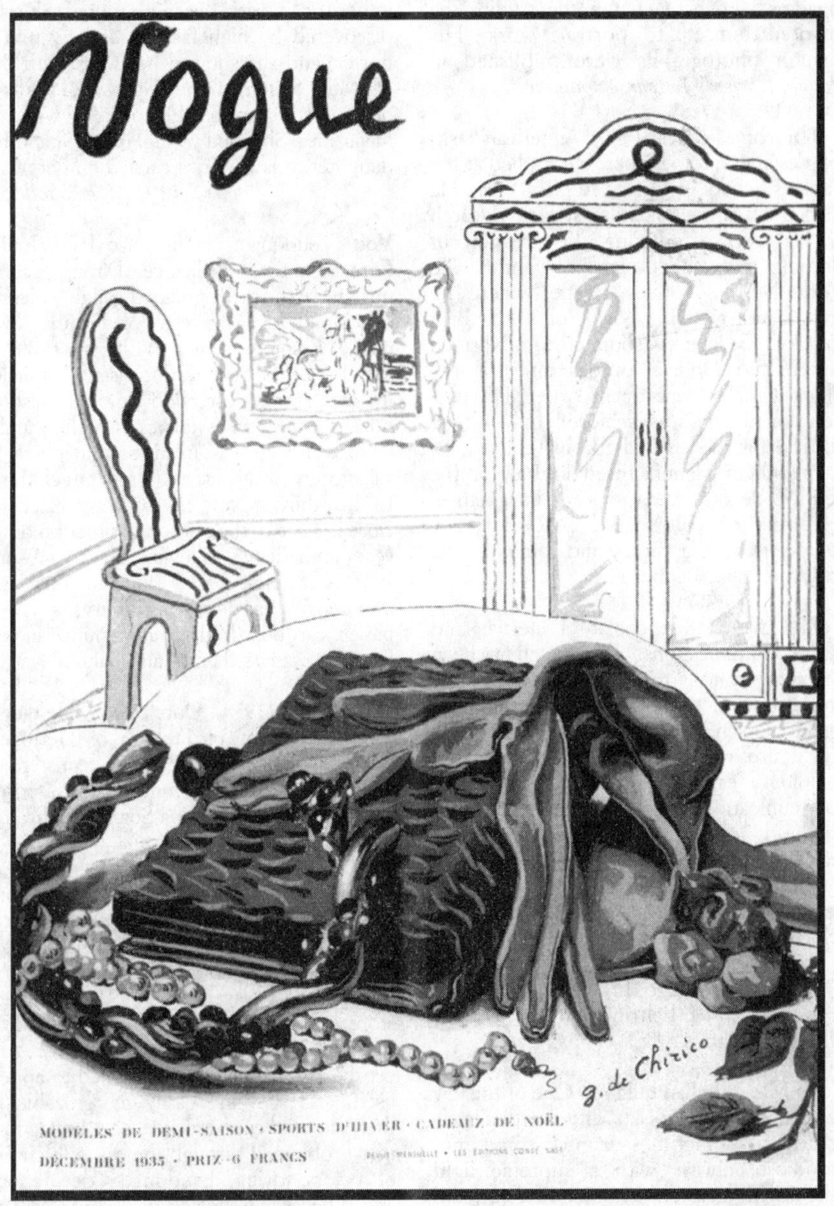

Giorgio De Chirico, cover of *Vogue*, 1935 (from *Art Fashion,* Biennial of Florence, Skira, 1996).

from 1931-1977, with the exception of the war years when, in disgust with the German invaders who actually ran the studios, he devoted himself to portrait work. His fashion photographs were published in *Vogue*, *Harper's Bazaar*, *Silhouette*.

Vollbracht Michael (1949). American fashion designer and designer. He studied at the Parsons School of Design in New York. He carried out at the same time stylistic research of his own, alternating the creation of clothing with the designs of fabrics. He worked for Geoffrey Beene, where he created the wedding gown for Linda Bird Johnson. He later collaborated with Norman Norell and Donald Brooks and for the Bloomingdales department stores. His passion for design was achieved fully in the fabrics that he created for his collections, having them manufactured in Italy at the Setificio Bellotti. Audacious and imaginative, in terms of colors and patterns, they characterized the tunics and kimono suits with their spare, sober lines.

Volli Ugo (1948). Scholar of lifestyle and mass communications. His research has been devoted primarily to the exploration of the linguistic and communicative experience: theater, kitsch, fashion and body, fascination and desire, relations between semiotics and sociology, especially concerning political communications and marketing. A professor at the University of Bologna, where he teaches Semiology of Fashion in the course for Fashion Professionals. He writes for newspapers and magazines and is a theater critic for *Grazia*. Among his books: *Contro la fashion* (Feltrinelli, 1988), *Jeans* (Lupetti, 1991), *Hair Language* (Proctor and Gamble, 1997), *Fascino* (Feltrinelli, 1997), *Block Modes* (Lupetti, 1998).

Volpi Maria. Italian milliner. One of the few genuine designers of hats, gifted with a lively creativity, sometimes ironic, sometimes grandiose, always with a supreme light touch, with an exquisite sense of color, and with demanding standards of workmanship. In her boutique, not far from Palazzo Carignano, the upper classes of Turin came to call; among those who frequented her, remaining loyal over time, were the actors on tour in the neighboring theater, such as the great Stoppa, who refused to wear anything but Volpi hats. Volpi excelled in particular in her fur busbies, her mink toques. She was discovered by high fashion and by prêt-à-porter, and she showed her work with that of Mila Schön, Irene Galitzine, Cadette, often winding up on the covers of women's magazines. She died young, in 1979, and her daughter-in-law Marisa carried on her work.

(*Lucia Sollazzo*)

Volt Pseudonym of Vincenzo Fani. Italian Futurist artist. "Brilliance, Daring Economy," were the three points through which he developed his Manifesto of Futurist Women's Fashion, signed Volt, in 1920. A member of the Second Futurism, Volt called for an artistic direction for the fashion houses: "Fashion is an art, just like architecture and music." In his second point, he calls for extravagance and daring in clothing. In his third point, he conceptualized, in close linkage to the economic situation of the years immediately following the First World War, a fashion based on new materials, inexpensive and revolutionary, such as paper, cardboard, glass, aluminum, tin foil, fish skin, canvas, hemp, and oakum.

Vos Edgard (1933). Dutch tailor. He taught at the Academy of Fashion of Hertogenbosch. He has an atelier in Amsterdam making custom items and a prêt-à-porter line with the *griffe* Sua-Sua sold through various boutiques.

Voyage "We want to be unique, we don't care if everyone likes us." This is the philosophy adopted by the Friuli-born Tiziano Mazzilli and his wife Louise, creators of the label Voyage. Since 1991 they have a store of their own in Fulham Road in London. The shop is quite exclusive. And yet the Voyage items are designed to appear used, and they are easily recognizable by their elevated economic value. A ragtag look that is obtained through the casual blending of colors, dying, hand-made decorations, and the washed effect.

❑ 2000. Opening of the I Love Voyage shop in Monmouth Street, near Covent Garden, and launch of the Passion and Amour lines. Rocky and Tatum, children of Tiziano and Louise, work respectively in the menswear and womenswear sectors and later they inaugurate and manage a new store in Conduit Street, in London's fashion district.

(*Lorenzo Leonarduzzi*)

Vreeland Diana (1903-1989). American journalist. Diana Dalziel was born and raised in Paris at the turn of the century by very sociable American parents. She married Reed Vreeland, a American banker with whom she had two children. They spent the first years of their marriage in Europe. They were both handsome, intelligent, and elegant, and they led an intense social life. These were the years of Francis Scott Fitzgerald's the beautiful and the damned. When they returned to America in 1936, Carmel Snow, then the editor at *Harper's Bazaar*, impressed by Diana's original elegance, offered her a job at the prestigious magazine. And so, at the age of 33, she began her career in the field of fashion that would make her one of the most famous people on the planet. She would never arrive in the office before noon, but by 8 in the morning she was already on the phone with the entire editorial staff by phone, from her bathtub. Her audacious and sophisticated column, *Why Don't You?* in which she would give advice, often patently absurd advice, to middle-class American women (wash your hair with champagne or sleep in a Chinese bed), actually constituted a subtle and highly intelligent idea: it was a way offering, in the heart of the Great Depression, a reassuring sense of continuity. In 1962 she became the editor-in-chief of *Vogue* and, as her first official act, she had the walls of her office painted bright red, her favorite color, then she completely modified her own physical appearance, and then finally hurled herself headfirst into the work of remaking the magazine. Diana had understood that times had changed, and that the way people dressed needed to take its inspiration from the street, and that the monthly should open up to an array of more relevant and up-to-date contents. She chose for this "youth-quake," as she described it with a newly coined term, a number of models with unusual forms of beauty, such as Veruschka, Twiggy and Jean Shrimpton, while such exotic landscapes as Turkey, Libya, or Israels served as the backgrounds for their clothing. She was never a fashion journalist, but she dictated fashion. In 1971 she resigned from *Vogue* to become a special consultant to the Costume Institute of the Metropolitan Museum where, for fifteen years she organized sensational exhibitions: among them, *The World of Balenciaga*; *Yves Saint-Laurent 25 Years of Creativity*; *The Glory of Russian Costume*. When she died, *The New York Times* ran the news on the front page, calling her "a legend." In 1994, the Metropolitan Musem recalled her life with a major retrospective show.

(*Adalberto Cremonese*)

Diana Vreeland portrayed by Cecil Beaton, 1954 (Prints Collection A. Bertarelli, Milan).

Vuarnet French brand of eyewear. It takes its name from the French Olympic champion skier, Jean Vuarnet, who won the gold medal in downhill freestyle in 1960 in Squaw Valley (USA). He used a pair of Skilynx lenses, patented by the Parisian optician Robert Pouilloux to protect himself against the glare and joined in the business. At first, things moved slowly: 200 pair of glasses. Thirty years later, 1.5 million have been sold and the turnover allowed the company to expand its manufacturing realm: apparel for sports, cosmetics for tanning, and watches.

Vuitton French luggage maker and fashion house. In 1835, Louis Vuitton (1821-1892) left his birthplace in the Jura region for Paris and, in the French capital, he specialized in making luggage for high society. Seventeen years later, he was summoned to construct a set of luggage for the Empress Eugénie, born Eugenia de Montijo. This experience allowed him to foresee the imminent extinction of the old traveling trunks with their convex covers – so much a part of the era of stagecoach travel – that were ill suited both to ocean liners and to trains. In 1854, he opened his first luggage shop in Paris in the Rue Neuve des Capucines, offering extremely light trunks made of poplar wood and luggage that was better suited to the new means of conveyance. His son Georges successfully created Monogram (1896), a cloth that featured the initials LV as a sort of certificate of authenticity and patented oilcloth bags as steamer bags, while his grandson Gaston, aside from overseeing production, collected travel objects and old luggage dating back to the period from the sixteenth to the nineteenth centuries. His collection still forms a valuable part of the holdings of the Musée des Arts Décoratifs in Paris. Trunks and suitcases won over the high aristocracy and the great figures of the century: the prince of Egypt Yusuf Kemal, the sultan Ismaïl Pasha, and many members of the royal houses of Europe would not travel without luggage created expressly for them. For Luigi Barzini and Scipione Borghese, who participated in the 1907 automobile race from Peking to Paris, the house designed special waterproof luggage. The trunk of the explorer Savorgnan de Brazza also contained a camp bed, and the trunk of the opera singer, Lily Pons, could hold no fewer than 36 pairs of shoes, while the trunk of the symphony conductor Léopold Stokowski contained a portable writing desk with shelves for books and scores. Even today, the *maison* is capable of fulfilling personal custom orders, created by the expert artisans who work in the Vuitton workshops. Since 1959, the line of production has expanded to include a line of bags, small leather goods, and accessories. Subsequently, the manufacturer entered the market for men's and women's prêt-à-porter: the American fashion designer Marc Jacobs is now in charge of that sector. It exports to about forty nations and has, around the world, some 150 sales outlets. It is no longer owned by the Vuitton family, but is now held by Bernard Arnault's LVMH Group.

(*Giuliana Parabiago*)

Vukmirovic Milan (1970). French designer of Yugoslavian descent. He began as a journalist at *Jardin des Modes*. He was a model and later an assistant to Lacroix on the runway presentations and, for style, to Erik Bergèr. He worked for the label of Emmanuelle Fouks. In 2000, Tom Ford summoned him to work as a creative for the Gucci group. He was hired by Prada as fashion designer for the Jil Sander *griffe*, a very challenging task that he performed without denaturing the house style.

Wacoal Label of Japanese women's underwear. It occupies a leading position in worldwide production. Turnover, continually increasing, was some 80 billion liras in 1992 for 100 million items a year. The company arrived in Europe in 1992, establishing a subsidiary in France, in order to reinforce the image of a high fashion lingerie in the European market as well. It later expanded to the American market, with investments in production in the free zones of the Caribbean.

Wada Emi (1937). Japanese costume designer. Winner of an Oscar for the extraordinary mediaeval costumes in *Ran* (1986) by Akira Kurosawa, a warrior saga in which the armies wear symbolic colors: red for violence, light blue for innocence, and yellow ambiguity. Born in Kyoto, she was also active in theatrical set design. In 1987 the festival of Cannes awarded her a prize for her creations.

Wadsworth Atheneum Hartford, Connecticut. An American museum with permanent collections of outfits and fabrics. The women's outfits date back to the mid-eighteenth century, with a collection of American high fashion. There is a unique collection of costumes from Diaghilev's Ballets Russes, along with sketches by the artists who worked on them. There is a varied collection of fabrics, ranging from fifteenth-century Italian tapestries to contemporary textile art. The collection of silks by the Cheney Brothers, the largest manufacturer in New England for over a hundred years, is available to scholars. The well stocked library is open to the public. The museum's collection is shown in special themed exhibits twice a year.

Waffle fabric Linen, cotton, or woolen fabric with a weave that creates a grid of lines in relief alternating with indentations. The resulting motif resembles the cells of a honeycomb. It is also used in knitwear.

Waikiki Hawaiian shirt, as loose-fitting as a kaftan, worn outside the belt, with side vents, broad, open neck, brightly colored tropical patterns. It takes its name from the beach in Honolulu and is also known as an "Aloha shirt."

Wainwright Janice (1937). British fashion designer. She studied at the Kingston College of Art in London and then enrolled in the Royal College of Art, where she now teaches. At the end of the 1960s she was considered one of the brightest talents in Swinging London. Her preferences range from dinner and evening wear to luxurious fabrics, bright colors, embroidered jersey enriched with precious appliqués. Her lines are always quite feminine, fluid and seductive. Her prêt-à-porter dates back to 1974.

Waistcoat One the three elements in a man's three-piece suit: sleeveless, buttoned in front with a V neck or lapels, it is worn over the shirt and under the jacket. It is the only element in a man's suit that allows a little personal fantasy. The front is made of cloth, the back of silk, with two strips at the back that tighten the waistcoat with a small buckle. It first appeared in its present form in the 1800s. Its first incarnation was under the name *gilet* in the second half of the 17th century, with sleeves and worn under a justicoat (from the French *just-au-corps* from the reign of King Louis XIV). In Venice in 1700 it was named *camiziola* or *camisola* and its transformation began. At the end of the 19th century it became part of a woman's wardrobe. In the late 1960s it often replaced the jacket in a pantsuit, and can be very long, almost to the knee. Other than in fabric, it can be manufactured also in knitwear, with or without sleeves, with or without buttons in the front, in the latter case rather similar to a cardigan. At the end of the 1980s, designers created elegant and sophisticated versions, reminiscent of the rich waistcoats of the 18th century. It is made in silk, jacquard, taffeta, velvet, or damask, and either plain dyed or decorated with floral patterns, enriched by embroideries and decorations.

Wakeley Amanda (1962). British fashion designer. The *Financial Times* called her the "English response to Donna Karan." She was born in Chester. After working as a model in America, she opened a high fashion boutique in London in 1990. In 2003 she had bridal shops in 11 British cities. There were three in London: in Knightsbridge, in Berner Street and in Fulham Road.

Wakeling Gwen (1901-1982). American costume designer. She specialized in kolossal costume films, and in 1950 she received an Oscar for her work on *Samson and Delilah*. Already, since the 1920s for that matter, after completing her studies in Paris, she had worked on the great sagas of Cecil B. De Mille, such as *The King of Kings* (1927). Her special love for period movies did not keep her from designing sophisticated outfits for starlets at Fox Pictures, the studio where she was in charge of the costume department. Her main star was Loretta Young (*Second Honeymoon*, 1937); among other actresses, she dressed Linda Darnell, Rosalind Russell, Alice Faye, and Simone Signoret. At the beginning of the 1940s she left Fox, but continued to work for the most important Hollywood studios: Columbia, Warner Bros., United Artists, RKO. She was definitely quite eclectic, and ended her career with a B movie, a musical called *Frankie and Johnny* (1966). She worked extensively in television, too. (*Roberto Nepoti*)

Walker André (1965). British fashion designer, of Jamaican descent. He studied at the Parsons School of Design and at the Fashion Institute of Technology in New York. In 1990-91 he designed the fall-Winter collection of the American house Williwear and, that same year, he began showing his own collections in Paris. He collaborated with Marc Jacobs. Vuitton put him in charge in 1999 of the stylistic direction of the menswear collection.

❑ For Spring-Summer 2001 Walker presented at the Nokia Fashion Hall, in the Petit Palais in Paris, along with Gilles Rosier, Jean Paul Knott, Enrique Oña Selfa.

Walker Catherine. French designer. She works in England. She began her career in 1975 with a company making clothing for children, in order to overcome the loss of her husband. She later founded The Chelsea Design Company and in 1991 she presented a prêt-à-porter line. She received in 1990 the title of Designer of the Year for British Couture and in 1991 the Designer of the Year for Glamour.

❑ In November 1998, Lady Di's favorite fashion designer published with Universe Books her autobiography and wrote about her friendship with the Princess of Wales.
❑ 2002. From May to November, the Victoria and Albert Museum in London celebrated her 25-year career, with a personal show in the Dress Gallery. On display were more than 50 sketches by the fashion designer, including sketches for outfits worn by Princess Diana, by the Viscountess Serena Linley, Lady Helen Taylor, and by Lady Gabriella Windsor. For the occasion a book also came out that described the career of the fashion designer, *Catherine Walker, 25 Years, British Couture*.

Walkjanker Tyrolean jacket made of boiled wool, trimmed in a contrasting color, with double button made of metal. Its particular feature is the absence of stitching. The traditional model (much loved by Grace Kelly) was developed by the Austrian Hofer company. The item was recently subjected to a restyling, entrusted to the Italian Olmes Caretti.

Wallabee Shoes in various colors with square toes and rubber soles.

Wallace Sewell English label of fashion accessories created in 1992 by Hariet Wallace-Jones (Dorset, 1965) and Emma Sewell (Norwich, 1964). Students together at Saint Martin's and then at the Royal College of Art (1990), they specialized in fabric design. After graduation, they began to work as a team, producing a line of scarves and stoles.

Wallace shirt A polo-neck men's shirt, in cotton or in wool, with a short central line of buttons. It was commonly used in the nineteenth century as an item of underwear, but it took its name from the Hollywood actor Wallace Beery, who wore it in the 1930s as an item of clothing in his films. In Italian, it is called a Serafino, from the name of the young Abruzzese shepherd, the protagonist of the film of that name by Pietro Germi (1968), played by Adriano Celentano.

Wallpaper (Subtitle: *The stuff that surrounds you*). British magazine of contemporary living. It was founded in 1996 based on an idea of Tyler Brulé, a young and brilliant London journalist. Despite its tiny budget (the four issues were assembled in the front room of Brulé's apartment) the magazine was enormously popular, and was purchased for well over a million pounds by Time Inc. (the American publishing branch of Time Warner). Fashion, architecture, design, travel, and food were treated equally with news and photography intended for a youthful, cosmopolitan audience, both men and women. The aspirations of the readers were reflected in the sophisticated graphics of the magazine, which made it a desirable object in and of itself. The journalism was minimalistic in its contents, humorous in its use of a refined English filled with wordplay, and it was in any case a worldwide success. Journalists from around the world worked on it, providing a sense of contact with what is happening in the places that count. At the furniture salon (Salone del Mobile) of Milan in 1999 it organized the event of the season, the Limitless Luxury Party, exhibiting all the mosst desirable objects, including an English butler. Shameless consumerism or British irony, whichever it was, it attracted all the names of fashion, design and architecture, thus establishing Brulé as a style guru for the twenty-first century.

Wang Vera. A *maison* specializing in wedding gowns for American high society. The exquisite creations are distinguished by the classic and linear cut and are made with cloths of the highest quality, such as silks and brocades. The fashion designer that founded the company was born into New York's prominent middle class. Her parents, despite her clear love of fashion, forbade her to attend the Fashion Institute of Technology. Vera began to work as a fashion editor for *Vogue*, but left the job after a few years to work as a designer and sketch artist. She was hired by Ralph Lauren and worked for him until 1990, the year that she decided to go into business on her own. In a few years, her creations became a status symbol for all young American brides. The *maison* had shops in the most important American cities. Aside from wedding gowns, the fashion designer is also famous for her work in the world of artistic skating, her old passion, for which she designed costumi glittering with beads and sequins. She designs the clothing for the American Olympic ice skating team and competitors. (*Priscilla Daroda*)

Wangenheim (von) Chris (1942-1981). American photographer of German descent. He moved to New York in 1965, and began to work in architectural photography under the supervision of James Moor. Attracted to the world of fashion, he distinguished himself by his sensual and aggressive style which evoked, as seems so often to be the case with German photographers, the Expressionism of the 1930s. He published in *Harper's Bazaar* and *Vogue*.

Warhol Andy (1930-1987). American photographer, graphic artist, and artist, whose real name was Andy Warhola (he was the son of Czech immigrants). He arrived in New York from Pittsburgh in 1960 and immediately

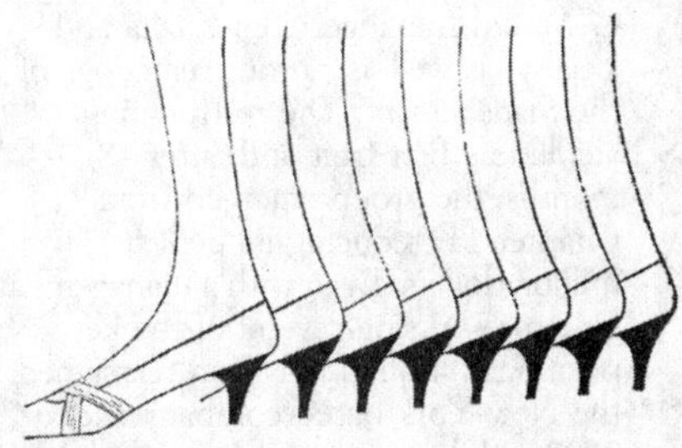

Andy Warhol, advertising for Miller shoes (from the *New York Times*).

made his way into the advertising world as an illustrator, and into the art world as a painter. His works, which reproduced in exaggerated terms everyday reality, consitute basic elements of the aesthetic of Pop Art. The use of photographic, cinematic, and silk-screen techniques characterized his research, which was presented to the broader public for the first time in 1966 in a famous exhibition in the Leo Castelli gallery. In the area of photography he used complex cameras such as the Leica rangefinder camera and simple cameras like the Polaroid, but his images were almost always the product of graphic processes. He was famous for his clothing creations: *Brillo* (a skirt with the image of the cleaning product of that name) and *Fragile, Handle with Care* – a long dress completely covered with the warning legend, transformed into a form of decoration – both created in 1962.

Warnaco American manufacturer of intimatewear and men's fashion. The company produces underwear for Calvin Klein, Olga, Valentino and Warner, and men's apparel for Ralph Lauren (Chaps line). It sells to over 16,000 stores. It is considered the second-largest American group in the sector of women's underwear, immediately behind Sara Lee Playtex. It employs some 20,000 people.

❑ In 2001, the American manufacturer, long insolvent toward the brands it licensed, went through its darkest moment: in June it was placed in Chapter 11, for bankruptcy protection, and was put under court administration. The debts amounted to 2.45 billion dollars. The first step out of Chapter 11 was the elimination of the sleep line GJM and the lingerie lines Izka and Lejaby, as well as various remixings of the management. The restructuing yielded its first fruit and, after 18 months, the group emerged from Chapter 11, reducing its debt to 247 million dollars. Even with a management structure missing several of the key positions that had not been reassigned, the New York-based company ended 2002 with less operating losses and debts than the year before.

❑ In Spring of 2003, the return to health could be said to be definitively underway when Nautica Apparel signed a multi-year agreement with Warnaco to license the production and sale of its lines of swimwear. Today Warnaco has become once again one of the leading names in the production of swimsuits, intimatewear, menswear, jeanswear and accessories with its own labels and with licensing agreements for Calvin Klein, Chaps and Polo by Ralph Lauren, Speedo-Authentic Fitness and others.

Warner Bros For decades, this company was a leader in the sector of corsetry. It was founded in 1874 by two American brothers, the Warners. They were doctors and at first they manufactured medical stays. They attained success in 1914, by manufacturing strapless brassieres, patented by Jacob. In 1932, they marketed bras with adjustable cups.

Wash and Wear All fabrics that, whether made from synthetic fibers or subjected to special treatments, can be washed and then dry rapidly, with no need of ironing.

Watanabe Junya (1962). Japanese designer, pupil and protégé of Rei Kawakubo, the founder of Comme de Garçons, with whom he still works. He lives and works in Tokyo, and leaves only to present his collections on the runways of Paris. He studied at the Bunka Fashion Institute, which graduated all the major Japanese fashion designers, from Kenzo to Yamamoto. He graduated in 1984. Three years later, he was already in charge of the tricot line of Comme des Garçons, a position that he continues to hold even though, ever since 1992, financed by his teacher, he has been designing a collection of his own within the fashion house. His motto is: "Push creativity forward, with no thought for the consequences." The next year, he won the Mainichi Newspaper Award for new designers and he presented twice in Paris. Since 1994 he has been designing his own line, characterized by destructured shoulders and colors that range from bright to dark. He often experiments with new and technological fabrics. He works with a vast array of materials and loves transformable outfits, often just with the use of a zipper. His sales volume is about 10 million Euros.

Wauchob Sharon (1969). British fashion designer. She moved from Northern Ireland to London, where she graduated from the Saint Martin's School, to the approval of the Japanese designer Koji Tatsuno whom she followed to Paris from 1993 to 1997. Then she worked for Louis Vuitton. In 1995 she created the costumes for the movie *The Pillow Book* by Peter Greenaway. Beginning from her very first personal collection, dated 1998, her style was inspired by the femininity of nomad women and is permeated with the spirituality of her Celtic roots.

❑ In October 2000, her creations were presented for the second year running at the south gallery of the Petit-Palais, in the Nokia Fashion Hall.
❑ The most recent collections by this Irish creative, like the one that she sent onto the runways in March 2003, have made the use of leather their common denominator: black, white, fake or real leather for stiletto pants and boots, in which we see once again the emergence of the "Celtic background" that marked the first collections and which continues to evoke the designer's origins.

Waxed Fabrics Fabrics soaked in synthetic resins to give a degree of waterproofing in sportswear, windcheaters, pants, and, especially, raincoats. They have a bright, smooth, almost plasticized surface.

We Swedish brand of streetwear. It was the creation, in 1999, and almost as a game, of a gropp of five young men who were passionately involved in skateboarding and snowboarding, and it reflected their aesthetic and functional philosophy. Today the collection consists of about 160 items, including apparel and accessories, and is distributed to specialty stores in Sweden, England, Japan and Canada. (*Gianluca Cantaro*)

Weave The way in which threads are intertwined to create a fabric. The most common weaves are cloth, twill (and its derivate *batavia*), and satin.

Web These sunglasses were created in Seattle, the city of Boeing airplanes. They have a distinctive bridge with a metal screw between the two lenses. They were first made in 1931, when they were adopted by the pilots of the U.S. Army Airforce. More than sixty years later, in 1993, Diego Della Valle and Luca di Montezemolo purchased the label. Today, these eyeglasses made of metal and celluloid are produced and distributed by Leonardo Del Vecchio's company, Luxottica. They are famous for having been immediately adopted by such celebrities as Ornella Muti, Sylvester Stallone and Sharon Stone. Beginning in fall 1997, a new line of eyeglasses was introduced. Some models hark back to the classic metal structure, while others are in 1950s retro style.

Webb David (1925-1975). American jeweler, Nature and mythology (Greek, Mesopotamian, Oriental, and Maya) are the sources for the imagination of this exuberant creative. He trained in the atelier of his uncle in Asheville, North Carolina, moving at the age of 16 to New York where, at the end of the 1940s, he began to produce, in collaboration with Nina Silberstein, jewelry in an exotic and whimsical style that in the 1960s, thanks to his customer Jackie Kennedy, enjoyed their period of greatest popularity and success.

Webber Tristan (1972). British fashion designer. He debuted in 1997. His psychedelic style, which attempted to shape bodies, considering them as "malleable forms of expression," enjoyed considerable success at the London Fashion Week of October 1998 with a collection entitled Sanctum, and inspired London's underground clubs.

❑ Beginning in 2001, he also worked in the team of designers for Debenhams, a chain of department stores.

Weber Bruce (1946). American photographer. He was responsible for the new image of beauty in fashion photography. Born in Greensburg, Pennsylvania, he studied in New York with Lisette Model. Here he met the photographer Diane Arbus, who would leave a deep impression upon his artistic sensibility. He began his career in the 1970s: his first personal show dates back to 1974, at the Staley-Wise gallery in New York. Weber presented a collection of photographs of body builders, showing that he had an avant-garde eye for male aesthetic trends. The physiques of men and boys depicted in the gym, with modeled muscles and glistening skin, would become standard fare only a decade later. In 1985, he took part in the major photography show at the Victoria and Albert Museum in London, entitled *Shots of Style*. His first fashion coverage was commissioned by *Vogue* (English edition) in 1980. Clothing takes on the value in his images of emphasizing bodies and faces. Expressions and movements took on life in his lens, and outfits became an integral part of a cinematic sentiment transferred to paper. Weber excels at portraits and in the depiction of male beauty, which he immortalized over the course of the years, establishing an evolutionary scale of men's aesthetics. It is no accident that in 1983 he photographed some 250 athletes who would be participating in the Olympics the following year. The first monographic work on the American photographer came out in 1989. He works frequently with the most important visual magazines on earth, from *Vogue America* to *Vanity Fair*. (*Marta Citacov*)

Wedge Footwear with a solid raised sole, which may be made from cork, wood, leather, straw or covered in fabric, and which has been fashionable from the 15th century onwards. A wedge with an arched high heel is also called a "Miranda" because Carmen Miranda wore this style in the 1940s. The famous wedge sandals designed by Ferragamo made fashion history. They came back into vogue in the 1960s, especially for Summer sandals, and again at the end of the century, after Madonna's role in Alan Parker's film *Evita* (1996). In 2000 they also appeared in Winter and sports shoes for young casual wear.

Weill French dynasty of the apparel industry. It dates back to 1892, when the Alsatian Albert Weill created in Paris, in the Sentier, the first house of non-custom ladies' wear. His grandson, Jean Claude, in 1949, after a trip to the America of ready-to-wear, convinced his father Robert to adopt the American systems and, the first to do so in Europe, to call his apparel prêt-à-porter,

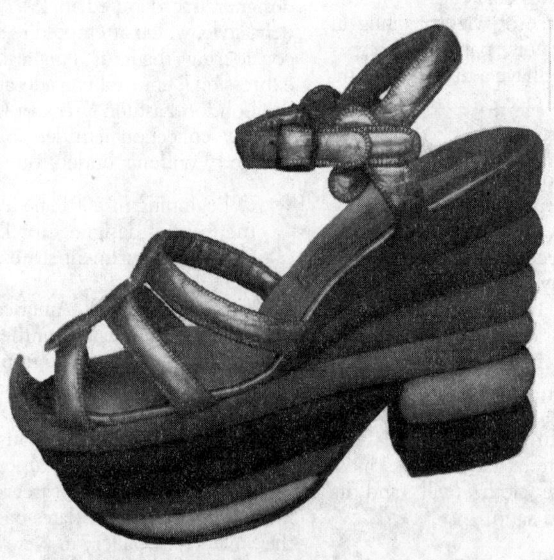

Wedge sandal, 1938. The heel is 13 centimeters high. Ferragamo Museum, Florence.

putting his name on them and adveristing them. The Weill company (two plants, in Lens and Provins) is still completely family operated. In 1972, Jean Claude took his father's place. His children, Bernard, Jean Pierre and Viviane, work for the company.

Weinberg Chester (1930). American fashion designer. For thirty years, he alternated his profession as a creative, known especially for evening wear, with that of a professor at the renowned Parsons School of Design, where he graduated at the age of 21.

Weinberg Sammy (1921). French apparel manufacturer. He is a child of the Sentier, the Parisian quarter that houses the largest number of fashion artisans. With his brother Maurice, in 1946, he industrialized the small womenswear business they had inherited from their father, where he had begun to work at the age of 15. The familyl business was specialized in overcoats and non-name *tailleurs*. In 1962, Sammy built a technologically advanced plant at Bourges, with warehouses in Chateauneuf, and expanded production, putting his name on the product (Weinberg and, from 1980 on, Rhapsodie as well), aiming at an up-market target. In 1989, he acquired Jean-Claude, a prêt-à-porter manufacturer. He is one of the first French industrialists to institute a policy of outsourcing overseas: Portugal and Eastern Europe. The company has about 700 employees.

Weisel Heidi (1967). American fashion designer. Her main focus is cashmere, which, far ahead of many other fashion designers, she used in evening wear, mixing it with silks or organdy. At the early age of 23, she opened her fashion house in New York and began to supply various Hollywood actresses. Fashion has long been her passion: as early as the age of 5 she was using old fabrics to stitch outfits for her dolls. After attending the prestigious Fashion Institute of Technology, she graduated in 1994 and began immediately to work in the Garment District, the general headquarters of fabrics.

❑ For Oscars Night 2003, the actress Lisa Kudrow chose to wear one of her red dresses.

Weitz John (1923). German fashion designer (naturalized American). He began his career in the 1950s, dedicating himself to women's sports apparel. Beginning in the early 1960s, he changed direction and decided to focus on menswear. He was one of the first to understand the growing importance of men's fashion. His was a classical style, in which the American concept of practicality and his own refined European were well combined.

Weitzman Stuart. He designs and produces two collections a year of shoes and bags, plus one collection for the Oscars. He is loved by actresses, internationally successful, and was born in New York, the son of a footwear manufacturer known as Mr. Seymour. At the age of twenty-four he replaced his father and continued production in Elda, near Alicante, in Spain, production that has now attained the volume of 2 million pairs per year. There are twelve single-label shops in the United States and twelve more around the world, while the headquarters is in New York. He is famous for having produced a million-dollar pair of shoes: a sandal-qua-jewelry made of platinum and 64-carat diamonds, worn by Laura Harring during the Oscar ceremonies in 2002. The value of the shoes were then donated to charity, a subject toward which Weitzman is especially sensitive: every year he organizes an event on behalf of breast cancer research. He sends various stars a white satin stiletto-heeled pair of shoes, which they paint, decorate, or simply sign. Then he auctions them off for charity.

❑ In 1998 he inaugurated his online boutique, for internet purchase of his shoes which, over the years, have become enriched with new materials such as vinyl, cork, and wallpaper. On the same website, it is possible to view and buy his line of handbags as well.
❑ In Summer 2003, he inaugurated a new single-label shop at Columbus Circle in New York. Weitzman shoes, distributed in 57 nations around the world through 24 boutiques and flagship stores, are present in Italy with 85 sales outlets.

Wendy Brigode American jewelry trademark. It takes its name from the company's designer. Brigode was born in New York, but she lives in Los Angeles. She makes the most sought-after pearl necklaces in Hollywood: her most famous model is a simple silk thread lined with pearls, each different from the others, a original and modern design. Her creations are always very youthful, even though she sells to the most classical department stores. She uses precious and semi-precious stones, which she sets elegantly in gold and silver.

Wessel Hannoh (1965). German fashion designer. He studied at the Academy of Fine Arts in Berlin. La Chambre Syndicale de la Couture in Paris, after a two-year apprenticeship with the high fashion *maison* of Lecoanet-Hemant, certified him as a women's clothing cutter. In 1993, he presented his first collection of prêt-à-porter womenswear. He successfully won a place for himself in the department stores of Printemps and Henry Bendel. Since 1997, he has had a place on the official calendar of the Paris runway presentations. He has often taken inspiration from military uniforms.

❑ In 2002, he won the competition for young talents at the Espace Créateurs of the Forum des Halles in Paris. What won the jury over was the German fashion designer's remarkable technique of breaking down and reassembling the traditional and artisanal lines.
❑ Wessel's new line was called H+ and was presented in an advance preview at the salon of prêt-à-porter in Paris in January 2003.
❑ The Hannoh collections are now distributed worldwide through a network of 35 sales outlets in Kuwait, Japan, Italy, United States, and Taiwan.

West Vera (1900-1947). American costume designer and fashion designer. Called "the high priestess of Universal," for her long career in science-fiction and B movies. Originally she was a fashion designer (just before her premature death, she reopened an atelier in Beverly Hills), from 1926 till 1947 she was in charge of the costumes for the production house, supervising the look of countless monstrous heroes: from the bandages of *The Mummy* (1932) to the cape worn by *The Phantom of the Opera* (1943), to Dracula's cape (*House of Horrors*, 1945). She created the exotic clothing worn by Maria Montez, and applied the same style (veils, costume jewelry, frills, and feathers) to Marlene Dietrich in *Destry Rides Again* (1939) or Mae West in *My Little Chickadee* (1940). When necessary, however, she was perfectly capable of designing sober, spare outfits like Ava Gardner's black suit, in which she played the legendary dark lady of *The Killers* (1946), or underscoring the adolescent innocence of Deanna Durbin at the height of her popularity.

Western Style A vernacular fashion. It triggered the most powerful peaceful revolution ever seen in the field of clothing. Blue jeans are the item of clothing that only a few people on earth have decided not to include in their wardrobe. They are also the first example of mass "dressing down" that became a tacitly accepted rule, in which the middle class adopted the clothing of the working class. If, along the span of the 1950s, jeans and "dressing down" expanded into the middle class, the western style, almost in form of compensation, evolved increasingly toward an ornate and glamorous elegance. For that matter, from the very beginning, the figure of the cowboy (as in the many Hollywood movies featuring singing cowboys in the 1930s and 1940s) is a figure from the mass imagination, rather than a genuine depiction of reality, the reality of the hard manual labor of the

Western Style, *Tex Willer* (Sergio Bonelli publisher).

prairies. In this sense the Las Vegas version of the cowboy, dressed in rhinestones and lamé, is the natural consequence of the process of self-legitimizaiton in stylistic terms. Nudie Cohen was one of the masterminds of this process. Much of the glamorous excesses, from Gene Autry and Roy Rogers to Elvis Presley and Dolly Parton, were the products of his inventive mind. He made an important contribution to the appropriation of an imaginative style as evident proof of success.

Weston French label of men's footwear created in 1926 by Eugène Blanchard. It has always distinguished itself for its painstaking manufacturing and the quality of materials used: only fine leathers, artisanal workmanship, and Goodyear components. One fan of these shoes was François Mitterand. Among the other admirers, we may list Jacques Chirac, Jean-Paul Belmondo, Johnny Hallyday and, since 1985, when the women's shoe line was founded, Catherine Deneuve and Vanessa Paradis. Weston shoes were worn by the student protesters of May 1968.

Westwood Vivienne (1941). British fashion designer. She changed the history of fashion as the "muse of punk." Born in Glossop, Derbyshire, she was the daughter of the textile factory workers Dora and Gordon Swire who named her Vivienne Isabel in homage to the actress Vivien Leigh; she was educated at the Glossop Grammar School. Prophetic, for her future career, was the school's motto: "Virtus, veritas, libertas." After a short marriage to Derek Westwood she began a relationship with the musician Malcolm McLaren, and they had a son in 1968, Joseph Ferdinand, now the owner of a fetish shop in London's Soho. In 1970, the couple opened a shop called Let it Rock at 430 King's Road. A forerunner of the cultural contaminations that were to come, the store sold 1950s records and outfits inspired by that period. In 1972, in the same store with a new sign, reading *Too Fast to Live, Too Young to Die*, she presented her first collection, dedicated to the Rockers. Among her first celebrity clients was Ringo Starr for whom the fashion designer invented the costumes for the movie *That'll Be the Day*. Decisive to her work and her

Trademark of Vivienne Westwood.

success, in any case, was certainly her ties with McLaren. With him, in 1974, she introduced leather outfits, rubber shirts, chains, and T-shirts with pornographic images. The setting for the succession of provocations: the usual boutique on King's Road, appropriately renamed "Sex." The police raided the place, in an attempt to shut down that den scandals. But behind the now shuttered windows of the shop, even more-revolutionary fermentations were bubbling away. Vivienne and Malcolm were getting ready to launch the band the Sex Pistols: an aesthetic and musical icon of the punk movement, which abhorred the hypocrisy of the time and which fought it, lambasting the codes of behavior of the establishment. For the occasion, the shop changed its name to Seditionaries: a play of words between seduction and sedition. As Giannino Malossi noted in his book *Liberi Tutti* (Mondadori) "The punks knew that clothing can be a weapon of subversion, just as books and manifestoes can be." And Seditionaries supplied, in terms of fashions and poses, the manual of the new anarchists who were playing at London's Roxy, piercing their cheeks with safety pins and combing and gelling their hair into menacing crests. The couple of "lost souls" reached the culmination of their greatest provocation and popularity in 1977, when the Sex Pistols – in tribute to the Silver Jubilee celebrating the 25th year of the reign of Queen Elizabeth II – recorded, on the Virgin lable, *God Save the Queen*. It was not exactly pleasant or pleasing. The song called Her Majesty a "moron": it immediately shot to the top of the hit parades and become an anthem of the punk movement, now a worldwide phenomenon. From the rebellion of the 1970s to the hedonism of the dawning 1980s, Westwood designed another epoch-making collection: the Pirates collection, which launched the New Romantic look, and also witnessing the entry of Vivienne's clothing into the Victoria and Albert Museum. Perhaps it was the decline of the punk rebellion that inspired the new name of World's End for her London shop and her move onto the runways of France. In 1982, after Mary Quant, she became the first English designer to be accepted into the calendar of French défilés. And even the fields of collaboration of "Lady Viv" changed, shifting from the world of music to the world of art. In 1983, she presented her Witches collection: the fruit of her increasingly close ties to the graffiti artist Keith Haring, corresponding to the end of her relationship with McLaren. Some thought that this transition also marked the end of the genius of Vivienne. In 1985, the fashion designer's farewell to the French runways only seemed to confirm this view. But she continued to enjoy success with her Crini Collection that year, with crinoline minis and incredibly high stacks, footwear, according to its creator, that was "designed to place feminine beauty high on a pedestal." And it was on those shoes, now called platforms, that the top model Naomi Campbell fell victim to an accident during a runway presentation, tripping over her dizzyingly high heels, she fell in a disastrous spread-eagle collapse. The increasingly dizzying ups and downs of the fashion designer, however, did nothing to undercut her prestige and her high consideration in the world of fashion. For her and for her fashion shows, always featuring a title as if there were pieces of conceptual theater, all the most famous top models were willing to work free of charge. While John Fairchild, publisher of WWD, in his 1989 book, *Chic Savages*, included Westwood as the only woman among the six best fashion designers on earth. She bgan to present in London again in 1987 with her collection Harris Tweed, and from 1989 to 1991 the fashion designer agreed to lecture at the Academy of the Applied Arts in Vienna, as a professor fashion. During this experience she developed her ideas for a menswear collection which she presented in a preview showing in 1990 in Florence, during Pitti Uomo. Her reputation by this point was so great that even Queen Elizabeth, forgiving the insult of *God Save the Queen*, awarded the fashion designer in 1992 the honor of naming her a member of the Order of the British Empire. But it was at the end of that ceremony, seemingly a marker of a truce with the establishment, that Vivienne flipped up her skirt for the cameras of the photographers, showing the world that she does not wear underwear. "Never," she added publicly, doubling the dose of provocation. And yet the Harris Tweed collection seems to have marked a new stylistic path, a nostaligic love of the past without the slightest avant-garde sneer or snicker, taking refuge in the period clothing of the eighteenth century. "As soon as I realized that the establishment requires opposition," she later explained, "I began to ignore them and focused my attention on more important things, like history." In fact, to the simpering notes Vivaldi, the former muse of punk brought out into the spotlight crinolines and white wigs. This did not prevent her from experimenting with new fields of contamination, however. In 1993, she was the first big fashion designer to design a Swatch wristwatch: the pop Putti with baroque angels, followed the next year by the Orb. This latter creation featured the fashion designer's logo, which summarizes her philosophy: a royal orb, symbol of tradition, surrounded by a ring of Saturn, emblem of the passage of time and the new creations that incessantly emerge from the past. And, in keeping with these concepts, in 1996, when – at the invitation of Nicola Trussardi – La Westwood launched her first menswear collection at the former Motta factory in Milan, the logo of the line, Man, was written in characters shaped like dolmens. Although she remained loyal "to the quality of stylistic research in opposition to the quantity of items manufactured," at the end of the 1990s, she reorganized and articulated her production. She added in 1997 to the Gold Label, produced in England with tailoring techniques and presented in Paris, the Red Label, a second line that she presented in London but manufactured in Italy, along with the Man Label; production was done by the Italiana Staff International. That same year Anglomania made its debut: men's and women's street-

From "Doppie Pagine" by Anna Piaggi for Vogue Italia: Vivienne Westwood, drawing by Richard Gray.

wear manufactured and distributed by the Italian company G.T.R. In conjunction with the rapidly proliferating number of products, she opened single-label boutiques around the world: from Tokyo to London (Conduit Street). It was inevitable that in this marketing strategy, a women's perfume would appear, launched in London in 1998; before 2002 a men's scent would join it. Among the many marketing strategies, Westwood artistic and provocative genius continued to prove its fertility. While in 1996 the fashion designer took part in the exhibition New Persona at the Stazione Leopolda in the context of the Biennale della Moda di Firenze, in 1998 she returned to the front pages of newspapers throughout the world, because one of her models was caught sniffing on the runway. "It was just snuff, tobacco," she claimed. "Something less legal," theorized the media. Always and in any case a gesture somewhere between "tradition and transgression," representative of this interpreter of highly discipline anarchy. Or, if you will, of the discipline of anarchy, however we choose to phrase it.

❑ An exhibition on the most delirious styles of British fashion could not fail to include items from Vivienne's production, and indeed, the creations of the London fashion designer were present in the exhibit "London Fashions," held by the Fashion Institute of Technology in New York. From 16 October 2001 to 12 January 2002 there were one hundred original creations on view, from the work of Mary Quant to Stella McCartney, based on the idea that "London is the only city on earth capable of creating street styles that wind up on runways."
❑ At the end of November 2002 the *griffe* was present during Moscow's fashion week at the "Rossia State Central Concert Hall," along with the names of Emilio Pucci, Julien MacDonald, and Emanuel Ungaro. For Christmas 2002, a collection of apparel and accessories for dogs was inaugurated, following in the footsteps of fashion designers who were the first to think of satisfying the needs of the four-footed "clientel": Hermès, Gucci and Burberry.
❑ 2003. One step backward in the United States and two steps forward in Paris and the Far East, with the closure of the New York flagship in the neighborhood of SoHo and the announcement of openings in Asia and in the French capital.
❑ For the Austrian Wolford group, she designed a line of body outfits with laces, knitwear, and jackets.

(*Gianluca Lo Vetro*)

Wexner Leslie (1937). American marketing entrepreneur. He was the founder of the Limited chain of stores. He was born in Dayton, Ohio to a family of businessmen, and at 26 he had started a business of his own, opening a discount sportswear store and offering well targeted items. He was one of the first to compete seriously against the department stores. Today his group controls 5,400 shops throughout the United States and includes, aside from The Limited, Limited Too for children, Structure for men's fashion, Victoria's Secret for women's underwear, Bath and Body Works for cosmetics, Bendel, Express, Lerner, and Lane Bryant. The entire company has 131,000 employees.

Whipcord Carded wool fabric used especially for uniforms. It is a variant on gabardine in which the diagonals are intertwined.

Whitaker Mark (1964). British fashion designer, born in Halifax, Yorkshire. After completing his studies in fashion at Newcastle-upon-Tyne College of Art, in 1986 he embarked on a career as a fashion editor, and worked with *The Sunday Times Magazine*, British *GQ* and the New York magazine *Details*. In 1995, he launched his own line of women's fashion. Each collection had a distinct identity and changed radically each time. He said of his outfits: "They are pleasantly shocking."

❑ The fashion designer-editor ushered in the new millennium with a procession of outfits cut on the bias, finished with patches of gleaming color. The manufacturing label consisted of small coins sewn in place of buttons.

Why Not Italian modeling agency. In

October 1976 Vittorio Zeviani and Tiziana Casali decide to set up a modeling agency. They began their business with a staff of four, two phone lines, and a telex. Today, they have 27 employees, 22 phone lines, and 3 fax lines. During Milan Collezioni, the staff rises to 67 with 57 phone lines. Why Not opened its Celebrity and Movie Division for special bookings and has worked with Brooke Shields, Uma Thurman, Greta Scacchi, Valeria Golino, and Claudia Koll.

Wiener Werkstätte (1903-1932). A workshop founded by the entrepreneur Fritz Waerndorfer, the architect Josef Hoffmann, and the painter Koloman Moser, the Wiener Werkstätte set itself the objective of reforming artistic craftsmanship, healing the hiatus between artisan and artist, between execution and design, according to rigorous standards of quality. The fashion section was officially founded on 9 March 1911, but already prior to that date we have documentation of interest on the part of the school in tailoring and clothing design, as shown by a number of drawings by Hoffmann himself, intended for special clients, and executed by the Viennese atelier of the Floge sisters, who were involved in the Wiener Werkstätte project as early as 1904. In the photographic albums of the workshop, we can see a number of photographs of Klimt's girlfriend, Emilie, in neo-Empire style outfits which are clear evidence of this collaboration. Among the many artists summoned to cooperate, such as Maria Likarz, Otto Lendecke, and Marianne Zels, we should make special mention of the figures of Eduard Josef Wimmer-Wisgrill (1882-1961), the artistic director of the fashion section from 1911 to 1922 and Max Snischek (1891-1968) who took his place, from 1922 until 1932. Fundamental to all the work in this section was the engagement for the creation of a rational, reformed type of clothing, with simplified lines, contrary to such constricting structures as the corset, refined in its decorations, inspired by the motifs of Austrian Art Nouveau. Following a nationalist parenthesis during the First World War, in the 1920s the fashion of the Wiener Werkstätte opened up to the international sphere, enjoying an especially successful period given a widespread trend toward the simplification of lines in that period. In 1917, a branch office was opened in Zurich, in 1929 in Berlin, and later also in New York: actresses and women from international high society purchased Wiener Werkstätte clothing for theater and for private life. Especially successful were the silk pajama-outfits shaped like capes or *robe-manteau*, and with destructured forms. Dating from this period, from the 'Teens to the 1920s, were contacts between Paul Poiret and the fashion section of the school of applied arts. In 1926 the economic crisis and the inflation that were gripping Austria forced the workshop to negotiate a special agreement to avoid bankruptcy. In 1928 the Wiener Werkstätte celebrated its 25th anniversary with a major runway presentation of clothing creations: despite this event, the constant financial difficulties caused by the general state of economic uncertainty of those years led, in 1932, to the closing of the company and its liquidation, through an auction of all its property. The great achievement of the fashion section of the Wiener Werkstätte remains, in any case, that of having brought a taste for artistica and avant-garde fashion to the larger public and for having transformed "elite-reformed" style into an "applied fashion."

(*Aurora Fiorentini*)

Wien Historisches Museum The clothing collection of this Viennese museum was begun after the Second World War at the behest of Alfred Kunz, director of the fashion school of Hetzendorf. Twenty thousand outfits and accessories, for men, women, and children. The W.F. Adlmuller, Gertrude Hochsman and Adele List collections formed the foundations of the textiles and apparel sectors. The library has about 12,000 volumes. There are also fashion journals, dating back to 1786 and to the present day, photographs, and 3,000 fashion prints from the mid-nineteenth century to the late-twentieth century.

Wilkens Emily (1920). American fashion designer. She was responsible for the invention of teenage style for American girls. An invention that long preceded the appearance rock 'n' roll and the films of James Dean, and which Spring from her remarkable ability to capture the moods and desires of the young people of the time. Her main goal was to show the fashion world that the wardrobe of young women needed to be conceived and designed with the same amount of care and dedication as for their mothers. Especially because the times and general prosperity were heralding the advent of a burgeoning consumerism among young people. (*Roberta Giordano*)

Willhelm Bernhard (1973). German fashion designer. He was born in Ulm. After studying at the Academy of Fine Arts in Antwerp, he began his career in intimatewear with the historic German house of Schiesser. Then, he began his important work in prêt-à-porter womenswear with Dirk Bikkenbergs, Vivienne Westwood and Alexander McQueen. The debut of his womenswear collection came in 1999 with the fall-Winter season. His style blends contemporary creativity with a memory of the past with the traditional costumes of the area of the Black Forest.

❑ The presentation of the prêt-à-porter Spring-Summer 2000 collections in Paris was the occasion to introduce some forty young European designers, including Bernhard and a handful of fashion designers from the Netherlands, all former students at the Arnhem Institute: Keupr Van Bentm, Mélanie Rozema, Niers Klavers.
❑ In Winter 2002-2003 the designer took over as the creative director of the *maison* of Roberto Capucci for prêt-à-porter. Willhem's more recente production waas characterized, on the other hand, by "Easter egg" motifs, marked by festive speckling which represented a reference to young children. Clogs and pastel shades complete the fashion designer's personal production.
❑ 2004. After his work with Capucci, the German designer continues to devote himself to his line.

Williamson Matthew (1971). Fashion designer. Born in Manchester. He founded his fashion house in 1996, two years after graduating from the St Martin's School in London and after working as a freelancer for Marni, Monsoon and Georgina von Ertzdorf. His very first runway presentation, Electric Angels, at the London Fashion Week in September 1997, won the acclaim of the international media. His refined and hyperfeminine collections, inspired by his friend and muse Jade Jagger and by his many trips to the Orient, were appreciated for the extraordinary, bright sense of color and his attention to detail. (*Mara Accettura*)

Winants Christian (1978). Belgian fashion designer. Recently graduated from the Academy of Fine Arts in Antwerp, he began to work with the guru of the Belgian school Dries van Noten, who at first put him in charge of the knitwear line, and progressively assigned him more and more important tasks. In 2001 he won the Jury Prize from the Hyères Festival and soon the doors of Bendel in New York and Via Bus Stop in Japan were swinging open for him.

Windsor Knot A prominent necktie knot, forming a perfect triangle, said to have been the creation of the Duke of Windsor before he renounced the throne, even though there are pictures of his father already wearing his tie knotted in this fashion. In any case, it was he, the former king Edward VIII, sensitive to all forms of elegance, who launched this knot in the world of men's fashion at the time. In Italy it was called, in an uninspired name, in the 1940s the "nodo Scappino" after the Turin tie manufacturer that had first explained how the know was done. In those years in Italy it was advisable not to use foreign words, and in particular terms that referred in any way "perfidious Albion" were especially taboo.

Winston Harry (1896-1978) American jeweler. The son of a modest watchmaker, he founded with capital of 2,000 dollars his first company, The Premier Diamond Company. He understood the importance of assembling unique and rare precious stones, to create a stock, which he recut and reset in a more modern style. During the war he obtained as many historic pieces of jewelry and important diamonds as he could. His collection was shown in the United States as "The Court of Jewels" and Winston was nicknamed the "King of Diamonds." A 45-carat blue diamond from a statue of Shiva, the "collier de l'inquisition" in emeralds and diamonds, whose history dates back to the

Incas, are among the most important items. In 1954, he opened his shop on the Fifth Avenue in New York. He donated to the Smithsonian Institute the renowned Hope Diamond. After his death, the company was taken over by his son Ronald, who had graduated from Harvard. He opened shops in Europe and became the most important jeweler in America. For his father's centennial, Ronald presented the American Rainbow Tiara (100 carats), worn by Brooke Shields and valued at over 40 million dollars. Currently, the company has five shops, in Tokyo, New York, Geneva, Paris, and Beverly Hills.It sells to wholesalers and retail. It has 1,200 employees, working with ultramodern processes of classification and cutting of the diamonds. It mines diamonds in Africa and in America. The company has handled some of the lovelist precious stones on earth. Winston's great innovation was in the art of setting stones, so as to allow the light from one stone to be reflected from another. The settings are so simple and discreet that it appears that the stones are directly on one's skin.

(*Gabriella Gregorietti*)

Wintour Anna (1949). Editor-in-chief of *Vogue America*. Born in London. She began her career in 1970 as a fashion editor for *Harpers Queen*. In 1976, she moved to the United States to became fashion editor for *Harper's Bazaar*. After a time at *New York Magazine*, as editor of the fashion and lifestyle sections, in 1983 she became the creative director of *Vogue America*. Three years later, she went back to London to become editor-in-chief of British *Vogue*. In November 1987, she published a memorable cover, which has since become part of the classical iconography of fashion: the model Christy Turlington dressed by Calvin Klein and photographed by David Bailey. In 1988 she returned to New York as editor-in-chief of *Vogue America*. In 1990, she was named "Editor of the Year" by *Adweek* for her unorthodox approach to fashion journalism and for her "imprint of fantasy in the realm of perfection." She had become one of the most powerful women in the world of fashion. Glacial, thread-thin in a sort of uniform (often a Chanel *tailleur*), impeccable, with enormous dark sunglasses, she has a steely personality, both at work and in her private life. She lives in Manhattan, and she gets up every morning at dawn to play tennis before going to work, dressed perfectly. She has two children by her first husband, David Schaffer, the chief of children's psychiatry at Columbia Presbyterian Hospital. (*Antonio Mancinelli*)

Wolfers Belgian jeweler. Founded in Brussels in 1850, where forty years later it opened a luxurious shop. In the 1940s and 1950s, its creations were inspired by French costume jewelry.

Wolford Austrian hosiery manufacturer. In 1998, it launched the pantyhose-outfit invented by the designer Philippe Starck. It was called Starcknaked Multiwear. It was made of microfiber. From a piece of clothing that extended from neck to toe, it could be converted into a minidress with plunging neckline. There were six combinations and it was produced in four color. Founded in Bregen in 1946, principally as a manufacturer for other labels, the company extended its realm of activity from hosiery and socks to pantyhose, from body stockings to clothing, all the way up to men's pantyhose. Since 1988, it has been held in shares. Eighty percent of its turnover derives from exports. It has subsidiaries in Europe and America and a number of sales outlets in Japan.

Women's Underwear Economic, political, social, and cultural events have undoubtedly influenced costume and every fashion: and clothing fashions have, in turn, influenced underwear. Once hoop skirts, *paniers* and crinolines had disappeared, in 1900 the first whole dress made its appearance; the elegant and simple *princesse* dress. This was followed by a two-piece with a rather masculine line, the *trotteur*, then called *tailleur*. Already in 1800, Bloomerism (the long clothing worn under skirts introduced to Europe by the American reformer Amelia Bloomer, who intended to start women's emancipation through clothing) had brought a natural evolution to underwear. But it was not until the 20th century that real progress was made. Every changed under outwear: baggy pants became tighter, underskirts were made in taffeta, satin, linen, madapolam (light and thin cloth), and bodices were made from elasticized fabric, strengthened with whalebone or strips of metal. It was custom made by bodice makers in the cities who visited their customers in their houses for fittings, while in the provinces a sales agent arrived with his case full of models, fabric samples, and whalebones. With the advent of art nouveau, came the corset (*sans ventre* for French, *gegen das Kim* for Germans) which needed someone else to tighten and fasten it behind. It emphasized the breasts, hips, and narrowed the waistline. Shortly after, the great Parisian clothes designer Paul Poiret replaced the flannel and muslin of the underskirt with cotton, batista, or silk to be worn under the new short, straight dresses: if not, how would it be possible to dance the Charleston, the One-step, or the Shimmy? By this time, underwear garments were starting to be purchased in haberdashers' shops, or by catalogue, rather than being made to measure. And after a few years, lingerie also became available in refined shops and department stores. Another garment joined the range of underwear, the sexy negligée, the nightdress in which the movie stars of the 1930s received their lovers. This later became a simple night robe for common use (without feathers or yards of lace), perhaps in satin or silk, or – in Winter – in knitwear or wool. During the 1940-45 war, the lack of raw materials and heating in the homes and schools meant that the jersey in soft white wool was replaced by coarse long sleeved sweaters in rough sheep's wool, a material that was also used, though reluctantly, for sheared or ribbed petticoats and long socks or culottes. The bodice was replaced by an elasticized girdle without whalebones, a "containing corset to hide curves," and suspenders and garters arrived on the scene. As a reaction to the sacrifices made during the war, in the

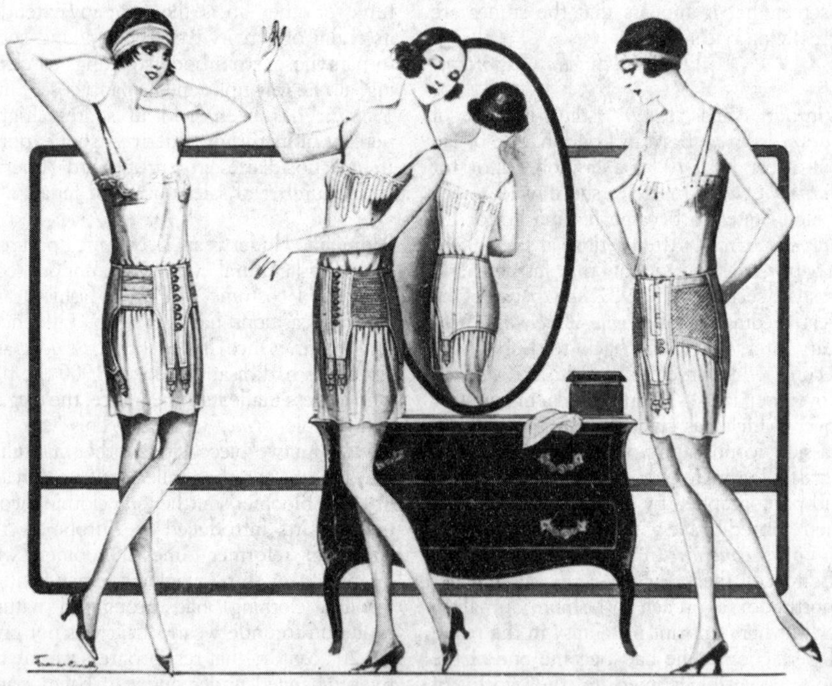

Illustrations of underwear pieces, 1920 (from *Anni Venti – La nascita dell'abito moderno*, Centro Di, Florence, catalogue for the exhibition held at the Galleria del Costume in the Pitti Palace, 1991).

LA LINGERIE

Guida pratica per la confezione della biancheria, tanto da casa che personale.

È un grosso album di oltre 40 pagine, riccamente illustrato, con artistica copertina a colori e una grande tavola interna pure a colori.

I figurini sono oltre 300 e sono tutti originali, recanti le ultime novità in fatto di biancheria. Sono completate da numerose e chiare spiegazioni ed informazioni scritte in lingua italiana.

PREZZO L. **8.—**

Di imminente pubblicazione:

LA BIANCHERIA

Nuovo album per la confezione della biancheria (L. 8.—).

SOCIETÀ EDITRICE " UNITAS „ — MILANO

VIALE MONFORTE, 12

Advertisement for lingerie, 1910 (Prints Collection A. Bertarelli, Milan).

postwar period younger women looked for the most feminine and sexiest underwear they could find.

During the 1950s-60s women reluctantly accepted the post-pregnancy elastic band around the tummy to get back into shape. Girdles made with nylon and rubber thread were abandoned in favor of light lingerie, likewise the hated high-necked, wide-shouldered petticoats that little girls had been forced to wear in the 1940s, though their mothers dressed in light petticoats and laces. The 1940s marked the magical moment when nylon stockings replaced their silk or wool forebears: the nylons arrived from America, where girls were photographed queuing to purchase their first pair, and who would then sit down on the sidewalk right outside the shop to put them on. Moving on from seams, baguettes, and the initial uniformity of color, stockings introduced a certain degree of fantasy: floral patterns, fishnet, lace, decorations to match a particular dress, etc. Shortly after came jersey leotards and, the next development, tights, popular due to their comfort, though they were not liked by men. Tights were made in various thicknesses and colors, sometimes in lurex, and decorated with strass, stripes and dots. The final development on the leg front was the self-supporting stocking (see Stockings).

During the 1950s Vionnet launched large women's panties, but the public preferred their tiny cousins, made with lace and inlays, matched to light, sheer bras, and sometimes forming an outfit with a nightgown and night robe.

Sexy bras – the antithesis of the brassiere, which made the breasts suffer – came on the market, worn perhaps under a very tight sweater, and perhaps fastened at the front rather than the traditional attachment at the back. Dresses were often so low-necked as to make bras useless, but some dresses were designed with a bra incorporated.

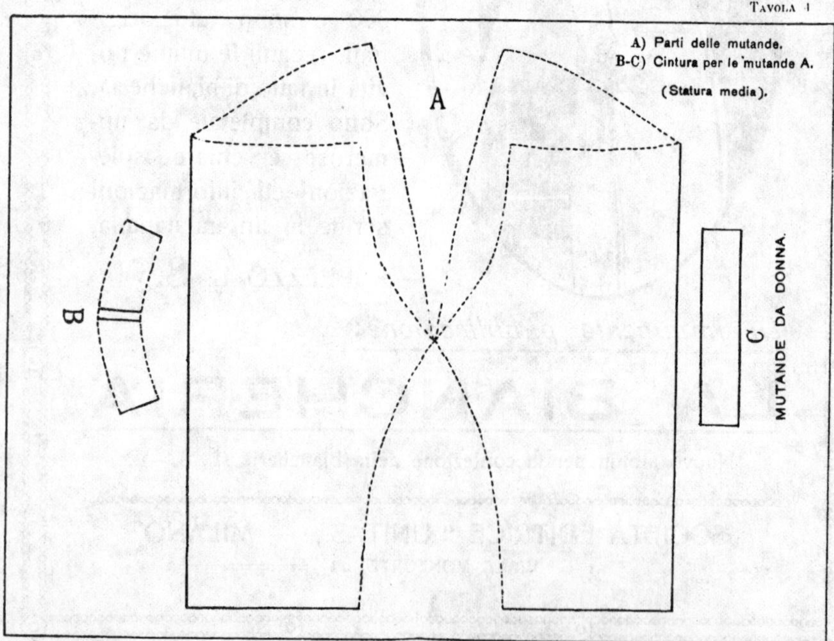

Paper pattern for woman's underwear by the firm Bonetti Biancheria (Hoepli Handbooks).

The next development in underwear was the leotard: the daughter – or grand-daughter – of the cami-knickers. Underwear became smaller and smaller, slips appeared and then the ultimate form: thongs.
Trade fairs dedicated to underwear become popular, and up-market shops dedicated purely to underwear were opened. Petticoats arrived in the stores that looked better than dresses, nightgowns as beautiful as evening outfits, leotards lovelier than swimming costumes. And all the time the boundary between what underwear hides and what it reveals became increasingly narrower. Marilyn Monroe took this to the limit, preferring to wear perfume in bed rather than a nightgown.
With the political events of 1968 and the 1970s, some women started to burn their bras, considering it an act of emancipation and freedom: what they either did not know or conveniently forgot was that their moms and grandmothers, in the 1930s and 1940s, had gained their own degree of emancipation, though without causing a scandal, by getting rid of an even more important garment, thick, baggy underpants. The younger women preferred not to go without any underwear for reasons of ethics and hygiene, and considered lace-up shorts or a slip sexier. Every now and then, depending on seasonal trends, there is a return to the guepière with whalebones, to show off a woman's hips and breasts, and it was even made fashionable to wear it as an outer garment.
Today there is a choice of everything: leotards with and without metal supports under the bra, see-through petticoats, two-piece bra-slip and panties combinations, and various items made from lace, satin, transparent muslin, and stretch tulle. Tank tops are also popular, and sweat suits, which are now also used for lounging around the house and as nightwear. And an eternal favorite is the long, baggy T-shirt, worn it seems on all occasions, but which is a favorite with women for nightwear.

(*Maria Vittoria Alfonsi*

Women's Wear Daily (*WWD*) American newspaper. It was the first daily publication on earth devoted entirely to the women's apparel industry, and for that reason, the most widely read and also the most greatly feared, in Europe as well. First published in 1910 by Fairchild Publications, it became over time the Bible of fashion designers, industrialists, and retailers, all over the world. A mirror of trends and markets, in 1960, under the direction of John B. Fairchild, grandson of the founder, it became even more important, publishing the designs of the most significant creations of each couturier on the same day that the collection was presented. The success of its formula lies in the alternating themes of the daily editions: textiles, prêt-à-porter, accessories, sportswear, intimatewear, beauty, and so on. But its real power comes from its love of indiscretion: not only society tidbits, but also hard news on the state of economic health of fashion designers and fashion houses, deals and commercial news involving manufacturers and distribution networks, marketing surveys and new trends. Over the years, many other publications have joined the daily, transforming the publishing house into a veritable empire of professional publications: the oldest one is the *Daily News Record* (*DNR*), founded in 1892 and devoted to men's apparel. Fairchild Publications, in 1999, was purchased by Condé Nast.

(*Lucia Serlenga*)

Wonderbra A brassiere. Created in 1963 by the Canadian fashion designer Louise Poirier, it made its official debut in 1994 in the United States, revolutionizing the world of lingerie. The Wonderbra enhanced a woman's cleavage with its special push-up system. It inspired many imitations and become something bordering on a cultural icon, in part thanks to the image of Eva Herzigova, the model used for its first advertising campaign. The Council of Fashion Designers of America called it "an unprecedented phenomenon in the fashion industry." (*Giulio Alberoni*)

Woodward Kirsten. English brand of hats, founded in 1984. After studying at the London College of Fashion, Kirsten began her career in 1983. She presented her models at Hyper-Hyper in London, where she was discovered by Karl Lagerfeld. From 1984 on she worked on the collections of Chanel and Fendi and, after 1988, with Alistair Blair, Betty Jackson, Victor Edelstein, David Fielden and Katharine Hamnett. She made hats with a Surrealist inspiration that resembled, variously, corsets or croissants. Beginning in 1984, she sold her creations in her boutique in Portobello Green.

Wool The most common animal fiber is obtained from the shearing of merino or crossbred sheep usually bred in New Zealand, Australia, Argentina, and South Africa, but also from Scotland, Italy, and many other countries. The transformation of the fleece into yarn involves the washing and spinning of the fleece. Spinning can be performed in either of two working cycles, depending on the quality of the fiber. One is the combing system, in which long fibers are set in parallel, to create a gathered yarn, and thus produce smooth, beaten fabrics; these are less warm but more expensive. The second method is the carding system which uses short fibers; this gives a more voluminous yarn and thus puffier, hairier fabrics, which are warmer and softer. The main characteristics of wool are that it is hygroscopic (i.e., it can absorb humidity up to 25% of its weight), non-conductive (which gives strong thermal protection), elastic (it returns to its original shape), and resistant to wear, fire, creasing, and pleating. The water in which the fleece is washed gives lanoline, which is used in cosmetics, adhesives, and oils. The "pure virgin wool" label, managed by Woolmark, certifies that the garments are 100% wool from shearing and not reused.

Woolman Chase Edna (1877-1957). American journalist. She was a crucial figure in the development of the magazine *Vogue*. Hired at the age of 18 as a circulation clerk, she joined the editorial staff in 1914. Six years later, she was already the editor-in-chief of the American, English, and French editions of *Vogue*. She was one of the promoters of American fashion. In 1935 she was awarded the French Legion of Honor. She retired in 1952, but continued to serve as the head of the editorial board. She wrote an autobiography, *Always in Vogue*.

Woolmark A promotional consortium comprising the leading wool producers and manufacturers of Great Britain, Australia, New Zealand, and South Africa. Its goal was to support and increase wool consumption. It established parameters of quality for production which it certified with its label.

Pure virgin wool for a double-face overcoat by Mila Schön, in a sketch by Brunetta (Biki Collection).

Woolrich American manufacturer of ready-to-wear fashion. It was founded in Pennsylvania by the Rich brothers, in 1830. At first it was just a small woolen mill. In 1845, the company moved to Woolrich where it is still based and soon afterward, it transformed itself definitively into a clothing manufacturer. In the 1930s it launched its first line of clothing for drives, and in the 1950s it launched its plaid TV Jackets. In the 1980s, the introduction of fabrics like Goretex and Cordura allowed the production of increasingly avant-garde items, a trend that continued in the 1990s as well, with the use of materials like Island Cotton, Riverwash and Canvas. In the 1990s, W.P. Lavori in Corso imported the label to Italy, giving rise to the phenomenon of the Parka windbreaker.

❑ 2002. In Italy, 48,000 Arctic Parka jackets were sold, in comparison with the 35,000 sold in 2000 and the 1,000 in 1990. From 1997 to 2002, the volume of sales of the U.S. label in Italy has increased by 73.6 percent.
❑ 2005. The American company

celebrates its 175th anniversary with a special collection, called *Anniversary Collection*, featuring a selection of historic articles.

Woolworth's American chain of department stores offereing popular prices. It was founded in 1879 by Frank Winfield Woolworth (1852-1919). After working as a shop clerk in a shop in Watertown (New York), he decided to open a store of his own, based on three principles: all items should cost 5 cents, payment should be in cash, and all articles should be in sight. A short while later he opened a second business in Lancaster, Pennsylvania, where he also offered items for 10 cents. This led to the famous slogan, "The five and dime department store." In 1886 he already had seven stores on the East Coast. The financial success was so great that, in 1913, Winfield built on Broadway the Woolworth Building, a steel skyscraper that remained until 1930 the tallest building on earth (architect, Cass Gilbert). In Europe there were many who followed his example: in France, we need only mention Prisunic and Monoprix, in Italy, Upim and Standa. Today, Woolworth's is part of the Venator Group Inc. which also owns a number of other distribution networks such as the Foot Locker (running and sports shoes), Kinney's shoes and Champs Sports (sports equipment). The headquarters of the group, however, is still in the legendary Woolworth Building. (*Eleonora Attolico*)

Wooyoungmi Woo Young. Korean fashion designer. Since 1988 she has been designing a menswear collection that is the top seller in South Korea. She uses cotton matelasse inspired by traditional fabrics, leather inserts with Chinese writing with political spiritual statements in her most recent collections. She has presented twice in Paris, the first time in 2002. In Korea her company is financed by CJ Group (a division of Samsung). Her items are sold in department stores in Seoul, and in the United States, England, Austria, Finland, Belgium, and Germany.

Workers for Freedom A men's fashion line created in 1984 in London by the fashion designer Richard Nott in partnership with the manager Graham Fraser. The following year, they also launched a woman's prêt-à-porter collection.

Worth Maison of high fashion created by Charles Frédérick Worth (1825-1895). A major and significant creator of fashion of the nineteenth century, the inventor of the concept of haute couture, he was a personality capable of overturning the age-old mechanism for the diffusion of fashions, by imposing his own tastes as a bourgeois man upon the most illustrious aristocracies of Europe and succeeding in establishing his own creations as emblems of value and uniqueness through his own label. He was born in Bourne, Lincolnshire, and began to work at the age of 12 anni as a shop clerk in London, first for Swan Edgar and later for Lewis Allemby, major specialty emporiums for the merchandising of cloths, upholstery, shawls, and silks. Young and ambitious, in 1845 he decided to move to Paris, the capital of taste and of international fashion, and there he undertook a career as a salesman in the renowned Gagelin "magasin de nouveautés" in the Rue Richelieu. After just five years, he succeeded in opening a dressmaking deparment and becoming its chief. The year 1853 was the year of the wedding of Napoleon III and Eugenia de Montijo, the

Worth, model of evening gown with ostrich plumes in a sketch by Drian (The Costume Institute, The Metropolitan Museum of Art, New York).

Corset designed by Gianfranco Bedin for the Couture Lingerie collection for the Maison of Worth, 2003.

new empress Eugenie: the maison Gagelin was the official purveyor of the empress's trousseau, and this placed it in the society pages, while at the same time it took part in the Universal Expositions of London in 1851 and Paris in 1855. It was here that Worth had an opportunity to exhibit an original creation of his own, a mantle for use in court, inspired by models from classical antiquity. In 1857-58 he decided to leave Gagelin and to go into business on his own, together with a partner of Swedish descent, Otto Bobergh, at number 7 in the Rue de la Paix, an ordinary Parisian street that Worth would make one of the best known addresses in the capital. The beginnings were difficult, with twenty seamstresses and the assistance of his wife, Marie Vernet, a mannequin that he met at Gagelin, but they were soon rewarded with success, thanks to an outfit created for Princess Pauline de Metternich, the wife of the Prussian ambassador to the French court. Pauline introduced Worth to the Empress Eugenie, and in 1859 he became the official court dressmaker, specializing in evening gowns and ball gowns in damasked tulle and lace, and interpreting in his own personal manner the Spanish tastes of Eugenia de Montijo through bolero jackets, laces, and mantillas in bright, confident colors. After taking the *cage-crinoline* to its greatest possible dimensions in 1859-60, with single specimens bedecked with hundreds of frills and ribbons, in 1865 he began to reduce it in size, sensing the imminent saturation of public taste. In its place he proposed the *demi-crinoline* and then the *tournure* (or *pouff*), definitively accepted in 1867-68, which relegated draperies and padding to the rear of the outfit, thus resulting in a flattening of the front of the skirt. It would be Worth who would establish a different rhythm in the alternations of fashions, introducing variants in form and other new developments, also inventing such new types of clothing as the *princesse*, created for the first time for the Empress Eugenie and for Alexandra of Wales. This style presented itself as a loose and comfortable dress, stitched without cuts in the waist, in contrast with the usual women's clothing of the time, composed of a separate skirt and corset. And so Worth introduced the concept of new developments into wardrobes that had become almost unchanged over time. By making use of sumptuous fabrics and exclusive workmanship, he contributed, after 1871, to the revival of the silkworks of Lyons, pushing textile manufacturers to develop increasingly varied designs and typologies, with the latest developments constituting the most desirable mode. He dissolved his partnership with Bobergh, in part due to the forced closure due to the Franco-Prussian war, and in 1874 his two sons Jean Philippe and Gaston joined the family company, with Jean Philippe assisting his father in the creative sector, and Gaston helping in the administration of the company, thus allowing the consolidation and expansion of the dressmaking business. Purveyor to the courts of France, Austria, Sweden, Italy, Spain and Russia, after the advent of the Republic the fashion house began to orient its production toward the new manfuacturing middle class, toward the world of politics and entertainement, and opening up to the social milieu of the Belle Epoque. Unrivaled master of taste and elegance in the second half of the nineteenth century, Worth would be the first to introduce innovative commercial and sartorial conceptions: he deserves credit for dividing fashion into seasons and for deciding to sell paper patterns of his creations on the international market, preferring to sell his own ideas himself, rather than falling victim to the inevitable imitations. The "*artiste en robe*" died in Paris in 1895, leaving his empire to his sons and heirs. After an initial series of successes, his sons faltered, unable to carry on the tradition in the face of an increasingly aggressive competition. The *maison* continued with varied fortunes for the entire first half of the twentieth century. In 1950, it was absorbed by Paquin. (*Aurora Fiorentini*)

Worth Gaston (1853-1924). The son of Charles F. Worth and Marie Vernet, he was born in Paris. He began working alongside his father as early as 1874, and after his father's death he took over the administrative and commercial side of the *maison*, helping it to expand. He became the first chairman of the Chambre Syndicale de la Confection et de la Couture of Paris, from 1895 to 1898, a position that was considered highly prestigious and which allowed him to gain a privilged view of the demands and possible developments of tailoring at the dawn of the new century. In 1902, he came to the conclusion that the Paris headquarters needed to be expanded to include new and luxurious sales outlets in other European capitals, he inaugurated an elegant and modern subsidiary in London, where the family had originated. Between 1900 and 1901 Gaston would hire the young Paul Poiret as designer and pattern-maker, soon to butt heads however with Gaston's brother Jean-Philippe who succeeded in ejecting Poiret from the atelier soon thereafter. In 1922, worn out by the war, Gaston handed over the administrative and commercial operations of the company to his son Jacques.

Worth Jacques. The youngest of the sons of Gaston Worth. In 1922 he took over from his father the administrative and financial control, while his brother Jean Jacques took over the artistic direction, replacing his uncle Jean-Philippe. In 1941 he handed over the position to his own sons, Roger and Maurice, who continued the company's two-headed tradition. Jacques played, like his father, an active role in the organization of the profession. He was the chairman of the Chambre Syndicale twice, in the years 1927-30 and 1933-35 and was also vice president of the Union Syndicale des Tissus. In 1930, he founded the school of the Chambre Syndicale de la Couture.

Worth Jean Philippe (1856-1926). The son of Charles F. Worth and Marie Vernet, he was born in Paris and from 1874 he worked with his father in the dressmaking atelier. In 1895 he took over the entire creative sector, focusing on preserving a high level of quality and the exclusive style of the creations. His work, especially intense and creative in the years of the Belle Epoque (among his clients were Sarah Bernhardt and Eleonora Duse), confermed the specialization of this dressmaking atelier in evening gowns and ball gowns and in any case in especially luxurious and refined creations. Forced to witness the progressiv triumph of a simpler, more linear fashion, after opposing the entry into the company of Poiret, in 1910 Jean Philippe retired, leaving his nephew Jean Charles the task of continuing the task of designing for Worth. The Worth atelier experienced great challenges during the two World Wars, and it continued its activity until 1950, the year it was purchased by the *maison* Paquin. Unfortunately, Paquin-Worth would close up shop definitively only three years later, in 1956.

❑ 2001. The Worth trademark was purchased, for perfumes, by the Indian Dilash Metha, who then extended the use of the trademark to fashion as well, by entrusting the revival of the maison to the Lebanese Mounir Moufarrige.
❑ 2002. Moufarrige hired the Italian fashion designer Giovanni Bedin for the "Couture Lingerie" collection which was presented in Paris in January 2003.

Wragge Sidney (1908-1978). American fashion designer. Like Ralph Lauren, to whom he has been compared in the context of contemporary fashion designers, he emphasized in his creations the epic aspects of America, often choosing country themes or themes that were inspired by typically American traditions. One of his distinctive features was the nonchalance with which he combined items of apparel in different styles.

Wrangler American western-style blue jeans brand, founded in 1947. Perhaps the name, a clear reference to a rodeo star, had already been adopted by the Globe Superior Manufacturing Company, a manufacturer based in Abdingdon, Illinois, founded in 1889. Others believe that it can be traced back to the Blue Bell Manufacturing Company which was based in Greensboro, North Carolina. The two companies produced work overalls blue denim trousers. In the first decades of the twentieth century, Blue Bell became the market leader through its merger with Big Ben Manufacturing and Jellico Clothing (1926). In 1931, it introduced a new process that limited the shrinking of the denim after the first washing, making the clothing more shapely and better suited to fashion wear. In 1936, it merged with Globe Superior. Ten years later, that merger gave birth to Wrangler, whose style was entrusted to Rodeo Ben, a Hollywood master of western wardrobes. Then collections were launched for children, inspired by Davie Crockett and other characters of Walt Disney. Then came the turn of the revolutionary model 13 MWZ with the zippered fly. In the 1960s and 1970s, a period marked by the advent of jeans as a symbol of rebellion, Wrangler increased the stitchings and pockets, entrusting one collection to Peter Max, an especially fanciful designer. In 1987 it was purchased by the VF Corporation, the American textile giant.

Wrap around Used by Coco Chanel, these are glasses with broad, curved arms, clinging close to the head. They came into fashion as sports sunglasses at the end of the 1990s.

Wrap Dress Pocket outfit designed by Diane von Fürstenberg in the 1970s.

Wurttembergisches Landesmuseum Stuttgart. The unusual collection of this museum comes from the former regional museum of arts and trades in Landesgewerbe which, in turn, began to collect specimens of local manufacturing in 1848. Aside from printed fabrics, threads and yarns of various sorts, embroideries and lace, outfits and types of apparel from the eighteenth century to the present day form part of the collection.

Wyatt David (1972). British fashion designer, born in Hampshire. His curriculum vitae includes a degree from the Manchester Polytechnic and important work with Enrica Massei, People Corporation, Alessandro Dell'Acqua, Alma, Thierry Mugler and Mark Jacobs (for whom he also designed Iceberg womenswear), before launching his own backward-looking collection, set in the 1920s and 1970s, especially in terms of form.

Wyatt Robert (1970). British photographer. He graduated in 1993 from the avant-garde West Surrey Institute of Art and Design. He lives and works in London, contributing fashion photography regularly to the *Guardian Weekend*. An artist and a documentarist by training, his photography with its delicate colors constructs situations in imaginary interiors from the 1960s, with an ironic and hyper-realistic style that clearly refers to the pictures of Martin Parr and Sophie Call.

Wyckman Jo (1946). Belgian fashion designer. After completing his studies at the Academy of Fine Arts of Antwerp, he was hired by Barton's to design a line of raincoats, and he became the director of the style office. With the help of Barton's, he launched a line of his own. Today he is a consultant for the Japanese Asahi Chemical Company and coordinator of Promostyl in Belgium. His first collection for men and women was called A Different Dialogue and was immediately successful, with its proper American college style, revisited with extreme irony. From his debut and throughout his career, his interest was not limited to the aesthetic side, but also extended to the technical, commercial, and marketing aspects.

Wynants Christian (1979). Belgian fashion designer. As soon as he graduated from the Academy of Fine Arts in Antwerp, he was noticed by Dries van Noten who, like a talent scout, immediately identified creative potential in this young man, and decided to allow him to design the line of knitwear and, over time, assigning him increasingly great responsibilities. Christian, with the appearance of a well-behaved boy and little Harry Potter spectacles, learned a great deal from his "master": he had plenty of imagination, so that in 2001 he won the Jury Prize of the Festival of Hyères and entered the Olympus of the new creatives from his country. His painstaking attention to details results in a style with a tailored aspect, personal and even nonconformist interventions: his name is linked to a prêt-à-porter already well known in the United States and in Japan.

(*Lucia Mari*)

Xiomara Katy (1974). Portuguese designer. She attended a course in fashion design at Citex in Porto and made an interesting study of the designer label Trussardi. She is very feminine, sensual and entertaining, and her clothes are youthful in style. She has shown her designs on the runways of Paris. She loves very personalized clothes, to which she adds her signature details. Cotton and lycra and favorite materials.

Xuly Bët (1962). Designer, born in Bamako Badian in Mali. His real name is Lamine Kouyate, but he has chosen this pseudonym for his label, which in the language of Mali means "he who opens his eyes, whose glance pierces appearances." He left Mali at the age of 14 to move first to Argentina and then to France, where he started to study architecture, but he abandoned his studies in favor of fashion. He founded the Funkin Fashion Factory in 1989 and presented his first collection of clothing in 1990. His most characteristic feature is his ability to recycle old clothes, creating new lines from old styles. "Just like the African tradition," he says, "where earrings are made from old tin cans." He opened a boutique in the Forum des Halles in Paris in 1996, and another one in Marseilles in 1998. He designed some of the costumes for the 1998 World Cup opening ceremony in the Stadium of France.

(*Valeria Vantaggi*)

Y

Yak A kind of ox that lives more than 4,000 meters up on the slopes of the Himalayas. Its undercoat is used to produce yarn with similar properties to cashmere and camel hair, which is used for luxury knitwear and very fine, light and warm blankets.

Yamamoto Kansai (1944). Japanese designer. After a degree at Nippon University, he worked for Junko Koshino. In 1971 he showed his first Collection in London and in 1974 in Paris, where he was praised for his innovation. Before closing his business, he was involved in various big art and fashion projects.

Yamamoto Yohji (1943). Japanese designer born in Tokyo. From the beginning his fashion has been characterized not only by inspiration and creativity, but also by intelligence and discipline. He started off in women's ready-to-wear with his Y's label in 1972 after studying at the University of Keio and gaining a diploma from the Bunka Gakuen Institute fashion course. He displayed his designs in Tokyo in 1977, and four years later left the Japanese capital which he sees as "dominated by the common sense of a boring bourgeoisie." He decided to make a start in Paris, where he arrived, with Rei Kawakubo of Comme des Garçons, with the declared intention of revolutionizing the rules of Western fashion. His Collection shocked fashion insiders, and the trade press referred to it as "post-atomic fashion": the clothes, made with indiscriminate cuts and big rips, brought to mind the threat of atomic war. In 1983, also on the Paris runways and still working with Kawakubo, his refined Pauperism Collection caught the media's attention for its lyricism, but above all it signaled the start of the influence of Eastern aesthetics on European fashion. His deconstructivism was the starting point for the new generation of fashion designers who, from the mid-1980s, rewrote the canons of European fashion. His research into fabrics (he mixes technological fibers with natural materials so that they look worn-in) led him to experiment with a highly innovative formal purism that earned him the title of "master" from his colleagues. In 1997, paying homage to the tradition of Dior and Chanel, he showed a Collection that borrowed from the past without looking dated. Whilst still showing his women's and men's Collections in Paris, he worked in a building-atelier in the center of Tokyo helped by his mother, who had been a dressmaker and his first teacher. He has over 300 employees. In 1989 the film director Wim Wenders documented his work in the film *Notebook on Cities and Clothes*. In 1996 he took part in the Florence Biennale *Il tempo e la moda* (Time and Fashion),

Yohji Yamamoto: clothes from Fall-Winter Collection.

contributing to the exhibition *New Persona e New Universe*. In an interview for *Elle* in 1999 he said: "Style is the art of mixing, of showing off and governing aesthetically the things you love. As for myself, I like to pair designer chic with things I find at the flea market. Choice is our ultimate freedom. Wearing certain designers' clothes is like changing your life. When somebody tells me: 'Yohji, I'd love to wear your clothes,' I reply 'Be careful, do not be so sure of yourself. It's not that simple.'" (*Michele Ciavarella*)

❑ 1998. As part of the celebrations for the 25th anniversary of the *Tanztheater Wuppertal Pina Bausch*, Yamamoto was asked to design the set for the meeting between several karate masters and the company's dancers.
❑ 2001, Fall. A wedding dress by Yamamoto was featured in the Radical Fashion exhibition at the Victoria & Albert Museum in London, where 50 dresses by nine of the most eccentric and exuberant designers were displayed.
❑ 2002, July. Yamamoto was appointed creative director of Adidas Sport Style. The line, previously called Equipment, specializes in sport fashion; the Collection consists of 50 men's items, as many again for women, and a line of accessories. Before taking up the position, the Japanese designer worked with Adidas Originals for three seasons: the shoes he designed became best sellers, notching up an estimated 500 million euros in sales. He increased his work with Adidas, creating a ready-to-wear line called Y3, which was completed in October 2002 and presented at Pitti Uomo the following January.
❑ 2003, Spring. The launch of a range of clothing designed by Yamamoto in about 290 outlets of the Japanese chain Muji.
❑ 2003, July. Yamamoto decided to show his Spring-Summer 2003 ready-to-wear Collection in July rather than October, ideally bringing it closer to *haute couture*, which traditionally shows in that period. His decision was motivated by a desire to keep his distance from the overcrowding during the ready-to-wear fashion week.

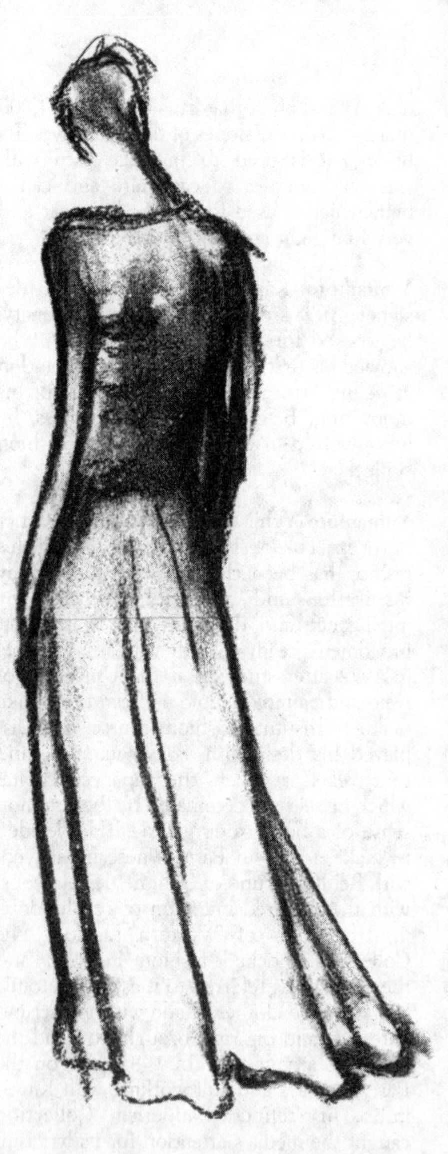
Yohji Yamamoto, sketch 1999.

Yantony A legendary figure in the world of footwear. Of Eastern origin, he opened an atelier in Paris at the beginning of the 1900s that produced footwear famous and coveted for both the elegance of its lines and its exquisite craftsmanship.

Yardley English brand of fragrances, with over two centuries of history and success. Its renowned lavender fragrance was launched in 1910, when the company (founded by Lord William Yardley in 1770) was the one of the leading soap manufacturers in England and France. In the last three decades of the 20th century, the company, whose products are distributed in 150 countries, changed ownership three times, first acquired by British American Tobacco, then the Beecham Group, and finally by the American Wasserstein Perella Group.

Yarmak Helen. Russian designer of furs. She was born in Kiev, but lives and works in Moscow in a building that bears her name. Here she produces her designs for the boutiques of Tverskaja Street and Kadasevskaja Embankment, and for her showroom on Fifth Avenue. Avid for luxury, she has a passion for sable. She is an active member of the New York Academy of Sciences and a member of the French Academy of Architecture and Design. She was named businesswoman of the year in 2000 by the International Association of Businesswomen in Washington. Eclectic, she also designs collectable jewelry and shawls, made of sable interwoven with gold and embroidered with natural pearls, inspired by dresses worn by the Tsarinas. She loves antique fabrics.

(*Lucia Mari*)

Yau Suet Ki Cecilia. Designer born in Hong Kong. She graduated from HK Polytechnic University and continued her training in design in Paris. She worked in the design studio of Biba Fashion Trading Co. In 1999 her first Collection, typified by precious fabrics and inspired by the concept of luxury, won first prize at the Hong Kong Fashion Designers Contest.

Yazbukey Sisters and designers. Emel was born in Cairo (1977), Yaz in Istanbul (1973). They are the grand-nieces of King Farouk, Egypt's last king. After living in different countries around the world, they moved to Paris. Yaz studied industrial and graphic design and, after internships at renowned houses such as Martin Margiela, Martin Sitbon, and Givenchy, she became the assistant of Jeremy Scott. In March 2000 the pair presented their first line of accessories together, followed by another in the fall of the same year. They worked with Gaspard Yurkievich for his ready-to-wear Fall-Winter 2002-2003 runway show in Paris. (*Maddalena Fossati*)

Yeohlee Malaysian designer who works in New York. She studied the relationship between fashion and architecture, and defines her clothes as portable constructions. In fact her clothes are often exhibited at architecture exhibitions to show the mutual influence of the two disciplines, and as examples of geometric design and functionalism. She attended Parson's School of Design, and in a few years was exhibiting her creations on important runways. She is also an advocate of comfort fabrics that are easy to wash and work for all seasons. One of her recent creations is a dress made of Teflon, the same material used for non-stick pans, that makes the cloth repellent to every type of stain.

Yé-Yé French name for the youth movement and its fashions in the 1960s. The Beatles, the undisputed leaders in the field of music, dominated the youth culture of that decade, with their haircuts and dress being widely imitated. In France, their chorus "Yeah Yeah Yeah" was abbreviated to yé-yé, and chosen to sum up the dress styles of that period. During the 1960s, the mass media had a fundamental role in the explosion of mass consumption, and to that end, used fashion as a marketing tool to continually direct and modify public taste, so as to always create new demands. Televisions and cars became more common. Clothing stores aimed at young people had great success, as they offered the young the opportunity to dress themselves. Chains with low and medium cost goods also become more widespread. Fashion saw the triumph of brightly colored Optical Art prints, the miniskirt created by Mary Quant and the soft-colored creations of Barbara Hulanicki, known as Biba. The names André Courrèges and Paco Rabanne appeared. The world of *haute couture* went into decline and ready-to-wear gained a stronger hold. Even men's clothing was invested with color. In 1969 the designer Rudy Geinrich stated: "*Haute couture* no longer holds the same meaning because money, status, and power no longer hold the same meaning. Now fashion starts in the street. I look at what the kids are wearing. I give shape to their style, I interpret it and add something of my own, and so it becomes fashion."

(*Gianluca Bauzano*)

YKK Leading multinational zip manufacturer. Founded by the Japanese Tadao Yoshida in the 1930s, they produce over 2 million kilometers of zips a year, and sell them in 62 countries. As well as a colossal fortune, Yoshida left his heirs a business philosophy: prosperity depends on creating well-being for those around you. Hence, for example, great attention is paid to the working environment.

Y.M.C. (You Must Create) English young fashion label. Created in London in 1996 by Fraser Moss (1966) and Jimmy Collins (1967). Neither studied fashion, but they both have experience working in the business: Moss worked for French Connection and subsequently launched the label Komodo; Collins was an apprentice to Vivienne Westwood before opening his own shop, Professor Head. Together they have created a modern unisex line, designed to be easily assimilated into their customers' wardrobes. The label's name is taken from a phrase by the American industrial designer Raymond Loewy: "You must create your own style." In 1999 they won the British Streetstyle Designers of the Year award.

❑ The brand opened a shop in London's Conduit Street, but this closed shortly after to make way for Boutique B. Other outlets were opened in Regent Street and Cardiff, Wales.

❑ In 2000 they created the Mini Millennium Capsule Collection in collaboration with the artist Andy Jordan, who creates clothes by making holes in cloth and embroidering around them. Y.M.C contributed to the T-shirt club organized by the rock band The Avalanches. The label produced a limited edition of 100 T-shirts, designed with the Australian Natalie Wood. They are sold on the internet and the proceeds go towards the NSPCC, an association for the protection of children.

Yon Women's clothing label. Created in 1984 by the Milanese Nicoletta Leo. She first designed a Collection of jewelry, then a line of women's fashion. The crux of her style is research into materials. The clothes from her first Collection for Fall-Winter 1999-2000 were all made from carbon fibers, PVC and glass-fiber.

Yonnet Paul (1948). French sociologist. He has made many studies of fashion, its messages, and the language of clothes, also investigating the phenomenon triggered by ready-to-wear clothes, jeans, and the influence of youth styles on adult dress. He published *Jeux, Modes et Masses* in 1985.

Yorke & Cole French ready-to-wear label created in 1984 by the models Bridget Yorke (Johannesburg, 1959) and Julie Cole (Pennsylvania, 1960). It disappeared in 1990 after an initial success, gained by distribution in over 50 sales points around the world.

Yoshiko Kajitani (1977). Japanese designer of women's clothing and accessories. She started studying fashion in Japan and then graduated from Studio Berçot in Paris in 1998. After an internship with Eric Halley, she also worked on her own Collection that was sold at the concept store Colette from 2000. She creates jewelry and clothes that are sold in the Parisian boutique Maria Luisa.

Young Fashion Award Italian competition for young designers first started in 2001. Organized by Moet & Chandon and the Italian National Chamber of Fashion, the Young Fashion Award allows the best pupils from six Italian fashion schools, selected by a jury of fashion experts, to show their own designs on the runway. The six chosen pupils, one from each school, can then proceed to the final phase of the competition: a runway show during Milan women's Fashion Week in September. At the end of the show the overall winner for the year is announced, who is then given the chance to work for one of the big Italian designers for six months. (*Sara Tieni*)

Yuba Wool and cotton yarn woven in a light sheer weave. Once processed, a two-tone effect with shiny and opaque touches is achieved.

Yudashkin Valentin (1964). Russian designer. He opened his fashion house in Moscow in 1990 and a year later made his debut at the Paris *haute couture* week. At the end of 1998 he signed a distribution agreement with Vision, which allowed him to sell his creations in the international market. In 1999 he held his first show at Milano Collezioni Donna.

Valentin Yudashkin, 1998.

❑ Late 1999. His first women's fragrance marked the launch of the cosmetics department of Valentin Yudashkin Trade Mark. The line is produced by the French "Parour Parfume" and is distributed in Russia and the rest of Europe.
❑ 2001, March. Yudashkin presented a series of hand-painted porcelain at Moscow's Central Concert Hall on the occasion of the runway show of his 19th *haute couture* Collection. The range was the result of a joint venture with Lucas International, a jewelry company with twenty-five years of experience.
❑ 2001, September. A line of underwear was launched.
❑ 2003. The Pakerson company signed an agreement for the manufacture and sale of "Pakerson by Valentin Yudashkin", a line of men's and women's hosiery presented at Micam in Milan at the end of March 2003.
(*Pierangelo Mastantuono*)

Yukata Cotton kimono. First appeared at the end of the 17th century in the bathhouses of Kyoto and Osaka because the heat and humidity of those environments made cotton more practical than silk. From then on they were worn by the merchant class, who were forbidden to wear silk kimonos.

Yulan Yong Joanne (1968). Scottish designer. Born in Scotland to a Chinese family, she graduated from the Royal College of Art in Edinburgh and then moved to Milan where she worked with the most important Italian fashion houses: Giorgio Armani, Max Mara, Marina Spadafora, and the Gilmar Group, where she was made head designer of the Gerani line in 1992. She launched her own line at London Fashion Week in 2000 with the Yulan label, combining an Oriental aesthetic with Western technical precision. The result is a discreet and delicate elegance based on very feminine and sexy details without any trace of vulgarity. She uses high-quality chiffon or silk crepe for the evening, and sporty tweed and wool herringbone for the daytime. Her clothes have a tailored cut, with soft simple lines that subtly drape the figure, underlining its sensuality with deep slits and clever asymmetric details.

Yuppies Youth movement and subsequent fashion, dating from the beginning of the 1980s. Term abbreviated from the phrase "young urban professional," coined to describe a generation of young managers and professionals totally dedicated to their careers. Money, luxurious living, and uncommitted relationships were the connotations of this lifestyle. The yuppy world was governed by strict codes of conduct. Clothing had to be from a designer label, preferably made in Italy, and all accessories, from watches to cars, were to be expensive. Yuppies frequented only the most fashionable restaurants and bars, and particular holiday resorts at certain times of the year. They attended international society events covered by the media. In contrast with the material consumerism of the 1980s, at the beginning of the 1990s the New Age movement gained an increasingly large number of advocates who looked to spirituality as a source of serenity and called for the rejection of all that the yuppies so frantically pursued.

Yurkievich Gaspard (1972). French designer. First noticed in 1998 at the 12th Hyéres festival on the Côte d'Azur, an event that showcases young designers and graduates from fashion schools. Immersed in pop culture, his first Collection was very visual and typically urban. It was graphic, asymmetric, sculptured, and played with contrasting materials to create glamour and humour.

❑ 1999. First show during Paris ready-to-wear fashion week. Yurkievich increased the impact of his clothes with a limited edition CD called *Yurkievich by Herbert.* The disc contained sounds recorded backstage during the show, from the screeching of clothes hangers being pulled along the rail, to the clicking of heels on the floor. Critics have likened him to Jeremy Scott and Jérome Dreyfuss for his aggressive and sexy style.

❑ Yurkievich did not neglect his outrageous side in his Spring-Summer 2002 show in Paris, when he sent girls from the Crazy Horse down the runway in the uniforms of the guards at Buckingham Palace, wearing corsets and bare-breasted. The ironic musical accompaniment was a track called *God Save our Bearskins.*

Yuzen The main Japanese printing technique used for kimonos from the beginning of the Edo period (1616-1867). Characterized by very intricate patterns and bright colors.

Z

Zaitsev Slava (1953) Russian designer. Graduated with top marks from the Moscow High School of Textiles and after a long experience with the Soviet Fashion House, he opened his own atelier in 1978. After a few years he earned the title as the "*perestroika*" designer for dressing Raisa Gorbachev. He left Russia for Paris in 1988. An admirer of Italian fashion, Slava has taken it as his inspiration. Using rougher materials – such as cotton, felt, and wool – he has recreated a style that is very close to Italian fashion, particularly when it comes to suits and footwear. (*Maria Vittoria Pozzi*)

❑ After winning various prestigious international fashion awards, Slava Zaitsev was made an honorary citizen of Paris for his creative contribution to the world of fashion.
❑ In the 1990s the designer was selected to design the robes of the judges of the Russian Constitutional Court and the uniforms of the Moscow Police.
❑ As well as being a fashion house, Slava Zaitsev is now also one of the most important model agencies in Russia, together with Prestige, Modus Vivendi and Abc.
❑ Zaitsev's fragrances, the sales of which kept the company afloat during the difficult years of the collapse of the Soviet Union, ideally echo Russian tradition. Maroussia, a woman's fragrance in a red bottle whose shape is similar to the outline of St Basil's Cathedral, is a homage to the designer's native country and his mother Maria.
❑ Slava's son Yegor, also a designer, started to assist Slava in the running of the fashion house.

Zamasport Italian clothing manufacturer. Founded in Novara in 1966 with the idea of renovating and transforming the *Maglificio Augusto Zanetti*, a family-run knitwear and underwear business. The Callaghan brand, whose knitwear is manufactured and distributed by Zamasport, was founded the same year. After two years Walter Albini was called in to redesign Callaghan's jersey ready-to-wear Collection. When Albini ended his relationship with Callaghan in 1972, a young Gianni Versace took his place, where he remained until 1986. Accustomed to working with avant-guarde designers, Zamasport then employed Romeo Gigli to bring a fresh ethnic edge to the company's new Collections, which met with international success at the end of the 1980s. Today Zamasport still produces and distributes the lines Gigli Donna, Gucci Donna, and Callaghan.

Zamponi Emanuele (1971). Born in Carnago, near Varese, he graduated from the Fine Arts Academy of Milan and set up a company specializing in leather and fur clothing. His constant research into and experimentation with new textures, effects, colors, and prints have made him a popular consultant to Italian and foreign designers, and also to tanneries. As a logical consequence, at the end of the 1990s he produced his own Collection, but in it the leather and fur were almost unrecognizable.

Zancan Italian jewelry company, founded near Vicenza by the owner Robertino Zancan in 1987. It soon became established on the national and international markets. Zancan's strength was to recognize the potential of color in jewelry. From the start their products played on the combination of colorful precious stones in geometric settings, then, 15 years later, they adopted more sinuous lines for their Liberty and Nouveau Collections. Several well known Italian actresses have provided testimonials for the brand, including Sabrina Febrilli.

(*Alessandra Quattordio*)

Zanini Marco (1971). Fashion designer born in Bergamo. After studying at Milan's

Academy of Fine Arts, he worked with Lawrence Steele, then Dolce & Gabbana. In 1999 he joined Donatella Versace's design team.

Zannier Leading children's fashion company in France and Europe. It produces the Kickers, 3 Pommers, Assorba, Z, Floriane, and Confetti brands. Founded by Roger Zannier in Saint Chamont in 1962, the group produces mid- and high-range Collections for a range of ages, from newborn to junior.

Zanone Alberto (1953). Italian designer, specialized in knitwear. He started out in the 1970s, working on product planning and quality research for the Della Rovere label. He achieved commercial success with the invention of reversible cashmere and lambswool pieces. He founded his own label in 1987 and started producing more modern, linear knitwear made from combed yarns, predicting a trend that subsequently materialized. For several years he was in charge of the "Tibet fibers" project run by the American Bridge Fund, which was set up to promote one of the Tibetan people's primary resources – yak hair. Since 2001 he has been collecting knitwear seconds, which he then repairs by hand and transforms into unique pieces to be sold through his Recycled Knit label. The label is distributed in Milan, Florence, New York, Tokyo, and Hong Kong. (*Sara Tieni*)

Zappieri Sanzio (1936). Italian fashion trader. He started out as a salesman at a very young age, and by the mid-1950s had already founded his own company in Turin. In the 1960s he started dealing with his first important brands: Ballantyne, Brioni, and Zanella (Zanella owns the UFO jeans brand). The 1970s saw the explosion of the fashion sector in Italy and Zappieri succeeded in obtaining the rights to represent Valentino, and Thierry Mugler, who was just entering the Italian market. In the 1980s Zappieri launched Moschino throughout the world and added labels like Krizia, Blumarine, and Oliver by Valentino to his stable, followed by lines from Dior, Ritz Sadler, and, more recently, Donna Karan Signature, plus high street labels like Kookai, L'Altra Moda, and Liu-Jo. His latest venture has been the opening of a 1,000 square-meter multi-brand franchising store called Zap in Milan's Galleria Passarella. The group is made up of various franchised companies, each with specific functions, and has about 120 employees. The annual turnover is about 103 million euros for about 1 million items. The company has 8 showrooms in Italy and 10 elsewhere in Europe.

Zara Brand and chain of clothing stores. The Spanish Inditex group, which was created in 1963 by the Cortega Gaona family, started with lingerie, then moved into men's ready-to-wear, then achieved great success with the creation of the Zara boutiques in the 1980s. There are now over 100 stores open in Spain, Italy, France, Greece, Portugal, the UK, and the USA. Using a direct link to 20 or so companies in Galicia, they can restock quickly using the "just in time" system. High quality fabrics, close attention to trends, and restricted prices make Zara appeal to a wide range of customers for women's, men's, and children's clothing.

❑ 2002, April. Opening of the first Italian megastore, Zara's 520th in the world. Located in Corso Vittorio Emanuele in Milan, it is the group's biggest European store, with four floors of women's, men's, and children's fashions. The opening is the first fruit of a joint venture created in 2001 between Inditex and Percassi, the property and trading group that holds a 49% share of Zara in Italy.
❑ 2002. Positive balance, with a 20% increase in sales.
❑ 2003. The chain had 531 stores around the world, and increased its selling space by 17% over 2003. Zara was launched in Russia with a store of about 1,500 square meters in Mega Mall, the country's biggest shopping mall. The launch was the result of a collaboration with the Stockman company from Finland. The English magazine *Retail Week*, which monitors the distibution sector, proclaimed Zara "International Retailer of the Year" at its annual Retail Week Awards.

Zazous Provocative French style and school of thought, circumscribed in German occupied Paris and Northern France from 1940 to 1944. It was a form of symbolic expression that summed up a whole world and way of thinking. The term comes from the name of an item of clothing, the American zoot suit, a fitted suit worn with high heels: the term was then reworked in French, and, inspired by the sound of jazz, it was translated onomatopoeically into "zazou-zazou-zazouhe." Despite being a movement with a limited number of followers, it played a central role in French culture, and was a forerunner of the existentialist current. As a style, it started from dandyism and gradually took shape as a political tendency contemporary to the Vichy regime. Rather like French punks of the occupation, as the Zazous have been defined, they adopted a rather provocative way of dressing. Presenting themselves as extraneous to their contemporary reality, they were always seen wearing sunglasses and playing with yo-yos. The Zazous' "uniform" consisted of a fitted suit with drainpipe pants and giant check patterns, and superfluous details like half-belts and raised shoulders. This was all worn with short white or mustard-colored socks and worn, deliberately unpolished, leather-soled shoes.

Zebrato Used to describe a pattern of irregular horizontal light-and-dark or black-and-white stripes that imitates the zebra's coat.

Zecca *Haute couture* dressmaker. Founded at the beginning of the 1920s by Nicola Zecca and his wife, and based at 46 Via Ludovisi in Rome. From the very start they had close links with couture and the French tradition. Two dresses made by Zecca for Princess Giovanelli, based on styles by Madame Vionnet and Chanel, can be admired today at the Costume Gallery in the Pitti Palace in Florence; they were donated by Umberto Tirelli. Zecca was credited as a supplier to the royal family, and the company was in constant contact with French fashion houses thanks to the contribution of Mario Vigolo, the dress designer, who regularly went to Paris and returned full of news, tips, information, and, above all, patterns which he gave to Nicola Zecca. In the years of economic self-sufficiency and the birth of the *Ente Moda*, Zecca found themselves firmly on the side of national fashion, becoming the promoter of 100% Italian products and gaining greater recognition for their craftsmanship. Their clothes were very coveted by the bourgeoisie of the time. But immediately after the war the company went back to buying French fashions in response to the demands of their new customers: especially through Rina Modelli in Milan. When the company closed at the end of the 1960s, its archive was acquired by Tirelli. Amongst the papers are a series of designs photographed thirty years earlier that were part of the *Ente Moda*'s examination to know if the designs were truly "Italian" or copied from French models: at the bottom you can see the printed gold mark that is to all extents the symbol of an authentic Italian creation. The majority of Zecca's clientele moved to Antonio De Luca who had the know-how required to continue the style and tradition of the great dressmakers.

(*Bonizza Giordani Aragno*)

1930s design. Zecca was one of the most esteemed dressmakers of the period (from *Anni Venti – La nascita dell'abito moderno*, Centro Di, Florence 1991, catalogue for the Galleria del Costume. Giovanni Battista Giorgini Archive).

Zeina Loredana. Italian model. Born in Venice, she was much in vogue from 1950 to 1954. Irving Penn dedicated a *Vogue* cover to her in September 1952 and she also graced the covers of *Bellezza*, *Grazia*, *Eva*, *Die Elegante Welt*, *Linea* and many other women's titles. Her first marriage was to Giorgio Pavone. She modeled for designers like Carosa, Simonetta Visconti, the Fontana sisters, and Galitzine.

Zelda American ready-to-wear label. From the name of Zelda Fitzgerland, wife of F. Scott Fitzgerald, and a protagonist of the wild years, the beautiful and damned era of the Wasp high society that divided its time between New York, Paris, and the Côte d'Azur. Quite deliberately, the specialty of this ready-to-wear label is recreating contemporary versions of 1920s, 1930s, and 1940s clothes. While the colors and fabrics may always follow the latest trends, the designs are always classic, with careful attention to details like hand embroidery, vintage buttons, and pockets sewn so that they remain hidden. The look has been defined as modern vintage.

Zephyr The ancient Greek word that meant a light spring breeze is here used to describe a light cotton striped or checked fabric. Once used for school tunics, Brigitte Bardot made the zephyr popular by wearing dresses in Saint-Tropez in the 1950s and 1960s whose childishness and ingenuity made them all the more sexy and provocative.

Zibeline Wool fabric with a combed warp and a carded weft. Produced in plain colors, it is dyed in rolls on spiked frames.

Zignone Wool mill specializing in pure wool worsted fabrics, cashmere blends, and extra fine merino that is machine washable. Their products are produced with classic and crêpe finishes. Located in 1968 in Strana (Biella), in recent years the mill's annual production has reached about 2 million meters, 78% of which is exported.

Zilkha Ronit. Ready-to-wear designer. Born in Israel, she lives and works in London. Tradition has made her shows the event that opens London Fashion Week. After graduating in Fashion Design, Ronit launched her first Collection in 1991 and held her first runway show in 1996. Her fashions have romantic, sinuous lines and intricate details. She has recently signed a license agreement with the Itoki Apparel Company for the production and distribution of her brand on the Japanese market. The successful results of this collaboration have also convinced Littlewoods to sign Zilkha up as a consultant. Today there are 4 London stores, and 23 own-brand stores, in-store sales points, and other outlets throughout the rest of Britain. (*Pierangelo Mastantuono*)

Zingone Corrado (1906). Children's clothing manufacturer in Rome. Starting in his premises in Via della Maddalena, Zingone built up a small empire that justifies the slogan "Zingone dresses the whole of Rome," but ambition altered this to become "Zingone dresses the whole world." Towards the end of the 1960s his sons Paolo (1941) and Giorgio (1942) joined the business. At that time they were the only representatives of children's clothing at the official *haute couture* shows. The company then created *Zingone Confezioni* for budget, standard, and luxury purses.

Zintala Handmade shoe company based in Casette d'Ete (Ascoli Piceno). The company was only founded in 1995, but it draws on 30 years of experience and tradition in the art of shoemaking. It has a showroom in Milan in Via Montenapoleone and in Rome in Via Bocca di Leone. The brand has three ranges: Silvano Lattanzi (made-to-measure items), Gerardo Fossati (limited runs using Goodyear technology) and Zintala (younger style shoes). The company has agents in the USA and Japan and also offers its foreign customers a made-to-measure service at home.

Zip In 1893 William Litcomb Judson from Chicago patented a fastening system with hooks that could be quickly opened and closed with a clasp. In 1913 a Swede, Gideon Sundback, perfected Judson's invention, making a zipper with metal teeth. Initially it was only used for belts with a hidden purse or tobacco pouches. The term "zip" was coined by B.G. Worth for a quick fastening system that was then in vogue for footwear. At the beginning of the 1930s the designer Elsa Schiaparelli was the first to use this accessory without hiding it under fabric. Halfway through the 20th century the zip was perfected and substituted button flies for men's pants.

Zohar Trendy shop that mixes fashion, furnishings, and antiques, in Milan's Via Brera. It opened in September 1999, selling silk ties, boxes, cases, leather goods, parchment, galuchat and zebra lampshades: all of the highest Italian craftsmanship. Even for the "antiques" (furniture from the 1920s to 1940s), the focus is still on unusual materials: parchment, galuchat, ceramic (*craquelure*), crystal, special woods (Macassar, venghè), ivory, crocodile, bone, and mother-of-pearl. In 2000 Salvatore Battello, the shop's director, had the first "pieces" of furniture made: the "*tagli&dettagli*" chair, upholstered entirely with parchment and galuchat, and the "*virgola*" chair, upholstered with parchment. He also presented a Collection of vintage drapery, and, in collaboration with a dressmaker, made-to-measure dresses and shirts cut from exclusive fabrics. In 2001 the "*happy hour*" armchair was created in parchment and natural horsehair, or parchment and natural washi (a very high-tech Japanese fabric made from paper). That same year Zohar started producing furniture for important companies, in particular for a big American and international men's fashion company. There has been a branch of Zohar in Rue Bonaparte in Paris since 2002.

Zooties The zoot-suiter style, brought back into vogue in the 1980s by Kid Creole and Sugar Coated, Hernandez, and Chris Sullivan with his Blue Rondo. The zoot suit style had its origins in New York jazz clubs like the Onyx and Famous Doors towards the end of the 1930s. It was reserved for the kind of men who frequented the clubs on 52nd Street, renamed Manhattan's "Swing Street," or Harlem's Savoy Ballroom where New York's black dandies used to parade. These were called Zoot-suiters or Zooties, from the style of suits they wore. Zoot is a distortion and phonetic doubling of suit, to underline the exaggeration and taste for excess that typified this new fashion. And everything really was exaggerated and oversized. Starting with the double-breasted jacket two or three sizes bigger than necessary that wraps around the chest and ends in swathes around the knees, and the pants with the waistband up around the chest as if a waistcoat had been grafted onto a pair of breeches with a very low crotch. Pastel hues and tartans were the preferred choices for the fabrics. Fancy accessories of all kinds and long hand-painted watch chains add to the whole effect. The principle of showy consumerism was pushed to the limit, given the profusion and waste of material involved whilst the USA was on the brink of involvement in World War II. Given that state of affairs, in 1941 the American War Production Board set out strict rules to regulate the manufacturing of garments to the millimeter. Paradoxically, as often happens, it was precisely this prohibition that sanctioned the use of a style that in principle was too radical to catch on through its use by a small minority.

Zoran (1947). American designer. The professional name of Zoran Ladicorbic, Zoran was born in Yugoslavia and studied architecture at the University of Belgrade before moving to New York in 1971. He worked in various fashion jobs, including as a salesman at the Balmain boutique, before launching his first Collection in 1977. A high priest of minimalism in fashion, which the designer hewed to throughout the flamboyance of the 1980s, Zoran creates his signature pieces in fine, often extravagantly priced cashmere. Many of his pieces are seamless and worn wrapped around the body, others are meant to be layered, as in skirts over skirts, T-shirts over T-shirts, tops over tops, all in a controlled palette of red, black, grey white and sand. Zoran has always been something of a designer's designer, with a loyal following of trend setters and initiates who collect his pieces for their distilled luxury. The Zoran brand is a business empire despite its limited production and the small number of sales outlets where it is distributed, including Saks Fifth Avenue and Neiman Marcus stores in the U.S., along with a handful of European boutiques.

Zorzi Alberto (1958). Italian artist and goldsmith. After graduating from the Pietro Selvatico School in Padua in 1978 he soon found his own style, based on the study of Constructivist and Futurist art. A lecturer at the European Institute of Design from 1991 to 1993, he has also taught on the fashion and design course at the University of Florence since 1994 and been professor of goldsmithery at Ravenna's Fine Arts Academy since 1998. His creations, which are often displayed at personal and collective exhibitions at galleries and museums all over Europe, reveal a strong bent for geometry and experimentation in form and materials. Gold is paired with silver, copper, and colored stones, transforming a piece of jewelry into a micro-sculpture. His works are exhibited at the American Craft Museum in New York, the Museum für Kunsthandewerk in Lipsia, and the Museum of Contemporary Design and Applied Arts (Mudac) in Lausanne. (*Alessandra Quattordio*)

Zouari Alexandre (1950). French hairdresser born in Tunisia. He worked for Lorca, the inventor of the blow dry, for 10 years from 1968 to 1978, and opened his first salon in Paris in partnership with Shiseido in 1987. During the 1990s he opened a further 4 salons in Japan and another in France. He works for famous designers, such as Gaultier, Mugler, Valentino, and Versace. His style is characterized by very sophisticated hairdos, with full chignons, and complicated plaiting.

Zubeldia Hélène. Designer. She trained at the Studio Berçot in France. She has worked for Chloé, for the women's Collections of Renoma, for the now defunct periodical *Jill* as fashion editor, for Lanvin, and for Vanessa Bruno. She launched her own line in 1996, whilst also designing for the Joseph boutique. Her style focuses on a strong femininity and is the opposite of minimalism. She is fascinated by dressmaking techniques and pays careful attention to details.

Zucca Label of the Japanese designer Akira Onozuca, the youngest of 6 siblings who learnt the art of dressmaking from his eldest sister. He was assistant to Miyake in his Tokyo and Paris ateliers but set up on his own in 1989, showing in the French capital but always staying within his teacher's orbit, since his business (30 stores in Japan and an annual turnover of 150 billion lire) is part of the Miyake Group. He opened a boutique, *La Cabane de Zucca*, in Paris in 1996. Whilst acknowledging that he has clearly been influenced by Miyake, he speaks of a fondness for the fashion of the Beatles and the Rolling Stones and for Biba's clothes.

❑ The company has 30 stores around the world, 8 of them called *La Cabane de Zucca*. The brand has become a leader in Japan and Europe. The designer has also developed a line of accessories, particularly watches, with new designs each season.

Zu' Elements Label founded in Summer 2002 by four people: Marco Del Bufalo, Alessandro Zuppa, Giancarlo Pancella, and Silvia Fabbo, who all work together on the style, from the designs and fabrics to the image. They offer an unconventional, sporty, trendy look aimed at men aged 18 to 30. They launched a women's Collection for Fall-Winter 2003-2004 called Zu4Girls. It is produced by Phard.

Zuffi Piero (1919-1998). Painter, set and costume designer. He had a long and happy collaboration with the dressmaker Germana Marucelli, who, in the postwar period and on the trail of Elsa Schiaparelli, stimulated the alliance between fashion and the arts by inviting painters to design fabrics and suggest lines. In the 1950s Zuffi became well-known for his set designs for Shakespeare's *Macbeth* and *Julius Caesar*, which were directed by Giorgio Strehler at Milan's Piccolo Teatro.

Zuhair Murad (1971). Lebanese *haute couture* designer. He made his debut "off the calendar" in January 2000 in Rome, with a Collection of dresses embellished with precious stones. He has a talent for combining humble materials, like raffia and jute, with rubies and diamonds. He has won a modest success with both the critics and public.

Printed in Italy by Mondadori Printing